# UNESCO

STATISTICAL YEARBOOK   ANNUAIRE STATISTIQUE   ANUARIO ESTADÍSTICO

## 1999

# ÉLAGUÉ

# UNESCO

## STATISTICAL YEARBOOK  ANNUAIRE STATISTIQUE  ANUARIO ESTADÍSTICO

## 1999

EDUCATION
Illiteracy
Enrolment
Graduates
Teaching staff
Expenditures
SCIENCE AND TECHNOLOGY
Manpower and expenditure in R&D
CULTURE AND COMMUNICATION
Libraries
Printed matter
Films and cinemas
Broadcasting

EDUCATION
Analphabétisme
Effectifs scolaires
Diplômés
Personnel enseignant
Dépenses
SCIENCE ET TECHNOLOGIE
Personnel et dépenses en R-D
CULTURE ET COMMUNICATION
Bibliothèques
Imprimés
Films et cinémas
Radiodiffusion

EDUCACION
Analfabetismo
Alumnos
Diplomados
Personal docente
Gastos
CIENCIA Y TECNOLOGIA
Personal y gastos en I y D
CULTURA Y COMUNICACION
Bibliotecas
Impresos
Películas y cines
Radiodifusión

# UNESCO Publishing & Bernan Press

Published jointly in 1999 by the United Nations Educational, Scientific and Cultural Organization 7, place Fontenoy, 75352 Paris 07 SP, France Email: uis.resource-centre@unesco.org

and

Bernan Press
4611-F Assembly Drive
Lanham, MD 20706-4391
U.S.A.
(800) 274-4447
Email: query@bernan.com

Photocomposition by
Automated Graphic Systems
4590 Graphics Drive
White Plains, Maryland 20695
U.S.A.

Publié conjointement en 1999 par l'Organisation des Nations Unies pour l'Education, la Science et la Culture 7, place Fontenoy, 75352 Paris 07 SP, France Email: uis.resource-centre@unesco.org

et

Bernan Press
4611-F Assembly Drive
Lanham, MD 20706-4391
U.S.A.
(800) 274-4447
Email: query@bernan.com

Photocomposition par
Automated Graphic Systems
4590 Graphics Drive
White Plains, Maryland 20695
U.S.A.

Publicado conjuntamente en 1999 por la Organización de las Naciones Unidas para la Educación, la Ciencia y la Cultura 7, place Fontenoy, 75352 Paris 07 SP, Francia Email: uis.resource-centre@unesco.org

y

Bernan Press
4611-F Assembly Drive
Lanham, MD 20706-4391
U.S.A.
(800) 274-4447
Email: query@bernan.com

Fotocomposición de
Automated Graphic Systems
4590 Graphics Drive
White Plains, Maryland 20695
U.S.A.

ISBN (UNESCO) 92-3-003635-8
ISBN (Bernan Press) 0-89059-245-4
ISSN 0082-7541

# Preface

The data contained in this *Yearbook* were gathered from official replies to UNESCO questionnaires and special surveys but also from official reports and publications, and were then processed and compiled by staff of the UNESCO Division of Statistics. We wish to take the opportunity to thank all those within countries who have devoted their time to completing UNESCO statistical enquiries and who have answered our further queries with efficiency and patience. We also wish to pay tribute to the National Commissions for UNESCO who assisted the Division of Statistics in bringing these data together. In addition we must thank the international agencies, particularly the Statistics and Population Divisions of the United Nations and other specialised agencies, who have provided information to supplement that collected directly by UNESCO. When using data from this *Yearbook* please credit UNESCO as the source: the citation should read *1999 Statistical Yearbook,* UNESCO Institute for Statistics.

The Division of Statistics, which has had responsibility for the *UNESCO Statistical Yearbook* since its first edition in 1963, was disbanded in June this year and on 1 July 1999 a new UNESCO Institute for Statistics was created. To signal this change and to mark the end of the millennium this *Yearbook* provides a longer time series of data, with the inclusion, wherever possible, of data from 1970 to the latest year available to UNESCO. Most of the data are presented at five-yearly intervals from 1970 to 1990 and yearly intervals thereafter. In order to make space for these time series some of the data collected by UNESCO have been omitted from this *Yearbook* (especially those for which long time series were not available or where no additional data had been received since the previous Yearbooks). If the data you require are missing from this edition please contact Ms. Souad El-Boustani at the address below or by e-mail at *s.aouad-el-boustani@unesco.org ,* who will be able to advise you as to their availability.

The transition to the new UNESCO Institute for Statistics is being overseen by a steering committee chaired by Mr. Jozef Ritzen, formerly Minister of Education in the Netherlands, now a Vice-President in the World Bank. A Director for the Institute, a statistician from the United Kingdom, Professor Denise Lievesley, has been appointed.

The UNESCO Institute for Statistics, although established as part of UNESCO, enjoys intellectual, administrative and functional autonomy. It provides statistical information on education, science, culture and communication to help countries improve the quality of life of their citizens through raising their intellectual capital. There are four main strands to this work:
-    the conceptual and methodological development of internationally comparable data and indicators;
-    the collection of high quality, timely and policy-relevant data from across the world and the dissemination of these data and indicators in ways which assure availability to all and promote their widespread and informed use;
-    the interpretation and analysis of data in order to inform policy debate, taking into account the needs of Member States;
-    capacity-building within countries to improve the scope and quality of data collections and assistance in forging links between users and producers of data of relevance to UNESCO's mission and in developing greater analytic skills.

The creation of the Institute for Statistics provides great opportunities for users of UNESCO's data. The Institute will be conducting fundamental reviews in order to determine what data it should collect and with what frequency. These reviews must be driven by user needs, especially by those users who have an interest in evaluating and determining policy. This is an excellent opportunity for you to influence the future programme of the Institute. We would love to hear about your research and analysis and how this influences your requirements in respect of the type of data, their frequency, the importance of time series, the disaggregation of data, the classification schema used, the creation of indicators, the value of explanatory metadata and the quality of data.

Similarly the creation of the new Institute will be used as an opportunity to evaluate the ways in which data should be disseminated. Is there a need for a *Yearbook* in the electronic age or can it be replaced by access to the full database over the Internet and on CD-ROMs supplemented by subsets of data on floppy disks? If paper publications are still required, should they be as comprehensive as the current *Yearbook* or would a series of smaller topic-focused publications be preferable? Users will appreciate that the production of the *Yearbook* is very resource-intensive. The time for compilation, checking, translation and publishing means that it contains data which are somewhat out of date before they reach users. Since we wish to promote the use of up-to-date data across the world - in both developed and developing countries - issues of access are crucial.

Please send your views on any of these issues to Denise Lievesley, Director, UNESCO Institute for Statistics, 7 place de Fontenoy, 75352 Paris 07 SP, France or e-mail *d.lievesley@unesco.org .*

# Préface

Les données présentées dans cet *Annuaire* ont été recueillies à partir des réponses aux questionnaires et aux enquêtes spéciales de l'UNESCO, mais aussi à partir de publications et rapports officiels. Elles ont été ensuite analysées et élaborées par le personnel de la Division des statistiques de l'UNESCO. A cette occasion nous souhaiterions remercier tous ceux qui, dans chaque pays, ont consacré de leur temps à répondre avec efficacité et patience aux enquêtes statistiques de l'UNESCO ainsi qu'à nos demandes de clarification. Nous voudrions également exprimer notre reconnaissance aux Commissions nationales pour l'UNESCO qui ont aidé la Division des statistiques à rassembler les données. Nos remerciements vont en outre aux organisations internationales, en particulier à la Division de statistique et à la Division de la population des Nations Unies et aux autres institutions spécialisées qui ont fourni les informations permettant de compléter celles collectées directement par l'UNESCO. Chaque fois que vous utiliserez les données de cet *Annuaire*, nous vous saurions gré de bien vouloir en indiquer la source à l'aide de la mention : *Annuaire statistique 1999*, Institut de statistique de l'UNESCO.

La Division des statistiques, sous la responsabilité de laquelle a été publié l'*Annuaire statistique* depuis sa première édition en 1963, a été dissoute en juin dernier, et un nouvel Institut de statistique de l'UNESCO a été créé le 1er juillet 1999. Pour marquer ce changement et aussi la fin du millénaire, nous avons présenté des séries chronologiques plus longues qu'à l'habitude en fournissant des données, lorsque cela était possible, depuis 1970 jusqu'à la dernière année disponible. La plupart des données sont présentées par intervalles de cinq ans de 1970 à 1990, et pour chaque année à partir de 1990. Du fait de l'extension de ces séries, certaines des données collectées par l'UNESCO n'ont pas été présentées dans cet *Annuaire* (en particulier celles pour lesquelles les séries chronologiques complètes n'étaient pas disponibles ou lorsque nous ne disposions pas de nouvelles données par rapport aux annuaires précédents). Si des données dont vous avez besoin ne figurent pas dans la présente édition, vous pouvez contacter Mme Souad El-Boustani à l'adresse ci-dessous ou par courrier électronique à l'adresse *s.aouad-el-boustani@unesco.org* . Elle pourra vous indiquer si elles sont disponibles.

La transition vers le nouvel Institut de statistique de l'UNESCO est suivie par un Comité directeur présidé par M. Jozef Ritzen, ancien Ministre de l'éducation des Pays-Bas et actuellement Vice-Président de la Banque mondiale. Le Professeur Denise Lievesley, statisticienne du Royaume-Uni, a été nommée Directrice de l'Institut.

L'Institut de statistique, bien que partie intégrante de l'UNESCO, jouit d'une autonomie intellectuelle, administrative et fonctionnelle. Il a pour objet de fournir des informations statistiques sur l'éducation, la science, la culture et la communication pour aider les pays à améliorer la qualité de vie de leurs citoyens en augmentant leur capital intellectuel. Cette tâche sera menée à bien suivant quatre directions principales :
- l'établissement conceptuel et méthodologique de données et d'indicateurs comparables sur le plan international ;
- la collecte, à travers le monde, de données actualisées, de haute qualité et axées sur les politiques, et la diffusion de ces données ainsi que d'indicateurs afin de les rendre accessibles à tous et en assurer l'utilisation la plus large et la plus judicieuse ;
- l'interprétation et l'analyse des données en vue de contribuer aux débats politiques, en tenant compte des besoins des Etats membres ;
- le renforcement des capacités, dans chaque pays, en vue d'améliorer l'étendue et la qualité des données, l'appui à la création de liens entre les utilisateurs et les producteurs de données pertinentes pour la mission de l'UNESCO et à la mise au point de meilleures techniques d'analyse.

La création de l'Institut de statistique de l'UNESCO offre de grandes opportunités pour les utilisateurs des données de l'UNESCO. L'Institut envisage de réaliser un examen de fond afin de déterminer la nature des données qu'il devra collecter et la fréquence de ces collectes. Cet examen devra être axé sur les besoins des utilisateurs, spécialement ceux qui participent à l'évaluation et à la définition des politiques. C'est une excellente possibilité qui vous est ainsi offerte d'influencer le futur programme de l'Institut. Nous serions très heureux de connaître vos recherches et analyses, dans la mesure où elles déterminent vos besoins quant au type de données, leur qualité, leur fréquence, l'importance des séries chronologiques, la ventilation des données, le type de classification utilisée, la création d'indicateurs et la valeur de la documentation rattachée aux données.

La création du nouvel Institut sera également l'occasion d'évaluer la façon dont les données doivent être diffusées. Un annuaire est-il toujours nécessaire à l'ère électronique ou peut-il être remplacé par l'accès à l'ensemble des bases de données via Internet et par des Cd-Rom, complété par la diffusion de données sélectionnées sur disquettes ? Si les textes imprimés sont encore nécessaires, doivent–ils pour autant être aussi complets que l'*Annuaire* actuel, ou une série de publications plus réduites sur des thèmes spécifiques serait-elle préférable ? Les utilisateurs ne peuvent ignorer que la production de l'*Annuaire* mobilise des ressources considérables. Vu le temps imparti à l'analyse, à la vérification, à la traduction et à la publication, les données sont nécessairement quelque peu dépassées au moment où elles parviennent aux utilisateurs. Dans la mesure où nous aspirons à promouvoir l'utilisation de données à jour dans le monde entier - tant dans les pays développés que dans les pays en développement - la question de leur accessibilité est cruciale.

Si vous le souhaitez, n'hésitez pas à faire parvenir vos observations ou suggestions sur toutes ces questions à Denise Lievesley, Directrice, Institut de statistique de l'UNESCO, 7, Place de Fontenoy, 75352 Paris 07 SP, France ou par courrier électronique ; *d.lievesley@unesco.org* .

# Prefacio

Los datos presentados en este *Anuario* provienen de las respuestas a los cuestionarios y encuestas especiales de la UNESCO así como de informes y publicaciones oficiales. Los datos han sido analizados y procesados por la División de Estadística de la UNESCO. Quisiéramos aprovechar esta oportunidad para agradecer a todos aquellos que, en cada país, han dedicado tiempo para responder con eficacia y paciencia a las encuestas estadísticas de la UNESCO y a nuestros pedidos de clarificación. También quisiéramos expresar nuestra gratitud a las Comisiones Nacionales para la UNESCO que han ayudado a la División de Estadística a reunir estos datos. Además, debemos agradecer a las organizaciones internacionales, particularmente a las Divisiones de Estadísticas y de Población de Naciones Unidas y a otras instituciones especializadas, que han proporcionado información necesaria para completar aquélla acopiada directamente por la UNESCO. Al utilizar los datos de este *Anuario*, sírvase citar a la UNESCO, utilizando la mención *Anuario estadístico de 1999*, Instituto de Estadística de la UNESCO.

La División de Estadística, bajo cuya responsabilidad se publicó el *Anuario Estadístico* desde su primera edición en 1963, ha sido disuelta en junio de este año y un nuevo Instituto de Estadística de la UNESCO ha sido creado el primero de julio de 1999. Para marcar este cambio y también el fin del milenio, este *Anuario* provee una serie cronológica larga, con la inclusión de datos, cuando ha sido posible, desde 1970 hasta el último año disponible. La mayoría de los datos se presenta por intervalos de cinco años de 1970 a 1990, y para cada año a partir de 1990. Debido a la extensión de estas series, algunos de los datos acopiados por la UNESCO han sido omitidos de este Anuario (especialmente cuando no se disponía de series cronológicas largas o cuando no se habían recibido nuevos datos con relación a los Anuarios anteriores). En caso de que los datos requeridos no se encuentren en esta edición, sírvase contactar a la Sra. Souad El-Boustani, en la dirección indicada más abajo o por correo electrónico *s.aouad-el-boustani@unesco.org* , quien podrá informarle acerca de su disponibilidad.

La transición hacia el nuevo Instituto de Estadística de la UNESCO se efectúa bajo la supervisión de un Comité Director presidido por el Sr. Jozef Ritzen, ex Ministro de Educación de los Países Bajos y actualmente Vicepresidente del Banco Mundial. La Profesora Denise Lievesley, especialista en estadísticas del Reino Unido, ha sido nombrada Directora de dicho Instituto.

El Instituto de Estadística de la UNESCO, a pesar de ser parte integrante de la UNESCO, goza de autonomía intelectual, administrativa y funcional. Proporciona información estadística sobre educación, ciencia, cultura y comunicación con el fin de ayudar a los países a mejorar la calidad de vida de sus ciudadanos a través del incremento del capital intelectual. Cuatro dimensiones principales constituyen la base de esta labor:
- el desarrollo conceptual y metodológico de datos e indicadores comparables internacionalmente;
- la recopilación de datos de alta calidad, recientes y relevantes a la acción política, así como la divulgación de esos datos e indicadores con el fin de asegurar su disponibilidad para todos y promover su utilización generalizada e informada;
- la interpretación y análisis de datos con el objeto de contribuir al debate sobre las políticas aplicadas, teniendo en cuenta las necesidades de los Estados Miembros;
- el fortalecimiento de las capacidades estadísticas y analíticas de los países para incrementar el alcance y la calidad de los datos acopiados, la creación de vínculos entre usuarios y productores de datos relevantes para la misión de la UNESCO.

La creación del Instituto de Estadística ofrece nuevas oportunidades a los usuarios de los datos de la UNESCO. El Instituto emprenderá análisis de fondo con el objeto de determinar qué datos deberán ser acopiados y con qué frecuencia. Estas análisis tendrán que guiarse por las necesidades de los usuarios, especialmente de aquellos que están directamente implicados en la evaluación y la definición de las acciones políticas. Esta es una excelente oportunidad para ustedes de orientar el futuro programa del Instituto. Nos gustaría mucho conocer sus investigaciones y análisis en la medida en que éstos determinan sus requerimientos con respecto al tipo de datos, su calidad, su frecuencia, la importancia de las series cronológicas, el desglose de los datos, el esquema de clasificación utilizado, la creación de indicadores y la utilidad de las notas explicativas adjuntas a los datos.

Al mismo tiempo, la creación del Instituto se utilizará como una oportunidad para evaluar la manera en que los datos tendrían que ser divulgados. ¿Es necesario un *Anuario* en la era electrónica, o puede ser reemplazado por el acceso al conjunto de la base de datos a través de Internet y los CD-ROM, completado con la difusión de datos seleccionados en disquetes? Si las publicaciones impresas son aún necesarias, ¿deben ser tan extensas como el actual *Anuario*? ¿No sería preferible una serie de publicaciones más reducidas y centradas en ciertos temas? Los usuarios del *Anuario* no pueden ignorar que su producción necesita recursos substanciales. Dado el tiempo necesario para compilar, verificar, traducir y publicar, los datos de este *Anuario* habrán perdido una parte de su actualidad cuando lleguen a los usuarios. En la medida en que deseamos favorecer el uso de datos actualizados en el mundo entero - trátese de países desarrollados o en desarrollo - la cuestión de la accesibilidad es crucial.

Por favor, dirijan sus comentarios y sugerencias sobre cualquiera de estos aspectos a Denise Lievesley, Directora del Instituto de Estadística de la UNESCO, 7 Place de Fontenoy, 75352 París 07 SP, Francia, o por correo electrónico: *d.lievesley@unesco.org* .

# Table of contents

# Table des matières

# Índice

# I.    Introduction

# Introduction

# Introducción

# Explanatory note

The data presented in this publication relate in general to territorial units within their present "de facto" boundaries. A complete list of countries and territories follows this note. Changes in country names during recent years are reflected in this list and used in the tables of the *Yearbook*.

It should be noted that:

-	data presented for *Jordan* refer to the *East Bank* only;

-	data for *Cyprus* refer to government controlled areas only;

-	statistics concerning *Palestine* are limited to the *Gaza Strip* and *West Bank*, and are to be found following the Asian countries in each of the relevant tables;

-	up to 1991, data for *Ethiopia* include *Eritrea*; however, when data for the latter are available for years prior to 1991, they are shown separately from Ethiopia;

-	as of 1 July 1997 Hong Kong became a Special Administrative Region (SAR) of China. However, for statistical purposes Hong Kong is still shown separetely straight after China.

Revised data may be presented in this edition of the *Yearbook* and thus differ from those published for the same year in earlier editions.

Owing to the rounding off of figures, the totals and sub-totals shown in the tables do not always correspond exactly to the sums of their component items.

The following symbols are used throughout this *Yearbook*:

| | |
|---|---|
| - | Magnitude nil |
| 0 or 0.0 | Magnitude less than half of unit employed |
| ... | Data not available |
| . | Category not applicable |
| * | Provisional or estimated data |
| ./. | Data included elsewhere under another category |
| ---> | The figure to the immediate left includes the data for the column(s) in which this symbol appears |
| <--- | The figure to the immediate right includes the data for the column(s) in which this symbol appears |

# Notice explicative

Les données présentées dans cette publication se rapportent, en général, aux territoires tels qu'ils sont délimités par les frontières de fait. Une liste complète des pays et territoires figure à la suite de cette note. Les changements de nom de pays survenus récemment dans certains pays sont reflétés dans cette liste et dans les tableaux de cet *Annuaire*.

Il convient de préciser que:

- les données relatives à la *Jordanie* se réfèrent à la rive orientale seulement;

- les données relatives à la *Chypre* se réfèrent aux zones contrôlées par le gouvernement;

- les statistiques relatives à *Palestine* concernent la *Bande de Gaza* et la *Cisjordanie* et se trouvent à la suite des pays asiatiques dans chacun des tableaux où ces données apparaissent;

- jusqu'en 1991, les données présentées pour l'Éthiopie incluent celles de l'Érythrée; cependant si des données pour les années antérieures à 1991 sont disponibles pour l'Érythrée, elles sont présentées séparément de l'Éthiopie;

- depuis juillet 1997, Hong Kong est devenu une Région Administrative Spéciale (RAS) de la Chine. Cependant, pour des raisons statistiques, Hong Kong est toujours présenté séparément, à la suite de la Chine.

Des données révisées peuvent être présentées dans cette édition de l'*Annuaire* et elles seront donc différentes des données correspondant à la même année qui figuraient dans les éditions précédentes.

Les chiffres et pourcentages ayant été arrondis, les totaux et les sous-totaux figurant dans les tableaux ne correspondent pas toujours exactement à la somme des éléments qui les composent.

Les symboles utilisés dans l'*Annuaire* sont les suivants:

| | |
|---|---|
| - | Chiffre nul |
| 0 ou 0.0 | Chiffre inférieur à la moitié de l'unité employée |
| ... | Données non disponibles |
| . | Catégorie sans objet |
| * | Chiffre provisoire ou estimé |
| ./. | Données comprises dans une autre rubrique |
| —> | Le chiffre immédiatement à gauche comprend les données de la (des) colonne(s) où figure ce symbole |
| <— | Le chiffre immédiatement à droite comprend les données de la (des) colonne(s) où figure ce symbole |

# Nota explicativa

En general, los datos que figuran en la presente publicación se refieren a los territorios delimitados por sus fronteras «de facto». A continuación de esta nota, se presenta una lista completa de países y territorios. Los cambios ocurridos en estos últimos años con respecto a la nomenclatura de algunos países se han reflejado en esta lista y en los cuadros del *Anuario*.

Se debe señalar que:

- los datos relativos a *Jordania* se refieren a la orilla oriental solamente;

- los datos relativos a *Chipre* se refieren solamente a aquellas zonas bajo control del gobierno;

- las estadísticas relativas a *Palestina* se refieren al *Estrecho de Gaza* y a *Cisjordania* y figuran inmediatamente después de los países de Asia en los cuadros correspondientes;

- hasta el año 1991, los datos presentados para *Etiopía* incluyen *Eritrea*; sin embargo, si para Eritrea se dispone de datos anteriores a 1991, éstos no se incluyen en los de Etiopía;

- desde julio de 1997, Hong Kong es una Región Administrativa Especial (RAE) de China. Sin embargo, por razones estadísticas, Hong Kong se sigue presentando aparte, inmediatamente después de China.

Esta edición del *Anuario* puede contener datos revisados y diferir de aquellos datos publicados en ediciones anteriores para el mismo año.

Como las cifras y porcentajes se han redondeado, los totales y subtotales que figuran en los cuadros no siempre corresponden exactamente a la suma de los elementos que los componen.

Los símbolos utilizados en el *Anuario* son los siguientes:

| | |
|---|---|
| - | Cifra nula |
| 0 ó 0.0 | Cifra inferior a la mitad de la unidad empleada |
| … | Datos no disponibles |
| . | Categoría sin objeto |
| * | Cifra provisional o estimada |
| ./. | Datos comprendidos en otra rúbrica |
| —> | La cifra situada inmediatamente a la izquierda comprende los datos relativos a la(s) columna(s) donde figura ese símbolo |
| <— | La cifra situada inmediatamente a la derecha comprende los datos relativos a la(s) columna(s) donde figura ese símbolo |

List of countries and territories I
Liste des pays et territoires
Lista de países y territorios

# List of countries and territories

# Liste des pays et territoires

# Lista de países y territorios

In the tables of this publication, the names of countries and territories are shown in English only. The names in French and Spanish are given in the following pages where they are grouped by continent and arranged in alphabetical order. The number preceding each one refers to the corresponding name in English.

Apart from the continental groupings, eight other groupings are used in the regional tables of Chapters II and IV of this **Yearbook**. The countries which compose these groupings can be found at the end of this list, in alphabetical order. There are no international standards on the use of the terms *developed* and *developing* countries, areas or regions. These designations are intended for statistical convenience and do not express a judgement on the stage reached by a particular country or area in the development process.

As in the previous edition of this **Yearbook**, the states of the former *U.S.S.R.* are included under either *Europe* or *Asia* and retained under the heading *Developed countries*. It should also be noted that countries may be included in more than one of the six groupings shown for *Developing countries*.

Dans les tableaux de cette publication, les noms des pays et des territoires sont donnés en anglais seulement. Les noms en français et en espagnol apparaissent dans la liste ci-après, où les pays ont été classés par continent et dans l'ordre alphabétique de chaque langue. Ils sont précédés d'un numéro qui les renvoie à leur équivalent en anglais.

Outre le groupement par continents, huit autres groupements sont utilisés dans les tableaux régionaux des chapitres II et IV de cet **Annuaire**. Les pays qui composent ces groupes se trouvent à la fin de cette liste, par ordre alphabétique. L'utilisation des expressions pays, zones ou régions *développés* ou en *développement* n'est pas normalisée à l'échelle internationale. Ces appellations sont employées pour des raisons de commodité statistique et n'expriment pas un jugement sur le stade de développement atteint par tel ou tel pays ou zone.

Comme dans l'édition précédente de cet **Annuaire**, les états de l'ancienne *U.R.S.S.* sont présentés en *Europe* ou en *Asie*, et dans le groupement des *Pays développés*. Il est à retenir que quelques pays peuvent appartenir à plus d'un des six groupes présentés sous l'intitulé *Pays en développement*.

En los cuadros de esta publicación, los nombres de los países y territorios figuran en inglés solamente. Los nombres en español y en francés se presentan en la lista a continuación, en la que los países se han clasificado por continente y de acuerdo con el orden alfabético de cada lengua. El número que precede a cada país corresponde a su nombre en inglés.

Además de la clasificación por continente, se han presentado también ocho grupos de países adicionales en los cuadros regionales de los capítulos II y IV de este **Anuario**. Los países que componen estos grupos figuran al final de esta lista, por orden alfabético. No existe una normalización internacional del empleo de las expresiones países, zonas o regiones *desarrolladas* o *en desarrollo*. Estas expresiones no deben interpretarse en el sentido de que expresen un juicio sobre el nivel de desarrollo alcanzado por un país o una zona.

Como en la edición precedente del **Anuario**, los estados de la ex *U.R.S.S.* figuran en *Europa* o *Asia* así como en los *Países desarrollados*. Cabe recordar que ciertos países pueden pertenecer a uno o más de los seis grupos que constituyen los *Países en desarrollo*.

I  List of countries and territories
Liste des pays et territoires
Lista de países y territorios

## Africa

| | |
|---|---|
| 101 | Algeria |
| 102 | Angola |
| 103 | Benin |
| 104 | Botswana |
| 105 | Burkina Faso |
| 106 | Burundi |
| 107 | Cameroon |
| 108 | Cape Verde |
| 109 | Central African Republic |
| 110 | Chad |
| 111 | Comoros |
| 112 | Congo |
| 113 | Côte d'Ivoire |
| 114 | Democratic Rep. of the Congo |
| 115 | Djibouti |
| 116 | Egypt |
| 117 | Equatorial Guinea |
| 118 | Eritrea |
| 119 | Ethiopia |
| 120 | Gabon |
| 121 | Gambia |
| 122 | Ghana |
| 123 | Guinea |
| 124 | Guinea-Bissau |
| 125 | Kenya |
| 126 | Lesotho |
| 127 | Liberia |
| 128 | Libyan Arab Jamahiriya |
| 129 | Madagascar |
| 130 | Malawi |
| 131 | Mali |
| 132 | Mauritania |
| 133 | Mauritius |
| 134 | Morocco |
| 135 | Mozambique |
| 136 | Namibia |
| 137 | Niger |
| 138 | Nigeria |
| 139 | Reunion |
| 140 | Rwanda |
| 141 | Sao Tome and Principe |
| 142 | Senegal |
| 143 | Seychelles |
| 144 | Sierra Leone |
| 145 | Somalia |
| 146 | South Africa |
| 147 | St. Helena |
| 148 | Sudan |
| 149 | Swaziland |
| 150 | Togo |
| 151 | Tunisia |
| 152 | Uganda |
| 153 | United Republic of Tanzania |
| 154 | Western Sahara |
| 155 | Zambia |
| 156 | Zimbabwe |

## Afrique

| | |
|---|---|
| 146 | Afrique du Sud |
| 101 | Algérie |
| 102 | Angola |
| 103 | Bénin |
| 104 | Botswana |
| 105 | Burkina Faso |
| 106 | Burundi |
| 107 | Cameroun |
| 108 | Cap-Vert |
| 111 | Comores |
| 112 | Congo |
| 113 | Côte d'Ivoire |
| 115 | Djibouti |
| 116 | Egypte |
| 118 | Erythrée |
| 119 | Ethiopie |
| 120 | Gabon |
| 121 | Gambie |
| 122 | Ghana |
| 123 | Guinée |
| 124 | Guinée-Bissau |
| 117 | Guinée équatoriale |
| 128 | Jamahiriya arabe libyenne |
| 125 | Kenya |
| 126 | Lesotho |
| 127 | Libéria |
| 129 | Madagascar |
| 130 | Malawi |
| 131 | Mali |
| 134 | Maroc |
| 133 | Maurice |
| 132 | Mauritanie |
| 135 | Mozambique |
| 136 | Namibie |
| 137 | Niger |
| 138 | Nigéria |
| 152 | Ouganda |
| 109 | République centrafricaine |
| 114 | Rép. démocratique du Congo |
| 153 | République-Unie de Tanzanie |
| 139 | Réunion |
| 140 | Rwanda |
| 154 | Sahara occidental |
| 147 | Sainte Hélène |
| 141 | Sao Tomé-et-Principe |
| 142 | Sénégal |
| 143 | Seychelles |
| 144 | Sierra Leone |
| 145 | Somalie |
| 148 | Soudan |
| 149 | Swaziland |
| 110 | Tchad |
| 150 | Togo |
| 151 | Tunisie |
| 155 | Zambie |
| 156 | Zimbabwe |

## Africa

| | |
|---|---|
| 102 | Angola |
| 101 | Argelia |
| 103 | Benín |
| 104 | Botswana |
| 105 | Burkina Faso |
| 106 | Burundi |
| 108 | Cabo Verde |
| 107 | Camerún |
| 110 | Chad |
| 111 | Comoras |
| 112 | Congo |
| 113 | Côte d'Ivoire |
| 115 | Djibouti |
| 116 | Egipto |
| 118 | Eritrea |
| 119 | Etiopía |
| 120 | Gabón |
| 121 | Gambia |
| 122 | Ghana |
| 123 | Guinea |
| 124 | Guinea-Bissau |
| 117 | Guinea Ecuatorial |
| 128 | Jamahiriya Árabe Libia |
| 125 | Kenya |
| 126 | Lesotho |
| 127 | Liberia |
| 129 | Madagascar |
| 130 | Malawi |
| 131 | Malí |
| 134 | Marruecos |
| 133 | Mauricio |
| 132 | Mauritania |
| 135 | Mozambique |
| 136 | Namibia |
| 137 | Níger |
| 138 | Nigeria |
| 139 | Reunión |
| 109 | República Centroafricana |
| 114 | Rep. Democrática del Congo |
| 153 | Rep. Unida de Tanzania |
| 140 | Rwanda |
| 154 | Sahara Occidental |
| 147 | Santa Elena |
| 141 | Santo Tomé y Príncipe |
| 142 | Senegal |
| 143 | Seychelles |
| 144 | Sierra Leona |
| 145 | Somalia |
| 146 | Sudáfrica |
| 148 | Sudán |
| 149 | Swazilandia |
| 150 | Togo |
| 151 | Túnez |
| 152 | Uganda |
| 155 | Zambia |
| 156 | Zimbabwe |

## North America

| | |
|---|---|
| 201 | Anguilla |
| 202 | Antigua and Barbuda |
| 203 | Aruba |

## Amérique du Nord

| | |
|---|---|
| 201 | Anguilla |
| 202 | Antigua-et-Barbuda |
| 226 | Antilles néerlandaises |

## América del Norte

| | |
|---|---|
| 201 | Anguilla |
| 202 | Antigua y Barbuda |
| 226 | Antillas Neerlandesas |

List of countries and territories
Liste des pays et territoires
Lista de países y territorios

| 204 Bahamas | 203 Aruba | 203 Aruba |
| 205 Barbados | 204 Bahamas | 204 Bahamas |
| 206 Belize | 205 Barbade | 205 Barbados |
| 207 Bermuda | 206 Belize | 206 Belice |
| 208 British Virgin Islands | 207 Bermudes | 207 Bermudas |
| 209 Canada | 209 Canada | 209 Canadá |
| 210 Cayman Islands | 211 Costa Rica | 211 Costa Rica |
| 211 Costa Rica | 212 Cuba | 212 Cuba |
| 212 Cuba | 213 Dominique | 213 Dominica |
| 213 Dominica | 215 El Salvador | 215 El Salvador |
| 214 Dominican Republic | 237 Etats-Unis d'Amérique | 237 Estados Unidos de América |
| 215 El Salvador | 217 Grenade | 217 Granada |
| 216 Greenland | 216 Groënland | 216 Groenlandia |
| 217 Grenada | 218 Guadeloupe | 218 Guadalupe |
| 218 Guadeloupe | 219 Guatemala | 219 Guatemala |
| 219 Guatemala | 220 Haïti | 220 Haití |
| 220 Haiti | 221 Honduras | 221 Honduras |
| 221 Honduras | 210 Îles Caïmanes | 210 Islas Caimán |
| 222 Jamaica | 235 Îles Turques et Caïques | 235 Islas Turcas y Caicos |
| 223 Martinique | 236 Îles Vierges américaines | 236 Islas Vírgenes Americanas |
| 224 Mexico | 208 Îles Vierges britaniques | 208 Islas Vírgenes Británicas |
| 225 Montserrat | 222 Jamaïque | 222 Jamaica |
| 226 Netherlands Antilles | 223 Martinique | 223 Martinica |
| 227 Nicaragua | 224 Mexique | 224 México |
| 228 Panama | 225 Montserrat | 225 Montserrat |
| 229 Puerto Rico | 227 Nicaragua | 227 Nicaragua |
| 230 St. Kitts and Nevis | 228 Panama | 228 Panamá |
| 231 St. Lucia | 229 Porto Rico | 229 Puerto Rico |
| 232 St. Pierre and Miquelon | 214 République dominicaine | 214 República Dominicana |
| 233 St. Vincent and the Grenadines | 230 Saint-Kitts-et-Nevis | 230 Saint Kitts y Nevis |
| 234 Trinidad and Tobago | 232 Saint-Pierre-et-Miquelon | 232 San Pedro y Miquelón |
| 235 Turks and Caicos Islands | 233 Saint-Vincent-et-Grenadines | 233 San Vicente y las Granadinas |
| 236 U. S. Virgin Islands | 231 Sainte-Lucie | 231 Santa Lucía |
| 237 United States of America | 234 Trinité-et-Tobago | 234 Trinidad y Tobago |

| **South America** | **Amérique du Sud** | **América del Sur** |
| 301 Argentina | 301 Argentine | 301 Argentina |
| 302 Bolivia | 302 Bolivie | 302 Bolivia |
| 303 Brazil | 303 Brésil | 303 Brasil |
| 304 Chile | 304 Chili | 304 Chile |
| 305 Colombia | 305 Colombie | 305 Colombia |
| 306 Ecuador | 306 Equateur | 306 Ecuador |
| 307 Falkland Islands (Malvinas) | 309 Guyana | 309 Guyana |
| 308 French Guiana | 308 Guyane française | 308 Guyana Francesa |
| 309 Guyana | 307 Îles Falkland (Malouines) | 307 Islas Falkland (Malvinas) |
| 310 Paraguay | 310 Paraguay | 310 Paraguay |
| 311 Peru | 311 Pérou | 311 Perú |
| 312 Suriname | 312 Suriname | 312 Suriname |
| 313 Uruguay | 313 Uruguay | 313 Uruguay |
| 314 Venezuela | 314 Venezuela | 314 Venezuela |

| **Asia** | **Asie** | **Asia** |
| 401 Afghanistan | 401 Afghanistan | 401 Afganistán |
| 402 Armenia | 438 Arabie saoudite | 438 Arabia Saudí |
| 403 Azerbaijan | 402 Arménie | 402 Armenia |
| 404 Bahrain | 403 Azerbaïdjan | 403 Azerbaiyán |
| 405 Bangladesh | 404 Bahreïn | 404 Bahrein |
| 406 Bhutan | 405 Bangladesh | 405 Bangladesh |
| 407 Brunei Darussalam | 406 Bhoutan | 406 Bhután |
| 408 Cambodia | 407 Brunéi Darussalam | 407 Brunei Darussalam |
| 409 China | 408 Cambodge | 408 Camboya |

I  List of countries and territories
Liste des pays et territoires
Lista de países y territorios

| 410 | China, Hong Kong SAR | 409 | Chine | 409 | China |
|---|---|---|---|---|---|
| 411 | Cyprus | 410 | Chine, Hong-Kong RAS | 410 | China, Hong-Kong RAE |
| 412 | East Timor | 411 | Chypre | 411 | Chipre |
| 413 | Georgia | 446 | Émirats arabes unis | 446 | Emiratos Árabes Unidos |
| 414 | India | 413 | Géorgie | 436 | Filipinas |
| 415 | Indonesia | 414 | Inde | 413 | Georgia |
| 416 | Iran, Islamic Republic of | 415 | Indonésie | 414 | India |
| 417 | Iraq | 416 | Iran, République islamique d' | 415 | Indonesia |
| 418 | Israel | 417 | Irak | 417 | Irak |
| 419 | Japan | 418 | Israël | 416 | Irán, República Islámica del |
| 420 | Jordan | 419 | Japon | 418 | Israel |
| 421 | Kazakstan | 420 | Jordanie | 419 | Japón |
| 422 | Korea, Democratic People's | 421 | Kazakstan | 420 | Jordania |
|  | Republic of | 425 | Kirghizistan | 421 | Kazajstán |
| 423 | Korea, Republic of | 424 | Koweït | 425 | Kirguistán |
| 424 | Kuwait | 427 | Liban | 424 | Kuwait |
| 425 | Kyrgyzstan | 428 | Macao | 427 | Líbano |
| 426 | Lao People's Democratic Republic | 429 | Malaisie | 428 | Macao |
| 427 | Lebanon | 430 | Maldives | 429 | Malasia |
| 428 | Macau | 431 | Mongolie | 430 | Maldivas |
| 429 | Malaysia | 432 | Myanmar | 431 | Mongolia |
| 430 | Maldives | 433 | Népal | 432 | Myanmar |
| 431 | Mongolia | 434 | Oman | 433 | Nepal |
| 432 | Myanmar | 447 | Ouzbékistan | 434 | Omán |
| 433 | Nepal | 435 | Pakistan | 435 | Pakistán |
| 434 | Oman | 436 | Philippines | 437 | Qatar |
| 435 | Pakistan | 437 | Qatar | 441 | República Árabe Siria |
| 436 | Philippines | 441 | République arabe syrienne | 423 | República de Corea |
| 437 | Qatar | 423 | République de Corée | 426 | Rep. Democrática Popular Lao |
| 438 | Saudi Arabia | 426 | Rép. démocratique populaire lao | 422 | República Popular Democrática |
| 439 | Singapore | 422 | Rép. populaire démocratique de |  | de Corea |
| 440 | Sri Lanka |  | Corée | 439 | Singapur |
| 441 | Syrian Arab Republic | 439 | Singapour | 440 | Sri Lanka |
| 442 | Tajikistan | 440 | Sri Lanka | 443 | Tailandia |
| 443 | Thailand | 442 | Tadjikistan | 442 | Tayikistán |
| 444 | Turkey | 443 | Thaïlande | 412 | Timor Oriental |
| 445 | Turkmenistan | 412 | Timor oriental | 445 | Turkmenistán |
| 446 | United Arab Emirates | 445 | Turkménistan | 444 | Turquía |
| 447 | Uzbekistan | 444 | Turquie | 447 | Uzbekistán |
| 448 | Viet Nam | 448 | Viet Nam | 448 | Viet Nam |
| 449 | Yemen | 449 | Yémen | 449 | Yemen |
|  |  |  |  |  |  |
| 450 | Palestine | 450 | Palestine | 450 | Palestina |

## Europe

## Europe

## Europa

| 501 | Albania | 501 | Albanie | 501 | Albania |
|---|---|---|---|---|---|
| 502 | Andorra | 516 | Allemagne | 516 | Alemania |
| 503 | Austria | 502 | Andorre | 502 | Andorra |
| 504 | Belarus | 503 | Autriche | 503 | Austria |
| 505 | Belgium | 504 | Bélarus | 504 | Belarrús |
| 506 | Bosnia and Herzegovina | 505 | Belgique | 505 | Bélgica |
| 507 | Bulgaria | 506 | Bosnie-Herzégovine | 506 | Bosnia y Herzegovina |
| 508 | Croatia | 507 | Bulgarie | 507 | Bulgaria |
| 509 | Czech Republic | 508 | Croatie | 508 | Croacia |
| 510 | Denmark | 510 | Danemark | 510 | Dinamarca |
| 511 | Estonia | 540 | Espagne | 538 | Eslovaquia |
| 512 | Faeroe Islands | 511 | Estonie | 539 | Eslovenia |
| 513 | Federal Republic of Yugoslavia | 536 | Fédération de Russie | 540 | España |
| 514 | Finland | 514 | Finlande | 511 | Estonia |
| 515 | France | 515 | France | 536 | Federación de Rusia |
| 516 | Germany | 517 | Gibraltar | 514 | Finlandia |
| 517 | Gibraltar | 518 | Grèce | 515 | Francia |
| 518 | Greece | 520 | Hongrie | 517 | Gibraltar |
| 519 | Holy See | 512 | Îles Féroé | 518 | Grecia |

List of countries and territories
Liste des pays et territoires
Lista de países y territorios

I

| 520 | Hungary | 522 | Irlande | 520 | Hungría |
|---|---|---|---|---|---|
| 521 | Iceland | 521 | Islande | 522 | Irlanda |
| 522 | Ireland | 523 | Italie | 521 | Islandia |
| 523 | Italy | 543 | L'ex-Rép. yougoslave de | 512 | Islas Feroé |
| 524 | Latvia | | Macédoine | 523 | Italia |
| 525 | Liechtenstein | 524 | Lettonie | 543 | La ex República Yugoslava |
| 526 | Lithuania | 525 | Liechtenstein | | de Macedonia |
| 527 | Luxembourg | 526 | Lithuanie | 524 | Letonia |
| 528 | Malta | 527 | Luxembourg | 525 | Liechtenstein |
| 529 | Moldova | 528 | Malte | 526 | Lituania |
| 530 | Monaco | 529 | Moldova | 527 | Luxemburgo |
| 531 | Netherlands | 530 | Monaco | 528 | Malta |
| 532 | Norway | 532 | Norvège | 529 | Moldova |
| 533 | Poland | 531 | Pays-Bas | 530 | Mónaco |
| 534 | Portugal | 533 | Pologne | 532 | Noruega |
| 535 | Romania | 534 | Portugal | 531 | Países Bajos |
| 536 | Russian Federation | 513 | Rép. fédérative de Yougoslavie | 533 | Polonia |
| 537 | San Marino | 509 | République tchèque | 534 | Portugal |
| 538 | Slovakia | 535 | Roumanie | 545 | Reino Unido |
| 539 | Slovenia | 545 | Royaume-Uni | 509 | República Checa |
| 540 | Spain | 537 | Saint-Marin | 513 | Rep. Federativa de Yugoslavia |
| 541 | Sweden | 519 | Saint-Siège | 535 | Rumania |
| 542 | Switzerland | 538 | Slovaquie | 537 | San Marino |
| 543 | The Former Yugoslav Rep. of | 539 | Slovenie | 519 | Santa Sede |
| | Macedonia | 541 | Suède | 541 | Suecia |
| 544 | Ukraine | 542 | Suisse | 542 | Suiza |
| 545 | United Kingdom | 544 | Ukraine | 544 | Ucrania |

## Oceania / Océanie / Oceanía

| 601 | American Samoa | 602 | Australie | 602 | Australia |
|---|---|---|---|---|---|
| 602 | Australia | 604 | Fidji | 604 | Fiji |
| 603 | Cook Islands | 606 | Guam | 606 | Guam |
| 604 | Fiji | 603 | Îles Cook | 603 | Islas Cook |
| 605 | French Polynesia | 608 | Îles Marshall | 608 | Islas Marshall |
| 606 | Guam | 613 | Îles Norfolk | 613 | Islas Norfolk |
| 607 | Kiribati | 614 | Îles du Pacifique (Palau) | 614 | Islas del Pacífico (Palau) |
| 608 | Marshall Islands | 617 | Îles Salomon | 617 | Islas Salomón |
| 609 | Nauru | 607 | Kiribati | 607 | Kiribati |
| 610 | New Caledonia | 609 | Nauru | 609 | Nauru |
| 611 | New Zealand | 612 | Nioué | 612 | Niue |
| 612 | Niue | 610 | Nouvelle-Calédonie | 610 | Nueva Caledonia |
| 613 | Norfolk Island | 611 | Nouvelle-Zélande | 611 | Nueva Zelandia |
| 614 | Pacific Islands (Palau) | 615 | Papouasie-Nouvelle-Guinée | 615 | Papua Nueva Guinea |
| 615 | Papua New Guinea | 605 | Polynésie française | 605 | Polinesia Francesa |
| 616 | Samoa | 616 | Samoa | 616 | Samoa |
| 617 | Solomon Islands | 601 | Samoa américaines | 601 | Samoa Americanas |
| 618 | Tokelau | 618 | Tokelaou | 618 | Tokelau |
| 619 | Tonga | 619 | Tonga | 619 | Tonga |
| 620 | Tuvalu | 620 | Tuvalu | 620 | Tuvalu |
| 621 | Vanuatu, Republic of | 621 | Vanuatu, Republique de | 621 | Vanuatu, República de |

| List of countries and territories
Liste des pays et territoires
Lista de países y territorios

## Continents, major areas and groups of countries
## Continents, grandes régions et groupes de pays
## Continentes, grandes regiones y grupos de países

### Developed countries / Pays développés / Países desarrollados

Albania, Andorra, Armenia, Australia, Austria, Azerbaijan, Belarus, Belgium, Bulgaria, Canada, Czech Republic, Denmark, Estonia, Faeroe Islands, Finland, France, Georgia, Germany, Gibraltar, Greece, Holy See, Hungary, Iceland, Ireland, Israel, Italy, Japan, Kazakstan, Kyrgyzstan, Latvia, Liechtenstein, Lithuania, Luxembourg, Moldova, Monaco, Netherlands, New Zealand, Norway, Poland, Portugal, Romania, Russian Federation, San Marino, Slovakia, Spain, Sweden, Switzerland, Tajikistan, Turkmenistan, Ukraine, United Kingdom, United States of America, Uzbekistan.

### Developing countries / Pays en développement / Países en desarrollo

All countries except the Developed countries listed above.
Tous les pays, sauf les Pays développés énumérés ci-dessus.
Todos los países, excepto los Países desarrollados indicados ariba.

*Sub-Saharan Africa / Afrique subsaharienne / Africa subsahariana*
Angola, Benin, Botswana, Burkina Faso, Burundi, Cameroon, Cape Verde, Central African Republic, Chad, Comoros, Congo, Democratic Republic of the Congo, Côte d'Ivoire, Djibouti, Equatorial Guinea, Eritrea, Ethiopia, Gabon, Gambia, Ghana, Guinea, Guinea-Bissau, Kenya, Lesotho, Liberia, Madagascar, Malawi, Mali, Mauritania, Mauritius, Mozambique, Namibia, Niger, Nigeria, Reunion, Rwanda, St. Helena, Sao Tome and Principe, Senegal, Seychelles, Sierra Leone, Somalia, South Africa, Sudan, Swaziland, Togo, Uganda, United Republic of Tanzania, Western Sahara, Zambia, Zimbabwe.

*Arab States / États arabes / Estados árabes*
Algeria, Bahrain, Djibouti, Egypt, Iraq, Jordan, Kuwait, Lebanon, Libyan Arab Jamahiriya, Mauritania, Morocco, Oman, Palestine: Gaza Strip and West Bank, Qatar, Saudi Arabia, Somalia, Sudan, Syrian Arab Republic, Tunisia, United Arab Emirates, Yemen.

*Latin America and the Caribbean / Amérique latine et les Caraïbes / América latina y el Caribe*
Anguilla, Antigua and Barbuda, Argentina, Aruba, Bahamas, Barbados, Belize, Bolivia, Brazil, British Virgin Islands, Cayman Islands, Chile, Colombia, Costa Rica, Cuba, Dominica, Dominican Republic, Ecuador, El Salvador, Falkland Islands (Malvinas), French Guiana, Grenada, Guadeloupe, Guatemala, Guyana, Haiti, Honduras, Jamaica, Martinique, Mexico, Montserrat, Netherlands Antilles, Nicaragua, Panama, Paraguay, Peru, Puerto Rico, St. Kitts and Nevis, St. Lucia, St. Vincent and the Grenadines, Suriname, Trinidad and Tobago, Turks and Caicos Islands, U.S. Virgin Islands, Uruguay, Venezuela,

*Eastern Asia and Oceania / Asie de l'est et Océanie / Asia del Este y Oceanía*
American Samoa, Brunei Darussalam, Cambodia, China, China, Hong Kong SAR, Cook Islands, East Timor, Fiji, French Polynesia, Guam, Indonesia, Kiribati, Democratic People's Republic of Korea, Republic of Korea, Lao People's Democratic Republic, Macau, Malaysia, Marshall Islands, Mongolia, Myanmar, Nauru, New Caledonia, Niue, Pacific Islands (Palau), Papua New Guinea, Philippines, Samoa, Singapore, Solomon Islands, Thailand, Tokelau, Tonga, Tuvalu, Vanuatu, Viet Nam.

*Southern Asia / Asie du Sud / Asia del Sur*
Afghanistan, Bangladesh, Bhutan, India, Islamic Republic of Iran, Maldives, Nepal, Pakistan, Sri Lanka.

*Other developing countries / Autres pays en développement / Otros países en desarrollo*
Bosnia and Herzegovina, Croatia, Cyprus, Federal Republic of Yugoslavia, Malta, Slovenia, The Former Yugoslav Republic of Macedonia and Turkey.

*Least Developed Countries / Pays les moins avancés / Países menos adelantados*
Afghanistan, Angola, Bangladesh, Benin, Bhutan, Burkina Faso, Burundi, Cambodia, Cape Verde, Central African Republic, Chad, Comoros, Congo, Democratic Republic of the Congo, Djibouti, Equatorial Guinea, Eritrea, Ethiopia, Gambia, Guinea, Guinea-Bissau, Haiti, Kiribati, Lao People's Democratic Republic, Lesotho, Liberia, Madagascar, Malawi, Maldives, Mali, Mauritania, Mozambique, Myanmar, Nepal, Niger, Rwanda, Samoa, Sao Tome and Principe, Sierra Leone, Solomon Islands, Somalia, Sudan, Togo, Tuvalu, Uganda, United Republic of Tanzania, Vanuatu, Yemen, Zambia.

# Fig.1 Estimated number of adult illiterates and distribution by gender and by region, 1980, 1990 and 2000

**Nombre estimé d'adultes analphabètes et distribution par sexe et par région,** 1980, 1990 et 2000

**Número estimado de adultos analfabetos y distribución por sexo y por región,** 1980, 1990 y 2000

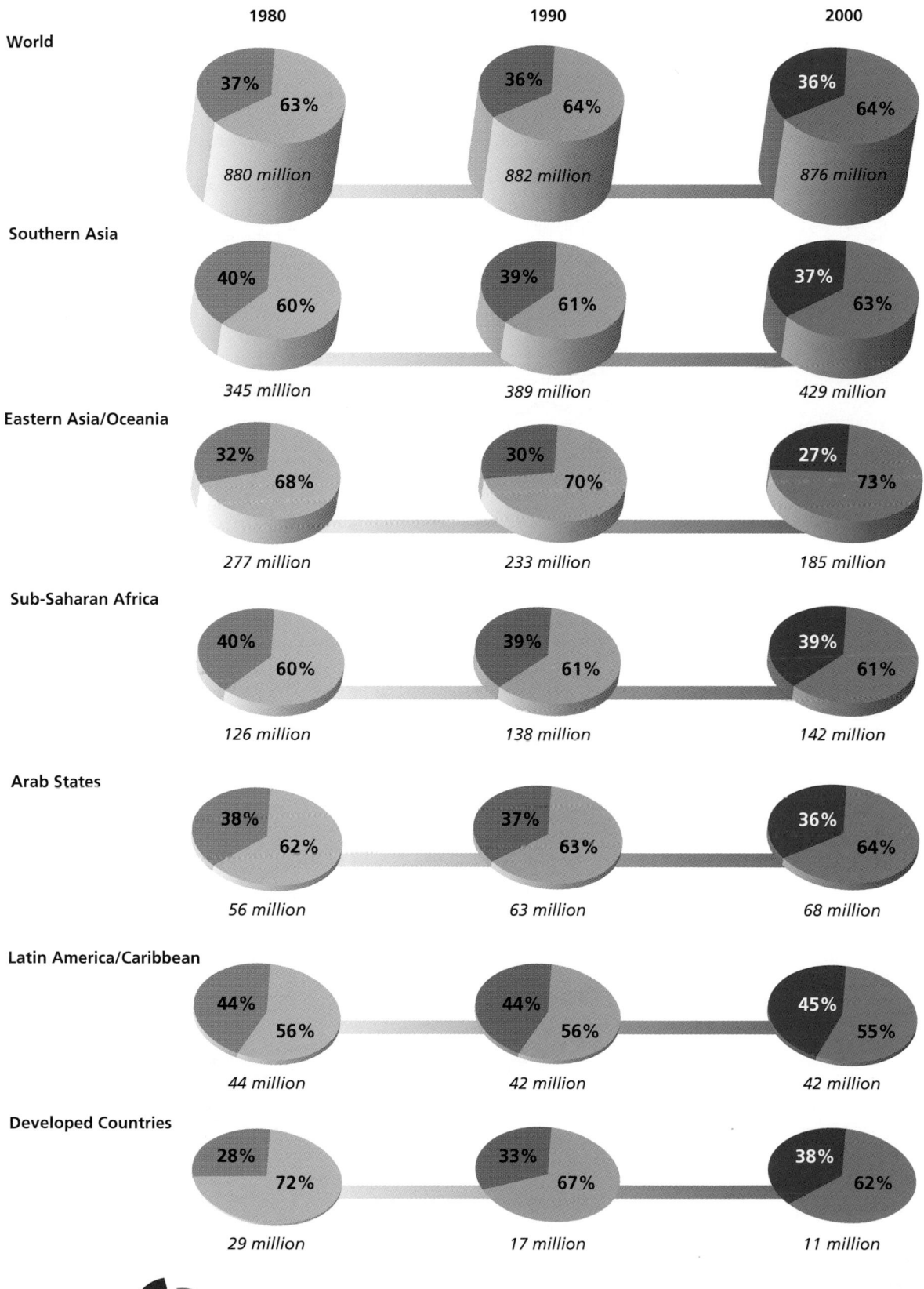

|  | 1980 | 1990 | 2000 |
|---|---|---|---|
| **World** | 37% 63% 880 million | 36% 64% 882 million | 36% 64% 876 million |
| **Southern Asia** | 40% 60% 345 million | 39% 61% 389 million | 37% 63% 429 million |
| **Eastern Asia/Oceania** | 32% 68% 277 million | 30% 70% 233 million | 27% 73% 185 million |
| **Sub-Saharan Africa** | 40% 60% 126 million | 39% 61% 138 million | 39% 61% 142 million |
| **Arab States** | 38% 62% 56 million | 37% 63% 63 million | 36% 64% 68 million |
| **Latin America/Caribbean** | 44% 56% 44 million | 44% 56% 42 million | 45% 55% 42 million |
| **Developed Countries** | 28% 72% 29 million | 33% 67% 17 million | 38% 62% 11 million |

Male

Female

Reference | Table II.S.1
Référence | Tableau II.S.1
Referencia | Cuadro II.S.1

# Fig.2  Estimated adult illiteracy rates by gender and by region, 1970 to 2000

Taux estimés d'analphabétisme des adultes par sexe et par région, 1970 à 2000

Tasas estimadas de analfabetismo de adultos por sexo y por región, 1970 a 2000

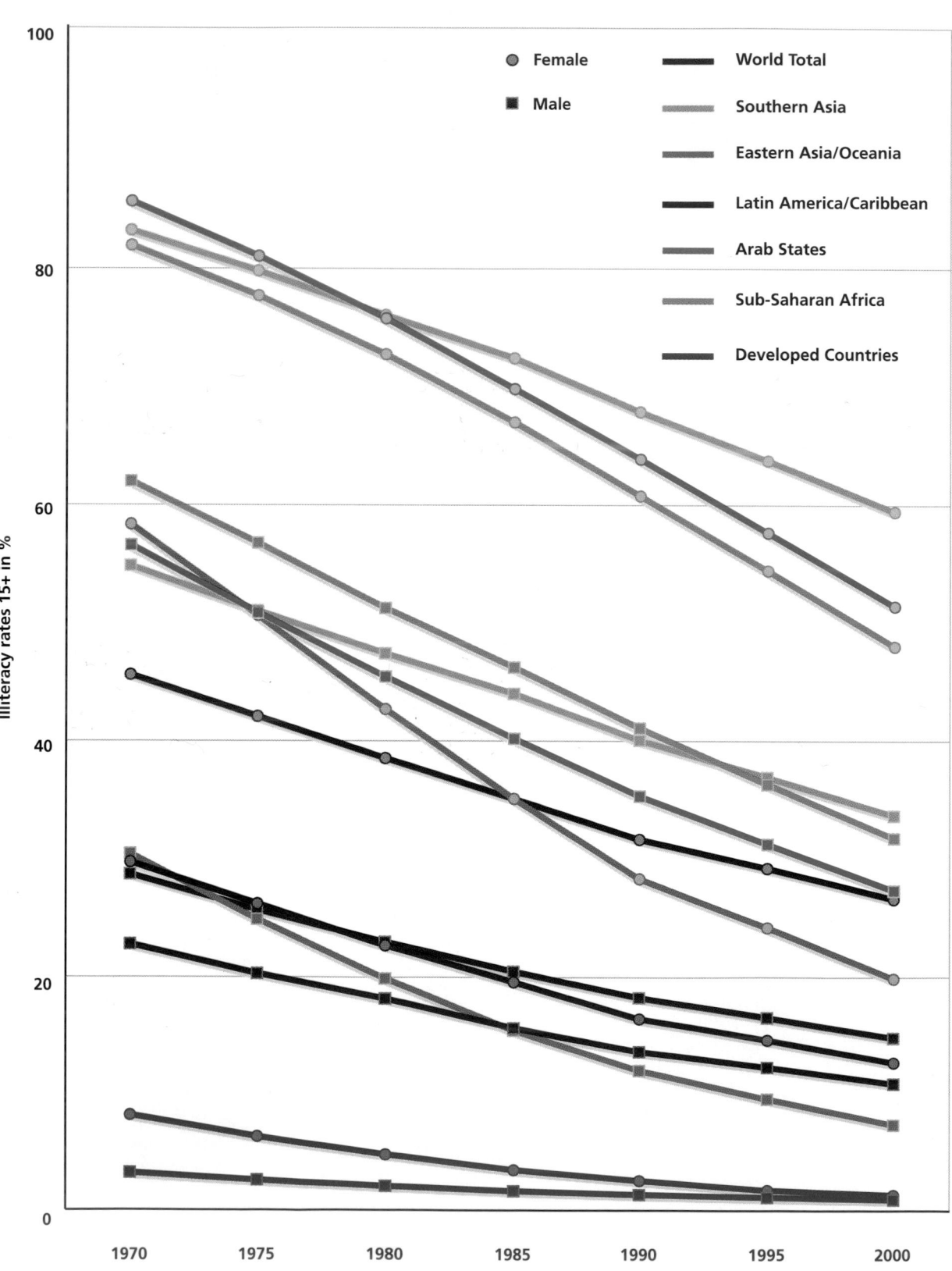

Reference | Table II.S.1
Référence | Tableau II.S.1
Referencia | Cuadro II.S.1

Fig.5

**Fig.3** **Estimated adult illiteracy rates, 2000**

Taux estimés d'analphabétisme des adultes, 2000

Tasas estimadas de analfabetismo de adultos, 2000

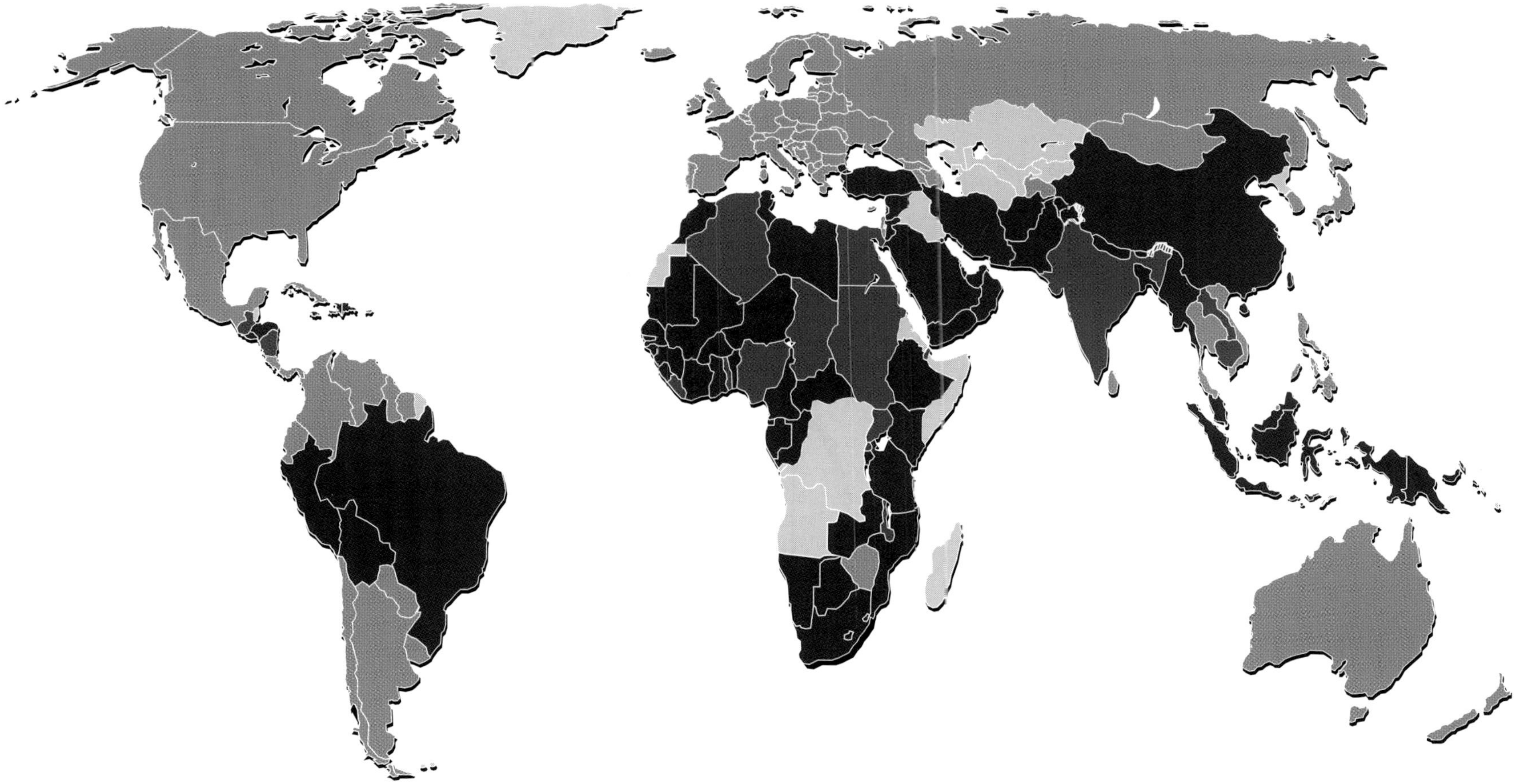

50% and more

30% to < 50%

10% to < 30%

less than 10%

data not avalaible

Reference | Table II.2
Référence | Tableau II.2
Referencia | Cuadro II.2

## Fig.14 Circulation of daily general-interest newspapers per 1 000 inhabitants, 1996

Diffusion des journaux quotidiens d'information générale pour 1 000 habitants, 1996

Difusión de la tirada de periódicos diaros de información general por 1 000 habitantes, 1996

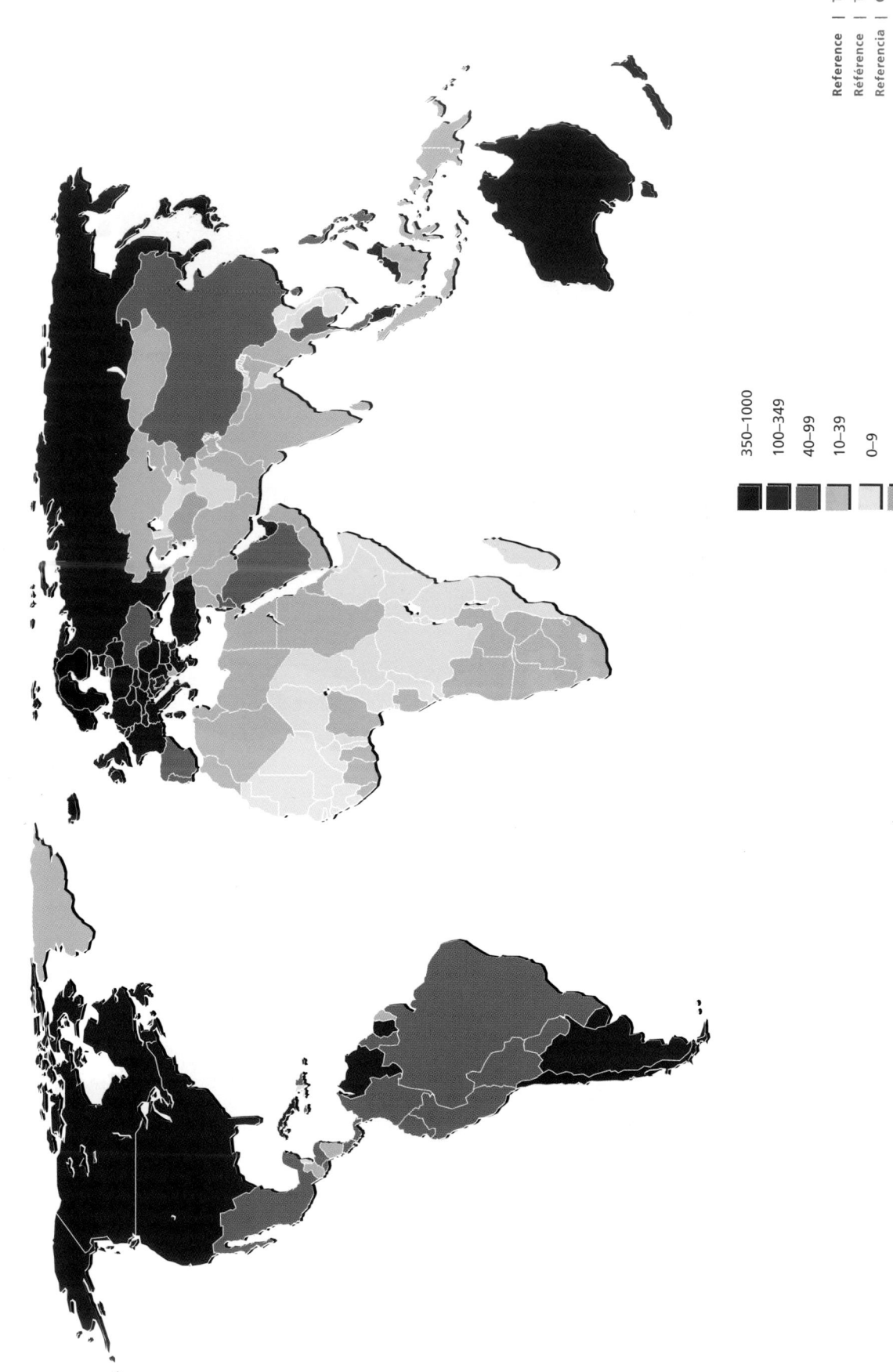

350–1000

100–349

40–99

10–39

0–9

No known daily publication

Reference | Table IV.8
Référence | Tableau IV.8
Referencia | Cuadro IV.8

**Fig.15  Number of television receivers, per 1 000 inhabitants, 1980**

Nombre de postes récepteurs de télévision pour 1 000 habitants, 1980

Número de receptores de televisión por 1 000 habitantes, 1980

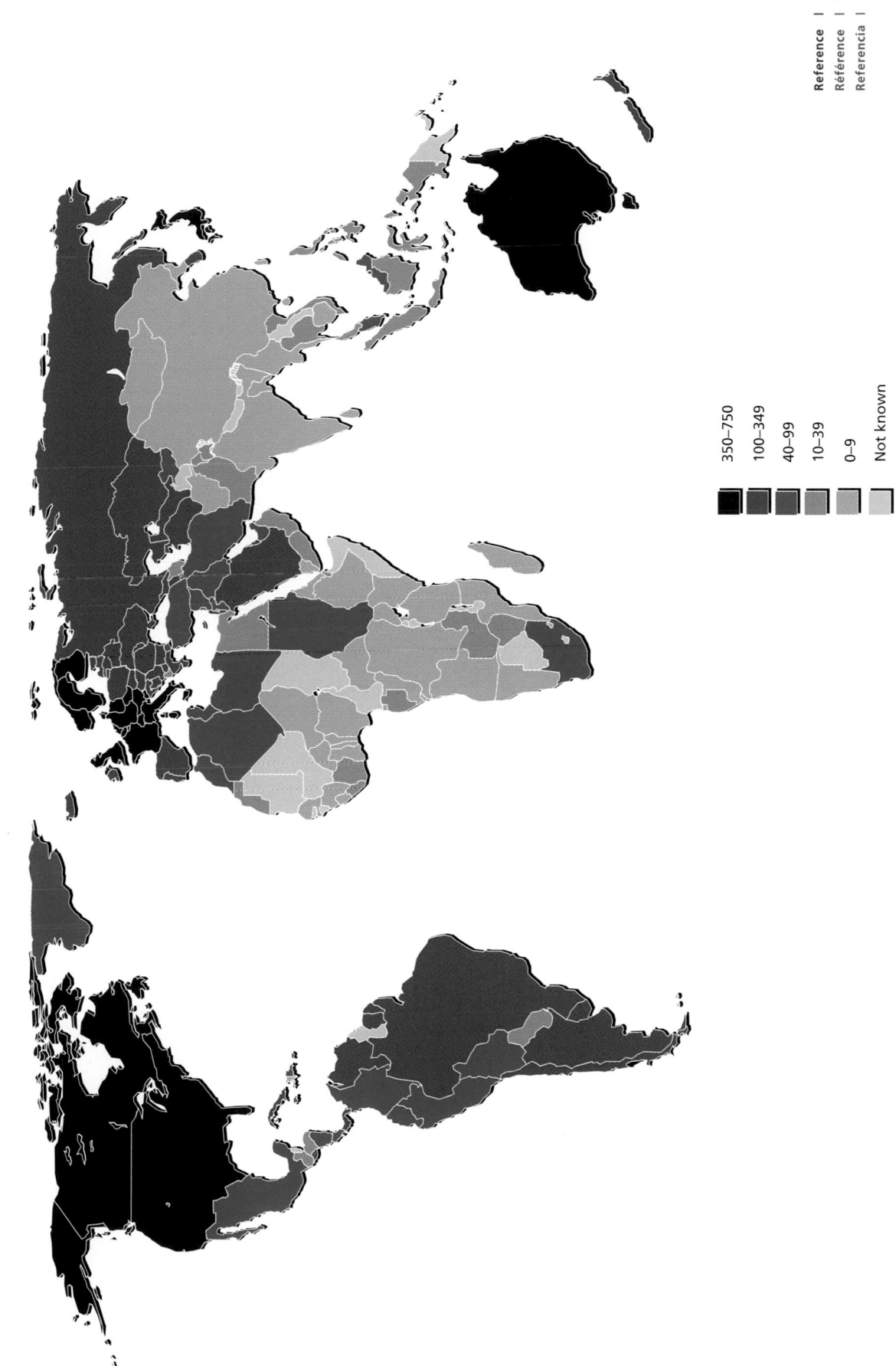

350–750

100–349

40–99

10–39

0–9

Not known

Reference  |  **Table IV.14**

Référence  |  Tableau IV.14

Referencia  |  Cuadro IV.14

**Fig. 16  Number of television receivers, per 1 000 inhabitants,** 1997

**Nombre de postes récepteurs de télévision pour 1 000 habitants,** 1997

**Número de receptores de televisión por 1 000 habitantes,** 1997

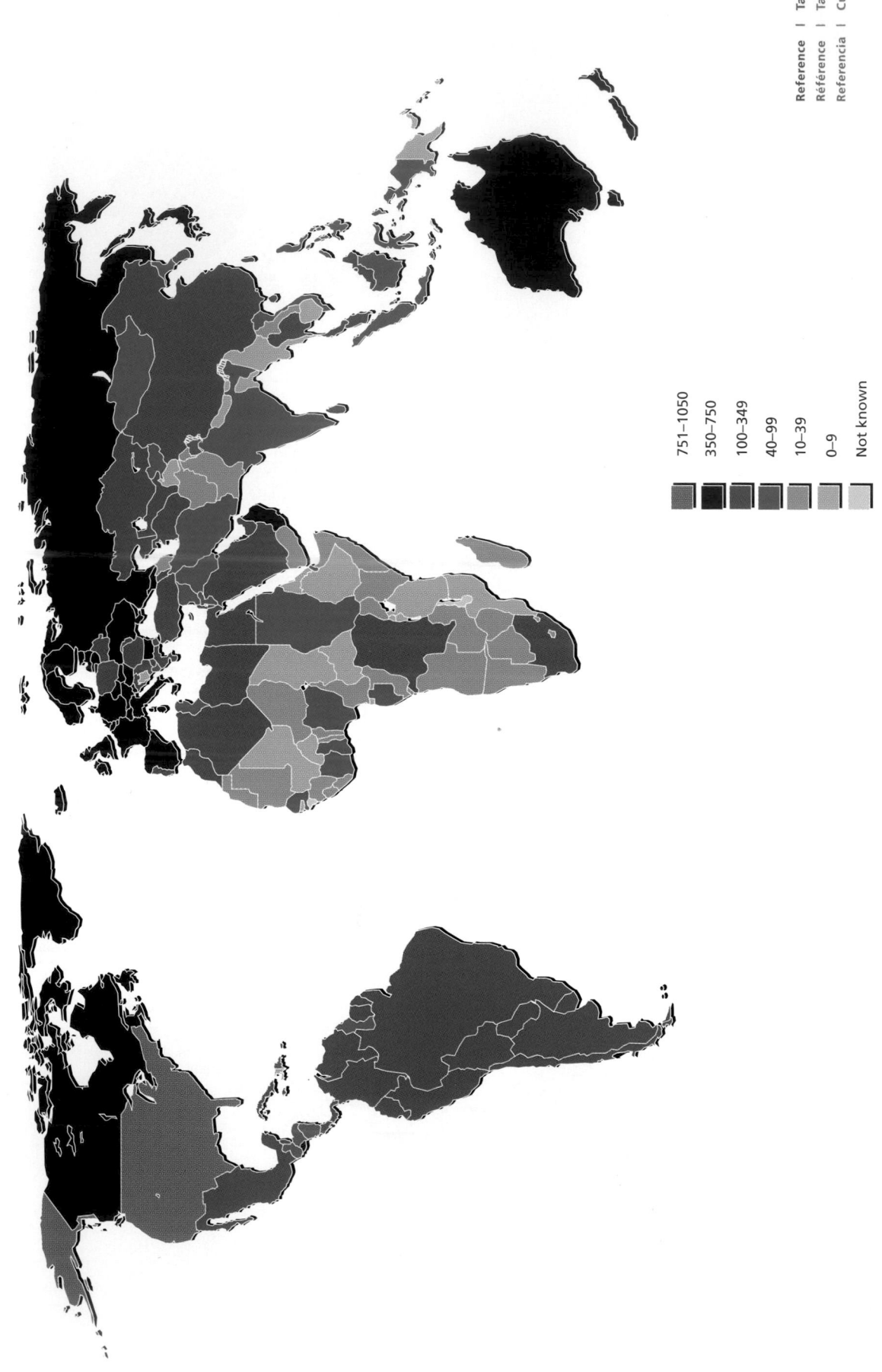

751–1050
350–750
100–349
40–99
10–39
0–9
Not known

Reference  |  Table IV.14
Référence  |  Tableau IV.14
Referencia  |  Cuadro IV.14

# II.   Education

# Éducation

# Educación

The education chapter of this *Yearbook* comprises five summary regional tables and twenty country tables that present statistics and indicators on literacy, educational attainment, students, graduates, teaching staff and expenditure on education.

For the purpose of these tables, the definitions and classifications applied are those set out in the Revised Recommendation concerning the International Standardization of Education Statistics (Paris, 1978) and those presented in the 1976 version of the International Standard Classification of Education (ISCED). In this context it should be noted that the revised version of ISCED (ISCED-97) was adopted by the General Conference of UNESCO in November 1997 and applied for the first time in the 1998 data collection.

As time series presented in this *Yearbook* relate to years preceding the adoption of the ISCED-97 the data reported for each level are based on the previous ISCED criteria. However, the revised ISCED terminology for the levels of education - 'pre-primary', 'primary', 'secondary', and 'tertiary' - is used in the present report in place of the old terms 'preceding the first level', 'first', 'second', and 'third level'.

According to ISCED these levels are defined as follows:

*Pre-primary education* (ISCED level 0) provided at e.g. nursery schools, kindergartens, infant schools, for children who are not old enough to enter school at the primary level.

*Primary education* (ISCED level 1), of which the main function is to provide the basic elements of education at such establishments as elementary schools, primary schools.

*Secondary education* (ISCED levels 2 and 3), providing general and/or specialized instruction at middle schools, secondary schools, high schools, teacher training schools and schools of a vocational or technical nature.

*Tertiary education* (ISCED levels 5, 6 and 7) provided at universities, teachers' colleges, higher professional schools, which requires, as a minimum condition of admission, the successful completion of secondary education or evidence of the attainment of an equivalent level of knowledge.

The statistics shown in this chapter refer in general to both public and private education.  Since 1994 special needs education is, in principle, included in the statistics reported.

Data on teaching staff refer to both full-time and part-time personnel with teaching functions, thus they exclude personnel without teaching functions such as librarians, guidance personnel, administrative staff, etc.

For countries taking part in the UNESCO/OECD/Eurostat (UOE) surveys there may have been breaks in the time series due to conceptual changes (extension of coverage regarding enrolment, teaching staff, etc. and inclusion of private spending in the statistics relating to expenditure on education).  These changes took effect in 1992 or later, depending on the country, and are indicated accordingly.

In the tables on basic data the year indicated represents the school or academic year (e.g. 1996 or 1996/97).  In tables on educational indicators, however, the year shown is that in which the school or academic year starts, e.g. 1996 refers to the school or academic year 1996 or 1996/97. In Tables II.18 to II.20 on expenditure, the year indicated refers to the calendar year in which the financial year begins.

Points specific to individual tables are set out below.

Le chapitre sur l'éducation de cet *Annuaire* comporte cinq tableaux régionaux récapitulatifs et vingt tableaux par pays qui présentent des statistiques et des indicateurs sur l'alphabétisme, le niveau d'instruction, les étudiants, les diplômés, le personnel enseignant et les dépenses d'éducation.

Pour ces tableaux, les définitions et classifications sont celles qui figurent dans la Recommandation révisée concernant la normalisation internationale des statistiques de l'éducation (Paris, 1978), ainsi que celles qui apparaissent dans la version de 1976 de la Classification Internationale Type de l'Education (CITE).

Dans ce sens, il faut noter que la version révisée de la CITE (CITE-97) a été adoptée par la Conférence Générale de l'UNESCO en novembre 1997 et utilisée pour la première fois lors de la collecte de données de 1998.

Dans la mesure où les séries temporelles se réfèrent aux années précédant l'adoption de la CITE-97, les critères sur lesquels reposent les données présentées dans cet *Annuaire* demeurent ceux de la version précédente. Cependant, la terminologie adoptée dans la version révisée de la CITE pour désigner les niveaux d'enseignement - "préprimaire", "primaire", "secondaire" et "supérieur" - a été reprise dans le présent rapport au lieu des anciennes appellations "précédant le premier degré", "premier degré", "second degré" et "troisième degré".

Conformément aux définitions de la CITE, ces niveaux d'enseignement sont classés de la façon suivante :

*Enseignement préprimaire* (Niveau 0 de la CITE) dispensé, par exemple, dans les écoles maternelles ou les jardins d'enfants, pour les enfants trop jeunes pour être admis à l'enseignement primaire.

*Enseignement primaire* (Niveau 1 de la CITE) dispensé, par exemple, dans les écoles élémentaires ou les écoles primaires et dont la fonction principale est de fournir les premiers éléments de l'instruction.

*Enseignement secondaire* (Niveaux 2 et 3 de la CITE) dispensé, par exemple, dans les écoles moyennes, les lycées, les collèges, les gymnases, les athénées, les écoles complémentaires, ainsi que dans les écoles destinées à la formation des maîtres et dans les écoles à caractère technique et professionnel ; cet enseignement donne une formation générale ou spécialisée.

*Enseignement supérieur* (Niveaux 5, 6 et 7 de la CITE) dispensé, par exemple, dans les universités, les grandes écoles et instituts supérieurs, y compris les écoles normales supérieures, exigeant comme condition minimale d'admission d'avoir suivi avec succès un enseignement complet du secondaire ou de faire preuve de connaissances équivalentes.

En règle générale, les statistiques présentées dans ce chapitre concernent à la fois l'enseignement public et privé. Depuis 1994, l'éducation répondant à des besoins spéciaux est en principe incluse dans les statistiques fournies par les pays.

Les données sur le personnel enseignant concernent à la fois le personnel à plein temps et à temps partiel chargé de fonctions d'enseignement, à l'exclusion donc du personnel dépourvu de ce type de fonctions tel que les bibliothécaires, les conseillers d'orientation professionnelle, le personnel administratif, etc.

Pour les pays qui ont pris part aux enquêtes de l'UNESCO/OCDE/EUROSTAT (UOE), on pourra trouver des discontinuités dans les séries temporelles en raison de changements conceptuels (extension de la couverture statistique au regard des effectifs scolaires, du personnel enseignant, etc., et l'inclusion des dépenses privées dans les données relatives aux dépenses d'éducation). Ces changements prennent effet en 1992 ou plus tard selon les pays, et sont indiqués le cas échéant.

Dans les tableaux sur les données de base, l'année indiquée se réfère à l'année scolaire ou universitaire (par exemple, 1996 ou 1996/97). Cependant, dans les tableaux sur les indicateurs de l'éducation, l'année indiquée est celle du début de l'année scolaire ou universitaire (ainsi, 1996 signifie l'année scolaire ou universitaire 1996 ou 1996/97). Dans les tableaux II.18 à II.20 sur les dépenses d'éducation, l'année indiquée est celle à laquelle commence l'exercice financier.

Les remarques spécifiques à chaque tableau sont présentées ci-dessous.

---

El capítulo sobre educación de este *Anuario* comprende cinco cuadros recapitulativos regionales y veinte cuadros por países que presentan estadísticas e indicadores sobre la alfabetización, el nivel de instrucción, los estudiantes, los diplomados, el personal docente y los gastos de educación.

En estos cuadros, las definiciones y clasificaciones son aquéllas presentadas en la Recomendación revisada sobre la normalización internacional de las estadísticas relativas a la educación (París, 1978), así como las definiciones que figuran en la versión de 1976 de la Clasificación Internacional Normalizada de la Educación (CINE).

En ese sentido, cabe observar que la versión revisada de la CINE (CINE-97) fue adoptada por la Conferencia General de la UNESCO en noviembre de 1997 y aplicada por primera vez en la colecta de datos estadísticos de 1998.

En la medida en que las series temporales se refieran a los años que preceden la adopción de la CINE-97, los datos facilitados en este *Anuario* sobre los distintos niveles se basan en los criterios de la antigua CINE. Sin embargo, en el presente informe se utiliza la terminología de la CINE revisada relativa a los niveles de enseñanza - "preprimaria", "primaria", "secundaria" y "superior" - en lugar de los términos anteriores "anterior al primer grado", "primer grado", "segundo grado" y "tercer grado".

Según las definiciones de la CINE, los niveles de enseñanza son los siguientes:

*Enseñanza preprimaria* (Nivel 0 de la CINE) la que se da, por ejemplo, en guarderías infantiles, escuelas de párvulos o jardines de la infancia, para los niños que no están aún en edad de ser admitidos en la enseñanza primaria.

*Enseñanza primaria* (Nivel 1 de la CINE) la que se da, por ejemplo, en escuelas elementales o en escuelas primarias, cuya función principal consiste en proporcionar los primeros elementos de la instrucción.

*Enseñanza secundaria* (Niveles 2 y 3 de la CINE) la que se da, por ejemplo, en escuelas de enseñanza media, secundarias, institutos, liceos, colegios, escuelas técnicas, escuelas normales y que da una formación general o especializada.

*Enseñanza superior* (Niveles 5, 6 y 7 de la CINE) la que se da, por ejemplo, en las universidades, escuelas técnicas superiores y escuelas normales superiores, y que requiere como condición mínima haber terminado con éxito la enseñanza secundaria o demostrar la posesión de conocimientos equivalentes.

En general, las estadísticas presentadas en este capítulo se refieren a la vez a la enseñanza pública y privada. Desde 1994, la educación para necesidades especiales está en principio incluida en los datos presentados.

Los datos sobre el personal docente se refieren a la vez al personal de jornada completa y de jornada parcial con funciones de enseñanza. Por lo tanto, se excluye al personal que no tiene funciones de enseñanza tal como los bibliotecarios, los consejeros de orientación profesional, el personal administrativo, etc.

En cuanto a los países que participaron en las encuestas de la UNESCO/OCDE/EUROSTAT (UOE), se podrán constatar discontinuidades en las series temporales, debido a cambios conceptuales (extensión de la cobertura estadística referente a la matrícula, al personal docente, etc., y la inclusión del gasto privado en las estadísticas relativas al gasto de educación). Estos cambios toman efecto en 1992 o más tarde según los países, y son indicados en cada caso.

En los cuadros sobre los datos de base, el año indicado representa el año escolar o universitario (por ejemplo, 1996 ó 1996/97). Sin embargo, en los cuadros sobre los indicadores de educación, el año indicado es el año en que comienza el año escolar o universitario (por ejemplo, 1996 significa el año escolar o universitario 1996 ó 1996/97). En los cuadros II.18 a II.20 relativos al gasto público destinado a la educación, el año indicado se refiere al año en que comienza el ejercicio económico.

Las observaciones específicas para cada cuadro se encuentran a continuación.

---

II.S    Summary tables on literacy and education by groups of countries
        Tableaux récapitulatifs sur l'alphabétisme et l'enseignement par groupes de pays
        Cuadros recapitulativos sobre la alfabetización y la enseñanza por grupos de países

# Summary tables on literacy and education by groups of countries

# Tableaux récapitulatifs sur l'alphabétisme et l'enseignement par groupes de pays

# Cuadros recapitulativos sobre la alfabetización y la enseñanza por grupos de países

These tables provide a summary presentation of data on literacy and education, thus conveying a general picture of the quantitative development since 1970 in adult illiteracy, enrolment, teaching staff and gross enrolment ratios, in the whole world and in each major area and group of countries (for their composition see the list on page I-10).

Ces tableaux présentent des données récapitulatives sur l'alphabétisme et l'enseignement. Ils donnent ainsi une idée générale sur l'évolution quantitative depuis 1970 de l'analphabétisme des adultes, des effectifs d'élèves et d'enseignants et des taux bruts d'inscription, dans le monde et dans chaque grande région et groupe de pays (en ce qui concerne leur composition, voir la liste, page I-10).

En estos cuadros se presentan datos recapitulativos sobre alfabetización y educación que dan una idea general del desarrollo cuantitativo, desde 1970, del analfabetismo de adultos, de la matrícula, del personal docente y de las tasas brutas de escolarización, en el mundo y en cada una de las grandes regiones y grupos de países (puede verse su composición en la página I-10).

Summary tables on literacy and education by groups of countries **II.S**
Tableaux récapitulatifs sur l'alphabétisme et l'enseignement par groupes de pays
Cuadros recapitulativos sobre la alfabetización y la enseñanza por grupos de países

## Notes and explanations on summary tables

## Notes et explications sur les tableaux récapitulatifs

## Notas y explicaciones de los cuadros recapitulativos

### Table II.S.1 Estimated illiteracy rate and illiterate population aged 15 years and over

This table provides trends of illiteracy rates and adult illiterate population aged 15 and over by major areas and groups of countries. The data presented in this table are the latest literacy estimates and projections of UNESCO, as assessed in 1998 based on statistics collected during national population censuses.

### Table II.S.2 Pre-primary education: teaching staff and enrolment

The data in this table are estimates based on the enrolment and teachers figures shown for each individual country and territory in Table II.4 of this *Yearbook*.

### Table II.S.3 Enrolment by level of education

Data in this table are estimates based on the enrolment figures shown for each country and territory in Tables II.5 to II.7 of this *Yearbook*. The definitions for each level of education are given in the introductory text to this Chapter. It should be noted that the breakdown by level of education is influenced by the length of schooling at each level, which in turn depends on the criteria applied in national definitions of levels. Please refer to Table II.1 for the duration of each level of education and to Table II.8, on enrolment ratios, for the changes in the education structures since 1970.

### Table II.S.4 Teaching staff by level of education

Data in this table are estimates based on the figures on teaching staff shown for each country and territory in Tables II.5 to II.7 of this *Yearbook*. The definitions for each level of education are given in the introductory text to this Chapter. It should be noted that the breakdown by level of education is influenced by the length of schooling at each level, which in turn depends on the criteria applied in national definitions of levels. Please refer to Table II.1 for the duration of each level of education and to Table II.8, on enrolment ratios, for the changes in the education structures since 1970.

### Table II.S.5 Gross enrolment ratios by level of education

This table presents adjusted gross enrolment ratios by level of education and by sex. The data are based on the enrolment estimates presented in Table II.S.3 and the medium variant of the population estimates and projections as assessed in 1998 by the United Nations Population Division. A gross enrolment ratio for a given level of education is derived by dividing the total enrolment for this level of education, regardless of age, by the population of the age group which according to national regulations, should be enrolled at this level. The term *adjusted* indicates that the population groups corresponding to the education system of each country have been used to derive the regional ratios. For tertiary education a duration of five years following the end of secondary general education was used for all countries. The ratios reflect all changes in the structure of the education systems, which occurred during the period. These are indicated in Table II.8 on enrolment ratios. All ratios are expressed as percentages and may exceed 100 because of early entry, repetition, etc.

---

### Tableau II.S.1 Estimations du taux d'analphabétisme et de la population analphabète âgée de 15 ans et plus

Ce tableau donne l'évolution des taux d'analphabétisme et du nombre d'adultes analphabètes âgés de 15 ans et plus, par grandes régions et groupes de pays. Les données présentées dans ce tableau sont les dernières estimations et projections de l'UNESCO sur l'alphabétisme, révisées en 1998 et basées sur les données collectées au cours des recensements nationaux de la population.

### Tableau II.S.2 Enseignement préprimaire : personnel enseignant et effectifs scolaires

Les données de ce tableau sont des estimations basées sur les chiffres des effectifs scolaires et du personnel enseignant présentés pour chaque pays et territoire dans le tableau II.4 de cet *Annuaire*.

### Tableau II.S.3 Effectifs scolaires par niveau d'enseignement

Les données dans ce tableau sont des estimations basées sur les chiffres des effectifs scolaires présentés par pays et par territoires dans les tableaux II.5 à II.7 de cet *Annuaire*. Les définitions pour chaque niveau d'enseignement sont présentées dans le texte d'introduction de ce chapitre. Il convient de noter que la répartition par niveau d'enseignement dépend de la durée de la scolarité à chaque niveau, qui dépend à son tour des critères adoptés dans les définitions nationales de ces niveaux. Pour la durée de chaque niveau d'enseignement on pourra consulter le tableau II.1 et, pour les changements dans les structures de l'enseignement depuis 1970, le tableau II.8 sur les taux de scolarisation.

### Tableau II.S.4 Personnel enseignant par niveau d'enseignement

Les données de ce tableau sont des estimations basées sur les chiffres du personnel enseignant présentées pour chaque pays et territoire dans les tableaux II.5 à II.7 de cet *Annuaire*. Les définitions pour chaque niveau d'enseignement sont présentées dans le texte d'introduction de ce chapitre. Il convient de noter que la répartition par niveau d'enseignement dépend de la durée de la scolarité à chaque niveau, qui dépend à son tour des critères adoptés dans les définitions nationales de ces niveaux. Pour la durée des niveaux d'enseignement on pourra consulter le tableau II.1 et, pour les changements dans les structures de l'enseignement depuis 1970, le tableau II.8 sur les taux de scolarisation.

**II.S**    Summary tables on literacy and education by groups of countries
Tableaux récapitulatifs sur l'alphabétisme et l'enseignement par groupes de pays
Cuadros recapitulativos sobre la alfabetización y la enseñanza por grupos de países

**Tableau II.S.5  Taux bruts de scolarisation par niveau d'enseignement**

Ce tableau présente les taux bruts de scolarisation ajustés par niveau d'enseignement et par sexe. Les données correspondent aux estimations des effectifs d'élèves présentées dans le tableau II.S.3 et à la variante moyenne des estimations et projections de la population effectuées par la Division de la Population des Nations Unies en 1998. Un taux brut de scolarisation pour un niveau d'enseignement donné est obtenu en divisant le total des effectifs scolaires de ce niveau d'enseignement, sans tenir compte de l'âge, par la population du groupe d'âge qui, suivant les systèmes nationaux, devrait être scolarisée à ce niveau. Le terme *ajusté* indique que les groupes de population utilisés pour calculer les taux régionaux correspondent au système d'éducation de chaque pays. Pour l'enseignement supérieur, une durée de 5 ans à partir de la fin de l'enseignement secondaire général a été utilisée pour tous les pays. Les taux reflètent les changements dans la structure du système de l'enseignement qui ont eu lieu pendant la période considérée. Ces changements sont indiqués dans le tableau II.8 sur les taux de scolarisation. Tous les taux sont exprimés en pourcentage et peuvent être supérieurs à 100, en raison des admissions précoces, des redoublements, etc.

---

**Cuadro II.S.1  Estimaciones de la tasa de analfabetismo y de la población analfabeta de 15 años y más**

Este cuadro presenta la evolución de las tasas de analfabetismo y del número de adultos analfabetos de 15 años y más, por grandes áreas y grupos de países. Los datos presentados en este cuadro son las últimas estimaciones y proyecciones de la UNESCO sobre la alfabetización, revisadas en 1998 y basadas en los datos acopiados en los censos nacionales de población.

**Cuadro II.S.2  Enseñanza preprimaria: personal docente y matrícula escolar**

Los datos de este cuadro son estimaciones basadas en las estadísticas sobre la matrícula escolar y el personal docente presentadas para cada país y territorio en el cuadro II.4 de este *Anuario*.

**Cuadro II.S.3  Matrícula escolar por nivel de enseñanza**

Los datos de este cuadro son estimaciones basadas en las cifras de la matrícula escolar por país y territorio que se presentan en los cuadros II.5 a II.7 de este *Anuario*. Las definiciones de los niveles de enseñanza se encuentran en el texto de introducción de este capítulo. Cabe señalar que la distribución por nivel de enseñanza depende de la duración de la escolaridad en cada nivel que, a su vez, depende de los criterios adoptados en las definiciones nacionales de dichos niveles. Se podrá consultar el cuadro II.1 referido a la duración de cada nivel de enseñanza y el cuadro II.8, sobre las tasas de escolarización, para los cambios en las estructuras de la enseñanza desde 1970.

**Cuadro II.S.4  Personal docente por nivel de enseñanza**

Los datos de este cuadro son estimaciones basadas en las cifras del personal docente presentadas por país y territorio en los cuadros II.5 a II.7 de este *Anuario*. Las definiciones de los niveles de enseñanza se encuentran en el texto de introducción de este capítulo. Cabe señalar que la distribución por nivel de enseñanza depende de la duración de la escolaridad en cada nivel que, a su vez, depende de los criterios adoptados en las definiciones nacionales de dichos niveles. Se podrá consultar el cuadro II.1 para la duración de cada nivel de enseñanza y el cuadro II.8 sobre las tasas de escolarización, para los cambios en las estructuras de la enseñanza desde 1970.

**Cuadro II.S.5  Tasas brutas de escolarización por nivel de enseñanza**

Este cuadro presenta las tasas brutas de escolarización ajustadas por nivel de enseñanza y por sexo. Los datos se refieren a las estimaciones de las matrículas escolares presentadas en el cuadro II.S.3 y a la variante media de las estimaciones y proyecciones de la población de la División de la Población de las Naciones Unidas, según la revisión de 1998. Una tasa bruta para un nivel de enseñanza dado se obtiene dividiendo el total de la matrícula del nivel de enseñanza en cuestión, independientemente de la edad, por la población del grupo de edad que, de acuerdo con las normas nacionales, debe de estar inscrita en ese nivel. El término *ajustado* indica que los grupos de población utilizados para calcular las tasas regionales corresponden al sistema de educación de cada país. Para la enseñanza superior, una duración de 5 años al final de la enseñanza secundaria general fue utilizada para todos los países. Las tasas reflejan los cambios ocurridos en la estructura del sistema de la enseñanza durante el periodo considerado. Estos cambios se indican en el cuadro II.8 sobre las tasas de escolarización. Todas las tasas están expresadas en porcentajes y pueden ser superiores al 100, debido a ingresos precoces, repetición, etc.

---

Estimated illiteracy rate and illiterate population    II.S.1
Estimations du taux d'analphabétisme et de la population analphabète
Estimaciones de la tasa de analfabetismo y de la población analfabeta

## II.S.1   Estimated illiteracy rate and illiterate population
### aged 15 years and over

### Estimations du taux d'analphabétisme et de la population analphabète
### âgée de 15 ans et plus

### Estimaciones de la tasa de analfabetismo y de la población analfabeta
### de 15 años y más

| Continents, major areas and groups of countries / Continents, grandes régions et groupes de pays / Continentes, grandes regiones y grupos de países | Year / Annóo / Año | Population aged 15 years and over / Population âgée de 15 ans et plus / Población de 15 años y más | | | | | |
|---|---|---|---|---|---|---|---|
| | | Illiteracy rate / Taux d'analphabetisme / Tasa de analfabetismo (%) | | | Illiterate population / Population analphabète / Población analfabeta (000 000) | | |
| | | MF | M | F | MF | M | F |
| World total | 1970 | 37.0 | 28.5 | 45.2 | 854 | 326 | 528 |
| | 1980 | 30.6 | 22.8 | 38.2 | 880 | 327 | 553 |
| | 1990 | 24.8 | 18.1 | 31.4 | 882 | 322 | 560 |
| | 1995 | 22.7 | 16.4 | 29.0 | 884 | 318 | 565 |
| | 2000 | 20.6 | 14.7 | 26.4 | 876 | 313 | 563 |
| Africa | 1970 | 71.6 | 60.6 | 82.2 | 141 | 58 | 83 |
| | 1980 | 61.8 | 50.0 | 73.1 | 159 | 63 | 96 |
| | 1990 | 51.0 | 40.2 | 61.5 | 174 | 68 | 107 |
| | 1995 | 45.6 | 35.6 | 55.4 | 179 | 69 | 110 |
| | 2000 | 40.3 | 31.3 | 49.1 | 182 | 70 | 112 |
| America | 1970 | 14.7 | 12.7 | 16.7 | 49 | 20 | 28 |
| | 1980 | 11.7 | 10.3 | 13.0 | 48 | 21 | 27 |
| | 1990 | 9.0 | 8.1 | 9.9 | 45 | 20 | 25 |
| | 1995 | 8.2 | 7.5 | 8.9 | 45 | 20 | 25 |
| | 2000 | 7.3 | 6.7 | 7.9 | 44 | 20 | 24 |
| Asia | 1970 | 49.1 | 36.7 | 61.9 | 629 | 239 | 390 |
| | 1980 | 39.4 | 28.2 | 50.9 | 648 | 236 | 412 |
| | 1990 | 30.5 | 21.2 | 40.1 | 648 | 230 | 418 |
| | 1995 | 27.7 | 18.9 | 36.7 | 648 | 225 | 423 |
| | 2000 | 24.9 | 16.8 | 33.2 | 641 | 220 | 421 |
| Europe | 1970 | 6.9 | 3.5 | 9.9 | 34 | 8 | 26 |
| | 1980 | 4.2 | 2.3 | 5.9 | 23 | 6 | 17 |
| | 1990 | 2.3 | 1.4 | 3.0 | 13 | 4 | 9 |
| | 1995 | 1.6 | 1.2 | 2.1 | 10 | 3 | 6 |
| | 2000 | 1.3 | 0.9 | 1.5 | 8 | 3 | 5 |
| Oceania | 1970 | 10.7 | 8.2 | 13.2 | 1.4 | 0.5 | 0.9 |
| | 1980 | 7.9 | 6.0 | 9.8 | 1.3 | 0.5 | 0.8 |
| | 1990 | 6.0 | 4.5 | 7.4 | 1.2 | 0.4 | 0.7 |
| | 1995 | 5.2 | 3.9 | 6.5 | 1.1 | 0.4 | 0.7 |
| | 2000 | 4.6 | 3.4 | 5.8 | 1.1 | 0.4 | 0.7 |
| Developing countries | 1970 | 51.9 | 39.8 | 64.2 | 812 | 315 | 497 |
| | 1980 | 41.8 | 30.9 | 52.9 | 851 | 319 | 532 |
| | 1990 | 32.6 | 23.5 | 41.9 | 865 | 316 | 549 |
| | 1995 | 29.5 | 21.0 | 38.1 | 870 | 314 | 557 |
| | 2000 | 26.3 | 18.6 | 34.2 | 865 | 309 | 556 |
| of which: | | | | | | | |
| Sub-Saharan Africa | 1970 | 71.6 | 61.5 | 81.3 | 113 | 47 | 66 |
| | 1980 | 61.7 | 50.8 | 72.2 | 126 | 51 | 75 |
| | 1990 | 50.7 | 40.7 | 60.3 | 138 | 54 | 83 |
| | 1995 | 45.2 | 36.0 | 54.0 | 141 | 55 | 86 |
| | 2000 | 39.7 | 31.5 | 47.6 | 142 | 55 | 86 |

**Estimated illiteracy rate and illiterate population**
Estimations du taux d'analphabétisme et de la population analphabète
Estimaciones de la tasa de analfabetismo y de la población analfabeta

| Continents, major areas and groups of countries / Continents, grandes régions et groupes de pays / Continentes, grandes regiones y grupos de países | Year / Année / Año | Population aged 15 years and over / Population âgée de 15 ans et plus / Población de 15 años y más | | | | | |
|---|---|---|---|---|---|---|---|
| | | Illiteracy rate / Taux d'analphabétisme / Tasa de analfabetismo (%) | | | Illiterate population / Population analphabète / Población analfabeta (000 000) | | |
| | | MF | M | F | MF | M | F |
| Arab States | 1970 | 70.7 | 56.1 | 85.0 | 49 | 19 | 29 |
| | 1980 | 60.0 | 45.0 | 75.2 | 56 | 21 | 35 |
| | 1990 | 48.8 | 35.0 | 63.4 | 63 | 23 | 40 |
| | 1995 | 43.8 | 31.0 | 57.2 | 66 | 24 | 42 |
| | 2000 | 38.8 | 27.1 | 51.0 | 68 | 24 | 44 |
| Latin America and the Caribbean | 1970 | 26.1 | 22.6 | 29.5 | 43 | 18 | 24 |
| | 1980 | 20.3 | 18.0 | 22.5 | 44 | 19 | 25 |
| | 1990 | 14.9 | 13.5 | 16.3 | 42 | 19 | 23 |
| | 1995 | 13.3 | 12.2 | 14.5 | 42 | 19 | 24 |
| | 2000 | 11.7 | 10.8 | 12.6 | 42 | 19 | 23 |
| Eastern Asia and Oceania | 1970 | 43.9 | 30.2 | 57.9 | 304 | 106 | 198 |
| | 1980 | 30.8 | 19.7 | 42.3 | 277 | 90 | 187 |
| | 1990 | 19.9 | 11.9 | 28.1 | 233 | 71 | 162 |
| | 1995 | 16.6 | 9.5 | 24.0 | 212 | 61 | 151 |
| | 2000 | 13.4 | 7.3 | 19.7 | 185 | 51 | 134 |
| Southern Asia | 1970 | 68.0 | 54.4 | 82.6 | 299 | 124 | 176 |
| | 1980 | 60.7 | 47.0 | 75.5 | 345 | 138 | 207 |
| | 1990 | 53.1 | 39.7 | 67.4 | 389 | 150 | 239 |
| | 1995 | 49.5 | 36.6 | 63.3 | 409 | 156 | 254 |
| | 2000 | 45.8 | 33.4 | 59.0 | 429 | 161 | 268 |
| Least developed countries | 1970 | 73.2 | 62.1 | 84.5 | 126 | 53 | 73 |
| | 1980 | 66.0 | 54.2 | 77.7 | 144 | 59 | 86 |
| | 1990 | 57.7 | 46.5 | 68.8 | 162 | 65 | 98 |
| | 1995 | 53.7 | 42.9 | 64.4 | 174 | 69 | 105 |
| | 2000 | 49.3 | 39.2 | 59.5 | 184 | 73 | 112 |
| Developed countries | 1970 | 5.7 | 3.1 | 8.0 | 42 | 11 | 31 |
| | 1980 | 3.4 | 2.0 | 4.7 | 29 | 8 | 21 |
| | 1990 | 1.9 | 1.3 | 2.5 | 17 | 6 | 12 |
| | 1995 | 1.4 | 1.1 | 1.7 | 13 | 5 | 9 |
| | 2000 | 1.1 | 0.9 | 1.3 | 11 | 4 | 7 |

**General note**
For general explanations and definitions, please refer to the beginning of this chapter.

**Note générale**
Pour les explications et définitions générales, prière de se référer au début de ce chapitre.

**Nota general**
Para las explicaciones y definiciones generales, referirse al comienzo de este capítulo.

Pre-primary education: teaching staff and enrolment | II.S.2
Enseignement préprimaire: personnel enseignant et effectifs scolaires
Enseñanza preprimaria: personal docente y matrícula escolar

## II.S.2 Pre-primary education: teaching staff and enrolment

### Enseignement préprimaire: personnel enseignant et effectifs scolaires

### Enseñanza preprimaria: personal docente y matrícula escolar

| Continents, major areas and groups of countries / Continents, grandes régions et groupes de pays / Continentes, grandes regiones y grupos de países | Year / Année / Año | Teaching staff / Personnel enseignant / Personal docente | | | Enrolment / Effectifs scolaires / Matrícula escolar | | | |
|---|---|---|---|---|---|---|---|---|
| | | Total (000) | Female Femmes Femenino (000) | % F | Total (000) | Female Femmes Femenina (000) | % F | Private Privé Privada % |
| World total | 1970 | ... | ... | ... | ... | ... | ... | ... |
| | 1975 | 2 140 | 2 041 | 95 | 43 742 | 21 893 | 50 | 20 |
| | 1980 | 2 962 | 2 789 | 94 | 58 430 | 28 102 | 48 | 19 |
| | 1985 | 3 830 | 3 618 | 94 | 72 533 | 34 770 | 48 | 21 |
| | 1990 | 4 588 | 4 336 | 94 | 85 374 | 41 008 | 48 | 22 |
| | 1991 | 4 656 | 4 384 | 94 | 88 398 | 42 333 | 48 | 21 |
| | 1992 | 4 607 | 4 342 | 94 | 89 923 | 42 939 | 48 | 20 |
| | 1993 | 4 619 | 4 341 | 94 | 92 106 | 43 993 | 48 | 21 |
| | 1994 | 4 670 | 4 393 | 94 | 93 824 | 44 709 | 48 | 22 |
| | 1995 | 4 710 | 4 422 | 94 | 95 245 | 45 427 | 48 | 22 |
| | 1996 | 4 801 | 4 494 | 94 | 95 789 | 45 677 | 48 | 22 |
| | 1997 | 4 854 | 4 549 | 94 | 95 624 | 45 643 | 48 | 23 |
| Africa (1) | 1970 | 7 | 7 | 94 | 274 | 123 | 45 | 76 |
| | 1975 | 33 | 13 | 40 | 920 | 345 | 38 | 76 |
| | 1980 | 72 | 38 | 53 | 2 237 | 892 | 40 | 58 |
| | 1985 | 94 | 56 | 60 | 2 753 | 1 174 | 43 | 64 |
| | 1990 | 126 | 84 | 67 | 3 465 | 1 514 | 44 | 63 |
| | 1991 | 134 | 95 | 71 | 3 696 | 1 608 | 44 | 61 |
| | 1992 | 138 | 100 | 73 | 3 837 | 1 685 | 44 | 61 |
| | 1993 | 142 | 107 | 75 | 3 924 | 1 716 | 44 | 61 |
| | 1994 | 146 | 110 | 76 | 4 051 | 1 776 | 44 | 60 |
| | 1995 | 154 | 117 | 76 | 4 152 | 1 823 | 44 | 61 |
| | 1996 | 160 | 125 | 78 | 4 256 | 1 872 | 44 | 60 |
| | 1997 | 164 | 128 | 78 | 4 359 | 1 923 | 44 | 60 |
| America | 1970 | 260 | 251 | 97 | 6 467 | 3 153 | 49 | 28 |
| | 1975 | 327 | 313 | 96 | 8 337 | 4 073 | 49 | 31 |
| | 1980 | 406 | 390 | 96 | 10 299 | 4 998 | 49 | 32 |
| | 1985 | 643 | 617 | 96 | 16 136 | 7 909 | 49 | 28 |
| | 1990 | 821 | 790 | 96 | 19 693 | 9 549 | 48 | 29 |
| | 1991 | 856 | 821 | 96 | 20 431 | 9 992 | 49 | 28 |
| | 1992 | 875 | 839 | 96 | 21 256 | 10 371 | 49 | 23 |
| | 1993 | 907 | 870 | 96 | 22 049 | 10 764 | 49 | 23 |
| | 1994 | 950 | 910 | 96 | 22 574 | 11 018 | 49 | 27 |
| | 1995 | 987 | 937 | 95 | 23 273 | 11 431 | 49 | 28 |
| | 1996 | 1 035 | 972 | 94 | 23 745 | 11 667 | 49 | 27 |
| | 1997 | 1 052 | 990 | 94 | 24 072 | 11 844 | 49 | 28 |
| Asia | 1970 | ... | ... | ... | ... | ... | ... | ... |
| | 1975 | 578 | 524 | 91 | 14 163 | 6 877 | 49 | 21 |
| | 1980 | 922 | 808 | 88 | 22 846 | 10 896 | 48 | 19 |
| | 1985 | 1 237 | 1 138 | 92 | 29 426 | 13 913 | 47 | 20 |
| | 1990 | 1 635 | 1 505 | 92 | 37 567 | 18 007 | 48 | 20 |
| | 1991 | 1 686 | 1 537 | 91 | 40 149 | 19 096 | 48 | 18 |
| | 1992 | 1 741 | 1 588 | 91 | 42 197 | 20 009 | 47 | 18 |
| | 1993 | 1 767 | 1 608 | 91 | 44 017 | 20 890 | 47 | 17 |
| | 1994 | 1 773 | 1 618 | 91 | 45 182 | 21 371 | 47 | 18 |
| | 1995 | 1 758 | 1 603 | 91 | 45 614 | 21 544 | 47 | 18 |
| | 1996 | 1 790 | 1 626 | 91 | 45 654 | 21 529 | 47 | 18 |
| | 1997 | 1 815 | 1 651 | 91 | 44 977 | 21 223 | 47 | 18 |

**II.S.2**    Pre-primary education: teaching staff and enrolment
Enseignement préprimaire: personnel enseignant et effectifs scolaires
Enseñanza preprimaria: personal docente y matrícula escolar

| Continents, major areas and groups of countries / Continents, grandes régions et groupes de pays / Continentes, grandes regiones y grupos de países | Year / Année / Año | Teaching staff / Personnel enseignant / Personal docente | | | Enrolment / Effectifs scolaires / Matrícula escolar | | | |
|---|---|---|---|---|---|---|---|---|
| | | Total (000) | Female Femmes Femenino (000) | % F | Total (000) | Female Femmes Femenina (000) | % F | Private Privé Privada % |
| Europe | 1970 | 912 | 909 | 100 | 15 873 | 7 839 | 49 | 14 |
| | 1975 | 1 192 | 1 181 | 99 | 20 047 | 10 462 | 52 | 13 |
| | 1980 | 1 553 | 1 543 | 99 | 22 770 | 11 179 | 49 | 11 |
| | 1985 | 1 845 | 1 796 | 97 | 23 926 | 11 633 | 49 | 13 |
| | 1990 | 1 991 | 1 942 | 98 | 24 288 | 11 762 | 48 | 13 |
| | 1991 | 1 966 | 1 917 | 98 | 23 751 | 11 457 | 48 | 14 |
| | 1992 | 1 838 | 1 798 | 98 | 22 247 | 10 686 | 48 | 15 |
| | 1993 | 1 787 | 1 740 | 97 | 21 729 | 10 436 | 48 | 17 |
| | 1994 | 1 783 | 1 736 | 97 | 21 627 | 10 355 | 48 | 18 |
| | 1995 | 1 791 | 1 745 | 97 | 21 753 | 10 407 | 48 | 18 |
| | 1996 | 1 797 | 1 752 | 98 | 21 723 | 10 407 | 48 | 17 |
| | 1997 | 1 804 | 1 759 | 97 | 21 798 | 10 448 | 48 | 17 |
| Oceania | 1970 | 8 | 6 | 83 | 234 | 113 | 49 | 23 |
| | 1975 | 10 | 9 | 98 | 276 | 135 | 49 | 18 |
| | 1980 | 10 | 10 | 99 | 279 | 136 | 49 | 19 |
| | 1985 | 11 | 11 | 98 | 292 | 142 | 49 | 21 |
| | 1990 | 15 | 15 | 99 | 361 | 176 | 49 | 21 |
| | 1991 | 15 | 15 | 99 | 371 | 180 | 49 | 20 |
| | 1992 | 16 | 16 | 99 | 385 | 187 | 49 | 19 |
| | 1993 | 17 | 16 | 98 | 386 | 188 | 49 | 20 |
| | 1994 | 18 | 17 | 98 | 389 | 190 | 49 | 21 |
| | 1995 | 20 | 20 | 98 | 453 | 222 | 49 | 27 |
| | 1996 | 20 | 20 | 98 | 411 | 202 | 49 | 27 |
| | 1997 | 21 | 20 | 98 | 418 | 206 | 49 | 29 |
| Developing Countries | 1970 | ... | ... | ... | ... | ... | ... | ... |
| | 1975 | 491 | 427 | 87 | 13 733 | 6 411 | 47 | 20 |
| | 1980 | 902 | 764 | 85 | 25 202 | 11 877 | 47 | 21 |
| | 1985 | 1 386 | 1 250 | 90 | 36 964 | 17 434 | 47 | 23 |
| | 1990 | 1 912 | 1 735 | 91 | 47 955 | 22 902 | 48 | 23 |
| | 1991 | 1 994 | 1 799 | 90 | 51 328 | 24 460 | 48 | 22 |
| | 1992 | 2 063 | 1 866 | 90 | 54 393 | 25 876 | 48 | 21 |
| | 1993 | 2 139 | 1 938 | 91 | 57 142 | 27 198 | 48 | 20 |
| | 1994 | 2 233 | 2 034 | 91 | 59 206 | 28 116 | 47 | 21 |
| | 1995 | 2 285 | 2 075 | 91 | 60 466 | 28 703 | 47 | 21 |
| | 1996 | 2 373 | 2 143 | 90 | 61 101 | 28 971 | 47 | 21 |
| | 1997 | 2 417 | 2 190 | 91 | 60 856 | 28 890 | 47 | 21 |
| of which: | | | | | | | | |
| Sub-Saharan Africa | 1970 | 5 | 5 | 95 | 220 | 96 | 44 | 72 |
| | 1975 | 11 | 10 | 91 | 470 | 212 | 45 | 57 |
| | 1980 | 38 | 33 | 86 | 1 540 | 692 | 45 | 39 |
| | 1985 | 55 | 47 | 86 | 1 848 | 870 | 47 | 49 |
| | 1990 | 75 | 65 | 87 | 2 386 | 1 136 | 48 | 49 |
| | 1991 | 83 | 73 | 89 | 2 608 | 1 235 | 47 | 48 |
| | 1992 | 87 | 79 | 90 | 2 721 | 1 293 | 48 | 48 |
| | 1993 | 91 | 83 | 91 | 2 784 | 1 313 | 47 | 50 |
| | 1994 | 95 | 86 | 90 | 2 885 | 1 356 | 47 | 48 |
| | 1995 | 99 | 90 | 91 | 2 950 | 1 383 | 47 | 50 |
| | 1996 | 103 | 94 | 91 | 3 014 | 1 413 | 47 | 49 |
| | 1997 | 105 | 96 | 92 | 3 081 | 1 449 | 47 | 49 |
| Arab States (1) | 1970 | 7 | 7 | 96 | 293 | 136 | 47 | 80 |
| | 1975 | 31 | 12 | 38 | 767 | 280 | 37 | 83 |
| | 1980 | 54 | 24 | 44 | 1 203 | 436 | 36 | 84 |
| | 1985 | 68 | 34 | 50 | 1 600 | 605 | 38 | 81 |
| | 1990 | 88 | 52 | 59 | 1 921 | 743 | 39 | 77 |
| | 1991 | 91 | 57 | 62 | 2 019 | 816 | 40 | 77 |
| | 1992 | 93 | 60 | 65 | 2 094 | 850 | 41 | 78 |
| | 1993 | 99 | 68 | 69 | 2 139 | 873 | 41 | 79 |
| | 1994 | 100 | 70 | 70 | 2 175 | 885 | 41 | 78 |
| | 1995 | 106 | 76 | 72 | 2 228 | 907 | 41 | 79 |
| | 1996 | 111 | 82 | 74 | 2 308 | 938 | 41 | 78 |
| | 1997 | 114 | 85 | 74 | 2 379 | 972 | 41 | 78 |
| Latin America and the Caribbean | 1970 | 66 | 65 | 98 | 1 815 | 905 | 50 | 27 |
| | 1975 | 98 | 97 | 99 | 2 795 | 1 395 | 50 | 30 |
| | 1980 | 177 | 174 | 98 | 4 737 | 2 355 | 50 | 30 |
| | 1985 | 366 | 355 | 97 | 9 406 | 4 590 | 49 | 25 |
| | 1990 | 518 | 504 | 97 | 11 918 | 5 807 | 49 | 25 |
| | 1991 | 549 | 532 | 97 | 12 392 | 6 140 | 50 | 24 |
| | 1992 | 567 | 549 | 97 | 12 972 | 6 417 | 49 | 24 |
| | 1993 | 594 | 577 | 97 | 13 557 | 6 701 | 49 | 24 |
| | 1994 | 635 | 615 | 97 | 13 839 | 6 847 | 49 | 24 |
| | 1995 | 666 | 637 | 96 | 14 290 | 7 078 | 50 | 25 |
| | 1996 | 713 | 671 | 94 | 14 738 | 7 301 | 50 | 24 |
| | 1997 | 729 | 689 | 95 | 15 050 | 7 466 | 50 | 24 |

Pre-primary education: teaching staff and enrolment
Enseignement préprimaire: personnel enseignant et effectifs scolaires
Enseñanza preprimaria: personal docente y matrícula escolar

II.S.2

| Continents, major areas and groups of countries / Continents, grandes régions et groupes de pays / Continentes, grandes regiones y grupos de países | Year / Année / Año | Teaching staff / Personnel enseignant / Personal docente | | | Enrolment / Effectifs scolaires / Matrícula escolar | | | |
|---|---|---|---|---|---|---|---|---|
| | | Total (000) | Female Femmes Femenino (000) | % F | Total (000) | Female Femmes Femenina (000) | % F | Private Privé Privada % |
| Eastern Asia and Oceania | 1970 | ... | ... | ... | ... | ... | ... | ... |
| | 1975 | 300 | 268 | 89 | 8 129 | 3 868 | 48 | 12 |
| | 1980 | 538 | 461 | 86 | 15 170 | 7 266 | 48 | 11 |
| | 1985 | 746 | 718 | 96 | 19 679 | 9 425 | 48 | 12 |
| | 1990 | 1 031 | 993 | 96 | 25 948 | 12 616 | 49 | 11 |
| | 1991 | 1 066 | 1 013 | 95 | 28 418 | 13 677 | 48 | 10 |
| | 1992 | 1 125 | 1 069 | 95 | 30 864 | 14 792 | 48 | 9 |
| | 1993 | 1 157 | 1 096 | 95 | 32 467 | 15 565 | 48 | 9 |
| | 1994 | 1 202 | 1 144 | 95 | 33 892 | 16 150 | 48 | 10 |
| | 1995 | 1 211 | 1 153 | 95 | 34 498 | 16 419 | 48 | 10 |
| | 1996 | 1 239 | 1 172 | 95 | 34 231 | 16 235 | 47 | 10 |
| | 1997 | 1 260 | 1 195 | 95 | 33 236 | 15 779 | 47 | 11 |
| Southern Asia | 1970 | 21 | 12 | 58 | 848 | 325 | 38 | 3 |
| | 1975 | 34 | 23 | 67 | 1 400 | 572 | 41 | 9 |
| | 1980 | 61 | 38 | 62 | 2 284 | 999 | 44 | 22 |
| | 1985 | 107 | 50 | 47 | 4 065 | 1 740 | 43 | 44 |
| | 1990 | 147 | 68 | 47 | 5 415 | 2 389 | 44 | 47 |
| | 1991 | 154 | 71 | 46 | 5 602 | 2 448 | 44 | 45 |
| | 1992 | 153 | 70 | 45 | 5 555 | 2 427 | 44 | 46 |
| | 1993 | 161 | 77 | 48 | 6 011 | 2 647 | 44 | 42 |
| | 1994 | 164 | 79 | 48 | 6 205 | 2 759 | 44 | 41 |
| | 1995 | 164 | 80 | 49 | 6 266 | 2 782 | 44 | 41 |
| | 1996 | 168 | 83 | 50 | 6 544 | 2 932 | 45 | 40 |
| | 1997 | 168 | 83 | 49 | 6 823 | 3 062 | 45 | 38 |
| Least Developed Countries | 1970 | 3 | 3 | 91 | 108 | 50 | 46 | 65 |
| | 1975 | 6 | 5 | 78 | 245 | 118 | 48 | 59 |
| | 1980 | 32 | 20 | 62 | 1 300 | 597 | 46 | 50 |
| | 1985 | 70 | 29 | 42 | 2 571 | 1 147 | 45 | 79 |
| | 1990 | 103 | 39 | 38 | 3 502 | 1 539 | 44 | 83 |
| | 1991 | 104 | 41 | 39 | 3 626 | 1 625 | 45 | 81 |
| | 1992 | 106 | 43 | 41 | 3 665 | 1 640 | 45 | 81 |
| | 1993 | 107 | 44 | 41 | 3 705 | 1 657 | 45 | 83 |
| | 1994 | 108 | 46 | 42 | 3 733 | 1 665 | 45 | 81 |
| | 1995 | 109 | 47 | 43 | 3 769 | 1 685 | 45 | 83 |
| | 1996 | 110 | 48 | 44 | 3 797 | 1 693 | 45 | 82 |
| | 1997 | 110 | 48 | 44 | 3 817 | 1 702 | 45 | 83 |
| Developed Countries | 1970 | 1 289 | 1 268 | 98 | 23 933 | 11 762 | 49 | 20 |
| | 1975 | 1 649 | 1 614 | 98 | 30 010 | 15 482 | 52 | 20 |
| | 1980 | 2 060 | 2 025 | 98 | 33 228 | 16 224 | 49 | 18 |
| | 1985 | 2 444 | 2 368 | 97 | 35 569 | 17 336 | 49 | 20 |
| | 1990 | 2 677 | 2 600 | 97 | 37 419 | 18 106 | 48 | 20 |
| | 1991 | 2 663 | 2 586 | 97 | 37 071 | 17 872 | 48 | 21 |
| | 1992 | 2 545 | 2 476 | 97 | 35 530 | 17 063 | 48 | 19 |
| | 1993 | 2 480 | 2 403 | 97 | 34 964 | 16 795 | 48 | 21 |
| | 1994 | 2 438 | 2 359 | 97 | 34 618 | 16 593 | 48 | 24 |
| | 1995 | 2 425 | 2 346 | 97 | 34 770 | 16 725 | 48 | 24 |
| | 1996 | 2 428 | 2 351 | 97 | 34 688 | 16 705 | 48 | 24 |
| | 1997 | 2 437 | 2 359 | 97 | 34 768 | 16 753 | 48 | 25 |

**General note**

For general explanations and definitions, please refer to the beginning of this chapter. For the year 1970, data for China are not available. Therefore data for World total, Asia, Developing countries and Eastern Asia and Oceania are not shown for this year. Data do not include the Democratic People's Republic of Korea. For 1970 and 1975 data do not include South Africa and Namibia.

**Note générale**

Pour les explications et définitions générales, prière de se référer au début de ce chapitre. Pour l'année 1970, les données pour la Chine ne sont pas disponibles. Ainsi, les données pour le Total mondial, l'Asie, les Pays en développement et l'Asie de l'est et Océanie ne sont pas présentées pour cette année. Les données n'incluent pas la République populaire démocratique de Corée. Pour 1970 et 1975 les données n'incluent pas l'Afrique du Sud et la Namibie.

**Nota general**

Para las explicaciones y definiciones generales, referirse al comienzo de este capítulo. Para el año 1970, no se dispone de los datos para China. Por esta razón no se presentan datos para el Total mundial, Asia, los Países en desarrollo y Asia del Este y Oceanía para este año. Los datos no incluyen la República Popular Democrática de Corea. Para 1970 y 1975 los datos no incluyen Sudáfrica y Namibia.

Notes

(1) The inclusion of Koranic schools from 1975 affects the comparability of this series.

Notes

(1) L'inclusion des écoles coraniques à partir de 1975 affecte la comparabilité de cette série.

Notas

(1) La inclusión de las escuelas coránicas a partir de 1975 afecta la comparabilidad de esta serie.

II.S.3    Enrolment by level of education
Effectifs scolaires par niveau d'enseignement
Matrícula escolar por nivel de enseñanza

## II.S.3   Enrolment by level of education

Effectifs scolaires par niveau d'enseignement

Matrícula escolar por nivel de enseñanza

| Continents, major areas and groups of countries / Continents, grandes régions et groupes de pays / Continentes, grandes regiones y grupos de países | Year / Année / Año | Total enrolment (thousands) Effectif scolaires (milliers) Matrícula escolar (miles) | | | | Female enrolment (thousands) Effectifs scolaires féminins (milliers) Matrícula escolar femenina (miles) | | | |
|---|---|---|---|---|---|---|---|---|---|
| | | Primary Primaire Primaria | Secondary Secondaire Secundaria | Tertiary Supérieur Superior | Total | Primary Primaire Primaria | Secondary Secondaire Secundaria | Tertiary Supérieur Superior | Total |
| World total | 1970 | 411 304 | 169 227 | 28 084 | 608 615 | 187 600 | 70 455 | 10 634 | 268 689 |
| | 1975 | 494 094 | 218 977 | 38 315 | 751 386 | 224 517 | 93 823 | 15 689 | 334 029 |
| | 1980 | 541 556 | 264 379 | 51 037 | 856 971 | 242 622 | 113 834 | 22 545 | 379 001 |
| | 1985 | 567 595 | 291 134 | 60 163 | 918 892 | 256 666 | 126 277 | 26 845 | 409 788 |
| | 1990 | 596 853 | 315 008 | 68 613 | 980 474 | 273 465 | 139 102 | 31 589 | 444 156 |
| | 1991 | 604 278 | 321 321 | 70 350 | 995 948 | 277 446 | 142 512 | 32 795 | 452 753 |
| | 1992 | 614 696 | 336 981 | 72 124 | 1 023 802 | 282 994 | 150 405 | 33 954 | 467 354 |
| | 1993 | 626 478 | 347 360 | 75 852 | 1 049 690 | 288 443 | 156 356 | 35 687 | 480 486 |
| | 1994 | 638 384 | 358 930 | 78 172 | 1 075 487 | 294 201 | 162 285 | 36 894 | 493 380 |
| | 1995 | 649 480 | 372 724 | 81 552 | 1 103 756 | 299 171 | 169 118 | 38 329 | 506 618 |
| | 1996 | 659 106 | 386 386 | 85 175 | 1 130 667 | 304 109 | 176 053 | 39 995 | 520 157 |
| | 1997 | 668 450 | 398 116 | 88 156 | 1 154 721 | 308 338 | 180 847 | 41 282 | 530 467 |
| Africa | 1970 | 33 461 | 4 874 | 483 | 38 819 | 13 374 | 1 549 | 111 | 15 033 |
| | 1975 | 43 777 | 8 533 | 922 | 53 232 | 18 149 | 2 983 | 236 | 21 368 |
| | 1980 | 62 134 | 14 360 | 1 542 | 78 036 | 26 999 | 5 297 | 417 | 32 712 |
| | 1985 | 72 162 | 19 816 | 2 187 | 94 164 | 31 979 | 7 997 | 614 | 40 590 |
| | 1990 | 80 640 | 24 378 | 2 853 | 107 871 | 36 229 | 10 480 | 949 | 47 657 |
| | 1991 | 82 316 | 25 295 | 3 005 | 110 616 | 37 236 | 10 896 | 1 033 | 49 164 |
| | 1992 | 85 308 | 26 138 | 3 240 | 114 686 | 38 705 | 11 416 | 1 119 | 51 240 |
| | 1993 | 88 957 | 27 667 | 3 413 | 120 038 | 40 268 | 12 207 | 1 228 | 53 703 |
| | 1994 | 93 127 | 29 320 | 3 619 | 126 066 | 42 169 | 13 046 | 1 327 | 56 543 |
| | 1995 | 95 928 | 30 899 | 3 966 | 130 794 | 43 373 | 13 821 | 1 477 | 58 672 |
| | 1996 | 98 356 | 32 127 | 4 360 | 134 843 | 44 425 | 14 436 | 1 632 | 60 493 |
| | 1997 | 100 226 | 33 708 | 4 780 | 138 714 | 45 265 | 15 148 | 1 802 | 62 215 |
| America | 1970 | 69 745 | 32 975 | 11 120 | 113 840 | 34 001 | 16 114 | 4 482 | 54 598 |
| | 1975 | 78 921 | 36 864 | 15 923 | 131 707 | 38 436 | 18 033 | 7 048 | 63 518 |
| | 1980 | 88 025 | 40 882 | 18 424 | 147 332 | 42 929 | 20 239 | 9 061 | 72 229 |
| | 1985 | 92 872 | 43 376 | 20 232 | 156 480 | 45 052 | 21 629 | 10 180 | 76 862 |
| | 1990 | 100 315 | 43 763 | 22 897 | 166 975 | 48 804 | 21 996 | 12 040 | 82 840 |
| | 1991 | 101 653 | 44 706 | 23 714 | 170 073 | 49 256 | 22 495 | 12 522 | 84 272 |
| | 1992 | 103 311 | 46 230 | 23 728 | 173 270 | 50 104 | 23 211 | 12 579 | 85 894 |
| | 1993 | 104 654 | 47 197 | 23 729 | 175 580 | 50 768 | 23 669 | 12 607 | 87 044 |
| | 1994 | 106 605 | 48 309 | 23 916 | 178 829 | 51 699 | 24 383 | 12 767 | 88 849 |
| | 1995 | 108 780 | 50 071 | 24 481 | 183 331 | 52 314 | 25 191 | 12 996 | 90 501 |
| | 1996 | 110 332 | 52 170 | 25 049 | 187 551 | 53 082 | 26 301 | 13 187 | 92 570 |
| | 1997 | 112 083 | 53 899 | 25 486 | 191 467 | 53 694 | 27 233 | 13 386 | 94 312 |
| Asia | 1970 | 250 537 | 82 551 | 7 223 | 340 312 | 107 367 | 29 245 | 2 146 | 138 758 |
| | 1975 | 316 583 | 114 504 | 9 552 | 440 639 | 137 425 | 43 936 | 3 023 | 184 384 |
| | 1980 | 336 174 | 144 755 | 14 227 | 495 155 | 145 819 | 56 576 | 4 753 | 207 148 |
| | 1985 | 349 103 | 163 379 | 20 004 | 532 486 | 153 629 | 64 809 | 7 040 | 225 478 |
| | 1990 | 364 213 | 181 652 | 23 314 | 569 179 | 163 225 | 74 287 | 8 748 | 246 260 |
| | 1991 | 368 836 | 186 195 | 23 748 | 578 779 | 165 859 | 76 712 | 9 163 | 251 734 |
| | 1992 | 375 349 | 195 310 | 24 660 | 595 319 | 169 497 | 81 098 | 9 723 | 260 318 |
| | 1993 | 382 737 | 200 815 | 27 074 | 610 627 | 173 025 | 84 676 | 10 708 | 268 410 |
| | 1994 | 388 446 | 209 331 | 28 702 | 626 479 | 175 964 | 88 901 | 11 390 | 276 255 |
| | 1995 | 394 304 | 219 415 | 30 890 | 644 609 | 178 992 | 93 959 | 12 218 | 285 169 |
| | 1996 | 400 405 | 229 981 | 33 008 | 663 394 | 182 320 | 99 339 | 13 143 | 294 802 |
| | 1997 | 406 661 | 237 861 | 34 844 | 679 366 | 185 324 | 102 234 | 13 914 | 301 473 |

Enrolment by level of education  II.S.3
Effectifs scolaires par niveau d'enseignement
Matrícula escolar por nivel de enseñanza

| Continents, major areas and groups of countries / Continents, grandes régions et groupes de pays / Continentes, grandes regiones y grupos de países | Year / Année / Año | Total enrolment (thousands) Effectif scolaires (milliers) Matrícula escolar (miles) | | | | Female enrolment (thousands) Effectifs scolaires féminins (milliers) Matrícula escolar femenina (miles) | | | |
|---|---|---|---|---|---|---|---|---|---|
| | | Primary Primaire Primaria | Secondary Secondaire Secundaria | Tertiary Supérieur Superior | Total | Primary Primaire Primaria | Secondary Secondaire Secundaria | Tertiary Supérieur Superior | Total |
| Europe | 1970 | 54 951 | 47 290 | 9 035 | 111 276 | 31 616 | 22 849 | 3 819 | 58 284 |
| | 1975 | 52 192 | 57 465 | 11 565 | 121 221 | 29 262 | 28 092 | 5 242 | 62 596 |
| | 1980 | 52 471 | 62 734 | 16 428 | 131 633 | 25 562 | 30 915 | 8 131 | 64 608 |
| | 1985 | 50 860 | 62 717 | 17 254 | 130 832 | 24 765 | 30 936 | 8 782 | 64 483 |
| | 1990 | 48 968 | 63 366 | 18 922 | 131 255 | 23 908 | 31 429 | 9 526 | 64 863 |
| | 1991 | 48 723 | 63 248 | 19 186 | 131 156 | 23 780 | 31 488 | 9 712 | 64 980 |
| | 1992 | 47 933 | 67 402 | 19 755 | 135 090 | 23 332 | 33 749 | 10 142 | 67 243 |
| | 1993 | 47 278 | 68 997 | 20 514 | 136 789 | 23 016 | 34 499 | 10 591 | 68 107 |
| | 1994 | 47 306 | 69 275 | 20 796 | 137 377 | 22 982 | 34 646 | 10 841 | 68 469 |
| | 1995 | 47 344 | 69 448 | 21 047 | 137 839 | 22 993 | 34 749 | 11 049 | 68 791 |
| | 1996 | 46 866 | 69 103 | 21 554 | 137 522 | 22 772 | 34 514 | 11 420 | 68 706 |
| | 1997 | 46 304 | 69 547 | 21 794 | 137 645 | 22 532 | 34 701 | 11 538 | 68 771 |
| Oceania | 1970 | 2 609 | 1 536 | 224 | 4 368 | 1 241 | 698 | 76 | 2 015 |
| | 1975 | 2 623 | 1 611 | 353 | 4 587 | 1 244 | 778 | 140 | 2 162 |
| | 1980 | 2 752 | 1 647 | 416 | 4 81 | 1 313 | 807 | 183 | 2 303 |
| | 1985 | 2 598 | 1 846 | 486 | 4 930 | 1 241 | 906 | 228 | 2 375 |
| | 1990 | 2 717 | 1 849 | 628 | 5 194 | 1 299 | 911 | 325 | 2 535 |
| | 1991 | 2 749 | 1 877 | 697 | 5 323 | 1 315 | 922 | 365 | 2 602 |
| | 1992 | 2 795 | 1 901 | 741 | 5 437 | 1 337 | 930 | 391 | 2 658 |
| | 1993 | 2 852 | 2 683 | 1 122 | 6 657 | 1 365 | 1 304 | 553 | 3 223 |
| | 1994 | 2 900 | 2 695 | 1 140 | 6 736 | 1 388 | 1 308 | 569 | 3 265 |
| | 1995 | 3 124 | 2 891 | 1 167 | 7 183 | 1 498 | 1 399 | 590 | 3 486 |
| | 1006 | 3 147 | 3 005 | 1 204 | 7 357 | 1 510 | 1 463 | 613 | 3 586 |
| | 1997 | 3 176 | 3 101 | 1 251 | 7 528 | 1 523 | 1 530 | 642 | 3 696 |
| Developing Countries | 1970 | 312 756 | 84 772 | 6 956 | 404 483 | 134 698 | 29 424 | 2 042 | 166 164 |
| | 1975 | 401 860 | 121 549 | 11 343 | 534 753 | 175 755 | 46 074 | 3 779 | 225 608 |
| | 1980 | 449 192 | 159 399 | 16 858 | 625 450 | 197 598 | 62 288 | 5 784 | 265 670 |
| | 1985 | 477 414 | 184 922 | 24 668 | 687 004 | 212 731 | 74 152 | 8 892 | 295 775 |
| | 1990 | 507 308 | 209 496 | 29 125 | 745 928 | 229 836 | 86 976 | 11 382 | 328 194 |
| | 1991 | 514 801 | 215 797 | 29 697 | 760 295 | 233 859 | 90 271 | 11 860 | 335 990 |
| | 1992 | 525 847 | 227 059 | 30 807 | 783 712 | 239 759 | 95 889 | 12 457 | 348 105 |
| | 1993 | 537 889 | 234 658 | 32 718 | 805 265 | 245 313 | 100 578 | 13 238 | 359 130 |
| | 1994 | 549 319 | 245 898 | 34 667 | 829 884 | 250 867 | 106 244 | 14 082 | 371 192 |
| | 1995 | 559 546 | 259 282 | 37 743 | 856 571 | 255 448 | 112 961 | 15 251 | 383 660 |
| | 1996 | 569 543 | 272 552 | 40 744 | 882 838 | 260 521 | 119 634 | 16 485 | 396 640 |
| | 1997 | 579 371 | 283 081 | 43 357 | 905 809 | 264 946 | 123 866 | 17 586 | 406 398 |
| of which: | | | | | | | | | |
| Sub-Saharan Africa | 1970 | 25 318 | 2 640 | 199 | 28 156 | 10 340 | 867 | 40 | 11 246 |
| | 1975 | 33 896 | 4 993 | 321 | 39 210 | 14 307 | 1 776 | 66 | 16 149 |
| | 1980 | 50 463 | 9 010 | 562 | 60 036 | 22 259 | 3 288 | 124 | 25 671 |
| | 1985 | 57 883 | 12 316 | 905 | 71 104 | 25 857 | 4 987 | 223 | 31 067 |
| | 1990 | 64 422 | 14 677 | 1 362 | 80 461 | 29 070 | 6 289 | 437 | 35 796 |
| | 1991 | 65 599 | 15 334 | 1 466 | 82 399 | 29 827 | 6 574 | 481 | 36 001 |
| | 1992 | 68 061 | 15 771 | 1 562 | 85 395 | 31 014 | 6 877 | 518 | 38 409 |
| | 1993 | 71 002 | 16 721 | 1 692 | 89 415 | 32 207 | 7 339 | 564 | 40 109 |
| | 1994 | 74 672 | 17 872 | 1 803 | 94 346 | 33 817 | 7 901 | 617 | 42 336 |
| | 1995 | 77 055 | 19 079 | 1 920 | 98 054 | 34 792 | 8 503 | 664 | 43 960 |
| | 1996 | 79 296 | 20 054 | 2 053 | 101 402 | 35 736 | 8 910 | 717 | 45 363 |
| | 1997 | 81 035 | 21 015 | 2 177 | 104 227 | 36 511 | 9 327 | 769 | 46 607 |
| Arab States | 1970 | 12 958 | 3 552 | 446 | 16 957 | 4 620 | 1 069 | 105 | 5 794 |
| | 1975 | 16 774 | 5 692 | 896 | 23 362 | 6 289 | 1 932 | 256 | 8 477 |
| | 1980 | 20 744 | 8 762 | 1 487 | 30 993 | 8 480 | 3 277 | 462 | 12 219 |
| | 1985 | 25 656 | 12 132 | 2 017 | 39 806 | 10 848 | 4 831 | 669 | 16 348 |
| | 1990 | 30 353 | 14 991 | 2 449 | 47 793 | 13 244 | 6 322 | 899 | 20 465 |
| | 1991 | 31 342 | 15 222 | 2 562 | 49 126 | 13 707 | 6 491 | 965 | 21 162 |
| | 1992 | 32 345 | 15 211 | 2 765 | 50 321 | 14 194 | 6 569 | 1 054 | 21 817 |
| | 1993 | 33 777 | 15 894 | 2 825 | 52 495 | 14 865 | 6 969 | 1 122 | 22 956 |
| | 1994 | 35 194 | 16 601 | 2 966 | 54 761 | 15 594 | 7 361 | 1 195 | 24 150 |
| | 1995 | 35 721 | 17 329 | 3 241 | 56 290 | 15 895 | 7 704 | 1 318 | 24 917 |
| | 1996 | 36 126 | 17 875 | 3 561 | 57 561 | 16 111 | 8 047 | 1 444 | 25 602 |
| | 1997 | 36 625 | 18 710 | 3 906 | 59 241 | 16 333 | 8 435 | 1 590 | 26 357 |
| Latin America and the Caribbean | 1970 | 43 963 | 10 740 | 1 639 | 56 343 | 21 431 | 5 184 | 581 | 27 196 |
| | 1975 | 56 260 | 12 588 | 3 658 | 72 507 | 27 384 | 6 090 | 1 527 | 35 001 |
| | 1980 | 65 414 | 16 969 | 4 908 | 87 291 | 31 903 | 8 459 | 2 127 | 42 488 |
| | 1985 | 70 397 | 20 486 | 6 345 | 97 228 | 34 113 | 10 435 | 2 860 | 47 408 |
| | 1990 | 75 505 | 22 194 | 7 269 | 104 968 | 36 798 | 11 402 | 3 530 | 51 729 |
| | 1991 | 76 552 | 22 656 | 7 410 | 106 617 | 37 108 | 11 667 | 3 641 | 52 417 |
| | 1992 | 77 930 | 23 306 | 7 494 | 108 730 | 37 825 | 12 042 | 3 692 | 53 559 |
| | 1993 | 79 035 | 23 681 | 7 647 | 110 362 | 38 317 | 12 246 | 3 793 | 54 356 |
| | 1994 | 80 362 | 24 712 | 7 852 | 112 926 | 38 950 | 12 806 | 3 917 | 55 673 |
| | 1995 | 82 279 | 26 087 | 8 455 | 116 821 | 39 459 | 13 499 | 4 138 | 57 095 |
| | 1996 | 83 596 | 27 815 | 9 018 | 120 429 | 40 059 | 14 354 | 4 326 | 58 738 |
| | 1997 | 85 177 | 29 153 | 9 448 | 123 778 | 40 590 | 15 096 | 4 525 | 60 211 |

II.S.3    Enrolment by level of education
Effectifs scolaires par niveau d'enseignement
Matrícula escolar por nivel de enseñanza

| Continents, major areas and groups of countries / Continents, grandes régions et groupes de pays / Continentes, grandes regiones y grupos de países | Year Année Año | Total enrolment (thousands) Effectif scolaires (milliers) Matrícula escolar (miles) | | | | Female enrolment (thousands) Effectifs scolaires féminins (milliers) Matrícula escolar femenina (miles) | | | |
|---|---|---|---|---|---|---|---|---|---|
| | | Primary Primaire Primaria | Secondary Secondaire Secundaria | Tertiary Supérieur Superior | Total | Primary Primaire Primaria | Secondary Secondaire Secundaria | Tertiary Supérieur Superior | Total |
| Eastern Asia and Oceania | 1970 | 152 767 | 38 167 | 1 435 | 192 370 | 69 644 | 13 681 | 591 | 83 916 |
| | 1975 | 203 441 | 61 347 | 2 261 | 267 048 | 93 201 | 24 835 | 902 | 118 938 |
| | 1980 | 210 902 | 79 037 | 5 293 | 295 232 | 95 713 | 32 492 | 1 809 | 130 013 |
| | 1985 | 203 162 | 79 987 | 9 111 | 292 260 | 93 178 | 33 569 | 3 251 | 129 999 |
| | 1990 | 194 867 | 81 963 | 10 603 | 287 433 | 91 595 | 35 579 | 4 082 | 131 255 |
| | 1991 | 194 786 | 83 670 | 10 612 | 289 068 | 92 005 | 36 760 | 4 200 | 132 965 |
| | 1992 | 195 682 | 85 851 | 11 055 | 292 589 | 92 445 | 37 958 | 4 561 | 134 964 |
| | 1993 | 198 288 | 87 994 | 12 253 | 298 534 | 93 954 | 39 814 | 4 969 | 138 737 |
| | 1994 | 201 875 | 93 750 | 13 521 | 309 146 | 95 903 | 42 877 | 5 430 | 144 211 |
| | 1995 | 205 778 | 101 147 | 14 479 | 321 404 | 97 943 | 46 674 | 5 736 | 150 353 |
| | 1996 | 210 428 | 107 885 | 15 796 | 334 108 | 100 547 | 49 832 | 6 375 | 156 755 |
| | 1997 | 214 682 | 113 404 | 16 790 | 344 876 | 102 821 | 52 248 | 6 827 | 161 896 |
| Southern Asia | 1970 | 71 905 | 26 472 | 2 818 | 101 195 | 26 054 | 7 367 | 592 | 34 013 |
| | 1975 | 85 759 | 33 259 | 3 545 | 122 563 | 31 819 | 9 931 | 811 | 42 561 |
| | 1980 | 96 138 | 42 212 | 4 063 | 142 414 | 36 583 | 13 379 | 1 041 | 51 003 |
| | 1985 | 114 028 | 56 021 | 5 555 | 175 604 | 45 603 | 18 733 | 1 592 | 65 928 |
| | 1990 | 136 041 | 70 995 | 6 453 | 213 489 | 56 117 | 25 479 | 2 050 | 83 645 |
| | 1991 | 140 558 | 74 042 | 6 618 | 221 218 | 58 275 | 26 782 | 2 169 | 87 227 |
| | 1992 | 146 156 | 81 241 | 6 787 | 234 184 | 61 486 | 30 093 | 2 179 | 93 758 |
| | 1993 | 150 452 | 84 539 | 6 945 | 241 936 | 63 318 | 31 768 | 2 232 | 97 318 |
| | 1994 | 152 635 | 86 908 | 7 134 | 246 677 | 64 300 | 32 782 | 2 337 | 99 419 |
| | 1995 | 154 327 | 89 455 | 8 108 | 251 890 | 65 192 | 33 975 | 2 769 | 101 937 |
| | 1996 | 155 865 | 92 756 | 8 625 | 257 246 | 65 982 | 35 872 | 2 959 | 104 812 |
| | 1997 | 157 695 | 94 607 | 9 303 | 261 605 | 66 642 | 36 130 | 3 192 | 105 964 |
| Least Developed Countries | 1970 | 22 677 | 4 076 | 263 | 27 017 | 8 254 | 1 054 | 45 | 9 354 |
| | 1975 | 30 953 | 5 998 | 379 | 37 331 | 11 575 | 1 649 | 66 | 13 291 |
| | 1980 | 41 151 | 8 217 | 652 | 50 020 | 16 718 | 2 452 | 166 | 19 336 |
| | 1985 | 46 105 | 10 214 | 1 023 | 57 342 | 19 242 | 3 463 | 267 | 22 973 |
| | 1990 | 53 755 | 12 110 | 1 169 | 67 034 | 23 405 | 4 382 | 310 | 28 097 |
| | 1991 | 55 603 | 12 493 | 1 311 | 69 408 | 24 288 | 4 584 | 343 | 29 215 |
| | 1992 | 57 451 | 12 503 | 1 433 | 71 387 | 25 070 | 4 593 | 392 | 30 054 |
| | 1993 | 59 409 | 13 013 | 1 497 | 73 919 | 25 825 | 4 782 | 401 | 31 007 |
| | 1994 | 62 806 | 14 007 | 1 582 | 78 395 | 27 293 | 5 249 | 426 | 32 969 |
| | 1995 | 64 774 | 14 896 | 1 672 | 81 342 | 28 012 | 5 691 | 448 | 34 151 |
| | 1996 | 66 904 | 15 729 | 1 776 | 84 409 | 28 906 | 6 028 | 474 | 35 409 |
| | 1997 | 68 740 | 16 430 | 1 857 | 87 027 | 29 675 | 6 296 | 496 | 36 467 |
| Developed Countries | 1970 | 98 548 | 84 455 | 21 129 | 204 132 | 52 902 | 41 031 | 8 591 | 102 524 |
| | 1975 | 92 234 | 97 427 | 26 972 | 216 633 | 48 762 | 47 748 | 11 910 | 108 421 |
| | 1980 | 92 363 | 104 979 | 34 179 | 231 522 | 45 024 | 51 546 | 16 761 | 113 331 |
| | 1985 | 90 181 | 106 212 | 35 494 | 231 888 | 43 935 | 52 125 | 17 953 | 114 014 |
| | 1990 | 89 545 | 105 512 | 39 488 | 234 546 | 43 629 | 52 126 | 20 206 | 115 962 |
| | 1991 | 89 477 | 105 524 | 40 653 | 235 653 | 43 587 | 52 241 | 20 935 | 116 762 |
| | 1992 | 88 850 | 109 923 | 41 317 | 240 090 | 43 236 | 54 516 | 21 497 | 119 249 |
| | 1993 | 88 589 | 112 701 | 43 135 | 244 425 | 43 130 | 55 778 | 22 449 | 121 357 |
| | 1994 | 89 066 | 113 031 | 43 506 | 245 603 | 43 335 | 56 041 | 22 813 | 122 188 |
| | 1995 | 89 933 | 113 443 | 43 809 | 247 185 | 43 723 | 56 157 | 23 078 | 122 958 |
| | 1996 | 89 563 | 113 834 | 44 432 | 247 829 | 43 588 | 56 419 | 23 510 | 123 517 |
| | 1997 | 89 078 | 115 035 | 44 798 | 248 912 | 43 393 | 56 981 | 23 696 | 124 070 |

**General note**
For general explanations and definitions, please refer to the beginning of this chapter. Data do not include the Democratic People's Republic of Korea.

**Note générale**
Pour les explications et définitions générales, prière de se référer au début de ce chapitre. Les données n'incluent pas la République populaire démocratique de Corée.

**Nota general**
Para las explicaciones y definiciones generales, referirse al comienzo de este capítulo. Los datos no incluyen la República Popular Democrática de Corea.

Teaching staff by level of education  II.S.4
Personnel enseignant par niveau d'enseignement
Personal docente por nivel de enseñanza

## II.S.4 Teaching staff by level of education

### Personnel enseignant par niveau d'enseignement

### Personal docente por nivel de enseñanza

| Continents, major areas and groups of countries / Continents, grandes régions et groupes de pays / Continentes, grandes regiones y grupos de países | Year / Année / Año | Total teaching staff (thousands) / Personnel enseignant total (milliers) / Personal docente total (miles) | | | | Female teaching staff (thousands) / Personnel enseignant féminin (milliers) / Personal docente femenino (miles) | |
|---|---|---|---|---|---|---|---|
| | | Primary / Primaire / Primaria | Secondary / Secondaire / Secundaria | Tertiary / Supérieur / Superior | Total | Primary / Primaire / Primaria | Secondary / Secondaire / Secundaria |
| World total | 1970 | 14 767 | 9 644 | 2 146 | 26 557 | 7 694 | 3 970 |
| | 1975 | 17 818 | 12 320 | 2 774 | 32 912 | 9 205 | 5 037 |
| | 1980 | 19 044 | 15 398 | 3 843 | 38 285 | 10 059 | 6 254 |
| | 1985 | 20 948 | 16 872 | 4 398 | 42 218 | 11 419 | 7 268 |
| | 1990 | 22 626 | 19 380 | 5 100 | 47 105 | 12 736 | 8 678 |
| | 1991 | 22 989 | 19 712 | 5 178 | 47 879 | 13 045 | 8 881 |
| | 1992 | 23 307 | 20 126 | 5 324 | 48 758 | 13 281 | 9 265 |
| | 1993 | 23 712 | 20 615 | 5 681 | 50 009 | 13 595 | 9 618 |
| | 1994 | 24 003 | 21 015 | 5 782 | 50 801 | 13 825 | 9 872 |
| | 1995 | 24 356 | 21 746 | 5 945 | 52 047 | 14 111 | 10 279 |
| | 1996 | 24 622 | 22 375 | 6 084 | 53 081 | 14 312 | 10 653 |
| | 1997 | 24 818 | 23 017 | 6 284 | 54 120 | 14 477 | 10 977 |
| Africa | 1970 | 837 | 225 | 36 | 1 097 | 262 | 70 |
| | 1975 | 1 148 | 348 | 56 | 1 551 | 384 | 106 |
| | 1980 | 1 661 | 584 | 94 | 2 338 | 597 | 196 |
| | 1985 | 2 029 | 892 | 132 | 3 054 | 799 | 301 |
| | 1990 | 2 390 | 1 241 | 160 | 3 791 | 1 000 | 433 |
| | 1991 | 2 494 | 1 257 | 166 | 3 917 | 1 067 | 405 |
| | 1992 | 2 572 | 1 271 | 171 | 4 015 | 1 126 | 448 |
| | 1993 | 2 665 | 1 315 | 182 | 4 162 | 1 185 | 472 |
| | 1994 | 2 711 | 1 367 | 192 | 4 270 | 1 199 | 496 |
| | 1995 | 2 811 | 1 471 | 205 | 4 486 | 1 285 | 509 |
| | 1996 | 2 881 | 1 538 | 223 | 4 642 | 1 302 | 533 |
| | 1997 | 2 927 | 1 585 | 242 | 4 754 | 1 319 | 549 |
| America | 1970 | 3 098 | 2 358 | 822 | 6 278 | 2 533 | 1 098 |
| | 1975 | 3 602 | 2 508 | 1 067 | 7 177 | 2 863 | 1 156 |
| | 1980 | 3 840 | 2 762 | 1 207 | 7 809 | 3 006 | 1 280 |
| | 1985 | 4 162 | 2 780 | 1 328 | 8 270 | 3 303 | 1 415 |
| | 1990 | 4 588 | 2 969 | 1 574 | 9 131 | 3 656 | 1 520 |
| | 1991 | 4 703 | 3 037 | 1 589 | 9 329 | 3 735 | 1 553 |
| | 1992 | 4 757 | 3 050 | 1 623 | 9 430 | 3 775 | 1 592 |
| | 1993 | 4 816 | 3 053 | 1 742 | 9 611 | 3 819 | 1 573 |
| | 1994 | 4 950 | 3 124 | 1 758 | 9 832 | 3 933 | 1 614 |
| | 1995 | 5 023 | 3 224 | 1 806 | 10 053 | 3 984 | 1 649 |
| | 1996 | 5 107 | 3 337 | 1 845 | 10 288 | 4 037 | 1 711 |
| | 1997 | 5 148 | 3 451 | 1 881 | 10 480 | 4 079 | 1 768 |
| Asia | 1970 | 7 838 | 3 897 | 620 | 12 355 | 2 807 | 1 159 |
| | 1975 | 10 030 | 5 557 | 750 | 16 337 | 3 780 | 1 675 |
| | 1980 | 10 874 | 7 554 | 1 213 | 19 641 | 4 395 | 2 317 |
| | 1985 | 11 913 | 8 400 | 1 530 | 21 843 | 5 063 | 2 863 |
| | 1990 | 12 692 | 9 947 | 1 816 | 24 455 | 5 705 | 3 709 |
| | 1991 | 12 842 | 10 106 | 1 855 | 24 803 | 5 825 | 3 810 |
| | 1992 | 12 999 | 10 320 | 1 887 | 25 207 | 5 952 | 3 943 |
| | 1993 | 13 219 | 10 526 | 2 056 | 25 800 | 6 109 | 4 117 |
| | 1994 | 13 351 | 10 807 | 2 079 | 26 236 | 6 230 | 4 290 |
| | 1995 | 13 499 | 11 273 | 2 183 | 26 955 | 6 361 | 4 573 |
| | 1996 | 13 630 | 11 719 | 2 247 | 27 596 | 6 510 | 4 853 |
| | 1997 | 13 763 | 12 185 | 2 339 | 28 288 | 6 637 | 5 089 |

II.S.4  Teaching staff by level of education
Personnel enseignant par niveau d'enseignement
Personal docente por nivel de enseñanza

| Continents, major areas and groups of countries / Continentes, grandes régions et groupes de pays / Continentes, grandes regiones y grupos de países | Year / Année / Año | Total teaching staff (thousands) / Personnel enseignant total (milliers) / Personal docente total (miles) | | | | Female teaching staff (thousands) / Personnel enseignant féminin (milliers) / Personal docente femenino (miles) | |
|---|---|---|---|---|---|---|---|
| | | Primary / Primaire / Primaria | Secondary / Secondaire / Secundaria | Tertiary / Supérieur / Superior | Total | Primary / Primaire / Primaria | Secondary / Secondaire / Secundaria |
| Europe | 1970 | 2 899 | 3 070 | 654 | 6 623 | 2 031 | 1 603 |
| | 1975 | 2 928 | 3 809 | 873 | 7 610 | 2 107 | 2 055 |
| | 1980 | 2 541 | 4 387 | 1 297 | 8 225 | 1 980 | 2 409 |
| | 1985 | 2 708 | 4 664 | 1 374 | 8 745 | 2 165 | 2 624 |
| | 1990 | 2 812 | 5 076 | 1 509 | 9 398 | 2 279 | 2 944 |
| | 1991 | 2 804 | 5 164 | 1 526 | 9 495 | 2 320 | 3 010 |
| | 1992 | 2 832 | 5 333 | 1 601 | 9 766 | 2 330 | 3 207 |
| | 1993 | 2 865 | 5 506 | 1 640 | 10 012 | 2 383 | 3 349 |
| | 1994 | 2 843 | 5 502 | 1 693 | 10 038 | 2 362 | 3 363 |
| | 1995 | 2 863 | 5 561 | 1 689 | 10 113 | 2 368 | 3 437 |
| | 1996 | 2 842 | 5 556 | 1 709 | 10 107 | 2 349 | 3 443 |
| | 1997 | 2 814 | 5 568 | 1 759 | 10 141 | 2 324 | 3 453 |
| Oceania | 1970 | 96 | 93 | 15 | 204 | 60 | 40 |
| | 1975 | 111 | 98 | 28 | 236 | 70 | 45 |
| | 1980 | 129 | 112 | 31 | 272 | 81 | 51 |
| | 1985 | 136 | 137 | 33 | 306 | 88 | 65 |
| | 1990 | 143 | 146 | 41 | 330 | 96 | 72 |
| | 1991 | 145 | 148 | 42 | 336 | 98 | 73 |
| | 1992 | 147 | 152 | 42 | 341 | 99 | 75 |
| | 1993 | 148 | 216 | 61 | 425 | 100 | 107 |
| | 1994 | 149 | 216 | 61 | 426 | 101 | 108 |
| | 1995 | 161 | 217 | 61 | 439 | 113 | 110 |
| | 1996 | 162 | 224 | 61 | 447 | 114 | 114 |
| | 1997 | 165 | 228 | 62 | 456 | 118 | 118 |
| Developing Countries | 1970 | 9 350 | 4 154 | 616 | 14 120 | 3 761 | 1 294 |
| | 1975 | 12 522 | 5 862 | 867 | 19 251 | 5 336 | 1 802 |
| | 1980 | 14 201 | 8 138 | 1 357 | 23 697 | 6 329 | 2 578 |
| | 1985 | 15 931 | 9 432 | 1 790 | 27 153 | 7 461 | 3 302 |
| | 1990 | 17 446 | 11 300 | 2 163 | 30 909 | 8 581 | 4 245 |
| | 1991 | 17 793 | 11 483 | 2 206 | 31 483 | 8 821 | 4 350 |
| | 1992 | 18 067 | 11 720 | 2 245 | 32 032 | 9 035 | 4 487 |
| | 1993 | 18 405 | 11 926 | 2 321 | 32 652 | 9 267 | 4 635 |
| | 1994 | 18 701 | 12 280 | 2 388 | 33 370 | 9 500 | 4 845 |
| | 1995 | 18 977 | 12 919 | 2 542 | 34 437 | 9 730 | 5 144 |
| | 1996 | 19 277 | 13 442 | 2 658 | 35 377 | 9 944 | 5 447 |
| | 1997 | 19 479 | 14 015 | 2 832 | 36 325 | 10 115 | 5 724 |
| of which: | | | | | | | |
| Sub-Saharan Africa | 1970 | 624 | 128 | 18 | 770 | 184 | 45 |
| | 1975 | 875 | 203 | 27 | 1 104 | 286 | 66 |
| | 1980 | 1 307 | 338 | 43 | 1 688 | 453 | 120 |
| | 1985 | 1 511 | 510 | 65 | 2 087 | 574 | 173 |
| | 1990 | 1 720 | 677 | 77 | 2 474 | 677 | 222 |
| | 1991 | 1 793 | 677 | 82 | 2 553 | 723 | 215 |
| | 1992 | 1 844 | 678 | 86 | 2 608 | 761 | 220 |
| | 1993 | 1 913 | 696 | 95 | 2 704 | 804 | 231 |
| | 1994 | 1 933 | 722 | 103 | 2 759 | 804 | 245 |
| | 1995 | 2 010 | 758 | 109 | 2 877 | 873 | 232 |
| | 1996 | 2 055 | 794 | 116 | 2 965 | 894 | 243 |
| | 1997 | 2 095 | 824 | 123 | 3 042 | 908 | 253 |
| Arab States | 1970 | 377 | 165 | 25 | 568 | 137 | 44 |
| | 1975 | 523 | 260 | 44 | 827 | 191 | 77 |
| | 1980 | 693 | 429 | 83 | 1 206 | 291 | 138 |
| | 1985 | 970 | 636 | 112 | 1 718 | 464 | 225 |
| | 1990 | 1 252 | 874 | 136 | 2 263 | 643 | 341 |
| | 1991 | 1 314 | 894 | 139 | 2 347 | 674 | 357 |
| | 1992 | 1 382 | 918 | 146 | 2 445 | 713 | 367 |
| | 1993 | 1 451 | 962 | 155 | 2 569 | 761 | 393 |
| | 1994 | 1 516 | 992 | 158 | 2 666 | 800 | 413 |
| | 1995 | 1 571 | 1 082 | 164 | 2 817 | 836 | 449 |
| | 1996 | 1 620 | 1 137 | 177 | 2 935 | 848 | 475 |
| | 1997 | 1 634 | 1 175 | 193 | 3 002 | 854 | 492 |
| Latin America and the Caribbean | 1970 | 1 363 | 788 | 158 | 2 309 | 1 101 | 384 |
| | 1975 | 2 023 | 812 | 304 | 3 139 | 1 586 | 382 |
| | 1980 | 2 260 | 1 083 | 387 | 3 730 | 1 725 | 513 |
| | 1985 | 2 601 | 1 338 | 507 | 4 447 | 2 001 | 643 |
| | 1990 | 3 006 | 1 520 | 605 | 5 131 | 2 319 | 738 |
| | 1991 | 3 119 | 1 556 | 615 | 5 291 | 2 393 | 754 |
| | 1992 | 3 179 | 1 594 | 631 | 5 404 | 2 440 | 767 |
| | 1993 | 3 221 | 1 575 | 652 | 5 448 | 2 471 | 737 |
| | 1994 | 3 327 | 1 621 | 675 | 5 623 | 2 559 | 762 |
| | 1995 | 3 374 | 1 696 | 714 | 5 784 | 2 587 | 784 |
| | 1996 | 3 446 | 1 785 | 752 | 5 983 | 2 631 | 832 |
| | 1997 | 3 474 | 1 874 | 789 | 6 138 | 2 664 | 876 |

Teaching staff by level of education    II.S.4
Personnel enseignant par niveau d'enseignement
Personal docente por nivel de enseñanza

| Continents, major areas and groups of countries / Continents, grandes régions et groupes de pays / Continentes, grandes regiones y grupos de países | Year / Année / Año | Total teaching staff (thousands) / Personnel enseignant total (milliers) / Personal docente total (miles) | | | | Female teaching staff (thousands) / Personnel enseignant féminin (milliers) / Personal docente femenino (miles) | |
|---|---|---|---|---|---|---|---|
| | | Primary / Primaire / Primaria | Secondary / Secondaire / Secundaria | Tertiary / Supérieur / Superior | Total | Primary / Primaire / Primaria | Secondary / Secondaire / Secundaria |
| Eastern Asia and Oceania | 1970 | 5 043 | 1 742 | 212 | 6 997 | 1 838 | 494 |
| | 1975 | 6 817 | 2 829 | 191 | 9 838 | 2 626 | 791 |
| | 1980 | 7 468 | 4 151 | 488 | 12 107 | 3 065 | 1 186 |
| | 1985 | 7 880 | 4 410 | 698 | 12 987 | 3 478 | 1 448 |
| | 1990 | 8 247 | 5 373 | 871 | 14 491 | 3 910 | 1 941 |
| | 1991 | 8 221 | 5 410 | 884 | 14 515 | 3 937 | 1 986 |
| | 1992 | 8 246 | 5 498 | 887 | 14 631 | 4 008 | 2 051 |
| | 1993 | 8 307 | 5 592 | 915 | 14 814 | 4 094 | 2 122 |
| | 1994 | 8 371 | 5 733 | 936 | 15 040 | 4 177 | 2 216 |
| | 1995 | 8 427 | 6 047 | 975 | 15 449 | 4 260 | 2 412 |
| | 1996 | 8 537 | 6 293 | 1 011 | 15 841 | 4 382 | 2 592 |
| | 1997 | 8 624 | 6 603 | 1 045 | 16 272 | 4 492 | 2 755 |
| Southern Asia | 1970 | 1 768 | 1 183 | 178 | 3 129 | 422 | 269 |
| | 1975 | 2 081 | 1 564 | 265 | 3 910 | 544 | 407 |
| | 1980 | 2 238 | 1 942 | 310 | 4 490 | 671 | 530 |
| | 1985 | 2 742 | 2 315 | 362 | 5 418 | 828 | 711 |
| | 1990 | 2 990 | 2 621 | 414 | 6 025 | 914 | 891 |
| | 1991 | 3 110 | 2 697 | 426 | 6 233 | 978 | 918 |
| | 1992 | 3 182 | 2 753 | 433 | 6 367 | 995 | 951 |
| | 1993 | 3 276 | 2 808 | 439 | 6 523 | 1 022 | 1 016 |
| | 1994 | 3 339 | 2 906 | 449 | 6 694 | 1 055 | 1 066 |
| | 1995 | 3 405 | 3 008 | 509 | 6 922 | 1 085 | 1 111 |
| | 1996 | 3 438 | 3 100 | 527 | 7 065 | 1 106 | 1 144 |
| | 1997 | 3 472 | 3 202 | 574 | 7 249 | 1 116 | 1 186 |
| Least Developed Countries | 1970 | 524 | 172 | 20 | 716 | 111 | 37 |
| | 1975 | 670 | 236 | 27 | 934 | 157 | 47 |
| | 1980 | 909 | 324 | 38 | 1 271 | 257 | 74 |
| | 1985 | 1 097 | 413 | 49 | 1 559 | 327 | 108 |
| | 1990 | 1 248 | 550 | 61 | 1 859 | 415 | 148 |
| | 1991 | 1 273 | 566 | 69 | 1 907 | 420 | 152 |
| | 1992 | 1 327 | 565 | 73 | 1 965 | 441 | 154 |
| | 1993 | 1 352 | 572 | 78 | 2 002 | 461 | 159 |
| | 1994 | 1 423 | 605 | 81 | 2 109 | 490 | 168 |
| | 1995 | 1 467 | 640 | 85 | 2 193 | 506 | 180 |
| | 1996 | 1 513 | 678 | 91 | 2 282 | 523 | 196 |
| | 1997 | 1 545 | 709 | 95 | 2 349 | 533 | 210 |
| Developed Countries | 1970 | 5 417 | 5 490 | 1 530 | 12 437 | 3 933 | 2 676 |
| | 1975 | 5 296 | 6 458 | 1 907 | 13 660 | 3 869 | 3 234 |
| | 1980 | 4 843 | 7 260 | 2 486 | 14 589 | 3 730 | 3 676 |
| | 1985 | 5 016 | 7 441 | 2 608 | 15 064 | 3 957 | 3 965 |
| | 1990 | 5 180 | 8 080 | 2 937 | 16 196 | 4 155 | 4 433 |
| | 1991 | 5 195 | 8 229 | 2 972 | 16 396 | 4 223 | 4 532 |
| | 1992 | 5 210 | 8 407 | 3 079 | 16 725 | 4 246 | 4 778 |
| | 1993 | 5 307 | 8 689 | 3 361 | 17 357 | 4 328 | 4 983 |
| | 1994 | 5 302 | 8 735 | 3 394 | 17 431 | 4 325 | 5 027 |
| | 1995 | 5 379 | 8 827 | 3 403 | 17 609 | 4 381 | 5 135 |
| | 1996 | 5 345 | 8 933 | 3 426 | 17 704 | 4 368 | 5 206 |
| | 1997 | 5 340 | 9 002 | 3 452 | 17 794 | 4 362 | 5 254 |

**General note**
For general explanations and definitions, please refer to the beginning of this chapter. Data do not include the Democratic People's Republic of Korea.

**Note générale**
Pour les explications et définitions générales, prière de se référer au début de ce chapitre. Les données n'incluent pas la République populaire démocratique de Corée.

**Nota general**
Para las explicaciones y definiciones generales, referirse al comienzo de este capítulo. Los datos no incluyen la República Popular Democrática de Corea.

II.S.5    Gross enrolment ratios by level of education
Taux bruts de scolarisation par niveau d'enseignement
Tasas brutas de escolarización por nivel de enseñanza

## II.S.5   Gross enrolment ratios by level of education

## Taux bruts de scolarisation par niveau d'enseignement

## Tasas brutas de escolarización por nivel de enseñanza

| Continents, major areas and groups of countries / Continents, grandes régions et groupes de pays / Continentes, grandes regiones y grupos de países | Year / Année / Año | Gross enrolment ratios / Taux bruts de scolarisation / Tasas brutas de escolarización (%) ||||||||||||
|---|---|---|---|---|---|---|---|---|---|---|---|---|---|
| | | Primary Primaire Primaria ||| Secondary Secondaire Secundaria ||| Tertiary Supérieur Superior ||| All levels Tous les niveaux Todos los niveles |||
| | | MF | M | F | MF | M | F | MF | M | F | MF | M | F |
| World total | 1970 | 89.9 | 97.5 | 81.9 | 36.4 | 41.8 | 30.7 | 9.2 | 11.2 | 7.1 | 50.3 | 55.8 | 44.6 |
| | 1975 | 97.7 | 105.6 | 89.5 | 44.4 | 49.8 | 38.8 | 10.7 | 12.4 | 8.9 | 56.2 | 61.6 | 50.6 |
| | 1980 | 95.9 | 103.3 | 88.1 | 46.5 | 51.6 | 41.1 | 12.3 | 13.4 | 11.1 | 55.3 | 60.2 | 50.2 |
| | 1985 | 99.6 | 106.5 | 92.3 | 48.6 | 53.6 | 43.3 | 12.9 | 14.0 | 11.8 | 56.2 | 60.7 | 51.4 |
| | 1990 | 99.2 | 105.0 | 93.0 | 51.8 | 56.5 | 46.9 | 13.8 | 14.6 | 13.0 | 57.5 | 61.4 | 53.3 |
| | 1991 | 98.9 | 104.5 | 93.0 | 52.6 | 57.1 | 47.8 | 14.1 | 14.7 | 13.5 | 57.9 | 61.7 | 53.9 |
| | 1992 | 98.9 | 104.2 | 93.3 | 54.7 | 59.1 | 50.1 | 14.4 | 14.9 | 13.9 | 58.9 | 62.6 | 55.1 |
| | 1993 | 99.2 | 104.5 | 93.6 | 55.8 | 59.9 | 51.5 | 15.2 | 15.7 | 14.6 | 59.8 | 63.4 | 56.1 |
| | 1994 | 99.7 | 105.0 | 94.3 | 57.0 | 60.9 | 52.8 | 15.6 | 16.1 | 15.1 | 60.7 | 64.2 | 57.1 |
| | 1995 | 100.3 | 105.5 | 94.7 | 58.3 | 62.1 | 54.3 | 16.2 | 16.8 | 15.6 | 61.7 | 65.2 | 58.1 |
| | 1996 | 100.9 | 106.0 | 95.5 | 59.4 | 63.1 | 55.6 | 16.9 | 17.5 | 16.3 | 62.6 | 65.9 | 59.0 |
| | 1997 | 101.8 | 106.9 | 96.4 | 60.1 | 64.0 | 56.0 | 17.4 | 18.1 | 16.7 | 63.3 | 66.7 | 59.6 |
| Africa | 1970 | 56.0 | 66.9 | 44.9 | 10.2 | 13.9 | 6.5 | 1.6 | 2.4 | 0.7 | 28.0 | 34.3 | 21.7 |
| | 1975 | 65.1 | 75.9 | 54.1 | 15.0 | 19.5 | 10.5 | 2.6 | 3.9 | 1.3 | 33.3 | 39.8 | 26.8 |
| | 1980 | 80.3 | 90.3 | 70.3 | 22.1 | 27.8 | 16.4 | 3.7 | 5.3 | 2.0 | 42.4 | 49.0 | 35.7 |
| | 1985 | 80.8 | 89.4 | 72.0 | 28.2 | 33.4 | 22.9 | 4.4 | 6.4 | 2.5 | 45.1 | 51.0 | 39.1 |
| | 1990 | 77.7 | 85.1 | 70.2 | 30.0 | 34.0 | 25.9 | 5.1 | 6.7 | 3.4 | 44.7 | 49.6 | 39.7 |
| | 1991 | 77.3 | 84.1 | 70.3 | 30.3 | 34.3 | 26.3 | 5.2 | 6.8 | 3.6 | 44.6 | 49.3 | 39.9 |
| | 1992 | 76.8 | 83.4 | 70.1 | 30.8 | 34.5 | 27.0 | 5.4 | 7.1 | 3.8 | 44.9 | 49.4 | 40.3 |
| | 1993 | 78.0 | 84.9 | 71.1 | 31.6 | 35.1 | 28.0 | 5.6 | 7.1 | 4.0 | 45.7 | 50.2 | 41.1 |
| | 1994 | 79.8 | 86.8 | 72.7 | 32.4 | 35.8 | 29.0 | 5.7 | 7.2 | 4.2 | 46.6 | 51.1 | 42.0 |
| | 1995 | 80.4 | 87.6 | 73.1 | 33.1 | 36.4 | 29.8 | 6.1 | 7.6 | 4.6 | 47.1 | 51.6 | 42.5 |
| | 1996 | 80.7 | 88.0 | 73.4 | 33.4 | 36.6 | 30.2 | 6.5 | 8.1 | 4.9 | 47.3 | 51.9 | 42.6 |
| | 1997 | 80.7 | 88.0 | 73.3 | 34.0 | 37.3 | 30.7 | 6.9 | 8.6 | 5.2 | 47.4 | 52.0 | 42.8 |
| America | 1970 | 99.1 | 100.1 | 98.1 | 49.4 | 49.9 | 48.9 | 24.2 | 28.9 | 19.5 | 62.2 | 64.0 | 60.2 |
| | 1975 | 95.4 | 96.6 | 94.2 | 58.5 | 58.9 | 58.0 | 29.7 | 32.9 | 26.5 | 66.1 | 67.6 | 64.5 |
| | 1980 | 102.8 | 103.9 | 101.7 | 63.4 | 63.1 | 63.6 | 30.7 | 30.9 | 30.4 | 70.1 | 70.6 | 69.6 |
| | 1985 | 103.4 | 105.0 | 101.7 | 67.1 | 66.3 | 67.8 | 32.1 | 31.6 | 32.6 | 71.9 | 72.3 | 71.6 |
| | 1990 | 104.3 | 105.5 | 103.2 | 65.8 | 64.5 | 67.1 | 36.1 | 33.9 | 38.2 | 73.8 | 73.4 | 74.2 |
| | 1991 | 104.6 | 106.1 | 103.1 | 66.4 | 65.1 | 67.9 | 37.1 | 34.7 | 39.5 | 74.5 | 74.1 | 74.8 |
| | 1992 | 105.3 | 106.6 | 103.9 | 67.9 | 66.6 | 69.2 | 36.8 | 34.3 | 39.3 | 75.1 | 74.7 | 75.5 |
| | 1993 | 105.8 | 107.0 | 104.4 | 68.5 | 67.2 | 69.8 | 36.4 | 33.8 | 38.9 | 75.3 | 74.9 | 75.8 |
| | 1994 | 106.9 | 108.1 | 105.6 | 69.2 | 67.5 | 71.0 | 36.2 | 33.5 | 38.9 | 75.9 | 75.3 | 76.5 |
| | 1995 | 108.3 | 110.4 | 106.1 | 70.9 | 69.4 | 72.6 | 36.6 | 34.0 | 39.2 | 77.0 | 76.9 | 77.2 |
| | 1996 | 109.2 | 111.2 | 107.1 | 73.1 | 71.3 | 75.0 | 37.0 | 34.7 | 39.3 | 78.1 | 77.9 | 78.3 |
| | 1997 | 110.4 | 112.8 | 107.8 | 74.8 | 72.8 | 76.9 | 37.1 | 34.9 | 39.4 | 79.0 | 79.0 | 79.1 |
| Asia | 1970 | 83.5 | 93.0 | 73.5 | 26.5 | 33.8 | 18.7 | 3.5 | 4.9 | 2.0 | 42.6 | 49.3 | 35.6 |
| | 1975 | 97.7 | 107.4 | 87.4 | 35.2 | 42.5 | 27.4 | 3.9 | 5.3 | 2.4 | 50.5 | 57.2 | 43.5 |
| | 1980 | 96.6 | 106.0 | 86.6 | 39.7 | 46.9 | 32.1 | 5.6 | 7.2 | 3.8 | 51.1 | 57.6 | 44.2 |
| | 1985 | 103.2 | 112.0 | 93.8 | 41.7 | 48.7 | 34.2 | 6.7 | 8.5 | 4.9 | 51.8 | 57.8 | 45.3 |
| | 1990 | 103.8 | 111.1 | 96.0 | 46.7 | 53.6 | 39.5 | 7.2 | 8.8 | 5.6 | 53.6 | 59.1 | 47.9 |
| | 1991 | 103.5 | 110.5 | 96.1 | 47.9 | 54.6 | 40.7 | 7.4 | 8.8 | 5.9 | 54.2 | 59.5 | 48.6 |
| | 1992 | 103.5 | 110.1 | 96.5 | 50.0 | 56.7 | 42.9 | 7.7 | 9.0 | 6.2 | 55.4 | 60.5 | 50.0 |
| | 1993 | 103.6 | 110.1 | 96.8 | 51.1 | 57.3 | 44.5 | 8.5 | 9.9 | 6.9 | 56.4 | 61.3 | 51.2 |
| | 1994 | 103.8 | 109.9 | 97.2 | 52.7 | 58.8 | 46.2 | 9.0 | 10.6 | 7.4 | 57.5 | 62.4 | 52.4 |
| | 1995 | 104.0 | 110.0 | 97.7 | 54.5 | 60.4 | 48.2 | 9.8 | 11.5 | 8.0 | 58.7 | 63.5 | 53.7 |
| | 1996 | 104.7 | 110.4 | 98.7 | 56.1 | 61.8 | 50.1 | 10.5 | 12.2 | 8.6 | 59.9 | 64.5 | 55.0 |
| | 1997 | 106.0 | 111.6 | 100.0 | 56.9 | 62.8 | 50.5 | 11.1 | 12.9 | 9.1 | 60.8 | 65.5 | 55.8 |

Gross enrolment ratios by level of education  II.S.5
Taux bruts de scolarisation par niveau d'enseignement
Tasas brutas de escolarización por nivel de enseñanza

| Continents, major areas and groups of countries / Continents, grandes régions et groupes de pays / Continentes, grandes regiones y grupos de países | Year / Année / Año | Gross enrolment ratios / Taux bruts de scolarisation / Tasas brutas de escolarización (%) | | | | | | | | | | | |
|---|---|---|---|---|---|---|---|---|---|---|---|---|---|
| | | Primary Primaire Primaria | | | Secondary Secondaire Secundaria | | | Tertiary Supérieur Superior | | | All levels Tous les niveaux Todos los niveles | | |
| | | MF | M | F | MF | M | F | MF | M | F | MF | M | F |
| Europe | 1970 | 106.4 | 106.6 | 106.2 | 67.5 | 69.9 | 65.1 | 14.4 | 17.7 | 11.0 | 66.5 | 68.4 | 64.6 |
| | 1975 | 105.0 | 104.8 | 105.3 | 77.3 | 78.6 | 76.0 | 19.9 | 22.6 | 17.1 | 70.9 | 72.1 | 69.5 |
| | 1980 | 102.2 | 102.5 | 101.9 | 86.9 | 86.3 | 87.6 | 29.3 | 29.0 | 29.7 | 73.3 | 73.1 | 73.6 |
| | 1985 | 102.1 | 102.4 | 101.8 | 90.5 | 89.6 | 91.3 | 31.7 | 30.6 | 33.0 | 75.4 | 74.8 | 76.0 |
| | 1990 | 101.1 | 101.1 | 101.1 | 92.4 | 91.1 | 93.7 | 35.9 | 35.0 | 36.9 | 77.3 | 76.6 | 78.1 |
| | 1991 | 100.5 | 100.5 | 100.4 | 92.6 | 91.0 | 94.3 | 36.6 | 35.4 | 37.8 | 77.5 | 76.5 | 78.5 |
| | 1992 | 101.8 | 102.1 | 101.6 | 97.0 | 94.7 | 99.3 | 37.9 | 36.2 | 39.8 | 80.1 | 78.7 | 81.5 |
| | 1993 | 101.6 | 101.9 | 101.3 | 98.8 | 96.6 | 101.0 | 39.6 | 37.5 | 41.7 | 81.3 | 79.9 | 82.8 |
| | 1994 | 101.9 | 102.4 | 101.5 | 99.3 | 97.2 | 101.6 | 40.3 | 37.8 | 42.9 | 81.9 | 80.4 | 83.5 |
| | 1995 | 103.4 | 103.8 | 102.9 | 99.3 | 97.1 | 101.6 | 41.0 | 38.1 | 43.9 | 82.5 | 80.8 | 84.2 |
| | 1996 | 103.8 | 104.2 | 103.4 | 98.7 | 96.7 | 100.9 | 42.1 | 38.8 | 45.6 | 82.7 | 81.0 | 84.5 |
| | 1997 | 104.7 | 104.9 | 104.4 | 99.2 | 97.2 | 101.3 | 42.8 | 39.5 | 46.3 | 83.3 | 81.5 | 85.1 |
| Oceania | 1970 | 104.3 | 106.3 | 102.1 | 68.7 | 73.3 | 64.0 | 13.7 | 17.7 | 9.5 | 67.6 | 71.0 | 64.0 |
| | 1975 | 99.1 | 101.5 | 96.7 | 63.5 | 63.9 | 63.1 | 19.7 | 23.2 | 15.9 | 64.7 | 66.7 | 62.6 |
| | 1980 | 101.1 | 102.9 | 99.1 | 62.7 | 61.8 | 63.6 | 21.3 | 23.2 | 19.4 | 65.4 | 66.2 | 64.5 |
| | 1985 | 101.2 | 102.9 | 99.4 | 67.4 | 66.8 | 68.0 | 23.3 | 24.0 | 22.7 | 66.7 | 67.2 | 66.2 |
| | 1990 | 103.1 | 104.9 | 101.3 | 68.0 | 67.2 | 68.9 | 28.8 | 27.1 | 30.7 | 69.0 | 68.8 | 69.2 |
| | 1991 | 102.9 | 104.7 | 101.1 | 69.1 | 68.5 | 69.8 | 31.9 | 29.7 | 34.4 | 70.3 | 70.0 | 70.6 |
| | 1992 | 102.9 | 104.8 | 100.9 | 70.1 | 69.6 | 70.6 | 33.9 | 31.3 | 36.7 | 71.4 | 71.2 | 71.7 |
| | 1993 | 103.2 | 105.1 | 101.2 | 98.9 | 98.8 | 98.9 | 51.4 | 50.9 | 51.9 | 86.9 | 87.4 | 86.4 |
| | 1994 | 103.2 | 105.2 | 101.2 | 99.1 | 99.2 | 98.9 | 52.3 | 51.2 | 53.4 | 87.4 | 87.8 | 86.9 |
| | 1995 | 100.4 | 102.1 | 98.6 | 106.0 | 106.6 | 105.4 | 54.1 | 52.3 | 55.9 | 89.8 | 90.2 | 89.4 |
| | 1996 | 100.1 | 101.7 | 98.4 | 108.9 | 108.9 | 108.9 | 55.4 | 53.1 | 57.8 | 91.1 | 91.1 | 91.1 |
| | 1997 | 100.2 | 101.0 | 99.5 | 111.0 | 109.7 | 112.4 | 57.7 | 54.9 | 60.7 | 92.6 | 92.0 | 93.2 |
| Developing Countries | 1970 | 81.2 | 90.3 | 71.7 | 22.7 | 29.1 | 16.0 | 2.9 | 4.0 | 1.7 | 40.8 | 47.0 | 34.4 |
| | 1975 | 92.6 | 101.7 | 83.0 | 30.9 | 37.5 | 24.0 | 3.9 | 5.1 | 2.7 | 48.3 | 54.5 | 41.8 |
| | 1980 | 94.9 | 103.7 | 85.7 | 35.3 | 41.9 | 28.3 | 5.2 | 6.7 | 3.7 | 50.2 | 56.3 | 43.8 |
| | 1985 | 99.3 | 107.5 | 90.7 | 38.0 | 44.4 | 31.4 | 6.6 | 8.2 | 4.9 | 51.2 | 56.9 | 45.3 |
| | 1990 | 98.8 | 105.6 | 91.7 | 42.2 | 48.2 | 36.0 | 7.1 | 8.5 | 5.7 | 52.7 | 57.6 | 47.5 |
| | 1991 | 98.6 | 105.1 | 91.7 | 43.2 | 49.1 | 37.1 | 7.2 | 8.5 | 5.9 | 53.1 | 57.9 | 48.1 |
| | 1992 | 98.5 | 104.7 | 92.0 | 45.2 | 50.9 | 39.1 | 7.5 | 8.7 | 6.2 | 54.1 | 58.7 | 49.3 |
| | 1993 | 98.9 | 105.0 | 92.5 | 46.1 | 51.4 | 40.6 | 7.9 | 9.2 | 6.6 | 55.0 | 59.4 | 50.3 |
| | 1994 | 99.4 | 105.4 | 93.2 | 47.6 | 52.8 | 42.2 | 8.4 | 9.7 | 7.0 | 56.0 | 60.4 | 51.4 |
| | 1995 | 100.0 | 106.0 | 93.7 | 49.3 | 54.3 | 44.1 | 9.1 | 10.6 | 7.5 | 57.1 | 61.5 | 52.5 |
| | 1996 | 100.7 | 106.5 | 94.5 | 50.9 | 55.6 | 45.8 | 9.8 | 11.4 | 8.1 | 58.2 | 62.5 | 53.6 |
| | 1997 | 101.6 | 107.5 | 95.4 | 51.7 | 56.6 | 46.4 | 10.3 | 12.0 | 8.6 | 58.9 | 63.4 | 54.3 |
| of which: | | | | | | | | | | | | | |
| Sub-Saharan Africa | 1970 | 52.5 | 62.3 | 42.8 | 7.1 | 9.6 | 4.6 | 0.8 | 1.3 | 0.3 | 25.6 | 30.8 | 20.3 |
| | 1975 | 62.1 | 71.9 | 52.3 | 11.2 | 14.5 | 7.9 | 1.2 | 1.8 | 0.5 | 30.8 | 36.4 | 25.3 |
| | 1980 | 79.5 | 88.7 | 70.2 | 17.5 | 22.2 | 12.8 | 1.7 | 2.7 | 0.7 | 40.6 | 46.4 | 34.7 |
| | 1985 | 78.9 | 87.2 | 70.6 | 22.1 | 26.3 | 17.9 | 2.3 | 3.5 | 1.1 | 42.3 | 47.6 | 37.0 |
| | 1990 | 74.8 | 81.9 | 67.6 | 22.4 | 25.5 | 19.2 | 3.0 | 4.1 | 1.9 | 40.9 | 45.4 | 36.4 |
| | 1991 | 74.1 | 80.6 | 67.5 | 22.8 | 26.0 | 19.6 | 3.2 | 4.3 | 2.1 | 40.8 | 45.0 | 36.5 |
| | 1992 | 73.3 | 79.6 | 67.0 | 23.1 | 26.1 | 20.2 | 3.3 | 4.4 | 2.2 | 40.9 | 45.0 | 36.8 |
| | 1993 | 74.4 | 81.1 | 67.6 | 23.7 | 26.6 | 20.9 | 3.4 | 4.6 | 2.3 | 41.6 | 45.8 | 37.4 |
| | 1994 | 76.2 | 83.1 | 69.2 | 24.6 | 27.4 | 21.7 | 3.5 | 4.7 | 2.4 | 42.6 | 46.9 | 38.3 |
| | 1995 | 76.6 | 83.8 | 69.4 | 25.4 | 28.1 | 22.7 | 3.7 | 4.8 | 2.5 | 43.0 | 47.4 | 38.6 |
| | 1996 | 76.9 | 84.3 | 69.5 | 25.8 | 28.7 | 23.0 | 3.8 | 5.0 | 2.7 | 43.2 | 47.7 | 38.7 |
| | 1997 | 76.8 | 84.1 | 69.4 | 26.2 | 29.1 | 23.3 | 3.9 | 5.1 | 2.8 | 43.2 | 47.7 | 38.7 |
| Arab States | 1970 | 64.3 | 79.5 | 48.4 | 20.2 | 27.6 | 12.5 | 4.3 | 6.6 | 2.1 | 34.9 | 44.5 | 24.9 |
| | 1975 | 74.6 | 89.9 | 58.6 | 28.1 | 36.0 | 19.7 | 7.0 | 9.8 | 4.1 | 41.7 | 51.2 | 31.6 |
| | 1980 | 79.0 | 90.1 | 67.5 | 38.5 | 47.1 | 29.6 | 9.6 | 12.9 | 6.1 | 47.8 | 56.0 | 39.2 |
| | 1985 | 81.8 | 90.7 | 72.4 | 47.0 | 54.9 | 38.7 | 11.3 | 14.7 | 7.6 | 52.5 | 59.7 | 45.0 |
| | 1990 | 81.4 | 90.0 | 72.4 | 52.2 | 59.1 | 44.9 | 11.4 | 14.1 | 8.6 | 54.6 | 61.1 | 47.8 |
| | 1991 | 81.8 | 90.3 | 72.9 | 51.5 | 57.8 | 44.8 | 11.6 | 14.1 | 9.0 | 54.6 | 60.9 | 48.1 |
| | 1992 | 79.5 | 87.7 | 71.0 | 52.8 | 58.7 | 46.6 | 12.2 | 14.7 | 9.5 | 54.5 | 60.5 | 48.3 |
| | 1993 | 81.1 | 89.3 | 72.7 | 53.6 | 58.9 | 48.0 | 12.1 | 14.2 | 9.8 | 55.4 | 61.1 | 49.5 |
| | 1994 | 84.2 | 92.1 | 76.1 | 54.7 | 59.7 | 49.6 | 12.5 | 14.6 | 10.3 | 57.1 | 62.6 | 51.5 |
| | 1995 | 84.2 | 91.7 | 76.4 | 55.5 | 60.4 | 50.4 | 13.2 | 15.4 | 11.0 | 57.4 | 62.7 | 51.9 |
| | 1996 | 84.2 | 91.6 | 76.5 | 55.8 | 60.1 | 51.3 | 14.1 | 16.4 | 11.7 | 57.4 | 62.5 | 52.1 |
| | 1997 | 84.7 | 92.1 | 76.9 | 56.9 | 61.2 | 52.3 | 14.9 | 17.3 | 12.4 | 57.9 | 63.0 | 52.6 |
| Latin America and the Caribbean | 1970 | 105.9 | 107.4 | 104.3 | 27.0 | 27.8 | 26.3 | 6.3 | 8.1 | 4.5 | 52.5 | 53.9 | 51.1 |
| | 1975 | 97.8 | 99.4 | 96.2 | 36.4 | 37.3 | 35.5 | 11.9 | 13.8 | 10.0 | 59.0 | 60.5 | 57.4 |
| | 1980 | 104.1 | 105.6 | 102.7 | 44.4 | 44.1 | 44.7 | 13.7 | 15.5 | 11.9 | 63.8 | 65.0 | 62.6 |
| | 1985 | 104.7 | 106.8 | 102.6 | 49.7 | 48.3 | 51.1 | 15.7 | 17.2 | 14.2 | 65.4 | 66.4 | 64.3 |
| | 1990 | 105.0 | 106.2 | 103.7 | 50.9 | 49.0 | 52.8 | 16.8 | 17.3 | 16.4 | 66.1 | 66.4 | 65.8 |
| | 1991 | 105.5 | 107.2 | 103.7 | 51.3 | 49.3 | 53.4 | 16.9 | 17.1 | 16.6 | 66.4 | 66.8 | 65.9 |
| | 1992 | 106.6 | 108.1 | 105.0 | 52.2 | 49.9 | 54.5 | 16.7 | 16.9 | 16.5 | 66.9 | 67.2 | 66.6 |
| | 1993 | 107.4 | 108.9 | 105.8 | 52.4 | 50.0 | 54.8 | 16.8 | 16.8 | 16.7 | 67.1 | 67.4 | 66.8 |
| | 1994 | 108.5 | 110.0 | 106.9 | 54.1 | 51.5 | 56.7 | 16.9 | 16.9 | 16.9 | 67.9 | 68.1 | 67.7 |
| | 1995 | 110.6 | 113.2 | 107.9 | 56.5 | 53.9 | 59.2 | 17.9 | 18.2 | 17.6 | 69.6 | 70.3 | 68.8 |
| | 1996 | 111.9 | 114.6 | 109.1 | 59.8 | 57.1 | 62.5 | 18.8 | 19.4 | 18.1 | 71.1 | 72.0 | 70.3 |
| | 1997 | 113.6 | 116.9 | 110.2 | 62.2 | 59.2 | 65.3 | 19.4 | 20.1 | 18.7 | 72.6 | 73.6 | 71.5 |

**Gross enrolment ratios by level of education**
Taux bruts de scolarisation par niveau d'enseignement
Tasas brutas de escolarización por nivel de enseñanza

| Continents, major areas and groups of countries / Continents, grandes régions et groupes de pays / Continentes, grandes regiones y grupos de países | Year / Année / Año | Gross enrolment ratios / Taux bruts de scolarisation / Tasas brutas de escolarización (%) | | | | | | | | | | | |
|---|---|---|---|---|---|---|---|---|---|---|---|---|---|
| | | Primary Primaire Primaria | | | Secondary Secondaire Secundaria | | | Tertiary Supérieur Superior | | | All levels Tous les niveaux Todos los niveles | | |
| | | MF | M | F | MF | M | F | MF | M | F | MF | M | F |
| Eastern Asia and Oceania | 1970 | 90.7 | 96.2 | 84.9 | 25.2 | 31.7 | 18.4 | 1.4 | 1.6 | 1.2 | 45.8 | 50.3 | 41.0 |
| | 1975 | 112.3 | 118.4 | 105.9 | 41.4 | 48.0 | 34.5 | 1.8 | 2.1 | 1.5 | 59.0 | 63.7 | 53.9 |
| | 1980 | 110.4 | 117.4 | 103.0 | 43.9 | 50.3 | 37.0 | 3.8 | 4.9 | 2.7 | 57.8 | 63.1 | 52.3 |
| | 1985 | 117.7 | 124.2 | 110.9 | 41.6 | 47.0 | 35.8 | 5.4 | 6.8 | 3.9 | 54.7 | 59.2 | 50.0 |
| | 1990 | 118.5 | 122.0 | 114.8 | 47.4 | 52.3 | 42.3 | 5.9 | 7.1 | 4.7 | 55.6 | 58.9 | 52.1 |
| | 1991 | 117.0 | 119.8 | 114.1 | 49.4 | 54.0 | 44.6 | 6.0 | 7.1 | 4.8 | 56.3 | 59.3 | 53.2 |
| | 1992 | 115.3 | 117.9 | 112.6 | 51.5 | 56.0 | 46.8 | 6.4 | 7.3 | 5.4 | 57.4 | 60.2 | 54.4 |
| | 1993 | 114.3 | 116.3 | 112.1 | 53.4 | 56.9 | 49.7 | 7.2 | 8.4 | 6.0 | 58.8 | 61.2 | 56.2 |
| | 1994 | 114.0 | 115.6 | 112.3 | 57.1 | 60.3 | 53.7 | 8.2 | 9.6 | 6.7 | 61.0 | 63.3 | 58.7 |
| | 1995 | 114.5 | 115.8 | 113.2 | 61.3 | 64.2 | 58.3 | 9.0 | 10.6 | 7.3 | 63.5 | 65.6 | 61.3 |
| | 1996 | 116.0 | 116.7 | 115.2 | 64.5 | 67.4 | 61.5 | 10.0 | 11.6 | 8.3 | 66.0 | 67.9 | 63.9 |
| | 1997 | 118.0 | 118.3 | 117.6 | 66.3 | 69.3 | 63.1 | 10.8 | 12.5 | 9.0 | 67.9 | 69.8 | 65.9 |
| Southern Asia | 1970 | 69.8 | 86.0 | 52.4 | 22.8 | 31.6 | 13.2 | 4.1 | 6.2 | 1.8 | 35.1 | 44.9 | 24.5 |
| | 1975 | 74.6 | 90.5 | 57.4 | 24.6 | 33.2 | 15.3 | 4.3 | 6.4 | 2.1 | 36.9 | 46.4 | 26.7 |
| | 1980 | 75.9 | 90.5 | 60.1 | 27.6 | 36.3 | 18.2 | 4.3 | 6.2 | 2.3 | 38.2 | 47.1 | 28.5 |
| | 1985 | 85.1 | 98.5 | 70.7 | 34.1 | 43.6 | 23.8 | 5.4 | 7.4 | 3.2 | 43.7 | 52.6 | 34.2 |
| | 1990 | 90.3 | 102.6 | 77.1 | 39.8 | 49.2 | 29.7 | 5.7 | 7.4 | 3.7 | 48.2 | 56.5 | 39.2 |
| | 1991 | 91.4 | 103.5 | 78.4 | 40.7 | 50.1 | 30.6 | 5.7 | 7.4 | 3.9 | 48.9 | 57.2 | 40.1 |
| | 1992 | 93.2 | 104.6 | 81.1 | 43.7 | 53.0 | 33.6 | 5.7 | 7.5 | 3.8 | 50.8 | 58.8 | 42.2 |
| | 1993 | 94.5 | 106.0 | 82.2 | 44.4 | 53.5 | 34.6 | 5.8 | 7.5 | 3.9 | 51.5 | 59.4 | 43.0 |
| | 1994 | 94.6 | 106.1 | 82.3 | 44.6 | 53.6 | 34.9 | 5.8 | 7.5 | 4.0 | 51.5 | 59.4 | 43.1 |
| | 1995 | 94.6 | 105.9 | 82.5 | 44.8 | 53.6 | 35.3 | 6.5 | 8.2 | 4.6 | 51.7 | 59.4 | 43.4 |
| | 1996 | 94.8 | 106.0 | 82.9 | 45.4 | 53.8 | 36.4 | 6.8 | 8.6 | 4.9 | 51.9 | 59.4 | 43.9 |
| | 1997 | 95.4 | 106.8 | 83.3 | 45.3 | 54.1 | 35.8 | 7.2 | 9.1 | 5.1 | 52.0 | 59.7 | 43.6 |
| Least Developed Countries | 1970 | 47.6 | 59.7 | 35.4 | 10.3 | 15.1 | 5.3 | 1.0 | 1.6 | 0.3 | 23.4 | 30.3 | 16.5 |
| | 1975 | 57.1 | 70.6 | 43.5 | 12.2 | 17.6 | 6.7 | 1.2 | 2.0 | 0.4 | 27.6 | 35.2 | 20.0 |
| | 1980 | 66.0 | 77.1 | 54.7 | 14.8 | 20.5 | 8.9 | 1.8 | 2.7 | 0.9 | 32.4 | 39.1 | 25.5 |
| | 1985 | 65.8 | 75.0 | 56.4 | 16.4 | 21.3 | 11.3 | 2.5 | 3.7 | 1.3 | 33.0 | 38.8 | 27.0 |
| | 1990 | 65.8 | 73.4 | 58.0 | 17.2 | 21.8 | 12.6 | 2.5 | 3.6 | 1.3 | 33.7 | 38.8 | 28.5 |
| | 1991 | 66.5 | 74.0 | 58.8 | 17.3 | 21.7 | 12.8 | 2.7 | 4.0 | 1.4 | 34.0 | 39.0 | 28.9 |
| | 1992 | 65.7 | 73.3 | 58.0 | 17.0 | 21.3 | 12.6 | 2.9 | 4.1 | 1.6 | 33.9 | 38.8 | 28.8 |
| | 1993 | 66.5 | 74.4 | 58.4 | 17.2 | 21.5 | 12.8 | 2.9 | 4.2 | 1.6 | 34.1 | 39.2 | 28.9 |
| | 1994 | 68.9 | 77.2 | 60.5 | 17.9 | 22.1 | 13.6 | 3.0 | 4.3 | 1.6 | 35.2 | 40.4 | 29.9 |
| | 1995 | 69.8 | 78.5 | 60.9 | 18.5 | 22.5 | 14.3 | 3.0 | 4.4 | 1.6 | 35.6 | 40.9 | 30.2 |
| | 1996 | 70.7 | 79.6 | 61.6 | 19.0 | 23.1 | 14.8 | 3.1 | 4.6 | 1.7 | 36.1 | 41.4 | 30.6 |
| | 1997 | 71.5 | 80.6 | 62.3 | 19.3 | 23.5 | 15.0 | 3.2 | 4.6 | 1.7 | 36.4 | 41.8 | 30.8 |
| Developed Countries | 1970 | 99.2 | 99.5 | 99.0 | 75.7 | 76.9 | 74.5 | 26.1 | 31.8 | 20.3 | 70.1 | 72.4 | 67.8 |
| | 1975 | 99.0 | 99.0 | 99.0 | 81.8 | 82.2 | 81.4 | 33.5 | 37.8 | 29.1 | 73.8 | 75.3 | 72.2 |
| | 1980 | 100.9 | 101.1 | 100.6 | 89.4 | 89.1 | 89.7 | 36.2 | 36.2 | 36.1 | 76.3 | 76.3 | 76.3 |
| | 1985 | 101.0 | 101.3 | 100.8 | 93.7 | 93.4 | 94.0 | 38.6 | 37.4 | 39.8 | 78.7 | 78.4 | 79.1 |
| | 1990 | 101.0 | 101.2 | 100.7 | 93.9 | 92.9 | 94.8 | 44.5 | 42.6 | 46.4 | 80.9 | 80.1 | 81.8 |
| | 1991 | 100.5 | 100.8 | 100.2 | 94.1 | 93.0 | 95.3 | 46.0 | 43.7 | 48.3 | 81.4 | 80.4 | 82.4 |
| | 1992 | 101.1 | 101.5 | 100.7 | 97.0 | 95.7 | 98.3 | 46.9 | 44.2 | 49.8 | 83.0 | 81.8 | 84.3 |
| | 1993 | 100.9 | 101.3 | 100.6 | 99.1 | 98.0 | 100.3 | 49.1 | 46.2 | 52.2 | 84.5 | 83.3 | 85.8 |
| | 1994 | 101.6 | 102.0 | 101.1 | 99.2 | 98.0 | 100.6 | 49.7 | 46.3 | 53.1 | 84.9 | 83.6 | 86.4 |
| | 1995 | 102.1 | 102.5 | 101.6 | 99.5 | 98.4 | 100.7 | 50.1 | 46.5 | 53.9 | 85.4 | 84.0 | 86.8 |
| | 1996 | 102.3 | 102.6 | 101.9 | 99.5 | 98.3 | 100.8 | 51.0 | 47.1 | 55.1 | 85.7 | 84.2 | 87.4 |
| | 1997 | 102.7 | 102.9 | 102.4 | 100.1 | 98.9 | 101.4 | 51.6 | 47.7 | 55.7 | 86.3 | 84.7 | 88.0 |

**General note**
For general explanations and definitions, please refer to the beginning of this chapter. Data do not include the Democratic People's Republic of Korea.

**Note générale**
Pour les explications et définitions générales, prière de se référer au début de ce chapitre. Les données n'incluent pas la République populaire démocratique de Corée.

**Nota general**
Para las explicaciones y definiciones generales, referirse al comienzo de este capítulo. Los datos no incluyen la República Popular Democrática de Corea.

Country tables on education II
Tableaux sur l'enseignement par pays
Cuadros sobre la enseñanza por países

# Country tables on education

# Tableaux sur l'enseignement par pays

# Cuadros sobre la enseñanza por países

The tables in this section can be grouped according to six categories. The first four cover national education systems, literacy and adult educational attainment, teaching staff and pupils by level of education, and indicators by level of education, such as enrolment ratios, intake rates and other selected indicators. The following group of tables covers exclusively tertiary education, with data and indicators on the distribution of students by ISCED level and by broad field of study and on foreign students. Finally, data and indicators are presented on public expenditure on education.

---

Les tableaux de cette section peuvent être groupés en six catégories. Les quatre premières portent sur les systèmes nationaux d'enseignement, l'alphabétisme et le niveau d'instruction des adultes, le personnel enseignant et les effectifs scolaires par niveau d'enseignement, et sur des indicateurs par niveau d'enseignement tels que les taux de scolarisation, les taux d'admission et autres indicateurs sélectionnés. Le groupe qui suit porte entièrement sur l'enseignement supérieur, avec des statistiques et des indicateurs sur la répartition des étudiants par niveaux de la CITE et par grands domaines d'études et sur les étudiants étrangers. Enfin, sont présentés des statistiques et des indicateurs sur les dépenses publiques destinées à l'éducation.

---

Los cuadros de esta sección pueden ser agrupados en seis categorías. Las cuatro primeras se refieren a los sistemas nacionales de enseñanza, la alfabetización y el nivel de instrucción de adultos, el personal docente y la matrícula escolar por nivel de enseñanza, así como indicadores por nivel de enseñanza tales como las tasas de escolarización, las tasas de ingreso y otros indicadores seleccionados. El grupo siguiente concierne únicamente la enseñanza superior, con estadísticas e indicadores sobre la distribución de los estudiantes por niveles de la CINE y por grandes sectores de estudios y sobre los estudiantes extranjeros. Para finalizar, se presentan estadísticas e indicadores sobre los gastos públicos destinados a la educación.

II  Country tables on education
Tableaux sur l'enseignement par pays
Cuadros sobre la enseñanza por países

# Notes and explanations on country tables

# Notes et explications sur les tableaux par pays

# Notas y explicaciones de los cuadros por países

### Table II.1  National education systems

This table provides a summary presentation of the education system currently in force in each country. The information given here is intended to facilitate the interpretation of the figures shown in the tables that follow.

The first two columns provide data on compulsory education regulations: the first column shows the lower and upper age limits while the second column shows the number of years of compulsory school attendance. The third column gives the age at which children are admitted to pre-primary education.

The coloured shading in the following columns indicates the duration and age of admission into primary and secondary general education. The blue shading represents the duration of primary education, the red the duration of lower secondary general education and the green the duration of upper secondary general education. Some countries and territories make no distinction between these two stages of secondary general education: in these cases the total duration is shown in yellow.

For a certain number of countries the entrance age and duration of education may vary according to administrative area or type of schools. These countries are shown with the symbol ‡.

The reader may consult Table II.8 on enrolment ratios to see the changes which occurred in the education systems since 1970.

### Table II. 2  Estimated illiteracy rate and illiterate population aged 15 years and over, and 15 to 24 years

Illiteracy rates and the illiterate population indicate respectively the proportion and number of persons within the population who cannot with understanding both read and write a short simple statement on their everyday life.  The data presented in this table are the latest illiteracy estimates and projections of UNESCO, as assessed in 1998 based on statistics collected during national population censuses.  Estimated illiteracy rate refers to the estimated number of illiterates (15 years and over or 15–24 years old) expressed as a percentage of the population in the corresponding age group.

### Table II.3  Percentage distribution of population aged 25 years and over by educational attainment

The percentage distribution of the population aged 25 years and over according to the highest level of education attained reflects both the outcomes of participation in education in the past and the educational composition of the population.  These data have been collected mainly during national population censuses and sample surveys.  The six levels of educational attainment presented here are based on the International Standard Classification of Education (ISCED) and are defined as follows:

*No schooling* refers to persons who have completed less than one year of primary education.

*Primary education incomplete* includes all persons who have completed at least one grade of primary education but who did not complete the final grade of this level of education as defined in Table II.1.

*Primary education completed* refers to all persons who have completed the final grade of primary education but did not enter secondary education.

*Attended lower secondary education* comprises all persons who have attended lower secondary education but not (upper) secondary education.

*Attended (upper) secondary education* includes all persons who have attended (upper) secondary education but not post-secondary education.

*Post-secondary education* refers to all persons who have completed secondary education and attended post-secondary education.

For the duration of the above levels in each country see Table II.1 on national education systems.

### Table II.4  Pre-primary education: schools, teaching staff and pupils

The data refer to pre-primary education i.e. education provided in kindergartens, nursery schools as well as infant classes attached to primary schools.  Day nurseries, childcare and play centres, etc. are excluded.  Table II.1 should be consulted for information on age of admission and theoretical duration of pre-primary education.

### Table II.5  Primary education: schools, teaching staff and pupils

Data in this table cover primary education as defined in the Introduction of this Chapter.  In consulting this table, reference should be made to the information given on the duration of schooling in Table II.1. The reader should also consult Table II.8, on enrolment ratios, which shows the changes which occurred in the education structures since 1970. Figures on teaching staff refer, in principle, to both full-time and part-time teachers.  Data comparability may thus be affected, particularly as regards the pupil/teacher ratio, as the proportion of part-time teachers varies greatly from one country to another.

### Table II.6  Secondary education: teaching staff and pupils in general, teacher training and vocational education

This tables gives the number of teaching staff and pupils in each of the three types of secondary education i.e. general, teacher training, and vocational/technical.

*Secondary general*: this term refers to education in secondary schools that provide general or specialized education based upon at least four years previous instruction at the primary level, and which do not aim at preparing the pupils directly for a given trade or occupation. Such schools may be called high schools, middle schools, lyceums, gymnasiums, etc., and offer programmes of which completion is a minimum condition for admission to tertiary education.  In many countries, because of the desire to broaden the curricula there has been the development of schools providing both general and vocational education.  These composite schools are also classified as secondary general.

*Secondary, Teacher training*: This term refers to educational programmes with the purpose of training students for the teaching profession.

*Secondary, Vocational/Technical*: This term covers education provided in those secondary schools which aim at preparing the pupils directly for a trade or occupation other than teaching.  The abbreviation 'vocational education' has been used in the table headings.

For international comparisons, this table should be consulted in conjunction with Table II.1 on national education systems.

Country tables on education    II
Tableaux sur l'enseignement par pays
Cuadros sobre la enseñanza por países

**Table II.7  Tertiary education: teaching staff and students**

The data in this table refer to teaching staff and students enrolled in tertiary institutions. The data are shown for 'All institutions' and for 'Universities and equivalent degree-granting institutions (shown as 'Universities')'. 'All institutions' includes: (a) universities and equivalent degree-granting institutions; (b) distance-learning university institutions; (c) other tertiary educational institutions such as teacher training colleges, technical colleges, etc.

It should be noted that the criteria applied for determining the three categories of institutions may not be exactly the same in each of the countries and territories covered. Moreover, following reforms in the educational system, some non-university institutions in a given country may be attached to universities or recognized as equivalent institutions from one year to the next.

**Table II.8  Gross enrolment ratios by level of education**

This table presents gross enrolment ratios for countries and territories whose population exceeds 150,000. For countries with a population of less than 150,000, population data by age are not available. Demographic data are based on estimates and projections of the United Nations Population Division, as assessed in 1998; the enrolment data used to calculate the gross enrolment ratios appear in Tables II.4 to II.7 of this *Yearbook*. When interpreting the enrolment ratios presented in this table, the reader should refer to notes indicating changes in coverage in the corresponding tables by level.

*Gross enrolment ratio in pre-primary education.* Number of children in pre-primary education, regardless of age, expressed as a percentage of the population of the age group corresponding to the national regulations for this level of education.

*Gross enrolment ratio in primary education.* Total enrolment in primary education, regardless of age, expressed as a percentage of the population of the age group which officially corresponds to primary schooling.

*Gross enrolment ratio in secondary education.* Total enrolment in secondary education, regardless of age, expressed as a percentage of the population of the age group which officially corresponds to the duration of general secondary schooling. It should be stressed that enrolment ratios for secondary education are based on the total enrolment (general education, teacher training and technical and vocational education).

*Gross enrolment ratio in tertiary education.* Total enrolment in tertiary education, regardless of age, expressed as a percentage of the population of the five-year age-group following on from the secondary-school leaving age.

*Gross enrolment ratio in primary and secondary (primary, secondary and tertiary) education combined.* The population age groups for the combined ratios are defined by the upper and lower limits of the age groups of the combined levels.

It should be emphasized that the gross enrolment ratios for pre-primary, primary and secondary education combined, include all pupils whatever their ages, whereas the population is limited to the range of official school ages. Therefore, for countries with almost universal education at a given level, the gross enrolment ratio will exceed 100 if the actual age distribution of pupils extends beyond the official school ages.

**Table II.9  Primary and secondary education: gross enrolment ratios and enrolment ratios by age groups**

*Gross enrolment ratios:* see definitions given for Table II.8.

*Net enrolment ratio (NER) in primary education.* Enrolment of the age group which officially corresponds to primary schooling, expressed as a percentage of the population of the same age group. Although theoretically the NER cannot exceed 100%, values up to 105% have been obtained, indicating inconsistencies in the enrolment and/or population data.

*Enrolment ratio in primary education for the under/over-age groups.* Number of under/over-age pupils enrolled in primary education, expressed as a percentage of the population of the age group which officially corresponds to primary schooling.

*Net enrolment ratio (NER) in secondary education.* Enrolment in total secondary education, for the age group which officially corresponds to secondary general education, expressed as a percentage of the population of the same age group.

*Enrolment ratio in secondary education for the under/over-age groups.* Number of under/over-age pupils enrolled in all secondary education, expressed as a percentage of the population of the age group which officially corresponds to general secondary schooling.

Note that the sum of enrolment ratios of the three age groups corresponds to the gross enrolment ratio. The figure '0' indicates that a negligible number of pupils are enrolled in the specified level and age group.

**Table II.10  Primary education: net intake rates by age**

*Net intake rate.* The net intake rate, or net admission rate, is the number of new entrants into first grade of primary education, of official admission age, expressed as a percentage of the population of the same age. The official admission age for each country can be seen in Table II.8.

*Intake rate, one year under/over age.* Number of new entrants, one year under/over the official admission age, expressed as a percentage of the population one year under/over the official admission age.

**Table II.11  Primary education: selected indicators**

*Apparent intake rate.* Number of new entrants into first grade of primary education, regardless of age, expressed as a percentage of the population of official admission age. The official admission age for each country can be seen in Table II.8.

*Percentage of repeaters.* Total number of pupils who are enrolled in the same grade as the previous year, expressed as a percentage of the total enrolment in primary education.

*Percentage of a cohort reaching grade 5 and final grade.* Percentage of children starting primary school who eventually attain grade 5 and final grade. The estimate is based on the Reconstructed Cohort Method, which uses data on enrolment and repeaters for two consecutive years. For countries where the duration of primary education is 4 years, only the percentage of the cohort reaching final grade has been shown.

*Coefficient of efficiency.* Ratio between the theoretical number of pupil-years that it would have taken the graduates to complete the cycle of education had there been no repetition or drop-out, and the number of pupil-years actually spent by the cohort. Theoretically it varies between '0' (complete inefficiency) and '1' (maximum efficiency). The coefficient is obtained through the Reconstructed Cohort Method.

*Transition rate from primary to secondary general education.* Number of new entrants into secondary general education, expressed as a percentage of the total number of pupils in the last grade of primary education in the previous year. The value of this rate is affected by the duration of primary education. In general, the longer the duration of primary education, the lower the rate is likely to be. The transition rate is not shown for countries where the duration of primary school exceeds seven years. It should be noted that in certain countries, some pupils enter directly to vocational secondary education. This infers a lower transition rate than if all pupils enter general secondary education.

*School life expectancy.* The school life expectancy, or expected number of years of education, is the number of years a child is expected to remain at school, or university, including years spent on repetition. It is the sum of the age-specific enrolment ratios for primary, secondary and tertiary education. In interpreting this indicator the reader should refer to Tables II.5 to II.7 on enrolment which indicate changes in data coverage which can be particularly significant for secondary and tertiary education.

**II**  Country tables on education
Tableaux sur l'enseignement par pays
Cuadros sobre la enseñanza por países

**Table II.12  Tertiary education: distribution of students by ISCED level and percentage female in each level**
*Percentage of students by ISCED level.* Enrolment in tertiary education at each ISCED level as a percentage of total enrolment.
*Percentage of female students in each ISCED level.* Female enrolment as a percentage of total enrolment at the level specified.
Definitions of ISCED level categories within tertiary education:
Level 5: first stage of tertiary education, of the type that leads to an award not equivalent to a first university degree.
Level 6: first stage of tertiary education, of the type that leads to a first university degree or equivalent.
Level 7: second stage of tertiary education, of the type that leads to a postgraduate degree or equivalent.

**Table II.13  Tertiary education: distribution of students by broad field of study**
*Percentage of students by broad field of study.* Enrolment in tertiary education, in the broad field of study specified, expressed as a percentage of the total enrolment in tertiary education. The distribution is shown only for countries where the percentage of students in the category 'others' is less than 25 per cent.
ISCED fields of study are grouped into the following broad fields of study:
*Education*: education science and teacher training.
*Humanities*: humanities; fine and applied arts; religion and theology.
*Social sciences*: law; social and behavioural sciences; commercial and business administration; home economics; mass communication and documentation; service trades.
*Natural sciences*: natural sciences; engineering; mathematics and computer sciences; architecture and town planning; transport and communications; trade, craft and industrial programmes; agriculture, forestry and fisheries.
*Medical sciences*: medical and health related sciences.

**Table II.14  Tertiary education: percentage of female students in each broad field of study**
*Percentage of female students in each broad field of study.* Number of female students in each broad field of study, expressed as a percentage of the total enrolment in each field.
Data are shown only for countries where the percentage of students in the category 'others' is less than 25 per cent.
For the composition of broad fields of study, see note to Table II.13 above.

**Table II.15  Tertiary education: distribution of graduates by ISCED level and percentage female in each level**
*Percentage of graduates by ISCED level.* Number of graduates in tertiary education at each ISCED level as a percentage of the total number of graduates.
*Percentage of female graduates in each ISCED level.* Number of female graduates as a percentage of total number of graduates, at the level specified.
Definitions of ISCED level categories within tertiary education:
Level 5: first stage of tertiary education, of the type that leads to an award not equivalent to a first university degree.
Level 6: first stage of tertiary education, of the type that leads to a first university degree or equivalent.
Level 7: second stage of tertiary education, of the type that leads to a postgraduate degree or equivalent.

**Table II.16  Tertiary education: distribution of graduates by broad field of study**
*Percentage of graduates by broad field of study.* Number of graduates from tertiary education, in the broad field of study specified, expressed as a percentage of the total number of graduates in tertiary education. The distribution is shown only for countries where the percentage of graduates in the category 'others' is less than 25 per cent.
ISCED fields of study are grouped into the following broad fields of study:
*Education*: education science and teacher training.
*Humanities*: humanities; fine and applied arts; religion and theology.
*Social sciences*: law; social and behavioural sciences; commercial and business administration; home economics; mass communication and documentation; service trades.
*Natural sciences*: natural sciences; engineering; mathematics and computer sciences; architecture and town planning; transport and communications; trade, craft and industrial programmes; agriculture, forestry and fisheries.
*Medical sciences*: medical and health related sciences.

**Table II.17  Tertiary education: distribution of foreign students by continent of origin**
This table presents the number and percentage of foreign students enrolled in institutions of tertiary education and their percentage distribution by continent of origin, based on the latest year for which such information is available. The data presented do not include some major host countries for which recent data are not available.
The distribution is not shown for countries with more than 25 per cent of foreign students from unspecified continents.

**Table II.18  Total and current public expenditure on education: percentage of GNP and government expenditure**
*Public expenditure on education as percentage of GNP.* Total and current public expenditure on education expressed as a percentage of the gross national product (1st and 3rd columns).
*Public expenditure on education as percentage of government expenditure.* Total and current public expenditure on education expressed as a percentage of total and current government expenditure respectively (2nd and 4th columns).
*Current expenditure as percentage of total.* Current public expenditure on education, expressed as a percentage of total public expenditure on education.
*Total* expenditure refers to current and capital expenditure on education. *Current* expenditure refers to expenditure for goods and services consumed within the year of reference, which should be renewed if there is need for prolongation the following year. *Capital* expenditure refers to expenditure for assets that last longer than one year.
*Public* expenditure on education refers to expenditure on education at every level of administration according to the constitution of the country, i.e. central, regional and local authorities.

**Table II.19  Current public expenditure on education: percentage distribution by level of education**
This table presents the percentage breakdown of current public expenditure by level of education. For several countries, expenditures on pre-primary and primary levels of education are combined due to the fact that it was not clearly indicated in the data reported whether expenditure on pre-primary level was nil or included with expenditure on primary level of education. Also, for countries where expenditure

Country tables on education II
Tableaux sur l'enseignement par pays
Cuadros sobre la enseñanza por países

for basic education cannot be distributed according to the corresponding levels, the table gives percentages of the combined pre-primary, primary and secondary levels of education.

The category 'other types' includes expenditure on special, adult and other types of education that cannot be distributed by level of education.

The category 'not distributed' while generally covering unspecified expenditure may sometimes include expenditure on administration and subsidies or transfers to educational institutions for which there is no breakdown by level of education.

### Table II.20 Current public expenditure on education: percentage of emoluments and teaching materials

This table presents the percentage breakdown of current public expenditure by the following categories:

*Emoluments of teaching staff.* Gross salaries and all other benefits, including contributions to pension funds and social security, paid to teachers and auxiliary teaching staff.

*Emoluments of non-teaching staff.* Gross salaries and all other benefits, including contributions to pension funds and social security, paid to administrative staff at all administrative levels and other personnel i.e. maintenance staff, security personnel, transportation workers, catering staff etc.

*Total emoluments.* The total of the two previous categories or expenditure on total emoluments for countries that cannot separate the emoluments of teaching and non-teaching staff.

*Teaching materials.* Expenditure for purchases directly related to instructional activities such as school books, textbooks, exercise books and other scholastic and teaching supplies.

---

### Tableau II.1 Systèmes nationaux d'enseignement

Ce tableau présente des informations sur le système d'enseignement le plus répandu dans chaque pays. Ces informations doivent aider à interpréter correctement les chiffres qui figurent dans les tableaux qui suivent.

Les deux premières colonnes présentent les données relatives à la scolarité obligatoire : dans la première colonne sont précisées les limites d'âge minimum et maximum tandis que la deuxième colonne indique le nombre d'années de scolarité obligatoire. La troisième colonne donne l'âge d'admission dans l'enseignement préprimaire.

Le diagramme des colonnes suivantes représente graphiquement la durée et l'âge d'admission dans l'enseignement primaire et dans l'enseignement secondaire général. La couleur bleue montre la durée de l'enseignement primaire, la couleur rouge celle du premier cycle de l'enseignement secondaire général et la couleur verte celle du deuxième cycle de l'enseignement secondaire général. Certains pays et territoires ne font pas distinction entre ces deux cycles de l'enseignement secondaire général : dans ces cas, la durée totale est indiquée en jaune.

Pour un certain nombre de pays, l'âge d'admission et la durée de l'enseignement peuvent varier selon la zone administrative ou le type d'école. Ces pays sont signalés par le symbole ‡.

Le lecteur peut consulter le tableau II.8 sur les taux de scolarisation pour connaître les changements survenus dans le système d'enseignement depuis 1970.

### Tableau II. 2 Estimations du taux d'analphabétisme et de la population analphabète âgée de 15 ans et plus, et de 15 à 24 ans

Les taux d'analphabétisme et la population analphabète indiquent respectivement la proportion et le nombre de personnes dans la population qui sont incapables de lire et d'écrire, en le comprenant, un exposé simple et bref de faits en rapport avec leur vie quotidienne. Les données présentées dans ce tableau sont les dernières estimations et projections de l'UNESCO sur l'analphabétisme, révisées en 1998 et basées sur les données collectées au cours des recensements nationaux de la population. Le taux estimé d'analphabétisme se réfère au nombre estimé d'analphabètes (âgés de 15 ans et plus ou de 15-24 ans) exprimé en pourcentage de la population dans le groupe d'âge correspondant.

### Tableau II.3 Répartition en pourcentage de la population âgée de 25 ans et plus selon le niveau d'instruction

La répartition en pourcentage de la population âgée de 25 ans et plus selon le plus haut niveau d'instruction atteint reflète à la fois les résultats de la participation de l'enseignement dans le passé et la composition de la population selon le niveau d'instruction. Ces données ont été tirées pour la plupart des recensements nationaux de population et des enquêtes par sondage. Les six niveaux d'instruction présentés ici ont été conçus à partir des catégories de la Classification Internationale Type de l'Education (CITE) et sont définis comme suit :

*Sans scolarité* se réfère aux personnes qui ont fait moins d'une année scolaire dans le primaire.

*Enseignement primaire incomplet* inclut toutes les personnes ayant fait au moins une année du primaire mais qui n'ont pas terminé la dernière année de ce niveau d'enseignement tel qu'il est défini dans le tableau II.1.

*Enseignement primaire complété* concerne ceux qui ont terminé la dernière année de l'enseignement primaire mais qui n'ont pas accédé à l'enseignement secondaire.

*Premier cycle de l'enseignement secondaire atteint* comprend ceux qui ont atteint le premier cycle de l'enseignement secondaire mais pas le deuxième cycle.

*Deuxième cycle de l'enseignement secondaire atteint* inclut ceux qui ont atteint le deuxième cycle de l'enseignement secondaire mais qui n'ont pas accédé à l'enseignement postsecondaire.

*Enseignement postsecondaire* concerne tous ceux qui ont complété l'enseignement secondaire et qui ont accédé à l'enseignement postsecondaire.

Pour la durée des différents niveaux d'enseignement dans chaque pays, voir le tableau II.1 sur les systèmes nationaux d'enseignement.

### Tableau II.4 Enseignement préprimaire : écoles, personnel enseignant et élèves

Les données se rapportent à l'enseignement préprimaire (jardins d'enfants, écoles maternelles et classes enfantines rattachées aux écoles primaires). Les centres de puériculture, garderies et crèches, etc. sont exclus. Voir le tableau II.1 pour des informations sur l'âge d'admission et la durée théorique de l'enseignement préprimaire.

### Tableau II.5 Enseignement primaire : écoles, personnel enseignant et élèves

Les données de ce tableau se rapportent à l'enseignement primaire tel qu'il a été défini dans l'introduction de ce chapitre. Il convient, en consultant ce tableau, de se reporter aux renseignements donnés au tableau II.1 sur la durée de la scolarité. Le lecteur pourra également consulter le tableau II.8 sur les taux de scolarisation qui montre les changements survenus dans les structures de l'enseignement depuis

II	Country tables on education
Tableaux sur l'enseignement par pays
Cuadros sobre la enseñanza por países

1970. Les chiffres relatifs au personnel enseignant présentent, en général, le nombre total de maîtres à plein temps et à temps partiel. Ceci peut affecter la comparabilité des données, surtout en ce qui concerne le nombre d'élèves par maître, car la proportion des enseignants à temps partiel peut varier considérablement d'un pays à l'autre.

### Tableau II.6  Enseignement secondaire : personnel enseignant et élèves dans les enseignements général, normal et technique

Ce tableau présente les données sur le personnel enseignant et les élèves inscrits dans chacun des trois types d'enseignement secondaire: général, normal et technique et professionnel.

*Enseignement secondaire général* : ce terme désigne l'enseignement général ou spécialisé, dispensé dans les écoles secondaires à des enfants ayant déjà fait au moins quatre années d'études dans le primaire, et qui ne vise pas à préparer directement les élèves à une profession ou à un emploi. Les écoles de ce type s'appellent collèges, lycées, gymnases, etc., et elles dispensent un enseignement qu'il faut obligatoirement avoir terminé pour pouvoir être admis dans l'enseignement supérieur. Dans de nombreux pays, où l'on souhaite dispenser des formations plus diversifiées aux élèves, on assiste au développement d'écoles qui offrent une formation tant générale que technique. Ces écoles composites sont également classées dans la catégorie de l'enseignement secondaire général.

*Enseignement secondaire normal* : cette formule désigne l'enseignement dispensé dans les écoles secondaires dont le but est de préparer à la profession d'enseignant.

*Enseignement technique et professionnel* : cette formule désigne l'enseignement dispensé dans des écoles secondaires qui visent à préparer directement les élèves à un emploi ou profession autre que l'enseignement. La formule abrégée "enseignement technique" est utilisée dans les en-têtes des tableaux.

Pour effectuer des comparaisons internationales, ce tableau doit être consulté conjointement avec le tableau II.1 sur les systèmes nationaux d'enseignement.

### Tableau II.7  Enseignement supérieur : personnel enseignant et étudiants

Ces données se rapportent au personnel enseignant et aux étudiants inscrits dans les établissements d'enseignement supérieur. Les données sont présentées pour le "Total des établissements" et pour les "Universités et établissements conférant des titres équivalents (indiqués par "Universités")". "Tous les établissements" comprend : (a) universités et établissements conférant des titres équivalents ; (b) établissements universitaires d'enseignement à distance ; (c) autres établissements d'enseignement supérieur tels que écoles normales supérieures, écoles techniques supérieures, etc.

Il faut souligner que le critère adopté pour déterminer ces trois catégories d'établissements peut ne pas être exactement le même dans chacun des pays et territoires concernés. De plus, il se peut que dans un même pays, à la suite des réformes du système d'enseignement, plusieurs établissements non universitaires soient, d'une année à l'autre, rattachés aux universités ou considérés comme des établissements équivalents.

### Tableau II.8  Taux bruts de scolarisation par niveau d'enseignement

Ce tableau présente les taux bruts de scolarisation pour les pays et territoires dont la population est supérieure à 150 000 habitants. Pour les pays dont la population est inférieure à 150 000 habitants, les données par âge ne sont pas disponibles. Les données démographiques sont basées sur les estimations et projections effectuées par la Division de la Population des Nations Unies en 1998. Les données sur les effectifs utilisées pour le calcul des taux bruts de scolarisation apparaissent dans les tableaux II.4 à II.7 de cet *Annuaire*. Pour l'interprétation du taux brut de scolarisation de ce tableau, le lecteur peut se référer aux notes indiquant les changements de couverture dans les tableaux par niveau correspondants.

*Taux brut de scolarisation dans l'enseignement préprimaire.* Nombre d'enfants dans l'enseignement préprimaire, quel que soit leur âge, exprimé en pourcentage de la population du groupe d'âge correspondant aux réglementations nationales à ce niveau d'enseignement.

*Taux brut de scolarisation dans l'enseignement primaire.* Total de l'effectif scolaire dans l'enseignement primaire, quel que soit l'âge des enfants, exprimé en pourcentage de la population du groupe d'âge officiellement scolarisable dans le primaire.

*Taux brut de scolarisation dans l'enseignement secondaire.* Total de l'effectif des élèves dans l'enseignement secondaire, quel que soit leur âge, exprimé en pourcentage de la population du groupe d'âge qui correspond officiellement à la durée de la scolarité dans le secondaire. Il est à noter que les taux de scolarisation dans l'enseignement secondaire sont basés sur le total des effectifs scolaires (enseignement secondaire général, normal et technique et professionnel).

*Taux brut de scolarisation dans l'enseignement supérieur.* Etudiants de l'enseignement supérieur, quel que soit leur âge, exprimé en pourcentage de la population du groupe d'âge quinquennal qui suit l'âge de la fin de la scolarité secondaire.

*Taux brut de scolarisation dans l'enseignement primaire et secondaire (primaire, secondaire et supérieur) combinés.* La population du groupe d'âge considéré pour le calcul du taux combiné est déterminée par les limites extrêmes de l'ensemble des groupes d'âge des niveaux combinés.

Il faut noter que le taux brut de scolarisation dans l'enseignement préprimaire, et dans le primaire et le secondaire combinés, inclut tous les élèves, quel que soit leur âge, alors que la population considérée est limitée à l'étendue des âges officiels de scolarité. Par conséquent, dans les pays où l'enseignement peut être considéré comme universel dans un niveau d'enseignement donné, le taux brut de scolarisation dépassera le chiffre 100 si la répartition effective des élèves par âge déborde les limites d'âge officielles.

### Tableau II.9  Enseignements primaire et secondaire : taux bruts de scolarisation et taux de scolarisation par groupes d'âge

*Taux bruts de scolarisation* : voir les définitions du tableau II.8.

*Taux net de scolarisation (TNS) dans l'enseignement primaire.* Effectif de l'enseignement primaire du groupe d'âge officiellement scolarisable à ce niveau d'enseignement, exprimé en pourcentage de la population du même groupe d'âge. Bien que théoriquement le TNS ne devrait pas dépasser 100%, des valeurs allant jusqu'à 105% ont été obtenues, indiquant des incohérences dans les données relatives aux effectifs et/ou à la population.

*Taux de scolarisation dans l'enseignement primaire pour le groupe d'âge en dessous/au-dessus de l'âge officiel.* Effectif scolaire dans le primaire dont l'âge est en dessous/au-dessus de l'âge officiel, exprimé en pourcentage de la population du groupe d'âge officiellement scolarisable dans le primaire.

*Taux net de scolarisation (TNS) dans l'enseignement secondaire.* Effectif scolaire dans l'enseignement secondaire, pour le groupe d'âge qui correspond officiellement à l'enseignement secondaire général, exprimé en pourcentage de la population du même groupe d'âge.

*Taux de scolarisation dans l'enseignement secondaire pour le groupe d'âge en dessous/au-dessus de l'âge officiel.* Effectif scolaire dans l'ensemble de l'enseignement secondaire dont l'âge est en dessous/au-dessus de l'âge officiel, exprimé en pourcentage de la population du groupe d'âge qui correspond officiellement à l'enseignement secondaire général.

Il faut noter que la somme des taux de scolarisation pour les trois groupes d'âge correspond au taux brut de scolarisation. Le chiffre '0' indique que l'effectif scolaire est négligeable pour le niveau et le groupe d'âge correspondants.

Country tables on education II
Tableaux sur l'enseignement par pays
Cuadros sobre la enseñanza por países

**Tableau II.10  Enseignement primaire : taux nets d'admission par âge**
*Taux net d'admission*. Le taux net d'admission, ou taux net d'accès, est le nombre de nouveaux entrants en première année de l'enseignement primaire qui ont l'âge officiel d'admission, exprimé en pourcentage de la population du même âge. Pour l'âge officiel d'accès dans chaque pays, voir le tableau II.8.
*Taux d'admission, un an en dessous/au-dessus de l'âge officiel*. Nombre de nouveaux entrants qui ont un an en dessous/au-dessus de l'âge officiel d'admission, exprimé en pourcentage de la population qui a un an en dessous/au-dessus de l'âge officiel d'admission.

**Tableau II.11  Enseignement primaire : indicateurs sélectionnés**
*Taux apparent d'admission*. Nouveaux entrants en première année de l'enseignement primaire, quel que soit leur âge, en pourcentage de la population ayant l'âge officiel d'admission. L'âge officiel d'admission pour chaque pays peut être consulté dans le tableau II.8.
*Pourcentage de redoublants*. Élèves inscrits dans la même classe que l'année précédente, en pourcentage des effectifs totaux de l'enseignement primaire.
*Pourcentage d'une cohorte atteignant la cinquième et la dernière année d'études*. Pourcentage d'enfants entrés à l'école primaire qui éventuellement atteignent la cinquième et la dernière année d'études. Cette estimation est obtenue par l'application de la méthode de la cohorte reconstituée, qui se fonde sur les chiffres des inscrits et des redoublants de deux années scolaires consécutives. Pour les pays où la durée de l'enseignement primaire est de 4 ans, seul est présenté le pourcentage de la cohorte atteignant la dernière année d'études.
*Coefficient d'efficacité*. Rapport entre le nombre théorique d'années-élèves nécessaires à l'achèvement du cycle d'études s'il n'y avait eu ni abandons ni redoublements et le nombre d'années-élèves que la cohorte y a effectivement consacré. Théoriquement, il est compris entre '0' (inefficacité totale) et '1' (efficacité maximale). Ce coefficient s'obtient par la méthode de la cohorte reconstituée.
*Taux de passage de l'enseignement primaire au secondaire général*. Nouveaux entrants dans l'enseignement secondaire général, en pourcentage du nombre total d'élèves qui étaient inscrits en dernière année d'école primaire l'année précédente. La valeur de ce taux dépend de la durée de l'enseignement primaire. En général, plus l'enseignement primaire sera long, plus le taux de passage sera bas. Le taux de passage n'est pas présenté pour les pays où la durée de l'enseignement primaire dépasse 7 ans. Il est à noter que dans certains pays les élèves peuvent entrer directement dans l'enseignement technique secondaire, ce qui entraîne un taux de passage inférieur que dans le cas où tous les élèves entreraient dans l'enseignement secondaire général.
*Espérance de vie scolaire*. Nombre d'années qu'un enfant est probablement appelé à passer à l'école et à l'université, années de redoublement comprises, calculé par addition des taux de scolarisation par âge dans l'enseignement primaire, secondaire et supérieur. Pour l'interprétation de cet indicateur, le lecteur peut consulter les tableaux II.5 à II.7 sur les effectifs scolaires où sont indiqués les changements de couverture qui peuvent être particulièrement importants pour l'enseignement secondaire et supérieur.

**Tableau II.12  Enseignement supérieur : répartition des étudiants par niveau de la CITE et pourcentage d'étudiantes dans chaque niveau**
*Répartition des étudiants par niveau de la CITE*. Étudiants de l'enseignement supérieur à chacun des niveaux de la CITE en pourcentage de l'effectif total des étudiants.
*Pourcentage d'étudiantes dans chaque niveau de la CITE*. Pourcentage de femmes dans l'effectif total des étudiants au niveau considéré.
Définitions des niveaux de la CITE dans l'enseignement supérieur :
Niveau 5: premier niveau de l'enseignement supérieur conduisant à un titre n'équivalant pas à un premier grade universitaire.
Niveau 6: premier niveau de l'enseignement supérieur conduisant à un premier grade universitaire ou à un titre équivalent.
Niveau 7: deuxième niveau de l'enseignement supérieur conduisant à un grade universitaire supérieur ou à un titre équivalent.

**Tableau II.13  Enseignement supérieur : répartition des étudiants par grand domaine d'études**
*Répartition des étudiants par grand domaine d'études*. Répartition des étudiants par grand domaine d'études, en pourcentage des effectifs totaux de l'enseignement supérieur. La répartition n'est indiquée que pour les pays où moins de 25% des étudiants sont inscrits dans la catégorie "autres".
Les différents domaines d'études de la CITE sont regroupés en cinq grands domaines.
*Education* : sciences de l'éducation et formation d'enseignants.
*Lettres*: lettres ; beaux-arts et arts appliqués ; religion et théologie.
*Sciences sociales* : droit ; sciences sociales et sciences du comportement ; enseignement commercial et préparation aux affaires ; enseignement ménager ; grande information et documentation ; formation pour le secteur tertiaire.
*Sciences naturelles* : sciences exactes et naturelles ; sciences de l'ingénieur ; mathématiques et informatique ; architecture et urbanisme ; transports et télécommunications ; formation aux métiers de la production industrielle et aux activités assimilées ; agriculture, sylviculture et halieutique.
*Sciences médicales* : sciences médicales, santé et hygiène.

**Tableau II.14  Enseignement supérieur : pourcentage d'étudiantes dans chaque grand domaine d'études**
*Pourcentage d'étudiantes dans chaque grand domaine d'études*. Pourcentage de femmes dans l'effectif total des étudiants dans chaque grand domaine d'études.
Les données sont présentées uniquement pour les pays où le pourcentage des étudiants inscrits dans la catégorie "autres" est inférieur à 25%.
Pour la composition des grands domaines d'études, voir les notes du tableau II.13 ci-dessus.

**Tableau II.15  Enseignement supérieur : répartition des diplômés par niveau de la CITE et pourcentage de femmes dans chaque niveau**
*Répartition des diplômés par niveau de la CITE*. Répartition des diplômés de l'enseignement supérieur à chaque niveau de la CITE en pourcentage du nombre total de diplômés.
*Répartition des femmes diplômées dans chaque niveau de la CITE*. Nombre de femmes diplômées en pourcentage du nombre total de diplômés dans le niveau spécifié.
Définitions des niveaux de la CITE correspondant à l'enseignement supérieur :
Niveau 5 :  premier niveau de l'enseignement supérieur conduisant à un titre n'équivalant pas à un premier grade universitaire.
Niveau 6 :  premier niveau de l'enseignement supérieur conduisant à un premier grade universitaire ou à un titre équivalent.
Niveau 7 : deuxième niveau de l'enseignement supérieur conduisant à un grade universitaire supérieur ou à un titre équivalent.

II   Country tables on education
     Tableaux sur l'enseignement par pays
     Cuadros sobre la enseñanza por países

**Tableau II.16  Enseignement supérieur : répartition des diplômés par grand domaine d'études**
*Répartition des diplômés par grand domaine d'études.* Répartition des diplômés par grand domaine d'études, en pourcentage des effectifs totaux de l'enseignement supérieur. La répartition n'est indiquée que pour les pays dont le pourcentage de diplômés dans la catégorie "autres" est inférieur à 25%.
Les différents domaines d'études de la CITE sont regroupés en cinq grands domaines:
*Education* :  sciences de l'éducation et formation d'enseignants.
*Lettres*: lettres ; beaux-arts et arts appliqués ; religion et théologie.
*Sciences sociales* :   droit ; sciences sociales et sciences du comportement ; enseignement commercial et préparation aux affaires ; enseignement ménager ; grande information et documentation ; formation pour le secteur tertiaire.
*Sciences naturelles* :   sciences exactes et naturelles ; sciences de l'ingénieur ; mathématiques et informatique ; architecture et urbanisme ; transports et télécommunications ; formation aux métiers de la production industrielle et aux activités assimilées ; agriculture, sylviculture et halieutique.
*Sciences médicales* : sciences médicales, santé et hygiène.

**Tableau II.17  Enseignement supérieur : répartition des étudiants étrangers par continent d'origine**
Ce tableau présente le nombre et le pourcentage d'étudiants étrangers inscrits dans des établissements d'enseignement supérieur et leur répartition en pourcentage par continent d'origine, sur la base de la dernière année pour laquelle ces données sont disponibles. Certains grands pays d'accueil ne sont pas présentés dans ce tableau, faute de données récentes disponibles.
La répartition n'est pas présentée pour les pays dont le pourcentage d'étudiants en provenance d'un continent d'origine "non spécifié" est supérieur à 25%.

**Tableau II.18  Dépenses publiques totales et ordinaires afférentes à l'éducation : pourcentage par rapport au PNB et aux dépenses du gouvernement**
*Dépenses publiques d'éducation en pourcentage du PNB.* Dépenses publiques totales et ordinaires d'éducation en pourcentage du produit national brut (1ère et 3ème colonnes).
*Dépenses publiques d'éducation en pourcentage des dépenses de l'Etat.* Dépenses publiques totales et ordinaires d'éducation en pourcentage des dépenses totales et ordinaires de l'Etat respectivement (2ème et 4ème colonnes).
*Dépenses ordinaires en pourcentage du total.* Dépenses publiques ordinaires d'éducation en pourcentage des dépenses publiques totales d'éducation.
Les dépenses *totales* concernent les dépenses d'éducation ordinaires et en capital. Les dépenses *ordinaires* concernent les dépenses en biens et en services consommés dans l'année en cours et qui doivent être renouvelées périodiquement pour assurer la production des services éducatifs. Les dépenses en *capital* concernent les dépenses qui couvrent l'achat de biens d'une durée supérieure à un an.
Les dépenses *publiques* d'éducation comprennent toutes les dépenses effectuées à quelque échelon administratif que ce soit, en fonction de l'organisation politique du pays : gouvernement central, autorités régionales et locales.

**Tableau II.19  Dépenses publiques ordinaires afférentes à l'éducation : répartition en pourcentage par niveau d'enseignement**
Ce tableau présente la répartition en pourcentage des dépenses publiques ordinaires par niveau d'enseignement. Pour un certain nombre de pays, les dépenses dans l'enseignement préprimaire et primaire sont combinées car les données notifiées n'indiquent pas de façon claire si les dépenses dans le préprimaire sont nulles ou comprises dans celles du primaire. Aussi, pour les pays où les dépenses ne peuvent pas être réparties selon les niveaux d'enseignement, le tableau présente les pourcentages combinés des niveaux d'enseignement préprimaire, primaire et secondaire.
La catégorie "autres types" regroupe les dépenses en éducation répondant à des besoins spéciaux, en éducation des adultes et autres types d'éducation ne pouvant être répartis par niveau d'enseignement.
La catégorie "non réparties" qui regroupe généralement les diverses dépenses non spécifiées peut parfois inclure les dépenses d'administration et les subventions ou transferts aux établissements d'enseignement pour lesquels on ne dispose pas de répartition par niveau d'enseignement.

**Tableau II.20   Dépenses publiques ordinaires afférentes à l'éducation : pourcentage des émoluments et du matériel pour l'enseignement**
Ce tableau présente la répartition en pourcentage des dépenses publiques ordinaires selon les catégories suivantes :
*Emoluments du personnel enseignant.* Traitements bruts et toutes sortes de primes additionnelles, y compris les contributions aux caisses de retraite et à la sécurité sociale, payés au personnel enseignant et enseignant auxiliaire.
*Emoluments du personnel non-enseignant.* Traitements bruts et toutes sortes de primes additionnelles, y compris les contributions aux caisses de retraite et à la sécurité sociale, payés au personnel administratif à tous les niveaux de l'administration et autre personnel tel que le personnel affecté aux travaux et à l'entretien des bâtiments, à la sécurité, au transport, à la restauration, etc.
*Total des émoluments.* Total des deux catégories précédentes ou dépenses totales des émoluments pour les pays qui ne peuvent pas séparer les émoluments du personnel enseignant et du personnel non-enseignant.
*Matériel pour l'enseignement.* Dépenses en rapport direct avec les activités scolaires tels que manuels, livres, cahiers et autres fournitures scolaires et didactiques.

---

**Cuadro II.1  Sistemas nacionales de enseñanza**
Este cuadro presenta informaciones sobre el sistema de enseñanza más corriente en cada país. Estas informaciones están destinadas a facilitar la interpretación de las cifras que figuran en los cuadros presentados a continuación.
Las dos primeras columnas presentan informaciones relativas a la escolaridad obligatoria. En la primera columna se precisan los límites de edad mínima y máxima mientras que en la segunda se señala el número de años de escolaridad obligatoria. La tercera columna indica la edad de admisión en la enseñanza preprimaria.
El diagrama que figura en las columnas siguientes representa gráficamente la duración y la edad de admisión en la enseñanza primaria y en la enseñanza secundaria general. El color azul indica la duración de la enseñanza primaria, el rojo, la duración del primer ciclo de la enseñanza secundaria general y el verde, la duración del segundo ciclo de la enseñanza secundaria general. Para algunos países y territorios no existe ninguna distinción entre los dos ciclos de enseñanza secundaria general: en tales casos, el color amarillo indica la duración total de este nivel de enseñanza.

Country tables on education
Tableaux sur l'enseignement par pays
Cuadros sobre la enseñanza por países

II

Para un cierto número de países, la edad de admisión y la duración de la enseñanza pueden variar según la zona administrativa o el tipo de escuela. Esos países se presentan con el símbolo ‡.

El lector puede consultar el cuadro II.8 sobre las tasas de escolarización para conocer los cambios introducidos en el sistema de enseñanza desde 1970.

### Cuadro II. 2  Estimaciones de la tasa de analfabetismo y de la población analfabeta de 15 años y más, y de 15 a 24 años

Las tasas de analfabetismo y la población analfabeta indican respectivamente la proporción y el número de personas en la población que son incapaces de leer y escribir, comprendiéndolo, un relato simple y breve relativo a su vida cotidiana. Los datos presentados en este cuadro son las últimas estimaciones y proyecciones de la UNESCO sobre el analfabetismo, revisadas en 1998 y basadas en los datos acopiados en los censos nacionales de población. La tasa estimada de analfabetismo se refiere al número estimado de analfabetos (de 15 años y más o de 15 a 24 años) expresado como porcentaje de la población del grupo de edad correspondiente.

### Cuadro II.3  Distribución porcentual de la población de 25 años y más según el nivel de instrucción

La distribución en porcentaje de la población de 25 años y más según el más alto nivel de instrucción alcanzado refleja a la vez los resultados de la participación de la enseñanza en el pasado y la composición de la población según el nivel de instrucción. Estos datos provienen por su mayor parte de censos nacionales de población y encuestas por el método de muestras.  Los seis niveles de instrucción definidos a continuación se basan en las categorías de la Clasificación Internacional Normalizada de la Educación (CINE):

*Sin escolaridad* se refiere a aquellas personas que no llegaron a completar un año de estudios en la enseñanza primaria.

*Enseñanza primaria sin completar* incluye a aquellas personas que terminaron al menos un año de la primaria pero no completaron el último año de ese nivel de enseñanza, tal como se define en el cuadro II.1.

*Enseñanza primaria completa* se refiere a aquellas personas que terminaron el último año de la primaria pero que no accedieron a la enseñanza secundaria.

*Primer ciclo de la enseñanza secundaria alcanzado* incluye a aquellas personas que alcanzaron el primer ciclo de la enseñanza secundaria sin acceder al segundo ciclo de ese nivel.

*Segundo ciclo de la enseñanza secundaria alcanzado* incluye a aquellas personas que alcanzaron el segundo ciclo de la enseñanza secundaria sin acceder a la enseñanza postsecundaria.

*Enseñanza postsecundaria* se refiere a aquellas personas que completaron la enseñanza secundaria y alcanzaron la enseñanza postsecundaria.

Para la duración de los niveles de enseñanza en cada país, ver el cuadro II.1 relativo a los sistemas nacionales de enseñanza.

### Cuadro II.4  Enseñanza preprimaria: escuelas, personal docente y alumnos

Los datos se refieren a la enseñanza preprimaria (jardines de la infancia, escuelas maternales y clases de párvulos adscritas a escuelas primarias). Se excluyen las guarderías, centros de juego, etc. Para toda información sobre la edad de admisión y la duración teórica de la enseñanza preprimaria, debe consultarse el cuadro II.1.

### Cuadro II.5  Enseñanza primaria: escuelas, personal docente y alumnos

Los datos de este cuadro se refieren a la enseñanza primaria tal como se ha definido en la introducción de este capítulo. Al consultar este cuadro, habrá que tener presentes los datos sobre la duración de la escolaridad que figuran en el cuadro II.1. Se podrá consultar asimismo el cuadro II.8 sobre las tasas de escolarización que muestra los cambios ocurridos en las estructuras de la enseñanza desde 1970. Las cifras relativas al personal docente presentan, en general, el número total de maestros de jornada completa y de jornada parcial. Esto puede afectar la comparabilidad de los datos, sobre todo en lo que concierne el número de alumnos por maestro, ya que la proporción de maestros de jornada parcial puede variar considerablemente de un país a otro.

### Cuadro II.6  Enseñanza secundaria: personal docente y alumnos en la enseñanza general, normal y técnica

Este cuadro indica el número de personal docente y de alumnos matriculados en cada uno de los tres tipos de enseñanza secundaria (general, normal y técnica/profesional).

*Enseñanza secundaria general*: esta categoría incluye las escuelas secundarias (es decir, las que dan una enseñanza general o especializada que implica cuatro años como mínimo de estudios previos en la primaria), cuya finalidad no consiste en preparar directamente a los alumnos para un oficio o una profesión determinada. Esas escuelas, que pueden llamarse escuelas secundarias, escuelas medias, liceos, gimnasios, etc., tienen un plan de estudios que conduce a la obtención de un diploma que es condición indispensable para el ingreso en la enseñanza superior. Bastantes países, para ofrecer otros tipos de formación a los alumnos, han creado escuelas donde se da una instrucción a la vez general y técnica. Esas escuelas de carácter mixto están agrupadas bajo la rúbrica enseñanza secundaria general.

*Enseñanza secundaria normal* (formación del personal docente): esta expresión se refiere a la enseñanza en escuelas secundarias destinadas a preparar para la profesión docente.

*Enseñanza secundaria técnica y profesional*: esta expresión designa las escuelas secundarias que tienen como finalidad preparar directamente a los alumnos para un oficio o una profesión determinada que no sea la docente. Por razones prácticas, se ha utilizado el término "enseñanza técnica" en los títulos de los cuadros.

Para efectuar comparaciones internacionales, este cuadro debe consultarse conjuntamente con el cuadro II.1 sobre los sistemas nacionales de enseñanza.

### Cuadro II.7  Enseñanza superior: personal docente y estudiantes

Estos datos se refieren al personal docente y a los estudiantes inscritos en los establecimientos de enseñanza superior. Los datos se presentan para "Todos los establecimientos" y para las "Universidades y establecimientos que conceden títulos equivalentes (indicados como "Universidades")". "Todos los establecimientos" incluye: (a) universidades e instituciones que conceden títulos equivalentes; (b) instituciones universitarias de enseñanza a distancia; (c) otros establecimientos de enseñanza superior como las escuelas normales superiores, las escuelas técnicas superiores, etc.

Cabe señalar que los criterios adoptados para determinar las tres categorías de establecimientos pueden no ser exactamente los mismos en cada uno de los países y territorios. Además, es posible que, en un mismo país, debido a una reforma del sistema de enseñanza, ciertos establecimientos no universitarios queden, de un año para el otro, adscritos a las universidades o considerados como establecimientos equivalentes.

### Cuadro II.8  Tasas brutas de escolarización por nivel de enseñanza

Este cuadro presenta las tasas brutas de escolarización para los países y territorios cuya población sobrepasa los 150.000 habitantes. Para los países cuya población es inferior a 150.000 habitantes, no se dispone de datos por edad. Los datos demográficos se refieren a las

II  Country tables on education
Tableaux sur l'enseignement par pays
Cuadros sobre la enseñanza por países

estimaciones y proyecciones de la División de la Población de las Naciones Unidas elaboradas en 1998. Los datos sobre la matrícula utilizados para el cálculo de las tasas brutas de escolarización aparecen en los cuadros II.4 a II.7 de este *Anuario*. Para la interpretación de las tasas brutas de escolarización, el lector puede referirse a las notas que indican los cambios de cobertura en los cuadros por nivel de enseñanza correspondientes.

*Tasa bruta de escolarización en la enseñanza preprimaria*. Número de niños en la enseñanza preprimaria, independientemente de la edad, expresado como porcentaje de la población del grupo de edad que, según la reglamentación nacional, debe matricularse en este nivel.

*Tasa bruta de escolarización en la enseñanza primaria*. Número total de alumnos escolarizados en la enseñanza primaria, independientemente de su edad, expresado como porcentaje de la población del grupo de edad que corresponde oficialmente a ese nivel de enseñanza.

*Tasa bruta de escolarización en la enseñanza secundaria*. Número total de alumnos en la enseñanza secundaria, independientemente de su edad, expresado en porcentaje de la población del grupo de edad que corresponde oficialmente a la duración de la escolaridad en la enseñanza secundaria general. Debe notarse que las tasas de escolarización para la enseñanza secundaria se basan en el total de alumnos, incluyendo la enseñanza general, normal y técnica y profesional.

*Tasa bruta de escolarización en la enseñanza superior*. Número de alumnos matriculados en la enseñanza superior, independientemente de su edad, expresado como porcentaje de la población del grupo de edad que corresponde a los cinco años siguientes a la conclusión de los estudios secundarios.

*Tasa bruta de escolarización en la enseñanza primaria y secundaria (primaria, secundaria y superior) combinadas*. La población del grupo de edad considerado para el cálculo de las tasas combinadas se determina a partir de los límites extremos del conjunto de los grupos de edad de los niveles combinados.

Debe observarse que las tasas brutas de escolarización en la enseñanza preprimaria, primaria y secundaria, incluyen a todos los alumnos, independientemente de su edad, mientras que la población considerada se limita a los grupos de edad oficialmente escolarizables, según la reglamentación ya mencionada. En consecuencia, en los países donde la enseñanza puede considerarse como universal para un nivel de enseñanza dado, la tasa bruta de escolarización será superior al 100 si la distribución de los alumnos por edad desborda los límites de edad oficiales.

### Cuadro II.9 Enseñanza primaria y secundaria: tasas brutas de escolarización y tasas de escolarización por grupos de edad

*Tasas brutas de escolarización*: ver las definiciones del cuadro II.8.

*Tasas netas de escolarización (TNE) en la enseñanza primaria*. Número de alumnos cuya edad corresponde a la edad oficial de escolarización en la enseñanza primaria, expresado como porcentaje de la población del mismo grupo de edad. Si bien teóricamente la TNE no puede ser superior al 100%, se han obtenido valores de hasta el 105%, lo que indica incoherencias en los datos sobre matrícula y/o población.

*Tasa de escolarización en la enseñanza primaria para los grupos de edad inferior/superior a la edad oficial*. Número de alumnos matriculados en la primaria cuya edad es inferior/superior a la edad oficial, expresado como porcentaje de la población del grupo de edad oficialmente escolarizable en la primaria.

*Tasa neta de escolarización (TNE) en la enseñanza secundaria*. Número de alumnos matriculados en la enseñanza secundaria del grupo de edad oficialmente escolarizable en la enseñanza secundaria general, expresado como porcentaje de la población del mismo grupo de edad.

*Tasa de escolarización en la enseñanza secundaria para los grupos de edad inferior/superior a la edad oficial*. Número de alumnos matriculados en el conjunto de la enseñanza secundaria cuya edad es inferior/superior a la edad oficial, expresado como porcentaje de la población del grupo de edad oficialmente escolarizable en la enseñanza secundaria general.

Cabe señalar que la suma de las tasas de escolarización para los tres grupos de edades corresponde a la tasa bruta de escolarización. La cifra '0' indica que el número de alumnos es insignificante para el nivel y el grupo de edad especificados.

### Cuadro II.10 Enseñanza primaria: tasas netas de ingreso por edad

*Tasa neta de ingreso*. La tasa neta de ingreso, o tasa neta de admisión, es igual al número de alumnos que ingresan al primer año de la enseñanza primaria, que tienen la edad oficial de ingreso, expresado como porcentaje de la población del mismo grupo de edad. La edad oficial de ingreso para cada país puede consultarse en el cuadro II.8.

*Tasa de ingreso, un año inferior/superior de la edad oficial*. Número de alumnos que ingresan con un año de edad inferior/superior a la edad oficial de admisión, expresado como porcentaje de la población cuya edad es de un año inferior/superior a la edad oficial de admisión.

### Cuadro II.11 Enseñanza primaria: indicadores seleccionados

*Tasa aparente de ingreso*. Número de alumnos que ingresan al primer año de la enseñanza primaria, independientemente de su edad, expresado como porcentaje del grupo de edad oficial de admisión. La edad oficial de admisión para cada país puede ser consultada en el cuadro II.8.

*Porcentaje de repetidores*. Número total de alumnos matriculados en el mismo grado que el año anterior, expresado como porcentaje del total de matrículas en la enseñanza primaria.

*Porcentaje de la cohorte que llega al quinto y último año de estudios*. Porcentaje de alumnos que ingresan en la escuela primaria y llegan al quinto y último año de estudios. La estimación se basa en el método de la cohorte reconstituida que utiliza datos sobre el número de alumnos matriculados y los repetidores de dos años consecutivos. En los países donde la duración de la enseñanza primaria es de 4 años, sólo se presenta el porcentaje de la cohorte que llega al último año de estudios.

*Coeficiente de eficiencia*. Relación entre el número teórico de años/alumno que habrían necesitado los graduados para completar este nivel de enseñanza (si no hubiera habido repetidores ni abandono escolar) y el número real de años/alumno de la cohorte. Teóricamente, varía entre '0' (ineficiencia total) y '1' (eficiencia máxima). Este coeficiente se obtiene con el método de la cohorte reconstituida.

*Tasa de transición de la enseñanza primaria a la secundaria general*. Número de alumnos que ingresan en la enseñanza secundaria, expresado como porcentaje del número total de alumnos matriculados en el último año de la enseñanza primaria en el año anterior. El valor de esta tasa depende de la duración de la enseñanza primaria. En general, cuanto más larga sea la duración de la enseñanza primaria, más baja va a ser la tasa de transición. La tasa de transición no se presenta para los países donde la duración de la enseñanza primaria excede los 7 años. Debe notarse que en ciertos países, los alumnos pueden entrar directamente a la enseñanza técnica secundaria. Esto produce una tasa de transición más baja que en el caso en que todos los alumnos entraran a la enseñanza secundaria general.

*Esperanza de vida escolar*. Número probable de años de educación, o número de años que se espera que un alumno va a pasar en la escuela o la universidad, comprendidos los años de repetición. Es la suma de la tasa de escolarización por edad en la enseñanza primaria, secundaria y superior. Para la interpretación de este indicador, el lector podrá consultar los cuadros II.5 a II.7 sobre la matrícula escolar, que indican los cambios de cobertura que pueden ser particularmente importantes para la enseñanza secundaria y superior.

Country tables on education
Tableaux sur l'enseignement par pays
Cuadros sobre la enseñanza por países

II

**Cuadro II.12  Enseñanza superior: distribución de los estudiantes por nivel de la CINE y porcentaje de mujeres en cada nivel**
*Porcentaje de estudiantes por niveles de la CINE.* Número de estudiantes de enseñanza superior en cada nivel de la CINE como porcentaje del número total de matriculados.
*Porcentaje de mujeres en cada nivel de la CINE.* Matrícula femenina como porcentaje del número total de estudiantes en cada nivel especificado.
Las definiciones de las categorías de niveles de la CINE en la enseñanza superior son:
Nivel 5: primer nivel de la enseñanza superior que permite obtener un certificado no equivalente a un primer título universitario.
Nivel 6: primer nivel de la enseñanza superior que permite obtener un primer título universitario o su equivalente.
Nivel 7: segundo nivel de la enseñanza superior que permite obtener un título universitario superior o su equivalente.

**Cuadro II.13  Enseñanza superior: distribución de los estudiantes por gran sector de estudios**
*Porcentaje de estudiantes por gran sector de estudios.* Número de estudiantes matriculados en la enseñanza superior, en el sector de estudios especificado, expresado como porcentaje del total de la matrícula de ese nivel. La distribución se muestra únicamente en los países cuyo porcentaje de estudiantes en la categoría "otros" es inferior al 25%.
Los campos de estudio de la CINE se agrupan en las siguientes categorías:
*Educación*: ciencias de la educación y formación docente.
*Humanidades*: estudios humanísticos, bellas artes y artes aplicadas, religión y teología.
*Ciencias sociales*: derecho; ciencias sociales y del comportamiento; estudios comerciales y administración de empresas; economía doméstica; comunicación de masas y documentación; y formación para el sector terciario.
*Ciencias naturales*: ciencias naturales, ingeniería, matemáticas e informática; arquitectura y urbanismo; transporte y comunicaciones; formación en actividades comerciales, artesanales e industriales; agricultura, silvicultura y pesca.
*Ciencias médicas*: medicina, salud e higiene.

**Cuadro II.14  Enseñanza superior: porcentaje de mujeres en cada gran sector de estudios**
*Porcentaje de mujeres en cada gran sector de estudios.* Número de alumnas en cada sector de estudios, expresado como porcentaje de la matrícula total de dicho sector.
Los datos se presentan únicamente para aquellos países cuyo porcentaje de estudiantes en la categoría "otros" es inferior al 25%.
Para la composición de los grandes sectores de estudio, véanse las notas del cuadro II.13.

**Cuadro II.15  Enseñanza superior: distribución de los diplomados por nivel de la CINE y porcentaje de mujeres en cada nivel**
*Porcentaje de diplomados por niveles de la CINE.* Número de diplomados de enseñanza superior en cada nivel de la CINE como porcentaje del número total de diplomados.
*Porcentaje de mujeres diplomadas en cada nivel de la CINE.* Número de mujeres diplomadas como porcentaje del número total de diplomados en el nivel especificado.
Las definiciones de las categorías de niveles de la CINE en la enseñanza superior son:
Nivel 5: primer nivel de la enseñanza superior que permite obtener un certificado no equivalente a un primer título universitario.
Nivel 6: primer nivel de la enseñanza superior que permite obtener un primer título universitario o su equivalente.
Nivel 7: segundo nivel de la enseñanza superior que permite obtener un título universitario superior o su equivalente.

**Cuadro II.16  Enseñanza superior: distribución de los diplomados por gran sector de estudios**
*Porcentaje de diplomados por gran sector de estudios.* Número de diplomados de la enseñanza superior en el sector de estudios especificado, expresado como porcentaje del total de diplomados en el mismo nivel de enseñanza. La distribución se muestra únicamente en los países cuyo porcentaje de diplomados en la categoría "otros" es inferior al 25%.
Los campos de estudio de la CINE se agrupan en las siguientes categorías:
*Educación*: ciencias de la educación y formación docente.
*Humanidades*: estudios humanísticos, bellas artes y artes aplicadas, religión y teología.
*Ciencias sociales*: derecho; ciencias sociales y del comportamiento; estudios comerciales y administración de empresas; economía doméstica; comunicación de masas y documentación; y formación para el sector terciario.
*Ciencias naturales*: ciencias naturales, ingeniería, matemáticas e informática; arquitectura y urbanismo; transporte y comunicaciones; formación en actividades comerciales, artesanales e industriales; agricultura, silvicultura y pesca.
*Ciencias médicas*: medicina, salud e higiene.

**Cuadro II.17  Enseñanza superior: distribución de los estudiantes extranjeros por continente de origen**
Este cuadro presenta el número y el porcentaje de los estudiantes extranjeros matriculados en establecimientos de enseñanza superior, así como el porcentaje de su distribución por continente de origen, sobre la base del último año para el que se dispone de datos. Los datos no incluyen algunos de los principales países huéspedes para los que no se dispone de datos recientes.
La distribución no se presenta en los países donde el porcentaje de estudiantes de continentes de origen "sin especificar" es superior al 25%.

**Cuadro II.18  Gastos públicos totales y ordinarios destinados a la educación: porcentaje en relación con el PNB y los gastos del gobierno**
*Gastos públicos en educación como porcentaje del PNB.* Gastos públicos totales y ordinarios en educación expresados como porcentaje del Producto nacional bruto (columnas 1ra y 3ra).
*Gastos públicos en educación como porcentaje de los gastos públicos.* Gastos públicos totales y ordinarios en educación expresados como porcentaje de los gastos públicos totales y ordinarios respectivamente (columnas 2da y 4ta).
*Gastos ordinarios como porcentaje del total.* Gastos públicos ordinarios de educación, expresados como porcentaje del total de los gastos públicos de educación.
Los gastos *totales* se refieren a los gastos ordinarios y de capital destinados a la educación. Los gastos *ordinarios* son aquéllos destinados a los bienes y servicios consumidos durante el año corriente, y que pueden ser acrecentados si se necesita una prolongación para el próximo año. Los gastos de *capital* son los gastos activos mayores a un año.
Los gastos *públicos* destinados a la educación comprenden todos los gastos efectuados a cualquier nivel administrativo, en función de la organización política del país: gobierno central, autoridades regionales y locales.

II Country tables on education
Tableaux sur l'enseignement par pays
Cuadros sobre la enseñanza por países

**Cuadro II.19  Gastos públicos ordinarios destinados a la educación: distribución en porcentaje por nivel de enseñanza**

Este cuadro presenta la distribución en porcentaje de los gastos públicos ordinarios por nivel de enseñanza. Para algunos países, los gastos de educación en la preprimaria y la primaria se presentan combinados ya que los datos proporcionados no indican claramente si los gastos en la primaria son nulos o si están incluidos con los de la primaria. De la misma manera, en los países para los cuales los gastos no pueden ser distribuidos según los niveles de enseñanza correspondientes, el cuadro presenta los porcentajes combinados de los niveles de enseñanza preprimaria, primaria y secundaria.

La categoría "otros tipos" agrupa la educación para necesidades especiales, la educación de adultos y los otros tipos de educación que no pueden clasificarse por nivel.

La categoría "sin distribución" comprende en general los diversos gastos no especificados e incluye a veces los gastos de administración y las subvenciones o transferencias a los establecimientos de enseñanza para los cuales no se dispone de la distribución por nivel de enseñanza.

**Cuadro II.20  Gastos públicos ordinarios destinados a la educación: porcentaje de emolumentos y de material educativo**

Este cuadro presenta la distribución en porcentaje de los gastos públicos ordinarios según las siguientes categorías:

*Emolumentos del personal docente.* Sueldos brutos y otras primas adicionales, incluyendo las contribuciones al fondo de pensiones y seguro social, relacionados con el personal docente y el personal docente auxiliar.

*Emolumentos del personal no docente.* Sueldos brutos y otras primas adicionales, incluyendo las contribuciones al fondo de pensiones y seguro social, relacionados con el personal administrativo a todos los niveles de la administración, y otro personal tal como el personal para el mantenimiento y la conservación de los edificios, personal de seguridad, personal del transporte, personal de la restauración, etc.

*Total de los emolumentos.* Total de las dos categorías anteriores o gastos totales de los emolumentos para los países que no pueden separar los emolumentos del personal docente y del personal no docente.

*Materiales de enseñanza.* Gastos para la compra de bienes ligados a las actividades de enseñanza tales como libros, libros de texto, libros de ejercicios y otros materiales escolares y de enseñanza.

National education systems **II.1**
Systèmes nationaux d'enseignement
Sistemas nacionales de enseñanza

## II.1 National education systems

## Systèmes nationaux d'enseignement

## Sistemas nacionales de enseñanza

| 1 2 3 = Primary education | 1 2 3 = Enseignement primaire | 1 2 3 = Enseñanza primaria |
|---|---|---|
| 1 2 3 = Secondary education | 1 2 3 = Enseignement secondaire | 1 2 3 = Enseñanza secundaria |
| 1 2 3 = Lower secondary education | 1 2 3 = Enseignement secondaire, premier cycle | 1 2 3 = Enseñanza secundaria, primer ciclo |
| 1 2 3 = Upper secondary education | 1 2 3 = Enseignement secondaire, deuxième cycle | 1 2 3 = Enseñanza secundaria, segundo ciclo |

For countries marked with the symbol ‡, the educational system allows for other alternatives.

Pour les pays signalés par le symbole ‡, le système d'enseignement permet d'autres structures.

En los países marcados con el símbolo ‡, el sistema de la enseñanza permite otras estructuras.

| Country / Pays / País | Compulsory education / Scolarité obligatoire / Escolaridad obligatoria — Age limits / Limites d'âge / Límites de edad | Duration (years) / Durée (années) / Duración (años) | Entrance age to pre-primary education / Age d'admission dans l'enseignement préprimaire / Edad de admisión en la enseñanza preprimaria | 4 | 5 | 6 | 7 | 8 | 9 | 10 | 11 | 12 | 13 | 14 | 15 | 16 | 17 | 18 | 19 | 20 |
|---|---|---|---|---|---|---|---|---|---|---|---|---|---|---|---|---|---|---|---|---|
| **Africa** | | | | | | | | | | | | | | | | | | | | |
| Algeria | 6-15 | 9 | 4 | | | 1 | 2 | 3 | 4 | 5 | 6 | 1 | 2 | 3 | 1 | 2 | 3 | | | |
| Angola | 7-15 | 8 | 5 | | | 1 | 2 | 3 | 4 | 1 | 2 | 3 | 4 | 1 | 2 | 3 | | | | |
| Benin | 6-11 | 6 | 3 | | | 1 | 2 | 3 | 4 | 5 | 6 | 1 | 2 | 3 | 4 | 1 | 2 | 3 | | |
| Botswana | ... | ... | - | | | 1 | 2 | 3 | 4 | 5 | 6 | 7 | 1 | 2 | 1 | 2 | 3 | | | |
| Burkina Faso | 7-14 | 7 | 4 | | | | 1 | 2 | 3 | 4 | 5 | 6 | 1 | 2 | 3 | 4 | 1 | 2 | 3 | |
| Burundi | 7-13 | 6 | 4 | | | | 1 | 2 | 3 | 4 | 5 | 6 | 1 | 2 | 3 | 4 | 1 | 2 | 3 | |
| Cameroon ‡ | 6-12 | 6 | 4 | | | 1 | 2 | 3 | 4 | 5 | 6 | 1 | 2 | 3 | 4 | 1 | 2 | 3 | | |
| Cape Verde | 7-13 | 6 | 5 | | | | 1 | 2 | 3 | 4 | 5 | 6 | 1 | 2 | 3 | 1 | 2 | 3 | | |
| Central African Republic | 6-14 | 6 | 3 | | | 1 | 2 | 3 | 4 | 5 | 6 | 1 | 2 | 3 | 4 | 1 | 2 | 3 | | |
| Chad | 6-12 | 6 | 3 | | | 1 | 2 | 3 | 4 | 5 | 6 | 1 | 2 | 3 | 4 | 1 | 2 | 3 | | |
| Comoros | 7-16 | 9 | 4 | | | | 1 | 2 | 3 | 4 | 5 | 6 | 1 | 2 | 3 | 4 | 1 | 2 | 3 | |
| Congo | 6-16 | 10 | 3 | | | 1 | 2 | 3 | 4 | 5 | 6 | 1 | 2 | 3 | 4 | 1 | 2 | 3 | | |
| Côte d'Ivoire | 7-13 | 6 | 3 | | | 1 | 2 | 3 | 4 | 5 | 6 | 1 | 2 | 3 | 4 | 1 | 2 | 3 | | |
| Democratic Rep. of the Congo | ... | ... | 3 | | | 1 | 2 | 3 | 4 | 5 | 6 | 1 | 2 | 1 | 2 | 3 | 4 | | | |
| Djibouti | 6-12 | 6 | 4 | | | 1 | 2 | 3 | 4 | 5 | 6 | 1 | 2 | 3 | 4 | 1 | 2 | 3 | | |
| Egypt | 6-14 | 8 | 4 | | | 1 | 2 | 3 | 4 | 5 | 1 | 2 | 3 | 1 | 2 | 3 | | | | |
| Equatorial Guinea | 6-11 | 5 | 3 | | | 1 | 2 | 3 | 4 | 5 | 1 | 2 | 3 | 4 | 1 | 2 | 3 | | | |
| Eritrea | 7-13 | 7 | 5 | | | | 1 | 2 | 3 | 4 | 5 | 1 | 2 | 1 | 2 | 3 | 4 | | | |
| Ethiopia | 7-13 | 6 | 4 | | | | 1 | 2 | 3 | 4 | 5 | 6 | 1 | 2 | 1 | 2 | 3 | 4 | | |
| Gabon | 6-16 | 10 | 3 | | | 1 | 2 | 3 | 4 | 5 | 6 | 1 | 2 | 3 | 4 | 1 | 2 | 3 | | |
| Gambia | ... | ... | 5 | | | | 1 | 2 | 3 | 4 | 5 | 6 | 1 | 2 | 3 | 1 | 2 | 3 | | |
| Ghana ‡ | 6-14 | 8 | 4 | | | 1 | 2 | 3 | 4 | 5 | 6 | 1 | 2 | 3 | 4 | 1 | 2 | 3 | | |

II.1   National education systems
Systèmes nationaux d'enseignement
Sistemas nacionales de enseñanza

| Country / Pays / País | Compulsory education — Age limits / Limites d'âge / Límites de edad | Compulsory education — Duration (years) / Durée (années) / Duración (años) | Entrance age to pre-primary education / Age d'admission dans l'enseignement préprimaire / Edad de admisión en la enseñanza preprimaria | 4 | 5 | 6 | 7 | 8 | 9 | 10 | 11 | 12 | 13 | 14 | 15 | 16 | 17 | 18 | 19 | 20 |
|---|---|---|---|---|---|---|---|---|---|---|---|---|---|---|---|---|---|---|---|---|
| Guinea | 7-13 | 6 | 4 | | | | 1 | 2 | 3 | 4 | 5 | 6 | 1 | 2 | 3 | 4 | 1 | 2 | 3 | |
| Guinea-Bissau | 7-13 | 6 | 4 | | | | 1 | 2 | 3 | 4 | 5 | 6 | 1 | 2 | 3 | 1 | 2 | | | |
| Kenya | 6-14 | 8 | 3 | | | 1 | 2 | 3 | 4 | 5 | 6 | 7 | 8 | 1 | 2 | 3 | 4 | | | |
| Lesotho | 6-13 | 7 | - | | | 1 | 2 | 3 | 4 | 5 | 6 | 7 | 1 | 2 | 3 | 1 | 2 | | | |
| Liberia | 6-16 | 10 | 4 | | | | 1 | 2 | 3 | 4 | 5 | 6 | 1 | 2 | 3 | 1 | 2 | 3 | | |
| Libyan Arab Jamahiriya | 6-15 | 9 | 4 | | | 1 | 2 | 3 | 4 | 5 | 6 | 7 | 8 | 9 | 1 | 2 | 3 | | | |
| Madagascar | 6-13 | 6 | 3 | | | 1 | 2 | 3 | 4 | 5 | 1 | 2 | 3 | 4 | 1 | 2 | 3 | | | |
| Malawi | 6-14 | 8 | - | | | 1 | 2 | 3 | 4 | 5 | 6 | 7 | 8 | 1 | 2 | 1 | 2 | | | |
| Mali ‡ | 7-16 | 9 | 3 | | | | 1 | 2 | 3 | 4 | 5 | 6 | 1 | 2 | 3 | 1 | 2 | 3 | | |
| Mauritania | 6-12 | 6 | 3 | | | 1 | 2 | 3 | 4 | 5 | 6 | 1 | 2 | 3 | 1 | 2 | 3 | | | |
| Mauritius | 5-12 | 7 | 3 | | 1 | 2 | 3 | 4 | 5 | 6 | 1 | 2 | 3 | 1 | 2 | 3 | 4 | | | |
| Morocco | 7-16 | 6 | 5 | | | | 1 | 2 | 3 | 4 | 5 | 6 | 1 | 2 | 3 | 1 | 2 | 3 | | |
| Mozambique ‡ | 7-14 | 7 | - | | | | 1 | 2 | 3 | 4 | 5 | 1 | 2 | 1 | 2 | 3 | 4 | 5 | | |
| Namibia ‡ | 6-16 | 10 | 6 | | | | 1 | 2 | 3 | 4 | 5 | 6 | 7 | 1 | 2 | 3 | 4 | 5 | | |
| Niger | 7-15 | 8 | 4 | | | | 1 | 2 | 3 | 4 | 5 | 6 | 1 | 2 | 3 | 4 | 1 | 2 | 3 | |
| Nigeria | 6-12 | 6 | 3 | | | 1 | 2 | 3 | 4 | 5 | 6 | 1 | 2 | 3 | 1 | 2 | 3 | | | |
| Reunion | 6-16 | 10 | 2 | | | 1 | 2 | 3 | 4 | 5 | 1 | 2 | 3 | 4 | 1 | 2 | 3 | | | |
| Rwanda | 7-13 | 6 | 4 | | | | 1 | 2 | 3 | 4 | 5 | 6 | 7 | 1 | 2 | 3 | 4 | 5 | 6 | |
| Sao Tome and Principe | 6-14 | 4 | 3 | | | | 1 | 2 | 3 | 4 | 1 | 2 | 3 | 4 | 5 | 1 | 2 | | | |
| Senegal ‡ | 7-13 | 6 | 4 | | | | 1 | 2 | 3 | 4 | 5 | 6 | 1 | 2 | 3 | 4 | 1 | 2 | 3 | |
| Seychelles | 6-16 | 10 | 4 | | | 1 | 2 | 3 | 4 | 5 | 6 | 1 | 2 | 3 | 4 | 5 | | | | |
| Sierra Leone | ... | ... | 3 | | 1 | 2 | 3 | 4 | 5 | 6 | 7 | 1 | 2 | 3 | 4 | 5 | 1 | 2 | | |
| Somalia | 6-14 | 8 | 4 | | | 1 | 2 | 3 | 4 | 5 | 6 | 7 | 8 | 1 | 2 | 3 | 4 | | | |
| South Africa | 6-14 | 9 | 5 | | | 1 | 2 | 3 | 4 | 5 | 6 | 7 | 1 | 2 | 3 | 1 | 2 | | | |
| St. Helena | 5-15 | 10 | 3 | | 1 | 2 | 3 | 4 | 5 | 6 | 1 | 2 | 3 | 4 | 1 | 2 | | | | |
| Sudan | 6-13 | 8 | 4 | | | 1 | 2 | 3 | 4 | 5 | 6 | 7 | 8 | 1 | 2 | 3 | | | | |
| Swaziland ‡ | 6-13 | 7 | 3 | | | 1 | 2 | 3 | 4 | 5 | 6 | 7 | 1 | 2 | 3 | 1 | 2 | | | |
| Togo | 6-12 | 6 | 3 | | | 1 | 2 | 3 | 4 | 5 | 6 | 1 | 2 | 3 | 4 | 1 | 2 | 3 | | |
| Tunisia | 6-16 | 9 | 3 | | | 1 | 2 | 3 | 4 | 5 | 6 | 1 | 2 | 3 | 1 | 2 | 3 | 4 | | |
| Uganda | ... | ... | ... | | | 1 | 2 | 3 | 4 | 5 | 6 | 7 | 1 | 2 | 3 | 4 | 1 | 2 | | |
| United Republic of Tanzania | 7-14 | 7 | 4 | | | | 1 | 2 | 3 | 4 | 5 | 6 | 7 | 1 | 2 | 3 | 4 | 1 | 2 | |
| Western Sahara | 6-16 | 8 | 4 | | | 1 | 2 | 3 | 4 | 5 | 1 | 2 | 3 | 1 | 2 | 3 | | | | |
| Zambia | 7-14 | 7 | 3 | | | | 1 | 2 | 3 | 4 | 5 | 6 | 7 | 1 | 2 | 1 | 2 | 3 | | |
| Zimbabwe | 7-15 | 8 | 5 | | | 1 | 2 | 3 | 4 | 5 | 6 | 7 | 1 | 2 | 3 | 4 | 5 | 6 | | |
| **North America** | | | | | | | | | | | | | | | | | | | | |
| Anguilla ‡ | 5-16 | 12 | 3 | | 1 | 2 | 3 | 4 | 5 | 6 | 7 | 1 | 2 | 3 | 4 | 5 | | | | |
| Antigua and Barbuda ‡ | 5-16 | 11 | 3 | | 1 | 2 | 3 | 4 | 5 | 6 | 7 | 1 | 2 | 3 | 1 | 2 | | | | |
| Bahamas | 5-14 | 9 | 3 | | 1 | 2 | 3 | 4 | 5 | 6 | 1 | 2 | 3 | 1 | 2 | 3 | | | | |
| Barbados | 5-16 | 11 | 3 | | 1 | 2 | 3 | 4 | 5 | 6 | 7 | 1 | 2 | 3 | 4 | 5 | 6 | | | |

National education systems
Systèmes nationaux d'enseignement
Sistemas nacionales de enseñanza

II.1

| Country / Pays / País | Compulsory education — Scolarité obligatoire — Escolaridad obligatoria | | Entrance age to pre-primary education — Age d'admission dans l'enseignement préprimaire — Edad de admisión en la enseñanza preprimaria | Entrance age and duration of primary and secondary general education — Age d'admission et durée des enseignements primaire et secondaire général — Edad de admisión y duración de las enseñanzas primaria y secundaria general — Age / Age / Edad | | | | | | | | | | | | | | | | | |
| | Age limits — Limites d'âge — Límites de edad | Duration (years) — Durée (années) — Duración (años) | | 4 | 5 | 6 | 7 | 8 | 9 | 10 | 11 | 12 | 13 | 14 | 15 | 16 | 17 | 18 | 19 | 20 |
|---|---|---|---|---|---|---|---|---|---|---|---|---|---|---|---|---|---|---|---|---|
| Belize | 5-14 | 10 | 3 | 1 | 2 | 3 | 4 | 5 | 6 | 7 | 8 | 1 | 2 | 3 | 4 | | | | | |
| Bermuda | 5-16 | 11 | 4 | 1 | 2 | 3 | 4 | 5 | 6 | 7 | 1 | 2 | 3 | 4 | 5 | | | | | |
| British Virgin Islands ‡ | 5-16 | 11 | 3 | 1 | 2 | 3 | 4 | 5 | 6 | 7 | 1 | 2 | 3 | 1 | 2 | | | | | |
| Canada ‡ | 6-16 | 10 | 4 | | 1 | 2 | 3 | 4 | 5 | 6 | 1 | 2 | 3 | 1 | 2 | 3 | | | | |
| Cayman Islands | 5-15 | 10 | - | | 1 | 2 | 3 | 4 | 5 | 6 | 1 | 2 | 3 | 4 | 5 | 6 | 7 | | | |
| Costa Rica ‡ | 6-18 | 10 | 5 | | 1 | 2 | 3 | 4 | 5 | 6 | 1 | 2 | 3 | 1 | 2 | | | | | |
| Cuba | 6-16 | 9 | 5 | | 1 | 2 | 3 | 4 | 5 | 6 | 1 | 2 | 3 | 1 | 2 | | | | | |
| Dominica ‡ | 5-16 | 11 | 3 | 1 | 2 | 3 | 4 | 5 | 6 | 7 | 1 | 2 | 3 | 4 | 5 | | | | | |
| Dominican Republic | 5-14 | 10 | 3 | 1 | 2 | 3 | 4 | 5 | 6 | 7 | 8 | 1 | 2 | 3 | 4 | | | | | |
| El Salvador | 7-15 | 9 | 4 | | | 1 | 2 | 3 | 4 | 5 | 6 | 7 | 8 | 9 | 1 | 2 | 3 | | | |
| Grenada ‡ | 5-16 | 11 | 3 | 1 | 2 | 3 | 4 | 5 | 6 | 7 | 1 | 2 | 3 | 4 | 5 | | | | | |
| Guadeloupe | 6-16 | 10 | 2 | | 1 | 2 | 3 | 4 | 5 | 1 | 2 | 3 | 4 | 1 | 2 | 3 | | | | |
| Guatemala | 7-14 | 6 | 5 | | | 1 | 2 | 3 | 4 | 5 | 6 | 1 | 2 | 3 | 1 | 2 | 3 | | | |
| Haiti ‡ | 6-12 | 6 | 3 | | | 1 | 2 | 3 | 4 | 5 | 6 | 1 | 2 | 3 | 1 | 2 | 3 | | | |
| Honduras | 7-12 | 6 | 4 | | | 1 | 2 | 3 | 4 | 5 | 6 | 1 | 2 | 3 | 1 | 2 | | | | |
| Jamaica | 6-12 | 6 | 3 | | 1 | 2 | 3 | 4 | 5 | 6 | 1 | 2 | 3 | 1 | 2 | 3 | 4 | | | |
| Martinique | 6-16 | 10 | 2 | | 1 | 2 | 3 | 4 | 5 | 1 | 2 | 3 | 4 | 1 | 2 | 3 | | | | |
| Mexico | 6-14 | 6 | 4 | | 1 | 2 | 3 | 4 | 5 | 6 | 1 | 2 | 3 | 1 | 2 | 3 | | | | |
| Montserrat | 5-14 | 9 | 3 | 1 | 2 | 3 | 4 | 5 | 6 | 7 | 1 | 2 | 3 | 4 | 5 | | | | | |
| Netherlands Antilles | 6-15 | 9 | 4 | | 1 | 2 | 3 | 4 | 5 | 6 | 1 | 2 | 3 | 4 | 5 | | | | | |
| Nicaragua | 6-12 | 6 | 3 | | | 1 | 2 | 3 | 4 | 5 | 6 | 1 | 2 | 3 | 1 | 2 | | | | |
| Panama | 6-15 | 6 | 5 | | | 1 | 2 | 3 | 4 | 5 | 6 | 1 | 2 | 3 | 1 | 2 | 3 | | | |
| Puerto Rico | 6-16 | 10 | 3 | 1 | 2 | 3 | 4 | 5 | 6 | 7 | 8 | 1 | 2 | 3 | 4 | | | | | |
| St. Kitts and Nevis | 5-17 | 12 | 3 | 1 | 2 | 3 | 4 | 5 | 6 | 7 | 1 | 2 | 3 | 4 | 1 | 2 | | | | |
| St. Lucia | 5-15 | 10 | 2 | 1 | 2 | 3 | 4 | 5 | 6 | 7 | 1 | 2 | 3 | 1 | 2 | | | | | |
| St. Pierre and Miquelon | 6-16 | 10 | 2 | | | 1 | 2 | 3 | 4 | 5 | 1 | 2 | 3 | 4 | 1 | 2 | 3 | | | |
| St. Vincent and the Grenadines | 5-15 | 10 | 3 | 1 | 2 | 3 | 4 | 5 | 6 | 7 | 1 | 2 | 3 | 4 | 5 | 1 | 2 | | | |
| Trinidad and Tobago | 5-12 | 7 | 3 | 1 | 2 | 3 | 4 | 5 | 6 | 7 | 1 | 2 | 3 | 1 | 2 | | | | | |
| Turks and Caicos Islands | 7-14 | 7 | 4 | | 1 | 2 | 3 | 4 | 5 | 6 | 1 | 2 | 3 | 4 | 5 | | | | | |
| U. S. Virgin Islands | 6-16 | 10 | 5 | | | 1 | 2 | 3 | 4 | 5 | 6 | 1 | 2 | 3 | 1 | 2 | 3 | | | |
| United States ‡ | 6-16 | 10 | 3 | | | 1 | 2 | 3 | 4 | 5 | 6 | 1 | 2 | 3 | 1 | 2 | 3 | | | |
| **South America** | | | | | | | | | | | | | | | | | | | | |
| Argentina ‡ | 5-14 | 10 | 3 | | 1 | 2 | 3 | 4 | 5 | 6 | 7 | 1 | 2 | 3 | 1 | 2 | | | | |
| Bolivia | 6-14 | 8 | 4 | | 1 | 2 | 3 | 4 | 5 | 6 | 7 | 8 | 1 | 2 | 3 | 4 | | | | |
| Brazil | 7-14 | 8 | 4 | | | 1 | 2 | 3 | 4 | 5 | 6 | 7 | 8 | 1 | 2 | 3 | | | | |
| Chile | 6-13 | 8 | 5 | | 1 | 2 | 3 | 4 | 5 | 6 | 7 | 8 | 1 | 2 | 1 | 2 | | | | |
| Colombia | 6-12 | 5 | 3 | | 1 | 2 | 3 | 4 | 5 | 1 | 2 | 3 | 4 | 1 | 2 | | | | | |
| Ecuador | 5-15 | 10 | 5 | | 1 | 2 | 3 | 4 | 5 | 6 | 1 | 2 | 3 | 1 | 2 | 3 | | | | |
| Falkland Islands (Malvinas) | 5-16 | 11 | 4 | 1 | 2 | 3 | 4 | 5 | 6 | 7 | 1 | 2 | 3 | 4 | 5 | | | | | |

II.1  National education systems
Systèmes nationaux d'enseignement
Sistemas nacionales de enseñanza

| Country / Pays / País | Compulsory education / Scolarité obligatoire / Escolaridad obligatoria — Age limits / Limites d'âge / Límites de edad | Duration (years) / Durée (années) / Duración (años) | Entrance age to pre-primary education / Age d'admission dans l'enseignement préprimaire / Edad de admisión en la enseñanza preprimaria | 4 | 5 | 6 | 7 | 8 | 9 | 10 | 11 | 12 | 13 | 14 | 15 | 16 | 17 | 18 | 19 | 20 |
|---|---|---|---|---|---|---|---|---|---|---|---|---|---|---|---|---|---|---|---|---|
| French Guiana | 6-16 | 10 | 2 | | | 1 | 2 | 3 | 4 | 5 | 1 | 2 | 3 | 4 | 1 | 2 | 3 | | | |
| Guyana ‡ | 6-14 | 8 | 4 | | | 1 | 2 | 3 | 4 | 5 | 6 | 1 | 2 | 3 | 1 | 2 | | | | |
| Paraguay | 6-12 | 6 | 5 | | | 1 | 2 | 3 | 4 | 5 | 6 | 1 | 2 | 3 | 1 | 2 | 3 | | | |
| Peru | 6-12 | 6 | 3 | | | 1 | 2 | 3 | 4 | 5 | 6 | 1 | 2 | 1 | 2 | 3 | | | | |
| Suriname | 7-12 | 6 | 4 | | | 1 | 2 | 3 | 4 | 5 | 6 | 1 | 2 | 3 | 4 | 1 | 2 | 3 | | |
| Uruguay | 6-14 | 6 | 3 | | | 1 | 2 | 3 | 4 | 5 | 6 | 1 | 2 | 3 | 1 | 2 | 3 | | | |
| Venezuela | 6-15 | 10 | 3 | | | 1 | 2 | 3 | 4 | 5 | 6 | 7 | 8 | 9 | 1 | 2 | | | | |
| **Asia** | | | | | | | | | | | | | | | | | | | | |
| Afghanistan | 7-13 | 6 | 3 | | | | 1 | 2 | 3 | 4 | 5 | 6 | 1 | 2 | 3 | 4 | 5 | 6 | | |
| Armenia | 6-17 | 11 | 3 | | | | 1 | 2 | 3 | 4 | 1 | 2 | 3 | 4 | 1 | 2 | | | | |
| Azerbaijan | 6-17 | 11 | 3 | | | 1 | 2 | 3 | 4 | 1 | 2 | 3 | 4 | 5 | 1 | 2 | | | | |
| Bahrain ‡ | 6-15 | 9 | 3 | | | 1 | 2 | 3 | 4 | 5 | 6 | 1 | 2 | 3 | 1 | 2 | 3 | | | |
| Bangladesh | 5-10 | 5 | 5 | | | 1 | 2 | 3 | 4 | 5 | 1 | 2 | 3 | 4 | 5 | 1 | 2 | | | |
| Bhutan | ... | ... | 5 | | | 1 | 2 | 3 | 4 | 5 | 6 | 7 | 1 | 2 | 1 | 2 | | | | |
| Brunei Darussalam ‡ | 5-16 | 12 | 3 | | | 1 | 2 | 3 | 4 | 5 | 6 | 1 | 2 | 3 | 4 | 5 | 1 | 2 | | |
| Cambodia | ... | ... | 3 | | | 1 | 2 | 3 | 4 | 5 | 6 | 1 | 2 | 3 | 1 | 2 | 3 | | | |
| China ‡ | 7-15 | 9 | 3 | | | | 1 | 2 | 3 | 4 | 5 | 1 | 2 | 3 | 1 | 2 | | | | |
| China, Hong Kong SAR ‡ | 7-15 | 9 | 3 | | | 1 | 2 | 3 | 4 | 5 | 6 | 1 | 2 | 3 | 4 | 5 | 1 | 2 | | |
| Cyprus ‡ | 5-15 | 9 | 2 | | | 1 | 2 | 3 | 4 | 5 | 6 | 1 | 2 | 3 | 1 | 2 | 3 | | | |
| East Timor | ... | ... | ... | | | 1 | 2 | 3 | 4 | 1 | 2 | 3 | 4 | 5 | 1 | 2 | | | | |
| Georgia | 6-14 | 9 | 3 | | | 1 | 2 | 3 | 4 | 1 | 2 | 3 | 4 | 5 | 1 | 2 | | | | |
| India | 6-14 | 8 | 4 | | | 1 | 2 | 3 | 4 | 5 | 1 | 2 | 3 | 1 | 2 | 3 | 4 | | | |
| Indonesia | 7-15 | 9 | 5 | | | | 1 | 2 | 3 | 4 | 5 | 6 | 1 | 2 | 3 | 1 | 2 | 3 | | |
| Iran, Islamic Republic of | 6-11 | 5 | 5 | | | 1 | 2 | 3 | 4 | 5 | 1 | 2 | 3 | 1 | 2 | 3 | 4 | | | |
| Iraq | 6-12 | 6 | 4 | | | 1 | 2 | 3 | 4 | 5 | 6 | 1 | 2 | 3 | 1 | 2 | 3 | | | |
| Israel | 5-15 | 11 | 2 | | | 1 | 2 | 3 | 4 | 5 | 6 | 1 | 2 | 3 | 1 | 2 | 3 | | | |
| Japan ‡ | 6-15 | 9 | 3 | | | 1 | 2 | 3 | 4 | 5 | 6 | 1 | 2 | 3 | 1 | 2 | 3 | | | |
| Jordan | 6-15 | 9 | 4 | | | 1 | 2 | 3 | 4 | 5 | 6 | 7 | 8 | 9 | 10 | 1 | 2 | | | |
| Kazakstan | 6-17 | 11 | 3 | | | | 1 | 2 | 3 | 4 | 1 | 2 | 3 | 4 | 5 | 1 | 2 | | | |
| Korea, Democratic People's Rep. | 5-15 | 10 | 4 | | | 1 | 2 | 3 | 4 | 1 | 2 | 3 | 4 | 5 | 6 | | | | | |
| Korea, Republic of | 6-15 | 9 | 5 | | | 1 | 2 | 3 | 4 | 5 | 6 | 1 | 2 | 3 | 1 | 2 | 3 | | | |
| Kuwait | 6-14 | 8 | 4 | | | 1 | 2 | 3 | 4 | 1 | 2 | 3 | 4 | 1 | 2 | 3 | 4 | | | |
| Kyrgyzstan ‡ | 7-16 | 10 | 3 | | | | 1 | 2 | 3 | 4 | 1 | 2 | 3 | 4 | 5 | 1 | 2 | | | |
| Lao People's Democratic Rep. | 6-15 | 5 | 3 | | | 1 | 2 | 3 | 4 | 5 | 1 | 2 | 3 | 1 | 2 | 3 | | | | |
| Lebanon | 7-15 | 9 | 3 | | | 1 | 2 | 3 | 4 | 5 | 1 | 2 | 3 | 4 | 1 | 2 | 3 | | | |
| Macau | 6-12 | 5 | 3 | | | 1 | 2 | 3 | 4 | 5 | 6 | 1 | 2 | 3 | 4 | 5 | 6 | | | |
| Malaysia ‡ | ... | ... | 4 | | | 1 | 2 | 3 | 4 | 5 | 6 | 1 | 2 | 3 | 1 | 2 | 3 | 4 | | |
| Maldives | ... | ... | 4 | | | 1 | 2 | 3 | 4 | 5 | 1 | 2 | 3 | 4 | 5 | 1 | 2 | | | |
| Mongolia | 8-16 | 8 | 4 | | | | 1 | 2 | 3 | 4 | 1 | 2 | 3 | 4 | 1 | 2 | | | | |

National education systems **II.1**
Systèmes nationaux d'enseignement
Sistemas nacionales de enseñanza

| Country / Pays / País | Compulsory education — Age limits / Limites d'âge / Límites de edad | Compulsory education — Duration (years) / Durée (années) / Duración (años) | Entrance age to pre-primary education / Age d'admission dans l'enseignement préprimaire / Edad de admisión en la enseñanza preprimaria | 4 | 5 | 6 | 7 | 8 | 9 | 10 | 11 | 12 | 13 | 14 | 15 | 16 | 17 | 18 | 19 | 20 |
|---|---|---|---|---|---|---|---|---|---|---|---|---|---|---|---|---|---|---|---|---|
| Myanmar | 5-10 | 5 | 4 |  | 1 | 2 | 3 | 4 | 5 | 1 | 2 | 3 | 4 | 1 | 2 |  |  |  |  |  |
| Nepal | 6-11 | 5 | 3 |  |  | 1 | 2 | 3 | 4 | 5 | 1 | 2 | 3 | 1 | 2 |  |  |  |  |  |
| Oman | ... | ... | 4 |  |  | 1 | 2 | 3 | 4 | 5 | 6 | 1 | 2 | 3 | 1 | 2 | 3 |  |  |  |
| Pakistan | ... | ... | 3 |  | 1 | 2 | 3 | 4 | 5 | 1 | 2 | 3 | 1 | 2 | 3 | 4 |  |  |  |  |
| Philippines | 6-12 | 6 | 5 |  |  |  | 1 | 2 | 3 | 4 | 5 | 6 | 1 | 2 | 3 | 4 |  |  |  |  |
| Qatar | ... | ... | 4 |  |  | 1 | 2 | 3 | 4 | 5 | 6 | 1 | 2 | 3 | 1 | 2 | 3 |  |  |  |
| Saudi Arabia | ... | ... | 4 |  |  | 1 | 2 | 3 | 4 | 5 | 6 | 1 | 2 | 3 | 1 | 2 | 3 |  |  |  |
| Singapore ‡ | ... | ... | 4 |  |  | 1 | 2 | 3 | 4 | 5 | 6 | 1 | 2 | 3 | 4 | 1 | 2 | 3 |  |  |
| Sri Lanka | 5-14 | 9 | 4 |  | 1 | 2 | 3 | 4 | 5 | 1 | 2 | 3 | 4 | 5 | 6 | 1 | 2 |  |  |  |
| Syrian Arab Republic | 6-12 | 6 | 3 |  |  | 1 | 2 | 3 | 4 | 5 | 6 | 1 | 2 | 3 | 1 | 2 | 3 |  |  |  |
| Tajikistan | 7-17 | 9 | 3 |  |  |  | 1 | 2 | 3 | 4 | 1 | 2 | 3 | 4 | 5 | 1 | 2 |  |  |  |
| Thailand | 7-15 | 6 | 3 |  |  | 1 | 2 | 3 | 4 | 5 | 6 | 1 | 2 | 3 | 1 | 2 | 3 |  |  |  |
| Turkey ‡ | 6-14 | 8 | 4 |  |  | 1 | 2 | 3 | 4 | 5 | 1 | 2 | 3 | 1 | 2 | 3 |  |  |  |  |
| Turkmenistan | ... | ... | 3 |  |  |  | 1 | 2 | 3 | 4 | 1 | 2 | 3 | 4 | 5 | 1 | 2 |  |  |  |
| United Arab Emirates | 6-12 | 6 | 4 |  |  | 1 | 2 | 3 | 4 | 5 | 6 | 1 | 2 | 3 | 1 | 2 | 3 |  |  |  |
| Uzbekistan | ... | ... | 3 |  |  | 1 | 2 | 3 | 4 | 1 | 2 | 3 | 4 | 5 | 1 | 2 |  |  |  |  |
| Viet Nam | 6-11 | 5 | 3 |  |  | 1 | 2 | 3 | 4 | 5 | 1 | 2 | 3 | 1 | 2 | 3 |  |  |  |  |
| Yemen | 6-15 | 9 | 3 |  |  | 1 | 2 | 3 | 4 | 5 | 6 | 7 | 8 | 9 | 1 | 2 | 3 |  |  |  |
| Palestine | ... | ... | 4 |  |  | 1 | 2 | 3 | 4 | 5 | 6 | 7 | 8 | 9 | 10 | 1 | 2 |  |  |  |
| **Europe** | | | | | | | | | | | | | | | | | | | | |
| Albania | 6-14 | 8 | 3 |  |  | 1 | 2 | 3 | 4 | 5 | 6 | 7 | 8 | 1 | 2 | 3 | 4 |  |  |  |
| Andorra ‡ | ... | ... | 3 |  |  | 1 | 2 | 3 | 4 | 5 | 1 | 2 | 3 | 4 | 1 | 2 | 3 |  |  |  |
| Austria ‡ | 6-15 | 9 | 3 |  |  | 1 | 2 | 3 | 4 | 1 | 2 | 3 | 4 | 1 | 2 | 3 | 4 |  |  |  |
| Belarus ‡ | 6-15 | 9 | 3 |  |  | 1 | 2 | 3 | 4 | 1 | 2 | 3 | 4 | 5 | 1 | 2 |  |  |  |  |
| Belgium | 6-18 | 12 | 3 |  |  | 1 | 2 | 3 | 4 | 5 | 6 | 1 | 2 | 1 | 2 | 3 | 4 |  |  |  |
| Bulgaria ‡ | 7-16 | 8 | 3 |  |  |  | 1 | 2 | 3 | 4 | 1 | 2 | 3 | 4 | 1 | 2 | 3 | 4 |  |  |
| Croatia | 7-15 | 8 | 3 |  |  |  | 1 | 2 | 3 | 4 | 1 | 2 | 3 | 4 | 1 | 2 | 3 | 4 |  |  |
| Czech Republic | 6-15 | 9 | 3 |  |  | 1 | 2 | 3 | 4 | 1 | 2 | 3 | 4 | 1 | 2 | 3 | 4 |  |  |  |
| Denmark | 7-16 | 9 | 3 |  |  |  | 1 | 2 | 3 | 4 | 5 | 6 | 1 | 2 | 3 | 1 | 2 | 3 |  |  |
| Estonia | 7-16 | 9 | 3 |  |  |  | 1 | 2 | 3 | 4 | 5 | 6 | 1 | 2 | 3 | 1 | 2 | 3 |  |  |
| Federal Republic of Yugoslavia | 7-15 | 8 | 3 |  |  |  | 1 | 2 | 3 | 4 | 1 | 2 | 3 | 4 | 1 | 2 | 3 | 4 |  |  |
| Finland | 7-16 | 9 | 3 |  |  |  | 1 | 2 | 3 | 4 | 5 | 6 | 1 | 2 | 3 | 1 | 2 | 3 |  |  |
| France | 6-16 | 10 | 2 |  | 1 | 2 | 3 | 4 | 5 | 1 | 2 | 3 | 4 | 1 | 2 | 3 |  |  |  |  |
| Germany | 6-18 | 12 | 3 |  |  | 1 | 2 | 3 | 4 | 1 | 2 | 3 | 4 | 5 | 6 | 1 | 2 | 3 |  |  |
| Gibraltar | 4-15 | 12 | 3 | 1 | 2 | 3 | 4 | 5 | 6 | 7 | 8 | 1 | 2 | 3 | 4 | 1 | 2 |  |  |  |
| Greece ‡ | 6-15 | 9 | 4 |  |  | 1 | 2 | 3 | 4 | 5 | 6 | 1 | 2 | 3 | 1 | 2 | 3 |  |  |  |
| Hungary | 6-16 | 10 | 3 |  |  | 1 | 2 | 3 | 4 | 1 | 2 | 3 | 4 | 1 | 2 | 3 | 4 |  |  |  |
| Iceland | 6-16 | 10 | 2 |  |  | 1 | 2 | 3 | 4 | 5 | 6 | 7 | 1 | 2 | 3 | 1 | 2 | 3 | 4 |  |

II.1    National education systems
Systèmes nationaux d'enseignement
Sistemas nacionales de enseñanza

| Country / Pays / País | Compulsory education — Age limits / Limites d'âge / Límites de edad | Duration (years) / Durée (années) / Duración (años) | Entrance age to pre-primary education / Age d'admission dans l'enseignement préprimaire / Edad de admisión en la enseñanza preprimaria | 4 | 5 | 6 | 7 | 8 | 9 | 10 | 11 | 12 | 13 | 14 | 15 | 16 | 17 | 18 | 19 | 20 |
|---|---|---|---|---|---|---|---|---|---|---|---|---|---|---|---|---|---|---|---|---|
| Ireland ‡ | 6-15 | 9 | 4 | | | 1 | 2 | 3 | 4 | 5 | 6 | 1 | 2 | 3 | 1 | 2 | | | | |
| Italy | 6-14 | 8 | 3 | | | 1 | 2 | 3 | 4 | 5 | 1 | 2 | 3 | 1 | 2 | 3 | 4 | 5 | | |
| Latvia | ... | ... | 3 | | | | 1 | 2 | 3 | 4 | 1 | 2 | 3 | 4 | 5 | 1 | 2 | 3 | | |
| Liechtenstein ‡ | 7-16 | 8 | 4 | | | 1 | 2 | 3 | 4 | 5 | 1 | 2 | 3 | 1 | 2 | 3 | | | | |
| Lithuania | 7-15 | 9 | 3 | | | | 1 | 2 | 3 | 4 | 1 | 2 | 3 | 4 | 5 | 1 | 2 | 3 | | |
| Luxembourg | 6-15 | 9 | 4 | | | 1 | 2 | 3 | 4 | 5 | 6 | 1 | 2 | 3 | 1 | 2 | 3 | 4 | | |
| Malta ‡ | 5-16 | 11 | 3 | | 1 | 2 | 3 | 4 | 5 | 6 | 1 | 2 | 1 | 2 | 3 | 4 | 5 | | | |
| Moldova ‡ | 6-17 | 11 | 3 | | | | 1 | 2 | 3 | 4 | 1 | 2 | 3 | 4 | 5 | 1 | 2 | | | |
| Monaco | 6-16 | 10 | 3 | | | 1 | 2 | 3 | 4 | 5 | 1 | 2 | 3 | 4 | 1 | 2 | 3 | | | |
| Netherlands ‡ | 5-18 | 13 | 4 | | | 1 | 2 | 3 | 4 | 5 | 6 | 1 | 2 | 3 | 1 | 2 | 3 | | | |
| Norway | 7-15 | 9 | 4 | | | | 1 | 2 | 3 | 4 | 5 | 6 | 1 | 2 | 3 | 1 | 2 | 3 | | |
| Poland | 7-15 | 8 | 3 | | | | 1 | 2 | 3 | 4 | 5 | 6 | 7 | 8 | 1 | 2 | 3 | 4 | | |
| Portugal | 6-15 | 9 | 3 | | | 1 | 2 | 3 | 4 | 5 | 6 | 1 | 2 | 3 | 1 | 2 | 3 | | | |
| Romania | 7-14 | 8 | 3 | | | | 1 | 2 | 3 | 4 | 1 | 2 | 3 | 4 | 1 | 2 | 3 | 4 | | |
| Russian Federation ‡ | 6-15 | 9 | 3 | | | | 1 | 2 | 3 | 1 | 2 | 3 | 4 | 5 | 1 | 2 | | | | |
| San Marino | 6-14 | 8 | 3 | | | 1 | 2 | 3 | 4 | 5 | 1 | 2 | 3 | 1 | 2 | 3 | 4 | 5 | | |
| Slovakia | 6-15 | 9 | 3 | | | 1 | 2 | 3 | 4 | 1 | 2 | 3 | 4 | 1 | 2 | 3 | 4 | | | |
| Slovenia | 7-15 | 8 | 3 | | | | 1 | 2 | 3 | 4 | 1 | 2 | 3 | 4 | 1 | 2 | 3 | 4 | | |
| Spain | 6-16 | 10 | 2 | | | 1 | 2 | 3 | 4 | 5 | 6 | 1 | 2 | 1 | 2 | 3 | 4 | | | |
| Sweden ‡ | 7-15 | 9 | 3 | | | | 1 | 2 | 3 | 4 | 5 | 6 | 1 | 2 | 3 | 1 | 2 | 3 | | |
| Switzerland ‡ | 6-16 | 9 | 5 | | | | 1 | 2 | 3 | 4 | 5 | 6 | 1 | 2 | 3 | 1 | 2 | 3 | 4 | |
| The Former Yugoslav Rep. of Macedonia | 7-15 | 8 | 3 | | | | 1 | 2 | 3 | 4 | 5 | 6 | 7 | 8 | 1 | 2 | 3 | 4 | | |
| Ukraine ‡ | 6-15 | 9 | 3 | | | | 1 | 2 | 3 | 4 | 1 | 2 | 3 | 4 | 5 | 1 | 2 | | | |
| United Kingdom | 5-16 | 11 | 3 | | 1 | 2 | 3 | 4 | 5 | 6 | 1 | 2 | 3 | 1 | 2 | 3 | 4 | | | |
| **Oceania** | | | | | | | | | | | | | | | | | | | | |
| American Samoa | 6-18 | 12 | 3 | | | 1 | 2 | 3 | 4 | 5 | 6 | 7 | 8 | 1 | 2 | 1 | 2 | | | |
| Australia ‡ | 6-15 | 10 | 4 | | 1 | 2 | 3 | 4 | 5 | 6 | 7 | 1 | 2 | 3 | 4 | 1 | 2 | | | |
| Cook Islands | 6-15 | 9 | 4 | | 1 | 2 | 3 | 4 | 5 | 6 | 1 | 2 | 3 | 1 | 2 | 3 | | | | |
| Fiji ‡ | 6-15 | 8 | 3 | | | 1 | 2 | 3 | 4 | 5 | 6 | 1 | 2 | 3 | 4 | 5 | 6 | | | |
| French Polynesia | 6-16 | 10 | 3 | | | 1 | 2 | 3 | 4 | 5 | 1 | 2 | 3 | 4 | 1 | 2 | 3 | | | |
| Guam | 5-16 | 11 | 5 | | | 1 | 2 | 3 | 4 | 5 | 6 | 7 | 8 | 1 | 2 | 3 | 4 | | | |
| Kiribati ‡ | 6-15 | 9 | 4 | | | 1 | 2 | 3 | 4 | 5 | 6 | 7 | 1 | 2 | 3 | 4 | 5 | | | |
| Nauru ‡ | 6-16 | 10 | 5 | | | 1 | 2 | 3 | 4 | 5 | 6 | 7 | 1 | 2 | 3 | 4 | | | | |
| New Caledonia | 6-16 | 10 | 3 | | | 1 | 2 | 3 | 4 | 5 | 1 | 2 | 3 | 4 | 1 | 2 | 3 | | | |
| New Zealand ‡ | 6-16 | 10 | 2 | | 1 | 2 | 3 | 4 | 5 | 6 | 1 | 2 | 3 | 4 | 1 | 2 | 3 | | | |
| Niue | 5-14 | 8 | 4 | | 1 | 2 | 3 | 4 | 5 | 6 | 1 | 2 | 3 | 4 | 5 | 6 | | | | |
| Norfolk Island | ... | ... | ... | | 1 | 2 | 3 | 4 | 5 | 6 | 7 | 1 | 2 | 3 | 4 | | | | | |
| Pacific Islands (Palau) | 6-14 | 8 | 4 | | | 1 | 2 | 3 | 4 | 5 | 6 | 7 | 8 | 1 | 2 | 1 | 2 | | | |

National education systems **II.1**
Systèmes nationaux d'enseignement
Sistemas nacionales de enseñanza

| Country / Pays / País | Compulsory education / Scolarité obligatoire / Escolaridad obligatoria | | Entrance age to pre-primary education / Age d'admission dans l'enseignement préprimaire / Edad de admisión en la enseñanza preprimaria | Entrance age and duration of primary and secondary general education / Age d'admission et durée des enseignements primaire et secondaire général / Edad de admisión y duración de las enseñanzas primaria y secundaria general — Age / Age / Edad | | | | | | | | | | | | | | | | | |
|---|---|---|---|---|---|---|---|---|---|---|---|---|---|---|---|---|---|---|---|---|---|
| | Age limits / Limites d'âge / Límites de edad | Duration (years) / Durée (années) / Duración (años) | | 4 | 5 | 6 | 7 | 8 | 9 | 10 | 11 | 12 | 13 | 14 | 15 | 16 | 17 | 18 | 19 | 20 |
| Papua New Guinea ‡ | ... | ... | 5 | | | | 1 | 2 | 3 | 4 | 5 | 6 | 1 | 2 | 3 | 4 | 1 | 2 | | |
| Samoa | 5-14 | 8 | 3 | | 1 | 2 | 3 | 4 | 5 | 6 | 7 | 8 | 1 | 2 | 3 | 1 | 2 | | | |
| Solomon Islands ‡ | ... | ... | 3 | | | | 1 | 2 | 3 | 4 | 5 | 6 | 1 | 2 | 3 | 1 | 2 | | | |
| Tokelau | 5-16 | 12 | 3 | | 1 | 2 | 3 | 4 | 5 | 6 | 7 | 8 | 9 | 1 | 2 | | | | | |
| Tonga ‡ | 6-14 | 8 | 3 | | | 1 | 2 | 3 | 4 | 5 | 6 | 1 | 2 | 3 | 4 | 5 | 6 | 7 | | |
| Tuvalu | 7-14 | 7 | 3 | | | 1 | 2 | 3 | 4 | 5 | 6 | 7 | 8 | 1 | 2 | 3 | 4 | | | |
| Vanuatu, Republic of | 6-12 | 6 | 3 | | | 1 | 2 | 3 | 4 | 5 | 6 | 1 | 2 | 3 | 4 | 1 | 2 | 3 | | |

**General note**
For general explanations and definitions, please refer to the beginning of this chapter.

**Note générale**
Pour les explications et définitions générales, prière de se référer au début de ce chapitre.

**Nota general**
Para las explicaciones y definiciones generales, referirse al comienzo de este capítulo.

## II.2 Estimated illiteracy rate and illiterate population aged 15 years and over, and 15 to 24 years old

Estimations du taux d'analphabétisme et de la population analphabète âgée de 15 ans et plus, et de 15 à 24 ans

Estimaciones de la tasa de analfabetismo y de la población analfabeta de 15 años y más, y de 15 a 24 años

| Country Pays País | Year Année Año | Population aged 15 years and over Population âgée de 15 ans et plus Población de 15 años y más | | | | | | Population aged 15 to 24 years Population âgée de 15 à 24 ans Población de 15 a 24 años | | | | | |
|---|---|---|---|---|---|---|---|---|---|---|---|---|---|
| | | Illiteracy rate Taux d'analphabétisme Tasa de analfabetismo ( % ) | | | Illiterate population Population analphabète Población analfabeta (000) | | | Illiteracy rate Taux d'analphabétisme Tasa de analfabetismo ( % ) | | | Illiterate population Population analphabète Población analfabeta (000) | | |
| | | MF | M | F | MF | M | F | MF | M | F | MF | M | F |
| **Africa** | | | | | | | | | | | | | |
| Algeria | 1980 | 59.9 | 44.8 | 74.1 | 6 009 | 2 181 | 3 828 | 40.1 | 25.8 | 55.0 | 1 472 | 484 | 988 |
| | 1985 | 53.2 | 39.2 | 67.2 | 6 521 | 2 407 | 4 113 | 33.9 | 21.0 | 47.2 | 1 542 | 482 | 1 060 |
| | 1990 | 47.2 | 33.6 | 60.9 | 6 830 | 2 450 | 4 380 | 28.9 | 17.8 | 40.5 | 1 484 | 466 | 1 017 |
| | 1995 | 41.6 | 28.9 | 54.6 | 7 110 | 2 486 | 4 624 | 24.6 | 15.4 | 34.3 | 1 456 | 464 | 991 |
| | 2000 | 36.7 | 24.9 | 48.7 | 7 331 | 2 506 | 4 824 | 20.6 | 12.9 | 28.6 | 1 381 | 440 | 941 |
| Benin | 1980 | 82.1 | 74.0 | 89.9 | 1 560 | 691 | 869 | 71.2 | 56.7 | 83.7 | 492 | 181 | 310 |
| | 1985 | 78.0 | 68.1 | 87.4 | 1 672 | 709 | 963 | 66.0 | 50.6 | 80.1 | 510 | 185 | 324 |
| | 1990 | 73.5 | 61.9 | 84.5 | 1 770 | 723 | 1 047 | 59.5 | 43.3 | 75.2 | 493 | 177 | 316 |
| | 1995 | 68.4 | 55.1 | 80.9 | 1 906 | 743 | 1 162 | 53.0 | 36.0 | 69.7 | 513 | 173 | 340 |
| | 2000 | 62.5 | 47.8 | 76.4 | 2 066 | 766 | 1 299 | 46.8 | 29.5 | 63.9 | 582 | 181 | 400 |
| Botswana | 1980 | 42.3 | 44.4 | 40.7 | 198 | 94 | 104 | 28.4 | 32.1 | 24.8 | 53 | 29 | 23 |
| | 1985 | 36.6 | 38.6 | 34.8 | 207 | 101 | 105 | 21.8 | 25.7 | 18.0 | 48 | 28 | 20 |
| | 1990 | 31.8 | 34.2 | 29.6 | 221 | 112 | 108 | 16.8 | 20.8 | 12.8 | 43 | 27 | 16 |
| | 1995 | 27.3 | 30.0 | 24.9 | 227 | 118 | 108 | 14.0 | 18.0 | 10.1 | 42 | 27 | 15 |
| | 2000 | 22.8 | 25.6 | 20.2 | 213 | 115 | 98 | 11.8 | 15.7 | 8.0 | 42 | 27 | 14 |
| Burkina Faso | 1980 | 89.2 | 82.4 | 95.7 | 3 242 | 1 467 | 1 774 | 82.8 | 73.4 | 92.2 | 1 023 | 453 | 570 |
| | 1985 | 86.8 | 79.0 | 94.3 | 3 590 | 1 606 | 1 984 | 79.6 | 69.4 | 89.9 | 1 185 | 518 | 667 |
| | 1990 | 84.0 | 75.3 | 92.4 | 3 996 | 1 763 | 2 233 | 76.0 | 65.1 | 86.9 | 1 330 | 571 | 758 |
| | 1995 | 80.8 | 71.3 | 90.0 | 4 413 | 1 921 | 2 492 | 71.8 | 60.5 | 83.3 | 1 454 | 614 | 839 |
| | 2000 | 77.0 | 66.8 | 86.9 | 4 845 | 2 081 | 2 763 | 67.1 | 55.5 | 78.8 | 1 598 | 664 | 933 |
| Burundi | 1980 | 72.4 | 59.4 | 83.7 | 1 653 | 632 | 1 021 | 60.4 | 49.2 | 71.5 | 524 | 211 | 312 |
| | 1985 | 67.8 | 55.4 | 78.8 | 1 782 | 685 | 1 096 | 54.4 | 45.3 | 63.5 | 523 | 217 | 306 |
| | 1990 | 62.2 | 51.5 | 72.0 | 1 847 | 727 | 1 120 | 47.5 | 41.1 | 53.7 | 493 | 212 | 280 |
| | 1995 | 57.7 | 47.8 | 66.8 | 1 913 | 759 | 1 154 | 41.9 | 37.4 | 46.4 | 482 | 213 | 268 |
| | 2000 | 51.9 | 43.7 | 59.5 | 1 867 | 754 | 1 112 | 35.8 | 33.7 | 37.9 | 470 | 219 | 250 |
| Cameroon | 1980 | 53.1 | 40.7 | 64.9 | 2 560 | 958 | 1 601 | 25.9 | 18.1 | 33.6 | 401 | 140 | 261 |
| | 1985 | 45.3 | 34.2 | 55.9 | 2 491 | 919 | 1 572 | 19.1 | 14.1 | 24.0 | 349 | 128 | 220 |
| | 1990 | 37.7 | 28.2 | 46.9 | 2 395 | 876 | 1 518 | 13.6 | 10.8 | 16.5 | 295 | 116 | 178 |
| | 1995 | 30.7 | 22.8 | 38.4 | 2 268 | 825 | 1 442 | 9.7 | 8.2 | 11.1 | 249 | 106 | 142 |
| | 2000 | 24.6 | 18.2 | 30.8 | 2 099 | 764 | 1 335 | 6.9 | 6.3 | 7.4 | 209 | 96 | 113 |
| Cape Verde | 1980 | 49.0 | 35.2 | 59.9 | 76 | 23 | 52 | 29.8 | 19.3 | 38.9 | 19 | 5 | 13 |
| | 1985 | 42.5 | 28.4 | 52.5 | 73 | 20 | 53 | 23.4 | 15.9 | 30.4 | 18 | 5 | 12 |
| | 1990 | 37.6 | 25.3 | 47.1 | 73 | 21 | 51 | 20.4 | 14.8 | 25.8 | 15 | 5 | 10 |
| | 1995 | 30.6 | 19.3 | 39.3 | 68 | 18 | 49 | 15.7 | 11.0 | 20.1 | 12 | 4 | 8 |
| | 2000 | 26.5 | 15.7 | 34.7 | 68 | 17 | 50 | 12.7 | 9.1 | 16.1 | 11 | 4 | 7 |
| Central African Republic | 1980 | 76.6 | 63.7 | 88.3 | 1 035 | 407 | 628 | 60.0 | 43.6 | 75.5 | 252 | 88 | 163 |
| | 1985 | 71.9 | 58.2 | 84.3 | 1 079 | 413 | 666 | 54.8 | 39.7 | 69.2 | 256 | 90 | 166 |
| | 1990 | 66.5 | 52.6 | 79.1 | 1 111 | 416 | 694 | 48.2 | 34.5 | 60.9 | 253 | 87 | 165 |
| | 1995 | 60.3 | 46.4 | 72.8 | 1 129 | 412 | 717 | 40.7 | 29.1 | 51.6 | 251 | 87 | 164 |
| | 2000 | 53.5 | 40.4 | 65.5 | 1 113 | 399 | 713 | 33.7 | 24.5 | 42.5 | 244 | 87 | 157 |
| Chad | 1980 | 67.3 | 53.2 | 80.6 | 1 749 | 672 | 1 076 | ... | ... | ... | ... | ... | ... |
| | 1985 | 62.3 | 47.9 | 76.0 | 1 806 | 677 | 1 128 | ... | ... | ... | ... | ... | ... |
| | 1990 | 57.2 | 42.8 | 70.9 | 1 794 | 655 | 1 139 | ... | ... | ... | ... | ... | ... |
| | 1995 | 51.8 | 37.8 | 65.2 | 1 874 | 668 | 1 205 | ... | ... | ... | ... | ... | ... |
| | 2000 | 46.4 | 33.1 | 59.2 | 1 937 | 675 | 1 262 | ... | ... | ... | ... | ... | ... |
| Comoros | 1980 | 51.7 | 43.8 | 59.5 | 104 | 43 | 60 | 47.8 | 40.5 | 55.1 | 34 | 14 | 19 |
| | 1985 | 47.5 | 39.5 | 55.1 | 112 | 45 | 66 | 43.9 | 36.7 | 51.1 | 38 | 16 | 22 |
| | 1990 | 46.2 | 38.6 | 53.6 | 129 | 53 | 76 | 42.8 | 35.8 | 49.8 | 45 | 19 | 26 |
| | 1995 | 45.0 | 37.5 | 52.4 | 150 | 61 | 88 | 41.6 | 34.9 | 48.6 | 52 | 22 | 30 |
| | 2000 | 43.8 | 36.5 | 50.9 | 175 | 72 | 102 | 40.6 | 34.0 | 47.3 | 61 | 25 | 35 |

| Country / Pays / País | Year / Année / Año | Population aged 15 years and over<br>Population âgée de 15 ans et plus<br>Población de 15 años y más | | | | | | Population aged 15 to 24 years<br>Population âgée de 15 à 24 ans<br>Población de 15 a 24 años | | | | | |
|---|---|---|---|---|---|---|---|---|---|---|---|---|---|
| | | Illiteracy rate<br>Taux d'analphabétisme<br>Tasa de analfabetismo<br>(%) | | | Illiterate population<br>Population analphabète<br>Población analfabeta<br>(000) | | | Illiteracy rate<br>Taux d'analphabétisme<br>Tasa de analfabetismo<br>(%) | | | Illiterate population<br>Population analphabète<br>Población analfabeta<br>(000) | | |
| | | MF | M | F | MF | M | F | MF | M | F | MF | M | F |
| Congo | 1980 | 49.6 | 36.3 | 61.7 | 454 | 159 | 294 | 19.9 | 12.1 | 27.3 | 60 | 18 | 42 |
| | 1985 | 40.9 | 29.2 | 51.7 | 431 | 148 | 283 | 12.4 | 7.8 | 16.9 | 44 | 13 | 31 |
| | 1990 | 32.8 | 22.7 | 42.1 | 396 | 132 | 264 | 7.5 | 5.1 | 9.9 | 31 | 10 | 21 |
| | 1995 | 25.6 | 17.3 | 33.2 | 354 | 115 | 239 | 4.4 | 3.1 | 5.7 | 22 | 7 | 14 |
| | 2000 | 19.3 | 12.5 | 25.6 | 305 | 94 | 210 | 2.6 | 1.8 | 3.3 | 15 | 5 | 9 |
| Côte d'Ivoire | 1980 | 76.9 | 67.6 | 87.0 | 3 370 | 1 542 | 1 827 | 63.5 | 51.8 | 75.5 | 929 | 383 | 545 |
| | 1985 | 72.1 | 62.6 | 82.4 | 3 745 | 1 685 | 2 059 | 57.1 | 46.2 | 68.1 | 998 | 406 | 591 |
| | 1990 | 66.6 | 57.2 | 76.6 | 4 070 | 1 802 | 2 268 | 49.9 | 40.4 | 59.5 | 1 054 | 428 | 626 |
| | 1995 | 60.0 | 51.3 | 69.4 | 4 468 | 1 976 | 2 492 | 42.4 | 34.8 | 50.1 | 1 145 | 475 | 669 |
| | 2000 | 53.2 | 45.4 | 61.5 | 4 457 | 1 952 | 2 505 | 35.2 | 29.7 | 40.7 | 1 119 | 473 | 646 |
| Djibouti | 1980 | 68.6 | 54.7 | 81.9 | 109 | 42 | 67 | ... | ... | ... | ... | ... | ... |
| | 1985 | 63.8 | 49.6 | 77.5 | 140 | 53 | 87 | ... | ... | ... | ... | ... | ... |
| | 1990 | 58.8 | 44.5 | 72.6 | 173 | 64 | 108 | ... | ... | ... | ... | ... | ... |
| | 1995 | 53.7 | 39.6 | 67.2 | 191 | 68 | 122 | ... | ... | ... | ... | ... | ... |
| | 2000 | 48.6 | 35.0 | 61.6 | 180 | 62 | 118 | ... | ... | ... | ... | ... | ... |
| Egypt | 1980 | 60.7 | 46.3 | 75.3 | 16 078 | 6 171 | 9 906 | 48.2 | 35.8 | 61.5 | 4 290 | 1 649 | 2 641 |
| | 1985 | 56.8 | 42.9 | 70.9 | 17 100 | 6 501 | 10 599 | 43.0 | 32.1 | 54.8 | 4 117 | 1 593 | 2 523 |
| | 1990 | 52.9 | 39.7 | 66.4 | 17 940 | 6 788 | 11 152 | 38.7 | 29.1 | 49.1 | 4 014 | 1 562 | 2 452 |
| | 1995 | 48.9 | 36.5 | 61.5 | 18 824 | 7 083 | 11 741 | 34.5 | 26.2 | 43.3 | 4 017 | 1 578 | 2 439 |
| | 2000 | 44.7 | 33.4 | 56.3 | 19 834 | 7 466 | 12 368 | 30.4 | 23.6 | 37.7 | 4 223 | 1 684 | 2 538 |
| Equatorial Guinea | 1980 | 40.4 | 24.0 | 55.9 | 51 | 14 | 36 | 15.4 | 6.5 | 24.4 | 5 | 1 | 4 |
| | 1985 | 33.5 | 18.9 | 47.4 | 61 | 16 | 44 | 10.8 | 4.7 | 16.9 | 6 | 1 | 4 |
| | 1990 | 26.9 | 14.6 | 38.8 | 54 | 14 | 40 | 7.2 | 3.2 | 11.3 | 4 | 1 | 3 |
| | 1995 | 22.2 | 10.7 | 32.8 | 51 | 11 | 39 | 4.8 | 2.2 | 7.3 | 3 | 0 | 2 |
| | 2000 | 16.8 | 7.5 | 25.5 | 42 | 9 | 33 | 3.1 | 1.5 | 4.6 | 2 | 0 | 1 |
| Ethiopia | 1980 | 80.3 | 71.9 | 88.5 | 16 190 | 7 205 | 8 984 | 67.9 | 58.4 | 77.8 | 4 647 | 2 056 | 2 590 |
| | 1985 | 76.2 | 67.9 | 84.4 | 17 236 | 7 670 | 9 566 | 62.7 | 54.6 | 71.2 | 4 846 | 2 164 | 2 682 |
| | 1990 | 71.7 | 64.0 | 79.4 | 18 816 | 8 422 | 10 394 | 57.5 | 51.9 | 63.3 | 5 150 | 2 375 | 2 774 |
| | 1995 | 66.8 | 60.1 | 73.5 | 20 057 | 9 079 | 10 977 | 51.6 | 48.5 | 54.8 | 5 315 | 2 551 | 2 764 |
| | 2000 | 61.3 | 56.1 | 66.6 | 20 664 | 9 497 | 11 166 | 45.5 | 44.9 | 46.0 | 5 426 | 2 703 | 2 722 |
| Gabon | 1980 | 59.2 | 45.7 | 72.0 | 269 | 101 | 168 | ... | ... | ... | ... | ... | ... |
| | 1985 | 51.5 | 38.6 | 63.6 | 266 | 97 | 168 | ... | ... | ... | ... | ... | ... |
| | 1990 | 44.0 | 32.3 | 55.1 | 258 | 93 | 165 | ... | ... | ... | ... | ... | ... |
| | 1995 | 36.7 | 26.3 | 46.6 | 243 | 84 | 159 | ... | ... | ... | ... | ... | ... |
| | 2000 | 29.2 | 20.2 | 37.8 | 214 | 72 | 142 | ... | ... | ... | ... | ... | ... |
| Gambia | 1980 | 83.6 | 78.9 | 88.2 | 308 | 142 | 165 | 71.4 | 64.2 | 78.4 | 80 | 35 | 44 |
| | 1985 | 79.5 | 73.9 | 84.8 | 334 | 152 | 182 | 64.9 | 56.9 | 72.7 | 85 | 37 | 47 |
| | 1990 | 74.4 | 68.3 | 80.3 | 397 | 179 | 218 | 57.9 | 49.5 | 66.1 | 96 | 40 | 55 |
| | 1995 | 69.1 | 62.2 | 75.6 | 451 | 199 | 251 | 50.5 | 42.0 | 58.8 | 99 | 41 | 58 |
| | 2000 | 63.5 | 56.2 | 70.4 | 494 | 214 | 279 | 43.0 | 34.8 | 51.0 | 99 | 40 | 59 |
| Ghana | 1980 | 56.8 | 42.9 | 70.2 | 3 389 | 1 258 | 2 131 | 34.8 | 22.0 | 47.5 | 734 | 232 | 502 |
| | 1985 | 49.7 | 36.5 | 62.5 | 3 513 | 1 269 | 2 244 | 27.1 | 17.1 | 37.1 | 670 | 211 | 459 |
| | 1990 | 42.7 | 30.6 | 54.4 | 3 534 | 1 246 | 2 287 | 20.3 | 13.0 | 27.6 | 585 | 187 | 398 |
| | 1995 | 36.1 | 25.3 | 46.6 | 3 518 | 1 217 | 2 301 | 14.9 | 9.8 | 19.9 | 503 | 167 | 336 |
| | 2000 | 29.8 | 20.5 | 38.8 | 3 426 | 1 166 | 2 260 | 10.6 | 7.4 | 13.8 | 428 | 149 | 278 |
| Guinea | 1980 | 77.5 | 65.5 | 89.3 | 1 752 | 719 | 1 033 | ... | ... | ... | ... | ... | ... |
| | 1985 | 73.4 | 60.5 | 86.2 | 1 934 | 779 | 1 154 | ... | ... | ... | ... | ... | ... |
| | 1990 | 68.9 | 55.3 | 82.4 | 2 083 | 815 | 1 267 | ... | ... | ... | ... | ... | ... |
| | 1995 | 64.1 | 50.0 | 78.0 | 2 132 | 815 | 1 316 | ... | ... | ... | ... | ... | ... |
| | 2000 | 58.9 | 44.9 | 73.0 | 2 186 | 816 | 1 370 | ... | ... | ... | ... | ... | ... |
| Guinea-Bissau | 1980 | 81.1 | 68.4 | 93.2 | 394 | 162 | 232 | 68.1 | 49.8 | 86.1 | 96 | 34 | 61 |
| | 1985 | 77.4 | 63.3 | 90.8 | 404 | 160 | 243 | 63.4 | 44.8 | 81.5 | 97 | 34 | 63 |
| | 1990 | 73.3 | 58.0 | 87.8 | 415 | 159 | 256 | 57.9 | 39.6 | 75.9 | 97 | 32 | 64 |
| | 1995 | 68.5 | 52.5 | 83.7 | 426 | 158 | 268 | 51.9 | 34.4 | 69.0 | 98 | 32 | 66 |
| | 2000 | 63.2 | 47.0 | 78.6 | 440 | 159 | 280 | 45.5 | 29.5 | 61.2 | 102 | 32 | 69 |
| Kenya | 1980 | 43.2 | 29.2 | 56.9 | 3 588 | 1 205 | 2 383 | 22.0 | 12.5 | 31.5 | 681 | 195 | 486 |
| | 1985 | 35.8 | 23.6 | 47.7 | 3 554 | 1 163 | 2 390 | 15.0 | 9.4 | 20.6 | 561 | 177 | 383 |
| | 1990 | 28.9 | 18.6 | 39.0 | 3 462 | 1 106 | 2 356 | 10.2 | 7.1 | 13.3 | 469 | 165 | 304 |
| | 1995 | 22.7 | 14.4 | 30.9 | 3 338 | 1 052 | 2 286 | 7.1 | 5.3 | 9.0 | 415 | 156 | 258 |
| | 2000 | 17.5 | 11.0 | 24.0 | 3 015 | 946 | 2 068 | 5.0 | 4.0 | 5.9 | 341 | 140 | 201 |
| Lesotho | 1980 | 28.5 | 41.7 | 16.8 | 223 | 153 | 69 | 16.4 | 28.4 | 5.0 | 40 | 34 | 6 |
| | 1985 | 24.9 | 37.7 | 13.4 | 222 | 159 | 62 | 14.2 | 24.8 | 3.8 | 40 | 34 | 5 |
| | 1990 | 21.6 | 33.7 | 10.5 | 219 | 163 | 55 | 12.1 | 21.5 | 2.8 | 39 | 34 | 4 |
| | 1995 | 18.6 | 29.9 | 8.1 | 214 | 165 | 48 | 10.3 | 18.5 | 2.0 | 39 | 35 | 3 |
| | 2000 | 16.1 | 26.4 | 6.4 | 208 | 165 | 42 | 8.8 | 16.0 | 1.5 | 38 | 34 | 3 |
| Liberia | 1980 | 72.2 | 58.1 | 86.4 | 753 | 305 | 447 | 55.5 | 37.5 | 74.2 | 191 | 65 | 125 |
| | 1985 | 66.5 | 51.3 | 82.0 | 795 | 309 | 486 | 48.7 | 30.8 | 67.1 | 198 | 63 | 134 |
| | 1990 | 60.8 | 44.7 | 77.1 | 836 | 309 | 526 | 42.8 | 24.9 | 61.2 | 204 | 60 | 144 |
| | 1995 | 54.8 | 38.4 | 71.6 | 512 | 181 | 331 | 35.9 | 19.3 | 53.7 | 144 | 40 | 104 |
| | 2000 | 46.6 | 30.1 | 63.2 | 849 | 276 | 572 | 31.4 | 15.5 | 47.4 | 239 | 59 | 180 |

| Country / Pays / País | Year / Année / Año | Population aged 15 years and over / Population âgée de 15 ans et plus / Población de 15 años y más | | | | | | Population aged 15 to 24 years / Population âgée de 15 à 24 ans / Población de 15 a 24 años | | | | | |
|---|---|---|---|---|---|---|---|---|---|---|---|---|---|
| | | Illiteracy rate / Taux d'analphabétisme / Tasa de analfabetismo ( % ) | | | Illiterate population / Population analphabète / Población analfabeta (000) | | | Illiteracy rate / Taux d'analphabétisme / Tasa de analfabetismo ( % ) | | | Illiterate population / Population analphabète / Población analfabeta (000) | | |
| | | MF | M | F | MF | M | F | MF | M | F | MF | M | F |
| Libyan Arab Jamahiriya | 1980 | 47.1 | 28.5 | 69.4 | 765 | 253 | 512 | 21.2 | 4.8 | 38.8 | 113 | 13 | 100 |
| | 1985 | 39.1 | 22.3 | 59.0 | 794 | 246 | 547 | 13.6 | 2.3 | 25.6 | 93 | 8 | 85 |
| | 1990 | 32.0 | 17.0 | 49.1 | 777 | 220 | 556 | 9.5 | 1.0 | 18.3 | 82 | 4 | 77 |
| | 1995 | 25.7 | 12.6 | 40.2 | 746 | 193 | 552 | 6.1 | 0.3 | 12.2 | 64 | 1 | 62 |
| | 2000 | 20.2 | 9.1 | 32.4 | 708 | 166 | 541 | 3.9 | 0.2 | 7.8 | 49 | 1 | 48 |
| Malawi | 1980 | 55.5 | 36.3 | 72.7 | 1 802 | 559 | 1 243 | 44.8 | 28.4 | 60.1 | 515 | 157 | 357 |
| | 1985 | 51.8 | 33.7 | 68.2 | 1 987 | 616 | 1 370 | 40.7 | 26.7 | 53.9 | 555 | 177 | 377 |
| | 1990 | 48.1 | 31.2 | 63.7 | 2 369 | 735 | 1 634 | 36.6 | 24.2 | 48.6 | 634 | 205 | 428 |
| | 1995 | 44.0 | 28.3 | 58.7 | 2 246 | 699 | 1 546 | 32.5 | 21.3 | 43.6 | 593 | 193 | 399 |
| | 2000 | 39.7 | 25.5 | 53.3 | 2 296 | 718 | 1 577 | 28.7 | 18.8 | 38.7 | 625 | 207 | 417 |
| Mali | 1980 | 86.4 | 80.8 | 91.5 | 3 158 | 1 415 | 1 743 | 74.4 | 66.2 | 82.5 | 987 | 433 | 554 |
| | 1985 | 81.1 | 74.5 | 87.2 | 3 427 | 1 515 | 1 911 | 66.0 | 57.1 | 74.7 | 1 021 | 437 | 583 |
| | 1990 | 75.0 | 67.7 | 81.8 | 3 503 | 1 527 | 1 976 | 56.1 | 47.3 | 64.8 | 962 | 404 | 557 |
| | 1995 | 67.7 | 60.0 | 74.9 | 3 562 | 1 531 | 2 030 | 45.7 | 37.8 | 53.6 | 904 | 373 | 531 |
| | 2000 | 59.7 | 52.1 | 66.8 | 3 604 | 1 532 | 2 072 | 35.7 | 29.3 | 42.1 | 828 | 338 | 489 |
| Mauritania | 1980 | 71.0 | 59.4 | 82.2 | 618 | 253 | 365 | 68.2 | 52.6 | 83.5 | 196 | 75 | 121 |
| | 1985 | 68.0 | 56.2 | 79.1 | 658 | 265 | 393 | 62.2 | 47.7 | 76.3 | 204 | 77 | 126 |
| | 1990 | 65.1 | 53.6 | 76.1 | 728 | 292 | 436 | 54.4 | 44.6 | 64.3 | 209 | 86 | 123 |
| | 1995 | 62.5 | 51.3 | 73.3 | 809 | 325 | 484 | 53.3 | 43.8 | 62.7 | 241 | 99 | 141 |
| | 2000 | 60.1 | 49.4 | 70.5 | 910 | 367 | 542 | 52.0 | 43.2 | 60.8 | 276 | 115 | 161 |
| Mauritius | 1980 | 25.8 | 18.7 | 32.6 | 161 | 57 | 104 | 13.5 | 11.2 | 15.7 | 27 | 11 | 16 |
| | 1985 | 22.8 | 16.9 | 28.5 | 158 | 58 | 100 | 10.9 | 10.0 | 11.8 | 23 | 11 | 12 |
| | 1990 | 20.0 | 14.8 | 25.3 | 148 | 54 | 94 | 8.9 | 8.4 | 9.4 | 17 | 8 | 9 |
| | 1995 | 17.8 | 13.6 | 21.8 | 143 | 55 | 88 | 7.8 | 7.8 | 7.8 | 16 | 8 | 7 |
| | 2000 | 15.7 | 12.3 | 19.0 | 136 | 53 | 83 | 6.7 | 6.9 | 6.5 | 14 | 7 | 6 |
| Morocco | 1980 | 71.4 | 58.0 | 84.5 | 7 869 | 3 151 | 4 717 | 57.7 | 42.8 | 72.3 | 2 274 | 835 | 1 439 |
| | 1985 | 66.5 | 52.6 | 80.0 | 8 426 | 3 291 | 5 134 | 51.7 | 37.8 | 65.6 | 2 278 | 836 | 1 442 |
| | 1990 | 61.3 | 47.3 | 75.0 | 8 977 | 3 422 | 5 554 | 44.7 | 31.9 | 58.0 | 2 248 | 818 | 1 430 |
| | 1995 | 56.0 | 42.3 | 69.5 | 9 464 | 3 546 | 5 918 | 38.4 | 27.3 | 50.0 | 2 182 | 790 | 1 391 |
| | 2000 | 51.1 | 38.1 | 64.0 | 9 786 | 3 621 | 6 165 | 32.7 | 23.8 | 41.9 | 1 970 | 730 | 1 240 |
| Mozambique | 1980 | 72.4 | 56.1 | 87.9 | 4 955 | 1 867 | 3 088 | 59.0 | 38.3 | 79.4 | 1 338 | 431 | 907 |
| | 1985 | 71.1 | 55.9 | 85.5 | 5 426 | 2 078 | 3 347 | 57.0 | 38.9 | 74.8 | 1 460 | 496 | 964 |
| | 1990 | 66.5 | 50.6 | 81.7 | 5 267 | 1 954 | 3 313 | 51.5 | 34.1 | 68.7 | 1 361 | 448 | 912 |
| | 1995 | 61.7 | 45.4 | 77.1 | 5 922 | 2 127 | 3 794 | 45.8 | 29.5 | 61.9 | 1 463 | 468 | 994 |
| | 2000 | 56.2 | 40.1 | 71.6 | 6 101 | 2 126 | 3 974 | 40.0 | 25.3 | 54.6 | 1 497 | 470 | 1 027 |
| Namibia | 1980 | 34.1 | 29.3 | 38.7 | 201 | 84 | 116 | 18.8 | 18.2 | 19.4 | 36 | 17 | 18 |
| | 1985 | 29.4 | 25.7 | 33.0 | 197 | 83 | 113 | 15.2 | 16.1 | 14.4 | 33 | 17 | 16 |
| | 1990 | 25.3 | 22.7 | 27.8 | 195 | 85 | 109 | 12.5 | 14.1 | 10.9 | 32 | 18 | 13 |
| | 1995 | 21.6 | 19.9 | 23.2 | 193 | 87 | 105 | 10.1 | 11.9 | 8.4 | 30 | 17 | 12 |
| | 2000 | 17.9 | 17.1 | 18.8 | 181 | 85 | 95 | 8.2 | 9.9 | 6.5 | 28 | 17 | 11 |
| Niger | 1980 | 91.9 | 86.3 | 97.3 | 2 735 | 1 247 | 1 487 | 88.4 | 81.9 | 94.8 | 937 | 430 | 507 |
| | 1985 | 90.3 | 84.3 | 96.1 | 3 150 | 1 429 | 1 720 | 85.8 | 78.7 | 92.7 | 1 069 | 486 | 582 |
| | 1990 | 88.6 | 82.0 | 94.9 | 3 584 | 1 616 | 1 968 | 83.1 | 75.3 | 90.8 | 1 209 | 544 | 665 |
| | 1995 | 86.6 | 79.4 | 93.4 | 4 091 | 1 832 | 2 259 | 80.5 | 72.1 | 88.9 | 1 383 | 615 | 768 |
| | 2000 | 84.3 | 76.5 | 91.7 | 4 688 | 2 083 | 2 605 | 77.6 | 68.5 | 86.6 | 1 584 | 695 | 888 |
| Nigeria | 1980 | 67.0 | 55.3 | 78.2 | 23 671 | 9 541 | 14 129 | 44.7 | 32.4 | 57.0 | 5 421 | 1 951 | 3 469 |
| | 1985 | 59.1 | 47.6 | 70.1 | 24 290 | 9 577 | 14 713 | 35.0 | 25.1 | 44.8 | 5 150 | 1 841 | 3 309 |
| | 1990 | 51.2 | 40.5 | 61.5 | 24 339 | 9 426 | 14 912 | 26.3 | 19.1 | 33.4 | 4 457 | 1 616 | 2 841 |
| | 1995 | 43.5 | 33.9 | 52.7 | 23 834 | 9 110 | 14 724 | 18.8 | 14.2 | 23.4 | 3 615 | 1 360 | 2 255 |
| | 2000 | 35.9 | 27.7 | 43.8 | 22 803 | 8 639 | 14 163 | 13.0 | 10.3 | 15.6 | 2 936 | 1 168 | 1 767 |
| Reunion | 1980 | 24.6 | 27.1 | 22.3 | 78 | 41 | 36 | 8.3 | 11.4 | 5.4 | 9 | 6 | 3 |
| | 1985 | 21.4 | 23.6 | 19.4 | 79 | 41 | 37 | 6.8 | 9.9 | 3.9 | 8 | 5 | 2 |
| | 1990 | 18.0 | 20.5 | 15.7 | 75 | 41 | 33 | 5.9 | 8.9 | 3.0 | 7 | 5 | 1 |
| | 1995 | 15.2 | 17.5 | 13.0 | 70 | 39 | 31 | 4.8 | 7.7 | 1.9 | 5 | 4 | 1 |
| | 2000 | 12.9 | 15.2 | 10.8 | 65 | 37 | 28 | 3.6 | 6.3 | 0.8 | 4 | 3 | 0 |
| Rwanda | 1980 | 60.1 | 48.5 | 71.2 | 1 589 | 628 | 960 | 41.3 | 31.6 | 50.8 | 394 | 149 | 244 |
| | 1985 | 53.3 | 42.5 | 63.7 | 1 660 | 649 | 1 011 | 33.9 | 26.3 | 41.3 | 390 | 150 | 239 |
| | 1990 | 46.6 | 37.0 | 55.8 | 1 708 | 664 | 1 043 | 27.1 | 21.8 | 32.4 | 370 | 147 | 222 |
| | 1995 | 39.6 | 31.3 | 47.6 | 1 103 | 424 | 678 | 21.2 | 17.8 | 24.5 | 224 | 93 | 130 |
| | 2000 | 33.0 | 26.3 | 39.4 | 1 394 | 543 | 851 | 16.4 | 14.6 | 18.1 | 270 | 119 | 151 |
| Senegal | 1980 | 78.7 | 69.2 | 88.1 | 2 384 | 1 040 | 1 343 | 68.5 | 58.4 | 78.6 | 718 | 307 | 411 |
| | 1985 | 75.3 | 65.6 | 85.0 | 2 612 | 1 130 | 1 481 | 65.1 | 55.2 | 75.1 | 780 | 331 | 448 |
| | 1990 | 71.5 | 61.6 | 81.3 | 2 860 | 1 225 | 1 635 | 59.9 | 50.1 | 69.9 | 833 | 349 | 483 |
| | 1995 | 67.2 | 57.2 | 77.0 | 3 063 | 1 289 | 1 773 | 54.8 | 45.4 | 64.3 | 892 | 370 | 522 |
| | 2000 | 62.7 | 52.8 | 72.4 | 3 290 | 1 368 | 1 921 | 49.6 | 40.8 | 58.4 | 932 | 385 | 547 |
| Sierra Leone | 1980 | 81.0 | 69.9 | 91.4 | 1 495 | 626 | 869 | ... | ... | ... | ... | ... | ... |
| | 1985 | 77.3 | 65.0 | 88.8 | 1 571 | 640 | 930 | ... | ... | ... | ... | ... | ... |
| | 1990 | 73.1 | 59.8 | 85.6 | 1 640 | 651 | 989 | ... | ... | ... | ... | ... | ... |
| | 1995 | 68.5 | 54.6 | 81.8 | 1 603 | 619 | 984 | ... | ... | ... | ... | ... | ... |
| | 2000 | 63.7 | 49.3 | 77.4 | 1 732 | 650 | 1 082 | ... | ... | ... | ... | ... | ... |

| Country / Pays / País | Year / Année / Año | Population aged 15 years and over / Population âgée de 15 ans et plus / Población de 15 años y más | | | | | | Population aged 15 to 24 years / Population âgée de 15 à 24 ans / Población de 15 a 24 años | | | | | |
|---|---|---|---|---|---|---|---|---|---|---|---|---|---|
| | | Illiteracy rate / Taux d'analphabétisme / Tasa de analfabetismo ( % ) | | | Illiterate population / Population analphabète / Población analfabeta (000) | | | Illiteracy rate / Taux d'analphabétisme / Tasa de analfabetismo ( % ) | | | Illiterate population / Population analphabète / Población analfabeta (000) | | |
| | | MF | M | F | MF | M | F | MF | M | F | MF | M | F |
| South Africa | 1980 | 23.5 | 22.1 | 24.8 | 3 926 | 1 827 | 2 098 | 15.1 | 14.8 | 15.3 | 843 | 423 | 420 |
| | 1985 | 20.9 | 19.8 | 22.1 | 3 969 | 1 848 | 2 120 | 13.3 | 13.2 | 13.5 | 828 | 413 | 415 |
| | 1990 | 18.7 | 17.7 | 19.7 | 3 995 | 1 856 | 2 139 | 11.8 | 11.7 | 11.9 | 797 | 394 | 402 |
| | 1995 | 16.7 | 15.9 | 17.5 | 4 009 | 1 859 | 2 150 | 10.4 | 10.3 | 10.5 | 769 | 379 | 389 |
| | 2000 | 14.9 | 14.2 | 15.5 | 3 916 | 1 814 | 2 102 | 9.1 | 9.1 | 9.1 | 728 | 360 | 367 |
| Sudan | 1980 | 67.0 | 52.0 | 81.7 | 6 903 | 2 663 | 4 239 | 50.8 | 35.9 | 66.0 | 1 797 | 641 | 1 155 |
| | 1985 | 61.3 | 46.9 | 75.8 | 7 366 | 2 820 | 4 545 | 43.0 | 30.1 | 56.3 | 1 738 | 618 | 1 119 |
| | 1990 | 55.1 | 41.4 | 68.8 | 7 523 | 2 830 | 4 692 | 35.3 | 24.8 | 46.2 | 1 625 | 580 | 1 044 |
| | 1995 | 49.2 | 36.5 | 61.7 | 7 592 | 2 807 | 4 785 | 28.7 | 20.7 | 36.8 | 1 472 | 533 | 938 |
| | 2000 | 42.9 | 31.7 | 54.0 | 7 675 | 2 820 | 4 855 | 22.9 | 17.3 | 28.5 | 1 407 | 534 | 873 |
| Swaziland | 1980 | 40.1 | 36.1 | 43.9 | 121 | 52 | 68 | 22.9 | 21.8 | 24.0 | 24 | 11 | 12 |
| | 1985 | 34.0 | 31.5 | 36.0 | 115 | 48 | 67 | 18.4 | 18.2 | 18.5 | 23 | 10 | 13 |
| | 1990 | 28.4 | 26.3 | 30.2 | 115 | 48 | 66 | 14.8 | 15.1 | 14.4 | 23 | 11 | 11 |
| | 1995 | 24.0 | 22.4 | 25.3 | 117 | 50 | 66 | 11.8 | 12.4 | 11.2 | 21 | 11 | 10 |
| | 2000 | 20.2 | 19.1 | 21.3 | 116 | 51 | 65 | 9.3 | 10.1 | 8.6 | 19 | 10 | 9 |
| Togo | 1980 | 67.3 | 51.8 | 82.0 | 978 | 367 | 611 | 49.8 | 31.5 | 67.7 | 243 | 76 | 166 |
| | 1985 | 61.6 | 45.6 | 76.9 | 1 029 | 371 | 657 | 43.2 | 26.0 | 60.2 | 245 | 73 | 172 |
| | 1990 | 55.6 | 39.5 | 71.1 | 1 065 | 369 | 695 | 36.7 | 21.0 | 52.2 | 239 | 68 | 171 |
| | 1995 | 49.3 | 33.5 | 64.6 | 1 081 | 359 | 721 | 30.4 | 16.7 | 44.0 | 232 | 63 | 168 |
| | 2000 | 42.9 | 27.8 | 57.4 | 1 073 | 341 | 732 | 24.7 | 13.2 | 36.2 | 224 | 59 | 164 |
| Tunisia | 1980 | 53.2 | 38.9 | 67.7 | 2 002 | 736 | 1 265 | 26.3 | 12.1 | 41.2 | 360 | 84 | 275 |
| | 1985 | 47.3 | 33.8 | 60.9 | 2 096 | 754 | 1 341 | 22.0 | 10.7 | 33.9 | 342 | 85 | 257 |
| | 1990 | 40.9 | 28.3 | 53.6 | 2 084 | 725 | 1 358 | 16.4 | 7.4 | 25.7 | 271 | 61 | 209 |
| | 1995 | 35.5 | 24.0 | 47.0 | 2 095 | 712 | 1 382 | 11.0 | 4.7 | 17.5 | 199 | 43 | 155 |
| | 2000 | 29.2 | 18.6 | 39.9 | 1 954 | 626 | 1 328 | 7.3 | 2.8 | 12.0 | 147 | 29 | 117 |
| Uganda | 1980 | 54.4 | 39.7 | 68.6 | 3 732 | 1 334 | 2 397 | 39.8 | 26.7 | 52.8 | 990 | 330 | 660 |
| | 1985 | 49.3 | 35.2 | 62.8 | 3 789 | 1 328 | 2 461 | 34.6 | 23.2 | 45.9 | 974 | 325 | 649 |
| | 1990 | 43.9 | 30.8 | 56.6 | 3 729 | 1 285 | 2 443 | 29.6 | 19.9 | 39.2 | 941 | 315 | 625 |
| | 1995 | 38.1 | 26.3 | 49.6 | 3 657 | 1 243 | 2 414 | 24.9 | 16.8 | 32.9 | 938 | 317 | 621 |
| | 2000 | 32.7 | 22.3 | 42.9 | 3 565 | 1 203 | 2 361 | 20.7 | 14.2 | 27.3 | 919 | 314 | 605 |
| United Republic of Tanzania | 1980 | 50.7 | 34.6 | 66.0 | 4 943 | 1 645 | 3 298 | 30.5 | 17.9 | 42.9 | 1 071 | 311 | 760 |
| | 1985 | 43.6 | 29.1 | 57.4 | 5 025 | 1 638 | 3 386 | 22.6 | 13.7 | 31.3 | 955 | 286 | 668 |
| | 1990 | 36.9 | 24.2 | 48.9 | 5 032 | 1 610 | 3 422 | 16.8 | 10.6 | 22.7 | 849 | 264 | 584 |
| | 1995 | 30.7 | 19.8 | 41.0 | 4 949 | 1 565 | 3 383 | 12.8 | 8.4 | 17.1 | 764 | 249 | 515 |
| | 2000 | 24.8 | 15.9 | 33.4 | 4 551 | 1 431 | 3 120 | 9.3 | 6.6 | 12.1 | 638 | 225 | 412 |
| Zambia | 1980 | 41.1 | 28.7 | 52.7 | 1 196 | 403 | 793 | 26.6 | 17.4 | 34.9 | 290 | 90 | 200 |
| | 1985 | 36.5 | 25.1 | 46.9 | 1 183 | 388 | 795 | 22.9 | 15.7 | 29.6 | 282 | 93 | 189 |
| | 1990 | 31.8 | 21.5 | 41.1 | 1 171 | 377 | 793 | 19.1 | 13.6 | 24.4 | 274 | 95 | 178 |
| | 1995 | 26.8 | 18.0 | 34.9 | 1 135 | 366 | 769 | 15.3 | 11.0 | 19.5 | 261 | 94 | 167 |
| | 2000 | 22.0 | 14.8 | 28.8 | 1 065 | 347 | 718 | 12.2 | 9.1 | 15.4 | 250 | 94 | 155 |
| Zimbabwe | 1980 | 20.5 | 14.4 | 26.4 | 763 | 264 | 498 | 10.4 | 6.5 | 14.2 | 151 | 47 | 104 |
| | 1985 | 16.6 | 11.4 | 21.7 | 752 | 254 | 498 | 6.5 | 3.6 | 9.3 | 112 | 31 | 81 |
| | 1990 | 13.2 | 8.7 | 17.5 | 726 | 235 | 490 | 3.4 | 1.5 | 5.4 | 71 | 15 | 56 |
| | 1995 | 10.2 | 6.5 | 13.9 | 631 | 197 | 433 | 1.8 | 0.4 | 3.1 | 40 | 4 | 35 |
| | 2000 | 7.3 | 4.5 | 10.1 | 504 | 153 | 350 | 0.6 | 0.2 | 1.0 | 16 | 2 | 13 |
| **North America** | | | | | | | | | | | | | |
| Bahamas | 1980 | 6.6 | 7.2 | 6.1 | 8 | 4 | 4 | 3.7 | 4.6 | 2.8 | 1 | 1 | 0 |
| | 1985 | 5.8 | 6.5 | 5.1 | 8 | 4 | 4 | 3.1 | 3.9 | 2.3 | 1 | 0 | 0 |
| | 1990 | 5.0 | 5.7 | 4.3 | 8 | 4 | 3 | 2.6 | 3.4 | 1.8 | 1 | 0 | 0 |
| | 1995 | 4.4 | 5.0 | 3.7 | 8 | 4 | 3 | 2.2 | 2.9 | 1.5 | 1 | 0 | 0 |
| | 2000 | 3.9 | 4.6 | 3.2 | 8 | 4 | 3 | 1.9 | 2.5 | 1.2 | 1 | 0 | 0 |
| Costa Rica | 1980 | 8.3 | 8.1 | 8.4 | 115 | 56 | 58 | 3.5 | 3.7 | 3.2 | 18 | 9 | 8 |
| | 1985 | 7.1 | 7.0 | 7.2 | 118 | 58 | 59 | 2.9 | 3.2 | 2.6 | 16 | 9 | 7 |
| | 1990 | 6.1 | 6.1 | 6.1 | 118 | 59 | 59 | 2.6 | 2.9 | 2.3 | 15 | 8 | 6 |
| | 1995 | 5.2 | 5.2 | 5.2 | 122 | 62 | 60 | 2.1 | 2.5 | 1.8 | 14 | 8 | 6 |
| | 2000 | 4.4 | 4.5 | 4.3 | 121 | 62 | 58 | 1.7 | 2.1 | 1.4 | 13 | 8 | 5 |
| Cuba | 1980 | 7.9 | 8.1 | 7.8 | 527 | 269 | 257 | 1.7 | 1.9 | 1.5 | 32 | 17 | 14 |
| | 1985 | 6.4 | 6.6 | 6.3 | 482 | 245 | 236 | 1.3 | 1.4 | 1.2 | 31 | 16 | 14 |
| | 1990 | 5.2 | 5.2 | 5.2 | 429 | 215 | 213 | 0.9 | 0.9 | 0.8 | 20 | 10 | 9 |
| | 1995 | 4.4 | 4.4 | 4.4 | 377 | 188 | 188 | 0.5 | 0.4 | 0.5 | 9 | 4 | 5 |
| | 2000 | 3.6 | 3.5 | 3.6 | 319 | 156 | 163 | 0.2 | 0.2 | 0.2 | 3 | 1 | 2 |
| Dominican Republic | 1980 | 26.2 | 25.2 | 27.3 | 863 | 421 | 442 | 17.3 | 17.8 | 16.8 | 214 | 111 | 102 |
| | 1985 | 23.1 | 22.4 | 23.9 | 899 | 443 | 456 | 14.6 | 15.0 | 14.1 | 207 | 108 | 98 |
| | 1990 | 20.5 | 20.0 | 21.0 | 920 | 457 | 463 | 12.2 | 12.6 | 11.8 | 184 | 96 | 87 |
| | 1995 | 18.2 | 17.9 | 18.5 | 927 | 463 | 464 | 10.2 | 10.6 | 9.8 | 159 | 84 | 74 |
| | 2000 | 16.2 | 16.0 | 16.3 | 921 | 463 | 458 | 8.5 | 8.9 | 8.1 | 138 | 73 | 64 |
| El Salvador | 1980 | 33.8 | 29.1 | 38.4 | 854 | 361 | 492 | 21.5 | 18.7 | 24.3 | 194 | 84 | 109 |
| | 1985 | 30.7 | 26.5 | 34.6 | 826 | 342 | 484 | 18.7 | 16.7 | 20.5 | 173 | 75 | 98 |
| | 1990 | 27.4 | 23.7 | 30.7 | 830 | 343 | 487 | 16.2 | 14.9 | 17.5 | 173 | 77 | 95 |
| | 1995 | 24.0 | 20.7 | 27.0 | 853 | 353 | 500 | 14.0 | 13.0 | 15.0 | 178 | 82 | 95 |
| | 2000 | 21.3 | 18.4 | 23.9 | 862 | 358 | 503 | 12.0 | 11.2 | 13.0 | 161 | 75 | 86 |

| Country / Pays / País | Year / Année / Año | Population aged 15 years and over / Population âgée de 15 ans et plus / Población de 15 años y más | | | | | | Population aged 15 to 24 years / Population âgée de 15 à 24 ans / Población de 15 a 24 años | | | | | |
|---|---|---|---|---|---|---|---|---|---|---|---|---|---|
| | | Illiteracy rate / Taux d'analphabétisme / Tasa de analfabetismo (%) | | | Illiterate population / Population analphabète / Población analfabeta (000) | | | Illiteracy rate / Taux d'analphabétisme / Tasa de analfabetismo (%) | | | Illiterate population / Population analphabète / Población analfabeta (000) | | |
| | | MF | M | F | MF | M | F | MF | M | F | MF | M | F |
| Guatemala | 1980 | 46.2 | 38.1 | 54.3 | 1 702 | 709 | 993 | 34.4 | 26.0 | 42.8 | 454 | 174 | 280 |
| | 1985 | 42.3 | 34.4 | 50.4 | 1 761 | 718 | 1 042 | 30.3 | 22.6 | 38.3 | 453 | 170 | 283 |
| | 1990 | 38.5 | 30.7 | 46.3 | 1 821 | 728 | 1 092 | 26.6 | 19.5 | 33.8 | 457 | 169 | 287 |
| | 1995 | 34.7 | 27.0 | 42.4 | 1 905 | 742 | 1 162 | 23.7 | 17.0 | 30.5 | 479 | 174 | 304 |
| | 2000 | 31.3 | 23.8 | 38.9 | 2 014 | 764 | 1 250 | 21.2 | 14.8 | 27.9 | 504 | 179 | 325 |
| Haiti | 1980 | 69.1 | 65.5 | 72.3 | 2 192 | 999 | 1 193 | 55.1 | 52.9 | 57.3 | 581 | 276 | 304 |
| | 1985 | 64.8 | 61.5 | 67.9 | 2 262 | 1 030 | 1 232 | 50.8 | 49.0 | 52.5 | 593 | 285 | 307 |
| | 1990 | 60.7 | 57.6 | 63.5 | 2 337 | 1 067 | 1 270 | 46.7 | 45.4 | 48.0 | 597 | 289 | 307 |
| | 1995 | 56.1 | 53.4 | 58.5 | 2 410 | 1 101 | 1 309 | 42.3 | 41.5 | 43.2 | 620 | 303 | 316 |
| | 2000 | 51.4 | 49.0 | 53.5 | 2 505 | 1 147 | 1 357 | 38.1 | 37.7 | 38.4 | 667 | 332 | 335 |
| Honduras | 1980 | 39.0 | 37.2 | 40.8 | 735 | 350 | 385 | 29.0 | 28.8 | 29.2 | 206 | 103 | 103 |
| | 1985 | 35.9 | 34.5 | 37.3 | 808 | 387 | 420 | 26.8 | 27.0 | 26.7 | 228 | 115 | 112 |
| | 1990 | 33.0 | 32.0 | 34.0 | 883 | 428 | 455 | 24.6 | 25.0 | 24.1 | 243 | 125 | 118 |
| | 1995 | 30.3 | 29.7 | 30.9 | 965 | 473 | 491 | 22.4 | 23.1 | 21.6 | 256 | 134 | 122 |
| | 2000 | 27.8 | 27.5 | 28.0 | 1 052 | 521 | 530 | 20.3 | 21.2 | 19.3 | 272 | 144 | 127 |
| Jamaica | 1980 | 22.5 | 26.8 | 18.5 | 287 | 165 | 122 | 12.2 | 16.9 | 7.6 | 54 | 37 | 17 |
| | 1985 | 19.5 | 23.8 | 15.4 | 284 | 169 | 115 | 10.7 | 15.2 | 6.3 | 55 | 39 | 16 |
| | 1990 | 17.3 | 21.7 | 13.1 | 265 | 161 | 104 | 9.3 | 13.6 | 5.1 | 45 | 32 | 12 |
| | 1995 | 15.2 | 19.5 | 11.1 | 251 | 157 | 94 | 8.0 | 11.9 | 4.0 | 39 | 29 | 9 |
| | 2000 | 13.3 | 17.5 | 9.3 | 238 | 152 | 85 | 6.8 | 10.5 | 3.0 | 33 | 26 | 7 |
| Martinique | 1980 | 7.6 | 8.4 | 6.9 | 17 | 9 | 8 | 1.2 | 1.6 | 0.8 | 0 | 0 | 0 |
| | 1985 | 5.9 | 6.6 | 5.4 | 14 | 7 | 6 | 0.7 | 1.0 | 0.4 | 0 | 0 | 0 |
| | 1990 | 4.5 | 5.2 | 3.9 | 12 | 6 | 5 | 0.3 | 0.4 | 0.2 | 0 | 0 | 0 |
| | 1995 | 3.5 | 4.0 | 2.9 | 10 | 5 | 4 | 0.2 | 0.2 | 0.2 | 0 | 0 | 0 |
| | 2000 | 2.6 | 3.0 | 2.1 | 8 | 4 | 3 | 0.2 | 0.2 | 0.2 | 0 | 0 | 0 |
| Mexico | 1980 | 17.0 | 13.8 | 20.2 | 6 320 | 2 520 | 3 800 | 7.6 | 6.3 | 8.8 | 1 017 | 425 | 591 |
| | 1985 | 14.9 | 11.7 | 18.0 | 6 512 | 2 504 | 4 008 | 6.5 | 5.2 | 7.8 | 1 019 | 406 | 613 |
| | 1990 | 12.3 | 9.6 | 15.0 | 6 320 | 2 401 | 3 919 | 5.0 | 4.0 | 5.9 | 920 | 368 | 551 |
| | 1995 | 10.5 | 8.2 | 12.8 | 6 212 | 2 355 | 3 856 | 4.2 | 3.4 | 5.0 | 851 | 343 | 507 |
| | 2000 | 9.0 | 6.9 | 10.9 | 5 965 | 2 247 | 3 718 | 3.4 | 2.7 | 4.1 | 687 | 278 | 409 |
| Netherlands Antilles | 1980 | 6.4 | 6.3 | 6.5 | 7 | 3 | 4 | 3.1 | 3.3 | 2.8 | 1 | 0 | 0 |
| | 1985 | 5.5 | 5.4 | 5.5 | 7 | 3 | 3 | 2.7 | 3.0 | 2.5 | 0 | 0 | 0 |
| | 1990 | 4.6 | 4.6 | 4.6 | 6 | 3 | 3 | 2.3 | 2.5 | 2.1 | 0 | 0 | 0 |
| | 1995 | 3.9 | 3.9 | 4.0 | 6 | 2 | 3 | 1.9 | 2.0 | 1.7 | 0 | 0 | 0 |
| | 2000 | 3.4 | 3.4 | 3.4 | 5 | 2 | 2 | 1.4 | 1.6 | 1.3 | 0 | 0 | 0 |
| Nicaragua | 1980 | 41.8 | 41.5 | 42.1 | 640 | 313 | 326 | 37.0 | 37.2 | 36.9 | 215 | 108 | 107 |
| | 1985 | 40.2 | 40.0 | 40.4 | 718 | 351 | 367 | 35.7 | 35.9 | 35.5 | 240 | 120 | 119 |
| | 1990 | 38.7 | 38.6 | 38.8 | 796 | 388 | 408 | 34.4 | 34.6 | 34.1 | 264 | 132 | 132 |
| | 1995 | 37.2 | 37.2 | 37.2 | 905 | 441 | 463 | 33.0 | 33.4 | 32.7 | 299 | 150 | 149 |
| | 2000 | 35.7 | 35.8 | 35.6 | 1 038 | 509 | 529 | 31.7 | 32.1 | 31.3 | 341 | 173 | 168 |
| Panama | 1980 | 14.3 | 13.7 | 15.1 | 167 | 80 | 86 | 6.0 | 5.3 | 6.7 | 23 | 10 | 13 |
| | 1985 | 12.8 | 12.1 | 13.5 | 173 | 82 | 90 | 5.5 | 5.0 | 6.1 | 25 | 11 | 13 |
| | 1990 | 11.2 | 10.7 | 11.8 | 174 | 83 | 90 | 4.9 | 4.6 | 5.3 | 24 | 11 | 13 |
| | 1995 | 9.4 | 8.7 | 10.0 | 165 | 77 | 87 | 3.9 | 3.5 | 4.4 | 20 | 9 | 11 |
| | 2000 | 8.1 | 7.4 | 8.7 | 159 | 73 | 85 | 3.2 | 2.8 | 3.6 | 17 | 7 | 9 |
| Puerto Rico | 1980 | 11.6 | 11.1 | 12.0 | 254 | 116 | 138 | 5.1 | 6.0 | 4.3 | 31 | 17 | 13 |
| | 1985 | 10.0 | 9.8 | 10.2 | 239 | 112 | 127 | 4.5 | 5.3 | 3.6 | 28 | 16 | 11 |
| | 1990 | 8.6 | 8.5 | 8.6 | 221 | 104 | 116 | 3.7 | 4.5 | 2.9 | 23 | 13 | 9 |
| | 1995 | 7.2 | 7.3 | 7.2 | 201 | 96 | 105 | 2.9 | 3.5 | 2.2 | 19 | 12 | 7 |
| | 2000 | 6.2 | 6.3 | 6.0 | 181 | 88 | 93 | 2.2 | 2.8 | 1.6 | 14 | 9 | 5 |
| Trinidad and Tobago | 1980 | 5.0 | 3.5 | 6.6 | 36 | 12 | 23 | 0.9 | 0.9 | 0.8 | 2 | 1 | 1 |
| | 1985 | 3.9 | 2.5 | 5.4 | 31 | 9 | 21 | 0.7 | 0.6 | 0.7 | 1 | 0 | 0 |
| | 1990 | 3.2 | 2.0 | 4.4 | 26 | 8 | 17 | 0.4 | 0.4 | 0.3 | 0 | 0 | 0 |
| | 1995 | 2.4 | 1.4 | 3.3 | 21 | 6 | 14 | 0.2 | 0.2 | 0.2 | 0 | 0 | 0 |
| | 2000 | 1.8 | 1.0 | 2.5 | 17 | 5 | 12 | 0.2 | 0.2 | 0.2 | 0 | 0 | 0 |
| **South America** | | | | | | | | | | | | | |
| Argentina | 1980 | 6.0 | 5.7 | 6.4 | 1 182 | 542 | 640 | 3.1 | 3.3 | 2.8 | 140 | 75 | 64 |
| | 1985 | 4.9 | 4.7 | 5.2 | 1 042 | 477 | 565 | 2.1 | 2.3 | 1.9 | 105 | 57 | 47 |
| | 1990 | 4.2 | 4.1 | 4.4 | 966 | 448 | 518 | 1.8 | 2.0 | 1.6 | 96 | 53 | 42 |
| | 1995 | 3.6 | 3.5 | 3.7 | 905 | 426 | 478 | 1.5 | 1.7 | 1.3 | 97 | 55 | 41 |
| | 2000 | 3.1 | 3.1 | 3.1 | 843 | 405 | 438 | 1.3 | 1.5 | 1.1 | 91 | 53 | 38 |
| Bolivia | 1980 | 30.9 | 19.9 | 41.3 | 950 | 298 | 652 | 13.7 | 6.8 | 20.5 | 142 | 35 | 107 |
| | 1985 | 26.1 | 16.2 | 35.5 | 890 | 269 | 621 | 10.1 | 5.1 | 15.1 | 114 | 28 | 85 |
| | 1990 | 21.6 | 12.9 | 29.9 | 835 | 243 | 592 | 7.4 | 3.8 | 11.0 | 96 | 24 | 71 |
| | 1995 | 17.7 | 10.1 | 24.9 | 781 | 218 | 562 | 5.6 | 2.8 | 8.3 | 82 | 21 | 61 |
| | 2000 | 14.4 | 7.9 | 20.6 | 725 | 195 | 530 | 4.2 | 2.0 | 6.3 | 68 | 16 | 51 |
| Brazil | 1980 | 25.4 | 23.7 | 27.2 | 19 185 | 8 867 | 10 318 | 13.7 | 14.6 | 12.8 | 3 522 | 1 883 | 1 639 |
| | 1985 | 21.7 | 20.4 | 22.9 | 18 623 | 8 677 | 9 946 | 11.2 | 12.6 | 9.8 | 3 125 | 1 765 | 1 360 |
| | 1990 | 18.3 | 17.9 | 18.8 | 17 720 | 8 488 | 9 231 | 9.5 | 11.4 | 7.6 | 2 766 | 1 657 | 1 109 |
| | 1995 | 16.8 | 16.6 | 17.0 | 18 310 | 8 836 | 9 473 | 9.0 | 10.7 | 7.2 | 2 832 | 1 693 | 1 139 |
| | 2000 | 14.7 | 14.9 | 14.6 | 17 909 | 8 802 | 9 106 | 7.5 | 9.2 | 5.7 | 2 545 | 1 578 | 966 |

| Country / Pays / País | Year / Année / Año | Population aged 15 years and over / Population âgée de 15 ans et plus / Población de 15 años y más | | | | | | Population aged 15 to 24 years / Population âgée de 15 à 24 ans / Población de 15 a 24 años | | | | | |
|---|---|---|---|---|---|---|---|---|---|---|---|---|---|
| | | Illiteracy rate / Taux d'analphabétisme / Tasa de analfabetismo (%) | | | Illiterate population / Population analphabète / Población analfabeta (000) | | | Illiteracy rate / Taux d'analphabétisme / Tasa de analfabetismo (%) | | | Illiterate population / Population analphabète / Población analfabeta (000) | | |
| | | MF | M | F | MF | M | F | MF | M | F | MF | M | F |
| Chile | 1980 | 8.5 | 7.9 | 9.1 | 635 | 286 | 348 | 3.2 | 3.3 | 3.1 | 77 | 40 | 37 |
| | 1985 | 7.2 | 6.7 | 7.6 | 597 | 271 | 326 | 2.5 | 2.7 | 2.3 | 64 | 34 | 29 |
| | 1990 | 6.0 | 5.6 | 6.4 | 556 | 254 | 301 | 1.9 | 2.1 | 1.7 | 48 | 27 | 21 |
| | 1995 | 5.1 | 4.8 | 5.4 | 518 | 239 | 278 | 1.5 | 1.7 | 1.3 | 37 | 21 | 15 |
| | 2000 | 4.3 | 4.1 | 4.5 | 470 | 220 | 250 | 1.1 | 1.3 | 0.9 | 29 | 17 | 11 |
| Colombia | 1980 | 15.6 | 14.7 | 16.4 | 2 633 | 1 217 | 1 415 | 7.4 | 7.7 | 7.1 | 458 | 239 | 218 |
| | 1985 | 13.2 | 12.5 | 13.7 | 2 600 | 1 214 | 1 385 | 6.0 | 6.4 | 5.5 | 420 | 228 | 192 |
| | 1990 | 11.3 | 10.9 | 11.6 | 2 528 | 1 195 | 1 332 | 5.0 | 5.6 | 4.4 | 367 | 207 | 160 |
| | 1995 | 9.6 | 9.4 | 9.7 | 2 437 | 1 166 | 1 270 | 4.0 | 4.6 | 3.3 | 302 | 177 | 125 |
| | 2000 | 8.2 | 8.2 | 8.2 | 2 344 | 1 140 | 1 203 | 3.1 | 3.8 | 2.5 | 255 | 155 | 100 |
| Ecuador | 1980 | 18.1 | 14.4 | 21.8 | 828 | 329 | 498 | 7.2 | 5.8 | 8.7 | 114 | 46 | 68 |
| | 1985 | 14.8 | 11.8 | 17.9 | 797 | 316 | 481 | 5.4 | 4.5 | 6.4 | 100 | 42 | 58 |
| | 1990 | 11.6 | 9.5 | 13.8 | 730 | 297 | 433 | 3.6 | 3.4 | 3.8 | 76 | 36 | 40 |
| | 1995 | 9.9 | 7.8 | 12.0 | 726 | 286 | 439 | 3.2 | 2.7 | 3.7 | 76 | 33 | 43 |
| | 2000 | 8.1 | 6.4 | 9.8 | 683 | 269 | 414 | 2.4 | 2.1 | 2.8 | 63 | 27 | 35 |
| Guyana | 1980 | 5.4 | 3.7 | 7.0 | 24 | 8 | 16 | 0.7 | 0.6 | 0.8 | 1 | 0 | 0 |
| | 1985 | 3.9 | 2.6 | 5.2 | 19 | 6 | 13 | 0.3 | 0.3 | 0.3 | 0 | 0 | 0 |
| | 1990 | 2.8 | 2.0 | 3.7 | 15 | 5 | 10 | 0.2 | 0.2 | 0.2 | 0 | 0 | 0 |
| | 1995 | 2.1 | 1.4 | 2.8 | 12 | 3 | 8 | 0.2 | 0.2 | 0.2 | 0 | 0 | 0 |
| | 2000 | 1.5 | 1.0 | 1.9 | 9 | 3 | 6 | 0.2 | 0.2 | 0.2 | 0 | 0 | 0 |
| Paraguay | 1980 | 14.1 | 10.6 | 17.5 | 254 | 94 | 159 | 6.4 | 5.5 | 7.2 | 41 | 18 | 23 |
| | 1985 | 11.6 | 8.9 | 14.3 | 243 | 93 | 150 | 5.3 | 4.7 | 5.8 | 38 | 17 | 21 |
| | 1990 | 9.7 | 7.7 | 11.7 | 238 | 94 | 143 | 4.4 | 4.0 | 4.7 | 36 | 17 | 19 |
| | 1995 | 8.1 | 6.6 | 9.6 | 229 | 93 | 135 | 3.6 | 3.4 | 3.8 | 32 | 15 | 16 |
| | 2000 | 6.7 | 5.6 | 7.8 | 223 | 93 | 129 | 2.9 | 2.8 | 2.9 | 31 | 15 | 15 |
| Peru | 1980 | 20.2 | 11.7 | 28.8 | 2 041 | 589 | 1 452 | 8.7 | 4.4 | 13.0 | 302 | 78 | 223 |
| | 1985 | 17.0 | 9.6 | 24.4 | 1 994 | 562 | 1 431 | 7.0 | 3.8 | 10.2 | 279 | 77 | 202 |
| | 1990 | 14.3 | 7.9 | 20.6 | 1 916 | 525 | 1 391 | 5.5 | 3.1 | 7.9 | 244 | 70 | 173 |
| | 1995 | 12.0 | 6.5 | 17.3 | 1 822 | 486 | 1 335 | 4.3 | 2.4 | 6.2 | 210 | 58 | 152 |
| | 2000 | 10.1 | 5.3 | 14.6 | 1 726 | 451 | 1 275 | 3.3 | 1.8 | 4.8 | 175 | 48 | 126 |
| Suriname | 1980 | 12.4 | 8.4 | 16.1 | 26 | 8 | 17 | ... | ... | ... | ... | ... | ... |
| | 1985 | 10.0 | 6.9 | 13.1 | 23 | 7 | 15 | ... | ... | ... | ... | ... | ... |
| | 1990 | 8.2 | 5.7 | 10.7 | 21 | 7 | 14 | ... | ... | ... | ... | ... | ... |
| | 1995 | 7.0 | 4.8 | 9.0 | 18 | 6 | 12 | ... | ... | ... | ... | ... | ... |
| | 2000 | 5.8 | 4.1 | 7.4 | 16 | 5 | 10 | ... | ... | ... | ... | ... | ... |
| Uruguay | 1980 | 5.3 | 5.7 | 4.8 | 112 | 59 | 53 | 1.5 | 2.0 | 1.0 | 7 | 4 | 2 |
| | 1985 | 4.6 | 5.2 | 4.2 | 103 | 54 | 48 | 1.6 | 2.0 | 1.2 | 7 | 4 | 2 |
| | 1990 | 3.4 | 3.9 | 3.0 | 79 | 43 | 36 | 0.9 | 1.3 | 0.6 | 4 | 3 | 1 |
| | 1995 | 2.7 | 3.1 | 2.3 | 66 | 36 | 29 | 0.7 | 1.0 | 0.4 | 4 | 2 | 1 |
| | 2000 | 2.2 | 2.6 | 1.8 | 55 | 31 | 24 | 0.6 | 0.8 | 0.3 | 3 | 2 | 0 |
| Venezuela | 1980 | 15.1 | 13.3 | 16.9 | 1 354 | 600 | 753 | 6.0 | 6.1 | 5.8 | 190 | 99 | 90 |
| | 1985 | 12.5 | 11.2 | 13.8 | 1 307 | 586 | 720 | 4.9 | 5.4 | 4.5 | 178 | 99 | 79 |
| | 1990 | 9.9 | 9.1 | 10.8 | 1 199 | 549 | 650 | 3.5 | 4.2 | 2.8 | 135 | 82 | 53 |
| | 1995 | 8.5 | 7.9 | 9.1 | 1 194 | 555 | 639 | 2.9 | 3.6 | 2.3 | 124 | 77 | 47 |
| | 2000 | 7.0 | 6.7 | 7.3 | 1 121 | 534 | 586 | 2.1 | 2.8 | 1.5 | 103 | 68 | 35 |
| **Asia** | | | | | | | | | | | | | |
| Afghanistan | 1980 | 81.9 | 69.9 | 94.5 | 7 500 | 3 289 | 4 211 | 70.6 | 53.9 | 88.4 | 2 110 | 829 | 1 281 |
| | 1985 | 77.9 | 64.7 | 91.9 | 6 585 | 2 818 | 3 766 | 65.4 | 48.2 | 83.7 | 1 877 | 715 | 1 161 |
| | 1990 | 73.5 | 59.6 | 88.4 | 6 068 | 2 543 | 3 524 | 59.1 | 42.3 | 77.3 | 1 739 | 650 | 1 089 |
| | 1995 | 68.5 | 53.8 | 83.9 | 7 972 | 3 215 | 4 757 | 53.2 | 37.0 | 70.1 | 2 081 | 744 | 1 337 |
| | 2000 | 63.7 | 49.0 | 79.2 | 8 146 | 3 213 | 4 933 | 45.7 | 31.6 | 60.8 | 1 782 | 633 | 1 148 |
| Bahrain | 1980 | 28.6 | 21.4 | 40.5 | 64 | 30 | 34 | 9.7 | 6.8 | 13.3 | 7 | 2 | 4 |
| | 1985 | 23.1 | 16.7 | 33.5 | 65 | 29 | 35 | 6.7 | 5.2 | 8.4 | 4 | 1 | 2 |
| | 1990 | 17.7 | 13.1 | 25.2 | 59 | 27 | 32 | 4.3 | 3.7 | 4.9 | 3 | 1 | 1 |
| | 1995 | 14.7 | 10.8 | 20.5 | 56 | 25 | 31 | 2.6 | 2.5 | 2.6 | 2 | 1 | 1 |
| | 2000 | 12.4 | 9.0 | 17.3 | 53 | 23 | 30 | 1.6 | 1.7 | 1.4 | 1 | 0 | 0 |
| Bangladesh | 1980 | 70.7 | 58.9 | 83.0 | 33 672 | 14 434 | 19 238 | 62.8 | 52.2 | 74.3 | 10 573 | 4 585 | 5 988 |
| | 1985 | 68.0 | 56.6 | 80.1 | 36 414 | 15 572 | 20 841 | 60.1 | 49.2 | 71.3 | 11 209 | 4 674 | 6 535 |
| | 1990 | 65.2 | 54.0 | 77.0 | 39 767 | 16 842 | 22 925 | 57.0 | 46.0 | 68.1 | 12 264 | 5 009 | 7 255 |
| | 1995 | 62.2 | 51.1 | 73.8 | 44 325 | 18 615 | 25 710 | 53.8 | 43.2 | 64.8 | 14 054 | 5 751 | 8 303 |
| | 2000 | 59.2 | 48.3 | 70.5 | 49 621 | 20 739 | 28 881 | 50.4 | 40.3 | 61.0 | 15 303 | 6 312 | 8 991 |
| Bhutan | 1980 | 71.9 | 58.9 | 85.0 | 556 | 227 | 329 | ... | ... | ... | ... | ... | ... |
| | 1985 | 67.5 | 53.8 | 81.2 | 585 | 233 | 352 | ... | ... | ... | ... | ... | ... |
| | 1990 | 62.7 | 48.7 | 76.8 | 615 | 239 | 376 | ... | ... | ... | ... | ... | ... |
| | 1995 | 57.8 | 43.7 | 71.8 | 613 | 233 | 380 | ... | ... | ... | ... | ... | ... |
| | 2000 | 52.7 | 38.9 | 66.4 | 642 | 237 | 404 | ... | ... | ... | ... | ... | ... |
| Brunei Darussalam | 1980 | 22.8 | 15.0 | 32.5 | 26 | 9 | 17 | 5.5 | 4.4 | 6.8 | 2 | 1 | 1 |
| | 1985 | 19.2 | 12.1 | 27.1 | 26 | 8 | 17 | 3.5 | 3.1 | 3.9 | 1 | 0 | 0 |
| | 1990 | 14.4 | 8.9 | 20.5 | 24 | 8 | 16 | 2.1 | 2.3 | 1.8 | 1 | 0 | 0 |
| | 1995 | 10.9 | 6.8 | 15.4 | 21 | 7 | 14 | 0.9 | 1.5 | 0.3 | 0 | 0 | 0 |
| | 2000 | 8.4 | 5.3 | 11.8 | 18 | 6 | 12 | 0.5 | 0.9 | 0.2 | 0 | 0 | 0 |

| Country / Pays / País | Year / Année / Año | Population aged 15 years and over / Population âgée de 15 ans et plus / Población de 15 años y más | | | | | | Population aged 15 to 24 years / Population âgée de 15 à 24 ans / Población de 15 a 24 años | | | | | |
|---|---|---|---|---|---|---|---|---|---|---|---|---|---|
| | | Illiteracy rate / Taux d'analphabétisme / Tasa de analfabetismo (%) | | | Illiterate population / Population analphabète / Población analfabeta (000) | | | Illiteracy rate / Taux d'analphabétisme / Tasa de analfabetismo (%) | | | Illiterate population / Population analphabète / Población analfabeta (000) | | |
| | | MF | M | F | MF | M | F | MF | M | F | MF | M | F |
| China | 1980 | 33.9 | 21.4 | 47.3 | 218 849 | 70 984 | 147 864 | 9.6 | 4.1 | 15.6 | 18 850 | 4 162 | 14 687 |
| | 1985 | 27.5 | 16.6 | 39.0 | 205 351 | 63 778 | 141 573 | 6.6 | 3.0 | 10.5 | 15 843 | 3 748 | 12 095 |
| | 1990 | 22.1 | 13.0 | 31.9 | 185 398 | 55 785 | 129 612 | 4.8 | 2.5 | 7.2 | 12 088 | 3 230 | 8 857 |
| | 1995 | 18.5 | 10.1 | 27.3 | 166 255 | 46 578 | 119 677 | 3.2 | 1.4 | 5.2 | 7 284 | 1 702 | 5 581 |
| | 2000 | 15.0 | 7.7 | 22.6 | 144 463 | 37 798 | 106 664 | 2.0 | 0.7 | 3.4 | 4 077 | 770 | 3 307 |
| China, Hong Kong SAR | 1980 | 14.4 | 5.9 | 23.7 | 543 | 117 | 425 | 3.2 | 2.7 | 3.7 | 36 | 16 | 20 |
| | 1985 | 12.1 | 5.2 | 19.4 | 507 | 113 | 394 | 2.2 | 2.3 | 2.2 | 23 | 12 | 11 |
| | 1990 | 10.0 | 4.6 | 15.6 | 449 | 106 | 342 | 1.4 | 1.9 | 0.9 | 12 | 8 | 4 |
| | 1995 | 8.2 | 4.0 | 12.6 | 405 | 103 | 302 | 0.9 | 1.5 | 0.3 | 8 | 7 | 1 |
| | 2000 | 6.6 | 3.5 | 10.0 | 353 | 96 | 256 | 0.7 | 1.2 | 0.2 | 6 | 6 | 0 |
| Cyprus | 1980 | 10.3 | 4.1 | 16.4 | 47 | 9 | 38 | 0.6 | 0.6 | 0.5 | 0 | 0 | 0 |
| | 1985 | 8.1 | 3.1 | 13.0 | 39 | 7 | 31 | 0.4 | 0.5 | 0.2 | 0 | 0 | 0 |
| | 1990 | 6.2 | 2.4 | 10.0 | 31 | 6 | 25 | 0.3 | 0.4 | 0.2 | 0 | 0 | 0 |
| | 1995 | 4.7 | 1.8 | 7.4 | 26 | 5 | 21 | 0.2 | 0.3 | 0.2 | 0 | 0 | 0 |
| | 2000 | 3.1 | 1.3 | 5.0 | 19 | 3 | 15 | 0.2 | 0.2 | 0.2 | 0 | 0 | 0 |
| India | 1980 | 59.1 | 44.7 | 74.7 | 250 592 | 97 862 | 152 730 | 46.1 | 32.4 | 61.1 | 61 650 | 22 666 | 38 984 |
| | 1985 | 55.3 | 41.0 | 70.6 | 265 774 | 101 807 | 163 967 | 42.0 | 29.2 | 56.1 | 63 030 | 22 925 | 40 105 |
| | 1990 | 51.5 | 37.6 | 66.5 | 279 006 | 105 054 | 173 952 | 38.0 | 26.3 | 50.9 | 62 544 | 22 642 | 39 901 |
| | 1995 | 47.9 | 34.5 | 62.3 | 289 513 | 107 497 | 182 016 | 34.2 | 23.6 | 45.8 | 59 769 | 21 542 | 38 226 |
| | 2000 | 44.2 | 31.4 | 57.9 | 299 327 | 109 681 | 189 645 | 30.3 | 20.9 | 40.5 | 57 997 | 20 850 | 37 146 |
| Indonesia | 1980 | 30.7 | 20.7 | 40.4 | 27 379 | 9 080 | 18 298 | 10.8 | 6.9 | 14.6 | 3 210 | 1 024 | 2 185 |
| | 1985 | 25.2 | 16.6 | 33.5 | 25 885 | 8 411 | 17 473 | 7.3 | 4.8 | 9.8 | 2 475 | 811 | 1 664 |
| | 1990 | 18.4 | 12.0 | 24.8 | 21 728 | 6 966 | 14 761 | 3.1 | 2.2 | 4.0 | 1 190 | 425 | 764 |
| | 1995 | 16.3 | 10.3 | 22.1 | 21 598 | 6 760 | 14 838 | 3.3 | 2.4 | 4.3 | 1 394 | 502 | 891 |
| | 2000 | 13.0 | 8.1 | 17.9 | 19 241 | 5 911 | 13 329 | 2.2 | 1.6 | 2.8 | 952 | 357 | 594 |
| Iran, Islamic Republic of | 1980 | 49.0 | 37.8 | 60.3 | 10 604 | 4 127 | 6 477 | 25.6 | 16.2 | 35.2 | 1 989 | 638 | 1 351 |
| | 1985 | 49.2 | 37.7 | 61.0 | 12 776 | 4 934 | 7 842 | 25.0 | 15.9 | 34.1 | 2 263 | 724 | 1 538 |
| | 1990 | 35.7 | 26.8 | 44.7 | 10 973 | 4 158 | 6 814 | 13.0 | 7.9 | 18.2 | 1 395 | 430 | 965 |
| | 1995 | 29.0 | 21.1 | 36.9 | 10 473 | 3 854 | 6 618 | 8.7 | 5.4 | 12.1 | 1 103 | 347 | 756 |
| | 2000 | 23.1 | 16.3 | 30.0 | 10 000 | 3 571 | 6 429 | 5.9 | 3.7 | 8.2 | 910 | 290 | 619 |
| Israel | 1980 | 8.7 | 5.0 | 12.2 | 225 | 64 | 161 | 2.2 | 1.3 | 3.1 | 14 | 4 | 10 |
| | 1985 | 7.3 | 4.1 | 10.4 | 209 | 58 | 151 | 1.5 | 0.9 | 2.2 | 11 | 3 | 7 |
| | 1990 | 5.9 | 3.3 | 8.5 | 191 | 52 | 138 | 1.1 | 0.7 | 1.6 | 9 | 3 | 6 |
| | 1995 | 4.9 | 2.6 | 7.0 | 194 | 52 | 142 | 0.7 | 0.4 | 0.9 | 6 | 2 | 4 |
| | 2000 | 3.9 | 2.1 | 5.7 | 178 | 46 | 132 | 0.3 | 0.2 | 0.4 | 3 | 1 | 2 |
| Jordan | 1980 | 31.6 | 18.0 | 46.0 | 467 | 137 | 330 | 8.9 | 4.1 | 14.3 | 50 | 12 | 38 |
| | 1985 | 25.0 | 14.4 | 36.6 | 547 | 164 | 382 | 5.1 | 2.8 | 7.7 | 43 | 13 | 30 |
| | 1990 | 18.8 | 10.1 | 28.3 | 461 | 131 | 330 | 2.7 | 1.9 | 3.6 | 27 | 10 | 16 |
| | 1995 | 14.4 | 9.5 | 19.9 | 471 | 161 | 310 | 2.1 | 3.6 | 0.5 | 27 | 23 | 3 |
| | 2000 | 10.2 | 5.1 | 15.6 | 396 | 104 | 292 | 0.5 | 0.7 | 0.2 | 6 | 5 | 1 |
| Korea, Republic of | 1980 | 7.2 | 3.2 | 11.2 | 1 824 | 403 | 1 421 | ... | ... | ... | ... | ... | ... |
| | 1985 | 5.5 | 2.2 | 8.8 | 1 596 | 324 | 1 271 | ... | ... | ... | ... | ... | ... |
| | 1990 | 4.1 | 1.6 | 6.6 | 1 328 | 261 | 1 067 | ... | ... | ... | ... | ... | ... |
| | 1995 | 3.1 | 1.2 | 5.0 | 1 073 | 207 | 865 | ... | ... | ... | ... | ... | ... |
| | 2000 | 2.2 | 0.8 | 3.6 | 843 | 162 | 680 | ... | ... | ... | ... | ... | ... |
| Kuwait | 1980 | 32.4 | 27.2 | 40.9 | 265 | 137 | 128 | 19.4 | 16.9 | 22.5 | 47 | 23 | 24 |
| | 1985 | 25.5 | 21.8 | 31.2 | 276 | 142 | 134 | 13.1 | 11.7 | 14.4 | 38 | 17 | 21 |
| | 1990 | 23.1 | 20.5 | 27.1 | 314 | 168 | 146 | 12.0 | 11.5 | 12.4 | 44 | 21 | 22 |
| | 1995 | 20.7 | 17.7 | 24.0 | 214 | 95 | 119 | 9.1 | 9.3 | 8.9 | 28 | 14 | 13 |
| | 2000 | 17.7 | 15.7 | 20.1 | 232 | 109 | 122 | 7.1 | 7.7 | 6.5 | 28 | 15 | 12 |
| Lao People's Democratic Republic | 1980 | 58.2 | 44.3 | 72.3 | 1 081 | 413 | 668 | ... | ... | ... | ... | ... | ... |
| | 1985 | 53.2 | 39.5 | 67.0 | 1 096 | 407 | 689 | ... | ... | ... | ... | ... | ... |
| | 1990 | 48.4 | 34.9 | 61.4 | 1 126 | 408 | 718 | ... | ... | ... | ... | ... | ... |
| | 1995 | 43.3 | 30.5 | 55.6 | 1 144 | 404 | 739 | ... | ... | ... | ... | ... | ... |
| | 2000 | 38.2 | 26.4 | 49.5 | 1 157 | 403 | 753 | ... | ... | ... | ... | ... | ... |
| Lebanon | 1980 | 27.6 | 17.4 | 37.0 | 441 | 134 | 306 | 12.4 | 6.7 | 17.8 | 67 | 17 | 50 |
| | 1985 | 23.6 | 14.4 | 31.7 | 395 | 113 | 281 | 9.9 | 5.4 | 14.2 | 57 | 15 | 42 |
| | 1990 | 19.6 | 11.5 | 26.8 | 327 | 91 | 235 | 7.8 | 4.3 | 11.4 | 45 | 12 | 32 |
| | 1995 | 16.6 | 9.5 | 23.0 | 329 | 89 | 239 | 6.2 | 3.4 | 9.0 | 37 | 10 | 26 |
| | 2000 | 13.9 | 7.7 | 19.6 | 308 | 82 | 225 | 4.7 | 2.5 | 7.0 | 28 | 7 | 20 |
| Macau | 1980 | 13.9 | 7.8 | 20.1 | 26 | 7 | 18 | 4.9 | 2.1 | 7.8 | 3 | 0 | 2 |
| | 1985 | 11.4 | 6.4 | 16.3 | 26 | 7 | 18 | 4.4 | 1.8 | 6.7 | 2 | 0 | 2 |
| | 1990 | 9.9 | 5.6 | 13.9 | 27 | 7 | 20 | 3.8 | 1.4 | 5.6 | 2 | 0 | 1 |
| | 1995 | 8.3 | 4.4 | 11.8 | 26 | 6 | 19 | 2.8 | 1.0 | 4.5 | 1 | 0 | 1 |
| | 2000 | 6.8 | 3.4 | 9.9 | 24 | 6 | 18 | 2.0 | 0.5 | 3.5 | 1 | 0 | 1 |
| Malaysia | 1980 | 30.3 | 20.4 | 40.3 | 2 537 | 848 | 1 688 | 11.6 | 7.9 | 15.2 | 340 | 114 | 226 |
| | 1985 | 23.5 | 15.9 | 30.9 | 2 260 | 765 | 1 495 | 7.3 | 6.0 | 8.6 | 237 | 98 | 138 |
| | 1990 | 19.1 | 13.0 | 25.4 | 2 171 | 742 | 1 428 | 5.3 | 4.8 | 5.8 | 182 | 83 | 98 |
| | 1995 | 15.5 | 10.5 | 20.6 | 2 004 | 686 | 1 318 | 3.6 | 3.6 | 3.7 | 137 | 69 | 68 |
| | 2000 | 12.5 | 8.5 | 16.4 | 1 836 | 633 | 1 202 | 2.5 | 2.7 | 2.3 | 105 | 58 | 47 |

| Country<br>Pays<br>País | Year<br>Année<br>Año | Population aged 15 years and over<br>Population âgée de 15 ans et plus<br>Población de 15 años y más | | | | | | Population aged 15 to 24 years<br>Population âgée de 15 à 24 ans<br>Población de 15 a 24 años | | | | | |
|---|---|---|---|---|---|---|---|---|---|---|---|---|---|
| | | Illiteracy rate<br>Taux d'analphabétisme<br>Tasa de analfabetismo<br>( % ) | | | Illiterate population<br>Population analphabète<br>Población analfabeta<br>(000) | | | Illiteracy rate<br>Taux d'analphabétisme<br>Tasa de analfabetismo<br>( % ) | | | Illiterate population<br>Population analphabète<br>Población analfabeta<br>(000) | | |
| | | MF | M | F | MF | M | F | MF | M | F | MF | M | F |
| Maldives | 1980 | 8.8 | 8.3 | 9.3 | 7 | 3 | 4 | 4.1 | 4.1 | 4.0 | 1 | 0 | 0 |
| | 1985 | 7.7 | 7.8 | 7.6 | 7 | 3 | 3 | 3.7 | 4.3 | 3.1 | 1 | 0 | 0 |
| | 1990 | 5.8 | 5.8 | 5.9 | 6 | 3 | 3 | 2.3 | 2.5 | 2.1 | 0 | 0 | 0 |
| | 1995 | 4.7 | 4.6 | 4.8 | 6 | 3 | 3 | 1.7 | 1.9 | 1.5 | 0 | 0 | 0 |
| | 2000 | 3.7 | 3.7 | 3.6 | 6 | 3 | 2 | 1.2 | 1.4 | 0.9 | 0 | 0 | 0 |
| Mongolia | 1980 | 1.7 | 1.2 | 2.2 | 21 | 7 | 14 | 0.9 | 0.9 | 0.9 | 2 | 1 | 1 |
| | 1985 | 1.5 | 1.1 | 1.8 | 21 | 8 | 13 | 0.9 | 1.0 | 0.8 | 3 | 1 | 1 |
| | 1990 | 1.2 | 1.0 | 1.3 | 20 | 9 | 11 | 0.7 | 0.9 | 0.6 | 3 | 2 | 1 |
| | 1995 | 0.9 | 0.9 | 1.0 | 18 | 9 | 9 | 0.5 | 0.7 | 0.3 | 2 | 1 | 0 |
| | 2000 | 0.7 | 0.8 | 0.7 | 17 | 9 | 8 | 0.4 | 0.6 | 0.2 | 2 | 1 | 0 |
| Myanmar | 1980 | 24.2 | 14.5 | 33.9 | 4 961 | 1 472 | 3 488 | 15.2 | 11.2 | 19.3 | 1 018 | 379 | 638 |
| | 1985 | 21.7 | 13.5 | 29.5 | 4 950 | 1 517 | 3 433 | 13.5 | 10.5 | 16.3 | 1 034 | 397 | 637 |
| | 1990 | 19.2 | 12.6 | 25.6 | 4 997 | 1 612 | 3 385 | 11.8 | 9.8 | 13.7 | 1 012 | 425 | 586 |
| | 1995 | 17.1 | 11.8 | 22.3 | 4 981 | 1 688 | 3 292 | 10.3 | 9.2 | 11.4 | 947 | 429 | 517 |
| | 2000 | 15.3 | 11.0 | 19.4 | 4 985 | 1 774 | 3 210 | 9.0 | 8.6 | 9.4 | 870 | 419 | 450 |
| Nepal | 1980 | 76.9 | 61.7 | 92.7 | 6 373 | 2 594 | 3 778 | 65.8 | 47.5 | 85.8 | 1 799 | 676 | 1 123 |
| | 1985 | 72.9 | 56.6 | 89.8 | 6 829 | 2 708 | 4 120 | 59.9 | 41.0 | 80.4 | 1 850 | 660 | 1 189 |
| | 1990 | 69.2 | 52.2 | 85.8 | 7 401 | 2 744 | 4 656 | 54.0 | 33.8 | 73.1 | 1 870 | 568 | 1 301 |
| | 1995 | 64.1 | 46.4 | 81.4 | 7 821 | 2 808 | 5 013 | 46.7 | 28.5 | 65.6 | 1 884 | 585 | 1 298 |
| | 2000 | 58.6 | 40.9 | 76.2 | 8 278 | 2 892 | 5 386 | 40.9 | 25.0 | 58.1 | 1 954 | 620 | 1 333 |
| Oman | 1980 | 63.2 | 47.6 | 83.6 | 395 | 169 | 226 | 39.7 | 17.6 | 64.2 | 78 | 18 | 60 |
| | 1985 | 54.0 | 39.4 | 73.2 | 422 | 174 | 247 | 25.9 | 9.4 | 43.4 | 64 | 12 | 52 |
| | 1990 | 45.0 | 32.1 | 61.6 | 430 | 173 | 257 | 14.3 | 4.5 | 24.5 | 44 | 7 | 37 |
| | 1995 | 36.0 | 25.4 | 49.3 | 420 | 164 | 255 | 5.9 | 1.4 | 10.4 | 22 | 2 | 19 |
| | 2000 | 28.1 | 19.6 | 38.3 | 398 | 152 | 246 | 2.0 | 0.3 | 3.7 | 10 | 0 | 9 |
| Pakistan | 1980 | 72.1 | 59.4 | 86.1 | 34 219 | 14 799 | 19 419 | 62.5 | 48.1 | 78.5 | 10 964 | 4 435 | 6 529 |
| | 1985 | 68.5 | 55.2 | 83.2 | 39 600 | 16 709 | 22 891 | 58.5 | 43.7 | 74.9 | 12 310 | 4 831 | 7 479 |
| | 1990 | 64.5 | 50.6 | 79.8 | 43 903 | 18 013 | 25 889 | 52.5 | 37.4 | 69.3 | 12 429 | 4 657 | 7 772 |
| | 1995 | 60.6 | 46.3 | 76.2 | 47 332 | 18 908 | 28 424 | 46.9 | 31.9 | 63.5 | 12 098 | 4 326 | 7 771 |
| | 2000 | 56.7 | 42.4 | 72.2 | 51 671 | 20 079 | 31 592 | 43.0 | 28.7 | 58.2 | 12 713 | 4 395 | 8 318 |
| Philippines | 1980 | 11.0 | 10.0 | 12.0 | 3 096 | 1 400 | 1 695 | 4.7 | 4.8 | 4.7 | 491 | 251 | 240 |
| | 1985 | 9.0 | 8.3 | 9.7 | 2 917 | 1 336 | 1 581 | 3.5 | 3.6 | 3.5 | 402 | 207 | 194 |
| | 1990 | 7.5 | 6.9 | 8.0 | 2 717 | 1 263 | 1 453 | 2.7 | 2.9 | 2.5 | 332 | 175 | 156 |
| | 1995 | 5.9 | 5.6 | 6.2 | 2 496 | 1 180 | 1 315 | 1.9 | 2.1 | 1.7 | 267 | 144 | 122 |
| | 2000 | 4.6 | 4.5 | 4.8 | 2 251 | 1 083 | 1 167 | 1.3 | 1.5 | 1.1 | 207 | 116 | 90 |
| Qatar | 1980 | 30.2 | 28.2 | 34.6 | 46 | 30 | 16 | 16.7 | 17.7 | 15.1 | 7 | 4 | 2 |
| | 1985 | 25.6 | 24.5 | 28.5 | 65 | 46 | 19 | 13.2 | 14.7 | 10.6 | 7 | 4 | 2 |
| | 1990 | 22.9 | 22.6 | 23.9 | 80 | 59 | 21 | 9.7 | 11.7 | 7.0 | 5 | 3 | 1 |
| | 1995 | 20.7 | 21.0 | 20.0 | 82 | 60 | 22 | 6.9 | 9.1 | 4.4 | 4 | 3 | 1 |
| | 2000 | 18.7 | 19.5 | 16.8 | 82 | 60 | 22 | 5.1 | 7.3 | 2.9 | 4 | 3 | 1 |
| Saudi Arabia | 1980 | 47.7 | 32.9 | 67.1 | 2 551 | 999 | 1 552 | 25.9 | 15.1 | 39.6 | 461 | 151 | 310 |
| | 1985 | 39.5 | 27.0 | 58.3 | 2 853 | 1 167 | 1 686 | 19.8 | 11.6 | 29.7 | 437 | 140 | 297 |
| | 1990 | 32.8 | 22.4 | 49.4 | 3 062 | 1 286 | 1 776 | 14.4 | 8.5 | 21.3 | 396 | 126 | 270 |
| | 1995 | 27.8 | 19.2 | 40.3 | 2 971 | 1 216 | 1 755 | 10.1 | 6.0 | 14.2 | 332 | 100 | 233 |
| | 2000 | 23.0 | 15.9 | 32.8 | 2 951 | 1 187 | 1 764 | 6.9 | 4.4 | 9.5 | 284 | 93 | 191 |
| Singapore | 1980 | 17.0 | 8.4 | 26.0 | 300 | 75 | 225 | 2.7 | 2.2 | 3.3 | 16 | 6 | 9 |
| | 1985 | 14.2 | 6.9 | 21.7 | 292 | 72 | 220 | 1.7 | 1.7 | 1.8 | 9 | 4 | 5 |
| | 1990 | 10.9 | 4.9 | 17.0 | 259 | 57 | 201 | 0.9 | 0.7 | 1.0 | 5 | 2 | 3 |
| | 1995 | 9.2 | 4.4 | 13.9 | 237 | 57 | 179 | 0.4 | 0.7 | 0.2 | 2 | 1 | 0 |
| | 2000 | 7.6 | 3.6 | 11.5 | 212 | 51 | 160 | 0.2 | 0.3 | 0.2 | 1 | 0 | 0 |
| Sri Lanka | 1980 | 14.6 | 9.0 | 20.5 | 1 409 | 440 | 969 | 7.4 | 5.7 | 9.2 | 233 | 90 | 143 |
| | 1985 | 12.8 | 8.0 | 17.8 | 1 358 | 423 | 934 | 6.1 | 4.8 | 7.4 | 197 | 78 | 118 |
| | 1990 | 11.3 | 7.1 | 15.4 | 1 298 | 405 | 893 | 5.0 | 4.0 | 5.9 | 163 | 67 | 96 |
| | 1995 | 9.8 | 6.3 | 13.1 | 1 237 | 390 | 847 | 4.0 | 3.4 | 4.6 | 138 | 59 | 78 |
| | 2000 | 8.4 | 5.5 | 11.1 | 1 171 | 377 | 794 | 3.2 | 2.9 | 3.6 | 122 | 55 | 66 |
| Syrian Arab Republic | 1980 | 46.7 | 27.9 | 66.1 | 2 095 | 636 | 1 458 | 29.4 | 12.5 | 47.1 | 504 | 109 | 394 |
| | 1985 | 40.6 | 22.4 | 59.2 | 2 184 | 612 | 1 572 | 24.5 | 9.9 | 40.0 | 521 | 108 | 412 |
| | 1990 | 35.1 | 18.1 | 52.5 | 2 275 | 592 | 1 682 | 20.2 | 7.8 | 33.2 | 502 | 99 | 403 |
| | 1995 | 30.1 | 14.6 | 45.9 | 2 363 | 576 | 1 786 | 16.3 | 6.0 | 26.9 | 480 | 90 | 390 |
| | 2000 | 25.6 | 11.7 | 39.6 | 2 447 | 564 | 1 883 | 12.9 | 4.6 | 21.4 | 464 | 85 | 379 |
| Tajikistan | 1980 | 5.8 | 3.2 | 8.3 | 132 | 35 | 96 | ... | ... | ... | ... | ... | ... |
| | 1985 | 3.6 | 1.9 | 5.3 | 95 | 24 | 71 | ... | ... | ... | ... | ... | ... |
| | 1990 | 2.2 | 1.1 | 3.2 | 66 | 16 | 49 | ... | ... | ... | ... | ... | ... |
| | 1995 | 1.3 | 0.7 | 1.9 | 44 | 11 | 33 | ... | ... | ... | ... | ... | ... |
| | 2000 | 0.8 | 0.4 | 1.1 | 30 | 8 | 22 | ... | ... | ... | ... | ... | ... |
| Thailand | 1980 | 12.6 | 7.7 | 17.4 | 3 532 | 1 071 | 2 461 | 3.3 | 2.5 | 4.2 | 335 | 126 | 208 |
| | 1985 | 9.8 | 6.0 | 13.5 | 3 237 | 987 | 2 249 | 2.5 | 1.9 | 3.1 | 287 | 110 | 176 |
| | 1990 | 6.6 | 4.4 | 8.8 | 2 503 | 827 | 1 675 | 0.7 | 1.0 | 0.4 | 92 | 63 | 29 |
| | 1995 | 5.8 | 3.6 | 8.0 | 2 465 | 765 | 1 700 | 1.3 | 0.8 | 1.8 | 164 | 54 | 110 |
| | 2000 | 4.4 | 2.8 | 6.0 | 2 047 | 641 | 1 405 | 0.9 | 0.5 | 1.4 | 115 | 30 | 85 |

| Country<br>Pays<br>País | Year<br>Année<br>Año | Population aged 15 years and over<br>Population âgée de 15 ans et plus<br>Población de 15 años y más | | | | | | Population aged 15 to 24 years<br>Population âgée de 15 à 24 ans<br>Población de 15 a 24 años | | | | | |
|---|---|---|---|---|---|---|---|---|---|---|---|---|---|
| | | Illiteracy rate<br>Taux d'analphabétisme<br>Tasa de analfabetismo<br>( % ) | | | Illiterate population<br>Population analphabète<br>Población analfabeta<br>(000) | | | Illiteracy rate<br>Taux d'analphabétisme<br>Tasa de analfabetismo<br>( % ) | | | Illiterate population<br>Population analphabète<br>Población analfabeta<br>(000) | | |
| | | MF | M | F | MF | M | F | MF | M | F | MF | M | F |
| Turkey | 1980 | 34.3 | 18.7 | 50.2 | 9 277 | 2 540 | 6 736 | 14.8 | 5.8 | 24.5 | 1 336 | 270 | 1 066 |
| | 1985 | 23.6 | 12.4 | 35.7 | 7 588 | 2 048 | 5 540 | 7.0 | 2.4 | 12.0 | 738 | 134 | 604 |
| | 1990 | 20.7 | 10.2 | 31.5 | 7 585 | 1 868 | 5 716 | 6.1 | 2.3 | 9.9 | 686 | 136 | 549 |
| | 1995 | 18.0 | 8.3 | 27.8 | 7 604 | 1 764 | 5 839 | 5.1 | 1.9 | 8.5 | 668 | 127 | 541 |
| | 2000 | 14.8 | 6.4 | 23.3 | 7 097 | 1 555 | 5 542 | 3.5 | 1.1 | 6.0 | 483 | 81 | 401 |
| United Arab Emirates | 1980 | 34.4 | 32.4 | 40.4 | 250 | 179 | 70 | 24.5 | 25.9 | 21.8 | 44 | 31 | 12 |
| | 1985 | 30.9 | 30.0 | 33.3 | 345 | 239 | 105 | 20.1 | 22.6 | 16.4 | 47 | 31 | 15 |
| | 1990 | 28.6 | 28.5 | 29.0 | 381 | 269 | 111 | 14.9 | 17.9 | 11.1 | 35 | 24 | 11 |
| | 1995 | 26.2 | 26.8 | 24.9 | 404 | 288 | 116 | 11.7 | 14.8 | 7.8 | 34 | 24 | 10 |
| | 2000 | 23.5 | 24.8 | 20.5 | 412 | 296 | 115 | 9.0 | 12.1 | 5.4 | 33 | 24 | 9 |
| Viet Nam | 1980 | 16.7 | 8.5 | 23.8 | 5 164 | 1 224 | 3 939 | 5.3 | 4.0 | 6.4 | 590 | 215 | 374 |
| | 1985 | 13.3 | 7.2 | 18.8 | 4 753 | 1 212 | 3 540 | 5.4 | 4.7 | 6.2 | 708 | 306 | 402 |
| | 1990 | 11.0 | 6.2 | 15.5 | 4 520 | 1 204 | 3 316 | 4.8 | 4.4 | 5.3 | 679 | 320 | 358 |
| | 1995 | 8.9 | 5.2 | 12.2 | 4 156 | 1 181 | 2 975 | 3.6 | 3.4 | 3.7 | 538 | 265 | 273 |
| | 2000 | 6.7 | 4.3 | 9.0 | 3 615 | 1 131 | 2 483 | 2.7 | 2.7 | 2.6 | 443 | 226 | 216 |
| Yemen | 1980 | 79.8 | 61.3 | 94.3 | 3 263 | 1 108 | 2 154 | 68.4 | 44.7 | 88.8 | 1 036 | 313 | 723 |
| | 1985 | 73.9 | 53.1 | 91.4 | 3 638 | 1 191 | 2 447 | 59.2 | 36.6 | 83.2 | 1 194 | 379 | 814 |
| | 1990 | 67.2 | 44.6 | 87.0 | 3 988 | 1 239 | 2 748 | 50.1 | 26.5 | 75.0 | 1 194 | 325 | 869 |
| | 1995 | 59.9 | 37.9 | 81.6 | 4 728 | 1 484 | 3 244 | 41.7 | 20.6 | 65.3 | 1 270 | 331 | 938 |
| | 2000 | 53.8 | 32.6 | 75.0 | 5 044 | 1 525 | 3 519 | 35.6 | 17.4 | 54.8 | 1 229 | 310 | 919 |
| **Europe** | | | | | | | | | | | | | |
| Belarus | 1980 | 5.6 | 1.4 | 9.0 | 419 | 48 | 371 | ... | ... | ... | ... | ... | ... |
| | 1985 | 3.5 | 0.9 | 5.7 | 276 | 32 | 243 | ... | ... | ... | ... | ... | ... |
| | 1990 | 2.1 | 0.6 | 3.3 | 167 | 22 | 144 | ... | ... | ... | ... | ... | ... |
| | 1995 | 1.2 | 0.4 | 1.8 | 98 | 16 | 82 | ... | ... | ... | ... | ... | ... |
| | 2000 | 0.6 | 0.3 | 0.8 | 51 | 12 | 39 | ... | ... | ... | ... | ... | ... |
| Bulgaria | 1980 | 4.7 | 2.6 | 6.8 | 330 | 91 | 239 | 0.6 | 0.5 | 0.8 | 8 | 3 | 4 |
| | 1985 | 3.5 | 2.1 | 5.0 | 253 | 73 | 180 | 0.6 | 0.5 | 0.7 | 7 | 3 | 4 |
| | 1990 | 2.6 | 1.6 | 3.6 | 185 | 55 | 129 | 0.5 | 0.4 | 0.7 | 7 | 2 | 4 |
| | 1995 | 2.0 | 1.2 | 2.6 | 138 | 42 | 96 | 0.4 | 0.3 | 0.6 | 6 | 2 | 3 |
| | 2000 | 1.5 | 0.9 | 2.0 | 105 | 33 | 72 | 0.3 | 0.2 | 0.5 | 4 | 1 | 3 |
| Croatia | 1980 | 7.5 | 2.7 | 11.8 | 259 | 45 | 214 | 0.5 | 0.4 | 0.5 | 3 | 1 | 1 |
| | 1985 | 5.3 | 1.9 | 8.5 | 189 | 32 | 157 | 0.4 | 0.4 | 0.4 | 2 | 1 | 1 |
| | 1990 | 3.7 | 1.3 | 5.8 | 134 | 23 | 110 | 0.3 | 0.3 | 0.4 | 2 | 1 | 1 |
| | 1995 | 2.6 | 0.9 | 4.0 | 94 | 17 | 77 | 0.3 | 0.2 | 0.3 | 1 | 0 | 1 |
| | 2000 | 1.7 | 0.6 | 2.7 | 66 | 12 | 53 | 0.2 | 0.2 | 0.2 | 1 | 0 | 0 |
| Greece | 1980 | 9.3 | 3.9 | 14.3 | 693 | 141 | 552 | 0.8 | 0.8 | 0.8 | 11 | 5 | 5 |
| | 1985 | 7.1 | 3.1 | 10.9 | 558 | 117 | 441 | 0.6 | 0.6 | 0.5 | 9 | 5 | 4 |
| | 1990 | 5.2 | 2.4 | 7.8 | 431 | 97 | 334 | 0.4 | 0.5 | 0.3 | 7 | 4 | 2 |
| | 1995 | 3.8 | 1.8 | 5.7 | 337 | 80 | 256 | 0.3 | 0.4 | 0.2 | 4 | 3 | 1 |
| | 2000 | 2.8 | 1.4 | 4.0 | 254 | 65 | 188 | 0.2 | 0.2 | 0.2 | 3 | 1 | 1 |
| Hungary | 1980 | 1.1 | 0.7 | 1.5 | 93 | 27 | 65 | ... | ... | ... | ... | ... | ... |
| | 1985 | 1.1 | 0.8 | 1.4 | 95 | 34 | 61 | ... | ... | ... | ... | ... | ... |
| | 1990 | 0.9 | 0.7 | 1.1 | 75 | 27 | 48 | ... | ... | ... | ... | ... | ... |
| | 1995 | 0.7 | 0.5 | 0.9 | 63 | 23 | 40 | ... | ... | ... | ... | ... | ... |
| | 2000 | 0.6 | 0.5 | 0.7 | 54 | 19 | 34 | ... | ... | ... | ... | ... | ... |
| Italy | 1980 | 3.9 | 2.8 | 4.9 | 1 728 | 608 | 1 119 | 0.3 | 0.2 | 0.4 | 31 | 12 | 18 |
| | 1985 | 3.0 | 2.1 | 3.7 | 1 379 | 481 | 898 | ... | ... | ... | ... | ... | ... |
| | 1990 | 2.3 | 1.6 | 2.9 | 1 115 | 388 | 727 | ... | ... | ... | ... | ... | ... |
| | 1995 | 1.8 | 1.3 | 2.2 | 889 | 310 | 579 | ... | ... | ... | ... | ... | ... |
| | 2000 | 1.5 | 1.1 | 1.9 | 764 | 263 | 500 | ... | ... | ... | ... | ... | ... |
| Latvia | 1980 | 1.1 | 0.3 | 1.8 | 23 | 3 | 20 | ... | ... | ... | ... | ... | ... |
| | 1985 | 0.8 | 0.3 | 1.3 | 17 | 2 | 14 | ... | ... | ... | ... | ... | ... |
| | 1990 | 0.6 | 0.2 | 0.9 | 13 | 2 | 10 | ... | ... | ... | ... | ... | ... |
| | 1995 | 0.4 | 0.2 | 0.6 | 9 | 2 | 7 | ... | ... | ... | ... | ... | ... |
| | 2000 | 0.3 | 0.2 | 0.4 | 6 | 1 | 4 | ... | ... | ... | ... | ... | ... |
| Lithuania | 1980 | 3.7 | 1.7 | 5.4 | 98 | 20 | 77 | ... | ... | ... | ... | ... | ... |
| | 1985 | 2.3 | 1.1 | 3.3 | 62 | 13 | 49 | ... | ... | ... | ... | ... | ... |
| | 1990 | 1.3 | 0.7 | 1.9 | 39 | 9 | 29 | ... | ... | ... | ... | ... | ... |
| | 1995 | 0.8 | 0.4 | 1.0 | 23 | 6 | 16 | ... | ... | ... | ... | ... | ... |
| | 2000 | 0.5 | 0.3 | 0.6 | 15 | 4 | 10 | ... | ... | ... | ... | ... | ... |
| Malta | 1980 | 16.4 | 16.7 | 16.1 | 41 | 20 | 20 | 4.6 | 6.3 | 2.9 | 2 | 1 | 0 |
| | 1985 | 13.8 | 14.0 | 13.6 | 36 | 17 | 18 | 3.2 | 4.7 | 1.7 | 1 | 1 | 0 |
| | 1990 | 11.5 | 12.0 | 10.9 | 31 | 16 | 15 | 2.4 | 3.8 | 1.0 | 1 | 0 | 0 |
| | 1995 | 9.5 | 10.1 | 8.9 | 27 | 14 | 13 | 1.8 | 3.1 | 0.4 | 1 | 0 | 0 |
| | 2000 | 7.9 | 8.6 | 7.2 | 24 | 13 | 11 | 1.3 | 2.4 | 0.2 | 0 | 0 | 0 |
| Moldova | 1980 | 8.1 | 3.6 | 12.0 | 240 | 49 | 191 | ... | ... | ... | ... | ... | ... |
| | 1985 | 5.5 | 2.2 | 8.3 | 170 | 32 | 138 | ... | ... | ... | ... | ... | ... |
| | 1990 | 3.5 | 1.3 | 5.3 | 110 | 19 | 90 | ... | ... | ... | ... | ... | ... |
| | 1995 | 2.0 | 0.8 | 3.1 | 66 | 12 | 54 | ... | ... | ... | ... | ... | ... |
| | 2000 | 1.1 | 0.4 | 1.7 | 39 | 7 | 31 | ... | ... | ... | ... | ... | ... |

| Country / Pays / País | Year / Année / Año | Population aged 15 years and over / Population âgée de 15 ans et plus / Población de 15 años y más | | | | | | Population aged 15 to 24 years / Population âgée de 15 à 24 ans / Población de 15 a 24 años | | | | | |
|---|---|---|---|---|---|---|---|---|---|---|---|---|---|
| | | Illiteracy rate / Taux d'analphabétisme / Tasa de analfabetismo (%) | | | Illiterate population / Population analphabète / Población analfabeta (000) | | | Illiteracy rate / Taux d'analphabétisme / Tasa de analfabetismo (%) | | | Illiterate population / Population analphabète / Población analfabeta (000) | | |
| | | MF | M | F | MF | M | F | MF | M | F | MF | M | F |
| Poland | 1980 | 1.0 | 0.6 | 1.3 | 283 | 87 | 196 | ... | ... | ... | ... | ... | ... |
| | 1985 | 0.6 | 0.4 | 0.8 | 184 | 62 | 121 | ... | ... | ... | ... | ... | ... |
| | 1990 | 0.4 | 0.3 | 0.5 | 122 | 47 | 74 | ... | ... | ... | ... | ... | ... |
| | 1995 | 0.3 | 0.2 | 0.3 | 96 | 40 | 55 | ... | ... | ... | ... | ... | ... |
| | 2000 | 0.2 | 0.2 | 0.2 | 83 | 37 | 45 | ... | ... | ... | ... | ... | ... |
| Portugal | 1980 | 18.2 | 13.3 | 22.6 | 1 323 | 456 | 866 | 2.0 | 1.8 | 2.3 | 35 | 16 | 19 |
| | 1985 | 15.7 | 11.2 | 19.6 | 1 193 | 405 | 787 | 1.1 | 1.1 | 1.1 | 20 | 10 | 9 |
| | 1990 | 12.7 | 9.0 | 16.1 | 1 008 | 340 | 668 | 0.4 | 0.5 | 0.4 | 7 | 4 | 3 |
| | 1995 | 10.0 | 6.9 | 12.8 | 815 | 268 | 546 | 0.2 | 0.2 | 0.2 | 3 | 1 | 1 |
| | 2000 | 7.8 | 5.2 | 10.0 | 645 | 207 | 438 | 0.2 | 0.2 | 0.2 | 2 | 1 | 1 |
| Romania | 1980 | 5.2 | 2.3 | 8.0 | 861 | 186 | 675 | 0.8 | 0.6 | 1.0 | 27 | 11 | 16 |
| | 1985 | 4.4 | 1.9 | 6.7 | 755 | 161 | 593 | 0.8 | 0.6 | 0.9 | 27 | 12 | 15 |
| | 1990 | 3.2 | 1.4 | 4.8 | 572 | 127 | 444 | 0.7 | 0.6 | 0.7 | 27 | 12 | 14 |
| | 1995 | 2.4 | 1.1 | 3.6 | 442 | 104 | 338 | 0.5 | 0.5 | 0.4 | 19 | 10 | 9 |
| | 2000 | 1.8 | 0.9 | 2.7 | 348 | 86 | 261 | 0.3 | 0.4 | 0.2 | 12 | 8 | 4 |
| Russian Federation | 1980 | 4.1 | 1.0 | 6.7 | 4 537 | 506 | 4 031 | ... | ... | ... | ... | ... | ... |
| | 1985 | 2.8 | 0.7 | 4.5 | 3 139 | 362 | 2 777 | ... | ... | ... | ... | ... | ... |
| | 1990 | 1.7 | 0.5 | 2.7 | 1 992 | 264 | 1 728 | ... | ... | ... | ... | ... | ... |
| | 1995 | 0.9 | 0.3 | 1.4 | 1 117 | 195 | 921 | ... | ... | ... | ... | ... | ... |
| | 2000 | 0.6 | 0.2 | 0.8 | 723 | 162 | 560 | ... | ... | ... | ... | ... | ... |
| Slovenia | 1980 | 0.6 | 0.5 | 0.7 | 9 | 3 | 5 | ... | ... | ... | ... | ... | ... |
| | 1985 | 0.5 | 0.4 | 0.6 | 8 | 3 | 5 | ... | ... | ... | ... | ... | ... |
| | 1990 | 0.4 | 0.4 | 0.5 | 7 | 3 | 4 | ... | ... | ... | ... | ... | ... |
| | 1995 | 0.4 | 0.3 | 0.4 | 6 | 2 | 3 | ... | ... | ... | ... | ... | ... |
| | 2000 | 0.3 | 0.3 | 0.4 | 6 | 2 | 3 | ... | ... | ... | ... | ... | ... |
| Spain | 1980 | 6.0 | 3.5 | 8.4 | 1 678 | 466 | 1 212 | 0.8 | 0.7 | 1.0 | 53 | 23 | 29 |
| | 1985 | 4.9 | 2.8 | 6.8 | 1 453 | 403 | 1 050 | 0.6 | 0.5 | 0.6 | 40 | 19 | 20 |
| | 1990 | 3.8 | 2.2 | 5.3 | 1 222 | 343 | 878 | 0.3 | 0.4 | 0.3 | 26 | 14 | 11 |
| | 1995 | 3.0 | 1.7 | 4.1 | 998 | 285 | 712 | 0.2 | 0.3 | 0.2 | 16 | 10 | 6 |
| | 2000 | 2.3 | 1.4 | 3.2 | 805 | 234 | 570 | 0.2 | 0.2 | 0.2 | 12 | 6 | 5 |
| **Oceania** | | | | | | | | | | | | | |
| Fiji | 1980 | 17.6 | 13.4 | 21.8 | 68 | 26 | 42 | 4.9 | 4.0 | 5.9 | 6 | 2 | 4 |
| | 1985 | 13.8 | 10.5 | 17.2 | 59 | 22 | 36 | 3.2 | 2.7 | 3.7 | 4 | 1 | 2 |
| | 1990 | 11.3 | 8.4 | 14.3 | 50 | 19 | 31 | 2.1 | 1.8 | 2.4 | 2 | 1 | 1 |
| | 1995 | 8.9 | 6.5 | 11.4 | 44 | 16 | 28 | 1.4 | 1.2 | 1.5 | 2 | 0 | 1 |
| | 2000 | 7.1 | 5.0 | 9.1 | 39 | 14 | 25 | 0.8 | 0.7 | 1.0 | 1 | 0 | 0 |
| Papua New Guinea | 1980 | 41.8 | 30.0 | 54.8 | 736 | 277 | 459 | ... | ... | ... | ... | ... | ... |
| | 1985 | 36.5 | 25.6 | 48.3 | 730 | 269 | 461 | ... | ... | ... | ... | ... | ... |
| | 1990 | 31.9 | 22.1 | 42.5 | 731 | 264 | 467 | ... | ... | ... | ... | ... | ... |
| | 1995 | 27.8 | 19.0 | 37.3 | 724 | 256 | 467 | ... | ... | ... | ... | ... | ... |
| | 2000 | 24.0 | 16.3 | 32.3 | 710 | 248 | 462 | ... | ... | ... | ... | ... | ... |

**General note**

For general explanations and definitions, please refer to the beginning of this chapter.

**Note générale**

Pour les explications et définitions générales, prière de se référer au début de ce chapitre.

**Nota general**

Para las explicaciones y definiciones generales, referirse al comienzo de este capítulo.

Educational attainment    II.3
Niveau d'instruction
Nivel de instrucción

## II.3   Percentage distribution of population aged 25 years and over by educational attainment

Répartition en pourcentage de la population âgée de 25 ans et plus selon le niveau d'instruction

Distribución porcentual de la población de 25 años y más según el nivel de instrucción

| Country / Pays / País | Yaer / Année / Año | | Sex / Sexe / Sexo | Population aged 25 years and over / Population âgée de 25 ans et plus / Población de 25 años y más | No schooling / Sans scolarité / Sin escolaridad | Primary / Primaire / Primaria Incomplete / Non complété / Incompleta | Primary Completed / Complété / Completa | Secondary Lower secondary / Premier cycle secondaire / Primer ciclo secundaria | Secondary Upper secondary / Deuxième cycle secondaire / Segundo ciclo secundaria | Post-secondary / Post-secondaire / Post-secundaria |
|---|---|---|---|---|---|---|---|---|---|---|
| **Africa** | | | | | | | | | | |
| Benin | 1992 | | MF | 1 700 914 | 78.5 | 10.8 | —> | 8.2 | —> | 1.3 |
| Botswana | (1) 1981 | Total | MF | 569 765 | 43.2 | 35.1 | 14.6 | 4.4 | 1.8 | 0.9 |
| | | | F | 311 706 | 39.8 | 38.4 | 15.6 | 4.3 | 1.4 | 0.5 |
| | | Urban | MF | 114 274 | 23.3 | 32.0 | 25.5 | 10.1 | 6.1 | 3.0 |
| | | | F | 54 253 | 19.4 | 35.3 | 27.3 | 10.6 | 5.5 | 2.0 |
| | | Rural | MF | 455 491 | 48.1 | 35.9 | 11.9 | 3.0 | 0.7 | 0.4 |
| | | | F | 257 453 | 44.1 | 39.1 | 13.1 | 3.0 | 0.5 | 0.2 |
| | (2) 1991 | Total | MF | 1 133 131 | 30.1 | 52.1 | —> | 16.0 | —> | 2.0 |
| | | Urban | MF | 255 134 | 16.1 | 50.4 | —> | 28.4 | —> | 5.2 |
| | | Rural | MF | 605 619 | 38.1 | 51.9 | —> | 9.5 | —> | 0.7 |
| | | Urban village | MF | 272 378 | 25.3 | 54.1 | —> | 18.8 | —> | 2.0 |
| | (3) 1993 | Total | MF | 1 350 899 | 20.4 | 44.1 | —> | 19.8 | —> | 1.4 |
| | | | F | 716 615 | 19.2 | 45.2 | —> | 21.6 | —> | 1.1 |
| | | Urban | MF | 316 139 | 11.2 | 42.1 | —> | 31.2 | —> | 3.8 |
| | | | F | 163 623 | 9.4 | 42.4 | —> | 34.1 | —> | 2.7 |
| | | Rural | MF | 704 317 | 26.5 | 44.4 | —> | 12.4 | —> | 0.5 |
| | | | F | 370 031 | 25.8 | 45.7 | —> | 13.6 | —> | 0.5 |
| | | Urban village | MF | 330 443 | 16.4 | 45.2 | —> | 24.7 | —> | 0.9 |
| | | | F | 182 961 | 14.5 | 46.7 | —> | 26.7 | —> | 0.8 |
| Burundi | 1990 | | MF | 1 897 323 | 75.4 | 19.9 | —> | 2.5 | —> | 0.6 |
| | | | F | 1 001 183 | 85.5 | 11.3 | —> | 1.6 | —> | 0.2 |
| Central African Republic | 1988 | | MF | 920 929 | 70.7 | 19.5 | —> | 7.3 | —> | 2.0 |
| | | | F | 481 154 | 82.6 | 12.9 | —> | 3.2 | —> | 0.8 |
| Congo | 1984 | | MF | 646 626 | 58.8 | 13.0 | 8.5 | 11.0 | 5.9 | 3.0 |
| | | | F | 345 173 | 72.0 | 10.0 | 5.6 | 8.2 | 3.0 | 1.1 |
| Côte d'Ivoire (4) | 1988 | | MF | 739 179 | - | 48.2 | —> | 43.1 | —> | 8.7 |
| | | | F | 217 251 | - | 58.2 | —> | 36.4 | —> | 5.4 |
| Democratic Rep. of the Congo | 1984 | | MF | 10 439 400 | 52.4 | 30.3 | —> | 14.6 | —> | 1.3 |
| | | | F | 5 489 500 | 70.4 | 21.2 | —> | 6.2 | —> | 0.3 |
| Egypt (5)(6) | 1986 | Total | MF | 19 441 903 | 64.1 | 16.5 | —> | 14.8 | —> | 4.6 |
| | | | F | 9 721 464 | 78.6 | 10.3 | —> | 9.3 | —> | 1.8 |
| | | Urban | MF | 9 089 987 | 47.8 | 21.6 | —> | 22.4 | —> | 8.2 |
| | | | F | 4 427 377 | 61.8 | 17.5 | —> | 17.1 | —> | 3.6 |
| | | Rural | MF | 10 351 916 | 78.4 | 12.0 | —> | 8.1 | —> | 1.5 |
| | | | F | 5 294 087 | 92.6 | 4.3 | —> | 2.8 | —> | 0.2 |
| Guinea-Bissau (7)(8) | 1979 | | MF | 483 336 | 91.1 | 7.5 | 0.5 | 0.6 | 0.2 | 0.1 |
| Kenya (9) | 1979 | | MF | 4 818 310 | 58.6 | 32.2 | —> | 7.9 | 1.3 | —> |
| | | | F | 2 442 417 | 73.0 | 23.0 | —> | 3.4 | 0.6 | —> |
| Ethiopia | 1994 | Total | MF | 18 716 940 | 80.1 | 6.3 | 1.5 | 2.1 | 3.4 | 1.0 |
| | | | F | 9 481 915 | 89.2 | 3.5 | 0.7 | 1.0 | 1.8 | 0.5 |
| | | Urban | MF | 2 726 527 | 42.5 | 14.5 | 4.3 | 7.3 | 17.3 | 6.2 |
| | | | F | 1 406 641 | 56.3 | 13.4 | 3.1 | 5.0 | 10.9 | 3.1 |
| | | Rural | MF | 15 990 413 | 86.5 | 4.9 | 1.0 | 1.2 | 1.0 | 0.1 |
| | | | F | 8 075 274 | 94.9 | 1.7 | 0.3 | 0.3 | 0.2 | 0.0 |

II.3  Educational attainment
Niveau d'instruction
Nivel de instrucción

| Country / Pays / País | | Year / Année / Año | | Sex / Sexe / Sexo | Population aged 25 years and over / Population âgée de 25 ans et plus / Población de 25 años y más | No schooling / Sans scolarité / Sin escolaridad | Highest level of education attained / Niveau d'instruction atteint / Nivel de instrucción alcanzado | | | | Post-secondary / Post-secondaire / Post-secundaria |
|---|---|---|---|---|---|---|---|---|---|---|---|
| | | | | | | | Primary / Primaire / Primaria | | Secondary / Secondaire / Secundaria | | |
| | | | | | | | Incomplete / Non complété / Incompleta | Completed / Complété / Completa | Lower secondary / Premier cycle secondaire / Primer ciclo secundaria | Upper secondary / Deuxième cycle secondaire / Segundo ciclo secundaria | |
| Libyan Arab Jamahiriya | (10) | 1984 | | MF | 966 774 | 59.7 | 15.4 | 8.5 | 5.2 | 8.5 | 2.7 |
| | | | | F | 493 212 | 79.4 | 6.4 | 3.0 | 1.6 | 4.3 | 5.2 |
| Malawi | | 1987 | | MF | 2 859 826 | 55.0 | 31.8 | 8.0 | 2.7 | 2.1 | 0.4 |
| | | | | F | 1 495 441 | 71.5 | 22.7 | 3.7 | 1.2 | 0.8 | 0.2 |
| Mauritania | | 1988 | | MF | 679 667 | 60.8 | 34.1 | —> | 3.8 | —> | 1.3 |
| | | | | F | 352 864 | 68.3 | 29.7 | —> | 1.7 | —> | 0.3 |
| Mauritius | | 1983 | | MF | 440 134 | 23.9 | 52.0 | —> | 20.6 | —> | 3.6 |
| | | | | F | 230 126 | 32.4 | 48.1 | —> | 17.5 | —> | 1.9 |
| | | 1990 | | MF | 540 244 | 18.3 | 42.6 | 6.1 | 7.2 | 23.9 | 1.9 |
| | | | | F | 274 291 | 25.8 | 42.1 | 6.1 | 5.9 | 19.2 | 0.9 |
| Mozambique | (6) | 1980 | | MF | 4 242 819 | 81.0 | 18.1 | —> | 0.8 | —> | 0.1 |
| | | | | F | 2 257 630 | 94.0 | 5.7 | —> | 0.3 | —> | 0.0 |
| Namibia | (11) | 1991 | Total | MF | 340 552 | ... | 49.1 | —> | 43.8 | —> | 4.0 |
| | | | | F | 172 581 | ... | 50.0 | —> | 43.7 | —> | 3.7 |
| | | | Urban | MF | 165 393 | ... | 33.2 | —> | 56.3 | —> | 5.8 |
| | | | | F | 76 869 | ... | 30.8 | —> | 59.4 | —> | 5.7 |
| | | | Rural | MF | 175 159 | ... | 64.2 | —> | 32.0 | —> | 2.2 |
| | | | | F | 95 712 | ... | 65.4 | —> | 31.2 | —> | 2.1 |
| Sao Tome and Principe | (6) | 1981 | | MF | 33 308 | 56.6 | 18.0 | 19.3 | 4.6 | 1.3 | 0.3 |
| | | | | F | 17 330 | 74.6 | 11.8 | 9.7 | 3.0 | 0.7 | 0.1 |
| Seychelles | | 1987 | | MF | 30 912 | 12.1 | 44.9 | —> | 35.7 | —> | 4.6 |
| Sierra Leone | (2) | 1985 | | MF | 1 315 897 | 64.5 | 18.7 | 1.8 | 9.7 | 3.8 | 1.5 |
| South Africa | (12) | 1980 | | MF | 10 460 159 | 32.0 | 28.0 | 11.8 | 16.8 | 10.0 | 1.3 |
| | (12) | 1985 | | MF | 10 388 428 | 24.8 | 41.6 | 4.8 | 20.6 | 5.9 | 2.3 |
| | | | | F | 5 288 066 | 26.9 | 40.7 | 4.6 | 20.0 | 6.2 | 1.5 |
| | (3) | 1994 | Total | MF | 40 316 996 | 24.6 | 28.0 | 6.6 | 21.3 | 18.0 | 1.5 |
| | | | Asian | MF | 1 038 852 | 14.6 | 19.7 | 5.7 | 27.3 | 30.8 | 2.1 |
| | | | Black | MF | 30 613 468 | 27.9 | 31.3 | 7.2 | 19.7 | 13.4 | 0.5 |
| | | | Coloured | MF | 3 472 178 | 19.7 | 28.0 | 9.2 | 27.9 | 14.9 | 0.5 |
| | | | White | MF | 5 192 498 | 10.4 | 9.8 | 1.8 | 25.1 | 44.5 | 8.3 |
| | (13) | 1995 | | MF | 22 100 000 | 13.0 | 17.1 | 6.9 | 26.7 | 25.7 | 8.8 |
| | | | | F | 11 519 000 | 15.1 | 17.3 | 7.2 | 26.6 | 23.9 | 8.0 |
| Sudan | (10)(14) | 1983 | Total | MF | 6 492 263 | 76.7 | 18.6 | —> | 1.9 | 2.0 | 0.8 |
| | | | | F | 3 351 247 | 88.8 | 9.1 | —> | 0.9 | 0.9 | 0.3 |
| | | | Urban | MF | 1 499 492 | 54.3 | 31.6 | —> | 5.4 | 6.1 | 2.7 |
| | | | | F | 695 700 | 71.3 | 21.0 | —> | 3.3 | 3.3 | 1.1 |
| | | | Rural | MF | 4 992 771 | 83.4 | 14.7 | —> | 0.9 | 0.8 | 0.2 |
| | | | | F | 2 655 547 | 93.4 | 5.9 | —> | 0.3 | 0.2 | 0.1 |
| Swaziland | | 1986 | | MF | 221 672 | 42.0 | 24.0 | 10.5 | 13.2 | 6.3 | 3.3 |
| | | | | F | 100 013 | 38.0 | 22.9 | 10.8 | 14.8 | 8.4 | 4.2 |
| Togo | | 1981 | | MF | 1 084 488 | 76.5 | 13.5 | —> | 8.7 | —> | 1.3 |
| | | | | F | 604 296 | 87.3 | 7.9 | —> | 4.2 | —> | 0.5 |
| Tunisia | | 1980 | | MF | 2 379 900 | 72.1 | 17.2 | —> | 4.1 | 4.8 | 1.8 |
| | | | | F | 1 205 800 | 85.0 | 9.5 | —> | 2.3 | 2.5 | 0.7 |
| | | 1984 | Total | MF | 2 714 100 | 66.3 | 18.9 | —> | 12.0 | —> | 2.8 |
| | | | | F | 1 347 700 | 79.0 | 12.7 | —> | 6.9 | —> | 1.3 |
| | | | Urban | MF | 1 504 300 | 53.4 | 23.7 | —> | 18.2 | —> | 4.7 |
| | | | | F | 746 600 | 67.9 | 18.2 | —> | 11.6 | —> | 2.3 |
| | | | Rural | MF | 1 209 800 | 82.3 | 12.8 | —> | 4.4 | —> | 0.6 |
| | | | | F | 601 100 | 92.7 | 5.9 | —> | 1.2 | —> | 0.2 |
| Uganda | | 1991 | | MF | 5 455 582 | 46.1 | 41.4 | —> | 8.9 | 1.3 | 0.5 |
| | | | | F | 2 791 949 | 60.8 | 32.4 | —> | 5.6 | 0.5 | 0.2 |
| United Rep. of Tanzania | (15) | 1988 | Total | MF | 3 598 169 | 0.0 | 89.7 | —> | 7.8 | 0.6 | 2.0 |
| | | | | F | 1 285 858 | 0.0 | 92.1 | —> | 6.4 | 0.3 | 1.2 |
| | | | Urban | MF | 1 055 633 | 0.0 | 78.2 | —> | 15.8 | 1.6 | 4.4 |
| | | | | F | 396 201 | 0.0 | 82.6 | —> | 13.9 | 0.8 | 2.8 |
| | | | Rural | MF | 2 542 536 | 0.0 | 94.4 | —> | 4.4 | 0.2 | 1.0 |
| | | | | F | 889 657 | 0.0 | 96.4 | —> | 3.1 | 0.1 | 0.5 |

Educational attainment II.3
Niveau d'instruction
Nivel de instrucción

| Country / Pays / País | Yaer / Année / Año | | Sex / Sexe / Sexo | Population aged 25 years and over / Population âgée de 25 ans et plus / Población de 25 años y más | Highest level of education attained / Niveau d'instruction atteint / Nivel de instrucción alcanzado | | | | | |
|---|---|---|---|---|---|---|---|---|---|---|
| | | | | | No schooling / Sans scolarité / Sin escolaridad | Primary / Primaire / Primaria | | Secondary / Secondaire / Secundaria | | Post-secondary / Post-secondaire / Post-secundaria |
| | | | | | | Incomplete / Non complété / Incompleta | Completed / Complété / Completa | Lower secondary / Premier cycle secondaire / Primer ciclo secundaria | Upper secondary / Deuxième cycle secondaire / Segundo ciclo secundaria | |
| Zambia | 1980 | Total | MF | 1 880 124 | 49.8 | 37.0 | —> | 12.8 | —> | 0.4 |
| | | | F | 961 086 | 64.2 | 29.6 | —> | 6.0 | —> | 0.2 |
| | | Urban | MF | 744 957 | 34.5 | 40.8 | —> | 23.8 | —> | 0.9 |
| | | | F | 314 509 | 45.1 | 40.5 | —> | 14.0 | —> | 0.4 |
| | | Rural | MF | 1 135 167 | 59.9 | 34.4 | —> | 5.6 | —> | 0.1 |
| | | | F | 646 577 | 73.6 | 24.3 | —> | 2.1 | —> | 0.0 |
| | (16)(17) 1993 | Total | MF | ... | 18.6 | 54.8 | —> | 12.9 | 12.2 | 1.5 |
| | | | F | ... | 18.3 | 57 6 | —> | 13.4 | 9.8 | 1.0 |
| | | Urban | MF | ... | 8.9 | 46.5 | —> | 19.1 | 22.4 | 3.1 |
| | | Rural | MF | ... | 26.7 | 59.6 | —> | 8.2 | 4.9 | 0.5 |
| Zimbabwe | 1992 | | MF | 3 445 195 | 22.3 | 53.2 | —> | 19.4 | —> | 4.9 |
| | | | F | 1 801 364 | 29.2 | 54.2 | —> | 13.1 | —> | 3.4 |
| **North America** | | | | | | | | | | |
| Aruba (18) | 1991 | | MF | 41 180 | 14.9 | 37.3 | —> | 37.7 | —> | 7.0 |
| | | | F | 18 751 | 14.9 | 36.9 | —> | 39.7 | —> | 5.5 |
| Bahamas | 1990 | | MF | 104 472 | 3.5 | 25.4 | —> | 57.7 | —> | 13.5 |
| | | | F | 54 844 | 3.2 | 25.6 | —> | 57.9 | —> | 13.4 |
| Barbados | 1980 | | MF | 116 874 | 0.8 | 63.5 | —> | 32.3 | —> | 3.3 |
| | | | MF | 68 807 | 0.9 | 65.2 | —> | 32.0 | —> | 1.9 |
| Belize | 1980 | | MF | 45 596 | 10.7 | 75.3 | —> | 11.7 | —> | 2.3 |
| | | | F | 22 632 | 10.5 | 76.6 | —> | 11.7 | —> | 1.2 |
| | 1991 | | MF | 66 520 | 13.0 | 64.3 | —> | 14.9 | —> | 6.6 |
| | | | F | 32 586 | 12.8 | 65.4 | —> | 15.1 | —> | 5.8 |
| Bermuda | 1991 | | MF | 38 873 | 0.5 | 18.2 | —> | 63.0 | —> | 18.4 |
| | | | F | 20 373 | 0.4 | 17.1 | —> | 65.0 | —> | 17.5 |
| British Virgin Islands | 1980 | | MF | 5 136 | 2.4 | 65.8 | —> | 23.3 | —> | 8.5 |
| | | | F | 2 437 | 2.4 | 64.7 | —> | 25.4 | —> | 7.4 |
| | 1991 | | MF | 8 986 | 0.7 | 43.2 | —> | 34.8 | 6.4 | 13.6 |
| | | | F | 4 297 | 0.6 | 39.4 | —> | 37.6 | 6.8 | 14.1 |
| Canada | 1981 | Total | MF | 13 971 280 | 2.0 | 14.2 | 9.5 | 36.8 | —> | 37.4 |
| | | | F | 7 161 655 | 2.2 | 14.2 | 9.4 | 39.6 | —> | 34.7 |
| | | Urban | MF | 10 743 370 | 1.9 | 13.1 | 8.5 | 39.4 | —> | 37.1 |
| | | | F | 5 597 975 | 2.2 | 13.6 | 8.7 | 39.1 | —> | 36.3 |
| | | Rural | MF | 3 227 895 | 2.3 | 18.1 | 12.7 | 37.6 | —> | 29.3 |
| | | | F | 1 563 690 | 2.0 | 16.2 | 11.9 | 41.0 | —> | 28.8 |
| | (19) 1986 | Total | MF | 15 472 920 | 1.2 | 5.0 | 14.9 | 34.7 | 24.8 | 19.3 |
| | | | F | 7 917 050 | 1.4 | 4.9 | 14.5 | 37.4 | 24.9 | 17.0 |
| | | Urban | MF | 11 984 850 | 1.2 | 4.8 | 13.4 | 33.8 | 25.5 | 21.4 |
| | | | F | 6 220 355 | 1.4 | 4.9 | 13.3 | 36.4 | 25.6 | 18.3 |
| | | Rural | MF | 3 488 070 | 1.2 | 5.9 | 20.3 | 37.9 | 22.3 | 12.3 |
| | | | F | 1 696 695 | 1.2 | 4.9 | 18.9 | 41.1 | 22.0 | 12.0 |
| | 1991 | Total | MF | 17 471 920 | 1.0 | 4.0 | 11.7 | 34.3 | 27.7 | 21.4 |
| | | | F | 8 996 970 | 1.1 | 4.0 | 11.6 | 35.7 | 28.0 | 19.6 |
| | | Urban | MF | 13 514 580 | 1.0 | 3.8 | 10.3 | 32.9 | 28.2 | 23.7 |
| | | | F | 7 056 000 | 1.2 | 4.0 | 10.8 | 34.3 | 28.5 | 21.2 |
| | | Rural | MF | 3 957 340 | 0.9 | 4.5 | 16.1 | 39.1 | 25.8 | 13.6 |
| | | | F | 1 940 970 | 0.8 | 3.7 | 14.7 | 40.6 | 26.2 | 13.9 |
| Cayman Islands | 1989 | | MF | 15 270 | 0.0 | 45.4 | —> | 40.6 | —> | 14.2 |
| | | | F | 7 922 | 0.0 | 45.8 | —> | 43.1 | —> | 11.3 |
| Cuba (20) | 1981 | Total | MF | 3 013 315 | 3.7 | 22.6 | 27.6 | 40.2 | —> | 5.9 |
| | | | F | 1 511 380 | 4.1 | 27.0 | 28.4 | 35.9 | —> | 4.5 |
| | | Urban | MF | 2 165 853 | 2.0 | 16.8 | 26.0 | 47.4 | —> | 7.8 |
| | | Rural | MF | 847 462 | 8.1 | 37.5 | 31.6 | 21.9 | —> | 1.0 |
| Dominica | 1981 | | MF | 27 508 | 6.6 | 80.5 | —> | 11.1 | —> | 1.7 |
| | | | F | 14 581 | 6.8 | 81.6 | —> | 10.6 | —> | 1.0 |
| El Salvador | (6)(21) 1980 | Total | MF | 3 132 400 | 30.2 | 60.7 | —> | 6.9 | —> | 2.3 |
| | | | F | 1 635 100 | 33.1 | 58.3 | —> | 6.6 | —> | 1.9 |
| | | Urban | MF | 1 405 000 | 15.5 | 66.2 | —> | 13.5 | —> | 4.8 |
| | | | F | 776 200 | 19.6 | 64.0 | —> | 12.5 | —> | 3.9 |
| | | Rural | MF | 1 727 400 | 42.2 | 56.2 | —> | 1.4 | —> | 0.2 |
| | | | F | 858 900 | 45.4 | 53.1 | —> | 1.3 | —> | 0.2 |

II.3   Educational attainment
Niveau d'instruction
Nivel de instrucción

| Country<br>Pays<br>País | Yaer<br>Année<br>Año | | Sex<br>Sexe<br>Sexo | Population aged 25 years and over<br>Population âgée de 25 ans et plus<br>Población de 25 años y más | Highest level of education attained<br>Niveau d'instruction atteint<br>Nivel de instrucción alcanzado | | | | | |
|---|---|---|---|---|---|---|---|---|---|---|
| | | | | | No schooling<br>Sans scolarité<br>Sin escolaridad | Primary / Primaire / Primaria | | Secondary / Secondaire / Secundaria | | Post-secondary<br>Post-secondaire<br>Post-secundaria |
| | | | | | | Incomplete<br>Non complété<br>Incompleta | Completed<br>Complété<br>Completa | Lower secondary<br>Premier cycle secondaire<br>Primer ciclo secundaria | Upper secondary<br>Deuxième cycle secondaire<br>Segundo ciclo secundaria | |
| El Salvador (cont) (6) | 1992 | | MF | 2 064 258 | 37.2 | 46.0 | —> | 9.8 | —> | 6.4 |
| | | | F | 1 102 301 | 38.6 | 45.8 | —> | 9.7 | —> | 5.3 |
| Grenada | 1981 | | MF | 33 401 | 2.2 | 87.8 | —> | 8.5 | —> | 1.5 |
| | | | F | 18 362 | 2.3 | 88.3 | —> | 8.5 | —> | 0.8 |
| Guadeloupe | 1982 | | MF | 150 253 | 10.7 | 54.6 | —> | 29.5 | —> | 5.2 |
| | | | F | 79 984 | 10.3 | 53.6 | —> | 31.8 | —> | 4.2 |
| Guatemala | 1981 | | MF | 2 060 399 | 55.0 | 27.3 | 8.6 | 2.9 | 4.0 | 2.2 |
| | | | F | 1 052 347 | 61.6 | 22.1 | 7.9 | 2.6 | 4.6 | 1.2 |
| Haiti | 1982 | | MF | 2 103 124 | 77.0 | 15.2 | —> | 7.2 | —> | 0.7 |
| | | | F | 1 093 992 | 81.3 | 12.3 | —> | 5.9 | —> | 0.4 |
| | 1986 | Total | MF | 2 229 501 | 59.5 | 30.5 | —> | 9.3 | —> | 0.7 |
| | | Urban | MF | 551 865 | 31.6 | 37.1 | —> | 28.9 | —> | 2.4 |
| | | Rural | MF | 1 677 636 | 68.6 | 28.4 | —> | 2.8 | —> | 0.2 |
| Honduras (23) | 1983 | Total | MF | ... | 33.5 | 51.3 | —> | 4.3 | 7.6 | 3.3 |
| | | | F | ... | 34.1 | 51.1 | —> | 4.4 | 8.3 | 2.2 |
| | | Urban | MF | ... | 17.3 | 51.8 | —> | 8.2 | 15.4 | 7.4 |
| | | | F | ... | 19.4 | 51.8 | —> | 8.4 | 15.8 | 4.6 |
| | | Rural | MF | ... | 46.1 | 51.0 | —> | 1.2 | 1.6 | 0.1 |
| | | | F | ... | 46.9 | 50.3 | —> | 1.0 | 1.7 | 0.1 |
| Jamaica | 1982 | | MF | 703 714 | 3.2 | 79.8 | —> | 15.0 | —> | 2.0 |
| | | | F | 365 612 | 3.0 | 79.4 | —> | 15.8 | —> | 1.8 |
| | (24) 1991 | | MF | 970 086 | 0.0 | 67.5 | —> | 29.9 | —> | 2.7 |
| | | | F | 507 293 | 0.0 | 65.6 | —> | 32.0 | —> | 2.6 |
| Martinique | 1982 | | MF | 157 574 | 8.1 | 55.5 | —> | 30.9 | —> | 5.6 |
| | | | F | 85 288 | 6.7 | 55.4 | —> | 33.2 | —> | 4.7 |
| Mexico | 1980 | | MF | 24 309 593 | 34.2 | 31.4 | 17.2 | 11.8 | —> | 5.3 |
| | | | F | 12 455 708 | 37.1 | 30.7 | 18.0 | 11.5 | —> | 2.7 |
| | 1990 | | MF | 31 188 180 | 18.8 | 28.6 | 19.9 | 12.7 | 10.7 | 9.2 |
| | | | F | 16 206 466 | 21.4 | 29.0 | 19.9 | 12.1 | 11.1 | 6.5 |
| Montserrat | 1980 | | MF | 5 544 | 1.7 | 84.6 | —> | 7.9 | —> | 5.8 |
| | | | F | 3 023 | 1.7 | 84.4 | —> | 9.9 | —> | 4.0 |
| Netherlands Antilles | 1981 | | MF | 115 087 | 61.3 | —> | —> | 32.2 | —> | 6.4 |
| | | | F | 62 076 | 67.3 | —> | —> | 27.8 | —> | 4.9 |
| | (18) 1992 | | MF | 111 592 | 1.7 | 34.4 | —> | 54.2 | —> | 8.8 |
| | | | F | 67 942 | 1.7 | 34.2 | —> | 56.6 | —> | 6.7 |
| Panama | 1980 | Total | MF | 725 878 | 18.3 | 27.1 | 23.2 | 11.7 | 11.5 | 8.3 |
| | | | F | 358 714 | 19.1 | 26.3 | 23.1 | 11.6 | 12.2 | 7.8 |
| | | Urban | MF | 391 047 | 7.0 | 17.9 | 25.1 | 17.7 | 18.2 | 14.1 |
| | | | F | 205 098 | 7.5 | 18.8 | 25.5 | 17.0 | 18.7 | 12.5 |
| | | Rural | MF | 334 831 | 31.5 | 37.7 | 20.9 | 4.7 | 3.6 | 1.5 |
| | | | F | 153 616 | 34.4 | 36.3 | 19.8 | 4.5 | 3.6 | 1.4 |
| | (25) 1990 | | MF | 1 035 339 | 11.7 | 20.2 | 21.8 | 12.6 | 16.4 | 13.2 |
| | | | F | 513 435 | 12.4 | 19.2 | 20.3 | 12.1 | 17.1 | 13.5 |
| Puerto Rico (19) | 1980 | | MF | 1 577 686 | 8.0 | 17.8 | 11.4 | 16.4 | 27.9 | 18.4 |
| | | | F | 839 399 | 9.1 | 17.8 | 11.9 | 15.7 | 27.2 | 18.3 |
| | 1990 | | MF | 1 952 297 | 4.6 | 31.0 | —> | 35.9 | —> | 28.7 |
| | | | F | 1 040 280 | 5.1 | 30.7 | —> | 34.2 | —> | 30.2 |
| St. Kitts and Nevis | 1980 | | MF | 16 771 | 1.1 | 29.0 | —> | 66.6 | —> | 2.3 |
| | | | F | 9 267 | 1.0 | 29.8 | —> | 67.0 | —> | 1.4 |
| St. Lucia | 1980 | | MF | 39 599 | 17.5 | 74.5 | —> | 6.8 | —> | 1.3 |
| | | | F | 21 756 | 16.8 | 75.6 | —> | 6.8 | —> | 0.7 |
| | 1991 | | MF | 49 031 | 0.0 | 75.5 | —> | 21.2 | —> | 3.4 |
| | | | F | 26 099 | 0.0 | 74.4 | —> | 23.3 | —> | 2.5 |
| St. Pierre and (26)<br>Miquelon | 1982 | | MF | 4 282 | 0.8 | 53.2 | —> | 40.8 | —> | 4.9 |
| | | | F | 2 172 | 0.9 | 55.0 | —> | 40.4 | —> | 3.5 |

Educational attainment II.3
Niveau d'instruction
Nivel de instrucción

| Country / Pays / País | | Yaer / Année / Año | Sex / Sexe / Sexo | Population aged 25 years and over / Population âgée de 25 ans et plus / Población de 25 años y más | No schooling / Sans scolarité / Sin escolaridad | Primary / Primaire / Primaria — Incomplete / Non complété / Incompleta | Primary — Completed / Complété / Completa | Secondary / Secondaire / Secundaria — Lower secondary / Premier cycle secondaire / Primer ciclo secundaria | Secondary — Upper secondary / Deuxième cycle secondaire / Segundo ciclo secundaria | Post-secondary / Post-secondaire / Post-secundaria |
|---|---|---|---|---|---|---|---|---|---|---|
| St. Vincent and the Grenadines | | 1980 | MF | 32 444 | 2.4 | 88.0 | —> | 8.2 | —> | 1.4 |
| | | | F | 17 893 | 2.5 | 88.6 | —> | 8.0 | —> | 0.9 |
| Trinidad and Tobago | | 1980 | MF | 408 215 | 1.3 | 29.4 | 42.6 | 19.7 | 4.0 | 2.9 |
| | | | F | 201 148 | 1.3 | 29.9 | 42.4 | 20.4 | 4.1 | 1.9 |
| | | 1990 | MF | 542 425 | 4.5 | 56.8 | —> | 32.3 | —> | 3.4 |
| | | | F | 275 195 | 5.9 | 55.2 | —> | 33.2 | —> | 2.7 |
| Turks and Caicos Islands | | 1980 | MF | 2 859 | 0.9 | 74.6 | —> | 16.9 | —> | 7.7 |
| | | | F | 1 545 | 1.0 | 77.5 | —> | 16.4 | —> | 5.1 |
| U. S. Virgin (28) Islands | | 1980 | MF | 44 986 | 1.5 | 26.3 | 7.8 | 14.4 | 25.7 | 24.4 |
| | | | F | 24 145 | 1.5 | 26.1 | 7.9 | 14.3 | 26.6 | 23.5 |
| United States | (7) | 1980 | MF | 132 835 687 | 1.0 | 2.6 | 3.7 | 15.5 | 45.2 | 31.9 |
| | | | F | 70 419 233 | 1.0 | 2.3 | 3.7 | 15.8 | 49.1 | 28.1 |
| | | 1981 | MF | 132 899 000 | 3.3 | —> | 64.6 | —> | —> | 32.2 |
| | | | F | 70 390 000 | 3.1 | —> | 68.8 | —> | —> | 28.0 |
| | (27) | 1990 | MF | 158 868 436 | 1.2 | 9.1 | —> | 44.4 | —> | 45.2 |
| | (27) | 1994 | MF | 164 511 000 | 0.6 | 8.2 | —> | 44.6 | —> | 46.5 |
| | | | F | 85 972 000 | 0.6 | 8.1 | —> | 46.8 | —> | 44.6 |
| **South America** | | | | | | | | | | |
| Argentina | | 1980 | MF | 14 913 575 | 7.1 | 33.4 | 33.0 | 20.4 | —> | 6.1 |
| | | | F | 7 711 356 | 6.7 | 32.1 | 35.2 | 20.1 | —> | 5.8 |
| | | 1991 | MF | 17 340 713 | 5.7 | 22.3 | 34.6 | 25.3 | —> | 12.0 |
| | | | F | 9 074 589 | 6.2 | 22.8 | 34.7 | 24.5 | —> | 11.8 |
| Bolivia (29) | | 1992 Total | MF | 2 533 393 | 23.5 | 20.4 | 6.6 | 15.2 | 15.7 | 9.9 |
| | | | F | 1 314 371 | 31.9 | 19.5 | 5.9 | 12.5 | 13.2 | 7.9 |
| | | Urban | MF | 1 454 355 | 13.1 | 15.6 | 7.0 | 16.1 | 23.7 | 15.7 |
| | | | F | 769 608 | 18.4 | 17.5 | 7.1 | 15.2 | 20.8 | 12.6 |
| | | Rural | MF | 1 079 038 | 37.5 | 26.9 | 6.1 | 14.0 | 4.9 | 2.0 |
| | | | F | 544 763 | 50.9 | 22.3 | 4.1 | 8.7 | 2.5 | 1.2 |
| Brazil | | 1980 Total | MF | 48 310 722 | 32.9 | 50.4 | 4.9 | 6.9 | —> | 5.0 |
| | | | F | 24 576 023 | 35.2 | 48.8 | 4.6 | 7.2 | —> | 4.1 |
| | | Urban | MF | 34 355 259 | 22.8 | 54.7 | 6.5 | 9.2 | > | 6.8 |
| | | | F | 17 928 564 | 25.9 | 53.1 | 6.0 | 9.4 | —> | 5.6 |
| | | Rural | MF | 13 955 463 | 57.7 | 40.0 | 0.9 | 1.0 | —> | 0.4 |
| | | | F | 6 647 459 | 60.5 | 37.3 | 0.9 | 1.1 | —> | 0.3 |
| | (30)(21) | 1989 Total | MF | 110 157 487 | 18.7 | 57.0 | 6.9 | 11.9 | 5.5 | —> |
| | | | F | 56 707 493 | 18.7 | 56.3 | 6.9 | 12.7 | 5.4 | —> |
| | | Urban | MF | 83 338 354 | 13.3 | 56.6 | 8.2 | 14.7 | 7.2 | —> |
| | | | F | 43 726 380 | 14.1 | 55.5 | 8.1 | 15.4 | 6.8 | —> |
| | | Rural | MF | 26 819 133 | 35.4 | 58.1 | 2.8 | 3.2 | 0.5 | —> |
| | | | F | 12 981 113 | 34.1 | 59.0 | 2.9 | 3.5 | 0.5 | —> |
| Chile | | 1982 | MF | 5 204 698 | 9.4 | 56.6 | —> | 26.9 | —> | 7.2 |
| | | | F | 2 724 739 | 10.0 | 56.9 | —> | 27.1 | —> | 5.9 |
| | | 1992 | MF | ... | 5.8 | 48.0 | —> | 33.9 | —> | 12.3 |
| | | | F | ... | 6.3 | 48.6 | —> | 33.5 | —> | 11.6 |
| Colombia | | 1993 | MF | 15 088 203 | 11.9 | 27.3 | 18.3 | 13.3 | 16.7 | 10.4 |
| Ecuador | | 1982 | MF | 2 887 330 | 25.4 | 17.0 | 34.1 | 8.1 | 7.9 | 7.6 |
| | | | F | 1 457 435 | 29.6 | 16.8 | 31.1 | 8.3 | 8.7 | 5.6 |
| | | 1990 | MF | 3 953 452 | 1.7 | 43.7 | —> | 22.6 | —> | 12.7 |
| | | | F | 2 014 479 | 1.8 | 42.6 | —> | 22.2 | —> | 11.1 |
| French Guiana | | 1982 | MF | 34 145 | 20.8 | 40.5 | —> | 32.4 | —> | 6.4 |
| Guyana | | 1980 | MF | 270 849 | 8.1 | 72.9 | —> | 17.3 | —> | 1.8 |
| | | | F | 138 083 | 10.6 | 73.0 | —> | 15.5 | —> | 0.9 |
| Paraguay | | 1982 | MF | 1 139 583 | 14.1 | 51.1 | 15.5 | 9.0 | 7.0 | 3.4 |
| | | | F | 573 256 | 17.9 | 49.5 | 15.3 | 7.7 | 7.0 | 2.5 |
| | (22) | 1992 | MF | 2 427 485 | 7.0 | 38.4 | 22.8 | 12.8 | 12.2 | 6.6 |
| | | | F | 1 219 289 | 8.6 | 38.1 | 23.0 | 11.4 | 11.8 | 6.6 |

**II.3** Educational attainment
Niveau d'instruction
Nivel de instrucción

| Country<br><br>Pays<br><br>País | | Yaer<br><br>Année<br><br>Año | | Sex<br><br>Sexe<br><br>Sexo | Population aged 25 years and over<br><br>Population âgée de 25 ans et plus<br><br>Población de 25 años y más | Highest level of education attained<br>Niveau d'instruction atteint<br>Nivel de instrucción alcanzado | | | | | |
|---|---|---|---|---|---|---|---|---|---|---|---|
| | | | | | | No schooling<br><br>Sans scolarité<br><br>Sin escolaridad | Primary / Primaire / Primaria | | Secondary / Secondaire / Secundaria | | Post-secondary<br><br>Post-secondaire<br><br>Post-secundaria |
| | | | | | | | Incomplete<br>Non complété<br>Incompleta | Completed<br>Complété<br>Completa | Lower secondary<br>Premier cycle secondaire<br>Primer ciclo secundaria | Upper secondary<br>Deuxième cycle secondaire<br>Segundo ciclo secundaria | |
| Peru | | 1981 | | MF | 6 526 328 | 20.1 | 27.3 | 17.2 | 10.7 | 10.7 | 10.1 |
| | | | | F | 3 308 370 | 28.8 | 24.4 | 15.5 | 8.6 | 9.7 | 7.7 |
| | | 1993 | | MF | 9 394 681 | 16.4 | 34.7 | —> | 27.2 | —> | 20.5 |
| | | | | F | 4 799 689 | 23.4 | 33.3 | —> | 23.8 | —> | 18.2 |
| Uruguay | (31) | 1985 | | MF | 1 701 705 | 4.7 | 58.0 | —> | 29.2 | —> | 8.1 |
| | | | | F | 903 318 | 3.6 | 57.5 | —> | 30.0 | —> | 8.9 |
| | | 1996 | Total | MF | 2 242 251 | 3.4 | 53.6 | —> | 31.7 | —> | 10.1 |
| | | | | F | 1 191 012 | 3.4 | 52.4 | —> | 32.0 | —> | 11.2 |
| | | | Urban | MF | 2 052 497 | 3.3 | 52.0 | —> | 33.2 | —> | 10.5 |
| | | | | F | 1 111 667 | 3.2 | 51.1 | —> | 33.0 | —> | 11.7 |
| | | | Rural | MF | 189 754 | 4.2 | 71.8 | —> | 16.0 | —> | 5.6 |
| | | | | F | 79 345 | 5.2 | 70.6 | —> | 17.6 | —> | 4.5 |
| Venezuela | | 1981 | | MF | 5 542 852 | *23.5 | *47.2 | —> | *22.3 | —> | *7 |
| | | | | F | 2 802 602 | *26.4 | *46.2 | —> | *21.9 | —> | *5.5 |
| | (9) | 1990 | Total | MF | 7 680 427 | 21.2 | 55.0 | —> | 12.0 | —> | 11.8 |
| | | | | F | 3 930 584 | 22.9 | 53.8 | —> | 12.1 | —> | 11.3 |
| | | | Urban | MF | 6 591 116 | 17.2 | 55.9 | —> | 13.4 | —> | 13.5 |
| | | | | F | 3 442 360 | 19.3 | 54.7 | —> | 13.3 | —> | 12.6 |
| | | | Rural | MF | 1 089 311 | 45.2 | 49.8 | —> | 3.5 | —> | 1.6 |
| | | | | F | 488 224 | 48.1 | 46.8 | —> | 3.6 | —> | 1.5 |
| | (21) | 1991 | Nat. estimates | MF | 14 789 619 | 9.0 | 45.4 | —> | 36.7 | —> | 9.1 |
| | (21) | 1991 | Nat. estimates | F | 7 353 817 | 10.0 | 43.2 | —> | 38.1 | —> | 8.9 |
| | (6)(21) | 1992 | Nat. estimates | MF | 15 201 949 | 8.5 | 44.5 | —> | 37.6 | —> | 9.5 |
| | (6)(21) | 1992 | Nat. estimates | F | 7 567 476 | 9.6 | 42.0 | —> | 39.1 | —> | 9.5 |
| | (6)(21) | 1993 | Nat. estimates | MF | 15 628 682 | 8.0 | 43.7 | —> | 38.3 | —> | 10.1 |
| | (6)(21) | 1993 | Nat. estimates | F | 7 778 295 | 9.0 | 41.2 | —> | 39.7 | —> | 10.2 |
| **Asia** | | | | | | | | | | | |
| Afghanistan | | 1979 | Total | MF | 4 891 473 | 89.0 | 6.5 | 0.3 | 1.1 | —> | 3.0 |
| | | | | F | 2 405 187 | 97.6 | 1.4 | 0.1 | 0.3 | —> | 0.6 |
| | | | Urban | MF | 717 983 | 72.1 | 12.0 | 1.1 | 3.5 | —> | 11.4 |
| | | | | F | 335 968 | 88.2 | 5.7 | 0.8 | 1.6 | —> | 3.7 |
| | | | Rural | MF | 4 173 490 | 92.0 | 5.5 | 0.2 | 0.7 | —> | 1.6 |
| | | | | F | 2 069 219 | 99.2 | 0.7 | 0.0 | 0.0 | —> | 0.0 |
| Bahrain | (21) | 1981 | Total | MF | 269 466 | 53.5 | 14.8 | —> | 10.2 | 13.4 | 8.3 |
| | | | | F | 105 749 | 59.7 | 12.8 | —> | 8.5 | 12.2 | 7.0 |
| | | | Nationals | MF | 99 143 | 46.7 | 11.9 | —> | 9.8 | 17.3 | 14.6 |
| | | | | F | 21 017 | 37.5 | 10.0 | —> | 9.3 | 23.1 | 20.3 |
| | | | Non-Nationals | MF | 170 323 | 57.5 | 16.5 | —> | 10.4 | 11.1 | 4.6 |
| | | | | F | 84 732 | 65.3 | 13.5 | —> | 8.3 | 9.5 | 3.7 |
| | | 1991 | | MF | 263 720 | 38.4 | 26.2 | —> | 25.1 | —> | 10.3 |
| | | | | F | 96 080 | 46.0 | 18.3 | —> | 25.3 | —> | 10.4 |
| Bangladesh | | 1981 | Total | MF | 31 593 122 | 70.4 | 16.7 | —> | 7.4 | 4.2 | 1.3 |
| | | | | F | 14 904 705 | 84.0 | 11.5 | —> | 3.3 | 0.8 | 0.3 |
| | | | Urban | MF | 5 036 383 | 52.0 | 18.4 | —> | 13.6 | 10.7 | 5.3 |
| | | | | F | 1 987 459 | 69.3 | 15.4 | —> | 9.5 | 4.1 | 1.7 |
| | | | Rural | MF | 26 556 739 | 73.9 | 16.3 | —> | 6.2 | 3.0 | 0.5 |
| | | | | F | 12 917 246 | 86.3 | 10.9 | —> | 2.4 | 0.3 | 0.0 |
| Brunei Darussalam | | 1981 | | MF | 75 283 | 32.1 | 28.3 | —> | 30.1 | —> | 9.4 |
| | | | | F | 33 701 | 45.8 | 21.7 | —> | 25.6 | —> | 6.9 |
| Cambodia | (2)(32) | 1993 | Total | MF | 8 664 920 | 30.5 | 47.0 | —> | 16.2 | 4.1 | 1.0 |
| | | | | F | 4 571 987 | 37.8 | 46.1 | —> | 12.1 | 2.7 | 0.5 |
| | | | Rural | MF | 7 303 746 | 32.2 | 48.0 | —> | 15.0 | 3.2 | 0.5 |
| | | | | F | 3 863 968 | 39.7 | 46.7 | —> | 10.4 | 2.0 | 0.2 |
| | | | Other Urban | MF | 713 628 | 25.9 | 43.0 | —> | 21.3 | 7.4 | 1.1 |
| | | | | F | 376 883 | 31.3 | 42.9 | —> | 18.7 | 5.5 | 0.6 |
| | | | Phnom Penh | MF | 647 546 | 16.8 | 40.2 | —> | 25.0 | 10.9 | 6.4 |
| | | | | F | 331 136 | 22.1 | 42.4 | —> | 23.7 | 7.5 | 3.4 |
| China | (33) | 1982 | | MF | 466 915 380 | 44.5 | —> | 32.7 | 16.1 | 5.6 | 1.0 |
| | | | | F | 227 191 450 | 62.3 | —> | 23.6 | 9.9 | 3.7 | 0.5 |
| | (34) | 1990 | | MF | 571 589 800 | 29.3 | 34.3 | —> | 34.4 | —> | 2.0 |

Educational attainment II.3
Niveau d'instruction
Nivel de instrucción

| Country / Pays / País | Yaer / Année / Año | Sex / Sexe / Sexo | Population aged 25 years and over / Population âgée de 25 ans et plus / Población de 25 años y más | Highest level of education attained / Niveau d'instruction atteint / Nivel de instrucción alcanzado | | | | | |
|---|---|---|---|---|---|---|---|---|---|
| | | | | No schooling / Sans scolarité / Sin escolaridad | Primary / Primaire / Primaria | | Secondary / Secondaire / Secundaria | | Post-secondary / Post-secondaire / Post-secundaria |
| | | | | | Incomplete / Non complété / Incompleta | Completed / Complété / Completa | Lower secondary / Premier cycle secondaire / Primer ciclo secundaria | Upper secondary / Deuxième cycle secondaire / Segundo ciclo secundaria | |
| China, Hong Kong SAR | (7) 1981 | MF | 2 601 296 | 22.5 | 16.7 | 23.1 | 13.2 | 17.3 | 7.1 |
| | | F | 1 239 697 | 35.9 | 15.3 | 19.5 | 9.9 | 14.4 | 5.0 |
| | 1986 | MF | 3 136 191 | 18.4 | 35.6 | —> | 38.3 | —> | 7.7 |
| | | F | 1 533 454 | 28.2 | 33.3 | —> | 32.7 | —> | 5.8 |
| | 1991 | MF | 3 530 524 | 15.7 | 30.3 | —> | 17.8 | 25.5 | 10.6 |
| | | F | 1 747 296 | 22.8 | 29.3 | —> | 14.6 | 25.0 | 8.3 |
| | 1996 | MF | 4 197 007 | 11.4 | 26.9 | —> | 18.7 | 28.7 | 14.5 |
| | | F | 2 125 797 | 16.6 | 26.8 | —> | 15.4 | 29.3 | 12.2 |
| Cyprus | (32)(13) 1980 | MF | ... | 8.0 | 55.0 | —> | 29.0 | —> | 8.0 |
| | | F | ... | 14.0 | 55.0 | —> | 25.0 | —> | 6.0 |
| | (32)(13) 1984 | MF | ... | 8.0 | 45.0 | —> | 34.0 | —> | 13.0 |
| | | F | ... | 13.0 | 47.0 | —> | 31.0 | —> | 9.0 |
| | (32)(13) 1987 | MF | ... | 6.0 | 46.0 | —> | 34.0 | —> | 14.0 |
| | | F | ... | 10.0 | 48.0 | —> | 30.0 | —> | 12.0 |
| | (32)(13) 1989 | MF | ... | 6.0 | 45.0 | —> | 35.0 | —> | 14.0 |
| | | F | ... | 9.0 | 47.0 | —> | 32.0 | —> | 12.0 |
| | (32)(13) 1991 | MF | ... | 6.0 | 39.0 | —> | 40.0 | —> | 15.0 |
| | | F | ... | 10.0 | 41.0 | —> | 36.0 | —> | 13.0 |
| | 1992 | MF | 363 573 | 5.1 | 13.0 | 30.6 | 34.2 | —> | 17.0 |
| | | F | 186 432 | 8.2 | 16.2 | 30.1 | 31.0 | —> | 14.4 |
| India | 1981 | MF | 280 599 720 | 72.5 | 11.3 | —> | 13.7 | —> | 2.5 |
| | | F | 135 517 843 | 85.2 | 7.2 | —> | 6.6 | —> | 1.1 |
| | (35) 1991 Total | MF | 368 000 483 | 57.5 | 28.0 | —> | 7.2 | —> | 7.3 |
| | | F | 176 970 663 | 72.8 | 19.6 | —> | 4.0 | —> | 3.7 |
| | Urban | MF | 97 278 399 | 33.9 | 33.9 | —> | 14.3 | —> | 17.9 |
| | | F | 45 211 753 | 47.0 | 31.4 | —> | 10.3 | —> | 11.3 |
| | Rural | MF | 270 722 084 | 66.0 | 25.8 | —> | 4.7 | —> | 3.5 |
| | | F | 131 758 910 | 81.6 | 15.5 | —> | 1.8 | —> | 1.1 |
| Indonesia | 1980 Total | MF | 58 441 240 | 41.1 | 31.6 | 16.8 | 4.7 | 4.9 | 0.8 |
| | | F | 29 764 530 | 53.9 | 26.6 | 12.9 | 3.3 | 3.0 | 0.4 |
| | Urban | MF | 12 518 959 | 21.9 | 26.0 | 23.1 | 12.1 | 14.1 | 2.9 |
| | | F | 6 288 212 | 34.8 | 24.2 | 20.3 | 9.8 | 9.5 | 1.4 |
| | Rural | MF | 45 922 281 | 45.9 | 33.6 | 15.1 | 2.7 | 2.5 | 0.2 |
| | | F | 23 476 318 | 59.0 | 27.3 | 10.8 | 1.5 | 1.3 | 0.1 |
| | 1990 | MF | 78 497 680 | 54.5 | 26.4 | —> | 16.8 | —> | 2.3 |
| | | F | 39 961 034 | 62.8 | 23.3 | —> | 12.4 | —> | 1.4 |
| Iraq (21) | 1987 Total | MF | 10 628 447 | 52.8 | 21.6 | —> | 11.6 | —> | 4.1 |
| | | F | 5 349 328 | 60.2 | 18.9 | —> | 8.8 | —> | 2.9 |
| | Urban | MF | 7 549 136 | 48.0 | 22.6 | —> | 14.0 | —> | 5.4 |
| | | F | 3 769 340 | 54.8 | 20.3 | —> | 11.7 | —> | 4.0 |
| | Rural | MF | 3 079 311 | 64.6 | 19.1 | —> | 5.6 | —> | 1.0 |
| | | F | 1 579 988 | 73.0 | 15.6 | —> | 2.1 | —> | 0.3 |
| Israel | 1982 Total | MF | 2 003 500 | 9.7 | 30.6 | —> | 36.6 | —> | 23.1 |
| | | F | 1 030 200 | 14.1 | 30.2 | —> | 34.8 | —> | 20.9 |
| | Jewish | MF | 1 785 400 | 7.4 | 28.3 | —> | 39.2 | —> | 25.1 |
| | | F | 918 500 | 10.5 | 28.8 | —> | 37.7 | —> | 23.0 |
| | Non Jewish | MF | 218 100 | 28.1 | 49.0 | —> | 15.6 | —> | 7.2 |
| | | F | 111 700 | 43.5 | 41.1 | —> | 11.2 | —> | 4.2 |
| | 1983 | MF | 2 043 720 | 10.5 | 42.4 | —> | 35.9 | —> | 11.2 |
| | | F | 1 059 465 | 14.2 | 41.5 | —> | 35.3 | —> | 9.0 |
| Japan | 1980 Total | MF | 73 368 684 | 0.4 | —> | 45.6 | —> | 39.7 | 14.3 |
| | | F | 38 110 839 | 0.6 | —> | 47.6 | —> | 42.1 | 9.5 |
| | Urban | MF | 55 235 050 | 0.3 | —> | 40.6 | —> | 42.5 | 16.5 |
| | | F | 28 596 309 | 0.4 | —> | 42.8 | —> | 45.8 | 11.0 |
| | Rural | MF | 18 133 634 | 0.7 | —> | 60.6 | —> | 31.0 | 7.6 |
| | | F | 9 514 530 | 0.9 | —> | 62.9 | —> | 30.9 | 5.1 |
| | (36) 1990 | MF | 81 991 363 | 0.3 | 33.6 | —> | 43.7 | —> | 20.7 |
| | | F | 42 625 628 | 0.3 | 35.7 | —> | 45.9 | —> | 16.4 |
| Kazakstan | 1989 | MF | 8 414 539 | 7.7 | 29.2 | —> | 50.7 | —> | 12.4 |
| | | F | 4 528 351 | 11.0 | 29.2 | —> | 48.1 | —> | 11.7 |

II.3 Educational attainment
Niveau d'instruction
Nivel de instrucción

| Country / Pays / País | Year / Année / Año | | Sex / Sexe / Sexo | Population aged 25 years and over / Population âgée de 25 ans et plus / Población de 25 años y más | Highest level of education attained / Niveau d'instruction atteint / Nivel de instrucción alcanzado | | | | | |
|---|---|---|---|---|---|---|---|---|---|---|
| | | | | | No schooling / Sans scolarité / Sin escolaridad | Primary / Primaire / Primaria | | Secondary / Secondaire / Secundaria | | Post-secondary / Post-secondaire / Post-secundaria |
| | | | | | | Incomplete / Non complété / Incompleta | Completed / Complété / Completa | Lower secondary / Premier cycle secondaire / Primer ciclo secundaria | Upper secondary / Deuxième cycle secondaire / Segundo ciclo secundaria | |
| Korea, Republic of | 1980 | | MF | 16 457 362 | 19.7 | 34.5 | —> | 18.2 | 18.7 | 8.9 |
| | 1980 | | F | 8 503 065 | 26.9 | 39.4 | —> | 16.7 | 12.9 | 4.0 |
| | 1985 | | MF | 19 760 111 | 15.4 | —> | 27.6 | —> | 45.3 | 11.7 |
| | 1985 | | F | 10 205 736 | 21.9 | —> | 32.1 | —> | 40.3 | 5.8 |
| | 1990 | | MF | 23 408 288 | 11.0 | 0.8 | 20.9 | 18.9 | 35.0 | 13.4 |
| | 1990 | | F | 11 983 259 | 16.3 | 1.0 | 25.2 | 20.3 | 30.0 | 7.2 |
| | 1995 | | MF | 26 217 862 | 8.7 | 0.9 | 17.3 | 15.7 | 36.2 | 21.1 |
| | 1995 | | F | 13 395 658 | 13.3 | 1.2 | 21.2 | 17.0 | 33.6 | 13.7 |
| Kuwait | 1980 | Total | MF | 568 086 | 58.0 | 7.6 | —> | 9.6 | 14.8 | 10.1 |
| | | | F | 205 573 | 62.7 | 6.4 | —> | 8.7 | 14.7 | 7.4 |
| | | Kuwaiti | MF | 176 011 | 69.5 | 7.8 | —> | 9.5 | 9.0 | 4.2 |
| | | | F | 89 718 | 80.0 | 4.5 | —> | 6.1 | 6.6 | 2.8 |
| | | Non Kuwaiti | MF | 392 075 | 52.8 | 7.5 | —> | 9.6 | 17.4 | 12.7 |
| | | | F | 115 855 | 49.3 | 7.9 | —> | 10.7 | 21.0 | 11.0 |
| | 1985 | | MF | 565 330 | 50.3 | 7.2 | —> | 10.7 | 19.0 | 12.7 |
| | | | F | 178 989 | 49.9 | 6.9 | —> | 10.7 | 20.9 | 11.6 |
| (6) | 1988 | Total | MF | 862 799 | 25.6 | 8.6 | —> | 15.1 | 15.1 | 16.4 |
| | | | F | 337 763 | 33.0 | 6.5 | —> | 11.8 | 14.2 | 15.8 |
| | | Kuwaiti | MF | 184 023 | 30.1 | 7.7 | —> | 19.4 | 10.6 | 21.3 |
| | | | F | 95 571 | 41.6 | 6.9 | —> | 15.6 | 7.3 | 19.1 |
| | | Non Kuwaiti | MF | 678 776 | 24.4 | 8.9 | —> | 13.9 | 16.3 | 15.1 |
| | | | F | 242 192 | 29.6 | 6.3 | —> | 10.2 | 16.9 | 14.5 |
| Macau | 1991 | | MF | 212 363 | 13.1 | 16.0 | 19.9 | 25.2 | 19.9 | 5.9 |
| | | | F | 108 515 | 18.8 | 16.7 | 20.2 | 22.3 | 17.3 | 4.7 |
| Malaysia | 1980 | | MF | 5 146 888 | 36.6 | 21.1 | 21.1 | 18.1 | 1.3 | 1.9 |
| | | | F | 2 587 961 | 49.0 | 18.8 | 16.9 | 13.5 | 0.8 | 1.0 |
| | 1996 | Total | MF | 9 654 600 | 16.7 | 13.0 | 20.7 | 19.4 | 23.6 | 6.9 |
| | | | F | 4 766 700 | 23.6 | 13.3 | 19.1 | 17.3 | 21.4 | 5.5 |
| | | Urban | MF | 5 160 400 | 11.4 | 10.0 | 18.0 | 21.5 | 29.6 | 9.8 |
| | | | F | 2 568 100 | 16.7 | 11.0 | 17.9 | 19.2 | 27.6 | 7.8 |
| | | Rural | MF | 4 494 200 | 22.9 | 16.5 | 23.7 | 17.0 | 16.7 | 3.5 |
| | | | F | 2 198 600 | 31.3 | 16.0 | 20.5 | 15.0 | 14.3 | 2.9 |
| Maldives | 1990 | | MF | 66 977 | 0.9 | 61.6 | 10.8 | 6.3 | 17.1 | 1.7 |
| | | | F | 31 553 | 0.9 | 66.6 | 11.6 | 5.1 | 13.4 | 1.0 |
| Mongolia | 1989 | Total | MF | 770 641 | 13.4 | 22.8 | —> | 13.9 | 26.5 | 23.4 |
| | | | F | 392 097 | 17.6 | 24.7 | —> | 13.0 | 21.6 | 23.1 |
| | | Urban | MF | 453 880 | 7.3 | 14.0 | —> | 19.2 | 27.3 | 32.2 |
| | | Rural | MF | 316 761 | 22.2 | 35.4 | —> | 6.2 | 25.4 | 10.8 |
| Myanmar | 1983 | | MF | 13 948 584 | 55.8 | 27.7 | —> | 14.5 | —> | 2.0 |
| | | | F | 7 122 177 | 60.4 | 28.9 | —> | 9.2 | —> | 1.5 |
| Nepal (6) | 1981 | Total | MF | 6 146 768 | 90.3 | 4.8 | —> | 3.7 | —> | 1.1 |
| | | | F | 3 010 119 | 95.9 | 2.8 | —> | 1.1 | —> | 0.3 |
| | | Urban | MF | 386 178 | 70.3 | 7.7 | —> | 13.4 | —> | 8.6 |
| | | | F | 176 471 | 82.3 | 6.2 | —> | 7.8 | —> | 3.7 |
| | | Rural | MF | 5 760 590 | 91.6 | 4.7 | —> | 3.1 | —> | 0.6 |
| | | | F | 2 833 648 | 96.7 | 2.5 | —> | 0.7 | —> | 0.1 |
| (36) | 1991 | Total | MF | ... | 69.7 | 16.2 | —> | 8.9 | 2.9 | 0.6 |
| | | | F | ... | 81.2 | 11.2 | —> | 5.0 | 1.3 | 0.2 |
| | | Urban | MF | ... | 44.9 | 18.7 | —> | 18.0 | 11.6 | 4.3 |
| | | | F | ... | 55.5 | 17.0 | —> | 15.0 | 8.4 | 2.1 |
| | | Rural | MF | ... | 72.2 | 15.9 | —> | 7.9 | 2.0 | 0.3 |
| | | | F | ... | 83.8 | 10.6 | —> | 4.0 | 0.6 | 0.0 |
| Oman (6) | 1996 | | MF | 461 115 | 71.7 | 11.5 | —> | 5.9 | 11.1 | —> |
| | | | F | 228 830 | 83.1 | 7.2 | —> | 3.1 | 6.7 | —> |
| Pakistan (14) | 1981 | Total | MF | 30 707 279 | 78.9 | 8.7 | —> | 10.5 | —> | 1.9 |
| | | | F | 14 400 805 | 90.4 | 4.7 | —> | 4.2 | —> | 0.7 |
| | | Urban | MF | 8 709 327 | 59.5 | 12.9 | —> | 22.1 | —> | 5.4 |
| | | | F | 3 901 096 | 73.9 | 10.8 | —> | 12.8 | —> | 2.6 |
| | | Rural | MF | 21 997 952 | 86.8 | 6.9 | —> | 5.9 | —> | 0.5 |
| | | | F | 10 499 709 | 96.5 | 2.4 | —> | 1.0 | —> | 0.1 |

Educational attainment  II.3
Niveau d'instruction
Nivel de instrucción

| Country / Pays / País | Yaer / Année / Año | | Sex / Sexe / Sexo | Population aged 25 years and over / Population âgée de 25 ans et plus / Población de 25 años y más | No schooling / Sans scolarité / Sin escolaridad | Primary / Primaire / Primaria Incomplete / Non complété / Incompleta | Primary Completed / Complété / Completa | Secondary Lower / Premier cycle secondaire / Primer ciclo secundaria | Secondary Upper / Deuxième cycle secondaire / Segundo ciclo secundaria | Post-secondary / Post-secondaire / Post-secundaria |
|---|---|---|---|---|---|---|---|---|---|---|
| Pakistan (cont) (38) | 1990 | Total | MF | ... | 73.8 | 9.7 | → | 5.8 | 8.2 | 2.5 |
| | | | F | ... | 87.9 | 5.3 | → | 2.2 | 3.8 | 0.9 |
| | | Urban | MF | ... | 59.2 | 11.8 | → | 8.8 | 14.5 | 5.7 |
| | | | F | ... | 74.9 | 8.4 | → | 4.9 | 9.2 | 2.6 |
| | | Rural | MF | ... | 80.4 | 8.0 | → | 4.4 | 5.4 | 1.1 |
| | | | F | ... | 94.1 | 3.0 | → | 1.0 | 1.2 | 0.0 |
| Philippines | 1980 | | MF | 17 865 290 | 11.7 | 31.3 | 22.8 | 18.9 | → | 15.2 |
| | | | F | 8 980 215 | 13.3 | 31.4 | 23.7 | 16.6 | → | 15.1 |
| | 1990 | | MF | 24 156 427 | 6.7 | 46.9 | → | 27.2 | → | 18.7 |
| | | | F | 12 167 641 | 7.5 | 47.8 | → | 25.3 | → | 18.9 |
| (22) | 1995 | Total | MF | 42 700 000 | 3.8 | 20.8 | 15.1 | 17.3 | 21.2 | 22.0 |
| | | | F | 21 339 000 | 4.3 | 19.5 | 15.4 | 17.0 | 20.3 | 23.8 |
| | | Urban | MF | 21 659 000 | 2.2 | 13.4 | 12.4 | 17.0 | 24.9 | 30.1 |
| | | | F | 10 904 000 | 2.5 | 12.5 | 12.5 | 16.7 | 23.6 | 32.4 |
| | | Rural | MF | 21 041 000 | 5.4 | 28.4 | 17.9 | 17.5 | 17.4 | 13.6 |
| | | | F | 10 435 000 | 6.2 | 26.7 | 18.4 | 17.4 | 16.7 | 14.9 |
| Qatar (6)(21) | 1981 | | MF | 188 940 | 48.9 | 15.0 | → | 11.7 | 12.8 | 11.6 |
| | | | F | 61 732 | 49.1 | 15.9 | → | 11.7 | 13.6 | 9.7 |
| | 1986 | | MF | 211 485 | 53.5 | 9.8 | → | 10.1 | 13.3 | 13.3 |
| | | | F | 50 673 | 56.0 | 6.7 | → | 7.5 | 14.6 | 15.3 |
| Singapore | 1980 | | MF | 1 176 282 | 43.7 | 38.3 | → | 9.6 | 5.0 | 3.4 |
| | | | F | 583 726 | 54.3 | 31.2 | → | 8.7 | 3.8 | 2.0 |
| (18) | 1990 | | MF | 1 596 600 | 64.0 | → | → | 23.2 | 8.1 | 4.7 |
| | | | F | 807 800 | 65.9 | → | → | 23.9 | 6.8 | 3.5 |
| (39) | 1995 | | MF | 1 860 878 | 14.3 | 11.2 | 16.5 | 36.9 | 13.7 | 7.6 |
| | | | F | 944 326 | 20.7 | 10.6 | 16.0 | 35.2 | 12.0 | 5.8 |
| Sri Lanka | 1981 | Total | MF | 6 490 502 | 15.9 | 48.9 | → | 34.1 | → | 1.1 |
| | | | F | 3 163 187 | 22.7 | 45.3 | → | 31.3 | → | 0.8 |
| | | Urban | MF | 1 471 818 | 8.8 | 39.5 | → | 49.2 | → | 2.4 |
| | | | F | 694 072 | 12.3 | 40.5 | → | 45.4 | → | 1.7 |
| | | Rural | MF | 5 018 684 | 18.0 | 51.6 | → | 29.7 | → | 0.7 |
| | | | F | 2 469 115 | 25.6 | 46.6 | → | 27.3 | → | 0.5 |
| Tajikistan | 1989 | | MF | 1 916 494 | 9.8 | 13.0 | → | 65.5 | → | 11.7 |
| | | | F | 984 302 | 13.5 | 15.3 | → | 63.1 | → | 8.1 |
| Thailand | 1980 | | MF | 17 491 470 | 20.5 | 67.3 | 2.4 | 4.5 | 2.3 | 2.9 |
| | | | F | 9 000 623 | 26.3 | 65.4 | 1.6 | 2.6 | 1.7 | 2.4 |
| (37) | 1990 | | MF | 49 076 100 | 10.7 | 69.6 | → | 13.7 | → | 5.1 |
| | | | F | 24 835 200 | 12.8 | 70.0 | → | 11.4 | → | 5.1 |
| Turkey | 1980 | | MF | 18 277 340 | 52.4 | 35.3 | → | 8.7 | → | 3.6 |
| | | | F | 9 207 179 | 68.3 | 24.5 | → | 5.7 | → | 1.5 |
| | 1985 | | MF | 21 366 259 | 40.0 | 44.5 | → | 4.6 | → | 10.8 |
| | | | F | 10 708 464 | 54.4 | 36.1 | → | 2.8 | → | 6.7 |
| (40) | 1993 | | MF | ... | 30.6 | 6.6 | 40.6 | 21.9 | → | → |
| | | | F | ... | 43.2 | 8.1 | 34.7 | 13.7 | → | → |
| Viet Nam | 1979 | | MF | 19 402 270 | 28.4 | → | 42.8 | → | 27.7 | 1.2 |
| | | | F | 10 564 766 | 37.1 | → | 43.8 | → | 18.5 | 0.6 |
| (32) | 1989 | | MF | 26 466 214 | 16.6 | 69.8 | → | 10.6 | → | 2.6 |
| | | | F | 14 315 859 | 23.4 | 66.2 | → | 8.4 | → | 1.7 |
| **Europe** | | | | | | | | | | |
| Austria | 1981 | | MF | 4 558 681 | ... | 49.3 | → | → | 47.5 | 3.3 |
| | | | F | 2 508 936 | ... | 61.9 | → | → | 36.6 | 1.6 |
| | 1991 | | MF | 5 288 032 | 0.0 | 0.0 | → | 94.0 | → | 6.1 |
| | | | F | 2 819 433 | 0.0 | 0.0 | → | 95.3 | → | 4.8 |
| Belarus (21) | 1979 | Total | MF | | ... 40.6 | → | → | 41.5 | 10.2 | 7.7 |
| | | | F | | ... 45.1 | → | → | 36.8 | 11.1 | 7.0 |
| | | Urban | MF | | ... 24.0 | → | → | 49.9 | 14.2 | 12.0 |
| | | | F | | ... 26.4 | → | → | 46.9 | 15.6 | 11.1 |
| | | Rural | MF | | ... 60.2 | → | → | 31.7 | 5.5 | 2.6 |
| | | | F | | ... 66.6 | → | → | 25.1 | 5.8 | 2.5 |

II.3 Educational attainment
Niveau d'instruction
Nivel de instrucción

| Country<br>Pays<br>País | Year<br>Année<br>Año | | Sex<br>Sexe<br>Sexo | Population aged 25 years and over<br>Population âgée de 25 ans et plus<br>Población de 25 años y más | Highest level of education attained<br>Niveau d'instruction atteint<br>Nivel de instrucción alcanzado | | | | | |
|---|---|---|---|---|---|---|---|---|---|---|
| | | | | | No schooling<br>Sans scolarité<br>Sin escolaridad | Primary / Primaire / Primaria | | Secondary / Secondaire / Secundaria | | Post-secondary<br>Post-secondaire<br>Post-secundaria |
| | | | | | | Incomplete<br>Non complété<br>Incompleta | Completed<br>Complété<br>Completa | Lower secondary<br>Premier cycle secondaire<br>Primer ciclo secundaria | Upper secondary<br>Deuxième cycle secondaire<br>Segundo ciclo secundaria | |
| Belarus (cont) | 1989 | | MF | 6 401 777 | 9.4 | 32.5 | —> | 45.8 | —> | 12.5 |
| | | | F | 3 548 670 | 13.4 | 32.5 | —> | 42.8 | —> | 11.5 |
| Bulgaria | (8) 1985 | Total | MF | 8 102 363 | ... | 63.6 | —> | 27.4 | —> | 9.1 |
| | | Urban | MF | 5 223 958 | ... | 52.6 | —> | 34.6 | —> | 12.9 |
| | | Rural | MF | 2 878 405 | ... | 83.6 | —> | 14.2 | —> | 2.3 |
| | (41) 1992 | Total | MF | 5 649 672 | 4.7 | 12.5 | 31.9 | 35.7 | —> | 15.0 |
| | | | F | 2 931 909 | 6.2 | 14.8 | 29.8 | 33.9 | —> | 15.2 |
| | | Urban | MF | 3 666 533 | 2.4 | 6.0 | 25.7 | 44.5 | —> | 21.2 |
| | | | F | 1 909 391 | 3.1 | 7.3 | 24.5 | 43.5 | —> | 21.5 |
| | | Rural | MF | 1 983 139 | 9.0 | 24.7 | 43.5 | 19.3 | —> | 3.5 |
| | | | F | 1 022 518 | 11.9 | 28.8 | 39.8 | 16.1 | —> | 3.4 |
| Croatia | (22) 1981 | | MF | 3 637 769 | 14.2 | 51.2 | —> | 31.0 | —> | 3.6 |
| | | | F | 1 904 061 | 18.7 | 55.3 | —> | 23.5 | —> | 2.5 |
| | (42) 1991 | Total | MF | 2 969 584 | 10.2 | 43.6 | —> | 39.5 | —> | 6.4 |
| | | | F | 1 587 468 | 14.4 | 48.8 | —> | 31.6 | —> | 4.9 |
| | | Urban(22) | MF | 2 083 869 | 4.5 | 34.9 | —> | 50.4 | —> | 8.8 |
| | | | F | 1 102 581 | 6.5 | 40.9 | —> | 44.2 | —> | 7.0 |
| | | Rural(22) | MF | 1 774 217 | 13.3 | 56.0 | —> | 27.8 | —> | 1.2 |
| | | | F | 911 371 | 18.6 | 58.4 | —> | 20.5 | —> | 0.9 |
| Czech Republic | 1991 | | MF | 6 580 525 | 0.3 | 31.4 | —> | 58.6 | —> | 8.5 |
| | | | F | 3 485 093 | 0.4 | 40.8 | —> | 51.7 | —> | 6.0 |
| Denmark (34) | 1991 | | MF | 2 742 734 | - | 38.7 | —> | 3.4 | 38.2 | 19.6 |
| | | | F | 1 363 396 | - | 44.3 | —> | 3.6 | 32.6 | 19.5 |
| Estonia | 1989 | Total | MF | 1 001 198 | 2.2 | 39.0 | —> | 45.1 | —> | 13.7 |
| | | | F | 559 294 | 2.9 | 38.5 | —> | 45.3 | —> | 13.2 |
| | | Urban | MF | 720 479 | 1.9 | 32.4 | —> | 49.6 | —> | 16.1 |
| | | | F | 406 333 | 2.7 | 32.2 | —> | 49.8 | —> | 15.4 |
| | | Rural | MF | 280 719 | 2.9 | 56.1 | —> | 33.6 | —> | 7.4 |
| | | | F | 152 961 | 3.6 | 55.5 | —> | 33.6 | —> | 7.3 |
| Finland | (43)(13) 1980 | | MF | 3 442 000 | - | 51.1 | —> | 7.7 | 29.2 | 11.9 |
| | | | F | 1 815 000 | - | 51.2 | —> | 8.9 | 28.5 | 10.4 |
| | 1985 | | MF | 3 235 017 | - | 55.6 | —> | 30.6 | —> | 13.8 |
| | | | F | 1 713 747 | - | 58.0 | —> | 30.3 | —> | 11.7 |
| | 1990 | | MF | 3 387 384 | - | 49.4 | —> | 35.3 | —> | 15.4 |
| | | | F | 1 784 166 | - | 51.4 | —> | 35.3 | —> | 13.3 |
| France (44) | 1990 | | MF | 37 354 255 | 0.6 | 51.1 | —> | 36.9 | —> | 11.4 |
| | | | F | 19 647 744 | 0.5 | 55.1 | —> | 34.2 | —> | 10.3 |
| Greece | 1981 | | MF | 5 966 511 | 11.5 | 16.9 | 44.3 | 6.1 | 13.6 | 7.6 |
| | | | F | 3 113 632 | 17.7 | 18.4 | 41.7 | 4.2 | 13.1 | 4.9 |
| | 1991 | Total | MF | 6 738 566 | 5.7 | 12.7 | 44.2 | 6.7 | 22.0 | 8.7 |
| | | Urban | MF | 4 269 892 | 3.6 | 8.7 | 37.9 | 7.8 | 29.6 | 12.4 |
| | | Rural | MF | 1 741 823 | 10.3 | 21.5 | 56.7 | 3.9 | 6.2 | 1.3 |
| | | Semi Urban | MF | 726 851 | 6.4 | 15.6 | 51.1 | 7.2 | 14.5 | 5.2 |
| Hungary | 1980 | | MF | 6 903 881 | 1.3 | 8.0 | 3.2 | 57.0 | 23.6 | 7.0 |
| | | | F | 3 670 474 | 1.7 | 8.7 | 3.4 | 61.5 | 19.6 | 5.0 |
| | (18) 1990 | | MF | 6 798 765 | 1.3 | 24.3 | 33.6 | —> | 30.7 | 10.1 |
| | | | F | 3 644 553 | 1.6 | 28.8 | 34.9 | —> | 26.0 | 8.7 |
| Ireland | 1981 | | MF | 1 793 855 | 52.3 | —> | —> | 39.8 | —> | 7.9 |
| | | | F | 909 047 | 50.2 | —> | —> | 43.2 | —> | 6.5 |
| | 1991 | | MF | 1 983 547 | 0.0 | 37.2 | —> | 19.1 | 27.2 | 13.1 |
| | | | F | 1 020 854 | 0.0 | 35.5 | —> | 19.7 | 29.0 | 12.3 |
| Italy | (6) 1981 | | MF | 35 596 616 | 19.3 | 47.4 | —> | 18.0 | 11.2 | 4.1 |
| | | | F | 18 790 372 | 23.2 | 48.8 | —> | 15.3 | 9.8 | 2.9 |
| | (45)(37) 1991 | | MF | 53 481 852 | 2.1 | 12.2 | 32.5 | 30.7 | 18.6 | 3.8 |
| Latvia | 1989 | | MF | 1 725 639 | 0.6 | 18.5 | 21.2 | 46.3 | —> | 13.4 |
| | | | F | 968 037 | 0.9 | 21.4 | 19.3 | 45.3 | —> | 13.0 |
| Lithuania | 1989 | | MF | 2 282 191 | 9.1 | 21.3 | —> | 57.0 | —> | 12.6 |
| | | | F | 1 255 511 | 11.7 | 22.8 | —> | 53.1 | —> | 12.3 |

Educational attainment II.3
Niveau d'instruction
Nivel de instrucción

| Country / Pays / País | Yaer / Année / Año | | Sex / Sexe / Sexo | Population aged 25 years and over / Population âgée de 25 ans et plus / Población de 25 años y más | Highest level of education attained / Niveau d'instruction atteint / Nivel de instrucción alcanzado | | | | | |
|---|---|---|---|---|---|---|---|---|---|---|
| | | | | | No schooling / Sans scolarité / Sin escolaridad | Primary / Primaire / Primaria | | Secondary / Secondaire / Secundaria | | Post-secondary / Post-secondaire / Post-secundaria |
| | | | | | | Incomplete / Non complété / Incompleta | Completed / Complété / Completa | Lower secondary / Premier cycle secondaire / Primer ciclo secundaria | Upper secondary / Deuxième cycle secondaire / Segundo ciclo secundaria | |
| Luxembourg | 1991 | | MF | 262 628 | ... | 39.7 | —> | 40.3 | —> | 10.8 |
| | | | F | 136 326 | ... | 44.4 | —> | 37.2 | —> | 7.9 |
| Moldova | 1989 | | MF | 2 499 613 | 12.7 | 17.1 | —> | 58.9 | —> | 11.3 |
| | | | F | 1 363 236 | 16.8 | 17.7 | —> | 55.0 | —> | 10.6 |
| Norway (9) | 1980 | | MF | 2 574 641 | 1.8 | 0.0 | —> | 60.0 | 26.2 | 11.9 |
| | | | F | 1 324 409 | 1.6 | 0.0 | —> | 65.7 | 23.8 | 8.8 |
| | 1990 | Total | MF | 2 803 030 | 0.1 | 0.1 | —> | 32.9 | 46.4 | 17.9 |
| | | | F | 1 442 854 | 0.1 | 0.1 | —> | 36.4 | 45.1 | 15.9 |
| | | Urban | MF | 2 024 051 | 0.1 | 0.1 | —> | 29.1 | 46.5 | 21.1 |
| | | | F | 1 060 370 | 0.1 | 0.1 | —> | 33.5 | 45.3 | 18.3 |
| | | Rural | MF | 762 807 | 0.0 | 0.0 | —> | 42.9 | 46.2 | 9.4 |
| | | | F | 375 419 | 0.0 | 0.0 | —> | 44.6 | 44.6 | 9.3 |
| (26) | 1994 | | MF | 3 460 669 | 0.0 | 0.0 | —> | 37.3 | 44.0 | 18.7 |
| | | | F | 1 765 751 | 0.0 | 0.0 | —> | 41.7 | 41.0 | 17.4 |
| Poland | 1988 | Total | MF | 22 986 018 | 1.5 | 5.6 | 37.2 | 47.8 | —> | 7.9 |
| | | | F | 12 120 238 | 2.0 | 6.8 | 40.6 | 43.5 | —> | 7.0 |
| | | Urban | MF | 14 284 765 | 0.9 | 2.4 | 29.3 | 56.2 | —> | 11.3 |
| | | | F | 7 673 764 | 1.2 | 3.1 | 33.7 | 52.3 | —> | 9.8 |
| | | Rural | MF | 8 701 253 | 2.5 | 10.9 | 50.2 | 34.1 | —> | 2.2 |
| | | | F | 4 446 474 | 3.4 | 13.3 | 52.6 | 28.5 | —> | 2.1 |
| Portugal | 1981 | | MF | 5 696 282 | 27.5 | 58.5 | —> | 10.6 | —> | 3.5 |
| | | | F | 3 057 786 | 33.4 | 55.1 | —> | 9.3 | —> | 2.2 |
| | 1991 | | MF | 6 280 792 | 16.1 | 61.5 | —> | 14.8 | —> | 7.7 |
| | | | F | 3 348 946 | 20.1 | 59.7 | —> | 12.9 | —> | 7.2 |
| Romania | 1992 | Total | MF | 13 602 159 | 5.4 | 24.4 | —> | 63.2 | —> | 6.9 |
| | | | F | 7 072 132 | 8.1 | 28.1 | —> | 58.4 | —> | 5.4 |
| | | Urban | MF | 7 143 727 | 1.8 | 12.9 | —> | 73.4 | —> | 12.0 |
| | | | F | 3 719 797 | 2.6 | 16.2 | —> | 71.7 | —> | 9.5 |
| | | Rural | MF | 6 458 432 | 9.5 | 37.2 | —> | 52.0 | —> | 1.4 |
| | | | F | 3 352 335 | 14.1 | 41.2 | —> | 43.7 | —> | 1.0 |
| (1) | 1996 | Nat. estimates | MF | 19 065 000 | 4.3 | 20.7 | —> | 69.4 | —> | 5.6 |
| Russian (46) Federation | 1989 | | MF | 86 016 990 | ... | 36.9 | —> | 49.0 | —> | 14.1 |
| | | | F | 46 006 781 | ... | 37.5 | —> | 48.7 | —> | 13.8 |
| Slovakia | 1991 | | MF | 3 144 143 | 0.7 | 37.9 | —> | 50.9 | —> | 9.5 |
| | | | F | 1 657 128 | 0.9 | 46.5 | —> | 44.1 | —> | 7.5 |
| Slovenia | 1991 | | MF | 1 272 409 | 0.7 | 45.1 | —> | 42.4 | —> | 10.4 |
| | | | F | 673 756 | 0.9 | 53.5 | —> | 35.0 | —> | 9.2 |
| Spain (14) | 1981 | Total | MF | 21 758 498 | 35.1 | 11.8 | 32.7 | 7.6 | 5.7 | 7.1 |
| | | | F | 11 411 664 | 38.9 | 11.8 | 32.5 | 7.2 | 4.1 | 5.5 |
| | | Urban | MF | 17 054 758 | 33.7 | 11.1 | 31.4 | 8.9 | 6.7 | 8.2 |
| | | | F | 9 023 931 | 37.6 | 11.2 | 31.7 | 8.5 | 4.8 | 6.2 |
| | | Rural | MF | 4 703 741 | 40.6 | 14.3 | 37.3 | 2.7 | 2.0 | 3.1 |
| | | | F | 2 387 733 | 44.1 | 14.0 | 35.7 | 2.4 | 1.4 | 2.5 |
| (14) | 1986 | | MF | 23 164 032 | 5.2 | 40.3 | 29.9 | 8.9 | 8.7 | 7.0 |
| | | | F | 12 123 167 | 7.3 | 42.0 | 29.8 | 8.5 | 6.6 | 5.8 |
| | 1991 | | MF | 24 667 414 | 65.3 | —> | —> | 25.5 | —> | 8.4 |
| | | | F | 12 906 677 | 68.9 | —> | —> | 22.9 | —> | 7.2 |
| Sweden (47) | 1986 | | MF | 6 114 449 | ... | 28.1 | —> | 15.6 | 37.0 | 13.8 |
| | | | F | 3 057 014 | ... | 28.8 | —> | 16.4 | 36.3 | 13.6 |
| | 1990 | | MF | 6 212 805 | ... | 23.2 | —> | 15.4 | 39.9 | 15.8 |
| | | | F | 3 099 034 | ... | 23.7 | —> | 16.1 | 39.5 | 15.8 |
| | 1995 | | MF | 6 329 913 | ... | 18.2 | —> | 14.7 | 44.1 | 21.0 |
| | | | F | 3 153 976 | ... | 18.1 | —> | 14.5 | 44.0 | 21.5 |
| Switzerland | 1980 | | MF | 3 232 206 | ... | 75.6 | —> | 8.9 | —> | 11.5 |
| | | | F | 1 626 305 | ... | 78.4 | —> | 11.7 | —> | 5.6 |
| The Former Yugoslav (22) Rep. of Macedonia | 1994 | | MF | 1 136 249 | 28.0 | 28.2 | —> | 30.6 | —> | 6.7 |

II.3 Educational attainment
Niveau d'instruction
Nivel de instrucción

| Country / Pays / País | Yaer / Année / Año | Sex / Sexe / Sexo | Population aged 25 years and over / Population âgée de 25 ans et plus / Población de 25 años y más | Highest level of education attained / Niveau d'instruction atteint / Nivel de instrucción alcanzado | | | | | |
|---|---|---|---|---|---|---|---|---|---|
| | | | | No schooling / Sans scolarité / Sin escolaridad | Primary / Primaire / Primaria Incomplete / Non complété / Incompleta | Completed / Complété / Completa | Secondary / Secondaire / Secundaria Lower secondary / Premier cycle secondaire / Primer ciclo secundaria | Upper secondary / Deuxième cycle secondaire / Segundo ciclo secundaria | Post-secondary / Post-secondaire / Post-secundaria |
| **Oceania** | | | | | | | | | |
| American Samoa (28) | 1980 | MF | 12 184 | 2.5 | 24.3 | 9.0 | 22.1 | 25.5 | 16.6 |
| | | F | 5 966 | 2.6 | 27.4 | 9.4 | 23.2 | 24.6 | 12.8 |
| | 1990 | MF | 19 570 | 1.9 | 16.8 | —> | 58.7 | —> | 22.6 |
| | | F | 9 578 | 2.0 | 17.5 | —> | 60.5 | —> | 20.0 |
| Fiji | 1986 | MF | 287 175 | 10.9 | 35.9 | 23.9 | 24.9 | —> | 4.5 |
| | | F | 147 154 | 14.8 | 35.0 | 24.9 | 21.9 | —> | 3.4 |
| Guam | 1980 | MF | 46 906 | 1.5 | 16.5 | 3.3 | 44.4 | —> | 34.4 |
| | | F | 22 366 | 2.1 | 19.4 | 3.5 | 44.2 | —> | 30.8 |
| (28) | 1990 | MF | 66 700 | ... | 13.9 | —> | 46.2 | —> | 39.9 |
| | | F | 30 956 | ... | 16.1 | —> | 46.2 | —> | 37.8 |
| New Caledonia | 1989 | MF | 69 922 | 6.5 | 51.2 | —> | 34.8 | —> | 7.5 |
| | | F | 33 800 | 7.8 | 51.9 | —> | 34.3 | —> | 6.0 |
| New Zealand | 1981 Total | MF | 1 720 383 | 1.2 | 41.5 | —> | —> | 26.6 | 30.6 |
| | | F | 884 310 | 1.2 | 42.3 | —> | —> | 28.9 | 27.6 |
| | Urban | MF | 1 450 758 | 1.2 | 41.3 | —> | —> | 26.0 | 31.5 |
| | | F | 757 791 | 1.3 | 42.8 | —> | —> | 28.3 | 27.6 |
| | Rural | MF | 269 625 | 1.0 | 42.8 | —> | —> | 30.1 | 26.1 |
| | | F | 126 519 | 0.9 | 39.1 | —> | —> | 32.3 | 27.7 |
| | 1991 | MF | 1 992 354 | 0.0 | 36.8 | —> | 16.3 | 7.8 | 39.1 |
| | | F | 1 029 375 | 0.0 | 39.5 | —> | 19.6 | 8.0 | 32.9 |
| Pacific Islands (28) | 1980 | MF | 46 177 | 17.8 | 36.8 | 10.9 | 10.1 | 13.5 | 10.9 |
| | | F | 22 398 | 21.7 | 41.8 | 11.7 | 8.3 | 10.2 | 6.3 |
| Papua New Guinea | 1980 | MF | 1 135 783 | 82.6 | 8.2 | 5.0 | 3.9 | 0.3 | —> |
| | | F | 551 886 | 87.3 | 7.2 | 3.6 | 1.8 | 0.0 | —> |
| Samoa | 1981 | MF | 48 872 | 3.0 | 53.7 | 2.4 | 12.9 | 25.4 | 2.7 |
| | | F | 24 633 | 3.0 | 53.6 | 1.8 | 13.2 | 25.4 | 2.8 |
| | 1991 | MF | 59 902 | 2.7 | 31.6 | —> | 31.4 | 26.0 | 5.6 |
| | | F | 29 489 | 3.5 | 30.6 | —> | 30.9 | 27.3 | 5.2 |
| Tonga | 1986 | MF | 33 911 | 9.6 | 34.6 | —> | 51.1 | —> | 2.8 |
| | | F | 17 737 | 10.2 | 36.2 | —> | 49.7 | —> | 2.0 |
| Tuvalu | 1991 | MF | 4 571 | 0.8 | 71.4 | —> | 16.2 | —> | 7.0 |
| | | F | 2 555 | 1.0 | 77.4 | —> | 13.2 | —> | 4.9 |
| Vanuatu, Republic of | 1979 | MF | 38 488 | 37.2 | 34.3 | 6.5 | 14.7 | 7.3 | —> |
| | | F | 17 612 | 43.5 | 33.7 | 5.8 | 11.8 | 5.2 | —> |

**General note**
For general explanations and definitions, please refer to the beginning of this chapter.

**Note générale**
Pour les explications et définitions générales, prière de se référer au début de ce chapitre.

**Nota general**
Para las explicaciones y definiciones generales, referirse al comienzo de este capítulo.

Notes

(1) Data refer to population aged 12 years and over.

(2) Data refer to population aged 5 years and over.

(3) Data refer to population of all ages.

(4) Not including persons with no schooling or less than one year of primary education.

(5) Nationals only.

Notes

(1) Les données se réfèrent à la population âgée de 12 ans et plus.

(2) Les données se réfèrent à la population âgée de 5 ans et plus.

(3) Les données se réfèrent à la population de tous les âges.

(4) Non compris les personnes sans scolarité ou ayant fait moins d'une année de l'enseignement primaire.

(5) Ressortissants du pays seulement.

Notas

(1) Los datos se refieren a la población de 12 años y más.

(2) Los datos de refieren a la población de 5 años y más.

(3) Los datos se refieren a la población de todas las edades.

(4) No incluyen a las personas sin escolaridad o con menos de un año de enseñanza primaria.

(5) Población nacional solamente.

Educational attainment **II.3**
Niveau d'instruction
Nivel de instrucción

(6) The category "No schooling" comprises illiterates.

(7) "Completed primary education" refers to the last two years of primary education.

(8) Data refer to population aged 7 years and over.

(9) The category "No schooling" comprises persons who did not state their level of education.

(10) Persons who can read and write have been counted with "Incomplete primary".

(11) Not including population attending and never attended schools.

(12) Not including Botphuthatwana, Transkei, Venda.

(13) Data refer to population aged 20 years and over.

(14) The category "No schooling" comprises illiterates and those who did not state their level of education.

(15) Data refer only to persons who have attended school but left school.

(16) Based on a sample survey of 35,502 persons.

(17) Data refer to population aged 14 years and over.

(18) Not including persons still in school.

(19) Based on a 20% sample of census returns.

(20) Data refer to population aged 25 to 49 years.

(21) Data refer to population aged 10 years and over.

(22) Data refer to population aged 15 years and over.

(23) Based on a sample survey of 51,372 persons.

(24) Post-secondary education refers to universities only.

(25) Not including transients and residents of former canal zone.

(26) Data refer to population aged 16 years and over.

(27) The category "No schooling" refers to those who have attended less than one grade of primary education.

(28) Not including armed forces stationed in the area

(29) Lower secondary education refers to "intermedio" level of education. (Upper) secondary education refers to "Media", "Técnica" and "Normal" education.

(30) Not including rural population of Northern Brazil.

(31) Based on a sample of census returns.

(32) Based on a sample survey.

(33) Based on a 10% sample of census returns.

(34) Not including persons whose level of education is unknown.

(35) Not including Jammu and Kashmir.

(36) Not including persons still attending school for whom the level is unknown.

(37) Data refer to population aged 6 years and over.

(38) Household survey results based on a sample of 6,393 households. The category of "No schooling" includes illiterates.

(39) (Upper) secondary education includes 'polytechnic'; post-secondary education refers to universities only.

(40) Data are based on a sample of 8,619 households(5,563 urban and 3,056 rural) from the 1993 Demographic and Health Survey.

(41) "Incomplete primary education" refers to grades 1 to 4 and "Completed primary education" refers to grades 5 to 8.

(42) Not including expatriate workers and their families.

(43) Data for secondary and post-secondary education refer to highest level completed.

(44) The category "No schooling" includes persons who are still in school.

(6) La catégorie "sans scolarité" comprend les analphabètes.

(7) "Enseignement primaire complété" se réfère aux deux dernières années de l'enseignement primaire.

(8) Les données se réfèrent à la population âgée de 7 ans et plus.

(9) La catégorie "sans scolarité" comprend les personnes dont le niveau d'instruction est inconnu.

(10)

(11) Non compris la population qui fréquente l'école et celle ne l'ayant jamais fréquentée.

(12) Non compris Botphuthatwana, Transkei, Venda.

(13) Les données se réfèrent à la population âgée de 20 ans et plus.

(14) La catégorie "sans scolarité" comprend les analphabètes et ceux dont le niveau d'instruction est inconnu.

(15) Les données se réfèrent seulement aux personnes qui ont fréquenté l'école mais qui ont abandonné leurs études.

(16) D'après une enquête par sondage portant sur 35 502 personnes.

(17) Les données se réfèrent à la population âgée de 14 ans et plus.

(18) Non compris les personnes qui fréquentent encore l'école.

(19) D'après un échantillon portant sur 20% du recensement.

(20) Les données se réfèrent à la population âgée de 25 à 49 ans.

(21) Les données se réfèrent à la population âgée de 10 ans et plus.

(22) Les données se réfèrent à la population âgée de 15 ans et plus.

(23) D'après une enquête par sondage portant sur 51 372 personnes.

(24) L'enseignement postsecondaire se réfère aux universités seulement.

(25) Non compris les personnes de passage et les résidants de l'ancienne Zone du Canal.

(26) Les données se réfèrent à la population âgée de 16 ans et plus.

(27) La catégorie "sans scolarité" se réfère à ceux qui ont fait moins d'une année scolaire dans l'enseignement primaire.

(28) Non compris les militaires en garnison sur le territoire.

(29) Le premier cycle de l'enseignement secondaire se réfère au niveau d'enseignement "intermedio". Le deuxième cycle de l'enseignement secondaire se réfère aux enseignements "Media", "Técnica" et "Normal".

(30) Non compris la population rurale du Nord du Brésil.

(31) D'après un échantillon du recensement.

(32) D'après une enquête par sondage.

(33) D'après un échantillon portant sur 10% du recensement.

(34) Non compris les personnes dont le niveau d'enseignement est inconnu.

(35) Non compris Jammu et Cachemire.

(36) Non compris les personnes qui fréquentent encore l'école et dont le niveau d'enseignement est inconnu.

(37) Les données se réfèrent à la population âgée de 6 ans et plus.

(38) D'après une enquête des ménages portant sur 6 393 ménages. La catégorie "sans scolarité" comprend les analphabètes.

(39) Le second cycle de l'enseignement secondaire inclut "polytechnic". L'enseignement postsecondaire se réfère aux universités seulement.

(40) Les données sont basées sur une enquête portant sur 8 619 ménages (dont 5 563 urbains et 3 056 ruraux) du Enquête Démographique et Santé de 1993.

(41) "Enseignement primaire non complété" se réfère aux 4 premières années d'études et "Enseignement primaire complété" comprend les 4 dernières années d'études.

(42) Non compris les travailleurs expatriés et leurs familles.

(43) Les données sur l'enseignement secondaire et le postsecondaire se réfèrent au plus haut niveau complété.

(44) La catégorie "sans scolarité" inclut les personnes qui poursuivent encore leurs études.

(6) La categoría "sin escolaridad" incluye a los analfabetas.

(7) "Enseñanza primaria completa" se refiere a los dos últimos años de la enseñanza primaria.

(8) Los datos se refieren a la población de 7 años y más.

(9) La categoría "sin escolaridad" comprende a las personas cuyo nivel de instrucción se desconoce.

(10) Las personas que saben leer y escribir están contabilizadas en "Enseñanza primaria incompleta".

(11) No incluyen a la población que frecuenta la escuela y a la que nunca la ha frecuentado.

(12) No incluyen Botphuthatwana, Transkei, Venda.

(13) Los datos se refieren a la población de 20 años y más.

(14) La categoría "sin escolaridad" comprende a los analfabetas y a aquellos cuyo nivel de instrucción se desconoce.

(15) Los datos se refieren solamente a las personas que frecuentaron la escuela y que abandonaron sus estudios.

(16) Según una encuesta por muestreo relativa a 35 502 personas.

(17) Los datos se refieren a la población de 14 años y más.

(18) No incluyen a las personas que aún frecuentan la escuela.

(19) Según una muestra relativa al 20% del censo.

(20) Los datos se refieren a la población de 25 a 49 años.

(21) Los datos se refieren a la población de 10 años y más.

(22) Los datos se refieren a la población de 15 años y más.

(23) Según una encuesta por muestreo relativa a 51 372 personas.

(24) La enseñanza postsecundaria se refiere a las universidades solamente.

(25) No incluyen a las personas de pasaje y a los residentes de la antigua Zona del Canal.

(26) Los datos se refieren a la población de 16 años y más.

(27) La categoría "sin escolaridad" se refiere a las personas que no completaron un año de enseñanza primaria.

(28) No incluyen a los militares destacados en la zona.

(29) El primer ciclo de la enseñanza secundaria se refiere al nivel de enseñanza "intermedio". El segundo ciclo de la enseñanza secundaria se refiere a las enseñanzas "Media", "Técnica" y "Normal".

(30) No incluyen a la población del Norte de Brasil.

(31) Según una muestra del censo.

(32) Según una encuesta por muestreo.

(33) Según una muestra relativa al 10% del censo.

(34) No incluyen a las personas cuyo nivel de enseñanza se desconoce.

(35) No incluyen Jammu y Cachemira.

(36) No incluyen a las personas que aún frecuentan la escuela y cuyo nivel de enseñanza se desconoce.

(37) Los datos se refieren a la población de 6 años y más.

(38) Según una encuesta de hogares relativa a 6 393 hogares. La categoría "sin escolaridad" incluye a los analfabetas.

(39) El segundo ciclo de la enseñanza secundaria incluye "polytechnic". La enseñanza postsecundaria se refiere a las universidades solamente.

(40) Los datos se basan en una encuesta relativa a 8 619 hogares (de los cuales 5 563 urbanos y 3 056 rurales) de la Encuesta Demográfica y Salud de 1993.

(41) "Enseñanza primaria sin completar" se refiere a los 4 primeros años de estudio. "Enseñanza primaria completa" incluye los 4 últimos años.

(42) No incluyen a los trabajadores expatriados y a sus familias.

(43) Los datos sobre la enseñanza secundaria y postsecundaria se refieren al más alto nivel completado.

(44) La categoría "sin escolaridad" incluye a las personas que todavía continúan sus estudios.

II.3    Educational attainment
Niveau d'instruction
Nivel de instrucción

(45) Data refer to the highest qualification obtained in any school and not to the highest class or course attended with profit. The category "No schooling" comprises illiterates.

(46) Secondary education includes persons with incomplete tertiary education. Post-secondary education refers to those who has completed tertiary education.

(47) Data refer to population aged 16 to 74 years.

(45) Les données se réfèrent au niveau de qualification le plus élevé obtenu dans quelque école que ce soit et non à l'année d'études ou au cours le plus élevé suivi avec succès. La catégorie "sans scolarité" comprend les analphabètes.

(46) L'enseignement secondaire inclut les personnes n'ayant pas complété l'enseignement supérieur. L'enseignement postsecondaire se réfère à ceux ayant complété l'enseignement supérieur.

(47) Les données se réfèrent à la population âgée de 16 à 74 ans.

(45) Los datos se refieren al nivel de calificación el más alto obtenido en cualquier tipo de escuela y no al año de estudios o al curso el más alto seguido con éxito. La categoría "sin escolaridad" incluye a los analfabetas.

(46) La enseñanza secundaria incluye a las personas que no han completado la enseñanza superior. La enseñanza postsecundaria se refiere a aquellos que han completado la enseñanza superior.

(47) Los datos se refieren a la población de 16 a 74 años.

## II.4 Pre-primary education:
schools, teaching staff and pupils

## Enseignement préprimaire:
écoles, personnel enseignant et élèves

## Enseñanza preprimaria:
escuelas, personal docente y alumnos

| Country<br>Pays<br>País | Year<br>Année<br>Año | Schools<br>Écoles<br>Escuelas | Teaching staff<br>Personnel enseignant<br>Personal docente | | | Pupils enrolled<br>Élèves inscrits<br>Alumnos matriculados | | | |
|---|---|---|---|---|---|---|---|---|---|
| | | | Total | Female<br>Féminin<br>Femenino | %<br>F | Total | Female<br>Féminin<br>Femenino | %<br>F | %<br>Private<br>Privé<br>Privada |
| **Africa** | | | | | | | | | |
| Algeria | 1970/71 | - | - | - | - | - | - | - | - |
| | 1975/76 | ... | - | - | - | - | - | - | - |
| | 1992/93 | ... | 1 042 | 836 | 80 | 21 120 | 10 399 | 49 | - |
| | 1993/94 | ... | 1 229 | 1 142 | 93 | 27 409 | 13 032 | 48 | - |
| | 1994/95 | ... | 1 280 | 1 085 | 85 | 27 657 | 13 309 | 48 | - |
| | 1995/96 | ... | 1 238 | 1 104 | 89 | 31 897 | 15 669 | 49 | - |
| | 1996/97 | ... | 1 333 | 1 179 | 88 | 33 503 | 16 403 | 49 | - |
| Angola | 1970/71 | 46 | 78 | ... | ... | 2 567 | 1 332 | 52 | ... |
| | 1980/81 | ... | ... | ... | ... | (1) 390 512 | (1) 157 803 | 40 | - |
| | 1985/86 | ... | ... | ... | ... | 230 154 | 103 139 | 45 | - |
| | 1990/91 | ... | ... | ... | ... | 164 146 | 55 817 | 34 | - |
| | 1991/92 | ... | ... | ... | ... | 214 867 | ... | ... | ... |
| Benin | 1975/76 | | | - | - | | ... | ... | - |
| | 1980/81 | 92 | 174 | ... | ... | 3 779 | ... | ... | - |
| | 1985/86 | 241 | 526 | 289 | 55 | 11 302 | 5 090 | 45 | - |
| | 1990/91 | 306 | 598 | 328 | 55 | 13 623 | 6 177 | 45 | 8 |
| | 1991/92 | 309 | 612 | 335 | 55 | 13 827 | 6 299 | 46 | 8 |
| | 1992/93 | 299 | 635 | 375 | 59 | 14 814 | 6 803 | 46 | 11 |
| | 1993/94 | 265 | 518 | 282 | 54 | 14 512 | 6 789 | 47 | ... |
| | 1994/95 | 277 | 603 | 358 | 59 | 15 979 | 7 600 | 48 | ... |
| | 1995/96 | 283 | 618 | 378 | 61 | 16 738 | 7 929 | 47 | 9 |
| | 1996/97 | ... | *622 | *389 | *63 | *17 441 | *8 335 | *48 | ... |
| Burkina Faso | 1970/71 | 3 | ... | ... | ... | 355 | 169 | 48 | 28 |
| | 1975/76 | ... | 19 | 19 | 100 | 497 | 239 | 48 | 87 |
| | 1980/81 | 5 | 15 | 14 | 93 | 382 | 179 | 47 | 79 |
| | 1985/86 | 45 | 135 | 115 | 85 | 3 543 | 1 773 | 50 | 29 |
| | 1990/91 | 80 | 240 | 204 | 85 | 6 781 | 3 402 | 50 | 29 |
| | 1991/92 | 85 | 255 | 220 | 86 | 7 593 | 3 817 | 50 | 35 |
| | 1992/93 | 90 | 270 | 235 | 87 | 7 943 | 3 921 | 49 | 38 |
| | 1993/94 | 117 | 351 | 307 | 87 | 9 958 | 4 979 | 50 | 34 |
| | 1994/95 | 117 | 351 | 307 | 87 | 10 067 | 5 067 | 50 | 35 |
| | 1995/96 | 127 | 381 | 336 | 88 | 13 695 | 6 969 | 51 | 37 |
| | 1996/97 | 141 | 423 | 377 | 89 | 17 005 | 8 658 | 51 | 35 |
| | 1997/98 | 147 | 441 | 394 | 89 | 18 045 | 9 124 | 51 | 37 |
| Burundi | 1970/71 | ... | 18 | 18 | 100 | 916 | 419 | 46 | 72 |
| | 1975/76 | ... | (2) 10 | ... | ... | (2) 594 | (2) 292 | 49 | ... |
| | 1980/81 | ... | (2) 15 | (2) 15 | 100 | (2) 1 004 | (2) 498 | 50 | ... |
| | 1985/86 | ... | 32 | 30 | 94 | 1 774 | 883 | 50 | 26 |
| Cameroon | 1970/71 | 14 | ... | ... | ... | 12 557 | 6 136 | 49 | 69 |
| | 1975/76 | ... | ... | ... | ... | 21 752 | 10 558 | 49 | 42 |
| | 1980/81 | 436 | 1 512 | 1 494 | 99 | 40 574 | 19 920 | 49 | 49 |
| | 1985/86 | 536 | 2 454 | 2 444 | 100 | 73 486 | 35 758 | 49 | 43 |
| | 1990/91 | 807 | 3 567 | 3 562 | 100 | 93 771 | 46 818 | 50 | 36 |
| | 1991/92 | 935 | 3 490 | 3 477 | 100 | 94 068 | 46 985 | 50 | 37 |
| | 1993/94 | 1 018 | 3 755 | *3 750 | *100 | 91 179 | 45 170 | 50 | 41 |
| | 1994/95 | 1 061 | 3 778 | 3 733 | 99 | 91 242 | 45 206 | 50 | 41 |
| | 1996/97 | 1 109 | 4 545 | ... | ... | 87 318 | ... | ... | 48 |
| Central African<br>Republic | 1970/71 | 107 | 180 | ... | ... | 7 779 | 3 558 | 46 | - |
| | 1975/76 | ... | 213 | 213 | 100 | 10 673 | *5 337 | *50 | 8 |
| | 1980/81 | ... | ... | ... | ... | 10 015 | ... | ... | ... |
| | 1990/91 | 162 | ... | ... | ... | 15 734 | ... | ... | ... |

| Country / Pays / País | Year / Année / Año | Schools / Écoles / Escuelas | Teaching staff / Personnel enseignant / Personal docente | | | Pupils enrolled / Élèves inscrits / Alumnos matriculados | | | |
|---|---|---|---|---|---|---|---|---|---|
| | | | Total | Female Féminin Femenino | % F | Total | Female Féminin Femenino | % F | % Private Privé Privada |
| Chad | 1994/95 | (2) 24 | (2) 67 | (2) 58 | 87 | (2) 1 673 | (2) 735 | 44 | ... |
| Comoros | 1980/81 | ... | 600 | 200 | 33 | 17 778 | 8 598 | 48 | - |
| Congo | 1970/71 | 1 | 10 | 10 | 100 | 355 | 153 | 43 | - |
| | 1980/81 | 36 | 334 | 334 | 100 | 3 498 | 1 736 | 50 | - |
| | 1985/86 | 51 | 537 | 537 | 100 | 5 595 | 2 756 | 49 | - |
| | 1990/91 | 56 | 645 | 645 | 100 | 5 810 | 2 897 | 50 | - |
| | 1991/92 | 63 | 685 | 685 | 100 | 6 836 | 3 511 | 51 | 9 |
| | 1992/93 | (2) 56 | (2) 599 | (2) 599 | 100 | (2) 4 673 | (2) 2 439 | 52 | ... |
| | 1993/94 | 53 | 619 | 619 | 100 | 4 415 | 2 301 | 52 | 8 |
| Côte d'Ivoire | 1970/71 | ... | ... | ... | ... | 4 110 | 2 120 | 52 | 57 |
| | 1975/76 | ... | 108 | 108 | 100 | 4 656 | 2 260 | 49 | 60 |
| | 1980/81 | ... | 179 | 179 | 100 | 6 291 | 2 953 | 47 | 76 |
| | 1985/86 | ... | ... | ... | ... | 8 570 | 4 104 | 48 | 63 |
| | 1990/91 | ... | ... | ... | ... | 11 624 | 5 624 | 48 | 67 |
| | 1991/92 | ... | ... | ... | ... | 11 217 | 5 422 | 48 | 67 |
| | 1992/93 | ... | ... | ... | ... | 17 949 | 8 594 | 48 | 51 |
| | 1993/94 | ... | ... | ... | ... | 22 458 | 10 981 | 49 | 49 |
| | 1994/95 | 281 | 1 192 | 1 113 | 93 | 25 638 | 12 323 | 48 | 54 |
| | 1995/96 | ... | ... | ... | ... | 30 885 | 14 959 | 48 | 52 |
| | 1996/97 | ... | ... | ... | ... | 32 141 | 15 551 | 48 | 49 |
| Democratic Rep. of the Congo | 1970/71 | ... | ... | ... | ... | 18 315 | ... | ... | ... |
| | 1992/93 | 429 | 768 | 404 | 53 | 33 235 | 17 279 | 52 | 86 |
| Djibouti | 1975/76 | 1 | 2 | 2 | 100 | 159 | 91 | 57 | 100 |
| | 1985/86 | 1 | ... | ... | ... | 234 | 116 | 50 | 100 |
| | 1990/91 | 1 | ... | ... | ... | 220 | 130 | 59 | 100 |
| | 1991/92 | 1 | ... | ... | ... | 210 | 123 | 59 | 100 |
| | 1992/93 | 1 | ... | ... | ... | 218 | 142 | 65 | 100 |
| | 1993/94 | 2 | ... | ... | ... | 236 | 150 | 64 | 100 |
| | 1994/95 | 2 | 6 | 6 | 100 | 259 | 148 | 57 | 100 |
| | 1995/96 | 2 | ... | ... | ... | 206 | 123 | 60 | 100 |
| | 1996/97 | 2 | ... | ... | ... | 247 | 132 | 53 | 100 |
| Egypt | 1970/71 | 35 | 632 | 607 | 96 | 24 558 | 12 469 | 51 | 100 |
| | 1975/76 | ... | ... | ... | ... | 41 948 | 20 719 | 49 | 100 |
| | 1980/81 | 433 | ... | ... | ... | 74 921 | 36 809 | 49 | 94 |
| | 1985/86 | 602 | ... | ... | ... | 128 272 | 62 368 | 49 | 93 |
| | 1990/91 | 1 075 | 8 015 | 7 649 | 95 | 198 742 | 96 749 | 49 | 87 |
| | 1991/92 | 1 196 | 9 384 | 8 758 | 93 | 223 051 | 108 204 | 49 | 84 |
| | 1992/93 | 1 335 | 9 184 | 8 818 | 96 | 235 733 | 113 995 | 48 | 83 |
| | 1993/94 | 1 569 | 9 692 | 9 344 | 96 | 246 100 | 118 432 | 48 | 77 |
| | 1994/95 | 1 790 | 9 216 | 8 976 | 97 | 257 815 | 124 092 | 48 | 72 |
| | 1995/96 | 2 060 | 10 913 | 10 773 | 99 | 266 502 | 127 670 | 48 | 69 |
| | 1996/97 | 2 367 | 12 050 | 11 889 | 99 | 289 995 | 138 618 | 48 | 64 |
| Equatorial Guinea | 1992/93 | (2) 72 | (2) 142 | (2) 142 | 100 | (2) 4 048 | ... | ... | ... |
| | 1993/94 | (2) 85 | (2) 171 | (2) 171 | 100 | (2) 3 788 | (2) 1 864 | 49 | ... |
| Eritrea | 1991/92 | 65 | 201 | 201 | 100 | 6 461 | 3 319 | 51 | 98 |
| | 1992/93 | 72 | 227 | 227 | 100 | 7 031 | 3 605 | 51 | 97 |
| | 1993/94 | 77 | 244 | 243 | 100 | 7 748 | 3 839 | 50 | 95 |
| | 1994/95 | 80 | 256 | 255 | 100 | 8 032 | 3 930 | 49 | 96 |
| | 1995/96 | 67 | 235 | 232 | 99 | 8 180 | 3 979 | 49 | 95 |
| | 1996/97 | 61 | 207 | 204 | 99 | 7 443 | 3 652 | 49 | 94 |
| Ethiopia | 1985/86 | 708 | 1 532 | ... | ... | 69 736 | ... | ... | 100 |
| | 1990/91 | 786 | 2 091 | 1 956 | 94 | 73 668 | 36 919 | 50 | 100 |
| | 1991/92 | 632 | 1 531 | 1 474 | 96 | 58 444 | 29 099 | 50 | 100 |
| | 1992/93 | 550 | 1 486 | 1 443 | 97 | 57 006 | 28 537 | 50 | 100 |
| | 1993/94 | 652 | 1 638 | 1 597 | 97 | 66 086 | 33 158 | 50 | 100 |
| | 1994/95 | 678 | 1 890 | 1 821 | 96 | 70 255 | 34 877 | 50 | 100 |
| | 1996/97 | 744 | 2 113 | 2 001 | 95 | 80 835 | 39 644 | 49 | 100 |
| Gabon | 1991/92 | 9 | 37 | 36 | 97 | 950 | 485 | 51 | 52 |
| Gambia | 1991/92 | ... | 408 | ... | ... | 13 118 | ... | ... | ... |
| Ghana | 1970/71 | ... | ... | ... | ... | 18 841 | 9 508 | 50 | 100 |
| | 1980/81 | 1 160 | ... | ... | ... | 158 395 | 72 682 | 46 | 11 |
| | 1985/86 | (2) 2 399 | (2) 10 218 | (2) 9 921 | 97 | (2) 171 182 | ... | ... | ... |
| Guinea | 1993/94 | 113 | 302 | 242 | 80 | 10 260 | 4 593 | 45 | 95 |
| | 1994/95 | *150 | *503 | ... | ... | *15 908 | *7 610 | *48 | *95 |
| | 1995/96 | 172 | 414 | 328 | 79 | 21 850 | 10 382 | 48 | 92 |
| | 1996/97 | 202 | 564 | 418 | 74 | 23 736 | 11 272 | 47 | 92 |
| | 1997/98 | ... | 594 | 438 | 74 | 30 857 | ... | ... | 93 |
| Guinea-Bissau | 1970/71 | 3 | 12 | ... | ... | 217 | 161 | 74 | 100 |
| | 1980/81 | 6 | 46 | 45 | 98 | (3) 459 | (3) 225 | 49 | - |
| Kenya | 1985 | 11 780 | 15 676 | 15 676 | 100 | 582 505 | 290 211 | 50 | ... |
| | 1990 | 17 000 | 22 000 | 21 800 | 99 | 850 000 | 450 000 | 53 | ... |
| | 1991 | 17 650 | 24 809 | ... | ... | 908 966 | ... | ... | ... |

| Country / Pays / País | Year / Année / Año | Schools / Écoles / Escuelas | Teaching staff / Personnel enseignant / Personal docente | | | Pupils enrolled / Élèves inscrits / Alumnos matriculados | | | |
|---|---|---|---|---|---|---|---|---|---|
| | | | Total | Female / Féminin / Femenino | % F | Total | Female / Féminin / Femenino | % F | % Private / Privé / Privada |
| Kenya (cont) | 1992 | ... | 25 681 | 25 000 | 97 | 931 826 | *465 000 | *50 | ... |
| | 1993 | 18 487 | 26 625 | ... | ... | 924 094 | 452 070 | 49 | ... |
| | 1994 | 19 083 | 27 829 | ... | ... | 951 997 | 466 645 | 49 | ... |
| Liberia | 1975 | ... | ... | ... | ... | 53 785 | 21 763 | 40 | ... |
| | 1980 | 60 | ... | ... | ... | 80 215 | 33 745 | 42 | 42 |
| Libyan Arab Jamahiriya | 1970/71 | 15 | 55 | 51 | 93 | 1 365 | 616 | 45 | 43 |
| | 1975/76 | 62 | 364 | 364 | 100 | 7 727 | 3 346 | 43 | 38 |
| | 1980/81 | ... | 515 | 515 | 100 | 9 008 | 4 146 | 46 | - |
| | 1985/86 | 78 | 1 051 | 1 051 | 100 | 15 028 | 7 243 | 48 | - |
| Madagascar | 1994/95 | ... | ... | ... | ... | 57 843 | 29 186 | 50 | ... |
| Mali | 1994/95 | ... | *503 | ... | ... | 15 908 | 7 610 | 48 | ... |
| | 1995/96 | ... | 531 | 471 | 89 | 17 165 | 8 211 | 48 | ... |
| | 1996/97 | 194 | ... | ... | ... | 20 322 | 9 944 | 49 | ... |
| | 1997/98 | 197 | 675 | 497 | 74 | 23 548 | 11 638 | 49 | ... |
| Mauritania | 1992/93 | 36 | 108 | 108 | 100 | 800 | ... | ... | 56 |
| Mauritius | 1970 | ... | 400 | 394 | 99 | 10 504 | 5 104 | 49 | 100 |
| | 1975 | 283 | 358 | 356 | 99 | 9 233 | 4 498 | 49 | 100 |
| | 1980 | 349 | 453 | 451 | 100 | 11 704 | 5 712 | 49 | 100 |
| | 1990 | 579 | 1 195 | 1 195 | 100 | 21 481 | 10 537 | 49 | ... |
| | 1993 | 848 | 1 704 | 1 704 | 100 | 33 071 | 16 260 | 49 | 90 |
| | 1996 | 1 131 | 2 469 | 2 469 | 100 | 34 444 | 16 981 | 49 | 82 |
| | 1997 | 1 145 | 2 588 | 2 588 | 100 | 42 904 | 21 241 | 50 | ... |
| Morocco | 1970/71 | ... | ... | ... | ... | (4) 9 552 | (4) 4 448 | 47 | 100 |
| | 1975/76 | ... | ... | ... | ... | (5) 375 567 | ... | ... | ... |
| | 1980/81 | (5) 27 245 | (5) 29 611 | (5) 1 532 | 5 | 579 547 | 143 127 | 25 | 100 |
| | 1985/86 | 30 180 | 33 919 | 3 491 | 10 | 723 770 | 216 025 | 30 | 100 |
| | 1990/91 | 33 345 | 39 805 | 8 080 | 20 | 812 487 | 248 574 | 31 | 100 |
| | 1991/92 | 31 071 | 38 289 | 8 979 | 23 | 788 326 | 227 980 | 29 | 100 |
| | 1992/93 | 31 928 | 36 464 | 8 125 | 22 | 779 043 | 229 694 | 29 | 100 |
| | 1993/94 | 31 898 | 36 203 | 9 623 | 27 | 783 456 | 232 334 | 30 | 100 |
| | 1994/95 | 32 021 | 36 553 | 10 692 | 29 | 796 669 | 241 277 | 30 | 100 |
| | 1995/96 | 33 063 | 38 383 | 11 431 | 30 | 816 619 | 254 404 | 31 | 100 |
| | 1996/97 | 33 617 | 39 469 | 13 504 | 34 | 829 384 | 261 371 | 32 | 100 |
| Mozambique | 1970/71 | 10 | 31 | 29 | 94 | 1 059 | 627 | 59 | 100 |
| | 1985 | ... | ... | ... | ... | (1) 62 940 | (1) 29 647 | 47 | - |
| Namibia | 1990 | ... | ... | ... | ... | 5 649 | 2 991 | 53 | ... |
| | 1991 | ... | ... | ... | ... | 5 780 | 2 874 | 50 | ... |
| | 1992 | 97 | 217 | 216 | 100 | 5 482 | 2 714 | 50 | 14 |
| | 1993 | ... | ... | ... | ... | 4 900 | 2 476 | 51 | ... |
| | 1994 | ... | ... | ... | ... | 4 579 | 2 306 | 50 | ... |
| Niger | 1975/76 | 6 | 19 | 19 | 100 | 874 | 424 | 49 | 100 |
| | 1980/81 | 21 | 85 | 85 | 100 | 2 561 | 1 268 | 50 | 54 |
| | 1985/86 | 24 | 115 | 115 | 100 | 3 980 | 1 967 | 49 | 44 |
| | 1990/91 | 81 | 317 | 317 | 100 | 11 696 | 5 593 | 48 | 22 |
| | 1991/92 | 87 | 317 | 317 | 100 | 13 182 | 6 363 | 48 | 21 |
| | 1992/93 | 88 | 367 | 367 | 100 | 12 600 | 6 366 | 51 | 22 |
| | 1994/95 | 98 | 400 | 400 | 100 | 9 939 | 4 833 | 49 | 29 |
| | 1995/96 | 105 | 417 | 417 | 100 | 9 203 | 4 467 | 49 | 30 |
| | 1996/97 | 117 | 446 | 442 | 99 | 10 638 | 5 192 | 49 | 23 |
| | 1997/98 | 123 | 494 | 490 | 99 | 11 764 | 5 919 | 50 | 21 |
| Reunion | 1970/71 | (2) 28 | (2) 298 | ... | ... | 13 125 | ... | ... | 16 |
| | 1975/76 | ... | (2) 514 | ... | ... | 26 700 | ... | ... | 10 |
| | 1980/81 | ... | ... | ... | ... | 33 816 | ... | ... | 8 |
| | 1985/86 | 142 | 1 212 | 1 181 | 97 | 37 694 | 18 651 | 49 | 8 |
| | 1990/91 | ... | ... | ... | ... | 41 294 | ... | ... | ... |
| | 1991/92 | ... | ... | ... | ... | 41 980 | ... | ... | 8 |
| | 1992/93 | ... | ... | ... | ... | 42 730 | ... | ... | 8 |
| | 1993/94 | 172 | ... | ... | ... | 43 737 | ... | ... | 8 |
| | 1994/95 | ... | ... | ... | ... | 44 312 | ... | ... | 7 |
| | 1995/96 | ... | ... | ... | ... | 45 015 | ... | ... | 7 |
| Sao Tome and Principe | 1970/71 | 2 | 5 | ... | ... | 224 | 120 | 54 | 100 |
| | 1980/81 | ... | ... | ... | ... | 2 430 | ... | ... | ... |
| Senegal | 1980/81 | 98 | (2) 85 | (2) 85 | 100 | 8 445 | 4 315 | 51 | 80 |
| | 1985/86 | 124 | 547 | ... | ... | 12 764 | 6 509 | 51 | 57 |
| | 1990/91 | 161 | 666 | 501 | 75 | 17 042 | 8 600 | 50 | 58 |
| | 1991/92 | 173 | 714 | 528 | 74 | 17 432 | 8 614 | 49 | 59 |
| | 1992/93 | ... | ... | ... | ... | 17 592 | 8 715 | 50 | 61 |
| | 1993/94 | 196 | 751 | 580 | 77 | 17 305 | 8 526 | 49 | 60 |
| | 1995/96 | 212 | 934 | 608 | 65 | 19 233 | 9 551 | 50 | 62 |
| | 1996/97 | 211 | 926 | 702 | 76 | 18 513 | 9 359 | 51 | 65 |
| | 1997/98 | 270 | 995 | 777 | 78 | 19 880 | 10 064 | 51 | 68 |
| Seychelles | 1970 | 33 | *40 | *40 | *100 | *390 | *250 | *64 | *100 |
| | 1980 | 34 | 91 | 91 | 100 | 2 568 | ... | ... | - |

| Country / Pays / País | Year / Année / Año | Schools / Écoles / Escuelas | | Teaching staff / Personnel enseignant / Personal docente | | | | Pupils enrolled / Élèves inscrits / Alumnos matriculados | | | | |
|---|---|---|---|---|---|---|---|---|---|---|---|---|
| | | | | Total | | Female Féminin Femenino | % F | | Total | | Female Féminin Femenino | % F | % Private Privé Privada |
| Seychelles (cont) | 1985 | | 38 | | 109 | 109 | 100 | | 3 180 | | ... | ... | - |
| | 1990 | | 34 | | *173 | *173 | *100 | | 3 412 | | *1 705 | *50 | - |
| | 1991 | | 35 | | 175 | 175 | 100 | | 3 257 | | 1 632 | 50 | 1 |
| | 1992 | | 35 | | 176 | 176 | 100 | | 3 199 | | 1 602 | 50 | 2 |
| | 1993 | | 34 | | 175 | 175 | 100 | | 3 125 | | 1 528 | 49 | 1 |
| | 1994 | | 35 | | 175 | 175 | 100 | | 3 167 | | 1 537 | 49 | 2 |
| | 1995 | | 35 | | 176 | 176 | 100 | | 3 250 | | 1 586 | 49 | 2 |
| | 1996 | | 35 | | 180 | 180 | 100 | | 3 262 | | 1 573 | 48 | 3 |
| Somalia | 1970/71 | | 8 | | 15 | 12 | 80 | | 595 | | 273 | 46 | 100 |
| | 1975/76 | | 9 | | 68 | 61 | 90 | | 1 080 | | 499 | 46 | - |
| | 1980/81 | | 17 | | 143 | 134 | 94 | | 2 089 | | 1 087 | 52 | - |
| | 1985/86 | | 16 | | 133 | 125 | 94 | | 1 558 | | 882 | 57 | - |
| South Africa | 1990 | | ... | | ... | ... | ... | (6) | 125 393 | (6) | 62 488 | 50 | |
| | 1991 | (6) | 1 336 | (6) | 6 957 | (6) 6 818 | 98 | (6) | 174 110 | (6) | 87 315 | 50 | 4 |
| | 1992 | | ... | | ... | ... | ... | (6) | 178 125 | (6) | 90 235 | 51 | ... |
| | 1993 | | ... | | ... | ... | ... | (6) | 193 176 | (6) | 96 126 | 50 | ... |
| | 1994 | | 3 060 | | 10 525 | 10 313 | 98 | | 286 663 | | 142 635 | 50 | 8 |
| | 1996 | | 4 596 | | 13 996 | 13 856 | 99 | | 329 070 | | 166 060 | 50 | |
| St. Helena | 1970 | | ... | | 6 | 6 | 100 | | 75 | | 50 | 67 | - |
| | 1980/81 | | 3 | | 9 | 9 | 100 | | 60 | | 36 | 60 | - |
| | 1985/86 | | 3 | | 6 | 6 | 100 | | 88 | | 60 | 68 | - |
| Sudan | 1970/71 | | ... | | 323 | 323 | 100 | | 16 508 | | 7 819 | 47 | 100 |
| | 1980/81 | (7) | 3 135 | (7) | 3 183 | ... | ... | (7) | 148 879 | | ... | ... | ... |
| | 1985/86 | (7) | 4 003 | (7) | 5 569 | (7) 2 278 | 41 | (7) | 235 943 | | ... | ... | ... |
| | 1990/91 | | 5 914 | | 8 055 | 3 770 | 47 | | 283 126 | | 100 279 | 35 | ... |
| | 1991/92 | | 6 525 | | 8 478 | 3 939 | 46 | | 350 306 | | 164 699 | 47 | ... |
| | 1996/97 | | 7 541 | | 8 897 | 6 662 | 75 | | 343 767 | | 138 149 | 40 | ... |
| Swaziland | 1990 | | 384 | | 623 | ... | ... | | 12 000 | | 7 757 | 65 | ... |
| | 1993 | | 446 | | 816 | ... | ... | | 19 182 | | ... | ... | ... |
| Togo | 1970/71 | | 114 | | 152 | 97 | 64 | | 9 414 | | 3 983 | 42 | 71 |
| | 1975/76 | | 94 | | 133 | 119 | 89 | | 6 723 | | 3 270 | 49 | 64 |
| | 1980/81 | | 148 | | 230 | 230 | 100 | | 7 726 | | 3 808 | 49 | 53 |
| | 1985/86 | | 212 | | 364 | 364 | 100 | | 9 740 | | 4 733 | 49 | 48 |
| | 1990/91 | | 252 | | 383 | 383 | 100 | | 10 949 | | 5 409 | 49 | 51 |
| | 1993/94 | | 241 | | 395 | 395 | 100 | | 10 526 | | 5 235 | 50 | 45 |
| | 1994/95 | | 232 | | 395 | 393 | 99 | | 10 098 | | 4 949 | 49 | 59 |
| | 1995/96 | | ... | | 446 | 441 | 99 | | 10 354 | | 5 074 | 49 | 51 |
| | 1996/97 | | ... | | 469 | 457 | 97 | | 10 489 | | 5 108 | 49 | 52 |
| Tunisia | 1991/92 | | 845 | | 2 192 | ... | ... | | 58 488 | | ... | ... | ... |
| | 1995/96 | | 1 115 | | ... | ... | ... | | 68 108 | | 32 561 | 48 | ... |
| **North America** | | | | | | | | | | | | |
| Anguilla | 1994/95 | | 10 | | 27 | 27 | 100 | | 391 | | ... | ... | 100 |
| | 1996/97 | | 10 | | 26 | 26 | 100 | | 417 | | 216 | 52 | 100 |
| Bahamas | 1991/92 | (2) | 5 | (2) | 19 | (2) 19 | 100 | (2) | 248 | (2) | 124 | 50 | ... |
| | 1992/93 | | 14 | | 47 | 47 | 100 | | 788 | | 390 | 49 | 69 |
| | 1993/94 | (2) | 7 | (2) | 21 | (2) 21 | 100 | (2) | 325 | (2) | 200 | 62 | ... |
| | 1994/95 | (2) | 7 | (2) | 22 | (2) 22 | 100 | (2) | 316 | (2) | 169 | 53 | ... |
| | 1996/97 | | 20 | | 76 | 76 | 100 | | 1 094 | | 544 | 50 | 57 |
| Barbados | 1975/76 | | *114 | | ... | ... | ... | | *2 661 | | *1 400 | *53 | *7 |
| | 1980/81 | | 132 | (2) | *151 | ... | ... | | 3 936 | | 1 962 | 50 | *20 |
| Belize | 1970/71 | | 3 | | ... | ... | ... | | *135 | | ... | ... | *100 |
| | 1975/76 | | 25 | | ... | ... | ... | | 1 084 | | ... | ... | 100 |
| | 1980/81 | | 55 | | 130 | ... | ... | | 2 000 | | ... | ... | ... |
| | 1990/91 | | 73 | | 155 | 154 | 99 | | 2 753 | | 1 443 | 52 | ... |
| | 1991/92 | | 81 | | 170 | 169 | 99 | | 3 250 | | 1 647 | 51 | ... |
| | 1992/93 | | 83 | | 176 | 175 | 99 | | 3 377 | | 1 661 | 49 | ... |
| | 1993/94 | | 83 | | 176 | 175 | 99 | | 3 162 | | 1 566 | 50 | ... |
| | 1994/95 | | 90 | | 190 | 189 | 99 | | 3 311 | | 1 704 | 51 | 88 |
| Bermuda | 1970/71 | | 30 | (2) | 27 | (2) 27 | 100 | | 1 205 | | 578 | 48 | 74 |
| | 1975/76 | (2) | 10 | | ... | ... | ... | (2) | 396 | (2) | 192 | 48 | ... |
| | 1980/81 | | 31 | | ... | ... | ... | | 1 067 | | 545 | 51 | 60 |
| | 1994/95 | (2) | 11 | (2) | 49 | (2) 49 | 100 | (2) | 491 | (2) | 237 | 48 | ... |
| | 1996/97 | (2) | 12 | (2) | 51 | (2) 51 | 100 | (2) | 432 | (2) | 235 | 52 | ... |
| British Virgin Islands | 1975/76 | | 6 | | 10 | 10 | 100 | | 155 | | 67 | 43 | 100 |
| | 1980/81 | | 8 | | 15 | 12 | 80 | | 299 | | 134 | 45 | 100 |
| | 1990/91 | | ... | | ... | ... | ... | | 228 | | ... | ... | 100 |
| | 1991/92 | | ... | | ... | ... | ... | | 320 | | 160 | 50 | 100 |
| | 1994/95 | | 5 | | 52 | 52 | 100 | | 482 | | ... | ... | 100 |
| Canada | 1970/71 | | ... | | ... | ... | ... | | 350 242 | | 170 219 | 49 | 3 |
| | 1975/76 | | ... | | ... | ... | ... | | 398 476 | | 193 620 | 49 | 2 |

| Country / Pays / País | Year / Année / Año | Schools / Écoles / Escuelas | Teaching staff — Personnel enseignant — Personal docente — Total | Female Féminin Femenino | % F | Pupils enrolled — Élèves inscrits — Alumnos matriculados — Total | Female Féminin Femenino | % F | % Private Privé Privada |
|---|---|---|---|---|---|---|---|---|---|
| Canada (cont) | 1980/81 | ... | ... | ... | ... | 397 266 | 193 807 | 49 | 3 |
| | 1985/86 | ... | (8) 12 625 | ... | ... | 422 085 | 205 391 | 49 | 3 |
| | 1990/91 | ... | (8) 15 471 | (8) 10 796 | 70 | 472 802 | 230 057 | 49 | 4 |
| | 1991/92 | ... | (8) 15 857 | (8) 10 947 | 69 | 486 609 | 237 183 | 49 | 4 |
| | 1992/93 | ... | 13 024 | 8 650 | 66 | 482 446 | 235 195 | 49 | 5 |
| | 1993/94 | ... | 13 127 | 8 690 | 66 | 491 140 | 239 442 | 49 | 4 |
| | 1994/95 | ... | 12 889 | 8 634 | 67 | 502 300 | 244 523 | 49 | 5 |
| | 1995/96 | ... | 12 880 | 8 628 | 67 | 509 589 | 248 071 | 49 | 5 |
| Costa Rica | 1970 | 106 | 256 | 251 | 98 | 7 483 | 3 879 | 52 | 17 |
| | 1975 | 318 | 500 | 500 | 100 | 15 608 | 7 789 | 50 | 11 |
| | 1980 | 370 | 673 | ... | ... | 21 857 | 10 792 | 49 | 13 |
| | 1985 | 536 | 1 302 | ... | ... | 36 356 | 18 020 | 50 | 11 |
| | 1990 | 791 | 1 989 | ... | ... | 46 638 | 22 912 | 49 | 11 |
| | 1991 | 845 | 2 170 | 2 115 | 97 | 52 040 | 25 612 | 49 | 11 |
| | 1992 | 879 | 2 090 | ... | ... | 52 644 | 25 884 | 49 | 10 |
| | 1993 | 913 | 2 284 | ... | ... | 53 774 | 26 327 | 49 | 10 |
| | 1994 | 964 | 2 435 | ... | ... | 55 125 | 27 035 | 49 | 11 |
| | 1995 | 1 048 | 2 584 | ... | ... | 58 371 | 28 575 | 49 | 9 |
| | 1996 | 1 128 | 2 894 | 2 812 | 97 | 60 710 | 29 457 | 49 | 10 |
| | 1997 | 1 128 | 3 348 | ... | ... | 63 585 | ... | ... | 9 |
| | 1998 | 1 387 | 3 327 | ... | ... | 67 325 | 32 977 | 49 | 9 |
| Cuba | 1970/71 | ... | 4 037 | ... | ... | 134 258 | 66 377 | 49 | - |
| | 1975/76 | ... | 4 358 | ... | ... | 126 565 | 61 951 | 49 | - |
| | 1980/81 | ... | 5 047 | 4 998 | 99 | 123 741 | 60 386 | 49 | - |
| | 1985/86 | ... | 4 635 | 4 635 | 100 | 108 881 | 47 347 | 43 | - |
| | 1990/91 | ... | 6 980 | 6 980 | 100 | 166 337 | 72 977 | 44 | - |
| | 1991/92 | ... | 6 813 | 6 813 | 100 | 147 550 | 63 467 | 43 | - |
| | 1992/93 | ... | 6 968 | 6 968 | 100 | 161 699 | 69 827 | 43 | - |
| | 1993/94 | ... | 6 933 | 6 933 | 100 | 165 278 | 68 968 | 42 | - |
| | 1994/95 | ... | 6 512 | 6 512 | 100 | 160 283 | 78 363 | 49 | - |
| | 1995/96 | ... | 7 087 | 7 087 | 100 | 169 369 | 82 073 | 48 | - |
| | 1996/97 | ... | 6 970 | 6 970 | 100 | 154 520 | 74 846 | 48 | - |
| Dominica | 1975/76 | 52 | 60 | 58 | 97 | 2 300 | 1 269 | 55 | ... |
| | 1985/86 | 54 | 86 | 86 | 100 | 2 500 | ... | ... | ... |
| | 1990/91 | 65 | 100 | 100 | 100 | 2 246 | 1 152 | 51 | 100 |
| | 1991/92 | 70 | 108 | 107 | 99 | 2 000 | 1 047 | 52 | 100 |
| | 1992/93 | 72 | 131 | 130 | 99 | 3 000 | ... | ... | 100 |
| Dominican Republic | 1970/71 | 249 | ... | ... | ... | 16 848 | ... | ... | ... |
| | 1975/76 | ... | ... | ... | ... | 24 015 | ... | ... | ... |
| | 1980/81 | 286 | ... | ... | ... | 27 278 | ... | ... | 87 |
| | 1985/86 | ... | ... | ... | ... | 67 615 | ... | ... | 79 |
| | 1992/93 | ... | ... | ... | ... | 134 603 | ... | ... | 64 |
| | 1993/94 | ... | ... | ... | ... | 148 435 | 75 380 | 51 | 55 |
| | 1994/95 | ... | ... | ... | ... | 143 475 | ... | ... | 50 |
| | 1995/96 | ... | ... | ... | ... | 179 351 | ... | ... | 45 |
| | 1996/97 | ... | ... | ... | ... | 189 085 | 92 930 | 49 | 41 |
| | 1997/98 | ... | 8 571 | 8 033 | 94 | 190 541 | 94 289 | 49 | 39 |
| El Salvador | 1970 | 235 | 737 | 712 | 97 | 24 211 | 12 793 | 53 | 15 |
| | 1975 | 320 | (2) 592 | (2) 592 | 100 | 42 227 | 22 101 | 52 | 13 |
| | 1980 | 459 | 1 036 | 1 036 | 100 | 48 684 | 25 350 | 52 | 20 |
| | 1991 | 1 271 | ... | ... | ... | 83 865 | 42 868 | 51 | 37 |
| | 1992 | 1 596 | ... | ... | ... | 97 700 | 49 623 | 51 | 33 |
| | 1993 | 2 312 | ... | ... | ... | 113 440 | 57 815 | 51 | 30 |
| | 1994 | ... | ... | ... | ... | 118 182 | ... | ... | ... |
| | 1995 | 2 412 | 5 129 | ... | ... | 134 074 | 67 800 | 51 | 31 |
| | 1996 | 3 679 | 6 009 | ... | ... | 150 749 | 76 463 | 51 | 25 |
| | 1997 | ... | ... | ... | ... | 179 046 | 90 599 | 51 | 22 |
| Grenada | 1970/71 | 85 | 117 | 117 | 100 | 2 101 | 1 135 | 54 | 100 |
| | 1980/81 | 67 | 115 | 113 | 98 | 2 500 | ... | ... | ... |
| Guadeloupe | 1970/71 | (2) 8 | (2) 93 | (2) 93 | 100 | 5 763 | ... | ... | 22 |
| | 1975/76 | ... | (2) 300 | ... | ... | 11 313 | ... | ... | 15 |
| | 1980/81 | ... | ... | ... | ... | 16 875 | ... | ... | 11 |
| | 1985/86 | 96 | 615 | ... | ... | 18 866 | 9 300 | 49 | 10 |
| | 1990/91 | 119 | 709 | ... | ... | 19 983 | 9 801 | 49 | 9 |
| | 1991/92 | 122 | 689 | ... | ... | 20 408 | 10 029 | 49 | 9 |
| | 1992/93 | 121 | 639 | 636 | 100 | 21 201 | 10 388 | 49 | 9 |
| | 1993/94 | 121 | 760 | ... | ... | 22 089 | 10 883 | 49 | 10 |
| | 1994/95 | ... | ... | ... | ... | 22 678 | ... | ... | 10 |
| Guatemala | 1970 | (9) 257 | (9) 678 | (9) 639 | 94 | (9) 21 463 | (9) 10 718 | 50 | 32 |
| | 1975 | (9) 342 | (9) 999 | (9) 927 | 93 | 63 869 | 27 796 | 44 | 21 |
| | 1980 | (9) 564 | (9) 1 700 | ... | ... | (9) 48 869 | (9) 24 464 | 50 | 38 |
| | 1985 | 2 864 | 4 407 | ... | ... | 133 726 | 63 522 | 48 | 25 |
| | 1991 | ... | ... | ... | ... | 145 719 | 70 496 | 48 | 31 |
| | 1993 | 4 553 | 7 708 | ... | ... | 193 061 | 92 745 | 48 | 32 |
| | 1995 | 5 135 | 6 567 | ... | ... | 208 882 | 100 688 | 48 | 33 |
| | 1996 | 5 548 | 7 025 | ... | ... | 217 748 | 105 150 | 48 | 32 |
| | 1997 | ... | ... | ... | ... | 222 703 | ... | ... | ... |
| Haiti | 1990/91 | ... | ... | ... | ... | 230 391 | 110 600 | 48 | 86 |

| Country<br><br>Pays<br><br>País | Year<br><br>Année<br><br>Año | Schools<br><br>Écoles<br><br>Escuelas | Teaching staff<br>Personnel enseignant<br>Personal docente<br><br>Total | | Female<br>Féminin<br>Femenino | %<br><br>F | | Pupils enrolled<br>Élèves inscrits<br>Alumnos matriculados<br><br>Total | | Female<br>Féminin<br>Femenino | %<br><br>F | %<br>Private<br>Privé<br>Privada |
|---|---|---|---|---|---|---|---|---|---|---|---|---|
| Honduras | 1970 | 123 | 217 | | 217 | 100 | | 9 720 | | 4 981 | 51 | *25 |
| | 1975 | 234 | 406 | | 406 | 100 | | 16 136 | | 8 073 | 50 | 16 |
| | 1980 | 441 | 833 | | ... | ... | | 33 034 | | 13 874 | 42 | 16 |
| | 1985 | ... | ... | | | | | 48 610 | | ... | ... | ... |
| | 1991 | 973 | 1 870 | | 1 870 | 100 | | 60 137 | | 30 413 | 51 | 18 |
| | 1993 | 1 210 | 2 220 | | 2 220 | 100 | | 64 876 | | 31 964 | 49 | 21 |
| | 1994 | 1 210 | ... | | ... | ... | | 69 776 | | 35 149 | 50 | 21 |
| Jamaica | 1975/76 | 1 705 | 3 163 | | ... | ... | | 126 217 | | 67 771 | 54 | 83 |
| | 1980/81 | ... | ... | | ... | ... | | 119 508 | | 61 592 | 52 | 85 |
| | 1985/86 | 1 581 | ... | | ... | ... | | 125 046 | | ... | ... | 84 |
| | 1990/91 | 1 681 | 4 158 | | ... | ... | | 133 687 | | 67 154 | 50 | 84 |
| | 1992/93 | ... | ... | | ... | ... | (10) | 114 427 | (10) | 53 567 | 47 | ... |
| Martinique | 1970/71 | 41 | (2) 405 | (2) | 405 | 100 | | 18 044 | | ... | ... | 5 |
| | 1975/76 | ... | (2) 574 | | ... | ... | | 21 459 | | ... | ... | 2 |
| | 1980/81 | ... | ... | | ... | ... | | 17 678 | | ... | ... | 4 |
| | 1990/91 | ... | ... | | ... | ... | | 20 122 | | ... | ... | 4 |
| | 1991/92 | 84 | ... | | ... | ... | | 20 435 | | 10 143 | 50 | 4 |
| | 1992/93 | 86 | ... | | ... | ... | | 21 285 | | 10 509 | 49 | 5 |
| | 1993/94 | 84 | 696 | | 655 | 94 | | 21 342 | | 10 524 | 49 | 4 |
| | 1994/95 | ... | ... | | ... | ... | | 21 475 | | ... | ... | 4 |
| | 1995/96 | 86 | 660 | | 622 | 94 | | 21 232 | | 10 554 | 50 | 4 |
| Mexico | 1970/71 | 3 237 | 11 968 | | 11 968 | 100 | | 422 682 | | 213 529 | 51 | 7 |
| | 1975/76 | 4 156 | 14 073 | | *14 073 | *100 | | 537 090 | | 265 705 | 49 | 8 |
| | 1980/81 | 13 021 | 32 368 | | 32 368 | 100 | | 1 071 619 | | 531 704 | 50 | 11 |
| | 1985/86 | 35 649 | 80 529 | | 80 529 | 100 | | 2 381 412 | | 1 188 108 | 50 | 6 |
| | 1990/91 | 46 736 | 104 972 | | *103 397 | *98 | | 2 734 054 | | 1 362 041 | 50 | 9 |
| | 1991/92 | 49 763 | 110 768 | | *109 106 | *98 | | 2 791 550 | | 1 389 748 | 50 | 9 |
| | 1992/93 | 51 554 | 114 335 | | *112 620 | *99 | | 2 858 890 | | 1 419 258 | 50 | 9 |
| | 1993/94 | 55 083 | 121 589 | | *119 765 | *98 | | 2 980 024 | | 1 480 944 | 50 | 8 |
| | 1994/95 | 58 868 | 129 576 | | *127 632 | *98 | | 3 092 834 | | 1 536 295 | 50 | 8 |
| | 1995/96 | 60 972 | 134 204 | | *132 190 | *98 | | 3 169 951 | | 1 575 209 | 50 | 7 |
| | 1996/97 | 63 319 | 146 247 | | *144 050 | *98 | | 3 238 337 | | 1 607 340 | 50 | 8 |
| Montserrat | 1993/94 | 12 | 31 | | 31 | 100 | | 407 | | 199 | 49 | 12 |
| Netherlands Antilles | 1991/92 | 74 | 314 | | ... | ... | | 7 462 | | ... | ... | 74 |
| Nicaragua | 1970 | ... | ... | | ... | ... | | 10 148 | | 5 335 | 53 | 68 |
| | 1975 | ... | ... | | ... | ... | | 8 986 | | ... | ... | 67 |
| | 1980 | 463 | 924 | | 915 | 99 | | 30 524 | | 15 649 | 51 | 43 |
| | 1985 | 686 | 1 983 | | 1 906 | 96 | | 62 784 | | 32 509 | 52 | 26 |
| | 1990 | 978 | 1 893 | | 1 868 | 99 | | 63 201 | | 32 514 | 51 | 24 |
| | 1991 | ... | 2 075 | | 2 044 | 99 | | 68 657 | | 35 214 | 51 | 26 |
| | 1992 | 1 152 | 2 102 | | ... | ... | | 66 727 | | 34 282 | 51 | 28 |
| | 1993 | 1 403 | 2 508 | | 2 472 | 99 | | 79 543 | | 40 391 | 51 | 36 |
| | 1994 | 2 100 | 3 409 | | 3 314 | 97 | | 97 163 | | 49 119 | 51 | 27 |
| | 1995 | 2 287 | ... | | ... | ... | | 99 145 | | 50 280 | 51 | 26 |
| | 1996 | ... | 3 672 | | ... | ... | | 115 532 | | 58 351 | 51 | ... |
| | 1997 | 3 443 | ... | | ... | ... | | 133 086 | | 67 171 | 50 | 22 |
| | 1998 | 3 968 | ... | | ... | ... | | 143 665 | | 71 958 | 50 | 20 |
| Panama | 1970 | 130 | 229 | | 227 | 99 | | 6 921 | | 3 532 | 51 | 58 |
| | 1975 | 224 | 457 | | 457 | 100 | | 12 398 | | 6 297 | 51 | 40 |
| | 1980 | 365 | 645 | | 644 | 100 | | 18 136 | | 9 063 | 50 | 34 |
| | 1985 | 637 | 1 121 | | 1 109 | 99 | | 27 501 | | 13 736 | 50 | 27 |
| | 1990 | 793 | 1 413 | | ... | ... | | 30 719 | | 15 033 | 49 | 27 |
| | 1991 | 848 | 1 516 | | ... | ... | | 33 530 | | ... | ... | 26 |
| | 1992 | 835 | 1 452 | | ... | ... | | 33 248 | | ... | ... | 30 |
| | 1993 | 887 | 1 544 | | ... | ... | | 35 582 | | ... | ... | 28 |
| | 1994 | 961 | 1 850 | | ... | ... | | 41 276 | | ... | ... | 28 |
| | 1995 | 985 | 1 888 | | ... | ... | | 41 520 | | ... | ... | 28 |
| | 1996 | 1 086 | 2 031 | | ... | ... | | 46 245 | | ... | ... | 26 |
| St. Kitts and Nevis | 1985/86 | 36 | 46 | | 45 | 98 | | 1 501 | | 740 | 49 | 75 |
| | 1991/92 | 56 | 89 | | 89 | 100 | | 1 693 | | ... | ... | 71 |
| | 1992/93 | ... | 116 | | 116 | 100 | | 1 706 | | 839 | 49 | 74 |
| | 1993/94 | 47 | 99 | | ... | ... | | 1 708 | | ... | ... | 73 |
| St. Lucia | 1985/86 | 105 | 202 | | ... | ... | | 3 711 | | ... | ... | 95 |
| | 1990/91 | ... | 340 | | ... | ... | | 5 366 | | ... | ... | 100 |
| | 1991/92 | 125 | 318 | | ... | ... | | 5 300 | | ... | ... | 100 |
| | 1992/93 | 150 | 310 | | 310 | 100 | | 4 566 | | ... | ... | 100 |
| | 1993/94 | 150 | 402 | | *402 | *100 | | 7 114 | | ... | ... | 100 |
| | 1996/97 | 150 | 456 | | ... | ... | | 8 483 | | ... | ... | 100 |
| St. Pierre and Miquelon | 1970/71 | 4 | 12 | | 12 | 100 | | 365 | | 176 | 48 | 67 |
| | 1980/81 | 4 | 18 | | 18 | 100 | | 356 | | 169 | 47 | 78 |
| | 1985/86 | 4 | 18 | | 18 | 100 | | 361 | | 186 | 52 | 76 |
| | 1990/91 | ... | ... | | ... | ... | | 343 | | ... | ... | ... |
| | 1992/93 | ... | ... | | ... | ... | | 307 | | ... | ... | ... |
| | 1994/95 | ... | ... | | ... | ... | | 298 | | ... | ... | ... |

| Country / Pays / País | Year / Année / Año | Schools / Écoles / Escuelas | Teaching staff / Personnel enseignant / Personal docente | | | Pupils enrolled / Élèves inscrits / Alumnos matriculados | | | |
|---|---|---|---|---|---|---|---|---|---|
| | | | Total | Female / Féminin / Femenino | % F | Total | Female / Féminin / Femenino | % F | % Private / Privé / Privada |
| St. Vincent and the | 1990/91 | 77 | 180 | 180 | 100 | 2 492 | 1 296 | 52 | 100 |
| Grenadines | 1993/94 | 97 | 175 | 174 | 99 | 2 500 | ... | ... | 100 |
| Trinidad and | 1980/81 | 39 | 117 | 117 | 100 | 1 739 | ... | ... | ... |
| Tobago (2) | 1985/86 | 49 | 147 | 147 | 100 | 2 035 | ... | ... | ... |
| | 1990/91 | 43 | 121 | 121 | 100 | 1 429 | 733 | 51 | ... |
| | 1992/93 | 50 | 126 | 126 | 100 | 1 418 | 691 | 49 | ... |
| Turks and Caicos | 1975/76 | 2 | 6 | 5 | 83 | 95 | ... | ... | 100 |
| Islands | 1996/97 | 21 | ... | ... | ... | 797 | 383 | 48 | 45 |
| U. S. Virgin Islands | 1980/81 | ... | ... | ... | ... | 2 561 | ... | ... | 31 |
| | 1985/86 | 58 | ... | ... | ... | 2 656 | ... | ... | 29 |
| | 1990/91 | 66 | 129 | ... | ... | 2 595 | ... | ... | 41 |
| | 1992/93 | 62 | 121 | ... | ... | 2 606 | ... | ... | 36 |
| United States | 1970/71 | ... | ... | ... | ... | 4 300 000 | ... | ... | 30 |
| | 1975/76 | ... | ... | ... | ... | (11) 5 141 000 | ... | ... | 33 |
| | 1980/81 | ... | ... | ... | ... | (11) 5 163 000 | (11) 2 449 000 | 47 | 36 |
| | 1985/86 | ... | ... | ... | ... | (11) 6 306 000 | (11) 3 113 000 | 49 | 35 |
| | 1990/91 | ... | ... | ... | ... | (11) 7 300 000 | (11) 3 511 000 | 48 | 38 |
| | 1994/95 | ... | 302 255 | 286 241 | 95 | 8 231 069 | 3 926 267 | 48 | 35 |
| | 1995/96 | ... | 307 752 | 291 448 | 95 | 8 470 918 | 4 103 862 | 48 | 35 |
| **South America** | | | | | | | | | |
| Argentina | 1970 | 3 808 | 11 639 | 11 558 | 99 | 223 251 | 112 949 | 51 | 31 |
| | 1975 | 5 694 | 18 991 | 18 928 | 100 | 369 082 | 185 743 | 50 | 30 |
| | 1980 | 6 622 | ... | ... | ... | 480 216 | ... | ... | 32 |
| | 1985 | 8 015 | 36 287 | 36 117 | 100 | 693 259 | 348 639 | 50 | 31 |
| | 1991 | ... | ... | ... | ... | 982 483 | ... | ... | ... |
| | 1994 | 12 378 | 65 708 | 63 387 | 96 | 1 009 610 | ... | ... | 31 |
| | 1996 | *13 800 | (12) *76 163 | ... | ... | 1 116 951 | 562 719 | 50 | 29 |
| Bolivia | 1970 | 199 | (13) 806 | ... | ... | 62 044 | *29 098 | *47 | 7 |
| | 1975 | 373 | 1 472 | ... | ... | (13) 40 242 | (13) 22 148 | 55 | 11 |
| | 1980 | ... | ... | ... | ... | 90 031 | 44 503 | 49 | ... |
| | 1990 | ... | 2 895 | 2 767 | 96 | 121 132 | 59 669 | 49 | 10 |
| Brazil | 1970 | 6 616 | 16 996 | 16 801 | 99 | 374 267 | 188 307 | 50 | 41 |
| | 1975 | 9 158 | 26 393 | 26 086 | 99 | 566 008 | 281 283 | 50 | 49 |
| | 1980 | 15 320 | 58 788 | 57 458 | 98 | 1 335 317 | 660 412 | 49 | 46 |
| | 1985 | (14) 38 418 | (14) 115 140 | ... | ... | (14) 2 650 490 | ... | ... | 34 |
| | 1990 | (14) 50 957 | (14) 155 358 | ... | ... | (14) 3 740 512 | ... | ... | 34 |
| | 1991 | 57 842 | 256 208 | ... | ... | 5 283 894 | ... | ... | 25 |
| | 1992 | 71 053 | 258 157 | ... | ... | 5 574 514 | ... | ... | 23 |
| | 1993 | 84 366 | 272 619 | ... | ... | 5 780 566 | ... | ... | 22 |
| | 1994 | 93 214 | 274 582 | ... | ... | 5 686 762 | ... | ... | 23 |
| | 1995 | ... | ... | ... | ... | 5 749 237 | ... | ... | 24 |
| | 1996 | ... | 295 517 | ... | ... | 5 714 303 | ... | ... | 22 |
| | 1997 | ... | 299 864 | ... | ... | 5 718 902 | ... | ... | 22 |
| Chile | 1970 | 1 092 | ... | ... | ... | 60 360 | 31 483 | 52 | 28 |
| | 1975 | 1 761 | 2 512 | 2 504 | 100 | 124 697 | ... | ... | 21 |
| | 1980 | ... | ... | ... | ... | 174 909 | ... | ... | 20 |
| | 1985 | ... | ... | ... | ... | 202 252 | 99 714 | 49 | 44 |
| | 1990 | 4 180 | ... | ... | ... | 220 396 | 108 786 | 49 | 48 |
| | 1991 | 4 302 | 8 542 | 8 363 | 98 | 205 283 | 101 532 | 49 | 49 |
| | 1992 | ... | ... | ... | ... | 241 759 | 119 010 | 49 | 47 |
| | 1993 | 4 235 | 9 415 | 9 140 | 97 | 256 348 | 126 129 | 49 | 48 |
| | 1994 | 4 389 | 9 415 | 9 140 | 97 | 263 337 | 129 654 | 49 | 48 |
| | 1995 | 4 779 | 9 576 | 9 296 | 97 | 283 061 | 139 142 | 49 | 49 |
| | 1996 | ... | ... | ... | ... | *289 762 | *142 640 | *49 | *51 |
| Colombia | 1975 | 2 013 | 3 887 | ... | ... | 95 908 | ... | ... | 70 |
| | 1980 | 3 281 | 6 742 | ... | ... | 174 369 | ... | ... | 64 |
| | 1985 | 5 127 | 10 891 | ... | ... | 285 286 | 142 380 | 50 | 61 |
| | 1991 | 7 269 | 14 435 | ... | ... | 342 514 | ... | ... | 52 |
| | 1992 | 9 737 | 19 763 | 19 022 | 96 | 468 379 | 237 468 | 51 | 58 |
| | 1993 | 9 886 | 20 770 | ... | ... | 506 080 | 249 194 | 49 | 57 |
| | 1994 | 12 914 | 28 946 | ... | ... | 627 782 | ... | ... | 55 |
| | 1995 | 14 872 | 35 031 | 33 586 | 96 | 726 721 | ... | ... | 56 |
| | 1996 | 16 591 | 45 888 | 43 736 | 95 | 919 680 | 456 715 | 50 | 51 |
| Ecuador | 1970/71 | 175 | 417 | 388 | 93 | 13 755 | 6 989 | 51 | 24 |
| | 1975/76 | 254 | 778 | 741 | 95 | 23 864 | 12 067 | 51 | 35 |
| | 1980/81 | 736 | 1 858 | 1 768 | 95 | 50 819 | 25 760 | 51 | 42 |
| | 1985/86 | ... | 3 846 | 3 652 | 95 | 93 665 | 47 249 | 50 | ... |
| | 1990/91 | 2 371 | 6 301 | ... | ... | 115 024 | ... | ... | ... |
| | 1991/92 | 2 449 | 5 799 | ... | ... | 123 074 | ... | ... | ... |
| | 1992/93 | 2 567 | 5 895 | 5 552 | 94 | 130 378 | 66 036 | 51 | 40 |
| | 1993/94 | 3 056 | 6 980 | 6 348 | 91 | 124 436 | 62 360 | 50 | 40 |
| | 1994/95 | 3 335 | (15) 8 246 | (15) 7 400 | 90 | (15) 136 158 | (15) 67 449 | 50 | 39 |
| | 1995/96 | ... | (15) 9 296 | (15) 8 274 | 89 | (15) 145 858 | (15) 72 918 | 50 | 39 |

| Country / Pays / País | Year / Année / Año | Schools / Écoles / Escuelas | Teaching staff / Personnel enseignant / Personal docente | | | | Pupils enrolled / Élèves inscrits / Alumnos matriculados | | | | |
|---|---|---|---|---|---|---|---|---|---|---|---|
| | | | | Total | Female Féminin Femenino | % F | | Total | Female Féminin Femenino | % F | % Private Privé Privada |
| Ecuador (cont) | 1996/97 | 3 723 | (15) | 9 980 | (15) 8 899 | 89 | (15) | 156 772 | (15) 78 280 | 50 | 38 |
| | 1997/98 | 4 009 | | 10 992 | ... | ... | | 167 582 | ... | ... | 39 |
| Falkland Islands (Malvinas) | 1995 | 1 | | ... | ... | ... | | 15 | 7 | 47 | 100 |
| French Guiana | 1970/71 | (2) 4 | (2) | 37 | ... | ... | | 2 370 | 1 288 | 54 | 32 |
| | 1975/76 | 8 | (2) | 56 | ... | ... | | 3 359 | ... | ... | ... |
| | 1980/81 | ... | | ... | ... | ... | | 3 879 | ... | ... | 12 |
| | 1990/91 | ... | | ... | ... | ... | | 7 231 | ... | ... | 10 |
| | 1991/92 | ... | | ... | ... | ... | | 7 406 | ... | ... | 10 |
| | 1992/93 | ... | | ... | ... | ... | | 7 786 | ... | ... | 10 |
| | 1993/94 | 42 | | ... | ... | ... | | 8 113 | 4 001 | 49 | 9 |
| | 1994/95 | ... | | ... | ... | ... | | 8 583 | ... | ... | 9 |
| | 1995/96 | ... | | ... | ... | ... | | 9 098 | 4 435 | 49 | 9 |
| Guyana | 1980/81 | 374 | | 2 018 | 1 975 | 98 | | 27 955 | 14 020 | 50 | - |
| | 1985/86 | ... | | 1 399 | 1 387 | 99 | | 25 685 | 12 984 | 51 | - |
| | 1990/91 | ... | | 1 149 | 1 136 | 99 | | 26 986 | 13 477 | 50 | - |
| | 1991/92 | 286 | | 1 438 | 1 428 | 99 | | 27 053 | 13 564 | 50 | - |
| | 1992/93 | ... | | 1 538 | 1 529 | 99 | | 30 019 | 14 844 | 49 | - |
| | 1993/94 | ... | | 1 516 | 1 497 | 99 | | 29 954 | 14 802 | 49 | - |
| | 1994/95 | 363 | | 1 545 | 1 523 | 99 | | 30 004 | 14 863 | 50 | - |
| | 1995/96 | 365 | | 1 795 | 1 782 | 99 | | 29 306 | 14 554 | 50 | - |
| | 1996/97 | 365 | | 1 831 | 1 822 | 100 | | 30 736 | 15 186 | 49 | - |
| Paraguay | 1970 | ... | | 257 | 257 | 100 | | 7 564 | 3 864 | 51 | 49 |
| | 1980 | ... | | ... | ... | ... | | 10 928 | ... | ... | ... |
| | 1985 | 70 | | ... | ... | ... | | 19 052 | 9 530 | 50 | 54 |
| | 1990 | ... | | ... | ... | ... | | 34 157 | 17 076 | 50 | 55 |
| | 1991 | ... | | ... | ... | ... | | 39 358 | 19 839 | 50 | 50 |
| | 1992 | 76 | | 2 255 | ... | ... | | 41 627 | *20 873 | *50 | 50 |
| | 1993 | ... | | 2 997 | 2 687 | 90 | | 55 318 | 27 738 | 50 | 47 |
| | 1994 | ... | | 2 447 | ... | ... | | 51 671 | 25 615 | 50 | 38 |
| | 1995 | ... | | ... | ... | ... | | 63 563 | 31 641 | 50 | 36 |
| | 1996 | ... | | 3 203 | ... | ... | | 74 713 | 37 336 | 50 | 28 |
| | 1997 | ... | | ... | ... | ... | | 87 666 | 50 181 | 57 | ... |
| Peru | 1970 | 639 | | 2 016 | ... | ... | | 74 318 | 38 557 | 52 | 28 |
| | 1975 | 2 098 | | 4 459 | 4 390 | 98 | | 172 051 | 85 062 | 49 | 27 |
| | 1980 | 3 271 | | 6 778 | 6 689 | 99 | | 228 168 | 114 940 | 50 | 27 |
| | 1985 | 5 268 | | 11 206 | 11 059 | 99 | | 342 779 | 172 141 | 50 | 23 |
| | 1990 | ... | | 20 469 | ... | ... | | 504 175 | ... | ... | 18 |
| | 1991 | ... | | 20 864 | 19 821 | 95 | | 518 429 | 259 059 | 50 | 19 |
| | 1992 | 10 644 | | 21 726 | ... | ... | | 536 607 | ... | ... | 20 |
| | 1993 | ... | | 20 572 | ... | ... | | 560 573 | ... | ... | 20 |
| | 1994 | 13 148 | | 27 219 | ... | ... | | 597 382 | ... | ... | 22 |
| | 1995 | 14 000 | | 27 378 | 26 898 | 98 | | 631 166 | 315 373 | 50 | 22 |
| | 1996 | ... | | 29 398 | ... | ... | | 668 588 | ... | ... | 22 |
| | 1997 | ... | | 30 736 | ... | ... | | 688 425 | ... | ... | 22 |
| Suriname | 1970/71 | 239 | | 736 | 736 | 100 | | 19 942 | 10 170 | 51 | 68 |
| | 1975/76 | 309 | | 589 | 589 | 100 | | 17 581 | 8 722 | 50 | 59 |
| | 1980/81 | ... | | 693 | 693 | 100 | | 17 314 | 8 467 | 49 | ... |
| | 1985/86 | ... | | 676 | 675 | 100 | | 17 226 | 8 441 | 49 | ... |
| | 1990/91 | ... | | 675 | 675 | 100 | | 16 968 | 8 281 | 49 | ... |
| | 1991/92 | ... | | 675 | 675 | 100 | | 17 827 | 8 787 | 49 | ... |
| | 1992/93 | ... | | 672 | 672 | 100 | | 18 720 | 9 079 | 48 | ... |
| | 1993/94 | ... | | ... | ... | ... | | 20 979 | 10 360 | 49 | ... |
| Uruguay | 1970 | ... | (2) | 650 | ... | ... | (2) | 20 131 | (2) 9 796 | 49 | ... |
| | 1975 | ... | (2) | 921 | ... | ... | | 40 239 | ... | ... | 32 |
| | 1980 | ... | (2) | 1 001 | ... | ... | | 42 444 | ... | ... | 25 |
| | 1985 | 968 | | 2 012 | ... | ... | | 55 092 | 27 457 | 50 | 26 |
| | 1990 | 1 495 | (2) | 1 479 | ... | ... | | 65 802 | ... | ... | 30 |
| | 1991 | 1 508 | | ... | ... | ... | | 66 841 | 32 994 | 49 | 29 |
| | 1992 | 1 567 | | 2 400 | ... | ... | | 68 048 | 33 792 | 50 | 29 |
| | 1993 | ... | (2) | 1 662 | ... | ... | | 67 209 | 33 331 | 50 | 31 |
| | 1994 | 1 668 | | 2 596 | ... | ... | | 68 999 | 33 392 | 48 | 30 |
| | 1995 | 1 693 | | 2 707 | 2 707 | 100 | | 69 464 | 34 609 | 50 | 29 |
| | 1996 | 1 961 | | 2 918 | ... | ... | | 75 580 | 37 554 | 50 | 26 |
| Venezuela | 1970/71 | ... | | 1 444 | 1 437 | 100 | | 50 159 | 24 687 | 49 | 49 |
| | 1975/76 | 327 | | 6 246 | 6 230 | 100 | | 224 600 | 112 272 | 50 | 21 |
| | 1980/81 | ... | | 16 487 | ... | ... | | 421 183 | ... | ... | 17 |
| | 1985/86 | 1 407 | | 22 102 | 21 747 | 98 | | 561 846 | 278 497 | 50 | 15 |
| | 1990/91 | ... | | 26 074 | 25 739 | 99 | | 634 812 | 314 457 | 50 | 15 |
| | 1991/92 | ... | | 27 792 | 27 424 | 99 | | 674 644 | 333 898 | 49 | 16 |
| | 1992/93 | ... | | 29 009 | 28 594 | 99 | | 683 495 | 338 149 | 49 | 17 |
| | 1993/94 | ... | | 29 942 | 29 436 | 98 | | 695 320 | 343 937 | 49 | 19 |
| | 1994/95 | ... | | 30 448 | 29 942 | 98 | | 716 529 | 351 383 | 49 | 19 |
| | 1995/96 | ... | | 31 945 | 31 439 | 98 | | 696 362 | 344 289 | 49 | 21 |
| | 1996/97 | ... | | 32 888 | 32 382 | 98 | | 738 845 | 364 511 | 49 | 19 |

| Country / Pays / País | Year / Année / Año | Schools / Écoles / Escuelas | Teaching staff / Personnel enseignant / Personal docente | | | | Pupils enrolled / Élèves inscrits / Alumnos matriculados | | | |
|---|---|---|---|---|---|---|---|---|---|---|
| | | | Total | Female / Féminin / Femenino | % F | | Total | Female / Féminin / Femenino | % F | % Private / Privé / Privada |
| **Asia** | | | | | | | | | | |
| Afghanistan | 1980 | 36 | 369 | 369 | 100 | | 4 470 | 2 010 | 45 | - |
| | 1985 | ... | 873 | 873 | 100 | | 17 000 | 7 545 | 44 | - |
| Armenia | 1980/81 | ... | 11 593 | ... | ... | | 134 839 | ... | ... | - |
| | 1985/86 | ... | 13 234 | ... | ... | | 149 768 | ... | ... | - |
| | 1990/91 | ... | 11 954 | ... | ... | | 113 303 | ... | ... | - |
| | 1991/92 | ... | 12 121 | ... | ... | | 114 964 | ... | ... | - |
| | 1992/93 | ... | 12 398 | ... | ... | | 105 325 | ... | ... | - |
| | 1993/94 | ... | 11 966 | ... | ... | | 93 052 | ... | ... | - |
| | 1994/95 | ... | 11 359 | ... | ... | | 81 594 | ... | ... | - |
| | 1995/96 | ... | ... | ... | ... | | 64 201 | ... | ... | - |
| | 1996/97 | 978 | 9 981 | ... | ... | | 68 426 | 41 901 | 61 | - |
| Azerbaijan | 1980/81 | ... | 13 628 | 13 628 | 100 | | 109 721 | 48 277 | 44 | - |
| | 1985/86 | ... | 15 331 | 15 331 | 100 | | 125 636 | 55 280 | 44 | - |
| | 1990/91 | ... | 18 516 | 18 516 | 100 | | 132 338 | 58 229 | 44 | - |
| | 1991/92 | ... | 19 193 | 19 193 | 100 | | 128 785 | 56 665 | 44 | - |
| | 1992/93 | 2 120 | 19 251 | 19 251 | 100 | | 123 094 | 54 161 | 44 | - |
| | 1993/94 | 2 115 | 20 140 | 20 140 | 100 | | 124 371 | 55 469 | 45 | - |
| | 1994/95 | ... | 14 863 | 14 863 | 100 | | 109 492 | 48 669 | 44 | - |
| | 1995/96 | (16) 1 921 | (16) 14 499 | (16) 14 499 | 100 | (16) | 103 608 | (16) 46 416 | 45 | - |
| | 1996/97 | (16) 1 867 | (16) 13 033 | (16) 13 033 | 100 | (16) | 96 318 | (16) 42 958 | 45 | - |
| Bahrain | 1970/71 | ... | ... | ... | ... | | 1 097 | ... | ... | 100 |
| | 1975/76 | ... | ... | ... | ... | | 1 983 | 964 | 49 | 100 |
| | 1980/81 | ... | ... | ... | ... | | 3 730 | 1 768 | 47 | 100 |
| | 1985/86 | 56 | 255 | 255 | 100 | | 7 608 | 3 599 | 47 | 100 |
| | 1990/91 | ... | 344 | 344 | 100 | | 9 056 | 4 412 | 49 | 100 |
| | 1991/92 | 72 | 387 | 386 | 100 | | 10 161 | 4 953 | 49 | 100 |
| | 1992/93 | 75 | 420 | 419 | 100 | | 11 492 | 5 519 | 48 | 100 |
| | 1993/94 | 79 | 464 | 464 | 100 | | 12 008 | 5 752 | 48 | 100 |
| | 1995/96 | 79 | 449 | 448 | 100 | | 12 277 | 5 825 | 47 | 100 |
| | 1996/97 | 90 | ... | ... | ... | | 12 308 | 5 991 | 49 | 100 |
| Brunei Darussalam | 1970 | 13 | 31 | 30 | 97 | | 1 214 | 545 | 45 | 100 |
| | 1975 | 14 | 39 | 39 | 100 | | 1 496 | 688 | 46 | 100 |
| | 1980 | 143 | 324 | 248 | 77 | | 6 760 | 3 251 | 48 | 51 |
| | 1985 | 141 | 366 | ... | ... | | 8 055 | ... | ... | ... |
| | 1991 | 161 | 451 | 404 | 90 | | 9 278 | 4 410 | 48 | 57 |
| | 1992 | 159 | 471 | 424 | 90 | | 9 869 | 4 673 | 47 | 57 |
| | 1993 | 165 | 538 | 495 | 92 | | 11 729 | 5 648 | 48 | 65 |
| | 1994 | 165 | 506 | 468 | 92 | | 10 717 | 5 172 | 48 | 64 |
| | 1995 | 170 | 510 | 476 | 93 | | 11 135 | 5 391 | 48 | 64 |
| | 1996 | ... | ... | ... | ... | | 11 703 | 5 685 | 49 | 69 |
| Cambodia | 1980/81 | 149 | 630 | ... | ... | | 15 077 | ... | ... | ... |
| | 1985/86 | 689 | 2 398 | ... | ... | | 56 165 | ... | ... | ... |
| | 1990/91 | 397 | 2 959 | 2 428 | 82 | | 49 277 | 23 138 | 47 | ... |
| | 1993/94 | 203 | 2 058 | 2 058 | 100 | | 53 080 | 26 848 | 51 | ... |
| | 1994/95 | 219 | 1 954 | 1 954 | 100 | | 49 542 | 24 810 | 50 | ... |
| | 1996/97 | 812 | 1 899 | 1 888 | 99 | | 44 814 | 22 315 | 50 | ... |
| | 1997/98 | *843 | *1 932 | *1 911 | *99 | | 46 460 | 22 971 | 49 | 7 |
| China | 1975/76 | 171 749 | 236 500 | ... | ... | | 6 200 000 | ... | ... | - |
| | 1980/81 | 170 419 | 410 700 | 335 100 | 82 | | 11 507 700 | ... | ... | - |
| | 1985/86 | 172 262 | 549 900 | 527 200 | 96 | | 14 796 900 | 6 971 700 | 47 | - |
| | 1990/91 | 172 322 | 749 600 | 721 700 | 96 | | 19 722 300 | 9 369 200 | 48 | - |
| | 1991/92 | 164 465 | 768 900 | 726 200 | 94 | | 22 092 900 | 10 383 600 | 47 | - |
| | 1992/93 | 172 506 | 815 000 | 770 200 | 95 | | 24 282 100 | 11 408 700 | 47 | - |
| | 1993/94 | 165 197 | 836 000 | 786 800 | 94 | | 25 525 400 | 11 975 900 | 47 | - |
| | 1994/95 | 174 657 | 861 756 | 815 570 | 95 | | 26 302 725 | 12 301 399 | 47 | - |
| | 1995/96 | 180 438 | 875 063 | 827 847 | 95 | | 27 112 328 | 12 676 034 | 47 | - |
| | 1996/97 | 187 324 | 888 596 | 833 592 | 94 | | 26 663 270 | 12 413 017 | 47 | - |
| | 1997/98 | 182 485 | 884 000 | ... | ... | | 25 189 600 | ... | ... | - |
| China, Hong Kong SAR | 1970/71 | 875 | 3 674 | 3 499 | 95 | | 140 960 | 67 214 | 48 | 100 |
| | 1975/76 | 839 | 4 168 | 4 025 | 97 | | 160 184 | 76 755 | 48 | 100 |
| | 1980/81 | 761 | 5 177 | 5 064 | 98 | | 197 410 | 94 788 | 48 | 100 |
| | 1985/86 | 828 | 6 959 | 6 850 | 98 | | 229 089 | 110 974 | 48 | 100 |
| | 1990/91 | 810 | 7 595 | ... | ... | | 196 466 | *95 480 | *49 | 100 |
| | 1991/92 | 793 | 7 814 | ... | ... | | 193 658 | *93 920 | *48 | 100 |
| | 1992/93 | 777 | 7 993 | ... | ... | | 189 730 | *92 020 | *49 | 100 |
| | 1993/94 | 761 | 8 222 | ... | ... | | 187 549 | *90 774 | *48 | 100 |
| | 1994/95 | 739 | ... | ... | ... | | 180 109 | 87 276 | 48 | 100 |
| | 1995/96 | 731 | 8 438 | 8 394 | 99 | | 180 317 | 87 104 | 48 | 100 |
| Cyprus (17) | 1970/71 | 109 | 236 | 231 | 98 | | 4 325 | 2 087 | 48 | 88 |
| | 1975/76 | 96 | 222 | 218 | 98 | | 4 229 | 2 067 | 49 | 74 |
| | 1980/81 | 259 | 418 | 416 | 100 | | 10 397 | 5 007 | 48 | 49 |
| | 1985/86 | 423 | 676 | 672 | 99 | | 16 810 | 7 985 | 48 | 58 |
| | 1990/91 | 572 | 1 030 | 1 022 | 99 | | 23 694 | 11 363 | 48 | 68 |
| | 1991/92 | 606 | 1 111 | 1 097 | 99 | | 24 793 | 12 104 | 49 | 68 |
| | 1992/93 | 608 | 1 242 | 1 226 | 99 | | 24 977 | 11 959 | 48 | 68 |
| | 1993/94 | 630 | 1 269 | 1 255 | 99 | | 25 236 | 12 062 | 48 | 66 |

| Country / Pays / País | Year / Année / Año | Schools / Écoles / Escuelas | Teaching staff / Personnel enseignant / Personal docente | | | Pupils enrolled / Élèves inscrits / Alumnos matriculados | | | |
|---|---|---|---|---|---|---|---|---|---|
| | | | Total | Female Féminin Femenino | % F | Total | Female Féminin Femenino | % F | % Private Privé Privada |
| Cyprus (cont) | 1994/95 | 642 | 1 308 | 1 295 | 99 | 25 819 | 12 271 | 48 | 66 |
| | 1995/96 | 647 | 1 323 | 1 306 | 99 | 26 254 | 12 718 | 48 | 66 |
| | 1996/97 | 659 | 1 453 | 1 442 | 99 | 25 996 | 12 607 | 48 | 66 |
| Georgia | 1980/81 | ... | 17 610 | *17 600 | *100 | 131 686 | ... | ... | - |
| | 1985/86 | ... | 19 358 | *19 353 | *100 | 113 338 | ... | ... | - |
| | 1990/91 | ... | 22 538 | *22 531 | *100 | 162 944 | ... | ... | - |
| | 1991/92 | ... | 21 874 | 21 874 | 100 | *147 997 | ... | ... | - |
| | 1992/93 | ... | 17 657 | *17 650 | *100 | 112 323 | ... | ... | ... |
| | 1993/94 | ... | *15 473 | *15 470 | *100 | 94 606 | ... | ... | ... |
| | 1994/95 | ... | *11 283 | *11 280 | *100 | 66 575 | ... | ... | ... |
| | 1995/96 | 1 322 | *10 491 | *10 490 | *100 | 81 938 | ... | ... | ... |
| | 1996/97 | ... | 9 368 | *9 368 | *100 | 71 407 | ... | ... | ... |
| India | 1970/71 | 3 895 | 8 338 | 7 339 | 88 | 357 749 | 167 538 | 47 | ... |
| | 1975/76 | 5 658 | ... | ... | ... | 569 296 | 256 187 | 45 | ... |
| | 1980/81 | 10 802 | ... | ... | ... | 918 238 | 416 848 | 45 | ... |
| | 1985/86 | 11 187 | ... | ... | ... | 1 235 750 | 560 150 | 45 | ... |
| | 1990/91 | 15 427 | ... | ... | ... | 1 510 090 | 687 278 | 46 | ... |
| | 1991/92 | 13 515 | ... | ... | ... | 1 435 724 | 639 116 | 45 | ... |
| | 1992/93 | 13 662 | ... | ... | ... | 1 463 486 | 652 090 | 45 | ... |
| | 1993/94 | 17 172 | ... | ... | ... | 1 940 692 | 882 886 | 45 | ... |
| | 1994/95 | 41 487 | ... | ... | ... | 2 115 751 | 986 055 | 47 | ... |
| | 1995/96 | 38 510 | ... | ... | ... | 2 139 200 | 981 279 | 46 | ... |
| | 1996/97 | 38 553 | ... | ... | ... | 2 382 401 | 1 115 307 | 47 | ... |
| Indonesia | 1970 | 9 220 | 15 030 | ... | ... | 394 100 | 191 800 | 49 | 88 |
| | 1975 | 12 795 | 22 203 | ... | ... | 525 775 | ... | ... | ... |
| | 1980/81 | 19 868 | 37 100 | ... | ... | 1 005 226 | ... | ... | 99 |
| | 1985/86 | 26 419 | 58 341 | ... | ... | 1 258 468 | ... | ... | 100 |
| | 1990/91 | 39 121 | 92 367 | ... | ... | 1 604 208 | ... | ... | 100 |
| | 1991/92 | 39 284 | 93 429 | ... | ... | 1 614 715 | ... | ... | 96 |
| | 1992/93 | 40 257 | 94 416 | ... | ... | 1 660 295 | ... | ... | 94 |
| | 1993/94 | 40 007 | 95 585 | ... | ... | 1 596 283 | ... | ... | 100 |
| | 1994/95 | 40 506 | 96 466 | ... | ... | 1 636 342 | 825 961 | 50 | 100 |
| | 1995/96 | ... | 98 094 | ... | ... | 1 649 145 | 836 134 | 51 | 99 |
| | 1996/97 | 40 215 | ... | ... | ... | 1 624 961 | ... | ... | 99 |
| Iran, Islamic Republic of | 1970/71 | 349 | 954 | 924 | 97 | 19 308 | 8 706 | 45 | 83 |
| | 1975/76 | 1 804 | 6 985 | 6 952 | 100 | 175 424 | 79 978 | 46 | 26 |
| | 1980/81 | 2 791 | 9 356 | ... | ... | 172 000 | ... | ... | ... |
| | 1985/86 | 1 732 | 5 795 | 5 791 | 100 | 106 986 | 50 376 | 47 | - |
| | 1990/91 | 3 586 | 8 520 | 8 504 | 100 | 227 492 | 108 151 | 48 | - |
| | 1991/92 | 4 114 | 8 841 | 8 821 | 100 | 252 513 | 119 959 | 48 | - |
| | 1992/93 | 3 003 | 6 885 | 6 860 | 100 | 168 864 | 81 307 | 48 | - |
| | 1993/94 | 2 483 | 6 469 | 6 446 | 100 | 132 653 | 63 534 | 48 | - |
| | 1994/95 | 2 715 | 6 151 | 6 131 | 100 | 141 728 | 67 782 | 48 | - |
| | 1996/97 | 3 322 | 6 025 | 5 949 | 99 | 195 181 | 95 339 | 49 | 19 |
| Iraq | 1970/71 | 123 | 614 | 609 | 99 | 13 686 | 5 955 | 44 | 33 |
| | 1975/76 | 245 | 1 913 | 1 913 | 100 | 44 413 | 20 578 | 46 | - |
| | 1980/81 | 387 | 3 235 | 3 235 | 100 | 76 507 | 36 671 | 48 | - |
| | 1985/86 | 584 | 4 657 | 4 657 | 100 | 81 431 | 38 604 | 47 | - |
| | 1990/91 | 646 | 4 908 | 4 908 | 100 | 86 508 | 41 225 | 48 | - |
| | 1992/93 | 578 | 4 778 | 4 778 | 100 | 90 836 | 43 656 | 48 | - |
| | 1995/96 | 571 | 4 841 | 4 841 | 100 | 85 024 | 41 135 | 48 | - |
| Israel | 1970/71 | 3 568 | 4 155 | ... | ... | 121 858 | ... | ... | ... |
| | 1975/76 | 5 289 | 6 122 | 6 118 | 100 | 200 710 | 96 483 | 48 | 19 |
| | 1980/81 | ... | ... | ... | ... | 269 506 | 127 832 | 47 | 17 |
| | 1985/86 | ... | ... | ... | ... | 292 000 | ... | ... | ... |
| | 1990/91 | ... | ... | ... | ... | 329 050 | ... | ... | ... |
| | 1991/92 | ... | ... | ... | ... | 336 500 | ... | ... | ... |
| | 1992/93 | ... | ... | ... | ... | 338 180 | ... | ... | ... |
| | 1993/94 | ... | ... | ... | ... | 344 900 | ... | ... | ... |
| | 1994/95 | ... | ... | ... | ... | (18) 315 000 | ... | ... | ... |
| | 1995/96 | ... | ... | ... | ... | (18) 315 200 | ... | ... | ... |
| Japan | 1970/71 | 10 920 | 73 913 | 64 223 | 87 | 1 690 404 | 827 000 | 49 | 75 |
| | 1975/76 | 13 108 | 93 853 | 82 255 | 88 | 2 292 591 | 1 121 244 | 49 | 75 |
| | 1980/81 | 14 893 | 110 037 | 97 083 | 88 | 2 407 093 | 1 177 453 | 49 | 73 |
| | 1985/86 | 15 220 | 107 606 | 94 762 | 88 | 2 067 951 | 1 012 435 | 49 | 75 |
| | 1990/91 | 15 076 | 109 753 | 97 419 | 89 | 2 007 964 | 987 014 | 49 | 78 |
| | 1991/92 | 15 041 | 110 351 | 98 148 | 89 | 1 977 611 | 972 458 | 49 | 79 |
| | 1992/93 | 15 006 | (19) 102 279 | (19) 95 974 | 94 | 1 948 868 | 958 956 | 49 | 80 |
| | 1993/94 | 14 958 | 113 081 | 100 601 | 89 | 1 909 136 | 939 051 | 49 | 80 |
| | 1994/95 | 14 901 | 112 416 | 99 770 | 89 | 1 853 922 | 912 877 | 49 | 80 |
| | 1995/96 | 14 856 | (19) 102 992 | (19) 96 757 | 94 | 1 808 432 | 890 594 | 49 | 80 |
| | 1996/97 | 14 790 | (19) 103 518 | (19) 97 283 | 94 | 1 798 050 | 885 940 | 49 | 80 |
| | 1997/98 | 14 690 | (19) 103 839 | (19) 97 624 | 94 | 1 789 523 | 881 625 | 49 | ... |
| Jordan (20) | 1970/71 | 35 | 298 | 284 | 95 | 10 674 | 4 674 | 44 | 100 |
| | 1975/76 | 158 | 453 | 451 | 100 | 14 952 | 6 343 | 42 | 99 |
| | 1980/81 | 207 | 737 | 731 | 99 | 19 598 | 8 372 | 43 | 99 |
| | 1985/86 | 358 | 1 336 | 1 332 | 100 | 27 954 | 12 554 | 45 | 98 |
| | 1990/91 | 546 | 1 933 | 1 932 | 100 | 44 856 | 20 406 | 45 | 99 |
| | 1991/92 | 575 | 2 115 | 2 113 | 100 | 49 422 | 22 530 | 46 | 98 |

| Country / Pays / País | Year / Année / Año | Schools / Écoles / Escuelas | Teaching staff / Personnel enseignant / Personal docente | | | | Pupils enrolled / Élèves inscrits / Alumnos matriculados | | | |
|---|---|---|---|---|---|---|---|---|---|---|
| | | | Total | Female Féminin Femenino | % F | | Total | Female Féminin Femenino | % F | % Private Privé Privada |
| Jordan (cont) | 1992/93 | 600 | 2 016 | 2 002 | 99 | | 52 284 | 23 848 | 46 | 96 |
| | 1993/94 | 666 | 2 422 | 2 417 | 100 | | 55 996 | 25 606 | 46 | 99 |
| | 1994/95 | 723 | 2 572 | ... | ... | | 57 050 | 26 505 | 46 | ... |
| | 1995/96 | 828 | 2 848 | 2 844 | 100 | | 63 250 | 29 001 | 46 | 100 |
| | 1996/97 | 905 | 3 108 | ... | ... | | 69 647 | 31 920 | 46 | ... |
| | 1997/98 | 932 | 3 346 | ... | ... | | 69 425 | 31 920 | 46 | ... |
| Kazakstan | 1980/81 | ... | 58 000 | ... | ... | | 814 900 | ... | ... | - |
| | 1985/86 | ... | 75 700 | ... | ... | | 965 100 | ... | ... | - |
| | 1990/91 | ... | 92 600 | ... | ... | | 1 055 600 | ... | ... | - |
| | 1991/92 | ... | 96 000 | ... | ... | | 1 013 000 | 471 800 | 47 | - |
| | 1992/93 | ... | 89 300 | ... | ... | | 861 000 | 398 800 | 46 | - |
| | 1993/94 | ... | 78 900 | ... | ... | | 741 900 | 345 900 | 47 | - |
| | 1994/95 | ... | ... | ... | ... | | 535 000 | ... | ... | - |
| | 1995/96 | 5 023 | ... | ... | ... | | 405 100 | 191 700 | 47 | - |
| Korea, Republic of | 1970/71 | 484 | 1 660 | 1 239 | 75 | | 22 271 | 9 837 | 44 | 100 |
| | 1975/76 | 611 | 2 153 | 1 689 | 78 | | 32 032 | 14 150 | 44 | 100 |
| | 1980/81 | 901 | 3 339 | 2 846 | 85 | | 66 433 | 30 041 | 45 | 97 |
| | 1985/86 | (18) 6 242 | (18) 9 281 | (18) 8 342 | 90 | (18) | 314 692 | (18) 148 371 | 47 | 54 |
| | 1990/91 | 8 354 | 18 511 | 17 309 | 94 | | 414 532 | 196 842 | 47 | 69 |
| | 1991/92 | 8 421 | 19 741 | 18 655 | 94 | | 425 535 | 203 772 | 48 | 72 |
| | 1992/93 | 8 498 | ... | ... | ... | | 450 882 | 214 341 | 48 | 74 |
| | 1993/94 | 8 515 | 18 176 | 18 135 | 100 | | 470 271 | 222 382 | 47 | 76 |
| | 1994/95 | 8 910 | 19 654 | 19 608 | 100 | | 511 043 | 240 487 | 47 | 78 |
| | 1995/96 | 8 960 | 21 098 | 21 044 | 100 | | 530 245 | 248 117 | 47 | 78 |
| | 1996/97 | 8 939 | 22 205 | 22 154 | 100 | | 552 755 | 260 160 | 47 | 79 |
| | 1997/98 | 9 005 | 22 893 | 22 871 | 100 | | 569 167 | 267 779 | 47 | 79 |
| Kuwait | 1970/71 | (2) 44 | 1 022 | 1 022 | 100 | | 19 273 | 9 001 | 47 | 33 |
| | 1975/76 | 101 | 1 299 | 1 299 | 100 | | 24 097 | 11 223 | 47 | 40 |
| | 1980/81 | 109 | 1 696 | 1 696 | 100 | | 29 965 | 14 262 | 48 | 41 |
| | 1985/86 | 161 | 2 539 | 2 539 | 100 | | 42 830 | 20 665 | 48 | 37 |
| | 1990/91 | ... | 2 343 | 2 343 | 100 | | 37 771 | 18 688 | 49 | 9 |
| | 1991/92 | 158 | 2 473 | 2 472 | 100 | | 39 246 | 19 412 | 49 | 12 |
| | 1992/93 | 169 | 2 634 | 2 632 | 100 | | 47 677 | 23 505 | 49 | 17 |
| | 1993/94 | 177 | 2 747 | 2 747 | 100 | | 46 482 | 22 648 | 49 | 21 |
| | 1994/95 | 193 | 2 927 | 2 925 | 100 | | 49 016 | 23 920 | 49 | 22 |
| | 1995/96 | 201 | 3 145 | 3 144 | 100 | | 49 393 | 24 276 | 49 | 25 |
| | 1996/97 | 208 | 3 295 | 3 293 | 100 | | 49 693 | 24 314 | 49 | 24 |
| | 1997/98 | 215 | 3 525 | 3 524 | 100 | | 54 572 | 26 568 | 49 | 23 |
| Kyrgyzstan | 1985/86 | ... | ... | ... | ... | | 122 900 | 61 500 | 50 | ... |
| | 1990/91 | ... | ... | ... | ... | | 158 500 | 79 300 | 50 | ... |
| | 1991/92 | ... | ... | ... | ... | | 147 400 | 73 700 | 50 | ... |
| | 1992/93 | ... | ... | ... | ... | | 113 500 | 56 800 | 50 | ... |
| | 1993/94 | ... | ... | ... | ... | | 68 700 | 34 400 | 50 | ... |
| | 1994/95 | 639 | ... | ... | ... | | 45 680 | ... | ... | ... |
| | 1995/96 | 453 | 4 013 | ... | ... | | 35 254 | ... | ... | ... |
| Lao People's Democratic Republic | 1980/81 | 153 | 252 | 252 | 100 | | 5 296 | 2 719 | 51 | - |
| | 1985/86 | 500 | 1 327 | 1 327 | 100 | | 21 625 | 9 534 | 44 | - |
| | 1990/91 | ... | 1 470 | 1 470 | 100 | | 28 802 | 13 205 | 46 | - |
| | 1991/92 | 608 | 1 618 | 1 618 | 100 | | 25 675 | 13 627 | 53 | 6 |
| | 1992/93 | 659 | 1 755 | 1 750 | 100 | | 27 389 | 14 498 | 53 | 8 |
| | 1993/94 | 750 | 1 883 | 1 883 | 100 | | 29 703 | 15 353 | 52 | 11 |
| | 1994/95 | ... | 1 974 | 1 958 | 99 | | 31 677 | 16 429 | 52 | 13 |
| | 1995/96 | ... | 2 007 | 2 001 | 100 | | 35 039 | 18 267 | 52 | 15 |
| | 1996/97 | 695 | 2 173 | 2 170 | 100 | | 37 851 | 19 349 | 51 | 15 |
| Lebanon | 1970/71 | ... | ... | ... | ... | | 137 744 | 64 160 | 47 | 81 |
| | 1980/81 | ... | 6 604 | ... | ... | | 123 530 | ... | ... | 81 |
| | 1991/92 | 1 757 | ... | ... | ... | | 131 074 | 63 707 | 49 | 83 |
| | 1993/94 | ... | ... | ... | ... | | 148 400 | 71 644 | 48 | 85 |
| | 1994/95 | 1 819 | ... | ... | ... | | 157 083 | 75 790 | 48 | 85 |
| | 1995/96 | 1 842 | ... | ... | ... | | 161 590 | 77 960 | 48 | 85 |
| | 1996/97 | 1 938 | ... | ... | ... | | *164 397 | *78 916 | *48 | *83 |
| Macau | 1970/71 | 68 | 176 | ... | ... | | 7 063 | 3 307 | 47 | ... |
| | 1975/76 | 41 | 130 | ... | ... | | 5 072 | ... | ... | 98 |
| | 1990/91 | ... | ... | ... | ... | | 20 814 | 10 090 | 48 | ... |
| | 1991/92 | ... | ... | ... | ... | | 21 573 | 10 419 | 48 | ... |
| | 1992/93 | ... | ... | ... | ... | | 21 600 | 10 352 | 48 | ... |
| Malaysia | 1980 | 3 087 | ... | ... | ... | | 170 955 | ... | ... | ... |
| | 1985 | 5 757 | 9 056 | 8 889 | 98 | | 293 801 | ... | ... | 45 |
| | 1990 | ... | 10 773 | ... | ... | | 328 813 | 161 704 | 49 | 60 |
| | 1991 | 6 502 | 10 918 | ... | ... | | 372 767 | 183 332 | 49 | ... |
| | 1992 | ... | 11 341 | ... | ... | | 383 715 | 188 216 | 49 | 43 |
| | 1993 | ... | 16 453 | 15 514 | 94 | | 395 611 | 193 878 | 49 | 39 |
| | 1994 | 9 743 | *20 352 | *20 176 | *99 | | 599 391 | 297 532 | 50 | 95 |
| | 1995 | ... | ... | ... | ... | | 459 015 | 227 273 | 50 | 94 |
| Maldives | 1970 | 3 | 30 | 30 | 100 | | 857 | 386 | 45 | ... |
| | 1992 | (21) 8 | ... | ... | ... | (21) | 3 298 | (21) 1 582 | 48 | 97 |
| | 1993 | ... | ... | ... | ... | | 9 592 | 4 695 | 49 | 93 |
| | 1995 | ... | ... | ... | ... | (21) | 11 198 | (21) 5 653 | 50 | 100 |

| Country<br>Pays<br>País | Year<br>Année<br>Año | Schools<br>Écoles<br>Escuelas | Teaching staff<br>Personnel enseignant<br>Personal docente | | | Pupils enrolled<br>Élèves inscrits<br>Alumnos matriculados | | | |
|---|---|---|---|---|---|---|---|---|---|
| | | | Total | Female<br>Féminin<br>Femenino | %<br>F | Total | Female<br>Féminin<br>Femenino | %<br>F | %<br>Private<br>Privé<br>Privada |
| Maldives (cont) | 1996 | ... | ... | ... | ... | 10 530 | 5 249 | 50 | 100 |
| | 1997 | ... | ... | ... | ... | 10 682 | 5 300 | 50 | 100 |
| | 1998 | 110 | 357 | 321 | 90 | 11 508 | 5 570 | 48 | 100 |
| Mongolia | 1970/71 | 546 | 1 440 | ... | ... | 32 000 | ... | ... | - |
| | 1975/76 | 542 | 1 699 | ... | ... | 36 974 | 19 497 | 53 | - |
| | 1980/81 | 617 | 1 813 | 1 813 | 100 | 49 800 | 26 203 | 53 | - |
| | 1985/86 | 680 | 2 205 | 2 203 | 100 | 62 470 | 34 321 | 55 | - |
| Mongolia (cont) | 1990/91 | 909 | 3 747 | ... | ... | 97 212 | 53 134 | 55 | - |
| | 1991/92 | 883 | 4 088 | ... | ... | 95 715 | 51 686 | 54 | - |
| | 1992/93 | 806 | 3 732 | ... | ... | 85 671 | 45 855 | 54 | - |
| | 1993/94 | ... | 3 154 | 3 139 | 100 | 59 909 | 31 616 | 53 | - |
| | 1994/95 | 696 | 5 309 | 5 294 | 100 | 60 959 | 33 581 | 55 | - |
| | 1995/96 | 660 | 5 274 | 5 249 | 100 | 64 086 | 34 314 | 54 | - |
| | 1996/97 | 667 | 5 541 | 5 524 | 100 | 67 972 | 36 489 | 54 | - |
| Oman | 1975/76 | 2 | 4 | 4 | 100 | 160 | 68 | 43 | 100 |
| | 1980/81 | 3 | 11 | 10 | 91 | 396 | 175 | 44 | 100 |
| | 1985/86 | 7 | 71 | 71 | 100 | 1 665 | 732 | 44 | 100 |
| | 1990/91 | 8 | 181 | 181 | 100 | 3 682 | 1 697 | 46 | 100 |
| | 1991/92 | 7 | 204 | 204 | 100 | 4 223 | 1 869 | 44 | 100 |
| | 1992/93 | 10 | 223 | 223 | 100 | 4 435 | 1 982 | 45 | 100 |
| | 1993/94 | 5 | 238 | 238 | 100 | 4 728 | 2 077 | 44 | 100 |
| | 1994/95 | 6 | 280 | 280 | 100 | 5 235 | 2 302 | 44 | 100 |
| | 1995/96 | 5 | 268 | 268 | 100 | 5 265 | 2 354 | 45 | 100 |
| | 1996/97 | 5 | 339 | 339 | 100 | 6 452 | 2 879 | 45 | 100 |
| | 1997/98 | 5 | 347 | 346 | 100 | 6 989 | 3 197 | 46 | 100 |
| Philippines | 1970/71 | ... | 1 500 | *1 500 | *100 | 51 857 | *25 000 | *48 | 97 |
| | 1975/76 | ... | ... | ... | ... | 86 443 | ... | ... | ... |
| | 1980/81 | ... | ... | ... | ... | *123 571 | ... | ... | ... |
| | 1985/86 | 2 334 | 4 636 | ... | ... | 189 654 | 98 020 | 52 | 61 |
| | 1990/91 | 4 201 | 9 644 | ... | ... | 397 364 | ... | ... | 58 |
| | 1991/92 | ... | 9 740 | ... | ... | 408 226 | ... | ... | 55 |
| | 1992/93 | ... | 9 610 | ... | ... | 415 483 | ... | ... | 49 |
| | 1993/94 | 5 035 | 10 646 | ... | ... | 416 894 | ... | ... | 53 |
| | 1995/96 | 6 362 | ... | ... | ... | 451 881 | ... | ... | 53 |
| | 1996/97 | 6 810 | ... | ... | ... | 401 799 | ... | ... | 60 |
| Qatar | 1970/71 | 11 | 47 | 47 | 100 | 686 | 310 | 45 | 100 |
| | 1975/76 | 12 | 38 | 38 | 100 | 1 434 | 635 | 44 | 100 |
| | 1980/81 | 19 | ... | ... | ... | 2 587 | 1 203 | 47 | 100 |
| | 1985/86 | 36 | 247 | 247 | 100 | 4 859 | 2 244 | 46 | 100 |
| | 1990/91 | 53 | 287 | 285 | 99 | 5 230 | 2 492 | 48 | 100 |
| | 1991/92 | 54 | 357 | 344 | 96 | 5 684 | 2 631 | 46 | 100 |
| | 1992/93 | 57 | 348 | 341 | 98 | 5 905 | 2 651 | 45 | 100 |
| | 1993/94 | 59 | 294 | 294 | 100 | 6 756 | 3 165 | 47 | 100 |
| | 1994/95 | 64 | 302 | 302 | 100 | 6 786 | 3 192 | 47 | 100 |
| | 1995/96 | 64 | 321 | 321 | 100 | 7 018 | 3 097 | 44 | 100 |
| Saudi Arabia | 1970/71 | 43 | 191 | 190 | 99 | 6 058 | 2 332 | 38 | 80 |
| | 1975/76 | 92 | 444 | 427 | 96 | 15 485 | 6 528 | 42 | 91 |
| | 1980/81 | 195 | 1 127 | 1 098 | 97 | 28 045 | 12 375 | 44 | 87 |
| | 1985/86 | 492 | 3 001 | 2 941 | 98 | 51 604 | 23 654 | 46 | 78 |
| | 1990/91 | 646 | 4 839 | 4 839 | 100 | 67 069 | 30 378 | 45 | 79 |
| | 1991/92 | 725 | 5 182 | 5 182 | 100 | 73 523 | 36 512 | 50 | 78 |
| | 1992/93 | 806 | 5 098 | 5 098 | 100 | 81 464 | 37 102 | 46 | 78 |
| | 1993/94 | 752 | 6 704 | 6 234 | 93 | 84 992 | 46 105 | 54 | 78 |
| | 1994/95 | 878 | 6 482 | ... | ... | 86 754 | ... | ... | 73 |
| | 1995/96 | 968 | 7 479 | 7 479 | 100 | 85 802 | ... | ... | 76 |
| | 1996/97 | 893 | 7 703 | 7 703 | 100 | 85 484 | 38 917 | 46 | 75 |
| Singapore | 1970 | 48 | 200 | 199 | 100 | 4 822 | 2 259 | 47 | 100 |
| | 1975 | 52 | 278 | 276 | 99 | 4 883 | 2 320 | 48 | 100 |
| | 1980 | 122 | ... | ... | ... | 11 142 | 5 240 | 47 | 63 |
| | 1985 | 108 | 684 | 684 | 100 | 15 658 | 7 344 | 47 | 69 |
| Syrian Arab Republic | 1970/71 | 259 | 723 | 696 | 96 | 26 438 | 11 550 | 44 | 100 |
| | 1975/76 | 323 | 1 012 | 980 | 97 | 33 477 | 14 940 | 45 | 100 |
| | 1980/81 | 351 | 1 082 | 1 052 | 97 | 33 611 | 14 985 | 45 | 100 |
| | 1985/86 | 610 | 2 028 | 2 018 | 100 | 61 988 | 28 056 | 45 | 62 |
| | 1990/91 | ... | 3 122 | 3 066 | 98 | 83 552 | 38 379 | 46 | 61 |
| | 1991/92 | 982 | 3 257 | 3 180 | 98 | 86 006 | 39 595 | 46 | 86 |
| | 1992/93 | 1 052 | 3 922 | 3 739 | 95 | 90 439 | 41 538 | 46 | 92 |
| | 1993/94 | 1 046 | 4 020 | 3 908 | 97 | 90 530 | 41 656 | 46 | 86 |
| | 1994/95 | 1 037 | 4 054 | 3 885 | 96 | 90 681 | 41 675 | 46 | 90 |
| | 1995/96 | 1 048 | 4 233 | 3 996 | 94 | 92 470 | 42 149 | 46 | 95 |
| | 1996/97 | 1 096 | 4 427 | 4 349 | 98 | 98 151 | 45 524 | 46 | 91 |
| Tajikistan | 1980/81 | ... | 7 391 | ... | ... | 61 558 | ... | ... | ... |
| | 1990/91 | ... | 10 827 | ... | ... | 105 527 | ... | ... | ... |
| | 1992/93 | ... | 9 988 | ... | ... | 81 839 | ... | ... | ... |
| | 1993/94 | ... | 9 345 | ... | ... | 80 848 | ... | ... | ... |
| | 1994/95 | ... | 8 879 | ... | ... | 76 087 | ... | ... | ... |
| | 1996/97 | 601 | 6 615 | ... | ... | 71 296 | 32 308 | 45 | ... |

| Country<br>Pays<br>País | Year<br>Année<br>Año | Schools<br>Écoles<br>Escuelas | Teaching staff<br>Personnel enseignant<br>Personal docente | | | Pupils enrolled<br>Élèves inscrits<br>Alumnos matriculados | | | |
|---|---|---|---|---|---|---|---|---|---|
| | | | Total | Female<br>Féminin<br>Femenino | %<br>F | Total | Female<br>Féminin<br>Femenino | %<br>F | %<br>Private<br>Privé<br>Privada |
| Thailand | 1970/71 | 395 | 2 857 | ... | ... | 134 355 | 64 499 | 48 | 56 |
| | 1975/76 | 2 864 | ... | ... | ... | 214 620 | 103 582 | 48 | 58 |
| | 1980/81 | ... | ... | ... | ... | 367 313 | 178 662 | 49 | 55 |
| | 1985/86 | 12 996 | 33 119 | ... | ... | 672 080 | ... | ... | 41 |
| | 1990/91 | ... | 64 628 | ... | ... | 1 463 660 | 721 530 | 49 | ... |
| | 1991/92 | ... | 72 586 | ... | ... | 1 528 525 | 751 675 | 49 | ... |
| | 1992/93 | 29 529 | 83 072 | ... | ... | 1 678 350 | 826 779 | 49 | 24 |
| | 1993/94 | ... | ... | ... | ... | 1 954 060 | ... | ... | 22 |
| | 1994/95 | ... | ... | ... | ... | 2 121 294 | ... | ... | 22 |
| | 1995/96 | ... | ... | ... | ... | 1 911 265 | ... | ... | 26 |
| | 1996/97 | ... | ... | ... | ... | 2 025 684 | ... | ... | 26 |
| | 1997/98 | ... | ... | ... | ... | 2 334 247 | ... | ... | 23 |
| Turkey | 1970/71 | (22) 112 | (22) 185 | (22) 176 | 95 | (22) 4 201 | (22) 1 902 | 45 | 96 |
| | 1980/81 | (22) 117 | (22) 262 | (22) 255 | 97 | (22) 4 691 | (22) 2 090 | 45 | 80 |
| | 1985/86 | 3 551 | 5 903 | 5 868 | 99 | 117 819 | 56 712 | 48 | 4 |
| | 1990/91 | 3 819 | 7 119 | 7 090 | 100 | 119 819 | 56 622 | 47 | 6 |
| | 1991/92 | 4 454 | 7 976 | 7 942 | 100 | 132 724 | 62 541 | 47 | 5 |
| | 1992/93 | 4 683 | 8 593 | 8 372 | 97 | 136 117 | 64 506 | 47 | 4 |
| | 1993/94 | 4 908 | 8 908 | 8 874 | 100 | 143 349 | 67 226 | 47 | 5 |
| | 1994/95 | 5 186 | 9 098 | 9 049 | 99 | 148 088 | 70 350 | 48 | ... |
| | 1996/97 | 6 082 | 9 971 | 9 930 | 100 | 174 710 | 82 038 | 47 | ... |
| United Arab Emirates | 1970/71 | (2) 2 | (2) 47 | ... | ... | (2) 1 114 | ... | ... | ... |
| | 1975/76 | (2) 11 | (2) 186 | (2) 186 | 100 | 7 603 | 3 895 | 51 | 51 |
| | 1980/81 | (2) 20 | (2) 359 | (2) 359 | 100 | 17 263 | 7 930 | 46 | 69 |
| | 1985/86 | (2) 32 | (2) 590 | (2) 590 | 100 | 35 360 | 16 668 | 47 | 62 |
| | 1990/91 | (2) 48 | 2 269 | 2 244 | 99 | 47 049 | 22 453 | 48 | 64 |
| | 1991/92 | (2) 48 | 2 374 | 2 344 | 99 | 49 064 | 23 479 | 48 | 66 |
| | 1992/93 | (2) 55 | 2 575 | 2 554 | 99 | 51 885 | 24 727 | 48 | 66 |
| | 1993/94 | (2) 65 | 2 760 | 2 737 | 99 | 55 566 | 26 393 | 47 | 67 |
| | 1994/95 | ... | 2 886 | 2 868 | 99 | 56 428 | 26 973 | 48 | 66 |
| | 1995/96 | ... | 2 828 | 2 818 | 100 | 56 202 | 26 755 | 48 | 66 |
| | 1996/97 | ... | 3 110 | 3 101 | 100 | 55 624 | 26 704 | 48 | 65 |
| Uzbekistan | 1980/81 | ... | 50 500 | ... | ... | 915 200 | ... | ... | ... |
| | 1985/86 | ... | 68 200 | ... | ... | 1 095 600 | ... | ... | ... |
| | 1990/91 | ... | 89 800 | ... | ... | 1 349 400 | ... | ... | ... |
| | 1991/92 | ... | 92 600 | ... | ... | 1 339 500 | 658 700 | 49 | ... |
| | 1992/93 | ... | 101 700 | ... | ... | 1 211 500 | 590 300 | 49 | ... |
| | 1993/94 | ... | 100 200 | ... | ... | 1 166 300 | 562 500 | 48 | ... |
| | 1994/95 | ... | 96 100 | ... | ... | 1 071 400 | 515 500 | 48 | ... |
| Viet Nam | 1975/76 | ... | *22 300 | ... | ... | *764 400 | ... | ... | ... |
| | 1980/81 | 6 121 | 57 605 | 57 605 | 100 | 1 595 724 | 823 806 | 52 | - |
| | 1985/86 | 6 446 | 65 718 | 65 718 | 100 | 1 701 681 | 885 567 | 52 | - |
| | 1990/91 | ... | 65 400 | ... | ... | 1 534 900 | ... | ... | - |
| | 1991/92 | ... | 69 800 | ... | ... | 1 496 100 | ... | ... | - |
| | 1992/93 | 6 806 | 69 300 | ... | ... | 1 521 000 | ... | ... | - |
| | 1993/94 | 6 870 | 66 300 | ... | ... | 1 655 500 | ... | ... | - |
| | 1994/95 | ... | 69 300 | ... | ... | 1 840 800 | ... | ... | - |
| | 1995/96 | 7 213 | 75 034 | ... | ... | 1 931 611 | ... | ... | - |
| | 1996/97 | ... | 84 400 | ... | ... | 2 092 700 | ... | ... | - |
| | 1997/98 | ... | 94 916 | ... | ... | 2 245 661 | ... | ... | - |
| Yemen | 1990/91 | 51 | 665 | ... | ... | 10 067 | 4 748 | 47 | ... |
| | 1991/92 | 61 | 645 | ... | ... | 10 283 | 4 836 | 47 | ... |
| | 1993/94 | 62 | 680 | ... | ... | 11 999 | 5 698 | 47 | ... |
| Palestine | 1975/76 | 153 | ... | ... | ... | 11 025 | ... | ... | 100 |
| | 1980/81 | 107 | ... | ... | ... | 12 050 | ... | ... | 100 |
| | 1985/86 | 199 | ... | ... | ... | 18 875 | ... | ... | 100 |
| | 1990/91 | 380 | ... | ... | ... | 30 158 | ... | ... | 100 |
| | 1991/92 | 382 | ... | ... | ... | 32 508 | ... | ... | 100 |
| | 1992/93 | 439 | ... | ... | ... | 38 643 | ... | ... | 100 |
| | 1993/94 | 466 | ... | ... | ... | 42 343 | ... | ... | 100 |
| | 1994/95 | 436 | 1 211 | 1 210 | 100 | 36 829 | 17 706 | 48 | 100 |
| | 1995/96 | 532 | 1 460 | 1 434 | 98 | 44 927 | 21 658 | 48 | 100 |
| | 1996/97 | 705 | 2 377 | 2 372 | 100 | 69 134 | 32 970 | 48 | 100 |
| **Europe** | | | | | | | | | |
| Albania | 1970/71 | ... | 2 460 | 2 460 | 100 | 47 524 | ... | ... | - |
| | 1980/81 | 2 667 | 4 162 | 4 162 | 100 | 92 490 | ... | ... | - |
| | 1985/86 | 3 064 | 4 850 | 4 850 | 100 | 110 603 | ... | ... | - |
| | 1990/91 | 3 426 | 5 664 | 5 664 | 100 | 130 007 | ... | ... | - |
| | 1993/94 | 2 656 | 4 578 | 4 578 | 100 | 80 395 | ... | ... | - |
| | 1994/95 | 2 668 | 4 428 | 4 428 | 100 | 80 348 | ... | ... | - |
| | 1995/96 | 2 670 | 4 416 | 4 416 | 100 | 84 536 | 42 244 | 50 | - |
| Austria | 1970/71 | 2 079 | 4 423 | 4 423 | 100 | (23)(24) 120 359 | (23)(24) 58 924 | 49 | 36 |
| | 1975/76 | 2 882 | 5 578 | 5 522 | 99 | (23)(24) 154 318 | (23)(24) 75 551 | 49 | 33 |
| | 1980/81 | 3 423 | 7 069 | 7 030 | 99 | 165 611 | 81 262 | 49 | 28 |

**Pre-primary education**
**Enseignement préprimaire**
**Enseñanza preprimaria**

| Country / Pays / País | Year / Année / Año | Schools / Écoles / Escuelas | Teaching staff — Personnel enseignant — Personal docente: Total | Female Féminin Femenino | % F | Pupils enrolled — Élèves inscrits — Alumnos matriculados: Total | Female Féminin Femenino | % F | % Private Privé Privada |
|---|---|---|---|---|---|---|---|---|---|
| Austria (cont) | 1985/86 | 3 667 | 8 159 | 8 113 | 99 | 181 582 | 88 540 | 49 | 27 |
| | 1990/91 | 3 915 | 9 329 | 9 295 | 100 | 194 829 | 94 633 | 49 | 26 |
| | 1991/92 | 3 983 | 9 634 | 9 615 | 100 | 197 186 | 95 703 | 49 | 26 |
| | 1992/93 | 4 084 | 9 981 | 9 961 | 100 | 202 294 | 97 962 | 48 | 26 |
| | 1993/94 | 4 212 | 11 536 | 11 317 | 98 | 209 743 | 101 570 | 48 | 26 |
| | 1994/95 | 4 308 | 12 803 | 12 561 | 98 | 214 951 | 104 067 | 48 | 26 |
| | 1995/96 | ... | 12 906 | 12 652 | 98 | 220 314 | 106 708 | 48 | 25 |
| | 1996/97 | 4 467 | 13 429 | 13 171 | 98 | 225 034 | 108 909 | 48 | 25 |
| Belarus | 1970/71 | 2 062 | ... | ... | ... | 220 191 | ... | ... | - |
| | 1980/81 | 3 488 | 36 400 | ... | ... | 345 300 | ... | ... | - |
| | 1985/86 | 4 476 | 52 000 | ... | ... | 407 100 | ... | ... | - |
| | 1990/91 | 5 215 | 62 300 | ... | ... | 419 600 | ... | ... | - |
| | 1991/92 | 5 207 | 62 700 | ... | ... | 416 000 | ... | ... | - |
| | 1992/93 | 4 938 | 56 100 | ... | ... | 380 200 | ... | ... | - |
| | 1993/94 | 4 811 | 54 800 | ... | ... | 367 600 | ... | ... | - |
| | 1994/95 | 4 674 | 55 300 | ... | ... | 368 700 | 166 000 | 45 | - |
| | 1995/96 | ... | 54 600 | ... | ... | 349 500 | 159 400 | 46 | - |
| | 1996/97 | 4 494 | 54 100 | ... | ... | 335 400 | 153 600 | 46 | - |
| Belgium | 1970/71 | ... | 17 916 | 17 916 | 100 | 458 702 | 224 709 | 49 | 59 |
| | 1975/76 | 5 226 | 17 460 | 17 460 | 100 | 437 838 | 214 159 | 49 | 57 |
| | 1980/81 | 4 325 | 17 116 | 17 075 | 100 | 383 955 | 188 248 | 49 | 58 |
| | 1985/86 | 4 087 | 19 793 | 19 691 | 99 | 391 848 | 191 208 | 49 | 58 |
| | 1990/91 | 4 058 | ... | ... | ... | 374 343 | 182 180 | 49 | 57 |
| | 1991/92 | 3 992 | ... | ... | ... | 398 005 | 193 641 | 49 | 57 |
| | 1992/93 | 4 001 | 24 332 | 24 052 | 99 | 410 183 | 199 788 | 49 | 57 |
| | 1993/94 | 4 156 | 24 170 | 23 876 | 99 | 421 409 | 205 087 | 49 | 57 |
| | 1994/95 | ... | ... | ... | ... | 429 726 | 208 341 | 48 | 57 |
| | 1995/96 | ... | ... | ... | ... | 428 134 | 208 239 | 49 | 57 |
| Bulgaria | 1970/71 | 8 037 | 18 185 | 18 185 | 100 | 331 960 | 164 847 | 50 | - |
| | 1975/76 | 7 550 | 24 137 | 24 137 | 100 | 392 625 | 191 806 | 49 | - |
| | 1980/81 | 6 185 | 28 996 | 28 996 | 100 | 420 804 | 204 002 | 48 | - |
| | 1985/86 | 5 054 | 28 864 | 28 864 | 100 | 360 395 | 174 649 | 48 | - |
| | 1990/91 | 4 590 | 28 776 | 28 776 | 100 | 303 779 | 148 397 | 49 | - |
| | 1991/92 | 4 465 | 28 045 | 28 045 | 100 | 258 995 | 126 214 | 49 | - |
| | 1992/93 | 4 429 | 27 400 | 27 400 | 100 | 263 004 | 127 750 | 49 | 0 |
| | 1993/94 | 3 856 | 25 623 | 25 516 | 100 | 247 472 | 119 892 | 48 | 0 |
| | 1994/95 | 3 659 | 24 091 | 24 018 | 100 | 246 608 | 119 550 | 48 | 0 |
| | 1995/96 | 3 762 | 23 890 | 23 846 | 100 | 254 234 | 123 370 | 49 | 0 |
| | 1996/97 | 3 713 | 23 353 | 22 043 | 94 | 247 015 | 118 909 | 48 | 0 |
| Croatia | 1980/81 | 738 | 3 758 | ... | ... | 62 937 | 30 238 | 48 | - |
| | 1985/86 | 839 | 4 395 | ... | ... | 69 374 | 33 250 | 48 | - |
| | 1990/91 | 930 | 5 619 | ... | ... | 70 396 | 34 097 | 48 | - |
| | 1991/92 | 763 | 4 759 | ... | ... | 52 140 | 25 010 | 48 | - |
| | 1992/93 | 814 | 4 820 | ... | ... | 54 715 | 26 072 | 48 | 0 |
| | 1993/94 | 846 | 5 081 | ... | ... | 59 767 | 28 499 | 48 | 2 |
| | 1994/95 | 871 | 5 320 | 5 308 | 100 | 65 395 | 31 098 | 48 | 2 |
| | 1995/96 | 902 | 5 531 | 5 521 | 100 | 66 105 | 31 580 | 48 | 3 |
| | 1996/97 | 960 | 5 842 | 5 831 | 100 | 81 893 | 39 103 | 48 | 5 |
| Czech Republic | 1970/71 | ... | 19 780 | 19 780 | 100 | 258 567 | 131 869 | 51 | - |
| | 1975/76 | ... | 23 449 | 23 449 | 100 | 316 991 | 161 665 | 51 | - |
| | 1980/81 | ... | 31 110 | 31 110 | 100 | 463 565 | 231 783 | 50 | - |
| | 1985/86 | ... | 29 625 | 29 625 | 100 | 432 067 | 216 034 | 50 | - |
| | 1990/91 | ... | 32 112 | 32 112 | 100 | 352 139 | 169 236 | 48 | - |
| | 1991/92 | ... | 29 888 | 29 888 | 100 | 323 270 | 187 326 | 58 | - |
| | 1992/93 | 6 816 | 30 700 | 30 700 | 100 | 325 576 | 163 388 | 50 | 0 |
| | 1993/94 | 6 836 | 28 148 | 28 148 | 100 | 338 498 | 165 294 | 49 | 1 |
| | 1994/95 | 6 710 | 30 731 | 30 731 | 100 | 345 553 | 170 664 | 49 | 2 |
| | 1995/96 | 6 622 | 29 329 | 29 262 | 100 | 342 161 | 166 772 | 49 | 2 |
| | 1996/97 | 6 935 | ... | ... | ... | 325 554 | 158 251 | 49 | 2 |
| Denmark | 1970/71 | ... | ... | ... | ... | 20 874 | 10 109 | 48 | ... |
| | 1975/76 | ... | ... | ... | ... | 44 859 | 21 776 | 49 | 7 |
| | 1980/81 | ... | ... | ... | ... | 62 936 | 30 864 | 49 | 8 |
| | 1985/86 | ... | (25) 3 592 | (25) 2 037 | 57 | (25) 56 735 | (25) 27 743 | 49 | 8 |
| | 1990/91 | ... | ... | ... | ... | 51 583 | 25 208 | 49 | 9 |
| | 1991/92 | ... | (25) 3 830 | ... | ... | 53 138 | 26 054 | 49 | 9 |
| | 1992/93 | ... | (26) 18 800 | (26) 17 300 | 92 | (26) 184 009 | (26) 90 165 | 49 | 3 |
| | 1993/94 | (26) 4 906 | (26) 18 800 | (26) 17 300 | 92 | (26) 196 605 | (26) 96 213 | 49 | 3 |
| | 1994/95 | (26) 4 395 | (26) 19 200 | (26) 17 700 | 92 | (26) 201 571 | (26) 98 634 | 49 | 3 |
| | 1995/96 | ... | ... | ... | ... | (26) 209 005 | (26) 101 705 | 49 | ... |
| Estonia | 1980/81 | ... | ... | ... | ... | 65 953 | ... | ... | - |
| | 1985/86 | ... | ... | ... | ... | 66 711 | ... | ... | - |
| | 1990/91 | ... | (27) 10 917 | ... | ... | 71 689 | 34 842 | 49 | - |
| | 1991/92 | ... | (27) 10 165 | (27) 10 152 | 100 | 64 718 | 31 533 | 49 | - |
| | 1992/93 | ... | (27) 8 698 | (27) 8 685 | 100 | 57 262 | 27 924 | 49 | - |
| | 1993/94 | ... | (27) 8 163 | (27) 8 144 | 100 | 57 212 | 28 060 | 49 | - |
| | 1994/95 | ... | (27) 8 093 | (27) 8 078 | 100 | 55 166 | 26 866 | 49 | 0 |
| | 1995/96 | 671 | (27) 8 090 | (27) 8 070 | 100 | 54 658 | 26 484 | 48 | ... |
| | 1996/97 | ... | (27) 8 070 | (27) 8 058 | 100 | 51 875 | 25 069 | 48 | ... |

| Country<br>Pays<br>País | Year<br>Année<br>Año | Schools<br>Écoles<br>Escuelas | Teaching staff<br>Personnel enseignant<br>Personal docente | | | Pupils enrolled<br>Élèves inscrits<br>Alumnos matriculados | | | |
|---|---|---|---|---|---|---|---|---|---|
| | | | Total | Female<br>Féminin<br>Femenino | %<br>F | Total | Female<br>Féminin<br>Femenino | %<br>F | %<br>Private<br>Privé<br>Privada |
| Federal Republic of | 1991/92 | 2 658 | 29 879 | 28 232 | 94 | 261 988 | 126 145 | 48 | - |
| Yugoslavia | 1992/93 | 1 682 | 16 306 | 15 367 | 94 | 159 719 | 77 015 | 48 | - |
| | 1993/94 | 1 638 | 15 622 | 14 633 | 94 | 146 212 | 70 659 | 48 | - |
| | 1994/95 | 1 674 | 15 774 | 14 859 | 94 | 165 860 | 80 805 | 49 | - |
| | 1995/96 | 1 725 | 16 704 | 15 813 | 95 | 177 350 | 85 709 | 48 | - |
| | 1996/97 | 1 748 | 17 198 | 16 274 | 95 | 182 125 | 87 986 | 48 | - |
| Finland | 1970/71 | 395 | 1 191 | 1 191 | 100 | 25 464 | 12 740 | 50 | - |
| | 1980/81 | ... | ... | ... | ... | 64 000 | ... | ... | ... |
| | 1985/86 | ... | ... | ... | ... | 76 097 | ... | ... | ... |
| | 1990/91 | ... | ... | ... | ... | 86 400 | ... | ... | ... |
| | 1991/92 | ... | ... | ... | ... | 88 492 | ... | ... | ... |
| | 1992/93 | 2 533 | ... | ... | ... | 89 670 | 43 676 | 49 | 7 |
| | 1993/94 | 2 377 | ... | ... | ... | 92 229 | 45 192 | 49 | 6 |
| | 1994/95 | 2 383 | 8 765 | 8 435 | 96 | 96 366 | 47 174 | 49 | 6 |
| | 1995/96 | 2 424 | 8 609 | 8 279 | 96 | 104 662 | 51 224 | 49 | 7 |
| | 1996/97 | 2 505 | 9 807 | 9 448 | 96 | 114 696 | 55 998 | 49 | 6 |
| France | 1970/71 | 9 617 | (2) 43 237 | (2) 43 220 | 100 | 2 213 346 | 1 083 050 | 49 | 15 |
| | 1975/76 | 13 051 | (2) 57 658 | (2) 57 514 | 100 | 2 591 142 | 1 275 000 | 49 | 14 |
| | 1980/81 | 16 080 | (2) 66 948 | ... | ... | 2 383 465 | 1 163 500 | 49 | 13 |
| | 1985/86 | 17 776 | (2) 71 705 | (2) 69 093 | 96 | 2 563 464 | 1 247 108 | 49 | 13 |
| | 1990/91 | 18 850 | ... | ... | ... | 2 555 684 | 1 246 014 | 49 | 12 |
| | 1991/92 | 18 993 | ... | ... | ... | 2 558 735 | 1 250 029 | 49 | 12 |
| | 1992/93 | 19 041 | 105 391 | 81 672 | 77 | 2 549 638 | 1 246 554 | 49 | 12 |
| | 1993/94 | | 106 550 | 82 611 | 78 | 2 548 490 | 1 244 451 | 49 | 12 |
| | 1994/95 | 18 989 | 106 297 | 82 427 | 78 | 2 530 856 | 1 235 741 | 49 | 12 |
| | 1995/96 | 18 844 | 105 925 | 82 996 | 78 | 2 500 867 | 1 220 391 | 49 | 12 |
| | 1996/97 | ... | 106 581 | 86 780 | 81 | 2 451 210 | 1 196 391 | 49 | 12 |
| Germany | 1992/93 | 43 552 | 137 330 | 132 787 | 97 | 2 404 776 | 1 171 666 | 49 | ... |
| | 1993/94 | 43 660 | 137 557 | 133 010 | 97 | 2 415 757 | 1 172 391 | 49 | ... |
| | 1994/95 | 43 786 | 116 723 | 112 832 | 97 | 2 233 768 | 1 071 943 | 48 | 62 |
| | 1995/96 | ... | 116 793 | 112 957 | 97 | 2 332 924 | 1 119 301 | 48 | 62 |
| | 1996/97 | 41 594 | 116 708 | 112 886 | 97 | 2 343 520 | 1 135 740 | 48 | 54 |
| Greece | 1970/71 | 2 402 | 2 747 | 2 747 | 100 | 87 087 | 42 239 | 49 | 15 |
| | 1975/76 | 3 279 | 4 137 | 4 137 | 100 | 108 357 | 52 459 | 48 | 15 |
| | 1980/81 | 4 576 | 6 514 | 6 514 | 100 | 145 924 | 71 173 | 49 | 9 |
| | 1985/86 | 5 203 | 7 617 | 7 617 | 100 | 160 079 | 78 152 | 49 | 4 |
| | 1990/91 | 5 518 | 8 400 | 8 384 | 100 | 136 536 | 66 497 | 49 | 5 |
| | 1991/92 | 5 529 | 8 377 | 8 357 | 100 | 135 014 | 66 147 | 49 | 5 |
| | 1992/93 | 5 544 | 8 179 | 8 103 | 99 | 134 991 | 66 692 | 49 | 4 |
| | 1993/94 | 5 588 | 8 400 | 8 376 | 100 | 132 818 | 65 352 | 49 | 4 |
| | 1994/95 | 5 603 | 8 428 | 8 406 | 100 | 131 138 | 64 327 | 49 | 4 |
| | 1995/96 | 5 603 | 8 573 | 8 549 | 100 | 127 947 | 62 794 | 49 | 4 |
| | 1996/97 | 5 542 | 8 789 | 8 752 | 100 | 132 746 | 65 016 | 49 | 3 |
| Hungary | 1970/71 | 3 457 | 12 481 | 12 481 | 100 | 227 279 | 109 368 | 48 | - |
| | 1975/76 | 4 077 | 20 512 | 20 512 | 100 | 329 408 | 159 052 | 48 | - |
| | 1980/81 | 4 690 | 29 437 | 29 437 | 100 | 478 100 | 230 493 | 48 | - |
| | 1985/86 | 4 823 | 33 548 | 33 548 | 100 | 424 678 | 206 606 | 49 | - |
| | 1990/91 | 4 718 | 33 635 | 33 534 | 100 | 391 129 | 187 805 | 48 | 0 |
| | 1991/92 | 4 706 | 33 159 | ... | ... | 394 091 | 189 791 | 48 | 0 |
| | 1992/93 | 4 730 | 33 140 | ... | ... | 394 420 | ... | ... | ... |
| | 1993/94 | 4 712 | 37 851 | 37 851 | 100 | 398 082 | 191 948 | 48 | 2 |
| | 1994/95 | 4 719 | 37 470 | 37 470 | 100 | 397 311 | 190 798 | 48 | 2 |
| | 1995/96 | ... | ... | ... | ... | 400 527 | 193 779 | 48 | 2 |
| Iceland | 1975/76 | ... | ... | ... | ... | (28) 3 502 | ... | ... | 8 |
| | 1980/81 | ... | ... | ... | ... | (28) 4 041 | ... | ... | ... |
| | 1985/86 | ... | ... | ... | ... | (28) 4 528 | (28) 2 222 | 49 | ... |
| | 1994/95 | 223 | (25)(29) 2 079 | ... | ... | (29) 13 869 | ... | ... | ... |
| | 1995/96 | 236 | (25) 2 186 | ... | ... | (29) 14 536 | (29) 7 087 | 49 | 6 |
| | 1996/97 | 257 | ... | ... | ... | 14 285 | 6 878 | 48 | 6 |
| Ireland | 1970/71 | ... | ... | ... | ... | 131 500 | 64 000 | 49 | ... |
| | 1975/76 | ... | 4 408 | 3 218 | 73 | 135 783 | 66 179 | 49 | ... |
| | 1980/81 | ... | 4 782 | 3 523 | 74 | 137 533 | 66 568 | 48 | ... |
| | 1985/86 | ... | 5 164 | 3 921 | 76 | 147 908 | 71 501 | 48 | ... |
| | 1990/91 | ... | 4 541 | 3 481 | 77 | 127 512 | 61 517 | 48 | ... |
| | 1991/92 | ... | 4 613 | 3 548 | 77 | 126 168 | 61 228 | 49 | ... |
| | 1992/93 | ... | 4 683 | 3 614 | 77 | 123 711 | 60 026 | 49 | ... |
| | 1993/94 | ... | 4 676 | 3 619 | 77 | 118 205 | 57 284 | 48 | ... |
| | 1994/95 | ... | 4 625 | 3 611 | 78 | 114 363 | 55 393 | 48 | ... |
| | 1995/96 | ... | 4 737 | 3 692 | 78 | 116 004 | 55 946 | 48 | ... |
| | 1996/97 | ... | 4 823 | 3 784 | 78 | 115 569 | 56 132 | 49 | ... |
| Italy | 1970/71 | 23 922 | 47 967 | 47 967 | 100 | 1 586 785 | 777 874 | 49 | ... |
| | 1975/76 | 27 485 | 63 523 | 63 523 | 100 | 1 822 527 | 892 143 | 49 | ... |
| | 1980/81 | 30 295 | 108 261 | ... | ... | 1 870 477 | 917 854 | 49 | 38 |
| | 1985/86 | 28 943 | 108 184 | ... | ... | 1 660 986 | 805 727 | 49 | 32 |
| | 1990/91 | 27 716 | 108 339 | 107 353 | 99 | 1 552 694 | 759 111 | 49 | 29 |
| | 1991/92 | 27 463 | 103 540 | 102 920 | 99 | 1 552 255 | 758 946 | 49 | 29 |
| | 1992/93 | 27 274 | 104 715 | 104 086 | 99 | 1 569 811 | 767 638 | 49 | 29 |
| | 1993/94 | ... | ... | ... | ... | 1 578 420 | 771 565 | 49 | 29 |
| | 1994/95 | ... | 114 951 | 114 469 | 100 | 1 582 338 | 762 640 | 48 | 30 |

| Country / Pays / País | Year / Année / Año | Schools / Écoles / Escuelas | Teaching staff / Personnel enseignant / Personal docente | | | Pupils enrolled / Élèves inscrits / Alumnos matriculados | | | |
|---|---|---|---|---|---|---|---|---|---|
| | | | Total | Female Féminin Femenino | % F | Total | Female Féminin Femenino | % F | % Private Privé Privada |
| Italy (cont) | 1995/96 | 26 296 | 114 230 | 113 539 | 99 | 1 582 556 | 757 931 | 48 | 26 |
| | 1996/97 | ... | ... | ... | | 1 584 283 | 764 227 | 48 | 28 |
| Latvia | 1980/81 | 865 | ... | ... | ... | 84 165 | 41 300 | 49 | - |
| | 1985/86 | 936 | ... | ... | ... | 95 684 | 46 885 | 49 | - |
| | 1990/91 | ... | 8 240 | ... | ... | 74 423 | 36 542 | 49 | - |
| | 1991/92 | ... | 7 699 | ... | ... | 60 926 | 29 793 | 49 | - |
| | 1992/93 | 750 | 6 829 | ... | ... | 44 659 | 21 794 | 49 | - |
| | 1993/94 | 647 | 6 902 | ... | ... | 49 188 | 23 955 | 49 | - |
| | 1994/95 | 608 | 7 226 | ... | ... | 56 806 | 27 040 | 48 | 0 |
| | 1995/96 | 608 | 7 789 | ... | ... | 62 942 | 30 213 | 48 | 0 |
| | 1996/97 | 611 | 7 988 | 7 951 | 100 | 62 673 | 29 966 | 48 | 0 |
| Lithuania | 1980/81 | ... | 14 335 | ... | ... | 110 778 | ... | ... | - |
| | 1985/86 | ... | (27) 18 902 | ... | ... | 136 210 | ... | ... | - |
| | 1990/91 | ... | (27) 22 026 | (27) 22 001 | 100 | 134 765 | 66 170 | 49 | - |
| | 1991/92 | 1 420 | (27) 18 494 | (27) 18 454 | 100 | 112 404 | 55 078 | 49 | - |
| | 1992/93 | 1 053 | (27) 14 472 | (27) 14 450 | 100 | 92 027 | 45 093 | 49 | - |
| | 1993/94 | 811 | (27) 11 676 | (27) 11 621 | 100 | 69 304 | 34 513 | 50 | - |
| | 1994/95 | 748 | (27) 11 511 | (27) 11 465 | 100 | 74 936 | 36 644 | 49 | 0 |
| | 1995/96 | 741 | (27) 11 795 | (27) 11 742 | 100 | 80 574 | 38 640 | 48 | 0 |
| | 1996/97 | 729 | (27) 11 974 | (27) 11 911 | 99 | 84 160 | 40 227 | 48 | 0 |
| Luxembourg | 1970/71 | ... | 317 | 317 | 100 | 7 814 | 3 891 | 50 | 1 |
| | 1975/76 | ... | 394 | 394 | 100 | 8 625 | 4 230 | 49 | 0 |
| | 1980/81 | ... | 415 | 411 | 99 | 7 621 | 3 703 | 49 | 1 |
| | 1985/86 | ... | 440 | ... | ... | 7 779 | ... | ... | ... |
| | 1990/91 | ... | ... | ... | ... | 8 354 | ... | ... | ... |
| | 1991/92 | ... | 499 | ... | ... | 8 689 | ... | ... | ... |
| | 1993/94 | ... | 491 | ... | ... | 9 408 | ... | ... | 1 |
| | 1994/95 | ... | 539 | ... | ... | 10 398 | ... | ... | ... |
| | 1995/96 | ... | ... | ... | ... | 9 882 | ... | ... | ... |
| | 1996/97 | ... | 584 | ... | ... | 9 932 | ... | ... | ... |
| Malta | 1970/71 | 21 | ... | ... | ... | 2 640 | 1 232 | 47 | 100 |
| | 1975/76 | 43 | 406 | 347 | 85 | 6 237 | 2 940 | 47 | 60 |
| | 1980/81 | 42 | 428 | 372 | 87 | 7 691 | 3 630 | 47 | 51 |
| | 1985/86 | 43 | 324 | 324 | 100 | 7 899 | 3 818 | 48 | 56 |
| | 1990/91 | 58 | 688 | 688 | 100 | 11 313 | 5 364 | 47 | 38 |
| | 1991/92 | 49 | 692 | 692 | 100 | 11 770 | 5 791 | 49 | 36 |
| | 1992/93 | 47 | 697 | 697 | 100 | 12 025 | 5 921 | 49 | 37 |
| | 1993/94 | 46 | 739 | 739 | 100 | 12 226 | 6 000 | 49 | 36 |
| | 1994/95 | 49 | 764 | 764 | 100 | 11 119 | 5 378 | 48 | 39 |
| | 1995/96 | 48 | 803 | 803 | 100 | 11 160 | 5 436 | 49 | 38 |
| | 1996/97 | 49 | ... | ... | ... | 11 171 | 5 461 | 49 | 37 |
| Moldova | 1980/81 | ... | 18 051 | 18 051 | 100 | 175 660 | 84 317 | 48 | ... |
| | 1985/86 | ... | 22 620 | 22 620 | 100 | 209 349 | 100 488 | 48 | ... |
| | 1990/91 | ... | 28 067 | 28 067 | 100 | 248 384 | 119 224 | 48 | ... |
| | 1991/92 | ... | 27 674 | 27 674 | 100 | 239 350 | 114 888 | 48 | ... |
| | 1992/93 | ... | 25 728 | 25 728 | 100 | 207 288 | 99 498 | 48 | ... |
| | 1993/94 | ... | 23 587 | 23 587 | 100 | 190 235 | 91 313 | 48 | ... |
| | 1994/95 | ... | (30) 21 680 | (30) 21 680 | 100 | (30) 162 062 | (30) 76 169 | 47 | ... |
| | 1995/96 | ... | *20 020 | *20 020 | *100 | *143 287 | *67 347 | *47 | *18 |
| | 1996/97 | ... | *18 395 | *18 395 | *100 | *133 426 | *62 719 | *47 | *17 |
| Monaco | 1980/81 | (2) 5 | ... | ... | ... | (2) 330 | (2) 151 | 46 | ... |
| | 1990/91 | 9 | 47 | 30 | 64 | 903 | 429 | 48 | 33 |
| | 1991/92 | 9 | 52 | 39 | 75 | 962 | 448 | 47 | 32 |
| | 1993/94 | 9 | 44 | ... | ... | 1 055 | 523 | 50 | 30 |
| | 1994/95 | 9 | 46 | ... | ... | 1 034 | 493 | 48 | 28 |
| | 1995/96 | 9 | 46 | ... | ... | 1 015 | 479 | 47 | 28 |
| | 1996/97 | 9 | ... | ... | ... | 996 | 470 | 47 | 26 |
| Netherlands | 1970/71 | ... | 15 954 | 15 954 | 100 | 491 732 | 239 680 | 49 | 75 |
| | 1975/76 | ... | 20 565 | 20 565 | 100 | 518 890 | 252 806 | 49 | 71 |
| | 1980/81 | (31) 8 727 | 22 361 | 22 361 | 100 | 409 576 | 198 795 | 49 | 70 |
| | 1985/86 | (31) 8 401 | 21 426 | 21 426 | 100 | 359 130 | 176 497 | 49 | 68 |
| | 1990/91 | (31) 8 450 | 21 019 | 21 019 | 100 | 360 880 | 177 951 | 49 | 69 |
| | 1991/92 | (31) 8 435 | 22 200 | 22 200 | 100 | 367 602 | 182 586 | 50 | 68 |
| | 1992/93 | (31) 8 331 | 22 700 | 22 700 | 100 | 368 473 | 180 491 | 49 | 68 |
| | 1993/94 | (31) 8 139 | (32) 24 871 | (32) 18 406 | 74 | 373 164 | 182 500 | 49 | 68 |
| | 1994/95 | (31) 7 860 | ... | ... | ... | 385 483 | 188 182 | 49 | 68 |
| | 1995/96 | (31) 7 411 | ... | ... | ... | 394 937 | 192 246 | 49 | 68 |
| | 1996/97 | (31) 7 287 | ... | ... | ... | 394 374 | 191 699 | 49 | 68 |
| Norway | 1975/76 | ... | 5 516 | ... | ... | 30 479 | ... | ... | ... |
| | 1980/81 | 2 554 | 16 866 | ... | ... | 78 189 | ... | ... | 41 |
| | 1985/86 | 3 281 | ... | ... | ... | 98 454 | ... | ... | 37 |
| | 1990/91 | 4 649 | 35 891 | 34 152 | 95 | 139 350 | ... | ... | 36 |
| | 1991/92 | 5 214 | 34 534 | 33 165 | 96 | 155 153 | ... | ... | 38 |
| | 1992/93 | 5 836 | 37 549 | 35 951 | 96 | 174 096 | ... | ... | 37 |
| | 1993/94 | 5 631 | ... | ... | ... | (33) 158 129 | (33) 79 064 | 50 | 37 |
| | 1994/95 | ... | ... | ... | ... | (33) 169 739 | (33) 84 869 | 50 | 36 |
| | 1995/96 | ... | ... | ... | ... | (33) 177 593 | (33) 88 796 | 50 | 35 |
| | 1996/97 | 6 409 | (25) 25 416 | ... | ... | 183 539 | 91 769 | 50 | 34 |

| Country / Pays / País | Year / Année / Año | Schools / Écoles / Escuelas | Teaching staff Personnel enseignant Personal docente | | | Pupils enrolled Élèves inscrits Alumnos matriculados | | | |
|---|---|---|---|---|---|---|---|---|---|
| | | | Total | Female Féminin Femenino | % F | Total | Female Féminin Femenino | % F | % Private Privé Privada |
| Poland | 1970/71 | 19 600 | 37 807 | ... | ... | 744 968 | ... | ... | - |
| | 1975/76 | 31 176 | 44 542 | 43 957 | 99 | 1 107 648 | ... | ... | |
| | 1980/81 | 31 014 | 57 730 | 57 137 | 99 | 1 349 528 | ... | ... | 0 |
| | 1985/86 | 26 344 | 78 092 | 76 798 | 98 | 1 360 044 | ... | ... | 0 |
| | 1990/91 | 25 732 | 89 864 | ... | ... | 1 226 101 | ... | ... | 0 |
| | 1991/92 | 24 101 | 80 517 | ... | ... | 1 098 279 | ... | ... | 0 |
| | 1992/93 | 21 310 | 71 117 | ... | ... | 1 019 171 | 499 394 | 49 | 1 |
| | 1993/94 | 21 326 | 69 688 | ... | ... | 986 996 | 483 628 | 49 | 1 |
| | 1994/95 | ... | ... | ... | ... | 984 545 | ... | ... | ... |
| | 1995/96 | ... | 73 867 | ... | ... | 983 489 | 475 741 | 48 | ... |
| Portugal | 1970/71 | 317 | 692 | 692 | 100 | 17 135 | 8 285 | 48 | 100 |
| | 1975/76 | 679 | 1 903 | 1 842 | 97 | 44 832 | 21 354 | 48 | 91 |
| | 1980/81 | 1 916 | 5 047 | 4 974 | 99 | 100 178 | 48 389 | 48 | ... |
| | 1985/86 | 2 547 | 6 408 | 6 323 | 99 | 128 089 | 62 226 | 49 | ... |
| | 1990/91 | 4 879 | 9 700 | 9 495 | 98 | 181 450 | 87 943 | 48 | 64 |
| | 1992/93 | 4 824 | ... | ... | ... | 179 135 | 85 743 | 48 | 58 |
| | 1993/94 | 4 911 | 9 668 | ... | ... | 183 298 | 88 500 | 48 | 58 |
| | 1994/95 | ... | ... | ... | ... | 184 384 | 89 680 | 49 | ... |
| | 1995/96 | ... | ... | ... | ... | 191 530 | 91 526 | 48 | ... |
| Romania | 1970/71 | 10 336 | 18 887 | 18 887 | 100 | 448 244 | 224 483 | 50 | - |
| | 1975/76 | 13 537 | 33 789 | 33 789 | 100 | 812 420 | 404 766 | 50 | - |
| | 1980/81 | 13 467 | 38 512 | 38 512 | 100 | 935 711 | 461 084 | 49 | - |
| | 1985/86 | 12 811 | 33 522 | 33 522 | 100 | 864 332 | 426 792 | 49 | - |
| | 1990/91 | 12 529 | 37 007 | 37 007 | 100 | 752 141 | 375 347 | 50 | - |
| | 1991/92 | 12 600 | 36 326 | 36 326 | 100 | 742 232 | 370 313 | 50 | - |
| | 1992/93 | 12 603 | 36 447 | 36 447 | 100 | 752 063 | 376 242 | 50 | 0 |
| | 1993/94 | 12 715 | 37 303 | 37 126 | 100 | 712 136 | 354 861 | 50 | 0 |
| | 1994/95 | 12 665 | 37 603 | 37 288 | 99 | 715 514 | 356 475 | 50 | 0 |
| | 1995/96 | 12 772 | 38 915 | 38 747 | 100 | 697 888 | 345 996 | 50 | 0 |
| | 1996/97 | 12 951 | 39 166 | 39 006 | 100 | 659 226 | 325 128 | 49 | 0 |
| Russian Federation | 1980/81 | ... | 532 000 | ... | ... | 5 703 000 | ... | ... | - |
| | 1985/86 | ... | 677 000 | ... | ... | 6 488 000 | ... | ... | - |
| | 1990/91 | ... | 770 000 | ... | ... | 7 042 000 | ... | ... | - |
| | 1991/92 | ... | 768 000 | ... | ... | 6 882 000 | 3 217 000 | 47 | - |
| | 1992/93 | ... | 687 000 | ... | ... | 6 058 000 | ... | ... | 0 |
| | 1993/94 | 78 333 | 646 000 | ... | ... | 5 696 000 | 2 657 000 | 47 | *7 |
| San Marino | 1970/71 | 14 | 30 | 30 | 100 | 684 | 313 | 46 | 51 |
| | 1975/76 | 16 | 68 | 68 | 100 | 735 | 356 | 48 | 31 |
| | 1980/81 | 17 | 91 | 91 | 100 | 877 | 430 | 49 | - |
| | 1985/86 | 16 | 109 | 109 | 100 | 814 | 388 | 48 | - |
| | 1990/91 | 15 | 108 | 108 | 100 | 759 | 373 | 49 | - |
| | 1991/92 | 15 | 103 | 103 | 100 | 750 | 346 | 46 | - |
| | 1992/93 | 15 | 103 | 103 | 100 | 785 | 363 | 46 | - |
| | 1993/94 | 15 | 102 | 102 | 100 | 811 | 377 | 46 | - |
| | 1995/96 | 15 | 94 | 94 | 100 | 867 | 406 | 47 | - |
| | 1996/97 | 15 | 96 | 96 | 100 | 854 | 409 | 48 | - |
| Slovakia | 1980/81 | 3 723 | 16 180 | ... | ... | 231 155 | ... | ... | - |
| | 1985/86 | 3 976 | 18 249 | ... | ... | 249 448 | ... | ... | - |
| | 1990/91 | 4 025 | 18 620 | ... | ... | 216 336 | ... | ... | - |
| | 1991/92 | 3 759 | 17 306 | ... | ... | 188 821 | ... | ... | - |
| | 1992/93 | 3 642 | 17 218 | ... | ... | 188 502 | ... | ... | - |
| | 1993/94 | 3 482 | 15 834 | ... | ... | 183 872 | ... | ... | 0 |
| | 1994/95 | 3 343 | 14 639 | ... | ... | 174 436 | ... | ... | 0 |
| | 1995/96 | 3 383 | 15 212 | 15 212 | 100 | 163 710 | ... | ... | 0 |
| | 1996/97 | 3 396 | *15 663 | *15 663 | *100 | 170 138 | ... | ... | 0 |
| Slovenia | 1980/81 | 711 | 5 002 | 4 695 | 94 | 61 432 | 29 354 | 48 | - |
| | 1985/86 | 793 | 5 674 | 5 532 | 97 | 68 544 | 32 441 | 47 | - |
| | 1990/91 | 785 | 5 869 | 5 811 | 99 | 66 484 | 31 575 | 47 | - |
| | 1991/92 | 776 | 5 539 | 5 439 | 98 | 56 081 | 30 098 | 54 | - |
| | 1992/93 | 774 | 4 809 | 4 719 | 98 | 53 543 | 25 666 | 48 | - |
| | 1993/94 | 773 | 4 803 | 4 780 | 100 | 55 460 | 26 599 | 48 | - |
| | 1994/95 | 776 | 4 944 | 4 902 | 99 | 55 233 | 26 263 | 48 | 0 |
| | 1995/96 | 793 | 4 989 | 4 894 | 98 | 54 716 | 25 942 | 47 | 0 |
| | 1996/97 | 800 | 4 923 | 4 838 | 98 | 54 191 | 25 852 | 48 | 1 |
| Spain | 1970/71 | ... | 20 745 | *20 745 | *100 | 819 914 | 419 583 | 51 | 56 |
| | 1975/76 | ... | 24 621 | 24 287 | 99 | 920 336 | 471 437 | 51 | 62 |
| | 1980/81 | ... | 35 588 | 34 386 | 97 | 1 182 425 | 593 030 | 50 | 45 |
| | 1985/86 | ... | 39 573 | 36 723 | 93 | 1 127 348 | 555 852 | 49 | 38 |
| | 1990/91 | 15 260 | 40 051 | 38 172 | 95 | 994 322 | 491 140 | 49 | 39 |
| | 1991/92 | 15 404 | 43 922 | 42 020 | 96 | 1 025 797 | 500 946 | 49 | 38 |
| | 1992/93 | ... | 50 598 | 48 211 | 95 | 1 056 221 | 514 960 | 49 | 36 |
| | 1993/94 | ... | 54 769 | 51 863 | 95 | 1 086 376 | 529 035 | 49 | 35 |
| | 1994/95 | ... | 55 254 | 52 700 | 95 | 1 095 973 | 534 244 | 49 | 34 |
| | 1995/96 | ... | 57 017 | 54 357 | 95 | 1 098 693 | 534 736 | 49 | 33 |
| | 1996/97 | ... | ... | ... | ... | 1 117 343 | 544 098 | 49 | 32 |
| | 1997/98 | ... | ... | ... | ... | *1 120 774 | ... | ... | *32 |
| | 1998/99 | ... | ... | ... | ... | *1 131 029 | ... | ... | ... |

| Country<br>Pays<br>País | Year<br>Année<br>Año | Schools<br>Écoles<br>Escuelas | Teaching staff<br>Personnel enseignant<br>Personal docente | | | | Pupils enrolled<br>Élèves inscrits<br>Alumnos matriculados | | | |
|---|---|---|---|---|---|---|---|---|---|---|
| | | | Total | Female<br>Féminin<br>Femenino | %<br>F | | Total | Female<br>Féminin<br>Femenino | %<br>F | %<br>Private<br>Privé<br>Privada |
| Sweden | 1975/76 | 5 913 | ... | ... | ... | | 206 726 | ... | ... | ... |
| | 1980/81 | 8 504 | ... | ... | ... | | 226 571 | ... | ... | ... |
| | 1985/86 | ... | ... | ... | ... | | 224 161 | ... | ... | ... |
| | 1990/91 | ... | ... | ... | ... | | 262 320 | ... | ... | ... |
| | 1991/92 | ... | ... | ... | ... | | 283 506 | ... | ... | ... |
| | 1992/93 | 8 847 | 17 374 | 16 888 | 97 | | 283 860 | ... | ... | 5 |
| | 1993/94 | 8 982 | 17 057 | 16 603 | 97 | | 295 529 | 147 766 | 50 | 8 |
| | 1994/95 | ... | 17 446 | 16 972 | 97 | | 312 978 | 156 489 | 50 | ... |
| | 1995/96 | 8 691 | ... | ... | ... | | 340 163 | 170 076 | 50 | 10 |
| | 1996/97 | 8 356 | 17 341 | 16 925 | 98 | | 345 045 | 172 059 | 50 | ... |
| Switzerland | 1980/81 | ... | ... | ... | ... | | 120 315 | 58 402 | 49 | 7 |
| | 1985/86 | ... | ... | ... | ... | | 123 128 | 59 848 | 49 | 3 |
| | 1990/91 | ... | ... | ... | ... | | 139 798 | 68 225 | 49 | 5 |
| | 1991/92 | ... | ... | ... | ... | | 141 360 | 68 832 | 49 | 5 |
| | 1992/93 | ... | ... | ... | ... | | 147 077 | 71 261 | 48 | 6 |
| | 1993/94 | ... | (2) 8 646 | (2) 8 592 | 99 | | 151 785 | 73 424 | 48 | 6 |
| | 1994/95 | ... | (2) 10 169 | (2) 10 108 | 99 | | 157 469 | 76 098 | 48 | 7 |
| | 1995/96 | ... | ... | ... | ... | | 160 987 | 77 999 | 48 | 7 |
| The Former Yugoslav<br>Rep. of Macedonia | 1992/93 | ... | 2 967 | 2 865 | 97 | | 30 946 | 14 956 | 48 | - |
| | 1993/94 | 49 | 2 938 | 2 913 | 99 | | 30 432 | 14 645 | 48 | - |
| | 1994/95 | ... | 3 027 | 3 000 | 99 | | 31 980 | 15 527 | 49 | - |
| | 1995/96 | ... | 3 059 | 3 031 | 99 | | 32 826 | 15 721 | 48 | - |
| | 1996/97 | 417 | 3 073 | 3 049 | 99 | | 32 466 | 15 555 | 48 | - |
| Ukraine | 1970/71 | 13 257 | 113 600 | ... | ... | | 1 208 200 | ... | ... | - |
| | 1975/76 | 17 707 | ... | ... | ... | | 1 886 000 | ... | ... | - |
| | 1980/81 | 21 200 | 194 700 | ... | ... | | 1 779 300 | ... | ... | - |
| | 1985/86 | 22 600 | 236 000 | ... | ... | | 1 902 600 | 894 200 | 47 | - |
| | 1990/91 | 23 600 | 212 600 | ... | ... | | 1 939 600 | 911 600 | 47 | - |
| | 1991/92 | 23 500 | 212 200 | ... | ... | | 1 875 000 | 892 600 | 48 | - |
| | 1992/93 | 23 700 | 201 400 | ... | ... | | 1 663 200 | 775 100 | 47 | - |
| | 1993/94 | 23 100 | 191 500 | ... | ... | | 1 566 600 | 728 500 | 47 | - |
| United Kingdom (34) | 1970/71 | ... | ... | ... | ... | | 302 347 | 147 145 | 49 | 6 |
| | 1975/76 | (2) 1 040 | ... | ... | ... | | 571 545 | 278 910 | 49 | 5 |
| | 1985/86 | (2) 1 262 | ... | ... | ... | | 665 000 | 315 000 | 47 | 5 |
| | 1990/91 | (2) 1 364 | 30 900 | 29 500 | 95 | | 792 700 | 388 100 | 49 | 6 |
| | 1991/92 | (2) 1 380 | 32 100 | 30 600 | 95 | | 810 600 | 396 500 | 49 | 6 |
| | 1992/93 | 1 406 | 12 102 | 12 102 | 100 | | 423 956 | 206 731 | 49 | - |
| | 1993/94 | ... | 12 280 | 12 280 | 100 | | 430 927 | 210 144 | 49 | - |
| | 1994/95 | ... | 14 329 | 14 329 | 100 | | 442 357 | 215 419 | 49 | - |
| | 1995/96 | ... | 15 191 | 15 191 | 100 | | 450 969 | 219 640 | 49 | - |
| | 1996/97 | 1 538 | 15 578 | 15 578 | 100 | | 455 849 | 221 765 | 49 | - |
| **Oceania** | | | | | | | | | | |
| American Samoa | 1980/81 | 111 | ... | ... | ... | | 1 922 | 891 | 46 | 7 |
| | 1985/86 | 97 | 98 | 98 | 100 | | 2 001 | 941 | 47 | 10 |
| | 1991/92 | 92 | 123 | 122 | 99 | | 2 694 | ... | ... | 11 |
| Australia | 1975 | ... | ... | ... | ... | (35) | 186 652 | (35) 90 903 | 49 | 19 |
| | 1980 | ... | ... | ... | ... | (35) | 165 742 | (35) 80 485 | 49 | 22 |
| | 1985 | ... | ... | ... | ... | (35) | 161 974 | (35) 78 433 | 48 | 26 |
| | 1990 | ... | ... | ... | ... | (35) | 180 470 | (35) 88 117 | 49 | 26 |
| | 1991 | ... | ... | ... | ... | (35) | 180 809 | (35) 88 040 | 49 | 26 |
| | 1992 | ... | ... | ... | ... | (35) | 181 358 | (35) 88 356 | 49 | 26 |
| | 1993 | ... | ... | ... | ... | (35) | 182 269 | (35) 88 878 | 49 | 26 |
| | 1994 | ... | ... | ... | ... | (35) | 186 163 | (35) 90 742 | 49 | 26 |
| | 1995 | ... | ... | ... | ... | (16) | 243 800 | ... | ... | ... |
| | 1996 | ... | ... | ... | ... | | 200 500 | ... | ... | ... |
| | 1997 | ... | ... | ... | ... | | 207 000 | ... | ... | ... |
| Cook Islands | 1985 | ... | ... | ... | ... | | 412 | ... | ... | ... |
| Fiji | 1975 | 117 | 256 | 256 | 100 | | 3 339 | 1 603 | 48 | 100 |
| | 1980 | 163 | 196 | 196 | 100 | | 4 493 | 2 201 | 49 | 100 |
| | 1985 | 244 | 308 | 306 | 99 | | 4 206 | ... | ... | 100 |
| | 1990 | 299 | 375 | ... | ... | | 7 506 | 3 760 | 50 | 100 |
| | 1991 | 327 | ... | ... | ... | | 7 839 | ... | ... | 100 |
| | 1992 | 334 | 422 | ... | ... | | 8 209 | 4 114 | 50 | 100 |
| French Polynesia | 1970/71 | ... | ... | ... | ... | | 6 512 | 3 232 | 50 | ... |
| | 1975/76 | 9 | 265 | 265 | 100 | | 8 117 | 3 949 | 49 | 26 |
| | 1990/91 | 75 | 626 | *616 | *98 | | 15 860 | 7 765 | 49 | 17 |
| | 1992/93 | 77 | 669 | 660 | 99 | | 16 472 | 7 905 | 48 | 16 |
| | 1994/95 | 71 | (2) 486 | ... | ... | | 16 545 | 7 936 | 48 | 16 |
| | 1995/96 | 59 | (2) 408 | (2) 402 | 99 | | 16 049 | 7 796 | 49 | 16 |
| Nauru | 1985 | 4 | 20 | 20 | 100 | | 383 | 187 | 49 | - |
| New Caledonia | 1970 | ... | 149 | 149 | 100 | | 3 044 | 1 527 | 50 | 52 |
| | 1975 | ... | ... | ... | ... | | 6 195 | ... | ... | ... |
| | 1980 | ... | ... | ... | ... | | 10 313 | 5 121 | 50 | 25 |

| Country / Pays / País | Year / Année / Año | Schools / Écoles / Escuelas | Teaching staff / Personnel enseignant / Personal docente | | | | | Pupils enrolled / Élèves inscrits / Alumnos matriculados | | | |
|---|---|---|---|---|---|---|---|---|---|---|---|
| | | | | Total | Female / Féminin / Femenino | % F | | | Total | Female / Féminin / Femenino | % F | % Private / Privé / Privada |
| New Caledonia (cont) | 1985 | 52 | | 355 | ... | ... | | | 8 647 | 4 280 | 49 | 33 |
| | 1990 | 73 | | 428 | ... | ... | | | 10 745 | 5 261 | 49 | 31 |
| | 1991 | 80 | | 461 | ... | ... | | | 11 431 | 5 531 | 48 | 31 |
| | 1994 | ... | | ... | ... | ... | | | 12 776 | ... | ... | ... |
| New Zealand | 1970 | 305 | | 619 | 619 | 100 | | | 24 336 | 12 053 | 50 | ... |
| | 1975 | 1 098 | (36) | 1 882 | (36) 1 881 | 100 | | (36) | 54 757 | (36) 26 964 | 49 | - |
| | 1980 | 1 208 | | ... | ... | ... | | (36) | 56 858 | (36) 27 653 | 49 | - |
| | 1985 | 1 388 | (36) | 1 459 | (36) 1 444 | 99 | | (36) | 60 666 | (36) 29 590 | 49 | - |
| | 1990 | 2 890 | | ... | ... | ... | | | 118 367 | 57 765 | 49 | 0 |
| | 1991 | 3 083 | | ... | ... | ... | | | 126 134 | 61 039 | 48 | 0 |
| | 1992 | 3 336 | | 5 567 | 5 448 | 98 | | | 135 732 | 65 778 | 48 | ... |
| | 1993 | 3 000 | | ... | ... | ... | | | 132 932 | 64 856 | 49 | ... |
| | 1994 | 3 720 | | 7 174 | 6 793 | 95 | | | 131 311 | 64 006 | 49 | ... |
| | 1995 | ... | | 9 236 | 8 845 | 96 | | | 135 935 | 65 935 | 49 | 18 |
| | 1996 | 3 924 | | ... | ... | ... | | | 135 904 | 65 560 | 48 | 20 |
| | 1997 | 3 789 | | ... | ... | ... | | | 134 040 | 64 950 | 48 | 22 |
| Niue | 1970 | 1 | | 2 | 2 | 100 | | | 30 | ... | ... | ... |
| | 1975 | 13 | | 45 | 45 | 100 | | | 352 | 171 | 49 | - |
| Papua New Guinea | 1975 | ... | | ... | ... | ... | | | 51 | 21 | 41 | ... |
| | 1990 | ... | | ... | ... | ... | | | 934 | 434 | 46 | 100 |
| | 1991 | ... | | ... | ... | ... | | | 698 | 328 | 47 | 100 |
| | 1992 | ... | | ... | ... | ... | | | 856 | 411 | 48 | 100 |
| | 1993 | ... | | ... | ... | ... | | | 1 404 | 610 | 43 | 60 |
| | 1994 | ... | (2) | 20 | (2) 15 | 75 | | | 1 524 | 703 | 46 | 60 |
| | 1995 | 29 | (?) | 53 | (2) 35 | 66 | | | 2 528 | 1 202 | 48 | 41 |
| Samoa | 1970 | 1 | | 5 | 5 | 100 | | | 80 | 39 | 49 | 100 |
| | 1975 | 21 | | 80 | 68 | 85 | | | 1 926 | 982 | 51 | 100 |
| | 1992 | ... | | 91 | ... | ... | | | 1 188 | ... | ... | 100 |
| | 1995 | ... | | ... | ... | ... | | | 2 347 | ... | ... | 100 |
| | 1996 | ... | | ... | ... | ... | | | 3 143 | ... | ... | 100 |
| Solomon Islands | 1970 | 2 | | 7 | 7 | 100 | | | 50 | 22 | 44 | 100 |
| | 1990 | ... | | ... | ... | ... | | (37) | 10 122 | (37) 4 711 | 47 | ... |
| | 1991 | ... | | ... | ... | ... | | (37) | 11 259 | (37) 5 303 | 47 | ... |
| | 1992 | ... | | ... | ... | ... | | (37) | 12 705 | (37) 5 900 | 46 | 9 |
| | 1993 | ... | | ... | ... | ... | | (37) | 12 839 | (37) 6 059 | 47 | 9 |
| | 1994 | ... | | ... | ... | ... | | (37) | 12 627 | (37) 5 950 | 47 | ... |
| Tokelau | 1991 | 3 | | 5 | 5 | 100 | | | 133 | 64 | 48 | - |
| Vanuatu, Republic of | 1970 | ... | | 23 | 12 | 52 | | | 336 | 222 | 66 | 51 |
| | 1980 | 34 | | 49 | 49 | 100 | | | 1 187 | 557 | 47 | 66 |
| | 1992 | 252 | | ... | ... | ... | | | 5 178 | *2 500 | *48 | 100 |

## General note
For general explanations and definitions, please refer to the beginning of this chapter.

## Note générale
Pour les explications et définitions générales, prière de se référer au début de ce chapitre.

## Nota general
Para las explicaciones y definiciones generales, referirse al comienzo de este capítulo.

### Notes

(1) Including initiation classes where pupils learn Portuguese.

(2) Public education only.

(3) Data refer to 'Sector autonomo Bissau' only.

(4) Not including Koranic schools.

(5) Koranic schools only.

(6) Not including the former independent states (Transkei, Bophuthatswana, Venda and Ciskei).

(7) Including Koranic schools Khalwas which accept pupils of all ages (161,882 pupils in 1985/86 ).

(8) Including administrative staff.

(9) Not including classes where pupils learn Spanish (la Castellanización).

(10) Public and aided education only.

(11) Nursery schools and kindergartens only.

(12) Data refer to posts and not to teaching staff.

(13) Not including public rural schools.

### Notes

(1) Y compris les classes d'initiation où les élèves apprennent le portugais.

(2) Enseignement public seulement.

(3) Les données se réfèrent au secteur autonome de 'Bissau' seulement.

(4) Non compris les écoles coraniques.

(5) Ecoles coraniques seulement.

(6) Non compris les anciens états indépendants (Transkei, Bophuthatswana, Venda et Ciskei).

(7) Y compris les écoles coraniques Khalwas qui acceptent les élèves de tous âges (161 882 élèves en 1985/86).

(8) Y compris le personnel administratif.

(9) Non compris les classes où les élèves apprennent l'espagnol (la Castellanización).

(10) Enseignement public et subventionné seulement.

(11) Ecoles maternelles et jardins d'enfants seulement.

(12) Les données se réfèrent au nombre de postes et non au nombre d'enseignants.

(13) Non compris les écoles publiques rurales.

### Notas

(1) Incluyen las clases de iniciación donde los alumnos aprenden el portugués.

(2) Enseñanza pública solamente.

(3) Los datos se refieren al sector autónomo de 'Bissau' solamente.

(4) No incluyen las escuelas coránicas.

(5) Escuelas coránicas solamente.

(6) No incluyen los antiguos estados independientes (Transkei, Bophuthatswana, Venda y Ciskei).

(7) Incluyen las escuelas coránicas Khalwas que admiten los alumnos de todas las edades (161 882 alumnos en 1985/86).

(8) Incluye el personal administrativo.

(9) No incluyen las clases donde los alumnos aprenden el español (la Castellanización).

(10) Enseñanza pública y subvencionada solamente.

(11) Escuelas maternales y jardines de infancia.

(12) Los datos se refieren al número de puestos y no al número de docentes.

(13) No incluidas las escuelas públicas rurales.

(14) Not including 'classes de Alfabetizaçao', which were created in 1985.

(15) Data refer to the end of school year.

(16) As from 1995, change in structure.

(17) Not including Turkish schools.

(18) As from this year, change in data coverage.

(19) Full-time only.

(20) East Bank only.

(21) The increase in enrolment since 1992 is due to the fact that pre-primary schools, which were exclusively found in the capital, then expanded to the atolls.

(22) Kindergartens only.

(23) Including special education.

(24) Not including "Vorschulklassen".

(25) Data are expressed in full-time equivalent.

(26) As from 1992, the coverage of pre-primary education was changed to include children aged 3 years and over.

(27) Data refer to classes for children aged 1-6.

(28) Data refer to 6 year old children.

(29) As from 1990, change in structure.

(30) As from 1994, including special education.

(31) Data refer to the total number of pre-primary and primary schools.

(32) In 1993/94, change in the method of estimating the breakdown of teaching staff by sex between the pre-primary and primary levels of education

(33) As from 1993, change in data coverage.

(34) From 1992/93 data refer only to nursery schools and nursery classes within primary schools. Small numbers of pupils in certain pre-primary programmes (such as playgroups) are excluded. In addition, pupils taught in infant classes in primary schools, and other pupils below compulsory age in independent and special schools are included within primary education.

(35) Data refer to preprimary classes in primary schools (pre-year 1).

(36) Not including licensed centres.

(37) Data refer to preparatory classes.

---

(14) Non compris les classes de 'Alfabetizaçao' qui ont été créées en 1985.

(15) Les données se réfèrent à la fin de l'année scolaire.

(16) A partir de 1995, changement de structure.

(17) Non compris les écoles turques.

(18) A partir de cette année, changement dans la couverture des données.

(19) Plein temps seulement.

(20) Rive orientale seulement.

(21) L'augmentation des effectifs en 1992 est due au fait que les écoles préprimaires qui n'existaient que dans la capitale, se sont maintenant développées dans les atolls.

(22) Jardins d'enfants seulement.

(23) Y compris l'enseignement spécial.

(24) Non compris les "Vorschulklassen".

(25) Les données sont exprimées en équivalents plein temps.

(26) A partir de 1992, l'enseignement préprimaire accueille les enfants dès l'âge de 3 ans.

(27) Les données se réfèrent aux classes pour enfants de 1 à 6 ans

(28) Les données se réfèrent aux enfants âgés de 6 ans.

(29) A partir de 1990, changement de structure.

(30) A partir 1994, y compris l'enseignement spécial.

(31) Les données se réfèrent au nombre total des écoles préprimaires et primaires.

(32) En 1993/94, changement de méthode d'estimation de la répartition par sexe du personnel enseignant entre les niveaux préprimaire et primaire.

(33) A partir de 1993, changement dans la couverture des données.

(34) A partir de 1992/93, les données se réfèrent seulement aux écoles maternelles et aux classes maternelles dans les écoles primaires. Un petit nombre d'élèves dans certains programmes du préprimaire (tels que les jardins d'enfants) ne sont pas inclus. De plus, les élèves inscrits dans les classes enfantines des écoles primaires et d'autres élèves en dessous de l'âge de la scolarité obligatoire inscrits dans les écoles indépendantes et spéciales sont compris dans l'enseignement primaire.

(35) Les données se réfèrent seulement aux classes du préprimaire rattachées aux écoles primaires (pre-year 1).

(36) Non compris les "licensed centres".

(37) Les données se réfèrent aux classes préparatoires.

---

(14) No incluyen las clases de 'Alfabetizaçao' que fueron creadas en 1985.

(15) Los datos se refieren al final del año escolar.

(16) A partir de 1995, cambio de estructura.

(17) No incluyen las escuelas turcas.

(18) A partir de este año, cambio en la cobertura de los datos.

(19) Jornada completa solamente.

(20) Orilla oriental solamente.

(21) El aumento de la matrícula en 1992 se debe a que las escuelas preprimarias, existentes solamente en la capital, se han ahora extendido a los atolones.

(22) Jardines de infancia solamente.

(23) Incluye la enseñanza especial.

(24) No incluyen las "Vorschulklassen".

(25) Los datos están expresados en equivalente de jornada completa.

(26) A partir de 1992, la enseñanza preprimaria incluye los niños desde los 3 años de edad.

(27) Los datos se refieren a las clases para los niños de 1 a 6 años.

(28) Los datos se refieren a los niños de 6 años de edad.

(29) A partir de 1990, cambio de estructura.

(30) A partir 1994, incluye la enseñanza especial.

(31) Los datos se refieren al número total de escuelas preprimarias y primarias.

(32) En 1993/94, cambio en el método de cálculo de la distribución por sexo del personal docente entre los niveles de enseñanza preprimaria y primaria.

(33) A partir de 1993, cambio en la cobertura de los datos.

(34) A partir de 1992/93, los datos se refieren solamente a las escuelas de párvulos y a las clases de párvulos en las escuelas preprimarias. Algunos alumnos en ciertos programas de preprimaria (como los jardines de infancia) no están incluidos. Además, los alumnos matriculados en las clases infantiles de las escuelas primarias y algunos alumnos que no han alcanzado la edad obligatoria de escolaridad adscritos en las escuelas privadas y especiales están incluidos en la enseñanza primaria.

(35) Los datos se refieren solamente a las clases de preprimara adscritas a las escuelas primarias (pre-year 1).

(36) No incluyen los "licensed centres".

(37) Los datos se refieren a las clases preparatorias.

Primary education: schools, teaching staff and pupils
Enseignement primaire: écoles, personnel enseignant et élèves
Enseñanza primaria: escuelas, personal docente y alumnos

II.5

## II.5 Primary education: schools, teaching staff and pupils

## Enseignement primaire: écoles, personnel enseignant et élèves

## Enseñanza primaria: escuelas, personal docente y alumnos

| Country / Pays / País | Year / Année / Año | Schools / Écoles / Escuelas | Teaching staff Personnel enseignant Personal docente | | | Pupils enrolled Élèves inscrits Alumnos matriculados | | | Pupil/ teacher ratio Nombre d'élèves par maître |
|---|---|---|---|---|---|---|---|---|---|
| | | | Total | Female Féminin Femenino | % F | Total | Female Féminin Femenino | % F | Número de alumnos por maestro |
| **Africa** | | | | | | | | | |
| Algeria | 1970/71 | 6 109 | 47 178 | 12 266 | 26 | 1 887 148 | 707 933 | 38 | 40 |
| | 1975/76 | 7 798 | 65 043 | ... | ... | 2 663 248 | 1 064 576 | 40 | 41 |
| | 1980/81 | 9 263 | 88 481 | 32 506 | 37 | 3 118 827 | 1 307 550 | 42 | 35 |
| | 1985/86 | 11 360 | 125 034 | 49 807 | 40 | 3 481 288 | 1 516 157 | 44 | 28 |
| | 1990/91 | 13 135 | 151 262 | 59 074 | 39 | 4 189 152 | 1 877 990 | 45 | 28 |
| | 1991/92 | 13 461 | 154 685 | 62 280 | 40 | 4 357 352 | 1 965 859 | 45 | 28 |
| | 1992/93 | 13 970 | 161 802 | 65 512 | 40 | 4 436 363 | 2 011 685 | 45 | 27 |
| | 1993/94 | 14 734 | 164 982 | 70 492 | 43 | 4 515 274 | 2 061 359 | 46 | 27 |
| | 1994/95 | 14 836 | 166 771 | 71 817 | 43 | 4 548 827 | 2 086 456 | 46 | 27 |
| | 1995/96 | 15 186 | 169 010 | 74 309 | 44 | 4 617 728 | 2 129 494 | 46 | 27 |
| | 1996/97 | 15 426 | 170 956 | 76 515 | 45 | 4 674 947 | 2 164 303 | 46 | 27 |
| Angola | 1970/71 | 4 418 | 9 786 | ... | ... | 434 370 | 154 932 | 36 | 44 |
| | 1980/81 | 6 090 | ... | ... | ... | 1 300 673 | ... | ... | ... |
| | 1985/86 | ... | 31 161 | ... | ... | 974 498 | 440 764 | 45 | 31 |
| | 1990/91 | ... | 31 062 | ... | ... | 990 155 | *475 500 | *48 | 32 |
| | 1991/92 | ... | ... | ... | ... | 989 443 | ... | ... | ... |
| Benin | 1970/71 | 904 | 3 753 | 1 088 | 29 | 155 255 | 48 040 | 31 | 41 |
| | 1975/76 | 1 325 | 4 864 | ... | ... | 259 880 | 81 623 | 31 | 53 |
| | 1980/81 | 2 275 | 7 994 | 1 848 | 23 | 379 926 | 121 745 | 32 | 48 |
| | 1985/86 | 2 715 | 13 452 | 3 284 | 24 | 444 163 | 148 882 | 34 | 33 |
| | 1990/91 | 2 864 | 13 556 | 3 354 | 25 | 490 129 | 163 048 | 33 | 36 |
| | 1991/92 | 2 904 | 13 422 | 3 323 | 25 | 534 810 | 179 612 | 34 | 40 |
| | 1992/93 | 2 982 | 13 184 | 3 346 | 25 | 599 830 | 204 213 | 34 | 45 |
| | 1993/94 | 2 984 | 12 924 | 3 288 | 25 | 624 778 | 219 766 | 35 | 48 |
| | 1994/95 | 3 064 | 13 586 | 3 355 | 25 | 677 900 | 242 458 | 36 | 50 |
| | 1995/96 | 3 088 | 13 889 | 3 338 | 24 | 722 161 | 263 256 | 36 | 52 |
| | 1996/97 | 3 072 | *13 957 | *3 335 | *24 | *779 329 | *286 503 | *37 | *56 |
| Botswana | 1970 | 282 | 2 275 | 1 231 | 54 | 83 002 | 44 053 | 53 | 36 |
| | 1975 | 323 | 3 509 | 2 333 | 66 | 116 293 | 63 949 | 55 | 33 |
| | 1980 | 415 | 5 316 | 3 827 | 72 | 171 914 | 93 793 | 55 | 32 |
| | 1985 | 528 | 6 980 | 5 435 | 78 | 223 608 | 117 185 | 52 | 32 |
| | 1990 | 602 | 8 956 | 7 150 | 80 | 283 516 | 146 299 | 52 | 32 |
| | 1991 | 626 | 9 833 | 7 687 | 78 | 298 812 | 153 546 | 51 | 30 |
| | 1992 | 643 | 10 463 | 8 057 | 77 | 301 482 | 154 068 | 51 | 29 |
| | 1993 | 657 | 11 190 | 8 582 | 77 | 305 479 | 154 728 | 51 | 27 |
| | 1994 | 670 | 11 731 | 8 971 | 76 | 310 128 | 156 339 | 50 | 26 |
| | 1995 | 681 | 12 306 | 9 547 | 78 | 313 693 | 157 133 | 50 | 25 |
| | 1996 | ... | *12 785 | *9 898 | *77 | *318 629 | *159 127 | *50 | *25 |
| Burkina Faso | 1970/71 | 603 | 2 370 | 386 | 16 | 105 351 | 38 322 | 36 | 44 |
| | 1975/76 | 712 | 2 997 | 544 | 18 | 141 177 | 52 275 | 37 | 47 |
| | 1980/81 | 936 | 3 700 | 747 | 20 | 201 595 | 74 367 | 37 | 54 |
| | 1985/86 | 1 758 (1) | 6 091 (1) | 1 522 | 25 | 351 807 | 129 838 | 37 | ... |
| | 1990/91 | 2 486 | 8 903 | 2 405 | 27 | 504 414 | 193 652 | 38 | 57 |
| | 1991/92 | 2 590 | 9 165 | ... | ... | 530 013 | 205 296 | 39 | 58 |
| | 1992/93 | 2 741 | 9 412 | 2 298 | 24 | 562 644 | 218 396 | 39 | 60 |
| | 1993/94 | 2 971 | 10 300 | 2 408 | 23 | 600 032 | 233 806 | 39 | 58 |
| | 1994/95 | 3 233 | 12 754 | 3 123 | 24 | 650 195 | 254 284 | 39 | 51 |
| | 1995/96 | ... | 14 037 | 3 412 | 24 | 700 995 | 274 830 | 39 | 50 |

II.5  Primary education: schools, teaching staff and pupils
Enseignement primaire: écoles, personnel enseignant et élèves
Enseñanza primaria: escuelas, personal docente y alumnos

| Country / Pays / País | Year / Année / Año | Schools / Écoles / Escuelas | Teaching staff / Personnel enseignant / Personal docente — Total | Female / Féminin / Femenino | % F | Pupils enrolled / Élèves inscrits / Alumnos matriculados — Total | Female / Féminin / Femenino | % F | Pupil/teacher ratio / Nombre d'élèves par maître / Número de alumnos por maestro |
|---|---|---|---|---|---|---|---|---|---|
| Burundi | 1970/71 | 970 | 4 955 | 1 267 | 26 | 181 758 | 59 843 | 33 | 37 |
| | 1975/76 | (2) 580 | (2) 4 199 | (2) 1 804 | 43 | (2) 129 597 | (2) 50 045 | 39 | 31 |
| | 1980/81 | 686 | (3) 4 805 | (3) 2 258 | 47 | 175 856 | 69 352 | 39 | ... |
| | 1985/86 | 1 023 | 6 866 | 3 260 | 47 | 385 936 | 161 473 | 42 | 56 |
| | 1990/91 | 1 342 | 9 465 | 4 376 | 46 | 633 203 | 288 896 | 46 | 67 |
| | 1991/92 | 1 373 | 9 582 | 4 498 | 47 | 631 039 | 283 768 | 45 | 66 |
| | 1992/93 | 1 418 | 10 400 | 4 865 | 47 | 651 086 | 292 906 | 45 | 63 |
| | 1994/95 | 1 254 | *9 442 | *4 480 | *47 | *541 085 | *234 582 | *43 | *57 |
| | 1995/96 | 1 501 | *10 316 | *5 146 | *50 | *518 144 | *234 628 | *45 | *50 |
| Cameroon | 1970/71 | ... | 19 359 | ... | ... | 923 234 | 392 788 | 43 | 48 |
| | 1975/76 | 4 506 | 22 209 | 3 055 | 14 | 1 122 900 | 500 049 | 45 | 51 |
| | 1980/81 | 4 971 | 26 763 | 5 248 | 20 | 1 379 205 | 626 966 | 45 | 52 |
| | 1985/86 | 5 856 | 33 598 | 8 993 | 27 | 1 705 319 | 777 820 | 46 | 51 |
| | 1990/91 | 6 709 | 38 430 | 11 534 | 30 | 1 964 146 | 904 179 | 46 | 51 |
| | 1991/92 | 6 890 | 40 012 | 12 647 | 32 | 1 915 148 | 913 132 | 48 | 48 |
| | 1993/94 | ... | ... | ... | ... | 1 892 778 | 891 530 | 47 | ... |
| | 1994/95 | 6 801 | 40 970 | 12 973 | 32 | 1 896 722 | 893 617 | 47 | 46 |
| | 1996/97 | 8 514 | 39 384 | ... | ... | 1 921 186 | ... | ... | 49 |
| Cape Verde | 1970/71 | 354 | 730 | ... | ... | 27 908 | ... | ... | 38 |
| | 1975/76 | 477 | (4) 1 243 | ... | ... | 64 794 | *31 000 | *48 | ... |
| | 1980/81 | ... | (4) 1 436 | ... | ... | 57 587 | 27 985 | 49 | ... |
| | 1985/86 | 436 | (4) 1 493 | ... | ... | 57 909 | 28 625 | 49 | ... |
| | 1990/91 | ... | ... | ... | ... | 69 832 | ... | ... | ... |
| | 1993/94 | ... | 2 657 | 1 560 | 59 | 78 173 | 38 336 | 49 | 29 |
| | 1997/98 | ... | 3 219 | 2 004 | 62 | 91 777 | 44 877 | 49 | 29 |
| Central African Republic | 1970/71 | 754 | 2 768 | 466 | 17 | 176 300 | 57 669 | 33 | 64 |
| | 1975/76 | 732 | 3 329 | 592 | 18 | 221 432 | 79 554 | 36 | 67 |
| | 1980/81 | 825 | 4 130 | 1 016 | 25 | 246 174 | 90 468 | 37 | 60 |
| | 1985/86 | ... | 4 718 | 1 178 | 25 | 309 656 | 120 968 | 39 | 66 |
| | 1990/91 | 1 040 | 4 004 | 996 | 25 | 308 409 | 121 742 | 39 | 77 |
| | 1991/92 | ... | ... | ... | ... | 277 961 | 111 353 | 40 | ... |
| Chad | 1970/71 | ... | 2 824 | 142 | 5 | (5) 183 250 | (5) 46 191 | 25 | ... |
| | 1975/76 | ... | (3) 2 512 | (3) 133 | 5 | 212 983 | 55 963 | 26 | ... |
| | 1985/86 | 1 243 | 4 779 | 168 | 4 | 337 616 | 95 323 | 28 | 71 |
| | 1990/91 | 2 073 | 7 980 | 470 | 6 | 525 165 | 162 857 | 31 | 66 |
| | 1991/92 | 2 437 | 9 126 | *566 | *6 | 568 630 | 182 258 | 32 | 62 |
| | 1992/93 | ... | ... | ... | ... | 553 205 | 177 592 | 32 | ... |
| | 1993/94 | 2 507 | 8 905 | 632 | 7 | 542 405 | 175 318 | 32 | 61 |
| | 1994/95 | 2 447 | 8 826 | 690 | 8 | 547 696 | 177 897 | 32 | 62 |
| | 1995/96 | 2 660 | 9 395 | 795 | 8 | 591 493 | 194 599 | 33 | 63 |
| | 1996/97 | ... | 10 151 | 837 | 8 | 680 909 | 233 224 | 34 | 67 |
| Comoros | 1970/71 | 100 | 361 | 41 | 11 | 15 047 | 4 749 | 32 | 42 |
| | 1975/76 | 161 | 756 | ... | ... | 35 818 | ... | ... | 47 |
| | 1980/81 | 236 | 1 292 | 95 | 7 | 59 709 | 24 777 | 41 | 46 |
| | 1985/86 | 253 | 1 901 | 393 | 21 | 66 084 | 28 241 | 43 | 35 |
| | 1990/91 | 257 | 1 995 | ... | ... | 72 824 | 30 300 | 42 | 37 |
| | 1991/92 | 255 | (3) 1 894 | ... | ... | 75 577 | 34 252 | 45 | ... |
| | 1992/93 | 268 | (3) 1 771 | ... | ... | 73 827 | 34 050 | 46 | ... |
| | 1993/94 | 275 | (3) 1 737 | ... | ... | 77 837 | 34 745 | 45 | ... |
| | 1995/96 | 327 | (3) 1 508 | ... | ... | 78 527 | ... | ... | ... |
| Congo | 1970/71 | 892 | 3 898 | *590 | *15 | 241 101 | 105 890 | 44 | 62 |
| | 1975/76 | 1 033 | 5 434 | 945 | 17 | 319 101 | 148 445 | 47 | 59 |
| | 1980/81 | 1 335 | 7 186 | 1 794 | 25 | 390 676 | 188 431 | 48 | 54 |
| | 1985/86 | 1 558 | 7 745 | 2 307 | 30 | 475 805 | 231 062 | 49 | 61 |
| | 1990/91 | 1 655 | 7 578 | 2 457 | 32 | 493 918 | 234 479 | 47 | 65 |
| | 1991/92 | 1 620 | 7 789 | 2 579 | 33 | 492 286 | 236 763 | 48 | 63 |
| | 1992/93 | 1 607 | 7 415 | 2 518 | 34 | 512 060 | 245 720 | 48 | 69 |
| | 1993/94 | 1 623 | 6 891 | 2 341 | 34 | 505 925 | 242 762 | 48 | 73 |
| | 1994/95 | ... | ... | ... | ... | *518 400 | *237 100 | *46 | ... |
| | 1995/96 | 1 612 | *7 060 | *2 565 | *36 | 497 305 | 239 139 | 48 | *70 |
| Côte d'Ivoire | 1970/71 | 2 252 | 11 170 | 1 492 | 13 | 502 865 | 182 950 | 36 | 45 |
| | 1975/76 | 2 904 | 15 358 | 1 906 | 12 | 672 707 | 253 582 | 38 | 44 |
| | 1980/81 | 4 807 | 26 460 | 4 070 | 15 | 1 024 585 | 409 859 | 40 | 39 |
| | 1985/86 | 5 796 | (6) 33 500 | (6) 6 289 | 19 | 1 214 511 | 502 672 | 41 | ... |
| | 1990/91 | 6 765 | (6) 39 002 | (6) 7 340 | 19 | 1 414 865 | 586 272 | 41 | ... |
| | 1991/92 | 6 844 | (6) 39 057 | (6) 7 387 | 19 | 1 447 785 | 603 492 | 42 | ... |
| | 1992/93 | 7 067 | (6) 41 067 | (6) 7 920 | 19 | 1 463 963 | 609 966 | 42 | ... |
| | 1993/94 | 7 249 | (6) 39 691 | (6) 7 976 | 20 | 1 553 540 | 650 608 | 42 | ... |
| | 1994/95 | 7 185 | 36 058 | 6 641 | 18 | 1 609 929 | 679 543 | 42 | 45 |
| | 1995/96 | 7 401 | 40 529 | 8 309 | 21 | 1 662 265 | 702 846 | 42 | 41 |
| | 1996/97 | 7 599 | ... | ... | ... | 1 735 814 | 735 633 | 42 | ... |
| Democratic Rep. of the Congo | 1970/71 | 4 756 | 72 546 | ... | ... | 3 088 011 | 1 135 556 | 37 | 43 |
| | 1975/76 | ... | ... | ... | ... | 3 544 498 | 1 405 657 | 40 | ... |
| | 1980/81 | 10 536 | ... | ... | ... | *4 195 699 | *1 745 385 | *42 | ... |
| | 1985/86 | 10 068 | ... | ... | ... | *4 650 756 | *1 827 111 | *39 | ... |
| | 1990/91 | 11 955 | *114 000 | 27 404 | 24 | 4 562 430 | 1 944 978 | 43 | *40 |
| | 1991/92 | 11 948 | 114 967 | 22 601 | 20 | 4 622 758 | 1 987 645 | 43 | 40 |
| | 1992/93 | 12 658 | 117 267 | 22 827 | 19 | 4 870 933 | 2 122 843 | 44 | 42 |

Primary education: schools, teaching staff and pupils  II.5
Enseignement primaire: écoles, personnel enseignant et élèves
Enseñanza primaria: escuelas, personal enseignante y alumnos

| Country / Pays / País | Year / Année / Año | Schools / Écoles / Escuelas | Teaching staff — Personnel enseignant — Personal docente | | | | Pupils enrolled — Élèves inscrits — Alumnos matriculados | | | | Pupil/teacher ratio — Nombre d'élèves par maître |
|---|---|---|---|---|---|---|---|---|---|---|---|
| | | | | Total | | Female Féminin Femenino | % F | | Total | Female Féminin Femenino | % F | Número de alumnos por maestro |
| Democratic Rep. of the Congo (cont) | 1993/94 | 12 987 | | 112 041 | | 26 934 | 24 | | 4 939 297 | 2 103 195 | 43 | 44 |
| | 1994/95 | 14 885 | | 121 054 | | 26 926 | 22 | | 5 417 506 | 2 198 684 | 41 | 45 |
| Djibouti | 1970/71 | 31 | | 180 | | 58 | 32 | | 6 422 | 1 926 | 30 | 36 |
| | 1975/76 | ... | | 268 | | 95 | 35 | | 9 764 | 3 464 | 35 | 36 |
| | 1980/81 | 45 | | 419 | | ... | ... | | 16 841 | ... | ... | 40 |
| | 1985/86 | 58 | | *585 | | ... | ... | | 25 212 | 10 423 | 41 | *43 |
| | 1990/91 | 69 | | 742 | | 275 | 37 | | 31 706 | 13 149 | 41 | 43 |
| | 1991/92 | 68 | | 769 | | ... | ... | | 33 251 | 13 887 | 42 | 43 |
| | 1992/93 | ... | | 714 | | ... | ... | | 30 589 | 13 287 | 43 | 43 |
| | 1993/94 | 74 | | 787 | | 294 | 37 | | 33 005 | 14 264 | 43 | 42 |
| | 1994/95 | 81 | | 881 | | ... | ... | | 35 024 | 15 153 | 43 | 40 |
| | 1995/96 | 81 | | 1 005 | | 329 | 33 | | 36 223 | 15 371 | 42 | 36 |
| | 1996/97 | 72 | | 1 096 | | 328 | 30 | | 36 896 | 15 599 | 42 | 34 |
| Egypt | 1970/71 | 8 606 | | 99 918 | | 52 991 | 53 | | 3 794 911 | 1 433 270 | 38 | 38 |
| | 1975/76 | 10 346 | (7) | 118 251 | (7) | 56 323 | 48 | | 4 181 198 | 1 601 608 | 38 | ... |
| | 1980/81 | 12 120 | | ... | | ... | ... | | 4 662 816 | 1 875 949 | 40 | ... |
| | 1985/86 | (7) 14 057 | (7) | 194 929 | (/) | 93 253 | 48 | | 6 214 250 | 2 684 574 | 43 | ... |
| | 1990/91 | (8) 16 481 | (7)(8) | 279 315 | (7)(8) | 144 200 | 52 | (8) | 6 964 306 | (8) 3 088 768 | 44 | ... |
| | 1991/92 | (7) 15 361 | (7) | 273 055 | (7) | 146 493 | 54 | (7) | 6 541 725 | (7) 2 942 755 | 45 | 24 |
| | 1992/93 | (7) 15 647 | (7) | 288 891 | (7) | 154 745 | 54 | (7) | 6 791 128 | (7) 3 069 511 | 45 | 24 |
| | 1993/94 | 17 799 | (7) | 288 939 | (7) | 155 075 | 54 | | 7 732 308 | 3 463 823 | 45 | ... |
| | 1994/95 | (7) 16 088 | (7) | 291 400 | (7) | 156 101 | 54 | (7) | 7 313 038 | (7) 3 344 785 | 46 | 25 |
| | 1995/96 | (7) 16 188 | (7) | 302 916 | (7) | 159 414 | 53 | (7) | 8 185 030 | (7) 3 436 972 | ... | ... |
| | 1996/97 | 18 522 | | 356 499 | | 176 347 | 49 | | 8 243 137 | 3 746 029 | 45 | 23 |
| | 1997/98 | | (7) | 310 116 | (7) | 161 054 | 52 | (7) | 7 499 303 | (7) 3 484 523 | 46 | 24 |
| Equatorial Guinea | 1970/71 | ... | | ... | | ... | ... | | 31 600 | 13 891 | 44 | ... |
| | 1975/76 | ... | | ... | | ... | ... | | *39 000 | ... | ... | ... |
| | 1980/81 | ... | | 647 | | ... | ... | | 44 499 | ... | ... | 69 |
| | 1992/93 | 749 | (3) | 1 352 | (3) | 371 | 27 | (3) | 72 725 | (3) 35 229 | 48 | 54 |
| | 1993/94 | 781 | | 1 381 | | 367 | 27 | | 75 751 | 37 127 | 49 | 55 |
| Eritrea | 1990/91 | 214 | | 2 895 | | 1 311 | 45 | | 109 087 | 53 020 | 49 | 38 |
| | 1991/92 | (9) 381 | (9) | 3 647 | (9) | 1 411 | 39 | (9) | 150 870 | (9) 69 324 | 46 | 41 |
| | 1992/93 | 447 | | 4 954 | | 1 841 | 37 | | 184 492 | 82 356 | 45 | 37 |
| | 1993/94 | 491 | | 5 272 | | 1 865 | 35 | | 207 099 | 91 988 | 44 | 39 |
| | 1994/95 | 507 | | 5 583 | | 1 974 | 35 | | 224 287 | 99 743 | 44 | 40 |
| | 1995/96 | 537 | | 5 828 | | 2 025 | 35 | | 241 725 | 108 254 | 45 | 41 |
| | 1996/97 | 549 | | 5 476 | | 1 977 | 36 | | 240 737 | 108 487 | 45 | 44 |
| Ethiopia | 1970/71 | 2 297 | | 13 514 | | 1 679 | 12 | | 655 427 | 205 676 | 31 | 48 |
| | 1975/76 | 3 706 | | 24 469 | | 3 779 | 15 | | 1 084 307 | 349 003 | 32 | 44 |
| | 1980/81 | 5 822 | | 33 322 | | 7 296 | 22 | | 2 130 716 | 744 068 | 35 | 64 |
| | 1985/86 | 7 900 | | 50 922 | | 13 056 | 26 | | 2 448 778 | 957 535 | 39 | 48 |
| | 1990/91 | 8 256 | | 68 370 | | 16 341 | 24 | | 2 466 464 | 980 634 | 40 | 36 |
| | 1991/92 | 8 434 | | 68 399 | | 17 078 | 25 | | 2 063 636 | 863 242 | 42 | 30 |
| | 1992/93 | 8 120 | | 69 743 | | 17 820 | 26 | | 1 855 894 | 757 054 | 41 | 27 |
| | 1993/94 | 8 674 | | 75 736 | | 20 162 | 27 | | 2 283 638 | 873 077 | 38 | 30 |
| | 1994/95 | 9 276 | | 83 113 | | 22 707 | 27 | | 2 722 192 | 1 007 757 | 37 | 33 |
| | 1995/96 | 9 704 | | 89 189 | | 24 637 | 28 | | 3 380 068 | 1 218 313 | 36 | 38 |
| | 1996/97 | *10 256 | | *92 775 | | *26 153 | *28 | | 4 007 694 | 1 429 676 | 36 | *43 |
| Gabon | 1970/71 | 676 | | 2 211 | | 327 | 15 | | 100 625 | 47 890 | 48 | 46 |
| | 1975/76 | 746 | | 2 664 | | 535 | 20 | | 128 552 | 62 736 | 49 | 48 |
| | 1980/81 | 864 | | 3 441 | | 939 | 27 | | 155 081 | 76 209 | 49 | 45 |
| | 1985/86 | 946 | | 4 008 | | 1 409 | 35 | | 183 607 | 90 480 | 49 | 46 |
| | 1991/92 | 1 024 | | 4 782 | | ... | ... | | 210 000 | 104 181 | 50 | 44 |
| | 1993/94 | ... | | ... | | ... | ... | | 229 713 | 113 883 | 50 | ... |
| | 1994/95 | 1 105 | | 4 709 | | 2 074 | 44 | | 247 018 | 122 374 | 50 | 52 |
| | 1995/96 | 1 147 | | 4 943 | | 1 938 | 39 | | 250 693 | 124 404 | 50 | 51 |
| Gambia | 1970/71 | 95 | | 624 | | 207 | 33 | | 17 140 | 5 251 | 31 | 27 |
| | 1975/76 | 103 | | 948 | | ... | ... | | 24 617 | 8 169 | 33 | 26 |
| | 1980/81 | (10) *182 | (10) | 1 932 | (10) | *616 | *32 | (10) | 47 101 | (10) 16 250 | 35 | 24 |
| | 1985/86 | (10) 189 | (10) | 2 979 | (10) | 1 078 | 36 | (10) | 69 017 | (10) 26 694 | 39 | 23 |
| | 1990/91 | 230 | | 2 757 | | *850 | *31 | | 86 307 | *35 000 | *41 | 31 |
| | 1991/92 | 231 | | 2 876 | | 880 | 31 | | 90 645 | 36 870 | 41 | 32 |
| | 1992/93 | 245 | | 3 193 | | 995 | 31 | | 97 262 | 40 314 | 41 | 30 |
| | 1993/94 | 250 | | 3 158 | | 979 | 31 | | 105 471 | 44 372 | 42 | 33 |
| | 1994/95 | 258 | | 3 370 | | 1 045 | 31 | | 113 241 | *48 271 | *43 | 34 |
| | 1995/96 | ... | | 4 118 | | 1 194 | 29 | | 124 513 | 54 343 | 44 | 30 |
| Ghana | 1970/71 | 10 759 | | 47 957 | | 12 720 | 27 | | 1 419 838 | 610 016 | 43 | 30 |
| | 1975/76 | (2)(3) 6 966 | (2)(3) | 38 381 | (2)(3) | 12 674 | 33 | (2)(3) | 1 156 758 | (2)(3) 502 479 | 43 | 30 |
| | 1980/81 | (3) 7 848 | (3) | 47 921 | (3) | 20 123 | 42 | (3) | 1 377 734 | (3) 611 328 | 44 | 29 |
| | 1985/86 | (3) 9 004 | (3) | 64 795 | (3) | 26 085 | 40 | (3) | 1 505 819 | ... | ... | 23 |
| | 1990/91 | 11 165 | | 66 946 | | 23 936 | 36 | | 1 945 422 | 879 430 | 45 | 29 |
| | 1991/92 | ... | | *72 925 | | *25 635 | *35 | | 2 011 602 | 918 411 | 46 | *28 |
| | 1992/93 | (3) 12 010 | (3) | 67 740 | (3) | 24 050 | 36 | (3) | 2 047 288 | (3) 940 503 | 46 | 30 |
| | 1993/94 | (3) 12 320 | (3) | 69 232 | (3) | 24 175 | 35 | (3) | 2 138 635 | (3) 985 935 | 46 | 31 |
| | 1994/95 | (3) 12 134 | (3) | 71 863 | (3) | 24 728 | 34 | (3) | 2 154 646 | (3) 998 860 | 46 | 30 |
| Guinea | 1970/71 | 1 984 | | 4 381 | | ... | ... | | 191 287 | 60 644 | 32 | 44 |
| | 1975/76 | 2 115 | | 4 977 | | 482 | 10 | | 198 849 | 66 909 | 34 | 40 |
| | 1980/81 | 2 555 | | 7 165 | | 985 | 14 | | 257 547 | 85 842 | 33 | 36 |

**Primary education: schools, teaching staff and pupils**
**Enseignement primaire: écoles, personnel enseignant et élèves**
**Enseñanza primaria: escuelas, personal docente y alumnos**

| Country / Pays / País | Year / Année / Año | Schools / Écoles / Escuelas | Teaching staff / Personnel enseignant / Personal docente | | | Pupils enrolled / Élèves inscrits / Alumnos matriculados | | | Pupil/teacher ratio / Nombre d'élèves par maître / Número de alumnos por maestro |
|---|---|---|---|---|---|---|---|---|---|
| | | | Total | Female Féminin Femenino | % F | Total | Female Féminin Femenino | % F | |
| **Guinea** (cont) | 1985/86 | 2 285 | 7 605 | 1 437 | 19 | 276 438 | 87 544 | 32 | 36 |
| | 1990/91 | 2 476 | 8 699 | 1 957 | 22 | 346 807 | 109 351 | 32 | 40 |
| | 1991/92 | 2 586 | 7 374 | 1 554 | 21 | 359 406 | 113 250 | 32 | 49 |
| | 1992/93 | 2 780 | 8 577 | 2 004 | 23 | 421 869 | 133 777 | 32 | 49 |
| | 1993/94 | 2 849 | 9 718 | 2 184 | 22 | 471 792 | 154 138 | 33 | 49 |
| | 1994/95 | 3 118 | 11 658 | 2 832 | 24 | 544 729 | 182 493 | 34 | 47 |
| | 1995/96 | 3 237 | 11 875 | 2 990 | 25 | 584 161 | 200 607 | 34 | 49 |
| | 1996/97 | 3 534 | 13 234 | 3 281 | 25 | 649 835 | 233 415 | 36 | 49 |
| | 1997/98 | 3 723 | 13 883 | 3 405 | 25 | 674 732 | 249 088 | 37 | 49 |
| **Guinea-Bissau** | 1970/71 | 261 | 616 | ... | ... | 27 974 | 8 428 | 30 | 45 |
| | 1975/76 | 550 | (6)(11) 2 163 | ... | ... | (12) 81 890 | (12) 28 819 | 35 | ... |
| | 1980/81 | ... | 3 257 | 782 | 24 | 74 539 | 23 549 | 32 | 23 |
| | 1991/92 | ... | ... | ... | ... | 79 882 | 28 478 | 36 | ... |
| | 1992/93 | ... | ... | ... | ... | 79 611 | 28 521 | 36 | ... |
| | 1993/94 | ... | ... | ... | ... | 91 103 | 33 030 | 36 | ... |
| | 1994/95 | ... | ... | ... | ... | 100 369 | 36 954 | 37 | ... |
| **Kenya** | 1970 | 6 123 | 41 479 | 11 344 | 27 | 1 427 589 | 591 282 | 41 | 34 |
| | 1975 | 8 161 | 86 107 | 24 594 | 29 | 2 881 155 | 1 319 654 | 46 | 33 |
| | 1980 | 10 268 | 102 489 | ... | ... | 3 926 629 | 1 864 014 | 47 | 38 |
| | 1985 | (13) 12 936 | (13) 138 374 | (13) 47 487 | 34 | (13) 4 702 414 | (13) 2 267 511 | 48 | 34 |
| | 1990 | 15 196 | 172 117 | 64 508 | 37 | 5 392 319 | 2 625 943 | 49 | 31 |
| | 1991 | 15 196 | 173 090 | 65 482 | 38 | 5 455 996 | 2 659 024 | 49 | 32 |
| | 1992 | 15 465 | 176 359 | 78 106 | 44 | 5 554 977 | 2 714 485 | 49 | 31 |
| | 1993 | 15 804 | *179 200 | *79 370 | *44 | *5 643 000 | *2 772 900 | *49 | *31 |
| | 1994 | 15 906 | 178 097 | 70 361 | 40 | 5 557 008 | 2 742 183 | 49 | 31 |
| | 1995 | ... | *181 975 | *72 672 | 40 | *5 544 998 | *2 742 693 | 49 | *30 |
| **Lesotho** | 1970 | 1 350 | 3 964 | 2 373 | 60 | 183 395 | 109 954 | 60 | 46 |
| | 1975 | (14) 1 079 | (14) 4 226 | (14) 2 939 | 70 | (14) 221 922 | (14) 131 014 | 59 | 53 |
| | 1980 | 1 074 | 5 097 | 3 818 | 75 | 244 838 | 143 472 | 59 | 48 |
| | 1985 | 1 141 | 5 663 | 4 343 | 77 | 314 003 | 174 701 | 56 | 55 |
| | 1990 | 1 190 | 6 448 | 5 154 | 80 | 351 632 | 192 433 | 55 | 55 |
| | 1991 | 1 198 | 6 685 | 5 360 | 80 | 361 144 | 197 716 | 55 | 54 |
| | 1992 | 1 201 | 7 051 | 5 592 | 79 | 362 657 | 196 158 | 54 | 51 |
| | 1993 | 1 209 | 7 292 | 5 817 | 80 | 354 275 | 189 571 | 54 | 49 |
| | 1994 | 1 234 | 7 433 | 5 892 | 79 | 366 935 | 194 218 | 53 | 49 |
| | 1995 | 1 240 | 7 923 | 6 270 | 79 | 378 011 | 198 604 | 53 | 48 |
| | 1996 | 1 249 | 7 898 | 6 249 | 79 | 374 628 | 196 147 | 52 | 47 |
| **Liberia** | 1970 | (6) 889 | (6) 3 384 | (6) 939 | 28 | (6) 120 245 | (6) 39 565 | 33 | 36 |
| | 1975 | ... | (6) 3 832 | (6) 1 140 | 30 | 104 056 | 34 987 | 34 | ... |
| | 1980 | ... | ... | ... | ... | 147 216 | 52 129 | 35 | ... |
| **Libyan Arab Jamahiriya** | 1970/71 | 1 324 | 12 304 | 2 978 | 24 | 350 225 | 129 595 | 37 | 28 |
| | 1975/76 | 2 042 | 24 331 | 7 086 | 29 | 556 169 | 256 065 | 46 | 23 |
| | 1980/81 | 2 607 | 36 591 | 17 160 | 47 | 662 843 | 314 570 | 47 | 18 |
| | 1985/86 | (13) 4 164 | (13) 63 122 | (13) 35 187 | 56 | (13) 1 011 952 | (13) 475 591 | 47 | 16 |
| | 1990/91 | ... | 85 537 | ... | ... | 1 175 229 | 558 477 | 48 | 14 |
| | 1991/92 | ... | 99 623 | 66 829 | 67 | 1 238 986 | 593 594 | 48 | 12 |
| | 1992/93 | ... | 103 791 | ... | ... | 1 254 242 | 604 948 | 48 | 12 |
| | 1993/94 | ... | ... | ... | ... | 1 357 040 | 666 920 | 49 | ... |
| **Madagascar** | 1970/71 | 5 845 | 14 424 | 4 117 | 29 | 938 015 | 433 105 | 46 | 65 |
| | 1975/76 | 7 960 | 20 134 | ... | ... | 1 210 841 | 526 201 | 43 | 60 |
| | 1980/81 | (15) 13 594 | (15) 39 474 | ... | ... | (15) 1 723 779 | (15) 844 822 | 49 | 44 |
| | 1990/91 | 13 791 | 38 933 | ... | ... | 1 570 721 | 773 797 | 49 | 40 |
| | 1991/92 | 13 686 | 39 637 | ... | ... | 1 496 845 | 713 328 | 48 | 38 |
| | 1992/93 | 13 508 | 38 743 | ... | ... | 1 490 317 | 726 412 | 49 | 38 |
| | 1993/94 | 13 624 | 37 676 | 21 029 | 56 | 1 504 668 | 737 641 | 49 | 40 |
| | 1994/95 | 13 266 | 39 713 | 20 356 | 51 | 1 511 408 | 768 220 | 51 | 38 |
| | 1995/96 | 13 325 | 44 145 | *22 700 | *51 | 1 638 187 | 801 681 | 49 | 37 |
| **Malawi** | 1970/71 | 1 990 | 8 382 | 1 987 | 24 | 362 561 | 134 763 | 37 | 43 |
| | 1975/76 | 2 140 | 10 588 | ... | ... | 641 709 | 253 563 | 40 | 61 |
| | 1980/81 | 2 340 | 12 540 | ... | ... | 809 862 | 333 495 | 41 | 65 |
| | 1985/86 | 2 520 | 15 440 | 5 124 | 33 | 942 539 | 408 727 | 43 | 61 |
| | 1990/91 | 2 906 | 22 942 | 7 176 | 31 | 1 400 682 | 633 127 | 45 | 61 |
| | 1991/92 | 3 056 | 23 294 | 8 018 | 34 | 1 662 583 | 760 718 | 46 | 71 |
| | 1992/93 | 3 118 | 26 333 | 9 064 | 34 | 1 795 451 | 847 974 | 47 | 68 |
| | 1993/94 | 3 319 | 27 948 | 9 620 | 34 | 1 895 423 | 912 126 | 48 | 68 |
| | 1994/95 | 3 425 | (16) 45 775 | (16) 17 489 | 38 | (16) 2 860 819 | (16) 1 345 317 | 47 | 62 |
| | 1995/96 | 3 706 | 49 138 | 19 165 | 39 | 2 887 107 | 1 358 543 | 47 | 59 |
| **Mali** | 1970/71 | ... | 5 086 | 977 | 19 | 203 703 | 72 658 | 36 | 40 |
| | 1975/76 | 1 063 | 6 213 | 1 148 | 18 | 252 393 | 90 033 | 36 | 41 |
| | 1980/81 | (17) 1 160 | (17) 6 862 | (17) 1 368 | 20 | (17) 291 159 | (17) 105 115 | 36 | 42 |
| | 1985/86 | (17) 1 259 | (17) 8 593 | (17) 1 850 | 22 | (17) 292 395 | (17) 108 875 | 37 | 34 |
| | 1990/91 | (17) 1 461 | (17) 8 156 | (17) 1 846 | 23 | 395 334 | 145 962 | 37 | ... |
| | 1991/92 | (17) 1 514 | (17) 7 963 | (17) 1 922 | 24 | 430 636 | 159 212 | 37 | ... |
| | 1992/93 | (17) 1 589 | (17) 8 688 | (17) 1 898 | 22 | 494 581 | 186 054 | 38 | ... |
| | 1993/94 | (17) 1 728 | (17) 8 363 | (17) 1 962 | 23 | 557 084 | 213 630 | 38 | ... |
| | 1994/95 | (17) 1 803 | (17) 8 274 | (17) 1 905 | 23 | 612 469 | 245 172 | 40 | ... |
| | 1995/96 | (17) 1 921 | (17) 8 718 | (17) 1 988 | 23 | 683 163 | 268 895 | 39 | ... |
| | 1996/97 | (17) 2 133 | (17) 9 677 | (17) 2 184 | 23 | 778 450 | 305 889 | 39 | ... |
| | 1997/98 | (17) 2 511 | (17) 10 853 | (17) 2 488 | 23 | 862 875 | 350 530 | 41 | ... |

Primary education: schools, teaching staff and pupils  II.5
Enseignement primaire: écoles, personnel enseignant et élèves
Enseñanza primaria: escuelas, personal docente y alumnos

| Country / Pays / País | Year / Année / Año | Schools / Écoles / Escuelas | | Teaching staff / Personnel enseignant / Personal docente | | | | Pupils enrolled / Élèves inscrits / Alumnos matriculados | | | | Pupil/teacher ratio / Nombre d'élèves par maître / Número de alumnos por maestro |
|---|---|---|---|---|---|---|---|---|---|---|---|---|
| | | | | Total | | Female Féminin Femenino | % F | | Total | Female Féminin Femenino | % F | |
| Mauritania | 1970/71 | | ... | 1 331 | | 93 | 7 | | 31 945 | 8 881 | 28 | 24 |
| | 1975/76 | | ... | 1 439 | | ... | ... | | 50 465 | 18 106 | 36 | 35 |
| | 1980/81 | (18) | 599 | (18) 2 183 | (18) | 198 | 9 | (18) | 90 530 | (18) 32 057 | 35 | 41 |
| | 1985/86 | | 875 | 2 785 | | 411 | 15 | | 140 871 | 56 362 | 40 | 51 |
| | 1990/91 | | 1 261 | 3 741 | | 667 | 18 | | 167 229 | 70 588 | 42 | 45 |
| | 1991/92 | | 1 320 | 4 039 | | 726 | 18 | | 188 580 | 81 235 | 43 | 47 |
| | 1992/93 | | 1 451 | 4 276 | | 765 | 18 | | 219 258 | 97 277 | 44 | 51 |
| | 1993/94 | | 1 635 | 4 686 | | 853 | 18 | | 248 048 | 111 058 | 45 | 53 |
| | 1994/95 | | 1 854 | 5 224 | | 1 052 | 20 | | 269 173 | 121 024 | 45 | 52 |
| | 1995/96 | | ... | ... | | ... | ... | | 289 945 | 132 683 | 46 | ... |
| | 1996/97 | | 2 392 | 6 225 | | ... | ... | | 312 671 | 146 828 | 47 | 50 |
| Mauritius | 1970 | | 347 | 4 731 | | 1 956 | 41 | | 150 402 | 73 042 | 49 | 32 |
| | 1975 | | ... | 5 791 | | ... | ... | | 150 573 | 73 711 | 49 | 26 |
| | 1980 | | 267 | 6 379 | | *2 770 | *43 | | 128 758 | 63 033 | 49 | 20 |
| | 1985 | | 280 | 6 450 | | 2 763 | 43 | | 140 714 | 69 528 | 49 | 22 |
| | 1990 | | 289 | 6 507 | | *2 870 | *44 | | 137 491 | 67 936 | 49 | 21 |
| | 1991 | | 290 | 6 369 | | 2 842 | 45 | | 135 233 | 66 720 | 49 | 21 |
| | 1992 | | 283 | 6 272 | | 2 888 | 46 | | 129 738 | 64 066 | 49 | 21 |
| | 1993 | | 281 | 5 931 | | 2 779 | 47 | | 125 543 | 62 000 | 49 | 21 |
| | 1994 | | 279 | 5 483 | | 2 666 | 49 | | 123 167 | 60 731 | 49 | 22 |
| | 1995 | | 279 | 5 137 | | 2 555 | 50 | | 122 895 | 60 595 | 49 | 24 |
| | 1996 | | 281 | 5 215 | | 2 674 | 51 | | 124 589 | 61 379 | 49 | 24 |
| | 1997 | | 283 | 6 434 | | 3 219 | 50 | | 127 109 | 62 723 | 49 | 20 |
| Morocco | 1970/71 | | 1 532 | (6) 34 277 | (6) | 6 262 | 18 | | 1 175 277 | 397 959 | 34 | ... |
| | 1975/76 | | 1 928 | (3) 37 226 | (3) | 7 725 | 21 | | 1 547 047 | 555 589 | 36 | ... |
| | 1980/81 | (3) | 2 332 | (3) 56 908 | (3) | 16 990 | 30 | | 2 172 289 | 804 056 | 37 | ... |
| | 1985/86 | | 3 570 | 81 867 | | 27 334 | 33 | | 2 279 887 | 871 164 | 38 | 28 |
| | 1990/91 | (3)(19) | 3 686 | (19) 91 680 | (19) | 34 128 | 37 | (19) | 2 483 691 | (19) 989 391 | 40 | 27 |
| | 1991/92 | (3) | 3 817 | 95 206 | | 36 460 | 38 | | 2 578 566 | 1 036 297 | 40 | 27 |
| | 1992/93 | | 4 420 | 98 734 | | 37 891 | 38 | | 2 727 833 | 1 105 995 | 41 | 28 |
| | 1993/94 | | 4 741 | 102 452 | | 39 186 | 38 | | 2 873 883 | 1 180 935 | 41 | 28 |
| | 1994/95 | | 5 144 | 106 393 | | 40 293 | 38 | | 3 006 631 | 1 249 589 | 42 | 28 |
| | 1995/96 | | 5 430 | 109 817 | | 41 743 | 38 | | 3 101 555 | 1 302 818 | 42 | 28 |
| | 1996/97 | | 5 806 | 114 406 | | 42 915 | 38 | | 3 160 907 | 1 340 439 | 42 | 28 |
| Mozambique | 1970/71 | | 4 088 | 7 220 | | ... | ... | | 496 910 | ... | ... | 69 |
| | 1980/81 | (12) | 5 730 | (12) 17 030 | (12) | 3 714 | 22 | (12) | 1 387 192 | (12) 590 101 | 43 | 81 |
| | 1985 | | 3 679 | (12) 20 286 | (12) | 4 390 | 22 | | 1 248 074 | 546 101 | 44 | ... |
| | 1990 | (20) | 3 441 | (20) 23 107 | (20) | ... | ... | (20) | 1 260 218 | (20) 542 908 | 43 | 55 |
| | 1991 | | 3 547 | 22 236 | | 5 136 | 23 | | 1 217 364 | 519 927 | 43 | 55 |
| | 1992 | | 3 384 | 22 474 | | 5 133 | 23 | | 1 199 476 | 514 162 | 43 | 53 |
| | 1993 | | 3 466 | 22 396 | | 5 127 | 23 | | 1 227 341 | 521 422 | 42 | 55 |
| | 1994 | | 3 765 | 22 544 | | 5 087 | 23 | | 1 301 833 | 547 066 | 42 | 58 |
| | 1995 | | 4 167 | 24 575 | | 5 591 | 23 | | 1 415 428 | 592 133 | 42 | 58 |
| Namibia | 1990 | | ... | ... | | ... | ... | | 314 105 | 163 336 | 52 | ... |
| | 1991 | | ... | ... | | ... | ... | | 341 701 | 173 601 | 51 | ... |
| | 1992 | | 1 213 | 10 912 | | 7 087 | 65 | | 349 167 | 176 160 | 50 | 32 |
| | 1993 | | ... | ... | | ... | ... | | 352 900 | 177 089 | 50 | ... |
| | 1994 | | ... | ... | | ... | ... | | 367 669 | 183 706 | 50 | ... |
| | 1995 | | ... | ... | | ... | ... | | 368 222 | 183 615 | 50 | ... |
| | 1996 | | ... | ... | | ... | ... | | 373 276 | 186 227 | 50 | ... |
| | 1997 | | ... | ... | | ... | ... | | 380 945 | 190 463 | 50 | ... |
| | 1998 | | ... | ... | | ... | ... | | 400 325 | 199 658 | 50 | ... |
| Niger | 1970/71 | | 699 | 2 275 | | 476 | 21 | | 88 594 | 30 563 | 34 | 39 |
| | 1975/76 | | 1 249 | 3 617 | | 1 124 | 31 | | 142 182 | 50 029 | 35 | 39 |
| | 1980/81 | | 1 686 | 5 518 | | 1 673 | 30 | | 228 855 | 80 784 | 35 | 41 |
| | 1985/86 | | 1 850 | 7 383 | | 2 421 | 33 | | 275 902 | 99 241 | 36 | 37 |
| | 1990/91 | | 2 307 | 8 835 | | 2 880 | 33 | | 368 732 | 133 252 | 36 | 42 |
| | 1991/92 | | 2 361 | 8 835 | | 2 880 | 33 | | 370 117 | 135 523 | 37 | 42 |
| | 1992/93 | | 2 422 | 10 027 | | 3 457 | 34 | | 386 056 | 142 257 | 37 | 39 |
| | 1993/94 | | 2 656 | ... | | ... | ... | | 410 929 | 146 515 | 36 | ... |
| | 1994/95 | | 2 817 | 10 820 | | ... | ... | | 426 929 | 159 974 | 37 | 39 |
| | 1995/96 | | 2 908 | 11 285 | | 3 772 | 33 | | 440 622 | 165 306 | 38 | 39 |
| | 1996/97 | | 3 063 | 11 376 | | 3 678 | 32 | | 464 267 | 177 136 | 38 | 41 |
| | 1997/98 | | 3 175 | 11 545 | | 3 651 | 32 | | 482 065 | 186 488 | 39 | 42 |
| Nigeria | 1970 | | 14 902 | 103 152 | | 24 409 | 24 | | 3 515 827 | 1 299 598 | 37 | 34 |
| | 1975/76 | | 14 676 | 144 351 | | 40 398 | 28 | | 4 889 857 | 1 964 038 | 40 | 34 |
| | 1980/81 | | 35 723 | 343 551 | | 118 491 | 34 | | 12 117 483 | 5 295 363 | 44 | 35 |
| | 1985/86 | | 35 281 | 308 072 | | 125 628 | 41 | | 13 025 287 | 5 768 791 | 44 | 42 |
| | 1990 | | 35 433 | 331 915 | | 142 416 | 43 | | 13 607 249 | 5 877 572 | 43 | 41 |
| | 1991 | | 35 446 | 353 600 | | 150 847 | 43 | | 13 776 854 | 6 034 957 | 44 | 39 |
| | 1992 | | 36 610 | 384 212 | | 172 562 | 45 | | 14 805 937 | 6 532 113 | 44 | 39 |
| | 1993 | | 38 254 | 428 097 | | 191 831 | 45 | | 15 870 280 | 6 939 680 | 44 | 37 |
| | 1994 | | 38 649 | 435 210 | | 201 905 | 46 | | 16 190 947 | 7 134 580 | 44 | 37 |
| Reunion | 1970/71 | | 368 | (3) 3 114 | | ... | ... | | 99 565 | ... | ... | 26 |
| | 1975/76 | | 371 | 3 661 | | ... | ... | | 95 810 | ... | ... | ... |
| | 1980/81 | | ... | ... | | ... | ... | | 79 143 | ... | ... | ... |
| | 1985/86 | | 349 | 3 811 | | 2 537 | 67 | | 73 985 | 35 516 | 48 | 19 |
| | 1990/91 | | ... | ... | | ... | ... | | 71 966 | ... | ... | ... |
| | 1991/92 | | ... | ... | | ... | ... | | 71 543 | ... | ... | ... |
| | 1992/93 | | ... | ... | | ... | ... | | 71 303 | ... | ... | ... |

**Primary education: schools, teaching staff and pupils**
Enseignement primaire: écoles, personnel enseignant et élèves
Enseñanza primaria: escuelas, personal docente y alumnos

| Country / Pays / País | Year / Année / Año | Schools / Écoles / Escuelas | Teaching staff / Personnel enseignant / Personal docente | | | Pupils enrolled / Élèves inscrits / Alumnos matriculados | | | Pupil/teacher ratio / Nombre d'élèves par maître / Número de alumnos por maestro |
|---|---|---|---|---|---|---|---|---|---|
| | | | Total | Female Féminin Femenino | % F | Total | Female Féminin Femenino | % F | |
| Reunion (cont) | 1993/94 | 343 | ... | ... | ... | 70 735 | 34 797 | 49 | ... |
| | 1994/95 | ... | ... | ... | ... | (21) 73 250 | ... | ... | ... |
| | 1995/96 | ... | ... | ... | ... | 73 702 | ... | ... | ... |
| Rwanda | 1970/71 | 2 022 | 7 025 | 1 627 | 23 | 419 059 | 184 877 | 44 | 60 |
| | 1975/76 | 1 668 | 8 022 | 2 355 | 29 | 401 521 | 184 814 | 46 | 50 |
| | 1980/81 | (22) 1 567 | (22) 11 912 | (22) 4 577 | 38 | (22) 704 924 | (22) 337 625 | 48 | 59 |
| | 1985/86 | 1 594 | 14 896 | 6 628 | 44 | 836 877 | 409 081 | 49 | 56 |
| | 1990/91 | 1 671 | 19 183 | 8 884 | 46 | 1 100 437 | 547 869 | 50 | 57 |
| | 1991/92 | (9) 1 710 | (9) 18 937 | (9) 8 986 | 47 | (9) 1 104 902 | (9) 548 171 | 50 | 58 |
| Sao Tome and Principe | 1970/71 | 44 | 271 | ... | ... | 9 018 | 3 980 | 44 | 33 |
| | 1975/76 | ... | (6) 422 | ... | ... | 14 290 | ... | ... | ... |
| | 1980/81 | ... | (6) 588 | ... | ... | 16 376 | ... | ... | ... |
| Senegal | 1970/71 | ... | 5 813 | ... | ... | 262 928 | 101 734 | 39 | 45 |
| | 1975/76 | ... | 7 577 | ... | ... | 311 913 | 131 315 | 42 | 41 |
| | 1980/81 | 1 672 | 9 175 | 2 202 | 24 | 419 748 | 166 913 | 40 | 46 |
| | 1985/86 | 2 322 | 12 559 | 3 347 | 27 | 583 890 | 235 319 | 40 | 46 |
| | 1990/91 | 2 458 | 13 394 | ... | ... | 708 448 | 297 375 | 42 | 53 |
| | 1991/92 | 2 434 | 12 307 | 3 317 | 27 | 725 496 | 307 353 | 42 | 59 |
| | 1992/93 | 2 454 | 12 693 | 3 324 | 26 | 738 556 | 314 020 | 43 | 58 |
| | 1993/94 | 2 559 | 13 394 | 3 457 | 26 | 773 386 | 329 081 | 43 | 58 |
| | 1994/95 | 2 657 | 13 483 | 3 473 | 26 | 805 437 | 345 418 | 43 | 60 |
| | 1995/96 | 3 051 | 15 045 | 3 927 | 26 | 875 661 | 384 413 | 44 | 58 |
| | 1996/97 | 3 530 | 16 567 | ... | ... | 954 758 | 425 200 | 45 | 58 |
| | 1997/98 | 3 884 | 18 373 | ... | ... | 1 026 570 | 463 612 | 45 | 56 |
| Seychelles | 1970 | 35 | 381 | 343 | 90 | 9 224 | 4 629 | 50 | 24 |
| | 1975 | 36 | 428 | 406 | 95 | 10 232 | 5 268 | 51 | 24 |
| | 1980 | (22) 27 | (22) 658 | (22) 529 | 80 | (22) 14 468 | (22) 7 356 | 51 | 22 |
| | 1985 | 25 | 652 | 555 | 85 | 14 368 | 7 073 | 49 | 22 |
| | 1990 | ... | ... | ... | ... | (3) 14 362 | ... | ... | ... |
| | 1991 | (9) 29 | ... | ... | ... | (9) 10 134 | (9) 4 968 | 49 | ... |
| | 1992 | 27 | ... | ... | ... | 9 931 | 4 836 | 49 | ... |
| | 1993 | 26 | 548 | 483 | 88 | 9 873 | 4 797 | 49 | 18 |
| | 1994 | 26 | 588 | 509 | 87 | 9 911 | 4 876 | 49 | 17 |
| | 1995 | 27 | 584 | 514 | 88 | (9) 9 885 | (9) 4 874 | 49 | ... |
| | 1996 | 26 | 577 | 509 | 88 | 9 886 | 4 888 | 49 | 17 |
| Sierra Leone | 1970/71 | 1 023 | 5 142 | ... | ... | 166 107 | 66 741 | 40 | 32 |
| | 1975/76 | 1 074 | 6 373 | 1 530 | 24 | 205 910 | 81 470 | 40 | 32 |
| | 1980/81 | 1 199 | 9 528 | ... | ... | 315 145 | 131 661 | 42 | 33 |
| | 1985/86 | 1 807 | 10 837 | ... | ... | 421 689 | ... | ... | 39 |
| | 1990/91 | 1 795 | 10 850 | ... | ... | (23) 367 426 | (23) 151 560 | 41 | ... |
| Somalia | 1970/71 | 204 | 981 | 139 | 14 | 32 610 | 8 071 | 25 | 33 |
| | 1975/76 | 730 | 3 481 | 565 | 16 | 197 706 | 70 122 | 35 | 57 |
| | 1980/81 | (22) 1 408 | (22) 8 122 | (22) 2 365 | 29 | (22) 271 704 | (22) 98 053 | 36 | 33 |
| | 1985/86 | 1 224 | 10 338 | 4 664 | 45 | 196 496 | 66 753 | 34 | 19 |
| South Africa | 1970 | ... | ... | ... | ... | 3 988 514 | 1 982 937 | 50 | ... |
| | 1975 | ... | ... | ... | ... | 4 635 315 | ... | ... | ... |
| | 1980 | ... | *160 286 | ... | ... | *4 352 916 | ... | ... | *27 |
| | 1990 | ... | ... | ... | ... | 6 951 777 | 3 448 868 | 50 | ... |
| | 1991 | 15 858 | 270 365 | 158 118 | 58 | 7 210 021 | 3 573 615 | 50 | 27 |
| | 1992 | ... | ... | ... | ... | (24) 5 643 707 | (24) 2 785 065 | 49 | ... |
| | 1993 | ... | ... | ... | ... | (24) 5 758 389 | (24) 2 850 973 | 50 | ... |
| | 1994 | 20 428 | 213 890 | 124 929 | 58 | 7 971 770 | 3 906 652 | 49 | 37 |
| | 1995 | 20 863 | 224 896 | 165 398 | 74 | 8 159 430 | 4 026 702 | 49 | 36 |
| St. Helena | 1970 | 8 | 40 | 39 | 98 | 780 | 420 | 54 | 20 |
| | 1975/76 | 8 | ... | ... | ... | 755 | 365 | 48 | ... |
| | 1980/81 | 8 | 39 | 37 | 95 | 717 | 369 | 51 | 18 |
| | 1985/86 | 8 | 32 | 31 | 97 | 582 | 318 | 55 | 18 |
| Sudan | 1970/71 | 4 061 | 17 740 | 6 788 | 38 | 825 620 | 311 864 | 38 | 47 |
| | 1975/76 | 4 719 | 31 695 | 9 990 | 32 | 1 169 279 | 416 156 | 36 | 37 |
| | 1980/81 | 6 027 | 43 451 | 13 497 | 31 | 1 464 227 | 591 173 | 40 | 34 |
| | 1985/86 | 6 775 | 50 089 | 22 038 | 44 | 1 738 341 | 702 987 | 40 | 35 |
| | 1990/91 | 7 939 | 60 047 | 30 651 | 51 | 2 042 743 | 872 174 | 43 | 34 |
| | 1991/92 | 8 016 | 64 227 | 33 263 | 52 | 2 168 180 | 932 517 | 43 | 34 |
| | 1993/94 | (25) 9 681 | (25) 66 268 | (25) 38 303 | 58 | (25) 2 377 437 | (25) 1 040 244 | 44 | 36 |
| | 1994/95 | 12 187 | 83 306 | 49 830 | 60 | 3 023 955 | 1 339 998 | 44 | 36 |
| | 1995/96 | 10 680 | 95 184 | 57 037 | 60 | 2 930 328 | 1 323 745 | 45 | 31 |
| | 1996/97 | 11 158 | 102 987 | 63 886 | 62 | 3 000 048 | 1 354 290 | 45 | 29 |
| Swaziland | 1970 | 351 | 1 706 | 1 041 | 61 | 69 055 | 33 484 | 48 | 40 |
| | 1975 | 412 | 2 363 | 1 805 | 76 | 89 528 | 43 984 | 49 | 38 |
| | 1980 | 450 | 3 278 | 2 590 | 79 | 112 019 | 55 937 | 50 | 34 |
| | 1985 | 466 | 4 107 | 3 278 | 80 | 139 345 | 69 042 | 50 | 34 |
| | 1990 | 497 | 5 083 | 4 025 | 79 | 166 454 | 82 665 | 50 | 33 |
| | 1991 | 514 | 5 347 | 4 157 | 78 | 172 908 | 85 663 | 50 | 32 |
| | 1992 | 515 | 5 504 | 4 271 | 78 | 180 285 | 89 111 | 49 | 33 |
| | 1993 | 520 | 5 696 | 4 387 | 77 | 186 271 | 91 630 | 49 | 33 |
| | 1994 | 521 | 5 887 | 4 547 | 77 | 192 599 | 94 792 | 49 | 33 |
| | 1995 | 529 | 5 917 | 4 510 | 76 | 201 307 | 98 814 | 49 | 34 |
| | 1996 | 529 | 5 975 | 4 657 | 78 | 202 439 | 99 016 | 49 | 34 |
| | 1997 | 529 | 6 094 | 4 598 | 75 | 205 829 | 100 696 | 49 | 34 |

Primary education: schools, teaching staff and pupils
Enseignement primaire: écoles, personnel enseignant et élèves
Enseñanza primaria: escuelas, personal docente y alumnos

II.5

| Country / Pays / País | Year / Année / Año | Schools / Écoles / Escuelas | Teaching staff / Personnel enseignant / Personal docente | | | Pupils enrolled / Élèves inscrits / Alumnos matriculados | | | Pupil/teacher ratio / Nombre d'élèves par maître / Número de alumnos por maestro |
|---|---|---|---|---|---|---|---|---|---|
| | | | Total | Female Féminin Femenino | % F | Total | Female Féminin Femenino | % F | |
| Togo | 1970/71 | 916 | 3 909 | 758 | 19 | 228 505 | 70 850 | 31 | 58 |
| | 1975/76 | 1 362 | 6 080 | 1 224 | 20 | 362 895 | 126 041 | 35 | 60 |
| | 1980/81 | 2 205 | 9 201 | 1 972 | 21 | 506 788 | 198 418 | 39 | 55 |
| | 1985/86 | 2 336 | 10 049 | 2 008 | 20 | 462 858 | 177 373 | 38 | 46 |
| | 1990/91 | 2 494 | 11 105 | 2 085 | 19 | 646 962 | 255 642 | 40 | 58 |
| | 1991/92 | ... | 10 230 | 1 491 | 15 | 652 548 | 260 853 | 40 | 64 |
| | 1993/94 | 2 594 | 12 487 | 2 007 | 16 | 663 126 | 265 252 | 40 | 53 |
| | 1994/95 | 2 730 | 13 892 | 2 225 | 16 | 762 137 | 308 642 | 40 | 55 |
| | 1995/96 | 3 283 | 16 217 | 2 349 | 14 | 824 626 | 337 198 | 41 | 51 |
| | 1996/97 | ... | 18 535 | 2 622 | 14 | 859 574 | 356 702 | 41 | 46 |
| Tunisia | 1970/71 | 2 208 | 19 712 | ... | ... | 935 738 | 364 867 | 39 | 47 |
| | 1975/76 | 2 319 | 23 320 | 5 597 | 24 | 932 787 | 364 370 | 39 | 40 |
| | 1980/81 | 2 661 | 27 375 | 8 003 | 29 | 1 054 027 | 438 252 | 42 | 39 |
| | 1985/86 | 3 373 | 40 887 | 15 641 | 38 | 1 291 490 | 574 817 | 45 | 32 |
| | 1990/91 | 3 866 | 50 609 | 22 659 | 45 | 1 405 665 | 643 910 | 46 | 28 |
| | 1991/92 | 3 971 | 54 013 | 24 669 | 46 | 1 426 215 | 657 029 | 46 | 26 |
| | 1992/93 | 4 080 | 55 013 | 26 005 | 47 | 1 440 960 | 668 436 | 46 | 26 |
| | 1993/94 | 4 201 | 56 154 | 26 867 | 48 | 1 476 329 | 688 292 | 47 | 26 |
| | 1994/95 | 4 321 | 58 738 | 28 300 | 48 | 1 481 759 | 694 360 | 47 | 25 |
| | 1995/96 | 4 384 | 59 887 | 29 081 | 49 | 1 468 998 | 692 018 | 47 | 25 |
| | 1996/97 | 4 428 | 60 101 | 29 456 | 49 | 1 450 916 | 685 946 | 47 | 24 |
| | 1997/98 | (3) 4 417 | (3) 59 708 | (3) 29 177 | 49 | (3) 1 440 479 | (3) 681 395 | 47 | 24 |
| Uganda | 1970 | (26) 2 755 | (26) 21 471 | ... | ... | (26) 720 127 | (26) 282 928 | 39 | 34 |
| | 1975 | 3 472 | (26) 28 681 | (26) 8 216 | 29 | (26) 973 604 | (26) 390 461 | 40 | 34 |
| | 1980 | (26) 4 276 | (26) 38 422 | (26) *11 410 | *30 | (26) 1 292 377 | (26) *558 300 | *43 | 34 |
| | 1985 | (26) 7 025 | (26) 61 424 | ... | ... | (26) 2 117 000 | | | 34 |
| | 1990 | (26) 8 080 | (26) 84 149 | (26) 25 117 | 30 | (26) *2 470 000 | (26) *1 096 000 | *44 | *29 |
| | 1991 | (26) 8 046 | (26) 78 259 | ... | ... | (26) 2 576 537 | (26) 1 175 151 | 46 | 33 |
| | 1992 | (26) 8 325 | (26) 86 821 | ... | ... | (26) 2 403 845 | (26) 1 054 092 | 44 | 28 |
| | 1993 | (26) 8 430 | (26) 91 905 | (26) 28 811 | 31 | (26) 2 674 965 | (26) 1 182 335 | 44 | 29 |
| | 1994 | 9 560 | (26) 84 043 | (26) 26 894 | 32 | 2 789 573 | 1 340 036 | 48 | ... |
| | 1995 | 10 000 | 82 745 | ... | ... | 2 912 473 | 1 328 146 | 46 | 35 |
| United Republic of Tanzania (27) | 1970 | 4 210 | 18 313 | 4 764 | 26 | 856 213 | 337 814 | 39 | 47 |
| | 1975 | 5 804 | 29 735 | 9 709 | 33 | 1 592 396 | 668 112 | 42 | 54 |
| | 1980 | 9 794 | *81 386 | *30 057 | *37 | 3 367 644 | 1 585 140 | 47 | *41 |
| | 1985 | 10 173 | 92 586 | ... | ... | 3 169 759 | 1 580 130 | 50 | 34 |
| | 1990 | 10 417 | 96 850 | 39 966 | 41 | 3 379 000 | 1 673 765 | 50 | 35 |
| | 1991 | 10 451 | 98 174 | 39 758 | 40 | 3 512 347 | 1 734 011 | 49 | 36 |
| | 1992 | 10 960 | 101 306 | 42 007 | 41 | 3 603 488 | 1 769 580 | 49 | 36 |
| | 1993 | 10 892 | 101 816 | ... | ... | 3 736 734 | 1 837 429 | 49 | 37 |
| | 1994 | 10 891 | 103 900 | 44 842 | 43 | 3 796 830 | 1 873 768 | 49 | 37 |
| | 1995 | 10 927 | 105 280 | 45 482 | 43 | 3 877 643 | 1 915 764 | 49 | 37 |
| | 1996 | 11 130 | 108 874 | 47 531 | 44 | 3 942 888 | 1 950 149 | 49 | 36 |
| | 1997 | 11 290 | 109 936 | 48 021 | 44 | 4 057 965 | 2 013 867 | 50 | 37 |
| Zambia | 1970 | 2 564 | 14 852 | 4 990 | 34 | 694 670 | 308 994 | 44 | 47 |
| | 1975 | 2 710 | 18 096 | 6 735 | 37 | 872 392 | 396 384 | 45 | 48 |
| | 1980 | 2 819 | 21 455 | 8 584 | 40 | 1 041 938 | 487 435 | 47 | 49 |
| | 1985 | 3 128 | 27 302 | 11 818 | 43 | 1 348 318 | 635 530 | 47 | 49 |
| | 1990 | 3 587 | 33 200 | ... | ... | 1 461 206 | ... | ... | 44 |
| | 1991 | ... | ... | ... | ... | 1 510 337 | ... | ... | ... |
| | 1994 | 3 715 | 36 697 | 16 234 | 44 | 1 507 660 | 720 122 | 48 | 41 |
| | 1995 | 3 883 | 38 528 | 16 695 | 43 | 1 506 349 | 720 604 | 48 | 39 |
| Zimbabwe | 1970 | 3 848 | ... | ... | ... | 735 782 | ... | ... | ... |
| | 1975 | 3 623 | (26) 21 202 | (26) 7 214 | 34 | 862 736 | 395 114 | 46 | ... |
| | 1980 | 3 157 | 28 118 | ... | ... | 1 235 036 | ... | ... | 44 |
| | 1985 | 4 216 | 56 067 | 24 347 | 43 | 2 214 963 | 1 073 658 | 48 | 40 |
| | 1990 | 4 534 | 59 154 | 23 213 | 39 | 2 116 414 | 1 052 869 | 50 | 36 |
| | 1991 | 4 549 | 58 436 | 23 597 | 40 | 2 289 309 | 1 124 109 | 49 | 39 |
| | 1992 | 4 567 | 60 834 | 24 874 | 41 | 2 301 642 | 1 141 553 | 50 | 38 |
| | 1993 | 4 578 | 61 506 | ... | ... | 2 430 198 | *1 175 600 | *48 | 40 |
| | 1995 | 4 633 | 63 475 | 27 852 | 44 | 2 482 508 | 1 222 686 | 49 | 39 |
| | 1996 | 4 659 | 63 718 | 28 109 | 44 | 2 493 791 | 1 227 900 | 49 | 39 |
| | 1997 | 4 670 | 63 900 | ... | ... | 2 510 605 | ... | ... | 39 |
| | 1998 | 4 706 | 64 538 | ... | ... | 2 507 098 | ... | ... | 39 |
| **North America** | | | | | | | | | |
| Anguilla | 1992/93 | 6 | 70 | 61 | 87 | 1 407 | 710 | 50 | 20 |
| | 1996/97 | 7 | 80 | 71 | 89 | 1 557 | 762 | 49 | 19 |
| Antigua and Barbuda | 1970/71 | 40 | (28) 538 | (28) 448 | 83 | 9 668 | 4 660 | 48 | ... |
| | 1975/76 | 59 | (28) 524 | (28) 443 | 85 | 11 340 | 5 507 | 49 | ... |
| | 1991/92 | ... | ... | ... | ... | 9 298 | 4 568 | 49 | ... |
| Bahamas | 1970/71 | 192 | 707 | (3) 487 | ... | (29) 32 142 | ... | ... | ... |
| | 1975/76 | ... | (3)(30) 1 294 | ... | ... | 31 707 | 15 915 | 50 | ... |
| | 1980/81 | ... | (3) 1 261 | ... | ... | 32 854 | ... | ... | ... |
| | 1985/86 | 88 | (30) 1 767 | ... | ... | 32 848 | 16 215 | 49 | ... |
| | 1990/91 | ... | ... | ... | ... | 32 873 | ... | ... | ... |
| | 1991/92 | ... | ... | ... | ... | 33 374 | *16 480 | *49 | ... |

**Primary education: schools, teaching staff and pupils**
**Enseignement primaire: écoles, personnel enseignant et élèves**
**Enseñanza primaria: escuelas, personal docente y alumnos**

| Country / Pays / País | Year / Année / Año | Schools / Écoles / Escuelas | Teaching staff / Personnel enseignant / Personal docente | | | Pupils enrolled / Élèves inscrits / Alumnos matriculados | | | Pupil/teacher ratio / Nombre d'élèves par maître / Número de alumnos por maestro |
|---|---|---|---|---|---|---|---|---|---|
| | | | Total | Female Féminin Femenino | % F | Total | Female Féminin Femenino | % F | |
| **Bahamas (cont)** | 1992/93 | ... | ... | ... | ... | 33 917 | *16 850 | *50 | ... |
| | 1993/94 | 115 | 1 581 | 1 446 | 91 | 33 343 | ... | ... | 21 |
| | 1994/95 | 111 | 1 485 | 1 344 | 91 | 32 684 | 16 126 | 49 | 22 |
| | 1996/97 | 113 | *1 540 | *1 351 | *88 | 34 199 | ... | ... | *22 |
| **Barbados** | 1970/71 | ... | ... | ... | ... | (26) 37 866 | (26) 18 539 | 49 | ... |
| | 1975/76 | ... | ... | ... | ... | 32 884 | 16 426 | 50 | ... |
| | 1980/81 | (22) 134 | (3)(22) *1 172 | ... | ... | (22) 31 147 | (22) 15 497 | 50 | ... |
| | 1991/92 | 106 | 1 553 | 1 120 | 72 | 26 662 | 13 164 | 49 | 17 |
| **Belize** | 1970/71 | (26) 181 | (26) 1 150 | (26) 800 | 70 | (26) 31 629 | (26) 15 511 | 49 | 28 |
| | 1975/76 | 194 | (26) 1 207 | (26) 871 | 72 | 33 444 | (26) 16 057 | ... | ... |
| | 1980/81 | (26) 197 | (26) 1 421 | ... | ... | (26) 34 615 | ... | ... | 24 |
| | 1985/86 | ... | (26) 1 555 | (26) 1 121 | 72 | (26) 39 212 | (26) 18 917 | 48 | 25 |
| | 1990/91 | (26) 236 | (26) 1 749 | (26) 1 224 | 70 | (26) 46 023 | (26) *22 297 | *48 | 26 |
| | 1991/92 | (26) 237 | (26) 1 776 | (26) 1 261 | 71 | (26) 46 874 | (26) 22 697 | 48 | 26 |
| | 1992/93 | (26) 270 | (26) 1 818 | (26) 1 292 | 71 | (26) 48 397 | (26) 23 418 | 48 | 27 |
| | 1993/94 | (26) 280 | (26) *1 939 | (26) *1 350 | *70 | (26) *50 291 | (26) *24 314 | *48 | *26 |
| | 1994/95 | (26) 277 | (26) 1 976 | (26) 1 390 | 70 | (26) 51 377 | (26) 24 835 | 48 | 26 |
| **Bermuda** | 1970/71 | 28 | 341 | 290 | 85 | 7 986 | 4 006 | 50 | 23 |
| | 1975/76 | 22 | ... | ... | ... | 6 808 | 3 288 | 48 | ... |
| | 1980/81 | 22 | 312 | (3) 227 | ... | 5 934 | 2 885 | 49 | 19 |
| | 1994/95 | (21) 30 | (21) 463 | (21) 406 | 88 | (21) 5 962 | (21) 2 941 | 49 | 13 |
| | 1996/97 | 26 | 478 | 421 | 88 | 5 883 | 2 902 | 49 | 12 |
| **British Virgin Islands** | 1970/71 | 20 | 94 | 77 | 82 | 2 156 | 976 | 45 | 23 |
| | 1975/76 | 22 | 113 | 102 | 90 | 2 096 | 1 042 | 50 | 19 |
| | 1980/81 | 18 | 109 | 92 | 84 | 1 974 | 982 | 50 | 18 |
| | 1990/91 | ... | 126 | ... | ... | 2 340 | 1 102 | 47 | 19 |
| | 1991/92 | 19 | 151 | ... | ... | 2 443 | 1 153 | 47 | 16 |
| | 1992/93 | ... | ... | ... | ... | 2 539 | ... | ... | ... |
| | 1993/94 | 20 | 166 | 147 | 89 | 2 502 | 1 204 | 48 | 15 |
| | 1994/95 | ... | 169 | 143 | 85 | 2 625 | 1 266 | 48 | 16 |
| **Canada** | 1970/71 | ... | 159 900 | ... | ... | 3 736 450 | 1 817 268 | 49 | 23 |
| | 1975/76 | ... | ... | ... | ... | 2 440 016 | 1 190 489 | 49 | ... |
| | 1980/81 | ... | ... | ... | ... | 2 184 919 | 1 064 543 | 49 | ... |
| | 1985/86 | ... | 135 010 | ... | ... | 2 254 887 | 1 086 611 | 48 | 17 |
| | 1990/91 | (31) 12 346 | 154 698 | 106 289 | 69 | 2 375 704 | 1 147 503 | 48 | 15 |
| | 1991/92 | (31) 12 456 | 156 432 | 107 586 | 69 | 2 394 115 | 1 156 674 | 48 | 15 |
| | 1992/93 | (31) 12 756 | 150 264 | 99 656 | 66 | 2 399 224 | 1 160 110 | 48 | 16 |
| | 1993/94 | (31) 12 721 | 151 436 | 100 101 | 66 | 2 400 819 | 1 160 898 | 48 | 16 |
| | 1994/95 | (31) 12 700 | 148 724 | 99 369 | 67 | 2 413 126 | 1 168 075 | 48 | 16 |
| | 1995/96 | (31) 12 685 | 148 565 | 99 241 | 67 | 2 448 144 | 1 185 025 | 48 | 16 |
| **Costa Rica** | 1970 | 2 523 | 11 720 | 8 735 | 75 | 349 378 | 170 892 | 49 | 30 |
| | 1975 | 2 770 | 12 429 | ... | ... | 361 303 | 176 792 | 49 | 29 |
| | 1980 | 2 936 | 12 596 | ... | ... | 348 674 | 169 403 | 49 | 28 |
| | 1985 | 3 091 | 11 526 | ... | ... | 362 877 | 175 721 | 48 | 31 |
| | 1990 | 3 268 | 13 651 | ... | ... | 435 205 | 211 251 | 49 | 32 |
| | 1991 | 3 317 | 14 078 | 11 225 | 80 | 453 297 | 220 386 | 49 | 32 |
| | 1992 | 3 359 | 14 584 | ... | ... | 471 049 | 228 900 | 49 | 32 |
| | 1993 | 3 442 | 14 949 | ... | ... | 484 958 | 235 688 | 49 | 32 |
| | 1994 | 3 472 | 15 806 | ... | ... | 495 879 | 240 941 | 49 | 31 |
| | 1995 | 3 544 | 16 565 | ... | ... | 507 037 | 246 465 | 49 | 31 |
| | 1996 | 3 607 | 17 554 | 13 755 | 78 | 518 603 | 252 402 | 49 | 30 |
| | 1997 | 3 671 | 18 358 | 14 905 | 81 | 525 273 | 254 761 | 49 | 29 |
| | 1998 | 3 711 | 19 235 | ... | ... | 529 637 | 256 955 | 49 | 28 |
| **Cuba** | 1970/71 | 15 190 | 56 555 | ... | ... | 1 530 376 | 748 676 | 49 | 27 |
| | 1975/76 | 14 886 | 77 472 | 55 543 | 72 | 1 795 752 | 862 687 | 48 | 23 |
| | 1980/81 | 12 196 | 84 041 | 63 339 | 75 | 1 468 538 | 698 138 | 48 | 17 |
| | 1985/86 | 10 187 | 77 111 | 59 359 | 77 | 1 077 213 | 509 055 | 47 | 14 |
| | 1990/91 | 9 375 | 70 962 | 55 987 | 79 | 887 737 | 426 609 | 48 | 13 |
| | 1991/92 | 9 346 | 74 354 | 57 870 | 78 | 917 889 | 445 071 | 48 | 12 |
| | 1992/93 | 9 368 | 76 161 | ... | ... | 942 431 | 457 961 | 49 | 12 |
| | 1993/94 | 9 440 | 76 193 | 59 646 | 78 | 983 459 | 478 746 | 49 | 12 |
| | 1994/95 | 9 425 | 74 225 | 60 288 | 81 | 1 007 769 | 490 621 | 49 | 13 |
| | 1995/96 | (21) 9 864 | (21) 90 565 | (21) 72 628 | 80 | (21) 1 074 153 | (21) 515 504 | 48 | 12 |
| | 1996/97 | 9 926 | 92 820 | 75 365 | 81 | 1 094 868 | 524 578 | 48 | 12 |
| **Dominica** | 1970/71 | ... | ... | ... | ... | 17 808 | 8 479 | 48 | ... |
| | 1975/76 | 57 | (32) 674 | (32) 477 | 71 | 17 166 | 8 276 | 48 | ... |
| | 1980/81 | ... | ... | ... | ... | 14 815 | 7 472 | 50 | ... |
| | 1985/86 | 66 | (32) 808 | (32) *541 | *67 | 12 340 | 5 940 | 48 | ... |
| | 1990/91 | 65 | 439 | 354 | 81 | 12 836 | 6 301 | 49 | 29 |
| | 1991/92 | 65 | (32) 605 | (32) 465 | 77 | 12 120 | 5 909 | 49 | ... |
| | 1992/93 | 64 | (32) 608 | (32) 440 | 72 | 12 795 | 6 325 | 49 | ... |
| | 1993/94 | 64 | (32) 674 | (32) 412 | 61 | 12 822 | 6 354 | 50 | ... |
| | 1994/95 | 64 | (32) 641 | (32) 469 | 73 | 12 627 | 6 266 | 50 | ... |
| **Dominican Republic** | 1970/71 | 5 214 | 13 796 | ... | ... | 764 085 | 380 086 | 50 | 55 |
| | 1975/76 | 5 487 | 17 932 | ... | ... | 911 142 | ... | ... | 51 |
| | 1980/81 | 4 606 | ... | ... | ... | 1 105 730 | ... | ... | ... |
| | 1985/86 | *6 299 | *27 952 | ... | ... | 1 219 681 | 614 514 | 50 | *44 |
| | 1990/91 | ... | (3)(20) 20 879 | ... | ... | (3)(20) 948 186 | ... | ... | 45 |

Primary education: schools, teaching staff and pupils
Enseignement primaire: écoles, personnel enseignant et élèves
Enseñanza primaria: escuelas, personal docente y alumnos

II.5

| Country / Pays / País | Year / Année / Año | Schools / Écoles / Escuelas | Teaching staff / Personnel enseignant / Personal docente | | | Pupils enrolled / Élèves inscrits / Alumnos matriculados | | | Pupil/teacher ratio / Nombre d'élèves par maître / Número de alumnos por maestro |
|---|---|---|---|---|---|---|---|---|---|
| | | | Total | Female Féminin Femenino | % F | Total | Female Féminin Femenino | % F | |
| Dominican Republic (cont) | 1991/92 | ... | (3) 22 530 | ... | ... | (3) 952 850 | ... | ... | 42 |
| | 1992/93 | ... | (3) 22 365 | ... | ... | 1 261 339 | ... | ... | |
| | 1993/94 | ... | 38 621 | ... | ... | 1 314 036 | ... | ... | 34 |
| | 1994/95 | ... | ... | ... | ... | 1 312 325 | ... | ... | |
| | 1995/96 | ... | ... | ... | ... | 1 369 456 | ... | ... | |
| | 1996/97 | ... | ... | ... | ... | 1 360 044 | 668 369 | 49 | |
| El Salvador | 1970 | 2 787 | (33) 14 193 | (33) 9 971 | 70 | 509 985 | 244 064 | 48 | |
| | 1975 | (14) 3 103 | ... | ... | ... | (14)(33) 759 460 | (14)(33) 366 612 | 48 | |
| | 1980 | 3 196 | 17 364 | 11 315 | 65 | 834 101 | 412 743 | 49 | 48 |
| | 1991 | 3 516 | ... | ... | ... | 1 000 671 | 496 199 | 50 | ... |
| | 1992 | 3 806 | ... | ... | ... | 1 028 877 | 510 001 | 50 | |
| | 1993 | 3 961 | ... | ... | ... | 1 042 256 | 515 378 | 49 | |
| | 1995 | 4 068 | 37 989 | ... | ... | 1 064 279 | 524 877 | 49 | 28 |
| | 1996 | 5 025 | 34 496 | ... | ... | 1 130 900 | 553 915 | 49 | 33 |
| | 1997 | ... | ... | ... | ... | 1 191 052 | 580 524 | 49 | |
| Grenada | 1970/71 | 58 | 800 | 466 | 58 | 30 355 | 14 990 | 49 | 38 |
| | 1975/76 | 63 | ... | ... | ... | (34) 21 195 | (34) 10 125 | 48 | ... |
| | 1980/81 | 57 | 776 | 506 | 65 | 18 076 | 8 647 | 48 | 23 |
| | 1985/86 | ... | ... | ... | ... | 16 538 | 7 343 | 44 | ... |
| | 1990/91 | ... | ... | ... | ... | 19 811 | *8 933 | *45 | ... |
| | 1991/92 | ... | ... | ... | ... | 21 365 | *9 415 | *44 | ... |
| | 1992/93 | ... | 963 | (3) 601 | ... | 22 345 | *10 895 | *49 | 23 |
| Guadeloupe | 1970/71 | 335 | (3) 2 058 | ... | ... | 70 288 | 34 241 | 49 | ... |
| | 1975/76 | 257 | 2 018 | ... | ... | 62 013 | ... | ... | 31 |
| | 1980/81 | ... | ... | ... | ... | 53 581 | ... | ... | ... |
| | 1985/86 | 230 | 1 927 | ... | ... | 42 734 | ... | ... | 22 |
| | 1990/91 | 222 | 2 064 | ... | ... | 38 531 | 18 902 | 49 | 19 |
| | 1991/92 | 218 | 1 972 | ... | ... | 38 255 | 18 771 | 49 | 19 |
| | 1992/93 | 219 | 1 920 | 1 232 | 64 | 37 765 | 18 512 | 49 | 20 |
| | 1993/94 | ... | ... | ... | ... | 37 330 | 18 209 | 49 | ... |
| | 1994/95 | ... | ... | ... | ... | (21) 38 332 | ... | ... | |
| Guatemala | 1970 | 5 250 | 14 058 | 9 070 | 65 | 505 691 | 223 636 | 44 | 36 |
| | 1975 | 6 122 | 18 129 | 11 162 | 62 | 627 126 | 280 719 | 45 | 35 |
| | 1980 | 6 959 | 23 770 | ... | ... | 803 404 | 362 083 | 45 | 34 |
| | 1985 | 8 016 | 27 809 | ... | ... | 1 016 474 | 458 469 | 45 | 37 |
| | 1990 | ... | ... | ... | ... | 1 164 937 | ... | ... | |
| | 1991 | 9 362 | 36 757 | ... | ... | 1 249 413 | 571 218 | 46 | 34 |
| | 1992 | ... | 37 677 | ... | ... | 1 340 657 | 612 613 | 46 | 36 |
| | 1993 | 10 770 | 44 220 | ... | ... | 1 393 921 | 637 548 | 46 | 32 |
| | 1994 | ... | 50 756 | ... | ... | 1 412 720 | 643 919 | 46 | 28 |
| | 1995 | 11 495 | 43 731 | ... | ... | 1 470 754 | 671 652 | 46 | 34 |
| | 1996 | 12 409 | 43 403 | ... | ... | 1 510 811 | 690 251 | 46 | 35 |
| | 1997 | ... | ... | ... | ... | 1 544 709 | 708 099 | 46 | ... |
| Haiti | 1970/71 | 2 191 | 7 833 | ... | ... | 366 846 | ... | ... | 47 |
| | 1975/76 | 2 788 | 11 816 | ... | ... | 487 135 | ... | ... | 41 |
| | 1980/81 | 3 271 | 14 581 | 7 124 | 49 | 642 391 | 294 712 | 46 | 44 |
| | 1985/86 | 3 734 | 23 200 | ... | ... | 872 500 | 407 002 | 47 | 38 |
| | 1990/91 | 7 306 | (6) 26 209 | (6) 11 681 | 45 | (35) 555 400 | (35) 207 120 | 48 | ... |
| Honduras | 1970 | 4 098 | 10 816 | ... | ... | 381 685 | 189 761 | 50 | 35 |
| | 1975 | 4 602 | 13 045 | ... | ... | 460 744 | 225 965 | 49 | 35 |
| | 1980 | 5 524 | 16 385 | 12 187 | 74 | 601 337 | 298 163 | 50 | 37 |
| | 1985 | ... | ... | ... | ... | 765 809 | 380 074 | 50 | ... |
| | 1991 | 7 593 | 23 872 | 17 646 | 74 | 908 446 | 456 751 | 50 | 38 |
| | 1993 | 8 127 | 26 561 | 19 475 | 73 | 990 352 | 490 580 | 50 | 37 |
| | 1994 | 8 114 | 28 888 | ... | ... | 1 008 181 | 499 178 | 50 | 35 |
| Jamaica | 1970/71 | (3) 748 | (3)(30) 8 053 | ... | ... | (3)(30) 376 075 | (3)(30) 187 661 | 50 | 47 |
| | 1975/76 | (14) 923 | (14)(30) 11 531 | ... | ... | (14) 371 876 | (14) 185 568 | 50 | ... |
| | 1980/81 | 894 | (3) 8 676 | (3) 7 506 | 87 | 359 488 | (3) 178 053 | ... | ... |
| | 1985/86 | ... | (3) 9 648 | (3) 8 474 | 88 | 340 059 | (3) 163 463 | ... | ... |
| | 1990/91 | ... | (3) 8 830 | ... | ... | (3) 323 378 | (3) 160 805 | 50 | 37 |
| | 1992/93 | ... | (3) 8 315 | (3) 7 705 | 93 | 333 104 | *163 200 | *49 | ... |
| | 1993/94 | ... | (3) 8 992 | (3) 8 165 | 91 | (3) 311 146 | (3) 152 663 | 49 | 35 |
| | 1994/95 | ... | (3) 9 712 | (3) 8 852 | 91 | (3) 305 238 | (3) 149 832 | 49 | 31 |
| | 1995/96 | ... | (3) 9 265 | (3) 8 407 | 91 | (3) 300 931 | (3) 148 349 | 49 | 32 |
| | 1996/97 | ... | (3) 9 512 | (3) 8 588 | 90 | (3) 293 863 | (3) 144 001 | 49 | 31 |
| Martinique | 1970/71 | 246 | (3) 2 425 | ... | ... | 68 785 | 33 694 | 49 | ... |
| | 1975/76 | 238 | 2 273 | ... | ... | 58 747 | ... | ... | 26 |
| | 1980/81 | ... | ... | ... | ... | 47 382 | ... | ... | ... |
| | 1990/91 | ... | ... | ... | ... | 32 744 | ... | ... | ... |
| | 1991/92 | 200 | ... | ... | ... | 32 747 | 15 786 | 48 | ... |
| | 1992/93 | 197 | ... | ... | ... | 32 585 | 15 955 | 49 | ... |
| | 1993/94 | 190 | 2 483 | 1 745 | 70 | 33 121 | 16 231 | 49 | 13 |
| | 1994/95 | ... | ... | ... | ... | (21) 33 917 | ... | ... | ... |
| | 1995/96 | 187 | 2 603 | 1 891 | 73 | 34 559 | 16 933 | 49 | 13 |
| Mexico | 1970/71 | 46 010 | 201 453 | 122 123 | 61 | 9 248 290 | 4 433 507 | 48 | 46 |
| | 1975/76 | 55 618 | 255 939 | 159 055 | 62 | 11 461 415 | 5 450 446 | 48 | 45 |
| | 1980/81 | 76 179 | 375 220 | ... | ... | 14 666 257 | 7 151 826 | 49 | 39 |
| | 1985/86 | 76 690 | 449 760 | ... | ... | 15 124 160 | 7 361 273 | 49 | 34 |

**Primary education: schools, teaching staff and pupils**
**Enseignement primaire: écoles, personnel enseignant et élèves**
**Enseñanza primaria: escuelas, personal docente y alumnos**

| Country Pays País | Year Année Año | Schools Écoles Escuelas | Teaching staff Personnel enseignant Personal docente | | | Pupils enrolled Élèves inscrits Alumnos matriculados | | | Pupil/ teacher ratio Nombre d'élèves par maître Número de alumnos por maestro |
|---|---|---|---|---|---|---|---|---|---|
| | | | Total | Female Féminin Femenino | % F | Total | Female Féminin Femenino | % F | |
| Mexico (cont) | 1990/91 | 82 280 | 471 625 | ... | ... | 14 401 588 | 6 989 433 | 49 | 31 |
| | 1991/92 | 84 606 | 479 616 | ... | ... | 14 396 993 | 6 984 375 | 49 | 30 |
| | 1992/93 | 85 249 | 486 686 | ... | ... | 14 425 669 | 6 996 240 | 48 | 30 |
| | 1993/94 | 87 271 | 496 472 | ... | ... | 14 469 450 | 6 997 719 | 48 | 29 |
| | 1994/95 | 91 857 | 507 669 | ... | ... | 14 574 202 | 7 059 946 | 48 | 29 |
| | 1995/96 | 94 844 | 516 051 | ... | ... | 14 623 438 | 7 080 967 | 48 | 28 |
| | 1996/97 | 95 855 | 524 927 | ... | ... | 14 650 521 | 7 102 544 | 48 | 28 |
| Montserrat | 1980/81 | 16 | ... | ... | ... | 1 846 | 892 | 48 | ... |
| | 1985/86 | ... | ... | ... | ... | 1 351 | 658 | 49 | ... |
| | 1990/91 | ... | ... | ... | ... | 1 593 | ... | ... | ... |
| | 1991/92 | 11 | *82 | ... | ... | 1 570 | 744 | 47 | *19 |
| | 1992/93 | ... | ... | ... | ... | 1 566 | ... | ... | ... |
| | 1993/94 | 11 | 85 | 64 | 75 | 1 525 | 704 | 46 | 18 |
| Netherlands Antilles | 1980/81 | ... | ... | ... | ... | 32 856 | 16 243 | 49 | ... |
| | 1991/92 | 86 | 1 077 | ... | ... | 22 410 | ... | ... | 21 |
| Nicaragua | 1970 | (6) 2 068 | (6) 7 645 | (6) 6 047 | 79 | 285 285 | 143 394 | 50 | ... |
| | 1975 | (6) 2 297 | (6) 8 817 | ... | ... | 341 533 | 174 182 | 51 | ... |
| | 1980 | 4 421 | 13 318 | 10 391 | 78 | 472 167 | 239 968 | 51 | 35 |
| | 1985 | 4 008 | 16 872 | 12 595 | 75 | 561 551 | 291 646 | 52 | 33 |
| | 1990 | 4 030 | 19 022 | 16 531 | 87 | 632 882 | 322 837 | 51 | 33 |
| | 1991 | 4 402 | 18 646 | 16 097 | 86 | 674 045 | 342 215 | 51 | 36 |
| | 1992 | 4 571 | 18 901 | ... | ... | 703 854 | 355 199 | 50 | 37 |
| | 1993 | 4 945 | 19 913 | 16 768 | 84 | 737 476 | 370 659 | 50 | 37 |
| | 1994 | 4 993 | 20 626 | 17 255 | 84 | 765 972 | 382 818 | 50 | 37 |
| | 1995 | 5 251 | 20 116 | 16 797 | 84 | 764 587 | 382 798 | 50 | 38 |
| | 1996 | ... | 21 020 | ... | ... | 762 712 | 381 213 | 50 | 36 |
| | 1997 | 7 098 | ... | ... | ... | 777 917 | 388 336 | 50 | ... |
| | 1998 | 7 224 | ... | ... | ... | 783 002 | 390 416 | 50 | ... |
| Panama | 1970 | 1 784 | 9 431 | 7 539 | 80 | 255 287 | 122 472 | 48 | 27 |
| | 1975 | 2 171 | 12 459 | 10 053 | 81 | 334 607 | 160 588 | 48 | 27 |
| | 1980 | 2 306 | 12 361 | 9 909 | 80 | 337 522 | 162 510 | 48 | 27 |
| | 1985 | 2 476 | 13 359 | 10 486 | 78 | 340 135 | 162 542 | 48 | 25 |
| | 1990 | 2 659 | 15 249 | ... | ... | 351 021 | 168 235 | 48 | 23 |
| | 1991 | 2 683 | ... | ... | ... | 350 104 | ... | ... | ... |
| | 1992 | 2 712 | ... | ... | ... | 353 154 | ... | ... | ... |
| | 1993 | 2 732 | ... | ... | ... | 357 402 | ... | ... | ... |
| | 1994 | 2 793 | ... | ... | ... | (21) 358 367 | ... | ... | ... |
| | 1995 | 2 823 | ... | ... | ... | 361 877 | ... | ... | ... |
| | 1996 | 2 849 | ... | ... | ... | 371 250 | ... | ... | ... |
| Puerto Rico | 1970/71 | 1 938 | (6) 15 930 | ... | ... | 472 742 | ... | ... | ... |
| | 1975/76 | ... | (3) 17 270 | ... | ... | (3) 385 903 | ... | ... | 22 |
| St. Kitts and Nevis | 1975/76 | ... | ... | ... | ... | 8 804 | 4 246 | 48 | ... |
| | 1980/81 | ... | ... | ... | ... | 7 149 | 3 488 | 49 | ... |
| | 1985/86 | 32 | 353 | (3) 214 | ... | 7 810 | (3) 3 287 | ... | 22 |
| | 1991/92 | 32 | 350 | 278 | 79 | 7 236 | 3 509 | 48 | 21 |
| | 1992/93 | ... | ... | ... | ... | 7 068 | 3 442 | 49 | ... |
| St. Lucia | 1970/71 | ... | ... | ... | ... | (30) 23 484 | (30) 12 092 | 51 | ... |
| | 1975/76 | 76 | 953 | ... | ... | 29 859 | 14 576 | 49 | 31 |
| | 1980/81 | 77 | 957 | 768 | 80 | 29 605 | 15 079 | 51 | 31 |
| | 1985/86 | 83 | (3) 1 084 | (3) 862 | 80 | 32 817 | 16 012 | 49 | ... |
| | 1990/91 | 87 | (3) 1 127 | (3) 931 | 83 | 33 006 | *16 061 | *49 | ... |
| | 1991/92 | 88 | (3) 1 181 | (3) 967 | 82 | 32 622 | *15 795 | *48 | ... |
| | 1992/93 | 88 | 1 204 | 998 | 83 | 32 545 | 15 765 | 48 | 27 |
| | 1995/96 | ... | 1 180 | *980 | *83 | *31 800 | *15 500 | *49 | *27 |
| | 1996/97 | 89 | 1 214 | 1 009 | 83 | 31 615 | 15 442 | 49 | 26 |
| St. Pierre and Miquelon | 1970/71 | 5 | 40 | 31 | 78 | 930 | 547 | 59 | 23 |
| | 1980/81 | 5 | 36 | 26 | 72 | 747 | 364 | 49 | 21 |
| | 1985/86 | 5 | 38 | 28 | 74 | 558 | 265 | 47 | 15 |
| | 1990/91 | ... | ... | ... | ... | 556 | ... | ... | ... |
| | 1992/93 | ... | ... | ... | ... | 529 | ... | ... | ... |
| | 1994/95 | ... | ... | ... | ... | 492 | ... | ... | ... |
| St. Vincent and the Grenadines | 1970/71 | 60 | 880 | 417 | 47 | (36) 28 225 | (36) 13 944 | 49 | ... |
| | 1975/76 | 61 | 1 210 | 518 | 43 | 21 854 | 10 605 | 49 | 18 |
| | 1980/81 | ... | ... | ... | ... | (36) 24 158 | ... | ... | ... |
| | 1985/86 | 61 | (36) 1 263 | (36) 801 | 63 | (36) 24 561 | (36) 11 918 | 49 | 19 |
| | 1990/91 | 64 | 1 119 | 746 | 67 | 22 030 | 10 845 | 49 | 20 |
| | 1993/94 | 65 | *1 080 | *725 | *67 | 21 386 | 10 374 | 49 | *20 |
| Trinidad and Tobago (26) | 1970/71 | (28) 469 | (28) 6 548 | (28) 3 873 | 59 | (28) 225 689 | (28) 111 242 | 49 | 34 |
| | 1975/76 | 473 | 6 471 | 4 022 | 62 | (28) 199 033 | (28) 98 990 | 50 | ... |
| | 1980/81 | 464 | 7 002 | 4 623 | 66 | (28) 167 039 | (28) 83 524 | 50 | ... |
| | 1985/86 | 468 | 7 627 | 5 357 | 70 | (28) 168 308 | (28) 83 708 | 50 | ... |
| | 1990/91 | 476 | 7 473 | 5 257 | 70 | (28) 193 992 | (28) 95 612 | 49 | ... |
| | 1991/92 | 475 | 7 512 | 5 374 | 72 | (28) 196 333 | (28) 96 854 | 49 | ... |
| | 1992/93 | ... | 7 647 | 5 483 | 72 | (28) 197 030 | (28) 97 180 | 49 | ... |
| | 1993/94 | 476 | 7 210 | 5 307 | 74 | (28) 195 013 | (28) 96 281 | 49 | ... |
| | 1995/96 | 476 | 7 296 | 5 387 | 74 | (28) 186 000 | (28) 91 468 | 49 | ... |
| | 1996/97 | 476 | 7 311 | 5 398 | 74 | (28) 181 030 | (28) 89 015 | 49 | ... |

II.5

...mary education: schools, teaching staff and pupils
...primaire: écoles, personnel enseignant et élèves
...primaria: escuelas, personal docente y alumnos

| Country / Pays / País | Year / Année / Año | Schools / Écoles / Escuelas | Teaching staff Personnel enseignant Personal docente Total | Female Féminin Femenino | % F | Pupils Total | F | % | Pupil/teacher ratio Nombre d'élèves par maître Número de alumnos por maestro |
|---|---|---|---|---|---|---|---|---|---|
| Turks and Caicos Islands | 1970/71 | 14 | 106 | 88 | 83 | 1 615 | ... | ... | 15 |
| | 1975/76 | 17 | 83 | 75 | 90 | 1 764 | ... | ... | 21 |
| | 1980/81 | (3) 17 | (3) 80 | (3) 74 | 93 | (3) 1 483 | (3) 712 | ... | 19 |
| | 1993/94 | (3) 10 | (3) 86 | (3) 78 | 91 | (3) 1 211 | (3) 604 | ... | 14 |
| | 1996/97 | 21 | ... | ... | ... | 1 573 | 773 | ... | ... |
| U. S. Virgin Islands | 1970/71 | (6) 36 | (6) 490 | ... | ... | (6) 12 800 | ... | ... | ... |
| | 1975/76 | 42 | 1 111 | ... | ... | 17 997 | ... | ... | ... |
| | 1980/81 | ... | ... | ... | ... | 12 641 | ... | ... | ... |
| | 1985/86 | 57 | (3) 711 | ... | ... | 14 948 | ... | ... | 6 |
| | 1990/91 | 57 | (3) 777 | (3) 671 | 86 | 14 319 | (3) 5 685 | ... | ... |
| | 1992/93 | 62 | (3) 790 | ... | ... | 14 544 | 6 778 | 47 | ... |
| United States | 1970/71 | ... | ... | ... | ... | 22 037 000 | ... | ... | ... |
| | 1975/76 | ... | ... | ... | ... | 20 213 000 | ... | ... | ... |
| | 1980/81 | ... | ... | ... | ... | 20 420 000 | 9 959 000 | 49 | ... |
| | 1985/86 | 76 000 | 1 425 000 | ... | ... | 20 214 000 | 9 850 000 | 49 | 14 |
| | 1990/91 | ... | ... | ... | ... | 22 429 000 | 10 856 000 | 48 | ... |
| | 1992/93 | ... | 1 427 387 | 1 234 581 | 86 | 22 976 240 | 11 115 649 | 48 | 16 |
| | 1993/94 | 72 000 | 1 442 913 | 1 247 819 | 86 | 23 212 276 | 11 287 559 | 49 | 16 |
| | 1994/95 | ... | 1 473 053 | 1 273 932 | 86 | 23 823 662 | 11 577 544 | 49 | 16 |
| | 1995/96 | ... | 1 499 697 | 1 296 974 | 86 | 24 045 967 | 11 667 481 | 49 | 16 |
| **South America** | | | | | | | | | |
| Argentina | 1970 | 19 847 | 175 929 | 161 401 | 92 | 3 385 790 | 1 672 717 | 49 | 19 |
| | 1975 | 20 646 | 195 997 | 181 141 | 92 | 3 571 180 | 1 758 729 | 49 | 18 |
| | 1980 | ... | ... | ... | ... | 3 917 449 | 1 927 389 | 49 | ... |
| | 1985 | 20 700 | 229 715 | 212 033 | 92 | 4 589 291 | 2 268 227 | 49 | 20 |
| | 1990 | ... | ... | ... | ... | 4 965 395 | ... | ... | ... |
| | 1991 | ... | ... | ... | ... | 5 044 398 | ... | ... | ... |
| | 1994 | (21) 25 646 | (21) 295 488 | (21) 263 947 | 89 | (21) 5 180 713 | ... | ... | 18 |
| | 1996 | *22 636 | (37) *326 570 | ... | ... | 5 250 329 | 2 569 706 | 49 | ... |
| | 1997 | 22 437 | (37) 309 081 | ... | ... | 5 153 256 | 2 536 118 | 49 | ... |
| Bolivia | 1970 | 8 217 | 25 509 | ... | ... | 679 123 | 276 556 | 41 | 27 |
| | 1975 | 9 519 | 38 737 | ... | ... | 859 413 | 383 882 | 45 | 22 |
| | 1980 | ... | 48 894 | 23 293 | 48 | 978 250 | 456 411 | 47 | 20 |
| | 1990 | ... | 51 763 | 29 663 | 57 | 1 278 775 | 604 245 | 47 | 25 |
| Brazil | 1970 | 146 136 | 457 406 | 433 542 | 95 | 12 812 029 | 6 368 913 | 50 | 28 |
| | 1975 | (14) 188 260 | (14) 890 052 | (14) 764 527 | 85 | (14) 19 549 249 | (14) 9 636 448 | 49 | 22 |
| | 1980 | 201 926 | 884 257 | 748 927 | 85 | 22 598 254 | 10 993 176 | 49 | 26 |
| | 1985 | 187 274 | 1 040 566 | ... | ... | 24 769 736 | ... | ... | 24 |
| | 1990 | 208 934 | 1 260 501 | ... | ... | 28 943 619 | ... | ... | 23 |
| | 1991 | 193 700 | 1 295 965 | ... | ... | 29 203 724 | ... | ... | 23 |
| | 1992 | 199 447 | 1 329 352 | ... | ... | 30 106 084 | ... | ... | 23 |
| | 1993 | 195 840 | 1 344 045 | ... | ... | 30 548 879 | ... | ... | 23 |
| | 1994 | 194 487 | 1 377 665 | ... | ... | 31 220 110 | ... | ... | 23 |
| | 1995 | ... | ... | ... | ... | 32 668 738 | ... | ... | ... |
| | 1996 | 195 767 | 1 388 247 | ... | ... | 33 131 270 | ... | ... | 24 |
| | 1997 | 196 479 | 1 413 607 | ... | ... | 34 229 388 | ... | ... | 24 |
| | 1998 | ... | ... | ... | ... | 35 838 372 | ... | ... | ... |
| Chile | 1970 | 7 387 | (3) 40 823 | (3) 28 132 | 69 | 2 040 071 | 1 010 613 | 50 | ... |
| | 1975 | 8 461 | 65 817 | 48 615 | 74 | 2 298 998 | 1 130 358 | 49 | 35 |
| | 1980 | ... | ... | ... | ... | 2 185 459 | 1 069 048 | 49 | ... |
| | 1985 | 8 586 | ... | ... | ... | 2 062 344 | 1 003 671 | 49 | ... |
| | 1990 | ... | ... | ... | ... | 1 991 178 | 971 962 | 49 | ... |
| | 1991 | 8 626 | 81 742 | 59 840 | 73 | 2 033 982 | 989 415 | 49 | 25 |
| | 1992 | 8 338 | ... | ... | ... | 2 034 839 | 994 152 | 49 | ... |
| | 1993 | ... | 78 813 | 56 999 | 72 | 2 066 046 | 1 009 396 | 49 | 26 |
| | 1994 | (21) 8 323 | (21) 78 813 | (21) 56 999 | 72 | (21) 2 119 737 | (21) 1 032 038 | 49 | 27 |
| | 1995 | 8 702 | 80 155 | 57 969 | 72 | 2 149 501 | 1 043 593 | 49 | 27 |
| | 1996 | ... | 73 960 | 53 593 | 72 | 2 241 536 | 1 086 734 | 48 | 30 |
| Colombia | 1970 | 27 094 | 86 005 | 66 370 | 77 | 3 286 052 | 1 652 884 | 50 | 38 |
| | 1975 | 33 202 | 121 957 | ... | ... | 3 911 244 | 1 974 005 | 50 | 32 |
| | 1980 | 33 557 | 136 381 | 107 744 | 79 | 4 168 200 | 2 083 500 | 50 | 31 |
| | 1985 | 34 004 | 132 940 | 105 014 | 79 | 4 039 533 | 2 019 305 | 50 | 30 |
| | 1990 | 40 340 | 141 936 | ... | ... | 4 246 658 | 2 233 368 | 53 | 30 |
| | 1991 | 41 044 | 143 193 | ... | ... | 4 310 970 | 2 136 292 | 50 | 30 |
| | 1992 | 44 139 | 162 445 | 129 566 | 80 | 4 525 959 | 2 282 377 | 50 | 28 |
| | 1993 | 44 693 | 166 123 | ... | ... | 4 599 132 | 2 281 437 | 50 | 28 |
| | 1994 | 46 458 | 179 776 | ... | ... | 4 648 335 | 2 272 745 | 49 | 26 |
| | 1995 | 47 663 | 189 123 | ... | ... | 4 692 614 | 2 292 948 | 49 | 25 |
| | 1996 | *48 933 | *193 911 | *149 777 | *77 | *4 916 934 | *2 406 524 | *49 | *25 |
| Ecuador | 1970/71 | (33) 7 692 | (33) 26 609 | (33) 16 899 | 64 | (33) 1 016 483 | (33) 490 379 | 48 | 38 |
| | 1975/76 | 9 479 | 32 279 | 20 960 | 65 | 1 216 233 | 591 241 | 49 | 38 |
| | 1980/81 | 11 451 | 42 415 | 27 696 | 65 | 1 534 258 | 746 014 | 49 | 36 |
| | 1985/86 | ... | 53 683 | 35 036 | 65 | 1 738 549 | 850 354 | 49 | 32 |
| | 1990/91 | ... | 61 039 | ... | ... | 1 846 338 | ... | ... | 30 |
| | 1991/92 | ... | 63 845 | ... | ... | 2 019 850 | ... | ... | 32 |

II.5 Primary education: schools, teach...
Enseignement primaire: écoles,...
Enseñanza primaria: escuelas,...

| Country / Pays / País | Year / Année / Año | Schools / Écoles / Escuelas | Teaching staff Personnel enseignant Personal docente | | | Pupils enrolled Élèves inscrits Alumnos matriculados | | | Pupil/ teacher ratio Nombre d'élèves par maître |
|---|---|---|---|---|---|---|---|---|---|
| | | | Total | Female Féminin Femenino | % F | Total | Female Féminin Femenino | % F | Número de alumnos por maestro |
| [Ecuador] | 1992/93 | ... | 63 347 | 41 173 | 65 | 1 986 753 | 971 411 | 49 | 31 |
| | 1993/94 | 16 838 | 63 500 | 42 532 | 67 | (38) 1 751 123 | (38) 858 216 | 49 | ... |
| | 1994/95 | (38) 17 194 | (38) 67 446 | (38) 45 817 | 68 | (38) 1 777 304 | (38) 871 017 | 49 | 26 |
| | 1995/96 | ... | (38) 70 162 | (38) 47 750 | 68 | (38) 1 812 255 | (38) 887 701 | 49 | 26 |
| | 1996/97 | (38) 17 367 | (38) 74 601 | (38) 50 160 | 67 | (38) 1 888 172 | (38) 924 561 | 49 | 25 |
| [...] Islands (Malvinas) | 1970 | (32) 42 | (32) 37 | (32) 15 | 41 | (32) 383 | (32) 198 | 52 | 10 |
| | 1975 | 18 | 23 | 11 | 48 | 206 | 99 | 48 | 9 |
| | 1980 | ... | 15 | 5 | 33 | 223 | 130 | 58 | 15 |
| | 1995 | 4 | ... | ... | ... | 199 | 93 | 47 | ... |
| French Guiana | 1970/71 | 51 | 343 | ... | ... | 8 322 | 4 137 | 50 | 24 |
| | 1975/76 | 46 | 259 | ... | ... | 7 594 | ... | ... | 29 |
| | 1980/81 | ... | ... | ... | ... | 9 276 | ... | ... | ... |
| | 1990/91 | ... | ... | ... | ... | 14 256 | ... | ... | ... |
| | 1991/92 | ... | ... | ... | ... | 14 924 | ... | ... | ... |
| | 1992/93 | ... | ... | ... | ... | 15 996 | ... | ... | ... |
| | 1993/94 | 78 | ... | ... | ... | 15 839 | 7 651 | 48 | ... |
| | 1994/95 | ... | ... | ... | ... | (21) 16 449 | ... | ... | ... |
| | 1995/96 | ... | 802 | 593 | 74 | 17 006 | 8 268 | 49 | 21 |
| Guyana | 1970/71 | (3) 388 | (3) 4 485 | (3) 2 460 | 55 | (3) 130 484 | (3) 63 914 | 49 | 29 |
| | 1975/76 | ... | 4 052 | 2 791 | 69 | 130 240 | 64 015 | 49 | 32 |
| | 1980/81 | 425 | 3 909 | 2 721 | 70 | 130 832 | 64 242 | 49 | 33 |
| | 1985/86 | ... | (36) 3 879 | (36) 2 663 | 69 | 113 857 | 56 072 | 49 | ... |
| | 1990/91 | 417 | 3 509 | 2 670 | 76 | 104 241 | 51 283 | 49 | 30 |
| | 1991/92 | 417 | 3 657 | 2 867 | 78 | 100 116 | 49 193 | 49 | 27 |
| | 1992/93 | 417 | 3 669 | 2 917 | 80 | 98 134 | 48 385 | 49 | 27 |
| | 1993/94 | ... | 3 453 | ... | ... | 98 132 | ... | ... | 28 |
| | 1994/95 | 422 | 3 417 | 2 742 | 80 | 99 664 | 48 974 | 49 | 29 |
| | 1995/96 | ... | 3 345 | ... | ... | 100 252 | 49 232 | 49 | 30 |
| | 1996/97 | 420 | 3 461 | 2 935 | 85 | 102 000 | 50 225 | 49 | 29 |
| Paraguay | 1970 | (6) 3 045 | (33) 13 135 | ... | ... | (33) 424 179 | (33) 199 480 | 47 | 32 |
| | 1975 | ... | 15 398 | ... | ... | 452 249 | 214 459 | 47 | 29 |
| | 1980 | ... | 18 948 | ... | ... | 518 968 | 246 876 | 48 | 27 |
| | 1985 | 3 923 | 22 764 | ... | ... | 570 775 | 272 656 | 48 | 25 |
| | 1990 | 4 602 | 27 831 | ... | ... | 687 331 | 331 801 | 48 | 25 |
| | 1991 | 4 649 | 29 172 | ... | ... | 720 983 | 348 760 | 48 | 25 |
| | 1992 | 4 807 | 32 732 | 18 034 | 55 | 749 336 | 361 929 | 48 | 23 |
| | 1993 | 5 172 | 33 061 | ... | ... | 798 981 | 386 548 | 48 | 24 |
| | 1994 | 5 318 | 34 580 | ... | ... | 835 089 | 403 900 | 48 | 24 |
| | 1995 | ... | ... | ... | ... | 862 940 | 418 151 | 48 | ... |
| | 1996 | 5 928 | 41 713 | ... | ... | 895 777 | 434 120 | 48 | 21 |
| | 1997 | ... | ... | ... | ... | 905 813 | 439 131 | 48 | ... |
| Peru | 1970 | 18 439 | 65 965 | ... | ... | 2 341 068 | 1 074 300 | 46 | 35 |
| | 1975 | 19 701 | 72 641 | ... | ... | 2 840 625 | ... | ... | 39 |
| | 1980 | 20 776 | 84 360 | 50 676 | 60 | 3 161 375 | 1 514 621 | 48 | 37 |
| | 1985 | 24 327 | 106 600 | 64 036 | 60 | 3 711 592 | 1 787 244 | 48 | 35 |
| | 1990 | 28 123 | 132 556 | ... | ... | 3 855 282 | ... | ... | 29 |
| | 1991 | 28 265 | 134 687 | ... | ... | 3 857 465 | 1 873 956 | 49 | 29 |
| | 1992 | 28 712 | 135 502 | ... | ... | 3 853 098 | ... | ... | 28 |
| | 1993 | 30 172 | 133 080 | ... | ... | 3 914 291 | ... | ... | 29 |
| | 1994 | (21) 31 315 | (21) 145 795 | ... | ... | (21) 4 031 359 | ... | ... | 28 |
| | 1995 | 31 939 | 146 242 | 84 372 | 58 | 4 131 085 | 2 006 951 | 49 | 28 |
| | 1996 | 32 383 | 151 664 | ... | ... | 4 159 935 | ... | ... | 27 |
| | 1997 | 33 017 | 153 951 | ... | ... | 4 163 180 | ... | ... | 27 |
| | 1998 | ... | ... | ... | ... | 4 185 489 | ... | ... | ... |
| Suriname | 1970/71 | 270 | 2 487 | 1 542 | 62 | 91 834 | 44 080 | 48 | 37 |
| | 1975/76 | 309 | 2 552 | 1 659 | 65 | 80 171 | 38 248 | 48 | 31 |
| | 1980/81 | ... | 2 803 | ... | ... | 74 538 | ... | ... | 27 |
| | 1985/86 | ... | 3 010 | 2 498 | 83 | 69 963 | 33 658 | 48 | 23 |
| | 1990/91 | ... | 2 686 | 2 258 | 84 | 60 085 | 29 489 | 49 | 22 |
| | 1991/92 | ... | 2 982 | 2 580 | 87 | 73 407 | 35 762 | 49 | 25 |
| | 1992/93 | ... | 3 695 | 3 223 | 87 | 79 162 | 37 878 | 48 | 21 |
| | 1993/94 | ... | ... | ... | ... | 87 882 | 43 359 | 49 | ... |
| Uruguay | 1970 | 2 312 | 12 009 | ... | ... | 354 096 | 169 175 | 48 | 29 |
| | 1975 | 2 308 | 13 572 | ... | ... | 322 602 | 156 947 | 49 | 24 |
| | 1980 | 2 294 | 14 768 | ... | ... | 331 247 | 161 293 | 49 | 22 |
| | 1985 | 2 360 | 14 193 | ... | ... | 356 002 | 173 382 | 49 | 25 |
| | 1990 | 2 393 | 15 827 | ... | ... | 346 416 | 168 783 | 49 | 22 |
| | 1991 | 2 413 | 15 747 | ... | ... | 340 789 | 165 939 | 49 | 22 |
| | 1992 | 2 419 | 16 376 | ... | ... | 338 020 | 164 322 | 49 | 21 |
| | 1993 | ... | ... | ... | ... | 338 204 | 164 433 | 49 | ... |
| | 1994 | 2 423 | 15 793 | ... | ... | 337 889 | 164 167 | 49 | 21 |
| | 1995 | 2 424 | 16 991 | ... | ... | 341 197 | 165 731 | 49 | 20 |
| | 1996 | 2 415 | 16 868 | ... | ... | 345 573 | 168 066 | 49 | 20 |
| Venezuela | 1970/71 | (6) 10 509 | 50 822 | 43 617 | 86 | 1 769 680 | 878 860 | 50 | 35 |
| | 1975/76 | 11 532 | 69 466 | ... | ... | 2 108 413 | 1 041 196 | 49 | 30 |
| | 1980/81 | ... | (39) 92 551 | ... | ... | (18) 3 158 466 | ... | ... | ... |
| | 1985/86 | 13 184 | (39) 108 125 | (39) 90 249 | 83 | 3 539 890 | 1 767 085 | 50 | ... |
| | 1990/91 | 15 445 | 177 049 | 131 855 | 74 | 4 052 947 | 2 018 163 | 50 | 23 |

Primary education: schools, teaching staff and pupils
Enseignement primaire: écoles, personnel enseignant et élèves
Enseñanza primaria: escuelas, personal docente y alumnos

II.5

| Country / Pays / País | Year / Année / Año | Schools / Écoles / Escuelas | Teaching staff / Personnel enseignant / Personal docente | | | Pupils enrolled / Élèves inscrits / Alumnos matriculados | | | Pupil/teacher ratio / Nombre d'élèves par maître / Número de alumnos por maestro |
|---|---|---|---|---|---|---|---|---|---|
| | | | Total | Female Féminin Femenino | % F | Total | Female Féminin Femenino | % F | |
| Venezuela (cont) | 1991/92 | 15 800 | 183 298 | 136 274 | 74 | 4 190 047 | 2 081 105 | 50 | 23 |
| | 1992/93 | 15 984 | 184 321 | 137 111 | 74 | 4 222 035 | 2 095 340 | 50 | 23 |
| | 1993/94 | ... | 185 748 | 138 450 | 75 | 4 217 283 | 2 094 806 | 50 | 23 |
| | 1994/95 | ... | 194 358 | 147 060 | 76 | 4 249 389 | 2 124 957 | 50 | 22 |
| | 1995/96 | ... | 198 231 | 151 023 | 76 | 4 120 418 | 2 051 357 | 50 | 21 |
| | 1996/97 | ... | 202 195 | 152 499 | 75 | 4 262 221 | 2 116 715 | 50 | 21 |
| **Asia** | | | | | | | | | |
| Afghanistan | 1970 | 3 020 | 13 116 | 2 183 | 17 | 540 685 | 76 143 | 14 | 41 |
| | 1975 | (40) 3 371 | (40)(41) 18 558 | (40)(41) 3 353 | 18 | (40) 784 568 | (40) 115 795 | 15 | ... |
| | 1980 | 3 824 | 35 364 | 7 413 | 21 | 1 115 993 | 198 580 | 18 | 32 |
| | 1985 | 792 | 15 581 | 8 223 | 53 | 580 499 | 179 027 | 31 | 37 |
| | 1990 | (19) 586 | (19) 15 106 | (19) 8 874 | 59 | (19) 622 513 | (19) 211 667 | 34 | 41 |
| | 1991 | 577 | ... | ... | ... | 627 888 | 212 488 | 34 | ... |
| | 1993 | 1 753 | 16 160 | 6 662 | 41 | 786 532 | 192 920 | 25 | 49 |
| | 1994 | ... | 20 055 | 7 557 | 38 | 1 161 444 | 367 866 | 32 | 58 |
| | 1995 | ... | ... | ... | ... | 1 312 197 | 420 270 | 32 | ... |
| Armenia | 1993/94 | ... | 12 908 | 12 340 | 96 | 266 076 | 134 505 | 51 | 21 |
| | 1995/96 | ... | 11 341 | 11 003 | 97 | 249 872 | ... | ... | 22 |
| | 1996/97 | 1 402 | 13 620 | ... | ... | 256 475 | ... | ... | 19 |
| Azerbaijan | 1980/81 | ... | ... | ... | ... | 473 298 | ... | ... | ... |
| | 1985/86 | ... | ... | ... | ... | 487 748 | ... | ... | ... |
| | 1990/91 | ... | ... | ... | ... | 527 370 | 255 820 | 49 | ... |
| | 1991/92 | ... | ... | ... | ... | 539 234 | 262 633 | 49 | ... |
| | 1992/93 | 4 368 | ... | ... | ... | 553 862 | 267 946 | 48 | ... |
| | 1993/94 | 4 406 | 30 098 | 23 000 | 76 | 580 266 | 275 589 | 47 | 19 |
| | 1994/95 | ... | 31 167 | 26 206 | 84 | 606 903 | 311 777 | 51 | 19 |
| | 1995/96 | (42) 4 462 | (42) 34 201 | (42) 28 415 | 83 | (42) 697 510 | (42) 352 154 | 50 | 20 |
| | 1996/97 | 4 454 | 35 514 | 28 352 | 80 | 719 013 | 344 305 | 48 | 20 |
| Bahrain | 1970/71 | 81 | ... | ... | ... | 38 711 | *16 313 | *42 | ... |
| | 1975/76 | ... | (43) 2 044 | (43) 946 | 46 | 44 857 | 19 569 | 44 | ... |
| | 1980/81 | ... | (3)(43) 2 577 | (3)(43) 1 242 | 48 | 48 451 | 22 439 | 46 | ... |
| | 1985/86 | ... | (3)(43) 2 856 | (3)(43) 1 359 | 48 | 57 330 | 28 181 | 49 | ... |
| | 1990/91 | (3)(43) 112 | (3)(43) 3 092 | (3)(43) 1 489 | 48 | 66 597 | 32 466 | 49 | ... |
| | 1991/92 | (3)(43) 114 | (3)(43) 3 085 | (3)(43) 1 483 | 48 | 66 694 | 32 490 | 49 | ... |
| | 1992/93 | (3)(43) 114 | (3)(43) 3 312 | (3)(43) 2 000 | 60 | 68 898 | 33 716 | 49 | ... |
| | 1993/94 | (3)(43) 118 | (3)(43) 3 386 | (3)(43) 2 100 | 62 | 70 513 | 34 612 | 49 | ... |
| | 1994/95 | (3)(43) 124 | (3)(43) 3 536 | (3)(43) 2 309 | 65 | 72 329 | 35 446 | 49 | ... |
| | 1995/96 | ... | ... | ... | ... | 72 526 | 35 443 | 49 | ... |
| | 1996/97 | ... | ... | ... | ... | 72 876 | 35 465 | 49 | ... |
| Bangladesh | 1970 | 29 082 | 113 673 | ... | ... | 5 283 787 | 1 693 057 | 32 | 46 |
| | 1975 | 39 914 | 164 717 | 8 397 | 5 | 8 349 834 | 2 839 021 | 34 | 51 |
| | 1980 | 43 936 | 153 859 | 12 128 | 8 | 8 240 169 | 3 044 989 | 37 | 54 |
| | 1985 | 44 180 | 189 900 | 15 192 | 8 | 8 920 292 | 3 568 116 | 40 | 47 |
| | 1990 | 45 917 | 189 508 | 36 727 | 19 | 11 939 949 | 5 346 707 | 45 | 63 |
| Bhutan | 1970 | ... | (32) 436 | (32) 60 | 14 | 9 039 | 456 | 5 | ... |
| | 1980 | ... | ... | ... | ... | 29 899 | ... | ... | ... |
| | 1985 | 145 | ... | ... | ... | 45 395 | 15 579 | 34 | ... |
| | 1992 | ... | ... | ... | ... | (44) 51 411 | ... | ... | ... |
| | 1993 | 235 | 1 859 | ... | ... | 56 773 | 24 207 | 43 | 31 |
| | 1994 | ... | ... | ... | ... | 60 089 | 25 924 | 43 | ... |
| Brunei Darussalam | 1970 | 128 | 1 190 | 481 | 40 | 27 941 | 13 356 | 48 | 23 |
| | 1975 | 139 | 1 582 | 684 | 43 | 30 109 | 14 324 | 48 | 19 |
| | 1980 | 137 | 1 671 | 760 | 45 | 30 513 | 14 550 | 48 | 18 |
| | 1985 | 140 | 2 165 | ... | ... | 34 815 | ... | ... | 16 |
| | 1991 | 149 | 2 543 | 1 444 | 57 | 38 933 | 18 368 | 47 | 15 |
| | 1992 | 151 | 2 561 | 1 477 | 58 | 39 782 | 18 820 | 47 | 16 |
| | 1993 | 158 | 2 646 | 1 570 | 59 | 41 134 | 19 537 | 47 | 16 |
| | 1994 | 158 | 2 772 | 1 666 | 60 | 42 270 | 19 991 | 47 | 15 |
| | 1995 | 158 | 2 924 | 1 700 | 58 | 42 672 | 20 059 | 47 | 15 |
| | 1996 | 160 | ... | ... | ... | 43 291 | 20 447 | 47 | ... |
| Cambodia | 1970/71 | 1 490 | 20 046 | (3) 2 945 | ... | 337 729 | (3) 138 884 | ... | 17 |
| | 1980/81 | ... | 30 316 | ... | ... | 1 328 053 | ... | ... | 44 |
| | 1985/86 | 4 294 | 35 080 | 8 704 | 25 | 1 315 531 | 596 487 | 45 | 38 |
| | 1990/91 | (44) 4 617 | (44) 40 820 | (44) 12 532 | 31 | (44) 1 329 573 | ... | ... | 33 |
| | 1993/94 | ... | 37 616 | 13 561 | 36 | 1 621 685 | 727 060 | 45 | 43 |
| | 1994/95 | ... | 37 827 | 14 071 | 37 | 1 703 316 | 756 135 | 44 | 45 |
| | 1996/97 | (45) 4 899 | (45) 43 205 | (45) 15 738 | 36 | (45) 1 918 985 | (45) 860 700 | 45 | 44 |
| | 1997/98 | 5 026 | 43 282 | 15 816 | 37 | 2 011 772 | 906 827 | 45 | 46 |
| China | 1970/71 | 961 131 | 3 612 000 | ... | ... | 105 280 000 | ... | ... | 29 |
| | 1975/76 | 1 093 317 | 5 203 000 | 1 888 500 | 36 | 150 941 000 | 68 243 000 | 45 | 29 |
| | 1980/81 | 917 316 | 5 499 400 | 2 039 100 | 37 | 146 270 000 | 65 174 000 | 45 | 27 |
| | 1985/86 | 832 309 | 5 376 800 | 2 127 900 | 40 | 133 701 800 | 59 862 200 | 45 | 25 |
| | 1990/91 | 766 072 | 5 581 810 | 2 408 800 | 43 | 122 413 800 | 56 555 200 | 46 | 22 |
| | 1991/92 | 729 158 | 5 532 300 | 2 422 700 | 44 | 121 641 500 | 56 546 400 | 46 | 22 |

II.5   Primary education: schools, teaching staff and pupils
Enseignement primaire: écoles, personnel enseignant et élèves
Enseñanza primaria: escuelas, personal docente y alumnos

| Country / Pays / País | Year / Année / Año | Schools / Écoles / Escuelas | Teaching staff / Personnel enseignant / Personal docente | | | Pupils enrolled / Élèves inscrits / Alumnos matriculados | | | Pupil/ teacher ratio / Nombre d'élèves par maître / Número de alumnos por maestro |
|---|---|---|---|---|---|---|---|---|---|
| | | | Total | Female Féminin Femenino | % F | Total | Female Féminin Femenino | % F | |
| China (cont) | 1992/93 | 712 973 | 5 526 500 | 2 458 500 | 44 | 122 012 800 | 56 856 000 | 47 | 22 |
| | 1993/94 | 696 681 | 5 551 600 | 2 506 900 | 45 | 124 212 400 | 58 159 000 | 47 | 22 |
| | 1994/95 | 685 588 | 5 611 324 | 2 569 827 | 46 | 128 226 233 | 60 353 001 | 47 | 23 |
| | 1995/96 | 668 685 | 5 664 057 | 2 640 040 | 47 | 131 951 477 | 62 410 771 | 47 | 23 |
| | 1996/97 | 645 983 | 5 735 790 | 2 718 842 | 47 | 136 150 042 | 64 670 134 | 47 | 24 |
| | 1997/98 | 628 840 | 5 794 000 | 2 797 000 | 48 | 139 954 000 | 66 660 000 | 48 | 24 |
| China, Hong Kong SAR | 1970/71 | 1 547 | 22 383 | 14 610 | 65 | 739 619 | 350 450 | 47 | 33 |
| | 1975/76 | 1 126 | 20 666 | 14 172 | 69 | 642 611 | 308 075 | 48 | 31 |
| | 1980/81 | 803 | 17 937 | 13 015 | 73 | 540 260 | 258 685 | 48 | 30 |
| | 1985/86 | 1 017 | 19 404 | ... | ... | 534 903 | 254 966 | 48 | 28 |
| | 1990/91 | 972 | 19 518 | ... | ... | 524 919 | *253 540 | *48 | 27 |
| | 1991/92 | 969 | 19 346 | ... | ... | 515 938 | *249 200 | *48 | 27 |
| | 1992/93 | 946 | 18 790 | ... | ... | 501 625 | *242 280 | *48 | 27 |
| | 1993/94 | 920 | 19 122 | ... | ... | 485 061 | *234 280 | *48 | 25 |
| | 1994/95 | 884 | ... | ... | ... | 476 847 | *232 220 | *49 | ... |
| | 1995/96 | 860 | 19 710 | 15 001 | 76 | 467 718 | 226 190 | 48 | 24 |
| Cyprus (46) | 1970/71 | 565 | 2 280 | 914 | 40 | 69 160 | 33 472 | 48 | 30 |
| | 1975/76 | 402 | 2 101 | 916 | 44 | 56 602 | 27 388 | 48 | 27 |
| | 1980/81 | 443 | 2 193 | 993 | 45 | 48 701 | 23 789 | 49 | 22 |
| | 1985/86 | 380 | 2 239 | 1 106 | 49 | 50 990 | 24 646 | 48 | 23 |
| | 1990/91 | 383 | 3 069 | 1 840 | 60 | 62 962 | 30 379 | 48 | 21 |
| | 1991/92 | 390 | 3 286 | 2 042 | 62 | 63 454 | 30 511 | 48 | 19 |
| | 1992/93 | 391 | 3 410 | 2 158 | 63 | 64 313 | 31 008 | 48 | 19 |
| | 1993/94 | 381 | 3 456 | 2 229 | 64 | 64 907 | 31 370 | 48 | 19 |
| | 1994/95 | 383 | 3 528 | 2 303 | 65 | 64 884 | 31 368 | 48 | 18 |
| | 1995/96 | 381 | 3 452 | 2 256 | 65 | 64 660 | 31 126 | 48 | 19 |
| | 1996/97 | 376 | 4 202 | 2 892 | 69 | 64 761 | 31 350 | 48 | 15 |
| Georgia | 1980/81 | ... | 16 944 | 15 049 | 89 | 322 292 | 158 361 | 49 | 19 |
| | 1985/86 | ... | 17 992 | 16 021 | 89 | 311 458 | 152 790 | 49 | 17 |
| | 1990/91 | ... | 20 473 | 18 888 | 92 | 352 393 | 172 879 | 49 | 17 |
| | 1991/92 | ... | 20 281 | 18 942 | 93 | 344 447 | 168 936 | 49 | 17 |
| | 1992/93 | ... | 18 400 | 16 980 | 92 | 309 153 | 151 564 | 49 | 17 |
| | 1993/94 | ... | 18 275 | 17 149 | 94 | 301 732 | 142 519 | 47 | 17 |
| | 1994/95 | 3 170 | 18 022 | 16 513 | 92 | 291 175 | 141 206 | 48 | 16 |
| | 1995/96 | 3 187 | 17 950 | 16 914 | 94 | 288 509 | 141 550 | 49 | 16 |
| | 1996/97 | 3 201 | 16 542 | 15 638 | 95 | 293 325 | 142 096 | 48 | 18 |
| India | 1970/71 | 408 378 | 1 376 176 | 334 852 | 24 | 57 045 441 | 21 306 280 | 37 | 41 |
| | 1975/76 | 453 530 | 1 559 137 | 387 122 | 25 | 65 660 022 | 25 010 985 | 38 | 42 |
| | 1980/81 | 485 538 | (6)(47) 1 345 376 | (6)(47) 343 399 | 26 | 73 873 184 | 28 537 132 | 39 | ... |
| | 1985/86 | 528 079 | (6)(47) 1 509 910 | (6)(47) 414 373 | 27 | 87 440 514 | 35 193 740 | 40 | ... |
| | 1990/91 | 558 392 | (6)(47) 1 636 898 | (6)(47) 470 414 | 29 | 99 118 320 | 41 023 604 | 41 | ... |
| | 1991/92 | 565 786 | (6)(47) 1 693 014 | (6)(47) 498 934 | 29 | 101 577 089 | 42 359 096 | 42 | ... |
| | 1992/93 | 572 541 | (6)(47) 1 681 970 | (6)(47) 492 966 | 29 | 105 370 216 | 44 915 896 | 43 | ... |
| | 1993/94 | 572 923 | (6)(47) 1 703 164 | (6)(47) 506 913 | 30 | 108 200 539 | 46 396 230 | 43 | ... |
| | 1994/95 | 581 305 | (6)(47) 1 714 395 | (6)(47) 533 117 | 31 | 109 043 663 | 46 786 705 | 43 | ... |
| | 1995/96 | 590 421 | (6)(47) 1 740 436 | (6)(47) 553 166 | 32 | 109 734 292 | 47 373 540 | 43 | ... |
| | 1996/97 | 598 354 | (6)(47) 1 789 733 | (6)(47) 584 953 | 33 | 110 390 406 | 47 891 749 | 43 | ... |
| Indonesia | 1970 | 64 040 | 514 007 | 163 454 | 32 | 14 870 220 | 6 780 820 | 46 | 29 |
| | 1975 | 72 760 | 603 327 | ... | ... | 17 776 617 | 8 088 266 | 45 | 29 |
| | 1980/81 | 128 875 | 787 400 | ... | ... | 25 537 053 | 11 786 487 | 46 | 32 |
| | 1985/86 | 168 555 | 1 181 807 | ... | ... | 29 897 115 | 14 320 934 | 48 | 25 |
| | 1990/91 | 169 133 | 1 281 407 | 647 583 | 51 | 29 753 576 | 14 479 304 | 49 | 23 |
| | 1991/92 | 170 780 | 1 261 089 | 636 590 | 50 | 29 577 704 | 14 461 795 | 49 | 23 |
| | 1992/93 | 171 455 | 1 276 217 | 656 338 | 51 | 29 598 790 | 14 354 056 | 48 | 23 |
| | 1993/94 | 173 921 | 1 296 103 | 674 701 | 52 | 29 876 196 | 14 464 611 | 48 | 23 |
| | 1994/95 | 173 696 | 1 311 571 | 685 354 | 52 | 29 721 859 | 14 363 989 | 48 | 23 |
| | 1995/96 | ... | 1 317 976 | 688 785 | 52 | 29 447 990 | 14 232 266 | 48 | 22 |
| | 1996/97 | 173 893 | 1 327 178 | ... | ... | 29 236 283 | 14 129 948 | 48 | 22 |
| Iran, Islamic Republic of | 1970/71 | 25 758 | 105 295 | 47 576 | 45 | 3 415 650 | 1 206 720 | 35 | 32 |
| | 1975/76 | (14) 36 738 | (14) 152 106 | (14) 79 492 | 52 | (14) 4 468 299 | (14) 1 685 364 | 38 | 29 |
| | 1980/81 | 39 213 | ... | ... | ... | 4 799 000 | ... | ... | ... |
| | 1985/86 | 50 432 | 309 736 | 160 231 | 52 | 6 788 323 | 2 960 218 | 44 | 22 |
| | 1990/91 | 59 280 | 298 759 | 158 109 | 53 | 9 369 646 | 4 328 327 | 46 | 31 |
| | 1991/92 | 60 672 | 312 273 | 168 787 | 54 | 9 787 593 | 4 563 250 | 47 | 31 |
| | 1992/93 | 61 323 | 311 839 | 172 679 | 55 | 9 937 369 | 4 666 836 | 47 | 32 |
| | 1993/94 | 61 683 | 311 531 | 172 564 | 55 | 9 862 817 | 4 652 405 | 47 | 32 |
| | 1994/95 | 61 889 | (3) 305 380 | (3) 167 611 | 55 | 9 745 600 | 4 594 053 | 47 | ... |
| | 1996/97 | 63 101 | 298 755 | 164 729 | 55 | 9 238 393 | 4 352 728 | 47 | 31 |
| Iraq | 1970/71 | 5 616 | 49 822 | 16 957 | 34 | 1 098 865 | 318 509 | 29 | 22 |
| | 1975/76 | 7 595 | 69 812 | 25 557 | 37 | 1 776 095 | 591 613 | 33 | 25 |
| | 1980/81 | 11 284 | 94 000 | 45 516 | 48 | 2 615 910 | 1 212 828 | 46 | 28 |
| | 1985/86 | 8 127 | 118 442 | 79 063 | 67 | 2 816 326 | 1 260 383 | 45 | 24 |
| | 1990/91 | 8 917 | 134 081 | 94 029 | 70 | 3 328 212 | 1 479 897 | 44 | 25 |
| | 1992/93 | 8 003 | 131 271 | 89 684 | 68 | 2 857 467 | 1 277 056 | 45 | 22 |
| | 1995/96 | 8 145 | 145 455 | 103 270 | 71 | 2 903 923 | 1 301 852 | 45 | 20 |
| Israel | 1970/71 | 1 587 | 27 780 | ... | ... | 478 951 | 229 917 | 48 | 17 |
| | 1975/76 | 1 503 | (48) 32 657 | ... | ... | 535 320 | 261 338 | 49 | ... |
| | 1980/81 | 1 576 | (48) 41 468 | ... | ... | 621 912 | ... | ... | ... |

Primary education: schools, teaching staff and pupils
Enseignement primaire: écoles, personnel enseignant et élèves
Enseñanza primaria: escuelas, personal docente y alumnos

II.5

| Country / Pays / País | Year / Année / Año | Schools / Écoles / Escuelas | | Teaching staff Personnel enseignant Personal docente | | | | Pupils enrolled Élèves inscrits Alumnos matriculados | | | | Pupil/ teacher ratio Nombre d'élèves par maître Número de alumnos por maestro |
|---|---|---|---|---|---|---|---|---|---|---|---|---|
| | | | | | Total | Female Féminin Femenino | % F | | Total | Female Féminin Femenino | % F | |
| Israel (cont) | 1985/86 | | 1 621 | (48) | 41 943 | ... | ... | | 699 476 | 345 943 | 49 | ... |
| | 1990/91 | | 1 514 | (48) | 40 571 | (48) 33 346 | 82 | | 724 502 | 357 997 | 49 | ... |
| | 1991/92 | | 1 525 | (48) | 43 248 | (48) 35 824 | 83 | | 748 069 | 365 124 | 49 | ... |
| | 1992/93 | | 1 533 | (48) | 47 299 | (48) 39 631 | 84 | | 763 511 | 372 667 | 49 | ... |
| | 1993/94 | | ... | (48) | 48 010 | (48) 40 255 | 84 | | 780 575 | 380 433 | 49 | ... |
| | 1994/95 | | ... | | ... | ... | ... | (49) | 618 513 | ... | ... | ... |
| | 1995/96 | | ... | | ... | ... | ... | (49) | 631 916 | ... | ... | ... |
| Japan | 1970/71 | | 25 034 | | 364 906 | 191 872 | 53 | | 9 630 815 | 4 706 222 | 49 | 26 |
| | 1975/76 | | 24 650 | | 402 553 | 228 728 | 57 | | 10 364 846 | 5 056 696 | 49 | 26 |
| | 1980/81 | | 24 945 | | 470 991 | 266 971 | 57 | | 11 826 573 | 5 764 765 | 49 | 25 |
| | 1985/86 | | 25 040 | | 464 173 | 260 169 | 56 | | 11 095 372 | 5 412 882 | 49 | 24 |
| | 1990/91 | | 24 827 | | 452 849 | 264 513 | 58 | | 9 373 295 | 4 575 098 | 49 | 21 |
| | 1991/92 | | 24 798 | | 453 379 | 268 663 | 59 | | 9 157 429 | 4 471 355 | 49 | 20 |
| | 1992/93 | | 24 730 | (50) | 440 769 | (50) 263 635 | 60 | | 8 947 226 | 4 369 221 | 49 | ... |
| | 1993/94 | | 24 676 | | 461 729 | 278 060 | 60 | | 8 798 082 | 4 293 958 | 49 | 19 |
| | 1994/95 | | 24 635 | | 464 431 | 276 887 | 60 | | 8 612 106 | 4 202 583 | 49 | 19 |
| | 1995/96 | | 24 548 | (50) | 430 958 | (50) 263 626 | 61 | | 8 370 246 | 4 087 655 | 49 | ... |
| | 1996/97 | | 24 482 | (50) | 425 714 | (50) 262 237 | 62 | | 8 105 629 | 3 957 411 | 49 | ... |
| | 1997/98 | | 24 376 | (50) | 420 901 | (50) 261 117 | 62 | | 7 855 387 | 3 835 146 | 49 | ... |
| Jordan (51) | 1970/71 | | 865 | | 7 150 | 3 278 | 46 | | 277 619 | 122 087 | 44 | 39 |
| | 1975/76 | | 1 165 | | 11 136 | 5 719 | 51 | | 386 012 | 179 394 | 46 | 35 |
| | 1980/81 | | 1 115 | | 14 303 | 8 416 | 59 | | 454 391 | 216 578 | 48 | 32 |
| | 1985/86 | | 1 239 | | 16 979 | 11 193 | 66 | | 530 906 | 253 437 | 48 | 31 |
| | 1990/91 | (8) | 2 457 | (8) | 36 930 | (8) 22 792 | 62 | (8) | 926 445 | (8) 448 098 | 48 | 25 |
| | 1991/92 | | 2 424 | | 40 694 | 24 197 | 59 | | 981 255 | 480 723 | 49 | 24 |
| | 1992/93 | | 2 441 | | 45 871 | 27 962 | 61 | | 1 014 295 | 497 866 | 49 | 22 |
| | 1993/94 | | 2 479 | | 48 150 | 29 128 | 60 | | 1 036 079 | 508 601 | 49 | 22 |
| | 1994/95 | | 2 492 | | 49 110 | 27 368 | 56 | | 1 074 855 | 528 760 | 49 | 22 |
| | 1995/96 | | 2 531 | | 51 721 | 31 491 | 61 | | 1 074 877 | 525 966 | 49 | 21 |
| | 1996/97 | | 2 575 | | 51 466 | 31 604 | 61 | | 1 086 641 | 532 214 | 49 | 21 |
| | 1997/98 | | 2 623 | | 45 367 | 28 164 | 62 | | 1 121 866 | 551 385 | 49 | 25 |
| Kazakstan | 1980/81 | | ... | | ... | ... | ... | | 1 064 000 | ... | ... | ... |
| | 1985/86 | | ... | | 44 700 | 42 800 | 96 | | 1 147 700 | ... | ... | 26 |
| | 1990/91 | | ... | | 56 300 | 54 200 | 96 | | 1 197 300 | ... | ... | 21 |
| | 1991/92 | | ... | | 60 900 | 59 200 | 97 | | 1 223 100 | ... | ... | 20 |
| | 1992/93 | | ... | | 64 100 | 62 300 | 97 | | 1 240 400 | ... | ... | 19 |
| | 1993/94 | | ... | | 66 700 | 64 800 | 97 | | 1 227 130 | 604 552 | 49 | 18 |
| | 1994/95 | | ... | | ... | ... | ... | | 1 252 000 | ... | ... | ... |
| | 1995/96 | | 8 611 | | ... | ... | ... | | 1 372 600 | 676 300 | 49 | ... |
| | 1996/97 | | ... | | ... | ... | ... | | 1 342 035 | 662 671 | 49 | ... |
| Korea, Republic of | 1970/71 | | 5 961 | | 101 095 | 29 428 | 29 | | 5 749 301 | 2 754 648 | 48 | 57 |
| | 1975/76 | | 6 367 | | 108 126 | 36 440 | 34 | | 5 599 074 | 2 709 133 | 48 | 52 |
| | 1980/81 | | 6 487 | | 119 064 | 43 792 | 37 | | 5 658 002 | 2 745 382 | 49 | 48 |
| | 1985/86 | | 6 519 | | 126 785 | 54 600 | 43 | (52) | 4 856 752 | (52) 2 357 028 | 49 | 38 |
| | 1990/91 | | 6 335 | | 136 800 | 68 604 | 50 | | 4 868 520 | 2 362 050 | 49 | 36 |
| | 1991/92 | | 6 245 | | 138 207 | 71 326 | 52 | | 4 758 505 | 2 306 271 | 48 | 34 |
| | 1992/93 | | 6 122 | | 138 945 | 73 249 | 53 | | 4 560 128 | 2 204 629 | 48 | 33 |
| | 1993/94 | | 6 058 | | 142 201 | 76 494 | 54 | | 4 347 317 | 2 095 930 | 48 | 31 |
| | 1994/95 | | 5 914 | | 123 905 | 72 561 | 59 | | 4 110 302 | 1 975 372 | 48 | 33 |
| | 1995/96 | | 5 881 | | 123 074 | 73 227 | 59 | | 3 915 848 | 1 873 071 | 48 | 32 |
| | 1996/97 | | 5 733 | | 122 265 | 74 659 | 61 | | 3 810 932 | 1 813 066 | 48 | 31 |
| | 1997/98 | | 5 721 | | 122 743 | 76 831 | 63 | | 3 794 447 | 1 799 449 | 47 | 31 |
| Kuwait | 1970/71 | (3) | 83 | | 3 555 | 1 967 | 55 | | 75 513 | 31 797 | 42 | 21 |
| | 1975/76 | | 177 | | 6 360 | 3 471 | 55 | | 111 820 | 51 099 | 46 | 18 |
| | 1980/81 | | 238 | | 8 035 | 4 466 | 56 | | 148 983 | 71 249 | 48 | 19 |
| | 1985/86 | | 270 | | 9 623 | 6 586 | 68 | | 172 975 | 84 175 | 49 | 18 |
| | 1990/91 | | ... | | 7 034 | 4 321 | 61 | | 124 996 | 59 920 | 48 | 18 |
| | 1991/92 | | 218 | | 6 967 | 4 401 | 63 | | 114 641 | 56 085 | 49 | 16 |
| | 1992/93 | | 230 | | 7 526 | 5 187 | 69 | | 122 930 | 60 687 | 49 | 16 |
| | 1993/94 | | 239 | | 8 229 | 5 799 | 70 | | 129 956 | 64 123 | 49 | 16 |
| | 1994/95 | | 247 | | 9 021 | 6 399 | 71 | | 131 264 | 65 944 | 50 | 15 |
| | 1995/96 | (21) | 266 | (21) | 9 747 | ... | ... | (21) | 141 841 | (21) 69 397 | 49 | 15 |
| | 1996/97 | | *275 | | 10 180 | 6 384 | 63 | | 143 286 | 70 100 | 49 | 14 |
| | 1997/98 | | 286 | | 10 798 | 6 414 | 59 | | 142 308 | 69 612 | 49 | 13 |
| Kyrgyzstan | 1980/81 | | ... | | 11 000 | 9 700 | 88 | | 306 000 | 149 900 | 49 | 28 |
| | 1985/86 | | ... | | 17 900 | 14 600 | 82 | | 342 600 | 169 400 | 49 | 19 |
| | 1990/91 | | ... | | 22 100 | 17 800 | 81 | | 354 700 | 176 100 | 50 | 16 |
| | 1991/92 | | ... | | 22 600 | 18 600 | 82 | | 361 700 | 180 400 | 50 | 16 |
| | 1992/93 | | ... | | 22 800 | 18 800 | 82 | | 368 500 | 183 500 | 50 | 16 |
| | 1993/94 | | ... | | 23 000 | 18 400 | 80 | | 380 100 | 189 700 | 50 | 17 |
| | 1994/95 | | 1 864 | | 23 259 | 18 964 | 82 | | 386 829 | 192 207 | 50 | 17 |
| | 1995/96 | (42) | 1 885 | (42) | 24 086 | (42) 20 054 | 83 | (42) | 473 077 | (42) 230 420 | 49 | 20 |
| Lao People's Democratic Republic | 1970/71 | | 3 264 | | 6 796 | 1 966 | 29 | | 244 803 | 90 546 | 37 | 36 |
| | 1975/76 | | ... | | 11 848 | ... | ... | | 317 126 | ... | ... | 27 |
| | 1980/81 | (15) | 6 339 | (15) | 16 109 | (15) 4 849 | 30 | (15) | 479 291 | (15) 217 297 | 45 | 30 |
| | 1985/86 | | 8 011 | | 21 033 | 6 744 | 32 | | 523 347 | 234 790 | 45 | 25 |
| | 1990/91 | | ... | | 21 039 | 7 962 | 38 | | 576 472 | 250 150 | 43 | 27 |
| | 1991/92 | | 7 140 | | 21 036 | 8 589 | 41 | | 580 792 | 253 261 | 44 | 28 |
| | 1992/93 | | 7 643 | | 21 652 | 8 988 | 42 | | 637 359 | 277 274 | 44 | 29 |

**Primary education: schools, teaching staff and pupils**
**Enseignement primaire: écoles, personnel enseignant et élèves**
**Enseñanza primaria: escuelas, personal docente y alumnos**

| Country / Pays / País | Year / Année / Año | Schools / Écoles / Escuelas | Teaching staff Personnel enseignant Personal docente | | | Pupils enrolled Élèves inscrits Alumnos matriculados | | | Pupil/ teacher ratio Nombre d'élèves par maître Número de alumnos por maestro |
|---|---|---|---|---|---|---|---|---|---|
| | | | Total | Female Féminin Femenino | % F | Total | Female Féminin Femenino | % F | |
| Lao People's Democratic | 1993/94 | 8 361 | 22 649 | 9 466 | 42 | 681 044 | 295 846 | 43 | 30 |
| Republic (cont) | 1994/95 | ... | 23 455 | 9 794 | 42 | 710 702 | 312 127 | 44 | 30 |
| | 1995/96 | ... | 24 455 | 10 554 | 43 | 757 551 | 333 332 | 44 | 31 |
| | 1996/97 | 7 896 | 25 831 | 10 970 | 42 | 786 335 | 348 094 | 44 | 30 |
| Lebanon | 1970/71 | 1 772 | (32) 34 735 | (32) 17 000 | 49 | 435 066 | 197 157 | 45 | ... |
| | 1980/81 | ... | 22 646 | ... | ... | 405 402 | ... | ... | 18 |
| | 1991/92 | 2 100 | ... | ... | ... | 345 662 | 167 607 | 48 | ... |
| | 1993/94 | ... | ... | ... | ... | 360 858 | 175 395 | 49 | ... |
| | 1994/95 | ... | ... | ... | ... | 365 174 | 176 829 | 48 | ... |
| | 1995/96 | ... | ... | ... | ... | 367 862 | 178 180 | 48 | ... |
| | 1996/97 | 2 160 | ... | ... | ... | *382 309 | *183 666 | *48 | ... |
| Macau | 1970/71 | 88 | 886 | ... | ... | 25 052 | 11 769 | 47 | 28 |
| | 1975/76 | 59 | 753 | ... | ... | 20 758 | ... | ... | 28 |
| | 1990/91 | ... | ... | ... | ... | 34 972 | 16 694 | 48 | ... |
| | 1991/92 | ... | ... | ... | ... | 37 872 | 18 229 | 48 | ... |
| | 1992/93 | ... | ... | ... | ... | 40 665 | 19 556 | 48 | ... |
| Malaysia | 1970 | 6 358 | 54 366 | ... | ... | 1 684 263 | 788 728 | 47 | 31 |
| | 1975 | 6 387 | 59 343 | ... | ... | 1 893 323 | 908 717 | 48 | 32 |
| | 1980 | 6 414 | 73 664 | 32 537 | 44 | 2 008 973 | 975 419 | 49 | 27 |
| | 1985 | 6 685 | 91 424 | 45 753 | 50 | 2 199 096 | 1 068 148 | 49 | 24 |
| | 1990 | ... | 120 505 | 68 490 | 57 | 2 455 525 | 1 194 161 | 49 | 20 |
| | 1991 | 6 922 | 126 139 | 72 097 | 57 | 2 540 623 | 1 235 034 | 49 | 20 |
| | 1992 | ... | 130 482 | 75 928 | 58 | 2 626 297 | 1 278 629 | 49 | 20 |
| | 1993 | ... | 134 579 | 79 280 | 59 | 2 693 632 | 1 311 490 | 49 | 20 |
| | 1994 | 7 021 | 139 343 | 82 408 | 59 | 2 744 993 | 1 338 351 | 49 | 20 |
| | 1995 | ... | (26) 140 430 | (26) 83 640 | 60 | (26) 2 799 744 | (26) 1 363 161 | 49 | 20 |
| | 1996 | ... | 147 128 | 88 754 | 60 | 2 856 613 | 1 390 790 | 49 | 19 |
| | 1997 | ... | *148 000 | *89 000 | *60 | *2 840 667 | *1 385 193 | *49 | *19 |
| Maldives | 1970 | (3) 2 | (3) 29 | (3) 24 | 83 | (3) 648 | (3) 336 | 52 | 22 |
| | 1975 | ... | ... | ... | ... | (3) 1 472 | (3) 728 | 49 | ... |
| | 1980 | ... | ... | ... | ... | 30 621 | ... | ... | ... |
| | 1992 | 134 | ... | ... | ... | 45 333 | 22 188 | 49 | ... |
| | 1993 | ... | ... | ... | ... | 48 321 | 23 586 | 49 | ... |
| | 1994 | ... | ... | ... | ... | 50 915 | 24 695 | 49 | ... |
| | 1995 | ... | ... | ... | ... | 50 733 | 24 513 | 48 | ... |
| | 1996 | ... | ... | ... | ... | 51 220 | 24 770 | 48 | ... |
| | 1997 | 230 | ... | ... | ... | 50 230 | 24 201 | 48 | ... |
| | 1998 | 228 | 1 992 | 1 344 | 67 | 48 895 | 23 435 | 48 | 25 |
| Mongolia | 1970/71 | ... | 4 800 | ... | ... | 146 014 | ... | ... | 30 |
| | 1975/76 | ... | ... | ... | ... | (53) 129 802 | (53) 63 420 | 49 | ... |
| | 1980/81 | ... | 4 496 | 3 921 | 87 | 145 200 | 71 200 | 49 | 32 |
| | 1985/86 | 590 | 5 064 | 4 462 | 88 | 153 100 | 76 453 | 50 | 30 |
| | 1990/91 | 638 | 5 917 | 5 306 | 90 | 166 349 | 83 254 | 50 | 28 |
| | 1991/92 | 643 | 6 230 | 5 638 | 90 | 154 588 | 77 758 | 50 | 25 |
| | 1992/93 | ... | 6 165 | 5 590 | 91 | 138 434 | 69 748 | 50 | 22 |
| | 1993/94 | ... | 6 299 | 5 691 | 90 | 142 132 | 72 264 | 51 | 23 |
| | 1994/95 | 638 | 6 704 | 6 052 | 90 | 158 990 | 80 400 | 51 | 24 |
| | 1995/96 | 650 | 7 088 | 6 439 | 91 | 176 036 | 88 486 | 50 | 25 |
| | 1996/97 | ... | (45) 7 587 | (45) 6 812 | 90 | (45) 234 193 | (45) 118 491 | 51 | 31 |
| Myanmar | 1970/71 | 17 399 | 68 156 | 28 919 | 42 | 3 177 739 | 1 492 027 | 47 | 47 |
| | 1975/76 | 18 670 | 66 251 | ... | ... | 3 475 749 | 1 658 078 | 48 | 52 |
| | 1980/81 | 21 999 | 80 343 | ... | ... | 4 148 342 | 1 994 086 | 48 | 52 |
| | 1985/86 | 31 499 | 87 482 | 51 747 | 59 | 4 710 616 | 2 266 693 | 48 | 54 |
| | 1990/91 | 33 305 | 111 470 | 68 934 | 62 | 5 384 539 | 2 612 608 | 49 | 48 |
| | 1991/92 | 35 468 | 115 793 | 72 969 | 63 | 5 869 297 | 2 845 037 | 48 | 51 |
| | 1992/93 | 35 657 | 118 684 | 75 912 | 64 | 5 919 339 | 2 864 030 | 48 | 50 |
| | 1993/94 | 35 727 | 119 725 | 78 371 | 65 | 5 896 026 | 2 862 322 | 49 | 49 |
| | 1994/95 | 35 741 | 119 942 | 79 963 | 67 | 5 530 502 | 2 677 743 | 48 | 46 |
| | 1995/96 | 35 752 | ... | ... | ... | 5 413 752 | ... | ... | ... |
| Nepal | 1970 | ... | 17 988 | ... | ... | 389 825 | 58 093 | 15 | 22 |
| | 1975 | (53) 8 314 | (53) 18 874 | ... | ... | (53) 542 524 | (53) 84 008 | 15 | 29 |
| | 1980 | 10 130 | 27 805 | 2 681 | 10 | 1 067 912 | 299 512 | 28 | 38 |
| | 1985 | (54) 11 946 | (54) 51 266 | ... | ... | (54) 1 812 098 | (54) 541 649 | 30 | 35 |
| | 1990 | 17 842 | 71 213 | ... | ... | 2 788 644 | 1 003 810 | 36 | 39 |
| | 1991 | 18 694 | 74 495 | 10 206 | 14 | 2 884 275 | 1 073 319 | 37 | 39 |
| | 1992 | 19 498 | 77 948 | 11 685 | 15 | 3 034 710 | 1 161 806 | 38 | 39 |
| | 1993 | 20 217 | 79 590 | 12 771 | 16 | 3 091 684 | 1 195 930 | 39 | 39 |
| | 1994 | 21 102 | 81 544 | ... | ... | 3 191 614 | 1 258 353 | 39 | 39 |
| | 1995 | 21 473 | 82 645 | ... | ... | 3 263 050 | 1 301 640 | 40 | 39 |
| | 1996 | 22 218 | 89 378 | ... | ... | 3 447 607 | 1 401 346 | 41 | 39 |
| Oman | 1970/71 | 16 | 196 | 30 | 15 | 3 478 | 470 | 14 | 18 |
| | 1975/76 | 181 | 2 055 | 550 | 27 | 54 611 | 14 901 | 27 | 27 |
| | 1980/81 | 178 | 3 959 | 1 362 | 34 | 91 895 | 31 455 | 34 | 23 |
| | 1985/86 | 349 | 6 681 | 2 923 | 44 | 177 541 | 78 360 | 44 | 27 |
| | 1990/91 | 431 | 9 551 | 4 486 | 47 | 262 989 | 123 604 | 47 | 28 |
| | 1991/92 | 436 | 10 184 | 4 853 | 48 | 277 370 | 130 783 | 47 | 27 |
| | 1992/93 | 416 | 10 839 | 5 216 | 48 | 289 911 | 137 568 | 47 | 27 |

Primary education: schools, teaching staff and pupils  II.5
Enseignement primaire: écoles, personnel enseignant et élèves
Enseñanza primaria: escuelas, personal docente y alumnos

| Country / Pays / País | Year / Année / Año | Schools / Écoles / Escuelas | Teaching staff / Personnel enseignant / Personal docente — Total | Female / Féminin / Femenino | % F | Pupils enrolled / Élèves inscrits / Alumnos matriculados — Total | Female / Féminin / Femenino | % F | Pupil/teacher ratio / Nombre d'élèves par maître / Número de alumnos por maestro |
|---|---|---|---|---|---|---|---|---|---|
| Oman (cont) | 1993/94 | 415 | 11 158 | 5 507 | 49 | 297 209 | 142 125 | 48 | 27 |
| | 1994/95 | 425 | 11 586 | 5 759 | 50 | 301 999 | 145 072 | 48 | 26 |
| | 1995/96 | 416 | 11 925 | 5 925 | 50 | 307 050 | 147 508 | 48 | 26 |
| | 1996/97 | 429 | ... | ... | ... | 311 955 | 149 580 | 48 | ... |
| | 1997/98 | 411 | 12 052 | 6 059 | 50 | 313 516 | 150 231 | 48 | 26 |
| Pakistan (6) | 1970/71 | 43 710 | 96 288 | 27 183 | 28 | 3 992 934 | 1 061 664 | 27 | 41 |
| | 1975/76 | 52 800 | 130 295 | 44 149 | 34 | 5 236 203 | 1 546 406 | 30 | 40 |
| | 1980/81 | 59 165 | 150 004 | 48 652 | 32 | 5 473 578 | 1 782 378 | 33 | 36 |
| | 1985/86 | 77 207 | 180 622 | 57 237 | 32 | 7 094 059 | 2 365 408 | 33 | 39 |
| | 1990/91 | ... | 271 100 | 71 900 | 27 | 11 451 000 | 3 689 000 | 32 | 42 |
| | 1991/92 | ... | 283 100 | ... | ... | 12 721 000 | 4 036 000 | 32 | 45 |
| | 1992/93 | ... | ... | ... | ... | 14 120 000 | 4 425 000 | 31 | ... |
| | 1993/94 | ... | ... | ... | ... | 15 532 000 | 4 771 000 | 31 | ... |
| Philippines | 1970/71 | 23 804 | 243 833 | 196 680 | 81 | 6 968 978 | ... | ... | 29 |
| | 1975/76 | 30 839 | 261 817 | ... | ... | 7 597 279 | ... | ... | 29 |
| | 1980/81 | (3) 30 595 | (3) 264 241 | (3) 211 271 | 80 | (3) 8 033 642 | (3) 3 905 036 | 49 | 30 |
| | 1985/86 | 33 104 | 289 251 | ... | ... | 8 925 959 | 4 367 764 | 49 | 31 |
| | 1990/91 | 34 081 | 317 023 | ... | ... | 10 427 077 | 5 088 286 | 49 | 33 |
| | 1991/92 | 34 081 | 316 182 | ... | ... | 10 558 105 | ... | ... | 33 |
| | 1992/93 | 34 570 | 316 602 | ... | ... | 10 679 748 | ... | ... | 34 |
| | 1993/94 | 35 087 | 320 634 | ... | ... | 10 731 453 | 5 316 112 | 50 | 33 |
| | 1994/95 | 35 671 | 324 418 | ... | ... | 10 903 529 | ... | ... | 34 |
| | 1995/96 | 35 871 | ... | ... | ... | 11 541 570 | 5 594 021 | 48 | ... |
| | 1996/97 | 37 645 | 341 183 | ... | ... | 11 902 501 | ... | ... | 35 |
| | 1997/98 | 38 631 | ... | ... | ... | 12 159 495 | ... | ... | ... |
| Qatar | 1970/71 | 89 | 772 | 355 | 46 | 15 025 | 6 727 | 45 | 19 |
| | 1975/76 | 100 | 1 252 | 678 | 54 | 23 615 | 11 246 | 48 | 19 |
| | 1980/81 | 101 | 2 029 | 1 159 | 57 | 30 078 | 14 472 | 48 | 15 |
| | 1985/86 | 113 | 3 154 | 2 070 | 66 | 40 636 | 19 359 | 48 | 13 |
| | 1990/91 | 153 | 4 286 | 3 103 | 72 | 48 650 | 23 144 | 48 | 11 |
| | 1991/92 | 157 | 4 598 | 3 354 | 73 | 48 785 | 23 150 | 47 | 11 |
| | 1992/93 | 160 | 4 917 | 3 567 | 73 | 49 059 | 23 548 | 48 | 10 |
| | 1993/94 | 158 | 5 656 | 4 327 | 77 | 52 016 | 24 871 | 48 | 9 |
| | 1994/95 | 169 | 5 853 | 4 595 | 79 | 52 130 | 25 088 | 48 | 9 |
| | 1995/96 | 174 | 5 864 | 4 659 | 79 | 53 631 | 26 279 | 49 | 9 |
| Saudi Arabia | 1970/71 | 1 877 | 17 435 | 4 716 | 27 | 422 744 | 132 277 | 31 | 24 |
| | 1975/76 | 3 460 | 34 481 | 10 568 | 31 | 677 803 | 246 559 | 36 | 20 |
| | 1980/81 | 5 719 | 50 511 | 19 645 | 39 | 926 531 | 360 030 | 39 | 18 |
| | 1985/86 | 7 813 | 83 420 | 35 393 | 42 | 1 344 076 | 584 190 | 43 | 16 |
| | 1990/91 | 9 097 | 119 881 | 56 990 | 48 | 1 876 916 | 857 208 | 46 | 16 |
| | 1991/92 | 9 490 | 124 698 | 58 730 | 47 | 1 922 254 | 893 276 | 46 | 15 |
| | 1992/93 | 10 228 | 141 930 | 67 627 | 48 | 2 025 948 | 951 065 | 47 | 14 |
| | 1993/94 | 11 244 | 153 556 | 74 917 | 49 | 2 110 893 | 996 536 | 47 | 14 |
| | 1994/95 | 10 871 | 160 932 | 80 734 | 50 | 2 168 637 | 1 033 090 | 48 | 13 |
| | 1995/96 | 11 217 | 169 321 | 86 260 | 51 | 2 248 122 | 1 069 626 | 40 | 13 |
| | 1996/97 | 11 506 | 175 458 | 90 668 | 52 | 2 256 185 | 1 081 774 | 48 | 13 |
| Singapore | 1970 | 427 | 12 259 | 8 094 | 66 | 363 518 | 169 693 | 47 | 30 |
| | 1975 | 391 | 10 777 | 7 223 | 67 | 328 401 | 154 995 | 47 | 30 |
| | 1980 | 335 | 9 463 | 6 289 | 66 | 291 722 | 139 276 | 48 | 31 |
| | 1985 | 236 | 10 363 | 7 192 | 69 | 278 060 | 130 977 | 47 | 27 |
| | 1990 | 200 | 10 006 | ... | ... | 257 932 | 122 269 | 47 | 26 |
| | 1991 | 202 | 9 843 | ... | ... | 260 286 | 123 292 | 47 | 26 |
| | 1992 | 194 | 10 188 | ... | ... | 262 599 | 124 628 | 47 | 26 |
| | 1993 | 193 | 10 711 | ... | ... | 261 534 | 123 772 | 47 | 24 |
| | 1994 | 194 | 10 553 | 8 039 | 76 | 251 097 | 119 508 | 48 | 24 |
| | 1995 | 199 | 10 356 | 7 983 | 77 | 261 648 | ... | ... | 25 |
| | 1996 | 198 | 10 618 | ... | ... | 269 668 | 128 300 | 48 | 25 |
| Sri Lanka | 1970 | ... | ... | ... | ... | 1 671 428 | 786 963 | 47 | ... |
| | 1975 | ... | (32) 99 067 | (32) 51 526 | 52 | (3) 1 367 860 | (3) 646 171 | 47 | ... |
| | 1980 | (55) 8 772 | ... | ... | ... | (55) 2 081 391 | (55) 999 173 | 48 | ... |
| | 1985 | 9 349 | ... | ... | ... | 2 242 645 | 1 082 127 | 48 | ... |
| | 1990 | (20) 9 574 | (20) *72 488 | ... | ... | (20) 2 112 023 | (20) 1 018 321 | 48 | *29 |
| | 1991 | 9 590 | *68 069 | ... | ... | 2 112 723 | 1 018 124 | 48 | *31 |
| | 1992 | ... | 69 965 | 56 245 | 80 | 2 059 203 | 992 377 | 48 | 29 |
| | 1993 | 9 664 | 70 008 | 56 195 | 80 | 2 012 702 | 971 905 | 48 | 29 |
| | 1994 | 9 648 | 70 108 | 57 695 | 82 | 1 960 495 | 945 919 | 48 | 28 |
| | 1995 | 9 657 | 70 537 | 58 832 | 83 | 1 962 498 | 946 665 | 48 | 28 |
| | 1996 | 9 554 | 66 339 | 63 420 | 96 | 1 843 848 | 891 334 | 48 | 28 |
| Syrian Arab Republic | 1970/71 | 5 500 | 25 134 | 9 949 | 40 | 924 969 | 335 940 | 36 | 37 |
| | 1975/76 | 7 018 | 37 621 | 17 035 | 45 | 1 273 944 | 504 939 | 40 | 34 |
| | 1980/81 | 7 846 | 55 346 | 29 616 | 54 | 1 555 921 | 667 780 | 43 | 28 |
| | 1985/86 | 9 039 | 78 388 | 47 750 | 61 | 2 029 752 | 930 821 | 46 | 26 |
| | 1990/91 | 9 683 | 97 811 | 62 730 | 64 | 2 452 086 | 1 140 131 | 46 | 25 |
| | 1991/92 | 9 934 | 102 617 | 65 441 | 64 | 2 539 081 | 1 180 712 | 47 | 25 |
| | 1992/93 | 10 079 | 106 164 | 68 073 | 64 | 2 573 181 | 1 200 147 | 47 | 24 |
| | 1993/94 | 10 219 | 110 580 | 70 537 | 64 | 2 624 594 | 1 224 642 | 47 | 24 |
| | 1994/95 | 10 420 | 113 384 | 72 584 | 64 | 2 651 247 | 1 237 336 | 47 | 23 |
| | 1995/96 | 10 564 | 113 530 | 73 330 | 65 | 2 672 960 | 1 246 830 | 47 | 24 |
| | 1996/97 | 10 783 | 114 689 | 74 761 | 65 | 2 690 205 | 1 256 820 | 47 | 23 |

**Primary education: schools, teaching staff and pupils**
**Enseignement primaire: écoles, personnel enseignant et élèves**
**Enseñanza primaria: escuelas, personal docente y alumnos**

| Country / Pays / País | Year / Année / Año | Schools / Écoles / Escuelas | Teaching staff Personnel enseignant Personal docente | | | Pupils enrolled Élèves inscrits Alumnos matriculados | | | Pupil/ teacher ratio Nombre d'élèves par maître Número de alumnos por maestro |
|---|---|---|---|---|---|---|---|---|---|
| | | | Total | Female Féminin Femenino | % F | Total | Female Féminin Femenino | % F | |
| Tajikistan | 1990/91 | ... | 23 807 | 11 581 | 49 | 507 354 | 247 959 | 49 | 21 |
| | 1991/92 | ... | 24 691 | 12 312 | 50 | 536 959 | 262 101 | 49 | 22 |
| | 1992/93 | ... | 24 977 | 12 017 | 48 | 519 701 | 251 842 | 48 | 21 |
| | 1993/94 | 625 | 25 664 | 12 946 | 50 | 570 916 | 277 049 | 49 | 22 |
| | 1994/95 | ... | 25 968 | 13 355 | 51 | 593 526 | 288 530 | 49 | 23 |
| | 1996/97 | 3 432 | 27 172 | 14 672 | 54 | 638 674 | 310 877 | 49 | 24 |
| Thailand | 1970/71 | ... | 162 512 | ... | ... | 5 634 782 | 2 637 599 | 47 | 35 |
| | 1975/76 | 42 179 | 239 128 | ... | ... | 6 686 477 | 3 161 807 | 47 | 28 |
| | 1980/81 | ... | ... | ... | ... | (55) 7 392 563 | (55) 3 562 975 | 48 | ... |
| | 1985/86 | 33 964 | *369 822 | ... | ... | 7 150 489 | ... | ... | *19 |
| | 1990/91 | ... | 314 684 | ... | ... | 6 956 717 | 3 378 159 | 49 | 22 |
| | 1991/92 | ... | 343 063 | ... | ... | 6 906 935 | 3 356 861 | 49 | 20 |
| | 1992/93 | 34 123 | 341 122 | ... | ... | 6 758 091 | 3 278 151 | 49 | 20 |
| | 1993/94 | ... | ... | ... | ... | 6 576 431 | ... | ... | ... |
| | 1994/95 | ... | ... | ... | ... | 6 291 945 | ... | ... | ... |
| | 1995/96 | 34 001 | ... | ... | ... | 5 961 855 | ... | ... | ... |
| | 1996/97 | ... | ... | ... | ... | 5 909 618 | ... | ... | ... |
| | 1997/98 | ... | ... | ... | ... | 5 927 902 | ... | ... | ... |
| Turkey | 1970/71 | 38 227 | 132 577 | 45 186 | 34 | 5 011 926 | 2 120 332 | 42 | 38 |
| | 1975/76 | 41 981 | 171 032 | 66 825 | 39 | 5 463 684 | 2 435 000 | 45 | 32 |
| | 1980/81 | 45 549 | 212 456 | 86 205 | 41 | 5 656 494 | 2 568 623 | 45 | 27 |
| | 1985/86 | 47 631 | 212 717 | 88 855 | 42 | 6 635 858 | 3 131 419 | 47 | 31 |
| | 1990/91 | 51 055 | 225 852 | 97 803 | 43 | 6 861 711 | 3 229 812 | 47 | 30 |
| | 1991/92 | 50 669 | 234 961 | 99 474 | 42 | 6 878 923 | 3 238 599 | 47 | 29 |
| | 1992/93 | 49 974 | 235 721 | 100 822 | 43 | 6 707 725 | 3 163 808 | 47 | 28 |
| | 1993/94 | 49 599 | 237 943 | 102 391 | 43 | 6 526 356 | 3 092 337 | 47 | 27 |
| | 1994/95 | 48 429 | 233 073 | 101 557 | 44 | 6 466 648 | 3 065 485 | 47 | 28 |
| | 1996/97 | 47 313 | ... | ... | ... | 6 389 060 | 3 013 550 | 47 | ... |
| United Arab Emirates | 1970/71 | ... | (3) 806 | ... | ... | (3) 22 009 | (3) 8 300 | 38 | 27 |
| | 1975/76 | ... | (3) 3 191 | (3) 1 563 | 49 | 52 207 | 23 694 | 45 | ... |
| | 1980/81 | (3) 200 | (3) 5 424 | (3) 2 949 | 54 | 88 617 | 42 343 | 48 | ... |
| | 1985/86 | ... | (3) 6 123 | (3) 3 310 | 54 | 152 125 | 73 308 | 48 | ... |
| | 1990/91 | ... | 12 526 | 8 049 | 64 | 228 980 | 110 274 | 48 | 18 |
| | 1991/92 | ... | 13 139 | 8 552 | 65 | 231 674 | 111 312 | 48 | 18 |
| | 1992/93 | ... | 13 940 | 9 450 | 68 | 238 469 | 114 895 | 48 | 17 |
| | 1993/94 | ... | 14 754 | 10 133 | 69 | 251 182 | 120 491 | 48 | 17 |
| | 1994/95 | ... | 15 449 | 10 670 | 69 | 262 628 | 125 695 | 48 | 17 |
| | 1995/96 | ... | 15 779 | 10 945 | 69 | 260 919 | 125 540 | 48 | 17 |
| | 1996/97 | ... | 16 148 | 11 258 | 70 | 259 509 | 124 692 | 48 | 16 |
| Uzbekistan | 1980/81 | ... | 57 700 | 44 900 | 78 | 1 391 000 | 676 000 | 49 | 24 |
| | 1985/86 | ... | 66 900 | 52 100 | 78 | 1 612 000 | 783 100 | 49 | 24 |
| | 1990/91 | ... | 73 800 | 58 100 | 79 | 1 777 900 | 872 300 | 49 | 24 |
| | 1991/92 | ... | 80 600 | 63 800 | 79 | 1 715 100 | 843 800 | 49 | 21 |
| | 1992/93 | ... | 87 700 | 69 800 | 80 | 1 769 300 | 875 300 | 49 | 20 |
| | 1993/94 | ... | 91 500 | 73 600 | 80 | 1 852 841 | 908 832 | 49 | 20 |
| | 1994/95 | ... | 92 400 | 76 200 | 82 | 1 905 693 | 925 205 | 49 | 21 |
| Viet Nam | 1975/76 | ... | 204 998 | 114 331 | 56 | 7 403 715 | 3 650 762 | 49 | 36 |
| | 1980/81 | ... | 204 104 | 133 652 | 65 | 7 887 439 | 3 732 913 | 47 | 39 |
| | 1985/86 | 12 511 | 235 791 | 165 825 | 70 | 8 125 836 | 3 864 348 | 48 | 34 |
| | 1990/91 | ... | 252 413 | ... | ... | 8 862 292 | ... | ... | 35 |
| | 1991/92 | ... | 259 000 | ... | ... | 9 090 800 | ... | ... | 35 |
| | 1992/93 | ... | 267 800 | ... | ... | 9 527 200 | ... | ... | 36 |
| | 1993/94 | 10 137 | 278 000 | ... | ... | 9 782 900 | ... | ... | 35 |
| | 1994/95 | ... | 288 200 | ... | ... | 10 029 000 | ... | ... | 35 |
| | 1995/96 | ... | 298 856 | ... | ... | 10 228 800 | ... | ... | 34 |
| | 1996/97 | ... | 311 500 | ... | ... | 10 431 300 | ... | ... | 33 |
| | 1997/98 | ... | 324 431 | 251 144 | 77 | 10 431 337 | 4 979 556 | 48 | 32 |
| Yemen | 1993/94 | 11 013 | ... | ... | ... | 2 678 863 | 743 851 | 28 | ... |
| | 1996/97 | ... | 90 478 | 15 015 | 17 | 2 699 788 | 758 024 | 28 | 30 |
| Palestine | 1994/95 | 1 141 | ... | ... | ... | 572 529 | 278 491 | 49 | ... |
| | 1995/96 | 1 098 | 14 624 | 7 052 | 48 | 611 857 | 298 497 | 49 | 42 |
| | 1996/97 | 1 118 | 15 903 | 7 785 | 49 | 656 353 | 321 951 | 49 | 41 |
| **Europe** | | | | | | | | | |
| Albania | 1970/71 | 1 374 | (56) 18 944 | (56) 9 094 | 48 | 496 523 | 235 429 | 47 | ... |
| | 1975/76 | ... | ... | ... | ... | 579 303 | 273 398 | 47 | ... |
| | 1980/81 | 1 559 | 25 980 | 13 060 | 50 | 552 651 | 260 895 | 47 | 21 |
| | 1985/86 | 1 641 | 27 167 | 14 075 | 52 | 543 775 | 258 600 | 48 | 20 |
| | 1990/91 | 1 726 | 28 798 | 15 826 | 55 | 551 294 | 265 552 | 48 | 19 |
| | 1993/94 | 1 777 | 32 098 | 19 367 | 60 | 535 713 | 260 396 | 49 | 17 |
| | 1994/95 | 1 782 | 30 893 | 18 492 | 60 | 550 737 | 265 582 | 48 | 18 |
| | 1995/96 | ... | 31 369 | 18 863 | 60 | 558 101 | 269 509 | 48 | 18 |
| Andorra | 1970/71 | ... | ... | ... | ... | (6) 3 334 | (6) 1 695 | 51 | ... |
| | 1975/76 | ... | ... | ... | ... | (6) 3 802 | (6) 1 802 | 47 | ... |

Primary education: schools, teaching staff and pupils  II.5
Enseignement primaire: écoles, personnel enseignant et élèves
Enseñanza primaria: escuelas, personal docente y alumnos

| Country / Pays / País | Year / Année / Año | Schools / Écoles / Escuelas | Teaching staff — Personnel enseignant — Personal docente — Total | Female Féminin Femenino | % F | Pupils enrolled — Élèves inscrits — Alumnos matriculados — Total | Female Féminin Femenino | % F | Pupil/teacher ratio — Nombre d'élèves par maître — Número de alumnos por maestro |
|---|---|---|---|---|---|---|---|---|---|
| **Austria** | 1970/71 | (57) 3 973 | (57) 24 815 | (57) 15 709 | 63 | 531 934 | 258 631 | 49 | ... |
| | 1975/76 | (57) 3 590 | (57) 26 374 | (57) 18 608 | 71 | 501 843 | 244 462 | 49 | ... |
| | 1980/81 | 3 450 | 27 525 | 20 776 | 75 | 400 397 | 195 074 | 49 | 15 |
| | 1985/86 | 3 760 | 32 806 | 25 899 | 79 | 343 823 | 166 176 | 48 | 10 |
| | 1990/91 | 3 721 | 34 232 | 27 975 | 82 | 370 210 | 180 416 | 49 | 11 |
| | 1991/92 | 3 716 | 34 902 | 28 767 | 82 | 378 676 | 184 195 | 49 | 11 |
| | 1992/93 | 3 715 | 33 507 | 27 661 | 83 | 382 663 | 186 133 | 49 | 11 |
| | 1993/94 | 3 723 | 32 059 | 26 838 | 84 | 381 628 | 185 464 | 49 | 12 |
| | 1994/95 | 3 718 | 32 634 | 27 367 | 84 | 381 363 | 184 986 | 49 | 12 |
| | 1995/96 | ... | 30 674 | 25 468 | 83 | 382 005 | 185 451 | 49 | 12 |
| | 1996/97 | 3 703 | 31 251 | 26 124 | 84 | 381 927 | 185 240 | 49 | 12 |
| **Belarus** | 1970/71 | (32) 10 650 | (32) 105 600 | ... | ... | 948 800 | ... | ... | ... |
| | 1975/76 | (32) 8 408 | (32) 106 893 | ... | ... | 770 500 | ... | ... | ... |
| | 1980/81 | ... | ... | ... | ... | 750 300 | ... | ... | ... |
| | 1985/86 | ... | ... | ... | ... | 796 600 | ... | ... | ... |
| | 1990/91 | ... | ... | ... | ... | (19) 614 800 | ... | ... | ... |
| | 1991/92 | 5 100 | 30 300 | | ... | 620 100 | ... | ... | 20 |
| | 1992/93 | 5 000 | 31 600 | | ... | 635 100 | 311 100 | 49 | 20 |
| | 1993/94 | 4 900 | 32 400 | ... | ... | 634 600 | 309 500 | 49 | 20 |
| | 1994/95 | 5 000 | 32 200 | ... | ... | 636 300 | 306 000 | 48 | 20 |
| | 1995/96 | ... | ... | ... | ... | 632 100 | 303 100 | 48 | ... |
| | 1996/97 | ... | ... | ... | ... | 625 000 | 298 300 | 48 | ... |
| **Belgium** | 1970/71 | ... | 51 692 | 29 053 | 56 | 1 021 511 | 495 752 | 49 | 20 |
| | 1975/76 | ... | 48 625 | 27 777 | 57 | 941 941 | 458 673 | 49 | 19 |
| | 1980/81 | 4 968 | 46 430 | 27 278 | 59 | 842 117 | 409 890 | 49 | 18 |
| | 1985/86 | 4 386 | 44 190 | 27 621 | 63 | 730 288 | 357 486 | 49 | 17 |
| | 1990/91 | 4 226 | ... | ... | ... | 719 372 | 353 668 | 49 | ... |
| | 1991/92 | 4 158 | ... | ... | ... | 711 521 | 349 289 | 49 | ... |
| | 1992/93 | 4 505 | 59 830 | 42 720 | 71 | 739 093 | 358 684 | 49 | 12 |
| | 1993/94 | 4 493 | 60 738 | 43 625 | 72 | 736 782 | 357 245 | 48 | 12 |
| | 1994/95 | ... | ... | ... | ... | 738 768 | 358 185 | 48 | ... |
| | 1995/96 | ... | ... | ... | ... | 742 796 | 360 419 | 49 | ... |
| **Bulgaria** | 1970/71 | 3 933 | 47 798 | 32 973 | 69 | 1 049 829 | 510 001 | 49 | 22 |
| | 1975/76 | 3 419 | 48 445 | 34 159 | 71 | 980 318 | 475 402 | 48 | 20 |
| | 1980/81 | 3 247 | 51 581 | 36 953 | 72 | 994 018 | 482 258 | 49 | 19 |
| | 1985/86 | 2 973 | 61 153 | 46 012 | 75 | 1 080 979 | 523 816 | 48 | 18 |
| | 1990/91 | 2 856 | 62 501 | 48 331 | 77 | 960 681 | 461 907 | 48 | 15 |
| | 1991/92 | 2 827 | 62 012 | 48 021 | 77 | 920 094 | 442 224 | 48 | 15 |
| | 1992/93 | 2 812 | 61 148 | 47 818 | 78 | 877 189 | 420 098 | 48 | 14 |
| | 1993/94 | 2 770 | 58 480 | 46 402 | 79 | 839 419 | 400 646 | 48 | 14 |
| | 1994/95 | 2 758 | 58 201 | 46 659 | 80 | 825 984 | 394 076 | 48 | 14 |
| | 1995/96 | ... | (42) 25 503 | (42) 22 730 | 89 | (42) 433 926 | (42) 209 193 | 48 | 17 |
| | 1996/97 | 3 170 | 25 860 | 23 098 | 89 | 431 790 | 208 089 | 48 | 17 |
| **Croatia** | 1985/86 | 2 724 | 27 165 | 19 921 | 73 | 520 576 | 253 823 | 49 | 19 |
| | 1990/91 | 2 026 | 23 262 | 17 511 | 75 | 431 586 | 209 524 | 49 | 19 |
| | 1991/92 | 1 859 | 22 187 | ... | ... | 415 750 | ... | ... | 19 |
| | 1992/93 | 1 891 | 23 077 | 17 269 | 75 | 436 755 | 212 035 | 49 | 19 |
| | 1993/94 | 1 930 | 24 067 | 18 101 | 75 | 441 837 | 214 856 | 49 | 18 |
| | 1994/95 | 1 980 | 24 879 | 18 796 | 76 | 434 418 | 210 829 | 49 | 17 |
| | 1995/96 | (42) 1 134 | (42) 10 605 | (42) 9 401 | 89 | (42) 207 890 | (42) 101 096 | 49 | 20 |
| | 1996/97 | 1 094 | 10 762 | 9 536 | 89 | 203 933 | 99 124 | 49 | 19 |
| **Czech Republic** | 1970/71 | ... | 24 881 | ... | ... | 672 455 | 329 503 | 49 | 27 |
| | 1975/76 | ... | 25 032 | ... | ... | 676 554 | 331 511 | 49 | 27 |
| | 1980/81 | ... | 21 999 | ... | ... | 647 029 | 317 044 | 49 | 29 |
| | 1985/86 | ... | 23 618 | ... | ... | 694 659 | 333 436 | 48 | 29 |
| | 1990/91 | ... | 23 630 | ... | ... | 545 814 | 266 845 | 49 | 23 |
| | 1991/92 | ... | 24 307 | ... | ... | 537 996 | 282 962 | 53 | 22 |
| | 1992/93 | 4 137 | 27 502 | 25 253 | 92 | 528 750 | 259 080 | 49 | 19 |
| | 1993/94 | 4 199 | 27 420 | 25 356 | 92 | 538 612 | 262 749 | 49 | 20 |
| | 1994/95 | 4 216 | 26 689 | 24 823 | 93 | 538 743 | 262 226 | 49 | 20 |
| | 1995/96 | 4 889 | 28 356 | 26 411 | 93 | 541 671 | 262 665 | 48 | 19 |
| **Denmark** | 1970/71 | 2 403 | ... | ... | ... | 443 031 | 218 569 | 49 | ... |
| | 1975/76 | ... | ... | ... | ... | 490 891 | 238 000 | 48 | ... |
| | 1980/81 | 2 346 | ... | ... | ... | 434 635 | 211 959 | 49 | ... |
| | 1985/86 | 2 556 | 34 744 | 19 677 | 57 | 402 707 | 196 825 | 49 | 12 |
| | 1990/91 | ... | ... | ... | ... | 340 267 | 166 582 | 49 | ... |
| | 1991/92 | ... | (58) 28 501 | ... | ... | 327 024 | 160 126 | 49 | ... |
| | 1992/93 | ... | 32 900 | 19 100 | 58 | 323 651 | 158 590 | 49 | 10 |
| | 1993/94 | 2 210 | 32 900 | 19 100 | 58 | 326 619 | 160 043 | 49 | 10 |
| | 1994/95 | ... | 33 100 | 19 200 | 58 | 328 875 | 161 372 | 49 | 10 |
| | 1995/96 | ... | ... | ... | ... | 336 690 | 164 181 | 49 | ... |
| **Estonia** | 1980/81 | ... | ... | ... | ... | 131 705 | 63 851 | 48 | ... |
| | 1985/86 | ... | ... | ... | ... | 138 573 | 67 084 | 48 | ... |
| | 1990/91 | ... | ... | ... | ... | 127 389 | 61 739 | 48 | ... |
| | 1991/92 | ... | ... | ... | ... | 126 050 | 61 157 | 49 | ... |
| | 1992/93 | ... | ... | ... | ... | 122 111 | 59 300 | 49 | ... |
| | 1993/94 | ... | 6 580 | 6 300 | 96 | 120 667 | 58 592 | 49 | 18 |
| | 1994/95 | ... | ... | ... | ... | 121 404 | 58 717 | 48 | ... |
| | 1995/96 | 727 | *7 276 | *6 496 | *89 | 125 718 | 60 763 | 48 | *17 |
| | 1996/97 | ... | ... | ... | ... | 126 800 | 61 282 | 48 | ... |

Primary education: schools, teaching staff and pupils
Enseignement primaire: écoles, personnel enseignant et élèves
Enseñanza primaria: escuelas, personal docente y alumnos

| Country / Pays / País | Year / Année / Año | Schools / Écoles / Escuelas | Teaching staff / Personnel enseignant / Personal docente | | | | Pupils enrolled / Élèves inscrits / Alumnos matriculados | | | | Pupil/teacher ratio / Nombre d'élèves par maître / Número de alumnos por maestro |
|---|---|---|---|---|---|---|---|---|---|---|---|
| | | | | Total | Female Féminin Femenino | % F | | Total | Female Féminin Femenino | % F | |
| Federal Republic of | 1990/91 | ... | | ... | ... | ... | (38) | 466 692 | (38) 227 175 | 49 | ... |
| Yugoslavia | 1991/92 | 4 424 | | 21 399 | 15 905 | 74 | | 470 669 | 229 078 | 49 | 22 |
| | 1992/93 | 4 433 | | 21 368 | 16 002 | 75 | | 473 902 | 230 426 | 49 | 22 |
| | 1993/94 | 4 421 | | ... | ... | ... | | 460 203 | 225 896 | 49 | ... |
| | 1994/95 | ... | | ... | ... | ... | | 448 533 | 218 998 | 49 | ... |
| | 1995/96 | ... | | ... | ... | ... | | 449 192 | 218 396 | 49 | |
| | 1996/97 | ... | | ... | ... | ... | | 437 780 | 212 893 | 49 | |
| Finland | 1970/71 | 4 507 | | 17 360 | *10 390 | *60 | | 386 230 | *183 459 | *47 | 22 |
| | 1975/76 | | (59) | 24 494 | (59) 14 990 | 61 | (59) | 453 737 | (59) 219 795 | 48 | 19 |
| | 1980/81 | 4 245 | | 25 949 | ... | ... | | 373 347 | 181 879 | 49 | 14 |
| | 1985/86 | ... | | ... | ... | ... | | 379 339 | 185 229 | 49 | ... |
| | 1990/91 | ... | | ... | ... | ... | | 390 587 | 190 330 | 49 | ... |
| | 1991/92 | (32) 5 316 | | ... | ... | ... | | 392 695 | 191 603 | 49 | ... |
| | 1992/93 | 4 137 | | ... | ... | ... | | 392 537 | 191 531 | 49 | ... |
| | 1993/94 | 3 986 | | ... | ... | ... | | 390 892 | 190 727 | 49 | ... |
| | 1994/95 | 3 912 | | ... | ... | ... | | 387 306 | 188 899 | 49 | ... |
| | 1995/96 | 3 851 | | 23 294 | 15 867 | 68 | | 384 369 | 187 922 | 49 | 17 |
| | 1996/97 | 3 766 | | 21 459 | 14 798 | 69 | | 380 932 | 186 207 | 49 | 18 |
| France | 1970/71 | 63 520 | (3) | 190 052 | ... | ... | | 4 939 683 | 2 412 399 | 49 | ... |
| | 1975/76 | 55 886 | (3) | 204 311 | (3) 139 877 | 68 | | 4 601 550 | 2 341 700 | 51 | ... |
| | 1980/81 | 51 448 | (3) | 192 438 | (3) 130 307 | 68 | | 4 610 361 | 2 235 963 | 48 | ... |
| | 1985/86 | 47 923 | | ... | ... | ... | | 4 115 846 | 1 986 129 | 48 | ... |
| | 1990/91 | 44 311 | | ... | ... | ... | | 4 149 143 | 2 010 219 | 48 | ... |
| | 1991/92 | 43 126 | (6) | 342 479 | (6) 262 700 | 77 | | 4 109 797 | 1 990 151 | 48 | ... |
| | 1992/93 | ... | | 219 182 | 169 555 | 77 | | 4 060 408 | 1 967 332 | 48 | 19 |
| | 1993/94 | ... | | 218 019 | 169 728 | 78 | | 4 078 370 | 1 971 292 | 48 | 19 |
| | 1994/95 | 41 244 | | 216 962 | 168 958 | 78 | | 4 071 599 | 1 970 033 | 48 | 19 |
| | 1995/96 | 41 000 | | 216 938 | 170 666 | 79 | | 4 065 005 | 1 969 585 | 48 | 19 |
| | 1996/97 | ... | | 211 192 | 166 038 | 79 | | 4 004 704 | 1 945 763 | 49 | 19 |
| Germany | 1990/91 | ... | | ... | ... | ... | | 3 431 385 | ... | ... | ... |
| | 1991/92 | ... | | ... | ... | ... | | 3 438 052 | 1 684 548 | 49 | ... |
| | 1992/93 | 17 941 | | 215 414 | 180 814 | 84 | | 3 582 582 | 1 739 892 | 49 | 17 |
| | 1993/94 | 17 911 | | 224 299 | 190 657 | 85 | | 3 639 717 | 1 767 681 | 49 | 16 |
| | 1994/95 | 17 895 | | 213 489 | 181 640 | 85 | | 3 727 157 | 1 810 540 | 49 | 17 |
| | 1995/96 | 17 910 | | 223 235 | 180 653 | 81 | | 3 804 887 | 1 847 085 | 49 | 17 |
| | 1996/97 | 17 892 | | 224 517 | 182 426 | 81 | | 3 859 490 | 1 872 778 | 49 | 17 |
| Gibraltar | 1970/71 | ... | | ... | ... | ... | | 3 382 | 1 658 | 49 | ... |
| | 1975/76 | 14 | | 158 | 139 | 88 | | 2 808 | 1 390 | 50 | 18 |
| | 1980/81 | 13 | | 157 | 131 | 83 | | 2 750 | 1 374 | 50 | 18 |
| | 1996/97 | 11 | | 172 | 119 | 69 | | 2 729 | 1 291 | 47 | 16 |
| Greece | 1970/71 | 9 513 | | 29 336 | 13 898 | 47 | | 907 446 | 435 422 | 48 | 31 |
| | 1975/76 | 9 633 | | 30 953 | 14 565 | 47 | | 935 730 | 450 506 | 48 | 30 |
| | 1980/81 | 9 461 | | 37 315 | 17 845 | 48 | | 900 641 | 435 000 | 48 | 24 |
| | 1985/86 | 8 675 | | 37 994 | 18 594 | 49 | | 887 735 | 429 906 | 48 | 23 |
| | 1990/91 | 7 653 | | 43 599 | 22 762 | 52 | | 813 353 | 394 228 | 48 | 19 |
| | 1991/92 | 7 526 | | 42 991 | 22 515 | 52 | | 784 707 | 380 614 | 49 | 18 |
| | 1992/93 | 7 257 | | 42 045 | 22 864 | 54 | | 749 312 | 363 214 | 48 | 18 |
| | 1993/94 | 7 193 | | 43 789 | 24 267 | 55 | | 723 701 | 350 276 | 48 | 17 |
| | 1994/95 | 7 066 | | 44 168 | 24 219 | 55 | | 710 774 | 346 877 | 49 | 16 |
| | 1995/96 | 6 853 | | 45 128 | 25 247 | 56 | | 675 267 | 327 141 | 48 | 15 |
| | 1996/97 | 6 651 | | 46 785 | 26 490 | 57 | | 652 040 | 316 199 | 48 | 14 |
| Hungary | 1970/71 | 5 480 | | 63 125 | 46 046 | 73 | | 1 115 993 | 538 310 | 48 | 18 |
| | 1975/76 | 4 468 | | 66 861 | ... | ... | | 1 051 095 | 510 180 | 49 | 16 |
| | 1980/81 | 3 633 | | 75 422 | 60 673 | 80 | | 1 162 203 | 565 243 | 49 | 15 |
| | 1985/86 | 3 546 | | 88 066 | 72 390 | 82 | | 1 297 818 | 632 567 | 49 | 15 |
| | 1990/91 | 3 548 | | 90 511 | 75 596 | 84 | | 1 130 656 | 551 952 | 49 | 12 |
| | 1991/92 | 3 641 | | 89 276 | 74 513 | 83 | | 1 081 213 | 528 461 | 49 | 12 |
| | 1992/93 | 3 717 | | 88 917 | 74 338 | 84 | | 1 044 164 | ... | ... | 12 |
| | 1993/94 | (60) 3 593 | (60) | 52 584 | (60) 42 511 | 81 | (60) | 507 617 | (60) 246 496 | 49 | 10 |
| | 1994/95 | 3 596 | | 44 585 | 40 819 | 92 | | 508 003 | 246 654 | 49 | 11 |
| | 1995/96 | ... | | ... | ... | ... | | 507 238 | 245 923 | 48 | ... |
| Iceland | 1970/71 | 187 | | 1 383 | 694 | 50 | | 27 066 | 13 187 | 49 | 20 |
| | 1975/76 | 183 | (6) | 1 380 | (6) 751 | 54 | | 26 418 | 12 912 | 49 | ... |
| | 1980/81 | ... | | ... | ... | ... | | 24 736 | ... | ... | ... |
| | 1985/86 | ... | | ... | ... | ... | | 24 603 | 11 994 | 49 | ... |
| | 1990/91 | ... | | ... | ... | ... | (19) | 29 816 | ... | ... | ... |
| | 1991/92 | ... | | ... | ... | ... | | 29 649 | ... | ... | ... |
| | 1992/93 | ... | | ... | ... | ... | | 29 351 | 14 315 | 49 | ... |
| | 1993/94 | ... | | ... | ... | ... | | 28 960 | 14 126 | 49 | ... |
| | 1994/95 | 195 | | ... | ... | ... | | 29 138 | 14 180 | 49 | ... |
| | 1995/96 | 196 | | ... | ... | ... | | 29 221 | 14 281 | 49 | ... |
| | 1996/97 | 193 | | ... | ... | ... | | 29 342 | 14 336 | 49 | ... |
| Ireland | 1970/71 | (6) 4 090 | (6) | 16 981 | ... | ... | | 399 700 | 195 700 | 49 | ... |
| | 1975/76 | (6) 3 558 | | 13 060 | 8 472 | 65 | | 404 818 | 197 491 | 49 | 31 |
| | 1980/81 | (6) 3 385 | | 14 636 | 10 795 | 74 | | 419 998 | 205 447 | 49 | 29 |
| | 1985/86 | (6) 3 334 | | 15 674 | 11 907 | 76 | | 420 236 | 205 236 | 49 | 27 |
| | 1990/91 | (6) 3 320 | | 15 614 | 11 965 | 77 | | 416 747 | 203 506 | 49 | 27 |
| | 1991/92 | (6) 3 308 | | 15 775 | 12 124 | 77 | | 408 567 | 198 995 | 49 | 26 |

Primary education: schools, teaching staff and pupils    II.5
Enseignement primaire: écoles, personnel enseignant et élèves
Enseñanza primaria: escuelas, personal docente y alumnos

| Country / Pays / País | Year / Année / Año | Schools / Écoles / Escuelas | | Teaching staff / Personnel enseignant / Personal docente | | | Pupils enrolled / Élèves inscrits / Alumnos matriculados | | | Pupil/teacher ratio / Nombre d'élèves par maître / Número de alumnos por maestro |
|---|---|---|---|---|---|---|---|---|---|---|
| | | | | Total | Female / Féminin / Femenino | % F | Total | Female / Féminin / Femenino | % F | |
| Ireland (cont) | 1992/93 | (6) | 3 288 | 16 212 | 12 484 | 77 | 402 226 | 195 500 | 49 | 25 |
| | 1993/94 | (6) | 3 391 | 16 212 | 12 530 | 77 | 391 998 | 190 467 | 49 | 24 |
| | 1994/95 | (6) | 3 387 | 16 339 | 12 736 | 78 | 380 983 | 185 213 | 49 | 23 |
| | 1995/96 | (6) | 3 391 | 16 311 | 12 708 | 78 | 367 689 | 178 827 | 49 | 23 |
| | 1996/97 | | ... | 16 202 | 12 708 | 78 | 358 830 | 174 406 | 49 | 22 |
| Italy | 1970/71 | | 37 095 | 224 646 | 173 312 | 77 | 4 856 953 | 2 351 309 | 48 | 22 |
| | 1975/76 | | 33 233 | 255 267 | 211 337 | 83 | 4 833 415 | 2 348 516 | 49 | 19 |
| | 1980/81 | | 30 305 | 273 744 | 238 299 | 87 | 4 422 888 | 2 150 146 | 49 | 16 |
| | 1985/86 | | 27 748 | 273 800 | 244 631 | 89 | 3 703 108 | 1 800 587 | 49 | 14 |
| | 1990/91 | | 24 268 | 265 553 | 240 466 | 91 | 3 055 883 | 1 485 252 | 49 | 12 |
| | 1991/92 | | 22 911 | 255 429 | 231 697 | 91 | 3 004 264 | 1 460 072 | 49 | 12 |
| | 1992/93 | | 22 710 | 251 621 | 228 233 | 91 | 2 959 564 | 1 459 066 | 49 | 12 |
| | 1993/94 | | 21 312 | 279 604 | 259 753 | 93 | 2 863 279 | 1 419 145 | 50 | 10 |
| | 1994/95 | | ... | 256 756 | 239 119 | 93 | 2 815 631 | 1 357 816 | 48 | 11 |
| | 1995/96 | | 20 361 | 251 827 | 235 677 | 94 | 2 816 128 | 1 360 754 | 48 | 11 |
| | 1996/97 | | ... | ... | ... | ... | 2 810 158 | 1 362 849 | 48 | ... |
| Latvia | 1980/81 | | 865 | 7 102 | ... | ... | 141 376 | ... | ... | 20 |
| | 1985/86 | | 856 | 7 788 | ... | ... | 140 744 | ... | ... | 18 |
| | 1990/91 | | 918 | 9 475 | ... | ... | 143 338 | 70 264 | 49 | 15 |
| | 1991/92 | | 947 | 9 468 | ... | ... | 146 250 | 71 882 | 49 | 15 |
| | 1992/93 | | 988 | 9 889 | ... | ... | 137 095 | 67 327 | 49 | 14 |
| | 1993/94 | | 1 010 | 9 329 | 8 586 | 92 | 132 059 | 64 541 | 49 | 14 |
| | 1994/95 | | 1 038 | 10 056 | 9 228 | 92 | 132 465 | 63 912 | 48 | 13 |
| | 1995/96 | | 1 056 | 10 357 | 10 003 | 97 | 139 925 | 67 510 | 48 | 14 |
| | 1996/97 | | 1 074 | (50) 10 883 | (50) 10 369 | 95 | 146 653 | 70 757 | 48 | ... |
| Lithuania | 1980/81 | | ... | 6 800 | 6 571 | 97 | 172 064 | 84 426 | 49 | 25 |
| | 1985/86 | | ... | 6 800 | 6 571 | 97 | 172 349 | 85 075 | 49 | 25 |
| | 1990/91 | | ... | 11 319 | (61) 10 590 | ... | 202 222 | (61) 95 947 | ... | 18 |
| | 1991/92 | | ... | 12 158 | (61) 11 284 | ... | 202 970 | (61) 96 869 | ... | 17 |
| | 1992/93 | | ... | 12 500 | (61) 11 764 | ... | 210 834 | (61) 100 569 | ... | 17 |
| | 1993/94 | | ... | 12 881 | (61) 12 058 | ... | 215 175 | (61) 100 965 | ... | 17 |
| | 1994/95 | | ... | 13 444 | (61) 12 673 | ... | 221 569 | 107 096 | 48 | 16 |
| | 1995/96 | | ... | 13 197 | (61) 12 915 | ... | 223 662 | 108 236 | 48 | 17 |
| | 1996/97 | | ... | 14 095 | (61) 12 895 | ... | 225 701 | 108 811 | 48 | 16 |
| Luxembourg | 1970/71 | | 1 605 | 1 750 | 930 | 53 | 34 530 | 16 973 | 49 | 20 |
| | 1975/76 | | ... | 1 521 | 810 | 53 | 29 430 | 14 468 | 49 | 19 |
| | 1980/81 | | ... | 1 765 | 882 | 50 | 24 628 | 11 954 | 49 | 14 |
| | 1985/86 | | ... | 1 745 | 855 | 49 | 22 003 | 10 721 | 49 | 13 |
| | 1990/91 | | 326 | 1 764 | 896 | 51 | 23 465 | 11 902 | 51 | 13 |
| | 1993/94 | | ... | ... | ... | ... | 28 205 | ... | ... | ... |
| | 1994/95 | | ... | ... | ... | ... | 27 082 | ... | ... | ... |
| | 1995/96 | | ... | ... | ... | ... | 27 844 | ... | ... | ... |
| | 1996/97 | | ... | 1 844 | ... | ... | 28 437 | ... | ... | 15 |
| Malta | 1970/71 | | 109 | 1 391 | 1 007 | 72 | 40 021 | 19 317 | 48 | 29 |
| | 1975/76 | | 104 | 1 421 | 974 | 69 | 29 834 | 14 465 | 48 | 21 |
| | 1980/81 | | 102 | 1 557 | 993 | 64 | 33 063 | 15 944 | 48 | 21 |
| | 1985/86 | | 107 | 1 665 | 1 123 | 67 | 36 240 | 17 108 | 47 | 22 |
| | 1990/91 | | 115 | 1 780 | 1 411 | 79 | 36 899 | 17 708 | 48 | 21 |
| | 1991/92 | | ... | 1 666 | 1 345 | 81 | 35 626 | 17 143 | 48 | 21 |
| | 1992/93 | | ... | 1 722 | 1 408 | 82 | 35 488 | 17 137 | 48 | 21 |
| | 1993/94 | | ... | 1 748 | 1 447 | 83 | 35 366 | 17 068 | 48 | 20 |
| | 1994/95 | | ... | 1 791 | 1 488 | 83 | 35 051 | 16 762 | 48 | 20 |
| | 1995/96 | | ... | 1 824 | 1 740 | 95 | 35 273 | 17 067 | 48 | 19 |
| | 1996/97 | | ... | ... | ... | ... | 35 374 | 17 116 | 48 | ... |
| Moldova | 1980/81 | | ... | 8 003 | 7 645 | 96 | 230 624 | 113 149 | 49 | 29 |
| | 1985/86 | | ... | 9 500 | 9 078 | 96 | 248 005 | 121 039 | 49 | 26 |
| | 1990/91 | | ... | 13 024 | 12 684 | 97 | 301 653 | 148 608 | 49 | 23 |
| | 1991/92 | | ... | 13 415 | 12 949 | 97 | 306 933 | 150 910 | 49 | 23 |
| | 1992/93 | | ... | 13 295 | 12 829 | 96 | 307 604 | 150 890 | 49 | 23 |
| | 1993/94 | | ... | 13 230 | 12 764 | 96 | 307 447 | 151 174 | 49 | 23 |
| | 1994/95 | | (21) ... | 13 322 | ... | ... | (21) 322 612 | (21) 158 080 | 49 | 24 |
| | 1995/96 | | ... | *14 209 | *13 791 | *97 | *320 055 | *155 708 | *49 | *23 |
| | 1996/97 | | ... | *14 097 | *13 731 | *97 | *320 725 | *156 417 | *49 | *23 |
| Monaco | 1970/71 | | 8 | (3) 48 | (3) 32 | 67 | 1 486 | 761 | 51 | ... |
| | 1980/81 | (3) | 3 | ... | ... | ... | (3) 1 017 | (3) 471 | 46 | ... |
| | 1990/91 | | 7 | ... | ... | ... | 1 773 | 897 | 51 | ... |
| | 1991/92 | (3) | 7 | (3) 60 | (3) 38 | 63 | 1 761 | 869 | 49 | ... |
| | 1993/94 | | 7 | ... | ... | ... | 1 815 | 889 | 49 | ... |
| | 1994/95 | | 7 | 106 | ... | ... | 1 838 | 866 | 47 | 17 |
| | 1995/96 | | 7 | 102 | ... | ... | 1 893 | 897 | 47 | 19 |
| | 1996/97 | | 7 | ... | ... | ... | 1 919 | 908 | 47 | ... |
| Netherlands | 1970/71 | | ... | (50) 49 243 | (50) 24 353 | 49 | 1 462 376 | 717 218 | 49 | ... |
| | 1975/76 | | ... | (50) 52 700 | (50) 24 216 | 46 | 1 453 467 | 714 053 | 49 | ... |
| | 1980/81 | (31) | 8 727 | 57 536 | 26 421 | 46 | 1 333 342 | 658 509 | 49 | 23 |
| | 1985/86 | (31) | 8 401 | 66 388 | 34 889 | 53 | 1 109 590 | 547 513 | 49 | 17 |
| | 1990/91 | (31) | 8 450 | 63 022 | 33 391 | 53 | 1 082 022 | 537 223 | 50 | 17 |
| | 1991/92 | (31) | 8 435 | 63 100 | 33 700 | 53 | 1 040 158 | 514 149 | 49 | 16 |
| | 1992/93 | (31) | 8 331 | 64 700 | 35 400 | 55 | 1 046 192 | 519 688 | 50 | 16 |

**Primary education: schools, teaching staff and pupils**
**Enseignement primaire: écoles, personnel enseignant et élèves**
**Enseñanza primaria: escuelas, personal docente y alumnos**

| Country / Pays / País | Year / Année / Año | Schools / Écoles / Escuelas | | Teaching staff / Personnel enseignant / Personal docente | | | Pupils enrolled / Élèves inscrits / Alumnos matriculados | | | Pupil/ teacher ratio / Nombre d'élèves par maître / Número de alumnos por maestro |
|---|---|---|---|---|---|---|---|---|---|---|
| | | | | Total | Female Féminin Femenino | % F | Total | Female Féminin Femenino | % F | |
| Netherlands (cont) | 1993/94 | (31) | 8 139 | (62) | 63 872 | (62) 41 224 | 65 | 1 172 534 | 568 254 | 48 | ... |
| | 1994/95 | (31) | 7 860 | | ... | ... | ... | 1 189 112 | 576 417 | 48 | ... |
| | 1995/96 | (31) | 7 411 | (6)(58) | 82 000 | (6)(58) 49 400 | 60 | 1 207 896 | 584 984 | 48 | ... |
| | 1996/97 | (31) | 7 287 | (6)(58) | 84 900 | (6)(58) 51 200 | 60 | 1 230 987 | 596 032 | 48 | ... |
| Norway | 1970/71 | | 3 060 | | 19 713 | 11 941 | 61 | 385 628 | 197 323 | 51 | 20 |
| | 1975/76 | | ... | | ... | ... | ... | 390 129 | 190 060 | 49 | ... |
| | 1980/81 | | ... | | ... | ... | ... | 390 186 | 190 252 | 49 | ... |
| | 1985/86 | | ... | | ... | ... | ... | 335 373 | 163 832 | 49 | ... |
| | 1990/91 | | ... | | ... | ... | ... | 309 432 | 150 737 | 49 | ... |
| | 1991/92 | | ... | | ... | ... | ... | 308 516 | 150 418 | 49 | ... |
| | 1992/93 | | ... | | ... | ... | ... | 307 461 | 150 144 | 49 | ... |
| | 1993/94 | | ... | | ... | ... | ... | 309 889 | 151 179 | 49 | ... |
| | 1994/95 | | ... | | ... | ... | ... | 314 062 | 152 993 | 49 | ... |
| | 1995/96 | | 2 129 | | ... | ... | ... | 320 752 | 156 366 | 49 | ... |
| | 1996/97 | | ... | | ... | ... | ... | 330 619 | 161 337 | 49 | ... |
| Poland | 1970/71 | | 26 126 | (56) | 228 743 | (56) 182 301 | 80 | 5 256 970 | 2 530 233 | 48 | ... |
| | 1975/76 | | 14 738 | (56) | 208 173 | (56) 167 976 | 81 | 4 309 823 | 2 081 313 | 48 | ... |
| | 1980/81 | | 12 593 | | 195 608 | ... | ... | 4 167 313 | 2 025 824 | 49 | 21 |
| | 1985/86 | | 16 254 | | 267 620 | ... | ... | 4 801 307 | 2 325 579 | 48 | 18 |
| | 1990/91 | | 17 788 | | 317 474 | ... | ... | 5 189 118 | 2 524 274 | 49 | 16 |
| | 1991/92 | | 17 892 | | 310 122 | ... | ... | 5 218 323 | 2 531 527 | 49 | 17 |
| | 1992/93 | | 20 397 | | 319 649 | ... | ... | 5 323 848 | 2 574 173 | 48 | 17 |
| | 1993/94 | | 20 326 | | 323 413 | ... | ... | 5 288 250 | 2 558 569 | 48 | 16 |
| | 1994/95 | (21) | 20 214 | (21) | 323 534 | ... | ... | (21) 5 124 477 | (21) 2 488 482 | 49 | 16 |
| | 1995/96 | | ... | | 325 601 | ... | ... | 5 021 378 | 2 431 802 | 48 | 15 |
| Portugal | 1970/71 | | 17 018 | | 29 554 | 26 274 | 89 | 992 446 | 482 955 | 49 | 34 |
| | 1975/76 | | 13 111 | | 59 485 | 48 074 | 81 | 1 204 567 | 581 147 | 48 | 20 |
| | 1980/81 | | 12 460 | | 68 746 | ... | ... | 1 240 307 | 594 090 | 48 | 18 |
| | 1985/86 | | 12 741 | | 73 343 | *60 800 | *83 | 1 235 312 | 588 646 | 48 | 17 |
| | 1990/91 | | 11 532 | | 72 140 | 58 781 | 81 | 1 019 794 | 485 324 | 48 | 14 |
| | 1991/92 | | 12 472 | | 71 105 | ... | ... | 1 004 848 | 480 385 | 48 | 14 |
| | 1992/93 | | ... | | 72 131 | ... | ... | 952 941 | 454 406 | 48 | 13 |
| | 1993/94 | | ... | | 76 444 | ... | ... | 929 471 | 441 507 | 48 | 12 |
| | 1994/95 | | ... | | ... | ... | ... | 896 681 | 426 993 | 48 | ... |
| | 1995/96 | | ... | | ... | ... | ... | 867 253 | 412 488 | 48 | ... |
| Romania | 1970/71 | | 14 927 | | 135 615 | 87 111 | 64 | 2 878 693 | 1 417 540 | 49 | 21 |
| | 1975/76 | | 14 695 | | 144 978 | 97 201 | 67 | 2 889 208 | 1 404 360 | 49 | 20 |
| | 1980/81 | | 14 381 | | 156 817 | 109 017 | 70 | 3 308 462 | 1 610 063 | 49 | 21 |
| | 1985/86 | | 14 076 | | 147 147 | 103 470 | 70 | 3 030 666 | 1 476 503 | 49 | 21 |
| | 1990/91 | (63) | 6 070 | (63) | 57 140 | (63) 47 989 | 84 | (63) 1 253 480 | (63) 613 352 | 49 | 22 |
| | 1991/92 | | 6 137 | | 56 938 | 47 228 | 83 | 1 211 239 | 590 891 | 49 | 21 |
| | 1992/93 | | 6 145 | | 57 014 | 47 358 | 83 | 1 201 229 | 584 917 | 49 | 21 |
| | 1993/94 | | 6 160 | | 58 195 | 48 642 | 84 | 1 237 655 | 602 685 | 49 | 21 |
| | 1994/95 | | 6 162 | | 61 960 | 52 004 | 84 | 1 335 973 | 650 697 | 49 | 22 |
| | 1995/96 | | 6 180 | | 69 536 | 58 697 | 84 | 1 391 951 | 677 613 | 49 | 20 |
| | 1996/97 | | 6 188 | | 71 829 | 61 076 | 85 | 1 405 308 | 683 727 | 49 | 20 |
| Russian Federation | 1980/81 | | ... | | 215 000 | 210 000 | 98 | 6 009 000 | 2 956 000 | 49 | 28 |
| | 1985/86 | | ... | | 248 000 | 244 000 | 98 | 6 579 000 | 3 244 000 | 49 | 27 |
| | 1990/91 | | ... | | 340 000 | 336 000 | 99 | 7 596 000 | 3 737 000 | 49 | 22 |
| | 1991/92 | | ... | | 363 000 | 358 000 | 99 | 7 738 000 | 3 807 000 | 49 | 21 |
| | 1992/93 | | ... | | 385 000 | 377 000 | 98 | 7 797 000 | 3 836 000 | 49 | 20 |
| | 1993/94 | | 66 235 | | 395 000 | 387 000 | 98 | 7 738 000 | 3 799 000 | 49 | 20 |
| | 1994/95 | | ... | | ... | ... | ... | 7 849 000 | 3 832 000 | 49 | ... |
| San Marino | 1970/71 | | 17 | | 89 | 72 | 81 | 1 639 | 751 | 46 | 18 |
| | 1975/76 | | 15 | | 116 | 100 | 86 | 1 692 | 789 | 47 | 15 |
| | 1980/81 | | 14 | | 145 | 128 | 88 | 1 509 | 733 | 49 | 10 |
| | 1985/86 | | 13 | | 158 | 138 | 87 | 1 411 | 691 | 49 | 9 |
| | 1990/91 | | 14 | | 208 | 186 | 89 | 1 212 | 564 | 47 | 6 |
| | 1991/92 | | 14 | | 218 | 187 | 86 | 1 200 | 579 | 48 | 6 |
| | 1992/93 | | 14 | | 221 | 195 | 88 | 1 190 | 574 | 48 | 5 |
| | 1993/94 | | 14 | | 219 | 192 | 88 | 1 166 | 566 | 49 | 5 |
| | 1995/96 | | 14 | | 217 | 192 | 88 | 1 134 | 541 | 48 | 5 |
| | 1996/97 | | 14 | | 221 | 197 | 89 | 1 170 | 561 | 48 | 5 |
| Slovakia | 1992/93 | | 2 472 | | 15 859 | 14 556 | 92 | 350 604 | 171 163 | 49 | 22 |
| | 1993/94 | | 2 483 | | 15 433 | 14 097 | 91 | 345 594 | 168 918 | 49 | 22 |
| | 1994/95 | | 2 481 | | 15 394 | 14 083 | 91 | 338 291 | 165 422 | 49 | 22 |
| | 1995/96 | | 2 485 | | ... | ... | ... | 338 767 | 165 713 | 49 | ... |
| | 1996/97 | | ... | | *16 820 | *15 375 | *91 | 329 880 | (61) 156 934 | ... | *20 |
| Slovenia | 1980/81 | | 842 | | ... | ... | ... | 109 500 | ... | ... | ... |
| | 1985/86 | | 830 | | ... | ... | ... | 116 016 | ... | ... | ... |
| | 1990/91 | | 822 | | ... | ... | ... | 112 134 | ... | ... | ... |
| | 1991/92 | | 818 | | ... | ... | ... | 111 663 | ... | ... | ... |
| | 1992/93 | (64) | 821 | | 5 935 | 5 487 | 92 | 104 441 | 50 983 | 49 | 18 |
| | 1993/94 | (64) | 821 | | 6 513 | 6 044 | 93 | 102 120 | 50 051 | 49 | 16 |
| | 1994/95 | (64) | 881 | | 6 780 | 6 259 | 92 | 102 184 | 49 988 | 49 | 15 |
| | 1995/96 | (64) | 822 | | 7 201 | 6 626 | 92 | 100 764 | 49 206 | 49 | 14 |
| | 1996/97 | (64) | 824 | | *7 283 | *6 700 | *92 | 98 866 | 48 060 | 49 | *14 |

Primary education: schools, teaching staff and pupils II.5
Enseignement primaire: écoles, personnel enseignant et élèves
Enseñanza primaria: escuelas, personal docente y alumnos

| Country / Pays / País | Year / Année / Año | Schools / Écoles / Escuelas | Teaching staff / Personnel enseignant / Personal docente — Total | Female / Féminin / Femenino | % F | Pupils enrolled / Élèves inscrits / Alumnos matriculados — Total | Female / Féminin / Femenino | % F | Pupil/teacher ratio / Nombre d'élèves par maître / Número de alumnos por maestro |
|---|---|---|---|---|---|---|---|---|---|
| Spain | 1970/71 | ... | 115 607 | 67 143 | 58 | 3 929 569 | 1 359 526 | 50 | 34 |
| | 1975/76 | ... | (64) 172 122 | (64) 100 477 | 58 | 3 653 320 | 1 786 175 | 49 | ... |
| | 1980/81 | ... | 127 679 | 86 135 | 67 | 3 609 623 | 1 753 535 | 49 | 28 |
| | 1985/86 | 18 851 | 137 807 | 94 585 | 69 | 3 483 948 | 1 681 536 | 48 | 25 |
| | 1990/91 | 18 672 | 128 034 | 93 098 | 73 | 2 820 497 | 1 366 826 | 48 | 22 |
| | 1991/92 | 18 561 | 125 828 | 94 364 | 75 | 2 662 490 | 1 286 059 | 48 | 21 |
| | 1992/93 | ... | 129 130 | 94 679 | 73 | 2 582 343 | 1 244 519 | 48 | 20 |
| | 1993/94 | ... | 128 559 | 92 570 | 72 | 2 471 084 | 1 190 278 | 48 | 19 |
| | 1994/95 | ... | 132 566 | 94 612 | 71 | 2 364 910 | 1 140 771 | 48 | 18 |
| | 1995/96 | ... | (42) *162 112 | (42) *106 716 | *66 | (42) 2 799 960 | (42) 1 348 298 | 48 | *17 |
| | 1996/97 | ... | ... | ... | ... | 2 702 553 | 1 305 266 | 48 | |
| | 1997/98 | ... | ... | ... | ... | *2 610 041 | ... | ... | |
| | 1998/99 | ... | ... | ... | ... | *2 567 012 | ... | ... | |
| Sweden | 1970/71 | ... | 30 800 | 25 600 | 83 | 615 331 | 302 153 | 49 | 20 |
| | 1975/76 | ... | 34 185 | 27 575 | 81 | 698 677 | 341 764 | 49 | 20 |
| | 1980/81 | 4 928 | ... | ... | ... | 666 679 | 325 121 | 49 | ... |
| | 1985/86 | ... | ... | ... | ... | 612 704 | ... | ... | ... |
| | 1990/91 | ... | (64) 92 843 | (64) 63 963 | 69 | 578 359 | 282 011 | 49 | ... |
| | 1991/92 | ... | (64) 92 924 | (64) 64 301 | 69 | 584 203 | 284 840 | 49 | ... |
| | 1992/93 | ... | 64 363 | 50 383 | 78 | 614 551 | 301 238 | 49 | 10 |
| | 1993/94 | ... | 61 635 | 48 606 | 79 | 626 254 | 306 955 | 49 | 10 |
| | 1994/95 | ... | 59 402 | 42 955 | 72 | 643 768 | 315 484 | 49 | 11 |
| | 1995/96 | ... | ... | ... | ... | 666 139 | 326 489 | 49 | ... |
| | 1996/97 | ... | 58 365 | 42 649 | 73 | 690 630 | 338 604 | 49 | 12 |
| Switzerland | 1970/71 | ... | ... | ... | ... | (3)(29) 500 492 | (3)(29) 247 094 | 49 | |
| | 1975/76 | ... | ... | ... | ... | (3)(29) 556 885 | (3)(29) 274 382 | 49 | |
| | 1980/81 | ... | ... | ... | ... | 450 942 | 220 942 | 49 | |
| | 1985/86 | ... | ... | ... | ... | 376 512 | 184 492 | 49 | |
| | 1990/91 | ... | ... | ... | ... | 404 154 | 198 385 | 49 | |
| | 1991/92 | ... | ... | ... | ... | 414 129 | 203 380 | 49 | |
| | 1992/93 | ... | ... | ... | ... | 443 512 | 215 311 | 49 | |
| | 1993/94 | ... | (3) 37 490 | (3) 25 460 | 68 | 447 240 | 217 365 | 49 | |
| | 1994/95 | ... | (3) 38 488 | (3) 26 686 | 69 | 461 805 | 224 357 | 49 | |
| | 1995/96 | ... | ... | ... | ... | 477 643 | 232 251 | 49 | ... |
| The Former Yugoslav Rep. of Macedonia | 1970/71 | 1 401 | 10 794 | ... | ... | 260 033 | ... | ... | 24 |
| | 1975/76 | 1 318 | 11 762 | ... | ... | 270 154 | ... | ... | 23 |
| | 1980/81 | 1 210 | 12 100 | ... | ... | 272 344 | ... | ... | 23 |
| | 1985/86 | 1 134 | 12 929 | ... | ... | 273 219 | ... | ... | 21 |
| | 1990/91 | 1 067 | 12 976 | ... | ... | 266 813 | 128 597 | 48 | 21 |
| | 1991/92 | 1 053 | 13 044 | 6 756 | 52 | 261 127 | 126 276 | 48 | 20 |
| | 1992/93 | 1 049 | 12 958 | 6 692 | 52 | 261 540 | 126 097 | 48 | 20 |
| | 1993/94 | 1 050 | 13 102 | 6 828 | 52 | 260 659 | 125 737 | 48 | 20 |
| | 1994/95 | 1 042 | 13 154 | 6 913 | 53 | 261 105 | 126 183 | 48 | 20 |
| | 1995/96 | 1 085 | 13 466 | 7 150 | 53 | 263 103 | 126 466 | 48 | 20 |
| | 1996/97 | 1 086 | 13 594 | 7 343 | 54 | 260 917 | 125 629 | 48 | 19 |
| Ukraine | 1970/71 | (32) 27 185 | (32) 445 300 | ... | ... | 6 668 000 | *3 270 000 | *49 | ... |
| | 1975/76 | (32) 23 435 | (32) 445 400 | ... | ... | 5 970 000 | ... | ... | ... |
| | 1980/81 | (32) 21 000 | (65) 79 500 | (65) 77 500 | 97 | 3 591 800 | 1 758 400 | 49 | ... |
| | 1985/86 | (32) 20 500 | (65) 88 200 | (65) 86 200 | 98 | 3 738 900 | ... | ... | ... |
| | 1990/91 | (32)(44)20 900 | (44)(65) 119 600 | (44)(65) 117 200 | 98 | (44) 3 990 500 | (44) 1 959 500 | 49 | ... |
| | 1991/92 | (32) 21 000 | (65) 125 300 | (65) 122 400 | 98 | 4 033 000 | 1 971 600 | 49 | ... |
| | 1992/93 | (25)(32)21 100 | (25) 130 600 | (25) 127 900 | 98 | (25) 2 682 600 | (25) 1 304 900 | 49 | 21 |
| | 1993/94 | (32) 21 720 | 133 600 | 130 600 | 98 | 2 658 800 | 1 300 000 | 49 | 20 |
| United Kingdom | 1970/71 | 29 504 | (6) 248 908 | (6) 192 409 | 77 | 5 806 349 | 2 833 864 | 49 | ... |
| | 1975/76 | (3) 26 981 | (6) 285 786 | (6) 230 659 | 81 | 5 725 167 | 2 793 625 | 49 | ... |
| | 1980/81 | (3) 26 504 | ... | ... | ... | 4 910 724 | 2 393 020 | 49 | ... |
| | 1985/86 | (3) 24 756 | ... | ... | ... | 4 296 000 | 2 096 000 | 49 | ... |
| | 1990/91 | (3) 24 135 | 229 100 | 178 800 | 78 | 4 532 500 | 2 221 200 | 49 | 20 |
| | 1991/92 | (3) 23 958 | 230 200 | 180 000 | 78 | 4 559 500 | 2 229 900 | 49 | 20 |
| | 1992/93 | ... | (66) 265 939 | (66) 205 677 | 77 | (66) 5 071 847 | (66) 2 474 662 | 49 | 19 |
| | 1993/94 | ... | 280 799 | 228 306 | 81 | 5 143 227 | 2 509 915 | 49 | 18 |
| | 1994/95 | ... | 279 036 | ... | ... | 5 208 961 | 2 542 307 | 49 | 19 |
| | 1995/96 | ... | 283 861 | 228 443 | 80 | 5 284 125 | 2 579 338 | 49 | 19 |
| | 1996/97 | 23 306 | 283 492 | 228 677 | 81 | 5 328 219 | 2 602 412 | 49 | 19 |
| **Oceania** | | | | | | | | | |
| American Samoa | 1970/71 | (6) 32 | (6) 350 | ... | ... | 8 100 | ... | ... | ... |
| | 1975/76 | ... | (3) 270 | ... | ... | (3) 6 052 | ... | ... | 22 |
| | 1985/86 | 31 | 454 | 284 | 63 | 7 704 | 3 614 | 47 | 17 |
| | 1991/92 | 30 | 524 | 341 | 65 | 7 884 | 3 769 | 48 | 15 |
| Australia | 1970 | 8 354 | (6) 64 670 | (6) 45 300 | 70 | (6) 1 812 000 | (6) 878 600 | 48 | 28 |
| | 1975 | 8 009 | (6) 78 390 | (6) 56 185 | 72 | 1 632 716 | 792 485 | 49 | ... |
| | 1980 | ... | ... | ... | ... | 1 718 352 | 835 617 | 49 | ... |
| | 1985 | ... | ... | ... | ... | 1 542 101 | 748 952 | 49 | ... |
| | 1990 | (6) 7 927 | ... | ... | ... | 1 583 024 | 769 337 | 49 | ... |
| | 1991 | (6) 7 916 | (6)(58) 96 779 | (6)(58) 71 363 | 74 | 1 605 720 | 780 406 | 49 | ... |
| | 1992 | (6) 7 923 | (6)(58) 97 955 | (6)(58) 72 652 | 74 | 1 623 012 | 789 407 | 49 | ... |

II.5 Primary education: schools, teaching staff and pupils
Enseignement primaire: écoles, personnel enseignant et élèves
Enseñanza primaria: escuelas, personal docente y alumnos

| Country / Pays / País | Year / Année / Año | Schools / Écoles / Escuelas | Teaching staff — Personnel enseignant — Personal docente | | | Pupils enrolled — Élèves inscrits — Alumnos matriculados | | | Pupil/teacher ratio / Nombre d'élèves par maître / Número de alumnos por maestro |
|---|---|---|---|---|---|---|---|---|---|
| | | | Total | Female Féminin Femenino | % F | Total | Female Féminin Femenino | % F | |
| Australia (cont) | 1993 | (6) 7 880 | (6)(58) 98 526 | (6)(58) 73 351 | 74 | 1 633 797 | 794 807 | 49 | ... |
| | 1994 | (6) 7 725 | ... | ... | ... | 1 639 577 | 797 944 | 49 | ... |
| | 1995 | (42) 7 730 | (42)(58) 101 035 | (42)(58) 76 875 | 76 | (42) 1 833 681 | (42) 891 994 | 49 | ... |
| | 1996 | 7 713 | (58) 102 267 | (58) 77 894 | 76 | 1 848 169 | 899 180 | 49 | ... |
| | 1997 | 8 123 | (58) 103 774 | (58) 79 796 | 77 | 1 855 789 | 902 670 | 49 | ... |
| Fiji | 1980 | 652 | 4 097 | 2 349 | 57 | 116 139 | 56 646 | 49 | 28 |
| | 1985 | 668 | 4 396 | 2 540 | 58 | 127 286 | 61 921 | 49 | 29 |
| | 1990 | 681 | 4 272 | ... | ... | 143 552 | ... | ... | 34 |
| | 1991 | 692 | 4 664 | 2 639 | 57 | 144 924 | 70 508 | 49 | 31 |
| | 1992 | 693 | 4 644 | 2 606 | 56 | 145 630 | 70 713 | 49 | 31 |
| French Polynesia | 1970/71 | 159 | 771 | 530 | 69 | 24 148 | 11 723 | 49 | 31 |
| | 1975/76 | 167 | 1 213 | 950 | 78 | 28 533 | 13 853 | 49 | 24 |
| | 1990/91 | 180 | 1 976 | (3) 1 264 | ... | 28 270 | 13 489 | 48 | 14 |
| | 1991/92 | ... | ... | ... | ... | 28 195 | ... | ... | ... |
| | 1992/93 | 176 | 1 741 | (3) 976 | ... | 29 132 | 13 996 | 48 | 17 |
| | 1994/95 | ... | 1 974 | 1 331 | 67 | 30 037 | 14 375 | 48 | 15 |
| | 1995/96 | 170 | 2 052 | 1 381 | 67 | 29 415 | 14 058 | 48 | 14 |
| Guam | 1970/71 | (6) 31 | (6) 713 | ... | ... | *17 927 | (3) 6 516 | ... | ... |
| | 1975/76 | 39 | 919 | ... | ... | 20 215 | ... | ... | 22 |
| | 1980/81 | ... | (3) 674 | ... | ... | 18 093 | ... | ... | ... |
| | 1985/86 | ... | (3) 711 | ... | ... | 16 783 | ... | ... | ... |
| Kiribati | 1970 | (30) 218 | (30) 546 | ... | ... | (30) 14 570 | ... | ... | 27 |
| | 1975 | 106 | 449 | ... | ... | 14 862 | ... | ... | 33 |
| | 1980 | 100 | 435 | 210 | 48 | 13 235 | 6 457 | 49 | 30 |
| | 1985 | 112 | 460 | 236 | 51 | 13 440 | 6 625 | 49 | 29 |
| | 1990 | 104 | 514 | 295 | 57 | 14 709 | 7 298 | 50 | 29 |
| | 1991 | 102 | 533 | 310 | 58 | 15 570 | 7 680 | 49 | 29 |
| | 1992 | 95 | 545 | 319 | 59 | 16 020 | 7 904 | 49 | 29 |
| | 1993 | 92 | 537 | 317 | 59 | 16 316 | 8 067 | 49 | 30 |
| | 1994 | 84 | 542 | ... | ... | 16 800 | 8 278 | 49 | 31 |
| | 1995 | 85 | 624 | 368 | 59 | 17 017 | 8 384 | 49 | 27 |
| | 1996 | 85 | 732 | 423 | 58 | 17 279 | 8 531 | 49 | 24 |
| | 1997 | 86 | 727 | 452 | 62 | 17 594 | 8 620 | 49 | 24 |
| Nauru | 1985 | 7 | 71 | 43 | 61 | 1 451 | 679 | 47 | 20 |
| New Caledonia | 1970 | 251 | 940 | 442 | 47 | 21 632 | 10 694 | 49 | 23 |
| | 1975 | (6) 235 | (6) 1 431 | ... | ... | 24 943 | 12 207 | 49 | ... |
| | 1985 | 211 | 1 131 | ... | ... | 22 517 | 10 838 | 48 | 20 |
| | 1990 | 205 | 1 147 | ... | ... | 22 958 | 11 098 | 48 | 20 |
| | 1991 | 200 | 1 096 | ... | ... | 22 325 | 10 780 | 48 | 20 |
| | 1992 | ... | ... | ... | ... | 21 865 | ... | ... | ... |
| | 1994 | ... | ... | ... | ... | 22 308 | ... | ... | ... |
| New Zealand | 1970 | ... | ... | ... | ... | (29) 400 445 | (29) 193 825 | 48 | ... |
| | 1975 | ... | ... | ... | ... | 391 399 | 190 087 | 49 | ... |
| | 1980 | ... | ... | ... | ... | 381 262 | 185 824 | 49 | ... |
| | 1985 | ... | ... | ... | ... | 329 337 | 160 197 | 49 | ... |
| | 1990 | 2 301 | 17 729 | 13 943 | 79 | 318 568 | 154 149 | 48 | 18 |
| | 1991 | 2 258 | 18 960 | 15 143 | 80 | 316 107 | 153 409 | 49 | 17 |
| | 1992 | 2 262 | 19 583 | 15 687 | 80 | 317 286 | 153 804 | 48 | 16 |
| | 1993 | ... | ... | ... | ... | 322 984 | 156 820 | 49 | ... |
| | 1994 | 2 324 | 19 443 | 15 742 | 81 | 331 666 | 161 221 | 49 | 17 |
| | 1995 | 2 316 | ... | ... | ... | 345 236 | 168 056 | 49 | ... |
| | 1996 | 2 302 | 18 146 | 14 839 | 82 | 348 098 | 169 468 | 49 | 19 |
| | 1997 | 2 296 | 19 523 | 15 978 | 82 | 357 569 | 173 728 | 49 | 18 |
| Niue | 1970 | 8 | (67) 71 | (67) 31 | 44 | (67) 1 299 | (67) 630 | 48 | 18 |
| | 1975 | 8 | 65 | 27 | 42 | 1 122 | 543 | 48 | 17 |
| | 1980 | ... | 45 | ... | ... | 666 | ... | ... | 15 |
| | 1985 | ... | 29 | ... | ... | 503 | ... | ... | 17 |
| | 1991 | ... | (9) 19 | ... | ... | (9) 371 | ... | ... | 20 |
| Papua New Guinea | 1970 | 1 620 | 6 439 | ... | ... | 191 083 | 69 739 | 36 | 30 |
| | 1975 | 1 762 | 7 544 | 1 721 | 23 | 238 267 | 88 994 | 37 | 32 |
| | 1980 | *2 130 | *9 549 | *2 559 | *27 | 299 823 | *123 805 | *41 | *31 |
| | 1990 | 2 606 | 13 105 | 4 227 | 32 | 415 195 | 184 128 | 44 | 32 |
| | 1991 | 2 603 | 13 417 | 4 531 | 34 | 422 348 | 188 244 | 45 | 31 |
| | 1992 | 2 821 | 14 117 | 4 770 | 34 | 443 552 | 197 720 | 45 | 31 |
| | 1993 | 2 726 | 14 378 | 5 089 | 35 | 478 040 | 215 197 | 45 | 33 |
| | 1994 | 2 864 | 15 298 | 5 542 | 36 | (68) 505 153 | (68) 226 966 | 45 | ... |
| | 1995 | (3) 2 790 | (3) 13 457 | (3) 4 910 | 36 | (68) 516 797 | (68) 233 979 | 45 | ... |
| Samoa | 1970 | 173 | 1 051 | ... | ... | 29 405 | 14 254 | 48 | 28 |
| | 1975 | 152 | (69) 1 216 | (69) 773 | 64 | 32 642 | 16 713 | 51 | ... |
| | 1980 | 152 | (69) 1 438 | (69) 1 026 | 71 | 33 012 | 15 694 | 48 | ... |
| | 1990 | ... | ... | ... | ... | 35 763 | 17 696 | 49 | ... |
| | 1991 | ... | 1 427 | 1 029 | 72 | 37 080 | 17 720 | 48 | 26 |
| | 1992 | ... | 1 488 | 1 078 | 72 | 35 447 | 16 895 | 48 | 24 |
| | 1993 | ... | 1 441 | 1 032 | 72 | 35 338 | 16 869 | 48 | 25 |
| | 1994 | ... | 1 476 | 1 060 | 72 | 35 750 | 17 102 | 48 | 24 |
| | 1995 | (42) 155 | (42) 1 475 | (42) 1 048 | 71 | (42) 35 811 | (42) 17 090 | 48 | 24 |
| | 1996 | ... | 1 479 | 1 063 | 72 | 35 378 | 16 761 | 47 | 24 |
| | 1997 | ... | ... | ... | ... | 35 649 | 17 063 | 48 | ... |

Primary education: schools, teaching staff and pupils  **II.5**
Enseignement primaire: écoles, personnel enseignant et élèves
Enseñanza primaria: escuelas, personal docente y alumnos

| Country<br>Pays<br>País | Year<br>Année<br>Año | Schools<br>Écoles<br>Escuelas | Teaching staff<br>Personnel enseignant<br>Personal docente | | | Pupils enrolled<br>Élèves inscrits<br>Alumnos matriculados | | | Pupil/<br>teacher ratio<br>Nombre<br>d'élèves<br>par maître<br>Número de<br>alumnos<br>por maestro |
|---|---|---|---|---|---|---|---|---|---|
| | | | Total | Female<br>Féminin<br>Femenino | %<br>F | Total | Female<br>Féminin<br>Femenino | %<br>F | |
| Solomon Islands | 1970 | 418 | 885 | 194 | 22 | 21 270 | 7 743 | 36 | 24 |
| | 1975 | 344 | 1 071 | 312 | 29 | 28 219 | 10 743 | 38 | 26 |
| | 1980 | (15) 370 | (15) 1 148 | (15) 303 | 26 | (15) 28 870 | (15) 11 980 | 41 | 25 |
| | 1985 | 423 | 1 496 | ... | ... | 38 716 | ... | ... | 26 |
| | 1990 | 518 | 2 457 | ... | ... | 47 598 | 21 107 | 44 | 19 |
| | 1991 | 520 | 2 388 | ... | ... | 49 000 | 21 758 | 44 | 21 |
| | 1992 | 521 | 2 490 | ... | ... | 53 320 | 23 581 | 44 | 21 |
| | 1993 | ... | 2 357 | ... | ... | 57 264 | 25 403 | 44 | 24 |
| | 1994 | ... | 2 514 | ... | ... | 60 493 | 27 089 | 45 | 24 |
| Tokelau | 1991 | ... | ... | ... | ... | 361 | 181 | 50 | ... |
| Tonga | 1970 | 128 | 658 | 288 | 44 | 17 865 | 8 548 | 48 | 27 |
| | 1975 | 126 | 688 | 368 | 53 | 19 260 | 9 176 | 48 | 28 |
| | 1980 | 110 | 781 | ... | ... | 19 012 | ... | ... | 24 |
| | 1985 | 112 | 744 | 460 | 62 | 17 019 | 8 162 | 48 | 23 |
| | 1990 | 115 | 689 | 475 | 69 | 16 522 | 7 915 | 48 | 24 |
| | 1991 | 115 | 714 | 481 | 67 | 16 728 | 7 985 | 48 | 23 |
| | 1992 | 115 | 784 | 503 | 64 | 16 658 | 7 960 | 48 | 21 |
| | 1993 | 115 | 754 | 495 | 66 | 16 792 | 7 994 | 48 | 22 |
| Tuvalu | 1980 | ... | ... | ... | ... | (70) 1 327 | ... | ... | ... |
| | 1990 | ... | (3) 72 | (3) 52 | 72 | (3)(70) 1 485 | (3)(70) 708 | 48 | ... |
| | 1993 | ... | ... | ... | ... | 1 752 | 838 | 48 | ... |
| | 1994 | 11 | ... | ... | ... | 1 906 | 932 | 49 | ... |
| Vanuatu, Republic of | 1970 | 275 | 778 | 229 | 29 | 18 250 | 7 983 | 44 | 23 |
| | 1975 | ... | ... | ... | ... | 20 095 | 9 029 | 45 | ... |
| | 1980 | 278 | 986 | ... | ... | 23 264 | 10 593 | 46 | 24 |
| | 1985 | 245 | ... | ... | ... | 22 897 | ... | ... | ... |
| | 1990 | 261 | ... | ... | ... | 24 471 | 11 518 | 47 | ... |
| | 1991 | 267 | 869 | 350 | 40 | 24 952 | 11 651 | 47 | 29 |
| | 1992 | 272 | 852 | ... | ... | 26 267 | 12 288 | 47 | 31 |

## General note
For general explanations and definitions, please refer to the beginning of this chapter.

## Note générale
Pour les explications et définitions générales, prière de se référer au début de ce chapitre.

## Nota general
Para las explicaciones y definiciones generales, referirse al comienzo de este capítulo.

Notes

(1) Including administrative staff.
(2) As from 1973, change in structure.
(3) Public education only.
(4) 'Ensino basico elementar' (grades 1 to 4) only
(5) Not including private Moslem education.
(6) Including pre-primary education.
(7) Not including Al Azhar university.
(8) As from 1989, change in structure.
(9) As from 1991, change in structure.
(10) Not including "Action aid schools".
(11) Not including the "Instituto Amizade".
(12) Including initiation classes where students learn portuguese.
(13) As from 1985, change in structure.
(14) As from 1971, change in structure.
(15) As from 1976, change in structure.
(16) In 1994/95, primary education became exempt of school fees.
(17) Not including recognised 'Medersas'.
(18) As from 1979, change in structure.
(19) As from 1990, change in structure.
(20) As from 1987, change in structure.
(21) As from this year, data reported include special education.
(22) As from 1980, change in structure.
(23) Data refer to approximately 95% of the total number of schools.
(24) Not including the former independent states (Transkei, Bophuthatswana, Venda and Ciskei).

Notes

(1) Y compris le personnel administratif.
(2) A partir de 1973, changement de structure.
(3) Enseignement public seulement.
(4) 'Ensino basico elementar' (années d'études de 1 à 4) seulement.
(5) Non compris l'enseignement privé musulman.
(6) Y compris l'enseignement préprimaire.
(7) Non compris l'université Al Azhar.
(8) A partir de 1989, changement de structure.
(9) A partir de 1991, changement de structure.
(10) Non compris "Action aid schools".
(11) Non compris l'"Instituto Amizade".
(12) Y compris les classes d'initiation où les élèves apprennent le portugais.
(13) A partir de 1985, changement de structure.
(14) A partir de 1971, changement de structure.
(15) A partir de 1976, changement de structure.
(16) En 1994/95, les frais de scolarité sont supprimés pour l'enseignement primaire.
(17) Non compris les écoles 'Medersas'.
(18) A partir de 1979, changement de structure.
(19) A partir de 1990, changement de structure.
(20) A partir de 1987, changement de structure.
(21) A partir de cette année, les données incluent l'enseignement spécial.
(22) A partir de 1980, changement de structure.
(23) Les données se réfèrent à environ 95% du nombre total des écoles.
(24) Non compris les anciens états indépendants (Transkei, Bophuthatswana, Venda et Ciskei).

Notas

(1) Incluye el personal administrativo.
(2) A partir de 1973, cambio de estructura.
(3) Enseñanza pública solamente.
(4) 'Ensino basico elementar' (años de estudios de 1 a 4) solamente.
(5) No incluye la enseñanza privada musulmana.
(6) Incluye la enseñanza preprimaria.
(7) No incluye la universidad Al Azhar.
(8) A partir de 1989, cambio de estructura.
(9) A partir de 1991, cambio de estructura.
(10) No incluye "Action aid schools".
(11) No incluye el Instituto Amizade.
(12) Incluyen las clases de iniciación donde los alumnos aprenden el portugués.
(13) A partir de 1985, cambio de estructura.
(14) A partir de 1971, cambio de estructura.
(15) A partir de 1976, cambio de estructura.
(16) En 1994/95, se suprimieron los gastos de inscripción de la enseñanza primaria.
(17) No incluyen las escuelas 'Medersas'
(18) A partir de 1979, cambio de estructura.
(19) A partir de 1990, cambio de estructura.
(20) A partir de 1987, cambio de estructura.
(21) A partir de este año, los datos incluyen la enseñanza especial.
(22) A partir de 1980, cambio de estructura.
(23) Los datos se refieren aproximadamente al 95% del total de las escuelas.
(24) No incluyen los antiguos estados independientes (Transkei, Bophuthatswana, Venda y Ciskei).

II.5    Primary education: schools, teaching staff and pupils
Enseignement primaire: écoles, personnel enseignant et élèves
Enseñanza primaria: escuelas, personal docente y alumnos

(25) As from 1992, change in structure.

(26) Public and aided education only.

(27) Tanzania mainland only.

(28) Including post-primary classes.

(29) Including special education.

(30) Including senior departments of all-age schools (secondary).

(31) Data refer to the total number of pre-primary and primary schools.

(32) Including secondary general education.

(33) Including evening schools.

(34) From 1974, forms I, II and III, previously classified as primary education are now included with general secondary education.

(35) Infant classes are classified at pre-primary education.

(36) Including secondary classes attached to primary schools.

(37) Data refer to posts and not to teaching staff.

(38) Data refer to the end of school year.

(39) Data refer to grades 1-6.

(40) As from 1975, change in structure.

(41) Not including primary classes attached to middle and secondary schools.

(42) As from 1995, change in structure.

(43) Including part of intermediate education.

(44) As from 1986, change in structure.

(45) As from 1996, change in structure.

(46) Not including Turkish schools.

(47) Not including teachers in primary classes attached to secondary schools.

(48) Not including intermediate sections in primary schools.

(49) From 1994, all intermediate schools are included in secondary education. Previously they were partly classified in primary education.

(50) Full-time only.

(51) East Bank only.

(52) As from 1981, change in data coverage.

(53) As from 1972, change in structure.

(54) As from 1981, change in structure.

(55) As from 1978, change in structure.

(56) Including evening and correspondence courses.

(57) Including grades 5-8 of the volksschulen classified under secondary general education.

(58) Data are expressed in full-time equivalent.

(59) As from 1975, change in data coverage.

(60) As from 1993, change in structure.

(61) Not including special education.

(62) In 1993/94, the national authorities of the Netherlands changed their method of estimating the breakdown of teaching staff by sex between the pre-primary and primary levels of education

(63) As from 1988, change in structure.

(64) Including the first stage of secondary general education.

(65) Data refer to grades 1 to 4 only.

(66) From 1992/93 data include pupils educated in infant classes in primary schools, previously considered as pre-primary education, as well as pupils below compulsory school age, in independent and special pre-primary schools.

(67) Data refer to grades 1-7.

(68) Grades VII and VIII refer to top up schools.

(69) Including intermediate education.

(70) Including 3 years of education provided in community training centres.

---

(25) A partir de 1992, changement de structure.

(26) Enseignement public et subventionné seulement.

(27) Tanzanie continentale seulement.

(28) Y compris les classes post-primaires.

(29) Y compris l'enseignement spécial.

(30) Y compris les sections supérieures des 'all-age schools' (secondaire).

(31) Les données se réfèrent au nombre total des écoles préprimaires et primaires.

(32) Y compris l'enseignement secondaire général.

(33) Y compris les écoles du soir.

(34) A partir de 1974, Les 'forms I, II and III' qui auparavant étaient classées comme enseignement primaire, sont maintenant comprises dans l'enseignement secondaire general.

(35) Les classes enfantines sont classées dans l'enseignement préprimaire.

(36) Y compris les classes secondaires rattachées aux écoles primaires.

(37) Les données se réfèrent au nombre de postes et non au nombre d'enseignants.

(38) Les données se réfèrent à la fin de l'année scolaire.

(39) Les données se réfèrent aux années d'études 1 à 6.

(40) A partir de 1975, changement de structure.

(41) Non compris les classes primaires rattachées aux écoles moyennes et secondaires.

(42) A partir de 1995, changement de structure.

(43) Y compris une partie de l'enseignement intermédiaire.

(44) A partir de 1986, changement de structure.

(45) A partir de 1996, changement de structure.

(46) Non compris les écoles turques.

(47) Non compris les enseignants des classes primaires rattachées aux écoles secondaires.

(48) Non compris les sections intermédiaires dans les écoles primaires.

(49) A partir de 1994, toutes les écoles intermédiaires sont incluses dans le secondaire. Auparavant elles étaient en partie comptées dans le primaire.

(50) Plein temps seulement.

(51) Rive orientale seulement.

(52) A partir de 1981, changement dans la couverture des données.

(53) A partir de 1972, changement de structure.

(54) A partir de 1981, changement de structure.

(55) A partir de 1978, changement de structure.

(56) Y compris les cours du soir et par correspondance.

(57) Y compris les années d'études 5 à 8 des "volksschulen" qui font partie de l'enseignement secondaire général.

(58) Les données sont exprimées en équivalents plein temps.

(59) A partir de 1975, changement dans la couverture des données.

(60) A partir de 1993, changement de structure.

(61) Non compris l'enseignement spécial.

(62) En 1993/94, les autorités nationales des Pays Bas ont changé de méthode d'estimation de la répartition par sexe du personnel enseignant entre les niveaux préprimaire et primaire.

(63) A partir de 1988, changement de structure.

(64) Y compris le premier cycle de l'enseignement secondaire général.

(65) les données se réfèrent aux années d'études de 1 à 4 seulement.

(66) A partir de 1992/93, les données incluent les élèves inscrits dans les classes enfantines des écoles primaires, considérées auparavant comme de l'enseignement préprimaire. Sont également inclus les élèves en dessous de l'âge de la scolarité obligatoire des écoles préprimaires indépendantes et spéciales.

(67) Les données se réfèrent aux années d'études de 1 à 7.

(68) Les septième et huitième années d'études se réfèrent aux 'top up schools'.

(69) Y compris l'enseignement intermédiaire.

(70) Y compris 3 années d'enseignement dispensé dans les 'community training centres'.

---

(25) A partir de 1992, cambio de estructura.

(26) Enseñanza pública y subvencionada solamente.

(27) Tanzania continental solamente.

(28) Incluyen las clases post-primarias.

(29) Incluye la enseñanza especial.

(30) Incluyen las secciones superiores de las 'all-age schools' (secundaria).

(31) Los datos se refieren al número total de escuelas preprimarias y primarias.

(32) Incluyen la enseñanza secundaria general.

(33) Incluyen las escuelas nocturnas.

(34) A partir de 1974, las 'forms I, II and III' que antes estaban consideradas como enseñanza primaria están ahora incluidas en la enseñanza secundaria general.

(35) Las clases de párvulos están clasificadas en la enseñanza preprimaria.

(36) Incluyen las clases secundarias dependientes de las escuelas primarias.

(37) Los datos se refieren al número de puestos y no al número de docentes.

(38) Los datos se refieren al final del año escolar.

(39) Los datos se refieren a los años de estudios de 1 a 6.

(40) A partir de 1975, cambio de estructura.

(41) No incluyen las clases primarias adscritas a las escuelas medias y secundarias.

(42) A partir de 1995, cambio de estructura.

(43) Incluye una parte de la enseñanza intermediaria.

(44) A partir de 1986, cambio de estructura.

(45) A partir de 1996, cambio de estructura.

(46) No incluyen las escuelas turcas.

(47) No incluyen los docentes de las clases primarias dependientes de las escuelas secundarias.

(48) No incluyen las secciones intermediarias en las escuelas primarias.

(49) A partir de 1994, todas las escuelas intermediarias están incluidas en la enseñanza secundaria. Antes estaban en parte incluidas en la enseñanza primaria.

(50) Jornada completa solamente.

(51) Orilla oriental solamente.

(52) A partir de 1981, cambio en la cobertura de los datos.

(53) A partir de 1972, cambio de estructura.

(54) A partir de 1981, cambio de estructura.

(55) A partir de 1978, cambio de estructura.

(56) Incluyen los cursos nocturnos y por correspondencia.

(57) Incluyen las clases 5 a 8 de las "volksschulen" que se clasifican en la enseñanza secundaria general.

(58) Los datos están expresados en equivalente de jornada completa.

(59) A partir de 1975, cambio en la cobertura de los datos.

(60) A partir de 1993, cambio de estructura.

(61) No incluye la enseñanza especial.

(62) En 1993/94, las autoridades nacionales de los Países Bajos cambiaron el método de cálculo de la distribución por sexo del personal docente entre los niveles de enseñanza preprimaria y primaria.

(63) A partir de 1988, cambio de estructura.

(64) Incluye el primer ciclo de la enseñanza secundaria general.

(65) Los datos se refieren a los años de estudios de 1 a 4 solamente.

(66) A partir de 1992/93, los datos incluyen los alumnos matriculados en las clases de párvulos de las escuelas primarias, consideradas antes como enseñanza preprimaria. Están igualmente incluidos los alumnos que no han alcanzado la edad de escolaridad obligatoria de las escuelas preprimarias independientes y especiales.

(67) Los datos se refieren a los años de estudios de 1 a 7.

(68) Los años de estudio séptimo y octavo se refieren a los 'top up schools'.

(69) Incluye la enseñanza intermediaria.

(70) Incluyen 3 años de enseñanza dispensada en los 'community training centres'.

Secondary education: teaching staff and pupils  II.6
Enseignement secondaire: personnel enseignant et élèves
Enseñanza secundaria: personal docente y alumnos

## II.6 Secondary education: teaching staff and pupils in general, teacher training and vocational education

## Enseignement secondaire: personnel enseignant et élèves dans les enseignements général, normal et technique

## Enseñanza secundaria: personal docente y alumnos en la enseñanza general, normal y técnica

| Total | = Total du secondaire | = Total enseñanza secundaria |
|---|---|---|
| General education | = Enseignement général | = Enseñanza general |
| Teacher training | = Enseignement normal | = Enseñanza normal |
| Vocational education | = Enseignement technique | = Enseñanza técnica |

| Country / Pays / País | Type of education / Type d'enseignement / Tipo de enseñanza | Year / Année / Año | Teaching staff Personnel enseignant Personal docente | | | Pupils enrolled Elèves inscrits Alumnos matriculados | | |
|---|---|---|---|---|---|---|---|---|
| | | | Total | Female Féminin Femenino | % F | Total | Female Féminin Femenino | % F |
| **Africa** | | | | | | | | |
| Algeria | Total | 1970/71 | 11 487 | *4 866 | *42 | 242 335 | 68 562 | 28 |
| | General education | | *7 837 | *3 021 | *39 | 186 261 | 53 480 | 29 |
| | Teacher training | | 484 | *97 | *20 | 8 333 | 2 926 | 35 |
| | Vocational education | | 3 166 | *1 748 | *55 | 47 741 | 12 156 | 25 |
| | Total | 1975/76 | 19 764 | ... | ... | 509 258 | 171 241 | 34 |
| | General education | | 18 205 | ... | ... | 487 648 | 165 672 | 34 |
| | Teacher training | | 792 | ... | ... | 8 809 | 2 891 | 33 |
| | Vocational education | | 767 | ... | ... | 12 801 | 2 678 | 21 |
| | Total | 1980/81 | 41 137 | ... | ... | 1 028 294 | 396 245 | 39 |
| | General education | | (1) 40 013 | ... | ... | 1 000 486 | 388 268 | 39 |
| | Teacher training | | 1 124 | ... | ... | 13 315 | 4 911 | 37 |
| | Vocational education | | ./. | ... | ... | 14 493 | 3 066 | 21 |
| | Total | 1985/86 | 82 218 | 29 883 | 36 | 1 823 392 | 757 511 | 42 |
| | General education | | 80 055 | 29 580 | 37 | 1 756 506 | 737 439 | 42 |
| | Teacher training | | - | - | - | - | - | - |
| | Vocational education | | 2 163 | 303 | 14 | 66 886 | 20 072 | 30 |
| | Total | 1990/91 | (2) 127 024 | (2) 49 600 | 39 | (2) 2 175 580 | (2) 943 357 | 43 |
| | General education | | (2) 120 706 | (2) 48 564 | 40 | (2) 2 022 220 | (2) 895 633 | 44 |
| | Teacher training | | - | - | - | - | - | - |
| | Vocational education | | 6 318 | 1 036 | 16 | 153 360 | 47 724 | 31 |
| | Total | 1991/92 | 131 232 | 52 560 | 40 | 2 232 780 | 981 917 | 44 |
| | General education | | 125 691 | 51 693 | 41 | 2 136 755 | 951 340 | 45 |
| | Teacher training | | - | - | - | - | - | - |
| | Vocational education | | 5 541 | 867 | 16 | (3) 96 025 | (3) 30 577 | 32 |
| | Total | 1992/93 | 135 730 | 56 891 | 42 | 2 305 198 | 1 027 489 | 45 |
| | General education | | 130 413 | 55 970 | 43 | 2 176 076 | 991 205 | 46 |
| | Teacher training | | - | - | - | - | - | - |
| | Vocational education | | 5 317 | 921 | 17 | 129 122 | 36 284 | 28 |
| | Total | 1993/94 | 143 887 | 61 892 | 43 | 2 412 079 | 1 093 221 | 45 |
| | General education | | 137 701 | 60 711 | 44 | 2 290 904 | 1 051 818 | 46 |
| | Teacher training | | - | - | - | - | - | - |
| | Vocational education | | 6 186 | 1 181 | 19 | 121 175 | 41 403 | 34 |
| | Total | 1994/95 | 146 792 | 63 284 | 43 | 2 472 569 | 1 136 941 | 46 |
| | General education | | 140 213 | 61 953 | 44 | 2 336 114 | 1 089 997 | 47 |
| | Teacher training | | - | - | - | - | - | - |
| | Vocational education | | 6 579 | 1 331 | 20 | 136 455 | 46 944 | 34 |
| | Total | 1995/96 | 150 397 | 66 332 | 44 | 2 544 864 | 1 181 439 | 46 |
| | General education | | 143 598 | 64 834 | 45 | 2 397 446 | 1 130 390 | 47 |
| | Teacher training | | - | - | - | - | - | - |
| | Vocational education | | 6 799 | 1 498 | 22 | 147 418 | 51 049 | 35 |
| | Total | 1996/97 | 151 948 | 68 677 | 45 | 2 618 242 | 1 253 576 | 48 |
| | General education | | 145 160 | 67 067 | 46 | 2 480 168 | 1 203 850 | 49 |
| | Teacher training | | - | - | - | - | - | - |
| | Vocational education | | 6 788 | 1 610 | 24 | 138 074 | 49 726 | 36 |

II.6 Secondary education: teaching staff and pupils
Enseignement secondaire: personnel enseignant et élèves
Enseñanza secundaria: personal docente y alumnos

| Country / Pays / País | Type of education / Type d'enseignement / Tipo de enseñanza | Year / Année / Año | Teaching staff Personnel enseignant Personal docente | | | Pupils enrolled Elèves inscrits Alumnos matriculados | | |
|---|---|---|---|---|---|---|---|---|
| | | | Total | Female Féminin Femenino | % F | Total | Female Féminin Femenino | % F |
| Angola | Total | 1970/71 | 3 814 | ... | ... | 57 829 | 24 131 | 42 |
| | General education | | 2 669 | ... | ... | 43 966 | 19 132 | 44 |
| | Teacher training | | 154 | ... | ... | 1 696 | 1 133 | 67 |
| | Vocational education | | 991 | ... | ... | 12 167 | 3 866 | 32 |
| | Total | 1980/81 | ... | ... | ... | 190 702 | ... | ... |
| | General education | | ... | ... | ... | 185 904 | ... | ... |
| | Teacher training | | ... | ... | ... | 2 086 | ... | ... |
| | Vocational education | | ... | ... | ... | 2 712 | ... | ... |
| | Total | 1985/86 | ... | ... | ... | 178 910 | ... | ... |
| | General education | | ... | ... | ... | 170 165 | ... | ... |
| | Teacher training | | ... | ... | ... | 4 070 | ... | ... |
| | Vocational education | | ... | ... | ... | 4 675 | ... | ... |
| | Total | 1990/91 | ... | ... | ... | 186 499 | ... | ... |
| | General education | | ... | ... | ... | 166 812 | ... | ... |
| | Teacher training | | ... | ... | ... | 8 753 | 3 657 | 42 |
| | Vocational education | | ... | ... | ... | 10 934 | ... | ... |
| | Total | 1991/92 | ... | ... | ... | 218 987 | ... | ... |
| | General education | | ... | ... | ... | 196 099 | ... | ... |
| | Teacher training | | ... | ... | ... | 10 772 | ... | ... |
| | Vocational education | | ... | ... | ... | 12 116 | ... | ... |
| Benin | Total | 1970/71 | ... | ... | ... | 17 889 | 5 330 | 30 |
| | General education | | 704 | ... | ... | 17 243 | 5 245 | 30 |
| | Teacher training | | 20 | 4 | 20 | 172 | 21 | 12 |
| | Vocational education | | ... | ... | ... | 474 | 64 | 14 |
| | Total | 1975/76 | ... | ... | ... | 43 123 | ... | ... |
| | General education | | 1 092 | ... | ... | 41 802 | 12 261 | 29 |
| | Teacher training | | 10 | 5 | 50 | 170 | 29 | 17 |
| | Vocational education | | ... | ... | ... | 1 151 | ... | ... |
| | Total | 1980/81 | ... | ... | ... | 89 969 | ... | ... |
| | General education | | 1 854 | ... | ... | 83 207 | 21 765 | 26 |
| | Teacher training | | ... | ... | ... | 788 | ... | ... |
| | Vocational education | | ... | ... | ... | 5 974 | ... | ... |
| | Total | 1985/86 | ... | ... | ... | 107 172 | 30 590 | 29 |
| | General education | | 2 722 | ... | ... | 99 345 | 27 824 | 28 |
| | Teacher training | | 57 | ... | ... | 1 332 | 394 | 30 |
| | Vocational education | | ... | ... | ... | 6 495 | 2 372 | 37 |
| | Total | 1990/91 | ... | ... | ... | ... | ... | ... |
| | General education | | ... | ... | ... | (4) 72 256 | (4) 19 686 | 27 |
| | Teacher training | | ... | ... | ... | ... | ... | ... |
| | Vocational education | | ... | ... | ... | ... | ... | ... |
| | Total | 1991/92 | ... | ... | ... | ... | ... | ... |
| | General education | | (4) 2 193 | (4) 508 | 23 | (4) 76 672 | (4) 21 363 | 28 |
| | Teacher training | | ... | ... | ... | ... | ... | ... |
| | Vocational education | | ... | ... | ... | ... | ... | ... |
| | Total | 1992/93 | ... | ... | ... | ... | ... | ... |
| | General education | | (4) 2 384 | (4) 476 | 20 | (4) 82 518 | (4) 22 792 | 28 |
| | Teacher training | | ... | ... | ... | ... | ... | ... |
| | Vocational education | | ... | ... | ... | ... | ... | ... |
| | Total | 1993/94 | ... | ... | ... | ... | ... | ... |
| | General education | | (4) 2 420 | (4) 486 | 20 | (4) 98 480 | (4) 27 649 | 28 |
| | Teacher training | | ... | ... | ... | ... | ... | ... |
| | Vocational education | | ... | ... | ... | ... | ... | ... |
| | Total | 1994/95 | ... | ... | ... | ... | ... | ... |
| | General education | | (4) 2 407 | (4) 469 | 19 | (4) 107 248 | (4) 30 535 | 28 |
| | Teacher training | | ... | ... | ... | ... | ... | ... |
| | Vocational education | | ... | ... | ... | ... | ... | ... |
| | Total | 1995/96 | ... | ... | ... | ... | ... | ... |
| | General education | | 3 799 | 830 | 22 | 128 256 | 38 189 | 30 |
| | Teacher training | | ... | ... | ... | ... | ... | ... |
| | Vocational education | | ... | ... | ... | ... | ... | ... |
| | Total | 1996/97 | ... | ... | ... | ... | ... | ... |
| | General education | | 5 352 | 871 | 16 | 146 135 | 44 124 | 30 |
| | Teacher training | | ... | ... | ... | ... | ... | ... |
| | Vocational education | | ... | ... | ... | ... | ... | ... |
| Botswana | Total | 1970 | 353 | 102 | 29 | 5 197 | 2 364 | 45 |
| | General education | | (5) 197 | (5) 56 | 28 | (5) 3 905 | (5) 1 831 | 47 |
| | Teacher training | | 32 | 7 | 22 | 283 | 151 | 53 |
| | Vocational education | | 124 | 39 | 31 | 1 009 | 382 | 38 |
| | Total | 1975 | 860 | 256 | 30 | 14 286 | 7 418 | 52 |
| | General education | | 570 | 167 | 29 | 12 098 | 6 392 | 53 |
| | Teacher training | | 48 | 20 | 42 | 489 | 373 | 76 |
| | Vocational education | | 242 | 69 | 29 | 1 699 | 653 | 38 |

Secondary education: teaching staff and pupils  II.6
Enseignement secondaire: personnel enseignant et élèves
Enseñanza secundaria: personal docente y alumnos

| Country / Pays / País | Type of education / Type d'enseignement / Tipo de enseñanza | Year / Année / Año | Teaching staff / Personnel enseignant / Personal docente | | | Pupils enrolled / Elèves inscrits / Alumnos matriculados | | |
|---|---|---|---|---|---|---|---|---|
| | | | Total | Female Féminin Femenino | % F | Total | Female Féminin Femenino | % F |
| Botswana (cont) | Total | 1980 | 1 137 | 417 | 37 | 20 969 | 11 434 | 55 |
| | General education | | 851 | 300 | 35 | 18 325 | 10 283 | 56 |
| | Teacher training | | 59 | 15 | 25 | 844 | 700 | 83 |
| | Vocational education | | 227 | 102 | 45 | 1 800 | 451 | 25 |
| | Total | 1985 | 1 675 | 662 | 40 | 36 144 | 19 163 | 53 |
| | General education | | 1 283 | 545 | 42 | 32 172 | 17 175 | 53 |
| | Teacher training | | 73 | 27 | 37 | 1 188 | 996 | 84 |
| | Vocational education | | 319 | 90 | 28 | 2 784 | 992 | 36 |
| | Total | 1990 | 3 716 | 1 482 | 40 | 61 767 | 32 444 | 53 |
| | General education | | 3 067 | 1 263 | 41 | 56 892 | 30 330 | 53 |
| | Teacher training | | 121 | 68 | 56 | 1 361 | 1 158 | 85 |
| | Vocational education | | 528 | 151 | 29 | 3 514 | 956 | 27 |
| | Total | 1991 | 4 312 | 1 740 | 40 | 77 998 | 42 068 | 54 |
| | General education | | 3 763 | 1 554 | 41 | 73 909 | 39 958 | 54 |
| | Teacher training | | 126 | 67 | 53 | 1 286 | 1 110 | 86 |
| | Vocational education | | 423 | 119 | 28 | 2 803 | 1 000 | 36 |
| | Total | 1992 | 4 467 | 1 791 | 40 | 80 358 | 43 021 | 54 |
| | General education | | 3 835 | 1 577 | 41 | 75 873 | 40 727 | 54 |
| | Teacher training | | 114 | 62 | 54 | 1 272 | 1 087 | 85 |
| | Vocational education | | 518 | 152 | 29 | *3 213 | *1 207 | *38 |
| | Total | 1993 | 5 084 | 2 179 | 43 | 90 658 | 48 114 | 53 |
| | General education | | 4 391 | 1 876 | 43 | 85 687 | 45 807 | 53 |
| | Teacher training | | 135 | 90 | 67 | 1 261 | 1 066 | 85 |
| | Vocational education | | 558 | 213 | 38 | 3 710 | 1 241 | 33 |
| | Total | 1994 | 5 475 | 2 408 | 44 | 91 862 | 47 953 | 52 |
| | General education | | 4 712 | 2 079 | 44 | 86 684 | 45 695 | 53 |
| | Teacher training | | 141 | 87 | 62 | 1 085 | 816 | 75 |
| | Vocational education | | 622 | 242 | 39 | 4 093 | 1 442 | 35 |
| | Total | 1995 | 6 670 | 2 846 | 43 | 111 134 | 58 040 | 52 |
| | General education | | 5 751 | 2 511 | 44 | 103 159 | 54 947 | 53 |
| | Teacher training | | 145 | 94 | 65 | 1 028 | 713 | 69 |
| | Vocational education | | 774 | 241 | 31 | 6 947 | 2 380 | 34 |
| | Total | 1996 | ... | ... | ... | ... | ... | ... |
| | General education | | 6 214 | 2 720 | 44 | 109 843 | 58 468 | 53 |
| | Teacher training | | 132 | 82 | 62 | 1 163 | 843 | 72 |
| | Vocational education | | ... | ... | ... | ... | ... | ... |
| Burkina Faso | Total | 1970/71 | 474 | ... | ... | 10 717 | 3 000 | 28 |
| | General education | | 296 | ... | ... | 8 803 | 2 202 | 25 |
| | Teacher training | | 39 | ... | ... | 337 | 37 | 11 |
| | Vocational education | | 139 | ... | ... | 1 577 | 761 | 48 |
| | Total | 1975/76 | 818 | ... | ... | 16 227 | 5 123 | 32 |
| | General education | | 580 | ... | ... | 13 167 | 4 037 | 31 |
| | Teacher training | | 28 | 14 | 50 | 391 | 117 | 30 |
| | Vocational education | | 210 | 40 | 19 | 2 669 | 969 | 36 |
| | Total | 1980/81 | ... | ... | ... | 27 539 | 9 224 | 33 |
| | General education | | 903 | ... | ... | 23 420 | 7 632 | 33 |
| | Teacher training | | ... | ... | ... | 248 | 57 | 23 |
| | Vocational education | | 194 | ... | ... | 3 871 | 1 535 | 40 |
| | Total | 1985/86 | ... | ... | ... | 53 565 | 17 991 | 34 |
| | General education | | ... | ... | ... | 48 938 | 15 667 | 32 |
| | Teacher training | | ... | ... | ... | 351 | 117 | 33 |
| | Vocational education | | ... | ... | ... | 4 276 | 2 207 | 52 |
| | Total | 1990/91 | ... | ... | ... | 98 929 | *34 003 | *34 |
| | General education | | 3 132 | ... | ... | 91 727 | 30 486 | 33 |
| | Teacher training | | ... | ... | ... | 350 | *130 | *37 |
| | Vocational education | | 474 | ... | ... | 6 852 | 3 387 | 49 |
| | Total | 1991/92 | ... | ... | ... | 105 542 | *36 342 | *34 |
| | General education | | 3 162 | ... | ... | 97 170 | 32 602 | 34 |
| | Teacher training | | ... | ... | ... | *350 | *130 | *37 |
| | Vocational education | | ... | ... | ... | 8 022 | 3 610 | 45 |
| | Total | 1992/93 | ... | ... | ... | 115 753 | *40 457 | *35 |
| | General education | | 3 864 | ... | ... | 107 024 | 36 306 | 34 |
| | Teacher training | | ... | ... | ... | *350 | *130 | *37 |
| | Vocational education | | 493 | ... | ... | 8 379 | 4 021 | 48 |
| | Total | 1993/94 | ... | ... | ... | ... | ... | ... |
| | General education | | 3 346 | 604 | 18 | 116 033 | 39 551 | 34 |
| | Teacher training | | ... | ... | ... | ... | ... | ... |
| | Vocational education | | 639 | 137 | 21 | 8 808 | 4 335 | 49 |

II.6    Secondary education: teaching staff and pupils
Enseignement secondaire: personnel enseignant et élèves
Enseñanza secundaria: personal docente y alumnos

| Country<br><br>Pays<br><br>País | Type of education<br><br>Type d'enseignement<br><br>Tipo de enseñanza | Year<br><br>Année<br><br>Año | Teaching staff<br>Personnel enseignant<br>Personal docente | | | Pupils enrolled<br>Elèves inscrits<br>Alumnos matriculados | | |
|---|---|---|---|---|---|---|---|---|
| | | | Total | Female<br>Féminin<br>Femenino | %<br><br>F | Total | Female<br>Féminin<br>Femenino | %<br><br>F |
| Burundi | Total | 1970/71 | ... | ... | ... | 8 169 | 1 632 | 20 |
| | General education | | 324 | 52 | 16 | 3 969 | 566 | 14 |
| | Teacher training | | 210 | 78 | 37 | 3 085 | 1 065 | 35 |
| | Vocational education | | ... | ... | ... | 1 115 | 1 | 0 |
| | Total | 1975/76 | (6) 731 | (6) 156 | 21 | (6) 13 623 | (6) 4 204 | 31 |
| | General education | | (6) 326 | (6) 71 | 22 | (6) 7 143 | (6) 1 934 | 27 |
| | Teacher training | | 302 | 85 | 28 | 5 381 | 2 245 | 42 |
| | Vocational education | | 103 | - | - | 1 099 | 25 | 2 |
| | Total | 1980/81 | ... | ... | ... | 19 013 | *6 079 | *32 |
| | General education | | ... | ... | ... | 8 899 | 2 265 | 25 |
| | Teacher training | | 412 | 84 | 20 | 6 849 | 3 213 | 47 |
| | Vocational education | | *239 | *25 | *10 | 3 265 | 601 | 18 |
| | Total | 1985/86 | 1 849 | 382 | 21 | 25 939 | 8 791 | 34 |
| | General education | | 785 | 181 | 23 | 13 037 | 3 918 | 30 |
| | Teacher training | | 498 | 138 | 28 | 8 032 | 3 830 | 48 |
| | Vocational education | | 566 | 63 | 11 | 4 870 | 1 043 | 21 |
| | Total | 1990/91 | 2 026 | 429 | 21 | 44 207 | 16 280 | 37 |
| | General education | | ... | ... | ... | 36 773 | 13 687 | 37 |
| | Teacher training | | ... | ... | ... | 1 532 | 708 | 46 |
| | Vocational education | | 493 | 67 | 14 | 5 902 | 1 885 | 32 |
| | Total | 1991/92 | 2 211 | 459 | 21 | 48 398 | 18 306 | 38 |
| | General education | | ... | ... | ... | 40 334 | 15 215 | 38 |
| | Teacher training | | ... | ... | ... | 1 890 | 914 | 48 |
| | Vocational education | | 510 | 91 | 18 | 6 174 | 2 177 | 35 |
| | Total | 1992/93 | 2 562 | 519 | 20 | 55 713 | 21 600 | 39 |
| | General education | | ... | ... | ... | 46 381 | 17 675 | 38 |
| | Teacher training | | ... | ... | ... | 2 470 | 1 233 | 50 |
| | Vocational education | | 502 | 70 | 14 | 6 862 | 2 692 | 39 |
| | Total | 1994/95 | ... | ... | ... | ... | ... | ... |
| | General education | | ... | ... | ... | 47 636 | ... | ... |
| | Teacher training | | ... | ... | ... | ... | ... | ... |
| | Vocational education | | ... | ... | ... | ... | ... | ... |
| Cameroon | Total | 1970/71 | ... | ... | ... | 76 461 | 21 896 | 29 |
| | General education | | 2 200 | 502 | 23 | 56 031 | 14 817 | 26 |
| | Teacher training | | ... | ... | ... | 3 030 | 703 | 23 |
| | Vocational education | | 900 | 250 | 28 | 17 400 | 6 376 | 37 |
| | Total | 1975/76 | 4 805 | 970 | 20 | 143 812 | 46 813 | 33 |
| | General education | | 3 309 | 628 | 19 | 106 266 | 33 398 | 31 |
| | Teacher training | | 132 | 22 | 17 | 1 284 | 327 | 25 |
| | Vocational education | | 1 364 | 320 | 23 | 36 262 | 13 088 | 36 |
| | Total | 1980/81 | 8 926 | ... | ... | 234 090 | 82 720 | 35 |
| | General education | | 5 944 | 1 044 | 18 | 169 298 | 57 438 | 34 |
| | Teacher training | | 218 | 47 | 22 | 2 118 | 768 | 36 |
| | Vocational education | | 2 764 | ... | ... | 62 674 | 24 514 | 39 |
| | Total | 1985/86 | 11 096 | 2 496 | 22 | 343 720 | 132 272 | 38 |
| | General education | | 7 510 | 1 571 | 21 | 256 453 | 96 027 | 37 |
| | Teacher training | | 502 | 115 | 23 | 4 058 | 1 692 | 42 |
| | Vocational education | | 3 084 | 810 | 26 | 83 209 | 34 553 | 42 |
| | Total | 1990/91 | 19 820 | ... | ... | 500 272 | 207 486 | 41 |
| | General education | | 13 893 | ... | ... | 409 729 | 169 841 | 41 |
| | Teacher training | | 232 | 69 | 30 | 515 | 283 | 55 |
| | Vocational education | | 5 695 | ... | ... | 90 028 | 37 362 | 42 |
| | Total | 1991/92 | ... | ... | ... | ... | ... | ... |
| | General education | | 14 765 | 2 936 | 20 | 443 244 | 182 694 | 41 |
| | Teacher training | | ... | ... | ... | ... | ... | ... |
| | Vocational education | | 5 658 | 1 414 | 25 | 91 207 | 39 721 | 44 |
| | Total | 1993/94 | ... | ... | ... | 550 480 | ... | ... |
| | General education | | ... | ... | ... | 458 141 | 185 057 | 40 |
| | Teacher training | | 123 | ... | ... | 435 | ... | ... |
| | Vocational education | | ... | ... | ... | 91 904 | 37 587 | 41 |
| | Total | 1994/95 | ... | ... | ... | ... | ... | ... |
| | General education | | 14 917 | 3 742 | 25 | 459 068 | 185 248 | 40 |
| | Teacher training | | ... | ... | ... | ... | ... | ... |
| | Vocational education | | 5 885 | 1 655 | 28 | 91 779 | 37 674 | 41 |
| Cape Verde | Total | 1970/71 | ... | ... | ... | ... | ... | ... |
| | General education | | ... | ... | ... | ... | ... | ... |
| | Teacher training | | 15 | ... | ... | 21 | 20 | 95 |
| | Vocational education | | 36 | ... | ... | 557 | 138 | 25 |
| | Total | 1975/76 | ... | ... | ... | ... | ... | ... |
| | General education | | ... | ... | ... | 2 025 | 957 | 47 |
| | Teacher training | | ... | ... | ... | ... | ... | ... |
| | Vocational education | | 33 | ... | ... | 409 | 191 | 47 |

Secondary education: teaching staff and pupils  II.6
Enseignement secondaire: personnel enseignant et élèves
Enseñanza secundaria: personal docente y alumnos

| Country / Pays / País | Type of education / Type d'enseignement / Tipo de enseñanza | Year / Année / Año | Teaching staff Personnel enseignant Personal docente | | | Pupils enrolled Elèves inscrits Alumnos matriculados | | |
|---|---|---|---|---|---|---|---|---|
| | | | Total | Female Féminin Femenino | % F | | Total | Female Féminin Femenino | % F |
| Cape Verde (cont) | Total | 1980/81 | 184 | ... | ... | | 3 341 | ... | ... |
| | General education | | 121 | ... | ... | | 2 733 | 1 167 | 43 |
| | Teacher training | | 23 | ... | ... | | 104 | ... | ... |
| | Vocational education | | 40 | ... | ... | | 504 | 198 | 39 |
| | Total | 1985/86 | ... | ... | ... | | ... | ... | ... |
| | General education | | 146 | 108 | 74 | | 4 941 | 2 211 | 45 |
| | Teacher training | | ... | ... | ... | | ... | ... | ... |
| | Vocational education | | ... | ... | ... | | 361 | 172 | 48 |
| | Total | 1991/92 | ... | ... | ... | | ... | ... | ... |
| | General education | | ... | ... | ... | (7) | 10 309 | ... | ... |
| | Teacher training | | ... | ... | ... | | ... | ... | ... |
| | Vocational education | | ... | ... | ... | | 1 149 | ... | ... |
| | Total | 1993/94 | ... | ... | ... | | 14 097 | 6 880 | 49 |
| | General education | | 438 | 158 | 36 | | 11 808 | 5 987 | 51 |
| | Teacher training | | ... | ... | ... | | 889 | 293 | 33 |
| | Vocational education | | 94 | 40 | 43 | | 1 400 | 600 | 43 |
| | Total | 1997/98 | 1 372 | 519 | 38 | | 31 602 | 16 125 | 51 |
| | General education | | ... | ... | ... | | ... | ... | ... |
| | Teacher training | | ... | ... | ... | | ... | ... | ... |
| | Vocational education | | ... | ... | ... | | ... | ... | ... |
| Central African Republic | Total | 1970/71 | 518 | ... | ... | | 11 279 | 2 134 | 19 |
| | General education | | 363 | ... | ... | | 9 691 | 1 606 | 17 |
| | Teacher training | | 26 | ... | ... | | 225 | 97 | 43 |
| | Vocational education | | 130 | *33 | *25 | | 1 363 | 431 | 32 |
| | Total | 1975/76 | ... | ... | ... | | 23 011 | 4 150 | 18 |
| | General education | | 515 | 134 | 26 | | 20 635 | 3 495 | 17 |
| | Teacher training | | (8) 47 | (8) 12 | 26 | | 404 | 194 | 48 |
| | Vocational education | | ... | ... | ... | | 1 972 | 461 | 23 |
| | Total | 1980/81 | 724 | 114 | 16 | | 45 211 | 11 936 | 26 |
| | General education | | 510 | 62 | 12 | | 41 811 | 10 396 | 25 |
| | Teacher training | | 88 | 21 | 24 | | 677 | 195 | 29 |
| | Vocational education | | 126 | 31 | 25 | | 2 723 | 1 345 | 49 |
| | Total | 1985/86 | 922 | ... | ... | | 59 273 | 15 985 | 27 |
| | General education | | 769 | 80 | 10 | | 56 941 | 14 936 | 26 |
| | Teacher training | | 28 | 9 | 32 | | 107 | 9 | 8 |
| | Vocational education | | 125 | ... | ... | | 2 225 | 1 040 | 47 |
| | Total | 1990/91 | ... | ... | ... | | 50 930 | 14 961 | 29 |
| | General education | | ... | ... | ... | | 49 068 | 14 073 | 29 |
| | Teacher training | | - | - | - | | - | - | - |
| | Vocational education | | ... | ... | ... | | 1 862 | 888 | 48 |
| | Total | 1991/92 | ... | ... | ... | (4) | 43 740 | (4) 12 851 | 29 |
| | General education | | ... | ... | ... | (4) | 42 263 | (4) 12 273 | 29 |
| | Teacher training | | - | - | - | | - | - | - |
| | Vocational education | | ... | ... | ... | | 1 477 | 578 | 39 |
| Chad | Total | 1970/71 | ... | ... | ... | | 10 556 | 802 | 8 |
| | General education | | 386 | 75 | 19 | | 9 105 | 738 | 8 |
| | Teacher training | | 29 | 12 | 41 | | 423 | 21 | 5 |
| | Vocational education | | ... | ... | ... | | 1 028 | 43 | 4 |
| | Total | 1975/76 | ... | ... | ... | | 16 391 | ... | ... |
| | General education | | ... | ... | ... | | 15 128 | ... | ... |
| | Teacher training | | ... | ... | ... | | 549 | ... | ... |
| | Vocational education | | ... | ... | ... | | 714 | ... | ... |
| | Total | 1985/86 | ... | ... | ... | | ... | ... | ... |
| | General education | | ... | ... | ... | | ... | ... | ... |
| | Teacher training | | ... | ... | ... | | 1 030 | ... | ... |
| | Vocational education | | ... | ... | ... | | 2 896 | 684 | 24 |
| | Total | 1990/91 | ... | ... | ... | | 59 565 | 9 382 | 16 |
| | General education | | 1 359 | 72 | 5 | | | | |
| | Teacher training | | ... | ... | ... | | ... | ... | ... |
| | Vocational education | | ... | ... | ... | | 3 093 | 967 | 31 |
| | Total | 1991/92 | ... | ... | ... | | ... | ... | ... |
| | General education | | 2 062 | ... | ... | | 72 641 | ... | ... |
| | Teacher training | | ... | ... | ... | | ... | ... | ... |
| | Vocational education | | ... | ... | ... | | 3 310 | 983 | 30 |
| | Total | 1992/93 | ... | ... | ... | | ... | ... | ... |
| | General education | | ... | ... | ... | | 79 458 | ... | ... |
| | Teacher training | | ... | ... | ... | | ... | ... | ... |
| | Vocational education | | ... | ... | ... | | ... | ... | ... |

II.6    Secondary education: teaching staff and pupils
Enseignement secondaire: personnel enseignant et élèves
Enseñanza secundaria: personal docente y alumnos

| Country<br>Pays<br>País | Type of education<br>Type d'enseignement<br>Tipo de enseñanza | Year<br>Année<br>Año | Teaching staff<br>Personnel enseignant<br>Personal docente | | | Pupils enrolled<br>Elèves inscrits<br>Alumnos matriculados | | |
|---|---|---|---|---|---|---|---|---|
| | | | Total | Female<br>Féminin<br>Femenino | %<br>F | Total | Female<br>Féminin<br>Femenino | %<br>F |
| Chad (cont) | Total | 1993/94 | 2 081 | ... | ... | 73 666 | 13 317 | 18 |
| | General education | | 1 893 | *85 | *4 | 69 784 | 12 187 | 17 |
| | Teacher training | | 67 | | | 635 | 153 | 24 |
| | Vocational education | | 121 | ... | ... | 3 247 | 977 | 30 |
| | Total | 1994/95 | 2 310 | 92 | 4 | 85 836 | 16 366 | 19 |
| | General education | | 2 128 | 82 | 4 | 82 559 | 15 464 | 19 |
| | Teacher training | | 67 | 1 | 1 | 513 | 149 | 29 |
| | Vocational education | | 115 | 9 | 8 | 2 764 | 753 | 27 |
| | Total | 1995/96 | 2 693 | 124 | 5 | 93 026 | 18 404 | 20 |
| | General education | | 2 468 | 112 | 5 | 90 100 | 17 456 | 19 |
| | Teacher training | | 65 | 3 | 5 | 806 | 309 | 38 |
| | Vocational education | | 160 | 9 | 6 | 2 120 | 639 | 30 |
| | Total | 1996/97 | 2 792 | 105 | 4 | 99 789 | 20 301 | 20 |
| | General education | | 2 598 | 98 | 4 | 97 011 | 19 389 | 20 |
| | Teacher training | | 46 | 1 | 2 | 625 | 265 | 42 |
| | Vocational education | | 148 | 6 | 4 | 2 153 | 647 | 30 |
| Comoros | Total | 1970/71 | 63 | 20 | 32 | 1 273 | 322 | 25 |
| | General education | | 61 | 20 | 33 | 1 249 | 316 | 25 |
| | Teacher training | | 2 | - | - | 24 | 6 | 25 |
| | Vocational education | | - | - | - | - | - | - |
| | Total | 1980/81 | 449 | 91 | 20 | 13 798 | 4 665 | 34 |
| | General education | | 432 | 88 | 20 | 13 528 | 4 597 | 34 |
| | Teacher training | | 8 | 2 | 25 | 119 | 29 | 24 |
| | Vocational education | | 9 | 1 | 11 | 151 | 39 | 26 |
| | Total | 1985/86 | ... | ... | ... | 21 056 | 8 169 | 39 |
| | General education | | ... | ... | ... | 20 541 | 8 032 | 39 |
| | Teacher training | | 11 | ... | ... | 94 | 13 | 14 |
| | Vocational education | | ... | ... | ... | 421 | 124 | 29 |
| | Total | 1991/92 | ... | ... | ... | 15 878 | ... | ... |
| | General education | | 613 | ... | ... | 15 647 | 6 129 | 39 |
| | Teacher training | | 11 | 1 | 9 | 129 | ... | ... |
| | Vocational education | | ... | ... | ... | 102 | ... | ... |
| | Total | 1992/93 | ... | ... | ... | ... | ... | ... |
| | General education | (4) | 551 | ... | ... | 15 068 | 6 285 | 42 |
| | Teacher training | | ... | ... | ... | 82 | ... | ... |
| | Vocational education | | ... | ... | ... | ... | ... | ... |
| | Total | 1993/94 | ... | ... | ... | 17 637 | ... | ... |
| | General education | (4) | 558 | ... | ... | 17 474 | 7 643 | 44 |
| | Teacher training | | ... | ... | ... | 37 | ... | ... |
| | Vocational education | | ... | ... | ... | 126 | 35 | 28 |
| | Total | 1995/96 | ... | ... | ... | ... | ... | ... |
| | General education | (4) | 591 | ... | ... | 21 192 | ... | ... |
| | Teacher training | | ... | ... | ... | ... | ... | ... |
| | Vocational education | | ... | ... | ... | ... | ... | ... |
| Congo | Total | 1970/71 | 1 037 | 226 | 22 | 34 267 | 10 298 | 30 |
| | General education | | 693 | 128 | 18 | 30 371 | 9 065 | 30 |
| | Teacher training | | 28 | 7 | 25 | 548 | 130 | 24 |
| | Vocational education | | 316 | 91 | 29 | 3 348 | 1 103 | 33 |
| | Total | 1975/76 | 2 413 | 266 | 11 | 102 110 | 36 782 | 36 |
| | General education | | 2 042 | 182 | 9 | 94 276 | 33 720 | 36 |
| | Teacher training | | 34 | 8 | 24 | 705 | 185 | 26 |
| | Vocational education | | 337 | 76 | 23 | 7 129 | 2 877 | 40 |
| | Total | 1980/81 | *5 117 | ... | ... | 187 585 | 77 222 | 41 |
| | General education | | 3 649 | ... | ... | 168 718 | 67 583 | 40 |
| | Teacher training | | 229 | ... | ... | 1 934 | 488 | 25 |
| | Vocational education | | *1 239 | ... | ... | 16 933 | 9 151 | 54 |
| | Total | 1985/86 | 6 322 | ... | ... | 222 633 | 96 908 | 44 |
| | General education | | 4 773 | ... | ... | 197 491 | 83 868 | 42 |
| | Teacher training | | 191 | 29 | 15 | 1 800 | 662 | 37 |
| | Vocational education | | 1 358 | ... | ... | 23 342 | 12 378 | 53 |
| | Total | 1990/91 | 6 851 | ... | ... | 182 967 | ... | ... |
| | General education | | 4 924 | ... | ... | 170 409 | 71 199 | 42 |
| | Teacher training | | 169 | ... | ... | 280 | ... | ... |
| | Vocational education | | 1 758 | 353 | 20 | 12 278 | 5 715 | 47 |
| | Total | 1991/92 | 7 230 | ... | ... | 191 459 | 82 382 | 43 |
| | General education | | 5 689 | ... | ... | 178 753 | 76 482 | 43 |
| | Teacher training | | 149 | 27 | 18 | 221 | 76 | 34 |
| | Vocational education | | 1 392 | 327 | 23 | 12 485 | 5 824 | 47 |

Secondary education: teaching staff and pupils II.6
Enseignement secondaire: personnel enseignant et élèves
Enseñanza secundaria: personal docente y alumnos

| Country / Pays / País | Type of education / Type d'enseignement / Tipo de enseñanza | Year / Année / Año | Teaching staff — Personnel enseignant — Personal docente | | | Pupils enrolled — Elèves inscrits — Alumnos matriculados | | |
|---|---|---|---|---|---|---|---|---|
| | | | Total | Female Féminin Femenino | % F | Total | Female Féminin Femenino | % F |
| Congo (cont) | Total | 1992/93 | ... | ... | ... | ... | ... | ... |
| | General education | | 5 464 | ... | ... | 176 303 | 74 462 | 42 |
| | Teacher training | | 144 | ... | ... | 704 | ... | ... |
| | Vocational education | | ... | ... | ... | ... | ... | ... |
| | Total | 1993/94 | 7 861 | ... | ... | 212 850 | ... | ... |
| | General education | | 6 048 | ... | ... | 192 229 | 79 463 | 41 |
| | Teacher training | | 143 | 18 | 13 | 769 | 475 | 62 |
| | Vocational education | | 1 670 | ... | ... | 19 852 | ... | ... |
| | Total | 1995/96 | *7 173 | *1 128 | *16 | 214 650 | 91 500 | 43 |
| | General education | | 5 710 | 862 | 15 | 189 381 | 80 308 | 42 |
| | Teacher training | | 67 | 22 | 33 | 78 | 59 | 76 |
| | Vocational education | | *1 396 | *244 | *17 | 25 191 | 11 133 | 44 |
| Côte d'Ivoire | Total | 1970/71 | 3 279 | ... | ... | 69 714 | 15 031 | 22 |
| | General education | | 2 579 | ... | ... | 62 969 | 13 488 | 21 |
| | Teacher training | | 87 | 16 | 18 | 1 622 | 475 | 29 |
| | Vocational education | | 613 | 144 | 23 | 5 123 | 1 068 | 21 |
| | Total | 1975/76 | ... | ... | ... | 119 482 | ... | ... |
| | General education | | (4) 3 247 | ... | ... | 102 387 | 25 207 | 25 |
| | Teacher training | | ... | ... | ... | 1 337 | 368 | 28 |
| | Vocational education | | ... | ... | ... | 15 758 | ... | ... |
| | Total | 1980/81 | ... | ... | ... | 198 190 | 55 826 | ... |
| | General education | | (4) 5 192 | ... | ... | | | 28 |
| | Teacher training | | ... | ... | ... | 2 454 | 423 | 17 |
| | Vocational education | | ... | ... | ... | (4)(9) 21 296 | (4)(9) 10 375 | 49 |
| | Total | 1985/86 | ... | ... | ... | ... | ... | ... |
| | General education | | (4) 7 188 | ... | ... | 260 330 | 76 364 | 29 |
| | Teacher training | | ... | ... | ... | ... | ... | ... |
| | Vocational education | | ... | ... | ... | (4)(9) 22 861 | (4)(9) 8 500 | 37 |
| | Total | 1990/91 | ... | ... | ... | ... | ... | ... |
| | General education | | (4) 10 788 | ... | ... | 361 032 | 114 832 | 32 |
| | Teacher training | | - | - | - | - | - | - |
| | Vocational education | | ... | ... | ... | ... | ... | ... |
| | Total | 1991/92 | ... | ... | ... | ... | ... | ... |
| | General education | | (4) 9 324 | ... | ... | 396 606 | 128 778 | 32 |
| | Teacher training | | - | - | - | - | - | - |
| | Vocational education | | ... | ... | ... | ... | ... | ... |
| | Total | 1992/93 | | ... | ... | ... | ... | ... |
| | General education | | ... | ... | ... | 414 504 | 135 911 | 33 |
| | Teacher training | | - | - | - | - | - | - |
| | Vocational education | | ... | ... | ... | ... | ... | ... |
| | Total | 1993/94 | ... | ... | ... | ... | ... | ... |
| | General education | | (4) 9 644 | ... | ... | 445 505 | 150 554 | 34 |
| | Teacher training | | - | - | - | - | - | - |
| | Vocational education | | (4)(9) 1 268 | ... | ... | (4)(9) 8 882 | (4)(9) 2 581 | 29 |
| | Total | 1994/95 | ... | ... | ... | ... | ... | ... |
| | General education | | (4) 9 505 | ... | ... | 463 810 | 150 365 | 32 |
| | Teacher training | | - | - | - | - | - | - |
| | Vocational education | | (4)(9) 1 424 | (4)(9) 250 | 18 | (4)(9) 11 037 | (4)(9) 2 449 | 22 |
| | Total | 1995/96 | ... | ... | ... | ... | ... | ... |
| | General education | | 15 959 | 2 310 | 14 | 489 740 | 161 961 | 33 |
| | Teacher training | | - | - | - | - | - | - |
| | Vocational education | | ... | ... | ... | ... | ... | ... |
| | Total | 1996/97 | ... | ... | ... | ... | ... | ... |
| | General education | | ... | ... | ... | 534 214 | 169 013 | 32 |
| | Teacher training | | - | - | - | - | - | - |
| | Vocational education | | ... | ... | ... | ... | ... | ... |
| Democratic Rep. of the Congo | Total | 1970/71 | ... | ... | ... | 248 318 | 53 350 | 21 |
| | General education | | ... | ... | ... | 185 370 | 38 615 | 21 |
| | Teacher training | | ... | ... | ... | 39 088 | 9 694 | 25 |
| | Vocational education | | ... | ... | ... | 23 860 | 5 041 | 21 |
| | Total | 1975/76 | ... | ... | ... | 511 481 | 135 341 | 26 |
| | General education | | ... | ... | ... | 360 888 | 89 484 | 25 |
| | Teacher training | | ... | ... | ... | 95 688 | 27 607 | 29 |
| | Vocational education | | ... | ... | ... | 54 905 | 18 250 | 33 |
| | Total | 1980/81 | ... | ... | ... | 861 774 | 235 610 | 27 |
| | General education | | ... | ... | ... | ... | ... | ... |
| | Teacher training | | ... | ... | ... | ... | ... | ... |
| | Vocational education | | ... | ... | ... | ... | ... | ... |

II.6  Secondary education: teaching staff and pupils
Enseignement secondaire: personnel enseignant et élèves
Enseñanza secundaria: personal docente y alumnos

| Country / Pays / País | Type of education / Type d'enseignement / Tipo de enseñanza | Year / Année / Año | Teaching staff / Personnel enseignant / Personal docente | | | Pupils enrolled / Elèves inscrits / Alumnos matriculados | | |
|---|---|---|---|---|---|---|---|---|
| | | | Total | Female / Féminin / Femenino | % F | Total | Female / Féminin / Femenino | % F |
| Democratic Rep. of the Congo (cont) | Total | 1985/86 | ... | ... | ... | 959 934 | 284 686 | 30 |
| | General education | | ... | ... | ... | ... | ... | ... |
| | Teacher training | | ... | ... | ... | ... | ... | ... |
| | Vocational education | | ... | ... | ... | ... | ... | ... |
| | Total | 1991/92 | 54 394 | 7 744 | 14 | 1 097 095 | 356 150 | 32 |
| | General education | | ... | ... | ... | 522 690 | 159 517 | 31 |
| | Teacher training | | ... | ... | ... | 279 721 | 91 966 | 33 |
| | Vocational education | | ... | ... | ... | 294 684 | 104 667 | 36 |
| | Total | 1992/93 | 59 879 | 8 996 | 15 | 1 218 760 | 389 110 | 32 |
| | General education | | ... | ... | ... | 585 005 | 175 100 | 30 |
| | Teacher training | | ... | ... | ... | 304 690 | 97 277 | 32 |
| | Vocational education | | ... | ... | ... | 329 065 | 116 733 | 35 |
| | Total | 1993/94 | 59 325 | 9 920 | 17 | 1 341 446 | 413 113 | 31 |
| | General education | | ... | ... | ... | 640 298 | 190 942 | 30 |
| | Teacher training | | ... | ... | ... | 360 249 | 111 589 | 31 |
| | Vocational education | | ... | ... | ... | 340 899 | 110 582 | 32 |
| | Total | 1994/95 | ... | ... | ... | 1 514 323 | 571 264 | 38 |
| | General education | | ... | ... | ... | (1) 1 155 517 | (1) 415 126 | 36 |
| | Teacher training | | ... | ... | ... | 358 806 | 156 138 | 44 |
| | Vocational education | | ... | ... | ... | ./. | ./. | ./. |
| Djibouti | Total | 1970/71 | ... | ... | ... | 1 385 | 376 | 27 |
| | General education | | 61 | 30 | 49 | 758 | 248 | 33 |
| | Teacher training | | 1 | 1 | 100 | 17 | 1 | 6 |
| | Vocational education | | ... | ... | ... | 610 | 127 | 21 |
| | Total | 1975/76 | 148 | 57 | 39 | 1 994 | 531 | 27 |
| | General education | | 85 | 41 | 48 | 1 398 | 443 | 32 |
| | Teacher training | | 4 | 1 | 25 | 36 | 7 | 19 |
| | Vocational education | | 59 | 15 | 25 | 560 | 81 | 14 |
| | Total | 1980/81 | 278 | ... | ... | 5 133 | ... | ... |
| | General education | | 179 | ... | ... | 3 812 | ... | ... |
| | Teacher training | | 11 | ... | ... | 42 | 17 | 40 |
| | Vocational education | | 88 | ... | ... | 1 279 | ... | ... |
| | Total | 1985/86 | (4) 306 | ... | ... | 7 041 | 2 718 | 39 |
| | General education | | (4) 221 | ... | ... | 5 057 | 1 688 | 33 |
| | Teacher training | | 13 | ... | ... | 107 | 19 | 18 |
| | Vocational education | | (4) 72 | ... | ... | 1 877 | 1 011 | 54 |
| | Total | 1990/91 | ... | ... | ... | 9 513 | ... | ... |
| | General education | | (4) 305 | ... | ... | 7 742 | 2 709 | 35 |
| | Teacher training | | 13 | ... | ... | 108 | 33 | 31 |
| | Vocational education | | ... | ... | ... | 1 663 | ... | ... |
| | Total | 1991/92 | (4) 400 | ... | ... | 10 026 | 3 990 | 40 |
| | General education | | (4) 265 | ... | ... | 8 130 | 2 853 | 35 |
| | Teacher training | | 14 | ... | ... | 103 | 34 | 33 |
| | Vocational education | | (4) 121 | ... | ... | 1 793 | 1 103 | 62 |
| | Total | 1992/93 | (4) 395 | ... | ... | 9 740 | 4 184 | 43 |
| | General education | | (4) 267 | ... | ... | 8 083 | 3 128 | 39 |
| | Teacher training | | ... | ... | ... | 112 | 38 | 34 |
| | Vocational education | | ... | ... | ... | 1 545 | 1 018 | 66 |
| | Total | 1993/94 | ... | ... | ... | 10 384 | 4 380 | 42 |
| | General education | | (4) 276 | ... | ... | 8 755 | 3 381 | 39 |
| | Teacher training | | ... | ... | ... | 108 | 37 | 34 |
| | Vocational education | | ... | ... | ... | 1 521 | 962 | 63 |
| | Total | 1994/95 | ... | ... | ... | 11 384 | 4 608 | 40 |
| | General education | | 409 | ... | ... | ... | ... | ... |
| | Teacher training | | ... | ... | ... | 110 | 28 | 25 |
| | Vocational education | | ... | ... | ... | 1 697 | 982 | 58 |
| | Total | 1995/96 | 628 | ... | ... | 11 860 | 4 958 | 42 |
| | General education | | 444 | 85 | 19 | 10 008 | 3 896 | 39 |
| | Teacher training | | 10 | ... | ... | 104 | 28 | 27 |
| | Vocational education | | 174 | ... | ... | 1 748 | 1 034 | 59 |
| | Total | 1996/97 | ... | ... | ... | 13 311 | 5 477 | 41 |
| | General education | | 403 | 80 | 20 | 11 367 | 4 380 | 39 |
| | Teacher training | | *13 | *4 | *31 | 103 | 20 | 19 |
| | Vocational education | | ... | ... | ... | 1 841 | 1 077 | 59 |
| Egypt | Total | 1970/71 | (10) 57 986 | (10) 13 687 | 24 | 1 448 242 | 465 901 | 32 |
| | General education | | (10) 41 947 | (10) 10 989 | 26 | 1 147 366 | 370 128 | 32 |
| | Teacher training | | (10) 2 351 | (10) 835 | 36 | 25 595 | 11 583 | 45 |
| | Vocational education | | 13 688 | 1 863 | 14 | 275 281 | 84 190 | 31 |

Secondary education: teaching staff and pupils II.6
Enseignement secondaire: personnel enseignant et élèves
Enseñanza secundaria: personal docente y alumnos

| Country / Pays / País | Type of education / Type d'enseignement / Tipo de enseñanza | Year / Année / Año | Teaching staff — Personnel enseignant — Personal docente | | | | Pupils enrolled — Elèves inscrits — Alumnos matriculados | | | |
|---|---|---|---|---|---|---|---|---|---|---|
| | | | | Total | | Female Féminin Femenino | % F | | Total | Female Féminin Femenino | % F |
| Egypt (cont) | Total | 1975/76 | (10) | 78 789 | (10) | 20 962 | 27 | | 2 176 362 | 744 997 | 34 |
| | General education | | (10) | 51 740 | (10) | 16 105 | 31 | | 1 765 853 | 603 618 | 34 |
| | Teacher training | | (10) | 2 755 | (10) | 1 048 | 38 | | 33 014 | 14 509 | 44 |
| | Vocational education | | | 24 294 | | 3 809 | 16 | | 377 495 | 126 870 | 34 |
| | Total | 1980/81 | (10) | 121 999 | (10) | 37 851 | 31 | | 2 929 168 | 1 081 504 | 37 |
| | General education | | (10) | 83 364 | (10) | 28 858 | 35 | | 2 238 882 | 813 072 | 36 |
| | Teacher training | | (10) | 4 148 | (10) | 1 766 | 43 | | 56 377 | 25 458 | 45 |
| | Vocational education | | | 34 487 | | 7 227 | 21 | | 633 909 | 242 974 | 38 |
| | Total | 1985/86 | (10) | 187 580 | (10) | 66 577 | 35 | | 3 826 601 | 1 514 049 | 40 |
| | General education | | (10) | 128 616 | (10) | 49 082 | 38 | | 2 864 615 | 1 112 459 | 39 |
| | Teacher training | | (10) | 6 727 | (10) | 3 020 | 45 | | 84 587 | 50 474 | 60 |
| | Vocational education | | | 52 237 | | 14 475 | 28 | | 877 399 | 351 116 | 40 |
| | Total | 1990/91 | (10) | 286 797 | | ... | ... | | 5 507 257 | 2 381 289 | 43 |
| | General education | | (10) | 203 073 | | ... | ... | | 4 434 748 | 1 916 367 | 43 |
| | Teacher training | | (10) | 6 072 | | ... | ... | (10) | 46 350 | (10) 28 262 | 61 |
| | Vocational education | | | 77 652 | | ... | ... | | 1 026 159 | 436 660 | 43 |
| | Total | 1991/92 | (10) | 283 170 | (10) | 113 894 | 40 | (10) | 5 284 174 | (10) 2 355 772 | 45 |
| | General education | | (10) | 201 040 | (10) | 86 341 | 43 | (10) | 4 148 655 | (10) 1 861 618 | 45 |
| | Teacher training | | (10) | 4 179 | (10) | 2 048 | 49 | (10) | 25 335 | (10) 15 051 | 59 |
| | Vocational education | | | 77 951 | | 25 505 | 33 | | 1 110 184 | 479 103 | 43 |
| | Total | 1992/93 | (10) | 296 668 | (10) | 118 399 | 40 | (10) | 5 515 092 | (10) 2 468 324 | 45 |
| | General education | | (10) | 204 371 | (10) | 86 380 | 42 | (10) | 4 058 834 | (10) 1 814 311 | 45 |
| | Teacher training | | (10) | 650 | (10) | 305 | 47 | (10) | 2 664 | (10) 954 | 36 |
| | Vocational education | | | 91 647 | | 31 714 | 35 | | 1 453 594 | 653 059 | 45 |
| | Total | 1993/94 | (10) | 309 131 | (10) | 123 371 | 40 | | 6 133 308 | 2 726 594 | 44 |
| | General education | | (10) | 209 519 | (10) | 87 652 | 42 | | 4 433 060 | 1 953 569 | 44 |
| | Teacher training | | | ... | | ... | ... | (10) | 109 | (10) 24 | 22 |
| | Vocational education | | | ... | | ... | ... | | 1 700 139 | 773 001 | 45 |
| | Total | 1994/95 | (10) | 333 706 | (10) | 133 914 | 40 | (10) | 6 147 263 | (10) 2 797 984 | 46 |
| | General education | | (10) | 219 132 | (10) | 91 582 | 42 | (10) | 4 153 435 | (10) 1 900 104 | 46 |
| | Teacher training | | | ... | | ... | ... | | ... | ... | ... |
| | Vocational education | | | 114 574 | | 42 332 | 37 | | 1 993 828 | 897 880 | 45 |
| | Total | 1995/96 | (10) | 369 107 | (10) | 148 034 | 40 | (10) | 6 142 651 | (10) 2 793 210 | 45 |
| | General education | | (10) | 235 313 | (10) | 97 527 | 41 | (10) | 4 242 245 | (10) 1 957 609 | 46 |
| | Teacher training | | | ... | | ... | ... | | ... | ... | ... |
| | Vocational education | | | 133 794 | | 50 507 | 38 | | 1 900 406 | 835 601 | 44 |
| | Total | 1996/97 | | 424 586 | | *163 994 | *39 | | 6 726 738 | 3 048 288 | 45 |
| | General education | | | 285 609 | | 111 940 | 39 | | 4 805 122 | 2 204 197 | 46 |
| | Teacher training | | | 750 | | 350 | 47 | | 9 576 | - | - |
| | Vocational education | | | 138 227 | | 51 704 | 37 | | 1 912 040 | 844 091 | 44 |
| | Total | 1997/98 | | ... | | ... | ... | | ... | ... | ... |
| | General education | | (10) | 259 618 | (10) | 106 507 | 41 | (10) | 4 835 938 | (10) 2 261 514 | 47 |
| | Teacher training | | | ... | | ... | ... | | ... | ... | ... |
| | Vocational education | | | ... | | ... | ... | | ... | ... | ... |
| Equatorial Guinea | Total | 1970/71 | | 175 | | ... | ... | | 6 014 | 1 556 | 26 |
| | General education | | | ... | | ... | ... | | 5 198 | 1 490 | 29 |
| | Teacher training | | | ... | | ... | ... | | 213 | 66 | 31 |
| | Vocational education | | | ... | | ... | ... | | 603 | - | - |
| | Total | 1975/76 | | 165 | | 18 | 11 | | 4 523 | 751 | 17 |
| | General education | | | 115 | | 14 | 12 | | 3 984 | 709 | 18 |
| | Teacher training | | | 21 | | 4 | 19 | | 169 | 42 | 25 |
| | Vocational education | | | 29 | | - | - | | 370 | - | - |
| | Total | 1992/93 | | ... | | ... | ... | | ... | ... | ... |
| | General education | | (4) | 461 | (4) | 57 | 12 | (4) | 15 180 | (4) 4 684 | 31 |
| | Teacher training | | | 18 | | 3 | 17 | | 269 | 53 | 20 |
| | Vocational education | | | 97 | | 4 | 4 | | 2 086 | 630 | 30 |
| | Total | 1993/94 | | 588 | | 67 | 11 | | 16 616 | 5 741 | 35 |
| | General education | | | 466 | | 58 | 12 | | 14 511 | 5 119 | 35 |
| | Teacher training | | | 44 | | 5 | 11 | | 609 | 150 | 25 |
| | Vocational education | | | 78 | | 4 | 5 | | 1 496 | 472 | 32 |
| Eritrea | Total | 1990/91 | | ... | | ... | 12 | | ... | ... | ... |
| | General education | | | 1 609 | | 198 | | | 59 696 | 29 042 | 49 |
| | Teacher training | | | ... | | ... | ... | | ... | ... | ... |
| | Vocational education | | | 43 | | ... | ... | | 333 | 40 | 12 |
| | Total | 1991/92 | | ... | | ... | ... | | ... | ... | ... |
| | General education | | | 1 541 | | 172 | 11 | | 55 544 | 27 111 | 49 |
| | Teacher training | | | ... | | ... | ... | | ... | ... | ... |
| | Vocational education | | | 67 | | ... | ... | | 480 | 61 | 13 |

II.6    Secondary education: teaching staff and pupils
Enseignement secondaire: personnel enseignant et élèves
Enseñanza secundaria: personal docente y alumnos

| Country / Pays / País | Type of education / Type d'enseignement / Tipo de enseñanza | Year / Année / Año | Teaching staff / Personnel enseignant / Personal docente | | | Pupils enrolled / Elèves inscrits / Alumnos matriculados | | |
|---|---|---|---|---|---|---|---|---|
| | | | Total | Female Féminin Femenino | % F | Total | Female Féminin Femenino | % F |
| Eritrea (cont) | Total | 1992/93 | 1 856 | 242 | 13 | 60 955 | 27 922 | 46 |
| | General education | | 1 759 | 236 | 13 | 59 958 | 27 765 | 46 |
| | Teacher training | | 22 | 2 | 9 | 460 | 99 | 22 |
| | Vocational education | | 75 | 4 | 5 | 537 | 58 | 11 |
| | Total | 1993/94 | 2 095 | 248 | 12 | 66 524 | 28 090 | 42 |
| | General education | | 1 993 | 244 | 12 | 65 537 | 27 976 | 43 |
| | Teacher training | | 39 | 4 | 10 | 398 | 54 | 14 |
| | Vocational education | | 63 | - | - | 589 | 60 | 10 |
| | Total | 1994/95 | 2 162 | 251 | 12 | 72 969 | 30 538 | 42 |
| | General education | | 2 029 | 245 | 12 | 71 723 | 30 316 | 42 |
| | Teacher training | | 44 | 3 | 7 | 427 | 133 | 31 |
| | Vocational education | | 89 | 3 | 3 | 819 | 89 | 11 |
| | Total | 1995/96 | 2 193 | 265 | 12 | 80 182 | 33 863 | 42 |
| | General education | | 2 031 | 259 | 13 | 78 902 | 33 578 | 43 |
| | Teacher training | | ... | ... | ... | ... | ... | ... |
| | Vocational education | | ... | ... | ... | ... | ... | ... |
| | Total | 1996/97 | 2 071 | 283 | 14 | 89 087 | 37 196 | 42 |
| | General education | | 1 959 | 276 | 14 | 88 054 | 37 053 | 42 |
| | Teacher training | | 33 | 6 | 18 | 359 | 52 | 14 |
| | Vocational education | | 79 | 1 | 1 | 674 | 91 | 14 |
| Ethiopia | Total | 1970/71 | 4 885 | 781 | 16 | 135 179 | 33 697 | 25 |
| | General education | | 4 124 | 594 | 14 | 126 357 | 30 620 | 24 |
| | Teacher training | | 158 | 28 | 18 | 2 802 | 483 | 17 |
| | Vocational education | | 603 | 159 | 26 | 6 020 | 2 594 | 43 |
| | Total | 1975/76 | ... | ... | | ... | ... | ... |
| | General education | | 6 791 | 714 | 11 | 230 908 | 68 904 | 30 |
| | Teacher training | | ... | ... | ... | ... | ... | ... |
| | Vocational education | | ... | ... | ... | ... | ... | ... |
| | Total | 1980/81 | ... | ... | ... | ... | ... | |
| | General education | | 9 962 | 1 003 | 10 | 426 277 | 151 542 | 36 |
| | Teacher training | | 240 | 26 | 11 | 4 610 | 1 307 | 28 |
| | Vocational education | | ... | ... | ... | ... | ... | ... |
| | Total | 1985/86 | 15 861 | | | 666 169 | | |
| | General education | | 15 218 | 1 700 | 11 | 655 517 | 255 719 | 39 |
| | Teacher training | | 253 | 27 | 11 | 5 683 | 850 | 15 |
| | Vocational education | | 390 | ... | ... | 4 969 | ... | ... |
| | Total | 1990/91 | 23 319 | 2 296 | 10 | 866 016 | 371 841 | 43 |
| | General education | | 22 721 | 2 254 | 10 | 858 846 | 370 262 | 43 |
| | Teacher training | | 293 | 42 | 14 | 3 823 | 998 | 26 |
| | Vocational education | | 305 | - | - | 3 347 | 581 | 17 |
| | Total | 1991/92 | 23 705 | 2 429 | 10 | 782 412 | 353 992 | 45 |
| | General education | | 23 110 | 2 387 | 10 | 775 211 | 352 063 | 45 |
| | Teacher training | | 293 | 42 | 14 | 4 527 | 1 395 | 31 |
| | Vocational education | | 302 | - | - | 2 674 | 534 | 20 |
| | Total | 1992/93 | 22 600 | 2 159 | 10 | 720 825 | 334 085 | 46 |
| | General education | | 21 970 | 2 136 | 10 | 712 489 | 331 798 | 47 |
| | Teacher training | | 320 | 23 | 7 | 5 747 | 1 818 | 32 |
| | Vocational education | | 310 | - | - | 2 589 | 469 | 18 |
| | Total | 1993/94 | 22 470 | 2 154 | 10 | 723 009 | 329 565 | 46 |
| | General education | | 21 598 | 2 130 | 10 | 714 622 | 327 277 | 46 |
| | Teacher training | | 365 | 24 | 7 | 5 782 | 1 865 | 32 |
| | Vocational education | | 507 | - | - | 2 605 | 423 | 16 |
| | Total | 1994/95 | 23 605 | 2 353 | 10 | 756 249 | 334 211 | 44 |
| | General education | | 22 779 | 2 328 | 10 | 747 146 | 331 344 | 44 |
| | Teacher training | | 372 | 25 | 7 | 6 469 | 2 442 | 38 |
| | Vocational education | | 454 | - | - | 2 634 | 425 | 16 |
| | Total | 1995/96 | 25 984 | 2 697 | 10 | 819 242 | 351 964 | 43 |
| | General education | | 25 075 | 2 684 | 11 | 810 604 | 349 330 | 43 |
| | Teacher training | | 274 | 13 | 5 | 5 900 | 2 160 | 37 |
| | Vocational education | | 635 | - | - | 2 738 | 474 | 17 |
| | Total | 1996/97 | ... | ... | ... | ... | ... | ... |
| | General education | | *25 402 | *2 662 | *10 | *889 650 | *374 122 | *42 |
| | Teacher training | | ... | ... | ... | ... | ... | ... |
| | Vocational education | | 633 | - | - | 2 924 | 415 | 14 |
| Gabon | Total | 1970/71 | 512 | 145 | 28 | 9 983 | 2 851 | 29 |
| | General education | | 369 | 116 | 31 | 8 244 | 2 488 | 30 |
| | Teacher training | | 22 | 5 | 23 | 131 | 29 | 22 |
| | Vocational education | | 121 | 24 | 20 | 1 608 | 334 | 21 |

Secondary education: teaching staff and pupils  II.6
Enseignement secondaire: personnel enseignant et élèves
Enseñanza secundaria: personal docente y alumnos

| Country / Pays / País | Type of education / Type d'enseignement / Tipo de enseñanza | Year / Année / Año | Teaching staff Personnel enseignant Personal docente | | | Pupils enrolled Elèves inscrits Alumnos matriculados | | |
|---|---|---|---|---|---|---|---|---|
| | | | Total | Female Féminin Femenino | % F | Total | Female Féminin Femenino | % F |
| Gabon (cont) | Total | 1975/76 | 1 016 | ... | ... | 22 542 | 7 870 | 35 |
| | General education | | 812 | 248 | 31 | 19 721 | 7 174 | 36 |
| | Teacher training | | 36 | ... | ... | 371 | 124 | 33 |
| | Vocational education | | 168 | 38 | 23 | 2 450 | 572 | 23 |
| | Total | 1980/81 | 1 587 | 387 | 24 | 29 406 | 11 776 | 40 |
| | General education | | 1 034 | 285 | 28 | 19 998 | 8 402 | 42 |
| | Teacher training | | 181 | 40 | 22 | 3 878 | 1 810 | 47 |
| | Vocational education | | 372 | 62 | 17 | 5 530 | 1 564 | 28 |
| | Total | 1985/86 | 2 074 | 460 | 22 | 44 124 | 18 668 | 42 |
| | General education | | 1 391 | 342 | 25 | 28 887 | 12 650 | 44 |
| | Teacher training | | 236 | 53 | 22 | 6 581 | 3 350 | 51 |
| | Vocational education | | 447 | 65 | 15 | 8 656 | 2 668 | 31 |
| | Total | 1991/92 | ... | ... | ... | 42 871 | ... | ... |
| | General education | | (4) 1 356 | (4) 360 | 27 | | ... | ... |
| | Teacher training | | ... | ... | ... | ... | ... | ... |
| | Vocational education | | 476 | ... | ... | 8 477 | ... | ... |
| | Total | 1993/94 | ... | ... | ... | 59 442 | 28 235 | 48 |
| | General education | | ... | ... | ... | ... | ... | ... |
| | Teacher training | | ... | ... | ... | ... | ... | ... |
| | Vocational education | | ... | ... | ... | ... | ... | ... |
| | Total | 1994/95 | 2 382 | 420 | 18 | 65 718 | 29 856 | 45 |
| | General education | | 1 897 | 361 | 19 | 56 457 | 26 162 | 46 |
| | Teacher training | | 10 | 1 | 10 | 52 | 11 | 21 |
| | Vocational education | | 475 | 58 | 12 | 9 209 | 3 683 | 40 |
| | Total | 1995/96 | 3 094 | 565 | 18 | 80 552 | 38 076 | 47 |
| | General education | | 2 683 | 514 | 19 | 72 888 | 35 402 | 49 |
| | Teacher training | | 10 | 1 | 10 | 76 | 36 | 47 |
| | Vocational education | | 401 | 50 | 12 | 7 588 | 2 638 | 35 |
| Gambia | Total | 1970/71 | 254 | 67 | 26 | 5 042 | 1 223 | 24 |
| | General education | | 224 | 61 | 27 | 4 712 | 1 175 | 25 |
| | Teacher training | | 12 | 4 | 33 | 149 | 31 | 21 |
| | Vocational education | | 18 | 2 | 11 | 181 | 17 | 9 |
| | Total | 1975/76 | (6) 347 | (6) 89 | 26 | (6) 6 618 | (6) 1 785 | 27 |
| | General education | | (6) 304 | (6) 78 | 26 | (6) 6 178 | (6) 1 690 | 27 |
| | Teacher training | | 13 | 5 | 38 | 111 | 45 | 41 |
| | Vocational education | | 30 | 6 | 20 | 329 | 50 | 15 |
| | Total | 1980/81 | 620 | 158 | 25 | 9 657 | 2 853 | 30 |
| | General education | | 536 | 144 | 27 | 9 081 | 2 740 | 30 |
| | Teacher training | | 30 | 3 | 10 | 262 | 53 | 20 |
| | Vocational education | | 54 | 11 | 20 | 314 | 60 | 19 |
| | Total | 1985/86 | 695 | ... | ... | 15 918 | 4 746 | 30 |
| | General education | | ... | ... | ... | ... | ... | ... |
| | Teacher training | | ... | ... | ... | 367 | 127 | 35 |
| | Vocational education | | ... | ... | ... | ... | ... | ... |
| | Total | 1990/91 | (7) 756 | ... | ... | (7) 20 400 | (7) 6 743 | 33 |
| | General education | | ... | ... | ... | ... | ... | ... |
| | Teacher training | | ... | ... | ... | ... | ... | ... |
| | Vocational education | | ... | ... | ... | ... | ... | ... |
| | Total | 1991/92 | 777 | ... | ... | 21 786 | 7 523 | 35 |
| | General education | | ... | ... | ... | ... | ... | ... |
| | Teacher training | | ... | ... | ... | ... | ... | ... |
| | Vocational education | | ... | ... | ... | ... | ... | ... |
| | Total | 1992/93 | 1 054 | 198 | 19 | 25 929 | 9 013 | 35 |
| | General education | | ... | ... | ... | ... | ... | ... |
| | Teacher training | | ... | ... | ... | ... | ... | ... |
| | Vocational education | | ... | ... | ... | ... | ... | ... |
| | Total | 1993/94 | 1 126 | 180 | 16 | 27 120 | 9 600 | 35 |
| | General education | | ... | ... | ... | ... | ... | ... |
| | Teacher training | | ... | ... | ... | ... | ... | ... |
| | Vocational education | | ... | ... | ... | ... | ... | ... |
| | Total | 1994/95 | 1 213 | 197 | 16 | 31 567 | *11 220 | *36 |
| | General education | | ... | ... | ... | ... | ... | ... |
| | Teacher training | | ... | ... | ... | ... | ... | ... |
| | Vocational education | | ... | ... | ... | ... | ... | ... |
| | Total | 1995/96 | 1 547 | 259 | 17 | 32 097 | 12 354 | 38 |
| | General education | | ... | ... | ... | ... | ... | ... |
| | Teacher training | | ... | ... | ... | ... | ... | ... |
| | Vocational education | | ... | ... | ... | ... | ... | ... |

II.6   Secondary education: teaching staff and pupils
Enseignement secondaire: personnel enseignant et élèves
Enseñanza secundaria: personal docente y alumnos

| Country / Pays / País | Type of education / Type d'enseignement / Tipo de enseñanza | Year / Année / Año | Teaching staff / Personnel enseignant / Personal docente | | | Pupils enrolled / Elèves inscrits / Alumnos matriculados | | |
|---|---|---|---|---|---|---|---|---|
| | | | Total | Female / Féminin / Femenino | % F | Total | Female / Féminin / Femenino | % F |
| Ghana | Total | 1970/71 | 5 842 | 1 009 | 17 | 99 299 | 27 473 | 28 |
| | General education | | 3 388 | 633 | 19 | 59 669 | 15 374 | 26 |
| | Teacher training | | 1 324 | 234 | 18 | 16 478 | 5 343 | 32 |
| | Vocational education | | 1 130 | 142 | 13 | 23 152 | 6 756 | 29 |
| | Total | 1975/76 | (6)(8) 25 142 | (6)(8) 5 443 | 22 | (6) 555 980 | (6) 212 667 | 38 |
| | General education | | (6) 23 181 | (6) 5 139 | 22 | (6) 532 520 | (6) 207 214 | 39 |
| | Teacher training | | (8) 939 | (8) 201 | 21 | 4 541 | 1 932 | 43 |
| | Vocational education | | 1 022 | 103 | 10 | 18 919 | 3 521 | 19 |
| | Total | 1980/81 | 31 636 | 6 656 | 21 | 693 159 | 263 097 | 38 |
| | General education | | 29 642 | 6 226 | 21 | 654 436 | 251 664 | 38 |
| | Teacher training | | 881 | 194 | 22 | 11 600 | 4 698 | 41 |
| | Vocational education | | 1 113 | 236 | 21 | 27 123 | 6 735 | 25 |
| | Total | 1985/86 | (4) 37 290 | (4) 9 615 | 26 | (4) 749 980 | ... | ... |
| | General education | | (4) 35 085 | (4) 9 287 | 26 | (4) 718 444 | ... | ... |
| | Teacher training | | 1 011 | 219 | 22 | 15 169 | ... | ... |
| | Vocational education | | (4) 1 194 | (4) 109 | 9 | (4) 16 367 | ... | ... |
| | Total | 1990/91 | ... | ... | ... | ... | ... | ... |
| | General education | | (4) 39 903 | (4) 9 760 | 24 | (4) 768 603 | (4) 297 914 | 39 |
| | Teacher training | | ... | ... | ... | ... | ... | ... |
| | Vocational education | | ... | ... | ... | ... | ... | ... |
| | Total | 1991/92 | ... | ... | ... | ... | ... | ... |
| | General education | | ... | ... | ... | 841 722 | 328 718 | 39 |
| | Teacher training | | ... | ... | ... | | | |
| | Vocational education | | ... | ... | ... | 22 578 | 6 914 | 31 |
| Guinea | Total | 1970/71 | 2 785 | ... | ... | 63 409 | 13 064 | 21 |
| | General education | | 2 360 | ... | ... | 59 918 | 12 430 | 21 |
| | Teacher training | | 275 | ... | ... | 1 478 | 232 | 16 |
| | Vocational education | | 150 | ... | ... | 2 013 | 402 | 20 |
| | Total | 1975/76 | ... | ... | ... | ... | ... | ... |
| | General education | | (1) 2 738 | (1) 133 | 5 | 69 908 | 18 064 | 26 |
| | Teacher training | | ... | ... | ... | ... | ... | ... |
| | Vocational education | | ./. | ./. | ./. | 1 260 | 150 | 12 |
| | Total | 1980/81 | ... | ... | ... | 98 305 | 27 599 | 28 |
| | General education | | 3 520 | ... | ... | 89 900 | 24 942 | 28 |
| | Teacher training | | ... | ... | ... | ... | ... | ... |
| | Vocational education | | ... | ... | ... | ... | ... | ... |
| | Total | 1985/86 | (11) 4 642 | (11) 323 | 7 | (11) 92 754 | (11) 24 493 | 26 |
| | General education | | (11) 3 764 | (11) 264 | 7 | (11) 86 474 | (11) 22 194 | 26 |
| | Teacher training | | 101 | 6 | 6 | 912 | 382 | 42 |
| | Vocational education | | 777 | 53 | 7 | 5 368 | 1 917 | 36 |
| | Total | 1990/91 | 5 976 | 725 | 12 | 85 942 | 20 929 | 24 |
| | General education | | 4 846 | 622 | 13 | 75 674 | 17 739 | 23 |
| | Teacher training | | 128 | 14 | 11 | 2 066 | 985 | 48 |
| | Vocational education | | 1 002 | 89 | 9 | 8 202 | 2 205 | 27 |
| | Total | 1991/92 | ... | ... | ... | ... | ... | ... |
| | General education | | 4 572 | 644 | 14 | 87 975 | 20 905 | 24 |
| | Teacher training | | ... | ... | ... | ... | ... | ... |
| | Vocational education | | ... | ... | ... | ... | ... | ... |
| | Total | 1992/93 | 4 719 | 614 | 13 | 106 811 | 26 443 | 25 |
| | General education | | 3 417 | 522 | 15 | 97 533 | 23 703 | 24 |
| | Teacher training | | 188 | ... | ... | 1 568 | 763 | 49 |
| | Vocational education | | 1 114 | ... | ... | 7 710 | 1 977 | 26 |
| | Total | 1993/94 | ... | ... | ... | 116 377 | 28 720 | 25 |
| | General education | | 3 629 | 510 | 14 | 108 459 | 26 444 | 24 |
| | Teacher training | | 194 | 13 | 7 | 1 329 | 615 | 46 |
| | Vocational education | | ... | ... | ... | 6 589 | 1 661 | 25 |
| | Total | 1994/95 | ... | ... | ... | 120 232 | 30 017 | 25 |
| | General education | | 4 198 | 493 | 12 | | | |
| | Teacher training | | ... | ... | ... | ... | ... | ... |
| | Vocational education | | ... | ... | ... | ... | ... | ... |
| | Total | 1995/96 | ... | ... | ... | 132 722 | 33 954 | 26 |
| | General education | | 4 690 | 580 | 12 | 127 517 | 32 046 | 25 |
| | Teacher training | | ... | ... | ... | 559 | 271 | 48 |
| | Vocational education | | ... | ... | ... | 4 646 | 1 637 | 35 |
| | Total | 1996/97 | ... | ... | ... | ... | ... | ... |
| | General education | | 4 958 | 524 | 11 | 143 243 | 36 817 | 26 |
| | Teacher training | | ... | ... | ... | ... | ... | ... |
| | Vocational education | | ... | ... | ... | ... | ... | ... |

Secondary education: teaching staff and pupils
Enseignement secondaire: personnel enseignant et élèves
Enseñanza secundaria: personal docente y alumnos

II.6

| Country / Pays / País | Type of education / Type d'enseignement / Tipo de enseñanza | Year / Année / Año | Teaching staff / Personnel enseignant / Personal docente | | | Pupils enrolled / Elèves inscrits / Alumnos matriculados | | |
|---|---|---|---|---|---|---|---|---|
| | | | Total | Female Féminin Femenino | % F | Total | Female Féminin Femenino | % F |
| Guinea (cont) | Total | 1997/98 | ... | ... | ... | ... | ... | ... |
| | General education | | 5 099 | 573 | 11 | 153 661 | 39 449 | 26 |
| | Teacher training | | ... | ... | ... | ... | ... | ... |
| | Vocational education | | ... | ... | ... | ... | ... | ... |
| Guinea-Bissau | Total | 1970/71 | 233 | ... | ... | 4 215 | 1 526 | 36 |
| | General education | | 141 | ... | ... | 3 268 | 1 245 | 38 |
| | Teacher training | | 37 | ... | ... | 390 | 143 | 37 |
| | Vocational education | | 55 | ... | ... | 557 | 138 | 25 |
| | Total | 1980/81 | 462 | 99 | 21 | 4 757 | 939 | 20 |
| | General education | | 387 | 78 | 20 | 4 068 | 876 | 22 |
| | Teacher training | | 46 | 20 | 43 | 412 | 25 | 6 |
| | Vocational education | | 29 | 1 | 3 | 277 | 38 | 14 |
| Kenya | Total | 1970 | (8) 6 599 | (8) 1 878 | 28 | 136 030 | 40 183 | 30 |
| | General education | | 5 881 | 1 690 | 29 | 126 855 | 37 528 | 30 |
| | Teacher training | | (8) 575 | (8) 188 | 33 | 6 749 | 2 655 | 39 |
| | Vocational education | | 143 | - | - | 2 426 | - | - |
| | Total | 1975 | 9 730 | ... | ... | 240 969 | 84 782 | 35 |
| | General education | | (1) 9 189 | ... | ... | 226 835 | 81 529 | 36 |
| | Teacher training | | 541 | 170 | 31 | 8 666 | 3 253 | 38 |
| | Vocational education | | ./. | ... | ... | 5 468 | - | - |
| | Total | 1980 | (8) 17 081 | ... | ... | 428 023 | 174 281 | 41 |
| | General education | | 15 916 | ... | ... | 407 322 (1) | 160 401 | ... |
| | Teacher training | | (8) 732 | ... | ... | 12 126 | 4 880 | 40 |
| | Vocational education | | 433 | ... | ... | 8 575 | ./. | ... |
| | Total | 1985 | (12) 23 055 | (12) 8 364 | 36 | (12) 457 767 | (12) 173 417 | 38 |
| | General education | | (12) 21 712 | (12) 8 027 | 37 | (12) 437 207 | (12) 167 174 | 38 |
| | Teacher training | | 808 | 242 | 30 | 12 720 | 5 162 | 41 |
| | Vocational education | | 535 | 95 | 18 | 7 840 | 1 081 | 14 |
| | Total | 1990 | ... | ... | ... | 618 461 | 264 766 | 43 |
| | General education | | 30 621 | 9 930 | 32 | 17 073 | 7 643 | 45 |
| | Teacher training | | ... | ... | ... | ... | ... | ... |
| | Vocational education | | ... | ... | ... | ... | ... | ... |
| | Total | 1991 | ... | ... | ... | ... | ... | ... |
| | General education | | (13) 35 097 | (13) 11 458 | 33 | (13) 614 161 | (13) 268 373 | 44 |
| | Teacher training | | ... | ... | ... | 17 504 | 7 696 | 44 |
| | Vocational education | | ... | ... | ... | ... | ... | ... |
| | Total | 1992 | ... | ... | ... | 629 062 | 275 690 | 44 |
| | General education | | 36 560 | 12 356 | 34 | 18 992 | 8 823 | 46 |
| | Teacher training | | ... | ... | ... | ... | ... | ... |
| | Vocational education | | ... | ... | ... | ... | ... | ... |
| | Total | 1993 | ... | ... | ... | ... | ... | ... |
| | General education | | *37 670 | *13 400 | *36 | *616 200 | *273 900 | *44 |
| | Teacher training | | ... | ... | ... | ... | ... | ... |
| | Vocational education | | ... | ... | ... | ... | ... | ... |
| | Total | 1994 | ... | ... | ... | ... | ... | ... |
| | General education | | 38 307 | 13 082 | 34 | 619 839 | 283 400 | 46 |
| | Teacher training | | ... | ... | ... | ... | ... | ... |
| | Vocational education | | ... | ... | ... | ... | ... | ... |
| | Total | 1995 | ... | ... | ... | ... | ... | ... |
| | General education | | *41 484 | *13 582 | *33 | *632 388 | *290 581 | *46 |
| | Teacher training | | ... | ... | ... | ... | ... | ... |
| | Vocational education | | ... | ... | ... | ... | ... | ... |
| Lesotho | Total | 1970 | 329 | 149 | 45 | 7 342 | 3 970 | 54 |
| | General education | | 256 | 115 | 45 | 6 028 | 3 168 | 53 |
| | Teacher training | | 40 | 23 | 57 | 695 | 459 | 66 |
| | Vocational education | | 33 | 11 | 33 | 619 | 343 | 55 |
| | Total | 1975 | (8) 698 | ... | ... | 16 476 | 9 161 | 56 |
| | General education | | 605 | 302 | 50 | 15 611 | 8 552 | 55 |
| | Teacher training | | (8) 27 | ... | ... | 318 | 228 | 72 |
| | Vocational education | | 66 | 39 | 59 | 547 | 381 | 70 |
| | Total | 1980 | (8) 1 299 | ... | ... | 25 292 | 15 239 | 60 |
| | General education | | 1 122 | 534 | 48 | 23 355 | 13 922 | 60 |
| | Teacher training | | (8) 55 | ... | ... | 701 | 624 | 89 |
| | Vocational education | | 122 | 57 | 47 | 1 236 | 693 | 56 |
| | Total | 1985 | (8) 1 897 | ... | ... | 37 343 | 22 274 | 60 |
| | General education | | 1 676 | 872 | 52 | 35 423 | 21 051 | 59 |
| | Teacher training | | (8) 93 | ... | ... | 657 | 572 | 87 |
| | Vocational education | | 128 | 61 | 48 | 1 263 | 651 | 52 |

II.6  Secondary education: teaching staff and pupils
Enseignement secondaire: personnel enseignant et élèves
Enseñanza secundaria: personal docente y alumnos

| Country<br><br>Pays<br><br>País | Type of education<br><br>Type d'enseignement<br><br>Tipo de enseñanza | Year<br><br>Année<br><br>Año | Teaching staff<br>Personnel enseignant<br>Personal docente | | | Pupils enrolled<br>Elèves inscrits<br>Alumnos matriculados | | |
|---|---|---|---|---|---|---|---|---|
| | | | Total | Female<br>Féminin<br>Femenino | %<br><br>F | Total | Female<br>Féminin<br>Femenino | %<br><br>F |
| Lesotho (cont) | Total | 1990 | ... | ... | ... | 48 209 | 28 769 | 60 |
| | General education | | 2 213 | 1 181 | 53 | 46 303 | 27 673 | 60 |
| | Teacher training | | ... | ... | ... | 346 | 309 | 89 |
| | Vocational education | | ... | ... | ... | 1 560 | 787 | 50 |
| | Total | 1991 (8) | 2 634 | ... | ... | 48 505 | 28 649 | 59 |
| | General education | | 2 407 | 1 235 | 51 | 46 572 | 27 577 | 59 |
| | Teacher training | (8) | 87 | ... | ... | 333 | 306 | 92 |
| | Vocational education | | 140 | ... | ... | 1 600 | 766 | 48 |
| | Total | 1992 | ... | ... | ... | 52 598 | 31 316 | 60 |
| | General education | | 2 443 | 1 211 | 50 | 51 895 | 30 789 | 59 |
| | Teacher training | | - | - | - | - | - | - |
| | Vocational education | | ... | ... | ... | 703 | 527 | 75 |
| | Total | 1993 | 2 580 | 1 296 | 50 | 55 984 | 33 267 | 59 |
| | General education | | 2 526 | 1 255 | 50 | 55 312 | 32 747 | 59 |
| | Teacher training | | - | - | - | - | - | - |
| | Vocational education | | 54 | 41 | 76 | 672 | 520 | 77 |
| | Total | 1994 | 2 655 | ... | ... | 62 399 | 37 271 | 60 |
| | General education | | 2 597 | 1 332 | 51 | 61 615 | 36 595 | 59 |
| | Teacher training | | - | - | - | - | - | - |
| | Vocational education | | 58 | ... | ... | 784 | 676 | 86 |
| | Total | 1995 | ... | ... | ... | 67 173 | ... | ... |
| | General education | | 2 709 | 1 411 | 52 | 66 454 | 39 479 | 59 |
| | Teacher training | | - | - | - | - | - | - |
| | Vocational education | | ... | ... | ... | 719 | ... | ... |
| | Total | 1996 | 2 878 | 1 517 | 53 | 68 132 | 40 149 | 59 |
| | General education | | 2 817 | 1 463 | 52 | 67 454 | 39 712 | 59 |
| | Teacher training | | - | - | - | - | - | - |
| | Vocational education | | 61 | 54 | 89 | 678 | 437 | 64 |
| Liberia | Total | 1970 | 1 016 | *193 | *19 | 16 771 | 3 860 | 23 |
| | General education | | 918 | 176 | 19 | 15 494 | 3 617 | 23 |
| | Teacher training | | 32 | 2 | 6 | 390 | 65 | 17 |
| | Vocational education | | 66 | *15 | *23 | 887 | 178 | 20 |
| | Total | 1975 | ... | ... | ... | 34 151 | 8 498 | 25 |
| | General education | | ... | ... | ... | 32 978 | 8 331 | 25 |
| | Teacher training | | 53 | 12 | 23 | 322 | 55 | 17 |
| | Vocational education | | ... | ... | ... | 851 | 112 | 13 |
| | Total | 1980 | ... | ... | ... | 54 623 | 15 343 | 28 |
| | General education | | ... | ... | ... | 51 666 | 14 632 | 28 |
| | Teacher training | | ... | ... | ... | 635 | 84 | 13 |
| | Vocational education | | ... | ... | ... | 2 322 | 627 | 27 |
| Libyan Arab<br>Jamahiriya | Total | 1970/71 | 4 343 | 455 | 10 | 53 953 | 9 819 | 18 |
| | General education | | 3 549 | 387 | 11 | 45 488 | 7 834 | 17 |
| | Teacher training | | 463 | 68 | 15 | 5 377 | 1 985 | 37 |
| | Vocational education | | 331 | - | - | 3 088 | - | - |
| | Total | 1975/76 | 11 819 | ... | ... | 166 122 | 55 722 | 34 |
| | General education | | 9 464 | 1 287 | 14 | 140 486 | 43 464 | 31 |
| | Teacher training | | 1 832 | 437 | 24 | 20 748 | 12 258 | 59 |
| | Vocational education | | 523 | ... | ... | 4 888 | - | - |
| | Total | 1980/81 | 24 323 | 5 750 | 24 | 296 197 | 118 953 | 40 |
| | General education | | 20 327 | 4 942 | 24 | 253 201 | 98 134 | 39 |
| | Teacher training | | 2 488 | 631 | 25 | 26 988 | 16 838 | 62 |
| | Vocational education | | 1 508 | 177 | 12 | 16 008 | 3 981 | 25 |
| | Total | 1985/86 | 10 765 | 2 064 | 19 | 143 113 | 67 644 | 47 |
| | General education | | 5 977 | 1 262 | 21 | 81 864 | 38 863 | 47 |
| | Teacher training | | 2 639 | 555 | 21 | 34 746 | 23 093 | 66 |
| | Vocational education | | 2 149 | 247 | 11 | 26 503 | 5 688 | 21 |
| | Total | 1990/91 | ... | ... | ... | 257 120 | ... | ... |
| | General education | | 9 219 | ... | ... | 148 406 | 78 268 | 53 |
| | Teacher training | | 3 306 | ... | ... | 43 142 | 30 193 | 70 |
| | Vocational education | | ... | ... | ... | 65 572 | ... | ... |
| | Total | 1991/92 | ... | ... | ... | 294 283 | ... | ... |
| | General education | | 14 941 | 5 920 | 40 | 181 368 | 95 809 | 53 |
| | Teacher training | | 3 688 | ... | ... | 34 289 | 25 690 | 75 |
| | Vocational education | | ... | ... | ... | 78 626 | ... | ... |
| | Total | 1992/93 | ... | ... | ... | 310 556 | ... | ... |
| | General education | | ... | ... | ... | 189 202 | ... | ... |
| | Teacher training | | 2 760 | ... | ... | 26 393 | 21 462 | 81 |
| | Vocational education | | ... | ... | ... | 94 961 | ... | ... |

Secondary education: teaching staff and pupils
Enseignement secondaire: personnel enseignant et élèves
Enseñanza secundaria: personal docente y alumnos

II.6

| Country / Pays / País | Type of education / Type d'enseignement / Tipo de enseñanza | Year / Année / Año | Teaching staff Personnel enseignant Personal docente | | | Pupils enrolled Elèves inscrits Alumnos matriculados | | |
|---|---|---|---|---|---|---|---|---|
| | | | Total | Female Féminin Femenino | % F | Total | Female Féminin Femenino | % F |
| Libyan Arab Jamahiriya (cont) | Total | 1993/94 | ... | ... | ... | ... | ... | ... |
| | General education | | ... | ... | ... | ... | ... | ... |
| | Teacher training | | ... | ... | ... | 29 125 | 23 595 | 81 |
| | Vocational education | | ... | ... | ... | 118 564 | ... | ... |
| Madagascar | Total | 1970/71 | 5 709 | ... | ... | 113 270 | 45 073 | 40 |
| | General education | | 4 757 | 1 632 | 34 | 101 412 | 41 902 | 41 |
| | Teacher training | | 224 | | ... | 2 009 | 676 | 34 |
| | Vocational education | | 728 | | ... | 9 849 | 2 495 | 25 |
| | Total | 1975/76 | ... | | ... | ... | | ... |
| | General education | | | | ... | (4) 78 954 | (4) 32 146 | 41 |
| | Teacher training | | ... | | ... | ... | ... | ... |
| | Vocational education | | 858 | | ... | 7 504 | ... | ... |
| | Total | 1980/81 | ... | | ... | ... | | ... |
| | General education | | | | ... | ... | ... | ... |
| | Teacher training | | 157 | | ... | 1 619 | ... | ... |
| | Vocational education | | 1 121 | | ... | 9 393 | 1 067 | 11 |
| | Total | 1990/91 | ... | | ... | ... | | ... |
| | General education | | 14 856 | ... | ... | 322 772 | 160 333 | 50 |
| | Teacher training | | ... | | ... | ... | ... | ... |
| | Vocational education | | 1 448 | | ... | 17 033 | 6 923 | 41 |
| | Total | 1991/92 | ... | | ... | ... | | ... |
| | General education | | 14 371 | ... | ... | 293 721 | 145 883 | 50 |
| | Teacher training | | ... | | ... | ... | ... | ... |
| | Vocational education | | ... | | ... | (4) 7 254 | (4) 2 324 | 32 |
| | Total | 1992/93 | ... | | ... | ... | | ... |
| | General education | | 14 770 | ... | ... | 304 796 | 150 891 | 50 |
| | Teacher training | | ... | | ... | ... | ... | ... |
| | Vocational education | | ... | | ... | ... | ... | ... |
| | Total | 1993/94 | ... | | ... | ... | | ... |
| | General education | | 15 118 | ... | ... | 298 241 | 149 900 | 50 |
| | Teacher training | | 58 | 18 | 31 | 341 | 142 | 42 |
| | Vocational education | | ... | | ... | ... | ... | ... |
| | Total | 1994/95 | ... | | ... | ... | | ... |
| | General education | | 16 491 | ... | ... | 293 579 | 146 351 | 50 |
| | Teacher training | | ... | | ... | ... | ... | ... |
| | Vocational education | | ... | | ... | ... | ... | ... |
| | Total | 1995/96 | ... | | ... | ... | | ... |
| | General education | | 16 795 | 6 982 | 42 | 302 035 | 151 493 | 50 |
| | Teacher training | | ... | | ... | ... | ... | ... |
| | Vocational education | | (4) 1 092 | (4) 359 | 33 | (4) 8 138 | (4) 2 430 | 30 |
| Malawi | Total | 1970/71 | ... | ... | ... | ... | | ... |
| | General education | | (14) 678 | (14) 170 | 25 | 13 166 | (14) 3 760 | ... |
| | Teacher training | | ... | ... | ... | ... | ... | ... |
| | Vocational education | | ... | ... | ... | 236 | - | - |
| | Total | 1975/76 | (14) 849 | | ... | 19 244 | (14) 4 178 | ... |
| | General education | | (14) 748 | | ... | 18 079 | (14) 4 117 | ... |
| | Teacher training | | 55 | ... | ... | 636 | 61 | 10 |
| | Vocational education | | 46 | - | - | 529 | - | - |
| | Total | 1980/81 | (14) 953 | | ... | 25 522 | (14) 5 704 | ... |
| | General education | | (14) 834 | | ... | 23 647 | (14) 5 248 | ... |
| | Teacher training | | *75 | ... | ... | 1 228 | 456 | 37 |
| | Vocational education | | 44 | - | - | 647 | - | - |
| | Total | 1985/86 | (14) 1 272 | | ... | 37 524 | (14) 8 629 | ... |
| | General education | | (14) 1 141 | | ... | 35 706 | (14) 8 136 | ... |
| | Teacher training | | *80 | ... | ... | 1 258 | 493 | 39 |
| | Vocational education | | 51 | - | - | 560 | - | - |
| | Total | 1990/91 | ... | ... | ... | 60 701 | (14) 11 589 | ... |
| | General education | | ... | ... | ... | 58 316 | (14) 10 923 | ... |
| | Teacher training | | *100 | ... | ... | 1 605 | 603 | 38 |
| | Vocational education | | ... | ... | ... | 780 | 63 | 8 |
| | Total | 1991/92 | (14) 1 299 | | ... | 71 567 | ... | ... |
| | General education | | (14) 1 141 | | ... | 68 956 | ... | ... |
| | Teacher training | | *100 | ... | ... | 1 771 | 623 | 35 |
| | Vocational education | | 58 | - | - | 840 | ... | ... |
| | Total | 1992/93 | (14) 1 393 | | ... | 75 372 | (14) 13 815 | ... |
| | General education | | (14) 1 212 | | ... | 72 329 | (14) 12 768 | ... |
| | Teacher training | | *120 | ... | ... | 2 180 | 982 | 45 |
| | Vocational education | | 61 | ... | ... | 863 | 65 | 8 |

II.6   Secondary education: teaching staff and pupils
Enseignement secondaire: personnel enseignant et élèves
Enseñanza secundaria: personal docente y alumnos

| Country / Pays / País | Type of education / Type d'enseignement / Tipo de enseñanza | Year / Année / Año | Teaching staff — Personnel enseignant — Personal docente | | | Pupils enrolled — Elèves inscrits — Alumnos matriculados | | |
|---|---|---|---|---|---|---|---|---|
| | | | Total | Female Féminin Femenino | % F | Total | Female Féminin Femenino | % F |
| Malawi (cont) | Total | 1993/94 | (14) 2 870 | ... | ... | 91 917 (14) | 19 163 | ... |
| | General education | | (14) 2 672 | ... | ... | 88 752 (14) | 18 179 | ... |
| | Teacher training | | *120 | ... | ... | 2 158 | 944 | 44 |
| | Vocational education | | 78 | ... | ... | 1 007 | 40 | 4 |
| | Total | 1994/95 | (14) 2 949 | ... | ... | 108 682 (14) | 19 430 | ... |
| | General education | | (14) 2 713 | ... | ... | 106 172 (14) | 18 918 | ... |
| | Teacher training | | *155 | ... | ... | 1 430 | 467 | 33 |
| | Vocational education | | 81 | ... | ... | 1 080 | 45 | 4 |
| | Total | 1995/96 | (14) 3 172 | ... | ... | 141 911 | ... | ... |
| | General education | | (14) 2 948 | ... | ... | 139 386 | 49 383 | 35 |
| | Teacher training | | *145 | ... | ... | 1 471 | 475 | 32 |
| | Vocational education | | 79 | ... | ... | 1 054 | ... | ... |
| Mali | Total | 1970/71 | 2 242 | 392 | 17 | 34 620 | 7 549 | 22 |
| | General education | | 1 818 | 317 | 17 | 29 683 | 6 614 | 22 |
| | Teacher training | | 92 | 20 | 22 | 1 551 | 269 | 17 |
| | Vocational education | | 332 | 55 | 17 | 3 386 | 666 | 20 |
| | Total | 1975/76 | ... | ... | ... | 55 444 | 14 287 | 26 |
| | General education | | 2 567 | 452 | 18 | 48 488 | 12 358 | 25 |
| | Teacher training | | ... | ... | ... | 1 948 | 359 | 18 |
| | Vocational education | | ... | ... | ... | 5 008 | 1 570 | 31 |
| | Total | 1990/91 | 5 748 | 802 | 14 | 84 220 | 28 203 | 33 |
| | General education | | 4 804 | 702 | 15 | 72 788 | 25 244 | 35 |
| | Teacher training | | 182 | 12 | 7 | 894 | 173 | 19 |
| | Vocational education | | 762 | 88 | 12 | 10 538 | 2 786 | 26 |
| | Total | 1991/92 | ... | ... | ... | 98 737 | 30 527 | 31 |
| | General education | | 4 854 | 803 | 17 | 86 065 | 27 492 | 32 |
| | Teacher training | | ... | ... | ... | 543 | 91 | 17 |
| | Vocational education | | ... | ... | ... | 12 129 | 2 944 | 24 |
| | Total | 1992/93 | ... | ... | ... | 102 781 | 33 978 | 33 |
| | General education | | ... | ... | ... | 92 866 | 30 795 | 33 |
| | Teacher training | | ... | ... | ... | 439 | 71 | 16 |
| | Vocational education | | ... | ... | ... | 9 476 | 3 112 | 33 |
| | Total | 1993/94 | ... | ... | ... | 120 912 | 39 382 | 33 |
| | General education | | ... | ... | ... | 107 105 | 35 264 | 33 |
| | Teacher training | | 75 | 6 | 8 | 427 | 63 | 15 |
| | Vocational education | | ... | ... | ... | 13 380 | 4 055 | 30 |
| | Total | 1994/95 | ... | ... | ... | 139 777 | 45 439 | 33 |
| | General education | | 4 549 | 799 | 18 | 120 997 | 39 833 | 33 |
| | Teacher training | | 48 | 3 | 6 | 323 | 59 | 18 |
| | Vocational education | | ... | ... | ... | 18 457 | 5 547 | 30 |
| | Total | 1995/96 | ... | ... | ... | 151 554 | 50 849 | 34 |
| | General education | | ... | ... | ... | 132 861 | 43 617 | 33 |
| | Teacher training | | ... | ... | ... | 787 | 213 | 27 |
| | Vocational education | | ... | ... | ... | 17 906 | 7 019 | 39 |
| | Total | 1996/97 | ... | ... | ... | 168 898 | 55 072 | 33 |
| | General education | | ... | ... | ... | 147 959 | 48 144 | 33 |
| | Teacher training | | 77 | ... | ... | 1 513 | 489 | 32 |
| | Vocational education | | (4) 526 | ... | ... | 19 426 | 6 439 | 33 |
| | Total | 1997/98 | ... | ... | ... | 188 109 | 62 460 | 33 |
| | General education | | ... | ... | ... | 166 372 | 55 260 | 33 |
| | Teacher training | | ... | ... | ... | 1 546 | 494 | 32 |
| | Vocational education | | ... | ... | ... | 20 191 | 6 706 | 33 |
| Mauritania | Total | 1970/71 | ... | ... | ... | 3 749 | ... | ... |
| | General education | | 148 | ... | ... | 3 408 | 382 | 11 |
| | Teacher training | | ... | ... | ... | 341 | ... | ... |
| | Vocational education | | - | - | - | - | - | - |
| | Total | 1975/76 | ... | ... | ... | ... | ... | ... |
| | General education | | ... | ... | ... | 6 571 | ... | ... |
| | Teacher training | | ... | ... | ... | 160 | ... | ... |
| | Vocational education | | ... | ... | ... | ... | ... | ... |
| | Total | 1980/81 | ... | ... | ... | 22 102 | 4 528 | 20 |
| | General education | | 646 | 54 | 8 | (15) 20 248 | (15) 4 291 | 21 |
| | Teacher training | | 51 | 6 | 12 | 850 | 164 | 19 |
| | Vocational education | | ... | ... | ... | 1 004 | 73 | 7 |
| | Total | 1985/86 | ... | ... | ... | 35 955 | ... | ... |
| | General education | | 1 378 | ... | ... | 33 148 | 9 398 | 28 |
| | Teacher training | | 66 | ... | ... | 953 | 266 | 28 |
| | Vocational education | | ... | ... | ... | 1 854 | ... | ... |

Secondary education: teaching staff and pupils   II.6
Enseignement secondaire: personnel enseignant et élèves
Enseñanza secundaria: personal docente y alumnos

| Country / Pays / País | Type of education / Type d'enseignement / Tipo de enseñanza | Year / Année / Año | Teaching staff Personnel enseignant Personal docente | | | Pupils enrolled Elèves inscrits Alumnos matriculados | | |
|---|---|---|---|---|---|---|---|---|
| | | | Total | Female Féminin Femenino | % F | Total | Female Féminin Femenino | % F |
| Mauritania (cont) | Total | 1990/91 | ... | ... | ... | (16) 37 653 | (16) 11 957 | 32 |
| | General education | | 2 091 | 224 | 11 | 36 177 | *11 773 | *33 |
| | Teacher training | | 47 | ... | ... | 676 | 174 | 26 |
| | Vocational education | | 115 | ... | ... | (16) 800 | (16) 10 | 1 |
| | Total | 1991/92 | 2 184 | ... | ... | (16) 39 821 | (16) *13 344 | *34 |
| | General education | | 2 015 | 198 | 10 | 38 039 | *13 006 | *34 |
| | Teacher training | | 51 | ... | ... | 752 | 193 | 26 |
| | Vocational education | | 118 | 16 | 14 | (16) 1 030 | (16) 145 | 14 |
| | Total | 1992/93 | 2 236 | ... | ... | (16) 43 034 | (16) 14 334 | 33 |
| | General education | | 2 071 | 202 | 10 | 41 071 | 13 909 | 34 |
| | Teacher training | | 49 | ... | ... | 791 | 231 | 29 |
| | Vocational education | | 116 | ... | ... | (16) 1 172 | (16) 194 | 17 |
| | Total | 1993/94 | 1 938 | 212 | 11 | (16) 45 810 | (16) 16 204 | 35 |
| | General education | | 1 776 | 204 | 11 | 43 861 | 15 667 | 36 |
| | Teacher training | | 57 | 4 | 7 | 820 | 276 | 34 |
| | Vocational education | | 105 | 4 | 4 | (16) 1 129 | (16) 261 | 23 |
| | Total | 1994/95 | 1 962 | 154 | 8 | (16) 49 008 | (16) 17 618 | 36 |
| | General education | | 1 777 | 154 | 9 | 46 917 | 17 042 | 36 |
| | Teacher training | | 41 | - | - | 873 | 253 | 29 |
| | Vocational education | | 144 | - | - | (16) 1 218 | (16) 323 | 27 |
| | Total | 1995/96 | 2 067 | ... | ... | (16) 51 765 | (16) 17 355 | 34 |
| | General education | | 1 865 | ... | ... | 49 221 | 16 613 | 34 |
| | Teacher training | | 43 | ... | ... | 1 130 | 327 | 29 |
| | Vocational education | | 150 | ... | ... | (16) 1 414 | (16) 415 | 29 |
| Mauritius | Total | 1970 | ... | ... | ... | ... | ... | ... |
| | General education | | 1 747 | 570 | 33 | 43 969 | 17 542 | 40 |
| | Teacher training | | ... | ... | ... | ... | ... | ... |
| | Vocational education | | ... | ... | ... | 538 | 245 | 46 |
| | Total | 1975 | 2 177 | ... | ... | 65 113 | 28 869 | 44 |
| | General education | | 2 065 | ... | ... | 63 492 | 28 195 | 44 |
| | Teacher training | | 19 | 8 | 42 | 569 | 245 | 42 |
| | Vocational education | | 93 | 26 | 28 | 1 032 | 429 | 42 |
| | Total | 1980 | ... | ... | ... | 81 926 | 39 602 | 48 |
| | General education | | 3 101 | ... | ... | 81 656 | 39 542 | 48 |
| | Teacher training | | - | - | - | - | - | - |
| | Vocational education | | ... | ... | ... | 270 | 60 | 22 |
| | Total | 1985 | ... | ... | ... | 72 551 | 34 232 | 47 |
| | General education | | 3 603 | 1 466 | 41 | 71 686 | 33 904 | 47 |
| | Teacher training | | - | - | - | - | - | - |
| | Vocational education | | ... | ... | ... | 865 | 328 | 38 |
| | Total | 1990 | ... | ... | ... | 79 229 | 39 357 | 50 |
| | General education | | 3 728 | 1 478 | 40 | 78 110 | 39 002 | 50 |
| | Teacher training | | - | - | - | - | - | - |
| | Vocational education | | ... | ... | ... | 1 119 | 355 | 32 |
| | Total | 1991 | ... | ... | ... | ... | ... | ... |
| | General education | | 3 949 | 1 635 | 41 | 81 090 | 41 312 | 51 |
| | Teacher training | | - | | - | - | | ... |
| | Vocational education | | ... | ... | ... | ... | | ... |
| | Total | 1992 | ... | ... | ... | 86 024 | ... | ... |
| | General education | | 4 050 | 1 719 | 42 | 83 591 | 42 345 | 51 |
| | Teacher training | | - | - | - | 2 433 | - | ... |
| | Vocational education | | ... | ... | ... | ... | | ... |
| | Total | 1993 | ... | ... | ... | ... | ... | ... |
| | General education | | 4 160 | 1 775 | 43 | 87 661 | 44 636 | 51 |
| | Teacher training | | - | | - | - | | - |
| | Vocational education | | ... | ... | ... | ... | | ... |
| | Total | 1994 | ... | ... | ... | ... | ... | ... |
| | General education | | 4 234 | 1 805 | 43 | 89 581 | 45 828 | 51 |
| | Teacher training | | - | | - | - | | - |
| | Vocational education | | ... | ... | ... | ... | | ... |
| | Total | 1995 | ... | ... | ... | ... | ... | ... |
| | General education | | 4 375 | 1 909 | 44 | 91 104 | 46 834 | 51 |
| | Teacher training | | - | | - | - | | - |
| | Vocational education | | ... | ... | ... | ... | | ... |
| | Total | 1996 | 4 737 | 2 112 | 45 | 95 932 | 48 309 | 50 |
| | General education | | 4 564 | 2 004 | 44 | 93 037 | 47 471 | 51 |
| | Teacher training | | - | | - | - | | - |
| | Vocational education | | 173 | 108 | 62 | 2 895 | 838 | 29 |

II.6 Secondary education: teaching staff and pupils
Enseignement secondaire: personnel enseignant et élèves
Enseñanza secundaria: personal docente y alumnos

| Country / Pays / País | Type of education / Type d'enseignement / Tipo de enseñanza | Year / Année / Año | Teaching staff / Personnel enseignant / Personal docente | | | Pupils enrolled / Elèves inscrits / Alumnos matriculados | | |
|---|---|---|---|---|---|---|---|---|
| | | | Total | Female Féminin Femenino | % F | Total | Female Féminin Femenino | % F |
| Mauritius (cont) | Total | 1997 | ... | ... | ... | ... | ... | ... |
| | General education | | 4 710 | 2 096 | 45 | 93 839 | 48 133 | 51 |
| | Teacher training | | - | - | - | | | - |
| | Vocational education | | | | ... | ... | ... | ... |
| Morocco | Total | 1970/71 | 14 680 | 4 378 | 30 | 298 880 | 84 499 | 28 |
| | General education | | 13 988 | 4 196 | 30 | (17) 289 327 | (17) 82 527 | 29 |
| | Teacher training | | 120 | 19 | 16 | 2 567 | 823 | 32 |
| | Vocational education | | 572 | 163 | 28 | 6 986 | 1 149 | 16 |
| | Total | 1975/76 | ... | ... | ... | 486 173 | 166 862 | 34 |
| | General education | | (1)(4) 19 613 | (1)(4) 5 381 | 27 | 468 870 | 160 119 | 34 |
| | Teacher training | | *486 | ... | ... | 3 953 | 1 716 | 43 |
| | Vocational education | | ./. | ./. | ./. | 13 350 | 5 027 | 38 |
| | Total | 1980/81 | 36 526 | ... | ... | (18) 797 110 | (18) 300 665 | 38 |
| | General education | | ... | ... | ... | 787 004 | 298 344 | 38 |
| | Teacher training | | - | | | | | |
| | Vocational education | | ... | ... | ... | (18) 10 106 | (18) 2 321 | 23 |
| | Total | 1985/86 | 67 733 | (18) 17 646 | ... | 1 248 702 | 487 526 | 39 |
| | General education | | 62 904 | 17 277 | 27 | 1 174 599 | 460 913 | 39 |
| | Teacher training | | - | - | - | - | - | - |
| | Vocational education | | 4 829 | (18) 369 | ... | 74 103 | 26 613 | 36 |
| | Total | 1990/91 | (7)(19) 79 657 | (7)(18) 23 240 | ... | (7) 1 194 377 | (7) 492 654 | 41 |
| | General education | | (7) 75 708 | (7) 22 982 | 30 | (7) 1 106 673 | (7) 452 491 | 41 |
| | Teacher training | | - | - | - | - | - | - |
| | Vocational education | | (19) 3 949 | (18) 258 | ... | 87 704 | 40 163 | 46 |
| | Total | 1991/92 | (19) 80 255 | (18) 23 983 | ... | 1 235 527 | 506 694 | 41 |
| | General education | | 75 922 | 23 706 | 31 | 1 151 771 | 467 979 | 41 |
| | Teacher training | | - | - | - | - | - | - |
| | Vocational education | | (19) 4 333 | (18) 277 | ... | 83 756 | 38 715 | 46 |
| | Total | 1992/93 | (19) 81 397 | (18) 24 720 | ... | 1 274 982 | 527 416 | 41 |
| | General education | | 77 297 | 24 420 | 32 | 1 191 716 | 489 180 | 41 |
| | Teacher training | | - | - | - | - | - | - |
| | Vocational education | | (19) 4 100 | (18) 300 | ... | 83 266 | 38 236 | 46 |
| | Total | 1993/94 | (19) 81 897 | (18) 25 088 | ... | 1 338 508 | 555 341 | 41 |
| | General education | | 77 753 | 24 759 | 32 | 1 248 324 | 515 597 | 41 |
| | Teacher training | | - | - | - | - | - | - |
| | Vocational education | | (19) 4 144 | (18) 329 | ... | 90 184 | 39 744 | 44 |
| | Total | 1994/95 | (19) 83 694 | (18) 25 757 | ... | 1 375 703 | 576 181 | 42 |
| | General education | | 79 474 | 25 391 | 32 | 1 280 135 | 533 356 | 42 |
| | Teacher training | | - | - | - | - | - | - |
| | Vocational education | | (19) 4 220 | (18) 366 | ... | 95 568 | 42 825 | 45 |
| | Total | 1995/96 | (19) 85 865 | (18) 26 531 | ... | 1 412 316 | 592 729 | 42 |
| | General education | | 80 817 | 25 918 | 32 | 1 315 342 | 548 147 | 42 |
| | Teacher training | | - | - | - | - | - | - |
| | Vocational education | | (19) 5 048 | (18) 613 | ... | 96 974 | 44 582 | 46 |
| | Total | 1996/97 | (18) 84 202 | (18) 27 045 | 32 | 1 442 049 | 610 727 | 42 |
| | General education | | ... | ... | ... | 1 345 589 | 566 648 | 42 |
| | Teacher training | | - | - | - | - | - | - |
| | Vocational education | | ... | ... | ... | 96 460 | 44 079 | 46 |
| Mozambique | Total | 1970/71 | 2 561 | ... | ... | 42 868 | ... | ... |
| | General education | | 1 431 | ... | | 26 668 | ... | |
| | Teacher training | | 114 | 56 | 49 | 1 169 | 510 | 44 |
| | Vocational education | | 1 016 | ... | ... | 15 031 | ... | ... |
| | Total | 1980/81 | ... | ... | ... | ... | ... | ... |
| | General education | | 2 151 | 590 | 27 | 90 041 | 25 979 | 29 |
| | Teacher training | | ... | ... | ... | ... | ... | ... |
| | Vocational education | | 680 | 102 | 15 | 12 704 | 2 127 | 17 |
| | Total | 1985 | 4 688 | 1 001 | 21 | 151 888 | 47 398 | 31 |
| | General education | | 3 377 | 799 | 24 | 135 068 | 44 452 | 33 |
| | Teacher training | | 350 | 40 | 11 | 5 177 | 842 | 16 |
| | Vocational education | | 961 | 162 | 17 | 11 643 | 2 104 | 18 |
| | Total | 1990 | 4 657 | ... | ... | 160 177 | 58 452 | 36 |
| | General education | | 3 437 | 611 | 18 | 145 341 | 54 975 | 38 |
| | Teacher training | | 324 | 35 | 11 | 4 904 | 1 365 | 28 |
| | Vocational education | | 896 | ... | ... | 9 932 | 2 112 | 21 |
| | Total | 1991 | 5 029 | ... | ... | 162 486 | 59 576 | 37 |
| | General education | | 3 888 | 718 | 18 | 148 409 | 56 468 | 38 |
| | Teacher training | | 295 | 24 | 8 | 4 348 | 1 228 | 28 |
| | Vocational education | | 846 | ... | ... | 9 729 | 1 880 | 19 |
| | Total | 1992 | ... | ... | ... | 159 202 | 61 194 | 38 |
| | General education | | 3 614 | 661 | 18 | 145 398 | 57 278 | 39 |
| | Teacher training | | 280 | 29 | 10 | 4 020 | 1 431 | 36 |
| | Vocational education | | ... | ... | ... | 9 784 | 2 485 | 25 |

Secondary education: teaching staff and pupils
Enseignement secondaire: personnel enseignant et élèves
Enseñanza secundaria: personal docente y alumnos

II.6

| Country<br>Pays<br>País | Type of education<br>Type d'enseignement<br>Tipo de enseñanza | Year<br>Année<br>Año | Teaching staff<br>Personnel enseignant<br>Personal docente | | | Pupils enrolled<br>Elèves inscrits<br>Alumnos matriculados | | |
|---|---|---|---|---|---|---|---|---|
| | | | Total | Female<br>Féminin<br>Femenino | %<br>F | Total | Female<br>Féminin<br>Femenino | %<br>F |
| Mozambique (cont) | Total | 1993 | 4 809 | 954 | 20 | 163 747 | 63 882 | 39 |
| | General education | | 3 924 | 773 | 20 | 147 201 | 59 013 | 40 |
| | Teacher training | | 231 | 24 | 10 | 4 902 | 1 917 | 39 |
| | Vocational education | | 654 | 157 | 24 | 11 644 | 2 952 | 25 |
| | Total | 1994 | 4 997 | 906 | 18 | 169 520 | 65 128 | 38 |
| | General education | | 3 909 | 727 | 19 | 150 683 | 59 555 | 40 |
| | Teacher training | | 262 | 32 | 12 | 5 021 | 2 086 | 42 |
| | Vocational education | | 826 | 147 | 18 | 13 816 | 3 487 | 25 |
| | Total | 1995 | 5 615 | 969 | 17 | 185 181 | 72 369 | 39 |
| | General education | | 4 376 | 846 | 19 | 165 868 | 66 549 | 40 |
| | Teacher training | | 254 | 22 | 9 | 4 731 | 2 051 | 43 |
| | Vocational education | | 985 | 101 | 10 | 14 582 | 3 769 | 26 |
| Namibia | Total | 1990 | ... | ... | ... | 62 399 | 34 732 | 56 |
| | General education | | ... | ... | ... | 61 801 | 34 599 | 56 |
| | Teacher training | | - | - | - | - | - | - |
| | Vocational education | | ... | ... | ... | 598 | 133 | 22 |
| | Total | 1991 | ... | ... | ... | 73 409 | 40 465 | 55 |
| | General education | | ... | ... | ... | 72 534 | 40 325 | 56 |
| | Teacher training | | - | - | - | - | - | - |
| | Vocational education | | ... | ... | ... | 875 | 140 | 16 |
| | Total | 1992 | 3 999 | 1 840 | 46 | 84 581 | 46 631 | 55 |
| | General education | | 3 943 | 1 829 | 46 | 83 862 | 46 476 | 55 |
| | Teacher training | | - | - | - | - | - | - |
| | Vocational education | | 56 | 11 | 20 | 719 | 155 | 22 |
| | Total | 1993 | ... | ... | ... | 92 725 | 50 844 | 55 |
| | General education | | ... | ... | ... | 92 136 | 50 718 | 55 |
| | Teacher training | | - | - | - | - | - | - |
| | Vocational education | | ... | ... | ... | 589 | 126 | 21 |
| | Total | 1994 | ... | ... | ... | 101 974 | 55 591 | 55 |
| | General education | | ... | ... | ... | 101 838 | 55 538 | 55 |
| | Teacher training | | - | - | - | - | - | - |
| | Vocational education | | ... | ... | ... | 136 | 53 | 39 |
| | Total | 1995 | ... | ... | ... | 103 308 | 55 704 | 54 |
| | General education | | ... | ... | ... | 103 212 | 55 675 | 54 |
| | Teacher training | | - | - | - | - | - | - |
| | Vocational education | | ... | ... | ... | 96 | 29 | 30 |
| | Total | 1996 | ... | ... | ... | 104 613 | 56 263 | 54 |
| | General education | | ... | ... | ... | 104 531 | 56 228 | 54 |
| | Teacher training | | - | - | - | - | - | - |
| | Vocational education | | ... | ... | ... | 82 | 35 | 43 |
| | Total | 1997 | ... | ... | ... | 108 888 | 58 144 | 53 |
| | General education | | ... | ... | ... | 108 791 | 58 094 | 53 |
| | Teacher training | | - | - | - | - | - | - |
| | Vocational education | | ... | ... | ... | 97 | 50 | 52 |
| | Total | 1998 | ... | ... | ... | 115 237 | 60 630 | 53 |
| | General education | | ... | ... | ... | 115 147 | 60 560 | 53 |
| | Teacher training | | - | - | - | - | - | - |
| | Vocational education | | ... | ... | ... | 90 | 70 | 78 |
| Niger | Total | 1970/71 | 346 | 75 | 22 | 6 999 | 1 876 | 27 |
| | General education | | 268 | 64 | 24 | 6 337 | 1 655 | 26 |
| | Teacher training | | 50 | 6 | 12 | 474 | 218 | 46 |
| | Vocational education | | 28 | 5 | 18 | 188 | 3 | 2 |
| | Total | 1975/76 | 637 | 146 | 23 | 14 462 | 3 983 | 28 |
| | General education | | 571 | 137 | 24 | 13 621 | 3 785 | 28 |
| | Teacher training | | 41 | 4 | 10 | 608 | 184 | 30 |
| | Vocational education | | 25 | 5 | 20 | 233 | 14 | 6 |
| | Total | 1980/81 | 1 284 | 267 | 21 | 38 861 | 11 334 | 29 |
| | General education | | 1 164 | 255 | 22 | 36 510 | 10 765 | 29 |
| | Teacher training | | 80 | 6 | 8 | 1 830 | 525 | 29 |
| | Vocational education | | 40 | 6 | 15 | 521 | 44 | 8 |
| | Total | 1985/86 | ... | ... | ... | ... | ... | ... |
| | General education | | 1 963 | 327 | 17 | 51 448 | 14 398 | 28 |
| | Teacher training | | ... | ... | ... | ... | ... | ... |
| | Vocational education | | ... | ... | ... | 615 | 72 | 12 |
| | Total | 1990/91 | 2 775 | 490 | 18 | 76 758 | 22 619 | 29 |
| | General education | | 2 534 | 455 | 18 | 74 337 | 21 884 | 29 |
| | Teacher training | | 122 | 19 | 16 | 1 578 | 661 | 42 |
| | Vocational education | | 119 | 16 | 13 | 843 | 74 | 9 |
| | Total | 1991/92 | 2 894 | 520 | 18 | 76 916 | 23 311 | 30 |
| | General education | | 2 653 | 485 | 18 | 74 944 | 22 772 | 30 |
| | Teacher training | | 122 | 19 | 16 | 1 176 | 464 | 39 |
| | Vocational education | | 119 | 16 | 13 | 796 | 75 | 9 |

II.6    Secondary education: teaching staff and pupils
Enseignement secondaire: personnel enseignant et élèves
Enseñanza secundaria: personal docente y alumnos

| Country / Pays / País | Type of education / Type d'enseignement / Tipo de enseñanza | Year / Année / Año | Teaching staff / Personnel enseignant / Personal docente | | | Pupils enrolled / Elèves inscrits / Alumnos matriculados | | |
|---|---|---|---|---|---|---|---|---|
| | | | Total | Female Féminin Femenino | % F | Total | Female Féminin Femenino | % F |
| Niger (cont) | Total | 1992/93 | ... | ... | ... | 80 009 | 26 003 | 33 |
| | General education | | ... | ... | ... | 77 899 | 25 514 | 33 |
| | Teacher training | | 76 | 6 | 8 | 1 322 | 389 | 29 |
| | Vocational education | | 99 | 12 | 12 | 788 | 100 | 13 |
| | Total | 1994/95 | 3 119 | ... | ... | 89 773 | 29 474 | 33 |
| | General education | | ... | ... | ... | ... | ... | ... |
| | Teacher training | | ... | ... | ... | ... | ... | ... |
| | Vocational education | | ... | ... | ... | ... | ... | ... |
| | Total | 1995/96 | 3 548 | 736 | 21 | 92 608 | 31 627 | 34 |
| | General education | | 3 348 | 713 | 21 | 90 470 | 31 261 | 35 |
| | Teacher training | | 87 | 12 | 14 | 1 357 | 250 | 18 |
| | Vocational education | | 113 | 11 | 10 | 781 | 116 | 15 |
| | Total | 1996/97 | 3 579 | 736 | 21 | 97 675 | 34 493 | 35 |
| | General education | | 3 364 | 717 | 21 | 95 530 | 34 016 | 36 |
| | Teacher training | | 101 | 7 | 7 | 1 340 | 333 | 25 |
| | Vocational education | | 114 | 12 | 11 | 805 | 144 | 18 |
| Nigeria | Total | 1970 | 16 794 | 3 064 | 18 | 356 565 | 114 272 | 32 |
| | General education | | 13 277 | 2 546 | 19 | 293 498 | 96 798 | 33 |
| | Teacher training | | 1 857 | 366 | 20 | 32 866 | 9 160 | 28 |
| | Vocational education | | 1 660 | 152 | 9 | 30 201 | 8 314 | 28 |
| | Total | 1980/81 | 41 581 | 12 242 | 29 | 1 864 713 | 623 257 | 33 |
| | General education | | 26 261 | 3 492 | 13 | 1 553 345 | 543 564 | 35 |
| | Teacher training | | 7 940 | 6 302 | 79 | 249 512 | 71 312 | 29 |
| | Vocational education | | 7 380 | 2 448 | 33 | 61 856 | 8 381 | 14 |
| | Total | 1985/86 | (20) 105 003 | (20) 29 902 | 28 | (20) 2 988 174 | (20) 1 231 139 | 41 |
| | General education | | ... | ... | ... | ... | ... | ... |
| | Teacher training | | ... | ... | ... | ... | ... | ... |
| | Vocational education | | ... | ... | ... | ... | ... | ... |
| | Total | 1990 | (21) 141 377 | (21) 46 074 | 33 | (21) 2 908 466 | (21) 1 243 669 | 43 |
| | General education | | ... | ... | ... | ... | ... | ... |
| | Teacher training | | ... | ... | ... | ... | ... | ... |
| | Vocational education | | ... | ... | ... | ... | ... | ... |
| | Total | 1991 | 141 491 | 44 936 | 32 | 3 123 277 | 1 301 970 | 42 |
| | General education | | ... | ... | ... | ... | ... | ... |
| | Teacher training | | ... | ... | ... | ... | ... | ... |
| | Vocational education | | ... | ... | ... | ... | ... | ... |
| | Total | 1992 | 147 530 | 49 427 | 34 | 3 600 620 | 1 621 575 | 45 |
| | General education | | ... | ... | ... | ... | ... | ... |
| | Teacher training | | ... | ... | ... | ... | ... | ... |
| | Vocational education | | ... | ... | ... | ... | ... | ... |
| | Total | 1993 | 151 722 | 52 363 | 35 | 4 032 083 | 1 850 049 | 46 |
| | General education | | ... | ... | ... | ... | ... | ... |
| | Teacher training | | ... | ... | ... | ... | ... | ... |
| | Vocational education | | ... | ... | ... | ... | ... | ... |
| | Total | 1994 | 152 596 | 54 949 | 36 | 4 451 329 | 2 031 547 | 46 |
| | General education | | ... | ... | ... | ... | ... | ... |
| | Teacher training | | ... | ... | ... | ... | ... | ... |
| | Vocational education | | ... | ... | ... | ... | ... | ... |
| Reunion | Total | 1970/71 | 1 312 | | ... | 30 853 | ... | ... |
| | General education | | ... | | ... | 28 086 | 16 192 | 58 |
| | Teacher training | | 19 | | ... | 669 | ... | ... |
| | Vocational education | | ... | ... | ... | 2 098 | ... | ... |
| | Total | 1975/76 | 2 363 | ... | ... | 50 467 | 27 954 | 55 |
| | General education | | ... | ... | ... | (22) 44 524 | (22) 25 134 | 56 |
| | Teacher training | | ... | ... | ./. | ./. | ./. | ./. |
| | Vocational education | | ... | ... | ... | 5 943 | 2 820 | 47 |
| | Total | 1980/81 | ... | ... | ... | 62 613 | ... | ... |
| | General education | | ... | ... | ... | ... | ... | ... |
| | Teacher training | | - | ... | - | - | - | ... |
| | Vocational education | | ... | ... | ... | ... | ... | ... |
| | Total | 1985/86 | 3 994 | ... | ... | 69 863 | 38 042 | 54 |
| | General education | | 2 978 | ... | ... | 46 550 | 27 090 | 58 |
| | Teacher training | | - | ... | - | - | - | - |
| | Vocational education | | 1 016 | ... | ... | 23 313 | 10 952 | 47 |
| | Total | 1993/94 | 5 699 | ... | ... | 88 605 | 44 885 | 51 |
| | General education | | 4 591 | 2 002 | 44 | 74 827 | 38 692 | 52 |
| | Teacher training | | - | | | - | - | - |
| | Vocational education | | 1 108 | ... | ... | 13 778 | 6 193 | 45 |
| | Total | 1994/95 | ... | ... | ... | 90 033 | 45 365 | 50 |
| | General education | | ... | ... | ... | 74 978 | 38 748 | 52 |
| | Teacher training | | - | ... | - | - | - | - |
| | Vocational education | | ... | ... | ... | 15 055 | 6 617 | 44 |

Secondary education: teaching staff and pupils  II.6
Enseignement secondaire: personnel enseignant et élèves
Enseñanza secundaria: personal docente y alumnos

| Country<br>Pays<br>País | Type of education<br>Type d'enseignement<br>Tipo de enseñanza | Year<br>Année<br>Año | Teaching staff<br>Personnel enseignant<br>Personal docente | | | Pupils enrolled<br>Elèves inscrits<br>Alumnos matriculados | | |
|---|---|---|---|---|---|---|---|---|
| | | | Total | Female<br>Féminin<br>Femenino | %<br>F | Total | Female<br>Féminin<br>Femenino | %<br>F |
| Reunion (cont) | Total | 1995/96 | 6 179 | 2 834 | 46 | 91 548 | 46 016 | 50 |
| | General education | | *5 059 | *2 359 | *47 | 78 001 | 39 996 | 51 |
| | Teacher training | | - | - | - | - | - | - |
| | Vocational education | | *1 120 | *475 | *42 | 13 547 | 6 020 | 44 |
| Rwanda | Total | 1970/71 | 1 005 | ... | ... | 13 752 | 6 833 | 50 |
| | General education | | ... | ... | ... | 7 398 | 2 247 | 30 |
| | Teacher training | | ... | ... | ... | 1 606 | 595 | 37 |
| | Vocational education | | ... | ... | ... | 4 748 | 3 991 | 84 |
| | Total | 1975/76 | 1 133 | (23) 194 | ... | 19 936 | 10 433 | 52 |
| | General education | | ... | ... | ... | 8 704 | 2 680 | 31 |
| | Teacher training | | ... | ... | ... | 1 552 | 665 | 43 |
| | Vocational education | | ... | ... | ... | 9 680 | 7 088 | 73 |
| | Total | 1980/81 | 1 454 | (23) 234 | ... | 20 672 | 9 602 | 46 |
| | General education | | ... | ... | ... | 5 022 | 1 388 | 28 |
| | Teacher training | | ... | ... | ... | 3 580 | 1 606 | 45 |
| | Vocational education | | ... | ... | ... | 12 070 | 6 608 | 55 |
| | Total | 1985/86 | 3 120 | (23) 288 | ... | 46 998 | 19 550 | 42 |
| | General education | | ... | ... | ... | 7 252 | 1 500 | 21 |
| | Teacher training | | ... | ... | ... | 6 101 | 2 757 | 45 |
| | Vocational education | | ... | ... | ... | 33 645 | 15 293 | 45 |
| | Total | 1990/91 | (23) 2 802 | (23) 565 | 20 | 70 400 | 30 523 | 43 |
| | General education | | ... | ... | ... | 16 173 | 5 784 | 36 |
| | Teacher training | | ... | ... | ... | 14 378 | 7 279 | 51 |
| | Vocational education | | ... | ... | ... | 39 849 | 17 460 | 44 |
| | Total | 1991/92 | (23) 3 413 | (23) 731 | 21 | 94 586 | 41 704 | 44 |
| | General education | | ... | ... | ... | 23 039 | 8 734 | 38 |
| | Teacher training | | ... | ... | ... | 20 171 | 10 331 | 51 |
| | Vocational education | | ... | ... | ... | 51 376 | 22 639 | 44 |
| Sao Tome and Principe | Total | 1970/71 | 107 | ... | ... | 1 669 | 693 | 42 |
| | General education | | 73 | ... | ... | 1 463 | 643 | 44 |
| | Teacher training | | - | - | - | - | - | - |
| | Vocational education | | 34 | ... | ... | 206 | 50 | 24 |
| | Total | 1975/76 | ... | ... | ... | 4 010 | ... | ... |
| | General education | | ... | ... | ... | 3 776 | ... | ... |
| | Teacher training | | - | - | - | - | - | - |
| | Vocational education | | ... | ... | ... | 234 | ... | ... |
| | Total | 1980/81 | ... | ... | ... | 3 815 | ... | ... |
| | General education | | ... | ... | ... | 3 685 | ... | ... |
| | Teacher training | | - | - | - | - | - | - |
| | Vocational education | | ... | ... | ... | 130 | ... | ... |
| Senegal | Total | 1970/71 | ... | ... | ... | 59 401 | 16 925 | 28 |
| | General education | | 1 838 | 471 | 26 | 53 298 | 14 942 | 28 |
| | Teacher training | | ... | ... | ... | 656 | 208 | 32 |
| | Vocational education | | ... | ... | ... | 5 447 | 1 775 | 33 |
| | Total | 1975/76 | ... | ... | ... | ... | ... | ... |
| | General education | | ... | ... | ... | 69 590 | ... | ... |
| | Teacher training | | ... | ... | ... | ... | ... | ... |
| | Vocational education | | ... | ... | ... | 8 182 | ... | ... |
| | Total | 1980/81 | 4 302 | ... | ... | 95 604 | 31 307 | 33 |
| | General education | | ... | ... | ... | 83 431 | 28 133 | 34 |
| | Teacher training | | ... | ... | ... | 2 241 | 724 | 32 |
| | Vocational education | | ... | ... | ... | 9 932 | 2 450 | 25 |
| | Total | 1985/86 | ... | ... | ... | 130 338 | 42 937 | 33 |
| | General education | | (4) 3 481 | (4) 597 | 17 | 121 104 | 40 450 | 33 |
| | Teacher training | | 93 | 6 | 6 | 464 | 80 | 17 |
| | Vocational education | | ... | ... | ... | 8 770 | 2 407 | 27 |
| | Total | 1990/91 | ... | ... | ... | ... | ... | ... |
| | General education | | (1)(4) 5 242 | ... | ... | 173 383 | 59 898 | 35 |
| | Teacher training | | ./. | ... | ... | ... | ... | ... |
| | Vocational education | | | ... | ... | 6 435 | 2 082 | 32 |
| | Total | 1991/92 | ... | ... | ... | 191 431 | 66 154 | 35 |
| | General education | | (1)(4) 5 374 | (1)(4) 748 | 14 | 183 071 | 63 442 | 35 |
| | Teacher training | | | ... | ... | 789 | 173 | 22 |
| | Vocational education | | ./. | ./. | ./. | 7 571 | 2 539 | 34 |
| | Total | 1992/93 | ... | ... | ... | ... | ... | ... |
| | General education | | ... | ... | ... | 182 140 | 64 252 | 35 |
| | Teacher training | | ... | ... | ... | ... | ... | ... |
| | Vocational education | | ... | ... | ... | 7 301 | 2 535 | 35 |
| | Total | 1993/94 | ... | ... | ... | 194 266 | 85 862 | 44 |
| | General education | | ... | ... | ... | (1) 193 071 | (1) 85 731 | 44 |
| | Teacher training | | ... | ... | ... | 495 | 131 | 26 |
| | Vocational education | | ... | ... | ... | ./. | ./. | ./. |

II.6 Secondary education: teaching staff and pupils
Enseignement secondaire: personnel enseignant et élèves
Enseñanza secundaria: personal docente y alumnos

| Country / Pays / País | Type of education / Type d'enseignement / Tipo de enseñanza | Year / Année / Año | Teaching staff / Personnel enseignant / Personal docente | | | Pupils enrolled / Elèves inscrits / Alumnos matriculados | | |
|---|---|---|---|---|---|---|---|---|
| | | | Total | Female Féminin Femenino | % F | Total | Female Féminin Femenino | % F |
| Senegal (cont) | Total | 1995/96 | ... | ... | ... | 208 786 | 78 225 | 37 |
| | General education | | (1)(4) 6 059 | (1)(4) 921 | 15 | 202 797 | 76 067 | 38 |
| | Teacher training | | ... | ... | ... | 528 | 108 | 20 |
| | Vocational education | | ./. | ./. | ./. | 5 461 | 2 050 | 38 |
| | Total | 1996/97 | ... | ... | ... | 211 558 | 78 992 | 37 |
| | General education | | (1)(4) 6 219 | (1)(4) 929 | 15 | 206 934 | 77 520 | 37 |
| | Teacher training | | ... | ... | ... | 566 | 92 | 16 |
| | Vocational education | | ./. | ./. | ./. | 4 058 | 1 380 | 34 |
| | Total | 1997/98 | ... | ... | ... | 215 988 | 81 661 | 38 |
| | General education | | ... | ... | ... | 210 798 | 79 862 | 38 |
| | Teacher training | | ... | ... | ... | 575 | 94 | 16 |
| | Vocational education | | ... | ... | ... | 4 615 | 1 705 | 37 |
| Seychelles | Total | 1970 | 120 | 74 | 62 | 2 359 | 1 308 | 55 |
| | General education | | 106 | 64 | 60 | 2 131 | 1 153 | 54 |
| | Teacher training | | - | - | - | - | - | - |
| | Vocational education | | 14 | 10 | 71 | 228 | 155 | 68 |
| | Total | 1975 | 177 | 102 | 58 | 3 778 | 2 125 | 56 |
| | General education | | 145 | 90 | 62 | 3 465 | 1 901 | 55 |
| | Teacher training | | - | - | - | - | - | - |
| | Vocational education | | 32 | 12 | 38 | 313 | 224 | 72 |
| | Total | 1980 | (24) 127 | (24) 47 | 37 | (24) 924 | (24) *438 | *47 |
| | General education | | (24) 67 | (24) 30 | 45 | (24) 478 | (24) 226 | 47 |
| | Teacher training | | - | - | - | - | - | - |
| | Vocational education | | 60 | 17 | 28 | 446 | 212 | 48 |
| | Total | 1985 | (11) 364 | (11) 107 | 29 | (11) 3 975 | (11) 1 997 | 50 |
| | General education | | (11) 193 | (11) 54 | 28 | (11) 2 435 | (11) 1 233 | 51 |
| | Teacher training | | 22 | 14 | 64 | 170 | 148 | 87 |
| | Vocational education | | 149 | 39 | 26 | 1 370 | 616 | 45 |
| | Total | 1990 | 328 | ... | ... | 4 396 | ... | ... |
| | General education | | 157 | ... | ... | 3 034 | ... | ... |
| | Teacher training | | ... | ... | ... | 294 | ... | ... |
| | Vocational education | | ... | ... | ... | 1 068 | ... | ... |
| | Total | 1991 | ... | ... | ... | (13) 9 020 | (13) 4 405 | 49 |
| | General education | | ... | ... | ... | (13) 7 642 | (13) 3 759 | 49 |
| | Teacher training | | 32 | 18 | 56 | 302 | 204 | 68 |
| | Vocational education | | 142 | 43 | 30 | 1 076 | 442 | 41 |
| | Total | 1992 | ... | ... | ... | 9 182 | 4 530 | 49 |
| | General education | | ... | ... | ... | 7 726 | 3 818 | 49 |
| | Teacher training | | 33 | 17 | 52 | 323 | 217 | 67 |
| | Vocational education | | 125 | 38 | 30 | 1 133 | 495 | 44 |
| | Total | 1993 | 735 | 382 | 52 | 9 111 | 4 530 | 50 |
| | General education | | 576 | 318 | 55 | 7 683 | 3 834 | 50 |
| | Teacher training | | 27 | 19 | 70 | 290 | 222 | 77 |
| | Vocational education | | 132 | 45 | 34 | 1 138 | 474 | 42 |
| | Total | 1994 | 757 | 380 | 50 | 9 280 | 4 621 | 50 |
| | General education | | 579 | 311 | 54 | 7 877 | 3 962 | 50 |
| | Teacher training | | 46 | 34 | 74 | 347 | 235 | 68 |
| | Vocational education | | 132 | 35 | 27 | 1 056 | 424 | 40 |
| | Total | 1995 | 711 | 342 | 48 | 8 931 | 4 376 | 49 |
| | General education | | 580 | 295 | 51 | 7 827 | 3 883 | 50 |
| | Teacher training | | 32 | 20 | 63 | 361 | 259 | 72 |
| | Vocational education | | 99 | 27 | 27 | 743 | 234 | 31 |
| | Total | 1996 | 689 | 346 | 50 | 9 099 | 4 497 | 49 |
| | General education | | 598 | 315 | 53 | 8 151 | 4 046 | 50 |
| | Teacher training | | 27 | 16 | 59 | 237 | 163 | 69 |
| | Vocational education | | 64 | 15 | 23 | 711 | 288 | 41 |
| Sierra Leone | Total | 1970/71 | 1 699 | 480 | 28 | 34 646 | 9 766 | 28 |
| | General education | | 1 495 | 438 | 29 | 33 318 | 9 455 | 28 |
| | Teacher training | | (8) 141 | (8) 37 | 26 | 792 | 219 | 28 |
| | Vocational education | | 63 | 5 | 8 | 536 | 92 | 17 |
| | Total | 1975/76 | 2 596 | 901 | 35 | 50 478 | 15 991 | 32 |
| | General education | | 2 378 | 854 | 36 | 48 534 | 15 589 | 32 |
| | Teacher training | | 120 | 34 | 28 | 1 145 | 355 | 31 |
| | Vocational education | | 98 | 13 | 13 | 799 | 47 | 6 |
| | Total | 1980/81 | ... | ... | ... | 68 199 | ... | ... |
| | General education | | 2 985 | ... | ... | 64 808 | 19 374 | 30 |
| | Teacher training | | ... | ... | ... | 1 500 | 523 | 35 |
| | Vocational education | | ... | ... | ... | 1 891 | ... | ... |
| | Total | 1985/86 | 3 006 | ... | ... | 94 717 | ... | ... |
| | General education | | 2 865 | ... | ... | 93 509 | ... | ... |
| | Teacher training | | - | - | - | - | - | - |
| | Vocational education | | 141 | ... | ... | 1 208 | ... | ... |

Secondary education: teaching staff and pupils  II.6
Enseignement secondaire: personnel enseignant et élèves
Enseñanza secundaria: personal docente y alumnos

| Country / Pays / País | Type of education / Type d'enseignement / Tipo de enseñanza | Year / Année / Año | Teaching staff — Personnel enseignant — Personal docente | | | Pupils enrolled — Elèves inscrits — Alumnos matriculados | | |
|---|---|---|---|---|---|---|---|---|
| | | | Total | Female Féminin Femenino | % F | Total | Female Féminin Femenino | % F |
| Sierra Leone (cont) | Total | 1990/91 | 5 969 | 1 049 | 18 | 102 474 | 37 660 | 37 |
| | General education | | 5 544 | 942 | 17 | 97 049 | 34 859 | 36 |
| | Teacher training | | - | - | - | - | - | - |
| | Vocational education | | 425 | 107 | 25 | 5 425 | 2 801 | 52 |
| Somalia | Total | 1970/71 | 1 022 | 103 | 10 | 24 862 | 5 151 | 21 |
| | General education | | 937 | 88 | 9 | 23 847 | 4 996 | 21 |
| | Teacher training | | 13 | 9 | 69 | 237 | 36 | 15 |
| | Vocational education | | 72 | 6 | 8 | 778 | 119 | 15 |
| | Total | 1975/76 | 1 529 | 130 | 9 | 31 857 | 7 566 | 24 |
| | General education | | 1 161 | 102 | 9 | 26 611 | 6 119 | 23 |
| | Teacher training | | 181 | - | - | 3 422 | 1 128 | 33 |
| | Vocational education | | 187 | 28 | 15 | 1 824 | 319 | 17 |
| | Total | 1980/81 | (24) 2 089 | (24) 153 | 7 | (24) 43 841 | (24) 11 689 | 27 |
| | General education | | (24) 1 345 | (24) 138 | 10 | (24) 33 132 | (24) 9 294 | 28 |
| | Teacher training | | 119 | 14 | 12 | 3 005 | 853 | 28 |
| | Vocational education | | 625 | 1 | 0 | 7 704 | 1 542 | 20 |
| | Total | 1985/86 | 2 786 | 320 | 11 | 45 686 | 16 036 | 35 |
| | General education | | 2 149 | 234 | 11 | 39 753 | 14 675 | 37 |
| | Teacher training | | - | - | - | - | - | - |
| | Vocational education | | 637 | 86 | 14 | 5 933 | 1 361 | 23 |
| South Africa | Total | 1970 | ... | ... | ... | ... | ... | ... |
| | General education | | ... | ... | ... | 542 194 | 264 461 | 49 |
| | Teacher training | | ... | ... | ... | (8) 21 000 | ... | ... |
| | Vocational education | | ... | ... | ... | ... | ... | ... |
| | Total | 1990 | ... | ... | ... | 2 742 105 | 1 474 611 | 54 |
| | General education | | ... | ... | ... | 2 701 024 | 1 458 772 | 54 |
| | Teacher training | | - | - | - | - | - | - |
| | Vocational education | | ... | ... | ... | 41 081 | 15 839 | 39 |
| | Total | 1991 | 113 215 | 71 452 | 63 | 2 939 270 | 1 589 180 | 54 |
| | General education | | 110 214 | 70 604 | 64 | 2 902 851 | 1 575 320 | 54 |
| | Teacher training | | - | - | - | - | - | - |
| | Vocational education | | 3 001 | 848 | 28 | 36 419 | 13 860 | 38 |
| | Total | 1992 | ... | ... | ... | ... | ... | ... |
| | General education | | ... | ... | ... | (25) 2 480 699 | (25) 1 322 178 | 53 |
| | Teacher training | | - | - | - | - | - | - |
| | Vocational education | | ... | ... | ... | ... | ... | ... |
| | Total | 1993 | ... | ... | ... | ... | ... | ... |
| | General education | | ... | ... | ... | (25) 2 658 726 | (25) 1 417 134 | 53 |
| | Teacher training | | - | - | - | - | - | - |
| | Vocational education | | ... | ... | ... | ... | ... | ... |
| | Total | 1994 | ... | ... | ... | 3 571 395 | 1 911 420 | 54 |
| | General education | | 128 099 | 81 682 | 64 | 3 523 594 | *1 891 974 | *54 |
| | Teacher training | | - | - | - | - | - | - |
| | Vocational education | | ... | ... | ... | 47 801 | 19 446 | 41 |
| | Total | 1995 | ... | ... | ... | 3 749 449 | 2 039 551 | 54 |
| | General education | | 128 611 | 60 258 | 47 | 3 749 449 | 2 039 551 | 54 |
| | Teacher training | | - | - | - | - | - | - |
| | Vocational education | | ... | ... | ... | ... | ... | ... |
| St. Helena | Total | 1970 | 35 | 24 | 69 | 413 | 230 | 56 |
| | General education | | 33 | 24 | 73 | 408 | 225 | 55 |
| | Teacher training | | 2 | - | - | 5 | 5 | 100 |
| | Vocational education | | - | - | - | - | - | - |
| | Total | 1975/76 | ... | ... | ... | 524 | 281 | 54 |
| | General education | | ... | ... | ... | 509 | 276 | 54 |
| | Teacher training | | ... | ... | ... | 5 | 5 | 100 |
| | Vocational education | | ... | ... | ... | 10 | - | - |
| | Total | 1980/81 | 47 | 35 | 74 | 638 | 304 | 48 |
| | General education | | 40 | 32 | 80 | 601 | 295 | 49 |
| | Teacher training | | 4 | 3 | 75 | 5 | 5 | 100 |
| | Vocational education | | 3 | - | - | 32 | 4 | 13 |
| | Total | 1985/86 | 54 | 37 | 69 | 513 | 252 | 49 |
| | General education | | 44 | 34 | 77 | 470 | 245 | 52 |
| | Teacher training | | 6 | 3 | 50 | 11 | 7 | 64 |
| | Vocational education | | 4 | - | - | 32 | - | - |
| Sudan | Total | 1970/71 | 8 006 | 1 459 | 18 | 132 626 | 37 416 | 28 |
| | General education | | 7 435 | 1 401 | 19 | 128 379 | 36 514 | 28 |
| | Teacher training | | 246 | 58 | 24 | 2 391 | 902 | 38 |
| | Vocational education | | 325 | - | - | 1 856 | - | - |
| | Total | 1975/76 | 13 166 | ... | ... | 281 839 | 86 806 | 31 |
| | General education | | 12 097 | 2 528 | 21 | 268 120 | *84 196 | *31 |
| | Teacher training | | 420 | ... | ... | 4 723 | 1 993 | 42 |
| | Vocational education | | 649 | - | - | 8 996 | 617 | 7 |

II.6   Secondary education: teaching staff and pupils
Enseignement secondaire: personnel enseignant et élèves
Enseñanza secundaria: personal docente y alumnos

| Country<br>Pays<br>País | Type of education<br>Type d'enseignement<br>Tipo de enseñanza | Year<br>Année<br>Año | Teaching staff<br>Personnel enseignant<br>Personal docente | | | Pupils enrolled<br>Elèves inscrits<br>Alumnos matriculados | | |
|---|---|---|---|---|---|---|---|---|
| | | | Total | Female<br>Féminin<br>Femenino | %<br><br>F | Total | Female<br>Féminin<br>Femenino | %<br><br>F |
| Sudan (cont) | Total | 1980/81 | 18 831 | ... | ... | 384 194 | 141 736 | 37 |
| | General education | | 17 452 | 4 487 | 26 | 362 992 | 136 016 | 37 |
| | Teacher training | | 695 | 180 | 26 | 5 657 | 2 429 | 43 |
| | Vocational education | | 684 | ... | ... | 15 545 | 3 291 | 21 |
| | Total | 1985/86 | 23 035 | 7 501 | 33 | 556 587 | 235 400 | 42 |
| | General education | | 21 342 | 7 140 | 33 | 525 533 | 226 445 | 43 |
| | Teacher training | | 479 | 168 | 35 | 5 444 | 2 851 | 52 |
| | Vocational education | | 1 214 | 193 | 16 | 25 610 | 6 104 | 24 |
| | Total | 1990/91 | 33 628 | *11 828 | *35 | 731 624 | 318 128 | 43 |
| | General education | | 31 535 | 11 366 | 36 | 695 964 | 308 573 | 44 |
| | Teacher training | | 683 | 265 | 39 | 5 328 | 2 876 | 54 |
| | Vocational education | | 1 410 | *197 | *14 | 30 332 | 6 679 | 22 |
| | Total | 1991/92 | 30 642 | 9 999 | 33 | 718 298 | 317 277 | 44 |
| | General education | | 29 208 | 9 755 | 33 | 683 982 | 309 333 | 45 |
| | Teacher training | | 640 | 128 | 20 | 5 328 | 2 876 | 54 |
| | Vocational education | | 794 | 116 | 15 | 28 988 | 5 068 | 17 |
| | Total | 1994/95 | ... | ... | ... | (26) 254 442 | (26) 117 829 | 46 |
| | General education | | ... | ... | ... | (26) 238 999 | (26) 115 377 | 48 |
| | Teacher training | | - | - | - | - | - | - |
| | Vocational education | | 621 | 99 | 16 | 15 443 | 2 452 | 16 |
| | Total | 1995/96 | ... | ... | ... | 378 139 | 174 120 | 46 |
| | General education | | 10 993 | 4 888 | 44 | 356 273 | 166 416 | 47 |
| | Teacher training | | - | - | - | - | - | - |
| | Vocational education | | ... | ... | ... | 21 866 | 7 704 | 35 |
| | Total | 1996/97 | 15 504 | 6 998 | 45 | 405 583 | 189 958 | 47 |
| | General education | | 14 743 | 6 742 | 46 | 379 162 | 179 981 | 47 |
| | Teacher training | | - | - | - | - | - | - |
| | Vocational education | | 761 | 256 | 34 | 26 421 | 9 977 | 38 |
| Swaziland | Total | 1970 | ... | ... | ... | 8 438 | 3 676 | 44 |
| | General education | | 432 | 148 | 34 | 8 027 | 3 458 | 43 |
| | Teacher training | | 215 | 169 | 79 | 215 | 169 | 79 |
| | Vocational education | | ... | ... | ... | 196 | 49 | 25 |
| | Total | 1975 | ... | ... | ... | 16 876 | 7 713 | 46 |
| | General education | | 739 | 291 | 39 | 16 227 | 7 378 | 45 |
| | Teacher training | | ... | ... | ... | 205 | 168 | 82 |
| | Vocational education | | ... | ... | ... | 444 | 167 | 38 |
| | Total | 1980 | ... | ... | ... | 23 665 | ... | ... |
| | General education | | 1 292 | 624 | 48 | 23 198 | 11 370 | 49 |
| | Teacher training | | ... | ... | ... | 283 | 218 | 77 |
| | Vocational education | | ... | ... | ... | 184 | ... | ... |
| | Total | 1985 | ... | ... | ... | 31 109 | ... | ... |
| | General education | | 1 561 | 725 | 46 | 29 914 | 14 717 | 49 |
| | Teacher training | | ... | ... | ... | 800 | ... | ... |
| | Vocational education | | ... | ... | ... | 395 | 58 | 15 |
| | Total | 1990 | 2 213 | 1 027 | 46 | 41 128 | 20 551 | 50 |
| | General education | | 2 213 | 1 027 | 46 | 41 128 | 20 551 | 50 |
| | Teacher training | | - | - | - | - | - | - |
| | Vocational education | | - | - | - | - | - | - |
| | Total | 1991 | 2 430 | 1 082 | 45 | 44 085 | 22 000 | 50 |
| | General education | | 2 430 | 1 082 | 45 | 44 085 | 22 000 | 50 |
| | Teacher training | | - | - | - | - | - | - |
| | Vocational education | | - | - | - | - | - | - |
| | Total | 1992 | 2 703 | ... | ... | 51 514 | 25 896 | 50 |
| | General education | | 2 703 | ... | ... | 51 514 | 25 896 | 50 |
| | Teacher training | | - | - | - | - | - | - |
| | Vocational education | | - | - | - | - | - | - |
| | Total | 1993 | 2 824 | ... | ... | 50 304 | 25 231 | 50 |
| | General education | | 2 824 | ... | ... | 50 304 | 25 231 | 50 |
| | Teacher training | | - | - | - | - | - | - |
| | Vocational education | | - | - | - | - | - | - |
| | Total | 1994 | 2 872 | 1 245 | 43 | 52 571 | 26 464 | 50 |
| | General education | | 2 872 | 1 245 | 43 | 52 571 | 26 464 | 50 |
| | Teacher training | | - | - | - | - | - | - |
| | Vocational education | | - | - | - | - | - | - |
| | Total | 1995 | 2 933 | 1 257 | 43 | 54 933 | 27 798 | 51 |
| | General education | | 2 933 | 1 257 | 43 | 54 933 | 27 798 | 51 |
| | Teacher training | | - | - | - | - | - | - |
| | Vocational education | | - | - | - | - | - | - |
| | Total | 1996 | 2 954 | 1 247 | 42 | 57 330 | 28 893 | 50 |
| | General education | | 2 954 | 1 247 | 42 | 57 330 | 28 893 | 50 |
| | Teacher training | | - | - | - | - | - | - |
| | Vocational education | | - | - | - | - | - | - |

Secondary education: teaching staff and pupils  II.6
Enseignement secondaire: personnel enseignant et élèves
Enseñanza secundaria: personal docente y alumnos

| Country / Pays / País | Type of education / Type d'enseignement / Tipo de enseñanza | Year / Année / Año | Teaching staff / Personnel enseignant / Personal docente | | | Pupils enrolled / Elèves inscrits / Alumnos matriculados | | |
|---|---|---|---|---|---|---|---|---|
| | | | Total | Female / Féminin / Femenino | % F | Total | Female / Féminin / Femenino | % F |
| Togo | Total | 1970/71 | 880 | 218 | 25 | 22 003 | 4 926 | 22 |
| | General education | | 663 | 157 | 24 | 19 746 | 4 099 | 21 |
| | Teacher training | | 16 | 2 | 13 | 153 | 22 | 14 |
| | Vocational education | | 201 | 59 | 29 | 2 104 | 805 | 38 |
| | Total | 1975/76 | 1 634 | *268 | *16 | 64 404 | 15 330 | 24 |
| | General education | | 1 358 | 204 | 15 | 59 162 | 13 760 | 23 |
| | Teacher training | | (8) 25 | (8) *5 | *20 | 124 | 26 | 21 |
| | Vocational education | | 251 | 59 | 24 | 5 118 | 1 544 | 30 |
| | Total | 1980/81 | ... | ... | ... | ... | ... | ... |
| | General education | | 3 166 | 427 | 13 | 125 122 | 30 066 | 24 |
| | Teacher training | | ... | ... | ... | | | ... |
| | Vocational education | | ... | ... | ... | 6 839 | 1 766 | 26 |
| | Total | 1985/86 | 4 351 | 559 | 13 | 97 120 | 23 025 | 24 |
| | General education | | 4 072 | 519 | 13 | 91 609 | 21 570 | 24 |
| | Teacher training | | - | - | - | - | - | - |
| | Vocational education | | 279 | 40 | 14 | 5 511 | 1 455 | 26 |
| | Total | 1990/91 | 4 492 | 529 | 12 | 125 545 | 31 766 | 25 |
| | General education | | 4 231 | 489 | 12 | 117 153 | 29 605 | 25 |
| | Teacher training | | - | - | - | - | - | - |
| | Vocational education | | 261 | 40 | 15 | 8 392 | 2 161 | 26 |
| | Total | 1991/92 | ... | ... | ... | 127 831 | 31 567 | 25 |
| | General education | | 3 922 | 427 | 11 | 120 289 | 29 785 | 25 |
| | Teacher training | | - | - | - | - | - | - |
| | Vocational education | | ... | ... | ... | 7 542 | 1 782 | 24 |
| | Total | 1993/94 | 3 513 | ... | ... | 134 559 | 34 397 | 26 |
| | General education | | 2 918 | 314 | 11 | 126 335 | 32 433 | 26 |
| | Teacher training | | - | - | - | - | - | - |
| | Vocational education | | 595 | ... | ... | 8 224 | 1 964 | 24 |
| | Total | 1994/95 | 4 847 | 579 | 12 | 153 348 | 40 088 | 26 |
| | General education | | 4 261 | 521 | 12 | 145 717 | 37 977 | 26 |
| | Teacher training | | - | - | - | - | - | - |
| | Vocational education | | 586 | 58 | 10 | 7 631 | 2 111 | 28 |
| | Total | 1995/96 | 5 389 | ... | ... | 169 481 | 44 256 | 26 |
| | General education | | 4 736 | 501 | 11 | 161 672 | 42 287 | 26 |
| | Teacher training | | - | - | - | - | - | - |
| | Vocational education | | 653 | ... | ... | 7 809 | 1 969 | 25 |
| | Total | 1996/97 | ... | ... | ... | 178 254 | 47 595 | 27 |
| | General education | | ... | ... | ... | 169 178 | 45 030 | 27 |
| | Teacher training | | - | - | - | - | - | - |
| | Vocational education | | 653 | ... | ... | 9 076 | 2 565 | 28 |
| Tunisia | Total | 1970/71 | (4) 6 883 | ... | ... | 191 445 | 52 928 | 28 |
| | General education | | ... | ... | ... | ... | ... | ... |
| | Teacher training | | ... | ... | ... | 11 677 | 3 868 | 33 |
| | Vocational education | | ... | ... | ... | ... | ... | ... |
| | Total | 1975/76 | (4) 8 769 | (4) 2 475 | 28 | 201 845 | 67 971 | 34 |
| | General education | | ... | ... | ... | 144 812 | 49 889 | 34 |
| | Teacher training | | ... | ... | ... | 1 059 | 554 | 52 |
| | Vocational education | | ... | ... | ... | 55 974 | 17 528 | 31 |
| | Total | 1980/81 | 14 328 | 4 091 | 29 | 293 351 | 107 074 | 37 |
| | General education | | ... | ... | ... | 209 060 | 80 493 | 39 |
| | Teacher training | | 148 | 36 | 24 | 4 101 | 2 557 | 62 |
| | Vocational education | | ... | ... | ... | 80 190 | 24 024 | 30 |
| | Total | 1985/86 | 25 245 | 7 918 | 31 | 457 630 | 183 580 | 40 |
| | General education | | ... | ... | ... | 366 995 | 149 825 | 41 |
| | Teacher training | | 232 | 64 | 28 | 3 935 | 2 758 | 70 |
| | Vocational education | | ... | ... | ... | 86 700 | 30 997 | 36 |
| | Total | 1990/91 | 33 058 | 10 512 | 32 | 564 540 | 243 427 | 43 |
| | General education | | ... | ... | ... | 526 245 | 228 766 | 43 |
| | Teacher training | | 191 | 48 | 25 | 1 497 | 949 | 63 |
| | Vocational education | | ... | ... | ... | 36 798 | 13 712 | 37 |
| | Total | 1991/92 | 34 808 | 11 156 | 32 | 589 674 | 260 679 | 44 |
| | General education | | ... | ... | ... | 568 555 | 252 242 | 44 |
| | Teacher training | | 66 | 23 | 35 | 616 | 496 | 81 |
| | Vocational education | | ... | ... | ... | 20 503 | 7 941 | 39 |
| | Total | 1992/93 | 36 535 | 11 913 | 33 | 639 403 | 287 456 | 45 |
| | General education | | ... | ... | - | 627 255 | 282 820 | 45 |
| | Teacher training | | - | - | - | - | - | - |
| | Vocational education | | ... | ... | ... | 12 148 | 4 636 | 38 |
| | Total | 1993/94 | (18) 38 891 | (18) 12 980 | 33 | 717 156 | 330 365 | 46 |
| | General education | | ... | ... | - | 671 975 | 308 473 | 46 |
| | Teacher training | | - | - | - | - | - | - |
| | Vocational education | | ... | ... | ... | 45 181 | 21 892 | 48 |

**Secondary education: teaching staff and pupils**
**Enseignement secondaire: personnel enseignant et élèves**
**Enseñanza secundaria: personal docente y alumnos**

| Country / Pays / País | Type of education / Type d'enseignement / Tipo de enseñanza | Year / Année / Año | Teaching staff — Personnel enseignant — Personal docente | | | Pupils enrolled — Elèves inscrits — Alumnos matriculados | | |
|---|---|---|---|---|---|---|---|---|
| | | | Total | Female / Féminin / Femenino | % F | Total | Female / Féminin / Femenino | % F |
| Tunisia (cont) | Total | 1994/95 | (18) 41 328 | (18) 14 195 | 34 | 783 169 | 364 665 | 47 |
| | General education | | ... | ... | ... | 733 002 | 341 038 | 47 |
| | Teacher training | | - | - | - | - | | - |
| | Vocational education | | ... | | ... | 50 167 | 23 627 | 47 |
| | Total | 1995/96 | ... | ... | ... | 849 359 | 400 298 | 47 |
| | General education | | 41 885 | 15 155 | 36 | 794 394 | 375 220 | 47 |
| | Teacher training | | - | - | - | - | | - |
| | Vocational education | | ... | | ... | 54 965 | 25 078 | 46 |
| | Total | 1996/97 | | | | (18) 882 730 | (18) 421 088 | 48 |
| | General education | | 45 411 | 17 191 | 38 | 864 999 | 414 168 | 48 |
| | Teacher training | | - | - | - | - | | - |
| | Vocational education | | ... | | ... | (18) 17 731 | (18) 6 920 | 39 |
| | Total | 1997/98 | | | | ... | ... | ... |
| | General education | | (4) 36 528 | (4) 16 172 | 44 | (4) 833 372 | (4) 418 409 | 50 |
| | Teacher training | | - | - | - | - | | - |
| | Vocational education | | (18) 1 944 | (18) 664 | 34 | (18) 15 186 | (18) 5 968 | 39 |
| Uganda | Total | 1970 | | | | ... | ... | ... |
| | General education | | (5) 1 816 | ... | ... | (5) 40 697 | (5) 9 720 | 24 |
| | Teacher training | | 309 | 74 | 24 | 3 967 | 1 192 | 30 |
| | Vocational education | | 310 | ... | ... | 3 557 | | ... |
| | Total | 1975 | | | | ... | ... | ... |
| | General education | | (5) 1 994 | (5) 392 | 20 | (5) 45 871 | (5) 12 112 | 26 |
| | Teacher training | | 330 | | ... | 6 096 | 2 160 | 35 |
| | Vocational education | | 275 | 1 | 0 | 3 296 | 85 | 3 |
| | Total | 1980 | 3 833 | | | ... | ... | |
| | General education | | (5) 3 202 | ... | ... | (5) 73 092 | (5) *21 123 | *29 |
| | Teacher training | | 388 | ... | ... | 10 027 | | ... |
| | Vocational education | | 243 | ... | ... | 3 441 | 294 | 9 |
| | Total | 1985 | ... | | | ... | ... | |
| | General education | | (5) 6 903 | ... | ... | (5) 159 702 | ... | ... |
| | Teacher training | | 906 | ... | ... | 12 551 | ... | ... |
| | Vocational education | | 443 | ... | ... | 6 932 | ... | ... |
| | Total | 1990 | ... | | | ... | ... | |
| | General education | | (5) 15 128 | (5) 2 450 | 16 | (5) 244 765 | (5) 90 988 | 37 |
| | Teacher training | | 1 022 | | ... | 14 206 | 5 833 | 41 |
| | Vocational education | | 731 | 22 | 3 | 8 549 | 447 | 5 |
| | Total | 1991 | ... | | | ... | ... | |
| | General education | | (5) 13 491 | ... | ... | (5) 228 857 | ... | ... |
| | Teacher training | | 1 439 | ... | ... | 14 305 | | ... |
| | Vocational education | | 708 | ... | ... | 10 889 | 834 | 8 |
| | Total | 1992 | ... | | | ... | ... | |
| | General education | | (5) 14 710 | ... | ... | (5) 226 805 | (5) 86 080 | 38 |
| | Teacher training | | 1 149 | ... | ... | 16 261 | 6 992 | 43 |
| | Vocational education | | 769 | ... | ... | 13 603 | 1 826 | 13 |
| | Total | 1993 | ... | | | ... | ... | |
| | General education | | (5) 14 620 | (5) 2 661 | 18 | (5) 231 430 | ... | ... |
| | Teacher training | | 830 | 181 | 22 | 17 541 | 7 429 | 42 |
| | Vocational education | | 716 | ... | ... | 12 791 | ... | ... |
| | Total | 1994 | ... | | | ... | ... | |
| | General education | | (5) 16 245 | (5) 3 214 | 20 | (5) 244 248 | (5) 95 257 | 39 |
| | Teacher training | | 922 | 213 | 23 | 18 790 | 8 145 | 43 |
| | Vocational education | | 826 | 63 | 8 | 12 552 | 1 415 | 11 |
| | Total | 1995 | ... | | | ... | ... | |
| | General education | | (5) 14 447 | ... | ... | (5) 256 258 | (5) 98 205 | 38 |
| | Teacher training | | 1 022 | ... | ... | 22 703 | ... | ... |
| | Vocational education | | 766 | ... | ... | 13 360 | ... | ... |
| United Republic of Tanzania | Total | 1970 | 2 449 | 677 | 28 | 44 941 | 12 934 | 29 |
| | General education | | (1) 2 122 | (1) 591 | 28 | (1) 41 179 | (1) 11 424 | 28 |
| | Teacher training | | 327 | 86 | 26 | 3 762 | 1 510 | 40 |
| | Vocational education | | ./. | ./. | ./. | ./. | ./. | ./. |
| | Total | 1975 | 3 218 | ... | ... | 62 031 | 19 439 | 31 |
| | General education | | (1) 2 606 | (1) 740 | 28 | (1) 52 290 | (1) 15 208 | 29 |
| | Teacher training | | 612 | ... | ... | 9 741 | 4 231 | 43 |
| | Vocational education | | ./. | ./. | ./. | ./. | ./. | ./. |
| | Total | 1980 | 3 837 | ... | ... | 78 715 | ... | ... |
| | General education | | 3 158 | ... | ... | 67 292 | 22 388 | 33 |
| | Teacher training | | 679 | ... | ... | 11 423 | ... | ... |
| | Vocational education | | - | - | - | - | ... | - |
| | Total | 1985 | 5 267 | ... | ... | 92 945 | ... | ... |
| | General education | | 4 329 | 1 081 | 25 | 83 098 | 30 558 | 37 |
| | Teacher training | | 938 | ... | ... | 9 847 | ... | ... |
| | Vocational education | | - | - | - | - | ... | - |

Secondary education: teaching staff and pupils II.6
Enseignement secondaire: personnel enseignant et élèves
Enseñanza secundaria: personal docente y alumnos

| Country<br>Pays<br>País | Type of education<br>Type d'enseignement<br>Tipo de enseñanza | Year<br>Année<br>Año | Teaching staff<br>Personnel enseignant<br>Personal docente | | | Pupils enrolled<br>Elèves inscrits<br>Alumnos matriculados | | |
|---|---|---|---|---|---|---|---|---|
| | | | Total | Female<br>Féminin<br>Femenino | %<br>F | Total | Female<br>Féminin<br>Femenino | %<br>F |
| United Republic of Tanzania (cont) | Total | 1990 | 7 944 | 1 931 | 24 | 167 150 | 70 337 | 42 |
| | General education | | 6 930 | 1 729 | 25 | 150 300 | 63 148 | 42 |
| | Teacher training | | 1 014 | 202 | 20 | 16 850 | 7 189 | 43 |
| | Vocational education | | - | - | - | - | - | - |
| | Total | 1991 | 9 904 | 2 256 | 23 | 183 109 | 79 430 | 43 |
| | General education | | 8 649 | 2 032 | 23 | 166 812 | 72 136 | 43 |
| | Teacher training | | 1 255 | 224 | 18 | 16 297 | 7 294 | 45 |
| | Vocational education | | - | - | - | - | - | - |
| | Total | 1992 | 10 251 | 2 308 | 23 | 189 827 | 83 258 | 44 |
| | General education | | 8 926 | 2 070 | 23 | 175 776 | 76 291 | 43 |
| | Teacher training | | 1 325 | 238 | 18 | 14 051 | 6 967 | 50 |
| | Vocational education | | - | - | - | - | - | - |
| | Total | 1993 | 10 735 | 2 190 | 20 | 196 723 | 86 392 | 44 |
| | General education | | 9 568 | 1 927 | 20 | 180 899 | 78 305 | 43 |
| | Teacher training | | 1 167 | 263 | 23 | 15 824 | 8 087 | 51 |
| | Vocational education | | - | - | - | - | - | - |
| | Total | 1994 | 11 956 | 2 975 | 25 | 202 498 | 89 957 | 44 |
| | General education | | 10 928 | 2 762 | 25 | 186 246 | 81 699 | 44 |
| | Teacher training | | 1 028 | 213 | 21 | 16 252 | 8 258 | 51 |
| | Vocational education | | - | - | - | - | - | - |
| | Total | 1995 | 12 198 | 3 046 | 25 | 212 763 | 95 986 | 45 |
| | General education | | 11 158 | 2 802 | 25 | 196 375 | 87 279 | 44 |
| | Teacher training | | 1 040 | 244 | 23 | 16 388 | 8 707 | 53 |
| | Vocational education | | - | - | - | - | - | - |
| | Total | 1996 | 12 751 | 3 366 | 26 | 211 664 | 98 201 | 46 |
| | General education | | 11 689 | 3 094 | 26 | 199 093 | 91 061 | 46 |
| | Teacher training | | 1 062 | 272 | 26 | 12 571 | 7 140 | 57 |
| | Vocational education | | - | - | - | - | - | - |
| | Total | 1997 | 12 496 | 3 303 | 26 | 234 743 | 104 782 | 45 |
| | General education | | 11 434 | 3 035 | 27 | 225 607 | 100 450 | 45 |
| | Teacher training | | 1 062 | 268 | 25 | 9 136 | 4 332 | 47 |
| | Vocational education | | - | - | - | - | - | - |
| Zambia | Total | 1970 | ... | ... | ... | 56 182 | 18 294 | 33 |
| | General education | | 2 465 | 824 | 33 | 52 472 | 17 267 | 33 |
| | Teacher training | | 167 | 49 | 29 | 1 934 | 710 | 37 |
| | Vocational education | | ... | ... | ... | 1 776 | *317 | *18 |
| | Total | 1975 | ... | | ... | 77 672 | | ... |
| | General education | | 3 202 | 1 042 | 33 | 73 049 | 25 066 | 34 |
| | Teacher training | | 220 | 49 | 22 | 2 246 | 1 022 | 46 |
| | Vocational education | | ... | ... | ... | 2 377 | ... | ... |
| | Total | 1980 | 4 882 | ... | ... | 102 019 | 35 718 | 35 |
| | General education | | 4 334 | ... | ... | 95 771 | 33 309 | 35 |
| | Teacher training | | 313 | 60 | 19 | 3 742 | 1 750 | 47 |
| | Vocational education | | 235 | 7 | 3 | 2 506 | 659 | 26 |
| | Total | 1985 | ... | ... | ... | 140 743 | ... | ... |
| | General education | | 5 758 | 1 419 | 25 | 131 502 | 48 366 | 37 |
| | Teacher training | | ... | ... | ... | 4 549 | ... | ... |
| | Vocational education | | ... | ... | ... | 4 692 | ... | ... |
| | Total | 1990 | ... | ... | ... | 189 796 | ... | ... |
| | General education | | ... | ... | ... | 181 814 | ... | ... |
| | Teacher training | | ... | ... | ... | 4 669 | ... | ... |
| | Vocational education | | ... | ... | ... | 3 313 | ... | ... |
| | Total | 1991 | ... | ... | ... | | ... | ... |
| | General education | | ... | ... | ... | (5) 195 419 | ... | ... |
| | Teacher training | | ... | ... | ... | ... | ... | ... |
| | Vocational education | | ... | ... | ... | ... | ... | ... |
| | Total | 1992 | ... | ... | ... | | ... | ... |
| | General education | | ... | ... | ... | (5) *197 962 | ... | ... |
| | Teacher training | | ... | ... | ... | ... | ... | ... |
| | Vocational education | | ... | ... | ... | ... | ... | ... |
| | Total | 1994 | ... | ... | ... | ... | ... | ... |
| | General education | | ... | ... | ... | (5) 199 154 | (5) 76 397 | 38 |
| | Teacher training | | ... | ... | ... | *4 598 | ... | ... |
| | Vocational education | | ... | ... | ... | *4 888 | ... | ... |
| Zimbabwe | Total | 1970 | ... | ... | ... | 49 845 | 19 622 | 39 |
| | General education | | ... | ... | ... | 49 079 | 19 048 | 39 |
| | Teacher training | | | - | | - | - | |
| | Vocational education | | ... | - | ... | 766 | 574 | 75 |
| | Total | 1975 | ... | ... | ... | 70 005 | 29 052 | 41 |
| | General education | | (5) 3 737 | (5) 1 477 | 40 | 68 693 | 27 984 | 41 |
| | Teacher training | | - | - | ... | - | - | |
| | Vocational education | | ... | ... | ... | 1 312 | 1 068 | 81 |

II.6   Secondary education: teaching staff and pupils
Enseignement secondaire: personnel enseignant et élèves
Enseñanza secundaria: personal docente y alumnos

| Country / Pays / País | Type of education / Type d'enseignement / Tipo de enseñanza | Year / Année / Año | Teaching staff / Personnel enseignant / Personal docente | | | Pupils enrolled / Elèves inscrits / Alumnos matriculados | | |
|---|---|---|---|---|---|---|---|---|
| | | | Total | Female Féminin Femenino | % F | Total | Female Féminin Femenino | % F |
| Zimbabwe (cont) | Total | 1980 | 3 782 | ... | ... | 74 746 | ... | ... |
| | General education | | 3 736 | ... | ... | 74 012 | ... | ... |
| | Teacher training | | - | - | - | - | - | - |
| | Vocational education | | 46 | ... | ... | 734 | 734 | 100 |
| | Total | 1985 | ... | ... | ... | 482 000 | ... | ... |
| | General education | | 17 315 | 5 139 | 30 | 481 708 | 194 784 | 40 |
| | Teacher training | | - | - | - | - | - | - |
| | Vocational education | | ... | ... | ... | 292 | ... | ... |
| | Total | 1990 | *24 547 | *7 106 | *29 | 661 066 | 308 677 | 47 |
| | General education | | *24 547 | *7 106 | *29 | 661 066 | 308 677 | 47 |
| | Teacher training | | - | - | - | - | - | - |
| | Vocational education | | - | - | - | - | - | - |
| | Total | 1991 | 25 225 | 8 010 | 32 | 710 619 | 312 665 | 44 |
| | General education | | 25 225 | 8 010 | 32 | 710 619 | 312 665 | 44 |
| | Teacher training | | - | - | - | - | - | - |
| | Vocational education | | - | - | - | - | - | - |
| | Total | 1992 | 23 233 | 7 706 | 33 | 657 344 | 289 274 | 44 |
| | General education | | 23 233 | 7 706 | 33 | 657 344 | 289 274 | 44 |
| | Teacher training | | - | - | - | - | - | - |
| | Vocational education | | - | - | - | - | - | - |
| | Total | 1993 | 21 403 | 6 767 | 32 | 639 559 | 283 971 | 44 |
| | General education | | 21 403 | 6 767 | 32 | 639 559 | 283 971 | 44 |
| | Teacher training | | - | - | - | - | - | - |
| | Vocational education | | - | - | - | - | - | - |
| | Total | 1994 | 25 702 | 10 326 | 40 | 660 986 | 297 488 | 45 |
| | General education | | 25 702 | 10 326 | 40 | 660 986 | 297 488 | 45 |
| | Teacher training | | - | - | - | - | - | - |
| | Vocational education | | - | - | - | - | - | - |
| | Total | 1995 | 27 458 | 9 843 | 36 | 711 094 | 324 319 | 46 |
| | General education | | 27 458 | 9 843 | 36 | 711 094 | 324 319 | 46 |
| | Teacher training | | - | - | - | - | - | - |
| | Vocational education | | - | - | - | - | - | - |
| | Total | 1996 | 28 254 | 10 215 | 36 | 751 349 | 346 944 | 46 |
| | General education | | 28 254 | 10 215 | 36 | 751 349 | 346 944 | 46 |
| | Teacher training | | - | - | - | - | - | - |
| | Vocational education | | - | - | - | - | - | - |
| | Total | 1997 | 29 074 | ... | ... | 806 126 | ... | ... |
| | General education | | 29 074 | ... | ... | 806 126 | ... | ... |
| | Teacher training | | - | - | - | - | - | - |
| | Vocational education | | - | - | - | - | - | - |
| | Total | 1998 | 30 482 | ... | ... | 847 296 | ... | ... |
| | General education | | 30 482 | ... | ... | 847 296 | ... | ... |
| | Teacher training | | - | - | - | - | - | - |
| | Vocational education | | - | - | - | - | - | - |
| **North America** | | | | | | | | |
| Anguilla | Total | 1992/93 | 59 | 34 | 58 | 836 | 446 | 53 |
| | General education | | 59 | 34 | 58 | 836 | 446 | 53 |
| | Teacher training | | - | - | - | - | - | - |
| | Vocational education | | - | - | - | - | - | - |
| | Total | 1996/97 | 75 | 39 | 52 | 1 062 | 581 | 55 |
| | General education | | 75 | 39 | 52 | 1 062 | 581 | 55 |
| | Teacher training | | - | - | - | - | - | - |
| | Vocational education | | - | - | - | - | - | - |
| Antigua and Barbuda | Total | 1970/71 | ... | ... | ... | ... | ... | ... |
| | General education | | (4) 47 | (4) 38 | 81 | 5 000 | 2 726 | 55 |
| | Teacher training | | 11 | 2 | 18 | 95 | *45 | *47 |
| | Vocational education | | ... | ... | ... | ... | ... | ... |
| | Total | 1975/76 | ... | ... | ... | 6 827 | ... | ... |
| | General education | | ... | ... | ... | 6 629 | 3 465 | 52 |
| | Teacher training | | 13 | 11 | 85 | 96 | 77 | 80 |
| | Vocational education | | 20 | 5 | 25 | 102 | ... | ... |
| | Total | 1991/92 | *400 | *348 | *87 | 5 845 | 2 937 | 50 |
| | General education | | *400 | *348 | *87 | 5 845 | 2 937 | 50 |
| | Teacher training | | - | - | - | - | - | - |
| | Vocational education | | - | - | - | - | - | - |
| Bahamas | Total | 1970/71 | 641 | ... | ... | 21 422 | ... | ... |
| | General education | | 548 | *310 | *57 | 20 495 | ... | ... |
| | Teacher training | | (8) 32 | (8) 19 | 59 | (8) 500 | ... | ... |
| | Vocational education | | 61 | 14 | 23 | 427 | ... | ... |

Secondary education: teaching staff and pupils
Enseignement secondaire: personnel enseignant et élèves
Enseñanza secundaria: personal docente y alumnos

II.6

| Country / Pays / País | Type of education / Type d'enseignement / Tipo de enseñanza | Year / Année / Año | Teaching staff / Personnel enseignant / Personal docente | | | Pupils enrolled / Elèves inscrits / Alumnos matriculados | | |
|---|---|---|---|---|---|---|---|---|
| | | | Total | Female Féminin Femenino | % F | Total | Female Féminin Femenino | % F |
| Bahamas (cont) | Total | 1975/76 | ... | ... | ... | 28 056 | ... | ... |
| | General education | | ... | ... | ... | 28 056 | 14 468 | 52 |
| | Teacher training | | 21 | ... | ... | (8) 731 | ... | ... |
| | Vocational education | | (27) 92 | ... | ... | (27) 1 823 | ... | ... |
| | Total | 1980/81 | (4) 1 018 | ... | ... | 28 136 | ... | ... |
| | General education | | (4) 1 018 | ... | ... | 28 136 | ... | ... |
| | Teacher training | | - | - | - | - | - | - |
| | Vocational education | | - | - | - | - | - | - |
| | Total | 1985/86 | ... | ... | ... | 27 604 | 14 448 | 52 |
| | General education | | ... | ... | ... | 27 604 | 14 448 | 52 |
| | Teacher training | | - | - | - | - | - | - |
| | Vocational education | | - | - | - | - | - | - |
| | Total | 1991/92 | ... | ... | ... | 29 559 | 14 678 | 50 |
| | General education | | ... | ... | ... | 29 559 | 14 678 | 50 |
| | Teacher training | | - | - | - | - | - | - |
| | Vocational education | | - | - | - | - | - | - |
| | Total | 1992/93 | ... | ... | ... | 29 863 | 14 792 | 50 |
| | General education | | ... | ... | ... | 29 863 | 14 792 | 50 |
| | Teacher training | | - | - | - | - | - | - |
| | Vocational education | | - | - | - | - | - | - |
| | Total | 1993/94 | 1 775 | 1 232 | 69 | 28 532 | ... | ... |
| | General education | | 1 775 | 1 232 | 69 | 28 532 | ... | ... |
| | Teacher training | | - | - | - | - | - | - |
| | Vocational education | | - | - | - | - | - | - |
| | Total | 1994/95 | (4) 1 379 | (4) 930 | 67 | 28 435 | 14 005 | 49 |
| | General education | | (4) 1 379 | (4) 930 | 67 | 28 435 | 14 005 | 49 |
| | Teacher training | | - | - | - | - | - | - |
| | Vocational education | | - | - | - | - | - | - |
| | Total | 1996/97 | (4) 1 352 | (4) 868 | 64 | 27 970 | ... | ... |
| | General education | | (4) 1 352 | (4) 868 | 64 | 27 970 | ... | ... |
| | Teacher training | | - | - | - | - | - | - |
| | Vocational education | | - | - | - | - | - | - |
| Barbados | Total | 1970/71 | ... | ... | ... | ... | ... | ... |
| | General education | | ... | ... | ... | (4) 19 007 | (4) 8 912 | 47 |
| | Teacher training | | - | - | - | - | - | - |
| | Vocational education | | ... | ... | ... | 806 | ... | ... |
| | Total | 1975/76 | (28) 1 421 | ... | ... | (28) 29 025 | (28) 14 963 | 52 |
| | General education | | (28) 1 421 | ... | ... | (28) 29 025 | (28) 14 963 | 52 |
| | Teacher training | | - | - | - | - | - | - |
| | Vocational education | | - | - | - | - | - | - |
| | Total | 1980/81 | (4) 1 231 | ... | ... | 28 818 | 14 363 | 50 |
| | General education | | (4) 1 231 | ... | ... | 28 818 | 14 363 | 50 |
| | Teacher training | | - | - | - | - | - | - |
| | Vocational education | | - | - | - | - | - | - |
| | Total | 1990/91 | ... | ... | ... | ... | ... | ... |
| | General education | | ... | ... | ... | ... | ... | ... |
| | Teacher training | | - | - | - | - | - | - |
| | Vocational education | | 14 | 6 | 43 | 161 | 40 | 25 |
| Belize | Total | 1970/71 | ... | ... | ... | ... | ... | ... |
| | General education | | 269 | 155 | 58 | 4 212 | 2 216 | 53 |
| | Teacher training | | 6 | 5 | 83 | 75 | 53 | 71 |
| | Vocational education | | ... | ... | ... | ... | ... | ... |
| | Total | 1975/76 | ... | ... | ... | ... | ... | ... |
| | General education | | ... | ... | ... | 5 008 | 2 759 | 55 |
| | Teacher training | | - | - | - | - | - | - |
| | Vocational education | | ... | ... | ... | ... | ... | ... |
| | Total | 1980/81 | ... | ... | ... | ... | ... | ... |
| | General education | | 338 | 159 | 47 | 5 435 | *2 989 | *55 |
| | Teacher training | | - | - | - | - | - | - |
| | Vocational education | | ... | ... | ... | ... | ... | ... |
| | Total | 1985/86 | 534 | 229 | 43 | 7 048 | 3 811 | 54 |
| | General education | | 528 | 228 | 43 | 6 947 | 3 798 | 55 |
| | Teacher training | | - | - | - | - | - | - |
| | Vocational education | | 6 | 1 | 17 | 101 | 13 | 13 |
| | Total | 1990/91 | 564 | 233 | 41 | 7 904 | 4 176 | 53 |
| | General education | | 556 | 231 | 42 | 7 799 | 4 172 | 53 |
| | Teacher training | | - | - | - | - | - | - |
| | Vocational education | | 8 | 2 | 25 | 105 | 4 | 4 |
| | Total | 1991/92 | ... | ... | ... | ... | ... | ... |
| | General education | | 622 | 287 | 46 | 8 901 | 4 896 | 55 |
| | Teacher training | | - | - | - | - | - | - |
| | Vocational education | | ... | ... | ... | ... | ... | ... |

II.6    Secondary education: teaching staff and pupils
Enseignement secondaire: personnel enseignant et élèves
Enseñanza secundaria: personal docente y alumnos

| Country / Pays / País | Type of education / Type d'enseignement / Tipo de enseñanza | Year / Année / Año | Teaching staff Personnel enseignant Personal docente | | | | Pupils enrolled Elèves inscrits Alumnos matriculados | | |
|---|---|---|---|---|---|---|---|---|---|
| | | | Total | Female Féminin Femenino | % F | | Total | Female Féminin Femenino | % F |
| Belize (cont) | Total | 1992/93 | ... | ... | ... | | ... | ... | ... |
| | General education | | 643 | 299 | 47 | | 9 457 | 4 812 | 51 |
| | Teacher training | | - | - | - | | | | |
| | Vocational education | | ... | ... | ... | | ... | ... | ... |
| | Total | 1993/94 | 719 | 331 | 46 | | 10 044 | 5 087 | 51 |
| | General education | | 702 | 327 | 47 | | 9 886 | 5 067 | 51 |
| | Teacher training | | - | - | - | | - | - | - |
| | Vocational education | | 17 | 4 | 24 | | 158 | 20 | 13 |
| | Total | 1994/95 | 758 | 352 | 46 | | 10 272 | 5 335 | 52 |
| | General education | | 740 | 346 | 47 | | 10 147 | 5 307 | 52 |
| | Teacher training | | - | - | - | | - | - | - |
| | Vocational education | | 18 | 6 | 33 | | 125 | 28 | 22 |
| Bermuda | Total | 1970/71 | 301 | 156 | 52 | | 4 268 | 2 284 | 54 |
| | General education | | 261 | 151 | 58 | | 3 844 | 2 077 | 54 |
| | Teacher training | | - | - | - | | - | - | - |
| | Vocational education | | 40 | 5 | 13 | | 424 | 207 | 49 |
| | Total | 1975/76 | ... | ... | ... | | ... | ... | ... |
| | General education | | ... | ... | ... | | 4 824 | 2 517 | 52 |
| | Teacher training | | ... | ... | ... | | - | - | - |
| | Vocational education | | ... | ... | ... | | ... | ... | ... |
| | Total | 1980/81 | ... | ... | ... | | ... | ... | ... |
| | General education | | 367 (4) | 151 | ... | | 4 347 | 2 165 | 50 |
| | Teacher training | | - | - | - | | - | - | - |
| | Vocational education | | ... | ... | ... | | ... | ... | ... |
| | Total | 1994/95 | ... | ... | ... | | ... | ... | ... |
| | General education | | 316 | 184 | 58 | | 3 553 | 1 783 | 50 |
| | Teacher training | | - | - | - | | - | - | - |
| | Vocational education | | ... | ... | ... | | ... | ... | ... |
| | Total | 1996/97 | ... | ... | ... | | ... | ... | ... |
| | General education | | 355 | 211 | 59 | | 3 726 | 1 890 | 51 |
| | Teacher training | | - | - | - | | - | - | - |
| | Vocational education | | ... | ... | ... | | ... | ... | ... |
| British Virgin Islands | Total | 1970/71 | ... | ... | ... | | 865 | 475 | 55 |
| | General education | | ... | ... | ... | | ... | ... | ... |
| | Teacher training | | - | - | - | | - | - | - |
| | Vocational education | | ... | ... | ... | | ... | ... | ... |
| | Total | 1975/76 | 48 | 25 | 52 | | 821 | 456 | 56 |
| | General education | | ... | ... | ... | | ... | ... | ... |
| | Teacher training | | - | - | - | | - | - | - |
| | Vocational education | | ... | ... | ... | | ... | ... | ... |
| | Total | 1980/81 | 55 | 33 | 60 | | 791 | 448 | 57 |
| | General education | | ... | ... | ... | | 510 | 279 | 55 |
| | Teacher training | | - | - | - | | - | - | - |
| | Vocational education | | ... | ... | ... | | 281 | 169 | 60 |
| | Total | 1990/91 | ... | ... | ... | | 1 124 | 596 | 53 |
| | General education | | ... | ... | ... | | 1 124 | 596 | 53 |
| | Teacher training | | - | - | - | | - | - | - |
| | Vocational education | | - | - | - | | - | - | - |
| | Total | 1991/92 | 98 | ... | ... | | 1 134 | 625 | 55 |
| | General education | | 98 | ... | ... | | 1 134 | 625 | 55 |
| | Teacher training | | - | - | - | | - | - | - |
| | Vocational education | | - | - | - | | - | - | - |
| | Total | 1993/94 | 115 | 75 | 65 | | 1 309 | 668 | 51 |
| | General education | | 115 | 75 | 65 | | 1 309 | 668 | 51 |
| | Teacher training | | - | - | - | | - | - | - |
| | Vocational education | | - | - | - | | - | - | - |
| Canada | Total | 1970/71 | 97 000 | ... | ... | | 1 636 913 | 799 141 | 49 |
| | General education | | 97 000 | ... | ... | | 1 636 913 | 799 141 | 49 |
| | Teacher training | | - | - | - | | - | - | - |
| | Vocational education | | - | - | - | | - | - | - |
| | Total | 1975/76 | 144 300 | 60 300 | 42 | | 2 589 862 | 1 276 542 | 49 |
| | General education | | 144 300 | 60 300 | 42 | | 2 589 862 | 1 276 542 | 49 |
| | Teacher training | | - | - | - | | - | - | - |
| | Vocational education | | - | - | - | | - | - | - |
| | Total | 1980/81 | ... | ... | ... | | 2 323 228 | 1 146 714 | 49 |
| | General education | | ... | ... | ... | | 2 323 228 | 1 146 714 | 49 |
| | Teacher training | | - | - | - | | - | - | - |
| | Vocational education | | - | - | - | | - | - | - |
| | Total | 1985/86 | 151 390 | ... | ... | | 2 250 941 | 1 097 002 | 49 |
| | General education | | 151 390 | ... | ... | | 2 250 941 | 1 097 002 | 49 |
| | Teacher training | | - | - | - | | - | - | - |
| | Vocational education | | - | - | - | | - | - | - |

Secondary education: teaching staff and pupils  II.6
Enseignement secondaire: personnel enseignant et élèves
Enseñanza secundaria: personal docente y alumnos

| Country / Pays / País | Type of education / Type d'enseignement / Tipo de enseñanza | Year / Année / Año | Teaching staff — Personnel enseignant — Personal docente | | | Pupils enrolled — Elèves inscrits — Alumnos matriculados | | |
|---|---|---|---|---|---|---|---|---|
| | | | Total | Female Féminin Femenino | % F | Total | Female Féminin Femenino | % F |
| Canada (cont) | Total | 1990/91 | 164 125 | 87 875 | 54 | 2 292 497 | 1 118 112 | 49 |
| | General education | | 164 125 | 87 875 | 54 | 2 292 497 | 1 118 112 | 49 |
| | Teacher training | | - | - | - | - | - | - |
| | Vocational education | | - | - | - | - | - | - |
| | Total | 1991/92 | 166 406 | 89 315 | 54 | 2 337 513 | 1 137 699 | 49 |
| | General education | | 166 406 | 89 315 | 54 | 2 337 513 | 1 137 699 | 49 |
| | Teacher training | | - | - | - | - | - | - |
| | Vocational education | | - | - | - | - | - | - |
| | Total | 1992/93 | (29) 134 799 | (29) 89 679 | 67 | (29) 2 402 531 | (29) 1 165 647 | 49 |
| | General education | | (29) 134 799 | (29) 89 679 | 67 | (29) 2 402 531 | (29) 1 165 647 | 49 |
| | Teacher training | | - | - | - | - | - | - |
| | Vocational education | | - | - | - | - | - | - |
| | Total | 1993/94 | 135 888 | 90 113 | 66 | 2 455 427 | 1 191 320 | 49 |
| | General education | | 135 888 | 90 113 | 66 | 2 455 427 | 1 191 320 | 49 |
| | Teacher training | | - | - | - | - | - | - |
| | Vocational education | | - | - | - | - | - | - |
| | Total | 1994/95 | 133 358 | 89 615 | 67 | 2 469 552 | 1 200 975 | 49 |
| | General education | | 133 358 | 89 615 | 67 | 2 469 552 | 1 200 975 | 49 |
| | Teacher training | | - | - | - | - | - | - |
| | Vocational education | | - | - | - | - | - | - |
| | Total | 1995/96 | 133 275 | 89 558 | 67 | 2 505 389 | 1 218 403 | 49 |
| | General education | | 133 275 | 89 558 | 67 | 2 505 389 | 1 218 403 | 40 |
| | Teacher training | | - | - | - | - | - | - |
| | Vocational education | | - | - | - | - | - | - |
| Costa Rica | Total | 1970 | 3 691 | 1 745 | 47 | 61 068 | 31 119 | 51 |
| | General education | | 3 285 | 1 659 | 51 | 55 079 | 28 990 | 53 |
| | Teacher training | | - | - | - | - | - | - |
| | Vocational education | | 406 | 86 | 21 | 5 989 | 2 129 | 36 |
| | Total | 1975 | 4 929 | ... | ... | 111 538 | 57 763 | 52 |
| | General education | | 3 866 | (4) 1 995 | ... | 91 227 | 48 736 | 53 |
| | Teacher training | | - | - | - | - | - | - |
| | Vocational education | | 1 063 | ... | ... | 20 311 | 9 027 | 44 |
| | Total | 1980 | 7 157 | ... | ... | 135 830 | 72 014 | 53 |
| | General education | | 4 903 | ... | ... | 105 220 | 56 586 | 54 |
| | Teacher training | | - | - | - | - | - | - |
| | Vocational education | | 2 254 | ... | ... | 30 610 | 15 428 | 50 |
| | Total | 1985 | 6 613 | ... | ... | 112 531 | 58 116 | 52 |
| | General education | | ... | ... | ... | 87 038 | 45 403 | 52 |
| | Teacher training | | - | - | - | - | - | - |
| | Vocational education | | ... | ... | ... | 25 493 | 12 713 | 50 |
| | Total | 1990 | 6 889 | ... | ... | 130 553 | 65 508 | 50 |
| | General education | | 4 671 | ... | ... | 101 451 | 51 518 | 51 |
| | Teacher training | | - | - | - | - | - | - |
| | Vocational education | | 2 218 | ... | ... | 29 102 | 13 990 | 48 |
| | Total | 1991 | 7 249 | ... | ... | 139 303 | 70 210 | 50 |
| | General education | | 4 968 | ... | ... | 108 344 | 55 266 | 51 |
| | Teacher training | | - | - | - | - | - | - |
| | Vocational education | | 2 281 | ... | ... | 30 959 | 14 944 | 48 |
| | Total | 1992 | 7 641 | ... | ... | 151 513 | 76 359 | 50 |
| | General education | | 5 281 | ... | ... | 117 975 | 60 193 | 51 |
| | Teacher training | | - | - | - | - | - | - |
| | Vocational education | | 2 360 | ... | ... | 33 538 | 16 166 | 48 |
| | Total | 1993 | 8 263 | ... | ... | 160 291 | 81 469 | 51 |
| | General education | | 5 892 | ... | ... | 124 660 | 64 009 | 51 |
| | Teacher training | | - | - | - | - | - | - |
| | Vocational education | | 2 371 | ... | ... | 35 631 | 17 460 | 49 |
| | Total | 1994 | 8 845 | ... | ... | 169 777 | 86 315 | 51 |
| | General education | | 6 316 | ... | ... | 132 914 | 68 460 | 52 |
| | Teacher training | | - | - | - | - | - | - |
| | Vocational education | | 2 529 | ... | ... | 36 863 | 17 855 | 48 |
| | Total | 1995 | 9 327 | ... | ... | 179 440 | 91 410 | 51 |
| | General education | | 6 697 | ... | ... | 139 268 | 71 795 | 52 |
| | Teacher training | | - | - | - | - | - | - |
| | Vocational education | | 2 630 | ... | ... | 40 172 | 19 615 | 49 |
| | Total | 1996 | 10 157 | 5 975 | 59 | 183 162 | 93 741 | 51 |
| | General education | | 7 305 | 4 350 | 60 | 143 163 | 74 097 | 52 |
| | Teacher training | | - | - | - | - | - | - |
| | Vocational education | | 2 852 | 1 625 | 57 | 39 999 | 19 644 | 49 |
| | Total | 1997 | 10 898 | ... | ... | 193 436 | ... | ... |
| | General education | | ... | ... | ... | 149 219 | 77 356 | 52 |
| | Teacher training | | ... | ... | ... | ... | ... | ... |
| | Vocational education | | ... | ... | ... | 44 217 | ... | ... |

II.6    Secondary education: teaching staff and pupils
Enseignement secondaire: personnel enseignant et élèves
Enseñanza secundaria: personal docente y alumnos

| Country / Pays / País | Type of education / Type d'enseignement / Tipo de enseñanza | Year / Année / Año | Teaching staff Personnel enseignant Personal docente | | | Pupils enrolled Elèves inscrits Alumnos matriculados | | |
|---|---|---|---|---|---|---|---|---|
| | | | Total | Female Féminin Femenino | % F | Total | Female Féminin Femenino | % F |
| Costa Rica (cont) | Total | 1998 | 10 943 | ... | ... | 202 415 | 104 081 | 51 |
| | General education | | ... | ... | ... | 158 092 | 82 071 | 52 |
| | Teacher training | | - | - | - | - | - | - |
| | Vocational education | | ... | ... | ... | 44 323 | 22 010 | 50 |
| Cuba | Total | 1970/71 | 21 781 | ... | ... | 272 526 | ... | ... |
| | General education | | 15 273 | 7 418 | 49 | 186 667 | 100 864 | 54 |
| | Teacher training | | 1 863 | 1 209 | 65 | 58 293 | ... | ... |
| | Vocational education | | 4 645 | ... | ... | 27 566 | 5 448 | 20 |
| | Total | 1975/76 | (30) 42 306 | (30) 20 032 | 47 | 629 398 | (30) 273 106 | ... |
| | General education | | 32 755 | 16 317 | 50 | 420 315 | 224 804 | 53 |
| | Teacher training | | (30) 2 640 | (30) 1 512 | 57 | 94 430 | (30) 23 494 | ... |
| | Vocational education | | (30) 6 911 | (30) 2 203 | 32 | 114 653 | (30) 24 808 | ... |
| | Total | 1980/81 | (15) 88 017 | (15)(30) 40 145 | ... | (15) 1 146 414 | (15) 577 396 | 50 |
| | General education | | (15) 63 685 | (15) 31 976 | 50 | (15) 837 261 | (15) 423 084 | 51 |
| | Teacher training | | 6 730 | 3 842 | 57 | 80 666 | 49 862 | 62 |
| | Vocational education | | 17 602 | (30) 4 327 | ... | 228 487 | 104 450 | 46 |
| | Total | 1985/86 | 100 673 | 48 444 | 48 | 1 156 555 | 585 507 | 51 |
| | General education | | 65 929 | 35 179 | 53 | 807 597 | 417 490 | 52 |
| | Teacher training | | 7 283 | 4 305 | 59 | 41 829 | 29 415 | 70 |
| | Vocational education | | 27 461 | 8 960 | 33 | 307 129 | 138 602 | 45 |
| | Total | 1990/91 | 100 118 | 51 112 | 51 | 1 002 338 | 524 488 | 52 |
| | General education | | 63 855 | 35 524 | 56 | 672 166 | 357 930 | 53 |
| | Teacher training | | 6 998 | 3 943 | 56 | 29 559 | 24 691 | 84 |
| | Vocational education | | 29 265 | 11 645 | 40 | 300 613 | 141 867 | 47 |
| | Total | 1991/92 | 95 696 | 44 582 | 47 | 912 165 | 480 419 | 53 |
| | General education | | 61 804 | 33 106 | 54 | 597 997 | 322 453 | 54 |
| | Teacher training | | 3 771 | 2 132 | 57 | 20 760 | 17 050 | 82 |
| | Vocational education | | 30 121 | 9 344 | 31 | 293 408 | 140 916 | 48 |
| | Total | 1992/93 | 92 813 | 45 679 | 49 | 819 712 | 427 038 | 52 |
| | General education | | 57 455 | 33 939 | 59 | 520 290 | 281 975 | 54 |
| | Teacher training | | 3 650 | 2 099 | 58 | 14 590 | 10 576 | 72 |
| | Vocational education | | 31 708 | 9 641 | 30 | 284 832 | 134 487 | 47 |
| | Total | 1993/94 | 85 094 | 43 302 | 51 | 725 800 | 374 630 | 52 |
| | General education | | 53 423 | 32 290 | 60 | 459 140 | 248 238 | 54 |
| | Teacher training | | 1 675 | 954 | 57 | 7 305 | 5 871 | 80 |
| | Vocational education | | 29 996 | 10 058 | 34 | 259 355 | 120 521 | 46 |
| | Total | 1994/95 | 68 960 | 35 244 | 51 | 674 152 | 349 664 | 52 |
| | General education | | 43 633 | 26 485 | 61 | 445 178 | 239 037 | 54 |
| | Teacher training | | 627 | 265 | 42 | 3 779 | 2 994 | 79 |
| | Vocational education | | 24 700 | 8 494 | 34 | 225 195 | 107 633 | 48 |
| | Total | 1995/96 | 74 139 | 39 025 | 53 | 704 601 | 353 177 | 50 |
| | General education | | 46 772 | 29 053 | 62 | 460 348 | 245 570 | 53 |
| | Teacher training | | 301 | 143 | 48 | 1 192 | 907 | 76 |
| | Vocational education | | 27 066 | 9 829 | 36 | 243 061 | 106 700 | 44 |
| | Total | 1996/97 | 70 628 | 40 016 | 57 | 712 897 | 367 943 | 52 |
| | General education | | 46 629 | 29 713 | 64 | 500 339 | 236 874 | 53 |
| | Teacher training | | 193 | 70 | 36 | 506 | 391 | 77 |
| | Vocational education | | 23 806 | 10 233 | 43 | 212 052 | 100 678 | 47 |
| Dominica | Total | 1975/76 | ... | ... | ... | 6 487 | 3 826 | 59 |
| | General education | | ... | ... | ... | 5 896 | 3 282 | 56 |
| | Teacher training | | 13 | 8 | 62 | 43 | 32 | 74 |
| | Vocational education | | ... | ... | ... | 548 | 512 | 93 |
| | Total | 1980/81 | ... | ... | ... | ... | ... | ... |
| | General education | | ... | ... | ... | 7 022 | 3 679 | 52 |
| | Teacher training | | - | - | - | - | - | - |
| | Vocational education | | ... | ... | ... | ... | ... | ... |
| | Total | 1985/86 | ... | ... | ... | 7 370 | 3 953 | 54 |
| | General education | | ... | ... | ... | 7 111 | 3 860 | 54 |
| | Teacher training | | - | - | - | - | - | - |
| | Vocational education | | 27 | 7 | 26 | 259 | 93 | 36 |
| | Total | 1990/91 | ... | ... | ... | ... | ... | ... |
| | General education | | ... | ... | ... | 4 749 | 2 471 | 52 |
| | Teacher training | | - | - | - | - | - | - |
| | Vocational education | | ... | ... | ... | ... | ... | ... |
| | Total | 1991/92 | ... | ... | ... | ... | ... | ... |
| | General education | | ... | ... | ... | 5 983 | 3 142 | 53 |
| | Teacher training | | ... | ... | ... | ... | ... | ... |
| | Vocational education | | ... | ... | ... | ... | ... | ... |
| | Total | 1992/93 | ... | ... | ... | ... | ... | ... |
| | General education | | ... | ... | ... | 6 179 | 3 289 | 53 |
| | Teacher training | | ... | ... | ... | ... | ... | ... |
| | Vocational education | | ... | ... | ... | ... | ... | ... |

Secondary education: teaching staff and pupils   II.6
Enseignement secondaire: personnel enseignant et élèves
Enseñanza secundaria: personal docente y alumnos

| Country / Pays / País | Type of education / Type d'enseignement / Tipo de enseñanza | Year / Année / Año | Teaching staff Personnel enseignant Personal docente | | | Pupils enrolled Elèves inscrits Alumnos matriculados | | |
|---|---|---|---|---|---|---|---|---|
| | | | Total | Female Féminin Femenino | % F | Total | Female Féminin Femenino | % F |
| Dominica (cont) | Total | 1993/94 | ... | ... | ... | ... | ... | ... |
| | General education | | ... | ... | ... | 6 431 | 3 174 | 49 |
| | Teacher training | | - | - | - | ... | ... | ... |
| | Vocational education | | ... | ... | ... | ... | ... | ... |
| | Total | 1994/95 | ... | ... | ... | ... | ... | ... |
| | General education | | ... | ... | ... | 6 493 | 3 334 | 51 |
| | Teacher training | | - | - | - | ... | ... | ... |
| | Vocational education | | ... | ... | ... | ... | ... | ... |
| Dominican Republic | Total | 1970/71 | 4 668 | 2 644 | 57 | 126 261 | ... | ... |
| | General education | | 4 393 | 2 576 | 59 | 113 616 | ... | ... |
| | Teacher training | | 45 | 35 | 78 | 600 | 419 | 70 |
| | Vocational education | | 230 | 33 | 14 | 12 045 | ... | ... |
| | Total | 1975/76 | ... | ... | ... | 260 133 | ... | ... |
| | General education | | ... | ... | ... | 239 424 | ... | ... |
| | Teacher training | | ... | ... | ... | 1 389 | ... | ... |
| | Vocational education | | ... | ... | ... | 19 320 | ... | ... |
| | Total | 1980/81 | ... | ... | ... | 356 091 | ... | ... |
| | General education | | ... | ... | ... | 331 471 | ... | ... |
| | Teacher training | | ... | ... | ... | 1 722 | ... | ... |
| | Vocational education | | ... | ... | ... | 22 898 | ... | ... |
| | Total | 1985/86 | ... | ... | ... | 463 511 | ... | ... |
| | General education | | 11 754 | ... | ... | 438 922 | 240 898 | 55 |
| | Teacher training | | ... | ... | ... | 3 433 | ... | ... |
| | Vocational education | | ... | ... | ... | 21 156 | ... | ... |
| | Total | 1992/93 | ... | ... | ... | ... | ... | ... |
| | General education | | ... | ... | ... | (21) 205 943 | ... | ... |
| | Teacher training | | ... | ... | ... | ... | ... | ... |
| | Vocational education | | ... | ... | ... | ... | ... | ... |
| | Total | 1993/94 | 11 605 | ... | ... | 232 999 | ... | ... |
| | General education | | 10 301 | ... | ... | 211 957 | 121 738 | 57 |
| | Teacher training | | 86 | ... | ... | 1 661 | 947 | 57 |
| | Vocational education | | 1 218 | ... | ... | 19 381 | 12 402 | 64 |
| | Total | 1994/95 | 12 054 | 5 934 | 49 | 263 236 | 151 261 | 57 |
| | General education | | 10 757 | 5 334 | 50 | 240 441 | 138 162 | 57 |
| | Teacher training | | 86 | 60 | 70 | 1 292 | 743 | 58 |
| | Vocational education | | 1 211 | 540 | 45 | 21 503 | 12 356 | 57 |
| | Total | 1996/97 | ... | ... | ... | ... | ... | ... |
| | General education | | ... | ... | ... | 313 840 | ... | ... |
| | Teacher training | | ... | ... | ... | ... | ... | ... |
| | Vocational education | | ... | ... | ... | ... | ... | ... |
| | Total | 1997/98 | ... | ... | ... | ... | ... | ... |
| | General education | | ... | ... | ... | 329 944 | 184 384 | 56 |
| | Teacher training | | ... | ... | ... | ... | ... | ... |
| | Vocational education | | ... | ... | ... | ... | ... | ... |
| El Salvador | Total | 1970 | 3 531 | 1 145 | 32 | 88 307 | 41 351 | 47 |
| | General education | | ... | ... | ... | 60 870 | 26 451 | 43 |
| | Teacher training | | - | - | - | ... | ... | - |
| | Vocational education | | ... | ... | ... | 27 437 | 14 900 | 54 |
| | Total | 1975 | (6) 2 869 | ... | ... | (6) 51 731 | (6) 22 987 | 44 |
| | General education | | ... | ... | ... | (6) 29 559 | (6) 13 037 | 44 |
| | Teacher training | | 25 | 13 | 52 | 620 | 374 | 60 |
| | Vocational education | | ... | ... | ... | 21 552 | 9 576 | 44 |
| | Total | 1980 | 3 080 | 844 | 27 | 73 030 | 34 929 | 48 |
| | General education | | 1 805 | 437 | 24 | 24 280 | 10 436 | 43 |
| | Teacher training | | 65 | 24 | 37 | 3 451 | 2 560 | 74 |
| | Vocational education | | 1 210 | 383 | 32 | 45 299 | 21 933 | 48 |
| | Total | 1991 | ... | ... | ... | 94 268 | 51 780 | 55 |
| | General education | | ... | ... | ... | 26 314 | 13 180 | 50 |
| | Teacher training | | ... | ... | ... | 2 314 | 1 649 | 71 |
| | Vocational education | | ... | ... | ... | 65 640 | 36 951 | 56 |
| | Total | 1992 | ... | ... | ... | 105 093 | 55 572 | 53 |
| | General education | | ... | ... | ... | 28 032 | 13 434 | 48 |
| | Teacher training | | ... | ... | ... | 1 961 | 1 437 | 73 |
| | Vocational education | | ... | ... | ... | 75 100 | 40 701 | 54 |
| | Total | 1993 | ... | ... | ... | 118 115 | 61 648 | 52 |
| | General education | | ... | ... | ... | 29 527 | 14 227 | 48 |
| | Teacher training | | ... | ... | ... | 1 623 | 1 204 | 74 |
| | Vocational education | | ... | ... | ... | 86 965 | 46 217 | 53 |
| | Total | 1995 | 7 286 | ... | ... | 144 078 | 75 375 | 52 |
| | General education | | ... | ... | ... | ... | ... | ... |
| | Teacher training | | ... | ... | ... | ... | ... | ... |
| | Vocational education | | ... | ... | ... | ... | ... | ... |

II.6 Secondary education: teaching staff and pupils
Enseignement secondaire: personnel enseignant et élèves
Enseñanza secundaria: personal docente y alumnos

| Country / Pays / País | Type of education / Type d'enseignement / Tipo de enseñanza | Year / Année / Año | Teaching staff — Personnel enseignant — Personal docente | | | Pupils enrolled — Élèves inscrits — Alumnos matriculados | | |
|---|---|---|---|---|---|---|---|---|
| | | | Total | Female Féminin Femenino | % F | Total | Female Féminin Femenino | % F |
| El Salvador (cont) | Total | 1996 | 9 255 | ... | ... | 143 588 | 75 361 | 52 |
| | General education | | ... | ... | ... | ... | ... | ... |
| | Teacher training | | ... | ... | ... | ... | ... | ... |
| | Vocational education | | ... | ... | ... | ... | ... | ... |
| | Total | 1997 | ... | ... | ... | 152 474 | 79 179 | 52 |
| | General education | | ... | ... | ... | ... | ... | ... |
| | Teacher training | | ... | ... | ... | ... | ... | ... |
| | Vocational education | | ... | ... | ... | ... | ... | ... |
| Grenada | Total | 1970/71 | 161 | 70 | 43 | 4 081 | 1 868 | 46 |
| | General education | | 129 | 54 | 42 | 3 039 | 1 696 | 56 |
| | Teacher training | | 12 | 5 | 42 | 57 | 36 | 63 |
| | Vocational education | | 20 | 11 | 55 | 985 | 136 | 14 |
| | Total | 1975/76 | ... | ... | ... | (31) 10 197 | ... | ... |
| | General education | | ... | ... | ... | (31) 10 197 | ... | ... |
| | Teacher training | | - | - | - | - | - | - |
| | Vocational education | | - | - | - | - | - | - |
| | Total | 1980/81 | ... | ... | ... | 8 626 | 5 056 | 59 |
| | General education | | ... | ... | ... | 8 626 | 5 056 | 59 |
| | Teacher training | | - | - | - | - | - | - |
| | Vocational education | | - | - | - | - | - | - |
| | Total | 1985/86 | ... | ... | ... | (20) 9 571 | (20) 5 110 | 53 |
| | General education | | ... | ... | ... | (20) 9 571 | (20) 5 110 | 53 |
| | Teacher training | | - | - | - | - | - | - |
| | Vocational education | | - | - | - | - | - | - |
| | Total | 1990/91 | ... | ... | ... | 9 776 | 5 215 | 53 |
| | General education | | ... | ... | ... | 9 776 | 5 215 | 53 |
| | Teacher training | | - | - | - | - | - | - |
| | Vocational education | | - | - | - | - | - | - |
| | Total | 1991/92 | ... | ... | ... | 9 896 | 5 374 | 54 |
| | General education | | ... | ... | ... | 9 896 | 5 374 | 54 |
| | Teacher training | | - | - | - | - | - | - |
| | Vocational education | | - | - | - | - | - | - |
| | Total | 1992/93 | 377 | 195 | 52 | 10 213 | 5 489 | 54 |
| | General education | | 377 | 195 | 52 | 10 213 | 5 489 | 54 |
| | Teacher training | | - | - | - | - | - | - |
| | Vocational education | | - | - | - | - | - | - |
| Guadeloupe | Total | 1970/71 | ... | ... | ... | 29 162 | ... | ... |
| | General education | | ... | ... | ... | 24 429 | 13 902 | 57 |
| | Teacher training | | ... | ... | ... | 334 | ... | ... |
| | Vocational education | | ... | ... | ... | 4 399 | 2 417 | 55 |
| | Total | 1975/76 | 2 147 | ... | ... | 43 805 | 23 291 | 53 |
| | General education | | ... | ... | ... | (22) 37 009 | (22) 19 947 | 54 |
| | Teacher training | | ... | ... | ... | ./. | ./. | ./. |
| | Vocational education | | ... | ... | ... | 6 796 | 3 344 | 49 |
| | Total | 1980/81 | ... | ... | ... | 49 398 | ... | ... |
| | General education | | ... | - | - | ... | - | ... |
| | Teacher training | | - | - | - | - | - | - |
| | Vocational education | | ... | - | - | ... | - | ... |
| | Total | 1985/86 | ... | ... | % | 51 634 | 27 460 | 53 |
| | General education | | ... | ... | ... | 38 510 | 21 043 | 55 |
| | Teacher training | | - | - | - | - | - | - |
| | Vocational education | | ... | ... | ... | 13 124 | 6 417 | 49 |
| | Total | 1990/91 | 3 237 | ... | ... | 49 846 | 26 480 | 53 |
| | General education | | ... | ... | ... | 39 208 | 21 255 | 54 |
| | Teacher training | | - | - | - | - | - | - |
| | Vocational education | | ... | ... | ... | 10 638 | 5 225 | 49 |
| | Total | 1991/92 | ... | ... | ... | 50 556 | 26 479 | 52 |
| | General education | | ... | ... | ... | 35 931 | 19 787 | 55 |
| | Teacher training | | - | - | - | - | - | - |
| | Vocational education | | ... | ... | ... | 14 625 | 6 692 | 46 |
| | Total | 1992/93 | 3 467 | ... | ... | 50 850 | 25 513 | 50 |
| | General education | | ... | ... | ... | 38 043 | 18 932 | 50 |
| | Teacher training | | - | - | - | - | - | - |
| | Vocational education | | ... | ... | ... | 12 807 | 6 581 | 51 |
| | Total | 1993/94 | ... | ... | ... | 50 174 | 26 002 | 52 |
| | General education | | ... | ... | ... | 41 139 | 21 652 | 53 |
| | Teacher training | | - | - | - | - | - | - |
| | Vocational education | | ... | ... | ... | 9 035 | 4 350 | 48 |
| | Total | 1994/95 | ... | ... | ... | 50 899 | 26 281 | 52 |
| | General education | | ... | ... | ... | 41 656 | 21 838 | 52 |
| | Teacher training | | - | - | - | - | - | - |
| | Vocational education | | ... | ... | ... | 9 243 | 4 443 | 48 |

Secondary education: teaching staff and pupils  II.6
Enseignement secondaire: personnel enseignant et élèves
Enseñanza secundaria: personal docente y alumnos

| Country / Pays / País | Type of education / Type d'enseignement / Tipo de enseñanza | Year / Année / Año | Teaching staff Personnel enseignant Personal docente | | | Pupils enrolled Elèves inscrits Alumnos matriculados | | |
|---|---|---|---|---|---|---|---|---|
| | | | Total | Female Féminin Femenino | % F | Total | Female Féminin Femenino | % F |
| Guatemala | Total | 1970 | 5 473 | 1 739 | 32 | 75 474 | 31 039 | 41 |
| | General education | | ... | ... | ... | 55 932 | 22 057 | 39 |
| | Teacher training | | ... | ... | ... | 8 192 | 4 563 | 56 |
| | Vocational education | | ... | ... | ... | 11 350 | 4 419 | 39 |
| | Total | 1975 | 5 994 | 2 252 | 38 | 99 233 | 45 749 | 46 |
| | General education | | ... | ... | ... | 73 947 | 32 387 | 44 |
| | Teacher training | | ... | ... | ... | 13 631 | 7 464 | 55 |
| | Vocational education | | ... | ... | ... | 11 655 | 5 898 | 51 |
| | Total | 1980 | 9 613 | ... | ... | 171 903 | 76 918 | 45 |
| | General education | | ... | ... | ... | 119 879 | 51 299 | 43 |
| | Teacher training | | ... | ... | ... | 22 256 | 13 880 | 62 |
| | Vocational education | | ... | ... | ... | 29 768 | 11 739 | 39 |
| | Total | 1985 | 14 629 | ... | ... | 204 049 | ... | ... |
| | General education | | ... | ... | ... | ... | ... | ... |
| | Teacher training | | ... | ... | ... | ... | ... | ... |
| | Vocational education | | ... | ... | ... | ... | ... | ... |
| | Total | 1991 | 20 717 | ... | ... | 294 907 | ... | ... |
| | General education | | ... | ... | ... | ... | ... | ... |
| | Teacher training | | ... | ... | ... | ... | ... | ... |
| | Vocational education | | ... | ... | ... | ... | ... | ... |
| | Total | 1993 | 20 942 | ... | ... | 334 383 | 156 370 | 47 |
| | General education | | ... | ... | ... | ... | ... | ... |
| | Teacher training | | ... | ... | ... | ... | ... | ... |
| | Vocational education | | ... | ... | ... | ... | ... | ... |
| | Total | 1994 | 22 499 | ... | ... | 357 878 | ... | ... |
| | General education | | ... | ... | ... | ... | ... | ... |
| | Teacher training | | ... | ... | ... | ... | ... | ... |
| | Vocational education | | ... | ... | ... | ... | ... | ... |
| | Total | 1995 | 23 807 | ... | ... | 372 006 | ... | ... |
| | General education | | ... | ... | ... | ... | ... | ... |
| | Teacher training | | ... | ... | ... | ... | ... | ... |
| | Vocational education | | ... | ... | ... | ... | ... | ... |
| | Total | 1996 | 22 624 | ... | ... | 375 528 | 175 923 | 47 |
| | General education | | ... | ... | ... | ... | ... | ... |
| | Teacher training | | ... | ... | ... | ... | ... | ... |
| | Vocational education | | ... | ... | ... | ... | ... | ... |
| | Total | 1997 | ... | ... | ... | 384 729 | ... | ... |
| | General education | | ... | ... | ... | ... | ... | ... |
| | Teacher training | | ... | ... | ... | ... | ... | ... |
| | Vocational education | | ... | ... | ... | ... | ... | ... |
| Haiti | Total | 1975/76 | ... | ... | ... | ... | ... | ... |
| | General education | | 3 388 | 311 | 9 | 55 213 | 25 630 | 46 |
| | Teacher training | | ... | ... | ... | ... | ... | ... |
| | Vocational education | | ... | ... | ... | ... | ... | ... |
| | Total | 1980/81 | 4 392 | ... | ... | 99 894 | ... | ... |
| | General education | | 4 034 | ... | ... | 96 596 | 45 867 | 47 |
| | Teacher training | | 123 | ... | ... | 723 | 519 | 72 |
| | Vocational education | | 235 | ... | ... | 2 575 | ... | ... |
| | Total | 1985/86 | ... | ... | ... | 143 758 | ... | ... |
| | General education | | 6 978 | 846 | 12 | 139 422 | 65 367 | 47 |
| | Teacher training | | 159 | 73 | 46 | 867 | 588 | 68 |
| | Vocational education | | ... | ... | ... | 3 469 | ... | ... |
| | Total | 1990/91 | ... | ... | ... | 184 968 | 90 534 | 49 |
| | General education | | 9 470 | ... | ... | ... | ... | ... |
| | Teacher training | | ... | ... | ... | ... | ... | ... |
| | Vocational education | | ... | ... | ... | ... | ... | ... |
| Honduras | Total | 1970 | ... | ... | ... | 39 839 | 18 693 | 47 |
| | General education | | ... | ... | ... | 28 949 | 12 740 | 44 |
| | Teacher training | | ... | ... | ... | 3 801 | 2 610 | 69 |
| | Vocational education | | ... | ... | ... | 7 089 | 3 343 | 47 |
| | Total | 1975 | 3 132 | ... | ... | 56 705 | ... | ... |
| | General education | | ... | ... | ... | 36 956 | 18 925 | 51 |
| | Teacher training | | ... | ... | ... | 2 004 | 1 415 | 71 |
| | Vocational education | | ... | ... | ... | 17 745 | ... | ... |
| | Total | 1980 | 4 489 | 2 152 | 48 | 127 293 | 64 182 | 50 |
| | General education | | ... | ... | ... | 93 806 | 46 534 | 50 |
| | Teacher training | | ... | ... | ... | 5 156 | 3 802 | 74 |
| | Vocational education | | ... | ... | ... | 28 331 | 13 846 | 49 |
| | Total | 1985 | ... | ... | ... | 184 112 | ... | ... |
| | General education | | ... | ... | ... | ... | ... | ... |
| | Teacher training | | ... | ... | ... | ... | ... | ... |
| | Vocational education | | ... | ... | ... | ... | ... | ... |

# II.6

Secondary education: teaching staff and pupils
Enseignement secondaire: personnel enseignant et élèves
Enseñanza secundaria: personal docente y alumnos

| Country / Pays / País | Type of education / Type d'enseignement / Tipo de enseñanza | Year / Année / Año | Teaching staff — Personnel enseignant — Personal docente | | | Pupils enrolled — Elèves inscrits — Alumnos matriculados | | |
|---|---|---|---|---|---|---|---|---|
| | | | Total | Female Féminin Femenino | % F | Total | Female Féminin Femenino | % F |
| Honduras (cont) | Total | 1991 | 8 507 | ... | ... | 194 083 | 106 503 | 55 |
| | General education | | ... | ... | ... | 126 582 | 67 033 | 53 |
| | Teacher training | | ... | ... | ... | 8 935 | 6 544 | 73 |
| | Vocational education | | ... | ... | ... | 58 566 | 32 926 | 56 |
| | Total | 1993 | 10 203 | ... | ... | 203 192 | ... | ... |
| | General education | | ... | ... | ... | ... | ... | ... |
| | Teacher training | | ... | ... | ... | ... | ... | ... |
| | Vocational education | | ... | ... | ... | ... | ... | ... |
| Jamaica | Total | 1975/76 | ... | ... | ... | ... | ... | ... |
| | General education | | (32) 6 181 | ... | ... | 211 309 | 113 379 | 54 |
| | Teacher training | | - | | - | - | | - |
| | Vocational education | | (5) 292 | ... | ... | (5) 4 939 | (5) 2 405 | 49 |
| | Total | 1980/81 | ... | ... | ... | ... | ... | ... |
| | General education | | (32) 7 110 | (32) 4 760 | 67 | 233 723 | 122 450 | 52 |
| | Teacher training | | - | | - | - | | - |
| | Vocational education | | (5) 415 | (5) 231 | 56 | 14 278 | 9 295 | 65 |
| | Total | 1985/86 | ... | ... | ... | 237 713 | 124 487 | 52 |
| | General education | | (5)(32) 7 485 | (5)(32) 5 041 | 67 | 229 023 | 120 111 | 52 |
| | Teacher training | | - | | - | - | | - |
| | Vocational education | | ... | ... | ... | ... | ... | ... |
| | Total | 1990/91 | ... | ... | ... | (5) 225 240 | (5) 115 999 | 52 |
| | General education | | ... | ... | ... | ... | ... | ... |
| | Teacher training | | - | | - | - | | - |
| | Vocational education | | ... | ... | ... | ... | ... | ... |
| | Total | 1992/93 | 10 931 | 7 333 | 67 | 235 071 | 120 640 | 51 |
| | General education | | ... | ... | ... | ... | ... | ... |
| | Teacher training | | - | | - | - | | - |
| | Vocational education | | - | | - | - | | - |
| Martinique | Total | 1970/71 | ... | ... | ... | 31 884 | ... | ... |
| | General education | | 1 691 | ... | ... | 29 454 | ... | ... |
| | Teacher training | | ... | ... | ... | 419 | ... | ... |
| | Vocational education | | ... | ... | ... | 2 011 | ... | ... |
| | Total | 1975/76 | 2 357 | ... | ... | 45 260 | 24 576 | 54 |
| | General education | | ... | ... | ... | (22) 39 234 | (22) 21 077 | 54 |
| | Teacher training | | ... | ... | ... | ./. | ./. | ./. |
| | Vocational education | | ... | ... | ... | 6 026 | 3 499 | 58 |
| | Total | 1980/81 | ... | ... | ... | 47 745 | ... | ... |
| | General education | | ... | ... | ... | ... | ... | ... |
| | Teacher training | | - | - | - | - | - | - |
| | Vocational education | | ... | ... | ... | ... | ... | ... |
| | Total | 1985/86 | ... | ... | ... | 47 500 | ... | ... |
| | General education | | ... | ... | ... | ... | ... | ... |
| | Teacher training | | - | | - | - | | - |
| | Vocational education | | ... | ... | ... | ... | ... | ... |
| | Total | 1991/92 | ... | ... | ... | 46 373 | 24 275 | 52 |
| | General education | | ... | ... | ... | 32 507 | 19 528 | 60 |
| | Teacher training | | - | | - | - | | - |
| | Vocational education | | ... | ... | ... | 13 866 | 4 747 | 34 |
| | Total | 1992/93 | ... | ... | ... | 43 928 | 23 657 | 54 |
| | General education | | ... | ... | ... | 30 912 | 16 952 | 55 |
| | Teacher training | | - | | - | - | | - |
| | Vocational education | | ... | ... | ... | 13 016 | 6 705 | 52 |
| | Total | 1993/94 | (4) 3 451 | (4) 1 813 | 53 | 46 108 | 23 517 | 51 |
| | General education | | - | - | - | 36 491 | 19 005 | 52 |
| | Teacher training | | - | | - | - | | - |
| | Vocational education | | ... | ... | ... | 9 617 | 4 512 | 47 |
| | Total | 1994/95 | ... | ... | ... | 46 178 | 23 258 | 50 |
| | General education | | ... | ... | ... | 36 810 | 18 991 | 52 |
| | Teacher training | | - | | - | - | | - |
| | Vocational education | | ... | ... | ... | 9 368 | 4 267 | 46 |
| | Total | 1995/96 | 3 784 | 2 035 | 54 | 47 706 | 24 093 | 51 |
| | General education | | 2 888 | 1 613 | 56 | 36 605 | 18 392 | 50 |
| | Teacher training | | - | - | - | - | - | - |
| | Vocational education | | 896 | 422 | 47 | 11 101 | 5 701 | 51 |
| Mexico | Total | 1970/71 | 109 470 | ... | ... | 1 584 342 | 609 669 | 38 |
| | General education | | ... | ... | ... | 1 107 906 | ... | ... |
| | Teacher training | | 5 131 | 2 232 | 44 | 52 852 | 34 657 | 66 |
| | Vocational education | | ... | ... | ... | 423 584 | ... | ... |
| | Total | 1975/76 | 169 781 | 55 218 | 33 | 2 938 972 | 1 159 319 | 39 |
| | General education | | 141 730 | 42 016 | 30 | 2 506 014 | 853 580 | 34 |
| | Teacher training | | 8 396 | 3 089 | 37 | 111 502 | 74 706 | 67 |
| | Vocational education | | 19 655 | 10 113 | 51 | 321 456 | 231 033 | 72 |

Secondary education: teaching staff and pupils
Enseignement secondaire: personnel enseignant et élèves
Enseñanza secundaria: personal docente y alumnos

II.6

| Country / Pays / País | Type of education / Type d'enseignement / Tipo de enseñanza | Year / Année / Año | Teaching staff / Personnel enseignant / Personal docente | | | Pupils enrolled / Elèves inscrits / Alumnos matriculados | | |
|---|---|---|---|---|---|---|---|---|
| | | | Total | Female Féminin Femenino | % F | Total | Female Féminin Femenino | % F |
| Mexico (cont) | Total | 1980/81 | 268 178 | ... | ... | 4 741 850 | 2 214 442 | 47 |
| | General education | | 226 532 | ... | ... | 4 042 188 | 1 750 873 | 43 |
| | Teacher training | | 12 988 | ... | ... | 207 997 | 138 669 | 67 |
| | Vocational education | | 28 658 | ... | ... | 491 665 | 324 900 | 66 |
| | Total | 1985/86 | 380 774 | ... | ... | 6 549 105 | 3 163 293 | 48 |
| | General education | | 321 459 | ... | ... | 5 717 572 | 2 645 629 | 46 |
| | Teacher training | | 8 491 | ... | ... | 64 700 | 47 117 | 73 |
| | Vocational education | | 50 824 | ... | ... | 766 833 | 470 547 | 61 |
| | Total | 1990/91 | 402 474 | ... | ... | 6 704 297 | 3 329 371 | 50 |
| | General education | | 344 293 | ... | ... | 5 911 816 | 2 827 425 | 48 |
| | Teacher training | | - | - | - | - | - | - |
| | Vocational education | | 58 181 | ... | ... | 792 481 | 501 946 | 63 |
| | Total | 1991/92 | 406 998 | ... | ... | 6 704 188 | 3 274 930 | 49 |
| | General education | | 348 448 | ... | ... | 5 885 986 | 2 835 341 | 48 |
| | Teacher training | | - | - | - | - | - | - |
| | Vocational education | | 58 550 | ... | ... | 818 202 | 439 589 | 54 |
| | Total | 1992/93 | 412 789 | ... | ... | 6 782 886 | 3 347 884 | 49 |
| | General education | | 353 072 | ... | ... | 5 970 118 | 2 884 530 | 48 |
| | Teacher training | | - | - | - | - | - | - |
| | Vocational education | | 59 717 | ... | ... | 812 768 | 463 354 | 57 |
| | Total | 1993/94 | 426 157 | ... | ... | 6 977 086 | 3 461 731 | 50 |
| | General education | | 365 908 | ... | ... | 6 179 579 | 2 988 739 | 48 |
| | Teacher training | | - | - | - | - | - | - |
| | Vocational education | | 60 249 | ... | ... | 797 507 | 472 992 | 59 |
| | Total | 1994/95 | 448 407 | ... | ... | 7 264 620 | 3 609 060 | 50 |
| | General education | | 386 182 | ... | ... | 6 429 571 | 3 120 916 | 49 |
| | Teacher training | | - | | | - | | |
| | Vocational education | | 62 225 | ... | ... | 835 049 | 488 144 | 58 |
| | Total | 1995/96 | 467 686 | ... | ... | 7 589 414 | 3 752 595 | 49 |
| | General education | | 403 028 | ... | ... | 6 738 024 | 3 260 028 | 48 |
| | Teacher training | | - | - | - | - | - | - |
| | Vocational education | | 64 658 | ... | ... | 851 390 | 492 567 | 58 |
| | Total | 1996/97 | 485 059 | ... | ... | 7 914 165 | 3 906 783 | 49 |
| | General education | | 421 385 | ... | ... | 7 031 605 | 3 407 756 | 48 |
| | Teacher training | | - | - | - | - | - | - |
| | Vocational education | | 63 674 | ... | ... | 882 560 | 499 027 | 57 |
| Montserrat | Total | 1975/76 | ... | ... | ... | 535 | ... | ... |
| | General education | | 35 | ... | ... | 482 | ... | ... |
| | Teacher training | | - | - | - | - | - | - |
| | Vocational education | | 8 | 3 | 38 | 53 | 24 | 45 |
| | Total | 1980/81 | 37 | ... | ... | 887 | ... | ... |
| | General education | | 32 | ... | ... | 828 | ... | ... |
| | Teacher training | | - | - | - | - | - | - |
| | Vocational education | | 5 | ... | ... | 59 | ... | ... |
| | Total | 1985/86 | ... | ... | ... | 1 069 | 545 | 51 |
| | General education | | ... | ... | ... | 1 016 | 521 | 51 |
| | Teacher training | | - | - | - | - | - | - |
| | Vocational education | | ... | ... | ... | 53 | 24 | 45 |
| | Total | 1990/91 | ... | ... | ... | ... | ... | ... |
| | General education | | ... | ... | ... | ... | ... | ... |
| | Teacher training | | - | - | - | - | - | - |
| | Vocational education | | ... | ... | ... | 43 | 14 | 33 |
| | Total | 1991/92 | ... | ... | ... | 837 | 414 | 49 |
| | General education | | ... | ... | ... | 747 | 385 | 52 |
| | Teacher training | | - | - | - | - | - | - |
| | Vocational education | | ... | ... | ... | 90 | 29 | 32 |
| | Total | 1992/93 | 72 | ... | ... | 888 | ... | ... |
| | General education | | ... | ... | ... | 785 | ... | ... |
| | Teacher training | | - | - | - | - | - | - |
| | Vocational education | | ... | ... | ... | 103 | 72 | 70 |
| | Total | 1993/94 | ... | ... | ... | ... | ... | ... |
| | General education | | 80 | 50 | 63 | 905 | 447 | 49 |
| | Teacher training | | - | - | - | - | - | - |
| | Vocational education | | ... | | | ... | | |
| Netherlands Antilles | Total | 1980/81 | ... | ... | ... | ... | | |
| | General education | | ... | ... | ... | 11 427 | 6 929 | 61 |
| | Teacher training | | ... | ... | ... | ... | | |
| | Vocational education | | ... | ... | ... | 10 532 | 4 472 | 42 |
| | Total | 1991/92 | ... | ... | ... | 14 987 | ... | ... |
| | General education | | ... | ... | ... | 8 740 | - | - |
| | Teacher training | | - | - | - | - | - | - |
| | Vocational education | | ... | ... | ... | 6 247 | ... | ... |

II.6 Secondary education: teaching staff and pupils
Enseignement secondaire: personnel enseignant et élèves
Enseñanza secundaria: personal docente y alumnos

| Country<br>Pays<br>País | Type of education<br>Type d'enseignement<br>Tipo de enseñanza | Year<br>Année<br>Año | Teaching staff<br>Personnel enseignant<br>Personal docente | | | | Pupils enrolled<br>Elèves inscrits<br>Alumnos matriculados | | |
|---|---|---|---|---|---|---|---|---|---|
| | | | Total | Female<br>Féminin<br>Femenino | %<br>F | | Total | Female<br>Féminin<br>Femenino | %<br>F |
| Nicaragua | Total | 1970 | 1 979 | ... | ... | | 51 383 | 24 347 | 47 |
| | General education | | 1 495 | ... | ... | | 45 185 | 21 253 | 47 |
| | Teacher training | | 110 | ... | ... | | 1 757 | 1 350 | 77 |
| | Vocational education | | 374 | ... | ... | | 4 441 | 1 744 | 39 |
| | Total | 1975 | 2 308 | ... | ... | | 80 202 | 40 434 | 50 |
| | General education | | 1 628 | ... | ... | | 66 958 | 32 875 | 49 |
| | Teacher training | | 55 | ... | ... | | 822 | 601 | 73 |
| | Vocational education | | 625 | ... | ... | | 12 422 | 6 958 | 56 |
| | Total | 1980 | (24) 4 221 | | ... | (24) | 139 743 | (24) 74 328 | 53 |
| | General education | | ... | ... | ... | (24) | 120 522 | (24) 63 000 | 52 |
| | Teacher training | | ... | ... | ... | | 2 560 | 2 027 | 79 |
| | Vocational education | | ... | ... | ... | | 16 661 | 9 301 | 56 |
| | Total | 1985 | 5 204 | 2 916 | 56 | | 128 499 | 86 324 | 67 |
| | General education | | 3 388 | 1 961 | 58 | | 99 984 | 64 627 | 65 |
| | Teacher training | | 296 | 173 | 58 | | 4 596 | 3 855 | 84 |
| | Vocational education | | 1 520 | 782 | 51 | | 23 919 | 17 842 | 75 |
| | Total | 1990 | ... | ... | ... | | 184 101 | ... | ... |
| | General education | | 3 948 | 2 292 | 58 | | 151 959 | 88 018 | 58 |
| | Teacher training | | 240 | 159 | 66 | | 1 597 | 1 302 | 82 |
| | Vocational education | | ... | ... | ... | | 30 545 | ... | ... |
| | Total | 1991 | ... | ... | ... | | 221 237 | ... | ... |
| | General education | | 4 136 | ... | ... | | 176 825 | 95 220 | 54 |
| | Teacher training | | 181 | 130 | 72 | | 2 454 | 1 954 | 80 |
| | Vocational education | | ... | ... | ... | | 41 958 | ... | ... |
| | Total | 1992 | ... | ... | ... | | 228 360 | ... | ... |
| | General education | | 4 465 | 2 522 | 56 | | 178 342 | 94 899 | 53 |
| | Teacher training | | ... | ... | ... | | 2 433 | 1 820 | 75 |
| | Vocational education | | ... | ... | ... | | 47 585 | ... | ... |
| | Total | 1993 | ... | ... | ... | | 238 399 | ... | ... |
| | General education | | 6 172 | 3 380 | 55 | | 186 722 | 98 099 | 53 |
| | Teacher training | | 175 | 99 | 57 | | 2 507 | 1 928 | 77 |
| | Vocational education | | ... | ... | ... | | 49 170 | ... | ... |
| | Total | 1994 | ... | ... | ... | | 249 091 | ... | ... |
| | General education | | 5 356 | 2 975 | 56 | | 205 716 | 108 412 | 53 |
| | Teacher training | | 202 | 133 | 66 | | 2 241 | 1 726 | 77 |
| | Vocational education | | ... | ... | ... | | 41 134 | ... | ... |
| | Total | 1995 | ... | ... | ... | | 265 515 | ... | ... |
| | General education | | 5 990 | 3 349 | 56 | | 220 670 | 118 508 | 54 |
| | Teacher training | | 205 | 139 | 68 | | 2 278 | 1 821 | 80 |
| | Vocational education | | ... | ... | ... | | 42 567 | ... | ... |
| | Total | 1996 | ... | ... | ... | | ... | ... | ... |
| | General education | | 5 970 | ... | ... | | 233 410 | 125 008 | 54 |
| | Teacher training | | ... | ... | ... | | ... | ... | ... |
| | Vocational education | | ... | ... | ... | | ... | ... | ... |
| | Total | 1997 | ... | ... | ... | | ... | ... | ... |
| | General education | | ... | ... | ... | | 268 438 | 144 153 | 54 |
| | Teacher training | | ... | ... | ... | | 2 018 | 1 636 | 81 |
| | Vocational education | | ... | ... | ... | | ... | ... | ... |
| | Total | 1998 | ... | ... | ... | | ... | ... | ... |
| | General education | | ... | ... | ... | | 287 476 | 154 263 | 54 |
| | Teacher training | | ... | ... | ... | | 2 120 | 1 659 | 78 |
| | Vocational education | | ... | ... | ... | | ... | ... | ... |
| Panama | Total | 1970 | 3 784 | 2 127 | 56 | | 78 466 | 40 799 | 52 |
| | General education | | 2 561 | 1 465 | 57 | | 50 920 | 25 377 | 50 |
| | Teacher training | | 94 | 51 | 54 | | 2 194 | 1 727 | 79 |
| | Vocational education | | 1 129 | 611 | 54 | | 25 352 | 13 695 | 54 |
| | Total | 1975 | 5 666 | 3 101 | 55 | | 133 181 | 68 848 | 52 |
| | General education | | 3 472 | 1 939 | 56 | | 89 364 | 45 242 | 51 |
| | Teacher training | | 244 | 141 | 58 | | 5 850 | 4 300 | 74 |
| | Vocational education | | 1 950 | 1 021 | 52 | | 37 967 | 19 306 | 51 |
| | Total | 1980 | 8 138 | 4 319 | 53 | | 171 273 | 89 328 | 52 |
| | General education | | 6 005 | 3 316 | 55 | | 130 496 | 67 037 | 51 |
| | Teacher training | | 48 | 26 | 54 | | 984 | 663 | 67 |
| | Vocational education | | 2 085 | 977 | 47 | | 39 793 | 21 628 | 54 |
| | Total | 1985 | 9 681 | 5 155 | 53 | | 184 536 | 95 750 | 52 |
| | General education | | 6 913 | 3 851 | 56 | | 134 470 | 68 782 | 51 |
| | Teacher training | | 41 | 18 | 44 | | 912 | 599 | 66 |
| | Vocational education | | 2 727 | 1 286 | 47 | | 49 154 | 26 369 | 54 |
| | Total | 1990 | 9 754 | 5 284 | 54 | | 195 903 | 99 634 | 51 |
| | General education | | 7 326 | 4 109 | 56 | | 144 690 | 73 416 | 51 |
| | Teacher training | | 69 | 36 | 52 | | 1 599 | 1 004 | 63 |
| | Vocational education | | 2 359 | 1 139 | 48 | | 49 614 | 25 214 | 51 |

Secondary education: teaching staff and pupils     II.6
Enseignement secondaire: personnel enseignant et élèves
Enseñanza secundaria: personal docente y alumnos

| Country / Pays / País | Type of education / Type d'enseignement / Tipo de enseñanza | Year / Année / Año | Teaching staff Personnel enseignant Personal docente | | | Pupils enrolled Elèves inscrits Alumnos matriculados | | |
|---|---|---|---|---|---|---|---|---|
| | | | Total | Female Féminin Femenino | % F | Total | Female Féminin Femenino | % F |
| Panama (cont) | Total | 1991 | 9 996 | ... | ... | 198 138 | ... | ... |
| | General education | | ... | ... | ... | ... | ... | ... |
| | Teacher training | | ... | ... | ... | ... | ... | ... |
| | Vocational education | | ... | ... | ... | ... | ... | ... |
| | Total | 1992 | 10 521 | ... | ... | 201 047 | ... | ... |
| | General education | | ... | ... | ... | ... | ... | ... |
| | Teacher training | | ... | ... | ... | ... | ... | ... |
| | Vocational education | | ... | ... | ... | ... | ... | ... |
| | Total | 1993 | 10 979 | ... | ... | 206 509 | ... | ... |
| | General education | | ... | ... | ... | ... | ... | ... |
| | Teacher training | | ... | ... | ... | ... | ... | ... |
| | Vocational education | | ... | ... | ... | ... | ... | ... |
| | Total | 1994 | 11 440 | ... | ... | 208 775 | ... | ... |
| | General education | | ... | ... | ... | ... | ... | ... |
| | Teacher training | | ... | ... | ... | ... | ... | ... |
| | Vocational education | | ... | ... | ... | ... | ... | ... |
| | Total | 1995 | 11 817 | ... | ... | 216 210 | ... | ... |
| | General education | | ... | ... | ... | ... | ... | ... |
| | Teacher training | | ... | ... | ... | ... | ... | ... |
| | Vocational education | | ... | ... | ... | ... | ... | ... |
| | Total | 1996 | 12 239 | ... | ... | 221 022 | ... | ... |
| | General education | | ... | ... | ... | ... | ... | ... |
| | Teacher training | | ... | ... | ... | ... | ... | ... |
| | Vocational education | | ... | ... | ... | ... | ... | ... |
| St. Kitts and Nevis | Total | 1975/76 | ... | ... | ... | ... | ... | ... |
| | General education | | ... | ... | ... | 4 740 | 2 430 | 51 |
| | Teacher training | | - | - | - | - | - | - |
| | Vocational education | | ... | | | | | |
| | Total | 1980/81 | ... | ... | ... | ... | ... | ... |
| | General education | | ... | ... | ... | 4 214 | 2 053 | 49 |
| | Teacher training | | - | - | - | - | - | - |
| | Vocational education | | ... | | | | | |
| | Total | 1985/86 | 275 | 148 | 54 | 4 197 | *2 046 | *49 |
| | General education | | 275 | 148 | 54 | 4 197 | *2 046 | *49 |
| | Teacher training | | - | - | - | - | - | - |
| | Vocational education | | - | - | - | - | - | - |
| | Total | 1991/92 | 294 | 164 | 56 | 4 396 | 2 225 | 51 |
| | General education | | 294 | 164 | 56 | 4 396 | 2 225 | 51 |
| | Teacher training | | - | - | - | - | - | - |
| | Vocational education | | - | - | - | - | - | - |
| | Total | 1992/93 | *322 | *190 | *59 | 4 402 | 2 242 | 51 |
| | General education | | *322 | *190 | *59 | 4 402 | 2 242 | 51 |
| | Teacher training | | - | - | - | - | - | - |
| | Vocational education | | - | - | - | - | - | - |
| St. Lucia | Total | 1975/76 | 297 | 115 | 39 | 4 522 | ... | ... |
| | General education | | 231 | 97 | 42 | 4 136 | 2 325 | 56 |
| | Teacher training | | 25 | 13 | 52 | 156 | ... | ... |
| | Vocational education | | 41 | 5 | 12 | 230 | 59 | 26 |
| | Total | 1980/81 | ... | ... | ... | 4 485 | 2 461 | 55 |
| | General education | | 229 | 120 | 52 | 4 306 | 2 400 | 56 |
| | Teacher training | | - | - | - | - | - | - |
| | Vocational education | | ... | ... | ... | 179 | 61 | 34 |
| | Total | 1985/86 | ... | ... | ... | 6 833 | 4 186 | 61 |
| | General education | | 331 | 193 | 58 | 6 239 | 3 592 | 58 |
| | Teacher training | | - | - | - | - | - | - |
| | Vocational education | | ... | ... | ... | 594 | 594 | 100 |
| | Total | 1990/91 | ... | ... | ... | 8 230 | *4 864 | *59 |
| | General education | | *427 | *264 | *62 | 7 959 | *4 604 | *58 |
| | Teacher training | | - | - | - | - | - | - |
| | Vocational education | | ... | ... | ... | 271 | *260 | *96 |
| | Total | 1991/92 | 514 | 318 | 62 | 9 419 | 5 713 | 61 |
| | General education | | 495 | 300 | 61 | 8 825 | 5 176 | 59 |
| | Teacher training | | - | - | - | - | - | - |
| | Vocational education | | 19 | 18 | 95 | 594 | 537 | 90 |
| | Total | 1992/93 | 558 | 350 | 63 | 10 356 | 6 476 | 63 |
| | General education | | 524 | 321 | 61 | 9 550 | 5 710 | 60 |
| | Teacher training | | - | - | - | - | - | - |
| | Vocational education | | 34 | 29 | 85 | 806 | 766 | 95 |
| | Total | 1996/97 | 682 | 405 | 59 | 11 753 | 6 605 | 56 |
| | General education | | - | - | - | ... | ... | ... |
| | Teacher training | | - | - | - | ... | ... | ... |
| | Vocational education | | ... | ... | ... | ... | ... | ... |

II.6
Secondary education: teaching staff and pupils
Enseignement secondaire: personnel enseignant et élèves
Enseñanza secundaria: personal docente y alumnos

| Country / Pays / País | Type of education / Type d'enseignement / Tipo de enseñanza | Year / Année / Año | Teaching staff Personnel enseignant Personal docente | | | Pupils enrolled Elèves inscrits Alumnos matriculados | | |
|---|---|---|---|---|---|---|---|---|
| | | | Total | Female Féminin Femenino | % F | Total | Female Féminin Femenino | % F |
| St. Pierre and Miquelon | Total | 1970/71 | 39 | 15 | 38 | 377 | 191 | 51 |
| | General education | | 28 | 11 | 39 | 302 | 159 | 53 |
| | Teacher training | | - | - | - | - | - | - |
| | Vocational education | | 11 | 4 | 36 | 75 | 32 | 43 |
| | Total | 1980/81 | 62 | 31 | 50 | 748 | 392 | 52 |
| | General education | | 49 | 28 | 57 | 527 | 278 | 53 |
| | Teacher training | | - | - | - | - | - | - |
| | Vocational education | | 13 | 3 | 23 | 221 | 114 | 52 |
| | Total | 1985/86 | 74 | 36 | 49 | 821 | 432 | 53 |
| | General education | | 58 | 32 | 55 | 556 | 297 | 53 |
| | Teacher training | | - | - | - | - | - | - |
| | Vocational education | | 16 | 4 | 25 | 265 | 135 | 51 |
| St. Vincent and the Grenadines | Total | 1970/71 | ... | ... | ... | 3 158 | 1 564 | 50 |
| | General education | | ... | ... | ... | 3 073 | 1 524 | 50 |
| | Teacher training | | 20 | 5 | 25 | 85 | 40 | 47 |
| | Vocational education | | - | - | - | - | - | - |
| | Total | 1975/76 | 243 | 104 | 43 | 5 084 | 2 974 | 58 |
| | General education | | 217 | 94 | 43 | 4 685 | 2 771 | 59 |
| | Teacher training | | 14 | 8 | 57 | 291 | 172 | 59 |
| | Vocational education | | 12 | 2 | 17 | 108 | 31 | 29 |
| | Total | 1990/91 | 431 | 226 | 52 | 10 719 | 5 867 | 55 |
| | General education | | 382 | 212 | 55 | 10 305 | 5 584 | 54 |
| | Teacher training | | 12 | 5 | 42 | 118 | 72 | 61 |
| | Vocational education | | 37 | 9 | 24 | 296 | 211 | 71 |
| | Total | 1993/94 | ... | ... | ... | ... | ... | ... |
| | General education | | 395 | 202 | 51 | 9 870 | 5 497 | 56 |
| | Teacher training | | ... | ... | ... | ... | ... | ... |
| | Vocational education | | ... | ... | ... | ... | ... | ... |
| Trinidad and Tobago | Total | 1970/71 | ... | ... | ... | 52 639 | 27 257 | 52 |
| | General education | | 1 894 | 866 | 46 | 49 810 | 26 430 | 53 |
| | Teacher training | | - | - | - | - | - | - |
| | Vocational education | | ... | ... | ... | 2 829 | 827 | 29 |
| | Total | 1975/76 | ... | ... | ... | ... | ... | ... |
| | General education | | ... | ... | ... | 64 039 | 32 134 | 50 |
| | Teacher training | | - | - | - | - | - | - |
| | Vocational education | | ... | ... | ... | ... | ... | ... |
| | Total | 1980/81 | 4 377 | ... | ... | 87 700 | ... | ... |
| | General education | | ... | ... | ... | 86 833 | ... | ... |
| | Teacher training | | - | - | - | - | - | - |
| | Vocational education | | ... | ... | ... | 867 | 327 | 38 |
| | Total | 1985/86 | ... | ... | ... | 95 302 | ... | ... |
| | General education | | ... | ... | ... | 94 564 | ... | ... |
| | Teacher training | | - | - | - | - | - | - |
| | Vocational education | | ... | ... | ... | 738 | 255 | 35 |
| | Total | 1990/91 | ... | ... | ... | 97 493 | 49 069 | 50 |
| | General education | | 4 839 | 2 605 | 54 | 96 599 | 48 810 | 50 |
| | Teacher training | | - | - | - | - | - | - |
| | Vocational education | | ... | ... | ... | 894 | 259 | 29 |
| | Total | 1991/92 | ... | ... | ... | 97 804 | 48 820 | 50 |
| | General education | | 4 844 | 2 602 | 54 | 97 253 | 48 710 | 50 |
| | Teacher training | | - | - | - | - | - | - |
| | Vocational education | | ... | ... | ... | 551 | 110 | 20 |
| | Total | 1992/93 | ... | ... | ... | 100 278 | 50 287 | 50 |
| | General education | | 4 920 | 2 712 | 55 | 99 590 | 50 174 | 50 |
| | Teacher training | | - | - | - | - | - | - |
| | Vocational education | | ... | ... | ... | 688 | 113 | 16 |
| | Total | 1993/94 | ... | ... | ... | ... | ... | ... |
| | General education | | 4 882 | 2 750 | 56 | 100 609 | 50 923 | 51 |
| | Teacher training | | ... | ... | ... | ... | ... | ... |
| | Vocational education | | ... | ... | ... | ... | ... | ... |
| | Total | 1995/96 | ... | ... | ... | ... | ... | ... |
| | General education | | 4 923 | 2 766 | 56 | 103 016 | 52 404 | 51 |
| | Teacher training | | - | - | - | - | - | - |
| | Vocational education | | ... | ... | ... | ... | ... | ... |
| | Total | 1996/97 | ... | ... | ... | ... | ... | ... |
| | General education | | 5 070 | 2 883 | 57 | 104 349 | 53 253 | 51 |
| | Teacher training | | - | - | - | - | - | - |
| | Vocational education | | ... | ... | ... | ... | ... | ... |
| Turks and Caicos Islands | Total | 1970/71 | 18 | 6 | 33 | 227 | ... | ... |
| | General education | | 18 | 6 | 33 | 227 | ... | ... |
| | Teacher training | | - | - | - | - | - | - |
| | Vocational education | | - | - | - | - | - | - |

Secondary education: teaching staff and pupils
Enseignement secondaire: personnel enseignant et élèves
Enseñanza secundaria: personal docente y alumnos

II.6

| Country<br>Pays<br>País | Type of education<br>Type d'enseignement<br>Tipo de enseñanza | Year<br>Année<br>Año | Teaching staff<br>Personnel enseignant<br>Personal docente | | | | Pupils enrolled<br>Elèves inscrits<br>Alumnos matriculados | | |
|---|---|---|---|---|---|---|---|---|---|
| | | | Total | Female<br>Féminin<br>Femenino | %<br>F | | Total | Female<br>Féminin<br>Femenino | %<br>F |
| Turks and Caicos Islands (cont) | Total | 1975/76 | 35 | *13 | *37 | | 671 | ... | ... |
| | General education | | 35 | *13 | *37 | | 671 | ... | ... |
| | Teacher training | | - | - | - | | - | - | - |
| | Vocational education | | - | - | - | | - | - | - |
| | Total | 1980/81 | 47 | 28 | 60 | | 691 | ... | ... |
| | General education | | 47 | 28 | 60 | | 691 | ... | ... |
| | Teacher training | | - | - | - | | - | - | - |
| | Vocational education | | - | - | - | | - | - | - |
| | Total | 1993/94 | 101 | 64 | 63 | | 1 032 | 519 | 50 |
| | General education | | 71 | 50 | 70 | | 943 | 460 | 49 |
| | Teacher training | | - | - | - | | - | - | - |
| | Vocational education | | 30 | 14 | 47 | | 89 | 59 | 66 |
| | Total | 1996/97 | ... | ... | ... | | ... | ... | ... |
| | General education | | ... | ... | ... | | 1 028 | 519 | 50 |
| | Teacher training | | - | - | - | | - | - | - |
| | Vocational education | | ... | ... | ... | | ... | ... | ... |
| U. S. Virgin Islands | Total | 1975/76 | 592 | ... | ... | | 10 590 | ... | ... |
| | General education | | ... | ... | ... | | ... | ... | ... |
| | Teacher training | | - | - | - | | - | - | - |
| | Vocational education | | ... | ... | ... | | ... | ... | ... |
| | Total | 1980/81 | (4) 617 | ... | ... | | 11 326 | ... | ... |
| | General education | | (4) 617 | ... | ... | | 11 326 | ... | ... |
| | Teacher training | | - | - | - | | - | - | - |
| | Vocational education | | - | - | - | | - | - | - |
| | Total | 1985/86 | ... | ... | ... | | 13 548 | ... | ... |
| | General education | | ... | ... | ... | | 13 548 | ... | ... |
| | Teacher training | | - | - | - | | - | - | - |
| | Vocational education | | - | - | - | | - | - | - |
| | Total | 1990/91 | ... | ... | ... | (4) | 10 050 | (4) 5 568 | 55 |
| | General education | | ... | ... | ... | (4) | 10 050 | (4) 5 568 | 55 |
| | Teacher training | | - | - | - | | - | - | - |
| | Vocational education | | - | - | - | | - | - | - |
| | Total | 1992/93 | ... | ... | ... | | 12 502 | 6 191 | 50 |
| | General education | | ... | ... | ... | | 12 502 | 6 191 | 50 |
| | Teacher training | | - | - | - | | - | - | - |
| | Vocational education | | - | - | - | | - | - | - |
| United States | Total | 1970/71 | ... | ... | ... | | 20 593 000 | ... | ... |
| | General education | | ... | ... | ... | | 20 593 000 | ... | ... |
| | Teacher training | | - | - | - | | - | - | - |
| | Vocational education | | - | - | - | | - | - | - |
| | Total | 1975/76 | ... | ... | ... | | 21 680 000 | ... | ... |
| | General education | | ... | ... | ... | | 21 680 000 | ... | ... |
| | Teacher training | | - | - | - | | - | - | - |
| | Vocational education | | - | - | - | | - | - | - |
| | Total | 1980/81 | ... | ... | ... | | 21 585 000 | 10 631 000 | 49 |
| | General education | | ... | ... | ... | | 21 585 000 | 10 631 000 | 49 |
| | Teacher training | | - | - | - | | - | - | - |
| | Vocational education | | - | - | - | | - | - | - |
| | Total | 1985/86 | ... | ... | ... | | 20 633 000 | 10 094 000 | 49 |
| | General education | | ... | ... | ... | | 20 633 000 | 10 094 000 | 49 |
| | Teacher training | | - | - | - | | - | - | - |
| | Vocational education | | - | - | - | | - | - | - |
| | Total | 1990/91 | ... | ... | ... | | 19 270 000 | 9 473 000 | 49 |
| | General education | | ... | ... | ... | | 19 270 000 | 9 473 000 | 49 |
| | Teacher training | | - | - | - | | - | - | - |
| | Vocational education | | - | - | - | | - | - | - |
| | Total | 1992/93 | 1 320 775 | 734 456 | 56 | | 20 516 146 | 10 000 943 | 49 |
| | General education | | 1 320 775 | 734 456 | 56 | | 20 516 146 | 10 000 943 | 49 |
| | Teacher training | | - | - | - | | - | - | - |
| | Vocational education | | - | - | - | | - | - | - |
| | Total | 1993/94 | 1 341 314 | 745 895 | 56 | | 21 055 473 | 10 228 972 | 49 |
| | General education | | 1 341 314 | 745 895 | 56 | | 21 055 473 | 10 228 972 | 49 |
| | Teacher training | | - | - | - | | - | - | - |
| | Vocational education | | - | - | - | | - | - | - |
| | Total | 1994/95 | 1 369 314 | 761 518 | 56 | | 21 122 633 | 10 373 671 | 49 |
| | General education | | 1 369 314 | 761 518 | 56 | | 21 122 633 | 10 373 671 | 49 |
| | Teacher training | | - | - | - | | - | - | - |
| | Vocational education | | - | - | - | | - | - | - |
| | Total | 1995/96 | 1 394 080 | 775 294 | 56 | | 21 473 692 | 10 471 227 | 49 |
| | General education | | 1 394 080 | 775 294 | 56 | | 21 473 692 | 10 471 227 | 49 |
| | Teacher training | | - | - | - | | - | - | - |
| | Vocational education | | - | - | - | | - | - | - |

II.6    Secondary education: teaching staff and pupils
Enseignement secondaire: personnel enseignant et élèves
Enseñanza secundaria: personal docente y alumnos

| Country / Pays / País | Type of education / Type d'enseignement / Tipo de enseñanza | Year / Année / Año | Teaching staff / Personnel enseignant / Personal docente | | | Pupils enrolled / Elèves inscrits / Alumnos matriculados | | |
|---|---|---|---|---|---|---|---|---|
| | | | Total | Female / Féminin / Femenino | % F | Total | Female / Féminin / Femenino | % F |
| **South America** | | | | | | | | |
| Argentina | Total | 1970 | 134 264 | 83 047 | 62 | 976 979 | 512 830 | 52 |
| | General education | | 57 785 | 41 849 | 72 | 405 435 | 246 911 | 61 |
| | Teacher training | | 192 | 149 | 78 | 566 | 549 | 97 |
| | Vocational education | | 76 287 | 41 049 | 54 | 570 978 | 265 370 | 46 |
| | Total | 1975 | 161 859 | 101 216 | 63 | 1 243 058 | 650 902 | 52 |
| | General education | | 62 334 | 45 526 | 73 | 454 194 | 275 784 | 61 |
| | Teacher training | | - | - | - | - | - | - |
| | Vocational education | | 99 525 | 55 690 | 56 | 788 864 | 375 118 | 48 |
| | Total | 1980 | ... | ... | ... | 1 326 680 | ... | ... |
| | General education | | ... | ... | ... | 510 080 | ... | ... |
| | Teacher training | | - | ... | ... | - | ... | ... |
| | Vocational education | | ... | ... | ... | 816 600 | ... | ... |
| | Total | 1985 | 230 093 | 151 168 | 66 | 1 800 049 | 942 768 | 52 |
| | General education | | 93 675 | 69 472 | 74 | 715 518 | 442 107 | 62 |
| | Teacher training | | - | - | - | - | - | - |
| | Vocational education | | 136 418 | 81 696 | 60 | 1 084 531 | 500 661 | 46 |
| | Total | 1990 | ... | ... | ... | 2 160 410 | ... | ... |
| | General education | | ... | ... | ... | ... | ... | ... |
| | Teacher training | | ... | ... | ... | ... | ... | ... |
| | Vocational education | | ... | ... | ... | ... | ... | ... |
| | Total | 1991 | ... | ... | ... | 2 263 263 | ... | ... |
| | General education | | ... | ... | ... | ... | ... | ... |
| | Teacher training | | ... | ... | ... | ... | ... | ... |
| | Vocational education | | ... | ... | ... | ... | ... | ... |
| | Total | 1994 | 238 791 | 156 668 | 66 | 2 307 821 | ... | ... |
| | General education | | ... | ... | ... | ... | ... | ... |
| | Teacher training | | ... | ... | ... | ... | ... | ... |
| | Vocational education | | ... | ... | ... | ... | ... | ... |
| | Total | 1996 (34) | 125 218 | ... | ... | 2 594 329 | 1 347 990 | 52 |
| | General education | | ... | ... | ... | ... | ... | ... |
| | Teacher training | | ... | ... | ... | ... | ... | ... |
| | Vocational education | | ... | ... | ... | ... | ... | ... |
| Bolivia | Total | 1970 | ... | ... | ... | 89 631 | ... | ... |
| | General education | | 4 370 | ... | ... | 75 146 | 29 462 | 39 |
| | Teacher training | | 344 | ... | ... | 4 356 | 1 679 | 39 |
| | Vocational education | | | | | 10 129 | ... | ... |
| | Total | 1975 | 7 143 | ... | ... | 130 029 | ... | ... |
| | General education | | ... | ... | ... | ... | ... | ... |
| | Teacher training | | ... | ... | ... | ... | ... | ... |
| | Vocational education | | ... | ... | ... | ... | ... | ... |
| | Total | 1980 | ... | ... | ... | 170 710 | 73 991 | 43 |
| | General education | | ... | ... | ... | ... | ... | ... |
| | Teacher training | | ... | ... | ... | ... | ... | ... |
| | Vocational education | | ... | ... | ... | ... | ... | ... |
| | Total | 1990 | 12 434 | 6 094 | 49 | 219 232 | 100 748 | 46 |
| | General education | | ... | ... | ... | ... | ... | ... |
| | Teacher training | | ... | ... | ... | ... | ... | ... |
| | Vocational education | | ... | ... | ... | ... | ... | ... |
| Brazil | Total | 1970 | 308 552 | 164 457 | 53 | 4 086 073 | 2 062 069 | 50 |
| | General education | | 208 312 | 114 244 | 55 | 3 055 652 | 1 516 877 | 50 |
| | Teacher training | | 39 423 | 28 174 | 71 | 347 873 | 289 055 | 83 |
| | Vocational education | | 60 817 | 22 039 | 36 | 682 548 | 256 137 | 38 |
| | Total | 1975 (35) | 133 070 | ... | ... | (35) 1 935 903 | (35) 1 033 096 | 53 |
| | General education | | ... | ... | ... | (35) 882 059 | (35) 563 427 | 64 |
| | Teacher training | | ... | ... | ... | 271 337 | 246 838 | 91 |
| | Vocational education | | ... | ... | ... | 782 507 | 222 831 | 28 |
| | Total | 1980 | 198 087 | 105 945 | 53 | 2 819 182 | 1 515 859 | 54 |
| | General education | | ... | ... | ... | ... | ... | ... |
| | Teacher training | | ... | ... | ... | ... | ... | ... |
| | Vocational education | | ... | ... | ... | ... | ... | ... |
| | Total | 1985 | 206 124 | ... | ... | 3 016 175 | ... | ... |
| | General education | | ... | ... | ... | 998 725 | ... | ... |
| | Teacher training | | ... | ... | ... | 536 453 | ... | ... |
| | Vocational education | | ... | ... | ... | 1 480 997 | ... | ... |
| | Total | 1990 | 243 246 | ... | ... | 3 498 777 | ... | ... |
| | General education | | ... | ... | ... | ... | ... | ... |
| | Teacher training | | ... | ... | ... | ... | ... | ... |
| | Vocational education | | ... | ... | ... | ... | ... | ... |

Secondary education: teaching staff and pupils
Enseignement secondaire: personnel enseignant et élèves
Enseñanza secundaria: personal docente y alumnos

II.6

| Country<br>Pays<br>País | Type of education<br>Type d'enseignement<br>Tipo de enseñanza | Year<br>Année<br>Año | Teaching staff<br>Personnel enseignant<br>Personal docente | | | Pupils enrolled<br>Elèves inscrits<br>Alumnos matriculados | | |
|---|---|---|---|---|---|---|---|---|
| | | | Total | Female<br>Féminin<br>Femenino | %<br>F | Total | Female<br>Féminin<br>Femenino | %<br>F |
| Brazil (cont) | Total | 1991 | 259 380 | ... | ... | 3 770 230 | ... | ... |
| | General education | | ... | ... | ... | ... | ... | ... |
| | Teacher training | | ... | ... | ... | ... | ... | ... |
| | Vocational education | | ... | ... | ... | ... | ... | ... |
| | Total | 1992 | ... | ... | ... | 4 085 631 | ... | ... |
| | General education | | ... | ... | ... | ... | ... | ... |
| | Teacher training | | ... | ... | ... | ... | ... | ... |
| | Vocational education | | ... | ... | ... | ... | ... | ... |
| | Total | 1993 | 273 539 | ... | ... | 4 183 847 | ... | ... |
| | General education | | ... | ... | ... | ... | ... | ... |
| | Teacher training | | ... | ... | ... | ... | ... | ... |
| | Vocational education | | ... | ... | ... | ... | ... | ... |
| | Total | 1994 | 295 542 | ... | ... | 4 510 199 | ... | ... |
| | General education | | ... | ... | ... | ... | ... | ... |
| | Teacher training | | ... | ... | ... | ... | ... | ... |
| | Vocational education | | ... | ... | ... | ... | ... | ... |
| | Total | 1996 | 326 827 | ... | ... | 5 739 077 | ... | ... |
| | General education | | ... | ... | ... | ... | ... | ... |
| | Teacher training | | ... | ... | ... | ... | ... | ... |
| | Vocational education | | ... | ... | ... | ... | ... | ... |
| | Total | 1997 | 352 894 | ... | ... | 6 405 057 | ... | ... |
| | General education | | ... | ... | ... | ... | ... | ... |
| | Teacher training | | ... | ... | ... | ... | ... | ... |
| | Vocational education | | ... | ... | ... | ... | ... | ... |
| | Total | 1998 | ... | ... | ... | 6 967 905 | ... | ... |
| | General education | | ... | ... | ... | ... | ... | ... |
| | Teacher training | | ... | ... | ... | ... | ... | ... |
| | Vocational education | | ... | ... | ... | ... | ... | ... |
| Chile | Total | 1970 | ... | ... | ... | 302 064 | 160 305 | 53 |
| | General education | | ... | ... | ... | 202 506 | 114 613 | 57 |
| | Teacher training | | - | - | - | - | - | - |
| | Vocational education | | ... | ... | ... | 99 558 | 45 692 | 46 |
| | Total | 1975 | 29 567 | 14 730 | 50 | 448 911 | 238 533 | 53 |
| | General education | | 17 799 | 9 802 | 55 | 285 806 | 166 363 | 58 |
| | Teacher training | | - | - | - | - | - | - |
| | Vocational education | | 11 768 | 4 928 | 42 | 163 105 | 72 170 | 44 |
| | Total | 1980 | ... | ... | ... | 538 309 | 284 784 | 53 |
| | General education | | ... | ... | ... | 369 180 | 204 802 | 55 |
| | Teacher training | | - | - | - | - | - | - |
| | Vocational education | | ... | ... | ... | 169 129 | 79 982 | 47 |
| | Total | 1985 | ... | ... | ... | 667 797 | 344 631 | 52 |
| | General education | | ... | ... | ... | 539 150 | 280 767 | 52 |
| | Teacher training | | - | - | - | - | - | - |
| | Vocational education | | ... | ... | ... | 128 647 | 63 864 | 50 |
| | Total | 1990 | ... | ... | ... | 719 819 | 369 855 | 51 |
| | General education | | ... | ... | ... | 464 423 | 247 932 | 53 |
| | Teacher training | | - | - | - | - | - | - |
| | Vocational education | | ... | ... | ... | 255 396 | 121 923 | 48 |
| | Total | 1991 | 49 082 | 26 049 | 53 | 699 455 | 357 440 | 51 |
| | General education | | ... | ... | ... | 436 892 | 232 116 | 53 |
| | Teacher training | | - | - | - | - | - | - |
| | Vocational education | | ... | ... | ... | 262 563 | 125 324 | 48 |
| | Total | 1992 | ... | ... | ... | 675 073 | 344 731 | 51 |
| | General education | | ... | ... | ... | 410 896 | 220 042 | 54 |
| | Teacher training | | - | - | - | - | - | - |
| | Vocational education | | ... | ... | ... | 264 177 | 124 689 | 47 |
| | Total | 1993 | ... | ... | ... | 652 815 | 334 298 | 51 |
| | General education | | ... | ... | ... | 391 457 | 210 283 | 54 |
| | Teacher training | | - | - | - | - | - | - |
| | Vocational education | | ... | ... | ... | 261 358 | 124 015 | 47 |
| | Total | 1994 | 50 187 | 26 314 | 52 | 664 498 | 338 177 | 51 |
| | General education | | ... | ... | ... | 387 272 | 209 116 | 54 |
| | Teacher training | | - | - | - | - | - | - |
| | Vocational education | | ... | ... | ... | 277 226 | 129 061 | 47 |
| | Total | 1995 | 51 042 | 26 762 | 52 | 679 165 | 349 703 | 51 |
| | General education | | ... | ... | ... | 388 117 | 209 871 | 54 |
| | Teacher training | | - | - | - | - | - | - |
| | Vocational education | | ... | ... | ... | 291 048 | 139 832 | 48 |
| | Total | 1996 | ... | ... | ... | 739 316 | 377 256 | 51 |
| | General education | | ... | ... | ... | 415 919 | 224 967 | 54 |
| | Teacher training | | - | - | - | - | - | - |
| | Vocational education | | ... | ... | ... | 323 397 | 152 289 | 47 |

II.6   Secondary education: teaching staff and pupils
Enseignement secondaire: personnel enseignant et élèves
Enseñanza secundaria: personal docente y alumnos

| Country / Pays / País | Type of education / Type d'enseignement / Tipo de enseñanza | Year / Année / Año | Teaching staff / Personnel enseignant / Personal docente | | | Pupils enrolled / Elèves inscrits / Alumnos matriculados | | |
|---|---|---|---|---|---|---|---|---|
| | | | Total | Female Féminin Femenino | % F | Total | Female Féminin Femenino | % F |
| Colombia | Total | 1970 | 43 695 | ... | ... | 750 055 | 365 652 | 49 |
| | General education | | 33 637 | ... | ... | 538 479 | 226 674 | 42 |
| | Teacher training | | ... | ... | ... | 59 990 | 46 192 | 77 |
| | Vocational education | | ... | ... | ... | 151 586 | 92 786 | 61 |
| | Total | 1975 | 70 451 | 29 237 | 41 | 1 370 567 | 683 639 | 50 |
| | General education | | 50 480 | 20 292 | 40 | 1 031 237 | 512 381 | 50 |
| | Teacher training | | 4 897 | 2 962 | 60 | 82 843 | 61 323 | 74 |
| | Vocational education | | 15 074 | 5 983 | 40 | 256 487 | 109 935 | 43 |
| | Total | 1980 | 85 135 | 35 756 | 42 | 1 733 192 | 870 276 | 50 |
| | General education | | 61 836 | 25 290 | 41 | 1 313 004 | 660 502 | 50 |
| | Teacher training | | 4 096 | 2 433 | 59 | 67 583 | 50 958 | 75 |
| | Vocational education | | 19 203 | 8 033 | 42 | 352 605 | 158 816 | 45 |
| | Total | 1985 | 95 981 | ... | ... | 1 934 032 | 965 082 | 50 |
| | General education | | 69 871 | ... | ... | 1 468 709 | 731 399 | 50 |
| | Teacher training | | 3 817 | ... | ... | 60 721 | 33 631 | 55 |
| | Vocational education | | 22 293 | ... | ... | 404 602 | 200 052 | 49 |
| | Total | 1991 | 119 742 | ... | ... | 2 377 947 | 1 274 580 | 54 |
| | General education | | 86 522 | ... | ... | 1 781 599 | 911 400 | 51 |
| | Teacher training | | 4 933 | ... | ... | 85 622 | 61 618 | 72 |
| | Vocational education | | 28 287 | ... | ... | 510 726 | 301 562 | 59 |
| | Total | 1992 | 130 514 | ... | ... | 2 686 515 | 1 442 659 | 54 |
| | General education | | 93 944 | ... | ... | 2 011 662 | ... | ... |
| | Teacher training | | 5 455 | ... | ... | 93 491 | ... | ... |
| | Vocational education | | 31 115 | ... | ... | 581 362 | ... | ... |
| | Total | 1993 | 134 161 | ... | ... | 2 796 007 | 1 498 660 | 54 |
| | General education | | 97 896 | ... | ... | 2 118 205 | ... | ... |
| | Teacher training | | 5 231 | ... | ... | 90 900 | ... | ... |
| | Vocational education | | 31 034 | ... | ... | 586 902 | ... | ... |
| | Total | 1994 | 140 181 | ... | ... | 2 935 830 | ... | ... |
| | General education | | ... | ... | ... | ... | ... | ... |
| | Teacher training | | ... | ... | ... | ... | ... | ... |
| | Vocational education | | ... | ... | ... | ... | ... | ... |
| | Total | 1995 | 143 731 | ... | ... | 3 025 350 | 1 596 506 | 53 |
| | General education | | ... | ... | ... | ... | ... | ... |
| | Teacher training | | ... | ... | ... | ... | ... | ... |
| | Vocational education | | ... | ... | ... | ... | ... | ... |
| | Total | 1996 | *169 816 | *81 661 | *48 | 3 317 782 | 1 687 248 | 51 |
| | General education | | ... | ... | ... | 2 403 118 | 1 179 407 | 49 |
| | Teacher training | | *3 840 | *2 220 | *58 | 65 654 | 47 352 | 72 |
| | Vocational education | | ... | ... | ... | 849 010 | 460 489 | 54 |
| Ecuador | Total | 1970/71 | 15 699 | 5 141 | 33 | 216 727 | 98 500 | 45 |
| | General education | | 11 160 | 3 512 | 31 | ... | ... | ... |
| | Teacher training | | 1 052 | 457 | 43 | 10 203 | 6 405 | 63 |
| | Vocational education | | 3 487 | 1 172 | 34 | ... | ... | ... |
| | Total | 1975/76 | 23 446 | 8 315 | 35 | 383 624 | 182 678 | 48 |
| | General education | | 18 335 | 6 514 | 36 | 339 771 | 156 333 | 46 |
| | Teacher training | | 130 | 31 | 24 | 913 | 488 | 53 |
| | Vocational education | | 4 981 | 1 770 | 36 | 42 940 | 25 857 | 60 |
| | Total | 1980/81 | 34 868 | ... | ... | 591 969 | ... | ... |
| | General education | | 27 048 | 10 278 | 38 | 516 548 | 246 141 | 48 |
| | Teacher training | | 258 | 65 | 25 | 4 945 | 3 452 | 70 |
| | Vocational education | | 7 562 | ... | ... | 70 476 | ... | ... |
| | Total | 1985/86 | 47 506 | 19 440 | 41 | 730 226 | 367 342 | 50 |
| | General education | | (22) 33 557 | (22) 13 728 | 41 | 488 078 | 230 458 | 47 |
| | Teacher training | | ./. | ./. | ./. | 7 677 | 5 007 | 65 |
| | Vocational education | | 13 949 | 5 712 | 41 | (36) 234 471 | (36) 131 877 | 56 |
| | Total | 1990/91 | ... | ... | ... | ... | ... | ... |
| | General education | | (1) 60 126 | ... | ... | (1) 785 844 | ... | ... |
| | Teacher training | | ... | ... | ... | ... | ... | ... |
| | Vocational education | | ./. | ... | ... | ./. | ... | ... |
| | Total | 1991/92 | ... | ... | ... | ... | ... | ... |
| | General education | | (1) 61 396 | ... | ... | (1) 811 666 | ... | ... |
| | Teacher training | | ... | ... | ... | ... | ... | ... |
| | Vocational education | | ./. | ... | ... | ./. | ... | ... |
| | Total | 1992/93 | ... | ... | ... | 814 359 | 405 655 | 50 |
| | General education | | (1) 62 630 | (1) 27 708 | 44 | 534 368 | 252 876 | 47 |
| | Teacher training | | ... | ... | ... | 802 | 427 | 53 |
| | Vocational education | | ./. | ./. | ./. | 279 189 | 152 352 | 55 |
| Falkland Islands (Malvinas) | Total | 1975 | ... | ... | ... | 126 | 55 | 44 |
| | General education | | ... | ... | ... | 126 | 55 | 44 |
| | Teacher training | | - | - | - | - | - | - |
| | Vocational education | | - | - | - | - | - | - |

Secondary education: teaching staff and pupils II.6
Enseignement secondaire: personnel enseignant et élèves
Enseñanza secundaria: personal docente y alumnos

| Country / Pays / País | Type of education / Type d'enseignement / Tipo de enseñanza | Year / Année / Año | Teaching staff / Personnel enseignant / Personal docente | | | Pupils enrolled / Elèves inscrits / Alumnos matriculados | | |
|---|---|---|---|---|---|---|---|---|
| | | | Total | Female Féminin Femenino | % F | Total | Female Féminin Femenino | % F |
| Falkland Islands (Malvinas) (cont) | Total | 1980 | 11 | 4 | 36 | 90 | 50 | 56 |
| | General education | | 11 | 4 | 36 | 90 | 50 | 56 |
| | Teacher training | | - | - | - | - | - | - |
| | Vocational education | | - | - | - | - | - | - |
| | Total | 1995 | ... | ... | ... | 147 | 72 | 49 |
| | General education | | ... | ... | ... | ... | ... | ... |
| | Teacher training | | ... | ... | ... | ... | ... | ... |
| | Vocational education | | ... | ... | ... | ... | ... | ... |
| French Guiana | Total | 1970/71 | 182 | ... | ... | 3 099 | *1 678 | *54 |
| | General education | | 114 | | ... | 2 213 | *1 298 | *59 |
| | Teacher training | | | - | - | | - | - |
| | Vocational education | | 68 | ... | ... | 886 | *380 | *43 |
| | Total | 1975/76 | 338 | ... | ... | 5 534 | 2 867 | 52 |
| | General education | | ... | ... | ... | (22) 3 998 | (22) 2 166 | 54 |
| | Teacher training | | ... | ... | ... | ./. | ./. | ./. |
| | Vocational education | | ... | ... | ... | 1 536 | 701 | 46 |
| | Total | 1980/81 | ... | ... | ... | 7 421 | ... | ... |
| | General education | | ... | ... | ... | ... | ... | ... |
| | Teacher training | | - | - | - | - | - | - |
| | Vocational education | | ... | ... | ... | ... | ... | ... |
| | Total | 1990/91 | ... | ... | ... | 10 722 | ... | ... |
| | General education | | ... | ... | ... | ... | ... | ... |
| | Teacher training | | - | - | - | - | - | - |
| | Vocational education | | ... | ... | ... | ... | ... | ... |
| | Total | 1993/94 | ... | ... | ... | 13 494 | 6 829 | 51 |
| | General education | | ... | ... | ... | 11 303 | 5 768 | 51 |
| | Teacher training | | - | | | - | | - |
| | Vocational education | | ... | ... | ... | 2 191 | 1 061 | 48 |
| | Total | 1994/95 | ... | ... | ... | 15 034 | 7 506 | 50 |
| | General education | | ... | ... | ... | 12 731 | 6 416 | 50 |
| | Teacher training | | - | - | - | - | - | - |
| | Vocational education | | ... | ... | ... | 2 303 | 1 090 | 47 |
| | Total | 1995/96 | 1 085 | 573 | 53 | 15 989 | 8 036 | 50 |
| | General education | | 875 | 474 | 54 | 13 585 | 6 849 | 50 |
| | Teacher training | | - | - | - | - | - | - |
| | Vocational education | | 210 | 99 | 47 | 2 404 | 1 187 | 49 |
| Guyana | Total | 1970/71 | ... | ... | ... | ... | ... | ... |
| | General education | | (5) 2 262 | (5) 1 063 | 47 | (5) 57 093 | (5) 28 958 | 51 |
| | Teacher training | | 30 | 17 | 57 | 259 | 136 | 53 |
| | Vocational education | | 72 | 16 | 22 | 3 060 | 1 442 | 47 |
| | Total | 1975/76 | ... | | ... | 71 327 | 36 021 | 51 |
| | General education | | 3 202 | 1 144 | 36 | 66 326 | 33 530 | 51 |
| | Teacher training | | - | - | - | - | - | - |
| | Vocational education | | ... | | ... | 5 001 | 2 491 | 50 |
| | Total | 1980/81 | ... | | | ... | ... | ... |
| | General education | | 4 236 | 1 897 | 45 | 75 335 | 38 504 | 51 |
| | Teacher training | | - | - | - | - | - | - |
| | Vocational education | | ... | ... | ... | ... | ... | ... |
| | Total | 1985/86 | ... | ... | ... | 76 546 | 39 289 | 51 |
| | General education | | ... | ... | ... | 72 679 | 37 984 | 52 |
| | Teacher training | | - | - | - | - | - | - |
| | Vocational education | | 237 | 46 | 19 | 3 867 | 1 305 | 34 |
| | Total | 1990/91 | 1 600 | 874 | 55 | 69 696 | 36 093 | 52 |
| | General education | | 1 600 | 874 | 55 | 69 696 | 36 093 | 52 |
| | Teacher training | | - | - | - | - | - | - |
| | Vocational education | | - | - | - | - | - | - |
| | Total | 1991/92 | 1 912 | 1 114 | 58 | 65 029 | 33 586 | 52 |
| | General education | | 1 912 | 1 114 | 58 | 65 029 | 33 586 | 52 |
| | Teacher training | | - | - | - | - | - | - |
| | Vocational education | | - | - | - | - | - | - |
| | Total | 1992/93 | 1 859 | 1 119 | 60 | 62 250 | 32 366 | 52 |
| | General education | | 1 859 | 1 119 | 60 | 62 250 | 32 366 | 52 |
| | Teacher training | | - | - | - | - | - | - |
| | Vocational education | | - | - | - | - | - | - |
| | Total | 1994/95 | 1 570 | 686 | 44 | 63 838 | 35 086 | 55 |
| | General education | | 1 570 | 686 | 44 | 63 838 | 35 086 | 55 |
| | Teacher training | | - | - | - | - | - | - |
| | Vocational education | | - | - | - | - | - | - |
| | Total | 1995/96 | 2 150 | 1 337 | 62 | 63 365 | 32 567 | 51 |
| | General education | | 2 150 | 1 337 | 62 | 63 365 | 32 567 | 51 |
| | Teacher training | | - | - | - | - | - | - |
| | Vocational education | | - | - | - | - | - | - |

II.6   Secondary education: teaching staff and pupils
       Enseignement secondaire: personnel enseignant et élèves
       Enseñanza secundaria: personal docente y alumnos

| Country / Pays / País | Type of education / Type d'enseignement / Tipo de enseñanza | Year / Année / Año | Teaching staff / Personnel enseignant / Personal docente | | | Pupils enrolled / Elèves inscrits / Alumnos matriculados | | |
|---|---|---|---|---|---|---|---|---|
| | | | Total | Female Féminin Femenino | % F | Total | Female Féminin Femenino | % F |
| Guyana (cont) | Total | 1996/97 | ... | ... | ... | 62 043 | 31 845 | 51 |
| | General education | | ... | ... | ... | 62 043 | 31 845 | 51 |
| | Teacher training | | - | - | - | - | - | - |
| | Vocational education | | - | - | - | - | - | - |
| Paraguay | Total | 1970 | 5 938 | 3 455 | 58 | 55 777 | 27 813 | 50 |
| | General education | | 4 170 | 2 366 | 57 | 48 742 | 23 157 | 48 |
| | Teacher training | | 1 003 | 776 | 77 | 3 545 | 3 170 | 89 |
| | Vocational education | | 765 | 313 | 41 | 3 490 | 1 486 | 43 |
| | Total | 1975 | ... | ... | ... | 75 424 | 37 363 | 50 |
| | General education | | | | | 70 048 | 36 107 | 52 |
| | Teacher training | | | | | - | - | - |
| | Vocational education | | ... | | ... | 5 376 | 1 256 | 23 |
| | Total | 1980 | | | | 118 828 | ... | ... |
| | General education | | ... | ... | ... | 111 905 | ... | ... |
| | Teacher training | | | | | - | - | - |
| | Vocational education | | ... | | ... | 6 923 | ... | ... |
| | Total | 1985 | | | | 150 736 | ... | ... |
| | General education | | ... | ... | ... | 141 461 | 69 997 | 49 |
| | Teacher training | | | | | - | - | - |
| | Vocational education | | ... | | ... | 9 275 | ... | ... |
| | Total | 1990 | ... | ... | ... | 163 734 | 82 123 | 50 |
| | General education | | ... | ... | ... | 153 206 | 77 382 | 51 |
| | Teacher training | | - | | - | - | - | - |
| | Vocational education | | ... | | ... | 10 528 | 4 741 | 45 |
| | Total | 1991 | 12 218 | 8 201 | 67 | 169 167 | 85 524 | 51 |
| | General education | | ... | ... | ... | 157 487 | 80 376 | 51 |
| | Teacher training | | | | | - | - | - |
| | Vocational education | | ... | | ... | 11 680 | 5 148 | 44 |
| | Total | 1992 | ... | ... | ... | 192 775 | 96 186 | 50 |
| | General education | | ... | ... | ... | 176 547 | ... | ... |
| | Teacher training | | | | | - | - | - |
| | Vocational education | | ... | | ... | 16 228 | ... | ... |
| | Total | 1993 | 20 793 | 13 711 | 66 | 214 272 | 108 463 | 51 |
| | General education | | - | - | - | 195 677 | ... | ... |
| | Teacher training | | | | | - | - | - |
| | Vocational education | | ... | | ... | 18 595 | ... | ... |
| | Total | 1994 | ... | ... | ... | 240 906 | 121 356 | 50 |
| | General education | | 17 668 | 11 430 | 65 | 220 512 | 112 536 | 51 |
| | Teacher training | | - | - | - | - | - | - |
| | Vocational education | | ... | ... | ... | 20 394 | 8 820 | 43 |
| | Total | 1995 | ... | ... | ... | 267 485 | 136 140 | 51 |
| | General education | | ... | ... | ... | 246 139 | ... | ... |
| | Teacher training | | - | - | - | - | - | - |
| | Vocational education | | ... | | ... | 21 346 | ... | ... |
| | Total | 1996 | ... | ... | ... | 293 651 | 148 592 | 51 |
| | General education | | ... | ... | ... | 270 207 | 136 385 | 50 |
| | Teacher training | | | | | - | - | - |
| | Vocational education | | ... | | ... | 23 444 | 12 207 | 52 |
| | Total | 1997 | ... | ... | ... | 327 775 | 165 780 | 51 |
| | General education | | ... | ... | ... | ... | ... | ... |
| | Teacher training | | ... | ... | ... | ... | ... | ... |
| | Vocational education | | ... | | ... | ... | ... | ... |
| Peru | Total | 1970 | 31 587 | ... | ... | 546 183 | 233 977 | 43 |
| | General education | | ... | ... | ... | 453 001 | 192 948 | 43 |
| | Teacher training | | - | | - | - | - | - |
| | Vocational education | | ... | | ... | 93 182 | 41 029 | 44 |
| | Total | 1980 | ... | ... | ... | 1 203 116 | 547 393 | 45 |
| | General education | | ... | ... | ... | 1 151 748 | 526 780 | 46 |
| | Teacher training | | - | | - | - | - | - |
| | Vocational education | | ... | | ... | 51 368 | 20 613 | 40 |
| | Total | 1985 | 68 541 | ... | ... | 1 427 261 | 667 399 | 47 |
| | General education | | 68 541 | ... | ... | 1 427 261 | 667 399 | 47 |
| | Teacher training | | - | | - | - | - | - |
| | Vocational education | | - | | - | - | - | - |
| | Total | 1990 | 86 247 | ... | ... | 1 697 943 | ... | ... |
| | General education | | 86 247 | ... | ... | 1 697 943 | ... | ... |
| | Teacher training | | - | | - | - | - | - |
| | Vocational education | | - | | - | - | - | - |
| | Total | 1991 | 86 918 | 41 286 | 47 | 1 710 715 | 814 813 | 48 |
| | General education | | 86 918 | 41 286 | 47 | 1 710 715 | 814 813 | 48 |
| | Teacher training | | - | | - | - | - | - |
| | Vocational education | | - | | - | - | - | - |

Secondary education: teaching staff and pupils  II.6
Enseignement secondaire: personnel enseignant et élèves
Enseñanza secundaria: personal docente y alumnos

| Country / Pays / País | Type of education / Type d'enseignement / Tipo de enseñanza | Year / Année / Año | Teaching staff / Personnel enseignant / Personal docente | | | Pupils enrolled / Elèves inscrits / Alumnos matriculados | | |
|---|---|---|---|---|---|---|---|---|
| | | | Total | Female Féminin Femenino | % F | Total | Female Féminin Femenino | % F |
| Peru (cont) | Total | 1992 | 87 624 | ... | ... | 1 703 997 | ... | ... |
| | General education | | 87 624 | ... | ... | 1 703 997 | ... | ... |
| | Teacher training | | - | - | - | - | - | - |
| | Vocational education | | - | - | - | - | - | - |
| | Total | 1993 | 85 023 | ... | ... | 1 719 854 | ... | ... |
| | General education | | 85 023 | ... | ... | 1 719 854 | ... | ... |
| | Teacher training | | - | - | - | - | - | - |
| | Vocational education | | - | - | - | - | - | - |
| | Total | 1994 | 100 698 | ... | ... | 1 833 783 | ... | ... |
| | General education | | 100 698 | ... | ... | 1 833 783 | ... | ... |
| | Teacher training | | - | - | - | - | - | - |
| | Vocational education | | - | - | - | - | - | - |
| | Total | 1995 | 97 873 | 38 288 | 39 | 1 862 728 | 887 256 | 48 |
| | General education | | 97 873 | 38 288 | 39 | 1 862 728 | 887 256 | 48 |
| | Teacher training | | - | - | - | - | - | - |
| | Vocational education | | - | - | - | - | - | - |
| | Total | 1996 | 102 952 | ... | ... | 1 930 917 | ... | ... |
| | General education | | 102 952 | ... | ... | 1 930 917 | ... | ... |
| | Teacher training | | - | - | - | - | ... | ... |
| | Vocational education | | - | - | - | - | ... | ... |
| | Total | 1997 | 106 614 | ... | ... | 1 969 501 | ... | ... |
| | General education | | 106 614 | ... | ... | 1 969 501 | ... | ... |
| | Teacher training | | - | ... | ... | - | ... | ... |
| | Vocational education | | - | ... | ... | - | ... | ... |
| Suriname | Total | 1970/71 | 1 367 | 641 | 47 | 23 504 | 12 784 | 54 |
| | General education | | ... | ... | ... | ... | ... | ... |
| | Teacher training | | 372 | 119 | 32 | 1 228 | 946 | 77 |
| | Vocational education | | ... | ... | ... | ... | ... | ... |
| | Total | 1975/76 | 1 793 | 901 | 50 | 30 603 | 16 726 | 55 |
| | General education | | ... | ... | ... | ... | ... | ... |
| | Teacher training | | 399 | 124 | 31 | 1 894 | 1 454 | 77 |
| | Vocational education | | ... | ... | ... | ... | ... | ... |
| | Total | 1980/81 | ... | ... | ... | (24) 24 027 | ... | ... |
| | General education | | ... | ... | ... | (24) 12 747 | ... | ... |
| | Teacher training | | 120 | ... | ... | 1 529 | ... | ... |
| | Vocational education | | ... | ... | ... | 9 751 | ... | ... |
| | Total | 1985/86 | 4 021 | 2 091 | 52 | 37 630 | 20 084 | 53 |
| | General education | | ... | ... | ... | 24 996 | 14 069 | 56 |
| | Teacher training | | ... | ... | ... | 2 320 | 2 095 | 90 |
| | Vocational education | | ... | ... | ... | 10 314 | 3 920 | 38 |
| | Total | 1990/91 | 2 482 | 1 539 | 62 | 33 561 | 17 793 | 53 |
| | General education | | ... | ... | ... | 19 902 | 11 245 | 57 |
| | Teacher training | | ... | ... | ... | 1 954 | 1 728 | 88 |
| | Vocational education | | ... | ... | ... | 11 705 | 4 820 | 41 |
| | Total | 1991/92 | 2 496 | ... | ... | 35 535 | 18 946 | 53 |
| | General education | | ... | ... | ... | 19 224 | 10 842 | 56 |
| | Teacher training | | ... | ... | ... | 1 900 | 1 677 | 88 |
| | Vocational education | | ... | ... | ... | 14 411 | 6 427 | 45 |
| | Total | 1992/93 | 2 487 | 1 500 | 60 | 30 016 | 15 999 | 53 |
| | General education | | ... | ... | ... | 17 709 | 9 386 | 53 |
| | Teacher training | | ... | ... | ... | 1 742 | 1 543 | 89 |
| | Vocational education | | ... | ... | ... | 10 565 | 5 070 | 48 |
| | Total | 1993/94 | ... | ... | ... | ... | ... | ... |
| | General education | | ... | ... | ... | 16 511 | 9 454 | 57 |
| | Teacher training | | ... | ... | ... | 1 654 | 1 372 | 83 |
| | Vocational education | | ... | ... | ... | ... | ... | ... |
| Uruguay | Total | 1970 | ... | ... | ... | 168 083 | 89 152 | 53 |
| | General education | | ... | ... | ... | 132 125 | 74 366 | 56 |
| | Teacher training | | ... | ... | ... | ... | ... | ... |
| | Vocational education | | ... | ... | ... | 35 958 | 14 786 | 41 |
| | Total | 1975 | ... | ... | ... | 182 195 | ... | ... |
| | General education | | ... | ... | ... | 144 497 | ... | ... |
| | Teacher training | | - | - | - | - | - | - |
| | Vocational education | | ... | ... | ... | 37 698 | 14 439 | 38 |
| | Total | 1980 | ... | ... | ... | (37) 148 294 | (37) 78 487 | 53 |
| | General education | | ... | ... | ... | (37) 125 438 | (37) 72 390 | 58 |
| | Teacher training | | - | - | - | - | - | - |
| | Vocational education | | ... | ... | ... | 22 856 | 6 097 | 27 |
| | Total | 1985 | ... | ... | ... | 213 774 | ... | ... |
| | General education | | ... | ... | ... | 188 176 | ... | ... |
| | Teacher training | | - | - | - | - | - | - |
| | Vocational education | | ... | ... | ... | 25 598 | 11 144 | 44 |

II.6　Secondary education: teaching staff and pupils
Enseignement secondaire: personnel enseignant et élèves
Enseñanza secundaria: personal docente y alumnos

| Country / Pays / País | Type of education / Type d'enseignement / Tipo de enseñanza | Year / Année / Año | Teaching staff / Personnel enseignant / Personal docente | | | Pupils enrolled / Elèves inscrits / Alumnos matriculados | | |
|---|---|---|---|---|---|---|---|---|
| | | | Total | Female Féminin Femenino | % F | Total | Female Féminin Femenino | % F |
| Uruguay (cont) | Total | 1990 | ... | ... | ... | 265 947 | ... | ... |
| | General education | | ... | ... | ... | 223 597 | ... | ... |
| | Teacher training | | - | - | - | - | | |
| | Vocational education | | | | ... | 42 350 | 20 327 | 48 |
| | Total | 1991 | ... | ... | ... | 276 482 | ... | ... |
| | General education | | ... | ... | ... | 231 455 | ... | ... |
| | Teacher training | | - | - | - | - | | |
| | Vocational education | | | | ... | 45 027 | 22 030 | 49 |
| | Total | 1992 | ... | ... | ... | 272 622 | ... | ... |
| | General education | | ... | ... | ... | 227 060 | ... | ... |
| | Teacher training | | - | - | - | - | - | - |
| | Vocational education | | | | ... | 45 562 | 21 726 | 48 |
| | Total | 1993 | ... | ... | ... | 266 840 | ... | ... |
| | General education | | ... | ... | ... | 221 260 | | |
| | Teacher training | | - | - | - | - | - | - |
| | Vocational education | | | | ... | 45 580 | | ... |
| | Total | 1994 | ... | ... | ... | 263 180 | 140 579 | 53 |
| | General education | | ... | ... | ... | 220 353 | 120 447 | 55 |
| | Teacher training | | - | - | - | - | - | - |
| | Vocational education | | | | ... | 42 827 | 20 132 | 47 |
| | Total | 1995 | ... | ... | ... | 263 616 | 141 569 | 54 |
| | General education | | ... | ... | ... | 220 289 | 121 465 | 55 |
| | Teacher training | | - | - | - | - | - | - |
| | Vocational education | | | | ... | 43 327 | 20 104 | 46 |
| | Total | 1996 | ... | ... | ... | 269 826 | ... | ... |
| | General education | | ... | ... | ... | 226 542 | ... | ... |
| | Teacher training | | - | - | - | - | - | - |
| | Vocational education | | | | ... | 43 284 | 19 348 | 45 |
| Venezuela | Total | 1970/71 | 22 983 | 8 998 | 39 | 425 146 | 215 443 | 51 |
| | General education | | 13 721 | 5 541 | 40 | 279 867 | 141 213 | 50 |
| | Teacher training | | 1 199 | 608 | 51 | 11 664 | 8 151 | 70 |
| | Vocational education | | 8 063 | 2 849 | 35 | 133 615 | 66 079 | 49 |
| | Total | 1975/76 | 37 232 | ... | ... | 669 138 | 351 890 | 53 |
| | General education | | ... | ... | ... | ... | ... | ... |
| | Teacher training | | ... | ... | ... | ... | ... | ... |
| | Vocational education | | ... | ... | ... | ... | ... | ... |
| | Total | 1980/81 | ... | ... | ... | (38) 222 267 | (38) 128 340 | 58 |
| | General education | | ... | ... | ... | (38) 154 626 | ... | ... |
| | Teacher training | | ... | ... | ... | 24 414 | | |
| | Vocational education | | ... | ... | ... | 43 227 | | |
| | Total | 1985/86 | ... | ... | ... | 268 580 | 151 002 | 56 |
| | General education | | ... | ... | ... | 213 697 | 120 860 | 57 |
| | Teacher training | | - | - | - | - | - | - |
| | Vocational education | | ... | ... | ... | 54 883 | 30 142 | 55 |
| | Total | 1990/91 | 30 844 | 15 860 | 51 | 281 419 | 160 587 | 57 |
| | General education | | ... | ... | ... | 231 659 | 133 852 | 58 |
| | Teacher training | | - | - | - | - | - | - |
| | Vocational education | | ... | ... | ... | 49 760 | 26 735 | 54 |
| | Total | 1991/92 | 32 572 | 16 905 | 52 | 289 430 | 164 685 | 57 |
| | General education | | ... | ... | ... | 238 417 | 137 308 | 58 |
| | Teacher training | | - | - | - | - | - | - |
| | Vocational education | | ... | ... | ... | 51 013 | 27 377 | 54 |
| | Total | 1992/93 | 34 183 | 17 861 | 52 | 298 534 | 171 018 | 57 |
| | General education | | ... | ... | ... | 245 770 | 142 198 | 58 |
| | Teacher training | | - | - | - | - | - | - |
| | Vocational education | | ... | ... | ... | 52 764 | 28 820 | 55 |
| | Total | 1993/94 | 33 692 | 17 903 | 53 | 311 209 | 179 920 | 58 |
| | General education | | ... | ... | ... | ... | ... | ... |
| | Teacher training | | - | - | - | - | - | - |
| | Vocational education | | ... | ... | ... | ... | ... | ... |
| | Total | 1995/96 | ... | ... | ... | 329 287 | 189 592 | 58 |
| | General education | | ... | ... | ... | ... | ... | ... |
| | Teacher training | | ... | ... | ... | ... | ... | ... |
| | Vocational education | | ... | ... | ... | ... | ... | ... |
| | Total | 1996/97 | ... | ... | ... | 377 984 | 217 894 | 58 |
| | General education | | ... | ... | ... | ... | ... | ... |
| | Teacher training | | ... | ... | ... | ... | ... | ... |
| | Vocational education | | ... | ... | ... | ... | ... | ... |

Secondary education: teaching staff and pupils II.6
Enseignement secondaire: personnel enseignant et élèves
Enseñanza secundaria: personal docente y alumnos

| Country / Pays / País | Type of education / Type d'enseignement / Tipo de enseñanza | Year / Année / Año | Teaching staff Personnel enseignant Personal docente | | | Pupils enrolled Elèves inscrits Alumnos matriculados | | |
|---|---|---|---|---|---|---|---|---|
| | | | Total | Female Féminin Femenino | % F | Total | Female Féminin Femenino | % F |
| **Asia** | | | | | | | | |
| Afghanistan | Total | 1970 | 5 021 | 618 | 12 | 116 174 | 15 253 | 13 |
| | General education | | 4 248 | 572 | 13 | 107 609 | 14 736 | 14 |
| | Teacher training | | (8) 341 | (8) 14 | 4 | 3 597 | 40 | 1 |
| | Vocational education | | 432 | 32 | 7 | 4 968 | 477 | 10 |
| | Total | 1975 | ... | ... | ... | (28) 93 497 | (28) 10 505 | 11 |
| | General education | | ... | ... | ... | (28) 87 537 | (28) 9 854 | 11 |
| | Teacher training | | - | - | - | - | - | - |
| | Vocational education | | 664 | 41 | 6 | 5 960 | 651 | 11 |
| | Total | 1980 | 7 532 | ... | ... | 136 898 | ... | ... |
| | General education | | 6 270 | 1 331 | 21 | 124 488 | 26 143 | 21 |
| | Teacher training | | - | - | - | - | - | - |
| | Vocational education | | 1 262 | ... | ... | 12 410 | ... | ... |
| | Total | 1985 | ... | ... | ... | ... | ... | ... |
| | General education | | 5 715 | 1 887 | 33 | 105 032 | 33 248 | 32 |
| | Teacher training | | - | - | - | - | - | - |
| | Vocational education | | ... | ... | ... | ... | ... | ... |
| | Total | 1990 | (7) 7 356 | (7) 3 269 | 44 | (7) 182 340 | ... | ... |
| | General education | | (7) 7 356 | (7) 3 269 | 44 | (7) 182 340 | ... | ... |
| | Teacher training | | - | - | - | - | - | - |
| | Vocational education | | - | - | - | - | - | - |
| | Total | 1991 | ... | ... | ... | 281 928 | 90 663 | 32 |
| | General education | | ... | ... | ... | 281 928 | 90 663 | 32 |
| | Teacher training | | - | - | - | - | - | - |
| | Vocational education | | - | - | - | - | - | - |
| | Total | 1993 | 12 448 | 6 522 | 52 | 332 170 | 85 692 | 26 |
| | General education | | 12 448 | 6 522 | 52 | 332 170 | 85 692 | 26 |
| | Teacher training | | - | - | - | - | - | - |
| | Vocational education | | - | - | - | - | - | - |
| | Total | 1994 | 17 548 | 6 042 | 34 | 497 762 | 101 282 | 20 |
| | General education | | 17 548 | 6 042 | 34 | 497 762 | 101 282 | 20 |
| | Teacher training | | - | - | - | - | - | - |
| | Vocational education | | - | - | - | - | - | - |
| | Total | 1995 | ... | ... | ... | 512 851 | 130 136 | 25 |
| | General education | | ... | ... | ... | 512 851 | 130 136 | 25 |
| | Teacher training | | - | - | - | - | - | - |
| | Vocational education | | - | - | - | - | - | - |
| Armenia | Total | 1993/94 | 32 674 | 14 442 | 44 | 343 096 | ... | ... |
| | General education | | ... | ... | ... | 322 067 | 164 452 | 51 |
| | Teacher training | | - | - | - | - | - | - |
| | Vocational education | | ... | ... | ... | 21 029 | ... | ... |
| | Total | 1995/96 | ... | ... | ... | 326 585 | ... | ... |
| | General education | | 31 898 | 27 059 | 85 | 319 233 | ... | ... |
| | Teacher training | | - | - | - | - | - | - |
| | Vocational education | | ... | ... | ... | 7 352 | ... | ... |
| | Total | 1996/97 | ... | ... | ... | 372 187 | ... | ... |
| | General education | | 57 325 | ... | ... | 365 025 | ... | ... |
| | Teacher training | | - | - | - | - | - | - |
| | Vocational education | | ... | ... | ... | 7 162 | ... | ... |
| Azerbaijan | Total | 1980/81 | ... | ... | ... | 1 008 831 | 487 633 | 48 |
| | General education | | ... | ... | ... | 941 742 | 467 104 | 50 |
| | Teacher training | | - | - | - | - | - | - |
| | Vocational education | | ... | ... | ... | 67 089 | 20 529 | 31 |
| | Total | 1985/86 | ... | ... | ... | 930 557 | 446 835 | 48 |
| | General education | | ... | ... | ... | 853 074 | 423 125 | 50 |
| | Teacher training | | - | - | - | - | - | - |
| | Vocational education | | ... | ... | ... | 77 483 | 23 710 | 31 |
| | Total | 1990/91 | ... | ... | ... | 867 386 | 421 451 | 49 |
| | General education | | ... | ... | ... | 816 869 | 405 488 | 50 |
| | Teacher training | | - | - | - | - | - | - |
| | Vocational education | | ... | ... | ... | 50 517 | 15 963 | 32 |
| | Total | 1991/92 | ... | ... | ... | 880 096 | 426 832 | 48 |
| | General education | | ... | ... | ... | 831 338 | 411 473 | 49 |
| | Teacher training | | - | - | - | - | - | - |
| | Vocational education | | ... | ... | ... | 48 758 | 15 359 | 32 |
| | Total | 1992/93 | ... | ... | ... | 887 952 | 427 647 | 48 |
| | General education | | ... | ... | ... | 843 440 | 412 068 | 49 |
| | Teacher training | | - | - | - | - | - | - |
| | Vocational education | | ... | ... | ... | 44 512 | 15 579 | 35 |

II.6    Secondary education: teaching staff and pupils
Enseignement secondaire: personnel enseignant et élèves
Enseñanza secundaria: personal docente y alumnos

| Country<br>Pays<br>País | Type of education<br>Type d'enseignement<br>Tipo de enseñanza | Year<br>Année<br>Año | Teaching staff<br>Personnel enseignant<br>Personal docente | | | | Pupils enrolled<br>Elèves inscrits<br>Alumnos matriculados | | | |
|---|---|---|---|---|---|---|---|---|---|---|
| | | | | Total | Female<br>Féminin<br>Femenino | %<br>F | | Total | Female<br>Féminin<br>Femenino | %<br>F |
| Azerbaijan (cont) | Total | 1993/94 | | ... | ... | ... | | 873 936 | 417 365 | 48 |
| | General education | | | 80 964 | 50 744 | 63 | | 838 546 | 405 155 | 48 |
| | Teacher training | | | - | - | - | | - | - | - |
| | Vocational education | | | ... | ... | ... | | 35 390 | 12 210 | 35 |
| | Total | 1994/95 | | ... | ... | ... | | 877 809 | 439 557 | 50 |
| | General education | | | 83 887 | 56 328 | 67 | | 851 059 | 431 157 | 51 |
| | Teacher training | | | - | - | - | | - | - | - |
| | Vocational education | | | ... | ... | ... | | 26 750 | 8 400 | 31 |
| | Total | 1995/96 | | ... | ... | ... | | 805 382 | 406 693 | 50 |
| | General education | | | 85 018 | 57 612 | 68 | | 786 025 | 401 836 | 51 |
| | Teacher training | | | - | - | - | | - | - | - |
| | Vocational education | | | ... | ... | ... | | 19 357 | 4 857 | 25 |
| | Total | 1996/97 | | ... | ... | ... | | 819 625 | 420 304 | 51 |
| | General education | | | 85 001 | 55 779 | 66 | | 802 338 | 414 651 | 52 |
| | Teacher training | | | - | - | - | | - | - | - |
| | Vocational education | | | ... | ... | ... | | 17 287 | 5 653 | 33 |
| Bahrain | Total | 1970/71 | | ... | ... | ... | | 13 652 | *5 569 | *41 |
| | General education | | | ... | ... | ... | | 12 697 | *5 531 | *44 |
| | Teacher training | | | - | - | - | | - | - | - |
| | Vocational education | | | ... | ... | ... | | 955 | 38 | 4 |
| | Total | 1975/76 | | ... | ... | ... | | 18 617 | 8 847 | 48 |
| | General education | | | ... | ... | ... | | 16 962 | 8 389 | 49 |
| | Teacher training | | | - | - | - | | - | - | - |
| | Vocational education | | | ... | ... | ... | | 1 655 | 458 | 28 |
| | Total | 1980/81 | (4)(38) | 1 184 | (4)(38) 603 | 51 | (38) | 26 528 | (38) 12 092 | 46 |
| | General education | | | ... | ... | ... | (38) | 23 718 | (38) 11 104 | 47 |
| | Teacher training | | | - | - | - | | - | - | - |
| | Vocational education | | | ... | ... | ... | | 2 810 | 988 | 35 |
| | Total | 1985/86 | | ... | ... | ... | | 38 577 | 18 567 | 48 |
| | General education | | | ... | ... | ... | | 30 707 | 15 813 | 51 |
| | Teacher training | | | - | - | - | | - | - | - |
| | Vocational education | | | 566 | 130 | 23 | | 7 870 | 2 754 | 35 |
| | Total | 1990/91 | (4) | 2 742 | (4) 1 370 | 50 | | 47 005 | 23 550 | 50 |
| | General education | | (4) | 1 982 | (4) 1 164 | 59 | | 40 778 | 21 934 | 54 |
| | Teacher training | | | - | - | - | | - | - | - |
| | Vocational education | | | 760 | 206 | 27 | | 6 227 | 1 616 | 26 |
| | Total | 1991/92 | (4) | 2 927 | (4) 1 473 | 50 | | 48 600 | 24 467 | 50 |
| | General education | | (4) | 2 118 | (4) 1 260 | 59 | | 42 435 | 22 883 | 54 |
| | Teacher training | | | - | - | - | | - | - | - |
| | Vocational education | | | 809 | 213 | 26 | | 6 165 | 1 584 | 26 |
| | Total | 1992/93 | (4) | 3 132 | (4) 1 599 | 51 | | 51 513 | 25 804 | 50 |
| | General education | | (4) | 2 309 | (4) 1 389 | 60 | | 45 120 | 24 214 | 54 |
| | Teacher training | | | - | - | - | | - | - | - |
| | Vocational education | | | 823 | 210 | 26 | | 6 393 | 1 590 | 25 |
| | Total | 1993/94 | (4) | 3 166 | (4) 1 594 | 50 | | 54 193 | 27 073 | 50 |
| | General education | | (4) | 2 343 | (4) 1 413 | 60 | | 47 417 | 25 345 | 53 |
| | Teacher training | | | - | - | - | | - | - | - |
| | Vocational education | | | 823 | 181 | 22 | | 6 776 | 1 728 | 26 |
| | Total | 1994/95 | (4) | 3 125 | (4) 1 580 | 51 | | 56 057 | 27 857 | 50 |
| | General education | | (4) | 2 305 | (4) 1 405 | 61 | | 48 944 | 26 089 | 53 |
| | Teacher training | | | - | - | - | | - | - | - |
| | Vocational education | | | 820 | 175 | 21 | | 7 113 | 1 768 | 25 |
| | Total | 1995/96 | | ... | ... | ... | | 57 222 | 28 698 | 50 |
| | General education | | | ... | ... | ... | | 49 794 | 26 652 | 54 |
| | Teacher training | | | - | - | - | | - | - | - |
| | Vocational education | | | ... | ... | ... | | 7 428 | 2 046 | 28 |
| | Total | 1996/97 | | ... | ... | ... | | 57 184 | 29 014 | 51 |
| | General education | | | ... | ... | ... | | 49 897 | 26 744 | 54 |
| | Teacher training | | | - | - | - | | - | - | - |
| | Vocational education | | | ... | ... | ... | | 7 287 | 2 270 | 31 |
| Bangladesh | Total | 1975 | | ... | ... | ... | | ... | ... | ... |
| | General education | | | ... | ... | ... | | 2 442 842 | 516 740 | 21 |
| | Teacher training | | | ... | ... | ... | | ... | ... | ... |
| | Vocational education | | | ... | ... | ... | | ... | ... | ... |
| | Total | 1980 | | 111 927 | 7 489 | 7 | | 2 659 208 | 636 584 | 24 |
| | General education | | | 110 096 | 7 314 | 7 | | 2 632 904 | 634 372 | 24 |
| | Teacher training | | | 772 | 127 | 16 | | 6 704 | 1 782 | 27 |
| | Vocational education | | | 1 059 | 48 | 5 | | 19 600 | 430 | 2 |
| | Total | 1985 | | 112 700 | 9 575 | 8 | | 3 125 219 | 875 353 | 28 |
| | General education | | | 110 757 | 9 426 | 9 | | 3 097 871 | 868 411 | 28 |
| | Teacher training | | | 516 | 101 | 20 | | 8 303 | 5 947 | 72 |
| | Vocational education | | | 1 427 | 48 | 3 | | 19 045 | 995 | 5 |

Secondary education: teaching staff and pupils
Enseignement secondaire: personnel enseignant et élèves
Enseñanza secundaria: personal docente y alumnos

II.6

| Country / Pays / País | Type of education / Type d'enseignement / Tipo de enseñanza | Year / Année / Año | Teaching staff / Personnel enseignant / Personal docente | | | Pupils enrolled / Elèves inscrits / Alumnos matriculados | | |
|---|---|---|---|---|---|---|---|---|
| | | | Total | Female Féminin Femenino | % F | Total | Female Féminin Femenino | % F |
| Bangladesh (cont) | Total | 1990 | 130 949 | 12 507 | 10 | 3 592 995 | *1 180 440 | *33 |
| | General education | | 128 389 | 12 368 | 10 | 3 562 194 | 1 176 122 | 33 |
| | Teacher training | | 502 | 91 | 18 | 5 010 | 2 348 | 47 |
| | Vocational education | | 2 058 | 48 | 2 | 25 791 | *1 970 | *8 |
| Bhutan | Total | 1970 | ... | ... | ... | 714 | 24 | 3 |
| | General education | | ... | ... | ... | 393 | 10 | 3 |
| | Teacher training | | 7 | 1 | 14 | 50 | 14 | 28 |
| | Vocational education | | 18 | - | - | 271 | - | - |
| | Total | 1985 | ... | ... | ... | 6 094 | ... | ... |
| | General education | | ... | ... | ... | 3 780 | 912 | 24 |
| | Teacher training | | ... | ... | ... | 95 | ... | ... |
| | Vocational education | | ... | ... | ... | 2 219 | ... | ... |
| | Total | 1993 | ... | ... | ... | ... | ... | ... |
| | General education | | ... | ... | ... | (39) 5 321 | (39) 1 917 | 36 |
| | Teacher training | | 16 | ... | ... | 119 | 46 | 39 |
| | Vocational education | | ... | ... | ... | ... | ... | ... |
| | Total | 1994 | ... | ... | ... | ... | ... | ... |
| | General education | | ... | ... | ... | 7 299 | 2 805 | 38 |
| | Teacher training | | 27 | ... | ... | 160 | 46 | 29 |
| | Vocational education | | ... | ... | ... | ... | ... | ... |
| Brunei Darussalam | Total | 1970 | 565 | 144 | 25 | 10 974 | 4 911 | 45 |
| | General education | | 532 | 138 | 26 | 10 421 | 4 721 | 45 |
| | Teacher training | | 24 | 0 | 25 | 434 | 190 | 44 |
| | Vocational education | | 9 | - | - | 119 | - | - |
| | Total | 1975 | 782 | 287 | 37 | 14 614 | 6 946 | 48 |
| | General education | | 684 | 276 | 40 | 13 687 | 6 666 | 49 |
| | Teacher training | | 37 | 11 | 30 | 613 | 273 | 45 |
| | Vocational education | | 61 | - | - | 314 | 7 | 2 |
| | Total | 1980 | 1 413 | 479 | 34 | 17 441 | 8 716 | 50 |
| | General education | | 1 214 | 453 | 37 | 16 532 | 8 349 | 51 |
| | Teacher training | | 81 | 23 | 28 | 450 | 296 | 66 |
| | Vocational education | | 118 | 3 | 3 | 459 | 71 | 15 |
| | Total | 1985 | 1 893 | ... | ... | 20 462 | ... | ... |
| | General education | | 1 572 | ... | ... | 18 889 | ... | ... |
| | Teacher training | | 100 | ... | ... | 598 | ... | ... |
| | Vocational education | | 221 | ... | ... | 975 | ... | ... |
| | Total | 1991 | 2 172 | 972 | 45 | 25 699 | 12 937 | 50 |
| | General education | | 1 865 | 901 | 48 | 24 142 | 12 306 | 51 |
| | Teacher training | | 25 | 11 | 44 | 369 | 207 | 56 |
| | Vocational education | | 282 | 60 | 21 | 1 188 | 424 | 36 |
| | Total | 1992 | 2 248 | 1 032 | 46 | 26 836 | 13 710 | 51 |
| | General education | | 1 922 | 952 | 50 | 25 115 | 13 011 | 52 |
| | Teacher training | | 26 | 12 | 46 | 358 | 202 | 56 |
| | Vocational education | | 300 | 68 | 23 | 1 363 | 497 | 36 |
| | Total | 1993 | 2 337 | 1 054 | 45 | 28 210 | 14 381 | 51 |
| | General education | | 1 948 | 962 | 49 | 26 199 | 13 522 | 52 |
| | Teacher training | | 25 | 12 | 48 | 418 | 225 | 54 |
| | Vocational education | | 364 | 80 | 22 | 1 593 | 634 | 40 |
| | Total | 1994 | 2 413 | 1 046 | 43 | 28 851 | 14 605 | 51 |
| | General education | | 1 975 | 942 | 48 | 26 700 | 13 691 | 51 |
| | Teacher training | | 58 | 18 | 31 | 506 | 253 | 50 |
| | Vocational education | | 380 | 86 | 23 | 1 645 | 661 | 40 |
| | Total | 1995 | 2 692 | 1 187 | 44 | 30 889 | 15 853 | 51 |
| | General education | | 2 346 | 1 117 | 48 | 29 265 | 15 243 | 52 |
| | Teacher training | | - | - | - | - | - | - |
| | Vocational education | | 346 | 70 | 20 | 1 624 | 610 | 38 |
| | Total | 1996 | 2 961 | 1 392 | 47 | 30 470 | 15 868 | 52 |
| | General education | | 2 505 | 1 280 | 51 | 28 274 | 14 949 | 53 |
| | Teacher training | | - | - | - | - | - | - |
| | Vocational education | | 456 | 112 | 25 | 2 196 | 919 | 42 |
| Cambodia | Total | 1970/71 | 3 937 | ... | ... | 86 999 | 26 872 | 31 |
| | General education | | 3 629 | ... | ... | 82 700 | 24 821 | 30 |
| | Teacher training | | 28 | 12 | 43 | 1 260 | 352 | 28 |
| | Vocational education | | 280 | ... | ... | 3 039 | 1 699 | 56 |
| | Total | 1980/81 | ... | ... | ... | ... | ... | ... |
| | General education | | 699 | ... | ... | 17 846 | ... | ... |
| | Teacher training | | ... | ... | ... | ... | ... | ... |
| | Vocational education | | ... | ... | ... | ... | ... | ... |
| | Total | 1985/86 | ... | ... | ... | 314 654 | ... | ... |
| | General education | | 8 033 | ... | ... | 311 795 | 116 721 | 37 |
| | Teacher training | | ... | ... | ... | ... | ... | ... |
| | Vocational education | | ... | ... | ... | ... | ... | ... |

II.6   Secondary education: teaching staff and pupils
Enseignement secondaire: personnel enseignant et élèves
Enseñanza secundaria: personal docente y alumnos

| Country<br><br>Pays<br><br>País | Type of education<br><br>Type d'enseignement<br><br>Tipo de enseñanza | Year<br><br>Année<br><br>Año | Teaching staff<br>Personnel enseignant<br>Personal docente | | | Pupils enrolled<br>Elèves inscrits<br>Alumnos matriculados | | |
|---|---|---|---|---|---|---|---|---|
| | | | Total | Female<br>Féminin<br>Femenino | %<br><br>F | Total | Female<br>Féminin<br>Femenino | %<br><br>F |
| Cambodia (cont) | Total | 1990/91 | ... | ... | ... | 264 419 | ... | ... |
| | General education | | 16 408 | 4 533 | 28 | 248 968 | ... | ... |
| | Teacher training | | ... | ... | ... | 7 356 | ... | ... |
| | Vocational education | | ... | ... | ... | 8 095 | 1 395 | 17 |
| | Total | 1993/94 | ... | ... | ... | 285 779 | 105 170 | 37 |
| | General education | | 16 622 | ... | ... | ... | ... | ... |
| | Teacher training | | ... | ... | ... | ... | ... | ... |
| | Vocational education | | ... | ... | ... | ... | ... | ... |
| | Total | 1994/95 | ... | ... | ... | 297 555 | 111 798 | 38 |
| | General education | | 16 349 | 4 513 | 28 | ... | ... | ... |
| | Teacher training | | ... | ... | ... | ... | ... | ... |
| | Vocational education | | ... | ... | ... | ... | ... | ... |
| | Total | 1996/97 | ... | ... | ... | ... | ... | ... |
| | General education | | 16 971 | 4 577 | 27 | 327 566 | 120 082 | 37 |
| | Teacher training | | ... | ... | ... | ... | ... | ... |
| | Vocational education | | 749 | 161 | 21 | 4 385 | 1 071 | 24 |
| | Total | 1997/98 | 19 135 | 5 232 | 27 | 312 934 | 108 917 | 35 |
| | General education | | 16 820 | 4 538 | 27 | 302 951 | 105 440 | 35 |
| | Teacher training | | 951 | 376 | 40 | 4 918 | 1 984 | 40 |
| | Vocational education | | 1 364 | 318 | 23 | 5 065 | 1 493 | 29 |
| China | Total | 1970/71 | 1 213 000 | | ... | 26 482 976 | | ... |
| | General education | | ... | ... | ... | 26 419 000 | | ... |
| | Teacher training | | ... | ... | ... | 32 308 | ... | ... |
| | Vocational education | | ... | ... | ... | 31 668 | ... | ... |
| | Total | 1975/76 | 2 164 601 | ... | ... | 45 368 318 | 17 781 000 | 39 |
| | General education | | 2 092 155 | 505 200 | 24 | 44 661 000 | 17 537 000 | 39 |
| | Teacher training | | 24 618 | ... | ... | 302 288 | ... | ... |
| | Vocational education | | 47 828 | ... | ... | 405 030 | ... | ... |
| | Total | 1980/81 | 3 171 564 | 787 700 | 25 | 56 778 008 | 22 341 014 | 39 |
| | General education | | 3 019 700 | 750 300 | 25 | 55 081 000 | 21 801 000 | 40 |
| | Teacher training | | 37 664 | 8 300 | 22 | 482 108 | 125 214 | 26 |
| | Vocational education | | 114 200 | 29 100 | 25 | 1 214 900 | 414 800 | 34 |
| | Total | 1985/86 | 3 039 100 | 854 800 | 28 | 51 663 800 | 20 578 100 | 40 |
| | General education | | 2 651 600 | 743 900 | 28 | 47 059 600 | 18 931 300 | 40 |
| | Teacher training | | 46 000 | 14 200 | 31 | 558 200 | 219 300 | 39 |
| | Vocational education | | *341 500 | *96 700 | *28 | 4 046 000 | *1 427 500 | *35 |
| | Total | 1990/91 | 3 631 500 | 1 128 900 | 31 | 52 385 600 | 21 706 500 | 41 |
| | General education | | 3 032 600 | 955 700 | 32 | 45 859 600 | 19 201 100 | 42 |
| | Teacher training | | 58 500 | 20 200 | 35 | 677 300 | 355 000 | 52 |
| | Vocational education | | *540 400 | *153 000 | *28 | 5 848 700 | *2 150 400 | *37 |
| | Total | 1991/92 | 3 696 400 | 1 175 600 | 32 | 53 690 000 | 22 636 900 | 42 |
| | General education | | 3 090 000 | 999 900 | 32 | 46 835 000 | 19 976 400 | 43 |
| | Teacher training | | 57 200 | 20 200 | 35 | 661 400 | 351 900 | 53 |
| | Vocational education | | *549 200 | *155 500 | *28 | 6 193 600 | *2 308 600 | *37 |
| | Total | 1992/93 | 3 776 750 | 1 230 050 | 33 | 55 100 000 | 23 481 100 | 43 |
| | General education | | 3 141 100 | 1 045 500 | 33 | 47 708 000 | 20 565 100 | 43 |
| | Teacher training | | 57 000 | 20 700 | 36 | 665 600 | 365 900 | 55 |
| | Vocational education | | *578 650 | *163 850 | *28 | 6 726 400 | *2 550 100 | *38 |
| | Total | 1993/94 | 3 836 100 | 1 272 900 | 33 | 55 548 100 | 24 397 800 | 44 |
| | General education | | 3 166 800 | 1 078 100 | 34 | 47 391 100 | 20 716 800 | 44 |
| | Teacher training | | 58 100 | 21 700 | 37 | 722 000 | 414 000 | 57 |
| | Vocational education | | *611 200 | *173 100 | *28 | 7 435 000 | *3 267 000 | *44 |
| | Total | 1994/95 | 3 910 232 | 1 321 680 | 34 | 58 941 484 | 26 277 732 | 45 |
| | General education | | 3 233 707 | 1 121 093 | 35 | 49 816 643 | 22 069 970 | 44 |
| | Teacher training | | 60 000 | *22 200 | *37 | 784 000 | *424 250 | *54 |
| | Vocational education | | 616 525 | *178 387 | *29 | 8 340 841 | *3 783 512 | *45 |
| | Total | 1995/96 | 4 099 272 | 1 431 683 | 35 | 63 800 417 | 28 834 526 | 45 |
| | General education | | 3 334 242 | 1 191 816 | 36 | 53 709 790 | 24 074 943 | 45 |
| | Teacher training | | 61 700 | 24 000 | 39 | 848 000 | 519 000 | 61 |
| | Vocational education | | 703 330 | 215 867 | 31 | 9 242 627 | 4 240 583 | 46 |
| | Total | 1996/97 | 4 217 947 | 1 537 605 | 36 | 68 275 438 | 30 960 739 | 45 |
| | General education | | 3 464 759 | 1 280 320 | 37 | 57 396 761 | 25 996 468 | 45 |
| | Teacher training | | 63 100 | 25 100 | 40 | 880 100 | 552 700 | 63 |
| | Vocational education | | 690 088 | 232 185 | 34 | 9 998 577 | 4 411 571 | 44 |
| | Total | 1997/98 | 4 437 000 | *1 650 000 | *37 | 71 883 000 | *32 530 000 | *45 |
| | General education | | 3 587 000 | 1 369 000 | 38 | 60 179 000 | 27 356 000 | 45 |
| | Teacher training | | 64 000 | ... | ... | 911 000 | ... | ... |
| | Vocational education | | *786 000 | ... | ... | 10 793 000 | ... | ... |
| China, Hong Kong SAR | Total | 1970/71 | 10 542 | 3 799 | 36 | 230 879 | 96 579 | 42 |
| | General education | | ... | ... | ... | 216 775 | 91 859 | 42 |
| | Teacher training | | - | - | - | - | - | - |
| | Vocational education | | ... | ... | ... | 14 104 | 4 720 | 33 |

Secondary education: teaching staff and pupils **II.6**
Enseignement secondaire: personnel enseignant et élèves
Enseñanza secundaria: personal docente y alumnos

| Country / Pays / País | Type of education / Type d'enseignement / Tipo de enseñanza | Year / Année / Año | Teaching staff Personnel enseignant Personal docente | | | Pupils enrolled Elèves inscrits Alumnos matriculados | | |
|---|---|---|---|---|---|---|---|---|
| | | | Total | Female Féminin Femenino | % F | Total | Female Féminin Femenino | % F |
| China, Hong Kong SAR (cont) | Total | 1975/76 | 15 149 | 6 198 | 41 | 368 655 | 172 405 | 47 |
| | General education | | ... | ... | ... | 347 146 | 166 083 | 48 |
| | Teacher training | | - | - | - | - | - | - |
| | Vocational education | | ... | ... | ... | 21 509 | 6 322 | 29 |
| | Total | 1980/81 | 15 986 | 7 784 | 49 | 468 975 | 231 238 | 49 |
| | General education | | ... | ... | ... | 437 956 | 221 280 | 51 |
| | Teacher training | | - | - | - | - | - | - |
| | Vocational education | | ... | ... | ... | 31 019 | 9 958 | 32 |
| | Total | 1985/86 | 18 773 | ... | ... | 450 367 | 222 954 | 50 |
| | General education | | ... | ... | ... | 411 388 | 211 197 | 51 |
| | Teacher training | | - | - | - | - | - | - |
| | Vocational education | | ... | ... | ... | 38 979 | 11 757 | 30 |
| | Total | 1990/91 | ... | ... | ... | ... | ... | ... |
| | General education | | (40) 20 159 | ... | ... | (41) 431 381 | ... | ... |
| | Teacher training | | - | - | - | - | - | - |
| | Vocational education | | ... | ... | ... | ... | ... | ... |
| | Total | 1991/92 | ... | ... | ... | ... | ... | ... |
| | General education | | (40) 20 360 | ... | ... | (41) 446 339 | ... | ... |
| | Teacher training | | - | - | - | - | - | - |
| | Vocational education | | ... | ... | ... | ... | ... | ... |
| | Total | 1992/93 | ... | ... | ... | ... | ... | ... |
| | General education | | (40) 20 900 | ... | ... | (41) 445 785 | ... | ... |
| | Teacher training | | - | - | - | - | - | - |
| | Vocational education | | ... | ... | ... | ... | ... | ... |
| | Total | 1993/94 | ... | ... | ... | ... | ... | ... |
| | General education | | (40) 21 391 | ... | ... | (41) 455 935 | ... | ... |
| | Teacher training | | - | - | - | - | - | - |
| | Vocational education | | ... | ... | ... | ... | ... | ... |
| | Total | 1994/95 | ... | ... | ... | ... | ... | ... |
| | General education | | (40) 21 444 | ... | - | (41) 458 199 | ... | - |
| | Teacher training | | - | - | - | - | - | - |
| | Vocational education | | ... | ... | ... | ... | ... | ... |
| | Total | 1995/96 | 23 536 | 11 852 | 50 | 473 817 | 232 505 | 49 |
| | General education | | 22 777 | 11 664 | 51 | 459 845 | 228 030 | 50 |
| | Teacher training | | - | - | - | - | - | - |
| | Vocational education | | 759 | 188 | 25 | 13 972 | 4 475 | 32 |
| Cyprus (42) | Total | 1970/71 | 2 011 | 768 | 38 | 42 305 | 19 590 | 46 |
| | General education | | 1 705 | 714 | 42 | 37 866 | 19 025 | 50 |
| | Teacher training | | - | - | - | - | - | - |
| | Vocational education | | 306 | 54 | 18 | 4 439 | 565 | 13 |
| | Total | 1975/76 | 2 451 | 985 | 40 | 49 373 | 23 435 | 47 |
| | General education | | 2 066 | 913 | 44 | 43 261 | 23 049 | 53 |
| | Teacher training | | - | - | - | - | - | - |
| | Vocational education | | 385 | 72 | 19 | 6 112 | 386 | 6 |
| | Total | 1980/81 | 2 953 | 1 237 | 42 | 47 599 | 23 286 | 49 |
| | General education | | 2 449 | 1 140 | 47 | 41 794 | 22 463 | 54 |
| | Teacher training | | - | - | - | - | - | - |
| | Vocational education | | 504 | 97 | 19 | 5 805 | 823 | 14 |
| | Total | 1985/86 | 3 138 | 1 367 | 44 | 46 159 | 22 829 | 49 |
| | General education | | ... | ... | ... | (43) 42 285 | (43) 22 362 | 53 |
| | Teacher training | | - | ... | ... | - | - | - |
| | Vocational education | | ... | ... | ... | (43) 3 874 | (43) 467 | 12 |
| | Total | 1990/91 | 3 735 | 1 710 | 46 | 44 614 | 21 971 | 49 |
| | General education | | 3 288 | 1 630 | 50 | (43) 41 584 | (43) 21 449 | 52 |
| | Teacher training | | - | - | - | - | - | - |
| | Vocational education | | 447 | 80 | 18 | (43) 3 030 | (43) 522 | 17 |
| | Total | 1991/92 | 3 952 | 1 859 | 47 | 47 908 | 23 622 | 49 |
| | General education | | 3 478 | 1 751 | 50 | (43) 44 736 | (43) 23 072 | 52 |
| | Teacher training | | - | - | - | - | - | - |
| | Vocational education | | 474 | 108 | 23 | (43) 3 172 | (43) 550 | 17 |
| | Total | 1992/93 | 4 217 | 2 037 | 48 | 51 641 | 25 514 | 49 |
| | General education | | 3 734 | 1 931 | 52 | (43) 48 123 | (43) 24 879 | 52 |
| | Teacher training | | - | - | - | - | - | - |
| | Vocational education | | 483 | 106 | 22 | (43) 3 518 | (43) 635 | 18 |
| | Total | 1993/94 | 4 459 | 2 169 | 49 | 54 687 | 26 933 | 49 |
| | General education | | 3 935 | 2 053 | 52 | (43) 50 870 | (43) 26 226 | 52 |
| | Teacher training | | - | - | - | - | - | - |
| | Vocational education | | 524 | 116 | 22 | (43) 3 817 | (43) 707 | 19 |
| | Total | 1994/95 | 4 641 | 2 323 | 50 | 57 804 | 28 390 | 49 |
| | General education | | 4 088 | 2 184 | 53 | (43) 53 738 | (43) 27 598 | 51 |
| | Teacher training | | - | - | - | - | - | - |
| | Vocational education | | 553 | 139 | 25 | (43) 4 066 | (43) 792 | 19 |

**Secondary education: teaching staff and pupils**
**Enseignement secondaire: personnel enseignant et élèves**
**Enseñanza secundaria: personal docente y alumnos**

| Country / Pays / País | Type of education / Type d'enseignement / Tipo de enseñanza | Year / Année / Año | Teaching staff — Personnel enseignant — Personal docente | | | Pupils enrolled — Elèves inscrits — Alumnos matriculados | | |
|---|---|---|---|---|---|---|---|---|
| | | | Total | Female Féminin Femenino | % F | Total | Female Féminin Femenino | % F |
| Cyprus (42) (cont) | Total | 1995/96 | 5 300 | 2 745 | 52 | 59 845 | 29 620 | 49 |
| | General education | | 4 656 | 2 574 | 55 | (43) 55 435 | (43) 28 723 | 52 |
| | Teacher training | | - | - | - | | | |
| | Vocational education | | 644 | 171 | 27 | (43) 4 410 | (43) 897 | 20 |
| | Total | 1996/97 | 4 934 | 2 537 | 51 | 61 266 | 30 303 | 49 |
| | General education | | 4 359 | 2 396 | 55 | (43) 56 652 | (43) 29 358 | 52 |
| | Teacher training | | - | - | - | | | |
| | Vocational education | | 575 | 141 | 25 | (43) 4 614 | (43) 945 | 20 |
| Georgia | Total | 1980/81 | 69 342 | 37 649 | 54 | 687 475 | 291 484 | 42 |
| | General education | | 67 625 | 37 134 | 55 | 626 553 | 273 208 | 44 |
| | Teacher training | | - | - | - | | | - |
| | Vocational education | | 1 717 | 515 | 30 | 60 922 | 18 276 | 30 |
| | Total | 1985/86 | 67 412 | 42 129 | 62 | 668 884 | 295 521 | 44 |
| | General education | | 64 597 | 41 325 | 64 | 597 229 | 274 025 | 46 |
| | Teacher training | | - | - | - | | | - |
| | Vocational education | | 2 815 | 804 | 29 | 71 655 | 21 496 | 30 |
| | Total | 1990/91 | 82 890 | 49 892 | 60 | 567 998 | 273 727 | 48 |
| | General education | | 80 465 | 49 164 | 61 | 525 803 | 259 803 | 49 |
| | Teacher training | | - | - | - | | | - |
| | Vocational education | | 2 425 | 728 | 30 | 42 195 | 13 924 | 33 |
| | Total | 1991/92 | 82 858 | 50 861 | 61 | 530 751 | 253 543 | 48 |
| | General education | | 80 509 | 50 180 | 62 | 494 354 | 242 624 | 49 |
| | Teacher training | | - | - | - | | | - |
| | Vocational education | | 2 349 | 681 | 29 | 36 397 | 10 919 | 30 |
| | Total | 1992/93 | 72 356 | 44 783 | 62 | 466 166 | 221 963 | 48 |
| | General education | | 70 145 | 44 045 | 63 | 431 793 | 211 651 | 49 |
| | Teacher training | | - | - | - | | | - |
| | Vocational education | | 2 211 | 738 | 33 | 34 373 | 10 312 | 30 |
| | Total | 1993/94 | 70 699 | 45 702 | 65 | 453 502 | 217 243 | 48 |
| | General education | | 68 610 | 45 015 | 66 | 425 347 | 208 796 | 49 |
| | Teacher training | | - | - | - | | | - |
| | Vocational education | | 2 089 | 687 | 33 | 28 155 | 8 447 | 30 |
| | Total | 1994/95 | 65 206 | 37 895 | 58 | 437 413 | 206 780 | 47 |
| | General education | | 63 141 | 37 284 | 59 | 418 332 | 200 483 | 48 |
| | Teacher training | | - | - | - | | | - |
| | Vocational education | | 2 065 | 611 | 30 | 19 081 | 6 297 | 33 |
| | Total | 1995/96 | 68 980 | 46 545 | 67 | 441 557 | 214 965 | 49 |
| | General education | | 66 851 | 45 886 | 69 | 422 383 | 206 567 | 49 |
| | Teacher training | | - | - | - | | | - |
| | Vocational education | | 2 129 | 659 | 31 | 19 174 | 8 398 | 44 |
| | Total | 1996/97 | 57 963 | 40 869 | 71 | 444 058 | 215 969 | 49 |
| | General education | | 55 817 | 40 154 | 72 | 424 465 | 206 611 | 49 |
| | Teacher training | | - | - | - | | | - |
| | Vocational education | | 2 146 | 715 | 33 | 19 593 | 9 358 | 48 |
| India | Total | 1970/71 | 964 445 | 222 280 | 23 | 21 143 698 | 5 904 829 | 28 |
| | General education | | 948 887 | 218 246 | 23 | 20 924 505 | 5 822 394 | 28 |
| | Teacher training | | 1 534 | 420 | 27 | 18 974 | 6 705 | 35 |
| | Vocational education | | 14 024 | 3 614 | 26 | 200 219 | 75 730 | 38 |
| | Total | 1975/76 | ... | ... | ... | (44) 25 196 115 | (44) 7 572 162 | 30 |
| | General education | | 1 180 233 | 303 644 | 26 | 24 952 526 | 7 478 613 | 30 |
| | Teacher training | | 19 379 | 8 704 | 45 | 19 379 | 8 704 | 45 |
| | Vocational education | | ... | ... | ... | (44) 224 210 | (44) 84 845 | 38 |
| | Total | 1980/81 | ... | ... | ... | 32 748 397 | 10 391 202 | 32 |
| | General education | | (45) 1 731 978 | (45) 511 841 | 30 | 32 323 173 | 10 253 252 | 32 |
| | Teacher training | | 977 | 351 | 36 | 15 349 | 8 300 | 54 |
| | Vocational education | | ... | ... | ... | 409 875 | 129 650 | 32 |
| | Total | 1985/86 | ... | ... | ... | 44 484 544 | 14 814 335 | 33 |
| | General education | | (45) 2 126 733 | (45) 660 079 | 31 | 43 807 380 | 14 614 475 | 33 |
| | Teacher training | | - | - | - | | | - |
| | Vocational education | | ... | ... | ... | 677 164 | 199 860 | 30 |
| | Total | 1990/91 | ... | ... | ... | 54 180 391 | 19 332 539 | 36 |
| | General education | | (45) 2 331 797 | (45) 768 315 | 33 | 54 180 391 | 19 332 539 | 36 |
| | Teacher training | | - | - | - | | | - |
| | Vocational education | | ... | ... | ... | ... | ... | ... |
| | Total | 1991/92 | ... | ... | ... | ... | ... | ... |
| | General education | | (45) 2 381 408 | (45) 783 517 | 33 | 55 673 664 | 20 041 128 | 36 |
| | Teacher training | | ... | ... | ... | | | ... |
| | Vocational education | | ... | ... | ... | ... | ... | ... |
| | Total | 1992/93 | ... | ... | ... | 62 245 635 | 22 819 986 | 37 |
| | General education | | (45) 2 435 293 | (45) 791 747 | 33 | 61 418 729 | 22 714 721 | 37 |
| | Teacher training | | - | ... | ... | | | |
| | Vocational education | | ... | ... | ... | 826 906 | 105 265 | 13 |

Secondary education: teaching staff and pupils  II.6
Enseignement secondaire: personnel enseignant et élèves
Enseñanza secundaria: personal docente y alumnos

| Country / Pays / País | Type of education / Type d'enseignement / Tipo de enseñanza | Year / Année / Año | Teaching staff Personnel enseignant Personal docente | | | Pupils enrolled Elèves inscrits Alumnos matriculados | | |
|---|---|---|---|---|---|---|---|---|
| | | | Total | Female Féminin Femenino | % F | Total | Female Féminin Femenino | % F |
| India (cont) | Total | 1993/94 | ... | ... | ... | 64 115 978 | 23 887 394 | 37 |
| | General education | | (45) 2 485 158 | (45) 836 754 | 34 | 63 262 226 | 23 775 784 | 38 |
| | Teacher training | | - | - | - | - | - | - |
| | Vocational education | | ... | ... | ... | 853 752 | 111 610 | 13 |
| | Total | 1994/95 | ... | ... | ... | 65 206 357 | 24 277 128 | 37 |
| | General education | | (45) 2 567 696 | (45) 879 812 | 34 | 64 425 675 | 24 167 941 | 38 |
| | Teacher training | | - | - | - | - | - | - |
| | Vocational education | | ... | ... | ... | 780 682 | 109 187 | 14 |
| | Total | 1995/96 | ... | ... | ... | 66 633 720 | 24 937 438 | 37 |
| | General education | | (45) 2 657 985 | (45) 919 782 | 35 | 65 902 708 | 24 824 243 | 38 |
| | Teacher training | | - | - | - | - | - | - |
| | Vocational education | | ... | ... | ... | 731 012 | 113 195 | 15 |
| | Total | 1996/97 | ... | ... | ... | 68 872 393 | 26 269 449 | 38 |
| | General education | | (45) 2 738 205 | (45) 966 743 | 35 | 68 101 705 | 26 150 336 | 38 |
| | Teacher training | | - | - | - | - | - | - |
| | Vocational education | | ... | ... | ... | 770 688 | 119 113 | 15 |
| Indonesia | Total | 1970 | 187 776 | *50 668 | *27 | 2 459 875 | 840 534 | 34 |
| | General education | | 130 826 | *35 453 | *27 | 1 815 645 | *673 604 | *37 |
| | Teacher training | | 8 170 | 1 580 | 19 | 99 400 | 46 700 | 47 |
| | Vocational education | | 48 780 | 13 635 | 28 | 544 830 | 120 230 | 22 |
| | Total | 1975 | | ... | ... | 3 570 080 | 1 366 151 | 38 |
| | General education | | ... | ... | ... | 2 709 953 | 1 088 838 | 40 |
| | Teacher training | | 8 311 | 1 830 | 22 | 102 847 | 59 865 | 58 |
| | Vocational education | | ... | ... | ... | 757 280 | 217 448 | 29 |
| | Total | 1980/81 | | ... | ... | 5 721 815 | ... | ... |
| | General education | | ... | ... | ... | 4 879 361 | ... | ... |
| | Teacher training | | 16 648 | ... | ... | 232 024 | 139 271 | 60 |
| | Vocational education | | ... | ... | ... | 610 430 | 166 872 | 27 |
| | Total | 1985/86 | 620 857 | ... | ... | 9 479 086 | ... | ... |
| | General education | | (46) 480 464 | ... | ... | 8 311 594 | ... | ... |
| | Teacher training | | 20 172 | ... | ... | 297 651 | ... | ... |
| | Vocational education | | (46) 120 221 | ... | ... | 869 841 | ... | ... |
| | Total | 1990/91 | ... | ... | ... | 10 965 430 | 4 882 717 | 45 |
| | General education | | (46) 624 407 | (46) 232 542 | 37 | 9 510 766 | 4 316 625 | 45 |
| | Teacher training | | ... | ... | ... | 40 297 | 20 154 | 50 |
| | Vocational education | | (46) 211 655 | (46) 57 818 | 27 | 1 414 367 | 545 938 | 39 |
| | Total | 1991/92 | 806 384 | 282 717 | 35 | 10 920 580 | 4 875 804 | 45 |
| | General education | | (46) 593 665 | (46) 224 335 | 38 | 9 506 882 | 4 320 819 | 45 |
| | Teacher training | | - | - | - | - | - | - |
| | Vocational education | | (46) 212 719 | (46) 58 382 | 27 | 1 413 698 | 554 985 | 39 |
| | Total | 1992/93 | 793 558 | 276 943 | 35 | 10 969 305 | 4 838 238 | 44 |
| | General education | | (46) 578 721 | (46) 218 387 | 38 | 9 538 778 | 4 269 629 | 45 |
| | Teacher training | | - | - | - | - | - | - |
| | Vocational education | | (46) 214 837 | (46) 58 556 | 27 | 1 430 527 | 568 609 | 40 |
| | Total | 1993/94 | 806 396 | 288 355 | 36 | 11 360 349 | 5 132 921 | 45 |
| | General education | | (46) 572 750 | (46) 224 564 | 39 | 9 919 480 | 4 557 307 | 46 |
| | Teacher training | | - | - | - | - | - | - |
| | Vocational education | | (46) 233 646 | (46) 63 791 | 27 | 1 440 869 | 575 614 | 40 |
| | Total | 1994/95 | 864 587 | 321 859 | 37 | 12 223 753 | 5 556 730 | 45 |
| | General education | | 747 115 | 288 423 | 39 | 10 631 996 | 4 881 082 | 46 |
| | Teacher training | | - | - | - | - | - | - |
| | Vocational education | | 117 472 | 33 436 | 28 | 1 591 757 | 675 648 | 42 |
| | Total | 1995/96 | 917 697 | 362 176 | 39 | 13 095 913 | 5 978 921 | 46 |
| | General education | | 794 852 | 309 252 | 39 | 11 430 633 | 5 269 110 | 46 |
| | Teacher training | | - | - | - | - | - | - |
| | Vocational education | | 122 845 | 52 924 | 43 | 1 665 280 | 709 811 | 43 |
| | Total | 1996/97 | 986 896 | ... | ... | 14 209 974 | ... | ... |
| | General education | | 863 389 | ... | ... | 12 442 813 | ... | ... |
| | Teacher training | | - | - | - | - | - | - |
| | Vocational education | | 123 507 | ... | ... | 1 767 161 | ... | ... |
| Iran, Islamic Republic of | Total | 1970/71 | 30 886 | 8 122 | 26 | 1 056 787 | 349 078 | 33 |
| | General education | | 28 244 | 7 574 | 27 | 1 012 920 | 334 757 | 33 |
| | Teacher training | | 461 | 157 | 34 | 13 288 | 8 060 | 61 |
| | Vocational education | | 2 181 | 391 | 18 | 30 579 | 6 261 | 20 |
| | Total | 1975/76 | 81 855 | 32 306 | 39 | 2 183 137 | 778 875 | 36 |
| | General education | | 73 056 | 30 560 | 42 | 1 988 670 | 727 458 | 37 |
| | Teacher training | | 1 733 | 485 | 28 | 43 958 | 22 352 | 51 |
| | Vocational education | | 7 066 | 1 261 | 18 | 150 509 | 29 065 | 19 |
| | Total | 1980/81 | ... | ... | ... | (15) 2 718 461 | (15) 1 016 145 | 37 |
| | General education | | ... | ... | ... | (15) 2 516 592 | (15) 984 496 | 39 |
| | Teacher training | | - | - | - | - | - | - |
| | Vocational education | | ... | ... | ... | 201 869 | 31 649 | 16 |

Secondary education: teaching staff and pupils
Enseignement secondaire: personnel enseignant et élèves
Enseñanza secundaria: personal docente y alumnos

| Country / Pays / País | Type of education / Type d'enseignement / Tipo de enseñanza | Year / Année / Año | Teaching staff Personnel enseignant Personal docente | | | Pupils enrolled Elèves inscrits Alumnos matriculados | | |
|---|---|---|---|---|---|---|---|---|
| | | | Total | Female Féminin Femenino | % F | Total | Female Féminin Femenino | % F |
| Iran, Islamic Republic of (cont) | Total | 1985/86 | ... | ... | ... | ... | ... | ... |
| | General education | | 195 319 | 75 689 | 39 | 3 204 445 | 1 297 482 | 40 |
| | Teacher training | | ... | ... | ... | ... | ... | ... |
| | Vocational education | | 20 665 | 2 778 | 13 | 195 352 | 45 942 | 24 |
| | Total | 1990/91 | 216 273 | 87 849 | 41 | 5 084 832 | 2 103 856 | 41 |
| | General education | | 197 630 | 85 054 | 43 | 4 822 087 | 2 047 677 | 42 |
| | Teacher training | | 959 | 226 | 24 | 32 684 | 10 871 | 33 |
| | Vocational education | | 17 684 | 2 569 | 15 | 230 061 | 45 308 | 20 |
| | Total | 1991/92 | 218 931 | 90 195 | 41 | 5 619 057 | 2 347 340 | 42 |
| | General education | | 199 451 | 86 452 | 43 | 5 311 988 | 2 277 063 | 43 |
| | Teacher training | | 1 222 | 969 | 79 | 46 493 | 17 823 | 38 |
| | Vocational education | | 18 258 | 2 774 | 15 | 260 576 | 52 454 | 20 |
| | Total | 1992/93 | 232 758 | 96 021 | 41 | 6 322 988 | 2 696 570 | 43 |
| | General education | | 211 711 | 92 524 | 44 | 5 995 051 | 2 619 306 | 44 |
| | Teacher training | | 1 590 | 514 | 32 | 48 256 | 19 618 | 41 |
| | Vocational education | | 19 457 | 2 983 | 15 | 279 681 | 57 646 | 21 |
| | Total | 1993/94 | 249 812 | 106 361 | 43 | 7 059 037 | 3 064 706 | 43 |
| | General education | | 227 961 | 102 648 | 45 | 6 683 832 | 2 969 164 | 44 |
| | Teacher training | | 1 159 | 334 | 29 | 34 721 | 13 339 | 38 |
| | Vocational education | | 20 692 | 3 379 | 16 | 340 484 | 82 203 | 24 |
| | Total | 1994/95 | 249 307 | 109 352 | 44 | 7 652 829 | 3 402 131 | 44 |
| | General education | | 228 889 | 105 882 | 46 | 7 284 611 | 3 310 470 | 45 |
| | Teacher training | | 538 | 158 | 29 | 21 210 | 7 605 | 36 |
| | Vocational education | | 19 880 | 3 312 | 17 | 347 008 | 84 056 | 24 |
| | Total | 1996/97 | 280 309 | 123 926 | 44 | 8 776 792 | 4 065 233 | 46 |
| | General education | | ... | ... | ... | ... | ... | ... |
| | Teacher training | | ... | ... | ... | ... | ... | ... |
| | Vocational education | | ... | ... | ... | ... | ... | ... |
| Iraq | Total | 1970/71 | 13 276 | 4 364 | 33 | 313 972 | 90 830 | 29 |
| | General education | | 12 309 | 4 124 | 34 | 304 240 | 88 595 | 29 |
| | Teacher training | | - | - | - | - | - | - |
| | Vocational education | | 967 | 240 | 25 | 9 732 | 2 235 | 23 |
| | Total | 1975/76 | 21 454 | 8 542 | 40 | 525 255 | 152 487 | 29 |
| | General education | | 19 397 | 8 008 | 41 | 493 384 | 141 497 | 29 |
| | Teacher training | | 403 | 262 | 65 | 8 096 | 5 485 | 68 |
| | Vocational education | | 1 654 | 272 | 16 | 23 775 | 5 505 | 23 |
| | Total | 1980/81 | 33 514 | 13 400 | 40 | 1 033 418 | 333 771 | 32 |
| | General education | | 28 552 | 11 890 | 42 | 954 536 | 303 154 | 32 |
| | Teacher training | | 814 | 517 | 64 | 21 958 | 13 939 | 63 |
| | Vocational education | | 4 148 | 993 | 24 | 56 924 | 16 678 | 29 |
| | Total | 1985/86 | 42 998 | 22 706 | 53 | 1 190 833 | 419 860 | 35 |
| | General education | | 35 143 | 19 238 | 55 | 1 038 627 | 372 096 | 36 |
| | Teacher training | | 1 110 | 605 | 55 | 26 767 | 15 764 | 59 |
| | Vocational education | | 6 745 | 2 863 | 42 | 125 439 | 32 000 | 26 |
| | Total | 1990/91 | ... | ... | ... | ... | ... | ... |
| | General education | | 44 772 | 27 269 | 61 | 1 023 710 | 398 765 | 39 |
| | Teacher training | | ... | ... | ... | ... | ... | ... |
| | Vocational education | | ... | ... | ... | ... | ... | ... |
| | Total | 1992/93 | 59 117 | 32 021 | 54 | 1 144 938 | 433 787 | 38 |
| | General education | | 48 496 | 26 551 | 55 | 992 617 | 386 522 | 39 |
| | Teacher training | | 1 303 | 633 | 49 | 22 018 | 13 571 | 62 |
| | Vocational education | | 9 318 | 4 837 | 52 | 130 303 | 33 694 | 26 |
| | Total | 1995/96 | 62 296 | 34 745 | 56 | 1 160 421 | 437 633 | 38 |
| | General education | | 52 393 | 29 477 | 56 | 1 037 482 | 406 025 | 39 |
| | Teacher training | | 1 392 | 777 | 56 | 23 534 | 14 120 | 60 |
| | Vocational education | | 8 511 | 4 491 | 53 | 99 405 | 17 488 | 18 |
| Israel | Total | 1970/71 | 14 031 | ... | ... | 142 521 | 73 073 | 51 |
| | General education | | ... | ... | ... | 76 264 | 43 203 | 57 |
| | Teacher training | | ... | ... | ... | 3 507 | 2 870 | 82 |
| | Vocational education | | ... | ... | ... | 62 750 | 27 000 | 43 |
| | Total | 1975/76 | ... | ... | ... | 170 168 | 89 229 | 52 |
| | General education | | ... | ... | ... | 96 625 | 55 509 | 57 |
| | Teacher training | | - | - | - | - | - | - |
| | Vocational education | | ... | ... | ... | 73 543 | 33 720 | 46 |
| | Total | 1980/81 | (47) 31 650 | (47) 18 150 | 57 | 199 859 | ... | ... |
| | General education | | ... | ... | ... | 117 527 | ... | ... |
| | Teacher training | | ... | ... | ... | - | - | - |
| | Vocational education | | ... | ... | ... | 82 332 | 38 236 | 46 |
| | Total | 1985/86 | (47) 37 735 | ... | ... | 251 466 | 129 110 | 51 |
| | General education | | ... | ... | ... | 150 996 | 84 118 | 56 |
| | Teacher training | | - | - | - | - | - | - |
| | Vocational education | | ... | ... | ... | 100 470 | 44 992 | 45 |

Secondary education: teaching staff and pupils   II.6
Enseignement secondaire: personnel enseignant et élèves
Enseñanza secundaria: personal docente y alumnos

| Country / Pays / País | Type of education / Type d'enseignement / Tipo de enseñanza | Year / Année / Año | Teaching staff Personnel enseignant Personal docente | | | Pupils enrolled Elèves inscrits Alumnos matriculados | | |
|---|---|---|---|---|---|---|---|---|
| | | | Total | Female Féminin Femenino | % F | Total | Female Féminin Femenino | % F |
| Israel (cont) | Total | 1990/91 | (47) 46 473 | (47) 29 256 | 63 | 309 098 | 156 653 | 51 |
| | General education | | ... | ... | ... | 194 022 | 104 377 | 54 |
| | Teacher training | | - | - | - | - | - | - |
| | Vocational education | | ... | ... | ... | 115 076 | 52 276 | 45 |
| | Total | 1991/92 | (47) 48 677 | (47) 30 802 | 63 | 326 319 | 165 370 | 51 |
| | General education | | ... | ... | ... | 204 581 | 110 570 | 54 |
| | Teacher training | | - | - | - | - | - | - |
| | Vocational education | | ... | ... | ... | 121 738 | 54 800 | 45 |
| | Total | 1992/93 | (47) 50 605 | (47) 32 650 | 65 | 334 290 | 169 589 | 51 |
| | General education | | ... | ... | ... | 212 597 | 114 887 | 54 |
| | Teacher training | | - | - | - | - | - | - |
| | Vocational education | | ... | ... | ... | 121 693 | 54 702 | 45 |
| | Total | 1993/94 | (47) 53 581 | (47) 34 682 | 65 | 338 288 | 170 029 | 50 |
| | General education | | ... | ... | ... | 215 938 | 114 667 | 53 |
| | Teacher training | | - | - | - | - | - | - |
| | Vocational education | | ... | ... | ... | 122 350 | 55 362 | 45 |
| | Total | 1994/95 | ... | ... | ... | (48) 533 797 | ... | ... |
| | General education | | ... | ... | ... | (48) 411 837 | ... | ... |
| | Teacher training | | ... | ... | ... | - | ... | ... |
| | Vocational education | | ... | ... | ... | 121 960 | ... | ... |
| | Total | 1995/96 | ... | ... | ... | 541 737 | ... | ... |
| | General education | | ... | ... | ... | 419 122 | ... | ... |
| | Teacher training | | ... | ... | ... | - | ... | ... |
| | Vocational education | | ... | ... | ... | 122 615 | ... | ... |
| Japan | Total | 1970/71 | 477 931 | 124 533 | 26 | 8 719 908 | 4 281 261 | 49 |
| | General education | | ... | ... | ... | 7 093 443 | 3 565 298 | 50 |
| | Teacher training | | - | - | - | - | - | - |
| | Vocational education | | ... | ... | ... | 1 626 465 | 715 963 | 44 |
| | Total | 1975/76 | 511 590 | 124 792 | 24 | 8 843 511 | 4 362 848 | 49 |
| | General education | | ... | ... | ... | 7 338 479 | 3 655 221 | 50 |
| | Teacher training | | - | - | - | - | - | - |
| | Vocational education | | ... | ... | ... | 1 505 032 | 707 627 | 47 |
| | Total | 1980/81 | 554 078 | 145 943 | 26 | 9 557 563 | 4 718 610 | 49 |
| | General education | | ... | ... | ... | 8 146 845 | 4 057 997 | 50 |
| | Teacher training | | - | - | - | - | - | - |
| | Vocational education | | ... | ... | ... | 1 410 718 | 660 613 | 47 |
| | Total | 1985/86 | 619 105 | 173 420 | 28 | 11 058 133 | 5 446 781 | 49 |
| | General education | | ... | ... | ... | 9 635 116 | 4 786 810 | 50 |
| | Teacher training | | - | - | - | - | - | - |
| | Vocational education | | ... | ... | ... | 1 423 017 | 659 971 | 46 |
| | Total | 1990/91 | 658 569 | 197 486 | 30 | 11 025 720 | 5 418 667 | 49 |
| | General education | | ... | ... | ... | 9 528 674 | 4 735 497 | 50 |
| | Teacher training | | - | - | - | - | - | - |
| | Vocational education | | ... | ... | ... | 1 497 046 | 683 170 | 46 |
| | Total | 1991/92 | 663 215 | 203 280 | 31 | 10 676 866 | 5 248 048 | 49 |
| | General education | | ... | ... | ... | 9 224 769 | 4 588 120 | 50 |
| | Teacher training | | - | - | - | - | - | - |
| | Vocational education | | ... | ... | ... | 1 452 097 | 659 928 | 45 |
| | Total | 1992/93 | ... | ... | ... | 10 255 337 | 5 054 022 | 49 |
| | General education | | ... | ... | ... | ... | ... | ... |
| | Teacher training | | - | - | - | - | - | - |
| | Vocational education | | ... | ... | ... | ... | ... | ... |
| | Total | 1993/94 | 695 707 | 230 677 | 33 | 10 202 510 | 5 013 127 | 49 |
| | General education | | 588 460 | 200 744 | 34 | 8 719 312 | 4 338 597 | 50 |
| | Teacher training | | - | - | - | - | - | - |
| | Vocational education | | 107 247 | 29 933 | 28 | 1 483 198 | 674 530 | 45 |
| | Total | 1994/95 | 702 575 | 229 645 | 33 | 9 878 568 | 4 852 217 | 49 |
| | General education | | 594 313 | 199 802 | 34 | 8 442 844 | 4 203 313 | 50 |
| | Teacher training | | - | - | - | - | - | - |
| | Vocational education | | 108 262 | 29 843 | 28 | 1 435 724 | 648 904 | 45 |
| Jordan (49) | Total | 1970/71 | 4 252 | 1 455 | 34 | 97 612 | 33 280 | 34 |
| | General education | | 4 093 | 1 427 | 35 | 94 659 | 32 601 | 34 |
| | Teacher training | | - | - | - | - | - | - |
| | Vocational education | | 159 | 28 | 18 | 2 953 | 679 | 23 |
| | Total | 1975/76 | 7 768 | 3 027 | 39 | 164 186 | 66 856 | 41 |
| | General education | | 7 410 | 2 945 | 40 | 157 745 | 64 963 | 41 |
| | Teacher training | | - | - | - | - | - | - |
| | Vocational education | | 358 | 82 | 23 | 6 441 | 1 893 | 29 |
| | Total | 1980/81 | 12 848 | 5 486 | 43 | 266 368 | 119 022 | 45 |
| | General education | | 11 999 | 5 248 | 44 | 252 367 | 114 833 | 46 |
| | Teacher training | | - | - | - | - | - | - |
| | Vocational education | | 849 | 238 | 28 | 14 001 | 4 189 | 30 |

II.6   Secondary education: teaching staff and pupils
Enseignement secondaire: personnel enseignant et élèves
Enseñanza secundaria: personal docente y alumnos

| Country<br>Pays<br>País | Type of education<br>Type d'enseignement<br>Tipo de enseñanza | Year<br>Année<br>Año | Teaching staff<br>Personnel enseignant<br>Personal docente | | | Pupils enrolled<br>Élèves inscrits<br>Alumnos matriculados | | |
|---|---|---|---|---|---|---|---|---|
| | | | Total | Female<br>Féminin<br>Femenino | %<br>F | Total | Female<br>Féminin<br>Femenino | %<br>F |
| Jordan (49) (cont) | Total | 1985/86 | 19 174 | 8 690 | 45 | 335 835 | 159 899 | 48 |
| | General education | | 17 074 | 7 897 | 46 | 305 046 | 147 809 | 48 |
| | Teacher training | | - | - | - | - | - | - |
| | Vocational education | | 2 100 | 793 | 38 | 30 789 | 12 090 | 39 |
| | Total | 1990/91 | (50) 6 940 | (50) 3 257 | 47 | (50) 100 953 | (50) 47 498 | 47 |
| | General education | | (50) 4 876 | (50) 2 477 | 51 | (50) 75 915 | (50) 38 845 | 51 |
| | Teacher training | | - | - | - | - | - | - |
| | Vocational education | | 2 064 | 780 | 38 | 25 038 | 8 653 | 35 |
| | Total | 1991/92 | 6 030 | 2 869 | 48 | 109 429 | 53 188 | 49 |
| | General education | | 3 983 | 2 067 | 52 | 83 930 | 43 727 | 52 |
| | Teacher training | | - | - | - | - | - | - |
| | Vocational education | | 2 047 | 802 | 39 | 25 499 | 9 461 | 37 |
| | Total | 1992/93 | 6 917 | 3 298 | 48 | 113 910 | 56 429 | 50 |
| | General education | | ... | ... | ... | 86 475 | 46 535 | 54 |
| | Teacher training | | - | - | - | - | - | - |
| | Vocational education | | 2 107 | 799 | 38 | 27 435 | 9 894 | 36 |
| | Total | 1993/94 | 7 150 | 3 378 | 47 | 123 825 | 61 710 | 50 |
| | General education | | 4 597 | 2 425 | 53 | 93 773 | 51 155 | 55 |
| | Teacher training | | - | - | - | - | - | - |
| | Vocational education | | 2 553 | 953 | 37 | 30 052 | 10 555 | 35 |
| | Total | 1994/95 | 7 661 | 3 616 | 47 | 132 319 | 66 500 | 50 |
| | General education | | ... | ... | ... | 100 834 | 55 758 | 55 |
| | Teacher training | | - | - | - | - | - | - |
| | Vocational education | | ... | ... | ... | 31 485 | 10 742 | 34 |
| | Total | 1995/96 | 8 615 | 4 160 | 48 | 143 014 | 71 980 | 50 |
| | General education | | 6 309 | 3 448 | 55 | 109 906 | 60 902 | 55 |
| | Teacher training | | - | - | - | - | - | - |
| | Vocational education | | 2 306 | 712 | 31 | 33 108 | 11 078 | 33 |
| | Total | 1996/97 | 8 972 | 4 339 | 48 | 149 063 | 74 870 | 50 |
| | General education | | ... | ... | ... | 113 484 | 62 557 | 55 |
| | Teacher training | | - | - | - | - | - | - |
| | Vocational education | | ... | ... | ... | 35 579 | 12 313 | 35 |
| | Total | 1997/98 | 9 300 | ... | ... | 155 008 | 77 240 | 50 |
| | General education | | ... | - | - | 115 307 | 62 930 | 55 |
| | Teacher training | | - | - | - | - | - | - |
| | Vocational education | | ... | - | - | 39 701 | 14 310 | 36 |
| Kazakstan | Total | 1980/81 | ... | ... | ... | 1 996 100 | ... | ... |
| | General education | | ... | ... | ... | 1 761 000 | ... | ... |
| | Teacher training | | - | - | - | - | - | - |
| | Vocational education | | ... | ... | ... | 235 100 | ... | ... |
| | Total | 1985/86 | ... | ... | ... | 2 173 900 | ... | ... |
| | General education | | 123 700 | 88 400 | 71 | 1 910 800 | ... | ... |
| | Teacher training | | - | - | - | - | - | - |
| | Vocational education | | ... | ... | ... | 263 100 | ... | ... |
| | Total | 1990/91 | ... | ... | ... | 2 144 400 | ... | ... |
| | General education | | 157 800 | 116 800 | 74 | 1 918 700 | ... | ... |
| | Teacher training | | - | - | - | - | - | - |
| | Vocational education | | ... | ... | ... | 225 700 | ... | ... |
| | Total | 1991/92 | ... | ... | ... | 2 115 400 | ... | ... |
| | General education | | 161 500 | 118 400 | 73 | 1 897 000 | ... | ... |
| | Teacher training | | - | - | - | - | - | - |
| | Vocational education | | ... | ... | ... | 218 400 | ... | ... |
| | Total | 1992/93 | ... | ... | ... | 2 064 100 | ... | ... |
| | General education | | 174 000 | 129 700 | 75 | 1 861 000 | ... | ... |
| | Teacher training | | - | - | - | - | - | - |
| | Vocational education | | ... | ... | ... | 203 100 | ... | ... |
| | Total | 1993/94 | ... | ... | ... | 2 019 700 | ... | ... |
| | General education | | 178 900 | 133 000 | 74 | 1 830 600 | 944 200 | 52 |
| | Teacher training | | - | - | - | - | - | - |
| | Vocational education | | ... | ... | ... | 189 100 | ... | ... |
| | Total | 1995/96 | ... | ... | ... | ... | ... | ... |
| | General education | | ... | ... | ... | 1 670 200 | 857 800 | 51 |
| | Teacher training | | - | - | - | - | - | - |
| | Vocational education | | ... | ... | ... | ... | ... | ... |
| | Total | 1996/97 | ... | ... | ... | 1 921 302 | 1 000 406 | 52 |
| | General education | | ... | ... | ... | 1 743 623 | 894 457 | 51 |
| | Teacher training | | ... | ... | ... | 23 009 | 21 769 | 95 |
| | Vocational education | | ... | ... | ... | 154 670 | 84 180 | 54 |
| Korea, Republic of | Total | 1970/71 | 52 232 | 7 953 | 15 | 1 906 918 | 723 568 | 38 |
| | General education | | 41 052 | 7 001 | 17 | 1 634 175 | 644 820 | 39 |
| | Teacher training | | - | - | - | - | - | - |
| | Vocational education | | 11 180 | 952 | 9 | 272 743 | 78 748 | 29 |

Secondary education: teaching staff and pupils
Enseignement secondaire: personnel enseignant et élèves
Enseñanza secundaria: personal docente y alumnos

II.6

| Country / Pays / País | Type of education / Type d'enseignement / Tipo de enseñanza | Year / Année / Año | Teaching staff Personnel enseignant Personal docente | | | Pupils enrolled Elèves inscrits Alumnos matriculados | | |
|---|---|---|---|---|---|---|---|---|
| | | | Total | Female Féminin Femenino | % F | Total | Female Féminin Femenino | % F |
| Korea, Republic of (cont) | Total | 1975/76 | 83 811 | 16 596 | 20 | 3 111 510 | 1 268 430 | 41 |
| | General education | | 67 332 | 14 659 | 22 | 2 674 972 | 1 126 247 | 42 |
| | Teacher training | | - | - | - | - | - | - |
| | Vocational education | | 16 479 | 1 937 | 12 | 436 538 | 142 183 | 33 |
| | Total | 1980/81 | 109 546 | 28 127 | 26 | 4 285 889 | 1 948 972 | 45 |
| | General education | | 82 338 | 22 744 | 28 | 3 404 602 | 1 561 667 | 46 |
| | Teacher training | | - | - | - | - | - | - |
| | Vocational education | | 27 208 | 5 383 | 20 | 881 287 | 387 305 | 44 |
| | Total | 1985/86 | 140 942 | 41 736 | 30 | (51) 4 934 975 | (51) 2 334 562 | 47 |
| | General education | | 109 123 | 34 547 | 32 | (51) 4 038 242 | (51) 1 890 076 | 47 |
| | Teacher training | | - | - | - | - | - | - |
| | Vocational education | | 31 819 | 7 189 | 23 | 896 733 | 444 486 | 50 |
| | Total | 1990/91 | 180 724 | 61 875 | 34 | 4 559 557 | 2 176 401 | 48 |
| | General education | | 145 613 | 53 379 | 37 | 3 735 151 | 1 738 762 | 47 |
| | Teacher training | | - | - | - | - | - | - |
| | Vocational education | | 35 111 | 8 496 | 24 | 824 406 | 437 639 | 53 |
| | Total | 1991/92 | 188 860 | 66 853 | 35 | 4 443 751 | 2 128 165 | 48 |
| | General education | | 151 055 | 57 364 | 38 | 3 624 482 | 1 690 674 | 47 |
| | Teacher training | | - | - | - | - | - | - |
| | Vocational education | | 37 805 | 9 489 | 25 | 819 269 | 437 491 | 53 |
| | Total | 1992/93 | 192 662 | 68 975 | 36 | 4 461 857 | 2 147 924 | 48 |
| | General education | | 151 790 | 58 657 | 39 | 3 626 259 | 1 701 519 | 47 |
| | Teacher training | | - | - | - | - | - | - |
| | Vocational education | | 40 872 | 10 318 | 25 | 835 598 | 446 405 | 53 |
| | Total | 1993/94 | (52) 192 703 | (52) 70 091 | 36 | (52) 4 580 040 | (52) 2 198 483 | 48 |
| | General education | | 151 616 | 59 586 | 39 | 3 664 573 | 1 723 086 | 47 |
| | Teacher training | | - | - | - | - | - | - |
| | Vocational education | | 41 087 | 10 505 | 26 | 915 467 | 475 397 | 52 |
| | Total | 1994/95 | 188 858 | 70 595 | 37 | 4 645 849 | 2 254 567 | 49 |
| | General education | | 147 640 | 59 769 | 40 | 3 732 006 | 1 765 036 | 47 |
| | Teacher training | | - | - | - | - | - | - |
| | Vocational education | | 41 218 | 10 826 | 26 | 913 843 | 489 531 | 54 |
| | Total | 1995/96 | 190 667 | 72 442 | 38 | 4 706 541 | 2 284 436 | 49 |
| | General education | | 148 382 | 61 058 | 41 | 3 744 442 | 1 769 734 | 47 |
| | Teacher training | | - | - | - | - | - | - |
| | Vocational education | | 42 285 | 11 384 | 27 | 962 099 | 514 702 | 53 |
| | Total | 1996/97 | 192 947 | 74 719 | 39 | 4 662 492 | 2 257 709 | 48 |
| | General education | | 150 508 | 63 071 | 42 | 3 712 742 | 1 763 794 | 48 |
| | Teacher training | | - | - | - | - | - | - |
| | Vocational education | | 42 439 | 11 648 | 27 | 949 750 | 493 915 | 52 |
| Kuwait | Total | 1970/71 | 5 476 | 2 435 | 44 | 70 734 | 30 185 | 43 |
| | General education | | 4 794 | 2 188 | 46 | 67 038 | 28 423 | 42 |
| | Teacher training | | 293 | 175 | 60 | 1 642 | 1 095 | 67 |
| | Vocational education | | 389 | 72 | 19 | 2 054 | 667 | 32 |
| | Total | 1975/76 | 9 371 | 4 564 | 49 | 108 219 | 49 127 | 45 |
| | General education | | 9 008 | 4 498 | 50 | 106 891 | 48 928 | 46 |
| | Teacher training | | - | - | - | - | - | - |
| | Vocational education | | 363 | 66 | 18 | 1 328 | 199 | 15 |
| | Total | 1980/81 | 15 342 | 7 607 | 50 | 181 882 | 83 227 | 46 |
| | General education | | 15 257 | 7 607 | 50 | 181 461 | 83 227 | 46 |
| | Teacher training | | - | - | - | - | - | - |
| | Vocational education | | 85 | - | - | 421 | - | - |
| | Total | 1985/86 | 18 795 | 9 726 | 52 | 239 581 | 112 780 | 47 |
| | General education | | 18 650 | 9 709 | 52 | 238 420 | 112 692 | 47 |
| | Teacher training | | - | - | - | - | - | - |
| | Vocational education | | 145 | 17 | 12 | 1 161 | 88 | 8 |
| | Total | 1990/91 | ... | ... | ... | ... | ... | ... |
| | General education | | 13 956 | 7 332 | 53 | 140 324 | 68 860 | 49 |
| | Teacher training | | - | - | - | - | - | - |
| | Vocational education | | ... | ... | ... | ... | ... | ... |
| | Total | 1991/92 | 15 062 | 7 963 | 53 | 167 331 | 82 698 | 49 |
| | General education | | 14 947 | 7 941 | 53 | 166 697 | 82 562 | 50 |
| | Teacher training | | - | - | - | - | - | - |
| | Vocational education | | 115 | 22 | 19 | 634 | 136 | 21 |
| | Total | 1992/93 | 16 081 | 8 517 | 53 | 177 675 | 87 383 | 49 |
| | General education | | 15 914 | 8 483 | 53 | 176 572 | 87 167 | 49 |
| | Teacher training | | - | - | - | - | - | - |
| | Vocational education | | 167 | 34 | 20 | 1 103 | 216 | 20 |
| | Total | 1993/94 | 17 424 | 9 294 | 53 | 187 941 | 92 507 | 49 |
| | General education | | 17 245 | 9 253 | 54 | 186 839 | 92 138 | 49 |
| | Teacher training | | - | - | - | - | - | - |
| | Vocational education | | 179 | 41 | 23 | 1 102 | 369 | 33 |

II.6    Secondary education: teaching staff and pupils
Enseignement secondaire: personnel enseignant et élèves
Enseñanza secundaria: personal docente y alumnos

| Country / Pays / País | Type of education / Type d'enseignement / Tipo de enseñanza | Year / Année / Año | Teaching staff / Personnel enseignant / Personal docente | | | Pupils enrolled / Elèves inscrits / Alumnos matriculados | | |
|---|---|---|---|---|---|---|---|---|
| | | | Total | Female Féminin Femenino | % F | Total | Female Féminin Femenino | % F |
| Kuwait (cont) | Total | 1994/95 | 18 405 | 9 850 | 54 | 198 661 | 97 775 | 49 |
| | General education | | 18 176 | 9 791 | 54 | 197 326 | 97 318 | 49 |
| | Teacher training | | - | - | - | - | - | - |
| | Vocational education | | 229 | 59 | 26 | 1 335 | 457 | 34 |
| | Total | 1995/96 | (53) 19 097 | ... | ... | (53) 206 934 | (53) 101 588 | 49 |
| | General education | | (53) 18 851 | ... | ... | (53) 204 959 | (53) 101 024 | 49 |
| | Teacher training | | - | - | - | - | - | - |
| | Vocational education | | 246 | 67 | 27 | 1 975 | 564 | 29 |
| | Total | 1996/97 | 19 878 | 10 860 | 55 | 216 223 | 106 313 | 49 |
| | General education | | 19 602 | 10 779 | 55 | 214 001 | 105 611 | 49 |
| | Teacher training | | - | - | - | - | - | - |
| | Vocational education | | 276 | 81 | 29 | 2 222 | 702 | 32 |
| | Total | 1997/98 | 21 187 | 11 791 | 56 | 224 293 | 111 744 | 50 |
| | General education | | 20 867 | 11 701 | 56 | 222 079 | 110 952 | 50 |
| | Teacher training | | - | - | - | - | - | - |
| | Vocational education | | 320 | 90 | 28 | 2 214 | 792 | 36 |
| Kyrgyzstan | Total | 1980/81 | ... | ... | ... | 631 400 | 308 500 | 49 |
| | General education | | 29 200 | 16 800 | 58 | 580 200 | 282 900 | 49 |
| | Teacher training | | - | - | - | - | - | - |
| | Vocational education | | ... | ... | ... | 51 200 | 25 600 | 50 |
| | Total | 1985/86 | ... | ... | ... | 657 300 | 320 700 | 49 |
| | General education | | 34 000 | 21 300 | 63 | 592 000 | 288 100 | 49 |
| | Teacher training | | - | - | - | - | - | - |
| | Vocational education | | ... | ... | ... | 65 300 | 32 600 | 50 |
| | Total | 1990/91 | ... | ... | ... | 651 200 | 327 400 | 50 |
| | General education | | 42 900 | 29 400 | 69 | 600 700 | 302 200 | 50 |
| | Teacher training | | - | - | - | - | - | - |
| | Vocational education | | ... | ... | ... | 50 500 | 25 200 | 50 |
| | Total | 1991/92 | 48 500 | 29 800 | 61 | 649 600 | 326 600 | 50 |
| | General education | | 43 200 | 28 100 | 65 | 600 300 | 302 000 | 50 |
| | Teacher training | | - | - | - | - | - | - |
| | Vocational education | | 5 300 | 1 700 | 32 | 49 300 | 24 600 | 50 |
| | Total | 1992/93 | 48 700 | 29 700 | 61 | 633 500 | 319 900 | 50 |
| | General education | | 43 600 | 28 000 | 64 | 586 200 | 296 300 | 51 |
| | Teacher training | | - | - | - | - | - | - |
| | Vocational education | | 5 100 | 1 700 | 33 | 47 300 | 23 600 | 50 |
| | Total | 1993/94 | 46 000 | 29 300 | 64 | 607 700 | 310 500 | 51 |
| | General education | | 41 500 | 27 800 | 67 | 565 600 | 289 500 | 51 |
| | Teacher training | | - | - | - | - | - | - |
| | Vocational education | | 4 500 | 1 500 | 33 | 42 100 | 21 000 | 50 |
| | Total | 1994/95 | 44 918 | 30 058 | 67 | 606 381 | ... | ... |
| | General education | | 40 718 | 28 458 | 70 | 565 681 | 289 151 | 51 |
| | Teacher training | | - | - | - | - | - | - |
| | Vocational education | | 4 200 | 1 600 | 38 | 40 700 | ... | ... |
| | Total | 1995/96 | 42 286 | ... | ... | 530 854 | ... | ... |
| | General education | | 38 915 | 27 806 | 71 | 498 849 | 261 482 | 52 |
| | Teacher training | | - | - | - | - | - | - |
| | Vocational education | | 3 371 | ... | ... | 32 005 | ... | ... |
| Lao People's Democratic Republic | Total | 1970/71 | 915 | 226 | 25 | 15 453 | 4 101 | 27 |
| | General education | | 436 | 103 | 24 | 10 026 | 2 659 | 27 |
| | Teacher training | | 218 | 46 | 21 | 3 283 | 901 | 27 |
| | Vocational education | | 261 | 77 | 30 | 2 144 | 541 | 25 |
| | Total | 1975/76 | ... | ... | ... | ... | ... | ... |
| | General education | | 1 209 | ... | ... | 29 523 | ... | ... |
| | Teacher training | | ... | ... | ... | ... | ... | ... |
| | Vocational education | | ... | ... | ... | ... | ... | ... |
| | Total | 1980/81 | (54) 4 703 | ... | ... | (54) 90 435 | (54) 34 913 | 39 |
| | General education | | (54) 3 764 | (54) 967 | 26 | (54) 78 925 | (54) 30 306 | 38 |
| | Teacher training | | 650 | 223 | 34 | 9 508 | 4 048 | 43 |
| | Vocational education | | 289 | ... | ... | 2 002 | 559 | 28 |
| | Total | 1985/86 | 10 146 | 3 510 | 35 | 113 630 | 46 490 | 41 |
| | General education | | 8 032 | 3 034 | 38 | 97 197 | 41 033 | 42 |
| | Teacher training | | 1 246 | 303 | 24 | 9 634 | 3 796 | 39 |
| | Vocational education | | 868 | 173 | 20 | 6 799 | 1 661 | 24 |
| | Total | 1990/91 | ... | ... | ... | ... | ... | ... |
| | General education | | 10 516 | 3 278 | 31 | 127 231 | 48 646 | 38 |
| | Teacher training | | ... | ... | ... | ... | ... | ... |
| | Vocational education | | ... | ... | ... | ... | ... | ... |
| | Total | 1991/92 | 10 198 | 2 877 | 28 | 125 702 | 48 964 | 39 |
| | General education | | 8 936 | 2 454 | 27 | 117 504 | 45 749 | 39 |
| | Teacher training | | 718 | 297 | 41 | 4 495 | 1 973 | 44 |
| | Vocational education | | 544 | 126 | 23 | 3 703 | 1 242 | 34 |

Secondary education: teaching staff and pupils   II.6
Enseignement secondaire: personnel enseignant et élèves
Enseñanza secundaria: personal docente y alumnos

| Country<br>Pays<br>País | Type of education<br>Type d'enseignement<br>Tipo de enseñanza | Year<br>Année<br>Año | Teaching staff<br>Personnel enseignant<br>Personal docente | | | Pupils enrolled<br>Elèves inscrits<br>Alumnos matriculados | | |
|---|---|---|---|---|---|---|---|---|
| | | | Total | Female<br>Féminin<br>Femenino | %<br>F | Total | Female<br>Féminin<br>Femenino | %<br>F |
| Lao People's<br>Democratic<br>Republic (cont) | Total<br>General education<br>Teacher training<br>Vocational education | 1992/93 | 12 838<br>10 956<br>660<br>1 222 | 4 889<br>4 322<br>248<br>319 | 38<br>39<br>38<br>26 | 139 819<br>126 976<br>4 440<br>8 403 | 53 176<br>48 717<br>1 857<br>2 602 | 38<br>38<br>42<br>31 |
| | Total<br>General education<br>Teacher training<br>Vocational education | 1993/94 | 12 713<br>11 066<br>611<br>1 036 | 4 831<br>4 331<br>228<br>272 | 38<br>39<br>37<br>26 | 155 366<br>143 673<br>4 065<br>7 628 | 60 023<br>55 942<br>1 720<br>2 361 | 39<br>39<br>42<br>31 |
| | Total<br>General education<br>Teacher training<br>Vocational education | 1994/95 | 11 635<br>10 149<br>476<br>1 010 | 4 370<br>3 936<br>154<br>280 | 38<br>39<br>32<br>28 | 163 657<br>154 176<br>3 123<br>6 358 | 64 073<br>60 830<br>1 201<br>2 042 | 39<br>39<br>38<br>32 |
| | Total<br>General education<br>Teacher training<br>Vocational education | 1995/96 | 11 269<br>10 117<br>344<br>808 | 4 260<br>3 918<br>116<br>226 | 38<br>39<br>34<br>28 | 169 691<br>161 934<br>2 098<br>5 659 | 66 711<br>63 943<br>840<br>1 928 | 39<br>39<br>40<br>34 |
| | Total<br>General education<br>Teacher training<br>Vocational education | 1996/97 | ...<br>10 717<br>197<br>... | ...<br>4 134<br>44<br>... | ...<br>39<br>22<br>... | *187 600<br>180 160<br>1 740<br>... | *73 944<br>71 164<br>780<br>... | *39<br>40<br>45<br>... |
| Lebanon | Total<br>General education<br>Teacher training<br>Vocational education | 1970/71 | ...<br>...<br>466<br>... | ...<br>...<br>168<br>... | ...<br>...<br>36<br>... | 165 854<br>159 871<br>3 393<br>2 590 | ...<br>64 141<br>1 644<br>... | ...<br>40<br>48<br>... |
| | Total<br>General education<br>Teacher training<br>Vocational education | 1980/81 | ...<br>21 344<br>392<br>... | ...<br>...<br>123<br>... | ...<br>...<br>31<br>... | 287 310<br>254 444<br>1 663<br>31 203 | ...<br>...<br>1 316<br>... | ...<br>...<br>79<br>... |
| | Total<br>General education<br>Teacher training<br>Vocational education | 1991/92 | ...<br>...<br>...<br>4 240 | ...<br>...<br>...<br>... | ...<br>...<br>...<br>... | ...<br>248 097<br>...<br>37 403 | ...<br>131 352<br>...<br>14 400 | ...<br>53<br>...<br>38 |
| | Total<br>General education<br>Teacher training<br>Vocational education | 1993/94 | ...<br>...<br>...<br>3 866 | ...<br>...<br>...<br>301 | ...<br>...<br>...<br>8 | ...<br>261 341<br>...<br>39 933 | ...<br>137 547<br>...<br>15 834 | ...<br>53<br>...<br>40 |
| | Total<br>General education<br>Teacher training<br>Vocational education | 1994/95 | ...<br>...<br>...<br>6 065 | ...<br>...<br>...<br>2 145 | ...<br>...<br>...<br>35 | ...<br>277 646<br>...<br>45 776 | ...<br>146 780<br>...<br>21 441 | ...<br>53<br>...<br>47 |
| | Total<br>General education<br>Teacher training<br>Vocational education | 1995/96 | ...<br>...<br>...<br>6 102 | ...<br>...<br>...<br>2 174 | ...<br>...<br>...<br>36 | ...<br>289 024<br>...<br>47 946 | ...<br>151 310<br>...<br>22 485 | ...<br>52<br>...<br>47 |
| | Total<br>General education<br>Teacher training<br>Vocational education | 1996/97 | ...<br>...<br>-<br>7 745 | ...<br>...<br>-<br>2 852 | ...<br>...<br>-<br>37 | 347 850<br>*292 002<br>-<br>*55 848 | 179 629<br>*154 244<br>-<br>*25 385 | 52<br>*53<br>-<br>*45 |
| Macau | Total<br>General education<br>Teacher training<br>Vocational education | 1970/71 | 725<br>556<br>16<br>153 | ...<br>...<br>65<br>... | ...<br>...<br>98<br>... | 10 007<br>8 960<br>65<br>982 | 4 491<br>4 183<br>64<br>244 | 45<br>47<br>98<br>25 |
| | Total<br>General education<br>Teacher training<br>Vocational education | 1975/76 | 564<br>382<br>6<br>176 | ...<br>...<br>...<br>... | ...<br>...<br>...<br>... | 11 758<br>7 867<br>61<br>3 830 | ...<br>...<br>...<br>... | ...<br>...<br>...<br>... |
| | Total<br>General education<br>Teacher training<br>Vocational education | 1991/92 | ...<br>...<br>...<br>... | ...<br>...<br>...<br>... | ...<br>...<br>...<br>... | 18 978<br>18 224<br>...<br>754 | 9 884<br>9 828<br>...<br>56 | 52<br>54<br>...<br>7 |
| | Total<br>General education<br>Teacher training<br>Vocational education | 1992/93 | ...<br>...<br>...<br>... | ...<br>...<br>...<br>... | ...<br>...<br>...<br>... | 20 383<br>19 526<br>...<br>857 | 10 721<br>10 635<br>...<br>86 | 53<br>54<br>...<br>10 |
| Malaysia | Total<br>General education<br>Teacher training<br>Vocational education | 1970 | 23 776<br>22 842<br>411<br>523 | ...<br>...<br>...<br>137 | ...<br>...<br>...<br>26 | 609 376<br>587 902<br>3 926<br>17 548 | 249 647<br>239 488<br>1 611<br>8 548 | 41<br>41<br>41<br>49 |
| | Total<br>General education<br>Teacher training<br>Vocational education | 1975 | 34 133<br>32 394<br>...<br>... | ...<br>...<br>...<br>... | ...<br>...<br>...<br>... | 933 411<br>899 669<br>...<br>... | ...<br>396 473<br>...<br>... | ...<br>44<br>...<br>... |

II.6  Secondary education: teaching staff and pupils
Enseignement secondaire: personnel enseignant et élèves
Enseñanza secundaria: personal docente y alumnos

| Country / Pays / País | Type of education / Type d'enseignement / Tipo de enseñanza | Year / Année / Año | Teaching staff — Personnel enseignant — Personal docente | | | Pupils enrolled — Elèves inscrits — Alumnos matriculados | | |
|---|---|---|---|---|---|---|---|---|
| | | | Total | Female / Féminin / Femenino | % F | Total | Female / Féminin / Femenino | % F |
| Malaysia (cont) | Total | 1980 | 47 625 | 21 436 | 45 | 1 083 818 | 516 114 | 48 |
| | General education | | 46 163 | 21 117 | 46 | 1 065 787 | 510 817 | 48 |
| | Teacher training | | - | - | - | - | - | - |
| | Vocational education | | 1 462 | 319 | 22 | 18 031 | 5 297 | 29 |
| | Total | 1985 | 58 630 | 27 728 | 47 | 1 294 990 | 635 995 | 49 |
| | General education | | 56 931 | 27 320 | 48 | 1 274 270 | 629 983 | 49 |
| | Teacher training | | - | - | - | - | - | - |
| | Vocational education | | 1 699 | 408 | 24 | 20 720 | 6 012 | 29 |
| | Total | 1990 | 75 328 | 38 682 | 51 | 1 456 497 | 740 060 | 51 |
| | General education | | 71 439 | 37 187 | 52 | 1 391 037 | 707 921 | 51 |
| | Teacher training | | - | - | - | - | - | - |
| | Vocational education | | 3 889 | 1 495 | 38 | 65 460 | 32 139 | 49 |
| | Total | 1991 | 80 573 | 42 379 | 53 | 1 511 084 | 761 619 | 50 |
| | General education | | 76 007 | 40 583 | 53 | 1 450 311 | 733 276 | 51 |
| | Teacher training | | - | - | - | - | - | - |
| | Vocational education | | 4 566 | 1 796 | 39 | 60 773 | 28 343 | 47 |
| | Total | 1992 | 86 192 | 46 400 | 54 | 1 566 790 | 794 246 | 51 |
| | General education | | 81 250 | 44 159 | 54 | 1 476 711 | 755 093 | 51 |
| | Teacher training | | - | - | - | - | - | - |
| | Vocational education | | 4 942 | 2 241 | 45 | 90 079 | 39 153 | 43 |
| | Total | 1993 | (55) 87 541 | ... | ... | (55) 1 572 837 | (55) 799 477 | 51 |
| | General education | | ... | ... | ... | 1 531 893 | 788 588 | 51 |
| | Teacher training | | - | - | - | - | - | - |
| | Vocational education | | (4) 4 185 | ... | ... | (4) 40 944 | (4) 10 889 | 27 |
| | Total | 1994 | (55) 86 697 | (55) 48 262 | 56 | 1 613 182 | 823 719 | 51 |
| | General education | | ... | ... | ... | 1 532 492 | 791 477 | 52 |
| | Teacher training | | - | - | - | - | - | - |
| | Vocational education | | (4) 4 490 | (4) 1 596 | 36 | 80 690 | 32 242 | 40 |
| | Total | 1995 | (4) 88 408 | (4) 47 020 | 53 | (4) 1 651 684 | (4) 845 747 | 51 |
| | General education | | (4) 83 564 | (4) 45 285 | 54 | (4) 1 603 322 | (4) 833 104 | 52 |
| | Teacher training | | - | - | - | - | - | - |
| | Vocational education | | (4) 4 844 | (4) 1 735 | 36 | (4) 48 362 | (4) 12 643 | 26 |
| | Total | 1996 | (4) 91 594 | (4) *54 985 | *60 | (4) 1 736 414 | (4) *892 643 | *51 |
| | General education | | (4) 86 605 | (4) 53 250 | 61 | (4) 1 690 691 | (4) 881 643 | 52 |
| | Teacher training | | - | - | - | - | - | - |
| | Vocational education | | (4) 4 989 | (4) *1 735 | *35 | (4) 45 723 | (4) *11 000 | *24 |
| | Total | 1997 | (4) 96 523 | (4) 56 905 | 59 | (4) 1 794 515 | (4) 910 866 | 51 |
| | General education | | ... | ... | ... | ... | ... | ... |
| | Teacher training | | - | - | - | - | - | .. |
| | Vocational education | | ... | ... | ... | ... | ... | ... |
| | Total | 1998 | (4) 102 139 | (4) 61 440 | 60 | (4) 1 889 592 | (4) 957 790 | 51 |
| | General education | | ... | ... | ... | ... | ... | ... |
| | Teacher training | | - | - | - | - | - | - |
| | Vocational education | | ... | ... | ... | ... | ... | ... |
| Maldives | Total | 1970 | 26 | 10 | 38 | 327 | 119 | 36 |
| | General education | | 26 | 10 | 38 | 327 | 119 | 36 |
| | Teacher training | | - | - | - | - | - | - |
| | Vocational education | | - | - | - | - | - | - |
| | Total | 1975 | ... | ... | ... | ... | ... | ... |
| | General education | | ... | ... | ... | 459 | 255 | 56 |
| | Teacher training | | - | - | - | - | - | - |
| | Vocational education | | ... | ... | ... | ... | ... | ... |
| | Total | 1980 | ... | ... | ... | 998 | ... | ... |
| | General education | | ... | ... | ... | 875 | ... | ... |
| | Teacher training | | - | - | - | - | - | - |
| | Vocational education | | ... | ... | ... | 123 | ... | ... |
| | Total | 1992 | ... | ... | ... | ... | ... | ... |
| | General education | | ... | ... | ... | 15 933 | 7 822 | 49 |
| | Teacher training | | ... | ... | ... | ... | ... | ... |
| | Vocational education | | ... | ... | ... | 154 | 5 | 3 |
| | Total | 1993 | ... | ... | ... | ... | ... | ... |
| | General education | | ... | ... | ... | 18 678 | 9 268 | 50 |
| | Teacher training | | ... | ... | ... | 298 | 190 | 64 |
| | Vocational education | | ... | ... | ... | ... | ... | ... |
| | Total | 1994 | ... | ... | ... | 21 409 | 10 703 | 50 |
| | General education | | ... | ... | ... | ... | ... | ... |
| | Teacher training | | ... | ... | ... | ... | ... | ... |
| | Vocational education | | ... | ... | ... | ... | ... | ... |
| | Total | 1995 | ... | ... | ... | 23 889 | 12 048 | 50 |
| | General education | | ... | ... | ... | ... | ... | ... |
| | Teacher training | | ... | ... | ... | ... | ... | ... |
| | Vocational education | | ... | ... | ... | ... | ... | ... |

Secondary education: teaching staff and pupils II.6
Enseignement secondaire: personnel enseignant et élèves
Enseñanza secundaria: personal docente y alumnos

| Country / Pays / País | Type of education / Type d'enseignement / Tipo de enseñanza | Year / Année / Año | Teaching staff Personnel enseignant Personal docente | | | Pupils enrolled Elèves inscrits Alumnos matriculados | | |
|---|---|---|---|---|---|---|---|---|
| | | | Total | Female Féminin Femenino | % F | Total | Female Féminin Femenino | % F |
| Maldives (cont) | Total | 1996 | ... | ... | ... | 26 701 | 13 401 | 50 |
| | General education | | ... | ... | ... | ... | ... | ... |
| | Teacher training | | ... | ... | ... | ... | ... | ... |
| | Vocational education | | ... | ... | ... | ... | ... | ... |
| | Total | 1997 | ... | ... | ... | 32 463 | 16 501 | 51 |
| | General education | | ... | ... | ... | ... | ... | ... |
| | Teacher training | | ... | ... | ... | ... | ... | ... |
| | Vocational education | | ... | ... | ... | ... | ... | ... |
| | Total | 1998 | ... | ... | ... | 36 905 | 18 885 | 51 |
| | General education | | ... | ... | ... | ... | ... | ... |
| | Teacher training | | ... | ... | ... | ... | ... | ... |
| | Vocational education | | ... | ... | ... | ... | ... | ... |
| Mongolia | Total | 1970/71 | ... | ... | ... | 96 543 | ... | ... |
| | General education | | 4 000 | ... | ... | 84 343 | ... | ... |
| | Teacher training | | ... | ... | ... | 1 600 | ... | ... |
| | Vocational education | | ... | ... | ... | 10 600 | ... | ... |
| | Total | 1975/76 | ... | ... | ... | (56) 184 688 | (56) 95 719 | 52 |
| | General education | | ... | ... | ... | (56) 172 134 | (56) 87 715 | 51 |
| | Teacher training | | 137 | 63 | 46 | 1 618 | 1 343 | 83 |
| | Vocational education | | ... | ... | ... | 10 936 | 6 661 | 61 |
| | Total | 1980/81 | ... | ... | ... | ... | ... | ... |
| | General education | | 9 456 | 5 629 | 60 | 227 418 | 117 032 | 51 |
| | Teacher training | | ... | ... | ... | ... | ... | ... |
| | Vocational education | | 1 272 | 651 | 51 | 18 651 | 8 529 | 46 |
| | Total | 1985/86 | 13 954 | 8 420 | 60 | 285 862 | ... | ... |
| | General education | | 12 027 | 7 405 | 62 | 262 626 | ... | ... |
| | Teacher training | | - | - | - | - | - | - |
| | Vocational education | | 1 927 | 1 015 | 53 | 23 236 | 11 402 | 49 |
| | Total | 1990/91 | 16 529 | 10 239 | 62 | 301 131 | 158 561 | 53 |
| | General education | | 14 712 | 9 253 | 63 | 274 700 | 145 710 | 53 |
| | Teacher training | | - | - | - | - | - | - |
| | Vocational education | | 1 817 | 986 | 54 | 26 431 | 12 851 | 49 |
| | Total | 1991/92 | 15 393 | 9 629 | 63 | 275 061 | ... | ... |
| | General education | | 14 251 | 8 945 | 63 | 257 100 | 137 218 | 53 |
| | Teacher training | | - | - | - | - | - | - |
| | Vocational education | | 1 142 | 684 | 60 | 17 961 | ... | ... |
| | Total | 1992/93 | 14 118 | 9 000 | 64 | 242 191 | 134 714 | 56 |
| | General education | | 13 276 | 8 525 | 64 | 230 700 | 134 144 | 58 |
| | Teacher training | | - | - | - | - | - | - |
| | Vocational education | | 842 | 475 | 56 | 11 491 | 570 | 5 |
| | Total | 1993/94 | 13 510 | 8 740 | 65 | 239 661 | 135 886 | 57 |
| | General education | | 12 858 | 8 366 | 65 | 228 170 | 130 177 | 57 |
| | Teacher training | | - | - | - | - | - | - |
| | Vocational education | | 652 | 374 | 57 | 11 491 | 5 709 | 50 |
| | Total | 1994/95 | 12 938 | 8 585 | 66 | 229 769 | 131 532 | 57 |
| | General education | | 12 353 | 8 255 | 67 | 222 214 | 127 868 | 58 |
| | Teacher training | | - | - | - | - | - | - |
| | Vocational education | | 585 | 330 | 56 | 7 555 | 3 664 | 48 |
| | Total | 1995/96 | 12 818 | 8 504 | 66 | 235 798 | 134 057 | 57 |
| | General education | | 12 323 | 8 213 | 67 | 227 811 | 129 898 | 57 |
| | Teacher training | | - | - | - | - | - | - |
| | Vocational education | | 495 | 291 | 59 | 7 987 | 4 159 | 52 |
| | Total | 1996/97 | (57) 13 171 | (57) 8 686 | 66 | (57) 195 408 | (57) 112 056 | 57 |
| | General education | | (57) 12 503 | (57) 8 311 | 66 | (57) 184 100 | (57) 106 110 | 58 |
| | Teacher training | | - | - | - | - | - | - |
| | Vocational education | | 668 | 375 | 56 | 11 308 | 5 946 | 53 |
| Myanmar | Total | 1970/71 | 24 636 | ... | ... | 791 059 | 309 100 | 39 |
| | General education | | 23 768 | 11 858 | 50 | 780 463 | 306 541 | 39 |
| | Teacher training | | 307 | ... | ... | 4 498 | 2 344 | 52 |
| | Vocational education | | 561 | ... | ... | 6 098 | 215 | 4 |
| | Total | 1975/76 | 24 911 | ... | ... | 933 486 | ... | ... |
| | General education | | 23 812 | ... | ... | 917 896 | 406 237 | 44 |
| | Teacher training | | 289 | ... | ... | 4 890 | 2 827 | 58 |
| | Vocational education | | 810 | ... | ... | 10 700 | ... | ... |
| | Total | 1980/81 | 31 248 | ... | ... | 1 066 300 | ... | ... |
| | General education | | 30 048 | ... | ... | 1 046 100 | ... | ... |
| | Teacher training | | 394 | ... | ... | 5 700 | ... | ... |
| | Vocational education | | 806 | ... | ... | 14 500 | ... | ... |
| | Total | 1985/86 | 55 363 | 37 885 | 68 | 1 273 073 | 593 849 | 47 |
| | General education | | 54 395 | 37 495 | 69 | 1 262 186 | 589 649 | 47 |
| | Teacher training | | 477 | *250 | *52 | 5 993 | *4 200 | *70 |
| | Vocational education | | 491 | *140 | *29 | 4 894 | - | - |

Secondary education: teaching staff and pupils
Enseignement secondaire: personnel enseignant et élèves
Enseñanza secundaria: personal docente y alumnos

| Country<br><br>Pays<br><br>País | Type of education<br><br>Type d'enseignement<br><br>Tipo de enseñanza | Year<br><br>Année<br><br>Año | Teaching staff<br>Personnel enseignant<br>Personal docente | | | Pupils enrolled<br>Elèves inscrits<br>Alumnos matriculados | | |
|---|---|---|---|---|---|---|---|---|
| | | | Total | Female<br>Féminin<br>Femenino | %<br><br>F | Total | Female<br>Féminin<br>Femenino | %<br><br>F |
| Myanmar (cont) | Total | 1990/91 | 99 964 | 70 992 | 71 | 1 281 165 | 629 795 | 49 |
| | General education | | 98 740 | 70 473 | 71 | 1 268 115 | 623 992 | 49 |
| | Teacher training | | 719 | *375 | *52 | 7 789 | 5 803 | 75 |
| | Vocational education | | 505 | 144 | 29 | 5 261 | - | - |
| | Total | 1991/92 | 101 874 | 73 016 | 72 | 1 408 030 | 700 508 | 50 |
| | General education | | 100 651 | 72 466 | 72 | 1 394 713 | 695 028 | 50 |
| | Teacher training | | 711 | *370 | *52 | 7 884 | *5 480 | *70 |
| | Vocational education | | 512 | *180 | *35 | 5 433 | - | - |
| | Total | 1992/93 | 104 402 | 75 345 | 72 | 1 439 735 | 717 920 | 50 |
| | General education | | 103 135 | 74 745 | 72 | 1 428 604 | 712 920 | 50 |
| | Teacher training | | 769 | *400 | *52 | 7 300 | *5 000 | *68 |
| | Vocational education | | 498 | *200 | *40 | 3 831 | - | - |
| | Total | 1993/94 | 104 740 | 76 725 | 73 | 1 530 378 | 761 944 | 50 |
| | General education | | 103 590 | 76 197 | 74 | 1 519 215 | 757 579 | 50 |
| | Teacher training | | 580 | *300 | *52 | 6 279 | 4 365 | 70 |
| | Vocational education | | 570 | 228 | 40 | 4 884 | - | - |
| | Total | 1994/95 | 106 515 | 78 257 | 73 | 1 752 510 | 878 168 | 50 |
| | General education | | 105 301 | 77 695 | 74 | 1 735 724 | 869 856 | 50 |
| | Teacher training | | 615 | *320 | *52 | 10 746 | 8 312 | 77 |
| | Vocational education | | 599 | 242 | 40 | 6 040 | - | - |
| | Total | 1995/96 | ... | ... | ... | ... | ... | ... |
| | General education | | ... | ... | ... | 1 923 323 | ... | ... |
| | Teacher training | | ... | ... | ... | ... | ... | ... |
| | Vocational education | | ... | ... | ... | ... | ... | ... |
| Nepal | Total | 1970 | ... | ... | ... | ... | ... | ... |
| | General education | | 5 484 | ... | ... | 115 614 | 15 824 | 14 |
| | Teacher training | | ... | ... | ... | ... | ... | ... |
| | Vocational education | | ... | ... | ... | ... | ... | ... |
| | Total | 1975 | 9 947 | ... | ... | 281 816 | 40 459 | 14 |
| | General education | | ... | ... | ... | ... | ... | ... |
| | Teacher training | | ... | ... | ... | ... | ... | ... |
| | Vocational education | | ... | ... | ... | ... | ... | ... |
| | Total | 1980 | 16 376 | 1 498 | 9 | 512 434 | 102 502 | 20 |
| | General education | | ... | ... | ... | ... | ... | ... |
| | Teacher training | | ... | ... | ... | ... | ... | ... |
| | Vocational education | | ... | ... | ... | ... | ... | ... |
| | Total | 1985 | (58) 18 362 | ... | ... | (58) 496 921 | (58) 113 162 | 23 |
| | General education | | ... | ... | ... | ... | ... | ... |
| | Teacher training | | ... | ... | ... | ... | ... | ... |
| | Vocational education | | ... | ... | ... | ... | ... | ... |
| | Total | 1990 | 22 820 | ... | ... | 708 663 | 205 288 | 29 |
| | General education | | ... | ... | ... | ... | ... | ... |
| | Teacher training | | ... | ... | ... | ... | ... | ... |
| | Vocational education | | ... | ... | ... | ... | ... | ... |
| | Total | 1991 | 24 632 | 2 423 | 10 | 773 808 | 232 742 | 30 |
| | General education | | ... | ... | ... | ... | ... | ... |
| | Teacher training | | ... | ... | ... | ... | ... | ... |
| | Vocational education | | ... | ... | ... | ... | ... | ... |
| | Total | 1992 | 25 357 | 2 969 | 12 | 855 137 | 272 237 | 32 |
| | General education | | ... | ... | ... | ... | ... | ... |
| | Teacher training | | ... | ... | ... | ... | ... | ... |
| | Vocational education | | ... | ... | ... | ... | ... | ... |
| | Total | 1993 | 26 303 | ... | ... | 910 114 | 300 395 | 33 |
| | General education | | ... | ... | ... | ... | ... | ... |
| | Teacher training | | ... | ... | ... | ... | ... | ... |
| | Vocational education | | ... | ... | ... | ... | ... | ... |
| | Total | 1994 | 29 503 | ... | ... | 944 509 | 325 157 | 34 |
| | General education | | ... | ... | ... | ... | ... | ... |
| | Teacher training | | ... | ... | ... | ... | ... | ... |
| | Vocational education | | ... | ... | ... | ... | ... | ... |
| | Total | 1995 | 31 406 | ... | ... | 1 016 443 | 365 157 | 36 |
| | General education | | ... | ... | ... | ... | ... | ... |
| | Teacher training | | ... | ... | ... | ... | ... | ... |
| | Vocational education | | ... | ... | ... | ... | ... | ... |
| | Total | 1996 | 36 127 | ... | ... | 1 121 335 | 419 909 | 37 |
| | General education | | ... | ... | ... | ... | ... | ... |
| | Teacher training | | ... | ... | ... | ... | ... | ... |
| | Vocational education | | ... | ... | ... | ... | ... | ... |
| Oman | Total | 1970/71 | - | - | - | - | - | - |
| | General education | | - | - | - | - | - | - |
| | Teacher training | | - | - | - | - | - | - |
| | Vocational education | | - | - | - | - | - | - |

Secondary education: teaching staff and pupils  II.6
Enseignement secondaire: personnel enseignant et élèves
Enseñanza secundaria: personal docente y alumnos

| Country / Pays / País | Type of education / Type d'enseignement / Tipo de enseñanza | Year / Année / Año | Teaching staff — Personnel enseignant — Personal docente | | | Pupils enrolled — Elèves inscrits — Alumnos matriculados | | |
|---|---|---|---|---|---|---|---|---|
| | | | Total | Female Féminin Femenino | % F | Total | Female Féminin Femenino | % F |
| Oman (cont) | Total | 1975/76 | (28) 208 | (28) 33 | 16 | (28) 1 379 | (28) 227 | 16 |
| | General education | | (28) 188 | (28) 33 | 18 | (28) 1 295 | (28) 227 | 18 |
| | Teacher training | | - | - | - | - | - | - |
| | Vocational education | | 20 | - | - | 84 | - | - |
| | Total | 1980/81 | ... | ... | ... | 16 776 | 4 058 | 24 |
| | General education | | 1 733 | 461 | 27 | 15 280 | 3 828 | 25 |
| | Teacher training | | 65 | 28 | 43 | 483 | 230 | 48 |
| | Vocational education | | ... | ... | ... | 1 013 | - | - |
| | Total | 1985/86 | 3 911 | ... | ... | 47 305 | 15 644 | 33 |
| | General education | | 3 416 | 1 117 | 33 | 44 931 | 15 227 | 34 |
| | Teacher training | | 102 | ... | ... | 657 | 314 | 48 |
| | Vocational education | | 393 | - | - | 1 717 | 103 | 6 |
| | Total | 1990/91 | 6 946 | 2 595 | 37 | 101 567 | 44 587 | 44 |
| | General education | | 6 059 | 2 595 | 43 | 99 176 | 44 587 | 45 |
| | Teacher training | | - | - | - | - | - | - |
| | Vocational education | | 887 | - | - | 2 391 | - | - |
| | Total | 1991/92 | 7 203 | 3 068 | 43 | 119 244 | 54 191 | 45 |
| | General education | | 6 841 | 3 068 | 45 | 116 817 | 54 191 | 46 |
| | Teacher training | | - | - | - | - | - | - |
| | Vocational education | | 362 | - | - | 2 427 | - | - |
| | Total | 1992/93 | 8 480 | 3 704 | 44 | 140 201 | 65 045 | 46 |
| | General education | | 8 112 | 3 704 | 46 | 137 947 | 65 045 | 47 |
| | Teacher training | | - | - | - | - | - | - |
| | Vocational education | | 368 | - | - | 2 254 | - | - |
| | Total | 1993/94 | 9 376 | 4 231 | 45 | 162 363 | 76 077 | 47 |
| | General education | | 9 127 | 4 231 | 46 | 160 654 | 76 077 | 47 |
| | Teacher training | | - | - | - | - | - | - |
| | Vocational education | | 249 | - | - | 1 709 | - | - |
| | Total | 1994/95 | 10 435 | 4 834 | 46 | 179 514 | 85 017 | 47 |
| | General education | | 10 193 | 4 834 | 47 | 178 226 | 85 017 | 48 |
| | Teacher training | | - | - | - | - | - | - |
| | Vocational education | | 242 | - | - | 1 288 | - | - |
| | Total | 1995/96 | 11 438 | 5 389 | 47 | 194 904 | 93 100 | 48 |
| | General education | | 11 231 | 5 389 | 48 | 193 113 | 93 100 | 48 |
| | Teacher training | | - | - | - | - | - | - |
| | Vocational education | | 207 | - | - | 1 791 | - | - |
| | Total | 1996/97 | 11 896 | 5 685 | 48 | 205 046 | 99 008 | 48 |
| | General education | | 11 712 | 5 685 | 49 | 203 346 | 99 008 | 49 |
| | Teacher training | | - | - | - | - | - | - |
| | Vocational education | | 184 | - | - | 1 700 | - | - |
| | Total | 1997/98 | 12 436 | 6 004 | 48 | 217 246 | 105 540 | 49 |
| | General education | | 12 251 | 6 004 | 49 | 215 673 | 105 540 | 49 |
| | Teacher training | | - | - | - | - | - | - |
| | Vocational education | | 185 | - | - | 1 573 | - | - |
| Pakistan | Total | 1970/71 | 73 846 | 19 343 | 26 | 1 462 644 | 291 101 | 20 |
| | General education | | 70 621 | 18 811 | 27 | 1 428 194 | 281 104 | 20 |
| | Teacher training | | 922 | 210 | 23 | 12 877 | 3 030 | 24 |
| | Vocational education | | 2 303 | 322 | 14 | 21 573 | 6 967 | 32 |
| | Total | 1975/76 | 106 960 | 31 492 | 29 | 1 935 849 | 451 729 | 23 |
| | General education | | 104 086 | 30 687 | 29 | 1 901 344 | 442 284 | 23 |
| | Teacher training | | 987 | 422 | 43 | 8 790 | 3 853 | 44 |
| | Vocational education | | 1 887 | 383 | 20 | 25 715 | 5 592 | 22 |
| | Total | 1980/81 | 123 817 | 36 815 | 30 | 2 165 832 | 558 029 | 26 |
| | General education | | 120 646 | 36 104 | 30 | 2 125 418 | 551 305 | 26 |
| | Teacher training | | 1 177 | 316 | 27 | 6 922 | 916 | 13 |
| | Vocational education | | 1 994 | 395 | 20 | 33 492 | 5 808 | 17 |
| | Total | 1985/86 | ... | ... | ... | 2 923 188 | 790 805 | 27 |
| | General education | | 157 600 | 49 300 | 31 | 2 871 520 | 779 490 | 27 |
| | Teacher training | | ... | ... | ... | 10 476 | 2 116 | 20 |
| | Vocational education | | ... | ... | ... | 41 192 | 9 199 | 22 |
| | Total | 1990/91 | ... | ... | ... | 4 345 464 | 1 350 117 | 31 |
| | General education | | ... | ... | ... | 4 254 998 | 1 325 998 | 31 |
| | Teacher training | | 3 309 | 1 439 | 43 | 36 295 | 13 927 | 38 |
| | Vocational education | | 4 093 | 1 127 | 28 | 54 171 | 10 192 | 19 |
| | Total | 1991/92 | ... | ... | ... | 5 022 416 | 1 613 275 | 32 |
| | General education | | ... | ... | ... | *4 933 000 | *1 588 000 | *32 |
| | Teacher training | | 2 654 | 1 408 | 53 | 33 149 | 13 305 | 40 |
| | Vocational education | | 4 047 | 1 269 | 31 | *56 267 | *11 970 | *21 |
| | Total | 1992/93 | ... | ... | ... | ... | ... | ... |
| | General education | | ... | ... | ... | ... | ... | ... |
| | Teacher training | | ... | ... | ... | ... | ... | ... |
| | Vocational education | | 6 772 | 2 790 | 41 | 91 000 | 29 000 | 32 |

II.6   Secondary education: teaching staff and pupils
       Enseignement secondaire: personnel enseignant et élèves
       Enseñanza secundaria: personal docente y alumnos

| Country / Pays / País | Type of education / Type d'enseignement / Tipo de enseñanza | Year / Année / Año | Teaching staff / Personnel enseignant / Personal docente | | | Pupils enrolled / Elèves inscrits / Alumnos matriculados | | |
|---|---|---|---|---|---|---|---|---|
| | | | Total | Female / Féminin / Femenino | % F | Total | Female / Féminin / Femenino | % F |
| Pakistan (cont) | Total | 1993/94 | ... | ... | ... | ... | ... | ... |
| | General education | | ... | ... | ... | ... | ... | ... |
| | Teacher training | | ... | ... | ... | ... | ... | ... |
| | Vocational education | | 6 850 | 2 860 | 42 | *92 000 | *30 000 | *33 |
| Philippines | Total | 1970/71 | 51 979 | ... | ... | 1 719 386 | ... | ... |
| | General education | | 51 979 | ... | ... | 1 719 386 | ... | ... |
| | Teacher training | | - | - | - | - | - | - |
| | Vocational education | | - | - | - | - | - | - |
| | Total | 1975/76 | 72 778 | ... | ... | 2 291 707 | ... | ... |
| | General education | | 72 778 | ... | ... | 2 291 707 | ... | ... |
| | Teacher training | | - | - | - | - | - | - |
| | Vocational education | | - | - | - | - | - | - |
| | Total | 1980/81 | 85 779 | ... | ... | 2 928 525 | 1 559 313 | 53 |
| | General education | | 85 779 | ... | ... | 2 928 525 | 1 559 313 | 53 |
| | Teacher training | | - | - | - | - | - | - |
| | Vocational education | | - | - | - | - | - | - |
| | Total | 1985/86 | 99 468 | ... | ... | 3 214 159 | 1 608 549 | 50 |
| | General education | | 99 468 | ... | ... | 3 214 159 | 1 608 549 | 50 |
| | Teacher training | | - | - | - | - | - | - |
| | Vocational education | | - | - | - | - | - | - |
| | Total | 1990/91 | 121 887 | ... | ... | 4 033 597 | ... | ... |
| | General education | | 121 887 | ... | ... | 4 033 597 | ... | ... |
| | Teacher training | | - | - | - | - | - | - |
| | Vocational education | | - | - | - | - | - | - |
| | Total | 1991/92 | 129 700 | ... | ... | 4 208 151 | ... | ... |
| | General education | | 129 700 | ... | ... | 4 208 151 | ... | ... |
| | Teacher training | | - | - | - | - | - | - |
| | Vocational education | | - | - | - | - | - | - |
| | Total | 1992/93 (4) | 89 063 | ... | ... | 4 421 649 | ... | ... |
| | General education | (4) | 89 063 | ... | ... | 4 421 649 | ... | ... |
| | Teacher training | | - | - | - | - | - | - |
| | Vocational education | | - | - | - | - | - | - |
| | Total | 1993/94 | 134 898 | ... | ... | 4 590 037 | ... | ... |
| | General education | | 134 898 | ... | ... | 4 590 037 | ... | ... |
| | Teacher training | | - | - | - | - | - | - |
| | Vocational education | | - | - | - | - | - | - |
| | Total | 1994/95 | 131 831 | ... | ... | 4 762 877 | ... | ... |
| | General education | | 131 831 | ... | ... | 4 762 877 | ... | ... |
| | Teacher training | | - | - | - | - | - | - |
| | Vocational education | | - | - | - | - | - | - |
| | Total | 1995/96 | ... | ... | ... | 4 809 863 | ... | ... |
| | General education | | ... | ... | ... | 4 809 863 | ... | ... |
| | Teacher training | | - | - | - | - | - | - |
| | Vocational education | | - | - | - | - | - | - |
| | Total | 1996/97 | 154 705 | ... | ... | 4 888 246 | ... | ... |
| | General education | | 154 705 | ... | ... | 4 888 246 | ... | ... |
| | Teacher training | | - | - | - | - | - | - |
| | Vocational education | | - | - | - | - | - | - |
| | Total | 1997/98 | ... | ... | ... | 4 979 795 | ... | ... |
| | General education | | ... | ... | ... | 4 979 795 | ... | ... |
| | Teacher training | | - | - | - | - | - | - |
| | Vocational education | | - | - | - | - | - | - |
| Qatar | Total | 1970/71 | 324 | 103 | 32 | 4 095 | 1 314 | 32 |
| | General education | | 250 | 96 | 38 | 3 649 | 1 200 | 33 |
| | Teacher training | | 30 | 7 | 23 | 237 | 114 | 48 |
| | Vocational education | | 44 | - | - | 209 | - | - |
| | Total | 1975/76 | 829 | 372 | 45 | 10 109 | 4 829 | 48 |
| | General education | | 698 | 335 | 48 | 9 416 | 4 560 | 48 |
| | Teacher training | | 56 | 37 | 66 | 324 | 269 | 83 |
| | Vocational education | | 75 | - | - | 369 | - | - |
| | Total | 1980/81 | 1 624 | 817 | 50 | 15 901 | 7 680 | 48 |
| | General education | | 1 538 | 817 | 53 | 15 461 | 7 680 | 50 |
| | Teacher training | | - | - | - | - | - | - |
| | Vocational education | | 86 | - | - | 440 | - | - |
| | Total | 1985/86 | 2 539 | 1 344 | 53 | 22 574 | 11 310 | 50 |
| | General education | | 2 434 | 1 344 | 55 | 21 874 | 11 310 | 52 |
| | Teacher training | | - | - | - | - | - | - |
| | Vocational education | | 105 | - | - | 700 | - | - |
| | Total | 1990/91 | 3 547 | 1 993 | 56 | 30 031 | 15 063 | 50 |
| | General education | | 3 420 | 1 993 | 58 | 29 154 | 15 063 | 52 |
| | Teacher training | | - | - | - | - | - | - |
| | Vocational education | | 127 | - | - | 877 | - | - |

Secondary education: teaching staff and pupils II.6
Enseignement secondaire: personnel enseignant et élèves
Enseñanza secundaria: personal docente y alumnos

| Country / Pays / País | Type of education / Type d'enseignement / Tipo de enseñanza | Year / Année / Año | Teaching staff / Personnel enseignant / Personal docente | | | Pupils enrolled / Elèves inscrits / Alumnos matriculados | | |
|---|---|---|---|---|---|---|---|---|
| | | | Total | Female / Féminin / Femenino | % F | Total | Female / Féminin / Femenino | % F |
| Qatar (cont) | Total | 1991/92 | 3 724 | 2 112 | 57 | 31 120 | 15 553 | 50 |
| | General education | | 3 593 | 2 112 | 59 | 30 277 | 15 553 | 51 |
| | Teacher training | | - | - | - | - | - | - |
| | Vocational education | | 131 | - | - | 843 | - | - |
| | Total | 1992/93 | 5 016 | 2 973 | 59 | 35 013 | 17 364 | 50 |
| | General education | | 4 888 | 2 973 | 61 | 34 231 | 17 364 | 51 |
| | Teacher training | | - | - | - | - | - | - |
| | Vocational education | | 128 | - | - | 782 | - | - |
| | Total | 1993/94 | 3 823 | 2 261 | 59 | 36 292 | 17 828 | 49 |
| | General education | | 3 695 | 2 261 | 61 | 35 518 | 17 828 | 50 |
| | Teacher training | | - | - | - | - | - | - |
| | Vocational education | | 128 | - | - | 774 | - | - |
| | Total | 1994/95 | 3 858 | 2 258 | 59 | 37 635 | 18 424 | 49 |
| | General education | | 3 738 | 2 258 | 60 | 36 964 | 18 424 | 50 |
| | Teacher training | | - | - | - | - | - | - |
| | Vocational education | | 120 | - | - | 671 | - | - |
| | Total | 1995/96 | ... | ... | ... | 38 594 | 18 804 | 49 |
| | General education | | 3 946 | 2 324 | 59 | 37 924 | 18 804 | 50 |
| | Teacher training | | - | - | - | - | - | - |
| | Vocational education | | ... | ... | ... | 670 | - | - |
| Saudi Arabia | Total | 1970/71 | 5 064 | 786 | 16 | 89 226 | 17 497 | 20 |
| | General education | | 3 993 | 369 | 9 | 74 691 | 10 501 | 14 |
| | Teacher training | | 762 | 359 | 47 | 12 827 | 6 286 | 49 |
| | Vocational education | | 309 | 58 | 19 | 1 708 | 710 | 42 |
| | Total | 1975/76 | 13 956 | 3 360 | 24 | 202 741 | 65 996 | 33 |
| | General education | | 12 154 | 3 038 | 25 | 184 404 | 61 673 | 33 |
| | Teacher training | | 1 156 | 288 | 25 | 14 015 | 4 064 | 29 |
| | Vocational education | | 646 | 34 | 5 | 4 322 | 259 | 6 |
| | Total | 1980/81 | 26 634 | 8 980 | 34 | 348 996 | 132 368 | 38 |
| | General education | | 24 254 | 8 058 | 33 | 328 328 | 122 307 | 37 |
| | Teacher training | | 1 619 | 922 | 57 | 15 562 | 10 061 | 65 |
| | Vocational education | | 761 | - | - | 5 106 | - | - |
| | Total | 1985/86 | ... | ... | ... | 603 127 | 229 633 | 38 |
| | General education | | 40 552 | 16 839 | 42 | 582 017 | 224 785 | 39 |
| | Teacher training | | 995 | 441 | 44 | 10 433 | 4 848 | 46 |
| | Vocational education | | 1 345 | - | - | 10 677 | - | - |
| | Total | 1990/91 | 71 149 | 29 123 | 41 | 892 585 | 392 136 | 44 |
| | General education | | 67 956 | 28 168 | 41 | 859 642 | 379 843 | 44 |
| | Teacher training | | 639 | 634 | 99 | 8 128 | 8 106 | 100 |
| | Vocational education | | 2 554 | 321 | 13 | 24 815 | 4 187 | 17 |
| | Total | 1991/92 | 73 230 | 33 263 | 45 | 965 305 | 426 961 | 44 |
| | General education | | 69 543 | 31 929 | 46 | 930 186 | 413 134 | 44 |
| | Teacher training | | 699 | 699 | 100 | 9 945 | 9 945 | 100 |
| | Vocational education | | 2 988 | 635 | 21 | 25 174 | 3 882 | 15 |
| | Total | 1992/93 | 92 975 | 37 553 | 40 | 1 073 361 | 472 972 | 44 |
| | General education | | 89 171 | 36 260 | 41 | 1 033 521 | 455 456 | 44 |
| | Teacher training | | 911 | 911 | 100 | 13 884 | 13 884 | 100 |
| | Vocational education | | 2 893 | 382 | 13 | 25 956 | 3 632 | 14 |
| | Total | 1993/94 | 106 981 | 45 474 | 43 | 1 197 079 | 530 214 | 44 |
| | General education | | 102 798 | 43 837 | 43 | 1 151 945 | 509 683 | 44 |
| | Teacher training | | 1 216 | 1 216 | 100 | 18 589 | 18 589 | 100 |
| | Vocational education | | 2 967 | 421 | 14 | 26 545 | 1 942 | 7 |
| | Total | 1994/95 | ... | ... | ... | ... | ... | ... |
| | General education | | 96 845 | 47 082 | 49 | 1 268 546 | 573 573 | 45 |
| | Teacher training | | ... | ... | ... | ... | ... | ... |
| | Vocational education | | ... | ... | ... | ... | ... | ... |
| | Total | 1995/96 | 109 529 | 53 581 | 49 | 1 424 785 | 652 344 | 46 |
| | General education | | 105 056 | 51 718 | 49 | 1 375 753 | 626 726 | 46 |
| | Teacher training | | 1 482 | 1 482 | 100 | 24 462 | 24 462 | 100 |
| | Vocational education | | 2 991 | 381 | 13 | 24 570 | 1 156 | 5 |
| | Total | 1996/97 | 119 881 | 59 852 | 50 | 1 542 989 | 707 073 | 46 |
| | General education | | 115 907 | 58 240 | 50 | 1 500 072 | 684 438 | 46 |
| | Teacher training | | 1 438 | 1 438 | 100 | 21 366 | 21 366 | 100 |
| | Vocational education | | 2 536 | 174 | 7 | 21 551 | 1 269 | 6 |
| Singapore | Total | 1970 | 7 513 | 3 061 | 41 | 149 143 | 71 005 | 48 |
| | General education | | 6 358 | 2 853 | 45 | 136 782 | 69 521 | 51 |
| | Teacher training | | - | - | - | - | - | - |
| | Vocational education | | 1 155 | 208 | 18 | 12 361 | 1 484 | 12 |
| | Total | 1975 | 7 951 | ... | ... | 183 364 | 89 980 | 49 |
| | General education | | 7 211 | *3 406 | *47 | 176 224 | 89 471 | 51 |
| | Teacher training | | - | - | - | - | - | - |
| | Vocational education | | 740 | ... | ... | 7 140 | 509 | 7 |

II.6 Secondary education: teaching staff and pupils
Enseignement secondaire: personnel enseignant et élèves
Enseñanza secundaria: personal docente y alumnos

| Country / Pays / País | Type of education / Type d'enseignement / Tipo de enseñanza | Year / Année / Año | Teaching staff — Personnel enseignant — Personal docente Total | Female Féminin Femenino | % F | Pupils enrolled — Elèves inscrits — Alumnos matriculados Total | Female Féminin Femenino | % F |
|---|---|---|---|---|---|---|---|---|
| Singapore (cont) | Total | 1980 | ... | ... | ... | 187 532 | 91 743 | 49 |
| | General education | | 8 275 | 4 613 | 56 | 173 693 | 89 483 | 52 |
| | Teacher training | | - | - | - | - | | |
| | Vocational education | | ... | ... | ... | 13 839 | 2 260 | 16 |
| | Total | 1985 | ... | ... | ... | (58) 211 489 | (58) 101 124 | 48 |
| | General education | | (58) 8 240 | (58) 4 743 | 58 | (58) 190 328 | (58) 96 503 | 51 |
| | Teacher training | | - | - | - | - | | |
| | Vocational education | | ... | ... | ... | 21 161 | 4 621 | 22 |
| | Total | 1990 | ... | ... | ... | 220 561 | 103 020 | 47 |
| | General education | | 9 197 | ... | ... | 191 459 | 95 898 | 50 |
| | Teacher training | | - | - | - | - | | |
| | Vocational education | | ... | ... | ... | 29 102 | 7 122 | 24 |
| | Total | 1991 | ... | ... | ... | 214 584 | 99 919 | 47 |
| | General education | | 9 200 | ... | ... | 185 713 | 92 963 | 50 |
| | Teacher training | | - | - | - | - | | |
| | Vocational education | | ... | ... | ... | 28 871 | 6 956 | 24 |
| | Total | 1992 | ... | ... | ... | 210 304 | 97 574 | 46 |
| | General education | | 9 278 | ... | ... | 182 149 | 90 631 | 50 |
| | Teacher training | | - | - | - | - | | |
| | Vocational education | | ... | ... | ... | 28 155 | 6 943 | 25 |
| | Total | 1993 | ... | ... | ... | 205 683 | 96 201 | 47 |
| | General education | | 9 606 | ... | ... | 180 729 | 90 071 | 50 |
| | Teacher training | | - | - | - | - | | |
| | Vocational education | | ... | ... | ... | 24 954 | 6 130 | 25 |
| | Total | 1994 | ... | ... | ... | ... | ... | ... |
| | General education | | 9 675 | ... | ... | 197 981 | 97 125 | 49 |
| | Teacher training | | - | - | - | - | | |
| | Vocational education | | (59) 1 310 | (59) 357 | 27 | (59) 12 492 | (59) 3 773 | 30 |
| | Total | 1995 | ... | ... | ... | ... | ... | ... |
| | General education | | 9 777 | 6 135 | 63 | 203 662 | ... | ... |
| | Teacher training | | - | - | - | - | | |
| | Vocational education | | (59) 1 382 | (59) 351 | 25 | (59) 9 476 | (59) 2 820 | 30 |
| | Total | 1996 | ... | ... | ... | ... | ... | ... |
| | General education | | 10 354 | ... | ... | 207 719 | ... | ... |
| | Teacher training | | - | - | - | - | | |
| | Vocational education | | (59) 1 212 | ... | ... | (59) 8 233 | ... | ... |
| Sri Lanka | Total | 1970 | ... | ... | ... | 941 322 | ... | ... |
| | General education | | ... | ... | ... | 930 897 | 467 982 | 50 |
| | Teacher training | | ... | ... | ... | 6 294 | ... | ... |
| | Vocational education | | ... | ... | ... | 4 131 | ... | ... |
| | Total | 1975 | ... | ... | ... | ... | ... | ... |
| | General education | | ... | ... | ... | (4) 1 063 766 | (4) 535 785 | 50 |
| | Teacher training | | ... | ... | ... | 8 855 | 5 852 | 66 |
| | Vocational education | | ... | ... | ... | ... | | |
| | Total | 1980 | ... | ... | ... | 1 267 323 | ... | ... |
| | General education | | ... | ... | ... | 1 258 002 | 641 045 | 51 |
| | Teacher training | | 689 | - | - | 9 321 | ... | ... |
| | Vocational education | | - | - | - | - | | |
| | Total | 1985 | ... | ... | ... | 1 462 794 | 757 738 | 52 |
| | General education | | ... | ... | ... | 1 462 794 | 757 738 | 52 |
| | Teacher training | | - | - | - | - | | |
| | Vocational education | | - | - | - | - | | |
| | Total | 1990 | (21) 108 944 | ... | ... | (21) 2 081 842 | (21) 1 064 399 | 51 |
| | General education | | (21) 108 944 | ... | ... | (21) 2 081 842 | (21) 1 064 399 | 51 |
| | Teacher training | | - | - | - | - | | |
| | Vocational education | | - | - | - | - | | |
| | Total | 1991 | 105 742 | ... | ... | 2 106 050 | 1 082 035 | 51 |
| | General education | | 105 742 | ... | ... | 2 106 050 | 1 082 035 | 51 |
| | Teacher training | | - | - | - | - | | |
| | Vocational education | | - | - | - | - | | |
| | Total | 1992 | 108 489 | 63 687 | 59 | 2 185 277 | 1 119 945 | 51 |
| | General education | | 108 489 | 63 687 | 59 | 2 185 277 | 1 119 945 | 51 |
| | Teacher training | | - | - | - | - | | |
| | Vocational education | | - | - | - | - | | |
| | Total | 1993 | 106 141 | 67 864 | 64 | 2 246 642 | 1 149 602 | 51 |
| | General education | | 106 141 | 67 864 | 64 | 2 246 642 | 1 149 602 | 51 |
| | Teacher training | | - | - | - | - | | |
| | Vocational education | | - | - | - | - | | |
| | Total | 1994 | 105 916 | 66 939 | 63 | 2 315 541 | 1 190 755 | 51 |
| | General education | | 105 916 | 66 939 | 63 | 2 315 541 | 1 190 755 | 51 |
| | Teacher training | | - | - | - | - | | |
| | Vocational education | | - | - | - | - | | |

Secondary education: teaching staff and pupils
Enseignement secondaire: personnel enseignant et élèves
Enseñanza secundaria: personal docente y alumnos

II.6

| Country / Pays / País | Type of education / Type d'enseignement / Tipo de enseñanza | Year / Année / Año | Teaching staff Personnel enseignant Personal docente | | | Pupils enrolled Elèves inscrits Alumnos matriculados | | |
|---|---|---|---|---|---|---|---|---|
| | | | Total | Female Féminin Femenino | % F | Total | Female Féminin Femenino | % F |
| Sri Lanka (cont) | Total | 1995 | 103 572 | 64 229 | 62 | 2 314 054 | 1 181 371 | 51 |
| | General education | | 103 572 | 64 229 | 62 | 2 314 054 | 1 181 371 | 51 |
| | Teacher training | | - | - | - | - | - | - |
| | Vocational education | | - | - | - | - | - | - |
| Syrian Arab Republic | Total | 1970/71 | (8) 15 045 | (8) 3 374 | 22 | 327 639 | 85 206 | 26 |
| | General education | | 13 483 | 3 219 | 24 | 315 803 | 84 170 | 27 |
| | Teacher training | | (8) 250 | (8) 93 | 37 | 653 | 357 | 55 |
| | Vocational education | | 1 312 | 62 | 5 | 11 183 | 679 | 6 |
| | Total | 1975/76 | (8) 24 895 | (8) 7 506 | 30 | 488 409 | 152 060 | 31 |
| | General education | | 22 704 | 7 062 | 31 | 463 348 | 146 925 | 32 |
| | Teacher training | | (8) 514 | (8) 253 | 49 | 3 015 | 1 371 | 45 |
| | Vocational education | | 1 677 | 191 | 11 | 22 046 | 3 764 | 17 |
| | Total | 1980/81 | ... | ... | ... | 604 327 | 220 939 | 37 |
| | General education | | 29 573 | 6 536 | 22 | 577 990 | 213 345 | 37 |
| | Teacher training | | ... | ... | ... | 147 | 88 | 60 |
| | Vocational education | | 3 280 | ... | ... | 26 190 | 7 506 | 29 |
| | Total | 1985/86 | 53 250 | 13 504 | 25 | 870 383 | 346 467 | 40 |
| | General education | | 45 912 | 12 326 | 27 | 814 917 | 332 455 | 41 |
| | Teacher training | | - | - | - | - | - | - |
| | Vocational education | | 7 338 | 1 178 | 16 | 55 466 | 14 012 | 25 |
| | Total | 1990/91 | 54 115 | 22 383 | 41 | 914 250 | 379 261 | 41 |
| | General education | | 44 875 | 20 151 | 45 | 847 783 | 352 975 | 42 |
| | Teacher training | | - | - | - | - | - | - |
| | Vocational education | | 9 240 | 2 232 | 24 | 66 467 | 26 286 | 40 |
| | Total | 1991/92 | 55 029 | 23 460 | 43 | 902 819 | 382 264 | 42 |
| | General education | | 46 218 | 21 015 | 45 | 849 530 | 361 890 | 43 |
| | Teacher training | | - | - | - | - | - | - |
| | Vocational education | | 8 811 | 2 445 | 28 | 53 289 | 20 374 | 38 |
| | Total | 1992/93 | 58 659 | 24 580 | 42 | 916 950 | 399 763 | 44 |
| | General education | | 47 889 | 21 418 | 45 | 845 631 | 369 642 | 44 |
| | Teacher training | | - | - | - | - | - | - |
| | Vocational education | | 10 770 | 3 162 | 29 | 71 319 | 30 121 | 42 |
| | Total | 1993/94 | 61 510 | 25 422 | 41 | 923 030 | 404 597 | 44 |
| | General education | | 49 951 | 21 683 | 43 | 846 550 | 370 997 | 44 |
| | Teacher training | | - | - | - | - | - | - |
| | Vocational education | | 11 559 | 3 739 | 32 | 76 480 | 33 600 | 44 |
| | Total | 1994/95 | 62 080 | 26 583 | 43 | 928 882 | 412 868 | 44 |
| | General education | | 50 779 | 22 720 | 45 | 841 964 | 373 481 | 44 |
| | Teacher training | | - | - | - | - | - | - |
| | Vocational education | | 11 301 | 3 863 | 34 | 86 918 | 39 387 | 45 |
| | Total | 1995/96 | 62 917 | 26 836 | 43 | 935 048 | 426 507 | 46 |
| | General education | | 51 477 | 22 496 | 44 | 846 778 | 381 750 | 45 |
| | Teacher training | | - | - | - | - | - | - |
| | Vocational education | | 11 440 | 4 340 | 38 | 88 270 | 44 757 | 51 |
| | Total | 1996/97 | 64 661 | 28 595 | 44 | 957 664 | 443 737 | 46 |
| | General education | | 52 182 | 23 697 | 45 | 865 042 | 396 010 | 46 |
| | Teacher training | | - | - | - | - | - | - |
| | Vocational education | | 12 479 | 4 898 | 39 | 92 622 | 47 727 | 52 |
| Tajikistan | Total | 1985/86 | ... | ... | ... | ... | ... | ... |
| | General education | | ... | ... | ... | ... | ... | ... |
| | Teacher training | | - | - | - | - | - | - |
| | Vocational education | | ... | ... | ... | 45 238 | ... | ... |
| | Total | 1990/91 | ... | ... | ... | 829 479 | ... | ... |
| | General education | | ... | ... | ... | 786 446 | ... | ... |
| | Teacher training | | - | - | - | - | - | - |
| | Vocational education | | ... | ... | ... | 43 033 | ... | ... |
| | Total | 1991/92 | ... | ... | ... | 830 302 | ... | ... |
| | General education | | ... | ... | ... | 788 441 | ... | ... |
| | Teacher training | | - | - | - | - | - | - |
| | Vocational education | | ... | ... | ... | 41 861 | ... | ... |
| | Total | 1992/93 | ... | ... | ... | 786 964 | ... | ... |
| | General education | | (43)(60) 64 000 | (43)(60) 22 000 | 34 | 752 999 | ... | ... |
| | Teacher training | | - | - | - | - | - | - |
| | Vocational education | | ... | ... | ... | 33 965 | ... | ... |
| | Total | 1993/94 | ... | ... | ... | 702 375 | ... | ... |
| | General education | | (43)(60) 62 700 | (43)(60) 21 900 | 35 | 669 584 | ... | ... |
| | Teacher training | | - | - | - | - | - | - |
| | Vocational education | | ... | ... | ... | 32 791 | ... | ... |
| | Total | 1994/95 | ... | ... | ... | 724 056 | ... | ... |
| | General education | | (43)(60) 58 189 | (43)(60) 20 756 | 36 | 694 574 | ... | ... |
| | Teacher training | | - | - | - | - | - | - |
| | Vocational education | | ... | ... | ... | 29 482 | ... | ... |

**Secondary education: teaching staff and pupils**
**Enseignement secondaire: personnel enseignant et élèves**
**Enseñanza secundaria: personal docente y alumnos**

| Country / Pays / País | Type of education / Type d'enseignement / Tipo de enseñanza | Year / Année / Año | Teaching staff Personnel enseignant Personal docente | | | Pupils enrolled Elèves inscrits Alumnos matriculados | | |
|---|---|---|---|---|---|---|---|---|
| | | | Total | Female Féminin Femenino | % F | Total | Female Féminin Femenino | % F |
| Tajikistan (cont) | Total | 1996/97 | ... | ... | ... | ... | ... | ... |
| | General education | | (60) 112 532 | (60) 39 730 | 35 | (60) 688 150 | (60) 322 468 | 47 |
| | Teacher training | | - | - | - | - | - | - |
| | Vocational education | | ... | ... | ... | ... | ... | ... |
| Thailand | Total | 1970/71 | ... | ... | ... | 695 023 | 290 207 | 42 |
| | General education | | 35 641 | (4) 6 631 | ... | 511 929 | 209 795 | 41 |
| | Teacher training | | ... | ... | ... | 28 253 | 14 409 | 51 |
| | Vocational education | | 6 010 | 2 371 | 39 | 154 841 | 66 003 | 43 |
| | Total | 1975/76 | ... | ... | ... | 1 193 741 | 523 203 | 44 |
| | General education | | (4) 29 527 | ... | ... | 956 427 | 414 461 | 43 |
| | Teacher training | | ... | ... | ... | 46 248 | 22 944 | 50 |
| | Vocational education | | 9 715 | 3 991 | 41 | 191 066 | 85 798 | 45 |
| | Total | 1980/81 | ... | ... | ... | (61) 1 919 967 | ... | ... |
| | General education | | (4)(61) 70 201 | (4)(61) 39 818 | 57 | (61) 1 617 465 | (61) 740 077 | 46 |
| | Teacher training | | ... | ... | ... | 5 388 | 2 746 | 51 |
| | Vocational education | | ... | ... | ... | 297 114 | ... | ... |
| | Total | 1985/86 | ... | ... | ... | ... | ... | ... |
| | General education | | 102 763 | ... | ... | 1 870 360 | ... | ... |
| | Teacher training | | ... | ... | ... | ... | ... | ... |
| | Vocational education | | *19 278 | ... | ... | 373 013 | ... | ... |
| | Total | 1990/91 | 133 882 | ... | ... | 2 230 403 | 1 076 896 | 48 |
| | General education | | 106 264 | ... | ... | 1 864 465 | 917 289 | 49 |
| | Teacher training | | - | - | - | - | - | - |
| | Vocational education | | 27 618 | ... | ... | 365 938 | 159 607 | 44 |
| | Total | 1991/92 | 134 087 | ... | ... | 2 444 092 | 1 183 778 | 48 |
| | General education | | 105 731 | ... | ... | 2 036 097 | 1 004 659 | 49 |
| | Teacher training | | - | - | - | - | - | - |
| | Vocational education | | 28 356 | ... | ... | 407 995 | 179 119 | 44 |
| | Total | 1992/93 | 141 632 | ... | ... | 2 717 672 | 1 323 630 | 49 |
| | General education | | 112 073 | ... | ... | 2 269 498 | 1 123 538 | 50 |
| | Teacher training | | - | - | - | - | - | - |
| | Vocational education | | 29 559 | ... | ... | 448 174 | 200 092 | 45 |
| | Total | 1993/94 | 151 008 | ... | ... | 3 044 069 | ... | ... |
| | General education | | 125 970 | ... | ... | 2 548 901 | ... | ... |
| | Teacher training | | - | - | - | - | - | - |
| | Vocational education | | 25 038 | ... | ... | 495 168 | ... | ... |
| | Total | 1994/95 | ... | ... | ... | 3 382 755 | ... | ... |
| | General education | | ... | ... | ... | 2 835 331 | ... | ... |
| | Teacher training | | - | - | - | - | - | - |
| | Vocational education | | ... | ... | ... | 547 424 | ... | ... |
| | Total | 1995/96 | ... | ... | ... | 3 794 290 | ... | ... |
| | General education | | ... | ... | ... | 3 144 482 | ... | ... |
| | Teacher training | | - | - | - | - | - | - |
| | Vocational education | | ... | ... | ... | 649 808 | ... | ... |
| | Total | 1996/97 | ... | ... | ... | 3 925 923 | ... | ... |
| | General education | | ... | ... | ... | 3 267 449 | ... | ... |
| | Teacher training | | - | - | - | - | - | - |
| | Vocational education | | ... | ... | ... | 658 474 | ... | ... |
| | Total | 1997/98 | ... | ... | ... | 4 097 331 | ... | ... |
| | General education | | ... | ... | ... | 3 358 470 | ... | ... |
| | Teacher training | | - | - | - | - | - | - |
| | Vocational education | | ... | ... | ... | 738 861 | ... | ... |
| Turkey | Total | 1970/71 | 47 452 | 17 368 | 37 | 1 308 779 | 373 167 | 29 |
| | General education | | 32 413 | 12 111 | 37 | 1 064 635 | 290 351 | 27 |
| | Teacher training | | 2 644 | 814 | 31 | 65 145 | 30 544 | 47 |
| | Vocational education | | 12 395 | 4 443 | 36 | 178 999 | 52 272 | 29 |
| | Total | 1975/76 | ... | ... | ... | 1 746 160 | 549 551 | 31 |
| | General education | | ... | ... | ... | 1 371 444 | 433 492 | 32 |
| | Teacher training | | ... | ... | ... | 53 445 | 25 181 | 47 |
| | Vocational education | | ... | ... | ... | 321 271 | 90 878 | 28 |
| | Total | 1980/81 | 112 178 | ... | ... | 2 217 909 | ... | ... |
| | General education | | 77 197 | 27 775 | 36 | 1 681 792 | 589 994 | 35 |
| | Teacher training | | 1 012 | ... | ... | 15 785 | ... | ... |
| | Vocational education | | 33 969 | ... | ... | 520 332 | ... | ... |
| | Total | 1985/86 | 138 640 | 49 601 | 36 | 2 927 692 | 1 030 948 | 35 |
| | General education | | 94 325 | 33 992 | 36 | 2 300 052 | 853 588 | 37 |
| | Teacher training | | 1 022 | 306 | 30 | 11 357 | 3 964 | 35 |
| | Vocational education | | 43 293 | 15 303 | 35 | 616 283 | 173 396 | 28 |
| | Total | 1990/91 | 159 401 | 61 696 | 39 | 3 808 142 | 1 426 071 | 37 |
| | General education | | 109 136 | 42 545 | 39 | 2 897 655 | 1 115 578 | 38 |
| | Teacher training | | 924 | 258 | 28 | 10 282 | 4 059 | 39 |
| | Vocational education | | 49 341 | 18 893 | 38 | 900 205 | 306 434 | 34 |

Secondary education: teaching staff and pupils **II.6**
Enseignement secondaire: personnel enseignant et élèves
Enseñanza secundaria: personal docente y alumnos

| Country<br>Pays<br>País | Type of education<br>Type d'enseignement<br>Tipo de enseñanza | Year<br>Année<br>Año | Teaching staff<br>Personnel enseignant<br>Personal docente | | | | Pupils enrolled<br>Elèves inscrits<br>Alumnos matriculados | | | |
|---|---|---|---|---|---|---|---|---|---|---|
| | | | | Total | Female<br>Féminin<br>Femenino | %<br>F | | Total | Female<br>Féminin<br>Femenino | %<br>F |
| Turkey (cont) | Total | 1991/92 | | 170 611 | 66 399 | 39 | | 3 987 423 | 1 514 908 | 38 |
| | General education | | | 114 496 | 44 897 | 39 | | 2 997 900 | 1 167 498 | 39 |
| | Teacher training | | | 1 116 | 341 | 31 | | 12 607 | 4 937 | 39 |
| | Vocational education | | | 54 999 | 21 161 | 38 | | 976 916 | 342 473 | 35 |
| | Total | 1992/93 | | 178 802 | 70 156 | 39 | | 4 299 810 | 1 653 221 | 38 |
| | General education | | | 119 291 | 47 129 | 40 | | 3 216 418 | 1 261 940 | 39 |
| | Teacher training | | | 1 239 | 366 | 30 | | 17 217 | 6 911 | 40 |
| | Vocational education | | | 58 272 | 22 661 | 39 | | 1 066 175 | 384 370 | 36 |
| | Total | 1993/94 | | 188 545 | 74 635 | 40 | | 4 476 086 | 1 756 393 | 39 |
| | General education | | | 126 627 | 50 640 | 40 | | 3 381 901 | 1 333 574 | 39 |
| | Teacher training | | | 1 435 | 414 | 29 | | 18 748 | 7 290 | 39 |
| | Vocational education | | | 60 483 | 23 581 | 39 | | 1 075 437 | 415 529 | 39 |
| | Total | 1994/95 | | 202 603 | 82 003 | 40 | | 4 725 551 | 1 842 245 | 39 |
| | General education | | | 133 359 | 55 321 | 41 | | 3 474 742 | 1 374 978 | 40 |
| | Teacher training | | | 1 453 | 417 | 29 | | 19 111 | 8 072 | 42 |
| | Vocational education | | | 67 791 | 26 265 | 39 | | 1 231 698 | 459 195 | 37 |
| | Total | 1996/97 | | 218 829 | 90 388 | 41 | | 4 760 892 | 1 900 870 | 40 |
| | General education | | | 143 322 | 60 968 | 43 | | 3 427 715 | 1 378 041 | 40 |
| | Teacher training | | | ./. | ./. | ./. | | ./. | ./. | ./. |
| | Vocational education | | (62) | 75 507 | (62) 29 420 | 39 | (62) | 1 333 177 | (62) 522 829 | 39 |
| United Arab<br>Emirates | Total | 1970/71 | (4) | 363 | ... | ... | (4) | 4 622 | ... | ... |
| | General education | | (4) | 302 | ... | ... | (4) | 4 008 | (4) 746 | 19 |
| | Teacher training | | | 18 | ... | ... | | 150 | ... | ... |
| | Vocational education | | | 43 | - | - | | 458 | - | - |
| | Total | 1975/76 | | ... | ... | ... | | 12 562 | 4 661 | 37 |
| | General education | | (4) | 1 389 | (4) 564 | 41 | | 12 148 | 4 569 | 38 |
| | Teacher training | | | ... | ... | ... | | 118 | 92 | 78 |
| | Vocational education | | | 90 | 1 | 1 | | 296 | - | - |
| | Total | 1980/81 | | ... | ... | ... | | 32 362 | 14 451 | 45 |
| | General education | | (4) | 2 829 | (4) 1 344 | 48 | | 31 940 | 14 451 | 45 |
| | Teacher training | | | - | - | - | | - | - | - |
| | Vocational education | | | ... | ... | ... | | 422 | - | - |
| | Total | 1985/86 | (4) | 4 237 | (4) 2 077 | 49 | | 62 082 | 29 880 | 48 |
| | General education | | | ... | ... | ... | | 61 478 | 29 880 | 49 |
| | Teacher training | | | - | - | - | | - | - | - |
| | Vocational education | | | ... | ... | ... | | 604 | - | - |
| | Total | 1990/91 | | 8 565 | 4 695 | 55 | | 107 881 | 54 342 | 50 |
| | General education | | | ... | ... | ... | | 107 115 | 54 342 | 51 |
| | Teacher training | | | - | - | - | | - | - | - |
| | Vocational education | | | ... | ... | ... | | 766 | - | - |
| | Total | 1991/92 | | 9 430 | 5 255 | 56 | | 118 011 | 59 754 | 51 |
| | General education | | | ... | ... | ... | | 117 118 | 59 754 | 51 |
| | Teacher training | | | - | - | - | | - | - | - |
| | Vocational education | | | ... | ... | ... | | 893 | - | - |
| | Total | 1992/93 | | 10 537 | 5 876 | 56 | | 129 683 | 65 756 | 51 |
| | General education | | | ... | ... | ... | | 128 643 | 65 756 | 51 |
| | Teacher training | | | - | - | - | | - | - | - |
| | Vocational education | | | ... | ... | ... | | 1 040 | - | - |
| | Total | 1993/94 | | 11 637 | 6 464 | 56 | | 145 143 | 73 403 | 51 |
| | General education | | | ... | ... | ... | | 144 000 | 73 403 | 51 |
| | Teacher training | | | - | - | - | | - | - | - |
| | Vocational education | | | ... | ... | ... | | 1 143 | - | - |
| | Total | 1994/95 | | 12 577 | 6 978 | 55 | | 159 840 | 80 380 | 50 |
| | General education | | | 12 388 | 6 978 | 56 | | 158 625 | 80 380 | 51 |
| | Teacher training | | | - | - | - | | - | - | - |
| | Vocational education | | | 189 | - | - | | 1 215 | - | - |
| | Total | 1995/96 | (4) | 10 061 | (4) 5 391 | 54 | (4) | 123 290 | (4) 63 790 | 52 |
| | General education | | (4) | 9 832 | (4) 5 391 | 55 | (4) | 121 736 | (4) 63 790 | 52 |
| | Teacher training | | | - | - | - | | - | - | - |
| | Vocational education | | | 229 | - | - | | 1 554 | - | - |
| | Total | 1996/97 | | ... | ... | ... | | 180 764 | 90 195 | 50 |
| | General education | | | ... | ... | ... | | 178 839 | 90 195 | 50 |
| | Teacher training | | | - | - | - | | - | - | - |
| | Vocational education | | | 249 | - | - | | 1 925 | - | - |
| Uzbekistan | Total | 1980/81 | | 192 100 | ... | ... | | 2 879 300 | ... | ... |
| | General education | | | 186 200 | 90 200 | 48 | | 2 656 200 | 1 211 500 | 46 |
| | Teacher training | | | - | - | - | | - | - | - |
| | Vocational education | | | 5 900 | ... | ... | | 223 100 | ... | ... |
| | Total | 1985/86 | | 226 300 | ... | ... | | 3 115 000 | ... | ... |
| | General education | | | 218 900 | 106 200 | 49 | | 2 824 400 | 1 331 900 | 47 |
| | Teacher training | | | - | - | - | | - | - | - |
| | Vocational education | | | 7 400 | ... | ... | | 290 600 | ... | ... |

II.6   Secondary education: teaching staff and pupils
Enseignement secondaire: personnel enseignant et élèves
Enseñanza secundaria: personal docente y alumnos

| Country<br>Pays<br>País | Type of education<br>Type d'enseignement<br>Tipo de enseñanza | Year<br>Année<br>Año | Teaching staff<br>Personnel enseignant<br>Personal docente | | | Pupils enrolled<br>Elèves inscrits<br>Alumnos matriculados | | |
|---|---|---|---|---|---|---|---|---|
| | | | Total | Female<br>Féminin<br>Femenino | %<br>F | Total | Female<br>Féminin<br>Femenino | %<br>F |
| Uzbekistan (cont) | Total | 1990/91 | 302 400 | ... | ... | 3 194 600 | ... | ... |
| | General education | | 293 900 | 141 200 | 48 | 2 965 800 | 1 456 300 | 49 |
| | Teacher training | | - | - | - | - | - | - |
| | Vocational education | | 8 500 | | ... | 228 800 | | ... |
| | Total | 1991/92 | 313 300 | ... | ... | 3 225 500 | ... | ... |
| | General education | | 305 700 | 143 300 | 47 | 3 006 200 | 1 473 100 | 49 |
| | Teacher training | | - | | - | - | | - |
| | Vocational education | | 7 600 | | ... | 219 300 | | ... |
| | Total | 1992/93 | 324 300 | ... | ... | 3 194 000 | ... | ... |
| | General education | | 316 300 | 152 900 | 48 | 2 979 800 | 1 443 700 | 48 |
| | Teacher training | | - | | - | - | | - |
| | Vocational education | | 8 000 | | ... | 214 200 | | ... |
| | Total | 1993/94 | 337 200 | ... | ... | 3 218 800 | ... | ... |
| | General education | | 328 900 | 158 900 | 48 | 2 992 800 | 1 454 400 | 49 |
| | Teacher training | | - | | - | - | | - |
| | Vocational education | | 8 300 | | ... | 226 000 | | ... |
| | Total | 1994/95 | 340 200 | ... | ... | 3 318 900 | ... | ... |
| | General education | | 332 300 | 162 400 | 49 | 3 104 400 | 1 492 300 | 48 |
| | Teacher training | | - | | - | - | | - |
| | Vocational education | | 7 900 | | ... | 214 500 | | ... |
| Viet Nam | Total | 1975/76 | 115 348 | 65 954 | 57 | 2 987 997 | 1 503 076 | 50 |
| | General education | | 108 454 | 64 209 | 59 | 2 915 753 | 1 462 826 | 50 |
| | Teacher training | | ... | ... | ... | ... | ... | ... |
| | Vocational education | | ... | ... | ... | ... | ... | ... |
| | Total | 1980/81 | ... | | ... | ... | | ... |
| | General education | | 148 973 | 86 182 | 58 | 3 846 737 | 1 808 028 | 47 |
| | Teacher training | | ... | ... | ... | 20 397 | 4 601 | 23 |
| | Vocational education | | ... | ... | ... | ... | ... | ... |
| | Total | 1985/86 | ... | | ... | ... | | ... |
| | General education | | 177 344 | 112 192 | 63 | 4 022 858 | 1 902 929 | 47 |
| | Teacher training | | ... | | ... | ... | | ... |
| | Vocational education | | 17 814 | | ... | 220 339 | | ... |
| | Total | 1990/91 | ... | | ... | ... | | ... |
| | General education | | 179 493 | ... | ... | 3 235 992 | ... | ... |
| | Teacher training | | ... | | ... | ... | | ... |
| | Vocational education | | 10 400 | | ... | 135 400 | | ... |
| | Total | 1991/92 | ... | | ... | ... | | ... |
| | General education | | 164 700 | ... | ... | 3 253 100 | ... | ... |
| | Teacher training | | ... | | ... | ... | | ... |
| | Vocational education | | 10 600 | | ... | 111 800 | | ... |
| | Total | 1992/93 | ... | | ... | ... | | ... |
| | General education | | 158 800 | ... | ... | 3 383 800 | ... | ... |
| | Teacher training | | ... | | ... | ... | | ... |
| | Vocational education | | 10 000 | | ... | 107 800 | | ... |
| | Total | 1993/94 | ... | | ... | ... | | ... |
| | General education | | 168 400 | ... | ... | 3 869 900 | ... | ... |
| | Teacher training | | ... | | ... | ... | | ... |
| | Vocational education | | 9 700 | | ... | 119 000 | | ... |
| | Total | 1994/95 | ... | | ... | ... | | ... |
| | General education | | 179 300 | ... | ... | 4 500 800 | ... | ... |
| | Teacher training | | ... | | ... | ... | | ... |
| | Vocational education | | 9 622 | 4 040 | 42 | 155 600 | ... | ... |
| | Total | 1995/96 | ... | | ... | ... | | ... |
| | General education | | 193 814 | ... | ... | 5 332 400 | ... | ... |
| | Teacher training | | ... | | ... | ... | | ... |
| | Vocational education | | 9 400 | | ... | 170 500 | | ... |
| | Total | 1996/97 | ... | | ... | ... | | ... |
| | General education | | 209 500 | ... | ... | 5 995 300 | ... | ... |
| | Teacher training | | ... | | ... | ... | | ... |
| | Vocational education | | 9 336 | 4 150 | 44 | 172 400 | ... | ... |
| | Total | 1997/98 | ... | | ... | ... | | ... |
| | General education | | 226 491 | 147 004 | 65 | 6 642 350 | 3 118 775 | 47 |
| | Teacher training | | ... | | ... | ... | | ... |
| | Vocational education | | ... | | ... | 179 907 | | ... |
| Yemen | Total | 1993/94 | ... | ... | ... | 212 129 | 37 791 | 18 |
| | General education | | ... | ... | ... | ... | ... | ... |
| | Teacher training | | ... | ... | ... | ... | ... | ... |
| | Vocational education | | ... | ... | ... | ... | ... | ... |
| | Total | 1996/97 | ... | | ... | 354 288 | 71 309 | 20 |
| | General education | | 13 787 | 3 192 | 23 | 286 405 | 60 939 | 21 |
| | Teacher training | | ... | | | 15 534 | 2 645 | 17 |
| | Vocational education | | ... | ... | ... | 52 349 | 7 725 | 15 |

Secondary education: teaching staff and pupils  II.6
Enseignement secondaire: personnel enseignant et élèves
Enseñanza secundaria: personal docente y alumnos

| Country Pays País | Type of education Type d'enseignement Tipo de enseñanza | Year Année Año | Teaching staff Personnel enseignant Personal docente | | | Pupils enrolled Elèves inscrits Alumnos matriculados | | |
|---|---|---|---|---|---|---|---|---|
| | | | Total | Female Féminin Femenino | % F | Total | Female Féminin Femenino | % F |
| Palestine | Total | 1994/95 | ... | ... | ... | 45 339 | 20 634 | 46 |
| | General education | | ... | ... | ... | 43 871 | 20 399 | 46 |
| | Teacher training | | - | - | - | - | - | - |
| | Vocational education | | 124 | ... | ... | 1 468 | 235 | 16 |
| | Total | 1995/96 | 6 937 | 2 870 | 41 | 50 770 | 23 538 | 46 |
| | General education | | 6 780 | 2 854 | 42 | 49 056 | 23 216 | 47 |
| | Teacher training | | - | - | - | - | - | - |
| | Vocational education | | 157 | 16 | 10 | 1 714 | 322 | 19 |
| | Total | 1996/97 | 7 950 | 3 401 | 43 | 56 467 | 26 833 | 48 |
| | General education | | 7 634 | 3 305 | 43 | 54 692 | 26 501 | 48 |
| | Teacher training | | - | - | - | - | - | - |
| | Vocational education | | 316 | 96 | 30 | 1 775 | 332 | 19 |
| **Europe** | | | | | | | | |
| Albania | Total | 1970/71 | ... | ... | ... | ... | ... | ... |
| | General education | | 1 157 | 333 | 29 | 20 514 | 9 832 | 48 |
| | Teacher training | | ... | ... | ... | ... | ... | ... |
| | Vocational education | | ... | ... | ... | ... | ... | ... |
| | Total | 1975/76 | ... | ... | ... | 110 519 | 50 707 | 46 |
| | General education | | ... | ... | ... | 32 796 | 16 936 | 52 |
| | Teacher training | | ... | ... | ... | 4 155 | 2 664 | 64 |
| | Vocational education | | ... | ... | ... | 73 568 | 31 107 | 42 |
| | Total | 1980/81 | 5 392 | 1 903 | 35 | 163 866 | 73 288 | 45 |
| | General education | | 1 008 | 468 | 46 | 30 780 | 18 070 | 59 |
| | Teacher training | | 21 | 19 | 90 | 604 | 532 | 88 |
| | Vocational education | | 4 363 | 1 416 | 32 | 132 482 | 54 686 | 41 |
| | Total | 1985/86 | 7 072 | 2 816 | 40 | 177 679 | 80 174 | 45 |
| | General education | | 1 470 | 845 | 57 | 42 133 | 24 049 | 57 |
| | Teacher training | | 102 | 56 | 55 | 2 417 | 1 621 | 67 |
| | Vocational education | | 5 500 | 1 915 | 35 | 133 129 | 54 504 | 41 |
| | Total | 1990/91 | 9 708 | ... | ... | 205 774 | 92 061 | 45 |
| | General education | | 3 318 | 1 231 | 37 | 67 589 | 37 415 | 55 |
| | Teacher training | | ... | ... | ... | 2 250 | 1 595 | 71 |
| | Vocational education | | ... | ... | ... | 135 935 | 53 051 | 39 |
| | Total | 1993/94 | 7 834 | 3 892 | 50 | 103 291 | 52 042 | 50 |
| | General education | | 4 149 | 2 417 | 58 | 73 259 | 40 896 | 56 |
| | Teacher training | | ... | ... | ... | 945 | 722 | 76 |
| | Vocational education | | ... | ... | ... | 29 087 | 10 424 | 36 |
| | Total | 1994/95 | 6 365 | 3 264 | 51 | 93 830 | 46 176 | 49 |
| | General education | | 4 965 | 2 564 | 52 | 73 216 | 39 813 | 54 |
| | Teacher training | | - | - | - | - | - | - |
| | Vocational education | | 1 400 | 700 | 50 | 20 614 | 6 363 | 31 |
| | Total | 1995/96 | 6 321 | 3 242 | 51 | 89 895 | 43 745 | 49 |
| | General education | | 4 147 | 2 134 | 51 | 71 391 | 37 999 | 53 |
| | Teacher training | | - | - | - | - | - | - |
| | Vocational education | | 2 174 | 1 108 | 51 | 18 504 | 5 746 | 31 |
| Andorra | Total | 1970/71 | ... | ... | ... | 724 | 317 | 44 |
| | General education | | ... | ... | ... | 724 | 317 | 44 |
| | Teacher training | | - | - | - | - | - | - |
| | Vocational education | | - | - | - | - | - | - |
| | Total | 1975/76 | ... | ... | ... | 1 753 | 1 092 | 62 |
| | General education | | ... | ... | ... | 1 753 | 1 092 | 62 |
| | Teacher training | | - | - | - | - | - | - |
| | Vocational education | | - | - | - | - | - | - |
| Austria | Total | 1970/71 | ... | ... | ... | 775 335 | 360 092 | 46 |
| | General education | | ... | ... | ... | 541 718 | 264 399 | 49 |
| | Teacher training | | 612 | 464 | 76 | 4 135 | 4 109 | 99 |
| | Vocational education | | 12 262 | 3 856 | 31 | 229 482 | 91 584 | 40 |
| | Total | 1975/76 | ... | ... | ... | 932 030 | 427 880 | 46 |
| | General education | | ... | ... | ... | 629 852 | 307 616 | 49 |
| | Teacher training | | ... | ... | ... | 6 283 | 6 247 | 99 |
| | Vocational education | | ... | ... | ... | 295 895 | 114 017 | 39 |
| | Total | 1980/81 | 68 492 | 33 594 | 49 | 937 484 | 433 494 | 46 |
| | General education | | 47 841 | 25 861 | 54 | 583 382 | 284 271 | 49 |
| | Teacher training | | 708 | 574 | 81 | 5 339 | 5 289 | 99 |
| | Vocational education | | 19 943 | 7 159 | 36 | 348 763 | 143 934 | 41 |
| | Total | 1985/86 | 74 014 | 38 883 | 53 | 847 188 | 394 872 | 47 |
| | General education | | 51 431 | 29 158 | 57 | 495 755 | 239 496 | 48 |
| | Teacher training | | 849 | 680 | 80 | 5 363 | 5 241 | 98 |
| | Vocational education | | 21 734 | 9 045 | 42 | 346 070 | 150 135 | 43 |

II.6 Secondary education: teaching staff and pupils
Enseignement secondaire: personnel enseignant et élèves
Enseñanza secundaria: personal docente y alumnos

| Country<br>Pays<br>País | Type of education<br>Type d'enseignement<br>Tipo de enseñanza | Year<br>Année<br>Año | Teaching staff<br>Personnel enseignant<br>Personal docente | | | Pupils enrolled<br>Elèves inscrits<br>Alumnos matriculados | | |
|---|---|---|---|---|---|---|---|---|
| | | | Total | Female<br>Féminin<br>Femenino | %<br>F | Total | Female<br>Féminin<br>Femenino | %<br>F |
| Austria (cont) | Total | 1990/91 | 76 295 | 41 451 | 54 | 746 272 | 349 612 | 47 |
| | General education | | 52 511 | 30 777 | 59 | 427 286 | 207 322 | 49 |
| | Teacher training | | 1 081 | 858 | 79 | 10 227 | 7 121 | 70 |
| | Vocational education | | 22 703 | 9 816 | 43 | 308 759 | 135 169 | 44 |
| | Total | 1991/92 | 78 069 | 42 711 | 55 | 756 385 | 354 667 | 47 |
| | General education | | 53 583 | 31 688 | 59 | 441 996 | 215 231 | 49 |
| | Teacher training | | 1 138 | 904 | 79 | 10 785 | 7 318 | 68 |
| | Vocational education | | 23 348 | 10 119 | 43 | 303 604 | 132 118 | 44 |
| | Total | 1992/93 | 80 980 | 45 182 | 56 | 768 176 | 361 570 | 47 |
| | General education | | 56 313 | 33 995 | 60 | 459 011 | 224 013 | 49 |
| | Teacher training | | 1 180 | 943 | 80 | 9 913 | 7 238 | 73 |
| | Vocational education | | 23 487 | 10 244 | 44 | 299 252 | 130 319 | 44 |
| | Total | 1993/94 | 82 696 | 46 594 | 56 | 778 006 | 367 347 | 47 |
| | General education | | 57 740 | 35 237 | 61 | 469 915 | 230 108 | 49 |
| | Teacher training | | 1 231 | 978 | 79 | 10 682 | 7 868 | 74 |
| | Vocational education | | 23 725 | 10 379 | 44 | 297 409 | 129 371 | 43 |
| | Total | 1994/95 | 83 608 | 47 368 | 57 | 786 156 | 371 435 | 47 |
| | General education | | 58 314 | 35 804 | 61 | 476 273 | 233 992 | 49 |
| | Teacher training | | 1 286 | 1 019 | 79 | 11 320 | 8 322 | 74 |
| | Vocational education | | 24 008 | 10 545 | 44 | 298 563 | 129 121 | 43 |
| | Total | 1995/96 | 80 168 | 44 436 | 55 | 791 453 | 375 011 | 47 |
| | General education | | 54 963 | 32 871 | 60 | 479 820 | 236 004 | 49 |
| | Teacher training | | 1 292 | 1 015 | 79 | 11 840 | 8 554 | 72 |
| | Vocational education | | 23 913 | 10 550 | 44 | 299 793 | 130 453 | 44 |
| | Total | 1996/97 | 79 806 | 44 382 | 56 | 793 485 | 377 559 | 48 |
| | General education | | 54 865 | 32 865 | 60 | 480 966 | 237 446 | 49 |
| | Teacher training | | ./. | ./. | ./. | 11 907 | 8 938 | 75 |
| | Vocational education | (62) 24 941 | (62) 11 517 | 46 | 300 612 | 131 175 | 44 |
| Belarus | Total | 1970/71 | ... | ... | ... | 818 300 | ... | ... |
| | General education | | ... | ... | ... | 767 400 | ... | ... |
| | Teacher training | | ... | ... | ... | 2 000 | ... | ... |
| | Vocational education | | ... | ... | ... | 48 900 | ... | ... |
| | Total | 1975/76 | ... | ... | ... | 882 600 | ... | ... |
| | General education | | ... | ... | ... | 800 000 | ... | ... |
| | Teacher training | | ... | ... | ... | 3 300 | ... | ... |
| | Vocational education | | ... | ... | ... | 79 300 | ... | ... |
| | Total | 1980/81 | ... | ... | ... | 759 700 | ... | ... |
| | General education | | ... | ... | ... | 645 200 | ... | ... |
| | Teacher training | | ... | ... | ... | 3 700 | ... | ... |
| | Vocational education | | ... | ... | ... | 110 800 | ... | ... |
| | Total | 1985/86 | ... | ... | ... | 716 700 | ... | ... |
| | General education | | ... | ... | ... | 586 700 | ... | ... |
| | Teacher training | | ... | ... | ... | 7 200 | ... | ... |
| | Vocational education | | ... | ... | ... | 122 800 | ... | ... |
| | Total | 1990/91 | ... | ... | ... | (7) 968 200 | ... | ... |
| | General education | | ... | ... | ... | (7) 843 700 | ... | ... |
| | Teacher training | | ... | ... | ... | 9 600 | ... | ... |
| | Vocational education | | ... | ... | ... | 114 900 | ... | ... |
| | Total | 1991/92 | 72 200 | | ... | 968 200 | ... | ... |
| | General education | | ... | | ... | 847 600 | ... | ... |
| | Teacher training | | ... | | ... | 9 500 | ... | ... |
| | Vocational education | | ... | | ... | 111 100 | ... | ... |
| | Total | 1992/93 | 75 200 | | ... | 970 300 | ... | ... |
| | General education | | ... | | ... | 851 100 | 433 400 | 51 |
| | Teacher training | | ... | | ... | 7 400 | ... | ... |
| | Vocational education | | ... | | ... | 111 800 | ... | ... |
| | Total | 1993/94 | 79 000 | | ... | 993 900 | ... | ... |
| | General education | | ... | | ... | 867 500 | 441 700 | 51 |
| | Teacher training | | ... | | ... | 6 800 | ... | ... |
| | Vocational education | | ... | | ... | 119 600 | ... | ... |
| | Total | 1994/95 | 81 700 | | ... | 1 024 600 | ... | ... |
| | General education | | ... | | ... | 902 100 | 454 200 | 50 |
| | Teacher training | | ... | | ... | 6 600 | ... | ... |
| | Vocational education | | ... | | ... | 115 900 | ... | ... |
| | Total | 1995/96 | ... | | ... | 1 055 200 | ... | ... |
| | General education | | ... | | ... | 929 000 | 465 000 | 50 |
| | Teacher training | | ... | | ... | 6 400 | ... | ... |
| | Vocational education | | ... | | ... | 119 800 | ... | ... |
| | Total | 1996/97 | ... | | ... | 1 064 700 | ... | ... |
| | General education | | ... | | ... | 946 100 | 472 600 | 50 |
| | Teacher training | | ... | | ... | 6 400 | ... | ... |
| | Vocational education | | ... | | ... | 112 200 | ... | ... |

Secondary education: teaching staff and pupils II.6
Enseignement secondaire: personnel enseignant et élèves
Enseñanza secundaria: personal docente y alumnos

| Country / Pays / País | Type of education / Type d'enseignement / Tipo de enseñanza | Year / Année / Año | Teaching staff — Personnel enseignant — Personal docente | | | Pupils enrolled — Elèves inscrits — Alumnos matriculados | | |
|---|---|---|---|---|---|---|---|---|
| | | | Total | Female Féminin Femenino | % F | Total | Female Féminin Femenino | % F |
| Belgium | Total | 1970/71 | ... | ... | ... | 723 703 | 350 036 | 48 |
| | General education | | ... | ... | ... | 334 891 | 156 258 | 47 |
| | Teacher training | | ... | ... | ... | 16 014 | 11 344 | 71 |
| | Vocational education | | ... | ... | ... | 372 798 | 182 434 | 49 |
| | Total | 1975/76 | ... | ... | ... | 795 203 | 387 798 | 49 |
| | General education | | ... | ... | ... | 494 684 | 232 727 | 47 |
| | Teacher training | | - | - | | - | | |
| | Vocational education | | ... | ... | ... | 300 519 | 155 071 | 52 |
| | Total | 1980/81 | ... | | | 835 524 | 415 108 | 50 |
| | General education | | ... | | | | | ... |
| | Teacher training | | - | | | | | ... |
| | Vocational education | | ... | | | | | |
| | Total | 1985/86 | ... | ... | ... | 824 997 | 405 651 | 49 |
| | General education | | ... | ... | ... | 450 662 | 228 164 | 51 |
| | Teacher training | | - | - | - | | | |
| | Vocational education | | ... | ... | ... | 374 335 | 177 487 | 47 |
| | Total | 1990/91 | 106 372 | 55 873 | 53 | 769 438 | 377 568 | 49 |
| | General education | | ... | ... | - | ... | | ... |
| | Teacher training | | - | - | - | | | |
| | Vocational education | | ... | | | ... | | ... |
| | Total | 1991/92 | 110 599 | 58 751 | 53 | 765 672 | 375 520 | 49 |
| | General education | | ... | ... | - | ... | | ... |
| | Teacher training | | - | - | - | | | |
| | Vocational education | | ... | | ... | ... | | ... |
| | Total | 1992/93 | (29) 128 500 | (29) 68 088 | 53 | (29) 1 040 586 | (29) 523 395 | 50 |
| | General education | | ... | ... | ... | (29) 493 591 | (29) 246 786 | 50 |
| | Teacher training | | - | - | - | | | - |
| | Vocational education | | ... | ... | ... | 546 995 | 276 609 | 51 |
| | Total | 1993/94 | 126 977 | 67 487 | 53 | 1 053 445 | 530 273 | 50 |
| | General education | | ... | ... | ... | 496 621 | 249 238 | 50 |
| | Teacher training | | - | - | | | | |
| | Vocational education | | ... | | ... | 556 824 | 281 035 | 50 |
| | Total | 1994/95 | ... | ... | ... | 1 061 790 | 537 673 | 51 |
| | General education | | ... | ... | ... | 495 560 | 248 932 | 50 |
| | Teacher training | | ... | ... | ... | | | - |
| | Vocational education | | ... | ... | ... | 566 230 | 288 741 | 51 |
| | Total | 1995/96 | ... | ... | ... | 1 058 998 | 535 324 | 51 |
| | General education | | ... | ... | ... | 489 957 | 246 775 | 50 |
| | Teacher training | | ... | ... | ... | | | |
| | Vocational education | | ... | ... | ... | 569 041 | 288 549 | 51 |
| Bulgaria | Total | 1970/71 | 23 053 | 11 206 | 49 | 318 725 | ... | ... |
| | General education | | 6 270 | 3 801 | 61 | 84 036 | ... | ... |
| | Teacher training | | ... | ... | ... | 65 | 65 | 100 |
| | Vocational education | | ... | ... | ... | 234 624 | 98 680 | 42 |
| | Total | 1975/76 | 27 045 | 14 079 | 52 | 344 015 | ... | ... |
| | General education | | 7 637 | 4 822 | 63 | 101 206 | ... | ... |
| | Teacher training | | - | - | | - | | |
| | Vocational education | | 19 408 | 9 257 | 48 | 242 809 | 101 406 | 42 |
| | Total | 1980/81 | 25 666 | 13 656 | 53 | 314 753 | 151 529 | 48 |
| | General education | | 7 159 | 4 604 | 64 | 91 863 | 62 673 | 68 |
| | Teacher training | | - | | | - | | |
| | Vocational education | | 18 507 | 9 052 | 49 | 222 890 | 88 856 | 40 |
| | Total | 1985/86 | 26 851 | 15 397 | 57 | 374 565 | 183 214 | 49 |
| | General education | | 9 392 | 6 318 | 67 | 163 417 | 104 400 | 64 |
| | Teacher training | | - | | | - | | |
| | Vocational education | | 17 459 | 9 079 | 52 | 211 148 | 78 814 | 37 |
| | Total | 1990/91 | 27 340 | 16 697 | 61 | 391 550 | 194 979 | 50 |
| | General education | | 9 873 | 7 154 | 72 | 152 683 | 101 432 | 66 |
| | Teacher training | | - | | | - | | |
| | Vocational education | | 17 467 | 9 543 | 55 | 238 867 | 93 547 | 39 |
| | Total | 1991/92 | 28 874 | 17 926 | 62 | 383 825 | 191 584 | 50 |
| | General education | | 10 790 | 7 911 | 73 | 150 297 | 101 875 | 68 |
| | Teacher training | | - | | | - | | |
| | Vocational education | | 18 084 | 10 015 | 55 | 233 528 | 89 709 | 38 |
| | Total | 1992/93 | 30 005 | 18 976 | 63 | 374 514 | 186 999 | 50 |
| | General education | | 11 329 | 8 477 | 75 | 152 801 | 103 648 | 68 |
| | Teacher training | | - | | | - | | |
| | Vocational education | | 18 676 | 10 499 | 56 | 221 713 | 83 351 | 38 |
| | Total | 1993/94 | 30 642 | 19 840 | 65 | 363 138 | 181 592 | 50 |
| | General education | | 11 806 | 8 861 | 75 | 151 903 | 102 046 | 67 |
| | Teacher training | | - | | | - | | |
| | Vocational education | | 18 836 | 10 979 | 58 | 211 235 | 79 546 | 38 |

**Secondary education: teaching staff and pupils**
**Enseignement secondaire: personnel enseignant et élèves**
**Enseñanza secundaria: personal docente y alumnos**

| Country / Pays / País | Type of education / Type d'enseignement / Tipo de enseñanza | Year / Année / Año | Teaching staff / Personnel enseignant / Personal docente | | | Pupils enrolled / Élèves inscrits / Alumnos matriculados | | |
|---|---|---|---|---|---|---|---|---|
| | | | Total | Female Féminin Femenino | % F | Total | Female Féminin Femenino | % F |
| Bulgaria (cont) | Total | 1994/95 | 31 305 | 20 770 | 66 | 371 102 | 186 732 | 50 |
| | General education | | 12 420 | 9 570 | 77 | 158 701 | 106 984 | 67 |
| | Teacher training | | - | - | - | - | - | - |
| | Vocational education | | 18 885 | 11 200 | 59 | 212 401 | 79 748 | 38 |
| | Total | 1995/96 | (63) 66 768 | (63) 47 564 | 71 | (63) 756 549 | (63) 366 315 | 48 |
| | General education | | (63) 47 627 | (63) 35 932 | 75 | (63) 543 212 | (63) 286 466 | 53 |
| | Teacher training | | - | - | - | - | - | - |
| | Vocational education | | 19 141 | 11 632 | 61 | 213 337 | 79 849 | 37 |
| | Total | 1996/97 | 67 088 | 48 545 | 72 | 733 362 | 356 083 | 49 |
| | General education | | 47 907 | 36 470 | 76 | 526 792 | 277 940 | 53 |
| | Teacher training | | - | - | - | - | - | - |
| | Vocational education | | 19 181 | 12 075 | 63 | 206 570 | 78 143 | 38 |
| Croatia | Total | 1980/81 | 13 387 | ... | ... | 194 395 | ... | ... |
| | General education | | ... | ... | ... | ... | ... | ... |
| | Teacher training | | - | - | - | - | - | - |
| | Vocational education | | ... | ... | ... | ... | ... | ... |
| | Total | 1985/86 | 12 403 | ... | ... | 189 946 | 95 451 | 50 |
| | General education | | ... | ... | ... | ... | ... | ... |
| | Teacher training | | - | - | - | - | - | - |
| | Vocational education | | ... | ... | ... | ... | ... | ... |
| | Total | 1990/91 | 13 858 | ... | ... | 186 090 | 95 012 | 51 |
| | General education | | ... | ... | ... | ... | ... | ... |
| | Teacher training | | - | - | - | - | - | - |
| | Vocational education | | ... | ... | ... | ... | ... | ... |
| | Total | 1991/92 | 11 705 | ... | ... | 173 727 | 90 088 | 52 |
| | General education | | ... | ... | ... | ... | ... | ... |
| | Teacher training | | - | - | - | - | - | - |
| | Vocational education | | ... | ... | ... | ... | ... | ... |
| | Total | 1992/93 | 12 278 | 7 382 | 60 | 190 926 | 98 053 | 51 |
| | General education | | ... | ... | ... | 43 205 | 28 124 | 65 |
| | Teacher training | | - | - | - | - | - | - |
| | Vocational education | | ... | ... | ... | 147 721 | 69 929 | 47 |
| | Total | 1993/94 | 14 965 | 9 022 | 60 | 207 013 | 104 634 | 51 |
| | General education | | 3 636 | 2 509 | 69 | 48 083 | 31 418 | 65 |
| | Teacher training | | - | - | - | - | - | - |
| | Vocational education | | 11 329 | 6 513 | 57 | 158 930 | 73 216 | 46 |
| | Total | 1994/95 | 15 338 | 9 226 | 60 | 197 027 | 99 988 | 51 |
| | General education | | 3 770 | 2 558 | 68 | 49 013 | 31 625 | 65 |
| | Teacher training | | - | - | - | - | - | - |
| | Vocational education | | 11 568 | 6 668 | 58 | 148 014 | 68 363 | 46 |
| | Total | 1995/96 | (63) 29 741 | (63) 18 880 | 63 | (63) 417 475 | (63) 206 433 | 49 |
| | General education | | (63) 17 781 | (63) 11 846 | 67 | (63) 265 467 | (63) 136 250 | 51 |
| | Teacher training | | - | - | - | - | - | - |
| | Vocational education | | 11 960 | 7 034 | 59 | 152 008 | 70 183 | 46 |
| | Total | 1996/97 | 31 070 | 19 771 | 64 | 416 829 | 205 490 | 49 |
| | General education | | 18 283 | 12 220 | 67 | 262 031 | 134 400 | 51 |
| | Teacher training | | - | - | - | - | - | - |
| | Vocational education | | 12 787 | 7 551 | 59 | 154 798 | 71 090 | 46 |
| Czech Republic | Total | 1970/71 | 83 008 | ... | ... | 1 025 567 | 512 334 | 50 |
| | General education | | 40 882 | ... | ... | 599 522 | 301 391 | 50 |
| | Teacher training | | ./. | ... | ... | ./. | ./. | ./. |
| | Vocational education | | (62) 42 126 | ... | ... | (62) 426 045 | (62) 210 943 | 50 |
| | Total | 1975/76 | 81 397 | ... | ... | 980 311 | 489 786 | 50 |
| | General education | | 39 191 | ... | ... | 580 029 | 293 908 | 51 |
| | Teacher training | | ./. | ... | ... | ./. | ./. | ./. |
| | Vocational education | | (62) 42 206 | ... | ... | (62) 400 282 | (62) 195 878 | 49 |
| | Total | 1985/86 | 88 302 | ... | ... | 1 160 863 | 583 895 | 50 |
| | General education | | 43 990 | ... | ... | 747 757 | 379 004 | 51 |
| | Teacher training | | ./. | ... | ... | ./. | ./. | ./. |
| | Vocational education | | (62) 44 312 | ... | ... | (62) 413 106 | (62) 204 891 | 50 |
| | Total | 1990/91 | 98 035 | ... | ... | 1 267 699 | 609 574 | 48 |
| | General education | | 47 412 | ... | ... | 756 643 | 387 844 | 51 |
| | Teacher training | | ./. | ... | ... | ./. | ./. | ./. |
| | Vocational education | | (62) 50 623 | ... | ... | (62) 511 056 | (62) 221 730 | 43 |
| | Total | 1991/92 | 97 624 | ... | ... | 1 201 149 | 599 092 | 50 |
| | General education | | 48 738 | ... | ... | 740 737 | 381 663 | 52 |
| | Teacher training | | ./. | ... | ... | ./. | ./. | ./. |
| | Vocational education | | (62) 48 886 | ... | ... | (62) 460 412 | (62) 217 429 | 47 |
| | Total | 1992/93 | 104 916 | 63 499 | 61 | 1 200 260 | 605 783 | 50 |
| | General education | | 54 252 | 39 779 | 73 | 687 124 | 346 821 | 50 |
| | Teacher training | | 593 | 408 | 69 | 4 465 | 4 274 | 96 |
| | Vocational education | | 50 071 | 23 312 | 47 | 508 671 | 254 688 | 50 |

Secondary education: teaching staff and pupils
Enseignement secondaire: personnel enseignant et élèves
Enseñanza secundaria: personal docente y alumnos

II.6

| Country / Pays / País | Type of education / Type d'enseignement / Tipo de enseñanza | Year / Année / Año | Teaching staff / Personnel enseignant / Personal docente | | | Pupils enrolled / Elèves inscrits / Alumnos matriculados | | |
|---|---|---|---|---|---|---|---|---|
| | | | Total | Female Féminin Femenino | % F | Total | Female Féminin Femenino | % F |
| Czech Republic (cont) | Total | 1993/94 | 105 167 | 64 273 | 61 | 1 189 988 | 584 600 | 49 |
| | General education | | 53 401 | 39 170 | 73 | 693 555 | 349 434 | 50 |
| | Teacher training | | 425 | 315 | 74 | 2 766 | 2 713 | 98 |
| | Vocational education | | 51 341 | 24 788 | 48 | 493 667 | 232 453 | 47 |
| | Total | 1994/95 | 101 251 (59) | 58 781 | ... | 1 193 245 | 591 390 | 50 |
| | General education | | 54 193 (59) | 38 054 | ... | 664 284 | 335 783 | 51 |
| | Teacher training | | 824 (59) | 455 | ... | 5 478 | 4 897 | 89 |
| | Vocational education | | 46 234 (59) | 20 272 | ... | 523 483 | 250 710 | 48 |
| | Total | 1995/96 | 114 373 | 70 178 | 61 | 1 190 725 | 591 073 | 50 |
| | General education | | 54 273 | 39 978 | 74 | 643 191 | 325 382 | 51 |
| | Teacher training | | 395 | 256 | 65 | 3 077 | 2 787 | 91 |
| | Vocational education | | 59 705 | 29 944 | 50 | 544 457 | 262 904 | 48 |
| Denmark | Total | 1970/71 | ... | ... | ... | 407 103 | | |
| | General education | | ... | ... | ... | 283 464 | 143 253 | 51 |
| | Teacher training | | - | - | - | - | - | - |
| | Vocational education | | ... | ... | ... | 123 639 | ... | - |
| | Total | 1975/76 | ... | ... | ... | ... | ... | |
| | General education | | ... | ... | ... | 327 588 | ... | - |
| | Teacher training | | - | - | - | - | - | - |
| | Vocational education | | ... | ... | ... | ... | ... | ... |
| | Total | 1980/81 | ... | ... | ... | 498 944 | 242 206 | 49 |
| | General education | | ... | ... | ... | 372 948 | 190 742 | 51 |
| | Teacher training | | - | | - | - | | - |
| | Vocational education | | ... | ... | ... | 125 996 | 51 464 | 41 |
| | Total | 1985/86 | ... | ... | ... | 487 526 | 237 437 | 49 |
| | General education | | 38 821 | ... | ... | 336 754 | 172 832 | 51 |
| | Teacher training | | - | | - | - | | - |
| | Vocational education | | ... | ... | ... | 150 772 | 64 605 | 43 |
| | Total | 1990/91 | ... | ... | ... | 464 555 | 228 598 | 49 |
| | General education | | ... | ... | ... | 316 748 | 163 022 | 51 |
| | Teacher training | | - | - | | - | | - |
| | Vocational education | | ... | ... | ... | 147 807 | 65 576 | 44 |
| | Total | 1991/92 | ... | ... | ... | 455 639 | 224 690 | 49 |
| | General education | | ... | ... | ... | 310 049 | 159 526 | 51 |
| | Teacher training | | - | - | | - | | - |
| | Vocational education | | ... | ... | ... | 145 590 | 65 164 | 45 |
| | Total | 1992/93 | 52 100 (29) | 25 900 (29) | 50 | 448 596 (29) | 222 056 (29) | 50 |
| | General education | | 39 300 | 20 800 | 53 | 326 175 | 168 106 | 52 |
| | Teacher training | | - | | - | - | | - |
| | Vocational education | | 12 800 | 5 100 | 40 | 122 421 | 53 950 | 44 |
| | Total | 1993/94 | 53 000 | 27 400 | 52 | 445 746 | 220 710 | 50 |
| | General education | | 39 700 | 21 500 | 54 | 325 108 | 167 495 | 52 |
| | Teacher training | | - | | - | - | | - |
| | Vocational education | | 13 300 | 5 900 | 44 | 120 638 | 53 215 | 44 |
| | Total | 1994/95 | 50 100 | 25 900 | 52 | 444 682 | 220 120 | 50 |
| | General education | | 37 000 | 20 100 | 54 | 321 448 | 165 324 | 51 |
| | Teacher training | | - | | - | - | | - |
| | Vocational education | | 13 100 | 5 800 | 44 | 123 234 | 54 796 | 44 |
| | Total | 1995/96 | ... | ... | ... | 438 809 | 217 156 | 49 |
| | General education | | ... | ... | ... | 316 750 | 163 033 | 51 |
| | Teacher training | | - | | - | - | | - |
| | Vocational education | | ... | ... | ... | 122 059 | 54 123 | 44 |
| Estonia | Total | 1980/81 | ... | ... | ... | ... | ... | ... |
| | General education | | ... | ... | ... | 85 873 | 43 808 | 51 |
| | Teacher training | | ... | ... | ... | ... | ... | ... |
| | Vocational education | | ... | ... | ... | ... | | |
| | Total | 1985/86 | ... | ... | ... | 126 440 | ... | ... |
| | General education | | ... | ... | ... | 84 504 | 43 659 | 52 |
| | Teacher training | | ... | ... | ... | 1 784 | 1 745 | 98 |
| | Vocational education | | ... | ... | ... | 40 152 | ... | ... |
| | Total | 1990/91 | ... | ... | ... | 134 463 | ... | ... |
| | General education | | ... | ... | ... | 98 014 | 51 581 | 53 |
| | Teacher training | | ... | ... | ... | 1 563 | ... | |
| | Vocational education | | ... | ... | ... | 34 886 | ... | |
| | Total | 1991/92 | ... | ... | ... | 132 020 | 67 119 | 51 |
| | General education | | ... | ... | ... | 97 625 | 51 348 | 53 |
| | Teacher training | | ... | ... | ... | 1 554 | 1 533 | 99 |
| | Vocational education | | ... | ... | ... | 32 841 | 14 238 | 43 |
| | Total | 1992/93 | 11 868 | 9 319 | 79 | 123 920 | 62 822 | 51 |
| | General education | | 10 169 | 8 440 | 83 | 94 307 | 49 692 | 53 |
| | Teacher training | | ./. | ./. | ./. | 945 | 914 | 97 |
| | Vocational education | | 1 699 (62) | 879 (62) | 52 | 28 668 | 12 216 | 43 |

II.6    Secondary education: teaching staff and pupils
Enseignement secondaire: personnel enseignant et élèves
Enseñanza secundaria: personal docente y alumnos

| Country / Pays / País | Type of education / Type d'enseignement / Tipo de enseñanza | Year / Année / Año | Teaching staff — Personnel enseignant — Personal docente | | | Pupils enrolled — Élèves inscrits — Alumnos matriculados | | |
|---|---|---|---|---|---|---|---|---|
| | | | Total | Female Féminin Femenino | % F | Total | Female Féminin Femenino | % F |
| Estonia (cont) | Total | 1993/94 | 11 896 | 9 732 | 82 | 122 894 | 63 995 | 52 |
| | General education | | 10 324 | 8 595 | 83 | 94 780 | 49 927 | 53 |
| | Teacher training | | ./. | ./. | ./. | 700 | 697 | 100 |
| | Vocational education | | (22) 1 572 | (22) 1 137 | 72 | 27 414 | 13 371 | 49 |
| | Total | 1994/95 | 14 183 | 11 194 | 79 | 125 052 | 64 856 | 52 |
| | General education | | 11 307 | 9 351 | 83 | 97 246 | 51 468 | 53 |
| | Teacher training | | 43 | 29 | 67 | 538 | 530 | 99 |
| | Vocational education | | 2 833 | 1 814 | 64 | 27 268 | 12 858 | 47 |
| | Total | 1995/96 | *11 098 | *8 903 | *80 | (64) 112 288 | (64) 57 911 | 52 |
| | General education | | *9 299 | *7 731 | *83 | 95 342 | 50 465 | 53 |
| | Teacher training | | *6 | *4 | *67 | 76 | 75 | 99 |
| | Vocational education | | *1 793 | *1 168 | *65 | (64) 16 870 | (64) 7 371 | 44 |
| | Total | 1996/97 | ... | ... | ... | ... | ... | ... |
| | General education | | ... | ... | ... | 95 877 | 50 412 | 53 |
| | Teacher training | | ... | ... | ... | ... | ... | ... |
| | Vocational education | | ... | ... | ... | ... | ... | ... |
| Federal Republic of Yugoslavia | Total | 1990/91 | | | | 788 170 | 386 756 | 49 |
| | General education | | ... | ... | ... | ... | ... | ... |
| | Teacher training | | ... | ... | ... | ... | ... | ... |
| | Vocational education | | ... | ... | ... | ... | ... | ... |
| | Total | 1991/92 | 55 165 | 30 165 | 55 | 816 143 | 398 081 | 49 |
| | General education | | ... | ... | ... | 540 426 | 272 912 | 50 |
| | Teacher training | | ... | ... | ... | 3 568 | 3 269 | 92 |
| | Vocational education | | ... | ... | ... | 272 149 | 121 900 | 45 |
| | Total | 1992/93 | 55 745 | 30 679 | 55 | 831 506 | 405 211 | 49 |
| | General education | | ... | ... | ... | 551 905 | 279 324 | 51 |
| | Teacher training | | ... | ... | ... | 1 783 | 1 619 | 91 |
| | Vocational education | | ... | ... | ... | 277 818 | 124 268 | 45 |
| | Total | 1993/94 | ... | ... | ... | 812 473 | 398 869 | 49 |
| | General education | | ... | ... | ... | 543 128 | 276 103 | 51 |
| | Teacher training | | ... | ... | ... | 1 338 | 787 | 59 |
| | Vocational education | | ... | ... | ... | 268 007 | 121 979 | 46 |
| | Total | 1994/95 | ... | ... | ... | 809 662 | 397 576 | 49 |
| | General education | | ... | ... | ... | 541 616 | 275 255 | 51 |
| | Teacher training | | ... | ... | ... | 311 | 241 | 77 |
| | Vocational education | | ... | ... | ... | 267 735 | 122 080 | 46 |
| | Total | 1995/96 | ... | ... | ... | 831 758 | 408 882 | 49 |
| | General education | | ... | ... | ... | 552 235 | 279 746 | 51 |
| | Teacher training | | ... | ... | ... | 346 | 251 | 73 |
| | Vocational education | | ... | ... | ... | 279 177 | 128 885 | 46 |
| | Total | 1996/97 | ... | ... | ... | 815 029 | 404 613 | 50 |
| | General education | | ... | ... | ... | 548 953 | 278 947 | 51 |
| | Teacher training | | ... | ... | ... | 327 | 239 | 73 |
| | Vocational education | | ... | ... | ... | 265 749 | 125 427 | 47 |
| Finland | Total | 1970/71 | 32 247 | 17 091 | 53 | 509 691 | 259 281 | 51 |
| | General education | | 22 099 | 13 491 | 61 | 407 978 | 215 680 | 53 |
| | Teacher training | | 392 | 267 | 68 | 1 521 | 1 130 | 74 |
| | Vocational education | | 9 756 | 3 333 | 34 | 100 192 | 42 471 | 42 |
| | Total | 1975/76 | ... | ... | ... | (65) 419 808 | (65) 218 933 | 52 |
| | General education | | ... | ... | ... | (65) 337 575 | (65) 180 566 | 53 |
| | Teacher training | | ... | ... | ... | 703 | 470 | 67 |
| | Vocational education | | ... | ... | ... | 81 530 | 37 897 | 46 |
| | Total | 1980/81 | (8) 33 958 | ... | ... | 449 322 | 232 244 | 52 |
| | General education | | 19 822 | ... | ... | 341 054 | 181 292 | 53 |
| | Teacher training | | (8) 188 | (8) 43 | 23 | 872 | 574 | 66 |
| | Vocational education | | 13 948 | 5 834 | 42 | 107 396 | 50 378 | 47 |
| | Total | 1985/86 | ... | ... | ... | 424 076 | 224 125 | 53 |
| | General education | | ... | ... | ... | 300 748 | 160 420 | 53 |
| | Teacher training | | ... | ... | ... | 954 | 631 | 66 |
| | Vocational education | | 15 700 | ... | ... | 122 374 | 63 074 | 52 |
| | Total | 1990/91 | ... | ... | ... | 426 864 | 227 534 | 53 |
| | General education | | ... | ... | ... | 305 979 | 161 089 | 53 |
| | Teacher training | | - | - | - | - | - | - |
| | Vocational education | | ... | ... | ... | 120 885 | 66 445 | 55 |
| | Total | 1991/92 | ... | ... | ... | 446 207 | 239 554 | 54 |
| | General education | | ... | ... | ... | 315 866 | 167 572 | 53 |
| | Teacher training | | - | - | - | - | - | - |
| | Vocational education | | ... | ... | ... | 130 341 | 71 982 | 55 |
| | Total | 1992/93 | ... | ... | ... | (29) 443 831 | (29) 235 604 | 53 |
| | General education | | ... | ... | ... | 314 242 | 165 135 | 53 |
| | Teacher training | | - | - | - | - | - | - |
| | Vocational education | | ... | ... | ... | 129 589 | 70 469 | 54 |

Secondary education: teaching staff and pupils
Enseignement secondaire: personnel enseignant et élèves
Enseñanza secundaria: personal docente y alumnos

II.6

| Country / Pays / País | Type of education / Type d'enseignement / Tipo de enseñanza | Year / Année / Año | Teaching staff — Personnel enseignant — Personal docente | | | Pupils enrolled — Elèves inscrits — Alumnos matriculados | | |
|---|---|---|---|---|---|---|---|---|
| | | | Total | Female Féminin Femenino | % F | Total | Female Féminin Femenino | % F |
| Finland (cont) | Total | 1993/94 | ... | ... | ... | 455 300 | 240 344 | 53 |
| | General education | | ... | ... | ... | 318 747 | 167 888 | 53 |
| | Teacher training | | - | - | - | - | | - |
| | Vocational education | | ... | ... | ... | 136 553 | 72 456 | 53 |
| | Total | 1994/95 | ... | ... | ... | 454 707 | 238 422 | 52 |
| | General education | | ... | ... | ... | 321 699 | 169 625 | 53 |
| | Teacher training | | - | - | - | - | | - |
| | Vocational education | | ... | ... | ... | 133 008 | 68 797 | 52 |
| | Total | 1995/96 | ... | ... | ... | 460 878 | 243 788 | 53 |
| | General education | | 22 232 | 14 863 | 67 | 325 661 | 170 978 | 53 |
| | Teacher training | | - | - | - | - | | - |
| | Vocational education | | ... | ... | ... | 135 217 | 72 810 | 54 |
| | Total | 1996/97 | ... | ... | ... | 469 933 | 244 760 | 52 |
| | General education | | 26 457 | 17 797 | 67 | 329 301 | 172 725 | 52 |
| | Teacher training | | - | - | - | - | | - |
| | Vocational education | | ... | ... | ... | 140 632 | 72 035 | 51 |
| France | Total | 1970/71 | 270 949 | (4) 109 683 | ... | 4 281 446 | 2 189 968 | 51 |
| | General education | | ... | ... | ... | 3 460 577 | 1 785 173 | 52 |
| | Teacher training | | 2 349 | 1 245 | 53 | 27 429 | 15 078 | 55 |
| | Vocational education | | ... | ... | ... | 793 440 | 389 717 | 49 |
| | Total | 1975/76 | ... | ... | ... | 4 890 152 | *2 389 816 | *49 |
| | General education | | ... | ... | ... | 3 864 720 | ... | ... |
| | Teacher training | | ... | ... | ... | 10 000 | ... | ... |
| | Vocational education | | ... | ... | ... | 1 009 432 | ... | ... |
| | Total | 1980/81 | (4) 256 369 | | ... | 5 013 666 | 2 677 574 | 53 |
| | General education | | ... | | ... | 3 911 054 | 1 929 406 | 49 |
| | Teacher training | | - | - | - | - | | - |
| | Vocational education | | ... | | ... | 1 102 612 | 748 168 | 68 |
| | Total | 1985/86 | ... | | ... | 5 371 593 | 2 730 395 | 51 |
| | General education | | ... | | ... | 4 043 246 | 2 116 554 | 52 |
| | Teacher training | | - | | - | - | | - |
| | Vocational education | | ... | | ... | 1 328 347 | 613 841 | 46 |
| | Total | 1990/91 | 441 452 | 253 119 | 57 | 5 521 862 | 2 770 286 | 50 |
| | General education | | ... | ... | ... | 4 275 891 | 2 196 794 | 51 |
| | Teacher training | | - | - | - | - | | - |
| | Vocational education | | ... | ... | ... | 1 245 971 | 573 492 | 46 |
| | Total | 1991/92 | 449 511 | 258 602 | 58 | 5 614 894 | 2 810 871 | 50 |
| | General education | | ... | ... | ... | 4 289 886 | 2 210 156 | 52 |
| | Teacher training | | - | - | - | - | | - |
| | Vocational education | | ... | ... | ... | 1 325 008 | 600 715 | 45 |
| | Total | 1992/93 | 458 870 | 267 036 | 58 | 5 573 582 | 2 779 489 | 50 |
| | General education | | ... | ... | ... | 4 355 952 | 2 241 029 | 51 |
| | Teacher training | | - | - | - | - | | - |
| | Vocational education | | ... | ... | ... | 1 217 630 | 538 460 | 44 |
| | Total | 1993/94 | (52) 467 848 | (52) 273 316 | 58 | (52) 5 983 059 | (52) 2 917 644 | 49 |
| | General education | | ... | ... | ... | 4 316 446 | 2 215 203 | 51 |
| | Teacher training | | - | - | - | - | | - |
| | Vocational education | | ... | ... | ... | 1 666 613 | 702 441 | 42 |
| | Total | 1994/95 | 473 673 | 278 667 | 59 | 6 003 797 | 2 916 793 | 49 |
| | General education | | ... | ... | ... | 4 300 032 | 2 207 750 | 51 |
| | Teacher training | | - | - | - | - | | - |
| | Vocational education | | ... | ... | ... | 1 703 765 | 709 043 | 42 |
| | Total | 1995/96 | 478 592 | 279 944 | 58 | 5 980 518 | 2 907 777 | 49 |
| | General education | | ... | ... | ... | 4 264 417 | 2 193 750 | 51 |
| | Teacher training | | - | - | - | - | | - |
| | Vocational education | | ... | ... | ... | 1 716 101 | 714 027 | 42 |
| | Total | 1996/97 | 483 493 | 283 186 | 59 | 5 979 690 | 2 910 884 | 49 |
| | General education | | ... | ... | ... | 4 333 313 | 2 215 880 | 51 |
| | Teacher training | | - | - | - | - | | - |
| | Vocational education | | ... | ... | ... | 1 646 377 | 695 004 | 42 |
| Germany | Total | 1990/91 | ... | ... | ... | 7 398 011 | ... | ... |
| | General education | | ... | ... | ... | 5 101 924 | ... | ... |
| | Teacher training | | - | - | - | - | | - |
| | Vocational education | | ... | ... | ... | 2 296 087 | ... | ... |
| | Total | 1991/92 | ... | ... | ... | 7 500 078 | 3 607 097 | 48 |
| | General education | | ... | ... | ... | 5 228 015 | 2 604 525 | 50 |
| | Teacher training | | - | - | - | - | | - |
| | Vocational education | | ... | ... | ... | 2 272 063 | 1 002 572 | 44 |
| | Total | 1992/93 | (29) 532 473 | (29) 242 668 | 46 | (29) 7 933 806 | (29) 3 791 437 | 48 |
| | General education | | 419 822 | 204 387 | 49 | 5 634 662 | 2 788 369 | 49 |
| | Teacher training | | - | - | - | - | | - |
| | Vocational education | | 112 651 | 38 281 | 34 | 2 299 144 | 1 003 068 | 44 |

II.6 Secondary education: teaching staff and pupils
Enseignement secondaire: personnel enseignant et élèves
Enseñanza secundaria: personal docente y alumnos

| Country<br>Pays<br>País | Type of education<br>Type d'enseignement<br>Tipo de enseñanza | Year<br>Année<br>Año | Teaching staff<br>Personnel enseignant<br>Personal docente | | | Pupils enrolled<br>Élèves inscrits<br>Alumnos matriculados | | |
|---|---|---|---|---|---|---|---|---|
| | | | Total | Female<br>Féminin<br>Femenino | %<br>F | Total | Female<br>Féminin<br>Femenino | %<br>F |
| Germany (cont) | Total | 1993/94 | 526 268 | 238 104 | 45 | 8 070 103 | 3 867 583 | 48 |
| | General education | | 413 621 | 199 114 | 48 | 5 783 786 | 2 865 529 | 50 |
| | Teacher training | | - | - | - | - | - | - |
| | Vocational education | | 112 647 | 38 990 | 35 | 2 286 317 | 1 002 054 | 44 |
| | Total | 1994/95 | 541 389 | 254 418 | 47 | 8 152 297 | 3 909 965 | 48 |
| | General education | | 430 139 | 215 145 | 50 | 5 891 319 | 2 922 084 | 50 |
| | Teacher training | | - | - | - | - | - | - |
| | Vocational education | | 111 250 | 39 273 | 35 | 2 260 978 | 987 881 | 44 |
| | Total | 1995/96 | 540 270 | 264 610 | 49 | 8 260 674 | 3 969 119 | 48 |
| | General education | | 428 280 | 224 054 | 52 | 5 986 050 | 2 972 690 | 50 |
| | Teacher training | | - | - | - | - | - | - |
| | Vocational education | | 111 990 | 40 556 | 36 | 2 274 624 | 996 429 | 44 |
| | Total | 1996/97 | 542 383 | 267 929 | 49 | 8 382 335 | 4 037 044 | 48 |
| | General education | | 428 246 | 225 909 | 53 | 6 061 870 | 3 012 743 | 50 |
| | Teacher training | | - | - | - | - | - | - |
| | Vocational education | | 114 137 | 42 020 | 37 | 2 320 465 | 1 024 301 | 44 |
| Gibraltar | Total | 1970/71 | ... | ... | ... | 1 794 | 898 | 50 |
| | General education | | ... | ... | ... | ... | ... | ... |
| | Teacher training | | - | - | - | - | - | - |
| | Vocational education | | ... | ... | ... | ... | ... | ... |
| | Total | 1975/76 | 132 | 53 | 40 | 1 629 | 824 | 51 |
| | General education | | 114 | 53 | 46 | 1 587 | 823 | 52 |
| | Teacher training | | - | - | - | - | - | - |
| | Vocational education | | 18 | - | - | 42 | 1 | 2 |
| | Total | 1980/81 | ... | ... | ... | 1 811 | 899 | 50 |
| | General education | | 123 | 52 | 42 | 1 770 | 899 | 51 |
| | Teacher training | | - | - | - | - | - | - |
| | Vocational education | | ... | ... | ... | 41 | | - |
| | Total | 1996/97 | ... | ... | ... | | | ... |
| | General education | | 128 | 53 | 41 | 1 781 | 862 | 48 |
| | Teacher training | | - | - | - | - | - | - |
| | Vocational education | | | | | - | | - |
| Greece | Total | 1970/71 | ... | ... | ... | 520 323 | 222 953 | 43 |
| | General education | | 12 958 | 6 315 | 49 | 422 022 | 209 064 | 50 |
| | Teacher training | | - | - | - | - | - | - |
| | Vocational education | | ... | ... | ... | 98 301 | 13 889 | 14 |
| | Total | 1975/76 | ... | ... | ... | 661 796 | 283 855 | 43 |
| | General education | | 18 719 | 9 952 | 53 | 529 205 | 266 493 | 50 |
| | Teacher training | | - | - | - | - | - | - |
| | Vocational education | | ... | ... | ... | 132 591 | 17 362 | 13 |
| | Total | 1980/81 | 39 571 | 19 429 | 49 | 740 058 | 337 816 | 46 |
| | General education | | 31 737 | 17 547 | 55 | 639 633 | 317 863 | 50 |
| | Teacher training | | - | - | - | - | - | - |
| | Vocational education | | 7 834 | 1 882 | 24 | 100 425 | 19 953 | 20 |
| | Total | 1985/86 | 50 388 | 26 475 | 53 | 813 534 | 387 134 | 48 |
| | General education | | 42 250 | 23 733 | 56 | 704 119 | 355 389 | 50 |
| | Teacher training | | - | - | - | - | - | - |
| | Vocational education | | 8 138 | 2 742 | 34 | 109 415 | 31 745 | 29 |
| | Total | 1990/91 | 60 303 | 32 057 | 53 | 851 353 | 408 580 | 48 |
| | General education | | 49 802 | 28 342 | 57 | 716 404 | 364 437 | 51 |
| | Teacher training | | - | - | - | - | - | - |
| | Vocational education | | 10 501 | 3 715 | 35 | 134 949 | 44 143 | 33 |
| | Total | 1991/92 | 62 798 | 33 405 | 53 | 870 235 | 418 384 | 48 |
| | General education | | 50 732 | 29 029 | 57 | 720 511 | 366 113 | 51 |
| | Teacher training | | - | - | - | - | - | - |
| | Vocational education | | 12 066 | 4 376 | 36 | 149 724 | 52 271 | 35 |
| | Total | 1992/93 | (29) 71 677 | (29) 38 504 | 54 | (29) 843 403 | (29) 410 840 | 49 |
| | General education | | 56 787 | 32 185 | 57 | 709 081 | 360 889 | 51 |
| | Teacher training | | - | - | - | - | - | - |
| | Vocational education | | 14 890 | 6 319 | 42 | 134 322 | 49 951 | 37 |
| | Total | 1993/94 | 75 270 | 40 495 | 54 | 851 294 | 403 086 | 47 |
| | General education | | 59 137 | 33 395 | 56 | 713 659 | 355 827 | 50 |
| | Teacher training | | - | - | - | - | - | - |
| | Vocational education | | 16 133 | 7 100 | 44 | 137 635 | 47 259 | 34 |
| | Total | 1994/95 | 66 479 | 35 905 | 54 | 842 633 | 409 124 | 49 |
| | General education | | 52 832 | 30 259 | 57 | 710 759 | 362 534 | 51 |
| | Teacher training | | - | - | - | - | - | - |
| | Vocational education | | 13 647 | 5 646 | 41 | 131 874 | 46 590 | 35 |
| | Total | 1995/96 | 85 474 | 46 820 | 55 | 835 158 | 407 285 | 49 |
| | General education | | 67 637 | 38 709 | 57 | 701 263 | 354 513 | 51 |
| | Teacher training | | - | - | - | - | - | - |
| | Vocational education | | 17 837 | 8 111 | 45 | 133 895 | 52 772 | 39 |

Secondary education: teaching staff and pupils
Enseignement secondaire: personnel enseignant et élèves
Enseñanza secundaria: personal docente y alumnos

II.6

| Country / Pays / País | Type of education / Type d'enseignement / Tipo de enseñanza | Year / Année / Año | Teaching staff / Personnel enseignant / Personal docente | | | Pupils enrolled / Elèves inscrits / Alumnos matriculados | | |
|---|---|---|---|---|---|---|---|---|
| | | | Total | Female Féminin Femenino | % F | Total | Female Féminin Femenino | % F |
| Greece (cont) | Total | 1996/97 | 70 682 | 39 260 | 56 | 817 566 | 400 097 | 49 |
| | General education | | 56 899 | 33 350 | 59 | 682 201 | 346 389 | 51 |
| | Teacher training | | - | - | - | - | - | - |
| | Vocational education | | 13 783 | 5 910 | 43 | 135 365 | 53 708 | 40 |
| Hungary | Total | 1970/71 | 22 442 | ... | ... | 465 324 | 198 219 | 43 |
| | General education | | 7 196 | ... | ... | 122 988 | 82 308 | 67 |
| | Teacher training | | - | - | - | - | - | - |
| | Vocational education | | 15 246 | ... | ... | 342 336 | 115 911 | 34 |
| | Total | 1975/76 | 22 781 | ... | ... | 371 898 | 168 126 | 45 |
| | General education | | 6 663 | ... | ... | 99 656 | 64 905 | 65 |
| | Teacher training | | ... | ... | ... | 4 913 | 4 913 | 100 |
| | Vocational education | | ... | ... | ... | 267 329 | 98 308 | 37 |
| | Total | 1980/81 | ... | ... | ... | 357 334 | 165 679 | 46 |
| | General education | | 6 639 | 4 027 | 61 | 89 400 | 58 286 | 65 |
| | Teacher training | | ... | ... | ... | 5 897 | 5 894 | 100 |
| | Vocational education | | ... | ... | ... | 262 037 | 101 499 | 39 |
| | Total | 1985/86 | ... | ... | ... | 422 323 | 205 114 | 49 |
| | General education | | 7 923 | 5 051 | 64 | 105 794 | 68 832 | 65 |
| | Teacher training | | ... | ... | ... | 5 081 | 5 079 | 100 |
| | Vocational education | | ... | ... | ... | 311 448 | 131 203 | 42 |
| | Total | 1990/91 | ... | ... | ... | 514 076 | 251 505 | 49 |
| | General education | | 10 246 | 6 747 | 66 | 123 427 | 81 991 | 66 |
| | Teacher training | | ... | ... | ... | 4 510 | 4 510 | 100 |
| | Vocational education | | ... | ... | ... | 386 139 | 165 004 | 43 |
| | Total | 1991/92 | ... | ... | ... | 531 051 | 259 450 | 49 |
| | General education | | 10 732 | 7 040 | 66 | 130 378 | 86 001 | 66 |
| | Teacher training | | ... | ... | ... | 3 865 | 3 862 | 100 |
| | Vocational education | | ... | ... | ... | 396 808 | 169 587 | 43 |
| | Total | 1993/94 | (52)(66) 111 317 | ... | ... | (52)(66) 1 156 874 | (52)(66) 574 213 | 50 |
| | General education | | (66) 67 792 | ... | ... | (66) 706 141 | (66) 365 920 | 52 |
| | Teacher training | | ./. | ... | ... | 4 151 | 4 045 | 97 |
| | Vocational education | | (62) 43 525 | ... | ... | (52) 446 582 | (52) 204 248 | 46 |
| | Total | 1994/95 | 109 902 | 72 506 | 66 | 1 128 911 | 561 107 | 50 |
| | General education | | 69 791 | 52 536 | 75 | 682 712 | 353 881 | 52 |
| | Teacher training | | ./. | ./. | ./. | 3 695 | 3 486 | 94 |
| | Vocational education | | (62) 40 111 | (62) 19 970 | 50 | 442 504 | 203 740 | 46 |
| | Total | 1995/96 | ... | ... | ... | 1 112 149 | 552 511 | 50 |
| | General education | | ... | ... | ... | 702 641 | 362 515 | 52 |
| | Teacher training | | ... | ... | ... | 3 379 | 3 161 | 94 |
| | Vocational education | | ... | ... | ... | 406 129 | 186 835 | 46 |
| Iceland | Total | 1970/71 | 2 207 | 618 | 28 | 23 144 | 10 176 | 44 |
| | General education | | 1 453 | 465 | 32 | 18 074 | 8 547 | 47 |
| | Teacher training | | 96 | 28 | 29 | 836 | 551 | 66 |
| | Vocational education | | 658 | 125 | 19 | 4 234 | 1 078 | 25 |
| | Total | 1975/76 | 2 387 | 699 | 29 | 25 853 | 11 566 | 45 |
| | General education | | 1 538 | 506 | 33 | 20 292 | 10 089 | 50 |
| | Teacher training | | 30 | 17 | 57 | 210 | 172 | 82 |
| | Vocational education | | 819 | 176 | 21 | 5 351 | 1 305 | 24 |
| | Total | 1980/81 | ... | ... | ... | 26 643 | 12 447 | 47 |
| | General education | | ... | ... | ... | 19 091 | ... | ... |
| | Teacher training | | ... | ... | ... | 168 | ... | ... |
| | Vocational education | | ... | ... | ... | 7 384 | ... | ... |
| | Total | 1985/86 | ... | ... | ... | 27 559 | 12 962 | 47 |
| | General education | | ... | ... | ... | 20 097 | 10 180 | 51 |
| | Teacher training | | ... | ... | ... | 297 | 249 | 84 |
| | Vocational education | | ... | ... | ... | 7 165 | 2 533 | 35 |
| | Total | 1990/91 | ... | ... | ... | 29 465 | 14 132 | 48 |
| | General education | | ... | ... | ... | 23 143 | 11 968 | 52 |
| | Teacher training | | ... | ... | ... | 373 | 333 | 89 |
| | Vocational education | | ... | ... | ... | 5 949 | 1 831 | 31 |
| | Total | 1991/92 | ... | ... | ... | 29 985 | 14 455 | 48 |
| | General education | | ... | ... | ... | 24 022 | 12 448 | 52 |
| | Teacher training | | ... | ... | ... | 462 | 407 | 88 |
| | Vocational education | | ... | ... | ... | 5 501 | 1 600 | 29 |
| | Total | 1992/93 | ... | ... | ... | 30 233 | 14 689 | 49 |
| | General education | | ... | ... | ... | 24 368 | 12 708 | 52 |
| | Teacher training | | ... | ... | ... | 481 | 423 | 88 |
| | Vocational education | | ... | ... | ... | 5 384 | 1 558 | 29 |
| | Total | 1993/94 | ... | ... | ... | 30 163 | 14 644 | 49 |
| | General education | | ... | ... | ... | 23 437 | 12 301 | 52 |
| | Teacher training | | ... | ... | ... | ./. | ./. | ./. |
| | Vocational education | | ... | ... | ... | (62) 6 726 | (62) 2 343 | 35 |

II.6 Secondary education: teaching staff and pupils
Enseignement secondaire: personnel enseignant et élèves
Enseñanza secundaria: personal docente y alumnos

| Country<br>Pays<br>País | Type of education<br>Type d'enseignement<br>Tipo de enseñanza | Year<br>Année<br>Año | Teaching staff<br>Personnel enseignant<br>Personal docente | | | | Pupils enrolled<br>Elèves inscrits<br>Alumnos matriculados | | | |
|---|---|---|---|---|---|---|---|---|---|---|
| | | | | Total | Female<br>Féminin<br>Femenino | %<br><br>F | | Total | Female<br>Féminin<br>Femenino | %<br><br>F |
| Iceland (cont) | Total | 1994/95 | | ... | ... | ... | | 30 253 | 14 625 | 48 |
| | General education | | | ... | ... | ... | | 24 083 | 12 522 | 52 |
| | Teacher training | | | ... | ... | ... | | ./. | ./. | ./. |
| | Vocational education | | | ... | ... | ... | (62) | 6 170 | (62) 2 103 | 34 |
| | Total | 1995/96 | | ... | ... | ... | | 30 463 | 14 716 | 48 |
| | General education | | | ... | ... | ... | | 24 404 | 12 604 | 52 |
| | Teacher training | | | ... | ... | ... | | ./. | ./. | ./. |
| | Vocational education | | | ... | ... | ... | (62) | 6 059 | (62) 2 112 | 35 |
| | Total | 1996/97 | | ... | ... | ... | | ... | ... | ... |
| | General education | | | ... | ... | ... | | 25 477 | 13 341 | 52 |
| | Teacher training | | | ... | ... | ... | | | | |
| | Vocational education | | | ... | ... | ... | | ... | ... | ... |
| Ireland | Total | 1970/71 | | ... | ... | ... | | 208 705 | 106 360 | 51 |
| | General education | | | 10 426 | 5 981 | 57 | | 154 575 | 85 541 | 55 |
| | Teacher training | | | | | | | - | | - |
| | Vocational education | | | ... | ... | ... | | 54 130 | 20 819 | 38 |
| | Total | 1975/76 | (67) | 18 913 | (67) 9 537 | 50 | | 270 956 | 138 851 | 51 |
| | General education | | | ... | ... | ... | | 260 999 | 130 601 | 50 |
| | Teacher training | | | - | - | | | - | | - |
| | Vocational education | | | ... | ... | ... | | 9 957 | 8 250 | 83 |
| | Total | 1980/81 | (67) | 19 878 | | ... | | 300 601 | 155 304 | 52 |
| | General education | | | ... | ... | ... | | 286 619 | 145 295 | 51 |
| | Teacher training | | | - | | | | - | | - |
| | Vocational education | | | ... | ... | ... | | 13 982 | 10 009 | 72 |
| | Total | 1985/86 | (67) | 20 611 | | ... | | 338 256 | 173 158 | 51 |
| | General education | | | ... | ... | ... | | 315 584 | 158 583 | 50 |
| | Teacher training | | | - | | | | - | | - |
| | Vocational education | | | ... | ... | ... | | 22 672 | 14 575 | 64 |
| | Total | 1990/91 | (67) | 20 830 | | ... | | 345 941 | 176 335 | 51 |
| | General education | | | ... | ... | ... | | 321 477 | 160 682 | 50 |
| | Teacher training | | | - | - | - | | - | | - |
| | Vocational education | | | ... | ... | ... | | 24 464 | 15 653 | 64 |
| | Total | 1991/92 | (67) | 21 371 | ... | ... | | 352 408 | 179 272 | 51 |
| | General education | | | ... | ... | ... | | 327 817 | 164 024 | 50 |
| | Teacher training | | | - | - | - | | - | | - |
| | Vocational education | | | ... | ... | ... | | 24 591 | 15 248 | 62 |
| | Total | 1992/93 | (29)(67) | 22 960 | ... | ... | (29) | 381 630 | (29) 189 909 | 50 |
| | General education | | | ... | ... | ... | | 336 826 | 168 323 | 50 |
| | Teacher training | | | ... | | | | - | | - |
| | Vocational education | | | ... | ... | ... | | 44 804 | 21 586 | 48 |
| | Total | 1993/94 | | 25 617 | 13 642 | 53 | | 387 813 | 193 565 | 50 |
| | General education | | | ... | ... | ... | | 346 742 | 173 354 | 50 |
| | Teacher training | | | - | - | - | | - | | - |
| | Vocational education | | | ... | ... | ... | | 41 071 | 20 211 | 49 |
| | Total | 1994/95 | | 26 317 | 14 112 | 54 | | 390 680 | 195 867 | 50 |
| | General education | | | ... | ... | ... | | 352 817 | 176 716 | 50 |
| | Teacher training | | | - | | | | - | | - |
| | Vocational education | | | ... | ... | ... | | 37 863 | 19 151 | 51 |
| | Total | 1995/96 | | 26 523 | 14 425 | 54 | | 389 374 | 196 451 | 50 |
| | General education | | | ... | ... | ... | | 352 820 | 176 885 | 50 |
| | Teacher training | | | - | - | | | - | | - |
| | Vocational education | | | ... | ... | ... | | 36 554 | 19 566 | 54 |
| | Total | 1996/97 | | 27 273 | 14 895 | 55 | | 389 353 | 197 386 | 51 |
| | General education | | | ... | ... | ... | | 353 270 | 177 469 | 50 |
| | Teacher training | | | - | - | | | - | | - |
| | Vocational education | | | ... | ... | ... | | 36 083 | 19 917 | 55 |
| Italy | Total | 1970/71 | | 332 106 | ... | ... | | 3 823 556 | 1 701 137 | 44 |
| | General education | | | 229 554 | ... | ... | | 2 625 667 | 1 210 448 | 46 |
| | Teacher training | | | 17 996 | ... | ... | | 221 623 | 197 546 | 89 |
| | Vocational education | | | 84 556 | ... | ... | | 976 266 | 293 143 | 30 |
| | Total | 1975/76 | | 432 867 | ... | ... | | 4 875 179 | 2 251 250 | 46 |
| | General education | | | 294 322 | ... | ... | | 3 343 085 | 1 587 955 | 47 |
| | Teacher training | | | 18 899 | ... | ... | | 198 426 | 183 161 | 92 |
| | Vocational education | | | 119 646 | ... | ... | | 1 333 668 | 480 134 | 36 |
| | Total | 1980/81 | | 519 128 | 302 040 | 58 | | 5 307 989 | 2 550 177 | 48 |
| | General education | | | 325 718 | 209 981 | 64 | | 3 484 339 | 1 680 440 | 48 |
| | Teacher training | | | 22 308 | 15 447 | 69 | | 237 471 | 223 310 | 94 |
| | Vocational education | | | 171 102 | 76 612 | 45 | | 1 586 179 | 646 427 | 41 |
| | Total | 1985/86 | | 562 196 | 341 719 | 61 | | 5 361 579 | 2 607 247 | 49 |
| | General education | | | 347 638 | 233 956 | 67 | | 3 381 434 | 1 649 137 | 49 |
| | Teacher training | | | 21 484 | 15 414 | 72 | | 197 349 | 185 144 | 94 |
| | Vocational education | | | 193 074 | 92 349 | 48 | | 1 782 796 | 772 966 | 43 |

Secondary education: teaching staff and pupils
Enseignement secondaire: personnel enseignant et élèves
Enseñanza secundaria: personal docente y alumnos

II.6

| Country<br>Pays<br>País | Type of education<br>Type d'enseignement<br>Tipo de enseñanza | Year<br>Année<br>Año | Teaching staff<br>Personnel enseignant<br>Personal docente | | | Pupils enrolled<br>Elèves inscrits<br>Alumnos matriculados | | |
|---|---|---|---|---|---|---|---|---|
| | | | Total | Female<br>Féminin<br>Femenino | %<br>F | Total | Female<br>Féminin<br>Femenino | %<br>F |
| Italy (cont) | Total | 1990/91 | 589 655 | 367 419 | 62 | 5 117 897 | 2 498 371 | 49 |
| | General education | | 336 215 | 234 965 | 70 | 2 994 957 | 1 477 109 | 49 |
| | Teacher training | | 21 618 | 15 804 | 73 | 184 802 | 171 988 | 93 |
| | Vocational education | | 231 822 | 116 650 | 50 | 1 938 138 | 849 274 | 44 |
| | Total | 1991/92 | 590 692 | 370 008 | 63 | 5 010 467 | 2 447 449 | 49 |
| | General education | | 333 137 | 234 013 | 70 | 2 900 114 | 1 434 986 | 49 |
| | Teacher training | | 22 281 | 16 435 | 74 | 183 711 | 170 944 | 93 |
| | Vocational education | | 235 274 | 119 560 | 51 | 1 926 642 | 841 519 | 44 |
| | Total | 1992/93 | 579 690 | 362 634 | 63 | 4 892 194 | 2 388 788 | 49 |
| | General education | | 324 506 | 227 890 | 70 | 2 805 158 | 1 391 426 | 50 |
| | Teacher training | | 22 073 | 16 282 | 74 | 181 040 | 168 451 | 93 |
| | Vocational education | | 233 111 | 118 462 | 51 | 1 905 996 | 828 911 | 43 |
| | Total | 1993/94 | (52) 603 830 | (52) 383 449 | 64 | (52) 4 938 465 | (52) 2 410 134 | 49 |
| | General education | | 322 673 | 228 432 | 71 | 2 788 666 | 1 396 931 | 50 |
| | Teacher training | | 21 910 | 16 235 | 74 | 190 225 | 175 522 | 92 |
| | Vocational education | | 259 247 | 138 782 | 54 | 1 959 574 | 837 681 | 43 |
| | Total | 1994/95 | 504 816 | 309 339 | 61 | 4 825 719 | 2 352 784 | 49 |
| | General education | | 267 828 | 180 160 | 67 | 2 744 266 | 1 377 953 | 50 |
| | Teacher training | | ./. | ./. | ./. | 195 487 | 180 552 | 92 |
| | Vocational education | | (62) 236 988 | (62) 129 179 | 55 | 1 885 966 | 794 279 | 42 |
| | Total | 1995/96 | 461 776 | 293 496 | 64 | 4 708 406 | 2 298 154 | 49 |
| | General education | | 249 521 | 183 561 | 74 | 2 696 097 | 1 349 973 | 50 |
| | Teacher training | | ./. | ./. | ./. | 205 944 | 190 426 | 92 |
| | Vocational education | | (62) 212 255 | (62) 109 935 | 52 | 1 806 365 | 757 756 | 42 |
| | Total | 1996/97 | ... | ... | ... | 4 602 243 | 2 244 975 | 49 |
| | General education | | ... | ... | ... | 2 642 456 | 1 324 401 | 50 |
| | Teacher training | | ... | ... | ... | ./. | ./. | ./. |
| | Vocational education | | ... | ... | ... | (62) 1 959 787 | (62) 920 574 | 47 |
| Latvia | Total | 1980/81 | 23 831 | ... | ... | 279 178 | ... | ... |
| | General education | | 16 571 | ... | ... | 204 326 | ... | ... |
| | Teacher training | | 163 | ... | ... | 1 452 | ... | ... |
| | Vocational education | | 7 097 | ... | ... | 73 400 | ... | ... |
| | Total | 1985/86 | 25 729 | ... | ... | 288 315 | ... | ... |
| | General education | | 18 172 | ... | ... | 209 216 | ... | ... |
| | Teacher training | | 195 | ... | ... | 1 741 | ... | ... |
| | Vocational education | | 7 362 | ... | ... | 77 358 | ... | ... |
| | Total | 1990/91 | 28 793 | ... | ... | 264 475 | 129 795 | 49 |
| | General education | | 22 108 | ... | ... | 197 066 | 98 533 | 50 |
| | Teacher training | | 352 | ... | ... | 3 067 | 2 952 | 96 |
| | Vocational education | | 6 333 | ... | ... | 64 342 | 28 310 | 44 |
| | Total | 1991/92 | 28 176 | ... | ... | 254 196 | 126 723 | 50 |
| | General education | | 22 093 | ... | ... | 192 673 | 98 263 | 51 |
| | Teacher training | | 299 | ... | ... | 2 662 | 2 561 | 96 |
| | Vocational education | | 5 784 | ... | ... | 58 861 | 25 899 | 44 |
| | Total | 1992/93 | 29 443 | ... | ... | 246 877 | 122 854 | 50 |
| | General education | | 23 075 | ... | ... | 191 565 | 97 421 | 51 |
| | Teacher training | | 323 | ... | ... | 2 108 | 2 033 | 96 |
| | Vocational education | | 6 045 | ... | ... | 53 204 | 23 400 | 44 |
| | Total | 1993/94 | 28 675 | ... | ... | 245 130 | 124 897 | 51 |
| | General education | | 23 710 | 19 005 | 80 | 195 686 | 102 023 | 52 |
| | Teacher training | | 95 | 79 | 83 | 788 | 781 | 99 |
| | Vocational education | | 4 870 | ... | ... | 48 656 | 22 093 | 45 |
| | Total | 1994/95 | 28 429 | ... | ... | 243 582 | 124 241 | 51 |
| | General education | | 23 288 | ... | ... | 198 470 | 103 723 | 52 |
| | Teacher training | | 26 | 23 | 88 | 137 | 136 | 99 |
| | Vocational education | | 5 115 | ... | ... | 44 975 | 20 382 | 45 |
| | Total | 1995/96 | 28 530 | 22 387 | 78 | 240 112 | 122 650 | 51 |
| | General education | | 23 490 | 19 076 | 81 | 197 735 | 103 395 | 52 |
| | Teacher training | | - | - | - | - | - | - |
| | Vocational education | | 5 040 | 3 311 | 66 | 42 377 | 19 255 | 45 |
| | Total | 1996/97 | 29 852 | 23 478 | 79 | 239 318 | 122 000 | 51 |
| | General education | | 24 112 | 19 773 | 82 | 196 148 | 102 320 | 52 |
| | Teacher training | | - | - | - | - | - | - |
| | Vocational education | | 5 740 | 3 705 | 65 | 43 170 | 19 680 | 46 |
| Lithuania | Total | 1980/81 | ... | ... | ... | ... | ... | ... |
| | General education | | 20 240 | 17 168 | 85 | 415 974 | ... | ... |
| | Teacher training | | - | - | - | - | ... | - |
| | Vocational education | | ... | ... | ... | ... | ... | ... |
| | Total | 1985/86 | ... | ... | ... | 466 166 | ... | ... |
| | General education | | 22 808 | 17 792 | 78 | 370 989 | ... | ... |
| | Teacher training | | - | - | - | - | ... | - |
| | Vocational education | | ... | ... | ... | 95 177 | ... | ... |

Secondary education: teaching staff and pupils
Enseignement secondaire: personnel enseignant et élèves
Enseñanza secundaria: personal docente y alumnos

| Country / Pays / País | Type of education / Type d'enseignement / Tipo de enseñanza | Year / Année / Año | Teaching staff Personnel enseignant Personal docente Total | Female Féminin Femenino | % F | Pupils enrolled Elèves inscrits Alumnos matriculados Total | Female Féminin Femenino | % F |
|---|---|---|---|---|---|---|---|---|
| Lithuania (cont) | Total | 1990/91 | (53) ... | (60) ... | ... | (53) 396 036 | ... | ... |
| | General education | | (53) 27 221 | (60) 21 242 | ... | (53) 322 987 | ... | ... |
| | Teacher training | | - | - | - | - | - | - |
| | Vocational education | | ... | ... | ... | 73 049 | ... | ... |
| | Total | 1991/92 | 33 836 | (60) 25 643 | ... | 379 162 | ... | ... |
| | General education | | *28 966 | (60) 22 926 | ... | 314 129 | ... | ... |
| | Teacher training | | - | - | - | - | - | - |
| | Vocational education | | 4 870 | 2 717 | 56 | 65 033 | 23 732 | 36 |
| | Total | 1992/93 | 34 269 | (60) 26 015 | ... | 356 678 | (60) 173 585 | ... |
| | General education | | *29 631 | (60) 23 394 | ... | 301 602 | (60) 152 556 | ... |
| | Teacher training | | - | - | - | - | - | - |
| | Vocational education | | 4 638 | 2 621 | 57 | 55 076 | 21 029 | 38 |
| | Total | 1993/94 | 34 679 | (60) 26 441 | ... | 347 434 | ... | ... |
| | General education | | 29 636 | (60) 23 574 | ... | 295 218 | ... | ... |
| | Teacher training | | - | - | - | - | - | - |
| | Vocational education | | 5 043 | 2 867 | 57 | 52 216 | 21 330 | 41 |
| | Total | 1994/95 | 35 957 | (60) 27 699 | ... | 351 517 | 177 399 | 50 |
| | General education | | 31 342 | (60) 24 979 | ... | 301 714 | 156 442 | 52 |
| | Teacher training | | - | - | - | - | - | - |
| | Vocational education | | 4 615 | 2 720 | 59 | 49 803 | 20 957 | 42 |
| | Total | 1995/96 | 36 185 | (60) 28 059 | ... | 365 351 | 183 158 | 50 |
| | General education | | 31 514 | (60) 25 272 | ... | 313 538 | 162 411 | 52 |
| | Teacher training | | - | - | - | - | - | - |
| | Vocational education | | 4 671 | 2 787 | 60 | 51 813 | 20 747 | 40 |
| | Total | 1996/97 | 36 932 | (60) 28 507 | ... | 378 754 | 189 096 | 50 |
| | General education | | 32 172 | (60) 25 591 | ... | 325 480 | 168 214 | 52 |
| | Teacher training | | - | - | - | - | - | - |
| | Vocational education | | 4 760 | 2 916 | 61 | 53 274 | 20 882 | 39 |
| Luxembourg | Total | 1970/71 | 1 451 | 367 | 25 | 16 430 | 7 764 | 47 |
| | General education | | 661 | 184 | 28 | 8 924 | 3 992 | 45 |
| | Teacher training | | - | - | - | - | - | - |
| | Vocational education | | 790 | 183 | 23 | 7 506 | 3 772 | 50 |
| | Total | 1975/76 | ... | ... | ... | 22 652 | 11 038 | 49 |
| | General education | | 959 | ... | ... | 15 191 | 7 573 | 50 |
| | Teacher training | | - | - | - | - | - | - |
| | Vocational education | | ... | ... | ... | 7 461 | 3 465 | 46 |
| | Total | 1980/81 | 1 944 | ... | ... | 27 487 | ... | ... |
| | General education | | ... | ... | ... | 9 037 | 4 910 | 54 |
| | Teacher training | | ... | ... | ... | 53 | 50 | 94 |
| | Vocational education | | ... | ... | ... | 18 397 | ... | ... |
| | Total | 1985/86 | 1 908 | ... | ... | 25 656 | 12 438 | 48 |
| | General education | | ... | ... | ... | 7 951 | 4 355 | 55 |
| | Teacher training | | ... | ... | ... | 86 | 67 | 78 |
| | Vocational education | | ... | ... | ... | 17 619 | 8 016 | 45 |
| | Total | 1990/91 | ... | ... | ... | ... | ... | ... |
| | General education | | ... | ... | ... | 7 594 | ... | ... |
| | Teacher training | | ... | ... | ... | ... | ... | ... |
| | Vocational education | | ... | ... | ... | ... | ... | ... |
| | Total | 1991/92 | ... | ... | ... | 20 817 | 10 285 | 49 |
| | General education | | ... | ... | ... | 8 420 | 4 510 | 54 |
| | Teacher training | | ... | ... | ... | - | - | - |
| | Vocational education | | ... | ... | ... | 12 397 | 5 775 | 47 |
| | Total | 1992/93 | ... | ... | ... | 21 989 | 11 013 | 50 |
| | General education | | ... | ... | ... | 8 806 | 4 804 | 55 |
| | Teacher training | | - | - | - | - | - | - |
| | Vocational education | | ... | ... | ... | 13 183 | 6 209 | 47 |
| | Total | 1993/94 | ... | ... | ... | 23 138 | 11 536 | 50 |
| | General education | | ... | ... | ... | 8 985 | 4 890 | 54 |
| | Teacher training | | ... | ... | ... | - | - | - |
| | Vocational education | | ... | ... | ... | 14 153 | 6 646 | 47 |
| | Total | 1994/95 | ... | ... | ... | 25 607 | 12 575 | 49 |
| | General education | | ... | ... | ... | 9 012 | 4 865 | 54 |
| | Teacher training | | ... | ... | ... | - | - | - |
| | Vocational education | | ... | ... | ... | 16 595 | 7 710 | 46 |
| | Total | 1995/96 | ... | ... | ... | 27 482 | 13 675 | 50 |
| | General education | | ... | ... | ... | 9 353 | 5 104 | 55 |
| | Teacher training | | ... | ... | ... | - | - | - |
| | Vocational education | | ... | ... | ... | 18 129 | 8 571 | 47 |
| | Total | 1996/97 | 2 836 | 1 108 | 39 | 28 796 | 14 509 | 50 |
| | General education | | 1 154 | 466 | 40 | 9 463 | 5 184 | 55 |
| | Teacher training | | - | - | - | - | - | - |
| | Vocational education | | 1 682 | 642 | 38 | 19 333 | 9 325 | 48 |

Secondary education: teaching staff and pupils  II.6
Enseignement secondaire: personnel enseignant et élèves
Enseñanza secundaria: personal docente y alumnos

| Country / Pays / País | Type of education / Type d'enseignement / Tipo de enseñanza | Year / Année / Año | Teaching staff / Personnel enseignant / Personal docente | | | Pupils enrolled / Elèves inscrits / Alumnos matriculados | | |
|---|---|---|---|---|---|---|---|---|
| | | | Total | Female Féminin Femenino | % F | Total | Female Féminin Femenino | % F |
| Malta | Total | 1970/71 | 1 662 | ... | ... | 24 388 | ... | ... |
| | General education | | 1 432 | 543 | 38 | 21 938 | 11 134 | 51 |
| | Teacher training | | - | - | - | - | - | - |
| | Vocational education | | *230 | ... | ... | 2 450 | ... | ... |
| | Total | 1975/76 | 2 498 | 934 | 37 | 32 409 | 14 927 | 46 |
| | General education | | 2 089 | 897 | 43 | 28 022 | 14 196 | 51 |
| | Teacher training | | - | - | - | - | - | - |
| | Vocational education | | 409 | 37 | 9 | 4 387 | 731 | 17 |
| | Total | 1980/81 | 2 141 | 783 | 37 | 25 501 | 11 458 | 45 |
| | General education | | 1 691 | 695 | 41 | 21 377 | 10 562 | 49 |
| | Teacher training | | - | - | - | - | - | - |
| | Vocational education | | 450 | 88 | 20 | 4 124 | 896 | 22 |
| | Total | 1985/86 | 2 315 | 779 | 34 | 27 779 | 13 294 | 48 |
| | General education | | 1 724 | 659 | 38 | 21 421 | 11 959 | 56 |
| | Teacher training | | - | - | - | - | - | - |
| | Vocational education | | 591 | 120 | 20 | 6 358 | 1 335 | 21 |
| | Total | 1990/91 | 2 688 | 956 | 36 | 32 544 | 15 196 | 47 |
| | General education | | 1 978 | 805 | 41 | 25 891 | 13 746 | 53 |
| | Teacher training | | - | - | - | - | - | - |
| | Vocational education | | 710 | 151 | 21 | 6 653 | 1 450 | 22 |
| | Total | 1991/92 | ... | ... | ... | 34 358 | 15 956 | 46 |
| | General education | | ... | ... | ... | 27 797 | 14 736 | 53 |
| | Teacher training | | - | - | - | - | - | - |
| | Vocational education | | 707 | 141 | 20 | 6 561 | 1 220 | 19 |
| | Total | 1992/93 | ... | ... | ... | 34 619 | 16 072 | 46 |
| | General education | | ... | ... | ... | 28 419 | 15 089 | 53 |
| | Teacher training | | - | - | - | - | - | - |
| | Vocational education | | 690 | 121 | 18 | 6 200 | 983 | 16 |
| | Total | 1993/94 | 3 268 | 1 403 | 43 | 34 955 | 16 027 | 46 |
| | General education | | 2 617 | 1 290 | 49 | 29 082 | 15 148 | 52 |
| | Teacher training | | - | - | - | - | - | - |
| | Vocational education | | 651 | 113 | 17 | 5 873 | 879 | 15 |
| | Total | 1994/95 | 3 357 | 1 405 | 42 | 35 527 | 16 649 | 47 |
| | General education | | 2 819 | 1 335 | 47 | 30 872 | 15 993 | 52 |
| | Teacher training | | - | - | - | - | - | - |
| | Vocational education | | 538 | 70 | 13 | 4 655 | 656 | 14 |
| | Total | 1995/96 | 3 180 | 1 418 | 45 | 34 128 | 16 003 | 47 |
| | General education | | 2 660 | 1 340 | 50 | 29 876 | 15 390 | 52 |
| | Teacher training | | - | - | - | - | - | - |
| | Vocational education | | 520 | 78 | 15 | 4 252 | 613 | 14 |
| | Total | 1996/97 | ... | ... | ... | 34 211 | 16 237 | 47 |
| | General education | | ... | ... | ... | 29 936 | 15 664 | 52 |
| | Teacher training | | - | - | - | - | - | - |
| | Vocational education | | ... | ... | ... | 4 275 | 573 | 13 |
| Moldova | Total | 1980/81 | ... | ... | ... | ... | ... | |
| | General education | | ... | ... | ... | 415 228 | 211 766 | 51 |
| | Teacher training | | ... | ... | ... | ... | ... | |
| | Vocational education | | ... | ... | ... | ... | ... | |
| | Total | 1985/86 | 31 857 | 21 664 | 68 | ... | ... | |
| | General education | | ... | ... | ... | 427 727 | 218 141 | 51 |
| | Teacher training | | ... | ... | ... | ... | ... | |
| | Vocational education | | ... | ... | ... | ... | ... | |
| | Total | 1990/91 | 36 299 | 25 116 | 69 | 459 701 | 237 626 | 52 |
| | General education | | ... | ... | ... | 419 153 | 213 768 | 51 |
| | Teacher training | | | | | 2 072 | 1 927 | 93 |
| | Vocational education | | ... | ... | ... | 38 476 | 21 931 | 57 |
| | Total | 1991/92 | 36 427 | 25 152 | 69 | 448 404 | 232 054 | 52 |
| | General education | | ... | ... | ... | 407 596 | 207 874 | 51 |
| | Teacher training | | | | | 2 555 | 2 376 | 93 |
| | Vocational education | | ... | ... | ... | 38 253 | 21 804 | 57 |
| | Total | 1992/93 | 37 888 | 26 531 | 70 | 441 955 | 229 857 | 52 |
| | General education | | ... | ... | ... | 399 586 | 203 789 | 51 |
| | Teacher training | | | | | 2 549 | 2 371 | 93 |
| | Vocational education | | ... | ... | ... | 39 820 | 23 697 | 60 |
| | Total | 1993/94 | 38 568 | 26 928 | 70 | 444 422 | 229 890 | 52 |
| | General education | | ... | ... | ... | 405 969 | 207 044 | 51 |
| | Teacher training | | | | | 2 576 | 2 396 | 93 |
| | Vocational education | | ... | ... | ... | 35 877 | 20 450 | 57 |
| | Total | 1994/95 | (53) 35 216 | ... | ... | (53) 441 573 | (53) 222 353 | 50 |
| | General education | | ... | ... | ... | 407 338 | 206 612 | 51 |
| | Teacher training | | ... | ... | ... | 2 354 | 2 166 | 92 |
| | Vocational education | | ... | ... | ... | 31 881 | 13 575 | 43 |

II.6 Secondary education: teaching staff and pupils
Enseignement secondaire: personnel enseignant et élèves
Enseñanza secundaria: personal docente y alumnos

| Country / Pays / País | Type of education / Type d'enseignement / Tipo de enseñanza | Year / Année / Año | Teaching staff / Personnel enseignant / Personal docente | | | Pupils enrolled / Elèves inscrits / Alumnos matriculados | | |
|---|---|---|---|---|---|---|---|---|
| | | | Total | Female Féminin Femenino | % F | Total | Female Féminin Femenino | % F |
| Moldova (cont) | Total | 1995/96 | *33 752 | *24 372 | *72 | *440 622 | *220 910 | *50 |
| | General education | | ... | ... | ... | *412 679 | *209 084 | *51 |
| | Teacher training | | ... | ... | ... | *2 276 | *2 116 | *93 |
| | Vocational education | | ... | ... | ... | *25 667 | *9 710 | *38 |
| | Total | 1996/97 | 28 615 | 20 832 | 73 | *445 501 | *223 162 | *50 |
| | General education | | ... | ... | ... | *419 256 | *211 931 | *51 |
| | Teacher training | | ... | ... | ... | *2 140 | *1 991 | *93 |
| | Vocational education | | ... | ... | ... | *24 105 | *9 240 | *38 |
| Monaco | Total | 1970/71 | 144 | ... | ... | 2 445 | ... | ... |
| | General education | | 116 | ... | ... | 2 033 | ... | ... |
| | Teacher training | | - | - | - | - | - | - |
| | Vocational education | | 28 | ... | ... | 412 | ... | ... |
| | Total | 1980/81 | ... | ... | ... | (4) 2 065 | ... | ... |
| | General education | | ... | ... | ... | (4) 1 314 | ... | ... |
| | Teacher training | | - | - | - | - | - | - |
| | Vocational education | | ... | ... | ... | (4) 751 | (4) 383 | 51 |
| | Total | 1990/91 | ... | ... | ... | 2 785 | 1 378 | 49 |
| | General education | | (4) 180 | (4) 103 | 57 | 2 415 | 1 242 | 51 |
| | Teacher training | | - | - | - | - | - | - |
| | Vocational education | | 145 | 63 | 43 | 370 | 136 | 37 |
| | Total | 1991/92 | ... | ... | ... | 2 858 | 1 391 | 49 |
| | General education | | (4) 181 | (4) 104 | 57 | 2 383 | 1 220 | 51 |
| | Teacher training | | - | - | - | - | - | - |
| | Vocational education | | 73 | 25 | 34 | 475 | 171 | 36 |
| | Total | 1993/94 | ... | ... | ... | 2 835 | 1 381 | 49 |
| | General education | | (4) 188 | (4) 121 | 64 | 2 385 | 1 199 | 50 |
| | Teacher training | | - | - | - | - | - | - |
| | Vocational education | | 61 | 38 | 62 | 450 | 182 | 40 |
| | Total | 1994/95 | 279 | 186 | 67 | 2 861 | 1 413 | 49 |
| | General education | | 195 | 141 | 72 | 2 358 | 1 202 | 51 |
| | Teacher training | | - | - | - | - | - | - |
| | Vocational education | | 84 | 45 | 54 | 503 | 211 | 42 |
| | Total | 1995/96 | 287 | 188 | 66 | 2 907 | 1 463 | 50 |
| | General education | | 196 | 140 | 71 | 2 387 | 1 241 | 52 |
| | Teacher training | | - | - | - | - | - | - |
| | Vocational education | | 91 | 48 | 53 | 520 | 222 | 43 |
| | Total | 1996/97 | 281 | 172 | 61 | 2 886 | 1 458 | 51 |
| | General education | | 192 | ... | ... | 2 358 | 1 217 | 52 |
| | Teacher training | | - | - | - | - | - | - |
| | Vocational education | | 89 | ... | ... | 528 | 241 | 46 |
| Netherlands | Total | 1970/71 | ... | ... | ... | 1 006 327 | 450 746 | 45 |
| | General education | | 38 849 | 8 677 | 22 | 591 311 | 281 282 | 48 |
| | Teacher training | | ... | ... | ... | 7 429 | 7 429 | 100 |
| | Vocational education | | ... | ... | ... | 407 587 | 162 035 | 40 |
| | Total | 1975/76 | ... | ... | ... | 1 283 585 | 600 323 | 47 |
| | General education | | 48 193 | 11 859 | 25 | 766 391 | 380 114 | 50 |
| | Teacher training | | ... | ... | ... | 10 830 | 10 789 | 100 |
| | Vocational education | | ... | ... | ... | 506 364 | 209 420 | 41 |
| | Total | 1980/81 | ... | ... | ... | 1 391 485 | 663 695 | 48 |
| | General education | | 54 369 | 13 997 | 26 | 823 730 | 428 252 | 52 |
| | Teacher training | | 1 124 | 583 | 52 | 7 190 | 7 119 | 99 |
| | Vocational education | | ... | ... | ... | 560 565 | 228 324 | 41 |
| | Total | 1985/86 | ... | ... | ... | (68) 1 620 011 | (68) 774 422 | 48 |
| | General education | | 53 361 | 14 377 | 27 | 803 782 | 425 118 | 53 |
| | Teacher training | | 234 | 95 | 41 | 2 138 | 2 097 | 98 |
| | Vocational education | | ... | ... | ... | (68) 814 091 | (68) 347 207 | 43 |
| | Total | 1990/91 | 89 370 | 25 900 | 29 | 1 401 739 | 657 882 | 47 |
| | General education | | ... | ... | ... | 683 662 | 356 407 | 52 |
| | Teacher training | | - | - | - | - | - | - |
| | Vocational education | | ... | ... | ... | 718 077 | 301 475 | 42 |
| | Total | 1991/92 | 87 200 | 25 800 | 30 | 1 377 768 | 649 622 | 47 |
| | General education | | ... | ... | ... | 673 592 | 351 418 | 52 |
| | Teacher training | | - | - | - | - | - | - |
| | Vocational education | | ... | ... | ... | 704 176 | 298 204 | 42 |
| | Total | 1992/93 | 86 000 | 25 800 | 30 | 1 369 507 | 653 200 | 48 |
| | General education | | ... | ... | ... | 668 094 | 349 283 | 52 |
| | Teacher training | | - | - | - | - | - | - |
| | Vocational education | | ... | ... | ... | 701 413 | 303 917 | 43 |
| | Total | 1993/94 | (52) 88 229 | (52) 27 010 | 31 | (52) 1 536 153 | (52) 724 595 | 47 |
| | General education | | 53 781 | 16 351 | 30 | 782 639 | 411 904 | 53 |
| | Teacher training | | - | - | - | - | - | - |
| | Vocational education | | 34 448 | 10 659 | 31 | 753 514 | 312 691 | 41 |

Secondary education: teaching staff and pupils
Enseignement secondaire: personnel enseignant et élèves
Enseñanza secundaria: personal docente y alumnos

II.6

| Country / Pays / País | Type of education / Type d'enseignement / Tipo de enseñanza | Year / Année / Año | Teaching staff / Personnel enseignant / Personal docente | | | Pupils enrolled / Elèves inscrits / Alumnos matriculados | | |
|---|---|---|---|---|---|---|---|---|
| | | | Total | Female Féminin Femenino | % F | Total | Female Féminin Femenino | % F |
| Netherlands (cont) | Total | 1994/95 | ... | ... | ... | 1 508 772 | 717 410 | 48 |
| | General education | | ... | ... | ... | 777 019 | 403 722 | 52 |
| | Teacher training | | - | - | - | - | - | - |
| | Vocational education | | ... | ... | ... | 731 753 | 313 688 | 43 |
| | Total | 1995/96 | (67) 67 800 | (67) 19 200 | 28 | 1 479 682 | 702 230 | 47 |
| | General education | | ... | ... | ... | 769 564 | 398 136 | 52 |
| | Teacher training | | - | - | - | - | - | - |
| | Vocational education | | ... | ... | ... | 710 118 | 304 094 | 43 |
| | Total | 1996/97 | (67) 69 000 | (67) 20 000 | 29 | 1 415 712 | 677 314 | 48 |
| | General education | | ... | ... | ... | 831 811 | 421 024 | 51 |
| | Teacher training | | - | - | - | - | - | - |
| | Vocational education | | ... | ... | ... | 583 901 | 256 290 | 44 |
| Norway | Total | 1970/71 | 31 459 | 10 351 | 33 | 302 792 | 147 053 | 49 |
| | General education | | 20 618 | 7 427 | 36 | 243 714 | 120 046 | 49 |
| | Teacher training | | - | - | - | - | - | - |
| | Vocational education | | 10 841 | 2 924 | 27 | 59 078 | 27 007 | 46 |
| | Total | 1975/76 | ... | ... | ... | 326 640 | 159 629 | 49 |
| | General education | | ... | ... | ... | 263 941 | 131 998 | 50 |
| | Teacher training | | - | - | - | - | - | - |
| | Vocational education | | 10 332 | 3 387 | 33 | 62 699 | 27 631 | 44 |
| | Total | 1980/81 | ... | ... | ... | 360 776 | 180 226 | 50 |
| | General education | | ... | ... | ... | 279 266 | 141 888 | 51 |
| | Teacher training | | ... | ... | ... | 345 | 288 | 83 |
| | Vocational education | | ... | ... | ... | 81 165 | 38 050 | 47 |
| | Total | 1985/86 | ... | ... | ... | 387 990 | 194 162 | 50 |
| | General education | | ... | ... | ... | 280 357 | 142 314 | 51 |
| | Teacher training | | ... | ... | ... | 630 | 577 | 92 |
| | Vocational education | | ... | ... | ... | 107 003 | 51 271 | 48 |
| | Total | 1990/91 | ... | ... | ... | 370 779 | 184 225 | 50 |
| | General education | | ... | ... | ... | 250 664 | 128 290 | 51 |
| | Teacher training | | ... | ... | ... | 1 154 | 1 081 | 94 |
| | Vocational education | | ... | ... | ... | 118 961 | 54 854 | 46 |
| | Total | 1991/92 | ... | ... | ... | 367 395 | 180 904 | 49 |
| | General education | | ... | ... | ... | 248 003 | 126 983 | 51 |
| | Teacher training | | ... | ... | ... | 1 336 | 1 255 | 94 |
| | Vocational education | | ... | ... | ... | 118 056 | 52 666 | 45 |
| | Total | 1992/93 | ... | ... | ... | 380 916 | 183 861 | 48 |
| | General education | | ... | ... | ... | 246 615 | 126 694 | 51 |
| | Teacher training | | ... | ... | ... | 1 888 | 1 799 | 95 |
| | Vocational education | | ... | ... | ... | 132 413 | 55 368 | 42 |
| | Total | 1993/94 | ... | ... | ... | (52) 408 418 | (52) 196 746 | 48 |
| | General education | | ... | ... | ... | 261 303 | 135 041 | 52 |
| | Teacher training | | ... | ... | ... | 2 192 | 2 046 | 93 |
| | Vocational education | | ... | ... | ... | 144 923 | 59 659 | 41 |
| | Total | 1994/95 | ... | ... | ... | 370 925 | 176 402 | 48 |
| | General education | | ... | ... | ... | 252 777 | 129 965 | 51 |
| | Teacher training | | ... | ... | ... | 2 379 | 2 218 | 93 |
| | Vocational education | | ... | ... | ... | 115 769 | 44 219 | 38 |
| | Total | 1995/96 | ... | ... | ... | 364 343 | 172 935 | 47 |
| | General education | | ... | ... | ... | 243 826 | 124 670 | 51 |
| | Teacher training | | ... | ... | ... | 265 | 201 | 76 |
| | Vocational education | | ... | ... | ... | 120 252 | 48 064 | 40 |
| | Total | 1996/97 | ... | ... | ... | 368 074 | 176 073 | 48 |
| | General education | | ... | ... | ... | 243 392 | 124 945 | 51 |
| | Teacher training | | - | - | - | - | - | - |
| | Vocational education | | ... | ... | ... | 124 682 | 51 128 | 41 |
| Poland | Total | 1970/71 | 170 457 | 67 796 | 40 | 1 734 193 | 883 193 | 51 |
| | General education | | 28 462 | 16 123 | 57 | 401 306 | 286 837 | 71 |
| | Teacher training | | ./. | ./. | ./. | 18 244 | 15 099 | 83 |
| | Vocational education | | (62) 141 995 | (62) 51 673 | 36 | 1 314 643 | 581 257 | 44 |
| | Total | 1975/76 | 169 635 | 78 403 | 46 | 1 946 366 | 980 709 | 50 |
| | General education | | 34 114 | 21 899 | 64 | 471 594 | 334 944 | 71 |
| | Teacher training | | ./. | ./. | ./. | 17 588 | 14 230 | 81 |
| | Vocational education | | (62) 135 521 | (62) 56 504 | 42 | 1 457 184 | 631 535 | 43 |
| | Total | 1980/81 | 93 346 | ... | ... | 1 673 869 | 840 888 | 50 |
| | General education | | 21 287 | ... | ... | 345 214 | 244 242 | 71 |
| | Teacher training | | 1 402 | ... | ... | 18 703 | 16 277 | 87 |
| | Vocational education | | 70 657 | ... | ... | 1 309 952 | 580 369 | 44 |
| | Total | 1985/86 | 95 552 | ... | ... | 1 567 641 | 793 568 | 51 |
| | General education | | 21 309 | ... | ... | 337 563 | 245 843 | 73 |
| | Teacher training | | 1 643 | ... | ... | 22 723 | 20 730 | 91 |
| | Vocational education | | 72 600 | ... | ... | 1 207 355 | 526 995 | 44 |

II.6 Secondary education: teaching staff and pupils
Enseignement secondaire: personnel enseignant et élèves
Enseñanza secundaria: personal docente y alumnos

| Country / Pays / País | Type of education / Type d'enseignement / Tipo de enseñanza | Year / Année / Año | Teaching staff — Personnel enseignant — Personal docente | | | Pupils enrolled — Elèves inscrits — Alumnos matriculados | | |
|---|---|---|---|---|---|---|---|---|
| | | | Total | Female / Féminin / Femenino | % F | Total | Female / Féminin / Femenino | % F |
| Poland (cont) | Total | 1990/91 | 103 814 | ... | ... | 1 887 667 | 945 044 | 50 |
| | General education | | 24 307 | ... | ... | 444 597 | 323 132 | 73 |
| | Teacher training | | 2 267 | ... | ... | 25 886 | 23 367 | 90 |
| | Vocational education | | 77 240 | ... | ... | 1 417 184 | 598 545 | 42 |
| | Total | 1991/92 | 105 372 | ... | ... | 1 965 021 | 983 322 | 50 |
| | General education | | 25 833 | ... | ... | 499 401 | 361 550 | 72 |
| | Teacher training | | 1 684 | ... | ... | 19 399 | 17 010 | 88 |
| | Vocational education | | 77 855 | ... | ... | 1 446 221 | 604 762 | 42 |
| | Total | 1992/93 | (29) 109 090 | ... | ... | (29) 2 258 970 | (29) 1 115 549 | 49 |
| | General education | | 28 302 | ... | ... | 607 138 | 432 819 | 71 |
| | Teacher training | | ./. | ... | ... | 2 966 | 1 412 | 48 |
| | Vocational education | | (29)(62) 80 788 | ... | ... | (29) 1 648 866 | (29) 681 318 | 41 |
| | Total | 1993/94 | 112 842 | ... | ... | 2 350 485 | 1 172 544 | 50 |
| | General education | | 30 304 | ... | ... | 659 524 | 474 897 | 72 |
| | Teacher training | | 167 | ... | ... | 1 832 | 885 | 48 |
| | Vocational education | | 82 371 | ... | ... | 1 689 129 | 696 762 | 41 |
| | Total | 1994/95 | 119 556 | ... | ... | 2 497 920 | 1 223 356 | 49 |
| | General education | | 34 758 | ... | ... | 756 023 | 504 014 | 67 |
| | Teacher training | | ./. | ... | ... | 30 | 22 | 73 |
| | Vocational education | | (62) 84 798 | ... | ... | 1 741 867 | 719 320 | 41 |
| | Total | 1995/96 | 121 301 | ... | ... | 2 539 138 | 1 239 331 | 49 |
| | General education | | 36 354 | ... | ... | 793 216 | 520 054 | 66 |
| | Teacher training | | ./. | ... | ... | 38 | 30 | 79 |
| | Vocational education | | (62) 84 947 | ... | ... | 1 745 884 | 719 247 | 41 |
| Portugal | Total | 1970/71 | 26 782 | 14 298 | 53 | 445 574 | 201 850 | 45 |
| | General education | | 17 018 | 9 972 | 59 | 290 969 | 143 644 | 49 |
| | Teacher training | | 342 | 175 | 51 | 5 313 | 4 845 | 91 |
| | Vocational education | | 9 422 | 4 151 | 44 | 149 292 | 53 361 | 36 |
| | Total | 1975/76 | 29 714 | 16 586 | 56 | 466 491 | 226 858 | 49 |
| | General education | | 14 903 | 8 816 | 59 | 330 008 | 171 949 | 52 |
| | Teacher training | | 826 | 501 | 61 | 9 166 | 7 841 | 86 |
| | Vocational education | | 13 985 | 7 269 | 52 | 127 317 | 47 068 | 37 |
| | Total | 1980/81 | (24) 32 028 | (24) 18 963 | 59 | (24) 398 320 | (4)(24) 190 612 | ... |
| | General education | | (24) 32 028 | (24) 18 963 | 59 | (24) 398 320 | (4)(24) 190 612 | ... |
| | Teacher training | | - | - | - | - | - | - |
| | Vocational education | | - | - | - | - | - | - |
| | Total | 1985/86 | ... | ... | ... | 580 248 | ... | ... |
| | General education | | 39 685 | 25 014 | 63 | 572 697 | 302 815 | 53 |
| | Teacher training | | - | - | - | - | - | - |
| | Vocational education | | ... | ... | ... | 7 551 | ... | ... |
| | Total | 1990/91 | 64 513 | 42 513 | 66 | 670 035 | 354 490 | 53 |
| | General education | | ... | - | ... | 637 761 | 342 712 | 54 |
| | Teacher training | | ... | - | - | - | - | - |
| | Vocational education | | ... | ... | ... | 32 274 | 11 778 | 36 |
| | Total | 1991/92 | ... | ... | ... | 759 639 | ... | ... |
| | General education | | ... | ... | ... | 728 283 | ... | ... |
| | Teacher training | | - | - | - | - | - | - |
| | Vocational education | | ... | ... | ... | 31 356 | ... | ... |
| | Total | 1992/93 | (29) 71 467 | ... | ... | (29) 898 483 | (29) 470 794 | 52 |
| | General education | | ... | ... | ... | 819 649 | 434 599 | 53 |
| | Teacher training | | - | - | - | - | - | - |
| | Vocational education | | ... | ... | ... | 78 834 | 36 195 | 46 |
| | Total | 1993/94 | ... | ... | ... | 938 653 | 480 751 | 51 |
| | General education | | ... | ... | ... | 827 099 | 430 384 | 52 |
| | Teacher training | | - | - | - | - | - | - |
| | Vocational education | | ... | ... | ... | 111 554 | 50 367 | 45 |
| | Total | 1994/95 | ... | ... | ... | 945 077 | 481 287 | 51 |
| | General education | | ... | ... | ... | 828 758 | 428 002 | 52 |
| | Teacher training | | - | - | - | - | - | - |
| | Vocational education | | ... | ... | ... | 116 319 | 53 285 | 46 |
| | Total | 1995/96 | ... | ... | ... | 947 478 | 484 773 | 51 |
| | General education | | ... | ... | ... | 821 474 | 426 779 | 52 |
| | Teacher training | | - | - | - | - | - | - |
| | Vocational education | | ... | ... | ... | 126 004 | 57 994 | 46 |
| Romania | Total | 1970/71 | 36 604 | 15 455 | 42 | 659 715 | 275 189 | 42 |
| | General education | | 13 831 | 7 407 | 54 | 255 667 | 153 929 | 60 |
| | Teacher training | | 1 280 | 735 | 57 | 23 732 | 20 229 | 85 |
| | Vocational education | | 21 493 | 7 313 | 34 | 380 316 | 101 031 | 27 |
| | Total | 1975/76 | 46 907 | 20 720 | 44 | 870 161 | 434 205 | 50 |
| | General education | | 14 713 | 8 120 | 55 | 256 135 | 177 639 | 69 |
| | Teacher training | | 1 248 | 728 | 58 | 18 898 | 16 958 | 90 |
| | Vocational education | | 30 946 | 11 872 | 38 | 595 128 | 239 608 | 40 |

Secondary education: teaching staff and pupils  
Enseignement secondaire: personnel enseignant et élèves  
Enseñanza secundaria: personal docente y alumnos

II.6

| Country<br>Pays<br>País | Type of education<br>Type d'enseignement<br>Tipo de enseñanza | Year<br>Année<br>Año | Teaching staff<br>Personnel enseignant<br>Personal docente | | | Pupils enrolled<br>Elèves inscrits<br>Alumnos matriculados | | |
|---|---|---|---|---|---|---|---|---|
| | | | Total | Female<br>Féminin<br>Femenino | %<br>F | Total | Female<br>Féminin<br>Femenino | %<br>F |
| Romania (cont) | Total | 1980/81 | 48 711 | 21 128 | 43 | 1 147 879 | 513 192 | 45 |
| | General education | | ... | ... | ... | ... | ... | ... |
| | Teacher training | | ... | ... | ... | ... | ... | ... |
| | Vocational education | | ... | ... | ... | ... | ... | ... |
| | Total | 1985/86 | 50 333 | 23 998 | 48 | 1 537 548 | 711 018 | 46 |
| | General education | | 7 383 | 3 945 | 53 | 103 268 | 72 024 | 70 |
| | Teacher training | | 699 | 423 | 61 | 4 286 | 4 078 | 95 |
| | Vocational education | | 42 251 | 19 630 | 46 | 1 429 994 | 634 916 | 44 |
| | Total | 1990/91 | (2) 157 474 | (2) 96 150 | 61 | (2) 2 837 948 | (2) 1 379 805 | 49 |
| | General education | | (2) 114 314 | (2) 74 704 | 65 | (2) 1 621 501 | (2) 821 089 | 51 |
| | Teacher training | | 1 208 | 764 | 63 | 10 716 | 10 169 | 95 |
| | Vocational education | | 41 952 | 20 682 | 49 | 1 205 731 | 548 547 | 45 |
| | Total | 1991/92 | 154 662 | 95 453 | 62 | 2 606 305 | 1 274 703 | 49 |
| | General education | | 113 040 | 73 422 | 65 | 1 646 423 | 848 698 | 52 |
| | Teacher training | | 1 596 | 1 014 | 64 | 13 026 | 12 328 | 95 |
| | Vocational education | | 40 026 | 21 017 | 53 | 946 856 | 413 677 | 44 |
| | Total | 1992/93 | 165 311 | 101 341 | 61 | 2 451 624 | 1 194 698 | 49 |
| | General education | | 119 460 | 77 125 | 65 | 1 659 362 | 860 764 | 52 |
| | Teacher training | | 1 796 | 1 150 | 64 | 16 598 | 15 736 | 95 |
| | Vocational education | | 44 055 | 23 066 | 52 | 775 664 | 318 198 | 41 |
| | Total | 1993/94 | 167 316 | 102 927 | 62 | 2 336 322 | 1 154 187 | 49 |
| | General education | | 118 427 | 77 402 | 65 | 1 559 075 | 817 637 | 52 |
| | Teacher training | | 2 035 | 1 285 | 63 | 18 909 | 17 010 | 95 |
| | Vocational education | | 46 854 | 24 240 | 52 | 758 338 | 318 631 | 42 |
| | Total | 1994/95 | 168 982 | 104 547 | 62 | 2 252 053 | 1 114 438 | 49 |
| | General education | | 118 675 | 77 010 | 65 | 1 468 039 | 774 916 | 53 |
| | Teacher training | | 2 270 | 1 465 | 65 | 19 967 | 18 873 | 95 |
| | Vocational education | | 48 037 | 26 072 | 54 | 764 047 | 320 649 | 42 |
| | Total | 1995/96 | 172 912 | 108 938 | 63 | 2 222 655 | 1 095 789 | 49 |
| | General education | | 121 639 | 79 666 | 65 | 1 461 422 | 769 587 | 53 |
| | Teacher training | | 2 207 | 1 487 | 67 | 18 693 | 17 631 | 94 |
| | Vocational education | | 49 066 | 27 785 | 57 | 742 540 | 308 571 | 42 |
| | Total | 1996/97 | 175 958 | 111 116 | 63 | 2 212 090 | 1 081 450 | 49 |
| | General education | | 123 487 | 81 812 | 66 | 1 457 608 | 764 985 | 52 |
| | Teacher training | | 2 231 | 1 498 | 67 | 17 928 | 16 936 | 94 |
| | Vocational education | | 50 240 | 27 806 | 55 | 736 554 | 299 529 | 41 |
| Russian Federation | Total | 1980/81 | ... | ... | ... | 12 991 000 | | |
| | General education | | 738 000 | 558 000 | 76 | 11 351 000 | 5 735 000 | 51 |
| | Teacher training | | | | | 241 000 | 220 000 | 91 |
| | Vocational education | | ... | ... | ... | 1 399 000 | ... | ... |
| | Total | 1985/86 | ... | ... | ... | 13 341 000 | | |
| | General education | | 775 000 | 596 000 | 77 | 11 675 000 | 5 836 000 | 50 |
| | Teacher training | | | | | 288 000 | 268 000 | 93 |
| | Vocational education | | ... | ... | ... | 1 378 000 | ... | ... |
| | Total | 1990/91 | ... | ... | ... | 13 956 000 | | ... |
| | General education | | 944 000 | 731 000 | 77 | 12 363 000 | 6 300 000 | 51 |
| | Teacher training | | | | | 341 000 | 318 000 | 93 |
| | Vocational education | | ... | ... | ... | 1 252 000 | | ... |
| | Total | 1991/92 | ... | ... | ... | 13 890 000 | | ... |
| | General education | | 983 000 | 764 000 | 78 | 12 313 000 | 6 317 000 | 51 |
| | Teacher training | | | | | 342 000 | 318 000 | 93 |
| | Vocational education | | ... | ... | ... | 1 235 000 | | ... |
| | Total | 1992/93 | ... | ... | ... | 13 724 000 | | ... |
| | General education | | 1 026 000 | 806 000 | 79 | 12 306 000 | 6 331 000 | 51 |
| | Teacher training | | | | | 322 000 | 298 000 | 93 |
| | Vocational education | | ... | ... | ... | 1 096 000 | | ... |
| | Total | 1993/94 | ... | ... | ... | 13 732 000 | | ... |
| | General education | | 1 070 000 | 844 000 | 79 | 12 424 000 | 6 399 000 | 52 |
| | Teacher training | | | | | 301 000 | 277 000 | 92 |
| | Vocational education | | ... | ... | ... | 1 007 000 | ... | ... |
| San Marino | Total | 1970/71 | 75 | 41 | 55 | 901 | 422 | 47 |
| | General education | | 75 | 41 | 55 | 901 | 422 | 47 |
| | Teacher training | | - | - | - | - | - | - |
| | Vocational education | | - | - | - | - | - | - |
| | Total | 1975/76 | 108 | 62 | 57 | 1 211 | 575 | 47 |
| | General education | | 108 | 62 | 57 | 1 211 | 575 | 47 |
| | Teacher training | | - | - | - | - | - | - |
| | Vocational education | | - | - | - | - | - | - |
| | Total | 1980/81 | 112 | 69 | 62 | 1 219 | 593 | 49 |
| | General education | | 112 | 69 | 62 | 1 219 | 593 | 49 |
| | Teacher training | | - | - | - | - | - | - |
| | Vocational education | | - | - | - | - | - | - |

II.6    Secondary education: teaching staff and pupils
Enseignement secondaire: personnel enseignant et élèves
Enseñanza secundaria: personal docente y alumnos

| Country<br>Pays<br>País | Type of education<br>Type d'enseignement<br>Tipo de enseñanza | Year<br>Année<br>Año | Teaching staff<br>Personnel enseignant<br>Personal docente | | | Pupils enrolled<br>Elèves inscrits<br>Alumnos matriculados | | |
|---|---|---|---|---|---|---|---|---|
| | | | Total | Female<br>Féminin<br>Femenino | %<br>F | Total | Female<br>Féminin<br>Femenino | %<br>F |
| San Marino (cont) | Total | 1985/86 | ... | ... | ... | 1 248 | 597 | 48 |
| | General education | | ... | ... | ... | 1 248 | 597 | 48 |
| | Teacher training | | - | - | - | - | - | - |
| | Vocational education | | - | - | - | - | - | - |
| | Total | 1990/91 | ... | ... | ... | 1 182 | 616 | 52 |
| | General education | | ... | ... | ... | 1 045 | 580 | 56 |
| | Teacher training | | - | - | - | - | - | - |
| | Vocational education | | ... | ... | ... | 137 | 36 | 26 |
| | Total | 1991/92 | ... | ... | ... | 1 158 | 571 | 49 |
| | General education | | ... | ... | ... | 1 021 | 535 | 52 |
| | Teacher training | | - | - | - | - | - | - |
| | Vocational education | | ... | ... | ... | 137 | 36 | 26 |
| | Total | 1992/93 | ... | ... | ... | 1 159 | 561 | 48 |
| | General education | | ... | ... | ... | 1 001 | 511 | 51 |
| | Teacher training | | - | - | - | - | - | - |
| | Vocational education | | ... | ... | ... | 158 | 50 | 32 |
| | Total | 1993/94 | ... | ... | ... | 1 157 | 550 | 48 |
| | General education | | ... | ... | ... | 994 | 495 | 50 |
| | Teacher training | | - | - | - | - | - | - |
| | Vocational education | | ... | ... | ... | 163 | 55 | 34 |
| | Total | 1995/96 | ... | ... | ... | 1 199 | 573 | 48 |
| | General education | | ... | ... | ... | 1 058 | 534 | 50 |
| | Teacher training | | - | - | - | - | - | - |
| | Vocational education | | ... | ... | ... | 141 | 39 | 28 |
| | Total | 1996/97 | ... | ... | ... | 1 192 | 578 | 48 |
| | General education | | ... | ... | ... | 1 063 | 541 | 51 |
| | Teacher training | | - | - | - | - | - | - |
| | Vocational education | | ... | ... | ... | 129 | 37 | 29 |
| Slovakia | Total | 1992/93 | 48 340 | 32 061 | 66 | 657 010 | 327 920 | 50 |
| | General education | | 29 386 | 21 582 | 73 | 416 982 | 212 618 | 51 |
| | Teacher training | | 308 | 237 | 77 | 2 730 | 2 651 | 97 |
| | Vocational education | | 18 646 | 10 242 | 55 | 237 298 | 112 651 | 47 |
| | Total | 1993/94 | 42 679 | 29 917 | 70 | 658 228 | 328 239 | 50 |
| | General education | | 28 256 | 21 100 | 75 | 412 575 | 210 376 | 51 |
| | Teacher training | | 244 | 184 | 75 | 2 787 | 2 666 | 96 |
| | Vocational education | | 14 179 | 8 633 | 61 | 242 866 | 115 197 | 47 |
| | Total | 1994/95 | 43 339 | 30 740 | 71 | 663 647 | 332 820 | 50 |
| | General education | | 28 493 | 21 421 | 75 | 409 594 | 208 479 | 51 |
| | Teacher training | | 227 | 171 | 75 | 2 832 | 2 669 | 94 |
| | Vocational education | | 14 619 | 9 148 | 63 | 251 221 | 121 672 | 48 |
| | Total | 1995/96 | ... | ... | ... | 684 306 (60) | 333 236 | ... |
| | General education | | ... | ... | ... | 422 311 (60) | 206 888 | ... |
| | Teacher training | | 319 | 246 | 77 | 2 708 | 2 534 | 94 |
| | Vocational education | | 20 415 | 12 660 | 62 | 259 287 (60) | 123 814 | ... |
| | Total | 1996/97 | *54 694 | *38 252 | *70 | 677 377 (60) | 329 135 | ... |
| | General education | | *32 478 | *24 648 | *76 | 418 199 (60) | 203 932 | ... |
| | Teacher training | | 331 | 259 | 78 | 2 817 | 2 627 | 93 |
| | Vocational education | | 21 885 | 13 345 | 61 | 256 361 (60) | 122 576 | ... |
| Slovenia | Total | 1985/86 | ... | ... | ... | 193 555 | ... | ... |
| | General education | | ... | ... | ... | 110 444 | ... | ... |
| | Teacher training | | ... | ... | ... | 4 610 | 4 116 | 89 |
| | Vocational education | | ... | ... | ... | 78 501 | 37 091 | 47 |
| | Total | 1990/91 | ... | ... | ... | 208 905 | ... | ... |
| | General education | | ... | ... | ... | 120 402 | ... | ... |
| | Teacher training | | ... | ... | ... | 3 936 | 3 295 | 84 |
| | Vocational education | | ... | ... | ... | 84 567 | 39 794 | 47 |
| | Total | 1991/92 | ... | ... | ... | 210 699 | ... | ... |
| | General education | | ... | ... | ... | 118 898 | ... | ... |
| | Teacher training | | ... | ... | ... | 2 815 | 2 400 | 85 |
| | Vocational education | | ... | ... | ... | 88 986 | 42 867 | 48 |
| | Total | 1992/93 | 13 749 | 9 384 | 68 | 211 426 | 104 544 | 49 |
| | General education | | 8 717 | 6 506 | 75 | 137 414 | 71 412 | 52 |
| | Teacher training | | 148 | 146 | 99 | 1 895 | 1 671 | 88 |
| | Vocational education | | 4 884 | 2 732 | 56 | 72 117 | 31 461 | 44 |
| | Total | 1993/94 | 13 605 | 9 331 | 69 | 211 739 | 104 415 | 49 |
| | General education | | 8 306 | 6 312 | 76 | 137 578 | 71 364 | 52 |
| | Teacher training | | 147 | 112 | 76 | 824 | 808 | 98 |
| | Vocational education | | 5 152 | 2 907 | 56 | 73 337 | 32 243 | 44 |
| | Total | 1994/95 | 13 919 | 9 600 | 69 | 214 042 | 105 637 | 49 |
| | General education | | 8 291 | 6 323 | 76 | 137 580 | 71 223 | 52 |
| | Teacher training | | 149 | 113 | 76 | 802 | 778 | 97 |
| | Vocational education | | 5 479 | 3 164 | 58 | 75 660 | 33 636 | 44 |

Secondary education: teaching staff and pupils **II.6**
Enseignement secondaire: personnel enseignant et élèves
Enseñanza secundaria: personal docente y alumnos

| Country / Pays / País | Type of education / Type d'enseignement / Tipo de enseñanza | Year / Année / Año | Teaching staff — Personnel enseignant — Personal docente |  |  | Pupils enrolled — Elèves inscrits — Alumnos matriculados |  |  |
|---|---|---|---|---|---|---|---|---|
|  |  |  | Total | Female / Féminin / Femenino | % F | Total | Female / Féminin / Femenino | % F |
| Slovenia (cont) | Total | 1995/96 | 14 941 | 9 933 | 66 | 212 038 | 104 736 | 49 |
|  | General education |  | 8 488 | 6 478 | 76 | 133 769 | 69 157 | 52 |
|  | Teacher training |  | 150 | 114 | 76 | 776 | 755 | 97 |
|  | Vocational education |  | 6 303 | 3 341 | 53 | 77 493 | 34 824 | 45 |
|  | Total | 1996/97 | 14 573 | 10 155 | 70 | 212 458 | 105 077 | 49 |
|  | General education |  | 8 665 | 6 591 | 76 | 131 573 | 67 257 | 51 |
|  | Teacher training |  | 53 | 44 | 83 | 745 | 725 | 97 |
|  | Vocational education |  | 5 855 | 3 520 | 60 | 80 140 | 37 095 | 46 |
| Spain | Total | 1970/71 | 90 770 | ... | ... | 1 950 496 | 814 673 | 42 |
|  | General education |  | 62 269 | ... | ... | 1 521 858 | 695 036 | 46 |
|  | Teacher training |  | 2 179 | 1 236 | 57 | 47 541 | 26 876 | 57 |
|  | Vocational education |  | 26 322 | ... | ... | 381 097 | 92 761 | 24 |
|  | Total | 1975/76 | ... | ... | ... | 3 188 619 | 1 530 843 | 48 |
|  | General education |  | ... | ... | ... | 2 638 551 | 1 295 197 | 49 |
|  | Teacher training |  | - | - | - | - | - | - |
|  | Vocational education |  | 37 744 | 10 283 | 27 | 550 068 | 235 646 | 43 |
|  | Total | 1980/81 | 190 251 | 76 767 | 40 | 3 976 747 | 1 979 208 | 50 |
|  | General education |  | 149 555 | 64 106 | 43 | 3 088 026 | 1 569 844 | 51 |
|  | Teacher training |  | - | - | - | - | - | - |
|  | Vocational education |  | 40 696 | 12 661 | 31 | 888 721 | 409 364 | 46 |
|  | Total | 1985/86 | 217 364 | 97 672 | 45 | 4 555 541 | 2 304 983 | 51 |
|  | General education |  | 160 723 | 77 838 | 48 | 3 349 211 | 1 687 735 | 50 |
|  | Teacher training |  | - | - | - | - | - | - |
|  | Vocational education |  | 56 641 | 19 834 | 35 | 1 206 330 | 617 248 | 51 |
|  | Total | 1990/91 | 285 557 | 145 444 | 51 | 4 755 322 | 2 396 541 | 50 |
|  | General education |  | 210 167 | 112 897 | 54 | 3 653 552 | 1 854 703 | 51 |
|  | Teacher training |  | - | - | - | - | - | - |
|  | Vocational education |  | 75 390 | 32 547 | 43 | 1 101 770 | 541 838 | 49 |
|  | Total | 1991/92 | 294 438 | 148 597 | 50 | 4 773 349 | 2 419 992 | 51 |
|  | General education |  | 212 640 | 113 359 | 53 | 3 618 326 | 1 828 102 | 51 |
|  | Teacher training |  | - | - | - | - | - | - |
|  | Vocational education |  | 81 798 | 35 238 | 43 | 1 155 023 | 591 890 | 51 |
|  | Total | 1992/93 | (29) 295 972 | (29) 147 962 | 50 | (29) 4 859 965 | (29) 2 469 605 | 51 |
|  | General education |  | ... | ... | ... | 3 632 828 | 1 837 202 | 51 |
|  | Teacher training |  | - | - | - | - | - | - |
|  | Vocational education |  | ... | ... | ... | 1 227 137 | 632 403 | 52 |
|  | Total | 1993/94 | 298 137 | 151 550 | 51 | 4 837 802 | 2 459 120 | 51 |
|  | General education |  | ... | ... | ... | 3 609 693 | 1 826 488 | 51 |
|  | Teacher training |  | - | - | - | - | - | - |
|  | Vocational education |  | ... | ... | ... | 1 228 109 | 632 632 | 52 |
|  | Total | 1994/95 | 299 056 | 153 042 | 51 | 4 744 829 | 2 410 276 | 51 |
|  | General education |  | ... | ... | ... | 3 557 852 | 1 794 710 | 50 |
|  | Teacher training |  | - | - | - | - | - | - |
|  | Vocational education |  | ... | ... | ... | 1 186 977 | 615 566 | 52 |
|  | Total | 1995/96 | (63) *270 866 | (63) *141 619 | *52 | (63) 4 117 052 | (63) 2 111 816 | 51 |
|  | General education |  | ... | ... | ... | (63) 2 972 766 | (63) 1 511 286 | 51 |
|  | Teacher training |  | - | - | - | - | - | - |
|  | Vocational education |  | ... | ... | ... | 1 144 286 | 600 530 | 52 |
|  | Total | 1996/97 | ... | ... | ... | 3 852 102 | 1 934 449 | 50 |
|  | General education |  | ... | ... | ... | 2 946 191 | 1 482 247 | 50 |
|  | Teacher training |  | - | - | - | - | - | - |
|  | Vocational education |  | ... | ... | ... | 905 911 | 452 202 | 50 |
| Sweden | Total | 1970/71 | *54 970 | *24 101 | *44 | 554 480 | 267 532 | 48 |
|  | General education |  | - | - | - | 416 001 | 198 781 | 48 |
|  | Teacher training |  | - | - | - | - | - | - |
|  | Vocational education |  | ... | ... | ... | 138 479 | 68 751 | 50 |
|  | Total | 1975/76 | ... | ... | ... | (65) 507 642 | (65) 258 556 | 51 |
|  | General education |  | ... | ... | ... | (65) 369 012 | (65) 189 047 | 51 |
|  | Teacher training |  | ... | ... | ... | 1 078 | 759 | 70 |
|  | Vocational education |  | ... | ... | ... | 137 552 | 68 750 | 50 |
|  | Total | 1980/81 | ... | ... | ... | 606 833 | 311 945 | 51 |
|  | General education |  | ... | ... | ... | 443 355 | 226 649 | 51 |
|  | Teacher training |  | ... | ... | ... | 73 | 43 | 59 |
|  | Vocational education |  | ... | ... | ... | 163 405 | 85 253 | 52 |
|  | Total | 1985/86 | ... | ... | ... | 624 835 | ... | ... |
|  | General education |  | ... | ... | ... | ... | ... | ... |
|  | Teacher training |  | ... | ... | ... | ... | ... | ... |
|  | Vocational education |  | ... | ... | ... | ... | ... | ... |
|  | Total | 1990/91 | ... | ... | ... | 588 474 | 293 856 | 50 |
|  | General education |  | ... | ... | ... | 377 191 | 196 586 | 52 |
|  | Teacher training |  | - | - | - | - | - | - |
|  | Vocational education |  | ... | ... | ... | 211 283 | 97 270 | 46 |

II.6    Secondary education: teaching staff and pupils
Enseignement secondaire: personnel enseignant et élèves
Enseñanza secundaria: personal docente y alumnos

| Country<br>Pays<br>País | Type of education<br>Type d'enseignement<br>Tipo de enseñanza | Year<br>Année<br>Año | Teaching staff<br>Personnel enseignant<br>Personal docente | | | Pupils enrolled<br>Elèves inscrits<br>Alumnos matriculados | | |
|---|---|---|---|---|---|---|---|---|
| | | | Total | Female<br>Féminin<br>Femenino | %<br>F | Total | Female<br>Féminin<br>Femenino | %<br>F |
| Sweden (cont) | Total | 1991/92 | ... | ... | ... | 585 527 | 292 138 | 50 |
| | General education | | ... | ... | ... | 373 132 | 195 474 | 52 |
| | Teacher training | | - | - | - | - | - | - |
| | Vocational education | | ... | ... | ... | 212 395 | 96 664 | 46 |
| | Total | 1992/93 | (29) 86 650 | (29) 45 587 | 53 | (29) 755 649 | (29) 393 393 | 52 |
| | General education | | 60 664 | 32 777 | 54 | 472 281 | 253 271 | 54 |
| | Teacher training | | - | - | - | - | - | - |
| | Vocational education | | 25 986 | 12 810 | 49 | 283 368 | 140 122 | 49 |
| | Total | 1993/94 | 87 545 | 46 082 | 53 | 778 838 | 404 089 | 52 |
| | General education | | 59 767 | 32 682 | 55 | 495 522 | 262 532 | 53 |
| | Teacher training | | - | - | - | - | - | - |
| | Vocational education | | 27 778 | 13 400 | 48 | 283 316 | 141 557 | 50 |
| | Total | 1994/95 | 81 385 | 47 498 | 58 | 791 848 | 413 747 | 52 |
| | General education | | 51 401 | 32 853 | 64 | 543 037 | 292 215 | 54 |
| | Teacher training | | - | - | - | - | - | - |
| | Vocational education | | 29 984 | 14 645 | 49 | 248 811 | 121 532 | 49 |
| | Total | 1995/96 | ... | ... | ... | 809 653 | 426 593 | 53 |
| | General education | | ... | ... | ... | 558 625 | 303 286 | 54 |
| | Teacher training | | - | - | - | - | - | - |
| | Vocational education | | ... | ... | ... | 251 028 | 123 307 | 49 |
| | Total | 1996/97 | 78 732 | 46 458 | 59 | 829 295 | 440 553 | 53 |
| | General education | | 51 348 | 33 078 | 64 | 571 956 | 312 636 | 55 |
| | Teacher training | | - | - | - | - | - | - |
| | Vocational education | | 27 384 | 13 380 | 49 | 257 339 | 127 917 | 50 |
| Switzerland | Total | 1970/71 | ... | ... | ... | (4) 345 786 | (4) 164 563 | 48 |
| | General education | | ... | ... | ... | (4) 316 337 | (4) 152 223 | 48 |
| | Teacher training | | ... | ... | ... | (4) 10 271 | (4) 6 340 | 62 |
| | Vocational education | | ... | ... | ... | (4) 19 178 | (4) 6 000 | 31 |
| | Total | 1975/76 | ... | ... | ... | (4) 371 978 | (4) 184 124 | 49 |
| | General education | | ... | ... | ... | (4) 334 629 | (4) 163 961 | 49 |
| | Teacher training | | ... | ... | ... | (4) 11 070 | (4) 7 564 | 68 |
| | Vocational education | | ... | ... | ... | (4) 26 279 | (4) 12 599 | 48 |
| | Total | 1980/81 | ... | ... | ... | 661 315 | 306 240 | 46 |
| | General education | | ... | ... | ... | 427 193 | 211 198 | 49 |
| | Teacher training | | ... | ... | ... | 9 882 | 7 717 | 78 |
| | Vocational education | | ... | ... | ... | 224 240 | 87 325 | 39 |
| | Total | 1985/86 | ... | ... | ... | 634 750 | 295 115 | 46 |
| | General education | | ... | ... | ... | 382 442 | 189 861 | 50 |
| | Teacher training | | ... | ... | ... | 9 221 | 7 465 | 81 |
| | Vocational education | | ... | ... | ... | 243 087 | 97 789 | 40 |
| | Total | 1990/91 | ... | ... | ... | 567 396 | 267 784 | 47 |
| | General education | | ... | ... | ... | 337 958 | 168 580 | 50 |
| | Teacher training | | ... | ... | ... | 8 119 | 6 413 | 79 |
| | Vocational education | | ... | ... | ... | 221 319 | 92 791 | 42 |
| | Total | 1991/92 | ... | ... | ... | 562 465 | 266 225 | 47 |
| | General education | | ... | ... | ... | 343 735 | 171 980 | 50 |
| | Teacher training | | ... | ... | ... | 8 803 | 6 979 | 79 |
| | Vocational education | | ... | ... | ... | 209 927 | 87 266 | 42 |
| | Total | 1992/93 | ... | ... | ... | 558 487 | 262 307 | 47 |
| | General education | | ... | ... | ... | 369 615 | 186 226 | 50 |
| | Teacher training | | ... | ... | ... | 9 162 | 5 966 | 65 |
| | Vocational education | | ... | ... | ... | 179 710 | 70 115 | 39 |
| | Total | 1993/94 | ... | ... | ... | 564 705 | 266 282 | 47 |
| | General education | | ... | ... | ... | 380 440 | 192 081 | 50 |
| | Teacher training | | ... | ... | ... | 9 474 | 7 221 | 76 |
| | Vocational education | | ... | ... | ... | 174 791 | 66 980 | 38 |
| | Total | 1994/95 | ... | ... | ... | 561 716 | 265 080 | 47 |
| | General education | | ... | ... | ... | 380 175 | 192 688 | 51 |
| | Teacher training | | ... | ... | ... | ./. | ./. | ./. |
| | Vocational education | | ... | ... | ... | (62) 181 541 | (62) 72 392 | 40 |
| | Total | 1995/96 | ... | ... | ... | 559 924 | 264 398 | 47 |
| | General education | | ... | ... | ... | 378 328 | 192 165 | 51 |
| | Teacher training | | ... | ... | ... | 9 330 | 7 491 | 80 |
| | Vocational education | | ... | ... | ... | 172 266 | 64 742 | 38 |
| The Former Yugoslav Rep. of Macedonia | Total | 1970/71 | 3 046 | ... | ... | 59 963 | ... | ... |
| | General education | | ... | ... | ... | ... | ... | ... |
| | Teacher training | | ... | ... | ... | ... | ... | ... |
| | Vocational education | | ... | ... | ... | ... | ... | ... |
| | Total | 1975/76 | 3 701 | ... | ... | 66 516 | ... | ... |
| | General education | | ... | ... | ... | ... | ... | ... |
| | Teacher training | | ... | ... | ... | ... | ... | ... |
| | Vocational education | | ... | ... | ... | ... | ... | ... |

Secondary education: teaching staff and pupils  II.6
Enseignement secondaire: personnel enseignant et élèves
Enseñanza secundaria: personal docente y alumnos

| Country / Pays / País | Type of education / Type d'enseignement / Tipo de enseñanza | Year / Année / Año | Teaching staff Personnel enseignant Personal docente | | | Pupils enrolled Elèves inscrits Alumnos matriculados | | |
|---|---|---|---|---|---|---|---|---|
| | | | Total | Female Féminin Femenino | % F | Total | Female Féminin Femenino | % F |
| The Former Yugoslav Rep. of Macedonia (cont) | Total | 1980/81 | 4 277 | ... | ... | 82 465 | ... | ... |
| | General education | | ... | ... | ... | ... | ... | ... |
| | Teacher training | | ... | ... | ... | ... | ... | ... |
| | Vocational education | | ... | ... | ... | ... | ... | ... |
| | Total | 1985/86 | 4 193 | ... | ... | 77 023 | ... | ... |
| | General education | | ... | ... | ... | ... | ... | ... |
| | Teacher training | | ... | ... | ... | ... | ... | ... |
| | Vocational education | | ... | ... | ... | ... | ... | ... |
| | Total | 1990/91 | 4 227 | ... | ... | 70 696 | ... | ... |
| | General education | | ... | ... | ... | ... | ... | ... |
| | Teacher training | | ... | ... | ... | ... | ... | ... |
| | Vocational education | | ... | ... | ... | ... | ... | ... |
| | Total | 1991/92 | 4 267 | ... | ... | 70 250 | ... | ... |
| | General education | | ... | ... | ... | ... | ... | ... |
| | Teacher training | | ... | ... | ... | ... | ... | ... |
| | Vocational education | | ... | ... | ... | ... | ... | ... |
| | Total | 1992/93 | 4 345 | 2 212 | 51 | 73 381 | 36 003 | 49 |
| | General education | | ... | ... | ... | 20 727 | 12 760 | 62 |
| | Teacher training | | - | - | - | - | - | - |
| | Vocational education | | ... | ... | ... | 52 654 | 23 243 | 44 |
| | Total | 1993/94 | 4 520 | 2 318 | 51 | 74 583 | 36 644 | 49 |
| | General education | | ... | ... | ... | 21 649 | 13 261 | 61 |
| | Teacher training | | ... | ... | ... | 000 | 136 | 35 |
| | Vocational education | | ... | ... | ... | 52 548 | 23 247 | 44 |
| | Total | 1994/95 | 4 682 | 2 401 | 51 | 77 804 | 37 857 | 49 |
| | General education | | ... | ... | ... | 23 181 | 13 915 | 60 |
| | Teacher training | | ... | ... | ... | 424 | 134 | 32 |
| | Vocational education | | ... | ... | ... | 54 199 | 23 808 | 44 |
| | Total | 1995/96 | 4 821 | 2 468 | 51 | 80 684 | 39 225 | 49 |
| | General education | | 1 427 | 742 | 52 | 24 252 | 14 677 | 61 |
| | Teacher training | | 29 | 18 | 62 | 436 | 139 | 32 |
| | Vocational education | | 3 365 | 1 708 | 51 | 55 996 | 24 409 | 44 |
| | Total | 1996/97 | 5 136 | 2 640 | 51 | 83 746 | 40 447 | 48 |
| | General education | | 1 536 | 798 | 52 | 25 359 | 15 030 | 59 |
| | Teacher training | | - | - | - | - | - | - |
| | Vocational education | | 3 600 | 1 842 | 51 | 58 387 | 25 417 | 44 |
| Ukraine | Total | 1970/71 | ... | ... | ... | (69) 1 627 700 | (69) 877 000 | 54 |
| | General education | | ... | ... | ... | 829 800 | 464 700 | 56 |
| | Teacher training | | ... | ... | ... | 45 700 | 36 800 | 81 |
| | Vocational education | | ... | ... | ... | (69) 752 200 | (69) 375 500 | 50 |
| | Total | 1975/76 | ... | ... | ... | (69) 1 821 900 | ... | ... |
| | General education | | ... | ... | ... | 1 038 100 | ... | ... |
| | Teacher training | | ... | ... | ... | ... | ... | ... |
| | Vocational education | | ... | ... | ... | ... | ... | ... |
| | Total | 1980/81 | ... | ... | ... | 3 406 400 | ... | ... |
| | General education | | ... | ... | ... | 2 904 000 | ... | ... |
| | Teacher training | | ... | ... | ... | 22 500 | ... | ... |
| | Vocational education | | ... | ... | ... | 479 900 | ... | ... |
| | Total | 1985/86 | ... | ... | ... | 3 401 100 | ... | ... |
| | General education | | (70) 316 600 | ... | ... | 2 824 400 | ... | ... |
| | Teacher training | | ... | ... | ... | 19 400 | ... | ... |
| | Vocational education | | ... | ... | ... | 557 300 | ... | ... |
| | Total | 1990/91 | ... | ... | ... | 3 407 500 | ... | ... |
| | General education | | (70) 353 500 | ... | ... | 2 863 900 | ... | ... |
| | Teacher training | | ... | ... | ... | 20 700 | ... | ... |
| | Vocational education | | ... | ... | ... | 522 900 | ... | ... |
| | Total | 1991/92 | ... | ... | ... | 3 354 400 | ... | ... |
| | General education | | (70) 359 800 | ... | ... | 2 803 600 | ... | ... |
| | Teacher training | | ... | ... | ... | 22 100 | ... | ... |
| | Vocational education | | ... | ... | ... | 528 700 | ... | ... |
| | Total | 1992/93 | ... | ... | ... | (26) 4 701 000 | ... | ... |
| | General education | | (26) 371 300 | ... | ... | (26) 4 156 700 | (26) 2 120 900 | 51 |
| | Teacher training | | ... | ... | ... | 22 600 | ... | ... |
| | Vocational education | | ... | ... | ... | 521 700 | ... | ... |
| | Total | 1993/94 | ... | ... | ... | 4 731 200 | ... | ... |
| | General education | | 377 000 | ... | ... | 4 202 200 | 2 139 400 | 51 |
| | Teacher training | | ... | ... | ... | 21 300 | ... | ... |
| | Vocational education | | ... | ... | ... | 507 700 | ... | ... |
| United Kingdom | Total | 1970/71 | ... | ... | ... | 4 149 067 | 2 009 046 | 48 |
| | General education | | 252 512 | 121 192 | 48 | 4 006 527 | 1 943 944 | 49 |
| | Teacher training | | - | - | - | - | - | - |
| | Vocational education | | ... | ... | ... | 142 540 | 65 102 | 46 |

II.6 Secondary education: teaching staff and pupils
Enseignement secondaire: personnel enseignant et élèves
Enseñanza secundaria: personal docente y alumnos

| Country<br>Pays<br>País | Type of education<br>Type d'enseignement<br>Tipo de enseñanza | Year<br>Année<br>Año | Teaching staff<br>Personnel enseignant<br>Personal docente | | | Pupils enrolled<br>Elèves inscrits<br>Alumnos matriculados | | |
|---|---|---|---|---|---|---|---|---|
| | | | Total | Female<br>Féminin<br>Femenino | %<br>F | Total | Female<br>Féminin<br>Femenino | %<br>F |
| United Kingdom (cont) | Total | 1975/76 | ... | ... | ... | 5 154 371 | 2 525 945 | 49 |
| | General education | | 308 827 | 147 810 | 48 | 4 945 770 | 2 413 008 | 49 |
| | Teacher training | | - | - | - | - | - | - |
| | Vocational education | | ... | ... | ... | 208 601 | 112 937 | 54 |
| | Total | 1980/81 | ... | ... | ... | 5 341 849 | 2 644 645 | 50 |
| | General education | | 332 585 | 162 490 | 49 | 5 087 036 | 2 498 999 | 49 |
| | Teacher training | | - | - | - | - | - | - |
| | Vocational education | | ... | ... | ... | 254 813 | 145 646 | 57 |
| | Total | 1985/86 | ... | ... | ... | 4 877 000 | 2 424 000 | 50 |
| | General education | | 321 000 | 160 000 | 50 | 4 474 000 | 2 193 000 | 49 |
| | Teacher training | | - | - | - | - | - | - |
| | Vocational education | | ... | ... | ... | 403 000 | 231 000 | 57 |
| | Total | 1990/91 | ... | ... | ... | 4 335 600 | 2 153 800 | 50 |
| | General education | | 286 900 | 153 200 | 53 | 3 855 200 | 1 892 900 | 49 |
| | Teacher training | | - | - | - | - | - | - |
| | Vocational education | | ... | ... | ... | 480 400 | 260 900 | 54 |
| | Total | 1991/92 | ... | ... | ... | 4 433 500 | 2 205 900 | 50 |
| | General education | | 288 600 | 155 300 | 54 | 3 883 500 | 1 912 800 | 49 |
| | Teacher training | | - | - | - | - | - | - |
| | Vocational education | | ... | ... | ... | 550 000 | 293 100 | 53 |
| | Total | 1992/93 | (29) 397 697 | (29) 214 121 | 54 | (29) 6 331 060 | (29) 3 270 499 | 52 |
| | General education | | 299 396 | 164 738 | 55 | 4 017 626 | 1 969 775 | 49 |
| | Teacher training | | - | - | - | - | - | - |
| | Vocational education | | 98 301 | 49 383 | 50 | 2 313 434 | 1 300 724 | 56 |
| | Total | 1993/94 | 404 307 | 218 182 | 54 | 6 491 190 | 3 371 071 | 52 |
| | General education | | 302 449 | 166 811 | 55 | 3 996 849 | 1 958 036 | 49 |
| | Teacher training | | - | - | - | - | - | - |
| | Vocational education | | 101 858 | 51 371 | 50 | 2 494 341 | 1 413 035 | 57 |
| | Total | 1994/95 | 452 464 | ... | ... | 6 677 836 | 3 492 940 | 52 |
| | General education | | 313 562 | 177 511 | 57 | 4 062 286 | 1 991 397 | 49 |
| | Teacher training | | - | - | - | - | - | - |
| | Vocational education | | 138 902 | | ... | 2 615 550 | 1 501 543 | 57 |
| | Total | 1995/96 | 476 337 | 264 208 | 55 | 6 696 772 | 3 509 029 | 52 |
| | General education | | 317 266 | 172 097 | 54 | 4 077 942 | 2 003 536 | 49 |
| | Teacher training | | - | - | - | - | - | - |
| | Vocational education | | 159 071 | 92 111 | 58 | 2 618 830 | 1 505 493 | 57 |
| | Total | 1996/97 | 464 134 | 255 669 | 55 | 6 548 786 | 3 405 483 | 52 |
| | General education | | 312 036 | 170 639 | 55 | 4 113 465 | 2 022 146 | 49 |
| | Teacher training | | - | - | - | - | - | - |
| | Vocational education | | 152 098 | 85 030 | 56 | 2 435 321 | 1 383 337 | 57 |
| **Oceania** | | | | | | | | |
| American Samoa | Total | 1970/71 | *120 | ... | ... | *2 300 | ... | ... |
| | General education | | ... | ... | ... | ... | ... | ... |
| | Teacher training | | - | - | - | - | - | - |
| | Vocational education | | ... | ... | ... | ... | ... | ... |
| | Total | 1975/76 | (4) *70 | ... | ... | (4) *2 097 | ... | ... |
| | General education | | ... | ... | ... | ... | ... | ... |
| | Teacher training | | - | - | - | - | - | - |
| | Vocational education | | ... | ... | ... | ... | ... | ... |
| | Total | 1980/81 | ... | ... | ... | 3 000 | ... | ... |
| | General education | | ... | ... | ... | ... | ... | ... |
| | Teacher training | | - | - | - | - | - | - |
| | Vocational education | | ... | ... | ... | ... | ... | ... |
| | Total | 1985/86 | 203 | 73 | 36 | 3 342 | 1 559 | 47 |
| | General education | | ... | ... | ... | ... | ... | ... |
| | Teacher training | | - | - | - | - | - | - |
| | Vocational education | | ... | ... | ... | ... | ... | ... |
| | Total | 1991/92 | 266 | 103 | 39 | 3 643 | 1 680 | 46 |
| | General education | | 245 | 99 | 40 | 3 483 | 1 673 | 48 |
| | Teacher training | | - | - | - | - | - | - |
| | Vocational education | | 21 | 4 | 19 | 160 | 7 | 4 |
| Australia | Total | 1975 | 74 041 | 34 463 | 47 | 1 099 922 | 535 965 | 49 |
| | General education | | 74 041 | 34 463 | 47 | 1 099 922 | 535 965 | 49 |
| | Teacher training | | - | - | - | - | - | - |
| | Vocational education | | - | - | - | - | - | - |
| | Total | 1980 | 85 340 | 38 604 | 45 | 1 100 468 | 545 897 | 50 |
| | General education | | 85 340 | 38 604 | 45 | 1 100 468 | 545 897 | 50 |
| | Teacher training | | - | - | - | - | - | - |
| | Vocational education | | - | - | - | - | - | - |

Secondary education: teaching staff and pupils    II.6
Enseignement secondaire: personnel enseignant et élèves
Enseñanza secundaria: personal docente y alumnos

| Country<br>Pays<br>País | Type of education<br>Type d'enseignement<br>Tipo de enseñanza | Year<br>Année<br>Año | Teaching staff<br>Personnel enseignant<br>Personal docente | | | Pupils enrolled<br>Elèves inscrits<br>Alumnos matriculados | | |
|---|---|---|---|---|---|---|---|---|
| | | | Total | Female<br>Féminin<br>Femenino | %<br><br>F | Total | Female<br>Féminin<br>Femenino | %<br><br>F |
| Australia (cont) | Total | 1985 | 105 955 | 50 960 | 48 | 1 278 272 | 632 578 | 49 |
| | General education | | 105 955 | 50 960 | 48 | 1 278 272 | 632 578 | 49 |
| | Teacher training | | - | - | - | - | - | - |
| | Vocational education | | - | - | - | - | - | - |
| | Total | 1990 | (67) 103 298 | (67) 51 743 | 50 | 1 278 163 | 635 691 | 50 |
| | General education | | (67) 103 298 | (67) 51 743 | 50 | 1 278 163 | 635 691 | 50 |
| | Teacher training | | - | - | - | - | - | - |
| | Vocational education | | - | - | - | - | - | - |
| | Total | 1991 | (67) 102 753 | (67) 51 803 | 50 | 1 288 691 | 638 213 | 50 |
| | General education | | (67) 102 753 | (67) 51 803 | 50 | 1 288 691 | 638 213 | 50 |
| | Teacher training | | - | - | - | - | - | - |
| | Vocational education | | - | - | - | - | - | - |
| | Total | 1992 | (67) 104 110 | (67) 52 710 | 51 | 1 294 596 | 639 470 | 49 |
| | General education | | (67) 104 110 | (67) 52 710 | 51 | 1 294 596 | 639 470 | 49 |
| | Teacher training | | - | - | - | - | - | - |
| | Vocational education | | - | - | - | - | - | - |
| | Total | 1993 | ... | ... | ... | (52) 2 029 407 | (52) 990 790 | 49 |
| | General education | | (67) 103 385 | (67) 52 881 | 51 | 1 282 309 | 634 060 | 49 |
| | Teacher training | | - | - | - | - | - | - |
| | Vocational education | | ... | ... | ... | 747 098 | 356 730 | 48 |
| | Total | 1994 | ... | ... | ... | 2 003 504 | 974 142 | 49 |
| | General education | | (67) 101 477 | (67) 52 101 | 51 | 1 273 640 | 631 453 | 50 |
| | Teacher training | | - | - | - | - | - | - |
| | Vocational education | | ... | ... | ... | 729 864 | 342 689 | 47 |
| | Total | 1995 | ... | ... | ... | 2 182 085 | 1 060 334 | 49 |
| | General education | | (67) 101 365 | (67) 52 996 | 52 | 1 275 656 | 633 420 | 50 |
| | Teacher training | | - | - | - | - | - | - |
| | Vocational education | | ... | ... | ... | 906 429 | 426 914 | 47 |
| | Total | 1996 | ... | ... | ... | 2 280 274 | 1 109 727 | 49 |
| | General education | | (67) 101 706 | (67) 53 514 | 53 | 1 294 846 | 643 092 | 50 |
| | Teacher training | | - | - | - | - | - | - |
| | Vocational education | | ... | ... | ... | 985 428 | 466 635 | 47 |
| | Total | 1997 | ... | ... | ... | 2 367 692 | 1 173 470 | 50 |
| | General education | | (67) 103 287 | (67) 54 879 | 53 | 1 315 835 | 654 182 | 50 |
| | Teacher training | | - | - | - | - | - | - |
| | Vocational education | | ... | ... | ... | 1 051 857 | 519 288 | 49 |
| Fiji | Total | 1980 | 2 564 | 1 043 | 41 | 49 963 | 25 380 | 51 |
| | General education | | 2 254 | 962 | 43 | 47 119 | 23 747 | 50 |
| | Teacher training | | 75 | 20 | 27 | 514 | 247 | 48 |
| | Vocational education | | 235 | 61 | 26 | 2 330 | 1 386 | 59 |
| | Total | 1985 | 2 954 | 1 256 | 43 | 45 093 | 22 421 | 50 |
| | General education | | 2 669 | 1 185 | 44 | 41 505 | 20 689 | 50 |
| | Teacher training | | - | - | - | - | - | - |
| | Vocational education | | 285 | 71 | 25 | 3 588 | 1 732 | 48 |
| | Total | 1991 | ... | ... | ... | 61 614 | 29 278 | 48 |
| | General education | | ... | ... | ... | 55 622 | 27 469 | 49 |
| | Teacher training | | - | - | - | - | - | - |
| | Vocational education | | ... | ... | ... | 5 992 | 1 809 | 30 |
| | Total | 1992 | 3 631 | 1 654 | 46 | 66 890 | 32 673 | 49 |
| | General education | | 3 045 | 1 438 | 47 | 60 237 | 30 950 | 51 |
| | Teacher training | | - | - | - | - | - | - |
| | Vocational education | | 586 | 216 | 37 | 6 653 | 1 723 | 26 |
| French Polynesia | Total | 1970/71 | 417 | 182 | 44 | 6 492 | 3 613 | 56 |
| | General education | | 341 | 150 | 44 | 5 383 | 3 030 | 56 |
| | Teacher training | | 5 | 2 | 40 | 76 | 54 | 71 |
| | Vocational education | | 71 | 30 | 42 | 1 033 | 529 | 51 |
| | Total | 1975/76 | 569 | 253 | 44 | 9 035 | 5 074 | 56 |
| | General education | | 434 | 190 | 44 | 7 280 | 4 164 | 57 |
| | Teacher training | | 6 | 3 | 50 | 111 | 85 | 77 |
| | Vocational education | | 129 | 60 | 47 | 1 644 | 825 | 50 |
| | Total | 1990/91 | 1 497 | 670 | 45 | 20 311 | 10 766 | 53 |
| | General education | | 1 174 | 577 | 49 | 16 806 | 9 444 | 56 |
| | Teacher training | | - | - | - | - | - | - |
| | Vocational education | | 323 | 93 | 29 | 3 505 | 1 322 | 38 |
| | Total | 1992/93 | 1 592 | 730 | 46 | 22 366 | 12 241 | 55 |
| | General education | | 1 276 | 631 | 49 | 18 636 | 10 492 | 56 |
| | Teacher training | | - | - | - | - | - | - |
| | Vocational education | | 316 | 99 | 31 | 3 730 | 1 749 | 47 |
| Guam | Total | 1970/71 | 495 | ... | ... | 10 055 | ... | ... |
| | General education | | ... | ... | ... | ... | ... | ... |
| | Teacher training | | - | - | - | - | - | - |
| | Vocational education | | ... | ... | ... | ... | ... | ... |

II.6  Secondary education: teaching staff and pupils
Enseignement secondaire: personnel enseignant et élèves
Enseñanza secundaria: personal docente y alumnos

| Country / Pays / País | Type of education / Type d'enseignement / Tipo de enseñanza | Year / Année / Año | Teaching staff — Personnel enseignant — Personal docente | | | Pupils enrolled — Elèves inscrits — Alumnos matriculados | | |
|---|---|---|---|---|---|---|---|---|
| | | | Total | Female Féminin Femenino | % F | Total | Female Féminin Femenino | % F |
| Guam (cont) | Total | 1975/76 | 595 | ... | ... | 13 242 | ... | ... |
| | General education | | ... | ... | ... | ... | ... | ... |
| | Teacher training | | - | - | - | - | - | - |
| | Vocational education | | ... | ... | ... | ... | ... | ... |
| | Total | 1980/81 (4) | 553 | ... | ... | 14 935 | ... | ... |
| | General education | | ... | ... | ... | ... | ... | ... |
| | Teacher training | | ... | ... | ... | ... | ... | ... |
| | Vocational education | | ... | ... | ... | ... | ... | ... |
| | Total | 1985/86 (4) | 589 | ... | ... | 14 557 | ... | ... |
| | General education | | ... | ... | ... | ... | ... | ... |
| | Teacher training | | ... | ... | ... | ... | ... | ... |
| | Vocational education | | ... | ... | ... | ... | ... | ... |
| Kiribati | Total | 1970 | 76 | 25 | 33 | 824 | 317 | 38 |
| | General education | | 44 | 16 | 36 | 622 | 264 | 42 |
| | Teacher training | | 16 | 6 | 38 | 112 | 33 | 29 |
| | Vocational education | | ... | ... | ... | 90 | 20 | 22 |
| | Total | 1975 | ... | ... | ... | ... | ... | ... |
| | General education | | ... | ... | ... | 795 | 378 | 48 |
| | Teacher training | | 13 | ... | ... | 55 | ... | ... |
| | Vocational education | | ... | ... | ... | ... | ... | ... |
| | Total | 1980 | 154 | 60 | 39 | 2 440 | 1 112 | 46 |
| | General education | | 70 | 30 | 43 | 957 | 490 | 51 |
| | Teacher training | | 13 | 4 | 31 | 107 | 56 | 52 |
| | Vocational education | | 71 | 26 | 37 | 1 376 | 566 | 41 |
| | Total | 1985 | 160 | 60 | 38 | 2 196 | 1 099 | 50 |
| | General education | | 88 | 44 | 50 | 1 437 | 734 | 51 |
| | Teacher training | | 12 | 4 | 33 | 97 | 68 | 70 |
| | Vocational education | | 60 | 12 | 20 | 662 | 297 | 45 |
| | Total | 1990 | 247 | 79 | 32 | 3 003 | 1 463 | 49 |
| | General education | | 172 | 69 | 40 | 2 713 | 1 399 | 52 |
| | Teacher training | | 16 | 4 | 25 | 39 | 24 | 62 |
| | Vocational education | | 59 | 6 | 10 | 251 | 40 | 16 |
| | Total | 1991 | 236 | 92 | 39 | 3 016 | 1 560 | 52 |
| | General education | | 182 | 78 | 43 | 2 795 | 1 497 | 54 |
| | Teacher training | | 15 | 4 | 27 | 51 | 31 | 61 |
| | Vocational education | | 39 | 10 | 26 | 170 | 32 | 19 |
| | Total | 1992 | 237 | 95 | 40 | 3 357 | 1 732 | 52 |
| | General education | | 194 | 83 | 43 | 3 069 | 1 601 | 52 |
| | Teacher training | | 12 | 3 | 25 | 54 | 33 | 61 |
| | Vocational education | | 31 | 9 | 29 | 234 | 98 | 42 |
| | Total | 1993 | ... | ... | ... | ... | ... | ... |
| | General education | | 179 | 79 | 44 | 3 152 | 1 688 | 54 |
| | Teacher training | | 9 | 3 | 33 | 63 | 38 | 60 |
| | Vocational education | | ... | ... | ... | ... | ... | ... |
| | Total | 1994 | 222 | ... | ... | 3 699 | ... | ... |
| | General education | | 206 | ... | ... | 3 347 | 1 753 | 52 |
| | Teacher training | | 10 | ... | ... | 84 | 57 | 68 |
| | Vocational education | | 6 | ... | ... | 268 | ... | ... |
| | Total | 1995 | 265 | 98 | 37 | 3 837 | 2 089 | 54 |
| | General education | | 245 | *92 | *38 | 3 532 | 1 918 | 54 |
| | Teacher training | | 12 | 4 | 33 | 110 | 76 | 69 |
| | Vocational education | | 8 | 2 | 25 | 195 | *95 | *49 |
| | Total | 1996 | 260 | 101 | 39 | 4 341 | 2 337 | 54 |
| | General education | | 240 | 95 | 40 | 4 023 | 2 159 | 54 |
| | Teacher training | | 12 | 4 | 33 | 123 | 83 | 67 |
| | Vocational education | | 8 | 2 | 25 | 195 | 95 | 49 |
| | Total | 1997 | ... | ... | ... | ... | ... | ... |
| | General education | | 215 | ... | ... | 4 403 | 2 335 | 53 |
| | Teacher training | | 15 | 6 | 40 | 138 | 97 | 70 |
| | Vocational education | | ... | ... | ... | ... | ... | ... |
| Nauru | Total | 1985 | 40 | 18 | 45 | 482 | 242 | 50 |
| | General education | | 36 | 18 | 50 | 465 | 234 | 50 |
| | Teacher training | | - | - | - | - | - | - |
| | Vocational education | | 4 | - | - | 17 | 8 | 47 |
| New Caledonia | Total | 1970 | 404 | 175 | 43 | 5 132 | 2 345 | 46 |
| | General education | | 251 | 128 | 51 | 3 745 | 1 858 | 50 |
| | Teacher training | | 26 | 8 | 31 | 41 | 30 | 73 |
| | Vocational education | | 127 | 39 | 31 | 1 346 | 457 | 34 |
| | Total | 1975 | ... | ... | ... | 7 960 | 3 995 | 50 |
| | General education | | 379 | 217 | 57 | 5 604 | 3 016 | 54 |
| | Teacher training | | 30 (4) | 6 | ... | 135 | 85 | 63 |
| | Vocational education | | ... | ... | ... | 2 221 | 894 | 40 |

Secondary education: teaching staff and pupils  II.6
Enseignement secondaire: personnel enseignant et élèves
Enseñanza secundaria: personal docente y alumnos

| Country / Pays / País | Type of education / Type d'enseignement / Tipo de enseñanza | Year / Année / Año | Teaching staff Personnel enseignant Personal docente | | | Pupils enrolled Elèves inscrits Alumnos matriculados | | |
|---|---|---|---|---|---|---|---|---|
| | | | Total | Female Féminin Femenino | % F | Total | Female Féminin Femenino | % F |
| New Caledonia (cont) | Total | 1980 | 839 | ... | ... | 11 945 | 6 449 | 54 |
| | General education | | 545 | ... | ... | 9 139 | 4 988 | 55 |
| | Teacher training | | - | - | - | - | - | - |
| | Vocational education | | 294 | 94 | 32 | 2 806 | 1 461 | 52 |
| | Total | 1985 | 1 265 | ... | ... | 18 351 | 9 530 | 52 |
| | General education | | ... | ... | ... | 12 922 | 7 017 | 54 |
| | Teacher training | | - | - | - | - | - | - |
| | Vocational education | | ... | ... | ... | 5 429 | 2 513 | 46 |
| | Total | 1990 | 1 544 | ... | ... | 20 673 | 10 673 | 52 |
| | General education | | ... | ... | ... | 14 011 | 7 688 | 55 |
| | Teacher training | | - | - | - | - | - | - |
| | Vocational education | | ... | ... | ... | 6 662 | 2 985 | 45 |
| | Total | 1991 | 1 669 | ... | ... | 21 908 | 11 307 | 52 |
| | General education | | ... | ... | ... | 14 889 | 8 149 | 55 |
| | Teacher training | | - | - | - | - | - | - |
| | Vocational education | | ... | ... | ... | 7 019 | 3 158 | 45 |
| | Total | 1997 | 1 940 | 805 | 41 | 25 560 | 13 230 | 52 |
| | General education | | 1 210 | 575 | 48 | 17 700 | 9 690 | 55 |
| | Teacher training | | - | - | - | - | - | - |
| | Vocational education | | 730 | 230 | 32 | 7 860 | 3 540 | 45 |
| New Zealand | Total | 1970 | | | | ... | ... | ... |
| | General education | | ... | ... | ... | 303 835 | 147 235 | 48 |
| | Teacher training | | - | - | * | - | - | - |
| | Vocational education | | ... | ... | ... | ... | ... | ... |
| | Total | 1975 | ... | ... | ... | (71) 354 107 | (71) 174 178 | 49 |
| | General education | | ... | ... | ... | 351 720 | 172 313 | 49 |
| | Teacher training | | - | - | - | - | - | - |
| | Vocational education | | ... | ... | ... | 2 387 | 1 865 | 78 |
| | Total | 1980 | ... | ... | ... | 352 427 | 174 175 | 49 |
| | General education | | ... | ... | ... | 349 356 | 171 668 | 49 |
| | Teacher training | | - | - | - | - | - | - |
| | Vocational education | | ... | ... | ... | 3 071 | 2 507 | 82 |
| | Total | 1985 | ... | ... | ... | 354 080 | 176 311 | 50 |
| | General education | | 18 663 | 8 502 | 46 | 351 618 | 174 299 | 50 |
| | Teacher training | | - | - | - | - | - | - |
| | Vocational education | | ... | ... | ... | 2 462 | 2 012 | 82 |
| | Total | 1990 | ... | ... | ... | 340 915 | 168 503 | 49 |
| | General education | | (4) 20 331 | (4) 10 702 | 53 | 332 014 | 164 123 | 49 |
| | Teacher training | | - | - | - | - | - | - |
| | Vocational education | | ... | ... | ... | 8 901 | 4 380 | 49 |
| | Total | 1991 | ... | ... | ... | 345 338 | 170 612 | 49 |
| | General education | | (4) 20 787 | (4) 11 039 | 53 | 332 801 | 164 189 | 49 |
| | Teacher training | | - | - | - | - | - | - |
| | Vocational education | | ... | ... | ... | 12 537 | 6 423 | 51 |
| | Total | 1992 | ... | ... | ... | 350 112 | 171 673 | 49 |
| | General education | | 22 195 | 11 938 | 54 | 331 962 | 163 439 | 49 |
| | Teacher training | | - | - | - | - | - | - |
| | Vocational education | | ... | ... | ... | 18 150 | 8 234 | 45 |
| | Total | 1993 | ... | ... | ... | (72) 376 947 | (72) 185 120 | 49 |
| | General education | | ... | ... | ... | 328 361 | 161 764 | 49 |
| | Teacher training | | - | - | - | - | - | - |
| | Vocational education | | ... | ... | ... | (72) 48 586 | (72) 23 356 | 48 |
| | Total | 1994 | 28 358 | 16 023 | 57 | 404 563 | 200 427 | 50 |
| | General education | | 24 569 | 14 172 | 58 | 340 905 | 170 246 | 50 |
| | Teacher training | | - | - | - | - | - | - |
| | Vocational education | | 3 789 | 1 851 | 49 | 63 658 | 30 181 | 47 |
| | Total | 1995 | ... | ... | ... | 420 070 | 203 282 | 48 |
| | General education | | ... | ... | ... | 339 660 | 169 600 | 50 |
| | Teacher training | | - | - | - | - | - | - |
| | Vocational education | | ... | ... | ... | 80 410 | 33 682 | 42 |
| | Total | 1996 | 27 481 | 15 659 | 57 | 430 526 | 215 447 | 50 |
| | General education | | 21 134 | 12 377 | 59 | 349 227 | 173 323 | 50 |
| | Teacher training | | - | - | - | - | - | - |
| | Vocational education | | 6 347 | 3 282 | 52 | 81 299 | 42 124 | 52 |
| | Total | 1997 | 28 548 | 16 553 | 58 | 433 347 | 216 630 | 50 |
| | General education | | 22 412 | 13 409 | 60 | 354 707 | 176 172 | 50 |
| | Teacher training | | - | - | - | - | - | - |
| | Vocational education | | 6 136 | 3 144 | 51 | 78 640 | 40 458 | 51 |
| Niue | Total | 1970 | 24 | 10 | 42 | 462 | 204 | 44 |
| | General education | | 24 | 10 | 42 | 462 | 204 | 44 |
| | Teacher training | | - | - | - | - | - | - |
| | Vocational education | | - | - | - | - | - | - |

II.6 Secondary education: teaching staff and pupils
Enseignement secondaire: personnel enseignant et élèves
Enseñanza secundaria: personal docente y alumnos

| Country<br>Pays<br>País | Type of education<br>Type d'enseignement<br>Tipo de enseñanza | Year<br>Année<br>Año | Teaching staff<br>Personnel enseignant<br>Personal docente | | | | Pupils enrolled<br>Elèves inscrits<br>Alumnos matriculados | | | |
|---|---|---|---|---|---|---|---|---|---|---|
| | | | | Total | Female<br>Féminin<br>Femenino | %<br>F | | Total | Female<br>Féminin<br>Femenino | %<br>F |
| Niue (cont) | Total | 1975 | | 22 | 9 | 41 | (73) | 271 | (73) 133 | 49 |
| | General education | | | 22 | 9 | 41 | (73) | 271 | (73) 133 | 49 |
| | Teacher training | | | - | - | - | | - | - | - |
| | Vocational education | | | - | | - | | - | | - |
| | Total | 1980 | | 25 | ... | ... | | 397 | ... | ... |
| | General education | | | 25 | ... | ... | | 397 | ... | ... |
| | Teacher training | | | - | - | - | | - | - | - |
| | Vocational education | | | - | | - | | - | | - |
| | Total | 1985 | | 31 | ... | ... | | 321 | ... | ... |
| | General education | | | 31 | ... | ... | | 321 | ... | ... |
| | Teacher training | | | - | - | - | | - | - | - |
| | Vocational education | | | - | | - | | - | | - |
| | Total | 1991 | (13) | 27 | ... | ... | (13) | 302 | (13) 159 | 53 |
| | General education | | (13) | 27 | ... | ... | (13) | 302 | (13) 159 | 53 |
| | Teacher training | | | - | - | - | | - | - | - |
| | Vocational education | | | - | | - | | - | | - |
| Papua New Guinea | Total | 1970 | | ... | | ... | | 24 365 | 6 472 | 27 |
| | General education | | | 807 | ... | ... | | 17 785 | 4 849 | 27 |
| | Teacher training | | | ... | ... | ... | | 1 865 | 559 | 30 |
| | Vocational education | | | ... | | ... | | 4 715 | 1 064 | 23 |
| | Total | 1975 | | 2 034 | 700 | 34 | | 41 391 | 11 731 | 28 |
| | General education | | | 1 282 | 482 | 38 | | 29 762 | 9 379 | 32 |
| | Teacher training | | | 166 | 76 | 46 | | 1 990 | 715 | 36 |
| | Vocational education | | | 586 | 142 | 24 | | 9 639 | 1 637 | 17 |
| | Total | 1980 | | ... | ... | | | ... | ... | ... |
| | General education | | | 1 586 | 533 | 34 | | 38 690 | 12 523 | 32 |
| | Teacher training | | | 154 | 64 | 42 | | 1 704 | 637 | 37 |
| | Vocational education | | | ... | | ... | | ... | | ... |
| | Total | 1990 | | ... | ... | ... | | 65 643 | 24 935 | 38 |
| | General education | | | ... | ... | ... | | 55 797 | 21 458 | 38 |
| | Teacher training | | | ... | ... | ... | | 2 232 | 850 | 38 |
| | Vocational education | | | ... | | ... | | 7 614 | 2 627 | 35 |
| | Total | 1991 | | 3 120 | 973 | 31 | | 68 506 | 26 421 | 39 |
| | General education | | | 2 285 | 713 | 31 | | 58 249 | 23 236 | 40 |
| | Teacher training | | | 159 | 42 | 26 | | 1 424 | 616 | 43 |
| | Vocational education | | | 676 | 218 | 32 | | 8 833 | 2 569 | 29 |
| | Total | 1992 | | 3 293 | 1 099 | 33 | | 69 596 | 26 811 | 39 |
| | General education | | | 2 415 | 838 | 35 | | 58 226 | 23 227 | 40 |
| | Teacher training | | | 144 | 37 | 26 | | 1 199 | 553 | 46 |
| | Vocational education | | | 734 | 224 | 31 | | 10 171 | 3 031 | 30 |
| | Total | 1993 | | ... | ... | ... | | 77 665 | 30 392 | 39 |
| | General education | | | ... | ... | ... | | 65 406 | 26 181 | 40 |
| | Teacher training | | | 142 | 31 | 22 | | 1 793 | 845 | 47 |
| | Vocational education | | | 555 | 190 | 34 | | 10 466 | 3 366 | 32 |
| | Total | 1994 | | ... | ... | ... | | 83 252 | 32 804 | 39 |
| | General education | | | ... | ... | ... | | 70 392 | 28 580 | 41 |
| | Teacher training | | | 143 | 30 | 21 | | 1 799 | 827 | 46 |
| | Vocational education | | | 618 | 194 | 31 | | 11 061 | 3 397 | 31 |
| | Total | 1995 | | ... | ... | ... | | 78 759 | 30 858 | 39 |
| | General education | | | ... | ... | ... | | 68 818 | 27 693 | 40 |
| | Teacher training | | | 155 | 33 | 21 | | 1 960 | 915 | 47 |
| | Vocational education | | | ... | ... | ... | | 7 981 | 2 250 | 28 |
| Samoa | Total | 1970 | | 460 | ... | ... | | 10 147 | 5 261 | 52 |
| | General education | | | 419 | ... | ... | | 9 717 | 5 097 | 52 |
| | Teacher training | | | 22 | 13 | 59 | | 303 | 164 | 54 |
| | Vocational education | | | 19 | - | - | | 127 | | - |
| | Total | 1975 | | ... | ... | ... | | 15 943 | 8 062 | 51 |
| | General education | | | ... | ... | ... | | 15 098 | 7 712 | 51 |
| | Teacher training | | | ... | ... | ... | | 490 | 263 | 54 |
| | Vocational education | | | ... | ... | ... | | 355 | 87 | 25 |
| | Total | 1980 | | ... | ... | ... | | 19 785 | 9 691 | 49 |
| | General education | | | ... | ... | ... | | 19 299 | 9 459 | 49 |
| | Teacher training | | | ... | ... | ... | | 222 | 124 | 56 |
| | Vocational education | | | ... | ... | ... | | 264 | 108 | 41 |
| | Total | 1990 | | ... | ... | ... | (7) | 10 450 | (7) 5 372 | 51 |
| | General education | | | ... | ... | ... | (7) | *10 450 | (7) 5 372 | *51 |
| | Teacher training | | | - | - | - | | - | - | - |
| | Vocational education | | | - | - | - | | - | - | - |
| | Total | 1991 | | 541 | 241 | 45 | | 9 843 | 6 197 | 63 |
| | General education | | | 541 | 241 | 45 | | 9 843 | 6 197 | 63 |
| | Teacher training | | | - | - | - | | - | - | - |
| | Vocational education | | | - | - | - | | - | - | - |

Secondary education: teaching staff and pupils
Enseignement secondaire: personnel enseignant et élèves
Enseñanza secundaria: personal docente y alumnos

II.6

| Country<br>Pays<br>País | Type of education<br>Type d'enseignement<br>Tipo de enseñanza | Year<br>Année<br>Año | Teaching staff<br>Personnel enseignant<br>Personal docente | | | | Pupils enrolled<br>Elèves inscrits<br>Alumnos matriculados | | | |
|---|---|---|---|---|---|---|---|---|---|---|
| | | | | Total | Female<br>Féminin<br>Femenino | %<br><br>F | | Total | Female<br>Féminin<br>Femenino | %<br><br>F |
| Samoa (cont) | Total | 1992 | | 625 | 283 | 45 | | 13 598 | 6 903 | 51 |
| | General education | | | 625 | 283 | 45 | | 13 598 | 6 903 | 51 |
| | Teacher training | | | - | - | - | | - | - | - |
| | Vocational education | | | - | - | - | | - | - | - |
| | Total | 1993 | | 641 | 295 | 46 | | 13 658 | 6 871 | 50 |
| | General education | | | 641 | 295 | 46 | | 13 658 | 6 871 | 50 |
| | Teacher training | | | - | - | - | | - | - | - |
| | Vocational education | | | - | - | - | | - | - | - |
| | Total | 1994 | | 696 | 311 | 45 | | 12 757 | 6 746 | 53 |
| | General education | | | 696 | 311 | 45 | | 12 757 | 6 746 | 53 |
| | Teacher training | | | - | - | - | | - | - | - |
| | Vocational education | | | - | - | - | | - | - | - |
| | Total | 1995 | (63) | 715 | (63) 323 | 45 | (63) | 13 241 | (63) 6 590 | 50 |
| | General education | | (63) | 715 | (63) 323 | 45 | (63) | 13 241 | (63) 6 590 | 50 |
| | Teacher training | | | - | - | - | | - | - | - |
| | Vocational education | | | - | - | - | | - | - | - |
| | Total | 1996 | | 665 | 312 | 47 | | 12 672 | 6 316 | 50 |
| | General education | | | 665 | 312 | 47 | | 12 672 | 6 316 | 50 |
| | Teacher training | | | - | - | - | | - | - | - |
| | Vocational education | | | - | - | - | | - | - | - |
| Solomon Islands | Total | 1970 | | 98 | 33 | 34 | | 1 400 | 358 | 26 |
| | General education | | | 64 | 19 | 30 | | 1 042 | 251 | 24 |
| | Teacher training | | | 11 | 6 | 55 | | 110 | 31 | 28 |
| | Vocational education | | | 23 | 8 | 35 | | 248 | 76 | 31 |
| | Total | 1975 | | 131 | 37 | 28 | | 2 014 | 503 | 25 |
| | General education | | | 87 | 28 | 32 | | 1 555 | 412 | 26 |
| | Teacher training | | | 18 | 5 | 28 | | 146 | 46 | 32 |
| | Vocational education | | | 26 | 4 | 15 | | 313 | 45 | 14 |
| | Total | 1980 | | 257 | 67 | 26 | | 4 030 | ... | ... |
| | General education | | | 196 | 61 | 31 | | 3 547 | 1 063 | 30 |
| | Teacher training | | | 24 | 3 | 13 | | 116 | ... | ... |
| | Vocational education | | | 37 | 3 | 8 | | 367 | 18 | 5 |
| | Total | 1985 | | ... | ... | ... | | ... | ... | ... |
| | General education | | | 270 | ... | ... | | 5 240 | ... | ... |
| | Teacher training | | | 28 | ... | ... | | 125 | ... | ... |
| | Vocational education | | | ... | ... | ... | | ... | ... | ... |
| | Total | 1990 | | ... | ... | ... | | 5 636 | 2 068 | 37 |
| | General education | | | ... | ... | ... | | 5 636 | 2 068 | 37 |
| | Teacher training | | | - | - | - | | - | - | - |
| | Vocational education | | | - | - | - | | - | - | - |
| | Total | 1991 | | 364 | ... | ... | | 6 363 | 2 269 | 36 |
| | General education | | | 364 | ... | ... | | 6 363 | 2 269 | 36 |
| | Teacher training | | | - | - | - | | - | - | - |
| | Vocational education | | | - | - | - | | - | - | - |
| | Total | 1992 | | ... | ... | ... | | 6 666 | 2 442 | 37 |
| | General education | | | ... | ... | ... | | 6 666 | 2 442 | 37 |
| | Teacher training | | | - | - | - | | - | - | - |
| | Vocational education | | | - | - | - | | - | - | - |
| | Total | 1993 | | ... | ... | ... | | 7 351 | 2 658 | 36 |
| | General education | | | ... | ... | ... | | 7 351 | 2 658 | 36 |
| | Teacher training | | | - | - | - | | - | - | - |
| | Vocational education | | | - | - | - | | - | - | - |
| | Total | 1994 | | ... | ... | ... | | 7 811 | 2 940 | 38 |
| | General education | | | ... | ... | ... | | 7 811 | 2 940 | 38 |
| | Teacher training | | | - | - | - | | - | - | - |
| | Vocational education | | | ... | ... | ... | | ... | ... | ... |
| Tokelau | Total | 1991 | | ... | ... | ... | | ... | ... | ... |
| | General education | | | ... | ... | ... | | 113 | 53 | 47 |
| | Teacher training | | | - | - | - | | - | - | - |
| | Vocational education | | | ... | ... | ... | | ... | ... | ... |
| Tonga | Total | 1970 | | 428 | 182 | 43 | | 10 159 | 4 869 | 48 |
| | General education | | | 417 | 176 | 42 | | 10 057 | 4 816 | 48 |
| | Teacher training | | | 11 | 6 | 55 | | 102 | 53 | 52 |
| | Vocational education | | | - | - | - | | - | - | - |
| | Total | 1975 | | ... | ... | ... | | 11 351 | 5 482 | 48 |
| | General education | | | ... | ... | ... | | 10 685 | 5 229 | 49 |
| | Teacher training | | | 11 | 7 | 64 | | 117 | 71 | 61 |
| | Vocational education | | | 23 | 4 | 17 | | 549 | 182 | 33 |
| | Total | 1985 | | 840 | 381 | 45 | | 15 232 | 7 694 | 51 |
| | General education | | | 770 | 347 | 45 | | 14 641 | 7 321 | 50 |
| | Teacher training | | | 12 | 9 | 75 | | 126 | 87 | 69 |
| | Vocational education | | | 58 | 25 | 43 | | 465 | 286 | 62 |

II.6    Secondary education: teaching staff and pupils
Enseignement secondaire: personnel enseignant et élèves
Enseñanza secundaria: personal docente y alumnos

| Country<br>Pays<br>País | Type of education<br>Type d'enseignement<br>Tipo de enseñanza | Year<br>Année<br>Año | Teaching staff<br>Personnel enseignant<br>Personal docente | | | Pupils enrolled<br>Elèves inscrits<br>Alumnos matriculados | | |
|---|---|---|---|---|---|---|---|---|
| | | | Total | Female<br>Féminin<br>Femenino | %<br>F | Total | Female<br>Féminin<br>Femenino | %<br>F |
| Tonga (cont) | Total | 1990 | 832 | 411 | 49 | 14 749 | 7 076 | 48 |
| | General education | | 767 | 375 | 49 | 13 877 | 6 681 | 48 |
| | Teacher training | | 20 | 13 | 65 | 210 | 104 | 50 |
| | Vocational education | | 45 | 23 | 51 | 662 | 291 | 44 |
| | Total | 1991 | 876 | 395 | 45 | 14 825 | 7 258 | 49 |
| | General education | | ... | ... | ... | 13 839 | 6 814 | 49 |
| | Teacher training | | ... | ... | ... | 223 | 110 | 49 |
| | Vocational education | | ... | ... | ... | 763 | 334 | 44 |
| | Total | 1992 | ... | ... | ... | ... | ... | ... |
| | General education | | ... | ... | ... | 13 318 | 6 352 | 48 |
| | Teacher training | | ... | ... | ... | 226 | 118 | 52 |
| | Vocational education | | ... | ... | ... | ... | ... | ... |
| | Total | 1993 | ... | ... | ... | 16 570 | 7 908 | 48 |
| | General education | | 847 | 265 | 31 | 15 573 | 7 450 | 48 |
| | Teacher training | | 18 | 11 | 61 | 210 | 128 | 61 |
| | Vocational education | | ... | ... | ... | 787 | 330 | 42 |
| Tuvalu | Total | 1980 | ... | ... | ... | 248 | ... | ... |
| | General education | | ... | ... | ... | ... | ... | ... |
| | Teacher training | | - | - | - | - | - | - |
| | Vocational education | | ... | ... | ... | ... | ... | ... |
| | Total | 1990 | 31 | 10 | 32 | 345 | 178 | 52 |
| | General education | | 21 | 10 | 48 | 314 | 178 | 57 |
| | Teacher training | | - | - | - | - | - | - |
| | Vocational education | | 10 | - | - | 31 | - | - |
| Vanuatu, Republic of | Total | 1970 | 71 | 28 | 39 | 784 | 331 | 42 |
| | General education | | 50 | 17 | 34 | 541 | 204 | 38 |
| | Teacher training | | 9 | 4 | 44 | 100 | 33 | 33 |
| | Vocational education | | 12 | 7 | 58 | 143 | 94 | 66 |
| | Total | 1975 | ... | ... | ... | 1 505 | 636 | 42 |
| | General education | | ... | ... | ... | 1 263 | 555 | 44 |
| | Teacher training | | ... | ... | ... | 103 | 50 | 49 |
| | Vocational education | | ... | ... | ... | 139 | 31 | 22 |
| | Total | 1980 | 185 | ... | ... | 2 426 | 1 018 | 42 |
| | General education | | (22) 140 | ... | ... | 1 970 | 866 | 44 |
| | Teacher training | | ./. | ... | ... | 106 | 59 | 56 |
| | Vocational education | | 45 | ... | ... | 350 | 93 | 27 |
| | Total | 1990 | ... | ... | ... | ... | ... | ... |
| | General education | | ... | ... | ... | ... | ... | ... |
| | Teacher training | | ... | ... | ... | 94 | 36 | 38 |
| | Vocational education | | ... | ... | ... | 199 | 76 | 38 |
| | Total | 1991 | ... | ... | ... | 4 184 | 1 797 | 43 |
| | General education | | 208 | 65 | 31 | 3 799 | 1 642 | 43 |
| | Teacher training | | 124 | ... | ... | 124 | 57 | 46 |
| | Vocational education | | ... | ... | ... | 261 | 98 | 38 |
| | Total | 1992 | ... | ... | ... | ... | ... | ... |
| | General education | | 220 | 79 | 36 | 4 269 | 1 894 | 44 |
| | Teacher training | | ... | ... | ... | ... | ... | ... |
| | Vocational education | | ... | ... | ... | 444 | 140 | 32 |

**General note**
For general explanations and definitions, please refer to the beginning of this chapter.

**Note générale**
Pour les explications et définitions générales, prière de se référer au début de ce chapitre.

**Nota general**
Para las explicaciones y definiciones generales, referirse al comienzo de este capítulo.

| Notes | Notes | Notas |
|---|---|---|
| (1) Including vocational education. | (1) Y compris l'enseignement technique. | (1) Incluida la enseñanza técnica. |
| (2) As from 1988, change in structure. | (2) A partir de 1988, changement de structure. | (2) A partir de 1988, cambio de estructura. |
| (3) As from 1991, change in data coverage. | (3) A partir de 1991, changement dans la couverture des données. | (3) A partir de 1991, cambio en la cobertura de los datos. |
| (4) Public education only. | (4) Enseignement public seulement. | (4) Enseñanza pública solamente. |
| (5) Public and aided education only. | (5) Enseignement public et subventionné seulement. | (5) Enseñanza pública y subvencionada solamente. |
| (6) As from 1973, change in structure. | (6) A partir de 1973, changement de structure. | (6) A partir de 1973, cambio de estructura. |
| (7) As from 1990, change in structure. | (7) A partir de 1990, changement de structure. | (7) A partir de 1990, cambio de estructura. |
| (8) Including teacher training at the third level of education. | (8) Y compris l'enseignement normal du troisième degré. | (8) Incluye la enseñanza normal de tercer grado. |

Secondary education: teaching staff and pupils  II.6
Enseignement secondaire: personnel enseignant et élèves
Enseñanza secundaria: personal docente y alumnos

(9) Data refer to vocational and technical schools attached to the Ministry of Education only.

(9) Les données se réfèrent aux écoles techniques et professionnelles rattachées au Ministère de l'Education seulement.

(9) Los datos se refieren a las escuelas técnicas y profesionales dependientes del Ministerio de Educación solamente.

(10) Not including Al Azhar university.

(10) Non compris l'université Al Azhar.

(10) No incluye la universidad Al Azhar.

(11) As from 1984, change in structure.

(11) A partir de 1984, changement de structure.

(11) A partir de 1984, cambio de estructura.

(12) As from 1985, change in structure.

(12) A partir de 1985, changement de structure.

(12) A partir de 1985, cambio de estructura.

(13) As from 1991, change in structure.

(13) A partir de 1991, changement de structure.

(13) A partir de 1991, cambio de estructura.

(14) Not including Malawi College of Distance Education.

(14) Non compris le collège Malawi d'enseignement à distance.

(14) No incluye el colegio Malawi de enseñanza a distancia.

(15) As from 1977, change in structure.

(15) A partir de 1977, changement de structure.

(15) A partir de 1977, cambio de estructura.

(16) Not including health-related programmes.

(16) Non compris les programmes relatifs à la santé.

(16) No incluyen los programas relativos a la salud.

(17) Including private vocational schools.

(17) Y compris les écoles privées d'enseignement technique.

(17) Incluye las escuelas privadas de enseñanza técnica.

(18) Not including professional schools.

(18) Non compris les écoles professionnelles.

(18) No incluyen las escuelas profesionales.

(19) Data do not include private professional schools.

(19) Les données n'incluent pas les écoles privées d'enseignement professionnel.

(19) Los datos no incluyen las escuelas privadas de enseñanza profesional.

(20) As from 1982, change in structure.

(20) A partir de 1982, changement de structure.

(20) A partir de 1982, cambio de estructura.

(21) As from 1987, change in structure.

(21) A partir de 1987, changement de structure.

(21) A partir de 1987, cambio de estructura.

(22) Including teacher training.

(22) Y compris l'enseignement normal.

(22) Incluye la enseñanza normal.

(23) Not including integrated rural and craft education.

(23) Non compris l'enseignement rural et artisanal intégré.

(23) No incluye la enseñanza rural y artesanal integrada.

(24) As from 1980, change in structure.

(24) A partir de 1980, changement de structure.

(24) A partir de 1980, cambio de estructura.

(25) Not including the former independent states (Transkei, Bophuthatswana, Venda and Ciskei).

(25) Non compris les anciens états indépandants (Transkei, Bophuthatswana, Venda et Ciskei).

(25) No incluyen los antiguos estados independientes (Transkei, Bophuthatswana, Venda y Ciskei).

(26) As from 1992, change in structure.

(26) A partir de 1992, changement de structure.

(26) A partir de 1992, cambio de estructura.

(27) Including part-time education.

(27) Y compris l'enseignement à temps partiel.

(27) Incluye la enseñanza de jornada parcial.

(28) As from 1975, change in structure.

(28) A partir de 1975, changement de structure.

(28) A partir de 1975, cambio de estructura.

(29) As from 1992, change in data coverage.

(29) A partir de 1992, changement dans la couverture des données.

(29) A partir de 1992, cambio en la cobertura de los datos.

(30) Not including evening schools.

(30) Non compris les cours du soir.

(30) No incluyen los cursos nocturnos.

(31) From 1974, forms I, II and III, previously classified as primary education are included with general secondary education.

(31) A partir de 1974, Les 'forms I, II and III' qui étaient classées comme enseignement primaire, sont comprises dans l'enseignement secondaire général.

(31) A partir de 1974, las 'forms I, II and III' que estaban consideradas como enseñanza primaria están incluidas en la enseñanza secundaria general.

(32) Not including senior departments of all age schools.

(32) Non compris les sections supérieures des 'all-age schools'.

(32) No incluyen las secciones superiores de las 'all-age schools'.

(33) Including courses in vocational and technical education.

(33) Y compris les cours d'enseignement professionnel et technique.

(33) Incluyen los cursos de enseñanza profesional y técnica.

(34) Data refer to posts and not to teaching staff.

(34) Les données se réfèrent au nombre de postes et non au nombre d'enseignants.

(34) Los datos se refieren al número de puestos y no al número de docentes.

(35) As from 1971, change in structure.

(35) A partir de 1971, changement de structure.

(35) A partir de 1971, cambio de estructura.

(36) From 1984, due to a change in classification, vocational education includes 6 grades instead of 3 grades previously.

(36) A partir de 1984, suite à un changement de classification, l'enseignement technique comprend 6 années d'études au lieu de 3 précédemment.

(36) A partir de 1984, debido a un cambio de clasificación, la enseñanza técnica comprende 6 años de estudios en lugar de 3 anteriormente.

(37) Not including courses of U.T.U. (Universidad del Trabajo del Uruguay).

(37) Non compris les cours de la U.T.U. (Universidad del Trabajo del Uruguay).

(37) No incluyen los cursos de la U.T.U. (Universidad del Trabajo del Uruguay).

(38) As from 1979, change in structure.

(38) A partir de 1979, changement de structure.

(38) A partir de 1979, cambio de estructura.

(39) As from 1986, change in structure.

(39) A partir de 1986, changement de structure.

(39) A partir de 1986, cambio de estructura.

(40) Not including international schools.

(40) Non compris les écoles internationales.

(40) No incluidas las escuelas internationales.

(41) Day schools only.

(41) Ecoles de jour seulement.

(41) Escuelas de jornada solamente.

(42) Not including Turkish schools.

(42) Non compris les écoles turques.

(42) No incluyen las escuelas turcas.

(43) Commercial schools are included with general education.

(43) Les écoles commerciales sont comprises avec l'enseignement général.

(43) Las escuelas comerciales están comprendidas en la enseñanza general.

(44) Not including oriental studies.

(44) Non compris les études orientales.

(44) No incluidos los estudios orientales.

(45) Including teachers in primary classes attached to secondary schools.

(45) Y compris les enseignants des classes primaires rattachés aux écoles secondaires.

(45) Incluyen los docentes de las clases primarias dependientes de las escuelas secundarias.

(46) Religious schools are included with vocational education.

(46) Les écoles religieuses sont comprises avec l'enseignement technique.

(46) Las escuelas religiosas están comprendidas en la enseñanza técnica.

(47) Including intermediate sections in primary schools.

(47) Y compris les classes intermédiaires de l'enseignement primaire.

(47) Incluyen las escuelas intermediarias de la enseñanza primaria.

(48) As from 1994, change in structure.

(48) A partir de 1994, changement de structure.

(48) A partir de 1994, cambio de estructura.

(49) East Bank only.

(49) Rive orientale seulement.

(49) Orilla oriental solamente.

(50) As from 1989, change in structure.

(50) A partir de 1989, changement de structure.

(50) A partir de 1989, cambio de estructura.

(51) As from 1981, change in data coverage.

(51) A partir de 1981, changement dans la couverture des données.

(51) A partir de 1981, cambio en la cobertura de los datos.

(52) As from 1993, change in data coverage.

(52) A partir de 1993, changement dans la couverture des données.

(52) A partir de 1993, cambio en la cobertura de los datos.

(53) As from this year, data reported include special education.

(53) A partir de cette année, les données incluent l'enseignement spécial.

(53) A partir de este año, los datos incluyen la enseñanza especial.

(54) As from 1976, change in structure.

(54) A partir de 1976, changement de structure.

(54) A partir de 1976, cambio de estructura.

(55) Data on vocational refer to public education only.

(55) Les données relatives a l'enseignement technique se réfèrent à l'enseignement public seulement.

(55) Los datos relativos a la enseñanza técnica se refieren a la enseñanza pública solamente.

(56) As from 1972, change in structure.

(56) A partir de 1972, changement de structure.

(56) A partir de 1972, cambio de estructura.

(57) As from 1996, change in structure.

(57) A partir de 1996, changement de structure.

(57) A partir de 1996, cambio de estructura.

(58) As from 1981, change in structure.

(58) A partir de 1981, changement de structure.

(58) A partir de 1981, cambio de estructura.

(59) Full-time only.

(59) Plein temps seulement.

(59) Jornada completa solamente.

(60) Not including special education.

(60) Non compris l'enseignement spécial.

(60) No incluye la enseñanza especial.

(61) As from 1978, change in structure.

(61) A partir de 1978, changement de structure.

(61) A partir de 1978, cambio de estructura.

(62) Vocational and teacher-training education are counted together.

(62) Les enseignements technique et normal sont regroupés.

(62) Las enseñanzas técnica y normal están reunidas.

(63) As from 1995, change in structure.

(63) A partir de 1995, changement de structure.

(63) A partir de 1995, cambio de estructura.

**II.6** Secondary education: teaching staff and pupils
Enseignement secondaire: personnel enseignant et élèves
Enseñanza secundaria: personal docente y alumnos

(64) From 1995, vocational schools previously classified as secondary education are included with tertiary education.

(65) As from 1975, change in data coverage.

(66) As from 1993, change in structure.

(67) Data are expressed in full-time equivalent.

(68) Including apprenticeships and health-care training.

(69) Including evening and correspondence courses.

(70) Data refer to grades 5-11.

(71) Including special education.

(72) As from 1993, data include part-time education.

(73) As from 1974, change in structure.

(64) A partir de 1995, les écoles techniques qui auparavant étaient classées dans le secondaire, sont comprises dans le supérieur.

(65) A partir de 1975, changement dans la couverture des données.

(66) A partir de 1993, changement de structure.

(67) Les données sont exprimées en équivalents plein temps.

(68) Y compris l'apprentissage et les programmes relatifs à la santé.

(69) Y compris les cours du soir et par correspondance.

(70) Les données se réfèrent aux années d'études de 5 à 11.

(71) Y compris l'enseignement spécial.

(72) A partie de 1993, les données incluent l'enseignement à temps partiel.

(73) A partir de 1974, changement de structure.

(64) A partir de 1995, las escuelas técnicas que antes estaban consideradas en la enseñanza secundaria están incluidas en la enseñanza superior.

(65) A partir de 1975, cambio en la cobertura de los datos.

(66) A partir de 1993, cambio de estructura.

(67) Los datos están expresados en equivalente de jornada completa.

(68) Incluyen el aprentizaje y los programas relativos a la salud.

(69) Incluyen los cursos nocturnos y por correspondencia.

(70) Los datos se refieren a los años de estudios de 5 a 11.

(71) Incluye la enseñanza especial.

(72) A partie de 1993, los datos incluyen la enseñanza de jornada parcial.

(73) A partir de 1974, cambio de estructura.

Tertiary education: teaching staff and students    II.7
Enseignement supérieur: personnel enseignant et étudiants
Enseñanza superior: personal docente y estudiantes

## II.7    Tertiary education: teaching staff and students

## Enseignement supérieur: personnel enseignant et étudiants

## Enseñanza superior: personal docente y estudiantes

All institutions
of which: Universities (and equiv. insts.)

= Total des établissements
= dont: Universités (et étab. équiv.)

= Todos los establecimientos
= de los cuales: Universidades (y estab. equiv.)

| Country / Pays / País | Type of institution / Type d'établissement / Tipo de establecimiento | Year / Année / Año | Teaching staff / Personnel enseignant / Personal docente | | | Students enrolled / Étudiants inscrits / Estudiantes matriculados | | |
|---|---|---|---|---|---|---|---|---|
| | | | Total | Female Féminin Femenino | % F | Total | Female Féminin Femenino | % F |
| **Africa** | | | | | | | | |
| Algeria | All institutions | 1970/71 | ... | ... | ... | (1) 19 531 | (1) 4 166 | 21 |
| | of which: Universities | | ... | ... | ... | (1) 19 531 | (1) 4 166 | 21 |
| | All institutions | 1975/76 | ... | ... | ... | (1) 41 847 | ... | ... |
| | of which: Universities | | ... | ... | ... | (1) 41 847 | ... | ... |
| | All institutions | 1980/81 | ... | ... | ... | ... | ... | ... |
| | of which: Universities | | (1) 8 962 | ... | ... | (1) 79 351 | (1) 21 014 | 26 |
| | All institutions | 1985/86 | ... | ... | ... | ... | ... | ... |
| | of which: Universities | | (1) 11 464 | ... | ... | (1) 132 057 | ... | ... |
| | All institutions | 1990/91 | ... | ... | ... | 285 930 | ... | ... |
| | of which: Universities | | 15 171 | ... | ... | 212 413 | ... | ... |
| | All institutions | 1991/92 | 20 336 | ... | ... | 298 117 | ... | ... |
| | of which: Universities | | 14 496 | ... | ... | 236 185 | 93 471 | 40 |
| | All institutions | 1992/93 | 19 291 | ... | ... | 303 111 | ... | ... |
| | of which: Universities | | 15 450 | 3 405 | 22 | 257 379 | 106 928 | 42 |
| | All institutions | 1993/94 | ... | ... | ... | 298 133 | ... | ... |
| | of which: Universities | | ... | ... | ... | 250 939 | *106 700 | *43 |
| | All institutions | 1994/95 | 20 026 | ... | ... | 298 767 | ... | ... |
| | of which: Universities | | 14 593 | 3 594 | 25 | 252 334 | 107 254 | 43 |
| | All institutions | 1995/96 | 19 910 | ... | ... | 347 410 | ... | ... |
| | of which: Universities | | 14 364 | 3 482 | 24 | 267 142 | 118 368 | 44 |
| Angola | All institutions | 1970/71 | 273 | ... | ... | 2 349 | 936 | 40 |
| | of which: Universities | | 273 | ... | ... | 2 349 | 936 | 40 |
| | All institutions | 1980/81 | 225 | ... | ... | 2 333 | ... | ... |
| | of which: Universities | | 225 | ... | ... | 2 333 | ... | ... |
| | All institutions | 1985/86 | 666 | ... | ... | 5 034 | ... | ... |
| | of which: Universities | | 666 | ... | ... | 5 034 | ... | ... |
| | All institutions | 1990/91 | 986 | ... | ... | 6 534 | ... | ... |
| | of which: Universities | | 986 | ... | ... | 6 534 | ... | ... |
| | All institutions | 1991/92 | 787 | ... | ... | 6 331 | ... | ... |
| | of which: Universities | | 787 | ... | ... | 6 331 | ... | ... |
| Benin | All institutions | 1970 | 33 | 4 | 12 | 311 | 23 | 7 |
| | of which: Universities | | 33 | 4 | 12 | 311 | 23 | 7 |
| | All institutions | 1975 | 153 | ... | ... | 2 118 | 315 | 15 |
| | of which: Universities | | 148 | ... | ... | 2 102 | 314 | 15 |
| | All institutions | 1980 | 649 | ... | ... | 4 822 | ... | ... |
| | of which: Universities | | ... | ... | ... | ... | ... | ... |

Tertiary education: teaching staff and students
Enseignement supérieur: personnel enseignant et étudiants
Enseñanza superior: personal docente y estudiantes

| Country / Pays / País | Type of institution / Type d'établissement / Tipo de establecimiento | Year / Année / Año | Teaching staff / Personnel enseignant / Personal docente | | | Students enrolled / Étudiants inscrits / Estudiantes matriculados | | |
|---|---|---|---|---|---|---|---|---|
| | | | Total | Female Féminin Femenino | % F | Total | Female Féminin Femenino | % F |
| Benin (cont) | All institutions | 1985 | 971 | ... | ... | 9 063 | 1 427 | 16 |
| | of which: Universities | | 971 | ... | ... | 9 063 | 1 427 | 16 |
| | All institutions | 1990 | 940 | ... | ... | 10 873 | 1 416 | 13 |
| | of which: Universities | | 940 | ... | ... | 10 873 | 1 416 | 13 |
| | All institutions | 1991 | 1 379 | 199 | 14 | 10 611 | 1 656 | 16 |
| | of which: Universities | | 1 379 | 199 | 14 | 10 611 | 1 656 | 16 |
| | All institutions | 1992 | 892 | 88 | 10 | 9 964 | 1 634 | 16 |
| | of which: Universities | | 892 | 88 | 10 | 9 964 | 1 634 | 16 |
| | All institutions | 1993 | 957 | 118 | 12 | 10 586 | 1 835 | 17 |
| | of which: Universities | | 957 | 118 | 12 | 10 586 | 1 835 | 17 |
| | All institutions | 1994 | *961 | ... | ... | 10 986 | 1 904 | 17 |
| | of which: Universities | | *961 | ... | ... | 10 986 | 1 904 | 17 |
| | All institutions | 1995 | *962 | ... | ... | 11 227 | 2 051 | 18 |
| | of which: Universities | | *962 | ... | ... | 11 227 | 2 051 | 18 |
| | All institutions | 1996 | ... | ... | ... | 14 055 | 2 657 | 19 |
| | of which: Universities | | ... | ... | ... | 14 055 | 2 657 | 19 |
| Botswana | All institutions | 1970/71 | - | - | - | - | - | - |
| | of which: Universities | | - | - | - | - | - | - |
| | All institutions | 1975/76 | 56 | 12 | 21 | 469 | 152 | 32 |
| | of which: Universities | | 56 | 12 | 21 | 469 | 152 | 32 |
| | All institutions | 1980/81 | 140 | ... | ... | 1 078 | 372 | 35 |
| | of which: Universities | | 140 | ... | ... | 1 078 | 372 | 35 |
| | All institutions | 1985/86 | 190 | ... | ... | 1 938 | 875 | 45 |
| | of which: Universities | | 178 | ... | ... | 1 773 | 801 | 45 |
| | All institutions | 1990/91 | ... | ... | ... | ... | ... | ... |
| | of which: Universities | | 300 | ... | ... | 3 365 | 1 481 | 44 |
| | All institutions | 1991/92 | 600 | ... | ... | 5 364 | 2 262 | 42 |
| | of which: Universities | | 376 | ... | ... | 3 567 | 1 605 | 45 |
| | All institutions | 1992/93 | ... | ... | ... | *6 036 | *2 731 | *45 |
| | of which: Universities | | 376 | ... | ... | 3 976 | 1 946 | 49 |
| | All institutions | 1993/94 | ... | ... | ... | 6 830 | 3 029 | 44 |
| | of which: Universities | | ... | ... | ... | 4 466 | 2 228 | 50 |
| | All institutions | 1994/95 | ... | ... | ... | 7 728 | 3 256 | 42 |
| | of which: Universities | | ... | ... | ... | 5 062 | 2 368 | 47 |
| | All institutions | 1995/96 | ... | ... | ... | 7 920 | 3 763 | 48 |
| | of which: Universities | | ... | ... | ... | 5 501 | 2 892 | 53 |
| | All institutions | 1996/97 | 765 | 212 | 28 | 8 850 | 4 197 | 47 |
| | of which: Universities | | 509 | 142 | 28 | 7 275 | 3 449 | 47 |
| Burkina Faso | All institutions | 1970/71 | ... | ... | ... | ... | ... | ... |
| | of which: Universities | (2) | 30 | ... | ... | 183 | 27 | 15 |
| | All institutions | 1975/76 | ... | ... | ... | ... | ... | ... |
| | of which: Universities | | 166 | 22 | 13 | 1 067 | 212 | 20 |
| | All institutions | 1980/81 | ... | ... | ... | 1 644 | 354 | 22 |
| | of which: Universities | | 140 | ... | ... | 1 520 | 285 | 19 |
| | All institutions | 1985/86 | ... | ... | ... | 4 085 | 946 | 23 |
| | of which: Universities | | ... | ... | ... | 3 856 | 844 | 22 |
| | All institutions | 1990/91 | 387 | ... | ... | 5 425 | 1 254 | 23 |
| | of which: Universities | | 381 | ... | ... | 5 089 | 1 108 | 22 |
| | All institutions | 1991/92 | ... | ... | ... | 7 387 | 1 666 | 23 |
| | of which: Universities | | ... | ... | ... | 6 912 | 1 429 | 21 |
| | All institutions | 1992/93 | 547 | 12 | 2 | 8 813 | 2 013 | 23 |
| | of which: Universities | | 525 | 10 | 2 | 8 276 | 1 777 | 21 |
| | All institutions | 1993/94 | 571 | ... | ... | 8 815 | 2 131 | 24 |
| | of which: Universities | | ... | ... | ... | ... | ... | ... |
| | All institutions | 1994/95 | 439 | ... | ... | 9 452 | 2 087 | 22 |
| | of which: Universities | | ... | ... | ... | ... | ... | ... |
| | All institutions | 1995/96 | 315 | ... | ... | 9 388 | 2 264 | 24 |
| | of which: Universities | | ... | ... | ... | ... | ... | ... |

Tertiary education: teaching staff and students
Enseignement supérieur: personnel enseignant et étudiants
Enseñanza superior: personal docente y estudiantes

II.7

| Country / Pays / País | Type of institution / Type d'établissement / Tipo de establecimiento | Year / Année / Año | Teaching staff / Personnel enseignant / Personal docente | | | Students enrolled / Étudiants inscrits / Estudiantes matriculados | | |
|---|---|---|---|---|---|---|---|---|
| | | | Total | Female / Féminin / Femenino | % F | Total | Female / Féminin / Femenino | % F |
| Burkina Faso (cont) | All institutions | 1996/97 | 352 | ... | ... | 8 911 | 2 022 | 23 |
| | of which: Universities | | ... | ... | ... | ... | ... | ... |
| Burundi | All institutions | 1970/71 | 102 | 7 | 7 | 466 | 26 | 6 |
| | of which: Universities | | 69 | 4 | 6 | 361 | 17 | 5 |
| | All institutions | 1975/76 | 223 | ... | ... | 1 002 | 112 | 11 |
| | of which: Universities | | 123 | ... | ... | 652 | 72 | 11 |
| | All institutions | 1980/81 | ... | ... | ... | 1 879 | 464 | 25 |
| | of which: Universities | | ... | ... | ... | 1 793 | 438 | 24 |
| | All institutions | 1985/86 | 467 | 31 | 7 | 2 783 | 676 | 24 |
| | of which: Universities | | 315 | 26 | 8 | 2 111 | 504 | 24 |
| | All institutions | 1990/91 | 436 | 36 | 8 | 3 592 | 957 | 27 |
| | of which: Universities | | 436 | 36 | 8 | 3 592 | 957 | 27 |
| | All institutions | 1991/92 | 539 | 60 | 11 | 3 830 | 1 013 | 26 |
| | of which: Universities | | 539 | 60 | 11 | 3 830 | 1 013 | 26 |
| | All institutions | 1992/93 | 556 | 61 | 11 | 4 256 | 1 127 | 26 |
| | of which: Universities | | 556 | 61 | 11 | 4 256 | 1 127 | 26 |
| Cameroon | All institutions | 1970/71 | 220 | 21 | 10 | 2 690 | 209 | 8 |
| | of which: Universities | | 158 | 14 | 9 | 2 120 | 158 | 7 |
| | All institutions | 1975/76 | ... | ... | ... | ... | ... | ... |
| | of which: Universities | | ... | ... | ... | 7 191 | 1 081 | 15 |
| | All institutions | 1980/81 | ... | ... | ... | (3) 11 686 | ... | ... |
| | of which: Universities | | ... | ... | ... | 10 631 | ... | ... |
| | All institutions | 1985/86 | ... | ... | ... | 17 071 | ... | ... |
| | of which: Universities | | 871 | ... | ... | | ... | ... |
| | All institutions | 1990/91 | 1 086 | ... | ... | 33 177 | ... | ... |
| | of which: Universities | | ... | ... | ... | 31 360 | ... | ... |
| Central African Republic | All institutions | 1970/71 | ... | ... | ... | 155 | ... | ... |
| | of which: Universities | | 6 | ... | ... | 88 | 3 | 3 |
| | All institutions | 1975/76 | 85 | ... | ... | 669 | ... | ... |
| | of which: Universities | | 85 | 20 | 24 | 555 | 31 | 6 |
| | All institutions | 1980/81 | 444 | 68 | 15 | 1 719 | 143 | 8 |
| | of which: Universities | | 379 | 63 | 17 | 1 394 | 119 | 9 |
| | All institutions | 1985/86 | 489 | 38 | 8 | 2 651 | 287 | 11 |
| | of which: Universities | | ... | ... | ... | 2 374 | 272 | 11 |
| | All institutions | 1990/91 | ... | ... | ... | 3 840 | 513 | 13 |
| | of which: Universities | | 410 | ... | ... | 3 116 | ... | ... |
| | All institutions | 1991/92 | ... | ... | ... | 3 684 | 545 | 15 |
| | of which: Universities | | ... | ... | ... | 2 923 | 276 | 9 |
| Chad | All institutions | 1970/71 | - | - | - | - | - | - |
| | of which: Universities | | - | - | - | - | - | - |
| | All institutions | 1975/76 | ... | ... | ... | 547 | 29 | 5 |
| | of which: Universities | | ... | ... | ... | 547 | 29 | 5 |
| | All institutions | 1992/93 | ... | ... | ... | ... | ... | ... |
| | of which: Universities | | 187 | ... | ... | 2 842 | 298 | 10 |
| | All institutions | 1993/94 | ... | ... | ... | ... | ... | ... |
| | of which: Universities | | 222 | 8 | 4 | 3 042 | 326 | 11 |
| | All institutions | 1994/95 | ... | ... | ... | ... | ... | ... |
| | of which: Universities | | 311 | 8 | 3 | 3 049 | 326 | 11 |
| | All institutions | 1995/96 | ... | ... | ... | 3 446 | 450 | 13 |
| | of which: Universities | | 288 | ... | ... | *3 274 | *406 | *12 |
| Comoros | All institutions | 1991/92 | ... | ... | ... | 223 | 63 | 28 |
| | of which: Universities | | - | - | - | - | - | - |
| | All institutions | 1992/93 | ... | ... | ... | 229 | ... | ... |
| | of which: Universities | | - | - | - | - | - | - |
| | All institutions | 1995/96 | ... | ... | ... | 348 | ... | ... |
| | of which: Universities | | - | - | - | - | - | - |

II.7   Tertiary education: teaching staff and students
Enseignement supérieur: personnel enseignant et étudiants
Enseñanza superior: personal docente y estudiantes

| Country / Pays / País | Type of institution / Type d'établissement / Tipo de establecimiento | Year / Année / Año | Teaching staff Personnel enseignant Personal docente | | | Students enrolled Étudiants inscrits Estudiantes matriculados | | | |
|---|---|---|---|---|---|---|---|---|---|
| | | | Total | Female Féminin Femenino | % F | | Total | Female Féminin Femenino | % F |
| Congo | All institutions | 1970/71 | 117 | 24 | 21 | | 1 788 | 87 | 5 |
| | of which: Universities | | 71 | 13 | 18 | | 1 436 | 75 | 5 |
| | All institutions | 1975/76 | 165 | 25 | 15 | | 3 249 | 321 | 10 |
| | of which: Universities | | 165 | 25 | 15 | | 3 249 | 321 | 10 |
| | All institutions | 1980/81 | 292 | 27 | 9 | | 7 255 | 1 079 | 15 |
| | of which: Universities | | 292 | 27 | 9 | | 7 255 | 1 079 | 15 |
| | All institutions | 1985/86 | ... | ... | ... | | 10 684 | 1 665 | 16 |
| | of which: Universities | | ... | ... | ... | | 10 684 | 1 665 | 16 |
| | All institutions | 1990/91 | 1 112 | 95 | 9 | | 10 671 | 1 885 | 18 |
| | of which: Universities | | 1 112 | 95 | 9 | | 10 671 | 1 885 | 18 |
| | All institutions | 1991/92 | 1 159 | 91 | 8 | | 12 045 | 2 241 | 19 |
| | of which: Universities | | 1 159 | 91 | 8 | | 12 045 | 2 241 | 19 |
| | All institutions | 1992/93 | 1 321 | ... | ... | | 13 806 | ... | ... |
| | of which: Universities | | 1 321 | ... | ... | | 13 806 | ... | ... |
| Côte d'Ivoire | All institutions | 1970/71 | 220 | ... | ... | (1) | 4 381 | (1) 615 | 14 |
| | of which: Universities | | 189 | ... | ... | | 4 001 | 590 | 15 |
| | All institutions | 1975/76 | ... | ... | ... | (1) | 7 174 | (1) 1 218 | 17 |
| | of which: Universities | | ... | ... | ... | | 6 274 | 1 123 | 18 |
| | All institutions | 1980/81 | ... | ... | ... | | 19 633 | ... | ... |
| | of which: Universities | | 625 | ... | ... | | 12 742 | 2 376 | 19 |
| | All institutions | 1985/86 | ... | ... | ... | | ... | ... | ... |
| | of which: Universities | | ... | ... | ... | (4) | 10 948 | (4) 2 237 | 20 |
| | All institutions | 1991/92 | ... | ... | ... | (5) | 30 064 | ... | ... |
| | of which: Universities | | 1 685 | ... | ... | | 29 147 | ... | ... |
| | All institutions | 1992/93 | ... | ... | ... | (5) | 37 811 | ... | ... |
| | of which: Universities | | 1 608 | ... | ... | | 36 005 | ... | ... |
| | All institutions | 1993/94 | ... | ... | ... | (5) | 51 215 | (5) 11 871 | 23 |
| | of which: Universities | | 1 594 | ... | ... | | 44 010 | 9 545 | 22 |
| | All institutions | 1994/95 | ... | ... | ... | (5) | 52 228 | (5) 12 776 | 24 |
| | of which: Universities | | 1 657 | ... | ... | | 43 147 | 9 078 | 21 |
| Democratic Rep. of the Congo | All institutions | 1970/71 | 1 315 | ... | ... | | 12 363 | 675 | 5 |
| | of which: Universities | | 695 | ... | ... | | 7 565 | 350 | 5 |
| | All institutions | 1975/76 | 2 010 | ... | ... | | 24 853 | ... | ... |
| | of which: Universities | | ... | ... | ... | | ... | ... | ... |
| | All institutions | 1980/81 | ... | ... | ... | | 28 493 | ... | ... |
| | of which: Universities | | ... | ... | ... | | 9 927 | ... | ... |
| | All institutions | 1985/86 | 3 272 | ... | ... | | 40 878 | ... | ... |
| | of which: Universities | | 1 387 | ... | % | | 16 239 | ... | ... |
| | All institutions | 1990/91 | ... | ... | ... | | 80 233 | ... | ... |
| | of which: Universities | | ... | ... | ... | | 35 448 | ... | ... |
| | All institutions | 1994/95 | ... | ... | ... | | 93 266 | ... | ... |
| | of which: Universities | | ... | ... | ... | | 40 765 | ... | ... |
| Djibouti | All institutions | 1990/91 | - | - | - | | - | - | - |
| | of which: Universities | | - | - | - | | - | - | - |
| | All institutions | 1991/92 | ... | ... | ... | | 53 | 16 | 30 |
| | of which: Universities | | - | - | - | | - | - | - |
| | All institutions | 1992/93 | ... | ... | ... | | 61 | 34 | 56 |
| | of which: Universities | | - | - | - | | - | - | - |
| | All institutions | 1993/94 | ... | ... | ... | | 75 | 38 | 51 |
| | of which: Universities | | - | - | - | | - | - | - |
| | All institutions | 1995/96 | ... | ... | ... | | 130 | 61 | 47 |
| | of which: Universities | | - | - | - | | - | - | - |
| | All institutions | 1996/97 | ... | ... | ... | | 161 | 71 | 44 |
| | of which: Universities | | - | - | - | | - | - | - |

Tertiary education: teaching staff and students
Enseignement supérieur: personnel enseignant et étudiants
Enseñanza superior: personal docente y estudiantes

II.7

| Country / Pays / País | Type of institution / Type d'établissement / Tipo de establecimiento | Year / Année / Año | Teaching staff Personnel enseignant Personal docente | | | Students enrolled Étudiants inscrits Estudiantes matriculados | | |
|---|---|---|---|---|---|---|---|---|
| | | | Total | Female Féminin Femenino | % F | Total | Female Féminin Femenino | % F |
| Egypt | All institutions | 1970/71 | 14 250 | ... | ... | 233 304 | 61 790 | 26 |
| | of which: Universities | | 11 959 | ... | ... | 213 404 | 55 840 | 26 |
| | All institutions | 1975/76 | ... | ... | ... | (6) 480 016 | (6) 144 096 | 30 |
| | of which: Universities | | ... | ... | ... | (6) 451 187 | (6) 136 422 | 30 |
| | All institutions | 1980/81 | ... | ... | ... | 715 701 | 225 562 | 32 |
| | of which: Universities | | ... | ... | ... | 663 418 | 210 072 | 32 |
| | All institutions | 1985/86 | (6) 31 903 | ... | ... | 854 584 | (7) 254 528 | ... |
| | of which: Universities | | (6) 29 889 | (6) 8 042 | 27 | 753 190 | (7) 225 873 | ... |
| | All institutions | 1990/91 | ... | ... | ... | (6)(7) 628 233 | (6)(7) 227 314 | 36 |
| | of which: Universities | | (6)(7) 34 553 | (6)(7) 10 006 | 29 | (6)(7) 520 496 | (6)(7) 192 773 | 37 |
| | All institutions | 1991/92 | ... | ... | ... | ... | ... | ... |
| | of which: Universities | | (6)(7) 36 609 | (6)(7) 10 627 | 29 | (6)(7) 518 645 | (6)(7) 191 263 | 37 |
| | All institutions | 1992/93 | ... | ... | ... | ... | ... | ... |
| | of which: Universities | | (6)(7) 37 608 | (6)(7) 10 999 | 29 | (6)(7) 562 658 | (6)(7) 210 154 | 37 |
| | All institutions | 1993/94 | ... | ... | ... | ... | ... | ... |
| | of which: Universities | | (6)(7) 38 828 | (6)(7) 11 596 | 30 | (6)(7) 620 145 | (6)(7) 240 099 | 39 |
| | All institutions | 1994/95 | ... | ... | ... | ... | ... | ... |
| | of which: Universities | | ... | ... | ... | (6)(7) 696 988 | (6)(7) 273 682 | 39 |
| | All institutions | 1995/96 | ... | ... | ... | ... | ... | ... |
| | of which: Universities | | ... | ... | ... | (6)(7) 850 051 | (6)(7) 352 902 | 42 |
| Equatorial Guinea | All institutions | 1990/91 | 58 | 7 | 12 | 578 | 73 | 13 |
| | of which: Universities | | 9 | 1 | 11 | 71 | 3 | 4 |
| Eritrea | All institutions | 1994/95 | 136 | 11 | 8 | 3 137 | 424 | 14 |
| | of which: Universities | | 136 | 11 | 8 | 3 137 | 424 | 14 |
| | All institutions | 1995/96 | 136 | 11 | 8 | 3 020 | 349 | 12 |
| | of which: Universities | | 136 | 11 | 8 | 3 020 | 349 | 12 |
| | All institutions | 1997/98 | 198 | 25 | 13 | 3 096 | 410 | 13 |
| | of which: Universities | | 198 | 25 | 13 | 3 096 | 410 | 13 |
| Ethiopia | All institutions | 1970/71 | 516 | 71 | 14 | 4 543 | 354 | 8 |
| | of which: Universities | | 516 | 71 | 14 | 4 543 | 354 | 8 |
| | All institutions | 1980/81 | 1 051 | ... | ... | 14 368 | ... | ... |
| | of which: Universities | | 787 | ... | ... | 9 291 | ... | ... |
| | All institutions | 1985/86 | 1 314 | 116 | 9 | 27 338 | 4 881 | 18 |
| | of which: Universities | | 1 034 | ... | ... | 21 601 | 3 055 | 14 |
| | All institutions | 1990/91 | 1 690 | 127 | 8 | 34 076 | 6 092 | 18 |
| | of which: Universities | | 1 439 | 109 | 8 | 29 066 | 4 485 | 15 |
| | All institutions | 1993/94 | 2 215 | 130 | 6 | 29 000 | 6 285 | 22 |
| | of which: Universities | | ... | ... | ... | 23 431 | 4 647 | 20 |
| | All institutions | 1994/95 | 1 937 | 123 | 6 | 32 671 | 6 558 | 20 |
| | of which: Universities | | ... | ... | ... | 26 415 | 4 764 | 18 |
| | All institutions | 1995/96 | ... | ... | ... | 35 027 | 6 682 | 19 |
| | of which: Universities | | ... | ... | ... | 28 614 | 4 977 | 17 |
| | All institutions | 1996/97 | ... | ... | ... | 42 226 | 8 524 | 20 |
| | of which: Universities | | ... | ... | ... | 36 678 | 6 823 | 19 |
| Gabon | All institutions | 1970/71 | ... | ... | ... | 172 | 26 | 15 |
| | of which: Universities | | ... | ... | ... | 172 | 26 | 15 |
| | All institutions | 1975/76 | ... | ... | ... | 1 014 | 207 | 20 |
| | of which: Universities | | ... | ... | ... | 651 | 148 | 23 |
| | All institutions | 1985/86 | ... | ... | ... | ... | ... | ... |
| | of which: Universities | | ... | ... | ... | 2 607 | ... | ... |
| | All institutions | 1991/92 | ... | ... | ... | ... | ... | ... |
| | of which: Universities | | 299 | ... | ... | 3 000 | 852 | 28 |
| | All institutions | 1993/94 | ... | ... | ... | ... | ... | ... |
| | of which: Universities | | ... | ... | ... | 3 977 | ... | ... |
| | All institutions | 1994/95 | ... | ... | ... | ... | ... | ... |
| | of which: Universities | | ... | ... | ... | 4 655 | ... | ... |

II.7    Tertiary education: teaching staff and students
Enseignement supérieur: personnel enseignant et étudiants
Enseñanza superior: personal docente y estudiantes

| Country / Pays / País | Type of institution / Type d'établissement / Tipo de establecimiento | Year / Année / Año | Teaching staff Personnel enseignant Personal docente | | | | Students enrolled Étudiants inscrits Estudiantes matriculados | | |
|---|---|---|---|---|---|---|---|---|---|
| | | | Total | Female Féminin Femenino | % F | | Total | Female Féminin Femenino | % F |
| Gambia | All institutions | 1994/95 | 155 | 36 | 23 | | 1 591 | 573 | 36 |
| | of which: Universities | | - | - | - | | - | - | - |
| Ghana | All institutions | 1970/71 | 902 | 83 | 9 | | 5 426 | 774 | 14 |
| | of which: Universities | | 825 | *65 | *8 | | 4 729 | 620 | 13 |
| | All institutions | 1975/76 | 1 103 | ... | ... | | 9 079 | 1 439 | 16 |
| | of which: Universities | | 963 | ... | ... | | 7 179 | 919 | 13 |
| | All institutions | 1980/81 | ... | ... | ... | | ... | ... | ... |
| | of which: Universities | | 987 | ... | ... | | 7 951 | 1 588 | 20 |
| | All institutions | 1985/86 | ... | ... | | | ... | ... | ... |
| | of which: Universities | | 1 097 | ... | | | 8 324 | 1 417 | 17 |
| | All institutions | 1990/91 | ... | ... | | | ... | ... | ... |
| | of which: Universities | | ... | ... | | | 9 609 | 2 158 | 22 |
| Guinea | All institutions | 1970/71 | ... | ... | ... | | 1 974 | 160 | 8 |
| | of which: Universities | | ... | ... | | | ... | ... | ... |
| | All institutions | 1975/76 | ... | ... | ... | | 12 411 | 2 237 | 18 |
| | of which: Universities | | ... | ... | | | ... | ... | ... |
| | All institutions | 1980/81 | 1 289 | 40 | 3 | | 18 270 | 3 497 | 19 |
| | of which: Universities | | 577 | 31 | 5 | | 5 319 | 726 | 14 |
| | All institutions | 1985/86 | 1 107 | 40 | 4 | | 8 801 | 1 267 | 14 |
| | of which: Universities | | 1 004 | 40 | 4 | | 8 393 | 1 195 | 14 |
| | All institutions | 1990/91 | ... | ... | ... | | 5 366 | 350 | 7 |
| | of which: Universities | | ... | ... | | | ... | ... | ... |
| | All institutions | 1991/92 | ... | ... | ... | | 5 213 | 334 | 6 |
| | of which: Universities | | ... | ... | | | 4 692 | 315 | 7 |
| | All institutions | 1992/93 | ... | ... | ... | | 7 398 | 515 | 7 |
| | of which: Universities | | ... | ... | | | 6 715 | 494 | 7 |
| | All institutions | 1993/94 | ... | ... | ... | | 7 129 | 451 | 6 |
| | of which: Universities | | ... | ... | | | 6 462 | 418 | 6 |
| | All institutions | 1994/95 | ... | ... | ... | | 8 096 | *499 | *6 |
| | of which: Universities | | ... | ... | | | 7 036 | 482 | 7 |
| | All institutions | 1995/96 | 1 070 | 37 | 3 | | 7 722 | 679 | 9 |
| | of which: Universities | | 865 | 34 | 4 | | 6 795 | 635 | 9 |
| | All institutions | 1996/97 | *947 | *34 | *4 | | 8 151 | 879 | 11 |
| | of which: Universities | | ... | ... | | | ... | ... | ... |
| Kenya | All institutions | 1970/71 | ... | ... | ... | | 7 795 | ... | ... |
| | of which: Universities | | ... | ... | ... | | 2 786 | ... | ... |
| | All institutions | 1975/76 | ... | ... | ... | | ... | ... | ... |
| | of which: Universities | | ... | ... | ... | | 6 327 | ... | ... |
| | All institutions | 1980/81 | ... | ... | ... | | 12 986 | ... | ... |
| | of which: Universities | | ... | ... | ... | | 9 155 | 2 302 | 25 |
| | All institutions | 1985/86 | ... | ... | ... | | 21 756 | 5 710 | 26 |
| | of which: Universities | | ... | ... | ... | | 9 148 | 2 635 | 29 |
| | All institutions | 1990/91 | ... | ... | ... | | ... | ... | ... |
| | of which: Universities | | 4 392 | ... | ... | | 35 421 | 9 769 | 28 |
| Lesotho | All institutions | 1970/71 | 61 | 5 | 8 | | 402 | 138 | 34 |
| | of which: Universities | | 61 | 5 | 8 | | 402 | 138 | 34 |
| | All institutions | 1975/76 | ... | ... | ... | | 529 | 222 | 42 |
| | of which: Universities | | 73 | ... | ... | | 502 | 212 | 42 |
| | All institutions | 1980/81 | ... | ... | ... | | 1 188 | ... | ... |
| | of which: Universities | | 137 | ... | ... | | 995 | ... | ... |
| | All institutions | 1985/86 | ... | ... | ... | | 1 771 | 935 | 53 |
| | of which: Universities | | 225 | ... | ... | | 1 504 | 779 | 52 |
| | All institutions | 1990/91 | ... | ... | ... | | 2 029 | 1 179 | 58 |
| | of which: Universities | | 273 | ... | ... | | 1 753 | 998 | 57 |
| | All institutions | 1991/92 | ... | ... | ... | | 2 112 | 1 244 | 59 |
| | of which: Universities | | 307 | ... | ... | | 1 878 | 1 098 | 58 |

Tertiary education: teaching staff and students
Enseignement supérieur: personnel enseignant et étudiants
Enseñanza superior: personal docente y estudiantes

II.7

| Country / Pays / País | Type of institution / Type d'établissement / Tipo de establecimiento | Year / Année / Año | Teaching staff Personnel enseignant Personal docente | | | Students enrolled Étudiants inscrits Estudiantes matriculados | | |
|---|---|---|---|---|---|---|---|---|
| | | | Total | Female Féminin Femenino | % F | Total | Female Féminin Femenino | % F |
| Lesotho (cont) | All institutions | 1992/93 | 490 | ... | ... | 3 704 | 2 013 | 54 |
| | of which: Universities | | 316 | ... | ... | 2 094 | 1 252 | 60 |
| | All institutions | 1993/94 | 492 | ... | ... | 4 001 | 2 223 | 56 |
| | of which: Universities | | 321 | ... | ... | 2 347 | 1 417 | 60 |
| | All institutions | 1994/95 | 467 | ... | ... | 4 365 | 2 398 | 55 |
| | of which: Universities | | 311 | ... | ... | 2 697 | 1 604 | 59 |
| | All institutions | 1995/96 | ... | ... | ... | 4 384 | 2 421 | 55 |
| | of which: Universities | | ... | ... | ... | 2 721 | 1 668 | 61 |
| | All institutions | 1996/97 | 574 | ... | ... | 4 614 | 2 509 | 54 |
| | of which: Universities | | 373 | ... | ... | 2 914 | 1 743 | 60 |
| Liberia | All institutions | 1970 | 164 | 18 | 11 | 1 109 | 238 | 21 |
| | of which: Universities | | 164 | 18 | 11 | 1 109 | 238 | 21 |
| | All institutions | 1975 | ... | ... | ... | 2 404 | 536 | 22 |
| | of which: Universities | | ... | ... | ... | 2 404 | 536 | 22 |
| Libyan Arab Jamahiriya | All institutions | 1970/71 | 394 | 17 | 4 | 5 222 | 561 | 11 |
| | of which: Universities | | 394 | 17 | 4 | 5 222 | 561 | 11 |
| | All institutions | 1975/76 | 951 | ... | ... | 13 427 | 2 358 | 18 |
| | of which: Universities | | 951 | ... | ... | 13 427 | 2 358 | 18 |
| | All institutions | 1980/81 | ... | ... | ... | 20 166 | 5 096 | 25 |
| | of which: Universities | | ... | ... | ... | 20 166 | 5 096 | 25 |
| | All institutions | 1985/86 | ... | ... | ... | *30 000 | ... | ... |
| | of which: Universities | | ... | ... | ... | *30 000 | ... | ... |
| | All institutions | 1991/92 | ... | ... | ... | 72 899 | 33 336 | 46 |
| | of which: Universities | | ... | ... | ... | 72 899 | 33 336 | 46 |
| Madagascar | All institutions | 1970/71 | 317 | 58 | 18 | 5 738 | 1 825 | 32 |
| | of which: Universities | | 155 | 32 | 21 | 4 025 | 1 275 | 32 |
| | All institutions | 1975/76 | ... | ... | ... | 8 385 | 4 350 | 52 |
| | of which: Universities | | ... | ... | ... | 8 385 | 4 350 | 52 |
| | All institutions | 1980/81 | 451 | ... | ... | 22 632 | ... | ... |
| | of which: Universities | | 451 | ... | ... | 22 632 | ... | ... |
| | All institutions | 1985/86 | 773 | ... | ... | 38 310 | 14 703 | 38 |
| | of which: Universities | | 773 | ... | ... | 38 310 | 14 703 | 38 |
| | All institutions | 1990/91 | 939 | 251 | 27 | 35 824 | 16 079 | 45 |
| | of which: Universities | | 939 | 251 | 27 | 35 824 | 16 079 | 45 |
| | All institutions | 1992/93 | 855 | ... | ... | 42 681 | ... | ... |
| | of which: Universities | | 808 | 243 | 30 | 33 202 | 14 866 | 45 |
| | All institutions | 1993/94 | 880 | ... | ... | 35 940 | ... | ... |
| | of which: Universities | | 880 | ... | ... | 27 319 | ... | ... |
| | All institutions | 1994/95 | ... | ... | ... | 29 998 | 13 639 | 45 |
| | of which: Universities | | ... | ... | ... | (8) 29 760 | (8) 13 596 | 46 |
| | All institutions | 1995/96 | 965 | 277 | 29 | 28 814 | 12 930 | 45 |
| | of which: Universities | | 909 | 265 | 29 | 20 763 | 9 460 | 46 |
| | All institutions | 1996/97 | ... | ... | ... | 26 715 | 12 004 | 45 |
| | of which: Universities | | 921 | 270 | 29 | 18 458 | 8 482 | 46 |
| Malawi | All institutions | 1970/71 | ... | ... | ... | ... | ... | ... |
| | of which: Universities | | 147 | 19 | 13 | 980 | 173 | 18 |
| | All institutions | 1975/76 | 232 | ... | ... | 1 903 | ... | ... |
| | of which: Universities | | 150 | 14 | 9 | 1 148 | 138 | 12 |
| | All institutions | 1980/81 | 256 | ... | ... | 2 591 | 697 | 27 |
| | of which: Universities | | 173 | 34 | 20 | 1 722 | 427 | 25 |
| | All institutions | 1985/86 | 427 | ... | ... | 3 057 | 699 | 23 |
| | of which: Universities | | 278 | ... | ... | 1 974 | 359 | 18 |
| | All institutions | 1990/91 | ... | ... | ... | 4 829 | 1 275 | 26 |
| | of which: Universities | | ... | ... | ... | 3 117 | 715 | 23 |
| | All institutions | 1991/92 | ... | ... | ... | 4 947 | 1 326 | 27 |
| | of which: Universities | | ... | ... | ... | 3 247 | 766 | 24 |

II.7 Tertiary education: teaching staff and students
Enseignement supérieur: personnel enseignant et étudiants
Enseñanza superior: personal docente y estudiantes

| Country / Pays / País | Type of institution / Type d'établissement / Tipo de establecimiento | Year / Année / Año | Teaching staff / Personnel enseignant / Personal docente | | | Students enrolled / Étudiants inscrits / Estudiantes matriculados | | |
|---|---|---|---|---|---|---|---|---|
| | | | Total | Female Féminin Femenino | % F | Total | Female Féminin Femenino | % F |
| Malawi (cont) | All institutions | 1992/93 | ... | ... | ... | 5 052 | 1 225 | 24 |
| | of which: Universities | | ... | ... | ... | 3 521 | 775 | 22 |
| | All institutions | 1993/94 | 447 | ... | ... | 5 346 | 1 450 | 27 |
| | of which: Universities | | 309 | 74 | 24 | 3 684 | 860 | 23 |
| | All institutions | 1994/95 | 533 | ... | ... | 5 358 | 1 588 | 30 |
| | of which: Universities | | 306 | 94 | 31 | 3 601 | 888 | 25 |
| | All institutions | 1995/96 | 531 | ... | ... | 5 561 | 1 685 | 30 |
| | of which: Universities | | 329 | 99 | 30 | 3 872 | 955 | 25 |
| Mali | All institutions | 1970/71 | 151 | 10 | 7 | 731 | 77 | 11 |
| | of which: Universities | | - | - | - | - | - | - |
| | All institutions | 1975/76 | ... | ... | ... | 2 936 | 302 | 10 |
| | of which: Universities | | ... | ... | ... | 2 936 | 302 | 10 |
| | All institutions | 1981/82 | 475 | ... | ... | 4 498 | 495 | 11 |
| | of which: Universities | | 475 | ... | ... | 4 498 | 495 | 11 |
| | All institutions | 1985/86 | ... | ... | ... | 6 768 | 874 | 13 |
| | of which: Universities | | ... | ... | ... | 6 768 | 874 | 13 |
| | All institutions | 1990/91 | ... | ... | ... | 4 780 | 651 | 14 |
| | of which: Universities | | ... | ... | ... | 4 780 | 651 | 14 |
| | All institutions | 1991/92 | ... | ... | ... | 6 273 | 862 | 14 |
| | of which: Universities | | ... | ... | ... | 6 273 | 862 | 14 |
| | All institutions | 1992/93 | ... | ... | ... | 7 507 | 1 126 | 15 |
| | of which: Universities | | ... | ... | ... | 7 507 | 1 126 | 15 |
| | All institutions | 1994/95 | ... | ... | ... | 8 249 | 1 221 | 15 |
| | of which: Universities | | ... | ... | ... | 8 249 | 1 221 | 15 |
| | All institutions | 1995/96 | ... | ... | ... | 9 595 | 1 602 | 17 |
| | of which: Universities | | ... | ... | ... | 9 595 | 1 602 | 17 |
| | All institutions | 1996/97 | 796 | ... | ... | 13 679 | 2 637 | 19 |
| | of which: Universities | | 796 | ... | ... | 13 679 | 2 637 | 19 |
| | All institutions | 1997/98 | ... | ... | ... | 13 847 | 2 762 | 20 |
| | of which: Universities | | ... | ... | ... | 13 847 | 2 762 | 20 |
| Mauritania | All institutions | 1985/86 | ... | ... | ... | 4 526 | ... | ... |
| | of which: Universities | | ... | ... | ... | ... | ... | ... |
| | All institutions | 1990/91 | 266 | ... | ... | 5 339 | 751 | 14 |
| | of which: Universities | | 110 | ... | ... | 4 495 | 640 | 14 |
| | All institutions | 1991/92 | 250 | ... | ... | 5 850 | 867 | 15 |
| | of which: Universities | | 135 | ... | ... | 4 948 | 696 | 14 |
| | All institutions | 1992/93 | 266 | ... | ... | 7 501 | 1 112 | 15 |
| | of which: Universities | | 115 | ... | ... | 6 681 | 998 | 15 |
| | All institutions | 1993/94 | 270 | ... | ... | 7 675 | 1 320 | 17 |
| | of which: Universities | | 152 | ... | ... | 6 861 | 1 204 | 18 |
| | All institutions | 1994/95 | 270 | ... | ... | 7 775 | 1 328 | 17 |
| | of which: Universities | | 152 | ... | ... | 6 965 | 1 215 | 17 |
| | All institutions | 1995/96 | 270 | ... | ... | 8 496 | 1 486 | 17 |
| | of which: Universities | | 214 | ... | ... | 8 171 | 1 463 | 18 |
| Mauritius | All institutions | 1970/71 | ... | ... | ... | 1 975 | 92 | 5 |
| | of which: Universities | | ... | ... | ... | ... | ... | ... |
| | All institutions | 1975/76 | 155 | 9 | 6 | 1 096 | 150 | 14 |
| | of which: Universities | | ... | ... | ... | ... | ... | ... |
| | All institutions | 1980/81 | 210 | 32 | 15 | 1 038 | 317 | 31 |
| | of which: Universities | | 125 | 8 | 6 | 470 | 88 | 19 |
| | All institutions | 1985/86 | 236 | 27 | 11 | 1 161 | 421 | 36 |
| | of which: Universities | | 130 | 8 | 6 | 507 | 114 | 22 |
| | All institutions | 1990/91 | 414 | 81 | 20 | 3 485 | 1 273 | 37 |
| | of which: Universities | | 274 | 42 | 15 | 1 658 | 530 | 32 |
| | All institutions | 1991/92 | 526 | 124 | 24 | 4 032 | 1 671 | 41 |
| | of which: Universities | | 306 | 51 | 17 | 1 799 | 588 | 33 |

Tertiary education: teaching staff and students  II.7
Enseignement supérieur: personnel enseignant et étudiants
Enseñanza superior: personal docente y estudiantes

| Country / Pays / País | Type of institution / Type d'établissement / Tipo de establecimiento | Year / Année / Año | Teaching staff / Personnel enseignant / Personal docente — Total | Female / Féminin / Femenino | % F | Students enrolled / Étudiants inscrits / Estudiantes matriculados — Total | Female / Féminin / Femenino | % F |
|---|---|---|---|---|---|---|---|---|
| Mauritius (cont) | All institutions | 1992/93 | ... | ... | ... | ... | ... | ... |
| | of which: Universities | | ... | ... | ... | 1 858 | 596 | 32 |
| | All institutions | 1993/94 | ... | ... | ... | 5 969 | ... | ... |
| | of which: Universities | | ... | ... | ... | 2 208 | 822 | 37 |
| | All institutions | 1994/95 | ... | ... | ... | 5 505 | 2 494 | 45 |
| | of which: Universities | | ... | ... | ... | 2 186 | 927 | 42 |
| | All institutions | 1995/96 | 474 | 122 | 26 | 6 141 | 3 040 | 50 |
| | of which: Universities | | ... | ... | ... | 2 344 | 1 122 | 48 |
| | All institutions | 1996/97 | ... | ... | ... | 7 098 | ... | ... |
| | of which: Universities | | ... | ... | ... | 2 496 | ... | ... |
| | All institutions | 1997/98 | ... | ... | ... | 6 419 | 3 229 | 50 |
| | of which: Universities | | ... | ... | ... | 3 135 | 1 458 | 47 |
| Morocco | All institutions | 1970/71 | (2) 620 | (2) 73 | 12 | 16 097 | 2 674 | 17 |
| | of which: Universities | | 503 | 67 | 13 | 15 199 | 2 635 | 17 |
| | All institutions | 1975/76 | 1 642 | ... | ... | 45 322 | 8 440 | 19 |
| | of which: Universities | | 937 | 160 | 17 | 35 081 | 6 726 | 19 |
| | All institutions | 1980/81 | ... | ... | ... | 112 405 | ... | ... |
| | of which: Universities | | 2 757 | (4) 486 | ... | 86 731 | 21 663 | 25 |
| | All institutions | 1985/86 | (9) 6 964 | ... | ... | 181 087 | 58 549 | 32 |
| | of which: Universities | | 5 310 | (4) 889 | ... | 150 795 | 49 545 | 33 |
| | All institutions | 1990/91 | ... | ... | ... | 255 667 | 92 878 | 36 |
| | of which: Universities | | ... | ... | ... | 206 725 | 76 763 | 37 |
| | All institutions | 1991/92 | (9)(10) 9 328 | ... | ... | (9) 253 390 | (9) 96 058 | 38 |
| | of which: Universities | | 6 865 | 1 432 | 21 | 216 873 | 82 066 | 38 |
| | All institutions | 1992/93 | (9)(10) 9 914 | ... | ... | (9) 267 671 | (9) 104 598 | 39 |
| | of which: Universities | | 7 327 | 1 560 | 21 | 230 081 | 89 593 | 39 |
| | All institutions | 1993/94 | (9)(10) 10 649 | ... | ... | (9) 276 402 | (9) 110 808 | 40 |
| | of which: Universities | | 7 777 | 1 678 | 22 | 234 946 | 94 260 | 40 |
| | All institutions | 1994/95 | (10) 13 155 | ... | ... | 294 502 | 121 042 | 41 |
| | of which: Universities | | 8 562 | 1 901 | 22 | 242 053 | 100 278 | 41 |
| | All institutions | 1996/97 | ... | ... | ... | 311 743 | 128 152 | 41 |
| | of which: Universities | | ... | ... | ... | ... | ... | ... |
| Mozambique | All institutions | 1970/71 | 210 | ... | ... | 1 982 | ... | ... |
| | of which: Universities | | 193 | 25 | 13 | 1 887 | 875 | 46 |
| | All institutions | 1980/81 | *300 | ... | ... | *1 000 | ... | ... |
| | of which: Universities | | *300 | ... | ... | *1 000 | ... | ... |
| | All institutions | 1985/86 | 331 | 70 | 21 | 1 442 | 332 | 23 |
| | of which: Universities | | 331 | 70 | 21 | 1 442 | 332 | 23 |
| | All institutions | 1992/93 | 720 | 182 | 25 | 4 600 | 1 211 | 26 |
| | of which: Universities | | 720 | 182 | 25 | 4 600 | 1 211 | 26 |
| | All institutions | 1993/94 | 877 | 173 | 20 | 5 250 | 1 357 | 26 |
| | of which: Universities | | 877 | 173 | 20 | 5 250 | 1 357 | 26 |
| | All institutions | 1994/95 | 833 | 186 | 22 | 6 129 | 1 601 | 26 |
| | of which: Universities | | 833 | 186 | 22 | 6 129 | 1 601 | 26 |
| | All institutions | 1995/96 | 715 | 152 | 21 | 6 639 | 1 682 | 25 |
| | of which: Universities | | 715 | 152 | 21 | 6 639 | 1 682 | 25 |
| | All institutions | 1996/97 | 915 | ... | ... | 7 143 | 1 747 | 24 |
| | of which: Universities | | 915 | ... | ... | 7 143 | 1 747 | 24 |
| Namibia | All institutions | 1991 | 331 | 165 | 50 | 4 157 | 2 664 | 64 |
| | of which: Universities | | 141 | 71 | 50 | 1 496 | 978 | 65 |
| | All institutions | 1994 | ... | ... | ... | 9 714 | 5 969 | 61 |
| | of which: Universities | | ... | ... | ... | ... | ... | ... |
| | All institutions | 1995 | ... | ... | ... | 11 344 | 6 904 | 61 |
| | of which: Universities | | ... | ... | ... | ... | ... | ... |

II.7 Tertiary education: teaching staff and students
Enseignement supérieur: personnel enseignant et étudiants
Enseñanza superior: personal docente y estudiantes

| Country<br>Pays<br>País | Type of institution<br>Type<br>d'établissement<br>Tipo de<br>establecimiento | Year<br>Année<br>Año | Teaching staff<br>Personnel enseignant<br>Personal docente | | | Students enrolled<br>Étudiants inscrits<br>Estudiantes matriculados | | | |
|---|---|---|---|---|---|---|---|---|---|
| | | | Total | Female<br>Féminin<br>Femenino | %<br>F | | Total | Female<br>Féminin<br>Femenino | %<br>F |
| Niger | All institutions<br>of which: Universities | 1970/71 | -<br>- | -<br>- | -<br>- | | -<br>- | -<br>- | -<br>- |
| | All institutions<br>of which: Universities | 1975/76 | 74<br>74 | 11<br>11 | 15<br>15 | | 541<br>541 | 56<br>56 | 10<br>10 |
| | All institutions<br>of which: Universities | 1980/81 | 224<br>224 | 29<br>29 | 13<br>13 | | 1 435<br>1 435 | 285<br>285 | 20<br>20 |
| | All institutions<br>of which: Universities | 1991/92 | 232<br>232 | 26<br>26 | 11<br>11 | | 4 513<br>4 513 | ...<br>... | ...<br>... |
| Nigeria | All institutions<br>of which: Universities | 1970 | ...<br>... | ...<br>... | ...<br>... | (11)<br> | 15 560<br>14 510 | (11) 2 286<br>2 066 | 15<br>14 |
| | All institutions<br>of which: Universities | 1975/76 | ...<br>5 019 | ...<br>... | ...<br>... | | 44 964<br>32 971 | ...<br>5 114 | ...<br>16 |
| | All institutions<br>of which: Universities | 1980/81 | 10 742<br>5 475 | ...<br>589 | ...<br>11 | | 150 072<br>70 395 | ...<br>... | ...<br>... |
| | All institutions<br>of which: Universities | 1985/86 | 18 010<br>11 016 | 2 326<br>1 359 | 13<br>12 | | 266 679<br>135 783 | 70 724<br>32 540 | 27<br>24 |
| | All institutions<br>of which: Universities | 1993/94 | ...<br>12 031 | ...<br>... | ...<br>... | | ...<br>207 982 | ...<br>... | ...<br>... |
| Rwanda | All institutions<br>of which: Universities | 1970/71 | 96<br>66 | 10<br>5 | 10<br>8 | | 571<br>411 | 53<br>38 | 9<br>9 |
| | All institutions<br>of which: Universities | 1975/76 | 175<br>89 | ...<br>... | ...<br>... | | 1 108<br>672 | ...<br>... | ...<br>... |
| | All institutions<br>of which: Universities | 1980/81 | 240<br>126 | 21<br>11 | 9<br>9 | | 1 243<br>920 | 122<br>101 | 10<br>11 |
| | All institutions<br>of which: Universities | 1985/86 | 331<br>284 | 20<br>19 | 6<br>7 | | 1 987<br>1 669 | 269<br>252 | 14<br>15 |
| Senegal | All institutions<br>of which: Universities | 1975/76 | ...<br>412 | ...<br>... | ...<br>... | | ...<br>8 213 | ...<br>1 428 | ...<br>17 |
| | All institutions<br>of which: Universities | 1980/81 | 1 085<br>652 | ...<br>... | ...<br>... | | 13 626<br>12 673 | 2 507<br>2 412 | 18<br>19 |
| | All institutions<br>of which: Universities | 1985/86 | ...<br>710 | ...<br>88 | ...<br>12 | | 13 354<br>12 711 | ...<br>2 640 | ...<br>21 |
| | All institutions<br>of which: Universities | 1990/91 | ...<br>... | ...<br>... | ...<br>... | | 18 689<br>... | ...<br>... | ...<br>... |
| | All institutions<br>of which: Universities | 1991/92 | 949<br>... | 124<br>... | 13<br>... | | 21 562<br>... | 5 262<br>... | 24<br>... |
| | All institutions<br>of which: Universities | 1992/93 | 965<br>... | ...<br>... | ...<br>... | | 23 001<br>... | ...<br>... | ...<br>... |
| | All institutions<br>of which: Universities | 1993/94 | ...<br>... | ...<br>... | ...<br>... | | 24 653<br>... | ...<br>... | ...<br>... |
| | All institutions<br>of which: Universities | 1994/95 | ...<br>... | ...<br>... | ...<br>... | | 24 081<br>... | ...<br>... | ...<br>... |
| Seychelles | All institutions<br>of which: Universities | 1970 | 7<br>- | 3<br>- | 43<br>- | | 87<br>- | 81<br>- | 93<br>- |
| | All institutions<br>of which: Universities | 1980 | 28<br>- | 16<br>- | 57<br>- | | 144<br>- | 128<br>- | 89<br>- |
| | All institutions<br>of which: Universities | 1985 | -<br>- | -<br>- | -<br>- | | -<br>- | -<br>- | -<br>- |
| Sierra Leone | All institutions<br>of which: Universities | 1980/81 | 270<br>270 | ...<br>... | ...<br>... | | 2 166<br>2 166 | ...<br>... | ...<br>... |
| | All institutions<br>of which: Universities | 1985/86 | ...<br>... | ...<br>... | ...<br>... | | 5 690<br>2 386 | ...<br>447 | ...<br>19 |
| | All institutions<br>of which: Universities | 1990/91 | 600<br>257 | ...<br>... | ...<br>... | | 4 742<br>2 571 | ...<br>... | ...<br>... |

Tertiary education: teaching staff and students
Enseignement supérieur: personnel enseignant et étudiants
Enseñanza superior: personal docente y estudiantes

II.7

| Country<br>Pays<br>País | Type of institution<br>Type d'établissement<br>Tipo de establecimiento | Year<br>Année<br>Año | Teaching staff<br>Personnel enseignant<br>Personal docente | | | | Students enrolled<br>Étudiants inscrits<br>Estudiantes matriculados | | | |
|---|---|---|---|---|---|---|---|---|---|---|
| | | | | Total | Female<br>Féminin<br>Femenino | %<br>F | | Total | Female<br>Féminin<br>Femenino | %<br>F |
| Somalia | All institutions<br>of which: Universities | 1970/71 | | 58<br>58 | -<br>- | -<br>- | | 964<br>964 | *125<br>*125 | *13<br>*13 |
| | All institutions<br>of which: Universities | 1975/76 | | 324<br>286 | ...<br>... | ...<br>... | | 2 040<br>1 936 | 218<br>192 | 11<br>10 |
| South Africa | All institutions<br>of which: Universities | 1970 | | ...<br>... | ...<br>... | ...<br>... | | 82 697<br>... | ...<br>... | ...<br>... |
| | All institutions<br>of which: Universities | 1990 | (12)<br> | 16 697<br>... | (12)<br> | 5 756<br>... | 34<br>... | (12)<br> | 439 007<br>... | (12)<br> | 195 043<br>... | 44<br>... |
| | All institutions<br>of which: Universities | 1991 | (12)<br> | 16 754<br>... | <br> | ...<br>... | ...<br>... | (12)<br> | 467 129<br>... | (12)<br> | 213 229<br>... | 46<br>... |
| | All institutions<br>of which: Universities | 1992 | (12)<br> | 16 861<br>... | <br> | ...<br>... | ...<br>... | (12)<br> | 490 112<br>... | (12)<br> | 227 712<br>... | 46<br>... |
| | All institutions<br>of which: Universities | 1993 | (12)<br> | 21 225<br>... | (12)<br> | 7 560<br>... | 36<br>... | (12)<br> | 552 948<br>... | (12)<br> | 255 572<br>... | 46<br>... |
| | All institutions<br>of which: Universities | 1994 | | 27 099<br>... | 10 132<br>... | 37<br>... | | 617 897<br>... | 296 844<br>... | 48<br>... |
| Sudan | All institutions<br>of which: Universities | 1970/71 | | 1 153<br>772 | ...<br>... | ...<br>... | | 14 308<br>12 057 | 1 852<br>1 491 | 13<br>12 |
| | All institutions<br>of which: Universities | 1975/76 | | 1 420<br>1 178 | 97<br>51 | 7<br>4 | | 21 342<br>19 208 | 3 408<br>2 973 | 16<br>15 |
| | All institutions<br>of which: Universities | 1980/81 | | 1 276<br>1 027 | 98<br>41 | 8<br>4 | | 28 788<br>25 699 | 7 791<br>7 026 | 27<br>27 |
| | All institutions<br>of which: Universities | 1985/86 | | 2 165<br>1 635 | 213<br>133 | 10<br>8 | | 37 367<br>33 934 | 13 742<br>13 090 | 37<br>39 |
| | All institutions<br>of which: Universities | 1990/91 | | ...<br>2 043 | ...<br>265 | ...<br>13 | | 59 824 | 28 615 | 48 |
| Swaziland | All institutions<br>of which: Universities | 198586 | | ...<br>115 | ...<br>... | ...<br>... | | 2 732<br>1 287 | ...<br>... | ...<br>... |
| | All institutions<br>of which: Universities | 1990/91 | | 447<br>231 | 168<br>61 | 38<br>26 | | 3 198<br>1 677 | 1 371<br>732 | 43<br>44 |
| | All institutions<br>of which: Universities | 1991/92 | | 452<br>240 | 183<br>71 | 40<br>30 | | 3 224<br>1 689 | 1 510<br>740 | 47<br>44 |
| | All institutions<br>of which: Universities | 1992/93 | | ...<br>247 | ...<br>71 | ...<br>29 | (13)<br> | 3 023<br>1 739 | (13)<br> | 1 280<br>777 | 42<br>45 |
| | All institutions<br>of which: Universities | 1993/94 | | 515<br>278 | ...<br>73 | ...<br>26 | (13)<br> | 4 183<br>2 466 | (13)<br> | 1 866<br>1 184 | 45<br>48 |
| | All institutions<br>of which: Universities | 1994/95 | | ...<br>273 | ...<br>76 | ...<br>28 | | ...<br>2 581 | ...<br>1 222 | ...<br>47 |
| | All institutions<br>of which: Universities | 1995/96 | | ...<br>269 | ...<br>78 | ...<br>29 | | ...<br>2 697 | ...<br>1 259 | ...<br>47 |
| | All institutions<br>of which: Universities | 1996/97 | | 467<br>257 | 187<br>81 | 40<br>32 | | 5 658<br>3 438 | 2 927<br>... | 52<br>... |
| Togo | All institutions<br>of which: Universities | 1970/71 | | ...<br>48 | ...<br>12 | ...<br>25 | | 886<br>845 | ....<br>102 | ...<br>12 |
| | All institutions<br>of which: Universities | 1975/76 | | ...<br>236 | ...<br>39 | ...<br>17 | | 2 353<br>2 167 | 323<br>308 | 14<br>14 |
| | All institutions<br>of which: Universities | 1980/81 | | 297<br>272 | 37<br>35 | 12<br>13 | | 4 750<br>4 345 | 703<br>664 | 15<br>15 |
| | All institutions<br>of which: Universities | 1985/86 | | ...<br>269 | ...<br>33 | ...<br>12 | | ...<br>5 055 | ...<br>678 | ...<br>13 |
| | All institutions<br>of which: Universities | 1990/91 | | 396<br>320 | 38<br>31 | 10<br>10 | | 8 969<br>8 755 | 1 252<br>1 241 | 14<br>14 |
| | All institutions<br>of which: Universities | 1991/92 | | 396<br>324 | 38<br>31 | 10<br>10 | | 10 224<br>10 018 | 1 219<br>1 210 | 12<br>12 |
| | All institutions<br>of which: Universities | 1992/93 | | 422<br>345 | 39<br>32 | 9<br>9 | | 8 925<br>8 699 | 1 092<br>1 084 | 12<br>12 |

Tertiary education: teaching staff and students
Enseignement supérieur: personnel enseignant et étudiants
Enseñanza superior: personal docente y estudiantes

| Country / Pays / País | Type of institution / Type d'établissement / Tipo de establecimiento | Year / Année / Año | Teaching staff Personnel enseignant Personal docente | | | Students enrolled Étudiants inscrits Estudiantes matriculados | | |
|---|---|---|---|---|---|---|---|---|
| | | | Total | Female Féminin Femenino | % F | Total | Female Féminin Femenino | % F |
| Togo (cont) | All institutions of which: Universities | 1993/94 | 392 328 | 37 33 | 9 10 | 9 320 9 122 | 1 127 1 119 | 12 12 |
| | All institutions of which: Universities | 1994/95 | 416 344 | 34 31 | 8 9 | 11 173 10 995 | 1 487 1 480 | 13 13 |
| | All institutions of which: Universities | 1995/96 | 443 374 | 36 32 | 8 9 | 11 639 11 462 | 1 745 1 737 | 15 15 |
| | All institutions of which: Universities | 1996/97 | 443 ... | 45 ... | 10 ... | 13 124 ... | 2 267 ... | 17 ... |
| Tunisia | All institutions of which: Universities | 1970/71 | ... ... | ... ... | ... ... | (1) 10 347 (1) 10 347 | (1) 2 136 (1) 2 136 | 21 21 |
| | All institutions of which: Universities | 1975/76 | 1 427 1 427 | 217 217 | 15 15 | 20 505 20 505 | 5 273 5 273 | 26 26 |
| | All institutions of which: Universities | 1980/81 | 4 031 4 031 | 357 357 | 9 9 | 31 827 31 827 | 9 437 9 437 | 30 30 |
| | All institutions of which: Universities | 1985/86 | 5 194 5 194 | ... ... | ... ... | 41 594 41 594 | 14 824 14 824 | 36 36 |
| | All institutions of which: Universities | 1990/91 | 4 550 ... | 984 ... | 22 ... | 68 535 ... | 26 989 ... | 39 ... |
| | All institutions of which: Universities | 1991/92 | 4 941 ... | ... ... | ... ... | 76 097 ... | 30 832 ... | 41 ... |
| | All institutions of which: Universities | 1992/93 | 5 360 ... | 1 284 ... | 24 ... | 87 780 ... | 36 121 ... | 41 ... |
| | All institutions of which: Universities | 1993/94 | 5 655 ... | 1 386 ... | 25 ... | 96 101 ... | 40 570 ... | 42 ... |
| | All institutions of which: Universities | 1994/95 | 5 944 ... | 1 519 ... | 26 ... | 102 682 ... | 44 230 ... | 43 ... |
| | All institutions of which: Universities | 1995/96 | 6 481 5 959 | 1 694 1 596 | 26 27 | 112 634 107 603 | 49 242 47 578 | 44 44 |
| | All institutions of which: Universities | 1996/97 | 6 641 ... | 1 766 ... | 27 ... | 121 787 115 485 | 54 278 52 457 | 45 45 |
| Uganda | All institutions of which: Universities | 197071 | 481 350 | ... ... | ... ... | 4 232 2 953 | 744 518 | 18 18 |
| | All institutions of which: Universities | 1975/76 | 617 444 | 58 33 | 9 7 | 5 474 3 914 | 988 619 | 18 16 |
| | All institutions of which: Universities | 1980/81 | ... ... | ... ... | ... ... | 5 856 4 035 | 1 323 795 | 23 20 |
| | All institutions of which: Universities | 1985/86 | ... *500 | ... ... | ... ... | 10 103 5 390 | 2 349 1 227 | 23 23 |
| | All institutions of which: Universities | 1990/91 | 1 555 725 | ... ... | ... ... | 17 578 7 618 | 4 949 1 919 | 28 25 |
| | All institutions of which: Universities | 1991/92 | 2 024 1 163 | 266 180 | 13 15 | 21 281 8 552 | 5 856 2 183 | 28 26 |
| | All institutions of which: Universities | 1992/93 | 2 327 1 351 | 344 244 | 15 18 | 21 489 9 017 | 6 132 2 516 | 29 28 |
| | All institutions of which: Universities | 1993/94 | 1 959 1 080 | 276 186 | 14 17 | 24 122 9 959 | 7 202 3 033 | 30 30 |
| | All institutions of which: Universities | 1994/95 | 2 029 1 073 | 297 *192 | 15 *18 | 27 586 10 869 | 8 721 3 484 | 32 32 |
| | All institutions of which: Universities | 1995/96 | 1 799 ... | 334 ... | 19 ... | 30 266 12 800 | 9 860 4 416 | 33 35 |
| | All institutions of which: Universities | 1996/97 | (14) 2 606 1 498 | (14) 463 319 | 18 21 | (14) 34 773 15 197 | (14) 11 542 5 591 | 33 37 |
| United Republic of Tanzania | All institutions of which: Universities | 1970/71 | ... ... | ... ... | ... ... | 2 027 1 823 | 335 294 | 17 16 |
| | All institutions of which: Universities | 1975/76 | ... 434 | ... ... | ... ... | 3 064 2 644 | 420 270 | 14 10 |

Tertiary education: teaching staff and students
Enseignement supérieur: personnel enseignant et étudiants
Enseñanza superior: personal docente y estudiantes

II.7

| Country | Type of institution | Year | Teaching staff Personnel enseignant Personal docente | | | Students enrolled Étudiants inscrits Estudiantes matriculados | | | |
| Pays | Type d'établissement | Année | | | | | | | |
| País | Tipo de establecimiento | Año | Total | Female Féminin Femenino | % F | | Total | Female Féminin Femenino | % F |
|---|---|---|---|---|---|---|---|---|---|
| United Republic of Tanzania (cont) | All institutions of which: Universities | 1985/86 | 1 239 1 025 | ... ... | ... ... | (2)(15) (2)(15) | 4 863 3 414 | (2)(15) 710 (2)(15) 547 | 15 16 |
| | All institutions of which: Universities | 1991/92 | ... ... | ... ... | ... ... | | 7 468 3 453 | 1 187 663 | 16 19 |
| | All institutions of which: Universities | 1992/93 | ... ... | ... ... | ... ... | | 7 981 3 735 | 1 303 695 | 16 19 |
| | All institutions of which: Universities | 1993/94 | ... ... | ... ... | ... ... | | 9 350 4 001 | 1 436 699 | 15 17 |
| | All institutions of which: Universities | 1994/95 | ... ... | ... ... | ... ... | | 10 457 4 198 | 1 811 817 | 17 19 |
| | All institutions of which: Universities | 1995/96 | 1 650 1 168 | 183 143 | 11 12 | | 12 776 5 881 | 2 075 1 012 | 16 17 |
| | All institutions of which: Universities | 1996/97 | 1 725 ... | ... ... | ... ... | | 14 882 ... | 2 612 ... | 18 ... |
| | All institutions of which: Universities | 1997/98 | 1 822 ... | ... ... | ... ... | | 17 812 ... | 3 510 ... | 20 ... |
| Zambia | All institutions of which: Universities | 1970 | 219 189 | ... 16 | ... 8 | | 1 433 1 231 | 214 182 | 15 15 |
| | All institutions of which: Universities | 1975 | ... ... | ... ... | ... ... | | 8 403 2 354 | 1 170 395 | 14 17 |
| | All institutions of which: Universities | 1980 | ... ... | ... ... | ... ... | | 3 425 | ... ... | ... ... |
| | All institutions of which: Universities | 1985 | ... 613 | ... 78 | ... 13 | | ... 4 680 | ... 810 | ... 17 |
| | All institutions of which: Universities | 1990 | ... ... | ... ... | ... ... | | 15 343 7 361 | ... ... | ... ... |
| Zimbabwe | All institutions of which: Universities | 1975 | ... ... | ... ... | ... ... | | 8 479 1 355 | ... ... | ... ... |
| | All institutions of which: Universities | 1980 | ... ... | ... ... | ... ... | | 8 339 1 873 | ... ... | ... ... |
| | All institutions of which: Universities | 1985 | ... ... | ... ... | ... ... | | 30 843 4 742 | ... ... | ... ... |
| | All institutions of which: Universities | 1990 | 2 308 558 | ... ... | ... ... | | 49 361 9 300 | ... ... | ... ... |
| | All institutions of which: Universities | 1991 | 2 585 585 | ... 153 | ... 26 | | 52 051 9 784 | *17 262 2 262 | *33 23 |
| | All institutions of which: Universities | 1992 | 3 076 976 | ... 153 | ... 16 | | 61 553 9 048 | 19 940 2 340 | 32 26 |
| | All institutions of which: Universities | 1993 | ... ... | ... ... | ... ... | (16) | 37 286 7 829 | ... ... | ... ... |
| | All institutions of which: Universities | 1994 | ... ... | ... ... | ... ... | (16) | 40 998 11 218 | (16) 14 738 3 084 | 36 27 |
| | All institutions of which: Universities | 1995 | (16) 3 581 (8) 1 618 | ... ... | ... ... | (16) (8) | 45 593 13 045 | (16) 15 867 (8) 2 673 | 35 20 |
| | All institutions of which: Universities | 1996 | ... ... | ... ... | ... ... | (16) | 46 673 10 322 | (16) 17 016 3 018 | 36 29 |
| **North America** | | | | | | | | | |
| Bahamas | All institutions of which: Universities | 1980/81 | 127 ... | ... ... | ... ... | | 4 093 ... | ... ... | ... ... |
| | All institutions of which: Universities | 1985/86 | ... ... | ... ... | ... ... | | 4 531 ... | ... ... | ... ... |
| Barbados | All institutions of which: Universities | 1970/71 | ... ... | ... ... | ... ... | | 763 459 | 349 179 | 46 39 |
| | All institutions of which: Universities | 1975/76 | ... ... | ... ... | ... ... | | 1 065 | ... ... | ... ... |

II.7    Tertiary education: teaching staff and students
Enseignement supérieur: personnel enseignant et étudiants
Enseñanza superior: personal docente y estudiantes

| Country / Pays / País | Type of institution / Type d'établissement / Tipo de establecimiento | Year / Année / Año | Teaching staff Personnel enseignant Personal docente | | | Students enrolled Étudiants inscrits Estudiantes matriculados | | |
|---|---|---|---|---|---|---|---|---|
| | | | Total | Female Féminin Femenino | % F | Total | Female Féminin Femenino | % F |
| Barbados (cont) | All institutions | 1980/81 | 317 | 90 | 28 | 4 033 | 2 170 | 54 |
| | of which: Universities | | 140 | 32 | 23 | 1 606 | 778 | 48 |
| | All institutions | 1990/91 | ... | ... | ... | 6 651 | ... | ... |
| | of which: Universities | | ... | ... | ... | 2 408 | ... | ... |
| | All institutions | 1991/92 | ... | ... | ... | 6 888 | 3 797 | 55 |
| | of which: Universities | | ... | ... | ... | 2 580 | 1 523 | 59 |
| | All institutions | 1992/93 | ... | ... | ... | 6 252 | ... | ... |
| | of which: Universities | | ... | ... | ... | 2 572 | ... | ... |
| | All institutions | 1993/94 | ... | ... | ... | ... | ... | ... |
| | of which: Universities | | ... | ... | ... | 2 811 | ... | ... |
| | All institutions | 1994/95 | ... | ... | ... | ... | ... | ... |
| | of which: Universities | | ... | ... | ... | 2 862 | 1 790 | 63 |
| | All institutions | 1995/96 | ... | ... | ... | ... | ... | ... |
| | of which: Universities | | 159 | ... | ... | 3 064 | 1 903 | 62 |
| | All institutions | 1996/97 | ... | ... | ... | ... | ... | ... |
| | of which: Universities | | ... | ... | ... | *3 275 | ... | ... |
| Bermuda | All institutions | 1980/81 | 67 | 22 | 33 | 608 | 312 | 51 |
| | of which: Universities | | - | - | - | - | - | - |
| Canada | All institutions | 1970/71 | ... | ... | ... | ... | ... | ... |
| | of which: Universities | | 24 612 | 3 140 | 13 | 477 292 | 174 543 | 37 |
| | All institutions | 1975/76 | ... | ... | ... | 1 079 960 | 484 800 | 45 |
| | of which: Universities | | 30 732 | 4 304 | 14 | 546 769 | 234 270 | 43 |
| | All institutions | 1980/81 | (2) 53 434 | (2) 12 565 | 24 | (17) 1 172 750 | (17) 587 720 | 50 |
| | of which: Universities | | (2) 33 015 | (2) 5 105 | 15 | 627 617 | 312 169 | 50 |
| | All institutions | 1985/86 | (2) 57 443 | (2) 13 655 | 24 | 1 639 410 | (17) 736 680 | ... |
| | of which: Universities | | (2) 35 245 | (2) 6 019 | 17 | 752 276 | 392 437 | 52 |
| | All institutions | 1990/91 | (2) 61 682 | (2) 16 085 | 26 | 1 916 801 | 1 038 194 | 54 |
| | of which: Universities | | 37 500 | 7 000 | 19 | 841 330 | 465 426 | 55 |
| | All institutions | 1991/92 | (2) 67 122 | (2) 18 679 | 28 | 1 942 814 | 1 053 723 | 54 |
| | of which: Universities | | 36 800 | 7 560 | 21 | 867 352 | 480 958 | 55 |
| | All institutions | 1992/93 | (18) 158 123 | (18) 53 349 | 34 | (18) 1 746 919 | (18) 924 107 | 53 |
| | of which: Universities | | ... | ... | ... | ... | ... | ... |
| | All institutions | 1993/94 | 174 684 | 59 060 | 34 | 1 776 792 | 935 739 | 53 |
| | of which: Universities | | ... | ... | ... | ... | ... | ... |
| | All institutions | 1994/95 | 176 783 | 59 708 | 34 | 1 783 716 | 942 735 | 53 |
| | of which: Universities | | ... | ... | ... | ... | ... | ... |
| | All institutions | 1995/96 | ... | ... | ... | 1 763 105 | 938 348 | 53 |
| | of which: Universities | | ... | ... | ... | ... | ... | ... |
| Costa Rica (19) | All institutions | 1970 | ... | ... | ... | 15 473 | 6 735 | 44 |
| | of which: Universities | | ... | ... | ... | 12 913 | 4 842 | 37 |
| | All institutions | 1975 | ... | ... | ... | ... | ... | ... |
| | of which: Universities | | ... | ... | ... | 32 794 | ... | ... |
| | All institutions | 1980 | ... | ... | ... | 55 593 | ... | ... |
| | of which: Universities | | 4 382 | ... | ... | 47 340 | ... | ... |
| | All institutions | 1985 | ... | ... | ... | 63 771 | ... | ... |
| | of which: Universities | | ... | ... | ... | 50 047 | ... | ... |
| | All institutions | 1990 | ... | ... | ... | (15) 74 681 | ... | ... |
| | of which: Universities | | ... | ... | ... | (15) 57 541 | ... | ... |
| | All institutions | 1991 | ... | ... | ... | 80 442 | ... | ... |
| | of which: Universities | | ... | ... | ... | 61 364 | ... | ... |
| | All institutions | 1992 | ... | ... | ... | 88 324 | ... | ... |
| | of which: Universities | | ... | ... | ... | 65 268 | ... | ... |
| | All institutions | 1994 | ... | ... | ... | ... | ... | ... |
| | of which: Universities | | ... | ... | ... | (8) 78 819 | ... | ... |
| Cuba | All institutions | 1970/71 | 4 129 | ... | ... | 26 342 | 10 366 | 39 |
| | of which: Universities | | 4 129 | ... | ... | 26 342 | 10 366 | 39 |

Tertiary education: teaching staff and students  II.7
Enseignement supérieur: personnel enseignant et étudiants
Enseñanza superior: personal docente y estudiantes

| Country / Pays / País | Type of institution / Type d'établissement / Tipo de establecimiento | Year / Année / Año | Teaching staff / Personnel enseignant / Personal docente | | | | Students enrolled / Étudiants inscrits / Estudiantes matriculados | | | |
|---|---|---|---|---|---|---|---|---|---|---|
| | | | | Total | Female Féminin Femenino | % F | | Total | Female Féminin Femenino | % F |
| Cuba (cont) | All institutions | 1975/76 | | 5 380 | ... | ... | | 82 688 | ... | ... |
| | of which: Universities | | | 5 380 | ... | ... | | 82 688 | ... | ... |
| | All institutions | 1980/81 | | 10 680 | ... | ... | | 151 733 | 73 413 | 48 |
| | of which: Universities | | | 10 680 | ... | ... | | 151 733 | 73 413 | 48 |
| | All institutions | 1985/86 | | 19 552 | 8 328 | 43 | | 235 224 | 127 054 | 54 |
| | of which: Universities | | | 19 552 | 8 328 | 43 | | 235 224 | 127 054 | 54 |
| | All institutions | 1990/91 | | 24 668 | 10 968 | 44 | | 242 434 | 139 171 | 57 |
| | of which: Universities | | | 24 668 | 10 968 | 44 | | 242 434 | 139 171 | 57 |
| | All institutions | 1991/92 | | 24 915 | 11 355 | 46 | | 224 568 | 130 615 | 58 |
| | of which: Universities | | | 24 915 | 11 355 | 46 | | 224 568 | 130 615 | 58 |
| | All institutions | 1992/93 | | 25 264 | 11 901 | 47 | | 198 474 | 114 584 | 58 |
| | of which: Universities | | | 25 264 | 11 901 | 47 | | 198 474 | 114 584 | 58 |
| | All institutions | 1993/94 | | 24 900 | ... | ... | | 176 228 | 100 199 | 57 |
| | of which: Universities | | | 24 900 | ... | ... | | 176 228 | 100 199 | 57 |
| | All institutions | 1994/95 | | 23 340 | 10 600 | 45 | | 140 815 | 82 164 | 58 |
| | of which: Universities | | | 23 340 | 10 600 | 45 | | 140 815 | 82 164 | 58 |
| | All institutions | 1995/96 | | 22 967 | 10 382 | 45 | | 122 346 | 72 967 | 60 |
| | of which: Universities | | | 22 967 | 10 382 | 45 | | 122 346 | 72 967 | 60 |
| | All institutions | 1996/97 | | 22 574 | 10 253 | 45 | | 111 587 | 67 134 | 60 |
| | of which: Universities | | | 22 574 | 10 253 | 45 | | 111 587 | 67 134 | 60 |
| Dominica | All institutions | 1980/81 | | 17 | 12 | 71 | | 63 | 14 | 22 |
| | of which: Universities | | | - | - | - | | - | - | - |
| | All institutions | 1990/91 | (9) | 34 | (9) 11 | 32 | (9) | 430 | (9) 177 | 41 |
| | of which: Universities | | | - | - | - | | - | - | - |
| | All institutions | 1991/92 | (9) | 40 | (9) 13 | 33 | (9) | 658 | (9) 364 | 55 |
| | of which: Universities | | | - | - | - | | - | - | - |
| | All institutions | 1992/93 | (9) | 34 | (9) 11 | 32 | (9) | 484 | (9) 227 | 47 |
| | of which: Universities | | | - | - | - | | - | - | - |
| Dominican Republic | All institutions | 1970/71 | | ... | ... | ... | | 23 546 | 10 143 | 43 |
| | of which: Universities | | | ... | ... | ... | | 23 098 | 9 883 | 43 |
| | All institutions | 1975/76 | | ... | ... | ... | | ... | ... | ... |
| | of which: Universities | | | 1 435 | ... | ... | | 28 628 | 11 773 | 41 |
| | All institutions | 1985/86 | | 6 539 | ... | ... | | 123 748 | ... | ... |
| | of which: Universities | | | ... | ... | ... | | ... | ... | ... |
| | All institutions | 1996/97 | | 9 041 | 2 863 | 32 | | 176 995 | 101 772 | 57 |
| | of which: Universities | | | ... | ... | ... | | ... | ... | ... |
| El Salvador | All institutions | 1970 | | 751 | 126 | 17 | | 9 515 | ... | ... |
| | of which: Universities | | | 680 | 107 | 16 | | 9 083 | ... | ... |
| | All institutions | 1975 | | 2 137 | 485 | 23 | | 28 281 | 9 468 | 33 |
| | of which: Universities | | | 1 880 | 379 | 20 | | 26 909 | 8 931 | 33 |
| | All institutions | 1982 | | ... | ... | ... | | 46 976 | 18 017 | 38 |
| | of which: Universities | | | ... | ... | ... | | ... | ... | ... |
| | All institutions | 1985 | | 4 197 | 1 054 | 25 | | 70 499 | 30 832 | 44 |
| | of which: Universities | | | 3 109 | 754 | 24 | | 57 131 | 24 019 | 42 |
| | All institutions | 1990 | | 4 216 | 1 097 | 26 | | 78 211 | ... | ... |
| | of which: Universities | | | 3 452 | 895 | 26 | | 66 092 | ... | ... |
| | All institutions | 1993 | | ... | ... | ... | | 95 451 | ... | ... |
| | of which: Universities | | | 4 643 | 3 346 | 72 | (8) | 92 662 | (8) 39 545 | 43 |
| | All institutions | 1994 | | 5 804 | 1 791 | 31 | | 106 795 | 52 876 | 50 |
| | of which: Universities | | (8) | 5 496 | (8) 1 715 | 31 | (8) | 102 725 | (8) 51 000 | 50 |
| | All institutions | 1995 | | 6 304 | 1 753 | 28 | | 114 998 | 58 133 | 51 |
| | of which: Universities | | (8) | 5 965 | (8) 1 685 | 28 | (8) | 110 774 | (8) 56 364 | 51 |
| | All institutions | 1996 | | 5 919 | 1 715 | 29 | | 112 266 | 56 336 | 50 |
| | of which: Universities | | (8) | 5 610 | (8) 1 636 | 29 | (8) | 107 475 | (8) 54 292 | 51 |
| Guatemala | All institutions | 1970 | | 1 314 | ... | ... | | 15 609 | 2 906 | 19 |
| | of which: Universities | | | 1 314 | ... | ... | | 15 609 | 2 906 | 19 |

II.7 Tertiary education: teaching staff and students
Enseignement supérieur: personnel enseignant et étudiants
Enseñanza superior: personal docente y estudiantes

| Country / Pays / País | Type of institution / Type d'établissement / Tipo de establecimiento | Year / Année / Año | Teaching staff Personnel enseignant Personal docente | | | Students enrolled Étudiants inscrits Estudiantes matriculados | | |
|---|---|---|---|---|---|---|---|---|
| | | | Total | Female Féminin Femenino | % F | Total | Female Féminin Femenino | % F |
| Guatemala (cont) | All institutions | 1980 | (20) 4 024 | ... | ... | 50 890 | ... | ... |
| | of which: Universities | | (20) 4 024 | ... | ... | 50 890 | ... | ... |
| | All institutions | 1992 | ... | ... | ... | 70 431 | ... | ... |
| | of which: Universities | | ... | ... | ... | ... | ... | ... |
| | All institutions | 1993 | | ... | ... | 71 567 | ... | ... |
| | of which: Universities | | | ... | ... | ... | ... | ... |
| | All institutions | 1994 | | ... | ... | 77 051 | ... | ... |
| | of which: Universities | | | ... | ... | ... | ... | ... |
| | All institutions | 1995 | | ... | ... | 80 228 | ... | ... |
| | of which: Universities | | | ... | ... | ... | ... | ... |
| Haiti | All institutions | 1975/76 | 408 | 48 | 12 | 2 881 | 691 | 24 |
| | of which: Universities | | 366 | 47 | 13 | 2 467 | 665 | 27 |
| | All institutions | 1980/81 | 690 | 75 | 11 | 4 671 | 1 410 | 30 |
| | of which: Universities | | 523 | 66 | 13 | 3 441 | 1 209 | 35 |
| | All institutions | 1985/86 | 654 | 243 | 37 | 6 288 | 1 625 | 26 |
| | of which: Universities | | 479 | 81 | 17 | 4 471 | 1 276 | 29 |
| Honduras | All institutions | 1970 | ... | ... | ... | ... | ... | ... |
| | of which: Universities | | ... | ... | ... | 4 047 | ... | ... |
| | All institutions | 1975 | 817 | ... | ... | 11 907 | 4 060 | 34 |
| | of which: Universities | | 648 | 116 | 18 | 10 635 | 3 408 | 32 |
| | All institutions | 1980 | 1 653 | ... | ... | 25 825 | 9 736 | 38 |
| | of which: Universities | | 1 439 | ... | ... | 24 021 | 9 025 | 38 |
| | All institutions | 1985 | 2 662 | 917 | 34 | 36 620 | ... | ... |
| | of which: Universities | | 2 274 | 762 | 34 | 30 623 | 12 721 | 42 |
| | All institutions | 1990 | 3 430 | ... | ... | 43 117 | 18 547 | 43 |
| | of which: Universities | | *3 258 | ... | ... | 35 641 | 14 691 | 41 |
| | All institutions | 1991 | ... | ... | ... | 44 365 | 19 590 | 44 |
| | of which: Universities | | ... | ... | ... | 40 388 | 17 390 | 43 |
| | All institutions | 1992 | ... | ... | ... | 47 262 | 20 323 | 43 |
| | of which: Universities | | ... | ... | ... | 43 319 | 18 037 | 42 |
| | All institutions | 1993 | ... | ... | ... | 47 562 | 21 201 | 45 |
| | of which: Universities | | ... | ... | ... | 44 042 | 18 824 | 43 |
| | All institutions | 1994 | 4 078 | 1 165 | 29 | 54 106 | 23 731 | 44 |
| | of which: Universities | | ... | ... | ... | 49 599 | 20 893 | 42 |
| Jamaica | All institutions | 1970/71 | 567 | ... | ... | 6 892 | 2 986 | 43 |
| | of which: Universities | | 291 | ... | ... | 2 886 | 1 271 | 44 |
| | All institutions | 1975/76 | ... | ... | ... | ... | ... | ... |
| | of which: Universities | | ... | ... | ... | 3 963 | ... | ... |
| | All institutions | 1980/81 | ... | ... | ... | 13 999 | ... | ... |
| | of which: Universities | | 397 | ... | ... | 4 548 | ... | ... |
| | All institutions | 1985/86 | ... | ... | ... | ... | ... | ... |
| | of which: Universities | | 295 | 87 | 29 | 5 126 | 2 914 | 57 |
| | All institutions | 1990/91 | ... | ... | ... | 16 018 | ... | ... |
| | of which: Universities | | 418 | ... | ... | 6 083 | 3 785 | 62 |
| | All institutions | 1991/92 | ... | ... | ... | 15 891 | ... | ... |
| | of which: Universities | | 395 | ... | ... | 6 284 | 3 958 | 63 |
| | All institutions | 1992/93 | ... | ... | ... | ... | ... | ... |
| | of which: Universities | | ... | ... | ... | 6 502 | ... | ... |
| | All institutions | 1993/94 | ... | ... | ... | ... | ... | ... |
| | of which: Universities | | ... | ... | ... | 7 229 | ... | ... |
| | All institutions | 1994/95 | ... | ... | ... | ... | ... | ... |
| | of which: Universities | | ... | ... | ... | 7 695 | ... | ... |
| | All institutions | 1995/96 | ... | ... | ... | ... | ... | ... |
| | of which: Universities | | 418 | ... | ... | 8 191 | 3 145 | 38 |

Tertiary education: teaching staff and students  II.7
Enseignement supérieur: personnel enseignant et étudiants
Enseñanza superior: personal docente y estudiantes

| Country / Pays / País | Type of institution / Type d'établissement / Tipo de establecimiento | Year / Année / Año | Teaching staff Personnel enseignant Personal docente | | | | Students enrolled Étudiants inscrits Estudiantes matriculados | | | |
|---|---|---|---|---|---|---|---|---|---|---|
| | | | | Total | Female Féminin Femenino | % F | | Total | Female Féminin Femenino | % F |
| Jamaica (cont) | All institutions | 1996/97 | | ... | ... | ... | | ... | ... | ... |
| | of which: Universities | | | ... | ... | ... | | *8 434 | ... | ... |
| Mexico | All institutions | 1970/71 | | ... | ... | ... | | 247 637 | 49 844 | 20 |
| | of which: Universities | | | ... | ... | ... | | | ... | ... |
| | All institutions | 1975/76 | | 47 529 | ... | ... | | 562 056 | ... | ... |
| | of which: Universities | | | 45 025 | ... | ... | | 520 194 | ... | ... |
| | All institutions | 1980/81 | | 77 653 | ... | ... | | 929 865 | 305 052 | 33 |
| | of which: Universities | | | 72 742 | ... | ... | | 817 558 | 248 062 | 30 |
| | All institutions | 1985/86 | | 108 002 | ... | ... | | 1 207 779 | ... | ... |
| | of which: Universities | | | ... | ... | ... | | 1 199 120 | 454 366 | 38 |
| | All institutions | 1990/91 | | 134 424 | ... | ... | | 1 310 835 | ... | ... |
| | of which: Universities | | | ... | ... | ... | | 1 252 027 | 536 070 | 43 |
| | All institutions | 1991/92 | | ... | ... | ... | | ... | ... | ... |
| | of which: Universities | | | ... | ... | ... | | 1 280 006 | 574 000 | 45 |
| | All institutions | 1992/93 | | ... | ... | ... | | 1 302 590 | 588 571 | 45 |
| | of which: Universities | | | ... | ... | ... | | ... | ... | ... |
| | All institutions | 1993/94 | (21) | 145 789 | ... | ... | (21) | 1 358 271 | (21) 625 736 | 46 |
| | of which: Universities | | | ... | ... | ... | | ... | ... | ... |
| | All institutions | 1994/95 | | 152 630 | ... | ... | | 1 420 461 | 663 396 | 47 |
| | of which: Universities | | | ... | ... | ... | | ... | ... | ... |
| | All institutions | 1995/96 | | 163 843 | ... | ... | | 1 532 846 | 726 526 | 47 |
| | of which: Universities | | | ... | ... | ... | | ... | ... | ... |
| | All institutions | 1996/97 | | 170 350 | ... | ... | | 1 612 318 | 769 394 | 48 |
| | of which: Universities | | | ... | ... | ... | | ... | ... | ... |
| Nicaragua | All institutions | 1970 | | 604 | ... | ... | | 9 385 | 2 987 | 32 |
| | of which: Universities | | | 492 | ... | ... | | 8 648 | 2 673 | 31 |
| | All institutions | 1975 | | 1 066 | ... | ... | | 18 282 | 6 216 | 34 |
| | of which: Universities | | | 911 | ... | ... | | 15 579 | 5 920 | 38 |
| | All institutions | 1980 | | ... | ... | ... | | 35 268 | ... | ... |
| | of which: Universities | | | ... | ... | ... | | 32 958 | ... | ... |
| | All institutions | 1985 | | 2 536 | ... | ... | | 29 001 | 16 355 | 56 |
| | of which: Universities | | | 2 151 | ... | ... | | 24 430 | 14 009 | 57 |
| | All institutions | 1990 | | ... | ... | ... | | 30 733 | 15 963 | 52 |
| | of which: Universities | | | 2 180 | ... | ... | | 29 780 | 15 615 | 52 |
| | All institutions | 1991 | | 2 130 | 635 | 30 | | 31 499 | 15 509 | 49 |
| | of which: Universities | | | 2 058 | 631 | 31 | | 30 483 | 15 103 | 50 |
| | All institutions | 1992 | | 2 274 | 566 | 25 | | 35 730 | 17 795 | 50 |
| | of which: Universities | | | ... | ... | ... | | ... | ... | ... |
| | All institutions | 1995 | | 3 062 | 1 097 | 36 | | 50 769 | 26 066 | 51 |
| | of which: Universities | | | 2 750 | 978 | 36 | | 42 157 | 22 183 | 53 |
| | All institutions | 1997 | | *3 840 | *1 432 | *37 | | *56 558 | *29 757 | *53 |
| | of which: Universities | | | 3 630 | 1 377 | 38 | | 48 758 | 26 317 | 54 |
| Panama | All institutions | 1970 | | 448 | 95 | 21 | | 8 947 | 3 800 | 42 |
| | of which: Universities | | | 448 | 95 | 21 | | 8 947 | 3 800 | 42 |
| | All institutions | 1975 | | 1 519 | ... | ... | | 26 289 | 13 090 | 50 |
| | of which: Universities | | | 1 519 | ... | ... | | 26 289 | 13 090 | 50 |
| | All institutions | 1980 | | 2 673 | ... | ... | | 40 369 | 22 168 | 55 |
| | of which: Universities | | | 2 673 | ... | ... | | 40 369 | 22 168 | 55 |
| | All institutions | 1985 | | 3 986 | ... | ... | | 55 303 | 31 856 | 58 |
| | of which: Universities | | | 3 986 | ... | ... | | 55 303 | 31 856 | 58 |
| | All institutions | 1990 | | 3 328 | ... | ... | | 53 235 | ... | ... |
| | of which: Universities | | | 3 270 | ... | ... | | 52 673 | ... | ... |
| | All institutions | 1991 | | 3 534 | ... | ... | | 58 625 | ... | ... |
| | of which: Universities | | | 3 452 | ... | ... | | 58 039 | ... | ... |
| | All institutions | 1992 | | 3 771 | ... | ... | | 63 848 | ... | ... |
| | of which: Universities | | | 3 724 | ... | ... | | 63 303 | ... | ... |

II.7    Tertiary education: teaching staff and students
Enseignement supérieur: personnel enseignant et étudiants
Enseñanza superior: personal docente y estudiantes

| Country / Pays / País | Type of Institution / Type d'établissement / Tipo de establecimiento | Year / Année / Año | Teaching staff / Personnel enseignant / Personal docente | | | Students enrolled / Étudiants inscrits / Estudiantes matriculados | | |
|---|---|---|---|---|---|---|---|---|
| | | | Total | Female Féminin Femenino | % F | Total | Female Féminin Femenino | % F |
| Panama (cont) | All institutions | 1993 | 4 108 | ... | ... | 69 451 | ... | ... |
| | of which: Universities | | 4 033 | ... | ... | 68 724 | ... | ... |
| | All institutions | 1994 | 4 652 | 1 690 | 36 | 69 437 | 41 169 | 59 |
| | of which: Universities | | 4 576 | 1 654 | 36 | 68 629 | 40 883 | 60 |
| | All institutions | 1995 | 4 747 | ... | ... | 76 798 | ... | ... |
| | of which: Universities | | 4 671 | ... | ... | 75 910 | ... | ... |
| | All institutions | 1996 | 4 979 | ... | ... | 80 980 | ... | ... |
| | of which: Universities | | 4 903 | ... | ... | 80 089 | ... | ... |
| St. Kitts and Nevis | All institutions | 1985/86 | 27 | 9 | 33 | 212 | 90 | 42 |
| | of which: Universities | | - | - | - | - | - | - |
| | All institutions | 1991/92 | 38 | 16 | 42 | 225 | 121 | 54 |
| | of which: Universities | | - | - | - | - | - | - |
| | All institutions | 1992/93 | 51 | 31 | 61 | 394 | 215 | 55 |
| | of which: Universities | | - | - | - | - | - | - |
| St. Lucia | All institutions | 1980/81 | ... | ... | ... | 301 | 157 | 52 |
| | of which: Universities | | - | - | - | - | - | - |
| | All institutions | 1992/93 | ... | ... | ... | 870 | 529 | 61 |
| | of which: Universities | | - | - | - | - | - | - |
| | All institutions | 1995/96 | 157 | 77 | 49 | 2 760 | 1 992 | 72 |
| | of which: Universities | | - | - | - | - | - | - |
| Trinidad and Tobago | All institutions | 1970/71 | 412 | 100 | 24 | 2 375 | 857 | 36 |
| | of which: Universities | | 329 | 64 | 19 | 1 671 | 464 | 28 |
| | All institutions | 1975/76 | ... | ... | ... | 4 940 | ... | ... |
| | of which: Universities | | 178 | ... | ... | 2 229 | ... | ... |
| | All institutions | 1980/81 | ... | ... | ... | 5 649 | ... | ... |
| | of which: Universities | | ... | ... | ... | 2 923 | ... | ... |
| | All institutions | 1985/86 | ... | ... | ... | 6 582 | 2 540 | 39 |
| | of which: Universities | | ... | ... | ... | 3 663 | 1 660 | 45 |
| | All institutions | 1990/91 | ... | ... | ... | 7 249 | 3 164 | 44 |
| | of which: Universities | | (2) 289 | ... | ... | 4 090 | 1 987 | 49 |
| | All institutions | 1991/92 | ... | ... | ... | (22) 7 513 | ... | ... |
| | of which: Universities | | (2) 292 | (2) 43 | 15 | 4 529 | ... | ... |
| | All institutions | 1992/93 | ... | ... | ... | (22) 8 170 | (22) 3 360 | 41 |
| | of which: Universities | | (2) 288 | (2) 39 | 14 | 4 947 | 2 402 | 49 |
| | All institutions | 1993/94 | ... | ... | ... | ... | ... | ... |
| | of which: Universities | | ... | ... | ... | 5 191 | 2 580 | 50 |
| | All institutions | 1994/95 | ... | ... | ... | ... | ... | ... |
| | of which: Universities | | ... | ... | ... | 5 231 | 2 731 | 52 |
| | All institutions | 1995/96 | ... | ... | ... | ... | ... | ... |
| | of which: Universities | | 421 | ... | ... | 5 348 | 2 882 | 54 |
| | All institutions | 1996/97 | ... | ... | ... | ... | ... | ... |
| | of which: Universities | | ... | ... | ... | 6 007 | 3 280 | 55 |
| U. S. Virgin Islands | All institutions | 1970/71 | *40 | ... | ... | 1 445 | 830 | 57 |
| | of which: Universities | | *40 | ... | ... | 1 445 | 830 | 57 |
| | All institutions | 1975/76 | ... | ... | ... | 2 069 | 1 301 | 63 |
| | of which: Universities | | ... | ... | ... | 2 069 | 1 301 | 63 |
| | All institutions | 1980/81 | ... | ... | ... | 2 148 | 1 533 | 71 |
| | of which: Universities | | ... | ... | ... | 2 148 | 1 533 | 71 |
| | All institutions | 1985/86 | 221 | 95 | 43 | 2 602 | 1 876 | 72 |
| | of which: Universities | | 221 | 95 | 43 | 2 602 | 1 876 | 72 |
| | All institutions | 1990/91 | 226 | 92 | 41 | 2 466 | 1 843 | 75 |
| | of which: Universities | | 226 | 92 | 41 | 2 466 | 1 843 | 75 |
| | All institutions | 1992/93 | 266 | 128 | 48 | 2 924 | 2 166 | 74 |
| | of which: Universities | | 266 | 128 | 48 | 2 924 | 2 166 | 74 |
| United States | All institutions | 1970/71 | 574 000 | ... | ... | 8 498 117 | 3 507 163 | 41 |
| | of which: Universities | | ... | ... | ... | 6 288 196 | 2 609 357 | 41 |

Tertiary education: teaching staff and students II.7
Enseignement supérieur: personnel enseignant et étudiants
Enseñanza superior: personal docente y estudiantes

| Country / Pays / País | Type of institution / Type d'établissement / Tipo de establecimiento | Year / Année / Año | Teaching staff Personnel enseignant Personal docente | | | Students enrolled Étudiants inscrits Estudiantes matriculados | | |
|---|---|---|---|---|---|---|---|---|
| | | | Total | Female Féminin Femenino | % F | Total | Female Féminin Femenino | % F |
| United States (cont) | All institutions | 1975/76 | 670 000 | ... | ... | 11 184 859 | 5 035 862 | 45 |
| | of which: Universities | | ... | ... | ... | 7 223 037 | 3 235 908 | 45 |
| | All institutions | 1980/81 | ... | ... | ... | 12 096 895 | 6 222 521 | 51 |
| | of which: Universities | | 305 982 | 71 980 | 24 | 7 572 657 | 3 745 958 | 49 |
| | All institutions | 1985/86 | 694 000 | ... | ... | 12 247 055 | 6 428 605 | 52 |
| | of which: Universities | | 494 000 | ... | ... | 7 715 978 | 3 899 762 | 51 |
| | All institutions | 1990/91 | 833 844 | 293 415 | 35 | 13 710 150 | 7 471 643 | 54 |
| | of which: Universities | | 589 799 | 182 640 | 31 | 8 529 132 | 4 498 360 | 53 |
| | All institutions | 1991/92 | 826 000 | ... | ... | 14 360 965 | ... | ... |
| | of which: Universities | | ... | ... | ... | ... | ... | ... |
| | All institutions | 1992/93 | 833 278 | 303 289 | 36 | 14 486 304 | 7 962 765 | 55 |
| | of which: Universities | | ... | ... | ... | ... | ... | ... |
| | All institutions | 1993/94 | 915 474 | 354 351 | 39 | 14 305 352 | 7 877 699 | 55 |
| | of which: Universities | | ... | ... | ... | ... | ... | ... |
| | All institutions | 1994/95 | 905 849 | 350 021 | 39 | 14 278 799 | 7 906 896 | 55 |
| | of which: Universities | | ... | ... | ... | ... | ... | ... |
| | All institutions | 1995/96 | 915 321 | 353 566 | 39 | 14 261 778 | 7 919 238 | 56 |
| | of which: Universities | | ... | ... | ... | ... | ... | ... |
| **South America** | | | | | | | | |
| Argentina | All institutions | 1970 | 22 477 | 6 889 | 31 | 274 634 | 117 251 | 43 |
| | of which: Universities | | 16 004 | 3 186 | 20 | 236 515 | 84 835 | 36 |
| | All institutions | 1975 | 45 204 | 17 665 | 39 | 596 736 | 283 762 | 48 |
| | of which: Universities | | 33 176 | 9 770 | 29 | 536 959 | 231 715 | 43 |
| | All institutions | 1980 | 46 267 | 20 039 | 43 | 491 473 | 247 656 | 50 |
| | of which: Universities | | 30 602 | 9 273 | 30 | 397 828 | 169 412 | 43 |
| | All institutions | 1985 | 70 699 | 32 694 | 46 | 846 145 | 444 636 | 53 |
| | of which: Universities | | 44 038 | 14 222 | 32 | 664 200 | 302 509 | 46 |
| | All institutions | 1991 | ... | ... | ... | 1 008 231 | ... | ... |
| | of which: Universities | | ... | ... | ... | 663 369 | ... | ... |
| | All institutions | 1994 | ... | ... | ... | 1 069 617 | ... | ... |
| | of which: Universities | | ... | ... | ... | 740 545 | ... | ... |
| Bolivia | All institutions | 1970 | ... | ... | ... | 35 250 | ... | ... |
| | of which: Universities | | ... | ... | ... | 28 662 | ... | ... |
| | All institutions | 1975 | ... | ... | ... | *49 850 | ... | ... |
| | of which: Universities | | ... | ... | ... | 34 350 | ... | ... |
| | All institutions | 1980 | ... | ... | ... | ... | ... | ... |
| | of which: Universities | | ... | ... | ... | 60 900 | ... | ... |
| | All institutions | 1985 | ... | ... | ... | ... | ... | ... |
| | of which: Universities | | 3 286 | ... | ... | 88 175 | ... | ... |
| | All institutions | 1990 | ... | ... | ... | ... | ... | ... |
| | of which: Universities | | 4 234 | ... | ... | 102 001 | ... | ... |
| | All institutions | 1991 | ... | ... | ... | ... | ... | ... |
| | of which: Universities | | 4 261 | ... | ... | 109 503 | ... | ... |
| Brazil | All institutions | 1970 | 42 968 | 8 898 | 21 | 430 473 | 162 176 | 38 |
| | of which: Universities | | 42 968 | 8 898 | 21 | 430 473 | 162 176 | 38 |
| | All institutions | 1975 | 92 546 | ... | ... | 1 089 808 | ... | ... |
| | of which: Universities | | 92 546 | ... | ... | 1 089 808 | ... | ... |
| | All institutions | 1980 | 109 788 | 33 238 | 30 | 1 409 243 (15) | (15) 680 445 | ... |
| | of which: Universities | | 109 788 | 33 238 | 30 | 1 409 243 (15) | (15) 680 445 | ... |
| | All institutions | 1990 | 131 641 | 53 503 | 41 | (15) 1 540 080 | (15) 806 547 | 52 |
| | of which: Universities | | 131 641 | 53 503 | 41 | (15) 1 540 080 | (15) 806 547 | 52 |
| | All institutions | 1991 | 133 135 | 49 994 | 38 | 1 619 310 | (15) 833 949 | ... |
| | of which: Universities | | 133 135 | 49 994 | 38 | 1 619 310 | (15) 833 949 | ... |
| | All institutions | 1992 | 134 403 | 50 144 | 37 | 1 591 176 | (15) 822 961 | ... |
| | of which: Universities | | 134 403 | 50 144 | 37 | 1 591 176 | (15) 822 961 | ... |
| | All institutions | 1993 | 137 156 | 52 672 | 38 | 1 652 333 | (15) 865 803 | ... |
| | of which: Universities | | 137 156 | 52 672 | 38 | 1 652 333 | (15) 865 803 | ... |

**II.7** Tertiary education: teaching staff and students
Enseignement supérieur: personnel enseignant et étudiants
Enseñanza superior: personal docente y estudiantes

| Country / Pays / País | Type of institution / Type d'établissement / Tipo de establecimiento | Year / Année / Año | Teaching staff / Personnel enseignant / Personal docente | | | Students enrolled / Étudiants inscrits / Estudiantes matriculados | | |
|---|---|---|---|---|---|---|---|---|
| | | | Total | Female Féminin Femenino | % F | Total | Female Féminin Femenino | % F |
| Brazil (cont) | All institutions | 1994 | 141 482 | 53 509 | 38 | (15) 1 716 263 | 907 677 | ... |
| | of which: Universities | | 141 482 | 53 509 | 38 | (15) 1 716 263 | 907 677 | ... |
| | All institutions | 1996 | 164 118 | ... | ... | (15) 1 868 529 | ... | ... |
| | of which: Universities | | 164 118 | ... | ... | (15) 1 868 529 | ... | ... |
| Chile | All institutions | 1970 | ... | ... | ... | 78 430 | 30 125 | 38 |
| | of which: Universities | | ... | ... | ... | 78 430 | 30 125 | 38 |
| | All institutions | 1975 | (2) 11 419 | ... | ... | 149 647 | 67 400 | 45 |
| | of which: Universities | | (2) 11 419 | ... | ... | 149 647 | 67 400 | 45 |
| | All institutions | 1980 | ... | ... | ... | 145 497 | 62 804 | 43 |
| | of which: Universities | | ... | ... | ... | 120 168 | 48 462 | 40 |
| | All institutions | 1985 | ... | ... | ... | 197 437 | 85 600 | 43 |
| | of which: Universities | | ... | ... | ... | ... | ... | ... |
| | All institutions | 1991 | ... | ... | ... | 261 800 | ... | ... |
| | of which: Universities | | ... | ... | ... | 195 813 | ... | ... |
| | All institutions | 1992 | ... | ... | ... | 297 122 | ... | ... |
| | of which: Universities | | (23) 17 945 | ... | ... | 223 218 | ... | ... |
| | All institutions | 1993 | ... | ... | ... | 324 594 | 147 596 | 45 |
| | of which: Universities | | (23) 18 084 | ... | ... | 241 499 | 107 932 | 45 |
| | All institutions | 1994 | ... | ... | ... | 334 808 | 153 226 | 46 |
| | of which: Universities | | ... | ... | ... | 257 664 | 116 421 | 45 |
| | All institutions | 1995 | ... | ... | ... | 342 788 | 156 614 | 46 |
| | of which: Universities | | ... | ... | ... | 271 899 | 123 390 | 45 |
| | All institutions | 1996 | ... | ... | ... | 367 094 | 166 887 | 45 |
| | of which: Universities | | ... | ... | ... | 305 193 | 138 282 | 45 |
| | All institutions | 1997 | ... | ... | ... | 380 603 | 175 242 | 46 |
| | of which: Universities | | ... | ... | ... | 325 614 | 149 064 | 46 |
| Colombia | All institutions | 1970 | 10 295 | ... | ... | 85 560 | 22 936 | 27 |
| | of which: Universities | | 10 295 | ... | ... | 85 560 | 22 936 | 27 |
| | All institutions | 1975 | 21 153 | 2 934 | 14 | 176 098 | 64 039 | 36 |
| | of which: Universities | | (8) 19 821 | (8) 2 585 | 13 | (8) 167 503 | (8) 59 309 | 35 |
| | All institutions | 1980 | 31 136 | 6 184 | 20 | 271 630 | 121 115 | 45 |
| | of which: Universities | | (8) 26 930 | (8) 5 181 | 19 | (8) 234 705 | (8) 100 587 | 43 |
| | All institutions | 1985 | (24) 43 227 | (24) 10 494 | 24 | 391 490 | 189 937 | 49 |
| | of which: Universities | | ... | ... | ... | (8) 342 036 | (8) 160 471 | 47 |
| | All institutions | 1990 | (24) 52 445 | (24) 13 965 | 27 | 487 448 | ... | ... |
| | of which: Universities | | ... | ... | ... | ... | ... | ... |
| | All institutions | 1991 | (24) 54 164 | (24) 14 074 | 26 | 510 649 | 261 237 | 51 |
| | of which: Universities | | ... | ... | ... | (8) 438 887 | (8) 220 700 | 50 |
| | All institutions | 1992 | (24) 54 414 | (24) 14 653 | 27 | 535 320 | ... | ... |
| | of which: Universities | | ... | ... | ... | ... | ... | ... |
| | All institutions | 1993 | (24) 55 796 | ... | ... | 547 468 | ... | ... |
| | of which: Universities | | ... | ... | ... | (8) 476 312 | ... | ... |
| | All institutions | 1994 | (24) 60 772 | (24) 16 887 | 28 | 576 540 | ... | ... |
| | of which: Universities | | ... | ... | ... | (8) 454 729 | ... | ... |
| | All institutions | 1995 | ... | ... | ... | 588 322 | 298 385 | 51 |
| | of which: Universities | | ... | ... | ... | ... | ... | ... |
| | All institutions | 1996 | (24) 66 538 | ... | ... | 644 188 | 334 204 | 52 |
| | of which: Universities | | ... | ... | ... | (8) 562 716 | (8) 292 269 | 52 |
| Ecuador | All institutions | 1970/71 | 2 867 | ... | ... | 38 692 | 11 629 | 30 |
| | of which: Universities | | 2 833 | ... | ... | 38 582 | 11 548 | 30 |
| | All institutions | 1975/76 | ... | ... | ... | 170 173 | ... | ... |
| | of which: Universities | | ... | ... | ... | 170 173 | ... | ... |
| | All institutions | 1980/81 | ... | ... | ... | 269 775 | ... | ... |
| | of which: Universities | | 11 326 | ... | ... | 264 136 | 97 350 | 37 |
| | All institutions | 1990/91 | 12 856 | ... | ... | 206 541 | ... | ... |
| | of which: Universities | | ... | ... | ... | ... | ... | ... |

Tertiary education: teaching staff and students
Enseignement supérieur: personnel enseignant et étudiants
Enseñanza superior: personal docente y estudiantes

II.7

| Country / Pays / País | Type of institution / Type d'établissement / Tipo de establecimiento | Year / Année / Año | Teaching staff Personnel enseignant Personal docente — Total | Female Féminin Femenino | % F | Students enrolled Étudiants inscrits Estudiantes matriculados — Total | Female Féminin Femenino | % F |
|---|---|---|---|---|---|---|---|---|
| Guyana | All institutions | 1970/71 | ... | ... | ... | 1 112 | 218 | 20 |
| | of which: Universities | | ... | ... | ... | 1 112 | 218 | 20 |
| | All institutions | 1975/76 | ... | ... | ... | 2 852 | 1 012 | 35 |
| | of which: Universities | | 172 | 37 | 22 | 1 749 | 486 | 28 |
| | All institutions | 1980/81 | 442 | 118 | 27 | 2 465 | 1 078 | 44 |
| | of which: Universities | | 322 | 68 | 21 | 1 681 | 535 | 32 |
| | All institutions | 1985/86 | 527 | 119 | 23 | 2 328 | 1 113 | 48 |
| | of which: Universities | | 390 | 65 | 17 | 1 598 | 640 | 40 |
| | All institutions | 1993/94 | 772 | ... | ... | 7 503 | 3 426 | 46 |
| | of which: Universities | | 418 | ... | ... | 3 607 | 1 951 | 54 |
| | All institutions | 1994/95 | 716 | 240 | 34 | 6 945 | 3 348 | 48 |
| | of which: Universities | | 329 | 94 | 29 | 3 311 | 1 838 | 56 |
| | All institutions | 1995/96 | 612 | 189 | 31 | 7 680 | 3 644 | 47 |
| | of which: Universities | | 352 | 103 | 29 | 3 511 | 1 957 | 56 |
| | All institutions | 1996/97 | ... | ... | ... | 8 965 | 4 540 | 51 |
| | of which: Universities | | ... | ... | ... | 3 701 | 2 154 | 58 |
| Paraguay | All institutions | 1970 | 956 | ... | ... | 8 172 | 3 442 | 42 |
| | of which: Universities | | 923 | ... | ... | 7 853 | 3 194 | 41 |
| | All institutions | 1975 | ... | ... | ... | 18 302 | ... | ... |
| | of which: Universities | | 1 741 | ... | ... | 17 153 | ... | ... |
| | All institutions | 1980 | ... | ... | ... | 26 915 | ... | ... |
| | of which: Universities | | 1 893 | ... | ... | 25 333 | ... | ... |
| | All institutions | 1985 | ... | ... | ... | 32 090 | ... | ... |
| | of which: Universities | | ... | ... | ... | 29 154 | ... | ... |
| | All institutions | 1990 | ... | ... | ... | 32 884 | ... | ... |
| | of which: Universities | | ... | ... | ... | 29 447 | 13 618 | 46 |
| | All institutions | 1993 | ... | ... | ... | 42 654 | (23) 19 295 | ... |
| | of which: Universities | | ... | ... | ... | 36 645 | (23) 14 691 | ... |
| | All institutions | 1995 | ... | ... | ... | (23) 40 913 | ... | ... |
| | of which: Universities | | ... | ... | ... | (23) 33 919 | ... | ... |
| | All institutions | 1996 | ... | ... | ... | (23) 42 302 | (23) 23 070 | 55 |
| | of which: Universities | | ... | ... | ... | (23) 32 520 | (23) 16 538 | 51 |
| Peru | All institutions | 1970 | 10 673 | 1 631 | 15 | 126 234 | 43 349 | 34 |
| | of which: Universities | | 8 573 | 891 | 10 | 100 505 | 32 973 | 30 |
| | All institutions | 1975 | 11 598 | 1 669 | 14 | 195 641 | 62 850 | 32 |
| | of which: Universities | | 10 844 | 1 321 | 12 | 186 511 | 59 684 | 32 |
| | All institutions | 1980 | 15 816 | ... | ... | 306 353 | 107 980 | 35 |
| | of which: Universities | | 14 384 | 2 343 | 16 | 246 510 | 83 791 | 34 |
| | All institutions | 1985 | 26 118 | ... | ... | 452 462 | ... | ... |
| | of which: Universities | | 20 123 | ... | ... | 354 888 | ... | ... |
| | All institutions | 1990 | 41 809 | ... | ... | 678 236 | ... | ... |
| | of which: Universities | | 27 579 | ... | ... | 442 932 | ... | ... |
| | All institutions | 1991 | 43 862 | ... | ... | 728 666 | ... | ... |
| | of which: Universities | | 28 719 | ... | ... | 475 709 | ... | ... |
| | All institutions | 1992 | 44 839 | ... | ... | 732 688 | ... | ... |
| | of which: Universities | | 28 781 | ... | ... | 463 499 | ... | ... |
| | All institutions | 1993 | 46 462 | ... | ... | 666 967 | ... | ... |
| | of which: Universities | | 29 313 | ... | ... | 403 091 | ... | ... |
| | All institutions | 1994 | 46 967 | ... | ... | 650 621 | ... | ... |
| | of which: Universities | | 28 801 | ... | ... | 366 027 | ... | ... |
| | All institutions | 1995 | 49 249 | ... | ... | 671 802 | ... | ... |
| | of which: Universities | | 30 186 | ... | ... | 372 908 | ... | ... |
| | All institutions | 1996 | 45 315 | ... | ... | 647 389 | ... | ... |
| | of which: Universities | | 25 795 | ... | ... | 346 532 | ... | ... |
| | All institutions | 1997 | 45 443 | ... | ... | 657 586 | ... | ... |
| | of which: Universities | | 25 795 | ... | ... | 352 909 | ... | ... |

II.7   Tertiary education: teaching staff and students
Enseignement supérieur: personnel enseignant et étudiants
Enseñanza superior: personal docente y estudiantes

| Country<br>Pays<br>País | Type of institution<br>Type d'établissement<br>Tipo de establecimiento | Year<br>Année<br>Año | Teaching staff<br>Personnel enseignant<br>Personal docente | | | Students enrolled<br>Étudiants inscrits<br>Estudiantes matriculados | | |
|---|---|---|---|---|---|---|---|---|
| | | | Total | Female<br>Féminin<br>Femenino | %<br>F | Total | Female<br>Féminin<br>Femenino | %<br>F |
| Suriname | All institutions<br>of which: Universities | 1970/71 | ...<br>... | ...<br>... | ...<br>... | 292 | ...<br>... | ...<br>... |
| | All institutions<br>of which: Universities | 1975/76 | ...<br>... | ...<br>... | ...<br>... | 465 | ...<br>54 | ...<br>12 |
| | All institutions<br>of which: Universities | 1980/81 | ...<br>... | ...<br>... | ...<br>... | 2 378<br>1 217 | ...<br>... | ...<br>... |
| | All institutions<br>of which: Universities | 1985/86 | ...<br>187 | ...<br>... | ...<br>... | 2 751<br>1 070 | 1 475<br>462 | 54<br>43 |
| Uruguay | All institutions<br>of which: Universities | 1975 | (23) 2 332<br>(23) 2 332 | (23) 530<br>(23) 530 | 23<br>23 | (23) 32 627<br>(23) 32 627 | (23) 14 313<br>(23) 14 313 | 44<br>44 |
| | All institutions<br>of which: Universities | 1980 | (23) 3 847<br>(23) 3 847 | (23) 1 141<br>(23) 1 141 | 30<br>30 | (23) 36 298<br>(23) 36 298 | (23) 19 236<br>(23) 19 236 | 53<br>53 |
| | All institutions<br>of which: Universities | 1990 | ...<br>6 808 | ...<br>... | ...<br>... | 71 612<br>62 433 | ...<br>... | ...<br>... |
| | All institutions<br>of which: Universities | 1991 | ...<br>6 899 | ...<br>... | ...<br>... | 73 660<br>62 587 | ...<br>... | ...<br>... |
| | All institutions<br>of which: Universities | 1992 | ...<br>6 442 | ...<br>... | ...<br>... | 68 227<br>56 760 | ...<br>... | ...<br>... |
| | All institutions<br>of which: Universities | 1996 | 9 907<br>8 035 | ...<br>... | ...<br>... | 79 691<br>67 474 | ...<br>... | ...<br>... |
| Venezuela | All institutions<br>of which: Universities | 1970/71 | 8 155<br>7 621 | 1 448<br>1 273 | 18<br>17 | 100 767<br>94 831 | *41 150<br>*37 800 | *41<br>*40 |
| | All institutions<br>of which: Universities | 1975/76 | 15 792<br>12 849 | ...<br>... | ...<br>... | 213 542<br>185 518 | ...<br>... | ...<br>... |
| | All institutions<br>of which: Universities | 1980/81 | 28 052<br>23 984 | ...<br>... | ...<br>... | 307 133<br>271 583 | ...<br>... | ...<br>... |
| | All institutions<br>of which: Universities | 1985/86 | 30 844<br>23 951 | ...<br>... | ...<br>... | 443 064<br>347 618 | 182 455<br>... | 41<br>... |
| | All institutions<br>of which: Universities | 1990/91 | 46 137<br>... | ...<br>... | ...<br>... | 550 030<br>... | ...<br>... | ...<br>... |
| | All institutions<br>of which: Universities | 1991/92 | 43 833<br>... | ...<br>... | ...<br>... | 550 783<br>... | ...<br>... | ...<br>... |
| **Asia** | | | | | | | | |
| Afghanistan | All institutions<br>of which: Universities | 1970 | 793<br>724 | 44<br>41 | 6<br>6 | 7 732<br>6 215 | 1 135<br>876 | 15<br>14 |
| | All institutions<br>of which: Universities | 1975 | ...<br>... | ...<br>... | ...<br>... | 12 256<br>8 681 | 1 681<br>800 | 14<br>9 |
| | All institutions<br>of which: Universities | 1990 | 1 342<br>444 | 323<br>97 | 24<br>22 | 24 333<br>9 367 | 7 469<br>3 970 | 31<br>42 |
| Armenia | All institutions<br>of which: Universities | 1995/96 | 5 606<br>... | 2 283<br>... | 41<br>... | 39 592<br>... | 20 033<br>... | 51<br>... |
| | All institutions<br>of which: Universities | 1996/97 | 4 065<br>... | ...<br>... | ...<br>... | 35 517<br>... | 19 928<br>... | 56<br>... |
| Azerbaijan | All institutions<br>of which: Universities | 1980/81 | 11 961<br>(8) 7 647 | ...<br>... | ...<br>... | 186 024<br>(8) 107 024 | 78 239<br>(8) 43 039 | 42<br>40 |
| | All institutions<br>of which: Universities | 1985/86 | 13 136<br>(8) 8 416 | ...<br>... | ...<br>... | 182 145<br>76 009 | 85 786<br>(8) 49 886 | 47<br>... |
| | All institutions<br>of which: Universities | 1990/91 | 13 809<br>(8) 8 935 | ...<br>... | ...<br>... | 163 901<br>77 063 | 64 342<br>(8) 39 807 | 39<br>... |
| | All institutions<br>of which: Universities | 1991/92 | 14 190<br>(8) 9 352 | ...<br>... | ...<br>... | 168 054<br>77 645 | 64 028<br>(8) 38 347 | 38<br>... |
| | All institutions<br>of which: Universities | 1992/93 | 14 853<br>(8) 9 917 | ...<br>... | ...<br>... | 147 909<br>(8) 100 985 | 59 401<br>(8) 38 655 | 40<br>38 |
| | All institutions<br>of which: Universities | 1993/94 | 15 149<br>(8) 9 831 | ...<br>... | ...<br>... | 128 242<br>(8) 94 345 | 55 032<br>(8) 39 489 | 43<br>42 |

Tertiary education: teaching staff and students
Enseignement supérieur: personnel enseignant et étudiants
Enseñanza superior: personal docente y estudiantes

II.7

| Country / Pays / País | Type of institution / Type d'établissement / Tipo de establecimiento | Year / Année / Año | Teaching staff — Personnel enseignant — Personal docente | | | Students enrolled — Étudiants inscrits — Estudiantes matriculados | | |
|---|---|---|---|---|---|---|---|---|
| | | | Total | Female Féminin Femenino | % F | Total | Female Féminin Femenino | % F |
| Azerbaijan (cont) | All institutions | 1994/95 | 15 537 | ... | ... | 120 870 | 56 005 | 46 |
| | of which: Universities | | (8) 10 934 | ... | ... | (8) 90 475 | (8) 39 256 | 43 |
| | All institutions | 1995/96 | *16 292 | ... | ... | 118 105 | 57 738 | 49 |
| | of which: Universities | | (8) *11 710 | ... | ... | (8) 87 587 | (8) 39 105 | 45 |
| | All institutions | 1996/97 | *15 929 | ... | ... | 115 116 | 56 996 | 50 |
| | of which: Universities | | (8) *11 395 | ... | ... | (8) 83 711 | (8) 36 992 | 44 |
| Bahrain | All institutions | 1970/71 | 32 | 12 | 38 | 289 | 151 | 52 |
| | of which: Universities | | - | - | - | - | - | - |
| | All institutions | 1975/76 | 79 | 11 | 14 | 703 | 371 | 53 |
| | of which: Universities | | - | - | - | - | - | - |
| | All institutions | 1980/81 | 159 | 21 | 13 | 1 908 | 786 | 41 |
| | of which: Universities | | 70 | 18 | 26 | 317 | 260 | 82 |
| | All institutions | 1985/86 | 434 | 159 | 37 | 4 180 | 2 490 | 60 |
| | of which: Universities | | 294 | 128 | 44 | 2 011 | 1 512 | 75 |
| | All institutions | 1990/91 | 557 | 163 | 29 | 6 868 | 3 824 | 56 |
| | of which: Universities | | 464 | 95 | 20 | 6 194 | 3 361 | 54 |
| | All institutions | 1991/92 | 605 | 169 | 28 | 7 147 | 4 157 | 58 |
| | of which: Universities | | 504 | 94 | 10 | 6 412 | 3 614 | 56 |
| | All institutions | 1992/93 | 582 | 165 | 28 | 7 763 | 4 424 | 57 |
| | of which: Universities | | 487 | 93 | 19 | 6 996 | 3 850 | 55 |
| | All institutions | 1993/94 | 655 | 189 | 29 | 7 676 | 4 444 | 58 |
| | of which: Universities | | 558 | 119 | 21 | 7 011 | 4 022 | 57 |
| Bangladesh | All institutions | 1970 | 7 201 | 581 | 8 | 117 603 | 11 453 | 10 |
| | of which: Universities | | 1 138 | 69 | 6 | 16 493 | 2 297 | 14 |
| | All institutions | 1980 | 12 428 | 1 305 | 11 | 240 181 | 33 348 | 14 |
| | of which: Universities | | 2 421 | 191 | 8 | 36 530 | 6 552 | 18 |
| | All institutions | 1985 | 16 187 | 2 941 | 18 | 461 073 | 87 755 | 19 |
| | of which: Universities | | 2 705 | 238 | 9 | 44 991 | 7 294 | 16 |
| | All institutions | 1990 | 22 447 | 2 861 | 13 | 434 309 | 68 866 | 16 |
| | of which: Universities | | 2 959 | 357 | 12 | 51 775 | 10 519 | 20 |
| Brunei Darussalam | All institutions | 1980/81 | 57 | 18 | 32 | 143 | 72 | 50 |
| | of which: Universities | | - | - | - | - | - | - |
| | All institutions | 1992/93 | 238 | 40 | 17 | 1 388 | 789 | 57 |
| | of which: Universities | | 199 | 38 | 19 | 1 181 | 677 | 57 |
| | All institutions | 1995/96 | ... | ... | ... | ... | ... | ... |
| | of which: Universities | | ... | ... | ... | 1 270 | 753 | 59 |
| Cambodia | All institutions | 1970/71 | ... | ... | ... | 9 228 | ... | ... |
| | of which: Universities | | ... | ... | ... | 9 228 | ... | ... |
| | All institutions | 1980/81 | ... | ... | ... | 601 | ... | ... |
| | of which: Universities | | ... | ... | ... | 601 | ... | ... |
| | All institutions | 1985/86 | ... | ... | ... | 2 213 | ... | ... |
| | of which: Universities | | ... | ... | ... | 2 213 | ... | ... |
| | All institutions | 1990/91 | ... | ... | ... | 6 659 | ... | ... |
| | of which: Universities | | ... | ... | ... | 6 659 | ... | ... |
| | All institutions | 1991/92 | ... | ... | ... | 8 764 | ... | ... |
| | of which: Universities | | ... | ... | ... | 8 764 | ... | ... |
| | All institutions | 1992/93 | ... | ... | ... | 10 837 | 1 882 | 17 |
| | of which: Universities | | ... | ... | ... | 10 837 | 1 882 | 17 |
| | All institutions | 1993/94 | 784 | 195 | 25 | 12 218 | 2 081 | 17 |
| | of which: Universities | | 784 | 195 | 25 | 12 218 | 2 081 | 17 |
| | All institutions | 1994/95 | 784 | 215 | 27 | 11 652 | 1 841 | 16 |
| | of which: Universities | | 784 | 215 | 27 | 11 652 | 1 841 | 16 |
| | All institutions | 1995/96 | ... | ... | ... | 13 401 | 2 116 | 16 |
| | of which: Universities | | ... | ... | ... | 13 401 | 2 116 | 16 |
| | All institutions | 1996/97 | 852 | 143 | 17 | 10 019 | 1 591 | 16 |
| | of which: Universities | | 852 | 143 | 17 | 10 019 | 1 591 | 16 |

II.7 Tertiary education: teaching staff and students
Enseignement supérieur: personnel enseignant et étudiants
Enseñanza superior: personal docente y estudiantes

| Country / Pays / País | Type of institution / Type d'établissement / Tipo de establecimiento | Year / Année / Año | Teaching staff — Personnel enseignant — Personal docente | | | | Students enrolled — Étudiants inscrits — Estudiantes matriculados | | | |
|---|---|---|---|---|---|---|---|---|---|---|
| | | | | Total | Female Féminin Femenino | % F | | Total | Female Féminin Femenino | % F |
| Cambodia (cont) | All institutions | 1997/98 | | 1 001 | 242 | 24 | | 8 901 | 1 719 | 19 |
| | of which: Universities | | | ... | ... | ... | | ... | ... | ... |
| China | All institutions | 1970/71 | | 128 617 | ... | ... | (25) | 47 815 | ... | ... |
| | of which: Universities | | | ... | ... | ... | | ... | ... | ... |
| | All institutions | 1975/76 | (2) | 155 723 | (2) 37 988 | 24 | (25) | 500 993 | (25) 163 290 | 33 |
| | of which: Universities | | | ... | ... | ... | | ... | ... | ... |
| | All institutions | 1980/81 | (2) | 281 765 | ... | ... | | 1 662 796 | ... | ... |
| | of which: Universities | | (2) | 246 862 | (2) 62 469 | 25 | | 1 165 316 | 270 255 | 23 |
| | All institutions | 1985/86 | (2) | 409 971 | ... | ... | | 3 515 485 | ... | ... |
| | of which: Universities | | (2) | 344 262 | (2) 91 879 | 27 | | 1 790 446 | 524 995 | 29 |
| | All institutions | 1990/91 | | ... | ... | ... | | 3 822 371 | ... | ... |
| | of which: Universities | | (2) | 394 567 | (2) 114 826 | 29 | | 2 155 713 | 713 370 | 33 |
| | All institutions | 1991/92 | | ... | ... | ... | | 3 660 248 | ... | ... |
| | of which: Universities | | (2) | 390 771 | (2) 115 778 | 30 | | 2 131 790 | 701 365 | 33 |
| | All institutions | 1992/93 | | ... | ... | ... | | 3 699 840 | ... | ... |
| | of which: Universities | | (2) | 387 585 | (2) 116 000 | 30 | | 2 278 540 | 757 815 | 33 |
| | All institutions | 1993/94 | | 522 086 | 157 640 | 30 | | 4 505 215 | 1 499 689 | 33 |
| | of which: Universities | | | 408 528 | 120 416 | 29 | | 2 642 288 | 879 689 | 33 |
| | All institutions | 1994/95 | | ... | ... | ... | | 5 278 935 | ... | ... |
| | of which: Universities | | (2) | 396 000 | (2) 127 000 | 32 | | 2 926 935 | ... | ... |
| | All institutions | 1995/96 | | ... | ... | ... | | 5 621 543 | ... | ... |
| | of which: Universities | | (2) | 401 000 | ... | ... | | 3 051 443 | ... | ... |
| | All institutions | 1996/97 | (2) | 510 570 | ... | ... | | 5 826 636 | ... | ... |
| | of which: Universities | | (2) | 411 970 | (2) *138 570 | *34 | | 3 170 936 | 1 144 844 | 36 |
| | All institutions | 1997/98 | (2) | 516 400 | ... | ... | | 6 075 215 | ... | ... |
| | of which: Universities | | (2) | *416 200 | (2) *143 270 | *34 | | 3 350 715 | ... | ... |
| China, Hong Kong SAR | All institutions | 1970/71 | | 1 677 | 252 | 15 | | 25 516 | 7 608 | 30 |
| | of which: Universities | | | 710 | 109 | 15 | | 5 610 | 1 842 | 33 |
| | All institutions | 1975/76 | | 3 043 | 446 | 15 | | 44 482 | 11 194 | 25 |
| | of which: Universities | | | 814 | 138 | 17 | | 8 264 | 2 435 | 29 |
| | All institutions | 1980/81 | | ... | ... | ... | | ... | ... | ... |
| | of which: Universities | | | 1 073 | 208 | 19 | | 11 689 | 4 021 | 34 |
| | All institutions | 1991/92 | | 5 978 | 1 481 | 25 | | 85 214 | 34 367 | 40 |
| | of which: Universities | | | 4 821 | 1 056 | 22 | | 63 177 | 23 992 | 38 |
| | All institutions | 1992/93 | | 6 027 | 1 489 | 25 | | 88 950 | 37 246 | 42 |
| | of which: Universities | | | 4 873 | 1 126 | 23 | | 68 238 | 27 433 | 40 |
| | All institutions | 1993/94 | | 6 504 | 1 656 | 25 | | 97 392 | 41 625 | 43 |
| | of which: Universities | | | 4 931 | 1 152 | 23 | | 69 907 | 29 657 | 42 |
| Cyprus (26) | All institutions | 1970/71 | | 64 | 14 | 22 | | 698 | 306 | 44 |
| | of which: Universities | | | - | - | - | | - | - | - |
| | All institutions | 1975/76 | | 69 | 17 | 25 | | 602 | 241 | 40 |
| | of which: Universities | | | - | - | - | | - | - | - |
| | All institutions | 1980/81 | (2) | 227 | (2) 57 | 25 | | 1 940 | 806 | 42 |
| | of which: Universities | | | - | - | - | | - | - | - |
| | All institutions | 1985/86 | (2) | 343 | (2) 108 | 31 | | 3 134 | 1 507 | 48 |
| | of which: Universities | | | - | - | - | | - | - | - |
| | All institutions | 1990/91 | | 688 | 283 | 41 | | 6 554 | 3 377 | 52 |
| | of which: Universities | | | - | - | - | | - | - | - |
| | All institutions | 1991/92 | (2) | 485 | (2) 182 | 38 | | 5 898 | 3 513 | 60 |
| | of which: Universities | | | - | - | - | | - | - | - |
| | All institutions | 1992/93 | | 700 | 256 | 37 | | 6 263 | 3 088 | 49 |
| | of which: Universities | | | 64 | 14 | 22 | | 548 | 443 | 81 |
| | All institutions | 1993/94 | | 725 | 276 | 38 | | 6 732 | 3 604 | 54 |
| | of which: Universities | | | 127 | 33 | 26 | | 1 043 | 862 | 83 |
| | All institutions | 1994/95 | | 815 | 314 | 39 | | 7 765 | 4 373 | 56 |
| | of which: Universities | | | 155 | 42 | 27 | | 1 741 | 1 318 | 76 |
| | All institutions | 1995/96 | | 922 | 359 | 39 | | 8 874 | 5 257 | 59 |
| | of which: Universities | | | 201 | 51 | 25 | | 2 174 | 1 668 | 77 |

Tertiary education: teaching staff and students II.7
Enseignement supérieur: personnel enseignant et étudiants
Enseñanza superior: personal docente y estudiantes

| Country / Pays / País | Type of institution / Type d'établissement / Tipo de establecimiento | Year / Année / Año | Teaching staff / Personnel enseignant / Personal docente | | | | | Students enrolled / Étudiants inscrits / Estudiantes matriculados | | | | |
|---|---|---|---|---|---|---|---|---|---|---|---|---|
| | | | | Total | | Female Féminin Femenino | % F | | | Total | | Female Féminin Femenino | % F |
| Cyprus (26) (cont) | All institutions | 1996/97 | | 1 061 | | 379 | 36 | | | 9 982 | | 5 559 | 56 |
| | of which: Universities | | | 241 | | 62 | 26 | | | 2 346 | | 1 750 | 75 |
| Georgia | All institutions | 1980/81 | (15) | 13 784 | | ... | ... | | | 140 578 | (15) | 65 401 | ... |
| | of which: Universities | | (15) | 7 743 | | ... | ... | | | 87 193 | (15) | 40 856 | ... |
| | All institutions | 1990/91 | (15) | 15 561 | | ... | ... | | | 148 391 | (15) | 68 539 | ... |
| | of which: Universities | | (15) | 10 277 | | ... | ... | | | 105 528 | (15) | 47 185 | ... |
| | All institutions | 1994/95 | | 24 430 | | ... | ... | | | 168 011 | | 94 367 | 56 |
| | of which: Universities | | | 19 084 | | ... | ... | | | 135 773 | | 75 496 | 56 |
| | All institutions | 1995/96 | | 24 358 | | ... | ... | | | 155 033 | | 81 558 | 53 |
| | of which: Universities | | | 19 168 | | ... | ... | | | 125 901 | | 66 168 | 53 |
| | All institutions | 1996/97 | | 25 549 | | ... | ... | | | 163 345 | (15) | 83 474 | ... |
| | of which: Universities | | | 20 016 | | 6 746 | 34 | | | 131 192 | (15) | 65 218 | ... |
| India | All institutions | 1970/71 | | ... | | ... | ... | | | 2 472 963 | | 527 113 | 21 |
| | of which: Universities | | | ... | | ... | ... | | | ... | | ... | ... |
| | All institutions | 1975/76 | | 235 822 | | 39 272 | 17 | | | 3 043 865 | | 709 023 | 23 |
| | of which: Universities | | | ... | | ... | ... | | | ... | | ... | ... |
| | All institutions | 1980/81 | | ... | | ... | ... | | | 3 515 318 | | 933 405 | 26 |
| | of which: Universities | | | ... | | ... | ... | | | ... | | ... | ... |
| | All institutions | 1985/86 | | 302 843 | | 63 517 | 21 | | | 4 470 844 | | 1 336 216 | 30 |
| | of which: Universities | | | ... | | ... | ... | | | ... | | ... | ... |
| | All institutions | 1990/91 | | ... | | ... | ... | | | 4 950 974 | | 1 637 610 | 33 |
| | of which: Universities | | | 263 125 | | 49 888 | 19 | | | 4 425 247 | | 1 436 887 | 32 |
| | All institutions | 1994/95 | | ... | | ... | ... | | | 4 932 669 | | 1 698 541 | 34 |
| | of which: Universities | | | ... | | ... | ... | | | ... | | ... | ... |
| | All institutions | 1995/96 | | ... | | ... | ... | | | 5 695 780 | | 2 053 083 | 36 |
| | of which: Universities | | | ... | | ... | ... | | | ... | | ... | ... |
| | All institutions | 1996/97 | | ... | | ... | ... | | | 6 060 418 | | 2 198 559 | 36 |
| | of which: Universities | | | ... | | ... | ... | | | ... | | ... | ... |
| Indonesia | All institutions | 1970 | | 20 018 | | ... | ... | | | 248 220 | | 62 400 | 25 |
| | of which: Universities | | | ... | | ... | ... | | | ... | | ... | ... |
| | All institutions | 1975 | | ... | | ... | ... | | | 278 200 | | ... | ... |
| | of which: Universities | | | ... | | ... | ... | | | ... | | ... | ... |
| | All institutions | 1980/81 | | ... | | ... | ... | | | 543 175 | | ... | ... |
| | of which: Universities | | | ... | | ... | ... | | | ... | | ... | ... |
| | All institutions | 1991/92 | | 134 949 | | ... | ... | | | 1 773 459 | | ... | ... |
| | of which: Universities | | | ... | | ... | ... | | | 1 661 880 | | ... | ... |
| | All institutions | 1992/93 | | 134 672 | | 10 887 | 8 | | | 1 795 453 | | 708 643 | 39 |
| | of which: Universities | | | 133 882 | | 10 600 | 8 | | | 1 617 812 | | 629 056 | 39 |
| | All institutions | 1993/94 | | ... | | ... | ... | | | 2 043 380 | | ... | ... |
| | of which: Universities | | | ... | | ... | ... | | | ... | | ... | ... |
| | All institutions | 1994/95 | | 150 608 | | ... | ... | | | 2 229 796 | | 854 465 | 38 |
| | of which: Universities | | | ... | | ... | ... | | | 1 844 621 | | 645 048 | 35 |
| | All institutions | 1995/96 | | 157 695 | | ... | ... | | | 2 303 469 | | 803 577 | 35 |
| | of which: Universities | | | ... | | ... | ... | | | 1 889 408 | | 578 455 | 31 |
| Iran, Islamic Republic of | All institutions | 1970/71 | | 6 474 | | 797 | 12 | | | 74 708 | | 19 027 | 25 |
| | of which: Universities | | | 3 828 | | 424 | 11 | | | 41 900 | | 9 520 | 23 |
| | All institutions | 1975/76 | | 13 392 | | 1 831 | 14 | | | 151 905 | | 42 789 | 28 |
| | of which: Universities | | | 6 253 | | 893 | 14 | | | 57 264 | | 17 368 | 30 |
| | All institutions | 1985/86 | (23) | 14 878 | (23) | 2 281 | 15 | (23) | | 184 442 | (23) | 52 780 | 29 |
| | of which: Universities | | (23) | 10 229 | (23) | 1 311 | 13 | (23) | | 121 459 | (23) | 37 010 | 30 |
| | All institutions | 1990/91 | (23) | 23 376 | | ... | ... | (23) | | 312 076 | (23) | 85 325 | 27 |
| | of which: Universities | | (23) | 19 320 | (23) | 3 988 | 21 | (23) | | 244 227 | (23) | 71 185 | 29 |
| | All institutions | 1991/92 | (23) | 29 828 | (23) | 4 285 | 14 | (23) | | 344 045 | (23) | 96 969 | 28 |
| | of which: Universities | | (23) | 24 184 | (23) | 3 798 | 16 | (23) | | 256 212 | (23) | 75 037 | 29 |
| | All institutions | 1992/93 | (23) | 30 262 | (23) | 5 539 | 18 | (23) | | 374 734 | (23) | 105 667 | 28 |
| | of which: Universities | | (23) | 25 167 | (23) | 4 992 | 20 | (23) | | 282 148 | (23) | 81 282 | 29 |

II.7    Tertiary education: teaching staff and students
Enseignement supérieur: personnel enseignant et étudiants
Enseñanza superior: personal docente y estudiantes

| Country / Pays / País | Type of institution / Type d'établissement / Tipo de establecimiento | Year / Année / Año | Teaching staff — Personnel enseignant — Personal docente — Total | Female Féminin Femenino | % F | Students enrolled — Étudiants Inscrits — Estudiantes matriculados — Total | Female Féminin Femenino | % F |
|---|---|---|---|---|---|---|---|---|
| Iran, Islamic Republic of (cont) | All institutions | 1993/94 | (23) 32 934 | (23) 5 800 | 18 | (23) 436 564 | (23) 124 350 | 28 |
| | of which: Universities | | (23) 25 947 | (23) 5 280 | 20 | (23) 306 667 | (23) 88 455 | 29 |
| | All institutions | 1994/95 | (23) 36 366 | (23) 6 490 | 18 | 909 476 | (23) 145 353 | ... |
| | of which: Universities | | (23) 27 981 | (23) 5 755 | 21 | 758 150 | (23) 99 544 | ... |
| | All institutions | 1995/96 | 52 812 | 12 359 | 23 | 1 048 093 | 384 461 | 37 |
| | of which: Universities | | 42 782 | 11 413 | 27 | 869 748 | 325 250 | 37 |
| | All institutions | 1996/97 | (23) 40 477 | (23) 7 171 | 18 | (23) 579 070 | (23) 209 163 | 36 |
| | of which: Universities | | (23) 28 343 | (23) 5 966 | 21 | (23) 367 296 | (23) 129 786 | 35 |
| Iraq | All institutions | 1970/71 | 1 822 | 155 | 9 | 42 431 | 9 439 | 22 |
| | of which: Universities | | 1 822 | 155 | 9 | 42 431 | 9 439 | 22 |
| | All institutions | 1975/76 | 3 801 | 748 | 20 | 86 111 | 28 267 | 33 |
| | of which: Universities | | 2 965 | 383 | 13 | 71 456 | 20 956 | 29 |
| | All institutions | 1980/81 | 6 703 | 1 107 | 17 | 106 709 | 33 869 | 32 |
| | of which: Universities | | 4 627 | 738 | 16 | 81 782 | 26 496 | 32 |
| | All institutions | 1985/86 | 8 818 | 2 089 | 24 | 169 665 | 61 749 | 36 |
| | of which: Universities | | ... | ... | ... | ... | ... | ... |
| Israel | All institutions | 1970/71 | 9 300 | ... | ... | 55 486 | *24 600 | *44 |
| | of which: Universities | | 6 783 | ... | ... | 40 087 | 17 340 | 43 |
| | All institutions | 1980/81 | ... | ... | ... | (27) 97 097 | 49 861 | ... |
| | of which: Universities | | 10 237 | 3 275 | 32 | 55 840 | 26 133 | 47 |
| | All institutions | 1985/86 | ... | ... | ... | 116 062 | 54 490 | 47 |
| | of which: Universities | | ... | ... | ... | 62 514 | 30 891 | 49 |
| | All institutions | 1990/91 | ... | ... | ... | 134 885 | 66 301 | 49 |
| | of which: Universities | | ... | ... | ... | 71 190 | 36 333 | 51 |
| | All institutions | 1991/92 | ... | ... | ... | ... | ... | ... |
| | of which: Universities | | ... | ... | ... | 78 640 | 41 267 | 52 |
| | All institutions | 1992/93 | ... | ... | ... | 162 219 | 83 227 | 51 |
| | of which: Universities | | ... | ... | ... | 84 990 | 45 574 | 54 |
| | All institutions | 1993/94 | ... | ... | ... | ... | ... | ... |
| | of which: Universities | | ... | ... | ... | 91 480 | *49 860 | *55 |
| | All institutions | 1994/95 | ... | ... | ... | 182 836 | ... | ... |
| | of which: Universities | | ... | ... | ... | 97 250 | 53 780 | 55 |
| | All institutions | 1995/96 | ... | ... | ... | 198 766 | ... | ... |
| | of which: Universities | | ... | ... | ... | 101 700 | ... | ... |
| Japan | All institutions | 1970/71 | 151 927 | 18 878 | 12 | 1 819 323 | 512 759 | 28 |
| | of which: Universities | | 118 971 | 9 250 | 8 | 1 503 286 | 287 823 | 19 |
| | All institutions | 1975/76 | 191 551 | 23 508 | 12 | 2 248 903 | 727 256 | 32 |
| | of which: Universities | | 149 349 | 12 375 | 8 | 1 840 708 | 412 072 | 22 |
| | All institutions | 1980/81 | 213 537 | 29 389 | 14 | 2 412 117 | 791 264 | 33 |
| | of which: Universities | | 168 739 | 16 002 | 9 | 1 937 124 | 447 256 | 23 |
| | All institutions | 1985/86 | 243 507 | 34 868 | 14 | 2 347 463 | 818 978 | 35 |
| | of which: Universities | | 191 533 | 19 166 | 10 | 1 932 785 | 470 914 | 24 |
| | All institutions | 1991/92 | 286 166 | 46 286 | 16 | 2 899 143 | 1 173 841 | 40 |
| | of which: Universities | | 221 311 | 26 102 | 12 | 2 311 618 | 675 766 | 29 |
| | All institutions | 1993/94 | (21) 413 861 | (21) 91 505 | 22 | (21) 3 841 134 | (21) 1 680 815 | 44 |
| | of which: Universities | | ... | ... | ... | ... | ... | ... |
| | All institutions | 1994/95 | 401 509 | 87 357 | 22 | 3 917 709 | 1 725 199 | 44 |
| | of which: Universities | | ... | ... | ... | ... | ... | ... |
| Jordan (28) | All institutions | 1970/71 | 314 | 55 | 18 | 4 518 | 1 349 | 30 |
| | of which: Universities | | 168 | 12 | 7 | 2 913 | 859 | 29 |
| | All institutions | 1975/76 | 797 | 169 | 21 | 11 873 | 3 969 | 33 |
| | of which: Universities | | 344 | 30 | 9 | 5 307 | 1 694 | 32 |
| | All institutions | 1980/81 | ... | ... | ... | 36 549 | 16 682 | 46 |
| | of which: Universities | | ... | ... | ... | 17 103 | 7 068 | 41 |
| | All institutions | 1985/86 | (2) 2 307 | (2) 468 | 20 | 53 753 | 24 162 | 45 |
| | of which: Universities | | (2) 1 295 | (2) 168 | 13 | 26 711 | 10 403 | 39 |

Tertiary education: teaching staff and students II.7
Enseignement supérieur: personnel enseignant et étudiants
Enseñanza superior: personal docente y estudiantes

| Country / Pays / País | Type of institution / Type d'établissement / Tipo de establecimiento | Year / Année / Año | Teaching staff / Personnel enseignant / Personal docente | | | Students enrolled / Étudiants inscrits / Estudiantes matriculados | | |
|---|---|---|---|---|---|---|---|---|
| | | | Total | Female Féminin Femenino | % F | Total | Female Féminin Femenino | % F |
| Jordan (28) (cont) | All institutions of which: Universities | 1990/91 | ... 1 931 | ... 242 | ... 13 | 80 442 39 668 | 38 890 16 581 | 48 42 |
| | All institutions of which: Universities | 1991/92 | 3 753 2 123 | 689 254 | 18 12 | 84 226 46 068 | 40 773 19 763 | 48 43 |
| | All institutions of which: Universities | 1992/93 | 4 014 2 457 | 737 302 | 18 12 | 88 506 56 530 | 43 394 23 653 | 49 42 |
| | All institutions of which: Universities | 1993/94 | 4 280 2 832 | 783 354 | 18 13 | 85 936 60 644 | 41 283 25 747 | 48 42 |
| | All institutions of which: Universities | 1994/95 | ... ... | ... ... | ... ... | 87 507 65 036 | ... ... | ... ... |
| | All institutions of which: Universities | 1995/96 | 4 821 3 511 | 825 423 | 17 12 | 99 020 76 375 | 45 697 31 003 | 46 41 |
| | All institutions of which: Universities | 1996/97 | 5 275 3 982 | 952 530 | 18 13 | 112 959 89 010 | 52 934 37 400 | 47 42 |
| Kazakstan | All institutions of which: Universities | 1980/81 | ... ... | ... ... | ... ... | 525 400 260 000 | ... ... | ... ... |
| | All institutions of which: Universities | 1985/86 | ... 19 500 | ... ... | ... ... | 551 000 273 400 | ... ... | ... ... |
| | All institutions of which: Universities | 1990/91 | ... 22 000 | ... ... | ... ... | 537 491 289 791 | ... ... | ... ... |
| | All institutions of which: Universities | 1991/92 | ... 23 200 | ... ... | ... ... | ... 290 840 | ... ... | ... ... |
| | All institutions of which: Universities | 1993/94 | ... 27 189 | ... ... | ... ... | (15) 494 152 272 091 | (15) 271 033 140 344 | 55 52 |
| | All institutions of which: Universities | 1994/95 | ... 27 189 | ... ... | ... ... | 482 690 268 410 | 266 241 *141 129 | 55 *53 |
| | All institutions of which: Universities | 1995/96 | ... ... | ... ... | ... ... | ... 260 043 | ... 137 560 | ... 53 |
| Korea, Republic of | All institutions of which: Universities | 1970/71 | 10 435 7 944 | 1 350 985 | 13 12 | 201 436 153 054 | 48 863 33 448 | 24 22 |
| | All institutions of which: Universities | 1975/76 | 15 317 11 578 | 2 266 1 654 | 15 14 | 318 683 222 856 | (29) 81 228 57 717 | ... 26 |
| | All institutions of which: Universities | 1980/81 | 21 173 14 969 | 3 270 2 289 | 15 15 | 647 505 436 918 | ... 96 420 | ... 22 |
| | All institutions of which: Universities | 1985/86 | 34 300 27 082 | 5 967 4 387 | 17 16 | 1 455 759 1 018 236 | 432 385 275 787 | 30 27 |
| | All institutions of which: Universities | 1990/91 | 72 954 57 179 | 16 236 11 918 | 22 21 | 1 691 429 1 143 037 | 534 053 325 979 | 32 29 |
| | All institutions of which: Universities | 1991/92 | 77 458 60 671 | 17 654 13 109 | 23 22 | 1 761 775 1 159 463 | 576 611 340 688 | 33 29 |
| | All institutions of which: Universities | 1992/93 | 82 870 64 730 | 19 499 14 551 | 24 22 | 1 911 765 1 203 009 | 674 454 363 710 | 35 30 |
| | All institutions of which: Universities | 1993/94 | (21) 85 669 ... | (21) 20 821 ... | 24 ... | (21) 1 950 306 ... | (21) 674 800 ... | 35 ... |
| | All institutions of which: Universities | 1994/95 | 93 275 ... | 23 462 ... | 25 ... | 2 065 579 ... | 722 853 ... | 35 ... |
| | All institutions of which: Universities | 1995/96 | 103 703 ... | 27 455 ... | 26 ... | 2 225 092 ... | 781 706 ... | 35 ... |
| | All institutions of which: Universities | 1996/97 | 114 231 ... | 31 708 ... | 28 ... | 2 541 659 1 556 949 | 940 175 497 012 | 37 32 |
| Kuwait | All institutions of which: Universities | 1970/71 | 244 189 | 28 15 | 11 8 | 2 686 2 225 | 1 300 1 078 | 48 48 |
| | All institutions of which: Universities | 1975/76 | 596 327 | 164 16 | 28 5 | 8 104 6 246 | 4 608 3 499 | 57 56 |
| | All institutions of which: Universities | 1980/81 | 1 151 608 | 270 61 | 23 10 | 13 630 9 388 | 7 807 5 466 | 57 58 |
| | All institutions of which: Universities | 1985/86 | ... 858 | ... ... | ... ... | 23 678 16 359 | 12 754 9 004 | 54 55 |

II.7    Tertiary education: teaching staff and students
Enseignement supérieur: personnel enseignant et étudiants
Enseñanza superior: personal docente y estudiantes

| Country<br><br>Pays<br><br>País | Type of institution<br><br>Type<br>d'établissement<br><br>Tipo de<br>establecimiento | Year<br><br>Année<br><br>Año | Teaching staff<br>Personnel enseignant<br>Personal docente | | | Students enrolled<br>Étudiants inscrits<br>Estudiantes matriculados | | |
|---|---|---|---|---|---|---|---|---|
| | | | Total | Female<br>Féminin<br>Femenino | %<br><br>F | Total | Female<br>Féminin<br>Femenino | %<br><br>F |
| Kuwait (cont) | All institutions<br>of which: Universities | 1991/92 | 1 771<br>677 | 383<br>152 | 22<br>22 | 21 171<br>10 031 | 13 734<br>6 614 | 65<br>66 |
| | All institutions<br>of which: Universities | 1992/93 | ...<br>... | ...<br>... | ...<br>... | 22 113<br>10 091 | 14 358<br>6 990 | 65<br>69 |
| | All institutions<br>of which: Universities | 1994/95 | 1 688<br>835 | ...<br>... | ...<br>... | 27 646<br>14 027 | 17 152<br>9 399 | 62<br>67 |
| | All institutions<br>of which: Universities | 1995/96 | 1 749<br>868 | ...<br>137 | ...<br>16 | 28 705<br>14 884 | 17 691<br>9 859 | 62<br>66 |
| | All institutions<br>of which: Universities | 1996/97 | 1 691<br>913 | ...<br>132 | ...<br>14 | 29 509<br>14 658 | 18 243<br>9 752 | 62<br>67 |
| Kyrgyzstan | All institutions<br>of which: Universities | 1980/81 | ...<br>... | ...<br>... | ...<br>... | (15) 64 595<br>... | ...<br>... | ...<br>... |
| | All institutions<br>of which: Universities | 1985/86 | ...<br>... | ...<br>... | ...<br>... | (15) 71 292<br>... | ...<br>... | ...<br>... |
| | All institutions<br>of which: Universities | 1990/91 | ...<br>... | ...<br>... | ...<br>... | 57 563<br>... | ...<br>... | ...<br>... |
| | All institutions<br>of which: Universities | 1991/92 | ...<br>... | ...<br>... | ...<br>... | 57 862<br>... | ...<br>... | ...<br>... |
| | All institutions<br>of which: Universities | 1993/94 | 4 918<br>... | ...<br>... | ...<br>... | 55 229<br>... | 28 652<br>... | 52<br>... |
| | All institutions<br>of which: Universities | 1995/96 | 3 691<br>... | ...<br>... | ...<br>... | 49 744<br>... | 26 041<br>... | 52<br>... |
| Lao People's Democratic<br>Republic | All institutions<br>of which: Universities | 1970/71 | 21<br>- | 3<br>- | 14<br>- | 424<br>- | 82<br>- | 19<br>- |
| | All institutions<br>of which: Universities | 1980/81 | 140<br>140 | 25<br>25 | 18<br>18 | 1 408<br>1 408 | 441<br>441 | 31<br>31 |
| | All institutions<br>of which: Universities | 1985/86 | 534<br>446 | 132<br>119 | 25<br>27 | 5 382<br>3 915 | 1 918<br>1 682 | 36<br>43 |
| | All institutions<br>of which: Universities | 1992/93 | 976<br>457 | 252<br>143 | 26<br>31 | 6 071<br>3 366 | 1 790<br>1 256 | 29<br>37 |
| | All institutions<br>of which: Universities | 1993/94 | 998<br>463 | 276<br>155 | 28<br>33 | 6 179<br>3 287 | 1 669<br>1 159 | 27<br>35 |
| | All institutions<br>of which: Universities | 1994/95 | 1 024<br>497 | 280<br>165 | 27<br>33 | 7 908<br>4 356 | 2 250<br>1 625 | 28<br>37 |
| | All institutions<br>of which: Universities | 1995/96 | 1 414<br>544 | 388<br>169 | 27<br>31 | 11 724<br>4 356 | 3 518<br>1 625 | 30<br>37 |
| | All institutions<br>of which: Universities | 1996/97 | 1 369<br>456 | 398<br>155 | 29<br>34 | 12 732<br>5 273 | 3 845<br>1 764 | 30<br>33 |
| Lebanon | All institutions<br>of which: Universities | 1970/71 | *2 300<br>*2 300 | ...<br>... | ...<br>... | 42 578<br>42 578 | *10 000<br>*10 000 | *23<br>*23 |
| | All institutions<br>of which: Universities | 1980/81 | ...<br>... | ...<br>... | 22<br>... | 79 073<br>79 073 | 28 531<br>28 531 | 36<br>36 |
| | All institutions<br>of which: Universities | 1985/86 | ...<br>... | ...<br>... | ...<br>... | *79 500<br>*79 500 | ...<br>... | ...<br>... |
| | All institutions<br>of which: Universities | 1991/92 | 5 400<br>5 400 | 1 318<br>1 318 | 24<br>24 | 85 495<br>85 495 | 40 923<br>40 923 | 48<br>48 |
| | All institutions<br>of which: Universities | 1995/96 | 10 444<br>10 444 | 3 448<br>3 448 | 33<br>33 | 81 588<br>81 588 | 40 160<br>40 160 | 49<br>49 |
| Macau | All institutions<br>of which: Universities | 1990/91 | 505<br>383 | 174<br>114 | 34<br>30 | 7 425<br>6 857 | 3 062<br>2 534 | 41<br>37 |
| | All institutions<br>of which: Universities | 1991/92 | 594<br>492 | 193<br>143 | 32<br>29 | 7 420<br>6 871 | 3 201<br>2 694 | 43<br>39 |
| | All institutions<br>of which: Universities | 1992/93 | 592<br>512 | 194<br>150 | 33<br>29 | 7 271<br>6 803 | 3 141<br>2 699 | 43<br>40 |
| | All institutions<br>of which: Universities | 1993/94 | 603<br>504 | 211<br>164 | 35<br>33 | 6 517<br>6 045 | 2 958<br>2 534 | 45<br>42 |

Tertiary education: teaching staff and students
Enseignement supérieur: personnel enseignant et étudiants
Enseñanza superior: personal docente y estudiantes

II.7

| Country<br>Pays<br>País | Type of institution<br>Type d'établissement<br>Tipo de establecimiento | Year<br>Année<br>Año | Teaching staff<br>Personnel enseignant<br>Personal docente | | | Students enrolled<br>Étudiants inscrits<br>Estudiantes matriculados | | |
|---|---|---|---|---|---|---|---|---|
| | | | Total | Female<br>Féminin<br>Femenino | %<br>F | Total | Female<br>Féminin<br>Femenino | %<br>F |
| Macau (cont) | All institutions | 1996/97 | 694 | 210 | 30 | 7 485 | 3 674 | 49 |
| | of which: Universities | | ... | ... | ... | ... | ... | ... |
| Malaysia | All institutions | 1980/81 | 5 541 | 1 415 | 26 | 57 650 | 22 199 | 39 |
| | of which: Universities | | 3 299 | 766 | 23 | 26 287 | 9 105 | 35 |
| | All institutions | 1985/86 | 8 213 | 1 801 | 22 | 93 249 | 41 468 | 44 |
| | of which: Universities | | 4 718 | 1 149 | 24 | 43 295 | 17 066 | 39 |
| | All institutions | 1990/91 | 10 169 | ... | ... | 121 412 | ... | ... |
| | of which: Universities | | 5 260 | ... | ... | 57 059 | 26 286 | 46 |
| | All institutions | 1991/92 | 11 239 | ... | ... | 137 826 | ... | ... |
| | of which: Universities | | 5 503 | ... | ... | 63 397 | ... | ... |
| | All institutions | 1992/93 | 13 590 | ... | ... | 160 566 | ... | ... |
| | of which: Universities | | 6 242 | ... | ... | 77 829 | ... | ... |
| | All institutions | 1993/94 | 11 490 | ... | ... | 170 145 | ... | ... |
| | of which: Universities | | 5 432 | ... | ... | 82 971 | ... | ... |
| | All institutions | 1994/95 | 12 247 | ... | ... | 191 290 | ... | ... |
| | of which: Universities | | ... | ... | ... | ... | ... | ... |
| | All institutions | 1995/96 | 14 960 | ... | ... | 210 724 | ... | ... |
| | of which: Universities | | ... | ... | ... | ... | ... | ... |
| Mongolia | All institutions | 1970/71 | ... | ... | ... | 6 874 | ... | ... |
| | of which: Universities | | ... | ... | ... | 5 176 | ... | ... |
| | All institutions | 1975/76 | 807 | ... | ... | 9 861 | 5 054 | 51 |
| | of which: Universities | | 625 | ... | ... | 7 677 | 3 777 | 49 |
| | All institutions | 1980/81 | (2) 2 180 | (2) 864 | 40 | 34 543 | 20 962 | 61 |
| | of which: Universities | | (2) 1 113 | (2) 342 | 31 | 17 152 | 8 927 | 52 |
| | All institutions | 1985/86 | (2) 2 747 | (2) 1 144 | 42 | 40 099 | 25 189 | 63 |
| | of which: Universities | | (2) 1 510 | (2) 526 | 35 | 18 487 | 10 051 | 54 |
| | All institutions | 1990/91 | (2) 2 725 | (2) 1 159 | 43 | 31 434 | 20 466 | 65 |
| | of which: Universities | | (2) 1 465 | (2) 504 | 34 | 13 825 | 7 659 | 55 |
| | All institutions | 1991/92 | (2) 2 601 | (2) 1 143 | 44 | 28 209 | 18 796 | 67 |
| | of which: Universities | | (2) 1 341 | (2) 463 | 35 | 13 223 | 7 540 | 57 |
| | All institutions | 1992/93 | (2) 2 424 | (2) 1 074 | 44 | 25 225 | 16 760 | 66 |
| | of which: Universities | | (2) 1 614 | (2) 630 | 39 | 17 109 | 10 820 | 63 |
| | All institutions | 1993/94 | (2) 2 886 | (2) 1 337 | 46 | 28 084 | 19 089 | 68 |
| | of which: Universities | | (2) 2 216 | (2) 903 | 41 | 22 518 | 14 866 | 66 |
| | All institutions | 1994/95 | (2) 2 826 | (2) 1 280 | 40 | 32 535 | 22 590 | 69 |
| | of which: Universities | | ... | ... | ... | ... | ... | ... |
| | All institutions | 1995/96 | (2) 3 076 | (2) 1 446 | 47 | 38 643 | 26 929 | 70 |
| | of which: Universities | | ... | ... | ... | ... | ... | ... |
| | All institutions | 1996/97 | 4 491 | (2) 1 611 | ... | 44 088 | 30 512 | 69 |
| | of which: Universities | | 2 343 | (2) 689 | ... | 20 846 | 12 643 | 61 |
| | All institutions | 1997/98 | (2) 3 331 | (2) 1 760 | 53 | 50 961 | 34 782 | 68 |
| | of which: Universities | | (2) 1 701 | (2) 725 | 43 | 23 785 | 14 248 | 60 |
| Myanmar | All institutions | 1970/71 | 3 509 | ... | ... | 46 150 | ... | ... |
| | of which: Universities | | ... | ... | ... | ... | ... | ... |
| | All institutions | 1975/76 | ... | ... | ... | 56 083 | ... | ... |
| | of which: Universities | | ... | ... | ... | ... | ... | ... |
| | All institutions | 1980/81 | 4 509 | ... | ... | 163 197 | ... | ... |
| | of which: Universities | | ... | ... | ... | 24 215 | ... | ... |
| | All institutions | 1985/86 | 4 758 | ... | ... | 179 366 | ... | ... |
| | of which: Universities | | ... | ... | ... | 63 262 | 33 771 | 53 |
| | All institutions | 1991/92 | 5 497 | ... | ... | 196 052 | 108 663 | 55 |
| | of which: Universities | | ... | ... | ... | 91 926 | 53 616 | 58 |
| | All institutions | 1992/93 | 5 442 | ... | ... | 243 870 | 140 432 | 58 |
| | of which: Universities | | ... | ... | ... | 89 768 | 54 236 | 60 |
| | All institutions | 1993/94 | 5 989 | ... | ... | 235 256 | ... | ... |
| | of which: Universities | | ... | ... | ... | 79 391 | ... | ... |
| | All institutions | 1994/95 | (13) 5 730 | ... | ... | (13) 245 317 | (13) 150 821 | 61 |
| | of which: Universities | | 4 888 | ... | ... | 89 717 | 57 558 | 64 |

II.7 Tertiary education: teaching staff and students
Enseignement supérieur: personnel enseignant et étudiants
Enseñanza superior: personal docente y estudiantes

| Country / Pays / País | Type of institution / Type d'établissement / Tipo de establecimiento | Year / Année / Año | Teaching staff Personnel enseignant Personal docente | | | | Students enrolled Étudiants inscrits Estudiantes matriculados | | | |
|---|---|---|---|---|---|---|---|---|---|---|
| | | | | Total | Female Féminin Femenino | % F | | Total | Female Féminin Femenino | % F |
| Nepal | All institutions | 1975 | | 1 516 | ... | ... | | 23 504 | ... | ... |
| | of which: Universities | | | 1 516 | ... | ... | | 23 504 | ... | ... |
| | All institutions | 1980 | (23) | 2 918 | (23) 480 | 16 | (23) | 34 094 | (23) 7 358 | 22 |
| | of which: Universities | | (23) | 2 918 | (23) 480 | 16 | (23) | 34 094 | (23) 7 358 | 22 |
| | All institutions | 1985 | | ... | ... | ... | (23) | 54 452 | ... | ... |
| | of which: Universities | | | ... | ... | ... | (23) | 54 452 | ... | ... |
| | All institutions | 1990 | | ... | ... | ... | | 93 753 | 21 654 | 23 |
| | of which: Universities | | | ... | ... | ... | | 93 753 | 21 654 | 23 |
| | All institutions | 1991 | | 4 925 | ... | ... | | 110 239 | 26 221 | 24 |
| | of which: Universities | | | 4 925 | ... | ... | | 110 239 | 26 221 | 24 |
| | All institutions | 1992 | | ... | ... | ... | | 103 840 | ... | ... |
| | of which: Universities | | | ... | ... | ... | | 103 840 | ... | ... |
| | All institutions | 1993 | | ... | ... | ... | | 102 882 | ... | ... |
| | of which: Universities | | | ... | ... | ... | | 102 882 | ... | ... |
| | All institutions | 1994 | | ... | ... | ... | | 98 731 | ... | ... |
| | of which: Universities | | | ... | ... | ... | | 98 731 | ... | ... |
| | All institutions | 1995 | | ... | ... | ... | | 93 176 | ... | ... |
| | of which: Universities | | | ... | ... | ... | | 93 176 | ... | ... |
| | All institutions | 1996 | | ... | ... | ... | | 105 694 | ... | ... |
| | of which: Universities | | | ... | ... | ... | | 105 694 | ... | ... |
| Oman | All institutions | 1975/76 | | - | - | - | | - | - | - |
| | of which: Universities | | | - | - | - | | - | - | - |
| | All institutions | 1980/81 | | 8 | ... | ... | | 18 | - | - |
| | of which: Universities | | | - | - | - | | - | - | - |
| | All institutions | 1985/86 | | 154 | ... | ... | | 990 | 358 | 36 |
| | of which: Universities | | | - | - | - | | - | - | - |
| | All institutions | 1990/91 | | 910 | ... | ... | | 6 208 | 2 808 | 45 |
| | of which: Universities | | | 433 | ... | ... | | 3 021 | 1 412 | 47 |
| | All institutions | 1991/92 | | 900 | ... | ... | | 7 351 | 3 577 | 49 |
| | of which: Universities | | | 461 | ... | ... | | 3 615 | 1 917 | 53 |
| | All institutions | 1992/93 | | 955 | ... | ... | | 7 646 | 3 711 | 49 |
| | of which: Universities | | | 515 | ... | ... | | 3 504 | 1 840 | 53 |
| | All institutions | 1993/94 | | 1 040 | ... | ... | | 8 155 | 4 150 | 51 |
| | of which: Universities | | | 563 | ... | ... | | 3 858 | 2 136 | 55 |
| | All institutions | 1994/95 | | 1 094 | ... | ... | | 9 761 | 4 768 | 49 |
| | of which: Universities | | | 563 | ... | ... | | 4 541 | 2 496 | 55 |
| | All institutions | 1995/96 | | 1 064 | ... | ... | | 9 664 | 4 540 | 47 |
| | of which: Universities | | | 581 | ... | ... | | 4 834 | 2 549 | 53 |
| | All institutions | 1996/97 | | 1 162 | ... | ... | | 12 251 | 5 638 | 46 |
| | of which: Universities | | | 593 | ... | ... | | 5 135 | 2 670 | 52 |
| | All institutions | 1997/98 | | 1 307 | ... | ... | | 16 032 | 7 138 | 45 |
| | of which: Universities | | | 606 | ... | ... | | 5 913 | 3 002 | 51 |
| Pakistan | All institutions | 1970/71 | (30) | 3 439 | (30) 372 | 11 | | 114 980 | 24 534 | 21 |
| | of which: Universities | | (30) | 3 439 | (30) 372 | 11 | | 114 980 | 24 534 | 21 |
| | All institutions | 1975/76 | (30) | 5 327 | (30) 750 | 14 | | 127 932 | 30 096 | 24 |
| | of which: Universities | | (30) | 5 327 | (30) 750 | 14 | | 127 932 | 30 096 | 24 |
| | All institutions | 1985/86 | (30) | 7 805 | (30) 1 303 | 17 | | 267 742 | 69 868 | 26 |
| | of which: Universities | | (30) | 7 744 | (30) 1 279 | 17 | | 233 989 | 61 774 | 26 |
| Philippines | All institutions | 1970/71 | | 28 977 | 14 300 | 49 | | 651 514 | 362 221 | 56 |
| | of which: Universities | | | ... | ... | ... | | ... | ... | ... |
| | All institutions | 1975/76 | | 31 783 | ... | ... | | 769 749 | ... | ... |
| | of which: Universities | | | ... | ... | ... | | ... | ... | ... |
| | All institutions | 1980/81 | | 43 770 | 23 381 | 53 | | 1 276 016 | 681 140 | 53 |
| | of which: Universities | | | ... | ... | ... | | 1 143 702 | 613 197 | 54 |
| | All institutions | 1985/86 | | 57 000 | ... | ... | | 1 402 000 | ... | ... |
| | of which: Universities | | | 50 821 | ... | ... | | 1 167 000 | ... | ... |
| | All institutions | 1990/91 | | ... | ... | ... | | 1 709 486 | ... | ... |
| | of which: Universities | | | ... | ... | ... | | 1 549 639 | 880 847 | 57 |

Tertiary education: teaching staff and students   II.7
Enseignement supérieur: personnel enseignant et étudiants
Enseñanza superior: personal docente y estudiantes

| Country / Pays / País | Type of institution / Type d'établissement / Tipo de establecimiento | Year / Année / Año | Teaching staff / Personnel enseignant / Personal docente | | | Students enrolled / Étudiants inscrits / Estudiantes matriculados | | |
|---|---|---|---|---|---|---|---|---|
| | | | Total | Female Féminin Femenino | % F | Total | Female Féminin Femenino | % F |
| Philippines (cont) | All institutions | 1991/92 | ... | ... | ... | 1 656 815 | 975 250 | 59 |
| | of which: Universities | | ... | ... | ... | 1 525 868 | ... | ... |
| | All institutions | 1992/93 | ... | ... | ... | ... | ... | ... |
| | of which: Universities | | ... | ... | ... | 1 532 152 | 863 153 | 56 |
| | All institutions | 1993/94 | ... | ... | ... | ... | ... | ... |
| | of which: Universities | | ... | ... | ... | 1 583 820 | 884 088 | 56 |
| | All institutions | 1994/95 | ... | ... | ... | ... | ... | ... |
| | of which: Universities | | ... | ... | ... | 1 832 553 | 1 041 287 | 57 |
| | All institutions | 1995/96 | ... | ... | ... | 2 022 106 | 1 146 794 | 57 |
| | of which: Universities | | 66 876 | 38 437 | 57 | 2 017 972 | 1 145 142 | 57 |
| Qatar | All institutions | 1970/71 | - | - | - | - | - | - |
| | of which: Universities | | - | - | - | - | - | - |
| | All institutions | 1975/76 | 69 | 13 | 19 | 779 | 447 | 57 |
| | of which: Universities | | 69 | 13 | 19 | 779 | 447 | 57 |
| | All institutions | 1980/81 | 283 | 87 | 31 | 2 269 | 1 403 | 62 |
| | of which: Universities | | 283 | 87 | 31 | 2 269 | 1 403 | 62 |
| | All institutions | 1985/86 | ... | ... | ... | 5 344 | 3 309 | 62 |
| | of which: Universities | | ... | ... | ... | 5 344 | 3 309 | 62 |
| | All institutions | 1000/01 | ... | ... | ... | 6 485 | 4 507 | 69 |
| | of which: Universities | | ... | ... | ... | 6 485 | 4 507 | 69 |
| | All institutions | 1991/92 | 558 | 183 | 33 | 6 548 | 4 720 | 72 |
| | of which: Universities | | 558 | 183 | 33 | 6 548 | 4 720 | 72 |
| | All institutions | 1992/93 | 605 | 193 | 32 | 7 283 | 5 204 | 71 |
| | of which: Universities | | 605 | 193 | 32 | 7 283 | 5 204 | 71 |
| | All institutions | 1993/94 | 637 | 207 | 32 | 7 351 | 5 195 | 71 |
| | of which: Universities | | 637 | 207 | 32 | 7 351 | 5 195 | 71 |
| | All institutions | 1994/95 | 637 | 202 | 32 | 7 794 | 5 558 | 71 |
| | of which: Universities | | 637 | 202 | 32 | 7 794 | 5 558 | 71 |
| | All institutions | 1995/96 | 645 | 206 | 32 | 8 271 | 5 967 | 72 |
| | of which: Universities | | 645 | 206 | 32 | 8 271 | 5 967 | 72 |
| | All institutions | 1996/97 | 643 | 209 | 33 | 8 475 | 6 195 | 73 |
| | of which: Universities | | 643 | 209 | 33 | 8 475 | 6 195 | 73 |
| Saudi Arabia | All institutions | 1970/71 | 697 | 45 | 6 | 8 492 | 691 | 8 |
| | of which: Universities | | 697 | 45 | 6 | 8 492 | 691 | 8 |
| | All institutions | 1975/76 | 2 133 | 325 | 15 | 26 437 | 5 010 | 20 |
| | of which: Universities | | 2 100 | 325 | 15 | 26 437 | 5 310 | 20 |
| | All institutions | 1980/81 | 7 448 | 1 419 | 19 | 62 074 | 17 311 | 28 |
| | of which: Universities | | 6 598 | 1 306 | 20 | 56 252 | 16 472 | 29 |
| | All institutions | 1985/86 | 10 923 | 2 732 | 25 | 113 529 | 44 697 | 39 |
| | of which: Universities | | 9 297 | 2 239 | 24 | 104 046 | 40 754 | 39 |
| | All institutions | 1990/91 | 13 260 | 3 331 | 25 | 153 967 | 66 417 | 43 |
| | of which: Universities | | ... | ... | ... | ... | ... | ... |
| | All institutions | 1991/92 | 11 682 | 3 049 | 26 | 163 688 | 64 732 | 40 |
| | of which: Universities | | 10 564 | 2 522 | 24 | 151 649 | 57 128 | 38 |
| | All institutions | 1992/93 | 14 803 | 3 938 | 27 | 192 625 | 88 484 | 46 |
| | of which: Universities | | 12 669 | 3 231 | 26 | 174 788 | 78 037 | 45 |
| | All institutions | 1993/94 | 14 394 | 2 824 | 20 | 201 090 | 90 602 | 45 |
| | of which: Universities | | 12 484 | 2 190 | 18 | 182 121 | 80 155 | 44 |
| | All institutions | 1994/95 | 18 039 | 5 421 | 30 | 233 710 | 110 331 | 47 |
| | of which: Universities | | ... | ... | ... | ... | ... | ... |
| | All institutions | 1995/96 | 14 986 | 4 481 | 30 | 251 945 | 121 366 | 48 |
| | of which: Universities | | 11 880 | 3 778 | 32 | 213 902 | 110 565 | 52 |
| | All institutions | 1996/97 | 15 868 | 4 687 | 30 | 273 992 | 127 462 | 47 |
| | of which: Universities | | 13 441 | 3 911 | 29 | 241 309 | 112 975 | 47 |
| Singapore | All institutions | 1970 | 1 157 | 186 | 16 | 13 771 | 4 167 | 30 |
| | of which: Universities | | 703 | 124 | 18 | 6 889 | 2 398 | 35 |
| | All institutions | 1975 | 1 448 | 254 | 18 | 22 607 | 8 933 | 40 |
| | of which: Universities | | 927 | 164 | 18 | 8 539 | 3 768 | 44 |

II.7 Tertiary education: teaching staff and students
Enseignement supérieur: personnel enseignant et étudiants
Enseñanza superior: personal docente y estudiantes

| Country / Pays / País | Type of institution / Type d'établissement / Tipo de establecimiento | Year / Année / Año | Teaching staff Personnel enseignant Personal docente | | | Students enrolled Étudiants inscrits Estudiantes matriculados | | |
|---|---|---|---|---|---|---|---|---|
| | | | Total | Female Féminin Femenino | % F | Total | Female Féminin Femenino | % F |
| Singapore (cont) | All institutions | 1980 | 2 270 | 422 | 19 | 23 256 | 9 087 | 39 |
| | of which: Universities | | 1 433 | 244 | 17 | 9 078 | 4 011 | 44 |
| | All institutions | 1985 | ... | ... | ... | 39 913 | 14 838 | 37 |
| | of which: Universities | | ... | ... | ... | 17 071 | 7 947 | 47 |
| | All institutions | 1990 | ... | ... | ... | 55 672 | 22 980 | 41 |
| | of which: Universities | | ... | ... | ... | 24 341 | 11 358 | 47 |
| | All institutions | 1991 | ... | ... | ... | 60 225 | 25 323 | 42 |
| | of which: Universities | | ... | ... | ... | 25 901 | 11 651 | 45 |
| | All institutions | 1992 | ... | ... | ... | 65 359 | 27 736 | 42 |
| | of which: Universities | | ... | ... | ... | 27 754 | 12 135 | 44 |
| | All institutions | 1993 | ... | ... | ... | 72 826 | 31 057 | 43 |
| | of which: Universities | | ... | ... | ... | 30 015 | 13 210 | 44 |
| | All institutions | 1994 | 5 603 | 1 791 | 32 | 75 985 | 33 729 | 44 |
| | of which: Universities | | 2 121 | 632 | 30 | 32 331 | 14 440 | 45 |
| | All institutions | 1995 | 6 902 | 2 143 | 31 | 83 914 | 37 155 | 44 |
| | of which: Universities | | 2 972 | 735 | 25 | 34 591 | 15 748 | 46 |
| | All institutions | 1996 | 6 689 | ... | ... | 92 140 | ... | ... |
| | of which: Universities | | 3 059 | ... | ... | 37 791 | ... | ... |
| Sri Lanka | All institutions | 1970 | 1 487 | 223 | 15 | 12 325 | 5 334 | 43 |
| | of which: Universities | | 1 487 | 223 | 15 | 12 325 | 5 334 | 43 |
| | All institutions | 1975 | ... | ... | ... | ... | ... | ... |
| | of which: Universities | | 2 000 | 338 | 17 | 15 426 | 5 506 | 36 |
| | All institutions | 1985 | 3 355 | ... | ... | 59 377 | 23 974 | 40 |
| | of which: Universities | | 2 189 | ... | ... | 24 222 | 10 378 | 43 |
| | All institutions | 1990 | ... | ... | ... | ... | ... | ... |
| | of which: Universities | | 2 013 | 600 | 30 | 38 424 | 15 256 | 40 |
| | All institutions | 1991 (31) | 2 358 | ... | ... | (31) 55 190 | (31) 17 483 | 32 |
| | of which: Universities | | 2 093 | 625 | 30 | 36 659 | 13 199 | 36 |
| | All institutions | 1994 | 3 511 | ... | ... | 80 704 | (31) 26 318 | ... |
| | of which: Universities | | 1 980 | 604 | 31 | 39 607 | 17 738 | 45 |
| | All institutions | 1995 (31) | 2 636 | (31) 900 | 34 | (31) 63 660 | (31) 28 008 | 44 |
| | of which: Universities | | 2 344 | 768 | 33 | 40 035 | 17 775 | 44 |
| Syrian Arab Republic | All institutions | 1970/71 | 1 192 | 71 | 6 | 42 667 | 8 464 | 20 |
| | of which: Universities | | 1 037 | 70 | 7 | 38 893 | 7 235 | 19 |
| | All institutions | 1975/76 | 1 406 | 117 | 8 | 73 660 | 18 641 | 25 |
| | of which: Universities | | 1 332 | 106 | 8 | 65 348 | 14 647 | 22 |
| | All institutions | 1980/81 | ... | ... | ... | 140 180 | 41 074 | 29 |
| | of which: Universities | | ... | ... | ... | 110 832 | 29 565 | 27 |
| | All institutions | 1985/86 | ... | ... | ... | 179 473 | 62 731 | 35 |
| | of which: Universities | | 4 504 | 756 | 17 | 135 191 | 42 968 | 32 |
| | All institutions | 1990/91 | ... | ... | ... | 221 628 | 85 734 | 39 |
| | of which: Universities | | ... | ... | ... | 169 913 | 62 657 | 37 |
| | All institutions | 1991/92 | ... | ... | ... | 219 587 | 86 530 | 39 |
| | of which: Universities | | 4 327 | 797 | 18 | 170 075 | *62 750 | *37 |
| | All institutions | 1992/93 | ... | ... | ... | 228 197 | 92 716 | 41 |
| | of which: Universities | | 5 997 | 1 196 | 20 | 178 526 | 67 993 | 38 |
| | All institutions | 1993/94 | ... | ... | ... | 216 211 | 88 361 | 41 |
| | of which: Universities | | ... | ... | ... | 170 830 | 66 707 | 39 |
| | All institutions | 1994/95 | ... | ... | ... | 215 734 | 88 748 | 41 |
| | of which: Universities | | 4 733 | 736 | 16 | 167 186 | 65 367 | 39 |
| Tajikistan | All institutions | 1980/81 | ... | ... | ... | 96 900 | ... | ... |
| | of which: Universities | | ... | ... | ... | ... | ... | ... |
| | All institutions | 1985/86 | ... | ... | ... | 95 247 | *40 003 | *42 |
| | of which: Universities | | ... | ... | ... | 55 056 | *23 123 | *42 |
| | All institutions | 1990/91 | ... | ... | ... | 109 653 | *42 207 | *38 |
| | of which: Universities | | ... | ... | ... | 68 760 | *25 441 | *37 |
| | All institutions | 1991/92 | ... | ... | ... | 110 064 | *41 493 | *38 |
| | of which: Universities | | ... | ... | ... | 69 345 | *23 577 | *34 |

Tertiary education: teaching staff and students
Enseignement supérieur: personnel enseignant et étudiants
Enseñanza superior: personal docente y estudiantes

II.7

| Country Pays País | Type of institution Type d'établissement Tipo de establecimiento | Year Année Año | Teaching staff Personnel enseignant Personal docente | | | Students enrolled Étudiants inscrits Estudiantes matriculados | | |
|---|---|---|---|---|---|---|---|---|
| | | | Total | Female Féminin Femenino | % F | Total | Female Féminin Femenino | % F |
| Tajikistan (cont) | All institutions of which: Universities | 1992/93 | ... ... | ... ... | ... ... | 109 016 70 633 | *38 016 *21 896 | *35 *31 |
| | All institutions of which: Universities | 1993/94 | ... ... | ... ... | ... ... | 107 402 69 002 | *34 680 *19 320 | *32 *28 |
| | All institutions of which: Universities | 1994/95 | ... 5 200 | ... ... | ... ... | 108 203 73 327 | *35 325 20 189 | *33 28 |
| | All institutions of which: Universities | 1996/97 | ... ... | ... ... | ... ... | ... 76 613 | ... 19 821 | ... 26 |
| Thailand | All institutions of which: Universities | 1970/71 | 7 506 6 532 | 2 866 2 458 | 38 38 | (29) 55 315 43 028 | (29) 23 136 17 977 | 42 42 |
| | All institutions of which: Universities | 1975/76 | 9 070 9 070 | 5 121 5 121 | 56 56 | 130 965 78 229 | 52 112 33 273 | 40 43 |
| | All institutions of which: Universities | 1981/82 | 35 281 ... | ... ... | ... ... | 911 166 (8) 712 650 | ... ... | ... ... |
| | All institutions of which: Universities | 1985/86 | 30 905 14 666 | ... ... | ... ... | 1 026 952 150 355 | ... ... | ... ... |
| | All institutions of which: Universities | 1992/93 | 49 466 18 336 | 21 471 9 391 | 43 51 | 1 156 174 266 107 | 607 822 139 940 | 53 53 |
| | All institutions of which: Universities | 1994/95 | 39 781 22 015 | ... ... | ... ... | 1 184 309 325 893 | ... ... | ... ... |
| | All institutions of which: Universities | 1995/96 | 38 423 25 171 | ... ... | ... ... | 1 220 481 481 936 | ... ... | ... ... |
| | All institutions of which: Universities | 1996/97 | ... ... | ... ... | ... ... | 1 332 767 ... | ... ... | ... ... |
| | All institutions of which: Universities | 1997/98 | ... ... | ... ... | ... ... | 1 522 142 ... | ... ... | ... ... |
| Turkey | All institutions of which: Universities | 1970/71 | 9 229 6 382 | 2 098 1 454 | 23 23 | 169 793 76 739 | 32 034 16 079 | 19 21 |
| | All institutions of which: Universities | 1975/76 | 15 560 (8) 9 596 | 3 759 (8) 2 279 | 24 24 | 327 082 93 541 | ... 21 160 | ... 23 |
| | All institutions of which: Universities | 1980/81 | 21 577 (8) 16 162 | 5 312 (8) 3 734 | 25 23 | 246 183 165 647 | ... 42 839 | ... 26 |
| | All institutions of which: Universities | 1985/86 | 22 968 (8) 20 430 | 6 950 (8) 5 888 | 30 29 | 469 992 300 836 | 152 047 101 601 | 32 34 |
| | All institutions of which: Universities | 1990/91 | 34 469 (8) 32 915 | 10 929 (8) 10 579 | 32 32 | 749 921 416 752 | 252 487 150 624 | 34 36 |
| | All institutions of which: Universities | 1991/92 | 35 123 (8) 33 455 | 11 200 (8) 10 835 | 32 32 | 810 781 444 018 | 276 677 163 422 | 34 37 |
| | All institutions of which: Universities | 1992/93 | 38 468 (8) 36 387 | 12 519 (8) 11 999 | 33 33 | 923 719 ... | 320 184 ... | 35 ... |
| | All institutions of which: Universities | 1993/94 | 42 475 (8) 40 041 | 13 761 (8) 13 135 | 32 33 | 1 143 083 570 672 | 427 290 214 106 | 37 38 |
| | All institutions of which: Universities | 1994/95 | 44 086 (8) 41 258 | 14 456 (8) 13 676 | 33 33 | 1 174 299 737 542 | 449 771 305 096 | 38 41 |
| | All institutions of which: Universities | 1996/97 | 50 313 ... | 16 616 ... | 33 ... | 1 434 033 ... | 504 088 ... | 35 ... |
| Turkmenistan | All institutions of which: Universities | 1980/81 | ... ... | ... ... | ... ... | (15) 69 800 ... | ... ... | ... ... |
| | All institutions of which: Universities | 1985/86 | ... ... | ... ... | ... ... | (15) 75 800 ... | ... ... | ... ... |
| | All institutions of which: Universities | 1990/91 | ... ... | ... ... | ... ... | (15) 76 000 ... | ... ... | ... ... |
| United Arab Emirates | All institutions of which: Universities | 1980/81 | 257 207 | 20 10 | 8 5 | 2 861 2 646 | 1 389 1 209 | 49 46 |
| | All institutions of which: Universities | 1985/86 | 445 295 | 47 15 | 11 5 | 7 772 7 248 | 4 541 4 057 | 58 56 |

II.7   Tertiary education: teaching staff and students
Enseignement supérieur: personnel enseignant et étudiants
Enseñanza superior: personal docente y estudiantes

| Country / Pays / País | Type of institution / Type d'établissement / Tipo de establecimiento | Year / Année / Año | Teaching staff — Personnel enseignant — Personal docente | | | Students enrolled — Étudiants inscrits — Estudiantes matriculados | | |
|---|---|---|---|---|---|---|---|---|
| | | | Total | Female Féminin Femenino | % F | Total | Female Féminin Femenino | % F |
| United Arab Emirates (cont) | All institutions | 1990/91 | 841 | 115 | 14 | 10 196 | 7 182 | 70 |
| | of which: Universities | | 494 | 28 | 6 | 8 496 | 6 063 | 71 |
| | All institutions | 1991/92 | 1 082 | 155 | 14 | 10 405 | 7 831 | 75 |
| | of which: Universities | | 728 | 64 | 9 | 8 668 | 6 721 | 78 |
| | All institutions | 1992/93 | ... | ... | ... | 10 641 | 7 429 | 70 |
| | of which: Universities | | ... | ... | ... | ... | ... | ... |
| | All institutions | 1996/97 | ... | ... | ... | ... | ... | ... |
| | of which: Universities | | ... | ... | ... | 16 213 | 11 694 | 72 |
| Uzbekistan | All institutions | 1980/81 | ... | ... | ... | 515 800 | ... | ... |
| | of which: Universities | | ... | ... | ... | ... | ... | ... |
| | All institutions | 1985/86 | ... | ... | ... | 567 200 | ... | ... |
| | of which: Universities | | ... | ... | ... | ... | ... | ... |
| | All institutions | 1990/91 | 23 062 | ... | ... | 602 700 | ... | ... |
| | of which: Universities | | ... | ... | ... | ... | ... | ... |
| | All institutions | 1991/92 | 24 787 | ... | ... | 638 200 | ... | ... |
| | of which: Universities | | ... | ... | ... | ... | ... | ... |
| Viet Nam | All institutions | 1975/76 | 9 642 | 1 705 | 18 | 80 323 | 31 702 | 39 |
| | of which: Universities | | 9 642 | 1 705 | 18 | 80 323 | 31 702 | 39 |
| | All institutions | 1980/81 | 17 242 | 3 857 | 22 | 114 701 | 27 090 | 24 |
| | of which: Universities | | 17 242 | 3 857 | 22 | 114 701 | 27 090 | 24 |
| | All institutions | 1985/86 | 18 614 | ... | ... | 121 159 | ... | ... |
| | of which: Universities | | ... | ... | ... | ... | ... | ... |
| | All institutions | 1990/91 | ... | ... | ... | 129 600 | ... | ... |
| | of which: Universities | | ... | ... | ... | ... | ... | ... |
| | All institutions | 1991/92 | 21 700 | ... | ... | 106 900 | ... | ... |
| | of which: Universities | | ... | ... | ... | ... | ... | ... |
| | All institutions | 1992/93 | 21 000 | ... | ... | 136 800 | ... | ... |
| | of which: Universities | | ... | ... | ... | ... | ... | ... |
| | All institutions | 1993/94 | 21 200 | ... | ... | 157 100 | ... | ... |
| | of which: Universities | | ... | ... | ... | ... | ... | ... |
| | All institutions | 1994/95 | 21 711 | 6 711 | 31 | 203 300 | ... | ... |
| | of which: Universities | | ... | ... | ... | ... | ... | ... |
| | All institutions | 1995/96 | 22 750 | ... | ... | 297 900 | ... | ... |
| | of which: Universities | | ... | ... | ... | ... | ... | ... |
| | All institutions | 1996/97 | 23 522 | 7 962 | 34 | 509 300 | ... | ... |
| | of which: Universities | | ... | ... | ... | ... | ... | ... |
| Yemen | All institutions | 1991/92 | 1 800 | 210 | 12 | 53 082 | 9 079 | 17 |
| | of which: Universities | | 1 800 | 210 | 12 | 53 082 | 9 079 | 17 |
| | All institutions | 1996/97 | ... | ... | ... | 65 675 | 8 224 | 13 |
| | of which: Universities | | ... | ... | ... | 65 675 | 8 224 | 13 |
| Palestine | All institutions | 1995/96 | 2 026 | 279 | 14 | 40 916 | 17 884 | 44 |
| | of which: Universities | | (8) 1 644 | (8) 203 | 12 | (8) 37 094 | (8) 15 904 | 43 |
| | All institutions | 1996/97 | 2 443 | 349 | 14 | 49 599 | 22 030 | 44 |
| | of which: Universities | | 1 966 | 258 | 13 | 36 921 | 16 072 | 44 |
| **Europe** | | | | | | | | |
| Albania | All institutions | 1980/81 | 1 103 | 222 | 20 | 14 568 | 7 221 | 50 |
| | of which: Universities | | 1 103 | 222 | 20 | 14 568 | 7 221 | 50 |
| | All institutions | 1985/86 | 1 468 | 347 | 24 | 21 995 | 9 995 | 45 |
| | of which: Universities | | 1 468 | 347 | 24 | 21 995 | 9 995 | 45 |
| | All institutions | 1990/91 | 1 806 | 513 | 28 | 22 059 | 11 384 | 52 |
| | of which: Universities | | 1 806 | 513 | 28 | 22 059 | 11 384 | 52 |
| | All institutions | 1991/92 | 1 805 | 489 | 27 | 28 001 | 14 536 | 52 |
| | of which: Universities | | 1 623 | 438 | 27 | 26 569 | 14 053 | 53 |

Tertiary education: teaching staff and students  II.7
Enseignement supérieur: personnel enseignant et étudiants
Enseñanza superior: personal docente y estudiantes

| Country / Pays / País | Type of institution / Type d'établissement / Tipo de establecimiento | Year / Année / Año | Teaching staff / Personnel enseignant / Personal docente | | | Students enrolled / Étudiants inscrits / Estudiantes matriculados | | |
|---|---|---|---|---|---|---|---|---|
| | | | Total | Female Féminin Femenino | % F | Total | Female Féminin Femenino | % F |
| Albania (cont) | All institutions | 1992/93 | 1 680 | 497 | 30 | 22 835 | 11 836 | 52 |
| | of which: Universities | | 1 523 | 449 | 29 | 21 666 | 11 447 | 53 |
| | All institutions | 1993/94 | 1 774 | 480 | 27 | 30 185 | 16 069 | 53 |
| | of which: Universities | | 1 596 | 440 | 28 | 28 519 | 15 546 | 55 |
| | All institutions | 1996/97 | 2 348 | 736 | 31 | 34 257 | 19 377 | 57 |
| | of which: Universities | | 2 304 | 702 | 30 | 33 962 | 19 121 | 56 |
| Austria | All institutions | 1970/71 | 6 980 | 832 | 12 | 59 778 | 17 547 | 29 |
| | of which: Universities | | 6 671 | 743 | 11 | 53 152 | 13 269 | 25 |
| | All institutions | 1975/76 | ... | ... | ... | 96 736 | 36 527 | 38 |
| | of which: Universities | | 10 001 | 1 282 | 13 | 86 123 | 28 931 | 34 |
| | All institutions | 1980/81 | 14 086 | 2 067 | 15 | 136 774 | 57 491 | 42 |
| | of which: Universities | | 12 572 | 1 599 | 13 | 127 423 | 50 200 | 39 |
| | All institutions | 1985/86 | ... | ... | ... | 173 215 | 78 593 | 45 |
| | of which: Universities | | (2) 10 252 | (2) 1 854 | 18 | 160 904 | 69 509 | 43 |
| | All institutions | 1990/91 | ... | ... | ... | 205 767 | 94 004 | 46 |
| | of which: Universities | | (2) 12 698 | (2) 2 812 | 22 | 191 793 | 84 306 | 44 |
| | All institutions | 1991/92 | ... | ... | ... | 216 529 | 99 917 | 46 |
| | of which: Universities | | (2) 13 315 | (2) 3 096 | 23 | 201 615 | 89 422 | 44 |
| | All institutions | 1992/93 | ... | ... | ... | 221 389 | 103 030 | 47 |
| | of which: Universities | | (2) 14 218 | (2) 3 481 | 24 | 205 769 | 91 847 | 45 |
| | All institutions | 1993/94 | (21) 24 732 | (21) 6 109 | 25 | (21) 227 444 | (21) 107 013 | 47 |
| | of which: Universities | | 22 609 | 5 239 | 23 | 210 639 | 94 988 | 45 |
| | All institutions | 1994/95 | 25 380 | 6 385 | 25 | 233 989 | 111 844 | 48 |
| | of which: Universities | | ... | ... | ... | ... | ... | ... |
| | All institutions | 1995/96 | 26 318 | 6 872 | 26 | 238 981 | 115 657 | 48 |
| | of which: Universities | | ... | ... | ... | ... | ... | ... |
| | All institutions | 1996/97 | 26 356 | 7 110 | 27 | 240 632 | 117 274 | 49 |
| | of which: Universities | | ... | ... | ... | ... | ... | ... |
| Belarus | All institutions | 1970/71 | ... | ... | ... | 286 134 | ... | ... |
| | of which: Universities | | ... | ... | ... | 140 034 | 72 568 | 52 |
| | All institutions | 1975/76 | ... | ... | ... | 314 603 | ... | ... |
| | of which: Universities | | ... | ... | ... | 159 903 | ... | ... |
| | All institutions | 1980/81 | ... | ... | ... | 339 800 | ... | ... |
| | of which: Universities | | 12 900 | ... | ... | 177 000 | ... | ... |
| | All institutions | 1985/86 | ... | ... | ... | 342 400 | ... | ... |
| | of which: Universities | | 13 500 | ... | ... | 181 900 | ... | ... |
| | All institutions | 1990/91 | *40 400 | ... | ... | 335 284 | ... | ... |
| | of which: Universities | | ... | ... | ... | 191 584 | 99 700 | 52 |
| | All institutions | 1991/92 | 39 800 | ... | ... | 313 500 | ... | ... |
| | of which: Universities | | ... | ... | ... | 187 435 | 98 400 | 52 |
| | All institutions | 1992/93 | 39 300 | ... | ... | 312 339 | ... | ... |
| | of which: Universities | | ... | ... | ... | 187 639 | 95 800 | 51 |
| | All institutions | 1993/94 | 39 200 | ... | ... | 299 640 | ... | ... |
| | of which: Universities | | ... | ... | ... | 178 016 | 91 800 | 52 |
| | All institutions | 1994/95 | 40 000 | ... | ... | 292 800 | ... | ... |
| | of which: Universities | | 17 300 | ... | ... | 176 508 | 91 100 | 52 |
| | All institutions | 1995/96 | 40 000 | ... | ... | 313 800 | 168 000 | 54 |
| | of which: Universities | | 17 600 | ... | ... | 200 500 | 105 400 | 53 |
| | All institutions | 1996/97 | 40 300 | ... | ... | 328 746 | 182 200 | 55 |
| | of which: Universities | | 18 000 | ... | ... | 212 446 | 112 000 | 53 |
| Belgium | All institutions | 1970/71 | ... | ... | ... | 124 857 | 45 231 | 36 |
| | of which: Universities | | ... | ... | ... | 75 106 | 21 483 | 29 |
| | All institutions | 1975/76 | ... | ... | ... | ... | ... | ... |
| | of which: Universities | | ... | ... | ... | 83 360 | 27 773 | 33 |
| | All institutions | 1980/81 | ... | ... | ... | 196 153 | 86 947 | 44 |
| | of which: Universities | | ... | ... | ... | 95 246 | 35 107 | 37 |
| | All institutions | 1985/86 | ... | ... | ... | 247 499 | 113 120 | 46 |
| | of which: Universities | | ... | ... | ... | 103 598 | 42 593 | 41 |

II.7 Tertiary education: teaching staff and students
Enseignement supérieur: personnel enseignant et étudiants
Enseñanza superior: personal docente y estudiantes

| Country<br>Pays<br>País | Type of institution<br>Type d'établissement<br>Tipo de establecimiento | Year<br>Année<br>Año | Teaching staff<br>Personnel enseignant<br>Personal docente | | | Students enrolled<br>Étudiants inscrits<br>Estudiantes matriculados | | |
|---|---|---|---|---|---|---|---|---|
| | | | Total | Female<br>Féminin<br>Femenino | %<br>F | Total | Female<br>Féminin<br>Femenino | %<br>F |
| Belgium (cont) | All institutions<br>of which: Universities | 1990/91 | 28 058<br>11 050 | 9 119<br>2 343 | 33<br>21 | 276 248<br>111 845 | 133 339<br>49 951 | 48<br>45 |
| | All institutions<br>of which: Universities | 1991/92 | ...<br>... | ...<br>... | ...<br>... | ...<br>116 250 | ...<br>... | ...<br>... |
| | All institutions<br>of which: Universities | 1992/93 | (18) 32 561<br>... | (18) 11 391<br>... | 35<br>... | (18) 307 130<br>... | (18) 150 246<br>... | 49<br>... |
| | All institutions<br>of which: Universities | 1993/94 | 32 938<br>... | 11 800<br>... | 36<br>... | 322 364<br>... | 159 138<br>... | 49<br>... |
| | All institutions<br>of which: Universities | 1994/95 | ...<br>... | ...<br>... | ...<br>... | 352 630<br>... | 174 332<br>... | 49<br>... |
| | All institutions<br>of which: Universities | 1995/96 | ...<br>... | ...<br>... | ...<br>... | 358 214<br>... | 178 833<br>... | 50<br>... |
| Bulgaria | All institutions<br>of which: Universities | 1970/71 | 7 680<br>7 125 | 2 006<br>1 752 | 26<br>25 | 99 596<br>89 331 | 50 445<br>43 508 | 51<br>49 |
| | All institutions<br>of which: Universities | 1975/76 | 12 230<br>11 248 | 3 937<br>3 411 | 32<br>30 | 128 593<br>108 814 | 73 806<br>57 957 | 57<br>53 |
| | All institutions<br>of which: Universities | 1980/81 | 14 412<br>12 622 | 5 592<br>4 638 | 39<br>37 | 101 359<br>87 335 | 56 946<br>46 491 | 56<br>53 |
| | All institutions<br>of which: Universities | 1985/86 | 15 252<br>14 409 | 5 592<br>5 157 | 37<br>36 | 113 795<br>104 259 | 62 035<br>54 950 | 55<br>53 |
| | All institutions<br>of which: Universities | 1990/91 | 23 663<br>20 716 | 9 353<br>7 781 | 40<br>38 | 188 479<br>156 536 | 96 807<br>75 689 | 51<br>48 |
| | All institutions<br>of which: Universities | 1991/92 | 23 954<br>20 940 | 9 392<br>7 775 | 39<br>37 | 185 914<br>156 247 | 99 125<br>79 228 | 53<br>51 |
| | All institutions<br>of which: Universities | 1992/93 | 21 976<br>18 895 | 8 459<br>6 950 | 38<br>37 | 195 447<br>165 186 | 111 759<br>90 715 | 57<br>55 |
| | All institutions<br>of which: Universities | 1993/94 | 21 148<br>18 158 | 8 049<br>6 561 | 38<br>36 | 206 179<br>178 388 | 121 250<br>101 031 | 59<br>57 |
| | All institutions<br>of which: Universities | 1994/95 | 24 274<br>21 227 | 9 913<br>8 360 | 41<br>39 | 223 030<br>197 869 | 134 958<br>116 263 | 61<br>59 |
| | All institutions<br>of which: Universities | 1995/96 | 25 339<br>22 228 | 10 447<br>8 868 | 41<br>40 | 250 336<br>225 025 | 155 226<br>136 230 | 62<br>61 |
| | All institutions<br>of which: Universities | 1996/97 | 26 303<br>23 285 | 10 765<br>9 143 | 41<br>39 | 262 757<br>237 776 | 161 049<br>142 404 | 61<br>60 |
| Croatia (32) | All institutions<br>of which: Universities | 1980/81 | 5 436<br>5 436 | ...<br>... | ...<br>... | 64 966<br>64 966 | ...<br>... | ...<br>... |
| | All institutions<br>of which: Universities | 1985/86 | 5 081<br>5 081 | ...<br>... | ...<br>... | 55 886<br>55 886 | ...<br>... | ...<br>... |
| | All institutions<br>of which: Universities | 1990/91 | 6 633<br>6 633 | ...<br>... | ...<br>... | 72 342<br>72 342 | ...<br>... | ...<br>... |
| | All institutions<br>of which: Universities | 1991/92 | 6 425<br>6 425 | ...<br>... | ...<br>... | 69 822<br>69 822 | ...<br>... | ...<br>... |
| | All institutions<br>of which: Universities | 1992/93 | 6 550<br>6 550 | 2 264<br>2 264 | 35<br>35 | 77 689<br>77 689 | 37 358<br>37 358 | 48<br>48 |
| | All institutions<br>of which: Universities | 1993/94 | 6 429<br>6 429 | 2 148<br>2 148 | 33<br>33 | 82 361<br>82 361 | 39 239<br>39 239 | 48<br>48 |
| | All institutions<br>of which: Universities | 1994/95 | 6 169<br>6 169 | 2 022<br>2 022 | 33<br>33 | 82 251<br>82 251 | 40 362<br>40 362 | 49<br>49 |
| | All institutions<br>of which: Universities | 1995/96 | 6 325<br>6 325 | 2 164<br>2 164 | 34<br>34 | 86 357<br>86 357 | 42 117<br>42 117 | 49<br>49 |
| | All institutions<br>of which: Universities | 1996/97 | 6 038<br>6 038 | 2 045<br>2 045 | 34<br>34 | 85 752<br>85 752 | 43 563<br>43 563 | 51<br>51 |
| Czech Republic | All institutions<br>of which: Universities | 1970/71 | 10 544<br>... | ...<br>... | ...<br>... | (2) 79 024<br>... | (2) 28 446<br>... | 36<br>... |
| | All institutions<br>of which: Universities | 1975/76 | 10 460<br>... | ...<br>... | ...<br>... | (2) 90 649<br>... | (2) 34 988<br>... | 39<br>... |

Tertiary education: teaching staff and students
Enseignement supérieur: personnel enseignant et étudiants
Enseñanza superior: personal docente y estudiantes

II.7

| Country<br>Pays<br>País | Type of institution<br>Type d'établissement<br>Tipo de establecimiento | Year<br>Année<br>Año | Teaching staff<br>Personnel enseignant<br>Personal docente | | | Students enrolled<br>Étudiants inscrits<br>Estudiantes matriculados | | |
|---|---|---|---|---|---|---|---|---|
| | | | Total | Female<br>Féminin<br>Femenino | %<br>F | Total | Female<br>Féminin<br>Femenino | %<br>F |
| Czech Republic (cont) | All institutions<br>of which: Universities | 1980/81 | 10 928<br>... | ...<br>... | ...<br>... | (2) 118 026<br>... | (2) 47 661<br>... | 40<br>... |
| | All institutions<br>of which: Universities | 1985/86 | 11 585<br>... | ...<br>... | ...<br>... | (2) 107 098<br>... | (2) 44 843<br>... | 42<br>... |
| | All institutions<br>of which: Universities | 1990/91 | 11 839<br>... | ...<br>... | ...<br>... | (2) 118 194<br>... | (2) 51 562<br>... | 44<br>... |
| | All institutions<br>of which: Universities | 1991/92 | 11 958<br>... | ...<br>... | ...<br>... | (2) 112 654<br>... | (2) 49 730<br>... | 44<br>... |
| | All institutions<br>of which: Universities | 1992/93 | 14 798<br>... | 4 321<br>... | 29<br>... | 116 560<br>60 431 | 51 502<br>33 558 | 44<br>56 |
| | All institutions<br>of which: Universities | 1993/94 | (21) 18 808<br>... | (21) 6 523<br>... | 35<br>... | (21) 163 394<br>... | (21) 78 530<br>... | 48<br>... |
| | All institutions<br>of which: Universities | 1994/95 | ...<br>... | ...<br>... | ...<br>... | 178 853<br>... | 85 743<br>... | 48<br>... |
| | All institutions<br>of which: Universities | 1995/96 | 19 769<br>... | 10 235<br>... | 52<br>... | 191 604<br>... | 89 654<br>... | 47<br>... |
| | All institutions<br>of which: Universities | 1996/97 | ...<br>... | ...<br>... | ...<br>... | 207 221<br>... | 100 315<br>... | 48<br>... |
| Denmark | All institutions<br>of which: Universities | 1970/71 | ...<br>... | ...<br>... | ...<br>... | 76 024<br>43 944 | 27 895<br>14 330 | 37<br>33 |
| | All institutions<br>of which: Universities | 1975/76 | ...<br>(2) 4 777 | ...<br>... | ...<br>... | 110 271<br>60 106 | 48 837<br>21 870 | 44<br>36 |
| | All institutions<br>of which: Universities | 1980/81 | ...<br>... | ...<br>... | ...<br>... | 106 241<br>85 388 | 51 923<br>36 318 | 49<br>43 |
| | All institutions<br>of which: Universities | 1985/86 | ...<br>... | ...<br>... | ...<br>... | 116 319<br>91 450 | 57 380<br>40 402 | 49<br>44 |
| | All institutions<br>of which: Universities | 1990/91 | ...<br>... | ...<br>... | ...<br>... | 142 968<br>120 125 | 74 385<br>61 019 | 52<br>51 |
| | All institutions<br>of which: Universities | 1991/92 | ...<br>... | ...<br>... | ...<br>... | 150 159<br>124 942 | 78 891<br>64 051 | 53<br>51 |
| | All institutions<br>of which: Universities | 1992/93 | (18) 8 700<br>... | (18) 3 300<br>... | 38<br>... | (18) 164 356<br>... | (18) 83 468<br>... | 51<br>... |
| | All institutions<br>of which: Universities | 1993/94 | 9 000<br>... | 2 700<br>... | 30<br>... | 169 619<br>... | 86 784<br>... | 51<br>... |
| | All institutions<br>of which: Universities | 1994/95 | 9 600<br>... | 2 900<br>... | 30<br>... | 160 783<br>... | 87 988<br>... | 52<br>... |
| | All institutions<br>of which: Universities | 1995/96 | ...<br>... | ...<br>... | ...<br>... | 174 975<br>... | 94 452<br>... | 54<br>... |
| Estonia | All institutions<br>of which: Universities | 1980/81 | ...<br>... | ...<br>... | ...<br>... | 25 500<br>... | 14 000<br>... | 55<br>... |
| | All institutions<br>of which: Universities | 1985/86 | ...<br>... | ...<br>... | ...<br>... | 23 500<br>... | 14 000<br>... | 60<br>... |
| | All institutions<br>of which: Universities | 1990/91 | ...<br>... | ...<br>... | ...<br>... | 25 900<br>... | 13 000<br>... | 50<br>... |
| | All institutions<br>of which: Universities | 1991/92 | ...<br>... | ...<br>... | ...<br>... | (15) 25 805<br>(15) 24 880 | (15) 12 771<br>(15) 12 375 | 49<br>50 |
| | All institutions<br>of which: Universities | 1992/93 | ...<br>... | ...<br>... | ...<br>... | (15) 24 464<br>(15) 22 875 | (15) 12 264<br>(15) 11 522 | 50<br>50 |
| | All institutions<br>of which: Universities | 1993/94 | ...<br>... | ...<br>... | ...<br>... | 24 768<br>21 261 | 12 676<br>11 051 | 51<br>52 |
| | All institutions<br>of which: Universities | 1994/95 | ...<br>... | ...<br>... | ...<br>... | 25 483<br>... | 13 162<br>... | 52<br>... |
| | All institutions<br>of which: Universities | 1995/96 | (33) 4 025<br>2 699 | (33) 1 923<br>1 059 | 48<br>39 | (33) 39 726<br>27 234 | (33) 20 889<br>14 168 | 53<br>52 |
| | All institutions<br>of which: Universities | 1996/97 | 4 435<br>3 052 | 2 168<br>1 273 | 49<br>42 | 43 468<br>30 072 | 23 233<br>15 953 | 53<br>53 |

II.7    Tertiary education: teaching staff and students
Enseignement supérieur: personnel enseignant et étudiants
Enseñanza superior: personal docente y estudiantes

| Country<br>Pays<br>País | Type of institution<br>Type d'établissement<br>Tipo de establecimiento | Year<br>Année<br>Año | Teaching staff<br>Personnel enseignant<br>Personal docente | | | Students enrolled<br>Étudiants inscrits<br>Estudiantes matriculados | | |
|---|---|---|---|---|---|---|---|---|
| | | | Total | Female<br>Féminin<br>Femenino | %<br>F | Total | Female<br>Féminin<br>Femenino | %<br>F |
| Federal Republic of Yugoslavia (32) | All institutions<br>of which: Universities | 1991/92 | 11 647<br>9 617 | 3 538<br>3 017 | 30<br>31 | 133 331<br>106 361 | 69 807<br>55 670 | 52<br>52 |
| | All institutions<br>of which: Universities | 1992/93 | 11 605<br>9 695 | 3 643<br>3 156 | 31<br>33 | 143 268<br>116 413 | 76 177<br>62 485 | 53<br>54 |
| | All institutions<br>of which: Universities | 1994/95 | 11 831<br>10 125 | 3 884<br>3 365 | 33<br>33 | 143 951<br>118 566 | 77 851<br>65 280 | 54<br>55 |
| | All institutions<br>of which: Universities | 1995/96 | 12 266<br>10 565 | 4 104<br>3 590 | 33<br>34 | 159 512<br>132 160 | 84 919<br>72 090 | 53<br>55 |
| | All institutions<br>of which: Universities | 1996/97 | 12 273<br>10 588 | 4 185<br>3 673 | 34<br>35 | 172 313<br>140 568 | 92 697<br>77 132 | 54<br>55 |
| Finland | All institutions<br>of which: Universities | 1970/71 | 6 267<br>5 749 | 1 194<br>937 | 19<br>16 | 59 769<br>57 739 | 28 916<br>27 391 | 48<br>47 |
| | All institutions<br>of which: Universities | 1975/76 | ...<br>5 225 | ...<br>... | ...<br>... | 114 272<br>75 765 | ...<br>37 151 | ...<br>49 |
| | All institutions<br>of which: Universities | 1980/81 | ...<br>6 194 | ...<br>... | ...<br>... | 123 165<br>84 176 | 59 356<br>41 746 | 48<br>50 |
| | All institutions<br>of which: Universities | 1985/86 | ...<br>7 169 | ...<br>... | ...<br>... | 127 976<br>92 230 | 62 467<br>46 704 | 49<br>51 |
| | All institutions<br>of which: Universities | 1990/91 | ...<br>7 798 | ...<br>... | ...<br>... | 165 714<br>112 921 | 86 468<br>58 401 | 52<br>52 |
| | All institutions<br>of which: Universities | 1991/92 | ...<br>7 802 | ...<br>... | ...<br>... | 173 702<br>115 358 | 91 574<br>59 692 | 53<br>52 |
| | All institutions<br>of which: Universities | 1992/93 | ...<br>(18) 7 917 | ...<br>... | ...<br>... | (18) 188 162<br>121 736 | (18) 99 791<br>63 210 | 53<br>52 |
| | All institutions<br>of which: Universities | 1993/94 | ...<br>7 905 | ...<br>... | ...<br>... | 197 367<br>124 370 | 104 713<br>64 627 | 53<br>52 |
| | All institutions<br>of which: Universities | 1994/95 | ...<br>... | ...<br>... | ...<br>... | 205 039<br>... | 108 471<br>... | 53<br>... |
| | All institutions<br>of which: Universities | 1995/96 | ...<br>... | ...<br>... | ...<br>... | 213 995<br>... | 112 748<br>... | 53<br>... |
| | All institutions<br>of which: Universities | 1996/97 | ...<br>... | ...<br>... | ...<br>... | 226 458<br>... | 119 653<br>... | 53<br>... |
| France | All institutions<br>of which: Universities | 1970/71 | ...<br>35 679 | ...<br>... | ...<br>... | 801 156<br>661 156 | ...<br>... | ...<br>... |
| | All institutions<br>of which: Universities | 1975/76 | ...<br>40 512 | ...<br>... | ...<br>... | 1 038 576<br>811 258 | *496 049<br>*386 000 | *48<br>*48 |
| | All institutions<br>of which: Universities | 1980/81 | ...<br>... | ...<br>... | ...<br>... | 1 076 717<br>869 788 | ...<br>... | ...<br>... |
| | All institutions<br>of which: Universities | 1985/86 | (34) 45 211<br>978 519 | (34) 11 620<br>510 275 | 26<br>52 | 1 278 581<br>978 519 | 643 429<br>510 275 | 50<br>52 |
| | All institutions<br>of which: Universities | 1990/91 | ...<br>48 248 | ...<br>... | ...<br>... | 1 698 938<br>1 191 823 | 902 557<br>645 442 | 53<br>54 |
| | All institutions<br>of which: Universities | 1991/92 | ...<br>50 331 | ...<br>13 992 | ...<br>28 | 1 840 307<br>1 246 989 | 989 443<br>679 928 | 54<br>55 |
| | All institutions<br>of which: Universities | 1992/93 | (18) 120 289<br>... | (18) 38 784<br>... | 32<br>... | (18) 1 951 994<br>1 296 459 | (18) 1 058 884<br>710 525 | 54<br>55 |
| | All institutions<br>of which: Universities | 1993/94 | 125 403<br>... | 40 613<br>... | 32<br>... | 2 083 232<br>1 395 103 | 1 138 302<br>772 135 | 55<br>55 |
| | All institutions<br>of which: Universities | 1994/95 | 131 664<br>... | 40 354<br>... | 31<br>... | 2 072 552<br>... | 1 138 397<br>... | 55<br>... |
| | All institutions<br>of which: Universities | 1995/96 | 132 140<br>... | 44 112<br>... | 33<br>... | 2 091 688<br>... | 1 147 202<br>... | 55<br>... |
| | All institutions<br>of which: Universities | 1996/97 | 141 410<br>... | 48 088<br>... | 34<br>... | 2 062 495<br>... | 1 133 990<br>... | 55<br>... |
| Germany (32) | All institutions<br>of which: Universities | 1990/91 | ...<br>... | ...<br>... | ...<br>... | 2 048 627<br>1 799 394 | ...<br>... | ...<br>... |

Tertiary education: teaching staff and students
Enseignement supérieur: personnel enseignant et étudiants
Enseñanza superior: personal docente y estudiantes

II.7

| Country / Pays / País | Type of institution / Type d'établissement / Tipo de establecimiento | Year / Année / Año | Teaching staff / Personnel enseignant / Personal docente | | | Students enrolled / Étudiants inscrits / Estudiantes matriculados | | |
|---|---|---|---|---|---|---|---|---|
| | | | Total | Female Féminin Femenino | % F | Total | Female Féminin Femenino | % F |
| Germany (32) (cont) | All institutions | 1991/92 | ... | ... | ... | 2 033 702 | 841 850 | 41 |
| | of which: Universities | | ... | ... | ... | 1 867 491 | ... | ... |
| | All institutions | 1992/93 | (18) 252 881 | (18) 67 739 | 27 | (18) 2 112 642 | (18) 886 737 | 42 |
| | of which: Universities | | 199 048 | 45 899 | 23 | 1 834 341 | 728 850 | 40 |
| | All institutions | 1993/94 | 259 991 | 70 275 | 27 | 2 132 162 | 902 390 | 42 |
| | of which: Universities | | 204 150 | 47 018 | 23 | 1 858 867 | 748 290 | 40 |
| | All institutions | 1994/95 | 264 062 | 73 316 | 28 | 2 155 728 | 935 446 | 43 |
| | of which: Universities | | 208 207 | 49 198 | 24 | 1 872 490 | 764 766 | 41 |
| | All institutions | 1995/96 | 270 997 | 77 756 | 29 | 2 144 169 | 955 856 | 45 |
| | of which: Universities | | 212 841 | 51 833 | 24 | 1 857 906 | 774 633 | 42 |
| | All institutions | 1996/97 | 274 963 | 80 958 | 29 | 2 131 907 | 975 448 | 46 |
| | of which: Universities | | 214 668 | 53 154 | 25 | 1 838 099 | 783 415 | 43 |
| Greece | All institutions | 1970/71 | ... | ... | ... | 85 776 | 26 976 | 31 |
| | of which: Universities | | 3 162 | 916 | 29 | 72 269 | 22 382 | 31 |
| | All institutions | 1975/76 | 6 326 | 2 238 | 35 | 117 246 | 43 361 | 37 |
| | of which: Universities | | 5 956 | 2 092 | 35 | 95 385 | 35 701 | 37 |
| | All institutions | 1980/81 | 10 542 | 3 372 | 32 | 121 116 | 50 204 | 41 |
| | of which: Universities | | 6 924 | 2 444 | 35 | 85 718 | 36 335 | 42 |
| | All institutions | 1985/86 | 11 878 | 3 563 | 30 | 181 901 | 88 963 | 49 |
| | of which: Universities | | 6 934 | 1 918 | 28 | 110 917 | 52 970 | 48 |
| | All institutions | 1990/91 | ... | ... | ... | (35) 283 415 | ... | ... |
| | of which: Universities | | ... | ... | ... | 201 505 | ... | ... |
| | All institutions | 1991/92 | 14 817 | 4 725 | 32 | 271 718 | 132 770 | 49 |
| | of which: Universities | | 9 124 | 2 554 | 28 | 191 070 | ... | ... |
| | All institutions | 1992/93 | 14 652 | 4 707 | 32 | 299 023 | 147 765 | 49 |
| | of which: Universities | | ... | ... | ... | ... | ... | ... |
| | All institutions | 1993/94 | 18 168 | 6 433 | 35 | 314 002 | 146 693 | 47 |
| | of which: Universities | | ... | ... | ... | ... | ... | ... |
| | All institutions | 1994/95 | 14 656 | 4 785 | 33 | 296 357 | 146 531 | 49 |
| | of which: Universities | | ... | ... | ... | ... | ... | ... |
| | All institutions | 1995/96 | 15 475 | 5 231 | 34 | 329 185 | 159 081 | 48 |
| | of which: Universities | | ... | ... | ... | ... | ... | ... |
| | All institutions | 1996/97 | 16 057 | 5 363 | 33 | 363 150 | 174 044 | 48 |
| | of which: Universities | | ... | ... | ... | ... | ... | ... |
| Holy See (36) | All institutions | 1970/71 | 978 | 7 | 1 | 8 128 | 1 207 | 15 |
| | of which: Universities | | 978 | 7 | 1 | 8 128 | 1 207 | 15 |
| | All institutions | 1975/76 | 1 280 | 37 | 3 | 7 758 | 2 099 | 27 |
| | of which: Universities | | 1 280 | 37 | 3 | 7 758 | 2 099 | 27 |
| | All institutions | 1980/81 | 1 349 | 90 | 7 | 9 104 | 3 538 | 39 |
| | of which: Universities | | 1 349 | 90 | 7 | 9 104 | 3 538 | 39 |
| | All institutions | 1985/86 | 1 498 | 111 | 7 | 9 775 | 3 219 | 33 |
| | of which: Universities | | 1 498 | 111 | 7 | 9 775 | 3 219 | 33 |
| | All institutions | 1990/91 | 1 502 | 117 | 8 | 10 938 | 3 502 | 32 |
| | of which: Universities | | 1 502 | 117 | 8 | 10 938 | 3 502 | 32 |
| | All institutions | 1991/92 | 1 584 | 131 | 8 | 11 681 | 3 594 | 31 |
| | of which: Universities | | 1 584 | 131 | 8 | 11 681 | 3 594 | 31 |
| | All institutions | 1992/93 | 1 588 | 131 | 8 | 12 253 | 3 886 | 32 |
| | of which: Universities | | 1 588 | 131 | 8 | 12 253 | 3 886 | 32 |
| | All institutions | 1995/96 | 1 872 | 129 | 7 | 14 403 | 3 580 | 25 |
| | of which: Universities | | 1 872 | 129 | 7 | 14 403 | 3 580 | 25 |
| Hungary | All institutions | 1970/71 | 9 791 | 2 200 | 22 | 80 536 | 34 432 | 43 |
| | of which: Universities | | 7 924 | 1 754 | 22 | 54 627 | 23 957 | 44 |
| | All institutions | 1975/76 | 12 135 | 3 244 | 27 | 107 555 | 51 952 | 48 |
| | of which: Universities | | 9 494 | 2 382 | 25 | 67 983 | 33 081 | 49 |
| | All institutions | 1980/81 | 13 890 | 4 046 | 29 | 101 166 | 50 314 | 50 |
| | of which: Universities | | 10 616 | 2 872 | 27 | 61 767 | 29 099 | 47 |

**II.7** Tertiary education: teaching staff and students
Enseignement supérieur: personnel enseignant et étudiants
Enseñanza superior: personal docente y estudiantes

| Country / Pays / País | Type of institution / Type d'établissement / Tipo de establecimiento | Year / Année / Año | Teaching staff — Personnel enseignant — Personal docente | | | Students enrolled — Étudiants inscrits — Estudiantes matriculados | | |
|---|---|---|---|---|---|---|---|---|
| | | | Total | Female Féminin Femenino | % F | Total | Female Féminin Femenino | % F |
| Hungary (cont) | All institutions<br>of which: Universities | 1985/86 | 14 850<br>11 460 | 4 496<br>3 200 | 30<br>28 | 99 344<br>61 163 | 53 188<br>30 172 | 54<br>49 |
| | All institutions<br>of which: Universities | 1990/91 | 17 302<br>12 949 | 5 592<br>3 830 | 32<br>30 | 102 387<br>67 384 | 51 507<br>32 767 | 50<br>49 |
| | All institutions<br>of which: Universities | 1991/92 | 17 477<br>13 036 | 5 604<br>3 830 | 32<br>29 | 107 079<br>71 452 | 53 791<br>34 771 | 50<br>49 |
| | All institutions<br>of which: Universities | 1992/93 | 17 743<br>13 349 | 5 824<br>4 117 | 33<br>31 | 117 460<br>76 096 | 59 457<br>37 549 | 51<br>49 |
| | All institutions<br>of which: Universities | 1993/94 | (21) 18 687<br>... | (21) 6 191<br>... | 33<br>... | (21) 144 428<br>... | (21) 74 765<br>... | 52<br>... |
| | All institutions<br>of which: Universities | 1994/95 | 19 103<br>... | 5 974<br>... | 31<br>... | 170 147<br>... | 88 379<br>... | 52<br>... |
| | All institutions<br>of which: Universities | 1995/96 | ...<br>... | ...<br>... | ...<br>... | 194 607<br>... | 103 536<br>... | 53<br>... |
| Iceland | All institutions<br>of which: Universities | 1970/71 | 237<br>237 | 20<br>20 | 8<br>8 | 1 706<br>1 706 | 422<br>422 | 25<br>25 |
| | All institutions<br>of which: Universities | 1975/76 | 575<br>527 | 68<br>54 | 12<br>10 | 2 970<br>2 789 | 1 094<br>965 | 37<br>35 |
| | All institutions<br>of which: Universities | 1980/81 | ...<br>... | ...<br>... | ...<br>... | 4 383<br>... | 2 179<br>... | 50<br>... |
| | All institutions<br>of which: Universities | 1985/86 | ...<br>... | ...<br>... | ...<br>... | 4 724<br>... | 2 621<br>... | 55<br>... |
| | All institutions<br>of which: Universities | 1990/91 | ...<br>... | ...<br>... | ...<br>... | 5 225<br>... | 3 001<br>... | 57<br>... |
| | All institutions<br>of which: Universities | 1991/92 | ...<br>... | ...<br>... | ...<br>... | 6 161<br>... | 3 608<br>... | 59<br>... |
| | All institutions<br>of which: Universities | 1992/93 | ...<br>... | ...<br>... | ...<br>... | 5 672<br>... | 3 266<br>... | 58<br>... |
| | All institutions<br>of which: Universities | 1993/94 | ...<br>... | ...<br>... | ...<br>... | 7 059<br>... | 4 088<br>... | 58<br>... |
| | All institutions<br>of which: Universities | 1994/95 | ...<br>... | ...<br>... | ...<br>... | 7 385<br>... | 4 250<br>... | 58<br>... |
| | All institutions<br>of which: Universities | 1995/96 | ...<br>... | ...<br>... | ...<br>... | 7 483<br>... | 4 401<br>... | 59<br>... |
| | All institutions<br>of which: Universities | 1996/97 | ...<br>... | ...<br>... | ...<br>... | 7 908<br>... | 4 626<br>... | 58<br>... |
| Ireland | All institutions<br>of which: Universities | 1970/71 | ...<br>... | ...<br>... | ...<br>... | 28 501<br>22 225 | 9 767<br>7 543 | 34<br>34 |
| | All institutions<br>of which: Universities | 1975/76 | 4 088<br>2 261 | ...<br>... | ...<br>... | 46 174<br>24 976 | 15 842<br>10 172 | 34<br>41 |
| | All institutions<br>of which: Universities | 1980/81 | ...<br>... | ...<br>... | ...<br>... | 54 746<br>33 173 | 22 248<br>15 819 | 41<br>48 |
| | All institutions<br>of which: Universities | 1985/86 | 6 002<br>3 332 | ...<br>... | ...<br>... | 70 301<br>39 120 | 30 385<br>18 912 | 43<br>48 |
| | All institutions<br>of which: Universities | 1990/91 | 5 598<br>2 695 | ...<br>... | ...<br>... | 90 296<br>47 955 | 41 440<br>24 409 | 46<br>51 |
| | All institutions<br>of which: Universities | 1991/92 | 5 929<br>2 837 | ...<br>... | ...<br>... | 101 108<br>52 288 | 47 568<br>26 941 | 47<br>52 |
| | All institutions<br>of which: Universities | 1992/93 | (18) 6 267<br>2 980 | ...<br>... | ...<br>... | (18) 108 394<br>56 190 | (18) 52 182<br>29 340 | 48<br>52 |
| | All institutions<br>of which: Universities | 1993/94 | 8 592<br>... | 1 906<br>... | 22<br>... | 117 641<br>... | 56 816<br>... | 48<br>... |
| | All institutions<br>of which: Universities | 1994/95 | 8 675<br>... | 2 585<br>... | 30<br>... | 121 401<br>... | 59 849<br>... | 49<br>... |
| | All institutions<br>of which: Universities | 1995/96 | 9 083<br>... | 3 359<br>... | 37<br>... | 128 284<br>... | 64 913<br>... | 51<br>... |
| | All institutions<br>of which: Universities | 1996/97 | 8 979<br>... | 2 783<br>... | 31<br>... | 134 566<br>... | 69 482<br>... | 52<br>... |

Tertiary education: teaching staff and students  II.7
Enseignement supérieur: personnel enseignant et étudiants
Enseñanza superior: personal docente y estudiantes

| Country / Pays / País | Type of institution / Type d'établissement / Tipo de establecimiento | Year / Année / Año | Teaching staff — Personnel enseignant — Personal docente | | | Students enrolled — Étudiants inscrits — Estudiantes matriculados | | |
|---|---|---|---|---|---|---|---|---|
| | | | Total | Female Féminin Femenino | % F | Total | Female Féminin Femenino | % F |
| Italy | All institutions | 1970/71 | ... | ... | ... | 687 242 | 259 015 | 38 |
| | of which: Universities | | 44 171 | ... | ... | 681 731 | 256 489 | 38 |
| | All institutions | 1975/76 | ... | ... | ... | 976 712 | 380 408 | 39 |
| | of which: Universities | | 41 824 | ... | ... | 968 119 | 376 323 | 39 |
| | All institutions | 1980/81 | ... | ... | ... | 1 117 742 | 476 028 | 43 |
| | of which: Universities | | 42 531 | ... | ... | 1 110 547 | 471 919 | 42 |
| | All institutions | 1985/86 | 51 539 | ... | ... | 1 185 304 | 545 902 | 46 |
| | of which: Universities | | 50 996 | ... | ... | 1 176 726 | 540 431 | 46 |
| | All institutions | 1990/91 | 55 766 | ... | ... | (15) 1 452 286 | (15) 690 490 | ... |
| | of which: Universities | | 54 991 | ... | ... | (15) 1 442 413 | (15) 683 855 | ... |
| | All institutions | 1991/92 | 57 283 | ... | ... | 1 533 202 | 759 521 | 50 |
| | of which: Universities | | 56 522 | ... | ... | 1 522 824 | 752 515 | 49 |
| | All institutions | 1992/93 | 58 359 | ... | ... | 1 615 150 | 816 632 | 51 |
| | of which: Universities | | 57 690 | ... | ... | 1 604 216 | 809 171 | 50 |
| | All institutions | 1993/94 | (21) 76 668 | ... | ... | (21) 1 770 253 | (21) 911 780 | 52 |
| | of which: Universities | | ... | ... | ... | ... | ... | ... |
| | All institutions | 1994/95 | 77 247 | 24 378 | 32 | 1 791 726 | 940 048 | 52 |
| | of which: Universities | | ... | ... | ... | ... | ... | ... |
| | All institutions | 1995/96 | 70 342 | 20 653 | 29 | 1 775 186 | 939 752 | 53 |
| | of which: Universities | | ... | ... | ... | ... | ... | ... |
| | All institutions | 1996/97 | ... | ... | ... | 1 892 542 | 1 021 815 | 54 |
| | of which: Universities | | ... | ... | ... | ... | ... | ... |
| Latvia | All institutions | 1980/81 | 4 923 | ... | ... | 47 230 | 26 763 | 57 |
| | of which: Universities | | ... | ... | ... | 33 930 | ... | ... |
| | All institutions | 1985/86 | 4 767 | ... | ... | 43 914 | 26 825 | 61 |
| | of which: Universities | | ... | ... | ... | ... | ... | ... |
| | All institutions | 1990/91 | 4 430 | ... | ... | 45 953 | 25 059 | 55 |
| | of which: Universities | | ... | ... | ... | ... | ... | ... |
| | All institutions | 1991/92 | 4 614 | ... | ... | 46 279 | 24 332 | 53 |
| | of which: Universities | | ... | ... | ... | ... | ... | ... |
| | All institutions | 1992/93 | (37) 4 478 | ... | ... | (37) 41 138 | (37) 21 886 | 53 |
| | of which: Universities | | ... | ... | ... | ... | ... | ... |
| | All institutions | 1993/94 | (37) 4 712 | ... | ... | (37) 37 907 | (37) 20 344 | 54 |
| | of which: Universities | | ... | ... | ... | ... | ... | ... |
| | All institutions | 1994/95 | (37) 4 229 | (37) 1 993 | 47 | (37) 38 046 | (37) 21 225 | 56 |
| | of which: Universities | | ... | ... | ... | ... | ... | ... |
| | All institutions | 1995/96 | (37) 3 825 | (37) 1 866 | 49 | (37) 44 064 | (37) 25 279 | 57 |
| | of which: Universities | | ... | ... | ... | ... | ... | ... |
| | All institutions | 1996/97 | 4 486 | 2 209 | 49 | 56 187 | 33 454 | 60 |
| | of which: Universities | | ... | ... | ... | ... | ... | ... |
| Lithuania | All institutions | 1985/86 | 10 324 | ... | ... | (15) 93 235 | (15) 59 973 | 64 |
| | of which: Universities | | ... | ... | ... | (15) 65 274 | (15) 40 592 | 62 |
| | All institutions | 1990/91 | 11 443 | ... | ... | (15) 88 668 | ... | ... |
| | of which: Universities | | ... | ... | ... | (15) 67 312 | ... | ... |
| | All institutions | 1991/92 | 11 271 | ... | ... | (15) 78 848 | (15) 44 343 | 56 |
| | of which: Universities | | ... | ... | ... | (15) 60 523 | (15) 31 891 | 53 |
| | All institutions | 1992/93 | 10 914 | ... | ... | (15) 72 148 | (15) 41 339 | 57 |
| | of which: Universities | | ... | ... | ... | (15) 55 138 | (15) 29 260 | 53 |
| | All institutions | 1993/94 | 11 366 | 5 305 | 47 | 70 460 | 41 043 | 58 |
| | of which: Universities | | 8 162 | 3 136 | 38 | 52 840 | 29 169 | 55 |
| | All institutions | 1994/95 | 11 799 | 5 476 | 46 | 70 863 | 41 258 | 58 |
| | of which: Universities | | 8 446 | 3 204 | 38 | 51 482 | 28 139 | 55 |
| | All institutions | 1995/96 | 12 690 | 6 038 | 48 | 75 559 | 44 954 | 59 |
| | of which: Universities | | 8 749 | 3 468 | 40 | 53 968 | 30 314 | 56 |
| | All institutions | 1996/97 | 13 136 | 6 196 | 47 | 83 645 | 49 566 | 59 |
| | of which: Universities | | 9 129 | 3 526 | 39 | 58 776 | 33 093 | 56 |

II.7    Tertiary education: teaching staff and students
Enseignement supérieur: personnel enseignant et étudiants
Enseñanza superior: personal docente y estudiantes

| Country<br>Pays<br>País | Type of institution<br>Type<br>d'établissement<br>Tipo de<br>establecimiento | Year<br>Année<br>Año | Teaching staff<br>Personnel enseignant<br>Personal docente | | | | Students enrolled<br>Étudiants inscrits<br>Estudiantes matriculados | | |
|---|---|---|---|---|---|---|---|---|---|
| | | | Total | Female<br>Féminin<br>Femenino | %<br>F | | Total | Female<br>Féminin<br>Femenino | %<br>F |
| Malta | All institutions<br>of which: Universities | 1980/81 | 129<br>129 | 7<br>7 | 5<br>5 | | 947<br>947 | 231<br>231 | 24<br>24 |
| | All institutions<br>of which: Universities | 1985/86 | 156<br>156 | 9<br>9 | 6<br>6 | | 1 474<br>1 474 | 482<br>482 | 33<br>33 |
| | All institutions<br>of which: Universities | 1990/91 | 252<br>252 | 27<br>27 | 11<br>11 | | 3 123<br>3 123 | 1 371<br>1 371 | 44<br>44 |
| | All institutions<br>of which: Universities | 1991/92 | 320<br>320 | 46<br>46 | 14<br>14 | | 3 602<br>3 602 | 1 685<br>1 685 | 47<br>47 |
| | All institutions<br>of which: Universities | 1992/93 | 330<br>330 | 46<br>46 | 14<br>14 | | 4 662<br>4 662 | 2 243<br>2 243 | 48<br>48 |
| | All institutions<br>of which: Universities | 1993/94 | 381<br>381 | 50<br>50 | 13<br>13 | | 5 177<br>5 177 | 2 525<br>2 525 | 49<br>49 |
| | All institutions<br>of which: Universities | 1994/95 | 470<br>470 | 80<br>80 | 17<br>17 | | 5 805<br>5 805 | 2 794<br>2 794 | 48<br>48 |
| | All institutions<br>of which: Universities | 1995/96 | 648<br>648 | 134<br>134 | 21<br>21 | | 7 179<br>7 179 | 3 581<br>3 581 | 50<br>50 |
| | All institutions<br>of which: Universities | 1996/97 | 709<br>709 | 154<br>154 | 22<br>22 | | 8 260<br>8 260 | 4 305<br>4 305 | 52<br>52 |
| Moldova | All institutions<br>of which: Universities | 1980/81 | ...<br>... | ...<br>... | ...<br>... | | 110 200<br>51 300 | ...<br>... | ...<br>... |
| | All institutions<br>of which: Universities | 1985/86 | ...<br>... | ...<br>... | ...<br>... | | 113 800<br>53 200 | ...<br>... | ...<br>... |
| | All institutions<br>of which: Universities | 1990/91 | ...<br>... | ...<br>... | ...<br>... | | 104 800<br>54 700 | ...<br>... | ...<br>... |
| | All institutions<br>of which: Universities | 1994/95 | 9 418<br>4 895 | 3 552<br>1 870 | 38<br>38 | | 100 833<br>56 969 | 54 003<br>30 931 | 54<br>54 |
| | All institutions<br>of which: Universities | 1995/96 | 8 846<br>4 807 | 3 241<br>1 735 | 37<br>36 | | 87 700<br>56 664 | 48 750<br>30 600 | 56<br>54 |
| | All institutions<br>of which: Universities | 1996/97 | 8 814<br>5 272 | 3 928<br>2 216 | 45<br>42 | | 93 759<br>60 445 | 51 411<br>32 669 | 55<br>54 |
| Netherlands | All institutions<br>of which: Universities | 1970/71 | ...<br>... | ...<br>... | ...<br>... | | 231 167<br>103 382 | 64 070<br>20 338 | 28<br>20 |
| | All institutions<br>of which: Universities | 1975/76 | ...<br>... | ...<br>... | ...<br>... | | 288 026<br>120 134 | 94 021<br>29 995 | 33<br>25 |
| | All institutions<br>of which: Universities | 1980/81 | ...<br>... | ...<br>... | ...<br>... | | 360 033<br>149 524 | 143 083<br>46 227 | 40<br>31 |
| | All institutions<br>of which: Universities | 1985/86 | ...<br>... | ...<br>... | ...<br>... | | 404 866<br>168 858 | 165 993<br>62 051 | 41<br>37 |
| | All institutions<br>of which: Universities | 1990/91 | ...<br>... | ...<br>... | ...<br>... | | 478 869<br>190 448 | 212 425<br>78 994 | 44<br>41 |
| | All institutions<br>of which: Universities | 1991/92 | 41 217<br>21 310 | 10 654<br>4 575 | 26<br>21 | | 493 563<br>198 442 | 224 205<br>85 096 | 45<br>43 |
| | All institutions<br>of which: Universities | 1992/93 | 40 288<br>20 355 | 10 446<br>4 251 | 26<br>21 | | 506 580<br>205 595 | 233 027<br>89 919 | 46<br>44 |
| | All institutions<br>of which: Universities | 1993/94 | (21) 48 185<br>... | (21) 11 587<br>... | 24<br>... | | (21) 532 405<br>... | (21) 245 721<br>... | 46<br>... |
| | All institutions<br>of which: Universities | 1994/95 | ...<br>... | ...<br>... | ...<br>... | | 502 928<br>... | 237 284<br>... | 47<br>... |
| | All institutions<br>of which: Universities | 1995/96 | ...<br>... | ...<br>... | ...<br>... | | 491 748<br>... | 233 441<br>... | 47<br>... |
| | All institutions<br>of which: Universities | 1996/97 | ...<br>... | ...<br>... | ...<br>... | | 468 970<br>... | 226 016<br>... | 48<br>... |
| Norway | All institutions<br>of which: Universities | 1970/71 | 5 118<br>2 673 | 847<br>298 | 17<br>11 | | 50 047<br>30 165 | 15 135<br>8 619 | 30<br>29 |
| | All institutions<br>of which: Universities | 1975/76 | 6 650<br>3 757 | 1 071<br>446 | 16<br>12 | | 66 628<br>40 774 | 25 088<br>14 695 | 38<br>36 |

Tertiary education: teaching staff and students II.7
Enseignement supérieur: personnel enseignant et étudiants
Enseñanza superior: personal docente y estudiantes

| Country Pays País | Type of institution Type d'établissement Tipo de establecimiento | Year Année Año | Teaching staff Personnel enseignant Personal docente | | | | Students enrolled Étudiants inscrits Estudiantes matriculados | | | |
|---|---|---|---|---|---|---|---|---|---|---|
| | | | | Total | Female Féminin Femenino | % F | | Total | Female Féminin Femenino | % F |
| Norway (cont) | All institutions of which: Universities | 1980/81 | | 7 763 3 903 | 1 490 511 | 19 13 | | 79 117 40 620 | 37 831 16 642 | 48 41 |
| | All institutions of which: Universities | 1985/86 | | 8 898 4 265 | 2 278 716 | 26 17 | | 94 658 41 658 | 49 233 19 533 | 52 47 |
| | All institutions of which: Universities | 1990/91 | | 9 504 4 516 | 3 702 951 | 39 21 | | 142 521 63 307 | 75 542 32 853 | 53 52 |
| | All institutions of which: Universities | 1991/92 | | ... ... | ... ... | ... ... | | 154 180 68 249 | 82 211 35 575 | 53 52 |
| | All institutions of which: Universities | 1992/93 | | ... ... | ... ... | ... ... | | 166 499 73 778 | 89 114 38 662 | 54 52 |
| | All institutions of which: Universities | 1993/94 | | ... ... | ... ... | ... ... | (21) | 176 722 77 951 | (21) 95 030 40 807 | 54 52 |
| | All institutions of which: Universities | 1994/95 | | ... ... | ... ... | ... ... | | 172 967 ... | 94 541 ... | 55 ... |
| | All institutions of which: Universities | 1995/96 | | ... ... | ... ... | ... ... | | 180 383 ... | 99 720 ... | 55 ... |
| | All institutions of which: Universities | 1996/97 | | 13 665 ... | 4 879 ... | 36 ... | | 185 320 ... | 104 224 ... | 56 ... |
| Poland | All institutions of which: Universities | 1970/71 | | ... 33 695 | ... 9 945 | ... 30 | | 397 897 330 789 | 188 734 139 835 | 47 42 |
| | All institutions of which: Universities | 1975/76 | | ... 50 272 | ... 17 068 | ... 34 | | 575 499 468 129 | 311 867 230 503 | 54 49 |
| | All institutions of which: Universities | 1980/81 | | ... 57 083 | ... 19 726 | ... 35 | | 589 134 453 652 | 328 416 226 658 | 56 50 |
| | All institutions of which: Universities | 1985/86 | | ... 57 280 | ... 20 113 | ... 35 | | 454 190 359 245 | 252 937 181 310 | 56 50 |
| | All institutions of which: Universities | 1990/91 | | ... 61 463 | ... ... | ... ... | | 544 893 436 608 | 305 279 222 073 | 56 51 |
| | All institutions of which: Universities | 1991/92 | | ... 60 528 | ... ... | ... ... | | 549 308 448 448 | 310 534 231 444 | 57 52 |
| | All institutions of which: Universities | 1992/93 | (18) | 66 390 ... | ... ... | ... ... | (18) | 616 400 520 550 | (18) 347 959 273 624 | 56 53 |
| | All institutions of which: Universities | 1993/94 | | 68 294 ... | ... ... | ... ... | | 747 638 635 777 | 424 107 341 525 | 57 54 |
| | All institutions of which: Universities | 1995/96 | | 75 432 ... | ... ... | ... ... | | 720 267 ... | 407 183 ... | 57 ... |
| Portugal | All institutions of which: Universities | 1970/71 | | 2 869 2 726 | 557 511 | 19 19 | | 50 095 43 191 | 22 248 19 797 | 44 46 |
| | All institutions of which: Universities | 1975/76 | | 7 891 4 168 | 2 527 1 060 | 32 25 | | 79 702 51 489 | 35 854 23 854 | 45 46 |
| | All institutions of which: Universities | 1980/81 | | 10 695 6 906 | 3 364 2 038 | 31 30 | | 92 152 67 652 | 44 549 32 269 | 48 48 |
| | All institutions of which: Universities | 1990/91 | (1) (1) | 14 432 11 239 | ... ... | ... ... | | 185 762 128 468 | 103 475 71 772 | 56 56 |
| | All institutions of which: Universities | 1991/92 | | ... ... | ... ... | ... ... | | 190 856 150 510 | 115 443 91 679 | 60 61 |
| | All institutions of which: Universities | 1992/93 | (18) | 21 901 ... | ... ... | ... ... | (18) | 247 523 ... | (18) 138 823 ... | 56 ... |
| | All institutions of which: Universities | 1993/94 | | 23 347 ... | ... ... | ... ... | | 276 534 ... | 157 204 ... | 57 ... |
| | All institutions of which: Universities | 1994/95 | | ... ... | ... ... | ... ... | | 300 573 ... | 170 205 ... | 57 ... |
| | All institutions of which: Universities | 1995/96 | | ... ... | ... ... | ... ... | | 319 525 ... | 180 506 ... | 56 ... |
| Romania | All institutions of which: Universities | 1970/71 | | 13 425 13 425 | 3 953 3 953 | 29 29 | | 151 885 151 885 | 65 353 65 353 | 43 43 |
| | All institutions of which: Universities | 1975/76 | | 14 066 14 066 | 4 105 4 105 | 29 29 | | 164 567 164 567 | 73 690 73 690 | 45 45 |

II.7    Tertiary education: teaching staff and students
Enseignement supérieur: personnel enseignant et étudiants
Enseñanza superior: personal docente y estudiantes

| Country / Pays / País | Type of institution / Type d'établissement / Tipo de establecimiento | Year / Année / Año | Teaching staff Personnel enseignant Personal docente | | | Students enrolled Étudiants inscrits Estudiantes matriculados | | |
|---|---|---|---|---|---|---|---|---|
| | | | Total | Female Féminin Femenino | % F | Total | Female Féminin Femenino | % F |
| Romania (cont) | All institutions | 1980/81 | 14 592 | 4 364 | 30 | 192 769 | 82 113 | 43 |
| | of which: Universities | | 14 592 | 4 364 | 30 | 192 769 | 82 113 | 43 |
| | All institutions | 1985/86 | 12 961 | 3 750 | 29 | 159 798 | 71 658 | 45 |
| | of which: Universities | | 12 961 | 3 750 | 29 | 159 798 | 71 658 | 45 |
| | All institutions | 1990/91 | 13 927 | 3 897 | 28 | 192 810 | 91 021 | 47 |
| | of which: Universities | | 13 927 | 3 897 | 28 | 192 810 | 91 021 | 47 |
| | All institutions | 1991/92 | 17 315 | 4 821 | 28 | 215 226 | 99 032 | 46 |
| | of which: Universities | | 17 315 | 4 821 | 28 | 215 226 | 99 032 | 46 |
| | All institutions | 1992/93 | (23) 18 123 | (23) 5 359 | 30 | 320 669 | (23) 110 035 | ... |
| | of which: Universities | | (23) 18 123 | (23) 5 359 | 30 | 320 669 | (23) 110 035 | ... |
| | All institutions | 1993/94 | (23) 19 130 | (23) 5 894 | 31 | 360 967 | (23) 116 511 | ... |
| | of which: Universities | | (23) 19 130 | (23) 5 894 | 31 | 360 967 | (23) 116 511 | ... |
| ... | All institutions | 1994/95 | (23) 20 452 | (23) 6 159 | 30 | 369 662 | (23) 120 258 | ... |
| | of which: Universities | | (23) 20 452 | (23) 6 159 | 30 | 369 662 | (23) 120 258 | ... |
| | All institutions | 1996/97 | 26 310 | 9 931 | 38 | 411 687 | 217 605 | 53 |
| | of which: Universities | | 23 477 | 8 148 | 35 | 354 488 | 176 811 | 50 |
| Russian Federation | All institutions | 1980/81 | ... | ... | ... | 5 700 000 | 3 200 000 | 56 |
| | of which: Universities | | ... | ... | ... | ... | ... | ... |
| | All institutions | 1985/86 | ... | ... | ... | 5 400 000 | 3 100 000 | 57 |
| | of which: Universities | | ... | ... | ... | ... | ... | ... |
| | All institutions | 1990/91 | ... | ... | ... | 5 100 000 | 2 800 000 | 55 |
| | of which: Universities | | ... | ... | ... | ... | ... | ... |
| | All institutions | 1991/92 | 423 000 | ... | ... | 4 965 000 | 2 700 000 | 54 |
| | of which: Universities | | (8) 259 000 | ... | ... | 1 918 000 | ... | ... |
| | All institutions | 1992/93 | ... | ... | ... | 4 692 000 | 2 600 000 | 55 |
| | of which: Universities | | (8) 247 000 | ... | ... | ... | ... | ... |
| | All institutions | 1993/94 | 363 508 | ... | ... | 4 587 045 | 2 505 048 | 55 |
| | of which: Universities | | (8) 247 218 | ... | ... | (8) 2 593 218 | (8) 1 333 927 | 51 |
| | All institutions | 1994/95 | 382 897 | ... | ... | 4 458 363 | 2 489 458 | 56 |
| | of which: Universities | | (8) 270 400 | ... | ... | (8) 2 587 510 | (8) 1 362 222 | 53 |
| Slovakia | All institutions | 1992/93 | ... | ... | ... | 66 002 | 31 782 | 48 |
| | of which: Universities | | 9 351 | 3 100 | 33 | 65 759 | 31 629 | 48 |
| | All institutions | 1993/94 | ... | ... | ... | 72 726 | 35 450 | 49 |
| | of which: Universities | | 8 392 | 2 873 | 34 | 71 916 | 34 979 | 49 |
| | All institutions | 1994/95 | ... | ... | ... | 82 223 | 40 344 | 49 |
| | of which: Universities | | 8 760 | 2 967 | 34 | 80 360 | 39 060 | 49 |
| | All institutions | 1995/96 | ... | ... | ... | 91 553 | 45 424 | 50 |
| | of which: Universities | | 9 155 | 3 310 | 36 | 88 508 | 43 140 | 49 |
| | All institutions | 1996/97 | *9 849 | *3 714 | *38 | 101 764 | 51 100 | 50 |
| | of which: Universities | | 9 560 | 3 526 | 37 | 97 600 | 47 874 | 49 |
| Slovenia | All institutions | 1980/81 | 2 625 | 479 | 18 | 27 707 | 14 934 | 54 |
| | of which: Universities | | 2 625 | 479 | 18 | 27 707 | 14 934 | 54 |
| | All institutions | 1985/86 | 2 668 | 549 | 21 | 29 601 | 15 643 | 53 |
| | of which: Universities | | 2 668 | 549 | 21 | 29 601 | 15 643 | 53 |
| | All institutions | 1990/91 | 2 558 | 615 | 24 | 33 565 | 18 668 | 56 |
| | of which: Universities | | 2 558 | 615 | 24 | 33 565 | 18 668 | 56 |
| | All institutions | 1991/92 | 2 609 | 609 | 23 | (38) 38 388 | (38) 20 257 | 53 |
| | of which: Universities | | 2 609 | 609 | 23 | (38) 38 388 | (38) 20 257 | 53 |
| | All institutions | 1992/93 | 2 783 | 703 | 25 | (38) 39 264 | (38) 21 338 | 54 |
| | of which: Universities | | 2 783 | 703 | 25 | (38) 39 264 | (38) 21 338 | 54 |
| | All institutions | 1993/94 | 3 172 | 819 | 26 | (38) 42 054 | (38) 23 155 | 55 |
| | of which: Universities | | 3 172 | 819 | 26 | (38) 42 054 | (38) 23 155 | 55 |
| | All institutions | 1994/95 | 3 229 | 843 | 26 | (38) 43 249 | (38) 24 346 | 56 |
| | of which: Universities | | 3 229 | 843 | 26 | (38) 43 249 | (38) 24 346 | 56 |

Tertiary education: teaching staff and students  II.7
Enseignement supérieur: personnel enseignant et étudiants
Enseñanza superior: personal docente y estudiantes

| Country / Pays / País | Type of institution / Type d'établissement / Tipo de establecimiento | Year / Année / Año | Teaching staff / Personnel enseignant / Personal docente | | | Students enrolled / Étudiants inscrits / Estudiantes matriculados | | |
|---|---|---|---|---|---|---|---|---|
| | | | Total | Female / Féminin / Femenino | % F | Total | Female / Féminin / Femenino | % F |
| Slovenia (cont) | All institutions | 1995/96 | 3 566 | 987 | 28 | (38) 47 908 | (38) 27 005 | 56 |
| | of which: Universities | | 3 566 | 987 | 28 | (38) 47 908 | (38) 27 005 | 56 |
| | All institutions | 1996/97 | 3 907 | 1 103 | 28 | (38) 51 009 | (38) 28 736 | 56 |
| | of which: Universities | | 3 846 | 1 080 | 28 | (38) 50 667 | (38) 28 660 | 57 |
| Spain | All institutions | 1975/76 | 29 701 | 5 538 | 19 | 540 238 | 195 616 | 36 |
| | of which: Universities | | 29 438 | 5 471 | 19 | 515 732 | 189 233 | 37 |
| | All institutions | 1980/81 | 42 831 | 8 997 | 21 | 697 789 | 304 838 | 44 |
| | of which: Universities | | (8) 42 260 | (8) 8 775 | 21 | (8) 690 801 | (8) 300 204 | 43 |
| | All institutions | 1985/86 | 47 504 | 12 552 | 26 | 935 126 | 459 105 | 49 |
| | of which: Universities | | 46 740 | 12 258 | 26 | 882 798 | 437 604 | 50 |
| | All institutions | 1990/91 | 65 736 | 19 318 | 29 | 1 222 089 | 623 868 | 51 |
| | of which: Universities | | 64 820 | 18 958 | 29 | 1 129 815 | 582 416 | 52 |
| | All institutions | 1991/92 | 70 410 | 21 630 | 31 | 1 301 748 | 667 143 | 51 |
| | of which: Universities | | 69 431 | 21 301 | 31 | 1 206 681 | 624 592 | 52 |
| | All institutions | 1992/93 | (18) 76 705 | (18) 23 642 | 31 | (18) 1 370 689 | (18) 708 791 | 52 |
| | of which: Universities | | ... | ... | ... | (18) 1 263 507 | (18) 662 004 | 52 |
| | All institutions | 1993/94 | 80 642 | 25 716 | 32 | 1 469 468 | 749 509 | 51 |
| | of which: Universities | | ... | ... | ... | 1 341 761 | 693 689 | 52 |
| | All institutions | 1994/95 | 82 234 | 26 075 | 32 | 1 526 985 | 802 033 | 53 |
| | of which: Universities | | ... | ... | ... | ... | ... | ... |
| | All institutions | 1995/96 | 88 223 | 28 514 | 32 | 1 591 863 | 840 524 | 53 |
| | of which: Universities | | ... | ... | ... | ... | ... | ... |
| | All institutions | 1996/97 | ... | ... | ... | 1 684 445 | 890 357 | 53 |
| | of which: Universities | | ... | ... | ... | ... | ... | ... |
| Sweden | All institutions | 1975/76 | ... | ... | ... | 162 640 | 65 626 | 40 |
| | of which: Universities | | ... | ... | ... | 113 348 | 41 529 | 37 |
| | All institutions | 1980/81 | ... | ... | ... | 171 356 | ... | ... |
| | of which: Universities | | ... | ... | ... | ... | ... | ... |
| | All institutions | 1985/86 | ... | ... | ... | 176 589 | 92 141 | 52 |
| | of which: Universities | | ... | ... | ... | ... | ... | ... |
| | All institutions | 1990/91 | ... | ... | ... | 192 611 | 103 552 | 54 |
| | of which: Universities | | ... | ... | ... | ... | ... | ... |
| | All institutions | 1991/92 | ... | ... | ... | 207 265 | 111 888 | 54 |
| | of which: Universities | | ... | ... | ... | ... | ... | ... |
| | All institutions | 1992/93 | 26 053 | 7 993 | 32 | 222 826 | 121 076 | 54 |
| | of which: Universities | | ... | ... | ... | ... | ... | ... |
| | All institutions | 1993/94 | 26 608 | 8 634 | 32 | 234 466 | 127 873 | 55 |
| | of which: Universities | | ... | ... | ... | ... | ... | ... |
| | All institutions | 1994/95 | 30 173 | 10 975 | 36 | 245 932 | 134 952 | 55 |
| | of which: Universities | | ... | ... | ... | ... | ... | ... |
| | All institutions | 1995/96 | ... | ... | ... | 261 209 | 144 455 | 55 |
| | of which: Universities | | ... | ... | ... | ... | ... | ... |
| | All institutions | 1996/97 | 33 498 | 11 849 | 35 | 275 217 | 153 600 | 56 |
| | of which: Universities | | ... | ... | ... | ... | ... | ... |
| Switzerland | All institutions | 1970/71 | ... | ... | ... | 51 426 | ... | ... |
| | of which: Universities | | 3 900 | 189 | 5 | 42 178 | 9 499 | 23 |
| | All institutions | 1975/76 | ... | ... | ... | 64 720 | ... | ... |
| | of which: Universities | | 5 414 | 356 | 7 | 52 623 | 14 088 | 27 |
| | All institutions | 1980/81 | ... | ... | ... | 85 127 | 25 766 | 30 |
| | of which: Universities | | 5 942 | 457 | 8 | 61 374 | 19 915 | 32 |
| | All institutions | 1985/86 | ... | ... | ... | 110 111 | 35 373 | 32 |
| | of which: Universities | | 6 236 | ... | ... | 74 806 | 26 774 | 36 |
| | All institutions | 1990/91 | ... | ... | ... | 137 486 | 47 647 | 35 |
| | of which: Universities | | 7 331 | 835 | 11 | 85 924 | 33 371 | 39 |
| | All institutions | 1991/92 | ... | ... | ... | 143 067 | 50 293 | 35 |
| | of which: Universities | | 7 344 | 851 | 12 | 89 031 | 35 201 | 40 |

II.7 Tertiary education: teaching staff and students
Enseignement supérieur: personnel enseignant et étudiants
Enseñanza superior: personal docente y estudiantes

| Country / Pays / País | Type of institution / Type d'établissement / Tipo de establecimiento | Year / Année / Año | Teaching staff Personnel enseignant Personal docente | | | Students enrolled Étudiants inscrits Estudiantes matriculados | | |
|---|---|---|---|---|---|---|---|---|
| | | | Total | Female Féminin Femenino | % F | Total | Female Féminin Femenino | % F |
| **Switzerland (cont)** | All institutions | 1992/93 | ... | ... | ... | (18) 146 266 | (18) 52 575 | 36 |
| | of which: Universities | | (18) 7 626 | (18) 934 | 12 | (18) 90 741 | (18) 36 377 | 40 |
| | All institutions | 1993/94 | ... | ... | ... | 148 664 | 54 571 | 37 |
| | of which: Universities | | 7 502 | 966 | 13 | 91 037 | 37 012 | 41 |
| | All institutions | 1994/95 | ... | ... | ... | 148 154 | 55 154 | 37 |
| | of which: Universities | | 7 709 | 1 045 | 14 | ... | ... | ... |
| | All institutions | 1995/96 | ... | ... | ... | 148 024 | 55 746 | 38 |
| | of which: Universities | | ... | ... | ... | ... | ... | ... |
| **The Former Yugoslav Rep. of Macedonia (32)** | All institutions | 1970/71 | ... | | | 30 337 | | |
| | of which: Universities | | ... | | | ... | ... | ... |
| | All institutions | 1975/76 | ... | ... | ... | 36 049 | | |
| | of which: Universities | | ... | | | ... | | |
| | All institutions | 1980/81 | ... | ... | ... | 46 281 | | |
| | of which: Universities | | ... | | | ... | ... | ... |
| | All institutions | 1985/86 | ... | ... | ... | 38 065 | | |
| | of which: Universities | | ... | | | ... | ... | ... |
| | All institutions | 1990/91 | 2 117 | ... | ... | 26 515 | 13 678 | 52 |
| | of which: Universities | | | ... | ... | ... | ... | ... |
| | All institutions | 1991/92 | 2 197 | ... | ... | 27 032 | 13 679 | 51 |
| | of which: Universities | | ... | | | ... | ... | ... |
| | All institutions | 1992/93 | 2 273 | 811 | 36 | 26 405 | 13 649 | 52 |
| | of which: Universities | | ... | ... | | 23 764 | 12 023 | 51 |
| | All institutions | 1993/94 | 2 320 | 850 | 37 | 27 340 | 14 434 | 53 |
| | of which: Universities | | 2 204 | 832 | 38 | 24 257 | 12 689 | 52 |
| | All institutions | 1994/95 | 2 394 | 909 | 38 | 29 057 | 15 692 | 54 |
| | of which: Universities | | 2 299 | 894 | 39 | 25 610 | 13 591 | 53 |
| | All institutions | 1995/96 | 2 493 | 968 | 39 | 29 583 | 16 079 | 54 |
| | of which: Universities | | 2 399 | 951 | 40 | 26 323 | 14 432 | 55 |
| | All institutions | 1996/97 | 2 462 | 1 008 | 41 | 30 754 | 16 738 | 54 |
| | of which: Universities | | 2 419 | 997 | 41 | 27 713 | 15 334 | 55 |
| **Ukraine** | All institutions | 1970/71 | ... | ... | ... | 1 604 500 | ... | ... |
| | of which: Universities | | 40 330 | ... | ... | 806 600 | 386 000 | 48 |
| | All institutions | 1975/76 | ... | ... | ... | 1 570 100 | ... | ... |
| | of which: Universities | | ... | ... | ... | 831 300 | 408 800 | 49 |
| | All institutions | 1980/81 | ... | ... | ... | 1 683 500 | ... | ... |
| | of which: Universities | | ... | ... | ... | 880 400 | ... | ... |
| | All institutions | 1985/86 | ... | ... | ... | 1 662 000 | ... | ... |
| | of which: Universities | | ... | ... | ... | 853 100 | ... | ... |
| | All institutions | 1990/91 | ... | | | 1 651 700 | ... | ... |
| | of which: Universities | | 72 300 | ... | ... | 894 700 | 443 200 | 50 |
| | All institutions | 1991/92 | 117 100 | ... | ... | 1 554 292 | ... | ... |
| | of which: Universities | | 75 900 | ... | ... | 890 192 | (15) 441 000 | ... |
| | All institutions | 1992/93 | ... | ... | ... | 1 530 200 | ... | ... |
| | of which: Universities | | ... | ... | ... | ... | ... | ... |
| | All institutions | 1993/94 | 121 300 | ... | ... | 1 460 600 | 822 000 | 56 |
| | of which: Universities | | 78 600 | ... | ... | 844 000 | *430 000 | *51 |
| | All institutions | 1994/95 | ... | ... | ... | 1 533 000 | ... | ... |
| | of which: Universities | | ... | ... | ... | 888 000 | ... | ... |
| | All institutions | 1995/96 | ... | ... | ... | 1 541 000 | ... | ... |
| | of which: Universities | | ... | ... | ... | 923 000 | ... | ... |
| **United Kingdom** | All institutions | 1970/71 | ... | ... | ... | 601 300 | 199 800 | 33 |
| | of which: Universities | | 286 670 | ... | ... | 258 700 | 73 900 | 29 |
| | All institutions | 1975/76 | ... | ... | ... | 732 947 | 264 254 | 36 |
| | of which: Universities | | 32 208 | ... | ... | 295 031 | 97 677 | 33 |
| | All institutions | 1980/81 | ... | ... | ... | 827 146 | 302 972 | 37 |
| | of which: Universities | | 34 297 | 6 107 | 18 | 339 925 | 126 438 | 37 |

Tertiary education: teaching staff and students II.7
Enseignement supérieur: personnel enseignant et étudiants
Enseñanza superior: personal docente y estudiantes

| Country / Pays / País | Type of institution / Type d'établissement / Tipo de establecimiento | Year / Année / Año | Teaching staff Personnel enseignant Personal docente | | | | Students enrolled Étudiants inscrits Estudiantes matriculados | | | |
|---|---|---|---|---|---|---|---|---|---|---|
| | | | | Total | Female Féminin Femenino | % F | | Total | Female Féminin Femenino | % F |
| United Kingdom (cont) | All institutions | 1985/86 | | 79 621 | 12 062 | 15 | | 1 032 491 | 469 948 | 46 |
| | of which: Universities | | | 31 412 | 3 666 | 12 | | 352 419 | 141 215 | 40 |
| | All institutions | 1990/91 | | 86 200 | 18 000 | 21 | | 1 258 188 | 607 040 | 48 |
| | of which: Universities | | | 36 500 | 7 100 | 19 | | 428 858 | 188 062 | 44 |
| | All institutions | 1991/92 | | 89 500 | 17 900 | 20 | | 1 385 072 | 675 345 | 49 |
| | of which: Universities | | | 37 200 | 5 900 | 16 | | 468 095 | 208 074 | 44 |
| | All institutions | 1992/93 | (18) | 92 067 | (18) 19 275 | 21 | (18) | 1 528 389 | (18) 757 937 | 50 |
| | of which: Universities | | | 37 969 | 6 339 | 17 | | 511 123 | 232 347 | 45 |
| | All institutions | 1993/94 | | ... | ... | ... | | 1 664 025 | 832 896 | 50 |
| | of which: Universities | | | ... | ... | ... | | ... | ... | ... |
| | All institutions | 1994/95 | | 82 203 | 22 711 | 28 | | 1 813 280 | 923 878 | 51 |
| | of which: Universities | | | ... | ... | ... | | ... | ... | ... |
| | All institutions | 1995/96 | | 89 241 | 26 374 | 30 | | 1 820 849 | 919 116 | 50 |
| | of which: Universities | | | ... | ... | ... | | ... | ... | ... |
| **Oceania** | | | | | | | | | | |
| American Samoa | All institutions | 1970/71 | | - | - | - | | - | - | - |
| | of which: Universities | | | - | - | - | | - | - | - |
| | All institutions | 1975/76 | | ... | ... | ... | | 689 | 337 | 49 |
| | of which: Universities | | | - | - | - | | - | - | - |
| | All institutions | 1980/81 | | ... | ... | ... | | 976 | 551 | 56 |
| | of which: Universities | | | - | - | - | | - | - | - |
| | All institutions | 1985/86 | | ... | ... | ... | | 758 | 392 | 52 |
| | of which: Universities | | | - | - | - | | - | - | - |
| Australia | All institutions | 1970 | | ... | | ... | (39) | 179 664 | (39) 58 771 | 33 |
| | of which: Universities | | (40) | 7 367 | | ... | | 116 778 | 34 931 | 30 |
| | All institutions | 1975 | (40) | 19 920 | | ... | (39) | 274 738 | (39) 111 596 | 41 |
| | of which: Universities | | (40) | 19 920 | | ... | | 274 738 | 111 596 | 41 |
| | All institutions | 1980 | (40) | 22 134 | | ... | (39) | 323 716 | (39) 146 676 | 45 |
| | of which: Universities | | (40) | 22 134 | | ... | | 323 716 | 146 676 | 45 |
| | All institutions | 1985 | (40) | 22 659 | (40) 5 114 | 23 | (39) | 370 048 | (39) 176 178 | 48 |
| | of which: Universities | | (40) | 22 659 | (40) 5 114 | 23 | | 370 048 | 176 178 | 48 |
| | All institutions | 1990 | (40) | 27 824 | (40) 9 203 | 33 | (39) | 485 075 | (39) 255 655 | 53 |
| | of which: Universities | | (40) | 27 824 | (40) 9 203 | 33 | | 485 075 | 255 655 | 53 |
| | All institutions | 1991 | | 28 671 | 9 542 | 33 | (39) | 534 530 | (39) 284 862 | 53 |
| | of which: Universities | | | 28 671 | 9 542 | 33 | | 534 530 | 284 862 | 53 |
| | All institutions | 1992 | | 27 442 | 8 626 | 31 | (39) | 559 365 | (39) 298 812 | 53 |
| | of which: Universities | | | 27 442 | 8 626 | 31 | | 559 365 | 298 812 | 53 |
| | All institutions | 1993 | | ... | ... | ... | (21) | 922 699 | (21) 450 561 | 49 |
| | of which: Universities | | | 27 774 | 8 875 | 32 | | ... | ... | ... |
| | All institutions | 1994 | | ... | ... | ... | | 932 969 | 460 307 | 49 |
| | of which: Universities | | | 27 604 | 8 886 | 32 | | ... | ... | ... |
| | All institutions | 1995 | | ... | ... | ... | | 964 998 | 483 596 | 50 |
| | of which: Universities | | | 26 876 | 8 863 | 33 | | ... | ... | ... |
| | All institutions | 1996 | | ... | ... | ... | | 1 002 476 | 507 091 | 51 |
| | of which: Universities | | | 26 920 | 8 991 | 33 | | ... | ... | ... |
| | All institutions | 1997 | | ... | ... | ... | | 1 041 648 | 529 335 | 51 |
| | of which: Universities | | | 26 407 | 8 871 | 34 | | ... | ... | ... |
| Fiji | All institutions | 1970 | | ... | ... | ... | | 359 | 119 | 33 |
| | of which: Universities | | | ... | ... | ... | | 359 | 119 | 33 |
| | All institutions | 1975 | | 166 | 29 | 17 | | 1 653 | 478 | 29 |
| | of which: Universities | | | 105 | 17 | 16 | | 1 229 | 385 | 31 |
| | All institutions | 1980 | | ... | ... | ... | | 1 666 | ... | ... |
| | of which: Universities | | | ... | ... | ... | | 1 391 | ... | ... |
| | All institutions | 1985 | | 249 | 44 | 18 | | 2 313 | 875 | 38 |
| | of which: Universities | | | 148 | 25 | 17 | | 1 932 | 710 | 37 |
| | All institutions | 1991 | | 277 | 92 | 33 | | 7 908 | ... | ... |
| | of which: Universities | | | 213 | 53 | 25 | | 3 621 | ... | ... |

II.7  Tertiary education: teaching staff and students
Enseignement supérieur: personnel enseignant et étudiants
Enseñanza superior: personal docente y estudiantes

| Country / Pays / País | Type of institution / Type d'établissement / Tipo de establecimiento | Year / Année / Año | Teaching staff / Personnel enseignant / Personal docente | | | Students enrolled / Étudiants inscrits / Estudiantes matriculados | | |
|---|---|---|---|---|---|---|---|---|
| | | | Total | Female Féminin Femenino | % F | Total | Female Féminin Femenino | % F |
| French Polynesia | All institutions | 1980/81 | 14 | 1 | 7 | 27 | 7 | 26 |
| | of which: Universities | | - | - | - | - | - | - |
| | All institutions | 1991/92 | ... | ... | ... | 301 | 150 | 50 |
| | of which: Universities | | - | - | - | - | - | - |
| Guam | All institutions | 1970/71 | *125 | ... | ... | 2 719 | 1 298 | 48 |
| | of which: Universities | | *125 | ... | ... | 2 719 | 1 298 | 48 |
| | All institutions | 1975/76 | ... | ... | ... | 3 800 | 1 616 | 43 |
| | of which: Universities | | ... | ... | ... | 3 800 | 1 616 | 43 |
| | All institutions | 1980/81 | ... | ... | ... | 3 217 | 1 768 | 55 |
| | of which: Universities | | ... | ... | ... | 3 217 | 1 768 | 55 |
| New Zealand | All institutions | 1970 | 3 483 | 506 | 15 | 39 816 | 15 608 | 39 |
| | of which: Universities | | 2 907 | 360 | 12 | 31 908 | 9 598 | 30 |
| | All institutions | 1975 | ... | ... | ... | 66 178 | 24 146 | 36 |
| | of which: Universities | | 4 108 | 454 | 11 | 36 931 | 13 801 | 37 |
| | All institutions | 1980 | 7 694 | 1 377 | 18 | 76 643 | 31 101 | 41 |
| | of which: Universities | | (8) 4 780 | (8) 647 | 14 | (8) 43 933 | (8) 18 379 | 42 |
| | All institutions | 1985 | 8 300 | 2 014 | 24 | 95 793 | 43 797 | 46 |
| | of which: Universities | | (8) 5 226 | (8) 1 062 | 20 | 47 799 | 22 135 | 46 |
| | All institutions | 1990 | 11 302 | 3 794 | 34 | 111 504 | 57 804 | 52 |
| | of which: Universities | | (8) 6 651 | (8) 1 840 | 28 | 65 606 | 32 589 | 50 |
| | All institutions | 1991 | 11 291 | 4 379 | 39 | 128 078 | 67 652 | 53 |
| | of which: Universities | | 4 623 | 1 129 | 24 | 72 381 | 36 233 | 50 |
| | All institutions | 1992 | 12 096 | 4 870 | 40 | 146 215 | 78 639 | 54 |
| | of which: Universities | | 4 521 | 1 172 | 26 | 93 113 | 48 639 | 52 |
| | All institutions | 1993 | 12 427 | 5 214 | 42 | 162 932 | 88 356 | 54 |
| | of which: Universities | | 4 740 | 1 277 | 27 | 105 555 | 55 611 | 53 |
| | All institutions | 1994 | ... | ... | ... | 169 421 | 93 725 | 55 |
| | of which: Universities | | ... | ... | ... | ... | ... | ... |
| | All institutions | 1995 | 10 512 | 4 284 | 41 | 163 923 | 90 895 | 55 |
| | of which: Universities | | ... | ... | ... | ... | ... | ... |
| | All institutions | 1996 | 10 250 | 4 139 | 40 | 162 350 | 90 885 | 56 |
| | of which: Universities | | ... | ... | ... | ... | ... | ... |
| | All institutions | 1997 | 10 833 | 4 517 | 42 | 169 656 | 97 223 | 57 |
| | of which: Universities | | ... | ... | ... | ... | ... | ... |
| Papua New Guinea | All institutions | 1970 | ... | ... | ... | ... | ... | ... |
| | of which: Universities | | ... | ... | ... | 1 032 | 165 | 16 |
| | All institutions | 1975 | ... | ... | ... | ... | ... | ... |
| | of which: Universities | | 353 | ... | ... | 2 869 | 338 | 12 |
| | All institutions | 1980 | 638 | ... | ... | 5 040 | 1 112 | 22 |
| | of which: Universities | | 473 | ... | ... | 2 872 | 305 | 11 |
| | All institutions | 1985 | ... | ... | ... | 5 068 | 1 174 | 23 |
| | of which: Universities | | ... | ... | ... | 3 181 | 515 | 16 |
| | All institutions | 1995 | ... | ... | ... | 13 663 | 4 353 | 32 |
| | of which: Universities | | 517 | ... | ... | 4 669 | 1 156 | 25 |
| Samoa | All institutions | 1970 | 24 | 1 | 4 | 114 | 1 | 1 |
| | of which: Universities | | - | - | - | - | - | - |
| | All institutions | 1975 | 40 | - | - | 249 | 13 | 5 |
| | of which: Universities | | - | - | - | - | - | - |
| | All institutions | 1981 | 79 | ... | ... | 644 | 45 | 7 |
| | of which: Universities | | 22 | ... | ... | 295 | 10 | 3 |

**General note**
For general explanations and definitions, please refer to the beginning of this chapter.

**Note générale**
Pour les explications et définitions générales, prière de se référer au début de ce chapitre.

**Nota general**
Para las explicaciones y definiciones generales, referirse al comienzo de este capítulo.

Tertiary education: teaching staff and students II.7
Enseignement supérieur: personnel enseignant et étudiants
Enseñanza superior: personal docente y estudiantes

| Notes | Notes | Notas |
|---|---|---|
| (1) Data refer only to institutions attached to the Ministry of Education. | (1) Les données se réfèrent seulement aux institutions attachées au Ministère de l'Education. | (1) Los datos se refieren solamente a las instituciones afectadas al Ministerio de la Educación. |
| (2) Full-time only. | (2) Plein temps seulement. | (2) Jornada completa solamente. |
| (3) Not including the 'Ecole Nationale d'Administration et de Magistrature'. | (3) Non compris l' 'Ecole Nationale d'Administration et de Magistrature'. | (3) No incluye la 'Ecole Nationale d'Administration et de Magistrature'. |
| (4) Universities only. | (4) Universités seulement. | (4) Universidades solamente. |
| (5) Data refer only to institutions under the authority of the Ministry of Higher Education and Scientific Research. | (5) Les données se réfèrent seulement aux institutions sous la tutelle du Ministère de l'Enseignement Supérieur et de la Recherche Scientifique. | (5) Los datos se refieren solamente a las instituciones bajo la tutela del Ministerio de Educación Superior y de Investigaciones Científicas. |
| (6) Not including Al Azhar university. | (6) Non compris l'université Al Azhar. | (6) No incluye la universidad Al Azhar. |
| (7) Not including private tertiary institutions. | (7) Non compris les institutions supérieures privées. | (7) No incluyen las instituciones superiores privadas. |
| (8) Including distance-learning university institutions. | (8) Y compris les institutions universitaires d'enseignement à distance. | (8) Incluyen las instituciones universitarias de enseñanza a distancia. |
| (9) Not including teacher training. | (9) Non compris la formation d'enseignants. | (9) No incluyen la formación de personal docente. |
| (10) Data do not include private professional schools. | (10) Les données n'incluent pas les écoles privées d'enseignement professionnel. | (10) Los datos no incluyen las escuelas privadas de enseñanza profesional. |
| (11) Not including non-university technical education. | (11) Non compris l'enseignement technique non universitaire. | (11) No incluye la enseñanza técnica no universitaria. |
| (12) Not including the former independent states (Transkei, Bophuthatswana, Venda and Ciskei). | (12) Non compris les anciens états indépendants (Transkei, Bophuthatswana, Venda et Ciskei). | (12) No incluyen los antiguos estados independientes (Transkei, Bophuthatswana, Venda y Ciskei). |
| (13) Not including medical science | (13) Non compris les science médicales. | (13) No incluyen las ciencias médicas. |
| (14) Not including private non-university institutions. | (14) Non compris les institutions privées non universitaires. | (14) No incluyen las instituciones no universitarias privadas. |
| (15) Not including ISCED level 7. | (15) Non compris le niveau 7 de la CITE. | (15) No incluye el nivel 7 de la CINE. |
| (16) Not including private colleges. | (16) Non compris les collèges privés. | (16) No incluyen los colegios privados. |
| (17) Not including part-time students at community colleges. | (17) Non compris les étudiants à temps partiel des 'community colleges'. | (17) No incluyen los estudiantes de jornada parcial de los 'community colleges'. |
| (18) As from 1992, change in data coverage. | (18) A partir de 1992, changement dans la couverture des données. | (18) A partir de 1992, cambio en la cobertura de los datos. |
| (19) Data refer only to institutions recognised by the national council for higher education. | (19) Les données se réfèrent seulement aux institutions reconnues par le Conseil National pour l'Education Supérieure. | (19) Los datos se refieren solamente a las instituciones reconocidas por el Consejo Nacional para la Educación Superior. |
| (20) University of San Carlos only. | (20) Université de San Carlos seulement. | (20) Universidad de San Carlos solamente. |
| (21) As from 1993, change in data coverage. | (21) A partir de 1993, changement dans la couverture des données. | (21) A partir de 1993, cambio en la cobertura de los datos. |
| (22) Not including teacher training at non-university institutions. | (22) Non compris la formation des enseignants dans les institutions non universitaires. | (22) No incluye la formación del personal docente en las instituciones no universitarias. |
| (23) Not including private universities. | (23) Non compris les universités privées. | (23) No incluyen las universidades privadas. |
| (24) Data refer to teaching posts. | (24) Les données se réfèrent aux postes d'enseignants. | (24) Los datos se refieren a los puestos de docente. |
| (25) Full-time national students only. | (25) Etudiants nationaux à plein temps seulement. | (25) Estudiantes nacionales de jornada completa solamente. |
| (26) Not including Turkish institutions. | (26) Non compris les institutions turques. | (26) No incluyen los instituciones turcas. |
| (27) Not including the Jewish studies institutes. | (27) Non compris les 'Jewish studies institutes'. | (27) No incluyen los 'Jewish studies institutes'. |
| (28) East Bank only. | (28) Rive orientale seulement. | (28) Orilla oriental solamente. |
| (29) Not including distance learning institutions. | (29) Non compris les institutions d'enseignement à distance. | (29) No incluyen las instituciones de enseñanza a distancia. |
| (30) Not including "arts and sciences colleges". | (30) Non compris "arts and sciences colleges". | (30) No incluyen "arts and sciences colleges". |
| (31) Not including some non-university institutions. | (31) Non compris quelques institutions supérieures non universitaires. | (31) No incluyen algunas instituciones de enseñanza superior no universitaria |
| (32) Not including students at ISCED level 7 for which registration is not required. | (32) Non compris les étudiants du niveau 7 de la CITE pour lequel l'inscription n'est pas exigée. | (32) No incluyen los estudiantes del nivel 7 de la CINE por el cual la inscripción no es exigida. |
| (33) From 1995, the vocational schools previously classified with secondary education are included at ISCED level 5. | (33) Depuis 1995, les écoles techniques précédemment classées dans le secondaire sont incluses dans le niveau 5 de la CITE. | (33) Desde 1995, las escuelas técnicas anteriormente clasificadas en la enseñanza secundaria están incluidas en el nivel 5 de la CINE. |
| (34) Public universities only. | (34) Universités publiques seulement. | (34) Universidades públicas solamente. |
| (35) As from 1990, change in data coverage. | (35) A partir de 1990, changement dans la couverture des données. | (35) A partir de 1990, cambio en la cobertura de los datos. |
| (36) Data refer to institutions under the authority of the Holy See. | (36) Les données se réfèrent aux institutions sous l'autorité du Saint -Siège. | (36) Los datos se refieren a las instituciones bajo la autoridad de la Santa Sede. |
| (37) Public education only. | (37) Enseignement public seulement. | (37) Enseñanza pública solamente. |
| (38) Not including students enrolled in doctoral studies. | (38) Non compris les étudiants inscrits en doctorat. | (38) No incluyen los estudiantes en doctorado. |
| (39) Data do not include Vocational Education and Training Institutes (VETS). | (39) Les données n'incluent pas l'Education Technique et les Instituts de Formation Professionnelle (VETS). | (39) Los datos no incluyen la Educación Técnica y los Institutos de Formación Profesional (VETS). |
| (40) Data are expressed in full-time equivalent. | (40) Les données sont exprimées en équivalents plein temps. | (40) Los datos están expresados en equivalente de jornada completa. |

II.8 Gross enrolment ratios by level of education
Taux bruts de scolarisation par niveau d'enseignement
Tasas brutas de escolarización por nivel de enseñanza

## II.8 Gross enrolment ratios by level of education

## Taux bruts de scolarisation par niveau d'enseignement

## Tasas brutas de escolarización por nivel de enseñanza

| Country<br><br>Pays<br><br>País | Year<br><br>Année<br><br>Año | Sex<br><br>Sexe<br><br>Sexo | Gross enrolment ratios / Taux bruts de scolarisation / Tasas brutas de escolarización (%) | | | | | |
|---|---|---|---|---|---|---|---|---|
| | | | Pre-primary<br><br>Préprimaire<br><br>Preprimaria | Primary<br><br>Primaire<br><br>Primaria | Secondary<br><br>Secondaire<br><br>Secundaria | Tertiary<br><br>Supérieur<br><br>Superior | Primary and secondary<br><br>Primaire et secondaire<br><br>Primaria y secundaria | Primary, secondary and tertiary<br><br>Primaire, secondaire et supérieur<br><br>Primaria, secundaria y superior |
| **Africa** | | | | | | | | |
| Algeria | 1970 | | | (6-11) | (12-18) | (19-23) | (6-18) | (6-23) |
| | | MF | - | 76 | 11 | 2 | 46 | 37 |
| | | M | - | 93 | 16 | 3 | 57 | 47 |
| | | F | - | 58 | 6 | 0.7 | 34 | 27 |
| | 1975 | | | | | | | |
| | | MF | - | 93 | 20 | 3 | 58 | 47 |
| | | M | - | 109 | 26 | ... | 70 | ... |
| | | F | - | 75 | 14 | ... | 46 | ... |
| | 1980 | | | | | | | |
| | | MF | - | 94 | 33 | 6 | 65 | 52 |
| | | M | - | 108 | 40 | 9 | 75 | 61 |
| | | F | - | 81 | 26 | 3 | 54 | 44 |
| | 1985 | | | | | | | |
| | | MF | - | 94 | 51 | 8 | 73 | 58 |
| | | M | - | 103 | 59 | 11 | 82 | 65 |
| | | F | - | 83 | 44 | 5 | 64 | 50 |
| | 1990 | | | (6-11) | (12-17) | (18-22) | (6-17) | (6-22) |
| | | MF | - | 100 | 61 | 11 | 82 | 65 |
| | | M | - | 108 | 67 | ... | 89 | ... |
| | | F | - | 92 | 54 | ... | 74 | ... |
| | 1991 | | | | | | | |
| | | MF | ... | 103 | 61 | 12 | 83 | 66 |
| | | M | ... | 111 | 66 | 15 | 90 | 72 |
| | | F | ... | 95 | 55 | 8 | 76 | 59 |
| | 1992 | | (4-5) | (6-11) | (12-17) | (18-22) | (6-17) | (6-22) |
| | | MF | 1 | 104 | 61 | 11 | 84 | 66 |
| | | M | 1 | 111 | 66 | 14 | 90 | 71 |
| | | F | 1 | 96 | 55 | 8 | 77 | 60 |
| | 1993 | | | | | | | |
| | | MF | 2 | 105 | 62 | 11 | 85 | 66 |
| | | M | 2 | 112 | 66 | ... | 90 | ... |
| | | F | 2 | 98 | 57 | ... | 79 | ... |
| | 1994 | | | | | | | |
| | | MF | 2 | 105 | 62 | 11 | 85 | 66 |
| | | M | 2 | 112 | 66 | 12 | 90 | 70 |
| | | F | 2 | 99 | 58 | 9 | 79 | 61 |
| | 1995 | | | | | | | |
| | | MF | 2 | 107 | 62 | 12 | 85 | 66 |
| | | M | 2 | 113 | 66 | 14 | 90 | 70 |
| | | F | 2 | 100 | 59 | 10 | 80 | 62 |
| | 1996 | | | | | | | |
| | | MF | 2 | 107 | 63 | ... | 86 | ... |
| | | M | 2 | 113 | 65 | ... | 90 | ... |
| | | F | 2 | 102 | 62 | ... | 82 | ... |

Gross enrolment ratios by level of education  II.8
Taux bruts de scolarisation par niveau d'enseignement
Tasas brutas de escolarización por nivel de enseñanza

| Country / Pays / País | Year / Année / Año | Sex / Sexe / Sexo | Gross enrolment ratios / Taux bruts de scolarisation / Tasas brutas de escolarización (%) | | | | | |
|---|---|---|---|---|---|---|---|---|
| | | | Pre-primary / Préprimaire / Preprimaria | Primary / Primaire / Primaria | Secondary / Secondaire / Secundaria | Tertiary / Supérieur / Superior | Primary and secondary / Primaire et secondaire / Primaria y secundaria | Primary, secondary and tertiary / Primaire, secondaire et supérieur / Primaria, secundaria y superior |
| Angola | 1970 | | (4-6) | (7-10) | (11-16) | (17-21) | (7-16) | (7-21) |
| | | MF | ... | 75 | 8 | 0.5 | 37 | 27 |
| | | M | ... | 98 | 9 | 0.5 | 48 | 35 |
| | | F | ... | 53 | 6 | 0.4 | 27 | 19 |
| | 1975 | | | | | | | |
| | | MF | ... | ... | 9 | ... | ... | ... |
| | | M | ... | ... | 13 | ... | ... | ... |
| | | F | ... | ... | 5 | ... | ... | ... |
| | 1980 | | | | | | | |
| | | MF | 59 | 175 | 21 | 0.4 | 89 | 64 |
| | | M | 71 | ... | ... | ... | ... | ... |
| | | F | 48 | ... | ... | ... | ... | ... |
| | 1990 | | (5-5) | (6-9) | (10-16) | (17-21) | (6-16) | (6-21) |
| | | MF | 54 | 92 | 12 | 0.8 | 45 | 34 |
| | | M | 71 | 95 | ... | ... | ... | ... |
| | | F | 37 | 88 | ... | ... | ... | ... |
| | 1991 | | | | | | | |
| | | MF | 68 | 88 | 14 | 0.7 | 45 | 34 |
| Benin | 1970 | | | (6-11) | (12-18) | (19-23) | (6-18) | (6-23) |
| | | MF | - | 32 | 4 | 0.1 | 20 | 16 |
| | | M | - | 45 | 6 | 0.3 | 27 | 22 |
| | | F | - | 20 | 3 | 0.0 | 12 | 9 |
| | 1975 | | | (5-10) | (11-17) | (18-22) | (5-17) | (5-22) |
| | | MF | - | 50 | 8 | 0.8 | 30 | 23 |
| | | M | - | 70 | 13 | 1 | 43 | 34 |
| | | F | - | 31 | 4 | 0.2 | 17 | 14 |
| | 1980 | | (3-4) | (5-10) | (11-17) | (18-22) | (5-17) | (5-22) |
| | | MF | 2 | 67 | 16 | 1 | 41 | 32 |
| | | M | ... | 91 | 24 | ... | 58 | ... |
| | | F | ... | 43 | 8 | ... | 25 | ... |
| | 1985 | | (3-5) | (6-11) | (12-18) | (19-23) | (6-18) | (6-23) |
| | | MF | 3 | 68 | 18 | 2 | 44 | 35 |
| | | M | 3 | 90 | 26 | 4 | 60 | 48 |
| | | F | 2 | 45 | 10 | 0.7 | 29 | 22 |
| | 1990 | | | | | | | |
| | | MF | 3 | 58 | 12 | 3 | 38 | 30 |
| | | M | 3 | 78 | 17 | 5 | 51 | 41 |
| | | F | 2 | 39 | 7 | 0.7 | 24 | 19 |
| | 1991 | | | | | | | |
| | | MF | 3 | 61 | 12 | 3 | 39 | 32 |
| | | M | 3 | 81 | 17 | 5 | 53 | 43 |
| | | F | 2 | 41 | 7 | 0.8 | 26 | 21 |
| | 1992 | | | | | | | |
| | | MF | 3 | 66 | 13 | 2 | 42 | 34 |
| | | M | 3 | 87 | 18 | 4 | 56 | 46 |
| | | F | 3 | 45 | 8 | 0.8 | 28 | 23 |
| | 1993 | | | | | | | |
| | | MF | 3 | 67 | 14 | 3 | 43 | 35 |
| | | M | 3 | 87 | 20 | 4 | 56 | 46 |
| | | F | 3 | 47 | 9 | 0.9 | 29 | 24 |
| | 1994 | | | | | | | |
| | | MF | 3 | 70 | 15 | 3 | 45 | 37 |
| | | M | 3 | 91 | 21 | 4 | 59 | 48 |
| | | F | 3 | 50 | 9 | 0.9 | 31 | 25 |
| | 1995 | | | | | | | |
| | | MF | 3 | 73 | 16 | 3 | 46 | 38 |
| | | M | 3 | 93 | 22 | 4 | 60 | 49 |
| | | F | 3 | 53 | 9 | 0.9 | 33 | 27 |
| | 1996 | | | | | | | |
| | | MF | 3 | 78 | 17 | 3 | 49 | 40 |
| | | M | 3 | 98 | 24 | 5 | 63 | 52 |
| | | F | 3 | 57 | 10 | 1 | 35 | 28 |
| | 1997 | | | | | | | |
| | | MF | ... | ... | 18 | ... | ... | ... |
| | | M | ... | ... | 26 | ... | ... | ... |
| | | F | ... | ... | 11 | ... | ... | ... |

Gross enrolment ratios by level of education
Taux bruts de scolarisation par niveau d'enseignement
Tasas brutas de escolarización por nivel de enseñanza

| Country<br>Pays<br>País | Year<br>Année<br>Año | Sex<br>Sexe<br>Sexo | Gross enrolment ratios / Taux bruts de scolarisation / Tasas brutas de escolarización (%) | | | | | |
|---|---|---|---|---|---|---|---|---|
| | | | Pre-primary<br>Préprimaire<br>Preprimaria | Primary<br>Primaire<br>Primaria | Secondary<br>Secondaire<br>Secundaria | Tertiary<br>Supérieur<br>Superior | Primary and secondary<br>Primaire et secondaire<br>Primaria y secundaria | Primary, secondary and tertiary<br>Primaire, secondaire et supérieur<br>Primaria, secundaria y superior |
| Botswana | 1970 | | | (7-13) | (14-18) | (19-23) | (7-18) | (7-23) |
| | | MF | - | 63 | 7 | - | 44 | 34 |
| | | M | - | 60 | 8 | - | 42 | 34 |
| | | F | - | 66 | 7 | - | 46 | 35 |
| | 1975 | | | (6-12) | (13-17) | (18-22) | (6-17) | (6-22) |
| | | MF | - | 71 | 15 | 0.7 | 51 | 40 |
| | | M | - | 64 | 15 | 0.9 | 46 | 36 |
| | | F | - | 78 | 16 | 0.4 | 56 | 43 |
| | 1980 | | | (6-12) | (13-17) | (18-22) | (6-17) | (6-22) |
| | | MF | - | 91 | 19 | 1 | 64 | 50 |
| | | M | - | 83 | 17 | 2 | 58 | 45 |
| | | F | - | 100 | 20 | 0.8 | 70 | 54 |
| | 1985 | | | (7-13) | (14-18) | (19-23) | (7-18) | (7-23) |
| | | MF | - | 105 | 29 | 2 | 77 | 59 |
| | | M | - | 100 | 27 | 2 | 73 | 56 |
| | | F | - | 111 | 31 | 2 | 81 | 62 |
| | 1990 | | | | | | | |
| | | MF | - | 113 | 43 | 3 | 87 | 67 |
| | | M | - | 109 | 41 | 3 | 84 | 65 |
| | | F | - | 117 | 45 | 3 | 91 | 70 |
| | 1991 | | | | | | | |
| | | MF | - | 116 | 52 | 4 | 92 | 72 |
| | | M | - | 112 | 48 | 5 | 89 | 69 |
| | | F | - | 119 | 56 | 4 | 96 | 74 |
| | 1992 | | | | | | | |
| | | MF | - | 114 | 52 | 5 | 91 | 70 |
| | | M | - | 111 | 48 | 5 | 88 | 68 |
| | | F | - | 117 | 56 | 4 | 94 | 73 |
| | 1993 | | | | | | | |
| | | MF | - | 112 | 57 | 5 | 92 | 71 |
| | | M | - | 110 | 53 | 6 | 89 | 69 |
| | | F | - | 114 | 60 | 5 | 94 | 73 |
| | 1994 | | | | | | | |
| | | MF | - | 111 | 55 | 6 | 90 | 70 |
| | | M | - | 110 | 53 | 6 | 89 | 69 |
| | | F | - | 113 | 58 | 5 | 92 | 71 |
| | 1995 | | | (6-12) | (13-17) | (18-22) | (6-17) | (6-22) |
| | | MF | - | 108 | 63 | 5 | 91 | 70 |
| | | M | - | 107 | 60 | 6 | 89 | 69 |
| | | F | - | 109 | 66 | 5 | 92 | 71 |
| | 1996 | | | | | | | |
| | | MF | - | 108 | 65 | 6 | 91 | 71 |
| | | M | - | 107 | 61 | 6 | 90 | 70 |
| | | F | - | 108 | 68 | 5 | 93 | 71 |
| Burkina Faso | 1970 | | (3-5) | (6-11) | (12-18) | (19-23) | (6-18) | (6-23) |
| | | MF | 0.1 | 12 | 1 | 0.0 | 7 | 6 |
| | | M | 0.1 | 15 | 2 | 0.1 | 9 | 7 |
| | | F | 0.1 | 9 | 0.8 | 0.0 | 5 | 4 |
| | 1975 | | (4-6) | (7-12) | (13-19) | (20-24) | (7-19) | (7-24) |
| | | MF | 0.1 | 14 | 2 | 0.2 | 9 | 7 |
| | | M | 0.1 | 18 | 3 | 0.4 | 11 | 9 |
| | | F | 0.1 | 11 | 1 | 0.1 | 6 | 5 |
| | 1980 | | | | | | | |
| | | MF | 0.1 | 17 | 3 | 0.3 | 11 | 9 |
| | | M | 0.1 | 22 | 4 | 0.5 | 13 | 11 |
| | | F | 0.1 | 13 | 2 | 0.1 | 8 | 6 |
| | 1985 | | | | | | | |
| | | MF | 0.4 | 27 | 4 | 0.6 | 16 | 13 |
| | | M | 0.4 | 34 | 6 | 0.9 | 20 | 16 |
| | | F | 0.5 | 20 | 3 | 0.3 | 12 | 9 |
| | 1990 | | | | | | | |
| | | MF | 0.7 | 33 | 7 | 0.7 | 21 | 16 |
| | | M | 0.7 | 41 | 9 | 1 | 26 | 21 |
| | | F | 0.7 | 26 | 5 | 0.3 | 16 | 12 |

Gross enrolment ratios by level of education   II.8
Taux bruts de scolarisation par niveau d'enseignement
Tasas brutas de escolarización por nivel de enseñanza

| Country / Pays / País | Year / Année / Año | Sex / Sexe / Sexo | Gross enrolment ratios / Taux bruts de scolarisation / Tasas brutas de escolarización (%) | | | | | |
|---|---|---|---|---|---|---|---|---|
| | | | Pre-primary / Préprimaire / Preprimaria | Primary / Primaire / Primaria | Secondary / Secondaire / Secundaria | Tertiary / Supérieur / Superior | Primary and secondary / Primaire et secondaire / Primaria y secundaria | Primary, secondary and tertiary / Primaire, secondaire et supérieur / Primaria, secundaria y superior |
| Burkina Faso (cont) | 1991 | | | | | | | |
| | | MF | 0.8 | 34 | 7 | 0.9 | 21 | 17 |
| | | M | 0.8 | 41 | 10 | 1 | 26 | 21 |
| | | F | 0.8 | 26 | 5 | 0.4 | 16 | 13 |
| | 1992 | | | | | | | |
| | | MF | 0.8 | 35 | 8 | 1 | 22 | 18 |
| | | M | 0.8 | 42 | 10 | 2 | 27 | 22 |
| | | F | 0.8 | 27 | 6 | 0.5 | 17 | 13 |
| | 1993 | | | | | | | |
| | | MF | 1 | 36 | 8 | 1 | 23 | 18 |
| | | M | 1 | 44 | 11 | 2 | 28 | 22 |
| | | F | 1 | 28 | 6 | 0.5 | 18 | 14 |
| | 1994 | | | | | | | |
| | | MF | 1 | 38 | ... | 1 | ... | ... |
| | | M | 1 | 46 | ... | 2 | ... | ... |
| | | F | 1 | 30 | ... | 0.5 | ... | ... |
| | 1995 | | | | | | | |
| | | MF | 1 | 40 | ... | 1 | ... | ... |
| | | M | 1 | 48 | ... | 2 | ... | ... |
| | | F | 1 | 31 | ... | 0.5 | ... | ... |
| | 1996 | | | | | | | |
| | | MF | 2 | ... | ... | 0.9 | ... | ... |
| | | M | 2 | ... | ... | 1 | ... | ... |
| | | F | 2 | ... | ... | 0.4 | ... | ... |
| Burundi | 1970 | | (4-5) | (6-12) | (13-18) | (19-23) | (6-18) | (6-23) |
| | | MF | 0.4 | 27 | 2 | 0.1 | 16 | 13 |
| | | M | 0.5 | 36 | 3 | 0.3 | 22 | 17 |
| | | F | 0.4 | 18 | 0.6 | 0.0 | 10 | 8 |
| | 1975 | | (4-5) | (6-11) | (12-18) | (19-23) | (6-18) | (6-23) |
| | | MF | 0.3 | 21 | 2 | 0.3 | 11 | 9 |
| | | M | 0.3 | 25 | 3 | 0.5 | 14 | 11 |
| | | F | 0.3 | 16 | 1 | 0.1 | 9 | 7 |
| | 1980 | | (4-6) | (7-12) | (13-19) | (20-24) | (7-19) | (7-24) |
| | | MF | 0.3 | 26 | 3 | 0.5 | 15 | 11 |
| | | M | 0.3 | 32 | 4 | 0.7 | 18 | 14 |
| | | F | 0.3 | 21 | 2 | 0.2 | 11 | 9 |
| | 1985 | | | | | | | |
| | | MF | 0.4 | 53 | 4 | 0.6 | 28 | 22 |
| | | M | 0.4 | 61 | 5 | 0.9 | 33 | 26 |
| | | F | 0.4 | 44 | 2 | 0.3 | 23 | 18 |
| | 1990 | | | | | | | |
| | | MF | ... | 73 | 6 | 0.7 | 41 | 32 |
| | | M | ... | 79 | 7 | 1 | 45 | 35 |
| | | F | ... | 66 | 4 | 0.4 | 37 | 28 |
| | 1991 | | | | | | | |
| | | MF | ... | 70 | 6 | 0.8 | 40 | 31 |
| | | M | ... | 77 | 7 | 1 | 44 | 35 |
| | | F | ... | 63 | 5 | 0.4 | 35 | 27 |
| | 1992 | | | | | | | |
| | | MF | ... | 70 | 7 | 0.8 | 40 | 31 |
| | | M | ... | 77 | 8 | 1 | 45 | 35 |
| | | F | ... | 63 | 5 | 0.4 | 36 | 28 |
| | 1993 | | | | | | | |
| | | MF | ... | 68 | 7 | ... | 39 | ... |
| | | M | ... | 75 | 8 | ... | 44 | ... |
| | | F | ... | 60 | 5 | ... | 34 | ... |
| | 1994 | | | | | | | |
| | | MF | ... | 54 | 7 | ... | 32 | ... |
| | | M | ... | 62 | ... | ... | ... | ... |
| | | F | ... | 47 | ... | ... | ... | ... |
| | 1995 | | | | | | | |
| | | MF | ... | 51 | ... | ... | ... | ... |
| | | M | ... | 55 | ... | ... | ... | ... |
| | | F | ... | 46 | ... | ... | ... | ... |

II.8    Gross enrolment ratios by level of education
       Taux bruts de scolarisation par niveau d'enseignement
       Tasas brutas de escolarización por nivel de enseñanza

| Country | Year | Sex | Gross enrolment ratios / Taux bruts de scolarisation / Tasas brutas de escolarización (%) | | | | | |
|---|---|---|---|---|---|---|---|---|
| | | | Pre-primary | Primary | Secondary | Tertiary | Primary and secondary | Primary, secondary and tertiary |
| Pays | Année | Sexe | Préprimaire | Primaire | Secondaire | Supérieur | Primaire et secondaire | Primaire, secondaire et supérieur |
| País | Año | Sexo | Preprimaria | Primaria | Secundaria | Superior | Primaria y secundaria | Primaria, secundaria y superior |
| Cameroon | 1970 | | (4-5) | (6-11) | (12-18) | (19-23) | (6-18) | (6-23) |
| | | MF | 3 | 92 | 8 | 0.5 | 51 | 40 |
| | | M | 3 | 105 | 12 | 0.9 | 60 | 47 |
| | | F | 3 | 78 | 5 | 0.1 | 42 | 33 |
| | 1975 | | | | | | | |
| | | MF | 5 | 95 | 13 | 1 | 56 | 44 |
| | | M | 5 | 105 | 18 | 2 | 63 | 50 |
| | | F | 5 | 84 | 9 | 0.4 | 48 | 38 |
| | 1980 | | | | | | | |
| | | MF | 7 | 98 | 18 | 2 | 60 | 48 |
| | | M | 7 | 107 | 24 | ... | 67 | ... |
| | | F | 7 | 89 | 13 | ... | 53 | ... |
| | 1985 | | | | | | | |
| | | MF | 11 | 102 | 23 | 2 | 65 | 51 |
| | | M | 12 | 111 | 28 | ... | 72 | ... |
| | | F | 11 | 93 | 18 | ... | 57 | ... |
| | 1990 | | | | | | | |
| | | MF | 13 | 101 | 28 | 3 | 66 | 53 |
| | | M | 13 | 109 | 33 | ... | 72 | ... |
| | | F | 13 | 93 | 23 | ... | 60 | ... |
| | 1991 | | | | | | | |
| | | MF | 13 | 96 | 29 | ... | 64 | ... |
| | | M | 12 | 100 | 34 | ... | 68 | ... |
| | | F | 13 | 92 | 24 | ... | 59 | ... |
| | 1992 | | | | | | | |
| | | MF | 12 | 93 | 28 | ... | 62 | ... |
| | | M | 12 | 98 | 34 | ... | 67 | ... |
| | | F | 12 | 88 | 23 | ... | 56 | ... |
| | 1993 | | | | | | | |
| | | MF | 12 | 90 | 28 | ... | 60 | ... |
| | | M | 12 | 95 | 33 | ... | 65 | ... |
| | | F | 12 | 86 | 22 | ... | 55 | ... |
| | 1994 | | | | | | | |
| | | MF | 11 | 88 | 27 | ... | 58 | ... |
| | | M | 11 | 93 | 32 | ... | 63 | ... |
| | | F | 11 | 84 | 22 | ... | 53 | ... |
| | 1995 | | | | | | | |
| | | MF | 11 | 87 | ... | ... | ... | ... |
| | 1996 | | | | | | | |
| | | MF | 10 | 85 | ... | ... | ... | ... |
| Cape Verde | 1970 | | (5-6) | (7-12) | (13-17) | (18-22) | (7-17) | (7-22) |
| | | MF | ... | 54 | 10 | - | 36 | 30 |
| | | M | ... | ... | 11 | - | ... | ... |
| | | F | ... | ... | 9 | - | ... | ... |
| | 1975 | | | | | | | |
| | | MF | ... | 127 | 7 | - | 75 | 58 |
| | | M | ... | 133 | 7 | - | 79 | 62 |
| | | F | ... | 120 | 6 | - | 71 | 55 |
| | 1980 | | | | | | | |
| | | MF | ... | 114 | 8 | - | 66 | 49 |
| | | M | ... | 119 | 9 | - | 69 | 52 |
| | | F | ... | 110 | 7 | - | 63 | 46 |
| | 1985 | | | | | | | |
| | | MF | ... | 116 | 13 | - | 70 | 49 |
| | | M | ... | 119 | 15 | - | 72 | 50 |
| | | F | ... | 112 | 12 | - | 68 | 47 |
| | 1990 | | (5-6) | (7-12) | (13-18) | (19-23) | (7-18) | (7-23) |
| | | MF | ... | 121 | 21 | - | 76 | 55 |
| | 1991 | | | | | | | |
| | | MF | ... | ... | 25 | - | ... | ... |
| | 1993 | | | | | | | |
| | | MF | ... | 131 | 27 | - | 83 | 62 |
| | | M | ... | 133 | 28 | - | 85 | 64 |
| | | F | ... | 129 | 26 | - | 80 | 60 |

Gross enrolment ratios by level of education
Taux bruts de scolarisation par niveau d'enseignement
Tasas brutas de escolarización por nivel de enseñanza

II.8

| Country / Pays / País | Year / Année / Año | Sex / Sexe / Sexo | Gross enrolment ratios / Taux bruts de scolarisation / Tasas brutas de escolarización (%) | | | | | |
|---|---|---|---|---|---|---|---|---|
| | | | Pre-primary / Préprimaire / Preprimaria | Primary / Primaire / Primaria | Secondary / Secondaire / Secundaria | Tertiary / Supérieur / Superior | Primary and secondary / Primaire et secondaire / Primaria y secundaria | Primary, secondary and tertiary / Primaire, secondaire et supérieur / Primaria, secundaria y superior |
| Cape Verde (cont) | 1997 | MF | ... | 148 | 55 | - | 103 | 77 |
| | | M | ... | 150 | 54 | - | 104 | 79 |
| | | F | ... | 147 | 56 | - | 103 | 76 |
| Central African Republic | 1970 | | (3-5) | (6-11) | (12-18) | (19-23) | (6-18) | (6-23) |
| | | MF | 5 | 65 | 4 | 0.1 | 35 | 27 |
| | | M | 5 | 90 | 7 | 0.2 | 48 | 38 |
| | | F | 4 | 41 | 2 | 0.0 | 21 | 17 |
| | 1975 | MF | 6 | 73 | 8 | 0.4 | 40 | 31 |
| | | M | 6 | 96 | 13 | 0.7 | 55 | 42 |
| | | F | 6 | 51 | 3 | 0.1 | 27 | 21 |
| | 1980 | MF | 5 | 71 | 14 | 0.9 | 43 | 33 |
| | | M | ... | 92 | 21 | 2 | 57 | 44 |
| | | F | ... | 51 | 7 | 0.1 | 20 | 20 |
| | 1985 | MF | ... | 75 | 16 | 1 | 47 | 37 |
| | | M | ... | 93 | 24 | 2 | 61 | 48 |
| | | F | ... | 57 | 8 | 0.2 | 34 | 27 |
| | 1990 | MF | 6 | 65 | 12 | 2 | 40 | 31 |
| | | M | ... | 80 | 17 | 3 | 50 | 40 |
| | | F | ... | 51 | 7 | 0.4 | 29 | 23 |
| | 1991 | MF | ... | 57 | 10 | 1 | 35 | 27 |
| | | M | ... | 69 | 15 | 3 | 43 | 35 |
| | | F | ... | 45 | 6 | 0.4 | 26 | 21 |
| Chad | 1970 | | (3-5) | (6-11) | (12-18) | (19-23) | (6-18) | (6-23) |
| | | MF | ... | 35 | 2 | - | 19 | 15 |
| | | M | ... | 52 | 4 | - | 28 | 22 |
| | | F | ... | 17 | 0.3 | - | 9 | 7 |
| | 1975 | MF | ... | 35 | 3 | 0.2 | 19 | 15 |
| | | M | ... | 51 | 5 | 0.3 | 28 | 22 |
| | | F | ... | 18 | 0.6 | 0.0 | 9 | 7 |
| | 1985 | MF | ... | 44 | 6 | 0.4 | 25 | 20 |
| | | M | ... | 63 | 10 | 0.8 | 37 | 29 |
| | | F | ... | 25 | 2 | 0.1 | 14 | 10 |
| | 1990 | MF | ... | 54 | 8 | ... | 33 | ... |
| | | M | ... | 75 | 13 | ... | 47 | ... |
| | | F | ... | 34 | 3 | ... | 19 | ... |
| | 1991 | MF | ... | 57 | 9 | ... | 35 | ... |
| | | M | ... | 77 | 15 | ... | 49 | ... |
| | | F | ... | 36 | 3 | ... | 21 | ... |
| | 1992 | MF | ... | 53 | 9 | 0.6 | 33 | 26 |
| | | M | ... | 72 | 16 | 1 | 46 | 37 |
| | | F | ... | 34 | 3 | 0.1 | 20 | 16 |
| | 1993 | MF | ... | 50 | 8 | 0.6 | 31 | 24 |
| | | M | ... | 68 | 13 | 1 | 43 | 34 |
| | | F | ... | 32 | 3 | 0.1 | 19 | 15 |
| | 1994 | MF | 0.5 | 49 | 9 | 0.6 | 31 | 24 |
| | | M | 0.5 | 66 | 15 | 1 | 43 | 34 |
| | | F | 0.4 | 32 | 3 | 0.1 | 19 | 15 |
| | 1995 | MF | ... | 51 | 9 | 0.6 | 32 | 25 |
| | | M | ... | 69 | 15 | 1 | 44 | 35 |
| | | F | ... | 34 | 4 | 0.2 | 20 | 16 |

II.8    Gross enrolment ratios by level of education
Taux bruts de scolarisation par niveau d'enseignement
Tasas brutas de escolarización por nivel de enseñanza

| Country<br>Pays<br>País | Year<br>Année<br>Año | Sex<br>Sexe<br>Sexo | Gross enrolment ratios / Taux bruts de scolarisation / Tasas brutas de escolarización (%) | | | | | |
|---|---|---|---|---|---|---|---|---|
| | | | Pre-primary<br>Préprimaire<br>Preprimaria | Primary<br>Primaire<br>Primaria | Secondary<br>Secondaire<br>Secundaria | Tertiary<br>Supérieur<br>Superior | Primary and secondary<br>Primaire et secondaire<br>Primaria y secundaria | Primary, secondary and tertiary<br>Primaire, secondaire et supérieur<br>Primaria, secundaria y superior |
| Chad (cont) | 1996 | | | 57 | 9 | ... | 35 | ... |
| | | MF | ... | 57 | 9 | ... | 35 | ... |
| | | M | ... | 76 | 15 | ... | 47 | ... |
| | | F | ... | 39 | 4 | ... | 23 | ... |
| Comoros | 1970 | | (4-5) | (6-11) | (12-18) | (19-23) | (6-18) | (6-23) |
| | | MF | ... | 33 | 3 | - | 19 | 15 |
| | | M | ... | 45 | 5 | - | 26 | 20 |
| | | F | ... | 21 | 2 | - | 12 | 9 |
| | 1975 | MF | ... | 64 | 13 | - | 40 | 32 |
| | | M | ... | ... | 18 | - | ... | ... |
| | | F | ... | ... | 7 | - | ... | ... |
| | 1980 | MF | 66 | 86 | 22 | - | 56 | 45 |
| | | M | 68 | 100 | 30 | - | 67 | 54 |
| | | F | 65 | 72 | 15 | - | 45 | 36 |
| | 1985 | MF | ... | 82 | 28 | - | 56 | 45 |
| | | M | ... | 93 | 34 | - | 65 | 52 |
| | | F | ... | 70 | 22 | - | 47 | 37 |
| | 1990 | MF | ... | 75 | 18 | ... | 48 | ... |
| | | M | ... | 87 | 21 | ... | 56 | ... |
| | | F | ... | 63 | 14 | ... | 40 | ... |
| | 1991 | | (4-6) | (7-12) | (13-19) | (20-24) | (7-19) | (7-24) |
| | | MF | ... | 79 | 18 | 0.4 | 50 | 39 |
| | | M | ... | 85 | 22 | 0.6 | 55 | 44 |
| | | F | ... | 72 | 14 | 0.3 | 44 | 35 |
| | 1992 | MF | ... | 75 | 17 | 0.4 | 47 | 37 |
| | | M | ... | 80 | 20 | 0.6 | 51 | 40 |
| | | F | ... | 70 | 14 | 0.3 | 43 | 34 |
| | 1993 | MF | ... | 77 | 19 | ... | 49 | ... |
| | | M | ... | 84 | 21 | ... | 54 | ... |
| | | F | ... | 69 | 16 | ... | 44 | ... |
| | 1994 | MF | ... | 76 | 20 | ... | 49 | ... |
| | | M | ... | ... | 22 | ... | ... | ... |
| | | F | ... | ... | 17 | ... | ... | ... |
| | 1995 | MF | ... | 75 | 21 | 0.6 | 48 | 38 |
| | | M | ... | ... | 24 | 0.9 | ... | ... |
| | | F | ... | ... | 19 | 0.4 | ... | ... |
| Congo | 1980 | | (3-5) | (6-11) | (12-18) | (19-23) | (6-18) | (6-23) |
| | | MF | 2 | 141 | 74 | 5 | 109 | 87 |
| | | M | 2 | 148 | 89 | 9 | 120 | 96 |
| | | F | 2 | 134 | 60 | 1 | 99 | 78 |
| | 1985 | MF | 3 | 147 | 75 | 6 | 113 | 90 |
| | | M | 3 | 154 | 87 | 11 | 122 | 98 |
| | | F | 3 | 141 | 64 | 2 | 104 | 82 |
| | 1990 | MF | 3 | 133 | 53 | 5 | 94 | 75 |
| | | M | 3 | 141 | 62 | 9 | 103 | 83 |
| | | F | 3 | 124 | 44 | 2 | 85 | 67 |
| | 1991 | MF | 3 | 128 | 54 | 6 | 92 | 74 |
| | | M | 3 | 135 | 62 | 10 | 100 | 80 |
| | | F | 3 | 122 | 45 | 2 | 85 | 67 |
| | 1992 | MF | 2 | 129 | 53 | 7 | 92 | 74 |
| | | M | 2 | 136 | 62 | ... | 101 | ... |
| | | F | 2 | 123 | 43 | ... | 84 | ... |

Gross enrolment ratios by level of education    II.8
Taux bruts de scolarisation par niveau d'enseignement
Tasas brutas de escolarización por nivel de enseñanza

| Country<br>Pays<br>País | Year<br>Année<br>Año | Sex<br>Sexe<br>Sexo | Gross enrolment ratios / Taux bruts de scolarisation / Tasas brutas de escolarización (%) | | | | | |
|---|---|---|---|---|---|---|---|---|
| | | | Pre-primary<br>Préprimaire<br>Preprimaria | Primary<br>Primaire<br>Primaria | Secondary<br>Secondaire<br>Secundaria | Tertiary<br>Supérieur<br>Superior | Primary and secondary<br>Primaire et secondaire<br>Primaria y secundaria | Primary, secondary and tertiary<br>Primaire, secondaire et supérieur<br>Primaria, secundaria y superior |
| Congo (cont) | 1993 | MF<br>M<br>F | 2<br>2<br>2 | 124<br>130<br>118 | 56<br>67<br>45 | ...<br>...<br>... | 91<br>100<br>83 | ...<br>...<br>... |
| | 1994 | MF<br>M<br>F | ...<br>...<br>... | 123<br>135<br>111 | 55<br>65<br>46 | ...<br>...<br>... | 90<br>101<br>80 | ...<br>...<br>... |
| | 1995 | MF<br>M<br>F | ...<br>...<br>... | 114<br>120<br>109 | 53<br>62<br>45 | ...<br>...<br>... | 85<br>92<br>78 | ...<br>...<br>... |
| Côte d'Ivoire | 1970 | <br>MF<br>M<br>F | (4-6)<br>1<br>1<br>1 | (7-12)<br>59<br>75<br>43 | (13-19)<br>9<br>14<br>4 | (20-24)<br>1<br>2<br>0.3 | (7-19)<br>35<br>46<br>24 | (7-24)<br>28<br>37<br>19 |
| | 1075 | <br>MF<br>M<br>F | (3-5)<br>0.7<br>0.7<br>0.6 | (6-11)<br>61<br>76<br>46 | (12-18)<br>12<br>18<br>7 | (19-23)<br>1<br>2<br>0.4 | (6-18)<br>38<br>49<br>28 | (6-23)<br>30<br>38<br>22 |
| | 1980 | MF<br>M<br>F | 0.7<br>0.8<br>0.7 | 75<br>90<br>60 | 19<br>26<br>11 | 3<br>5<br>1 | 49<br>60<br>37 | 39<br>48<br>30 |
| | 1985 | MF<br>M<br>F | 0.8<br>0.8<br>0.8 | 72<br>84<br>59 | 20<br>28<br>12 | 3<br>4<br>1 | 48<br>58<br>37 | 38<br>47<br>30 |
| | 1990 | MF<br>M<br>F | 0.9<br>1<br>0.9 | 67<br>79<br>56 | 22<br>30<br>14 | ...<br>...<br>... | 46<br>56<br>37 | ...<br>...<br>... |
| | 1991 | MF<br>M<br>F | 0.9<br>0.9<br>0.9 | 66<br>77<br>55 | 23<br>31<br>15 | 4<br>...<br>... | 46<br>56<br>37 | 38<br>...<br>... |
| | 1992 | MF<br>M<br>F | 1<br>1<br>1 | 65<br>76<br>54 | 23<br>31<br>15 | 5<br>...<br>... | 45<br>55<br>36 | 37<br>...<br>... |
| | 1993 | MF<br>M<br>F | 2<br>2<br>2 | 67<br>78<br>56 | 23<br>30<br>16 | 6<br>9<br>3 | 46<br>55<br>37 | 38<br>46<br>30 |
| | 1994 | MF<br>M<br>F | 2<br>2<br>2 | 68<br>78<br>57 | 23<br>30<br>15 | 6<br>9<br>3 | 46<br>55<br>37 | 38<br>46<br>30 |
| | 1995 | MF<br>M<br>F | 2<br>2<br>2 | 69<br>79<br>58 | 23<br>31<br>15 | ...<br>...<br>... | 47<br>56<br>38 | ...<br>...<br>... |
| | 1996 | MF<br>M<br>F | 2<br>3<br>2 | 71<br>82<br>60 | 24<br>33<br>16 | ...<br>...<br>... | 48<br>58<br>38 | ...<br>...<br>... |
| | 1997 | MF<br>M<br>F | ...<br>...<br>... | ...<br>...<br>... | 25<br>34<br>16 | ...<br>...<br>... | ...<br>...<br>... | ...<br>...<br>... |
| Democratic Rep. of the Congo | 1970 | <br>MF<br>M<br>F | (3-5)<br>0.9<br>...<br>... | (6-11)<br>95<br>120<br>70 | (12-17)<br>9<br>15<br>4 | (18-22)<br>0.7<br>1<br>0.1 | (6-17)<br>57<br>73<br>40 | (6-22)<br>43<br>56<br>30 |

II.8 Gross enrolment ratios by level of education
Taux bruts de scolarisation par niveau d'enseignement
Tasas brutas de escolarización por nivel de enseñanza

| Country / Pays / País | Year / Année / Año | Sex / Sexe / Sexo | Gross enrolment ratios / Taux bruts de scolarisation / Tasas brutas de escolarización (%) | | | | | |
|---|---|---|---|---|---|---|---|---|
| | | | Pre-primary / Préprimaire / Preprimaria | Primary / Primaire / Primaria | Secondary / Secondaire / Secundaria | Tertiary / Supérieur / Superior | Primary and secondary / Primaire et secondaire / Primaria y secundaria | Primary, secondary and tertiary / Primaire, secondaire et supérieur / Primaria, secundaria y superior |
| Democratic Rep. of the Congo (cont) | 1975 | MF | ... | 93 | 17 | 1 | 59 | 46 |
| | | M | ... | 112 | 25 | ... | 73 | ... |
| | | F | ... | 73 | 9 | ... | 45 | ... |
| | 1980 | MF | ... | 92 | 24 | 1 | 62 | 48 |
| | | M | ... | 108 | 35 | ... | 76 | ... |
| | | F | ... | 77 | 13 | ... | 49 | ... |
| | 1985 | MF | ... | 87 | 23 | 1 | 58 | 45 |
| | | M | ... | 105 | 32 | ... | 73 | ... |
| | | F | ... | 68 | 13 | ... | 44 | ... |
| | 1990 | MF | ... | 70 | ... | 2 | ... | ... |
| | | M | ... | 81 | ... | ... | ... | ... |
| | | F | ... | 60 | ... | ... | ... | ... |
| | 1991 | MF | ... | 69 | 21 | ... | 48 | ... |
| | | M | ... | 78 | 28 | ... | 57 | ... |
| | | F | ... | 59 | 14 | ... | 39 | ... |
| | 1992 | MF | 0.8 | 70 | 22 | ... | 49 | ... |
| | | M | 0.7 | 79 | 31 | ... | 58 | ... |
| | | F | 0.8 | 61 | 14 | ... | 40 | ... |
| | 1993 | MF | ... | 68 | 24 | ... | 49 | ... |
| | | M | ... | 78 | 33 | ... | 58 | ... |
| | | F | ... | 58 | 15 | ... | 39 | ... |
| | 1994 | MF | ... | 72 | 26 | 2 | 52 | 40 |
| | | M | ... | 86 | 32 | ... | 62 | ... |
| | | F | ... | 59 | 19 | ... | 41 | ... |
| Djibouti | 1970 | | (4-5) | (6-11) | (12-18) | (19-23) | (6-18) | (6-23) |
| | | MF | 2 | 28 | 7 | - | 18 | 13 |
| | | M | 2 | 39 | 10 | - | 25 | 19 |
| | | F | 3 | 17 | 4 | - | 10 | 8 |
| | 1975 | MF | 1 | 30 | 7 | - | 19 | 15 |
| | | M | 1 | 39 | 10 | - | 25 | 20 |
| | | F | 1 | 21 | 4 | - | 13 | 10 |
| | 1980 | MF | ... | 37 | 12 | - | 25 | 20 |
| | | M | ... | ... | 15 | - | ... | ... |
| | | F | ... | ... | 9 | - | ... | ... |
| | 1985 | MF | 1 | 40 | 12 | - | 26 | 20 |
| | | M | 1 | 47 | 14 | - | 31 | 24 |
| | | F | 1 | 33 | 9 | - | 21 | 17 |
| | 1990 | MF | 0.7 | 38 | 12 | - | 25 | 20 |
| | | M | 0.6 | 45 | 14 | - | 30 | 23 |
| | | F | 0.8 | 32 | 9 | - | 21 | 16 |
| | 1991 | MF | 0.6 | 39 | 12 | 0.1 | 26 | 20 |
| | | M | 0.5 | 45 | 15 | 0.2 | 30 | 23 |
| | | F | 0.7 | 32 | 10 | 0.1 | 21 | 16 |
| | 1992 | MF | 0.7 | 34 | 11 | 0.1 | 23 | 18 |
| | | M | 0.5 | 39 | 13 | 0.1 | 26 | 20 |
| | | F | 0.8 | 30 | 10 | 0.1 | 20 | 15 |
| | 1993 | MF | 0.7 | 36 | 12 | 0.1 | 24 | 19 |
| | | M | 0.5 | 41 | 14 | 0.1 | 28 | 21 |
| | | F | 0.9 | 31 | 10 | 0.1 | 21 | 16 |

Gross enrolment ratios by level of education    II.8
Taux bruts de scolarisation par niveau d'enseignement
Tasas brutas de escolarización por nivel de enseñanza

| Country / Pays / País | Year / Année / Año | Sex / Sexe / Sexo | Gross enrolment ratios / Taux bruts de scolarisation / Tasas brutas de escolarización (%) | | | | | |
|---|---|---|---|---|---|---|---|---|
| | | | Pre-primary / Préprimaire / Preprimaria | Primary / Primaire / Primaria | Secondary / Secondaire / Secundaria | Tertiary / Supérieur / Superior | Primary and secondary / Primaire et secondaire / Primaria y secundaria | Primary, secondary and tertiary / Primaire, secondaire et supérieur / Primaria, secundaria y superior |
| Djibouti (cont) | 1994 | | | | | | | |
| | | MF | 0.8 | 38 | 13 | 0.2 | 25 | 20 |
| | | M | 0.6 | 43 | 15 | 0.2 | 29 | 23 |
| | | F | 0.9 | 33 | 10 | 0.2 | 22 | 17 |
| | 1995 | | | | | | | |
| | | MF | 0.6 | 38 | 13 | 0.2 | 26 | 20 |
| | | M | 0.5 | 44 | 15 | 0.2 | 30 | 23 |
| | | F | 0.7 | 33 | 11 | 0.2 | 22 | 17 |
| | 1996 | | | | | | | |
| | | MF | 0.7 | 39 | 14 | 0.3 | 26 | 20 |
| | | M | 0.6 | 44 | 17 | 0.3 | 31 | 24 |
| | | F | 0.7 | 33 | 12 | 0.2 | 22 | 17 |
| Egypt | 1970 | | (4-5) | (6-11) | (12-17) | (18-22) | (6-17) | (6-22) |
| | | MF | 1 | 68 | 28 | 7 | 49 | 39 |
| | | M | 1 | 81 | 38 | 10 | 61 | 49 |
| | | F | 1 | 53 | 19 | 4 | 36 | 29 |
| | 1975 | | | | | | | |
| | | MF | 2 | 70 | 40 | 12 | 56 | 44 |
| | | M | 2 | 83 | 51 | 16 | 68 | 54 |
| | | F | 2 | 56 | 29 | 7 | 43 | 33 |
| | 1980 | | | | | | | |
| | | MF | 3 | 73 | 50 | 16 | 62 | 50 |
| | | M | 3 | 84 | 61 | 21 | 73 | 60 |
| | | F | 3 | 61 | 39 | 11 | 50 | 40 |
| | 1985 | | | | | | | |
| | | MF | 5 | 85 | 61 | 18 | 74 | 60 |
| | | M | 5 | 94 | 72 | 24 | 84 | 68 |
| | | F | 5 | 76 | 50 | 11 | 64 | 51 |
| | 1990 | | (4-5) | (6-10) | (11-16) | (17-21) | (6-16) | (6-21) |
| | | MF | 6 | 94 | 76 | 16 | 85 | 67 |
| | | M | 6 | 101 | 84 | 20 | 93 | 74 |
| | | F | 6 | 86 | 68 | 11 | 77 | 60 |
| | 1991 | | | | | | | |
| | | MF | 7 | 93 | 75 | 16 | 84 | 66 |
| | | M | 7 | 101 | 82 | 20 | 92 | 73 |
| | | F | 7 | 85 | 67 | 11 | 76 | 59 |
| | 1992 | | | | | | | |
| | | MF | 7 | 94 | 75 | 17 | 85 | 67 |
| | | M | 7 | 101 | 82 | 22 | 92 | 74 |
| | | F | 7 | 87 | 67 | 12 | 77 | 60 |
| | 1993 | | | | | | | |
| | | MF | 7 | 97 | 76 | 17 | 86 | 68 |
| | | M | 7 | 104 | 82 | 21 | 93 | 74 |
| | | F | 7 | 89 | 69 | 13 | 79 | 62 |
| | 1994 | | | | | | | |
| | | MF | 8 | 98 | 77 | 18 | 87 | 70 |
| | | M | 8 | 104 | 82 | 22 | 93 | 75 |
| | | F | 8 | 91 | 71 | 14 | 81 | 64 |
| | 1995 | | | | | | | |
| | | MF | 8 | 100 | 77 | 20 | 88 | 70 |
| | | M | 8 | 106 | 82 | 24 | 94 | 76 |
| | | F | 8 | 93 | 70 | 16 | 81 | 65 |
| | 1996 | | | | | | | |
| | | MF | 9 | 100 | 75 | ... | 87 | ... |
| | | M | 9 | 107 | 80 | ... | 93 | ... |
| | | F | 9 | 94 | 70 | ... | 81 | ... |
| | 1997 | | | | | | | |
| | | MF | ... | 101 | 78 | ... | 89 | ... |
| | | M | ... | 108 | 83 | ... | 94 | ... |
| | | F | ... | 94 | 73 | ... | 83 | ... |
| Equatorial Guinea (1) | | | (3-5) | (6-10) | (11-17) | (18-22) | (6-17) | (6-22) |

Gross enrolment ratios by level of education
Taux bruts de scolarisation par niveau d'enseignement
Tasas brutas de escolarización por nivel de enseñanza

| Country<br><br>Pays<br><br>País | Year<br><br>Année<br><br>Año | Sex<br><br>Sexe<br><br>Sexo | Gross enrolment ratios / Taux bruts de scolarisation / Tasas brutas de escolarización (%) | | | | | |
|---|---|---|---|---|---|---|---|---|
| | | | Pre-primary<br><br>Préprimaire<br><br>Preprimaria | Primary<br><br>Primaire<br><br>Primaria | Secondary<br><br>Secondaire<br><br>Secundaria | Tertiary<br><br>Supérieur<br><br>Superior | Primary and secondary<br><br>Primaire et secondaire<br><br>Primaria y secundaria | Primary, secondary and tertiary<br><br>Primaire, secondaire et supérieur<br><br>Primaria, secundaria y superior |
| Eritrea | 1992 | | (5-6) | (7-11) | (12-17) | (18-22) | (7-17) | (7-22) |
| | | MF | 4 | 46 | 15 | ... | 31 | ... |
| | | M | 4 | 51 | 17 | ... | 34 | ... |
| | | F | 4 | 41 | 14 | ... | 28 | ... |
| | 1993 | | | | | | | |
| | | MF | 4 | 51 | 17 | ... | 34 | ... |
| | | M | 4 | 57 | 19 | ... | 38 | ... |
| | | F | 4 | 45 | 14 | ... | 30 | ... |
| | 1994 | | | | | | | |
| | | MF | 4 | 54 | 18 | 1 | 36 | 27 |
| | | M | 4 | 60 | 21 | 2 | 40 | 30 |
| | | F | 4 | 48 | 15 | 0.3 | 31 | 23 |
| | 1995 | | | | | | | |
| | | MF | 4 | 56 | 19 | 1 | 38 | 28 |
| | | M | 4 | 62 | 22 | 2 | 42 | 32 |
| | | F | 4 | 50 | 16 | 0.2 | 33 | 25 |
| | 1996 | | | | | | | |
| | | MF | 4 | 53 | 20 | ... | 37 | ... |
| | | M | 4 | 59 | 24 | ... | 41 | ... |
| | | F | 4 | 48 | 17 | ... | 33 | ... |
| | 1997 | | | | | | | |
| | | MF | ... | ... | ... | 1 | ... | ... |
| | | M | ... | ... | ... | 2 | ... | ... |
| | | F | ... | ... | ... | 0.3 | ... | ... |
| Ethiopia | 1970 | | (4-6) | (7-12) | (13-18) | (19-23) | (7-18) | (7-23) |
| | | MF | ... | 14 | 4 | 0.2 | 10 | 7 |
| | | M | ... | 20 | 5 | 0.3 | 13 | 10 |
| | | F | ... | 9 | 2 | 0.0 | 6 | 4 |
| | 1975 | | | | | | | |
| | | MF | ... | 21 | 6 | ... | 14 | ... |
| | | M | ... | 28 | 8 | ... | 19 | ... |
| | | F | ... | 13 | 3 | ... | 9 | ... |
| | 1980 | | | | | | | |
| | | MF | ... | 37 | 9 | 0.4 | 25 | 19 |
| | | M | ... | 48 | 12 | 0.7 | 31 | 24 |
| | | F | ... | 27 | 7 | 0.2 | 18 | 14 |
| | 1985 | | | | | | | |
| | | MF | 2 | 38 | 13 | 0.7 | 26 | 20 |
| | | M | ... | 45 | 15 | 1 | 31 | 24 |
| | | F | ... | 30 | 10 | 0.3 | 21 | 16 |
| | 1990 | | | | | | | |
| | | MF | 2 | 33 | 14 | 0.8 | 24 | 19 |
| | | M | 2 | 39 | 16 | 1 | 29 | 22 |
| | | F | 2 | 26 | 13 | 0.3 | 20 | 15 |
| | 1991 | | | | | | | |
| | | MF | 1 | 26 | 13 | 0.7 | 20 | 16 |
| | | M | 1 | 31 | 13 | 1 | 23 | 18 |
| | | F | 1 | 22 | 12 | 0.3 | 18 | 13 |
| | 1992 | | | | | | | |
| | | MF | 1 | 23 | 11 | ... | 18 | ... |
| | | M | 1 | 27 | 12 | ... | 20 | ... |
| | | F | 1 | 19 | 11 | ... | 15 | ... |
| | 1993 | | | | | | | |
| | | MF | 1 | 27 | 11 | 0.6 | 20 | 15 |
| | | M | 1 | 34 | 12 | 1 | 24 | 18 |
| | | F | 1 | 21 | 10 | 0.3 | 16 | 12 |
| | 1994 | | | | | | | |
| | | MF | 1 | 31 | 11 | 0.7 | 22 | 17 |
| | | M | 1 | 39 | 12 | 1 | 27 | 21 |
| | | F | 1 | 23 | 10 | 0.3 | 17 | 13 |
| | 1995 | | | | | | | |
| | | MF | 1 | 37 | 12 | 0.7 | 26 | 20 |
| | | M | 1 | 48 | 13 | 1 | 33 | 25 |
| | | F | 1 | 27 | 10 | 0.3 | 20 | 15 |

Gross enrolment ratios by level of education  II.8
Taux bruts de scolarisation par niveau d'enseignement
Tasas brutas de escolarización por nivel de enseñanza

| Country / Pays / País | Year / Année / Año | Sex / Sexe / Sexo | Gross enrolment ratios / Taux bruts de scolarisation / Tasas brutas de escolarización (%) | | | | | |
|---|---|---|---|---|---|---|---|---|
| | | | Pre-primary / Préprimaire / Preprimaria | Primary / Primaire / Primaria | Secondary / Secondaire / Secundaria | Tertiary / Supérieur / Superior | Primary and secondary / Primaire et secondaire / Primaria y secundaria | Primary, secondary and tertiary / Primaire, secondaire et supérieur / Primaria, secundaria y superior |
| Ethiopia (cont) | 1996 | MF | 1 | 43 | 12 | 0.8 | 29 | 23 |
| | | M | 1 | 55 | 14 | 1 | 37 | 29 |
| | | F | 1 | 30 | 10 | 0.3 | 22 | 17 |
| Gabon (1) | | | (3-5) | (6-11) | (12-18) | (19-23) | (6-18) | (6-23) |
| Gambia | 1970 | | (3-5) | (6-11) | (12-18) | (19-23) | (6-18) | (6-23) |
| | | MF | ... | 25 | 8 | ... | 17 | ... |
| | | M | ... | 35 | 13 | ... | 24 | ... |
| | | F | ... | 15 | 4 | ... | 10 | ... |
| | 1975 | | (6-7) | (8-13) | (14-20) | (21-25) | (8-20) | (8-25) |
| | | MF | ... | 33 | 9 | ... | 21 | ... |
| | | M | ... | 44 | 14 | ... | 29 | ... |
| | | F | ... | 21 | 5 | ... | 13 | ... |
| | 1980 | | | | | | | |
| | | MF | ... | 53 | 11 | ... | 33 | ... |
| | | M | ... | 70 | 16 | ... | 44 | ... |
| | | Γ | ... | 36 | 7 | ... | 22 | ... |
| | 1985 | | | | | | | |
| | | MF | ... | 68 | 16 | ... | 43 | ... |
| | | M | ... | 84 | 23 | ... | 55 | ... |
| | | F | ... | 52 | 10 | ... | 32 | ... |
| | 1990 | | (5-6) | (7-12) | (13-18) | (19-23) | (7-18) | (7-23) |
| | | MF | ... | 64 | 19 | ... | 44 | ... |
| | | M | ... | 76 | 25 | ... | 54 | ... |
| | | F | ... | 52 | 12 | ... | 34 | ... |
| | 1991 | | | | | | | |
| | | MF | 24 | 65 | 19 | ... | 44 | ... |
| | | M | ... | 77 | 25 | ... | 54 | ... |
| | | F | ... | 52 | 13 | ... | 35 | ... |
| | 1992 | | | | | | | |
| | | MF | ... | 67 | 22 | ... | 47 | ... |
| | | M | ... | 79 | 29 | ... | 57 | ... |
| | | F | ... | 55 | 15 | ... | 37 | ... |
| | 1993 | | | | | | | |
| | | MF | ... | 70 | 22 | ... | 49 | ... |
| | | M | ... | 81 | 29 | ... | 58 | ... |
| | | F | ... | 59 | 16 | ... | 40 | ... |
| | 1994 | | | | | | | |
| | | MF | ... | 73 | 25 | 2 | 51 | 39 |
| | | M | ... | 84 | 32 | 2 | 61 | 46 |
| | | F | ... | 62 | 18 | 1 | 42 | 32 |
| | 1995 | | | | | | | |
| | | MF | ... | 77 | 25 | ... | 54 | ... |
| | | M | ... | 87 | 30 | ... | 62 | ... |
| | | F | ... | 67 | 19 | ... | 46 | ... |
| Ghana | 1970 | | (4-5) | (6-15) | (16-19) | (20-24) | (6-19) | (6-24) |
| | | MF | 3 | 62 | 14 | 0.7 | 51 | 41 |
| | | M | 3 | 71 | 20 | 1 | 59 | 48 |
| | | F | 3 | 54 | 8 | 0.2 | 43 | 34 |
| | 1975 | | (4-5) | (6-11) | (12-18) | (19-23) | (6-18) | (6-23) |
| | | MF | ... | 72 | 36 | 1 | 54 | 43 |
| | | M | ... | 81 | 44 | 2 | 63 | 50 |
| | | F | ... | 63 | 27 | 0.3 | 45 | 36 |
| | 1980 | | | | | | | |
| | | MF | 22 | 79 | 41 | 2 | 61 | 48 |
| | | M | 24 | 88 | 50 | 2 | 70 | 55 |
| | | F | 21 | 71 | 31 | 0.6 | 51 | 40 |
| | 1985 | | | | | | | |
| | | MF | 24 | 75 | 40 | 1 | 58 | 45 |
| | | M | ... | ... | 49 | 2 | ... | ... |
| | | F | ... | ... | 30 | 0.6 | ... | ... |
| | 1990 | | | | | | | |
| | | MF | ... | 75 | 36 | 1 | 57 | 45 |
| | | M | ... | 82 | 45 | 2 | 64 | 51 |
| | | F | ... | 68 | 28 | 0.6 | 49 | 39 |

II.8   Gross enrolment ratios by level of education
Taux bruts de scolarisation par niveau d'enseignement
Tasas brutas de escolarización por nivel de enseñanza

| Country / Pays / País | Year / Année / Año | Sex / Sexe / Sexo | Gross enrolment ratios / Taux bruts de scolarisation / Tasas brutas de escolarización (%) | | | | | |
|---|---|---|---|---|---|---|---|---|
| | | | Pre-primary / Préprimaire / Preprimaria | Primary / Primaire / Primaria | Secondary / Secondaire / Secundaria | Tertiary / Supérieur / Superior | Primary and secondary / Primaire et secondaire / Primaria y secundaria | Primary, secondary and tertiary / Primaire, secondaire et supérieur / Primaria, secundaria y superior |
| Ghana (cont) | 1991 | | | | | | | |
| | | MF | ... | 75 | 36 | ... | 57 | ... |
| | | M | ... | 81 | 44 | ... | 64 | ... |
| | | F | ... | 69 | 28 | ... | 50 | ... |
| | 1992 | | | | | | | |
| | | MF | ... | 80 | ... | ... | ... | ... |
| | | M | ... | 85 | ... | ... | ... | ... |
| | | F | ... | 74 | ... | ... | ... | ... |
| | 1993 | | | | | | | |
| | | MF | ... | 80 | ... | ... | ... | ... |
| | | M | ... | 86 | ... | ... | ... | ... |
| | | F | ... | 75 | ... | ... | ... | ... |
| | 1994 | | | | | | | |
| | | MF | ... | 79 | ... | ... | ... | ... |
| | | M | ... | 84 | ... | ... | ... | ... |
| | | F | ... | 74 | ... | ... | ... | ... |
| Guinea | 1970 | | (4-6) | (7-12) | (13-18) | (19-23) | (7-18) | (7-23) |
| | | MF | ... | 31 | 12 | 0.6 | 23 | 18 |
| | | M | ... | 42 | 19 | 1 | 32 | 25 |
| | | F | ... | 20 | 5 | 0.1 | 13 | 10 |
| | 1975 | | | | | | | |
| | | MF | ... | 30 | 14 | 3 | 23 | 18 |
| | | M | ... | 40 | 20 | 5 | 31 | 25 |
| | | F | ... | 21 | 7 | 1 | 15 | 11 |
| | 1980 | | | | | | | |
| | | MF | ... | 36 | 17 | 5 | 28 | 22 |
| | | M | ... | 48 | 24 | 7 | 37 | 30 |
| | | F | ... | 25 | 10 | 2 | 18 | 14 |
| | 1985 | | (4-6) | (7-12) | (13-19) | (20-24) | (7-19) | (7-24) |
| | | MF | ... | 34 | 13 | 2 | 24 | 19 |
| | | M | ... | 47 | 18 | 3 | 33 | 27 |
| | | F | ... | 22 | 7 | 0.6 | 15 | 12 |
| | 1990 | | | | | | | |
| | | MF | ... | 37 | 10 | 1 | 24 | 19 |
| | | M | ... | 50 | 15 | 2 | 33 | 27 |
| | | F | ... | 24 | 5 | 0.1 | 15 | 12 |
| | 1991 | | | | | | | |
| | | MF | ... | 36 | 11 | 1 | 24 | 19 |
| | | M | ... | 49 | 16 | 2 | 33 | 27 |
| | | F | ... | 23 | 5 | 0.1 | 15 | 12 |
| | 1992 | | | | | | | |
| | | MF | ... | 40 | 11 | 1 | 26 | 21 |
| | | M | ... | 54 | 17 | 2 | 36 | 29 |
| | | F | ... | 26 | 6 | 0.2 | 16 | 13 |
| | 1993 | | | | | | | |
| | | MF | 2 | 42 | 12 | 1 | 28 | 22 |
| | | M | 2 | 56 | 17 | 2 | 38 | 30 |
| | | F | 1 | 28 | 6 | 0.2 | 17 | 14 |
| | 1994 | | | | | | | |
| | | MF | 2 | 46 | 12 | 1 | 30 | 24 |
| | | M | 2 | 61 | 18 | 2 | 40 | 32 |
| | | F | 2 | 31 | 6 | 0.2 | 19 | 15 |
| | 1995 | | | | | | | |
| | | MF | 3 | 48 | 12 | 1 | 31 | 25 |
| | | M | 3 | 62 | 18 | 2 | 41 | 33 |
| | | F | 3 | 33 | 6 | 0.2 | 20 | 16 |
| | 1996 | | | | | | | |
| | | MF | 3 | 53 | 13 | 1 | 34 | 27 |
| | | M | 3 | 66 | 19 | 2 | 44 | 35 |
| | | F | 3 | 38 | 7 | 0.3 | 23 | 18 |
| | 1997 | | | | | | | |
| | | MF | 4 | 54 | 14 | ... | 35 | ... |
| | | M | ... | 68 | 20 | ... | 45 | ... |
| | | F | ... | 41 | 7 | ... | 25 | ... |

Gross enrolment ratios by level of education II.8
Taux bruts de scolarisation par niveau d'enseignement
Tasas brutas de escolarización por nivel de enseñanza

| Country / Pays / País | Year / Année / Año | Sex / Sexe / Sexo | Gross enrolment ratios / Taux bruts de scolarisation / Tasas brutas de escolarización (%) | | | | | |
| | | | Pre-primary / Préprimaire / Preprimaria | Primary / Primaire / Primaria | Secondary / Secondaire / Secundaria | Tertiary / Supérieur / Superior | Primary and secondary / Primaire et secondaire / Primaria y secundaria | Primary, secondary and tertiary / Primaire, secondaire et supérieur / Primaria, secundaria y superior |
|---|---|---|---|---|---|---|---|---|
| Guinea-Bissau | 1970 | | (4-6) | (7-12) | (13-17) | (18-22) | (7-17) | (7-22) |
| | | MF | 0.5 | 40 | 8 | ... | 27 | ... |
| | | M | 0.3 | 57 | 11 | ... | 37 | ... |
| | | F | 0.8 | 24 | 6 | ... | 16 | ... |
| | 1975 | | | | | | | |
| | | MF | ... | 65 | 4 | ... | 39 | ... |
| | | M | ... | 90 | 5 | ... | 54 | ... |
| | | F | ... | 41 | 2 | ... | 25 | ... |
| | 1980 | | | | | | | |
| | | MF | 2 | 68 | 6 | ... | 42 | ... |
| | | M | 2 | 94 | 10 | ... | 59 | ... |
| | | F | 2 | 43 | 2 | ... | 26 | ... |
| | 1985 | | | | | | | |
| | | MF | ... | 64 | 9 | ... | 41 | ... |
| | | M | ... | 85 | 14 | ... | 55 | ... |
| | | F | ... | 43 | 4 | ... | 27 | ... |
| | 1991 | | | | | | | |
| | | MF | ... | 54 | ... | ... | ... | ... |
| | | M | ... | 70 | ... | ... | ... | ... |
| | | F | ... | 38 | ... | ... | ... | ... |
| | 1992 | | | | | | | |
| | | MF | ... | 52 | ... | ... | ... | ... |
| | | M | ... | 67 | ... | ... | ... | ... |
| | | F | ... | 37 | ... | ... | ... | ... |
| | 1993 | | | | | | | |
| | | MF | ... | 58 | ... | ... | ... | ... |
| | | M | ... | 74 | ... | ... | ... | ... |
| | | F | ... | 42 | ... | ... | ... | ... |
| | 1994 | | | | | | | |
| | | MF | ... | 62 | ... | ... | ... | ... |
| | | M | ... | 79 | ... | ... | ... | ... |
| | | F | ... | 45 | ... | ... | ... | ... |
| Kenya | 1970 | | | (6-12) | (13-18) | (19-23) | (6-18) | (6-23) |
| | | MF | ... | 62 | 9 | 0.8 | 41 | 33 |
| | | M | ... | 72 | 13 | ... | 49 | ... |
| | | F | ... | 52 | 5 | ... | 33 | ... |
| | 1975 | | | | | | | |
| | | MF | ... | 104 | 13 | 0.8 | 68 | 54 |
| | | M | ... | 112 | 17 | ... | 75 | ... |
| | | F | ... | 96 | 9 | ... | 62 | ... |
| | 1980 | | | | | | | |
| | | MF | ... | 115 | 20 | 0.9 | 78 | 62 |
| | | M | ... | 120 | 23 | 1 | 82 | 66 |
| | | F | ... | 110 | 16 | 0.3 | 73 | 58 |
| | 1985 | | (3-5) | (6-13) | (14-18) | (19-23) | (6-18) | (6-23) |
| | | MF | 26 | 99 | 21 | 1 | 75 | 60 |
| | | M | 25 | 102 | 26 | 2 | 78 | 63 |
| | | F | 26 | 96 | 16 | 0.7 | 71 | 57 |
| | 1990 | | | | | | | |
| | | MF | 34 | 95 | 24 | 2 | 72 | 58 |
| | | M | 32 | 97 | 28 | 2 | 75 | 60 |
| | | F | 36 | 93 | 21 | 0.9 | 70 | 56 |
| | 1991 | | (3-5) | (6-13) | (14-17) | (18-22) | (6-17) | (6-22) |
| | | MF | 35 | 93 | 28 | ... | 75 | ... |
| | | M | ... | 95 | 31 | ... | 77 | ... |
| | | F | ... | 91 | 24 | ... | 73 | ... |
| | 1992 | | | | | | | |
| | | MF | 36 | 92 | 27 | ... | 73 | ... |
| | | M | 35 | 93 | 31 | ... | 75 | ... |
| | | F | 36 | 91 | 24 | ... | 71 | ... |
| | 1993 | | | | | | | |
| | | MF | 35 | 90 | 26 | ... | 72 | ... |
| | | M | 35 | 91 | 29 | ... | 73 | ... |
| | | F | 34 | 90 | 23 | ... | 70 | ... |

II.8    Gross enrolment ratios by level of education
Taux bruts de scolarisation par niveau d'enseignement
Tasas brutas de escolarización por nivel de enseñanza

| Country | Year | Sex | Gross enrolment ratios / Taux bruts de scolarisation / Tasas brutas de escolarización (%) | | | | | |
|---|---|---|---|---|---|---|---|---|
| | | | Pre-primary | Primary | Secondary | Tertiary | Primary and secondary | Primary, secondary and tertiary |
| Pays | Année | Sexe | Préprimaire | Primaire | Secondaire | Supérieur | Primaire et secondaire | Primaire, secondaire et supérieur |
| País | Año | Sexo | Preprimaria | Primaria | Secundaria | Superior | Primaria y secundaria | Primaria, secundaria y superior |
| Kenya (cont) | 1994 | | | | | | | |
| | | MF | 35 | 87 | 25 | ... | 69 | ... |
| | | M | 35 | 87 | 27 | ... | 70 | ... |
| | | F | 35 | 87 | 23 | ... | 68 | ... |
| | 1995 | | | | | | | |
| | | MF | ... | 85 | 24 | ... | 67 | ... |
| | | M | ... | 85 | 26 | ... | 68 | ... |
| | | F | ... | 85 | 22 | ... | 66 | ... |
| Lesotho | 1970 | | | (6-13) | (14-18) | (19-23) | (6-18) | (6-23) |
| | | MF | - | 87 | 7 | 0.4 | 60 | 46 |
| | | M | - | 72 | 7 | 0.6 | 50 | 39 |
| | | F | - | 102 | 7 | 0.3 | 70 | 53 |
| | 1975 | | | (6-12) | (13-17) | (18-22) | (6-17) | (6-22) |
| | | MF | - | 106 | 13 | 0.5 | 71 | 54 |
| | | M | - | 87 | 12 | 0.6 | 60 | 46 |
| | | F | - | 123 | 14 | 0.4 | 82 | 62 |
| | 1980 | | | | | | | |
| | | MF | - | 103 | 18 | 1 | 72 | 54 |
| | | M | - | 85 | 14 | 0.7 | 59 | 45 |
| | | F | - | 122 | 21 | 1 | 84 | 63 |
| | 1985 | | | | | | | |
| | | MF | - | 112 | 23 | 1 | 80 | 61 |
| | | M | - | 98 | 19 | 1 | 69 | 53 |
| | | F | - | 125 | 28 | 1 | 90 | 68 |
| | 1990 | | | | | | | |
| | | MF | - | 112 | 25 | 1 | 79 | 61 |
| | | M | - | 100 | 20 | 1 | 70 | 54 |
| | | F | - | 123 | 30 | 2 | 88 | 68 |
| | 1991 | | | | | | | |
| | | MF | - | 113 | 25 | 1 | 79 | 61 |
| | | M | - | 101 | 20 | 1 | 70 | 54 |
| | | F | - | 125 | 29 | 2 | 88 | 67 |
| | 1992 | | | | | | | |
| | | MF | - | 112 | 26 | 2 | 79 | 60 |
| | | M | - | 102 | 21 | 2 | 71 | 54 |
| | | F | - | 122 | 31 | 2 | 87 | 66 |
| | 1993 | | | | | | | |
| | | MF | - | 108 | 27 | 2 | 76 | 58 |
| | | M | - | 99 | 22 | 2 | 69 | 53 |
| | | F | - | 116 | 32 | 3 | 83 | 64 |
| | 1994 | | | | | | | |
| | | MF | - | 110 | 29 | 2 | 78 | 60 |
| | | M | - | 102 | 23 | 2 | 72 | 54 |
| | | F | - | 117 | 35 | 3 | 85 | 65 |
| | 1995 | | | | | | | |
| | | MF | - | 111 | 31 | 2 | 80 | 60 |
| | | M | - | 104 | 25 | 2 | 73 | 56 |
| | | F | - | 117 | 37 | 3 | 86 | 65 |
| | 1996 | | | | | | | |
| | | MF | - | 108 | 31 | 2 | 78 | 59 |
| | | M | - | 102 | 25 | 2 | 72 | 54 |
| | | F | - | 114 | 36 | 3 | 84 | 63 |
| Liberia | 1970 | | (4-5) | (6-11) | (12-17) | (18-22) | (6-17) | (6-22) |
| | | MF | ... | ... | 10 | 0.9 | ... | ... |
| | | M | ... | ... | 15 | 1 | ... | ... |
| | | F | ... | ... | 5 | 0.4 | ... | ... |
| | 1975 | | | | | | | |
| | | MF | 53 | 40 | 16 | 2 | 29 | 23 |
| | | M | 62 | 52 | 24 | 3 | 40 | 31 |
| | | F | 43 | 27 | 8 | 0.8 | 19 | 15 |
| | 1980 | | | | | | | |
| | | MF | 67 | 48 | 22 | ... | 36 | ... |
| | | M | 77 | 61 | 31 | ... | 48 | ... |
| | | F | 58 | 34 | 12 | ... | 25 | ... |

Gross enrolment ratios by level of education II.8
Taux bruts de scolarisation par niveau d'enseignement
Tasas brutas de escolarización por nivel de enseñanza

| Country / Pays / País | Year / Année / Año | Sex / Sexe / Sexo | Gross enrolment ratios / Taux bruts de scolarisation / Tasas brutas de escolarización (%) | | | | | |
|---|---|---|---|---|---|---|---|---|
| | | | Pre-primary / Préprimaire / Preprimaria | Primary / Primaire / Primaria | Secondary / Secondaire / Secundaria | Tertiary / Supérieur / Superior | Primary and secondary / Primaire et secondaire / Primaria y secundaria | Primary, secondary and tertiary / Primaire, secondaire et supérieur / Primaria, secundaria y superior |
| Libyan Arab Jamahiriya | 1970 | | (4-5) | (6-11) | (12-17) | (18-22) | (6-17) | (6-22) |
| | | MF | 1 | 111 | 21 | 3 | 70 | 54 |
| | | M | 1 | 136 | 33 | 5 | 90 | 69 |
| | | F | 1 | 84 | 8 | 0.6 | 50 | 38 |
| | 1975 | | | | | | | |
| | | MF | 5 | 137 | 55 | 6 | 102 | 79 |
| | | M | 5 | 145 | 71 | 9 | 113 | 88 |
| | | F | 4 | 130 | 38 | 2 | 90 | 69 |
| | 1980 | | | | | | | |
| | | MF | 4 | 125 | 76 | 8 | 104 | 83 |
| | | M | 5 | 129 | 89 | 11 | 112 | 89 |
| | | F | 4 | 121 | 63 | 4 | 96 | 76 |
| | 1985 | | (4-5) | (6-14) | (15-17) | (18-22) | (6-17) | (6-22) |
| | | MF | 6 | 109 | 59 | 9 | 98 | 79 |
| | | M | 6 | 113 | 61 | ... | 102 | ... |
| | | F | 6 | 104 | 57 | ... | 94 | ... |
| | 1990 | | | | | | | |
| | | MF | ... | 105 | 86 | 15 | 101 | 81 |
| | | M | ... | 108 | ... | ... | ... | ... |
| | | F | ... | 102 | ... | ... | ... | ... |
| | 1991 | | | | | | | |
| | | MF | ... | 107 | 95 | 17 | 105 | 84 |
| | | M | ... | 110 | ... | 18 | ... | ... |
| | | F | ... | 105 | ... | 15 | ... | ... |
| | 1992 | | | | | | | |
| | | MF | ... | 105 | 98 | ... | 104 | ... |
| | | M | ... | 107 | ... | ... | ... | ... |
| | | F | ... | 103 | ... | ... | ... | ... |
| | 1993 | | | | | | | |
| | | MF | ... | 111 | ... | ... | ... | ... |
| | | M | ... | 110 | ... | ... | ... | ... |
| | | F | ... | 111 | ... | ... | ... | ... |
| Madagascar | 1970 | | (3-5) | (6-11) | (12-18) | (19-23) | (6-18) | (6-23) |
| | | MF | ... | 81 | 10 | 1 | 47 | 37 |
| | | M | ... | 88 | 12 | 1 | 51 | 41 |
| | | F | ... | 75 | 8 | 0.6 | 42 | 34 |
| | 1975 | | | | | | | |
| | | MF | ... | 92 | 13 | 1 | 53 | 42 |
| | | M | ... | 104 | 15 | 1 | 61 | 48 |
| | | F | ... | 80 | 11 | 1 | 46 | 36 |
| | 1980 | | (3-5) | (6-10) | (11-17) | (18-22) | (6-17) | (6-22) |
| | | MF | ... | 130 | ... | 3 | ... | ... |
| | | M | ... | 131 | ... | ... | ... | ... |
| | | F | ... | 129 | ... | ... | ... | ... |
| | 1985 | | | | | | | |
| | | MF | ... | ... | ... | 4 | ... | ... |
| | | M | ... | ... | ... | 5 | ... | ... |
| | | F | ... | ... | ... | 3 | ... | ... |
| | 1990 | | | | | | | |
| | | MF | ... | 103 | 18 | 3 | 56 | 42 |
| | | M | ... | 103 | 18 | 3 | 56 | 42 |
| | | F | ... | 103 | 18 | 3 | 56 | 42 |
| | 1991 | | | | | | | |
| | | MF | ... | 96 | 16 | 3 | 52 | 39 |
| | | M | ... | 98 | 16 | 4 | 54 | 40 |
| | | F | ... | 93 | 16 | 3 | 50 | 38 |
| | 1992 | | | | | | | |
| | | MF | ... | 93 | 17 | 3 | 51 | 39 |
| | | M | ... | 94 | 17 | 4 | 52 | 39 |
| | | F | ... | 93 | 16 | 3 | 51 | 38 |
| | 1993 | | | | | | | |
| | | MF | ... | 91 | 16 | 3 | 50 | 38 |
| | | M | ... | 91 | 16 | ... | 51 | ... |
| | | F | ... | 92 | 16 | ... | 50 | ... |

II.8    Gross enrolment ratios by level of education
Taux bruts de scolarisation par niveau d'enseignement
Tasas brutas de escolarización por nivel de enseñanza

| Country / Pays / País | Year / Année / Año | Sex / Sexe / Sexo | Gross enrolment ratios / Taux bruts de scolarisation / Tasas brutas de escolarización (%) | | | | | |
|---|---|---|---|---|---|---|---|---|
| | | | Pre-primary / Préprimaire / Preprimaria | Primary / Primaire / Primaria | Secondary / Secondaire / Secundaria | Tertiary / Supérieur / Superior | Primary and secondary / Primaire et secondaire / Primaria y secundaria | Primary, secondary and tertiary / Primaire, secondaire et supérieur / Primaria, secundaria y superior |
| Madagascar (cont) | 1994 | MF | 5 | 89 | 16 | 2 | 49 | 37 |
| | | M | 4 | 85 | 16 | 2 | 48 | 36 |
| | | F | 5 | 92 | 15 | 2 | 50 | 38 |
| | 1995 | MF | ... | 92 | 16 | 2 | 51 | 39 |
| | | M | ... | 92 | 16 | 2 | 51 | 39 |
| | | F | ... | 91 | 16 | 2 | 51 | 38 |
| | 1996 | MF | ... | ... | ... | 2 | ... | ... |
| | | M | ... | ... | ... | 2 | ... | ... |
| | | F | ... | ... | ... | 2 | ... | ... |
| Malawi | 1970 | | | (6-13) | (14-17) | (18-22) | (6-17) | (6-22) |
| | | MF | - | 37 | 4 | 0.4 | 28 | 21 |
| | | M | - | 48 | 5 | 0.6 | 36 | 28 |
| | | F | - | 27 | 2 | 0.1 | 20 | 15 |
| | 1975 | MF | - | 56 | 4 | 0.4 | 41 | 32 |
| | | M | - | 69 | 6 | 0.7 | 52 | 40 |
| | | F | - | 43 | 2 | 0.1 | 31 | 24 |
| | 1980 | MF | - | 60 | 5 | 0.5 | 44 | 34 |
| | | M | - | 72 | 7 | 0.7 | 54 | 42 |
| | | F | - | 48 | 3 | 0.2 | 35 | 27 |
| | 1985 | MF | - | 60 | 6 | 0.5 | 45 | 34 |
| | | M | - | 69 | 8 | 0.7 | 52 | 40 |
| | | F | - | 52 | 4 | 0.2 | 38 | 29 |
| | 1990 | MF | - | 68 | 8 | 0.6 | 51 | 40 |
| | | M | - | 74 | 11 | 0.9 | 57 | 44 |
| | | F | - | 62 | 5 | 0.3 | 46 | 35 |
| | 1991 | MF | - | 79 | 9 | 0.6 | 60 | 46 |
| | | M | - | 85 | 12 | 0.9 | 65 | 51 |
| | | F | - | 73 | 6 | 0.3 | 54 | 42 |
| | 1992 | MF | - | 84 | 9 | 0.6 | 64 | 49 |
| | | M | - | 88 | 12 | 0.9 | 67 | 52 |
| | | F | - | 80 | 6 | 0.3 | 60 | 46 |
| | 1993 | MF | - | 89 | 11 | 0.6 | 67 | 52 |
| | | M | - | 92 | 15 | 0.9 | 70 | 55 |
| | | F | - | 86 | 8 | 0.3 | 64 | 50 |
| | 1994 | MF | - | 134 | 13 | 0.6 | 100 | 77 |
| | | M | - | 141 | 16 | 0.9 | 106 | 82 |
| | | F | - | 127 | 9 | 0.4 | 94 | 72 |
| | 1995 | MF | - | 134 | 17 | 0.6 | 100 | 78 |
| | | M | - | 140 | 21 | 0.9 | 106 | 83 |
| | | F | - | 127 | 12 | 0.4 | 94 | 73 |
| Mali | 1970 | | (5-6) | (7-12) | (13-18) | (19-23) | (7-18) | (7-23) |
| | | MF | ... | 23 | 5 | 0.2 | 15 | 12 |
| | | M | ... | 30 | 8 | 0.3 | 20 | 15 |
| | | F | ... | 16 | 2 | 0.0 | 10 | 8 |
| | 1975 | MF | ... | 25 | 7 | 0.5 | 17 | 13 |
| | | M | ... | 33 | 10 | 1 | 23 | 18 |
| | | F | ... | 18 | 3 | 0.1 | 11 | 9 |
| | 1980 | MF | ... | 26 | 8 | 0.8 | 18 | 14 |
| | | M | ... | 34 | 12 | 1 | 24 | 19 |
| | | F | ... | 19 | 5 | 0.2 | 13 | 10 |

Gross enrolment ratios by level of education  II.8
Taux bruts de scolarisation par niveau d'enseignement
Tasas brutas de escolarización por nivel de enseñanza

| Country / Pays / País | Year / Année / Año | Sex / Sexe / Sexo | Gross enrolment ratios / Taux bruts de scolarisation / Tasas brutas de escolarización (%) | | | | | |
| | | | Pre-primary / Préprimaire / Preprimaria | Primary / Primaire / Primaria | Secondary / Secondaire / Secundaria | Tertiary / Supérieur / Superior | Primary and secondary / Primaire et secondaire / Primaria y secundaria | Primary, secondary and tertiary / Primaire, secondaire et supérieur / Primaria, secundaria y superior |
|---|---|---|---|---|---|---|---|---|
| Mali (cont) | 1985 | | | | | | | |
| | | MF | ... | 25 | ... | 0.9 | ... | ... |
| | | M | ... | 31 | ... | 2 | ... | ... |
| | | F | ... | 18 | ... | 0.2 | ... | ... |
| | 1990 | | | | | | | |
| | | MF | ... | 26 | 7 | 0.6 | 18 | 14 |
| | | M | ... | 34 | 9 | 1 | 23 | 18 |
| | | F | ... | 19 | 5 | 0.2 | 13 | 10 |
| | 1991 | | | | | | | |
| | | MF | ... | 28 | 8 | 0.8 | 19 | 15 |
| | | M | ... | 36 | 11 | 1 | 25 | 19 |
| | | F | ... | 21 | 5 | 0.2 | 14 | 11 |
| | 1992 | | | | | | | |
| | | MF | ... | 31 | 8 | 0.9 | 21 | 16 |
| | | M | ... | 39 | 11 | 2 | 27 | 21 |
| | | F | ... | 24 | 5 | 0.3 | 15 | 12 |
| | 1993 | | (3-6) | (7-12) | (13-18) | (19-23) | (7-18) | (7-23) |
| | | MF | ... | 35 | 9 | ... | 23 | ... |
| | | M | ... | 43 | 12 | ... | 29 | ... |
| | | F | ... | 26 | 6 | ... | 17 | ... |
| | 1994 | | | | | | | |
| | | MF | 2 | 37 | 10 | 0.9 | 25 | 19 |
| | | M | 2 | 45 | 14 | 2 | 31 | 24 |
| | | F | 2 | 30 | 7 | 0.3 | 19 | 15 |
| | 1995 | | | | | | | |
| | | MF | 2 | 41 | 11 | 1 | 27 | 21 |
| | | M | 2 | 49 | 14 | 2 | 33 | 26 |
| | | F | 2 | 32 | 7 | 0.3 | 21 | 16 |
| | 1996 | | | | | | | |
| | | MF | 2 | 45 | 12 | 1 | 30 | 23 |
| | | M | 2 | 55 | 16 | 2 | 37 | 29 |
| | | F | 2 | 35 | 8 | 0.6 | 23 | 18 |
| | 1997 | | | | | | | |
| | | MF | 2 | 49 | 13 | 1 | 32 | 25 |
| | | M | 2 | 58 | 17 | 2 | 39 | 31 |
| | | F | 2 | 40 | 8 | 0.6 | 25 | 20 |
| Mauritania | 1970 | | (3-5) | (6-12) | (13-19) | (20-24) | (6-19) | (6-24) |
| | | MF | ... | 15 | 2 | ... | 9 | ... |
| | | M | ... | 21 | 4 | ... | 13 | ... |
| | | F | ... | 8 | 0.5 | ... | 5 | ... |
| | 1975 | | | | | | | |
| | | MF | ... | 20 | 4 | ... | 13 | ... |
| | | M | ... | 26 | 7 | ... | 18 | ... |
| | | F | ... | 15 | 0.8 | ... | 8 | ... |
| | 1980 | | (3-5) | (6-11) | (12-17) | (18-22) | (6-17) | (6-22) |
| | | MF | ... | 37 | 11 | ... | 25 | ... |
| | | M | ... | 47 | 17 | ... | 34 | ... |
| | | F | ... | 26 | 4 | ... | 16 | ... |
| | 1985 | | | | | | | |
| | | MF | ... | 48 | 15 | 3 | 33 | 26 |
| | | M | ... | 58 | 22 | ... | 42 | ... |
| | | F | ... | 39 | 8 | ... | 25 | ... |
| | 1990 | | | | | | | |
| | | MF | ... | 49 | 14 | 3 | 33 | 26 |
| | | M | ... | 56 | 19 | 5 | 39 | 31 |
| | | F | ... | 41 | 9 | 0.8 | 27 | 21 |
| | 1991 | | | | | | | |
| | | MF | ... | 53 | 14 | 3 | 36 | 28 |
| | | M | ... | 61 | 19 | 5 | 42 | 33 |
| | | F | ... | 46 | 9 | 0.9 | 30 | 23 |
| | 1992 | | | | | | | |
| | | MF | 0.4 | 61 | 15 | 4 | 40 | 31 |
| | | M | ... | 67 | 19 | 6 | 46 | 37 |
| | | F | ... | 54 | 10 | 1 | 34 | 26 |

II.8    Gross enrolment ratios by level of education
Taux bruts de scolarisation par niveau d'enseignement
Tasas brutas de escolarización por nivel de enseñanza

| Country / Pays / País | Year / Année / Año | Sex / Sexe / Sexo | Gross enrolment ratios / Taux bruts de scolarisation / Tasas brutas de escolarización (%) | | | | | |
|---|---|---|---|---|---|---|---|---|
| | | | Pre-primary / Préprimaire / Preprimaria | Primary / Primaire / Primaria | Secondary / Secondaire / Secundaria | Tertiary / Supérieur / Superior | Primary and secondary / Primaire et secondaire / Primaria y secundaria | Primary, secondary and tertiary / Primaire, secondaire et supérieur / Primaria, secundaria y superior |
| Mauritania (cont) | 1993 | | | | | | | |
| | | MF | ... | 67 | 15 | 4 | 44 | 34 |
| | | M | ... | 74 | 19 | 6 | 49 | 39 |
| | | F | ... | 60 | 11 | 1 | 38 | 29 |
| | 1994 | | | | | | | |
| | | MF | ... | 71 | 16 | 4 | 46 | 36 |
| | | M | ... | 78 | 20 | 6 | 52 | 41 |
| | | F | ... | 64 | 11 | 1 | 40 | 31 |
| | 1995 | | | | | | | |
| | | MF | ... | 75 | 16 | 4 | 48 | 38 |
| | | M | ... | 81 | 21 | 6 | 54 | 42 |
| | | F | ... | 69 | 11 | 1 | 42 | 33 |
| | 1996 | | | | | | | |
| | | MF | ... | 79 | ... | ... | ... | ... |
| | | M | ... | 84 | ... | ... | ... | ... |
| | | F | ... | 75 | ... | ... | ... | ... |
| Mauritius | 1970 | | (3-4) | (5-10) | (11-17) | (18-22) | (5-17) | (5-22) |
| | | MF | 21 | 96 | 31 | 2 | 64 | 52 |
| | | M | 21 | 97 | 36 | 5 | 67 | 54 |
| | | F | 20 | 95 | 25 | 0.2 | 61 | 49 |
| | 1975 | | | | | | | |
| | | MF | 22 | 105 | 38 | 1 | 68 | 53 |
| | | M | 22 | 106 | 41 | 2 | 70 | 55 |
| | | F | 22 | 103 | 34 | 0.3 | 66 | 51 |
| | 1980 | | | | | | | |
| | | MF | 27 | 93 | 50 | 1 | 70 | 52 |
| | | M | 27 | 94 | 51 | 1 | 71 | 53 |
| | | F | 26 | 91 | 49 | 0.6 | 69 | 51 |
| | 1985 | | | | | | | |
| | | MF | ... | 109 | 49 | 1 | 77 | 55 |
| | | M | ... | 110 | 51 | 1 | 78 | 56 |
| | | F | ... | 109 | 46 | 0.8 | 76 | 54 |
| | 1990 | | | | | | | |
| | | MF | 56 | 109 | 53 | 4 | 79 | 59 |
| | | M | 56 | 109 | 53 | 4 | 78 | 59 |
| | | F | 56 | 109 | 53 | 3 | 79 | 59 |
| | 1991 | | | | | | | |
| | | MF | ... | 109 | 55 | 4 | 79 | 60 |
| | | M | ... | 109 | 54 | 5 | 79 | 59 |
| | | F | ... | 109 | 56 | 3 | 80 | 60 |
| | 1992 | | | | | | | |
| | | MF | ... | 107 | 57 | 5 | 79 | 60 |
| | | M | ... | 107 | 56 | 6 | 79 | 59 |
| | | F | ... | 107 | 57 | 4 | 80 | 60 |
| | 1993 | | | | | | | |
| | | MF | 86 | 107 | 59 | 6 | 80 | 60 |
| | | M | 86 | 107 | 58 | 7 | 79 | 60 |
| | | F | 86 | 106 | 60 | 5 | 80 | 60 |
| | 1994 | | | | | | | |
| | | MF | ... | 106 | 60 | 6 | 80 | 60 |
| | | M | ... | 107 | 59 | 6 | 79 | 60 |
| | | F | ... | 106 | 62 | 5 | 81 | 60 |
| | 1995 | | | | | | | |
| | | MF | ... | 107 | 62 | 6 | 81 | 61 |
| | | M | ... | 107 | 60 | 6 | 80 | 60 |
| | | F | ... | 106 | 64 | 6 | 82 | 61 |
| | 1996 | | | | | | | |
| | | MF | 85 | 107 | 64 | 7 | 83 | 62 |
| | | M | 85 | 107 | 63 | 8 | 82 | 62 |
| | | F | 85 | 106 | 66 | 6 | 84 | 62 |
| | 1997 | | | | | | | |
| | | MF | 104 | 106 | ... | 6 | ... | ... |
| | | M | 104 | 106 | ... | 6 | ... | ... |
| | | F | 104 | 106 | ... | 6 | ... | ... |

Gross enrolment ratios by level of education    II.8
Taux bruts de scolarisation par niveau d'enseignement
Tasas brutas de escolarización por nivel de enseñanza

| Country<br>Pays<br>País | Year<br>Année<br>Año | Sex<br>Sexe<br>Sexo | Gross enrolment ratios / Taux bruts de scolarisation / Tasas brutas de escolarización (%) | | | | | |
|---|---|---|---|---|---|---|---|---|
| | | | Pre-primary<br>Préprimaire<br>Preprimaria | Primary<br>Primaire<br>Primaria | Secondary<br>Secondaire<br>Secundaria | Tertiary<br>Supérieur<br>Superior | Primary and secondary<br>Primaire et secondaire<br>Primaria y secundaria | Primary, secondary and tertiary<br>Primaire, secondaire et supérieur<br>Primaria, secundaria y superior |
| Morocco | 1970 | | (5-6) | (7-11) | (12-18) | (19-23) | (7-18) | (7-23) |
| | | MF | ... | 51 | 13 | 1 | 32 | 26 |
| | | M | ... | 66 | 17 | 2 | 41 | 34 |
| | | F | ... | 36 | 7 | 0.5 | 21 | 17 |
| | 1975 | | | | | | | |
| | | MF | 35 | 62 | 16 | 3 | 37 | 30 |
| | | M | 51 | 78 | 21 | 5 | 47 | 38 |
| | | F | 18 | 45 | 12 | 1 | 27 | 22 |
| | 1980 | | | | | | | |
| | | MF | 50 | 83 | 26 | 6 | 52 | 41 |
| | | M | 74 | 102 | 32 | 9 | 65 | 51 |
| | | F | 25 | 63 | 20 | 3 | 39 | 30 |
| | 1985 | | | | | | | |
| | | MF | 57 | 77 | 35 | 9 | 54 | 43 |
| | | M | 79 | 93 | 42 | 12 | 66 | 53 |
| | | F | 35 | 60 | 28 | 6 | 43 | 34 |
| | 1990 | | (5-6) | (7-12) | (13-18) | (19-23) | (7-18) | (7-23) |
| | | MF | 66 | 67 | 35 | 11 | 52 | 41 |
| | | M | 90 | 79 | 41 | 13 | 61 | 49 |
| | | F | 41 | 54 | 30 | 8 | 43 | 34 |
| | 1991 | | | | | | | |
| | | MF | 64 | 69 | 36 | 11 | 53 | 42 |
| | | M | 89 | 81 | 41 | 13 | 62 | 49 |
| | | F | 38 | 57 | 30 | 9 | 44 | 35 |
| | 1992 | | | | | | | |
| | | MF | 63 | 73 | 36 | 11 | 55 | 44 |
| | | M | 87 | 85 | 42 | 13 | 64 | 51 |
| | | F | 38 | 60 | 31 | 9 | 46 | 36 |
| | 1993 | | | | | | | |
| | | MF | 63 | 77 | 37 | 11 | 58 | 45 |
| | | M | 87 | 89 | 43 | 13 | 66 | 52 |
| | | F | 38 | 64 | 32 | 9 | 48 | 38 |
| | 1994 | | | | | | | |
| | | MF | 64 | 81 | 38 | 11 | 60 | 47 |
| | | M | 88 | 93 | 43 | 13 | 68 | 53 |
| | | F | 40 | 68 | 32 | 9 | 51 | 40 |
| | 1995 | | | | | | | |
| | | MF | 66 | 84 | 39 | 11 | 61 | 48 |
| | | M | 90 | 95 | 44 | 13 | 70 | 54 |
| | | F | 42 | 72 | 33 | 9 | 52 | 41 |
| | 1996 | | | | | | | |
| | | MF | 68 | 86 | 39 | 11 | 62 | 48 |
| | | M | 92 | 97 | 44 | 13 | 71 | 55 |
| | | F | 44 | 74 | 34 | 9 | 54 | 42 |
| Mozambique | 1970 | | (4-5) | (6-10) | (11-15) | (16-20) | (6-15) | (6-20) |
| | | MF | ... | 40 | 4 | 0.2 | 24 | 17 |
| | | M | ... | ... | 5 | 0.3 | ... | ... |
| | | F | ... | ... | 3 | 0.2 | ... | ... |
| | 1975 | | (4-5) | (6-9) | (10-16) | (17-21) | (6-16) | (6-21) |
| | | MF | ... | ... | 3 | ... | ... | ... |
| | | M | ... | ... | 4 | ... | ... | ... |
| | | F | ... | ... | 2 | ... | ... | ... |
| | 1980 | | | | | | | |
| | | MF | ... | ... | 5 | 0.1 | ... | ... |
| | | M | ... | ... | 8 | ... | ... | ... |
| | | F | ... | ... | 3 | ... | ... | ... |
| | 1985 | | (6-6) | (7-10) | (11-17) | (18-22) | (7-17) | (7-22) |
| | | MF | 16 | 87 | 7 | 0.1 | 40 | 29 |
| | | M | 17 | 99 | 10 | 0.2 | 46 | 34 |
| | | F | 15 | 76 | 5 | 0.1 | 34 | 25 |
| | 1990 | | | (7-11) | (12-18) | (19-23) | (7-18) | (7-23) |
| | | MF | - | 67 | 8 | ... | 36 | ... |
| | | M | - | 77 | 10 | ... | 41 | ... |
| | | F | - | 57 | 6 | ... | 30 | ... |

Gross enrolment ratios by level of education
Taux bruts de scolarisation par niveau d'enseignement
Tasas brutas de escolarización por nivel de enseñanza

| Country / Pays / País | Year / Année / Año | Sex / Sexe / Sexo | Gross enrolment ratios / Taux bruts de scolarisation / Tasas brutas de escolarización (%) | | | | | |
|---|---|---|---|---|---|---|---|---|
| | | | Pre-primary / Préprimaire / Preprimaria | Primary / Primaire / Primaria | Secondary / Secondaire / Secundaria | Tertiary / Supérieur / Superior | Primary and secondary / Primaire et secondaire / Primaria y secundaria | Primary, secondary and tertiary / Primaire, secondaire et supérieur / Primaria, secundaria y superior |
| Mozambique (cont) | 1991 | | | | | | | |
| | | MF | - | 62 | 7 | ... | 33 | ... |
| | | M | - | 72 | 10 | ... | 39 | ... |
| | | F | - | 53 | 5 | ... | 28 | ... |
| | 1992 | | | | | | | |
| | | MF | - | 59 | 7 | 0.3 | 31 | 24 |
| | | M | - | 67 | 9 | 0.5 | 36 | 28 |
| | | F | - | 50 | 5 | 0.2 | 27 | 20 |
| | 1993 | | | | | | | |
| | | MF | - | 57 | 7 | 0.4 | 31 | 24 |
| | | M | - | 66 | 8 | 0.6 | 36 | 27 |
| | | F | - | 48 | 5 | 0.2 | 26 | 20 |
| | 1994 | | | | | | | |
| | | MF | - | 58 | 7 | 0.4 | 31 | 24 |
| | | M | - | 67 | 8 | 0.6 | 36 | 28 |
| | | F | - | 48 | 5 | 0.2 | 26 | 20 |
| | 1995 | | | | | | | |
| | | MF | - | 60 | 7 | 0.4 | 32 | 25 |
| | | M | - | 70 | 9 | 0.7 | 38 | 29 |
| | | F | - | 50 | 5 | 0.2 | 27 | 20 |
| | 1996 | | | | | | | |
| | | MF | - | ... | ... | 0.5 | ... | ... |
| | | M | - | ... | ... | 0.7 | ... | ... |
| | | F | - | ... | ... | 0.2 | ... | ... |
| Namibia | 1990 | | (6-6) | (7-13) | (14-18) | (19-23) | (7-18) | (7-23) |
| | | MF | 14 | 129 | 44 | ... | 98 | ... |
| | | M | 13 | 123 | 39 | ... | 92 | ... |
| | | F | 15 | 135 | 49 | ... | 103 | ... |
| | 1991 | | | | | | | |
| | | MF | 14 | 137 | 50 | 3 | 105 | 80 |
| | | M | 14 | 134 | 45 | 2 | 101 | 77 |
| | | F | 14 | 140 | 55 | 4 | 109 | 84 |
| | 1992 | | | | | | | |
| | | MF | 13 | 136 | 56 | ... | 106 | ... |
| | | M | 13 | 134 | 50 | ... | 103 | ... |
| | | F | 13 | 139 | 62 | ... | 110 | ... |
| | 1993 | | | | | | | |
| | | MF | 12 | 134 | 59 | ... | 106 | ... |
| | | M | 11 | 133 | 53 | ... | 103 | ... |
| | | F | 12 | 136 | 65 | ... | 110 | ... |
| | 1994 | | | | | | | |
| | | MF | 11 | 136 | 63 | 7 | 109 | 84 |
| | | M | 10 | 135 | 57 | 5 | 106 | 82 |
| | | F | 11 | 137 | 69 | 9 | 112 | 87 |
| | 1995 | | | | | | | |
| | | MF | ... | 133 | 62 | 8 | 106 | 83 |
| | | M | ... | 132 | 57 | 6 | 104 | 81 |
| | | F | ... | 134 | 68 | 10 | 109 | 85 |
| | 1996 | | | | | | | |
| | | MF | ... | 131 | 61 | ... | 105 | ... |
| | | M | ... | 130 | 56 | ... | 103 | ... |
| | | F | ... | 132 | 66 | ... | 108 | ... |
| | 1997 | | | | | | | |
| | | MF | ... | 131 | 62 | ... | 105 | ... |
| | | M | ... | 129 | 58 | ... | 102 | ... |
| | | F | ... | 132 | 67 | ... | 107 | ... |
| Niger | 1970 | | (5-6) | (7-12) | (13-19) | (20-24) | (7-19) | (7-24) |
| | | MF | ... | 13 | 1 | - | 7 | 6 |
| | | M | ... | 18 | 2 | - | 10 | 8 |
| | | F | ... | 9 | 0.6 | - | 5 | 4 |
| | 1975 | | | | | | | |
| | | MF | 0.3 | 19 | 2 | 0.1 | 11 | 8 |
| | | M | 0.3 | 24 | 3 | 0.2 | 14 | 11 |
| | | F | 0.3 | 13 | 1 | 0.0 | 7 | 6 |

Gross enrolment ratios by level of education
Taux bruts de scolarisation par niveau d'enseignement
Tasas brutas de escolarización por nivel de enseñanza

II.8

| Country<br><br>Pays<br><br>País | Year<br><br>Année<br><br>Año | Sex<br><br>Sexe<br><br>Sexo | Gross enrolment ratios / Taux bruts de scolarisation / Tasas brutas de escolarización (%) | | | | | |
|---|---|---|---|---|---|---|---|---|
| | | | Pre-primary<br><br>Préprimaire<br><br>Preprimaria | Primary<br><br>Primaire<br><br>Primaria | Secondary<br><br>Secondaire<br><br>Secundaria | Tertiary<br><br>Supérieur<br><br>Superior | Primary and secondary<br><br>Primaire et secondaire<br><br>Primaria y secundaria | Primary, secondary and tertiary<br><br>Primaire, secondaire et supérieur<br><br>Primaria, secundaria y superior |
| Niger (cont) | 1980 | | (4-6) | (7-12) | (13-19) | (20-24) | (7-19) | (7-24) |
| | | MF | 0.5 | 25 | 5 | 0.3 | 15 | 12 |
| | | M | 0.5 | 33 | 7 | 0.5 | 20 | 16 |
| | | F | 0.5 | 18 | 3 | 0.1 | 11 | 8 |
| | 1985 | | | | | | | |
| | | MF | 0.6 | 26 | 5 | 0.5 | 16 | 13 |
| | | M | 0.6 | 33 | 8 | 0.9 | 21 | 17 |
| | | F | 0.6 | 18 | 3 | 0.2 | 11 | 9 |
| | 1990 | | | | | | | |
| | | MF | 1 | 29 | 7 | 0.7 | 18 | 15 |
| | | M | 2 | 37 | 9 | ... | 24 | ... |
| | | F | 1 | 21 | 4 | ... | 13 | ... |
| | 1991 | | | | | | | |
| | | MF | 2 | 28 | 6 | 0.7 | 18 | 14 |
| | | M | 2 | 36 | 9 | ... | 23 | ... |
| | | F | 2 | 20 | 4 | ... | 13 | ... |
| | 1992 | | | | | | | |
| | | MF | 2 | 28 | 8 | ... | 18 | ... |
| | | M | 1 | 36 | 9 | ... | 23 | ... |
| | | F | 2 | 21 | 4 | ... | 13 | ... |
| | 1993 | | | | | | | |
| | | MF | 1 | 29 | 7 | ... | 18 | ... |
| | | M | 1 | 37 | 9 | ... | 24 | ... |
| | | F | 1 | 21 | 4 | ... | 13 | ... |
| | 1994 | | | | | | | |
| | | MF | 1 | 29 | 7 | ... | 18 | ... |
| | | M | 1 | 36 | 9 | ... | 23 | ... |
| | | F | 1 | 22 | 4 | ... | 14 | ... |
| | 1995 | | | | | | | |
| | | MF | 1 | 29 | 7 | ... | 18 | ... |
| | | M | 1 | 36 | 9 | ... | 23 | ... |
| | | F | 1 | 22 | 5 | ... | 14 | ... |
| | 1996 | | | | | | | |
| | | MF | 1 | 29 | 7 | ... | 19 | ... |
| | | M | 1 | 36 | 9 | ... | 23 | ... |
| | | F | 1 | 22 | 5 | ... | 14 | ... |
| | 1997 | | | | | | | |
| | | MF | 1 | 29 | ... | ... | ... | ... |
| | | M | 1 | 36 | ... | ... | ... | ... |
| | | F | 1 | 23 | ... | ... | ... | ... |
| Nigeria | 1970 | | (3-5) | (6-11) | (12-18) | (19-23) | (6-18) | (6-23) |
| | | MF | ... | 44 | 5 | 0.5 | 26 | 20 |
| | | M | ... | 55 | 7 | 0.9 | 33 | 26 |
| | | F | ... | 32 | 3 | 0.1 | 19 | 15 |
| | 1975 | | | | | | | |
| | | MF | ... | 50 | 8 | 1 | 31 | 25 |
| | | M | ... | 60 | 10 | 2 | 37 | 30 |
| | | F | ... | 40 | 6 | 0.3 | 24 | 19 |
| | 1980 | | | | | | | |
| | | MF | ... | 109 | 18 | 3 | 65 | 52 |
| | | M | ... | 123 | 24 | ... | 75 | ... |
| | | F | ... | 95 | 12 | ... | 55 | ... |
| | 1985 | | (3-5) | (6-11) | (12-16) | (17-21) | (6-16) | (6-21) |
| | | MF | ... | 104 | 34 | 4 | 75 | 56 |
| | | M | ... | 115 | 40 | 5 | 84 | 64 |
| | | F | ... | 92 | 28 | 2 | 65 | 49 |
| | 1990 | | (3-5) | (6-11) | (12-17) | (18-22) | (6-17) | (6-22) |
| | | MF | ... | 91 | 25 | ... | 62 | ... |
| | | M | ... | 104 | 29 | ... | 71 | ... |
| | | F | ... | 79 | 21 | ... | 54 | ... |
| | 1991 | | | | | | | |
| | | MF | ... | 90 | 26 | ... | 62 | ... |
| | | M | ... | 101 | 30 | ... | 70 | ... |
| | | F | ... | 79 | 22 | ... | 54 | ... |

II.8 Gross enrolment ratios by level of education
Taux bruts de scolarisation par niveau d'enseignement
Tasas brutas de escolarización por nivel de enseñanza

| Country / Pays / País | Year / Année / Año | Sex / Sexe / Sexo | Gross enrolment ratios / Taux bruts de scolarisation / Tasas brutas de escolarización (%) | | | | | |
|---|---|---|---|---|---|---|---|---|
| | | | Pre-primary / Préprimaire / Preprimaria | Primary / Primaire / Primaria | Secondary / Secondaire / Secundaria | Tertiary / Supérieur / Superior | Primary and secondary / Primaire et secondaire / Primaria y secundaria | Primary, secondary and tertiary / Primaire, secondaire et supérieur / Primaria, secundaria y superior |
| Nigeria (cont) | 1992 | | | | | | | |
| | | MF | ... | 94 | 29 | ... | 65 | ... |
| | | M | ... | 105 | 32 | ... | 73 | ... |
| | | F | ... | 83 | 26 | ... | 58 | ... |
| | 1993 | | | | | | | |
| | | MF | ... | 98 | 31 | 4 | 68 | 53 |
| | | M | ... | 110 | 34 | ... | 76 | ... |
| | | F | ... | 86 | 29 | ... | 60 | ... |
| | 1994 | | | | | | | |
| | | MF | ... | 98 | 33 | ... | 69 | ... |
| | | M | ... | 109 | 36 | ... | 77 | ... |
| | | F | ... | 87 | 30 | ... | 61 | ... |
| Reunion (1) | | | (2-5) | (6-10) | (11-17) | (18-22) | (6-17) | (6-22) |
| Rwanda | 1970 | | (4-6) | (7-12) | (13-18) | (19-23) | (7-18) | (7-23) |
| | | MF | ... | 70 | 3 | 0.2 | 41 | 31 |
| | | M | ... | 78 | 3 | 0.3 | 46 | 35 |
| | | F | ... | 61 | 3 | 0.0 | 36 | 27 |
| | 1975 | | | | | | | |
| | | MF | ... | 55 | 4 | 0.3 | 33 | 26 |
| | | M | ... | 60 | 3 | 0.5 | 35 | 28 |
| | | F | ... | 50 | 4 | 0.1 | 30 | 24 |
| | 1980 | | (4-6) | (7-14) | (15-20) | (21-25) | (7-20) | (7-25) |
| | | MF | ... | 63 | 3 | 0.3 | 42 | 34 |
| | | M | ... | 66 | 4 | 0.6 | 44 | 36 |
| | | F | ... | 60 | 3 | 0.1 | 40 | 32 |
| | 1985 | | | | | | | |
| | | MF | ... | 63 | 6 | 0.4 | 43 | 35 |
| | | M | ... | 65 | 7 | 0.7 | 44 | 36 |
| | | F | ... | 61 | 5 | 0.1 | 41 | 33 |
| | 1990 | | | | | | | |
| | | MF | ... | 70 | 8 | ... | 48 | ... |
| | | M | ... | 70 | 9 | ... | 49 | ... |
| | | F | ... | 69 | 7 | ... | 47 | ... |
| | 1991 | | (4-6) | (7-13) | (14-19) | (20-24) | (7-19) | (7-24) |
| | | MF | ... | 81 | 11 | ... | 53 | ... |
| | | M | ... | 82 | 12 | ... | 55 | ... |
| | | F | ... | 80 | 9 | ... | 52 | ... |
| Sao Tome and Principe (1) | | | (3-6) | (7-10) | (11-17) | (18-22) | (7-17) | (7-22) |
| Senegal | 1970 | | (3-5) | (6-11) | (12-18) | (19-23) | (6-18) | (6-23) |
| | | MF | ... | 39 | 9 | 1 | 24 | 20 |
| | | M | ... | 47 | 13 | 2 | 31 | 25 |
| | | F | ... | 30 | 5 | 0.5 | 18 | 14 |
| | 1975 | | | | | | | |
| | | MF | ... | 40 | 11 | 2 | 26 | 20 |
| | | M | ... | 46 | 15 | 3 | 31 | 25 |
| | | F | ... | 34 | 6 | 0.7 | 20 | 16 |
| | 1980 | | | | | | | |
| | | MF | 2 | 46 | 11 | 3 | 29 | 24 |
| | | M | 1 | 55 | 15 | 4 | 36 | 29 |
| | | F | 2 | 37 | 7 | 1 | 23 | 18 |
| | 1985 | | (4-6) | (7-12) | (13-19) | (20-24) | (7-19) | (7-24) |
| | | MF | 2 | 56 | 14 | 2 | 36 | 29 |
| | | M | 2 | 67 | 18 | 4 | 44 | 35 |
| | | F | 2 | 46 | 9 | 1 | 28 | 22 |
| | 1990 | | | | | | | |
| | | MF | 2 | 59 | 16 | 3 | 38 | 31 |
| | | M | 2 | 68 | 21 | 5 | 45 | 37 |
| | | F | 2 | 50 | 11 | 1 | 31 | 25 |
| | 1991 | | | | | | | |
| | | MF | 2 | 59 | 17 | 3 | 39 | 31 |
| | | M | 2 | 67 | 22 | 5 | 45 | 37 |
| | | F | 2 | 50 | 12 | 2 | 32 | 25 |

Gross enrolment ratios by level of education
Taux bruts de scolarisation par niveau d'enseignement
Tasas brutas de escolarización por nivel de enseñanza

II.8

| Country / Pays / País | Year / Année / Año | Sex / Sexe / Sexo | Gross enrolment ratios / Taux bruts de scolarisation / Tasas brutas de escolarización (%) | | | | | |
|---|---|---|---|---|---|---|---|---|
| | | | Pre-primary / Préprimaire / Preprimaria | Primary / Primaire / Primaria | Secondary / Secondaire / Secundaria | Tertiary / Supérieur / Superior | Primary and secondary / Primaire et secondaire / Primaria y secundaria | Primary, secondary and tertiary / Primaire, secondaire et supérieur / Primaria, secundaria y superior |
| Senegal (cont) | 1992 | | | | | | | |
| | | MF | 2 | 58 | 16 | 3 | 38 | 31 |
| | | M | 2 | 67 | 21 | ... | 44 | ... |
| | | F | 2 | 50 | 11 | ... | 31 | ... |
| | 1993 | | | | | | | |
| | | MF | 2 | 60 | 16 | 4 | 38 | 31 |
| | | M | 2 | 68 | 18 | ... | 44 | ... |
| | | F | 2 | 51 | 14 | ... | 33 | ... |
| | 1994 | | | | | | | |
| | | MF | 2 | 61 | 16 | 3 | 39 | 31 |
| | | M | 2 | 69 | 20 | ... | 45 | ... |
| | | F | 2 | 52 | 12 | ... | 33 | ... |
| | 1995 | | | | | | | |
| | | MF | 2 | 64 | 16 | ... | 41 | ... |
| | | M | 2 | 72 | 20 | ... | 47 | ... |
| | | F | 2 | 57 | 12 | ... | 35 | ... |
| | 1996 | | | | | | | |
| | | MF | 2 | 68 | 16 | ... | 43 | ... |
| | | M | 2 | 75 | 20 | ... | 48 | ... |
| | | F | 2 | 61 | 12 | ... | 37 | ... |
| | 1997 | | | | | | | |
| | | MF | 2 | 71 | 16 | ... | 44 | ... |
| | | M | 2 | 78 | 20 | ... | 49 | ... |
| | | F | 2 | 65 | 12 | ... | 39 | ... |
| Seychelles (1) | | | (4-5) | (6-11) | (12-16) | (17-21) | (6-16) | (6-21) |
| Sierra Leone | 1970 | | (3-4) | (5-11) | (12-18) | (19-23) | (5-18) | (5-23) |
| | | MF | ... | 35 | 9 | 0.5 | 23 | 18 |
| | | M | ... | 42 | 13 | 0.9 | 29 | 23 |
| | | F | ... | 28 | 5 | 0.2 | 18 | 14 |
| | 1975 | | | | | | | |
| | | MF | ... | 38 | 12 | 0.6 | 27 | 21 |
| | | M | ... | 47 | 16 | 1 | 33 | 27 |
| | | F | ... | 30 | 7 | 0.2 | 20 | 16 |
| | 1980 | | | | | | | |
| | | MF | ... | 52 | 14 | 0.8 | 35 | 28 |
| | | M | ... | 61 | 20 | ... | 43 | ... |
| | | F | ... | 43 | 8 | ... | 28 | ... |
| | 1985 | | | | | | | |
| | | MF | ... | 63 | 18 | 2 | 43 | 34 |
| | | M | ... | ... | 24 | 3 | ... | ... |
| | | F | ... | ... | 12 | 0.6 | ... | ... |
| | 1990 | | | | | | | |
| | | MF | ... | 50 | 17 | 1 | 36 | 29 |
| | | M | ... | 60 | 22 | ... | 43 | ... |
| | | F | ... | 41 | 13 | ... | 29 | ... |
| Somalia | 1970 | | (4-5) | (6-9) | (10-17) | (18-22) | (6-17) | (6-22) |
| | | MF | 0.3 | 8 | 4 | 0.3 | 5 | 4 |
| | | M | 0.3 | 12 | 6 | 0.5 | 8 | 6 |
| | | F | 0.2 | 4 | 2 | 0.1 | 2 | 2 |
| | 1975 | | | | | | | |
| | | MF | 0.4 | 42 | 4 | 0.5 | 19 | 14 |
| | | M | 0.4 | 54 | 6 | 0.9 | 25 | 19 |
| | | F | 0.4 | 30 | 2 | 0.1 | 12 | 10 |
| | 1980 | | (4-5) | (6-13) | (14-17) | (18-22) | (6-17) | (6-22) |
| | | MF | 0.5 | 21 | 9 | ... | 18 | ... |
| | | M | 0.5 | 28 | 13 | ... | 23 | ... |
| | | F | 0.5 | 15 | 5 | ... | 12 | ... |
| | 1985 | | | | | | | |
| | | MF | 0.3 | 14 | 8 | ... | 12 | ... |
| | | M | 0.3 | 18 | 10 | ... | 16 | ... |
| | | F | 0.4 | 9 | 6 | ... | 8 | ... |

II.8   Gross enrolment ratios by level of education
       Taux bruts de scolarisation par niveau d'enseignement
       Tasas brutas de escolarización por nivel de enseñanza

| Country / Pays / País | Year / Année / Año | Sex / Sexe / Sexo | Gross enrolment ratios / Taux bruts de scolarisation / Tasas brutas de escolarización (%) | | | | | |
|---|---|---|---|---|---|---|---|---|
| | | | Pre-primary / Préprimaire / Preprimaria | Primary / Primaire / Primaria | Secondary / Secondaire / Secundaria | Tertiary / Supérieur / Superior | Primary and secondary / Primaire et secondaire / Primaria y secundaria | Primary, secondary and tertiary / Primaire, secondaire et supérieur / Primaria, secundaria y superior |
| South Africa | 1970 | | (5-5) | (6-12) | (13-17) | (18-22) | (6-17) | (6-22) |
| | | MF | ... | 92 | ... | 4 | ... | ... |
| | | M | ... | 85 | ... | ... | ... | ... |
| | | F | ... | 100 | ... | ... | ... | ... |
| | 1975 | | | | | | | |
| | | MF | ... | 104 | ... | ... | ... | ... |
| | 1980 | | | | | | | |
| | | MF | ... | 90 | ... | ... | ... | ... |
| | 1990 | | | | | | | |
| | | MF | 19 | 122 | 74 | 13 | 103 | 80 |
| | | M | 19 | 123 | 69 | 15 | 102 | 79 |
| | | F | 19 | 121 | 80 | 12 | 104 | 80 |
| | 1991 | | | | | | | |
| | | MF | 20 | 124 | 78 | 14 | 106 | 82 |
| | | M | 20 | 126 | 72 | 15 | 105 | 81 |
| | | F | 20 | 123 | 84 | 13 | 108 | 83 |
| | 1992 | | | | | | | |
| | | MF | 25 | 127 | 81 | 14 | 109 | 84 |
| | | M | 24 | 128 | 75 | 15 | 107 | 83 |
| | | F | 25 | 126 | 87 | 13 | 111 | 85 |
| | 1993 | | | | | | | |
| | | MF | 27 | 129 | 86 | 16 | 112 | 87 |
| | | M | 27 | 131 | 79 | 17 | 110 | 86 |
| | | F | 28 | 128 | 92 | 14 | 114 | 88 |
| | 1994 | | | | | | | |
| | | MF | 31 | 132 | 91 | 17 | 116 | 90 |
| | | M | 31 | 134 | 85 | 18 | 115 | 89 |
| | | F | 31 | 129 | 97 | 16 | 116 | 90 |
| | 1995 | | | | | | | |
| | | MF | 33 | 133 | 95 | 19 | 118 | 92 |
| | | M | 33 | 135 | 88 | ... | 116 | ... |
| | | F | 33 | 131 | 103 | ... | 120 | ... |
| | 1996 | | | | | | | |
| | | MF | 35 | ... | ... | ... | ... | ... |
| | | M | 35 | ... | ... | ... | ... | ... |
| | | F | 35 | ... | ... | ... | ... | ... |
| St. Helena (1) | | | (3-4) | (5-10) | (11-16) | (17-21) | (5-16) | (5-21) |
| Sudan | 1970 | | (5-6) | (7-12) | (13-18) | (19-23) | (7-18) | (7-23) |
| | | MF | 2 | 38 | 7 | 1 | 24 | 19 |
| | | M | 2 | 47 | 10 | 2 | 30 | 24 |
| | | F | 2 | 29 | 4 | 0.3 | 18 | 14 |
| | 1975 | | | | | | | |
| | | MF | ... | 47 | 14 | 1 | 32 | 24 |
| | | M | ... | 59 | 19 | 2 | 41 | 32 |
| | | F | ... | 34 | 8 | 0.5 | 22 | 17 |
| | 1980 | | | | | | | |
| | | MF | 13 | 50 | 16 | 2 | 35 | 27 |
| | | M | ... | 59 | 20 | 2 | 41 | 32 |
| | | F | ... | 41 | 12 | 0.9 | 28 | 21 |
| | 1985 | | | | | | | |
| | | MF | 17 | 52 | 21 | 2 | 38 | 29 |
| | | M | ... | 61 | 24 | 2 | 45 | 34 |
| | | F | ... | 42 | 18 | 1 | 31 | 24 |
| | 1990 | | | | | | | |
| | | MF | 18 | 53 | 24 | 3 | 40 | 31 |
| | | M | 23 | 60 | 27 | 3 | 46 | 35 |
| | | F | 13 | 45 | 21 | 3 | 35 | 27 |
| | 1991 | | | | | | | |
| | | MF | 23 | 54 | 23 | ... | 40 | ... |
| | | M | 24 | 62 | 25 | ... | 46 | ... |
| | | F | 22 | 47 | 20 | ... | 35 | ... |
| | 1993 | | (4-5) | (6-13) | (14-16) | (17-21) | (6-16) | (6-21) |
| | | MF | ... | 42 | ... | ... | ... | ... |
| | | M | ... | 47 | ... | ... | ... | ... |
| | | F | ... | 37 | ... | ... | ... | ... |

Gross enrolment ratios by level of education   II.8
Taux bruts de scolarisation par niveau d'enseignement
Tasas brutas de escolarización por nivel de enseñanza

| Country / Pays / País | Year / Année / Año | Sex / Sexe / Sexo | Gross enrolment ratios / Taux bruts de scolarisation / Tasas brutas de escolarización (%) | | | | | |
|---|---|---|---|---|---|---|---|---|
| | | | Pre-primary / Préprimaire / Preprimaria | Primary / Primaire / Primaria | Secondary / Secondaire / Secundaria | Tertiary / Supérieur / Superior | Primary and secondary / Primaire et secondaire / Primaria y secundaria | Primary, secondary and tertiary / Primaire, secondaire et supérieur / Primaria, secundaria y superior |
| Sudan (cont) | 1994 | MF | ... | 53 | 14 | ... | 44 | ... |
| | | M | ... | 58 | 15 | ... | 48 | ... |
| | | F | ... | 47 | 13 | ... | 39 | ... |
| | 1995 | MF | ... | 50 | 21 | ... | 43 | ... |
| | | M | ... | 54 | 22 | ... | 47 | ... |
| | | F | ... | 46 | 19 | ... | 39 | ... |
| | 1996 | MF | 23 | 51 | 21 | ... | 44 | ... |
| | | M | 27 | 55 | 23 | ... | 47 | ... |
| | | F | 19 | 47 | 20 | ... | 40 | ... |
| Swaziland | 1970 | | (3-5) | (6-12) | (13-17) | (18-22) | (6-17) | (6-22) |
| | | MF | | 87 | 19 | 0.5 | 62 | 48 |
| | | M | | 90 | 21 | 0.7 | 65 | 50 |
| | | F | | 84 | 16 | 0.4 | 59 | 45 |
| | 1975 | MF | ... | 97 | 32 | 2 | 73 | 57 |
| | | M | ... | 100 | 35 | ... | 76 | ... |
| | | F | ... | 95 | 29 | ... | 71 | ... |
| | 1980 | MF | ... | 103 | 38 | 4 | 79 | 62 |
| | | M | ... | 104 | 39 | 4 | 80 | 63 |
| | | F | ... | 102 | 37 | 3 | 78 | 61 |
| | 1985 | MF | ... | 102 | 39 | 4 | 79 | 62 |
| | | M | ... | 104 | 40 | ... | 81 | ... |
| | | F | ... | 100 | 38 | ... | 77 | ... |
| | 1990 | MF | 17 | 111 | 44 | 4 | 85 | 66 |
| | | M | 12 | 114 | 44 | 5 | 87 | 67 |
| | | F | 21 | 109 | 43 | 3 | 84 | 64 |
| | 1991 | MF | ... | 113 | 46 | 4 | 87 | 67 |
| | | M | ... | 116 | 47 | 4 | 89 | 68 |
| | | F | ... | 111 | 45 | 4 | 86 | 65 |
| | 1992 | MF | ... | 116 | 53 | 4 | 91 | 70 |
| | | M | ... | 119 | 53 | 4 | 93 | 71 |
| | | F | ... | 113 | 52 | 4 | 90 | 68 |
| | 1993 | MF | 24 | 117 | 50 | 5 | 91 | 70 |
| | | M | ... | 121 | 51 | 6 | 94 | 72 |
| | | F | ... | 114 | 50 | 4 | 89 | 68 |
| | 1994 | MF | ... | 118 | 52 | 5 | 93 | 71 |
| | | M | ... | 121 | 52 | 6 | 95 | 72 |
| | | F | ... | 115 | 51 | 5 | 91 | 69 |
| | 1995 | MF | ... | 121 | 53 | 5 | 95 | 72 |
| | | M | ... | 124 | 53 | 6 | 97 | 74 |
| | | F | ... | 118 | 53 | 5 | 93 | 70 |
| | 1996 | MF | ... | 118 | 54 | 6 | 94 | 72 |
| | | M | ... | 122 | 55 | 6 | 96 | 73 |
| | | F | ... | 115 | 54 | 6 | 92 | 70 |
| | 1997 | MF | ... | 117 | ... | ... | ... | ... |
| | | M | ... | 120 | ... | ... | ... | ... |
| | | F | ... | 114 | ... | ... | ... | ... |
| Togo | 1970 | | (3-5) | (6-11) | (12-18) | (19-23) | (6-18) | (6-23) |
| | | MF | 5 | 71 | 7 | 0.5 | 40 | 31 |
| | | M | 6 | 99 | 11 | 0.9 | 57 | 44 |
| | | F | 4 | 44 | 3 | 0.1 | 24 | 19 |

**Gross enrolment ratios by level of education**
**Taux bruts de scolarisation par niveau d'enseignement**
**Tasas brutas de escolarización por nivel de enseñanza**

| Country / Pays / País | Year / Année / Año | Sex / Sexe / Sexo | Gross enrolment ratios / Taux bruts de scolarisation / Tasas brutas de escolarización (%) | | | | | |
|---|---|---|---|---|---|---|---|---|
| | | | Pre-primary / Préprimaire / Preprimaria | Primary / Primaire / Primaria | Secondary / Secondaire / Secundaria | Tertiary / Supérieur / Superior | Primary and secondary / Primaire et secondaire / Primaria y secundaria | Primary, secondary and tertiary / Primaire, secondaire et supérieur / Primaria, secundaria y superior |
| Togo (cont) | 1975 | MF | 3 | 98 | 19 | 1 | 60 | 47 |
| | | M | 3 | 128 | 29 | 2 | 80 | 63 |
| | | F | 3 | 68 | 9 | 0.3 | 39 | 31 |
| | 1980 | MF | 3 | 118 | 33 | 2 | 77 | 61 |
| | | M | 3 | 144 | 50 | 4 | 99 | 78 |
| | | F | 3 | 93 | 16 | 0.6 | 55 | 43 |
| | 1985 | MF | 3 | 93 | 21 | 2 | 58 | 46 |
| | | M | 3 | 115 | 32 | 3 | 75 | 60 |
| | | F | 3 | 71 | 10 | 0.5 | 42 | 33 |
| | 1990 | MF | 3 | 109 | 24 | 3 | 69 | 54 |
| | | M | 3 | 132 | 35 | 5 | 86 | 69 |
| | | F | 3 | 86 | 12 | 0.8 | 51 | 40 |
| | 1991 | MF | ... | 107 | 23 | 3 | 67 | 53 |
| | | M | ... | 128 | 35 | 6 | 84 | 67 |
| | | F | ... | 85 | 11 | 0.8 | 50 | 40 |
| | 1992 | MF | ... | 104 | 24 | 3 | 66 | 52 |
| | | M | ... | 125 | 35 | 5 | 82 | 66 |
| | | F | ... | 83 | 12 | 0.7 | 49 | 39 |
| | 1993 | MF | 3 | 102 | 23 | 3 | 64 | 51 |
| | | M | 3 | 122 | 34 | 5 | 80 | 64 |
| | | F | 3 | 82 | 12 | 0.7 | 48 | 38 |
| | 1994 | MF | 3 | 113 | 25 | 3 | 71 | 57 |
| | | M | 3 | 135 | 37 | 6 | 88 | 71 |
| | | F | 2 | 92 | 13 | 0.9 | 54 | 43 |
| | 1995 | MF | 3 | 119 | 27 | 3 | 75 | 60 |
| | | M | 3 | 140 | 40 | 6 | 92 | 74 |
| | | F | 2 | 97 | 14 | 1 | 57 | 45 |
| | 1996 | MF | 2 | 120 | 27 | 4 | 76 | 60 |
| | | M | 3 | 140 | 40 | 6 | 92 | 74 |
| | | F | 2 | 99 | 14 | 1 | 59 | 47 |
| Tunisia | 1970 | | (3-5) | (6-11) | (12-18) | (19-23) | (6-18) | (6-23) |
| | | MF | ... | 100 | 23 | 3 | 63 | 52 |
| | | M | ... | 121 | 33 | 4 | 79 | 66 |
| | | F | ... | 80 | 13 | 1 | 48 | 39 |
| | 1975 | MF | ... | 96 | 21 | 4 | 59 | 47 |
| | | M | ... | 115 | 27 | 6 | 71 | 58 |
| | | F | ... | 77 | 15 | 2 | 46 | 36 |
| | 1980 | MF | ... | 102 | 27 | 5 | 64 | 50 |
| | | M | ... | 117 | 34 | 7 | 74 | 58 |
| | | F | ... | 87 | 20 | 3 | 53 | 41 |
| | 1985 | MF | ... | 115 | 39 | 6 | 76 | 59 |
| | | M | ... | 124 | 46 | 7 | 84 | 65 |
| | | F | ... | 105 | 32 | 4 | 68 | 52 |
| | 1990 | MF | 8 | 113 | 45 | 9 | 79 | 62 |
| | | M | ... | 120 | 50 | 10 | 85 | 67 |
| | | F | ... | 107 | 40 | 7 | 73 | 56 |
| | 1991 | MF | 9 | 114 | 46 | 9 | 79 | 62 |
| | | M | ... | 120 | 50 | 11 | 85 | 67 |
| | | F | ... | 108 | 41 | 8 | 74 | 58 |

Gross enrolment ratios by level of education
Taux bruts de scolarisation par niveau d'enseignement
Tasas brutas de escolarización por nivel de enseñanza

II.8

| Country / Pays / País | Year / Année / Año | Sex / Sexe / Sexo | Gross enrolment ratios / Taux bruts de scolarisation / Tasas brutas de escolarización (%) | | | | | |
|---|---|---|---|---|---|---|---|---|
| | | | Pre-primary / Préprimaire / Preprimaria | Primary / Primaire / Primaria | Secondary / Secondaire / Secundaria | Tertiary / Supérieur / Superior | Primary and secondary / Primaire et secondaire / Primaria y secundaria | Primary, secondary and tertiary / Primaire, secondaire et supérieur / Primaria, secundaria y superior |
| Tunisia (cont) | 1992 | MF | ... | 114 | 49 | 11 | 81 | 64 |
| | | M | ... | 119 | 52 | 12 | 85 | 68 |
| | | F | ... | 109 | 45 | 9 | 76 | 59 |
| | 1993 | MF | ... | 117 | 53 | 12 | 84 | 66 |
| | | M | ... | 122 | 56 | 13 | 88 | 70 |
| | | F | ... | 111 | 50 | 10 | 80 | 63 |
| | 1994 | MF | ... | 117 | 57 | 12 | 86 | 68 |
| | | M | ... | 122 | 59 | 14 | 89 | 71 |
| | | F | ... | 112 | 54 | 11 | 82 | 65 |
| | 1995 | MF | 11 | 117 | 60 | 13 | 87 | 69 |
| | | M | 12 | 121 | 62 | 14 | 90 | 72 |
| | | F | 11 | 113 | 58 | 12 | 84 | 66 |
| | 1996 | MF | ... | 116 | 65 | 14 | 89 | 70 |
| | | M | ... | 120 | 66 | 15 | 91 | 72 |
| | | F | ... | 113 | 63 | 12 | 86 | 68 |
| | 1997 | MF | ... | 118 | 64 | ... | 89 | ... |
| | | M | ... | 122 | 66 | ... | 91 | ... |
| | | F | ... | 114 | 63 | ... | 86 | ... |
| Uganda | 1970 | | | (6-12) | (13-18) | (19-23) | (6-18) | (6-23) |
| | | MF | ... | 38 | 4 | 0.5 | 24 | 19 |
| | | M | ... | 46 | 6 | 0.8 | 30 | 24 |
| | | F | ... | 30 | 2 | 0.2 | 18 | 14 |
| | 1975 | MF | ... | 44 | 4 | 0.5 | 28 | 22 |
| | | M | ... | 53 | 6 | 0.9 | 34 | 27 |
| | | F | ... | 35 | 2 | 0.2 | 22 | 17 |
| | 1980 | MF | ... | 50 | 5 | 0.5 | 32 | 25 |
| | | M | ... | 56 | 7 | 0.8 | 37 | 29 |
| | | F | ... | 43 | 3 | 0.2 | 27 | 21 |
| | 1985 | MF | ... | 70 | 10 | 0.8 | 48 | 38 |
| | | M | ... | ... | 13 | 1 | ... | ... |
| | | F | ... | ... | 7 | 0.4 | ... | ... |
| | 1990 | MF | ... | 74 | 13 | 1 | 50 | 40 |
| | | M | ... | 83 | 17 | 2 | 57 | 45 |
| | | F | ... | 66 | 10 | 0.7 | 44 | 34 |
| | 1991 | MF | ... | 75 | 12 | 1 | 50 | 40 |
| | | M | ... | 82 | 15 | 2 | 56 | 44 |
| | | F | ... | 69 | 9 | 0.8 | 45 | 36 |
| | 1992 | MF | ... | 74 | 12 | 1 | 49 | 39 |
| | | M | ... | 82 | 15 | 2 | 55 | 44 |
| | | F | ... | 65 | 9 | 0.8 | 43 | 34 |
| | 1993 | MF | ... | 74 | 11 | 1 | 49 | 39 |
| | | M | ... | 80 | 14 | 2 | 54 | 43 |
| | | F | ... | 68 | 8 | 0.9 | 44 | 35 |
| | 1994 | MF | ... | 73 | 12 | 2 | 49 | 39 |
| | | M | ... | 76 | 15 | 2 | 51 | 41 |
| | | F | ... | 70 | 9 | 1 | 46 | 36 |
| | 1995 | MF | ... | 74 | 12 | 2 | 49 | 39 |
| | | M | ... | 81 | 15 | 2 | 54 | 43 |
| | | F | ... | 68 | 9 | 1 | 44 | 35 |

II.8    Gross enrolment ratios by level of education
        Taux bruts de scolarisation par niveau d'enseignement
        Tasas brutas de escolarización por nivel de enseñanza

| Country / Pays / País | Year / Année / Año | Sex / Sexe / Sexo | Gross enrolment ratios / Taux bruts de scolarisation / Tasas brutas de escolarización (%) | | | | | |
|---|---|---|---|---|---|---|---|---|
| | | | Pre-primary / Préprimaire / Preprimaria | Primary / Primaire / Primaria | Secondary / Secondaire / Secundaria | Tertiary / Supérieur / Superior | Primary and secondary / Primaire et secondaire / Primaria y secundaria | Primary, secondary and tertiary / Primaire, secondaire et supérieur / Primaria, secundaria y superior |
| Uganda (cont) | 1996 | MF | ... | ... | ... | 2 | ... | ... |
| | | M | ... | ... | ... | 3 | ... | ... |
| | | F | ... | ... | ... | 1 | ... | ... |
| United Republic of Tanzania | 1970 | | (4-6) | (7-13) | (14-19) | (20-24) | (7-19) | (7-24) |
| | | MF | ... | 33 | 3 | 0.2 | 21 | 17 |
| | | M | ... | 41 | 4 | 0.3 | 26 | 21 |
| | | F | ... | 26 | 2 | 0.1 | 16 | 13 |
| | 1975 | MF | ... | 53 | 3 | 0.2 | 33 | 26 |
| | | M | ... | 62 | 4 | 0.4 | 39 | 31 |
| | | F | ... | 44 | 2 | 0.1 | 27 | 22 |
| | 1980 | MF | ... | 93 | 3 | 0.3 | 57 | 45 |
| | | M | ... | 99 | 4 | 0.4 | 62 | 49 |
| | | F | ... | 86 | 2 | 0.1 | 53 | 42 |
| | 1985 | MF | ... | 75 | 3 | 0.3 | 46 | 36 |
| | | M | ... | 76 | 4 | 0.4 | 47 | 37 |
| | | F | ... | 74 | 2 | 0.1 | 45 | 36 |
| | 1990 | MF | ... | 70 | 5 | 0.3 | 43 | 34 |
| | | M | ... | 70 | 6 | ... | 44 | ... |
| | | F | ... | 69 | 4 | ... | 42 | ... |
| | 1991 | MF | ... | 70 | 5 | 0.3 | 43 | 34 |
| | | M | ... | 71 | 6 | 0.5 | 45 | 35 |
| | | F | ... | 69 | 4 | 0.1 | 42 | 33 |
| | 1992 | MF | ... | 69 | 5 | 0.3 | 43 | 34 |
| | | M | ... | 70 | 6 | 0.5 | 44 | 35 |
| | | F | ... | 68 | 5 | 0.1 | 42 | 33 |
| | 1993 | MF | ... | 69 | 5 | 0.4 | 43 | 34 |
| | | M | ... | 70 | 6 | 0.6 | 44 | 35 |
| | | F | ... | 68 | 5 | 0.1 | 42 | 33 |
| | 1994 | MF | ... | 68 | 5 | 0.4 | 42 | 33 |
| | | M | ... | 68 | 6 | 0.7 | 43 | 34 |
| | | F | ... | 67 | 5 | 0.1 | 42 | 32 |
| | 1995 | MF | ... | 67 | 5 | 0.5 | 42 | 33 |
| | | M | ... | 68 | 6 | 0.8 | 43 | 34 |
| | | F | ... | 66 | 5 | 0.1 | 41 | 32 |
| | 1996 | MF | ... | 66 | 5 | 0.5 | 42 | 33 |
| | | M | ... | 67 | 6 | 0.9 | 42 | 33 |
| | | F | ... | 65 | 5 | 0.2 | 41 | 32 |
| | 1997 | MF | ... | 66 | 6 | 0.6 | 42 | 33 |
| | | M | ... | 67 | 6 | 1 | 42 | 33 |
| | | F | ... | 66 | 5 | 0.2 | 41 | 32 |
| Zambia | 1970 | | (3-6) | (7-13) | (14-18) | (19-23) | (7-18) | (7-23) |
| | | MF | ... | 90 | 13 | 0.4 | 62 | 47 |
| | | M | ... | 99 | 17 | 0.7 | 70 | 53 |
| | | F | ... | 80 | 8 | 0.1 | 54 | 41 |
| | 1975 | MF | ... | 97 | 15 | 2 | 67 | 52 |
| | | M | ... | 105 | 20 | 3 | 74 | 58 |
| | | F | ... | 88 | 10 | 0.6 | 60 | 46 |
| | 1980 | MF | ... | 90 | 16 | 1 | 64 | 50 |
| | | M | ... | 97 | 22 | 2 | 71 | 56 |
| | | F | ... | 83 | 11 | 0.6 | 57 | 44 |

Gross enrolment ratios by level of education    II.8
Taux bruts de scolarisation par niveau d'enseignement
Tasas brutas de escolarización por nivel de enseñanza

| Country<br><br>Pays<br><br>País | Year<br><br>Année<br><br>Año | Sex<br><br>Sexe<br><br>Sexo | Gross enrolment ratios / Taux bruts de scolarisation / Tasas brutas de escolarización (%) | | | | | |
|---|---|---|---|---|---|---|---|---|
| | | | Pre-primary<br><br>Préprimaire<br><br>Preprimaria | Primary<br><br>Primaire<br><br>Primaria | Secondary<br><br>Secondaire<br><br>Secundaria | Tertiary<br><br>Supérieur<br><br>Superior | Primary and secondary<br><br>Primaire et secondaire<br><br>Primaria y secundaria | Primary, secondary and tertiary<br><br>Primaire, secondaire et supérieur<br><br>Primaria, secundaria y superior |
| Zambia (cont) | 1985 | MF<br>M<br>F | ...<br>...<br>... | 105<br>111<br>98 | 19<br>25<br>14 | 2<br>4<br>0.6 | 74<br>81<br>68 | 58<br>64<br>52 |
| | 1990 | MF | ... | 99 | 24 | 2 | 72 | 56 |
| | 1991 | MF | ... | 99 | 25 | ... | 73 | ... |
| | 1994 | MF<br>M<br>F | ...<br>...<br>... | 91<br>94<br>88 | 27<br>34<br>21 | 2<br>4<br>1 | 68<br>72<br>63 | 53<br>57<br>49 |
| | 1995 | MF<br>M<br>F | ...<br>...<br>... | 89<br>91<br>86 | ...<br>...<br>... | ...<br>...<br>... | ...<br>...<br>... | ...<br>...<br>... |
| Zimbabwe | 1970 | <br>MF<br>M<br>F | (5-6)<br>...<br>...<br>... | (7-13)<br>70<br>78<br>63 | (14-19)<br>7<br>9<br>6 | (20-24)<br>...<br>...<br>... | (7-19)<br>46<br>51<br>41 | (7-24)<br>...<br>...<br>... |
| | 1975 | MF<br>M<br>F | ...<br>...<br>... | 70<br>76<br>64 | 8<br>10<br>7 | 2<br>...<br>... | 45<br>50<br>41 | 37<br>...<br>... |
| | 1980 | MF<br>M<br>F | ...<br>...<br>... | 85<br>...<br>... | 8<br>9<br>6 | 1<br>...<br>... | 54<br>...<br>... | 43<br>...<br>... |
| | 1985 | MF<br>M<br>F | ...<br>...<br>... | 136<br>141<br>131 | 42<br>50<br>33 | 4<br>...<br>... | 97<br>103<br>91 | 76<br>...<br>... |
| | 1990 | MF<br>M<br>F | ...<br>...<br>... | 116<br>117<br>115 | 50<br>53<br>46 | 5<br>...<br>... | 88<br>90<br>86 | 69<br>...<br>... |
| | 1991 | MF<br>M<br>F | ...<br>...<br>... | 122<br>124<br>119 | 52<br>59<br>46 | 5<br>7<br>4 | 93<br>97<br>88 | 72<br>76<br>69 |
| | 1992 | MF<br>M<br>F | ...<br>...<br>... | 118<br>120<br>117 | 48<br>54<br>42 | 6<br>8<br>4 | 89<br>92<br>86 | 70<br>73<br>67 |
| | 1993 | <br>MF<br>M<br>F | (5-5)<br>...<br>...<br>... | (6-12)<br>117<br>121<br>113 | (13-18)<br>45<br>50<br>39 | (19-23)<br>6<br>8<br>4 | (6-18)<br>88<br>92<br>83 | (6-23)<br>69<br>73<br>65 |
| | 1994 | MF<br>M<br>F | ...<br>...<br>... | ...<br>...<br>... | 45<br>50<br>40 | 6<br>9<br>4 | ...<br>...<br>... | ...<br>...<br>... |
| | 1995 | MF<br>M<br>F | ...<br>...<br>... | 114<br>116<br>113 | 47<br>52<br>43 | 6<br>9<br>4 | 87<br>90<br>84 | 69<br>72<br>66 |
| | 1996 | MF<br>M<br>F | ...<br>...<br>... | 113<br>115<br>111 | 49<br>52<br>45 | 7<br>9<br>4 | 86<br>89<br>84 | 68<br>71<br>66 |
| | 1997 | MF | ... | 112 | 50 | ... | 86 | ... |

II.8 Gross enrolment ratios by level of education
Taux bruts de scolarisation par niveau d'enseignement
Tasas brutas de escolarización por nivel de enseñanza

| Country / Pays / País | Year / Année / Año | Sex / Sexe / Sexo | Gross enrolment ratios / Taux bruts de scolarisation / Tasas brutas de escolarización (%) | | | | | |
|---|---|---|---|---|---|---|---|---|
| | | | Pre-primary / Préprimaire / Preprimaria | Primary / Primaire / Primaria | Secondary / Secondaire / Secundaria | Tertiary / Supérieur / Superior | Primary and secondary / Primaire et secondaire / Primaria y secundaria | Primary, secondary and tertiary / Primaire, secondaire et supérieur / Primaria, secundaria y superior |
| **North America** | | | | | | | | |
| Bahamas | 1980 | | (3-4) | (5-10) | (11-16) | (17-21) | (5-16) | (5-21) |
| | | MF | ... | 99 | 88 | 17 | 93 | 72 |
| | | M | ... | 96 | ... | ... | ... | ... |
| | | F | ... | 101 | ... | ... | ... | ... |
| | 1985 | | | | | | | |
| | | MF | ... | 100 | 87 | 18 | 93 | 72 |
| | | M | ... | 100 | 83 | ... | 92 | ... |
| | | F | ... | 99 | 91 | ... | 95 | ... |
| | 1990 | | | | | | | |
| | | MF | ... | 101 | ... | ... | ... | ... |
| | 1991 | | | | | | | |
| | | MF | 7 | 102 | 94 | ... | 98 | ... |
| | | M | 6 | 102 | 94 | ... | 98 | ... |
| | | F | 7 | 103 | 94 | ... | 99 | ... |
| | 1992 | | | | | | | |
| | | MF | 7 | 103 | 95 | ... | 99 | ... |
| | | M | 7 | 102 | 95 | ... | 99 | ... |
| | | F | 7 | 104 | 95 | ... | 100 | ... |
| | 1993 | | | | | | | |
| | | MF | 7 | 100 | 90 | ... | 95 | ... |
| | | M | 7 | ... | 90 | ... | ... | ... |
| | | F | 7 | ... | 90 | ... | ... | ... |
| | 1994 | | | | | | | |
| | | MF | 7 | 97 | 90 | ... | 93 | ... |
| | | M | 7 | 97 | 90 | ... | 93 | ... |
| | | F | 8 | 97 | 90 | ... | 93 | ... |
| | 1995 | | | | | | | |
| | | MF | ... | 98 | 88 | ... | 93 | ... |
| | 1996 | | | | | | | |
| | | MF | 9 | 98 | 87 | ... | 93 | ... |
| | | M | 9 | ... | ... | ... | ... | ... |
| | | F | 9 | ... | ... | ... | ... | ... |
| Barbados | 1970 | | (3-4) | (5-10) | (11-17) | (18-22) | (5-17) | (5-22) |
| | | MF | ... | 102 | 68 | 3 | 85 | 67 |
| | | M | ... | 104 | 67 | 4 | 85 | 67 |
| | | F | ... | 101 | 69 | 3 | 84 | 66 |
| | 1975 | | (3-4) | (5-10) | (11-16) | (17-21) | (5-16) | (5-21) |
| | | MF | 31 | 108 | 79 | 9 | 92 | 69 |
| | | M | 29 | 108 | 75 | ... | 90 | ... |
| | | F | 33 | 108 | 83 | ... | 94 | ... |
| | 1980 | | (3-4) | (5-11) | (12-17) | (18-22) | (5-17) | (5-22) |
| | | MF | 40 | 85 | 88 | 15 | 87 | 66 |
| | | M | 40 | 86 | 88 | 14 | 87 | 66 |
| | | F | 40 | 85 | 88 | 16 | 87 | 66 |
| | 1990 | | | | | | | |
| | | MF | ... | 93 | ... | 27 | ... | ... |
| | | M | ... | 93 | ... | 24 | ... | ... |
| | | F | ... | 93 | ... | 30 | ... | ... |
| | 1991 | | | | | | | |
| | | MF | ... | 90 | ... | 28 | ... | ... |
| | | M | ... | 90 | ... | 25 | ... | ... |
| | | F | ... | 90 | ... | 32 | ... | ... |
| | 1992 | | | | | | | |
| | | MF | ... | ... | ... | 26 | ... | ... |
| | 1993 | | | | | | | |
| | | MF | ... | ... | ... | 26 | ... | ... |
| | 1994 | | | | | | | |
| | | MF | ... | ... | ... | 27 | ... | ... |
| | | M | ... | ... | ... | 22 | ... | ... |
| | | F | ... | ... | ... | 33 | ... | ... |

Gross enrolment ratios by level of education    II.8
Taux bruts de scolarisation par niveau d'enseignement
Tasas brutas de escolarización por nivel de enseñanza

| Country / Pays / País | Year / Année / Año | Sex / Sexe / Sexo | Gross enrolment ratios / Taux bruts de scolarisation / Tasas brutas de escolarización (%) | | | | | |
|---|---|---|---|---|---|---|---|---|
| | | | Pre-primary / Préprimaire / Preprimaria | Primary / Primaire / Primaria | Secondary / Secondaire / Secundaria | Tertiary / Supérieur / Superior | Primary and secondary / Primaire et secondaire / Primaria y secundaria | Primary, secondary and tertiary / Primaire, secondaire et supérieur / Primaria, secundaria y superior |
| Barbados (cont) | 1995 | | | | | | | |
| | | MF | ... | ... | ... | 29 | ... | ... |
| | | M | ... | ... | ... | 23 | ... | ... |
| | | F | ... | ... | ... | 34 | ... | ... |
| Belize | 1980 | | (3-5) | (6-13) | (14-17) | (18-22) | (6-17) | (6-22) |
| | | MF | 14 | 106 | 38 | ... | 85 | ... |
| | | M | ... | ... | 34 | ... | ... | ... |
| | | F | ... | ... | 42 | ... | ... | ... |
| | 1985 | | (3-4) | (5-12) | (13-16) | (17-21) | (5-16) | (5-21) |
| | | MF | ... | 103 | 43 | ... | 85 | ... |
| | | M | ... | 106 | 39 | ... | 86 | ... |
| | | F | ... | 100 | 46 | ... | 84 | ... |
| | 1990 | | | | | | | |
| | | MF | 24 | 112 | 41 | ... | 90 | ... |
| | | M | 22 | 113 | 39 | ... | 91 | ... |
| | | F | 26 | 110 | 44 | ... | 89 | ... |
| | 1991 | | | | | | | |
| | | MF | 28 | 112 | 46 | ... | 92 | ... |
| | | M | 27 | 114 | 42 | ... | 92 | ... |
| | | F | 28 | 111 | 50 | ... | 92 | ... |
| | 1992 | | | | | | | |
| | | MF | 29 | 116 | 48 | ... | 94 | ... |
| | | M | 29 | 118 | 47 | ... | 96 | ... |
| | | F | 28 | 114 | 48 | ... | 93 | ... |
| | 1993 | | | | | | | |
| | | MF | 26 | 119 | 49 | ... | 97 | ... |
| | | M | 27 | 121 | 48 | ... | 98 | ... |
| | | F | 26 | 117 | 50 | ... | 96 | ... |
| | 1994 | | | | | | | |
| | | MF | 27 | 121 | 49 | ... | 98 | ... |
| | | M | 26 | 123 | 47 | ... | 99 | ... |
| | | F | 28 | 119 | 52 | ... | 97 | ... |
| Canada | 1970 | | (4-5) | (6-13) | (14-19) | (20-24) | (6-19) | (6-24) |
| | | MF | 41 | 101 | 65 | 53 | 87 | 79 |
| | | M | 41 | 102 | 65 | 63 | 87 | 82 |
| | | F | 41 | 101 | 65 | 43 | 86 | 76 |
| | 1975 | | (4-5) | (6-11) | (12-17) | (18-22) | (6-17) | (6-22) |
| | | MF | 56 | 98 | 90 | 48 | 94 | 80 |
| | | M | 57 | 98 | 89 | 52 | 93 | 81 |
| | | F | 56 | 98 | 91 | 43 | 94 | 79 |
| | 1980 | | | | | | | |
| | | MF | 55 | 99 | 88 | 57 | 93 | 81 |
| | | M | 55 | 99 | 87 | 56 | 92 | 80 |
| | | F | 55 | 99 | 89 | 58 | 93 | 81 |
| | 1985 | | | | | | | |
| | | MF | 57 | 103 | 99 | 70 | 101 | 90 |
| | | M | 57 | 104 | 99 | 62 | 102 | 88 |
| | | F | 58 | 102 | 99 | 78 | 100 | 93 |
| | 1990 | | | | | | | |
| | | MF | 60 | 103 | 101 | 95 | 102 | 100 |
| | | M | 61 | 104 | 101 | 85 | 102 | 97 |
| | | F | 60 | 102 | 101 | 104 | 101 | 102 |
| | 1991 | | | | | | | |
| | | MF | 62 | 103 | 102 | 97 | 102 | 101 |
| | | M | 62 | 104 | 102 | 88 | 103 | 98 |
| | | F | 62 | 102 | 102 | 107 | 102 | 103 |
| | 1992 | | | | | | | |
| | | MF | 61 | 102 | 104 | 88 | 103 | 98 |
| | | M | 61 | 103 | 104 | 82 | 104 | 97 |
| | | F | 61 | 101 | 103 | 95 | 102 | 100 |
| | 1993 | | | | | | | |
| | | MF | 62 | 102 | 105 | 89 | 103 | 99 |
| | | M | 62 | 103 | 105 | 83 | 104 | 98 |
| | | F | 62 | 100 | 104 | 96 | 102 | 100 |

II.8   Gross enrolment ratios by level of education
Taux bruts de scolarisation par niveau d'enseignement
Tasas brutas de escolarización por nivel de enseñanza

| Country / Pays / País | Year / Année / Año | Sex / Sexe / Sexo | Gross enrolment ratios / Taux bruts de scolarisation / Tasas brutas de escolarización (%) | | | | | |
|---|---|---|---|---|---|---|---|---|
| | | | Pre-primary / Préprimaire / Preprimaria | Primary / Primaire / Primaria | Secondary / Secondaire / Secundaria | Tertiary / Supérieur / Superior | Primary and secondary / Primaire et secondaire / Primaria y secundaria | Primary, secondary and tertiary / Primaire, secondaire et supérieur / Primaria, secundaria y superior |
| Canada (cont) | 1994 | MF | 63 | 101 | 104 | 89 | 103 | 99 |
| | | M | 64 | 102 | 105 | 83 | 103 | 97 |
| | | F | 63 | 100 | 104 | 96 | 102 | 100 |
| | 1995 | MF | 64 | 102 | 105 | 88 | 103 | 99 |
| | | M | 64 | 103 | 105 | 81 | 104 | 97 |
| | | F | 64 | 101 | 105 | 95 | 103 | 101 |
| Costa Rica | 1970 | | (5-5) | (6-11) | (12-16) | (17-21) | (6-16) | (6-21) |
| | | MF | 13 | 110 | 28 | 9 | 76 | 60 |
| | | M | 12 | 110 | 27 | 10 | 76 | 60 |
| | | F | 14 | 109 | 29 | 8 | 76 | 60 |
| | 1975 | MF | 28 | 107 | 43 | 15 | 79 | 62 |
| | | M | 27 | 107 | 40 | ... | 78 | ... |
| | | F | 28 | 107 | 45 | ... | 80 | ... |
| | 1980 | MF | 39 | 105 | 47 | 21 | 78 | 61 |
| | | M | 39 | 106 | 44 | ... | 77 | ... |
| | | F | 39 | 104 | 51 | ... | 80 | ... |
| | 1985 | MF | 52 | 97 | 40 | 22 | 73 | 57 |
| | | M | 51 | 98 | 38 | ... | 72 | ... |
| | | F | 53 | 96 | 42 | ... | 73 | ... |
| | 1990 | MF | 61 | 101 | 42 | 27 | 76 | 62 |
| | | M | 61 | 101 | 41 | ... | 76 | ... |
| | | F | 61 | 100 | 43 | ... | 76 | ... |
| | 1991 | MF | 66 | 102 | 43 | 28 | 77 | 63 |
| | | M | 66 | 102 | 42 | ... | 77 | ... |
| | | F | 67 | 101 | 44 | ... | 77 | ... |
| | 1992 | MF | 66 | 103 | 45 | 29 | 78 | 65 |
| | | M | 65 | 103 | 43 | ... | 78 | ... |
| | | F | 66 | 102 | 46 | ... | 78 | ... |
| | 1993 | MF | 65 | 103 | 46 | 30 | 78 | 65 |
| | | M | 65 | 103 | 44 | ... | 78 | ... |
| | | F | 65 | 102 | 48 | ... | 79 | ... |
| | 1994 | MF | 65 | 102 | 47 | 30 | 78 | 65 |
| | | M | 65 | 103 | 45 | 33 | 78 | 65 |
| | | F | 66 | 102 | 49 | 28 | 79 | 65 |
| | 1995 | MF | 68 | 102 | 48 | ... | 79 | ... |
| | | M | 68 | 103 | 46 | ... | 78 | ... |
| | | F | 68 | 102 | 50 | ... | 79 | ... |
| | 1996 | MF | 71 | 103 | 47 | ... | 79 | ... |
| | | M | 71 | 104 | 45 | ... | 78 | ... |
| | | F | 70 | 103 | 49 | ... | 80 | ... |
| | 1997 | MF | 74 | 104 | 48 | ... | 79 | ... |
| | | M | ... | 104 | 47 | ... | 79 | ... |
| | | F | ... | 103 | 50 | ... | 80 | ... |
| | 1998 | MF | 79 | 104 | 49 | ... | 80 | ... |
| | | M | 79 | 104 | 47 | ... | 79 | ... |
| | | F | 79 | 103 | 52 | ... | 80 | ... |
| Cuba | 1970 | | (5-5) | (6-11) | (12-18) | (19-23) | (6-18) | (6-23) |
| | | MF | 52 | 123 | 26 | 4 | 78 | 60 |
| | | M | 52 | 124 | 24 | 4 | 78 | 61 |
| | | F | 53 | 122 | 28 | 3 | 78 | 60 |

Gross enrolment ratios by level of education  II.8
Taux bruts de scolarisation par niveau d'enseignement
Tasas brutas de escolarización por nivel de enseñanza

| Country / Pays / País | Year / Année / Año | Sex / Sexe / Sexo | Gross enrolment ratios / Taux bruts de scolarisation / Tasas brutas de escolarización (%) | | | | | |
|---|---|---|---|---|---|---|---|---|
| | | | Pre-primary / Préprimaire / Preprimaria | Primary / Primaire / Primaria | Secondary / Secondaire / Secundaria | Tertiary / Supérieur / Superior | Primary and secondary / Primaire et secondaire / Primaria y secundaria | Primary, secondary and tertiary / Primaire, secondaire et supérieur / Primaria, secundaria y superior |
| Cuba (cont) | 1975 | | | | | | | |
| | | MF | 54 | 124 | 49 | 11 | 89 | 72 |
| | | M | 54 | 127 | 46 | 13 | 89 | 73 |
| | | F | 54 | 122 | 52 | 8 | 89 | 71 |
| | 1980 | | (5-5) | (6-11) | (12-17) | (18-22) | (6-17) | (6-22) |
| | | MF | 59 | 106 | 81 | 17 | 93 | 75 |
| | | M | 59 | 109 | 79 | 18 | 94 | 76 |
| | | F | 59 | 103 | 83 | 17 | 93 | 74 |
| | 1985 | | | | | | | |
| | | MF | 79 | 101 | 82 | 20 | 91 | 68 |
| | | M | 87 | 105 | 80 | 18 | 90 | 67 |
| | | F | 71 | 98 | 85 | 22 | 91 | 69 |
| | 1990 | | | | | | | |
| | | MF | 101 | 98 | 89 | 21 | 93 | 67 |
| | | M | 111 | 99 | 83 | 17 | 90 | 64 |
| | | F | 91 | 96 | 95 | 25 | 96 | 70 |
| | 1991 | | | | | | | |
| | | MF | 86 | 100 | 86 | 20 | 92 | 66 |
| | | M | 96 | 100 | 79 | 16 | 89 | 63 |
| | | F | 76 | 99 | 92 | 24 | 95 | 69 |
| | 1992 | | | | | | | |
| | | MF | 92 | 100 | 82 | 18 | 91 | 64 |
| | | M | 102 | 100 | 77 | 15 | 88 | 62 |
| | | F | 81 | 99 | 87 | 21 | 93 | 67 |
| | 1993 | | | | | | | |
| | | MF | 92 | 101 | 77 | 17 | 89 | 63 |
| | | M | 105 | 101 | 73 | 14 | 87 | 61 |
| | | F | 79 | 101 | 81 | 19 | 91 | 65 |
| | 1994 | | | | | | | |
| | | MF | 89 | 100 | 74 | 14 | 88 | 62 |
| | | M | 88 | 101 | 70 | 11 | 86 | 60 |
| | | F | 89 | 100 | 79 | 17 | 90 | 65 |
| | 1995 | | | | | | | |
| | | MF | 94 | 105 | 80 | 13 | 93 | 66 |
| | | M | 95 | 107 | 78 | 10 | 93 | 65 |
| | | F | 94 | 103 | 82 | 16 | 93 | 67 |
| | 1996 | | | | | | | |
| | | MF | 88 | 106 | 81 | 12 | 94 | 68 |
| | | M | 00 | 108 | 76 | 10 | 93 | 67 |
| | | F | 87 | 104 | 85 | 15 | 96 | 70 |
| Dominican Republic | 1970 | | (3-6) | (7-12) | (13-18) | (19-23) | (7-18) | (7-23) |
| | | MF | 3 | 98 | 21 | 6 | 65 | 52 |
| | | M | ... | 98 | ... | 7 | ... | ... |
| | | F | ... | 99 | ... | 5 | ... | ... |
| | 1975 | | | | | | | |
| | | MF | 4 | 102 | 36 | 9 | 72 | 58 |
| | | M | ... | ... | ... | 10 | ... | ... |
| | | F | ... | ... | ... | 8 | ... | ... |
| | 1980 | | | | | | | |
| | | MF | 4 | 118 | 42 | ... | 81 | ... |
| | 1985 | | | | | | | |
| | | MF | 10 | 126 | 51 | 18 | 89 | 70 |
| | | M | ... | 123 | 44 | ... | 85 | ... |
| | | F | ... | 129 | 57 | ... | 94 | ... |
| | 1992 | | (3-6) | (7-14) | (15-18) | (19-23) | (7-18) | (7-23) |
| | | MF | 18 | 93 | 36 | ... | 75 | ... |
| | 1993 | | | | | | | |
| | | MF | 20 | 96 | 37 | ... | 77 | ... |
| | | M | 19 | 96 | 30 | ... | 75 | ... |
| | | F | 20 | 95 | 43 | ... | 79 | ... |
| | 1994 | | (3-5) | (6-13) | (14-17) | (18-22) | (6-17) | (6-22) |
| | | MF | 25 | 93 | 41 | ... | 76 | ... |
| | | M | ... | 93 | 34 | ... | 74 | ... |
| | | F | ... | 93 | 47 | ... | 79 | ... |

II.8    Gross enrolment ratios by level of education
Taux bruts de scolarisation par niveau d'enseignement
Tasas brutas de escolarización por nivel de enseñanza

| Country / Pays / País | Year / Année / Año | Sex / Sexe / Sexo | Gross enrolment ratios / Taux bruts de scolarisation / Tasas brutas de escolarización (%) | | | | | |
|---|---|---|---|---|---|---|---|---|
| | | | Pre-primary / Préprimaire / Preprimaria | Primary / Primaire / Primaria | Secondary / Secondaire / Secundaria | Tertiary / Supérieur / Superior | Primary and secondary / Primaire et secondaire / Primaria y secundaria | Primary, secondary and tertiary / Primaire, secondaire et supérieur / Primaria, secundaria y superior |
| Dominican Republic (cont) | 1995 | MF | 31 | 96 | ... | ... | ... | ... |
| | 1996 | MF | 33 | 94 | 52 | 23 | 81 | 65 |
| | | M | 33 | 94 | ... | 19 | ... | ... |
| | | F | 33 | 94 | ... | 27 | ... | ... |
| | 1997 | MF | 33 | ... | 54 | ... | ... | ... |
| | | M | 33 | ... | 47 | ... | ... | ... |
| | | F | 33 | ... | 61 | ... | ... | ... |
| El Salvador | 1970 | | (4-6) | (7-12) | (13-17) | (18-22) | (7-17) | (7-22) |
| | | MF | 7 | 84 | 22 | 3 | 59 | 45 |
| | | M | 6 | 86 | 23 | ... | 61 | ... |
| | | F | 7 | 82 | 20 | ... | 57 | ... |
| | 1975 | | (4-6) | (7-15) | (16-18) | (19-23) | (7-18) | (7-23) |
| | | MF | 11 | 74 | 19 | 8 | 63 | 50 |
| | | M | 10 | 75 | 21 | 10 | 64 | 52 |
| | | F | 11 | 73 | 17 | 5 | 61 | 49 |
| | 1980 | MF | 11 | 75 | 24 | 9 | 64 | 52 |
| | | M | 11 | 75 | 25 | 12 | 64 | 52 |
| | | F | 12 | 75 | 23 | 7 | 64 | 51 |
| | 1985 | MF | ... | ... | ... | 17 | ... | ... |
| | | M | ... | ... | ... | 20 | ... | ... |
| | | F | ... | ... | ... | 14 | ... | ... |
| | 1990 | MF | ... | 81 | 26 | 16 | 69 | 56 |
| | | M | ... | 81 | 26 | 19 | 69 | 57 |
| | | F | ... | 82 | 27 | 13 | 69 | 56 |
| | 1991 | MF | 21 | 81 | 25 | 17 | 68 | 55 |
| | | M | 20 | 80 | 23 | ... | 67 | ... |
| | | F | 22 | 81 | 28 | ... | 69 | ... |
| | 1992 | MF | 24 | 83 | 27 | 17 | 70 | 57 |
| | | M | 23 | 83 | 25 | ... | 69 | ... |
| | | F | 25 | 84 | 29 | ... | 71 | ... |
| | 1993 | MF | 28 | 85 | 29 | 17 | 71 | 57 |
| | | M | 27 | 85 | 28 | 17 | 71 | 57 |
| | | F | 29 | 85 | 31 | 17 | 72 | 57 |
| | 1994 | MF | 28 | 87 | 32 | 18 | 73 | 58 |
| | | M | 27 | 87 | 30 | 19 | 72 | 58 |
| | | F | 29 | 87 | 34 | 18 | 73 | 58 |
| | 1995 | MF | 31 | 88 | 34 | 19 | 74 | 59 |
| | | M | 30 | 87 | 32 | 19 | 73 | 59 |
| | | F | 32 | 88 | 36 | 19 | 74 | 59 |
| | 1996 | MF | 35 | 93 | 34 | 18 | 78 | 61 |
| | | M | 33 | 93 | 32 | 18 | 78 | 61 |
| | | F | 36 | 92 | 36 | 18 | 78 | 61 |
| | 1997 | MF | 40 | 97 | 37 | ... | 82 | ... |
| | | M | 39 | 98 | 35 | ... | 82 | ... |
| | | F | 42 | 96 | 39 | ... | 82 | ... |
| Guadeloupe (1) | | | (2-5) | (6-10) | (11-17) | (18-22) | (6-17) | (6-22) |
| Guatemala | 1970 | | (5-6) | (7-12) | (13-18) | (19-23) | (7-18) | (7-23) |
| | | MF | 12 | 58 | 8 | 3 | 36 | 28 |
| | | M | 17 | 64 | 9 | 5 | 39 | 32 |
| | | F | 7 | 52 | 8 | 1 | 32 | 25 |

Gross enrolment ratios by level of education **II.8**
Taux bruts de scolarisation par niveau d'enseignement
Tasas brutas de escolarización por nivel de enseñanza

| Country / Pays / País | Year / Année / Año | Sex / Sexe / Sexo | Gross enrolment ratios / Taux bruts de scolarisation / Tasas brutas de escolarización (%) | | | | | |
|---|---|---|---|---|---|---|---|---|
| | | | Pre-primary / Préprimaire / Preprimaria | Primary / Primaire / Primaria | Secondary / Secondaire / Secundaria | Tertiary / Supérieur / Superior | Primary and secondary / Primaire et secondaire / Primaria y secundaria | Primary, secondary and tertiary / Primaire, secondaire et supérieur / Primaria, secundaria y superior |
| Guatemala (cont) | 1975 | | | | | | | |
| | | MF | 17 | 63 | 12 | 5 | 40 | 32 |
| | | M | 19 | 69 | 13 | 9 | 44 | 35 |
| | | F | 15 | 58 | 11 | 2 | 37 | 28 |
| | 1980 | | | | | | | |
| | | MF | 21 | 71 | 19 | 8 | 48 | 38 |
| | | M | 22 | 77 | 20 | ... | 52 | ... |
| | | F | 20 | 65 | 17 | ... | 43 | ... |
| | 1985 | | | | | | | |
| | | MF | 27 | 78 | 19 | 9 | 52 | 42 |
| | | M | 28 | 84 | ... | ... | ... | ... |
| | | F | 26 | 72 | ... | ... | ... | ... |
| | 1990 | | | | | | | |
| | | MF | ... | 78 | ... | ... | ... | ... |
| | 1991 | | | | | | | |
| | | MF | 26 | 81 | 23 | ... | 55 | ... |
| | | M | 26 | 86 | ... | ... | ... | ... |
| | | F | 25 | 76 | ... | ... | ... | ... |
| | 1992 | | | | | | | |
| | | MF | 29 | 85 | 24 | 8 | 57 | 46 |
| | | M | 30 | 91 | ... | ... | ... | ... |
| | | F | 29 | 79 | ... | ... | ... | ... |
| | 1993 | | | | | | | |
| | | MF | 33 | 87 | 25 | 8 | 59 | 47 |
| | | M | 33 | 92 | 26 | ... | 62 | ... |
| | | F | 32 | 81 | 24 | ... | 55 | ... |
| | 1994 | | | | | | | |
| | | MF | 33 | 86 | 26 | 8 | 59 | 47 |
| | | M | 34 | 92 | ... | ... | ... | ... |
| | | F | 33 | 80 | ... | ... | ... | ... |
| | 1995 | | | | | | | |
| | | MF | 34 | 87 | 26 | 8 | 59 | 48 |
| | | M | 35 | 93 | ... | ... | ... | ... |
| | | F | 34 | 82 | ... | ... | ... | ... |
| | 1996 | | | | | | | |
| | | MF | 35 | 88 | 26 | ... | 59 | ... |
| | | M | 35 | 94 | 27 | ... | 63 | ... |
| | | F | 34 | 82 | 25 | ... | 56 | ... |
| | 1997 | | | | | | | |
| | | MF | 35 | 88 | 26 | ... | 59 | ... |
| | | M | 35 | 93 | ... | ... | ... | ... |
| | | F | 34 | 82 | ... | ... | ... | ... |
| Haiti (2) | 1980 | | (4-5) | (6-11) | (12-17) | (18-22) | (6-17) | (6-22) |
| | | MF | ... | 77 | 14 | 0.9 | 47 | 36 |
| | | M | ... | 83 | 14 | 1 | 51 | 39 |
| | | F | ... | 71 | 13 | 0.5 | 44 | 33 |
| | 1985 | | (3-5) | (6-11) | (12-17) | (18-22) | (6-17) | (6-22) |
| | | MF | ... | 90 | 18 | 1 | 58 | 44 |
| | | M | ... | 95 | 19 | 2 | 61 | 47 |
| | | F | ... | 84 | 17 | 0.6 | 54 | 41 |
| | 1990 | | | | | | | |
| | | MF | 34 | 48 | 21 | ... | 36 | ... |
| | | M | 35 | 49 | 21 | ... | 37 | ... |
| | | F | 33 | 46 | 20 | ... | 35 | ... |
| Honduras | 1970 | | (4-6) | (7-12) | (13-17) | (18-22) | (7-17) | (7-22) |
| | | MF | 4 | 87 | 13 | 2 | 57 | 44 |
| | | M | 4 | 86 | 14 | ... | 57 | ... |
| | | F | 4 | 87 | 13 | ... | 57 | ... |
| | 1975 | | | | | | | |
| | | MF | 5 | 88 | 16 | 4 | 59 | 46 |
| | | M | 5 | 89 | 16 | 5 | 59 | 46 |
| | | F | 5 | 87 | 17 | 3 | 59 | 45 |
| | 1980 | | | | | | | |
| | | MF | 9 | 98 | 30 | 7 | 70 | 55 |
| | | M | 11 | 98 | 29 | 9 | 70 | 55 |
| | | F | 8 | 99 | 31 | 6 | 71 | 54 |

II.8   Gross enrolment ratios by level of education
Taux bruts de scolarisation par niveau d'enseignement
Tasas brutas de escolarización por nivel de enseñanza

| Country / Pays / País | Year / Année / Año | Sex / Sexe / Sexo | Gross enrolment ratios / Taux bruts de scolarisation / Tasas brutas de escolarización (%) | | | | | |
|---|---|---|---|---|---|---|---|---|
| | | | Pre-primary / Préprimaire / Preprimaria | Primary / Primaire / Primaria | Secondary / Secondaire / Secundaria | Tertiary / Supérieur / Superior | Primary and secondary / Primaire et secondaire / Primaria y secundaria | Primary, secondary and tertiary / Primaire, secondaire et supérieur / Primaria, secundaria y superior |
| Honduras (cont) | 1985 | MF | 12 | 108 | 37 | 9 | 79 | 61 |
| | | M | 11 | 108 | ... | 11 | ... | ... |
| | | F | 12 | 109 | ... | 7 | ... | ... |
| | 1990 | MF | ... | ... | ... | 9 | ... | ... |
| | | M | ... | ... | ... | 10 | ... | ... |
| | | F | ... | ... | ... | 8 | ... | ... |
| | 1991 | MF | 13 | 108 | 33 | 9 | 77 | 59 |
| | | M | 12 | 105 | 29 | 10 | 74 | 58 |
| | | F | 13 | 110 | 37 | 8 | 80 | 61 |
| | 1992 | MF | 13 | 110 | 33 | 9 | 78 | 60 |
| | | M | 12 | 108 | ... | 10 | ... | ... |
| | | F | 13 | 111 | ... | 8 | ... | ... |
| | 1993 | MF | 13 | 112 | 32 | 9 | 79 | 61 |
| | | M | 13 | 111 | ... | 10 | ... | ... |
| | | F | 13 | 112 | ... | 8 | ... | ... |
| | 1994 | MF | 14 | 111 | ... | 10 | ... | ... |
| | | M | 13 | 110 | ... | 11 | ... | ... |
| | | F | 14 | 112 | ... | 9 | ... | ... |
| Jamaica | 1970 | | (3-5) | (6-10) | (11-17) | (18-22) | (6-17) | (6-22) |
| | | MF | ... | 119 | 46 | 5 | 82 | 68 |
| | | M | ... | 119 | 46 | 6 | 82 | 69 |
| | | F | ... | 119 | 45 | 4 | 82 | 67 |
| | 1975 | | (3-5) | (6-11) | (12-18) | (19-23) | (6-18) | (6-23) |
| | | MF | 69 | 99 | 59 | 6 | 79 | 66 |
| | | M | 63 | 99 | 54 | ... | 76 | ... |
| | | F | 75 | 99 | 64 | ... | 82 | ... |
| | 1980 | MF | 70 | 103 | 67 | 7 | 84 | 67 |
| | | M | 67 | 103 | 63 | ... | 82 | ... |
| | | F | 73 | 104 | 71 | ... | 87 | ... |
| | 1985 | MF | 77 | 100 | 59 | 4 | 78 | 60 |
| | | M | ... | 99 | 56 | 5 | 76 | 59 |
| | | F | ... | 102 | 63 | 4 | 80 | 61 |
| | 1990 | MF | 78 | 101 | 65 | 7 | 82 | 63 |
| | | M | 77 | 102 | 63 | 8 | 82 | 64 |
| | | F | 79 | 101 | 67 | 6 | 83 | 63 |
| | 1991 | MF | ... | ... | 65 | 7 | ... | ... |
| | | M | ... | ... | 63 | 8 | ... | ... |
| | | F | ... | ... | 67 | 6 | ... | ... |
| | 1992 | MF | 75 | 101 | 65 | 7 | 82 | 63 |
| | | M | 79 | 102 | 63 | ... | 82 | ... |
| | | F | 72 | 99 | 67 | ... | 83 | ... |
| | 1993 | MF | ... | 104 | ... | 7 | ... | ... |
| | | M | ... | 105 | ... | ... | ... | ... |
| | | F | ... | 102 | ... | ... | ... | ... |
| | 1994 | MF | ... | 102 | ... | 7 | ... | ... |
| | | M | ... | 103 | ... | ... | ... | ... |
| | | F | ... | 101 | ... | ... | ... | ... |
| | 1995 | MF | ... | 102 | ... | 8 | ... | ... |
| | | M | ... | 102 | ... | 9 | ... | ... |
| | | F | ... | 101 | ... | 7 | ... | ... |

Gross enrolment ratios by level of education II.8
Taux bruts de scolarisation par niveau d'enseignement
Tasas brutas de escolarización por nivel de enseñanza

| Country / Pays / País | Year / Année / Año | Sex / Sexe / Sexo | Gross enrolment ratios / Taux bruts de scolarisation / Tasas brutas de escolarización (%) | | | | | |
|---|---|---|---|---|---|---|---|---|
| | | | Pre-primary / Préprimaire / Preprimaria | Primary / Primaire / Primaria | Secondary / Secondaire / Secundaria | Tertiary / Supérieur / Superior | Primary and secondary / Primaire et secondaire / Primaria y secundaria | Primary, secondary and tertiary / Primaire, secondaire et supérieur / Primaria, secundaria y superior |
| Jamaica (cont) | 1996 | MF | ... | 100 | ... | ... | ... | ... |
| | | M | ... | 100 | ... | ... | ... | ... |
| | | F | ... | 99 | ... | ... | ... | ... |
| Martinique (1) | | | (2-5) | (6-10) | (11-17) | (18-22) | (6-17) | (6-22) |
| Mexico | 1970 | | (4-5) | (6-11) | (12-17) | (18-22) | (6-17) | (6-22) |
| | | MF | 13 | 106 | 23 | 5 | 69 | 55 |
| | | M | 12 | 109 | 27 | 9 | 73 | 58 |
| | | F | 13 | 103 | 18 | 2 | 65 | 51 |
| | 1975 | MF | 13 | 111 | 35 | 10 | 77 | 62 |
| | | M | 13 | 115 | 43 | ... | 83 | ... |
| | | F | 14 | 107 | 28 | ... | 72 | ... |
| | 1980 | MF | 24 | 120 | 49 | 14 | 88 | 71 |
| | | M | 24 | 122 | 51 | 19 | 90 | 74 |
| | | F | 24 | 119 | 46 | 9 | 86 | 69 |
| | 1985 | MF | 56 | 118 | 57 | 16 | 89 | 71 |
| | | M | 55 | 119 | 58 | 20 | 90 | 74 |
| | | F | 56 | 116 | 55 | 12 | 87 | 69 |
| | 1990 | MF | 64 | 114 | 53 | 15 | 84 | 65 |
| | | M | 64 | 115 | 53 | 17 | 84 | 67 |
| | | F | 65 | 112 | 54 | 12 | 83 | 64 |
| | 1991 | MF | 66 | 114 | 53 | 14 | 84 | 65 |
| | | M | 65 | 115 | 54 | 16 | 85 | 66 |
| | | F | 66 | 113 | 53 | 13 | 82 | 63 |
| | 1992 | MF | 67 | 114 | 54 | 14 | 84 | 65 |
| | | M | 66 | 116 | 54 | 15 | 85 | 66 |
| | | F | 67 | 113 | 54 | 12 | 83 | 63 |
| | 1993 | MF | 69 | 114 | 56 | 14 | 85 | 65 |
| | | M | 68 | 116 | 55 | 15 | 86 | 66 |
| | | F | 70 | 113 | 56 | 13 | 84 | 64 |
| | 1994 | MF | 71 | 115 | 58 | 14 | 87 | 66 |
| | | M | 70 | 116 | 58 | 15 | 87 | 67 |
| | | F | 72 | 113 | 59 | 13 | 86 | 65 |
| | 1995 | MF | 72 | 115 | 61 | 15 | 88 | 67 |
| | | M | 71 | 116 | 61 | 16 | 89 | 68 |
| | | F | 73 | 113 | 61 | 14 | 88 | 66 |
| | 1996 | MF | 73 | 114 | 64 | 16 | 90 | 69 |
| | | M | 72 | 116 | 64 | 17 | 90 | 69 |
| | | F | 74 | 113 | 64 | 15 | 89 | 68 |
| Netherlands Antilles (1) | | | (4-5) | (6-11) | (12-16) | (17-21) | (6-16) | (6-21) |
| Nicaragua | 1970 | | (3-6) | (7-12) | (13-18) | (19-23) | (7-18) | (7-23) |
| | | MF | 3 | 78 | 17 | 5 | 51 | 41 |
| | | M | 3 | 76 | 18 | 7 | 50 | 41 |
| | | F | 4 | 79 | 16 | 3 | 51 | 40 |
| | 1975 | MF | 3 | 80 | 23 | 8 | 54 | 43 |
| | | M | ... | 77 | 23 | 10 | 53 | 43 |
| | | F | ... | 82 | 23 | 5 | 56 | 44 |
| | 1980 | | (3-6) | (7-12) | (13-17) | (18-22) | (7-17) | (7-22) |
| | | MF | 8 | 94 | 41 | 12 | 73 | 57 |
| | | M | 7 | 92 | 38 | ... | 70 | ... |
| | | F | 8 | 97 | 44 | ... | 75 | ... |

II.8   Gross enrolment ratios by level of education
       Taux bruts de scolarisation par niveau d'enseignement
       Tasas brutas de escolarización por nivel de enseñanza

| Country / Pays / País | Year / Année / Año | Sex / Sexe / Sexo | Gross enrolment ratios / Taux bruts de scolarisation / Tasas brutas de escolarización (%) | | | | | |
|---|---|---|---|---|---|---|---|---|
| | | | Pre-primary / Préprimaire / Preprimaria | Primary / Primaire / Primaria | Secondary / Secondaire / Secundaria | Tertiary / Supérieur / Superior | Primary and secondary / Primaire et secondaire / Primaria y secundaria | Primary, secondary and tertiary / Primaire, secondaire et supérieur / Primaria, secundaria y superior |
| Nicaragua (cont) | 1985 | MF | 14 | 97 | 32 | 9 | 71 | 55 |
| | | M | 13 | 92 | 21 | 8 | 63 | 50 |
| | | F | 14 | 101 | 44 | 10 | 78 | 61 |
| | 1990 | MF | 12 | 94 | 40 | 8 | 72 | 56 |
| | | M | 12 | 91 | 34 | 8 | 68 | 53 |
| | | F | 13 | 96 | 47 | 8 | 76 | 59 |
| | 1991 | MF | 13 | 97 | 47 | 8 | 77 | 60 |
| | | M | 13 | 95 | 43 | 8 | 74 | 58 |
| | | F | 14 | 100 | 51 | 8 | 80 | 62 |
| | 1992 | MF | 13 | 99 | 47 | 9 | 78 | 61 |
| | | M | 12 | 98 | 43 | 9 | 75 | 59 |
| | | F | 13 | 101 | 50 | 9 | 80 | 62 |
| | 1993 | MF | 15 | 102 | 47 | ... | 79 | ... |
| | | M | 15 | 101 | 44 | ... | 77 | ... |
| | | F | 16 | 104 | 50 | ... | 82 | ... |
| | 1994 | MF | 19 | 104 | 47 | ... | 81 | ... |
| | | M | 18 | 103 | 44 | ... | 79 | ... |
| | | F | 19 | 106 | 50 | ... | 82 | ... |
| | 1995 | MF | 19 | 103 | 49 | 11 | 80 | 62 |
| | | M | 18 | 101 | 45 | 11 | 78 | 61 |
| | | F | 19 | 104 | 53 | 12 | 82 | 64 |
| | 1996 | MF | 21 | 101 | 50 | 12 | 79 | 62 |
| | | M | 21 | 100 | 46 | 11 | 77 | 60 |
| | | F | 22 | 102 | 54 | 12 | 82 | 63 |
| | 1997 | MF | 23 | 102 | 55 | 12 | 82 | 63 |
| | | M | 23 | 100 | 50 | 11 | 79 | 61 |
| | | F | 24 | 103 | 60 | 12 | 84 | 65 |
| | 1998 | MF | 24 | 101 | 57 | ... | 82 | ... |
| | | M | 24 | 100 | 52 | ... | 79 | ... |
| | | F | 25 | 102 | 62 | ... | 85 | ... |
| Panama | 1970 | | (5-5) | (6-11) | (12-17) | (18-22) | (6-17) | (6-22) |
| | | MF | 15 | 101 | 39 | 7 | 73 | 58 |
| | | M | 14 | 104 | 37 | 7 | 74 | 58 |
| | | F | 15 | 99 | 41 | 6 | 73 | 57 |
| | 1975 | MF | 24 | 116 | 56 | 16 | 89 | 72 |
| | | M | 23 | 118 | 53 | 16 | 89 | 72 |
| | | F | 25 | 113 | 58 | 16 | 88 | 71 |
| | 1980 | MF | 33 | 106 | 61 | 21 | 85 | 69 |
| | | M | 33 | 108 | 58 | 19 | 85 | 69 |
| | | F | 34 | 104 | 65 | 23 | 86 | 70 |
| | 1985 | MF | 51 | 106 | 60 | 25 | 84 | 68 |
| | | M | 50 | 109 | 57 | 21 | 84 | 67 |
| | | F | 52 | 104 | 63 | 29 | 84 | 69 |
| | 1990 | MF | 53 | 106 | 63 | 21 | 85 | 67 |
| | | M | 53 | 108 | 60 | ... | 85 | ... |
| | | F | 53 | 104 | 65 | ... | 85 | ... |
| | 1991 | MF | 57 | 105 | 63 | 23 | 85 | 68 |
| | 1992 | MF | 56 | 105 | 64 | 25 | 85 | 68 |

Gross enrolment ratios by level of education II.8
Taux bruts de scolarisation par niveau d'enseignement
Tasas brutas de escolarización por nivel de enseñanza

| Country / Pays / País | Year / Année / Año | Sex / Sexe / Sexo | Pre-primary / Préprimaire / Preprimaria | Primary / Primaire / Primaria | Secondary / Secondaire / Secundaria | Tertiary / Supérieur / Superior | Primary and secondary / Primaire et secondaire / Primaria y secundaria | Primary, secondary and tertiary / Primaire, secondaire et supérieur / Primaria, secundaria y superior |
|---|---|---|---|---|---|---|---|---|
| Panama (cont) | 1993 | MF | 59 | 105 | 65 | 27 | 86 | 69 |
| | 1994 | MF | 69 | 104 | 66 | 27 | 86 | 69 |
| | 1995 | MF | 69 | 104 | 68 | 30 | 86 | 71 |
| | 1996 | MF | 76 | 105 | 69 | 32 | 88 | 72 |
| Trinidad and Tobago | 1970 | | (3-4) | (5-11) | (12-16) | (17-21) | (5-16) | (5-21) |
| | | MF | ... | 109 | 43 | 2 | 85 | 65 |
| | | M | ... | 110 | 42 | 3 | 85 | 66 |
| | | F | ... | 108 | 44 | 2 | 84 | 65 |
| | 1975 | MF | ... | 113 | 48 | 4 | 85 | 64 |
| | | M | ... | 113 | 48 | 6 | 85 | 64 |
| | | F | ... | 113 | 48 | 3 | 85 | 63 |
| | 1980 | MF | 8 | 99 | 69 | 4 | 86 | 61 |
| | | M | ... | 98 | ... | 5 | ... | ... |
| | | F | ... | 100 | ... | 4 | ... | ... |
| | 1985 | MF | 8 | 96 | 81 | 5 | 90 | 65 |
| | | M | ... | 95 | 81 | 6 | 90 | 65 |
| | | F | ... | 97 | 81 | 4 | 90 | 64 |
| | 1990 | MF | 9 | 97 | 80 | 7 | 91 | 69 |
| | | M | 9 | 97 | 78 | 7 | 90 | 69 |
| | | F | 9 | 96 | 82 | 6 | 91 | 70 |
| | 1991 | MF | ... | 97 | 78 | 7 | 90 | 69 |
| | | M | ... | 98 | 77 | 8 | 90 | 69 |
| | | F | ... | 97 | 80 | 6 | 90 | 69 |
| | 1992 | MF | 10 | 98 | 78 | 7 | 90 | 69 |
| | | M | 10 | 98 | 76 | 9 | 90 | 69 |
| | | F | 10 | 98 | 79 | 6 | 91 | 70 |
| | 1993 | MF | ... | 98 | 76 | 8 | 89 | 69 |
| | | M | ... | 99 | 74 | 9 | 89 | 69 |
| | | F | ... | 98 | 78 | 7 | 90 | 69 |
| | 1994 | MF | ... | 98 | 75 | 8 | 88 | 68 |
| | | M | ... | 99 | 73 | 9 | 88 | 68 |
| | | F | ... | 98 | 76 | 7 | 89 | 68 |
| | 1995 | MF | ... | 98 | 74 | 8 | 88 | 67 |
| | | M | ... | 99 | 72 | 9 | 88 | 67 |
| | | F | ... | 98 | 75 | 7 | 88 | 67 |
| | 1996 | MF | ... | 99 | ... | 8 | ... | ... |
| | | M | ... | 99 | ... | 9 | ... | ... |
| | | F | ... | 98 | ... | 7 | ... | ... |
| United States | 1970 | | (3-5) | (6-11) | (12-17) | (18-22) | (6-17) | (6-22) |
| | | MF | 37 | 88 | 84 | 47 | 86 | 75 |
| | | M | ... | ... | ... | 56 | ... | ... |
| | | F | ... | ... | ... | 38 | ... | ... |
| | 1975 | MF | 51 | 89 | 84 | 55 | 87 | 77 |
| | | M | ... | ... | ... | 59 | ... | ... |
| | | F | ... | ... | ... | 50 | ... | ... |
| | 1980 | MF | 52 | 99 | 91 | 56 | 95 | 82 |
| | | M | 53 | 99 | 91 | 53 | 95 | 81 |
| | | F | 50 | 99 | 92 | 58 | 95 | 83 |

II.8 Gross enrolment ratios by level of education
Taux bruts de scolarisation par niveau d'enseignement
Tasas brutas de escolarización por nivel de enseñanza

| Country<br><br>Pays<br><br>País | Year<br><br>Année<br><br>Año | Sex<br><br>Sexe<br><br>Sexo | Gross enrolment ratios / Taux bruts de scolarisation / Tasas brutas de escolarización (%) | | | | | |
|---|---|---|---|---|---|---|---|---|
| | | | Pre-primary<br><br>Préprimaire<br><br>Preprimaria | Primary<br><br>Primaire<br><br>Primaria | Secondary<br><br>Secondaire<br><br>Secundaria | Tertiary<br><br>Supérieur<br><br>Superior | Primary and secondary<br><br>Primaire et secondaire<br><br>Primaria y secundaria | Primary, secondary and tertiary<br><br>Primaire, secondaire et supérieur<br><br>Primaria, secundaria y superior |
| United States (cont) | 1985 | MF<br>M<br>F | 60<br>59<br>60 | 99<br>99<br>99 | 97<br>97<br>97 | 60<br>56<br>64 | 98<br>98<br>98 | 86<br>85<br>87 |
| | 1990 | MF<br>M<br>F | 63<br>63<br>62 | 102<br>103<br>101 | 93<br>93<br>94 | 75<br>67<br>84 | 98<br>98<br>98 | 91<br>89<br>94 |
| | 1991 | MF<br>M<br>F | ...<br>...<br>... | 102<br>103<br>101 | 95<br>94<br>95 | 80<br>71<br>89 | 98<br>98<br>98 | 93<br>90<br>95 |
| | 1992 | MF<br>M<br>F | ...<br>...<br>... | 101<br>102<br>101 | 97<br>97<br>97 | 82<br>72<br>92 | 99<br>100<br>99 | 94<br>92<br>97 |
| | 1993 | MF<br>M<br>F | ...<br>...<br>... | 101<br>101<br>101 | 99<br>99<br>98 | 81<br>71<br>91 | 100<br>100<br>99 | 94<br>92<br>97 |
| | 1994 | MF<br>M<br>F | 68<br>70<br>67 | 102<br>103<br>102 | 97<br>97<br>98 | 81<br>71<br>92 | 100<br>100<br>100 | 95<br>92<br>98 |
| | 1995 | MF<br>M<br>F | 70<br>71<br>70 | 102<br>102<br>101 | 97<br>98<br>97 | 81<br>71<br>92 | 100<br>100<br>99 | 94<br>92<br>97 |
| **South America** | | | | | | | | |
| Argentina | 1970 | <br>MF<br>M<br>F | (4-5)<br>23<br>23<br>24 | (6-12)<br>105<br>105<br>106 | (13-17)<br>44<br>42<br>47 | (18-22)<br>13<br>15<br>12 | (6-17)<br>81<br>79<br>82 | (6-22)<br>62<br>62<br>63 |
| | 1975 | MF<br>M<br>F | 36<br>35<br>36 | 106<br>106<br>106 | 54<br>51<br>57 | 27<br>28<br>26 | 85<br>84<br>86 | 68<br>68<br>69 |
| | 1980 | MF<br>M<br>F | 40<br>...<br>... | 106<br>106<br>106 | 56<br>52<br>60 | 22<br>22<br>22 | 87<br>85<br>88 | 69<br>68<br>70 |
| | 1985 | MF<br>M<br>F | 50<br>49<br>51 | 105<br>105<br>105 | 70<br>66<br>74 | 36<br>34<br>38 | 92<br>90<br>94 | 78<br>76<br>80 |
| | 1990 | MF | ... | 106 | 71 | ... | 92 | ... |
| | 1991 | <br>MF | (3-5)<br>50 | (6-12)<br>108 | (13-17)<br>72 | (18-22)<br>38 | (6-17)<br>94 | (6-22)<br>80 |
| | 1994 | MF | 50 | 112 | 69 | 36 | 94 | 78 |
| | 1996 | MF<br>M<br>F | 54<br>53<br>56 | 113<br>114<br>113 | 77<br>73<br>81 | ...<br>...<br>... | 98<br>97<br>99 | ...<br>...<br>... |
| Bolivia | 1970 | <br>MF<br>M<br>F | (4-5)<br>24<br>26<br>23 | (6-13)<br>78<br>93<br>63 | (14-17)<br>25<br>29<br>21 | (18-22)<br>9<br>...<br>... | (6-17)<br>62<br>74<br>51 | (6-22)<br>49<br>...<br>... |
| | 1975 | MF<br>M<br>F | 26<br>25<br>27 | 88<br>97<br>78 | 31<br>36<br>27 | 11<br>...<br>... | 71<br>79<br>63 | 56<br>...<br>... |

Gross enrolment ratios by level of education II.8
Taux bruts de scolarisation par niveau d'enseignement
Tasas brutas de escolarización por nivel de enseñanza

| Country / Pays / País | Year / Année / Año | Sex / Sexe / Sexo | Gross enrolment ratios / Taux bruts de scolarisation / Tasas brutas de escolarización (%) | | | | | |
|---|---|---|---|---|---|---|---|---|
| | | | Pre-primary / Préprimaire / Preprimaria | Primary / Primaire / Primaria | Secondary / Secondaire / Secundaria | Tertiary / Supérieur / Superior | Primary and secondary / Primaire et secondaire / Primaria y secundaria | Primary, secondary and tertiary / Primaire, secondaire et supérieur / Primaria, secundaria y superior |
| Bolivia (cont) | 1980 | | | | | | | |
| | | MF | 27 | 87 | 37 | 15 | 72 | 58 |
| | | M | 28 | 92 | 42 | ... | 78 | ... |
| | | F | 27 | 81 | 32 | ... | 66 | ... |
| | 1985 | | | | | | | |
| | | MF | 39 | 95 | 39 | 19 | 79 | 65 |
| | | M | 39 | 101 | 42 | ... | 84 | ... |
| | | F | 38 | 90 | 36 | ... | 74 | ... |
| | 1990 | | | | | | | |
| | | MF | 32 | 95 | 37 | 21 | 77 | 63 |
| | | M | 32 | 99 | 40 | ... | 81 | ... |
| | | F | 32 | 90 | 34 | ... | 73 | ... |
| | 1991 | | | | | | | |
| | | MF | ... | ... | ... | 22 | ... | ... |
| Brazil | 1970 | | (4-6) | (7-10) | (11-17) | (18-22) | (7-17) | (7-22) |
| | | MF | 4 | 119 | 26 | 5 | 64 | 49 |
| | | M | 4 | 119 | 26 | 6 | 64 | 49 |
| | | F | 4 | 119 | 26 | 4 | 64 | 48 |
| | 1975 | | (4-6) | (7-14) | (15-17) | (18-22) | (7-17) | (7-22) |
| | | MF | 6 | 87 | 26 | 10 | 72 | 56 |
| | | M | 6 | 88 | 24 | ... | 72 | ... |
| | | F | 6 | 87 | 28 | ... | 72 | ... |
| | 1980 | | | | | | | |
| | | MF | 14 | 98 | 33 | 11 | 81 | 61 |
| | | M | 14 | 100 | 31 | 11 | 82 | 61 |
| | | F | 14 | 96 | 36 | 11 | 80 | 60 |
| | 1985 | | | | | | | |
| | | MF | 36 | 100 | 35 | ... | 83 | ... |
| | 1990 | | | | | | | |
| | | MF | 48 | 106 | 38 | 11 | 89 | 67 |
| | 1991 | | | | | | | |
| | | MF | 50 | 106 | 41 | 11 | 90 | 68 |
| | 1992 | | | | | | | |
| | | MF | 54 | 109 | 43 | 11 | 92 | 69 |
| | 1993 | | | | | | | |
| | | MF | 56 | 110 | 43 | 11 | 92 | 69 |
| | 1994 | | | | | | | |
| | | MF | 56 | 112 | 45 | 11 | 94 | 71 |
| | 1995 | | | | | | | |
| | | MF | 57 | 118 | ... | ... | ... | ... |
| | 1996 | | | | | | | |
| | | MF | 58 | 120 | 56 | 15 | 102 | 77 |
| | 1997 | | | | | | | |
| | | MF | 58 | 125 | 62 | ... | 107 | ... |
| Chile | 1970 | | (5-5) | (6-13) | (14-17) | (18-22) | (6-17) | (6-22) |
| | | MF | 23 | 104 | 37 | 9 | 85 | 67 |
| | | M | 22 | 104 | 35 | 11 | 84 | 67 |
| | | F | 24 | 104 | 40 | 7 | 85 | 67 |
| | 1975 | | | | | | | |
| | | MF | 50 | 112 | 47 | 15 | 92 | 72 |
| | | M | ... | 113 | 44 | 16 | 91 | 72 |
| | | F | ... | 111 | 51 | 13 | 92 | 72 |
| | 1980 | | | | | | | |
| | | MF | 71 | 109 | 53 | 12 | 90 | 68 |
| | | M | ... | 110 | 49 | 14 | 89 | 68 |
| | | F | ... | 108 | 56 | 11 | 90 | 68 |
| | 1985 | | | | | | | |
| | | MF | 82 | 105 | 67 | 16 | 92 | 69 |
| | | M | 82 | 106 | 64 | 18 | 92 | 70 |
| | | F | 83 | 104 | 70 | 14 | 92 | 69 |

II.8    Gross enrolment ratios by level of education
Taux bruts de scolarisation par niveau d'enseignement
Tasas brutas de escolarización por nivel de enseñanza

| Country<br>Pays<br>País | Year<br>Année<br>Año | Sex<br>Sexe<br>Sexo | Gross enrolment ratios / Taux bruts de scolarisation / Tasas brutas de escolarización (%) | | | | | |
|---|---|---|---|---|---|---|---|---|
| | | | Pre-primary<br>Préprimaire<br>Preprimaria | Primary<br>Primaire<br>Primaria | Secondary<br>Secondaire<br>Secundaria | Tertiary<br>Supérieur<br>Superior | Primary and secondary<br>Primaire et secondaire<br>Primaria y secundaria | Primary, secondary and tertiary<br>Primaire, secondaire et supérieur<br>Primaria, secundaria y superior |
| Chile (cont) | 1990 | | | | | | | |
| | | MF | 82 | 100 | 73 | ... | 91 | ... |
| | | M | 82 | 101 | 71 | ... | 91 | ... |
| | | F | 83 | 99 | 76 | ... | 92 | ... |
| | 1991 | | | | | | | |
| | | MF | 75 | 101 | 72 | 21 | 91 | 71 |
| | | M | 74 | 102 | 69 | ... | 91 | ... |
| | | F | 76 | 100 | 74 | ... | 91 | ... |
| | 1992 | | | | | | | |
| | | MF | 86 | 99 | 69 | 24 | 89 | 71 |
| | | M | 86 | 100 | 67 | ... | 89 | ... |
| | | F | 86 | 98 | 72 | ... | 90 | ... |
| | 1993 | | | | | | | |
| | | MF | 89 | 99 | 67 | 27 | 89 | 71 |
| | | M | 89 | 99 | 65 | 29 | 88 | 71 |
| | | F | 90 | 98 | 70 | 24 | 89 | 71 |
| | 1994 | | | | | | | |
| | | MF | 90 | 99 | 68 | 27 | 90 | 72 |
| | | M | 90 | 100 | 66 | 29 | 90 | 73 |
| | | F | 91 | 98 | 71 | 25 | 90 | 71 |
| | 1995 | | | | | | | |
| | | MF | 96 | 99 | 69 | 28 | 90 | 73 |
| | | M | 96 | 100 | 66 | 30 | 90 | 73 |
| | | F | 96 | 98 | 73 | 26 | 90 | 72 |
| | 1996 | | | | | | | |
| | | MF | 98 | 101 | 75 | 30 | 93 | 76 |
| | | M | 97 | 103 | 72 | 33 | 93 | 77 |
| | | F | 98 | 100 | 78 | 28 | 93 | 75 |
| | 1997 | | | | | | | |
| | | MF | ... | ... | ... | 31 | ... | ... |
| | | M | ... | ... | ... | 34 | ... | ... |
| | | F | ... | ... | ... | 29 | ... | ... |
| Colombia | 1970 | | | (7-11) | (12-17) | (18-22) | (7-17) | (7-22) |
| | | MF | ... | 101 | 23 | 4 | 62 | 47 |
| | | M | ... | 99 | 23 | 6 | 61 | 47 |
| | | F | ... | 103 | 23 | 2 | 62 | 47 |
| | 1975 | | | | | | | |
| | | MF | ... | 106 | 36 | 7 | 71 | 54 |
| | | M | ... | 104 | 36 | 9 | 69 | 54 |
| | | F | ... | 109 | 36 | 5 | 72 | 54 |
| | 1980 | | (3-5) | (6-10) | (11-16) | (17-21) | (6-16) | (6-21) |
| | | MF | 8 | 112 | 39 | 9 | 73 | 55 |
| | | M | ... | 110 | 39 | 9 | 71 | 54 |
| | | F | ... | 114 | 40 | 8 | 74 | 55 |
| | 1985 | | | | | | | |
| | | MF | 11 | 102 | 44 | 11 | 71 | 53 |
| | | M | 11 | 100 | 43 | 11 | 70 | 53 |
| | | F | 11 | 104 | 44 | 11 | 72 | 54 |
| | 1990 | | | | | | | |
| | | MF | 13 | 102 | 50 | 13 | 74 | 57 |
| | | M | ... | 95 | 47 | 13 | 70 | 53 |
| | | F | ... | 109 | 53 | 14 | 79 | 60 |
| | 1991 | | | | | | | |
| | | MF | 13 | 103 | 50 | 14 | 75 | 57 |
| | | M | ... | 102 | 46 | 14 | 72 | 55 |
| | | F | ... | 104 | 55 | 14 | 78 | 59 |
| | 1992 | | | | | | | |
| | | MF | 18 | 108 | 56 | 15 | 80 | 61 |
| | | M | 17 | 105 | 51 | ... | 76 | ... |
| | | F | 18 | 110 | 61 | ... | 84 | ... |
| | 1993 | | | | | | | |
| | | MF | 19 | 109 | 58 | 15 | 81 | 62 |
| | | M | 19 | 108 | 53 | ... | 78 | ... |
| | | F | 19 | 110 | 63 | ... | 85 | ... |

Gross enrolment ratios by level of education   **II.8**
Taux bruts de scolarisation par niveau d'enseignement
Tasas brutas de escolarización por nivel de enseñanza

| Country<br>Pays<br>País | Year<br>Année<br>Año | Sex<br>Sexe<br>Sexo | Gross enrolment ratios / Taux bruts de scolarisation / Tasas brutas de escolarización (%) | | | | | |
|---|---|---|---|---|---|---|---|---|
| | | | Pre-primary<br>Préprimaire<br>Preprimaria | Primary<br>Primaire<br>Primaria | Secondary<br>Secondaire<br>Secundaria | Tertiary<br>Supérieur<br>Superior | Primary and secondary<br>Primaire et secondaire<br>Primaria y secundaria | Primary, secondary and tertiary<br>Primaire, secondaire et supérieur<br>Primaria, secundaria y superior |
| Colombia (cont) | 1994 | | | | | | | |
| | | MF | 23 | 109 | 60 | 15 | 83 | 63 |
| | | M | ... | 109 | 55 | ... | 80 | ... |
| | | F | ... | 109 | 65 | ... | 85 | ... |
| | 1995 | | | | | | | |
| | | MF | 27 | 109 | 61 | 15 | 83 | 64 |
| | | M | ... | 109 | 57 | 15 | 81 | 62 |
| | | F | ... | 108 | 66 | 16 | 86 | 65 |
| | 1996 | | | | | | | |
| | | MF | 33 | 113 | 67 | 17 | 88 | 67 |
| | | M | 33 | 113 | 64 | 16 | 87 | 66 |
| | | F | 34 | 112 | 69 | 17 | 89 | 68 |
| Ecuador | 1970 | | (5-5) | (6-11) | (12-17) | (18-22) | (6-17) | (6-22) |
| | | MF | 7 | 99 | 26 | 7 | 66 | 53 |
| | | M | 7 | 101 | 28 | 10 | 68 | 55 |
| | | F | 8 | 97 | 24 | 4 | 64 | 50 |
| | 1075 | | | | | | | |
| | | MF | 11 | 106 | 40 | 25 | 76 | 64 |
| | | M | 11 | 107 | 42 | ... | 78 | ... |
| | | F | 11 | 104 | 39 | ... | 74 | ... |
| | 1980 | | | | | | | |
| | | MF | 21 | 117 | 53 | 35 | 88 | 75 |
| | | M | 21 | 119 | 53 | 43 | 89 | 78 |
| | | F | 22 | 116 | 53 | 26 | 87 | 72 |
| | 1985 | | | | | | | |
| | | MF | 36 | 119 | 58 | ... | 91 | ... |
| | | M | 35 | 120 | 57 | ... | 91 | ... |
| | | F | 37 | 118 | 59 | ... | 91 | ... |
| | 1990 | | | | | | | |
| | | MF | 42 | 116 | 55 | 20 | 88 | 70 |
| | 1991 | | | | | | | |
| | | MF | 45 | 126 | 56 | ... | 93 | ... |
| | 1992 | | | | | | | |
| | | MF | 47 | 123 | 55 | ... | 90 | ... |
| | | M | 46 | 124 | 54 | ... | 91 | ... |
| | | F | 48 | 122 | 56 | ... | 90 | ... |
| | 1993 | | | | | | | |
| | | MF | 45 | 122 | 49 | ... | 87 | ... |
| | | M | 44 | 123 | 48 | ... | 87 | ... |
| | | F | 46 | 121 | 49 | ... | 86 | ... |
| | 1994 | | | | | | | |
| | | MF | 49 | 121 | 50 | ... | 87 | ... |
| | | M | 48 | 120 | 50 | ... | 86 | ... |
| | | F | 49 | 122 | 50 | ... | 87 | ... |
| | 1995 | | | | | | | |
| | | MF | 52 | 123 | ... | ... | ... | ... |
| | | M | 51 | 123 | ... | ... | ... | ... |
| | | F | 53 | 122 | ... | ... | ... | ... |
| | 1996 | | | | | | | |
| | | MF | 56 | 127 | ... | ... | ... | ... |
| | | M | 55 | 134 | ... | ... | ... | ... |
| | | F | 56 | 119 | ... | ... | ... | ... |
| French Guiana (1) | | | (2-5) | (6-10) | (11-17) | (18-22) | (6-17) | (6-22) |
| Guyana | 1970 | | (4-5) | (6-11) | (12-16) | (17-21) | (6-16) | (6-21) |
| | | MF | ... | 98 | 64 | 2 | 84 | 65 |
| | | M | ... | 100 | 64 | 3 | 85 | 66 |
| | | F | ... | 96 | 65 | 0.6 | 83 | 64 |
| | 1975 | | | | | | | |
| | | MF | ... | 99 | 72 | 4 | 88 | 66 |
| | | M | ... | 101 | 72 | 5 | 88 | 67 |
| | | F | ... | 98 | 73 | 2 | 87 | 65 |

II.8   Gross enrolment ratios by level of education
Taux bruts de scolarisation par niveau d'enseignement
Tasas brutas de escolarización por nivel de enseñanza

| Country<br>Pays<br>País | Year<br>Année<br>Año | Sex<br>Sexe<br>Sexo | Gross enrolment ratios / Taux bruts de scolarisation / Tasas brutas de escolarización (%) | | | | | |
|---|---|---|---|---|---|---|---|---|
| | | | Pre-primary<br>Préprimaire<br>Preprimaria | Primary<br>Primaire<br>Primaria | Secondary<br>Secondaire<br>Secundaria | Tertiary<br>Supérieur<br>Superior | Primary and secondary<br>Primaire et secondaire<br>Primaria y secundaria | Primary, secondary and tertiary<br>Primaire, secondaire et supérieur<br>Primaria, secundaria y superior |
| Guyana (cont) | 1980 | | | | | | | |
| | | MF | 67 | 102 | 77 | 3 | 91 | 66 |
| | | M | 67 | 103 | 76 | 3 | 91 | 67 |
| | | F | 67 | 100 | 77 | 2 | 90 | 65 |
| | 1985 | | | | | | | |
| | | MF | 71 | 103 | 76 | 2 | 90 | 63 |
| | | M | 70 | 104 | 73 | 3 | 89 | 62 |
| | | F | 72 | 101 | 78 | 2 | 90 | 63 |
| | 1990 | | | | | | | |
| | | MF | 69 | 98 | 83 | ... | 91 | ... |
| | | M | 68 | 98 | 81 | ... | 91 | ... |
| | | F | 70 | 97 | 86 | ... | 92 | ... |
| | 1991 | | | | | | | |
| | | MF | 70 | 94 | 79 | ... | 87 | ... |
| | | M | 68 | 95 | 77 | ... | 87 | ... |
| | | F | 71 | 93 | 81 | ... | 88 | |
| | 1992 | | | | | | | |
| | | MF | 79 | 92 | 76 | ... | 85 | ... |
| | | M | 79 | 93 | 73 | ... | 84 | ... |
| | | F | 79 | 92 | 79 | ... | 86 | ... |
| | 1993 | | | | | | | |
| | | MF | 81 | 92 | 76 | 9 | 85 | 62 |
| | | M | 81 | 92 | 70 | 10 | 83 | 60 |
| | | F | 82 | 92 | 82 | 8 | 88 | 63 |
| | 1994 | | | | | | | |
| | | MF | 85 | 94 | 76 | 9 | 86 | 63 |
| | | M | 85 | 94 | 69 | 9 | 83 | 61 |
| | | F | 84 | 93 | 84 | 8 | 89 | 65 |
| | 1995 | | | | | | | |
| | | MF | 84 | 95 | 75 | 10 | 86 | 64 |
| | | M | 84 | 95 | 73 | 10 | 85 | 63 |
| | | F | 84 | 94 | 78 | 9 | 87 | 64 |
| | 1996 | | | | | | | |
| | | MF | 89 | 96 | 73 | 11 | 86 | 64 |
| | | M | 89 | 97 | 71 | 11 | 85 | 64 |
| | | F | 89 | 96 | 76 | 12 | 87 | 65 |
| Paraguay | 1970 | | (6-6) | (7-12) | (13-18) | (19-23) | (7-18) | (7-23) |
| | | MF | 11 | 108 | 16 | 4 | 65 | 52 |
| | | M | 10 | 113 | 16 | 5 | 67 | 54 |
| | | F | 11 | 104 | 16 | 4 | 62 | 50 |
| | 1975 | | | | | | | |
| | | MF | ... | 103 | 20 | 7 | 65 | 50 |
| | | M | ... | 106 | 20 | ... | 66 | ... |
| | | F | ... | 99 | 20 | ... | 63 | ... |
| | 1980 | | | | | | | |
| | | MF | 12 | 106 | 27 | 9 | 69 | 54 |
| | | M | ... | 109 | ... | ... | ... | ... |
| | | F | ... | 102 | ... | ... | ... | ... |
| | 1985 | | | | | | | |
| | | MF | 19 | 105 | 31 | 9 | 71 | 55 |
| | | M | 19 | 108 | 32 | ... | 72 | ... |
| | | F | 19 | 102 | 31 | ... | 69 | ... |
| | 1990 | | | | | | | |
| | | MF | 27 | 105 | 31 | 8 | 72 | 56 |
| | | M | 27 | 107 | 30 | 9 | 73 | 57 |
| | | F | 28 | 103 | 32 | 8 | 71 | 55 |
| | 1991 | | | | | | | |
| | | MF | 30 | 106 | 31 | ... | 73 | ... |
| | | M | 30 | 108 | 30 | ... | 73 | ... |
| | | F | 31 | 105 | 32 | ... | 72 | ... |
| | 1992 | | | | | | | |
| | | MF | 32 | 107 | 34 | ... | 75 | ... |
| | | M | 31 | 108 | 34 | ... | 75 | ... |
| | | F | 32 | 105 | 35 | ... | 74 | ... |

Gross enrolment ratios by level of education
Taux bruts de scolarisation par niveau d'enseignement
Tasas brutas de escolarización por nivel de enseñanza

II.8

| Country<br>Pays<br>País | Year<br>Année<br>Año | Sex<br>Sexe<br>Sexo | Gross enrolment ratios / Taux bruts de scolarisation / Tasas brutas de escolarización<br>(%) | | | | | |
|---|---|---|---|---|---|---|---|---|
| | | | Pre-primary<br>Préprimaire<br>Preprimaria | Primary<br>Primaire<br>Primaria | Secondary<br>Secondaire<br>Secundaria | Tertiary<br>Supérieur<br>Superior | Primary and secondary<br>Primaire et secondaire<br>Primaria y secundaria | Primary, secondary and tertiary<br>Primaire, secondaire et supérieur<br>Primaria, secundaria y superior |
| Paraguay (cont) | 1993 | MF | 41 | 110 | 37 | 10 | 78 | 61 |
| | | M | 41 | 112 | 36 | 10 | 78 | 62 |
| | | F | 42 | 108 | 38 | 10 | 77 | 61 |
| | 1994 | | (5-5) | (6-11) | (12-17) | (18-22) | (6-17) | (6-22) |
| | | MF | 38 | 109 | 38 | 10 | 77 | 61 |
| | | M | 37 | 110 | 38 | ... | 78 | ... |
| | | F | 38 | 107 | 39 | ... | 77 | ... |
| | 1995 | MF | 46 | 110 | 41 | 10 | 79 | 63 |
| | | M | 45 | 111 | 40 | ... | 79 | ... |
| | | F | 46 | 108 | 43 | ... | 78 | ... |
| | 1996 | MF | 53 | 112 | 43 | 10 | 80 | 64 |
| | | M | 52 | 113 | 42 | 10 | 81 | 64 |
| | | F | 54 | 110 | 45 | 11 | 80 | 64 |
| | 1997 | MF | 61 | 111 | 47 | ... | 81 | ... |
| | | M | 51 | 112 | 46 | ... | 82 | ... |
| | | F | 71 | 109 | 48 | ... | 81 | ... |
| Peru | 1970 | | (3-5) | (6-11) | (12-17) | (18-22) | (6-17) | (6-22) |
| | | MF | 6 | 107 | 31 | 11 | 73 | 58 |
| | | M | 6 | 114 | 35 | 14 | 78 | 63 |
| | | F | 6 | 99 | 27 | 7 | 67 | 53 |
| | 1975 | | (3-5) | (6-11) | (12-16) | (17-21) | (6-16) | (6-21) |
| | | MF | 12 | 114 | 46 | 13 | 85 | 67 |
| | | M | 12 | ... | 50 | 18 | ... | ... |
| | | F | 12 | ... | 41 | 9 | ... | ... |
| | 1980 | MF | 15 | 114 | 59 | 17 | 90 | 71 |
| | | M | 14 | 117 | 63 | 22 | 94 | 75 |
| | | F | 15 | 111 | 54 | 12 | 87 | 67 |
| | 1985 | MF | 21 | 120 | 63 | 22 | 96 | 76 |
| | | M | 20 | 123 | 66 | ... | 99 | ... |
| | | F | 21 | 118 | 60 | ... | 93 | ... |
| | 1990 | MF | 30 | 118 | 67 | 30 | 90 | 78 |
| | 1991 | MF | 31 | 118 | 67 | 32 | 95 | 78 |
| | | M | 30 | 119 | 69 | ... | 97 | ... |
| | | F | 31 | 116 | 64 | ... | 93 | ... |
| | 1992 | MF | 31 | 117 | 66 | 31 | 94 | 76 |
| | 1993 | MF | 33 | 118 | 66 | 28 | 95 | 76 |
| | 1994 | MF | 35 | 121 | 69 | 27 | 98 | 77 |
| | 1995 | MF | 36 | 123 | 70 | 27 | 99 | 78 |
| | | M | 36 | 125 | 72 | ... | 101 | ... |
| | | F | 37 | 121 | 67 | ... | 97 | ... |
| | 1996 | MF | 39 | 123 | 72 | 26 | 100 | 78 |
| | 1997 | MF | 40 | 123 | 72 | 26 | 100 | 78 |
| Suriname (1) | | | (4-5) | (6-11) | (12-18) | (19-23) | (6-18) | (6-23) |
| Uruguay | 1970 | | (2-5) | (6-11) | (12-17) | (18-22) | (6-17) | (6-22) |
| | | MF | 15 | 112 | 59 | ... | 87 | ... |
| | | M | 15 | 115 | 54 | ... | 86 | ... |
| | | F | 15 | 109 | 63 | ... | 87 | ... |

II.8    Gross enrolment ratios by level of education
Taux bruts de scolarisation par niveau d'enseignement
Tasas brutas de escolarización por nivel de enseñanza

| Country<br><br>Pays<br><br>País | Year<br><br>Année<br><br>Año | Sex<br><br>Sexe<br><br>Sexo | Gross enrolment ratios / Taux bruts de scolarisation / Tasas brutas de escolarización<br>(%) | | | | | |
|---|---|---|---|---|---|---|---|---|
| | | | Pre-primary<br><br>Préprimaire<br><br>Preprimaria | Primary<br><br>Primaire<br><br>Primaria | Secondary<br><br>Secondaire<br><br>Secundaria | Tertiary<br><br>Supérieur<br><br>Superior | Primary and secondary<br><br>Primaire et secondaire<br><br>Primaria y secundaria | Primary, secondary and tertiary<br>Primaire, secondaire et supérieur<br>Primaria, secundaria y superior |
| Uruguay (cont) | 1975 | | | | | | | |
| | | MF | 19 | 107 | 61 | 15 | 84 | 66 |
| | | M | ... | 107 | ... | 17 | ... | ... |
| | | F | ... | 106 | ... | 13 | ... | ... |
| | 1980 | | | | | | | |
| | | MF | 19 | 107 | 62 | 17 | 85 | 66 |
| | | M | ... | 107 | 61 | 16 | 85 | 66 |
| | | F | ... | 107 | 62 | 17 | 85 | 66 |
| | 1985 | | | | | | | |
| | | MF | 25 | 107 | 72 | ... | 90 | ... |
| | | M | 25 | 107 | ... | ... | ... | ... |
| | | F | 25 | 106 | ... | ... | ... | ... |
| | 1990 | | (3-5) | (6-11) | (12-17) | (18-22) | (6-17) | (6-22) |
| | | MF | 43 | 109 | 81 | 30 | 95 | 77 |
| | | M | 42 | 109 | ... | ... | ... | ... |
| | | F | 43 | 108 | ... | ... | ... | ... |
| | 1991 | | | | | | | |
| | | MF | 43 | 108 | 84 | 30 | 96 | 78 |
| | | M | 43 | 108 | ... | ... | ... | ... |
| | | F | 43 | 107 | ... | ... | ... | ... |
| | 1992 | | | | | | | |
| | | MF | 43 | 107 | 83 | 27 | 95 | 76 |
| | | M | 42 | 108 | ... | ... | ... | ... |
| | | F | 44 | 106 | ... | ... | ... | ... |
| | 1993 | | | | | | | |
| | | MF | 42 | 108 | 82 | ... | 94 | ... |
| | | M | 41 | 108 | ... | ... | ... | ... |
| | | F | 42 | 107 | ... | ... | ... | ... |
| | 1994 | | | | | | | |
| | | MF | 42 | 107 | 82 | ... | 94 | ... |
| | | M | 43 | 108 | 75 | ... | 91 | ... |
| | | F | 42 | 107 | 89 | ... | 98 | ... |
| | 1995 | | | | | | | |
| | | MF | 42 | 108 | 82 | ... | 95 | ... |
| | | M | 41 | 109 | 75 | ... | 92 | ... |
| | | F | 43 | 107 | 90 | ... | 99 | ... |
| | 1996 | | | | | | | |
| | | MF | 45 | 109 | 85 | 30 | 97 | 77 |
| | | M | 44 | 109 | ... | ... | ... | ... |
| | | F | 46 | 108 | ... | ... | ... | ... |
| Venezuela | 1970 | | (4-6) | (7-12) | (13-17) | (18-22) | (7-17) | (7-22) |
| | | MF | 5 | 97 | 35 | 10 | 72 | 57 |
| | | M | 5 | 96 | 34 | 12 | 71 | 56 |
| | | F | 5 | 98 | 36 | 8 | 73 | 57 |
| | 1975 | | | | | | | |
| | | MF | 20 | 98 | 44 | 17 | 76 | 61 |
| | | M | 19 | 97 | 41 | ... | 74 | ... |
| | | F | 20 | 99 | 47 | ... | 77 | ... |
| | 1980 | | (4-6) | (7-15) | (16-18) | (19-23) | (7-18) | (7-23) |
| | | MF | 34 | 93 | 21 | 21 | 76 | 62 |
| | | M | ... | 91 | 18 | ... | 74 | ... |
| | | F | ... | 95 | 25 | ... | 79 | ... |
| | 1985 | | | | | | | |
| | | MF | 39 | 97 | 24 | 25 | 80 | 65 |
| | | M | 39 | 95 | 21 | 29 | 78 | 65 |
| | | F | 40 | 98 | 27 | 21 | 82 | 65 |
| | 1990 | | (3-5) | (6-14) | (15-16) | (17-21) | (6-16) | (6-21) |
| | | MF | 41 | 96 | 35 | 29 | 86 | 70 |
| | | M | 40 | 94 | 29 | ... | 84 | ... |
| | | F | 41 | 97 | 40 | ... | 88 | ... |
| | 1991 | | | | | | | |
| | | MF | 43 | 97 | 35 | 28 | 87 | 71 |
| | | M | 42 | 96 | 29 | ... | 85 | ... |
| | | F | 43 | 98 | 40 | ... | 89 | ... |

Gross enrolment ratios by level of education  II.8
Taux bruts de scolarisation par niveau d'enseignement
Tasas brutas de escolarización por nivel de enseñanza

| Country / Pays / País | Year / Année / Año | Sex / Sexe / Sexo | Gross enrolment ratios / Taux bruts de scolarisation / Tasas brutas de escolarización (%) | | | | | |
|---|---|---|---|---|---|---|---|---|
| | | | Pre-primary / Préprimaire / Preprimaria | Primary / Primaire / Primaria | Secondary / Secondaire / Secundaria | Tertiary / Supérieur / Superior | Primary and secondary / Primaire et secondaire / Primaria y secundaria | Primary, secondary and tertiary / Primaire, secondaire et supérieur / Primaria, secundaria y superior |
| Venezuela (cont) | 1992 | | | | | | | |
| | | MF | 43 | 96 | 35 | ... | 86 | ... |
| | | M | 42 | 95 | 29 | ... | 84 | ... |
| | | F | 43 | 97 | 41 | ... | 88 | ... |
| | 1993 | | | | | | | |
| | | MF | 43 | 94 | 35 | ... | 85 | ... |
| | | M | 42 | 93 | 29 | ... | 83 | ... |
| | | F | 43 | 96 | 41 | ... | 87 | ... |
| | 1994 | | | | | | | |
| | | MF | 44 | 94 | 35 | ... | 84 | ... |
| | | M | 44 | 92 | 29 | ... | 81 | ... |
| | | F | 44 | 96 | 41 | ... | 86 | ... |
| | 1995 | | | | | | | |
| | | MF | 42 | 90 | 35 | ... | 80 | ... |
| | | M | 42 | 88 | 29 | ... | 78 | ... |
| | | F | 42 | 91 | 41 | ... | 83 | ... |
| | 1996 | | | | | | | |
| | | MF | 44 | 91 | 40 | ... | 83 | ... |
| | | M | 44 | 00 | 33 | ... | 80 | ... |
| | | F | 45 | 93 | 46 | ... | 85 | ... |
| **Asia** | | | | | | | | |
| Afghanistan | 1970 | | (3-6) | (7-12) | (13-18) | (19-23) | (7-18) | (7-23) |
| | | MF | 0.1 | 27 | 7 | 0.6 | 18 | 14 |
| | | M | 0.1 | 45 | 13 | 1 | 31 | 23 |
| | | F | 0.1 | 8 | 2 | 0.2 | 5 | 4 |
| | 1975 | | (3-5) | (6-13) | (14-17) | (18-22) | (6-17) | (6-22) |
| | | MF | 0.1 | 25 | 7 | 1 | 20 | 16 |
| | | M | 0.1 | 41 | 13 | 2 | 33 | 26 |
| | | F | 0.1 | 8 | 2 | 0.3 | 6 | 5 |
| | 1980 | | (3-6) | (7-14) | (15-18) | (19-23) | (7-18) | (7-23) |
| | | MF | 0.2 | 34 | 10 | ... | 27 | ... |
| | | M | 0.2 | 54 | 16 | ... | 43 | ... |
| | | F | 0.2 | 12 | 4 | ... | 10 | ... |
| | 1985 | | | | | | | |
| | | MF | 1 | 20 | 8 | ... | 16 | ... |
| | | M | 1 | 27 | 11 | ... | 22 | ... |
| | | F | 1 | 13 | 5 | ... | 11 | ... |
| | 1990 | | (3-6) | (7-12) | (13-18) | (19-23) | (7-18) | (7-23) |
| | | MF | ... | 27 | 9 | 2 | 19 | 15 |
| | | M | ... | 35 | ... | 2 | ... | ... |
| | | F | ... | 19 | ... | 1 | ... | ... |
| | 1991 | | | | | | | |
| | | MF | ... | 27 | 13 | ... | 20 | ... |
| | | M | ... | 34 | 18 | ... | 26 | ... |
| | | F | ... | 19 | 9 | ... | 14 | ... |
| | 1992 | | | | | | | |
| | | MF | ... | 29 | 14 | ... | 22 | ... |
| | | M | ... | 40 | 20 | ... | 31 | ... |
| | | F | ... | 17 | 8 | ... | 13 | ... |
| | 1993 | | | | | | | |
| | | MF | ... | 31 | 15 | ... | 24 | ... |
| | | M | ... | 46 | 21 | ... | 34 | ... |
| | | F | ... | 16 | 8 | ... | 12 | ... |
| | 1994 | | | | | | | |
| | | MF | ... | 45 | 22 | ... | 34 | ... |
| | | M | ... | 59 | 34 | ... | 47 | ... |
| | | F | ... | 29 | 9 | ... | 20 | ... |
| | 1995 | | | | | | | |
| | | MF | ... | 49 | 22 | ... | 36 | ... |
| | | M | ... | 64 | 32 | ... | 49 | ... |
| | | F | ... | 32 | 11 | ... | 22 | ... |
| | 1996 | | | | | | | |
| | | MF | ... | ... | 22 | ... | ... | ... |
| | | M | ... | ... | 32 | ... | ... | ... |
| | | F | ... | ... | 12 | ... | ... | ... |

II.8  Gross enrolment ratios by level of education
Taux bruts de scolarisation par niveau d'enseignement
Tasas brutas de escolarización por nivel de enseñanza

| Country / Pays / País | Year / Année / Año | Sex / Sexe / Sexo | Gross enrolment ratios / Taux bruts de scolarisation / Tasas brutas de escolarización (%) | | | | | |
| --- | --- | --- | --- | --- | --- | --- | --- | --- |
| | | | Pre-primary / Préprimaire / Preprimaria | Primary / Primaire / Primaria | Secondary / Secondaire / Secundaria | Tertiary / Supérieur / Superior | Primary and secondary / Primaire et secondaire / Primaria y secundaria | Primary, secondary and tertiary / Primaire, secondaire et supérieur / Primaria, secundaria y superior |
| Armenia | 1980 | | (3-6) | (7-9) | (10-16) | (17-21) | (7-16) | (7-21) |
| | | MF | 54 | ... | ... | ... | ... | ... |
| | 1985 | MF | 54 | ... | ... | ... | ... | ... |
| | 1990 | MF | 37 | ... | ... | ... | ... | ... |
| | 1991 | MF | 37 | ... | ... | ... | ... | ... |
| | 1992 | MF | 34 | ... | ... | ... | ... | ... |
| | 1993 | | (3-6) | (7-10) | (11-16) | (17-21) | (7-16) | (7-21) |
| | | MF | 31 | 89 | 88 | ... | 88 | ... |
| | | M | ... | 87 | 85 | ... | 86 | ... |
| | | F | ... | 91 | 91 | ... | 91 | ... |
| | 1994 | MF | 28 | 86 | 85 | ... | 85 | ... |
| | | M | ... | ... | 84 | ... | ... | ... |
| | | F | ... | ... | 86 | ... | ... | ... |
| | 1995 | MF | 23 | 84 | 80 | 14 | 82 | 62 |
| | | M | ... | ... | 89 | 13 | ... | ... |
| | | F | ... | ... | 71 | 14 | ... | ... |
| | 1996 | MF | 26 | 87 | 90 | 12 | 89 | 66 |
| | | M | 20 | ... | 100 | 11 | ... | ... |
| | | F | 32 | ... | 79 | 14 | ... | ... |
| Azerbaijan | 1980 | | (3-6) | (7-9) | (10-16) | (17-21) | (7-16) | (7-21) |
| | | MF | 20 | 115 | 95 | 24 | 100 | 74 |
| | | M | 23 | ... | 96 | 27 | ... | ... |
| | | F | 18 | ... | 93 | 21 | ... | ... |
| | 1985 | MF | 21 | 118 | 97 | 24 | 103 | 76 |
| | | M | 23 | ... | 99 | 26 | ... | ... |
| | | F | 19 | ... | 95 | 23 | ... | ... |
| | 1990 | MF | 20 | 114 | 90 | 24 | 98 | 74 |
| | | M | 21 | 114 | 90 | 29 | 98 | 75 |
| | | F | 18 | 113 | 90 | 20 | 97 | 73 |
| | 1991 | MF | 19 | 114 | 90 | 25 | 98 | 75 |
| | | M | 20 | 114 | 90 | 30 | 98 | 76 |
| | | F | 17 | 114 | 90 | 20 | 98 | 73 |
| | 1992 | MF | 18 | 115 | 89 | 22 | 98 | 74 |
| | | M | 19 | 115 | 90 | 26 | 98 | 76 |
| | | F | 16 | 114 | 89 | 19 | 97 | 73 |
| | 1993 | MF | 18 | 118 | 87 | 20 | 97 | 73 |
| | | M | 19 | 121 | 88 | 22 | 99 | 75 |
| | | F | 16 | 115 | 85 | 17 | 95 | 71 |
| | 1994 | MF | 16 | 122 | 85 | 18 | 97 | 74 |
| | | M | 17 | 115 | 83 | 19 | 94 | 71 |
| | | F | 15 | 129 | 88 | 18 | 101 | 76 |
| | 1995 | | (3-5) | (6-9) | (10-16) | (17-21) | (6-16) | (6-21) |
| | | MF | 20 | 103 | 77 | 18 | 87 | 68 |
| | | M | 22 | 100 | 74 | 18 | 84 | 66 |
| | | F | 19 | 108 | 80 | 18 | 90 | 71 |
| | 1996 | MF | 19 | 106 | 77 | 17 | 88 | 69 |
| | | M | 21 | 108 | 73 | 17 | 87 | 67 |
| | | F | 18 | 105 | 81 | 18 | 90 | 70 |

Gross enrolment ratios by level of education **II.8**
Taux bruts de scolarisation par niveau d'enseignement
Tasas brutas de escolarización por nivel de enseñanza

| Country / Pays / País | Year / Année / Año | Sex / Sexe / Sexo | Gross enrolment ratios / Taux bruts de scolarisation / Tasas brutas de escolarización (%) | | | | | |
|---|---|---|---|---|---|---|---|---|
| | | | Pre-primary / Préprimaire / Preprimaria | Primary / Primaire / Primaria | Secondary / Secondaire / Secundaria | Tertiary / Supérieur / Superior | Primary and secondary / Primaire et secondaire / Primaria y secundaria | Primary, secondary and tertiary / Primaire, secondaire et supérieur / Primaria, secundaria y superior |
| **Bahrain** | 1970 | | (3-5) | (6-11) | (12-16) | (17-21) | (6-16) | (6-21) |
| | | MF | 5 | 98 | 51 | 1 | 79 | 61 |
| | | M | ... | 113 | 60 | 1 | 91 | 69 |
| | | F | ... | 84 | 43 | 2 | 67 | 53 |
| | 1975 | | | | | | | |
| | | MF | 8 | 96 | 52 | 2 | 77 | 55 |
| | | M | 8 | 106 | 51 | 2 | 82 | 57 |
| | | F | 8 | 85 | 54 | 3 | 72 | 54 |
| | 1980 | | (3-5) | (6-11) | (12-17) | (18-22) | (6-17) | (6-22) |
| | | MF | 15 | 104 | 64 | 5 | 85 | 61 |
| | | M | 15 | 111 | 70 | 5 | 92 | 64 |
| | | F | 14 | 98 | 58 | 5 | 79 | 58 |
| | 1985 | | | | | | | |
| | | MF | 27 | 113 | 97 | 13 | 106 | 81 |
| | | M | 27 | 110 | 98 | 10 | 104 | 79 |
| | | F | 27 | 116 | 97 | 16 | 107 | 84 |
| | 1990 | | | | | | | |
| | | MF | 27 | 110 | 100 | 18 | 106 | 82 |
| | | M | 27 | 110 | 98 | 15 | 105 | 81 |
| | | F | 28 | 110 | 101 | 21 | 106 | 84 |
| | 1991 | | | | | | | |
| | | MF | 30 | 108 | 98 | 18 | 103 | 81 |
| | | M | 30 | 108 | 96 | 15 | 103 | 79 |
| | | F | 30 | 108 | 100 | 22 | 104 | 83 |
| | 1992 | | | | | | | |
| | | MF | 33 | 109 | 99 | 20 | 105 | 83 |
| | | M | 33 | 108 | 97 | 17 | 103 | 81 |
| | | F | 33 | 110 | 101 | 24 | 106 | 85 |
| | 1993 | | | | | | | |
| | | MF | 34 | 110 | 99 | 20 | 105 | 84 |
| | | M | 34 | 108 | 98 | 16 | 104 | 82 |
| | | F | 33 | 111 | 101 | 24 | 106 | 86 |
| | 1994 | | | | | | | |
| | | MF | 34 | 110 | 98 | ... | 105 | ... |
| | | M | 34 | 109 | 97 | ... | 103 | ... |
| | | F | 33 | 112 | 100 | ... | 106 | ... |
| | 1995 | | | | | | | |
| | | MF | 33 | 108 | 97 | ... | 103 | ... |
| | | M | 34 | 107 | 95 | ... | 101 | ... |
| | | F | 32 | 109 | 99 | ... | 105 | ... |
| | 1996 | | | | | | | |
| | | MF | 33 | 106 | 94 | ... | 100 | ... |
| | | M | 33 | 105 | 91 | ... | 98 | ... |
| | | F | 32 | 106 | 98 | ... | 102 | ... |
| **Bangladesh** | 1970 | | (4-4) | (5-9) | (10-14) | (15-19) | (5-14) | (5-19) |
| | | MF | ... | 54 | ... | 2 | ... | ... |
| | | M | ... | 72 | ... | 3 | ... | ... |
| | | F | ... | 35 | ... | 0.4 | ... | ... |
| | 1975 | | (4-4) | (5-9) | (10-16) | (17-21) | (5-16) | (5-21) |
| | | MF | ... | 73 | 19 | 2 | 44 | 35 |
| | | M | ... | 95 | ... | 4 | ... | ... |
| | | F | ... | 51 | ... | 0.5 | ... | ... |
| | 1980 | | | | | | | |
| | | MF | ... | 61 | 18 | 3 | 38 | 30 |
| | | M | ... | 75 | 26 | 5 | 49 | 39 |
| | | F | ... | 46 | 9 | 0.8 | 26 | 21 |
| | 1985 | | (5-5) | (6-10) | (11-17) | (18-22) | (6-17) | (6-22) |
| | | MF | ... | 62 | 19 | 5 | 39 | 31 |
| | | M | ... | 72 | 27 | 8 | 48 | 39 |
| | | F | ... | 52 | 11 | 2 | 30 | 23 |
| | 1990 | | | | | | | |
| | | MF | ... | 72 | 19 | 4 | 44 | 35 |
| | | M | ... | 77 | 25 | 7 | 49 | 40 |
| | | F | ... | 66 | 13 | 1 | 38 | 29 |

II.8 Gross enrolment ratios by level of education
Taux bruts de scolarisation par niveau d'enseignement
Tasas brutas de escolarización por nivel de enseñanza

| Country<br><br>Pays<br><br>País | Year<br><br>Année<br><br>Año | Sex<br><br>Sexe<br><br>Sexo | Gross enrolment ratios / Taux bruts de scolarisation / Tasas brutas de escolarización (%) | | | | | |
|---|---|---|---|---|---|---|---|---|
| | | | Pre-primary<br><br>Préprimaire<br><br>Preprimaria | Primary<br><br>Primaire<br><br>Primaria | Secondary<br><br>Secondaire<br><br>Secundaria | Tertiary<br><br>Supérieur<br><br>Superior | Primary and secondary<br><br>Primaire et secondaire<br><br>Primaria y secundaria | Primary, secondary and tertiary<br><br>Primaire, secondaire et supérieur<br><br>Primaria, secundaria y superior |
| Bhutan (1) | | | (5-5) | (6-12) | (13-16) | (17-21) | (6-16) | (6-21) |
| Brunei Darussalam | 1980 | | (3-5) | (6-11) | (12-18) | (19-23) | (6-18) | (6-23) |
| | | MF | 42 | 109 | 61 | 0.6 | 84 | 61 |
| | | M | 42 | 111 | 59 | 0.6 | 85 | 60 |
| | | F | 42 | 106 | 63 | 0.7 | 84 | 62 |
| | 1985 | | | | | | | |
| | | MF | 44 | 106 | 65 | 3 | 86 | 66 |
| | | M | 44 | 107 | 63 | 2 | 85 | 65 |
| | | F | 43 | 105 | 67 | 3 | 86 | 67 |
| | 1990 | | | | | | | |
| | | MF | 47 | 115 | 69 | ... | 92 | ... |
| | | M | 48 | 119 | 66 | ... | 93 | ... |
| | | F | 46 | 112 | 71 | ... | 92 | ... |
| | 1991 | | | | | | | |
| | | MF | 48 | 112 | 77 | ... | 95 | ... |
| | | M | 49 | 116 | 73 | ... | 95 | ... |
| | | F | 46 | 109 | 80 | ... | 95 | ... |
| | 1992 | | | | | | | |
| | | MF | 49 | 111 | 77 | 6 | 95 | 72 |
| | | M | 50 | 114 | 73 | 5 | 94 | 71 |
| | | F | 48 | 109 | 82 | 7 | 96 | 72 |
| | 1993 | | | | | | | |
| | | MF | 57 | 111 | 79 | ... | 95 | ... |
| | | M | 56 | 113 | 75 | ... | 94 | ... |
| | | F | 58 | 109 | 83 | ... | 96 | ... |
| | 1994 | | | | | | | |
| | | MF | 51 | 110 | 78 | ... | 94 | ... |
| | | M | 51 | 113 | 74 | ... | 94 | ... |
| | | F | 51 | 108 | 81 | ... | 95 | ... |
| | 1995 | | | | | | | |
| | | MF | 51 | 108 | 80 | 7 | 94 | 74 |
| | | M | 51 | 111 | 76 | 5 | 94 | 73 |
| | | F | 52 | 105 | 85 | 8 | 95 | 75 |
| | 1996 | | | | | | | |
| | | MF | 53 | 106 | 77 | ... | 92 | ... |
| | | M | 53 | 109 | 72 | ... | 90 | ... |
| | | F | 53 | 104 | 82 | ... | 93 | ... |
| Cambodia | 1970 | | (5-5) | (6-11) | (12-18) | (19-23) | (6-18) | (6-23) |
| | | MF | ... | 30 | 8 | 1 | 20 | 16 |
| | | M | ... | 35 | 11 | ... | 23 | ... |
| | | F | ... | 26 | 5 | ... | 16 | ... |
| | 1990 | | (3-5) | (6-10) | (11-16) | (17-21) | (6-16) | (6-21) |
| | | MF | 5 | 121 | 32 | 0.7 | 83 | 56 |
| | | M | 6 | ... | 45 | ... | ... | ... |
| | | F | 5 | ... | 19 | ... | ... | ... |
| | 1993 | | | | | | | |
| | | MF | 6 | 121 | 30 | 2 | 82 | 62 |
| | | M | 5 | 133 | 38 | 3 | 92 | 70 |
| | | F | 6 | 110 | 22 | 0.5 | 72 | 54 |
| | 1994 | | | | | | | |
| | | MF | 5 | 122 | 28 | 2 | 80 | 63 |
| | | M | 5 | 135 | 35 | 3 | 90 | 71 |
| | | F | 5 | 110 | 21 | 0.5 | 70 | 54 |
| | 1995 | | | | | | | |
| | | MF | 5 | 126 | 26 | 2 | 80 | 64 |
| | | M | 5 | 138 | 33 | 3 | 90 | 72 |
| | | F | 5 | 113 | 20 | 0.6 | 70 | 56 |
| | 1996 | | (3-5) | (6-11) | (12-17) | (18-22) | (6-17) | (6-22) |
| | | MF | 5 | 110 | 29 | 1 | 77 | 61 |
| | | M | 5 | 119 | 37 | 2 | 86 | 69 |
| | | F | 5 | 100 | 21 | 0.4 | 68 | 54 |

Gross enrolment ratios by level of education
Taux bruts de scolarisation par niveau d'enseignement
Tasas brutas de escolarización por nivel de enseñanza

II.8

| Country Pays País | Year Année Año | Sex Sexe Sexo | Gross enrolment ratios / Taux bruts de scolarisation / Tasas brutas de escolarización (%) | | | | | |
|---|---|---|---|---|---|---|---|---|
| | | | Pre-primary Préprimaire Preprimaria | Primary Primaire Primaria | Secondary Secondaire Secundaria | Tertiary Supérieur Superior | Primary and secondary Primaire et secondaire Primaria y secundaria | Primary, secondary and tertiary Primaire, secondaire et supérieur Primaria, secundaria y superior |
| Cambodia (cont) | 1997 | | 5 | 113 | 24 | 1 | 76 | 61 |
| | | MF | 5 | 123 | 31 | 2 | 85 | 68 |
| | | M | 5 | 104 | 17 | 0.5 | 67 | 54 |
| | | F | | | | | | |
| China | 1970 | | (3-6) | (7-12) | (13-18) | (19-23) | (7-18) | (7-23) |
| | | MF | ... | 91 | 24 | 0.1 | 59 | 44 |
| | | M | ... | ... | 32 | ... | ... | ... |
| | | F | ... | ... | 16 | ... | ... | ... |
| | 1975 | | (3-6) | (7-11) | (12-16) | (17-21) | (7-16) | (7-21) |
| | | MF | 6 | 122 | 46 | 0.6 | 88 | 63 |
| | | M | ... | 129 | 54 | 0.7 | 96 | 69 |
| | | F | ... | 114 | 38 | 0.4 | 80 | 58 |
| | 1980 | | | | | | | |
| | | MF | 13 | 113 | 46 | 2 | 80 | 58 |
| | | M | ... | 121 | 54 | 3 | 88 | 64 |
| | | F | ... | 104 | 37 | 0.8 | 71 | 52 |
| | 1985 | | | | | | | |
| | | MF | 20 | 123 | 40 | 3 | 78 | 52 |
| | | M | 20 | 132 | 46 | 4 | 85 | 58 |
| | | F | 19 | 114 | 33 | 2 | 70 | 46 |
| | 1990 | | | | | | | |
| | | MF | 23 | 125 | 49 | 3 | 85 | 53 |
| | | M | 23 | 130 | 55 | 4 | 91 | 58 |
| | | F | 23 | 120 | 42 | 2 | 79 | 49 |
| | 1991 | | | | | | | |
| | | MF | 25 | 122 | 52 | 3 | 86 | 54 |
| | | M | 25 | 126 | 58 | 4 | 91 | 58 |
| | | F | 24 | 119 | 45 | 2 | 81 | 51 |
| | 1992 | | | | | | | |
| | | MF | 26 | 119 | 55 | 3 | 87 | 56 |
| | | M | 26 | 122 | 61 | 4 | 92 | 59 |
| | | F | 26 | 116 | 49 | 2 | 82 | 52 |
| | 1993 | | | | | | | |
| | | MF | 27 | 117 | 57 | 4 | 88 | 57 |
| | | M | 27 | 119 | 62 | 5 | 92 | 60 |
| | | F | 27 | 115 | 52 | 3 | 84 | 54 |
| | 1994 | | | | | | | |
| | | MF | 28 | 117 | 61 | 5 | 91 | 61 |
| | | M | 28 | 118 | 65 | ... | 94 | ... |
| | | F | 27 | 115 | 56 | ... | 88 | ... |
| | 1995 | | | | | | | |
| | | MF | 29 | 118 | 66 | 5 | 94 | 64 |
| | | M | 29 | 118 | 69 | ... | 96 | ... |
| | | F | 28 | 117 | 62 | ... | 91 | ... |
| | 1996 | | | | | | | |
| | | MF | 29 | 120 | 69 | 6 | 96 | 67 |
| | | M | 29 | 120 | 72 | 7 | 98 | 69 |
| | | F | 28 | 120 | 65 | 4 | 94 | 64 |
| | 1997 | | | | | | | |
| | | MF | 28 | 123 | 70 | 6 | 98 | 69 |
| | | M | ... | 122 | 74 | ... | 99 | ... |
| | | F | ... | 123 | 66 | ... | 96 | ... |
| China, Hong Kong SAR | 1970 | | (3-5) | (6-11) | (12-18) | (19-23) | (6-18) | (6-23) |
| | | MF | 48 | 117 | 36 | 7 | 76 | 60 |
| | | M | 48 | 118 | 40 | 9 | 79 | 63 |
| | | F | 47 | 115 | 31 | 4 | 73 | 58 |
| | 1975 | | | | | | | |
| | | MF | 73 | 120 | 49 | 10 | 78 | 60 |
| | | M | 74 | 122 | 51 | 14 | 80 | 63 |
| | | F | 72 | 117 | 47 | 5 | 76 | 58 |

II.8    Gross enrolment ratios by level of education
Taux bruts de scolarisation par niveau d'enseignement
Tasas brutas de escolarización por nivel de enseñanza

| Country<br><br>Pays<br><br>País | Year<br><br>Année<br><br>Año | Sex<br><br>Sexe<br><br>Sexo | Gross enrolment ratios / Taux bruts de scolarisation / Tasas brutas de escolarización (%) | | | | | |
|---|---|---|---|---|---|---|---|---|
| | | | Pre-primary<br><br>Préprimaire<br><br>Preprimaria | Primary<br><br>Primaire<br><br>Primaria | Secondary<br><br>Secondaire<br><br>Secundaria | Tertiary<br><br>Supérieur<br><br>Superior | Primary and secondary<br><br>Primaire et secondaire<br><br>Primaria y secundaria | Primary, secondary and tertiary<br><br>Primaire, secondaire et supérieur<br><br>Primaria, secundaria y superior |
| China, Hong Kong SAR (cont) | 1980 | | | | | | | |
| | | MF | 81 | 107 | 64 | 10 | 81 | 59 |
| | | M | 81 | 107 | 63 | 14 | 81 | 59 |
| | | F | 80 | 106 | 65 | 7 | 82 | 58 |
| | 1985 | | | | | | | |
| | | MF | 92 | 105 | 71 | ... | 86 | ... |
| | | M | 92 | 106 | 69 | ... | 85 | ... |
| | | F | 92 | 105 | 73 | ... | 87 | ... |
| | 1990 | | | | | | | |
| | | MF | 80 | 102 | 80 | ... | 90 | ... |
| | | M | 79 | 102 | 78 | ... | 89 | ... |
| | | F | 81 | 103 | 82 | ... | 91 | ... |
| | 1991 | | | | | | | |
| | | MF | 81 | 101 | 82 | 19 | 90 | 70 |
| | | M | 80 | 100 | 80 | 22 | 89 | 70 |
| | | F | 81 | 102 | 84 | 16 | 92 | 70 |
| | 1992 | | | | | | | |
| | | MF | 81 | 99 | 80 | 20 | 89 | 69 |
| | | M | 81 | 98 | 78 | 23 | 87 | 69 |
| | | F | 82 | 99 | 83 | 18 | 90 | 70 |
| | 1993 | | | | | | | |
| | | MF | 82 | 96 | 81 | 22 | 88 | 69 |
| | | M | 82 | 95 | 78 | 24 | 86 | 68 |
| | | F | 83 | 97 | 83 | 20 | 89 | 70 |
| | 1994 | | | | | | | |
| | | MF | 81 | 95 | 80 | ... | 87 | ... |
| | | M | 81 | 94 | 77 | ... | 84 | ... |
| | | F | 82 | 97 | 82 | ... | 89 | ... |
| | 1995 | | | | | | | |
| | | MF | 83 | 94 | 73 | ... | 82 | ... |
| | | M | 82 | 93 | 71 | ... | 80 | ... |
| | | F | 83 | 95 | 76 | ... | 84 | ... |
| Cyprus (3) | 1975 | | (2-5) | (6-11) | (12-17) | (18-22) | (6-17) | (6-22) |
| | | MF | ... | 112 | 78 | 2 | 93 | 74 |
| | | M | ... | 112 | 80 | 2 | 94 | 72 |
| | | F | ... | 112 | 76 | 2 | 92 | 76 |
| | 1980 | | | | | | | |
| | | MF | ... | 104 | 90 | 4 | 97 | 66 |
| | | M | ... | 105 | 90 | 5 | 97 | 70 |
| | | F | ... | 103 | 90 | 3 | 96 | 63 |
| | 1985 | | | | | | | |
| | | MF | ... | 96 | 87 | 6 | 92 | 63 |
| | | M | ... | 96 | 85 | 6 | 91 | 63 |
| | | F | ... | 96 | 89 | 6 | 93 | 64 |
| | 1990 | | | | | | | |
| | | MF | 57 | 105 | 83 | 15 | 95 | 73 |
| | | M | 58 | 105 | 83 | 15 | 95 | 73 |
| | | F | 57 | 105 | 83 | 15 | 94 | 72 |
| | 1991 | | | | | | | |
| | | MF | ... | 103 | 87 | 13 | 95 | 72 |
| | | M | ... | 103 | 86 | 13 | 95 | 76 |
| | | F | ... | 103 | 88 | 13 | 96 | 69 |
| | 1992 | | | | | | | |
| | | MF | ... | 101 | 93 | 14 | 97 | 75 |
| | | M | ... | 101 | 92 | 14 | 97 | 74 |
| | | F | ... | 101 | 94 | 14 | 98 | 75 |
| | 1993 | | | | | | | |
| | | MF | ... | 101 | 95 | 15 | 98 | 76 |
| | | M | ... | 101 | 94 | 14 | 98 | 76 |
| | | F | ... | 101 | 96 | 16 | 99 | 76 |

Gross enrolment ratios by level of education
Taux bruts de scolarisation par niveau d'enseignement
Tasas brutas de escolarización por nivel de enseñanza

II.8

| Country<br><br>Pays<br><br>País | Year<br><br>Année<br><br>Año | Sex<br><br>Sexe<br><br>Sexo | Gross enrolment ratios / Taux bruts de scolarisation / Tasas brutas de escolarización (%) | | | | | |
|---|---|---|---|---|---|---|---|---|
| | | | Pre-primary<br><br>Préprimaire<br><br>Preprimaria | Primary<br><br>Primaire<br><br>Primaria | Secondary<br><br>Secondaire<br><br>Secundaria | Tertiary<br><br>Supérieur<br><br>Superior | Primary and secondary<br><br>Primaire et secondaire<br><br>Primaria y secundaria | Primary, secondary and tertiary<br><br>Primaire, secondaire et supérieur<br><br>Primaria, secundaria y superior |
| Cyprus (3) (cont) | 1994 | | | | | | | |
| | | MF | 59 | 100 | 97 | 17 | 99 | 77 |
| | | M | 60 | 100 | 96 | 15 | 98 | 76 |
| | | F | 58 | 100 | 98 | 19 | 99 | 77 |
| | 1995 | | | | | | | |
| | | MF | ... | 100 | 97 | 20 | 99 | 78 |
| | | M | ... | 100 | 96 | 16 | 98 | 77 |
| | | F | ... | 100 | 99 | 24 | 100 | 80 |
| | 1996 | | | | | | | |
| | | MF | ... | 100 | 97 | 23 | 99 | 79 |
| | | M | ... | 100 | 95 | 20 | 98 | 78 |
| | | F | ... | 100 | 99 | 25 | 100 | 80 |
| Georgia | 1980 | | (3-5) | (6-9) | (10-16) | (17-21) | (6-16) | (6-21) |
| | | MF | 50 | 93 | 109 | 30 | 104 | 80 |
| | | M | ... | 93 | 124 | 28 | 113 | 86 |
| | | F | ... | 92 | 94 | 32 | 93 | 73 |
| | 1985 | | | | | | | |
| | | MF | 43 | 90 | 111 | ... | 103 | ... |
| | | M | ... | 90 | 121 | ... | 110 | ... |
| | | F | ... | 89 | 100 | ... | 96 | ... |
| | 1990 | | | | | | | |
| | | MF | 59 | 97 | 95 | 37 | 96 | 78 |
| | | M | ... | 97 | 96 | 34 | 97 | 78 |
| | | F | ... | 97 | 94 | 40 | 95 | 79 |
| | 1991 | | | | | | | |
| | | MF | 54 | 95 | 89 | ... | 91 | ... |
| | | M | ... | 95 | 91 | ... | 93 | ... |
| | | F | ... | 95 | 87 | ... | 90 | ... |
| | 1992 | | | | | | | |
| | | MF | 42 | 86 | 78 | ... | 81 | ... |
| | | M | ... | 86 | 80 | ... | 83 | ... |
| | | F | ... | 87 | 76 | ... | 80 | ... |
| | 1993 | | | | | | | |
| | | MF | 36 | 86 | 77 | ... | 80 | ... |
| | | M | ... | 88 | 78 | ... | 82 | ... |
| | | F | ... | 83 | 75 | ... | 78 | ... |
| | 1994 | | | | | | | |
| | | MF | 26 | 84 | 74 | 43 | 78 | 68 |
| | | M | ... | 85 | 77 | 37 | 80 | 67 |
| | | F | ... | 84 | 71 | 49 | 76 | 68 |
| | 1995 | | | | | | | |
| | | MF | 33 | 85 | 76 | 40 | 79 | 67 |
| | | M | ... | 84 | 76 | 37 | 79 | 67 |
| | | F | ... | 86 | 75 | 43 | 79 | 68 |
| | 1996 | | | | | | | |
| | | MF | 30 | 88 | 77 | 42 | 81 | 69 |
| | | M | ... | 89 | 78 | 40 | 82 | 69 |
| | | F | ... | 88 | 76 | 44 | 80 | 70 |
| India | 1970 | | (4-4) | (5-9) | (10-16) | (17-21) | (5-16) | (5-21) |
| | | MF | 2 | 78 | 24 | 5 | 49 | 38 |
| | | M | 2 | 94 | 33 | 7 | 61 | 48 |
| | | F | 2 | 61 | 14 | 2 | 35 | 27 |
| | 1975 | | | | | | | |
| | | MF | 3 | 81 | 26 | 5 | 51 | 39 |
| | | M | 3 | 96 | 34 | 7 | 62 | 49 |
| | | F | 3 | 64 | 16 | 2 | 38 | 29 |

II.8 Gross enrolment ratios by level of education
Taux bruts de scolarisation par niveau d'enseignement
Tasas brutas de escolarización por nivel de enseñanza

| Country / Pays / País | Year / Année / Año | Sex / Sexe / Sexo | Gross enrolment ratios / Taux bruts de scolarisation / Tasas brutas de escolarización (%) | | | | | |
|---|---|---|---|---|---|---|---|---|
| | | | Pre-primary / Préprimaire / Preprimaria | Primary / Primaire / Primaria | Secondary / Secondaire / Secundaria | Tertiary / Supérieur / Superior | Primary and secondary / Primaire et secondaire / Primaria y secundaria | Primary, secondary and tertiary / Primaire, secondaire et supérieur / Primaria, secundaria y superior |
| India (cont) | 1980 | MF | 5 | 83 | 30 | 5 | 54 | 41 |
| | | M | 5 | 98 | 39 | 7 | 65 | 51 |
| | | F | 5 | 67 | 20 | 3 | 41 | 31 |
| | 1985 | | (4-5) | (6-10) | (11-17) | (18-22) | (6-17) | (6-22) |
| | | MF | 3 | 96 | 38 | 6 | 63 | 48 |
| | | M | 3 | 111 | 48 | 8 | 75 | 58 |
| | | F | 3 | 80 | 26 | 4 | 50 | 38 |
| | 1990 | MF | 3 | 97 | 44 | 6 | 68 | 52 |
| | | M | 4 | 110 | 55 | 8 | 80 | 60 |
| | | F | 3 | 84 | 33 | 4 | 56 | 42 |
| | 1991 | MF | 3 | 98 | 45 | ... | 69 | ... |
| | | M | 3 | 110 | 55 | ... | 80 | ... |
| | | F | 3 | 85 | 33 | ... | 57 | ... |
| | 1992 | MF | 3 | 100 | 49 | ... | 72 | ... |
| | | M | 3 | 111 | 59 | ... | 82 | ... |
| | | F | 3 | 88 | 37 | ... | 60 | ... |
| | 1993 | MF | 4 | 101 | 49 | ... | 72 | ... |
| | | M | 5 | 111 | 59 | ... | 83 | ... |
| | | F | 4 | 90 | 38 | ... | 61 | ... |
| | 1994 | MF | 5 | 101 | 49 | 6 | 72 | 55 |
| | | M | 5 | 111 | 59 | 7 | 82 | 62 |
| | | F | 4 | 90 | 38 | 4 | 61 | 46 |
| | 1995 | MF | 5 | 100 | 49 | 7 | 72 | 55 |
| | | M | 5 | 110 | 59 | 8 | 81 | 62 |
| | | F | 4 | 90 | 38 | 5 | 61 | 47 |
| | 1996 | MF | 5 | 100 | 49 | 7 | 72 | 55 |
| | | M | 5 | 109 | 59 | 8 | 81 | 62 |
| | | F | 5 | 90 | 39 | 5 | 62 | 47 |
| Indonesia | 1970 | | (5-6) | (7-12) | (13-18) | (19-23) | (7-18) | (7-23) |
| | | MF | 6 | 80 | 16 | 3 | 51 | 40 |
| | | M | 6 | 87 | 21 | 4 | 58 | 46 |
| | | F | 6 | 73 | 11 | 1 | 45 | 35 |
| | 1975 | MF | 7 | 86 | 20 | 2 | 55 | 43 |
| | | M | 6 | 94 | 25 | ... | 62 | ... |
| | | F | 7 | 78 | 15 | ... | 49 | ... |
| | 1980 | MF | 12 | 107 | 29 | 4 | 72 | 55 |
| | | M | ... | 115 | 35 | ... | 79 | ... |
| | | F | ... | 100 | 23 | ... | 65 | ... |
| | 1985 | MF | 15 | 117 | 41 | ... | 81 | ... |
| | | M | ... | 120 | 47 | ... | 86 | ... |
| | | F | ... | 114 | 35 | ... | 76 | ... |
| | 1990 | MF | 18 | 115 | 44 | 9 | 80 | 61 |
| | | M | ... | 117 | 48 | ... | 83 | ... |
| | | F | ... | 114 | 40 | ... | 77 | ... |
| | 1991 | MF | 18 | 114 | 43 | 9 | 79 | 60 |
| | | M | ... | 115 | 48 | ... | 82 | ... |
| | | F | ... | 113 | 39 | ... | 77 | ... |
| | 1992 | MF | 19 | 114 | 43 | 9 | 79 | 60 |
| | | M | ... | 116 | 48 | 11 | 83 | 63 |
| | | F | ... | 112 | 39 | 7 | 76 | 57 |

Gross enrolment ratios by level of education II.8
Taux bruts de scolarisation par niveau d'enseignement
Tasas brutas de escolarización por nivel de enseñanza

| Country / Pays / País | Year / Année / Año | Sex / Sexe / Sexo | Pre-primary Préprimaire Preprimaria | Primary Primaire Primaria | Secondary Secondaire Secundaria | Tertiary Supérieur Superior | Primary and secondary Primaire et secondaire Primaria y secundaria | Primary, secondary and tertiary Primaire, secondaire et supérieur Primaria, secundaria y superior |
|---|---|---|---|---|---|---|---|---|
| Indonesia (cont) | 1993 | MF | 18 | 115 | 45 | 10 | 80 | 61 |
| | | M | ... | 117 | 49 | 13 | 83 | 64 |
| | | F | ... | 113 | 41 | 8 | 77 | 58 |
| | 1994 | MF | 19 | 114 | 48 | 11 | 82 | 62 |
| | | M | 18 | 117 | 52 | 14 | 85 | 65 |
| | | F | 19 | 112 | 44 | 9 | 79 | 59 |
| | 1995 | MF | 19 | 113 | 51 | 11 | 83 | 62 |
| | | M | 18 | 116 | 55 | 15 | 86 | 66 |
| | | F | 20 | 111 | 48 | 8 | 80 | 59 |
| | 1996 | MF | 19 | 113 | 56 | 11 | 84 | 64 |
| | | M | ... | 115 | ... | ... | ... | ... |
| | | F | ... | 110 | ... | ... | ... | ... |
| Iran, Islamic Republic of | 1970 | | | (7-12) | (13-18) | (19-23) | (7-18) | (7-23) |
| | | MF | ... | 70 | 27 | 3 | 52 | 41 |
| | | M | ... | 93 | 36 | 4 | 67 | 53 |
| | | F | ... | 52 | 18 | 2 | 37 | 29 |
| | 1975 | | (5-5) | (6-10) | (11-16) | (17-21) | (6-16) | (6-21) |
| | | MF | 17 | 93 | 45 | 4 | 69 | 52 |
| | | M | 18 | 114 | 57 | 6 | 86 | 65 |
| | | F | 15 | 71 | 33 | 3 | 52 | 39 |
| | 1985 | | (5-5) | (6-10) | (11-17) | (18-22) | (6-17) | (6-22) |
| | | MF | ... | 98 | 45 | 5 | 70 | 55 |
| | | M | ... | 109 | 54 | 7 | 80 | 63 |
| | | F | ... | 87 | 36 | 3 | 60 | 47 |
| | 1990 | MF | 12 | 112 | 55 | 10 | 82 | 66 |
| | | M | 13 | 118 | 64 | 14 | 90 | 72 |
| | | F | 12 | 106 | 46 | 6 | 75 | 59 |
| | 1991 | MF | 14 | 113 | 59 | 11 | 85 | 68 |
| | | M | 14 | 118 | 67 | 14 | 92 | 74 |
| | | F | 13 | 108 | 50 | 8 | 77 | 61 |
| | 1992 | MF | 9 | 112 | 64 | 13 | 86 | 70 |
| | | M | 9 | 116 | 72 | 17 | 93 | 76 |
| | | F | 9 | 107 | 55 | 8 | 80 | 63 |
| | 1993 | MF | 7 | 108 | 69 | 14 | 87 | 71 |
| | | M | 7 | 111 | 76 | 19 | 93 | 76 |
| | | F | 7 | 104 | 61 | 9 | 81 | 65 |
| | 1994 | MF | 7 | 105 | 72 | 15 | 87 | 71 |
| | | M | 7 | 108 | 78 | 20 | 92 | 76 |
| | | F | 7 | 101 | 65 | 11 | 82 | 66 |
| | 1995 | MF | 9 | 101 | 75 | 17 | 87 | 71 |
| | | M | 9 | 104 | 81 | 21 | 92 | 76 |
| | | F | 9 | 98 | 69 | 13 | 82 | 66 |
| | 1996 | MF | 11 | 98 | 77 | 18 | 86 | 70 |
| | | M | 11 | 102 | 81 | 22 | 90 | 74 |
| | | F | 11 | 95 | 73 | 13 | 83 | 66 |
| Iraq | 1970 | | (4-5) | (6-11) | (12-17) | (18-22) | (6-17) | (6-22) |
| | | MF | 2 | 69 | 24 | 5 | 49 | 39 |
| | | M | 2 | 95 | 34 | 7 | 68 | 54 |
| | | F | 2 | 41 | 14 | 2 | 29 | 23 |
| | 1975 | MF | 6 | 94 | 35 | 8 | 67 | 54 |
| | | M | 6 | 122 | 48 | 11 | 89 | 71 |
| | | F | 6 | 64 | 21 | 6 | 45 | 36 |

Gross enrolment ratios by level of education
Taux bruts de scolarisation par niveau d'enseignement
Tasas brutas de escolarización por nivel de enseñanza

| Country<br><br>Pays<br><br>País | Year<br><br>Année<br><br>Año | Sex<br><br>Sexe<br><br>Sexo | Gross enrolment ratios / Taux bruts de scolarisation / Tasas brutas de escolarización (%) | | | | | |
|---|---|---|---|---|---|---|---|---|
| | | | Pre-primary<br><br>Préprimaire<br><br>Preprimaria | Primary<br><br>Primaire<br><br>Primaria | Secondary<br><br>Secondaire<br><br>Secundaria | Tertiary<br><br>Supérieur<br><br>Superior | Primary and secondary<br><br>Primaire et secondaire<br><br>Primaria y secundaria | Primary, secondary and tertiary<br><br>Primaire, secondaire et supérieur<br><br>Primaria, secundaria y superior |
| Iraq (cont) | 1980 | | | | | | | |
| | | MF | 9 | 113 | 57 | 9 | 89 | 70 |
| | | M | 9 | 119 | 76 | 12 | 100 | 80 |
| | | F | 9 | 107 | 38 | 6 | 77 | 60 |
| | 1985 | | | | | | | |
| | | MF | 8 | 108 | 54 | 12 | 83 | 66 |
| | | M | 9 | 116 | 68 | 14 | 94 | 76 |
| | | F | 8 | 99 | 39 | 9 | 71 | 57 |
| | 1990 | | | | | | | |
| | | MF | 8 | 111 | 47 | ... | 82 | ... |
| | | M | 8 | 120 | 57 | ... | 91 | ... |
| | | F | 7 | 102 | 36 | ... | 72 | ... |
| | 1991 | | | | | | | |
| | | MF | 7 | 101 | 45 | ... | 75 | ... |
| | | M | 8 | 109 | 54 | ... | 84 | ... |
| | | F | 7 | 92 | 35 | ... | 66 | ... |
| | 1992 | | | | | | | |
| | | MF | 8 | 90 | 44 | ... | 69 | ... |
| | | M | 8 | 97 | 53 | ... | 77 | ... |
| | | F | 7 | 83 | 34 | ... | 61 | ... |
| | 1995 | | | | | | | |
| | | MF | 7 | 85 | 42 | ... | 66 | ... |
| | | M | 7 | 92 | 51 | ... | 73 | ... |
| | | F | 7 | 78 | 32 | ... | 58 | ... |
| Israel | 1970 | | (2-5) | (6-13) | (14-17) | (18-22) | (6-17) | (6-22) |
| | | MF | 44 | 96 | 57 | 18 | 83 | 64 |
| | | M | ... | 97 | 54 | 20 | 82 | 65 |
| | | F | ... | 95 | 60 | 17 | 83 | 64 |
| | 1975 | | | | | | | |
| | | MF | 61 | 97 | 66 | 23 | 87 | 68 |
| | | M | 62 | 96 | 61 | 25 | 85 | 67 |
| | | F | 60 | 97 | 71 | 22 | 89 | 69 |
| | 1980 | | | | | | | |
| | | MF | 71 | 95 | 73 | 29 | 88 | 73 |
| | | M | 73 | ... | 67 | 28 | ... | ... |
| | | F | 69 | ... | 79 | 31 | ... | ... |
| | 1985 | | | | | | | |
| | | MF | 77 | 97 | 80 | 33 | 92 | 77 |
| | | M | ... | 95 | 76 | 34 | 90 | 75 |
| | | F | ... | 98 | 85 | 32 | 94 | 79 |
| | 1990 | | | | | | | |
| | | MF | 83 | 95 | 85 | 34 | 92 | 76 |
| | | M | ... | 93 | 82 | 33 | 90 | 75 |
| | | F | ... | 96 | 89 | 34 | 94 | 78 |
| | 1991 | | | | | | | |
| | | MF | 83 | 96 | 88 | 36 | 93 | 78 |
| | | M | ... | 96 | 85 | 35 | 92 | 77 |
| | | F | ... | 96 | 91 | 37 | 95 | 79 |
| | 1992 | | | | | | | |
| | | MF | 81 | 96 | 88 | 37 | 93 | 78 |
| | | M | ... | 96 | 84 | 35 | 92 | 77 |
| | | F | ... | 96 | 91 | 39 | 95 | 79 |
| | 1993 | | | | | | | |
| | | MF | 81 | 96 | 87 | 38 | 93 | 78 |
| | | M | ... | 96 | 84 | 35 | 92 | 76 |
| | | F | ... | 96 | 89 | 40 | 94 | 79 |
| | 1994 | | (2-5) | (6-11) | (12-17) | (18-22) | (6-17) | (6-22) |
| | | MF | 72 | 98 | 88 | 39 | 93 | 78 |
| | | M | ... | ... | 89 | 36 | ... | ... |
| | | F | ... | ... | 88 | 41 | ... | ... |
| | 1995 | | | | | | | |
| | | MF | 71 | 98 | 88 | 41 | 93 | 79 |
| | | M | ... | ... | 89 | ... | ... | ... |
| | | F | ... | ... | 87 | ... | ... | ... |

Gross enrolment ratios by level of education  II.8
Taux bruts de scolarisation par niveau d'enseignement
Tasas brutas de escolarización por nivel de enseñanza

| Country / Pays / País | Year / Année / Año | Sex / Sexe / Sexo | Gross enrolment ratios / Taux bruts de scolarisation / Tasas brutas de escolarización (%) | | | | | |
|---|---|---|---|---|---|---|---|---|
| | | | Pre-primary / Préprimaire / Preprimaria | Primary / Primaire / Primaria | Secondary / Secondaire / Secundaria | Tertiary / Supérieur / Superior | Primary and secondary / Primaire et secondaire / Primaria y secundaria | Primary, secondary and tertiary / Primaire, secondaire et supérieur / Primaria, secundaria y superior |
| Japan | 1970 | | (3-5) | (6-11) | (12-17) | (18-22) | (6-17) | (6-22) |
| | | MF | 33 | 100 | 87 | 18 | 93 | 67 |
| | | M | 32 | 100 | 87 | 25 | 93 | 70 |
| | | F | 33 | 99 | 86 | 10 | 93 | 64 |
| | 1975 | | | | | | | |
| | | MF | 40 | 99 | 92 | 26 | 96 | 75 |
| | | M | 40 | 99 | 91 | 35 | 95 | 78 |
| | | F | 41 | 100 | 92 | 17 | 96 | 72 |
| | 1980 | | | | | | | |
| | | MF | 41 | 101 | 93 | 31 | 97 | 80 |
| | | M | 41 | 101 | 92 | 40 | 97 | 82 |
| | | F | 41 | 101 | 94 | 20 | 98 | 77 |
| | 1985 | | | | | | | |
| | | MF | 46 | 102 | 95 | 28 | 98 | 79 |
| | | M | 45 | 102 | 94 | 35 | 98 | 81 |
| | | F | 46 | 102 | 96 | 20 | 99 | 77 |
| | 1990 | | | | | | | |
| | | MF | 48 | 100 | 97 | 30 | 98 | 77 |
| | | M | 48 | 100 | 96 | 36 | 98 | 79 |
| | | F | 49 | 100 | 98 | 23 | 99 | 75 |
| | 1991 | | | | | | | |
| | | MF | 48 | 100 | 96 | 30 | 98 | 77 |
| | | M | 48 | 100 | 96 | 35 | 98 | 78 |
| | | F | 49 | 101 | 97 | 25 | 99 | 75 |
| | 1992 | | | | | | | |
| | | MF | 49 | 101 | 96 | 31 | 98 | 76 |
| | | M | 49 | 101 | 95 | 35 | 97 | 77 |
| | | F | 49 | 101 | 97 | 27 | 99 | 75 |
| | 1993 | | | | | | | |
| | | MF | 49 | 102 | 99 | 40 | 100 | 80 |
| | | M | 49 | 102 | 98 | 44 | 100 | 81 |
| | | F | 50 | 102 | 100 | 35 | 101 | 79 |
| | 1994 | | | | | | | |
| | | MF | 49 | 103 | 100 | 41 | 101 | 80 |
| | | M | 49 | 103 | 99 | 44 | 101 | 81 |
| | | F | 50 | 103 | 100 | 36 | 101 | 79 |
| | 1995 | | | | | | | |
| | | MF | 49 | 103 | 103 | ... | 103 | ... |
| | | M | 49 | 102 | 103 | ... | 103 | ... |
| | | F | 50 | 103 | 104 | ... | 103 | ... |
| | 1996 | | | | | | | |
| | | MF | 50 | 102 | ... | ... | ... | ... |
| | | M | 49 | 102 | ... | ... | ... | ... |
| | | F | 50 | 102 | ... | ... | ... | ... |
| | 1997 | | | | | | | |
| | | MF | ... | 101 | ... | ... | ... | ... |
| | | M | ... | 101 | ... | ... | ... | ... |
| | | F | ... | 101 | ... | ... | ... | ... |
| Jordan (4) | 1980 | | (4-5) | (6-11) | (12-17) | (18-22) | (6-17) | (6-22) |
| | | MF | 12 | 104 | 75 | 27 | 91 | ... |
| | | M | 14 | 105 | 79 | 29 | 93 | ... |
| | | F | 21 | 97 | 63 | 24 | 93 | ... |
| | 1992 | | (4-5) | (6-15) | (16-17) | (18-22) | (6-17) | (6-22) |
| | | MF | 25 | 94 | ... | ... | ... | ... |
| | | M | 27 | 94 | ... | ... | ... | ... |
| | | F | 24 | 95 | ... | ... | ... | ... |
| Kazakstan | 1980 | | (3-6) | (7-10) | (11-17) | (18-22) | (7-17) | (7-22) |
| | | MF | 61 | 84 | 93 | 34 | 90 | 72 |
| | | M | ... | ... | 92 | ... | ... | ... |
| | | F | ... | ... | 93 | ... | ... | ... |
| | 1985 | | | | | | | |
| | | MF | 70 | 88 | 103 | 37 | 97 | 79 |
| | | M | ... | ... | 102 | ... | ... | ... |
| | | F | ... | ... | 104 | ... | ... | ... |

II.8    Gross enrolment ratios by level of education
Taux bruts de scolarisation par niveau d'enseignement
Tasas brutas de escolarización por nivel de enseñanza

| Country<br><br>Pays<br><br>País | Year<br><br>Année<br><br>Año | Sex<br><br>Sexe<br><br>Sexo | Gross enrolment ratios / Taux bruts de scolarisation / Tasas brutas de escolarización (%) | | | | | |
|---|---|---|---|---|---|---|---|---|
| | | | Pre-primary<br><br>Préprimaire<br><br>Preprimaria | Primary<br><br>Primaire<br><br>Primaria | Secondary<br><br>Secondaire<br><br>Secundaria | Tertiary<br><br>Supérieur<br><br>Superior | Primary and secondary<br><br>Primaire et secondaire<br><br>Primaria y secundaria | Primary, secondary and tertiary<br><br>Primaire, secondaire et supérieur<br><br>Primaria, secundaria y superior |
| Kazakstan (cont) | 1990 | MF | 72 | 87 | 98 | 40 | 94 | 79 |
| | | M | ... | ... | 97 | ... | ... | ... |
| | | F | ... | ... | 99 | ... | ... | ... |
| | 1991 | MF | 69 | 88 | 96 | 39 | 93 | 78 |
| | | M | 73 | ... | 95 | ... | ... | ... |
| | | F | 66 | ... | 98 | ... | ... | ... |
| | 1992 | MF | 59 | 89 | 94 | ... | 92 | ... |
| | | M | 62 | ... | 93 | ... | ... | ... |
| | | F | 56 | ... | 95 | ... | ... | ... |
| | 1993 | MF | 51 | 87 | 92 | 36 | 90 | 75 |
| | | M | 54 | 87 | 91 | 32 | 89 | 73 |
| | | F | 49 | 87 | 93 | 40 | 91 | 77 |
| | 1994 | MF | 38 | 89 | 88 | 34 | 88 | 73 |
| | | M | 39 | 89 | 88 | 30 | 88 | 72 |
| | | F | 36 | 89 | 89 | 39 | 89 | 75 |
| | 1995 | MF | 29 | 98 | 84 | 33 | 90 | 74 |
| | | M | 30 | 98 | 84 | 29 | 89 | 72 |
| | | F | 28 | 98 | 85 | 37 | 90 | 75 |
| | 1996 | MF | ... | 98 | 87 | ... | 91 | ... |
| | | M | ... | 97 | 82 | ... | 88 | ... |
| | | F | ... | 98 | 91 | ... | 94 | ... |
| Korea, Republic of | 1970 | | (5-5) | (6-11) | (12-17) | (18-22) | (6-17) | (6-22) |
| | | MF | 2 | 103 | 42 | 7 | 75 | 61 |
| | | M | 3 | 104 | 50 | 11 | 80 | 65 |
| | | F | 2 | 103 | 32 | 4 | 71 | 57 |
| | 1975 | MF | 4 | 107 | 56 | 9 | 81 | 63 |
| | | M | 4 | 107 | 64 | 12 | 85 | 67 |
| | | F | 3 | 107 | 48 | 5 | 77 | 58 |
| | 1980 | MF | 8 | 110 | 78 | 15 | 94 | 70 |
| | | M | 8 | 109 | 82 | 21 | 95 | 74 |
| | | F | 7 | 111 | 74 | 8 | 92 | 67 |
| | 1985 | MF | 42 | 97 | 92 | 34 | 94 | 77 |
| | | M | 43 | 96 | 93 | 46 | 94 | 80 |
| | | F | 41 | 98 | 91 | 21 | 94 | 73 |
| | 1990 | MF | 55 | 105 | 90 | 39 | 97 | 79 |
| | | M | 56 | 105 | 91 | 51 | 98 | 83 |
| | | F | 55 | 105 | 88 | 25 | 96 | 74 |
| | 1991 | MF | 58 | 105 | 89 | 40 | 97 | 79 |
| | | M | 59 | 105 | 90 | 53 | 97 | 83 |
| | | F | 58 | 105 | 88 | 27 | 96 | 74 |
| | 1992 | MF | 65 | 103 | 91 | 44 | 97 | 80 |
| | | M | 65 | 103 | 91 | 55 | 97 | 84 |
| | | F | 64 | 104 | 90 | 32 | 96 | 76 |
| | 1993 | MF | 71 | 101 | 95 | 45 | 98 | 81 |
| | | M | 71 | 101 | 96 | 57 | 98 | 85 |
| | | F | 71 | 102 | 94 | 32 | 97 | 76 |
| | 1994 | MF | 80 | 98 | 98 | 48 | 98 | 82 |
| | | M | 80 | 98 | 98 | 60 | 98 | 85 |
| | | F | 80 | 99 | 98 | 34 | 98 | 77 |

Gross enrolment ratios by level of education   II.8
Taux bruts de scolarisation par niveau d'enseignement
Tasas brutas de escolarización por nivel de enseñanza

| Country<br><br>Pays<br><br>País | Year<br><br>Année<br><br>Año | Sex<br><br>Sexe<br><br>Sexo | Gross enrolment ratios / Taux bruts de scolarisation / Tasas brutas de escolarización (%) | | | | | |
|---|---|---|---|---|---|---|---|---|
| | | | Pre-primary<br><br>Préprimaire<br><br>Preprimaria | Primary<br><br>Primaire<br><br>Primaria | Secondary<br><br>Secondaire<br><br>Secundaria | Tertiary<br><br>Supérieur<br><br>Superior | Primary and secondary<br><br>Primaire et secondaire<br><br>Primaria y secundaria | Primary, secondary and tertiary<br><br>Primaire, secondaire et supérieur<br><br>Primaria, secundaria y superior |
| Korea, Republic of (cont) | 1995 | | | | | | | |
| | | MF | 85 | 95 | 101 | 52 | 98 | 83 |
| | | M | 84 | 95 | 101 | 66 | 98 | 87 |
| | | F | 85 | 96 | 101 | 38 | 99 | 79 |
| | 1996 | | | | | | | |
| | | MF | 88 | 94 | 102 | 60 | 98 | 86 |
| | | M | 87 | 94 | 102 | 74 | 98 | 90 |
| | | F | 89 | 94 | 102 | 46 | 99 | 81 |
| | 1997 | | | | | | | |
| | | MF | 88 | 94 | ... | 68 | ... | ... |
| | | M | 87 | 94 | ... | 82 | ... | ... |
| | | F | 89 | 95 | ... | 52 | ... | ... |
| Kuwait | 1970 | | (4-5) | (6-9) | (10-17) | (18-22) | (6-17) | (6-22) |
| | | MF | 37 | 88 | 63 | 4 | 74 | 56 |
| | | M | 39 | 100 | 70 | 4 | 83 | 61 |
| | | F | 36 | 76 | 57 | 4 | 65 | 50 |
| | 1975 | | | | | | | |
| | | MF | 34 | 93 | 66 | 9 | 78 | 61 |
| | | M | 36 | 99 | 71 | 7 | 83 | 64 |
| | | F | 32 | 86 | 62 | 11 | 72 | 58 |
| | 1980 | | | | | | | |
| | | MF | 37 | 102 | 80 | 11 | 89 | 70 |
| | | M | 38 | 105 | 84 | 9 | 92 | 70 |
| | | F | 36 | 100 | 76 | 15 | 85 | 69 |
| | 1985 | | | | | | | |
| | | MF | 46 | 103 | 91 | 17 | 96 | 76 |
| | | M | 47 | 104 | 95 | 15 | 99 | 78 |
| | | F | 45 | 102 | 87 | 18 | 92 | 74 |
| | 1990 | | | | | | | |
| | | MF | 33 | 60 | 43 | ... | 50 | ... |
| | | M | 33 | 62 | 43 | ... | 50 | ... |
| | | F | 33 | 59 | 43 | ... | 49 | ... |
| | 1991 | | | | | | | |
| | | MF | 34 | 55 | 51 | 12 | 52 | 42 |
| | | M | 34 | 55 | 51 | 9 | 52 | 42 |
| | | F | 35 | 54 | 51 | 16 | 52 | 43 |
| | 1992 | | | | | | | |
| | | MF | 43 | 59 | 54 | 13 | 56 | 46 |
| | | M | 43 | 59 | 54 | 9 | 56 | 45 |
| | | F | 43 | 59 | 54 | 17 | 56 | 47 |
| | 1993 | | | | | | | |
| | | MF | 44 | 64 | 58 | 16 | 60 | 50 |
| | | M | 44 | 64 | 58 | 13 | 60 | 49 |
| | | F | 43 | 64 | 58 | 19 | 60 | 51 |
| | 1994 | | | | | | | |
| | | MF | 48 | 66 | 62 | 18 | 63 | 53 |
| | | M | 49 | 65 | 62 | 14 | 63 | 52 |
| | | F | 48 | 67 | 62 | 23 | 64 | 54 |
| | 1995 | | | | | | | |
| | | MF | 52 | 73 | 64 | 19 | 67 | 57 |
| | | M | 52 | 74 | 64 | 15 | 68 | 56 |
| | | F | 51 | 72 | 64 | 24 | 67 | 57 |
| | 1996 | | | | | | | |
| | | MF | 55 | 76 | 65 | 19 | 69 | 58 |
| | | M | 55 | 76 | 65 | 15 | 69 | 57 |
| | | F | 54 | 75 | 65 | 24 | 69 | 58 |
| | 1997 | | | | | | | |
| | | MF | 63 | 77 | 65 | ... | 69 | ... |
| | | M | 64 | 78 | 64 | ... | 69 | ... |
| | | F | 62 | 77 | 66 | ... | 69 | ... |
| Kyrgyzstan | 1980 | | (3-6) | (7-9) | (10-16) | (17-21) | (7-16) | (7-21) |
| | | MF | ... | 116 | 110 | 16 | 112 | 81 |
| | | M | ... | 117 | 112 | ... | 113 | ... |
| | | F | ... | 114 | 108 | ... | 110 | ... |

II.8    Gross enrolment ratios by level of education
Taux bruts de scolarisation par niveau d'enseignement
Tasas brutas de escolarización por nivel de enseñanza

| Country<br>Pays<br>País | Year<br>Année<br>Año | Sex<br>Sexe<br>Sexo | Gross enrolment ratios / Taux bruts de scolarisation / Tasas brutas de escolarización (%) | | | | | |
|---|---|---|---|---|---|---|---|---|
| | | | Pre-primary<br>Préprimaire<br>Preprimaria | Primary<br>Primaire<br>Primaria | Secondary<br>Secondaire<br>Secundaria | Tertiary<br>Supérieur<br>Superior | Primary and secondary<br>Primaire et secondaire<br>Primaria y secundaria | Primary, secondary and tertiary<br>Primaire, secondaire et supérieur<br>Primaria, secundaria y superior |
| Kyrgyzstan (cont) | 1985 | | | | | | | |
| | | MF | 30 | 122 | 109 | 18 | 113 | 84 |
| | | M | 30 | 123 | 111 | ... | 115 | ... |
| | | F | 31 | 122 | 107 | ... | 112 | ... |
| | 1990 | | | | | | | |
| | | MF | 34 | 111 | 100 | 14 | 104 | 78 |
| | | M | 33 | 111 | 99 | ... | 103 | ... |
| | | F | 34 | 111 | 101 | ... | 105 | ... |
| | 1991 | | | | | | | |
| | | MF | 31 | 111 | 98 | 14 | 103 | 77 |
| | | M | 30 | 110 | 97 | ... | 101 | ... |
| | | F | 31 | 111 | 100 | ... | 104 | ... |
| | 1992 | | | | | | | |
| | | MF | 23 | 110 | 95 | 14 | 100 | 75 |
| | | M | 23 | 110 | 93 | ... | 99 | ... |
| | | F | 24 | 111 | 96 | ... | 101 | ... |
| | 1993 | | | | | | | |
| | | MF | 14 | 112 | 90 | 13 | 97 | 73 |
| | | M | 14 | 111 | 87 | 13 | 95 | 71 |
| | | F | 14 | 113 | 92 | 14 | 99 | 75 |
| | 1994 | | | | | | | |
| | | MF | 9 | 113 | 88 | 13 | 97 | 72 |
| | | M | 10 | 112 | 86 | 12 | 95 | 71 |
| | | F | 8 | 113 | 91 | 13 | 98 | 74 |
| | 1995 | | (3-6) | (7-10) | (11-17) | (18-22) | (7-17) | (7-22) |
| | | MF | 7 | 104 | 79 | 12 | 89 | 68 |
| | | M | 9 | 105 | 75 | 11 | 87 | 67 |
| | | F | 6 | 103 | 83 | 13 | 91 | 70 |
| Lao People's Democratic Republic | 1970 | | (3-5) | (6-11) | (12-18) | (19-23) | (6-18) | (6-23) |
| | | MF | ... | 57 | 4 | 0.2 | 31 | 24 |
| | | M | ... | 71 | 5 | 0.3 | 39 | 30 |
| | | F | ... | 43 | 2 | 0.1 | 22 | 18 |
| | 1975 | | | | | | | |
| | | MF | ... | 67 | 8 | ... | 37 | ... |
| | | M | ... | ... | 11 | ... | ... | ... |
| | | F | ... | ... | 5 | ... | ... | ... |
| | 1980 | | (3-5) | (6-10) | (11-16) | (17-21) | (6-16) | (6-21) |
| | | MF | 2 | 113 | 21 | 0.4 | 66 | 49 |
| | | M | 2 | 123 | 25 | 0.6 | 73 | 54 |
| | | F | 2 | 104 | 16 | 0.3 | 59 | 43 |
| | 1985 | | | | | | | |
| | | MF | 6 | 111 | 23 | 2 | 67 | 49 |
| | | M | 7 | 121 | 27 | 2 | 74 | 55 |
| | | F | 6 | 100 | 19 | 1 | 59 | 44 |
| | 1990 | | | | | | | |
| | | MF | 7 | 105 | 25 | ... | 65 | ... |
| | | M | 8 | 118 | 31 | ... | 74 | ... |
| | | F | 7 | 92 | 19 | ... | 56 | ... |
| | 1991 | | | | | | | |
| | | MF | 6 | 102 | 22 | ... | 62 | ... |
| | | M | 6 | 113 | 27 | ... | 71 | ... |
| | | F | 7 | 90 | 18 | ... | 54 | ... |
| | 1992 | | | | | | | |
| | | MF | 6 | 107 | 24 | 1 | 66 | 50 |
| | | M | 6 | 119 | 30 | 2 | 75 | 56 |
| | | F | 7 | 94 | 19 | 0.9 | 57 | 42 |
| | 1993 | | | | | | | |
| | | MF | 7 | 109 | 26 | 1 | 69 | 52 |
| | | M | 6 | 122 | 32 | 2 | 78 | 59 |
| | | F | 7 | 96 | 20 | 0.8 | 59 | 44 |
| | 1994 | | | | | | | |
| | | MF | 7 | 109 | 27 | 2 | 69 | 52 |
| | | M | 6 | 120 | 32 | 3 | 78 | 59 |
| | | F | 7 | 97 | 21 | 1 | 60 | 45 |

Gross enrolment ratios by level of education   II.8
Taux bruts de scolarisation par niveau d'enseignement
Tasas brutas de escolarización por nivel de enseñanza

| Country / Pays / País | Year / Année / Año | Sex / Sexe / Sexo | Gross enrolment ratios / Taux bruts de scolarisation / Tasas brutas de escolarización (%) | | | | | |
|---|---|---|---|---|---|---|---|---|
| | | | Pre-primary / Préprimaire / Preprimaria | Primary / Primaire / Primaria | Secondary / Secondaire / Secundaria | Tertiary / Supérieur / Superior | Primary and secondary / Primaire et secondaire / Primaria y secundaria | Primary, secondary and tertiary / Primaire, secondaire et supérieur / Primaria, secundaria y superior |
| Lao People's Democratic Republic (cont) | 1995 | MF | 7 | 112 | 27 | 3 | 71 | 54 |
| | | M | 7 | 123 | 32 | 4 | 79 | 60 |
| | | F | 8 | 100 | 21 | 2 | 62 | 47 |
| | 1996 | MF | 8 | 112 | 28 | 3 | 72 | 54 |
| | | M | 7 | 123 | 34 | 4 | 80 | 61 |
| | | F | 8 | 101 | 23 | 2 | 63 | 48 |
| Lebanon | 1970 | | | (6-10) | (11-17) | (18-22) | (6-17) | (6-22) |
| | | MF | ... | 121 | 41 | 21 | 79 | 67 |
| | | M | ... | 131 | 49 | 31 | 88 | 76 |
| | | F | ... | 112 | 33 | 10 | 71 | 58 |
| | 1975 | | (3-5) | (6-10) | (11-17) | (18-22) | (6-17) | (6-22) |
| | | MF | ... | ... | 47 | ... | ... | ... |
| | | M | ... | ... | 47 | ... | ... | ... |
| | | F | ... | ... | 46 | ... | ... | ... |
| | 1980 | MF | 59 | 111 | 50 | 30 | 82 | 69 |
| | | M | ... | ... | 61 | 41 | ... | ... |
| | | F | ... | ... | 57 | 21 | ... | ... |
| | 1985 | MF | 59 | 112 | 61 | 28 | 81 | 67 |
| | | M | ... | ... | 61 | ... | ... | ... |
| | | F | ... | ... | 60 | ... | ... | ... |
| | 1991 | MF | 68 | 118 | 74 | 29 | 93 | 74 |
| | | M | 69 | 120 | 71 | 30 | 92 | 73 |
| | | F | 68 | 116 | 76 | 28 | 93 | 74 |
| | 1992 | MF | 71 | 117 | ... | ... | ... | ... |
| | | M | 72 | 119 | ... | ... | ... | ... |
| | | F | 70 | 115 | ... | ... | ... | ... |
| | 1993 | MF | 73 | 115 | 76 | ... | 93 | ... |
| | | M | 74 | 117 | 73 | ... | 92 | ... |
| | | F | 72 | 114 | 78 | ... | 94 | ... |
| | 1994 | MF | 74 | 112 | 79 | ... | 94 | ... |
| | | M | 75 | 114 | 75 | ... | 92 | ... |
| | | F | 73 | 110 | 83 | ... | 95 | ... |
| | 1995 | MF | 75 | 109 | 81 | 27 | 93 | 74 |
| | | M | 76 | 111 | 77 | 27 | 92 | 74 |
| | | F | 73 | 108 | 84 | 27 | 95 | 75 |
| | 1996 | MF | 75 | 111 | 81 | ... | 94 | ... |
| | | M | 76 | 113 | 78 | ... | 93 | ... |
| | | F | 73 | 108 | 84 | ... | 95 | ... |
| Macau | 1990 | | (3-5) | (6-11) | (12-17) | (18-22) | (6-17) | (6-22) |
| | | MF | 89 | 99 | 65 | 25 | 84 | 65 |
| | | M | 90 | 101 | 62 | 37 | 84 | 71 |
| | | F | 88 | 96 | 68 | 18 | 84 | 60 |
| | 1991 | MF | 89 | 99 | 68 | 26 | 86 | 68 |
| | | M | 88 | 100 | 64 | 35 | 85 | 72 |
| | | F | 89 | 97 | 72 | 19 | 87 | 64 |
| | 1992 | MF | 87 | 99 | 71 | 26 | 87 | 70 |
| | | M | 88 | 100 | 66 | 34 | 86 | 73 |
| | | F | 86 | 97 | 76 | 20 | 89 | 67 |
| | 1993 | MF | ... | ... | ... | 24 | ... | ... |
| | | M | ... | ... | ... | 28 | ... | ... |
| | | F | ... | ... | ... | 20 | ... | ... |

II.8  Gross enrolment ratios by level of education
Taux bruts de scolarisation par niveau d'enseignement
Tasas brutas de escolarización por nivel de enseñanza

| Country<br><br>Pays<br><br>País | Year<br><br>Année<br><br>Año | Sex<br><br>Sexe<br><br>Sexo | Gross enrolment ratios / Taux bruts de scolarisation / Tasas brutas de escolarización (%) | | | | | |
|---|---|---|---|---|---|---|---|---|
| | | | Pre-primary<br><br>Préprimaire<br><br>Preprimaria | Primary<br><br>Primaire<br><br>Primaria | Secondary<br><br>Secondaire<br><br>Secundaria | Tertiary<br><br>Supérieur<br><br>Superior | Primary and secondary<br><br>Primaire et secondaire<br><br>Primaria y secundaria | Primary, secondary and tertiary<br><br>Primaire, secondaire et supérieur<br><br>Primaria, secundaria y superior |
| Macau (cont) | 1996 | | | | | | | |
| | | MF | ... | ... | ... | 28 | ... | ... |
| | | M | ... | ... | ... | 28 | ... | ... |
| | | F | ... | ... | ... | 28 | ... | ... |
| Malaysia | 1970 | | (4-5) | (6-11) | (12-18) | (19-23) | (6-18) | (6-23) |
| | | MF | ... | 89 | 34 | ... | 62 | ... |
| | | M | ... | 94 | 41 | ... | 68 | ... |
| | | F | ... | 83 | 28 | ... | 56 | ... |
| | 1975 | | | | | | | |
| | | MF | ... | 94 | 46 | ... | 70 | ... |
| | | M | ... | 97 | 53 | ... | 75 | ... |
| | | F | ... | 92 | 39 | ... | 65 | ... |
| | 1980 | | | | | | | |
| | | MF | 23 | 93 | 48 | 4 | 70 | 54 |
| | | M | ... | 93 | 50 | 5 | 71 | 56 |
| | | F | ... | 92 | 46 | 3 | 68 | 52 |
| | 1985 | | | | | | | |
| | | MF | 37 | 101 | 53 | 6 | 75 | 58 |
| | | M | ... | 101 | 53 | 7 | 76 | 58 |
| | | F | ... | 100 | 53 | 5 | 75 | 57 |
| | 1990 | | | | | | | |
| | | MF | 35 | 94 | 56 | 7 | 75 | 59 |
| | | M | 35 | 94 | 55 | 8 | 74 | 59 |
| | | F | 35 | 94 | 58 | 7 | 76 | 59 |
| | 1991 | | | | | | | |
| | | MF | 39 | 95 | 57 | 8 | 76 | 60 |
| | | M | 39 | 96 | 56 | ... | 76 | ... |
| | | F | 40 | 95 | 59 | ... | 77 | ... |
| | 1992 | | | | | | | |
| | | MF | 41 | 98 | 58 | 9 | 78 | 61 |
| | | M | 40 | 98 | 56 | ... | 77 | ... |
| | | F | 41 | 98 | 60 | ... | 79 | ... |
| | 1993 | | | | | | | |
| | | MF | 42 | 101 | 58 | 10 | 79 | 62 |
| | | M | 42 | 100 | 55 | ... | 77 | ... |
| | | F | 43 | 101 | 60 | ... | 80 | ... |
| | 1994 | | | | | | | |
| | | MF | 64 | 102 | 56 | 11 | 78 | 62 |
| | | M | 63 | 102 | 54 | ... | 77 | ... |
| | | F | 66 | 103 | 59 | ... | 80 | ... |
| | 1995 | | | | | | | |
| | | MF | 49 | 103 | 59 | 12 | 80 | 64 |
| | | M | 48 | 103 | 55 | ... | 78 | ... |
| | | F | 50 | 104 | 63 | ... | 83 | ... |
| | 1996 | | | | | | | |
| | | MF | 42 | 103 | 61 | ... | 81 | ... |
| | | M | 41 | 103 | 57 | ... | 79 | ... |
| | | F | 44 | 103 | 66 | ... | 84 | ... |
| | 1997 | | | | | | | |
| | | MF | ... | 101 | 64 | ... | 82 | ... |
| | | M | ... | 101 | 59 | ... | 80 | ... |
| | | F | ... | 101 | 69 | ... | 85 | ... |
| Maldives | 1992 | | (4-5) | (6-10) | (11-17) | (18-22) | (6-17) | (6-22) |
| | | MF | 21 | 129 | 44 | ... | 85 | ... |
| | | M | 22 | 130 | 44 | ... | 86 | ... |
| | | F | 20 | 127 | 44 | ... | 84 | ... |
| | 1993 | | | | | | | |
| | | MF | 60 | 132 | 49 | ... | 89 | ... |
| | | M | 61 | 134 | 49 | ... | 90 | ... |
| | | F | 59 | 130 | 49 | ... | 89 | ... |
| | 1994 | | | | | | | |
| | | MF | 59 | 135 | 52 | ... | 92 | ... |
| | | M | 58 | 137 | 52 | ... | 93 | ... |
| | | F | 60 | 133 | 53 | ... | 91 | ... |

Gross enrolment ratios by level of education    II.8
Taux bruts de scolarisation par niveau d'enseignement
Tasas brutas de escolarización por nivel de enseñanza

| Country / Pays / País | Year / Année / Año | Sex / Sexe / Sexo | Gross enrolment ratios / Taux bruts de scolarisation / Tasas brutas de escolarización (%) | | | | | |
|---|---|---|---|---|---|---|---|---|
| | | | Pre-primary / Préprimaire / Preprimaria | Primary / Primaire / Primaria | Secondary / Secondaire / Secundaria | Tertiary / Supérieur / Superior | Primary and secondary / Primaire et secondaire / Primaria y secundaria | Primary, secondary and tertiary / Primaire, secondaire et supérieur / Primaria, secundaria y superior |
| Maldives (cont) | 1995 | MF | 69 | 132 | 56 | ... | 92 | ... |
| | | M | 66 | 134 | 55 | ... | 92 | ... |
| | | F | 72 | 130 | 57 | ... | 91 | ... |
| | 1996 | MF | 64 | 131 | 59 | ... | 93 | ... |
| | | M | 62 | 133 | 59 | ... | 93 | ... |
| | | F | 67 | 130 | 60 | ... | 92 | ... |
| | 1997 | MF | 66 | 128 | 69 | ... | 96 | ... |
| | | M | 64 | 130 | 67 | ... | 96 | ... |
| | | F | 68 | 127 | 71 | ... | 96 | ... |
| Mongolia | 1970 | | (4-7) | (8-11) | (12-15) | (16-20) | (8-15) | (8-20) |
| | | MF | 21 | 110 | 83 | 5 | 98 | 67 |
| | | M | ... | ... | 83 | ... | ... | ... |
| | | F | ... | ... | 84 | ... | ... | ... |
| | 1975 | | (4-7) | (8-10) | (11-17) | (18-22) | (8-17) | (8-22) |
| | | MF | 21 | 111 | 79 | 7 | 90 | 67 |
| | | M | 20 | 112 | 75 | 7 | 88 | 65 |
| | | F | 23 | 110 | 83 | 8 | 92 | 68 |
| | 1980 | MF | 25 | 107 | 92 | 22 | 97 | 76 |
| | | M | 23 | 108 | 88 | 17 | 94 | 73 |
| | | F | 27 | 107 | 95 | 27 | 99 | 79 |
| | 1985 | MF | 28 | 101 | 91 | 22 | 94 | 74 |
| | | M | 25 | 99 | 87 | 16 | 91 | 70 |
| | | F | 32 | 102 | 95 | 28 | 98 | 78 |
| | 1990 | MF | 39 | 97 | 82 | 14 | 87 | 65 |
| | | M | 35 | 96 | 77 | 10 | 83 | 62 |
| | | F | 43 | 98 | 88 | 18 | 91 | 70 |
| | 1991 | MF | 37 | 87 | 74 | 12 | 78 | 59 |
| | | M | 34 | 86 | 68 | 8 | 74 | 54 |
| | | F | 41 | 89 | 80 | 16 | 82 | 63 |
| | 1992 | MF | 32 | 75 | 61 | 11 | 68 | 51 |
| | | M | 30 | 74 | 56 | 7 | 62 | 46 |
| | | F | 35 | 77 | 72 | 14 | 74 | 56 |
| | 1993 | MF | 22 | 75 | 63 | 11 | 67 | 50 |
| | | M | 20 | 73 | 54 | 7 | 60 | 44 |
| | | F | 23 | 77 | 72 | 16 | 73 | 56 |
| | 1994 | MF | 22 | 81 | 59 | 13 | 66 | 50 |
| | | M | 19 | 79 | 50 | 8 | 60 | 44 |
| | | F | 24 | 83 | 68 | 18 | 73 | 57 |
| | 1995 | MF | 23 | 88 | 59 | 15 | 69 | 53 |
| | | M | 21 | 87 | 51 | 9 | 63 | 47 |
| | | F | 25 | 90 | 68 | 21 | 75 | 59 |
| | 1996 | | (4-7) | (8-11) | (12-17) | (18-22) | (8-17) | (8-22) |
| | | MF | 25 | 88 | 56 | 17 | 70 | 54 |
| | | M | 23 | 86 | 48 | 10 | 64 | 48 |
| | | F | 27 | 91 | 65 | 24 | 76 | 61 |
| Myanmar | 1970 | | (4-4) | (5-9) | (10-15) | (16-20) | (5-15) | (5-20) |
| | | MF | ... | 88 | 21 | 2 | 53 | 40 |
| | | M | ... | 92 | 25 | ... | 57 | ... |
| | | F | ... | 83 | 16 | ... | 49 | ... |
| | 1975 | MF | ... | 85 | 22 | 2 | 53 | 39 |
| | | M | ... | 88 | 24 | ... | 55 | ... |
| | | F | ... | 82 | 20 | ... | 50 | ... |

II.8    Gross enrolment ratios by level of education
Taux bruts de scolarisation par niveau d'enseignement
Tasas brutas de escolarización por nivel de enseñanza

| Country<br><br>Pays<br><br>País | Year<br><br>Année<br><br>Año | Sex<br><br>Sexe<br><br>Sexo | Gross enrolment ratios / Taux bruts de scolarisation / Tasas brutas de escolarización (%) | | | | | |
|---|---|---|---|---|---|---|---|---|
| | | | Pre-primary<br><br>Préprimaire<br><br>Preprimaria | Primary<br><br>Primaire<br><br>Primaria | Secondary<br><br>Secondaire<br><br>Secundaria | Tertiary<br><br>Supérieur<br><br>Superior | Primary and secondary<br><br>Primaire et secondaire<br><br>Primaria y secundaria | Primary, secondary and tertiary<br><br>Primaire, secondaire et supérieur<br><br>Primaria, secundaria y superior |
| Myanmar (cont) | 1980 | | | | | | | |
| | | MF | ... | 91 | 22 | 5 | 56 | 42 |
| | | M | ... | 93 | 25 | ... | 58 | ... |
| | | F | ... | 89 | 19 | ... | 53 | ... |
| | 1985 | | | | | | | |
| | | MF | ... | 98 | 23 | 5 | 58 | 43 |
| | | M | ... | 101 | 24 | 4 | 60 | 45 |
| | | F | ... | 96 | 22 | 5 | 56 | 42 |
| | 1990 | | | | | | | |
| | | MF | ... | 106 | 23 | 4 | 62 | 45 |
| | | M | ... | 108 | 23 | ... | 63 | ... |
| | | F | ... | 105 | 23 | ... | 61 | ... |
| | 1991 | | | | | | | |
| | | MF | ... | 117 | 25 | 4 | 68 | 49 |
| | | M | ... | 120 | 25 | 4 | 69 | 49 |
| | | F | ... | 115 | 25 | 5 | 67 | 48 |
| | 1992 | | | | | | | |
| | | MF | ... | 121 | 25 | 5 | 69 | 50 |
| | | M | ... | 123 | 25 | 4 | 70 | 50 |
| | | F | ... | 118 | 25 | 6 | 68 | 49 |
| | 1993 | | | | | | | |
| | | MF | ... | 124 | 26 | 5 | 70 | 50 |
| | | M | ... | 126 | 26 | 4 | 71 | 51 |
| | | F | ... | 122 | 26 | 6 | 69 | 50 |
| | 1994 | | | | | | | |
| | | MF | ... | 120 | 30 | 5 | 69 | 50 |
| | | M | ... | 122 | 29 | 4 | 70 | 50 |
| | | F | ... | 117 | 30 | 7 | 68 | 50 |
| | 1995 | | | | | | | |
| | | MF | ... | 121 | ... | ... | ... | ... |
| Nepal | 1970 | | (3-5) | (6-10) | (11-15) | (16-20) | (6-15) | (6-20) |
| | | MF | ... | 26 | 9 | ... | 18 | ... |
| | | M | ... | 43 | 16 | ... | 30 | ... |
| | | F | ... | 8 | 3 | ... | 6 | ... |
| | 1975 | | (3-5) | (6-8) | (9-15) | (16-20) | (6-15) | (6-20) |
| | | MF | ... | 53 | 13 | 2 | 26 | 19 |
| | | M | ... | 86 | 22 | ... | 43 | ... |
| | | F | ... | 17 | 4 | ... | 8 | ... |
| | 1980 | | | | | | | |
| | | MF | ... | 86 | 22 | 3 | 44 | 32 |
| | | M | ... | 119 | 33 | 4 | 63 | 46 |
| | | F | ... | 50 | 9 | 1 | 23 | 17 |
| | 1985 | | (3-5) | (6-10) | (11-15) | (16-20) | (6-15) | (6-20) |
| | | MF | ... | 80 | 25 | 4 | 55 | 41 |
| | | M | ... | 108 | 37 | ... | 75 | ... |
| | | F | ... | 50 | 12 | ... | 32 | ... |
| | 1990 | | | | | | | |
| | | MF | ... | 108 | 33 | 5 | 74 | 55 |
| | | M | ... | 132 | 46 | 8 | 94 | 71 |
| | | F | ... | 81 | 20 | 2 | 53 | 38 |
| | 1991 | | | | | | | |
| | | MF | ... | 108 | 35 | 6 | 75 | 56 |
| | | M | ... | 130 | 48 | 9 | 93 | 71 |
| | | F | ... | 84 | 22 | 3 | 56 | 40 |
| | 1992 | | | | | | | |
| | | MF | ... | 110 | 37 | 5 | 77 | 57 |
| | | M | ... | 130 | 49 | ... | 94 | ... |
| | | F | ... | 88 | 25 | ... | 59 | ... |
| | 1993 | | | | | | | |
| | | MF | ... | 109 | 38 | 5 | 77 | 57 |
| | | M | ... | 128 | 50 | ... | 92 | ... |
| | | F | ... | 88 | 26 | ... | 60 | ... |
| | 1994 | | | | | | | |
| | | MF | ... | 109 | 38 | 5 | 77 | 57 |
| | | M | ... | 127 | 48 | ... | 91 | ... |
| | | F | ... | 90 | 27 | ... | 61 | ... |

Gross enrolment ratios by level of education    II.8
Taux bruts de scolarisation par niveau d'enseignement
Tasas brutas de escolarización por nivel de enseñanza

| Country / Pays / País | Year / Année / Año | Sex / Sexe / Sexo | Gross enrolment ratios / Taux bruts de scolarisation / Tasas brutas de escolarización (%) | | | | | |
|---|---|---|---|---|---|---|---|---|
| | | | Pre-primary / Préprimaire / Preprimaria | Primary / Primaire / Primaria | Secondary / Secondaire / Secundaria | Tertiary / Supérieur / Superior | Primary and secondary / Primaire et secondaire / Primaria y secundaria | Primary, secondary and tertiary / Primaire, secondaire et supérieur / Primaria, secundaria y superior |
| Nepal (cont) | 1995 | MF | ... | 109 | 40 | 4 | 77 | 57 |
| | | M | ... | 126 | 49 | ... | 90 | ... |
| | | F | ... | 91 | 30 | ... | 63 | ... |
| | 1996 | MF | ... | 113 | 42 | 5 | 80 | 59 |
| | | M | ... | 129 | 51 | ... | 92 | ... |
| | | F | ... | 96 | 33 | ... | 67 | ... |
| Oman | 1975 | | (4-5) | (6-11) | (12-17) | (18-22) | (6-17) | (6-22) |
| | | MF | 0.3 | 37 | 1 | - | 22 | 16 |
| | | M | 0.3 | 53 | 2 | - | 32 | 23 |
| | | F | 0.2 | 20 | 0.4 | - | 12 | 9 |
| | 1980 | MF | 0.6 | 51 | 12 | 0.0 | 33 | 26 |
| | | M | 0.6 | 67 | 17 | 0.0 | 45 | 34 |
| | | F | 0.5 | 35 | 6 | - | 22 | 17 |
| | 1985 | MF | 2 | 76 | 27 | 0.8 | 55 | 42 |
| | | M | 2 | 85 | 35 | 1 | 64 | 49 |
| | | F | 2 | 68 | 18 | 0.6 | 46 | 36 |
| | 1990 | MF | 3 | 86 | 46 | 4 | 69 | 55 |
| | | M | 3 | 90 | 51 | 4 | 74 | 58 |
| | | F | 3 | 82 | 40 | 4 | 64 | 51 |
| | 1991 | MF | 3 | 86 | 51 | 5 | 71 | 57 |
| | | M | 4 | 90 | 55 | 5 | 76 | 60 |
| | | F | 3 | 82 | 46 | 5 | 67 | 53 |
| | 1992 | MF | 3 | 85 | 57 | 5 | 73 | 58 |
| | | M | 4 | 89 | 61 | 5 | 77 | 61 |
| | | F | 3 | 82 | 53 | 5 | 70 | 56 |
| | 1993 | MF | 3 | 83 | 62 | 5 | 74 | 60 |
| | | M | 4 | 86 | 66 | 5 | 77 | 62 |
| | | F | 3 | 81 | 58 | 5 | 71 | 57 |
| | 1994 | MF | 4 | 81 | 65 | 6 | 74 | 60 |
| | | M | 4 | 83 | 68 | 6 | 77 | 62 |
| | | F | 3 | 79 | 62 | 6 | 72 | 58 |
| | 1995 | MF | 4 | 79 | 67 | 5 | 74 | 59 |
| | | M | 4 | 81 | 69 | 6 | 76 | 61 |
| | | F | 3 | 77 | 64 | 5 | 72 | 57 |
| | 1996 | MF | 4 | 78 | 67 | 6 | 73 | 59 |
| | | M | 5 | 80 | 68 | 7 | 75 | 61 |
| | | F | 4 | 76 | 65 | 6 | 71 | 57 |
| | 1997 | MF | 5 | 76 | 67 | 8 | 72 | 58 |
| | | M | 5 | 78 | 68 | 9 | 74 | 60 |
| | | F | 4 | 74 | 66 | 7 | 70 | 57 |
| Pakistan | 1970 | | (3-4) | (5-9) | (10-16) | (17-21) | (5-16) | (5-21) |
| | | MF | ... | 36 | 13 | 2 | 23 | 19 |
| | | M | ... | 51 | 20 | 3 | 34 | 27 |
| | | F | ... | 19 | 5 | 0.8 | 12 | 9 |
| | 1975 | MF | ... | 40 | 15 | 2 | 26 | 20 |
| | | M | ... | 53 | 22 | 2 | 36 | 28 |
| | | F | ... | 25 | 7 | 0.8 | 16 | 12 |
| | 1980 | MF | ... | 40 | 14 | ... | 26 | ... |
| | | M | ... | 52 | 20 | ... | 34 | ... |
| | | F | ... | 27 | 8 | ... | 16 | ... |

II.8    Gross enrolment ratios by level of education
Taux bruts de scolarisation par niveau d'enseignement
Tasas brutas de escolarización por nivel de enseñanza

| Country / Pays / País | Year / Année / Año | Sex / Sexe / Sexo | Gross enrolment ratios / Taux bruts de scolarisation / Tasas brutas de escolarización (%) | | | | | |
|---|---|---|---|---|---|---|---|---|
| | | | Pre-primary / Préprimaire / Preprimaria | Primary / Primaire / Primaria | Secondary / Secondaire / Secundaria | Tertiary / Supérieur / Superior | Primary and secondary / Primaire et secondaire / Primaria y secundaria | Primary, secondary and tertiary / Primaire, secondaire et supérieur / Primaria, secundaria y superior |
| Pakistan (cont) | 1985 | | | | | | | |
| | | MF | ... | 44 | 17 | 2 | 29 | 22 |
| | | M | ... | 56 | 24 | 4 | 38 | 29 |
| | | F | ... | 30 | 10 | 1 | 19 | 15 |
| | 1990 | | | | | | | |
| | | MF | ... | 61 | 23 | 3 | 40 | 31 |
| | | M | ... | 82 | 30 | 4 | 53 | 41 |
| | | F | ... | 39 | 15 | 2 | 26 | 20 |
| | 1991 | | | | | | | |
| | | MF | ... | 65 | 26 | 3 | 44 | 34 |
| | | M | ... | 87 | 33 | 4 | 58 | 44 |
| | | F | ... | 42 | 17 | 2 | 29 | 22 |
| Philippines | 1970 | | (5-6) | (7-12) | (13-16) | (17-21) | (7-16) | (7-21) |
| | | MF | 2 | 108 | 46 | 17 | 85 | 66 |
| | | M | 2 | ... | 47 | 15 | ... | ... |
| | | F | 2 | ... | 44 | 19 | ... | ... |
| | 1975 | | | | | | | |
| | | MF | 3 | 109 | 54 | 16 | 88 | 67 |
| | | M | ... | 106 | 54 | ... | 86 | ... |
| | | F | ... | 112 | 54 | ... | 90 | ... |
| | 1980 | | | | | | | |
| | | MF | 4 | 112 | 64 | 24 | 94 | 73 |
| | | M | ... | 114 | 60 | 23 | 94 | 72 |
| | | F | ... | 110 | 69 | 26 | 94 | 74 |
| | 1985 | | | | | | | |
| | | MF | 6 | 107 | 64 | 25 | 91 | 72 |
| | | M | 6 | 108 | 64 | ... | 91 | ... |
| | | F | 7 | 107 | 65 | ... | 91 | ... |
| | 1990 | | | | | | | |
| | | MF | 12 | 111 | 73 | 28 | 97 | 77 |
| | | M | ... | 113 | 74 | 24 | 99 | 77 |
| | | F | ... | 109 | 73 | 33 | 96 | 77 |
| | 1991 | | | | | | | |
| | | MF | 12 | 111 | 75 | 27 | 97 | 77 |
| | | M | ... | ... | 75 | 22 | ... | ... |
| | | F | ... | ... | 74 | 31 | ... | ... |
| | 1992 | | | | | | | |
| | | MF | 12 | 110 | 76 | 27 | 98 | 77 |
| | | M | ... | ... | 77 | 23 | ... | ... |
| | | F | ... | ... | 76 | 31 | ... | ... |
| | 1993 | | | | | | | |
| | | MF | 12 | 109 | 77 | 27 | 97 | 76 |
| | | M | ... | 108 | 77 | 23 | 97 | 75 |
| | | F | ... | 110 | 77 | 31 | 97 | 78 |
| | 1994 | | | | | | | |
| | | MF | 12 | 109 | 78 | 27 | 98 | 77 |
| | | M | ... | ... | 78 | 23 | ... | ... |
| | | F | ... | ... | 79 | 31 | ... | ... |
| | 1995 | | | | | | | |
| | | MF | 12 | 114 | 77 | 29 | 100 | 79 |
| | | M | ... | 115 | 77 | 25 | 101 | 78 |
| | | F | ... | 113 | 78 | 33 | 100 | 79 |
| | 1996 | | | | | | | |
| | | MF | 11 | 116 | 77 | ... | 101 | ... |
| | | M | ... | ... | 77 | ... | ... | ... |
| | | F | ... | ... | 78 | ... | ... | ... |
| | 1997 | | | | | | | |
| | | MF | ... | 117 | 78 | ... | 102 | ... |
| Qatar | 1970 | | (4-5) | (6-11) | (12-17) | (18-22) | (6-17) | (6-22) |
| | | MF | 11 | 96 | 36 | - | 71 | 52 |
| | | M | 12 | 104 | 41 | - | 75 | 50 |
| | | F | 10 | 88 | 30 | - | 67 | 54 |

Gross enrolment ratios by level of education  II.8
Taux bruts de scolarisation par niveau d'enseignement
Tasas brutas de escolarización por nivel de enseñanza

| Country / Pays / País | Year / Année / Año | Sex / Sexe / Sexo | Gross enrolment ratios / Taux bruts de scolarisation / Tasas brutas de escolarización (%) | | | | | |
|---|---|---|---|---|---|---|---|---|
| | | | Pre-primary / Préprimaire / Preprimaria | Primary / Primaire / Primaria | Secondary / Secondaire / Secundaria | Tertiary / Supérieur / Superior | Primary and secondary / Primaire et secondaire / Primaria y secundaria | Primary, secondary and tertiary / Primaire, secondaire et supérieur / Primaria, secundaria y superior |
| Qatar (cont) | 1975 | MF | 18 | 112 | 54 | 4 | 84 | 60 |
| | | M | 20 | 114 | 49 | 3 | 81 | 52 |
| | | F | 16 | 109 | 61 | 9 | 88 | 72 |
| | 1980 | MF | 25 | 105 | 66 | 10 | 87 | 65 |
| | | M | 26 | 107 | 65 | 6 | 87 | 60 |
| | | F | 23 | 102 | 68 | 17 | 87 | 70 |
| | 1985 | MF | 32 | 108 | 82 | 21 | 97 | 76 |
| | | M | 34 | 110 | 79 | 13 | 97 | 70 |
| | | F | 31 | 107 | 86 | 34 | 98 | 83 |
| | 1990 | MF | 27 | 97 | 81 | 27 | 90 | 77 |
| | | M | 28 | 101 | 77 | 15 | 90 | 73 |
| | | F | 26 | 94 | 85 | 43 | 90 | 81 |
| | 1991 | MF | 29 | 92 | 79 | 27 | 87 | 74 |
| | | M | 30 | 96 | 76 | 13 | 87 | 71 |
| | | F | 27 | 89 | 82 | 43 | 86 | 78 |
| | 1992 | MF | 28 | 88 | 84 | 29 | 87 | 74 |
| | | M | 31 | 91 | 82 | 15 | 87 | 71 |
| | | F | 26 | 86 | 86 | 45 | 86 | 78 |
| | 1993 | MF | 31 | 89 | 83 | 27 | 87 | 74 |
| | | M | 33 | 92 | 82 | 15 | 88 | 72 |
| | | F | 30 | 86 | 84 | 42 | 85 | 77 |
| | 1994 | MF | 31 | 86 | 82 | 27 | 84 | 72 |
| | | M | 32 | 88 | 82 | 15 | 85 | 70 |
| | | F | 29 | 84 | 82 | 42 | 83 | 75 |
| | 1995 | MF | 32 | 86 | 80 | 27 | 83 | 71 |
| | | M | 35 | 87 | 80 | 14 | 84 | 69 |
| | | F | 28 | 86 | 79 | 42 | 83 | 74 |
| | 1996 | MF | ... | ... | ... | 27 | ... | ... |
| | | M | ... | ... | ... | 14 | ... | ... |
| | | F | ... | ... | ... | 41 | ... | ... |
| Saudi Arabia | 1970 | | (4-5) | (6-11) | (12-17) | (18-22) | (6-17) | (6-22) |
| | | MF | 2 | 45 | 12 | 2 | 31 | 24 |
| | | M | 2 | 61 | 19 | 3 | 42 | 33 |
| | | F | 1 | 29 | 5 | 0.3 | 18 | 14 |
| | 1975 | MF | 3 | 58 | 22 | 4 | 42 | 32 |
| | | M | 4 | 72 | 28 | 6 | 52 | 40 |
| | | F | 3 | 43 | 15 | 2 | 30 | 24 |
| | 1980 | MF | 5 | 61 | 29 | 7 | 47 | 37 |
| | | M | 5 | 74 | 36 | 9 | 57 | 44 |
| | | F | 4 | 49 | 23 | 5 | 37 | 30 |
| | 1985 | MF | 6 | 65 | 40 | 11 | 54 | 44 |
| | | M | 7 | 73 | 48 | 12 | 62 | 50 |
| | | F | 6 | 57 | 31 | 9 | 46 | 38 |
| | 1990 | MF | 7 | 73 | 44 | 12 | 60 | 49 |
| | | M | 8 | 78 | 49 | 12 | 65 | 53 |
| | | F | 7 | 68 | 39 | 11 | 55 | 46 |
| | 1991 | MF | 8 | 73 | 45 | 12 | 61 | 50 |
| | | M | 7 | 77 | 50 | 13 | 65 | 53 |
| | | F | 8 | 69 | 41 | 10 | 57 | 47 |

II.8   Gross enrolment ratios by level of education
Taux bruts de scolarisation par niveau d'enseignement
Tasas brutas de escolarización por nivel de enseñanza

| Country / Pays / País | Year / Année / Año | Sex / Sexe / Sexo | Gross enrolment ratios / Taux bruts de scolarisation / Tasas brutas de escolarización (%) | | | | | |
|---|---|---|---|---|---|---|---|---|
| | | | Pre-primary / Préprimaire / Preprimaria | Primary / Primaire / Primaria | Secondary / Secondaire / Secundaria | Tertiary / Supérieur / Superior | Primary and secondary / Primaire et secondaire / Primaria y secundaria | Primary, secondary and tertiary / Primaire, secondaire et supérieur / Primaria, secundaria y superior |
| Saudi Arabia (cont) | 1992 | MF | 8 | 75 | 48 | 14 | 63 | 52 |
| | | M | 9 | 78 | 53 | 14 | 67 | 55 |
| | | F | 8 | 72 | 43 | 13 | 59 | 49 |
| | 1993 | MF | 8 | 77 | 52 | 14 | 65 | 54 |
| | | M | 7 | 79 | 57 | 15 | 69 | 57 |
| | | F | 9 | 74 | 47 | 13 | 62 | 51 |
| | 1994 | MF | 8 | 77 | 55 | 15 | 67 | 55 |
| | | M | ... | 78 | 59 | 16 | 70 | 58 |
| | | F | ... | 76 | 51 | 15 | 64 | 53 |
| | 1995 | MF | 8 | 78 | 58 | 16 | 69 | 57 |
| | | M | ... | 79 | 62 | 16 | 71 | 59 |
| | | F | ... | 76 | 54 | 15 | 66 | 54 |
| | 1996 | MF | 8 | 76 | 61 | 16 | 69 | 57 |
| | | M | 8 | 77 | 65 | 17 | 71 | 59 |
| | | F | 7 | 75 | 57 | 15 | 67 | 54 |
| Singapore | 1970 | | (4-5) | (6-11) | (12-17) | (18-22) | (6-17) | (6-22) |
| | | MF | 5 | 105 | 46 | 6 | 77 | 59 |
| | | M | 5 | 110 | 47 | 8 | 79 | 62 |
| | | F | 4 | 101 | 45 | 4 | 74 | 56 |
| | 1975 | MF | 6 | 110 | 52 | 8 | 78 | 58 |
| | | M | 6 | 113 | 51 | 10 | 80 | 59 |
| | | F | 5 | 106 | 53 | 7 | 77 | 57 |
| | 1980 | MF | 13 | 108 | 60 | 8 | 82 | 57 |
| | | M | 13 | 109 | 60 | 9 | 83 | 58 |
| | | F | 13 | 106 | 60 | 6 | 82 | 56 |
| | 1985 | | (4-5) | (6-11) | (12-18) | (19-23) | (6-18) | (6-23) |
| | | MF | 20 | 108 | 62 | 14 | 82 | 59 |
| | | M | 20 | 110 | 63 | 17 | 83 | 61 |
| | | F | 19 | 106 | 61 | 10 | 80 | 57 |
| | 1990 | MF | ... | 104 | 68 | 19 | 84 | 61 |
| | | M | ... | 105 | 70 | 22 | 86 | 64 |
| | | F | ... | 102 | 66 | 15 | 81 | 58 |
| | 1991 | MF | ... | 104 | 67 | 21 | 83 | 62 |
| | | M | ... | 105 | 70 | 24 | 86 | 65 |
| | | F | ... | 102 | 65 | 17 | 81 | 59 |
| | 1992 | MF | ... | 103 | 67 | 23 | 84 | 63 |
| | | M | ... | 105 | 70 | 27 | 86 | 66 |
| | | F | ... | 102 | 65 | 20 | 81 | 60 |
| | 1993 | MF | ... | 101 | 67 | 27 | 83 | 65 |
| | | M | ... | 103 | 69 | 31 | 85 | 67 |
| | | F | ... | 99 | 65 | 23 | 81 | 62 |
| | 1994 | MF | ... | 94 | 72 | 29 | 83 | 66 |
| | | M | ... | 95 | 74 | 25 | 84 | 66 |
| | | F | ... | 93 | 70 | 34 | 81 | 66 |
| | 1995 | MF | ... | 95 | 73 | 34 | 84 | 69 |
| | | M | ... | 96 | ... | 37 | ... | ... |
| | | F | ... | 94 | ... | 31 | ... | ... |
| | 1996 | MF | ... | 94 | 74 | 39 | 84 | 71 |
| | | M | ... | 95 | ... | ... | ... | ... |
| | | F | ... | 93 | ... | ... | ... | ... |

Gross enrolment ratios by level of education  II.8
Taux bruts de scolarisation par niveau d'enseignement
Tasas brutas de escolarización por nivel de enseñanza

| Country / Pays / País | Year / Année / Año | Sex / Sexe / Sexo | Gross enrolment ratios / Taux bruts de scolarisation / Tasas brutas de escolarización (%) | | | | | |
|---|---|---|---|---|---|---|---|---|
| | | | Pre-primary / Préprimaire / Preprimaria | Primary / Primaire / Primaria | Secondary / Secondaire / Secundaria | Tertiary / Supérieur / Superior | Primary and secondary / Primaire et secondaire / Primaria y secundaria | Primary, secondary and tertiary / Primaire, secondaire et supérieur / Primaria, secundaria y superior |
| Sri Lanka | 1970 | | | (6-10) | (11-17) | (18-22) | (6-17) | (6-22) |
| | | MF | ... | 99 | 47 | ... | 71 | ... |
| | | M | ... | 104 | 46 | ... | 72 | ... |
| | | F | ... | 94 | 48 | ... | 69 | ... |
| | 1975 | | | | | | | |
| | | MF | ... | ... | 48 | ... | ... | ... |
| | | M | ... | ... | 47 | ... | ... | ... |
| | | F | ... | ... | 49 | ... | ... | ... |
| | 1980 | | (4-4) | (5-10) | (11-17) | (18-22) | (5-17) | (5-22) |
| | | MF | ... | 103 | 55 | 3 | 77 | 57 |
| | | M | ... | 105 | 52 | 3 | 77 | 58 |
| | | F | ... | 100 | 57 | 2 | 77 | 57 |
| | 1985 | | | | | | | |
| | | MF | ... | 103 | 63 | 4 | 82 | 62 |
| | | M | ... | 104 | 60 | 4 | 81 | 61 |
| | | F | ... | 101 | 66 | 3 | 83 | 62 |
| | 1990 | | (4-4) | (5-9) | (10-17) | (18-22) | (5-17) | (5-22) |
| | | MF | ... | 106 | 74 | 5 | 87 | 66 |
| | | M | ... | 107 | 71 | 6 | 86 | 66 |
| | | F | ... | 105 | 77 | 4 | 88 | 67 |
| | 1991 | | | | | | | |
| | | MF | ... | 107 | 73 | 5 | 87 | 66 |
| | | M | ... | 109 | 70 | 6 | 85 | 66 |
| | | F | ... | 106 | 77 | 3 | 89 | 67 |
| | 1992 | | | | | | | |
| | | MF | ... | 107 | 74 | ... | 87 | ... |
| | | M | ... | 109 | 71 | ... | 86 | ... |
| | | F | ... | 106 | 78 | ... | 89 | ... |
| | 1993 | | | | | | | |
| | | MF | ... | 109 | 75 | ... | 87 | ... |
| | | M | ... | 110 | 71 | ... | 86 | ... |
| | | F | ... | 108 | 78 | ... | 89 | ... |
| | 1994 | | | | | | | |
| | | MF | ... | 110 | 76 | 5 | 88 | 67 |
| | | M | ... | 111 | 72 | 6 | 86 | 66 |
| | | F | ... | 109 | 80 | 4 | 90 | 68 |
| | 1995 | | | | | | | |
| | | MF | ... | 113 | 75 | 5 | 89 | 67 |
| | | M | ... | 115 | 72 | 6 | 87 | 66 |
| | | F | ... | 112 | 78 | 4 | 90 | 68 |
| | 1996 | | | | | | | |
| | | MF | ... | 109 | ... | ... | ... | ... |
| | | M | ... | 110 | ... | ... | ... | ... |
| | | F | ... | 108 | ... | ... | ... | ... |
| Syrian Arab Republic | 1970 | | (3-5) | (6-11) | (12-17) | (18-22) | (6-17) | (6-22) |
| | | MF | 4 | 78 | 38 | 8 | 61 | 50 |
| | | M | 4 | 95 | 54 | 13 | 78 | 65 |
| | | F | 3 | 59 | 21 | 3 | 43 | 35 |
| | 1975 | | | | | | | |
| | | MF | 4 | 96 | 43 | 11 | 71 | 58 |
| | | M | 5 | 112 | 57 | 15 | 86 | 71 |
| | | F | 4 | 78 | 28 | 6 | 55 | 45 |
| | 1980 | | | | | | | |
| | | MF | 4 | 100 | 46 | 17 | 75 | 62 |
| | | M | 4 | 111 | 57 | 23 | 86 | 72 |
| | | F | 3 | 88 | 35 | 10 | 64 | 52 |
| | 1985 | | | | | | | |
| | | MF | 6 | 110 | 58 | 17 | 87 | 70 |
| | | M | 6 | 117 | 68 | 22 | 95 | 77 |
| | | F | 5 | 102 | 48 | 12 | 78 | 62 |
| | 1990 | | | | | | | |
| | | MF | 6 | 108 | 52 | 18 | 84 | 68 |
| | | M | 7 | 114 | 60 | 22 | 90 | 74 |
| | | F | 6 | 102 | 44 | 14 | 77 | 62 |

II.8     Gross enrolment ratios by level of education
Taux bruts de scolarisation par niveau d'enseignement
Tasas brutas de escolarización por nivel de enseñanza

| Country / Pays / País | Year / Année / Año | Sex / Sexe / Sexo | Gross enrolment ratios / Taux bruts de scolarisation / Tasas brutas de escolarización (%) | | | | | |
|---|---|---|---|---|---|---|---|---|
| | | | Pre-primary / Préprimaire / Preprimaria | Primary / Primaire / Primaria | Secondary / Secondaire / Secundaria | Tertiary / Supérieur / Superior | Primary and secondary / Primaire et secondaire / Primaria y secundaria | Primary, secondary and tertiary / Primaire, secondaire et supérieur / Primaria, secundaria y superior |
| Syrian Arab Republic (cont) | 1991 | | | | | | | |
| | | MF | 6 | 108 | 49 | 18 | 82 | 67 |
| | | M | 7 | 114 | 56 | 21 | 88 | 73 |
| | | F | 6 | 102 | 42 | 14 | 76 | 62 |
| | 1992 | | | | | | | |
| | | MF | 7 | 105 | 48 | 18 | 80 | 66 |
| | | M | 7 | 110 | 54 | 21 | 86 | 71 |
| | | F | 6 | 99 | 43 | 15 | 75 | 61 |
| | 1993 | | | | | | | |
| | | MF | 7 | 103 | 47 | 16 | 78 | 64 |
| | | M | 7 | 109 | 52 | 19 | 84 | 69 |
| | | F | 6 | 98 | 41 | 14 | 73 | 60 |
| | 1994 | | | | | | | |
| | | MF | 7 | 102 | 45 | 16 | 77 | 63 |
| | | M | 7 | 107 | 49 | 18 | 81 | 67 |
| | | F | 6 | 96 | 40 | 13 | 72 | 58 |
| | 1995 | | | | | | | |
| | | MF | 7 | 101 | 43 | ... | 75 | ... |
| | | M | 7 | 106 | 46 | ... | 79 | ... |
| | | F | 6 | 96 | 40 | ... | 71 | ... |
| | 1996 | | | | | | | |
| | | MF | 7 | 101 | 42 | ... | 74 | ... |
| | | M | 8 | 106 | 45 | ... | 78 | ... |
| | | F | 7 | 96 | 40 | ... | 70 | ... |
| Tajikistan | 1980 | | (3-6) | (7-10) | (11-17) | (18-22) | (7-17) | (7-22) |
| | | MF | 13 | ... | ... | 24 | ... | ... |
| | 1985 | | | | | | | |
| | | MF | ... | ... | ... | 20 | ... | ... |
| | | M | ... | ... | ... | 23 | ... | ... |
| | | F | ... | ... | ... | 17 | ... | ... |
| | 1990 | | | | | | | |
| | | MF | 16 | 91 | 102 | 22 | 98 | 77 |
| | | M | ... | 92 | ... | 27 | ... | ... |
| | | F | ... | 90 | ... | 17 | ... | ... |
| | 1991 | | | | | | | |
| | | MF | 14 | 92 | 100 | 22 | 97 | 77 |
| | | M | ... | 93 | ... | 27 | ... | ... |
| | | F | ... | 91 | ... | 16 | ... | ... |
| | 1992 | | | | | | | |
| | | MF | 12 | 86 | 94 | 21 | 90 | 72 |
| | | M | ... | 87 | 97 | 28 | 93 | 76 |
| | | F | ... | 84 | 91 | 15 | 88 | 69 |
| | 1993 | | | | | | | |
| | | MF | 11 | 90 | 82 | 21 | 86 | 69 |
| | | M | ... | 92 | 86 | 28 | 89 | 73 |
| | | F | ... | 89 | 78 | 13 | 83 | 65 |
| | 1994 | | | | | | | |
| | | MF | 10 | 91 | 83 | 21 | 86 | 69 |
| | | M | ... | 93 | 87 | 27 | 89 | 74 |
| | | F | ... | 90 | 78 | 14 | 83 | 65 |
| | 1995 | | | | | | | |
| | | MF | 10 | 93 | 81 | ... | 86 | ... |
| | | M | ... | 94 | ... | ... | ... | ... |
| | | F | ... | 91 | ... | ... | ... | ... |
| | 1996 | | | | | | | |
| | | MF | 10 | 95 | 78 | 20 | 85 | 69 |
| | | M | 11 | 96 | 83 | 27 | 88 | 73 |
| | | F | 9 | 94 | 74 | 13 | 82 | 65 |
| Thailand | 1970 | | (4-6) | (7-13) | (14-18) | (19-23) | (7-18) | (7-23) |
| | | MF | 4 | 81 | 17 | 3 | 58 | 46 |
| | | M | 4 | 85 | 20 | 4 | 62 | 50 |
| | | F | 4 | 77 | 14 | 2 | 54 | 43 |

Gross enrolment ratios by level of education    II.8
Taux bruts de scolarisation par niveau d'enseignement
Tasas brutas de escolarización por nivel de enseñanza

| Country / Pays / País | Year / Année / Año | Sex / Sexe / Sexo | Gross enrolment ratios / Taux bruts de scolarisation / Tasas brutas de escolarización (%) | | | | | |
|---|---|---|---|---|---|---|---|---|
| | | | Pre-primary / Préprimaire / Preprimaria | Primary / Primaire / Primaria | Secondary / Secondaire / Secundaria | Tertiary / Supérieur / Superior | Primary and secondary / Primaire et secondaire / Primaria y secundaria | Primary, secondary and tertiary / Primaire, secondaire et supérieur / Primaria, secundaria y superior |
| Thailand (cont) | 1975 | MF | 5 | 84 | 25 | 3 | 62 | 48 |
| | | M | 6 | 87 | 28 | 4 | 65 | 51 |
| | | F | 5 | 80 | 22 | 3 | 58 | 45 |
| | 1980 | | (4-6) | (7-12) | (13-18) | (19-23) | (7-18) | (7-23) |
| | | MF | 10 | 99 | 29 | 15 | 66 | 53 |
| | | M | 10 | 100 | 30 | ... | 67 | ... |
| | | F | 10 | 97 | 28 | ... | 65 | ... |
| | 1985 | MF | 18 | 96 | 30 | 19 | 63 | 52 |
| | 1990 | | (3-5) | (6-11) | (12-17) | (18-22) | (6-17) | (6-22) |
| | | MF | 43 | 99 | 30 | ... | 64 | ... |
| | | M | 43 | 100 | 31 | ... | 64 | ... |
| | | F | 44 | 98 | 30 | ... | 63 | ... |
| | 1991 | MF | 45 | 99 | 33 | ... | 65 | ... |
| | | M | 45 | 100 | 34 | ... | 66 | ... |
| | | F | 45 | 08 | 33 | ... | 65 | ... |
| | 1992 | MF | 50 | 97 | 37 | 19 | 67 | 52 |
| | | M | 49 | 98 | 38 | 17 | 67 | 52 |
| | | F | 50 | 96 | 37 | 20 | 66 | 52 |
| | 1993 | MF | 58 | 94 | 42 | 19 | 68 | 53 |
| | 1994 | MF | 63 | 91 | 48 | 19 | 69 | 54 |
| | 1995 | MF | 57 | 86 | 54 | 20 | 70 | 55 |
| | 1996 | MF | 62 | 87 | 56 | 22 | 71 | 56 |
| Turkey | 1980 | | (4-5) | (6-10) | (11-16) | (17-21) | (6-16) | (6-21) |
| | | MF | ... | 96 | 35 | 5 | 64 | 48 |
| | | M | ... | 102 | 44 | 8 | 72 | 54 |
| | | F | ... | 90 | 24 | 3 | 56 | 42 |
| | 1985 | MF | 6 | 113 | 42 | 9 | 74 | 55 |
| | | M | 5 | 117 | 52 | 12 | 81 | 61 |
| | | F | 5 | 110 | 30 | 6 | 67 | 49 |
| | 1990 | MF | 5 | 99 | 47 | 13 | 71 | 55 |
| | | M | 5 | 102 | 57 | 17 | 78 | 61 |
| | | F | 4 | 96 | 37 | 9 | 64 | 49 |
| | 1991 | MF | 5 | 100 | 49 | 14 | 72 | 56 |
| | | M | 5 | 103 | 59 | 18 | 79 | 62 |
| | | F | 5 | 97 | 38 | 10 | 65 | 49 |
| | 1992 | MF | 5 | 100 | 52 | 15 | 73 | 57 |
| | | M | 6 | 103 | 62 | 20 | 80 | 63 |
| | | F | 5 | 97 | 41 | 11 | 66 | 50 |
| | 1993 | MF | 6 | 102 | 53 | 18 | 74 | 58 |
| | | M | 6 | 104 | 63 | 22 | 81 | 63 |
| | | F | 6 | 99 | 43 | 14 | 67 | 51 |
| | 1994 | MF | 6 | 105 | 56 | 18 | 77 | 59 |
| | | M | 7 | 107 | 67 | 22 | 84 | 65 |
| | | F | 6 | 102 | 45 | 14 | 69 | 52 |
| | 1995 | MF | 7 | 107 | 57 | 19 | 78 | 59 |
| | | M | 7 | 110 | 67 | 24 | 85 | 66 |
| | | F | 7 | 103 | 46 | 15 | 70 | 53 |

II.8  Gross enrolment ratios by level of education
Taux bruts de scolarisation par niveau d'enseignement
Tasas brutas de escolarización por nivel de enseñanza

| Country / Pays / País | Year / Année / Año | Sex / Sexe / Sexo | Gross enrolment ratios / Taux bruts de scolarisation / Tasas brutas de escolarización (%) | | | | | |
|---|---|---|---|---|---|---|---|---|
| | | | Pre-primary / Préprimaire / Preprimaria | Primary / Primaire / Primaria | Secondary / Secondaire / Secundaria | Tertiary / Supérieur / Superior | Primary and secondary / Primaire et secondaire / Primaria y secundaria | Primary, secondary and tertiary / Primaire, secondaire et supérieur / Primaria, secundaria y superior |
| Turkey (cont) | 1996 | MF | 8 | 107 | 58 | 21 | 79 | 60 |
| | | M | 8 | 111 | 68 | 27 | 86 | 67 |
| | | F | 7 | 104 | 48 | 15 | 71 | 53 |
| Turkmenistan | 1980 | | (3-6) | (7-10) | (11-17) | (18-22) | (7-17) | (7-22) |
| | | MF | ... | ... | ... | 22 | ... | ... |
| | 1985 | MF | ... | ... | ... | 22 | ... | ... |
| | 1990 | MF | ... | ... | ... | 22 | ... | ... |
| United Arab Emirates | 1970 | | (4-5) | (6-11) | (12-17) | (18-22) | (6-17) | (6-22) |
| | | MF | ... | 95 | 22 | ... | 61 | ... |
| | | M | ... | 115 | 30 | ... | 73 | ... |
| | | F | ... | 72 | 10 | ... | 47 | ... |
| | 1980 | MF | 38 | 89 | 52 | 3 | 75 | 49 |
| | | M | 40 | 90 | 55 | 2 | 76 | 45 |
| | | F | 35 | 88 | 49 | 5 | 73 | 54 |
| | 1985 | MF | 56 | 98 | 55 | 7 | 80 | 58 |
| | | M | 58 | 98 | 55 | 5 | 80 | 55 |
| | | F | 54 | 97 | 55 | 9 | 80 | 61 |
| | 1990 | MF | 52 | 104 | 67 | 9 | 89 | 71 |
| | | M | 53 | 106 | 63 | 5 | 87 | 67 |
| | | F | 51 | 103 | 72 | 15 | 90 | 74 |
| | 1991 | MF | 52 | 99 | 69 | 9 | 86 | 69 |
| | | M | 53 | 100 | 65 | 4 | 85 | 66 |
| | | F | 51 | 97 | 74 | 16 | 88 | 73 |
| | 1992 | MF | 53 | 95 | 72 | 9 | 86 | 69 |
| | | M | 55 | 96 | 68 | 5 | 84 | 66 |
| | | F | 51 | 94 | 77 | 14 | 87 | 72 |
| | 1993 | MF | 56 | 94 | 77 | ... | 87 | ... |
| | | M | 57 | 96 | 72 | ... | 86 | ... |
| | | F | 54 | 92 | 81 | ... | 88 | ... |
| | 1994 | MF | 56 | 94 | 80 | ... | 88 | ... |
| | | M | 57 | 96 | 76 | ... | 88 | ... |
| | | F | 55 | 92 | 84 | ... | 89 | ... |
| | 1995 | MF | 56 | 91 | 78 | ... | 85 | ... |
| | | M | 58 | 92 | 74 | ... | 85 | ... |
| | | F | 54 | 89 | 81 | ... | 86 | ... |
| | 1996 | MF | 57 | 89 | 80 | 12 | 85 | 68 |
| | | M | 58 | 91 | 77 | 5 | 85 | 65 |
| | | F | 56 | 87 | 82 | 21 | 85 | 71 |
| Uzbekistan | 1980 | | (3-5) | (6-9) | (10-16) | (17-21) | (6-16) | (6-21) |
| | | MF | 66 | 81 | 105 | 28 | 96 | 77 |
| | | M | ... | 83 | 117 | ... | 104 | ... |
| | | F | ... | 80 | 94 | ... | 88 | ... |
| | 1985 | MF | 70 | 87 | 107 | 30 | 99 | 79 |
| | | M | ... | 88 | 117 | ... | 105 | ... |
| | | F | ... | 85 | 97 | ... | 92 | ... |
| | 1990 | MF | 73 | 81 | 99 | 30 | 92 | 76 |
| | | M | ... | 82 | 104 | ... | 95 | ... |
| | | F | ... | 81 | 95 | ... | 89 | ... |

Gross enrolment ratios by level of education    II.8
Taux bruts de scolarisation par niveau d'enseignement
Tasas brutas de escolarización por nivel de enseñanza

| Country / Pays / País | Year / Année / Año | Sex / Sexe / Sexo | Gross enrolment ratios / Taux bruts de scolarisation / Tasas brutas de escolarización (%) | | | | | |
|---|---|---|---|---|---|---|---|---|
| | | | Pre-primary / Préprimaire / Preprimaria | Primary / Primaire / Primaria | Secondary / Secondaire / Secundaria | Tertiary / Supérieur / Superior | Primary and secondary / Primaire et secondaire / Primaria y secundaria | Primary, secondary and tertiary / Primaire, secondaire et supérieur / Primaria, secundaria y superior |
| Uzbekistan (cont) | 1991 | MF | 71 | 76 | 98 | 32 | 89 | 74 |
| | | M | 71 | 76 | 102 | ... | 92 | ... |
| | | F | 71 | 76 | 94 | ... | 86 | ... |
| | 1992 | MF | 63 | 76 | 95 | ... | 87 | ... |
| | | M | 64 | 76 | 100 | ... | 90 | ... |
| | | F | 62 | 76 | 90 | ... | 84 | ... |
| | 1993 | MF | 60 | 77 | 93 | ... | 87 | ... |
| | | M | 61 | 78 | 98 | ... | 90 | ... |
| | | F | 59 | 77 | 88 | ... | 84 | ... |
| | 1994 | MF | 55 | 78 | 94 | ... | 87 | ... |
| | | M | 56 | 79 | 100 | ... | 91 | ... |
| | | F | 54 | 76 | 88 | ... | 83 | ... |
| Viet Nam | 1975 | | (3-5) | (6-10) | (11-16) | (17-21) | (6-16) | (6-21) |
| | | MF | ... | 107 | 39 | 2 | 72 | 54 |
| | | M | ... | 106 | 38 | 2 | 71 | 54 |
| | | F | | 108 | 41 | 1 | 73 | 55 |
| | 1980 | | (3-5) | (6-10) | (11-17) | (18-22) | (6-17) | (6-22) |
| | | MF | 35 | 109 | 42 | 2 | 71 | 54 |
| | | M | 33 | 111 | 44 | 3 | 73 | 57 |
| | | F | 37 | 106 | 40 | 0.9 | 68 | 51 |
| | 1985 | MF | 33 | 103 | 43 | 2 | 69 | 51 |
| | | M | 31 | 106 | 44 | ... | 71 | ... |
| | | F | 35 | 100 | 41 | ... | 67 | ... |
| | 1990 | MF | 28 | 103 | 32 | 2 | 64 | 47 |
| | | M | ... | ... | 33 | ... | ... | ... |
| | | F | ... | ... | 31 | ... | ... | ... |
| | 1991 | MF | 27 | 104 | 31 | 2 | 64 | 48 |
| | | M | ... | ... | 32 | ... | ... | ... |
| | | F | ... | ... | 31 | ... | ... | ... |
| | 1992 | MF | 28 | 109 | 32 | 2 | 66 | 49 |
| | | M | ... | !!! | 32 | ... | ... | ... |
| | | F | ... | ... | 31 | ... | ... | ... |
| | 1993 | MF | 30 | 111 | 35 | 2 | 69 | 51 |
| | | M | ... | ... | 36 | ... | ... | ... |
| | | F | ... | ... | 35 | ... | ... | ... |
| | 1994 | MF | 33 | 113 | 41 | 3 | 72 | 54 |
| | | M | ... | ... | 41 | ... | ... | ... |
| | | F | ... | ... | 40 | ... | ... | ... |
| | 1995 | MF | 35 | 114 | 47 | 4 | 76 | 57 |
| | | M | ... | ... | 48 | ... | ... | ... |
| | | F | ... | ... | 46 | ... | ... | ... |
| | 1996 | MF | 38 | 115 | 52 | 7 | 79 | 60 |
| | 1997 | MF | 40 | 113 | 57 | ... | 81 | ... |
| | | M | ... | 115 | ... | ... | ... | ... |
| | | F | ... | 111 | ... | ... | ... | ... |
| Yemen | 1991 | | (3-5) | (6-14) | (15-17) | (18-22) | (6-17) | (6-22) |
| | | MF | 0.8 | ... | ... | 4 | ... | ... |
| | | M | 0.8 | ... | ... | 7 | ... | ... |
| | | F | 0.8 | ... | ... | 2 | ... | ... |
| | 1993 | MF | 0.8 | 79 | 23 | ... | 67 | ... |
| | | M | 0.9 | 113 | 36 | ... | 96 | ... |
| | | F | 0.8 | 45 | 8 | ... | 37 | ... |

II.8　Gross enrolment ratios by level of education
Taux bruts de scolarisation par niveau d'enseignement
Tasas brutas de escolarización por nivel de enseñanza

| Country / Pays / País | Year / Année / Año | Sex / Sexe / Sexo | Gross enrolment ratios / Taux bruts de scolarisation / Tasas brutas de escolarización (%) | | | | | |
|---|---|---|---|---|---|---|---|---|
| | | | Pre-primary / Préprimaire / Preprimaria | Primary / Primaire / Primaria | Secondary / Secondaire / Secundaria | Tertiary / Supérieur / Superior | Primary and secondary / Primaire et secondaire / Primaria y secundaria | Primary, secondary and tertiary / Primaire, secondaire et supérieur / Primaria, secundaria y superior |
| Yemen (cont) | 1996 | | | | | | | |
| | | MF | ... | 70 | 34 | 4 | 63 | 49 |
| | | M | ... | 100 | 53 | 7 | 90 | 69 |
| | | F | ... | 40 | 14 | 1 | 35 | 27 |
| **Europe** | | | | | | | | |
| Albania | 1970 | | (3-5) | (6-13) | (14-17) | (18-22) | (6-17) | (6-22) |
| | | MF | 25 | 106 | 35 | ... | 86 | ... |
| | | M | ... | 109 | 42 | ... | 90 | ... |
| | | F | ... | 102 | 27 | ... | 81 | ... |
| | 1975 | | | | | | | |
| | | MF | ... | 115 | 48 | ... | 94 | ... |
| | | M | ... | 119 | 51 | ... | 98 | ... |
| | | F | ... | 111 | 45 | ... | 90 | ... |
| | 1980 | | | | | | | |
| | | MF | 46 | 113 | 67 | 5 | 98 | 72 |
| | | M | ... | 116 | 70 | 5 | 100 | 73 |
| | | F | ... | 111 | 63 | 5 | 95 | 70 |
| | 1985 | | | | | | | |
| | | MF | 52 | 103 | 72 | 7 | 93 | 69 |
| | | M | ... | 104 | 75 | 7 | 95 | 70 |
| | | F | ... | 102 | 68 | 7 | 91 | 67 |
| | 1990 | | | | | | | |
| | | MF | 59 | 100 | 78 | 7 | 93 | 69 |
| | | M | ... | 100 | 84 | 7 | 95 | 70 |
| | | F | ... | 100 | 72 | 7 | 91 | 68 |
| | 1991 | | | | | | | |
| | | MF | ... | ... | ... | 9 | ... | ... |
| | | M | ... | ... | ... | 8 | ... | ... |
| | | F | ... | ... | ... | 9 | ... | ... |
| | 1992 | | | | | | | |
| | | MF | ... | ... | ... | 7 | ... | ... |
| | | M | ... | ... | ... | 7 | ... | ... |
| | | F | ... | ... | ... | 8 | ... | ... |
| | 1993 | | | | | | | |
| | | MF | 37 | 100 | 41 | 10 | 81 | 61 |
| | | M | ... | 99 | 40 | 9 | 80 | 60 |
| | | F | ... | 102 | 43 | 11 | 83 | 63 |
| | 1994 | | | | | | | |
| | | MF | 37 | 104 | 38 | ... | 84 | ... |
| | | M | ... | 104 | 38 | ... | 83 | ... |
| | | F | ... | 105 | 39 | ... | 84 | ... |
| | 1995 | | | | | | | |
| | | MF | 40 | 107 | 38 | ... | 85 | ... |
| | | M | 39 | 106 | 37 | ... | 85 | ... |
| | | F | 41 | 108 | 38 | ... | 86 | ... |
| | 1996 | | | | | | | |
| | | MF | ... | ... | ... | 12 | ... | ... |
| | | M | ... | ... | ... | 10 | ... | ... |
| | | F | ... | ... | ... | 14 | ... | ... |
| Austria | 1970 | | (3-5) | (6-9) | (10-17) | (18-22) | (6-17) | (6-22) |
| | | MF | 32 | 104 | 89 | 12 | 94 | 73 |
| | | M | 32 | 105 | 93 | 17 | 97 | 76 |
| | | F | 32 | 104 | 84 | 7 | 91 | 69 |
| | 1975 | | | | | | | |
| | | MF | 47 | 101 | 91 | 18 | 94 | 74 |
| | | M | 47 | 101 | 96 | 22 | 98 | 78 |
| | | F | 47 | 101 | 85 | 14 | 90 | 70 |
| | 1980 | | | | | | | |
| | | MF | 63 | 99 | 93 | 22 | 94 | 72 |
| | | M | 63 | 99 | 98 | 25 | 98 | 76 |
| | | F | 63 | 98 | 87 | 19 | 90 | 68 |

Gross enrolment ratios by level of education  II.8
Taux bruts de scolarisation par niveau d'enseignement
Tasas brutas de escolarización por nivel de enseñanza

| Country<br><br>Pays<br><br>País | Year<br><br>Année<br><br>Año | Sex<br><br>Sexe<br><br>Sexo | Gross enrolment ratios / Taux bruts de scolarisation / Tasas brutas de escolarización<br>(%) | | | | | |
|---|---|---|---|---|---|---|---|---|
| | | | Pre-primary<br><br>Préprimaire<br><br>Preprimaria | Primary<br><br>Primaire<br><br>Primaria | Secondary<br><br>Secondaire<br><br>Secundaria | Tertiary<br><br>Supérieur<br><br>Superior | Primary and<br>secondary<br><br>Primaire<br>et secondaire<br><br>Primaria y<br>secundaria | Primary,<br>secondary<br>and tertiary<br><br>Primaire,<br>secondaire et<br>supérieur<br><br>Primaria,<br>secundaria y<br>superior |
| Austria (cont) | 1985 | | | | | | | |
| | | MF | 71 | 100 | 99 | 26 | 99 | 73 |
| | | M | 71 | 101 | 103 | 28 | 102 | 76 |
| | | F | 71 | 99 | 94 | 24 | 95 | 70 |
| | 1990 | | | | | | | |
| | | MF | 70 | 102 | 104 | 35 | 103 | 79 |
| | | M | 71 | 102 | 107 | 37 | 105 | 82 |
| | | F | 69 | 102 | 100 | 33 | 101 | 77 |
| | 1991 | | | | | | | |
| | | MF | 70 | 103 | 106 | 38 | 105 | 82 |
| | | M | 70 | 103 | 109 | 40 | 107 | 84 |
| | | F | 70 | 103 | 102 | 36 | 102 | 80 |
| | 1992 | | | | | | | |
| | | MF | 72 | 103 | 107 | 40 | 105 | 84 |
| | | M | 72 | 103 | 109 | 42 | 107 | 86 |
| | | F | 72 | 103 | 104 | 39 | 103 | 82 |
| | 1993 | | | | | | | |
| | | MF | 75 | 102 | 106 | 43 | 105 | 85 |
| | | M | 75 | 102 | 109 | 44 | 106 | 86 |
| | | F | 74 | 102 | 104 | 42 | 103 | 83 |
| | 1994 | | | | | | | |
| | | MF | 77 | 102 | 105 | 45 | 104 | 86 |
| | | M | 77 | 101 | 108 | 46 | 106 | 87 |
| | | F | 77 | 102 | 103 | 45 | 102 | 84 |
| | 1995 | | | | | | | |
| | | MF | 79 | 101 | 104 | 47 | 103 | 86 |
| | | M | 78 | 101 | 106 | 47 | 104 | 87 |
| | | F | 79 | 101 | 102 | 47 | 102 | 85 |
| | 1996 | | | | | | | |
| | | MF | 80 | 100 | 103 | 48 | 102 | 86 |
| | | M | 80 | 100 | 105 | 48 | 103 | 86 |
| | | F | 81 | 100 | 102 | 49 | 101 | 85 |
| Belarus | 1980 | | (3-6) | (7-11) | (12-16) | (17-21) | (7-16) | (7-21) |
| | | MF | 58 | 104 | 98 | 39 | 101 | 78 |
| | 1985 | | | | | | | |
| | | MF | 66 | 108 | 99 | 45 | 104 | 83 |
| | 1990 | | (3-5) | (6-9) | (10-16) | (17-21) | (6 10) | (6-21) |
| | | MF | 84 | 95 | 93 | 48 | 94 | 80 |
| | | M | ... | ... | ... | 45 | ... | ... |
| | | F | ... | ... | ... | 50 | ... | ... |
| | 1991 | | | | | | | |
| | | MF | 84 | 94 | 92 | 44 | 93 | 79 |
| | | M | ... | ... | ... | 43 | ... | ... |
| | | F | ... | ... | ... | 46 | ... | ... |
| | 1992 | | | | | | | |
| | | MF | 78 | 95 | 90 | 44 | 92 | 78 |
| | | M | ... | 95 | 87 | 41 | 90 | 76 |
| | | F | ... | 95 | 94 | 47 | 94 | 80 |
| | 1993 | | | | | | | |
| | | MF | 77 | 94 | 91 | 42 | 92 | 78 |
| | | M | ... | 95 | 88 | 40 | 90 | 76 |
| | | F | ... | 94 | 94 | 43 | 94 | 79 |
| | 1994 | | | | | | | |
| | | MF | 80 | 95 | 92 | 40 | 93 | 78 |
| | | M | 86 | 97 | 90 | 38 | 92 | 76 |
| | | F | 74 | 93 | 95 | 43 | 94 | 79 |
| | 1995 | | | | | | | |
| | | MF | 80 | 96 | 93 | 42 | 94 | 79 |
| | | M | 85 | 98 | 91 | 39 | 94 | 78 |
| | | F | 75 | 94 | 95 | 46 | 95 | 81 |
| | 1996 | | | | | | | |
| | | MF | 82 | 98 | 93 | 44 | 95 | 80 |
| | | M | 86 | 100 | 91 | 39 | 94 | 78 |
| | | F | 77 | 96 | 95 | 49 | 95 | 82 |

II.8   Gross enrolment ratios by level of education
Taux bruts de scolarisation par niveau d'enseignement
Tasas brutas de escolarización por nivel de enseñanza

| Country / Pays / País | Year / Année / Año | Sex / Sexe / Sexo | Gross enrolment ratios / Taux bruts de scolarisation / Tasas brutas de escolarización (%) | | | | | |
|---|---|---|---|---|---|---|---|---|
| | | | Pre-primary / Préprimaire / Preprimaria | Primary / Primaire / Primaria | Secondary / Secondaire / Secundaria | Tertiary / Supérieur / Superior | Primary and secondary / Primaire et secondaire / Primaria y secundaria | Primary, secondary and tertiary / Primaire, secondaire et supérieur / Primaria, secundaria y superior |
| Belgium | 1970 | | (3-5) | (6-11) | (12-17) | (18-22) | (6-17) | (6-22) |
| | | MF | 100 | 108 | 81 | 17 | 95 | 73 |
| | | M | 99 | 109 | 82 | 21 | 96 | 75 |
| | | F | 100 | 107 | 80 | 13 | 94 | 71 |
| | 1975 | | | | | | | |
| | | MF | 108 | 105 | 84 | 22 | 94 | 73 |
| | | M | 107 | 105 | 84 | 26 | 94 | 74 |
| | | F | 108 | 104 | 83 | 19 | 93 | 72 |
| | 1980 | | | | | | | |
| | | MF | 103 | 104 | 91 | 26 | 97 | 75 |
| | | M | 103 | 104 | 90 | 29 | 97 | 75 |
| | | F | 104 | 104 | 92 | 23 | 98 | 74 |
| | 1985 | | | | | | | |
| | | MF | 110 | 99 | 101 | 32 | 100 | 78 |
| | | M | 110 | 99 | 101 | 34 | 100 | 78 |
| | | F | 110 | 99 | 102 | 30 | 101 | 77 |
| | 1990 | | | | | | | |
| | | MF | 105 | 101 | 103 | 40 | 102 | 82 |
| | | M | 105 | 100 | 103 | 41 | 101 | 82 |
| | | F | 105 | 101 | 103 | 40 | 102 | 82 |
| | 1991 | | | | | | | |
| | | MF | 111 | 99 | 104 | 43 | 102 | 83 |
| | | M | 111 | 99 | 103 | 43 | 101 | 83 |
| | | F | 111 | 100 | 104 | 43 | 102 | 83 |
| | 1992 | | | | | | | |
| | | MF | 114 | 103 | 142 | 46 | 123 | 99 |
| | | M | 114 | 104 | 138 | 46 | 121 | 98 |
| | | F | 114 | 103 | 146 | 46 | 125 | 100 |
| | 1993 | | | | | | | |
| | | MF | 116 | 103 | 144 | 49 | 124 | 101 |
| | | M | 117 | 103 | 140 | 49 | 122 | 99 |
| | | F | 116 | 102 | 149 | 50 | 126 | 102 |
| | 1994 | | | | | | | |
| | | MF | 118 | 103 | 146 | 55 | 125 | 103 |
| | | M | 119 | 103 | 141 | 54 | 122 | 101 |
| | | F | 117 | 102 | 151 | 55 | 127 | 105 |
| | 1995 | | | | | | | |
| | | MF | 118 | 103 | 146 | 56 | 125 | 104 |
| | | M | 118 | 104 | 142 | 55 | 123 | 102 |
| | | F | 117 | 102 | 151 | 57 | 127 | 106 |
| Bulgaria | 1970 | | (4-6) | (7-14) | (15-17) | (18-22) | (7-17) | (7-22) |
| | | MF | 88 | 101 | 79 | 14 | 95 | 69 |
| | | M | 86 | 101 | 80 | 14 | 95 | 69 |
| | | F | 90 | 100 | 78 | 15 | 94 | 68 |
| | 1975 | | | | | | | |
| | | MF | 102 | 99 | 89 | 19 | 96 | 71 |
| | | M | 102 | 99 | 89 | 16 | 96 | 70 |
| | | F | 102 | 99 | 89 | 23 | 96 | 72 |
| | 1980 | | | | | | | |
| | | MF | 104 | 98 | 84 | 16 | 94 | 70 |
| | | M | 105 | 98 | 85 | 14 | 95 | 70 |
| | | F | 104 | 98 | 84 | 19 | 94 | 70 |
| | 1985 | | | | | | | |
| | | MF | 93 | 102 | 102 | 19 | 102 | 77 |
| | | M | 94 | 103 | 101 | 17 | 102 | 77 |
| | | F | 92 | 102 | 102 | 21 | 102 | 78 |
| | 1990 | | (3-5) | (6-13) | (14-17) | (18-22) | (6-17) | (6-22) |
| | | MF | 92 | 98 | 75 | 31 | 90 | 73 |
| | | M | 91 | 99 | 74 | 30 | 90 | 73 |
| | | F | 92 | 96 | 77 | 33 | 90 | 73 |
| | 1991 | | | | | | | |
| | | MF | 80 | 95 | 74 | 30 | 88 | 71 |
| | | M | 79 | 97 | 72 | 28 | 88 | 70 |
| | | F | 80 | 94 | 75 | 33 | 87 | 72 |

Gross enrolment ratios by level of education    II.8
Taux bruts de scolarisation par niveau d'enseignement
Tasas brutas de escolarización por nivel de enseñanza

| Country / Pays / País | Year / Année / Año | Sex / Sexe / Sexo | Gross enrolment ratios / Taux bruts de scolarisation / Tasas brutas de escolarización (%) | | | | | |
|---|---|---|---|---|---|---|---|---|
| | | | Pre-primary / Préprimaire / Preprimaria | Primary / Primaire / Primaria | Secondary / Secondaire / Secundaria | Tertiary / Supérieur / Superior | Primary and secondary / Primaire et secondaire / Primaria y secundaria | Primary, secondary and tertiary / Primaire, secondaire et supérieur / Primaria, secundaria y superior |
| Bulgaria (cont) | 1992 | | | | | | | |
| | | MF | 82 | 92 | 72 | 31 | 85 | 69 |
| | | M | 82 | 94 | 71 | 26 | 86 | 68 |
| | | F | 82 | 91 | 74 | 37 | 85 | 70 |
| | 1993 | | (3-6) | (7-14) | (15-18) | (19-23) | (7-18) | (7-23) |
| | | MF | 58 | 89 | 70 | 33 | 82 | 68 |
| | | M | 58 | 90 | 68 | 27 | 83 | 66 |
| | | F | 57 | 87 | 72 | 40 | 81 | 69 |
| | 1994 | | | | | | | |
| | | MF | 58 | 89 | 72 | 35 | 83 | 69 |
| | | M | 59 | 91 | 70 | 27 | 83 | 66 |
| | | F | 58 | 87 | 74 | 44 | 83 | 71 |
| | 1995 | | (3-6) | (7-10) | (11-18) | (19-23) | (7-18) | (7-23) |
| | | MF | 62 | 97 | 78 | 39 | 84 | 70 |
| | | M | 63 | 98 | 78 | 29 | 85 | 68 |
| | | F | 61 | 96 | 77 | 50 | 83 | 73 |
| | 1996 | | | | | | | |
| | | MF | 63 | 99 | 77 | 41 | 84 | 70 |
| | | M | 64 | 100 | 77 | 31 | 84 | 68 |
| | | F | 62 | 98 | 76 | 52 | 83 | 73 |
| Croatia | 1980 | | (3-6) | (7-14) | (15-18) | (19-23) | (7-18) | (7-23) |
| | | MF | 26 | ... | 77 | 19 | ... | ... |
| | | M | 26 | ... | ... | ... | ... | ... |
| | | F | 25 | ... | ... | ... | ... | ... |
| | 1985 | | | | | | | |
| | | MF | 27 | 105 | 78 | 18 | 96 | 73 |
| | | M | 27 | 105 | 77 | 18 | 96 | ... |
| | | F | 27 | 106 | 80 | ... | 97 | ... |
| | 1990 | | | | | | | |
| | | MF | 28 | 85 | 76 | 24 | 82 | 65 |
| | | M | 29 | 85 | 73 | ... | 81 | ... |
| | | F | 28 | 84 | 80 | ... | 83 | ... |
| | 1991 | | | | | | | |
| | | MF | 21 | 81 | 71 | 23 | 78 | 62 |
| | | M | 22 | 82 | 66 | ... | 77 | ... |
| | | F | 21 | 81 | 75 | ... | 79 | ... |
| | 1992 | | | | | | | |
| | | MF | 23 | 86 | 77 | 26 | 83 | 67 |
| | | M | 24 | 86 | 73 | 26 | 82 | 66 |
| | | F | 23 | 85 | 81 | 25 | 84 | 67 |
| | 1993 | | | | | | | |
| | | MF | 26 | 87 | 83 | 27 | 86 | 69 |
| | | M | 27 | 87 | 80 | 28 | 85 | 69 |
| | | F | 25 | 87 | 86 | 26 | 86 | 69 |
| | 1994 | | | | | | | |
| | | MF | 30 | 86 | 78 | 27 | 84 | 67 |
| | | M | 30 | 87 | 75 | 27 | 83 | 67 |
| | | F | 29 | 86 | 81 | 27 | 84 | 68 |
| | 1995 | | (3-6) | (7-10) | (11-18) | (19-23) | (7-18) | (7-23) |
| | | MF | 31 | 86 | 82 | 28 | 83 | 67 |
| | | M | 32 | 87 | 81 | 28 | 83 | 67 |
| | | F | 30 | 86 | 83 | 28 | 84 | 68 |
| | 1996 | | | | | | | |
| | | MF | 40 | 87 | 82 | 28 | 83 | 67 |
| | | M | 41 | 88 | 81 | 27 | 83 | 67 |
| | | F | 39 | 87 | 83 | 29 | 84 | 68 |
| Czech Republic | 1980 | | (3-5) | (6-9) | (10-17) | (18-22) | (6-17) | (6-22) |
| | | MF | 84 | 95 | 99 | 17 | 97 | 75 |
| | | M | 82 | 95 | 96 | 20 | 96 | 75 |
| | | F | 86 | 96 | 102 | 14 | 99 | 76 |
| | 1985 | | | | | | | |
| | | MF | 91 | 99 | 91 | 16 | 94 | 74 |
| | | M | 89 | 101 | 88 | 18 | 93 | 74 |
| | | F | 93 | 97 | 93 | 14 | 95 | 74 |

II.8    Gross enrolment ratios by level of education
Taux bruts de scolarisation par niveau d'enseignement
Tasas brutas de escolarización por nivel de enseñanza

| Country / Pays / País | Year / Année / Año | Sex / Sexe / Sexo | Gross enrolment ratios / Taux bruts de scolarisation / Tasas brutas de escolarización (%) | | | | | |
|---|---|---|---|---|---|---|---|---|
| | | | Pre-primary / Préprimaire / Preprimaria | Primary / Primaire / Primaria | Secondary / Secondaire / Secundaria | Tertiary / Supérieur / Superior | Primary and secondary / Primaire et secondaire / Primaria y secundaria | Primary, secondary and tertiary / Primaire, secondaire et supérieur / Primaria, secundaria y superior |
| Czech Republic (cont) | 1990 | MF | 95 | 96 | 91 | 16 | 93 | 72 |
| | | M | 96 | 96 | 93 | 18 | 94 | 73 |
| | | F | 94 | 97 | 90 | 14 | 92 | 70 |
| | 1991 | MF | 88 | 98 | 87 | 15 | 90 | 69 |
| | | M | ... | ... | 86 | 16 | ... | ... |
| | | F | ... | ... | 89 | 13 | ... | ... |
| | 1992 | MF | 89 | 98 | 90 | 15 | 92 | 69 |
| | | M | 86 | 98 | 87 | 16 | 90 | 68 |
| | | F | 91 | 99 | 93 | 13 | 94 | 70 |
| | 1993 | MF | 91 | 101 | 92 | 20 | 95 | 71 |
| | | M | 91 | 101 | 91 | 20 | 94 | 71 |
| | | F | 91 | 101 | 92 | 19 | 95 | 71 |
| | 1994 | MF | 92 | 102 | 95 | 21 | 98 | 72 |
| | | M | 91 | 103 | 94 | 21 | 97 | 72 |
| | | F | 93 | 102 | 97 | 20 | 98 | 73 |
| | 1995 | MF | 91 | 104 | 99 | 22 | 100 | 74 |
| | | M | 91 | 105 | 97 | 23 | 99 | 74 |
| | | F | 91 | 103 | 100 | 21 | 101 | 74 |
| | 1996 | MF | ... | ... | ... | 24 | ... | ... |
| | | M | ... | ... | ... | 24 | ... | ... |
| | | F | ... | ... | ... | 23 | ... | ... |
| Denmark | 1970 | | | (6-11) | (12-17) | (18-22) | (6-17) | (6-22) |
| | | MF | ... | 96 | 93 | 19 | 95 | 71 |
| | | M | ... | 95 | 101 | 23 | 98 | 75 |
| | | F | ... | 97 | 85 | 14 | 91 | 67 |
| | 1975 | MF | ... | 104 | 95 | 30 | 100 | 80 |
| | | M | ... | 105 | 101 | 33 | 103 | 83 |
| | | F | ... | 104 | 89 | 27 | 96 | 77 |
| | 1980 | | (6-6) | (7-12) | (13-18) | (19-23) | (7-18) | (7-23) |
| | | MF | 88 | 95 | 105 | 28 | 100 | 80 |
| | | M | 88 | 96 | 105 | 28 | 101 | 80 |
| | | F | 88 | 95 | 104 | 28 | 100 | 79 |
| | 1985 | MF | 94 | 99 | 105 | 29 | 102 | 79 |
| | | M | 93 | 99 | 106 | 29 | 102 | 79 |
| | | F | 94 | 98 | 105 | 29 | 102 | 79 |
| | 1990 | MF | 99 | 98 | 109 | 36 | 104 | 81 |
| | | M | 99 | 98 | 109 | 34 | 104 | 80 |
| | | F | 99 | 98 | 110 | 39 | 105 | 83 |
| | 1991 | MF | 101 | 97 | 110 | 39 | 104 | 82 |
| | | M | 101 | 97 | 109 | 36 | 104 | 80 |
| | | F | 101 | 97 | 111 | 42 | 105 | 83 |
| | 1992 | | (3-6) | (7-12) | (13-18) | (19-23) | (7-18) | (7-23) |
| | | MF | 82 | 97 | 112 | 43 | 105 | 84 |
| | | M | 82 | 97 | 111 | 41 | 105 | 83 |
| | | F | 83 | 98 | 113 | 45 | 106 | 85 |
| | 1993 | MF | 84 | 99 | 115 | 45 | 108 | 86 |
| | | M | 83 | 99 | 114 | 43 | 107 | 85 |
| | | F | 85 | 100 | 116 | 47 | 109 | 87 |
| | 1994 | MF | 83 | 100 | 119 | 46 | 110 | 88 |
| | | M | 82 | 100 | 117 | 43 | 109 | 86 |
| | | F | 83 | 100 | 120 | 48 | 111 | 89 |

Gross enrolment ratios by level of education    II.8
Taux bruts de scolarisation par niveau d'enseignement
Tasas brutas de escolarización por nivel de enseñanza

| Country / Pays / País | Year / Année / Año | Sex / Sexe / Sexo | Gross enrolment ratios / Taux bruts de scolarisation / Tasas brutas de escolarización (%) | | | | | |
|---|---|---|---|---|---|---|---|---|
| | | | Pre-primary / Préprimaire / Preprimaria | Primary / Primaire / Primaria | Secondary / Secondaire / Secundaria | Tertiary / Supérieur / Superior | Primary and secondary / Primaire et secondaire / Primaria y secundaria | Primary, secondary and tertiary / Primaire, secondaire et supérieur / Primaria, secundaria y superior |
| Denmark (cont) | 1995 | | | | | | | |
| | | MF | 83 | 101 | 121 | 48 | 112 | 90 |
| | | M | 83 | 102 | 120 | 43 | 111 | 88 |
| | | F | 83 | 101 | 122 | 53 | 112 | 92 |
| Estonia | 1980 | | (3-5) | (6-11) | (12-16) | (17-21) | (6-16) | (6-21) |
| | | MF | 97 | 103 | 127 | 25 | 113 | 84 |
| | | M | ... | 104 | 126 | 22 | 114 | 83 |
| | | F | ... | 102 | 127 | 27 | 113 | 85 |
| | 1985 | | | | | | | |
| | | MF | 99 | 103 | 119 | 24 | 110 | 84 |
| | | M | ... | 104 | 116 | 20 | 109 | 83 |
| | | F | ... | 101 | 122 | 29 | 111 | 86 |
| | 1990 | | (3-6) | (7-11) | (12-17) | (18-22) | (7-17) | (7-22) |
| | | MF | 75 | 111 | 102 | 26 | 106 | 82 |
| | | M | 76 | 112 | 98 | 25 | 104 | 80 |
| | | F | 75 | 109 | 107 | 27 | 108 | 84 |
| | 1991 | | | | | | | |
| | | MF | 68 | 109 | 100 | 26 | 104 | 81 |
| | | M | 68 | 110 | 96 | 25 | 102 | 79 |
| | | F | 68 | 107 | 104 | 27 | 106 | 83 |
| | 1992 | | | | | | | |
| | | MF | 61 | 105 | 94 | 25 | 99 | 77 |
| | | M | 61 | 106 | 91 | 24 | 98 | 75 |
| | | F | 61 | 103 | 98 | 25 | 100 | 78 |
| | 1993 | | | | | | | |
| | | MF | 63 | 103 | 94 | 24 | 98 | 76 |
| | | M | 62 | 104 | 88 | 22 | 96 | 73 |
| | | F | 63 | 102 | 100 | 25 | 101 | 79 |
| | 1994 | | | | | | | |
| | | MF | 63 | 104 | 96 | 24 | 100 | 77 |
| | | M | 63 | 105 | 91 | 23 | 98 | 75 |
| | | F | 63 | 102 | 101 | 26 | 102 | 79 |
| | 1995 | | (3-6) | (7-12) | (13-17) | (18-22) | (7-17) | (7-22) |
| | | MF | 66 | 91 | 104 | 38 | 97 | 79 |
| | | M | 66 | 92 | 99 | 35 | 95 | 77 |
| | | F | 66 | 90 | 109 | 41 | 98 | 81 |
| | 1996 | | | | | | | |
| | | MF | 68 | 94 | 104 | 42 | 98 | 81 |
| | | M | 69 | 95 | 100 | 38 | 97 | 80 |
| | | F | 67 | 93 | 108 | 46 | 99 | 83 |
| Federal Republic of Yugoslavia | 1990 | | (3-6) | (7-10) | (11-18) | (19-23) | (7-18) | (7-23) |
| | | MF | ... | 72 | 63 | ... | 66 | ... |
| | | M | ... | 71 | 62 | ... | 66 | ... |
| | | F | ... | 73 | 64 | ... | 67 | ... |
| | 1991 | | | | | | | |
| | | MF | ... | 72 | 65 | 18 | 67 | 54 |
| | | M | ... | 72 | 64 | 17 | 67 | 53 |
| | | F | ... | 73 | 66 | 19 | 68 | 54 |
| | 1992 | | | | | | | |
| | | MF | 25 | 73 | 65 | 19 | 68 | 54 |
| | | M | 25 | 72 | 65 | 17 | 67 | 53 |
| | | F | 25 | 73 | 66 | 21 | 68 | 55 |
| | 1993 | | | | | | | |
| | | MF | 24 | 71 | 63 | 19 | 66 | 52 |
| | | M | 24 | 69 | 62 | 17 | 64 | 51 |
| | | F | 24 | 72 | 64 | 21 | 67 | 54 |
| | 1994 | | | | | | | |
| | | MF | 27 | 69 | 62 | 19 | 65 | 52 |
| | | M | 27 | 68 | 61 | 17 | 64 | 50 |
| | | F | 27 | 70 | 63 | 21 | 66 | 53 |
| | 1995 | | | | | | | |
| | | MF | 30 | 70 | 64 | 20 | 66 | 53 |
| | | M | 30 | 69 | 62 | 19 | 65 | 52 |
| | | F | 30 | 71 | 65 | 23 | 67 | 54 |

II.8    Gross enrolment ratios by level of education
Taux bruts de scolarisation par niveau d'enseignement
Tasas brutas de escolarización por nivel de enseñanza

| Country / Pays / País | Year / Année / Año | Sex / Sexe / Sexo | Gross enrolment ratios / Taux bruts de scolarisation / Tasas brutas de escolarización (%) | | | | | |
|---|---|---|---|---|---|---|---|---|
| | | | Pre-primary / Préprimaire / Preprimaria | Primary / Primaire / Primaria | Secondary / Secondaire / Secundaria | Tertiary / Supérieur / Superior | Primary and secondary / Primaire et secondaire / Primaria y secundaria | Primary, secondary and tertiary / Primaire, secondaire et supérieur / Primaria, secundaria y superior |
| Federal Republic of Yugoslavia (cont) | 1996 | | | | | | | |
| | | MF | 31 | 69 | 62 | 22 | 64 | 52 |
| | | M | 31 | 69 | 60 | 20 | 63 | 51 |
| | | F | 31 | 70 | 64 | 24 | 66 | 54 |
| Finland | 1970 | | (5-6) | (7-12) | (13-18) | (19-23) | (7-18) | (7-23) |
| | | MF | 17 | 82 | 102 | 13 | 92 | 67 |
| | | M | 17 | 84 | 98 | 13 | 91 | 66 |
| | | F | 17 | 79 | 106 | 13 | 93 | 68 |
| | 1975 | | (3-6) | (7-12) | (13-18) | (19-23) | (7-18) | (7-23) |
| | | MF | ... | 102 | 89 | 28 | 95 | 74 |
| | | M | ... | 103 | 83 | 28 | 93 | 73 |
| | | F | ... | 101 | 94 | 27 | 98 | 76 |
| | 1980 | | | | | | | |
| | | MF | 27 | 96 | 100 | 32 | 98 | 77 |
| | | M | ... | 97 | 94 | 33 | 95 | 76 |
| | | F | ... | 96 | 105 | 32 | 101 | 79 |
| | 1985 | | | | | | | |
| | | MF | 28 | 102 | 106 | 34 | 104 | 81 |
| | | M | ... | 103 | 98 | 34 | 100 | 78 |
| | | F | ... | 102 | 114 | 34 | 109 | 84 |
| | 1990 | | | | | | | |
| | | MF | 34 | 99 | 116 | 49 | 107 | 89 |
| | | M | ... | 99 | 106 | 46 | 103 | 85 |
| | | F | ... | 99 | 127 | 52 | 112 | 94 |
| | 1991 | | | | | | | |
| | | MF | 35 | 99 | 121 | 53 | 110 | 92 |
| | | M | ... | 99 | 109 | 49 | 104 | 88 |
| | | F | ... | 99 | 133 | 57 | 115 | 98 |
| | 1992 | | | | | | | |
| | | MF | 35 | 99 | 118 | 59 | 108 | 94 |
| | | M | 36 | 100 | 108 | 54 | 104 | 89 |
| | | F | 35 | 99 | 128 | 64 | 113 | 99 |
| | 1993 | | | | | | | |
| | | MF | 37 | 100 | 118 | 63 | 109 | 96 |
| | | M | 37 | 100 | 109 | 58 | 105 | 91 |
| | | F | 37 | 100 | 128 | 69 | 114 | 101 |
| | 1994 | | | | | | | |
| | | MF | 38 | 99 | 116 | 67 | 108 | 96 |
| | | M | 38 | 100 | 108 | 62 | 104 | 92 |
| | | F | 38 | 99 | 124 | 72 | 112 | 101 |
| | 1995 | | | | | | | |
| | | MF | 42 | 99 | 116 | 70 | 108 | 97 |
| | | M | 42 | 99 | 107 | 65 | 103 | 92 |
| | | F | 42 | 99 | 125 | 76 | 113 | 102 |
| | 1996 | | | | | | | |
| | | MF | 45 | 99 | 118 | 74 | 108 | 99 |
| | | M | 45 | 98 | 110 | 68 | 104 | 94 |
| | | F | 45 | 99 | 125 | 80 | 112 | 103 |
| France | 1970 | | (2-5) | (6-10) | (11-17) | (18-22) | (6-17) | (6-22) |
| | | MF | 65 | 117 | 73 | 19 | 92 | 70 |
| | | M | 65 | 117 | 70 | ... | 90 | ... |
| | | F | 65 | 116 | 76 | ... | 93 | ... |
| | 1975 | | | | | | | |
| | | MF | 79 | 109 | 82 | 25 | 93 | 73 |
| | | M | 78 | 105 | 82 | 25 | 91 | 72 |
| | | F | 79 | 114 | 81 | 24 | 95 | 74 |
| | 1980 | | | | | | | |
| | | MF | 76 | 111 | 85 | 25 | 95 | 75 |
| | | M | 77 | 112 | 77 | 27 | 92 | 73 |
| | | F | 76 | 110 | 92 | 24 | 99 | 77 |
| | 1985 | | | | | | | |
| | | MF | 89 | 109 | 90 | 30 | 97 | 77 |
| | | M | 89 | 110 | 86 | 29 | 95 | 75 |
| | | F | 88 | 107 | 94 | 30 | 99 | 78 |

Gross enrolment ratios by level of education II.8
Taux bruts de scolarisation par niveau d'enseignement
Tasas brutas de escolarización por nivel de enseñanza

| Country / Pays / País | Year / Année / Año | Sex / Sexe / Sexo | Gross enrolment ratios / Taux bruts de scolarisation / Tasas brutas de escolarización (%) | | | | | |
|---|---|---|---|---|---|---|---|---|
| | | | Pre-primary / Préprimaire / Preprimaria | Primary / Primaire / Primaria | Secondary / Secondaire / Secundaria | Tertiary / Supérieur / Superior | Primary and secondary / Primaire et secondaire / Primaria y secundaria | Primary, secondary and tertiary / Primaire, secondaire et supérieur / Primaria, secundaria y superior |
| France (cont) | 1990 | | | | | | | |
| | | MF | 83 | 108 | 99 | 40 | 103 | 83 |
| | | M | 83 | 109 | 96 | 37 | 101 | 81 |
| | | F | 83 | 108 | 101 | 43 | 104 | 85 |
| | 1991 | | | | | | | |
| | | MF | 83 | 107 | 101 | 43 | 104 | 85 |
| | | M | 83 | 108 | 99 | 39 | 103 | 83 |
| | | F | 83 | 106 | 104 | 47 | 105 | 87 |
| | 1992 | | | | | | | |
| | | MF | 83 | 106 | 102 | 46 | 103 | 85 |
| | | M | 83 | 107 | 100 | 41 | 102 | 83 |
| | | F | 83 | 105 | 104 | 51 | 104 | 88 |
| | 1993 | | | | | | | |
| | | MF | 84 | 106 | 110 | 50 | 108 | 90 |
| | | M | 84 | 107 | 110 | 44 | 109 | 89 |
| | | F | 84 | 105 | 110 | 55 | 108 | 91 |
| | 1994 | | | | | | | |
| | | MF | 84 | 106 | 111 | 50 | 109 | 91 |
| | | M | 84 | 107 | 112 | 44 | 110 | 89 |
| | | F | 84 | 105 | 111 | 56 | 108 | 92 |
| | 1995 | | | | | | | |
| | | MF | 84 | 106 | 111 | 51 | 109 | 91 |
| | | M | 84 | 107 | 112 | 45 | 110 | 90 |
| | | F | 84 | 105 | 111 | 57 | 108 | 93 |
| | 1996 | | | | | | | |
| | | MF | 83 | 105 | 111 | 51 | 109 | 91 |
| | | M | 83 | 106 | 112 | 45 | 109 | 90 |
| | | F | 83 | 104 | 111 | 57 | 108 | 93 |
| Germany | 1990 | | (3-5) | (6-9) | (10-18) | (19-23) | (6-18) | (6-23) |
| | | MF | ... | 101 | 98 | 34 | 99 | 76 |
| | | M | ... | ... | 100 | ... | ... | ... |
| | | F | ... | ... | 97 | ... | ... | ... |
| | 1991 | | | | | | | |
| | | MF | ... | 99 | 100 | 35 | 100 | 78 |
| | | M | ... | 98 | 101 | 40 | 100 | 80 |
| | | F | ... | 99 | 99 | 30 | 99 | 75 |
| | 1992 | | | | | | | |
| | | MF | 89 | 100 | 106 | 39 | 104 | 82 |
| | | M | 89 | 101 | 107 | 44 | 105 | 85 |
| | | F | 89 | 100 | 104 | 33 | 103 | 80 |
| | 1993 | | | | | | | |
| | | MF | 89 | 100 | 106 | 41 | 104 | 84 |
| | | M | 89 | 100 | 107 | 47 | 105 | 87 |
| | | F | 89 | 99 | 104 | 36 | 103 | 82 |
| | 1994 | | | | | | | |
| | | MF | 82 | 100 | 105 | 44 | 103 | 86 |
| | | M | 83 | 101 | 106 | 49 | 104 | 88 |
| | | F | 81 | 100 | 103 | 39 | 102 | 84 |
| | 1995 | | | | | | | |
| | | MF | 87 | 102 | 104 | 46 | 103 | 87 |
| | | M | 88 | 102 | 105 | 50 | 104 | 89 |
| | | F | 85 | 102 | 103 | 42 | 102 | 85 |
| | 1996 | | | | | | | |
| | | MF | 89 | 104 | 104 | 47 | 104 | 88 |
| | | M | 89 | 104 | 105 | 50 | 104 | 89 |
| | | F | 88 | 104 | 103 | 44 | 103 | 87 |
| Greece | 1970 | | (4-5) | (6-11) | (12-17) | (18-22) | (6-17) | (6-22) |
| | | MF | 31 | 107 | 63 | 13 | 85 | 65 |
| | | M | 31 | 108 | 70 | 17 | 89 | 69 |
| | | F | 31 | 106 | 55 | 9 | 81 | 61 |
| | 1975 | | | | | | | |
| | | MF | 36 | 104 | 78 | 18 | 91 | 71 |
| | | M | 36 | 105 | 87 | 21 | 96 | 75 |
| | | F | 36 | 104 | 69 | 14 | 87 | 67 |

Gross enrolment ratios by level of education
Taux bruts de scolarisation par niveau d'enseignement
Tasas brutas de escolarización por nivel de enseñanza

| Country | Year | Sex | Gross enrolment ratios / Taux bruts de scolarisation / Tasas brutas de escolarización (%) | | | | | |
|---|---|---|---|---|---|---|---|---|
| Pays | Année | Sexe | Pre-primary Préprimaire Preprimaria | Primary Primaire Primaria | Secondary Secondaire Secundaria | Tertiary Supérieur Superior | Primary and secondary Primaire et secondaire Primaria y secundaria | Primary, secondary and tertiary Primaire, secondaire et supérieur Primaria, secundaria y superior |
| País | Año | Sexo | | | | | | |
| Greece (cont) | 1980 | MF | 54 | 103 | 81 | 17 | 92 | 71 |
| | | M | 53 | 103 | 85 | 20 | 94 | 73 |
| | | F | 54 | 103 | 77 | 14 | 89 | 68 |
| | 1985 | MF | 57 | 104 | 90 | 24 | 97 | 75 |
| | | M | 56 | 104 | 92 | 24 | 98 | 75 |
| | | F | 57 | 104 | 89 | 25 | 97 | 75 |
| | 1990 | MF | 56 | 98 | 93 | 36 | 95 | 77 |
| | | M | 56 | 98 | 94 | 36 | 96 | 78 |
| | | F | 57 | 98 | 92 | 36 | 95 | 76 |
| | 1991 | MF | 58 | 96 | 95 | 35 | 96 | 77 |
| | | M | 57 | 97 | 96 | 35 | 96 | 77 |
| | | F | 58 | 96 | 95 | 34 | 95 | 76 |
| | 1992 | MF | 60 | 95 | 93 | 38 | 94 | 76 |
| | | M | 59 | 95 | 93 | 38 | 94 | 76 |
| | | F | 60 | 94 | 93 | 38 | 94 | 76 |
| | 1993 | MF | 60 | 94 | 94 | 40 | 94 | 77 |
| | | M | 60 | 95 | 97 | 42 | 96 | 79 |
| | | F | 61 | 94 | 92 | 38 | 93 | 75 |
| | 1994 | MF | 61 | 96 | 95 | 38 | 95 | 77 |
| | | M | 60 | 96 | 95 | 37 | 95 | 76 |
| | | F | 61 | 96 | 94 | 39 | 95 | 77 |
| | 1995 | MF | 61 | 94 | 95 | 42 | 95 | 78 |
| | | M | 60 | 94 | 95 | 42 | 95 | 78 |
| | | F | 61 | 94 | 96 | 42 | 95 | 77 |
| | 1996 | MF | 64 | 93 | 95 | 47 | 94 | 79 |
| | | M | 63 | 93 | 95 | 47 | 94 | 79 |
| | | F | 64 | 93 | 96 | 46 | 95 | 79 |
| Hungary | 1970 | | (3-5) | (6-13) | (14-17) | (18-22) | (6-17) | (6-22) |
| | | MF | 60 | 98 | 63 | 9 | 84 | 61 |
| | | M | 60 | 98 | 71 | 11 | 88 | 64 |
| | | F | 59 | 97 | 55 | 8 | 81 | 58 |
| | 1975 | MF | 71 | 99 | 63 | 12 | 86 | 60 |
| | | M | 71 | 99 | 67 | 12 | 88 | 61 |
| | | F | 71 | 99 | 59 | 12 | 84 | 59 |
| | 1980 | MF | 96 | 96 | 70 | 14 | 88 | 67 |
| | | M | 97 | 96 | 72 | 14 | 89 | 67 |
| | | F | 95 | 97 | 67 | 14 | 88 | 66 |
| | 1985 | MF | 91 | 99 | 72 | 15 | 91 | 72 |
| | | M | 91 | 99 | 72 | 14 | 91 | 71 |
| | | F | 91 | 99 | 72 | 17 | 91 | 72 |
| | 1990 | MF | 113 | 95 | 79 | 14 | 89 | 68 |
| | | M | 115 | 95 | 78 | 14 | 89 | 67 |
| | | F | 111 | 95 | 79 | 14 | 89 | 68 |
| | 1991 | MF | 116 | 94 | 80 | 14 | 89 | 67 |
| | | M | 117 | 94 | 80 | 14 | 89 | 67 |
| | | F | 114 | 94 | 81 | 15 | 89 | 67 |
| | 1992 | MF | 115 | 94 | 84 | 15 | 90 | 67 |
| | | M | 116 | 94 | 83 | 15 | 90 | 67 |
| | | F | 113 | 94 | 86 | 16 | 91 | 68 |

Gross enrolment ratios by level of education
Taux bruts de scolarisation par niveau d'enseignement
Tasas brutas de escolarización por nivel de enseñanza

II.8

| Country / Pays / País | Year / Année / Año | Sex / Sexe / Sexo | Gross enrolment ratios / Taux bruts de scolarisation / Tasas brutas de escolarización (%) | | | | | |
|---|---|---|---|---|---|---|---|---|
| | | | Pre-primary / Préprimaire / Preprimaria | Primary / Primaire / Primaria | Secondary / Secondaire / Secundaria | Tertiary / Supérieur / Superior | Primary and secondary / Primaire et secondaire / Primaria y secundaria | Primary, secondary and tertiary / Primaire, secondaire et supérieur / Primaria, secundaria y superior |
| Hungary (cont) | 1993 | | (3-5) | (6-9) | (10-17) | (18-22) | (6-17) | (6-22) |
| | | MF | 113 | 102 | 94 | 18 | 97 | 72 |
| | | M | 114 | 103 | 93 | 17 | 96 | 71 |
| | | F | 111 | 102 | 96 | 19 | 98 | 73 |
| | 1994 | | | | | | | |
| | | MF | 110 | 103 | 96 | 21 | 98 | 73 |
| | | M | 111 | 104 | 94 | 20 | 97 | 71 |
| | | F | 108 | 102 | 97 | 22 | 99 | 74 |
| | 1995 | | | | | | | |
| | | MF | 109 | 103 | 98 | 24 | 99 | 74 |
| | | M | 110 | 104 | 96 | 22 | 99 | 73 |
| | | F | 108 | 102 | 99 | 26 | 100 | 75 |
| Iceland | 1970 | | (6-6) | (7-12) | (13-19) | (20-24) | (7-19) | (7-24) |
| | | MF | ... | 98 | 80 | 10 | 89 | 70 |
| | | M | ... | 98 | 87 | 14 | 93 | 74 |
| | | F | ... | 99 | 72 | 5 | 85 | 67 |
| | 1975 | | | | | | | |
| | | MF | 84 | 100 | 82 | 15 | 90 | 71 |
| | | M | ... | 100 | 88 | 18 | 93 | 74 |
| | | F | ... | 99 | 75 | 12 | 86 | 67 |
| | 1980 | | | | | | | |
| | | MF | 96 | 99 | 86 | 20 | 92 | 72 |
| | | M | ... | ... | 90 | 20 | ... | ... |
| | | F | ... | ... | 82 | 21 | ... | ... |
| | 1985 | | | | | | | |
| | | MF | 109 | 98 | 91 | 21 | 94 | 73 |
| | | M | 109 | 99 | 94 | 18 | 96 | 74 |
| | | F | 109 | 98 | 87 | 24 | 92 | 73 |
| | 1990 | | (2-5) | (6-12) | (13-19) | (20-24) | (6-19) | (6-24) |
| | | MF | ... | 101 | 100 | 25 | 100 | 81 |
| | | M | ... | ... | 101 | 21 | ... | ... |
| | | F | ... | ... | 98 | 29 | ... | ... |
| | 1991 | | | | | | | |
| | | MF | ... | 100 | 102 | 30 | 101 | 82 |
| | | M | ... | ... | 103 | 24 | ... | ... |
| | | F | ... | ... | 100 | 35 | ... | ... |
| | 1992 | | | | | | | |
| | | MF | ... | 99 | 103 | 27 | 101 | 82 |
| | | M | ... | 100 | 103 | 23 | 102 | 81 |
| | | F | ... | 99 | 102 | 32 | 101 | 82 |
| | 1993 | | | | | | | |
| | | MF | ... | 98 | 103 | 34 | 100 | 83 |
| | | M | ... | 98 | 104 | 28 | 101 | 82 |
| | | F | ... | 97 | 102 | 40 | 100 | 84 |
| | 1994 | | | | | | | |
| | | MF | 80 | 98 | 103 | 35 | 101 | 83 |
| | | M | ... | 99 | 104 | 29 | 101 | 82 |
| | | F | ... | 98 | 102 | 41 | 100 | 84 |
| | 1995 | | | | | | | |
| | | MF | 84 | 98 | 104 | 35 | 101 | 84 |
| | | M | 84 | 98 | 105 | 29 | 102 | 82 |
| | | F | 83 | 98 | 102 | 43 | 100 | 85 |
| | 1996 | | | | | | | |
| | | MF | 80 | 98 | 109 | 37 | 103 | 86 |
| | | M | 84 | 98 | 109 | 30 | 103 | 84 |
| | | F | 77 | 98 | 108 | 45 | 103 | 88 |
| Ireland | 1970 | | (4-5) | (6-11) | (12-16) | (17-21) | (6-16) | (6-21) |
| | | MF | 104 | 107 | 74 | 12 | 93 | 71 |
| | | M | 104 | 107 | 71 | 15 | 92 | 71 |
| | | F | 104 | 107 | 77 | 8 | 94 | 71 |
| | 1975 | | | | | | | |
| | | MF | 102 | 104 | 87 | 17 | 97 | 74 |
| | | M | 102 | 104 | 83 | 22 | 95 | 74 |
| | | F | 102 | 104 | 91 | 12 | 98 | 74 |

II.8    Gross enrolment ratios by level of education
Taux bruts de scolarisation par niveau d'enseignement
Tasas brutas de escolarización por nivel de enseñanza

| Country / Pays / País | Year / Année / Año | Sex / Sexe / Sexo | Gross enrolment ratios / Taux bruts de scolarisation / Tasas brutas de escolarización (%) | | | | | |
|---|---|---|---|---|---|---|---|---|
| | | | Pre-primary / Préprimaire / Preprimaria | Primary / Primaire / Primaria | Secondary / Secondaire / Secundaria | Tertiary / Supérieur / Superior | Primary and secondary / Primaire et secondaire / Primaria y secundaria | Primary, secondary and tertiary / Primaire, secondaire et supérieur / Primaria, secundaria y superior |
| Ireland (cont) | 1980 | | | | | | | |
| | | MF | 97 | 100 | 90 | 18 | 95 | 73 |
| | | M | 98 | 100 | 85 | 21 | 93 | 73 |
| | | F | 96 | 100 | 95 | 15 | 98 | 74 |
| | 1985 | | | | | | | |
| | | MF | 106 | 100 | 98 | 22 | 99 | 77 |
| | | M | 107 | 100 | 93 | 25 | 97 | 76 |
| | | F | 105 | 100 | 103 | 20 | 101 | 78 |
| | 1990 | | | | | | | |
| | | MF | 101 | 103 | 101 | 29 | 102 | 81 |
| | | M | 102 | 103 | 96 | 31 | 100 | 80 |
| | | F | 101 | 103 | 105 | 28 | 104 | 82 |
| | 1991 | | | | | | | |
| | | MF | 104 | 103 | 103 | 33 | 103 | 82 |
| | | M | 104 | 103 | 98 | 34 | 101 | 81 |
| | | F | 104 | 103 | 107 | 32 | 105 | 83 |
| | 1992 | | | | | | | |
| | | MF | 106 | 104 | 111 | 35 | 107 | 86 |
| | | M | 106 | 104 | 109 | 35 | 106 | 85 |
| | | F | 106 | 104 | 114 | 34 | 108 | 86 |
| | 1993 | | | | | | | |
| | | MF | 105 | 104 | 113 | 37 | 109 | 87 |
| | | M | 105 | 104 | 111 | 38 | 107 | 86 |
| | | F | 105 | 104 | 116 | 37 | 110 | 87 |
| | 1994 | | | | | | | |
| | | MF | 106 | 104 | 115 | 38 | 109 | 87 |
| | | M | 106 | 104 | 112 | 38 | 108 | 86 |
| | | F | 106 | 104 | 118 | 38 | 111 | 88 |
| | 1995 | | | | | | | |
| | | MF | 111 | 104 | 116 | 40 | 110 | 87 |
| | | M | 112 | 104 | 112 | 38 | 108 | 86 |
| | | F | 110 | 104 | 120 | 41 | 112 | 89 |
| | 1996 | | | | | | | |
| | | MF | 114 | 104 | 118 | 41 | 111 | 88 |
| | | M | 114 | 105 | 113 | 39 | 109 | 86 |
| | | F | 114 | 104 | 122 | 43 | 113 | 90 |
| Italy | 1970 | | (3-5) | (6-10) | (11-18) | (19-23) | (6-18) | (6-23) |
| | | MF | 56 | 109 | 61 | 17 | 81 | 63 |
| | | M | 56 | 109 | 66 | 21 | 84 | 67 |
| | | F | 57 | 108 | 55 | 13 | 77 | 59 |
| | 1975 | | | | | | | |
| | | MF | 69 | 105 | 71 | 26 | 84 | 70 |
| | | M | 68 | 106 | 74 | 31 | 87 | 73 |
| | | F | 69 | 105 | 67 | 20 | 82 | 66 |
| | 1980 | | | | | | | |
| | | MF | 78 | 100 | 72 | 27 | 82 | 68 |
| | | M | 78 | 100 | 73 | 31 | 83 | 70 |
| | | F | 79 | 100 | 70 | 23 | 81 | 66 |
| | 1985 | | | | | | | |
| | | MF | 85 | 96 | 73 | 25 | 81 | 65 |
| | | M | 85 | 97 | 74 | 27 | 82 | 66 |
| | | F | 85 | 96 | 73 | 24 | 81 | 64 |
| | 1990 | | | | | | | |
| | | MF | 93 | 103 | 83 | 32 | 89 | 70 |
| | | M | 93 | 103 | 83 | 33 | 90 | 71 |
| | | F | 94 | 103 | 83 | 31 | 89 | 70 |
| | 1991 | | | | | | | |
| | | MF | 94 | 105 | 85 | 34 | 91 | 72 |
| | | M | 94 | 105 | 85 | 34 | 91 | 72 |
| | | F | 95 | 104 | 85 | 34 | 91 | 72 |
| | 1992 | | | | | | | |
| | | MF | 96 | 105 | 86 | 36 | 93 | 73 |
| | | M | 95 | 104 | 86 | 35 | 92 | 73 |
| | | F | 96 | 106 | 86 | 37 | 93 | 74 |

Gross enrolment ratios by level of education  II.8
Taux bruts de scolarisation par niveau d'enseignement
Tasas brutas de escolarización por nivel de enseñanza

| Country / Pays / País | Year / Année / Año | Sex / Sexe / Sexo | Gross enrolment ratios / Taux bruts de scolarisation / Tasas brutas de escolarización (%) | | | | | |
|---|---|---|---|---|---|---|---|---|
| | | | Pre-primary / Préprimaire / Preprimaria | Primary / Primaire / Primaria | Secondary / Secondaire / Secundaria | Tertiary / Supérieur / Superior | Primary and secondary / Primaire et secondaire / Primaria y secundaria | Primary, secondary and tertiary / Primaire, secondaire et supérieur / Primaria, secundaria y superior |
| Italy (cont) | 1993 | MF | 96 | 102 | 91 | 40 | 95 | 76 |
| | | M | 95 | 100 | 91 | 38 | 94 | 75 |
| | | F | 96 | 104 | 91 | 42 | 96 | 77 |
| | 1994 | MF | 95 | 101 | 93 | 42 | 96 | 77 |
| | | M | 96 | 102 | 93 | 39 | 96 | 76 |
| | | F | 95 | 100 | 93 | 44 | 95 | 77 |
| | 1995 | MF | 95 | 101 | 94 | 42 | 96 | 78 |
| | | M | 96 | 101 | 94 | 39 | 97 | 77 |
| | | F | 94 | 100 | 94 | 46 | 96 | 79 |
| | 1996 | MF | 95 | 101 | 95 | 47 | 97 | 80 |
| | | M | 95 | 101 | 94 | 42 | 97 | 78 |
| | | F | 94 | 100 | 95 | 52 | 97 | 81 |
| Latvia | 1980 | | (3-6) | (7-10) | (11-18) | (19-23) | (7-18) | (7-23) |
| | | MF | 58 | 102 | 99 | 24 | 100 | 75 |
| | | M | 57 | ... | ... | 20 | ... | ... |
| | | F | 58 | ... | ... | 27 | ... | ... |
| | 1985 | MF | 67 | 100 | 103 | 23 | 102 | 77 |
| | | M | 67 | ... | ... | 17 | ... | ... |
| | | F | 67 | ... | ... | 28 | ... | ... |
| | 1990 | MF | 45 | 94 | 93 | 25 | 93 | 73 |
| | | M | 45 | 95 | 93 | 22 | 93 | 72 |
| | | F | 45 | 94 | 93 | 28 | 93 | 74 |
| | 1991 | MF | 37 | 94 | 89 | 25 | 91 | 72 |
| | | M | 37 | 95 | 88 | 23 | 90 | 71 |
| | | F | 37 | 94 | 90 | 28 | 92 | 73 |
| | 1992 | MF | 28 | 87 | 87 | 24 | 87 | 69 |
| | | M | 28 | 87 | 87 | 22 | 87 | 68 |
| | | F | 27 | 87 | 88 | 27 | 87 | 70 |
| | 1993 | MF | 31 | 83 | 87 | 23 | 85 | 67 |
| | | M | 32 | 84 | 85 | 21 | 84 | 66 |
| | | F | 31 | 82 | 89 | 25 | 87 | 69 |
| | 1994 | MF | 38 | 83 | 87 | 23 | 85 | 68 |
| | | M | 39 | 85 | 84 | 20 | 85 | 66 |
| | | F | 36 | 81 | 89 | 26 | 86 | 69 |
| | 1995 | MF | 44 | 89 | 85 | 27 | 86 | 70 |
| | | M | 45 | 91 | 83 | 23 | 86 | 68 |
| | | F | 43 | 86 | 87 | 31 | 87 | 71 |
| | 1996 | MF | 47 | 96 | 84 | 33 | 88 | 73 |
| | | M | 49 | 98 | 82 | 27 | 88 | 71 |
| | | F | 46 | 93 | 85 | 40 | 88 | 75 |
| Lithuania | 1980 | | (3-6) | (7-10) | (11-18) | (19-23) | (7-18) | (7-23) |
| | | MF | 51 | 79 | 114 | 35 | 102 | 82 |
| | | M | ... | 79 | ... | 28 | ... | ... |
| | | F | ... | 79 | ... | 41 | ... | ... |
| | 1985 | MF | 64 | 80 | 105 | 33 | 97 | 77 |
| | | M | ... | 80 | ... | 23 | ... | ... |
| | | F | ... | 81 | ... | 42 | ... | ... |
| | 1990 | MF | 58 | 91 | 92 | 34 | 91 | 74 |
| | | M | 57 | 93 | ... | 30 | ... | ... |
| | | F | 58 | 88 | ... | 38 | ... | ... |

Gross enrolment ratios by level of education
Taux bruts de scolarisation par niveau d'enseignement
Tasas brutas de escolarización por nivel de enseñanza

| Country<br><br>Pays<br><br>País | Year<br><br>Année<br><br>Año | Sex<br><br>Sexe<br><br>Sexo | Gross enrolment ratios / Taux bruts de scolarisation / Tasas brutas de escolarización<br>(%) | | | | | |
|---|---|---|---|---|---|---|---|---|
| | | | Pre-primary<br><br>Préprimaire<br><br>Preprimaria | Primary<br><br>Primaire<br><br>Primaria | Secondary<br><br>Secondaire<br><br>Secundaria | Tertiary<br><br>Supérieur<br><br>Superior | Primary and secondary<br><br>Primaire et secondaire<br><br>Primaria y secundaria | Primary, secondary and tertiary<br><br>Primaire, secondaire et supérieur<br><br>Primaria, secundaria y superior |
| Lithuania (cont) | 1991 | MF | 48 | 90 | 88 | 31 | 89 | 72 |
| | | M | 48 | 91 | ... | 26 | ... | ... |
| | | F | 48 | 88 | ... | 35 | ... | ... |
| | 1992 | MF | 39 | 92 | 83 | 28 | 86 | 69 |
| | | M | 39 | 93 | 83 | 24 | 86 | 68 |
| | | F | 39 | 91 | 84 | 33 | 86 | 71 |
| | 1993 | MF | ... | 93 | 81 | 26 | 85 | 68 |
| | | M | ... | 95 | 79 | 21 | 85 | 67 |
| | | F | ... | 90 | 82 | 31 | 85 | 70 |
| | 1994 | MF | 33 | 95 | 82 | 26 | 86 | 69 |
| | | M | 33 | 96 | 80 | 22 | 85 | 67 |
| | | F | 33 | 93 | 84 | 31 | 87 | 71 |
| | 1995 | MF | 37 | 96 | 84 | 28 | 88 | 71 |
| | | M | 37 | 97 | 83 | 22 | 88 | 69 |
| | | F | 36 | 95 | 86 | 34 | 89 | 73 |
| | 1996 | MF | 40 | 98 | 86 | 31 | 90 | 74 |
| | | M | 41 | 99 | 85 | 25 | 90 | 72 |
| | | F | 39 | 96 | 88 | 38 | 91 | 76 |
| Luxembourg (5) | 1970 | | (4-5) | (6-11) | (12-18) | (19-23) | (6-18) | (6-23) |
| | | MF | 77 | 112 | 48 | ... | 78 | ... |
| | | M | 77 | 112 | 49 | ... | 79 | ... |
| | | F | 76 | 112 | 46 | ... | 77 | ... |
| | 1975 | MF | 85 | 89 | 59 | ... | 73 | ... |
| | | M | 81 | 89 | 59 | ... | 73 | ... |
| | | F | 89 | 90 | 59 | ... | 73 | ... |
| | 1980 | MF | 94 | 87 | 71 | ... | 78 | ... |
| | | M | 95 | 87 | 80 | ... | 83 | ... |
| | | F | 92 | 87 | 62 | ... | 72 | ... |
| | 1985 | MF | 96 | 89 | 75 | ... | 81 | ... |
| | | M | ... | 89 | 75 | ... | 81 | ... |
| | | F | ... | 89 | 74 | ... | 80 | ... |
| | 1990 | MF | 92 | 91 | 75 | ... | 82 | ... |
| | | M | ... | 87 | ... | ... | ... | ... |
| | | F | ... | 94 | ... | ... | ... | ... |
| | 1991 | MF | 95 | ... | 69 | ... | ... | ... |
| | | M | ... | ... | 68 | ... | ... | ... |
| | | F | ... | ... | 70 | ... | ... | ... |
| | 1992 | MF | 95 | ... | 72 | ... | ... | ... |
| | | M | ... | ... | 70 | ... | ... | ... |
| | | F | ... | ... | 74 | ... | ... | ... |
| | 1993 | MF | 99 | 105 | 74 | ... | 88 | ... |
| | | M | ... | ... | 73 | ... | ... | ... |
| | | F | ... | ... | 76 | ... | ... | ... |
| | 1994 | MF | 107 | 99 | 81 | ... | 89 | ... |
| | | M | ... | ... | 80 | ... | ... | ... |
| | | F | ... | ... | 81 | ... | ... | ... |
| | 1995 | MF | 99 | 100 | 85 | 9 | 92 | 66 |
| | | M | ... | ... | 83 | 12 | ... | ... |
| | | F | ... | ... | 86 | 6 | ... | ... |

Gross enrolment ratios by level of education    II.8
Taux bruts de scolarisation par niveau d'enseignement
Tasas brutas de escolarización por nivel de enseñanza

| Country / Pays / País | Year / Année / Año | Sex / Sexe / Sexo | Gross enrolment ratios / Taux bruts de scolarisation / Tasas brutas de escolarización (%) | | | | | |
|---|---|---|---|---|---|---|---|---|
| | | | Pre-primary / Préprimaire / Preprimaria | Primary / Primaire / Primaria | Secondary / Secondaire / Secundaria | Tertiary / Supérieur / Superior | Primary and secondary / Primaire et secondaire / Primaria y secundaria | Primary, secondary and tertiary / Primaire, secondaire et supérieur / Primaria, secundaria y superior |
| Luxembourg (5) (cont) | 1996 | | 98 | 99 | 88 | 10 | 93 | 68 |
| | | MF | ... | ... | 85 | 12 | ... | ... |
| | | M | ... | ... | 90 | 7 | ... | ... |
| | | F | | | | | | |
| Malta | 1970 | | (4-4) | (5-10) | (11-17) | (18-22) | (5-17) | (5-22) |
| | | MF | 53 | 116 | 54 | 6 | 81 | 59 |
| | | M | 56 | 116 | 55 | 8 | 82 | 61 |
| | | F | 49 | 116 | 53 | 4 | 80 | 57 |
| | 1975 | MF | 139 | 106 | 85 | 5 | 94 | 68 |
| | | M | 143 | 107 | 90 | 8 | 97 | 73 |
| | | F | 134 | 106 | 79 | 3 | 90 | 64 |
| | 1980 | MF | 145 | 114 | 75 | 3 | 93 | 64 |
| | | M | 150 | 115 | 79 | 5 | 96 | 67 |
| | | F | 140 | 112 | 70 | 2 | 89 | 61 |
| | 1985 | MF | 141 | 107 | 78 | 6 | 92 | 69 |
| | | M | 146 | 109 | 79 | 8 | 94 | 71 |
| | | F | 136 | 104 | 77 | 4 | 90 | 67 |
| | 1990 | | (3-4) | (5-10) | (11-17) | (18-22) | (5-17) | (5-22) |
| | | MF | 104 | 110 | 84 | 13 | 96 | 75 |
| | | M | 108 | 112 | 87 | 14 | 98 | 77 |
| | | F | 99 | 108 | 81 | 12 | 94 | 73 |
| | 1991 | MF | 107 | 106 | 88 | 15 | 96 | 76 |
| | | M | 107 | 108 | 91 | 15 | 99 | 78 |
| | | F | 107 | 104 | 84 | 14 | 94 | 74 |
| | 1992 | MF | 111 | 106 | 87 | 18 | 96 | 76 |
| | | M | 113 | 108 | 90 | 19 | 98 | 78 |
| | | F | 110 | 105 | 84 | 18 | 93 | 74 |
| | 1993 | MF | 113 | 106 | 87 | 20 | 96 | 76 |
| | | M | 115 | 108 | 92 | 20 | 99 | 78 |
| | | F | 111 | 105 | 82 | 20 | 93 | 74 |
| | 1994 | MF | ... | 106 | 00 | 22 | 96 | 76 |
| | | M | ... | 108 | 91 | 22 | 98 | 78 |
| | | F | ... | 103 | 85 | 21 | 93 | 74 |
| | 1995 | MF | 107 | 107 | 84 | 26 | 94 | 76 |
| | | M | 106 | 108 | 87 | 25 | 96 | 77 |
| | | F | 109 | 106 | 81 | 27 | 92 | 74 |
| | 1996 | MF | 107 | 107 | 84 | 29 | 95 | 77 |
| | | M | 106 | 108 | 86 | 27 | 96 | 77 |
| | | F | 109 | 107 | 82 | 32 | 93 | 76 |
| Moldova | 1980 | | (3-6) | (7-10) | (11-18) | (19-23) | (7-18) | (7-23) |
| | | MF | 58 | 83 | 78 | 30 | 80 | 64 |
| | | M | 60 | 83 | 78 | ... | 80 | ... |
| | | F | 57 | 82 | 79 | ... | 80 | ... |
| | 1985 | MF | 66 | 84 | 86 | 33 | 85 | 70 |
| | | M | 68 | 85 | 83 | ... | 84 | ... |
| | | F | 65 | 84 | 89 | ... | 87 | ... |
| | 1990 | MF | 73 | 93 | 80 | 36 | 85 | 73 |
| | | M | 74 | 93 | 77 | ... | 83 | ... |
| | | F | 71 | 93 | 83 | ... | 87 | ... |
| | 1991 | MF | 70 | 93 | 77 | ... | 83 | ... |
| | | M | 72 | 93 | 74 | ... | 81 | ... |
| | | F | 68 | 93 | 80 | ... | 85 | ... |

II.8 Gross enrolment ratios by level of education
Taux bruts de scolarisation par niveau d'enseignement
Tasas brutas de escolarización por nivel de enseñanza

| Country<br><br>Pays<br><br>País | Year<br><br>Année<br><br>Año | Sex<br><br>Sexe<br><br>Sexo | Gross enrolment ratios / Taux bruts de scolarisation / Tasas brutas de escolarización (%) | | | | | |
|---|---|---|---|---|---|---|---|---|
| | | | Pre-primary<br><br>Préprimaire<br><br>Preprimaria | Primary<br><br>Primaire<br><br>Primaria | Secondary<br><br>Secondaire<br><br>Secundaria | Tertiary<br><br>Supérieur<br><br>Superior | Primary and secondary<br><br>Primaire et secondaire<br><br>Primaria y secundaria | Primary, secondary and tertiary<br><br>Primaire, secondaire et supérieur<br><br>Primaria, secundaria y superior |
| Moldova (cont) | 1992 | | | | | | | |
| | | MF | 61 | 92 | 75 | ... | 81 | ... |
| | | M | 62 | 92 | 71 | ... | 79 | ... |
| | | F | 60 | 92 | 79 | ... | 83 | ... |
| | 1993 | | (3-6) | (7-10) | (11-17) | (18-22) | (7-17) | (7-22) |
| | | MF | 57 | 91 | 84 | 31 | 87 | 72 |
| | | M | 58 | 91 | 80 | ... | 84 | ... |
| | | F | 56 | 91 | 88 | ... | 89 | ... |
| | 1994 | | | | | | | |
| | | MF | 50 | 96 | 82 | 30 | 87 | 71 |
| | | M | 52 | 96 | 81 | 28 | 87 | 70 |
| | | F | 48 | 95 | 84 | 32 | 88 | 73 |
| | 1995 | | | | | | | |
| | | MF | 46 | 96 | 81 | 25 | 86 | 69 |
| | | M | 47 | 96 | 80 | 22 | 86 | 68 |
| | | F | 44 | 95 | 82 | 28 | 87 | 70 |
| | 1996 | | | | | | | |
| | | MF | 45 | 97 | 80 | 27 | 87 | 70 |
| | | M | 46 | 98 | 79 | 24 | 86 | 68 |
| | | F | 43 | 97 | 82 | 29 | 87 | 71 |
| Netherlands | 1970 | | | (6-11) | (12-17) | (18-22) | (6-17) | (6-22) |
| | | MF | ... | 102 | 75 | 20 | 89 | 68 |
| | | M | ... | 101 | 81 | 28 | 91 | 72 |
| | | F | ... | 102 | 69 | 11 | 86 | 64 |
| | 1975 | | | | | | | |
| | | MF | ... | 99 | 89 | 25 | 94 | 75 |
| | | M | ... | 99 | 92 | 34 | 96 | 78 |
| | | F | ... | 100 | 85 | 17 | 92 | 71 |
| | 1980 | | (4-5) | (6-11) | (12-17) | (18-22) | (6-17) | (6-22) |
| | | MF | 107 | 100 | 93 | 29 | 96 | 76 |
| | | M | 108 | 99 | 95 | 35 | 97 | 78 |
| | | F | 106 | 101 | 90 | 24 | 95 | 74 |
| | 1985 | | | | | | | |
| | | MF | 106 | 99 | 117 | 32 | 109 | 83 |
| | | M | 105 | 98 | 120 | 37 | 110 | 85 |
| | | F | 107 | 100 | 114 | 27 | 108 | 81 |
| | 1990 | | | | | | | |
| | | MF | 99 | 102 | 120 | 40 | 111 | 86 |
| | | M | 99 | 101 | 124 | 43 | 113 | 89 |
| | | F | 100 | 104 | 115 | 36 | 110 | 84 |
| | 1991 | | | | | | | |
| | | MF | 99 | 98 | 121 | 42 | 110 | 86 |
| | | M | 98 | 97 | 125 | 45 | 111 | 88 |
| | | F | 101 | 99 | 116 | 39 | 108 | 84 |
| | 1992 | | | | | | | |
| | | MF | 98 | 97 | 123 | 45 | 110 | 88 |
| | | M | 98 | 96 | 126 | 47 | 111 | 89 |
| | | F | 98 | 99 | 120 | 42 | 110 | 86 |
| | 1993 | | | | | | | |
| | | MF | 97 | 108 | 140 | 48 | 124 | 99 |
| | | M | 97 | 108 | 145 | 51 | 127 | 102 |
| | | F | 97 | 107 | 135 | 45 | 121 | 96 |
| | 1994 | | | | | | | |
| | | MF | 99 | 107 | 139 | 47 | 123 | 98 |
| | | M | 100 | 108 | 143 | 49 | 125 | 101 |
| | | F | 99 | 106 | 136 | 45 | 121 | 96 |
| | 1995 | | | | | | | |
| | | MF | 101 | 107 | 137 | 48 | 122 | 99 |
| | | M | 101 | 108 | 141 | 50 | 124 | 101 |
| | | F | 100 | 106 | 134 | 46 | 120 | 96 |
| | 1996 | | | | | | | |
| | | MF | 100 | 108 | 132 | 47 | 119 | 97 |
| | | M | 100 | 109 | 134 | 48 | 121 | 99 |
| | | F | 99 | 107 | 129 | 46 | 117 | 95 |

Gross enrolment ratios by level of education   II.8
Taux bruts de scolarisation par niveau d'enseignement
Tasas brutas de escolarización por nivel de enseñanza

| Country / Pays / País | Year / Année / Año | Sex / Sexe / Sexo | Gross enrolment ratios / Taux bruts de scolarisation / Tasas brutas de escolarización (%) | | | | | |
|---|---|---|---|---|---|---|---|---|
| | | | Pre-primary / Préprimaire / Preprimaria | Primary / Primaire / Primaria | Secondary / Secondaire / Secundaria | Tertiary / Supérieur / Superior | Primary and secondary / Primaire et secondaire / Primaria y secundaria | Primary, secondary and tertiary / Primaire, secondaire et supérieur / Primaria, secundaria y superior |
| Norway | 1970 | | (4-6) | (7-13) | (14-19) | (20-24) | (7-19) | (7-24) |
| | | MF | ... | 89 | 83 | 16 | 87 | 67 |
| | | M | ... | 85 | 84 | 22 | 84 | 67 |
| | | F | ... | 93 | 83 | 10 | 89 | 67 |
| | 1975 | | (4-6) | (7-12) | (13-18) | (19-23) | (7-18) | (7-23) |
| | | MF | 15 | 101 | 88 | 22 | 95 | 74 |
| | | M | ... | 101 | 88 | 27 | 94 | 75 |
| | | F | ... | 101 | 88 | 17 | 95 | 73 |
| | 1980 | MF | 44 | 99 | 94 | 25 | 97 | 76 |
| | | M | ... | 99 | 92 | 26 | 96 | 76 |
| | | F | ... | 99 | 96 | 25 | 98 | 77 |
| | 1985 | MF | 66 | 97 | 97 | 30 | 97 | 77 |
| | | M | ... | 97 | 95 | 28 | 96 | 75 |
| | | F | ... | 97 | 100 | 32 | 98 | 78 |
| | 1990 | MF | 88 | 100 | 103 | 42 | 102 | 82 |
| | | M | ... | 100 | 101 | 39 | 101 | 80 |
| | | F | ... | 100 | 105 | 46 | 103 | 84 |
| | 1991 | MF | 96 | 100 | 105 | 46 | 103 | 84 |
| | | M | ... | 100 | 104 | 42 | 103 | 82 |
| | | F | ... | 101 | 106 | 50 | 103 | 85 |
| | 1992 | MF | 105 | 100 | 113 | 50 | 106 | 87 |
| | | M | ... | 99 | 114 | 46 | 107 | 86 |
| | | F | ... | 100 | 111 | 55 | 106 | 89 |
| | 1993 | MF | 94 | 99 | 125 | 55 | 112 | 93 |
| | | M | 91 | 99 | 126 | 49 | 113 | 92 |
| | | F | 96 | 99 | 123 | 60 | 111 | 94 |
| | 1994 | MF | 98 | 99 | 116 | 55 | 107 | 90 |
| | | M | 96 | 99 | 119 | 49 | 109 | 89 |
| | | F | 101 | 99 | 113 | 61 | 106 | 91 |
| | 1995 | MF | 101 | 99 | 116 | 59 | 108 | 92 |
| | | M | 99 | 99 | 119 | 51 | 109 | 90 |
| | | F | 104 | 99 | 113 | 66 | 106 | 93 |
| | 1996 | MF | 103 | 100 | 118 | 62 | 109 | 94 |
| | | M | 101 | 100 | 121 | 53 | 110 | 92 |
| | | F | 106 | 100 | 116 | 71 | 108 | 96 |
| Poland | 1970 | | (3-6) | (7-14) | (15-18) | (19-23) | (7-18) | (7-23) |
| | | MF | 37 | 101 | 62 | 13 | 88 | 67 |
| | | M | ... | 103 | 60 | 14 | 88 | 68 |
| | | F | ... | 100 | 64 | 13 | 87 | 67 |
| | 1975 | MF | 53 | 100 | 72 | 17 | 89 | 65 |
| | | M | ... | 102 | 70 | 15 | 89 | 65 |
| | | F | ... | 99 | 74 | 18 | 89 | 66 |
| | 1980 | MF | 55 | 100 | 77 | 18 | 92 | 67 |
| | | M | ... | 100 | 75 | 16 | 91 | 66 |
| | | F | ... | 99 | 80 | 21 | 92 | 68 |
| | 1985 | MF | 51 | 101 | 78 | 17 | 94 | 72 |
| | | M | ... | 102 | 76 | 15 | 94 | 72 |
| | | F | ... | 100 | 81 | 20 | 94 | 73 |
| | 1990 | MF | 47 | 98 | 81 | 22 | 93 | 75 |
| | | M | ... | 99 | 80 | 19 | 93 | 74 |
| | | F | ... | 98 | 83 | 25 | 93 | 76 |

II.8 Gross enrolment ratios by level of education
Taux bruts de scolarisation par niveau d'enseignement
Tasas brutas de escolarización por nivel de enseñanza

| Country / Pays / País | Year / Année / Año | Sex / Sexe / Sexo | Gross enrolment ratios / Taux bruts de scolarisation / Tasas brutas de escolarización (%) | | | | | |
|---|---|---|---|---|---|---|---|---|
| | | | Pre-primary / Préprimaire / Preprimaria | Primary / Primaire / Primaria | Secondary / Secondaire / Secundaria | Tertiary / Supérieur / Superior | Primary and secondary / Primaire et secondaire / Primaria y secundaria | Primary, secondary and tertiary / Primaire, secondaire et supérieur / Primaria, secundaria y superior |
| Poland (cont) | 1991 | | | | | | | |
| | | MF | 43 | 98 | 82 | 21 | 93 | 75 |
| | | M | ... | 99 | 80 | 18 | 93 | 74 |
| | | F | ... | 97 | 84 | 25 | 93 | 76 |
| | 1992 | | | | | | | |
| | | MF | 42 | 100 | 92 | 23 | 97 | 79 |
| | | M | 41 | 101 | 91 | 20 | 98 | 78 |
| | | F | 42 | 99 | 93 | 27 | 97 | 79 |
| | 1993 | | | | | | | |
| | | MF | 42 | 99 | 94 | 27 | 98 | 79 |
| | | M | 42 | 100 | 92 | 23 | 98 | 78 |
| | | F | 42 | 98 | 96 | 32 | 97 | 80 |
| | 1994 | | | | | | | |
| | | MF | 44 | 97 | 98 | 26 | 97 | 78 |
| | | M | 44 | 98 | 98 | 22 | 98 | 78 |
| | | F | 44 | 96 | 98 | 30 | 97 | 79 |
| | 1995 | | | | | | | |
| | | MF | 46 | 96 | 98 | 25 | 97 | 77 |
| | | M | 46 | 97 | 98 | 21 | 97 | 77 |
| | | F | 46 | 95 | 97 | 28 | 96 | 78 |
| Portugal | 1970 | | (3-5) | (6-11) | (12-16) | (17-21) | (6-16) | (6-21) |
| | | MF | 3 | 95 | 56 | 7 | 78 | 57 |
| | | M | 3 | 95 | 60 | 7 | 80 | 59 |
| | | F | 3 | 95 | 52 | 6 | 76 | 55 |
| | 1975 | | | | | | | |
| | | MF | 9 | 117 | 55 | 10 | 89 | 66 |
| | | M | 9 | 118 | 55 | 11 | 90 | 67 |
| | | F | 9 | 116 | 54 | 9 | 88 | 65 |
| | 1980 | | (3-5) | (6-11) | (12-17) | (18-22) | (6-17) | (6-22) |
| | | MF | 20 | 123 | 37 | 11 | 79 | 59 |
| | | M | 20 | 124 | 34 | 11 | 78 | 58 |
| | | F | 20 | 123 | 40 | 11 | 80 | 60 |
| | 1985 | | | | | | | |
| | | MF | 30 | 129 | 57 | 12 | 92 | 68 |
| | | M | 30 | 132 | 53 | 11 | 92 | 68 |
| | | F | 30 | 125 | 62 | 13 | 93 | 69 |
| | 1990 | | | | | | | |
| | | MF | 53 | 123 | 67 | 23 | 93 | 72 |
| | | M | 53 | 126 | 62 | 20 | 92 | 70 |
| | | F | 53 | 120 | 72 | 26 | 94 | 73 |
| | 1991 | | | | | | | |
| | | MF | 55 | 127 | 78 | 24 | 100 | 76 |
| | | M | 55 | 129 | 71 | 19 | 97 | 73 |
| | | F | 55 | 124 | 85 | 29 | 102 | 79 |
| | 1992 | | | | | | | |
| | | MF | 55 | 125 | 94 | 31 | 108 | 83 |
| | | M | 56 | 128 | 88 | 26 | 106 | 81 |
| | | F | 54 | 123 | 101 | 35 | 110 | 86 |
| | 1993 | | | | | | | |
| | | MF | 57 | 128 | 102 | 34 | 113 | 87 |
| | | M | 58 | 131 | 97 | 29 | 112 | 85 |
| | | F | 57 | 124 | 106 | 39 | 114 | 89 |
| | 1994 | | | | | | | |
| | | MF | 58 | 128 | 106 | 36 | 116 | 89 |
| | | M | 58 | 131 | 102 | 31 | 115 | 86 |
| | | F | 58 | 125 | 111 | 42 | 117 | 91 |
| | 1995 | | | | | | | |
| | | MF | 61 | 128 | 111 | 39 | 118 | 91 |
| | | M | 62 | 131 | 106 | 33 | 117 | 88 |
| | | F | 59 | 124 | 116 | 44 | 120 | 93 |
| Romania | 1970 | | (3-5) | (6-13) | (14-17) | (18-22) | (6-17) | (6-22) |
| | | MF | 49 | 113 | 45 | 9 | 88 | 65 |
| | | M | 47 | 112 | 51 | 10 | 89 | 67 |
| | | F | 50 | 114 | 38 | 8 | 86 | 63 |

Gross enrolment ratios by level of education **II.8**
Taux bruts de scolarisation par niveau d'enseignement
Tasas brutas de escolarización por nivel de enseñanza

| Country / Pays / País | Year / Année / Año | Sex / Sexe / Sexo | Gross enrolment ratios / Taux bruts de scolarisation / Tasas brutas de escolarización (%) | | | | | |
|---|---|---|---|---|---|---|---|---|
| | | | Pre-primary / Préprimaire / Preprimaria | Primary / Primaire / Primaria | Secondary / Secondaire / Secundaria | Tertiary / Supérieur / Superior | Primary and secondary / Primaire et secondaire / Primaria y secundaria | Primary, secondary and tertiary / Primaire, secondaire et supérieur / Primaria, secundaria y superior |
| Romania (cont) | 1975 | | | | | | | |
| | | MF | 61 | 107 | 65 | 9 | 93 | 67 |
| | | M | 60 | 108 | 64 | 10 | 93 | 67 |
| | | F | 63 | 107 | 67 | 8 | 93 | 67 |
| | 1980 | | | | | | | |
| | | MF | 83 | 104 | 94 | 12 | 101 | 77 |
| | | M | 83 | 104 | 102 | 14 | 104 | 80 |
| | | F | 84 | 103 | 86 | 11 | 98 | 75 |
| | 1985 | | | | | | | |
| | | MF | 75 | 98 | 94 | 10 | 97 | 75 |
| | | M | 74 | 98 | 99 | 11 | 99 | 76 |
| | | F | 76 | 98 | 89 | 9 | 95 | 73 |
| | 1990 | | (3-5) | (6-9) | (10-17) | (18-22) | (6-17) | (6-22) |
| | | MF | 76 | 91 | 92 | 10 | 92 | 66 |
| | | M | 75 | 91 | 92 | 10 | 92 | 67 |
| | | F | 78 | 91 | 92 | 9 | 92 | 66 |
| | 1991 | | | | | | | |
| | | MF | 75 | 88 | 86 | 11 | 87 | 63 |
| | | M | 74 | 89 | 86 | 11 | 87 | 63 |
| | | F | 77 | 88 | 86 | 10 | 87 | 63 |
| | 1992 | | | | | | | |
| | | MF | 76 | 87 | 83 | 16 | 84 | 63 |
| | | M | 74 | 87 | 83 | 17 | 84 | 63 |
| | | F | 77 | 86 | 82 | 15 | 83 | 62 |
| | 1993 | | (3-6) | (7-10) | (11-18) | (19-23) | (7-18) | (7-23) |
| | | MF | 53 | 87 | 79 | 19 | 82 | 63 |
| | | M | 52 | 88 | 79 | 19 | 82 | 63 |
| | | F | 54 | 87 | 80 | 18 | 82 | 63 |
| | 1994 | | | | | | | |
| | | MF | 53 | 95 | 78 | 20 | 83 | 64 |
| | | M | 52 | 95 | 77 | 20 | 83 | 64 |
| | | F | 54 | 94 | 79 | 19 | 84 | 64 |
| | 1995 | | | | | | | |
| | | MF | 53 | 100 | 78 | 18 | 85 | 65 |
| | | M | 52 | 101 | 77 | ... | 85 | ... |
| | | F | 53 | 99 | 78 | ... | 85 | ... |
| | 1996 | | | | | | | |
| | | MF | 53 | 103 | 78 | 23 | 87 | 67 |
| | | M | 53 | 104 | 70 | 21 | 87 | 67 |
| | | F | 53 | 103 | 78 | 24 | 86 | 67 |
| Russian Federation | 1980 | | (3-6) | (7-9) | (10-16) | (17-21) | (7-16) | (7-21) |
| | | MF | 67 | 102 | 96 | 46 | 98 | 78 |
| | | M | ... | 102 | 95 | 40 | 97 | 75 |
| | | F | ... | 102 | 97 | 53 | 98 | 81 |
| | 1985 | | | | | | | |
| | | MF | 73 | 104 | 97 | 54 | 99 | 84 |
| | | M | ... | 103 | 96 | 45 | 98 | 81 |
| | | F | ... | 104 | 98 | 63 | 100 | 87 |
| | 1990 | | | | | | | |
| | | MF | 74 | 109 | 93 | 52 | 98 | 84 |
| | | M | ... | 109 | 91 | 46 | 96 | 81 |
| | | F | ... | 109 | 96 | 58 | 100 | 87 |
| | 1991 | | | | | | | |
| | | MF | 73 | 109 | 91 | 50 | 97 | 83 |
| | | M | 76 | 109 | 88 | 45 | 95 | 79 |
| | | F | 69 | 109 | 94 | 56 | 99 | 86 |
| | 1992 | | | | | | | |
| | | MF | 65 | 108 | 88 | 47 | 95 | 80 |
| | | M | 68 | 108 | 85 | 41 | 92 | 76 |
| | | F | 62 | 108 | 92 | 53 | 97 | 83 |
| | 1993 | | | | | | | |
| | | MF | 63 | 106 | 87 | 45 | 93 | 78 |
| | | M | 65 | 106 | 83 | 40 | 91 | 75 |
| | | F | 60 | 106 | 91 | 50 | 95 | 81 |

II.8 Gross enrolment ratios by level of education
Taux bruts de scolarisation par niveau d'enseignement
Tasas brutas de escolarización por nivel de enseñanza

| Country / Pays / País | Year / Année / Año | Sex / Sexe / Sexo | Gross enrolment ratios / Taux bruts de scolarisation / Tasas brutas de escolarización (%) | | | | | |
|---|---|---|---|---|---|---|---|---|
| | | | Pre-primary / Préprimaire / Preprimaria | Primary / Primaire / Primaria | Secondary / Secondaire / Secundaria | Tertiary / Supérieur / Superior | Primary and secondary / Primaire et secondaire / Primaria y secundaria | Primary, secondary and tertiary / Primaire, secondaire et supérieur / Primaria, secundaria y superior |
| Russian Federation (cont) | 1994 | MF | ... | 107 | ... | 43 | ... | ... |
| | | M | ... | 108 | ... | 37 | ... | ... |
| | | F | ... | 107 | ... | 49 | ... | ... |
| Slovakia | 1992 | | (3-5) | (6-9) | (10-17) | (18-22) | (6-17) | (6-22) |
| | | MF | 78 | 101 | 88 | 16 | 92 | 71 |
| | | M | ... | 101 | 86 | 16 | 91 | 71 |
| | | F | ... | 101 | 90 | 16 | 93 | 72 |
| | 1993 | MF | 77 | 101 | 89 | 17 | 93 | 71 |
| | | M | ... | 101 | 87 | 17 | 92 | 71 |
| | | F | ... | 101 | 90 | 17 | 94 | 72 |
| | 1994 | MF | 74 | 101 | 90 | 19 | 93 | 72 |
| | | M | ... | 101 | 88 | 19 | 92 | 71 |
| | | F | ... | 101 | 92 | 19 | 95 | 73 |
| | 1995 | MF | 71 | 103 | 94 | 20 | 97 | 74 |
| | | M | ... | 103 | 92 | 20 | 95 | 73 |
| | | F | ... | 103 | 96 | 20 | 98 | 75 |
| | 1996 | MF | 76 | 102 | 94 | 22 | 96 | 74 |
| | | M | ... | 102 | 92 | 22 | 95 | 73 |
| | | F | ... | 102 | 96 | 23 | 98 | 75 |
| Slovenia | 1980 | | (3-6) | (7-10) | (11-18) | (19-23) | (7-18) | (7-23) |
| | | MF | 54 | 98 | ... | 20 | ... | ... |
| | | M | 55 | ... | ... | 18 | ... | ... |
| | | F | 53 | ... | ... | 22 | ... | ... |
| | 1985 | MF | 58 | 99 | 86 | 21 | 91 | 71 |
| | | M | 59 | ... | ... | 20 | ... | ... |
| | | F | 57 | ... | ... | 23 | ... | ... |
| | 1990 | MF | 74 | 108 | 91 | 24 | 96 | 75 |
| | | M | 76 | ... | ... | 21 | ... | ... |
| | | F | 72 | ... | ... | 28 | ... | ... |
| | 1991 | MF | 63 | 109 | 91 | 28 | 97 | 77 |
| | | M | 58 | ... | ... | 26 | ... | ... |
| | | F | 69 | ... | ... | 30 | ... | ... |
| | 1992 | MF | 60 | 101 | 91 | 28 | 94 | 75 |
| | | M | 61 | 101 | 89 | 25 | 93 | 73 |
| | | F | 59 | 101 | 92 | 31 | 95 | 76 |
| | 1993 | MF | 62 | 98 | 90 | 30 | 93 | 74 |
| | | M | 62 | 98 | 89 | 26 | 92 | 73 |
| | | F | 61 | 99 | 92 | 33 | 94 | 76 |
| | 1994 | MF | 61 | 98 | 91 | 32 | 93 | 75 |
| | | M | 62 | 98 | 90 | 27 | 92 | 73 |
| | | F | 59 | 98 | 92 | 36 | 94 | 77 |
| | 1995 | MF | 60 | 98 | 91 | 34 | 93 | 75 |
| | | M | 62 | 98 | 89 | 30 | 92 | 73 |
| | | F | 59 | 98 | 92 | 39 | 94 | 77 |
| | 1996 | MF | 61 | 98 | 92 | 36 | 94 | 76 |
| | | M | 62 | 98 | 90 | 31 | 93 | 74 |
| | | F | 60 | 98 | 93 | 41 | 94 | 78 |
| Spain | 1970 | | (2-5) | (6-10) | (11-16) | (17-21) | (6-16) | (6-21) |
| | | MF | 32 | 123 | 56 | 9 | 88 | 66 |
| | | M | 30 | 121 | 64 | 13 | 91 | 70 |
| | | F | 33 | 125 | 48 | 5 | 85 | 62 |

Gross enrolment ratios by level of education    II.8
Taux bruts de scolarisation par niveau d'enseignement
Tasas brutas de escolarización por nivel de enseñanza

| Country / Pays / País | Year / Année / Año | Sex / Sexe / Sexo | Gross enrolment ratios / Taux bruts de scolarisation / Tasas brutas de escolarización (%) | | | | | |
|---|---|---|---|---|---|---|---|---|
| | | | Pre-primary / Préprimaire / Preprimaria | Primary / Primaire / Primaria | Secondary / Secondaire / Secundaria | Tertiary / Supérieur / Superior | Primary and secondary / Primaire et secondaire / Primaria y secundaria | Primary, secondary and tertiary / Primaire, secondaire et supérieur / Primaria, secundaria y superior |
| Spain (cont) | 1975 | | (2-5) | (6-10) | (11-17) | (18-22) | (6-17) | (6-22) |
| | | MF | 35 | 111 | 73 | 20 | 89 | 71 |
| | | M | 33 | 111 | 74 | 25 | 90 | 73 |
| | | F | 37 | 111 | 71 | 14 | 89 | 69 |
| | 1980 | | | | | | | |
| | | MF | 44 | 109 | 87 | 23 | 96 | 76 |
| | | M | 43 | 110 | 85 | 26 | 95 | 76 |
| | | F | 46 | 109 | 89 | 21 | 97 | 76 |
| | 1985 | | | | | | | |
| | | MF | 51 | 110 | 98 | 29 | 103 | 81 |
| | | M | 51 | 111 | 95 | 29 | 101 | 80 |
| | | F | 52 | 109 | 102 | 29 | 105 | 82 |
| | 1990 | | | | | | | |
| | | MF | 59 | 109 | 104 | 37 | 106 | 84 |
| | | M | 59 | 109 | 101 | 35 | 104 | 82 |
| | | F | 60 | 108 | 108 | 38 | 108 | 86 |
| | 1991 | | | | | | | |
| | | MF | 64 | 107 | 107 | 39 | 107 | 85 |
| | | M | 63 | 108 | 103 | 37 | 105 | 83 |
| | | F | 64 | 106 | 111 | 41 | 109 | 87 |
| | 1992 | | | | | | | |
| | | MF | 67 | 109 | 112 | 41 | 111 | 88 |
| | | M | 67 | 110 | 108 | 39 | 109 | 85 |
| | | F | 67 | 108 | 117 | 43 | 114 | 90 |
| | 1993 | | | | | | | |
| | | MF | 70 | 109 | 116 | 44 | 113 | 89 |
| | | M | 70 | 110 | 111 | 42 | 111 | 87 |
| | | F | 70 | 108 | 121 | 46 | 116 | 92 |
| | 1994 | | | | | | | |
| | | MF | 71 | 109 | 118 | 45 | 115 | 90 |
| | | M | 71 | 110 | 114 | 42 | 112 | 88 |
| | | F | 71 | 108 | 123 | 49 | 118 | 93 |
| | 1995 | | (2-5) | (6-11) | (12-17) | (18-22) | (6-17) | (6-22) |
| | | MF | 72 | 109 | 122 | 48 | 116 | 92 |
| | | M | 72 | 110 | 116 | 44 | 114 | 89 |
| | | F | 72 | 108 | 128 | 52 | 120 | 95 |
| | 1996 | | | | | | | |
| | | MF | 74 | 109 | 120 | 51 | 115 | 92 |
| | | M | 73 | 109 | 116 | 47 | 113 | 89 |
| | | F | 74 | 108 | 123 | 56 | 116 | 94 |
| Sweden | 1970 | | (4-6) | (7-12) | (13-18) | (19-23) | (7-18) | (7-23) |
| | | MF | ... | 94 | 86 | 22 | 90 | 67 |
| | | M | ... | 93 | 87 | 25 | 90 | 68 |
| | | F | ... | 95 | 85 | 19 | 90 | 66 |
| | 1975 | | | | | | | |
| | | MF | 60 | 101 | 78 | 30 | 90 | 72 |
| | | M | ... | 101 | 75 | 35 | 88 | 73 |
| | | F | ... | 102 | 82 | 24 | 92 | 72 |
| | 1980 | | | | | | | |
| | | MF | 71 | 97 | 88 | 31 | 92 | 75 |
| | | M | ... | 96 | 83 | ... | 90 | ... |
| | | F | ... | 97 | 93 | ... | 95 | ... |
| | 1985 | | (3-6) | (7-12) | (13-18) | (19-23) | (7-18) | (7-23) |
| | | MF | 62 | 98 | 91 | 30 | 94 | 74 |
| | | M | ... | 97 | 89 | 28 | 93 | 73 |
| | | F | ... | 99 | 93 | 32 | 95 | 76 |
| | 1990 | | | | | | | |
| | | MF | 65 | 100 | 90 | 32 | 95 | 74 |
| | | M | ... | 100 | 88 | 29 | 94 | 72 |
| | | F | ... | 100 | 92 | 35 | 96 | 76 |
| | 1991 | | | | | | | |
| | | MF | 67 | 100 | 92 | 35 | 96 | 76 |
| | | M | ... | 100 | 90 | 31 | 95 | 74 |
| | | F | ... | 101 | 94 | 38 | 97 | 78 |

II.8   Gross enrolment ratios by level of education
       Taux bruts de scolarisation par niveau d'enseignement
       Tasas brutas de escolarización por nivel de enseñanza

| Country<br><br>Pays<br><br>País | Year<br><br>Année<br><br>Año | Sex<br><br>Sexe<br><br>Sexo | Gross enrolment ratios / Taux bruts de scolarisation / Tasas brutas de escolarización (%) | | | | | |
|---|---|---|---|---|---|---|---|---|
| | | | Pre-primary<br><br>Préprimaire<br><br>Preprimaria | Primary<br><br>Primaire<br><br>Primaria | Secondary<br><br>Secondaire<br><br>Secundaria | Tertiary<br><br>Supérieur<br><br>Superior | Primary and secondary<br><br>Primaire et secondaire<br><br>Primaria y secundaria | Primary, secondary and tertiary<br><br>Primaire, secondaire et supérieur<br><br>Primaria, secundaria y superior |
| Sweden (cont) | 1992 | | | | | | | |
| | | MF | 65 | 104 | 121 | 38 | 113 | 88 |
| | | M | ... | 104 | 113 | 34 | 109 | 84 |
| | | F | ... | 105 | 129 | 42 | 117 | 93 |
| | 1993 | | | | | | | |
| | | MF | 66 | 105 | 127 | 40 | 116 | 91 |
| | | M | 64 | 104 | 120 | 36 | 112 | 87 |
| | | F | 67 | 105 | 135 | 45 | 121 | 96 |
| | 1994 | | | | | | | |
| | | MF | 68 | 105 | 132 | 43 | 118 | 94 |
| | | M | 66 | 104 | 123 | 38 | 114 | 89 |
| | | F | 69 | 106 | 141 | 48 | 123 | 99 |
| | 1995 | | | | | | | |
| | | MF | 72 | 106 | 137 | 47 | 121 | 97 |
| | | M | 70 | 105 | 126 | 41 | 115 | 92 |
| | | F | 74 | 107 | 148 | 53 | 126 | 103 |
| | 1996 | | | | | | | |
| | | MF | 73 | 107 | 140 | 50 | 123 | 100 |
| | | M | 71 | 106 | 128 | 43 | 117 | 94 |
| | | F | 74 | 107 | 153 | 57 | 129 | 107 |
| Switzerland | 1980 | | (4-6) | (7-12) | (13-19) | (20-24) | (7-19) | (7-24) |
| | | MF | 53 | ... | ... | 18 | 90 | 70 |
| | | M | 53 | ... | ... | 26 | 92 | 74 |
| | | F | 53 | ... | ... | 11 | 87 | 66 |
| | 1985 | | | | | | | |
| | | MF | 57 | ... | ... | 21 | 91 | 68 |
| | | M | 57 | ... | ... | 28 | 93 | 72 |
| | | F | 56 | ... | ... | 14 | 88 | 64 |
| | 1990 | | | | | | | |
| | | MF | 60 | ... | ... | 26 | 95 | 71 |
| | | M | 60 | ... | ... | 33 | 96 | 74 |
| | | F | 60 | ... | ... | 18 | 94 | 68 |
| | 1991 | | | | | | | |
| | | MF | 59 | ... | ... | 27 | 96 | 73 |
| | | M | 59 | ... | ... | 34 | 97 | 76 |
| | | F | 59 | ... | ... | 20 | 95 | 70 |
| | 1992 | | | | | | | |
| | | MF | 61 | ... | ... | 29 | 98 | 75 |
| | | M | 61 | ... | ... | 36 | 100 | 79 |
| | | F | 60 | ... | ... | 21 | 96 | 72 |
| | 1993 | | (5-6) | (7-12) | (13-19) | (20-24) | (7-19) | (7-24) |
| | | MF | 93 | ... | ... | 30 | 98 | 77 |
| | | M | 93 | ... | ... | 37 | 100 | 80 |
| | | F | 92 | ... | ... | 23 | 97 | 73 |
| | 1994 | | | | | | | |
| | | MF | 94 | ... | ... | 32 | 98 | 78 |
| | | M | 95 | ... | ... | 38 | 100 | 81 |
| | | F | 93 | ... | ... | 24 | 97 | 74 |
| | 1995 | | | | | | | |
| | | MF | 95 | ... | ... | 33 | 99 | 79 |
| | | M | 96 | ... | ... | 40 | 100 | 82 |
| | | F | 94 | ... | ... | 25 | 97 | 75 |
| The Former Yugoslav Rep. of Macedonia | 1980 | | (3-6) | (7-14) | (15-18) | (19-23) | (7-18) | (7-23) |
| | | MF | ... | 100 | 61 | 28 | 87 | 70 |
| | | M | ... | ... | 65 | ... | ... | ... |
| | | F | ... | ... | 57 | ... | ... | ... |
| | 1985 | | | | | | | |
| | | MF | ... | 105 | 60 | 24 | 90 | 71 |
| | | M | ... | ... | 65 | ... | ... | ... |
| | | F | ... | ... | 55 | ... | ... | ... |
| | 1990 | | | | | | | |
| | | MF | ... | 99 | 56 | 17 | 85 | 66 |
| | | M | ... | 100 | 56 | 16 | 86 | 66 |
| | | F | ... | 98 | 55 | 18 | 85 | 65 |

Gross enrolment ratios by level of education    II.8
Taux bruts de scolarisation par niveau d'enseignement
Tasas brutas de escolarización por nivel de enseñanza

| Country<br>Pays<br>País | Year<br>Année<br>Año | Sex<br>Sexe<br>Sexo | Gross enrolment ratios / Taux bruts de scolarisation / Tasas brutas de escolarización (%) | | | | | |
|---|---|---|---|---|---|---|---|---|
| | | | Pre-primary<br>Préprimaire<br>Preprimaria | Primary<br>Primaire<br>Primaria | Secondary<br>Secondaire<br>Secundaria | Tertiary<br>Supérieur<br>Superior | Primary and secondary<br>Primaire et secondaire<br>Primaria y secundaria | Primary, secondary and tertiary<br>Primaire, secondaire et supérieur<br>Primaria, secundaria y superior |
| The Former Yugoslav Rep. of Macedonia (cont) | 1991 | | | | | | | |
| | | MF | ... | 97 | 55 | 17 | 83 | 65 |
| | | M | ... | 97 | 56 | 17 | 84 | 65 |
| | | F | ... | 96 | 55 | 18 | 83 | 64 |
| | 1992 | | | | | | | |
| | | MF | 24 | 97 | 57 | 17 | 84 | 65 |
| | | M | 24 | 98 | 57 | 16 | 85 | 65 |
| | | F | 24 | 96 | 57 | 18 | 84 | 65 |
| | 1993 | | | | | | | |
| | | MF | 24 | 97 | 57 | 17 | 84 | 65 |
| | | M | 24 | 98 | 57 | 16 | 84 | 65 |
| | | F | 23 | 96 | 58 | 19 | 84 | 65 |
| | 1994 | | | | | | | |
| | | MF | 25 | 98 | 59 | 19 | 85 | 66 |
| | | M | 25 | 98 | 59 | 17 | 86 | 66 |
| | | F | 25 | 97 | 59 | 21 | 84 | 66 |
| | 1995 | | | | | | | |
| | | MF | 26 | 99 | 61 | 19 | 86 | 67 |
| | | M | 27 | 100 | 61 | 17 | 87 | 67 |
| | | F | 26 | 98 | 61 | 21 | 85 | 67 |
| | 1996 | | | | | | | |
| | | MF | 26 | 99 | 63 | 20 | 87 | 68 |
| | | M | 26 | 100 | 64 | 17 | 88 | 68 |
| | | F | 26 | 98 | 62 | 22 | 86 | 68 |
| Ukraine | 1980 | | (3-6) | (7-11) | (12-16) | (17-21) | (7-16) | (7-21) |
| | | MF | 60 | 102 | 94 | 42 | 98 | 78 |
| | | M | ... | 103 | ... | ... | ... | ... |
| | | F | ... | 102 | ... | ... | ... | ... |
| | 1985 | | | | | | | |
| | | MF | 65 | 103 | 96 | 47 | 100 | 82 |
| | | M | 68 | ... | ... | ... | ... | ... |
| | | F | 62 | ... | ... | ... | ... | ... |
| | 1990 | | (3-5) | (6-11) | (12-16) | (17-21) | (6-16) | (6-21) |
| | | MF | 85 | 89 | 93 | 47 | 91 | 77 |
| | | M | 88 | 89 | ... | 46 | ... | ... |
| | | F | 81 | 89 | ... | 47 | ... | ... |
| | 1991 | | | | | | | |
| | | MF | 83 | 89 | 91 | 44 | 90 | 76 |
| | | M | 85 | 90 | ... | 43 | ... | ... |
| | | F | 81 | 89 | ... | 44 | ... | ... |
| | 1992 | | (3-6) | (7-10) | (11-17) | (18-22) | (7-17) | (7-22) |
| | | MF | 56 | 88 | 91 | 43 | 90 | 76 |
| | | M | 58 | 89 | 87 | ... | 88 | ... |
| | | F | 53 | 87 | 94 | ... | 92 | ... |
| | 1993 | | | | | | | |
| | | MF | 54 | 87 | 91 | 41 | 90 | 75 |
| | | M | 56 | 87 | 88 | 35 | 88 | 72 |
| | | F | 51 | 86 | 94 | 47 | 92 | 78 |
| | 1994 | | | | | | | |
| | | MF | ... | ... | ... | 42 | ... | ... |
| | 1995 | | | | | | | |
| | | MF | ... | ... | ... | 42 | ... | ... |
| United Kingdom | 1970 | | (3-4) | (5-10) | (11-17) | (18-22) | (5-17) | (5-22) |
| | | MF | 16 | 104 | 73 | 14 | 88 | 68 |
| | | M | 16 | 103 | 73 | 19 | 88 | 70 |
| | | F | 16 | 104 | 73 | 10 | 88 | 67 |
| | 1975 | | | | | | | |
| | | MF | 34 | 105 | 82 | 19 | 93 | 74 |
| | | M | 34 | 105 | 82 | 23 | 93 | 75 |
| | | F | 34 | 105 | 83 | 14 | 93 | 73 |
| | 1980 | | | | | | | |
| | | MF | 42 | 103 | 83 | 19 | 92 | 71 |
| | | M | 42 | 103 | 82 | 24 | 91 | 72 |
| | | F | 42 | 103 | 85 | 14 | 93 | 71 |

Gross enrolment ratios by level of education
Taux bruts de scolarisation par niveau d'enseignement
Tasas brutas de escolarización por nivel de enseñanza

| Country / Pays / País | Year / Année / Año | Sex / Sexe / Sexo | Gross enrolment ratios / Taux bruts de scolarisation / Tasas brutas de escolarización (%) | | | | | |
|---|---|---|---|---|---|---|---|---|
| | | | Pre-primary / Préprimaire / Preprimaria | Primary / Primaire / Primaria | Secondary / Secondaire / Secundaria | Tertiary / Supérieur / Superior | Primary and secondary / Primaire et secondaire / Primaria y secundaria | Primary, secondary and tertiary / Primaire, secondaire et supérieur / Primaria, secundaria y superior |
| United Kingdom (cont) | 1985 | MF | 49 | 104 | 84 | 22 | 92 | 69 |
| | | M | 50 | 104 | 82 | 23 | 91 | 69 |
| | | F | 48 | 105 | 86 | 20 | 93 | 70 |
| | 1990 | MF | 52 | 104 | 85 | 30 | 94 | 74 |
| | | M | 52 | 103 | 83 | 31 | 92 | 74 |
| | | F | 53 | 106 | 88 | 29 | 96 | 75 |
| | 1991 | MF | 53 | 103 | 89 | 34 | 95 | 77 |
| | | M | 52 | 102 | 86 | 35 | 94 | 76 |
| | | F | 53 | 104 | 91 | 34 | 98 | 78 |
| | 1992 | MF | 27 | 113 | 127 | 39 | 121 | 97 |
| | | M | 27 | 112 | 119 | 39 | 116 | 93 |
| | | F | 28 | 114 | 136 | 39 | 126 | 100 |
| | 1993 | MF | 28 | 114 | 130 | 43 | 122 | 100 |
| | | M | 28 | 113 | 121 | 42 | 117 | 96 |
| | | F | 28 | 115 | 140 | 45 | 128 | 104 |
| | 1994 | MF | 29 | 114 | 134 | 48 | 124 | 103 |
| | | M | 29 | 113 | 123 | 46 | 119 | 98 |
| | | F | 29 | 115 | 145 | 51 | 130 | 108 |
| | 1995 | MF | 29 | 115 | 133 | 50 | 124 | 104 |
| | | M | 29 | 114 | 123 | 47 | 119 | 99 |
| | | F | 29 | 116 | 144 | 52 | 131 | 109 |
| | 1996 | MF | 30 | 116 | 129 | 52 | 123 | 104 |
| | | M | 30 | 115 | 120 | 49 | 118 | 99 |
| | | F | 30 | 116 | 139 | 56 | 128 | 109 |
| **Oceania** | | | | | | | | |
| Australia | 1970 | | (5-5) | (6-11) | (12-17) | (18-22) | (6-17) | (6-22) |
| | | MF | 79 | 115 | 82 | 16 | 99 | 76 |
| | | M | ... | 115 | 88 | 21 | 102 | 79 |
| | | F | ... | 115 | 76 | 11 | 96 | 72 |
| | 1975 | MF | 74 | 107 | 72 | 23 | 89 | 71 |
| | | M | 74 | 107 | 72 | 27 | 89 | 72 |
| | | F | 74 | 106 | 72 | 19 | 89 | 69 |
| | 1980 | MF | 68 | 112 | 71 | 25 | 92 | 72 |
| | | M | 68 | 113 | 70 | 27 | 91 | 73 |
| | | F | 67 | 111 | 72 | 24 | 92 | 72 |
| | 1985 | MF | 71 | 107 | 80 | 28 | 93 | 73 |
| | | M | 72 | 107 | 79 | 28 | 93 | 73 |
| | | F | 71 | 106 | 81 | 27 | 93 | 73 |
| | 1990 | MF | 71 | 108 | 82 | 35 | 94 | 76 |
| | | M | 71 | 108 | 80 | 33 | 94 | 75 |
| | | F | 71 | 107 | 83 | 38 | 95 | 77 |
| | 1991 | MF | 71 | 108 | 83 | 39 | 95 | 78 |
| | | M | 71 | 108 | 82 | 36 | 95 | 76 |
| | | F | 70 | 108 | 84 | 43 | 96 | 79 |
| | 1992 | MF | 70 | 108 | 84 | 41 | 96 | 79 |
| | | M | 71 | 108 | 83 | 38 | 95 | 78 |
| | | F | 70 | 108 | 85 | 45 | 96 | 80 |

Gross enrolment ratios by level of education  II.8
Taux bruts de scolarisation par niveau d'enseignement
Tasas brutas de escolarización por nivel de enseñanza

| Country / Pays / País | Year / Année / Año | Sex / Sexe / Sexo | Gross enrolment ratios / Taux bruts de scolarisation / Tasas brutas de escolarización (%) | | | | | |
|---|---|---|---|---|---|---|---|---|
| | | | Pre-primary / Préprimaire / Preprimaria | Primary / Primaire / Primaria | Secondary / Secondaire / Secundaria | Tertiary / Supérieur / Superior | Primary and secondary / Primaire et secondaire / Primaria y secundaria | Primary, secondary and tertiary / Primaire, secondaire et supérieur / Primaria, secundaria y superior |
| Australia (cont) | 1993 | MF | 71 | 107 | 132 | 69 | 120 | 104 |
| | | M | 71 | 107 | 132 | 69 | 120 | 104 |
| | | F | 71 | 107 | 132 | 68 | 120 | 104 |
| | 1994 | MF | 72 | 106 | 131 | 70 | 119 | 104 |
| | | M | 72 | 106 | 131 | 69 | 119 | 104 |
| | | F | 72 | 106 | 131 | 70 | 118 | 104 |
| | 1995 | | (4-4) | (5-11) | (12-17) | (18-22) | (5-17) | (5-22) |
| | | MF | 95 | 101 | 142 | 73 | 120 | 107 |
| | | M | ... | 101 | 143 | 71 | 120 | 106 |
| | | F | ... | 101 | 142 | 75 | 120 | 107 |
| | 1996 | MF | 78 | 101 | 148 | 76 | 123 | 110 |
| | | M | ... | 101 | 149 | 74 | 123 | 109 |
| | | F | ... | 101 | 148 | 79 | 122 | 110 |
| | 1997 | MF | 80 | 101 | 153 | 80 | 125 | 112 |
| | | M | ... | 101 | 150 | 77 | 124 | 111 |
| | | F | ... | 101 | 155 | 83 | 125 | 114 |
| Fiji | 1970 | | (3-5) | (6-11) | (12-17) | (18-22) | (6-17) | (6-22) |
| | | MF | ... | 125 | 28 | 0.7 | 80 | 61 |
| | | M | ... | 127 | 32 | 0.9 | 83 | 64 |
| | | F | ... | 122 | 25 | 0.5 | 77 | 59 |
| | 1975 | MF | 7 | 138 | 44 | 3 | 91 | 68 |
| | | M | 8 | 138 | 44 | 4 | 91 | 69 |
| | | F | 7 | 137 | 44 | 1 | 90 | 67 |
| | 1980 | MF | 9 | 119 | 55 | 2 | 88 | 66 |
| | | M | 9 | 120 | 53 | ... | 88 | ... |
| | | F | 9 | 119 | 57 | ... | 89 | ... |
| | 1985 | MF | 7 | 122 | 51 | 3 | 89 | 66 |
| | | M | ... | 122 | 50 | 4 | 89 | 66 |
| | | F | ... | 122 | 51 | 2 | 89 | 65 |
| | 1990 | MF | 13 | 125 | 56 | 8 | 93 | 73 |
| | | M | 13 | ... | ... | ... | ... | ... |
| | | F | 14 | ... | ... | ... | ... | ... |
| | 1991 | MF | 14 | 126 | 61 | 12 | 96 | 76 |
| | | M | 14 | 126 | 62 | ... | 96 | ... |
| | | F | 15 | 126 | 60 | ... | 95 | ... |
| | 1992 | MF | 15 | 128 | 64 | ... | 97 | ... |
| | | M | 15 | 128 | 64 | ... | 97 | ... |
| | | F | 16 | 128 | 65 | ... | 98 | ... |
| French Polynesia | 1980 | | (3-5) | (6-11) | (12-18) | (19-23) | (6-18) | (6-23) |
| | | MF | 76 | 121 | 50 | 0.2 | 84 | 65 |
| | | M | 76 | 124 | ... | 0.2 | ... | ... |
| | | F | 76 | 118 | ... | 0.1 | ... | ... |
| | 1985 | | (3-5) | (6-10) | (11-17) | (18-22) | (6-17) | (6-22) |
| | | MF | ... | ... | 60 | ... | ... | ... |
| | | M | ... | ... | 53 | ... | ... | ... |
| | | F | ... | ... | 67 | ... | ... | ... |
| | 1990 | MF | 111 | 130 | 71 | ... | 96 | ... |
| | | M | 114 | 132 | 65 | ... | 94 | ... |
| | | F | 108 | 127 | 76 | ... | 98 | ... |
| | 1991 | MF | 109 | 126 | 74 | 1 | 97 | 69 |
| | | M | 111 | 128 | 68 | 1 | 95 | 67 |
| | | F | 107 | 123 | 80 | 2 | 99 | 72 |

II.8 Gross enrolment ratios by level of education
Taux bruts de scolarisation par niveau d'enseignement
Tasas brutas de escolarización por nivel de enseñanza

| Country<br><br>Pays<br><br>País | Year<br><br>Année<br><br>Año | Sex<br><br>Sexe<br><br>Sexo | Gross enrolment ratios / Taux bruts de scolarisation / Tasas brutas de escolarización (%) | | | | | |
|---|---|---|---|---|---|---|---|---|
| | | | Pre-primary<br><br>Préprimaire<br><br>Preprimaria | Primary<br><br>Primaire<br><br>Primaria | Secondary<br><br>Secondaire<br><br>Secundaria | Tertiary<br><br>Supérieur<br><br>Superior | Primary and secondary<br><br>Primaire et secondaire<br><br>Primaria y secundaria | Primary, secondary and tertiary<br><br>Primaire, secondaire et supérieur<br><br>Primaria, secundaria y superior |
| French Polynesia (cont) | 1992 | | | | | | | |
| | | MF | 107 | 125 | 78 | ... | 99 | ... |
| | | M | 111 | 127 | 69 | ... | 95 | ... |
| | | F | 103 | 124 | 86 | ... | 103 | ... |
| | 1993 | | | | | | | |
| | | MF | 104 | 123 | ... | ... | ... | ... |
| | | M | 106 | 125 | ... | ... | ... | ... |
| | | F | 102 | 121 | ... | ... | ... | ... |
| | 1994 | | | | | | | |
| | | MF | 102 | 121 | ... | ... | ... | ... |
| | | M | 102 | 123 | ... | ... | ... | ... |
| | | F | 103 | 118 | ... | ... | ... | ... |
| | 1995 | | | | | | | |
| | | MF | 99 | 116 | ... | ... | ... | ... |
| | | M | 101 | 118 | ... | ... | ... | ... |
| | | F | 97 | 113 | ... | ... | ... | ... |
| New Caledonia | 1985 | | (3-5) | (6-11) | (12-18) | (19-23) | (6-18) | (6-23) |
| | | MF | 82 | 122 | 73 | 5 | 94 | 71 |
| | | M | 84 | 125 | 69 | 6 | 92 | 71 |
| | | F | 80 | 119 | 78 | 5 | 96 | 72 |
| | 1990 | | | | | | | |
| | | MF | 98 | 129 | 79 | ... | 99 | ... |
| | | M | 97 | 130 | 76 | ... | 98 | ... |
| | | F | 98 | 127 | 83 | ... | 101 | ... |
| | 1991 | | | | | | | |
| | | MF | 103 | 125 | 84 | ... | 101 | ... |
| | | M | 104 | 127 | 80 | ... | 99 | ... |
| | | F | 103 | 123 | 88 | ... | 102 | ... |
| | 1992 | | | | | | | |
| | | MF | ... | 122 | ... | ... | ... | ... |
| | 1993 | | | | | | | |
| | | MF | ... | 122 | ... | ... | ... | ... |
| | 1994 | | | | | | | |
| | | MF | 107 | 122 | ... | ... | ... | ... |
| | 1997 | | | | | | | |
| | | MF | ... | ... | 100 | ... | ... | ... |
| | | M | ... | ... | 95 | ... | ... | ... |
| | | F | ... | ... | 106 | ... | ... | ... |
| New Zealand | 1970 | | (3-4) | (5-10) | (11-17) | (18-22) | (5-17) | (5-22) |
| | | MF | 20 | 110 | 77 | 16 | 93 | 74 |
| | | M | 20 | 111 | 77 | 19 | 94 | 75 |
| | | F | 21 | 109 | 76 | 13 | 92 | 73 |
| | 1975 | | | | | | | |
| | | MF | 52 | 107 | 81 | 24 | 93 | 75 |
| | | M | 51 | 108 | 80 | 30 | 93 | 77 |
| | | F | 52 | 106 | 81 | 18 | 92 | 74 |
| | 1980 | | | | | | | |
| | | MF | 73 | 111 | 83 | 27 | 96 | 77 |
| | | M | 73 | 111 | 82 | 31 | 95 | 78 |
| | | F | 74 | 111 | 84 | 22 | 96 | 76 |
| | 1985 | | | | | | | |
| | | MF | 91 | 107 | 85 | 33 | 94 | 77 |
| | | M | 90 | 108 | 84 | 35 | 94 | 77 |
| | | F | 92 | 106 | 87 | 31 | 95 | 77 |
| | 1990 | | (2-4) | (5-10) | (11-17) | (18-22) | (5-17) | (5-22) |
| | | MF | 75 | 106 | 89 | 40 | 96 | 80 |
| | | M | 75 | 106 | 88 | 38 | 96 | 79 |
| | | F | 74 | 105 | 90 | 42 | 96 | 80 |
| | 1991 | | | | | | | |
| | | MF | 77 | 102 | 91 | 46 | 96 | 82 |
| | | M | 78 | 103 | 91 | 43 | 96 | 81 |
| | | F | 77 | 102 | 92 | 49 | 96 | 83 |

Gross enrolment ratios by level of education    II.8
Taux bruts de scolarisation par niveau d'enseignement
Tasas brutas de escolarización por nivel de enseñanza

| Country / Pays / País | Year / Année / Año | Sex / Sexe / Sexo | Gross enrolment ratios / Taux bruts de scolarisation / Tasas brutas de escolarización (%) | | | | | |
|---|---|---|---|---|---|---|---|---|
| | | | Pre-primary / Préprimaire / Preprimaria | Primary / Primaire / Primaria | Secondary / Secondaire / Secundaria | Tertiary / Supérieur / Superior | Primary and secondary / Primaire et secondaire / Primaria y secundaria | Primary, secondary and tertiary / Primaire, secondaire et supérieur / Primaria, secundaria y superior |
| New Zealand (cont) | 1992 | | | | | | | |
| | | MF | 81 | 99 | 94 | 53 | 96 | 84 |
| | | M | 81 | 100 | 93 | 48 | 96 | 83 |
| | | F | 81 | 99 | 94 | 57 | 96 | 85 |
| | 1993 | | | | | | | |
| | | MF | 78 | 98 | 101 | 59 | 100 | 88 |
| | | M | 77 | 98 | 101 | 53 | 99 | 87 |
| | | F | 78 | 97 | 102 | 64 | 100 | 89 |
| | 1995 | | | | | | | |
| | | MF | 77 | 99 | 112 | 60 | 106 | 93 |
| | | M | 77 | 99 | 113 | 53 | 106 | 92 |
| | | F | 77 | 99 | 112 | 66 | 106 | 95 |
| | 1996 | | | | | | | |
| | | MF | 77 | 99 | 114 | 59 | 107 | 94 |
| | | M | 77 | 99 | 111 | 52 | 105 | 91 |
| | | F | 76 | 99 | 117 | 67 | 108 | 97 |
| | 1997 | | | | | | | |
| | | MF | 76 | 101 | 113 | 63 | 107 | 95 |
| | | M | 77 | 101 | 110 | 53 | 106 | 92 |
| | | F | 76 | 101 | 116 | 73 | 109 | 99 |
| Papua New Guinea | 1970 | | (5-6) | (7-12) | (13-18) | (19-23) | (7-18) | (7-23) |
| | | MF | - | 52 | 8 | 0.5 | 32 | 25 |
| | | M | - | 63 | 11 | 0.8 | 40 | 31 |
| | | F | - | 39 | 4 | 0.2 | 24 | 18 |
| | 1975 | | | | | | | |
| | | MF | 0.0 | 56 | 12 | 2 | 36 | 28 |
| | | M | 0.0 | 68 | 16 | 3 | 44 | 34 |
| | | F | 0.0 | 44 | 7 | 1 | 27 | 21 |
| | 1980 | | | | | | | |
| | | MF | 0.2 | 59 | 12 | 2 | 38 | 30 |
| | | M | 0.2 | 66 | 15 | 3 | 43 | 34 |
| | | F | 0.1 | 51 | 8 | 0.9 | 32 | 25 |
| | 1985 | | | | | | | |
| | | MF | 0.5 | 66 | 11 | 2 | 40 | 31 |
| | | M | 0.6 | 71 | 15 | 2 | 44 | 34 |
| | | F | 0.4 | 60 | 8 | 0.8 | 36 | 28 |
| | 1990 | | | | | | | |
| | | MF | 0.4 | 72 | 12 | ... | 44 | ... |
| | | M | 0.5 | 78 | 15 | ... | 48 | ... |
| | | F | 0.4 | 66 | 10 | ... | 39 | ... |
| | 1991 | | | | | | | |
| | | MF | 0.3 | 72 | 13 | ... | 44 | ... |
| | | M | 0.3 | 78 | 15 | ... | 48 | ... |
| | | F | 0.3 | 66 | 10 | ... | 40 | ... |
| | 1992 | | | | | | | |
| | | MF | 0.4 | 74 | 13 | ... | 45 | ... |
| | | M | 0.4 | 80 | 15 | ... | 49 | ... |
| | | F | 0.4 | 67 | 10 | ... | 41 | ... |
| | 1993 | | | | | | | |
| | | MF | 0.6 | 78 | 14 | ... | 48 | ... |
| | | M | 0.7 | 84 | 17 | ... | 52 | ... |
| | | F | 0.5 | 71 | 12 | ... | 44 | ... |
| | 1994 | | | | | | | |
| | | MF | 0.7 | 80 | 15 | ... | 50 | ... |
| | | M | 0.7 | 87 | 18 | ... | 54 | ... |
| | | F | 0.6 | 73 | 12 | ... | 45 | ... |
| | 1995 | | | | | | | |
| | | MF | 1 | 80 | 14 | 3 | 49 | 37 |
| | | M | 1 | 87 | 17 | 4 | 54 | 41 |
| | | F | 1 | 74 | 11 | 2 | 45 | 34 |
| Samoa | 1990 | | (3-4) | (5-11) | (12-18) | (19-23) | (5-18) | (5-23) |
| | | MF | ... | 122 | 50 | ... | 92 | ... |
| | | M | ... | 117 | 46 | ... | 87 | ... |
| | | F | ... | 127 | 56 | ... | 98 | ... |

II.8    Gross enrolment ratios by level of education
Taux bruts de scolarisation par niveau d'enseignement
Tasas brutas de escolarización por nivel de enseñanza

| Country<br>Pays<br>País | Year<br>Année<br>Año | Sex<br>Sexe<br>Sexo | Gross enrolment ratios / Taux bruts de scolarisation / Tasas brutas de escolarización (%) | | | | | |
|---|---|---|---|---|---|---|---|---|
| | | | Pre-primary<br>Préprimaire<br>Preprimaria | Primary<br>Primaire<br>Primaria | Secondary<br>Secondaire<br>Secundaria | Tertiary<br>Supérieur<br>Superior | Primary and secondary<br>Primaire et secondaire<br>Primaria y secundaria | Primary, secondary and tertiary<br>Primaire, secondaire et supérieur<br>Primaria, secundaria y superior |
| Samoa (cont) | 1991 | MF<br>M<br>F | ...<br>...<br>... | 126<br>125<br>127 | 48<br>33<br>65 | ...<br>...<br>... | 94<br>87<br>101 | ...<br>...<br>... |
| | 1992 | MF<br>M<br>F | 13<br>...<br>... | 119<br>119<br>119 | 67<br>62<br>72 | ...<br>...<br>... | 98<br>95<br>100 | ...<br>...<br>... |
| | 1993 | MF<br>M<br>F | ...<br>...<br>... | 117<br>117<br>117 | 67<br>63<br>72 | ...<br>...<br>... | 97<br>95<br>99 | ...<br>...<br>... |
| | 1994 | MF<br>M<br>F | ...<br>...<br>... | 117<br>117<br>117 | 63<br>56<br>71 | ...<br>...<br>... | 95<br>92<br>99 | ...<br>...<br>... |
| | 1995 | MF<br>M<br>F | (3-4)<br>26<br>...<br>... | (5-12)<br>102<br>102<br>102 | (13-17)<br>...<br>...<br>... | (18-22)<br>...<br>...<br>... | (5-17)<br>...<br>...<br>... | (5-22)<br>...<br>...<br>... |
| | 1996 | MF<br>M<br>F | 33<br>...<br>... | 100<br>101<br>99 | 62<br>59<br>66 | ...<br>...<br>... | 86<br>86<br>87 | ...<br>...<br>... |
| | 1997 | MF<br>M<br>F | ...<br>...<br>... | 100<br>101<br>100 | ...<br>...<br>... | ...<br>...<br>... | ...<br>...<br>... | ...<br>...<br>... |
| Solomon Islands | 1980 | MF<br>M<br>F | (3-6)<br>...<br>... | (7-12)<br>76<br>85<br>65 | (13-17)<br>16<br>22<br>9 | (18-22)<br>...<br>...<br>... | (7-17)<br>52<br>60<br>43 | (7-22)<br>...<br>...<br>... |
| | 1985 | MF<br>M<br>F | (3-5)<br>...<br>...<br>... | (6-11)<br>79<br>...<br>... | (12-16)<br>19<br>24<br>14 | (17-21)<br>...<br>...<br>... | (6-16)<br>55<br>...<br>... | (6-21)<br>...<br>...<br>... |
| | 1990 | MF<br>M<br>F | 32<br>32<br>32 | 84<br>91<br>78 | 14<br>17<br>11 | ...<br>...<br>... | 55<br>60<br>50 | ...<br>...<br>... |
| | 1991 | MF<br>M<br>F | 35<br>35<br>34 | 85<br>91<br>78 | 15<br>19<br>11 | ...<br>...<br>... | 56<br>61<br>50 | ...<br>...<br>... |
| | 1992 | MF<br>M<br>F | 38<br>40<br>36 | 90<br>97<br>82 | 16<br>19<br>12 | ...<br>...<br>... | 59<br>64<br>53 | ...<br>...<br>... |
| | 1993 | MF<br>M<br>F | 37<br>38<br>36 | 94<br>101<br>86 | 17<br>21<br>13 | ...<br>...<br>... | 62<br>67<br>56 | ...<br>...<br>... |
| | 1994 | MF<br>M<br>F | 36<br>37<br>35 | 97<br>103<br>89 | 17<br>21<br>14 | ...<br>...<br>... | 64<br>69<br>58 | ...<br>...<br>... |
| Vanuatu, Republic of | 1985 | MF | (3-5)<br>... | (6-11)<br>100 | (12-18)<br>... | (19-23)<br>... | (6-18)<br>... | (6-23)<br>... |
| | 1990 | MF<br>M<br>F | ...<br>...<br>... | 96<br>98<br>94 | 17<br>19<br>14 | ...<br>...<br>... | 59<br>62<br>56 | ...<br>...<br>... |

Gross enrolment ratios by level of education    II.8
Taux bruts de scolarisation par niveau d'enseignement
Tasas brutas de escolarización por nivel de enseñanza

| Country / Pays / País | Year / Année / Año | Sex / Sexe / Sexo | Gross enrolment ratios / Taux bruts de scolarisation / Tasas brutas de escolarización (%) | | | | | |
|---|---|---|---|---|---|---|---|---|
| | | | Pre-primary / Préprimaire / Preprimaria | Primary / Primaire / Primaria | Secondary / Secondaire / Secundaria | Tertiary / Supérieur / Superior | Primary and secondary / Primaire et secondaire / Primaria y secundaria | Primary, secondary and tertiary / Primaire, secondaire et supérieur / Primaria, secundaria y superior |
| Vanuatu, Republic of (cont) | 1991 | MF | ... | 95 | 18 | ... | 59 | ... |
| | | M | ... | 99 | 21 | ... | 62 | ... |
| | | F | ... | 92 | 16 | ... | 56 | ... |
| | 1992 | MF | 35 | 98 | 20 | ... | 61 | ... |
| | | M | 36 | 101 | 23 | ... | 64 | ... |
| | | F | 34 | 94 | 18 | ... | 58 | ... |

## General note

For general explanations and definitions, please refer to the beginning of this chapter.

## Note générale

Pour les explications et définitions générales, prière de se référer au début de ce chapitre.

## Nota general

Para las explicaciones y definiciones generales, referirse al comienzo de este capítulo.

### Notes

(1) Enrolment ratios are not shown for certain countries because of inconsistencies between enrolment and population data and/or the unavailability of population data by age.

(2) Until 1985 primary education includes infant classes.

(3) Not including Turkish institutions.

(4) East Bank only.

(5) Some students from Luxembourg pursue their studies in neighbouring countries.

### Notes

(1) Les taux de scolarisation n'ont pas été calculés pour certains pays à cause du manque de cohérence entre les chiffres des effectifs scolaires ou universitaires et les données démographiques, ou de l'absence de données démographiques par âge.

(2) Jusqu'à 1985 l'enseignement primaire inclut les classes enfantines.

(3) Non compris les institutions turques.

(4) Rive orientale seulement.

(5) Une partie des étudiants luxembourgeois poursuit ses études dans les pays voisins.

### Notas

(1) Las tasas de escolarización no se calcularon para algunos países debido a las incongruencias observadas entre los datos de la escolarización y de la población y/o por no disponerse de datos de población por edad.

(2) Hasta 1985 la enseñanza primaria incluye las clases infantiles.

(3) No incluyen las instituciones turcas.

(4) Orilla oriental solamente.

(5) Una parte de los estudiantes de Luxemburgo cursa estudios en los países vecinos.

**II.9** Primary and secondary education: enrolment ratios by age groups
Enseignements primaire et secondaire: taux de scolarisation par groupes d'âge
Enseñanza primaria y secundaria: tasas de escolarización por grupos de edad

## II.9 Primary and secondary education: gross enrolment ratios and enrolment ratios by age groups

## Enseignements primaire et secondaire: taux bruts de scolarisation et taux de scolarisation par groupes d'âge

## Enseñanza primaria y secundaria: tasas brutas de escolarización y tasas de escolarización por grupos de edad

| Country / Pays / País | Year / Année / Año | Sex / Sexe / Sexo | Primary education — Enseignement primaire — Enseñanza primaria | | | | Secondary education — Enseignement secondaire — Enseñanza secundaria | | | |
|---|---|---|---|---|---|---|---|---|---|---|
| | | | Gross enrolment ratios / Taux bruts de scolarisation / Tasas brutas de escolarización (%) | Enrolment ratios by age groups / Taux de scolarisation par groupes d'âge / Tasas de escolarización por grupos de edad | | | Gross enrolment ratios / Taux bruts de scolarisation / Tasas brutas de escolarización (%) | Enrolment ratios by age groups / Taux de scolarisation par groupes d'âge / Tasas de escolarización por grupos de edad | | |
| | | | | Under-age / En dessous de l'âge officiel / Inferior a la edad oficial (%) | Official age group (NER) / Groupe d'âge officiel (TNS) / Grupo de edad oficial (TNE) (%) | Over-age / Au-dessus de l'âge officiel / Superior a la edad oficial (%) | | Under-age / En dessous de l'âge officiel / Inferior a la edad oficial (%) | Official age group (NER) / Groupe d'âge officiel (TNS) / Grupo de edad oficial (TNE) (%) | Over-age / Au-dessus de l'âge officiel / Superior a la edad oficial (%) |
| **Africa** | | | | | | | | | | |
| Algeria | 1970 | | (6-11) | (<6) | (6-11) | (>11) | (12-18) | (<12) | (12-18) | (>18) |
| | | MF | 76 | ... | ... | ... | 11 | 0.0 | 10 | 0.8 |
| | | M | 93 | ... | ... | ... | 16 | 0.0 | 14 | 1 |
| | | F | 58 | ... | ... | ... | 6 | 0.0 | 6 | 0.4 |
| | 1975 | MF | 93 | 1 | 77 | 15 | 20 | ... | ... | ... |
| | | M | 109 | 2 | 89 | 19 | 26 | ... | ... | ... |
| | | F | 75 | 1 | 64 | 11 | 14 | ... | ... | ... |
| | 1980 | MF | 94 | 1 | 81 | 12 | 33 | 0.7 | 31 | 2 |
| | | M | 108 | 2 | 91 | 15 | 40 | 0.9 | 37 | 2 |
| | | F | 81 | 1 | 71 | 9 | 26 | 0.6 | 24 | 1 |
| | 1985 | MF | 94 | 2 | 86 | 6 | 51 | 1 | 45 | 6 |
| | | M | 103 | 2 | 94 | 8 | 59 | 1 | 51 | 6 |
| | | F | 83 | 1 | 78 | 4 | 44 | 1 | 38 | 5 |
| | 1990 | | (6-11) | (<6) | (6-11) | (>11) | (12-17) | (<12) | (12-17) | (>17) |
| | | MF | 100 | 1 | 93 | 6 | 61 | 1 | 54 | 6 |
| | | M | 108 | 1 | 99 | 8 | 67 | 1 | 60 | 6 |
| | | F | 92 | 1 | 87 | 4 | 54 | 1 | 48 | 5 |
| | 1991 | MF | 103 | 2 | 95 | 6 | 61 | 1 | 54 | 5 |
| | | M | 111 | 2 | 100 | 8 | 66 | 1 | 59 | 6 |
| | | F | 95 | 2 | 89 | 4 | 55 | 1 | 49 | 5 |
| | 1992 | MF | 104 | 2 | 95 | 7 | 61 | 1 | 55 | 5 |
| | | M | 111 | 2 | 100 | 9 | 66 | 1 | 59 | 5 |
| | | F | 96 | 2 | 89 | 5 | 55 | 1 | 50 | 4 |
| | 1993 | MF | 105 | 2 | 95 | 8 | 62 | 2 | 55 | 5 |
| | | M | 112 | 3 | 100 | 10 | 66 | 2 | 59 | 6 |
| | | F | 98 | 2 | 90 | 5 | 57 | 2 | 51 | 5 |
| | 1994 | MF | 105 | 2 | 96 | 8 | 62 | 1 | 55 | 5 |
| | | M | 112 | 2 | 100 | 10 | 66 | 1 | 59 | 5 |
| | | F | 99 | 2 | 91 | 5 | 58 | 1 | 52 | 5 |

Primary and secondary education: enrolment ratios by age groups II.9
Enseignements primaire et secondaire: taux de scolarisation par groupes d'âge
Enseñanza primaria y secundaria: tasas de escolarización por grupos de edad

| Country / Pays / País | Year / Année / Año | Sex / Sexe / Sexo | Primary education — Enseignement primaire — Enseñanza primaria | | | | Secondary education — Enseignement secondaire — Enseñanza secundaria | | | |
|---|---|---|---|---|---|---|---|---|---|---|
| | | | Gross enrolment ratios / Taux bruts de scolarisation / Tasas brutas de escolarización (%) | Under-age / En dessous de l'âge officiel / Inferior a la edad oficial (%) | Official age group (NER) / Groupe d'âge officiel (TNS) / Grupo de edad oficial (TNE) (%) | Over-age / Au-dessus de l'âge officiel / Superior a la edad oficial (%) | Gross enrolment ratios / Taux bruts de scolarisation / Tasas brutas de escolarización (%) | Under-age / En dessous de l'âge officiel / Inferior a la edad oficial (%) | Official age group (NER) / Groupe d'âge officiel (TNS) / Grupo de edad oficial (TNE) (%) | Over-age / Au-dessus de l'âge officiel / Superior a la edad oficial (%) |
| Algeria (cont) | 1995 | MF | 107 | 2 | 95 | 9 | 62 | 1 | 56 | 5 |
| | | M | 113 | 2 | 99 | 11 | 66 | 1 | 59 | 5 |
| | | F | 100 | 2 | 91 | 7 | 59 | 1 | 53 | 5 |
| | 1996 | MF | 107 | 3 | 94 | 11 | 63 | 1 | 56 | 6 |
| | | M | 113 | 3 | 97 | 13 | 65 | 1 | 58 | 6 |
| | | F | 102 | 3 | 91 | 8 | 62 | 1 | 54 | 6 |
| Benin | 1985 | | (6-11) | (<6) | (6-11) | (>11) | (12-18) | (<12) | (12-18) | (>18) |
| | | MF | 68 | 2 | 53 | 13 | 18 | ... | ... | ... |
| | | M | 90 | 2 | 71 | 17 | 26 | ... | ... | ... |
| | | F | 45 | 1 | 36 | 8 | 10 | ... | ... | ... |
| | 1991 | MF | 61 | 1 | 49 | 11 | 12 | ... | ... | ... |
| | | M | 81 | 2 | 65 | 14 | 17 | ... | ... | ... |
| | | F | 41 | 1 | 32 | 7 | 7 | ... | ... | ... |
| | 1992 | MF | 66 | 2 | 53 | 11 | 13 | ... | ... | ... |
| | | M | 87 | 2 | 70 | 15 | 18 | ... | ... | ... |
| | | F | 45 | 1 | 36 | 8 | 8 | ... | ... | ... |
| | 1993 | MF | 67 | 1 | 54 | 11 | 14 | ... | ... | ... |
| | | M | 87 | 2 | 70 | 15 | 20 | ... | ... | ... |
| | | F | 47 | 1 | 38 | 7 | 9 | ... | ... | ... |
| | 1994 | MF | 70 | 2 | 57 | 12 | 15 | ... | ... | ... |
| | | M | 91 | 2 | 73 | 16 | 21 | ... | ... | ... |
| | | F | 50 | 1 | 41 | 8 | 9 | ... | ... | ... |
| | 1995 | MF | 73 | 2 | 60 | 12 | 16 | ... | ... | ... |
| | | M | 93 | 2 | 75 | 16 | 22 | ... | ... | ... |
| | | F | 53 | 2 | 44 | 8 | 9 | ... | ... | ... |
| | 1996 | MF | 78 | 2 | 63 | 12 | 17 | ... | ... | ... |
| | | M | 98 | 2 | 80 | 16 | 24 | ... | ... | ... |
| | | F | 57 | 2 | 47 | 8 | 10 | ... | ... | ... |
| Botswana | 1970 | | (7-13) | (<7) | (7-13) | (>13) | (14-18) | (<14) | (14-18) | (>18) |
| | | MF | 63 | 3 | 46 | 14 | 7 | ... | ... | ... |
| | | M | 60 | 3 | 42 | 14 | 8 | ... | ... | ... |
| | | F | 66 | 4 | 50 | 13 | 7 | ... | ... | ... |
| | 1975 | | (6-12) | (<6) | (6-12) | (>12) | (13-17) | (<13) | (13-17) | (>17) |
| | | MF | 71 | 1 | 57 | 13 | 15 | 0.2 | 11 | 4 |
| | | M | 64 | 1 | 52 | 11 | 15 | 0.1 | 9 | 5 |
| | | F | 78 | 1 | 63 | 14 | 16 | 0.3 | 12 | 3 |
| | 1980 | MF | 91 | 0.9 | 76 | 15 | 19 | 0.2 | 14 | 4 |
| | | M | 83 | 0.8 | 69 | 13 | 17 | 0.1 | 12 | 5 |
| | | F | 100 | 0.9 | 82 | 17 | 20 | 0.3 | 17 | 3 |
| | 1985 | | (7-13) | (<7) | (7-13) | (>13) | (14-18) | (<14) | (14-18) | (>18) |
| | | MF | 105 | 3 | 89 | 13 | 29 | 1 | 23 | 5 |
| | | M | 100 | 3 | 84 | 13 | 27 | 1 | 21 | 6 |
| | | F | 111 | 3 | 94 | 13 | 31 | 2 | 25 | 5 |
| | 1990 | MF | 113 | 4 | 93 | 16 | 43 | 1 | 34 | 8 |
| | | M | 109 | 3 | 90 | 16 | 41 | 0.9 | 31 | 9 |
| | | F | 117 | 4 | 97 | 16 | 45 | 2 | 36 | 7 |
| | 1991 | MF | 116 | 3 | 96 | 17 | 52 | 2 | 42 | 9 |
| | | M | 112 | 3 | 92 | 18 | 48 | 1 | 38 | 9 |
| | | F | 119 | 3 | 99 | 17 | 56 | 2 | 46 | 8 |

Primary and secondary education: enrolment ratios by age groups
Enseignements primaire et secondaire: taux de scolarisation par groupes d'âge
Enseñanza primaria y secundaria: tasas de escolarización por grupos de edad

| Country / Pays / País | Year / Année / Año | Sex / Sexe / Sexo | Primary education — Gross enrolment ratios / Taux bruts de scolarisation / Tasas brutas de escolarización (%) | Primary — Under-age / En dessous de l'âge officiel / Inferior a la edad oficial (%) | Primary — Official age group (NER) / Groupe d'âge officiel (TNS) / Grupo de edad oficial (TNE) (%) | Primary — Over-age / Au-dessus de l'âge officiel / Superior a la edad oficial (%) | Secondary education — Gross enrolment ratios / Taux bruts de scolarisation / Tasas brutas de escolarización (%) | Secondary — Under-age / En dessous de l'âge officiel / Inferior a la edad oficial (%) | Secondary — Official age group (NER) / Groupe d'âge officiel (TNS) / Grupo de edad oficial (TNE) (%) | Secondary — Over-age / Au-dessus de l'âge officiel / Superior a la edad oficial (%) |
|---|---|---|---|---|---|---|---|---|---|---|
| Botswana (cont) | 1992 | | | | | | | | | |
| | | MF | 114 | 3 | 95 | 16 | 52 | 2 | 42 | 8 |
| | | M | 111 | 3 | 92 | 16 | 48 | 1 | 39 | 8 |
| | | F | 117 | 3 | 98 | 15 | 56 | 2 | 46 | 8 |
| | 1993 | | | | | | | | | |
| | | MF | 112 | 3 | 94 | 15 | 57 | 2 | 46 | 9 |
| | | M | 110 | 3 | 91 | 16 | 53 | 1 | 42 | 10 |
| | | F | 114 | 3 | 96 | 14 | 60 | 2 | 49 | 9 |
| | 1994 | | | | | | | | | |
| | | MF | 111 | 3 | 93 | 15 | 55 | 2 | 45 | 9 |
| | | M | 110 | 3 | 90 | 16 | 53 | 1 | 42 | 10 |
| | | F | 113 | 4 | 95 | 14 | 58 | 2 | 48 | 8 |
| | 1995 | | (6-12) | (<6) | (6-12) | (>12) | (13-17) | (<13) | (13-17) | (>17) |
| | | MF | 108 | 0.3 | 81 | 26 | 63 | 0.2 | 44 | 18 |
| | | M | 107 | 0.3 | 79 | 28 | 60 | 0.1 | 40 | 19 |
| | | F | 109 | 0.3 | 83 | 25 | 66 | 0.2 | 49 | 17 |
| | 1996 | | | | | | | | | |
| | | MF | 108 | 0.3 | 81 | 27 | 65 | ... | ... | ... |
| | | M | 107 | 0.2 | 79 | 28 | 61 | ... | ... | ... |
| | | F | 108 | 0.3 | 83 | 25 | 68 | ... | ... | ... |
| Burkina Faso | 1970 | | (6-11) | (<6) | (6-11) | (>11) | (12-18) | (<12) | (12-18) | (>18) |
| | | MF | 12 | 0.0 | 9 | 3 | 1 | 0.0 | 1 | 0.2 |
| | | M | 15 | 0.0 | 12 | 4 | 2 | 0.0 | 2 | 0.3 |
| | | F | 9 | 0.0 | 7 | 2 | 0.8 | 0.0 | 0.7 | 0.1 |
| | 1980 | | (7-12) | (<7) | (7-12) | (>12) | (13-19) | (<13) | (13-19) | (>19) |
| | | MF | 17 | 0.6 | 15 | 2 | 3 | ... | ... | ... |
| | | M | 22 | 0.8 | 18 | 3 | 4 | ... | ... | ... |
| | | F | 13 | 0.5 | 11 | 2 | 2 | ... | ... | ... |
| | 1985 | | | | | | | | | |
| | | MF | 27 | 1 | 23 | 3 | 4 | 0.0 | 3 | 1 |
| | | M | 34 | 1 | 29 | 4 | 6 | 0.0 | 5 | 1 |
| | | F | 20 | 0.8 | 17 | 2 | 3 | 0.0 | 2 | 0.6 |
| | 1990 | | | | | | | | | |
| | | MF | 33 | 2 | 27 | 5 | 7 | ... | ... | ... |
| | | M | 41 | 2 | 33 | 6 | 9 | ... | ... | ... |
| | | F | 26 | 1 | 21 | 3 | 5 | ... | ... | ... |
| | 1991 | | | | | | | | | |
| | | MF | 34 | 2 | 27 | 5 | 7 | 0.2 | 7 | 0.6 |
| | | M | 41 | 2 | 33 | 6 | 10 | 0.2 | 9 | 0.8 |
| | | F | 26 | 2 | 21 | 4 | 5 | 0.2 | 5 | 0.4 |
| | 1992 | | | | | | | | | |
| | | MF | 35 | 2 | 28 | 5 | 8 | 0.2 | 7 | 0.9 |
| | | M | 42 | 3 | 34 | 6 | 10 | 0.2 | 9 | 1 |
| | | F | 27 | 2 | 22 | 3 | 6 | 0.2 | 5 | 0.7 |
| | 1993 | | | | | | | | | |
| | | MF | 36 | 2 | 29 | 5 | 8 | 0.0 | 7 | 1 |
| | | M | 44 | 3 | 36 | 6 | 11 | 0.0 | 9 | 2 |
| | | F | 28 | 2 | 23 | 3 | 6 | 0.0 | 5 | 1 |
| | 1994 | | | | | | | | | |
| | | MF | 38 | 2 | 31 | 5 | ... | ... | ... | ... |
| | | M | 46 | 3 | 37 | 6 | ... | ... | ... | ... |
| | | F | 30 | 2 | 24 | 4 | ... | ... | ... | ... |
| Burundi | 1975 | | (6-11) | (<6) | (6-11) | (>11) | (12-18) | (<12) | (12-18) | (>18) |
| | | MF | 21 | ... | ... | ... | 2 | 0.0 | 2 | 0.4 |
| | | M | 25 | ... | ... | ... | 3 | 0.0 | 2 | 0.7 |
| | | F | 16 | ... | ... | ... | 1 | 0.0 | 1 | 0.2 |
| | 1980 | | (7-12) | (<7) | (7-12) | (>12) | (13-19) | (<13) | (13-19) | (>19) |
| | | MF | 26 | 0.5 | 20 | 6 | 3 | ... | ... | ... |
| | | M | 32 | 0.5 | 23 | 8 | 4 | ... | ... | ... |
| | | F | 21 | 0.4 | 16 | 5 | 2 | ... | ... | ... |

Primary and secondary education: enrolment ratios by age groups
Enseignements primaire et secondaire: taux de scolarisation par groupes d'âge
Enseñanza primaria y secundaria: tasas de escolarización por grupos de edad

II.9

| Country / Pays / País | Year / Année / Año | Sex / Sexe / Sexo | Primary education / Enseignement primaire / Enseñanza primaria | | | | Secondary education / Enseignement secondaire / Enseñanza secundaria | | | |
|---|---|---|---|---|---|---|---|---|---|---|
| | | | Gross enrolment ratios / Taux bruts de scolarisation / Tasas brutas de escolarización (%) | Enrolment ratios by age groups / Taux de scolarisation par groupes d'âge / Tasas de escolarización por grupos de edad | | | Gross enrolment ratios / Taux bruts de scolarisation / Tasas brutas de escolarización (%) | Enrolment ratios by age groups / Taux de scolarisation par groupes d'âge / Tasas de escolarización por grupos de edad | | |
| | | | | Under-age / En dessous de l'âge officiel / Inferior a la edad oficial (%) | Official age group (NER) / Groupe d'âge officiel (TNS) / Grupo de edad oficial (TNE) (%) | Over-age / Au-dessus de l'âge officiel / Superior a la edad oficial (%) | | Under-age / En dessous de l'âge officiel / Inferior a la edad oficial (%) | Official age group (NER) / Groupe d'âge officiel (TNS) / Grupo de edad oficial (TNE) (%) | Over-age / Au-dessus de l'âge officiel / Superior a la edad oficial (%) |
| Burundi (cont) | 1985 | | | | | | | | | |
| | | MF | 53 | 1 | 41 | 10 | 4 | 0.0 | 3 | 0.9 |
| | | M | 61 | 1 | 47 | 13 | 5 | 0.0 | 3 | 1 |
| | | F | 44 | 1 | 36 | 7 | 2 | 0.0 | 2 | 0.5 |
| | 1992 | | | | | | | | | |
| | | MF | 70 | 2 | 52 | 16 | 7 | 0.0 | 5 | 2 |
| | | M | 77 | 2 | 56 | 19 | 8 | 0.0 | 6 | 2 |
| | | F | 63 | 2 | 48 | 13 | 5 | 0.0 | 4 | 1 |
| Cameroon | 1970 | | (6-11) | (<6) | (6-11) | (>11) | (12-18) | (<12) | (12-18) | (>18) |
| | | MF | 92 | 5 | 64 | 23 | 8 | 0.1 | 7 | 1 |
| | | M | 105 | 5 | 72 | 28 | 12 | 0.1 | 10 | 2 |
| | | F | 78 | 4 | 56 | 18 | 5 | 0.1 | 4 | 0.5 |
| | 1975 | | | | | | | | | |
| | | MF | 95 | 4 | 67 | 23 | 13 | 0.2 | 11 | 2 |
| | | M | 105 | 5 | 74 | 27 | 18 | 0.2 | 15 | 3 |
| | | F | 84 | 4 | 61 | 19 | 9 | 0.2 | 7 | 1 |
| | 1980 | | | | | | | | | |
| | | MF | 98 | ... | ... | ... | 18 | 0.3 | 15 | 3 |
| | | M | 107 | ... | ... | ... | 24 | 0.3 | 19 | 4 |
| | | F | 89 | ... | ... | ... | 13 | 0.3 | 11 | 2 |
| Cape Verde | 1980 | | (7-12) | (<7) | (7-12) | (>12) | (13-17) | (<13) | (13-17) | (>17) |
| | | MF | 114 | 2 | 90 | 22 | 8 | ... | ... | ... |
| | | M | 119 | 2 | 93 | 23 | 9 | ... | ... | ... |
| | | F | 110 | 2 | 88 | 20 | 7 | ... | ... | ... |
| | 1985 | | | | | | | | | |
| | | MF | 116 | 3 | 95 | 18 | 13 | ... | ... | ... |
| | | M | 119 | 3 | 97 | 19 | 15 | ... | ... | ... |
| | | F | 112 | 3 | 93 | 16 | 12 | ... | ... | ... |
| | 1997 | | (7-12) | (<7) | (7-12) | (>12) | (13-18) | (<13) | (13-18) | (>18) |
| | | MF | 148 | ... | ... | ... | 55 | 5 | 48 | 2 |
| | | M | 150 | ... | ... | ... | 54 | 5 | 47 | 2 |
| | | F | 147 | ... | ... | ... | 56 | 6 | 48 | 2 |
| Central African Republic | 1970 | | (6-11) | (<6) | (6-11) | (>11) | (12-18) | (<12) | (12-18) | (>18) |
| | | MF | 65 | 0.8 | 50 | 14 | 4 | 0.0 | 4 | 0.4 |
| | | M | 90 | 1 | 67 | 22 | 7 | 0.1 | 6 | 0.7 |
| | | F | 41 | 0.7 | 33 | 7 | 2 | 0.0 | 1 | 0.1 |
| | 1980 | | | | | | | | | |
| | | MF | 71 | 0.0 | 56 | 14 | 14 | ... | ... | ... |
| | | M | 92 | 0.0 | 73 | 20 | 21 | ... | ... | ... |
| | | F | 51 | 0.0 | 41 | 9 | 7 | ... | ... | ... |
| | 1985 | | | | | | | | | |
| | | MF | 75 | 0.0 | 61 | 14 | 16 | ... | ... | ... |
| | | M | 93 | 0.0 | 75 | 19 | 24 | ... | ... | ... |
| | | F | 57 | 0.0 | 47 | 10 | 8 | ... | ... | ... |
| | 1990 | | | | | | | | | |
| | | MF | 65 | 0.1 | 53 | 12 | 12 | ... | ... | ... |
| | | M | 80 | 0.2 | 64 | 15 | 17 | ... | ... | ... |
| | | F | 51 | 0.1 | 42 | 8 | 7 | ... | ... | ... |
| Chad | 1995 | | (6-11) | (<6) | (6-11) | (>11) | (12-18) | (<12) | (12-18) | (>18) |
| | | MF | 51 | 0.9 | 40 | 11 | 9 | 0.0 | 6 | 4 |
| | 1996 | | | | | | | | | |
| | | MF | 57 | 0.9 | 46 | 11 | 9 | ... | ... | ... |
| | | M | 76 | 1 | 59 | 16 | 15 | ... | ... | ... |
| | | F | 39 | 0.6 | 33 | 6 | 4 | ... | ... | ... |
| Comoros | 1985 | | (6-11) | (<6) | (6-11) | (>11) | (12-18) | (<12) | (12-18) | (>18) |
| | | MF | 82 | 0.2 | 61 | 21 | 28 | ... | ... | ... |
| | 1993 | | (7-12) | (<7) | (7-12) | (>12) | (13-19) | (<13) | (13-19) | (>19) |
| | | MF | 77 | 3 | 52 | 21 | 19 | ... | ... | ... |
| | | M | 84 | 4 | 57 | 23 | 21 | ... | ... | ... |
| | | F | 69 | 3 | 47 | 19 | 16 | ... | ... | ... |

II.9   Primary and secondary education: enrolment ratios by age groups
Enseignements primaire et secondaire: taux de scolarisation par groupes d'âge
Enseñanza primaria y secundaria: tasas de escolarización por grupos de edad

| Country / Pays / País | Year / Année / Año | Sex / Sexe / Sexo | Primary education — Enseignement primaire — Enseñanza primaria | | | | Secondary education — Enseignement secondaire — Enseñanza secundaria | | | |
|---|---|---|---|---|---|---|---|---|---|---|
| | | | Gross enrolment ratios / Taux bruts de scolarisation / Tasas brutas de escolarización (%) | Under-age / En dessous de l'âge officiel / Inferior a la edad oficial (%) | Official age group (NER) / Groupe d'âge officiel (TNS) / Grupo de edad oficial (TNE) (%) | Over-age / Au-dessus de l'âge officiel / Superior a la edad oficial (%) | Gross enrolment ratios / Taux bruts de scolarisation / Tasas brutas de escolarización (%) | Under-age / En dessous de l'âge officiel / Inferior a la edad oficial (%) | Official age group (NER) / Groupe d'âge officiel (TNS) / Grupo de edad oficial (TNE) (%) | Over-age / Au-dessus de l'âge officiel / Superior a la edad oficial (%) |
| Congo | 1980 | | (6-11) | (<6) | (6-11) | (>11) | (12-18) | (<12) | (12-18) | (>18) |
| | | MF | 141 | 0.0 | 96 | 45 | 74 | ... | ... | ... |
| | | M | 148 | 0.0 | 99 | 49 | 89 | ... | ... | ... |
| | | F | 134 | 0.0 | 93 | 41 | 60 | ... | ... | ... |
| Côte d'Ivoire | 1970 | | (7-12) | (<7) | (7-12) | (>12) | (13-19) | (<13) | (13-19) | (>19) |
| | | MF | 59 | ... | ... | ... | 9 | 0.5 | 8 | 0.7 |
| | | M | 75 | ... | ... | ... | 14 | 0.7 | 12 | 1 |
| | | F | 43 | ... | ... | ... | 4 | 0.2 | 3 | 0.3 |
| | 1990 | | (6-11) | (<6) | (6-11) | (>11) | (12-18) | (<12) | (12-18) | (>18) |
| | | MF | 67 | 0.2 | 47 | 20 | 22 | ... | ... | ... |
| | 1991 | | | | | | | | | |
| | | MF | 66 | 0.8 | 47 | 18 | 23 | ... | ... | ... |
| | 1995 | | | | | | | | | |
| | | MF | 69 | 4 | 53 | 12 | 23 | ... | ... | ... |
| | | M | 79 | 4 | 61 | 15 | 31 | ... | ... | ... |
| | | F | 58 | 3 | 45 | 10 | 15 | ... | ... | ... |
| | 1996 | | | | | | | | | |
| | | MF | 71 | 4 | 55 | 12 | 24 | ... | ... | ... |
| | | M | 82 | 5 | 63 | 14 | 33 | ... | ... | ... |
| | | F | 60 | 4 | 47 | 9 | 16 | ... | ... | ... |
| Democratic Rep. of the Congo | 1970 | | (6-11) | (<6) | (6-11) | (>11) | (12-17) | (<12) | (12-17) | (>17) |
| | | MF | 95 | 0.7 | 68 | 26 | 9 | ... | ... | ... |
| | | M | 120 | 0.8 | 83 | 36 | 15 | ... | ... | ... |
| | | F | 70 | 0.6 | 53 | 16 | 4 | ... | ... | ... |
| | 1990 | | | | | | | | | |
| | | MF | 70 | 0.6 | 54 | 15 | ... | ... | ... | ... |
| | | M | 81 | 0.7 | 61 | 19 | ... | ... | ... | ... |
| | | F | 60 | 0.6 | 48 | 12 | ... | ... | ... | ... |
| | 1991 | | | | | | | | | |
| | | MF | 69 | 0.6 | 53 | 15 | 21 | 0.2 | 15 | 6 |
| | | M | 78 | 0.6 | 59 | 19 | 28 | 0.2 | 19 | 9 |
| | | F | 59 | 0.6 | 47 | 12 | 14 | 0.2 | 11 | 2 |
| | 1992 | | | | | | | | | |
| | | MF | 70 | 0.6 | 52 | 17 | 22 | 0.2 | 16 | 6 |
| | | M | 79 | 0.6 | 58 | 20 | 31 | 0.2 | 21 | 9 |
| | | F | 61 | 0.5 | 47 | 14 | 14 | 0.2 | 12 | 3 |
| | 1993 | | | | | | | | | |
| | | MF | 68 | 1 | 54 | 13 | 24 | 0.2 | 17 | 7 |
| | | M | 78 | 1 | 60 | 17 | 33 | 0.2 | 22 | 10 |
| | | F | 58 | 1 | 47 | 10 | 15 | 0.2 | 11 | 3 |
| Djibouti | 1985 | | (6-11) | (<6) | (6-11) | (>11) | (12-18) | (<12) | (12-18) | (>18) |
| | | MF | 40 | 0.2 | 31 | 8 | 12 | 0.2 | 11 | 0.9 |
| | | M | 47 | 0.3 | 37 | 10 | 14 | 0.3 | 13 | 1 |
| | | F | 33 | 0.1 | 26 | 7 | 9 | 0.1 | 8 | 0.6 |
| | 1990 | | | | | | | | | |
| | | MF | 38 | 0.1 | 32 | 6 | 12 | ... | ... | ... |
| | 1991 | | | | | | | | | |
| | | MF | 39 | 0.1 | 32 | 6 | 12 | ... | ... | ... |
| | | M | 45 | 0.1 | 37 | 8 | 15 | ... | ... | ... |
| | | F | 32 | 0.1 | 27 | 5 | 10 | ... | ... | ... |
| | 1992 | | | | | | | | | |
| | | MF | 34 | 0.0 | 29 | 5 | 11 | ... | ... | ... |
| | | M | 39 | 0.1 | 33 | 6 | 13 | ... | ... | ... |
| | | F | 30 | 0.0 | 25 | 4 | 10 | ... | ... | ... |
| | 1993 | | | | | | | | | |
| | | MF | 36 | 0.2 | 30 | 6 | 12 | ... | ... | ... |
| | | M | 41 | 0.2 | 34 | 7 | 14 | ... | ... | ... |
| | | F | 31 | 0.2 | 26 | 5 | 10 | ... | ... | ... |

Primary and secondary education: enrolment ratios by age groups **II.9**
Enseignements primaire et secondaire: taux de scolarisation par groupes d'âge
Enseñanza primaria y secundaria: tasas de escolarización por grupos de edad

| Country / Pays / País | Year / Année / Año | Sex / Sexe / Sexo | Primary education / Enseignement primaire / Enseñanza primaria | | | | Secondary education / Enseignement secondaire / Enseñanza secundaria | | | |
|---|---|---|---|---|---|---|---|---|---|---|
| | | | Gross enrolment ratios / Taux bruts de scolarisation / Tasas brutas de escolarización (%) | Enrolment ratios by age groups / Taux de scolarisation par groupes d'âge / Tasas de escolarización por grupos de edad | | | Gross enrolment ratios / Taux bruts de scolarisation / Tasas brutas de escolarización (%) | Enrolment ratios by age groups / Taux de scolarisation par groupes d'âge / Tasas de escolarización por grupos de edad | | |
| | | | | Under-age / En dessous de l'âge officiel / Inferior a la edad oficial (%) | Official age group (NER) / Groupe d'âge officiel (TNS) / Grupo de edad oficial (TNE) (%) | Over-age / Au-dessus de l'âge officiel / Superior a la edad oficial (%) | | Under-age / En dessous de l'âge officiel / Inferior a la edad oficial (%) | Official age group (NER) / Groupe d'âge officiel (TNS) / Grupo de edad oficial (TNE) (%) | Over-age / Au-dessus de l'âge officiel / Superior a la edad oficial (%) |
| Djibouti (cont) | 1994 | | | | | | | | | |
| | | MF | 38 | 0.1 | 32 | 6 | 13 | ... | ... | ... |
| | | M | 43 | 0.1 | 36 | 7 | 15 | ... | ... | ... |
| | | F | 33 | 0.1 | 28 | 5 | 10 | ... | ... | ... |
| | 1995 | | | | | | | | | |
| | | MF | 38 | 0.2 | 32 | 6 | 13 | ... | ... | ... |
| | | M | 44 | 0.2 | 37 | 7 | 15 | ... | ... | ... |
| | | F | 33 | 0.1 | 28 | 5 | 11 | ... | ... | ... |
| | 1996 | | | | | | | | | |
| | | MF | 39 | 0.1 | 32 | 7 | 14 | 0.1 | 12 | 2 |
| | | M | 44 | 0.2 | 36 | 8 | 17 | 0.2 | 15 | 2 |
| | | F | 33 | 0.1 | 27 | 5 | 12 | 0.1 | 10 | 1 |
| Egypt | 1970 | | (6-11) | (<6) | (6-11) | (>11) | (12-17) | (<12) | (12-17) | (>17) |
| | | MF | 68 | 1 | 63 | 4 | 28 | 0.4 | 24 | 5 |
| | | M | 81 | 1 | 75 | 5 | 38 | 0.4 | 31 | 6 |
| | | F | 53 | 1 | 49 | 2 | 19 | 0.3 | 15 | 3 |
| | 1993 | | (6-10) | (<6) | (6-10) | (>10) | (11-16) | (<11) | (11-16) | (>16) |
| | | MF | 97 | 3 | 88 | 5 | 76 | 2 | 65 | 8 |
| | | M | 104 | 3 | 94 | 6 | 82 | 2 | 70 | 10 |
| | | F | 89 | 3 | 82 | 4 | 69 | 2 | 60 | 7 |
| | 1996 | | | | | | | | | |
| | | MF | 100 | 0.4 | 93 | 7 | 75 | 2 | 67 | 6 |
| | | M | 107 | 0.4 | 98 | 8 | 80 | 2 | 71 | 7 |
| | | F | 94 | 0.4 | 88 | 6 | 70 | 2 | 64 | 5 |
| Eritrea | 1993 | | (7-11) | (<7) | (7-11) | (>11) | (12-17) | (<12) | (12-17) | (>17) |
| | | MF | 51 | 0.4 | 28 | 23 | 17 | 0.1 | 12 | 4 |
| | | M | 57 | 0.4 | 29 | 27 | 19 | 0.1 | 13 | 6 |
| | | F | 45 | 0.4 | 26 | 18 | 14 | 0.1 | 12 | 2 |
| | 1994 | | | | | | | | | |
| | | MF | 54 | 0.2 | 29 | 24 | 18 | 0.1 | 13 | 4 |
| | | M | 60 | 0.2 | 31 | 29 | 21 | 0.1 | 14 | 7 |
| | | F | 48 | 0.2 | 28 | 20 | 15 | 0.1 | 12 | 2 |
| | 1995 | | | | | | | | | |
| | | MF | 56 | 0.2 | 31 | 25 | 19 | 0.2 | 14 | 4 |
| | | M | 62 | 0.2 | 32 | 29 | 22 | 0.2 | 15 | 6 |
| | | F | 50 | 0.2 | 29 | 20 | 16 | 0.1 | 13 | 2 |
| | 1996 | | | | | | | | | |
| | | MF | 53 | 0.3 | 30 | 23 | 20 | 0.3 | 16 | 4 |
| | | M | 59 | 0.3 | 32 | 26 | 24 | 0.3 | 17 | 6 |
| | | F | 48 | 0.2 | 29 | 19 | 17 | 0.2 | 14 | 2 |
| Ethiopia | 1993 | | (7-12) | (<7) | (7-12) | (>12) | (13-18) | (<13) | (13-18) | (>18) |
| | | MF | 27 | 0.4 | 20 | 6 | 11 | ... | ... | ... |
| | | M | 34 | 0.5 | 24 | 9 | 12 | ... | ... | ... |
| | | F | 21 | 0.4 | 16 | 4 | 10 | ... | ... | ... |
| | 1994 | | | | | | | | | |
| | | MF | 31 | 0.5 | 23 | 7 | 11 | ... | ... | ... |
| | | M | 39 | 0.6 | 29 | 10 | 12 | ... | ... | ... |
| | | F | 23 | 0.4 | 18 | 4 | 10 | ... | ... | ... |
| | 1995 | | | | | | | | | |
| | | MF | 37 | 0.5 | 28 | 9 | 12 | ... | ... | ... |
| | | M | 48 | 0.6 | 35 | 13 | 13 | ... | ... | ... |
| | | F | 27 | 0.4 | 21 | 5 | 10 | ... | ... | ... |
| | 1996 | | | | | | | | | |
| | | MF | 43 | 0.5 | 32 | 10 | 12 | ... | ... | ... |
| | | M | 55 | 0.6 | 39 | 15 | 14 | ... | ... | ... |
| | | F | 30 | 0.4 | 24 | 6 | 10 | ... | ... | ... |
| Gambia | 1970 | | (6-11) | (<6) | (6-11) | (>11) | (12-18) | (<12) | (12-18) | (>18) |
| | | MF | 25 | 0.6 | 21 | 3 | 8 | ... | ... | ... |
| | | M | 35 | 0.7 | 29 | 5 | 13 | ... | ... | ... |
| | | F | 15 | 0.5 | 13 | 2 | 4 | ... | ... | ... |

II.9    Primary and secondary education: enrolment ratios by age groups
Enseignements primaire et secondaire: taux de scolarisation par groupes d'âge
Enseñanza primaria y secundaria: tasas de escolarización por grupos de edad

| Country / Pays / País | Year / Année / Año | Sex / Sexe / Sexo | Primary education — Gross enrolment ratios (%) | Primary — Under-age (%) | Primary — Official age group (NER) (%) | Primary — Over-age (%) | Secondary education — Gross enrolment ratios (%) | Secondary — Under-age (%) | Secondary — Official age group (NER) (%) | Secondary — Over-age (%) |
|---|---|---|---|---|---|---|---|---|---|---|
| Gambia (cont) | 1975 | | (8-13) | (<8) | (8-13) | (>13) | (14-20) | (<14) | (14-20) | (>20) |
| | | MF | 33 | 11 | 21 | 0.2 | 9 | ... | ... | ... |
| | | M | 44 | 15 | 29 | 0.4 | 14 | ... | ... | ... |
| | | F | 21 | 8 | 13 | 0.1 | 5 | ... | ... | ... |
| | 1980 | | | | | | | | | |
| | | MF | 53 | 2 | 50 | 1 | 11 | ... | ... | ... |
| | | M | 70 | 2 | 66 | 2 | 16 | ... | ... | ... |
| | | F | 36 | 1 | 34 | 0.6 | 7 | ... | ... | ... |
| | 1985 | | | | | | | | | |
| | | MF | 68 | 3 | 62 | 3 | 16 | 2 | 13 | 0.4 |
| | | M | 84 | 3 | 77 | 4 | 23 | 3 | 19 | 0.5 |
| | | F | 52 | 2 | 48 | 2 | 10 | 1 | 8 | 0.3 |
| | 1991 | | (7-12) | (<7) | (7-12) | (>12) | (13-18) | (<13) | (13-18) | (>18) |
| | | MF | 65 | 2 | 51 | 12 | 19 | 0.6 | 18 | 0.7 |
| | | M | 77 | 2 | 60 | 15 | 25 | 0.7 | 24 | 1 |
| | | F | 52 | 2 | 42 | 9 | 13 | 0.6 | 12 | 0.3 |
| | 1992 | | | | | | | | | |
| | | MF | 67 | 3 | 55 | 10 | 22 | 0.3 | 20 | 2 |
| | | M | 79 | 3 | 64 | 12 | 29 | 0.3 | 26 | 3 |
| | | F | 55 | 2 | 46 | 7 | 15 | 0.3 | 14 | 1 |
| | 1995 | | | | | | | | | |
| | | MF | 77 | 3 | 65 | 9 | 25 | ... | ... | ... |
| | | M | 87 | 4 | 72 | 11 | 30 | ... | ... | ... |
| | | F | 67 | 3 | 57 | 7 | 19 | ... | ... | ... |
| Guinea | 1985 | | (7-12) | (<7) | (7-12) | (>12) | (13-19) | (<13) | (13-19) | (>19) |
| | | MF | 34 | 0.5 | 27 | 7 | 13 | 0.1 | 9 | 4 |
| | | M | 47 | 0.6 | 36 | 9 | 18 | 0.2 | 13 | 5 |
| | | F | 22 | 0.4 | 18 | 4 | 7 | 0.1 | 5 | 2 |
| | 1993 | | | | | | | | | |
| | | MF | 42 | 2 | 37 | 4 | 12 | ... | ... | ... |
| | 1997 | | | | | | | | | |
| | | MF | 54 | 1 | 42 | 12 | 14 | ... | ... | ... |
| | | M | 68 | 1 | 50 | 16 | 20 | ... | ... | ... |
| | | F | 41 | 1 | 33 | 7 | 7 | ... | ... | ... |
| Guinea-Bissau | 1980 | | (7-12) | (<7) | (7-12) | (>12) | (13-17) | (<13) | (13-17) | (>17) |
| | | MF | 68 | 2 | 47 | 19 | 6 | 0.0 | 3 | 3 |
| | | M | 94 | 3 | 63 | 27 | 10 | 0.0 | 4 | 6 |
| | | F | 43 | 2 | 31 | 10 | 2 | 0.0 | 1 | 1 |
| Kenya | 1975 | | (6-12) | (<6) | (6-12) | (>12) | (13-18) | (<13) | (13-18) | (>18) |
| | | MF | 104 | 0.0 | 88 | 16 | 13 | 0.0 | 11 | 2 |
| | | M | 112 | 0.0 | 93 | 19 | 17 | 0.0 | 13 | 4 |
| | | F | 96 | 0.0 | 83 | 13 | 9 | 0.0 | 9 | 0.8 |
| | 1980 | | | | | | | | | |
| | | MF | 115 | 0.0 | 91 | 25 | 20 | ... | ... | ... |
| | | M | 120 | 0.0 | 92 | 28 | 23 | ... | ... | ... |
| | | F | 110 | 0.0 | 89 | 21 | 16 | ... | ... | ... |
| Lesotho | 1970 | | (6-13) | (<6) | (6-13) | (>13) | (14-18) | (<14) | (14-18) | (>18) |
| | | MF | 87 | 1 | 66 | 20 | 7 | 0.2 | 5 | 2 |
| | | M | 72 | 0.8 | 53 | 18 | 7 | 0.2 | 4 | 2 |
| | | F | 102 | 1 | 79 | 22 | 7 | 0.2 | 6 | 1 |
| | 1980 | | (6-12) | (<6) | (6-12) | (>12) | (13-17) | (<13) | (13-17) | (>17) |
| | | MF | 103 | 1 | 67 | 36 | 18 | 0.8 | 13 | 4 |
| | | M | 85 | 1 | 55 | 30 | 14 | 0.6 | 9 | 5 |
| | | F | 122 | 1 | 79 | 42 | 21 | 1 | 17 | 4 |
| | 1985 | | | | | | | | | |
| | | MF | 112 | 2 | 72 | 38 | 23 | 0.3 | 13 | 10 |
| | | M | 98 | 1 | 62 | 35 | 19 | 0.2 | 9 | 10 |
| | | F | 125 | 2 | 82 | 41 | 28 | 0.4 | 18 | 10 |
| | 1990 | | | | | | | | | |
| | | MF | 112 | 2 | 73 | 37 | 25 | ... | ... | ... |
| | | M | 100 | 2 | 65 | 34 | 20 | ... | ... | ... |
| | | F | 123 | 2 | 81 | 40 | 30 | ... | ... | ... |

Primary and secondary education: enrolment ratios by age groups
Enseignements primaire et secondaire: taux de scolarisation par groupes d'âge
Enseñanza primaria y secundaria: tasas de escolarización por grupos de edad

II.9

| Country / Pays / País | Year / Année / Año | Sex / Sexe / Sexo | Primary education — Enseignement primaire — Enseñanza primaria | | | | Secondary education — Enseignement secondaire — Enseñanza secundaria | | | |
|---|---|---|---|---|---|---|---|---|---|---|
| | | | Gross enrolment ratios / Taux bruts de scolarisation / Tasas brutas de escolarización (%) | Under-age / En dessous de l'âge officiel / Inferior a la edad oficial (%) | Official age group (NER) / Groupe d'âge officiel (TNS) / Grupo de edad oficial (TNE) (%) | Over-age / Au-dessus de l'âge officiel / Superior a la edad oficial (%) | Gross enrolment ratios / Taux bruts de scolarisation / Tasas brutas de escolarización (%) | Under-age / En dessous de l'âge officiel / Inferior a la edad oficial (%) | Official age group (NER) / Groupe d'âge officiel (TNS) / Grupo de edad oficial (TNE) (%) | Over-age / Au-dessus de l'âge officiel / Superior a la edad oficial (%) |
| Lesotho (cont) | 1991 | MF | 113 | 2 | 74 | 37 | 25 | 0.2 | 15 | 10 |
| | | M | 101 | 1 | 66 | 34 | 20 | 0.1 | 10 | 10 |
| | | F | 125 | 2 | 83 | 40 | 29 | 0.3 | 20 | 9 |
| | 1992 | MF | 112 | 2 | 75 | 36 | 26 | 0.7 | 17 | 9 |
| | | M | 102 | 1 | 67 | 34 | 21 | 0.4 | 11 | 9 |
| | | F | 122 | 2 | 82 | 38 | 31 | 1 | 22 | 8 |
| | 1993 | MF | 108 | 2 | 72 | 34 | 27 | 0.5 | 17 | 9 |
| | | M | 99 | 2 | 65 | 33 | 22 | 0.2 | 12 | 9 |
| | | F | 116 | 2 | 79 | 35 | 32 | 0.7 | 23 | 8 |
| | 1994 | MF | 110 | 0.4 | 73 | 37 | 29 | 0.2 | 16 | 13 |
| | | M | 102 | 0.4 | 66 | 36 | 23 | 0.1 | 11 | 12 |
| | | F | 117 | 0.5 | 79 | 37 | 35 | 0.3 | 22 | 13 |
| | 1995 | MF | 111 | 0.3 | 71 | 40 | 31 | ... | ... | ... |
| | | M | 104 | 0.3 | 65 | 39 | 25 | ... | ... | ... |
| | | F | 117 | 0.3 | 76 | 41 | 37 | ... | ... | ... |
| | 1996 | MF | 108 | 0.4 | 70 | 37 | 31 | 0.3 | 18 | 12 |
| | | M | 102 | 0.3 | 64 | 37 | 25 | 0.2 | 13 | 12 |
| | | F | 114 | 0.4 | 76 | 38 | 36 | 0.5 | 24 | 12 |
| Libyan Arab Jamahiriya | 1970 | | (6-11) | (<6) | (6-11) | (>11) | (12-17) | (<12) | (12-17) | (>17) |
| | | MF | 111 | 0.0 | 86 | 25 | 21 | 0.2 | 13 | 7 |
| | | M | 136 | 0.0 | 100 | 36 | 33 | 0.3 | 20 | 13 |
| | | F | 84 | 0.0 | 71 | 13 | 8 | 0.1 | 6 | 2 |
| | 1975 | MF | 137 | ... | ... | ... | 55 | 0.0 | 45 | 10 |
| | | M | 145 | ... | ... | ... | 71 | 0.0 | 56 | 14 |
| | | F | 130 | ... | ... | ... | 38 | 0.0 | 32 | 5 |
| | 1980 | MF | 126 | ... | ... | ... | 76 | 0.0 | 62 | 14 |
| | | M | 129 | ... | ... | ... | 89 | 0.0 | 71 | 17 |
| | | F | 121 | ... | ... | ... | 63 | 0.0 | 53 | 10 |
| | 1992 | | (6-14) | (<6) | (6-14) | (>14) | (15-17) | (<15) | (15-17) | (>17) |
| | | MF | 105 | 0.4 | 96 | 8 | 98 | ... | ... | ... |
| | | M | 107 | 0.4 | 97 | 9 | ... | ... | ... | ... |
| | | F | 103 | 0.4 | 96 | 7 | ... | ... | ... | ... |
| Madagascar | 1994 | | (6-10) | (<6) | (6-10) | (>10) | (11-17) | (<11) | (11-17) | (>17) |
| | | MF | 89 | 2 | 59 | 27 | 16 | ... | ... | ... |
| | | M | 85 | 2 | 55 | 28 | 16 | ... | ... | ... |
| | | F | 92 | 2 | 64 | 26 | 15 | ... | ... | ... |
| | 1995 | MF | 92 | 4 | 61 | 27 | 16 | ... | ... | ... |
| | | M | 92 | 4 | 59 | 28 | 16 | ... | ... | ... |
| | | F | 91 | 4 | 62 | 25 | 16 | ... | ... | ... |
| Malawi | 1980 | | (6-13) | (<6) | (6-13) | (>13) | (14-17) | (<14) | (14-17) | (>17) |
| | | MF | 60 | 2 | 43 | 15 | 5 | ... | ... | ... |
| | | M | 72 | 2 | 48 | 23 | 7 | ... | ... | ... |
| | | F | 48 | 2 | 38 | 9 | 3 | ... | ... | ... |
| | 1985 | MF | 60 | 0.9 | 43 | 16 | 6 | ... | ... | ... |
| | | M | 69 | 0.8 | 46 | 22 | 8 | ... | ... | ... |
| | | F | 52 | 0.9 | 41 | 10 | 4 | ... | ... | ... |
| | 1990 | MF | 68 | 0.0 | 50 | 18 | 8 | ... | ... | ... |
| | | M | 74 | 0.0 | 52 | 22 | 11 | ... | ... | ... |
| | | F | 62 | 0.0 | 48 | 14 | 5 | ... | ... | ... |

II.9    Primary and secondary education: enrolment ratios by age groups
Enseignements primaire et secondaire: taux de scolarisation par groupes d'âge
Enseñanza primaria y secundaria: tasas de escolarización por grupos de edad

| | | | Primary education / Enseignement primaire / Enseñanza primaria | | | | Secondary education / Enseignement secondaire / Enseñanza secundaria | | | |
|---|---|---|---|---|---|---|---|---|---|---|
| Country / Pays / País | Year / Année / Año | Sex / Sexe / Sexo | Gross enrolment ratios / Taux bruts de scolarisation / Tasas brutas de escolarización (%) | Enrolment ratios by age groups / Taux de scolarisation par groupes d'âge / Tasas de escolarización por grupos de edad | | | Gross enrolment ratios / Taux bruts de scolarisation / Tasas brutas de escolarización (%) | Enrolment ratios by age groups / Taux de scolarisation par groupes d'âge / Tasas de escolarización por grupos de edad | | |
| | | | | Under-age / En dessous de l'âge officiel / Inferior a la edad oficial (%) | Official age group (NER) / Groupe d'âge officiel (TNS) / Grupo de edad oficial (TNE) (%) | Over-age / Au-dessus de l'âge officiel / Superior a la edad oficial (%) | | Under-age / En dessous de l'âge officiel / Inferior a la edad oficial (%) | Official age group (NER) / Groupe d'âge officiel (TNS) / Grupo de edad oficial (TNE) (%) | Over-age / Au-dessus de l'âge officiel / Superior a la edad oficial (%) |
| Malawi (cont) | 1992 | | | | | | | | | |
| | | MF | 84 | 0.2 | 55 | 30 | 9 | ... | ... | ... |
| | | M | 88 | 0.2 | 53 | 36 | 12 | ... | ... | ... |
| | | F | 80 | 0.3 | 57 | 23 | 6 | ... | ... | ... |
| | 1993 | | | | | | | | | |
| | | MF | 89 | 2 | 68 | 19 | 11 | ... | ... | ... |
| | | M | 92 | 2 | 66 | 24 | 15 | ... | ... | ... |
| | | F | 86 | 2 | 71 | 14 | 8 | ... | ... | ... |
| | 1994 | | | | | | | | | |
| | | MF | 134 | 3 | 103 | 28 | 13 | ... | ... | ... |
| | | M | 141 | 3 | 102 | 36 | 16 | ... | ... | ... |
| | | F | 127 | 3 | 104 | 20 | 9 | ... | ... | ... |
| Mali | 1970 | | (7-12) | (<7) | (7-12) | (>12) | (13-18) | (<13) | (13-18) | (>18) |
| | | MF | 23 | 0.5 | 17 | 6 | 5 | 0.1 | 4 | 0.9 |
| | | M | 30 | 0.6 | 21 | 8 | 8 | 0.1 | 6 | 2 |
| | | F | 16 | 0.4 | 12 | 4 | 2 | 0.0 | 2 | 0.3 |
| | 1980 | | | | | | | | | |
| | | MF | 26 | 3 | 20 | 4 | 8 | ... | ... | ... |
| | 1990 | | | | | | | | | |
| | | MF | 26 | 2 | 21 | 3 | 7 | 0.3 | 5 | 1 |
| | | M | 34 | 2 | 27 | 5 | 9 | 0.3 | 7 | 2 |
| | | F | 19 | 1 | 16 | 2 | 5 | 0.2 | 4 | 0.7 |
| | 1991 | | | | | | | | | |
| | | MF | 28 | 2 | 22 | 4 | 8 | ... | ... | ... |
| | | M | 36 | 2 | 28 | 6 | 11 | ... | ... | ... |
| | | F | 21 | 1 | 16 | 3 | 5 | ... | ... | ... |
| | 1992 | | | | | | | | | |
| | | MF | 31 | 2 | 24 | 5 | 8 | ... | ... | ... |
| | | M | 39 | 2 | 31 | 7 | 11 | ... | ... | ... |
| | | F | 24 | 2 | 19 | 3 | 5 | ... | ... | ... |
| | 1993 | | | | | | | | | |
| | | MF | 35 | 2 | 27 | 6 | 9 | ... | ... | ... |
| | | M | 43 | 2 | 33 | 8 | 12 | ... | ... | ... |
| | | F | 26 | 2 | 21 | 4 | 6 | ... | ... | ... |
| | 1994 | | | | | | | | | |
| | | MF | 37 | 2 | 29 | 6 | 10 | ... | ... | ... |
| | | M | 45 | 3 | 34 | 8 | 14 | ... | ... | ... |
| | | F | 30 | 2 | 23 | 4 | 7 | ... | ... | ... |
| | 1995 | | | | | | | | | |
| | | MF | 41 | 3 | 31 | 7 | 11 | ... | ... | ... |
| | | M | 49 | 3 | 38 | 8 | 14 | ... | ... | ... |
| | | F | 32 | 2 | 25 | 5 | 7 | ... | ... | ... |
| Mauritania | 1993 | | (6-11) | (<6) | (6-11) | (>11) | (12-17) | (<12) | (12-17) | (>17) |
| | | MF | 67 | 0.0 | 47 | 20 | 15 | ... | ... | ... |
| | | M | 74 | 0.0 | 52 | 22 | 19 | ... | ... | ... |
| | | F | 60 | 0.0 | 43 | 18 | 11 | ... | ... | ... |
| | 1994 | | | | | | | | | |
| | | MF | 71 | 0.0 | 54 | 18 | 16 | ... | ... | ... |
| | | M | 78 | 0.0 | 59 | 20 | 20 | ... | ... | ... |
| | | F | 64 | 0.0 | 49 | 16 | 11 | ... | ... | ... |
| | 1995 | | | | | | | | | |
| | | MF | 75 | 0.0 | 57 | 18 | 16 | ... | ... | ... |
| | | M | 81 | 0.0 | 61 | 20 | 21 | ... | ... | ... |
| | | F | 69 | 0.0 | 53 | 16 | 11 | ... | ... | ... |
| Mauritius | 1975 | | (5-10) | (<5) | (5-10) | (>10) | (11-17) | (<11) | (11-17) | (>17) |
| | | MF | 105 | 0.2 | 80 | 24 | 38 | 0.0 | 33 | 4 |
| | | M | 106 | 0.2 | 81 | 25 | 41 | 0.0 | 36 | 5 |
| | | F | 103 | 0.2 | 79 | 24 | 34 | 0.0 | 31 | 4 |
| | 1980 | | | | | | | | | |
| | | MF | 93 | 0.1 | 79 | 13 | 50 | ... | ... | ... |
| | | M | 94 | 0.1 | 80 | 14 | 51 | ... | ... | ... |
| | | F | 91 | 0.1 | 79 | 13 | 49 | ... | ... | ... |

Primary and secondary education: enrolment ratios by age groups II.9
Enseignements primaire et secondaire: taux de scolarisation par groupes d'âge
Enseñanza primaria y secundaria: tasas de escolarización por grupos de edad

| Country<br>Pays<br>País | Year<br>Année<br>Año | Sex<br>Sexe<br>Sexo | Primary education<br>Enseignement primaire<br>Enseñanza primaria | | | | Secondary education<br>Enseignement secondaire<br>Enseñanza secundaria | | | |
|---|---|---|---|---|---|---|---|---|---|---|
| | | | Gross enrolment ratios<br>Taux bruts de scolarisation<br>Tasas brutas de escolarización<br>(%) | Enrolment ratios by age groups<br>Taux de scolarisation par groupes d'âge<br>Tasas de escolarización por grupos de edad | | | Gross enrolment ratios<br>Taux bruts de scolarisation<br>Tasas brutas de escolarización<br>(%) | Enrolment ratios by age groups<br>Taux de scolarisation par groupes d'âge<br>Tasas de escolarización por grupos de edad | | |
| | | | | Under-age<br>En dessous de l'âge officiel<br>Inferior a la edad oficial<br>(%) | Official age group (NER)<br>Groupe d'âge officiel (TNS)<br>Grupo de edad oficial (TNE)<br>(%) | Over-age<br>Au-dessus de l'âge officiel<br>Superior a la edad oficial<br>(%) | | Under-age<br>En dessous de l'âge officiel<br>Inferior a la edad oficial<br>(%) | Official age group (NER)<br>Groupe d'âge officiel (TNS)<br>Grupo de edad oficial (TNE)<br>(%) | Over-age<br>Au-dessus de l'âge officiel<br>Superior a la edad oficial<br>(%) |
| Mauritius (cont) | 1985 | MF | 109 | 0.0 | 100 | 9 | 49 | ... | ... | ... |
| | | M | 110 | 0.0 | 100 | 9 | 51 | ... | ... | ... |
| | | F | 109 | 0.0 | 101 | 9 | 46 | ... | ... | ... |
| | 1990 | MF | 109 | 0.0 | 95 | 14 | 53 | ... | ... | ... |
| | | M | 109 | 0.0 | 95 | 14 | 53 | ... | ... | ... |
| | | F | 109 | 0.0 | 95 | 14 | 53 | ... | ... | ... |
| | 1991 | MF | 109 | 0.0 | 91 | 18 | 55 | ... | ... | ... |
| | | M | 109 | 0.0 | 91 | 18 | 54 | ... | ... | ... |
| | | F | 109 | 0.0 | 92 | 18 | 56 | ... | ... | ... |
| | 1993 | MF | 107 | 0.0 | 94 | 13 | 59 | ... | ... | ... |
| | | M | 107 | 0.0 | 94 | 13 | 58 | ... | ... | ... |
| | | F | 106 | 0.0 | 94 | 12 | 60 | ... | ... | ... |
| | 1994 | MF | 106 | 0.0 | 95 | 11 | 60 | ... | ... | ... |
| | | M | 107 | 0.0 | 96 | 11 | 59 | ... | ... | ... |
| | | F | 106 | 0.0 | 95 | 11 | 62 | ... | ... | ... |
| | 1995 | MF | 107 | 0.0 | 96 | 10 | 62 | ... | ... | ... |
| | | M | 107 | 0.0 | 96 | 11 | 60 | ... | ... | ... |
| | | F | 106 | 0.0 | 96 | 10 | 64 | ... | ... | ... |
| | 1996 | MF | 107 | 0.0 | 98 | 9 | 64 | ... | ... | ... |
| | | M | 107 | 0.0 | 98 | 9 | 63 | ... | ... | ... |
| | | F | 106 | 0.0 | 98 | 9 | 66 | ... | ... | ... |
| | 1997 | MF | 106 | 0.0 | 98 | 8 | ... | ... | ... | ... |
| | | M | 106 | 0.0 | 98 | 9 | ... | ... | ... | ... |
| | | F | 106 | 0.0 | 98 | 8 | ... | ... | ... | ... |
| Morocco | 1970 | | (7-11) | (<7) | (7-11) | (>11) | (12-18) | (<12) | (12-18) | (>18) |
| | | MF | 51 | 1 | 39 | 11 | 13 | ... | ... | ... |
| | 1975 | MF | 62 | 1 | 47 | 14 | 16 | 0.3 | 14 | 2 |
| | | M | 78 | 2 | 58 | 19 | 21 | 0.4 | 17 | 3 |
| | | F | 45 | 0.8 | 35 | 9 | 12 | 0.2 | 10 | 1 |
| | 1980 | MF | 83 | 2 | 62 | 19 | 26 | 0.5 | 20 | 5 |
| | | M | 102 | 3 | 75 | 24 | 32 | 0.6 | 25 | 7 |
| | | F | 63 | 2 | 47 | 13 | 20 | 0.4 | 16 | 4 |
| | 1985 | MF | 77 | 2 | 61 | 14 | 35 | ... | ... | ... |
| | | M | 93 | 3 | 73 | 18 | 42 | ... | ... | ... |
| | | F | 60 | 2 | 48 | 10 | 28 | ... | ... | ... |
| | 1990 | | (7-12) | (<7) | (7-12) | (>12) | (13-18) | (<13) | (13-18) | (>18) |
| | | MF | 67 | 4 | 58 | 5 | 35 | ... | ... | ... |
| | | M | 79 | 4 | 68 | 7 | 41 | ... | ... | ... |
| | | F | 54 | 3 | 48 | 3 | 30 | ... | ... | ... |
| | 1991 | MF | 69 | 4 | 60 | 6 | 36 | ... | ... | ... |
| | | M | 81 | 4 | 70 | 7 | 41 | ... | ... | ... |
| | | F | 57 | 3 | 50 | 4 | 30 | ... | ... | ... |
| | 1992 | MF | 73 | 5 | 63 | 6 | 36 | ... | ... | ... |
| | | M | 85 | 5 | 73 | 7 | 42 | ... | ... | ... |
| | | F | 60 | 4 | 53 | 4 | 31 | ... | ... | ... |
| | 1993 | MF | 77 | 5 | 66 | 6 | 37 | ... | ... | ... |
| | | M | 89 | 5 | 76 | 8 | 43 | ... | ... | ... |
| | | F | 64 | 4 | 56 | 4 | 32 | ... | ... | ... |

II.9 Primary and secondary education: enrolment ratios by age groups
Enseignements primaire et secondaire: taux de scolarisation par groupes d'âge
Enseñanza primaria y secundaria: tasas de escolarización por grupos de edad

| Country / Pays / País | Year / Année / Año | Sex / Sexe / Sexo | Primary education — Enseignement primaire — Enseñanza primaria | | | | Secondary education — Enseignement secondaire — Enseñanza secundaria | | | |
|---|---|---|---|---|---|---|---|---|---|---|
| | | | Gross enrolment ratios / Taux bruts de scolarisation / Tasas brutas de escolarización (%) | Under-age / En dessous de l'âge officiel / Inferior a la edad oficial (%) | Official age group (NER) / Groupe d'âge officiel (TNS) / Grupo de edad oficial (TNE) (%) | Over-age / Au-dessus de l'âge officiel / Superior a la edad oficial (%) | Gross enrolment ratios / Taux bruts de scolarisation / Tasas brutas de escolarización (%) | Under-age / En dessous de l'âge officiel / Inferior a la edad oficial (%) | Official age group (NER) / Groupe d'âge officiel (TNS) / Grupo de edad oficial (TNE) (%) | Over-age / Au-dessus de l'âge officiel / Superior a la edad oficial (%) |
| Morocco (cont) | 1994 | | | | | | | | | |
| | | MF | 81 | 5 | 70 | 6 | 38 | ... | ... | ... |
| | | M | 93 | 5 | 79 | 8 | 43 | ... | ... | ... |
| | | F | 68 | 4 | 60 | 4 | 32 | ... | ... | ... |
| | 1995 | | | | | | | | | |
| | | MF | 84 | 5 | 72 | 6 | 39 | ... | ... | ... |
| | | M | 95 | 5 | 81 | 9 | 44 | ... | ... | ... |
| | | F | 72 | 5 | 63 | 4 | 33 | ... | ... | ... |
| | 1996 | | | | | | | | | |
| | | MF | 86 | 5 | 74 | 7 | 39 | ... | ... | ... |
| | | M | 97 | 6 | 83 | 9 | 44 | ... | ... | ... |
| | | F | 74 | 5 | 65 | 5 | 34 | ... | ... | ... |
| Mozambique | 1985 | | (7-10) | (<7) | (7-10) | (>10) | (11-17) | (<11) | (11-17) | (>17) |
| | | MF | 87 | 1 | 51 | 35 | 7 | ... | ... | ... |
| | | M | 99 | 1 | 56 | 41 | 10 | ... | ... | ... |
| | | F | 76 | 1 | 47 | 28 | 5 | ... | ... | ... |
| | 1990 | | (7-11) | (<7) | (7-11) | (>11) | (12-18) | (<12) | (12-18) | (>18) |
| | | MF | 67 | 0.7 | 47 | 19 | 8 | ... | ... | ... |
| | 1991 | | | | | | | | | |
| | | MF | 62 | 0.6 | 44 | 18 | 7 | ... | ... | ... |
| | | M | 72 | 0.6 | 49 | 22 | 10 | ... | ... | ... |
| | | F | 53 | 0.5 | 38 | 14 | 5 | ... | ... | ... |
| | 1992 | | | | | | | | | |
| | | MF | 59 | 0.6 | 41 | 17 | 7 | 0.2 | 7 | 0.3 |
| | | M | 67 | 0.6 | 46 | 21 | 9 | 0.2 | 8 | 0.4 |
| | | F | 50 | 0.6 | 36 | 14 | 5 | 0.1 | 5 | 0.2 |
| | 1993 | | | | | | | | | |
| | | MF | 57 | 2 | 39 | 16 | 7 | 0.2 | 6 | 0.3 |
| | | M | 66 | 2 | 44 | 20 | 8 | 0.2 | 8 | 0.4 |
| | | F | 48 | 2 | 34 | 13 | 5 | 0.2 | 5 | 0.2 |
| | 1994 | | | | | | | | | |
| | | MF | 58 | 2 | 39 | 17 | 7 | 0.1 | 6 | 0.6 |
| | | M | 67 | 2 | 44 | 21 | 8 | 0.2 | 7 | 0.9 |
| | | F | 48 | 2 | 33 | 13 | 5 | 0.1 | 5 | 0.3 |
| | 1995 | | | | | | | | | |
| | | MF | 60 | 2 | 40 | 18 | 7 | 0.2 | 6 | 0.7 |
| | | M | 70 | 2 | 45 | 23 | 9 | 0.2 | 7 | 1 |
| | | F | 50 | 2 | 34 | 14 | 5 | 0.1 | 5 | 0.4 |
| Namibia | 1992 | | (7-13) | (<7) | (7-13) | (>13) | (14-18) | (<14) | (14-18) | (>18) |
| | | MF | 136 | 9 | 89 | 38 | 56 | 1 | 31 | 24 |
| | | M | 134 | 9 | 86 | 39 | 50 | 0.8 | 26 | 23 |
| | | F | 139 | 10 | 93 | 36 | 62 | 1 | 36 | 25 |
| | 1994 | | | | | | | | | |
| | | MF | 136 | 9 | 91 | 36 | 63 | 2 | 35 | 26 |
| | 1995 | | | | | | | | | |
| | | MF | 133 | 7 | 92 | 34 | 62 | 2 | 36 | 25 |
| | 1996 | | | | | | | | | |
| | | MF | 131 | 7 | 91 | 33 | 61 | 2 | 36 | 23 |
| Niger | 1975 | | (7-12) | (<7) | (7-12) | (>12) | (13-19) | (<13) | (13-19) | (>19) |
| | | MF | 19 | ... | ... | ... | 2 | 0.1 | 2 | 0.1 |
| | | M | 24 | ... | ... | ... | 3 | 0.1 | 3 | 0.2 |
| | | F | 13 | ... | ... | ... | 1 | 0.0 | 1 | 0.0 |
| | 1980 | | | | | | | | | |
| | | MF | 25 | 1 | 21 | 3 | 5 | 0.5 | 4 | 0.5 |
| | | M | 33 | ... | ... | ... | 7 | 0.7 | 5 | 0.8 |
| | | F | 18 | ... | ... | ... | 3 | 0.3 | 2 | 0.2 |
| | 1985 | | | | | | | | | |
| | | MF | 26 | 0.0 | 25 | 0.9 | 5 | ... | ... | ... |
| | | M | 33 | 0.0 | 32 | 0.6 | 8 | ... | ... | ... |
| | | F | 18 | 0.0 | 17 | 1 | 3 | ... | ... | ... |

Primary and secondary education: enrolment ratios by age groups    II.9
Enseignements primaire et secondaire: taux de scolarisation par groupes d'âge
Enseñanza primaria y secundaria: tasas de escolarización por grupos de edad

| Country / Pays / País | Year / Année / Año | Sex / Sexe / Sexo | Primary education — Enseignement primaire — Enseñanza primaria | | | | Secondary education — Enseignement secondaire — Enseñanza secundaria | | | |
|---|---|---|---|---|---|---|---|---|---|---|
| | | | Gross enrolment ratios / Taux bruts de scolarisation / Tasas brutas de escolarización (%) | Under-age / En dessous de l'âge officiel / Inferior a la edad oficial (%) | Official age group (NER) / Groupe d'âge officiel (TNS) / Grupo de edad oficial (TNE) (%) | Over-age / Au-dessus de l'âge officiel / Superior a la edad oficial (%) | Gross enrolment ratios / Taux bruts de scolarisation / Tasas brutas de escolarización (%) | Under-age / En dessous de l'âge officiel / Inferior a la edad oficial (%) | Official age group (NER) / Groupe d'âge officiel (TNS) / Grupo de edad oficial (TNE) (%) | Over-age / Au-dessus de l'âge officiel / Superior a la edad oficial (%) |
| Niger (cont) | 1990 | | | | | | | | | |
| | | MF | 29 | 0.6 | 25 | 3 | 7 | 0.1 | 6 | 0.7 |
| | | M | 37 | 0.7 | 32 | 4 | 9 | 0.2 | 8 | 1 |
| | | F | 21 | 0.5 | 18 | 2 | 4 | 0.1 | 3 | 0.3 |
| | 1991 | | | | | | | | | |
| | | MF | 28 | 0.4 | 23 | 5 | 6 | ... | ... | ... |
| | | M | 36 | 0.5 | 29 | 6 | 9 | ... | ... | ... |
| | | F | 20 | 0.4 | 17 | 4 | 4 | ... | ... | ... |
| | 1996 | | | | | | | | | |
| | | MF | 29 | 1 | 24 | 3 | 7 | 0.1 | 6 | 1 |
| | | M | 36 | 2 | 30 | 4 | 9 | 0.2 | 7 | 1 |
| | | F | 22 | 1 | 19 | 3 | 5 | 0.1 | 4 | 0.6 |
| Rwanda | 1980 | | (7-14) | (<7) | (7-14) | (>14) | (15-20) | (<15) | (15-20) | (>20) |
| | | MF | 63 | 0.1 | 59 | 4 | 3 | ... | ... | ... |
| | | M | 08 | 0.1 | 62 | 4 | 4 | ... | ... | ... |
| | | F | 60 | 0.1 | 57 | 3 | 3 | ... | ... | ... |
| | 1985 | | | | | | | | | |
| | | MF | 63 | 0.1 | 60 | 3 | 6 | ... | ... | ... |
| | | M | 65 | 0.1 | 61 | 4 | 7 | ... | ... | ... |
| | | F | 61 | 0.1 | 59 | 3 | 5 | ... | ... | ... |
| | 1990 | | | | | | | | | |
| | | MF | 70 | 0.4 | 66 | 3 | 8 | 0.1 | 7 | 0.8 |
| | | M | 70 | 0.4 | 66 | 4 | 9 | 0.1 | 8 | 1 |
| | | F | 69 | 0.4 | 66 | 3 | 7 | 0.1 | 6 | 0.7 |
| | 1991 | | (7-13) | (<7) | (7-13) | (>13) | (14-19) | (<14) | (14-19) | (>19) |
| | | MF | 81 | 0.4 | 75 | 5 | 11 | 0.0 | 8 | 2 |
| | | M | 82 | 0.4 | 76 | 6 | 12 | 0.0 | 9 | 3 |
| | | F | 80 | 0.5 | 75 | 5 | 9 | 0.0 | 7 | 2 |
| Senegal | 1980 | | (6-11) | (<6) | (6-11) | (>11) | (12-18) | (<12) | (12-18) | (>18) |
| | | MF | 46 | 0.3 | 37 | 9 | 11 | ... | ... | ... |
| | | M | 55 | 0.3 | 44 | 11 | 15 | ... | ... | ... |
| | | F | 37 | 0.3 | 30 | 7 | 7 | ... | ... | ... |
| | 1985 | | (7-12) | (<7) | (7-12) | (>12) | (13-19) | (<13) | (13-19) | (>19) |
| | | MF | 56 | 2 | 48 | 6 | 14 | ... | ... | ... |
| | | M | 67 | 2 | 57 | 8 | 10 | ... | ... | ... |
| | | F | 46 | 2 | 39 | 5 | 9 | ... | ... | ... |
| | 1991 | | | | | | | | | |
| | | MF | 59 | 2 | 48 | 9 | 17 | ... | ... | ... |
| | | M | 67 | 2 | 55 | 10 | 22 | ... | ... | ... |
| | | F | 50 | 2 | 41 | 7 | 12 | ... | ... | ... |
| | 1993 | | | | | | | | | |
| | | MF | 60 | 2 | 50 | 8 | 16 | ... | ... | ... |
| | 1995 | | | | | | | | | |
| | | MF | 64 | 3 | 54 | 8 | 16 | ... | ... | ... |
| | | M | 72 | 3 | 60 | 9 | 20 | ... | ... | ... |
| | | F | 57 | 2 | 48 | 7 | 12 | ... | ... | ... |
| | 1996 | | | | | | | | | |
| | | MF | 68 | 3 | 58 | 7 | 16 | ... | ... | ... |
| | | M | 75 | 3 | 64 | 8 | 20 | ... | ... | ... |
| | | F | 61 | 3 | 52 | 6 | 12 | ... | ... | ... |
| | 1997 | | | | | | | | | |
| | | MF | 71 | 3 | 60 | 8 | 16 | ... | ... | ... |
| | | M | 78 | 3 | 65 | 9 | 20 | ... | ... | ... |
| | | F | 65 | 3 | 55 | 7 | 12 | ... | ... | ... |
| Somalia | 1975 | | (6-9) | (<6) | (6-9) | (>9) | (10-17) | (<10) | (10-17) | (>17) |
| | | MF | 42 | 0.0 | 16 | 26 | 4 | ... | ... | ... |
| | | M | 54 | 0.0 | 19 | 36 | 6 | ... | ... | ... |
| | | F | 30 | 0.0 | 13 | 17 | 2 | ... | ... | ... |
| | 1980 | | (6-13) | (<6) | (6-13) | (>13) | (14-17) | (<14) | (14-17) | (>17) |
| | | MF | 21 | 0.0 | 16 | 6 | 9 | 0.0 | 5 | 4 |
| | | M | 28 | 0.0 | 20 | 7 | 13 | 0.0 | 7 | 6 |
| | | F | 15 | 0.0 | 12 | 4 | 5 | 0.0 | 3 | 2 |

II.9　Primary and secondary education: enrolment ratios by age groups
Enseignements primaire et secondaire: taux de scolarisation par groupes d'âge
Enseñanza primaria y secundaria: tasas de escolarización por grupos de edad

| Country / Pays / País | Year / Année / Año | Sex / Sexe / Sexo | Primary education — Enseignement primaire — Enseñanza primaria | | | | Secondary education — Enseignement secondaire — Enseñanza secundaria | | | |
|---|---|---|---|---|---|---|---|---|---|---|
| | | | Gross enrolment ratios / Taux bruts de scolarisation / Tasas brutas de escolarización (%) | Under-age / En dessous de l'âge officiel / Inferior a la edad oficial (%) | Official age group (NER) / Groupe d'âge officiel (TNS) / Grupo de edad oficial (TNE) (%) | Over-age / Au-dessus de l'âge officiel / Superior a la edad oficial (%) | Gross enrolment ratios / Taux bruts de scolarisation / Tasas brutas de escolarización (%) | Under-age / En dessous de l'âge officiel / Inferior a la edad oficial (%) | Official age group (NER) / Groupe d'âge officiel (TNS) / Grupo de edad oficial (TNE) (%) | Over-age / Au-dessus de l'âge officiel / Superior a la edad oficial (%) |
| Somalia (cont) | 1985 | MF | 14 | 0.0 | 10 | 4 | 8 | 0.0 | 3 | 5 |
| | | M | 18 | 0.0 | 13 | 5 | 10 | 0.0 | 4 | 6 |
| | | F | 9 | 0.0 | 7 | 2 | 6 | 0.0 | 2 | 3 |
| South Africa | 1970 | | (6-12) | (<6) | (6-12) | (>12) | (13-17) | (<13) | (13-17) | (>17) |
| | | MF | 92 | 0.1 | 67 | 26 | ... | ... | ... | ... |
| | | M | 85 | 0.1 | 65 | 20 | ... | ... | ... | ... |
| | | F | 100 | 0.1 | 69 | 31 | ... | ... | ... | ... |
| | 1991 | MF | 124 | 3 | 103 | 19 | 78 | 1 | 51 | 26 |
| | | M | 126 | 3 | 101 | 22 | 72 | 1 | 47 | 24 |
| | | F | 123 | 3 | 104 | 17 | 84 | 1 | 54 | 29 |
| | 1994 | MF | 132 | ... | ... | ... | 91 | 1 | 58 | 32 |
| | | M | 134 | ... | ... | ... | 85 | 1 | 53 | 31 |
| | | F | 129 | ... | ... | ... | 97 | 2 | 63 | 33 |
| Swaziland | 1970 | | (6-12) | (<6) | (6-12) | (>12) | (13-17) | (<13) | (13-17) | (>17) |
| | | MF | 87 | 2 | 62 | 23 | 19 | 0.2 | 12 | 6 |
| | | M | 90 | 2 | 62 | 27 | 21 | 0.2 | 13 | 8 |
| | | F | 84 | 2 | 62 | 19 | 16 | 0.2 | 12 | 4 |
| | 1975 | MF | 97 | 2 | 72 | 23 | 32 | 0.9 | 21 | 10 |
| | | M | 100 | 2 | 72 | 26 | 35 | 0.6 | 20 | 14 |
| | | F | 95 | 2 | 73 | 20 | 29 | 1 | 22 | 6 |
| | 1980 | MF | 103 | 2 | 80 | 20 | 38 | ... | ... | ... |
| | 1985 | MF | 102 | 2 | 79 | 21 | 39 | ... | ... | ... |
| | | M | 104 | 2 | 78 | 24 | 40 | ... | ... | ... |
| | | F | 100 | 2 | 80 | 18 | 38 | ... | ... | ... |
| | 1990 | MF | 111 | 2 | 88 | 21 | 44 | ... | ... | ... |
| | | M | 114 | 2 | 87 | 24 | 44 | ... | ... | ... |
| | | F | 109 | 2 | 88 | 18 | 43 | ... | ... | ... |
| | 1991 | MF | 113 | 2 | 90 | 22 | 46 | 1 | 33 | 11 |
| | | M | 116 | 2 | 89 | 25 | 47 | 0.8 | 30 | 15 |
| | | F | 111 | 2 | 90 | 18 | 45 | 2 | 36 | 7 |
| | 1992 | MF | 116 | 2 | 92 | 22 | 53 | 2 | 39 | 12 |
| | | M | 119 | 2 | 92 | 25 | 53 | 2 | 36 | 15 |
| | | F | 113 | 2 | 92 | 19 | 52 | 3 | 41 | 8 |
| | 1993 | MF | 117 | 2 | 91 | 24 | 50 | 0.9 | 37 | 13 |
| | | M | 121 | 2 | 91 | 28 | 51 | 0.6 | 34 | 17 |
| | | F | 114 | 2 | 91 | 21 | 50 | 1 | 39 | 9 |
| | 1994 | MF | 118 | 2 | 92 | 24 | 52 | 0.9 | 37 | 14 |
| | | M | 121 | 2 | 92 | 28 | 52 | 0.7 | 34 | 18 |
| | | F | 115 | 2 | 93 | 21 | 51 | 1 | 40 | 10 |
| | 1995 | MF | 121 | 2 | 94 | 25 | 53 | 1 | 38 | 14 |
| | | M | 124 | 2 | 93 | 29 | 53 | 0.8 | 34 | 18 |
| | | F | 118 | 3 | 94 | 21 | 53 | 1 | 41 | 10 |
| | 1996 | MF | 118 | 2 | 91 | 25 | 54 | ... | ... | ... |
| | | M | 122 | 2 | 90 | 29 | 55 | ... | ... | ... |
| | | F | 115 | 3 | 91 | 21 | 54 | ... | ... | ... |
| Togo | 1970 | | (6-11) | (<6) | (6-11) | (>11) | (12-18) | (<12) | (12-18) | (>18) |
| | | MF | 71 | 2 | 55 | 14 | 7 | 0.1 | 6 | 0.9 |
| | | M | 99 | 3 | 75 | 20 | 11 | 0.1 | 10 | 1 |
| | | F | 44 | 2 | 34 | 8 | 3 | 0.0 | 3 | 0.4 |

Primary and secondary education: enrolment ratios by age groups
Enseignements primaire et secondaire: taux de scolarisation par groupes d'âge
Enseñanza primaria y secundaria: tasas de escolarización por grupos de edad

II.9

| Country / Pays / País | Year / Année / Año | Sex / Sexe / Sexo | Primary education / Enseignement primaire / Enseñanza primaria | | | | Secondary education / Enseignement secondaire / Enseñanza secundaria | | | |
|---|---|---|---|---|---|---|---|---|---|---|
| | | | Gross enrolment ratios / Taux bruts de scolarisation / Tasas brutas de escolarización (%) | Enrolment ratios by age groups / Taux de scolarisation par groupes d'âge / Tasas de escolarización por grupos de edad | | | Gross enrolment ratios / Taux bruts de scolarisation / Tasas brutas de escolarización (%) | Enrolment ratios by age groups / Taux de scolarisation par groupes d'âge / Tasas de escolarización por grupos de edad | | |
| | | | | Under-age / En dessous de l'âge officiel / Inferior a la edad oficial (%) | Official age group (NER) / Groupe d'âge officiel (TNS) / Grupo de edad oficial (TNE) (%) | Over-age / Au-dessus de l'âge officiel / Superior a la edad oficial (%) | | Under-age / En dessous de l'âge officiel / Inferior a la edad oficial (%) | Official age group (NER) / Groupe d'âge officiel (TNS) / Grupo de edad oficial (TNE) (%) | Over-age / Au-dessus de l'âge officiel / Superior a la edad oficial (%) |
| Togo (cont) | 1985 | MF | 93 | 3 | 61 | 30 | 21 | ... | ... | ... |
| | | M | 115 | 3 | 72 | 39 | 32 | ... | ... | ... |
| | | F | 71 | 2 | 49 | 20 | 10 | ... | ... | ... |
| | 1990 | MF | 109 | 2 | 75 | 32 | 24 | 0.3 | 18 | 5 |
| | | M | 132 | 2 | 87 | 43 | 35 | 0.3 | 26 | 8 |
| | | F | 86 | 2 | 62 | 22 | 12 | 0.2 | 10 | 2 |
| | 1993 | MF | 102 | 2 | 69 | 30 | 23 | ... | ... | ... |
| | | M | 122 | 2 | 80 | 39 | 34 | ... | ... | ... |
| | | F | 82 | 2 | 58 | 22 | 12 | ... | ... | ... |
| | 1994 | MF | 113 | 3 | 78 | 32 | 25 | | | ... |
| | | M | 135 | 3 | 90 | 42 | 37 | | | ... |
| | | F | 92 | 3 | 66 | 23 | 13 | | | ... |
| | 1995 | MF | 119 | 4 | 85 | 30 | 27 | ... | ... | ... |
| | | M | 140 | 4 | 98 | 38 | 40 | ... | ... | ... |
| | | F | 97 | 3 | 72 | 22 | 14 | ... | ... | ... |
| | 1996 | MF | 120 | 5 | 81 | 33 | 27 | ... | ... | ... |
| | | M | 140 | 6 | 93 | 41 | 40 | ... | ... | ... |
| | | F | 99 | 5 | 69 | 25 | 14 | ... | ... | ... |
| Tunisia | 1970 | | (6-11) | (<6) | (6-11) | (>11) | (12-18) | (<12) | (12-18) | (>18) |
| | | MF | 100 | 0.6 | 76 | 24 | 23 | ... | ... | ... |
| | | M | 121 | 0.8 | 89 | 31 | 33 | ... | ... | ... |
| | | F | 80 | 0.5 | 62 | 17 | 13 | ... | ... | ... |
| | 1975 | MF | 96 | ... | ... | ... | 21 | 0.9 | 16 | 4 |
| | | M | 115 | ... | ... | ... | 27 | 2 | 20 | 5 |
| | | F | 77 | ... | ... | ... | 15 | 0.2 | 12 | 2 |
| | 1980 | MF | 102 | 2 | 82 | 18 | 27 | 0.4 | 23 | 4 |
| | | M | 117 | 2 | 92 | 23 | 34 | 0.4 | 28 | 5 |
| | | F | 87 | 1 | 72 | 14 | 20 | 0.3 | 17 | 3 |
| | 1985 | MF | 115 | 3 | 93 | 19 | 39 | ... | ... | ... |
| | | M | 124 | 3 | 99 | 22 | 46 | ... | ... | ... |
| | | F | 105 | 3 | 87 | 16 | 32 | ... | ... | ... |
| | 1990 | MF | 113 | 1 | 94 | 19 | 45 | ... | ... | ... |
| | | M | 120 | 1 | 97 | 21 | 50 | ... | ... | ... |
| | | F | 107 | 1 | 90 | 16 | 40 | ... | ... | ... |
| | 1991 | MF | 114 | 1 | 94 | 18 | 46 | 1 | 43 | 2 |
| | | M | 120 | 1 | 98 | 21 | 50 | 2 | 46 | 3 |
| | | F | 108 | 1 | 91 | 16 | 41 | 1 | 39 | 1 |
| | 1992 | MF | 114 | 1 | 96 | 17 | 49 | ... | ... | ... |
| | | M | 119 | 1 | 99 | 19 | 52 | ... | ... | ... |
| | | F | 109 | 1 | 93 | 15 | 45 | ... | ... | ... |
| | 1993 | MF | 117 | 2 | 97 | 18 | 53 | ... | ... | ... |
| | | M | 122 | 2 | 100 | 20 | 56 | ... | ... | ... |
| | | F | 111 | 2 | 94 | 16 | 50 | ... | ... | ... |
| | 1994 | MF | 117 | 1 | 98 | 18 | 57 | ... | ... | ... |
| | | M | 122 | 1 | 100 | 20 | 59 | ... | ... | ... |
| | | F | 112 | 1 | 95 | 16 | 54 | ... | ... | ... |

II.9　Primary and secondary education: enrolment ratios by age groups
Enseignements primaire et secondaire: taux de scolarisation par groupes d'âge
Enseñanza primaria y secundaria: tasas de escolarización por grupos de edad

| Country / Pays / País | Year / Année / Año | Sex / Sexe / Sexo | Primary education — Enseignement primaire — Enseñanza primaria | | | | Secondary education — Enseignement secondaire — Enseñanza secundaria | | | |
|---|---|---|---|---|---|---|---|---|---|---|
| | | | Gross enrolment ratios — Taux bruts de scolarisation — Tasas brutas de escolarización (%) | Under-age — En dessous de l'âge officiel — Inferior a la edad oficial (%) | Official age group (NER) — Groupe d'âge officiel (TNS) — Grupo de edad oficial (TNE) (%) | Over-age — Au-dessus de l'âge officiel — Superior a la edad oficial (%) | Gross enrolment ratios — Taux bruts de scolarisation — Tasas brutas de escolarización (%) | Under-age — En dessous de l'âge officiel — Inferior a la edad oficial (%) | Official age group (NER) — Groupe d'âge officiel (TNS) — Grupo de edad oficial (TNE) (%) | Over-age — Au-dessus de l'âge officiel — Superior a la edad oficial (%) |
| Tunisia (cont) | 1995 | MF | 117 | 2 | 98 | 17 | 60 | ... | ... | ... |
| | | M | 121 | 2 | 100 | 19 | 62 | ... | ... | ... |
| | | F | 113 | 2 | 95 | 16 | 58 | ... | ... | ... |
| | 1996 | MF | 116 | 2 | 98 | 17 | 65 | ... | ... | ... |
| | | M | 120 | 2 | 99 | 19 | 66 | ... | ... | ... |
| | | F | 113 | 2 | 96 | 15 | 63 | ... | ... | ... |
| United Republic of Tanzania | 1980 | | (7-13) | (<7) | (7-13) | (>13) | (14-19) | (<14) | (14-19) | (>19) |
| | | MF | 93 | 0.3 | 68 | 24 | 3 | ... | ... | ... |
| | 1985 | MF | 75 | 0.1 | 56 | 19 | 3 | ... | ... | ... |
| | | M | 76 | 0.1 | 55 | 21 | 4 | ... | ... | ... |
| | | F | 74 | 0.1 | 56 | 18 | 2 | ... | ... | ... |
| | 1990 | MF | 70 | 0.0 | 51 | 18 | 5 | ... | ... | ... |
| | | M | 70 | 0.0 | 51 | 19 | 6 | ... | ... | ... |
| | | F | 69 | 0.0 | 52 | 17 | 4 | ... | ... | ... |
| | 1991 | MF | 70 | 0.0 | 51 | 19 | 5 | ... | ... | ... |
| | | M | 71 | 0.0 | 50 | 20 | 6 | ... | ... | ... |
| | | F | 69 | 0.0 | 51 | 18 | 4 | ... | ... | ... |
| | 1992 | MF | 69 | 0.0 | 50 | 19 | 5 | ... | ... | ... |
| | | M | 70 | 0.0 | 50 | 20 | 6 | ... | ... | ... |
| | | F | 68 | 0.0 | 51 | 17 | 5 | ... | ... | ... |
| | 1993 | MF | 69 | 0.0 | 49 | 19 | 5 | ... | ... | ... |
| | | M | 70 | 0.0 | 49 | 21 | 6 | ... | ... | ... |
| | | F | 68 | 0.0 | 50 | 18 | 5 | ... | ... | ... |
| | 1994 | MF | 68 | 0.0 | 48 | 20 | 5 | ... | ... | ... |
| | | M | 68 | 0.0 | 47 | 21 | 6 | ... | ... | ... |
| | | F | 67 | 0.0 | 49 | 18 | 5 | ... | ... | ... |
| | 1995 | MF | 67 | 0.0 | 48 | 19 | 5 | ... | ... | ... |
| | | M | 68 | 0.0 | 47 | 20 | 6 | ... | ... | ... |
| | | F | 66 | 0.0 | 48 | 18 | 5 | ... | ... | ... |
| | 1996 | MF | 66 | 0.0 | 48 | 18 | 5 | ... | ... | ... |
| | | M | 67 | 0.0 | 47 | 19 | 6 | ... | ... | ... |
| | | F | 65 | 0.0 | 48 | 17 | 5 | ... | ... | ... |
| | 1997 | MF | 66 | 0.0 | 48 | 18 | 6 | ... | ... | ... |
| | | M | 67 | 0.0 | 48 | 19 | 6 | ... | ... | ... |
| | | F | 66 | 0.0 | 49 | 17 | 5 | ... | ... | ... |
| Zambia | 1980 | | (7-13) | (<7) | (7-13) | (>13) | (14-18) | (<14) | (14-18) | (>18) |
| | | MF | 90 | 0.6 | 77 | 12 | 16 | ... | ... | ... |
| | | M | 97 | 0.6 | 81 | 16 | 22 | ... | ... | ... |
| | | F | 83 | 0.7 | 73 | 9 | 11 | ... | ... | ... |
| | 1994 | MF | 91 | 0.8 | 77 | 13 | ... | ... | ... | ... |
| | | M | 94 | 0.7 | 78 | 15 | ... | ... | ... | ... |
| | | F | 88 | 0.9 | 76 | 11 | ... | ... | ... | ... |
| | 1995 | MF | 89 | 0.9 | 75 | 13 | ... | ... | ... | ... |
| | | M | 91 | 0.8 | 76 | 15 | ... | ... | ... | ... |
| | | F | 86 | 1 | 74 | 11 | ... | ... | ... | ... |

Primary and secondary education: enrolment ratios by age groups
Enseignements primaire et secondaire: taux de scolarisation par groupes d'âge
Enseñanza primaria y secundaria: tasas de escolarización por grupos de edad

II.9

| Country / Pays / País | Year / Année / Año | Sex / Sexe / Sexo | Primary education — Enseignement primaire — Enseñanza primaria | | | | Secondary education — Enseignement secondaire — Enseñanza secundaria | | | |
|---|---|---|---|---|---|---|---|---|---|---|
| | | | Gross enrolment ratios / Taux bruts de scolarisation / Tasas brutas de escolarización (%) | Enrolment ratios by age groups — Taux de scolarisation par groupes d'âge — Tasas de escolarización por grupos de edad | | | Gross enrolment ratios / Taux bruts de scolarisation / Tasas brutas de escolarización (%) | Enrolment ratios by age groups — Taux de scolarisation par groupes d'âge — Tasas de escolarización por grupos de edad | | |
| | | | | Under-age / En dessous de l'âge officiel / Inferior a la edad oficial (%) | Official age group (NER) / Groupe d'âge officiel (TNS) / Grupo de edad oficial (TNE) (%) | Over-age / Au-dessus de l'âge officiel / Superior a la edad oficial (%) | | Under-age / En dessous de l'âge officiel / Inferior a la edad oficial (%) | Official age group (NER) / Groupe d'âge officiel (TNS) / Grupo de edad oficial (TNE) (%) | Over-age / Au-dessus de l'âge officiel / Superior a la edad oficial (%) |
| **North America** | | | | | | | | | | |
| Bahamas | 1980 | | (5-10) | (<5) | (5-10) | (>10) | (11-16) | (<11) | (11-16) | (>16) |
| | | MF | 99 | 0.0 | 99 | 0.0 | 88 | 0.0 | 88 | 0.0 |
| | 1985 | MF | 100 | 0.0 | 100 | 0.0 | 87 | 0.0 | 83 | 3 |
| | | M | 100 | 0.0 | 100 | 0.0 | 83 | 0.0 | 80 | 3 |
| | | F | 99 | 0.0 | 99 | 0.0 | 91 | 0.0 | 87 | 4 |
| | 1991 | MF | 102 | 0.0 | 96 | 6 | 94 | 0.0 | 87 | 6 |
| | | M | 102 | 0.0 | 96 | 6 | 94 | 0.0 | 87 | 7 |
| | | F | 103 | 0.0 | 97 | 6 | 94 | 0.0 | 88 | 6 |
| | 1992 | MF | 103 | 0.0 | 96 | 7 | 95 | 0.0 | 89 | 6 |
| | | M | 102 | 0.0 | 95 | 7 | 95 | 0.0 | 88 | 7 |
| | | F | 104 | 0.0 | 97 | 7 | 95 | 0.0 | 89 | 6 |
| | 1993 | MF | 100 | 0.0 | 98 | 2 | 90 | 0.0 | 86 | 4 |
| Barbados | 1970 | | (5-10) | (<5) | (5-10) | (>10) | (11-17) | (<11) | (11-17) | (>17) |
| | | MF | 102 | 0.0 | 87 | 16 | 68 | ... | ... | ... |
| | | M | 104 | 0.0 | 87 | 16 | 67 | ... | ... | ... |
| | | F | 101 | 0.0 | 86 | 15 | 69 | ... | ... | ... |
| | 1975 | | (5-10) | (<5) | (5-10) | (>10) | (11-16) | (<11) | (11-16) | (>16) |
| | | MF | 108 | 8 | 99 | 0.3 | 79 | 2 | 73 | 4 |
| | | M | 108 | 8 | 100 | 0.2 | 75 | 2 | 69 | 4 |
| | | F | 108 | 9 | 99 | 0.5 | 83 | 2 | 77 | 4 |
| | 1980 | | (5-11) | (<5) | (5-11) | (>11) | (12-17) | (<12) | (12-17) | (>17) |
| | | MF | 85 | 0.7 | 84 | 0.4 | 88 | 14 | 74 | 0.5 |
| | | M | 86 | 0.6 | 84 | 0.6 | 88 | 14 | 73 | 0.7 |
| | | F | 85 | 0.8 | 84 | 0.3 | 88 | 13 | 75 | 0.4 |
| | 1991 | MF | 90 | 12 | 78 | 0.0 | | ... | ... | ... |
| | | M | 90 | 12 | 78 | 0.0 | ... | ... | ... | ... |
| | | F | 90 | 13 | 77 | 0.0 | ... | ... | ... | ... |
| Belize | 1990 | | (5-12) | (<5) | (5-12) | (>12) | (13-16) | (<13) | (13-16) | (>16) |
| | | MF | 112 | ... | ... | ... | 41 | 1 | 29 | 11 |
| | | M | 113 | ... | ... | ... | 39 | 0.9 | 27 | 11 |
| | | F | 110 | ... | ... | ... | 44 | 1 | 30 | 12 |
| Canada | 1985 | | (6-11) | (<6) | (6-11) | (>11) | (12-17) | (<12) | (12-17) | (>17) |
| | | MF | 103 | 4 | 95 | 4 | 99 | 2 | 88 | 8 |
| | | M | 104 | 5 | 95 | 5 | 99 | 2 | 88 | 9 |
| | | F | 102 | 4 | 95 | 3 | 99 | 3 | 89 | 8 |
| | 1990 | MF | 103 | 3 | 97 | 3 | 101 | 2 | 89 | 10 |
| | | M | 104 | 3 | 97 | 3 | 101 | 2 | 88 | 11 |
| | | F | 102 | 4 | 97 | 2 | 101 | 2 | 89 | 9 |
| | 1991 | MF | 103 | 3 | 97 | 3 | 102 | 2 | 90 | 10 |
| | | M | 104 | 3 | 98 | 3 | 102 | 2 | 89 | 11 |
| | | F | 102 | 3 | 97 | 2 | 102 | 2 | 90 | 9 |
| | 1992 | MF | 102 | 4 | 96 | 3 | 104 | 2 | 91 | 10 |
| | | M | 103 | 4 | 97 | 3 | 104 | 2 | 91 | 11 |
| | | F | 101 | 3 | 95 | 3 | 103 | 2 | 91 | 10 |
| | 1993 | MF | 102 | 3 | 96 | 3 | 105 | 2 | 90 | 12 |
| | | M | 103 | 3 | 97 | 3 | 105 | 2 | 92 | 11 |
| | | F | 100 | 4 | 94 | 3 | 104 | 3 | 88 | 13 |

II.9  Primary and secondary education: enrolment ratios by age groups
Enseignements primaire et secondaire: taux de scolarisation par groupes d'âge
Enseñanza primaria y secundaria: tasas de escolarización por grupos de edad

| Country / Pays / País | Year / Année / Año | Sex / Sexe / Sexo | Primary education — Gross enrolment ratios (Taux bruts de scolarisation / Tasas brutas de escolarización) (%) | Primary — Under-age (En dessous de l'âge officiel / Inferior a la edad oficial) (%) | Primary — Official age group (NER) (Groupe d'âge officiel (TNS) / Grupo de edad oficial (TNE)) (%) | Primary — Over-age (Au-dessus de l'âge officiel / Superior a la edad oficial) (%) | Secondary education — Gross enrolment ratios (Taux bruts de scolarisation / Tasas brutas de escolarización) (%) | Secondary — Under-age (En dessous de l'âge officiel / Inferior a la edad oficial) (%) | Secondary — Official age group (NER) (Groupe d'âge officiel (TNS) / Grupo de edad oficial (TNE)) (%) | Secondary — Over-age (Au-dessus de l'âge officiel / Superior a la edad oficial) (%) |
|---|---|---|---|---|---|---|---|---|---|---|
| Canada (cont) | 1994 | MF | 101 | 5 | 94 | 3 | 104 | 4 | 91 | 10 |
|  |  | M | 102 | 5 | 95 | 3 | 105 | 3 | 91 | 10 |
|  |  | F | 100 | 5 | 93 | 2 | 104 | 5 | 90 | 9 |
|  | 1995 | MF | 102 | 5 | 95 | 3 | 105 | 4 | 91 | 10 |
|  |  | M | 103 | 5 | 96 | 3 | 105 | 3 | 92 | 10 |
|  |  | F | 101 | 5 | 94 | 2 | 105 | 5 | 90 | 9 |
| Costa Rica | 1970 |  | (6-11) | (<6) | (6-11) | (>11) | (12-16) | (<12) | (12-16) | (>16) |
|  |  | MF | 110 | 0.0 | 89 | 21 | 28 | 0.1 | 22 | 6 |
|  |  | M | 110 | 0.1 | 90 | 21 | 27 | 0.1 | 22 | 5 |
|  |  | F | 109 | 0.0 | 89 | 21 | 29 | 0.1 | 23 | 6 |
|  | 1975 | MF | 107 | 0.1 | 92 | 15 | 43 | 0.5 | 35 | 7 |
|  |  | M | 107 | 0.1 | 92 | 16 | 40 | 0.4 | 33 | 7 |
|  |  | F | 107 | 0.0 | 93 | 14 | 45 | 0.5 | 37 | 7 |
|  | 1980 | MF | 105 | 0.0 | 89 | 16 | 47 | 0.9 | 39 | 7 |
|  |  | M | 106 | 0.0 | 89 | 17 | 44 | 0.8 | 36 | 7 |
|  |  | F | 104 | 0.0 | 90 | 14 | 51 | 1 | 43 | 8 |
|  | 1985 | MF | 97 | 0.2 | 84 | 13 | 40 | 0.5 | 34 | 6 |
|  |  | M | 98 | 0.2 | 83 | 14 | 38 | 0.4 | 32 | 6 |
|  |  | F | 96 | 0.1 | 84 | 12 | 42 | 0.6 | 36 | 6 |
|  | 1990 | MF | 101 | 0.0 | 86 | 14 | 42 | 0.2 | 36 | 6 |
|  |  | M | 101 | 0.0 | 86 | 15 | 41 | 0.3 | 34 | 6 |
|  |  | F | 100 | 0.0 | 87 | 13 | 43 | 0.2 | 37 | 6 |
|  | 1991 | MF | 102 | 0.0 | 87 | 15 | 43 | 0.1 | 36 | 6 |
|  |  | M | 102 | 0.0 | 86 | 16 | 42 | 0.1 | 35 | 7 |
|  |  | F | 101 | 0.0 | 87 | 14 | 44 | 0.0 | 38 | 6 |
|  | 1992 | MF | 103 | 0.0 | 88 | 14 | 45 | 0.2 | 38 | 6 |
|  | 1993 | MF | 103 | 0.0 | 88 | 14 | 46 | 0.1 | 39 | 6 |
|  | 1994 | MF | 102 | 0.0 | 87 | 15 | 47 | 0.0 | 41 | 6 |
|  | 1995 | MF | 102 | 0.0 | 88 | 14 | 48 | 0.1 | 41 | 7 |
|  | 1996 | MF | 103 | 0.0 | 91 | 13 | 47 | 0.1 | 40 | 7 |
|  | 1997 | MF | 104 | 0.0 | 89 | 15 | 48 | ... | ... | ... |
|  |  | M | 104 | 0.0 | 89 | 16 | 47 | ... | ... | ... |
|  |  | F | 103 | 0.0 | 89 | 14 | 50 | ... | ... | ... |
| Cuba | 1980 |  | (6-11) | (<6) | (6-11) | (>11) | (12-17) | (<12) | (12-17) | (>17) |
|  |  | MF | 106 | 0.9 | 95 | 10 | 81 | ... | ... | ... |
|  |  | M | 109 | 0.8 | 95 | 12 | 79 | ... | ... | ... |
|  |  | F | 103 | 0.9 | 95 | 7 | 83 | ... | ... | ... |
|  | 1985 | MF | 101 | 1 | 91 | 9 | 82 | 2 | 67 | 14 |
|  |  | M | 105 | 0.9 | 91 | 12 | 80 | 2 | 63 | 15 |
|  |  | F | 98 | 1 | 91 | 6 | 85 | 2 | 71 | 12 |
|  | 1990 | MF | 98 | 1 | 92 | 5 | 89 | 2 | 69 | 18 |
|  |  | M | 99 | 1 | 92 | 6 | 83 | 1 | 64 | 17 |
|  |  | F | 96 | 2 | 92 | 3 | 95 | 2 | 74 | 20 |

II.9

Primary and secondary education: enrolment ratios by age groups
Enseignements primaire et secondaire: taux de scolarisation par groupes d'âge
Enseñanza primaria y secundaria: tasas de escolarización por grupos de edad

| Country / Pays / País | Year / Année / Año | Sex / Sexe / Sexo | Primary education — Enseignement primaire — Enseñanza primaria | | | | Secondary education — Enseignement secondaire — Enseñanza secundaria | | | |
|---|---|---|---|---|---|---|---|---|---|---|
| | | | Gross enrolment ratios — Taux bruts de scolarisation — Tasas brutas de escolarización (%) | Under-age — En dessous de l'âge officiel — Inferior a la edad oficial (%) | Official age group (NER) — Groupe d'âge officiel (TNS) — Grupo de edad oficial (TNE) (%) | Over-age — Au-dessus de l'âge officiel — Superior a la edad oficial (%) | Gross enrolment ratios — Taux bruts de scolarisation — Tasas brutas de escolarización (%) | Under-age — En dessous de l'âge officiel — Inferior a la edad oficial (%) | Official age group (NER) — Groupe d'âge officiel (TNS) — Grupo de edad oficial (TNE) (%) | Over-age — Au-dessus de l'âge officiel — Superior a la edad oficial (%) |
| Cuba (cont) | 1991 | | | | | | | | | |
| | | MF | 100 | 2 | 94 | 4 | 86 | 2 | 66 | 19 |
| | | M | 100 | 2 | 94 | 5 | 79 | 1 | 61 | 18 |
| | | F | 99 | 2 | 95 | 2 | 92 | 2 | 71 | 20 |
| | 1992 | | | | | | | | | |
| | | MF | 100 | 2 | 95 | 3 | 82 | ... | ... | ... |
| | | M | 100 | 2 | 94 | 4 | 77 | ... | ... | ... |
| | | F | 99 | 2 | 95 | 2 | 87 | ... | ... | ... |
| | 1993 | | | | | | | | | |
| | | MF | 101 | 2 | 97 | 2 | 77 | 2 | 59 | 16 |
| | | M | 101 | 2 | 96 | 3 | 73 | 2 | 55 | 16 |
| | | F | 101 | 2 | 97 | 2 | 81 | 2 | 63 | 16 |
| | 1994 | | | | | | | | | |
| | | MF | 100 | 2 | 96 | 2 | 74 | ... | ... | ... |
| | | M | 101 | 2 | 96 | 3 | 70 | ... | ... | ... |
| | | F | 100 | 2 | 97 | 2 | 79 | ... | ... | ... |
| | 1995 | | | | | | | | | |
| | | MF | 105 | 1 | 99 | 5 | 80 | ... | ... | ... |
| | | M | 107 | 1 | 99 | 6 | 78 | ... | ... | ... |
| | | F | 103 | 1 | 99 | 3 | 82 | ... | ... | ... |
| | 1996 | | | | | | | | | |
| | | MF | 106 | 0.9 | 101 | 5 | 81 | ... | ... | ... |
| | | M | 108 | 0.8 | 101 | 6 | 76 | ... | ... | ... |
| | | F | 104 | 0.9 | 100 | 3 | 85 | ... | ... | ... |
| Dominican Republic | 1993 | | (7-14) | (<7) | (7-14) | (>14) | (15-18) | (<15) | (15-18) | (>18) |
| | | MF | 96 | ... | ... | ... | 37 | 6 | 24 | 6 |
| | | M | 96 | ... | ... | ... | 30 | 6 | 20 | 5 |
| | | F | 95 | ... | ... | ... | 43 | 7 | 29 | 7 |
| | 1994 | | (6-13) | (<6) | (6-13) | (>13) | (14-17) | (<14) | (14-17) | (>17) |
| | | MF | 93 | ... | ... | ... | 41 | 0.9 | 22 | 18 |
| | | M | 93 | ... | ... | ... | 34 | 0.6 | 18 | 15 |
| | | F | 93 | ... | ... | ... | 47 | 1 | 26 | 20 |
| El Salvador | 1970 | | (7-12) | (<7) | (7-12) | (>12) | (13-17) | (<13) | (13-17) | (>17) |
| | | MF | 84 | 2 | 66 | 17 | 22 | 0.6 | 14 | 7 |
| | | M | 86 | 2 | 66 | 18 | 23 | 0.6 | 13 | 9 |
| | | F | 82 | 2 | 65 | 15 | 20 | 0.6 | 14 | 6 |
| | 1992 | | (7-15) | (<7) | (7-15) | (>15) | (16-18) | (<16) | (16-18) | (>18) |
| | | MF | 83 | 3 | 75 | 6 | 27 | ... | ... | ... |
| | | M | 83 | 3 | 74 | 6 | 25 | ... | ... | ... |
| | | F | 84 | 3 | 75 | 6 | 29 | ... | ... | ... |
| | 1995 | | | | | | | | | |
| | | MF | 88 | 4 | 78 | 5 | 34 | 5 | 22 | 8 |
| | | M | 87 | 4 | 78 | 6 | 32 | 4 | 21 | 8 |
| | | F | 88 | 4 | 78 | 5 | 36 | 5 | 23 | 8 |
| Guatemala | 1970 | | (7-12) | (<7) | (7-12) | (>12) | (13-18) | (<13) | (13-18) | (>18) |
| | | MF | 58 | 0.7 | 49 | 9 | 8 | 0.3 | 9 | ...0.5 |
| | | M | 64 | 0.7 | 53 | 10 | 9 | ... | ... | ... |
| | | F | 52 | 0.7 | 45 | 7 | 8 | ... | ... | ... |
| | 1975 | | | | | | | | | |
| | | MF | 63 | 1 | 53 | 9 | 12 | 0.5 | 10 | 2 |
| | | M | 69 | 1 | 57 | 11 | 13 | 0.5 | 10 | 2 |
| | | F | 58 | 1 | 49 | 8 | 11 | 0.5 | 9 | 1 |
| | 1980 | | | | | | | | | |
| | | MF | 71 | 1 | 59 | 11 | 19 | 0.5 | 13 | 5 |
| | 1997 | | | | | | | | | |
| | | MF | 88 | 2 | 72 | 13 | 26 | ... | ... | ... |
| | | M | 93 | 2 | 76 | 16 | ... | ... | ... | ... |
| | | F | 82 | 2 | 69 | 11 | ... | ... | ... | ... |
| Haiti | 1990 | | (6-11) | (<6) | (6-11) | (>11) | (12-17) | (<12) | (12-17) | (>17) |
| | | MF | 48 | 0.3 | 22 | 25 | 21 | ... | ... | ... |
| | | M | 49 | 0.2 | 22 | 27 | 21 | ... | ... | ... |
| | | F | 46 | 0.3 | 23 | 23 | 20 | ... | ... | ... |

II.9    Primary and secondary education: enrolment ratios by age groups
Enseignements primaire et secondaire: taux de scolarisation par groupes d'âge
Enseñanza primaria y secundaria: tasas de escolarización por grupos de edad

| | | | Primary education — Enseignement primaire — Enseñanza primaria | | | | Secondary education — Enseignement secondaire — Enseñanza secundaria | | | |
| | | | Gross enrolment ratios | Enrolment ratios by age groups — Taux de scolarisation par groupes d'âge — Tasas de escolarización por grupos de edad | | | Gross enrolment ratios | Enrolment ratios by age groups — Taux de scolarisation par groupes d'âge — Tasas de escolarización por grupos de edad | | |
| Country | Year | Sex | | Under-age | Official age group (NER) | Over-age | | Under-age | Official age group (NER) | Over-age |
| Pays | Année | Sexe | Taux bruts de scolarisation | En dessous de l'âge officiel | Groupe d'âge officiel (TNS) | Au-dessus de l'âge officiel | Taux bruts de scolarisation | En dessous de l'âge officiel | Groupe d'âge officiel (TNS) | Au-dessus de l'âge officiel |
| País | Año | Sexo | Tasas brutas de escolarización (%) | Inferior a la edad oficial (%) | Grupo de edad oficial (TNE) (%) | Superior a la edad oficial (%) | Tasas brutas de escolarización (%) | Inferior a la edad oficial (%) | Grupo de edad oficial (TNE) (%) | Superior a la edad oficial (%) |
|---|---|---|---|---|---|---|---|---|---|---|
| Honduras | 1980 | | (7-12) | (<7) | (7-12) | (>12) | (13-17) | (<13) | (13-17) | (>17) |
| | | MF | 98 | 5 | 78 | 15 | 30 | ... | ... | ... |
| | | M | 98 | 5 | 78 | 15 | 29 | ... | ... | ... |
| | | F | 99 | 6 | 78 | 15 | 31 | ... | ... | ... |
| | 1991 | | | | | | | | | |
| | | MF | 108 | 7 | 89 | 12 | 33 | 3 | 21 | 10 |
| | 1993 | | | | | | | | | |
| | | MF | 112 | 9 | 90 | 12 | 32 | ... | ... | ... |
| | | M | 111 | 9 | 89 | 13 | ... | ... | ... | ... |
| | | F | 112 | 9 | 91 | 12 | ... | ... | ... | ... |
| Jamaica | 1975 | | (6-11) | (<6) | (6-11) | (>11) | (12-18) | (<12) | (12-18) | (>18) |
| | | MF | 99 | 0.0 | 91 | 8 | 59 | 0.8 | 57 | 0.9 |
| | | M | 99 | 0.0 | 90 | 8 | 54 | 0.7 | 53 | 0.2 |
| | | F | 99 | 0.0 | 92 | 8 | 64 | 0.9 | 62 | 2 |
| | 1980 | | | | | | | | | |
| | | MF | 103 | 0.1 | 96 | 7 | 67 | 1 | 64 | 1 |
| | | M | 103 | 0.1 | 95 | 7 | 63 | 1 | 61 | 0.7 |
| | | F | 104 | 0.1 | 97 | 6 | 71 | 2 | 68 | 2 |
| | 1985 | | | | | | | | | |
| | | MF | 100 | 0.3 | 94 | 6 | 59 | 2 | 58 | 0.0 |
| | | M | 99 | 0.3 | 92 | 6 | 56 | 2 | 55 | 0.0 |
| | | F | 102 | 0.2 | 96 | 6 | 63 | 2 | 60 | 0.0 |
| | 1990 | | | | | | | | | |
| | | MF | 101 | 0.3 | 96 | 5 | 65 | 1 | 64 | 0.0 |
| | | M | 102 | 0.3 | 96 | 6 | 63 | 1 | 62 | 0.0 |
| | | F | 101 | 0.3 | 96 | 5 | 67 | 2 | 65 | 0.0 |
| | 1992 | | | | | | | | | |
| | | MF | 101 | 0.3 | 95 | 5 | 65 | 1 | 64 | 0.0 |
| | | M | 102 | 0.3 | 96 | 6 | 63 | 1 | 62 | 0.0 |
| | | F | 99 | 0.2 | 94 | 5 | 67 | 2 | 66 | 0.0 |
| Mexico | 1970 | | (6-11) | (<6) | (6-11) | (>11) | (12-17) | (<12) | (12-17) | (>17) |
| | | MF | 106 | 0.0 | 83 | 23 | 23 | 0.3 | 17 | 5 |
| | | M | 109 | 0.0 | 83 | 26 | 27 | ... | ... | ... |
| | | F | 103 | 0.0 | 82 | 21 | 18 | ... | ... | ... |
| | 1985 | | | | | | | | | |
| | | MF | 118 | 0.0 | 100 | 18 | 57 | 1 | 46 | 9 |
| | 1990 | | | | | | | | | |
| | | MF | 114 | 0.7 | 100 | 13 | 53 | 2 | 45 | 6 |
| | 1991 | | | | | | | | | |
| | | MF | 114 | 0.7 | 101 | 12 | 53 | ... | ... | ... |
| | 1992 | | | | | | | | | |
| | | MF | 114 | 0.7 | 101 | 12 | 54 | ... | ... | ... |
| | 1993 | | | | | | | | | |
| | | MF | 114 | 1 | 101 | 12 | 56 | 2 | 47 | 7 |
| | 1994 | | | | | | | | | |
| | | MF | 115 | 1 | 101 | 12 | 58 | 2 | 49 | 7 |
| | 1995 | | | | | | | | | |
| | | MF | 115 | 1 | 101 | 12 | 61 | 2 | 51 | 8 |
| | 1996 | | | | | | | | | |
| | | MF | 114 | 2 | 101 | 11 | 64 | ... | ... | ... |
| | | M | 116 | 2 | 101 | 13 | 64 | ... | ... | ... |
| | | F | 113 | 2 | 102 | 10 | 64 | ... | ... | ... |
| Nicaragua | 1970 | | (7-12) | (<7) | (7-12) | (>12) | (13-18) | (<13) | (13-18) | (>18) |
| | | MF | 78 | 2 | 61 | 15 | 17 | ... | ... | ... |
| | 1975 | | | | | | | | | |
| | | MF | 80 | 2 | 63 | 15 | 23 | ... | ... | ... |

Primary and secondary education: enrolment ratios by age groups    II.9
Enseignements primaire et secondaire: taux de scolarisation par groupes d'âge
Enseñanza primaria y secundaria: tasas de escolarización por grupos de edad

| Country / Pays / País | Year / Année / Año | Sex / Sexe / Sexo | Primary education / Enseignement primaire / Enseñanza primaria | | | | Secondary education / Enseignement secondaire / Enseñanza secundaria | | | |
|---|---|---|---|---|---|---|---|---|---|---|
| | | | Gross enrolment ratios / Taux bruts de scolarisation / Tasas brutas de escolarización (%) | Enrolment ratios by age groups / Taux de scolarisation par groupes d'âge / Tasas de escolarización por grupos de edad | | | Gross enrolment ratios / Taux bruts de scolarisation / Tasas brutas de escolarización (%) | Enrolment ratios by age groups / Taux de scolarisation par groupes d'âge / Tasas de escolarización por grupos de edad | | |
| | | | | Under-age / En dessous de l'âge officiel / Inferior a la edad oficial (%) | Official age group (NER) / Groupe d'âge officiel (TNS) / Grupo de edad oficial (TNE) (%) | Over-age / Au-dessus de l'âge officiel / Superior a la edad oficial (%) | | Under-age / En dessous de l'âge officiel / Inferior a la edad oficial (%) | Official age group (NER) / Groupe d'âge officiel (TNS) / Grupo de edad oficial (TNE) (%) | Over-age / Au-dessus de l'âge officiel / Superior a la edad oficial (%) |
| Nicaragua (cont) | 1980 | | (7-12) | (<7) | (7-12) | (>12) | (13-17) | (<13) | (13-17) | (>17) |
| | | MF | 94 | 4 | 70 | 20 | 41 | 0.7 | 22 | 18 |
| | | M | 92 | 4 | 70 | 19 | 38 | 0.6 | 20 | 17 |
| | | F | 97 | 4 | 71 | 22 | 44 | 0.7 | 24 | 19 |
| | 1985 | | | | | | | | | |
| | | MF | 97 | 6 | 73 | 17 | 32 | 0.6 | 18 | 14 |
| | | M | 92 | 6 | 71 | 15 | 21 | 0.5 | 13 | 7 |
| | | F | 101 | 7 | 75 | 20 | 44 | 0.7 | 23 | 20 |
| | 1990 | | | | | | | | | |
| | | MF | 94 | 7 | 72 | 14 | 40 | ... | ... | ... |
| | | M | 91 | 7 | 71 | 13 | 34 | ... | ... | ... |
| | | F | 96 | 7 | 73 | 15 | 47 | ... | ... | ... |
| | 1991 | | | | | | | | | |
| | | MF | 97 | 7 | 75 | 15 | 47 | ... | ... | ... |
| | | M | 95 | 7 | 74 | 14 | 43 | ... | ... | ... |
| | | F | 100 | 7 | 76 | 17 | 51 | ... | ... | ... |
| | 1992 | | | | | | | | | |
| | | MF | 99 | 7 | 79 | 14 | 47 | ... | ... | ... |
| | | M | 98 | 6 | 77 | 14 | 43 | ... | ... | ... |
| | | F | 101 | 7 | 80 | 15 | 50 | ... | ... | ... |
| | 1993 | | | | | | | | | |
| | | MF | 102 | 7 | 79 | 16 | 47 | ... | ... | ... |
| | | M | 101 | 6 | 78 | 16 | 44 | ... | ... | ... |
| | | F | 104 | 7 | 80 | 16 | 50 | ... | ... | ... |
| | 1994 | | | | | | | | | |
| | | MF | 104 | 7 | 80 | 17 | 47 | ... | ... | ... |
| | | M | 103 | 7 | 79 | 18 | 44 | ... | ... | ... |
| | | F | 106 | 7 | 81 | 17 | 50 | ... | ... | ... |
| | 1995 | | | | | | | | | |
| | | MF | 103 | 8 | 78 | 17 | 49 | ... | ... | ... |
| | | M | 101 | 8 | 76 | 17 | 45 | ... | ... | ... |
| | | F | 104 | 8 | 79 | 17 | 53 | ... | ... | ... |
| | 1996 | | | | | | | | | |
| | | MF | 101 | 9 | 76 | 16 | 50 | ... | ... | ... |
| | 1997 | | | | | | | | | |
| | | MF | 102 | 9 | 77 | 15 | 55 | ... | ... | ... |
| Panama | 1970 | | (6-11) | (<6) | (6-11) | (>11) | (12-17) | (<12) | (12-17) | (>17) |
| | | MF | 101 | 0.0 | 76 | 26 | 39 | 0.1 | 28 | 10 |
| | | M | 104 | 0.0 | 75 | 28 | 37 | 0.1 | 26 | 10 |
| | | F | 99 | 0.0 | 76 | 23 | 41 | 0.1 | 30 | 10 |
| | 1975 | | | | | | | | | |
| | | MF | 116 | 0.6 | 89 | 26 | 56 | 0.1 | 40 | 16 |
| | | M | 118 | 0.6 | 89 | 29 | 53 | 0.1 | 37 | 16 |
| | | F | 113 | 0.6 | 89 | 23 | 58 | 0.1 | 42 | 16 |
| | 1980 | | | | | | | | | |
| | | MF | 106 | 0.8 | 89 | 17 | 61 | 0.7 | 46 | 14 |
| | | M | 108 | 0.7 | 88 | 19 | 58 | 0.7 | 43 | 14 |
| | | F | 104 | 0.8 | 89 | 15 | 65 | 0.7 | 49 | 15 |
| | 1985 | | | | | | | | | |
| | | MF | 106 | 0.3 | 90 | 16 | 60 | 0.7 | 48 | 12 |
| | | M | 109 | 0.3 | 90 | 19 | 57 | 0.7 | 45 | 11 |
| | | F | 104 | 0.4 | 90 | 13 | 63 | 0.7 | 51 | 12 |
| | 1990 | | | | | | | | | |
| | | MF | 106 | 0.5 | 91 | 14 | 63 | 0.6 | 51 | 11 |
| | | M | 108 | 0.5 | 91 | 17 | 60 | 0.5 | 48 | 12 |
| | | F | 104 | 0.6 | 92 | 12 | 65 | 0.6 | 53 | 11 |
| Trinidad and Tobago | 1970 | | (5-11) | (<5) | (5-11) | (>11) | (12-16) | (<12) | (12-16) | (>16) |
| | | MF | 109 | 0.0 | 89 | 20 | 43 | 0.8 | 33 | 9 |
| | | M | 110 | 0.0 | 88 | 21 | 42 | 0.9 | 32 | 9 |
| | | F | 108 | 0.0 | 89 | 19 | 44 | 0.7 | 35 | 9 |

**II.9** Primary and secondary education: enrolment ratios by age groups
Enseignements primaire et secondaire: taux de scolarisation par groupes d'âge
Enseñanza primaria y secundaria: tasas de escolarización por grupos de edad

| Country / Pays / País | Year / Année / Año | Sex / Sexe / Sexo | Primary education / Enseignement primaire / Enseñanza primaria | | | | Secondary education / Enseignement secondaire / Enseñanza secundaria | | | |
|---|---|---|---|---|---|---|---|---|---|---|
| | | | Gross enrolment ratios / Taux bruts de scolarisation / Tasas brutas de escolarización (%) | Enrolment ratios by age groups / Taux de scolarisation par groupes d'âge / Tasas de escolarización por grupos de edad | | | Gross enrolment ratios / Taux bruts de scolarisation / Tasas brutas de escolarización (%) | Enrolment ratios by age groups / Taux de scolarisation par groupes d'âge / Tasas de escolarización por grupos de edad | | |
| | | | | Under-age / En dessous de l'âge officiel / Inferior a la edad oficial (%) | Official age group (NER) / Groupe d'âge officiel (TNS) / Grupo de edad oficial (TNE) (%) | Over-age / Au-dessus de l'âge officiel / Superior a la edad oficial (%) | | Under-age / En dessous de l'âge officiel / Inferior a la edad oficial (%) | Official age group (NER) / Groupe d'âge officiel (TNS) / Grupo de edad oficial (TNE) (%) | Over-age / Au-dessus de l'âge officiel / Superior a la edad oficial (%) |
| **Trinidad and Tobago (cont)** | 1975 | | | | | | | | | |
| | | MF | 113 | 0.0 | 94 | 19 | 48 | ... | ... | ... |
| | | M | 113 | 0.0 | 93 | 20 | 48 | ... | ... | ... |
| | | F | 113 | 0.0 | 94 | 18 | 48 | ... | ... | ... |
| | 1980 | | | | | | | | | |
| | | MF | 99 | 0.0 | 90 | 10 | 69 | ... | ... | ... |
| | | M | 98 | 0.0 | 89 | 10 | ... | ... | ... | ... |
| | | F | 100 | 0.0 | 91 | 10 | ... | ... | ... | ... |
| | 1985 | | | | | | | | | |
| | | MF | 96 | 0.0 | 92 | 5 | 81 | ... | ... | ... |
| | | M | 95 | 0.0 | 91 | 5 | 81 | ... | ... | ... |
| | | F | 97 | 0.0 | 92 | 5 | 81 | ... | ... | ... |
| | 1990 | | | | | | | | | |
| | | MF | 97 | 1 | 91 | 4 | 80 | ... | ... | ... |
| | | M | 97 | 1 | 91 | 5 | 78 | ... | ... | ... |
| | | F | 96 | 1 | 91 | 4 | 82 | ... | ... | ... |
| | 1991 | | | | | | | | | |
| | | MF | 97 | 1 | 92 | 5 | 78 | ... | ... | ... |
| | | M | 98 | 1 | 92 | 5 | 77 | ... | ... | ... |
| | | F | 97 | 1 | 91 | 5 | 80 | ... | ... | ... |
| | 1992 | | | | | | | | | |
| | | MF | 98 | 1 | 91 | 5 | 78 | 7 | 65 | 6 |
| | | M | 98 | 1 | 91 | 6 | 76 | 7 | 64 | 5 |
| | | F | 98 | 1 | 91 | 5 | 79 | 7 | 66 | 6 |
| | 1995 | | | | | | | | | |
| | | MF | 98 | 1 | 90 | 7 | 74 | ... | ... | ... |
| | | M | 99 | 1 | 90 | 8 | 72 | ... | ... | ... |
| | | F | 98 | 1 | 89 | 7 | 75 | ... | ... | ... |
| | 1996 | | | | | | | | | |
| | | MF | 99 | 2 | 88 | 9 | ... | ... | ... | ... |
| | | M | 99 | 2 | 88 | 9 | ... | ... | ... | ... |
| | | F | 98 | 1 | 88 | 8 | ... | ... | ... | ... |
| **United States** | 1985 | | (6-11) | (<6) | (6-11) | (>11) | (12-17) | (<12) | (12-17) | (>17) |
| | | MF | 99 | 1 | 93 | 5 | 97 | 1 | 91 | 5 |
| | | M | 99 | 1 | 92 | 6 | 97 | 0.9 | 91 | 6 |
| | | F | 99 | 1 | 93 | 5 | 97 | 1 | 92 | 4 |
| | 1990 | | | | | | | | | |
| | | MF | 102 | 0.8 | 96 | 6 | 93 | 1 | 86 | 6 |
| | | M | 103 | 0.7 | 96 | 6 | 93 | 1 | 85 | 6 |
| | | F | 101 | 0.8 | 96 | 4 | 94 | 1 | 87 | 6 |
| | 1992 | | | | | | | | | |
| | | MF | 101 | 0.9 | 95 | 6 | 97 | 0.9 | 89 | 7 |
| | | M | 102 | 0.9 | 95 | 7 | 97 | 0.8 | 89 | 8 |
| | | F | 101 | 0.9 | 95 | 5 | 97 | 1 | 90 | 6 |
| | 1993 | | | | | | | | | |
| | | MF | 101 | 1 | 94 | 6 | 99 | 1 | 90 | 7 |
| | | M | 101 | 1 | 94 | 7 | 99 | 0.9 | 90 | 8 |
| | | F | 101 | 1 | 95 | 5 | 98 | 1 | 91 | 6 |
| | 1994 | | | | | | | | | |
| | | MF | 102 | 1 | 95 | 6 | 97 | 1 | 91 | 6 |
| | | M | 103 | 0.9 | 95 | 6 | 97 | 0.7 | 90 | 6 |
| | | F | 102 | 1 | 96 | 5 | 98 | 1 | 91 | 5 |
| | 1995 | | | | | | | | | |
| | | MF | 102 | 1 | 95 | 6 | 97 | 0.9 | 90 | 7 |
| | | M | 102 | 1 | 94 | 7 | 98 | 0.7 | 90 | 7 |
| | | F | 101 | 1 | 95 | 5 | 97 | 1 | 90 | 6 |
| **South America** | | | | | | | | | | |
| Argentina | 1970 | | (6-12) | (<6) | (6-12) | (>12) | (13-17) | (<13) | (13-17) | (>17) |
| | | MF | 105 | 0.9 | 95 | 10 | 44 | 2 | 34 | 8 |
| | | M | 105 | 0.8 | 94 | 10 | 42 | 2 | 32 | 7 |
| | | F | 106 | 0.9 | 96 | 9 | 47 | 3 | 37 | 8 |

Primary and secondary education: enrolment ratios by age groups II.9
Enseignements primaire et secondaire: taux de scolarisation par groupes d'âge
Enseñanza primaria y secundaria: tasas de escolarización por grupos de edad

| Country / Pays / País | Year / Année / Año | Sex / Sexe / Sexo | Primary education — Enseignement primaire — Enseñanza primaria | | | | Secondary education — Enseignement secondaire — Enseñanza secundaria | | | |
|---|---|---|---|---|---|---|---|---|---|---|
| | | | Gross enrolment ratios / Taux bruts de scolarisation / Tasas brutas de escolarización (%) | Under-age / En dessous de l'âge officiel / Inferior a la edad oficial (%) | Official age group (NER) / Groupe d'âge officiel (TNS) / Grupo de edad oficial (TNE) (%) | Over-age / Au-dessus de l'âge officiel / Superior a la edad oficial (%) | Gross enrolment ratios / Taux bruts de scolarisation / Tasas brutas de escolarización (%) | Under-age / En dessous de l'âge officiel / Inferior a la edad oficial (%) | Official age group (NER) / Groupe d'âge officiel (TNS) / Grupo de edad oficial (TNE) (%) | Over-age / Au-dessus de l'âge officiel / Superior a la edad oficial (%) |
| Argentina (cont) | 1975 | MF | 106 | 0.6 | 96 | 9 | 54 | 3 | 42 | 9 |
| | | M | 106 | 0.6 | 96 | 10 | 51 | 2 | 39 | 9 |
| | | F | 106 | 0.6 | 97 | 9 | 57 | 3 | 44 | 10 |
| Bolivia | 1975 | | (6-13) | (<6) | (6-13) | (>13) | (14-17) | (<14) | (14-17) | (>17) |
| | | MF | 88 | 0.7 | 75 | 11 | 31 | 0.5 | 21 | 10 |
| | 1980 | MF | 87 | 0.0 | 79 | 8 | 37 | 0.0 | 16 | 21 |
| | | M | 92 | 0.0 | 84 | 9 | 42 | 0.0 | 18 | 24 |
| | | F | 81 | 0.0 | 74 | 7 | 32 | 0.0 | 14 | 18 |
| | 1990 | MF | 95 | 0.6 | 91 | 3 | 37 | 1 | 29 | 6 |
| | | M | 99 | 0.6 | 95 | 4 | 40 | 1 | 32 | 7 |
| | | F | 90 | 0.6 | 87 | 3 | 34 | 1 | 27 | 6 |
| Brazil | 1970 | | (7-10) | (<7) | (7-10) | (>10) | (11-17) | (<11) | (11-17) | (>17) |
| | | MF | 119 | 4 | 70 | 45 | 26 | 0.0 | 17 | 8 |
| | 1975 | | (7-14) | (<7) | (7-14) | (>14) | (15-17) | (<15) | (15-17) | (>17) |
| | | MF | 87 | 3 | 70 | 14 | 26 | 0.5 | 9 | 17 |
| | 1980 | MF | 98 | 3 | 80 | 15 | 33 | 1 | 14 | 18 |
| | 1985 | MF | 100 | 3 | 81 | 16 | 35 | 1 | 14 | 20 |
| | 1990 | MF | 106 | 3 | 86 | 17 | 38 | 1 | 15 | 22 |
| | 1991 | MF | 106 | 2 | 86 | 17 | 41 | 1 | 17 | 22 |
| | 1992 | MF | 109 | 3 | 88 | 18 | 43 | 1 | 18 | 23 |
| | 1993 | MF | 110 | 2 | 88 | 19 | 43 | 1 | 18 | 23 |
| | 1994 | MF | 112 | 3 | 90 | 20 | 45 | 2 | 19 | 24 |
| Chile | 1970 | | (6-13) | (<6) | (6-13) | (>13) | (14-17) | (<14) | (14-17) | (>17) |
| | | MF | 104 | 0.3 | 90 | 14 | 37 | 1 | 28 | 8 |
| | 1975 | MF | 112 | 0.4 | 94 | 18 | 47 | 0.5 | 33 | 13 |
| | | M | 113 | 0.4 | 94 | 19 | 44 | 0.5 | 31 | 13 |
| | | F | 111 | 0.4 | 95 | 16 | 51 | 0.6 | 36 | 14 |
| | 1990 | MF | 100 | 0.0 | 88 | 12 | 73 | 0.2 | 55 | 19 |
| | 1991 | MF | 101 | 0.2 | 89 | 12 | 72 | 0.2 | 55 | 17 |
| | | M | 102 | 0.2 | 90 | 12 | 69 | 0.2 | 53 | 16 |
| | | F | 100 | 0.2 | 88 | 11 | 74 | 0.2 | 57 | 17 |
| | 1992 | MF | 99 | 0.0 | 86 | 13 | 69 | 0.1 | 52 | 17 |
| | | M | 100 | 0.0 | 87 | 12 | 67 | 0.1 | 50 | 17 |
| | | F | 98 | 0.0 | 85 | 14 | 72 | 0.1 | 55 | 17 |
| | 1993 | MF | 99 | 0.0 | 88 | 11 | 67 | 0.1 | 53 | 14 |
| | | M | 99 | 0.0 | 88 | 11 | 65 | 0.1 | 51 | 14 |
| | | F | 98 | 0.0 | 87 | 11 | 70 | 0.1 | 55 | 15 |
| | 1994 | MF | 99 | 0.0 | 86 | 13 | 68 | 0.1 | 54 | 15 |
| | | M | 100 | 0.0 | 87 | 13 | 66 | 0.1 | 52 | 14 |
| | | F | 98 | 0.0 | 85 | 13 | 71 | 0.1 | 55 | 15 |

II.9    Primary and secondary education: enrolment ratios by age groups
Enseignements primaire et secondaire: taux de scolarisation par groupes d'âge
Enseñanza primaria y secundaria: tasas de escolarización por grupos de edad

| Country / Pays / País | Year / Année / Año | Sex / Sexe / Sexo | Primary education — Enseignement primaire — Enseñanza primaria — Gross enrolment ratios / Taux bruts de scolarisation / Tasas brutas de escolarización (%) | Under-age / En dessous de l'âge officiel / Inferior a la edad oficial (%) | Official age group (NER) / Groupe d'âge officiel (TNS) / Grupo de edad oficial (TNE) (%) | Over-age / Au-dessus de l'âge officiel / Superior a la edad oficial (%) | Secondary education — Enseignement secondaire — Enseñanza secundaria — Gross enrolment ratios / Taux bruts de scolarisation / Tasas brutas de escolarización (%) | Under-age / En dessous de l'âge officiel / Inferior a la edad oficial (%) | Official age group (NER) / Groupe d'âge officiel (TNS) / Grupo de edad oficial (TNE) (%) | Over-age / Au-dessus de l'âge officiel / Superior a la edad oficial (%) |
|---|---|---|---|---|---|---|---|---|---|---|
| Chile (cont) | 1995 | | | | | | | | | |
| | | MF | 99 | 0.0 | 87 | 12 | 69 | 0.1 | 55 | 15 |
| | | M | 100 | 0.0 | 88 | 12 | 66 | 0.1 | 52 | 14 |
| | | F | 98 | 0.0 | 86 | 11 | 73 | 0.1 | 57 | 15 |
| | 1996 | | | | | | | | | |
| | | MF | 101 | 0.0 | 89 | 12 | 75 | 0.0 | 58 | 17 |
| | | M | 103 | 0.0 | 91 | 12 | 72 | 0.0 | 56 | 16 |
| | | F | 100 | 0.0 | 88 | 12 | 78 | 0.0 | 60 | 17 |
| Colombia | 1985 | | (6-10) | (<6) | (6-10) | (>10) | (11-16) | (<11) | (11-16) | (>16) |
| | | MF | 102 | 0.0 | 65 | 36 | 44 | ... | ... | ... |
| | 1991 | | | | | | | | | |
| | | MF | 103 | 0.0 | 69 | 34 | 50 | 0.0 | 34 | 16 |
| | 1992 | | | | | | | | | |
| | | MF | 108 | 2 | 77 | 29 | 56 | 1 | 40 | 15 |
| | 1993 | | | | | | | | | |
| | | MF | 109 | 2 | 77 | 29 | 58 | 1 | 38 | 19 |
| | 1994 | | | | | | | | | |
| | | MF | 109 | 1 | 78 | 30 | 60 | 2 | 43 | 16 |
| | 1995 | | | | | | | | | |
| | | MF | 109 | 3 | 81 | 25 | 61 | 2 | 46 | 14 |
| | | M | 109 | ... | ... | ... | 57 | 1 | 42 | 13 |
| | | F | 108 | ... | ... | ... | 66 | 2 | 49 | 15 |
| | 1996 | | | | | | | | | |
| | | MF | 113 | 2 | 85 | 26 | 67 | ... | ... | ... |
| Guyana | 1970 | | (6-11) | (<6) | (6-11) | (>11) | (12-16) | (<12) | (12-16) | (>16) |
| | | MF | 98 | 0.3 | 86 | 11 | 64 | 3 | 54 | 8 |
| | | M | 100 | 0.3 | 87 | 13 | 64 | 3 | 53 | 8 |
| | | F | 96 | 0.3 | 86 | 10 | 65 | 3 | 54 | 7 |
| | 1975 | | | | | | | | | |
| | | MF | 99 | 0.4 | 88 | 11 | 72 | ... | ... | ... |
| | | M | 101 | 0.4 | 88 | 12 | 72 | ... | ... | ... |
| | | F | 98 | 0.3 | 88 | 10 | 73 | ... | ... | ... |
| | 1990 | | | | | | | | | |
| | | MF | 98 | 0.0 | 93 | 5 | 83 | 9 | 71 | 4 |
| | | M | 98 | 0.0 | 93 | 6 | 81 | 9 | 68 | 4 |
| | | F | 97 | 0.0 | 93 | 4 | 86 | 9 | 73 | 5 |
| | 1991 | | | | | | | | | |
| | | MF | 94 | 0.0 | 90 | 4 | 79 | 7 | 69 | 3 |
| | | M | 95 | 0.0 | 91 | 4 | 77 | 6 | 67 | 3 |
| | | F | 93 | 0.0 | 90 | 3 | 81 | 7 | 70 | 4 |
| | 1992 | | | | | | | | | |
| | | MF | 92 | 0.0 | 88 | 4 | 76 | 6 | 66 | 4 |
| | | M | 93 | 0.0 | 89 | 4 | 73 | 6 | 64 | 3 |
| | | F | 92 | 0.0 | 88 | 3 | 79 | 6 | 68 | 4 |
| | 1994 | | | | | | | | | |
| | | MF | 94 | 0.0 | 90 | 4 | 76 | ... | ... | ... |
| | | M | 94 | 0.0 | 90 | 5 | 69 | ... | ... | ... |
| | | F | 93 | 0.0 | 89 | 4 | 84 | ... | ... | ... |
| | 1995 | | | | | | | | | |
| | | MF | 95 | 0.0 | 87 | 7 | 75 | 6 | 66 | 4 |
| | | M | 95 | 0.0 | 87 | 8 | 73 | 6 | 64 | 3 |
| | | F | 94 | 0.0 | 87 | 7 | 78 | 6 | 68 | 4 |
| Paraguay | 1970 | | (7-12) | (<7) | (7-12) | (>12) | (13-18) | (<13) | (13-18) | (>18) |
| | | MF | 108 | 3 | 88 | 17 | 16 | ... | ... | ... |
| | | M | 113 | 3 | 89 | 21 | 16 | ... | ... | ... |
| | | F | 104 | 3 | 86 | 14 | 16 | ... | ... | ... |
| | 1975 | | | | | | | | | |
| | | MF | 103 | 4 | 86 | 14 | 20 | 2 | 16 | 2 |
| | | M | 106 | 3 | 87 | 16 | 20 | 2 | 16 | 2 |
| | | F | 99 | 4 | 85 | 11 | 20 | 2 | 17 | 2 |

Primary and secondary education: enrolment ratios by age groups    II.9
Enseignements primaire et secondaire: taux de scolarisation par groupes d'âge
Enseñanza primaria y secundaria: tasas de escolarización por grupos de edad

| Country / Pays / País | Year / Année / Año | Sex / Sexe / Sexo | Primary education / Enseignement primaire / Enseñanza primaria | | | | Secondary education / Enseignement secondaire / Enseñanza secundaria | | | |
|---|---|---|---|---|---|---|---|---|---|---|
| | | | Gross enrolment ratios / Taux bruts de scolarisation / Tasas brutas de escolarización (%) | Enrolment ratios by age groups / Taux de scolarisation par groupes d'âge / Tasas de escolarización por grupos de edad | | | Gross enrolment ratios / Taux bruts de scolarisation / Tasas brutas de escolarización (%) | Enrolment ratios by age groups / Taux de scolarisation par groupes d'âge / Tasas de escolarización por grupos de edad | | |
| | | | | Under-age / En dessous de l'âge officiel / Inferior a la edad oficial (%) | Official age group (NER) / Groupe d'âge officiel (TNS) / Grupo de edad oficial (TNE) (%) | Over-age / Au-dessus de l'âge officiel / Superior a la edad oficial (%) | | Under-age / En dessous de l'âge officiel / Inferior a la edad oficial (%) | Official age group (NER) / Groupe d'âge officiel (TNS) / Grupo de edad oficial (TNE) (%) | Over-age / Au-dessus de l'âge officiel / Superior a la edad oficial (%) |
| Paraguay (cont) | 1980 | MF | 106 | 4 | 89 | 13 | 27 | ... | ... | ... |
| | | M | 109 | 4 | 90 | 15 | ... | ... | ... | ... |
| | | F | 102 | 4 | 88 | 10 | ... | ... | ... | ... |
| | 1985 | MF | 105 | 4 | 89 | 12 | 31 | ... | ... | ... |
| | | M | 108 | 4 | 90 | 14 | 32 | ... | ... | ... |
| | | F | 102 | 4 | 89 | 9 | 31 | ... | ... | ... |
| | 1990 | MF | 105 | 5 | 93 | 8 | 31 | 3 | 26 | 2 |
| | | M | 107 | 5 | 94 | 9 | 30 | 3 | 25 | 2 |
| | | F | 103 | 5 | 92 | 6 | 32 | 3 | 26 | 2 |
| | 1991 | MF | 106 | 4 | 94 | 8 | 31 | 2 | 26 | 2 |
| | | M | 108 | 4 | 95 | 9 | 30 | 2 | 26 | 2 |
| | | F | 105 | 5 | 94 | 6 | 32 | 3 | 27 | 2 |
| | 1992 | MF | 107 | 4 | 95 | 8 | 34 | 3 | 29 | 2 |
| | | M | 108 | 4 | 95 | 9 | 34 | 3 | 29 | 2 |
| | | F | 105 | 4 | 94 | 7 | 35 | 3 | 29 | 2 |
| | 1993 | MF | 110 | 7 | 94 | 8 | 37 | 3 | 32 | 2 |
| | | M | 112 | 7 | 95 | 10 | 36 | 3 | 31 | 2 |
| | | F | 108 | 7 | 94 | 7 | 38 | 3 | 32 | 2 |
| | 1994 | | (6-11) | (<6) | (6-11) | (>11) | (12-17) | (<12) | (12-17) | (>17) |
| | | MF | 109 | 0.0 | 89 | 20 | 38 | 0.0 | 33 | 5 |
| | | M | 110 | 0.0 | 89 | 21 | 38 | 0.0 | 32 | 5 |
| | | F | 107 | 0.0 | 89 | 18 | 39 | 0.0 | 34 | 5 |
| | 1995 | MF | 110 | 0.1 | 88 | 21 | 41 | 0.0 | 38 | 5 |
| | 1996 | MF | 112 | 0.0 | 91 | 21 | 43 | 0.0 | 38 | 6 |
| | | M | 113 | 0.0 | 91 | 22 | 42 | 0.0 | 37 | 6 |
| | | F | 110 | 0.0 | 91 | 19 | 45 | 0.0 | 39 | 6 |
| Peru | 1970 | | (6-11) | (<6) | (6-11) | (>11) | (12-17) | (<12) | (12-17) | (>17) |
| | | MF | 107 | 0.4 | 78 | 28 | 31 | 0.9 | 27 | 3 |
| | | M | 114 | 0.5 | 81 | 32 | 35 | 0.8 | 30 | 4 |
| | | F | 99 | 0.4 | 74 | 25 | 27 | 0.9 | 24 | 2 |
| | 1980 | | (6-11) | (<6) | (6-11) | (>11) | (12-16) | (<12) | (12-16) | (>16) |
| | | MF | 114 | 1 | 86 | 26 | 59 | ... | ... | ... |
| | 1985 | MF | 120 | ... | ... | ... | 63 | 1 | 49 | 12 |
| | 1993 | MF | 118 | 0.9 | 87 | 30 | 66 | 0.8 | 46 | 19 |
| | 1995 | MF | 123 | 2 | 91 | 31 | 70 | 1 | 53 | 15 |
| | | M | 125 | 1 | 91 | 32 | 72 | 1 | 54 | 17 |
| | | F | 121 | 2 | 90 | 29 | 67 | 1 | 52 | 14 |
| | 1996 | MF | 123 | 2 | 91 | 31 | 72 | 1 | 55 | 16 |
| | 1997 | MF | 123 | 2 | 91 | 30 | 72 | 1 | 55 | 16 |
| Uruguay | 1985 | | (6-11) | (<6) | (6-11) | (>11) | (12-17) | (<12) | (12-17) | (>17) |
| | | MF | 107 | 0.0 | 88 | 19 | 72 | ... | ... | ... |
| | 1991 | MF | 108 | 0.0 | 91 | 17 | 84 | ... | ... | ... |
| | | M | 108 | 0.0 | 91 | 18 | ... | ... | ... | ... |
| | | F | 107 | 0.0 | 92 | 15 | ... | ... | ... | ... |

II.9    Primary and secondary education: enrolment ratios by age groups
Enseignements primaire et secondaire: taux de scolarisation par groupes d'âge
Enseñanza primaria y secundaria: tasas de escolarización por grupos de edad

| Country / Pays / País | Year / Année / Año | Sex / Sexe / Sexo | Primary education — Enseignement primaire — Enseñanza primaria | | | | Secondary education — Enseignement secondaire — Enseñanza secundaria | | | |
|---|---|---|---|---|---|---|---|---|---|---|
| | | | Gross enrolment ratios / Taux bruts de scolarisation / Tasas brutas de escolarización (%) | Under-age / En dessous de l'âge officiel / Inferior a la edad oficial (%) | Official age group (NER) / Groupe d'âge officiel (TNS) / Grupo de edad oficial (TNE) (%) | Over-age / Au-dessus de l'âge officiel / Superior a la edad oficial (%) | Gross enrolment ratios / Taux bruts de scolarisation / Tasas brutas de escolarización (%) | Under-age / En dessous de l'âge officiel / Inferior a la edad oficial (%) | Official age group (NER) / Groupe d'âge officiel (TNS) / Grupo de edad oficial (TNE) (%) | Over-age / Au-dessus de l'âge officiel / Superior a la edad oficial (%) |
| Uruguay (cont) | 1992 | MF | 107 | 0.0 | 92 | 15 | 83 | ... | ... | ... |
| | | M | 108 | 0.0 | 92 | 16 | ... | ... | ... | ... |
| | | F | 106 | 0.0 | 93 | 14 | ... | ... | ... | ... |
| | 1993 | MF | 108 | 0.0 | 93 | 14 | 82 | ... | ... | ... |
| | | M | 108 | 0.0 | 93 | 15 | ... | ... | ... | ... |
| | | F | 107 | 0.0 | 94 | 13 | ... | ... | ... | ... |
| | 1994 | MF | 107 | 0.0 | 92 | 15 | 82 | ... | ... | ... |
| | | M | 108 | 0.0 | 92 | 16 | 75 | ... | ... | ... |
| | | F | 107 | 0.0 | 93 | 14 | 89 | ... | ... | ... |
| | 1995 | MF | 108 | 0.0 | 93 | 16 | 82 | ... | ... | ... |
| | | M | 109 | 0.0 | 92 | 17 | 75 | ... | ... | ... |
| | | F | 107 | 0.0 | 93 | 14 | 90 | ... | ... | ... |
| | 1996 | MF | 109 | 0.0 | 93 | 16 | 85 | ... | ... | ... |
| | | M | 109 | 0.0 | 92 | 17 | ... | ... | ... | ... |
| | | F | 108 | 0.0 | 93 | 15 | ... | ... | ... | ... |
| Venezuela | 1970 | | (7-12) | (<7) | (7-12) | (>12) | (13-17) | (<13) | (13-17) | (>17) |
| | | MF | 97 | 5 | 80 | 13 | 35 | 3 | 27 | 5 |
| | | M | 96 | ... | ... | ... | 34 | 3 | 26 | 5 |
| | | F | 98 | ... | ... | ... | 36 | 3 | 28 | 5 |
| | 1975 | MF | 98 | 7 | 80 | 11 | 44 | 4 | 35 | 5 |
| | | M | 97 | ... | ... | ... | 41 | 4 | 33 | 5 |
| | | F | 99 | ... | ... | ... | 47 | 5 | 37 | 6 |
| | 1980 | | (7-15) | (<7) | (7-15) | (>15) | (16-18) | (<16) | (16-18) | (>18) |
| | | MF | 93 | 7 | 82 | 4 | 21 | 4 | 14 | 4 |
| | 1985 | MF | 97 | 9 | 84 | 4 | 24 | 5 | 16 | 3 |
| | | M | 95 | ... | ... | ... | 21 | 5 | 14 | 3 |
| | | F | 98 | ... | ... | ... | 27 | 6 | 18 | 3 |
| | 1990 | | (6-14) | (<6) | (6-14) | (>14) | (15-16) | (<15) | (15-16) | (>16) |
| | | MF | 96 | 1 | 88 | 6 | 35 | 2 | 19 | 14 |
| | | M | 94 | 1 | 87 | 6 | 29 | 1 | 15 | 13 |
| | | F | 97 | 1 | 89 | 7 | 40 | 2 | 22 | 16 |
| | 1991 | MF | 97 | 1 | 89 | 7 | 35 | 2 | 19 | 14 |
| | | M | 96 | 1 | 88 | 6 | 29 | 1 | 15 | 13 |
| | | F | 98 | 1 | 90 | 7 | 40 | 2 | 23 | 15 |
| | 1992 | MF | 96 | 1 | 88 | 6 | 35 | 2 | 20 | 13 |
| | | M | 95 | 1 | 87 | 6 | 29 | 1 | 16 | 12 |
| | | F | 97 | 1 | 90 | 6 | 41 | 3 | 24 | 14 |
| | 1995 | MF | 90 | 1 | 82 | 6 | 35 | 2 | 19 | 14 |
| | 1996 | MF | 91 | 1 | 84 | 6 | 40 | 2 | 22 | 15 |
| | | M | 90 | 1 | 83 | 6 | 33 | 2 | 18 | 14 |
| | | F | 93 | 1 | 85 | 7 | 46 | 3 | 27 | 17 |
| **Asia** | | | | | | | | | | |
| Afghanistan | 1980 | | (7-14) | (<7) | (7-14) | (>14) | (15-18) | (<15) | (15-18) | (>18) |
| | | MF | 34 | 1 | 29 | 3 | 10 | ... | ... | ... |
| | | M | 54 | 2 | 46 | 6 | 16 | ... | ... | ... |
| | | F | 12 | 0.5 | 11 | 0.8 | 4 | ... | ... | ... |

Primary and secondary education: enrolment ratios by age groups II.9
Enseignements primaire et secondaire: taux de scolarisation par groupes d'âge
Enseñanza primaria y secundaria: tasas de escolarización por grupos de edad

| Country / Pays / País | Year / Année / Año | Sex / Sexe / Sexo | Primary education / Enseignement primaire / Enseñanza primaria | | | | Secondary education / Enseignement secondaire / Enseñanza secundaria | | | |
|---|---|---|---|---|---|---|---|---|---|---|
| | | | Gross enrolment ratios / Taux bruts de scolarisation / Tasas brutas de escolarización (%) | Enrolment ratios by age groups / Taux de scolarisation par groupes d'âge / Tasas de escolarización por grupos de edad | | | Gross enrolment ratios / Taux bruts de scolarisation / Tasas brutas de escolarización (%) | Enrolment ratios by age groups / Taux de scolarisation par groupes d'âge / Tasas de escolarización por grupos de edad | | |
| | | | | Under-age / En dessous de l'âge officiel / Inferior a la edad oficial (%) | Official age group (NER) / Groupe d'âge officiel (TNS) / Grupo de edad oficial (TNE) (%) | Over-age / Au-dessus de l'âge officiel / Superior a la edad oficial (%) | | Under-age / En dessous de l'âge officiel / Inferior a la edad oficial (%) | Official age group (NER) / Groupe d'âge officiel (TNS) / Grupo de edad oficial (TNE) (%) | Over-age / Au-dessus de l'âge officiel / Superior a la edad oficial (%) |
| Afghanistan (cont) | 1985 | | | | | | | | | |
| | | MF | 20 | 0.2 | 17 | 2 | 8 | ... | ... | ... |
| | | M | 27 | 0.4 | 23 | 3 | 11 | ... | ... | ... |
| | | F | 13 | 0.1 | 11 | 1 | 5 | ... | ... | ... |
| | 1993 | | (7-12) | (<7) | (7-12) | (>12) | (13-18) | (<13) | (13-18) | (>18) |
| | | MF | 31 | 0.3 | 29 | 2 | 15 | 0.2 | 14 | 0.7 |
| | | M | 46 | 0.4 | 42 | 3 | 21 | 0.2 | 20 | 1 |
| | | F | 16 | 0.1 | 15 | 1 | 8 | 0.2 | 7 | 0.4 |
| Bahrain | 1970 | | (6-11) | (<6) | (6-11) | (>11) | (12-16) | (<12) | (12-16) | (>16) |
| | | MF | 98 | 0.2 | 71 | 28 | 51 | 0.9 | 36 | 14 |
| | | M | 113 | 0.1 | 78 | 35 | 60 | 0.7 | 40 | 19 |
| | | F | 84 | 0.2 | 63 | 21 | 43 | 1 | 33 | 9 |
| | 1975 | | | | | | | | | |
| | | MF | 96 | 0.1 | 70 | 26 | 52 | 0.4 | 36 | 10 |
| | | M | 100 | 0.0 | 75 | 31 | 51 | 0.2 | 34 | 17 |
| | | F | 85 | 0.1 | 64 | 21 | 54 | 0.7 | 38 | 15 |
| | 1980 | | (6-11) | (<6) | (6-11) | (>11) | (12-17) | (<12) | (12-17) | (>17) |
| | | MF | 104 | 0.8 | 80 | 24 | 64 | 0.8 | 55 | 9 |
| | | M | 111 | 1 | 84 | 26 | 70 | 0.9 | 57 | 12 |
| | | F | 98 | 0.6 | 76 | 21 | 58 | 0.7 | 52 | 6 |
| | 1985 | | | | | | | | | |
| | | MF | 113 | 2 | 96 | 14 | 97 | 4 | 77 | 16 |
| | | M | 110 | 2 | 95 | 13 | 98 | 4 | 76 | 18 |
| | | F | 116 | 2 | 98 | 16 | 97 | 5 | 77 | 15 |
| | 1990 | | | | | | | | | |
| | | MF | 110 | 2 | 99 | 9 | 100 | 2 | 85 | 12 |
| | | M | 110 | 2 | 99 | 9 | 98 | 2 | 84 | 12 |
| | | F | 110 | 2 | 99 | 9 | 101 | 3 | 86 | 13 |
| | 1991 | | | | | | | | | |
| | | MF | 108 | 2 | 97 | 9 | 98 | 3 | 84 | 11 |
| | | M | 108 | 2 | 96 | 9 | 96 | 2 | 83 | 11 |
| | | F | 108 | 2 | 97 | 8 | 100 | 3 | 86 | 11 |
| | 1992 | | | | | | | | | |
| | | MF | 109 | 3 | 99 | 7 | 99 | 3 | 86 | 10 |
| | | M | 100 | 3 | 99 | 7 | 97 | 3 | 85 | 10 |
| | | F | 110 | 3 | 100 | 7 | 101 | 3 | 87 | 11 |
| | 1993 | | | | | | | | | |
| | | MF | 110 | 3 | 100 | 7 | 99 | 3 | 85 | 11 |
| | | M | 108 | 3 | 99 | 7 | 98 | 3 | 84 | 11 |
| | | F | 111 | 3 | 102 | 7 | 101 | 3 | 87 | 11 |
| | 1994 | | | | | | | | | |
| | | MF | 110 | 2 | 102 | 6 | 98 | 3 | 85 | 10 |
| | | M | 109 | 2 | 100 | 6 | 97 | 3 | 84 | 10 |
| | | F | 112 | 2 | 103 | 6 | 100 | 3 | 87 | 10 |
| | 1995 | | | | | | | | | |
| | | MF | 108 | 2 | 101 | 5 | 97 | 3 | 84 | 9 |
| | | M | 107 | 2 | 99 | 5 | 95 | 3 | 82 | 9 |
| | | F | 109 | 2 | 102 | 5 | 99 | 3 | 87 | 10 |
| | 1996 | | | | | | | | | |
| | | MF | 106 | 2 | 98 | 5 | 94 | 3 | 83 | 8 |
| | | M | 105 | 2 | 97 | 6 | 91 | 3 | 79 | 8 |
| | | F | 106 | 2 | 99 | 5 | 98 | 3 | 87 | 8 |
| Bangladesh | 1970 | | (5-9) | (<5) | (5-9) | (>9) | (10-14) | (<10) | (10-14) | (>14) |
| | | MF | 54 | 1 | 50 | 3 | ... | ... | ... | ... |
| | | M | 72 | 2 | 66 | 5 | ... | ... | ... | ... |
| | | F | 35 | 0.3 | 33 | 2 | ... | ... | ... | ... |
| | 1985 | | (6-10) | (<6) | (6-10) | (>10) | (11-17) | (<11) | (11-17) | (>17) |
| | | MF | 62 | 3 | 56 | 3 | 19 | 0.0 | 18 | 0.8 |
| | | M | 72 | 4 | 65 | 4 | 27 | ... | ... | ... |
| | | F | 52 | 2 | 47 | 3 | 11 | ... | ... | ... |

II.9 Primary and secondary education: enrolment ratios by age groups
Enseignements primaire et secondaire: taux de scolarisation par groupes d'âge
Enseñanza primaria y secundaria: tasas de escolarización por grupos de edad

| Country / Pays / País | Year / Année / Año | Sex / Sexe / Sexo | Primary education — Enseignement primaire — Enseñanza primaria | | | | Secondary education — Enseignement secondaire — Enseñanza secundaria | | | |
|---|---|---|---|---|---|---|---|---|---|---|
| | | | Gross enrolment ratios / Taux bruts de scolarisation / Tasas brutas de escolarización (%) | Under-age / En dessous de l'âge officiel / Inferior a la edad oficial (%) | Official age group (NER) / Groupe d'âge officiel (TNS) / Grupo de edad oficial (TNE) (%) | Over-age / Au-dessus de l'âge officiel / Superior a la edad oficial (%) | Gross enrolment ratios / Taux bruts de scolarisation / Tasas brutas de escolarización (%) | Under-age / En dessous de l'âge officiel / Inferior a la edad oficial (%) | Official age group (NER) / Groupe d'âge officiel (TNS) / Grupo de edad oficial (TNE) (%) | Over-age / Au-dessus de l'âge officiel / Superior a la edad oficial (%) |
| Bangladesh (cont) | 1990 | | | | | | | | | |
| | | MF | 72 | 4 | 64 | 4 | 19 | 0.0 | 18 | 0.9 |
| | | M | 77 | 4 | 68 | 5 | 25 | 0.0 | 24 | 1 |
| | | F | 66 | 3 | 60 | 3 | 13 | 0.0 | 12 | 0.5 |
| Brunei Darussalam | 1980 | | (6-11) | (<6) | (6-11) | (>11) | (12-18) | (<12) | (12-18) | (>18) |
| | | MF | 109 | 0.8 | 82 | 26 | 61 | 0.3 | 51 | 9 |
| | | M | 111 | 0.9 | 83 | 28 | 59 | 0.3 | 49 | 10 |
| | | F | 106 | 0.8 | 82 | 24 | 63 | 0.4 | 54 | 8 |
| | 1991 | | | | | | | | | |
| | | MF | 112 | 4 | 91 | 18 | 77 | 1 | 71 | 4 |
| | | M | 116 | 4 | 92 | 20 | 73 | 1 | 67 | 5 |
| | | F | 109 | 4 | 90 | 15 | 80 | 1 | 75 | 3 |
| | 1992 | | | | | | | | | |
| | | MF | 111 | 3 | 92 | 17 | 77 | 2 | 67 | 9 |
| | | M | 114 | 3 | 92 | 19 | 73 | 1 | 63 | 9 |
| | | F | 109 | 3 | 92 | 14 | 82 | 2 | 72 | 8 |
| | 1993 | | | | | | | | | |
| | | MF | 111 | 4 | 92 | 15 | 79 | 2 | 67 | 9 |
| | | M | 113 | 3 | 92 | 18 | 75 | 2 | 65 | 8 |
| | | F | 109 | 4 | 93 | 12 | 83 | 2 | 70 | 10 |
| | 1994 | | | | | | | | | |
| | | MF | 110 | 4 | 91 | 15 | 78 | 2 | 68 | 8 |
| | | M | 113 | 4 | 90 | 18 | 74 | 2 | 64 | 9 |
| | | F | 108 | 4 | 91 | 12 | 81 | 2 | 71 | 7 |
| Cambodia | 1996 | | (6-11) | (<6) | (6-11) | (>11) | (12-17) | (<12) | (12-17) | (>17) |
| | | MF | 110 | 0.5 | 98 | 11 | 29 | ... | ... | ... |
| | 1997 | | | | | | | | | |
| | | MF | 113 | 0.3 | 100 | 13 | 24 | ... | ... | ... |
| China | 1990 | | (7-11) | (<7) | (7-11) | (>11) | (12-16) | (<12) | (12-16) | (>16) |
| | | MF | 125 | 5 | 97 | 23 | 49 | ... | ... | ... |
| | | M | 130 | 5 | 99 | 25 | 55 | ... | ... | ... |
| | | F | 120 | 5 | 95 | 20 | 42 | ... | ... | ... |
| | 1991 | | | | | | | | | |
| | | MF | 122 | 4 | 96 | 22 | 52 | ... | ... | ... |
| | | M | 126 | 5 | 98 | 23 | 58 | ... | ... | ... |
| | | F | 119 | 4 | 95 | 20 | 45 | ... | ... | ... |
| | 1992 | | | | | | | | | |
| | | MF | 119 | 5 | 95 | 19 | 55 | ... | ... | ... |
| | | M | 122 | 5 | 96 | 21 | 61 | ... | ... | ... |
| | | F | 116 | 4 | 94 | 17 | 49 | ... | ... | ... |
| | 1993 | | | | | | | | | |
| | | MF | 117 | 5 | 95 | 18 | 57 | ... | ... | ... |
| | | M | 119 | 5 | 96 | 19 | 62 | ... | ... | ... |
| | | F | 115 | 5 | 94 | 16 | 52 | ... | ... | ... |
| | 1994 | | | | | | | | | |
| | | MF | 117 | 4 | 95 | 17 | 61 | ... | ... | ... |
| | | M | 118 | 4 | 96 | 18 | 65 | ... | ... | ... |
| | | F | 115 | 4 | 95 | 16 | 56 | ... | ... | ... |
| | 1995 | | | | | | | | | |
| | | MF | 118 | 4 | 98 | 15 | 66 | ... | ... | ... |
| | | M | 118 | 4 | 98 | 16 | 69 | ... | ... | ... |
| | | F | 117 | 4 | 98 | 14 | 62 | ... | ... | ... |
| | 1996 | | | | | | | | | |
| | | MF | 120 | 4 | 101 | 14 | 69 | ... | ... | ... |
| | | M | 120 | 4 | 101 | 14 | 72 | ... | ... | ... |
| | | F | 120 | 4 | 102 | 13 | 65 | ... | ... | ... |
| China, Hong Kong SAR | 1970 | | (6-11) | (<6) | (6-11) | (>11) | (12-18) | (<12) | (12-18) | (>18) |
| | | MF | 117 | 0.8 | 87 | 29 | 36 | 0.1 | 33 | 2 |
| | | M | 118 | 0.8 | 87 | 30 | 40 | 0.1 | 37 | 3 |
| | | F | 115 | 0.8 | 86 | 27 | 31 | 0.0 | 29 | 2 |

Primary and secondary education: enrolment ratios by age groups II.9
Enseignements primaire et secondaire: taux de scolarisation par groupes d'âge
Enseñanza primaria y secundaria: tasas de escolarización por grupos de edad

| Country / Pays / País | Year / Année / Año | Sex / Sexe / Sexo | Primary education / Enseignement primaire / Enseñanza primaria | | | | Secondary education / Enseignement secondaire / Enseñanza secundaria | | | |
|---|---|---|---|---|---|---|---|---|---|---|
| | | | Gross enrolment ratios / Taux bruts de scolarisation / Tasas brutas de escolarización (%) | Enrolment ratios by age groups / Taux de scolarisation par groupes d'âge / Tasas de escolarización por grupos de edad | | | Gross enrolment ratios / Taux bruts de scolarisation / Tasas brutas de escolarización (%) | Enrolment ratios by age groups / Taux de scolarisation par groupes d'âge / Tasas de escolarización por grupos de edad | | |
| | | | | Under-age / En dessous de l'âge officiel / Inferior a la edad oficial (%) | Official age group (NER) / Groupe d'âge officiel (TNS) / Grupo de edad oficial (TNE) (%) | Over-age / Au-dessus de l'âge officiel / Superior a la edad oficial (%) | | Under-age / En dessous de l'âge officiel / Inferior a la edad oficial (%) | Official age group (NER) / Groupe d'âge officiel (TNS) / Grupo de edad oficial (TNE) (%) | Over-age / Au-dessus de l'âge officiel / Superior a la edad oficial (%) |
| China, Hong Kong SAR (cont) | 1975 | MF | 120 | 0.6 | 92 | 27 | 49 | 0.1 | 46 | 3 |
| | | M | 122 | 0.5 | 93 | 29 | 51 | 0.2 | 48 | 3 |
| | | F | 117 | 0.6 | 91 | 25 | 47 | 0.1 | 44 | 2 |
| | 1980 | MF | 107 | 2 | 95 | 9 | 64 | 2 | 61 | 2 |
| | | M | 107 | 2 | 95 | 10 | 63 | 1 | 59 | 2 |
| | | F | 106 | 2 | 96 | 8 | 65 | 2 | 62 | 1 |
| | 1994 | MF | 95 | 1 | 91 | 3 | 80 | ... | ... | ... |
| | | M | 94 | 1 | 89 | 3 | 77 | ... | ... | ... |
| | | F | 97 | 2 | 93 | 3 | 82 | ... | ... | ... |
| | 1995 | MF | 94 | 2 | 90 | 3 | 73 | 1 | 69 | 3 |
| | | M | 93 | 2 | 88 | 3 | 71 | 1 | 67 | 3 |
| | | F | 95 | 2 | 91 | 2 | 76 | 1 | 71 | 3 |
| Georgia | 1994 | | (6-9) | (<6) | (6-9) | (>9) | (10-16) | (<10) | (10-16) | (>16) |
| | | MF | 84 | 0.1 | 84 | 0.1 | 74 | 0.0 | 70 | 4 |
| | | M | 85 | 0.1 | 84 | 0.1 | 77 | 0.0 | 72 | 5 |
| | | F | 84 | 0.1 | 83 | 0.1 | 71 | 0.0 | 69 | 3 |
| | 1995 | MF | 85 | 0.0 | 85 | 0.1 | 76 | 0.0 | 73 | 2 |
| | | M | 84 | 0.0 | 84 | 0.1 | 76 | 0.0 | 74 | 2 |
| | | F | 86 | 0.0 | 86 | 0.1 | 75 | 0.0 | 73 | 2 |
| | 1996 | MF | 88 | 0.0 | 87 | 1 | 77 | 0.0 | 74 | 3 |
| | | M | 89 | 0.0 | 87 | 1 | 78 | 0.0 | 75 | 3 |
| | | F | 88 | 0.0 | 87 | 1 | 76 | 0.0 | 74 | 3 |
| Indonesia | 1975 | | (7-12) | (<7) | (7-12) | (>12) | (13-18) | (<13) | (13-18) | (>18) |
| | | MF | 86 | 4 | 72 | 10 | 20 | 0.6 | 17 | 2 |
| | | M | 94 | 4 | 78 | 12 | 25 | 0.6 | 21 | 3 |
| | | F | 78 | 3 | 67 | 8 | 15 | 0.5 | 14 | 1 |
| | 1980 | MF | 107 | 5 | 88 | 14 | 29 | ... | ... | ... |
| | | M | 115 | 6 | 90 | 16 | 35 | ... | ... | ... |
| | | F | 100 | 5 | 83 | 12 | 23 | ... | ... | ... |
| | 1985 | MF | 117 | 6 | 98 | 13 | 41 | ... | ... | ... |
| | | M | 120 | 5 | 101 | 14 | 47 | ... | ... | ... |
| | | F | 114 | 6 | 95 | 13 | 35 | ... | ... | ... |
| | 1990 | MF | 115 | 8 | 97 | 10 | 44 | 3 | 38 | 3 |
| | | M | 117 | 8 | 100 | 9 | 48 | 3 | 40 | 5 |
| | | F | 114 | 8 | 95 | 10 | 40 | 2 | 35 | 2 |
| | 1991 | MF | 114 | 8 | 97 | 9 | 43 | 3 | 38 | 3 |
| | | M | 115 | 8 | 100 | 8 | 48 | 3 | 42 | 3 |
| | | F | 113 | 8 | 95 | 10 | 39 | 3 | 34 | 3 |
| | 1992 | MF | 114 | 8 | 97 | 9 | 43 | 3 | 37 | 3 |
| | | M | 116 | 8 | 99 | 9 | 48 | 3 | 41 | 4 |
| | | F | 112 | 8 | 95 | 9 | 39 | 3 | 34 | 2 |
| | 1993 | MF | 115 | 8 | 97 | 9 | 45 | ... | ... | ... |
| | | M | 117 | 9 | 99 | 8 | 49 | ... | ... | ... |
| | | F | 113 | 8 | 95 | 10 | 41 | ... | ... | ... |
| | 1994 | MF | 114 | 9 | 97 | 9 | 48 | 3 | 42 | 2 |
| | | M | 117 | 10 | 99 | 8 | 52 | 4 | 45 | 3 |
| | | F | 112 | 8 | 95 | 10 | 44 | 3 | 39 | 2 |

**Primary and secondary education: enrolment ratios by age groups**
**Enseignements primaire et secondaire: taux de scolarisation par groupes d'âge**
**Enseñanza primaria y secundaria: tasas de escolarización por grupos de edad**

| Country / Pays / País | Year / Année / Año | Sex / Sexe / Sexo | Primary education / Enseignement primaire / Enseñanza primaria | | | | Secondary education / Enseignement secondaire / Enseñanza secundaria | | | |
|---|---|---|---|---|---|---|---|---|---|---|
| | | | Gross enrolment ratios / Taux bruts de scolarisation / Tasas brutas de escolarización (%) | Enrolment ratios by age groups / Taux de scolarisation par groupes d'âge / Tasas de escolarización por grupos de edad | | | Gross enrolment ratios / Taux bruts de scolarisation / Tasas brutas de escolarización (%) | Enrolment ratios by age groups / Taux de scolarisation par groupes d'âge / Tasas de escolarización por grupos de edad | | |
| | | | | Under-age / En dessous de l'âge officiel / Inferior a la edad oficial (%) | Official age group (NER) / Groupe d'âge officiel (TNS) / Grupo de edad oficial (TNE) (%) | Over-age / Au-dessus de l'âge officiel / Superior a la edad oficial (%) | | Under-age / En dessous de l'âge officiel / Inferior a la edad oficial (%) | Official age group (NER) / Groupe d'âge officiel (TNS) / Grupo de edad oficial (TNE) (%) | Over-age / Au-dessus de l'âge officiel / Superior a la edad oficial (%) |
| Indonesia (cont) | 1995 | | | | | | | | | |
| | | MF | 113 | 9 | 95 | 9 | 51 | ... | ... | ... |
| | | M | 116 | 11 | 97 | 8 | 55 | ... | ... | ... |
| | | F | 111 | 8 | 94 | 10 | 48 | ... | ... | ... |
| | 1996 | | | | | | | | | |
| | | MF | 113 | 9 | 95 | 9 | 56 | ... | ... | ... |
| | | M | 115 | 11 | 96 | 8 | ... | ... | ... | ... |
| | | F | 110 | 8 | 93 | 9 | ... | ... | ... | ... |
| Iran, Islamic Republic of | 1970 | | (7-12) | (<7) | (7-12) | (>12) | (13-18) | (<13) | (13-18) | (>18) |
| | | MF | 73 | 7 | 60 | 6 | 27 | ... | ... | ... |
| | 1985 | | (6-10) | (<6) | (6-10) | (>10) | (11-17) | (<11) | (11-17) | (>17) |
| | | MF | 98 | 0.0 | 81 | 17 | 45 | ... | ... | ... |
| | | M | 109 | 0.0 | 88 | 21 | 54 | ... | ... | ... |
| | | F | 87 | 0.0 | 74 | 13 | 36 | ... | ... | ... |
| | 1991 | | | | | | | | | |
| | | MF | 113 | 0.2 | 99 | 14 | 59 | ... | ... | ... |
| | | M | 118 | 0.3 | 102 | 16 | 67 | ... | ... | ... |
| | | F | 108 | 0.2 | 96 | 12 | 50 | ... | ... | ... |
| | 1996 | | | | | | | | | |
| | | MF | 98 | 0.0 | 90 | 9 | 77 | 0.2 | 71 | 5 |
| | | M | 102 | 0.0 | 91 | 10 | 81 | 0.2 | 74 | 6 |
| | | F | 95 | 0.0 | 88 | 7 | 73 | 0.2 | 68 | 4 |
| Iraq | 1970 | | (6-11) | (<6) | (6-11) | (>11) | (12-17) | (<12) | (12-17) | (>17) |
| | | MF | 69 | 0.0 | 55 | 13 | 24 | 0.0 | 19 | 5 |
| | | M | 95 | 0.0 | 76 | 20 | 34 | 0.0 | 27 | 7 |
| | | F | 41 | 0.0 | 34 | 7 | 14 | 0.0 | 12 | 3 |
| | 1975 | | | | | | | | | |
| | | MF | 94 | 0.0 | 79 | 15 | 35 | 0.0 | 25 | 9 |
| | | M | 122 | 0.0 | 101 | 21 | 48 | 0.0 | 34 | 14 |
| | | F | 64 | 0.0 | 55 | 8 | 21 | 0.0 | 16 | 5 |
| | 1980 | | | | | | | | | |
| | | MF | 113 | 0.0 | 99 | 15 | 57 | 0.0 | 47 | 10 |
| | | M | 119 | 0.0 | 103 | 16 | 76 | 0.0 | 62 | 14 |
| | | F | 107 | 0.0 | 94 | 14 | 38 | 0.0 | 31 | 7 |
| | 1985 | | | | | | | | | |
| | | MF | 108 | 0.0 | 93 | 15 | 54 | ... | ... | ... |
| | | M | 116 | 0.0 | 99 | 17 | 68 | ... | ... | ... |
| | | F | 99 | 0.0 | 87 | 12 | 39 | ... | ... | ... |
| | 1992 | | | | | | | | | |
| | | MF | 90 | 1 | 79 | 10 | 44 | 0.0 | 37 | 6 |
| | | M | 97 | 1 | 83 | 13 | 53 | 0.0 | 44 | 8 |
| | | F | 83 | 1 | 74 | 7 | 34 | 0.0 | 30 | 4 |
| | 1995 | | | | | | | | | |
| | | MF | 85 | 2 | 76 | 7 | 42 | ... | ... | ... |
| | | M | 92 | 2 | 81 | 9 | 51 | ... | ... | ... |
| | | F | 78 | 1 | 71 | 6 | 32 | ... | ... | ... |
| Japan | 1970 | | (6-11) | (<6) | (6-11) | (>11) | (12-17) | (<12) | (12-17) | (>17) |
| | | MF | 100 | 0.0 | 100 | 0.0 | 87 | 0.0 | 86 | 0.9 |
| | | M | 100 | 0.0 | 100 | 0.0 | 87 | 0.0 | 86 | 1 |
| | | F | 99 | 0.0 | 99 | 0.0 | 86 | 0.0 | 86 | 0.8 |
| | 1975 | | | | | | | | | |
| | | MF | 99 | 0.0 | 99 | 0.0 | 92 | ... | ... | ... |
| | | M | 99 | 0.0 | 99 | 0.0 | 91 | ... | ... | ... |
| | | F | 100 | 0.0 | 100 | 0.0 | 92 | ... | ... | ... |
| | 1980 | | | | | | | | | |
| | | MF | 101 | 0.0 | 101 | 0.0 | 93 | 0.0 | 93 | 0.4 |
| | | M | 101 | 0.0 | 101 | 0.0 | 92 | 0.0 | 92 | 0.4 |
| | | F | 101 | 0.0 | 101 | 0.0 | 94 | 0.0 | 94 | 0.3 |
| | 1985 | | | | | | | | | |
| | | MF | 102 | 0.0 | 102 | 0.0 | 95 | 0.0 | 95 | 0.0 |
| | | M | 102 | 0.0 | 102 | 0.0 | 94 | ... | ... | ... |
| | | F | 102 | 0.0 | 102 | 0.0 | 96 | ... | ... | ... |

Primary and secondary education: enrolment ratios by age groups  II.9
Enseignements primaire et secondaire: taux de scolarisation par groupes d'âge
Enseñanza primaria y secundaria: tasas de escolarización por grupos de edad

| Country / Pays / País | Year / Année / Año | Sex / Sexe / Sexo | Primary education — Enseignement primaire — Enseñanza primaria | | | | Secondary education — Enseignement secondaire — Enseñanza secundaria | | | |
|---|---|---|---|---|---|---|---|---|---|---|
| | | | Gross enrolment ratios / Taux bruts de scolarisation / Tasas brutas de escolarización (%) | Under-age / En dessous de l'âge officiel / Inferior a la edad oficial (%) | Official age group (NER) / Groupe d'âge officiel (TNS) / Grupo de edad oficial (TNE) (%) | Over-age / Au-dessus de l'âge officiel / Superior a la edad oficial (%) | Gross enrolment ratios / Taux bruts de scolarisation / Tasas brutas de escolarización (%) | Under-age / En dessous de l'âge officiel / Inferior a la edad oficial (%) | Official age group (NER) / Groupe d'âge officiel (TNS) / Grupo de edad oficial (TNE) (%) | Over-age / Au-dessus de l'âge officiel / Superior a la edad oficial (%) |
| Japan (cont) | 1990 | | | | | | | | | |
| | | MF | 100 | 0.0 | 100 | 0.0 | 97 | 0.0 | 97 | 0.3 |
| | | M | 100 | 0.0 | 100 | 0.0 | 96 | ... | ... | ... |
| | | F | 100 | 0.0 | 100 | 0.0 | 98 | ... | ... | ... |
| | 1991 | | | | | | | | | |
| | | MF | 100 | 0.0 | 100 | 0.0 | 96 | 0.0 | 96 | 0.3 |
| | | M | 100 | 0.0 | 100 | 0.0 | 96 | ... | ... | ... |
| | | F | 101 | 0.0 | 101 | 0.0 | 97 | ... | ... | ... |
| | 1993 | | | | | | | | | |
| | | MF | 102 | 0.0 | 102 | 0.0 | 99 | 0.0 | 97 | 2 |
| | | M | 102 | 0.0 | 102 | 0.0 | 98 | 0.0 | 96 | 2 |
| | | F | 102 | 0.0 | 102 | 0.0 | 100 | 0.0 | 98 | 2 |
| | 1994 | | | | | | | | | |
| | | MF | 103 | 0.0 | 103 | 0.0 | 100 | 0.0 | 99 | 1 |
| | | M | 103 | 0.0 | 103 | 0.0 | 99 | ... | ... | ... |
| | | F | 103 | 0.0 | 103 | 0.0 | 100 | ... | ... | ... |
| Korea, Republic of | 1970 | | (6-11) | (<6) | (6-11) | (>11) | (12-17) | (<12) | (12-17) | (>17) |
| | | MF | 103 | 0.0 | 94 | 9 | 42 | 0.7 | 38 | 3 |
| | | M | 104 | 0.0 | 95 | 9 | 50 | 0.9 | 45 | 4 |
| | | F | 103 | 0.0 | 94 | 9 | 32 | 0.5 | 30 | 2 |
| | 1975 | | | | | | | | | |
| | | MF | 107 | 0.0 | 99 | 7 | 56 | 0.6 | 52 | 4 |
| | | M | 107 | 0.0 | 99 | 7 | 64 | 0.7 | 58 | 5 |
| | | F | 107 | 0.0 | 100 | 8 | 48 | 0.6 | 45 | 2 |
| | 1980 | | | | | | | | | |
| | | MF | 110 | 0.0 | 104 | 6 | 78 | 1 | 70 | 7 |
| | | M | 109 | 0.0 | 104 | 5 | 82 | 0.9 | 73 | 8 |
| | | F | 111 | 0.0 | 105 | 6 | 74 | 1 | 67 | 6 |
| | 1985 | | | | | | | | | |
| | | MF | 97 | 0.0 | 94 | 3 | 92 | 0.6 | 84 | 7 |
| | | M | 96 | 0.0 | 94 | 2 | 93 | 0.6 | 85 | 8 |
| | | F | 98 | 0.0 | 95 | 3 | 91 | 0.7 | 84 | 6 |
| | 1990 | | | | | | | | | |
| | | MF | 105 | 0.0 | 104 | 1 | 90 | 0.2 | 86 | 4 |
| | | M | 105 | 0.0 | 103 | 1 | 91 | 0.2 | 87 | 4 |
| | | F | 105 | 0.0 | 104 | 1 | 88 | 0.2 | 85 | 4 |
| | 1991 | | | | | | | | | |
| | | MF | 105 | 0.0 | 104 | 1 | 89 | 0.3 | 84 | 5 |
| | | M | 105 | 0.0 | 103 | 1 | 90 | 0.3 | 85 | 5 |
| | | F | 105 | 0.0 | 104 | 2 | 88 | 0.3 | 83 | 4 |
| | 1992 | | | | | | | | | |
| | | MF | 103 | 0.0 | 102 | 2 | 91 | 0.3 | 85 | 5 |
| | | M | 103 | 0.0 | 101 | 2 | 91 | 0.3 | 85 | 6 |
| | | F | 104 | 0.0 | 102 | 2 | 90 | 0.3 | 85 | 5 |
| | 1993 | | | | | | | | | |
| | | MF | 101 | 0.0 | 99 | 2 | 95 | ... | ... | ... |
| | | M | 101 | 0.0 | 99 | 2 | 96 | ... | ... | ... |
| | | F | 102 | 0.0 | 100 | 2 | 94 | ... | ... | ... |
| | 1994 | | | | | | | | | |
| | | MF | 98 | 0.0 | 96 | 2 | 98 | ... | ... | ... |
| | | M | 98 | 0.0 | 95 | 2 | 98 | ... | ... | ... |
| | | F | 99 | 0.0 | 97 | 2 | 98 | ... | ... | ... |
| | 1995 | | | | | | | | | |
| | | MF | 95 | 0.0 | 93 | 2 | 101 | 0.3 | 96 | 5 |
| | | M | 95 | 0.0 | 93 | 2 | 101 | 0.3 | 96 | 5 |
| | | F | 96 | 0.0 | 94 | 2 | 101 | 0.3 | 96 | 5 |
| | 1996 | | | | | | | | | |
| | | MF | 94 | 0.0 | 92 | 2 | 102 | 0.2 | 97 | 4 |
| | | M | 94 | 0.0 | 92 | 2 | 102 | 0.3 | 97 | 4 |
| | | F | 94 | 0.0 | 93 | 2 | 102 | 0.2 | 98 | 4 |

II.9    Primary and secondary education: enrolment ratios by age groups
Enseignements primaire et secondaire: taux de scolarisation par groupes d'âge
Enseñanza primaria y secundaria: tasas de escolarización por grupos de edad

| | | | Primary education Enseignement primaire Enseñanza primaria | | | | Secondary education Enseignement secondaire Enseñanza secundaria | | | |
|---|---|---|---|---|---|---|---|---|---|---|
| Country | Year | Sex | Gross enrolment ratios | Enrolment ratios by age groups Taux de scolarisation par groupes d'âge Tasas de escolarización por grupos de edad | | | Gross enrolment ratios | Enrolment ratios by age groups Taux de scolarisation par groupes d'âge Tasas de escolarización por grupos de edad | | |
| | | | | Under-age | Official age group (NER) | Over-age | | Under-age | Official age group (NER) | Over-age |
| Pays | Année | Sexe | Taux bruts de scolarisation | En dessous de l'âge officiel | Groupe d'âge officiel (TNS) | Au-dessus de l'âge officiel | Taux bruts de scolarisation | En dessous de l'âge officiel | Groupe d'âge officiel (TNS) | Au-dessus de l'âge officiel |
| País | Año | Sexo | Tasas brutas de escolarización (%) | Inferior a la edad oficial (%) | Grupo de edad oficial (TNE) (%) | Superior a la edad oficial (%) | Tasas brutas de escolarización (%) | Inferior a la edad oficial (%) | Grupo de edad oficial (TNE) (%) | Superior a la edad oficial (%) |
| Korea, Republic of (cont) | 1997 | | | | | | | | | |
| | | MF | 94 | 0.1 | 93 | 1 | ... | ... | ... | ... |
| | | M | 94 | 0.1 | 92 | 1 | ... | ... | ... | ... |
| | | F | 95 | 0.2 | 93 | 1 | ... | ... | ... | ... |
| Kuwait | 1970 | | (6-9) | (<6) | (6-9) | (>9) | (10-17) | (<10) | (10-17) | (>17) |
| | | MF | 88 | 0.3 | 61 | 27 | 63 | 0.0 | 53 | 10 |
| | | M | 100 | 0.0 | 67 | 33 | 70 | 0.0 | 57 | 12 |
| | | F | 76 | 0.5 | 54 | 22 | 57 | 0.0 | 48 | 8 |
| | 1975 | | | | | | | | | |
| | | MF | 93 | 0.0 | 69 | 24 | 66 | 0.0 | 57 | 9 |
| | | M | 99 | 0.0 | 72 | 27 | 71 | 0.0 | 61 | 10 |
| | | F | 86 | 0.0 | 65 | 21 | 62 | 0.0 | 54 | 8 |
| | 1980 | | | | | | | | | |
| | | MF | 102 | 4 | 85 | 14 | 80 | ... | ... | ... |
| | | M | 105 | 5 | 89 | 11 | 84 | ... | ... | ... |
| | | F | 100 | 3 | 80 | 17 | 76 | ... | ... | ... |
| | 1985 | | | | | | | | | |
| | | MF | 103 | 7 | 87 | 9 | 91 | ... | ... | ... |
| | | M | 104 | 7 | 88 | 9 | 95 | ... | ... | ... |
| | | F | 102 | 6 | 85 | 10 | 87 | ... | ... | ... |
| | 1991 | | | | | | | | | |
| | | MF | 55 | 4 | 45 | 7 | 51 | 0.0 | 45 | 5 |
| | | M | 55 | 3 | 45 | 7 | 51 | 0.0 | 46 | 5 |
| | | F | 54 | 4 | 44 | 6 | 51 | 0.0 | 45 | 6 |
| | 1993 | | | | | | | | | |
| | | MF | 64 | 5 | 54 | 5 | 58 | 0.0 | 54 | 4 |
| | | M | 64 | 5 | 54 | 4 | 58 | 0.0 | 54 | 4 |
| | | F | 64 | 6 | 53 | 5 | 58 | 0.0 | 54 | 4 |
| | 1995 | | | | | | | | | |
| | | MF | 73 | 6 | 62 | 5 | 64 | 0.0 | 62 | 2 |
| | | M | 74 | 6 | 62 | 5 | 64 | 0.0 | 62 | 2 |
| | | F | 72 | 6 | 62 | 5 | 64 | 0.0 | 62 | 2 |
| | 1996 | | | | | | | | | |
| | | MF | 76 | 10 | 62 | 4 | 65 | 0.0 | 61 | 4 |
| | | M | 76 | 11 | 62 | 4 | 65 | 0.0 | 62 | 4 |
| | | F | 75 | 9 | 61 | 4 | 65 | 0.0 | 61 | 4 |
| Kyrgyzstan | 1995 | | (7-10) | (<7) | (7-10) | (>10) | (11-17) | (<11) | (11-17) | (>17) |
| | | MF | 104 | 10 | 95 | 0.0 | 79 | ... | ... | ... |
| | | M | 105 | 9 | 96 | 0.0 | 75 | ... | ... | ... |
| | | F | 103 | 10 | 93 | 0.0 | 83 | ... | ... | ... |
| Lao People's Democratic Republic | 1991 | | (6-10) | (<6) | (6-10) | (>10) | (11-16) | (<11) | (11-16) | (>16) |
| | | MF | 102 | 0.0 | 61 | 40 | 22 | 0.0 | 15 | 7 |
| | | M | 113 | 0.0 | 66 | 47 | 27 | 0.0 | 17 | 10 |
| | | F | 90 | 0.0 | 57 | 33 | 18 | 0.0 | 13 | 4 |
| | 1992 | | | | | | | | | |
| | | MF | 107 | 0.0 | 66 | 41 | 24 | 0.0 | 16 | 8 |
| | | M | 119 | 0.0 | 71 | 48 | 30 | 0.0 | 18 | 12 |
| | | F | 94 | 0.0 | 61 | 33 | 19 | 0.0 | 14 | 5 |
| | 1993 | | | | | | | | | |
| | | MF | 109 | 0.0 | 69 | 40 | 26 | 0.0 | 19 | 7 |
| | | M | 122 | 0.0 | 74 | 48 | 32 | 0.0 | 21 | 11 |
| | | F | 96 | 0.0 | 64 | 32 | 20 | 0.0 | 16 | 4 |
| | 1995 | | | | | | | | | |
| | | MF | 112 | 0.0 | 70 | 42 | 27 | ... | ... | ... |
| | | M | 123 | 0.0 | 74 | 49 | 32 | ... | ... | ... |
| | | F | 100 | 0.0 | 66 | 34 | 21 | ... | ... | ... |
| | 1996 | | | | | | | | | |
| | | MF | 112 | 0.0 | 72 | 40 | 28 | 0.0 | 22 | 6 |
| | | M | 123 | 0.0 | 76 | 47 | 34 | 0.0 | 25 | 9 |
| | | F | 101 | 0.0 | 68 | 32 | 23 | 0.0 | 19 | 4 |

Primary and secondary education: enrolment ratios by age groups
Enseignements primaire et secondaire: taux de scolarisation par groupes d'âge
Enseñanza primaria y secundaria: tasas de escolarización por grupos de edad

II.9

| Country / Pays / País | Year / Année / Año | Sex / Sexe / Sexo | Primary education — Enseignement primaire — Enseñanza primaria | | | | Secondary education — Enseignement secondaire — Enseñanza secundaria | | | |
|---|---|---|---|---|---|---|---|---|---|---|
| | | | Gross enrolment ratios / Taux bruts de scolarisation / Tasas brutas de escolarización (%) | Under-age / En dessous de l'âge officiel / Inferior a la edad oficial (%) | Official age group (NER) / Groupe d'âge officiel (TNS) / Grupo de edad oficial (TNE) (%) | Over-age / Au-dessus de l'âge officiel / Superior a la edad oficial (%) | Gross enrolment ratios / Taux bruts de scolarisation / Tasas brutas de escolarización (%) | Under-age / En dessous de l'âge officiel / Inferior a la edad oficial (%) | Official age group (NER) / Groupe d'âge officiel (TNS) / Grupo de edad oficial (TNE) (%) | Over-age / Au-dessus de l'âge officiel / Superior a la edad oficial (%) |
| Lebanon | 1996 | | (6-10) | (<6) | (6-10) | (>10) | (11-17) | (<11) | (11-17) | (>17) |
| | | MF | 111 | 0.0 | 76 | 35 | 81 | ... | ... | ... |
| Macau | 1991 | | (6-11) | (<6) | (6-11) | (>11) | (12-17) | (<12) | (12-17) | (>17) |
| | | MF | 99 | 0.4 | 81 | 17 | 68 | 0.4 | 53 | 15 |
| | | M | 100 | 0.4 | 81 | 18 | 64 | 0.2 | 50 | 14 |
| | | F | 97 | 0.4 | 81 | 16 | 72 | 0.5 | 56 | 15 |
| Malaysia | 1970 | | (6-11) | (<6) | (6-11) | (>11) | (12-18) | (<12) | (12-18) | (>18) |
| | | MF | 89 | 0.1 | 88 | 0.6 | 34 | 0.7 | 33 | 0.4 |
| | | M | 94 | 0.1 | 93 | 0.7 | 41 | 0.7 | 39 | 0.5 |
| | | F | 83 | 0.0 | 83 | 0.4 | 28 | 0.6 | 27 | 0.3 |
| | 1994 | | | | | | | | | |
| | | MF | 102 | 0.0 | 102 | 0.1 | 56 | ... | ... | ... |
| | | M | 102 | 0.0 | 102 | 0.1 | 54 | ... | ... | ... |
| | | F | 103 | 0.0 | 102 | 0.1 | 59 | ... | ... | ... |
| Mongolia | 1994 | | (8-10) | (<8) | (8-10) | (>10) | (11-17) | (<11) | (11-17) | (>17) |
| | | MF | 81 | 3 | 75 | 3 | 59 | 2 | 56 | 0.8 |
| | | M | 79 | 3 | 74 | 3 | 50 | 2 | 47 | 0.7 |
| | | F | 83 | 4 | 77 | 2 | 68 | 3 | 65 | 0.8 |
| | 1995 | | | | | | | | | |
| | | MF | 88 | 3 | 80 | 5 | 59 | 2 | 57 | 0.8 |
| | | M | 87 | 3 | 78 | 6 | 51 | 1 | 48 | 0.6 |
| | | F | 90 | 4 | 81 | 5 | 68 | 2 | 65 | 0.9 |
| | 1996 | | (8-11) | (<8) | (8-11) | (>11) | (12-17) | (<12) | (12-17) | (>17) |
| | | MF | 88 | 3 | 81 | 5 | 56 | 2 | 53 | 1 |
| | | M | 86 | 2 | 79 | 5 | 48 | 2 | 45 | 1 |
| | | F | 91 | 3 | 83 | 4 | 65 | 2 | 61 | 2 |
| Oman | 1975 | | (6-11) | (<6) | (6-11) | (>11) | (12-17) | (<12) | (12-17) | (>17) |
| | | MF | 37 | 0.1 | 27 | 10 | 1 | 0.0 | 0.9 | 0.4 |
| | | M | 53 | 0.1 | 37 | 16 | 2 | 0.0 | 1 | 0.7 |
| | | F | 20 | 0.1 | 17 | 4 | 0.4 | 0.0 | 0.3 | 0.1 |
| | 1980 | | | | | | | | | |
| | | MF | 51 | 0.2 | 43 | 8 | 12 | 0.0 | 10 | 2 |
| | | M | 67 | 0.2 | 54 | 12 | 17 | 0.0 | 15 | 3 |
| | | F | 35 | 0.1 | 31 | 4 | 6 | 0.0 | 5 | 0.6 |
| | 1985 | | | | | | | | | |
| | | MF | 76 | 1 | 66 | 9 | 27 | ... | ... | ... |
| | | M | 85 | 1 | 70 | 14 | 35 | ... | ... | ... |
| | | F | 68 | 0.8 | 63 | 4 | 18 | ... | ... | ... |
| | 1990 | | | | | | | | | |
| | | MF | 86 | 2 | 70 | 14 | 46 | ... | ... | ... |
| | | M | 90 | 2 | 73 | 16 | 51 | ... | ... | ... |
| | | F | 82 | 2 | 68 | 12 | 40 | ... | ... | ... |
| | 1991 | | | | | | | | | |
| | | MF | 86 | 3 | 70 | 13 | 51 | ... | ... | ... |
| | | M | 90 | 3 | 72 | 15 | 55 | ... | ... | ... |
| | | F | 82 | 2 | 68 | 12 | 46 | ... | ... | ... |
| | 1992 | | | | | | | | | |
| | | MF | 85 | 2 | 72 | 11 | 57 | 0.7 | 49 | 7 |
| | | M | 89 | 2 | 74 | 13 | 61 | 0.7 | 52 | 8 |
| | | F | 82 | 2 | 71 | 9 | 53 | 0.8 | 46 | 6 |
| | 1993 | | | | | | | | | |
| | | MF | 83 | 3 | 72 | 9 | 62 | ... | ... | ... |
| | | M | 86 | 3 | 73 | 10 | 66 | ... | ... | ... |
| | | F | 81 | 2 | 71 | 8 | 58 | ... | ... | ... |
| | 1994 | | | | | | | | | |
| | | MF | 81 | 2 | 71 | 8 | 65 | ... | ... | ... |
| | | M | 83 | 2 | 72 | 9 | 68 | ... | ... | ... |
| | | F | 79 | 2 | 70 | 7 | 62 | ... | ... | ... |
| | 1995 | | | | | | | | | |
| | | MF | 79 | 1 | 70 | 8 | 67 | ... | ... | ... |
| | | M | 81 | 1 | 71 | 8 | 69 | ... | ... | ... |
| | | F | 77 | 1 | 69 | 7 | 64 | ... | ... | ... |

II.9   Primary and secondary education: enrolment ratios by age groups
Enseignements primaire et secondaire: taux de scolarisation par groupes d'âge
Enseñanza primaria y secundaria: tasas de escolarización por grupos de edad

| Country / Pays / País | Year / Année / Año | Sex / Sexe / Sexo | Primary education — Enseignement primaire — Enseñanza primaria | | | | Secondary education — Enseignement secondaire — Enseñanza secundaria | | | |
|---|---|---|---|---|---|---|---|---|---|---|
| | | | Gross enrolment ratios / Taux bruts de scolarisation / Tasas brutas de escolarización (%) | Under-age / En dessous de l'âge officiel / Inferior a la edad oficial (%) | Official age group (NER) / Groupe d'âge officiel (TNS) / Grupo de edad oficial (TNE) (%) | Over-age / Au-dessus de l'âge officiel / Superior a la edad oficial (%) | Gross enrolment ratios / Taux bruts de scolarisation / Tasas brutas de escolarización (%) | Under-age / En dessous de l'âge officiel / Inferior a la edad oficial (%) | Official age group (NER) / Groupe d'âge officiel (TNS) / Grupo de edad oficial (TNE) (%) | Over-age / Au-dessus de l'âge officiel / Superior a la edad oficial (%) |
| Oman (cont) | 1996 | | | | | | | | | |
| | | MF | 78 | 1 | 69 | 8 | 67 | ... | ... | ... |
| | | M | 80 | 2 | 70 | 9 | 68 | ... | ... | ... |
| | | F | 76 | 1 | 68 | 7 | 65 | ... | ... | ... |
| Philippines | 1975 | | (7-12) | (<7) | (7-12) | (>12) | (13-16) | (<13) | (13-16) | (>16) |
| | | MF | 109 | 0.1 | 97 | 12 | 54 | ... | ... | ... |
| | | M | 106 | 0.1 | 94 | 11 | 54 | ... | ... | ... |
| | | F | 112 | 0.1 | 99 | 12 | 54 | ... | ... | ... |
| | 1980 | | | | | | | | | |
| | | MF | 112 | 1 | 94 | 17 | 64 | 3 | 45 | 16 |
| | | M | 114 | 1 | 95 | 18 | 60 | 3 | 42 | 15 |
| | | F | 110 | 1 | 92 | 17 | 69 | 3 | 48 | 18 |
| | 1985 | | | | | | | | | |
| | | MF | 107 | 0.7 | 96 | 10 | 64 | 3 | 50 | 12 |
| | | M | 108 | 0.8 | 97 | 11 | 64 | 3 | 49 | 12 |
| | | F | 107 | 0.7 | 96 | 10 | 65 | 3 | 50 | 12 |
| | 1991 | | | | | | | | | |
| | | MF | 111 | 1 | 97 | 12 | 75 | 4 | 57 | 14 |
| | 1992 | | | | | | | | | |
| | | MF | 110 | 1 | 97 | 12 | 76 | 4 | 58 | 14 |
| | 1993 | | | | | | | | | |
| | | MF | 109 | 1 | 96 | 12 | 77 | 4 | 59 | 14 |
| | 1995 | | | | | | | | | |
| | | MF | 114 | 1 | 101 | 13 | 77 | 4 | 59 | 14 |
| Qatar | 1970 | | (6-11) | (<6) | (6-11) | (>11) | (12-17) | (<12) | (12-17) | (>17) |
| | | MF | 96 | 0.1 | 72 | 24 | 36 | 0.6 | 25 | 11 |
| | | M | 104 | 0.1 | 78 | 26 | 41 | 0.9 | 27 | 13 |
| | | F | 88 | 0.1 | 66 | 22 | 30 | 0.1 | 23 | 7 |
| | 1975 | | | | | | | | | |
| | | MF | 112 | 0.1 | 81 | 31 | 54 | 0.5 | 35 | 18 |
| | | M | 114 | 0.1 | 80 | 34 | 49 | 0.5 | 30 | 18 |
| | | F | 109 | 0.0 | 82 | 27 | 61 | 0.5 | 43 | 18 |
| | 1980 | | | | | | | | | |
| | | MF | 105 | 4 | 85 | 16 | 66 | 2 | 51 | 13 |
| | | M | 107 | 4 | 87 | 16 | 65 | 2 | 50 | 13 |
| | | F | 102 | 4 | 82 | 16 | 68 | 2 | 52 | 14 |
| | 1985 | | | | | | | | | |
| | | MF | 108 | 5 | 91 | 12 | 82 | 3 | 66 | 13 |
| | | M | 110 | 5 | 88 | 17 | 79 | 3 | 64 | 12 |
| | | F | 107 | 5 | 94 | 8 | 86 | 3 | 69 | 14 |
| | 1990 | | | | | | | | | |
| | | MF | 97 | 2 | 87 | 8 | 81 | 4 | 67 | 10 |
| | | M | 101 | 2 | 87 | 11 | 77 | 3 | 64 | 10 |
| | | F | 94 | 2 | 86 | 6 | 85 | 4 | 70 | 10 |
| | 1991 | | | | | | | | | |
| | | MF | 92 | 3 | 82 | 7 | 79 | 4 | 66 | 9 |
| | | M | 96 | 3 | 84 | 9 | 76 | 4 | 63 | 9 |
| | | F | 89 | 3 | 81 | 5 | 82 | 4 | 69 | 9 |
| | 1992 | | | | | | | | | |
| | | MF | 88 | 3 | 79 | 6 | 84 | 5 | 70 | 9 |
| | | M | 91 | 3 | 80 | 8 | 82 | 4 | 68 | 9 |
| | | F | 86 | 3 | 78 | 4 | 86 | 5 | 72 | 9 |
| | 1993 | | | | | | | | | |
| | | MF | 89 | 4 | 80 | 6 | 83 | 5 | 69 | 9 |
| | | M | 92 | 4 | 81 | 7 | 82 | 5 | 68 | 9 |
| | | F | 86 | 3 | 79 | 4 | 84 | 5 | 71 | 8 |
| Saudi Arabia | 1970 | | (6-11) | (<6) | (6-11) | (>11) | (12-17) | (<12) | (12-17) | (>17) |
| | | MF | 45 | 2 | 32 | 11 | 12 | 0.4 | 9 | 3 |
| | | M | 61 | 0.7 | 44 | 17 | 19 | 0.5 | 14 | 4 |
| | | F | 29 | 3 | 21 | 5 | 5 | 0.4 | 4 | 0.6 |

Primary and secondary education: enrolment ratios by age groups
Enseignements primaire et secondaire: taux de scolarisation par groupes d'âge
Enseñanza primaria y secundaria: tasas de escolarización por grupos de edad

II.9

| Country / Pays / País | Year / Année / Año | Sex / Sexe / Sexo | Primary education / Enseignement primaire / Enseñanza primaria | | | | Secondary education / Enseignement secondaire / Enseñanza secundaria | | | |
|---|---|---|---|---|---|---|---|---|---|---|
| | | | Gross enrolment ratios / Taux bruts de scolarisation / Tasas brutas de escolarización (%) | Enrolment ratios by age groups / Taux de scolarisation par groupes d'âge / Tasas de escolarización por grupos de edad | | | Gross enrolment ratios / Taux bruts de scolarisation / Tasas brutas de escolarización (%) | Enrolment ratios by age groups / Taux de scolarisation par groupes d'âge / Tasas de escolarización por grupos de edad | | |
| | | | | Under-age / En dessous de l'âge officiel / Inferior a la edad oficial (%) | Official age group (NER) / Groupe d'âge officiel (TNS) / Grupo de edad oficial (TNE) (%) | Over-age / Au-dessus de l'âge officiel / Superior a la edad oficial (%) | | Under-age / En dessous de l'âge officiel / Inferior a la edad oficial (%) | Official age group (NER) / Groupe d'âge officiel (TNS) / Grupo de edad oficial (TNE) (%) | Over-age / Au-dessus de l'âge officiel / Superior a la edad oficial (%) |
| Saudi Arabia (cont) | 1975 | MF | 58 | 0.3 | 42 | 15 | 22 | 0.2 | 13 | 8 |
| | | M | 72 | 0.5 | 54 | 18 | 28 | 0.3 | 17 | 11 |
| | | F | 43 | 0.2 | 29 | 13 | 15 | 0.1 | 9 | 5 |
| | 1980 | MF | 61 | 0.6 | 49 | 12 | 29 | 0.5 | 21 | 8 |
| | | M | 74 | 0.8 | 60 | 13 | 36 | 0.7 | 26 | 9 |
| | | F | 49 | 0.4 | 37 | 12 | 23 | 0.2 | 16 | 7 |
| | 1985 | MF | 65 | 0.5 | 51 | 13 | 40 | 0.4 | 27 | 12 |
| | | M | 73 | 0.7 | 60 | 13 | 48 | 0.7 | 32 | 15 |
| | | F | 57 | 0.3 | 42 | 14 | 31 | 0.2 | 22 | 9 |
| | 1990 | MF | 73 | 0.6 | 59 | 14 | 44 | 0.3 | 31 | 12 |
| | | M | 78 | 0.7 | 65 | 12 | 49 | 0.5 | 34 | 14 |
| | | F | 68 | 0.6 | 53 | 15 | 39 | 0.2 | 28 | 11 |
| | 1991 | MF | 73 | 0.6 | 59 | 13 | 45 | 0.3 | 32 | 13 |
| | | M | 77 | 0.7 | 64 | 12 | 50 | ... | ... | ... |
| | | F | 69 | 0.6 | 54 | 15 | 41 | ... | ... | ... |
| | 1992 | MF | 75 | 0.7 | 61 | 13 | 48 | 0.2 | 34 | 14 |
| | | M | 78 | 0.7 | 65 | 12 | 53 | ... | ... | ... |
| | | F | 72 | 0.6 | 57 | 15 | 43 | ... | ... | ... |
| | 1993 | MF | 77 | 0.7 | 62 | 14 | 52 | 0.2 | 37 | 15 |
| | | M | 79 | 0.8 | 66 | 12 | 57 | ... | ... | ... |
| | | F | 74 | 0.5 | 59 | 15 | 47 | ... | ... | ... |
| | 1995 | MF | 78 | 0.8 | 63 | 14 | 58 | 0.7 | 48 | 10 |
| | | M | 79 | 0.6 | 66 | 13 | 62 | 1 | 54 | 7 |
| | | F | 76 | 1 | 60 | 15 | 54 | 0.3 | 41 | 12 |
| | 1996 | MF | 76 | 0.5 | 61 | 14 | 61 | 0.4 | 42 | 18 |
| | | M | 77 | 0.3 | 63 | 14 | 65 | ... | ... | ... |
| | | F | 75 | 0.7 | 60 | 15 | 57 | ... | ... | ... |
| Singapore | 1970 | | (6-11) | (<6) | (6-11) | (>11) | (12-17) | (<12) | (12-17) | (>17) |
| | | MF | 105 | 0.0 | 94 | 11 | 46 | 0.1 | 44 | 2 |
| | | M | 110 | 0.0 | 96 | 13 | 47 | 0.1 | 43 | 3 |
| | | F | 101 | 0.0 | 92 | 9 | 45 | 0.0 | 44 | 1 |
| | 1975 | MF | 110 | 0.1 | 101 | 9 | 52 | ... | ... | ... |
| | | M | 113 | 0.2 | 101 | 11 | 51 | ... | ... | ... |
| | | F | 106 | 0.1 | 100 | 6 | 53 | ... | ... | ... |
| | 1980 | MF | 108 | 0.0 | 99 | 8 | 60 | ... | ... | ... |
| | | M | 109 | 0.0 | 100 | 10 | 60 | ... | ... | ... |
| | | F | 106 | 0.0 | 99 | 7 | 60 | ... | ... | ... |
| | 1994 | | (6-11) | (<6) | (6-11) | (>11) | (12-18) | (<12) | (12-18) | (>18) |
| | | MF | 94 | 0.0 | 92 | 2 | 72 | ... | ... | ... |
| | | M | 95 | 0.0 | 93 | 3 | 74 | ... | ... | ... |
| | | F | 93 | 0.0 | 92 | 2 | 70 | ... | ... | ... |
| | 1995 | MF | 95 | 0.3 | 93 | 2 | 73 | ... | ... | ... |
| Syrian Arab Republic | 1970 | | (6-11) | (<6) | (6-11) | (>11) | (12-17) | (<12) | (12-17) | (>17) |
| | | MF | 78 | 0.5 | 70 | 7 | 38 | 0.0 | 29 | 9 |
| | | M | 95 | 0.6 | 84 | 10 | 54 | 0.0 | 40 | 14 |
| | | F | 59 | 0.5 | 54 | 5 | 21 | 0.0 | 17 | 4 |
| | 1975 | MF | 96 | 0.0 | 87 | 8 | 43 | 0.8 | 37 | 5 |
| | | M | 112 | 0.0 | 101 | 11 | 57 | 1 | 48 | 8 |
| | | F | 78 | 0.0 | 72 | 6 | 28 | 0.5 | 25 | 2 |

II.9   Primary and secondary education: enrolment ratios by age groups
Enseignements primaire et secondaire: taux de scolarisation par groupes d'âge
Enseñanza primaria y secundaria: tasas de escolarización por grupos de edad

| Country / Pays / País | Year / Année / Año | Sex / Sexe / Sexo | Primary education — Enseignement primaire — Enseñanza primaria | | | | Secondary education — Enseignement secondaire — Enseñanza secundaria | | | |
|---|---|---|---|---|---|---|---|---|---|---|
| | | | Gross enrolment ratios / Taux bruts de scolarisation / Tasas brutas de escolarización (%) | Enrolment ratios by age groups / Taux de scolarisation par groupes d'âge / Tasas de escolarización por grupos de edad | | | Gross enrolment ratios / Taux bruts de scolarisation / Tasas brutas de escolarización (%) | Enrolment ratios by age groups / Taux de scolarisation par groupes d'âge / Tasas de escolarización por grupos de edad | | |
| | | | | Under-age / En dessous de l'âge officiel / Inferior a la edad oficial (%) | Official age group (NER) / Groupe d'âge officiel (TNS) / Grupo de edad oficial (TNE) (%) | Over-age / Au-dessus de l'âge officiel / Superior a la edad oficial (%) | | Under-age / En dessous de l'âge officiel / Inferior a la edad oficial (%) | Official age group (NER) / Groupe d'âge officiel (TNS) / Grupo de edad oficial (TNE) (%) | Over-age / Au-dessus de l'âge officiel / Superior a la edad oficial (%) |
| Syrian Arab Republic (cont) | 1980 | MF | 100 | 3 | 89 | 7 | 46 | 0.0 | 39 | 7 |
| | | M | 111 | 3 | 99 | 9 | 57 | 0.0 | 48 | 9 |
| | | F | 88 | 3 | 80 | 5 | 35 | 0.0 | 30 | 5 |
| | 1985 | MF | 110 | 5 | 98 | 7 | 58 | 1 | 51 | 6 |
| | | M | 117 | 5 | 103 | 8 | 68 | 2 | 59 | 8 |
| | | F | 102 | 4 | 92 | 6 | 48 | 1 | 42 | 4 |
| | 1990 | MF | 108 | 5 | 98 | 5 | 52 | 2 | 46 | 4 |
| | | M | 114 | 6 | 103 | 6 | 60 | 3 | 52 | 5 |
| | | F | 102 | 5 | 93 | 4 | 44 | 2 | 39 | 3 |
| | 1991 | MF | 108 | 5 | 98 | 5 | 49 | 3 | 45 | 2 |
| | | M | 114 | 5 | 102 | 6 | 56 | 3 | 50 | 3 |
| | | F | 102 | 4 | 93 | 4 | 42 | 2 | 39 | 2 |
| | 1992 | MF | 105 | 5 | 95 | 5 | 48 | 2 | 44 | 2 |
| | | M | 110 | 6 | 99 | 6 | 54 | 3 | 48 | 2 |
| | | F | 99 | 5 | 91 | 4 | 43 | 2 | 39 | 1 |
| | 1993 | MF | 103 | 5 | 94 | 5 | 47 | 3 | 42 | 2 |
| | | M | 109 | 5 | 98 | 5 | 52 | 3 | 46 | 2 |
| | | F | 98 | 5 | 90 | 4 | 41 | 2 | 38 | 1 |
| | 1994 | MF | 102 | 5 | 92 | 5 | 45 | 3 | 40 | 2 |
| | | M | 107 | 5 | 96 | 5 | 49 | 4 | 43 | 2 |
| | | F | 96 | 4 | 88 | 4 | 40 | 2 | 37 | 1 |
| | 1995 | MF | 101 | 5 | 91 | 4 | 43 | 3 | 39 | 1 |
| | | M | 106 | 6 | 95 | 5 | 46 | 3 | 41 | 2 |
| | | F | 96 | 5 | 87 | 4 | 40 | 3 | 36 | 1 |
| | 1996 | MF | 101 | 5 | 91 | 4 | 42 | 3 | 38 | 1 |
| | | M | 106 | 6 | 95 | 5 | 45 | 3 | 40 | 2 |
| | | F | 96 | 5 | 87 | 3 | 40 | 3 | 36 | 1 |
| Turkey | 1985 | | (6-10) | (<6) | (6-10) | (>10) | (11-16) | (<11) | (11-16) | (>16) |
| | | MF | 113 | 2 | 98 | 13 | 42 | 0.8 | 36 | 5 |
| | 1990 | MF | 99 | 1 | 89 | 9 | 47 | 1 | 41 | 5 |
| | 1991 | MF | 100 | 1 | 91 | 8 | 49 | 0.9 | 43 | 5 |
| | 1992 | MF | 100 | 1 | 91 | 8 | 52 | 0.8 | 45 | 6 |
| | 1993 | MF | 102 | 0.9 | 94 | 7 | 53 | 0.6 | 47 | 5 |
| | | M | 104 | 0.8 | 96 | 8 | 63 | 0.7 | 55 | 7 |
| | | F | 99 | 0.9 | 92 | 6 | 43 | 0.5 | 39 | 4 |
| | 1994 | MF | 105 | 1 | 96 | 7 | 56 | 0.6 | 50 | 6 |
| | | M | 107 | 1 | 98 | 8 | 67 | 0.6 | 58 | 8 |
| | | F | 102 | 1 | 94 | 7 | 45 | 0.5 | 41 | 4 |
| | 1996 | MF | 107 | 1 | 99 | 7 | 58 | 0.6 | 51 | 6 |
| | | M | 111 | 1 | 102 | 8 | 68 | 0.7 | 59 | 8 |
| | | F | 104 | 1 | 96 | 6 | 48 | 0.5 | 43 | 4 |
| United Arab Emirates | 1980 | | (6-11) | (<6) | (6-11) | (>11) | (12-17) | (<12) | (12-17) | (>17) |
| | | MF | 89 | 4 | 74 | 12 | 52 | ... | ... | ... |
| | | M | 90 | 4 | 72 | 13 | 55 | ... | ... | ... |
| | | F | 88 | 3 | 75 | 10 | 49 | ... | ... | ... |

Primary and secondary education: enrolment ratios by age groups
Enseignements primaire et secondaire: taux de scolarisation par groupes d'âge
Enseñanza primaria y secundaria: tasas de escolarización por grupos de edad

II.9

| Country<br>Pays<br>País | Year<br>Année<br>Año | Sex<br>Sexe<br>Sexo | Primary education<br>Enseignement primaire<br>Enseñanza primaria | | | | Secondary education<br>Enseignement secondaire<br>Enseñanza secundaria | | | |
|---|---|---|---|---|---|---|---|---|---|---|
| | | | Gross enrolment ratios<br>Taux bruts de scolarisation<br>Tasas brutas de escolarización<br>(%) | Enrolment ratios by age groups<br>Taux de scolarisation par groupes d'âge<br>Tasas de escolarización por grupos de edad | | | Gross enrolment ratios<br>Taux bruts de scolarisation<br>Tasas brutas de escolarización<br>(%) | Enrolment ratios by age groups<br>Taux de scolarisation par groupes d'âge<br>Tasas de escolarización por grupos de edad | | |
| | | | | Under-age<br>En dessous de l'âge officiel<br>Inferior a la edad oficial<br>(%) | Official age group (NER)<br>Groupe d'âge officiel (TNS)<br>Grupo de edad oficial (TNE)<br>(%) | Over-age<br>Au-dessus de l'âge officiel<br>Superior a la edad oficial<br>(%) | | Under-age<br>En dessous de l'âge officiel<br>Inferior a la edad oficial<br>(%) | Official age group (NER)<br>Groupe d'âge officiel (TNS)<br>Grupo de edad oficial (TNE)<br>(%) | Over-age<br>Au-dessus de l'âge officiel<br>Superior a la edad oficial<br>(%) |
| United Arab Emirates (cont) | 1990 | | | | | | | | | |
| | | MF | 104 | 3 | 94 | 7 | 67 | 3 | 59 | 5 |
| | | M | 106 | 3 | 95 | 7 | 63 | 3 | 56 | 4 |
| | | F | 103 | 3 | 93 | 7 | 72 | 3 | 63 | 5 |
| | 1991 | | | | | | | | | |
| | | MF | 99 | 2 | 90 | 7 | 69 | 3 | 61 | 5 |
| | | M | 100 | 1 | 92 | 7 | 65 | 3 | 57 | 4 |
| | | F | 97 | 3 | 88 | 6 | 74 | 3 | 66 | 5 |
| | 1992 | | | | | | | | | |
| | | MF | 95 | 3 | 86 | 6 | 72 | 3 | 64 | 5 |
| | | M | 96 | 3 | 87 | 7 | 68 | 3 | 61 | 4 |
| | | F | 94 | 3 | 85 | 6 | 77 | 4 | 68 | 5 |
| | 1993 | | | | | | | | | |
| | | MF | 94 | 4 | 83 | 7 | 77 | 4 | 68 | 4 |
| | | M | 96 | 3 | 84 | 9 | 72 | 4 | 65 | 4 |
| | | F | 92 | 6 | 82 | 4 | 81 | 5 | 72 | 5 |
| | 1994 | | | | | | | | | |
| | | MF | 94 | 6 | 83 | 5 | 80 | 4 | 71 | 4 |
| | | M | 96 | 6 | 84 | 6 | 76 | 5 | 67 | 4 |
| | | F | 92 | 6 | 82 | 4 | 84 | 3 | 75 | 5 |
| | 1995 | | | | | | | | | |
| | | MF | 91 | 6 | 80 | 5 | 78 | ... | ... | ... |
| | | M | 92 | 6 | 80 | 5 | 74 | ... | ... | ... |
| | | F | 89 | 6 | 79 | 4 | 81 | ... | ... | ... |
| | 1996 | | | | | | | | | |
| | | MF | 89 | 6 | 78 | 5 | 80 | 4 | 71 | 5 |
| | | M | 91 | 6 | 79 | 6 | 77 | 4 | 68 | 5 |
| | | F | 87 | 6 | 78 | 4 | 82 | 4 | 74 | 4 |
| **Europe** | | | | | | | | | | |
| Albania | 1995 | | (6-13) | (<6) | (6-13) | (>13) | (14-17) | (<14) | (14-17) | (>17) |
| | | MF | 107 | 0.0 | 102 | 6 | 38 | ... | ... | ... |
| | | M | 106 | 0.0 | 100 | 6 | 37 | ... | ... | ... |
| | | F | 108 | 0.0 | 103 | 5 | 38 | ... | ... | ... |
| Austria | 1970 | | (6-9) | (<6) | (6-9) | (>9) | (10-17) | (<10) | (10-17) | (>17) |
| | | MF | 104 | 0.0 | 92 | 12 | 89 | 0.0 | 69 | 20 |
| | 1975 | | | | | | | | | |
| | | MF | 101 | 0.0 | 89 | 12 | 91 | 0.0 | 70 | 20 |
| | 1980 | | | | | | | | | |
| | | MF | 99 | 0.0 | 87 | 11 | 93 | ... | ... | ... |
| | | M | 99 | 0.0 | 87 | 12 | 98 | ... | ... | ... |
| | | F | 98 | 0.0 | 88 | 11 | 87 | ... | ... | ... |
| | 1992 | | | | | | | | | |
| | | MF | 103 | 0.0 | 90 | 13 | 107 | 0.0 | 91 | 15 |
| | | M | 103 | 0.0 | 89 | 14 | 109 | 0.0 | 91 | 18 |
| | | F | 103 | 0.0 | 91 | 12 | 104 | 0.0 | 91 | 13 |
| | 1993 | | | | | | | | | |
| | | MF | 102 | 0.0 | 89 | 13 | 106 | 0.0 | 91 | 15 |
| | | M | 102 | 0.0 | 88 | 14 | 109 | 0.0 | 91 | 18 |
| | | F | 102 | 0.0 | 90 | 12 | 104 | 0.0 | 91 | 12 |
| | 1994 | | | | | | | | | |
| | | MF | 102 | 0.0 | 89 | 13 | 105 | 0.0 | 91 | 14 |
| | | M | 101 | 0.0 | 88 | 14 | 108 | 0.0 | 91 | 17 |
| | | F | 102 | 0.0 | 90 | 12 | 103 | 0.0 | 91 | 12 |
| | 1995 | | | | | | | | | |
| | | MF | 101 | 0.0 | 88 | 13 | 104 | 0.0 | 89 | 15 |
| | | M | 101 | 0.0 | 87 | 14 | 106 | 0.0 | 89 | 18 |
| | | F | 101 | 0.0 | 90 | 12 | 102 | 0.0 | 89 | 13 |
| | 1996 | | | | | | | | | |
| | | MF | 100 | 0.0 | 87 | 13 | 103 | 0.0 | 88 | 15 |
| | | M | 100 | 0.0 | 86 | 14 | 105 | 0.0 | 88 | 17 |
| | | F | 100 | 0.0 | 89 | 12 | 102 | 0.0 | 89 | 13 |

II.9　Primary and secondary education: enrolment ratios by age groups
Enseignements primaire et secondaire: taux de scolarisation par groupes d'âge
Enseñanza primaria y secundaria: tasas de escolarización por grupos de edad

| Country / Pays / País | Year / Année / Año | Sex / Sexe / Sexo | Primary education / Enseignement primaire / Enseñanza primaria | | | | Secondary education / Enseignement secondaire / Enseñanza secundaria | | | |
|---|---|---|---|---|---|---|---|---|---|---|
| | | | Gross enrolment ratios / Taux bruts de scolarisation / Tasas brutas de escolarización (%) | Under-age / En dessous de l'âge officiel / Inferior a la edad oficial (%) | Official age group (NER) / Groupe d'âge officiel (TNS) / Grupo de edad oficial (TNE) (%) | Over-age / Au-dessus de l'âge officiel / Superior a la edad oficial (%) | Gross enrolment ratios / Taux bruts de scolarisation / Tasas brutas de escolarización (%) | Under-age / En dessous de l'âge officiel / Inferior a la edad oficial (%) | Official age group (NER) / Groupe d'âge officiel (TNS) / Grupo de edad oficial (TNE) (%) | Over-age / Au-dessus de l'âge officiel / Superior a la edad oficial (%) |
| Belarus | 1994 | | (6-9) | (<6) | (6-9) | (>9) | (10-16) | (<10) | (10-16) | (>16) |
| | | MF | 95 | 0.1 | 85 | 10 | 92 | ... | ... | ... |
| | | M | 97 | 0.1 | 87 | 10 | 90 | ... | ... | ... |
| | | F | 93 | 0.1 | 84 | 10 | 95 | ... | ... | ... |
| Belgium | 1980 | | (6-11) | (<6) | (6-11) | (>11) | (12-17) | (<12) | (12-17) | (>17) |
| | | MF | 104 | 0.4 | 97 | 6 | 91 | ... | ... | ... |
| | | M | 104 | 0.4 | 97 | 7 | 90 | ... | ... | ... |
| | | F | 104 | 0.4 | 98 | 5 | 92 | ... | ... | ... |
| | 1985 | MF | 99 | 0.3 | 94 | 4 | 101 | 0.3 | 89 | 13 |
| | | M | 99 | 0.3 | 94 | 5 | 101 | 0.2 | 87 | 14 |
| | | F | 99 | 0.4 | 95 | 4 | 102 | 0.3 | 90 | 11 |
| | 1990 | MF | 101 | 0.3 | 97 | 3 | 103 | 0.3 | 88 | 15 |
| | | M | 100 | 0.2 | 96 | 4 | 103 | 0.2 | 86 | 16 |
| | | F | 101 | 0.3 | 98 | 3 | 103 | 0.3 | 89 | 14 |
| | 1991 | MF | 99 | 0.3 | 96 | 4 | 104 | 0.3 | 88 | 15 |
| | | M | 99 | 0.3 | 95 | 4 | 103 | 0.2 | 87 | 16 |
| | | F | 100 | 0.4 | 96 | 3 | 104 | 0.3 | 90 | 14 |
| | 1992 | MF | 103 | 0.2 | 98 | 5 | 142 | 0.2 | 96 | 45 |
| | | M | 104 | 0.2 | 98 | 5 | 138 | 0.2 | 96 | 41 |
| | | F | 103 | 0.3 | 98 | 4 | 146 | 0.3 | 96 | 49 |
| | 1993 | MF | 103 | 0.2 | 98 | 5 | 144 | 0.2 | 98 | 46 |
| | | M | 103 | 0.2 | 98 | 5 | 140 | 0.2 | 98 | 42 |
| | | F | 102 | 0.3 | 98 | 4 | 149 | 0.3 | 98 | 50 |
| | 1994 | MF | 103 | 0.2 | 98 | 5 | 146 | 0.2 | 99 | 47 |
| | | M | 103 | 0.2 | 98 | 5 | 141 | 0.2 | 99 | 42 |
| | | F | 102 | 0.3 | 98 | 4 | 151 | 0.3 | 99 | 52 |
| | 1995 | MF | 103 | 0.2 | 98 | 4 | 146 | 13 | 88 | 45 |
| | | M | 104 | 0.2 | 99 | 5 | 142 | 13 | 89 | 40 |
| | | F | 102 | 0.3 | 98 | 4 | 151 | 13 | 87 | 51 |
| Bulgaria | 1970 | | (7-14) | (<7) | (7-14) | (>14) | (15-17) | (<15) | (15-17) | (>17) |
| | | MF | 101 | 1 | 97 | 3 | 79 | 2 | 55 | 22 |
| | | M | 101 | 1 | 97 | 4 | 80 | 1 | 52 | 26 |
| | | F | 100 | 1 | 96 | 3 | 78 | 2 | 59 | 17 |
| | 1975 | MF | 99 | 0.2 | 96 | 2 | 89 | 3 | 68 | 18 |
| | | M | 99 | 0.2 | 96 | 3 | 89 | ... | ... | ... |
| | | F | 99 | 0.3 | 97 | 2 | 89 | ... | ... | ... |
| | 1980 | MF | 98 | 0.6 | 96 | 0.9 | 84 | 4 | 73 | 8 |
| | | M | 98 | 0.5 | 96 | 1 | 85 | 3 | 73 | 9 |
| | | F | 98 | 0.6 | 96 | 0.7 | 84 | 4 | 72 | 8 |
| | 1990 | | (6-13) | (<6) | (6-13) | (>13) | (14-17) | (<14) | (14-17) | (>17) |
| | | MF | 98 | 0.0 | 86 | 11 | 75 | 0.3 | 63 | 12 |
| | | M | 99 | 0.0 | 86 | 12 | 74 | 0.2 | 62 | 12 |
| | | F | 96 | 0.0 | 86 | 10 | 77 | 0.4 | 65 | 12 |
| | 1991 | MF | 95 | 0.0 | 84 | 11 | 74 | 0.5 | 64 | 10 |
| | | M | 97 | 0.0 | 85 | 11 | 72 | 0.3 | 62 | 10 |
| | | F | 94 | 0.0 | 83 | 10 | 75 | 0.6 | 65 | 10 |
| | 1992 | MF | 92 | 0.0 | 82 | 10 | 72 | 0.8 | 63 | 9 |
| | | M | 94 | 0.0 | 83 | 11 | 71 | 0.5 | 61 | 9 |
| | | F | 91 | 0.0 | 82 | 9 | 74 | 1 | 64 | 9 |

Primary and secondary education: enrolment ratios by age groups  II.9
Enseignements primaire et secondaire: taux de scolarisation par groupes d'âge
Enseñanza primaria y secundaria: tasas de escolarización por grupos de edad

| Country / Pays / País | Year / Année / Año | Sex / Sexe / Sexo | Primary education / Enseignement primaire / Enseñanza primaria | | | | Secondary education / Enseignement secondaire / Enseñanza secundaria | | | |
|---|---|---|---|---|---|---|---|---|---|---|
| | | | Gross enrolment ratios / Taux bruts de scolarisation / Tasas brutas de escolarización (%) | Enrolment ratios by age groups — Under-age / En dessous de l'âge officiel / Inferior a la edad oficial (%) | Official age group (NER) / Groupe d'âge officiel (TNS) / Grupo de edad oficial (TNE) (%) | Over-age / Au-dessus de l'âge officiel / Superior a la edad oficial (%) | Gross enrolment ratios / Taux bruts de scolarisation / Tasas brutas de escolarización (%) | Under-age / En dessous de l'âge officiel / Inferior a la edad oficial (%) | Official age group (NER) / Groupe d'âge officiel (TNS) / Grupo de edad oficial (TNE) (%) | Over-age / Au-dessus de l'âge officiel / Superior a la edad oficial (%) |
| Bulgaria (cont) | 1993 | | (7-14) | (<7) | (7-14) | (>14) | (15-18) | (<15) | (15-18) | (>18) |
| | | MF | 89 | 1 | 85 | 2 | 70 | 9 | 59 | 2 |
| | | M | 90 | 1 | 86 | 3 | 68 | 8 | 59 | 2 |
| | | F | 87 | 2 | 84 | 1 | 72 | 11 | 60 | 1 |
| | 1994 | | | | | | | | | |
| | | MF | 89 | 1 | 86 | 2 | 72 | 10 | 60 | 2 |
| | | M | 91 | 1 | 87 | 3 | 70 | 9 | 59 | 2 |
| | | F | 07 | I | 84 | 1 | 74 | 12 | 60 | 3 |
| | 1995 | | (7-10) | (<7) | (7-10) | (>10) | (11-18) | (<11) | (11-18) | (>18) |
| | | MF | 97 | 3 | 90 | 4 | 78 | 2 | 75 | 1 |
| | | M | 98 | 2 | 91 | 4 | 78 | ... | ... | ... |
| | | F | 96 | 3 | 89 | 4 | 77 | ... | ... | ... |
| | 1996 | | | | | | | | | |
| | | MF | 99 | 2 | 92 | 5 | 77 | 1 | 74 | 1 |
| | | M | 100 | 2 | 93 | 5 | 77 | ... | ... | ... |
| | | F | 98 | 2 | 91 | 4 | 76 | ... | ... | ... |
| Croatia | 1990 | | (7-14) | (<7) | (7-14) | (>14) | (15-18) | (<15) | (15-18) | (>18) |
| | | MF | 85 | 0.0 | 79 | 6 | 76 | 2 | 63 | 11 |
| | | M | 85 | 0.0 | 79 | 6 | 73 | 2 | 60 | 10 |
| | | F | 84 | 0.0 | 79 | 6 | 80 | 3 | 66 | 11 |
| | 1994 | | | | | | | | | |
| | | MF | 86 | 3 | 82 | 0.8 | 78 | 12 | 66 | 0.6 |
| | | M | 87 | 3 | 83 | 0.9 | 75 | 11 | 63 | 0.7 |
| | | F | 86 | 3 | 82 | 0.6 | 81 | 13 | 68 | 0.4 |
| Czech Republic | 1993 | | (6-9) | (<6) | (6-9) | (>9) | (10-17) | (<10) | (10-17) | (>17) |
| | | MF | 101 | 0.0 | 91 | 10 | 92 | 0.0 | 86 | 6 |
| | | M | 101 | 0.0 | 91 | 10 | 91 | 0.0 | 86 | 5 |
| | | F | 101 | 0.0 | 91 | 10 | 92 | 0.0 | 86 | 6 |
| | 1994 | | | | | | | | | |
| | | MF | 102 | 0.0 | 91 | 11 | 95 | 0.0 | 88 | 7 |
| | | M | 103 | 0.0 | 92 | 11 | 94 | 0.0 | 87 | 7 |
| | | F | 102 | 0.0 | 91 | 11 | 97 | 0.0 | 89 | 8 |
| | 1995 | | | | | | | | | |
| | | MF | 104 | ... | ... | ... | 99 | 0.0 | 87 | 12 |
| | | M | 105 | ... | ... | ... | 97 | 0.0 | 86 | 11 |
| | | F | 103 | ... | ... | ... | 100 | 0.0 | 89 | 12 |
| Denmark | 1980 | | (7-12) | (<7) | (7-12) | (>12) | (13-18) | (<13) | (13-18) | (>18) |
| | | MF | 95 | 0.0 | 95 | 0.0 | 105 | 0.7 | 88 | 16 |
| | | M | 96 | 0.0 | 96 | 0.0 | 105 | 0.6 | 87 | 18 |
| | | F | 95 | 0.0 | 95 | 0.0 | 104 | 0.7 | 89 | 14 |
| | 1985 | | | | | | | | | |
| | | MF | 99 | 0.0 | 99 | 0.0 | 105 | 1 | 83 | 21 |
| | | M | 99 | 0.0 | 99 | 0.0 | 106 | 1 | 82 | 22 |
| | | F | 98 | 0.0 | 98 | 0.0 | 105 | 2 | 84 | 20 |
| | 1990 | | | | | | | | | |
| | | MF | 98 | 0.0 | 98 | 0.0 | 109 | 0.6 | 87 | 22 |
| | | M | 98 | 0.0 | 98 | 0.0 | 109 | 0.5 | 86 | 22 |
| | | F | 98 | 0.0 | 98 | 0.0 | 110 | 0.8 | 88 | 21 |
| | 1991 | | | | | | | | | |
| | | MF | 97 | 0.0 | 97 | 0.0 | 110 | 0.6 | 87 | 23 |
| | | M | 97 | 0.0 | 97 | 0.0 | 109 | 0.5 | 86 | 23 |
| | | F | 97 | 0.0 | 97 | 0.0 | 111 | 0.8 | 88 | 22 |
| | 1992 | | | | | | | | | |
| | | MF | 97 | 0.6 | 96 | 1 | 112 | 0.6 | 87 | 25 |
| | | M | 97 | 0.6 | 96 | 1 | 111 | 0.6 | 86 | 24 |
| | | F | 98 | 0.6 | 96 | 1 | 113 | 0.6 | 88 | 25 |
| | 1993 | | | | | | | | | |
| | | MF | 99 | 0.7 | 98 | 1 | 115 | 0.6 | 88 | 27 |
| | | M | 99 | 0.7 | 98 | 1 | 114 | 0.6 | 86 | 27 |
| | | F | 100 | 0.7 | 98 | 1 | 116 | 0.6 | 89 | 27 |

II.9    Primary and secondary education: enrolment ratios by age groups
Enseignements primaire et secondaire: taux de scolarisation par groupes d'âge
Enseñanza primaria y secundaria: tasas de escolarización por grupos de edad

| Country / Pays / País | Year / Année / Año | Sex / Sexe / Sexo | Primary education / Enseignement primaire / Enseñanza primaria | | | | Secondary education / Enseignement secondaire / Enseñanza secundaria | | | |
|---|---|---|---|---|---|---|---|---|---|---|
| | | | Gross enrolment ratios / Taux bruts de scolarisation / Tasas brutas de escolarización (%) | Enrolment ratios by age groups / Taux de scolarisation par groupes d'âge / Tasas de escolarización por grupos de edad | | | Gross enrolment ratios / Taux bruts de scolarisation / Tasas brutas de escolarización (%) | Enrolment ratios by age groups / Taux de scolarisation par groupes d'âge / Tasas de escolarización por grupos de edad | | |
| | | | | Under-age / En dessous de l'âge officiel / Inferior a la edad oficial (%) | Official age group (NER) / Groupe d'âge officiel (TNS) / Grupo de edad oficial (TNE) (%) | Over-age / Au-dessus de l'âge officiel / Superior a la edad oficial (%) | | Under-age / En dessous de l'âge officiel / Inferior a la edad oficial (%) | Official age group (NER) / Groupe d'âge officiel (TNS) / Grupo de edad oficial (TNE) (%) | Over-age / Au-dessus de l'âge officiel / Superior a la edad oficial (%) |
| Denmark (cont) | 1994 | | | | | | | | | |
| | | MF | 100 | 0.8 | 98 | 1 | 119 | 0.7 | 87 | 31 |
| | | M | 100 | 0.6 | 98 | 2 | 117 | 0.5 | 86 | 31 |
| | | F | 100 | 1 | 98 | 1 | 120 | 0.8 | 89 | 31 |
| | 1995 | | | | | | | | | |
| | | MF | 101 | 0.8 | 99 | 2 | 121 | 0.7 | 88 | 33 |
| | | M | 102 | 0.5 | 99 | 2 | 120 | 0.5 | 87 | 33 |
| | | F | 101 | 1 | 99 | 1 | 122 | 1 | 89 | 33 |
| Estonia | 1992 | | (7-11) | (<7) | (7-11) | (>11) | (12-17) | (<12) | (12-17) | (>17) |
| | | MF | 105 | 4 | 94 | 6 | 94 | 0.5 | 82 | 11 |
| | | M | 106 | 4 | 94 | 7 | 91 | 0.5 | 79 | 11 |
| | | F | 103 | 5 | 94 | 4 | 98 | 0.5 | 85 | 12 |
| | 1993 | | | | | | | | | |
| | | MF | 103 | 4 | 93 | 6 | 94 | 0.6 | 82 | 11 |
| | | M | 104 | 4 | 92 | 8 | 88 | 0.6 | 79 | 9 |
| | | F | 102 | 5 | 93 | 4 | 100 | 0.7 | 86 | 13 |
| | 1994 | | | | | | | | | |
| | | MF | 104 | 3 | 92 | 9 | 96 | ... | ... | ... |
| | | M | 105 | 2 | 92 | 11 | 91 | ... | ... | ... |
| | | F | 102 | 4 | 92 | 6 | 101 | ... | ... | ... |
| | 1995 | | (7-12) | (<7) | (7-12) | (>12) | (13-17) | (<13) | (13-17) | (>17) |
| | | MF | 91 | 2 | 87 | 2 | 104 | 10 | 83 | 10 |
| | | M | 92 | 2 | 87 | 3 | 99 | 9 | 80 | 9 |
| | | F | 90 | 3 | 86 | 1 | 109 | 12 | 86 | 11 |
| Federal Republic of Yugoslavia | 1990 | | (7-10) | (<7) | (7-10) | (>10) | (11-18) | (<11) | (11-18) | (>18) |
| | | MF | 72 | 2 | 69 | 0.6 | 63 | 1 | 62 | 0.2 |
| | | M | 71 | 2 | 69 | 0.6 | 62 | 1 | 61 | 0.2 |
| | | F | 73 | 2 | 70 | 0.6 | 64 | 1 | 63 | 0.1 |
| Finland | 1970 | | (7-12) | (<7) | (7-12) | (>12) | (13-18) | (<13) | (13-18) | (>18) |
| | | MF | 82 | ... | ... | ... | 102 | 15 | 71 | 16 |
| | 1990 | | | | | | | | | |
| | | MF | 99 | ... | ... | ... | 116 | 0.1 | 93 | 23 |
| | | M | 99 | ... | ... | ... | 106 | 0.0 | 92 | 14 |
| | | F | 99 | ... | ... | ... | 127 | 0.1 | 94 | 33 |
| | 1992 | | | | | | | | | |
| | | MF | 99 | 0.2 | 99 | 0.4 | 118 | 0.1 | 96 | 22 |
| | | M | 100 | 0.2 | 99 | 0.4 | 108 | 0.1 | 95 | 13 |
| | | F | 99 | 0.1 | 99 | 0.3 | 128 | 0.1 | 97 | 31 |
| | 1993 | | | | | | | | | |
| | | MF | 100 | 0.1 | 99 | 0.5 | 118 | 0.1 | 96 | 23 |
| | | M | 100 | 0.1 | 99 | 0.7 | 109 | 0.0 | 95 | 14 |
| | | F | 100 | 0.1 | 99 | 0.3 | 128 | 0.1 | 96 | 31 |
| | 1994 | | | | | | | | | |
| | | MF | 99 | 0.1 | 99 | 0.5 | 116 | 0.1 | 93 | 23 |
| | | M | 100 | 0.1 | 99 | 0.7 | 108 | 0.0 | 92 | 16 |
| | | F | 99 | 0.1 | 99 | 0.4 | 124 | 0.1 | 93 | 31 |
| | 1995 | | | | | | | | | |
| | | MF | 99 | 0.1 | 99 | 0.5 | 116 | 0.1 | 93 | 23 |
| | | M | 99 | 0.1 | 98 | 0.7 | 107 | 0.0 | 92 | 15 |
| | | F | 99 | 0.1 | 99 | 0.4 | 125 | 0.1 | 94 | 32 |
| | 1996 | | | | | | | | | |
| | | MF | 99 | 0.1 | 98 | 0.3 | 118 | 0.1 | 93 | 24 |
| | | M | 98 | 0.2 | 98 | 0.3 | 110 | 0.1 | 93 | 18 |
| | | F | 99 | 0.1 | 98 | 0.3 | 125 | 0.1 | 94 | 31 |
| France | 1970 | | (6-10) | (<6) | (6-10) | (>10) | (11-17) | (<11) | (11-17) | (>17) |
| | | MF | 117 | 1 | 98 | 18 | 73 | 0.8 | 66 | 6 |
| | | M | 117 | 1 | 98 | 19 | 70 | 0.8 | 63 | 6 |
| | | F | 116 | 1 | 98 | 17 | 76 | 0.9 | 70 | 6 |
| | 1975 | | | | | | | | | |
| | | MF | 109 | 0.8 | 98 | 11 | 82 | 0.7 | 76 | 5 |

Primary and secondary education: enrolment ratios by age groups
Enseignements primaire et secondaire: taux de scolarisation par groupes d'âge
Enseñanza primaria y secundaria: tasas de escolarización por grupos de edad

II.9

| Country / Pays / País | Year / Année / Año | Sex / Sexe / Sexo | Primary education / Enseignement primaire / Enseñanza primaria | | | | Secondary education / Enseignement secondaire / Enseñanza secundaria | | | |
|---|---|---|---|---|---|---|---|---|---|---|
| | | | Gross enrolment ratios / Taux bruts de scolarisation / Tasas brutas de escolarización (%) | Enrolment ratios by age groups / Taux de scolarisation par groupes d'âge / Tasas de escolarización por grupos de edad | | | Gross enrolment ratios / Taux bruts de scolarisation / Tasas brutas de escolarización (%) | Enrolment ratios by age groups / Taux de scolarisation par groupes d'âge / Tasas de escolarización por grupos de edad | | |
| | | | | Under-age / En dessous de l'âge officiel / Inferior a la edad oficial (%) | Official age group (NER) / Groupe d'âge officiel (TNS) / Grupo de edad oficial (TNE) (%) | Over-age / Au-dessus de l'âge officiel / Superior a la edad oficial (%) | | Under-age / En dessous de l'âge officiel / Inferior a la edad oficial (%) | Official age group (NER) / Groupe d'âge officiel (TNS) / Grupo de edad oficial (TNE) (%) | Over-age / Au-dessus de l'âge officiel / Superior a la edad oficial (%) |
| France (cont) | 1980 | MF | 111 | 0.5 | 100 | 11 | 85 | 0.5 | 79 | 5 |
| | 1985 | MF | 109 | 0.5 | 97 | 11 | 90 | 0.3 | 82 | 8 |
| | | M | 110 | 0.4 | 97 | 12 | 86 | 0.3 | 78 | 8 |
| | | F | 107 | 0.6 | 97 | 10 | 94 | 0.4 | 85 | 9 |
| | 1990 | MF | 108 | 0.4 | 101 | 7 | 99 | ... | ... | ... |
| | | M | 109 | 0.3 | 101 | 8 | 96 | ... | ... | ... |
| | | F | 108 | 0.5 | 101 | 6 | 101 | ... | ... | ... |
| | 1991 | MF | 107 | 0.4 | 100 | 7 | 101 | 0.4 | 86 | 15 |
| | | M | 108 | 0.3 | 100 | 8 | 99 | 0.4 | 84 | 15 |
| | | F | 106 | 0.5 | 100 | 6 | 104 | 0.5 | 88 | 15 |
| | 1992 | MF | 106 | 0.3 | 99 | 6 | 102 | 0.4 | 87 | 15 |
| | | M | 107 | 0.3 | 99 | 7 | 100 | 0.4 | 85 | 15 |
| | | F | 105 | 0.4 | 99 | 5 | 104 | 0.5 | 89 | 15 |
| | 1993 | MF | 106 | 0.4 | 99 | 7 | 110 | 0.5 | 92 | 17 |
| | | M | 107 | 0.4 | 99 | 8 | 110 | 0.4 | 92 | 18 |
| | | F | 105 | 0.5 | 99 | 6 | 110 | 0.5 | 93 | 16 |
| | 1994 | MF | 106 | 0.4 | 100 | 6 | 111 | 0.5 | 94 | 17 |
| | | M | 107 | 0.3 | 100 | 7 | 112 | 0.4 | 93 | 18 |
| | | F | 105 | 0.4 | 99 | 5 | 111 | 0.5 | 94 | 16 |
| | 1995 | MF | 106 | 0.3 | 100 | 6 | 111 | 0.5 | 94 | 16 |
| | | M | 107 | 0.2 | 100 | 7 | 112 | 0.4 | 94 | 17 |
| | | F | 105 | 0.4 | 100 | 5 | 111 | 0.6 | 95 | 15 |
| | 1996 | MF | 105 | 0.3 | 100 | 5 | 111 | 0.5 | 95 | 16 |
| | | M | 106 | 0.2 | 100 | 6 | 112 | 0.4 | 94 | 17 |
| | | F | 104 | 0.4 | 100 | 4 | 111 | 0.6 | 95 | 15 |
| Germany | 1992 | | (6-9) | (<6) | (6-9) | (>9) | (10-18) | (<10) | (10-18) | (>18) |
| | | MF | 100 | 0.0 | 84 | 17 | 106 | 0.0 | 89 | 17 |
| | | M | 101 | 0.0 | 83 | 18 | 107 | 0.0 | 89 | 18 |
| | | F | 100 | 0.0 | 84 | 16 | 104 | 0.0 | 89 | 15 |
| | 1993 | MF | 100 | 0.0 | 83 | 17 | 106 | 0.0 | 90 | 16 |
| | | M | 100 | 0.0 | 82 | 18 | 107 | 0.0 | 90 | 18 |
| | | F | 99 | 0.0 | 84 | 16 | 104 | 0.0 | 90 | 15 |
| | 1994 | MF | 100 | 0.0 | 83 | 17 | 105 | 0.0 | 89 | 15 |
| | | M | 101 | 0.0 | 83 | 18 | 106 | 0.0 | 89 | 17 |
| | | F | 100 | 0.0 | 84 | 16 | 103 | 0.0 | 89 | 14 |
| | 1995 | MF | 102 | 0.0 | 85 | 17 | 104 | 0.0 | 89 | 15 |
| | | M | 102 | 0.0 | 84 | 18 | 105 | 0.0 | 89 | 16 |
| | | F | 102 | 0.0 | 86 | 16 | 103 | 0.0 | 89 | 14 |
| | 1996 | MF | 104 | 0.0 | 86 | 18 | 104 | 0.0 | 88 | 15 |
| | | M | 104 | 0.0 | 86 | 19 | 105 | 0.0 | 88 | 16 |
| | | F | 104 | 0.0 | 87 | 16 | 103 | 0.0 | 89 | 14 |
| Greece | 1970 | | (6-11) | (<6) | (6-11) | (>11) | (12-17) | (<12) | (12-17) | (>17) |
| | | MF | 107 | 5 | 97 | 5 | 63 | 2 | 52 | 9 |
| | | M | 108 | 5 | 97 | 6 | 70 | 2 | 56 | 12 |
| | | F | 106 | 5 | 97 | 4 | 55 | 2 | 48 | 5 |
| | 1975 | MF | 104 | 4 | 97 | 3 | 78 | 3 | 64 | 11 |
| | | M | 105 | 4 | 97 | 4 | 87 | 3 | 68 | 15 |
| | | F | 104 | 4 | 97 | 3 | 69 | 3 | 59 | 6 |

II.9    Primary and secondary education: enrolment ratios by age groups
Enseignements primaire et secondaire: taux de scolarisation par groupes d'âge
Enseñanza primaria y secundaria: tasas de escolarización por grupos de edad

| Country / Pays / País | Year / Année / Año | Sex / Sexe / Sexo | Primary education / Enseignement primaire / Enseñanza primaria | | | | Secondary education / Enseignement secondaire / Enseñanza secundaria | | | |
|---|---|---|---|---|---|---|---|---|---|---|
| | | | Gross enrolment ratios / Taux bruts de scolarisation / Tasas brutas de escolarización (%) | Under-age / En dessous de l'âge officiel / Inferior a la edad oficial (%) | Official age group (NER) / Groupe d'âge officiel (TNS) / Grupo de edad oficial (TNE) (%) | Over-age / Au-dessus de l'âge officiel / Superior a la edad oficial (%) | Gross enrolment ratios / Taux bruts de scolarisation / Tasas brutas de escolarización (%) | Under-age / En dessous de l'âge officiel / Inferior a la edad oficial (%) | Official age group (NER) / Groupe d'âge officiel (TNS) / Grupo de edad oficial (TNE) (%) | Over-age / Au-dessus de l'âge officiel / Superior a la edad oficial (%) |
| Greece (cont) | 1980 | | | | | | | | | |
| | | MF | 103 | 4 | 96 | 2 | 81 | ... | ... | ... |
| | | M | 103 | 4 | 96 | 2 | 85 | ... | ... | ... |
| | | F | 103 | 4 | 97 | 2 | 77 | ... | ... | ... |
| | 1985 | | | | | | | | | |
| | | MF | 104 | 4 | 99 | 0.9 | 90 | 4 | 81 | 6 |
| | | M | 104 | 4 | 99 | 1 | 92 | 4 | 81 | 7 |
| | | F | 104 | 4 | 99 | 0.8 | 89 | 4 | 81 | 4 |
| | 1990 | | | | | | | | | |
| | | MF | 98 | 3 | 94 | 0.4 | 93 | 4 | 83 | 7 |
| | | M | 98 | 3 | 94 | 0.4 | 94 | 4 | 82 | 8 |
| | | F | 98 | 3 | 94 | 0.4 | 92 | 4 | 83 | 5 |
| | 1991 | | | | | | | | | |
| | | MF | 96 | 3 | 93 | 0.4 | 95 | 4 | 84 | 8 |
| | | M | 97 | 3 | 93 | 0.5 | 96 | 4 | 83 | 9 |
| | | F | 96 | 3 | 92 | 0.4 | 95 | 4 | 84 | 6 |
| | 1992 | | | | | | | | | |
| | | MF | 95 | 3 | 91 | 0.4 | 93 | 4 | 82 | 7 |
| | | M | 95 | 3 | 92 | 0.5 | 93 | 4 | 81 | 8 |
| | | F | 94 | 3 | 91 | 0.4 | 93 | 4 | 84 | 6 |
| | 1993 | | | | | | | | | |
| | | MF | 94 | 3 | 91 | 0.6 | 94 | 4 | 83 | 7 |
| | | M | 95 | 3 | 92 | 0.6 | 97 | 4 | 84 | 9 |
| | | F | 94 | 3 | 90 | 0.5 | 92 | 4 | 83 | 6 |
| | 1994 | | | | | | | | | |
| | | MF | 96 | 3 | 92 | 0.5 | 95 | 4 | 85 | 6 |
| | | M | 96 | 3 | 91 | 0.6 | 95 | 4 | 86 | 5 |
| | | F | 96 | 3 | 92 | 0.4 | 94 | 4 | 84 | 7 |
| | 1995 | | | | | | | | | |
| | | MF | 94 | 3 | 90 | 0.4 | 95 | 3 | 86 | 6 |
| | | M | 94 | 3 | 90 | 0.5 | 95 | 3 | 85 | 7 |
| | | F | 94 | 3 | 90 | 0.3 | 96 | 3 | 88 | 5 |
| | 1996 | | | | | | | | | |
| | | MF | 93 | 2 | 90 | 1 | 95 | 3 | 87 | 6 |
| | | M | 93 | 2 | 90 | 1 | 95 | 3 | 85 | 7 |
| | | F | 93 | 2 | 90 | 1 | 96 | 3 | 88 | 5 |
| Hungary | 1970 | | (6-13) | (<6) | (6-13) | (>13) | (14-17) | (<14) | (14-17) | (>17) |
| | | MF | 98 | 0.3 | 94 | 4 | 63 | 0.0 | 31 | 33 |
| | | M | 98 | 0.0 | 94 | 4 | 71 | 0.0 | 25 | 46 |
| | | F | 97 | 0.0 | 94 | 3 | 55 | 0.0 | 37 | 18 |
| | 1980 | | | | | | | | | |
| | | MF | 96 | 0.2 | 95 | 2 | 70 | ... | ... | ... |
| | | M | 96 | 0.2 | 94 | 2 | 72 | ... | ... | ... |
| | | F | 97 | 0.2 | 95 | 1 | 67 | ... | ... | ... |
| | 1985 | | | | | | | | | |
| | | MF | 99 | 0.0 | 97 | 2 | 72 | 0.1 | 70 | 2 |
| | | M | 99 | 0.0 | 97 | 2 | 72 | 0.1 | 69 | 3 |
| | | F | 99 | 0.1 | 98 | 1 | 72 | 0.2 | 70 | 2 |
| | 1990 | | | | | | | | | |
| | | MF | 95 | 0.6 | 91 | 3 | 79 | 0.1 | 75 | 4 |
| | | M | 95 | 0.5 | 91 | 3 | 78 | 0.1 | 73 | 5 |
| | | F | 95 | 0.7 | 92 | 2 | 79 | 0.2 | 76 | 2 |
| | 1991 | | | | | | | | | |
| | | MF | 94 | 0.6 | 90 | 3 | 80 | 0.1 | 76 | 4 |
| | | M | 94 | 0.5 | 90 | 4 | 80 | 0.1 | 75 | 5 |
| | | F | 94 | 0.7 | 91 | 2 | 81 | 0.1 | 78 | 3 |
| | 1993 | | (6-9) | (<6) | (6-9) | (>9) | (10-17) | (<10) | (10-17) | (>17) |
| | | MF | 102 | ... | ... | ... | 94 | 0.0 | 83 | 11 |
| | 1994 | | | | | | | | | |
| | | MF | 103 | ... | ... | ... | 96 | 0.0 | 83 | 13 |

Primary and secondary education: enrolment ratios by age groups  II.9
Enseignements primaire et secondaire: taux de scolarisation par groupes d'âge
Enseñanza primaria y secundaria: tasas de escolarización por grupos de edad

| Country | Year | Sex | Primary education Enseignement primaire Enseñanza primaria | | | | Secondary education Enseignement secondaire Enseñanza secundaria | | | |
| | | | | Enrolment ratios by age groups Taux de scolarisation par groupes d'âge Tasas de escolarización por grupos de edad | | | | Enrolment ratios by age groups Taux de scolarisation par groupes d'âge Tasas de escolarización por grupos de edad | | |
| | | | Gross enrolment ratios | Under-age | Official age group (NER) | Over-age | Gross enrolment ratios | Under-age | Official age group (NER) | Over-age |
| Pays | Année | Sexe | Taux bruts de scolarisation | En dessous de l'âge officiel | Groupe d'âge officiel (TNS) | Au-dessus de l'âge officiel | Taux bruts de scolarisation | En dessous de l'âge officiel | Groupe d'âge officiel (TNS) | Au-dessus de l'âge officiel |
| País | Año | Sexo | Tasas brutas de escolarización | Inferior a la edad oficial | Grupo de edad oficial (TNE) | Superior a la edad oficial | Tasas brutas de escolarización | Inferior a la edad oficial | Grupo de edad oficial (TNE) | Superior a la edad oficial |
| | | | (%) | (%) | (%) | (%) | (%) | (%) | (%) | (%) |
|---|---|---|---|---|---|---|---|---|---|---|
| Hungary (cont) | 1995 | | | | | | | | | |
| | | MF | 103 | 0.6 | 97 | 6 | 98 | 0.0 | 86 | 12 |
| | | M | 104 | 0.5 | 97 | 6 | 96 | 0.0 | 85 | 11 |
| | | F | 102 | 0.8 | 96 | 6 | 99 | 0.0 | 87 | 12 |
| Iceland | 1993 | | (6-12) | (<6) | (6-12) | (>12) | (13-19) | (<13) | (13-19) | (>19) |
| | | MF | 98 | 0.1 | 98 | 0.0 | 103 | 0.0 | 85 | 18 |
| | | M | 98 | 0.1 | 98 | 0.0 | 104 | 0.0 | 84 | 20 |
| | | F | 97 | 0.0 | 97 | 0.0 | 102 | 0.0 | 87 | 15 |
| | 1995 | | | | | | | | | |
| | | MF | 98 | 0.0 | 98 | 0.0 | 104 | 0.0 | 87 | 17 |
| | | M | 98 | 0.0 | 98 | 0.0 | 105 | 0.0 | 86 | 19 |
| | | F | 98 | 0.0 | 98 | 0.0 | 102 | 0.0 | 88 | 15 |
| | 1996 | | | | | | | | | |
| | | MF | 98 | 0.0 | 98 | 0.0 | 109 | ... | ... | ... |
| | | M | 98 | 0.0 | 98 | 0.0 | 109 | ... | ... | ... |
| | | F | 98 | 0.0 | 98 | 0.0 | 108 | ... | ... | ... |
| Ireland | 1970 | | (6-11) | (<6) | (6-11) | (>11) | (12-16) | (<12) | (12-16) | (>16) |
| | | MF | 107 | 0.0 | 93 | 14 | 74 | 0.5 | 63 | 10 |
| | | M | 107 | 0.0 | 93 | 15 | 71 | 0.5 | 62 | 9 |
| | | F | 107 | 0.0 | 94 | 13 | 77 | 0.5 | 65 | 11 |
| | 1975 | | | | | | | | | |
| | | MF | 104 | 0.2 | 92 | 12 | 87 | 0.4 | 75 | 12 |
| | | M | 104 | 0.2 | 92 | 12 | 83 | 0.4 | 73 | 10 |
| | | F | 104 | 0.3 | 93 | 11 | 91 | 0.4 | 77 | 13 |
| | 1980 | | | | | | | | | |
| | | MF | 100 | 0.1 | 90 | 10 | 90 | 0.3 | 78 | 12 |
| | | M | 100 | 0.1 | 89 | 10 | 85 | 0.3 | 75 | 9 |
| | | F | 100 | 0.2 | 91 | 9 | 95 | 0.2 | 80 | 15 |
| | 1985 | | | | | | | | | |
| | | MF | 100 | 0.1 | 89 | 11 | 98 | 0.1 | 81 | 16 |
| | | M | 100 | 0.1 | 88 | 12 | 93 | 0.2 | 79 | 14 |
| | | F | 100 | 0.2 | 89 | 10 | 103 | 0.1 | 84 | 19 |
| | 1990 | | | | | | | | | |
| | | MF | 103 | 0.0 | 91 | 12 | 101 | 0.1 | 80 | 21 |
| | | M | 103 | 0.0 | 90 | 13 | 96 | 0.1 | 78 | 18 |
| | | F | 103 | 0.0 | 91 | 12 | 105 | 0.0 | 82 | 23 |
| | 1991 | | | | | | | | | |
| | | MF | 103 | 0.0 | 90 | 12 | 103 | 0.0 | 81 | 22 |
| | | M | 103 | 0.0 | 90 | 13 | 98 | 0.0 | 79 | 19 |
| | | F | 103 | 0.0 | 91 | 12 | 107 | 0.0 | 83 | 24 |
| | 1992 | | | | | | | | | |
| | | MF | 104 | 0.0 | 91 | 13 | 111 | 0.0 | 85 | 27 |
| | | M | 104 | 0.0 | 90 | 14 | 109 | 0.0 | 82 | 27 |
| | | F | 104 | 0.0 | 91 | 12 | 114 | 0.0 | 87 | 27 |
| | 1993 | | | | | | | | | |
| | | MF | 104 | 0.0 | 91 | 13 | 113 | 0.0 | 85 | 29 |
| | | M | 104 | 0.0 | 90 | 14 | 111 | 0.0 | 83 | 28 |
| | | F | 104 | 0.0 | 91 | 12 | 116 | 0.0 | 87 | 30 |
| | 1994 | | | | | | | | | |
| | | MF | 104 | 0.0 | 91 | 13 | 115 | 0.0 | 86 | 29 |
| | | M | 104 | 0.0 | 90 | 14 | 112 | 0.0 | 84 | 28 |
| | | F | 104 | 0.0 | 92 | 13 | 118 | 0.0 | 88 | 31 |
| | 1995 | | | | | | | | | |
| | | MF | 104 | 0.0 | 91 | 13 | 116 | 0.0 | 86 | 29 |
| | | M | 104 | 0.0 | 90 | 14 | 112 | 0.0 | 84 | 27 |
| | | F | 104 | 0.0 | 92 | 12 | 120 | 0.0 | 89 | 31 |
| | 1996 | | | | | | | | | |
| | | MF | 104 | 0.0 | 92 | 13 | 118 | 0.0 | 86 | 32 |
| | | M | 105 | 0.0 | 91 | 13 | 113 | 0.0 | 84 | 29 |
| | | F | 104 | 0.0 | 93 | 12 | 122 | 0.0 | 88 | 35 |

II.9   Primary and secondary education: enrolment ratios by age groups
Enseignements primaire et secondaire: taux de scolarisation par groupes d'âge
Enseñanza primaria y secundaria: tasas de escolarización por grupos de edad

| Country / Pays / País | Year / Année / Año | Sex / Sexe / Sexo | Primary education — Enseignement primaire — Enseñanza primaria | | | | Secondary education — Enseignement secondaire — Enseñanza secundaria | | | |
|---|---|---|---|---|---|---|---|---|---|---|
| | | | Gross enrolment ratios / Taux bruts de scolarisation / Tasas brutas de escolarización (%) | Enrolment ratios by age groups / Taux de scolarisation par groupes d'âge / Tasas de escolarización por grupos de edad | | | Gross enrolment ratios / Taux bruts de scolarisation / Tasas brutas de escolarización (%) | Enrolment ratios by age groups / Taux de scolarisation par groupes d'âge / Tasas de escolarización por grupos de edad | | |
| | | | | Under-age / En dessous de l'âge officiel / Inferior a la edad oficial (%) | Official age group (NER) / Groupe d'âge officiel (TNS) / Grupo de edad oficial (TNE) (%) | Over-age / Au-dessus de l'âge officiel / Superior a la edad oficial (%) | | Under-age / En dessous de l'âge officiel / Inferior a la edad oficial (%) | Official age group (NER) / Groupe d'âge officiel (TNS) / Grupo de edad oficial (TNE) (%) | Over-age / Au-dessus de l'âge officiel / Superior a la edad oficial (%) |
| Italy | 1975 | | (6-10) | (<6) | (6-10) | (>10) | (11-18) | (<11) | (11-18) | (>18) |
| | | MF | 105 | 0.2 | 97 | 8 | 71 | 0.6 | 67 | 3 |
| | | M | 106 | 0.2 | 97 | 9 | 74 | 0.7 | 69 | 5 |
| | | F | 105 | 0.2 | 98 | 7 | 67 | 0.6 | 64 | 2 |
| | 1994 | | | | | | | | | |
| | | MF | 101 | 0.0 | 100 | 1 | 93 | ... | ... | ... |
| | 1995 | | | | | | | | | |
| | | MF | 101 | 0.1 | 100 | 0.8 | 94 | ... | ... | ... |
| | | M | 101 | 0.1 | 100 | 1 | 94 | ... | ... | ... |
| | | F | 100 | 0.1 | 100 | 0.7 | 94 | ... | ... | ... |
| | 1996 | | | | | | | | | |
| | | MF | 101 | 0.1 | 100 | 0.8 | 95 | ... | ... | ... |
| | | M | 101 | 0.1 | 100 | 1 | 94 | ... | ... | ... |
| | | F | 100 | 0.1 | 100 | 0.7 | 95 | ... | ... | ... |
| Latvia | 1992 | | (7-10) | (<7) | (7-10) | (>10) | (11-18) | (<11) | (11-18) | (>18) |
| | | MF | 87 | 4 | 83 | 0.0 | 87 | | ... | ... |
| | | M | 87 | 4 | 84 | 0.0 | 87 | | ... | ... |
| | | F | 87 | 4 | 82 | 0.0 | 88 | | ... | ... |
| | 1993 | | | | | | | | | |
| | | MF | 83 | ... | ... | ... | 87 | 7 | 77 | 4 |
| | 1994 | | | | | | | | | |
| | | MF | 83 | 2 | 81 | 0.0 | 87 | 5 | 78 | 4 |
| | | M | 85 | 1 | 83 | 0.0 | 84 | ... | ... | ... |
| | | F | 81 | 2 | 79 | 0.0 | 89 | ... | ... | ... |
| | 1995 | | | | | | | | | |
| | | MF | 89 | 1 | 84 | 4 | 85 | 4 | 77 | 3 |
| | | M | 91 | 0.9 | 85 | 5 | 83 | 4 | 77 | 2 |
| | | F | 86 | 1 | 82 | 4 | 87 | 5 | 78 | 4 |
| | 1996 | | | | | | | | | |
| | | MF | 96 | 1 | 89 | 5 | 84 | 2 | 79 | 3 |
| | | M | 98 | 0.8 | 92 | 5 | 82 | 1 | 78 | 3 |
| | | F | 93 | 1 | 87 | 5 | 85 | 3 | 79 | 4 |
| Malta | 1970 | | (5-10) | (<5) | (5-10) | (>10) | (11-17) | (<11) | (11-17) | (>17) |
| | | MF | 116 | 2 | 90 | 24 | 54 | 0.2 | 51 | 3 |
| | | M | 116 | 2 | 89 | 25 | 55 | 0.1 | 52 | 3 |
| | | F | 116 | 2 | 91 | 24 | 53 | 0.2 | 50 | 2 |
| | 1975 | | | | | | | | | |
| | | MF | 106 | 0.0 | 95 | 12 | 85 | 0.4 | 80 | 4 |
| | | M | 107 | 0.0 | 95 | 12 | 90 | 0.4 | 84 | 6 |
| | | F | 106 | 0.0 | 94 | 11 | 79 | 0.4 | 77 | 2 |
| | 1980 | | | | | | | | | |
| | | MF | 114 | 0.0 | 99 | 15 | 75 | 0.1 | 71 | 4 |
| | | M | 115 | 0.0 | 100 | 15 | 79 | 0.1 | 72 | 7 |
| | | F | 112 | 0.0 | 97 | 15 | 70 | 0.1 | 69 | 0.9 |
| | 1985 | | | | | | | | | |
| | | MF | 107 | 0.0 | 96 | 10 | 78 | 0.0 | 74 | 4 |
| | | M | 109 | 0.0 | 96 | 13 | 79 | 0.1 | 73 | 7 |
| | | F | 104 | 0.0 | 97 | 8 | 77 | 0.0 | 75 | 2 |
| | 1990 | | | | | | | | | |
| | | MF | 110 | 0.0 | 99 | 11 | 84 | 0.0 | 80 | 5 |
| | | M | 112 | 0.0 | 99 | 13 | 87 | 0.0 | 80 | 7 |
| | | F | 108 | 0.0 | 98 | 9 | 81 | 0.0 | 79 | 2 |
| | 1991 | | | | | | | | | |
| | | MF | 106 | 0.0 | 99 | 8 | 88 | 0.0 | 82 | 5 |
| | | M | 108 | 0.0 | 100 | 9 | 91 | 0.0 | 83 | 8 |
| | | F | 104 | 0.0 | 98 | 7 | 84 | 0.0 | 82 | 2 |
| | 1992 | | | | | | | | | |
| | | MF | 106 | 0.0 | 99 | 7 | 87 | 0.0 | 82 | 5 |
| | | M | 108 | 0.0 | 100 | 8 | 90 | 0.0 | 83 | 8 |
| | | F | 105 | 0.0 | 98 | 7 | 84 | 0.1 | 81 | 2 |

Primary and secondary education: enrolment ratios by age groups
Enseignements primaire et secondaire: taux de scolarisation par groupes d'âge
Enseñanza primaria y secundaria: tasas de escolarización por grupos de edad

II.9

| Country / Pays / País | Year / Année / Año | Sex / Sexe / Sexo | Primary education / Enseignement primaire / Enseñanza primaria | | | | Secondary education / Enseignement secondaire / Enseñanza secundaria | | | |
|---|---|---|---|---|---|---|---|---|---|---|
| | | | Gross enrolment ratios / Taux bruts de scolarisation / Tasas brutas de escolarización (%) | Enrolment ratios by age groups / Taux de scolarisation par groupes d'âge / Tasas de escolarización por grupos de edad | | | Gross enrolment ratios / Taux bruts de scolarisation / Tasas brutas de escolarización (%) | Enrolment ratios by age groups / Taux de scolarisation par groupes d'âge / Tasas de escolarización por grupos de edad | | |
| | | | | Under-age / En dessous de l'âge officiel / Inferior a la edad oficial (%) | Official age group (NER) / Groupe d'âge officiel (TNS) / Grupo de edad oficial (TNE) (%) | Over-age / Au-dessus de l'âge officiel / Superior a la edad oficial (%) | | Under-age / En dessous de l'âge officiel / Inferior a la edad oficial (%) | Official age group (NER) / Groupe d'âge officiel (TNS) / Grupo de edad oficial (TNE) (%) | Over-age / Au-dessus de l'âge officiel / Superior a la edad oficial (%) |
| **Malta** (cont) | 1993 | | | | | | | | | |
| | | MF | 106 | 0.0 | 97 | 9 | 87 | 0.1 | 82 | 5 |
| | | M | 108 | 0.0 | 98 | 9 | 92 | 0.1 | 83 | 8 |
| | | F | 105 | 0.0 | 96 | 8 | 82 | 0.0 | 80 | 3 |
| | 1994 | | | | | | | | | |
| | | MF | 106 | 0.0 | 98 | 7 | 88 | 0.0 | 82 | 6 |
| | | M | 108 | 0.0 | 100 | 8 | 91 | 0.0 | 83 | 8 |
| | | F | 103 | 0.0 | 97 | 7 | 85 | 0.0 | 82 | 3 |
| | 1995 | | | | | | | | | |
| | | MF | 107 | 0.0 | 100 | 7 | 84 | 0.0 | 79 | 5 |
| | | M | 108 | 0.0 | 100 | 7 | 87 | 0.0 | 79 | 8 |
| | | F | 106 | 0.0 | 100 | 6 | 81 | 0.0 | 78 | 3 |
| | 1996 | | | | | | | | | |
| | | MF | 107 | 0.0 | 100 | 7 | 04 | 0.0 | 79 | 5 |
| | | M | 108 | 0.0 | 100 | 8 | 86 | 0.0 | 79 | 7 |
| | | F | 107 | 0.0 | 100 | 6 | 82 | 0.0 | 79 | 3 |
| **Netherlands** | 1970 | | (6-11) | (<6) | (6-11) | (>11) | (12-17) | (<12) | (12-17) | (>17) |
| | | MF | 102 | 0.0 | 93 | 9 | 75 | 0.0 | 69 | 6 |
| | | M | 101 | 0.0 | 92 | 9 | 81 | 0.0 | 72 | 9 |
| | | F | 102 | 0.0 | 94 | 8 | 69 | 0.0 | 65 | 3 |
| | 1975 | | | | | | | | | |
| | | MF | 99 | 0.0 | 92 | 7 | 89 | 0.0 | 80 | 9 |
| | | M | 99 | 0.0 | 91 | 8 | 92 | 0.0 | 81 | 12 |
| | | F | 100 | 0.0 | 93 | 7 | 85 | 0.0 | 80 | 5 |
| | 1980 | | | | | | | | | |
| | | MF | 100 | 0.0 | 93 | 8 | 93 | 0.0 | 81 | 11 |
| | | M | 99 | 0.0 | 91 | 8 | 95 | 0.0 | 80 | 14 |
| | | F | 101 | 0.0 | 94 | 7 | 90 | 0.0 | 82 | 8 |
| | 1985 | | | | | | | | | |
| | | MF | 99 | 0.0 | 92 | 7 | 117 | 0.0 | 89 | 28 |
| | | M | 98 | 0.0 | 91 | 8 | 120 | 0.0 | 87 | 32 |
| | | F | 100 | 0.0 | 94 | 7 | 114 | 0.0 | 90 | 24 |
| | 1990 | | | | | | | | | |
| | | MF | 102 | 0.0 | 95 | 7 | 120 | 0.1 | 84 | 36 |
| | | M | 101 | 0.0 | 93 | 7 | 124 | 0.1 | 83 | 41 |
| | | F | 104 | 0.0 | 97 | 7 | 115 | 0.0 | 85 | 30 |
| | 1991 | | | | | | | | | |
| | | MF | 98 | ... | ... | ... | 121 | 0.0 | 84 | 37 |
| | | M | 97 | ... | ... | ... | 125 | 0.0 | 83 | 42 |
| | | F | 99 | ... | ... | ... | 116 | 0.0 | 86 | 31 |
| | 1992 | | | | | | | | | |
| | | MF | 97 | ... | ... | ... | 123 | 0.0 | 86 | 37 |
| | | M | 96 | ... | ... | ... | 126 | 0.0 | 84 | 42 |
| | | F | 99 | ... | ... | ... | 120 | 0.0 | 87 | 33 |
| | 1993 | | | | | | | | | |
| | | MF | 108 | 0.2 | 99 | 8 | 140 | ... | ... | ... |
| | | M | 108 | 0.3 | 99 | 9 | 145 | ... | ... | ... |
| | | F | 107 | 0.1 | 99 | 7 | 135 | ... | ... | ... |
| | 1994 | | | | | | | | | |
| | | MF | 107 | 0.2 | 99 | 8 | 139 | 0.1 | 91 | 49 |
| | | M | 108 | 0.3 | 100 | 9 | 143 | 0.1 | 90 | 52 |
| | | F | 106 | 0.1 | 99 | 7 | 136 | 0.1 | 91 | 44 |
| | 1995 | | | | | | | | | |
| | | MF | 107 | 0.2 | 99 | 8 | 137 | 0.1 | 91 | 47 |
| | | M | 108 | 0.3 | 100 | 8 | 141 | 0.1 | 90 | 51 |
| | | F | 106 | 0.2 | 99 | 7 | 134 | 0.1 | 91 | 42 |
| | 1996 | | | | | | | | | |
| | | MF | 108 | 0.2 | 100 | 8 | 132 | 0.3 | 90 | 42 |
| | | M | 109 | 0.3 | 100 | 8 | 134 | 0.3 | 89 | 44 |
| | | F | 107 | 0.2 | 99 | 7 | 129 | 0.3 | 91 | 38 |

II.9
Primary and secondary education: enrolment ratios by age groups
Enseignements primaire et secondaire: taux de scolarisation par groupes d'âge
Enseñanza primaria y secundaria: tasas de escolarización por grupos de edad

| Country / Pays / País | Year / Année / Año | Sex / Sexe / Sexo | Primary education — Enseignement primaire — Enseñanza primaria | | | | Secondary education — Enseignement secondaire — Enseñanza secundaria | | | |
|---|---|---|---|---|---|---|---|---|---|---|
| | | | Gross enrolment ratios — Taux bruts de scolarisation — Tasas brutas de escolarización (%) | Under-age — En dessous de l'âge officiel — Inferior a la edad oficial (%) | Official age group (NER) — Groupe d'âge officiel (TNS) — Grupo de edad oficial (TNE) (%) | Over-age — Au-dessus de l'âge officiel — Superior a la edad oficial (%) | Gross enrolment ratios — Taux bruts de scolarisation — Tasas brutas de escolarización (%) | Under-age — En dessous de l'âge officiel — Inferior a la edad oficial (%) | Official age group (NER) — Groupe d'âge officiel (TNS) — Grupo de edad oficial (TNE) (%) | Over-age — Au-dessus de l'âge officiel — Superior a la edad oficial (%) |
| Norway | 1970 | MF | (7-13) 89 | (<7) 0.2 | (7-13) 88 | (>13) 0.4 | (14-19) 83 | (<14) 11 | (14-19) 65 | (>19) 7 |
| | 1975 | MF | (7-12) 101 | (<7) 0.3 | (7-12) 100 | (>12) 0.8 | (13-18) 88 | (<13) 0.0 | (13-18) 79 | (>18) 9 |
| | | M | 101 | 0.3 | 99 | 1 | 88 | 0.0 | 79 | 9 |
| | | F | 101 | 0.4 | 100 | 0.6 | 88 | 0.0 | 80 | 8 |
| | 1980 | MF | 99 | 0.3 | 98 | 0.8 | 94 | 0.2 | 84 | 10 |
| | | M | 99 | 0.2 | 98 | 1 | 92 | 0.1 | 82 | 10 |
| | | F | 99 | 0.3 | 99 | 0.6 | 96 | 0.3 | 86 | 11 |
| | 1985 | MF | 97 | 0.2 | 96 | 0.2 | 97 | 0.2 | 86 | 11 |
| | | M | 97 | 0.1 | 97 | 0.3 | 95 | 0.1 | 84 | 10 |
| | | F | 97 | 0.2 | 96 | 0.2 | 100 | 0.2 | 88 | 12 |
| | 1990 | MF | 100 | 0.2 | 100 | 0.2 | 103 | 0.2 | 88 | 15 |
| | | M | 100 | 0.1 | 100 | 0.3 | 101 | 0.1 | 87 | 14 |
| | | F | 100 | 0.2 | 100 | 0.1 | 105 | 0.2 | 88 | 16 |
| | 1991 | MF | 100 | 0.2 | 100 | 0.2 | 105 | 0.2 | 89 | 16 |
| | | M | 100 | 0.1 | 100 | 0.3 | 104 | 0.1 | 88 | 16 |
| | | F | 101 | 0.2 | 100 | 0.1 | 106 | 0.2 | 89 | 17 |
| | 1992 | MF | 100 | 0.2 | 99 | 0.2 | 113 | 0.2 | 90 | 22 |
| | | M | 99 | 0.2 | 99 | 0.2 | 114 | 0.1 | 90 | 24 |
| | | F | 100 | 0.3 | 99 | 0.1 | 111 | 0.2 | 91 | 20 |
| | 1993 | MF | 99 | 0.2 | 99 | 0.2 | 125 | 0.2 | 92 | 32 |
| | | M | 99 | 0.1 | 99 | 0.2 | 126 | 0.1 | 92 | 34 |
| | | F | 99 | 0.2 | 99 | 0.1 | 123 | 0.2 | 92 | 30 |
| | 1994 | MF | 99 | 0.2 | 99 | 0.1 | 116 | 0.1 | 94 | 22 |
| | | M | 99 | 0.1 | 99 | 0.2 | 119 | 0.1 | 94 | 25 |
| | | F | 99 | 0.2 | 98 | 0.1 | 113 | 0.2 | 94 | 19 |
| | 1995 | MF | 99 | 0.1 | 99 | 0.2 | 116 | 0.1 | 95 | 21 |
| | | M | 99 | 0.1 | 99 | 0.2 | 119 | 0.1 | 95 | 24 |
| | | F | 99 | 0.2 | 99 | 0.1 | 113 | 0.2 | 96 | 17 |
| | 1996 | MF | 100 | 0.1 | 100 | 0.2 | 118 | 0.2 | 97 | 21 |
| | | M | 100 | 0.1 | 100 | 0.2 | 121 | 0.1 | 97 | 23 |
| | | F | 100 | 0.2 | 100 | 0.1 | 116 | 0.2 | 98 | 18 |
| Poland | 1970 | MF | (7-14) 101 | (<7) 0.4 | (7-14) 95 | (>14) 6 | (15-18) 62 | (<15) ... | (15-18) ... | (>18) ... |
| | | M | 103 | 0.4 | 95 | 8 | 60 | ... | ... | ... |
| | | F | 100 | 0.5 | 95 | 4 | 64 | ... | ... | ... |
| | 1975 | MF | 100 | 0.4 | 96 | 4 | 72 | ... | ... | ... |
| | | M | 102 | 0.4 | 96 | 5 | 70 | ... | ... | ... |
| | | F | 99 | 0.5 | 96 | 2 | 74 | ... | ... | ... |
| | 1980 | MF | 100 | 0.2 | 98 | 1 | 77 | 1 | 70 | 5 |
| | | M | 100 | 0.2 | 98 | 2 | 75 | 1 | 68 | 6 |
| | | F | 99 | 0.2 | 98 | 0.9 | 80 | 1 | 74 | 5 |
| | 1985 | MF | 101 | 0.1 | 99 | 2 | 78 | 0.8 | 73 | 5 |
| | | M | 102 | 0.1 | 100 | 2 | 76 | 0.6 | 70 | 5 |
| | | F | 100 | 0.1 | 99 | 1 | 81 | 1 | 76 | 4 |
| | 1990 | MF | 98 | 0.1 | 97 | 2 | 81 | 0.4 | 76 | 5 |
| | | M | 99 | 0.1 | 97 | 2 | 80 | 0.4 | 73 | 6 |
| | | F | 98 | 0.2 | 97 | 1 | 83 | 0.5 | 79 | 4 |

Primary and secondary education: enrolment ratios by age groups
Enseignements primaire et secondaire: taux de scolarisation par groupes d'âge
Enseñanza primaria y secundaria: tasas de escolarización por grupos de edad

II.9

| Country / Pays / País | Year / Année / Año | Sex / Sexe / Sexo | Primary education — Enseignement primaire — Enseñanza primaria | | | | Secondary education — Enseignement secondaire — Enseñanza secundaria | | | |
|---|---|---|---|---|---|---|---|---|---|---|
| | | | Gross enrolment ratios / Taux bruts de scolarisation / Tasas brutas de escolarización (%) | Under-age / En dessous de l'âge officiel / Inferior a la edad oficial (%) | Official age group (NER) / Groupe d'âge officiel (TNS) / Grupo de edad oficial (TNE) (%) | Over-age / Au-dessus de l'âge officiel / Superior a la edad oficial (%) | Gross enrolment ratios / Taux bruts de scolarisation / Tasas brutas de escolarización (%) | Under-age / En dessous de l'âge officiel / Inferior a la edad oficial (%) | Official age group (NER) / Groupe d'âge officiel (TNS) / Grupo de edad oficial (TNE) (%) | Over-age / Au-dessus de l'âge officiel / Superior a la edad oficial (%) |
| Poland (cont) | 1991 | | | | | | | | | |
| | | MF | 98 | 0.1 | 96 | 2 | 82 | 0.4 | 77 | 5 |
| | | M | 99 | 0.1 | 97 | 2 | 80 | 0.3 | 73 | 7 |
| | | F | 97 | 0.2 | 96 | 0.9 | 84 | 0.4 | 80 | 4 |
| | 1992 | | | | | | | | | |
| | | MF | 100 | 0.2 | 97 | 2 | 92 | 0.3 | 81 | 11 |
| | | M | 101 | 0.2 | 98 | 3 | 91 | 0.2 | 78 | 13 |
| | | F | 99 | 0.2 | 97 | 1 | 93 | 0.4 | 84 | 9 |
| | 1993 | | | | | | | | | |
| | | MF | 99 | 0.1 | 97 | 2 | 94 | 0.4 | 82 | 12 |
| | | M | 100 | 0.1 | 97 | 3 | 92 | ... | ... | ... |
| | | F | 98 | 0.2 | 97 | 1 | 96 | ... | ... | ... |
| | 1994 | | | | | | | | | |
| | | MF | 97 | 0.1 | 95 | 2 | 98 | 0.2 | 86 | 13 |
| | | M | 98 | 0.1 | 95 | 3 | 98 | 0.2 | 81 | 16 |
| | | F | 96 | 0.1 | 95 | 1 | 98 | 0.2 | 88 | 10 |
| | 1995 | | | | | | | | | |
| | | MF | 96 | 0.1 | 95 | 2 | 98 | ... | ... | ... |
| | | M | 97 | 0.1 | 95 | 3 | 98 | ... | ... | ... |
| | | F | 95 | 0.1 | 94 | 1 | 97 | ... | ... | ... |
| Portugal | 1970 | | (6-11) | (<6) | (6-11) | (>11) | (12-16) | (<12) | (12-16) | (>16) |
| | | MF | 95 | 0.0 | 80 | 15 | 56 | 7 | 30 | 18 |
| | | M | 95 | 0.0 | 80 | 15 | 60 | 7 | 32 | 21 |
| | | F | 95 | 0.0 | 81 | 14 | 52 | 8 | 28 | 16 |
| | 1975 | | | | | | | | | |
| | | MF | 117 | 0.0 | 90 | 27 | 55 | 0.4 | 29 | 25 |
| | | M | 118 | 0.0 | 90 | 28 | 55 | 0.4 | 28 | 27 |
| | | F | 116 | 0.0 | 90 | 25 | 54 | 0.4 | 30 | 24 |
| | 1980 | | (6-11) | (<6) | (6-11) | (>11) | (12-17) | (<12) | (12-17) | (>17) |
| | | MF | 123 | 0.0 | 98 | 25 | 37 | ... | ... | ... |
| | | M | 124 | 0.0 | 97 | 27 | 34 | ... | ... | ... |
| | | F | 123 | 0.0 | 100 | 23 | 40 | ... | ... | ... |
| | 1985 | | | | | | | | | |
| | | MF | 129 | 0.0 | 105 | 24 | 57 | ... | ... | ... |
| | | M | 132 | 0.0 | 105 | 27 | 53 | ... | ... | ... |
| | | F | 125 | 0.0 | 104 | 21 | 62 | ... | ... | ... |
| | 1990 | | | | | | | | | |
| | | MF | 123 | 0.0 | 102 | 21 | 67 | ... | ... | ... |
| | | M | 126 | 0.0 | 102 | 25 | 62 | ... | ... | ... |
| | | F | 120 | 0.0 | 102 | 18 | 72 | ... | ... | ... |
| | 1992 | | | | | | | | | |
| | | MF | 125 | ... | ... | ... | 94 | 0.0 | 70 | 25 |
| | | M | 128 | ... | ... | ... | 88 | 0.0 | 64 | 24 |
| | | F | 123 | ... | ... | ... | 101 | 0.0 | 76 | 25 |
| | 1993 | | | | | | | | | |
| | | MF | 128 | 0.0 | 104 | 23 | 102 | 0.0 | 78 | 24 |
| | | M | 131 | ... | ... | ... | 97 | 0.0 | 74 | 23 |
| | | F | 124 | ... | ... | ... | 106 | 0.0 | 82 | 24 |
| | 1994 | | | | | | | | | |
| | | MF | 128 | ... | ... | ... | 106 | 0.0 | 78 | 29 |
| | | M | 131 | ... | ... | ... | 102 | 0.0 | 74 | 28 |
| | | F | 125 | ... | ... | ... | 111 | 0.0 | 81 | 29 |
| Romania | 1992 | | (6-9) | (<6) | (6-9) | (>9) | (10-17) | (<10) | (10-17) | (>17) |
| | | MF | 87 | 0.0 | 77 | 10 | 83 | ... | ... | ... |
| | | M | 87 | 0.0 | 77 | 9 | 83 | ... | ... | ... |
| | | F | 86 | 0.0 | 76 | 10 | 82 | ... | ... | ... |
| | 1993 | | (7-10) | (<7) | (7-10) | (>10) | (11-18) | (<11) | (11-18) | (>18) |
| | | MF | 87 | 5 | 80 | 2 | 79 | 4 | 73 | 3 |
| | | M | 88 | 5 | 81 | 2 | 79 | 4 | 72 | 3 |
| | | F | 87 | 5 | 80 | 2 | 80 | 4 | 74 | 3 |

II.9 Primary and secondary education: enrolment ratios by age groups
Enseignements primaire et secondaire: taux de scolarisation par groupes d'âge
Enseñanza primaria y secundaria: tasas de escolarización por grupos de edad

| | | | Primary education Enseignement primaire Enseñanza primaria | | | | Secondary education Enseignement secondaire Enseñanza secundaria | | | |
|---|---|---|---|---|---|---|---|---|---|---|
| Country | Year | Sex | Gross enrolment ratios | Enrolment ratios by age groups Taux de scolarisation par groupes d'âge Tasas de escolarización por grupos de edad | | | Gross enrolment ratios | Enrolment ratios by age groups Taux de scolarisation par groupes d'âge Tasas de escolarización por grupos de edad | | |
| | | | | Under-age | Official age group (NER) | Over-age | | Under-age | Official age group (NER) | Over-age |
| Pays | Année | Sexe | Taux bruts de scolarisation | En dessous de l'âge officiel | Groupe d'âge officiel (TNS) | Au-dessus de l'âge officiel | Taux bruts de scolarisation | En dessous de l'âge officiel | Groupe d'âge officiel (TNS) | Au-dessus de l'âge officiel |
| País | Año | Sexo | Tasas brutas de escolarización | Inferior a la edad oficial | Grupo de edad oficial (TNE) | Superior a la edad oficial | Tasas brutas de escolarización | Inferior a la edad oficial | Grupo de edad oficial (TNE) | Superior a la edad oficial |
| | | | (%) | (%) | (%) | (%) | (%) | (%) | (%) | (%) |
| Romania (cont) | 1994 | | | | | | | | | |
| | | MF | 95 | 5 | 87 | 2 | 78 | 3 | 72 | 3 |
| | | M | 95 | 5 | 88 | 3 | 77 | 3 | 71 | 3 |
| | | F | 94 | 5 | 87 | 2 | 79 | 3 | 73 | 3 |
| | 1995 | | | | | | | | | |
| | | MF | 100 | 4 | 92 | 3 | 78 | 3 | 73 | 2 |
| | | M | 101 | 4 | 92 | 4 | 77 | 3 | 72 | 3 |
| | | F | 99 | 5 | 92 | 3 | 78 | 3 | 74 | 2 |
| | 1996 | | | | | | | | | |
| | | MF | 103 | 4 | 95 | 4 | 78 | 2 | 73 | 3 |
| | | M | 104 | 4 | 96 | 5 | 79 | 2 | 72 | 4 |
| | | F | 103 | 4 | 95 | 3 | 78 | 2 | 74 | 2 |
| Russian Federation | 1993 | | (7-9) | (<7) | (7-9) | (>9) | (10-16) | (<10) | (10-16) | (>16) |
| | | MF | 106 | 10 | 95 | 0.0 | 87 | ... | ... | ... |
| | | M | 106 | 10 | 96 | 0.0 | 83 | ... | ... | ... |
| | | F | 106 | 10 | 95 | 0.0 | 91 | ... | ... | ... |
| | 1994 | | | | | | | | | |
| | | MF | 107 | 6 | 93 | 9 | ... | ... | ... | ... |
| | | M | 108 | 5 | 93 | 10 | ... | ... | ... | ... |
| | | F | 107 | 6 | 93 | 8 | ... | ... | ... | ... |
| Slovenia | 1994 | | (7-10) | (<7) | (7-10) | (>10) | (11-18) | (<11) | (11-18) | (>18) |
| | | MF | 98 | 2 | 95 | 2 | 91 | ... | ... | ... |
| | | M | 98 | 2 | 94 | 2 | 90 | ... | ... | ... |
| | | F | 98 | 2 | 95 | 1 | 92 | ... | ... | ... |
| | 1995 | | | | | | | | | |
| | | MF | 98 | 2 | 95 | 1 | 91 | ... | ... | ... |
| | | M | 98 | 1 | 95 | 2 | 89 | ... | ... | ... |
| | | F | 98 | 2 | 95 | 1 | 92 | ... | ... | ... |
| | 1996 | | | | | | | | | |
| | | MF | 98 | 2 | 95 | 2 | 92 | ... | ... | ... |
| | | M | 98 | 1 | 95 | 2 | 90 | ... | ... | ... |
| | | F | 98 | 2 | 94 | 1 | 93 | ... | ... | ... |
| Spain | 1970 | | (6-10) | (<6) | (6-10) | (>10) | (11-16) | (<11) | (11-16) | (>16) |
| | | MF | 123 | 0.0 | 94 | 29 | 56 | 4 | 40 | 12 |
| | | M | 121 | 0.0 | 93 | 28 | 64 | 5 | 45 | 15 |
| | | F | 125 | 0.0 | 95 | 30 | 48 | 4 | 35 | 9 |
| | 1975 | | (6-10) | (<6) | (6-10) | (>10) | (11-17) | (<11) | (11-17) | (>17) |
| | | MF | 111 | 0.0 | 103 | 8 | 73 | 3 | 63 | 7 |
| | | M | 111 | 0.0 | 103 | 8 | 74 | 2 | 65 | 7 |
| | | F | 111 | 0.0 | 103 | 8 | 71 | 3 | 61 | 7 |
| | 1980 | | | | | | | | | |
| | | MF | 109 | 0.0 | 102 | 7 | 87 | 1 | 74 | 12 |
| | | M | 110 | 0.0 | 102 | 8 | 85 | 0.8 | 74 | 11 |
| | | F | 109 | 0.0 | 102 | 6 | 89 | 1 | 74 | 13 |
| | 1985 | | | | | | | | | |
| | | MF | 110 | 0.0 | 104 | 6 | 98 | ... | ... | ... |
| | | M | 111 | 0.0 | 104 | 7 | 95 | ... | ... | ... |
| | | F | 109 | 0.0 | 104 | 5 | 102 | ... | ... | ... |
| | 1990 | | | | | | | | | |
| | | MF | 109 | 0.0 | 103 | 5 | 104 | ... | ... | ... |
| | | M | 109 | 0.0 | 103 | 6 | 101 | ... | ... | ... |
| | | F | 108 | 0.0 | 103 | 5 | 108 | ... | ... | ... |
| | 1991 | | | | | | | | | |
| | | MF | 107 | 0.0 | 102 | 5 | 107 | ... | ... | ... |
| | | M | 108 | 0.0 | 102 | 6 | 103 | ... | ... | ... |
| | | F | 106 | 0.0 | 102 | 4 | 111 | ... | ... | ... |
| | 1992 | | | | | | | | | |
| | | MF | 109 | 0.0 | 103 | 6 | 112 | ... | ... | ... |
| | | M | 110 | 0.0 | 103 | 7 | 108 | ... | ... | ... |
| | | F | 108 | 0.0 | 103 | 5 | 117 | ... | ... | ... |

Primary and secondary education: enrolment ratios by age groups    II.9
Enseignements primaire et secondaire: taux de scolarisation par groupes d'âge
Enseñanza primaria y secundaria: tasas de escolarización por grupos de edad

| Country / Pays / País | Year / Année / Año | Sex / Sexe / Sexo | Primary education — Gross enrolment ratios / Taux bruts de scolarisation / Tasas brutas de escolarización (%) | Primary — Under-age / En dessous de l'âge officiel / Inferior a la edad oficial (%) | Primary — Official age group (NER) / Groupe d'âge officiel (TNS) / Grupo de edad oficial (TNE) (%) | Primary — Over-age / Au-dessus de l'âge officiel / Superior a la edad oficial (%) | Secondary education — Gross enrolment ratios / Taux bruts de scolarisation / Tasas brutas de escolarización (%) | Secondary — Under-age / En dessous de l'âge officiel / Inferior a la edad oficial (%) | Secondary — Official age group (NER) / Groupe d'âge officiel (TNS) / Grupo de edad oficial (TNE) (%) | Secondary — Over-age / Au-dessus de l'âge officiel / Superior a la edad oficial (%) |
|---|---|---|---|---|---|---|---|---|---|---|
| Spain | 1993 | MF | 109 | 0.0 | 104 | 5 | 116 | ... | ... | ... |
| | | M | 110 | 0.0 | 104 | 6 | 111 | ... | ... | ... |
| | | F | 108 | 0.0 | 103 | 4 | 121 | ... | ... | ... |
| | 1994 | MF | 109 | 0.0 | 104 | 5 | 118 | ... | ... | ... |
| | | M | 110 | 0.0 | 104 | 5 | 114 | ... | ... | ... |
| | | F | 108 | 0.0 | 104 | 4 | 123 | ... | ... | ... |
| | 1995 | | (6-11) | (<6) | (6-11) | (>11) | (12-17) | (<12) | (12-17) | (>17) |
| | | MF | 109 | 0.0 | 105 | 5 | 122 | ... | ... | ... |
| | | M | 110 | 0.0 | 105 | 5 | 116 | ... | ... | ... |
| | | F | 108 | 0.0 | 104 | 4 | 128 | ... | ... | ... |
| Sweden | 1975 | | (7-12) | (<7) | (7-12) | (>12) | (13-18) | (<13) | (13-18) | (>18) |
| | | MF | 101 | 0.1 | 101 | 0.5 | 78 | ... | ... | ... |
| | | M | 101 | 0.1 | 100 | 0.7 | 75 | ... | ... | ... |
| | | F | 102 | 0.2 | 101 | 0.3 | 82 | ... | ... | ... |
| | 1990 | MF | 100 | 0.0 | 100 | 0.0 | 90 | 0.0 | 85 | 5 |
| | | M | 100 | 0.0 | 100 | 0.0 | 88 | 0.0 | 85 | 3 |
| | | F | 100 | 0.0 | 100 | 0.0 | 92 | 0.0 | 86 | 6 |
| | 1991 | MF | 100 | 0.0 | 100 | 0.0 | 92 | 0.0 | 86 | 5 |
| | | M | 100 | 0.0 | 100 | 0.0 | 90 | 0.0 | 86 | 4 |
| | | F | 101 | 0.0 | 101 | 0.0 | 94 | 0.0 | 87 | 7 |
| | 1992 | MF | 104 | 0.6 | 101 | 3 | 121 | 0.0 | 91 | 30 |
| | | M | 104 | 0.5 | 101 | 2 | 113 | 0.0 | 90 | 23 |
| | | F | 105 | 0.8 | 100 | 4 | 129 | 0.0 | 91 | 38 |
| | 1993 | MF | 105 | 1 | 101 | 3 | 127 | 0.0 | 94 | 33 |
| | | M | 104 | 0.8 | 101 | 2 | 120 | 0.0 | 94 | 26 |
| | | F | 105 | 1 | 100 | 4 | 135 | 0.0 | 94 | 41 |
| | 1994 | MF | 105 | 1 | 101 | 3 | 132 | 0.0 | 96 | 35 |
| | | M | 104 | 1 | 100 | 3 | 123 | 0.0 | 90 | 27 |
| | | F | 106 | 1 | 102 | 2 | 141 | 0.0 | 97 | 45 |
| | 1995 | MF | 106 | 1 | 102 | 3 | 137 | 0.0 | 98 | 38 |
| | | M | 105 | 1 | 102 | 2 | 126 | 0.0 | 98 | 28 |
| | | F | 107 | 2 | 102 | 3 | 148 | 0.0 | 99 | 49 |
| | 1996 | MF | 107 | 2 | 102 | 3 | 140 | 0.0 | 99 | 42 |
| | | M | 106 | 1 | 103 | 2 | 128 | 0.0 | 99 | 30 |
| | | F | 107 | 2 | 102 | 3 | 153 | 0.0 | 99 | 54 |
| The Former Yugoslav Rep. of Macedonia | 1990 | | (7-14) | (<7) | (7-14) | (>14) | (15-18) | (<15) | (15-18) | (>18) |
| | | MF | 99 | 4 | 94 | 0.6 | 56 | ... | ... | ... |
| | | M | 100 | 4 | 95 | 0.7 | 56 | ... | ... | ... |
| | | F | 98 | 4 | 94 | 0.4 | 55 | ... | ... | ... |
| | 1994 | MF | 98 | 3 | 94 | 0.5 | 59 | 6 | 53 | 0.8 |
| | | M | 98 | 3 | 95 | 0.7 | 59 | 6 | 53 | 1 |
| | | F | 97 | 3 | 94 | 0.4 | 59 | 6 | 53 | 0.7 |
| | 1995 | MF | 99 | 3 | 95 | 0.8 | 61 | 6 | 55 | 0.6 |
| | | M | 100 | 3 | 96 | 1 | 61 | 6 | 55 | 0.8 |
| | | F | 98 | 3 | 94 | 0.6 | 61 | 6 | 55 | 0.4 |
| | 1996 | MF | 99 | 3 | 95 | 0.8 | 63 | 6 | 56 | 0.6 |
| | | M | 100 | 3 | 96 | 0.9 | 64 | 6 | 57 | 0.6 |
| | | F | 98 | 3 | 94 | 0.6 | 62 | 7 | 55 | 0.6 |

II.9    Primary and secondary education: enrolment ratios by age groups
Enseignements primaire et secondaire: taux de scolarisation par groupes d'âge
Enseñanza primaria y secundaria: tasas de escolarización por grupos de edad

| Country / Pays / País | Year / Année / Año | Sex / Sexe / Sexo | Primary education / Enseignement primaire / Enseñanza primaria | | | | Secondary education / Enseignement secondaire / Enseñanza secundaria | | | |
|---|---|---|---|---|---|---|---|---|---|---|
| | | | Gross enrolment ratios / Taux bruts de scolarisation / Tasas brutas de escolarización (%) | Enrolment ratios by age groups / Taux de scolarisation par groupes d'âge / Tasas de escolarización por grupos de edad | | | Gross enrolment ratios / Taux bruts de scolarisation / Tasas brutas de escolarización (%) | Enrolment ratios by age groups / Taux de scolarisation par groupes d'âge / Tasas de escolarización por grupos de edad | | |
| | | | | Under-age / En dessous de l'âge officiel / Inferior a la edad oficial (%) | Official age group (NER) / Groupe d'âge officiel (TNS) / Grupo de edad oficial (TNE) (%) | Over-age / Au-dessus de l'âge officiel / Superior a la edad oficial (%) | | Under-age / En dessous de l'âge officiel / Inferior a la edad oficial (%) | Official age group (NER) / Groupe d'âge officiel (TNS) / Grupo de edad oficial (TNE) (%) | Over-age / Au-dessus de l'âge officiel / Superior a la edad oficial (%) |
| United Kingdom | 1970 | | (5-10) | (<5) | (5-10) | (>10) | (11-17) | (<11) | (11-17) | (>17) |
| | | MF | 104 | 0.0 | 98 | 6 | 73 | 0.4 | 67 | 6 |
| | | M | 103 | 0.0 | 98 | 6 | 73 | 0.3 | 67 | 6 |
| | | F | 104 | 0.0 | 98 | 6 | 73 | 0.4 | 67 | 5 |
| | 1975 | | | | | | | | | |
| | | MF | 105 | 0.0 | 97 | 8 | 82 | 0.9 | 77 | 4 |
| | | M | 105 | 0.0 | 97 | 8 | 82 | 0.9 | 77 | 4 |
| | | F | 105 | 0.0 | 98 | 8 | 83 | 0.9 | 78 | 4 |
| | 1980 | | | | | | | | | |
| | | MF | 103 | 3 | 97 | 3 | 83 | 1 | 79 | 3 |
| | | M | 103 | 3 | 96 | 3 | 82 | 1 | 78 | 3 |
| | | F | 103 | 3 | 97 | 3 | 85 | 1 | 81 | 3 |
| | 1985 | | | | | | | | | |
| | | MF | 104 | 7 | 94 | 2 | 84 | 1 | 80 | 3 |
| | | M | 104 | 7 | 94 | 3 | 82 | 1 | 78 | 3 |
| | | F | 105 | 7 | 95 | 2 | 86 | 1 | 82 | 3 |
| | 1990 | | | | | | | | | |
| | | MF | 104 | 5 | 97 | 3 | 85 | 2 | 79 | 4 |
| | | M | 103 | 4 | 96 | 3 | 83 | 2 | 77 | 4 |
| | | F | 106 | 5 | 98 | 3 | 88 | 2 | 81 | 5 |
| | 1991 | | | | | | | | | |
| | | MF | 103 | 5 | 96 | 3 | 89 | 1 | 81 | 6 |
| | | M | 102 | 5 | 95 | 3 | 86 | 1 | 79 | 6 |
| | | F | 104 | 5 | 97 | 3 | 91 | 1 | 84 | 7 |
| | 1992 | | | | | | | | | |
| | | MF | 113 | 15 | 96 | 2 | 127 | 2 | 89 | 36 |
| | | M | 112 | 15 | 96 | 2 | 119 | 2 | 88 | 29 |
| | | F | 114 | 15 | 97 | 2 | 136 | 2 | 91 | 44 |
| | 1993 | | | | | | | | | |
| | | MF | 114 | 15 | 97 | 2 | 130 | 2 | 91 | 38 |
| | | M | 113 | 15 | 96 | 2 | 121 | 2 | 89 | 30 |
| | | F | 115 | 15 | 98 | 2 | 140 | 2 | 92 | 47 |
| | 1994 | | | | | | | | | |
| | | MF | 114 | 15 | 97 | 2 | 134 | 2 | 92 | 40 |
| | | M | 113 | 15 | 97 | 2 | 123 | 2 | 90 | 31 |
| | | F | 115 | 15 | 98 | 2 | 145 | 2 | 93 | 50 |
| | 1995 | | | | | | | | | |
| | | MF | 115 | 15 | 98 | 2 | 133 | 2 | 91 | 40 |
| | | M | 114 | 15 | 97 | 2 | 123 | 2 | 90 | 31 |
| | | F | 116 | 15 | 99 | 2 | 144 | 2 | 93 | 50 |
| | 1996 | | | | | | | | | |
| | | MF | 116 | 15 | 99 | 2 | 129 | ... | ... | ... |
| | | M | 115 | 15 | 98 | 2 | 120 | ... | ... | ... |
| | | F | 116 | 15 | 99 | 2 | 139 | ... | ... | ... |
| **Oceania** | | | | | | | | | | |
| Australia | 1975 | | (6-11) | (<6) | (6-11) | (>11) | (12-17) | (<12) | (12-17) | (>17) |
| | | MF | 107 | 3 | 96 | 8 | 72 | 0.3 | 70 | 1 |
| | | M | 107 | 3 | 96 | 8 | 72 | 0.3 | 70 | 2 |
| | | F | 106 | 3 | 96 | 7 | 72 | 0.3 | 70 | 1 |
| | 1980 | | | | | | | | | |
| | | MF | 112 | 3 | 102 | 7 | 71 | 0.3 | 70 | 1 |
| | | M | 113 | 3 | 102 | 7 | 70 | 0.2 | 69 | 1 |
| | | F | 111 | 3 | 102 | 6 | 72 | 0.3 | 71 | 1 |
| | 1985 | | | | | | | | | |
| | | MF | 107 | 3 | 98 | 6 | 80 | 0.3 | 78 | 1 |
| | | M | 107 | 3 | 98 | 7 | 79 | 0.2 | 77 | 2 |
| | | F | 106 | 3 | 98 | 5 | 81 | 0.3 | 79 | 1 |
| | 1990 | | | | | | | | | |
| | | MF | 108 | 3 | 99 | 6 | 82 | 0.3 | 79 | 3 |
| | | M | 108 | 3 | 99 | 6 | 80 | 0.2 | 77 | 3 |
| | | F | 107 | 3 | 99 | 5 | 83 | 0.3 | 80 | 3 |

Primary and secondary education: enrolment ratios by age groups II.9
Enseignements primaire et secondaire: taux de scolarisation par groupes d'âge
Enseñanza primaria y secundaria: tasas de escolarización por grupos de edad

| Country / Pays / País | Year / Année / Año | Sex / Sexe / Sexo | Primary education / Enseignement primaire / Enseñanza primaria | | | | Secondary education / Enseignement secondaire / Enseñanza secundaria | | | |
|---|---|---|---|---|---|---|---|---|---|---|
| | | | Gross enrolment ratios / Taux bruts de scolarisation / Tasas brutas de escolarización (%) | Under-age / En dessous de l'âge officiel / Inferior a la edad oficial (%) | Official age group (NER) / Groupe d'âge officiel (TNS) / Grupo de edad oficial (TNE) (%) | Over-age / Au-dessus de l'âge officiel / Superior a la edad oficial (%) | Gross enrolment ratios / Taux bruts de scolarisation / Tasas brutas de escolarización (%) | Under-age / En dessous de l'âge officiel / Inferior a la edad oficial (%) | Official age group (NER) / Groupe d'âge officiel (TNS) / Grupo de edad oficial (TNE) (%) | Over-age / Au-dessus de l'âge officiel / Superior a la edad oficial (%) |
| Australia (cont) | 1991 | | | | | | | | | |
| | | MF | 108 | 2 | 99 | 6 | 83 | 0.2 | 79 | 3 |
| | | M | 108 | 2 | 99 | 7 | 82 | 0.2 | 78 | 3 |
| | | F | 108 | 2 | 99 | 6 | 84 | 0.2 | 81 | 3 |
| | 1992 | | | | | | | | | |
| | | MF | 108 | 2 | 99 | 7 | 84 | 0.2 | 80 | 4 |
| | | M | 108 | 2 | 99 | 7 | 83 | 0.1 | 79 | 4 |
| | | F | 108 | 2 | 99 | 6 | 85 | 0.2 | 81 | 4 |
| | 1993 | | | | | | | | | |
| | | MF | 107 | 2 | 98 | 7 | 132 | 0.2 | 86 | 46 |
| | | M | 107 | 2 | 98 | 7 | 132 | 0.1 | 85 | 47 |
| | | F | 107 | 2 | 98 | 6 | 132 | 0.2 | 87 | 45 |
| | 1994 | | | | | | | | | |
| | | MF | 106 | 2 | 97 | 7 | 131 | 0.2 | 86 | 45 |
| | | M | 106 | 2 | 97 | 8 | 131 | 0.2 | 85 | 46 |
| | | F | 106 | 2 | 97 | 6 | 131 | 0.2 | 87 | 43 |
| | 1995 | | (5-11) | (<5) | (5-11) | (>11) | (12-17) | (<12) | (12-17) | (>17) |
| | | MF | 101 | 0.2 | 95 | 6 | 142 | 0.2 | 87 | 55 |
| | | M | 101 | 0.2 | 94 | 7 | 143 | 0.2 | 86 | 56 |
| | | F | 101 | 0.2 | 95 | 6 | 142 | 0.2 | 88 | 54 |
| | 1996 | | | | | | | | | |
| | | MF | 101 | 0.2 | 95 | 6 | 148 | 0.2 | 89 | 59 |
| | | M | 101 | 0.2 | 95 | 6 | 149 | 0.2 | 88 | 60 |
| | | F | 101 | 0.2 | 95 | 5 | 148 | 0.2 | 89 | 58 |
| | 1997 | | | | | | | | | |
| | | MF | 101 | 0.3 | 95 | 6 | 153 | ... | ... | ... |
| | | M | 101 | 0.2 | 95 | 6 | 150 | ... | ... | ... |
| | | F | 101 | 0.3 | 95 | 5 | 155 | ... | ... | ... |
| Fiji | 1980 | | (6-11) | (<6) | (6-11) | (>11) | (12-17) | (<12) | (12-17) | (>17) |
| | | MF | 119 | 7 | 92 | 20 | 55 | ... | ... | ... |
| | | M | 120 | 7 | 92 | 20 | 53 | ... | ... | ... |
| | | F | 119 | 8 | 92 | 19 | 57 | ... | ... | ... |
| | 1985 | | | | | | | | | |
| | | MF | 122 | 7 | 97 | 18 | 51 | ... | ... | ... |
| | | M | 122 | 7 | 90 | 19 | 50 | ... | ... | ... |
| | | F | 122 | 7 | 97 | 18 | 51 | ... | ... | ... |
| | 1991 | | | | | | | | | |
| | | MF | 126 | 6 | 101 | 19 | 61 | ... | ... | ... |
| | | M | 126 | 6 | 100 | 20 | 62 | ... | ... | ... |
| | | F | 126 | 7 | 101 | 18 | 60 | ... | ... | ... |
| | 1992 | | | | | | | | | |
| | | MF | 128 | 6 | 99 | 22 | 64 | ... | ... | ... |
| | | M | 128 | 6 | 99 | 23 | 64 | ... | ... | ... |
| | | F | 128 | 6 | 100 | 21 | 65 | ... | ... | ... |
| French Polynesia | 1992 | | (6-10) | (<6) | (6-10) | (>10) | (11-17) | (<11) | (11-17) | (>17) |
| | | MF | 125 | 0.6 | 105 | 20 | 78 | ... | ... | ... |
| | 1994 | | | | | | | | | |
| | | MF | 121 | 0.5 | 104 | 16 | ... | ... | ... | ... |
| | | M | 123 | 0.4 | 104 | 19 | ... | ... | ... | ... |
| | | F | 118 | 0.6 | 105 | 13 | ... | ... | ... | ... |
| | 1995 | | | | | | | | | |
| | | MF | 116 | 0.0 | 103 | 13 | ... | ... | ... | ... |
| | | M | 118 | 0.0 | 103 | 15 | ... | ... | ... | ... |
| | | F | 113 | 0.0 | 103 | 11 | ... | ... | ... | ... |
| New Caledonia | 1985 | | (6-10) | (<6) | (6-10) | (>10) | (11-17) | (<11) | (11-17) | (>17) |
| | | MF | 122 | 7 | 89 | 26 | 73 | 6 | 62 | 5 |
| | | M | 125 | 7 | 89 | 29 | 69 | 5 | 59 | 4 |
| | | F | 119 | 8 | 89 | 22 | 78 | 7 | 66 | 5 |
| | 1990 | | | | | | | | | |
| | | MF | 129 | 9 | 97 | 22 | 79 | 1 | 69 | 9 |
| | | M | 130 | 9 | 97 | 24 | 76 | 1 | 65 | 9 |
| | | F | 127 | 9 | 97 | 20 | 83 | 2 | 73 | 9 |

II.9　Primary and secondary education: enrolment ratios by age groups
Enseignements primaire et secondaire: taux de scolarisation par groupes d'âge
Enseñanza primaria y secundaria: tasas de escolarización por grupos de edad

| Country / Pays / País | Year / Année / Año | Sex / Sexe / Sexo | Primary education — Enseignement primaire — Enseñanza primaria | | | | Secondary education — Enseignement secondaire — Enseñanza secundaria | | | |
|---|---|---|---|---|---|---|---|---|---|---|
| | | | Gross enrolment ratios — Taux bruts de scolarisation — Tasas brutas de escolarización (%) | Under-age — En dessous de l'âge officiel — Inferior a la edad oficial (%) | Official age group (NER) — Groupe d'âge officiel (TNS) — Grupo de edad oficial (TNE) (%) | Over-age — Au-dessus de l'âge officiel — Superior a la edad oficial (%) | Gross enrolment ratios — Taux bruts de scolarisation — Tasas brutas de escolarización (%) | Under-age — En dessous de l'âge officiel — Inferior a la edad oficial (%) | Official age group (NER) — Groupe d'âge officiel (TNS) — Grupo de edad oficial (TNE) (%) | Over-age — Au-dessus de l'âge officiel — Superior a la edad oficial (%) |
| New Caledonia (cont) | 1991 | MF | 125 | 9 | 98 | 18 | 84 | 1 | 72 | 11 |
| | | M | 127 | 9 | 99 | 20 | 80 | 1 | 68 | 11 |
| | | F | 123 | 9 | 98 | 16 | 88 | 2 | 76 | 10 |
| New Zealand | 1970 | | (5-10) | (<5) | (5-10) | (>10) | (11-17) | (<11) | (11-17) | (>17) |
| | | MF | 110 | 0.0 | 104 | 6 | 77 | 0.5 | 76 | 0.7 |
| | | M | 111 | 0.0 | 104 | 7 | 77 | 0.3 | 76 | 1 |
| | | F | 109 | 0.0 | 103 | 5 | 76 | 0.6 | 75 | 0.3 |
| | 1975 | MF | 107 | 0.0 | 100 | 7 | 81 | 0.3 | 79 | 1 |
| | | M | 108 | 0.0 | 100 | 7 | 80 | 0.2 | 79 | 1 |
| | | F | 106 | 0.0 | 100 | 6 | 81 | 0.4 | 80 | 0.7 |
| | 1980 | MF | 111 | ... | ... | ... | 83 | 0.2 | 81 | 1 |
| | | M | 111 | ... | ... | ... | 82 | 0.2 | 81 | 1 |
| | | F | 111 | ... | ... | ... | 84 | 0.3 | 82 | 1 |
| | 1985 | MF | 107 | 0.0 | 102 | 5 | 85 | 0.2 | 84 | 1 |
| | | M | 108 | 0.0 | 102 | 5 | 84 | 0.1 | 83 | 1 |
| | | F | 106 | 0.0 | 102 | 4 | 87 | 0.2 | 85 | 1 |
| | 1990 | MF | 106 | 0.0 | 101 | 4 | 89 | 0.2 | 85 | 4 |
| | | M | 106 | 0.0 | 102 | 5 | 88 | 0.2 | 84 | 4 |
| | | F | 105 | 0.0 | 101 | 4 | 90 | 0.2 | 86 | 4 |
| | 1991 | MF | 102 | 0.0 | 99 | 4 | 91 | 0.2 | 86 | 5 |
| | | M | 103 | 0.0 | 99 | 4 | 91 | 0.2 | 85 | 5 |
| | | F | 102 | 0.0 | 99 | 3 | 92 | 0.2 | 87 | 5 |
| | 1992 | MF | 99 | 0.0 | 96 | 3 | 94 | 0.2 | 87 | 6 |
| | | M | 100 | 0.0 | 96 | 4 | 93 | 0.1 | 86 | 7 |
| | | F | 99 | 0.0 | 96 | 3 | 94 | 0.2 | 88 | 6 |
| | 1995 | MF | 99 | 0.0 | 96 | 3 | 112 | 0.2 | 89 | 23 |
| | | M | 99 | 0.0 | 96 | 3 | 113 | 0.2 | 88 | 24 |
| | | F | 99 | 0.0 | 96 | 3 | 112 | 0.2 | 90 | 22 |
| | 1996 | MF | 99 | 0.0 | 98 | 1 | 114 | 0.2 | 92 | 22 |
| | | M | 99 | 0.0 | 97 | 1 | 111 | 0.2 | 91 | 20 |
| | | F | 99 | 0.0 | 98 | 1 | 117 | 0.3 | 93 | 24 |
| | 1997 | MF | 101 | 0.0 | 100 | 1 | 113 | 0.2 | 90 | 23 |
| | | M | 101 | 0.0 | 100 | 1 | 110 | 0.2 | 89 | 21 |
| | | F | 101 | 0.0 | 100 | 1 | 116 | 0.2 | 91 | 25 |
| Samoa | 1995 | | (5-12) | (<5) | (5-12) | (>12) | (13-17) | (<13) | (13-17) | (>17) |
| | | MF | 102 | 0.0 | 97 | 5 | ... | ... | ... | ... |
| | | M | 102 | 0.0 | 97 | 5 | ... | ... | ... | ... |
| | | F | 102 | 0.0 | 97 | 5 | ... | ... | ... | ... |
| | 1996 | MF | 100 | 0.0 | 96 | 5 | 62 | ... | ... | ... |
| | | M | 101 | 0.0 | 96 | 5 | 59 | ... | ... | ... |
| | | F | 99 | 0.0 | 95 | 4 | 66 | ... | ... | ... |

**General note**

For general explanations and definitions, please refer to the beginning of this chapter.

**Note générale**

Pour les explications et définitions générales, prière de se référer au début de ce chapitre.

**Nota general**

Para las explicaciones y definiciones generales, referirse al comienzo de este capítulo.

Primary education: net intake rates by age  II.10
Enseignement primaire: taux nets d'admission par âge
Enseñanza primaria: tasas netas de ingreso por edad

## II.10 Primary education: net intake rates by age

## Enseignement primaire: taux nets d'admission par âge

## Enseñanza primaria: tasas netas de ingreso por edad

| Country / Pays / País | Year / Année / Año | Net intake rates by age / Taux nets d'admission par âge / Tasas netas de ingreso por edad (%) | | | | | | | | |
|---|---|---|---|---|---|---|---|---|---|---|
| | | One year under age Un an en dessous de l'âge officiel Un año inferior a la edad oficial | | | Official entrance age Age officiel d'ontróo Edad oficial de ingreso | | | One year over age Un an au-dessus de l'âge officiel Un año superior a la edad oficial | | |
| | | MF | M | F | MF | M | F | MF | M | F |
| **Africa** | | | | | | | | | | |
| Algeria | 1992 | 12.7 | 13.2 | 12.1 | 79.9 | 83.1 | 76.4 | 4.9 | 4.8 | 5.0 |
| | 1994 | 13.1 | 13.5 | 12.7 | 79.9 | 82.6 | 77.2 | 3.6 | 3.3 | 3.9 |
| | 1996 | 16.6 | 16.7 | 16.5 | 77.3 | 79.6 | 75.0 | 4.9 | 5.0 | 4.8 |
| Burundi | 1992 | 7.7 | 8.5 | 6.9 | 33.9 | 36.7 | 31.1 | 17.1 | 18.7 | 15.5 |
| Eritrea | 1996 | 1.0 | 1.0 | 0.9 | 14.5 | 15.4 | 13.6 | 9.6 | 10.4 | 8.9 |
| Lesotho | 1991 | 9.1 | 8.2 | 10.0 | 36.4 | 33.7 | 39.1 | 31.5 | 29.5 | 33.5 |
| | 1992 | 8.5 | 7.6 | 9.4 | 34.8 | 32.0 | 37.7 | 30.5 | 28.2 | 32.8 |
| | 1993 | 9.5 | 8.7 | 10.2 | 28.8 | 26.6 | 31.0 | 30.5 | 29.1 | 31.9 |
| | 1994 | 2.4 | 2.1 | 2.8 | 34.0 | 31.4 | 36.7 | 34.1 | 32.8 | 35.5 |
| | 1996 | 2.0 | 1.9 | 2.1 | 30.2 | 29.1 | 31.4 | 34.8 | 33.6 | 36.0 |
| Malawi | 1993 | 11.9 | 10.6 | 13.3 | 45.5 | 42.4 | 48.7 | 31.6 | 30.2 | 33.1 |
| | 1994 | 19.0 | 17.6 | 20.4 | 72.4 | 69.9 | 75.0 | 51.2 | 50.6 | 51.7 |
| Mauritius | 1993 | - | - | - | 76.8 | 75.5 | 78.1 | 25.2 | 25.0 | 25.3 |
| | 1994 | - | - | - | 80.5 | 81.2 | 79.8 | 25.9 | 25.3 | 26.6 |
| | 1995 | - | - | - | 79.3 | 78.8 | 79.9 | 30.2 | 31.4 | 28.9 |
| | 1996 | - | - | - | 82.2 | 81.7 | 82.7 | 28.2 | 28.3 | 28.1 |
| | 1997 | - | - | - | 77.7 | 78.1 | 77.3 | 28.1 | 28.6 | 27.6 |
| Morocco | 1991 | 22.5 | 25.3 | 19.6 | 48.8 | 55.2 | 42.2 | 5.4 | 6.3 | 4.4 |
| | 1992 | 23.6 | 26.6 | 20.5 | 53.6 | 60.4 | 46.5 | 6.9 | 8.0 | 5.6 |
| | 1993 | 24.9 | 27.5 | 22.1 | 54.5 | 60.4 | 48.3 | 7.1 | 8.0 | 6.2 |
| | 1994 | 24.7 | 26.9 | 22.3 | 55.2 | 60.9 | 49.4 | 6.9 | 7.6 | 6.2 |
| | 1995 | 25.7 | 27.8 | 23.6 | 54.5 | 59.4 | 49.4 | 7.1 | 7.6 | 6.5 |
| | 1996 | 27.1 | 29.0 | 25.1 | 55.3 | 60.2 | 50.3 | 6.7 | 7.4 | 6.1 |
| Niger | 1996 | 7.6 | 8.4 | 6.7 | 19.3 | 23.4 | 15.2 | 4.2 | 5.3 | 3.2 |
| Swaziland | 1991 | 11.7 | 11.5 | 12.0 | 51.6 | 50.6 | 52.6 | 34.0 | 35.5 | 32.5 |
| | 1993 | 10.3 | 9.1 | 11.5 | 49.2 | 49.0 | 49.4 | 34.5 | 36.6 | 32.3 |
| | 1994 | 10.4 | 9.6 | 11.3 | 53.7 | 52.3 | 55.1 | 31.7 | 33.1 | 30.3 |
| | 1996 | 13.9 | 12.8 | 15.0 | 54.6 | 53.8 | 55.5 | 27.9 | 29.0 | 26.7 |
| Togo | 1994 | 16.5 | 17.7 | 15.3 | 58.6 | 64.1 | 53.1 | 23.5 | 25.2 | 21.7 |
| Tunisia | 1991 | 7.4 | 7.7 | 7.1 | 92.1 | 94.3 | 89.8 | 3.1 | 2.8 | 3.5 |
| | 1992 | 7.5 | 7.7 | 7.2 | 91.9 | 94.0 | 89.8 | 3.3 | 3.0 | 3.7 |
| | 1994 | 8.9 | 9.2 | 8.6 | 86.5 | 88.1 | 84.9 | 3.4 | 2.9 | 3.9 |
| | 1995 | 10.1 | 10.2 | 9.9 | 83.0 | 84.1 | 81.9 | 2.5 | 2.2 | 2.7 |
| | 1996 | 11.8 | 12.1 | 11.6 | 87.8 | 88.7 | 86.8 | 2.0 | 1.7 | 2.3 |
| **North America** | | | | | | | | | | |
| Costa Rica | 1994 | - | - | - | 46.5 | ... | ... | 46.7 | ... | ... |
| | 1995 | - | - | - | 52.8 | ... | ... | 41.2 | ... | ... |
| | 1996 | - | - | - | 55.5 | ... | ... | 42.7 | ... | ... |

**Primary education: net intake rates by age**
**Enseignement primaire: taux nets d'admission par âge**
**Enseñanza primaria: tasas netas de ingreso por edad**

| Country | Year | Net intake rates by age / Taux nets d'admission par âge / Tasas netas de ingreso por edad (%) | | | | | | | | |
|---------|------|------|------|------|------|------|------|------|------|------|
| Pays | Année | One year under age Un an en dessous de l'âge officiel Un año inferior a la edad oficial | | | Official entrance age Age officiel d'entrée Edad oficial de ingreso | | | One year over age Un an au-dessus de l'âge officiel Un año superior a la edad oficial | | |
| País | Año | MF | M | F | MF | M | F | MF | M | F |
| Cuba | 1996 | 5.0 | 4.8 | 5.2 | 99.7 | 100.0 | 97.7 | 1.3 | 1.6 | 1.0 |
| El Salvador | 1995 | 30.0 | 28.8 | 31.3 | 51.8 | 52.8 | 50.8 | 20.3 | 21.1 | 19.5 |
| **South America** | | | | | | | | | | |
| Bolivia | 1990 | 4.5 | 4.5 | 4.5 | 84.7 | 85.3 | 84.2 | 34.5 | 34.6 | 34.4 |
| Chile | 1996 | 0.2 | 0.2 | 0.2 | 38.2 | 38.8 | 37.6 | 59.5 | 60.4 | 58.6 |
| Paraguay | 1996 | - | - | - | 70.4 | 69.1 | 71.8 | 35.9 | 36.9 | 34.7 |
| Venezuela | 1991 | 10.4 | 9.8 | 11.0 | 65.1 | 65.1 | 65.1 | 22.4 | 23.5 | 21.2 |
| | 1992 | 10.8 | 10.2 | 11.5 | 65.4 | 65.4 | 65.4 | 19.8 | 21.0 | 18.5 |
| | 1996 | 8.7 | 8.2 | 9.2 | 62.0 | 61.9 | 62.2 | 21.9 | 22.8 | 20.8 |
| **Asia** | | | | | | | | | | |
| Bahrain | 1992 | 14.3 | 13.6 | 15.0 | 84.9 | 84.8 | 84.9 | 5.5 | 4.2 | 6.8 |
| | 1993 | 14.3 | 14.2 | 14.4 | 88.2 | 86.9 | 89.5 | 3.3 | 3.7 | 2.9 |
| | 1994 | 13.8 | 13.7 | 13.8 | 85.0 | 81.7 | 88.6 | 6.7 | 7.4 | 5.9 |
| Cambodia | 1996 | 2.7 | 2.8 | 2.6 | 78.9 | 81.5 | 76.2 | 30.4 | 31.9 | 28.9 |
| | 1997 | 2.0 | 2.1 | 2.0 | 73.5 | 75.8 | 71.1 | 28.9 | 30.2 | 27.5 |
| Indonesia | 1992 | 43.4 | ... | ... | 51.7 | ... | ... | 11.3 | ... | ... |
| | 1994 | 46.3 | 48.5 | 44.1 | 47.8 | 49.4 | 46.2 | 11.3 | 10.6 | 11.9 |
| Iraq | 1992 | 7.0 | 7.6 | 6.3 | 65.4 | 67.3 | 63.4 | 7.9 | 8.3 | 7.4 |
| Japan | 1990 | - | - | - | 100.0 | 100.0 | 100.0 | - | - | - |
| | 1991 | - | - | - | 100.0 | 100.0 | 100.0 | - | - | - |
| | 1994 | - | - | - | 100.0 | 100.0 | 100.0 | - | - | - |
| Korea, Republic of | 1992 | - | - | - | 86.0 | 86.0 | 86.0 | 5.4 | 5.4 | 5.4 |
| | 1993 | - | - | - | 85.7 | 85.0 | 86.3 | 6.7 | 6.8 | 6.5 |
| | 1994 | - | - | - | 88.6 | 87.6 | 89.6 | 7.1 | 7.1 | 7.1 |
| | 1995 | - | - | - | 91.5 | 90.8 | 92.3 | 7.0 | 7.1 | 7.0 |
| | 1996 | - | - | - | 93.7 | 93.2 | 94.3 | 8.4 | 8.8 | 7.9 |
| Lao People's Democratic Republic | 1991 | - | - | - | 29.1 | 30.0 | 28.2 | 29.5 | 31.1 | 27.8 |
| | 1992 | - | - | - | 32.4 | 32.8 | 32.0 | 32.7 | 34.3 | 31.0 |
| | 1993 | - | - | - | 35.5 | 35.8 | 35.2 | 31.9 | 34.1 | 29.6 |
| Mongolia | 1994 | 8.5 | 7.2 | 9.8 | 73.1 | 72.8 | 73.5 | 7.9 | 8.7 | 7.0 |
| | 1995 | 8.7 | 7.4 | 9.9 | 74.2 | 74.1 | 74.4 | 8.4 | 9.1 | 7.6 |
| | 1996 | 9.1 | 7.8 | 10.4 | 76.9 | 76.1 | 77.8 | 8.5 | 9.1 | 7.9 |
| Oman | 1996 | 7.9 | 8.4 | 7.3 | 55.9 | 56.2 | 55.6 | 4.3 | 4.2 | 4.4 |
| Saudi Arabia | 1992 | 3.6 | 3.8 | 3.4 | 43.1 | 54.1 | 31.4 | 21.4 | 12.7 | 30.5 |
| | 1993 | 3.6 | 4.4 | 2.7 | 43.2 | 54.2 | 31.6 | 21.2 | 12.5 | 30.5 |
| | 1995 | 4.3 | 2.6 | 6.1 | 41.2 | 45.3 | 36.9 | 21.8 | 18.4 | 25.3 |
| | 1996 | 2.7 | 1.7 | 3.8 | 41.0 | 46.5 | 35.1 | 19.0 | 15.9 | 22.3 |
| Syrian Arab Republic | 1990 | 28.4 | 30.1 | 26.6 | 62.3 | 63.6 | 60.9 | 6.2 | 6.4 | 6.0 |
| | 1991 | 25.8 | 28.0 | 23.7 | 69.2 | 70.4 | 67.9 | 5.5 | 5.6 | 5.4 |
| | 1992 | 28.7 | 30.4 | 27.0 | 63.9 | 65.9 | 61.8 | 5.2 | 5.1 | 5.2 |
| | 1993 | 27.8 | 29.8 | 25.7 | 62.9 | 64.4 | 61.3 | 4.6 | 4.6 | 4.7 |
| | 1994 | 26.6 | 28.9 | 24.2 | 62.7 | 63.7 | 61.6 | 5.1 | 5.1 | 5.0 |
| | 1996 | 30.7 | 32.6 | 28.8 | 57.7 | 58.7 | 56.7 | 5.4 | 5.5 | 5.3 |
| **Europe** | | | | | | | | | | |
| Croatia | 1994 | 26.4 | 25.4 | 27.5 | 57.7 | 58.5 | 56.9 | 3.5 | 3.7 | 3.3 |
| Denmark | 1992 | 3.9 | 3.9 | 3.9 | 89.3 | 87.0 | 91.8 | 8.1 | 10.1 | 5.9 |
| Malta | 1991 | - | - | - | 72.6 | 74.8 | 70.4 | 29.4 | 31.8 | 27.0 |
| | 1992 | - | - | - | 74.9 | 75.7 | 74.0 | 28.4 | 27.8 | 29.0 |
| | 1993 | - | - | - | 70.1 | 69.6 | 70.7 | 28.7 | 29.9 | 27.4 |
| | 1994 | - | - | - | 76.6 | 74.9 | 78.3 | 30.8 | 31.2 | 30.5 |
| | 1995 | - | - | - | 79.7 | 79.9 | 79.5 | 25.8 | 24.8 | 27.0 |
| | 1996 | - | - | - | 77.7 | 77.7 | 77.7 | 29.7 | 28.4 | 31.1 |
| Norway | 1992 | 1.2 | 0.9 | 1.5 | 94.9 | 94.7 | 95.1 | 1.0 | 1.3 | 0.7 |
| | 1993 | 0.9 | 0.7 | 1.1 | 95.6 | 96.1 | 95.0 | 1.0 | 1.2 | 0.8 |
| Russian Federation | 1993 | 23.6 | 23.7 | 23.5 | 72.4 | 73.0 | 71.9 | 2.7 | 2.6 | 2.7 |
| Sweden | 1991 | - | - | - | 99.7 | 99.6 | 99.8 | - | - | - |
| The Former Yugoslav Rep. of Macedonia | 1996 | 24.6 | 24.1 | 25.1 | 75.2 | 76.7 | 73.5 | 1.9 | 1.9 | 2.0 |

Primary education: net intake rates by age    **II.10**
Enseignement primaire: taux nets d'admission par âge
Enseñanza primaria: tasas netas de ingreso por edad

| Country | Year | Net intake rates by age / Taux nets d'admission par âge / Tasas netas de ingreso por edad (%) | | | | | | | | |
|---------|------|------|------|------|------|------|------|------|------|------|
| Pays | Année | One year under age Un an en dessous de l'âge officiel Un año inferior a la edad oficial | | | Official entrance age Age officiel d'entrée Edad oficial de ingreso | | | One year over age Un an au-dessus de l'âge officiel Un año superior a la edad oficial | | |
| País | Año | MF | M | F | MF | M | F | MF | M | F |
| Ukraine | 1993 | 36.9 | 37.2 | 36.6 | 62.8 | 63.4 | 62.3 | - | - | - |
| **Oceania** | | | | | | | | | | |
| New Zealand | 1990 | 0.1 | 0.1 | 0.1 | 100.0 | 100.0 | 100.0 | 2.6 | 2.7 | 2.6 |
| | 1991 | - | - | - | 99.2 | 98.5 | 99.9 | 1.9 | 2.0 | 1.9 |
| | 1992 | - | - | - | 96.6 | 97.4 | 95.7 | 0.9 | 0.9 | 0.9 |
| | 1993 | - | - | - | 98.0 | 96.2 | 99.8 | 2.5 | 2.7 | 2.3 |
| | 1995 | 0.1 | 0.1 | 0.1 | 100.0 | 99.9 | 100.0 | 3.3 | 3.4 | 3.1 |
| | 1996 | - | - | - | 100.0 | 100.0 | 100.0 | 5.7 | 5.8 | 5.6 |

**General note**

For general explanations and definitions, please refer to the beginning of this chapter.

**Note générale**

Pour les explications et définitions générales, prière de se référer au début de ce chapitre.

**Nota general**

Para las explicaciones y definiciones generales, referirse al comienzo de este capítulo.

II.11    Primary education: selected indicators
Enseignement primaire: indicateurs selectionnés
Enseñanza primaria: indicadores seleccionados

## II.11    Primary education: selected indicators

## Enseignement primaire: indicateurs selectionnés

## Enseñanza primaria: indicadores seleccionados

| Country Pays País | Year Année Año | Sex Sexe Sexo | Apparent intake rate / Taux d'admission apparent / Tasa aparente de ingreso (%) | Percentage repeaters / Pourcentage de redoublants / Porcentaje de repetidores | Percentage of cohort reaching: Pourcentage de la cohorte atteignant: Porcentaje de la cohorte que llega al: | | Coefficient of efficiency / Coefficient d'efficacité / Coeficiente de eficacia | Transition rate (Prim. to Sec. gen.) / Taux de transition (Prim. au sec. gén.) / Tasa de transición (Prim. a la Sec. gen.) (%) | School life expectancy (in years) / Espérance de vie scolaire (années) / Esperanza de vida escolar (en años) |
|---|---|---|---|---|---|---|---|---|---|
| | | | | | Grade 5 5e année Quinto año | Final grade Dernière année Ultimo año | | | |
| **Africa** | | | | | | | | | |
| Algeria | 1975 | MF | 88 | 13 | 85 | 71 | 0.70 | 45 | ... |
| | | M | 100 | 13 | 87 | 73 | 0.71 | 46 | ... |
| | | F | 76 | 12 | 84 | 68 | 0.68 | 44 | ... |
| | 1980 | MF | 87 | 12 | 88 | 77 | 0.75 | 58 | 8.3 |
| | | M | 96 | 12 | 90 | 79 | 0.76 | 55 | 9.8 |
| | | F | 77 | 11 | 85 | 74 | 0.75 | 62 | 6.8 |
| | 1985 | MF | 95 | 8 | 94 | 90 | 0.87 | ... | 9.6 |
| | | M | 102 | 9 | 95 | 93 | 0.88 | ... | 10.9 |
| | | F | 88 | 6 | 92 | 87 | 0.87 | ... | 8.3 |
| | 1990 | MF | 101 | 9 | 94 | 91 | 0.85 | 81 | 10.3 |
| | | M | 106 | 11 | 95 | 92 | 0.84 | 79 | ... |
| | | F | 96 | 7 | 93 | 89 | 0.86 | 83 | ... |
| | 1991 | MF | 105 | 9 | 92 | 89 | 0.84 | 80 | 10.4 |
| | | M | 109 | 10 | 92 | 89 | 0.83 | 78 | 11.3 |
| | | F | 100 | 7 | 92 | 88 | 0.86 | 83 | 9.4 |
| | 1992 | MF | 99 | 9 | 93 | 90 | 0.85 | 79 | 10.4 |
| | | M | 102 | 11 | 93 | 90 | 0.84 | 77 | 11.3 |
| | | F | 95 | 7 | 93 | 90 | 0.87 | 83 | 9.5 |
| | 1993 | MF | 100 | 9 | 92 | 88 | 0.84 | 80 | 10.6 |
| | | M | 103 | 11 | 93 | 89 | 0.83 | 77 | ... |
| | | F | 97 | 7 | 91 | 87 | 0.86 | 82 | ... |
| | 1994 | MF | 98 | 9 | 94 | 90 | 0.85 | 80 | 10.6 |
| | | M | 100 | 11 | 94 | 90 | 0.83 | 77 | 11.2 |
| | | F | 95 | 6 | 95 | 90 | 0.87 | 82 | 9.9 |
| | 1995 | MF | 103 | 9 | 94 | 90 | 0.84 | 78 | 10.8 |
| | | M | 106 | 11 | 93 | 89 | 0.81 | 74 | 11.4 |
| | | F | 101 | 6 | 95 | 92 | 0.87 | 82 | 10.1 |
| | 1996 | MF | 101 | 10 | ... | ... | ... | ... | ... |
| | | M | 103 | 13 | ... | ... | ... | ... | ... |
| | | F | 99 | 8 | ... | ... | ... | ... | ... |
| Angola | 1990 | MF | 76 | 33 | ... | ... | ... | ... | ... |
| Benin | 1970 | MF | 43 | 19 | 66 | 65 | 0.68 | 28 | ... |
| | | M | 59 | 18 | 67 | 66 | 0.69 | 27 | ... |
| | | F | 27 | 20 | 65 | 63 | 0.65 | 31 | ... |

Primary education: selected indicators II.11
Enseignement primaire: indicateurs selectionnés
Enseñanza primaria: indicadores seleccionados

| Country / Pays / País | Year / Année / Año | Sex / Sexe / Sexo | Apparent intake rate / Taux d'admission apparent / Tasa aparente de ingreso (%) | Percentage repeaters / Pourcentage de redoublants / Porcentaje de repetidores | Percentage of cohort reaching: / Pourcentage de la cohorte atteignant: / Porcentaje de la cohorte que llega al: | | Coefficient of efficiency / Coefficient d'efficacité / Coeficiente de eficacia | Transition rate (Prim. to Sec. gen.) / Taux de transition (Prim. au sec. gén.) / Tasa de transición (Prim. a la Sec. gen.) (%) | School life expectancy (in years) / Espérance de vie scolaire (années) / Esperanza de vida escolar (en años) |
|---|---|---|---|---|---|---|---|---|---|
| | | | | | Grade 5 / 5e année / Quinto año | Final grade / Dernière année / Ultimo año | | | |
| Benin (cont) | 1975 | MF | 60 | 21 | 52 | 48 | 0.56 | 29 | ... |
| | | M | 80 | 20 | 54 | 52 | 0.59 | 30 | ... |
| | | F | 40 | 23 | 47 | 40 | 0.48 | 27 | ... |
| | 1980 | MF | 85 | 20 | 60 | 56 | 0.63 | | ... |
| | | M | 115 | 19 | 59 | 54 | 0.63 | ... | ... |
| | | F | 54 | 22 | 62 | 58 | 0.63 | ... | ... |
| | 1985 | MF | ... | 27 | 50 | 43 | 0.47 | 38 | ... |
| | | M | ... | 26 | 50 | 44 | 0.48 | ... | ... |
| | | F | ... | 28 | 49 | 40 | 0.43 | ... | ... |
| | 1990 | MF | 76 | 21 | 55 | 45 | 0.47 | ... | ... |
| | | M | 103 | 21 | 55 | 46 | 0.49 | ... | ... |
| | | F | 49 | 22 | 56 | 44 | 0.45 | ... | ... |
| | 1991 | MF | 71 | 23 | 67 | 60 | 0.56 | ... | ... |
| | | M | 93 | 23 | 67 | 62 | 0.57 | ... | ... |
| | | F | 48 | 24 | 68 | 58 | 0.53 | ... | ... |
| | 1992 | MF | 76 | 24 | 55 | 47 | 0.50 | ... | ... |
| | | M | 99 | 24 | 56 | 48 | 0.51 | ... | ... |
| | | F | 54 | 24 | 55 | 44 | 0.46 | ... | ... |
| | 1993 | MF | 71 | 25 | 65 | 55 | 0.53 | ... | ... |
| | | M | 86 | 25 | 67 | 58 | 0.55 | ... | ... |
| | | F | 57 | 25 | 61 | 50 | 0.49 | ... | ... |
| | 1994 | MF | 77 | 24 | 61 | 51 | 0.50 | ... | ... |
| | | M | 94 | 24 | 64 | 54 | 0.52 | ... | ... |
| | | F | 61 | 25 | 57 | 45 | 0.46 | ... | ... |
| | 1995 | MF | 80 | 25 | ... | ... | ... | ... | ... |
| | | M | 95 | 25 | ... | ... | ... | ... | ... |
| | | F | 65 | 25 | ... | ... | ... | ... | ... |
| Botswana | 1970 | MF | 59 | 0 | 64 | 50 | 0.67 | ... | ... |
| | | M | 56 | 0 | 61 | 49 | 0.67 | ... | ... |
| | | F | 63 | 0 | 67 | 50 | 0.67 | ... | ... |
| | 1975 | MF | 98 | 3 | 88 | 82 | 0.86 | ... | 6.0 |
| | | M | ... | ... | ... | ... | ... | ... | 5.5 |
| | | F | ... | ... | ... | ... | ... | ... | 6.5 |
| | 1980 | MF | 108 | 3 | 82 | 73 | 0.79 | ... | 7.6 |
| | | M | ... | ... | 80 | 70 | 0.76 | ... | 7.0 |
| | | F | ... | ... | 84 | 76 | 0.82 | ... | 8.3 |
| | 1985 | MF | 112 | 6 | 90 | 89 | 0.91 | 36 | 9.0 |
| | | M | 110 | 6 | 88 | 88 | 0.90 | 38 | 8.6 |
| | | F | 113 | 6 | 91 | 91 | 0.92 | 35 | 9.3 |
| | 1990 | MF | 118 | 5 | 97 | 91 | 0.90 | 76 | 10.4 |
| | | M | 117 | 5 | 94 | 87 | 0.87 | 75 | 10.1 |
| | | F | 118 | 5 | 98 | 93 | 0.91 | 76 | 10.6 |
| | 1991 | MF | 122 | 5 | ... | ... | ... | 76 | 11.0 |
| | | M | 122 | 5 | ... | ... | ... | 74 | 10.7 |
| | | F | 121 | 4 | ... | ... | ... | 77 | 11.3 |
| | 1992 | MF | 120 | 3 | 89 | 83 | 0.89 | 84 | 10.9 |
| | | M | 121 | 4 | 88 | 80 | 0.86 | 84 | 10.7 |
| | | F | 119 | 3 | 91 | 86 | 0.91 | 85 | 11.1 |
| | 1993 | MF | 113 | 3 | 89 | 84 | 0.90 | 84 | 11.1 |
| | | M | 115 | 3 | 86 | 79 | 0.87 | 84 | 10.9 |
| | | F | 111 | 2 | 92 | 88 | 0.93 | 85 | 11.3 |
| | 1994 | MF | 113 | 3 | 87 | 81 | 0.88 | 90 | 10.9 |
| | | M | 115 | 3 | 85 | 78 | 0.84 | 89 | 10.8 |
| | | F | 111 | 2 | 88 | 85 | 0.91 | 91 | 11.0 |
| | 1995 | MF | 114 | 3 | 90 | 86 | 0.91 | ... | 11.3 |
| | | M | 115 | 4 | 87 | 81 | 0.87 | ... | 11.1 |
| | | F | 113 | 3 | 93 | 91 | 0.94 | ... | 11.4 |
| | 1996 | MF | 114 | 3 | ... | ... | ... | ... | ... |
| | | M | 116 | 4 | ... | ... | ... | ... | ... |
| | | F | 112 | 3 | ... | ... | ... | ... | ... |
| Burkina Faso | 1970 | MF | 13 | 16 | 56 | 50 | 0.56 | 13 | 0.9 |
| | | M | 17 | 16 | 57 | 50 | 0.58 | 14 | 1.1 |
| | | F | 10 | 17 | 55 | 49 | 0.53 | 13 | 0.6 |

II.11   Primary education: selected indicators
Enseignement primaire: indicateurs selectionnés
Enseñanza primaria: indicadores seleccionados

| Country / Pays / País | Year / Année / Año | Sex / Sexe / Sexo | Apparent intake rate / Taux d'admission apparent / Tasa aparente de ingreso (%) | Percentage repeaters / Pourcentage de redoublants / Porcentaje de repetidores | Percentage of cohort reaching: / Pourcentage de la cohorte atteignant: / Porcentaje de la cohorte que llega al: Grade 5 / 5e année / Quinto año | Final grade / Dernière année / Ultimo año | Coefficient of efficiency / Coefficient d'efficacité / Coeficiente de eficacia | Transition rate (Prim. to Sec. gen.) / Taux de transition (Prim. au sec. gén.) / Tasa de transición (Prim. a la Sec. gen.) (%) | School life expectancy (in years) / Espérance de vie scolaire (années) / Esperanza de vida escolar (en años) |
|---|---|---|---|---|---|---|---|---|---|
| Burkina Faso (cont) | 1975 | MF | 16 | 17 | 64 | 61 | 0.62 | 18 | ... |
| | | M | 20 | 17 | 66 | 63 | 0.64 | 19 | ... |
| | | F | 11 | 19 | 61 | 58 | 0.60 | 17 | ... |
| | 1980 | MF | 20 | 17 | 75 | 75 | 0.69 | 21 | ... |
| | | M | 26 | 17 | 76 | 76 | 0.71 | ... | ... |
| | | F | 15 | 18 | 74 | 70 | 0.65 | ... | ... |
| | 1985 | MF | ... | ... | 75 | 73 | 0.67 | ... | 2.0 |
| | | M | ... | ... | 75 | 74 | 0.68 | ... | 2.5 |
| | | F | ... | ... | 75 | 71 | 0.65 | ... | 1.4 |
| | 1990 | MF | 33 | 18 | 70 | 69 | 0.69 | 30 | ... |
| | | M | 40 | 18 | 71 | 71 | 0.70 | ... | ... |
| | | F | 25 | 18 | 68 | 67 | 0.67 | ... | ... |
| | 1991 | MF | 31 | 17 | 70 | 70 | 0.65 | 27 | 2.6 |
| | | M | 38 | 16 | 65 | 65 | 0.62 | ... | 3.3 |
| | | F | 24 | 17 | 78 | 78 | 0.69 | ... | 2.0 |
| | 1992 | MF | 35 | 17 | ... | ... | ... | 27 | 2.7 |
| | | M | 43 | 16 | ... | ... | ... | 27 | 3.4 |
| | | F | 27 | 17 | ... | ... | ... | 27 | 2.1 |
| | 1993 | MF | 34 | 16 | 79 | 77 | 0.71 | ... | 2.8 |
| | | M | 41 | 16 | 78 | 77 | 0.72 | ... | 3.5 |
| | | F | 26 | 16 | 80 | 76 | 0.69 | ... | 2.2 |
| | 1994 | MF | 44 | 16 | ... | ... | ... | ... | ... |
| | | M | 54 | 16 | ... | ... | ... | ... | ... |
| | | F | 34 | 17 | ... | ... | ... | ... | ... |
| | 1995 | MF | 43 | 16 | ... | ... | ... | ... | ... |
| | | M | 53 | 16 | ... | ... | ... | ... | ... |
| | | F | 34 | 16 | ... | ... | ... | ... | ... |
| Burundi | 1975 | MF | 20 | 26 | 57 | 45 | 0.48 | 6 | ... |
| | | M | 24 | 27 | 57 | 47 | 0.49 | 6 | ... |
| | | F | 17 | 24 | 57 | 43 | 0.46 | 5 | ... |
| | 1980 | MF | 27 | 30 | ... | ... | ... | 8 | ... |
| | | M | 32 | 30 | ... | ... | ... | 8 | ... |
| | | F | 21 | 30 | ... | ... | ... | 7 | ... |
| | 1985 | MF | 61 | 18 | 87 | 87 | 0.73 | 9 | 3.5 |
| | | M | 68 | 18 | 87 | 87 | 0.73 | 9 | 4.2 |
| | | F | 54 | 18 | 87 | 86 | 0.72 | 9 | 2.9 |
| | 1990 | MF | 68 | 22 | ... | ... | ... | 10 | ... |
| | | M | 73 | 22 | ... | ... | ... | 11 | ... |
| | | F | 63 | 21 | ... | ... | ... | 9 | ... |
| | 1991 | MF | 59 | 23 | 74 | 74 | 0.68 | 11 | ... |
| | | M | 64 | 23 | 74 | 74 | 0.68 | 12 | ... |
| | | F | 53 | 23 | 75 | 73 | 0.67 | 11 | ... |
| | 1992 | MF | 62 | 24 | ... | ... | ... | ... | 4.9 |
| | | M | 67 | 24 | ... | ... | ... | ... | 5.5 |
| | | F | 56 | 23 | ... | ... | ... | ... | 4.3 |
| Cameroon | 1975 | MF | 96 | 25 | 57 | 53 | 0.56 | 22 | 6.9 |
| | | M | 104 | 26 | 57 | 54 | 0.57 | 24 | 8.0 |
| | | F | 89 | 24 | 57 | 51 | 0.54 | 20 | 5.9 |
| | 1980 | MF | 91 | 30 | 70 | 63 | 0.55 | 22 | ... |
| | | M | 99 | 30 | 70 | 65 | 0.56 | 24 | ... |
| | | F | 84 | 29 | 69 | 62 | 0.55 | 19 | ... |
| | 1985 | MF | 88 | 29 | 76 | 70 | 0.59 | 29 | ... |
| | | M | 94 | 30 | 76 | 70 | 0.58 | 31 | ... |
| | | F | 82 | 28 | 77 | 70 | 0.59 | 28 | ... |
| | 1990 | MF | 85 | 29 | ... | ... | ... | ... | ... |
| | | M | 90 | 30 | ... | ... | ... | ... | ... |
| | | F | 80 | 28 | ... | ... | ... | ... | ... |
| Cape Verde | 1980 | MF | 111 | 29 | ... | ... | ... | 30 | ... |
| | | M | 115 | 29 | ... | ... | ... | 31 | ... |
| | | F | 107 | 29 | ... | ... | ... | 28 | ... |
| | 1985 | MF | 103 | 28 | 51 | 39 | 0.36 | ... | ... |
| | | M | 111 | 29 | 53 | 42 | 0.37 | ... | ... |
| | | F | 96 | 26 | 48 | 37 | 0.34 | ... | ... |

Primary education: selected indicators II.11
Enseignement primaire: indicateurs selectionnés
Enseñanza primaria: indicadores seleccionados

| Country / Pays / País | Year / Année / Año | Sex / Sexe / Sexo | Apparent intake rate / Taux d'admission apparent / Tasa aparente de ingreso (%) | Percentage repeaters / Pourcentage de redoublants / Porcentaje de repetidores | Percentage of cohort reaching: Pourcentage de la cohorte atteignant: Porcentaje de la cohorte que llega al: | | Coefficient of efficiency / Coefficient d'efficacité / Coeficiente de eficacia | Transition rate (Prim. to Sec. gen.) / Taux de transition (Prim. au sec. gén.) / Tasa de transición (Prim. a la Sec. gen.) (%) | School life expectancy (in years) / Espérance de vie scolaire (années) / Esperanza de vida escolar (en años) |
|---|---|---|---|---|---|---|---|---|---|
| | | | | | Grade 5 / 5e année / Quinto año | Final grade / Dernière année / Ultimo año | | | |
| Cape Verde (cont) | 1993 | MF | 136 | 17 | ... | ... | ... | ... | ... |
| | | M | 136 | 18 | ... | ... | ... | ... | ... |
| | | F | 135 | 16 | ... | ... | ... | ... | ... |
| Central African Republic | 1970 | MF | 80 | 28 | 36 | 29 | 0.38 | 23 | 4.3 |
| | | M | 105 | 27 | 42 | 36 | 0.44 | 23 | 6.0 |
| | | F | 56 | 30 | 26 | 19 | 0.27 | 21 | 2.6 |
| | 1975 | MF | 64 | 35 | 57 | 53 | 0.48 | ... | ... |
| | | M | 79 | 36 | ... | ... | ... | ... | ... |
| | | F | 49 | 34 | ... | ... | ... | ... | ... |
| | 1980 | MF | 69 | 35 | 58 | 52 | 0.45 | 37 | ... |
| | | M | 86 | 34 | 63 | 60 | 0.49 | 38 | ... |
| | | F | 52 | 37 | 50 | 40 | 0.37 | 35 | ... |
| | 1985 | MF | 65 | 29 | ... | ... | ... | 26 | ... |
| | | M | 77 | 30 | ... | ... | ... | 25 | ... |
| | | F | 54 | 29 | ... | ... | ... | 26 | ... |
| | 1990 | MF | 59 | 32 | ... | ... | ... | ... | ... |
| | | M | 69 | 32 | ... | ... | ... | ... | ... |
| | | F | 51 | 32 | ... | ... | ... | ... | ... |
| | 1991 | MF | 51 | 37 | ... | ... | ... | ... | ... |
| | | M | 58 | 38 | ... | ... | ... | ... | ... |
| | | F | 45 | 37 | ... | ... | ... | ... | ... |
| Chad | 1970 | MF | 50 | 27 | ... | ... | ... | ... | ... |
| | 1975 | MF | 39 | 37 | 34 | 27 | 0.32 | ... | ... |
| | | M | 55 | 37 | 37 | 31 | 0.34 | ... | ... |
| | | F | 23 | 35 | 26 | 19 | 0.25 | ... | ... |
| | 1990 | MF | 55 | 32 | 53 | 44 | 0.40 | | ... |
| | | M | 69 | 32 | 58 | 49 | 0.42 | | ... |
| | | F | 41 | 34 | 43 | 34 | 0.33 | | ... |
| | 1991 | MF | 58 | 34 | ... | ... | ... | ... | ... |
| | | M | 72 | 33 | ... | ... | ... | ... | ... |
| | | F | 43 | 34 | ... | ... | ... | ... | ... |
| | 1993 | MF | 57 | 29 | 29 | 21 | 0.26 | 41 | ... |
| | | M | 73 | 29 | 33 | 25 | 0.30 | 41 | ... |
| | | F | 41 | 29 | 21 | 13 | 0.19 | 40 | ... |
| | 1994 | MF | 60 | 35 | 41 | 31 | 0.32 | 46 | ... |
| | | M | 76 | 34 | 47 | 37 | 0.36 | 46 | ... |
| | | F | 43 | 35 | 30 | 20 | 0.24 | 46 | ... |
| | 1995 | MF | 66 | 00 | 59 | 50 | 0.43 | ... | 3.9 |
| | | M | 82 | 33 | 62 | 53 | 0.46 | ... | ... |
| | | F | 49 | 33 | 53 | 41 | 0.37 | ... | ... |
| | 1996 | MF | 74 | 32 | ... | ... | ... | ... | ... |
| | | M | 91 | 32 | ... | ... | ... | ... | ... |
| | | F | 57 | 32 | ... | ... | ... | ... | ... |
| Comoros | 1980 | MF | 83 | 25 | ... | ... | ... | ... | ... |
| | 1985 | MF | 67 | 33 | 39 | 31 | 0.34 | 30 | ... |
| | | M | 76 | 32 | 33 | 26 | 0.30 | ... | ... |
| | | F | 58 | 33 | 46 | 39 | 0.39 | ... | ... |
| | 1991 | MF | ... | 39 | 46 | 32 | 0.31 | 18 | ... |
| | 1992 | MF | 60 | 41 | 79 | 74 | 0.53 | ... | ... |
| | 1993 | MF | 65 | 36 | ... | ... | ... | ... | ... |
| Congo | 1970 | MF | 103 | 33 | 76 | 71 | 0.56 | ... | ... |
| | 1975 | MF | 119 | 26 | 77 | 71 | 0.63 | 75 | ... |
| | | M | 124 | 27 | 79 | 74 | 0.64 | 76 | ... |
| | | F | 115 | 26 | 74 | 67 | 0.60 | 74 | ... |
| | 1980 | MF | 119 | 26 | 82 | 75 | 0.61 | 83 | ... |
| | | M | 124 | 26 | 81 | 76 | 0.61 | 86 | ... |
| | | F | 115 | 25 | 83 | 74 | 0.61 | 80 | ... |
| | 1985 | MF | 112 | 30 | 80 | 72 | 0.55 | 62 | ... |
| | | M | 117 | 31 | 82 | 72 | 0.53 | 65 | ... |
| | | F | 108 | 29 | 73 | 66 | 0.56 | 60 | ... |

II.11   Primary education: selected indicators
Enseignement primaire: indicateurs selectionnés
Enseñanza primaria: indicadores seleccionados

| Country / Pays / País | Year / Année / Año | Sex / Sexe / Sexo | Apparent intake rate / Taux d'admission apparent / Tasa aparente de ingreso (%) | Percentage repeaters / Pourcentage de redoublants / Porcentaje de repetidores | Percentage of cohort reaching: / Pourcentage de la cohorte atteignant: / Porcentaje de la cohorte que llega al: | | Coefficient of efficiency / Coefficient d'efficacité / Coeficiente de eficacia | Transition rate (Prim. to Sec. gen.) / Taux de transition (Prim. au sec. gén.) / Tasa de transición (Prim. a la Sec. gen.) (%) | School life expectancy (in years) / Espérance de vie scolaire (années) / Esperanza de vida escolar (en años) |
|---|---|---|---|---|---|---|---|---|---|
| | | | | | Grade 5 / 5e année / Quinto año | Final grade / Dernière année / Ultimo año | | | |
| Congo (cont) | 1990 | MF | 94 | 37 | 62 | 51 | 0.44 | ... | ... |
| | | M | 100 | 37 | 58 | 47 | 0.41 | ... | ... |
| | | F | 88 | 37 | 67 | 57 | 0.48 | ... | ... |
| | 1991 | MF | 102 | 33 | 80 | 70 | 0.53 | 46 | ... |
| | | M | 106 | 34 | 77 | 67 | 0.51 | 47 | ... |
| | | F | 98 | 32 | 82 | 74 | 0.54 | 46 | ... |
| | 1992 | MF | 96 | 34 | 65 | 52 | 0.42 | 48 | ... |
| | | M | 101 | 34 | 66 | 54 | 0.43 | 57 | ... |
| | | F | 92 | 34 | 63 | 50 | 0.42 | 39 | ... |
| | 1993 | MF | 90 | 36 | ... | ... | ... | ... | ... |
| | | M | 91 | 37 | ... | ... | ... | ... | ... |
| | | F | 90 | 35 | ... | ... | ... | ... | ... |
| | 1994 | MF | ... | ... | 55 | 37 | 0.34 | 51 | ... |
| | | M | ... | ... | 40 | 25 | 0.27 | 47 | ... |
| | | F | ... | ... | 78 | 56 | 0.44 | 56 | ... |
| | 1995 | MF | 87 | 33 | ... | ... | ... | ... | ... |
| | | M | 91 | 35 | ... | ... | ... | ... | ... |
| | | F | 83 | 32 | ... | ... | ... | ... | ... |
| Côte d'Ivoire | 1970 | MF | ... | ... | ... | ... | ... | 27 | ... |
| | | M | ... | ... | ... | ... | ... | 30 | ... |
| | | F | ... | ... | ... | ... | ... | 22 | ... |
| | 1975 | MF | 55 | 21 | 96 | 95 | 0.75 | 25 | ... |
| | | M | 65 | 21 | 100 | 99 | 0.76 | 26 | ... |
| | | F | 44 | 21 | 87 | 82 | 0.69 | 22 | ... |
| | 1980 | MF | 67 | 20 | 83 | 82 | 0.68 | 27 | ... |
| | | M | 77 | 20 | ... | ... | ... | ... | ... |
| | | F | 56 | 20 | ... | ... | ... | ... | ... |
| | 1985 | MF | 61 | 28 | 75 | 73 | 0.63 | 23 | ... |
| | | M | 70 | 29 | 80 | 78 | 0.65 | 23 | ... |
| | | F | 53 | 28 | 68 | 63 | 0.57 | 23 | ... |
| | 1990 | MF | 57 | 24 | 73 | 70 | 0.61 | 33 | ... |
| | | M | 65 | 24 | 75 | 74 | 0.63 | ... | ... |
| | | F | 49 | 24 | 70 | 63 | 0.56 | ... | ... |
| | 1992 | MF | 61 | 27 | 84 | 82 | 0.67 | 37 | ... |
| | | M | 69 | 27 | 86 | 84 | 0.67 | 37 | ... |
| | | F | 53 | 26 | 82 | 76 | 0.63 | 37 | ... |
| | 1993 | MF | 64 | 25 | 74 | 72 | 0.62 | 37 | ... |
| | | M | 72 | 26 | 77 | 76 | 0.65 | ... | ... |
| | | F | 55 | 25 | 71 | 64 | 0.57 | ... | ... |
| | 1994 | MF | 64 | 27 | 73 | 68 | 0.62 | 40 | ... |
| | | M | 72 | 27 | 76 | 74 | 0.66 | 42 | ... |
| | | F | 56 | 27 | 68 | 61 | 0.58 | 36 | ... |
| | 1995 | MF | 67 | 24 | 75 | 74 | 0.66 | 39 | ... |
| | | M | 76 | 23 | 77 | 77 | 0.67 | 42 | ... |
| | | F | 59 | 24 | 71 | 67 | 0.61 | 34 | ... |
| | 1996 | MF | 70 | 24 | ... | ... | ... | ... | ... |
| | | M | 79 | 24 | ... | ... | ... | ... | ... |
| | | F | 61 | 25 | ... | ... | ... | ... | ... |
| Democratic Rep. of the Congo | 1970 | MF | 112 | 23 | 46 | 41 | 0.49 | 40 | ... |
| | | M | 129 | 23 | 51 | 46 | 0.53 | 40 | ... |
| | | F | 95 | 23 | 38 | 31 | 0.40 | 37 | ... |
| | 1975 | MF | 98 | 21 | 59 | 56 | 0.62 | ... | ... |
| | | M | 112 | 21 | 61 | 60 | 0.65 | ... | ... |
| | | F | 84 | 22 | 55 | 50 | 0.56 | ... | ... |
| | 1980 | MF | 103 | 19 | 61 | 59 | 0.67 | ... | ... |
| | | M | 117 | 19 | 56 | 55 | 0.67 | ... | ... |
| | | F | 90 | 19 | 59 | 55 | 0.63 | ... | ... |
| | 1990 | MF | ... | ... | 55 | 47 | 0.59 | 27 | ... |
| | | M | ... | ... | 58 | 53 | 0.64 | 26 | ... |
| | | F | ... | ... | 50 | 40 | 0.53 | 29 | ... |
| | 1991 | MF | 80 | 12 | 64 | 64 | 0.77 | 32 | ... |
| | | M | 86 | 12 | 68 | 68 | 0.80 | 31 | ... |
| | | F | 74 | 12 | 58 | 58 | 0.73 | 34 | ... |

Primary education: selected indicators  II.11
Enseignement primaire: indicateurs selectionnés
Enseñanza primaria: indicadores seleccionados

| Country<br>Pays<br>País | Year<br>Année<br>Año | Sex<br>Sexe<br>Sexo | Apparent<br>intake rate<br>Taux<br>d'admission<br>apparent<br>Tasa<br>aparente de<br>ingreso<br>(%) | Percentage<br>repeaters<br>Pourcentage<br>de<br>redoublants<br>Porcentaje<br>de<br>repetidores | Percentage of cohort reaching:<br>Pourcentage de la cohorte atteignant:<br>Porcentaje de la cohorte que llega al: | | Coefficient of<br>efficiency<br>Coefficient<br>d'efficacité<br>Coeficiente<br>de eficacia | Transition rate<br>(Prim. to Sec. gen.)<br>Taux de transition<br>(Prim. au sec. gén.)<br>Tasa de transición<br>(Prim. a la Sec.<br>gen.)<br>(%) | School life<br>expectancy<br>(in years)<br>Espérance de<br>vie scolaire<br>(années)<br>Esperanza de<br>vida escolar<br>(en años) |
|---|---|---|---|---|---|---|---|---|---|
| | | | | | Grade 5<br>5e année<br>Quinto año | Final grade<br>Dernière année<br>Ultimo año | | | |
| Democratic Rep. of the Congo (cont) | 1992 | MF | 81 | 9 | 64 | 57 | 0.58 | 27 | ... |
| | | M | 89 | 8 | 73 | 67 | 0.64 | 25 | ... |
| | | F | 73 | 11 | 54 | 45 | 0.51 | 30 | ... |
| | 1993 | MF | 70 | 21 | ... | ... | ... | ... | ... |
| | | M | 78 | 21 | ... | ... | ... | ... | ... |
| | | F | 61 | 21 | ... | ... | ... | ... | ... |
| Djibouti | 1970 | MF | 24 | 11 | 81 | 81 | 0.78 | ... | ... |
| | | M | 34 | 11 | 81 | 81 | 0.79 | ... | ... |
| | | F | 14 | 10 | 79 | 79 | 0.74 | ... | ... |
| | 1975 | MF | 31 | 19 | ... | ... | ... | ... | ... |
| | | M | 43 | 21 | ... | ... | ... | ... | ... |
| | | F | 20 | 16 | ... | ... | ... | ... | ... |
| | 1985 | MF | 37 | 12 | 92 | 88 | 0.77 | 30 | ... |
| | 1990 | MF | 36 | 13 | 87 | 87 | 0.80 | 34 | ... |
| | 1991 | MF | 36 | 14 | ... | ... | ... | 31 | ... |
| | 1992 | MF | 31 | 14 | 98 | 98 | 0.84 | ... | ... |
| | 1993 | MF | 35 | 13 | 94 | 94 | 0.84 | ... | ... |
| | 1994 | MF | 38 | 12 | 82 | 82 | 0.77 | 36 | ... |
| | 1995 | MF | 38 | 15 | 79 | 77 | 0.73 | 39 | ... |
| | 1996 | MF | 35 | 16 | ... | ... | ... | ... | 3.4 |
| | | M | ... | ... | ... | ... | ... | ... | 3.9 |
| | | F | ... | ... | ... | ... | ... | ... | 2.8 |
| Egypt | 1970 | MF | 78 | 4 | 81 | 78 | 0.82 | ... | 6.2 |
| | | M | 91 | 4 | 85 | 83 | 0.85 | ... | 7.7 |
| | | F | 64 | 6 | 74 | 70 | 0.78 | ... | 4.5 |
| | 1975 | MF | 73 | 7 | 86 | 84 | 0.87 | 70 | ... |
| | | M | 84 | 7 | 88 | 87 | 0.89 | 70 | ... |
| | | F | 61 | 7 | 81 | 79 | 0.84 | 69 | ... |
| | 1980 | MF | 80 | 8 | 91 | 85 | 0.88 | ... | ... |
| | | M | 89 | 7 | 92 | 87 | 0.89 | ... | ... |
| | | F | 69 | 9 | 88 | 82 | 0.87 | ... | ... |
| | 1985 | MF | 88 | 2 | 97 | 95 | 0.94 | ... | ... |
| | | M | 95 | 2 | ... | ... | ... | ... | ... |
| | | F | 81 | 1 | ... | ... | ... | ... | ... |
| | 1993 | MF | ... | ... | ... | ... | ... | ... | 10.3 |
| | | M | ... | ... | ... | ... | ... | ... | 11.2 |
| | | F | ... | ... | ... | ... | ... | ... | 9.3 |
| | 1996 | MF | 90 | 6 | ... | ... | ... | ... | ... |
| | | M | 93 | 7 | ... | ... | ... | ... | ... |
| | | F | 85 | 5 | ... | ... | ... | ... | ... |
| Eritrea | 1992 | MF | ... | 25 | 83 | 83 | 0.73 | 77 | ... |
| | | M | ... | 22 | 85 | 85 | 0.77 | 84 | ... |
| | | F | ... | 29 | 80 | 80 | 0.69 | 70 | ... |
| | 1993 | MF | 52 | 20 | 79 | 79 | 0.73 | 80 | ... |
| | | M | 58 | 18 | 81 | 81 | 0.76 | 85 | ... |
| | | F | 46 | 23 | 76 | 76 | 0.70 | 74 | ... |
| | 1994 | MF | 49 | 19 | 79 | 79 | 0.70 | 79 | 4.1 |
| | | M | 53 | 17 | 78 | 78 | 0.74 | 83 | 4.7 |
| | | F | 44 | 21 | 79 | 79 | 0.66 | 74 | 3.5 |
| | 1995 | MF | 50 | 19 | 70 | 70 | 0.67 | 76 | 4.3 |
| | | M | 56 | 15 | 73 | 73 | 0.69 | 79 | 4.9 |
| | | F | 44 | 23 | 67 | 67 | 0.63 | 73 | 3.7 |
| | 1996 | MF | 42 | 20 | ... | ... | ... | ... | ... |
| | | M | 46 | 19 | ... | ... | ... | ... | ... |
| | | F | 38 | 22 | ... | ... | ... | ... | ... |
| Ethiopia | 1980 | MF | ... | ... | 50 | 50 | 0.69 | ... | ... |
| | | M | ... | ... | 50 | 49 | 0.69 | ... | ... |
| | | F | ... | ... | 51 | 51 | 0.68 | ... | ... |
| | 1985 | MF | ... | ... | 52 | 50 | 0.70 | 80 | ... |
| | | M | ... | ... | 56 | 54 | 0.73 | 84 | ... |
| | | F | ... | ... | 46 | 44 | 0.65 | 75 | ... |

II.11   Primary education: selected indicators
Enseignement primaire: indicateurs selectionnés
Enseñanza primaria: indicadores seleccionados

| Country<br>Pays<br>País | Year<br>Année<br>Año | Sex<br>Sexe<br>Sexo | Apparent intake rate<br>Taux d'admission apparent<br>Tasa aparente de ingreso (%) | Percentage repeaters<br>Pourcentage de redoublants<br>Porcentaje de repetidores | Percentage of cohort reaching:<br>Pourcentage de la cohorte atteignant:<br>Porcentaje de la cohorte que llega al: | | Coefficient of efficiency<br>Coefficient d'efficacité<br>Coeficiente de eficacia | Transition rate (Prim. to Sec. gen.)<br>Taux de transition (Prim. au sec. gén.)<br>Tasa de transición (Prim. a la Sec. gen.) (%) | School life expectancy (in years)<br>Espérance de vie scolaire (années)<br>Esperanza de vida escolar (en años) |
|---|---|---|---|---|---|---|---|---|---|
| | | | | | Grade 5<br>5e année<br>Quinto año | Final grade<br>Dernière année<br>Ultimo año | | | |
| Ethiopia (cont) | 1992 | MF | ... | ... | 58 | 56 | 0.74 | 80 | ... |
| | | M | ... | ... | 61 | 59 | 0.75 | 82 | ... |
| | | F | ... | ... | 54 | 52 | 0.71 | 77 | ... |
| | 1993 | MF | 52 | 9 | 51 | 51 | 0.74 | 77 | ... |
| | | M | 67 | 8 | 51 | 51 | 0.76 | 81 | ... |
| | | F | 36 | 10 | 51 | 49 | 0.70 | 72 | ... |
| | 1994 | MF | 60 | 9 | 55 | 55 | 0.75 | 82 | ... |
| | | M | 79 | 7 | 57 | 57 | 0.77 | 85 | ... |
| | | F | 42 | 11 | 53 | 53 | 0.72 | 77 | ... |
| | 1995 | MF | 73 | 10 | 51 | 47 | ... | 88 | ... |
| | | M | 95 | 9 | 51 | 47 | ... | 88 | ... |
| | | F | 50 | 12 | 50 | 46 | ... | 88 | ... |
| | 1996 | MF | 82 | 8 | ... | ... | ... | ... | ... |
| | | M | 105 | 7 | ... | ... | ... | ... | ... |
| | | F | 58 | 9 | ... | ... | ... | ... | ... |
| Gabon | 1970 | MF | ... | ... | 56 | 48 | 0.47 | 19 | ... |
| | | M | ... | ... | 58 | 52 | 0.50 | 19 | ... |
| | | F | ... | ... | 53 | 43 | 0.44 | 20 | ... |
| | 1975 | MF | ... | 34 | 50 | 49 | 0.50 | ... | ... |
| | | M | ... | 34 | 53 | 53 | 0.52 | ... | ... |
| | | F | ... | 34 | 46 | 45 | 0.48 | ... | ... |
| | 1980 | MF | ... | 35 | 56 | 55 | 0.52 | 23 | ... |
| | | M | ... | 35 | 57 | 56 | 0.52 | ... | ... |
| | | F | ... | 34 | 56 | 55 | 0.53 | ... | ... |
| | 1985 | MF | ... | ... | 61 | 55 | 0.49 | 35 | ... |
| | | M | ... | ... | 58 | 54 | 0.49 | ... | ... |
| | | F | ... | ... | 65 | 56 | 0.49 | ... | ... |
| | 1994 | MF | ... | 39 | 59 | 51 | 0.47 | ... | ... |
| | | M | ... | 40 | 58 | 50 | 0.46 | ... | ... |
| | | F | ... | 38 | 61 | 52 | 0.47 | ... | ... |
| Gambia | 1970 | MF | 21 | 13 | 89 | 89 | 0.84 | ... | ... |
| | | M | 27 | 15 | 92 | 92 | 0.84 | ... | ... |
| | | F | 15 | 11 | 85 | 85 | 0.85 | ... | ... |
| | 1975 | MF | 34 | 10 | 90 | 83 | 0.66 | 41 | ... |
| | | M | 45 | 11 | 95 | 88 | 0.68 | 39 | ... |
| | | F | 23 | 10 | 75 | 67 | 0.58 | 46 | ... |
| | 1980 | MF | 74 | 12 | 74 | 73 | 0.77 | 41 | ... |
| | | M | 91 | 13 | 74 | 74 | 0.78 | 41 | ... |
| | | F | 57 | 12 | 71 | 67 | 0.73 | 42 | ... |
| | 1985 | MF | ... | 17 | 97 | 95 | 0.80 | 32 | ... |
| | | M | ... | 18 | 97 | 97 | 0.80 | 31 | ... |
| | | F | ... | 16 | 93 | 86 | 0.76 | 34 | ... |
| | 1991 | MF | 69 | 16 | 87 | 82 | 0.78 | ... | ... |
| | | M | 80 | 17 | 85 | 81 | 0.77 | ... | ... |
| | | F | 59 | 15 | 89 | 82 | 0.78 | ... | ... |
| | 1992 | MF | 76 | 14 | 81 | 76 | 0.76 | ... | ... |
| | | M | 89 | 15 | 79 | 77 | 0.78 | ... | ... |
| | | F | 64 | 14 | 85 | 74 | 0.73 | ... | ... |
| | 1993 | MF | 83 | 13 | 76 | 70 | 0.73 | ... | ... |
| | | M | 95 | 13 | 76 | 71 | 0.74 | ... | ... |
| | | F | 70 | 13 | 77 | 68 | 0.72 | ... | ... |
| | 1994 | MF | 81 | 13 | 80 | 74 | 0.76 | ... | ... |
| | | M | 90 | 14 | 78 | 71 | 0.75 | ... | ... |
| | | F | 72 | 13 | 83 | 78 | 0.78 | ... | ... |
| | 1995 | MF | 95 | 13 | ... | ... | ... | ... | ... |
| | | M | 105 | 13 | ... | ... | ... | ... | ... |
| | | F | 85 | 12 | ... | ... | ... | ... | ... |
| Ghana | 1970 | MF | 75 | 3 | 75 | 72 | 0.83 | ... | ... |
| | | M | 82 | 3 | 79 | 77 | 0.87 | ... | ... |
| | | F | 68 | 3 | 70 | 65 | 0.80 | ... | ... |
| | 1975 | MF | 87 | 2 | 78 | 76 | 0.87 | ... | ... |
| | | M | 96 | 2 | 82 | 81 | 0.89 | ... | ... |
| | | F | 78 | 2 | 74 | 70 | 0.83 | ... | ... |

Primary education: selected indicators  II.11
Enseignement primaire: indicateurs selectionnés
Enseñanza primaria: indicadores seleccionados

| Country / Pays / País | Year / Année / Año | Sex / Sexe / Sexo | Apparent intake rate / Taux d'admission apparent / Tasa aparente de ingreso (%) | Percentage repeaters / Pourcentage de redoublants / Porcentaje de repetidores | Percentage of cohort reaching: / Pourcentage de la cohorte atteignant: / Porcentaje de la cohorte que llega al: | | Coefficient of efficiency / Coefficient d'efficacité / Coeficiente de eficacia | Transition rate (Prim. to Sec. gen.) / Taux de transition (Prim. au sec. gén.) / Tasa de transición (Prim. a la Sec. gen.) (%) | School life expectancy (in years) / Espérance de vie scolaire (années) / Esperanza de vida escolar (en años) |
|---|---|---|---|---|---|---|---|---|---|
| | | | | | Grade 5 / 5e année / Quinto año | Final grade / Dernière année / Ultimo año | | | |
| Ghana (cont) | 1980 | MF | 90 | 2 | ... | ... | ... | ... | ... |
| | | M | 96 | 2 | ... | ... | ... | ... | ... |
| | | F | 83 | 2 | ... | ... | ... | ... | ... |
| | 1990 | MF | 82 | 3 | 80 | 78 | 0.88 | ... | ... |
| | | M | 87 | 3 | 81 | 80 | 0.89 | ... | ... |
| | | F | 77 | 3 | 79 | 76 | 0.85 | ... | ... |
| | 1991 | MF | 80 | 3 | ... | ... | ... | ... | ... |
| | | M | 84 | 3 | ... | ... | ... | ... | ... |
| | | F | 76 | 3 | ... | ... | ... | ... | ... |
| Guinea | 1980 | MF | 33 | 22 | 55 | 46 | 0.48 | ... | ... |
| | 1985 | MF | 26 | 27 | 57 | 44 | 0.44 | 27 | 3.2 |
| | | M | 33 | 25 | 63 | 51 | 0.49 | 28 | 4.4 |
| | | F | 18 | 31 | 45 | 30 | 0.34 | 25 | 1.9 |
| | 1990 | MF | 43 | 20 | 59 | 52 | 0.55 | 61 | ... |
| | | M | 57 | 18 | 64 | 57 | 0.59 | 63 | ... |
| | | F | 28 | 23 | 48 | 40 | 0.46 | 56 | ... |
| | 1991 | MF | 38 | 20 | 80 | 72 | 0.61 | 48 | ... |
| | | M | 50 | 18 | 84 | 77 | 0.65 | 49 | ... |
| | | F | 26 | 22 | 70 | 60 | 0.52 | 44 | ... |
| | 1992 | MF | 50 | 21 | 80 | 72 | 0.61 | 50 | ... |
| | | M | 66 | 19 | 82 | 75 | 0.64 | 51 | ... |
| | | F | 34 | 23 | 75 | 66 | 0.56 | 47 | ... |
| | 1993 | MF | 46 | 22 | 80 | 70 | 0.58 | ... | ... |
| | | M | 58 | 21 | 85 | 79 | 0.64 | ... | ... |
| | | F | 33 | 24 | 68 | 52 | 0.44 | ... | ... |
| | 1994 | MF | 49 | 22 | 54 | 54 | 0.60 | ... | ... |
| | | M | 57 | 21 | ... | ... | ... | ... | ... |
| | | F | 40 | 24 | ... | ... | ... | ... | ... |
| | 1995 | MF | 48 | 24 | | | | | |
| | 1997 | MF | 41 | 28 | ... | ... | ... | ... | ... |
| | | M | 47 | 27 | ... | ... | ... | ... | ... |
| | | F | 36 | 29 | ... | ... | ... | ... | ... |
| Guinea-Bissau | 1980 | MF | 84 | 29 | ... | ... | ... | 65 | ... |
| | | M | 108 | 28 | ... | ... | ... | 71 | ... |
| | | F | 61 | 30 | ... | ... | ... | 46 | ... |
| Kenya | 1970 | MF | 77 | 5 | 74 | 74 | 0.85 | ... | ... |
| | | M | 85 | 5 | 73 | 73 | 0.84 | ... | ... |
| | | F | 68 | 5 | 76 | 69 | 0.79 | ... | ... |
| | 1975 | MF | ... | 5 | ... | ... | ... | ... | 8.3 |
| | 1980 | MF | 138 | 13 | 61 | 51 | 0.64 | ... | ... |
| | | M | 140 | 13 | 60 | 53 | 0.67 | ... | ... |
| | | F | 135 | 13 | 62 | 48 | 0.60 | ... | ... |
| Lesotho | 1970 | MF | ... | ... | 41 | ... | ... | ... | 7.7 |
| | | M | ... | ... | ... | ... | ... | ... | 6.5 |
| | | F | ... | ... | ... | ... | ... | ... | 8.8 |
| | 1975 | MF | 139 | 6 | 52 | 34 | 0.49 | ... | ... |
| | | M | 131 | 6 | 40 | 25 | 0.41 | ... | ... |
| | | F | 147 | 6 | 63 | 42 | 0.54 | ... | ... |
| | 1980 | MF | 129 | 21 | 60 | 48 | 0.54 | ... | 8.8 |
| | | M | 121 | 22 | 50 | 39 | 0.47 | ... | 7.3 |
| | | F | 137 | 20 | 68 | 56 | 0.59 | ... | 10.2 |
| | 1985 | MF | 126 | 23 | 60 | 46 | 0.51 | ... | 9.8 |
| | | M | 121 | 25 | 49 | 35 | 0.43 | ... | 8.6 |
| | | F | 132 | 21 | 70 | 56 | 0.58 | ... | 11.0 |
| | 1990 | MF | 113 | 22 | 71 | 57 | 0.57 | ... | ... |
| | | M | 111 | 25 | 58 | 42 | 0.46 | ... | ... |
| | | F | 115 | 19 | 83 | 70 | 0.66 | ... | ... |
| | 1991 | MF | 117 | 22 | 66 | 51 | 0.55 | ... | 9.7 |
| | | M | 114 | 25 | 59 | 44 | 0.49 | ... | 8.7 |
| | | F | 119 | 20 | 73 | 58 | 0.61 | ... | 10.8 |
| | 1992 | MF | 114 | 21 | 61 | 47 | 0.54 | ... | 9.7 |
| | | M | 111 | 24 | 54 | 40 | 0.48 | ... | 8.7 |
| | | F | 116 | 19 | 66 | 53 | 0.60 | ... | 10.6 |

II.11 Primary education: selected indicators
Enseignement primaire: indicateurs selectionnés
Enseñanza primaria: indicadores seleccionados

| Country / Pays / País | Year / Année / Año | Sex / Sexe / Sexo | Apparent intake rate / Taux d'admission apparent / Tasa aparente de ingreso (%) | Percentage repeaters / Pourcentage de redoublants / Porcentaje de repetidores | Percentage of cohort reaching: / Pourcentage de la cohorte atteignant: / Porcentaje de la cohorte que llega al: Grade 5 / 5e année / Quinto año | Percentage of cohort reaching: Final grade / Dernière année / Ultimo año | Coefficient of efficiency / Coefficient d'efficacité / Coeficiente de eficacia | Transition rate (Prim. to Sec. gen.) / Taux de transition (Prim. au sec. gén.) / Tasa de transición (Prim. a la Sec. gen.) (%) | School life expectancy (in years) / Espérance de vie scolaire (années) / Esperanza de vida escolar (en años) |
|---|---|---|---|---|---|---|---|---|---|
| Lesotho (cont) | 1993 | MF | 103 | 20 | 80 | 68 | 0.67 | ... | 9.4 |
| | | M | 101 | 22 | 72 | 58 | 0.59 | ... | 8.5 |
| | | F | 105 | 17 | 87 | 77 | 0.73 | ... | 10.2 |
| | 1994 | MF | 112 | 18 | ... | ... | ... | ... | 9.7 |
| | | M | 111 | 21 | ... | ... | ... | ... | 8.9 |
| | | F | 113 | 16 | ... | ... | ... | ... | 10.5 |
| | 1996 | MF | 103 | 20 | ... | ... | ... | ... | 9.6 |
| | | M | 102 | 23 | ... | ... | ... | ... | 8.9 |
| | | F | 103 | 18 | ... | ... | ... | ... | 10.4 |
| Libyan Arab Jamahiriya | 1970 | MF | 120 | 26 | 91 | 89 | 0.85 | 59 | 8.4 |
| | | M | 130 | 26 | 94 | 93 | 0.87 | 59 | 10.8 |
| | | F | 110 | 25 | 86 | 83 | 0.82 | 60 | 5.6 |
| | 1975 | MF | 123 | 16 | 89 | 83 | 0.77 | 75 | 11.6 |
| | | M | 124 | 17 | 93 | 88 | 0.79 | 75 | 13.0 |
| | | F | 121 | 16 | 85 | 77 | 0.73 | 74 | 10.1 |
| | 1980 | MF | 116 | 9 | ... | ... | ... | ... | 12.3 |
| | | M | 117 | 10 | ... | ... | ... | ... | 13.4 |
| | | F | 115 | 8 | ... | ... | ... | ... | 11.1 |
| Madagascar | 1990 | MF | 103 | 36 | 22 | 22 | ... | ... | ... |
| | | M | 99 | 37 | 22 | 22 | ... | ... | ... |
| | | F | 107 | 34 | 21 | 21 | ... | ... | ... |
| | 1991 | MF | 102 | 34 | 31 | 31 | 0.37 | ... | ... |
| | | M | 111 | 34 | 29 | 29 | 0.35 | ... | ... |
| | | F | 93 | 33 | 34 | 34 | 0.38 | ... | ... |
| | 1992 | MF | 97 | 33 | 28 | 28 | 0.33 | 35 | ... |
| | | M | 96 | 34 | 26 | 26 | 0.31 | 35 | ... |
| | | F | 99 | 32 | 30 | 30 | 0.35 | 35 | ... |
| | 1993 | MF | 102 | 32 | 27 | 27 | 0.33 | ... | ... |
| | | M | 101 | 34 | 23 | 23 | 0.31 | ... | ... |
| | | F | 103 | 31 | 32 | 32 | 0.35 | ... | ... |
| | 1994 | MF | 100 | 32 | 40 | 40 | 0.38 | 42 | ... |
| | | M | 94 | 33 | 49 | 49 | 0.40 | 41 | ... |
| | | F | 106 | 30 | 33 | 33 | 0.36 | 43 | ... |
| | 1995 | MF | 102 | 34 | ... | ... | ... | ... | ... |
| | | M | 102 | 35 | ... | ... | ... | ... | ... |
| | | F | 102 | 33 | ... | ... | ... | ... | ... |
| Malawi | 1975 | MF | 91 | 16 | 37 | 30 | 0.49 | ... | ... |
| | | M | 103 | 16 | 40 | 33 | 0.53 | ... | ... |
| | | F | 80 | 17 | 33 | 24 | 0.42 | ... | ... |
| | 1980 | MF | 100 | 17 | 44 | 34 | 0.52 | ... | ... |
| | | M | 109 | 18 | 48 | 40 | 0.58 | ... | ... |
| | | F | 91 | 17 | 40 | 22 | 0.38 | ... | ... |
| | 1985 | MF | 86 | 18 | 57 | 45 | 0.54 | ... | ... |
| | | M | 90 | 18 | 60 | 49 | 0.56 | ... | ... |
| | | F | 82 | 17 | 54 | 37 | 0.46 | ... | ... |
| | 1990 | MF | 101 | 19 | 64 | 38 | 0.45 | ... | ... |
| | | M | 105 | 19 | 71 | 42 | 0.46 | ... | ... |
| | | F | 97 | 19 | 57 | 35 | 0.45 | ... | ... |
| Mali | 1970 | MF | 27 | 26 | 54 | 44 | 0.43 | 33 | 1.8 |
| | | M | ... | ... | ... | ... | ... | ... | 2.4 |
| | | F | ... | ... | ... | ... | ... | ... | 1.2 |
| | 1975 | MF | 28 | 23 | 66 | 58 | 0.56 | ... | ... |
| | 1980 | MF | 23 | 30 | ... | ... | ... | 39 | ... |
| | | M | 29 | 29 | ... | ... | ... | 41 | ... |
| | | F | 16 | 30 | ... | ... | ... | 36 | ... |
| | 1985 | MF | 22 | 30 | 53 | 39 | 0.40 | 43 | ... |
| | | M | ... | ... | 55 | 42 | 0.42 | 45 | ... |
| | | F | ... | ... | 50 | 36 | 0.37 | 40 | ... |
| | 1990 | MF | 27 | 27 | 72 | 65 | 0.54 | ... | 2.1 |
| | | M | 34 | 27 | 73 | 65 | 0.56 | ... | 2.7 |
| | | F | 20 | 28 | 70 | 64 | 0.51 | ... | 1.4 |
| | 1991 | MF | 28 | 31 | 76 | 63 | 0.53 | 58 | ... |
| | | M | 35 | 30 | 81 | 66 | 0.54 | 63 | ... |
| | | F | 20 | 31 | 69 | 58 | 0.50 | 51 | ... |

Primary education: selected indicators  II.11
Enseignement primaire: indicateurs selectionnés
Enseñanza primaria: indicadores seleccionados

| Country<br><br>Pays<br><br>País | Year<br><br>Année<br><br>Año | Sex<br><br>Sexe<br><br>Sexo | Apparent intake rate<br>Taux d'admission apparent<br>Tasa aparente de ingreso (%) | Percentage repeaters<br>Pourcentage de redoublants<br>Porcentaje de repetidores | Percentage of cohort reaching:<br>Pourcentage de la cohorte atteignant:<br>Porcentaje de la cohorte que llega al:<br>Grade 5<br>5e année<br>Quinto año | Final grade<br>Dernière année<br>Ultimo año | Coefficient of efficiency<br>Coefficient d'efficacité<br>Coeficiente de eficacia | Transition rate (Prim. to Sec. gen.)<br>Taux de transition (Prim. au sec. gén.)<br>Tasa de transición (Prim. a la Sec. gen.) (%) | School life expectancy (in years)<br>Espérance de vie scolaire (années)<br>Esperanza de vida escolar (en años) |
|---|---|---|---|---|---|---|---|---|---|
| Mali (cont) | 1992 | MF | 38 | 27 | 82 | 75 | 0.60 | 61 | ... |
|  |  | M | 45 | 27 | 85 | 77 | 0.61 | 64 | ... |
|  |  | F | 31 | 26 | 77 | 70 | 0.58 | 56 | ... |
|  | 1993 | MF | 36 | 25 | 77 | 65 | 0.50 | ... | ... |
|  |  | M | 42 | 25 | 71 | 59 | 0.51 | ... | ... |
|  |  | F | 31 | 25 | 86 | 75 | 0.49 | ... | ... |
|  | 1994 | MF | 37 | 28 | 84 | 77 | 0.67 | 55 | ... |
|  |  | M | 42 | 28 | 92 | 86 | 0.68 | 57 | ... |
|  |  | F | 32 | 27 | 70 | 61 | 0.64 | 51 | ... |
|  | 1995 | MF | 42 | 18 | 84 | 77 | 0.66 | ... | ... |
|  |  | M | 49 | 18 | ... | ... | ... | ... | ... |
|  |  | F | 35 | 18 | ... | ... | ... | ... | ... |
|  | 1996 | MF | 52 | 16 | ... | ... | ... | ... | ... |
| Mauritania | 1975 | MF | 31 | 15 | 92 | 84 | 0.71 | ... | ... |
|  |  | M | 40 | 13 | 99 | 99 | 0.80 | ... | ... |
|  |  | F | 21 | 18 | 77 | 41 | 0.40 | ... | ... |
|  | 1980 | MF | 35 | 14 | ... | ... | ... | ... | ... |
|  |  | M | 45 | 13 | ... | ... | ... | ... | ... |
|  |  | F | 25 | 17 | ... | ... | ... | ... | ... |
|  | 1985 | MF | 48 | 18 | 92 | 92 | 0.74 | 29 | ... |
|  |  | M | 58 | 17 | 97 | 96 | 0.77 | ... | ... |
|  |  | F | 38 | 20 | 82 | 77 | 0.65 | ... | ... |
|  | 1990 | MF | 53 | 18 | 75 | 75 | 0.70 | 31 | ... |
|  |  | M | 60 | 17 | 75 | 75 | 0.71 | 33 | ... |
|  |  | F | 46 | 19 | 75 | 74 | 0.67 | 27 | ... |
|  | 1991 | MF | 69 | 17 | 75 | 75 | 0.71 | 34 | ... |
|  |  | M | 76 | 17 | 73 | 73 | 0.71 | 37 | ... |
|  |  | F | 62 | 18 | 79 | 79 | 0.70 | 29 | ... |
|  | 1992 | MF | 86 | 16 | 72 | 69 | 0.67 | 32 | ... |
|  |  | M | 94 | 15 | 74 | 71 | 0.70 | 34 | ... |
|  |  | F | 78 | 17 | 69 | 65 | 0.64 | 28 | ... |
|  | 1993 | MF | 89 | 16 | 66 | 62 | 0.65 | 35 | ... |
|  |  | M | 96 | 16 | 68 | 66 | 0.69 | 38 | ... |
|  |  | F | 83 | 17 | 63 | 57 | 0.60 | 30 | ... |
|  | 1994 | MF | 86 | 16 | 63 | 56 | 0.60 | ... | ... |
|  |  | M | 93 | 16 | 63 | 56 | 0.62 | ... | ... |
|  |  | F | 79 | 17 | 62 | 56 | 0.59 | ... | ... |
|  | 1995 | MF | 92 | 16 | 64 | 58 | 0.61 | ... | ... |
|  |  | M | 97 | 15 | 61 | 56 | 0.61 | ... | ... |
|  |  | F | 86 | 17 | 68 | 62 | 0.61 | ... | ... |
|  | 1996 | MF | 92 | 16 | ... | ... | ... | ... | ... |
|  |  | M | 95 | 15 | ... | ... | ... | ... | ... |
|  |  | F | 89 | 17 | ... | ... | ... | ... | ... |
| Mauritius | 1975 | MF | ... | ... | ... | ... | ... | 40 | 8.9 |
|  |  | M | ... | ... | ... | ... | ... | 42 | 9.2 |
|  |  | F | ... | ... | ... | ... | ... | 37 | 8.5 |
|  | 1985 | MF | 112 | 6 | 97 | 96 | 0.90 | 43 | ... |
|  |  | M | 112 | 6 | 97 | 95 | 0.89 | ... | ... |
|  |  | F | 111 | 6 | 97 | 96 | 0.91 | ... | ... |
|  | 1990 | MF | 99 | 5 | 98 | 97 | 0.91 | 50 | ... |
|  |  | M | 99 | 5 | 98 | 97 | 0.91 | 47 | ... |
|  |  | F | 99 | 5 | 98 | 97 | 0.91 | 53 | ... |
|  | 1991 | MF | 95 | 7 | 97 | 97 | 0.91 | 46 | ... |
|  |  | M | 95 | 8 | 97 | 96 | 0.91 | 45 | ... |
|  |  | F | 96 | 7 | 98 | 98 | 0.92 | 48 | ... |
|  | 1992 | MF | 96 | 8 | 99 | 99 | 0.93 | 51 | ... |
|  |  | M | 97 | 8 | 100 | 99 | 0.93 | 49 | ... |
|  |  | F | 95 | 8 | 99 | 99 | 0.93 | 54 | ... |
|  | 1993 | MF | 102 | 8 | 99 | 99 | 0.94 | 51 | ... |
|  |  | M | 101 | 8 | 99 | 98 | 0.93 | 49 | ... |
|  |  | F | 104 | 8 | 99 | 99 | 0.94 | 54 | ... |
|  | 1994 | MF | 106 | 7 | 99 | 98 | 0.93 | 56 | ... |
|  |  | M | 106 | 7 | 98 | 97 | 0.93 | 52 | ... |
|  |  | F | 106 | 6 | 99 | 98 | 0.94 | 60 | ... |

II.11    Primary education: selected indicators
Enseignement primaire: indicateurs sélectionnés
Enseñanza primaria: indicadores seleccionados

| Country / Pays / País | Year / Année / Año | Sex / Sexe / Sexo | Apparent intake rate / Taux d'admission apparent / Tasa aparente de ingreso (%) | Percentage repeaters / Pourcentage de redoublants / Porcentaje de repetidores | Percentage of cohort reaching: / Pourcentage de la cohorte atteignant: / Porcentaje de la cohorte que llega al: | | Coefficient of efficiency / Coefficient d'efficacité / Coeficiente de eficacia | Transition rate (Prim. to Sec. gen.) / Taux de transition (Prim. au sec. gén.) / Tasa de transición (Prim. a la Sec. gen.) (%) | School life expectancy (in years) / Espérance de vie scolaire (années) / Esperanza de vida escolar (en años) |
|---|---|---|---|---|---|---|---|---|---|
| | | | | | Grade 5 / 5e année / Quinto año | Final grade / Dernière année / Ultimo año | | | |
| Mauritius (cont) | 1995 | MF | 109 | 6 | 99 | 99 | 0.95 | 61 | ... |
| | | M | 110 | 6 | 98 | 98 | 0.94 | 57 | ... |
| | | F | 109 | 5 | 99 | 99 | 0.95 | 65 | ... |
| | 1996 | MF | 110 | 4 | 99 | 98 | ... | 61 | ... |
| | | M | 110 | 5 | 98 | 96 | ... | 57 | ... |
| | | F | 111 | 4 | 99 | 98 | ... | 65 | ... |
| Morocco | 1970 | MF | 46 | 30 | 66 | 66 | 0.55 | 27 | ... |
| | 1975 | MF | 58 | 28 | 78 | 78 | 0.60 | 36 | 4.5 |
| | | M | ... | ... | 78 | 78 | 0.59 | 35 | 5.8 |
| | | F | ... | ... | 79 | 79 | 0.61 | 39 | 3.2 |
| | 1980 | MF | 71 | 29 | 79 | 79 | 0.61 | ... | 6.4 |
| | | M | 85 | 30 | 79 | 79 | 0.60 | ... | 8.1 |
| | | F | 57 | 28 | 78 | 78 | 0.62 | ... | 4.8 |
| | 1985 | MF | 76 | 20 | 69 | 69 | 0.66 | 54 | ... |
| | | M | 89 | 21 | 70 | 70 | 0.65 | 51 | ... |
| | | F | 62 | 18 | 67 | 67 | 0.67 | 59 | ... |
| | 1990 | MF | 76 | 11 | 75 | 68 | 0.71 | 87 | ... |
| | | M | 87 | 12 | 75 | 67 | 0.69 | 86 | ... |
| | | F | 65 | 10 | 76 | 69 | 0.74 | 88 | ... |
| | 1991 | MF | 79 | 12 | 80 | 74 | 0.74 | 81 | ... |
| | | M | 89 | 14 | 80 | 74 | 0.72 | 79 | ... |
| | | F | 68 | 10 | 80 | 74 | 0.76 | 84 | ... |
| | 1992 | MF | 87 | 12 | 79 | 73 | 0.74 | 82 | ... |
| | | M | 99 | 14 | 79 | 73 | 0.73 | 81 | ... |
| | | F | 75 | 10 | 80 | 74 | 0.77 | 85 | ... |
| | 1993 | MF | 91 | 12 | 80 | 74 | 0.75 | 82 | ... |
| | | M | 101 | 14 | 80 | 75 | 0.74 | 80 | ... |
| | | F | 80 | 10 | 79 | 74 | 0.77 | 85 | ... |
| | 1994 | MF | 90 | 12 | 78 | 72 | 0.74 | ... | ... |
| | | M | 99 | 13 | 79 | 73 | 0.73 | ... | ... |
| | | F | 81 | 10 | 77 | 71 | 0.75 | ... | ... |
| | 1995 | MF | 91 | 12 | 75 | 68 | 0.71 | 79 | ... |
| | | M | 98 | 13 | 76 | 69 | 0.70 | 77 | ... |
| | | F | 83 | 10 | 74 | 68 | 0.73 | 82 | ... |
| | 1996 | MF | 92 | 12 | ... | ... | ... | ... | ... |
| | | M | 100 | 14 | ... | ... | ... | ... | ... |
| | | F | 84 | 10 | ... | ... | ... | ... | ... |
| Mozambique | 1985 | MF | ... | 24 | . | 40 | 0.45 | 34 | ... |
| | | M | ... | 23 | . | 44 | 0.49 | 34 | ... |
| | | F | ... | 24 | . | 34 | 0.41 | 34 | ... |
| | 1990 | MF | 73 | 26 | 33 | 33 | 0.41 | ... | ... |
| | | M | 81 | 25 | 37 | 37 | 0.43 | ... | ... |
| | | F | 65 | 27 | 28 | 28 | 0.37 | ... | ... |
| | 1991 | MF | 63 | 24 | 34 | 34 | 0.40 | 39 | ... |
| | | M | 70 | 24 | 37 | 37 | 0.42 | 39 | ... |
| | | F | 56 | 26 | 32 | 32 | 0.38 | 39 | ... |
| | 1992 | MF | 60 | 25 | 35 | 35 | 0.40 | 39 | 3.6 |
| | | M | 67 | 25 | 39 | 39 | 0.42 | 39 | 4.2 |
| | | F | 53 | 26 | 31 | 31 | 0.37 | 39 | 3.0 |
| | 1993 | MF | 64 | 26 | 43 | 43 | 0.45 | 40 | 3.5 |
| | | M | 72 | 25 | 48 | 48 | 0.48 | 41 | 4.1 |
| | | F | 57 | 26 | 36 | 36 | 0.40 | 38 | 2.9 |
| | 1994 | MF | 65 | 26 | 46 | 46 | 0.46 | 41 | 3.5 |
| | | M | 74 | 25 | 52 | 52 | 0.49 | 41 | 4.2 |
| | | F | 57 | 27 | 39 | 39 | 0.42 | 41 | 2.9 |
| | 1995 | MF | 69 | 26 | ... | ... | ... | ... | 3.7 |
| | | M | 77 | 25 | ... | ... | ... | ... | 4.3 |
| | | F | 61 | 27 | ... | ... | ... | ... | 3.0 |
| Namibia | 1991 | MF | ... | ... | 63 | 52 | 0.56 | 74 | ... |
| | | M | ... | ... | 61 | 51 | 0.55 | 76 | ... |
| | | F | ... | ... | 65 | 54 | 0.57 | 72 | ... |
| | 1992 | MF | 142 | 25 | ... | ... | ... | ... | ... |
| | | M | 141 | 26 | ... | ... | ... | ... | ... |
| | | F | 142 | 23 | ... | ... | ... | ... | ... |

Primary education: selected indicators    II.11
Enseignement primaire: indicateurs selectionnés
Enseñanza primaria: indicadores seleccionados

| Country / Pays / País | Year / Année / Año | Sex / Sexe / Sexo | Apparent intake rate / Taux d'admission apparent / Tasa aparente de ingreso (%) | Percentage repeaters / Pourcentage de redoublants / Porcentaje de repetidores | Percentage of cohort reaching: Grade 5 / 5e année / Quinto año | Percentage of cohort reaching: Final grade / Dernière année / Ultimo año | Coefficient of efficiency / Coefficient d'efficacité / Coeficiente de eficacia | Transition rate (Prim. to Sec. gen.) / Taux de transition (Prim. au sec. gén.) / Tasa de transición (Prim. a la Sec. gen.) (%) | School life expectancy (in years) / Espérance de vie scolaire (années) / Esperanza de vida escolar (en años) |
|---|---|---|---|---|---|---|---|---|---|
| Namibia (cont) | 1993 | MF | ... | ... | 82 | 74 | 0.67 | 74 | ... |
| | | M | ... | ... | 80 | 72 | 0.65 | ... | ... |
| | | F | ... | ... | 84 | 76 | 0.69 | ... | ... |
| | 1994 | MF | 125 | 23 | 76 | 64 | 0.65 | 74 | 13.7 |
| | | M | 126 | 24 | ... | ... | ... | ... | ... |
| | | F | 125 | 21 | ... | ... | ... | ... | ... |
| | 1995 | MF | 110 | 18 | 79 | 67 | 0.69 | 77 | 12.9 |
| | | M | ... | ... | 76 | 63 | ... | 78 | ... |
| | | F | ... | ... | 82 | 70 | ... | 77 | ... |
| | 1996 | MF | 117 | 13 | 86 | 75 | ... | 81 | ... |
| | | M | 118 | 14 | ... | ... | ... | ... | ... |
| | | F | 117 | 12 | ... | ... | ... | ... | ... |
| | 1997 | MF | 117 | 12 | ... | ... | ... | ... | ... |
| Niger | 1970 | MF | 15 | 19 | 55 | 51 | 0.55 | 24 | ... |
| | | M | 20 | 19 | 57 | 54 | 0.58 | 26 | ... |
| | | F | 11 | 20 | 51 | 47 | 0.51 | 20 | ... |
| | 1975 | MF | 27 | 13 | 70 | 66 | 0.67 | 34 | ... |
| | | M | 36 | 13 | 72 | 68 | 0.69 | 35 | ... |
| | | F | 18 | 13 | 67 | 63 | 0.65 | 30 | ... |
| | 1980 | MF | 28 | 14 | 73 | 73 | 0.75 | ... | 1.9 |
| | | M | 37 | 15 | 74 | 74 | 0.75 | ... | ... |
| | | F | 20 | 14 | 72 | 72 | 0.74 | ... | ... |
| | 1985 | MF | 26 | 15 | 76 | 76 | 0.74 | ... | ... |
| | | M | 33 | 15 | 76 | 76 | 0.74 | ... | ... |
| | | F | 19 | 15 | 75 | 75 | 0.74 | ... | ... |
| | 1990 | MF | 27 | 14 | 62 | 57 | 0.62 | 27 | 2.3 |
| | | M | 35 | 14 | 61 | 56 | 0.61 | 28 | ... |
| | | F | 20 | 14 | 65 | 59 | 0.63 | 24 | ... |
| | 1991 | MF | 27 | 15 | 77 | 61 | 0.57 | ... | ... |
| | | M | 34 | 15 | 76 | 58 | 0.55 | ... | ... |
| | | F | 20 | 16 | 78 | 66 | 0.62 | ... | ... |
| | 1992 | MF | 27 | 18 | ... | ... | ... | ... | ... |
| | | M | 34 | 18 | ... | ... | ... | ... | ... |
| | | F | 20 | 16 | ... | ... | ... | ... | ... |
| | 1995 | MF | 31 | 16 | 73 | 67 | 0.69 | 29 | ... |
| | | M | 39 | 19 | 72 | 66 | 0.68 | 28 | ... |
| | | F | 24 | 12 | 73 | 68 | 0.69 | 29 | ... |
| | 1996 | MF | 32 | 13 | ... | ... | ... | ... | ... |
| | | M | 38 | 13 | ... | ... | ... | ... | ... |
| | | F | 25 | 13 | ... | ... | ... | ... | ... |
| Reunion | 1975 | MF | 102 | 22 | 89 | 89 | 0.72 | 67 | ... |
| | 1985 | MF | 103 | 16 | 96 | 96 | 0.82 | 71 | ... |
| Rwanda | 1970 | MF | 67 | 30 | 40 | 30 | 0.37 | 37 | ... |
| | | M | 73 | 30 | 42 | 34 | 0.40 | 40 | ... |
| | | F | 62 | 29 | 37 | 26 | 0.33 | 33 | ... |
| | 1975 | MF | ... | ... | 58 | 48 | 0.54 | 54 | ... |
| | | M | ... | ... | 58 | 50 | 0.55 | 55 | ... |
| | | F | ... | ... | 58 | 46 | 0.52 | 52 | ... |
| | 1980 | MF | 78 | 6 | 71 | 47 | 0.54 | ... | ... |
| | | M | 80 | 6 | 69 | 50 | 0.58 | ... | ... |
| | | F | 76 | 6 | 74 | 44 | 0.50 | ... | ... |
| | 1985 | MF | 85 | 12 | 69 | 49 | 0.59 | ... | ... |
| | | M | 86 | 12 | 68 | 52 | 0.62 | ... | ... |
| | | F | 84 | 12 | 70 | 45 | 0.55 | ... | ... |
| | 1990 | MF | 94 | 12 | 60 | ... | ... | ... | ... |
| | | M | 95 | 13 | 61 | ... | ... | ... | ... |
| | | F | 94 | 12 | 59 | ... | ... | ... | ... |
| | 1991 | MF | 106 | 14 | ... | ... | ... | ... | ... |
| | | M | 107 | 15 | ... | ... | ... | ... | ... |
| | | F | 105 | 14 | ... | ... | ... | ... | ... |

II.11  Primary education: selected indicators
Enseignement primaire: indicateurs selectionnés
Enseñanza primaria: indicadores seleccionados

| Country<br>Pays<br>País | Year<br>Année<br>Año | Sex<br>Sexe<br>Sexo | Apparent intake rate<br>Taux d'admission apparent<br>Tasa aparente de ingreso (%) | Percentage repeaters<br>Pourcentage de redoublants<br>Porcentaje de repetidores | Percentage of cohort reaching:<br>Pourcentage de la cohorte atteignant:<br>Porcentaje de la cohorte que llega al:<br>Grade 5 / 5e année / Quinto año | Final grade<br>Dernière année<br>Ultimo año | Coefficient of efficiency<br>Coefficient d'efficacité<br>Coeficiente de eficacia | Transition rate (Prim. to Sec. gen.)<br>Taux de transition (Prim. au sec. gén.)<br>Tasa de transición (Prim. a la Sec. gen.) (%) | School life expectancy (in years)<br>Espérance de vie scolaire (années)<br>Esperanza de vida escolar (en años) |
|---|---|---|---|---|---|---|---|---|---|
| Senegal | 1970 | MF | 36 | 20 | 73 | 71 | 0.68 | 32 | ... |
|  |  | M | 44 | 20 | 74 | 74 | 0.70 | ... | ... |
|  |  | F | 29 | 20 | 71 | 66 | 0.64 | ... | ... |
|  | 1980 | MF | 45 | 16 | 86 | 86 | 0.76 | 29 | ... |
|  |  | M | 53 | 15 | 89 | 89 | 0.78 | ... | ... |
|  |  | F | 37 | 16 | 82 | 79 | 0.72 | ... | ... |
|  | 1985 | MF | 47 | 16 | ... | ... | ... | ... | ... |
|  |  | M | 54 | 16 | ... | ... | ... | ... | ... |
|  |  | F | 40 | 17 | ... | ... | ... | ... | ... |
|  | 1990 | MF | ... | ... | 85 | 79 | 0.73 | 26 | ... |
|  | 1991 | MF | 55 | 16 | ... | ... | ... | ... | ... |
|  |  | M | 61 | 16 | ... | ... | ... | ... | ... |
|  |  | F | 49 | 16 | ... | ... | ... | ... | ... |
|  | 1992 | MF | ... | ... | 87 | 83 | 0.76 | ... | ... |
|  | 1993 | MF | 59 | 15 | 81 | 75 | ... | ... | ... |
|  |  | M | 65 | 15 | 83 | 80 | ... | ... | ... |
|  |  | F | 52 | 15 | 78 | 69 | ... | ... | ... |
|  | 1994 | MF | 61 | 15 | 81 | 76 | 0.73 | 31 | ... |
|  |  | M | 67 | 15 | 81 | 78 | ... | 32 | ... |
|  |  | F | 55 | 15 | 81 | 73 | ... | 29 | ... |
|  | 1995 | MF | 76 | 14 | 85 | 81 | 0.76 | 30 | ... |
|  |  | M | 80 | 14 | 89 | 87 | 0.80 | 31 | ... |
|  |  | F | 71 | 14 | 81 | 74 | 0.72 | 29 | ... |
|  | 1996 | MF | 78 | 13 | 87 | 84 | ... | 30 | ... |
|  |  | M | 82 | 13 | 89 | 87 | ... | 32 | ... |
|  |  | F | 75 | 13 | 85 | 80 | ... | 29 | ... |
|  | 1997 | MF | 74 | 13 | ... | ... | ... | ... | ... |
|  |  | M | 77 | 13 | ... | ... | ... | ... | ... |
|  |  | F | 71 | 13 | ... | ... | ... | ... | ... |
| Seychelles | 1975 | MF | ... | 1 | 88 | 86 | 0.93 | ... | ... |
|  |  | M | ... | 1 | 90 | 86 | 0.93 | ... | ... |
|  |  | F | ... | 1 | 82 | 81 | 0.89 | ... | ... |
|  | 1980 | MF | ... | - | 100 | 89 | 0.92 | ... | ... |
|  |  | M | ... | - | 98 | 86 | 0.90 | ... | ... |
|  |  | F | ... | - | 100 | 90 | 0.93 | ... | ... |
|  | 1985 | MF | ... | - | 96 | 93 | 0.96 | ... | ... |
|  |  | M | ... | - | 97 | 93 | 0.96 | ... | ... |
|  |  | F | ... | - | 95 | 92 | 0.96 | ... | ... |
|  | 1991 | MF | ... | - | 93 | 92 | 0.96 | 99 | ... |
|  |  | M | ... | - | 91 | 91 | 0.97 | 99 | ... |
|  |  | F | ... | - | 94 | 91 | 0.94 | 100 | ... |
|  | 1992 | MF | ... | - | 97 | 97 | 0.99 | ... | ... |
|  |  | M | ... | - | 99 | 99 | 1.00 | ... | ... |
|  |  | F | ... | - | 92 | 90 | 0.94 | ... | ... |
|  | 1993 | MF | ... | - | 99 | 99 | 1.00 | ... | ... |
|  |  | M | ... | - | 96 | 93 | 0.96 | ... | ... |
|  |  | F | ... | - | 99 | 99 | 1.00 | ... | ... |
|  | 1994 | MF | ... | - | 97 | 97 | 0.99 | ... | ... |
|  |  | M | ... | - | 99 | 99 | 1.00 | ... | ... |
|  |  | F | ... | - | 96 | 95 | 0.98 | ... | ... |
|  | 1995 | MF | ... | - | 99 | 99 | 0.99 | ... | ... |
|  |  | M | ... | - | 98 | 98 | 0.99 | ... | ... |
|  |  | F | ... | - | 99 | 99 | 0.99 | ... | ... |
| South Africa | 1990 | MF | ... | ... | 75 | 68 | 0.75 | 90 | ... |
|  |  | M | ... | ... | 72 | 63 | 0.71 | 87 | ... |
|  |  | F | ... | ... | 79 | 73 | 0.79 | 91 | ... |
|  | 1991 | MF | ... | 12 | ... | ... | ... | ... | 13.3 |
|  |  | M | ... | 14 | ... | ... | ... | ... | 13.2 |
|  |  | F | ... | 11 | ... | ... | ... | ... | 13.4 |
|  | 1994 | MF | ... | ... | ... | ... | ... | ... | 14.1 |
|  |  | M | ... | ... | ... | ... | ... | ... | 14.1 |
|  |  | F | ... | ... | ... | ... | ... | ... | 14.1 |

Primary education: selected indicators   II.11
Enseignement primaire: indicateurs selectionnés
Enseñanza primaria: indicadores seleccionados

| Country / Pays / País | Year / Année / Año | Sex / Sexe / Sexo | Apparent intake rate / Taux d'admission apparent / Tasa aparente de ingreso (%) | Percentage repeaters / Pourcentage de redoublants / Porcentaje de repetidores | Percentage of cohort reaching: Grade 5 / 5e année / Quinto año | Percentage of cohort reaching: Final grade / Dernière année / Ultimo año | Coefficient of efficiency / Coefficient d'efficacité / Coeficiente de eficacia | Transition rate (Prim. to Sec. gen.) / Taux de transition (Prim. au sec. gén.) / Tasa de transición (%) | School life expectancy (in years) / Espérance de vie scolaire (années) / Esperanza de vida escolar (en años) |
|---|---|---|---|---|---|---|---|---|---|
| Sudan | 1980 | MF | 60 | - | 69 | 69 | 0.85 | ... | ... |
| | | M | 71 | - | 68 | 68 | 0.84 | ... | ... |
| | | F | 48 | - | 71 | 71 | 0.86 | ... | ... |
| | 1985 | MF | 57 | - | ... | ... | ... | ... | ... |
| | | M | 69 | - | ... | ... | ... | ... | ... |
| | | F | 46 | - | ... | ... | ... | ... | ... |
| | 1990 | MF | 56 | - | 94 | 81 | 0.86 | ... | ... |
| | | M | 64 | - | 90 | 78 | 0.84 | ... | ... |
| | | F | 48 | - | 95 | 82 | 0.86 | ... | ... |
| | 1991 | MF | 62 | - | ... | ... | ... | ... | ... |
| | | M | 70 | - | ... | ... | ... | ... | ... |
| | | F | 54 | - | ... | ... | ... | ... | ... |
| | 1994 | MF | 70 | - | ... | ... | ... | ... | ... |
| | | M | 78 | - | ... | ... | ... | ... | ... |
| | | F | 61 | - | ... | ... | ... | ... | ... |
| | 1995 | MF | 69 | - | ... | ... | ... | ... | ... |
| | | M | 75 | - | ... | ... | ... | ... | ... |
| | | F | 63 | - | ... | ... | ... | ... | ... |
| | 1996 | MF | 66 | - | ... | ... | ... | ... | ... |
| | | M | 73 | - | ... | ... | ... | ... | ... |
| | | F | 59 | - | ... | ... | ... | ... | ... |
| Swaziland | 1970 | MF | 101 | 11 | 66 | 50 | 0.56 | 47 | 7.5 |
| | | M | 106 | 11 | 66 | 52 | 0.57 | 49 | 8.0 |
| | | F | 96 | 10 | 67 | 49 | 0.56 | 45 | 7.0 |
| | 1975 | MF | 108 | 10 | 72 | 59 | 0.66 | 60 | 9.0 |
| | | M | 111 | 11 | 70 | 54 | 0.63 | 61 | ... |
| | | F | 105 | 9 | 75 | 65 | 0.70 | 60 | ... |
| | 1980 | MF | 119 | 11 | 79 | 69 | 0.71 | 70 | ... |
| | | M | 121 | 12 | 77 | 67 | 0.69 | 69 | ... |
| | | F | 118 | 9 | 81 | 70 | 0.73 | 70 | ... |
| | 1985 | MF | 109 | 14 | 74 | 61 | 0.64 | 67 | ... |
| | | M | 112 | 16 | 70 | 57 | 0.61 | 68 | ... |
| | | F | 106 | 12 | 78 | 64 | 0.67 | 66 | ... |
| | 1990 | MF | 127 | 15 | 76 | 65 | 0.67 | 76 | ... |
| | | M | 130 | 17 | 74 | 63 | 0.64 | 77 | ... |
| | | F | 124 | 13 | 78 | 66 | 0.70 | 75 | ... |
| | 1991 | MF | 126 | 15 | 77 | 67 | 0.68 | ... | 10.7 |
| | | M | 129 | 18 | 74 | 64 | 0.66 | ... | 11.0 |
| | | F | 124 | 13 | 80 | 60 | 0.71 | ... | 10.4 |
| | 1992 | MF | 126 | 15 | 77 | 67 | 0.68 | 80 | 11.2 |
| | | M | 129 | 17 | 74 | 64 | 0.65 | 81 | 11.5 |
| | | F | 123 | 13 | 80 | 69 | 0.71 | 79 | 10.9 |
| | 1993 | MF | 118 | 16 | 79 | 69 | 0.70 | 79 | 11.2 |
| | | M | 122 | 18 | 76 | 66 | 0.67 | 79 | 11.6 |
| | | F | 115 | 14 | 82 | 73 | 0.74 | 79 | 10.9 |
| | 1994 | MF | 118 | 15 | 87 | 76 | 0.71 | 77 | 11.4 |
| | | M | 119 | 17 | 85 | 74 | 0.68 | 76 | 11.7 |
| | | F | 116 | 13 | 89 | 77 | 0.74 | 78 | 11.0 |
| | 1995 | MF | 117 | 16 | ... | ... | ... | 77 | 11.6 |
| | | M | 119 | 18 | ... | ... | ... | ... | 12.0 |
| | | F | 116 | 13 | ... | ... | ... | ... | 11.3 |
| | 1996 | MF | 115 | 15 | 76 | 65 | ... | ... | ... |
| | | M | 117 | 18 | 73 | 62 | ... | ... | ... |
| | | F | 113 | 13 | 79 | 68 | ... | ... | ... |
| | 1997 | MF | 112 | 16 | ... | ... | ... | ... | ... |
| | | M | 113 | 18 | ... | ... | ... | ... | ... |
| | | F | 111 | 13 | ... | ... | ... | ... | ... |
| Togo | 1970 | MF | 75 | 34 | 75 | 67 | 0.53 | 29 | 4.9 |
| | | M | 100 | 34 | 78 | 71 | 0.55 | ... | 7.0 |
| | | F | 51 | 35 | 69 | 58 | 0.49 | ... | 2.9 |
| | 1975 | MF | 100 | 29 | ... | ... | ... | ... | ... |
| | | M | 122 | 28 | ... | ... | ... | ... | ... |
| | | F | 77 | 30 | ... | ... | ... | ... | ... |

II.11 Primary education: selected indicators
Enseignement primaire: indicateurs selectionnés
Enseñanza primaria: indicadores seleccionados

| Country / Pays / País | Year / Année / Año | Sex / Sexe / Sexo | Apparent intake rate / Taux d'admission apparent / Tasa aparente de ingreso (%) | Percentage repeaters / Pourcentage de redoublants / Porcentaje de repetidores | Percentage of cohort reaching: / Pourcentage de la cohorte atteignant: / Porcentaje de la cohorte que llega al: Grade 5 / 5e année / Quinto año | Final grade / Dernière année / Ultimo año | Coefficient of efficiency / Coefficient d'efficacité / Coeficiente de eficacia | Transition rate (Prim. to Sec. gen.) / Taux de transition (Prim. au sec. gén.) / Tasa de transición (Prim. a la Sec. gen.) (%) | School life expectancy (in years) / Espérance de vie scolaire (années) / Esperanza de vida escolar (en años) |
|---|---|---|---|---|---|---|---|---|---|
| Togo (cont) | 1980 | MF | 97 | 36 | 53 | 42 | 0.40 | 37 | ... |
| | | M | 112 | 35 | 59 | 49 | 0.44 | 39 | ... |
| | | F | 82 | 37 | 44 | 33 | 0.33 | 34 | ... |
| | 1985 | MF | 90 | 35 | 72 | 58 | 0.44 | 34 | ... |
| | | M | 107 | 34 | 80 | 67 | 0.49 | 36 | ... |
| | | F | 73 | 36 | 61 | 44 | 0.36 | 30 | ... |
| | 1990 | MF | 96 | 36 | ... | ... | ... | 38 | 8.9 |
| | | M | 109 | 35 | ... | ... | ... | 40 | 11.4 |
| | | F | 83 | 37 | ... | ... | ... | 35 | 6.4 |
| | 1991 | MF | 89 | 37 | ... | ... | ... | ... | ... |
| | | M | 100 | 37 | ... | ... | ... | ... | ... |
| | | F | 78 | 38 | ... | ... | ... | ... | ... |
| | 1993 | MF | 88 | 46 | 94 | 84 | 0.55 | 45 | ... |
| | | M | 99 | 46 | 98 | 91 | 0.58 | 47 | ... |
| | | F | 77 | 46 | 82 | 69 | 0.48 | 39 | ... |
| | 1994 | MF | 109 | 33 | 71 | 61 | 0.56 | 52 | ... |
| | | M | 122 | 33 | 79 | 71 | 0.62 | 55 | ... |
| | | F | 97 | 34 | 60 | 47 | 0.46 | 47 | ... |
| | 1995 | MF | 128 | 24 | ... | ... | ... | ... | ... |
| | | M | 141 | 24 | ... | ... | ... | ... | ... |
| | | F | 115 | 25 | ... | ... | ... | ... | ... |
| Tunisia | 1970 | MF | 79 | 29 | 68 | 55 | 0.48 | ... | ... |
| | 1975 | MF | 84 | 19 | 86 | 79 | 0.64 | 16 | ... |
| | | M | 96 | 20 | 90 | 84 | 0.65 | 15 | ... |
| | | F | 72 | 18 | 82 | 73 | 0.63 | 16 | ... |
| | 1980 | MF | 93 | 21 | 87 | 78 | 0.69 | 31 | 8.4 |
| | | M | 100 | 22 | 89 | 80 | 0.69 | 31 | 9.8 |
| | | F | 86 | 19 | 84 | 75 | 0.68 | 31 | 6.8 |
| | 1985 | MF | 101 | 20 | 87 | 77 | 0.64 | 31 | ... |
| | | M | 104 | 21 | 89 | 80 | 0.64 | 30 | ... |
| | | F | 98 | 19 | 83 | 74 | 0.64 | 31 | ... |
| | 1990 | MF | 101 | 20 | 87 | 76 | 0.66 | 48 | ... |
| | | M | 103 | 21 | 92 | 80 | 0.71 | 48 | ... |
| | | F | 99 | 18 | 78 | 70 | 0.60 | 48 | ... |
| | 1991 | MF | 103 | 20 | 88 | 78 | 0.69 | 60 | 10.6 |
| | | M | 108 | 16 | 88 | 78 | 0.68 | 60 | 11.3 |
| | | F | 98 | 26 | 87 | 79 | 0.71 | 60 | 9.8 |
| | 1992 | MF | 103 | 19 | 90 | 84 | 0.73 | 58 | ... |
| | | M | 105 | 20 | 91 | 83 | 0.71 | 57 | ... |
| | | F | 101 | 17 | 90 | 84 | 0.74 | 59 | ... |
| | 1993 | MF | 103 | 18 | 92 | 86 | 0.76 | 62 | ... |
| | | M | 104 | 19 | 91 | 85 | 0.74 | 62 | ... |
| | | F | 101 | 16 | 92 | 87 | 0.78 | 63 | ... |
| | 1994 | MF | 99 | 16 | 92 | 87 | 0.76 | 61 | ... |
| | | M | 100 | 18 | 92 | 86 | 0.74 | 60 | ... |
| | | F | 98 | 15 | 93 | 88 | 0.78 | 62 | ... |
| | 1995 | MF | 96 | 17 | 91 | 85 | 0.76 | 65 | ... |
| | | M | 97 | 19 | 90 | 84 | 0.74 | 64 | ... |
| | | F | 95 | 16 | 92 | 87 | 0.78 | 66 | ... |
| | 1996 | MF | 102 | 16 | ... | ... | ... | ... | ... |
| | | M | 103 | 17 | ... | ... | ... | ... | ... |
| | | F | 101 | 15 | ... | ... | ... | ... | ... |
| United Republic of Tanzania | 1970 | MF | ... | ... | 64 | 59 | 0.73 | ... | ... |
| | 1975 | MF | 95 | 0 | 86 | 84 | 0.92 | ... | ... |
| | | M | 107 | 1 | 88 | 87 | 0.94 | ... | ... |
| | | F | 84 | 0 | 82 | 76 | 0.86 | ... | ... |
| | 1980 | MF | ... | ... | 89 | 82 | 0.88 | ... | ... |
| | | M | ... | ... | 89 | 83 | 0.89 | ... | ... |
| | | F | ... | ... | 90 | 80 | 0.86 | ... | ... |
| | 1985 | MF | 78 | 1 | 86 | 81 | 0.89 | ... | ... |
| | | M | ... | ... | 85 | 80 | 0.89 | ... | ... |
| | | F | ... | ... | 87 | 82 | 0.90 | ... | ... |

Primary education: selected indicators  II.11
Enseignement primaire: indicateurs selectionnés
Enseñanza primaria: indicadores seleccionados

| Country / Pays / País | Year / Année / Año | Sex / Sexe / Sexo | Apparent intake rate / Taux d'admission apparent / Tasa aparente de ingreso (%) | Percentage repeaters / Pourcentage de redoublants / Porcentaje de repetidores | Percentage of cohort reaching: / Pourcentage de la cohorte atteignant: / Porcentaje de la cohorte que llega al: | | Coefficient of efficiency / Coefficient d'efficacité / Coeficiente de eficacia | Transition rate (Prim. to Sec. gen.) / Taux de transition (Prim. au sec. gén.) / Tasa de transición (Prim. a la Sec. gen.) (%) | School life expectancy (in years) / Espérance de vie scolaire (années) / Esperanza de vida escolar (en años) |
|---|---|---|---|---|---|---|---|---|---|
| | | | | | Grade 5 / 5e année / Quinto año | Final grade / Dernière année / Ultimo año | | | |
| United Republic of Tanzania (cont) | 1990 | MF | ... | 4 | 79 | 73 | 0.83 | ... | ... |
| | | M | ... | 4 | 77 | 72 | 0.82 | ... | ... |
| | | F | ... | 5 | 81 | 73 | 0.83 | ... | ... |
| | 1991 | MF | 75 | 4 | 81 | 74 | 0.82 | ... | ... |
| | | M | 77 | 4 | 81 | 74 | 0.83 | ... | ... |
| | | F | 72 | 4 | 82 | 74 | 0.82 | ... | ... |
| | 1992 | MF | 77 | 3 | 83 | 77 | 0.85 | ... | ... |
| | | M | 79 | 3 | 81 | 75 | 0.85 | ... | ... |
| | | F | 75 | 4 | 85 | 78 | 0.86 | ... | ... |
| | 1993 | MF | 74 | 3 | ... | ... | ... | ... | ... |
| | | M | 76 | 3 | ... | ... | ... | ... | ... |
| | | F | 73 | 3 | ... | ... | ... | ... | ... |
| | 1996 | MF | ... | ... | 81 | 71 | ... | ... | ... |
| | | M | ... | ... | 78 | 68 | ... | ... | ... |
| | | F | ... | ... | 84 | 75 | ... | ... | ... |
| | 1997 | MF | 74 | 2 | ... | ... | ... | ... | ... |
| | | M | 76 | 2 | ... | ... | ... | ... | ... |
| | | F | 73 | 2 | ... | ... | ... | ... | ... |
| Zambia | 1975 | MF | 101 | 2 | 82 | 80 | 0.86 | 22 | ... |
| | | M | 103 | 2 | 84 | 84 | 0.89 | 23 | ... |
| | | F | 99 | 2 | 77 | 68 | 0.76 | 21 | ... |
| | 1980 | MF | 91 | 2 | 86 | 83 | 0.88 | 20 | ... |
| | | M | 94 | 2 | 88 | 88 | 0.91 | ... | ... |
| | | F | 88 | 2 | 82 | 73 | 0.80 | ... | ... |
| | 1985 | MF | ... | ... | 86 | 84 | 0.89 | ... | ... |
| | | M | ... | ... | 88 | 88 | 0.91 | ... | ... |
| | | F | ... | ... | 84 | 75 | 0.82 | ... | ... |
| | 1994 | MF | ... | 2 | ... | ... | ... | ... | 7.8 |
| | | M | ... | 3 | ... | ... | ... | ... | 8.3 |
| | | F | ... | 2 | ... | ... | ... | ... | 7.2 |
| Zimbabwe | 1990 | MF | 133 | - | ... | ... | ... | ... | ... |
| | | M | 133 | - | ... | ... | ... | ... | ... |
| | | F | 132 | - | ... | ... | ... | ... | ... |
| | 1991 | MF | 137 | - | 76 | 69 | 0.85 | ... | ... |
| | | M | 141 | - | 72 | 65 | 0.83 | ... | ... |
| | | F | 133 | - | 81 | 74 | 0.87 | ... | ... |
| | 1992 | MF | 133 | - | 80 | 80 | 0.94 | ... | ... |
| | | M | 134 | - | ... | ... | ... | ... | ... |
| | | F | 131 | - | ... | ... | ... | ... | ... |
| | 1995 | MF | 127 | - | 79 | 76 | 0.91 | ... | ... |
| | | M | 130 | - | 78 | 76 | 0.91 | ... | ... |
| | | F | 125 | - | 79 | 76 | 0.91 | ... | ... |
| | 1996 | MF | 129 | - | ... | ... | ... | ... | ... |
| | | M | 130 | - | ... | ... | ... | ... | ... |
| | | F | 127 | - | ... | ... | ... | ... | ... |
| **North America** | | | | | | | | | |
| Bahamas | 1980 | MF | ... | ... | ... | ... | ... | ... | 12.0 |
| | 1985 | MF | ... | ... | ... | ... | ... | ... | 11.9 |
| | 1992 | MF | ... | ... | 78 | 76 | 0.89 | ... | ... |
| | 1993 | MF | 111 | - | ... | ... | ... | ... | ... |
| | 1996 | MF | 109 | - | ... | ... | ... | ... | ... |
| | | M | 97 | - | ... | ... | ... | ... | ... |
| | | F | 121 | - | ... | ... | ... | ... | ... |
| Barbados | 1975 | MF | ... | ... | ... | ... | ... | ... | 11.6 |
| | 1980 | MF | ... | ... | ... | ... | ... | ... | 12.0 |
| | | M | ... | ... | ... | ... | ... | ... | 12.0 |
| | | F | ... | ... | ... | ... | ... | ... | 12.1 |
| Belize | 1990 | MF | ... | ... | 67 | 56 | 0.72 | ... | ... |
| | | M | ... | ... | 69 | 56 | 0.72 | ... | ... |
| | | F | ... | ... | 66 | 56 | 0.73 | ... | ... |

II.11   Primary education: selected indicators
Enseignement primaire: indicateurs selectionnés
Enseñanza primaria: indicadores seleccionados

| Country<br>Pays<br>País | Year<br>Année<br>Año | Sex<br>Sexe<br>Sexo | Apparent intake rate<br>Taux d'admission apparent<br>Tasa aparente de ingreso (%) | Percentage repeaters<br>Pourcentage de redoublants<br>Porcentaje de repetidores | Percentage of cohort reaching:<br>Pourcentage de la cohorte atteignant:<br>Porcentaje de la cohorte que llega al: | | Coefficient of efficiency<br>Coefficient d'efficacité<br>Coeficiente de eficacia | Transition rate (Prim. to Sec. gen.)<br>Taux de transition (Prim. au sec. gén.)<br>Tasa de transición (Prim. a la Sec. gen.) (%) | School life expectancy (in years)<br>Espérance de vie scolaire (années)<br>Esperanza de vida escolar (en años) |
|---|---|---|---|---|---|---|---|---|---|
| | | | | | Grade 5<br>5e année<br>Quinto año | Final grade<br>Dernière année<br>Ultimo año | | | |
| Belize (cont) | 1993 | MF | ... | ... | 70 | 58 | 0.71 | ... | ... |
| | | M | ... | ... | 70 | 57 | 0.69 | ... | ... |
| | | F | ... | ... | 71 | 58 | 0.72 | ... | ... |
| Canada | 1985 | MF | ... | ... | ... | ... | ... | ... | 15.6 |
| | | M | ... | ... | ... | ... | ... | ... | 15.2 |
| | | F | ... | ... | ... | ... | ... | ... | 15.9 |
| | 1990 | MF | | ... | ... | ... | ... | ... | 16.9 |
| | | M | | ... | ... | ... | ... | ... | 16.5 |
| | | F | | ... | ... | ... | ... | ... | 17.4 |
| | 1991 | MF | | ... | ... | ... | ... | ... | 17.1 |
| | | M | | ... | ... | ... | ... | ... | 16.7 |
| | | F | | ... | ... | ... | ... | ... | 17.6 |
| | 1992 | MF | | ... | ... | ... | ... | ... | 16.7 |
| | | M | | ... | ... | ... | ... | ... | 16.5 |
| | | F | | ... | ... | ... | ... | ... | 17.0 |
| | 1993 | MF | | ... | ... | ... | ... | ... | 16.8 |
| | | M | | ... | ... | ... | ... | ... | 16.6 |
| | | F | | ... | ... | ... | ... | ... | 17.1 |
| | 1994 | MF | | ... | ... | ... | ... | ... | 16.8 |
| | | M | | ... | ... | ... | ... | ... | 16.5 |
| | | F | | ... | ... | ... | ... | ... | 17.0 |
| | 1995 | MF | | ... | ... | ... | ... | ... | 16.8 |
| | | M | | ... | ... | ... | ... | ... | 16.5 |
| | | F | | ... | ... | ... | ... | ... | 17.1 |
| Costa Rica | 1970 | MF | 113 | 10 | 77 | 71 | 0.74 | 49 | 8.7 |
| | | M | 114 | 12 | 76 | 70 | 0.72 | 49 | 8.7 |
| | | F | 113 | 9 | 79 | 73 | 0.76 | 50 | 8.6 |
| | 1975 | MF | 116 | 6 | 81 | 77 | 0.81 | ... | 9.4 |
| | | M | 119 | 8 | 78 | 74 | 0.78 | ... | ... |
| | | F | 114 | 5 | 85 | 81 | 0.84 | ... | ... |
| | 1980 | MF | 113 | 8 | 80 | 75 | 0.80 | 55 | 9.7 |
| | | M | 116 | 9 | 77 | 72 | 0.78 | 55 | ... |
| | | F | 110 | 7 | 82 | 78 | 0.82 | 56 | ... |
| | 1985 | MF | 99 | 11 | 86 | 81 | 0.80 | 57 | 9.1 |
| | | M | 100 | 12 | 85 | 79 | 0.78 | 57 | ... |
| | | F | 98 | 9 | 87 | 82 | 0.82 | 57 | ... |
| | 1990 | MF | 101 | 11 | 82 | 77 | 0.78 | 63 | 9.6 |
| | | M | ... | ... | 81 | 75 | 0.76 | 62 | ... |
| | | F | ... | ... | 84 | 79 | 0.80 | 64 | ... |
| | 1991 | MF | 110 | 11 | 84 | 79 | 0.80 | 66 | 9.8 |
| | | M | 110 | 12 | 83 | 78 | 0.78 | 66 | ... |
| | | F | 110 | 9 | 85 | 80 | 0.81 | 67 | ... |
| | 1992 | MF | 111 | 10 | 85 | 81 | 0.82 | 66 | 10.0 |
| | | M | 111 | 11 | 84 | 79 | 0.80 | 66 | ... |
| | | F | 111 | 8 | 87 | 82 | 0.84 | 67 | ... |
| | 1993 | MF | 106 | 8 | 88 | 83 | 0.83 | 67 | 10.0 |
| | | M | 107 | 9 | 87 | 82 | 0.81 | 66 | ... |
| | | F | 106 | 7 | 89 | 85 | 0.84 | 69 | ... |
| | 1994 | MF | 102 | 9 | 89 | 84 | 0.82 | 68 | 10.1 |
| | | M | 102 | 10 | 87 | 82 | 0.81 | 68 | ... |
| | | F | 101 | 8 | 90 | 86 | 0.84 | 69 | ... |
| | 1995 | MF | 101 | 9 | 88 | 83 | 0.80 | 68 | ... |
| | | M | 101 | 11 | 86 | 81 | 0.78 | 67 | ... |
| | | F | 100 | 8 | 89 | 85 | 0.82 | 69 | ... |
| | 1996 | MF | 102 | 11 | 87 | 83 | ... | ... | ... |
| | | M | 102 | 13 | ... | ... | ... | ... | ... |
| | | F | 102 | 10 | ... | ... | ... | ... | ... |
| | 1997 | MF | 102 | 10 | 90 | 85 | ... | ... | ... |
| | 1998 | MF | 100 | 10 | ... | ... | ... | ... | ... |
| | | M | ... | 11 | ... | ... | ... | ... | ... |
| | | F | ... | 9 | ... | ... | ... | ... | ... |
| Cuba | 1970 | MF | 122 | 22 | 71 | 59 | 0.51 | ... | ... |
| | | M | 125 | 24 | 67 | 55 | 0.48 | ... | ... |
| | | F | 118 | 19 | 75 | 63 | 0.55 | ... | ... |

Primary education: selected indicators II.11
Enseignement primaire: indicateurs selectionnés
Enseñanza primaria: indicadores seleccionados

| Country<br>Pays<br>País | Year<br>Année<br>Año | Sex<br>Sexe<br>Sexo | Apparent intake rate<br>Taux d'admission apparent<br>Tasa aparente de ingreso (%) | Percentage repeaters<br>Pourcentage de redoublants<br>Porcentaje de repetidores | Percentage of cohort reaching:<br>Pourcentage de la cohorte atteignant:<br>Porcentaje de la cohorte que llega al: | | Coefficient of efficiency<br>Coefficient d'efficacité<br>Coeficiente de eficacia | Transition rate (Prim. to Sec. gen.)<br>Taux de transition (Prim. au sec. gén.)<br>Tasa de transición (Prim. a la Sec. gen.) (%) | School life expectancy (in years)<br>Espérance de vie scolaire (années)<br>Esperanza de vida escolar (en años) |
|---|---|---|---|---|---|---|---|---|---|
| | | | | | Grade 5<br>5e année<br>Quinto año | Final grade<br>Dernière année<br>Ultimo año | | | |
| Cuba (cont) | 1975 | MF | 104 | 8 | 88 | 83 | 0.88 | 81 | ... |
| | 1980 | MF | 96 | 6 | 89 | 86 | 0.86 | 91 | ... |
| | 1985 | MF | 98 | 3 | 94 | 92 | 0.92 | 93 | 12.0 |
| | | M | ... | ... | ... | ... | ... | ... | 11.9 |
| | | F | ... | ... | ... | ... | ... | ... | 12.1 |
| | 1990 | MF | 100 | 3 | 92 | 90 | 0.92 | 95 | 12.1 |
| | | M | ... | ... | ... | ... | ... | ... | 11.6 |
| | | F | ... | ... | ... | ... | ... | ... | 12.5 |
| | 1991 | MF | 110 | 3 | 94 | 92 | 0.93 | 95 | 11.9 |
| | | M | ... | ... | ... | ... | ... | ... | 11.4 |
| | | F | ... | ... | ... | ... | ... | ... | 12.4 |
| | 1992 | MF | 94 | 3 | 95 | 93 | 0.94 | 94 | ... |
| | 1993 | MF | 100 | 3 | 94 | 92 | 0.94 | 95 | 11.3 |
| | | M | ... | ... | ... | ... | ... | ... | 10.9 |
| | | F | ... | ... | ... | ... | ... | ... | 11.6 |
| | 1994 | MF | 101 | 3 | 100 | 100 | 0.97 | 96 | ... |
| | 1995 | MF | 103 | 3 | ... | ... | | 94 | ... |
| El Salvador | 1970 | MF | ... | ... | 36 | 29 | 0.43 | ... | 6.5 |
| | | M | ... | ... | 35 | 27 | 0.41 | ... | ... |
| | | F | ... | ... | 37 | 30 | 0.44 | ... | ... |
| | 1975 | MF | 143 | 7 | 44 | 29 | 0.53 | ... | ... |
| | | M | ... | ... | 42 | 28 | 0.52 | ... | ... |
| | | F | ... | ... | 45 | 30 | 0.55 | ... | ... |
| | 1991 | MF | 130 | 8 | 58 | 37 | 0.57 | ... | ... |
| | | M | 131 | 9 | 56 | 35 | 0.55 | ... | ... |
| | | F | 128 | 7 | 60 | 40 | 0.59 | ... | ... |
| | 1992 | MF | 142 | 7 | 58 | 39 | 0.59 | ... | ... |
| | | M | 144 | 7 | 58 | 37 | 0.56 | ... | ... |
| | | F | 140 | 6 | 59 | 41 | 0.62 | ... | ... |
| | 1993 | MF | 131 | 8 | ... | ... | ... | ... | ... |
| | | M | 133 | 8 | ... | ... | ... | ... | ... |
| | | F | 130 | 7 | ... | ... | ... | ... | ... |
| | 1995 | MF | 127 | 6 | 77 | 49 | 0.63 | ... | 9.8 |
| | | M | 129 | 7 | 76 | 49 | 0.63 | ... | 9.7 |
| | | F | 125 | 5 | 77 | 49 | 0.64 | ... | 9.9 |
| Guadeloupe | 1970 | MF | 129 | 25 | ... | ... | ... | ... | ... |
| | | M | 128 | 28 | ... | ... | ... | ... | ... |
| | | F | 130 | 22 | ... | ... | ... | ... | ... |
| | 1975 | MF | 112 | 20 | 94 | 94 | 0.83 | 85 | ... |
| | 1990 | MF | 103 | 8 | ... | ... | ... | 96 | ... |
| Guatemala | 1970 | MF | 91 | 16 | 34 | 31 | 0.48 | 60 | 4.4 |
| | | M | ... | ... | ... | ... | ... | 61 | ... |
| | | F | ... | ... | ... | ... | ... | 59 | ... |
| | 1975 | MF | 97 | 15 | 35 | 32 | 0.50 | 67 | 4.9 |
| | | M | ... | ... | 35 | 32 | 0.49 | 67 | 5.5 |
| | | F | ... | ... | 36 | 33 | 0.51 | 67 | 4.3 |
| | 1980 | MF | 105 | 15 | 46 | 41 | 0.55 | ... | 5.9 |
| | 1985 | MF | 106 | 13 | 39 | 36 | 0.59 | ... | ... |
| | 1995 | MF | ... | ... | 50 | 45 | 0.57 | ... | ... |
| | | M | ... | ... | 52 | 46 | 0.58 | ... | ... |
| | | F | ... | ... | 47 | 42 | 0.56 | ... | ... |
| | 1996 | MF | 113 | 15 | ... | ... | ... | ... | ... |
| | | M | 117 | 16 | ... | ... | ... | ... | ... |
| | | F | 109 | 14 | ... | ... | ... | ... | ... |
| Haiti | 1985 | MF | ... | 9 | ... | ... | ... | 68 | ... |
| | | M | ... | 9 | ... | ... | ... | 66 | ... |
| | | F | ... | 9 | ... | ... | ... | 71 | ... |
| | 1990 | MF | 59 | 13 | ... | ... | ... | ... | ... |
| | | M | 61 | 13 | ... | ... | ... | ... | ... |
| | | F | 58 | 13 | ... | ... | ... | ... | ... |

II.11    Primary education: selected indicators
Enseignement primaire: indicateurs selectionnés
Enseñanza primaria: indicadores seleccionados

| Country<br><br>Pays<br><br>País | Year<br><br>Année<br><br>Año | Sex<br><br>Sexe<br><br>Sexo | Apparent intake rate<br>Taux d'admission apparent<br>Tasa aparente de ingreso (%) | Percentage repeaters<br>Pourcentage de redoublants<br>Porcentaje de repetidores | Percentage of cohort reaching:<br>Pourcentage de la cohorte atteignant:<br>Porcentaje de la cohorte que llega al:<br>Grade 5 5e année Quinto año | Final grade Dernière année Ultimo año | Coefficient of efficiency<br>Coefficient d'efficacité<br>Coeficiente de eficacia | Transition rate (Prim. to Sec. gen.)<br>Taux de transition (Prim. au sec. gén.)<br>Tasa de transición (Prim. a la Sec. gen.) (%) | School life expectancy (in years)<br>Espérance de vie scolaire (années)<br>Esperanza de vida escolar (en años) |
|---|---|---|---|---|---|---|---|---|---|
| Honduras | 1980 | MF | 142 | 16 | ... | ... | ... | ... | ... |
| | | M | 145 | 17 | ... | ... | ... | ... | ... |
| | | F | 138 | 15 | ... | ... | ... | ... | ... |
| | 1991 | MF | 139 | 12 | ... | ... | ... | ... | 8.7 |
| | | M | 132 | 11 | ... | ... | ... | ... | ... |
| | | F | 146 | 13 | ... | ... | ... | ... | ... |
| | 1993 | MF | 133 | 12 | 60 | 54 | 0.65 | ... | ... |
| | | M | 135 | 13 | ... | ... | ... | ... | ... |
| | | F | 131 | 11 | ... | ... | ... | ... | ... |
| | 1994 | MF | 129 | 12 | ... | ... | ... | ... | ... |
| Jamaica | 1975 | MF | 96 | 4 | 88 | 75 | 0.77 | ... | 10.2 |
| | | M | 97 | 4 | 88 | 71 | 0.73 | ... | ... |
| | | F | 95 | 3 | 88 | 78 | 0.80 | ... | ... |
| | 1980 | MF | 96 | 4 | ... | ... | ... | ... | 10.9 |
| | | M | 97 | 4 | ... | ... | ... | ... | ... |
| | | F | 96 | 4 | ... | ... | ... | ... | ... |
| | 1985 | MF | 99 | 3 | 95 | 88 | 0.87 | ... | 10.3 |
| | | M | ... | ... | | | | ... | 10.1 |
| | | F | ... | ... | | | | ... | 10.5 |
| | 1990 | MF | 95 | 4 | ... | ... | ... | ... | 10.9 |
| | | M | 97 | 4 | ... | ... | ... | ... | 10.8 |
| | | F | 94 | 4 | ... | ... | ... | ... | 11.0 |
| | 1992 | MF | 93 | 3 | ... | ... | ... | ... | 10.9 |
| | | M | 95 | 4 | ... | ... | ... | ... | ... |
| | | F | 90 | 3 | ... | ... | ... | ... | ... |
| Martinique | 1970 | MF | 123 | 23 | ... | ... | ... | ... | ... |
| | | M | 122 | 25 | ... | ... | ... | ... | ... |
| | | F | 123 | 21 | ... | ... | ... | ... | ... |
| | 1975 | MF | 111 | 18 | 89 | 89 | 0.78 | 85 | ... |
| | 1991 | MF | 106 | 5 | ... | ... | ... | ... | ... |
| Mexico | 1975 | MF | 138 | 11 | 68 | 65 | 0.75 | 75 | ... |
| | | M | 141 | 12 | 64 | 60 | 0.71 | ... | ... |
| | | F | 134 | 10 | 73 | 70 | 0.78 | ... | ... |
| | 1980 | MF | 139 | 10 | 71 | 66 | 0.74 | 85 | ... |
| | 1985 | MF | 122 | 10 | 77 | 72 | 0.77 | 81 | 11.2 |
| | 1990 | MF | 120 | 9 | 80 | 76 | 0.80 | 80 | 10.6 |
| | 1991 | MF | 118 | 9 | 82 | 78 | 0.81 | 81 | ... |
| | | M | ... | ... | 81 | 77 | 0.79 | 84 | ... |
| | | F | ... | ... | 82 | 79 | 0.83 | 79 | ... |
| | 1992 | MF | 117 | 9 | 84 | 81 | 0.84 | 83 | ... |
| | | M | 118 | 10 | 85 | 81 | 0.83 | 86 | ... |
| | | F | 116 | 7 | 84 | 81 | 0.85 | 81 | ... |
| | 1993 | MF | 114 | 7 | 85 | 82 | 0.85 | 85 | 10.7 |
| | | M | 115 | 8 | 83 | 80 | 0.83 | 88 | ... |
| | | F | 114 | 6 | 86 | 84 | 0.87 | 83 | ... |
| | 1994 | MF | 117 | 7 | 86 | 84 | 0.86 | ... | 10.8 |
| | | M | 117 | 8 | 85 | 83 | 0.85 | ... | ... |
| | | F | 116 | 6 | 86 | 85 | 0.88 | ... | ... |
| | 1995 | MF | 114 | 7 | 86 | 83 | ... | 84 | 11.1 |
| | | M | 114 | 8 | 85 | 82 | ... | 87 | ... |
| | | F | 114 | 6 | 86 | 84 | ... | 82 | ... |
| | 1996 | MF | 115 | 7 | ... | ... | ... | ... | ... |
| | | M | 115 | 8 | ... | ... | ... | ... | ... |
| | | F | 115 | 6 | ... | ... | ... | ... | ... |
| Nicaragua | 1970 | MF | 137 | 13 | 33 | 30 | 0.52 | ... | ... |
| | | M | 139 | 13 | 31 | 27 | 0.50 | ... | ... |
| | | F | 136 | 12 | 35 | 32 | 0.55 | ... | ... |
| | 1980 | MF | ... | 17 | ... | ... | ... | ... | 8.7 |
| | | M | ... | 18 | ... | ... | ... | ... | ... |
| | | F | ... | 16 | ... | ... | ... | ... | ... |

Primary education: selected indicators    II.11
Enseignement primaire: indicateurs selectionnés
Enseñanza primaria: indicadores seleccionados

| Country<br>Pays<br>País | Year<br>Année<br>Año | Sex<br>Sexe<br>Sexo | Apparent intake rate<br>Taux d'admission apparent<br>Tasa aparente de ingreso (%) | Percentage repeaters<br>Pourcentage de redoublants<br>Porcentaje de repetidores | Percentage of cohort reaching:<br>Pourcentage de la cohorte atteignant:<br>Porcentaje de la cohorte que llega al:<br>Grade 5<br>5e année<br>Quinto año | Final grade<br>Dernière année<br>Ultimo año | Coefficient of efficiency<br>Coefficient d'efficacité<br>Coeficiente de eficacia | Transition rate (Prim. to Sec. gen.)<br>Taux de transition (Prim. au sec. gén.)<br>Tasa de transición (Prim. a la Sec. gen.) (%) | School life expectancy (in years)<br>Espérance de vie scolaire (années)<br>Esperanza de vida escolar (en años) |
|---|---|---|---|---|---|---|---|---|---|
| Nicaragua (cont) | 1985 | MF | 129 | 15 | ... | ... | ... | ... | 8.1 |
| | | M | 129 | 16 | ... | ... | ... | ... | 7.2 |
| | | F | 129 | 15 | ... | ... | ... | ... | 9.1 |
| | 1990 | MF | 130 | 17 | 46 | 44 | 0.58 | ... | ... |
| | 1991 | MF | 135 | 16 | 44 | 40 | 0.54 | ... | ... |
| | 1992 | MF | 138 | 17 | 54 | 51 | 0.61 | ... | ... |
| | | M | ... | ... | 51 | 48 | 0.59 | ... | ... |
| | | F | ... | ... | 57 | 54 | 0.64 | ... | ... |
| | 1993 | MF | 128 | 17 | 54 | 53 | 0.64 | ... | ... |
| | | M | 130 | 18 | 52 | 51 | 0.62 | ... | ... |
| | | F | 127 | 16 | 56 | 55 | 0.66 | ... | ... |
| | 1994 | MF | 132 | 15 | ... | ... | ... | 95 | ... |
| | | M | 132 | 16 | ... | ... | ... | 97 | ... |
| | | F | 131 | 14 | ... | ... | ... | 93 | ... |
| | 1995 | MF | 132 | 15 | ... | ... | ... | ... | ... |
| | | M | 133 | 16 | ... | ... | ... | ... | ... |
| | | F | 130 | 14 | ... | ... | ... | ... | ... |
| | 1996 | MF | ... | ... | 51 | 45 | ... | 101 | ... |
| | 1997 | MF | 136 | 13 | ... | ... | ... | ... | ... |
| Panama | 1970 | MF | 109 | 15 | 88 | 86 | 0.78 | ... | 9.2 |
| | | M | 112 | 17 | 88 | 86 | 0.77 | ... | 9.3 |
| | | F | 106 | 14 | 88 | 85 | 0.79 | ... | 9.1 |
| | 1975 | MF | 109 | 13 | 78 | 75 | 0.78 | 63 | 11.6 |
| | | M | 110 | 14 | 75 | 72 | 0.76 | ... | 11.6 |
| | | F | 107 | 11 | 82 | 79 | 0.82 | ... | 11.5 |
| | 1980 | MF | 107 | 13 | 77 | 73 | 0.76 | ... | 11.4 |
| | | M | 109 | 15 | 74 | 70 | 0.73 | ... | 11.2 |
| | | F | 105 | 11 | 79 | 76 | 0.79 | ... | 11.5 |
| | 1985 | MF | 106 | 13 | 84 | 82 | 0.81 | 84 | 11.3 |
| | | M | 107 | 15 | 82 | 80 | 0.79 | ... | 11.1 |
| | | F | 106 | 11 | 86 | 83 | 0.84 | ... | 11.5 |
| St. Lucia | 1991 | MF | ... | - | 95 | 95 | 0.98 | ... | ... |
| | | M | ... | - | 91 | 91 | 0.97 | ... | ... |
| | | F | ... | - | 97 | 96 | 0.98 | ... | ... |
| St. Pierre and Miquelon | 1985 | MF | ... | 3 | 90 | 00 | 0.07 | ... | ... |
| Trinidad and Tobago | 1980 | MF | ... | ... | 86 | 78 | 0.86 | ... | ... |
| | | M | ... | ... | 85 | 75 | 0.85 | ... | ... |
| | | F | ... | ... | 87 | 80 | 0.87 | ... | ... |
| | 1990 | MF | 88 | 3 | 96 | 94 | 0.94 | ... | ... |
| | | M | 90 | 3 | 96 | 93 | 0.93 | ... | ... |
| | | F | 86 | 3 | 96 | 94 | 0.94 | ... | ... |
| | 1991 | MF | 85 | 3 | 95 | 94 | 0.94 | 64 | ... |
| | | M | 87 | 3 | 95 | 93 | 0.93 | 66 | ... |
| | | F | 84 | 3 | 95 | 93 | 0.93 | 63 | ... |
| | 1992 | MF | 86 | 4 | ... | ... | ... | ... | 11.1 |
| | | M | 86 | 4 | ... | ... | ... | ... | 11.1 |
| | | F | 85 | 4 | ... | ... | ... | ... | 11.1 |
| | 1995 | MF | 87 | 6 | 97 | 97 | ... | 68 | ... |
| | | M | 88 | 6 | 98 | 97 | ... | 69 | ... |
| | | F | 86 | 5 | 97 | 97 | ... | 67 | ... |
| | 1996 | MF | 89 | 6 | ... | ... | ... | ... | ... |
| | | M | 90 | 6 | ... | ... | ... | ... | ... |
| | | F | 88 | 5 | ... | ... | ... | ... | ... |
| United States | 1985 | MF | ... | ... | ... | ... | ... | ... | 14.7 |
| | | M | ... | ... | ... | ... | ... | ... | 14.5 |
| | | F | ... | ... | ... | ... | ... | ... | 14.9 |
| | 1990 | MF | ... | ... | ... | ... | ... | ... | 15.5 |
| | | M | ... | ... | ... | ... | ... | ... | 15.1 |
| | | F | ... | ... | ... | ... | ... | ... | 15.9 |

Primary education: selected indicators
Enseignement primaire: indicateurs sélectionnés
Enseñanza primaria: indicadores seleccionados

| Country<br><br>Pays<br><br>País | Year<br><br>Année<br><br>Año | Sex<br><br>Sexe<br><br>Sexo | Apparent intake rate<br><br>Taux d'admission apparent<br><br>Tasa aparente de ingreso (%) | Percentage repeaters<br><br>Pourcentage de redoublants<br><br>Porcentaje de repetidores | Percentage of cohort reaching:<br>Pourcentage de la cohorte atteignant:<br>Porcentaje de la cohorte que llega al:<br>Grade 5<br>5e année<br>Quinto año | Final grade<br>Dernière année<br>Ultimo año | Coefficient of efficiency<br><br>Coefficient d'efficacité<br><br>Coeficiente de eficacia | Transition rate (Prim. to Sec. gen.)<br><br>Taux de transition (Prim. au sec. gén.)<br><br>Tasa de transición (Prim. a la Sec. gen.) (%) | School life expectancy (in years)<br><br>Espérance de vie scolaire (années)<br><br>Esperanza de vida escolar (en años) |
|---|---|---|---|---|---|---|---|---|---|
| United States (cont) | 1992 | MF<br>M<br>F | ...<br>...<br>... | ...<br>...<br>... | ...<br>...<br>... | ...<br>...<br>... | ...<br>...<br>... | ...<br>...<br>... | 16.0<br>15.6<br>16.5 |
|  | 1993 | MF<br>M<br>F | ...<br>...<br>... | ...<br>...<br>... | ...<br>...<br>... | ...<br>...<br>... | ...<br>...<br>... | ...<br>...<br>... | 16.0<br>15.6<br>16.3 |
|  | 1994 | MF<br>M<br>F | ...<br>...<br>... | ...<br>...<br>... | ...<br>...<br>... | ...<br>...<br>... | ...<br>...<br>... | ...<br>...<br>... | 15.9<br>15.4<br>16.4 |
|  | 1995 | MF<br>M<br>F | ...<br>...<br>... | ...<br>...<br>... | ...<br>...<br>... | ...<br>...<br>... | ...<br>...<br>... | ...<br>...<br>... | 15.9<br>15.5<br>16.4 |
| **South America** | | | | | | | | | |
| Argentina | 1970 | MF<br>M<br>F | 119<br>120<br>118 | 11<br>13<br>10 | 75<br>73<br>77 | 64<br>61<br>67 | 0.71<br>0.68<br>0.74 | ...<br>...<br>... | 10.3<br>10.2<br>10.4 |
|  | 1975 | MF<br>M<br>F | 116<br>116<br>115 | 9<br>10<br>8 | 76<br>75<br>77 | 66<br>63<br>68 | 0.74<br>0.72<br>0.77 | ...<br>...<br>... | 11.5<br>11.4<br>11.6 |
|  | 1994 | MF | 116 | 6 | ... | ... | ... | ... | ... |
|  | 1996 | MF<br>M<br>F | 117<br>117<br>117 | 6<br>6<br>5 | ...<br>...<br>... | ...<br>...<br>... | ...<br>...<br>... | ...<br>...<br>... | ...<br>...<br>... |
| Bolivia | 1975 | MF | ... | ... | ... | ... | ... | ... | 9.0 |
|  | 1980 | MF | ... | ... | ... | ... | ... | ... | 8.6 |
|  | 1990 | MF<br>M<br>F | 140<br>140<br>139 | 3<br>3<br>3 | ...<br>...<br>... | ...<br>...<br>... | ...<br>...<br>... | ...<br>...<br>... | 9.9<br>...<br>... |
| Brazil | 1970 | MF | 149 | 19 | 28 | 50 | 0.64 | ... | 7.2 |
|  | 1975 | MF | 166 | 15 | 35 | 21 | 0.40 | ... | 8.2 |
|  | 1980 | MF | 166 | 20 | 37 | 20 | 0.35 | ... | 9.5 |
|  | 1985 | MF | 151 | 20 | ... | ... | ... | ... | ... |
|  | 1990 | MF | ... | ... | ... | ... | ... | ... | 10.4 |
|  | 1991 | MF | ... | ... | ... | ... | ... | ... | 10.5 |
|  | 1992 | MF | 136 | 17 | 70 | 37 | 0.45 | ... | 10.7 |
|  | 1993 | MF | 141 | 18 | 71 | 38 | 0.44 | ... | 10.8 |
|  | 1994 | MF | 147 | 18 | ... | ... | ... | ... | 11.1 |
| Chile | 1970 | MF<br>M<br>F | 125<br>125<br>126 | 10<br>11<br>9 | 82<br>82<br>81 | 66<br>67<br>64 | 0.74<br>0.74<br>0.73 | ...<br>...<br>... | 10.5<br>...<br>... |
|  | 1975 | MF<br>M<br>F | 119<br>120<br>117 | 12<br>14<br>11 | 74<br>72<br>76 | 49<br>46<br>51 | 0.57<br>0.54<br>0.59 | ...<br>...<br>... | 11.7<br>11.7<br>11.6 |
|  | 1991 | MF | ... | ... | ... | ... | ... | ... | 12.0 |
|  | 1992 | MF | ... | ... | ... | ... | ... | ... | 12.0 |
|  | 1993 | MF<br>M<br>F | ...<br>...<br>... | ...<br>...<br>... | ...<br>...<br>... | ...<br>...<br>... | ...<br>...<br>... | ...<br>...<br>... | 12.0<br>12.0<br>12.0 |
|  | 1994 | MF<br>M<br>F | ...<br>...<br>... | ...<br>...<br>... | ...<br>...<br>... | ...<br>...<br>... | ...<br>...<br>... | ...<br>...<br>... | 12.1<br>12.2<br>12.0 |
|  | 1995 | MF<br>M<br>F | 100<br>100<br>99 | 6<br>7<br>5 | 100<br>100<br>100 | 97<br>94<br>99 | 0.92<br>0.89<br>0.95 | ...<br>...<br>... | 12.1<br>12.2<br>12.1 |

Primary education: selected indicators II.11
Enseignement primaire: indicateurs selectionnés
Enseñanza primaria: indicadores seleccionados

| Country<br><br>Pays<br><br>País | Year<br><br>Année<br><br>Año | Sex<br><br>Sexe<br><br>Sexo | Apparent intake rate<br><br>Taux d'admission apparent<br><br>Tasa aparente de ingreso<br>(%) | Percentage repeaters<br><br>Pourcentage de redoublants<br><br>Porcentaje de repetidores | Percentage of cohort reaching:<br>Pourcentage de la cohorte atteignant:<br>Porcentaje de la cohorte que llega al: | | Coefficient of efficiency<br><br>Coefficient d'efficacité<br><br>Coeficiente de eficacia | Transition rate (Prim. to Sec. gen.)<br><br>Taux de transition (Prim. au sec. gén.)<br><br>Tasa de transición (Prim. a la Sec. gen.)<br>(%) | School life expectancy (in years)<br><br>Espérance de vie scolaire (années)<br><br>Esperanza de vida escolar (en años) |
|---|---|---|---|---|---|---|---|---|---|
| | | | | | Grade 5<br>5e année<br>Quinto año | Final grade<br>Dernière année<br>Ultimo año | | | |
| Chile (cont) | 1996 | MF | 103 | 5 | ... | ... | ... | ... | 12.6 |
| | | M | 104 | 6 | ... | ... | ... | ... | 12.7 |
| | | F | 102 | 4 | ... | ... | ... | ... | 12.5 |
| Colombia | 1970 | MF | 140 | 17 | 41 | 41 | 0.55 | ... | ... |
| | | M | 144 | 17 | 48 | 48 | 0.64 | ... | ... |
| | | F | 135 | 16 | 35 | 35 | 0.48 | ... | ... |
| | 1985 | MF | 114 | 17 | 57 | 57 | 0.66 | 60 | ... |
| | | M | 116 | 17 | 55 | 55 | 0.66 | 61 | ... |
| | | F | 112 | 17 | 58 | 58 | 0.64 | 60 | ... |
| | 1990 | MF | 125 | 11 | 62 | 62 | 0.73 | ... | ... |
| | | M | 118 | 15 | 71 | 71 | 0.78 | ... | ... |
| | | F | 133 | 9 | 50 | 50 | 0.63 | ... | ... |
| | 1991 | MF | 122 | 11 | 74 | 74 | 0.81 | ... | 9.0 |
| | | M | 123 | 12 | 74 | 74 | 0.78 | ... | ... |
| | | F | 121 | 11 | 74 | 74 | 0.84 | ... | ... |
| | 1992 | MF | 121 | 12 | ... | ... | ... | ... | 9.6 |
| | | M | 108 | 17 | ... | ... | ... | ... | ... |
| | | F | 135 | 8 | ... | ... | ... | ... | ... |
| | 1993 | MF | ... | 7 | ... | | ... | ... | 9.8 |
| | 1995 | MF | 136 | 9 | 73 | 73 | 0.85 | ... | 10.0 |
| | | M | 140 | 10 | 70 | 70 | 0.83 | ... | ... |
| | | F | 132 | 9 | 76 | 76 | 0.86 | ... | ... |
| | 1996 | MF | 140 | 7 | ... | ... | ... | ... | ... |
| | | M | 142 | 8 | ... | ... | ... | ... | ... |
| | | F | 137 | 7 | ... | ... | ... | ... | ... |
| Ecuador | 1970 | MF | 133 | 12 | 51 | 46 | 0.60 | 68 | ... |
| | | M | 134 | 13 | 52 | 47 | 0.60 | 71 | ... |
| | | F | 131 | 12 | 50 | 46 | 0.60 | 64 | ... |
| | 1975 | MF | 131 | 11 | 59 | 57 | 0.70 | 84 | 10.4 |
| | | M | 133 | 12 | 59 | 57 | 0.70 | 86 | ... |
| | | F | 130 | 11 | 60 | 58 | 0.71 | 82 | ... |
| | 1980 | MF | 144 | 10 | 67 | 65 | 0.77 | 86 | ... |
| | 1993 | MF | 127 | 5 | 77 | 74 | 0.85 | ... | ... |
| | | M | 128 | 5 | 75 | 73 | 0.84 | ... | ... |
| | | F | 126 | 4 | 78 | 76 | 0.86 | ... | ... |
| | 1994 | MF | 129 | 4 | 78 | 75 | 0.86 | ... | ... |
| | | M | 130 | 5 | 77 | 76 | 0.05 | ... | ... |
| | | F | 128 | 4 | 78 | 76 | 0.87 | ... | ... |
| | 1995 | MF | 130 | 4 | 85 | 85 | 0.92 | ... | ... |
| | | M | 131 | 4 | 84 | 84 | 0.91 | ... | ... |
| | | F | 129 | 4 | 86 | 86 | 0.93 | ... | ... |
| | 1996 | MF | 133 | 3 | ... | ... | ... | ... | ... |
| | | M | 134 | 4 | ... | ... | ... | ... | ... |
| | | F | 132 | 3 | ... | ... | ... | ... | ... |
| Guyana | 1970 | MF | 89 | 9 | 92 | 90 | 0.83 | 82 | 9.4 |
| | | M | 90 | 10 | 91 | 87 | 0.81 | 82 | 9.5 |
| | | F | 88 | 9 | 93 | 93 | 0.86 | 82 | 9.2 |
| | 1975 | MF | 88 | 8 | 97 | 97 | 0.90 | ... | ... |
| | | M | 89 | 9 | 97 | 97 | 0.90 | ... | ... |
| | | F | 86 | 8 | 97 | 97 | 0.91 | ... | ... |
| | 1980 | MF | 98 | 3 | 91 | 84 | 0.85 | ... | ... |
| | | M | ... | ... | 88 | 81 | 0.83 | ... | ... |
| | | F | ... | ... | 95 | 87 | 0.87 | ... | ... |
| | 1991 | MF | ... | 6 | 93 | 91 | 0.90 | 89 | ... |
| | | M | ... | 7 | 93 | 88 | 0.86 | 89 | ... |
| | | F | ... | 5 | 93 | 93 | 0.92 | 88 | ... |
| | 1994 | MF | 99 | 4 | 91 | 84 | 0.85 | 97 | ... |
| | | M | 98 | 5 | 88 | 80 | 0.82 | 97 | ... |
| | | F | 101 | 3 | 94 | 89 | 0.88 | 96 | ... |
| | 1995 | MF | 94 | 4 | 91 | 88 | ... | 95 | 9.9 |
| | | M | 98 | 5 | 91 | 87 | ... | 98 | 9.8 |
| | | F | 91 | 3 | 92 | 89 | ... | 93 | 9.9 |

II.11   Primary education: selected indicators
        Enseignement primaire: indicateurs selectionnés
        Enseñanza primaria: indicadores seleccionados

| Country Pays País | Year Année Año | Sex Sexe Sexo | Apparent intake rate<br>Taux d'admission apparent<br>Tasa aparente de ingreso (%) | Percentage repeaters<br>Pourcentage de redoublants<br>Porcentaje de repetidores | Percentage of cohort reaching: Pourcentage de la cohorte atteignant: Porcentaje de la cohorte que llega al: | | Coefficient of efficiency<br>Coefficient d'efficacité<br>Coeficiente de eficacia | Transition rate (Prim. to Sec. gen.)<br>Taux de transition (Prim. au sec. gén.)<br>Tasa de transición (Prim. a la Sec. gen.) (%) | School life expectancy (in years)<br>Espérance de vie scolaire (années)<br>Esperanza de vida escolar (en años) |
|---|---|---|---|---|---|---|---|---|---|
| | | | | | Grade 5 5e année Quinto año | Final grade Dernière année Ultimo año | | | |
| Guyana (cont) | 1996 | MF | 96 | 4 | ... | ... | ... | ... | ... |
| | | M | 97 | 5 | ... | ... | ... | ... | ... |
| | | F | 95 | 3 | ... | ... | ... | ... | ... |
| Paraguay | 1970 | MF | 134 | 18 | 49 | 40 | 0.48 | ... | ... |
| | | M | 135 | 20 | ... | ... | ... | ... | ... |
| | | F | 133 | 15 | ... | ... | ... | ... | ... |
| | 1975 | MF | 120 | 15 | 55 | 45 | 0.54 | ... | 7.8 |
| | | M | 122 | 17 | 55 | 45 | 0.53 | ... | ... |
| | | F | 118 | 14 | 54 | 45 | 0.55 | ... | ... |
| | 1980 | MF | 124 | 14 | 58 | 51 | 0.60 | ... | ... |
| | | M | 125 | 15 | 58 | 51 | 0.58 | ... | ... |
| | | F | 123 | 12 | 58 | 51 | 0.61 | ... | ... |
| | 1985 | MF | 122 | 11 | 59 | 50 | 0.61 | ... | ... |
| | | M | 123 | 12 | 59 | 49 | 0.59 | ... | ... |
| | | F | 121 | 9 | 59 | 51 | 0.62 | ... | ... |
| | 1990 | MF | 120 | 9 | 70 | 63 | 0.70 | ... | 8.6 |
| | | M | 122 | 10 | 69 | 61 | 0.68 | ... | 8.7 |
| | | F | 117 | 7 | 72 | 65 | 0.73 | ... | 8.4 |
| | 1991 | MF | 117 | 9 | 74 | 67 | 0.73 | ... | ... |
| | | M | 119 | 10 | 73 | 66 | 0.71 | ... | ... |
| | | F | 116 | 8 | 75 | 68 | 0.74 | ... | ... |
| | 1992 | MF | 111 | 9 | 76 | 69 | 0.74 | ... | ... |
| | | M | 113 | 10 | 75 | 67 | 0.72 | ... | ... |
| | | F | 110 | 8 | 78 | 71 | 0.76 | ... | ... |
| | 1993 | MF | 130 | 8 | 71 | 65 | 0.73 | ... | 9.3 |
| | | M | 131 | 9 | 70 | 63 | 0.71 | ... | 9.3 |
| | | F | 129 | 7 | 73 | 67 | 0.75 | ... | 9.2 |
| | 1994 | MF | 129 | 8 | 73 | 66 | ... | ... | 9.6 |
| | | M | 130 | 9 | 71 | 64 | ... | ... | ... |
| | | F | 127 | 7 | 75 | 69 | ... | ... | ... |
| | 1995 | MF | 125 | 8 | 78 | 72 | ... | 80 | 9.8 |
| | | M | 127 | 9 | 77 | 71 | ... | 82 | ... |
| | | F | 123 | 7 | 80 | 74 | ... | 78 | ... |
| | 1996 | MF | 122 | 9 | ... | ... | ... | ... | 10.0 |
| | | M | 123 | 10 | ... | ... | ... | ... | 10.0 |
| | | F | 121 | 8 | ... | ... | ... | ... | 10.0 |
| Peru | 1970 | MF | 123 | 17 | ... | ... | ... | ... | 9.2 |
| | | M | 132 | 18 | ... | ... | ... | ... | 10.1 |
| | | F | 114 | 16 | ... | ... | ... | ... | 8.3 |
| | 1975 | MF | 131 | 10 | 71 | 66 | 0.75 | 66 | ... |
| | 1980 | MF | 117 | 19 | 76 | 70 | 0.69 | 80 | ... |
| | | M | 118 | 19 | 78 | 72 | 0.70 | 81 | ... |
| | | F | 117 | 18 | 74 | 68 | 0.67 | 78 | ... |
| | 1985 | MF | 139 | 14 | ... | ... | ... | ... | 11.7 |
| | 1993 | MF | ... | ... | ... | ... | ... | ... | 11.9 |
| | 1995 | MF | 124 | 15 | ... | ... | ... | ... | 12.4 |
| | | M | 124 | 16 | ... | ... | ... | ... | ... |
| | | F | 123 | 15 | ... | ... | ... | ... | ... |
| | 1996 | MF | ... | ... | ... | ... | ... | ... | 12.4 |
| | 1997 | MF | ... | ... | ... | ... | ... | ... | 12.4 |
| Suriname | 1975 | MF | 97 | 24 | 100 | 100 | 0.76 | 75 | ... |
| | | M | 101 | 26 | 100 | 98 | 0.73 | 72 | ... |
| | | F | 93 | 21 | 98 | 98 | 0.78 | 77 | ... |
| | 1980 | MF | 108 | 22 | 92 | 89 | 0.73 | | ... |
| Uruguay | 1970 | MF | 76 | 18 | 88 | 84 | 0.75 | | ... |
| | 1975 | MF | ... | ... | 90 | 84 | 0.73 | | ... |
| | 1980 | MF | 73 | 15 | ... | ... | ... | ... | ... |
| | | M | 73 | 17 | ... | ... | ... | ... | ... |
| | | F | 73 | 13 | ... | ... | ... | ... | ... |

Primary education: selected indicators II.11
Enseignement primaire: indicateurs selectionnés
Enseñanza primaria: indicadores seleccionados

| Country<br>Pays<br>País | Year<br>Année<br>Año | Sex<br>Sexe<br>Sexo | Apparent<br>intake rate<br>Taux<br>d'admission<br>apparent<br>Tasa<br>aparente de<br>ingreso<br>(%) | Percentage<br>repeaters<br>Pourcentage<br>de<br>redoublants<br>Porcentaje<br>de<br>repetidores | Percentage of cohort reaching:<br>Pourcentage de la cohorte atteignant:<br>Porcentaje de la cohorte que llega al: Grade 5<br>5e année<br>Quinto año | Final grade<br>Dernière année<br>Ultimo año | Coefficient of<br>efficiency<br>Coefficient<br>d'efficacité<br>Coeficiente<br>de eficacia | Transition rate<br>(Prim. to Sec. gen.)<br>Taux de transition<br>(Prim. au sec. gén.)<br>Tasa de transición<br>(Prim. a la Sec.<br>gen.)<br>(%) | School life<br>expectancy<br>(in years)<br>Espérance de<br>vie scolaire<br>(années)<br>Esperanza de<br>vida escolar<br>(en años) |
|---|---|---|---|---|---|---|---|---|---|
| Uruguay (cont) | 1985 | MF | 97 | 11 | 90 | 86 | 0.82 | ... | ... |
| | | M | 96 | 13 | 89 | 84 | 0.80 | ... | ... |
| | | F | 98 | 9 | 91 | 88 | 0.85 | ... | ... |
| | 1990 | MF | 101 | 9 | 94 | 92 | 0.86 | ... | ... |
| | | M | 100 | 11 | 93 | 90 | 0.83 | ... | ... |
| | | F | 101 | 8 | 96 | 94 | 0.89 | ... | ... |
| | 1991 | MF | 100 | 10 | 95 | 92 | 0.85 | ... | ... |
| | | M | 99 | 12 | 94 | 90 | 0.82 | ... | ... |
| | | F | 101 | 8 | 97 | 95 | 0.88 | ... | ... |
| | 1992 | MF | 100 | 10 | 96 | 93 | 0.86 | ... | ... |
| | | M | 100 | 12 | 94 | 91 | 0.83 | ... | ... |
| | | F | 100 | 8 | 97 | 95 | 0.89 | ... | ... |
| | 1993 | MF | 101 | 10 | 94 | 91 | 0.86 | ... | ... |
| | | M | 101 | 11 | 93 | 89 | 0.83 | ... | ... |
| | | F | 102 | 8 | 96 | 94 | 0.88 | ... | ... |
| | 1994 | MF | 99 | 10 | 96 | 94 | 0.87 | ... | ... |
| | | M | 99 | 12 | 96 | 93 | 0.85 | ... | ... |
| | | F | 99 | 8 | 97 | 96 | 0.89 | ... | ... |
| | 1995 | MF | 100 | 10 | 98 | 96 | 0.88 | ... | ... |
| | | M | 99 | 11 | 96 | 94 | 0.86 | ... | ... |
| | | F | 101 | 8 | 99 | 97 | 0.90 | ... | ... |
| | 1996 | MF | 99 | 9 | ... | ... | ... | ... | ... |
| | | M | 98 | 11 | ... | ... | ... | ... | ... |
| | | F | 100 | 8 | ... | ... | ... | ... | ... |
| Venezuela | 1970 | MF | 116 | 2 | 65 | 59 | ... | ... | 8.2 |
| | 1975 | MF | 133 | 3 | 65 | 61 | ... | ... | 9.0 |
| | 1980 | MF | 124 | 11 | 74 | 37 | 0.47 | ... | 10.0 |
| | 1985 | MF | 115 | 10 | 80 | 41 | 0.49 | ... | 10.5 |
| | 1990 | MF | 115 | 11 | 86 | 46 | 0.50 | ... | 10.8 |
| | | M | 117 | 13 | 83 | 39 | 0.44 | ... | ... |
| | | F | 112 | 9 | 90 | 52 | 0.57 | ... | ... |
| | 1991 | MF | 113 | 11 | 78 | 39 | 0.46 | ... | 10.9 |
| | | M | 115 | 13 | 75 | 32 | 0.40 | ... | ... |
| | | F | 110 | 9 | 82 | 46 | 0.53 | ... | ... |
| | 1992 | MF | 108 | 11 | ... | ... | ... | ... | ... |
| | | M | 110 | 13 | ... | ... | ... | ... | ... |
| | | F | 106 | 9 | ... | ... | ... | ... | ... |
| | 1995 | MF | 101 | 11 | 89 | 56 | 0.60 | ... | ... |
| | | M | 102 | 12 | 86 | 49 | 0.53 | ... | ... |
| | | F | 100 | 9 | 92 | 64 | 0.67 | ... | ... |
| | 1996 | MF | 103 | 10 | ... | ... | ... | ... | ... |
| | | M | 105 | 12 | ... | ... | ... | ... | ... |
| | | F | 102 | 9 | ... | ... | ... | ... | ... |
| **Asia** | | | | | | | | | |
| Afghanistan | 1980 | MF | 42 | 15 | 62 | 54 | 0.71 | ... | ... |
| | | M | 67 | 15 | 62 | 49 | 0.65 | ... | ... |
| | | F | 16 | 16 | 61 | 61 | 0.78 | ... | ... |
| | 1985 | MF | 28 | 6 | ... | ... | ... | ... | ... |
| | | M | 36 | 6 | ... | ... | ... | ... | ... |
| | | F | 19 | 6 | ... | ... | ... | ... | ... |
| | 1993 | MF | 28 | 9 | ... | ... | ... | ... | ... |
| | | M | 42 | 9 | ... | ... | ... | ... | ... |
| | | F | 14 | 9 | ... | ... | ... | ... | ... |
| Armenia | 1995 | MF | ... | ... | . | 100 | 1.00 | ... | ... |
| | 1996 | MF | 90 | 0 | ... | ... | ... | ... | ... |
| Azerbaijan | 1992 | MF | 102 | 0 | . | 93 | 0.97 | 97 | ... |
| | | M | 102 | 0 | . | ... | 0.98 | 99 | ... |
| | | F | 102 | 0 | . | ... | 0.96 | 94 | ... |
| | 1993 | MF | 115 | 0 | ... | ... | ... | ... | ... |
| | | M | 119 | 0 | ... | ... | ... | ... | ... |
| | | F | 111 | 0 | ... | ... | ... | ... | ... |

II.11   Primary education: selected indicators
Enseignement primaire: indicateurs selectionnés
Enseñanza primaria: indicadores seleccionados

| Country<br>Pays<br>País | Year<br>Année<br>Año | Sex<br>Sexe<br>Sexo | Apparent intake rate<br>Taux d'admission apparent<br>Tasa aparente de ingreso<br>(%) | Percentage repeaters<br>Pourcentage de redoublants<br>Porcentaje de repetidores | Percentage of cohort reaching:<br>Pourcentage de la cohorte atteignant:<br>Porcentaje de la cohorte que llega al: | | Coefficient of efficiency<br>Coefficient d'efficacité<br>Coeficiente de eficacia | Transition rate (Prim. to Sec. gen.)<br>Taux de transition (Prim. au sec. gén.)<br>Tasa de transición (Prim. a la Sec. gen.)<br>(%) | School life expectancy (in years)<br>Espérance de vie scolaire (années)<br>Esperanza de vida escolar (en años) |
|---|---|---|---|---|---|---|---|---|---|
| | | | | | Grade 5<br>5e année<br>Quinto año | Final grade<br>Dernière année<br>Ultimo año | | | |
| Azerbaijan (cont) | 1995 | MF | 105 | 0 | . | 93 | 0.97 | 98 | ... |
| | | M | 104 | 0 | . | ... | 0.99 | 102 | ... |
| | | F | 106 | 0 | . | ... | 0.88 | 95 | ... |
| | 1996 | MF | 106 | 0 | ... | ... | ... | ... | ... |
| | | M | 108 | 0 | ... | ... | ... | ... | ... |
| | | F | 104 | 0 | ... | ... | ... | ... | ... |
| Bahrain | 1970 | MF | ... | ... | ... | ... | ... | 66 | 9.1 |
| | | M | ... | ... | ... | ... | ... | 58 | 10.5 |
| | | F | ... | ... | ... | ... | ... | 75 | 7.6 |
| | 1975 | MF | ... | ... | ... | ... | ... | 71 | 8.7 |
| | | M | ... | ... | ... | ... | ... | 66 | 9.1 |
| | | F | ... | ... | ... | ... | ... | 78 | 8.2 |
| | 1980 | MF | ... | ... | 97 | 95 | 0.85 | 82 | 10.5 |
| | | M | ... | ... | 100 | 100 | 0.88 | 80 | 11.2 |
| | | F | ... | ... | 85 | 81 | 0.80 | 84 | 9.7 |
| | 1985 | MF | 112 | 9 | ... | ... | ... | ... | 13.5 |
| | | M | 110 | 8 | ... | ... | ... | ... | 13.1 |
| | | F | 115 | 9 | ... | ... | ... | ... | 13.7 |
| | 1990 | MF | 108 | 5 | 89 | 81 | 0.84 | 99 | 13.5 |
| | | M | 107 | 5 | 89 | 81 | 0.83 | 98 | 13.3 |
| | | F | 109 | 5 | 90 | 82 | 0.84 | 100 | 13.8 |
| | 1991 | MF | 105 | 5 | 100 | 94 | 0.90 | 101 | 13.3 |
| | | M | 106 | 4 | 100 | 94 | 0.90 | 100 | 13.0 |
| | | F | 105 | 5 | 100 | 94 | 0.90 | 103 | 13.6 |
| | 1992 | MF | 107 | 5 | 99 | 90 | 0.87 | ... | 13.5 |
| | | M | 105 | 5 | 98 | 89 | 0.86 | ... | 13.2 |
| | | F | 109 | 5 | 100 | 91 | 0.88 | ... | 13.8 |
| | 1993 | MF | 107 | 5 | 99 | 92 | 0.88 | ... | 13.5 |
| | | M | 107 | 5 | 99 | 92 | 0.88 | ... | 13.2 |
| | | F | 108 | 5 | 98 | 91 | 0.88 | ... | 13.8 |
| | 1994 | MF | 107 | 5 | ... | ... | ... | ... | ... |
| | | M | 105 | 6 | ... | ... | ... | ... | ... |
| | | F | 109 | 5 | ... | ... | ... | ... | ... |
| | 1995 | MF | 104 | 5 | 95 | 85 | 0.85 | ... | ... |
| | | M | 103 | 6 | 94 | 84 | 0.84 | ... | ... |
| | | F | 105 | 5 | 95 | 86 | 0.86 | ... | ... |
| | 1996 | MF | 100 | 5 | ... | ... | ... | ... | ... |
| | | M | 101 | 5 | ... | ... | ... | ... | ... |
| | | F | 99 | 5 | ... | ... | ... | ... | ... |
| Bangladesh | 1980 | MF | ... | ... | 21 | 21 | 0.34 | ... | ... |
| | | M | ... | ... | 18 | 18 | 0.32 | ... | ... |
| | | F | ... | ... | 26 | 26 | 0.38 | ... | ... |
| | 1985 | MF | ... | ... | | | | | 4.7 |
| | 1990 | MF | ... | ... | ... | ... | ... | ... | 5.1 |
| | | M | ... | ... | ... | ... | ... | ... | 5.9 |
| | | F | ... | ... | ... | ... | ... | ... | 4.2 |
| Bhutan | 1993 | MF | ... | 19 | 82 | 71 | 0.66 | 76 | ... |
| | | M | ... | 19 | 81 | 69 | 0.64 | 77 | ... |
| | | F | ... | 18 | 84 | 74 | 0.67 | 74 | ... |
| | 1994 | MF | ... | 19 | ... | ... | ... | ... | ... |
| | | M | ... | 20 | ... | ... | ... | ... | ... |
| | | F | ... | 18 | ... | ... | ... | ... | ... |
| Brunei Darussalam | 1980 | MF | 101 | 13 | 93 | 83 | 0.79 | 83 | 11.0 |
| | | M | 102 | 15 | 91 | 79 | 0.74 | 77 | 11.0 |
| | | F | 100 | 10 | 94 | 86 | 0.84 | 90 | 11.0 |
| | 1991 | MF | 105 | 10 | 95 | 92 | 0.86 | ... | ... |
| | 1992 | MF | 102 | 10 | 100 | 94 | 0.85 | 81 | 12.5 |
| | 1993 | MF | 104 | 10 | 95 | 92 | 0.87 | 81 | ... |
| | 1994 | MF | 104 | 9 | 92 | 88 | ... | ... | ... |
| | 1995 | MF | 100 | 8 | ... | ... | ... | ... | ... |

Primary education: selected indicators II.11
Enseignement primaire: indicateurs selectionnés
Enseñanza primaria: indicadores seleccionados

| Country<br><br>Pays<br><br>País | Year<br><br>Année<br><br>Año | Sex<br><br>Sexe<br><br>Sexo | Apparent<br>intake rate<br><br>Taux<br>d'admission<br>apparent<br><br>Tasa<br>aparente de<br>ingreso<br>(%) | Percentage<br>repeaters<br><br>Pourcentage<br>de<br>redoublants<br><br>Porcentaje<br>de<br>repetidores | Percentage of cohort reaching:<br>Pourcentage de la cohorte atteignant:<br>Porcentaje de la cohorte que llega al: | | Coefficient of<br>efficiency<br><br>Coefficient<br>d'efficacité<br><br>Coeficiente<br>de eficacia | Transition rate<br>(Prim. to Sec. gen.)<br><br>Taux de transition<br>(Prim. au sec. gén.)<br><br>Tasa de transición<br>(Prim. a la Sec.<br>gen.)<br>(%) | School life<br>expectancy<br>(in years)<br><br>Espérance de<br>vie scolaire<br>(années)<br><br>Esperanza de<br>vida escolar<br>(en años) |
|---|---|---|---|---|---|---|---|---|---|
| | | | | | Grade 5<br>5e année<br>Quinto año | Final grade<br>Dernière année<br>Ultimo año | | | |
| Cambodia | 1993 | MF | 133 | 27 | 49 | 49 | 0.47 | ... | ... |
| | | M | ... | ... | 56 | 56 | 0.51 | ... | ... |
| | | F | ... | ... | 42 | 42 | 0.42 | ... | ... |
| | 1994 | MF | 115 | 30 | ... | ... | ... | ... | ... |
| | | M | 122 | 31 | ... | ... | ... | ... | ... |
| | | F | 109 | 30 | ... | ... | ... | ... | ... |
| | 1996 | MF | 133 | 27 | 49 | 39 | ... | 79 | ... |
| | | M | 139 | 27 | 51 | 42 | ... | 82 | ... |
| | | F | 127 | 26 | 46 | 36 | ... | 74 | ... |
| | 1997 | MF | 124 | 26 | ... | ... | ... | ... | ... |
| | | M | 129 | 27 | ... | ... | ... | ... | ... |
| | | F | 119 | 25 | ... | ... | ... | ... | ... |
| China | 1990 | MF | 107 | 6 | 86 | 86 | 0.87 | 70 | |
| | 1991 | MF | 103 | 5 | 88 | 88 | 0.89 | 75 | |
| | 1992 | MF | 103 | 5 | 88 | 88 | 0.89 | 74 | ... |
| | 1993 | MF | 106 | 4 | 91 | 91 | 0.91 | 79 | |
| | | M | ... | ... | ... | ... | ... | 80 | |
| | | F | ... | ... | ... | ... | ... | 77 | |
| | 1994 | MF | 110 | 3 | 92 | 92 | 0.93 | 88 | ... |
| | | M | ... | ... | 92 | 92 | 0.93 | 89 | |
| | | F | ... | ... | 92 | 92 | 0.93 | 86 | |
| | 1995 | MF | 108 | 2 | 94 | 94 | 0.94 | 88 | ... |
| | | M | 107 | 2 | 93 | 93 | 0.94 | 89 | |
| | | F | 109 | 2 | 94 | 94 | 0.95 | 86 | |
| | 1996 | MF | 108 | 2 | ... | ... | ... | ... | ... |
| | | M | 107 | 2 | ... | ... | ... | ... | |
| | | F | 109 | 1 | ... | ... | ... | ... | |
| China, Hong Kong SAR | 1970 | MF | ... | ... | ... | ... | ... | ... | 10.0 |
| | | M | ... | ... | ... | ... | ... | ... | 10.5 |
| | | F | ... | ... | ... | ... | ... | ... | 9.4 |
| | 1975 | MF | ... | ... | ... | ... | ... | ... | 10.7 |
| | | M | ... | ... | ... | ... | ... | ... | 11.2 |
| | | F | ... | ... | ... | ... | ... | ... | 10.2 |
| | 1980 | MF | 108 | 4 | 99 | 98 | 0.95 | 90 | 11.4 |
| | | M | 107 | 4 | 98 | 97 | 0.93 | 87 | 11.6 |
| | | F | 109 | 3 | 99 | 99 | 0.96 | 93 | 11.3 |
| | 1990 | MF | 93 | 1 | 100 | 99 | 0.98 | 99 | ... |
| | 1991 | MF | 93 | 1 | 100 | 98 | 0.98 | 99 | ... |
| | 1992 | MF | 90 | 1 | 100 | 99 | 0.98 | 99 | ... |
| | 1993 | MF | 90 | 1 | 100 | 99 | 0.98 | 99 | ... |
| | 1994 | MF | ... | 1 | 100 | 99 | 0.98 | 99 | ... |
| | 1995 | MF | 98 | 1 | ... | ... | ... | ... | ... |
| Cyprus | 1970 | MF | ... | 2 | 97 | 97 | 0.96 | 74 | |
| | | M | ... | 3 | 96 | 96 | 0.96 | 70 | |
| | | F | ... | 2 | 99 | 97 | 0.96 | 77 | |
| | 1975 | MF | ... | 1 | 99 | 99 | 0.99 | 86 | |
| | | M | ... | 1 | 99 | 99 | 0.99 | 81 | |
| | | F | ... | 1 | 99 | 98 | 0.99 | 92 | |
| | 1980 | MF | ... | 1 | 100 | 100 | 0.99 | 90 | ... |
| | | M | ... | 1 | 100 | 100 | 0.99 | 88 | |
| | | F | ... | 0 | 100 | 100 | 1.00 | 91 | |
| | 1985 | MF | ... | 0 | 99 | 98 | 0.99 | 98 | |
| | | M | ... | 0 | 99 | 99 | 0.99 | 99 | |
| | | F | ... | 0 | 99 | 98 | 0.99 | 97 | |
| | 1990 | MF | ... | 0 | 100 | 100 | 0.99 | ... | |
| | | M | ... | 0 | 100 | 100 | 1.00 | ... | |
| | | F | ... | 0 | 100 | 100 | 0.99 | ... | |
| | 1991 | MF | ... | 0 | 100 | 100 | 1.00 | 101 | ... |
| | | M | ... | 0 | 100 | 100 | 1.00 | 101 | |
| | | F | ... | 0 | 100 | 100 | 1.00 | 101 | ... |

Primary education: selected indicators
Enseignement primaire: indicateurs selectionnés
Enseñanza primaria: indicadores seleccionados

| Country<br><br>Pays<br><br>País | Year<br><br>Année<br><br>Año | Sex<br><br>Sexe<br><br>Sexo | Apparent intake rate<br><br>Taux d'admission apparent<br><br>Tasa aparente de ingreso (%) | Percentage repeaters<br><br>Pourcentage de redoublants<br><br>Porcentaje de repetidores | Percentage of cohort reaching:<br>Pourcentage de la cohorte atteignant:<br>Porcentaje de la cohorte que llega al: Grade 5<br>5e année<br>Quinto año | Final grade<br>Dernière année<br>Ultimo año | Coefficient of efficiency<br><br>Coefficient d'efficacité<br><br>Coeficiente de eficacia | Transition rate (Prim. to Sec. gen.)<br><br>Taux de transition (Prim. au sec. gén.)<br><br>Tasa de transición (Prim. a la Sec. gen.) (%) | School life expectancy (in years)<br><br>Espérance de vie scolaire (années)<br><br>Esperanza de vida escolar (en años) |
|---|---|---|---|---|---|---|---|---|---|
| Cyprus (cont) | 1992 | MF<br>M<br>F | ...<br>...<br>... | 0<br>0<br>0 | 100<br>100<br>99 | 100<br>100<br>99 | 1.00<br>1.00<br>1.00 | 100<br>101<br>99 | ...<br><br>... |
| | 1993 | MF<br>M<br>F | ...<br>...<br>... | 0<br>0<br>0 | 100<br>100<br>100 | 100<br>100<br>100 | 1.00<br>1.00<br>1.00 | 101<br>101<br>100 | ...<br><br>... |
| | 1994 | MF<br>M<br>F | ...<br>...<br>... | 0<br>0<br>0 | 100<br>100<br>100 | 100<br>100<br>100 | 1.00<br>1.00<br>1.00 | 100<br>100<br>101 | ...<br><br>... |
| | 1995 | MF<br>M<br>F | <br><br> | 0<br>0<br>0 | 100<br>99<br>100 | 100<br>99<br>100 | 1.00<br>0.99<br>1.00 | 101<br>101<br>100 | ...<br><br>... |
| Georgia | 1994 | MF<br>M<br>F | ...<br>...<br>... | 0<br>...<br>... | .<br>...<br>... | 98<br>...<br>... | 0.98<br>...<br>... | 98<br>...<br>... | 10.5<br>10.3<br>10.6 |
| | 1995 | MF<br>M<br>F | ...<br>...<br>... | 0<br>...<br>... | .<br>...<br>... | 98<br>...<br>... | 0.99<br>...<br>... | 98<br>...<br>... | 10.7<br>10.5<br>10.8 |
| | 1996 | MF<br>M<br>F | 96<br>...<br>... | 0<br>...<br>... | ...<br>...<br>... | ...<br>...<br>... | <br><br> | ...<br>...<br>... | 11.0<br>11.0<br>11.1 |
| India | 1970 | MF<br>M<br>F | 98<br>116<br>79 | 21<br>21<br>21 | ...<br>...<br>... | ...<br>...<br>... | ...<br>...<br>... | ...<br>...<br>... | 5.9<br>7.5<br>4.2 |
| | 1985 | MF<br>M<br>F | ...<br>...<br>... | ...<br>...<br>... | 53<br>55<br>50 | 53<br>55<br>50 | 0.69<br>0.71<br>0.67 | 83<br>86<br>78 | ...<br><br>... |
| | 1993 | MF<br>M<br>F | ...<br>...<br>... | ...<br>...<br>... | 59<br>61<br>55 | 59<br>61<br>55 | 0.75<br>0.77<br>0.72 | ...<br>...<br>... | ...<br><br>... |
| | 1994 | MF<br>M<br>F | 126<br>137<br>114 | 4<br>3<br>4 | ...<br>...<br>... | ...<br>...<br>... | ...<br>...<br>... | ...<br>...<br>... | ...<br><br>... |
| Indonesia | 1975 | MF | 110 | 11 | 60 | 50 | 0.59 | 43 | 6.5 |
| | 1980 | MF | 116 | 8 | 76 | 68 | 0.72 | 58 | ... |
| | 1985 | MF | 110 | 11 | 85 | 80 | 0.79 | 54 | ... |
| | 1990 | MF<br>M<br>F | 111<br>...<br>... | 10<br>...<br>... | 84<br>...<br>... | 78<br>...<br>... | 0.78<br>...<br>... | 50<br>53<br>48 | 9.7<br>...<br>... |
| | 1991 | MF<br>M<br>F | 110<br>...<br>... | 9<br>...<br>... | 86<br>...<br>... | 82<br>...<br>... | 0.81<br>...<br>... | 51<br>54<br>49 | 9.6<br>...<br>... |
| | 1992 | MF<br>M<br>F | 110<br>...<br>... | 9<br>...<br>... | 93<br>...<br>... | 89<br>...<br>... | 0.86<br>...<br>... | 54<br>54<br>54 | 9.6<br>10.1<br>9.2 |
| | 1993 | MF<br>M<br>F | 110<br>...<br>... | 8<br>...<br>... | 89<br>96<br>81 | 86<br>86<br>81 | 0.85<br>0.82<br>0.85 | 68<br>69<br>67 | ...<br><br>... |
| | 1994 | MF<br>M<br>F | 109<br>112<br>106 | 8<br>8<br>7 | 91<br>90<br>92 | 85<br>82<br>88 | ...<br>...<br>... | ...<br>...<br>... | 10.0<br>10.4<br>9.6 |
| | 1995 | MF<br>M<br>F | 108<br>111<br>105 | 7<br>7<br>7 | 88<br>88<br>89 | 83<br>82<br>84 | ...<br>...<br>... | ...<br>...<br>... | ...<br><br>... |
| | 1996 | MF<br>M<br>F | 112<br>114<br>111 | 6<br>6<br>6 | ...<br>...<br>... | ...<br>...<br>... | ...<br>...<br>... | ...<br>...<br>... | ...<br><br>... |
| Iran, Islamic Republic of | 1970 | MF<br>M<br>F | 84<br>104<br>63 | 9<br>10<br>7 | ...<br>...<br>... | ...<br>...<br>... | ...<br>...<br>... | ...<br>...<br>... | ...<br><br>... |
| | 1985 | MF<br>M<br>F | 103<br>...<br>... | 10<br>...<br>... | 83<br>86<br>79 | 83<br>86<br>79 | 0.81<br>0.81<br>0.81 | 69<br>70<br>68 | ...<br><br>... |

Primary education: selected indicators II.11
Enseignement primaire: indicateurs selectionnés
Enseñanza primaria: indicadores seleccionados

| Country / Pays / País | Year / Année / Año | Sex / Sexe / Sexo | Apparent intake rate / Taux d'admission apparent / Tasa aparente de ingreso (%) | Percentage repeaters / Pourcentage de redoublants / Porcentaje de repetidores | Percentage of cohort reaching: / Pourcentage de la cohorte atteignant: / Porcentaje de la cohorte que llega al: | | Coefficient of efficiency / Coefficient d'efficacité / Coeficiente de eficacia | Transition rate (Prim. to Sec. gen.) / Taux de transition (Prim. au sec. gén.) / Tasa de transición (Prim. a la Sec. gen.) (%) | School life expectancy (in years) / Espérance de vie scolaire (années) / Esperanza de vida escolar (en años) |
|---|---|---|---|---|---|---|---|---|---|
| | | | | | Grade 5 5e année Quinto año | Final grade Dernière année Ultimo año | | | |
| Iran, Islamic Republic of (cont) | 1990 | MF | 112 | 9 | 90 | 90 | 0.86 | ... | ... |
| | | M | 114 | 11 | 91 | 91 | 0.85 | ... | ... |
| | | F | 111 | 8 | 89 | 89 | 0.87 | ... | ... |
| | 1991 | MF | 110 | 10 | 91 | 91 | 0.89 | 82 | ... |
| | | M | 111 | 11 | 91 | 91 | 0.88 | 83 | ... |
| | | F | 109 | 8 | 90 | 90 | 0.89 | 82 | ... |
| | 1992 | MF | 103 | 7 | 89 | 89 | 0.88 | 84 | ... |
| | | M | 104 | 8 | 90 | 90 | 0.87 | 85 | ... |
| | | F | 102 | 6 | 88 | 88 | 0.89 | 83 | ... |
| | 1993 | MF | 96 | 7 | 90 | 90 | 0.88 | ... | ... |
| | | M | 96 | 8 | 92 | 92 | 0.88 | ... | ... |
| | | F | 95 | 6 | 89 | 89 | 0.89 | ... | ... |
| | 1994 | MF | 91 | 7 | ... | ... | ... | ... | ... |
| | | M | 93 | 9 | ... | ... | ... | ... | ... |
| | | F | 90 | 6 | ... | ... | ... | ... | ... |
| | 1996 | MF | 92 | 6 | ... | ... | ... | ... | 11.3 |
| | | M | 93 | 7 | ... | ... | ... | ... | 12.0 |
| | | F | 91 | 4 | ... | ... | ... | ... | 10.5 |
| Iraq | 1970 | MF | 77 | 21 | 74 | 61 | 0.57 | 50 | 6.0 |
| | | M | 104 | 20 | 81 | 67 | 0.60 | 46 | 8.4 |
| | | F | 48 | 22 | 58 | 47 | 0.50 | 62 | 3.5 |
| | 1975 | MF | 110 | 16 | 89 | 88 | 0.81 | 71 | 8.4 |
| | | M | 133 | 16 | 89 | 89 | 0.82 | 65 | 11.0 |
| | | F | 87 | 15 | 89 | 83 | 0.78 | 86 | 5.5 |
| | 1980 | MF | ... | ... | ... | ... | ... | ... | 10.8 |
| | | M | ... | ... | ... | ... | ... | ... | 12.2 |
| | | F | ... | ... | ... | ... | ... | ... | 9.1 |
| | 1985 | MF | 104 | 21 | 84 | 71 | 0.62 | 51 | ... |
| | | M | 107 | 22 | 89 | 77 | 0.62 | 52 | ... |
| | | F | 101 | 19 | 79 | 66 | 0.61 | 49 | ... |
| | 1992 | MF | 83 | 16 | ... | ... | ... | ... | ... |
| | | M | 86 | 19 | ... | ... | ... | ... | ... |
| | | F | 80 | 13 | ... | ... | ... | ... | ... |
| Japan | 1970 | MF | 98 | - | 100 | 100 | 1.00 | 98 | 12.0 |
| | | M | 98 | - | 100 | 100 | 1.00 | 98 | 12.4 |
| | | F | 98 | - | 100 | 100 | 1.00 | 98 | 11.6 |
| | 1975 | MF | 104 | - | 100 | 100 | 1.00 | 100 | ... |
| | | M | 104 | - | 100 | 100 | 1.00 | ... | ... |
| | | F | 104 | - | 100 | 100 | 1.00 | ... | ... |
| | 1980 | MF | 102 | - | 100 | 100 | 1.00 | 100 | 13.1 |
| | | M | 102 | - | 100 | 100 | 1.00 | 100 | 13.5 |
| | | F | 102 | - | 100 | 100 | 1.00 | 100 | 12.6 |
| | 1985 | MF | 103 | - | 100 | 100 | 1.00 | 100 | 13.1 |
| | | M | 103 | - | 100 | 100 | 1.00 | 100 | ... |
| | | F | 104 | - | 100 | 100 | 1.00 | 100 | ... |
| | 1990 | MF | 102 | - | 100 | 100 | 1.00 | 100 | 13.2 |
| | | M | 102 | - | 100 | 100 | 1.00 | 100 | ... |
| | | F | 103 | - | 100 | 100 | 1.00 | 100 | ... |
| | 1991 | MF | 102 | - | ... | ... | ... | ... | 13.3 |
| | | M | 102 | - | ... | ... | ... | ... | ... |
| | | F | 102 | - | ... | ... | ... | ... | ... |
| | 1993 | MF | 101 | - | 100 | 100 | 1.00 | 100 | 13.9 |
| | | M | 101 | - | 100 | 100 | 1.00 | ... | 14.0 |
| | | F | 102 | - | 100 | 100 | 1.00 | ... | 13.7 |
| | 1994 | MF | 102 | - | ... | ... | ... | ... | 13.2 |
| | | M | 102 | - | ... | ... | ... | ... | ... |
| | | F | 101 | - | ... | ... | ... | ... | ... |
| Jordan | 1970 | MF | ... | ... | 79 | 71 | 0.76 | 79 | ... |
| | | M | ... | ... | 82 | 75 | 0.79 | 79 | ... |
| | | F | ... | ... | 75 | 66 | 0.73 | 79 | ... |
| | 1975 | MF | ... | 4 | 91 | 87 | 0.88 | 87 | ... |
| | | M | ... | 4 | 92 | 89 | 0.90 | 88 | ... |
| | | F | ... | 4 | 90 | 84 | 0.86 | 85 | ... |

II.11   Primary education: selected indicators
Enseignement primaire: Indicateurs sélectionnés
Enseñanza primaria: Indicadores seleccionados

| Country<br>Pays<br>País | Year<br>Année<br>Año | Sex<br>Sexe<br>Sexo | Apparent intake rate<br>Taux d'admission apparent<br>Tasa aparente de ingreso (%) | Percentage repeaters<br>Pourcentage de redoublants<br>Porcentaje de repetidores | Percentage of cohort reaching:<br>Pourcentage de la cohorte atteignant:<br>Porcentaje de la cohorte que llega al: | | Coefficient of efficiency<br>Coefficient d'efficacité<br>Coeficiente de eficacia | Transition rate (Prim. to Sec. gen.)<br>Taux de transition (Prim. au sec. gén.)<br>Tasa de transición (Prim. a la Sec. gen.) (%) | School life expectancy (in years)<br>Espérance de vie scolaire (années)<br>Esperanza de vida escolar (en años) |
|---|---|---|---|---|---|---|---|---|---|
| | | | | | Grade 5<br>5e année<br>Quinto año | Final grade<br>Dernière année<br>Ultimo año | | | |
| Jordan (cont) | 1980 | MF | ... | 3 | 100 | 97 | 0.93 | 88 | ... |
| | | M | ... | 3 | 100 | 98 | 0.94 | 88 | ... |
| | | F | ... | 3 | 98 | 94 | 0.92 | 88 | ... |
| | 1990 | MF | ... | 5 | 100 | 87 | 0.84 | ... | ... |
| | | M | ... | 6 | 100 | 77 | 0.76 | ... | ... |
| | | F | ... | 5 | 100 | 97 | 0.92 | ... | ... |
| | 1991 | MF | ... | 6 | 100 | 80 | 0.80 | ... | ... |
| | | M | ... | 6 | 100 | 74 | 0.75 | ... | ... |
| | | F | ... | 5 | 100 | 86 | 0.85 | ... | ... |
| | 1992 | MF | ... | 4 | 98 | 79 | 0.83 | ... | ... |
| | | M | ... | 5 | 98 | 76 | 0.81 | ... | ... |
| | | F | ... | 4 | 99 | 82 | 0.85 | ... | ... |
| Kazakstan | 1993 | MF | 99 | 1 | ... | ... | ... | ... | ... |
| | | M | 100 | 1 | ... | ... | ... | ... | ... |
| | | F | 99 | 1 | ... | ... | ... | ... | ... |
| | 1995 | MF | ... | ... | . | 92 | 0.95 | 99 | ... |
| | 1996 | MF | 95 | 1 | ... | ... | ... | ... | ... |
| Korea, Republic of | 1970 | MF | 112 | 0 | 96 | 95 | 0.98 | 70 | 9.1 |
| | | M | 112 | 0 | 96 | 96 | 0.98 | 80 | 9.9 |
| | | F | 112 | 0 | 96 | 95 | 0.97 | 58 | 8.3 |
| | 1975 | MF | 116 | - | 94 | 92 | 0.97 | 79 | 10.2 |
| | | M | 116 | - | 94 | 93 | 0.97 | 85 | 10.8 |
| | | F | 116 | - | 94 | 92 | 0.96 | 71 | 9.5 |
| | 1980 | MF | 109 | - | 94 | 94 | 0.97 | 97 | 11.7 |
| | | M | 108 | - | 94 | 94 | 0.97 | 99 | 12.3 |
| | | F | 109 | - | 94 | 94 | 0.97 | 96 | 11.1 |
| | 1985 | MF | 99 | - | 99 | 99 | 1.00 | 99 | 13.0 |
| | | M | 98 | - | 99 | 99 | 0.99 | 99 | 13.6 |
| | | F | 100 | - | 99 | 99 | 1.00 | 99 | 12.3 |
| | 1990 | MF | 98 | - | 99 | 99 | 1.00 | ... | 13.3 |
| | | M | 98 | - | 99 | 99 | 0.99 | ... | 14.0 |
| | | F | 98 | - | 100 | 99 | 1.00 | ... | 12.5 |
| | 1991 | MF | 88 | - | 100 | 100 | 1.00 | ... | 13.2 |
| | | M | 88 | - | 100 | 100 | 1.00 | ... | 13.9 |
| | | F | 88 | - | 100 | 100 | 1.00 | ... | 12.5 |
| | 1992 | MF | 92 | - | 100 | 100 | 1.00 | ... | 13.5 |
| | | M | 92 | - | 100 | 100 | 1.00 | ... | 14.1 |
| | | F | 92 | - | 100 | 100 | 1.00 | ... | 12.8 |
| | 1993 | MF | 93 | - | 99 | 99 | 1.00 | 99 | ... |
| | | M | 92 | - | 99 | 99 | 0.99 | 100 | ... |
| | | F | 93 | - | 100 | 99 | 1.00 | 99 | ... |
| | 1994 | MF | 96 | - | 100 | 100 | 1.00 | ... | ... |
| | | M | 95 | - | 100 | 100 | 1.00 | ... | ... |
| | | F | 97 | - | 100 | 99 | 1.00 | ... | ... |
| | 1995 | MF | 99 | - | 98 | 98 | ... | 100 | 14.2 |
| | | M | 98 | - | 98 | 98 | ... | 100 | 14.9 |
| | | F | 100 | - | 99 | 98 | ... | 100 | 13.6 |
| | 1996 | MF | 102 | - | ... | ... | ... | ... | 14.6 |
| | | M | 102 | - | ... | ... | ... | ... | 15.3 |
| | | F | 103 | - | ... | ... | ... | ... | 13.9 |
| Kuwait | 1970 | MF | 54 | 16 | | 98 | 0.79 | ... | 9.4 |
| | | M | 59 | 16 | | 96 | 0.78 | ... | 10.4 |
| | | F | 48 | 15 | | 100 | 0.79 | ... | 8.3 |
| | 1975 | MF | 88 | 11 | ... | ... | ... | 79 | 10.1 |
| | | M | 95 | 11 | ... | ... | ... | 78 | 10.6 |
| | | F | 81 | 11 | ... | ... | ... | 80 | 9.5 |
| | 1980 | MF | 99 | 6 | . | 96 | 0.93 | 98 | ... |
| | | M | 99 | 6 | . | 97 | 0.93 | 98 | ... |
| | | F | 99 | 6 | . | 96 | 0.92 | 98 | ... |
| | 1985 | MF | 96 | 5 | . | 90 | 0.90 | ... | ... |
| | | M | 97 | 5 | . | 91 | 0.90 | ... | ... |
| | | F | 95 | 5 | . | 90 | 0.90 | ... | ... |

Primary education: selected indicators  II.11
Enseignement primaire: indicateurs selectionnés
Enseñanza primaria: indicadores seleccionados

| Country<br><br>Pays<br><br>País | Year<br><br>Année<br><br>Año | Sex<br><br>Sexe<br><br>Sexo | Apparent intake rate<br><br>Taux d'admission apparent<br><br>Tasa aparente de ingreso (%) | Percentage repeaters<br><br>Pourcentage de redoublants<br><br>Porcentaje de repetidores | Percentage of cohort reaching:<br>Pourcentage de la cohorte atteignant:<br>Porcentaje de la cohorte que llega al: | | Coefficient of efficiency<br><br>Coefficient d'efficacité<br><br>Coeficiente de eficacia | Transition rate (Prim. to Sec. gen.)<br><br>Taux de transition (Prim. au sec. gén.)<br><br>Tasa de transición (Prim. a la Sec. gen.) (%) | School life expectancy (in years)<br><br>Espérance de vie scolaire (années)<br><br>Esperanza de vida escolar (en años) |
|---|---|---|---|---|---|---|---|---|---|
| | | | | | Grade 5<br>5e année<br>Quinto año | Final grade<br>Dernière année<br>Ultimo año | | | |
| Kuwait (cont) | 1991 | MF | 46 | 3 | ... | ... | ... | ... | 7.0 |
| | | M | 46 | 3 | ... | ... | ... | ... | 6.8 |
| | | F | 46 | 3 | ... | ... | ... | ... | 7.1 |
| | 1993 | MF | 62 | 4 | . | 92 | 0.91 | 97 | 8.0 |
| | | M | 62 | 4 | . | 84 | 0.85 | 97 | 7.9 |
| | | F | 62 | 4 | . | 99 | 0.96 | 97 | 8.2 |
| | 1994 | MF | 68 | 4 | . | 100 | 0.96 | 106 | ... |
| | | M | 69 | 4 | . | 100 | 0.96 | 115 | ... |
| | | F | 68 | 4 | . | 100 | 0.96 | 99 | ... |
| | 1995 | MF | 72 | 3 | . | 96 | 0.94 | 104 | 9.0 |
| | | M | 73 | 3 | . | 94 | 0.93 | 107 | 8.8 |
| | | F | 70 | 4 | . | 97 | 0.95 | 101 | 9.0 |
| | 1996 | MF | 77 | 3 | ... | ... | ... | ... | 9.2 |
| | | M | 79 | 3 | ... | ... | ... | ... | 9.0 |
| | | F | 76 | 3 | ... | ... | ... | ... | 9.3 |
| Kyrgyzstan | 1994 | MF | 104 | 1 | . | 97 | 0.98 | ... | ... |
| | 1995 | MF | 103 | 0 | ... | ... | ... | ... | ... |
| Lao People's Democratic Republic | 1991 | MF | 111 | 31 | 53 | 53 | 0.54 | 63 | ... |
| | | M | 121 | 32 | 56 | 56 | 0.54 | 65 | ... |
| | | F | 100 | 29 | 50 | 50 | 0.53 | 60 | ... |
| | 1992 | MF | 122 | 27 | 53 | 53 | 0.56 | 69 | 7.4 |
| | | M | 133 | 29 | 55 | 55 | 0.56 | 70 | 8.6 |
| | | F | 111 | 26 | 51 | 51 | 0.55 | 66 | 6.3 |
| | 1993 | MF | 119 | 26 | ... | ... | ... | ... | 7.7 |
| | | M | 130 | 27 | ... | ... | ... | ... | 8.8 |
| | | F | 108 | 25 | ... | ... | ... | ... | 6.5 |
| | 1995 | MF | 114 | ... | 55 | 55 | ... | 64 | ... |
| | | M | 121 | ... | 57 | 57 | ... | 65 | ... |
| | | F | 106 | ... | 54 | 54 | ... | 62 | ... |
| | 1996 | MF | 115 | 23 | ... | ... | ... | ... | 8.0 |
| | | M | 121 | 25 | ... | ... | ... | ... | 9.1 |
| | | F | 108 | 22 | ... | ... | ... | ... | 6.9 |
| Lebanon | 1996 | MF | 100 | 13 | ... | ... | ... | ... | ... |
| Macau | 1991 | MF | 97 | 7 | 97 | 97 | 0.91 | 85 | 11.6 |
| | | M | 96 | 8 | 93 | 93 | 0.90 | 78 | 12.1 |
| | | F | 97 | 6 | 96 | 96 | 0.00 | 92 | 11.3 |
| | 1992 | MF | 94 | 7 | ... | ... | ... | ... | ... |
| | | M | 96 | 5 | ... | ... | ... | ... | ... |
| | | F | 93 | 8 | ... | ... | ... | ... | ... |
| Malaysia | 1980 | MF | 93 | - | 97 | 96 | 0.98 | ... | ... |
| | | M | 94 | - | 97 | 95 | 0.97 | ... | ... |
| | | F | 93 | - | 97 | 96 | 0.98 | ... | ... |
| | 1985 | MF | 103 | - | ... | ... | ... | ... | ... |
| | | M | 103 | - | ... | ... | ... | ... | ... |
| | | F | 104 | - | ... | ... | ... | ... | ... |
| | 1990 | MF | 95 | - | 98 | 96 | 0.98 | ... | ... |
| | | M | 95 | - | 98 | 96 | 0.97 | ... | ... |
| | | F | 95 | - | 98 | 97 | 0.98 | ... | ... |
| | 1991 | MF | 99 | - | 97 | 96 | 0.97 | ... | ... |
| | | M | 100 | - | 97 | 95 | 0.97 | ... | ... |
| | | F | 99 | - | 97 | 96 | 0.98 | ... | ... |
| | 1992 | MF | 105 | - | 97 | 95 | 0.97 | ... | ... |
| | | M | 104 | - | 97 | 95 | 0.97 | ... | ... |
| | | F | 106 | - | 97 | 96 | 0.98 | ... | ... |
| | 1993 | MF | 106 | - | 99 | 97 | 0.98 | ... | ... |
| | | M | 106 | - | 98 | 96 | 0.98 | ... | ... |
| | | F | 106 | - | 100 | 99 | 0.99 | ... | ... |
| | 1994 | MF | 106 | - | ... | ... | ... | ... | ... |
| | | M | 106 | - | ... | ... | ... | ... | ... |
| | | F | 106 | - | ... | ... | ... | ... | ... |

II.11    Primary education: selected indicators
Enseignement primaire: indicateurs selectionnés
Enseñanza primaria: indicadores seleccionados

| Country<br>Pays<br>País | Year<br>Année<br>Año | Sex<br>Sexe<br>Sexo | Apparent intake rate<br>Taux d'admission apparent<br>Tasa aparente de ingreso (%) | Percentage repeaters<br>Pourcentage de redoublants<br>Porcentaje de repetidores | Percentage of cohort reaching: / Pourcentage de la cohorte atteignant: / Porcentaje de la cohorte que llega al: | | Coefficient of efficiency<br>Coefficient d'efficacité<br>Coeficiente de eficacia | Transition rate (Prim. to Sec. gen.)<br>Taux de transition (Prim. au sec. gén.)<br>Tasa de transición (Prim. a la Sec. gen.) (%) | School life expectancy (in years)<br>Espérance de vie scolaire (années)<br>Esperanza de vida escolar (en años) |
|---|---|---|---|---|---|---|---|---|---|
| | | | | | Grade 5<br>5e année<br>Quinto año | Final grade<br>Dernière année<br>Ultimo año | | | |
| Mongolia | 1994 | MF | 94 | 1 | . | 92 | 0.95 | 95 | 7.2 |
| | | M | 94 | 1 | . | 90 | 0.94 | 94 | 6.2 |
| | | F | 95 | 1 | . | 94 | 0.96 | 96 | 8.1 |
| | 1995 | MF | 95 | 1 | . | 90 | 0.95 | ... | 7.5 |
| | | M | 95 | 1 | . | 89 | 0.93 | ... | 6.6 |
| | | F | 95 | 1 | . | 92 | 0.96 | ... | 8.5 |
| | 1996 | MF | 96 | 1 | ... | ... | ... | ... | 7.7 |
| | | M | 95 | 1 | ... | ... | ... | ... | 6.8 |
| | | F | 97 | 1 | ... | ... | ... | ... | 8.7 |
| Nepal | 1991 | MF | 123 | 27 | 52 | 52 | 0.58 | 78 | ... |
| | | M | ... | ... | 52 | 52 | 0.56 | 79 | ... |
| | | F | ... | ... | 52 | 52 | 0.60 | 77 | ... |
| | 1992 | MF | 124 | 27 | ... | ... | ... | ... | ... |
| | | M | 136 | 28 | ... | ... | ... | ... | ... |
| | | F | 111 | 24 | ... | ... | ... | ... | ... |
| Oman | 1975 | MF | 40 | 9 | 74 | 64 | 0.64 | 65 | ... |
| | | M | 50 | 9 | ... | ... | ... | ... | ... |
| | | F | 30 | 9 | ... | ... | ... | ... | ... |
| | 1985 | MF | 81 | 12 | 93 | 89 | 0.81 | 82 | ... |
| | | M | 81 | 13 | 95 | 91 | 0.80 | 80 | ... |
| | | F | 80 | 9 | 91 | 86 | 0.82 | 86 | ... |
| | 1990 | MF | ... | ... | 96 | 93 | 0.86 | 86 | ... |
| | | M | ... | ... | 95 | 94 | 0.86 | 84 | ... |
| | | F | ... | ... | 96 | 91 | 0.86 | 88 | ... |
| | 1991 | MF | 81 | 9 | ... | ... | ... | ... | ... |
| | | M | 82 | 10 | ... | ... | ... | ... | ... |
| | | F | 80 | 8 | ... | ... | ... | ... | ... |
| | 1992 | MF | ... | ... | 96 | 93 | 0.87 | 90 | 9.1 |
| | | M | ... | ... | 96 | 93 | 0.86 | 88 | 9.6 |
| | | F | ... | ... | 96 | 93 | 0.88 | 93 | 8.5 |
| | 1993 | MF | 75 | 9 | 95 | 93 | 0.88 | 94 | ... |
| | | M | 75 | 10 | 95 | 93 | 0.87 | 93 | ... |
| | | F | 74 | 7 | 95 | 93 | 0.90 | 95 | ... |
| | 1994 | MF | 68 | 8 | 96 | 94 | 0.88 | 93 | ... |
| | | M | 70 | 9 | 96 | 94 | 0.87 | 91 | ... |
| | | F | 67 | 7 | 96 | 94 | 0.90 | 95 | ... |
| | 1995 | MF | 68 | 8 | 96 | 94 | 0.87 | 91 | ... |
| | | M | 68 | 10 | 96 | 94 | 0.86 | 88 | ... |
| | | F | 67 | 7 | 96 | 93 | 0.88 | 94 | ... |
| | 1996 | MF | 69 | 9 | ... | ... | ... | ... | ... |
| | | M | 69 | 11 | ... | ... | ... | ... | ... |
| | | F | 68 | 7 | ... | ... | ... | ... | ... |
| Philippines | 1980 | MF | 130 | 2 | ... | ... | ... | ... | 10.7 |
| | | M | 134 | 3 | ... | ... | ... | ... | 10.5 |
| | | F | 125 | 2 | ... | ... | ... | ... | 10.8 |
| | 1985 | MF | 133 | 2 | 79 | 75 | 0.87 | ... | 10.3 |
| | | M | 136 | 2 | 79 | 75 | 0.87 | ... | ... |
| | | F | 129 | 2 | 79 | 75 | 0.87 | ... | ... |
| | 1991 | MF | ... | ... | ... | ... | ... | ... | 10.9 |
| | 1992 | MF | ... | ... | ... | ... | ... | ... | 11.0 |
| | 1993 | MF | ... | ... | ... | ... | ... | ... | 11.0 |
| | 1995 | MF | ... | ... | ... | ... | ... | ... | 11.2 |
| Qatar | 1970 | MF | 77 | 24 | 97 | 93 | 0.72 | ... | ... |
| | | M | 79 | 24 | 96 | 90 | 0.71 | ... | ... |
| | | F | 74 | 24 | 96 | 94 | 0.73 | ... | ... |
| | 1975 | MF | 89 | 22 | 96 | 93 | 0.73 | 84 | 10.3 |
| | | M | 88 | 23 | 96 | 92 | 0.72 | 74 | 9.7 |
| | | F | 90 | 21 | 95 | 93 | 0.74 | 96 | 11.6 |
| | 1980 | MF | ... | 13 | ... | ... | ... | ... | 10.9 |
| | | M | ... | 12 | ... | ... | ... | ... | 10.6 |
| | | F | ... | 13 | ... | ... | ... | ... | 11.4 |

Primary education: selected indicators  II.11
Enseignement primaire: indicateurs selectionnés
Enseñanza primaria: indicadores seleccionados

| Country<br><br>Pays<br><br>País | Year<br><br>Année<br><br>Año | Sex<br><br>Sexe<br><br>Sexo | Apparent intake rate<br><br>Taux d'admission apparent<br><br>Tasa aparente de ingreso<br>(%) | Percentage repeaters<br><br>Pourcentage de redoublants<br><br>Porcentaje de repetidores | Percentage of cohort reaching:<br>Pourcentage de la cohorte atteignant:<br>Porcentaje de la cohorte que llega al: | | Coefficient of efficiency<br><br>Coefficient d'efficacité<br><br>Coeficiente de eficacia | Transition rate (Prim. to Sec. gen.)<br><br>Taux de transition (Prim. au sec. gén.)<br><br>Tasa de transición (Prim. a la Sec. gen.)<br>(%) | School life expectancy (in years)<br><br>Espérance de vie scolaire (années)<br><br>Esperanza de vida escolar (en años) |
| | | | | | Grade 5<br>5e année<br>Quinto año | Final grade<br>Dernière année<br>Ultimo año | | | |
|---|---|---|---|---|---|---|---|---|---|
| Qatar (cont) | 1985 | MF | 75 | 11 | 99 | 96 | 0.84 | 81 | 12.6 |
| | | M | 73 | 13 | 98 | 94 | 0.80 | 74 | 11.8 |
| | | F | 78 | 8 | 99 | 97 | 0.88 | 88 | 13.2 |
| | 1990 | MF | 54 | 7 | 64 | 57 | 0.69 | 85 | 12.3 |
| | | M | 54 | 10 | 63 | 56 | 0.65 | 82 | 11.6 |
| | | F | 55 | 5 | 65 | 58 | 0.72 | 89 | 13.1 |
| | 1991 | MF | 58 | 7 | 94 | 91 | 0.89 | 93 | 11.8 |
| | | M | 57 | 9 | 91 | 88 | 0.85 | 89 | 11.2 |
| | | F | 60 | 4 | 96 | 94 | 0.93 | 97 | 12.6 |
| | 1992 | MF | 57 | 6 | 98 | 96 | 0.92 | 98 | 11.9 |
| | | M | 55 | 7 | 96 | 94 | 0.89 | 95 | 11.3 |
| | | F | 59 | 4 | 100 | 98 | 0.95 | 100 | 12.7 |
| | 1993 | MF | 54 | 5 | 95 | 92 | 0.90 | 97 | 11.8 |
| | | M | 53 | 7 | 92 | 88 | 0.86 | 94 | 11.4 |
| | | F | 54 | 3 | 98 | 96 | 0.94 | 99 | 12.4 |
| | 1994 | MF | 53 | 5 | 99 | 98 | 0.93 | 97 | ... |
| | | M | 51 | 7 | 97 | 94 | 0.90 | 94 | ... |
| | | F | 55 | 3 | 99 | 99 | 0.96 | 100 | ... |
| | 1995 | MF | 54 | 5 | ... | ... | ... | ... | ... |
| | | M | 51 | 6 | ... | ... | ... | ... | ... |
| | | F | 57 | 3 | ... | ... | ... | ... | ... |
| Saudi Arabia | 1970 | MF | ... | ... | 83 | 77 | 0.67 | 70 | 3.7 |
| | | M | ... | ... | 81 | 75 | 0.65 | 70 | 5.2 |
| | | F | ... | ... | 86 | 82 | 0.73 | 71 | 2.1 |
| | 1975 | MF | 61 | 15 | 83 | 78 | 0.79 | ... | 5.3 |
| | | M | 74 | 17 | 82 | 78 | 0.79 | ... | 6.6 |
| | | F | 47 | 12 | 80 | 76 | 0.78 | ... | 3.8 |
| | 1980 | MF | 64 | 16 | 84 | 79 | 0.76 | 88 | 6.0 |
| | | M | 71 | 19 | 82 | 78 | 0.73 | 85 | 7.2 |
| | | F | 57 | 10 | 86 | 82 | 0.82 | 94 | 4.8 |
| | 1985 | MF | 64 | 12 | ... | ... | ... | ... | 7.2 |
| | | M | 70 | 15 | ... | ... | ... | ... | 8.2 |
| | | F | 59 | 9 | ... | ... | ... | ... | 6.2 |
| | 1990 | MF | 73 | 9 | 83 | 77 | 0.81 | 95 | 8.0 |
| | | M | 75 | 11 | 82 | 76 | 0.79 | 96 | 8.6 |
| | | F | 71 | 7 | 84 | 79 | 0.84 | 94 | 7.4 |
| | 1991 | MF | 75 | 7 | 96 | 93 | 0.84 | 95 | 8.1 |
| | | M | 74 | 8 | 96 | 93 | 0.82 | 96 | ... |
| | | F | 77 | 5 | 95 | 92 | 0.87 | 94 | ... |
| | 1992 | MF | 76 | 11 | 94 | 91 | 0.86 | ... | 8.5 |
| | | M | 74 | 13 | 95 | 92 | 0.84 | ... | ... |
| | | F | 78 | 8 | 93 | 90 | 0.89 | ... | ... |
| | 1993 | MF | 75 | 9 | ... | ... | ... | ... | 8.8 |
| | | M | 74 | 11 | ... | ... | ... | ... | ... |
| | | F | 76 | 6 | ... | ... | ... | ... | ... |
| | 1995 | MF | 75 | 8 | 89 | 88 | 0.87 | 99 | 9.2 |
| | | M | 74 | 11 | 87 | 87 | 0.85 | 102 | 9.5 |
| | | F | 76 | 5 | 92 | 89 | 0.90 | 95 | 8.8 |
| | 1996 | MF | ... | 8 | ... | ... | ... | ... | 9.0 |
| | | M | ... | 11 | ... | ... | ... | ... | ... |
| | | F | ... | 1 | ... | ... | ... | ... | ... |
| Singapore | 1970 | MF | ... | ... | ... | ... | ... | ... | 9.4 |
| | | M | ... | ... | ... | ... | ... | ... | 9.8 |
| | | F | ... | ... | ... | ... | ... | ... | 8.9 |
| | 1975 | MF | 99 | 8 | 97 | 95 | 0.88 | 58 | ... |
| | | M | 99 | 10 | 96 | 95 | 0.86 | 52 | ... |
| | | F | 99 | 6 | 97 | 95 | 0.90 | 65 | ... |
| | 1980 | MF | 104 | 7 | 97 | 90 | 0.88 | 82 | ... |
| | | M | 103 | 8 | ... | ... | ... | ... | ... |
| | | F | 104 | 6 | ... | ... | ... | ... | ... |
| Sri Lanka | 1970 | MF | 86 | 22 | ... | ... | ... | 77 | ... |
| | | M | 88 | 24 | ... | ... | ... | ... | ... |
| | | F | 84 | 20 | ... | ... | ... | ... | ... |

**Primary education: selected indicators**
**Enseignement primaire: indicateurs sélectionnés**
**Enseñanza primaria: indicadores seleccionados**

| Country / Pays / País | Year / Année / Año | Sex / Sexe / Sexo | Apparent intake rate / Taux d'admission apparent / Tasa aparente de ingreso (%) | Percentage repeaters / Pourcentage de redoublants / Porcentaje de repetidores | Percentage of cohort reaching: / Pourcentage de la cohorte atteignant: / Porcentaje de la cohorte que llega al: — Grade 5 / 5e année / Quinto año | Final grade / Dernière année / Ultimo año | Coefficient of efficiency / Coefficient d'efficacité / Coeficiente de eficacia | Transition rate (Prim. to Sec. gen.) / Taux de transition (Prim. au sec. gén.) / Tasa de transición (Prim. a la Sec. gen.) (%) | School life expectancy (in years) / Espérance de vie scolaire (années) / Esperanza de vida escolar (en años) |
|---|---|---|---|---|---|---|---|---|---|
| Sri Lanka (cont) | 1980 | MF | 99 | 10 | 96 | 91 | 0.83 | 84 | ... |
| | 1985 | MF | 98 | 8 | 93 | 88 | 0.84 | 88 | ... |
| | | M | 99 | 8 | 92 | 87 | 0.82 | 86 | ... |
| | | F | 97 | 9 | 93 | 89 | 0.87 | 90 | ... |
| | 1990 | MF | 99 | 8 | 94 | 94 | 0.89 | 90 | ... |
| | | M | 99 | 9 | 94 | 94 | 0.88 | 88 | ... |
| | | F | 99 | 7 | 95 | 95 | 0.91 | 92 | ... |
| | 1991 | MF | 102 | 8 | 92 | 92 | 0.89 | 90 | ... |
| | | M | 101 | 9 | 92 | 92 | 0.88 | 88 | ... |
| | | F | 102 | 6 | 93 | 93 | 0.91 | 92 | ... |
| | 1992 | MF | 98 | 7 | ... | ... | ... | ... | ... |
| | | M | 98 | 8 | ... | ... | ... | ... | ... |
| | | F | 99 | 6 | ... | ... | ... | ... | ... |
| | 1996 | MF | 107 | 2 | ... | ... | ... | ... | ... |
| | | M | 107 | 3 | ... | ... | ... | ... | ... |
| | | F | 107 | 2 | ... | ... | ... | ... | ... |
| Syrian Arab Republic | 1970 | MF | 85 | 11 | 89 | 82 | 0.80 | 82 | 7.7 |
| | | M | 98 | 12 | 91 | 86 | 0.82 | 82 | 10.1 |
| | | F | 72 | 10 | 86 | 77 | 0.76 | 82 | 5.1 |
| | 1975 | MF | 98 | 10 | 86 | 79 | 0.78 | 76 | 9.0 |
| | | M | 112 | 10 | 89 | 84 | 0.81 | 76 | 10.8 |
| | | F | 84 | 10 | 80 | 71 | 0.73 | 76 | 6.7 |
| | 1980 | MF | 104 | 8 | 91 | 86 | 0.84 | 76 | 9.7 |
| | | M | 111 | 9 | 93 | 89 | 0.85 | 76 | 11.4 |
| | | F | 96 | 7 | 88 | 83 | 0.83 | 76 | 8.0 |
| | 1985 | MF | 108 | 7 | 95 | 93 | 0.89 | 76 | 10.9 |
| | | M | 112 | 8 | 96 | 95 | 0.90 | 80 | 12.0 |
| | | F | 104 | 7 | 95 | 91 | 0.89 | 72 | 9.6 |
| | 1990 | MF | 103 | 7 | 94 | 91 | 0.87 | 69 | 10.3 |
| | | M | 106 | 8 | 94 | 93 | 0.88 | 73 | 11.2 |
| | | F | 100 | 6 | 94 | 89 | 0.87 | 64 | 9.4 |
| | 1991 | MF | 103 | 7 | 92 | 87 | 0.85 | 65 | 10.1 |
| | | M | 107 | 8 | 92 | 87 | 0.85 | 68 | 10.8 |
| | | F | 99 | 6 | 92 | 87 | 0.86 | 61 | 9.3 |
| | 1992 | MF | 99 | 7 | 92 | 87 | 0.85 | 66 | 10.0 |
| | | M | 103 | 8 | 94 | 89 | 0.85 | 69 | 10.6 |
| | | F | 96 | 6 | 91 | 85 | 0.85 | 62 | 9.2 |
| | 1993 | MF | 97 | 7 | 90 | 84 | 0.83 | ... | 9.7 |
| | | M | 101 | 8 | 91 | 85 | 0.82 | ... | 10.4 |
| | | F | 94 | 6 | 89 | 83 | 0.83 | ... | 9.0 |
| | 1994 | MF | 95 | 8 | 91 | 85 | 0.84 | ... | 9.5 |
| | | M | 99 | 9 | 92 | 86 | 0.83 | ... | 10.1 |
| | | F | 92 | 6 | 90 | 84 | 0.84 | ... | 8.8 |
| | 1995 | MF | 97 | 7 | 94 | 89 | 0.86 | ... | ... |
| | | M | 101 | 8 | 93 | 89 | 0.86 | ... | ... |
| | | F | 93 | 6 | 94 | 89 | 0.87 | ... | ... |
| | 1996 | MF | 95 | 7 | ... | ... | ... | ... | ... |
| | | M | 98 | 8 | ... | ... | ... | ... | ... |
| | | F | 92 | 6 | ... | ... | ... | ... | ... |
| Tajikistan | 1994 | MF | 102 | 0 | ... | ... | ... | ... | ... |
| | 1996 | MF | 99 | 0 | ... | ... | ... | ... | ... |
| Thailand | 1975 | MF | 100 | 10 | 49 | 40 | 0.51 | 77 | ... |
| | | M | 102 | 11 | 51 | 42 | 0.52 | 79 | ... |
| | | F | 98 | 9 | 47 | 38 | 0.49 | 76 | ... |
| | 1980 | MF | 98 | 8 | ... | ... | ... | ... | ... |
| | | M | 98 | 9 | ... | ... | ... | ... | ... |
| | | F | 97 | 7 | ... | ... | ... | ... | ... |
| Turkey | 1985 | MF | 103 | 8 | 96 | 96 | 0.90 | 46 | 8.5 |
| | | M | 107 | 8 | 97 | 97 | 0.90 | 56 | ... |
| | | F | 100 | 8 | 95 | 95 | 0.89 | 36 | ... |
| | 1990 | MF | 93 | 7 | 98 | 98 | 0.92 | 54 | 8.5 |
| | | M | 96 | 7 | 98 | 98 | 0.92 | 62 | ... |
| | | F | 90 | 7 | 97 | 97 | 0.91 | 44 | ... |

Primary education: selected indicators  II.11
Enseignement primaire: indicateurs selectionnés
Enseñanza primaria: indicadores seleccionados

| Country / Pays / País | Year / Année / Año | Sex / Sexe / Sexo | Apparent intake rate / Taux d'admission apparent / Tasa aparente de ingreso (%) | Percentage repeaters / Pourcentage de redoublants / Porcentaje de repetidores | Percentage of cohort reaching: / Pourcentage de la cohorte atteignant: / Porcentaje de la cohorte que llega al: Grade 5 / 5e année / Quinto año | Final grade / Dernière année / Ultimo año | Coefficient of efficiency / Coefficient d'efficacité / Coeficiente de eficacia | Transition rate (Prim. to Sec. gen.) / Taux de transition (Prim. au sec. gén.) / Tasa de transición (Prim. a la Sec. gen.) (%) | School life expectancy (in years) / Espérance de vie scolaire (années) / Esperanza de vida escolar (en años) |
|---|---|---|---|---|---|---|---|---|---|
| Turkey (cont) | 1991 | MF | 96 | 7 | 92 | 92 | 0.90 | ... | 8.6 |
| | | M | 99 | 7 | 92 | 92 | 0.90 | ... | ... |
| | | F | 93 | 7 | 93 | 93 | 0.90 | ... | ... |
| | 1992 | MF | 98 | 6 | ... | ... | ... | ... | 8.9 |
| | | M | 101 | 6 | ... | ... | ... | ... | ... |
| | | F | 94 | 6 | ... | ... | ... | ... | ... |
| | 1993 | MF | 99 | 5 | 95 | 95 | 0.92 | ... | 9.2 |
| | | M | 102 | 5 | 93 | 93 | 0.92 | ... | 10.1 |
| | | F | 96 | 5 | 96 | 96 | 0.92 | ... | 8.2 |
| | 1994 | MF | 105 | 5 | ... | ... | ... | ... | 9.5 |
| | | M | 108 | 4 | ... | ... | ... | ... | 10.4 |
| | | F | 102 | 5 | ... | ... | ... | ... | 8.5 |
| United Arab Emirates | 1975 | MF | ... | 15 | 100 | 95 | 0.81 | 89 | ... |
| | | M | ... | 15 | 98 | 92 | 0.79 | 87 | ... |
| | | F | ... | 15 | 100 | 97 | 0.83 | 91 | ... |
| | 1985 | MF | ... | 6 | 88 | 82 | 0.83 | 91 | ... |
| | | M | ... | 6 | 85 | 78 | 0.80 | 90 | ... |
| | | F | ... | 5 | 91 | 86 | 0.86 | 91 | ... |
| | 1990 | MF | 99 | 4 | ... | ... | 0.82 | 91 | 10.8 |
| | | M | 101 | 5 | ... | ... | 0.81 | 89 | 10.4 |
| | | Г | 97 | 4 | ... | ... | 0.83 | 93 | 11.3 |
| | 1991 | MF | 96 | 4 | 89 | 85 | 0.88 | 94 | 10.7 |
| | | M | 97 | 5 | 88 | 84 | 0.87 | 92 | 10.2 |
| | | F | 94 | 4 | 90 | 87 | 0.90 | 96 | 11.2 |
| | 1992 | MF | 92 | 4 | 100 | 98 | 0.94 | 96 | 10.6 |
| | | M | 93 | 4 | 100 | 98 | 0.93 | 94 | 10.2 |
| | | F | 92 | 3 | 99 | 97 | 0.95 | 97 | 11.1 |
| | 1993 | MF | 90 | 5 | 98 | 96 | 0.92 | 94 | ... |
| | | M | 91 | 6 | 98 | 95 | 0.91 | 92 | ... |
| | | F | 89 | 4 | 98 | 96 | 0.93 | 97 | ... |
| | 1994 | MF | 94 | 5 | ... | ... | ... | ... | ... |
| | | M | 96 | 6 | ... | ... | ... | ... | ... |
| | | F | 92 | 4 | ... | ... | ... | ... | ... |
| | 1995 | MF | 90 | 5 | ... | ... | ... | 95 | ... |
| | | M | 90 | 5 | ... | ... | ... | 93 | ... |
| | | F | 89 | 4 | ... | ... | ... | 97 | ... |
| | 1996 | MF | 89 | 4 | ... | ... | ... | ... | 10.7 |
| | | M | 91 | 5 | ... | ... | ... | ... | 10.3 |
| | | F | 88 | 3 | ... | ... | ... | ... | 11.2 |
| Uzbekistan | 1993 | MF | 100 | 0 | ... | ... | ... | ... | ... |
| | 1994 | MF | 99 | 0 | ... | ... | ... | ... | ... |
| Palestine | 1994 | MF | ... | 5 | 100 | 73 | 0.74 | ... | ... |
| | | M | ... | 5 | 100 | 71 | 0.72 | ... | ... |
| | | F | ... | 5 | 100 | 75 | 0.76 | ... | ... |
| | 1995 | MF | ... | 4 | 100 | 78 | 0.78 | ... | ... |
| | | M | ... | 5 | 99 | 73 | 0.75 | ... | ... |
| | | F | ... | 4 | 100 | 82 | 0.82 | ... | ... |
| **Europe** | | | | | | | | | |
| Albania | 1994 | MF | ... | ... | 82 | 81 | 0.89 | ... | ... |
| | | M | ... | ... | 81 | 77 | 0.85 | ... | ... |
| | | F | ... | ... | 83 | 83 | 0.92 | ... | ... |
| | 1995 | MF | 100 | 5 | ... | ... | ... | ... | ... |
| | | M | 99 | 7 | ... | ... | ... | ... | ... |
| | | F | 101 | 4 | ... | ... | ... | ... | ... |
| Austria | 1970 | MF | 100 | 6 | . | 95 | 0.93 | ... | 10.5 |
| | | M | 100 | 7 | . | 94 | 0.92 | ... | ... |
| | | F | 101 | 5 | . | 96 | 0.95 | ... | ... |
| | 1975 | MF | | | | | | ... | 10.9 |
| | 1992 | MF | | | | | | ... | 14.5 |
| | | M | ... | ... | ... | ... | ... | ... | 14.8 |
| | | F | ... | ... | ... | ... | ... | ... | 14.1 |

II.11 Primary education: selected indicators
Enseignement primaire: indicateurs selectionnés
Enseñanza primaria: indicadores seleccionados

| Country<br>Pays<br>País | Year<br>Année<br>Año | Sex<br>Sexe<br>Sexo | Apparent intake rate<br>Taux d'admission apparent<br>Tasa aparente de ingreso<br>(%) | Percentage repeaters<br>Pourcentage de redoublants<br>Porcentaje de repetidores | Percentage of cohort reaching:<br>Pourcentage de la cohorte atteignant:<br>Porcentaje de la cohorte que llega al: | | Coefficient of efficiency<br>Coefficient d'efficacité<br>Coeficiente de eficacia | Transition rate (Prim. to Sec. gen.)<br>Taux de transition (Prim. au sec. gén.)<br>Tasa de transición (Prim. a la Sec. gen.)<br>(%) | School life expectancy (in years)<br>Espérance de vie scolaire (années)<br>Esperanza de vida escolar (en años) |
|---|---|---|---|---|---|---|---|---|---|
| | | | | | Grade 5<br>5e année<br>Quinto año | Final grade<br>Dernière année<br>Ultimo año | | | |
| Austria (cont) | 1993 | MF | ... | ... | ... | ... | ... | ... | 14.3 |
| | | M | ... | ... | ... | ... | ... | ... | 14.5 |
| | | F | ... | ... | ... | ... | ... | ... | 14.2 |
| | 1994 | MF | ... | ... | ... | ... | ... | ... | 14.4 |
| | | M | ... | ... | ... | ... | ... | ... | 14.5 |
| | | F | ... | ... | ... | ... | ... | ... | 14.3 |
| | 1995 | MF | ... | ... | ... | ... | ... | ... | 14.4 |
| | | M | ... | ... | ... | ... | ... | ... | 14.5 |
| | | F | ... | ... | ... | ... | ... | ... | 14.3 |
| | 1996 | MF | ... | ... | ... | ... | ... | ... | 14.5 |
| | | M | ... | ... | ... | ... | ... | ... | 14.5 |
| | | F | ... | ... | ... | ... | ... | ... | 14.4 |
| Belarus | 1990 | MF | 97 | 1 | . | 98 | 0.98 | 100 | ... |
| | 1991 | MF | 93 | 1 | . | 99 | 0.99 | 100 | |
| | 1992 | MF | 93 | 1 | . | 98 | 0.98 | 100 | ... |
| | | M | 94 | 1 | . | 98 | 0.98 | 101 | |
| | | F | 93 | 1 | . | 99 | 0.98 | 100 | |
| | 1993 | MF | 94 | 1 | . | 100 | 0.99 | 101 | ... |
| | | M | 94 | 1 | . | 100 | 0.99 | 103 | ... |
| | | F | 93 | 1 | . | 98 | 0.98 | 99 | |
| | 1994 | MF | 96 | 1 | . | 98 | 0.98 | 98 | |
| | | M | 98 | 1 | . | 98 | 0.98 | 97 | |
| | | F | 95 | 1 | . | 98 | 0.98 | 99 | |
| | 1995 | MF | 98 | 1 | . | 98 | 0.98 | 99 | |
| | | M | 100 | 1 | . | 98 | 0.98 | 99 | |
| | | F | 96 | 1 | . | 98 | 0.98 | 99 | |
| | 1996 | MF | 100 | 1 | ... | ... | ... | ... | |
| | | M | 102 | 1 | ... | ... | ... | ... | |
| | | F | 97 | 1 | ... | ... | ... | ... | |
| Belgium | 1985 | MF | 99 | 17 | ... | ... | ... | ... | 13.6 |
| | | M | 99 | 18 | ... | ... | ... | ... | 13.6 |
| | | F | 99 | 15 | ... | ... | ... | ... | 13.5 |
| | 1990 | MF | ... | ... | ... | ... | ... | ... | 14.2 |
| | | M | ... | ... | ... | ... | ... | ... | 14.1 |
| | | F | ... | ... | ... | ... | ... | ... | 14.2 |
| | 1991 | MF | ... | ... | ... | ... | ... | ... | 14.3 |
| | | M | ... | ... | ... | ... | ... | ... | 14.2 |
| | | F | ... | ... | ... | ... | ... | ... | 14.3 |
| | 1992 | MF | ... | ... | ... | ... | ... | ... | 15.4 |
| | | M | ... | ... | ... | ... | ... | ... | 15.5 |
| | | F | ... | ... | ... | ... | ... | ... | 15.3 |
| | 1993 | MF | ... | ... | ... | ... | ... | ... | 15.6 |
| | | M | ... | ... | ... | ... | ... | ... | 15.6 |
| | | F | ... | ... | ... | ... | ... | ... | 15.5 |
| | 1994 | MF | ... | ... | ... | ... | ... | ... | 15.8 |
| | | M | ... | ... | ... | ... | ... | ... | 15.9 |
| | | F | ... | ... | ... | ... | ... | ... | 15.8 |
| | 1995 | MF | ... | ... | ... | ... | ... | ... | 16.8 |
| | | M | ... | ... | ... | ... | ... | ... | 16.7 |
| | | F | ... | ... | ... | ... | ... | ... | 16.9 |
| Bulgaria | 1970 | MF | 107 | 6 | 94 | 78 | 0.81 | ... | 11.1 |
| | | M | ... | ... | ... | ... | ... | ... | 11.2 |
| | | F | ... | ... | ... | ... | ... | ... | 11.1 |
| | 1975 | MF | 107 | 2 | 94 | 83 | 0.87 | ... | 11.5 |
| | | M | ... | 3 | ... | ... | ... | ... | ... |
| | | F | ... | 1 | ... | ... | ... | ... | ... |
| | 1980 | MF | 103 | 2 | 95 | 87 | 0.90 | ... | 11.1 |
| | | M | ... | 2 | ... | ... | ... | ... | 11.0 |
| | | F | ... | 1 | ... | ... | ... | ... | 11.2 |
| | 1985 | MF | 106 | 2 | 96 | 90 | 0.92 | ... | ... |
| | | M | 105 | 3 | 97 | 92 | 0.93 | ... | ... |
| | | F | 107 | 1 | 95 | 88 | 0.91 | ... | ... |

Primary education: selected indicators II.11
Enseignement primaire: indicateurs selectionnés
Enseñanza primaria: indicadores seleccionados

| Country / Pays / País | Year / Année / Año | Sex / Sexe / Sexo | Apparent intake rate / Taux d'admission apparent / Tasa aparente de ingreso (%) | Percentage repeaters / Pourcentage de redoublants / Porcentaje de repetidores | Percentage of cohort reaching: Grade 5 / 5e année / Quinto año | Final grade / Dernière année / Ultimo año | Coefficient of efficiency / Coefficient d'efficacité / Coeficiente de eficacia | Transition rate (Prim. to Sec. gen.) / Taux de transition / Tasa de transición (%) | School life expectancy (in years) / Espérance de vie scolaire / Esperanza de vida escolar (en años) |
|---|---|---|---|---|---|---|---|---|---|
| Bulgaria (cont) | 1990 | MF | 96 | 4 | 91 | 74 | 0.78 | ... | 12.3 |
| | | M | 95 | 6 | 91 | 75 | 0.78 | ... | 12.3 |
| | | F | 97 | 3 | 90 | 73 | 0.79 | ... | 12.3 |
| | 1991 | MF | 94 | 5 | 88 | 67 | 0.73 | ... | 12.0 |
| | | M | 93 | 6 | 88 | 69 | 0.73 | ... | 11.9 |
| | | F | 94 | 3 | 88 | 66 | 0.72 | ... | 12.0 |
| | 1992 | MF | 95 | 5 | 84 | 62 | 0.70 | ... | 11.8 |
| | | M | 94 | 7 | 81 | 62 | 0.71 | ... | 11.5 |
| | | F | 95 | 4 | 87 | 62 | 0.69 | ... | 12.0 |
| | 1993 | MF | 96 | 5 | 93 | 75 | 0.78 | ... | 11.6 |
| | | M | 96 | 6 | 93 | 78 | 0.80 | ... | 11.3 |
| | | F | 96 | 3 | 90 | 69 | 0.75 | ... | 11.9 |
| | 1994 | MF | 97 | 4 | ... | ... | ... | ... | 11.8 |
| | | M | 97 | 5 | ... | ... | ... | ... | 11.5 |
| | | F | 97 | 3 | ... | ... | ... | ... | 12.2 |
| | 1995 | MF | 102 | 4 | ... | 89 | 0.93 | 94 | 12.1 |
| | | M | 103 | 4 | ... | 90 | 0.92 | 94 | ... |
| | | F | 100 | 3 | ... | 89 | 0.93 | 95 | ... |
| | 1996 | MF | 102 | 3 | ... | ... | ... | ... | 12.2 |
| | | M | 103 | 4 | ... | ... | ... | ... | ... |
| | | F | 101 | 3 | ... | ... | ... | ... | ... |
| Croatia | 1990 | MF | ... | ... | ... | ... | ... | | 11.0 |
| | 1992 | MF | ... | ... | 100 | 100 | 0.99 | | ... |
| | 1993 | MF | 86 | 1 | 98 | 97 | 0.97 | ... | ... |
| | | M | ... | ... | 98 | 97 | 0.97 | ... | ... |
| | | F | ... | ... | 98 | 97 | 0.98 | ... | ... |
| | 1994 | MF | 87 | 1 | ... | ... | ... | ... | 11.4 |
| | | M | 87 | 2 | ... | ... | ... | ... | 11.3 |
| | | F | 87 | 1 | ... | ... | ... | ... | 11.5 |
| | 1995 | MF | 86 | 1 | . | 100 | 1.00 | 100 | ... |
| | | M | 86 | 1 | . | 100 | 0.99 | 100 | ... |
| | | F | 85 | 0 | . | 100 | 0.99 | 100 | ... |
| | 1996 | MF | 87 | 0 | ... | ... | ... | ... | ... |
| | | M | 87 | 1 | ... | ... | ... | ... | ... |
| | | F | 87 | 0 | ... | ... | ... | ... | ... |
| Czech Republic | 1991 | MF | ... | ... | . | 95 | 0.96 | ... | ... |
| | 1992 | MF | 104 | 1 | . | 100 | 0.99 | ... | ... |
| | | M | 104 | 1 | . | 100 | 0.99 | ... | ... |
| | | F | 104 | 1 | . | 100 | 0.99 | ... | ... |
| | 1993 | MF | 105 | 1 | . | 99 | 0.99 | 102 | 12.3 |
| | | M | 105 | 1 | ... | ... | ... | ... | 12.3 |
| | | F | 105 | 1 | ... | ... | ... | ... | 12.3 |
| | 1994 | MF | 103 | 1 | . | 98 | 0.98 | 97 | 12.7 |
| | | M | ... | ... | . | 98 | 0.98 | 95 | 12.6 |
| | | F | ... | ... | . | 98 | 0.98 | 100 | 12.7 |
| | 1995 | MF | 101 | 1 | ... | ... | ... | ... | 12.8 |
| | | M | 102 | 1 | ... | ... | ... | ... | 12.8 |
| | | F | 101 | 1 | ... | ... | ... | ... | 12.9 |
| Denmark | 1970 | MF | 102 | - | 96 | 96 | 0.99 | | ... |
| | | M | 102 | - | 95 | 95 | 0.98 | | ... |
| | | F | 102 | - | 98 | 98 | 0.99 | | ... |
| | 1980 | MF | 98 | - | 99 | 99 | 1.00 | ... | 13.4 |
| | | M | 98 | - | 99 | 99 | 1.00 | ... | 13.4 |
| | | F | 98 | - | 99 | 99 | 1.00 | ... | 13.3 |
| | 1985 | MF | 99 | - | 100 | 100 | 1.00 | ... | 13.6 |
| | | M | 99 | - | 100 | 99 | 1.00 | ... | 13.6 |
| | | F | 99 | - | 100 | 100 | 1.00 | ... | 13.6 |
| | 1990 | MF | 99 | - | ... | ... | ... | ... | 14.2 |
| | | M | 99 | - | ... | ... | ... | ... | 14.0 |
| | | F | 100 | - | ... | ... | ... | ... | 14.3 |
| | 1991 | MF | 99 | - | 100 | 100 | 1.00 | ... | 14.2 |
| | | M | 100 | - | 100 | 100 | 1.00 | ... | 14.0 |
| | | F | 99 | - | 100 | 100 | 1.00 | ... | 14.4 |

II.11    Primary education: selected indicators
Enseignement primaire: indicateurs selectionnés
Enseñanza primaria: indicadores seleccionados

| Country<br><br>Pays<br><br>País | Year<br><br>Année<br><br>Año | Sex<br><br>Sexe<br><br>Sexo | Apparent<br>intake rate<br><br>Taux<br>d'admission<br>apparent<br><br>Tasa<br>aparente de<br>ingreso<br>(%) | Percentage<br>repeaters<br><br>Pourcentage<br>de<br>redoublants<br><br>Porcentaje<br>de<br>repetidores | Percentage of cohort reaching:<br>Pourcentage de la cohorte atteignant:<br>Porcentaje de la cohorte que llega al:<br>Grade 5<br>5e année<br>Quinto año | Final grade<br>Dernière année<br>Ultimo año | Coefficient of<br>efficiency<br><br>Coefficient<br>d'efficacité<br><br>Coeficiente<br>de eficacia | Transition rate<br>(Prim. to Sec. gen.)<br><br>Taux de transition<br>(Prim. au sec. gén.)<br><br>Tasa de transición<br>(Prim. a la Sec.<br>gen.)<br>(%) | School life<br>expectancy<br>(in years)<br><br>Espérance de<br>vie scolaire<br>(années)<br><br>Esperanza de<br>vida escolar<br>(en años) |
|---|---|---|---|---|---|---|---|---|---|
| Denmark (cont) | 1992 | MF | 101 | - | 100 | 100 | 1.00 | ... | 14.2 |
|  |  | M | 101 | - | 100 | 100 | 1.00 | ... | 14.1 |
|  |  | F | 102 | - | 100 | 100 | 1.00 | ... | 14.3 |
|  | 1993 | MF | 103 | - | 99 | 98 | 0.99 | ... | 14.5 |
|  |  | M | 103 | - | 98 | 97 | 0.99 | ... | 14.4 |
|  |  | F | 103 | - | 99 | 99 | 1.00 | ... | 14.6 |
|  | 1994 | MF | 101 | - | 100 | 100 | 1.00 | ... | 14.6 |
|  |  | M | 101 | - | 100 | 100 | 1.00 | ... | 14.5 |
|  |  | F | 102 | - | 99 | 99 | 1.00 | ... | 14.8 |
|  | 1995 | MF | 102 | - | ... | ... | ... | ... | 14.8 |
|  |  | M | 102 | - | ... | ... | ... | ... | 14.6 |
|  |  | F | 102 | - | ... | ... | ... | ... | 15.0 |
| Estonia | 1992 | MF | ... | 3 | ... | ... | ... | 98 | 12.1 |
|  |  | M | ... | 4 | ... | ... | ... | 96 | 12.0 |
|  |  | F | ... | 1 | ... | ... | ... | 100 | 12.3 |
|  | 1993 | MF | ... | 3 | 95 | 95 | 0.97 | 99 | 12.0 |
|  |  | M | ... | 4 | 95 | 95 | 0.96 | 99 | 11.6 |
|  |  | F | ... | 1 | 95 | 95 | 0.98 | 99 | 12.4 |
|  | 1994 | MF | ... | 3 | 96 | 96 | 0.96 | ... | ... |
|  |  | M | ... | 5 | 96 | 96 | 0.94 | ... | ... |
|  |  | F | ... | 2 | 97 | 97 | 0.97 | ... | ... |
|  | 1995 | MF | 97 | 3 | ... | ... | ... | ... | 12.6 |
|  |  | M | 97 | 4 | ... | ... | ... | ... | 12.3 |
|  |  | F | 97 | 1 | ... | ... | ... | ... | 12.9 |
| Federal Republic of Yugoslavia | 1990 | MF | 72 | 2 | ... | ... | ... | ... | ... |
|  | 1993 | MF | 68 | 1 | . | 97 | 0.97 | ... | ... |
|  | 1994 | MF | 68 | 1 | . | 100 | 0.99 | ... | ... |
|  | 1995 | MF | 70 | 1 | . | 98 | 0.98 | ... | ... |
| Finland | 1985 | MF | ... | ... | 98 | 98 | 0.99 | 102 | ... |
|  |  | M | ... | ... | 98 | 98 | 0.99 | 101 | ... |
|  |  | F | ... | ... | 98 | 98 | 0.99 | 103 | ... |
|  | 1990 | MF | 102 | 0 | 100 | 100 | 0.99 | 103 | ... |
|  |  | M | 102 | 0 | 100 | 99 | 0.99 | 101 | ... |
|  |  | F | 102 | 0 | 100 | 100 | 1.00 | 104 | ... |
|  | 1991 | MF | 101 | 0 | 100 | 100 | 1.00 | 101 | ... |
|  |  | M | 101 | 1 | 100 | 100 | 0.99 | 101 | ... |
|  |  | F | 101 | 0 | 100 | 100 | 1.00 | 102 | ... |
|  | 1992 | MF | 99 | 0 | 100 | 100 | 1.00 | 102 | 15.1 |
|  |  | M | 98 | 1 | 100 | 100 | 0.99 | 101 | 14.6 |
|  |  | F | 99 | 0 | 100 | 100 | 1.00 | 103 | 15.6 |
|  | 1993 | MF | 97 | 0 | 100 | 100 | 1.00 | ... | 15.4 |
|  |  | M | 97 | 1 | 100 | 100 | 0.99 | ... | 14.9 |
|  |  | F | 97 | 0 | 100 | 100 | 1.00 | ... | 15.9 |
|  | 1994 | MF | 96 | 0 | 100 | 100 | 1.00 | ... | 15.5 |
|  |  | M | 96 | 1 | 100 | 99 | 0.99 | ... | 15.0 |
|  |  | F | 96 | 0 | 100 | 100 | 1.00 | ... | 16.0 |
|  | 1995 | MF | 102 | 0 | 100 | 100 | ... | ... | 15.6 |
|  |  | M | 102 | 1 | ... | ... | ... | ... | 15.1 |
|  |  | F | 102 | 0 | ... | ... | ... | ... | 16.2 |
|  | 1996 | MF | 101 | 0 | ... | ... | ... | ... | 16.0 |
|  |  | M | ... | ... | ... | ... | ... | ... | 15.4 |
|  |  | F | ... | ... | ... | ... | ... | ... | 16.5 |
| France | 1970 | MF | 106 | 13 | ... | ... | ... | ... | 11.9 |
|  |  | M | 106 | 14 | ... | ... | ... | ... | ... |
|  |  | F | 106 | 12 | ... | ... | ... | ... | ... |
|  | 1975 | MF | 104 | 9 | 91 | 91 | 0.86 | 91 | 12.4 |
|  | 1980 | MF | ... | ... | ... | ... | ... | 87 | 12.6 |
|  | 1985 | MF | 108 | 8 | 95 | 95 | 0.90 | 89 | 13.1 |
|  |  | M | ... | ... | ... | ... | ... | ... | 12.9 |
|  |  | F | ... | ... | ... | ... | ... | ... | 13.4 |

Primary education: selected indicators II.11
Enseignement primaire: indicateurs selectionnés
Enseñanza primaria: indicadores seleccionados

| Country / Pays / País | Year / Année / Año | Sex / Sexe / Sexo | Apparent intake rate / Taux d'admission apparent / Tasa aparente de ingreso (%) | Percentage repeaters / Pourcentage de redoublants / Porcentaje de repetidores | Percentage of cohort reaching: / Pourcentage de la cohorte atteignant: / Porcentaje de la cohorte que llega al: Grade 5 / 5e année / Quinto año | Final grade / Dernière année / Ultimo año | Coefficient of efficiency / Coefficient d'efficacité / Coeficiente de eficacia | Transition rate (Prim. to Sec. gen.) / Taux de transition (Prim. au sec. gén.) / Tasa de transición (Prim. a la Sec. gen.) (%) | School life expectancy (in years) / Espérance de vie scolaire (années) / Esperanza de vida escolar (en años) |
|---|---|---|---|---|---|---|---|---|---|
| France (cont) | 1990 | MF | 101 | 5 | 96 | 96 | 0.94 | 95 | ... |
| | 1991 | MF | 101 | 4 | ... | ... | ... | 95 | 14.5 |
| | | M | ... | ... | ... | ... | ... | ... | 14.2 |
| | | F | ... | ... | ... | ... | ... | ... | 14.8 |
| | 1992 | MF | ... | ... | ... | ... | ... | 95 | 14.6 |
| | | M | ... | ... | ... | ... | ... | ... | 14.3 |
| | | F | ... | ... | ... | ... | ... | ... | 15.0 |
| | 1993 | MF | ... | ... | ... | ... | ... | 92 | 15.4 |
| | | M | ... | ... | ... | ... | ... | ... | 15.2 |
| | | F | ... | ... | ... | ... | ... | ... | 15.6 |
| | 1994 | MF | ... | ... | ... | ... | ... | 93 | 15.4 |
| | | M | ... | ... | ... | ... | ... | ... | 15.2 |
| | | F | ... | ... | ... | ... | ... | ... | 15.6 |
| | 1995 | MF | ... | ... | ... | ... | ... | ... | 15.5 |
| | | M | ... | ... | ... | ... | ... | ... | 15.3 |
| | | F | ... | ... | ... | ... | ... | ... | 15.7 |
| | 1996 | MF | ... | ... | ... | ... | ... | ... | 15.5 |
| | | M | ... | ... | ... | ... | ... | ... | 15.2 |
| | | F | ... | ... | ... | ... | ... | ... | 15.7 |
| Germany | 1992 | MF | 99 | 2 | . | 100 | 0.98 | 100 | 14.9 |
| | | M | 99 | 2 | . | 99 | 0.98 | 99 | 15.3 |
| | | F | 99 | 2 | . | 100 | 0.98 | 100 | 14.5 |
| | 1993 | MF | 101 | 2 | . | 99 | 0.98 | 100 | 15.1 |
| | | M | 101 | 2 | . | 99 | 0.97 | 100 | 15.4 |
| | | F | 100 | 2 | . | 100 | 0.98 | 100 | 14.7 |
| | 1994 | MF | 103 | 2 | . | 100 | 0.98 | 100 | 15.2 |
| | | M | 103 | 2 | . | 99 | 0.97 | 100 | 15.5 |
| | | F | 102 | 2 | . | 100 | 0.98 | 100 | 14.8 |
| | 1995 | MF | 103 | 2 | . | 99 | ... | 99 | 15.3 |
| | | M | 103 | 2 | . | 99 | ... | 99 | 15.6 |
| | | F | 102 | 1 | . | 100 | ... | 100 | 15.1 |
| | 1996 | MF | 104 | ... | ... | ... | ... | ... | 15.8 |
| | | M | 104 | ... | ... | ... | ... | ... | 15.9 |
| | | F | 104 | ... | ... | ... | ... | ... | 15.5 |
| Greece | 1970 | MF | 106 | 5 | 95 | 93 | 0.92 | 63 | 10.8 |
| | | M | 107 | 6 | 94 | 93 | 0.90 | 63 | 11.5 |
| | | F | 105 | 4 | 96 | 94 | 0.93 | 64 | 10.1 |
| | 1975 | MF | 99 | 3 | 98 | 98 | 0.97 | 80 | 11.8 |
| | | M | 99 | 3 | 98 | 97 | 0.96 | 80 | 12.6 |
| | | F | 99 | 2 | 99 | 98 | 0.97 | 81 | 11.0 |
| | 1980 | MF | 111 | 1 | 98 | 98 | 0.99 | 101 | ... |
| | | M | 111 | 1 | 99 | 99 | 0.99 | 103 | ... |
| | | F | 111 | 1 | 98 | 97 | 0.99 | 100 | ... |
| | 1985 | MF | 104 | 0 | ... | ... | ... | 102 | 12.8 |
| | | M | 103 | 0 | ... | ... | ... | 103 | 12.9 |
| | | F | 104 | 0 | ... | ... | ... | 101 | 12.7 |
| | 1990 | MF | ... | ... | 99 | 99 | 1.00 | 104 | 13.3 |
| | | M | ... | ... | 99 | 99 | 1.00 | 106 | 13.4 |
| | | F | ... | ... | 100 | 100 | 1.00 | 103 | 13.2 |
| | 1991 | MF | ... | 0 | ... | ... | ... | ... | 13.3 |
| | | M | ... | 0 | ... | ... | ... | ... | 13.3 |
| | | F | ... | 0 | ... | ... | ... | ... | 13.2 |
| | 1992 | MF | ... | ... | ... | ... | ... | ... | 13.2 |
| | | M | ... | ... | ... | ... | ... | ... | 13.1 |
| | | F | ... | ... | ... | ... | ... | ... | 13.2 |
| | 1993 | MF | ... | ... | ... | ... | ... | ... | 13.3 |
| | | M | ... | ... | ... | ... | ... | ... | 13.5 |
| | | F | ... | ... | ... | ... | ... | ... | 13.1 |
| | 1994 | MF | ... | ... | ... | ... | ... | ... | 13.3 |
| | 1995 | MF | ... | ... | ... | ... | ... | ... | 13.5 |
| | | M | ... | ... | ... | ... | ... | ... | 13.5 |
| | | F | ... | ... | ... | ... | ... | ... | 13.5 |

II.11  Primary education: selected indicators
Enseignement primaire: indicateurs selectionnés
Enseñanza primaria: indicadores seleccionados

| Country / Pays / País | Year / Année / Año | Sex / Sexe / Sexo | Apparent intake rate / Taux d'admission apparent / Tasa aparente de ingreso (%) | Percentage repeaters / Pourcentage de redoublants / Porcentaje de repetidores | Percentage of cohort reaching: Grade 5 / 5e année / Quinto año | Final grade / Dernière année / Ultimo año | Coefficient of efficiency / Coefficient d'efficacité / Coeficiente de eficacia | Transition rate (Prim. to Sec. gen.) / Taux de transition / Tasa de transición (%) | School life expectancy (in years) / Espérance de vie scolaire (années) / Esperanza de vida escolar (en años) |
|---|---|---|---|---|---|---|---|---|---|
| Greece (cont) | 1996 | MF | ... | ... | ... | ... | ... | ... | 13.7 |
|  |  | M | ... | ... | ... | ... | ... | ... | 13.7 |
|  |  | F | ... | ... | ... | ... | ... | ... | 13.7 |
| Hungary | 1970 | MF | 104 | 4 | 93 | 85 | 0.88 | ... | 9.5 |
|  |  | M | ... | ... | ... | ... | ... | ... | 9.3 |
|  |  | F | ... | ... | ... | ... | ... | ... | 9.7 |
|  | 1975 | MF | 101 | 3 | 95 | 91 | 0.93 | ... | ... |
|  |  | M | 100 | 3 | 95 | 89 | 0.92 | ... | ... |
|  |  | F | 101 | 2 | 96 | 93 | 0.95 | ... | ... |
|  | 1980 | MF | 102 | 2 | 97 | 93 | 0.94 | ... | ... |
|  |  | M | 101 | 3 | 96 | 93 | 0.94 | ... | ... |
|  |  | F | 102 | 2 | 97 | 94 | 0.95 | ... | ... |
|  | 1985 | MF | 92 | 3 | 96 | 92 | 0.93 | ... | 11.4 |
|  |  | M | 92 | 4 | 96 | 91 | 0.92 | ... | 11.3 |
|  |  | F | 93 | 2 | 97 | 94 | 0.95 | ... | 11.5 |
|  | 1990 | MF | 99 | 3 | 98 | 93 | 0.93 | ... | 11.4 |
|  |  | M | ... | ... | ... | ... | ... | ... | 11.3 |
|  |  | F | ... | ... | ... | ... | ... | ... | 11.4 |
|  | 1991 | MF | 102 | 3 | 98 | 93 | 0.94 | ... | 11.4 |
|  |  | M | ... | ... | ... | ... | ... | ... | 11.4 |
|  |  | F | ... | ... | ... | ... | ... | ... | 11.5 |
|  | 1992 | MF | 106 | 3 | ... | ... | ... | ... | ... |
|  | 1993 | MF | ... | ... | ... | ... | ... | ... | 12.2 |
|  | 1994 | MF | ... | ... | ... | ... | ... | ... | 12.5 |
|  | 1995 | MF | ... | ... | ... | ... | ... | ... | 12.9 |
|  |  | M | ... | ... | ... | ... | ... | ... | 12.7 |
|  |  | F | ... | ... | ... | ... | ... | ... | 13.1 |
| Iceland | 1993 | MF | 97 | - | 99 | 99 | 0.99 | 99 | 14.8 |
|  |  | M | 100 | - | 99 | 99 | 1.00 | 99 | 14.5 |
|  |  | F | 93 | - | 99 | 98 | 0.99 | 99 | 15.2 |
|  | 1994 | MF | 107 | - | 99 | 99 | 0.99 | 100 | ... |
|  |  | M | 109 | - | 99 | 99 | 0.99 | 100 | ... |
|  |  | F | 104 | - | 99 | 99 | 0.99 | 100 | ... |
|  | 1995 | MF | 103 | - | ... | ... | ... | ... | 15.2 |
|  |  | M | 102 | - | ... | ... | ... | ... | 14.7 |
|  |  | F | 104 | - | ... | ... | ... | ... | 15.5 |
| Ireland | 1970 | MF | ... | ... | ... | ... | ... | ... | 10.8 |
|  |  | M | ... | ... | ... | ... | ... | ... | 10.9 |
|  |  | F | ... | ... | ... | ... | ... | ... | 10.8 |
|  | 1975 | MF | ... | ... | ... | ... | ... | ... | 11.5 |
|  |  | M | ... | ... | ... | ... | ... | ... | 11.5 |
|  |  | F | ... | ... | ... | ... | ... | ... | 11.4 |
|  | 1980 | MF | ... | ... | ... | ... | ... | ... | 11.4 |
|  |  | M | ... | ... | ... | ... | ... | ... | 11.3 |
|  |  | F | ... | ... | ... | ... | ... | ... | 11.6 |
|  | 1985 | MF | ... | ... | ... | ... | ... | ... | 12.0 |
|  |  | M | ... | ... | ... | ... | ... | ... | 11.9 |
|  |  | F | ... | ... | ... | ... | ... | ... | 12.2 |
|  | 1990 | MF | ... | ... | 100 | 100 | 0.98 | ... | 12.6 |
|  |  | M | ... | ... | 100 | 100 | 0.98 | ... | 12.4 |
|  |  | F | ... | ... | 100 | 100 | 0.98 | ... | 12.8 |
|  | 1991 | MF | 96 | 2 | 100 | 100 | 0.98 | ... | 12.8 |
|  |  | M | 97 | 2 | 100 | 100 | 0.98 | ... | 12.7 |
|  |  | F | 96 | 2 | 100 | 100 | 0.98 | ... | 13.0 |
|  | 1992 | MF | 100 | 2 | 100 | 100 | 0.98 | ... | 13.4 |
|  |  | M | 100 | 2 | 100 | 100 | 0.98 | ... | 13.3 |
|  |  | F | 100 | 2 | 100 | 100 | 0.98 | ... | 13.4 |
|  | 1993 | MF | 103 | 2 | 100 | 100 | 0.98 | ... | 13.7 |
|  |  | M | 102 | 2 | 99 | 99 | 0.98 | ... | 13.6 |
|  |  | F | 103 | 2 | 100 | 100 | 0.98 | ... | 13.8 |
|  | 1994 | MF | 103 | 2 | ... | ... | ... | 97 | 13.7 |
|  |  | M | 104 | 2 | ... | ... | ... | 97 | 13.5 |
|  |  | F | 103 | 2 | ... | ... | ... | 97 | 13.8 |

Primary education: selected indicators II.11
Enseignement primaire: indicateurs selectionnés
Enseñanza primaria: indicadores seleccionados

| Country<br><br>Pays<br><br>País | Year<br><br>Année<br><br>Año | Sex<br><br>Sexe<br><br>Sexo | Apparent<br>intake rate<br><br>Taux<br>d'admission<br>apparent<br><br>Tasa<br>aparente de<br>ingreso<br>(%) | Percentage<br>repeaters<br><br>Pourcentage<br>de<br>redoublants<br><br>Porcentaje<br>de<br>repetidores | Percentage of cohort reaching:<br>Pourcentage de la cohorte atteignant:<br>Porcentaje de la cohorte que llega al: | | Coefficient of<br>efficiency<br><br>Coefficient<br>d'efficacité<br><br>Coeficiente<br>de eficacia | Transition rate<br>(Prim. to Sec. gen.)<br><br>Taux de transition<br>(Prim. au sec. gén.)<br><br>Tasa de transición<br>(Prim. a la Sec.<br>gen.)<br>(%) | School life<br>expectancy<br>(in years)<br><br>Espérance de<br>vie scolaire<br>(années)<br><br>Esperanza de<br>vida escolar<br>(en años) |
|---|---|---|---|---|---|---|---|---|---|
| | | | | | Grade 5<br>5e année<br>Quinto año | Final grade<br>Dernière année<br>Ultimo año | | | |
| Ireland (cont) | 1995 | MF | ... | ... | ... | ... | ... | 98 | 13.7 |
| | | M | ... | ... | ... | ... | ... | 98 | 13.5 |
| | | F | ... | ... | ... | ... | ... | 98 | 13.9 |
| | 1996 | MF | ... | ... | ... | ... | ... | ... | 13.9 |
| | | M | ... | ... | ... | ... | ... | ... | 13.6 |
| | | F | ... | ... | ... | ... | ... | ... | 14.2 |
| Italy | 1970 | MF | 104 | 7 | 96 | 96 | 0.92 | 91 | ... |
| | | M | 104 | 8 | 96 | 96 | 0.91 | 92 | ... |
| | | F | 104 | 6 | 96 | 96 | 0.92 | 89 | ... |
| | 1975 | MF | 96 | 3 | 99 | 99 | 0.97 | 97 | 12.1 |
| | | M | 96 | 4 | 99 | 99 | 0.96 | 98 | 12.8 |
| | | F | 97 | 2 | 98 | 98 | 0.97 | 95 | 11.5 |
| | 1980 | MF | 95 | 1 | 99 | 99 | 0.98 | 98 | ... |
| | | M | 96 | 1 | 99 | 99 | 0.98 | 98 | ... |
| | | F | 95 | 1 | 99 | 99 | 0.98 | 98 | ... |
| | 1985 | MF | 89 | 1 | 100 | 100 | 0.99 | 100 | ... |
| | | M | 89 | 1 | 100 | 100 | 0.99 | 100 | ... |
| | | F | 89 | 1 | 99 | 99 | 0.99 | 99 | ... |
| | 1990 | MF | 99 | 1 | 100 | 100 | 0.99 | 00 | ... |
| | | M | 99 | 1 | 100 | 100 | 0.99 | 99 | ... |
| | | F | 98 | 1 | 100 | 100 | 0.99 | 99 | ... |
| | 1991 | MF | 100 | 1 | ... | ... | ... | 99 | ... |
| | | M | 100 | 1 | ... | ... | ... | 99 | ... |
| | | F | 99 | 1 | ... | ... | ... | 100 | ... |
| | 1993 | MF | 97 | 1 | ... | ... | ... | 101 | ... |
| | | M | 94 | 1 | ... | ... | ... | 103 | ... |
| | | F | 99 | 0 | ... | ... | ... | 98 | ... |
| | 1994 | MF | 99 | 1 | 100 | 100 | 1.00 | 101 | ... |
| | | M | 100 | 1 | 100 | 100 | 0.99 | 101 | ... |
| | | F | 98 | 0 | 100 | 100 | 1.00 | 102 | ... |
| | 1995 | MF | 98 | 0 | 99 | 99 | ... | 100 | ... |
| | | M | 99 | 1 | 98 | 98 | ... | 100 | ... |
| | | F | 98 | 0 | 99 | 99 | ... | 99 | ... |
| | 1996 | MF | 100 | 0 | ... | ... | ... | ... | ... |
| | | M | 100 | 1 | ... | ... | ... | ... | ... |
| | | F | 99 | 0 | ... | ... | ... | ... | ... |
| Latvia | 1994 | MF | ... | 3 | . | 96 | 0.95 | 98 | 11.3 |
| | 1995 | MF | ... | 3 | . | 97 | 0.96 | 97 | 11.6 |
| | | M | ... | ... | . | ... | ... | ... | 11.3 |
| | | F | ... | ... | ... | ... | ... | ... | 11.9 |
| | 1996 | MF | 96 | 2 | ... | ... | ... | ... | 12.1 |
| | | M | ... | ... | ... | ... | ... | ... | 11.8 |
| | | F | ... | ... | ... | ... | ... | ... | 12.5 |
| Lithuania | 1992 | MF | ... | ... | . | 93 | 0.95 | 99 | ... |
| | 1993 | MF | ... | 2 | . | 98 | 0.98 | 98 | ... |
| | | M | ... | ... | . | ... | 0.96 | 97 | ... |
| | | F | ... | ... | . | ... | 0.99 | 99 | ... |
| | 1994 | MF | 96 | 2 | . | 98 | 0.98 | 99 | ... |
| | | M | 97 | 3 | . | 98 | 0.97 | 99 | ... |
| | | F | 95 | 1 | . | 99 | 0.99 | 100 | ... |
| | 1995 | MF | ... | 1 | . | 99 | 0.98 | 99 | ... |
| | | M | ... | 2 | . | 99 | 0.98 | 99 | ... |
| | | F | ... | 1 | . | 98 | 0.99 | 99 | ... |
| | 1996 | MF | 100 | 1 | ... | ... | ... | ... | ... |
| | | M | 101 | 2 | ... | ... | ... | ... | ... |
| | | F | 100 | 1 | ... | ... | ... | ... | ... |
| Malta | 1970 | MF | 92 | 2 | 76 | 76 | 0.93 | 98 | 10.8 |
| | | M | 94 | 2 | 74 | 74 | 0.92 | 102 | 11.0 |
| | | F | 89 | 1 | 78 | 78 | 0.95 | 95 | 10.5 |
| | 1975 | MF | 136 | 1 | 97 | 97 | 0.98 | 101 | 12.0 |
| | | M | 142 | 1 | 92 | 92 | 0.96 | 101 | 12.5 |
| | | F | 130 | 1 | 100 | 100 | 0.99 | 100 | 11.5 |

II.11 Primary education: selected indicators
Enseignement primaire: indicateurs selectionnés
Enseñanza primaria: indicadores seleccionados

| Country Pays País | Year Année Año | Sex Sexe Sexo | Apparent intake rate Taux d'admission apparent Tasa aparente de ingreso (%) | Percentage repeaters Pourcentage de redoublants Porcentaje de repetidores | Percentage of cohort reaching: Pourcentage de la cohorte atteignant: Porcentaje de la cohorte que llega al: Grade 5 5e année Quinto año | Final grade Dernière année Ultimo año | Coefficient of efficiency Coefficient d'efficacité Coeficiente de eficacia | Transition rate (Prim. to Sec. gen.) Taux de transition (Prim. au sec. gén.) Tasa de transición (Prim. a la Sec. gen.) (%) | School life expectancy (in years) Espérance de vie scolaire (années) Esperanza de vida escolar (en años) |
|---|---|---|---|---|---|---|---|---|---|
| Malta (cont) | 1980 | MF | 107 | 2 | 98 | 97 | 0.97 | 99 | 11.9 |
| | | M | 110 | 2 | 97 | 96 | 0.97 | 99 | 12.2 |
| | | F | 105 | 2 | 97 | 97 | 0.97 | 99 | 11.4 |
| | 1985 | MF | 99 | 3 | 98 | 98 | 0.97 | ... | 12.1 |
| | | M | 97 | 3 | 98 | 98 | 0.96 | ... | 12.4 |
| | | F | 100 | 2 | 98 | 98 | 0.97 | ... | 11.7 |
| | 1990 | MF | 103 | 1 | 100 | 100 | 0.99 | 98 | 12.9 |
| | | M | 105 | 1 | 100 | 100 | 0.98 | 98 | 13.3 |
| | | F | 100 | 1 | 100 | 100 | 0.99 | 98 | 12.5 |
| | 1991 | MF | 103 | 1 | 100 | 100 | 0.98 | 98 | 12.9 |
| | | M | 107 | 2 | 98 | 98 | 0.98 | 98 | 13.2 |
| | | F | 98 | 1 | 100 | 100 | 0.99 | 97 | 12.6 |
| | 1992 | MF | 104 | 2 | 98 | 98 | 0.97 | 95 | 13.1 |
| | | M | 104 | 2 | 97 | 97 | 0.97 | 99 | 13.3 |
| | | F | 104 | 1 | 99 | 98 | 0.97 | 90 | 12.9 |
| | 1993 | MF | 108 | 2 | 97 | 97 | 0.96 | 95 | 13.2 |
| | | M | 106 | 2 | 99 | 99 | 0.97 | 93 | 13.4 |
| | | F | 109 | 2 | 92 | 91 | 0.94 | 96 | 12.9 |
| | 1994 | MF | 108 | 2 | 100 | 100 | 0.98 | 94 | 13.4 |
| | | M | 107 | 2 | 100 | 100 | 0.98 | 93 | 13.6 |
| | | F | 110 | 1 | 100 | 100 | 0.99 | 96 | 13.0 |
| | 1995 | MF | 106 | 2 | 100 | 100 | 0.98 | ... | 13.4 |
| | | M | 106 | 2 | 99 | 99 | 0.97 | ... | 13.6 |
| | | F | 107 | 1 | 99 | 99 | 0.98 | ... | 13.1 |
| | 1996 | MF | 108 | 2 | ... | ... | ... | ... | 13.4 |
| | | M | 107 | 2 | ... | ... | ... | ... | 13.5 |
| | | F | 110 | 1 | ... | ... | ... | ... | 13.3 |
| Moldova | 1993 | MF | ... | ... | . | 97 | 0.98 | 97 | ... |
| | | M | ... | ... | . | 95 | 0.97 | 96 | ... |
| | | F | ... | ... | . | 99 | 0.98 | 97 | ... |
| | 1994 | MF | 97 | 1 | . | 93 | 0.96 | 98 | ... |
| | | M | 99 | 1 | . | 95 | 0.97 | 99 | ... |
| | | F | 96 | 1 | . | 91 | 0.95 | 97 | ... |
| | 1995 | MF | 99 | 1 | . | 95 | 0.97 | 98 | ... |
| | | M | 99 | 1 | . | 93 | 0.96 | 98 | ... |
| | | F | 98 | 1 | . | 97 | 0.98 | 99 | ... |
| | 1996 | MF | 98 | 1 | ... | ... | ... | ... | ... |
| | | M | 99 | 1 | ... | ... | ... | ... | ... |
| | | F | 97 | 1 | ... | ... | ... | ... | ... |
| Netherlands | 1970 | MF | 100 | 3 | 97 | 95 | 0.95 | ... | 11.6 |
| | | M | 100 | 4 | 95 | 93 | 0.93 | ... | 12.3 |
| | | F | 100 | 3 | 98 | 97 | 0.96 | ... | 10.8 |
| | 1975 | MF | 103 | 2 | 97 | 96 | 0.96 | ... | 12.6 |
| | | M | 103 | 3 | 96 | 94 | 0.94 | ... | 13.2 |
| | | F | 104 | 2 | 99 | 98 | 0.97 | ... | 11.9 |
| | 1980 | MF | 93 | 3 | 96 | 95 | 0.95 | ... | 13.0 |
| | | M | 92 | 3 | 94 | 93 | 0.94 | ... | 13.3 |
| | | F | 93 | 2 | 98 | 97 | 0.97 | ... | 12.6 |
| | 1985 | MF | ... | ... | ... | ... | ... | ... | 14.3 |
| | | M | ... | ... | ... | ... | ... | ... | 14.7 |
| | | F | ... | ... | ... | ... | ... | ... | 14.0 |
| | 1990 | MF | ... | ... | ... | ... | ... | ... | 14.9 |
| | | M | ... | ... | ... | ... | ... | ... | 15.2 |
| | | F | ... | ... | ... | ... | ... | ... | 14.6 |
| | 1991 | MF | ... | ... | ... | ... | ... | ... | 14.8 |
| | | M | ... | ... | ... | ... | ... | ... | 15.1 |
| | | F | ... | ... | ... | ... | ... | ... | 14.6 |
| | 1992 | MF | ... | ... | ... | ... | ... | ... | 15.1 |
| | | M | ... | ... | ... | ... | ... | ... | 15.2 |
| | | F | ... | ... | ... | ... | ... | ... | 14.9 |
| | 1994 | MF | ... | ... | ... | ... | ... | ... | 15.8 |
| | | M | ... | ... | ... | ... | ... | ... | 16.1 |
| | | F | ... | ... | ... | ... | ... | ... | 15.5 |

Primary education: selected Indicators II.11
Enseignement primaire: indicateurs selectionnés
Enseñanza primaria: Indicadores seleccionados

| Country / Pays / País | Year / Année / Año | Sex / Sexe / Sexo | Apparent intake rate / Taux d'admission apparent / Tasa aparente de ingreso (%) | Percentage repeaters / Pourcentage de redoublants / Porcentaje de repetidores | Percentage of cohort reaching: / Pourcentage de la cohorte atteignant: / Porcentaje de la cohorte que llega al: Grade 5 / 5e année / Quinto año | Final grade / Dernière année / Ultimo año | Coefficient of efficiency / Coefficient d'efficacité / Coeficiente de eficacia | Transition rate (Prim. to Sec. gen.) / Taux de transition (Prim. au sec. gén.) / Tasa de transición (Prim. a la Sec. gen.) (%) | School life expectancy (in years) / Espérance de vie scolaire (années) / Esperanza de vida escolar (en años) |
|---|---|---|---|---|---|---|---|---|---|
| Netherlands (cont) | 1995 | MF | ... | ... | ... | ... | ... | ... | 16.3 |
| | 1995 | MF | ... | ... | ... | ... | ... | ... | 15.9 |
| | | M | ... | ... | ... | ... | ... | ... | 16.0 |
| | | F | ... | ... | ... | ... | ... | ... | 15.6 |
| Norway | 1975 | MF | 101 | - | 100 | 100 | 1.00 | ... | 12.4 |
| | | M | 101 | - | 100 | 100 | 1.00 | ... | 12.7 |
| | | F | 101 | - | 100 | 100 | 1.00 | ... | 12.2 |
| | 1980 | MF | 98 | - | 100 | 100 | 1.00 | ... | 12.9 |
| | | M | 99 | - | 100 | 100 | 1.00 | ... | 12.7 |
| | | F | 97 | - | 100 | 100 | 1.00 | ... | 13.0 |
| | 1985 | MF | 100 | - | 100 | 100 | 1.00 | ... | 13.2 |
| | | M | 100 | - | 99 | 99 | 1.00 | ... | 12.9 |
| | | F | 99 | - | 100 | 100 | 1.00 | ... | 13.4 |
| | 1990 | MF | 98 | - | 100 | 100 | 1.00 | ... | 14.2 |
| | | M | 99 | - | 100 | 100 | 1.00 | ... | 14.0 |
| | | F | 98 | - | 100 | 100 | 1.00 | ... | 14.5 |
| | 1991 | MF | 98 | - | 100 | 99 | 0.99 | ... | 14.5 |
| | | M | 97 | - | 99 | 99 | 0.99 | ... | 14.2 |
| | | F | 98 | - | 100 | 99 | 0.99 | ... | 14.8 |
| | 1992 | MF | 97 | - | 100 | 100 | 1.00 | ... | 15.1 |
| | | M | 97 | - | 100 | 100 | 1.00 | ... | 14.9 |
| | | F | 97 | - | 100 | 100 | 1.00 | ... | 15.2 |
| | 1993 | MF | 98 | - | 100 | 100 | 1.00 | ... | 15.0 |
| | | M | 98 | - | 100 | 100 | 1.00 | ... | 14.7 |
| | | F | 97 | - | 100 | 100 | 1.00 | ... | 15.2 |
| | 1994 | MF | 98 | - | 100 | 100 | 1.00 | ... | 14.9 |
| | | M | 98 | - | 100 | 100 | 1.00 | ... | 14.7 |
| | | F | 99 | - | 100 | 100 | 1.00 | ... | 15.2 |
| | 1995 | MF | 102 | - | ... | ... | ... | ... | 15.2 |
| | | M | 102 | - | ... | ... | ... | ... | 14.9 |
| | | F | 102 | - | ... | ... | ... | ... | 15.5 |
| | 1996 | MF | ... | ... | ... | ... | ... | ... | 15.6 |
| | | M | ... | ... | ... | ... | ... | ... | 15.2 |
| | | F | ... | ... | ... | ... | ... | ... | 16.0 |
| Poland | 1970 | MF | 98 | 5 | 97 | 89 | 0.88 | ... | ... |
| | 1975 | MF | 99 | 3 | 98 | 92 | 0.93 | ... | ... |
| | 1980 | MF | 100 | 2 | 98 | 94 | 0.93 | ... | 12.0 |
| | | M | ... | ... | ... | ... | ... | ... | 11.8 |
| | | F | ... | ... | ... | ... | ... | ... | 12.1 |
| | 1985 | MF | 99 | 3 | 98 | 94 | 0.93 | ... | 12.0 |
| | | M | ... | ... | ... | ... | ... | ... | 11.9 |
| | | F | ... | ... | ... | ... | ... | ... | 12.2 |
| | 1990 | MF | 100 | 2 | 98 | 96 | 0.96 | ... | 12.2 |
| | | M | ... | ... | ... | ... | ... | ... | 12.0 |
| | | F | ... | ... | ... | ... | ... | ... | 12.4 |
| | 1991 | MF | 99 | 2 | 100 | 100 | 0.99 | ... | 12.2 |
| | | M | ... | ... | ... | ... | ... | ... | 12.1 |
| | | F | ... | ... | ... | ... | ... | ... | 12.4 |
| | 1992 | MF | 99 | 1 | 99 | 98 | 0.97 | ... | 12.9 |
| | | M | ... | ... | ... | ... | ... | ... | 12.7 |
| | | F | ... | ... | ... | ... | ... | ... | 13.0 |
| | 1993 | MF | 96 | 1 | ... | ... | ... | ... | 13.1 |
| | 1994 | MF | 94 | 1 | 97 | 95 | 0.96 | ... | 12.9 |
| | | M | ... | ... | ... | ... | ... | ... | 12.8 |
| | | F | ... | ... | ... | ... | ... | ... | 13.1 |
| | 1995 | MF | 95 | 1 | ... | ... | ... | ... | ... |
| Portugal | 1970 | MF | ... | ... | ... | ... | ... | ... | 8.9 |
| | | M | ... | ... | ... | ... | ... | ... | 9.2 |
| | | F | ... | ... | ... | ... | ... | ... | 8.6 |
| | 1975 | MF | ... | 11 | ... | ... | ... | 71 | 10.4 |
| | | M | ... | 13 | ... | ... | ... | 70 | 10.5 |
| | | F | ... | 10 | ... | ... | ... | 73 | 10.2 |

II.11 Primary education: selected indicators
Enseignement primaire: indicateurs selectionnés
Enseñanza primaria: indicadores seleccionados

| Country / Pays / País | Year / Année / Año | Sex / Sexe / Sexo | Apparent intake rate / Taux d'admission apparent / Tasa aparente de ingreso (%) | Percentage repeaters / Pourcentage de redoublants / Porcentaje de repetidores | Percentage of cohort reaching: / Pourcentage de la cohorte atteignant: / Porcentaje de la cohorte que llega al: | | Coefficient of efficiency / Coefficient d'efficacité / Coeficiente de eficacia | Transition rate (Prim. to Sec. gen.) / Taux de transition (Prim. au sec. gén.) / Tasa de transición (Prim. a la Sec. gen.) (%) | School life expectancy (in years) / Espérance de vie scolaire (années) / Esperanza de vida escolar (en años) |
|---|---|---|---|---|---|---|---|---|---|
| | | | | | Grade 5 / 5e année / Quinto año | Final grade / Dernière année / Ultimo año | | | |
| Portugal (cont) | 1990 | MF | ... | 14 | ... | ... | ... | ... | ... |
| | | M | ... | 16 | ... | ... | ... | ... | ... |
| | | F | ... | 12 | ... | ... | ... | ... | ... |
| | 1992 | MF | ... | ... | ... | ... | ... | ... | 13.6 |
| | | M | ... | ... | ... | ... | ... | ... | 13.2 |
| | | F | ... | ... | ... | ... | ... | ... | 14.0 |
| | 1993 | MF | ... | ... | ... | ... | ... | ... | 14.1 |
| | | M | ... | ... | ... | ... | ... | ... | 13.8 |
| | | F | ... | ... | ... | ... | ... | ... | 14.5 |
| | 1994 | MF | ... | ... | ... | ... | ... | ... | 14.5 |
| | | M | ... | ... | ... | ... | ... | ... | 14.2 |
| | | F | ... | ... | ... | ... | ... | ... | 14.9 |
| Romania | 1991 | MF | ... | ... | . | 93 | 0.93 | 95 | ... |
| | | M | ... | ... | . | 93 | 0.92 | 94 | ... |
| | | F | ... | ... | . | 93 | 0.94 | 96 | ... |
| | 1992 | MF | 94 | 4 | ... | ... | ... | ... | 10.8 |
| | | M | 94 | 5 | ... | ... | ... | ... | 10.9 |
| | | F | 94 | 3 | ... | ... | ... | ... | 10.7 |
| | 1993 | MF | ... | ... | . | 96 | 0.95 | ... | 10.9 |
| | | M | ... | ... | ... | ... | ... | ... | 10.9 |
| | | F | ... | ... | ... | ... | ... | ... | 10.8 |
| | 1994 | MF | 100 | 3 | . | 99 | 0.97 | 100 | 11.1 |
| | | M | ... | ... | ... | ... | ... | 104 | 11.1 |
| | | F | ... | ... | ... | ... | ... | 96 | 11.1 |
| | 1995 | MF | 100 | 3 | . | 95 | 0.95 | 98 | 11.3 |
| | 1996 | MF | 100 | 3 | ... | ... | ... | ... | 11.6 |
| | | M | ... | ... | ... | ... | ... | ... | 11.5 |
| | | F | ... | ... | ... | ... | ... | ... | 11.6 |
| Russian Federation | 1993 | MF | 98 | 2 | . | 97 | 0.97 | ... | ... |
| | | M | 99 | 2 | . | 96 | 0.97 | ... | ... |
| | | F | 98 | 2 | . | 97 | 0.97 | ... | ... |
| | 1994 | MF | 101 | 2 | ... | ... | ... | ... | ... |
| | | M | 103 | 2 | ... | ... | ... | ... | ... |
| | | F | 99 | 2 | ... | ... | ... | ... | ... |
| San Marino | 1985 | MF | ... | 0 | 97 | 97 | 0.98 | ... | ... |
| | 1990 | MF | ... | 0 | 100 | 100 | 1.00 | ... | ... |
| | | M | ... | ... | 92 | 92 | 0.95 | ... | ... |
| | | F | ... | ... | 100 | 100 | 1.00 | ... | ... |
| | 1991 | MF | ... | 0 | 100 | 100 | 1.00 | ... | ... |
| | | M | ... | 0 | 100 | 100 | 0.99 | ... | ... |
| | | F | ... | - | 87 | 87 | 0.93 | ... | ... |
| | 1992 | MF | ... | 0 | 100 | 100 | 1.00 | 100 | ... |
| | | M | ... | 1 | 98 | 98 | 0.97 | ... | ... |
| | | F | ... | - | 97 | 97 | 0.99 | ... | ... |
| | 1995 | MF | ... | 0 | 100 | 100 | 1.00 | ... | ... |
| | | M | ... | 0 | 100 | 100 | 1.00 | ... | ... |
| | | F | ... | - | 100 | 100 | 1.00 | ... | ... |
| Slovakia | 1992 | MF | 101 | 2 | . | 97 | 0.97 | 98 | ... |
| | | M | 102 | 2 | . | 97 | 0.97 | 98 | ... |
| | | F | 101 | 2 | . | 97 | 0.97 | 99 | ... |
| | 1993 | MF | 101 | 2 | . | 97 | 0.97 | ... | ... |
| | | M | 101 | 2 | . | 97 | 0.96 | ... | ... |
| | | F | 101 | 2 | . | 97 | 0.97 | ... | ... |
| | 1994 | MF | 100 | 2 | . | 96 | 0.97 | ... | ... |
| | | M | 100 | 2 | . | 96 | 0.96 | ... | ... |
| | | F | 100 | 2 | . | 97 | 0.97 | ... | ... |
| | 1995 | MF | 99 | 2 | . | 96 | 0.97 | 98 | ... |
| | | M | 99 | 2 | . | 96 | 0.96 | 98 | ... |
| | | F | 99 | 2 | . | 97 | 0.97 | 98 | ... |
| | 1996 | MF | 98 | 2 | ... | ... | ... | ... | ... |
| | | M | 98 | 2 | ... | ... | ... | ... | ... |
| | | F | 97 | 2 | ... | ... | ... | ... | ... |

Primary education: selected indicators    II.11
Enseignement primaire: indicateurs selectionnés
Enseñanza primaria: indicadores seleccionados

| Country / Pays / País | Year / Année / Año | Sex / Sexe / Sexo | Apparent intake rate / Taux d'admission apparent / Tasa aparente de ingreso (%) | Percentage repeaters / Pourcentage de redoublants / Porcentaje de repetidores | Percentage of cohort reaching: / Pourcentage de la cohorte atteignant: / Porcentaje de la cohorte que llega al: Grade 5 / 5e année / Quinto año | Final grade / Dernière année / Ultimo año | Coefficient of efficiency / Coefficient d'efficacité / Coeficiente de eficacia | Transition rate (Prim. to Sec. gen.) / Taux de transition (Prim. au sec. gén.) / Tasa de transición (Prim. a la Sec. gen.) (%) | School life expectancy (in years) / Espérance de vie scolaire (années) / Esperanza de vida escolar (en años) |
|---|---|---|---|---|---|---|---|---|---|
| Slovenia | 1992 | MF | 102 | 1 | . | 99 | 0.99 | 99 | ... |
|  | 1993 | MF | 100 | 1 | . | 100 | 0.99 | 101 | ... |
|  | 1994 | MF | 101 | 1 | . | 98 | 0.98 | 98 | ... |
|  | 1995 | MF | 100 | 1 | . | 100 | 0.99 | ... | ... |
|  |  | M | ... | ... | . | 100 | 0.99 | ... | ... |
|  |  | F | ... | ... | . | 100 | 0.99 | ... | ... |
|  | 1996 | MF | 95 | 1 | ... | ... | ... | ... | ... |
|  |  | M | 96 | 1 | ... | ... | ... | ... | ... |
|  |  | F | 94 | 1 | ... | ... | ... | ... | ... |
| Spain | 1970 | MF | ... | ... | ... | ... | ... | ... | 10.0 |
|  |  | M | ... | ... | ... | ... | ... | ... | 10.7 |
|  |  | F | ... | ... | ... | ... | ... | ... | 9.4 |
|  | 1975 | MF | ... | ... | ... | ... | ... | ... | 11.4 |
|  |  | M | ... | ... | ... | ... | ... | ... | 11.8 |
|  |  | F | ... | ... | ... | ... | ... | ... | 11.0 |
|  | 1980 | MF | 107 | 6 | 95 | 95 | 0.91 | 90 | 12.5 |
|  |  | M | 107 | 7 | 95 | 95 | 0.90 | 89 | 12.6 |
|  |  | F | 107 | 6 | 94 | 94 | 0.92 | 91 | 12.5 |
|  | 1985 | MF | 103 | 5 | 98 | 98 | 0.93 | 88 | ... |
|  |  | M | 103 | 6 | 96 | 96 | 0.92 | 87 | ... |
|  |  | F | 103 | 4 | 100 | 100 | 0.95 | 90 | ... |
|  | 1991 | MF | ... | ... | 100 | 100 | 0.96 | 92 | ... |
|  |  | M | ... | ... | 100 | 100 | 0.95 | 91 | ... |
|  |  | F | ... | ... | 100 | 100 | 0.97 | 93 | ... |
|  | 1992 | MF | 106 | 4 | 98 | 98 | 0.97 | 93 | ... |
|  |  | M | 107 | 5 | 98 | 98 | 0.96 | 91 | ... |
|  |  | F | 106 | 3 | 99 | 99 | 0.97 | 94 | ... |
|  | 1993 | MF | 104 | 3 | ... | ... | ... | ... | ... |
|  |  | M | 104 | 3 | ... | ... | ... | ... | ... |
|  |  | F | 105 | 2 | ... | ... | ... | ... | ... |
| Sweden | 1970 | MF | 99 | - | 99 | 99 | 1.00 | ... | ... |
|  |  | M | 99 | - | 98 | 98 | 1.00 | ... | ... |
|  |  | F | 99 | - | 99 | 99 | 1.00 | ... | ... |
|  | 1975 | MF | 96 | - | 100 | 100 | 1.00 | ... | ... |
|  |  | M | 96 | - | 100 | 100 | 1.00 | ... | ... |
|  |  | F | 97 | - | 100 | 100 | 1.00 | ... | ... |
|  | 1980 | MF | 99 | - | 98 | 98 | 0.99 | ... | ... |
|  |  | M | 99 | - | 98 | 98 | 0.99 | ... | ... |
|  |  | F | 99 | - | 98 | 98 | 0.99 | ... | ... |
|  | 1990 | MF | 98 | - | 100 | 100 | 1.00 | ... | 13.0 |
|  |  | M | 99 | - | 100 | 100 | 1.00 | ... | 12.7 |
|  |  | F | 98 | - | 100 | 100 | 1.00 | ... | 13.2 |
|  | 1991 | MF | 100 | - | 100 | 100 | 1.00 | ... | 13.2 |
|  |  | M | 100 | - | 100 | 100 | 1.00 | ... | 12.9 |
|  |  | F | 100 | - | 100 | 100 | 1.00 | ... | 13.5 |
|  | 1992 | MF | 103 | - | 98 | 98 | 0.99 | ... | 13.7 |
|  |  | M | 104 | - | 99 | 99 | 1.00 | ... | 13.4 |
|  |  | F | 103 | - | 97 | 97 | 0.99 | ... | 14.0 |
|  | 1993 | MF | 103 | - | 98 | 98 | 0.99 | ... | 14.1 |
|  |  | M | 103 | - | 99 | 99 | 1.00 | ... | 13.8 |
|  |  | F | 103 | - | 97 | 97 | 0.99 | ... | 14.4 |
|  | 1994 | MF | 104 | - | 98 | 98 | 0.99 | ... | 14.4 |
|  |  | M | 104 | - | 98 | 98 | 0.99 | ... | 13.9 |
|  |  | F | 104 | - | 97 | 97 | 0.99 | ... | 14.5 |
|  | 1995 | MF | 111 | - | 97 | 97 | ... | ... | 14.7 |
|  |  | M | 110 | - | 97 | 97 | ... | ... | 14.4 |
|  |  | F | 111 | - | 97 | 97 | ... | ... | 15.1 |
|  | 1996 | MF | 111 | - | ... | ... | ... | ... | 15.0 |
|  |  | M | 110 | - | ... | ... | ... | ... | 14.5 |
|  |  | F | 111 | - | ... | ... | ... | ... | 14.4 |
| Switzerland | 1980 | MF | 92 | 2 | ... | ... | ... | ... | 12.6 |
|  |  | M | 91 | 2 | ... | ... | ... | ... | 13.3 |
|  |  | F | 92 | 2 | ... | ... | ... | ... | 11.9 |

II.11 Primary education: selected indicators
Enseignement primaire: Indicateurs sélectionnés
Enseñanza primaria: Indicadores seleccionados

| Country<br>Pays<br>País | Year<br>Année<br>Año | Sex<br>Sexe<br>Sexo | Apparent intake rate<br>Taux d'admission apparent<br>Tasa aparente de ingreso (%) | Percentage repeaters<br>Pourcentage de redoublants<br>Porcentaje de repetidores | Percentage of cohort reaching:<br>Pourcentage de la cohorte atteignant:<br>Porcentaje de la cohorte que llega al: | | Coefficient of efficiency<br>Coefficient d'efficacité<br>Coeficiente de eficacia | Transition rate (Prim. to Sec. gen.)<br>Taux de transition (Prim. au sec. gén.)<br>Tasa de transición (Prim. a la Sec. gen.) (%) | School life expectancy (in years)<br>Espérance de vie scolaire (années)<br>Esperanza de vida escolar (en años) |
|---|---|---|---|---|---|---|---|---|---|
| | | | | | Grade 5<br>5e année<br>Quinto año | Final grade<br>Dernière année<br>Ultimo año | | | |
| Switzerland (cont) | 1985 | MF | 93 | 2 | ... | ... | ... | ... | 12.9 |
| | | M | 92 | 2 | ... | ... | ... | ... | 13.5 |
| | | F | 93 | 2 | ... | ... | ... | ... | 12.3 |
| | 1990 | MF | 98 | 2 | ... | ... | ... | ... | 13.6 |
| | | M | 97 | 2 | ... | ... | ... | ... | 14.1 |
| | | F | 99 | 1 | ... | ... | ... | ... | 13.1 |
| | 1991 | MF | 98 | 2 | ... | ... | ... | ... | 13.8 |
| | | M | 96 | 2 | ... | ... | ... | ... | 14.3 |
| | | F | 100 | 2 | ... | ... | ... | ... | 13.3 |
| | 1992 | MF | 101 | 2 | ... | ... | ... | ... | 13.9 |
| | | M | 100 | 2 | ... | ... | ... | ... | 14.3 |
| | | F | 102 | 1 | ... | ... | ... | ... | 13.4 |
| | 1993 | MF | 99 | 2 | ... | ... | ... | ... | 13.9 |
| | | M | 99 | 2 | ... | ... | ... | ... | 14.3 |
| | | F | 99 | 1 | ... | ... | ... | ... | 13.4 |
| | 1994 | MF | ... | ... | ... | ... | ... | ... | 14.1 |
| | | M | ... | ... | ... | ... | ... | ... | 14.6 |
| | | F | ... | ... | ... | ... | ... | ... | 13.5 |
| | 1995 | MF | 101 | 2 | ... | ... | ... | ... | 14.1 |
| | | M | 101 | 2 | ... | ... | ... | ... | 14.7 |
| | | F | 101 | 1 | ... | ... | ... | ... | 13.5 |
| The Former Yugoslav Rep. of Macedonia | 1992 | MF | 100 | 2 | 95 | 86 | 0.90 | ... | ... |
| | 1993 | MF | 102 | 2 | 95 | 88 | 0.91 | ... | ... |
| | | M | ... | ... | 95 | 87 | 0.90 | ... | ... |
| | | F | ... | ... | 95 | 89 | 0.92 | ... | ... |
| | 1994 | MF | 105 | 1 | 99 | 95 | 0.96 | ... | 11.1 |
| | | M | 107 | 2 | 99 | 96 | 0.96 | ... | 11.1 |
| | | F | 104 | 1 | 97 | 93 | 0.94 | ... | 11.1 |
| | 1995 | MF | 104 | 1 | 95 | 88 | 0.92 | ... | 11.3 |
| | | M | 106 | 2 | 95 | 87 | 0.91 | ... | 11.2 |
| | | F | 103 | 1 | 95 | 89 | 0.93 | ... | 11.3 |
| | 1996 | MF | 102 | 0 | ... | ... | ... | ... | 11.4 |
| | | M | 103 | 1 | ... | ... | ... | ... | 11.4 |
| | | F | 101 | 0 | ... | ... | ... | ... | 11.4 |
| Ukraine | 1980 | MF | ... | ... | 89 | 89 | 0.96 | 99 | ... |
| | 1990 | MF | 101 | 1 | 59 | 59 | 0.74 | 99 | ... |
| | 1991 | MF | 97 | 1 | ... | ... | ... | 105 | ... |
| | 1992 | MF | 96 | 1 | ... | ... | ... | ... | ... |
| | | M | 98 | 1 | ... | ... | ... | ... | ... |
| | | F | 94 | 1 | ... | ... | ... | ... | ... |
| | 1993 | MF | 99 | 1 | ... | ... | ... | ... | ... |
| | | M | 100 | 1 | ... | ... | ... | ... | ... |
| | | F | 99 | 1 | ... | ... | ... | ... | ... |
| United Kingdom | 1970 | MF | ... | - | ... | ... | ... | ... | 12.0 |
| | | M | ... | | ... | ... | ... | ... | 12.3 |
| | | F | ... | - | ... | ... | ... | ... | 11.8 |
| | 1975 | MF | ... | - | ... | ... | ... | ... | 12.9 |
| | | M | ... | | ... | ... | ... | ... | 13.1 |
| | | F | ... | - | ... | ... | ... | ... | 12.7 |
| | 1980 | MF | ... | - | ... | ... | ... | ... | 12.9 |
| | | M | ... | | ... | ... | ... | ... | 13.1 |
| | | F | ... | - | ... | ... | ... | ... | 12.8 |
| | 1985 | MF | ... | - | ... | ... | ... | ... | 13.1 |
| | | M | ... | | ... | ... | ... | ... | 13.1 |
| | | F | ... | - | ... | ... | ... | ... | 13.2 |
| | 1990 | MF | ... | - | ... | ... | ... | ... | 13.7 |
| | | M | ... | | ... | ... | ... | ... | 13.5 |
| | | F | ... | | ... | ... | ... | ... | 13.9 |
| | 1991 | MF | ... | - | ... | ... | ... | ... | 13.8 |
| | | M | ... | | ... | ... | ... | ... | 13.5 |
| | | F | ... | - | ... | ... | ... | ... | 14.0 |

Primary education: selected indicators  II.11
Enseignement primaire: indicateurs selectionnés
Enseñanza primaria: indicadores seleccionados

| Country / Pays / País | Year / Année / Año | Sex / Sexe / Sexo | Apparent intake rate / Taux d'admission apparent / Tasa aparente de ingreso (%) | Percentage repeaters / Pourcentage de redoublants / Porcentaje de repetidores | Percentage of cohort reaching: / Pourcentage de la cohorte atteignant: / Porcentaje de la cohorte que llega al: | | Coefficient of efficiency / Coefficient d'efficacité / Coeficiente de eficacia | Transition rate (Prim. to Sec. gen.) / Taux de transition (Prim. au sec. gén.) / Tasa de transición (Prim. a la Sec. gen.) (%) | School life expectancy (in years) / Espérance de vie scolaire (années) / Esperanza de vida escolar (en años) |
|---|---|---|---|---|---|---|---|---|---|
| | | | | | Grade 5 / 5e année / Quinto año | Final grade / Dernière année / Ultimo año | | | |
| United Kingdom (cont) | 1992 | MF | ... | - | ... | ... | ... | ... | 15.7 |
| | | M | ... | - | ... | ... | ... | | 15.6 |
| | | F | ... | - | ... | ... | ... | | 15.8 |
| | 1993 | MF | ... | - | ... | ... | ... | ... | 16.0 |
| | | M | ... | - | ... | ... | ... | | 15.9 |
| | | F | ... | - | ... | ... | ... | | 16.2 |
| | 1994 | MF | ... | - | ... | ... | ... | ... | 16.4 |
| | | M | ... | - | ... | ... | ... | | 16.1 |
| | | F | ... | - | ... | ... | ... | | 16.6 |
| | 1995 | MF | ... | - | ... | ... | ... | ... | 16.5 |
| | | M | ... | - | ... | ... | ... | | 16.2 |
| | | F | ... | - | ... | ... | ... | | 16.7 |
| **Oceania** | | | | | | | | | |
| Australia | 1975 | MF | ... | ... | ... | ... | ... | ... | 11.8 |
| | | M | ... | ... | ... | ... | ... | | 12.1 |
| | | F | ... | ... | ... | ... | ... | ... | 11.6 |
| | 1980 | MF | ... | ... | ... | ... | ... | ... | 12.1 |
| | | M | ... | ... | ... | ... | ... | | 12.1 |
| | | F | ... | ... | ... | ... | ... | | 12.0 |
| | 1985 | MF | ... | ... | ... | ... | ... | ... | 12.5 |
| | | M | ... | ... | ... | ... | ... | | 12.5 |
| | | F | ... | ... | ... | ... | ... | | 12.5 |
| | 1990 | MF | ... | ... | ... | ... | ... | ... | 13.1 |
| | | M | ... | ... | ... | ... | ... | | 12.9 |
| | | F | ... | ... | ... | ... | ... | | 13.3 |
| | 1991 | MF | ... | ... | ... | ... | ... | ... | 13.4 |
| | | M | ... | ... | ... | ... | ... | | 13.1 |
| | | F | ... | ... | ... | ... | ... | | 13.6 |
| | 1992 | MF | ... | ... | ... | ... | ... | ... | 13.5 |
| | | M | ... | ... | ... | ... | ... | | 13.3 |
| | | F | ... | ... | ... | ... | ... | | 13.8 |
| | 1993 | MF | ... | ... | ... | ... | ... | ... | 15.8 |
| | | M | ... | ... | ... | ... | ... | | 16.0 |
| | | F | ... | ... | ... | ... | ... | | 15.7 |
| | 1994 | MF | ... | ... | ... | ... | ... | ... | 15.9 |
| | | M | ... | ... | ... | ... | ... | | 15.9 |
| | | F | ... | ... | ... | ... | ... | | 15.8 |
| | 1995 | MF | ... | ... | ... | ... | ... | ... | 16.8 |
| | | M | ... | ... | ... | ... | ... | | 16.8 |
| | | F | ... | ... | ... | ... | ... | | 16.7 |
| | 1996 | MF | ... | ... | ... | ... | ... | ... | 17.1 |
| | | M | ... | ... | ... | ... | ... | | 17.1 |
| | | F | ... | ... | ... | ... | ... | | 17.1 |
| Fiji | 1975 | MF | ... | ... | 93 | 90 | 0.91 | ... | ... |
| | 1980 | MF | 103 | 5 | 94 | 90 | 0.91 | ... | ... |
| | | M | 104 | 5 | 92 | 88 | 0.89 | ... | ... |
| | | F | 103 | 4 | 95 | 93 | 0.93 | ... | ... |
| | 1985 | MF | 109 | 3 | 94 | 90 | 0.92 | ... | ... |
| | | M | 110 | 4 | 93 | 88 | 0.90 | ... | ... |
| | | F | 108 | 2 | 96 | 92 | 0.93 | ... | ... |
| Kiribati | 1985 | MF | ... | 3 | 85 | 85 | 0.94 | ... | ... |
| | | M | ... | 3 | 84 | 83 | 0.93 | ... | ... |
| | | F | ... | 3 | 84 | 84 | 0.94 | ... | ... |
| | 1990 | MF | ... | 1 | 98 | 98 | 0.99 | ... | ... |
| | | M | ... | 1 | 93 | 93 | 0.98 | ... | ... |
| | | F | ... | 1 | 99 | 95 | 0.96 | ... | ... |
| | 1991 | MF | ... | 1 | 90 | 89 | 0.97 | ... | ... |
| | | M | ... | 1 | 86 | 86 | 0.96 | ... | ... |
| | | F | ... | 1 | 92 | 88 | 0.95 | ... | ... |
| | 1993 | MF | ... | 0 | 90 | 90 | 0.97 | ... | ... |
| | | M | ... | 1 | 89 | 89 | 0.96 | ... | ... |
| | | F | ... | 0 | 91 | 87 | 0.94 | ... | ... |

II.11 Primary education: selected indicators
Enseignement primaire: indicateurs selectionnés
Enseñanza primaria: indicadores seleccionados

| Country<br><br>Pays<br><br>País | Year<br><br>Année<br><br>Año | Sex<br><br>Sexe<br><br>Sexo | Apparent<br>intake rate<br><br>Taux<br>d'admission<br>apparent<br><br>Tasa<br>aparente de<br>ingreso<br>(%) | Percentage<br>repeaters<br><br>Pourcentage<br>de<br>redoublants<br><br>Porcentaje<br>de<br>repetidores | Percentage of cohort reaching:<br>Pourcentage de la cohorte atteignant:<br>Porcentaje de la cohorte que llega al: | | Coefficient of<br>efficiency<br><br>Coefficient<br>d'efficacité<br><br>Coeficiente<br>de eficacia | Transition rate<br>(Prim. to Sec. gen.)<br><br>Taux de transition<br>(Prim. au sec. gén.)<br><br>Tasa de transición<br>(Prim. a la Sec.<br>gen.)<br>(%) | School life<br>expectancy<br>(in years)<br><br>Espérance de<br>vie scolaire<br>(années)<br><br>Esperanza de<br>vida escolar<br>(en años) |
|---|---|---|---|---|---|---|---|---|---|
| | | | | | Grade 5<br>5e année<br>Quinto año | Final grade<br>Dernière année<br>Ultimo año | | | |
| Kiribati (cont) | 1994 | MF | ... | 0 | 90 | 90 | 0.97 | ... | ... |
| | | M | ... | 0 | 85 | 84 | 0.94 | ... | ... |
| | | F | ... | 0 | 92 | 92 | 0.98 | ... | ... |
| | 1995 | MF | ... | 0 | 89 | 89 | 0.96 | ... | ... |
| | | M | ... | 0 | 86 | 86 | 0.95 | ... | ... |
| | | F | ... | 0 | 86 | 86 | 0.96 | ... | ... |
| | 1996 | MF | ... | 0 | 95 | 93 | ... | ... | ... |
| | | M | ... | 0 | 95 | 94 | ... | ... | ... |
| | | F | ... | 0 | 93 | 89 | ... | ... | ... |
| New Caledonia | 1985 | MF | 97 | 17 | 94 | 94 | 0.79 | 67 | 11.4 |
| | | M | 95 | 19 | 91 | 91 | 0.75 | 64 | 11.3 |
| | | F | 99 | 15 | 96 | 96 | 0.83 | 70 | 11.6 |
| | 1990 | MF | 108 | 13 | ... | ... | ... | ... | ... |
| | | M | 108 | 15 | ... | ... | ... | ... | ... |
| | | F | 108 | 12 | ... | ... | ... | ... | ... |
| New Zealand | 1970 | MF | ... | - | ... | ... | ... | ... | 12.5 |
| | | M | ... | - | ... | ... | ... | ... | 12.8 |
| | | F | ... | - | ... | ... | ... | ... | 12.2 |
| | 1975 | MF | ... | - | ... | ... | ... | 101 | 13.1 |
| | | M | ... | - | ... | ... | ... | 101 | 13.4 |
| | | F | ... | - | ... | ... | ... | 101 | 12.7 |
| | 1980 | MF | 104 | 4 | ... | ... | ... | 100 | 13.4 |
| | | M | 104 | 4 | ... | ... | ... | 100 | 13.6 |
| | | F | 104 | 3 | ... | ... | ... | 100 | 13.2 |
| | 1985 | MF | 109 | 3 | ... | ... | ... | ... | 13.7 |
| | | M | 109 | 3 | ... | ... | ... | ... | 13.8 |
| | | F | 109 | 3 | ... | ... | ... | ... | 13.7 |
| | 1990 | MF | 104 | 3 | ... | ... | ... | 102 | 14.5 |
| | | M | 105 | 3 | ... | ... | ... | 102 | 14.4 |
| | | F | 104 | 3 | ... | ... | ... | 101 | 14.6 |
| | 1991 | MF | 101 | 3 | ... | ... | ... | 102 | 14.8 |
| | | M | 101 | 4 | ... | ... | ... | 103 | 14.7 |
| | | F | 102 | 3 | ... | ... | ... | 102 | 15.0 |
| | 1992 | MF | 98 | 4 | ... | ... | ... | 103 | 15.1 |
| | | M | 98 | 4 | ... | ... | ... | 104 | 14.9 |
| | | F | 97 | 4 | ... | ... | ... | 103 | 15.3 |
| | 1994 | MF | 98 | ... | ... | ... | ... | 102 | 16.5 |
| | | M | 98 | ... | ... | ... | ... | 102 | 16.0 |
| | | F | 98 | ... | ... | ... | ... | 102 | 16.9 |
| | 1995 | MF | 104 | ... | ... | ... | ... | ... | 16.0 |
| | | M | 103 | ... | ... | ... | ... | ... | 15.7 |
| | | F | 105 | ... | ... | ... | ... | ... | 16.4 |
| | 1996 | MF | 107 | - | ... | ... | ... | ... | 15.9 |
| | | M | 107 | - | ... | ... | ... | ... | 15.5 |
| | | F | 106 | - | ... | ... | ... | ... | 16.3 |
| | 1997 | MF | 107 | - | ... | ... | ... | ... | 16.2 |
| | | M | 108 | - | ... | ... | ... | ... | 15.6 |
| | | F | 106 | - | ... | ... | ... | ... | 16.7 |
| Papua New Guinea | 1990 | MF | 98 | - | 59 | 52 | 0.72 | ... | ... |
| | | M | 106 | - | 60 | 52 | 0.71 | ... | ... |
| | | F | 90 | - | 58 | 52 | 0.72 | ... | ... |
| | 1991 | MF | 98 | - | 69 | 62 | 0.78 | ... | ... |
| | | M | 105 | - | 70 | 64 | 0.79 | ... | ... |
| | | F | 90 | - | 68 | 60 | 0.77 | ... | ... |
| | 1992 | MF | 97 | - | 73 | 66 | 0.80 | ... | ... |
| | | M | 104 | - | 72 | 65 | 0.80 | ... | ... |
| | | F | 89 | - | 74 | 67 | 0.80 | ... | ... |
| | 1993 | MF | 105 | - | ... | ... | ... | ... | ... |
| | 1994 | MF | 104 | - | ... | ... | ... | ... | ... |
| | | M | 110 | - | ... | ... | ... | ... | ... |
| | | F | 97 | - | ... | ... | ... | ... | ... |
| | 1995 | MF | 104 | - | ... | ... | ... | ... | ... |
| | | M | 110 | - | ... | ... | ... | ... | ... |
| | | F | 97 | - | ... | ... | ... | ... | ... |

Primary education: selected indicators    II.11
Enseignement primaire: indicateurs selectionnés
Enseñanza primaria: indicadores seleccionados

| Country / Pays / País | Year / Année / Año | Sex / Sexe / Sexo | Apparent intake rate / Taux d'admission apparent / Tasa aparente de ingreso (%) | Percentage repeaters / Pourcentage de redoublants / Porcentaje de repetidores | Percentage of cohort reaching: / Pourcentage de la cohorte atteignant: / Porcentaje de la cohorte que llega al: | | Coefficient of efficiency / Coefficient d'efficacité / Coeficiente de eficacia | Transition rate (Prim. to Sec. gen.) / Taux de transition (Prim. au sec. gén.) / Tasa de transición (Prim. a la Sec. gen.) (%) | School life expectancy (in years) / Espérance de vie scolaire (années) / Esperanza de vida escolar (en años) |
|---|---|---|---|---|---|---|---|---|---|
| | | | | | Grade 5 / 5e année / Quinto año | Final grade / Dernière année / Ultimo año | | | |
| Samoa | 1995 | MF | 106 | 2 | 86 | 79 | 0.89 | ... | ... |
| | 1996 | MF | 105 | ... | 85 | 82 | 0.93 | ... | ... |
| Solomon Islands | 1980 | MF | 91 | 5 | 69 | 60 | 0.73 | ... | ... |
| | | M | 98 | 5 | 75 | 66 | 0.77 | ... | ... |
| | | F | 84 | 5 | 62 | 53 | 0.69 | ... | ... |
| | 1990 | MF | 86 | 10 | 85 | 80 | 0.84 | ... | ... |
| | 1991 | MF | 96 | 6 | 88 | 78 | 0.80 | ... | ... |
| | 1992 | MF | 110 | 6 | 84 | 71 | 0.77 | ... | ... |
| | 1993 | MF | 115 | 6 | 81 | 73 | 0.76 | ... | ... |
| | 1994 | MF | 108 | 9 | ... | ... | ... | ... | ... |
| Tonga | 1985 | MF | ... | 8 | 92 | 92 | 0.90 | ... | ... |
| | | M | ... | 8 | 96 | 94 | 0.90 | ... | ... |
| | | F | ... | 7 | 87 | 87 | 0.89 | ... | ... |
| | 1990 | MF | ... | 4 | 84 | 81 | 0.80 | ... | ... |
| | | M | ... | 4 | 85 | 84 | 0.84 | ... | ... |
| | | F | ... | 4 | 75 | 70 | 0.71 | ... | ... |
| | 1992 | MF | ... | ... | 92 | 90 | 0.88 | 76 | ... |
| | | M | ... | ... | 93 | 90 | 0.88 | 71 | ... |
| | | F | ... | ... | 84 | 84 | 0.84 | 83 | ... |
| Tuvalu | 1992 | MF | ... | - | 96 | 96 | 0.99 | ... | ... |
| | | M | ... | - | 89 | 89 | 0.98 | ... | ... |
| | | F | ... | - | 98 | 98 | 1.00 | ... | ... |
| Vanuatu, Republic of | 1991 | MF | ... | ... | 90 | 87 | 0.79 | ... | ... |
| | | M | ... | ... | 89 | 89 | 0.80 | ... | ... |
| | | F | ... | ... | 91 | 85 | 0.79 | ... | ... |
| | 1992 | MF | 100 | 13 | ... | ... | ... | ... | ... |
| | | M | 101 | 14 | ... | ... | ... | ... | ... |
| | | F | 98 | 11 | ... | ... | ... | ... | ... |

**General note**
For general explanations and definitions, please refer to the beginning of this chapter.

**Note générale**
Pour les explications et définitions générales, prière de se référer au début de ce chapitre.

**Nota general**
Para las explicaciones y definiciones generales, referirse al comienzo de este capítulo.

II.12    Tertiary education: students (total and female) by ISCED level
Enseignement supérieur: étudiants (total et femmes) par niveau de la CITE
Enseñanza superior: estudiantes (total y mujeres) por nivel de la CINE

## II.12    Tertiary education: distribution of students by ISCED level and percentage female in each level

### Enseignement supérieur: répartition des étudiants par niveau de la CITE et pourcentage d'étudiantes dans chaque niveau

### Enseñanza superior: distribución de los estudiantes por nivel de la CINE y porcentaje de mujeres en cada nivel

| Country / Pays / País | Year / Année / Año | | Total of students / Total des étudiants / Total de estudiantes | Percentage of students by ISCED level / Pourcentage d'étudiants par niveau de la CITE / Porcentaje de estudiantes por nivel de la CINE | | | | Female students / Femmes étudiantes / Mujeres estudiantes | Percentage female in each level / Pourcentage de femmes dans chaque niveau / Porcentaje de mujeres en cada nivel | | |
|---|---|---|---|---|---|---|---|---|---|---|---|
| | | | | ISCED 5 CITE 5 CINE 5 | ISCED 6 CITE 6 CINE 6 | ISCED 7 CITE 7 CINE 7 | | | ISCED 5 CITE 5 CINE 5 | ISCED 6 CITE 6 CINE 6 | ISCED 7 CITE 7 CINE 7 |
| **Africa** | | | | | | | | | | | |
| Algeria | 1995/96 | (1) | 267 142 | 14.6 | 79.8 | 5.6 | (1) | 118 368 | 36.8 | 46.9 | 27.4 |
| Botswana | 1996/97 | (2) | 7 275 | 29.9 | 64.5 | 5.6 | (2) | 3 449 | 54.0 | 44.1 | 50.1 |
| Burkina Faso | 1994/95 | | 9 452 | 4.0 | 96.0 | —> | | 2 087 | 34.1 | 21.6 | —> |
| Djibouti | 1995/96 | | 130 | 100.0 | - | - | | 61 | 46.9 | . | . |
| Egypt | 1995/96 | (3)(4) | 850 051 | - | 88.5 | 11.5 | (3)(4) | 352 902 | . | 42.6 | 33.5 |
| Eritrea | 1997/98 | | 3 096 | 14.0 | 86.0 | - | | 410 | 7.9 | 14.1 | . |
| Ethiopia | 1996/97 | | 42 226 | 52.1 | 46.1 | 1.9 | | 8 524 | 24.6 | 15.7 | 7.0 |
| Lesotho | 1996/97 | | 4 614 | 55.0 | 44.5 | 0.5 | | 2 509 | 53.2 | 55.9 | 50.0 |
| Morocco | 1994/95 | (5) | 250 919 | 4.2 | 89.1 | 6.6 | (5) | 102 720 | 29.4 | 42.3 | 30.1 |
| South Africa | 1994 | (6) | 468 086 | 46.8 | 45.6 | 7.7 | (6) | 230 600 | 48.0 | 51.5 | 43.2 |
| Swaziland | 1996/97 | | 5 658 | 59.7 | 36.1 | 4.2 | | 2 927 | 53.9 | 48.3 | 50.8 |
| Togo | 1994/95 | | 11 173 | 43.7 | 56.3 | - | | 1 487 | 15.7 | 11.4 | . |
| Tunisia | 1996/97 | | 121 787 | 9.1 | 84.6 | 6.3 | | 54 278 | 33.6 | 46.5 | 34.3 |
| Uganda | 1996/97 | (7) | 34 773 | 54.0 | 43.4 | 2.6 | (7) | 11 542 | 30.9 | 36.5 | 26.2 |
| United Republic of Tanzania | 1995/96 | | 12 776 | 31.8 | 63.6 | 4.6 | | 2 075 | 19.3 | 14.7 | 15.7 |
| Zimbabwe | 1996 | (8) | 46 673 | 70.8 | 25.4 | 3.8 | (8) | 17 016 | 39.7 | 29.4 | 24.2 |
| **North America** | | | | | | | | | | | |
| Barbados | 1995/96 | (2) | 3 064 | - | 92.1 | 7.9 | (2) | 1 903 | . | 62.6 | 56.8 |
| Canada | 1995/96 | | 1 763 105 | 44.4 | 49.0 | 6.7 | | 938 348 | 49.3 | 57.5 | 48.1 |
| Costa Rica | 1994 | (2) | 78 819 | - | 100.0 | —> | | ... | . | ... | ... |
| Cuba | 1996/97 | | 111 587 | - | 100.0 | - | | 67 134 | . | 60.2 | . |
| Dominican Republic | 1996/97 | | 176 995 | 9.5 | 89.9 | 0.6 | | ... | ... | ... | ... |
| Honduras | 1994 | | 54 106 | 1.6 | 97.9 | 0.5 | | 23 731 | 42.8 | 43.9 | 37.9 |

Tertiary education: students (total and female) by ISCED level
Enseignement supérieur: étudiants (total et femmes) par niveau de la CITE
Enseñanza superior: estudiantes (total y mujeres) por nivel de la CINE

II.12

| Country<br><br>Pays<br><br>País | Year<br><br>Année<br><br>Año | | Total<br>of students<br><br>Total des<br>étudiants<br><br>Total de<br>estudiantes | Percentage of students<br>by ISCED level<br>Pourcentage d'étudiants<br>par niveau de la CITE<br>Porcentaje de estudiantes<br>por nivel de la CINE | | | | Female<br>students<br><br>Femmes<br>étudiantes<br><br>Mujeres<br>estudiantes | Percentage female<br>in each level<br>Pourcentage de femmes<br>dans chaque niveau<br>Porcentaje de mujeres<br>en cada nivel | | |
|---|---|---|---|---|---|---|---|---|---|---|---|
| | | | | ISCED 5<br>CITE 5<br>CINE 5 | ISCED 6<br>CITE 6<br>CINE 6 | ISCED 7<br>CITE 7<br>CINE 7 | | | ISCED 5<br>CITE 5<br>CINE 5 | ISCED 6<br>CITE 6<br>CINE 6 | ISCED 7<br>CITE 7<br>CINE 7 |
| Mexico | 1996/97 | | 1 612 318 | <— | 94.2 | 5.8 | | 769 394 | <— | 48.1 | 41.0 |
| Nicaragua | 1995 | | 50 769 | 8.6 | 89.8 | 1.6 | | 26 066 | 57.7 | 50.8 | 46.3 |
| Panama | 1994 | (2) | 68 629 | 9.0 | 89.6 | 1.4 | (2) | 40 883 | 32.7 | 62.3 | 60.5 |
| Trinidad and Tobago | 1994/95 | (2) | 5 231 | 8.5 | 73.9 | 17.6 | (2) | 2 731 | 69.1 | 52.0 | 44.7 |
| United States | 1995/96 | | 14 261 778 | 38.5 | 47.3 | 14.2 | | 7 919 238 | 57.6 | 54.4 | 53.6 |
| **South America** | | | | | | | | | | | |
| Brazil | 1994 | (9) | 1 661 034 | <— | 100.0 | ... | (9) | 907 677 | <— | 54.6 | ... |
| Chile | 1997 | | 380 603 | 20.1 | 77.3 | 2.6 | | 175 242 | 44.7 | 46.4 | 45.5 |
| Colombia | 1996 | | 644 188 | 19.9 | 74.3 | 5.8 | | 334 204 | 51.3 | 52.1 | 51.1 |
| Guyana | 1996/97 | (2) | 3 701 | 41.0 | 56.3 | 2.7 | (2) | 2 154 | 55.9 | 59.7 | 62.4 |
| Paraguay | 1996 | (10) | 42 302 | 23.1 | 76.7 | 0.2 | (10) | 23 070 | 66.8 | 50.9 | 41.5 |
| Uruguay | 1996 | | 79 691 | 15.3 | 84.7 | —> | | ... | ... | ... | ... |
| **Asia** | | | | | | | | | | | |
| Azerbaijan | 1996 | | 115 116 | 27.3 | 71.6 | 1.1 | (9) | 56 631 | 63.7 | 44.4 | ... |
| Cambodia | 1996/97 | | 10 019 | - | 100.0 | - | | 1 591 | . | 15.9 | . |
| China | 1994/95 | (2) | 2 926 935 | 43.8 | 51.8 | 4.4 | | ... | ... | ... | ... |
| Cyprus (11) | 1996/97 | | 9 982 | 76.5 | 21.0 | 2.5 | | 5 559 | 49.9 | 78.4 | 42.2 |
| Georgia | 1995/96 | | 155 033 | 18.8 | 80.1 | 1.1 | | 81 558 | 53.0 | 52.5 | 55.0 |
| Indonesia | 1995/96 | | 2 303 469 | 28.6 | 71.4 | —> | | 803 577 | 41.6 | 32.2 | —> |
| Iran, Islamic Republic of | 1995/96 | | 1 048 093 | 6.9 | 89.1 | 4.0 | | 384 461 | 28.3 | 37.9 | 23.7 |
| Japan | 1994/95 | | 3 917 709 | 32.4 | 64.1 | 3.5 | | 1 725 199 | 68.0 | 33.2 | 20.3 |
| Jordan (12) | 1996/97 | | 112 959 | 21.2 | 73.9 | 4.9 | | 52 934 | 64.9 | 43.0 | 26.5 |
| Kazakstan | 1994/95 | | 482 690 | 44.4 | 55.3 | 0.3 | (9) | 265 341 | 58.4 | 52.6 | ... |
| Korea, Republic of | 1996/97 | | 2 541 659 | 25.9 | 69.1 | 5.0 | | 940 175 | 39.1 | 36.8 | 28.5 |
| Kuwait | 1995/96 | | 28 705 | 27.5 | 70.8 | 1.7 | | 17 691 | 47.0 | 67.6 | 48.8 |
| Lao People's<br>Democratic Republic | 1996/97 | | 12 732 | 58.6 | 41.4 | - | | 3 845 | 27.9 | 33.5 | . |
| Lebanon | 1995/96 | | 81 588 | 1.4 | 98.6 | —> | | 40 160 | 60.7 | 49.1 | —> |
| Macau | 1996/97 | | 7 485 | 19.3 | 58.7 | 22.0 | | 3 674 | 50.6 | 51.9 | 40.3 |
| Mongolia | 1996/97 | | 44 088 | 11.9 | 85.4 | 2.7 | | 30 512 | 78.7 | 68.1 | 61.7 |
| Myanmar | 1994/95 | (13) | 245 317 | <— | 96.1 | 3.9 | (13) | 150 821 | <— | 60.7 | 79.6 |
| Philippines | 1995/96 | (2) | 2 017 972 | <— | 95.3 | 4.7 | (2) | 1 145 142 | <— | 56.1 | 70.3 |
| Qatar | 1996/97 | | 8 475 | 5.0 | 92.6 | 2.3 | | 6 195 | 72.4 | 72.9 | 83.3 |
| Saudi Arabia | 1995/96 | | 251 945 | 15.3 | 81.6 | 3.1 | | 121 366 | 28.3 | 52.4 | 36.0 |
| Sri Lanka | 1995 | (14) | 63 660 | 27.6 | 59.7 | 12.7 | (14) | 28 008 | 38.0 | 46.2 | 46.6 |
| Syrian Arab Republic | 1994/95 | (14) | 196 753 | 15.0 | 83.0 | 1.9 | (14) | 76 245 | 36.8 | 39.2 | 34.3 |
| Tajikistan | 1994/95 | | 108 203 | 32.2 | 67.8 | —> | | 35 325 | 43.4 | 27.5 | —> |
| Thailand | 1995/96 | | 1 220 481 | 23.1 | 72.8 | 4.1 | | ... | ... | ... | ... |
| Turkey | 1994/95 | | 1 174 299 | 25.2 | 69.1 | 5.7 | | 449 771 | 44.6 | 36.2 | 35.6 |
| United Arab Emirates | 1996/97 | (2) | 16 213 | - | 99.5 | 0.5 | (2) | 11 694 | . | 72.2 | 51.3 |
| Palestine | 1996/97 | | 49 599 | 8.5 | 89.0 | 2.5 | | 22 030 | 56.0 | 43.8 | 26.3 |

II.12    Tertiary education: students (total and female) by ISCED level
Enseignement supérieur: étudiants (total et femmes) par niveau de la CITE
Enseñanza superior: estudiantes (total y mujeres) por nivel de la CINE

| Country<br>Pays<br>País | Year<br>Année<br>Año | | Total<br>of students<br>Total des<br>étudiants<br>Total de<br>estudiantes | Percentage of students by ISCED level<br>Pourcentage d'étudiants par niveau de la CITE<br>Porcentaje de estudiantes por nivel de la CINE | | | | Female<br>students<br>Femmes<br>étudiantes<br>Mujeres<br>estudiantes | Percentage female in each level<br>Pourcentage de femmes dans chaque niveau<br>Porcentaje de mujeres en cada nivel | | |
|---|---|---|---|---|---|---|---|---|---|---|---|
| | | | | ISCED 5<br>CITE 5<br>CINE 5 | ISCED 6<br>CITE 6<br>CINE 6 | ISCED 7<br>CITE 7<br>CINE 7 | | | ISCED 5<br>CITE 5<br>CINE 5 | ISCED 6<br>CITE 6<br>CINE 6 | ISCED 7<br>CITE 7<br>CINE 7 |
| **Europe** | | | | | | | | | | | |
| Austria | 1996/97 | (15) | 293 172 | 6.3 | 85.7 | 8.0 | (15) | 136 501 | 68.5 | 45.8 | 37.9 |
| Belarus | 1996/97 | (1) | 212 446 | - | 98.3 | 1.7 | | ... | . | 52.8 | ... |
| Bulgaria | 1996/97 | | 262 757 | 9.5 | 89.7 | 0.8 | | 161 049 | 74.6 | 60.1 | 41.3 |
| Croatia | 1996/97 | (16) | 85 752 | 22.4 | 77.6 | - | (16) | 43 563 | 37.1 | 54.8 | . |
| Czech Republic | 1996/97 | | 207 221 | 13.1 | 82.0 | 5.0 | | 100 315 | 68.2 | 46.4 | 30.0 |
| Denmark | 1995/96 | | 174 975 | 10.5 | 89.5 | —> | | 94 452 | 47.5 | 54.7 | —> |
| Estonia | 1996/97 | | 43 468 | 30.8 | 61.1 | 8.1 | | 23 233 | 54.3 | 53.1 | 52.9 |
| Federal Republic of Yugoslavia | 1996/97 | (16) | 172 313 | 18.4 | 81.6 | - | (16) | 92 697 | 49.0 | 54.9 | . |
| Finland | 1996/97 | | 226 458 | 16.5 | 75.0 | 8.4 | | 119 653 | 62.7 | 51.4 | 46.0 |
| Germany | 1996/97 | (16) | 2 131 907 | 13.8 | 86.2 | - | (16) | 975 448 | 65.4 | 42.6 | . |
| Greece | 1994/95 | | 296 357 | 30.6 | 69.4 | —> | | ... | ... | ... | ... |
| Holy See | 1995/96 | (17) | 14 403 | 22.3 | 42.8 | 34.9 | (17) | 3 580 | 25.6 | 27.6 | 21.0 |
| Iceland | 1996/97 | | 7 908 | 16.2 | 80.8 | 3.0 | | 4 626 | 59.1 | 58.3 | 59.2 |
| Italy | 1996/97 | | 1 892 542 | 2.9 | 93.7 | 3.4 | | 1 021 815 | 65.7 | 53.7 | 53.3 |
| Latvia | 1996/97 | | 56 187 | - | 86.5 | 13.5 | | 33 454 | - | 59.8 | 57.9 |
| Lithuania | 1996/97 | | 83 645 | 29.7 | 59.0 | 11.3 | | 49 566 | 66.2 | 57.0 | 52.8 |
| Malta | 1994/95 | | 5 805 | 24.2 | 66.1 | 9.7 | | 2 794 | 47.0 | 49.5 | 41.9 |
| Moldova | 1996/97 | | 93 759 | 35.5 | 63.5 | 1.0 | | ... | ... | ... | ... |
| Netherlands | 1994/95 | | 502 928 | <— | 56.6 | 43.4 | | 237 284 | <— | 49.3 | 44.4 |
| Norway | 1996/97 | | 185 320 | 29.2 | 70.8 | —> | | 104 224 | 54.5 | 57.0 | —> |
| Portugal | 1995/96 | | 319 525 | 22.0 | 74.2 | 3.8 | | 180 506 | 53.6 | 57.5 | 52.8 |
| Romania | 1996/97 | | 411 687 | 13.9 | 86.1 | —> | | 217 605 | 71.3 | 49.9 | —> |
| Russian Federation | 1994/95 | | 4 458 363 | 42.0 | 56.8 | 1.2 | (9) | 2 463 912 | 60.3 | 52.8 | ... |
| Slovakia | 1996/97 | | 101 764 | 4.1 | 91.5 | 4.4 | | 51 100 | 77.5 | 49.5 | 39.7 |
| Slovenia | 1996/97 | (9) | 51 009 | 12.8 | 87.2 | - | (9) | 28 736 | 48.5 | 57.5 | . |
| Spain | 1995/96 | | 1 591 863 | 2.3 | 94.0 | 3.7 | | 840 524 | 47.5 | 53.1 | 47.8 |
| Sweden | 1996/97 | | 275 217 | <— | 94.2 | 5.8 | | 153 600 | <— | 56.9 | 38.4 |
| Switzerland | 1995/96 | | 148 024 | 42.4 | 48.4 | 9.3 | | 55 746 | 32.3 | 43.3 | 32.6 |
| The Former Yugoslav Rep. of Macedonia | 1996/97 | (16) | 30 754 | 9.9 | 90.1 | - | (16) | 16 738 | 46.2 | 55.3 | . |
| United Kingdom | 1996/97 | | 1 891 450 | 25.0 | 56.2 | 18.8 | | 979 659 | 56.0 | 51.6 | 46.8 |
| **Oceania** | | | | | | | | | | | |
| Australia | 1997 | | 1 041 648 | 39.1 | 47.7 | 13.2 | | 529 335 | 44.8 | 55.5 | 51.8 |
| New Zealand | 1997 | | 169 656 | 26.6 | 60.2 | 13.2 | | 97 223 | 60.2 | 57.4 | 51.0 |

**General note**

For general explanations and definitions, please refer to the beginning of this chapter.

**Note générale**

Pour les explications et définitions générales, prière de se référer au début de ce chapitre.

**Nota general**

Para las explicaciones y definiciones generales, referirse al comienzo de este capítulo.

Tertiary education: students (total and female) by ISCED level    II.12
Enseignement supérieur: étudiants (total et femmes) par niveau de la CITE
Enseñanza superior: estudiantes (total y mujeres) por nivel de la CINE

## Notes

(1) Universities and equivalent degree-granting institutions only.
(2) Universities only.
(3) Not including private tertiary institutions.
(4) Universities and degree-granting institutions only, excluding al Azhar.
(5) Not including professional schools.
(6) Data are expressed in full-time equivalent.
(7) Not including private non-university institutions.
(8) Not including private colleges.
(9) Not including ISCED level 7.
(10) Not including private universities.
(11) Not including Turkish institutions.
(12) East Bank only.
(13) Not including medical science.
(14) Not including some non-university institutions.
(15) Including multiple counting of students enrolled in more than one field of study.
(16) Not including students at ISCED level 7 for which registration is not required.
(17) Data refer to institutions under the authority of the Holy See.

## Notes

(1) Universités et établissements conférant des grades équivalents seulement.
(2) Universités seulement.
(3) Non compris les institutions supérieures privées.
(4) Universités et établissements conférant des titres équivalents seulement, à l'exception d'Al Azhar.
(5) Non compris les écoles professionnelles.
(6) Les données sont exprimées en équivalents plein temps.
(7) Non compris les institutions privées non universitaires.
(8) Non compris les collèges privés.
(9) Non compris le niveau 7 de la CITE.
(10) Non compris les universités privées.
(11) Non compris les institutions turques.
(12) Rive orientale seulement.
(13) Non compris les science médicales.
(14) Non compris quelques institutions supérieures non universitaires.
(15) Y compris les doubles comptes dus aux étudiants inscrits dans plus d'un domaine d'études.
(16) Non compris les étudiants du niveau 7 de la CITE pour lequel l'inscription n'est pas exigée.
(17) Les données se réfèrent aux institutions sous l'autorité du Saint-Siège.

## Notas

(1) Universidades y establecimientos que otorgan títulos equivalentes solamente.
(2) Universidades solamente.
(3) No incluyen las instituciones superiores privadas.
(4) Universidades y establecimientos que otorgan títulos equivalentes solamente, con excepción de Al Azhar.
(5) No incluyen las escuelas profesionales.
(6) Los datos están expresados en equivalente de jornada completa.
(7) No incluyen las instituciones no universitarias privadas.
(8) No incluyen los colegios privados.
(9) No incluye el nivel 7 de la CINE.
(10) No incluyen las universidades privadas.
(11) No incluyen las instituciones turcas.
(12) Orilla oriental solamente.
(13) No incluyen las ciencias médicas.
(14) No incluyen algunas instituciones de enseñanza superior no universitaria.
(15) Incluyen los estudiantes inscritos en diversos sectores de estudios.
(16) No incluyen los estudiantes del nivel 7 de la CINE para el cual la inscripción no es exigida.
(17) Los datos se refieren a las instituciones bajo la autoridad de la Santa Sede.

II.13  Tertiary education: students by broad field of study
Enseignement supérieur: étudiants par grand domaine d'études
Enseñanza superior: estudiantes por gran sector de estudios

## II.13  Tertiary education: distribution of students by broad field of study

### Enseignement supérieur: répartition des étudiants par grand domaine d'études

### Enseñanza superior: distribución de los estudiantes por gran sector de estudios

| Country | Year | Total enrolment | | Percentage of students by broad field of study Pourcentage d'étudiants par grand domaine d'études Porcentaje de estudiantes por gran sector de estudios | | | | | |
| --- | --- | --- | --- | --- | --- | --- | --- | --- | --- |
| | | | | Education | Humanities | Social sciences | Natural sciences | Medical sciences | Others |
| Pays | Année | Effectifs totaux | | Education | Lettres | Sciences sociales | Sciences naturelles | Sciences médicales | Autres |
| País | Año | Matrícula total | | Educación | Humanidades | Ciencias sociales | Ciencias naturales | Ciencias médicas | Otros |
| **Africa** | | | | | | | | | |
| Algeria | 1995/96 | (1) | 267 142 | 0.7 | 13.4 | 25.0 | 49.8 | 10.0 | 1.1 |
| Benin | 1996 | | 14 055 | 28.6 | <— | 48.9 | 18.2 | 3.7 | 0.6 |
| Botswana | 1996/97 | (2) | 7 275 | 10.7 | 13.3 | 43.8 | 26.7 | 1.2 | 4.3 |
| Burkina Faso | 1994/95 | | 9 452 | 7.4 | 30.5 | 35.2 | 18.5 | 8.5 | - |
| Chad | 1995/96 | (1) | 3 274 | 3.8 | 49.4 | 29.9 | 13.7 | 3.3 | - |
| Djibouti | 1995/96 | | 130 | 27.7 | - | 72.3 | - | - | - |
| Egypt | 1995/96 | (3)(4) | 850 051 | 15.9 | 19.2 | 41.2 | 14.6 | 7.4 | 1.7 |
| Ethiopia | 1996/97 | | 42 226 | 24.5 | 2.7 | 31.5 | 35.5 | 5.8 | - |
| Gabon | 1994/95 | (1) | 4 655 | 7.9 | 25.5 | 47.5 | - | 19.2 | - |
| Guinea | 1996/97 | | 8 151 | 3.6 | (5) 17.4 | (5) 21.7 | 41.9 | 14.4 | 1.0 |
| Lesotho | 1996/97 | | 4 614 | 33.9 | 6.5 | 46.4 | 13.2 | - | - |
| Madagascar | 1996/97 | | 26 715 | 2.5 | 11.0 | 54.3 | 20.0 | 12.2 | - |
| Mauritius | 1996/97 | | 7 098 | 43.2 | (5) 26.3 | (5) 9.3 | 16.6 | - | 4.6 |
| Morocco | 1994/95 | (6) | 250 919 | 0.1 | (5) 30.3 | (5) 37.1 | 28.8 | 3.0 | 0.7 |
| Mozambique | 1996/97 | | 7 143 | 18.3 | 7.9 | 21.3 | 46.1 | 6.4 | - |
| Namibia | 1995 | | 11 344 | 25.9 | 12.1 | 13.8 | 4.4 | 19.1 | 24.7 |
| Nigeria | 1993/94 | (2) | 207 982 | 14.9 | 10.9 | 22.4 | 41.2 | 10.6 | - |
| South Africa | 1994 | (7) | 468 086 | 20.7 | 12.4 | 44.1 | 17.7 | 4.0 | 0.9 |
| Swaziland | 1996/97 | | 5 658 | 20.8 | 8.5 | 35.2 | 21.7 | 6.6 | 7.2 |
| Togo | 1996/97 | | 13 124 | 1.3 | 41.1 | 38.6 | 11.2 | 6.7 | 1.1 |
| Tunisia | 1996/97 | | 121 787 | 1.9 | 23.6 | 31.9 | 26.9 | 8.4 | 7.3 |
| Uganda | 1996/97 | (8) | 34 773 | 34.7 | 6.3 | 36.2 | 14.8 | 2.0 | 5.8 |
| United Republic of Tanzania | 1995/96 | | 12 776 | 14.3 | <— | 41.4 | 39.3 | 3.2 | 1.7 |
| Zimbabwe | 1996 | (9) | 46 673 | 47.4 | 3.9 | 22.1 | 23.4 | 2.4 | 0.7 |

Tertiary education: students by broad field of study II.13
Enseignement supérieur: étudiants par grand domaine d'études
Enseñanza superior: estudiantes por gran sector de estudios

| Country<br><br>Pays<br><br>País | Year<br><br>Année<br><br>Año | Total enrolment<br><br>Effectifs totaux<br><br>Matrícula total | | Percentage of students by broad field of study<br>Pourcentage d'étudiants par grand domaine d'études<br>Porcentaje de estudiantes por gran sector de estudios | | | | | |
|---|---|---|---|---|---|---|---|---|---|
| | | | | Education<br><br>Education<br><br>Educación | Humanities<br><br>Lettres<br><br>Humanidades | Social<br>sciences<br>Sciences<br>sociales<br>Ciencias<br>sociales | Natural<br>sciences<br>Sciences<br>naturelles<br>Ciencias<br>naturales | Medical<br>sciences<br>Sciences<br>médicales<br>Ciencias<br>médicas | Others<br><br>Autres<br><br>Otros |
| **North America** | | | | | | | | | |
| Barbados | 1995/96 | (2) | 3 064 | 1.4 | 22.7 | 52.6 | 21.1 | 2.3 | - |
| Costa Rica | 1994 | (2) | 78 819 | 15.6 | 5.9 | 32.3 | 18.1 | 6.1 | 22.0 |
| Cuba | 1996/97 | | 111 587 | 34.2 | 2.3 | 8.5 | 20.9 | 26.3 | 7.8 |
| Dominican Republic | 1996/97 | | 176 995 | 13.1 | 4.2 | 48.4 | 24.6 | 9.7 | - |
| El Salvador | 1996 | | 112 266 | 0.2 | (10) 6.8 | 40.6 | (10) 19.9 | 12.6 | - |
| Honduras | 1994 | | 54 106 | 12.6 | 1.5 | 40.5 | 26.0 | 11.7 | 7.7 |
| Jamaica | 1995/96 | (2) | 8 191 | 6.6 | 19.3 | 44.5 | 19.5 | 10.0 | - |
| Mexico | 1996/97 | | 1 612 318 | 14.2 | 2.0 | 40.9 | 31.1 | 8.3 | 3.5 |
| Nicaragua | 1995 | | 50 769 | 11.6 | 1.8 | 43.0 | 31.3 | 11.1 | 1.2 |
| Panama | 1994 | (2) | 68 629 | 12.1 | 10.9 | 46.3 | 26.5 | 4.2 | 0.1 |
| Trinidad and Tobago | 1995/96 | (2) | 5 348 | 6.1 | 14.6 | 25.3 | 40.9 | 13.1 | - |
| **South America** | | | | | | | | | |
| Argentina | 1994 | (2) | 740 545 | 1.6 | 11.4 | 42.2 | 29.7 | 13.7 | 1.4 |
| Brazil | 1994 | (11) | 1 661 034 | 11.6 | 9.0 | 44.0 | 22.5 | 9.3 | 3.7 |
| Chile | 1997 | | 380 603 | 7.8 | (5) 6.4 | (5) 37.3 | 42.6 | 5.8 | - |
| Colombia | 1996 | | 644 188 | 13.7 | 3.4 | 43.2 | 30.6 | 9.1 | - |
| Guyana | 1996/97 | (2) | 3 701 | 9.1 | 4.8 | 49.9 | 24.6 | 9.2 | 2.5 |
| Paraguay | 1996 | (12) | 42 302 | 23.8 | 3.7 | 40.4 | 21.9 | 4.7 | 5.6 |
| Uruguay | 1996 | | 79 691 | 17.0 | 2.2 | 42.1 | 24.4 | 13.5 | 0.8 |
| **Asia** | | | | | | | | | |
| Armenia | 1995/96 | (13) | 35 903 | 24.6 | 12.3 | 16.8 | 33.0 | 10.5 | 2.8 |
| Brunei Darussalam | 1995/96 | (2) | 1 270 | 61.6 | 1.4 | 19.2 | 5.7 | - | 12.1 |
| Cambodia | 1996/97 | | 10 019 | 26.4 | 2.2 | 28.8 | 22.6 | 20.1 | - |
| China | 1994/95 | (2) | 2 926 935 | 16.4 | 6.4 | 9.4 | 53.2 | 8.9 | 5.6 |
| Cyprus (14) | 1996/97 | | 9 982 | 13.1 | 6.3 | 43.1 | 17.2 | 9.2 | 11.1 |
| Georgia | 1995/96 | | 155 033 | 11.2 | 14.1 | 16.4 | 48.1 | 10.2 | - |
| India | 1996/97 | | 6 060 418 | 3.9 | (5) 48.8 | (5) 20.7 | 24.6 | 2.0 | - |
| Indonesia | 1995/96 | | 2 303 469 | 17.2 | 6.4 | 46.3 | 28.2 | 1.9 | - |
| Iran, Islamic Republic of | 1995/96 | | 1 048 093 | 13.5 | 12.9 | 20.6 | 36.2 | 11.9 | 4.9 |
| Japan | 1994/95 | | 3 917 709 | 7.9 | (5) 18.1 | (5) 37.9 | 22.9 | 8.1 | 5.0 |
| Jordan (15) | 1996/97 | | 112 959 | 11.7 | 17.8 | 31.5 | 27.2 | 10.6 | 1.3 |
| Kazakstan | 1994/95 | | 482 690 | 16.4 | 12.2 | 15.0 | 41.6 | 9.6 | 5.2 |
| Korea, Republic of | 1996/97 | | 2 541 659 | 5.9 | 16.5 | 25.2 | 34.1 | 5.1 | 13.2 |
| Kuwait | 1995/96 | | 28 705 | 30.5 | 7.7 | 34.1 | 23.2 | 4.4 | - |
| Lebanon | 1995/96 | | 81 588 | 0.6 | 26.3 | 51.8 | 16.7 | 3.4 | 1.2 |
| Macau | 1996/97 | | 7 485 | 9.3 | 10.4 | 63.7 | 9.8 | - | 6.9 |
| Mongolia | 1996/97 | | 44 088 | 22.1 | 16.3 | 26.4 | 24.8 | 10.3 | 0.1 |
| Myanmar | 1994/95 | (16) | 245 317 | 0.3 | 41.5 | 21.5 | 36.6 | - | - |

II.13    Tertiary education: students by broad field of study
Enseignement supérieur: étudiants par grand domaine d'études
Enseñanza superior: estudiantes por gran sector de estudios

| Country<br>Pays<br>País | Year<br>Année<br>Año | Total enrolment<br>Effectifs totaux<br>Matrícula total | Percentage of students by broad field of study<br>Pourcentage d'étudiants par grand domaine d'études<br>Porcentaje de estudiantes por gran sector de estudios | | | | | |
|---|---|---|---|---|---|---|---|---|
| | | | Education<br>Education<br>Educación | Humanities<br>Lettres<br>Humanidades | Social sciences<br>Sciences sociales<br>Ciencias sociales | Natural sciences<br>Sciences naturelles<br>Ciencias naturales | Medical sciences<br>Sciences médicales<br>Ciencias médicas | Others<br>Autres<br>Otros |
| Nepal | 1996 | 105 694 | 10.4 | (5) 40.7 | (5) 33.6 | 14.2 | 1.1 | - |
| Oman | 1997/98 | 16 032 | 39.1 | 18.7 | 6.1 | 30.5 | 4.9 | 0.8 |
| Saudi Arabia | 1995/96 | 251 945 | 35.9 | 19.4 | 22.7 | 17.6 | 3.4 | 1.1 |
| Sri Lanka | 1995 | (17) 63 660 | 9.9 | 18.1 | 33.2 | 28.5 | 9.9 | 0.4 |
| Syrian Arab Republic | 1994/95 | (17) 196 753 | 2.4 | (5) 26.8 | (5) 28.2 | 31.0 | 11.5 | 0.1 |
| Tajikistan | 1994/95 | 108 203 | 38.3 | 1.5 | 4.9 | 23.4 | 13.8 | 18.2 |
| Thailand | 1995/96 | 1 220 481 | 8.7 | 3.5 | 59.7 | 20.9 | 5.9 | 1.3 |
| Turkey | 1994/95 | 1 174 299 | 9.6 | 4.9 | 52.7 | 22.3 | 9.7 | 0.7 |
| United Arab Emirates | 1996/97 | (2) 16 213 | 30.7 | 27.2 | 13.6 | 26.9 | 1.7 | - |
| Yemen | 1996/97 | 65 675 | 26.2 | 19.7 | 44.2 | 5.8 | 4.1 | - |
| Palestine | 1996/97 | 49 599 | 24.3 | 10.9 | 29.6 | 10.2 | 3.9 | 21.1 |
| **Europe** | | | | | | | | |
| Albania | 1996/97 | 34 257 | 12.4 | 21.0 | 36.2 | 22.2 | 7.3 | 0.9 |
| Austria | 1996/97 | (18) 293 172 | 6.5 | 15.0 | 40.9 | 28.3 | 8.1 | 1.2 |
| Belarus | 1996/97 | (1) 212 446 | 17.3 | 22.0 | 21.7 | 32.8 | 4.2 | 1.9 |
| Bulgaria | 1996/97 | 262 757 | 14.2 | 8.3 | 38.9 | 25.2 | 7.2 | 6.2 |
| Croatia | 1996/97 | (19) 85 752 | 10.3 | 8.2 | 32.3 | 37.9 | 7.0 | 4.4 |
| Czech Republic | 1996/97 | 207 221 | 16.5 | 8.0 | 26.1 | 34.0 | 9.8 | 5.6 |
| Denmark | 1995/96 | 174 975 | 17.5 | 17.7 | 23.8 | 21.0 | 11.3 | 8.7 |
| Estonia | 1996/97 | 43 468 | 8.1 | 11.9 | 36.0 | 32.0 | 7.2 | 4.8 |
| Federal Republic of Yugoslavia | 1996/97 | (19) 172 313 | 6.0 | 12.7 | 28.8 | 40.7 | 10.3 | 1.5 |
| Finland | 1996/97 | 226 458 | 9.1 | 13.5 | 23.8 | 37.0 | 16.2 | 0.4 |
| France | 1995/96 | 2 091 688 | 4.2 | 15.0 | 39.6 | 24.7 | 10.6 | 6.0 |
| Germany | 1996/97 | (19) 2 131 907 | 5.8 | 15.8 | 30.5 | 30.7 | 10.8 | 6.4 |
| Holy See | 1995/96 | (20) 14 403 | 6.7 | 83.4 | 9.9 | - | - | - |
| Hungary | 1994/95 | 170 147 | 20.7 | 11.6 | 25.9 | 32.0 | 7.2 | 2.7 |
| Iceland | 1996/97 | 7 908 | 17.6 | 19.2 | 27.0 | 20.0 | 16.3 | - |
| Ireland | 1996/97 | 134 566 | 2.8 | 17.7 | 27.0 | 30.1 | 5.1 | 17.4 |
| Italy | 1996/97 | 1 892 542 | 3.4 | 15.4 | 41.9 | 27.7 | 8.7 | 3.0 |
| Latvia | 1996/97 | 56 187 | 23.0 | 8.5 | 30.2 | 28.7 | 4.1 | 5.6 |
| Lithuania | 1996/97 | 83 645 | 17.3 | 8.9 | 24.8 | 37.8 | 8.8 | 2.4 |
| Malta | 1994/95 | 5 805 | 19.1 | 23.5 | 24.1 | 13.4 | 17.5 | 2.3 |
| Moldova | 1994/95 | 100 833 | 23.5 | 3.8 | 11.8 | 44.4 | 11.0 | 5.4 |
| Netherlands | 1996/97 | 468 970 | 12.0 | 8.3 | 47.9 | 20.3 | 10.0 | 1.5 |
| Norway | 1996/97 | 185 320 | 16.6 | 12.1 | 29.9 | 18.0 | 11.2 | 12.1 |
| Portugal | 1995/96 | 319 525 | 11.8 | 8.4 | 40.9 | 30.8 | 5.6 | 2.5 |
| Romania | 1996/97 | 411 687 | 1.4 | 9.4 | 40.4 | 31.5 | 14.4 | 3.0 |
| Russian Federation | 1994/95 | 4 458 363 | 10.2 | 7.3 | 22.3 | 48.5 | 8.5 | 3.3 |
| Slovakia | 1996/97 | 101 764 | 17.4 | 8.0 | 22.5 | 43.0 | 8.6 | 0.5 |
| Slovenia | 1996/97 | (11) 51 009 | 11.3 | 7.7 | 43.3 | 29.4 | 6.0 | 2.4 |

Tertiary education: students by broad field of study
Enseignement supérieur: étudiants par grand domaine d'études
Enseñanza superior: estudiantes por gran sector de estudios

II.13

| Country<br><br>Pays<br><br>País | Year<br><br>Année<br><br>Año | Total enrolment<br><br>Effectifs totaux<br><br>Matrícula total | Percentage of students by broad field of study<br>Pourcentage d'étudiants par grand domaine d'études<br>Porcentaje de estudiantes por gran sector de estudios | | | | | |
|---|---|---|---|---|---|---|---|---|
| | | | Education<br><br>Education<br><br>Educación | Humanities<br><br>Lettres<br><br>Humanidades | Social sciences<br><br>Sciences sociales<br><br>Ciencias sociales | Natural sciences<br><br>Sciences naturelles<br><br>Ciencias naturales | Medical sciences<br><br>Sciences médicales<br><br>Ciencias médicas | Others<br><br>Autres<br><br>Otros |
| Spain | 1996/97 | 1 684 445 | 8.0 | 9.9 | 42.2 | 30.5 | 7.1 | 2.3 |
| Sweden | 1996/97 | 275 217 | 14.1 | 15.6 | 25.9 | 30.6 | 13.2 | 0.5 |
| Switzerland | 1995/96 | 148 024 | 5.1 | 14.2 | 41.3 | 31.3 | 8.1 | 0.1 |
| The Former Yugoslav Rep. of Macedonia | 1996/97 | (19) 30 754 | 7.4 | 11.1 | 31.8 | 38.1 | 9.9 | 1.7 |
| United Kingdom | 1994/95 | 1 813 280 | 9.4 | 14.9 | 30.8 | 28.7 | 16.2 | - |
| **Oceania** | | | | | | | | |
| Australia | 1997 | 1 041 648 | 8.2 | 13.3 | 32.7 | 31.6 | 11.6 | 2.6 |
| New Zealand | 1997 | 169 656 | 12.7 | 21.1 | 32.7 | 20.8 | 7.6 | 5.1 |

**General note**
For general explanations and definitions, please refer to the beginning of this chapter.

**Note générale**
Pour les explications et définitions générales, prière de se référer au début de ce chapitre.

**Nota general**
Para las explicaciones y definiciones generales, referirse al comienzo de este capítulo.

Notes
(1) Universities and equivalent degree-granting institutions only.
(2) Universities only.
(3) Not including private tertiary institutions.
(4) Universities and degree-granting institutions only, excluding al Azhar.
(5) Humanities include part of Social sciences.
(6) Not including professional schools.
(7) Data are expressed in full-time equivalent.
(8) Not including private non-university institutions.
(9) Not including private colleges.
(10) Humanities include part of Natural sciences.
(11) Not including ISCED level 7.
(12) Not including private universities.
(13) Full-time only.
(14) Not including Turkish institutions.
(15) East Bank only.
(16) Not including medical science.
(17) Not including some non-university institutions.
(18) Including multiple counting of students enrolled in more than one field of study.
(19) Not including students at ISCED level 7 for which registration is not required.
(20) Data refer to institutions under the authority of the Holy See.

Notes
(1) Universités et établissements conférant des grades équivalents seulement.
(2) Universités seulement.
(3) Non compris les institutions supérieures privées.
(4) Universités et établissements conférant des titres équivalents seulement, à l'exception d'Al Azhar.
(5) Les Lettres incluent une partie des Sciences sociales
(6) Non compris les écoles professionnelles.
(7) Les données sont exprimées en équivalents plein temps.
(8) Non compris les institutions privées non universitaires.
(9) Non compris les collèges privés.
(10) Les Lettres incluent une partie des Sciences naturelles.
(11) Non compris le niveau 7 de la CITE.
(12) Non compris les universités privées.
(13) Plein temps seulement.
(14) Non compris les institutions turques.
(15) Rive orientale seulement.
(16) Non compris les science médicales.
(17) Non compris quelques institutions supérieures non universitaires.
(18) Y compris les doubles comptes dus aux étudiants inscrits dans plus d'un domaine d'études.
(19) Non compris les étudiants du niveau 7 de la CITE pour lequel l'inscription n'est pas exigée.
(20) Les données se réfèrent aux institutions sous l'autorité du Saint-Siège.

Notas
(1) Universidades y establecimientos que otorgan títulos equivalentes solamente.
(2) Universidades solamente.
(3) No incluyen las instituciones superiores privadas.
(4) Universidades y establecimientos que otorgan títulos equivalentes solamente, con excepción de Al Azhar.
(5) Las Humanidades incluyen parte de las Ciencias sociales.
(6) No incluyen las escuelas profesionales.
(7) Los datos están expresados en equivalente de jornada completa.
(8) No incluyen las instituciones no universitarias privadas.
(9) No incluyen los colegios privados.
(10) Las Humanidades incluyen parte de las Ciencias naturales.
(11) No incluye el nivel 7 de la CINE.
(12) No incluyen las universidades privadas.
(13) Jornada completa solamente.
(14) No incluyen las instituciones turcas.
(15) Orilla oriental solamente.
(16) No incluyen las ciencias médicas.
(17) No incluyen algunas instituciones de enseñanza superior no universitaria.
(18) Incluyen los estudiantes inscritos en diversos sectores de estudios.
(19) No incluyen los estudiantes del nivel 7 de la CINE para el cual la inscripción no es exigida.
(20) Los datos se refieren a las instituciones bajo la autoridad de la Santa Sede.

II.14   Tertiary education: female students in each broad field of study
Enseignement supérieur: étudiantes dans chaque grand domaine d'études
Enseñanza superior: mujeres en cada gran sector de estudios

## II.14   Tertiary education: percentage of female students in each broad field of study

### Enseignement supérieur: pourcentage d'étudiantes dans chaque grand domaine d'études

### Enseñanza superior: porcentaje de mujeres en cada gran sector de estudios

| Country / Pays / País | Year / Année / Año | | Female enrolment / Effectifs féminins / Matrícula femenina | Percentage of female students in each broad field of study / Pourcentage d'étudiantes dans chaque grand domaine d'études / Porcentaje de mujeres en cada gran sector de estudios | | | | | |
|---|---|---|---|---|---|---|---|---|---|
| | | | | Education / Education / Educación | Humanities / Lettres / Humanidades | Social sciences / Sciences sociales / Ciencias sociales | Natural sciences / Sciences naturelles / Ciencias naturales | Medical sciences / Sciences médicales / Ciencias médicas | Others / Autres / Otros |
| **Africa** | | | | | | | | | |
| Algeria | 1995/96 | (1) | 118 368 | 25.8 | 65.4 | 46.7 | 36.3 | 49.9 | 54.9 |
| Benin | 1996 | | 2 657 | 20.6 | <— | 19.9 | 12.6 | 24.3 | 13.2 |
| Botswana | 1996/97 | (2) | 3 449 | 49.1 | 55.6 | 59.9 | 23.9 | 90.8 | 24.9 |
| Burkina Faso | 1994/95 | | 2 087 | 13.6 | 32.0 | 22.4 | 7.7 | 23.8 | . |
| Chad | 1995/96 | (1) | 397 | 4.9 | 14.8 | 12.9 | 5.6 | - | . |
| Djibouti | 1995/96 | | 61 | 61.1 | . | 41.5 | . | . | . |
| Egypt | 1995/96 | (3)(4) | 352 902 | 53.9 | 53.4 | 35.8 | 29.4 | 43.1 | 27.0 |
| Ethiopia | 1996/97 | | 8 524 | 22.7 | 34.6 | 26.7 | 12.1 | 17.1 | . |
| Gabon | 1994/95 | (1) | 1 785 | 22.3 | 32.6 | 35.9 | . | 58.5 | . |
| Guinea | 1996/97 | | 879 | 9.2 | (5)  14.1 | (5)  13.0 | 6.5 | 17.0 | - |
| Lesotho | 1996/97 | | 2 509 | 70.9 | 64.6 | 47.5 | 31.3 | . | . |
| Madagascar | 1996/97 | | 12 004 | 35.8 | 65.5 | 46.2 | 29.9 | 47.2 | . |
| Morocco | 1994/95 | (6) | 102 720 | 30.6 | (5)  51.2 | (5)  41.7 | 28.4 | 49.3 | 34.1 |
| Mozambique | 1996/97 | | 1 747 | 30.2 | 27.4 | 18.5 | 20.0 | 56.1 | . |
| Namibia | 1995 | | 6 904 | 57.7 | 51.5 | 42.5 | 35.2 | 83.3 | 66.2 |
| South Africa | 1994 | (7) | 230 600 | 63.7 | 60.9 | 46.0 | 29.4 | 61.2 | 54.6 |
| Swaziland | 1996/97 | | 2 927 | 55.3 | 56.8 | 59.5 | 12.3 | 84.9 | 85.8 |
| Togo | 1996/97 | | 2 267 | 27.9 | 20.0 | 16.5 | 6.6 | 21.2 | 16.1 |
| Tunisia | 1996/97 | | 54 278 | 41.9 | 61.0 | 43.7 | 32.4 | 55.0 | 28.5 |
| Uganda | 1996/97 | (8) | 11 542 | 29.1 | 38.3 | 40.4 | 16.7 | 31.0 | 50.2 |
| United Republic of Tanzania | 1995/96 | | 2 075 | 18.1 | <— | 19.9 | 9.1 | 28.3 | 53.7 |
| Zimbabwe | 1996 | (9) | 17 016 | 46.0 | 28.1 | 41.5 | 14.0 | 38.5 | 20.7 |

Tertiary education: female students in each broad field of study
Enseignement supérieur: étudiantes dans chaque grand domaine d'études
Enseñanza superior: mujeres en cada gran sector de estudios

II.14

| Country / Pays / País | Year / Année / Año | | Female enrolment / Effectifs féminins / Matrícula femenina | Percentage of female students in each broad field of study / Pourcentage d'étudiantes dans chaque grand domaine d'études / Porcentaje de mujeres en cada gran sector de estudios | | | | | |
|---|---|---|---|---|---|---|---|---|---|
| | | | | Education / Education / Educación | Humanities / Lettres / Humanidades | Social sciences / Sciences sociales / Ciencias sociales | Natural sciences / Sciences naturelles / Ciencias naturales | Medical sciences / Sciences médicales / Ciencias médicas | Others / Autres / Otros |
| **North America** | | | | | | | | | |
| Barbados | 1995/96 | (2) | 1 903 | 58.1 | 75.5 | 63.5 | 46.2 | 44.9 | . |
| Cuba | 1996/97 | | 67 134 | 76.0 | 62.8 | 61.6 | 29.8 | 72.3 | 28.9 |
| El Salvador | 1996 | | 56 336 | 60.8 (10) | 61.4 | 48.8 (10) | 28.7 | 65.3 | . |
| Honduras | 1994 | | 23 731 | 68.2 | 47.1 | 42.8 | 25.9 | 57.6 | 48.3 |
| Jamaica | 1995/96 | (2) | 5 449 | 83.3 | 80.3 | 67.8 | 50.3 | 54.9 | |
| Mexico | 1996/97 | | 769 394 | 63.6 | 57.6 | 54.1 | 28.4 | 58.0 | 50.7 |
| Nicaragua | 1995 | | 26 066 | 68.4 | 56.3 | 54.9 | 34.7 | 64.2 | 65.7 |
| Panama | 1994 | (2) | 40 883 | 76.8 | 65.3 | 65.9 | 35.9 | 74.5 | 77.5 |
| Trinidad and Tobago | 1995/96 | (2) | 2 882 | 73.0 | 75.5 | 65.9 | 38.2 | 46.9 | |
| **South America** | | | | | | | | | |
| Brazil | 1994 | (11) | 907 677 | 81.2 | 72.8 | 51.3 | 34.0 | 66.1 | 64.7 |
| Chile | 1997 | | 175 242 | 78.4 (5) | 70.8 (5) | 51.1 | 29.1 | 66.7 | |
| Colombia | 1996 | | 334 204 | 67.1 | 53.0 | 56.2 | 33.5 | 69.8 | . |
| Guyana | 1996/97 | (2) | 2 154 | 78.3 | 68.2 | 67.9 | 27.4 | 61.4 | 64.8 |
| Paraguay | 1996 | (12) | 23 070 | 68.4 | 52.9 | 50.8 | 47.0 | 61.7 | 47.1 |
| **Asia** | | | | | | | | | |
| Armenia | 1995/96 | (13) | 19 875 | 79.8 | 77.0 | 40.9 | 36.7 | 65.7 | 13.2 |
| Brunei Darussalam | 1995/96 | (2) | 753 | 73.9 | 55.6 | 52.9 | 36.1 | . | 6.5 |
| Cambodia | 1996/97 | | 1 591 | 20.8 | 24.4 | 12.4 | 11.0 | 19.0 | . |
| Cyprus (14) | 1996/97 | | 5 559 | 92.2 | 76.3 | 57.4 | 27.4 | 73.9 | 23.0 |
| Georgia | 1995/96 | | 81 558 | 74.4 | 76.7 | 46.8 | 39.6 | 66.0 | |
| India | 1996/97 | | 2 198 559 | 46.1 (5) | 41.4 (5) | 29.3 | 30.4 | 35.4 | . |
| Indonesia | 1995/96 | | 803 577 | 43.7 | 42.1 | 36.8 | 23.8 | 48.5 | . |
| Iran, Islamic Republic of | 1995/96 | | 384 461 | 48.9 | 58.3 | 30.9 | 21.2 | 57.9 | 33.2 |
| Japan | 1994/95 | | 1 725 199 | 71.4 (5) | 71.3 (5) | 38.9 | 13.0 | 65.5 | 48.2 |
| Jordan (15) | 1996/97 | | 52 934 | 64.8 | 63.7 | 37.5 | 35.5 | 54.1 | 60.5 |
| Kazakstan | 1994/95 | (11) | 265 341 | 68.4 | 74.8 | 44.2 | 39.2 | 77.0 | 82.5 |
| Korea, Republic of | 1996/97 | | 940 175 | 73.1 | 57.8 | 40.9 | 17.1 | 56.4 | 31.2 |
| Kuwait | 1995/96 | | 17 691 | 73.9 | 70.2 | 60.2 | 42.7 | 72.4 | |
| Lebanon | 1995/96 | | 40 160 | 38.1 | 53.6 | 50.5 | 36.9 | 52.5 | 68.4 |
| Macau | 1996/97 | | 3 674 | 71.9 | 61.5 | 49.7 | 15.1 | . | 42.4 |
| Mongolia | 1996/97 | | 30 512 | 78.0 | 74.6 | 66.2 | 53.6 | 87.4 | 8.0 |
| Myanmar | 1994/95 | (16) | 150 821 | 68.6 | 63.6 | 58.7 | 60.6 | . | |
| Oman | 1997/98 | | 7 138 | 42.3 | 65.8 | 42.8 | 32.5 | 57.5 | 50.8 |
| Saudi Arabia | 1995/96 | | 121 366 | 62.4 | 37.0 | 42.5 | 43.8 | 36.8 | - |
| Sri Lanka | 1995 | (17) | 28 008 | 60.4 | 56.9 | 43.1 | 31.4 | 45.4 | - |
| Syrian Arab Republic | 1994/95 | (17) | 76 245 | 53.0 (5) | 56.9 (5) | 30.2 | 31.0 | 35.4 | 59.2 |
| Tajikistan | 1994/95 | | 35 325 | 38.8 | 20.9 | 20.9 | 12.6 | 67.2 | 23.2 |

Tertiary education: female students in each broad field of study
Enseignement supérieur: étudiantes dans chaque grand domaine d'études
Enseñanza superior: mujeres en cada gran sector de estudios

| Country / Pays / País | Year / Année / Año | | Female enrolment / Effectifs féminins / Matrícula femenina | Percentage of female students in each broad field of study / Pourcentage d'étudiantes dans chaque grand domaine d'études / Porcentaje de mujeres en cada gran sector de estudios | | | | | |
|---|---|---|---|---|---|---|---|---|---|
| | | | | Education / Education / Educación | Humanities / Lettres / Humanidades | Social sciences / Sciences sociales / Ciencias sociales | Natural sciences / Sciences naturelles / Ciencias naturales | Medical sciences / Sciences médicales / Ciencias médicas | Others / Autres / Otros |
| Turkey | 1994/95 | | 449 771 | 41.5 | 47.3 | 36.7 | 28.7 | 63.9 | 3.3 |
| United Arab Emirates | 1996/97 | (2) | 11 694 | 95.1 | 84.0 | 56.1 | 42.3 | 67.4 | |
| Yemen | 1996/97 | | 8 224 | 22.6 | 19.7 | 3.6 | 16.7 | 4.6 | . |
| Palestine | 1996/97 | | 22 030 | 57.0 | 56.8 | 31.3 | 31.7 | 54.1 | 46.3 |
| **Europe** | | | | | | | | | |
| Albania | 1996/97 | | 19 377 | 81.6 | 70.1 | 46.9 | 44.7 | 63.2 | 24.4 |
| Austria | 1996/97 | (18) | 136 501 | 75.1 | 63.2 | 48.6 | 25.6 | 60.2 | 16.1 |
| Bulgaria | 1996/97 | | 161 049 | 80.3 | 72.0 | 65.7 | 45.7 | 70.4 | 28.7 |
| Croatia | 1996/97 | (19) | 43 563 | 81.3 | 69.8 | 63.2 | 26.8 | 68.5 | 32.0 |
| Czech Republic | 1996/97 | | 100 315 | 70.2 | 57.7 | 53.8 | 24.8 | 67.9 | 55.0 |
| Denmark | 1995/96 | | 94 452 | 75.0 | 67.7 | 42.7 | 29.3 | 81.2 | 38.7 |
| Estonia | 1996/97 | | 23 233 | 85.2 | 70.2 | 60.2 | 26.2 | 84.0 | 43.6 |
| Federal Republic of Yugoslavia | 1996/97 | (19) | 92 697 | 71.4 | 76.3 | 60.2 | 37.0 | 68.3 | 26.0 |
| Finland | 1996/97 | | 119 653 | 76.4 | 70.2 | 58.6 | 23.8 | 83.4 | 38.2 |
| France | 1995/96 | | 1 147 202 | 72.8 | 75.2 | 60.4 | 30.9 | 62.9 | 39.0 |
| Germany | 1996/97 | (19) | 975 448 | 71.3 | 61.4 | 44.1 | 22.9 | 64.5 | 70.1 |
| Holy See | 1995/96 | (20) | 3 580 | 68.6 | 21.1 | 26.8 | . | . | . |
| Hungary | 1994/95 | | 88 379 | 79.5 | 65.2 | 50.8 | 27.6 | 60.3 | 60.5 |
| Iceland | 1996/97 | | 4 626 | 82.3 | 64.6 | 52.2 | 27.4 | 74.2 | . |
| Ireland | 1996/97 | | 69 482 | 69.4 | 66.6 | 57.1 | 33.9 | 63.6 | 52.3 |
| Italy | 1996/97 | | 1 021 815 | 88.9 | 77.5 | 54.5 | 34.5 | 56.6 | 59.1 |
| Latvia | 1996/97 | | 33 454 | 82.2 | 75.9 | 62.7 | 36.4 | 71.0 | 34.7 |
| Lithuania | 1996/97 | | 49 566 | 82.0 | 74.7 | 64.5 | 37.9 | 77.1 | 55.0 |
| Malta | 1994/95 | | 2 794 | 64.0 | 51.7 | 44.1 | 20.8 | 55.7 | 25.2 |
| Moldova | 1994/95 | (11) | 53 662 | 80.5 | 48.4 | 49.6 | 36.8 | 77.0 | 32.4 |
| Netherlands | 1996/97 | | 226 016 | 66.5 | 60.0 | 50.0 | 18.7 | 69.6 | 35.0 |
| Norway | 1996/97 | | 104 224 | 75.0 | 63.2 | 52.8 | 28.9 | 78.8 | 51.7 |
| Portugal | 1995/96 | | 180 506 | 79.1 | 70.2 | 59.6 | 37.3 | 72.0 | 54.7 |
| Romania | 1996/97 | | 217 605 | 87.7 | 65.3 | 58.0 | 33.6 | 73.7 | 31.5 |
| Russian Federation | 1994/95 | (11) | 2 463 912 | 87.5 | 75.3 | 72.3 | 34.3 | 78.5 | 46.1 |
| Slovakia | 1996/97 | | 51 100 | 74.3 | 57.0 | 55.4 | 32.9 | 69.0 | 31.2 |
| Slovenia | 1996/97 | (11) | 28 736 | 79.5 | 70.9 | 63.0 | 30.3 | 75.6 | 50.4 |
| Spain | 1996/97 | | 890 357 | 74.7 | 64.1 | 57.4 | 32.9 | 70.2 | 56.0 |
| Sweden | 1996/97 | | 153 600 | 75.4 | 64.7 | 57.9 | 31.0 | 76.9 | 76.5 |
| Switzerland | 1995/96 | | 55 746 | 70.0 | 57.1 | 40.2 | 15.8 | 54.9 | 20.3 |
| The Former Yugoslav Rep. of Macedonia | 1996/97 | (19) | 16 738 | 85.6 | 71.2 | 60.3 | 35.9 | 70.0 | 23.0 |
| United Kingdom | 1994/95 | | 923 878 | 71.1 | 60.5 | 50.2 | 25.3 | 77.4 | . |

Tertiary education: female students in each broad field of study **II.14**
Enseignement supérieur: étudiantes dans chaque grand domaine d'études
Enseñanza superior: mujeres en cada gran sector de estudios

| Country / Pays / País | Year / Année / Año | Female enrolment / Effectifs féminins / Matrícula femenina | Percentage of female students in each broad field of study / Pourcentage d'étudiantes dans chaque grand domaine d'études / Porcentaje de mujeres en cada gran sector de estudios | | | | | |
|---|---|---|---|---|---|---|---|---|
| | | | Education / Education / Educación | Humanities / Lettres / Humanidades | Social sciences / Sciences sociales / Ciencias sociales | Natural sciences / Sciences naturelles / Ciencias naturales | Medical sciences / Sciences médicales / Ciencias médicas | Others / Autres / Otros |
| **Oceania** | | | | | | | | |
| Australia | 1997 | 529 335 | 70.7 | 66.6 | 52.4 | 28.2 | 73.8 | 60.1 |
| New Zealand | 1997 | 97 223 | 82.1 | 62.0 | 56.2 | 33.0 | 78.2 | 51.4 |

## General note

For general explanations and definitions, please refer to the beginning of this chapter.

## Note générale

Pour les explications et définitions générales, prière de se référer au début de ce chapitre.

## Nota general

Para las explicaciones y definiciones generales, referirse al comienzo de este capítulo.

Notes

(1) Universities and equivalent degree-granting institutions only.
(2) Universities only.
(3) Not including private tertiary institutions.
(4) Universities and degree-granting institutions only, excluding al Azhar.
(5) Humanities include part of Social sciences.
(6) Not including professional schools.
(7) Data are expressed in full-time equivalent.
(8) Not including private non-university institutions.
(9) Not including private colleges.
(10) Humanities include part of Natural sciences.
(11) Not including ISCED level 7.
(12) Not including private universities.
(13) Full-time only.
(14) Not including Turkish institutions.
(15) East Bank only.
(16) Not including medical science.
(17) Not including some non-university institutions.
(18) Including multiple counting of students enrolled in more than one field of study.
(19) Not including students at ISCED level 7 for which registration is not required.
(20) Data refer to institutions under the authority of the Holy See.

Notes

(1) Universités et établissements conférant des grades équivalents seulement.
(2) Universités seulement.
(3) Non compris les institutions supérieures privées.
(4) Universités et établissements conférant des titres équivalents seulement, à l'exception d'Al Azhar.
(5) Les Lettres incluent une partie des Sciences sociales
(6) Non compris les écoles professionnelles.
(7) Les données sont exprimées en équivalents plein temps.
(8) Non compris les institutions privées non universitaires.
(9) Non compris les collèges privés.
(10) Les Lettres incluent une partie des Sciences naturelles.
(11) Non compris le niveau 7 de la CITE.
(12) Non compris les universités privées.
(13) Plein temps seulement.
(14) Non compris les institutions turques.
(15) Rive orientale seulement.
(16) Non compris les science médicales.
(17) Non compris quelques institutions supérieures non universitaires.
(18) Y compris les doubles comptes dus aux étudiants inscrits dans plus d'un domaine d'études.
(19) Non compris les étudiants du niveau 7 de la CITE pour lequel l'inscription n'est pas exigée.
(20) Les données se réfèrent aux institutions sous l'autorité du Saint-Siège.

Notas

(1) Universidades y establecimientos que otorgan títulos equivalentes solamente.
(2) Universidades solamente.
(3) No incluyen las instituciones superiores privadas.
(4) Universidades y establecimientos que otorgan títulos equivalentes solamente, con excepción de Al Azhar.
(5) Las Humanidades incluyen parte de las Ciencias sociales
(6) No incluyen las escuelas profesionales.
(7) Los datos están expresados en equivalente de jornada completa.
(8) No incluyen las instituciones no universitarias privadas.
(9) No incluyen los colegios privados.
(10) Las Humanidades incluyen parte de las Ciencias naturales.
(11) No incluye el nivel 7 de la CINE.
(12) No incluyen las universidades privadas.
(13) Jornada completa solamente.
(14) No incluyen las instituciones turcas.
(15) Orilla oriental solamente.
(16) No incluyen las ciencias médicas.
(17) No incluyen algunas instituciones de enseñanza superior no universitaria.
(18) Incluyen los estudiantes inscritos en diversos sectores de estudios.
(19) No incluyen los estudiantes del nivel 7 de la CINE para el cual la inscripción no es exigida.
(20) Los datos se refieren a las instituciones bajo la autoridad de la Santa Sede.

II.15    Tertiary education: graduates (total and female) by ISCED level
Enseignement supérieur: diplômés (total et femmes) par niveau de la CITE
Enseñanza superior: diplomados (total y mujeres) por nivel de la CINE

## II.15    Tertiary education: distribution of graduates by ISCED level and percentage female in each level

Enseignement supérieur: répartition des diplômés par niveau de la CITE et pourcentage de femmes dans chaque niveau

Enseñanza superior: distribución de los diplomados por nivel de la CINE y porcentaje de mujeres en cada nivel

| Country<br><br>Pays<br><br>País | Year<br><br>Année<br><br>Año | Total graduates<br><br>Total des diplômés<br><br>Total de diplomados | Percentage of graduates by ISCED level<br><br>Pourcentage de diplômés par niveau de la CITE<br><br>Porcentaje de diplomados por nivel de la CINE | | | Female graduates<br><br>Femmes diplômées<br><br>Mujeres diplomadas | Percentage female in each level<br><br>Pourcentage de femmes dans chaque niveau<br><br>Porcentaje de mujeres en cada nivel | | |
|---|---|---|---|---|---|---|---|---|---|
| | | | ISCED 5<br>CITE 5<br>CINE 5 | ISCED 6<br>CITE 6<br>CINE 6 | ISCED 7<br>CITE 7<br>CINE 7 | | ISCED 5<br>CITE 5<br>CINE 5 | ISCED 6<br>CITE 6<br>CINE 6 | ISCED 7<br>CITE 7<br>CINE 7 |
| **Africa** | | | | | | | | | |
| Algeria | 1995 | (1) 32 557 | 23.1 | 76.9 | —> | (1) 15 974 | 40.5 | 51.6 | —> |
| Botswana | 1997 | (2) 1 971 | 54.4 | 40.4 | 5.1 | (2) 888 | 41.1 | 50.2 | 46.5 |
| Egypt | 1995 | (3)(4) 107 512 | - | 79.6 | 20.4 | (3)(4) 43 829 | . | 41.4 | 38.2 |
| Eritrea | 1998 | 559 | 32.9 | 67.1 | - | 55 | 10.3 | 9.6 | . |
| Ethiopia | 1997 | 7 448 | 63.9 | 32.8 | 3.3 | 1 348 | 20.5 | 14.5 | 7.3 |
| Lesotho | 1996 | 1 930 | 78.2 | 21.1 | 0.7 | ... | ... | ... | ... |
| Malawi | 1994 | 3 815 | 80.8 | 18.7 | 0.4 | 1 352 | 39.3 | 18.3 | 52.9 |
| Mauritania | 1994 | 733 | 6.1 | 93.9 | - | ... | 2.2 | ... | . |
| Morocco | 1994 | (1) 24 501 | 1.7 | 96.1 | 2.2 | (1) 9 592 | 32.8 | 39.6 | 26.4 |
| Mozambique | 1994 | 249 | 15.7 | 84.3 | - | 81 | 28.2 | 33.3 | . |
| South Africa | 1994 | 147 391 | 62.6 | 22.1 | 15.3 | 79 358 | 54.9 | 53.9 | 49.5 |
| Swaziland | 1995 | (5) 988 | 60.1 | 34.3 | 5.6 | (5) 361 | 29.3 | 48.1 | 43.6 |
| Togo | 1995 | (6) 5 254 | 39.7 | 60.3 | - | (6) 789 | 17.4 | 13.4 | . |
| Tunisia | 1994 | 11 654 | 29.1 | 61.5 | 9.4 | 4 984 | 48.2 | 41.2 | 36.3 |
| Uganda | 1996 | (7) 9 959 | 68.3 | 26.0 | 5.7 | (7) 3 094 | 30.3 | 34.2 | 26.1 |
| United Republic of Tanzania | 1996 | 2 413 | 58.7 | 37.2 | 4.1 | 425 | 15.8 | 21.0 | 13.0 |
| **North America** | | | | | | | | | |
| Canada | 1996 | 383 946 | 60.3 | 33.2 | 6.5 | 197 405 | 48.2 | 57.9 | 47.6 |
| Cuba | 1996 | 27 502 | - | 100.0 | - | 15 566 | . | 56.6 | . |
| Dominican Republic | 1997 | 19 276 | 10.9 | 87.1 | 2.0 | ... | ... | ... | ... |
| Mexico | 1997 | 238 553 | <— | 91.2 | 8.8 | 119 834 | <— | 51.2 | 40.3 |
| Nicaragua | 1997 | 6 915 | 6.9 | 90.8 | 2.3 | 4 160 | 53.6 | 61.0 | 45.2 |
| Panama | 1994 | (2) 5 744 | 15.1 | 81.5 | 3.4 | (2) 3 730 | 38.5 | 69.7 | 68.5 |
| United States | 1995 | 2 454 932 | 31.6 | 47.3 | 21.1 | 1 354 800 | 58.3 | 54.6 | 51.7 |

Tertiary education: graduates (total and female) by ISCED level
Enseignement supérieur: diplômés (total et femmes) par niveau de la CITE
Enseñanza superior: diplomados (total y mujeres) por nivel de la CINE

II.15

| Country / Pays / País | Year / Année / Año | Total graduates / Total des diplômés / Total de diplomados | Percentage of graduates by ISCED level / Pourcentage de diplômés par niveau de la CITE / Porcentaje de diplomados por nivel de la CINE | | | Female graduates / Femmes diplômées / Mujeres diplomadas | Percentage female in each level / Pourcentage de femmes dans chaque niveau / Porcentaje de mujeres en cada nivel | | |
|---|---|---|---|---|---|---|---|---|---|
| | | | ISCED 5 CITE 5 CINE 5 | ISCED 6 CITE 6 CINE 6 | ISCED 7 CITE 7 CINE 7 | | ISCED 5 CITE 5 CINE 5 | ISCED 6 CITE 6 CINE 6 | ISCED 7 CITE 7 CINE 7 |
| **South America** | | | | | | | | | |
| Chile | 1997 | 41 458 | 39.9 | 55.5 | 4.6 | 21 927 | 54.7 | 52.7 | 39.4 |
| Colombia | 1996 | 92 219 | 25.6 | 58.8 | 15.6 | 51 454 | 54.3 | 56.3 | 56.4 |
| Guyana | 1995 | 1 554 | 76.0 | 21.4 | 2.6 | 838 | 54.7 | 50.0 | 63.4 |
| Uruguay | 1996 | 5 930 | 39.8 | 60.2 | —> | ... | ... | ... | ... |
| **Asia** | | | | | | | | | |
| Azerbaijan | 1996 | 27 249 | 30.2 | 68.7 | 1.1 | ... | ... | ... | ... |
| China | 1994 | 1 040 135 | 63.9 | 33.4 | 2.7 | ... | ... | ... | ... |
| China, Hong Kong SAR | 1994 | 23 515 | 36.5 | 48.3 | 15.2 | 9 989 | 41.6 | 45.4 | 35.6 |
| Cyprus (8) | 1996 | 2 482 | 96.4 | - | 3.6 | 1 491 | 61.1 | . | 31.5 |
| Georgia | 1997 | 28 431 | 25.9 | 72.5 | 1.6 | ... | 48.6 | 53.2 | ... |
| Indonesia | 1997 (9) | 200 583 | 28.1 | 71.9 | —> | (9) 94 151 | 57.5 | 42.8 | —> |
| Iran, Islamic Republic of | 1997 (10) | 83 385 | 25.9 | 59.1 | 15.0 | (10) 26 938 | 28.9 | 35.2 | 26.6 |
| Japan | 1996 | 1 127 500 | 48.9 | 46.1 | 5.0 | 568 212 | 69.2 | 33.8 | 19.8 |
| Jordan (11) | 1996 | 22 395 | 38.5 | 56.4 | 5.1 | 11 921 | 68.1 | 45.3 | 29.0 |
| Kazakstan | 1995 | 106 008 | 56.7 | 43.0 | 0.3 | ... | ... | ... | ... |
| Korea, Republic of | 1997 | 380 571 | 41.1 | 50.1 | 8.8 | 174 328 | 54.1 | 42.2 | 27.8 |
| Lao People's Democratic Republic | 1996 | 2 817 | 67.1 | 32.9 | ... | 808 | 29.1 | 27.8 | ... |
| Lebanon | 1995 | 9 653 | 3.4 | 96.6 | —> | 4 234 | 46.2 | 43.8 | —> |
| Macau | 1997 | 1 656 | 28.1 | 57.7 | 14.2 | 954 | 62.2 | 56.3 | 54.0 |
| Mongolia | 1997 | 7 394 | 21.8 | 73.2 | 5.0 | 5 318 | 86.5 | 68.5 | 57.9 |
| Myanmar | 1995 (5) | 35 898 | <— | 98.6 | 1.4 | (5) 22 296 | <— | 62.2 | 58.7 |
| Philippines | 1996 (2) | 286 545 | <— | 96.8 | 3.2 | (2) 179 785 | <— | 62.3 | 74.5 |
| Qatar | 1997 | 1 360 | 5.2 | 88.8 | 6.0 | 957 | 56.3 | 70.9 | 74.4 |
| Saudi Arabia | 1996 | 37 901 | 27.5 | 70.3 | 2.3 | 18 863 | 33.2 | 57.0 | 26.1 |
| Sri Lanka | 1994 | 7 995 | 21.1 | 72.6 | 6.3 | 3 515 | 53.9 | 42.6 | 26.3 |
| Syrian Arab Republic | 1995 (13) | 24 202 | 26.8 | 68.6 | 4.6 | (13) 10 477 | 46.8 | 41.6 | 47.6 |
| Tajikistan | 1995 (1) | 10 198 | ... | 100.0 | —> | (1) 3 218 | ... | 31.6 | —> |
| Thailand | 1995 (1) | 130 223 | 1.5 | 91.6 | 6.9 | ... | ... | ... | ... |
| Turkey | 1994 | 124 861 | 29.2 | 64.4 | 6.4 | 51 256 | 51.0 | 36.7 | 38.7 |
| United Arab Emirates | 1997 (2) | 1 638 | - | 98.4 | 1.6 | (2) 1 329 | . | 82.1 | 25.9 |
| Palestine | 1995 (12) | 4 510 | 33.7 | 66.3 | ... | (12) 2 296 | 57.6 | 47.5 | ... |
| **Europe** | | | | | | | | | |
| Albania | 1994 | 3 963 | - | 100.0 | - | 2 106 | . | 53.1 | . |
| Austria | 1997 | 21 357 | 24.9 | 65.0 | 10.0 | 11 106 | 75.2 | 45.9 | 33.9 |
| Belarus | 1996 | 68 663 | 51.3 | 47.8 | 1.0 | ... | ... | ... | ... |
| Bulgaria | 1997 | 36 463 | 22.0 | 77.3 | 0.8 | 23 538 | 79.0 | 60.7 | 35.0 |
| Croatia | 1996 | 12 467 | 30.7 | 61.6 | 7.7 | 6 500 | 48.9 | 55.0 | 42.4 |
| Czech Republic | 1997 | 30 640 | 22.2 | 76.2 | 1.6 | 16 604 | 71.5 | 49.7 | 28.3 |
| Denmark | 1995 | 30 243 | 20.1 | 72.8 | 7.1 | 15 308 | 37.3 | 55.4 | 39.1 |

**II.15**  Tertiary education: graduates (total and female) by ISCED level
Enseignement supérieur: diplômés (total et femmes) par niveau de la CITE
Enseñanza superior: diplomados (total y mujeres) por nivel de la CINE

| Country / Pays / País | Year / Année / Año | Total graduates / Total des diplômés / Total de diplomados | Percentage of graduates by ISCED level / Pourcentage de diplômés par niveau de la CITE / Porcentaje de diplomados por nivel de la CINE | | | Female graduates / Femmes diplômées / Mujeres diplomadas | Percentage female in each level / Pourcentage de femmes dans chaque niveau / Porcentaje de mujeres en cada nivel | | |
|---|---|---|---|---|---|---|---|---|---|
| | | | ISCED 5 / CITE 5 / CINE 5 | ISCED 6 / CITE 6 / CINE 6 | ISCED 7 / CITE 7 / CINE 7 | | ISCED 5 / CITE 5 / CINE 5 | ISCED 6 / CITE 6 / CINE 6 | ISCED 7 / CITE 7 / CINE 7 |
| Estonia | 1996 | 6 236 | 47.1 | 45.8 | 7.2 | 3 829 | 62.3 | 60.7 | 59.6 |
| Federal Republic of Yugoslavia | 1997 | 19 050 | 29.4 | 62.2 | 8.4 | 10 484 | 59.1 | 54.8 | 42.8 |
| Finland | 1996 | 28 625 | 36.3 | 58.7 | 5.0 | 16 645 | 65.3 | 54.6 | 47.6 |
| Germany | 1996 | 336 473 | 29.6 | 63.6 | 6.8 | 153 710 | 57.5 | 41.7 | 31.1 |
| Greece | 1996 | 29 268 | 27.5 | 68.6 | 3.8 | 15 985 | 53.6 | 56.0 | 37.3 |
| Holy See | 1996 (14) | 3 047 | 17.0 | 45.4 | 37.6 | (14) 544 | 35.6 | 15.5 | 12.6 |
| Iceland | 1996 | 1 624 | 35.3 | 62.0 | 2.7 | 948 | 51.7 | 62.6 | 50.0 |
| Ireland | 1997 | 35 380 | 37.5 | 51.7 | 10.8 | 18 259 | 48.0 | 55.0 | 47.7 |
| Italy | 1996 | 175 489 | 18.0 | 75.6 | 6.4 | 97 996 | 64.5 | 54.5 | 47.3 |
| Latvia | 1997 | 8 188 | - | 83.0 | 17.0 | ... | ... | ... | ... |
| Lithuania | 1997 | 17 704 | 30.6 | 49.5 | 19.9 | 10 191 | 70.2 | 54.9 | 44.8 |
| Malta | 1995 | 1 332 | 14.6 | 68.7 | 16.7 | 671 | 55.2 | 51.4 | 42.2 |
| Moldova | 1997 | 11 810 | 39.2 | 59.1 | 1.7 | ... | ... | ... | ... |
| Netherlands | 1994 | 77 951 | <— | 62.0 | 38.0 | 37 748 | <— | 51.1 | 44.0 |
| Norway | 1997 | 52 990 | 56.8 | 29.6 | 13.6 | 30 370 | 56.6 | 64.2 | 45.3 |
| Poland | 1994 | 134 367 | 30.6 | 44.8 | 24.6 | 83 097 | 79.4 | 51.7 | 58.4 |
| Portugal | 1996 | 39 116 | 27.4 | 66.6 | 6.0 | 25 103 | 67.6 | 63.8 | 53.3 |
| Romania | 1996 | 70 841 | 19.0 | 81.0 | —> | 37 956 | 62.9 | 51.4 | —> |
| Russian Federation | 1995 | 950 488 | 55.9 | 42.8 | 1.3 | (12) 560 224 | 65.0 | 52.8 | ... |
| Slovakia | 1997 | 12 799 | 7.6 | 90.9 | 1.5 | 6 855 | 75.6 | 51.9 | 40.2 |
| Slovenia | 1997 | 8 557 | 37.6 | 52.7 | 9.7 | 5 033 | 58.5 | 61.6 | 45.0 |
| Spain | 1995 | 177 737 | 7.3 | 89.5 | 3.2 | 101 310 | 49.1 | 58.3 | 39.8 |
| Sweden | 1997 | 35 243 | 10.2 | 72.6 | 17.2 | 20 530 | 48.8 | 62.3 | 46.6 |
| Switzerland | 1996 | 37 210 | 63.6 | 26.6 | 9.8 | 12 734 | 32.3 | 39.4 | 32.3 |
| The Former Yugoslav Rep. of Macedonia | 1997 | 3 292 | 20.4 | 76.8 | 2.9 | 1 890 | 64.8 | 56.0 | 42.6 |
| United Kingdom | 1997 | 456 180 | 19.1 | 56.6 | 24.3 | 239 913 | 57.8 | 52.1 | 49.7 |
| **Oceania** | | | | | | | | | |
| Australia | 1997 (2) | 141 478 | - | 69.2 | 30.8 | (2) 80 491 | . | 58.7 | 52.8 |
| New Zealand | 1997 | 34 218 | 26.3 | 53.9 | 19.8 | 20 141 | 64.6 | 59.2 | 50.4 |

**General note**
For general explanations and definitions, please refer to the beginning of this chapter.

**Note générale**
Pour les explications et définitions générales, prière de se référer au début de ce chapitre.

**Nota general**
Para las explicaciones y definiciones generales, referirse al comienzo de este capítulo.

Notes

(1) Universities and equivalent degree-granting institutions only.
(2) Universities only.
(3) Not including private tertiary institutions.
(4) Universities and degree-granting institutions only, excluding al Azhar.

Notes

(1) Universités et établissements conférant des grades équivalents seulement.
(2) Universités seulement.
(3) Non compris les institutions supérieures privées.
(4) Universités et établissements conférant des titres équivalents seulement, à l'exception d'Al Azhar.

Notas

(1) Universidades y establecimientos que otorgan títulos equivalentes solamente.
(2) Universidades solamente.
(3) No incluyen las instituciones superiores privadas.
(4) Universidades y establecimientos que otorgan títulos equivalentes solamente, con excepción de Al Azhar.

Tertiary education: graduates (total and female) by ISCED level    **II.15**
Enseignement supérieur: diplômés (total et femmes) par niveau de la CITE
Enseñanza superior: diplomados (total y mujeres) por nivel de la CINE

(5) Not including medical science.

(6) Not including "l'école Africaine et Mauricienne d'architecture et d'urbanisme, l'école normale supérieure d'Atakpame et le centre régionale d'action culturelle".

(7) Not including private non-university institutions.

(8) Not including Turkish institutions.

(9) Data refer to private universities only.

(10) Public universities only.

(11) East Bank only.

(12) Not including ISCED level 7.

(13) Not including some non-university institutions.

(14) Data refer to institutions under the authority of the Holy See.

(5) Non compris les science médicales.

(6) Non compris "l'école Africaine et Mauricienne d'architecture et d'urbanisme, l'école normale supérieure d'Atakpame et le centre régionale d'action culturelle".

(7) Non compris les institutions privées non universitaires.

(8) Non compris les institutions turques.

(9) Les données se réfèrent aux universités privées seulement.

(10) Universités publiques seulement.

(11) Rive orientale seulement.

(12) Non compris le niveau 7 de la CITE.

(13) Non compris quelques institutions supérieures non universitaires.

(14) Les données se réfèrent aux institutions sous l'autorité du Saint-Siège.

(5) No incluyen las ciencias médicas.

(6) No incluyen "l'école Africaine et Mauricienne d'architecture et d'urbanisme, l'école normale supérieure d'Atakpame et le centre régionale d'action culturelle".

(7) No incluyen las instituciones no universitarias privadas.

(8) No incluyen las instituciones turcas.

(9) Los datos se refieren a las universidades privadas solamente.

(10) Universidades públicas solamente.

(11) Orilla oriental solamente.

(12) No incluye el nivel 7 de la CINE.

(13) No incluyen algunas instituciones de enseñanza superior no universitaria.

(14) Los datos se refieren a las instituciones bajo la autoridad de la Santa Sede.

II.16    Tertiary education: graduates by broad field of study
Enseignement supérieur: diplômés par grand domaine d'études
Enseñanza superior: diplomados por gran sector de estudios

## II.16   Tertiary education: distribution of graduates by broad field of study

### Enseignement supérieur: répartition des diplômés par grand domaine d'études

### Enseñanza superior: distribución de los diplomados por gran sector de estudios

| Country<br><br>Pays<br><br>País | Year<br><br>Année<br><br>Año | | Total<br>graduates<br><br>Total des<br>diplômés<br><br>Total de<br>diplomados | Percentage of graduates by broad field of study<br>Pourcentage de diplômés par grand domaine d'études<br>Porcentaje de diplomados por gran sector de estudios | | | | | |
|---|---|---|---|---|---|---|---|---|---|
| | | | | Education<br><br>Education<br><br>Educación | Humanities<br><br>Lettres<br><br>Humanidades | Social<br>sciences<br><br>Sciences<br>sociales<br><br>Ciencias<br>sociales | Natural<br>sciences<br><br>Sciences<br>naturelles<br><br>Ciencias<br>naturales | Medical<br>sciences<br><br>Sciences<br>médicales<br><br>Ciencias<br>médicas | Others<br><br>Autres<br><br>Otros |
| **Africa** | | | | | | | | | |
| Algeria | 1995 | (1) | 32 557 | 1.0 | 15.8 | 24.5 | 51.8 | 6.0 | 0.9 |
| Botswana | 1997 | (2) | 1 971 | 6.6 | 10.6 | 46.3 | 34.5 | 1.4 | 0.6 |
| Egypt | 1995 | (3)(4) | 107 512 | 23.8 | 15.9 | 32.5 | 15.0 | 10.3 | 2.5 |
| Eritrea | 1998 | | 559 | 15.6 | 10.6 | 32.4 | 41.5 | - | - |
| Ethiopia | 1997 | | 7 448 | 27.5 | 1.5 | 28.9 | 32.1 | 9.9 | - |
| Lesotho | 1996 | | 1 930 | 36.5 | 2.8 | 49.2 | 11.5 | - | - |
| Madagascar | 1996 | | 6 341 | 2.8 | 18.4 | 51.0 | 22.5 | 5.4 | - |
| Malawi | 1994 | | 3 815 | 72.8 | 0.4 | 10.9 | 12.2 | 3.9 | - |
| Mauritania | 1994 | | 733 | 11.5 | 23.2 | 49.5 | 15.8 | - | - |
| Morocco | 1995 | (5) | 26 859 | 0.2 | (6) 33.3 | (6) 28.5 | 32.9 | 2.8 | 2.2 |
| Mozambique | 1995 | | 300 | 36.7 | 8.3 | 10.3 | 35.7 | 9.0 | - |
| South Africa | 1994 | | 147 391 | 43.1 | 7.4 | 31.1 | 13.5 | 3.9 | 1.0 |
| Swaziland | 1995 | (7) | 988 | 19.0 | 5.5 | 39.1 | 34.9 | ... | 1.5 |
| Togo | 1995 | (8) | 5 254 | - | 47.9 | 36.9 | 8.2 | 7.0 | - |
| Tunisia | 1996 | (9) | 14 565 | 9.6 | 17.5 | 34.9 | 22.8 | 10.2 | 5.0 |
| Uganda | 1996 | (10) | 9 959 | 53.0 | 4.9 | 26.1 | 13.5 | 2.0 | 0.5 |
| United Republic of<br>Tanzania | 1996 | | 2 413 | 3.6 | - | 55.8 | 25.9 | 14.6 | - |
| **North America** | | | | | | | | | |
| Canada | 1996 | | 383 946 | 6.8 | 11.8 | 28.6 | 27.8 | 8.1 | 16.9 |
| Cuba | 1996 | | 27 502 | 32.3 | 1.4 | 6.6 | 25.8 | 23.8 | 10.1 |
| Dominican Republic | 1997 | | 19 276 | 16.5 | 4.5 | 50.2 | 17.2 | 11.7 | - |
| El Salvador | 1996 | | 7 897 | 0.2 | (11) 47.7 | 24.5 | (11) 15.6 | 12.0 | - |
| Mexico | 1994 | | 152 316 | 3.2 | 3.0 | 51.4 | 32.7 | 9.6 | 0.2 |
| Nicaragua | 1997 | | 6 915 | 8.9 | 1.6 | 46.8 | 25.9 | 16.8 | - |
| Panama | 1994 | (2) | 5 744 | 22.1 | 6.3 | 34.7 | 26.8 | 10.1 | - |

Tertiary education: graduates by broad field of study  II.16
Enseignement supérieur: diplômés par grand domaine d'études
Enseñanza superior: diplomados por gran sector de estudios

| Country / Pays / País | Year / Année / Año | Total graduates / Total des diplômés / Total de diplomados | Percentage of graduates by broad field of study Pourcentage de diplômés par grand domaine d'études Porcentaje de diplomados por gran sector de estudios | | | | | |
|---|---|---|---|---|---|---|---|---|
| | | | Education / Education / Educación | Humanities / Lettres / Humanidades | Social sciences / Sciences sociales / Ciencias sociales | Natural sciences / Sciences naturelles / Ciencias naturales | Medical sciences / Sciences médicales / Ciencias médicas | Others / Autres / Otros |
| St. Lucia | 1996 | 313 | 53.4 | 37.4 | - | 4.8 | 4.5 | - |
| United States | 1995 | 2 454 932 | 9.2 | 16.1 | 36.3 | 18.9 | 12.6 | 6.9 |
| **South America** | | | | | | | | |
| Chile | 1997 | 41 458 | 11.5 | (6) 4.6 | (6) 42.8 | 34.0 | 7.1 | - |
| Colombia | 1996 | 92 219 | 20.3 | 3.0 | 41.5 | 26.2 | 9.0 | - |
| Guyana | 1995 | 1 554 | 27.7 | 1.9 | 26.6 | 33.0 | 4.8 | 6.0 |
| Uruguay | 1996 | 5 930 | 35.5 | 0.4 | 30.0 | 17.2 | 11.9 | 5.0 |
| **Asia** | | | | | | | | |
| Armenia | 1996 | 9 055 | 17.5 | 11.7 | 15.6 | 33.0 | 19.9 | 2.4 |
| Bahrain | 1994 | 1 382 | 22.9 | 8.2 | 26.9 | 25.1 | 16.9 | - |
| Brunei Darussalam | 1996 | (2) 420 | 79.8 | 3.3 | 12.9 | 4.0 | - | - |
| China | 1994 | 1 040 135 | 28.3 | 7.6 | 22.1 | 35.0 | 6.4 | 0.6 |
| China, Hong Kong SAR | 1994 | 23 515 | 9.0 | 9.3 | 34.4 | 41.9 | 4.4 | 1.1 |
| Cyprus (12) | 1996 | 2 482 | 15.8 | 5.8 | 48.2 | 17.0 | 3.5 | 9.7 |
| Georgia | 1996 | 25 470 | 6.3 | 13.0 | 17.7 | 50.8 | 12.1 | - |
| Indonesia | 1996 | 388 672 | 14.2 | 6.7 | 49.9 | 27.4 | 1.8 | - |
| Iran, Islamic Republic of | 1997 | (13) 83 385 | 13.7 | 9.0 | 14.2 | 34.1 | 29.0 | - |
| Japan | 1996 | 1 127 500 | 8.2 | (6) 17.7 | (6) 37.6 | 23.2 | 8.2 | 5.0 |
| Jordan (14) | 1996 | 22 395 | 14.3 | 20.3 | 28.4 | 23.7 | 11.4 | 1.9 |
| Kazakstan | 1995 | 106 008 | 19.4 | 8.9 | 14.9 | 40.2 | 13.8 | 2.8 |
| Korea, Republic of | 1997 | 380 571 | 7.7 | 18.3 | 28.1 | 38.3 | 6.1 | 1.5 |
| Lao People's Democratic Republic | 1994 | 1 645 | 28.0 | 7.1 | 12.5 | 37.8 | 11.4 | 3.2 |
| Lebanon | 1995 | 9 653 | 0.7 | 23.1 | 52.0 | 18.5 | 5.7 | - |
| Macau | 1997 | 1 656 | 12.4 | 15.6 | 45.0 | 8.1 | - | 18.8 |
| Mongolia | 1997 | 7 394 | 30.6 | 15.0 | 19.0 | 18.4 | 17.0 | - |
| Myanmar | 1995 | (7) 35 898 | - | 61.3 | 8.6 | 30.1 | - | - |
| Oman | 1995 | (2) 733 | 51.4 | —> | 16.4 | 26.1 | 6.1 | - |
| Philippines | 1995 | 309 645 | 14.8 | 6.0 | 30.5 | 28.0 | 19.1 | 1.6 |
| Qatar | 1997 | 1 360 | 41.2 | (6) 26.2 | (6) 8.4 | 19.0 | —> | 5.2 |
| Saudi Arabia | 1996 | 37 901 | 38.8 | 19.0 | 17.4 | 21.4 | 3.0 | 0.3 |
| Singapore | 1995 | 20 603 | 6.9 | (6) 8.4 | (6) 24.3 | 57.9 | 2.5 | - |
| Sri Lanka | 1994 | 7 995 | 6.3 | 29.1 | 28.1 | 28.9 | 7.4 | 0.3 |
| Syrian Arab Republic | 1995 | (15) 24 202 | 4.4 | (6) 18.0 | (6) 20.7 | 40.6 | 16.3 | 0.1 |
| Tajikistan | 1995 | (1) 10 198 | 47.8 | 19.3 | 1.0 | 17.9 | 9.7 | 4.4 |
| Thailand | 1995 | (1) 130 223 | 6.6 | 6.6 | 55.9 | 17.9 | 11.3 | 1.7 |
| Turkey | 1994 | 124 861 | 12.7 | 6.1 | 31.9 | 29.8 | 18.0 | 1.5 |
| United Arab Emirates | 1997 | (2) 1 638 | 47.1 | 14.8 | 13.4 | 23.1 | 1.6 | - |
| Palestine | 1995 | (9) 4 510 | 26.1 | 30.2 | 16.3 | 19.6 | 7.2 | 0.6 |

II.16    Tertiary education: graduates by broad field of study
Enseignement supérieur: diplômés par grand domaine d'études
Enseñanza superior: diplomados por gran sector de estudios

| Country | Year | | Total graduates | Percentage of graduates by broad field of study Pourcentage de diplômés par grand domaine d'études Porcentaje de diplomados por gran sector de estudios | | | | | |
| Pays | Année | | Total des diplômés | Education | Humanities | Social sciences | Natural sciences | Medical sciences | Others |
| | | | | Education | Lettres | Sciences sociales | Sciences naturelles | Sciences médicales | Autres |
| País | Año | | Total de diplomados | Educación | Humanidades | Ciencias sociales | Ciencias naturales | Ciencias médicas | Otros |
|---|---|---|---|---|---|---|---|---|---|
| **Europe** | | | | | | | | | |
| Albania | 1996 | | 3 845 | 6.2 | 24.6 | 25.0 | 32.9 | 11.2 | - |
| Austria | 1997 | | 21 357 | 16.8 | 12.5 | 31.6 | 27.7 | 10.6 | 0.8 |
| Belarus | 1996 | | 68 663 | 13.5 | 14.8 | 17.2 | 44.2 | 9.4 | 0.9 |
| Bulgaria | 1997 | | 36 463 | 20.0 | 6.1 | 28.9 | 26.0 | 13.4 | 5.7 |
| Croatia | 1996 | | 12 467 | 9.1 | 5.9 | 30.9 | 37.2 | 12.6 | 4.4 |
| Czech Republic | 1997 | | 30 640 | 16.6 | 7.8 | 33.0 | 28.4 | 13.5 | 0.8 |
| Denmark | 1995 | | 30 243 | 12.7 | 9.0 | 28.5 | 28.2 | 16.1 | 5.5 |
| Estonia | 1996 | | 6 236 | 10.3 | 10.2 | 31.4 | 27.4 | 11.1 | 9.6 |
| Federal Republic of Yugoslavia | 1997 | | 19 050 | 9.5 | 11.6 | 22.7 | 42.8 | 11.9 | 1.5 |
| Finland | 1996 | | 28 625 | 10.4 | 8.3 | 19.5 | 33.7 | 27.6 | 0.5 |
| Germany | 1996 | | 336 473 | 3.6 | 8.7 | 26.5 | 34.7 | 16.0 | 10.5 |
| Holy See | 1996 | (16) | 3 047 | 8.0 | 77.6 | 14.4 | - | - | - |
| Iceland | 1996 | | 1 624 | 26.3 | 16.5 | 23.3 | 23.0 | 10.9 | - |
| Hungary | 1995 | | 32 393 | 23.9 | 7.6 | 27.2 | 25.6 | 13.2 | 2.5 |
| Ireland | 1997 | | 35 380 | 5.7 | 16.7 | 36.4 | 36.1 | 3.6 | 1.6 |
| Italy | 1996 | | 175 489 | 2.2 | 13.6 | 31.5 | 23.0 | 11.5 | 18.2 |
| Latvia | 1997 | | 8 188 | 27.5 | 11.1 | 24.3 | 28.4 | 6.0 | 2.7 |
| Lithuania | 1997 | | 17 704 | 17.2 | 8.9 | 24.5 | 33.8 | 13.2 | 2.3 |
| Malta | 1995 | | 1 332 | 23.2 | 16.7 | 37.2 | 11.5 | 11.2 | 0.2 |
| Moldova | 1997 | (17) 9.7 | 11 810 | (17) | 6.5 | 32.6 | 29.5 | 18.5 | 3.1 |
| Netherlands | 1996 | | 87 271 | 14.1 | 8.0 | 43.5 | 22.3 | 12.1 | - |
| Norway | 1997 | | 52 990 | 13.1 | 21.4 | 37.4 | 11.4 | 9.3 | 7.3 |
| Poland | 1994 | | 134 367 | 17.4 | 8.0 | 25.5 | 21.6 | 24.8 | 2.6 |
| Portugal | 1996 | | 39 116 | 18.4 | 9.6 | 40.2 | 19.8 | 9.2 | 2.7 |
| Romania | 1996 | | 70 841 | 1.8 | 8.7 | 33.8 | 39.8 | 12.1 | 3.9 |
| Russian Federation | 1995 | | 950 488 | 11.9 | 5.5 | 21.7 | 44.8 | 13.2 | 2.9 |
| Slovakia | 1997 | | 12 799 | 20.6 | 7.6 | 21.4 | 37.4 | 12.7 | 0.3 |
| Slovenia | 1997 | | 8 557 | 11.5 | 4.4 | 43.5 | 29.1 | 8.1 | 3.4 |
| Spain | 1995 | | 177 737 | 11.5 | 9.9 | 42.1 | 22.5 | 11.3 | 2.8 |
| Sweden | 1997 | | 35 243 | 22.3 | 6.3 | 22.9 | 28.0 | 20.5 | - |
| The Former Yugoslav Rep. of Macedonia | 1997 | | 3 292 | 10.4 | 11.1 | 29.1 | 35.9 | 11.6 | 1.9 |
| United Kingdom | 1997 | | 456 180 | 11.5 | 17.1 | 33.3 | 27.7 | 10.4 | - |
| **Oceania** | | | | | | | | | |
| Australia | 1997 | (2) | 141 478 | 15.3 | 13.7 | 31.9 | 22.6 | 14.1 | 2.3 |
| New Zealand | 1997 | | 34 218 | 14.4 | 18.8 | 33.4 | 19.9 | 9.9 | 3.6 |

Tertiary education: graduates by broad field of study II.16
Enseignement supérieur: diplômés par grand domaine d'études
Enseñanza superior: diplomados por gran sector de estudios

**General note**

For general explanations and definitions, please refer to the beginning of this chapter.

**Note générale**

Pour les explications et définitions générales, prière de se référer au début de ce chapitre.

**Nota general**

Para las explicaciones y definiciones generales, referirse al comienzo de este capítulo.

| Notes | Notes | Notas |
|---|---|---|
| (1) Universities and equivalent degree-granting institutions only. | (1) Universités et établissements conférant des grades équivalents seulement. | (1) Universidades y establecimientos que otorgan títulos equivalentes solamente. |
| (2) Universities only. | (2) Universités seulement. | (2) Universidades solamente. |
| (3) Not including private tertiary institutions. | (3) Non compris les institutions supérieures privées. | (3) No incluyen las instituciones superiores privadas. |
| (4) Universities and degree-granting institutions only, excluding al Azhar. | (4) Universités et établissements conférant des titres équivalents seulement, à l'exception d'Al Azhar. | (4) Universidades y establecimientos que otorgan títulos equivalentes solamente, con excepción de Al Azhar. |
| (5) Not including professional schools. | (5) Non compris les écoles professionnelles. | (5) No incluyen las escuelas profesionales. |
| (6) Humanities include part of Social sciences. | (6) Les Lettres incluent une partie des Sciences sociales. | (6) Las Humanidades incluyen parte de las Ciencias sociales. |
| (7) Not including medical science. | (7) Non compris les science médicales. | (7) No incluyen las ciencias médicas. |
| (8) Not including "l'école Africaine et Mauricienne d'architecture et d'urbanisme, l'école normale supérieure d'Atakpame et le centre régionale d'action culturelle". | (8) Non compris "l'école Africaine et Mauricienne d'architecture et d'urbanisme, l'école normale supérieure d'Atakpame et le centre régionale d'action culturelle". | (8) No incluyen "l'école Africaine et Mauricienne d'architecture et d'urbanisme, l'école normale supérieure d'Atakpame et le centre régionale d'action culturelle". |
| (9) Not including ISCED level 7. | (9) Non compris le niveau 7 de la CITE. | (9) No incluye el nivel 7 de la CINE. |
| (10) Not including private non-university institutions. | (10) Non compris les institutions privées non universitaires. | (10) No incluyen las instituciones no universitarias privadas. |
| (11) Humanities include part of Natural sciences. | (11) Les Lettres incluent une partie des Sciences naturelles. | (11) Las Humanidades incluyen parte de las Ciencias naturales. |
| (12) Not including Turkish institutions. | (12) Non compris les institutions turques. | (12) No incluyen las instituciones turcas. |
| (13) Public universities only. | (13) Universités publiques seulement. | (13) Universidades públicas solamente. |
| (14) East Bank only. | (14) Rive orientale seulement. | (14) Orilla oriental solamente. |
| (15) Not including some non-university institutions. | (15) Non compris quelques institutions supérieures non universitaires. | (15) No incluyen algunas instituciones de enseñanza superior no universitaria. |
| (16) Data refer to institutions under the authority of the Holy See. | (16) Les données se réfèrent aux institutions sous l'autorité du Saint-Siège. | (16) Los datos se refieren a las instituciones bajo la autoridad de la Santa Sede. |
| (17) Education includes part of Humanities. | (17) L'Education inclue une partie des Lettres. | (17) La Educación incluye parte de las Humanidades. |

II.17    Tertiary education: foreign students by continent of origin
Enseignement supérieur: étudiants étrangers par continent d'origine
Enseñanza superior: estudiantes extranjeros por continente de origen

II.17    Tertiary education: distribution of foreign students by continent of origin

Enseignement supérieur: répartition des étudiants étrangers par continent d'origine

Enseñanza superior: distribución de los estudiantes extranjeros por continente de origen

| Host country / Pays d'accueil / País huésped | Year / Année / Año | Total foreign students / Total des etudiants étrangers / Total de estudiantes extranjeros | Foreign students as % of total students / Etudiants étrangers en % du total des étudiants / Estudiantes extranjeros en % del total de estudiantes | Percentage distribution of foreign students by continent of origin / Répartition en pourcentage des étudiants étrangers par continent d'origine / Distribución en porcentaje de estudiantes extranjeros por continente de origen | | | | | | |
|---|---|---|---|---|---|---|---|---|---|---|
| | | | | Africa / Afrique / Africa | North America / Amérique du Nord / América del Norte | South America / Amérique du Sud / América del Sur | Asia / Asie / Asia | Europe / Europe / Europa | Oceania / Océanie / Oceanía | Not specified / Non spécifié / Sin especificar |
| **Africa** | | | | | | | | | | |
| Benin | 1996 | 740 | 5.3 | 93.4 | - | - | - | 0.4 | - | 6.2 |
| Burkina Faso | 1994/95 | 755 | 8.0 | ... | ... | ... | ... | ... | ... | ... |
| Egypt (1)(2) | 1995/96 | 6 726 | 0.8 | 23.3 | 0.1 | - | 75.1 | 1.5 | - | - |
| Eritrea | 1997/98 | 117 | 3.8 | 99.1 | - | - | 0.9 | - | - | - |
| Gabon (3) | 1994/95 | 227 | 4.9 | ... | ... | ... | ... | ... | ... | ... |
| Guinea | 1996/97 | 45 | 0.6 | 100.0 | - | - | - | - | - | - |
| Lesotho (3) | 1996/97 | 133 | 2.5 | 100.0 | - | - | - | - | - | - |
| Madagascar | 1996/97 | 678 | 2.5 | 99.3 | - | - | 0.4 | 0.3 | - | - |
| Morocco (3) | 1994/95 | 3 617 | 1.5 | 73.2 | - | - | 12.1 | 1.2 | - | 13.5 |
| South Africa | 1994 | 12 625 | 2.0 | 61.0 | 2.8 | 1.2 | 5.2 | 28.6 | 1.3 | - |
| Swaziland (3) | 1996/97 | 196 | 5.7 | 97.4 | - | - | 1.0 | 1.5 | - | - |
| Togo | 1996/97 | 480 | 3.7 | 97.1 | 1.0 | - | - | 1.3 | - | 0.6 |
| Tunisia | 1996/97 | 2 861 | 2.3 | ... | ... | ... | ... | ... | ... | ... |
| **North America** | | | | | | | | | | |
| Cuba | 1996/97 | 4 243 | 3.8 | 76.4 | 10.0 | 8.3 | 4.8 | 0.5 | - | - |
| El Salvador (4) | 1996 | 473 | 0.4 | - | 86.9 | 9.7 | 2.1 | 1.3 | - | - |
| Honduras | 1994 | 521 | 1.0 | ... | ... | ... | ... | ... | ... | ... |
| Nicaragua | 1997 | 279 | 0.5 | - | 83.2 | 7.9 | 1.1 | 5.7 | - | 2.2 |
| Panama | 1994 | 708 | 1.0 | 0.1 | 36.7 | 47.5 | 6.9 | 8.8 | - | - |
| Trinidad and Tobago (3) | 1996/97 | 142 | 2.4 | 8.5 | 35.2 | 4.2 | 37.3 | 14.1 | 0.7 | - |
| United States | 1995/96 | 453 785 | 3.2 | 4.6 | 10.7 | 4.9 | 64.1 | 14.8 | 0.9 | - |
| **South America** | | | | | | | | | | |
| Argentina (5) | 1994 | 12 678 | ... | - | - | 75.0 | - | 4.4 | - | 20.7 |
| Guyana | 1994/95 | 38 | 0.5 | ... | ... | ... | ... | ... | ... | ... |

Tertiary education: foreign students by continent of origin  II.17
Enseignement supérieur: étudiants étrangers par continent d'origine
Enseñanza superior: estudiantes extranjeros por continente de origen

| Host country / Pays d'accueil / País huésped | Year / Année / Año | Total foreign students / Total des etudiants étrangers / Total de estudiantes extranjeros | Foreign students as % of total students / Etudiants étrangers en % du total des étudiants / Estudiantes extranjeros en % del total de estudiantes | Percentage distribution of foreign students by continent of origin / Répartition en pourcentage des étudiants étrangers par continent d'origine / Distribución en porcentaje de estudiantes extranjeros por continente de origen | | | | | | |
|---|---|---|---|---|---|---|---|---|---|---|
| | | | | Africa / Afrique / Africa | North America / Amérique du Nord / América del Norte | South America / Amérique du Sud / América del Sur | Asia / Asie / Asia | Europe / Europe / Europa | Oceania / Océanie / Oceanía | Not specified / Non spécifié / Sin especificar |
| **Asia** | | | | | | | | | | |
| Armenia | 1995/96 | 869 | 2.2 | - | 0.7 | - | 87.7 | 11.6 | - | - |
| Azerbaijan | 1996/97 | 3 986 | 3.5 | 0.1 | 0.0 | 0.9 | 88.0 | 11.0 | - | - |
| Cyprus (6) | 1996/97 | 1 675 | 16.8 | 3.8 | 0.5 | 0.1 | 44.1 | 44.7 | 0.2 | 6.5 |
| Georgia | 1996/97 | 69 | 0.0 | ... | ... | ... | ... | ... | ... | ... |
| Indonesia | 1995/96 | 1 147 | 0.0 | 0.8 | 8.2 | - | 67.8 | 13.7 | 9.5 | - |
| Iran, Islamic Republic of (7) | 1996/97 | 622 | 0.1 | 3.5 | - | - | 96.1 | 0.3 | - | - |
| Japan | 1994/95 | 53 511 | 1.4 | 0.8 | 2.7 | 1.2 | 92.1 | 2.5 | 0.6 | - |
| Kazakstan (8) | 1995/96 | 2 928 | 0.7 | 1.4 | 0.0 | 0.3 | 72.4 | 22.6 | - | 3.3 |
| Korea, Republic of | 1996/97 | 2 143 | 0.1 | 0.7 | 16.8 | 4.7 | 72.8 | 3.7 | 1.3 | - |
| Kuwait | 1995/96 | 2 694 | 9.4 | 8.9 | 0.1 | - | 85.3 | 0.3 | 0.0 | 5.3 |
| Kyrgyzstan | 1995/96 | 125 | 0.3 | - | 0.8 | 0.8 | 98.4 | - | - | - |
| Lao People's Democratic Republic | 1996/97 | 56 | 0.4 | - | - | - | 100.0 | - | - | - |
| Lebanon | 1995/96 | 18 253 | 22.4 | 21.2 | - | - | 78.8 | - | - | - |
| Macau | 1996/97 | 1 224 | 16.4 | 5.4 | 0.2 | 1.1 | 64.9 | 18.5 | 0.1 | 9.8 |
| Mongolia | 1996/97 | 283 | 0.6 | - | 1.1 | - | 54.4 | 44.5 | - | - |
| Philippines | 1995/96 | 4 864 | 0.2 | 2.8 | 24.4 | 0.0 | 68.7 | 3.6 | 0.5 | - |
| Qatar | 1996/97 | 1 360 | 16.0 | 13.6 | 0.3 | - | 86.0 | 0.1 | - | - |
| Saudi Arabia | 1995/96 | 5 361 | 2.1 | ... | ... | ... | ... | ... | ... | ... |
| Sri Lanka | 1994 | 55 | 0.1 | - | 3.6 | - | 94.5 | 1.8 | - | - |
| Syrian Arab Republic (3) | 1994/95 | 11 790 | 7.1 | 13.2 | 0.1 | 0.2 | 86.1 | 0.4 | - | - |
| Tajikistan (3) | 1996/97 | 6 726 | 8.8 | - | - | - | 65.4 | 34.6 | - | - |
| Turkey | 1994/95 | 14 719 | 1.3 | 4.4 | 0.2 | 0.0 | 55.0 | 20.6 | 0.1 | 19.6 |
| United Arab Emirates (3) | 1996/97 | 1 584 | 9.8 | 16.5 | 0.3 | - | 80.3 | 0.6 | - | 2.4 |
| **Europe** | | | | | | | | | | |
| Austria (9) | 1996/97 | 27 172 | ... | 3.7 | 2.3 | 1.2 | 15.4 | 77.3 | 0.2 | - |
| Belarus | 1996/97 | 3 714 | 1.1 | 14.1 | 0.7 | 0.4 | 58.0 | 26.8 | - | - |
| Belgium | 1994/95 | 34 966 | 9.9 | 31.3 | 1.3 | 2.2 | 8.3 | 55.0 | 0.0 | 1.9 |
| Bulgaria | 1996/97 | 8 496 | 3.2 | 3.2 | 0.4 | 0.2 | 14.8 | 81.5 | - | - |
| Croatia (10) | 1996/97 | 725 | 0.8 | 1.4 | 2.6 | - | 1.4 | 81.8 | - | 12.8 |
| Czech Republic | 1996/97 | 3 901 | 1.9 | 7.9 | 1.6 | 1.3 | 15.7 | 53.7 | - | 19.9 |
| Denmark | 1995/96 | 8 982 | 5.1 | ... | ... | ... | ... | ... | ... | ... |
| Federal Republic of Yugoslavia (10) | 1996/97 | 1 180 | 0.7 | 0.6 | 0.4 | 0.2 | 11.1 | 87.7 | - | - |
| Finland | 1996/97 | 3 829 | 1.7 | 13.4 | 6.3 | 1.6 | 25.6 | 50.8 | 0.5 | 1.8 |
| France (5) | 1995/96 | 138 191 | ... | 51.7 | 3.6 | 2.7 | 13.4 | 27.6 | 0.1 | 0.9 |
| Germany (10) | 1996/97 | 165 977 | 7.8 | 9.1 | 3.3 | 2.3 | 36.2 | 47.2 | 0.2 | 1.6 |
| Holy See (11) | 1995/96 | 14 403 | 100.0 | 7.5 | 8.9 | 8.9 | 9.9 | 64.3 | 0.4 | - |
| Hungary (12) | 1994/95 | 6 399 | 5.4 | 5.4 | 3.8 | 0.5 | 20.4 | 69.9 | 0.0 | - |

II.17 Tertiary education: foreign students by continent of origin
Enseignement supérieur: étudiants étrangers par continent d'origine
Enseñanza superior: estudiantes extranjeros por continente de origen

| Host country / Pays d'accueil / País huésped | Year / Année / Año | Total foreign students / Total des etudiants étrangers / Total de estudiantes extranjeros | Foreign students as % of total students / Etudiants étrangers en % du total des étudiants / Estudiantes extranjeros en % del total de estudiantes | Percentage distribution of foreign students by continent of origin / Répartition en pourcentage des étudiants étrangers par continent d'origine / Distribución en porcentaje de estudiantes extranjeros por continente de origen | | | | | | |
|---|---|---|---|---|---|---|---|---|---|---|
| | | | | Africa / Afrique / Africa | North America / Amérique du Nord / América del Norte | South America / Amérique du Sud / América del Sur | Asia / Asie / Asia | Europe / Europe / Europa | Oceania / Océanie / Oceanía | Not specified / Non spécifié / Sin especificar |
| Iceland | 1996/97 | 185 | 2.3 | 1.6 | 13.0 | 1.6 | 4.9 | 76.8 | 1.6 | 0.5 |
| Ireland | 1996/97 | 5 975 | 4.4 | 4.3 | 19.3 | 0.1 | 21.1 | 52.8 | 1.2 | 1.2 |
| Italy | 1996/97 | 24 858 | 1.3 | 12.2 | 2.7 | 3.6 | 12.1 | 65.9 | 0.2 | 3.3 |
| Latvia | 1996/97 | 850 | 1.5 | 4.0 | 0.6 | 0.4 | 38.9 | 56.1 | - | - |
| Lithuania (3) | 1996/97 | 370 | 0.6 | - | 1.9 | 0.3 | 72.4 | 24.3 | 1.1 | - |
| Malta | 1994/95 | 62 | 1.1 | 16.1 | 24.2 | 1.6 | 17.7 | 33.9 | 6.5 | - |
| Moldova | 1996/97 | 1 187 | 1.3 | 4.6 | 0.3 | 0.1 | 49.9 | 45.2 | - | - |
| Norway | 1995/96 | 11 225 | 6.2 | 9.0 | 6.4 | 3.0 | 31.5 | 36.3 | 0.3 | 13.5 |
| Poland | 1995/96 | 5 202 | 0.7 | 11.7 | 3.3 | 1.7 | 21.6 | 61.5 | 0.2 | - |
| Portugal | 1994/95 | 6 140 | 2.0 | 49.8 | 6.2 | 22.0 | 0.6 | 19.1 | 0.3 | 2.0 |
| Romania (3) | 1996/97 | 14 181 | 4.0 | 7.0 | 1.1 | 0.2 | 15.9 | 75.3 | 0.1 | 0.5 |
| Russian Federation | 1994/95 | 73 172 | 1.6 | 5.1 | 0.4 | 0.7 | 53.6 | 40.2 | - | - |
| Slovakia | 1996/97 | 1 725 | 1.7 | 13.2 | 0.9 | 0.5 | 25.0 | 60.3 | 0.1 | - |
| Slovenia (13) | 1996/97 | 425 | 0.8 | 0.7 | 0.7 | 1.2 | 3.1 | 94.4 | - | - |
| Spain | 1994/95 | 21 403 | 1.4 | 10.3 | 7.2 | 15.3 | 4.1 | 62.7 | 0.2 | 0.2 |
| Sweden | 1996/97 | 12 189 | 4.4 | 3.5 | 5.3 | 3.2 | 19.1 | 67.7 | 0.5 | 0.7 |
| Switzerland | 1995/96 | 24 093 | 16.3 | 5.4 | 2.7 | 3.1 | 6.5 | 74.3 | 0.2 | 7.7 |
| The Former Yugoslav Rep. of Macedonia (10) | 1996/97 | 313 | 1.0 | 1.0 | - | - | 10.2 | 83.7 | - | 5.1 |
| Ukraine | 1994/95 | 18 302 | 1.2 | 21.1 | 0.7 | 2.2 | 43.8 | 32.2 | 0.0 | - |
| United Kingdom | 1996/97 | 198 839 | 10.5 | 7.1 | 7.8 | 1.2 | 34.2 | 46.2 | 0.9 | 2.6 |
| **Oceania** | | | | | | | | | | |
| Australia | 1997 | 102 284 | 9.8 | ... | ... | ... | ... | ... | ... | ... |
| New Zealand | 1997 | 6 415 | 3.8 | 0.8 | 4.2 | 0.7 | 70.8 | 5.5 | 16.6 | 1.4 |
| Papua New Guinea | 1995 | 281 | 2.1 | ... | ... | ... | ... | ... | ... | ... |

**General note**
For general explanations and definitions, please refer to the beginning of this chapter.

**Note générale**
Pour les explications et définitions générales, prière de se référer au début de ce chapitre.

**Nota general**
Para las explicaciones y definiciones generales, referirse al comienzo de este capítulo.

| Notes | Notes | Notas |
|---|---|---|
| (1) Not including private tertiary institutions. | (1) Non compris les institutions supérieures privées. | (1) No incluyen las instituciones superiores privadas. |
| (2) Universities and degree-granting institutions only, excluding al Azhar. | (2) Universités et établissements conférant des titres équivalents seulement, à l'exception d'Al Azhar. | (2) Universidades y establecimientos que otorgan títulos equivalentes solamente, con excepción de Al Azhar. |
| (3) Universities only. | (3) Universités seulement. | (3) Universidades solamente. |
| (4) Not including non-university institutions. | (4) Non compris les institutions supérieures non universitaires. | (4) No incluyen las instituciones de enseñanza superior no universitaria. |
| (5) Public universities only. | (5) Universités publiques seulement. | (5) Universidades públicas solamente. |
| (6) Not including Turkish institutions. | (6) Non compris les institutions turques. | (6) No incluyen las instituciones turcas. |
| (7) Not including private universities. | (7) Non compris les universités privées. | (7) No incluyen las universidades privadas. |
| (8) Not including some non-university institutions. | (8) Non compris quelques institutions supérieures non universitaires. | (8) No incluyen algunas instituciones de enseñanza superior no universitaria |
| (9) Universities and equivalent degree-granting institutions only. | (9) Universités et établissements conférant des grades équivalents seulement. | (9) Universidades y establecimientos que otorgan títulos equivalentes solamente. |

(10) Not including students at ISCED level 7 for which registration is not required.

(11) Data refer to institutions under the authority of the Holy See.

(12) Full-time only.

(13) Not including students enrolled in doctoral studies.

(10) Non compris les étudiants du niveau 7 de la CITE pour lequel l'inscription n'est pas exigée.

(11) Les données se réfèrent aux institutions sous l'autorité du Saint-Siège.

(12) Plein temps seulement.

(13) Non compris les étudiants inscrits en doctorat.

(10) No incluyen los estudiantes del nivel 7 de la CINE para el cual la inscripción no es exigida.

(11) Los datos se refieren a las instituciones bajo la autoridad de la Santa Sede.

(12) Jornada completa solamente.

(13) No incluyen los estudiantes en doctorado.

II.18 Total and current public expenditure on education
Dépenses publiques totales et ordinaires afférentes à l'éducation
Gastos públicos totales y ordinarios destinados a la educación

## II.18 Total and current public expenditure on education: percentage of GNP and government expenditure

## Dépenses publiques totales et ordinaires afférentes à l'éducation: pourcentage par rapport au PNB et aux dépenses du gouvernement

## Gastos públicos totales y ordinarios destinados a la educación: porcentaje en relación con el PNB y los gastos del gobierno

| Country / Pays / País | Year / Année / Año | Total expenditure on education / Dépenses totales d'éducation / Gastos totales de educación | | Current expenditure on education / Dépenses ordinaires d'éducation / Gastos ordinarios de educación | | |
|---|---|---|---|---|---|---|
| | | As % of Gross National Product / En % du Produit National Brut / En % del Producto Nacional Bruto | As % of total government expenditure / En % des dépenses totales du gouvernement / En % de los gastos totales del gobierno | As % of Gross National Product / En % du Produit National Brut / En % del Producto Nacional Bruto | As % of current government expenditure / En % des dépenses ordinaires du gouvernement / En % de los gastos ordinarios del gobierno | As % of total expenditure on education / En % des dépenses totales d'éducation / En % de los gastos totales de educación |
| **Africa** | | | | | | |
| Algeria | 1970 | 7.9 | 31.6 | 4.8 | 26.8 | 61.4 |
| | 1975 | 6.7 | 23.0 | 4.8 | 23.9 | 72.3 |
| | 1980 | 7.8 | 24.3 | 5.2 | 29.8 | 66.9 |
| | 1985 | 8.5 | 20.7 | 5.9 | 26.2 | 69.3 |
| (1) | 1990 | 5.5 | 21.1 | 4.7 | 29.7 | 84.6 |
| (1) | 1991 | 5.3 | 22.0 | 4.7 | 32.1 | 88.1 |
| (1) | 1992 | 6.1 | 19.1 | 5.2 | 26.2 | 85.3 |
| (1) | 1993 | 6.8 | 18.4 | 5.8 | 21.5 | 85.9 |
| (1) | 1994 | 6.0 | 18.8 | 5.3 | 23.3 | 88.1 |
| (1) | 1995 | 5.8 | 14.7 | 5.2 | 21.9 | 88.7 |
| (1) | 1996 | 5.1 | 16.4 | 4.5 | 35.4 | 87.3 |
| Angola | 1970 | ... | | ... | 10.5 | ... |
| (2) | 1985 | 5.1 | 10.8 | 5.0 | 14.0 | 97.7 |
| (2) | 1990 | 4.9 | 10.7 | 4.4 | ... | 89.9 |
| Benin | 1970 | ... | ... | 3.2 | 29.8 | ... |
| | 1975 | ... | ... | 3.9 | 38.9 | ... |
| | 1980 | ... | ... | 4.2 | 36.8 | ... |
| | 1995 | 3.2 | 15.2 | 2.7 | 21.1 | 85.6 |
| Botswana | 1970 | 4.7 | ... | 4.0 | ... | 84.6 |
| | 1975 | 7.4 | 18.8 | 4.0 | 17.6 | 54.5 |
| | 1980 | 6.0 | 16.0 | 4.5 | 20.8 | 75.8 |
| | 1985 | 6.2 | 15.4 | 4.9 | 18.6 | 79.3 |
| | 1990 | 6.9 | 17.0 | 4.9 | 21.1 | 71.3 |
| | 1991 | 7.3 | 18.7 | 5.6 | 22.9 | 77.1 |
| | 1992 | 7.1 | 17.5 | 5.7 | 21.7 | 80.7 |
| | 1993 | 7.8 | 17.6 | 6.2 | 21.8 | 79.3 |
| | 1994 | 8.2 | 19.3 | 6.4 | 21.6 | 77.7 |
| | 1995 | 8.6 | 20.5 | 6.6 | 23.1 | 76.5 |
| | 1996 | 10.3 | 21.8 | 7.7 | 24.8 | 74.8 |
| | 1997 | 8.6 | 20.6 | 6.9 | 24.6 | 79.9 |
| Burkina Faso | 1970 | ... | ... | 1.8 | 25.9 | ... |
| | 1975 | ... | ... | 1.7 | 23.0 | ... |
| | 1980 | 2.2 | 19.8 | 2.1 | 21.1 | 93.0 |
| | 1985 | 2.0 | 21.0 | 1.9 | 22.4 | 95.3 |
| | 1990 | 2.7 | ... | ... | ... | ... |
| | 1991 | 2.9 | ... | ... | ... | ... |
| | 1992 | 3.0 | ... | 2.8 | ... | 93.3 |
| | 1994 | 3.6 | 11.1 | 2.9 | 17.4 | 82.7 |
| | 1997 | ... | | 2.4 | ... | ... |
| Burundi | 1970 | | | 2.3 | 25.8 | ... |
| | 1975 | ... | | 2.2 | 22.7 | ... |
| | 1981 | 3.4 | 15.6 | 3.0 | 20.8 | 89.1 |
| | 1985 | 2.5 | 15.5 | 2.4 | 17.1 | 92.7 |
| | 1990 | 3.4 | 16.7 | 3.3 | 19.4 | 97.0 |

Total and current public expenditure on education    II.18
Dépenses publiques totales et ordinaires afférentes à l'éducation
Gastos públicos totales y ordinarios destinados a la educación

| Country / Pays / País | Year / Année / Año | Total expenditure on education / Dépenses totales d'éducation / Gastos totales de educación | | Current expenditure on education / Dépenses ordinaires d'éducation / Gastos ordinarios de educación | | |
|---|---|---|---|---|---|---|
| | | As % of Gross National Product / En % du Produit National Brut / En % del Producto Nacional Bruto | As % of total government expenditure / En % des dépenses totales du gouvernement / En % de los gastos totales del gobierno | As % of Gross National Product / En % du Produit National Brut / En % del Producto Nacional Bruto | As % of current government expenditure / En % des dépenses ordinaires du gouverment / En % de los gastos ordinarios del gobierno | As % of total expenditure on education / En % des dépenses totales d'éducation / En % de los gastos totales de educación |
| Burundi (cont) | 1991 | 3.5 | 17.7 | 3.4 | 20.2 | 97.4 |
| | 1992 | 3.8 | 12.2 | 3.6 | 24.2 | 93.4 |
| | 1994 | 4.6 | ... | 4.5 | ... | 97.8 |
| | 1995 | 5.1 | ... | 4.7 | ... | 91.7 |
| | 1996 | 4.0 | 18.3 | 3.9 | 20.3 | 97.2 |
| Cameroon | 1970 | 3.7 | 19.6 | 3.4 | 20.6 | 92.2 |
| | 1975 | 4.0 | 21.3 | 3.4 | 22.7 | 83.5 |
| | 1980 | 3.8 | 20.3 | 3.1 | ... | 81.3 |
| | 1985 | 2.9 | 14.8 | 2.4 | 20.9 | 82.4 |
| | 1990 | 3.4 | 19.6 | 3.1 | 26.9 | 90.7 |
| | 1991 | 2.9 | 16.9 | 2.6 | 21.6 | 88.9 |
| | 1996 | ... | ... | 2.3 | 12.8 | ... |
| Cape Verde | 1970 | ... | ... | ... | 13.4 | ... |
| | 1976 | ... | ... | ... | 20.2 | ... |
| | 1985 | 3.6 | ... | 3.5 | 15.2 | 95.3 |
| | 1991 | 4.0 | 19.9 | 3.0 | 20.0 | 98.6 |
| Central African Republic | 1970 | ... | ... | 3.6 | 16.1 | ... |
| | 1975 | 4.8 | 20.1 | 4.2 | ... | 86.9 |
| | 1980 | ... | ... | 3.7 | 21.5 | ... |
| (2) | 1985 | 2.1 | ... | ... | ... | ... |
| (2) | 1990 | 2.2 | ... | 2.1 | 23.7 | 96.9 |
| (2) | 1991 | 2.3 | ... | 2.2 | 25.7 | 98.0 |
| (2) | 1992 | ... | ... | 2.2 | ... | ... |
| (2) | 1993 | ... | ... | 2.2 | ... | ... |
| (2) | 1994 | ... | ... | 1.7 | ... | ... |
| (2) | 1995 | ... | ... | 1.6 | ... | ... |
| Chad | 1970 | ... | ... | 1.5 | 13.0 | ... |
| | 1975 | ... | ... | 1.2 | 11.9 | ... |
| | 1991 | 1.7 | ... | 1.6 | ... | 99.1 |
| | 1993 | ... | ... | 2.3 | 18.7 | ... |
| | 1994 | 1.7 | ... | 1.7 | 15.1 | 99.0 |
| | 1996 | ... | ... | 1.4 | 15.8 | ... |
| Comoros (2) | 1985 | ... | ... | 4.1 | 23.1 | ... |
| | 1990 | ... | ... | 3.9 | 24.3 | ... |
| | 1991 | ... | ... | 4.0 | 23.2 | ... |
| | 1992 | ... | ... | 4.0 | 22.0 | ... |
| | 1993 | ... | ... | 3.9 | 20.5 | ... |
| | 1994 | ... | ... | 4.2 | 21.6 | ... |
| | 1995 | ... | ... | 4.2 | 21.1 | ... |
| Congo | 1970 | 5.9 | 23.7 | 5.7 | 25.4 | 96.6 |
| | 1975 | 8.1 | 18.2 | 6.7 | 24.7 | 82.6 |
| | 1980 | 7.0 | 23.6 | 6.6 | 24.1 | 93.8 |
| | 1990 | 6.0 | 14.4 | 5.8 | 18.0 | 97.4 |
| | 1991 | 8.9 | ... | 8.8 | 19.3 | 99.0 |
| | 1992 | 9.6 | ... | 9.5 | 20.4 | 99.2 |
| | 1993 | 9.1 | ... | 8.9 | ... | 97.9 |
| | 1994 | 7.5 | 15.5 | 7.0 | 18.2 | 92.8 |
| | 1995 | 6.1 | 14.7 | 5.9 | 15.0 | 97.6 |
| Côte d'Ivoire | 1970 | 5.3 | 19.3 | 4.6 | 30.7 | 85.6 |
| | 1975 | 6.3 | 19.0 | 5.4 | 33.7 | 84.7 |
| | 1980 | 7.2 | 22.6 | 6.0 | 36.4 | 83.5 |
| | 1985 | ... | ... | 6.3 | ... | ... |
| | 1992 | 7.7 | 35.6 | 7.7 | ... | 99.2 |
| | 1993 | 7.9 | 34.8 | 7.8 | ... | 98.3 |
| | 1994 | 5.8 | 30.7 | 5.4 | ... | 93.9 |
| | 1995 | 5.3 | 28.8 | 4.7 | ... | 90.0 |
| | 1996 | 5.0 | 24.0 | 4.6 | ... | 91.9 |
| | 1997 | 5.0 | 24.9 | 4.5 | ... | 90.8 |
| Democratic Rep. of the Congo | 1970 | ... | ... | 2.3 | 20.4 | ... |
| | 1975 | ... | ... | 2.1 | 27.0 | ... |
| | 1980 | 2.6 | 24.2 | 2.6 | 25.3 | 98.3 |
| | 1985 | 1.0 | 7.3 | 1.0 | 7.3 | 98.4 |
| Djibouti | 1970 | ... | ... | ... | ... | 78.3 |
| | 1979 | ... | 11.5 | ... | 9.6 | 76.5 |
| (2) | 1985 | ... | 7.5 | ... | ... | ... |
| | 1990 | ... | 10.5 | ... | ... | ... |
| | 1991 | 3.6 | 11.1 | ... | ... | ... |

II.18 Total and current public expenditure on education
Dépenses publiques totales et ordinaires afférentes à l'éducation
Gastos públicos totales y ordinarios destinados a la educación

| Country<br><br>Pays<br><br>País | Year<br><br>Année<br><br>Año | Total expenditure on education<br>Dépenses totales d'éducation<br>Gastos totales de educación | | Current expenditure on education<br>Dépenses ordinaires d'éducation<br>Gastos ordinarios de educación | | |
|---|---|---|---|---|---|---|
| | | As % of Gross National Product<br><br>En % du Produit National Brut<br><br>En % del Producto Nacional Bruto | As % of total government expenditure<br><br>En % des dépenses totales du gouvernement<br><br>En % de los gastos totales del gobierno | As % of Gross National Product<br><br>En % du Produit National Brut<br><br>En % del Producto Nacional Bruto | As % of current government expenditure<br><br>En % des dépenses ordinaires du gouvernment<br><br>En % de los gastos ordinarios del gobierno | As % of total expenditure on education<br><br>En % des dépenses totales d'éducation<br><br>En % de los gastos totales de educación |
| Egypt | 1970 | 4.8 | 15.8 | 4.4 | 23.8 | 92.7 |
| | 1975 | 5.1 | ... | 4.4 | ... | 86.4 |
| | 1981 | 5.7 | 9.4 | 4.5 | 10.1 | 78.6 |
| | 1985 | 6.3 | ... | 5.9 | 10.8 | 94.5 |
| | 1990 | 3.8 | ... | 3.3 | ... | 86.4 |
| | 1991 | 4.7 | 9.7 | 4.0 | 11.0 | 86.5 |
| | 1992 | 4.4 | 11.0 | 3.5 | 11.0 | 80.2 |
| | 1993 | 4.7 | 13.9 | 3.9 | 13.4 | 82.7 |
| | 1994 | 4.7 | 13.8 | 4.2 | 15.0 | 89.4 |
| | 1995 | 4.8 | 14.9 | 4.4 | 16.7 | 92.0 |
| | 1996 | ... | | 4.4 | ... | ... |
| Equatorial Guinea | 1993 | 1.7 | 5.6 | 1.7 | 5.8 | 98.2 |
| Eritrea (1) | 1992 | ... | ... | 1.4 | ... | ... |
| | 1993 | ... | ... | 1.5 | ... | ... |
| | 1994 | ... | ... | 1.3 | ... | ... |
| | 1995 | ... | ... | 1.9 | ... | ... |
| | 1996 | 1.8 | ... | 1.4 | ... | 76.6 |
| Ethiopia | 1970 | ... | 14.1 | ... | 14.4 | 81.3 |
| | 1975 | ... | 14.5 | ... | 16.5 | 82.2 |
| | 1981 | 3.1 | 11.4 | 2.4 | 13.9 | 77.9 |
| | 1985 | 3.0 | 9.5 | 2.6 | 14.3 | 84.3 |
| | 1990 | 3.4 | 9.4 | 2.8 | 11.1 | 82.4 |
| | 1991 | 3.1 | 13.1 | 2.7 | 16.7 | 86.9 |
| | 1992 | 3.4 | 11.9 | 2.7 | 17.8 | 80.1 |
| | 1993 | 4.2 | 13.1 | 3.0 | ... | 71.4 |
| | 1994 | 4.6 | 13.0 | 3.2 | 16.5 | 68.2 |
| | 1995 | 4.0 | 13.9 | 2.8 | 16.6 | 70.6 |
| | 1996 | 4.0 | 13.7 | 2.7 | ... | 67.9 |
| Gabon | 1970 | 3.2 | 16.2 | 3.1 | 24.2 | 95.6 |
| | 1975 | 2.1 | ... | 1.8 | ... | 85.0 |
| | 1980 | 2.7 | ... | 2.0 | ... | 72.3 |
| | 1985 | 5.0 | 9.4 | 3.4 | 21.7 | 68.3 |
| (1) | 1992 | 3.2 | ... | 2.7 | ... | 82.9 |
| (1) | 1994 | 2.8 | ... | 2.2 | ... | 80.7 |
| (1) | 1995 | 2.9 | ... | 2.2 | ... | 75.2 |
| Gambia | 1970 | 2.3 | 10.8 | 2.2 | 12.4 | 94.4 |
| | 1975 | 3.4 | ... | 2.6 | ... | 78.1 |
| | 1980 | 3.2 | ... | 2.8 | ... | 88.1 |
| | 1985 | 3.7 | ... | 2.9 | 16.4 | 80.1 |
| | 1990 | 4.1 | 14.6 | 3.2 | ... | 77.1 |
| | 1993 | 5.1 | ... | 3.2 | ... | 64.0 |
| | 1994 | 5.3 | 16.0 | 3.3 | 12.9 | 61.4 |
| | 1995 | 5.6 | ... | 3.4 | ... | 60.2 |
| | 1996 | 4.9 | 21.2 | 3.5 | ... | 71.6 |
| Ghana | 1970 | 4.3 | 19.6 | 3.8 | 24.1 | 87.8 |
| | 1975 | 5.9 | 21.5 | 4.6 | 24.1 | 77.9 |
| | 1980 | 3.1 | 17.1 | ... | ... | ... |
| | 1985 | 2.6 | 19.0 | 2.5 | 21.2 | 97.1 |
| | 1990 | 3.3 | 24.3 | 2.8 | 27.1 | 86.7 |
| | 1992 | 4.5 | 25.0 | 4.3 | 31.5 | 95.5 |
| | 1993 | 4.3 | 21.7 | 4.2 | 25.7 | 95.9 |
| | 1994 | 4.3 | 19.2 | 4.2 | 25.3 | 97.7 |
| | 1995 | 4.8 | 21.4 | 4.3 | 25.4 | 91.1 |
| | 1996 | 4.2 | 19.9 | 4.0 | 24.1 | 97.2 |
| Guinea | 1970 | ... | ... | ... | 28.3 | ... |
| | 1986 | 1.8 | 13.0 | ... | ... | ... |
| | 1991 | 2.1 | 25.7 | ... | ... | ... |
| | 1992 | 2.1 | 25.2 | ... | ... | ... |
| | 1993 | 2.2 | 26.0 | ... | ... | ... |
| | 1994 | 1.9 | 23.3 | ... | ... | ... |
| | 1995 | 2.0 | 27.7 | ... | ... | ... |
| | 1996 | 1.9 | 25.6 | ... | ... | ... |
| | 1997 | 1.9 | 26.8 | ... | ... | ... |
| Guinea-Bissau | 1970 | ... | ... | 0.4 | 5.5 | ... |
| | 1976 | ... | ... | 2.5 | ... | ... |
| | 1980 | ... | ... | 2.6 | ... | ... |
| | 1984 | ... | ... | 2.1 | 11.2 | ... |

Total and current public expenditure on education
Dépenses publiques totales et ordinaires afférentes à l'éducation
Gastos públicos totales y ordinarios destinados a la educación

II.18

| Country / Pays / País | Year / Année / Año | Total expenditure on education / Dépenses totales d'éducation / Gastos totales de educación | | Current expenditure on education / Dépenses ordinaires d'éducation / Gastos ordinarios de educación | | |
|---|---|---|---|---|---|---|
| | | As % of Gross National Product / En % du Produit National Brut / En % del Producto Nacional Bruto | As % of total government expenditure / En % des dépenses totales du gouvernement / En % de los gastos totales del gobierno | As % of Gross National Product / En % du Produit National Brut / En % del Producto Nacional Bruto | As % of current government expenditure / En % des dépenses ordinaires du gouvernement / En % de los gastos ordinarios del gobierno | As % of total expenditure on education / En % des dépenses totales d'éducation / En % de los gastos totales de educación |
| Kenya | 1970 | 5.0 | 17.6 | 4.7 | 23.3 | 93.9 |
| | 1975 | 6.3 | 19.4 | 6.0 | 27.7 | 95.4 |
| | 1980 | 6.8 | 18.1 | 6.2 | 23.6 | 92.1 |
| | 1985 | 6.4 | ... | 6.0 | ... | 93.8 |
| | 1990 | 7.1 | 17.0 | 6.4 | 20.5 | 90.4 |
| | 1991 | 6.7 | 15.7 | 6.1 | ... | 92.0 |
| | 1992 | 6.7 | 13.4 | 6.1 | ... | 91.8 |
| | 1993 | 6.5 | 11.3 | 6.2 | ... | 94.1 |
| | 1994 | 7.1 | 16.4 | 6.7 | ... | 94.4 |
| | 1995 | 6.7 | 16.9 | 6.4 | ... | 94.5 |
| | 1996 | 6.5 | 16.7 | 6.1 | ... | 93.4 |
| Lesotho | 1970 | 3.0 | 16.2 | 2.8 | 17.4 | 91.3 |
| | 1975 | 4.5 | 23.5 | 3.4 | 26.8 | 76.0 |
| | 1980 | 5.1 | 14.8 | 4.1 | 19.0 | 79.9 |
| | 1985 | 4.3 | ... | ... | ... | ... |
| | 1990 | 3.7 | 12.2 | 3.1 | 17.4 | 82.1 |
| | 1991 | 6.2 | 17.6 | 5.4 | 25.3 | 86.2 |
| | 1992 | 0.0 | ... | 5.1 | ... | 77.9 |
| | 1993 | 5.4 | ... | 5.3 | ... | 98.8 |
| | 1994 | 6.7 | ... | 6.0 | ... | 88.6 |
| | 1995 | ... | ... | 7.3 | ... | ... |
| | 1996 | 8.4 | ... | 6.4 | ... | 75.5 |
| Liberia | 1970 | 2.0 | 9.5 | ... | ... | ... |
| | 1975 | 1.9 | 11.6 | ... | ... | ... |
| | 1980 | 5.7 | 24.3 | 4.9 | 27.0 | 85.9 |
| Libyan Arab Jamahiriya | 1975 | 5.9 | 14.5 | 3.2 | ... | 54.5 |
| | 1980 | 3.4 | ... | 2.1 | ... | 63.0 |
| | 1985 | 7.1 | 19.8 | 5.7 | ... | 79.6 |
| Madagascar | 1970 | ... | ... | 2.9 | 18.9 | ... |
| | 1975 | 2.5 | 18.5 | 2.4 | 23.0 | 95.2 |
| | 1980 | 4.4 | ... | 3.7 | ... | 85.5 |
| | 1985 | 2.9 | ... | 2.8 | ... | 95.4 |
| | 1990 | 2.2 | ... | 2.0 | ... | 90.8 |
| | 1991 | 2.7 | ... | ... | ... | ... |
| | 1992 | 2.3 | ... | ... | ... | ... |
| | 1993 | 2.2 | 16.1 | ... | ... | ... |
| | 1997 | 1.9 | ... | ... | ... | ... |
| Malawi | 1970 | 4.6 | 13.2 | 3.4 | 16.4 | 73.7 |
| | 1975 | 2.4 | 9.6 | 2.2 | 18.3 | 91.9 |
| | 1980 | 3.4 | 8.4 | 2.6 | ... | 75.6 |
| | 1985 | 3.5 | 9.6 | 2.5 | ... | 72.2 |
| | 1990 | 3.4 | 11.1 | 2.6 | 11.1 | 75.3 |
| | 1991 | 3.2 | 12.1 | 2.2 | 11.3 | 69.7 |
| | 1992 | 4.8 | 17.4 | 3.7 | 17.5 | 75.9 |
| | 1993 | 4.4 | 20.0 | 3.5 | 20.7 | 79.1 |
| | 1994 | 4.3 | 18.3 | 3.4 | 20.8 | 79.2 |
| | 1995 | 5.4 | ... | 4.4 | ... | 82.3 |
| Mali | 1975 | ... | ... | 3.5 | 30.6 | ... |
| | 1980 | 3.7 | 30.8 | 3.6 | 32.1 | 98.8 |
| | 1985 | 3.1 | ... | 3.1 | ... | 99.2 |
| | 1991 | ... | ... | 3.2 | ... | ... |
| | 1992 | ... | ... | 2.6 | 22.0 | ... |
| | 1993 | ... | ... | 2.6 | 19.9 | ... |
| | 1994 | ... | ... | 2.3 | 20.1 | ... |
| | 1995 | 2.2 | ... | 2.1 | 21.2 | 97.7 |
| | 1996 | 2.2 | ... | ... | ... | ... |
| Mauritania | 1970 | 3.3 | 21.9 | 3.2 | ... | 95.0 |
| | 1975 | ... | ... | 3.7 | 16.1 | ... |
| (2) | 1980 | ... | ... | 5.0 | ... | ... |
| (2) | 1986 | ... | ... | 6.4 | 26.8 | ... |
| (2) | 1990 | ... | ... | 4.5 | ... | ... |
| (2) | 1991 | 4.9 | 13.9 | 4.2 | ... | 85.6 |
| (2) | 1992 | 4.9 | 13.4 | 4.0 | ... | 80.9 |
| (2) | 1993 | 5.1 | 14.5 | 4.0 | ... | 78.6 |
| (2) | 1994 | 5.2 | 16.2 | 3.9 | ... | 74.1 |
| (2) | 1995 | 5.1 | 16.2 | 3.7 | 22.1 | 73.7 |
| (2) | 1996 | ... | ... | 3.7 | 24.9 | ... |
| Mauritius | 1970 | 3.1 | 11.5 | 2.9 | 14.0 | 92.0 |
| | 1975 | 3.6 | 9.6 | 3.1 | 11.7 | 87.4 |
| | 1980 | 5.3 | 11.6 | 4.8 | 15.5 | 89.9 |

II.18　Total and current public expenditure on education
Dépenses publiques totales et ordinaires afférentes à l'éducation
Gastos públicos totales y ordinarios destinados a la educación

| Country / Pays / País | Year / Année / Año | Total expenditure on education / Dépenses totales d'éducation / Gastos totales de educación | | Current expenditure on education / Dépenses ordinaires d'éducation / Gastos ordinarios de educación | | |
|---|---|---|---|---|---|---|
| | | As % of Gross National Product / En % du Produit National Brut / En % del Producto Nacional Bruto | As % of total government expenditure / En % des dépenses totales du gouvernement / En % de los gastos totales del gobierno | As % of Gross National Product / En % du Produit National Brut / En % del Producto Nacional Bruto | As % of current government expenditure / En % des dépenses ordinaires du gouvernment / En % de los gastos ordinarios del gobierno | As % of total expenditure on education / En % des dépenses totales d'éducation / En % de los gastos totales de educación |
| Mauritius (cont) | 1985 | 3.8 | 9.8 | 3.5 | 12.4 | 92.8 |
| | 1990 | 3.6 | 11.8 | 3.3 | 14.0 | 93.0 |
| | 1991 | 3.8 | 14.6 | 3.3 | 15.7 | 86.3 |
| | 1992 | 3.6 | 15.0 | 3.2 | 16.2 | 87.2 |
| | 1993 | 4.1 | 16.2 | 3.6 | 17.8 | 89.2 |
| | 1994 | 4.4 | 17.8 | 3.8 | 18.3 | 85.2 |
| | 1995 | 4.2 | 16.8 | 3.5 | 16.9 | 84.3 |
| | 1996 | 4.6 | 17.4 | 3.6 | 16.3 | 78.5 |
| Morocco (2) | 1970 | 3.5 | 16.6 | 3.3 | 21.3 | 93.6 |
| | 1975 | 5.3 | 12.5 | 3.7 | 13.9 | 69.5 |
| | 1980 | 6.1 | 18.5 | 4.9 | 23.3 | 80.8 |
| | 1985 | 6.3 | 22.9 | 5.0 | 28.6 | 79.0 |
| | 1990 | 5.5 | 26.1 | 5.0 | 33.6 | 90.8 |
| | 1991 | 5.2 | 26.3 | 4.6 | 32.5 | 88.9 |
| | 1992 | 5.8 | 26.7 | 5.1 | 32.0 | 88.1 |
| | 1993 | 6.1 | 25.6 | 5.4 | 30.9 | 88.7 |
| | 1994 | 5.6 | 22.6 | 5.0 | 28.4 | 89.4 |
| | 1995 | 5.8 | 24.7 | 5.3 | ... | 91.1 |
| | 1996 | 5.3 | 24.9 | 4.9 | 29.9 | 92.4 |
| Mozambique | 1980 | 3.1 | 12.1 | 2.7 | 17.7 | 86.2 |
| | 1985 | 2.9 | 10.6 | 2.7 | 12.3 | 93.2 |
| | 1990 | 4.1 | 12.0 | 2.6 | 17.5 | 63.7 |
| Namibia | 1981 | 1.5 | ... | ... | ... | ... |
| | 1990 | 7.5 | ... | ... | ... | ... |
| | 1991 | 9.1 | 23.1 | 8.9 | ... | 97.9 |
| | 1992 | 9.8 | 23.2 | 9.7 | ... | 98.8 |
| | 1993 | 9.4 | 25.5 | 9.3 | ... | 99.0 |
| | 1994 | 9.1 | 27.2 | 8.7 | ... | 95.9 |
| | 1995 | 8.5 | 24.6 | 7.9 | ... | 93.3 |
| | 1996 | 9.3 | 25.6 | 8.6 | ... | 93.0 |
| | 1997 | 9.1 | ... | 8.5 | ... | 93.2 |
| Niger | 1970 | 1.1 | 17.7 | 1.1 | 17.5 | 93.8 |
| | 1975 | 2.4 | 18.7 | 2.1 | 17.9 | 87.0 |
| | 1980 | 3.2 | 22.9 | 1.5 | 16.8 | 47.0 |
| (1) | 1990 | 3.2 | 18.6 | ... | ... | ... |
| (1) | 1991 | 3.1 | 18.4 | 3.0 | ... | 96.8 |
| (1) | 1992 | 4.1 | 19.9 | ... | ... | ... |
| (1) | 1993 | 2.9 | 14.7 | ... | ... | ... |
| (1) | 1994 | 2.9 | 14.6 | ... | ... | ... |
| (1) | 1995 | 2.9 | 16.4 | ... | ... | ... |
| (1) | 1996 | 2.6 | 15.2 | ... | ... | ... |
| (1) | 1997 | 2.3 | 12.8 | ... | ... | ... |
| Nigeria (3) | 1976 | 4.1 | 16.5 | 2.1 | 27.3 | 51.0 |
| | 1979 | 3.6 | 16.2 | 2.4 | ... | 65.8 |
| | 1985 | 1.2 | 8.7 | 1.0 | 19.7 | 85.9 |
| | 1990 | 1.0 | ... | 0.8 | ... | 85.0 |
| | 1991 | 0.5 | ... | 0.4 | ... | 79.3 |
| | 1992 | 0.5 | ... | 0.4 | ... | 75.3 |
| | 1993 | 0.9 | ... | 0.7 | ... | 80.5 |
| | 1994 | 0.9 | 14.8 | 0.7 | ... | 76.6 |
| | 1995 | 0.7 | 11.5 | 0.5 | ... | 76.5 |
| Rwanda | 1970 | 2.3 | 26.6 | 2.2 | 28.3 | 98.8 |
| | 1975 | 2.3 | 25.3 | 2.3 | 28.4 | 99.9 |
| | 1980 | 2.7 | 21.6 | 2.3 | 21.5 | 84.7 |
| | 1984 | 3.1 | 25.1 | 3.1 | 28.1 | 97.8 |
| | 1989 | 3.8 | 25.4 | 3.5 | 29.1 | 94.1 |
| Sao Tome and Principe | 1970 | ... | ... | 2.4 | 11.3 | ... |
| | 1981 | 8.0 | ... | ... | ... | ... |
| | 1986 | 3.8 | 18.8 | ... | ... | ... |
| Senegal | 1970 | 3.8 | 21.3 | 3.7 | 22.3 | 97.8 |
| | 1975 | ... | ... | 4.1 | 21.4 | ... |
| | 1980 | ... | ... | 4.4 | 23.2 | ... |
| | 1985 | ... | ... | 4.2 | 23.1 | ... |
| | 1990 | 4.1 | 26.9 | 4.0 | 30.9 | 99.4 |
| | 1992 | 4.3 | 33.0 | 4.3 | 37.8 | 99.2 |
| | 1993 | 4.4 | 26.8 | 4.3 | 30.5 | 98.2 |
| | 1994 | 4.0 | 31.4 | 4.0 | 36.3 | 98.8 |
| | 1995 | 4.0 | 33.1 | 3.9 | 38.6 | 98.5 |
| | 1996 | 3.7 | ... | 3.7 | ... | 98.8 |
| | 1997 | ... | ... | 3.4 | ... | ... |

Total and current public expenditure on education
Dépenses publiques totales et ordinaires afférentes à l'éducation
Gastos públicos totales y ordinarios destinados a la educación

II.18

| Country / Pays / País | Year / Année / Año | Total expenditure on education / Dépenses totales d'éducation / Gastos totales de educación | | Current expenditure on education / Dépenses ordinaires d'éducation / Gastos ordinarios de educación | | |
|---|---|---|---|---|---|---|
| | | As % of Gross National Product / En % du Produit National Brut / En % del Producto Nacional Bruto | As % of total government expenditure / En % des dépenses totales du gouvernement / En % de los gastos totales del gobierno | As % of Gross National Product / En % du Produit National Brut / En % del Producto Nacional Bruto | As % of current government expenditure / En % des dépenses ordinaires du gouvernment / En % de los gastos ordinarios del gobierno | As % of total expenditure on education / En % des dépenses totales d'éducation / En % de los gastos totales de educación |
| Seychelles | 1970 | 4.2 | 11.5 | 3.8 | 15.1 | 89.9 |
| | 1975 | 4.4 | 9.5 | 3.9 | 15.1 | 88.7 |
| | 1980 | 5.8 | 14.4 | 5.5 | 14.0 | 95.7 |
| | 1985 | 10.7 | 21.3 | 10.3 | 21.9 | 96.4 |
| | 1990 | 8.1 | 14.8 | 8.1 | 18.5 | 100.0 |
| | 1992 | 8.4 | 14.6 | 7.2 | 15.4 | 85.6 |
| | 1994 | 9.3 | 16.8 | 7.6 | 16.0 | 81.4 |
| | 1995 | 8.0 | 16.3 | 6.5 | 15.7 | 81.6 |
| | 1996 | 7.9 | 24.1 | 6.3 | 25.6 | 79.9 |
| Sierra Leone | 1970 | 3.2 | 17.5 | 2.8 | 18.4 | 89.0 |
| | 1975 | 3.3 | ... | 3.0 | 16.3 | 90.2 |
| | 1980 | 3.5 | 11.8 | 3.3 | 14.5 | 95.3 |
| | 1985 | 1.9 | 12.4 | 1.8 | 15.5 | 94.9 |
| | 1989 | 0.9 | ... | 0.9 | ... | 95.5 |
| Somalia | 1970 | 1.0 | 7.6 | 1.0 | 7.6 | 100.0 |
| | 1975 | 2.1 | 12.5 | 1.7 | 12.8 | 83.7 |
| (1) | 1979 | 1.7 | 8.4 | 1.5 | ... | 87.3 |
| (1) | 1981 | 1.1 | 8.1 | 1.0 | ... | 87.5 |
| (1) | 1984 | 0.6 | 5.3 | 0.5 | ... | 82.7 |
| (1) | 1985 | 0.5 | 4.1 | 0.3 | ... | 73.8 |
| (1) | 1986 | 0.4 | 2.8 | 0.3 | ... | 66.9 |
| South Africa | 1986 | 6.0 | ... | 5.0 | ... | 84.4 |
| | 1989 | 5.9 | ... | 5.1 | ... | 87.3 |
| | 1990 | 6.5 | ... | 5.8 | ... | 89.0 |
| | 1992 | 7.0 | 22.1 | 6.4 | ... | 92.1 |
| | 1993 | 7.1 | 22.9 | 6.4 | ... | 90.6 |
| | 1994 | 7.3 | 21.6 | ... | ... | ... |
| | 1995 | 6.8 | 20.5 | 6.4 | ... | 94.0 |
| | 1996 | 8.0 | 23.9 | 7.5 | ... | 94.9 |
| Sudan | 1970 | 3.7 | 12.6 | 3.5 | 14.2 | 93.4 |
| | 1974 | 5.0 | 14.8 | 4.5 | ... | 89.6 |
| | 1980 | 4.3 | 9.1 | 3.9 | 12.6 | 92.2 |
| | 1995 | 1.4 | ... | 1.4 | ... | 99.4 |
| Swaziland | 1970 | 4.9 | 17.3 | 4.2 | 20.1 | 85.7 |
| | 1975 | 3.8 | ... | 3.0 | ... | 78.1 |
| | 1980 | 5.6 | ... | 4.3 | 23.1 | 76.4 |
| | 1985 | 5.5 | 19.3 | 4.6 | ... | 83.6 |
| | 1990 | 5.5 | 19.5 | 4.5 | ... | 81.9 |
| | 1991 | 7.2 | 23.0 | 5.9 | ... | 82.5 |
| | 1992 | 7.3 | 20.6 | 6.0 | ... | 81.6 |
| | 1993 | 6.7 | 17.5 | 5.5 | 21.0 | 82.0 |
| | 1994 | 7.7 | 18.3 | 6.5 | ... | 84.5 |
| | 1995 | 6.3 | 19.9 | 5.5 | 23.5 | 86.7 |
| | 1996 | 5.7 | 18.1 | 5.1 | ... | 89.0 |
| Togo | 1970 | 2.2 | 19.0 | 2.0 | ... | 88.8 |
| | 1975 | 3.5 | 15.1 | 3.4 | 21.3 | 96.3 |
| | 1980 | 5.6 | 19.4 | 5.4 | 21.0 | 96.4 |
| | 1985 | 4.9 | 19.4 | 4.6 | 19.2 | 94.6 |
| | 1990 | 5.6 | 26.4 | 5.2 | ... | 93.0 |
| | 1991 | ... | ... | 5.2 | ... | ... |
| | 1992 | 6.1 | 21.6 | 6.0 | 29.0 | 97.4 |
| | 1995 | ... | ... | 4.3 | ... | ... |
| | 1996 | 4.5 | 24.7 | 4.2 | 24.1 | 92.9 |
| Tunisia | 1970 | 7.1 | 23.2 | 6.0 | 27.5 | 84.4 |
| | 1975 | 5.2 | 16.4 | 4.6 | 22.5 | 89.2 |
| | 1980 | 5.4 | 16.4 | 4.7 | 23.5 | 87.6 |
| | 1985 | 5.8 | 14.1 | 5.2 | 20.8 | 90.2 |
| | 1990 | 6.2 | 13.5 | 5.4 | 16.3 | 87.8 |
| | 1991 | 6.3 | 14.3 | 5.5 | 17.4 | 88.2 |
| | 1992 | 6.0 | 14.2 | 5.4 | 17.6 | 88.9 |
| | 1993 | 6.4 | 15.8 | 5.5 | ... | 86.4 |
| | 1994 | 6.6 | 16.4 | 5.8 | 20.9 | 88.0 |
| | 1995 | 6.8 | 17.4 | 5.9 | ... | 86.9 |
| | 1996 | 6.7 | 17.4 | 5.7 | 25.9 | 85.8 |
| | 1997 | 7.7 | 19.9 | 6.6 | 30.4 | 86.3 |
| Uganda | 1970 | 4.1 | 17.7 | 3.4 | 22.3 | 82.4 |
| (2) | 1975 | 2.7 | 17.0 | 2.5 | 22.0 | 93.0 |
| (2) | 1980 | 1.2 | 11.3 | 1.1 | 12.8 | 88.3 |
| (2) | 1984 | 3.5 | ... | 2.5 | ... | 71.1 |

II.18 Total and current public expenditure on education
Dépenses publiques totales et ordinaires afférentes à l'éducation
Gastos públicos totales y ordinarios destinados a la educación

| Country / Pays / País | Year / Année / Año | Total expenditure on education / Dépenses totales d'éducation / Gastos totales de educación | | Current expenditure on education / Dépenses ordinaires d'éducation / Gastos ordinarios de educación | | |
|---|---|---|---|---|---|---|
| | | As % of Gross National Product / En % du Produit National Brut / En % del Producto Nacional Bruto | As % of total government expenditure / En % des dépenses totales du gouvernement / En % de los gastos totales del gobierno | As % of Gross National Product / En % du Produit National Brut / En % del Producto Nacional Bruto | As % of current government expenditure / En % des dépenses ordinaires du gouvernment / En % de los gastos ordinarios del gobierno | As % of total expenditure on education / En % des dépenses totales d'éducation / En % de los gastos totales de educación |
| Uganda (cont) (2) | 1990 | 1.5 | 11.5 | 1.4 | 15.1 | 91.8 |
| (2) | 1991 | 1.9 | 15.0 | 1.8 | 16.5 | 94.2 |
| | 1995 | 2.6 | 21.4 | 2.4 | 22.8 | 95.5 |
| United Republic of Tanzania | 1970 | ... | 16.0 | ... | 19.7 | 82.8 |
| | 1975 | ... | 17.8 | ... | 22.5 | 80.4 |
| | 1980 | ... | 11.2 | ... | 16.3 | 82.7 |
| | 1985 | ... | 14.0 | ... | 15.6 | 86.0 |
| | 1990 | 3.4 | 11.4 | 3.0 | ... | 87.9 |
| | 1991 | ... | ... | 2.9 | ... | ... |
| | 1992 | ... | ... | 3.0 | 14.6 | ... |
| | 1993 | ... | ... | 3.1 | 17.9 | ... |
| | 1994 | ... | ... | 3.7 | 23.0 | ... |
| Zambia | 1970 | 4.5 | 9.0 | 3.6 | 11.7 | 79.2 |
| | 1975 | 6.7 | 11.5 | 5.2 | 12.4 | 76.9 |
| | 1980 | 4.5 | 7.6 | 4.2 | 11.1 | 95.1 |
| | 1985 | 4.7 | 13.4 | 4.4 | 14.3 | 92.9 |
| | 1990 | 2.6 | 8.7 | 2.3 | 8.7 | 87.0 |
| | 1991 | 3.1 | 7.1 | 2.8 | ... | 89.8 |
| | 1992 | 2.3 | 7.7 | 2.2 | ... | 93.1 |
| | 1993 | 2.1 | 9.2 | 2.0 | ... | 94.7 |
| | 1994 | 2.1 | 6.5 | 1.8 | ... | 86.0 |
| | 1995 | 2.2 | 7.1 | 2.0 | ... | 92.6 |
| Zimbabwe | 1970 | 2.7 | ... | 2.6 | 16.1 | 96.1 |
| | 1975 | 2.9 | ... | 2.7 | 14.2 | 91.8 |
| | 1980 | 5.3 | 13.7 | 5.1 | 14.1 | 97.4 |
| | 1985 | 7.0 | 16.0 | ... | ... | ... |
| | 1990 | 8.0 | ... | ... | ... | ... |
| | 1991 | 6.7 | ... | ... | ... | ... |
| | 1992 | 7.4 | ... | ... | ... | ... |
| | 1993 | 7.1 | ... | ... | ... | ... |
| | 1994 | ... | ... | 7.5 | ... | ... |
| **North America** | | | | | | |
| Antigua and Barbuda | 1970 | ... | 10.4 | ... | ... | 99.3 |
| | 1975 | ... | 14.4 | ... | 15.9 | 89.5 |
| | 1980 | 3.0 | ... | 3.0 | ... | 98.9 |
| | 1984 | 2.7 | ... | 2.6 | ... | 95.8 |
| Aruba | 1990 | 5.0 | 18.0 | 4.0 | 19.4 | 81.2 |
| | 1991 | 4.5 | 15.9 | 3.5 | 16.8 | 78.4 |
| | 1992 | 4.8 | 15.5 | 3.7 | 16.3 | 75.7 |
| | 1993 | 4.7 | 16.6 | 3.8 | 17.0 | 79.8 |
| | 1994 | 4.9 | 16.9 | 3.6 | 16.0 | 74.6 |
| | 1995 | ... | 16.2 | ... | 15.8 | 80.9 |
| | 1996 | ... | 11.8 | ... | 12.2 | 87.3 |
| | 1997 | ... | 12.8 | ... | 14.0 | 87.2 |
| Bahamas | 1970 | 4.8 | 19.4 | 3.8 | 18.6 | 79.3 |
| | 1975 | 6.2 | ... | 5.7 | 22.2 | 92.1 |
| | 1980 | ... | ... | 4.4 | 22.1 | ... |
| | 1985 | 4.0 | 18.0 | 3.8 | ... | 94.5 |
| | 1990 | 4.3 | 17.8 | 3.8 | ... | 89.2 |
| | 1991 | 4.0 | 16.3 | 3.6 | ... | 90.8 |
| | 1996 | ... | 13.2 | ... | 14.4 | 92.6 |
| Barbados | 1970 | 5.8 | 21.2 | 5.5 | 23.6 | 94.3 |
| | 1975 | 6.0 | 20.9 | 5.2 | ... | 86.5 |
| | 1980 | 6.5 | 20.5 | 5.3 | ... | 82.8 |
| | 1984 | 6.1 | ... | 5.4 | ... | 88.2 |
| | 1990 | 7.9 | 22.2 | 6.4 | 22.1 | 81.0 |
| | 1991 | 7.6 | 18.4 | 6.5 | 18.7 | 85.4 |
| | 1992 | 6.9 | 16.9 | 6.2 | 17.5 | 89.3 |
| | 1993 | 7.5 | 18.6 | 7.3 | 20.0 | 96.8 |
| | 1994 | 7.2 | 19.0 | ... | ... | ... |
| Belize | 1970 | 3.8 | ... | 3.7 | ... | 98.6 |
| | 1974 | 3.3 | ... | 3.0 | ... | 90.9 |
| | 1980 | 2.4 | 14.5 | 2.3 | ... | 98.5 |
| | 1985 | 4.7 | 15.4 | 4.6 | ... | 98.2 |
| | 1990 | 4.8 | 18.5 | 4.5 | ... | 94.4 |
| | 1991 | 4.8 | 16.6 | 4.4 | ... | 91.5 |
| | 1992 | 5.3 | 17.9 | 4.8 | ... | 90.0 |
| | 1993 | 5.6 | 19.6 | 5.6 | ... | 99.5 |

| Country<br><br>Pays<br><br>País | Year<br><br>Année<br><br>Año | Total expenditure on education<br>Dépenses totales d'éducation<br>Gastos totales de educación | | Current expenditure on education<br>Dépenses ordinaires d'éducation<br>Gastos ordinarios de educación | | |
|---|---|---|---|---|---|---|
| | | As % of Gross National Product<br><br>En % du Produit National Brut<br><br>En % del Producto Nacional Bruto | As % of total government expenditure<br><br>En % des dépenses totales du gouvernement<br><br>En % de los gastos totales del gobierno | As % of Gross National Product<br><br>En % du Produit National Brut<br><br>En % del Producto Nacional Bruto | As % of current government expenditure<br><br>En % des dépenses ordinaires du gouvernement<br><br>En % de los gastos ordinarios del gobiemo | As % of total expenditure on education<br><br>En % des dépenses totales d'éducation<br><br>En % de los gastos totales de educación |
| Belize (cont) | 1994 | 5.9 | 19.9 | 5.7 | ... | 96.6 |
| | 1995 | 5.3 | 19.6 | 5.1 | ... | 96.9 |
| | 1996 | 5.0 | 19.5 | 4.8 | ... | 96.0 |
| Bermuda | 1970 | 3.6 | 18.8 | 2.9 | | 82.6 |
| | 1975 | 3.0 | ... | 2.8 | | 95.8 |
| | 1980 | 4.0 | | 3.9 | | 98.0 |
| | 1984 | 3.1 | 18.4 | 3.0 | 19.9 | 95.2 |
| | 1990 | 3.3 | 14.5 | 3.1 | 15.7 | 92.5 |
| | 1991 | 3.7 | ... | 3.3 | | 89.2 |
| British Virgin Islands | 1970 | ... | 15.0 | ... | 19.9 | 51.2 |
| | 1976 | ... | 13.2 | ... | 13.6 | 81.3 |
| | 1980 | ... | ... | ... | 13.3 | ... |
| | 1985 | ... | 16.7 | ... | | 90.5 |
| | 1990 | ... | 12.2 | ... | | 89.2 |
| | 1991 | ... | 15.4 | ... | ... | 80.0 |
| Canada @ | 1970 | 8.6 | ... | 7.3 | | 84.9 |
| | 1975 | 7.6 | 17.8 | 6.8 | ... | 90.1 |
| | 1980 | 6.9 | 16.3 | 6.4 | ... | 92.6 |
| | 1985 | 6.5 | 11.9 | 6.1 | ... | 93.1 |
| | 1990 | 6.8 | 14.2 | 6.3 | ... | 92.6 |
| | 1991 | 7.3 | ... | 6.8 | ... | 92.9 |
| | _1992_ | 7.5 | 14.3 | 7.0 | ... | 93.1 |
| | 1993 | 7.2 | 13.2 | ... | ... | ... |
| | 1994 | 6.9 | 12.9 | 6.4 | | 92.4 |
| Costa Rica | 1970 | 5.2 | 31.8 | 5.0 | ... | 96.1 |
| | 1975 | 6.9 | 31.1 | 6.4 | 39.7 | 93.5 |
| | 1980 | 7.8 | 22.2 | 7.1 | 26.7 | 91.3 |
| | 1985 | 4.5 | 22.7 | 4.2 | 26.2 | 95.2 |
| | 1990 | 4.6 | 20.8 | 4.4 | 26.3 | 96.9 |
| | 1991 | 4.5 | 21.8 | 4.3 | ... | 96.4 |
| | 1992 | 4.4 | 21.4 | ... | ... | ... |
| | 1993 | 4.6 | 20.2 | ... | ... | ... |
| | 1994 | 4.6 | 19.2 | ... | ... | ... |
| | 1995 | 4.6 | 19.8 | ... | ... | ... |
| | 1996 | 5.4 | 22.8 | ... | ... | ... |
| Cuba | (4) 1970 | 4.2 | 18.4 | ... | ... | ... |
| | (4) 1975 | 5.7 | | ... | ... | ... |
| | (4) 1980 | 7.2 | ... | 6.4 | ... | 89.5 |
| | (4) 1985 | 6.3 | | 6.0 | ... | 93.9 |
| | (4) 1990 | 6.6 | 12.3 | 6.1 | 14.4 | 93.1 |
| | 1991 | 9.7 | 10.8 | 9.3 | 13.6 | 95.5 |
| | 1992 | ... | | 9.6 | 12.1 | ... |
| | 1993 | 9.5 | 9.8 | 9.2 | 11.1 | 97.3 |
| | 1994 | 7.5 | 10.2 | 7.5 | 12.5 | 99.3 |
| | 1995 | 6.8 | 10.9 | 6.7 | 12.5 | 99.2 |
| | 1996 | 6.7 | 12.6 | 6.7 | 15.0 | 99.1 |
| Dominica | 1986 | 5.8 | 16.7 | 5.5 | 18.5 | 95.9 |
| | 1989 | 5.5 | 10.6 | 5.0 | 19.9 | 91.0 |
| Dominican Republic | 1970 | 2.9 | 15.9 | 2.7 | 22.7 | 93.1 |
| | 1976 | 1.9 | 14.3 | 1.6 | 19.7 | 82.4 |
| | 1980 | 2.2 | 16.0 | ... | ... | ... |
| | 1985 | 1.6 | 14.0 | ... | ... | ... |
| | 1992 | 1.4 | 8.9 | ... | ... | ... |
| | 1993 | 1.7 | 9.8 | ... | ... | ... |
| | 1994 | 2.0 | 12.2 | ... | ... | ... |
| | 1995 | 1.9 | 13.2 | ... | ... | ... |
| | 1996 | 2.0 | 13.4 | 1.7 | 21.8 | 87.9 |
| | 1997 | 2.3 | 13.8 | 2.1 | 19.3 | 91.7 |
| El Salvador | 1970 | 2.6 | 27.6 | 2.5 | 29.9 | 93.7 |
| | 1975 | 3.3 | 22.2 | 3.0 | 28.1 | 91.7 |
| | 1980 | 3.9 | 17.1 | 3.7 | 22.9 | 94.1 |
| | 1984 | 3.1 | 12.5 | 2.7 | 16.3 | 87.3 |
| | 1990 | 2.0 | 16.6 | ... | ... | ... |
| | 1991 | 1.8 | 15.2 | ... | ... | ... |
| | 1992 | 1.9 | 13.8 | ... | ... | ... |
| | 1993 | 1.8 | 14.5 | ... | ... | ... |
| | 1994 | 2.0 | 14.7 | ... | ... | ... |
| | 1995 | 2.2 | 15.3 | 2.2 | ... | 99.3 |
| | 1996 | 2.3 | 14.1 | ... | ... | ... |
| | 1997 | 2.5 | 16.0 | ... | ... | ... |

II.18    Total and current public expenditure on education
Dépenses publiques totales et ordinaires afférentes à l'éducation
Gastos públicos totales y ordinarios destinados a la educación

| Country / Pays / País | Year / Année / Año | Total expenditure on education — Dépenses totales d'éducation — Gastos totales de educación | | Current expenditure on education — Dépenses ordinaires d'éducation — Gastos ordinarios de educación | | |
|---|---|---|---|---|---|---|
| | | As % of Gross National Product — En % du Produit National Brut — En % del Producto Nacional Bruto | As % of total government expenditure — En % des dépenses totales du gouvernement — En % de los gastos totales del gobierno | As % of Gross National Product — En % du Produit National Brut — En % del Producto Nacional Bruto | As % of current government expenditure — En % des dépenses ordinaires du gouvernement — En % de los gastos ordinarios del gobierno | As % of total expenditure on education — En % des dépenses totales d'éducation — En % de los gastos totales de educación |
| Grenada | 1975 | ... | 12.5 | ... | 23.4 | 99.5 |
| | 1981 | 6.1 | 9.5 | ... | ... | ... |
| | 1985 | 5.8 | 7.7 | ... | ... | ... |
| | 1990 | 5.4 | 13.2 | ... | ... | ... |
| | 1991 | 5.0 | 11.9 | ... | ... | ... |
| | 1992 | 4.7 | 13.4 | ... | ... | ... |
| | 1993 | 4.7 | 11.8 | ... | ... | ... |
| | 1994 | 4.6 | 12.5 | ... | ... | ... |
| | 1995 | 4.6 | 11.2 | ... | ... | ... |
| | 1996 | 4.7 | 10.6 | ... | ... | ... |
| Guatemala | 1970 | 2.0 | 17.5 | 1.7 | 21.0 | 88.3 |
| | 1975 | 1.6 | 15.7 | ... | ... | ... |
| | (2) 1980 | 1.8 | 11.9 | ... | ... | ... |
| | (2) 1985 | 1.6 | 14.5 | ... | ... | ... |
| | (2) 1990 | 1.4 | 11.8 | ... | ... | ... |
| | (2) 1991 | 1.3 | 13.0 | ... | ... | ... |
| | (2) 1992 | 1.4 | 11.5 | ... | ... | ... |
| | (2) 1993 | 1.6 | 12.8 | ... | ... | ... |
| | (2) 1994 | 1.5 | 14.7 | 1.4 | ... | 93.5 |
| | (2) 1995 | 1.7 | 16.0 | 1.6 | ... | 94.8 |
| | (2) 1996 | 1.7 | 15.8 | 1.6 | ... | 94.7 |
| Haiti | 1970 | ... | ... | 1.3 | 17.8 | ... |
| | 1975 | ... | ... | 1.0 | 15.8 | ... |
| | 1980 | 1.5 | 14.9 | 1.2 | 17.2 | 80.1 |
| | 1985 | 1.2 | 16.5 | 1.2 | 16.7 | 99.8 |
| | 1990 | 1.5 | 20.0 | 1.5 | 20.1 | 99.9 |
| Honduras | 1970 | 3.1 | 18.4 | 3.0 | ... | 95.3 |
| | 1975 | 3.7 | 20.3 | ... | ... | ... |
| | 1980 | 3.2 | 14.2 | 2.9 | 19.5 | 91.0 |
| | 1985 | 4.2 | 13.8 | 4.1 | ... | 98.6 |
| | 1991 | 4.1 | ... | 4.0 | ... | 97.7 |
| | 1994 | 3.5 | 16.0 | 3.4 | ... | 98.3 |
| | 1995 | 3.6 | 16.5 | 3.5 | ... | 98.1 |
| Jamaica | 1970 | 3.6 | ... | 2.6 | ... | 71.5 |
| | 1975 | 5.9 | 16.0 | 4.7 | ... | 78.8 |
| | 1980 | 7.0 | 13.1 | 6.9 | 19.4 | 99.6 |
| | 1985 | 5.4 | 12.1 | 5.1 | 15.8 | 93.7 |
| | 1990 | 5.4 | 12.8 | 4.7 | 17.3 | 86.7 |
| | 1991 | 4.7 | 7.9 | 4.1 | 18.2 | 87.9 |
| | 1992 | 4.6 | 11.8 | 4.1 | 17.9 | 87.9 |
| | 1993 | 5.8 | 12.9 | 5.3 | 15.6 | 92.1 |
| | 1994 | 5.7 | 10.4 | 5.0 | 16.1 | 88.1 |
| | 1995 | 6.4 | 7.7 | 5.8 | 17.9 | 90.9 |
| | 1996 | 7.5 | 12.9 | 6.8 | 20.6 | 91.4 |
| Mexico @ | 1970 | 2.3 | ... | ... | ... | ... |
| | 1975 | 3.5 | 20.4 | ... | ... | ... |
| | 1980 | 4.7 | 20.4 | ... | ... | ... |
| | 1985 | 3.9 | 13.6 | ... | ... | ... |
| | 1990 | 3.7 | 12.8 | ... | ... | ... |
| | 1991 | 3.9 | 15.3 | ... | ... | ... |
| | 1992 | 4.4 | 18.1 | ... | ... | ... |
| | 1993 | 5.1 | 22.3 | ... | ... | ... |
| | 1994 | 4.7 | 26.0 | 4.5 | ... | 94.9 |
| | 1995 | 4.9 | 23.0 | 4.6 | ... | 94.1 |
| Montserrat | 1971 | ... | ... | ... | 15.3 | ... |
| | 1990 | ... | ... | ... | 18.9 | ... |
| | 1991 | ... | ... | ... | 19.5 | ... |
| | 1992 | ... | ... | ... | 19.3 | ... |
| | 1993 | ... | ... | ... | 18.8 | ... |
| Nicaragua | 1970 | 2.5 | 18.1 | 2.4 | ... | 98.7 |
| | 1975 | 2.5 | 13.1 | 2.0 | ... | 79.8 |
| | 1980 | 3.4 | 10.4 | 3.0 | ... | 87.5 |
| | 1985 | 5.9 | 10.2 | 5.7 | 12.2 | 96.7 |
| | (1) 1990 | 3.4 | 9.7 | ... | ... | ... |
| | (1) 1991 | 4.3 | 12.1 | ... | ... | ... |
| | (1) 1992 | 4.1 | 10.6 | 4.0 | ... | 98.4 |
| | (1) 1993 | 3.5 | 9.8 | ... | ... | ... |
| | (1) 1994 | 3.9 | 9.0 | 3.8 | ... | 96.1 |
| | (1) 1995 | 3.7 | 9.9 | 3.0 | ... | 80.5 |
| | (1) 1996 | 3.7 | 10.2 | 2.6 | ... | 72.4 |
| | (1) 1997 | 3.9 | 8.8 | ... | ... | ... |

Total and current public expenditure on education  II.18
Dépenses publiques totales et ordinaires afférentes à l'éducation
Gastos públicos totales y ordinarios destinados a la educación

| Country / Pays / País | Year / Année / Año | Total expenditure on education / Dépenses totales d'éducation / Gastos totales de educación | | Current expenditure on education / Dépenses ordinaires d'éducation / Gastos ordinarios de educación | | |
|---|---|---|---|---|---|---|
| | | As % of Gross National Product / En % du Produit National Brut / En % del Producto Nacional Bruto | As % of total government expenditure / En % des dépenses totales du gouvernement / En % de los gastos totales del gobierno | As % of Gross National Product / En % du Produit National Brut / En % del Producto Nacional Bruto | As % of current government expenditure / En % des dépenses ordinaires du gouvernment / En % de los gastos ordinarios del gobierno | As % of total expenditure on education / En % des dépenses totales d'éducation / En % de los gastos totales de educación |
| Panama | 1970 | 5.3 | 22.1 | 4.9 | 28.9 | 92.3 |
| | 1975 | 5.4 | 21.3 | 5.1 | 31.6 | 93.6 |
| | 1980 | 4.9 | 19.0 | 4.6 | 19.8 | 93.7 |
| | 1985 | 4.6 | 18.7 | 4.4 | 19.9 | 97.7 |
| | 1990 | 4.9 | 20.9 | 4.8 | 22.2 | 97.3 |
| | 1991 | 5.0 | 18.9 | 4.8 | 21.1 | 97.5 |
| | 1992 | 5.3 | 18.9 | 5.0 | 21.9 | 93.2 |
| | 1993 | 5.0 | 22.9 | 4.7 | 24.5 | 93.8 |
| | 1994 | 5.0 | 22.2 | 4.7 | 24.5 | 95.3 |
| | 1995 | 5.2 | 22.1 | 4.8 | 23.9 | 91.2 |
| | 1996 | 5.3 | 20.9 | 5.0 | 22.3 | 93.3 |
| | 1997 | 5.1 | 16.3 | 4.8 | 17.2 | 92.9 |
| Puerto Rico | 1970 | 7.8 | ... | 7.3 | ... | 94.2 |
| | 1975 | 8.2 | ... | 7.9 | ... | 97.1 |
| St. Kitts and Nevis | 1970 | ... | 9.7 | ... | ... | ... |
| | 1975 | ... | 10.5 | ... | 12.4 | 99.3 |
| | 1980 | 5.3 | 9.4 | 5.2 | 13.6 | 99.5 |
| | 1985 | 5.8 | 18.5 | 5.8 | 19.1 | 99.7 |
| | 1992 | 3.2 | ... | 3.1 | ... | 95.2 |
| | 1995 | 3.7 | 9.8 | 3.6 | 14.9 | 96.1 |
| | 1996 | 3.8 | 8.8 | 3.5 | 13.8 | 92.5 |
| St. Lucia | 1975 | ... | 16.8 | ... | 20.0 | 87.8 |
| | 1980 | ... | ... | 6.9 | ... | ... |
| | 1986 | 5.5 | ... | 5.2 | ... | 94.4 |
| | 1990 | ... | ... | 5.4 | 22.8 | ... |
| | 1991 | ... | ... | 5.1 | 20.8 | ... |
| | 1992 | ... | ... | 5.2 | 23.2 | ... |
| | 1993 | ... | ... | 5.7 | 23.7 | ... |
| | 1994 | 9.8 | 22.2 | 6.5 | 24.9 | 65.9 |
| St. Vincent and the Grenadines | 1970 | 5.8 | ... | 4.9 | ... | 83.8 |
| | 1976 | 6.7 | ... | ... | ... | ... |
| | 1986 | 6.0 | 11.6 | 5.6 | 16.8 | 93.4 |
| | 1991 | 6.3 | 13.8 | 4.7 | 17.2 | 75.3 |
| Trinidad and Tobago | 1970 | 3.4 | 14.0 | 3.0 | 16.9 | 88.3 |
| | 1975 | 3.1 | 14.7 | 2.7 | 17.7 | 88.1 |
| | 1980 | 4.0 | 11.5 | 3.0 | 17.6 | 76.4 |
| | 1985 | 6.1 | ... | 5.3 | ... | 87.5 |
| | 1990 | 4.0 | 11.6 | 3.7 | 13.5 | 92.2 |
| | 1991 | 4.5 | 12.4 | 4.2 | 13.0 | 92.1 |
| | 1992 | 3.8 | 10.3 | 3.6 | 10.7 | 95.2 |
| | 1993 | 3.7 | ... | 3.5 | ... | 96.3 |
| | 1994 | 4.4 | ... | 4.0 | ... | 90.7 |
| U. S. Virgin Islands | 1970 | 6.5 | ... | 6.4 | ... | 97.9 |
| | 1975 | 9.5 | ... | 9.4 | ... | 98.9 |
| | 1984 | 7.5 | ... | ... | ... | ... |
| United States @ | 1985 | 4.9 | 15.5 | 4.5 | 16.3 | 91.7 |
| | 1990 | 5.2 | 12.3 | 4.7 | 12.3 | 90.5 |
| | 1992 | 5.4 | 14.1 | ... | ... | ... |
| | 1993 | 5.3 | 14.0 | ... | ... | ... |
| | 1994 | 5.4 | 14.4 | ... | ... | ... |
| **South America** | | | | | | |
| Argentina | 1971 | 2.5 | 16.0 | ... | ... | ... |
| | 1975 | 1.8 | 9.5 | 1.7 | 10.9 | 93.8 |
| | 1980 | 2.7 | 15.1 | 2.3 | 18.8 | 84.5 |
| | 1984 | 2.7 | ... | 2.4 | 23.8 | 88.2 |
| | 1991 | 3.4 | ... | ... | ... | ... |
| | 1992 | 3.1 | 15.7 | ... | ... | ... |
| | 1993 | 3.3 | 12.4 | ... | ... | ... |
| | 1994 | 3.8 | 14.0 | ... | ... | ... |
| | 1996 | 3.5 | 12.6 | 3.2 | ... | 91.8 |
| Bolivia | 1970 | 3.3 | 28.4 | 3.3 | ... | 99.7 |
| | 1975 | 3.5 | ... | 3.5 | ... | 99.9 |
| | 1980 | 4.4 | 25.3 | 4.2 | 27.0 | 96.0 |
| | 1985 | 2.0 | ... | ... | ... | ... |
| | 1994 | 4.9 | 11.2 | 4.8 | 15.1 | 97.8 |
| | 1995 | 5.9 | ... | 5.1 | ... | 86.6 |
| | 1996 | 4.9 | 11.1 | 4.8 | 14.2 | 99.0 |

II.18    Total and current public expenditure on education
Dépenses publiques totales et ordinaires afférentes à l'éducation
Gastos públicos totales y ordinarios destinados a la educación

| Country / Pays / País | | Year / Année / Año | Total expenditure on education / Dépenses totales d'éducation / Gastos totales de educación | | Current expenditure on education / Dépenses ordinaires d'éducation / Gastos ordinarios de educación | | |
|---|---|---|---|---|---|---|---|
| | | | As % of Gross National Product / En % du Produit National Brut / En % del Producto Nacional Bruto | As % of total government expenditure / En % des dépenses totales du gouvernement / En % de los gastos totales del gobierno | As % of Gross National Product / En % du Produit National Brut / En % del Producto Nacional Bruto | As % of current government expenditure / En % des dépenses ordinaires du gouvernement / En % de los gastos ordinarios del gobierno | As % of total expenditure on education / En % des dépenses totales d'éducation / En % de los gastos totales de educación |
| Brazil | | 1970 | 2.9 | 10.6 | ... | ... | ... |
| | | 1975 | 3.0 | ... | ... | ... | ... |
| | | 1980 | 3.6 | ... | ... | ... | ... |
| | | 1985 | 3.8 | 19.1 | ... | ... | ... |
| | | 1989 | 4.5 | ... | ... | ... | ... |
| | | 1995 | 5.1 | ... | 4.7 | ... | 93.1 |
| Chile | | 1970 | 5.1 | 22.0 | ... | ... | ... |
| | | 1975 | 4.1 | 12.0 | 3.9 | 16.0 | 94.4 |
| | | 1980 | 4.6 | 11.9 | 4.4 | 13.4 | 94.9 |
| | | 1985 | 4.4 | 15.3 | ... | ... | ... |
| | | 1991 | 2.7 | 10.0 | 2.6 | ... | 96.8 |
| | | 1992 | 2.8 | 12.9 | 2.7 | 15.0 | 96.3 |
| | | 1993 | 2.8 | ... | 2.7 | ... | 98.1 |
| | | 1994 | 3.1 | 13.4 | 2.9 | 14.7 | 94.4 |
| | | 1995 | 3.1 | 14.0 | 2.9 | 15.6 | 94.7 |
| | | 1996 | 3.4 | 14.8 | 3.2 | 16.5 | 93.9 |
| | | 1997 | 3.6 | 15.5 | 3.4 | 17.8 | 95.6 |
| Colombia | (2) | 1970 | 1.9 | 13.6 | 1.5 | 17.3 | 78.6 |
| | | 1975 | 2.2 | 16.4 | 1.9 | 25.0 | 85.4 |
| | | 1980 | 2.4 | 19.2 | 2.2 | ... | 92.2 |
| | | 1985 | 2.8 | 19.5 | 2.7 | ... | 94.1 |
| | | 1990 | 2.6 | 16.0 | 2.3 | ... | 89.8 |
| | | 1991 | 2.6 | 15.0 | 2.2 | ... | 84.2 |
| | | 1992 | 3.7 | 16.4 | 3.3 | ... | 89.3 |
| | | 1993 | 3.1 | 17.4 | 2.7 | ... | 87.4 |
| | | 1994 | 3.6 | 16.7 | 2.9 | ... | 82.0 |
| | | 1995 | 4.0 | 18.6 | 3.0 | ... | 76.4 |
| | | 1996 | 4.4 | 19.0 | 3.2 | ... | 72.3 |
| Ecuador | | 1970 | 4.2 | 23.2 | 3.3 | ... | 78.4 |
| | | 1975 | 3.2 | 25.9 | ... | ... | ... |
| | | 1980 | 5.6 | 33.3 | 5.3 | 36.0 | 94.0 |
| | | 1985 | 3.7 | 20.6 | 3.5 | 25.8 | 93.7 |
| | | 1990 | 3.1 | 17.2 | 2.8 | ... | 92.4 |
| | | 1991 | 2.6 | 17.5 | 2.3 | 23.9 | 87.3 |
| | | 1992 | 2.7 | 19.2 | 2.3 | 24.0 | 84.6 |
| | | 1993 | 2.7 | 18.1 | 2.4 | ... | 90.2 |
| | | 1994 | 3.4 | 19.2 | 3.4 | ... | 98.1 |
| | | 1995 | 3.4 | 15.2 | 3.1 | ... | 89.7 |
| | | 1996 | 3.5 | 13.0 | 3.2 | ... | 91.3 |
| Falkland Islands (Malvinas) | | 1970 | ... | 12.2 | ... | ... | 98.4 |
| | | 1975 | ... | 13.5 | ... | ... | 93.4 |
| | | 1996 | ... | 5.4 | ... | 9.6 | 92.9 |
| Guyana | | 1970 | 4.7 | 13.2 | 3.9 | 15.4 | 82.2 |
| | | 1975 | 4.9 | 9.8 | 4.2 | 14.9 | 84.0 |
| | | 1979 | 9.7 | 14.0 | 7.2 | 15.2 | 73.6 |
| | | 1985 | 9.8 | 10.4 | 8.1 | 13.0 | 83.1 |
| | | 1990 | 4.8 | ... | 4.0 | ... | 82.7 |
| | | 1991 | 3.5 | 6.5 | 2.8 | 8.0 | 81.0 |
| | | 1992 | 5.4 | 6.0 | 4.0 | 5.3 | 74.6 |
| | | 1993 | 4.8 | 7.4 | 3.5 | 7.2 | 72.0 |
| | | 1994 | 4.5 | 7.1 | 3.3 | 7.1 | 72.8 |
| | | 1995 | 4.3 | 8.1 | 3.3 | 8.9 | 77.9 |
| | | 1996 | 5.0 | 10.0 | 3.3 | 9.9 | 65.9 |
| Paraguay | | 1970 | 2.2 | 15.3 | 1.9 | ... | 88.8 |
| | | 1975 | 1.6 | 14.0 | ... | ... | ... |
| | | 1980 | 1.5 | 16.4 | ... | ... | ... |
| | | 1985 | 1.5 | 16.7 | 1.2 | 18.8 | 81.4 |
| | (2) | 1990 | 1.1 | 9.1 | 1.1 | ... | 97.4 |
| | (2) | 1991 | 1.9 | 10.3 | 1.8 | ... | 94.2 |
| | (2) | 1992 | 2.6 | 12.4 | 2.4 | ... | 89.3 |
| | (2) | 1993 | 2.9 | 16.9 | 2.6 | 17.1 | 92.5 |
| | (2) | 1994 | 2.9 | 18.6 | 2.7 | ... | 92.7 |
| | (2) | 1995 | 3.4 | 18.0 | ... | ... | ... |
| | (2) | 1996 | 3.9 | 18.6 | 3.5 | 25.0 | 87.9 |
| | (2) | 1997 | 4.0 | 19.8 | ... | ... | ... |
| Peru | | 1970 | 3.3 | 18.8 | 3.2 | 27.1 | 96.7 |
| | | 1975 | 3.3 | 16.6 | 3.2 | 23.2 | 96.4 |
| | | 1980 | 3.1 | 15.2 | 2.9 | 18.5 | 94.4 |
| | | 1985 | 2.9 | 15.7 | 2.7 | 17.9 | 96.3 |
| | | 1990 | 2.3 | ... | ... | ... | ... |

Total and current public expenditure on education
Dépenses publiques totales et ordinaires afférentes à l'éducation
Gastos públicos totales y ordinarios destinados a la educación

II.18

| Country<br>Pays<br>País | Year<br>Année<br>Año | Total expenditure on education<br>Dépenses totales d'éducation<br>Gastos totales de educación | | Current expenditure on education<br>Dépenses ordinaires d'éducation<br>Gastos ordinarios de educación | | |
|---|---|---|---|---|---|---|
| | | As % of<br>Gross<br>National<br>Product<br><br>En % du<br>Produit<br>National<br>Brut<br><br>En % del<br>Producto<br>Nacional<br>Bruto | As %<br>of total<br>government<br>expenditure<br><br>En % des<br>dépenses<br>totales du<br>gouvernement<br><br>En % de<br>los gastos<br>totales del<br>gobierno | As % of<br>Gross<br>National<br>Product<br><br>En % du<br>Produit<br>National<br>Brut<br><br>En % del<br>Producto<br>Nacional<br>Bruto | As % of<br>current<br>government<br>expenditure<br><br>En % des<br>dépenses<br>ordinaires du<br>gouvernement<br><br>En % de<br>los gastos<br>ordinarios<br>del gobierno | As % of<br>total<br>expenditure on<br>education<br><br>En % des<br>dépenses<br>totales<br>d'éducation<br><br>En % de<br>los gastos<br>totales<br>de educación |
| Peru (cont) | 1991 | 2.4 | ... | ... | ... | ... |
| | 1992 | 2.4 | ... | ... | ... | ... |
| | 1993 | 2.6 | ... | ... | ... | ... |
| | 1994 | 3.9 | ... | 3.6 | ... | 93.2 |
| | 1996 | 2.9 | 19.2 | 2.6 | 26.9 | 88.4 |
| Suriname | 1970 | 7.3 | 17.9 | 6.4 | 21.5 | 87.2 |
| | 1975 | 5.6 | 14.1 | 4.9 | 17.9 | 88.4 |
| | 1980 | 6.7 | 22.5 | 6.7 | 22.8 | 100.0 |
| | 1985 | 9.4 | ... | ... | ... | ... |
| | 1990 | 8.3 | ... | 8.2 | ... | 99.6 |
| | 1991 | 7.5 | ... | 7.4 | ... | 99.6 |
| | 1992 | 7.2 | ... | 7.1 | ... | 99.4 |
| | 1993 | 3.5 | ... | 3.4 | ... | 99.0 |
| Uruguay | 1970 | 3.9 | ... | ... | ... | ... |
| | 1980 | 2.3 | 10.0 | 2.2 | ... | 94.7 |
| | 1985 | 2.8 | 9.3 | 2.7 | 0.3 | 96.0 |
| | 1990 | 3.1 | 15.9 | 2.8 | 16.7 | 91.8 |
| | 1991 | 2.9 | 16.6 | 2.7 | 17.0 | 92.6 |
| | 1992 | 2.7 | 15.4 | 2.5 | 15.5 | 91.1 |
| | 1994 | 2.5 | 13.3 | 2.5 | 13.3 | 96.7 |
| | 1995 | 2.8 | ... | 2.5 | ... | 88.1 |
| | 1996 | 3.3 | 15.5 | 3.0 | 15.8 | 91.1 |
| Venezuela | 1970 | 4.1 | 22.9 | 3.9 | 34.0 | 94.3 |
| | 1975 | 4.5 | ... | 4.3 | ... | 95.8 |
| | 1980 | 4.4 | 14.7 | 4.2 | 24.3 | 95.1 |
| | 1985 | 5.1 | 20.3 | ... | ... | ... |
| | 1990 | 3.1 | 12.0 | ... | ... | ... |
| | 1992 | 5.3 | 23.5 | ... | ... | ... |
| | 1993 | 4.6 | 22.0 | ... | ... | ... |
| | 1994 | 5.2 | 22.4 | 5.0 | 31.2 | 96.6 |
| | 1995 | ... | ... | 5.0 | 23.5 | ... |
| **Asia** | | | | | | |
| Afghanistan | 1970 | 1.1 | ... | 1.0 | 15.9 | 89.5 |
| | 1974 | 1.3 | ... | 1.2 | 15.3 | 90.4 |
| | 1980 | 2.0 | 12.7 | 1.8 | 14.4 | 90.0 |
| Armenia | 1990 | 7.3 | 20.5 | ... | ... | ... |
| | 1993 | ... | ... | 3.5 | ... | ... |
| | 1996 | 2.0 | 10.3 | 1.8 | 11.5 | 93.6 |
| Azerbaijan | 1985 | ... | 26.7 | ... | ... | ... |
| | 1990 | 7.0 | 23.5 | ... | ... | ... |
| | 1991 | 7.0 | 24.7 | ... | ... | ... |
| | 1992 | 5.8 | 23.5 | 5.7 | ... | 96.9 |
| | 1993 | 6.8 | 18.3 | ... | ... | ... |
| | 1994 | 4.4 | 13.7 | 4.2 | ... | 94.9 |
| | 1995 | 2.9 | 17.5 | 2.7 | 16.9 | 91.1 |
| | 1996 | 3.3 | 21.3 | 3.0 | 21.0 | 91.2 |
| | 1997 | 3.0 | 18.8 | ... | ... | ... |
| Bahrain | 1970 | ... | 20.0 | ... | 21.3 | 97.8 |
| | 1975 | ... | 8.8 | ... | 14.2 | 91.1 |
| | 1980 | 2.9 | 9.4 | 2.5 | ... | 86.5 |
| | 1985 | 4.1 | 10.4 | 3.9 | 14.6 | 94.2 |
| | 1990 | 5.0 | 14.6 | 4.7 | ... | 94.3 |
| | 1991 | 5.0 | 12.8 | 4.8 | 14.9 | 94.6 |
| | 1992 | 4.6 | 12.3 | 4.4 | 14.4 | 94.2 |
| | 1993 | 4.3 | 13.9 | 4.2 | ... | 97.1 |
| | 1994 | 4.6 | 11.8 | 4.3 | 13.8 | 93.9 |
| | 1995 | 4.3 | 12.8 | 4.0 | 14.1 | 91.9 |
| | 1996 | 4.2 | 12.8 | 4.0 | ... | 94.8 |
| | 1997 | 4.4 | 12.0 | 4.2 | 14.8 | 96.4 |
| Bangladesh (2) | 1975 | 0.8 | 13.6 | 0.5 | 18.9 | 67.4 |
| | 1980 | 1.1 | 7.8 | 0.7 | 13.6 | 66.8 |
| | 1985 | 1.4 | 9.7 | 1.1 | 15.3 | 77.2 |
| | 1990 | 1.5 | 10.3 | 1.2 | 14.4 | 79.1 |
| | 1991 | 1.6 | 11.3 | 1.2 | 15.9 | 76.0 |
| | 1992 | 1.7 | 8.7 | 1.4 | 10.4 | 79.7 |
| | 1996 | 2.2 | ... | 1.3 | ... | 58.5 |

II.18 Total and current public expenditure on education
Dépenses publiques totales et ordinaires afférentes à l'éducation
Gastos públicos totales y ordinarios destinados a la educación

| | | Total expenditure on education Dépenses totales d'éducation Gastos totales de educación | | Current expenditure on education Dépenses ordinaires d'éducation Gastos ordinarios de educación | | |
|---|---|---|---|---|---|---|
| Country Pays País | Year Année Año | As % of Gross National Product En % du Produit National Brut En % del Producto Nacional Bruto | As % of total government expenditure En % des dépenses totales du gouvernement En % de los gastos totales del gobierno | As % of Gross National Product En % du Produit National Brut En % del Producto Nacional Bruto | As % of current government expenditure En % des dépenses ordinaires du gouvernement En % de los gastos ordinarios del gobierno | As % of total expenditure on education En % des dépenses totales d'éducation En % de los gastos totales de educación |
| Bhutan | 1992 | ... | ... | 3.3 | ... | ... |
| | 1993 | ... | ... | 3.0 | ... | ... |
| | 1994 | ... | ... | 2.9 | ... | ... |
| | 1995 | ... | ... | 2.9 | ... | ... |
| | 1996 | ... | ... | 2.8 | ... | ... |
| | 1997 | 4.1 | 7.0 | 2.4 | 8.8 | 57.5 |
| Brunei Darussalam | 1970 | ... | 13.9 | ... | 13.8 | 55.6 |
| | 1975 | ... | 12.2 | ... | 12.8 | 84.7 |
| | 1980 | ... | 11.8 | ... | 12.5 | 88.8 |
| | 1990 | 2.5 | | 2.3 | | 90.4 |
| Cambodia | 1970 | 5.8 | 23.5 | ... | ... | ... |
| | 1996 | 2.9 | ... | 1.8 | ... | 63.5 |
| China | 1970 | 1.3 | 4.3 | 1.2 | ... | 97.8 |
| | 1975 | 1.7 | 6.3 | 1.6 | ... | 92.9 |
| | 1980 | 2.5 | 9.3 | 2.3 | ... | 90.7 |
| | 1985 | 2.5 | 12.2 | 2.2 | ... | 87.9 |
| | 1990 | 2.3 | 12.8 | 2.2 | ... | 93.2 |
| | 1991 | 2.2 | 12.7 | 2.1 | ... | 93.9 |
| | 1992 | 2.0 | 12.2 | 1.8 | 13.5 | 90.9 |
| | 1993 | 1.9 | 12.2 | 1.7 | ... | 91.7 |
| | 1994 | 2.4 | ... | 2.1 | ... | 89.6 |
| | 1995 | 2.3 | ... | 2.0 | ... | 88.2 |
| | 1996 | 2.3 | ... | 2.0 | ... | 87.5 |
| China, Hong Kong SAR | 1970 | 2.4 | 22.8 | 2.1 | 25.4 | 86.4 |
| | 1975 | 2.5 | 20.7 | 2.3 | 25.7 | 91.8 |
| | 1980 | 2.4 | 14.6 | 2.1 | 25.5 | 88.1 |
| | 1985 | 2.8 | 18.4 | 2.6 | ... | 92.0 |
| | 1990 | 2.8 | 17.4 | ... | ... | ... |
| | 1991 | 2.9 | 18.1 | 2.5 | ... | 86.5 |
| | 1992 | 2.8 | 17.4 | 2.6 | ... | 91.7 |
| | 1993 | 2.8 | 17.0 | ... | ... | ... |
| | 1995 | 2.9 | ... | 2.8 | ... | 95.1 |
| Cyprus (5) | 1970 | ... | 17.4 | ... | 17.7 | 80.5 |
| | 1975 | 4.4 | 14.3 | 4.0 | 15.2 | 90.4 |
| | 1980 | 3.5 | 12.9 | 3.3 | 16.2 | 94.0 |
| | 1985 | 3.7 | 12.2 | 3.6 | 13.4 | 95.4 |
| | 1990 | 3.4 | 11.3 | 3.3 | 12.3 | 94.9 |
| | 1991 | 3.7 | 11.6 | 3.5 | 12.4 | 94.0 |
| | 1992 | 3.8 | 12.5 | 3.6 | 13.1 | 92.6 |
| | 1993 | 4.2 | 13.5 | 3.9 | 13.8 | 91.0 |
| | 1994 | 4.4 | 13.8 | 4.0 | 14.1 | 91.2 |
| | 1995 | 4.5 | 13.2 | 4.1 | 13.7 | 91.5 |
| Georgia | 1994 | 5.2 | 6.9 | 4.3 | 7.5 | 82.8 |
| India | 1970 | 2.6 | 10.7 | 2.5 | 16.1 | 94.6 |
| | 1975 | 2.7 | 8.6 | 2.7 | 15.1 | 99.1 |
| | 1980 | 3.0 | 11.2 | 2.9 | ... | 98.9 |
| | 1985 | 3.5 | 13.7 | 3.5 | ... | 98.6 |
| | 1990 | 3.9 | 12.2 | 3.9 | ... | 98.7 |
| | 1991 | 3.7 | 11.6 | 3.7 | ... | 98.9 |
| | 1992 | 3.6 | 11.4 | 3.6 | ... | 98.9 |
| | 1993 | 3.6 | 11.8 | 3.5 | ... | 98.9 |
| | 1994 | 3.5 | 11.8 | 3.5 | ... | 99.0 |
| | 1995 | 3.3 | 11.6 | 3.3 | 12.7 | 99.0 |
| | 1996 | 3.2 | ... | ... | ... | ... |
| Indonesia | 1970 | 2.6 | ... | 2.3 | ... | 89.8 |
| | 1975 | 2.7 | 13.1 | 2.1 | ... | 77.6 |
| | 1980 | 1.7 | 8.9 | ... | ... | ... |
| (2) | 1990 | 1.0 | ... | 0.7 | ... | 69.0 |
| (2) | 1991 | 1.1 | 5.2 | 0.7 | ... | 63.2 |
| (2) | 1992 | 1.3 | 6.3 | 0.7 | 5.7 | 54.1 |
| (3) | 1993 | 1.8 | 9.1 | 0.7 | 5.6 | 36.9 |
| (3) | 1994 | 1.4 | 7.5 | 0.6 | 5.3 | 43.2 |
| (3) | 1995 | 1.4 | 7.8 | 0.6 | 5.9 | 46.0 |
| (3) | 1996 | 1.4 | 7.9 | 0.6 | 5.8 | 46.0 |
| Iran, Islamic Republic of | 1970 | ... | 9.6 | ... | ... | 84.7 |
| | 1976 | 5.7 | 14.1 | 5.1 | ... | 88.8 |
| | 1980 | 7.5 | 15.7 | 6.6 | 20.1 | 88.4 |
| | 1985 | 3.6 | 17.2 | 3.2 | 20.6 | 88.6 |
| | 1990 | 4.1 | 22.4 | 3.4 | 28.8 | 82.5 |

Total and current public expenditure on education
Dépenses publiques totales et ordinaires afférentes à l'éducation
Gastos públicos totales y ordinarios destinados a la educación

II.18

| Country / Pays / País | Year / Année / Año | Total expenditure on education<br>Dépenses totales d'éducation<br>Gastos totales de educación | | Current expenditure on education<br>Dépenses ordinaires d'éducation<br>Gastos ordinarios de educación | | |
|---|---|---|---|---|---|---|
| | | As % of Gross National Product<br>En % du Produit National Brut<br>En % del Producto Nacional Bruto | As % of total government expenditure<br>En % des dépenses totales du gouvernement<br>En % de los gastos totales del gobierno | As % of Gross National Product<br>En % du Produit National Brut<br>En % del Producto Nacional Bruto | As % of current government expenditure<br>En % des dépenses ordinaires du gouvernment<br>En % de los gastos ordinarios del gobierno | As % of total expenditure on education<br>En % des dépenses totales d'éducation<br>En % de los gastos totales de educación |
| Iran, Islamic Republic of (cont) | 1991 | 4.0 | 22.1 | 3.2 | 24.7 | 80.5 |
| | 1992 | 4.8 | 28.2 | 3.9 | 31.4 | 82.2 |
| | 1993 | 5.4 | 22.8 | 4.4 | 26.4 | 81.7 |
| | 1994 | 4.7 | 18.1 | 3.8 | 22.7 | 82.1 |
| | 1995 | 4.0 | 17.8 | 3.3 | 21.6 | 82.9 |
| Iraq | 1970 | ... | ... | 4.7 | 19.8 | ... |
| | 1976 | 3.6 | 6.9 | 2.7 | 10.5 | 76.2 |
| | 1980 | 3.0 | ... | ... | ... | ... |
| | 1985 | 4.0 | 6.5 | ... | ... | ... |
| Israel @ | 1970 | 5.7 | 8.1 | ... | ... | ... |
| | 1975 | 7.3 | 7.6 | 6.2 | 8.3 | 84.2 |
| | 1980 | 8.2 | 7.3 | 7.6 | 8.9 | 92.3 |
| | 1985 | 7.5 | 9.3 | 6.9 | 9.0 | 92.3 |
| | 1990 | 6.5 | 11.3 | 6.0 | 11.2 | 92.2 |
| | 1991 | 6.6 | 11.4 | 6.0 | 11.8 | 91.6 |
| | 1992 | 6.8 | 11.8 | 6.3 | 12.0 | 91.0 |
| | 1993 | 7.0 | 12.3 | 6.4 | 13.0 | 91.2 |
| | 1994 | 7.6 | ... | 6.9 | ... | 91.4 |
| Japan @ | 1992 | 3.6 | 10.4 | ... | ... | ... |
| | 1993 | 3.8 | 10.8 | ... | ... | ... |
| | 1994 | 3.6 | 9.9 | ... | ... | ... |
| Jordan | 1970 | 3.7 | 9.3 | 3.1 | 11.3 | 83.1 |
| | 1980 | 6.6 | 14.4 | 4.1 | ... | 62.3 |
| | 1985 | 6.8 | 15.8 | 4.8 | ... | 71.1 |
| | 1990 | 8.9 | 17.1 | 6.3 | ... | 70.7 |
| | 1991 | 8.6 | 19.1 | 6.3 | ... | 72.6 |
| | 1992 | 7.2 | 17.6 | 5.2 | ... | 72.8 |
| | 1993 | 8.2 | 20.8 | 5.9 | ... | 72.2 |
| | 1994 | 7.7 | 19.6 | 5.9 | ... | 77.2 |
| | 1995 | 8.7 | 21.4 | 6.1 | ... | 70.1 |
| | 1996 | 7.9 | 19.8 | 6.4 | ... | 80.8 |
| Kazakstan | 1985 | ... | 18.9 | ... | ... | ... |
| | 1990 | 3.2 | 17.6 | ... | ... | ... |
| | 1991 | 3.9 | 19.1 | ... | ... | ... |
| | 1992 | 2.8 | 25.2 | 2.6 | ... | 92.8 |
| | 1995 | 4.6 | 17.6 | 4.6 | 18.2 | 99.9 |
| | 1996 | 4.7 | ... | 4.6 | ... | 98.0 |
| | 1997 | 4.4 | ... | ... | ... | ... |
| Korea, Republic of @ | 1970 | 3.4 | ... | 2.6 | ... | 77.1 |
| | 1975 | 2.2 | 13.9 | 1.6 | ... | 74.4 |
| | 1980 | 3.7 | 14.1 | 3.1 | ... | 84.3 |
| | 1985 | 4.5 | ... | 3.5 | ... | 79.7 |
| | 1990 | 3.5 | ... | 3.1 | ... | 89.2 |
| | 1991 | 4.0 | ... | 3.1 | ... | 78.8 |
| | 1992 | 4.2 | 14.8 | 3.3 | 15.3 | 79.8 |
| | 1993 | 4.4 | 16.0 | 3.5 | 17.7 | 79.5 |
| | 1994 | 3.7 | 17.4 | ... | ... | ... |
| | 1995 | 3.7 | 17.5 | ... | ... | ... |
| Kuwait | 1970 | 4.2 | 11.2 | 4.1 | 14.0 | 96.6 |
| | 1975 | 3.0 | 10.0 | 2.4 | 10.8 | 80.4 |
| | 1980 | 2.4 | 8.1 | 2.3 | 11.2 | 93.1 |
| | 1985 | 4.5 | 11.4 | 4.3 | ... | 95.6 |
| | 1990 | 3.5 | ... | ... | ... | ... |
| | 1991 | 9.7 | 7.4 | ... | ... | ... |
| | 1992 | 6.1 | 11.4 | ... | ... | ... |
| | 1993 | 5.4 | 10.6 | ... | ... | ... |
| | 1994 | 5.5 | 10.9 | ... | ... | ... |
| | 1995 | 5.2 | 11.7 | ... | ... | ... |
| | 1996 | 4.8 | 13.5 | ... | ... | ... |
| | 1997 | 5.0 | 14.0 | ... | ... | ... |
| Kyrgyzstan | 1980 | ... | 22.2 | ... | ... | ... |
| | 1985 | ... | 22.4 | ... | ... | 92.6 |
| | 1990 | 8.3 | 22.5 | 7.4 | ... | 88.5 |
| | 1991 | 6.0 | 22.7 | 5.8 | ... | 96.6 |
| | 1993 | 4.3 | 20.7 | 4.1 | 21.0 | 94.7 |
| | 1994 | 6.2 | 25.6 | 5.9 | 25.2 | 95.4 |
| | 1995 | 6.7 | 23.1 | 6.5 | 24.2 | 96.8 |
| | 1996 | 5.3 | 23.5 | 5.1 | 24.1 | 95.9 |

Total and current public expenditure on education
Dépenses publiques totales et ordinaires afférentes à l'éducation
Gastos públicos totales y ordinarios destinados a la educación

| Country / Pays / País | Year / Année / Año | Total expenditure on education — Dépenses totales d'éducation — Gastos totales de educación | | Current expenditure on education — Dépenses ordinaires d'éducation — Gastos ordinarios de educación | | |
|---|---|---|---|---|---|---|
| | | As % of Gross National Product / En % du Produit National Brut / En % del Producto Nacional Bruto | As % of total government expenditure / En % des dépenses totales du gouvernement / En % de los gastos totales del gobierno | As % of Gross National Product / En % du Produit National Brut / En % del Producto Nacional Bruto | As % of current government expenditure / En % des dépenses ordinaires du gouvernement / En % de los gastos ordinarios del gobierno | As % of total expenditure on education / En % des dépenses totales d'éducation / En % de los gastos totales de educación |
| Lao People's Democratic Republic | 1980 | ... | 1.3 | ... | ... | ... |
| | 1985 | 0.4 | 4.5 | ... | ... | ... |
| | 1992 | 2.5 | ... | 1.9 | ... | 75.8 |
| | 1993 | 1.9 | ... | 1.6 | ... | 84.7 |
| | 1994 | 2.8 | ... | 2.4 | ... | 85.0 |
| | 1995 | 2.3 | ... | 2.0 | ... | 85.2 |
| | 1996 | 2.5 | 10.3 | 2.1 | 17.8 | 84.7 |
| | 1997 | 2.1 | 8.7 | 1.8 | 16.0 | 85.8 |
| Lebanon (2) | 1970 | ... | 16.8 | ... | ... | 93.1 |
| | 1975 | ... | 16.1 | ... | ... | ... |
| | 1980 | ... | 13.2 | ... | ... | ... |
| | 1985 | ... | 16.8 | ... | ... | ... |
| | 1989 | 2.6 | ... | ... | ... | ... |
| | 1992 | 2.1 | 12.5 | 2.1 | ... | 98.8 |
| | 1993 | 1.9 | 6.6 | 1.7 | ... | 90.1 |
| | 1994 | 2.0 | 7.5 | 1.5 | ... | 75.8 |
| | 1995 | 2.6 | 8.7 | ... | ... | ... |
| | 1996 | 2.5 | 8.2 | ... | ... | ... |
| Macau | 1990 | ... | 10.7 | ... | ... | ... |
| | 1991 | ... | 10.4 | ... | ... | ... |
| | 1992 | ... | 8.9 | ... | ... | ... |
| Malaysia | 1970 | 4.2 | 17.7 | 3.8 | 21.5 | 91.5 |
| | 1975 | 6.0 | 19.3 | 5.1 | 23.6 | 84.9 |
| | 1980 | 6.0 | 14.7 | 5.0 | 18.4 | 83.0 |
| | 1985 | 6.6 | 16.3 | 5.6 | ... | 85.4 |
| | 1990 | 5.5 | 18.3 | 4.2 | 19.3 | 77.3 |
| | 1991 | 5.6 | 18.0 | 4.5 | 19.1 | 80.2 |
| | 1992 | 5.5 | 16.9 | 4.7 | 19.6 | 86.4 |
| | 1993 | 5.1 | 15.7 | 4.5 | 17.2 | 87.8 |
| | 1994 | 5.2 | 15.5 | 4.3 | 15.9 | 83.5 |
| | 1995 | 4.7 | ... | 3.8 | ... | 81.2 |
| | 1996 | 5.2 | 15.4 | 4.3 | ... | 81.2 |
| | 1997 | 4.9 | ... | 4.1 | ... | 82.8 |
| Maldives | 1975 | ... | ... | ... | 11.5 | ... |
| | 1986 | 4.4 | 7.2 | 3.7 | ... | 82.4 |
| | 1990 | 6.3 | 10.0 | ... | ... | ... |
| | 1991 | 11.5 | 16.0 | ... | ... | ... |
| | 1992 | 11.9 | 16.0 | ... | ... | ... |
| | 1993 | 8.4 | 13.6 | 6.1 | 18.0 | 72.3 |
| | 1995 | 6.4 | 10.5 | 4.9 | 16.5 | 76.4 |
| Mongolia | 1970 | ... | 15.6 | ... | ... | 92.7 |
| | 1980 | ... | 19.1 | ... | ... | ... |
| | 1985 | 11.7 | 17.1 | ... | ... | ... |
| | 1990 | 12.9 | 17.6 | ... | ... | ... |
| | 1991 | 11.3 | 22.7 | ... | ... | ... |
| | 1992 | 7.1 | 26.2 | ... | ... | ... |
| | 1993 | 6.3 | 15.7 | ... | ... | ... |
| | 1994 | 6.0 | 16.2 | ... | ... | ... |
| | 1995 | 6.0 | 17.0 | ... | ... | ... |
| | 1996 | 6.4 | 15.9 | ... | ... | ... |
| | 1997 | 5.7 | 15.1 | ... | ... | ... |
| Myanmar | 1970 | 3.1 | 17.9 | 2.9 | 19.6 | 93.1 |
| (2) | 1975 | 1.7 | 15.3 | 1.6 | 16.3 | 95.2 |
| (2) | 1980 | 1.7 | ... | 1.5 | ... | 88.5 |
| (2) | 1985 | 2.0 | ... | 1.5 | ... | 77.6 |
| (2) | 1994 | 1.2 | 14.4 | 0.9 | 19.0 | 78.0 |
| Nepal | 1970 | 0.6 | 6.7 | ... | ... | ... |
| | 1975 | 1.5 | 11.5 | ... | ... | ... |
| | 1980 | 1.8 | 10.5 | ... | ... | ... |
| | 1985 | 2.6 | 12.7 | ... | ... | ... |
| | 1990 | 2.0 | 8.5 | ... | ... | ... |
| | 1991 | 2.7 | 12.3 | ... | ... | ... |
| | 1992 | 2.9 | 13.2 | ... | ... | ... |
| | 1993 | 3.3 | 13.3 | 2.2 | ... | 65.4 |
| | 1994 | 2.8 | 14.0 | 1.8 | ... | 65.1 |
| | 1995 | 3.3 | 14.0 | 2.2 | ... | 65.4 |
| | 1996 | 3.1 | 13.5 | 2.0 | ... | 65.5 |
| | 1997 | 3.2 | ... | ... | ... | ... |

Total and current public expenditure on education II.18
Dépenses publiques totales et ordinaires afférentes à l'éducation
Gastos públicos totales y ordinarios destinados a la educación

| Country<br><br>Pays<br><br>País | Year<br><br>Année<br><br>Año | Total expenditure on education<br>Dépenses totales d'éducation<br>Gastos totales de educación | | Current expenditure on education<br>Dépenses ordinaires d'éducation<br>Gastos ordinarios de educación | | |
|---|---|---|---|---|---|---|
| | | As % of Gross National Product<br><br>En % du Produit National Brut<br><br>En % del Producto Nacional Bruto | As % of total government expenditure<br><br>En % des dépenses totales du gouvernement<br><br>En % de los gastos totales del gobierno | As % of Gross National Product<br><br>En % du Produit National Brut<br><br>En % del Producto Nacional Bruto | As % of current government expenditure<br><br>En % des dépenses ordinaires du gouverment<br><br>En % de los gastos ordinarios del gobierno | As % of total expenditure on education<br><br>En % des dépenses totales d'éducation<br><br>En % de los gastos totales de educación |
| Oman | 1975 | 1.6 | 1.9 | 1.1 | 2.0 | 70.3 |
| | 1980 | 2.1 | 4.1 | 1.7 | 4.6 | 81.3 |
| | 1985 | 4.0 | ... | 2.5 | ... | 62.7 |
| | 1990 | 3.5 | 11.1 | 3.2 | 18.8 | 92.0 |
| | 1991 | 3.8 | 15.8 | 3.4 | 18.4 | 91.4 |
| | 1992 | 4.0 | 16.2 | 3.6 | 19.3 | 89.8 |
| | 1993 | 4.6 | 15.2 | 4.1 | 19.1 | 89.1 |
| | 1995 | 4.5 | 16.7 | 4.1 | 19.8 | 89.7 |
| | 1996 | ... | 18.9 | ... | 20.8 | 94.1 |
| | 1997 | ... | 16.4 | ... | 22.1 | 93.3 |
| Pakistan | 1970 | 1.7 | 4.2 | 1.0 | 3.6 | 60.8 |
| | 1975 | 2.2 | 5.2 | 1.6 | ... | 69.6 |
| | 1980 | 2.1 | 5.0 | 1.5 | 5.2 | 73.1 |
| | 1985 | 2.9 | 8.2 | 2.1 | 8.1 | 74.3 |
| | 1990 | 2.7 | 7.4 | 2.2 | 7.4 | 80.9 |
| | 1991 | 2.6 | 6.1 | 2.2 | 6.6 | 85.0 |
| | 1992 | 2.4 | 6.5 | 2.1 | 6.7 | 85.7 |
| | 1993 | 2.6 | 7.9 | 2.3 | 8.3 | 87.7 |
| | 1994 | 2.8 | 7.4 | 2.4 | 7.4 | 85.7 |
| | 1995 | 2.8 | 7.1 | 2.4 | 7.1 | 85.7 |
| | 1996 | 3.0 | 8.1 | 2.4 | 7.6 | 80.4 |
| | 1997 | 2.7 | 7.1 | 2.3 | 7.1 | 86.1 |
| Philippines | 1970 | 2.8 | 24.4 | 2.8 | ... | 98.8 |
| | 1975 | 2.0 | 11.4 | ... | ... | ... |
| | 1980 | 1.7 | 9.1 | 1.7 | 13.0 | 96.0 |
| | 1985 | 1.4 | 7.4 | 1.3 | 10.0 | 93.4 |
| | 1990 | 2.9 | 10.1 | 2.7 | 11.1 | 92.4 |
| | 1991 | 3.0 | 10.5 | 2.6 | 11.1 | 88.8 |
| | 1995 | 3.0 | 15.6 | 2.5 | ... | 85.1 |
| | 1996 | 3.2 | 17.6 | 2.8 | ... | 86.4 |
| | 1997 | 3.4 | 15.7 | 2.9 | 17.4 | 85.0 |
| Qatar | 1970 | 3.3 | 8.9 | 3.0 | ... | 91.5 |
| | 1975 | 1.9 | 4.0 | 1.3 | 4.1 | 69.7 |
| | 1980 | 2.6 | 7.2 | 2.0 | 7.8 | 75.5 |
| | 1985 | 4.1 | ... | 3.1 | ... | 75.7 |
| | 1990 | 3.4 | ... | 3.3 | ... | 97.3 |
| | 1991 | 3.6 | ... | 3.4 | ... | 97.1 |
| | 1992 | 3.3 | ... | 3.1 | ... | 93.6 |
| | 1993 | 3.6 | ... | 3.3 | ... | 91.3 |
| | 1994 | 3.4 | ... | 3.1 | ... | 91.8 |
| Saudi Arabia | 1970 | 3.5 | 9.8 | 3.3 | 15.1 | 95.0 |
| | 1975 | 7.9 | 11.7 | 3.4 | 15.1 | 42.7 |
| | 1980 | 4.1 | 8.7 | 2.6 | ... | 63.5 |
| | 1985 | 6.7 | 11.8 | 5.5 | ... | 81.9 |
| | 1990 | 6.0 | 17.8 | 5.7 | ... | 94.4 |
| | 1991 | 5.5 | 17.8 | 5.1 | ... | 94.5 |
| | 1992 | 6.3 | 17.0 | 6.0 | ... | 95.5 |
| | 1993 | 6.8 | 16.0 | 6.4 | ... | 93.9 |
| | 1994 | 6.2 | 18.0 | 5.9 | ... | 95.0 |
| | 1995 | 5.4 | 17.7 | 5.2 | ... | 95.5 |
| | 1996 | 5.1 | 17.0 | 4.8 | ... | 93.4 |
| | 1997 | 7.5 | 22.8 | 7.2 | ... | 95.3 |
| Singapore | 1970 | 3.1 | 11.7 | 3.0 | 14.4 | 94.1 |
| | 1975 | 2.9 | 8.6 | 2.5 | 11.4 | 86.9 |
| | 1980 | 2.8 | 7.3 | 2.4 | 10.3 | 85.6 |
| | 1985 | 4.4 | ... | 3.4 | ... | 78.2 |
| | 1990 | 3.0 | 18.2 | 2.6 | 25.4 | 87.3 |
| | 1991 | 3.7 | 24.9 | 3.1 | 30.2 | 83.7 |
| | 1992 | 3.2 | 21.2 | 2.5 | 24.1 | 78.6 |
| | 1993 | 3.1 | 23.1 | 2.4 | 24.2 | 76.1 |
| | 1994 | 3.0 | 23.5 | 2.3 | 25.6 | 74.9 |
| | 1995 | 3.0 | 23.4 | 2.3 | 25.4 | 76.0 |
| Sri Lanka | 1970 | 4.0 | 13.6 | 3.8 | 15.9 | 93.0 |
| | 1975 | 2.8 | 10.1 | 2.6 | 13.0 | 93.6 |
| | 1980 | 2.7 | 7.7 | 2.3 | 13.5 | 85.3 |
| | 1985 | 2.6 | 6.9 | 2.2 | 11.4 | 84.4 |
| | 1990 | 2.7 | 8.1 | 2.2 | 10.7 | 81.5 |
| | 1991 | 3.3 | 8.4 | 2.4 | 11.3 | 73.6 |
| | 1992 | 3.3 | 8.8 | 2.5 | 10.6 | 76.3 |
| | 1993 | 3.1 | 9.0 | 2.6 | 12.2 | 81.2 |

II.18   Total and current public expenditure on education
Dépenses publiques totales et ordinaires afférentes à l'éducation
Gastos públicos totales y ordinarios destinados a la educación

| Country / Pays / País | Year / Année / Año | Total expenditure on education — Dépenses totales d'éducation — Gastos totales de educación | | Current expenditure on education — Dépenses ordinaires d'éducation — Gastos ordinarios de educación | | |
|---|---|---|---|---|---|---|
| | | As % of Gross National Product — En % du Produit National Brut — En % del Producto Nacional Bruto | As % of total government expenditure — En % des dépenses totales du gouvernement — En % de los gastos totales del gobierno | As % of Gross National Product — En % du Produit National Brut — En % del Producto Nacional Bruto | As % of current government expenditure — En % des dépenses ordinaires du gouvernement — En % de los gastos ordinarios del gobierno | As % of total expenditure on education — En % des dépenses totales d'éducation — En % de los gastos totales de educación |
| Sri Lanka (cont) | 1994 | 3.2 | 9.4 | 2.7 | 13.2 | 83.9 |
| | 1995 | 3.0 | 8.1 | 2.4 | 11.5 | 80.3 |
| | 1996 | 3.4 | 8.9 | 2.9 | 11.6 | 82.9 |
| Syrian Arab Republic | 1970 | 3.9 | 9.4 | ... | ... | ... |
| | 1975 | 3.9 | 7.8 | ... | ... | ... |
| | 1980 | 4.6 | 8.1 | ... | ... | ... |
| | 1985 | 6.1 | 11.8 | ... | ... | ... |
| | 1990 | 4.3 | 17.3 | ... | ... | ... |
| | 1991 | 4.1 | 14.2 | ... | ... | ... |
| (1) | 1992 | 3.2 | 11.7 | ... | ... | ... |
| (1) | 1994 | 3.8 | 12.5 | ... | ... | ... |
| (1) | 1995 | 3.3 | 11.2 | ... | ... | ... |
| | 1996 | 4.2 | 13.6 | ... | ... | ... |
| (1) | 1997 | 3.1 | ... | ... | ... | ... |
| Tajikistan | 1980 | ... | 29.2 | ... | | 92.4 |
| | 1985 | ... | 29.5 | ... | ... | 94.1 |
| | 1990 | 9.7 | 24.7 | 8.9 | ... | 91.8 |
| | 1991 | 8.2 | 24.4 | 8.0 | ... | 97.0 |
| | 1992 | 9.3 | 19.2 | 9.0 | ... | 96.8 |
| | 1993 | 8.6 | 17.8 | 7.8 | 18.8 | 90.2 |
| | 1995 | 2.4 | 16.1 | 2.3 | 18.5 | 95.3 |
| | 1996 | 2.2 | 11.5 | 2.0 | 12.1 | 94.8 |
| Thailand | 1970 | 3.2 | 17.3 | 2.3 | ... | 73.1 |
| | 1975 | 3.5 | 21.0 | 2.6 | 18.9 | 73.3 |
| | 1980 | 3.4 | 20.6 | 2.4 | 19.1 | 70.6 |
| | 1985 | 3.8 | 18.5 | 3.3 | 19.2 | 85.9 |
| | 1990 | 3.6 | 20.0 | 3.0 | 21.0 | 83.6 |
| | 1991 | 3.6 | 19.1 | 2.9 | 19.9 | 82.0 |
| | 1992 | 4.0 | 19.6 | ... | | ... |
| | 1993 | 4.1 | 20.6 | 3.4 | 22.7 | 81.2 |
| | 1994 | 3.8 | 18.9 | 3.0 | 21.1 | 80.1 |
| | 1995 | 4.1 | 20.1 | 3.2 | 25.8 | 78.6 |
| | 1996 | 4.8 | ... | 3.6 | ... | 75.2 |
| Turkey @ | 1970 | 2.1 | 13.7 | 1.5 | ... | 71.0 |
| | 1980 | 2.2 | 10.5 | 1.9 | ... | 83.7 |
| | 1985 | 1.8 | ... | 1.5 | ... | 83.4 |
| (1) | 1990 | 2.1 | ... | 1.9 | ... | 89.1 |
| (1) | 1991 | 2.4 | ... | 2.1 | ... | 91.0 |
| (1) | 1992 | 2.8 | ... | 2.5 | ... | 91.9 |
| | 1993 | 3.3 | ... | 3.2 | ... | 94.4 |
| | 1994 | 3.4 | 14.7 | 3.2 | ... | 93.3 |
| | 1995 | 2.2 | ... | ... | | ... |
| Turkmenistan | 1985 | ... | 28.0 | ... | ... | ... |
| | 1990 | 4.3 | 21.0 | ... | ... | ... |
| | 1991 | 3.9 | 19.7 | ... | ... | ... |
| United Arab Emirates | 1975 | 0.9 | ... | 0.7 | | 78.3 |
| | 1980 | 1.3 | ... | 1.0 | ... | 79.0 |
| | 1985 | 1.7 | 10.4 | 1.6 | 10.6 | 94.2 |
| | 1990 | 1.7 | 14.6 | 1.7 | 14.3 | 95.4 |
| | 1991 | 1.9 | 15.0 | 1.8 | 14.9 | 95.0 |
| | 1992 | 2.0 | 15.2 | 1.8 | 15.1 | 93.3 |
| | 1993 | 2.0 | 15.1 | 1.8 | 14.9 | 92.5 |
| | 1994 | 1.8 | 17.3 | 1.7 | 17.3 | 92.7 |
| | 1995 | 1.8 | 16.3 | 1.7 | 15.9 | 92.3 |
| | 1996 | ... | 16.7 | ... | 16.1 | 92.2 |
| Uzbekistan | 1980 | ... | 23.0 | ... | ... | 85.7 |
| | 1985 | ... | 25.1 | ... | ... | 84.1 |
| | 1990 | 9.5 | 20.4 | 7.6 | ... | 79.8 |
| | 1991 | 9.4 | 17.8 | 8.0 | ... | 84.8 |
| | 1992 | 10.2 | 23.3 | 9.6 | ... | 93.4 |
| | 1993 | 9.6 | 24.4 | 9.4 | ... | 97.8 |
| | 1994 | 8.3 | 24.9 | 8.0 | ... | 95.8 |
| | 1995 | 7.4 | 22.8 | 6.9 | ... | 92.5 |
| | 1996 | 7.7 | 21.1 | 7.4 | ... | 96.5 |
| Viet Nam | 1990 | 2.1 | 7.5 | 1.9 | 8.4 | 90.3 |
| | 1991 | 1.8 | 9.7 | 1.6 | 10.4 | 90.8 |
| | 1992 | 2.0 | 7.3 | 1.8 | 8.6 | 92.4 |
| | 1993 | 2.7 | 7.4 | 2.5 | 8.6 | 92.7 |
| | 1994 | 2.6 | ... | 2.4 | ... | 92.8 |

Total and current public expenditure on education
Dépenses publiques totales et ordinaires afférentes à l'éducation
Gastos públicos totales y ordinarios destinados a la educación

II.18

| Country / Pays / País | | Year / Année / Año | Total expenditure on education / Dépenses totales d'éducation / Gastos totales de educación | | Current expenditure on education / Dépenses ordinaires d'éducation / Gastos ordinarios de educación | | |
|---|---|---|---|---|---|---|---|
| | | | As % of Gross National Product / En % du Produit National Brut / En % del Producto Nacional Bruto | As % of total government expenditure / En % des dépenses totales du gouvernement / En % de los gastos totales del gobierno | As % of Gross National Product / En % du Produit National Brut / En % del Producto Nacional Bruto | As % of current government expenditure / En % des dépenses ordinaires du gouvernment / En % de los gastos ordinarios del gobierno | As % of total expenditure on education / En % des dépenses totales d'éducation / En % de los gastos totales de educación |
| Viet Nam (cont) | | 1995 | 3.0 | ... | 2.8 | ... | 94.6 |
| | | 1996 | 2.9 | ... | 2.7 | ... | 93.4 |
| | | 1997 | 3.0 | ... | 2.8 | ... | 92.9 |
| Yemen | | 1993 | 6.2 | 20.9 | 6.0 | ... | 95.6 |
| | | 1994 | 6.3 | 21.6 | 6.1 | ... | 97.3 |
| | | 1995 | 5.4 | ... | 5.1 | ... | 94.7 |
| | | 1996 | 6.3 | ... | 5.7 | ... | 89.9 |
| | | 1997 | 7.0 | ... | 5.6 | ... | 80.1 |
| **Europe** | | | | | | | |
| Albania | | 1971 | ... | 11.6 | ... | ... | ... |
| | | 1980 | ... | 10.3 | ... | ... | ... |
| | | 1990 | 5.8 | ... | ... | ... | ... |
| | | 1994 | 3.1 | ... | 2.8 | ... | 90.8 |
| Austria @ | | 1970 | 4.5 | 8.1 | 3.5 | 8.6 | 77.8 |
| | | 1975 | 5.6 | 8.5 | 4.4 | 9.8 | 78.5 |
| | | 1980 | 5.5 | 8.0 | 4.7 | 8.4 | 85.3 |
| | | 1985 | 5.8 | 7.9 | 5.2 | 8.6 | 90.1 |
| | | 1990 | 5.4 | 7.6 | 5.0 | 8.8 | 92.4 |
| | | 1991 | 5.6 | 7.6 | 5.1 | 8.6 | 91.4 |
| | | 1992 | 5.7 | 7.7 | 5.1 | 8.6 | 88.2 |
| | | 1993 | 5.5 | ... | 4.8 | ... | 88.3 |
| | | 1995 | 5.6 | 10.6 | 5.2 | ... | 91.4 |
| | | 1996 | 5.4 | 10.4 | 5.0 | ... | 91.2 |
| Belarus | | 1970 | ... | 18.7 | ... | ... | 82.5 |
| | | 1990 | 4.9 | ... | 4.1 | ... | 84.0 |
| | | 1991 | 5.7 | ... | 4.8 | ... | 84.5 |
| | | 1992 | 6.6 | 19.3 | 5.4 | 20.0 | 81.8 |
| | | 1993 | 6.8 | 15.9 | 5.4 | ... | 79.5 |
| | | 1994 | 7.0 | 17.3 | 5.8 | ... | 83.0 |
| | | 1995 | 5.6 | 17.1 | 5.3 | ... | 95.5 |
| | | 1996 | 5.9 | 17.8 | 5.4 | 18.5 | 91.1 |
| Belgium @ | (2) | 1970 | ... | ... | 4.2 | 18.3 | ... |
| | (2) | 1975 | 6.2 | 22.2 | 5.7 | 23.0 | 91.7 |
| | (2) | 1980 | 6.0 | 16.3 | 5.9 | 18.6 | 98.9 |
| | (2) | 1985 | 6.0 | 15.2 | 5.7 | 16.0 | 94.9 |
| | (2) | 1990 | 5.0 | ... | 4.9 | ... | 98.8 |
| | (2) | 1991 | 5.0 | ... | 4.9 | ... | 98.9 |
| | (2) | 1992 | 5.0 | 9.0 | 5.0 | ... | 99.2 |
| | | 1993 | 5.5 | 10.0 | 5.5 | ... | 98.6 |
| | | 1994 | 5.6 | 10.4 | 5.6 | ... | 99.1 |
| | (6) | 1995 | 3.1 | 5.8 | 3.0 | ... | 97.8 |
| | (6) | 1996 | 3.1 | 6.0 | 3.0 | ... | 97.9 |
| Bulgaria | | 1970 | ... | 9.1 | ... | ... | 86.0 |
| | | 1975 | ... | 8.5 | ... | ... | 92.1 |
| | | 1980 | 4.5 | ... | 4.3 | ... | 95.9 |
| | | 1985 | 5.5 | ... | 4.9 | ... | 89.6 |
| | | 1990 | 5.6 | ... | 5.2 | ... | 92.6 |
| | | 1991 | 6.0 | ... | 5.7 | ... | 93.8 |
| | | 1992 | 5.9 | ... | 5.7 | ... | 95.6 |
| | | 1993 | 5.6 | ... | 5.2 | ... | 93.3 |
| | | 1994 | 4.7 | ... | 4.4 | ... | 94.3 |
| | | 1995 | 3.9 | ... | 3.7 | ... | 93.9 |
| | | 1996 | 3.2 | 7.0 | 3.0 | 6.9 | 95.5 |
| Croatia | | 1991 | 6.0 | ... | ... | ... | ... |
| | | 1992 | 4.1 | ... | ... | ... | ... |
| | | 1994 | 5.0 | ... | ... | ... | ... |
| | | 1995 | 5.3 | ... | ... | ... | ... |
| Czech Republic @ | | 1992 | 4.7 | ... | 4.3 | ... | 91.1 |
| | | 1993 | 5.9 | 12.7 | 5.4 | ... | 92.1 |
| | | 1994 | 5.6 | 13.8 | 5.0 | ... | 89.6 |
| | | 1995 | 5.4 | 13.6 | 4.7 | ... | 88.1 |
| | | 1996 | 5.1 | ... | 4.4 | ... | 86.4 |
| Denmark @ | | 1970 | 6.7 | 16.9 | 5.2 | ... | 77.4 |
| | | 1975 | 7.6 | 15.2 | 6.6 | ... | 86.9 |
| | | 1980 | 6.7 | 9.5 | 5.9 | 9.0 | 88.7 |
| | | 1985 | 7.0 | ... | ... | ... | ... |

**Total and current public expenditure on education**
**Dépenses publiques totales et ordinaires afférentes à l'éducation**
**Gastos públicos totales y ordinarios destinados a la educación**

| Country / Pays / País | Year / Année / Año | Total expenditure on education / Dépenses totales d'éducation / Gastos totales de educación — As % of Gross National Product / En % du Produit National Brut / En % del Producto Nacional Bruto | As % of total government expenditure / En % des dépenses totales du gouvernement / En % de los gastos totales del gobierno | Current expenditure on education / Dépenses ordinaires d'éducation / Gastos ordinarios de educación — As % of Gross National Product / En % du Produit National Brut / En % del Producto Nacional Bruto | As % of current government expenditure / En % des dépenses ordinaires du gouvernment / En % de los gastos ordinarios del gobierno | As % of total expenditure on education / En % des dépenses totales d'éducation / En % de los gastos totales de educación |
|---|---|---|---|---|---|---|
| Denmark @ (cont) | 1991 | 7.1 | 11.8 | 6.6 | 11.5 | 93.1 |
|  | 1993 | 8.1 | 12.9 | 7.6 | ... | 94.0 |
|  | 1994 | 7.8 | 12.5 | 7.4 | ... | 94.0 |
|  | 1995 | 7.7 | 13.1 | 7.3 | ... | 94.3 |
|  | 1996 | 8.1 | ... | 7.7 | ... | 94.1 |
| Estonia | 1992 | 6.1 | 31.3 | 5.6 | ... | 91.7 |
|  | 1993 | 7.0 | 20.1 | 6.1 | 20.9 | 87.3 |
|  | 1994 | 6.7 | 23.8 | 5.8 | 25.7 | 87.9 |
|  | 1995 | 7.0 | 25.5 | 6.2 | 26.7 | 88.7 |
|  | 1996 | 7.3 | 22.3 | 6.3 | 22.5 | 87.3 |
|  | 1997 | 7.2 | 25.5 | 6.4 | 26.2 | 88.4 |
| Finland @ | 1970 | 5.9 | ... | 5.3 | ... | 89.8 |
|  | 1975 | 6.4 | 13.0 | 5.5 | 14.3 | 86.1 |
|  | 1980 | 5.3 | ... | 4.9 | 12.0 | 91.5 |
|  | 1985 | 5.4 | 11.8 | 5.0 | 11.9 | 92.5 |
|  | 1990 | 5.7 | 11.9 | 5.3 | 12.1 | 93.0 |
|  | 1991 | 6.8 | 11.9 | 6.5 | 12.2 | 94.6 |
|  | 1992 | 7.2 | 11.6 | 7.0 | 11.9 | 96.1 |
|  | 1993 | 8.3 | 12.8 | 7.8 | ... | 94.1 |
|  | 1994 | 7.6 | 11.9 | 7.1 | ... | 94.4 |
|  | 1995 | 7.5 | 12.2 | 7.1 | ... | 94.5 |
|  | 1996 | 7.5 | 12.2 | 7.0 | ... | 93.4 |
| France @ | 1970 | 4.8 | 24.9 | ... | ... | ... |
|  | 1975 | 5.2 | ... | 4.5 | ... | 87.6 |
|  | 1980 | 5.0 | ... | 4.7 | ... | 92.5 |
|  | 1985 | 5.8 | ... | 5.4 | ... | 94.5 |
|  | 1990 | 5.4 | ... | 5.1 | ... | 93.1 |
|  | 1991 | 5.8 | ... | 5.3 | ... | 91.6 |
|  | 1992 | 5.7 | ... | 5.2 | ... | 92.3 |
|  | 1993 | 5.8 | 10.4 | 5.3 | ... | 90.8 |
|  | 1994 | 5.9 | 10.8 | 5.4 | ... | 91.4 |
|  | 1995 | 6.1 | 11.1 | 5.5 | ... | 91.0 |
|  | 1996 | 6.0 | 10.9 | 5.6 | ... | 92.3 |
| Germany @ | 1993 | 4.8 | 9.5 | 4.3 | ... | 90.9 |
|  | 1994 | 4.7 | 9.4 | 4.2 | ... | 90.6 |
|  | 1995 | 4.8 | 8.4 | 4.3 | ... | 90.8 |
|  | 1996 | 4.8 | 9.6 | 4.4 | ... | 90.8 |
| Gibraltar | 1970 | 3.6 | ... | 3.3 | ... | 92.6 |
|  | 1975 | 3.3 | ... | 3.0 | ... | 91.2 |
|  | 1980 | 9.0 | ... | 5.5 | ... | 61.0 |
|  | 1984 | 6.0 | ... | ... | ... | ... |
| Greece @ | 1970 | 1.7 | 9.6 | 1.4 | 9.8 | 81.6 |
|  | 1975 | 1.7 | 8.0 | 1.5 | 9.0 | 91.0 |
|  | 1979 | 1.8 | 8.4 | 1.7 | 9.6 | 94.3 |
|  | 1985 | 2.4 | 7.5 | 2.3 | 8.5 | 95.2 |
|  | 1990 | 2.5 | ... | 2.3 | ... | 94.1 |
|  | 1991 | 2.3 | ... | 2.2 | ... | 94.6 |
|  | 1993 | 2.8 | 8.7 | ... | ... | ... |
|  | 1994 | 2.4 | 7.0 | ... | ... | ... |
|  | 1995 | 2.9 | 8.2 | ... | ... | ... |
|  | 1996 | 3.1 | ... | ... | ... | ... |
| Hungary @ | 1970 | ... | 6.9 | ... | ... | 87.2 |
|  | 1975 | 4.1 | 4.2 | 3.5 | 5.3 | 86.5 |
|  | 1980 | 4.7 | 5.2 | 3.9 | 6.4 | 83.1 |
|  | 1985 | 5.5 | 6.4 | 4.9 | 7.4 | 89.0 |
|  | 1990 | 6.1 | 7.8 | 5.5 | 8.6 | 90.4 |
|  | 1991 | 6.4 | 7.8 | 5.8 | 8.5 | 91.0 |
|  | 1992 | 6.8 | 7.7 | 6.3 | 8.6 | 92.4 |
|  | 1993 | 6.7 | 7.4 | 6.3 | 8.3 | 94.0 |
|  | 1994 | 6.6 | 6.9 | 6.2 | 7.9 | 94.5 |
|  | 1995 | 5.3 | ... | 4.9 | ... | 93.0 |
|  | 1996 | 4.6 | ... | 4.3 | ... | 92.0 |
| Iceland @ | 1971 | 4.4 | 18.8 | ... | ... | ... |
|  | 1980 | 4.4 | 14.0 | ... | ... | ... |
|  | 1985 | 4.9 | 13.8 | ... | ... | ... |
|  | 1990 | 5.6 | ... | 4.1 | ... | 73.9 |
|  | 1993 | 5.4 | 12.8 | 4.8 | ... | 88.8 |
|  | 1994 | 5.0 | 12.0 | 4.4 | ... | 87.9 |
|  | 1995 | 5.0 | 12.3 | 4.5 | ... | 89.2 |
|  | 1996 | 5.4 | 13.6 | 4.8 | ... | 87.6 |

Total and current public expenditure on education II.18
Dépenses publiques totales et ordinaires afférentes à l'éducation
Gastos públicos totales y ordinarios destinados a la educación

| Country / Pays / País | | Year / Année / Año | Total expenditure on education / Dépenses totales d'éducation / Gastos totales de educación | | Current expenditure on education / Dépenses ordinaires d'éducation / Gastos ordinarios de educación | | |
|---|---|---|---|---|---|---|---|
| | | | As % of Gross National Product / En % du Produit National Brut / En % del Producto Nacional Bruto | As % of total government expenditure / En % des dépenses totales du gouvernement / En % de los gastos totales del gobierno | As % of Gross National Product / En % du Produit National Brut / En % del Producto Nacional Bruto | As % of current government expenditure / En % des dépenses ordinaires du gouvernment / En % de los gastos ordinarios del gobierno | As % of total expenditure on education / En % des dépenses totales d'éducation / En % de los gastos totales de educación |
| Ireland @ | | 1970 | 4.8 | 10.8 | 4.0 | 12.1 | 83.9 |
| | | 1975 | 5.8 | 10.8 | 5.0 | 12.8 | 86.6 |
| | | 1980 | 6.3 | ... | 5.5 | ... | 86.6 |
| | | 1985 | 6.4 | 8.9 | 5.8 | 10.5 | 91.0 |
| | | 1990 | 5.6 | 10.2 | 5.3 | 12.1 | 95.0 |
| | | 1991 | 5.7 | 9.7 | 5.5 | 12.2 | 95.7 |
| | | 1992 | 6.0 | 10.9 | 5.7 | 13.6 | 95.3 |
| | | 1993 | 6.2 | 13.1 | 5.9 | ... | 95.5 |
| | | 1994 | 6.3 | 13.3 | 6.0 | ... | 94.9 |
| | | 1995 | 6.0 | 13.5 | 5.7 | ... | 95.1 |
| | | 1996 | 6.0 | ... | 5.7 | ... | 95.0 |
| Italy @ | | 1970 | 3.7 | 11.9 | 3.6 | 17.2 | 97.2 |
| | | 1975 | 4.1 | 9.4 | 3.7 | 12.6 | 89.2 |
| | | 1979 | 4.4 | 11.1 | 3.8 | 10.7 | 86.5 |
| | | 1985 | 5.0 | 8.3 | 4.6 | 10.0 | 90.9 |
| | | 1993 | 5.2 | 9.0 | 4.9 | ... | 93.7 |
| | | 1994 | 4.9 | 8.7 | 4.7 | ... | 95.8 |
| | | 1995 | 4.7 | 8.9 | 4.5 | ... | 95.6 |
| | | 1996 | 4.9 | 9.1 | 4.6 | ... | 95.3 |
| Latvia | | 1980 | 3.3 | 15.3 | 3.2 | ... | 95.4 |
| | | 1985 | 3.4 | 12.4 | 3.2 | ... | 95.4 |
| | | 1990 | 3.8 | 10.8 | 3.4 | ... | 91.1 |
| | | 1991 | 4.1 | 16.9 | 3.8 | ... | 94.0 |
| | | 1992 | 4.5 | 22.1 | 4.4 | ... | 97.4 |
| | | 1993 | 6.0 | 16.8 | 5.9 | 16.8 | 97.4 |
| | | 1994 | 6.1 | 16.1 | 6.0 | 16.2 | 98.8 |
| | | 1995 | 6.7 | 16.8 | 6.7 | 17.0 | 99.1 |
| | | 1996 | 6.3 | 14.1 | 6.1 | 14.3 | 96.6 |
| Lithuania | | 1980 | ... | 15.4 | ... | ... | 92.0 |
| | | 1985 | ... | 12.9 | ... | ... | 90.3 |
| | | 1990 | 4.6 | 13.8 | 4.3 | ... | 93.9 |
| | | 1991 | 5.5 | 20.6 | 5.2 | ... | 94.7 |
| | | 1992 | 5.3 | 22.1 | 5.0 | 23.5 | 95.5 |
| | | 1993 | 4.6 | 20.1 | 4.3 | 32.2 | 94.1 |
| | | 1994 | 5.6 | 21.8 | 5.2 | 23.9 | 93.5 |
| | | 1995 | 5.6 | 21.8 | 5.2 | 24.0 | 93.5 |
| | | 1996 | 5.5 | 22.8 | 5.2 | 24.3 | 95.1 |
| Luxembourg @ | | 1970 | 3.6 | 14.8 | 2.7 | ... | 74.2 |
| | | 1975 | 4.7 | 15.0 | 3.7 | 15.8 | 77.7 |
| | | 1980 | 5.7 | 14.9 | 5.4 | 19.8 | 95.0 |
| | | 1986 | 3.8 | 15.7 | 3.3 | 15.4 | 87.3 |
| | | 1989 | 4.0 | 16.0 | 3.3 | ... | 82.1 |
| | (2) | 1990 | 2.6 | 10.4 | ... | ... | ... |
| | (2) | 1991 | 2.6 | 10.8 | ... | ... | ... |
| | (2) | 1992 | 2.8 | 11.2 | ... | ... | ... |
| | (2) | 1993 | 3.1 | 11.7 | ... | ... | ... |
| | (2) | 1994 | 3.1 | 11.5 | ... | ... | ... |
| | | 1995 | 4.1 | 15.1 | 3.7 | 15.0 | 90.1 |
| | | 1996 | 4.0 | ... | 3.7 | ... | 93.4 |
| Malta | | 1970 | 6.3 | 13.0 | 5.8 | 16.0 | 91.9 |
| | | 1975 | 3.9 | 7.6 | 3.7 | 11.9 | 96.8 |
| | | 1980 | 3.0 | 7.8 | 3.0 | 9.7 | 99.3 |
| | | 1985 | 3.4 | 7.7 | 3.3 | 9.1 | 98.2 |
| | | 1990 | 4.0 | 8.3 | 3.8 | 10.9 | 94.4 |
| | | 1991 | 4.1 | 8.5 | 3.9 | 11.1 | 94.4 |
| | | 1992 | 4.6 | 10.9 | 4.5 | 12.5 | 97.1 |
| | | 1993 | 5.2 | 11.8 | 4.9 | 13.0 | 94.9 |
| | | 1994 | 5.2 | 11.4 | 4.9 | 12.3 | 93.4 |
| | | 1995 | 5.2 | 11.4 | 4.8 | 12.3 | 93.5 |
| | | 1996 | 5.1 | 10.8 | 4.7 | 11.3 | 91.9 |
| Moldova | | 1980 | 3.4 | ... | 2.9 | ... | 83.8 |
| | | 1985 | 3.6 | ... | 3.1 | ... | 84.3 |
| | | 1990 | 5.6 | 17.2 | 4.4 | ... | 78.9 |
| | | 1991 | 5.4 | 21.6 | 4.7 | ... | 87.4 |
| | | 1992 | 7.3 | 26.4 | 6.0 | 25.4 | 81.8 |
| | | 1993 | 7.0 | ... | 6.5 | ... | 93.1 |
| | | 1994 | 9.0 | 28.9 | 8.6 | 25.1 | 94.7 |
| | | 1995 | 9.2 | 22.9 | 8.7 | 24.3 | 95.2 |
| | | 1996 | 10.6 | 28.1 | 10.3 | 29.7 | 96.7 |

II.18   Total and current public expenditure on education
Dépenses publiques totales et ordinaires afférentes à l'éducation
Gastos públicos totales y ordinarios destinados a la educación

| Country / Pays / País | | Year / Année / Año | Total expenditure on education<br>Dépenses totales d'éducation<br>Gastos totales de educación | | Current expenditure on education<br>Dépenses ordinaires d'éducation<br>Gastos ordinarios de educación | | |
|---|---|---|---|---|---|---|---|
| | | | As % of Gross National Product<br>En % du Produit National Brut<br>En % del Producto Nacional Bruto | As % of total government expenditure<br>En % des dépenses totales du gouvernement<br>En % de los gastos totales del gobierno | As % of Gross National Product<br>En % du Produit National Brut<br>En % del Producto Nacional Bruto | As % of current government expenditure<br>En % des dépenses ordinaires du gouvernement<br>En % de los gastos ordinarios del gobierno | As % of total expenditure on education<br>En % des dépenses totales d'éducation<br>En % de los gastos totales de educación |
| Monaco | | 1974 | ... | 10.4 | ... | ... | 58.2 |
| | | 1989 | ... | 5.3 | ... | 7.8 | 91.1 |
| | | 1992 | ... | 5.6 | ... | 7.7 | 91.4 |
| | | 1995 | ... | 6.7 | ... | 8.4 | 92.6 |
| | | 1996 | ... | 6.3 | ... | 7.9 | 92.5 |
| | | 1997 | ... | 5.3 | ... | 7.0 | 91.2 |
| Netherlands @ | | 1970 | 7.2 | ... | 5.7 | ... | 79.7 |
| | | 1975 | 8.1 | ... | 6.7 | ... | 82.2 |
| | | 1980 | 7.6 | ... | 7.0 | ... | 92.0 |
| | | 1985 | 6.4 | ... | 6.0 | ... | 93.9 |
| | | 1990 | 6.0 | ... | 5.7 | ... | 95.1 |
| | | 1991 | 5.9 | ... | 5.6 | ... | 95.6 |
| | | 1993 | 5.4 | 9.2 | 5.2 | ... | 96.1 |
| | | 1994 | 5.2 | 9.4 | 5.1 | ... | 96.7 |
| | | 1995 | 5.2 | 8.7 | 5.0 | ... | 96.7 |
| | | 1996 | 5.1 | 9.8 | 4.9 | ... | 96.0 |
| Norway @ | | 1970 | 5.4 | 15.5 | 4.1 | ... | 77.5 |
| | | 1975 | 6.3 | 14.7 | 5.1 | 13.9 | 80.6 |
| | | 1980 | 6.5 | 13.7 | 5.4 | 14.4 | 83.4 |
| | | 1985 | 5.9 | 14.6 | 5.2 | 15.3 | 88.3 |
| | | 1990 | 7.3 | 14.6 | 6.3 | 14.5 | 86.3 |
| | | 1991 | 7.4 | 14.6 | 6.5 | 15.7 | 87.4 |
| | | 1992 | 7.7 | 14.1 | 6.7 | 15.8 | 86.4 |
| | | 1993 | 8.2 | 15.0 | 7.7 | ... | 93.8 |
| | | 1994 | 8.2 | 15.7 | 7.7 | ... | 93.1 |
| | | 1995 | 8.1 | 16.2 | 7.3 | ... | 90.8 |
| | | 1996 | 7.4 | 15.8 | 6.9 | ... | 92.1 |
| Poland @ | | 1971 | 4.0 | 8.7 | 3.6 | 9.2 | 91.7 |
| | | 1975 | ... | ... | 3.7 | 8.7 | ... |
| | | 1980 | ... | ... | 3.3 | 7.0 | ... |
| | | 1985 | 4.9 | 12.2 | 4.0 | 11.6 | 81.5 |
| | | 1990 | ... | ... | 5.3 | 16.4 | ... |
| | | 1991 | 5.4 | 14.6 | 5.0 | 15.0 | 92.9 |
| | | 1992 | 5.5 | 14.0 | 5.2 | 14.2 | 93.6 |
| | | 1993 | 5.5 | 14.0 | 5.1 | 15.5 | 93.1 |
| | | 1994 | 5.3 | 13.2 | 5.0 | 13.5 | 94.1 |
| | | 1995 | 5.2 | 16.4 | ... | ... | ... |
| | | 1996 | 7.5 | 24.8 | ... | ... | ... |
| Portugal @ | (2) | 1970 | 1.5 | 6.6 | 1.3 | 7.9 | 90.8 |
| | | 1975 | 3.5 | 11.2 | 3.3 | 13.9 | 93.8 |
| | | 1980 | 3.8 | ... | 3.3 | ... | 85.4 |
| | | 1985 | 4.0 | ... | 3.6 | ... | 88.7 |
| | (2) | 1990 | 4.2 | ... | 3.9 | ... | 91.7 |
| | (2) | 1991 | 4.8 | ... | 4.5 | ... | 94.1 |
| | | 1992 | 5.1 | ... | 4.8 | ... | 93.7 |
| | | 1993 | 5.5 | ... | 5.1 | ... | 93.1 |
| | | 1994 | 5.3 | 12.1 | 5.0 | ... | 93.7 |
| | | 1995 | 5.3 | 11.7 | 4.8 | ... | 91.4 |
| | | 1996 | 5.8 | ... | 5.3 | ... | 92.8 |
| Romania | | 1970 | ... | 8.0 | ... | ... | 88.6 |
| | | 1975 | 3.5 | 6.4 | 3.0 | ... | 84.8 |
| | | 1980 | 3.3 | 6.7 | 2.9 | ... | 88.8 |
| | | 1985 | 2.2 | ... | 2.1 | ... | 96.7 |
| | | 1990 | 2.8 | 7.3 | 2.8 | 9.0 | 98.4 |
| | (3) | 1991 | 3.5 | ... | ... | ... | ... |
| | | 1992 | 3.6 | 14.2 | 3.5 | 15.5 | 96.5 |
| | | 1993 | 3.2 | 9.1 | 3.0 | 9.8 | 95.2 |
| | (3) | 1994 | 3.0 | 13.6 | ... | ... | ... |
| | | 1996 | 3.6 | 10.5 | 3.3 | 11.5 | 92.5 |
| Russian Federation @ | | 1970 | 3.9 | ... | ... | ... | ... |
| | | 1975 | 3.9 | ... | ... | ... | ... |
| | | 1980 | 3.5 | ... | ... | ... | ... |
| | | 1985 | 3.2 | ... | ... | ... | ... |
| | | 1990 | 3.5 | ... | ... | ... | ... |
| | | 1991 | 3.6 | ... | ... | ... | ... |
| | | 1992 | 3.7 | ... | ... | ... | ... |
| | | 1993 | 4.1 | 9.6 | 3.9 | 10.0 | 95.5 |
| | | 1995 | 3.5 | | | | |
| San Marino | | 1970 | ... | 13.4 | ... | ... | 73.9 |
| | | 1975 | ... | 13.1 | ... | 15.0 | 90.0 |

Total and current public expenditure on education II.18
Dépenses publiques totales et ordinaires afférentes à l'éducation
Gastos públicos totales y ordinarios destinados a la educación

| Country / Pays / País | Year / Année / Año | Total expenditure on education / Dépenses totales d'éducation / Gastos totales de educación | | Current expenditure on education / Dépenses ordinaires d'éducation / Gastos ordinarios de educación | | |
|---|---|---|---|---|---|---|
| | | As % of Gross National Product / En % du Produit National Brut / En % del Producto Nacional Bruto | As % of total government expenditure / En % des dépenses totales du gouvernement / En % de los gastos totales del gobierno | As % of Gross National Product / En % du Produit National Brut / En % del Producto Nacional Bruto | As % of current government expenditure / En % des dépenses ordinaires du gouvernement / En % de los gastos ordinarios del gobierno | As % of total expenditure on education / En % des dépenses totales d'éducation / En % de los gastos totales de educación |
| San Marino (cont) | 1980 | ... | 7.5 | ... | 9.5 | 86.4 |
| | 1984 | ... | 10.7 | ... | 10.3 | 91.3 |
| Slovakia | 1990 | 5.1 | ... | ... | ... | ... |
| | 1991 | 5.6 | ... | ... | ... | ... |
| | 1992 | 6.0 | ... | 5.3 | ... | 88.6 |
| | 1993 | 5.3 | ... | 4.6 | ... | 87.5 |
| | 1994 | 4.5 | ... | 3.9 | ... | 88.0 |
| | 1995 | 5.1 | ... | 4.0 | ... | 78.5 |
| | 1996 | 5.0 | ... | 4.6 | ... | 92.9 |
| Slovenia | 1991 | 4.8 | 16.1 | 4.4 | | 91.9 |
| | 1992 | 5.5 | 12.0 | 5.2 | | 94.2 |
| | 1993 | 5.8 | 12.4 | 5.4 | | 92.1 |
| | 1994 | 5.5 | 12.0 | 4.9 | | 90.5 |
| | 1995 | 5.7 | 12.6 | 5.4 | | 93.4 |
| Spain @ | 1970 | 2.0 | | 1.4 | | 66.6 |
| | 1975 | 1.8 | ... | ... | | ... |
| | 1979 | 2.6 | ... | 2.3 | | 86.3 |
| | 1985 | 3.3 | ... | 2.9 | | 89.5 |
| | 1990 | 4.4 | 9.4 | 3.9 | | 88.7 |
| | 1991 | 4.5 | ... | 4.0 | | 88.5 |
| | 1992 | 4.6 | 9.3 | 4.1 | | 90.4 |
| | 1993 | 4.7 | 11.6 | 4.3 | | 91.1 |
| | 1994 | 5.0 | 10.5 | 4.6 | | 92.1 |
| | 1995 | 4.9 | 10.6 | 4.5 | | 92.0 |
| | 1996 | 5.0 | 11.0 | 4.6 | | 91.9 |
| Sweden @ | 1970 | 7.6 | | 6.2 | ... | 82.0 |
| | 1975 | 7.0 | 13.4 | 6.3 | 13.9 | 90.8 |
| | 1980 | 9.0 | 14.1 | 7.7 | | 86.4 |
| | 1985 | 7.7 | 12.6 | 6.8 | | 88.8 |
| | 1990 | 7.7 | 13.8 | 7.1 | | 91.8 |
| | 1991 | 8.0 | 14.0 | 7.4 | | 91.9 |
| | 1992 | 8.4 | 12.7 | 7.6 | | 91.0 |
| | 1994 | 8.0 | 11.0 | ... | ... | ... |
| | 1995 | 8.1 | 11.6 | ... | ... | ... |
| | 1996 | 8.3 | 12.2 | ... | | ... |
| Switzerland @ | 1970 | 3.8 | 18.4 | 2.8 | 17.7 | 74.2 |
| | 1975 | 4.8 | 19.4 | 3.9 | 19.8 | 80.9 |
| | 1980 | 4.7 | 18.8 | 4.2 | 20.0 | 89.5 |
| | 1985 | 4.7 | 18.6 | 4.2 | 19.9 | 91.0 |
| | 1990 | 4.9 | 18.7 | 4.4 | ... | 88.8 |
| | 1991 | 5.2 | 18.8 | 4.6 | 19.5 | 88.7 |
| | 1993 | 5.4 | 16.1 | 4.8 | ... | 88.9 |
| | 1994 | 5.5 | 15.2 | 4.9 | ... | 89.5 |
| | 1995 | 5.4 | 15.3 | 4.9 | ... | 89.8 |
| | 1996 | 5.4 | 15.4 | 4.9 | ... | 90.5 |
| The Former Yugoslav Rep. of Macedonia | 1992 | 5.3 | ... | 5.2 | ... | 97.7 |
| | 1993 | 5.1 | 21.5 | 5.0 | 21.3 | 97.4 |
| | 1994 | 5.2 | 18.3 | 5.1 | 18.5 | 97.6 |
| | 1995 | 5.0 | 18.7 | 4.8 | 18.5 | 95.6 |
| | 1996 | 5.1 | 20.0 | 4.9 | 20.2 | 95.8 |
| Ukraine | 1970 | 5.5 | 28.1 | 4.6 | ... | 83.4 |
| | 1975 | 5.8 | 27.4 | 5.0 | ... | 86.0 |
| | 1980 | 5.6 | 24.5 | 4.8 | ... | 86.3 |
| | 1985 | 5.2 | 21.2 | 4.4 | ... | 84.9 |
| | 1990 | 5.0 | 19.7 | 4.0 | ... | 80.2 |
| | 1991 | 6.1 | 18.9 | 5.3 | ... | 86.6 |
| | 1992 | 6.5 | 17.1 | 5.6 | ... | 85.6 |
| | 1993 | 6.2 | 15.7 | 5.1 | ... | 82.5 |
| | 1994 | 7.1 | ... | 5.9 | ... | 83.0 |
| | 1995 | 7.3 | ... | 6.4 | ... | 87.5 |
| United Kingdom @ | 1970 | 5.3 | 14.1 | 4.5 | ... | 85.2 |
| | 1975 | 6.6 | 14.3 | 6.0 | ... | 89.6 |
| | 1980 | 5.6 | 13.9 | 5.2 | ... | 94.1 |
| | 1985 | 4.9 | ... | 4.7 | ... | 95.8 |
| | 1990 | 4.9 | ... | 4.7 | ... | 94.9 |
| | 1991 | 5.2 | ... | 4.9 | ... | 95.0 |
| | 1992 | 5.4 | 11.2 | ... | ... | ... |
| | 1993 | 5.5 | 11.4 | ... | ... | ... |
| | 1994 | 5.4 | 11.4 | ... | ... | ... |
| | 1995 | 5.3 | 11.6 | ... | ... | ... |

II.18    Total and current public expenditure on education
Dépenses publiques totales et ordinaires afférentes à l'éducation
Gastos públicos totales y ordinarios destinados a la educación

| Country / Pays / País | Year / Année / Año | Total expenditure on education / Dépenses totales d'éducation / Gastos totales de educación | | Current expenditure on education / Dépenses ordinaires d'éducation / Gastos ordinarios de educación | | |
|---|---|---|---|---|---|---|
| | | As % of Gross National Product / En % du Produit National Brut / En % del Producto Nacional Bruto | As % of total government expenditure / En % des dépenses totales du gouvernement / En % de los gastos totales del gobierno | As % of Gross National Product / En % du Produit National Brut / En % del Producto Nacional Bruto | As % of current government expenditure / En % des dépenses ordinaires du gouvernment / En % de los gastos ordinarios del gobiemo | As % of total expenditure on education / En % des dépenses totales d'éducation / En % de los gastos totales de educación |
| **Oceania** | | | | | | |
| American Samoa | 1975 | 14.2 | ... | 11.8 | ... | 82.6 |
| | 1981 | 8.2 | 16.0 | 8.1 | 17.9 | 98.1 |
| Australia @ | 1970 | 4.1 | 13.3 | 3.3 | 15.9 | 81.1 |
| | 1975 | 5.9 | 14.8 | 4.9 | 18.4 | 83.1 |
| | 1980 | 5.5 | 14.8 | 5.0 | 16.8 | 90.9 |
| | 1985 | 5.6 | 12.8 | 5.1 | 14.2 | 91.7 |
| | 1990 | 5.3 | 14.8 | 4.9 | 14.8 | 92.4 |
| | 1991 | 5.5 | 14.1 | 5.1 | 14.6 | 93.0 |
| | 1992 | 5.9 | 14.2 | 5.4 | ... | 91.2 |
| | 1993 | 5.6 | 13.2 | 5.3 | ... | 95.8 |
| | 1994 | 5.4 | 12.9 | 5.1 | ... | 95.5 |
| | 1995 | 5.5 | 13.5 | 5.2 | ... | 95.6 |
| Cook Islands | 1986 | ... | 9.5 | ... | 9.5 | 99.1 |
| | 1991 | ... | 12.4 | ... | 12.7 | 99.9 |
| Fiji | 1970 | 4.2 | 15.6 | 3.7 | 17.0 | 88.5 |
| | 1975 | 4.7 | 19.5 | 4.3 | 23.2 | 92.3 |
| | 1980 | 5.1 | ... | 4.9 | 21.5 | 96.4 |
| | 1986 | 6.0 | ... | 5.9 | ... | 98.0 |
| (2) | 1990 | 4.7 | ... | 4.7 | ... | 99.1 |
| (2) | 1991 | 4.8 | ... | 4.5 | ... | 93.5 |
| (2) | 1992 | 5.4 | 18.6 | 5.2 | ... | 96.9 |
| French Polynesia | 1984 | 9.8 | ... | 8.9 | ... | 90.7 |
| Guam | 1975 | 13.3 | ... | 13.2 | ... | 99.7 |
| | 1981 | 8.0 | ... | 7.9 | ... | 98.2 |
| | 1985 | 8.5 | ... | 8.3 | ... | 97.7 |
| Kiribati | 1980 | ... | ... | 7.6 | 17.4 | ... |
| | 1985 | ... | ... | 5.1 | 18.5 | ... |
| | 1990 | ... | ... | 5.4 | 18.3 | ... |
| | 1991 | ... | ... | 5.2 | 18.3 | ... |
| | 1992 | ... | ... | 6.2 | ... | ... |
| | 1994 | ... | ... | 6.3 | 17.6 | ... |
| | 1995 | ... | ... | 9.9 | ... | ... |
| | 1996 | ... | ... | 11.4 | ... | ... |
| New Caledonia | 1970 | 4.2 | ... | 3.8 | ... | 89.5 |
| | 1981 | 11.9 | ... | 11.2 | ... | 94.9 |
| | 1985 | 13.5 | ... | 12.3 | ... | 91.2 |
| New Zealand @ | 1970 | 4.7 | ... | 3.7 | ... | 79.4 |
| | 1975 | 5.8 | 17.1 | 4.6 | ... | 79.7 |
| | 1980 | 5.8 | 23.1 | 5.2 | 27.9 | 89.9 |
| | 1985 | 4.7 | 18.4 | 4.3 | 25.5 | 91.2 |
| | 1990 | 6.5 | ... | 6.3 | ... | 95.5 |
| | 1991 | 7.4 | ... | 7.1 | ... | 96.2 |
| | 1992 | 7.4 | 16.9 | 7.1 | ... | 96.2 |
| | 1993 | 7.0 | 17.1 | 6.6 | ... | 94.9 |
| | 1994 | 6.8 | ... | 6.5 | ... | 95.4 |
| | 1995 | 7.5 | ... | 7.1 | ... | 93.7 |
| | 1996 | 7.3 | ... | 6.9 | ... | 93.7 |
| Niue | 1970 | ... | ... | ... | ... | 93.7 |
| | 1975 | ... | 18.6 | ... | 28.7 | 94.3 |
| | 1980 | ... | 13.2 | ... | 15.9 | 97.2 |
| | 1991 | ... | 10.2 | ... | 10.8 | 98.0 |
| Norfolk Island | 1970 | ... | 14.3 | ... | ... | 94.5 |
| | 1975 | ... | 13.7 | ... | 17.7 | 95.0 |
| | 1980 | ... | 15.1 | ... | 17.3 | 100.0 |
| Papua New Guinea | 1970 | 4.5 | 13.2 | 3.7 | 13.9 | 82.0 |
| | 1976 | 7.7 | ... | 6.9 | ... | 90.2 |
| | 1979 | 4.7 | 14.2 | 4.5 | ... | 96.7 |
| Samoa | 1970 | ... | 20.0 | ... | 19.7 | 87.3 |
| | 1976 | ... | 8.5 | ... | 16.7 | 100.0 |
| | 1990 | 4.2 | 10.7 | 4.0 | 15.8 | 94.0 |

Total and current public expenditure on education II.18
Dépenses publiques totales et ordinaires afférentes à l'éducation
Gastos públicos totales y ordinarios destinados a la educación

| | | Total expenditure on education<br>Dépenses totales d'éducation<br>Gastos totales de educación | | Current expenditure on education<br>Dépenses ordinaires d'éducation<br>Gastos ordinarios de educación | | |
|---|---|---|---|---|---|---|
| Country<br><br>Pays<br><br>País | Year<br><br>Année<br><br>Año | As % of<br>Gross<br>National<br>Product<br>En % du<br>Produit<br>National<br>Brut<br>En % del<br>Producto<br>Nacional<br>Bruto | As %<br>of total<br>government<br>expenditure<br>En % des<br>dépenses<br>totales du<br>gouvernement<br>En % de<br>los gastos<br>totales del<br>gobierno | As % of<br>Gross<br>National<br>Product<br>En % du<br>Produit<br>National<br>Brut<br>En % del<br>Producto<br>Nacional<br>Bruto | As % of<br>current<br>government<br>expenditure<br>En % des<br>dépenses<br>ordinaires du<br>gouvernement<br>En % de<br>los gastos<br>ordinarios<br>del gobierno | As % of<br>total<br>expenditure on<br>education<br>En % des<br>dépenses<br>totales<br>d'éducation<br>En % de<br>los gastos<br>totales<br>de educación |
| Solomon Islands | 1970 | ... | 13.8 | ... | 13.0 | 70.0 |
| | 1975 | 5.5 | 14.7 | 4.3 | 17.6 | 79.0 |
| | 1980 | 5.6 | 11.2 | 4.3 | 14.1 | 76.2 |
| | 1984 | 4.7 | 12.4 | 1.9 | 8.0 | 40.2 |
| | 1991 | 3.8 | 7.9 | ... | ... | ... |
| Tonga | 1971 | ... | 15.7 | ... | 19.0 | 89.0 |
| | 1975 | ... | 12.7 | ... | 14.4 | 96.8 |
| | 1980 | ... | 11.6 | ... | 13.3 | 89.8 |
| | 1985 | 4.1 | 16.1 | ... | ... | ... |
| | 1992 | 4.7 | 17.3 | ... | ... | ... |
| Tuvalu | 1990 | ... | 16.2 | ... | ... | ... |
| Vanuatu, Republic of | 1990 | 4.4 | 19.2 | ... | ... | ... |
| | 1991 | 4.8 | 18.8 | ... | ... | ... |
| | 1994 | 5.0 | ... | ... | ... | ... |
| | 1995 | 4.0 | ... | ... | ... | ... |

**General note**
For general explanations and definitions, please refer to the beginning of this chapter.

**Note générale**
Pour les explications et définitions générales, prière de se référer au début de ce chapitre.

**Nota general**
Para las explicaciones y definiciones generales, referirse al comienzo de este capítulo.

| Notes | Notes | Notas |
|---|---|---|
| @ For countries participating in the UNESCO/OECD/Eurostat survey there may be a break in the series due to methodological changes. This is indicated by a line that separates the relevant years from the previous ones. | @ Pour les pays qui participent à l'enquête de l'UNESCO/OCDE/Eurostat, il peut y avoir une rupture dans les séries temporelles due à des changements méthodologiques. Ceci est indiqué par une ligne qui sépare les années concernées des années antérieures. | @ Para los países que participan en la encuesta de UNESCO/OCDE/Eurostat puede haber una ruptura de serie debido a la introducción de algunos cambios metodológicos. Esto está indicado por una línea que separa los años correspondientes de los años anteriores. |
| (1) Not including expenditure on tertiary education. | (1) Non compris les dépenses de l'enseignement supérieur. | (1) No incluyen los gastos de la enseñanza superior. |
| (2) Ministry of Education only. | (2) Ministère de l'Education seulement. | (2) Ministerio de Educación solamente. |
| (3) Central government only. | (3) Gouvernement central seulement. | (3) Gobierno central solamente. |
| (4) Expenditure on Education as % of Global Social Product | (4) Les dépenses d'enseignement en pourcentage du Produit Social Global | (4) Los gastos relativos a la enseñanza en porcentaje del Producto Social Global. |
| (5) Expenditure of the Office of Greek Education only. | (5) Les dépenses du bureau grec de l'éducation seulement. | (5) Los gastos del servicio griego de educación solamente. |
| (6) Flemish Community only. | (6) Communauté flamande seulement. | (6) Comunidad flamenca solamente. |

II.19 Current public expenditure by level of education
Dépenses publiques ordinaires par niveau d'enseignement
Gastos públicos ordinarios por nivel de enseñanza

## II.19 Current public expenditure on education: percentage distribution by level of education

Dépenses publiques ordinaires afférentes à l'éducation: répartition en pourcentage par niveau d'enseignement

Gastos públicos ordinarios destinados a la educación: distribución en porcentaje por nivel de enseñanza

| Country<br>Pays<br>País | Year<br>Année<br>Año | Pre-primary<br>Pré-primaire<br>Pre-primaria<br>(%) | Primary<br>Primaire<br>Primaria<br>(%) | Preprimary + Primary<br>Préprimaire + Primaire<br>Preprimaria + Primaria<br>(%) | Secondary<br>Secondaire<br>Secundaria<br>(%) | Preprimary + Primary + Secondary<br>Préprimaire + Primaire + Secondaire<br>Preprimaria + Primaria + Secundaria<br>(%) | Tertiary<br>Supérieur<br>Superior<br>(%) | Other types<br>Autres types<br>Otros tipos<br>(%) | Not distributed<br>Non réparties<br>Sin distribución<br>(%) |
|---|---|---|---|---|---|---|---|---|---|
| **Africa** | | | | | | | | | |
| Algeria | 1980 | - | 28.4 | 28.4 | 25.2 | 53.6 | 17.3 | 19.8 | 9.3 |
| (1) | 1991 | - | ... | ... | ... | 95.4 | (1) ... | 2.4 | 2.2 |
| (1) | 1992 | ... | ... | ... | ... | 95.6 | (1) ... | 2.2 | 2.2 |
| (1) | 1993 | ... | ... | ... | ... | 96.3 | (1) ... | 1.7 | 2.0 |
| (1) | 1994 | ... | ... | ... | ... | 94.5 | (1) ... | 2.5 | 3.0 |
| (1) | 1995 | ... | ... | ... | ... | 95.0 | (1) ... | 2.1 | 2.8 |
| (1) | 1996 | ... | ... | ... | ... | 95.3 | (1) ... | 1.8 | 2.9 |
| Angola (2) | 1985 | ... | ... | ... | ... | 86.8 | 5.0 | 8.2 | - |
| | 1990 | ... | ... | ... | ... | 96.3 | 3.7 | - | - |
| Benin | 1970 | ... | ... | 49.8 | 24.9 | 74.7 | 13.3 | 2.8 | 9.3 |
| | 1975 | ... | ... | 44.9 | 26.1 | 70.9 | 18.5 | 4.8 | 5.8 |
| | 1995 | 1.5 | 57.6 | 59.1 | 21.7 | 80.8 | 18.8 | 0.4 | - |
| Botswana | 1970 | - | 57.6 | 57.6 | 29.8 | 87.3 | 8.8 | - | 3.9 |
| | 1975 | - | 46.5 | 46.5 | 33.5 | 79.9 | 13.6 | - | 6.5 |
| | 1979 | - | 52.1 | 52.1 | 29.2 | 81.3 | 13.2 | - | 5.6 |
| | 1985 | - | 36.3 | 36.3 | 40.7 | 77.0 | 17.2 | 0.9 | 4.8 |
| | 1991 | - | 31.1 | 31.1 | 48.8 | 79.8 | 12.2 | 1.8 | 6.1 |
| Burkina Faso | 1975 | ... | ... | 43.3 | 26.2 | 69.6 | 24.8 | - | 5.6 |
| | 1980 | ... | ... | 32.3 | 19.8 | 52.0 | 33.7 | 9.2 | 5.1 |
| | 1985 | ... | ... | 38.1 | 20.3 | 58.5 | 30.7 | 4.9 | 6.0 |
| | 1989 | ... | ... | 41.7 | 25.8 | 67.5 | 32.1 | 0.4 | - |
| | 1994 | 0.0 | 48.1 | 48.1 | 27.0 | 75.1 | 19.5 | 5.4 | - |
| | 1997 | ... | ... | 56.6 | 25.1 | 81.7 | 18.3 | - | - |
| Burundi | 1975 | ... | ... | 45.0 | 33.3 | 78.3 | 19.5 | 0.9 | 1.2 |
| | 1979 | ... | ... | 42.7 | 31.0 | 73.7 | 20.6 | 5.1 | 0.6 |
| | 1985 | ... | ... | 45.0 | 32.2 | 77.3 | 19.8 | 1.4 | 1.5 |
| | 1990 | ... | ... | 46.8 | 29.1 | 75.8 | 22.0 | 0.9 | 1.3 |
| | 1991 | ... | ... | 43.0 | 28.1 | 71.1 | 27.2 | - | 1.7 |
| | 1992 | ... | ... | 44.5 | 28.2 | 72.7 | 24.6 | - | 2.8 |
| | 1994 | ... | ... | 43.0 | 35.9 | 78.8 | 18.3 | - | 2.9 |
| | 1995 | ... | ... | 41.5 | 39.9 | 81.4 | 15.6 | - | 3.0 |
| | 1996 | ... | ... | 42.7 | 36.7 | 79.4 | 17.1 | - | 3.5 |
| Cameroon | 1970 | ... | ... | 40.7 | 28.4 | 69.1 | 15.8 | 6.9 | 8.2 |
| | 1981 | ... | ... | ... | ... | 76.0 | 24.0 | - | 0.0 |
| | 1985 | ... | ... | ... | ... | 72.6 | 27.4 | - | - |
| | 1990 | ... | ... | ... | ... | 70.5 | 29.5 | - | - |
| | 1991 | ... | ... | ... | ... | 86.6 | 13.4 | - | - |
| | 1996 | ... | ... | ... | ... | 86.8 | 13.2 | - | - |
| Cape Verde | 1985 | ... | ... | 61.5 | 15.9 | 77.4 | - | 3.7 | 18.9 |
| | 1991 | ... | ... | 54.7 | 17.5 | 72.2 | (3) 2.7 | 9.7 | 15.4 |
| Central African Republic | 1975 | ... | ... | 56.9 | 14.5 | 71.3 | 9.9 | 1.1 | 17.7 |
| | 1981 | ... | ... | 54.9 | 13.9 | 68.8 | 16.3 | 0.2 | 14.7 |
| (2) | 1986 | ... | ... | 55.2 | 17.6 | 72.8 | 18.8 | - | 8.4 |
| (2) | 1990 | ... | ... | 52.7 | 14.6 | 67.2 | 21.5 | - | 11.3 |

Current public expenditure by level of education    II.19
Dépenses publiques ordinaires par niveau d'enseignement
Gastos públicos ordinarios por nivel de enseñanza

| Country<br>Pays<br>País | | Year<br>Année<br>Año | Pre-<br>primary<br>Pré-<br>primaire<br>Pre-<br>primaria<br>(%) | Primary<br>Primaire<br>Primaria<br>(%) | Preprimary<br>+ Primary<br>Préprimaire<br>+ Primaire<br>Preprimaria<br>+ Primaria<br>(%) | Secondary<br>Secondaire<br>Secundaria<br>(%) | Preprimary<br>+ Primary<br>+ Secondary<br>Préprimaire<br>+ Primaire<br>+ Secondaire<br>Preprimaria<br>+ Primaria<br>+ Secundaria<br>(%) | Tertiary<br>Supérieur<br>Superior<br>(%) | Other<br>types<br>Autres<br>types<br>Otros<br>tipos<br>(%) | Not<br>distributed<br>Non<br>réparties<br>Sin<br>distribución<br>(%) |
|---|---|---|---|---|---|---|---|---|---|---|
| Central African Republic | (2) | 1991 | ... | ... | 54.5 | 16.7 | 71.2 | 23.7 | - | 5.1 |
| (cont) | (2) | 1992 | ... | ... | 56.6 | 16.6 | 73.1 | 21.9 | - | 4.9 |
| | (2) | 1993 | ... | ... | 56.3 | 16.4 | 72.7 | 21.7 | - | 5.6 |
| | (2) | 1994 | ... | ... | 53.0 | 16.6 | 69.6 | 23.7 | - | 6.7 |
| | (2) | 1995 | ... | ... | 53.2 | 16.5 | 69.6 | 24.0 | - | 6.4 |
| Chad | | 1991 | 3.6 | 43.6 | 47.1 | 20.9 | 68.0 | 8.2 | 0.4 | 23.4 |
| | | 1993 | 3.0 | 41.6 | 44.6 | 21.3 | 65.9 | 9.1 | 1.5 | 23.5 |
| | | 1994 | 3.2 | 38.9 | 42.1 | 21.7 | 63.7 | 7.6 | 0.9 | 27.8 |
| | | 1996 | 0.1 | 43.4 | 43.5 | 24.2 | 67.7 | 9.0 | 0.7 | 22.6 |
| Comoros (2) | | 1990 | ... | ... | 42.4 | 28.2 | 70.6 | 17.3 | - | 12.1 |
| | | 1991 | ... | ... | 43.1 | 31.3 | 74.5 | 17.4 | - | 8.1 |
| | | 1992 | ... | ... | 39.5 | 33.6 | 73.1 | 16.3 | - | 10.6 |
| | | 1993 | ... | ... | 40.8 | 32.8 | 73.6 | 11.9 | - | 14.4 |
| | | 1995 | ... | ... | 36.6 | 35.1 | 71.7 | 17.2 | - | 11.1 |
| Congo | | 1970 | 0.2 | 48.7 | 48.9 | 36.3 | 85.2 | 9.6 | 0.4 | 4.8 |
| | | 1975 | 0.8 | 34.3 | 35.1 | 31.9 | 67.0 | 28.6 | 0.2 | 4.3 |
| | | 1980 | ... | ... | 35.8 | 29.1 | 64.9 | 24.3 | 0.1 | 10.7 |
| | | 1984 | ... | ... | 30.0 | 35.6 | 65.6 | 34.4 | - | - |
| | | 1993 | 0.2 | 48.6 | 48.7 | 11.6 | 60.4 | 29.3 | 0.7 | 9.6 |
| | | 1994 | 0.2 | 46.6 | 48.8 | 12.3 | 61.0 | 28.5 | 0.7 | 9.8 |
| | | 1995 | 0.2 | 50.2 | 50.4 | 11.6 | 62.0 | 28.0 | 0.8 | 9.2 |
| Côte d'Ivoire | | 1980 | ... | ... | 46.8 | 37.2 | 84.0 | 14.9 | - | 1.0 |
| | | 1985 | ... | ... | 40.2 | 42.7 | 82.9 | 17.1 | - | - |
| | | 1992 | ... | ... | 49.7 | 35.6 | 85.4 | 14.6 | - | - |
| | | 1993 | ... | ... | 50.5 | 34.9 | 85.4 | 14.6 | - | - |
| | | 1994 | ... | ... | 50.7 | 33.9 | 84.6 | 15.4 | - | - |
| | | 1995 | ... | ... | 49.8 | 33.8 | 83.6 | 16.4 | - | - |
| | | 1996 | ... | ... | 45.7 | 36.9 | 82.6 | 17.4 | - | - |
| | | 1997 | ... | ... | 45.2 | 36.2 | 81.4 | 18.6 | - | - |
| Democratic Rep. of the | | 1975 | ... | ... | 44.1 | 35.3 | 79.4 | 20.6 | - | ... |
| Congo | | 1980 | ... | ... | ... | ... | 69.2 | 30.8 | - | - |
| | | 1985 | ... | ... | ... | ... | 71.3 | 28.7 | - | - |
| | | 1988 | ... | ... | ... | ... | 64.6 | 35.4 | - | - |
| Djibouti | | 1970 | - | 48.3 | 48.3 | 50.9 | 99.2 | - | - | 0.8 |
| | | 1979 | - | 58.4 | 58.4 | 18.1 | 76.6 | (3) 19.1 | 3.6 | 0.7 |
| | | 1990 | - | 58.0 | 58.0 | 21.7 | 79.6 | (3) 11.5 | 2.6 | 6.3 |
| | | 1991 | - | 53.4 | 53.4 | 21.1 | 74.5 | (3) 13.9 | 5.8 | 5.7 |
| Egypt | | 1970 | ... | ... | ... | ... | 79.6 | 20.4 | - | - |
| | | 1975 | ... | ... | ... | ... | 70.0 | 30.0 | - | - |
| | | 1980 | ... | ... | ... | ... | 69.1 | 30.9 | - | - |
| | | 1990 | ... | ... | ... | ... | 64.0 | 36.0 | - | - |
| | | 1991 | ... | ... | ... | ... | 62.9 | 37.1 | - | - |
| | | 1992 | ... | ... | ... | ... | 63.5 | 36.5 | - | - |
| | | 1993 | ... | ... | ... | ... | 64.7 | 35.3 | - | - |
| | | 1994 | ... | ... | ... | ... | 64.3 | 35.7 | - | - |
| | | 1995 | ... | ... | ... | ... | 64.6 | 35.4 | - | - |
| | | 1996 | ... | ... | ... | ... | 66.7 | 33.3 | - | - |
| Eritrea (1) | | 1993 | ... | ... | 49.9 | 20.4 | 70.3 | (1) ... | 5.8 | 23.9 |
| | | 1994 | ... | ... | 51.4 | 16.7 | 68.0 | (1) ... | ←— | 32.0 |
| | | 1996 | ... | ... | 44.5 | 17.6 | 62.1 | (1) ... | ←— | 37.9 |
| Ethiopia | | 1970 | ... | ... | 45.1 | 29.0 | 74.1 | 18.6 | 0.4 | 6.9 |
| | | 1975 | ... | ... | 36.6 | 38.7 | 75.3 | 14.3 | 1.1 | 9.3 |
| | | 1980 | ... | ... | 42.0 | 29.8 | 71.8 | 19.0 | 4.0 | 5.2 |
| | | 1986 | ... | ... | 51.5 | 28.3 | 79.8 | 14.4 | 2.4 | 3.5 |
| | | 1990 | ... | ... | 53.9 | 28.1 | 82.0 | 12.1 | 1.8 | 4.0 |
| | | 1992 | ... | ... | 53.2 | 26.6 | 79.8 | 12.4 | 2.0 | 5.7 |
| | | 1993 | ... | ... | 53.6 | 27.7 | 81.3 | 10.5 | 1.7 | 6.4 |
| | (4) | 1995 | ... | ... | 50.8 | 26.1 | 76.9 | 14.9 | 0.7 | 7.5 |
| | (4) | 1996 | ... | ... | 46.2 | 23.7 | 69.9 | 15.9 | 0.5 | 13.8 |
| Gambia | | 1970 | ... | ... | 43.3 | 26.0 | 69.4 | - | - | 30.6 |
| | | 1975 | ... | ... | 44.0 | 21.3 | 65.4 | - | - | 34.6 |
| | | 1980 | ... | ... | 49.2 | 23.5 | 72.6 | (5) 10.8 | 1.5 | 15.1 |
| | | 1985 | ... | ... | 49.0 | 21.3 | 70.3 | (5) 13.8 | 0.9 | 15.0 |
| | | 1990 | ... | ... | 41.6 | 21.2 | 62.9 | (5) 17.8 | 0.6 | 18.7 |
| | | 1994 | ... | ... | 42.5 | 24.6 | 67.1 | (5) 12.1 | 0.5 | 20.2 |
| | | 1995 | ... | ... | 45.4 | 25.0 | 70.4 | (5) 10.9 | 0.5 | 18.2 |
| | | 1996 | ... | ... | 48.9 | 31.6 | 80.5 | (5) 12.9 | 1.5 | 5.1 |
| Ghana | | 1975 | ... | ... | 24.5 | 37.0 | 61.4 | 16.8 | 0.5 | 21.3 |
| | | 1984 | ... | ... | 24.5 | 29.5 | 53.9 | 12.5 | 0.8 | 32.7 |
| | | 1990 | ... | ... | 29.2 | 34.3 | 63.5 | 11.0 | 1.1 | 24.4 |

Current public expenditure by level of education
Dépenses publiques ordinaires par niveau d'enseignement
Gastos públicos ordinarios por nivel de enseñanza

| Country / Pays / País | Year / Année / Año | Pre-primary / Pré-primaire / Pre-primaria (%) | Primary / Primaire / Primaria (%) | Preprimary + Primary / Préprimaire + Primaire / Preprimaria + Primaria (%) | Secondary / Secondaire / Secundaria (%) | Preprimary + Primary + Secondary / Préprimaire + Primaire + Secondaire / Preprimaria + Primaria + Secundaria (%) | Tertiary / Supérieur / Superior (%) | Other types / Autres types / Otros tipos (%) | Not distributed / Non réparties / Sin distribución (%) |
|---|---|---|---|---|---|---|---|---|---|
| Guinea | 1979 | ... | ... | 24.7 | 28.9 | 53.6 | 31.9 | 0.7 | 13.8 |
| | 1984 | ... | ... | 30.8 | 36.9 | 67.7 | 23.5 | 0.3 | 8.5 |
| (4) | 1991 | ... | ... | 32.5 | 28.3 | 60.8 | 25.0 | - | 14.2 |
| (4) | 1992 | ... | ... | 36.1 | 30.5 | 66.6 | 20.7 | - | 12.7 |
| (4) | 1993 | ... | ... | 35.0 | 29.1 | 64.2 | 23.3 | - | 12.5 |
| (4) | 1995 | ... | ... | 35.1 | 29.6 | 64.7 | 26.1 | - | 9.2 |
| Guinea-Bissau | 1980 | 0.5 | 75.8 | 76.3 | 16.2 | 92.5 | - | - | 7.5 |
| Kenya | 1970 | ... | ... | ... | ... | 80.8 | 13.6 | 0.5 | 5.1 |
| | 1975 | ... | ... | 65.4 | 18.8 | 84.2 | 11.0 | 0.4 | 4.4 |
| | 1981 | 0.0 | 64.4 | 64.4 | 14.9 | 79.3 | 13.8 | 1.9 | 5.0 |
| | 1985 | 0.1 | 59.8 | 59.9 | 17.7 | 77.5 | 12.4 | 1.9 | 8.2 |
| | 1990 | | | 50.3 | 18.8 | 69.0 | 21.6 | 0.6 | 8.8 |
| | 1991 | 0.1 | 55.7 | 55.8 | 18.9 | 74.7 | 17.2 | 0.8 | 7.2 |
| | 1992 | 0.1 | 53.9 | 54.0 | 19.6 | 73.6 | 17.7 | 0.9 | 7.8 |
| | 1993 | 0.1 | 58.9 | 59.0 | 19.6 | 78.6 | 15.8 | 0.7 | 4.9 |
| Lesotho | 1970 | - | 59.3 | 59.3 | 20.7 | 80.0 | 14.7 | - | 5.3 |
| | 1975 | - | 47.7 | 47.7 | 23.1 | 70.8 | 20.6 | - | 8.6 |
| | 1980 | - | 38.6 | 38.6 | 33.4 | 72.0 | 21.7 | - | 4.3 |
| | 1984 | - | 39.1 | 39.1 | 32.7 | 71.8 | 22.3 | 1.9 | 5.9 |
| | 1992 | - | 51.0 | 51.0 | 27.4 | 78.4 | 18.9 | 0.9 | 1.8 |
| | 1993 | - | 48.8 | 48.8 | 27.6 | 76.4 | 18.8 | 1.3 | 3.4 |
| | 1994 | - | 50.8 | 50.8 | 33.1 | 83.9 | 14.8 | 1.2 | - |
| | 1996 | - | 41.2 | 41.2 | 29.2 | 70.4 | 28.7 | 0.9 | - |
| Liberia | 1975 | ... | ... | 27.3 | 28.4 | 55.8 | 20.4 | 1.2 | 22.6 |
| | 1979 | ... | ... | 17.6 | 26.6 | 44.2 | 19.0 | 3.9 | 32.9 |
| Madagascar | 1970 | ... | ... | 48.5 | 19.3 | 67.7 | 25.0 | 1.6 | 5.7 |
| | 1975 | ... | ... | 42.9 | 30.5 | 73.4 | 13.9 | - | 12.7 |
| | 1980 | ... | ... | 41.4 | 25.5 | 66.9 | 27.5 | - | 5.6 |
| | 1985 | ... | ... | 42.3 | 26.5 | 68.8 | 27.2 | - | 3.9 |
| | 1990 | ... | ... | 36.0 | 26.1 | 62.0 | 26.8 | - | 11.1 |
| (4) | 1993 | ... | ... | 27.2 | 34.3 | 61.6 | 24.6 | - | 13.8 |
| | 1997 | ... | ... | 30.0 | 33.4 | 63.4 | 21.1 | - | 15.5 |
| Malawi | 1970 | - | 42.3 | 42.3 | 24.5 | 66.8 | 25.5 | 1.8 | 6.0 |
| | 1975 | - | 44.6 | 44.6 | 23.2 | 67.8 | 22.8 | 1.8 | 7.5 |
| | 1980 | - | 38.9 | 38.9 | 15.7 | 54.6 | 30.2 | - | 15.2 |
| | 1985 | - | 41.3 | 41.3 | 15.2 | 56.5 | 23.3 | 4.4 | 15.8 |
| | 1989 | - | 48.1 | 48.1 | 13.3 | 61.4 | 22.0 | 2.2 | 14.3 |
| | 1990 | - | 44.7 | 44.7 | 13.1 | 57.8 | 20.2 | 2.8 | 19.2 |
| | 1991 | - | 46.1 | 46.1 | 12.6 | 58.7 | 22.3 | 2.0 | 17.1 |
| | 1992 | - | 54.1 | 54.1 | 10.4 | 64.5 | 18.9 | 1.3 | 15.3 |
| | 1993 | - | 51.1 | 51.1 | 11.5 | 62.6 | 21.3 | 2.1 | 13.9 |
| | 1994 | - | 43.3 | 43.3 | 12.2 | 55.5 | 26.9 | 2.4 | 15.2 |
| | 1995 | - | 58.8 | 58.8 | 8.9 | 67.7 | 20.5 | 1.4 | 10.3 |
| Mali | 1975 | 0.1 | 39.7 | 39.8 | 25.5 | 65.3 | 22.9 | 0.9 | 11.0 |
| | 1980 | 0.2 | 38.8 | 39.0 | 25.1 | 64.1 | (6) 24.9 | - | 11.0 |
| | 1986 | ... | ... | 48.4 | 22.6 | 71.0 | 13.4 | 0.5 | 15.1 |
| | 1993 | ... | ... | 47.2 | 25.5 | 72.7 | 23.2 | 0.5 | 3.6 |
| | 1995 | 0.5 | 45.4 | 45.9 | 21.6 | 67.4 | 17.7 | - | 14.8 |
| Mauritania | 1975 | ... | ... | 45.3 | 39.5 | 84.8 | 14.6 | 0.3 | 0.3 |
| (2) | 1980 | ... | ... | 35.4 | 50.3 | 85.7 | 13.5 | - | 0.8 |
| (2) | 1986 | ... | ... | 32.6 | 36.2 | 68.8 | 27.4 | - | 3.8 |
| (2) | 1990 | ... | ... | 33.3 | 37.7 | 71.0 | 24.9 | - | 4.2 |
| (2) | 1991 | ... | ... | 34.2 | 37.0 | 71.1 | 24.2 | - | 4.6 |
| (2) | 1992 | ... | ... | 35.9 | 37.7 | 73.6 | 22.0 | - | 4.4 |
| (2) | 1993 | ... | ... | 36.9 | 39.1 | 76.0 | 19.9 | - | 4.2 |
| (2) | 1994 | ... | ... | 38.5 | 36.8 | 75.3 | 20.8 | - | 3.9 |
| (2) | 1995 | ... | ... | 40.0 | 36.0 | 75.9 | 20.1 | - | 3.9 |
| (2) | 1996 | ... | ... | 39.4 | 35.3 | 74.6 | 21.2 | - | 4.2 |
| Mauritius | 1970 | ... | ... | ... | ... | 89.9 | 6.2 | 0.2 | 3.7 |
| | 1980 | | | 44.1 | 36.5 | 80.6 | 7.7 | 3.5 | 8.1 |
| | 1985 | 0.1 | 45.1 | 45.2 | 37.6 | 82.8 | 5.6 | 3.4 | 8.3 |
| | 1990 | 0.1 | 37.5 | 37.7 | 36.4 | 74.0 | 16.6 | 2.4 | 7.0 |
| | 1994 | 0.4 | 31.6 | 32.0 | 38.3 | 70.3 | 20.9 | <— | 8.8 |
| | 1996 | 1.2 | 29.8 | 31.0 | 36.3 | 67.3 | 24.7 | <— | 8.1 |
| Morocco (2) | 1970 | ... | ... | 44.8 | 44.7 | 89.4 | 10.6 | - | - |
| | 1975 | ... | ... | 44.1 | 43.4 | 87.6 | 12.4 | - | - |
| | 1980 | ... | ... | 35.4 | 46.3 | 81.7 | 18.3 | - | - |
| | 1985 | ... | ... | 35.3 | 47.6 | 82.9 | 17.1 | - | - |
| | 1990 | ... | ... | 34.8 | 48.9 | 83.8 | 16.2 | - | - |
| | 1991 | ... | ... | 35.0 | 48.7 | 83.7 | 16.3 | - | - |
| | 1992 | ... | ... | 33.0 | 50.7 | 83.7 | 16.3 | - | - |
| | 1993 | ... | ... | 35.0 | 48.8 | 83.8 | 16.2 | - | - |

Current public expenditure by level of education II.19
Dépenses publiques ordinaires par niveau d'enseignement
Gastos públicos ordinarios por nivel de enseñanza

| Country / Pays / País | Year / Année / Año | Pre-primary / Pré-primaire / Pre-primaria (%) | Primary / Primaire / Primaria (%) | Preprimary + Primary / Préprimaire + Primaire / Preprimaria + Primaria (%) | Secondary / Secondaire / Secundaria (%) | Preprimary + Primary + Secondary / Préprimaire + Primaire + Secondaire / Preprimaria + Primaria + Secundaria (%) | Tertiary / Supérieur / Superior (%) | Other types / Autres types / Otros tipos (%) | Not distributed / Non réparties / Sin distribución (%) |
|---|---|---|---|---|---|---|---|---|---|
| Morocco (cont) (2) | 1994 | ... | ... | 35.0 | 48.5 | 83.5 | 16.5 | - | - |
| | 1995 | ... | ... | 36.5 | 47.7 | 84.2 | 15.8 | - | - |
| | 1996 | ... | ... | 34.6 | 48.8 | 83.5 | 16.5 | - | - |
| Mozambique | 1990 | - | 49.8 | 49.8 | 15.7 | 65.5 | 9.9 | 4.1 | 20.5 |
| Namibia | 1991 | ... | ... | 42.1 | 29.1 | 71.2 | 8.5 | 6.3 | 14.0 |
| | 1992 | ... | ... | 53.5 | 28.7 | 82.2 | 7.2 | 6.4 | 4.2 |
| | 1993 | ... | ... | 52.8 | 27.7 | 80.4 | 7.3 | 7.5 | 4.8 |
| | 1994 | ... | ... | 49.2 | 28.0 | 77.2 | 9.1 | 9.7 | 4.0 |
| | 1995 | ... | ... | 47.2 | 28.8 | 76.0 | 9.4 | 11.1 | 3.4 |
| | 1997 | ... | ... | 58.0 | 28.9 | 86.9 | 13.1 | - | - |
| Niger | 1970 | ... | ... | 60.5 | 25.2 | 85.8 | 2.6 | 1.8 | 9.8 |
| | 1981 | ... | ... | ... | ... | 83.0 | 17.0 | - | - |
| (1)(4) | 1990 | ... | ... | 60.6 | 33.1 | 93.8 | (1) ... | - | 6.2 |
| (1)(4) | 1992 | ... | ... | 54.1 | 29.6 | 83.7 | (1) ... | - | 16.3 |
| (1)(4) | 1993 | ... | ... | 62.1 | 31.6 | 93.7 | (1) ... | - | 6.3 |
| (1)(4) | 1994 | ... | ... | 60.6 | 33.1 | 93.7 | (1) ... | - | 6.3 |
| (1)(4) | 1995 | ... | ... | 62.0 | 31.6 | 93.7 | (1) ... | - | 6.3 |
| (1)(4) | 1996 | ... | ... | 59.7 | 32.3 | 92.1 | (1) ... | - | 7.9 |
| (1)(4) | 1997 | ... | ... | 59.7 | 32.3 | 92.1 | (1) ... | - | 7.9 |
| Nigeria | 1970 | ... | ... | 40.4 | 23.9 | 64.2 | 20.0 | 2.4 | 13.4 |
| | 1981 | ... | ... | ... | ... | 57.1 | 25.0 | 0.6 | 17.4 |
| Reunion | 1985 | ... | ... | 32.8 | 57.1 | 89.9 | 0.0 | - | 10.1 |
| | 1990 | 14.4 | 25.8 | 40.1 | 53.1 | 93.2 | 3.0 | - | 3.8 |
| | 1991 | 14.5 | 25.2 | 39.7 | 54.7 | 94.4 | 3.5 | - | 2.1 |
| | 1993 | 12.8 | 23.4 | 36.3 | 57.0 | 93.2 | 1.7 | 3.0 | 2.1 |
| Rwanda | 1970 | ... | ... | 66.4 | 19.0 | 85.4 | 9.9 | - | 4.7 |
| | 1975 | ... | ... | 69.0 | 16.6 | 85.6 | 10.8 | - | 3.7 |
| | 1980 | ... | ... | 67.1 | 19.9 | 87.0 | 9.6 | - | 3.3 |
| | 1986 | ... | ... | 67.6 | 15.3 | 82.9 | 11.5 | - | 5.6 |
| | 1989 | ... | ... | 67.7 | 14.1 | 81.8 | 16.2 | - | 2.0 |
| Sao Tome and Principe | 1986 | 5.6 | 50.0 | 55.7 | 27.0 | 82.6 | - | 17.4 | - |
| Senegal | 1976 | ... | ... | 47.8 | 29.1 | 76.9 | 20.7 | - | 2.4 |
| | 1980 | ... | ... | 42.8 | 27.8 | 70.7 | 25.0 | - | 4.3 |
| | 1985 | 0.9 | 49.1 | 50.1 | 25.1 | 75.2 | 19.0 | 0.4 | 5.3 |
| | 1990 | 0.9 | 43.0 | 43.9 | 25.7 | 69.5 | 24.0 | 0.3 | 6.1 |
| | 1996 | ... | ... | 34.2 | 42.5 | 76.8 | 23.2 | - | - |
| Seychelles | 1970 | ... | ... | 44.4 | 50.1 | 94.5 | - | - | 5.5 |
| | 1975 | ... | ... | 53.1 | 45.9 | 99.0 | - | 1.0 | ... |
| | 1985 | ... | ... | 29.5 | 54.3 | 83.8 | - | 1.1 | 15.1 |
| | 1990 | ... | ... | 28.2 | 40.7 | 68.9 | (3) 9.5 | 1.6 | 20.1 |
| | 1992 | ... | ... | ... | ... | 66.2 | (3) 10.7 | 0.8 | 22.2 |
| | 1995 | 9.1 | 28.8 | 37.8 | 30.9 | 68.7 | (3) 13.1 | 0.1 | 18.0 |
| | 1996 | 6.7 | 20.2 | 27.0 | 38.7 | 65.7 | (3) 16.2 | 0.2 | 17.9 |
| Sierra Leone | 1975 | ... | ... | 26.5 | 29.3 | 55.7 | 26.0 | - | 18.3 |
| | 1986 | ... | ... | 33.2 | 29.3 | 62.5 | 24.2 | - | 13.2 |
| | 1989 | ... | ... | 21.2 | 31.6 | 52.8 | 34.8 | - | 12.5 |
| South Africa | 1986 | ... | ... | ... | ... | (7) 73.1 | (8) 24.8 | 2.0 | - |
| | 1990 | ... | ... | ... | ... | (7) 75.6 | (8) 21.5 | 2.9 | - |
| | 1992 | ... | ... | ... | ... | (7) 83.7 | (8) 13.3 | 3.0 | - |
| | 1993 | ... | ... | ... | ... | (7) 81.4 | (8) 15.0 | 3.6 | - |
| | 1995 | ... | ... | ... | ... | (7) 81.8 | (8) 15.4 | 2.7 | - |
| | 1996 | 1.4 | 42.1 | 43.5 | 29.5 | 73.1 | 14.3 | 5.5 | 7.1 |
| Sudan | 1970 | 0.2 | 40.1 | 40.3 | 22.4 | 62.7 | 17.8 | 3.4 | 16.2 |
| | 1980 | ... | ... | 48.0 | 31.0 | 79.0 | 20.7 | 0.3 | - |
| Swaziland | 1975 | ... | ... | 32.2 | 40.6 | 72.9 | 18.7 | - | 8.5 |
| | 1980 | ... | ... | 45.8 | 34.3 | 80.2 | 10.7 | 1.8 | 7.4 |
| | 1985 | 0.0 | 39.4 | 39.4 | 29.6 | 69.0 | 19.5 | <— | 11.5 |
| | 1990 | 0.1 | 31.1 | 31.2 | 24.5 | 55.7 | 26.0 | <— | 18.4 |
| | 1993 | 0.1 | 31.5 | 31.6 | 25.7 | 57.3 | 31.3 | 2.7 | 8.8 |
| | 1994 | 0.1 | 33.4 | 33.5 | 26.5 | 60.0 | 29.6 | 2.4 | 8.0 |
| | 1995 | 0.1 | 36.5 | 36.6 | 26.4 | 63.0 | 27.5 | 1.5 | 8.0 |
| | 1996 | 0.1 | 35.7 | 35.8 | 27.1 | 62.9 | 26.6 | <— | 10.6 |
| Togo | 1980 | 0.7 | 29.5 | 30.2 | 31.0 | 61.2 | 29.8 | 0.2 | 8.7 |
| | 1986 | ... | ... | 34.0 | 29.1 | 63.1 | 22.8 | <— | 14.2 |
| | 1990 | ... | ... | 30.4 | 25.8 | 56.2 | 29.0 | 10.7 | 4.0 |
| | 1992 | ... | ... | 31.8 | 28.1 | 59.9 | 30.6 | 6.0 | 3.5 |
| | 1995 | ... | ... | 36.4 | 27.8 | 64.2 | 32.9 | - | 2.9 |
| | 1996 | ... | ... | 45.9 | 26.9 | 72.7 | 24.7 | - | 2.5 |

Current public expenditure by level of education
Dépenses publiques ordinaires par niveau d'enseignement
Gastos públicos ordinarios por nivel de enseñanza

| Country<br><br>Pays<br><br>País | Year<br><br>Année<br><br>Año | Pre-<br>primary<br><br>Pré-<br>primaire<br><br>Pre-<br>primaria<br>(%) | Primary<br><br>Primaire<br><br>Primaria<br><br>(%) | Preprimary<br>+ Primary<br><br>Préprimaire<br>+ Primaire<br><br>Preprimaria<br>+ Primaria<br>(%) | Secondary<br><br>Secondaire<br><br>Secundaria<br><br>(%) | Preprimary<br>+ Primary<br>+ Secondary<br>Préprimaire<br>+ Primaire<br>+ Secondaire<br>Preprimaria<br>+ Primaria<br>+ Secundaria<br>(%) | Tertiary<br><br>Supérieur<br><br>Superior<br><br>(%) | Other<br>types<br><br>Autres<br>types<br><br>Otros<br>tipos<br>(%) | Not<br>distributed<br><br>Non<br>réparties<br><br>Sin<br>distribución<br>(%) |
|---|---|---|---|---|---|---|---|---|---|
| Tunisia (2) | 1975 | ... | ... | 42.3 | 38.2 | 80.5 | 17.7 | - | 1.9 |
| (2) | 1980 | ... | ... | 41.2 | 36.6 | 77.8 | 20.5 | - | 1.8 |
| (2) | 1985 | ... | ... | 44.0 | 37.0 | 80.9 | 18.2 | - | 0.9 |
| | 1990 | ... | ... | 39.8 | 36.4 | 76.2 | 18.5 | 3.7 | 1.6 |
| (2) | 1991 | ... | ... | ... | ... | 80.6 | 19.4 | - | - |
| (2) | 1992 | ... | ... | 42.7 | 36.2 | 79.0 | 18.8 | - | 2.3 |
| (2) | 1993 | ... | ... | 42.5 | 36.0 | 78.5 | 19.3 | - | 2.2 |
| | 1994 | ... | ... | 42.3 | 36.4 | 78.7 | 19.2 | 0.6 | 1.5 |
| | 1995 | ... | ... | 42.6 | 36.8 | 79.4 | 18.8 | 0.5 | 1.2 |
| | 1996 | ... | ... | 42.5 | 37.2 | 79.7 | 18.5 | 0.7 | 1.1 |
| Uganda | 1970 | ... | ... | 48.8 | 30.7 | 79.5 | 20.5 | - | - |
| (2) | 1975 | ... | ... | 41.1 | 33.4 | 74.5 | 21.9 | - | 3.6 |
| (2) | 1981 | ... | ... | ... | ... | 74.2 | 18.0 | - | 7.8 |
| (2) | 1984 | ... | ... | 44.5 | 33.4 | 77.9 | 13.2 | - | 8.9 |
| United Republic of Tanzania | 1970 | ... | ... | 41.5 | 22.5 | 64.0 | 12.0 | 16.8 | 7.2 |
| | 1981 | ... | ... | 54.4 | 21.1 | 75.5 | 11.1 | 6.8 | 6.6 |
| | 1985 | ... | ... | 57.5 | 20.5 | 78.0 | 12.7 | 3.9 | 5.4 |
| | 1989 | ... | ... | 41.6 | 32.1 | 73.7 | 17.1 | 3.4 | 5.8 |
| Zambia | 1970 | ... | ... | 44.2 | 30.3 | 74.5 | 13.0 | - | 12.5 |
| | 1975 | ... | ... | 45.3 | 25.0 | 70.3 | 16.7 | - | 13.0 |
| | 1980 | 0.0 | 45.3 | 45.3 | 25.5 | 70.8 | 18.0 | 0.2 | 11.0 |
| | 1985 | ... | ... | 43.9 | 26.9 | 70.7 | 18.3 | - | 11.0 |
| | 1991 | ... | ... | 42.9 | 20.2 | 63.0 | 18.4 | 0.6 | 17.9 |
| | 1992 | ... | ... | 36.0 | 20.3 | 56.3 | 23.7 | 0.6 | 19.5 |
| | 1993 | ... | ... | 39.0 | 14.8 | 53.9 | 29.6 | 0.5 | 16.0 |
| | 1994 | ... | ... | 39.6 | 18.5 | 58.1 | 23.3 | 1.1 | 17.5 |
| | 1995 | ... | ... | 41.5 | 18.4 | 59.8 | 23.2 | 0.9 | 16.1 |
| Zimbabwe | 1970 | ... | ... | 47.6 | 34.4 | 82.1 | 6.5 | - | 11.5 |
| | 1975 | ... | ... | 49.4 | 33.7 | 83.1 | 8.4 | - | 8.4 |
| | 1980 | ... | ... | 66.5 | 21.4 | 87.9 | 7.5 | - | 4.6 |
| | 1991 | ... | ... | 54.7 | 27.6 | 82.3 | 13.5 | 0.2 | 4.0 |
| | 1992 | ... | ... | 52.7 | 26.9 | 79.5 | 16.5 | 0.1 | 3.8 |
| | 1993 | ... | ... | 51.6 | 27.7 | 79.2 | 17.5 | 0.1 | 3.2 |
| | 1994 | ... | ... | 51.7 | 26.4 | 78.1 | 17.3 | - | 4.7 |
| **North America** | | | | | | | | | |
| Antigua and Barbuda | 1970 | ... | ... | 63.6 | 27.6 | 91.2 | 2.4 | 1.9 | 4.5 |
| | 1975 | ... | ... | 29.2 | 35.2 | 64.5 | 16.7 | 3.5 | 15.3 |
| | 1980 | 0.2 | 33.2 | 33.3 | 24.1 | 57.5 | 13.8 | - | 28.8 |
| | 1984 | ... | ... | 36.6 | 30.6 | 67.2 | 12.7 | - | 20.1 |
| Barbados | 1970 | ... | ... | 34.7 | 33.9 | 68.7 | 13.0 | 2.6 | 15.7 |
| | 1975 | ... | ... | 27.3 | 29.7 | 57.0 | 18.5 | 1.3 | 23.2 |
| | 1980 | ... | ... | 32.0 | 32.0 | 64.0 | 18.1 | 1.1 | 16.8 |
| | 1984 | ... | ... | 31.0 | 32.5 | 63.5 | 22.3 | 0.9 | 13.3 |
| | 1990 | ... | ... | 37.5 | 37.6 | 75.1 | 19.2 | 0.2 | 5.5 |
| Belize | 1985 | 0.7 | 55.0 | 55.7 | 27.7 | 83.4 | 2.3 | <— | 14.2 |
| | 1990 | 0.6 | 60.3 | 61.0 | 20.2 | 81.1 | 8.1 | <— | 10.7 |
| | 1991 | 0.7 | 61.1 | 61.9 | 22.0 | 83.8 | 8.2 | <— | 7.9 |
| | 1992 | 0.8 | 60.5 | 61.2 | 22.8 | 84.0 | 9.2 | <— | 6.8 |
| | 1993 | 1.0 | 56.5 | 57.5 | 22.9 | 80.5 | 7.5 | <— | 12.0 |
| | 1994 | 1.1 | 58.6 | 59.8 | 25.8 | 85.6 | 7.7 | <— | 6.7 |
| | 1995 | 1.0 | 58.5 | 59.5 | 26.6 | 86.2 | 7.4 | <— | 6.4 |
| | 1996 | 0.8 | 62.1 | 62.8 | 25.8 | 88.6 | 6.9 | 0.9 | 3.6 |
| Bermuda | 1974 | 3.3 | 36.1 | 39.3 | 37.4 | 76.8 | 11.7 | 4.7 | 6.9 |
| | 1984 | 4.4 | 31.1 | 35.4 | 33.8 | 69.2 | 21.4 | 9.4 | - |
| | 1990 | 4.3 | 35.7 | 40.0 | 33.6 | 73.6 | 20.2 | 6.2 | - |
| | 1991 | 4.4 | 32.9 | 37.3 | 26.9 | 64.2 | 18.5 | 6.3 | 11.0 |
| British Virgin Islands | 1970 | ... | ... | 48.0 | 39.0 | 87.0 | (3) 2.8 | 3.1 | 7.0 |
| | 1975 | ... | ... | 43.4 | 40.0 | 83.5 | (3) 6.3 | 0.3 | 9.9 |
| | 1980 | ... | ... | 45.1 | 42.7 | 87.8 | (3) 4.3 | - | 8.0 |
| | 1985 | ... | ... | 38.9 | 35.8 | 74.8 | (3) 9.7 | - | 15.6 |
| | 1990 | ... | ... | 35.5 | 35.3 | 70.8 | 14.8 | - | 14.4 |
| | 1991 | ... | ... | 30.5 | 31.2 | 61.6 | 25.3 | - | 13.1 |
| | 1992 | ... | ... | 27.8 | 31.3 | 59.1 | 24.7 | - | 16.2 |
| Canada @ | 1970 | ... | ... | ... | ... | 65.0 | 27.4 | 7.6 | - |
| | 1975 | ... | ... | ... | ... | 63.2 | 28.9 | 7.9 | - |
| | 1980 | ... | ... | ... | ... | 65.3 | 27.4 | 7.4 | - |
| | 1985 | ... | ... | ... | ... | 63.6 | 28.7 | 7.7 | - |
| | 1990 | ... | ... | ... | ... | 62.2 | 28.6 | 9.2 | - |
| | 1991 | ... | ... | ... | ... | 61.6 | 28.1 | 10.3 | - |
| | 1992 | ... | ... | ... | ... | 60.8 | 27.9 | 11.3 | - |
| (4) | 1993 | ... | ... | ... | ... | 65.4 | 34.6 | - | - |
| (4) | 1994 | ... | ... | ... | ... | 64.7 | 35.3 | - | - |

Current public expenditure by level of education II.19
Dépenses publiques ordinaires par niveau d'enseignement
Gastos públicos ordinarios por nivel de enseñanza

| Country Pays País | Year Année Año | Pre-primary Pré-primaire Pre-primaria (%) | Primary Primaire Primaria (%) | Preprimary + Primary Préprimaire + Primaire Preprimaria + Primaria (%) | Secondary Secondaire Secundaria (%) | Preprimary + Primary + Secondary Préprimaire + Primaire + Secondaire Preprimaria + Primaria + Secundaria (%) | Tertiary Supérieur Superior (%) | Other types Autres types Otros tipos (%) | Not distributed Non réparties Sin distribución (%) |
|---|---|---|---|---|---|---|---|---|---|
| Costa Rica | 1970 | ... | ... | 51.2 | 18.9 | 70.1 | 10.5 | - | 19.4 |
| | 1975 | ... | ... | 37.2 | 22.4 | 59.6 | 24.4 | 1.0 | 15.1 |
| | 1980 | ... | ... | 28.0 | 21.5 | 49.6 | 26.1 | 1.0 | 23.4 |
| | 1985 | ... | ... | 35.1 | 22.3 | 57.4 | 41.4 | 1.2 | - |
| | 1991 | 3.6 | 34.5 | 38.2 | 21.6 | 59.8 | 36.1 | 1.5 | 2.7 |
| | 1992 | 1.8 | 35.6 | 37.5 | 20.1 | 57.6 | 34.3 | 2.3 | 5.8 |
| | 1993 | 3.2 | 36.3 | 39.5 | 21.4 | 60.9 | 33.8 | 2.5 | 2.8 |
| | 1994 | ... | ... | 38.6 | 22.9 | 61.5 | 31.1 | 2.8 | 4.6 |
| | 1995 | ... | ... | 38.3 | 23.3 | 61.6 | 30.9 | 2.7 | 4.8 |
| | 1996 | ... | ... | 40.2 | 24.3 | 64.5 | 28.3 | 2.9 | 4.3 |
| Cuba | 1980 | 5.1 | 24.4 | 29.4 | 40.8 | 70.3 | 6.9 | 5.9 | 16.9 |
| | 1985 | 5.6 | 20.7 | 26.3 | 42.0 | 68.2 | 12.9 | 10.2 | 8.7 |
| | 1990 | 7.4 | 18.2 | 25.7 | 39.0 | 64.7 | 14.4 | 20.9 | - |
| | 1991 | 7.8 | 19.3 | 27.1 | 37.2 | 64.3 | 15.2 | 20.5 | - |
| | 1992 | 8.0 | 20.9 | 28.9 | 35.5 | 64.3 | 16.1 | 19.6 | - |
| | 1993 | 8.3 | 22.2 | 30.5 | 35.1 | 65.6 | 15.8 | 18.6 | - |
| | 1994 | 7.9 | 23.3 | 31.2 | 34.9 | 66.1 | 15.7 | 18.2 | - |
| | 1995 | 7.8 | 24.0 | 31.8 | 33.4 | 65.2 | 15.4 | 19.3 | - |
| | 1996 | 7.6 | 24.3 | 31.9 | 33.0 | 64.8 | 14.9 | 20.3 | - |
| Dominica | 1986 | 0.1 | 62.3 | 62.4 | 26.2 | 88.6 | 2.6 | 2.6 | 6.2 |
| | 1989 | 0.2 | 59.3 | 59.5 | 27.1 | 86.6 | 2.5 | 3.3 | 7.6 |
| Dominican Republic | 1970 | ... | ... | 41.1 | 18.3 | 59.4 | 20.7 | 7.6 | 12.3 |
| | 1976 | ... | ... | 37.5 | 20.4 | 57.9 | 19.6 | 3.8 | 18.6 |
| | 1980 | ... | ... | 36.8 | 22.9 | 59.7 | 23.9 | 10.6 | 5.8 |
| | 1985 | 0.7 | 46.6 | 47.3 | 19.7 | 67.0 | 20.8 | 7.7 | 4.5 |
| | 1992 | 1.2 | 48.2 | 49.4 | 14.8 | 64.2 | 13.7 | 6.0 | 16.0 |
| | 1993 | 0.7 | 46.8 | 47.5 | 15.9 | 63.3 | 13.0 | 6.7 | 16.9 |
| | 1994 | ... | ... | 51.4 | 12.4 | 63.8 | 10.5 | 5.8 | 19.9 |
| | 1995 | ... | ... | 53.5 | 13.3 | 66.8 | 9.0 | 6.1 | 18.0 |
| | 1996 | ... | ... | 49.5 | 12.5 | 62.0 | 13.0 | 4.3 | 20.7 |
| El Salvador | 1970 | ... | ... | 57.9 | 11.8 | 69.7 | 21.4 | 2.5 | 6.4 |
| | 1975 | ... | ... | 57.5 | 6.6 | 64.1 | 23.7 | 1.3 | 10.9 |
| | 1980 | ... | ... | 61.9 | 6.2 | 68.1 | 14.2 | 1.9 | 15.9 |
| | 1995 | 2.5 | 61.0 | 63.5 | 6.5 | 69.9 | 7.2 | 7.6 | 15.3 |
| Grenada | 1970 | ... | ... | | | 91.5 | 8.5 | - | |
| | 1975 | ... | ... | 53.5 | 19.9 | 73.4 | 19.3 | - | 7.3 |
| Guadeloupe | 1990 | 13.0 | 25.6 | 38.6 | 54.4 | 92.9 | 3.2 | - | 3.8 |
| | 1991 | 13.4 | 25.7 | 39.1 | 56.0 | 95.1 | 3.4 | - | 1.6 |
| | 1993 | 12.4 | 25.0 | 37.4 | 56.6 | 94.0 | 1.1 | 3.6 | 1.3 |
| Guatemala | 1970 | 2.8 | 55.2 | 58.0 | 16.9 | 75.0 | 13.1 | 4.5 | 7.4 |
| | 1976 | 2.5 | 51.3 | 53.7 | 15.5 | 69.2 | 19.9 | 3.3 | 7.5 |
| (2) | 1993 | 5.0 | 50.4 | 55.4 | 10.7 | 66.1 | 19.5 | 5.8 | 8.7 |
| (2) | 1994 | 3.6 | 50.9 | 54.5 | 13.2 | 67.7 | 14.8 | 6.0 | 11.5 |
| (2) | 1995 | 3.4 | 55.5 | 58.9 | 11.5 | 70.4 | 15.5 | 4.6 | 9.5 |
| (2) | 1996 | 4.9 | 58.1 | 63.0 | 12.1 | 75.2 | 15.2 | 4.5 | 5.1 |
| Haiti | 1970 | ... | ... | 65.1 | 17.8 | 82.9 | 9.1 | <— | 8.0 |
| | 1975 | ... | ... | 63.0 | 17.5 | 80.5 | 11.4 | <— | 8.1 |
| | 1980 | ... | ... | 59.3 | 20.4 | 79.7 | 9.6 | <— | 10.7 |
| | 1985 | ... | ... | 51.0 | 18.1 | 69.1 | 10.8 | 7.7 | 12.4 |
| | 1990 | 0.2 | 53.0 | 53.1 | 19.0 | 72.1 | 9.1 | 10.1 | 8.7 |
| Honduras | 1970 | ... | ... | 64.2 | 15.4 | 79.6 | 12.2 | 1.7 | 6.5 |
| | 1980 | ... | ... | 61.9 | 17.9 | 79.8 | 19.3 | 0.9 | - |
| | 1985 | ... | ... | 49.1 | 16.7 | 65.7 | 21.3 | 0.7 | 12.3 |
| | 1991 | ... | ... | 49.1 | 17.2 | 66.3 | 18.2 | 0.6 | 14.9 |
| | 1994 | ... | ... | 48.5 | 16.9 | 65.3 | 19.8 | 0.7 | 14.1 |
| | 1995 | ... | ... | 52.5 | 21.5 | 74.0 | 16.6 | 0.8 | 8.7 |
| Jamaica | 1970 | ... | ... | 44.7 | 35.6 | 80.4 | 8.8 | 1.0 | 9.8 |
| | 1975 | 2.2 | 33.5 | 35.7 | 32.3 | 68.0 | 19.8 | 1.9 | 10.3 |
| | 1980 | 1.0 | 33.7 | 34.7 | 36.9 | 71.6 | 19.2 | 4.3 | 5.0 |
| | 1985 | 2.0 | 29.9 | 31.9 | 34.0 | 65.9 | 19.4 | 2.4 | 12.3 |
| | 1990 | 2.7 | 34.7 | 37.4 | 33.2 | 70.6 | 21.1 | 2.0 | 6.3 |
| | 1991 | 2.7 | 33.3 | 36.1 | 32.6 | 68.7 | 23.8 | 1.5 | 6.0 |
| | 1992 | 2.2 | 32.7 | 35.0 | 31.1 | 66.1 | 26.3 | 1.5 | 6.0 |
| | 1993 | 3.1 | 34.8 | 37.9 | 35.5 | 73.4 | 20.3 | 1.5 | 4.7 |
| | 1994 | 3.1 | 24.7 | 27.7 | 37.4 | 65.1 | 25.7 | 1.7 | 7.5 |
| | 1995 | 2.9 | 28.6 | 31.5 | 37.7 | 69.1 | 23.1 | 1.5 | 6.3 |
| | 1996 | 3.2 | 28.1 | 31.3 | 37.4 | 68.7 | 22.4 | 1.7 | 7.2 |
| Martinique | 1990 | 14.3 | 23.9 | 38.2 | 55.6 | 93.8 | 2.8 | - | 3.4 |
| | 1991 | 14.3 | 23.8 | 38.0 | 57.3 | 95.4 | 3.2 | - | 1.4 |
| | 1993 | 13.4 | 23.8 | 37.2 | 55.1 | 92.3 | 1.5 | 4.6 | 1.7 |

Current public expenditure by level of education
Dépenses publiques ordinaires par niveau d'enseignement
Gastos públicos ordinarios por nivel de enseñanza

| Country / Pays / País | | Year / Année / Año | Pre-primary / Pré-primaire / Pre-primaria (%) | Primary / Primaire / Primaria (%) | Preprimary + Primary / Préprimaire + Primaire / Preprimaria + Primaria (%) | Secondary / Secondaire / Secundaria (%) | Preprimary + Primary + Secondary / Préprimaire + Primaire + Secondaire / Preprimaria + Primaria + Secundaria (%) | Tertiary / Supérieur / Superior (%) | Other types / Autres types / Otros tipos (%) | Not distributed / Non réparties / Sin distribución (%) |
|---|---|---|---|---|---|---|---|---|---|---|
| Mexico @ | (2) | 1980 | 1.9 | 31.7 | 33.6 | 24.2 | 57.8 | 12.1 | <— | 30.1 |
| | (2) | 1985 | 4.1 | 27.4 | 31.5 | 26.8 | 58.3 | 17.6 | <— | 24.2 |
| | (2) | 1990 | 5.6 | 26.7 | 32.3 | 29.6 | 61.9 | 16.5 | <— | 21.6 |
| | (2) | 1991 | 5.8 | 33.5 | 39.4 | 27.6 | 67.0 | 16.7 | <— | 16.3 |
| | (2) | 1992 | 6.1 | 28.6 | 34.7 | 26.6 | 61.3 | 14.7 | <— | 23.9 |
| | (2) | 1993 | 6.4 | 30.8 | 37.2 | 25.9 | 63.1 | 13.7 | <— | 23.3 |
| | | 1994 | 8.7 | 39.8 | 48.5 | 32.1 | 80.7 | 19.3 | - | - |
| | | 1995 | 8.9 | 41.4 | 50.3 | 32.5 | 82.8 | 17.2 | - | - |
| Montserrat | | 1990 | 1.9 | 23.8 | 25.7 | 38.3 | 64.0 | - | - | 36.0 |
| | | 1991 | 2.2 | 26.6 | 28.9 | 38.9 | 67.7 | - | - | 32.3 |
| | | 1992 | 2.3 | 27.5 | 29.8 | 38.4 | 68.1 | - | - | 31.9 |
| | | 1993 | 2.3 | 29.1 | 31.4 | 38.8 | 70.2 | - | - | 29.8 |
| Netherlands Antilles | | 1971 | 3.7 | ... | ... | ... | 80.9 | (3) 7.1 | 6.5 | 5.5 |
| | (4) | 1991 | 7.9 | 35.1 | 43.0 | 46.9 | 89.9 | (3) 4.6 | 5.5 | - |
| | (4) | 1992 | 8.7 | 35.9 | 44.6 | 44.7 | 89.3 | (3) 4.8 | 5.9 | - |
| | (4) | 1993 | 8.9 | 36.2 | 45.0 | 44.8 | 89.8 | (3) 4.2 | 6.0 | - |
| Nicaragua | | 1970 | ... | ... | 57.9 | 17.6 | 75.5 | 10.0 | 9.7 | 4.8 |
| | | 1975 | ... | ... | 55.1 | 17.5 | 72.6 | 16.5 | 10.8 | - |
| | | 1980 | 0.4 | 44.7 | 45.1 | 25.1 | 70.2 | 10.5 | 7.7 | 11.5 |
| | | 1985 | 2.4 | 43.3 | 45.6 | 16.7 | 62.3 | 23.2 | 5.0 | 9.5 |
| | (1) | 1992 | 3.9 | 57.6 | 61.4 | 18.2 | 79.6 | (1) ... | 2.6 | 17.8 |
| | (1) | 1994 | 3.8 | 60.2 | 64.0 | 18.1 | 82.1 | (1) ... | 2.3 | 15.6 |
| | (1) | 1995 | 3.0 | 53.0 | 56.0 | 12.3 | 68.4 | (1) ... | 3.3 | 28.3 |
| | (1) | 1996 | 2.2 | 66.4 | 68.6 | 13.9 | 82.5 | (1) ... | 3.1 | 14.4 |
| Panama | | 1970 | ... | ... | 38.9 | 25.1 | 64.0 | 10.8 | 0.9 | 24.3 |
| | | 1975 | ... | ... | 39.1 | 23.5 | 62.6 | 12.6 | <— | 24.8 |
| | | 1980 | ... | ... | 46.3 | 22.0 | 68.2 | 13.4 | 1.9 | 16.4 |
| | | 1985 | ... | ... | 38.3 | 25.2 | 63.5 | 20.4 | 2.9 | 13.3 |
| | | 1990 | ... | ... | 37.0 | 23.3 | 60.3 | 21.3 | 4.6 | 13.9 |
| | | 1991 | ... | ... | 35.9 | 22.4 | 58.3 | 20.2 | 4.8 | 16.7 |
| | | 1992 | ... | ... | 31.5 | 20.4 | 51.9 | 26.1 | 5.8 | 16.2 |
| | | 1994 | ... | ... | 30.3 | 20.7 | 51.0 | 24.8 | 5.8 | 18.4 |
| | | 1995 | ... | ... | 29.8 | 19.7 | 49.5 | 23.5 | <— | 27.0 |
| | | 1996 | ... | ... | 29.8 | 19.2 | 49.0 | 24.5 | <— | 26.5 |
| | | 1997 | ... | ... | 31.1 | 19.8 | 50.9 | 26.1 | <— | 23.1 |
| Puerto Rico | | 1970 | ... | ... | ... | ... | 75.2 | 24.8 | - | - |
| | | 1975 | ... | ... | ... | ... | 68.4 | 31.6 | - | - |
| St. Kitts and Nevis | | 1970 | ... | ... | 65.2 | 31.6 | 96.8 | 3.2 | - | - |
| | | 1975 | ... | ... | 48.0 | 42.5 | 90.5 | 3.1 | 0.1 | 6.3 |
| | | 1980 | 0.4 | 49.6 | 50.0 | 40.6 | 90.6 | 2.9 | 0.2 | 6.3 |
| | | 1985 | 1.2 | 49.1 | 50.3 | 40.1 | 90.4 | 2.1 | 0.4 | 7.1 |
| | | 1992 | 3.7 | 31.0 | 34.7 | 45.4 | 80.1 | 12.2 | 0.1 | 7.6 |
| | | 1995 | 3.9 | 33.7 | 37.6 | 43.0 | 80.5 | 11.6 | 1.0 | 6.8 |
| | | 1996 | 4.9 | 33.2 | 38.1 | 42.5 | 80.6 | 11.4 | 1.0 | 7.0 |
| St. Lucia | | 1975 | ... | ... | 46.6 | 34.9 | 81.5 | 10.0 | 0.1 | 8.4 |
| | | 1980 | ... | ... | 45.6 | 23.7 | 69.2 | 14.7 | 0.7 | 15.3 |
| | | 1990 | 0.3 | 47.9 | 48.2 | 23.3 | 71.6 | 12.8 | 0.6 | 15.0 |
| | | 1991 | 0.4 | 48.1 | 48.5 | 23.0 | 71.4 | 13.2 | 0.8 | 14.6 |
| | | 1992 | 0.2 | 47.6 | 47.9 | 26.1 | 74.0 | 12.1 | 1.2 | 12.8 |
| | | 1994 | 0.2 | 44.7 | 44.9 | 24.4 | 69.3 | 12.5 | 2.8 | 15.5 |
| St. Pierre and Miquelon | | 1970 | ... | ... | 45.4 | 54.1 | 99.5 | - | - | 0.5 |
| | | 1986 | ... | ... | 35.3 | 56.3 | 91.6 | - | 0.6 | 7.8 |
| | | 1990 | 15.6 | 25.9 | 41.6 | 54.5 | 96.0 | - | - | 4.0 |
| | | 1991 | 14.8 | 26.3 | 41.1 | 57.2 | 98.3 | - | - | 1.7 |
| | | 1992 | 13.8 | 24.7 | 38.5 | 59.5 | 98.0 | - | - | 2.0 |
| | | 1993 | 13.4 | 24.8 | 38.2 | 60.2 | 98.4 | - | - | 1.6 |
| St. Vincent and the Grenadines | | 1970 | ... | ... | 75.6 | 20.1 | 95.7 | - | 0.8 | 3.6 |
| | | 1975 | ... | ... | 67.2 | 28.6 | 95.8 | - | 1.4 | 2.7 |
| | | 1986 | 1.2 | 72.1 | 73.3 | 26.6 | 99.9 | - | 0.1 | - |
| | | 1991 | ... | ... | 64.1 | 31.7 | 95.8 | - | 1.8 | 2.4 |
| Trinidad and Tobago | | 1980 | ... | ... | 46.9 | 34.9 | 81.8 | 10.2 | - | 8.0 |
| | | 1985 | ... | ... | 47.5 | 36.8 | 84.4 | 8.9 | - | 6.8 |
| | | 1990 | 0.1 | 42.4 | 42.5 | 36.8 | 79.3 | 11.9 | 0.2 | 8.7 |
| | | 1994 | 0.2 | 40.3 | 40.5 | 33.1 | 73.5 | 13.3 | 0.1 | 13.0 |
| Turks and Caicos Islands | | 1975 | ... | ... | 52.2 | 22.8 | 75.0 | - | - | 25.0 |
| | | 1980 | ... | ... | 58.2 | 40.6 | 98.8 | (3) 1.2 | - | - |
| U. S. Virgin Islands | | 1970 | ... | ... | ... | ... | 75.6 | 24.4 | - | - |
| | | 1975 | ... | ... | ... | ... | 84.6 | 15.4 | - | - |

Current public expenditure by level of education    II.19
Dépenses publiques ordinaires par niveau d'enseignement
Gastos públicos ordinarios por nivel de enseñanza

| Country<br>Pays<br>País | Year<br>Année<br>Año | Pre-<br>primary<br>Pré-<br>primaire<br>Pre-<br>primaria<br>(%) | Primary<br>Primaire<br>Primaria<br>(%) | Preprimary<br>+ Primary<br>Préprimaire<br>+ Primaire<br>Preprimaria<br>+ Primaria<br>(%) | Secondary<br>Secondaire<br>Secundaria<br>(%) | Preprimary<br>+ Primary<br>+ Secondary<br>Préprimaire<br>+ Primaire<br>+ Secondaire<br>Preprimaria<br>+ Primaria<br>+ Secundaria<br>(%) | Tertiary<br>Supérieur<br>Superior<br>(%) | Other<br>types<br>Autres<br>types<br>Otros<br>tipos<br>(%) | Not<br>distributed<br>Non<br>réparties<br>Sin<br>distribución<br>(%) |
|---|---|---|---|---|---|---|---|---|---|
| United States @ | 1985 | ... | ... | 44.7 | 30.3 | 74.9 | 25.1 | - | - |
| | 1990 | ... | ... | 38.9 | 37.0 | 75.9 | 24.1 | - | ... |
| (4) | 1992 | 3.7 | 34.7 | 38.4 | 36.5 | 74.8 | 25.2 | - | - |
| (4) | 1993 | 7.2 | 33.0 | 40.1 | 36.6 | 76.7 | 23.3 | - | - |
| (4) | 1994 | 7.0 | 31.7 | 38.7 | 36.1 | 74.8 | 25.2 | | - |
| **South America** | | | | | | | | | |
| Argentina | 1970 | 1.2 | 29.0 | 30.2 | 30.2 | 60.5 | 21.0 | 2.5 | 16.0 |
| | 1980 | ... | ... | 40.1 | 25.6 | 65.6 | 22.7 | 1.9 | 9.7 |
| | 1984 | ... | ... | 37.7 | 27.4 | 65.1 | 19.2 | 0.7 | 15.0 |
| (4) | 1992 | ... | ... | 50.5 | 26.1 | 76.7 | 17.6 | - | 5.8 |
| (4) | 1993 | ... | ... | ... | ... | 72.2 | 18.1 | | 9.7 |
| (4) | 1994 | ... | ... | ... | ... | 72.3 | 16.5 | - | 11.3 |
| | 1996 | 6.7 | 39.1 | 45.7 | 34.8 | 80.5 | 19.5 | | - |
| Bolivia | 1970 | 2.0 | 60.1 | 62.1 | 12.9 | 75.0 | 10.9 | 2.0 | 12.1 |
| | 1975 | 2.1 | 60.3 | 62.4 | 7.2 | 69.7 | 15.1 | 2.3 | 13.0 |
| | 1980 | ... | ... | 58.9 | 11.4 | 70.3 | 17.1 | 2.9 | 9.7 |
| | 1994 | 2.4 | 39.5 | 41.9 | 11.8 | 53.7 | 29.5 | 2.3 | 14.5 |
| | 1995 | 2.7 | 41.6 | 44.2 | 8.7 | 52.9 | 28.7 | 2.5 | 15.8 |
| | 1996 | 2.8 | 47.9 | 50.7 | 9.8 | 60.5 | 27.7 | 3.6 | 8.2 |
| Brazil | 1976 | ... | ... | 45.4 | 10.9 | 56.3 | 22.8 | 2.1 | 18.8 |
| (4) | 1980 | ... | ... | 44.8 | 7.1 | 51.9 | 18.9 | <— | 29.3 |
| (4) | 1985 | ... | ... | 45.9 | 7.7 | 53.7 | 19.6 | <— | 26.8 |
| (4) | 1989 | ... | ... | 48.8 | 6.9 | 55.7 | 25.6 | 1.3 | 17.5 |
| | 1995 | 5.1 | 48.4 | 53.5 | 20.3 | 73.8 | 26.2 | - | |
| Chile | 1975 | ... | ... | 34.9 | 13.5 | 48.3 | 25.2 | 4.1 | 22.4 |
| | 1980 | 1.9 | 42.7 | 44.7 | 18.0 | 62.6 | 33.2 | 0.4 | 3.8 |
| | 1985 | 6.0 | 51.0 | 57.0 | 19.5 | 76.5 | 20.3 | - | 3.2 |
| | 1991 | 7.2 | 49.2 | 56.4 | 15.3 | 71.7 | 21.6 | 2.1 | 4.6 |
| | 1992 | 6.7 | 49.4 | 56.0 | 14.9 | 70.9 | 20.6 | 2.0 | 6.5 |
| | 1993 | 7.6 | 48.6 | 56.3 | 13.4 | 69.7 | 21.0 | 0.5 | 8.8 |
| | 1994 | 8.1 | 50.3 | 58.4 | 17.2 | 75.7 | 19.7 | 3.1 | 1.5 |
| | 1995 | 8.9 | 53.8 | 62.7 | 16.2 | 78.8 | 18.1 | 2.6 | 0.4 |
| | 1996 | 7.5 | 52.9 | 60.4 | 18.9 | 79.3 | 16.4 | 3.0 | 1.3 |
| | 1997 | 7.3 | 50.9 | 58.3 | 18.8 | 77.1 | 16.1 | 3.3 | 3.5 |
| Colombia (2) | 1980 | ... | ... | 44.2 | 27.0 | 71.3 | 24.4 | 4.4 | - |
| | 1985 | ... | ... | 42.0 | 32.5 | 74.4 | 21.2 | 4.4 | - |
| | 1990 | ... | ... | 39.3 | 30.9 | 70.2 | 20.7 | 2.4 | 6.7 |
| | 1991 | ... | ... | 39.9 | 32.9 | 72.8 | 21.4 | 2.7 | 3.1 |
| | 1992 | ... | ... | 30.7 | 24.7 | 55.3 | 14.5 | 2.1 | 28.1 |
| | 1993 | ... | ... | 36.2 | 30.6 | 66.8 | 18.1 | 1.8 | 13.4 |
| | 1994 | ... | ... | 37.1 | 31.0 | 68.0 | 20.9 | 1.2 | 9.1 |
| | 1995 | ... | ... | 36.2 | 29.6 | 65.9 | 18.5 | 1.3 | 14.3 |
| | 1996 | ... | ... | 40.5 | 31.5 | 72.0 | 19.2 | 1.3 | 7.6 |
| Ecuador | 1970 | ... | ... | 45.9 | 41.0 | 86.9 | 9.9 | 1.1 | 2.0 |
| | 1985 | ... | ... | 45.5 | 35.8 | 81.3 | 17.8 | 0.9 | - |
| | 1990 | ... | ... | 34.4 | 34.2 | 68.5 | 18.3 | 3.0 | 10.2 |
| | 1991 | ... | ... | 31.3 | 30.8 | 62.1 | 28.2 | 0.9 | 8.8 |
| | 1992 | ... | ... | 32.1 | 33.7 | 65.8 | 22.7 | 1.8 | 9.7 |
| | 1993 | ... | ... | 39.4 | 36.1 | 75.5 | 18.0 | 1.1 | 5.5 |
| | 1995 | ... | ... | 36.9 | 36.7 | 73.6 | 23.0 | 0.7 | 2.7 |
| | 1996 | ... | ... | 38.4 | 36.0 | 74.4 | 21.3 | 0.5 | 3.7 |
| Falkland Islands (Malvinas) | 1996 | ... | ... | 27.8 | 32.6 | 60.5 | (3) 18.4 | 12.2 | 8.9 |
| French Guiana | 1990 | 14.7 | 28.8 | 43.5 | 52.2 | 95.7 | 1.2 | - | 3.1 |
| | 1991 | 13.7 | 28.8 | 42.5 | 54.2 | 96.7 | 0.8 | - | 2.5 |
| | 1993 | 13.6 | 29.7 | 43.2 | 51.0 | 94.2 | 0.2 | 3.7 | 1.8 |
| Guyana | 1970 | ... | ... | 46.5 | 34.4 | 81.0 | 14.7 | 0.1 | 4.2 |
| | 1975 | ... | ... | 44.8 | 33.3 | 78.1 | 15.9 | 1.5 | 4.5 |
| | 1979 | 8.5 | 33.1 | 41.6 | 33.1 | 74.7 | 15.2 | 4.2 | 6.0 |
| | 1985 | 7.6 | 31.1 | 38.8 | 23.8 | 62.6 | 17.8 | 0.1 | 19.6 |
| | 1995 | ... | ... | ... | ... | 71.3 | 7.7 | 1.9 | 19.1 |
| Paraguay | 1970 | ... | ... | 64.8 | 17.1 | 81.8 | 16.5 | 1.7 | - |
| | 1985 | ... | ... | 36.6 | 29.7 | 66.3 | 23.8 | 2.8 | 7.1 |
| (2)(4) | 1990 | ... | ... | 43.9 | 22.6 | 66.5 | 25.8 | <— | 7.7 |
| (2)(4) | 1991 | ... | ... | 41.4 | 21.8 | 63.2 | 20.4 | <— | 16.4 |
| (2)(4) | 1992 | ... | ... | 45.6 | 19.4 | 65.0 | 21.4 | <— | 13.6 |
| (2)(4) | 1993 | ... | ... | 48.9 | 19.6 | 68.5 | 19.8 | <— | 11.8 |
| (2)(4) | 1994 | ... | ... | 47.9 | 19.8 | 67.7 | 17.5 | <— | 14.7 |
| (2)(4) | 1996 | ... | ... | 50.0 | 18.1 | 68.1 | 19.7 | <— | 12.2 |

II.19    Current public expenditure by level of education
Dépenses publiques ordinaires par niveau d'enseignement
Gastos públicos ordinarios por nivel de enseñanza

| Country / Pays / País | Year / Année / Año | Pre-primary / Pré-primaire / Pre-primaria (%) | Primary / Primaire / Primaria (%) | Preprimary + Primary / Préprimaire + Primaire / Preprimaria + Primaria (%) | Secondary / Secondaire / Secundaria (%) | Preprimary + Primary + Secondary / Préprimaire + Primaire + Secondaire / Preprimaria + Primaria + Secundaria (%) | Tertiary / Supérieur / Superior (%) | Other types / Autres types / Otros tipos (%) | Not distributed / Non réparties / Sin distribución (%) |
|---|---|---|---|---|---|---|---|---|---|
| Peru | 1970 | 1.1 | 39.8 | 40.9 | 20.8 | 61.8 | (9) 1.9 | 4.8 | (9) 31.6 |
|  | 1975 | 2.0 | 40.7 | 42.7 | 20.8 | 63.5 | (9) 1.8 | 4.4 | (9) 30.3 |
|  | 1980 | 2.8 | 45.1 | 47.9 | 19.9 | 67.8 | (9) 3.1 | 3.8 | (9) 25.2 |
|  | 1985 | 4.0 | 35.6 | 39.5 | 20.5 | 60.1 | (9) 2.7 | 5.0 | (9) 32.2 |
|  | 1996 | 4.9 | 30.3 | 35.2 | 21.2 | 56.4 | 16.0 | 1.2 | 26.3 |
| Suriname | 1980 | ... | ... | 64.0 | 8.4 | 72.4 | 7.4 | 1.1 | 19.1 |
|  | 1986 | ... | ... | 63.7 | 13.5 | 77.2 | 7.7 | 1.3 | 13.9 |
|  | 1990 | ... | ... | 60.5 | 14.5 | 75.0 | 8.8 | 0.5 | 15.6 |
|  | 1991 | ... | ... | 59.0 | 15.2 | 74.2 | 9.1 | 0.5 | 16.2 |
|  | 1992 | ... | ... | 60.0 | 14.7 | 74.7 | 8.1 | 0.5 | 16.7 |
|  | 1993 | ... | ... | 60.4 | 14.8 | 75.2 | 7.6 | 0.4 | 16.7 |
| Uruguay | 1970 | ... | ... | 45.1 | 30.4 | 75.5 | 19.0 | - | 5.5 |
|  | 1980 | ... | ... | 48.4 | 33.2 | 81.6 | 16.1 | 2.3 | - |
|  | 1985 | ... | ... | 37.7 | 28.4 | 66.1 | 22.4 | 2.3 | 9.2 |
|  | 1990 | ... | ... | 37.5 | 30.3 | 67.8 | 22.6 | 2.0 | 7.5 |
|  | 1991 | ... | ... | 36.4 | 29.3 | 65.7 | 24.4 | 2.2 | 7.6 |
|  | 1992 | ... | ... | 35.7 | 29.9 | 65.6 | 24.6 | 2.3 | 7.6 |
|  | 1994 | ... | ... | 35.6 | 31.9 | 67.6 | 24.9 | 2.4 | 5.1 |
|  | 1995 | ... | ... | 29.8 | 26.7 | 56.5 | 27.0 | 1.2 | 15.3 |
|  | 1996 | ... | ... | 32.6 | 29.0 | 61.6 | 19.6 | 1.9 | 16.9 |
| Venezuela | 1970 | ... | ... | 38.3 | 20.6 | 59.0 | 25.5 | 8.5 | 7.0 |
|  | 1975 | ... | ... | 22.1 | 18.4 | 40.5 | 37.0 | 1.4 | 21.0 |
|  | 1980 | 3.6 | ... | ... | ... | 36.1 | 39.2 | 4.6 | 20.2 |
|  | 1994 | 3.7 | ... | ... | ... | 29.5 | 34.7 | 2.8 | 33.0 |
| **Asia** | | | | | | | | | |
| Afghanistan | 1970 | ... | ... | 28.6 | 41.7 | 70.3 | 20.4 | - | 9.3 |
|  | 1980 | 1.6 | 41.9 | 43.5 | 22.3 | 65.8 | 18.4 | 4.8 | 11.0 |
|  | 1990 | ... | ... | ... | ... | 87.6 | 12.4 | - | - |
| Armenia | 1993 | ... | ... | 19.8 | 57.7 | 77.4 | 22.6 | - | - |
|  | 1996 | ... | ... | 15.8 | 63.0 | 78.8 | 13.2 | 8.0 | - |
| Azerbaijan | 1992 | ... | ... | 13.1 | 66.1 | 79.2 | 10.4 | 9.6 | 0.8 |
|  | 1995 | ... | ... | 17.9 | 61.1 | 79.0 | 7.8 | 5.5 | 7.8 |
|  | 1996 | ... | ... | 14.6 | 63.9 | 78.6 | 7.5 | 5.9 | 8.0 |
| Bahrain | 1970 | ... | ... | 48.7 | 40.6 | 89.3 | 4.7 | - | 6.0 |
|  | 1990 | ... | ... | 30.4 | 45.8 | 76.3 | (10) ... | 1.2 | (10) 22.5 |
|  | 1991 | ... | ... | 29.0 | 46.7 | 75.7 | (10) ... | 1.2 | (10) 23.1 |
|  | 1992 | ... | ... | 28.9 | 47.2 | 76.1 | (10) ... | 1.2 | (10) 22.7 |
|  | (4) 1993 | ... | ... | 27.9 | 45.1 | 73.0 | (10) ... | 1.2 | (10) 25.8 |
|  | (4) 1994 | ... | ... | 27.9 | 45.1 | 73.0 | (10) ... | 0.6 | (10) 26.4 |
|  | (4) 1995 | ... | ... | 27.9 | 45.1 | 73.0 | (10) ... | 1.2 | (10) 25.8 |
|  | (4) 1996 | ... | ... | 27.9 | 45.1 | 73.0 | (10) ... | 1.2 | (10) 25.8 |
|  | (4) 1997 | ... | ... | 30.1 | 34.5 | 64.7 | (10) ... | - | (10) 35.3 |
| Bangladesh (2) | 1975 | ... | ... | 57.0 | 16.5 | 73.5 | 17.4 | 9.1 | - |
|  | 1980 | ... | ... | 45.3 | 39.2 | 84.5 | 12.9 | - | 2.5 |
|  | 1985 | ... | ... | 46.1 | 34.7 | 80.8 | 10.4 | - | 8.8 |
|  | 1990 | ... | ... | 45.6 | 42.2 | 87.7 | 8.7 | 1.0 | 2.5 |
|  | 1991 | ... | ... | 48.2 | 39.3 | 87.4 | 8.5 | 1.1 | 3.0 |
|  | 1992 | ... | ... | 44.2 | 43.3 | 87.5 | 7.9 | 4.6 | - |
|  | 1996 | ... | ... | 44.8 | 43.8 | 88.6 | 7.9 | 3.5 | - |
| Bhutan | 1970 | ... | ... | 22.0 | 70.0 | 92.0 | - | 1.7 | 6.3 |
|  | 1974 | ... | ... | 13.6 | 56.2 | 69.8 | (3) 20.5 | - | 9.6 |
|  | 1997 | ... | ... | 44.0 | 35.6 | 79.6 | 20.4 | - | - |
| Brunei Darussalam | 1970 | ... | ... | 44.0 | 42.9 | 86.9 | 9.7 | 3.4 | - |
|  | 1975 | ... | ... | 33.0 | 53.2 | 86.2 | 8.9 | 3.3 | 1.6 |
|  | 1980 | ... | ... | 31.4 | 46.0 | 77.4 | 16.7 | 3.2 | 2.6 |
|  | 1990 | 0.0 | 24.1 | 24.1 | 26.1 | 50.2 | 9.5 | 0.2 | 40.1 |
| Cambodia | 1970 | ... | ... | 56.1 | 26.5 | 82.6 | 12.5 | - | 4.9 |
| China | 1971 | ... | ... | ... | ... | 86.2 | 13.8 | - | - |
|  | 1975 | ... | ... | ... | ... | 85.2 | 14.8 | - | - |
|  | (11) 1980 | 0.5 | 27.1 | 27.6 | 34.3 | 61.9 | 20.0 | 18.1 | - |
|  | (11) 1985 | 0.9 | 28.6 | 29.5 | 33.2 | 62.7 | 21.8 | 15.5 | - |
|  | (11) 1989 | 1.2 | 31.5 | 32.7 | 34.4 | 67.1 | 18.6 | 14.3 | - |
|  | (11) 1992 | 1.3 | 33.3 | 34.5 | 34.7 | 69.2 | 19.1 | 11.7 | - |
|  | 1993 | 1.3 | 34.0 | 35.3 | 38.0 | 73.2 | 17.8 | 9.0 | - |
|  | 1994 | 1.4 | 35.5 | 36.8 | 31.5 | 68.4 | 16.5 | 15.2 | - |
|  | 1996 | 1.3 | 36.1 | 37.4 | 32.2 | 69.6 | 15.6 | 14.8 | - |

Current public expenditure by level of education  II.19
Dépenses publiques ordinaires par niveau d'enseignement
Gastos públicos ordinarios por nivel de enseñanza

| Country / Pays / País | Year / Année / Año | Pre-primary / Pré-primaire / Pre-primaria (%) | Primary / Primaire / Primaria (%) | Preprimary + Primary / Préprimaire + Primaire / Preprimaria + Primaria (%) | Secondary / Secondaire / Secundaria (%) | Preprimary + Primary + Secondary / Préprimaire + Primaire + Secondaire / Preprimaria + Primaria + Secundaria (%) | Tertiary / Supérieur / Superior (%) | Other types / Autres types / Otros tipos (%) | Not distributed / Non réparties / Sin distribución (%) |
|---|---|---|---|---|---|---|---|---|---|
| China, Hong Kong SAR | 1970 | ... | ... | 54.9 | 21.2 | 76.2 | 19.2 | 2.6 | 2.1 |
| | 1975 | ... | ... | 48.7 | 26.3 | 75.0 | 20.6 | 3.5 | 0.9 |
| | 1980 | ... | ... | 33.7 | 35.7 | 69.4 | 24.6 | 6.1 | - |
| | 1984 | 0.1 | 31.4 | 31.5 | 37.9 | 69.4 | 25.1 | 4.6 | 0.9 |
| | 1990 | 0.6 | 25.9 | 26.6 | 38.8 | 65.4 | 30.8 | 3.2 | 0.7 |
| | 1991 | 0.7 | 26.3 | 26.9 | 39.3 | 66.2 | 30.0 | 3.2 | 0.5 |
| | 1995 | 0.5 | 21.4 | 21.9 | 35.0 | 56.9 | 37.1 | 2.9 | 3.2 |
| Cyprus (12) | 1970 | 0.5 | 46.5 | 47.1 | 40.2 | 87.2 | 6.9 | 3.5 | 2.4 |
| | 1975 | 0.5 | 42.7 | 43.2 | 48.8 | 92.0 | 3.4 | 2.7 | 1.9 |
| | 1980 | 2.5 | 35.4 | 37.9 | 50.5 | 88.4 | 4.1 | 4.0 | 3.5 |
| | 1985 | 3.7 | 34.0 | 37.6 | 50.7 | 88.4 | 4.2 | 4.2 | 3.2 |
| | 1990 | 4.3 | 34.2 | 38.5 | 50.3 | 88.8 | 3.8 | 4.2 | 3.2 |
| | 1991 | 4.4 | 34.5 | 38.8 | 49.7 | 88.5 | 3.9 | 4.3 | 3.4 |
| | 1992 | 4.3 | 34.3 | 38.6 | 49.6 | 88.2 | 6.0 | 2.8 | 3.0 |
| | 1993 | 3.9 | 33.3 | 37.2 | 50.4 | 87.6 | 5.3 | 4.0 | 3.1 |
| | 1994 | 4.2 | 33.2 | 37.3 | 50.7 | 88.0 | 5.9 | 3.0 | 3.0 |
| | 1995 | 4.3 | 32.5 | 36.7 | 50.8 | 87.5 | 6.5 | 3.1 | 2.9 |
| Georgia | 1994 | ... | ... | 22.0 | 45.1 | 67.0 | 18.5 | 11.8 | 2.7 |
| India | 1970 | 0.2 | ... | ... | ... | 64.8 | 24.6 | 1.4 | 9.2 |
| | 1975 | ... | ... | 40.0 | 26.6 | 66.6 | 12.1 | 2.0 | 19.3 |
| | 1980 | ... | ... | 38.2 | 25.8 | 64.0 | 15.4 | 4.5 | 16.1 |
| | 1985 | ... | ... | 38.0 | 25.3 | 63.3 | 15.3 | 3.6 | 17.8 |
| | 1990 | ... | ... | 38.9 | 27.0 | 65.9 | 14.9 | 3.1 | 16.1 |
| | 1991 | ... | ... | 38.8 | 27.7 | 66.5 | 14.5 | 2.8 | 16.2 |
| | 1992 | ... | ... | 37.9 | 28.7 | 66.5 | 14.4 | 2.8 | 16.3 |
| | 1993 | ... | ... | 38.3 | 27.4 | 65.7 | 14.6 | 2.5 | 17.2 |
| | 1994 | ... | ... | 38.9 | 26.6 | 65.5 | 14.4 | 2.7 | 17.3 |
| | 1995 | ... | ... | 39.5 | 26.5 | 66.0 | 13.7 | 3.9 | 16.4 |
| Indonesia | 1971 | 2.3 | 45.5 | 47.8 | 33.6 | 81.4 | 7.9 | - | 10.7 |
| (2) | 1993 | ... | ... | ... | ... | 76.6 | 21.9 | 1.5 | - |
| (2) | 1994 | ... | ... | ... | ... | 72.5 | 25.6 | 1.9 | - |
| (2) | 1995 | ... | ... | ... | ... | 72.9 | 25.1 | 1.9 | - |
| (2) | 1996 | ... | ... | ... | ... | 73.5 | 24.4 | 2.1 | - |
| Iran, Islamic Republic of | 1970 | ... | ... | 50.9 | 23.3 | 74.2 | 12.9 | 1.2 | 11.7 |
| | 1974 | 0.6 | 31.3 | 31.9 | 26.8 | 58.7 | 17.7 | 1.4 | 22.3 |
| | 1980 | 2.0 | 41.7 | 43.7 | 38.1 | 81.7 | 7.1 | 3.8 | 7.4 |
| | 1985 | 1.1 | 40.9 | 42.0 | 37.9 | 80.0 | 10.7 | 2.2 | 7.2 |
| | 1990 | ... | ... | 33.2 | 39.2 | 72.4 | 13.6 | 5.8 | 8.2 |
| | 1991 | 0.1 | 34.6 | 34.7 | 40.1 | 74.8 | 15.4 | 1.9 | 7.8 |
| | 1992 | 0.1 | 32.6 | 32.7 | 42.6 | 75.2 | 15.0 | 1.6 | 8.2 |
| | 1993 | 0.0 | 31.8 | 31.8 | 40.9 | 72.7 | 15.6 | <— | 11.8 |
| | 1994 | ... | ... | 27.7 | 36.1 | 63.8 | 22.0 | <— | 14.2 |
| | 1995 | ... | ... | 29.0 | 33.9 | 62.9 | 22.9 | 3.5 | 10.6 |
| Iraq | 1970 | ... | ... | 60.1 | 20.3 | 80.4 | 17.0 | - | 2.7 |
| | 1976 | ... | ... | 45.3 | 16.2 | 61.5 | 18.1 | 1.5 | 18.9 |
| (4) | 1980 | ... | ... | 47.5 | 17.3 | 64.8 | 24.1 | 11.1 | - |
| (4) | 1985 | ... | ... | 46.5 | 19.5 | 66.0 | 25.0 | 9.0 | - |
| | 1991 | 2.5 | 53.2 | 55.8 | 23.6 | 79.4 | 20.6 | - | - |
| Israel @ | 1970 | 6.3 | 32.2 | 38.5 | 26.3 | 64.9 | 26.1 | 2.9 | 6.2 |
| | 1975 | 6.1 | 32.7 | 38.8 | 25.5 | 64.3 | 30.1 | 0.8 | 4.8 |
| | 1980 | 6.6 | 33.7 | 40.4 | 29.2 | 69.6 | 24.8 | 1.5 | 4.1 |
| | 1985 | 8.3 | 34.5 | 42.8 | 30.8 | 73.6 | 18.9 | 2.8 | 4.7 |
| | 1990 | 9.2 | 33.7 | 43.0 | 31.3 | 74.3 | 16.2 | 4.2 | 5.3 |
| | 1991 | 9.2 | 33.6 | 42.8 | 31.4 | 74.2 | 15.8 | 4.6 | 5.3 |
| | 1992 | 9.1 | 33.2 | 42.3 | 30.9 | 73.2 | 16.7 | 4.8 | 5.3 |
| | 1993 | 8.5 | 33.7 | 42.2 | 31.7 | 73.9 | 17.2 | - | 8.9 |
| | 1994 | 8.2 | 34.1 | 42.3 | 31.2 | 73.5 | 18.2 | - | 8.3 |
| Japan @ (4) | 1992 | 2.3 | 38.1 | 40.4 | 43.1 | 83.4 | 10.2 | - | 6.4 |
| | 1993 | 2.2 | 36.0 | 38.2 | 42.2 | 80.3 | 13.5 | - | 6.1 |
| | 1994 | 2.3 | 37.0 | 39.3 | 41.8 | 81.2 | 12.1 | - | 6.8 |
| Jordan | 1970 | ... | ... | ... | ... | 78.2 | 10.8 | 5.7 | 5.3 |
| | 1980 | ... | ... | ... | ... | 72.8 | 24.4 | 0.6 | 2.2 |
| | 1985 | ... | ... | ... | ... | 62.9 | 34.1 | 0.5 | 2.5 |
| | 1990 | ... | ... | ... | ... | 62.4 | 35.1 | 0.4 | 2.0 |
| | 1991 | ... | ... | ... | ... | 61.3 | 36.6 | 0.4 | 1.7 |
| | 1992 | ... | ... | ... | ... | 61.2 | 36.2 | 0.5 | 2.1 |
| | 1993 | ... | ... | ... | ... | 58.0 | 39.6 | 0.5 | 1.9 |
| | 1994 | ... | ... | ... | ... | 62.8 | 34.6 | 0.5 | 2.1 |
| | 1995 | ... | ... | ... | ... | 62.6 | 34.9 | 0.6 | 1.9 |
| | 1996 | ... | ... | ... | ... | 64.5 | 33.0 | 0.7 | 1.8 |
| Kazakstan | 1995 | ... | ... | 14.1 | 60.4 | 74.5 | 12.5 | 10.7 | 2.2 |
| | 1996 | ... | ... | 10.4 | 61.1 | 71.5 | 13.4 | 15.1 | - |
| (4) | 1997 | ... | ... | 7.2 | 63.0 | 70.2 | 13.9 | 10.5 | 5.4 |

II.19  Current public expenditure by level of education
Dépenses publiques ordinaires par niveau d'enseignement
Gastos públicos ordinarios por nivel de enseñanza

| Country / Pays / País | | Year / Année / Año | Pre-primary / Pré-primaire / Pre-primaria (%) | Primary / Primaire / Primaria (%) | Preprimary + Primary / Préprimaire + Primaire / Preprimaria + Primaria (%) | Secondary / Secondaire / Secundaria (%) | Preprimary + Primary + Secondary / Préprimaire + Primaire + Secondaire / Preprimaria + Primaria + Secundaria (%) | Tertiary / Supérieur / Superior (%) | Other types / Autres types / Otros tipos (%) | Not distributed / Non réparties / Sin distribución (%) |
|---|---|---|---|---|---|---|---|---|---|---|
| Korea, Republic of @ | | 1970 | ... | ... | 64.3 | 23.1 | 87.4 | 8.3 | 0.3 | 4.1 |
| | | 1975 | ... | ... | 62.4 | 25.5 | 87.8 | 12.2 | - | - |
| | | 1980 | ... | ... | 49.9 | 33.2 | 83.1 | 8.7 | 0.1 | 8.2 |
| | | 1985 | 0.3 | 46.7 | 47.0 | 36.7 | 83.7 | 10.9 | 0.6 | 4.8 |
| | | 1990 | 0.1 | 44.3 | 44.4 | 34.1 | 78.6 | 7.4 | 1.2 | 12.8 |
| | | 1991 | 0.9 | 43.6 | 44.5 | 38.6 | 83.1 | 7.2 | 1.2 | 8.4 |
| | | 1992 | 1.3 | 42.2 | 43.5 | 39.4 | 82.8 | 6.9 | 1.1 | 9.1 |
| | | 1993 | 1.0 | 40.9 | 41.9 | 39.0 | 80.9 | 7.6 | 1.1 | 10.4 |
| | (4) | 1994 | 1.0 | 44.5 | 45.5 | 34.4 | 79.9 | 7.9 | - | 12.2 |
| | (4) | 1995 | 0.9 | 44.5 | 45.3 | 36.6 | 82.0 | 8.0 | - | 10.0 |
| Kuwait | | 1970 | 6.4 | ... | ... | ... | 74.8 | 9.4 | 6.0 | 9.7 |
| | | 1975 | 5.8 | ... | ... | ... | 72.1 | 17.7 | 3.8 | 6.4 |
| | | 1980 | 6.3 | ... | ... | ... | 77.7 | 16.5 | 4.1 | 1.6 |
| | (4) | 1990 | 10.4 | ... | ... | ... | 67.0 | 16.0 | 3.2 | 13.9 |
| | (4) | 1991 | 6.2 | ... | ... | ... | 44.2 | 38.1 | 1.5 | 16.1 |
| | (4) | 1995 | 8.0 | ... | ... | ... | 56.6 | 34.3 | 1.8 | 7.3 |
| | (4) | 1996 | ... | ... | ... | ... | 68.5 | 31.5 | - | - |
| | (4) | 1997 | ... | ... | ... | ... | 69.8 | 30.2 | - | - |
| Kyrgyzstan | | 1985 | ... | ... | 10.9 | 60.4 | 71.3 | 8.8 | 6.4 | 13.5 |
| | | 1990 | ... | ... | 8.5 | 57.9 | 66.4 | 10.0 | 7.1 | 16.6 |
| | | 1991 | ... | ... | 8.3 | 65.4 | 73.7 | 12.6 | 7.8 | 6.0 |
| | | 1993 | ... | ... | 10.9 | 66.8 | 77.7 | 9.5 | 7.4 | 5.5 |
| | | 1994 | ... | ... | 7.3 | 68.8 | 76.0 | 10.8 | 8.5 | 4.7 |
| | | 1995 | ... | ... | 7.1 | 73.1 | 80.2 | 8.3 | 6.7 | 4.8 |
| | | 1996 | ... | ... | 6.6 | 68.0 | 74.6 | 14.1 | 6.2 | 5.0 |
| Lao People's Democratic Republic | | 1970 | ... | ... | 62.5 | 23.6 | 86.0 | 7.0 | 1.4 | 5.6 |
| | | 1992 | 2.7 | 39.5 | 42.2 | 43.5 | 85.7 | 3.9 | 5.3 | 5.2 |
| | | 1995 | 3.7 | 49.5 | 53.2 | 32.6 | 85.8 | 5.4 | 3.0 | 5.8 |
| | | 1996 | 3.3 | 51.6 | 54.9 | 26.4 | 81.3 | 7.9 | 4.0 | 6.8 |
| | | 1997 | 3.5 | 44.8 | 48.3 | 30.7 | 78.9 | 7.4 | - | 13.7 |
| Lebanon (2)(4) | | 1993 | ... | ... | 50.8 | 16.9 | 67.7 | 23.8 | 8.5 | - |
| | | 1994 | ... | ... | 55.4 | 18.5 | 73.8 | 24.5 | 1.6 | - |
| | | 1995 | ... | ... | ... | ... | 68.7 | 17.3 | 14.0 | - |
| | | 1996 | ... | ... | ... | ... | 68.9 | 16.2 | 14.9 | - |
| Malaysia | | 1971 | ... | ... | 44.9 | 29.7 | 74.5 | 10.3 | 0.4 | 14.8 |
| | | 1980 | ... | ... | 35.0 | 34.0 | 69.1 | 12.4 | 2.0 | 16.5 |
| | | 1985 | ... | ... | 37.8 | 37.1 | 74.8 | 14.6 | 0.5 | 10.1 |
| | | 1990 | ... | ... | 34.3 | 34.4 | 68.8 | 19.9 | 0.2 | 11.1 |
| | | 1991 | ... | ... | 34.0 | 34.9 | 68.8 | 19.9 | 0.4 | 10.9 |
| | | 1992 | 0.1 | 38.5 | 38.6 | 37.4 | 76.0 | 16.1 | 1.1 | 6.8 |
| | | 1993 | 0.2 | 34.3 | 34.5 | 38.7 | 73.2 | 17.3 | 0.8 | 8.7 |
| | | 1994 | 0.3 | 35.1 | 35.4 | 41.2 | 76.6 | 16.8 | 2.1 | 4.5 |
| | | 1995 | 0.3 | 31.7 | 32.0 | 39.7 | 71.7 | 15.4 | 0.5 | 12.3 |
| | | 1996 | 1.1 | 36.2 | 37.3 | 35.5 | 72.8 | 20.2 | - | 7.0 |
| | | 1997 | 1.2 | 31.5 | 32.7 | 30.6 | 63.3 | 25.5 | - | 11.2 |
| Maldives | | 1993 | ... | ... | 66.7 | 31.9 | 98.6 | - | 1.4 | - |
| Mongolia | | 1970 | ... | ... | 11.5 | 60.3 | 71.8 | 13.9 | 11.7 | 2.5 |
| | | 1980 | ... | ... | 10.4 | 52.6 | 62.9 | 16.6 | 20.5 | - |
| | (4) | 1985 | ... | ... | 10.7 | 51.2 | 61.9 | 17.3 | 20.8 | - |
| | (4) | 1990 | ... | ... | 13.9 | 48.8 | 62.8 | 14.5 | 22.8 | - |
| | (4) | 1991 | ... | ... | 16.4 | 45.3 | 61.7 | 17.1 | 21.2 | - |
| | (4) | 1992 | ... | ... | 17.6 | 52.3 | 69.9 | 15.2 | 14.9 | - |
| | (4) | 1993 | ... | ... | 20.5 | 58.1 | 78.6 | 14.9 | 6.5 | - |
| | (4) | 1994 | ... | ... | 19.5 | 54.9 | 74.5 | 16.7 | 8.9 | - |
| | (4) | 1995 | ... | ... | 20.1 | 56.7 | 76.8 | 17.9 | 5.3 | - |
| | (4) | 1996 | ... | ... | 19.9 | 56.0 | 75.9 | 14.3 | 9.8 | - |
| Myanmar (2) | | 1971 | ... | ... | 33.9 | 42.8 | 76.7 | 16.8 | - | 6.5 |
| | | 1975 | ... | ... | ... | ... | 87.7 | 10.7 | - | 1.5 |
| | | 1994 | ... | ... | 47.7 | 40.3 | 88.0 | 11.7 | - | 0.3 |
| Nepal | | 1971 | ... | ... | 23.0 | 23.2 | 46.2 | 31.6 | 5.1 | 17.1 |
| | | 1975 | ... | ... | ... | ... | 48.8 | 40.7 | 1.5 | 9.0 |
| | | 1980 | ... | ... | ... | ... | 58.8 | 35.0 | 2.1 | 4.2 |
| | | 1985 | ... | ... | 35.7 | 19.9 | 55.6 | 33.4 | <— | 11.0 |
| | | 1990 | ... | ... | 48.2 | 15.7 | 64.0 | 23.3 | <— | 12.7 |
| | | 1991 | ... | ... | 48.6 | 14.7 | 63.2 | 27.6 | <— | 9.1 |
| | | 1992 | ... | ... | 44.5 | 17.7 | 62.2 | 28.1 | <— | 9.7 |
| | | 1993 | ... | ... | 49.1 | 15.7 | 64.7 | 21.8 | 6.4 | 7.1 |
| | | 1994 | ... | ... | 49.8 | 14.7 | 64.5 | 22.2 | 5.5 | 7.8 |
| | | 1995 | ... | ... | 49.2 | 16.7 | 65.9 | 17.3 | 5.8 | 11.1 |
| | | 1996 | ... | ... | 49.3 | 20.9 | 70.1 | 17.9 | 6.5 | 5.5 |
| | | 1997 | ... | ... | 45.1 | 19.0 | 64.1 | 19.0 | - | 16.8 |

Current public expenditure by level of education  II.19
Dépenses publiques ordinaires par niveau d'enseignement
Gastos públicos ordinarios por nivel de enseñanza

| Country<br>Pays<br>País | | Year<br>Année<br>Año | Pre-<br>primary<br>Pré-<br>primaire<br>Pre-<br>primaria<br>(%) | Primary<br>Primaire<br>Primaria<br>(%) | Preprimary<br>+ Primary<br>Préprimaire<br>+ Primaire<br>Preprimaria<br>+ Primaria<br>(%) | Secondary<br>Secondaire<br>Secundaria<br>(%) | Preprimary<br>+ Primary<br>+ Secondary<br>Préprimaire<br>+ Primaire<br>+ Secondaire<br>Preprimaria<br>+ Primaria<br>+ Secundaria<br>(%) | Tertiary<br>Supérieur<br>Superior<br>(%) | Other<br>types<br>Autres<br>types<br>Otros<br>tipos<br>(%) | Not<br>distributed<br>Non<br>réparties<br>Sin<br>distribución<br>(%) |
|---|---|---|---|---|---|---|---|---|---|---|
| Oman | | 1974 | ... | ... | ... | ... | 91.9 | 8.1 | - | - |
| | | 1990 | ... | ... | 54.1 | 37.0 | 91.1 | 7.4 | 1.2 | 0.4 |
| | | 1991 | ... | ... | 52.3 | 39.7 | 92.0 | 6.6 | 1.1 | 0.2 |
| | | 1992 | ... | ... | 50.4 | 42.6 | 93.0 | 5.7 | 1.1 | 0.2 |
| | | 1993 | ... | ... | 47.8 | 45.3 | 93.1 | 5.8 | 1.0 | 0.2 |
| | | 1996 | ... | ... | 42.1 | 51.1 | 93.3 | 5.6 | 1.1 | - |
| | | 1997 | ... | ... | 40.9 | 51.3 | 92.3 | 7.0 | - | 0.7 |
| Pakistan | | 1970 | ... | ... | 39.7 | 32.5 | 72.2 | 16.4 | | 11.4 |
| | | 1975 | ... | ... | 41.1 | 30.3 | 71.4 | 17.2 | - | 11.5 |
| | | 1980 | ... | ... | 39.4 | 31.0 | 70.5 | 18.8 | <— | 10.7 |
| | | 1985 | ... | ... | 36.0 | 33.3 | 69.3 | 18.2 | <— | 12.5 |
| | | 1990 | ... | ... | 45.4 | 28.1 | 73.6 | 16.6 | 0.8 | 9.0 |
| | | 1991 | ... | ... | 47.5 | 28.5 | 75.9 | 14.2 | 0.3 | 9.5 |
| | | 1992 | ... | ... | 45.5 | 27.7 | 73.1 | 15.6 | 0.8 | 10.5 |
| | | 1993 | ... | ... | 46.5 | 29.4 | 75.9 | 14.3 | 0.3 | 9.5 |
| | | 1994 | ... | ... | 45.9 | 29.9 | 75.7 | 13.9 | 0.2 | 10.1 |
| | | 1995 | ... | ... | 46.9 | 29.4 | 76.3 | 13.5 | 0.3 | 9.9 |
| | | 1996 | ... | ... | 47.7 | 29.6 | 77.3 | 13.2 | 0.2 | 9.3 |
| | | 1997 | ... | ... | 51.8 | 27.9 | 79.8 | 13.0 | - | 7.2 |
| Philippines | | 1970 | ... | ... | ... | ... | 87.0 | 13.0 | | - |
| | | 1976 | ... | ... | ... | ... | 72.3 | 22.4 | | 5.3 |
| | | 1980 | ... | ... | 61.4 | 15.7 | 77.1 | 22.1 | 0.1 | 0.7 |
| | | 1985 | ... | ... | 63.9 | 10.1 | 74.0 | 22.5 | - | 3.5 |
| | | 1995 | 0.2 | 58.8 | 59.0 | 20.7 | 79.8 | 16.9 | - | 3.3 |
| | | 1996 | 0.2 | 54.6 | 54.7 | 23.5 | 78.3 | 17.8 | - | 3.9 |
| | | 1997 | 0.1 | 55.9 | 56.1 | 23.3 | 79.3 | 18.0 | - | 2.7 |
| Qatar | | 1970 | 0.1 | 40.7 | 40.7 | 23.2 | 63.9 | 7.2 | 4.2 | 24.7 |
| | | 1975 | 0.0 | 32.8 | 32.9 | 32.5 | 65.3 | 9.4 | 3.7 | 21.5 |
| Saudi Arabia | (4) | 1974 | ... | ... | 43.3 | 15.9 | 59.1 | 39.8 | 1.0 | - |
| | | 1980 | ... | ... | ... | ... | 72.1 | 27.9 | - | - |
| | | 1985 | ... | ... | ... | ... | 72.9 | 27.1 | - | - |
| | | 1990 | ... | ... | ... | ... | 78.8 | 21.2 | - | - |
| | | 1991 | ... | ... | ... | ... | 78.8 | 21.2 | - | - |
| | | 1992 | ... | ... | ... | ... | 80.3 | 19.7 | - | - |
| | | 1993 | ... | ... | ... | ... | 80.4 | 19.6 | - | - |
| | | 1994 | ... | ... | ... | ... | 82.0 | 18.0 | - | - |
| | | 1995 | ... | ... | ... | ... | 82.2 | 17.8 | - | - |
| | | 1996 | ... | ... | ... | ... | 82.2 | 17.8 | - | - |
| | | 1997 | ... | ... | ... | ... | 84.4 | 15.6 | - | - |
| Singapore | | 1970 | ... | ... | 44.2 | 33.5 | 77.7 | 14.7 | 1.0 | 6.6 |
| | | 1975 | ... | ... | 38.1 | 34.3 | 72.3 | 17.6 | 6.4 | 3.7 |
| | | 1980 | ... | ... | 35.8 | 41.1 | 76.9 | 17.1 | 3.1 | 3.0 |
| | | 1985 | ... | ... | 30.5 | 36.9 | 67.3 | 27.9 | - | 4.8 |
| | | 1990 | ... | ... | 29.6 | 36.5 | 66.1 | 29.3 | 0.4 | 4.1 |
| | | 1991 | ... | ... | 23.4 | 29.1 | 52.4 | 44.1 | 0.4 | 3.1 |
| | | 1992 | ... | ... | 27.8 | 34.5 | 62.3 | 31.3 | 0.5 | 5.9 |
| | | 1993 | ... | ... | 27.2 | 34.7 | 61.9 | 32.9 | - | 5.2 |
| | | 1994 | ... | ... | 25.9 | 34.8 | 60.7 | 34.7 | - | 4.6 |
| | | 1995 | ... | ... | 25.7 | 34.6 | 60.3 | 34.8 | - | 4.9 |
| Sri Lanka | | 1970 | ... | ... | ... | ... | 85.8 | 7.1 | 2.7 | 4.4 |
| | | 1975 | ... | ... | ... | ... | 84.5 | 6.5 | - | 9.0 |
| | | 1980 | ... | ... | ... | ... | 91.1 | 8.9 | - | - |
| | | 1985 | ... | ... | ... | ... | 90.2 | 9.8 | - | - |
| | | 1990 | ... | ... | ... | ... | 84.3 | 13.4 | - | 2.4 |
| | | 1991 | ... | ... | ... | ... | 85.7 | 12.1 | - | 2.2 |
| | | 1992 | ... | ... | ... | ... | 81.6 | 13.7 | 2.1 | 2.5 |
| | | 1993 | ... | ... | ... | ... | 76.0 | 11.0 | 1.6 | 11.4 |
| | | 1994 | ... | ... | ... | ... | 72.1 | 11.3 | 1.7 | 14.9 |
| | | 1995 | ... | ... | ... | ... | 72.7 | 12.2 | 1.9 | 13.2 |
| | | 1996 | ... | ... | ... | ... | 74.8 | 9.3 | 1.7 | 14.2 |
| Syrian Arab Republic | | 1970 | ... | ... | 43.0 | 28.2 | 71.1 (13) | 22.1 | - | 6.8 |
| | | 1975 | ... | ... | 38.4 | 30.0 | 68.3 (13) | 25.8 | 0.3 | 5.6 |
| | | 1980 | ... | ... | 38.8 | 28.5 | 67.3 (13) | 32.7 | 0.1 | - |
| | | 1985 | ... | ... | 38.4 | 25.3 | 63.8 (13) | 33.6 | 0.2 | 2.4 |
| | (4) | 1990 | ... | ... | 38.5 | 28.2 | 66.8 | 21.3 | 0.1 | 11.8 |
| | (4) | 1991 | ... | ... | 40.5 | 26.7 | 67.2 | 20.0 | 0.1 | 12.7 |
| | | 1996 | ... | ... | 41.9 | 29.8 | 71.7 (13) | 25.9 | - | 2.4 |
| Tajikistan | | 1980 | ... | ... | 8.7 | 52.5 | 61.2 | 9.6 | 14.5 | 14.8 |
| | | 1985 | ... | ... | 9.2 | 55.7 | 64.9 | 7.7 | 13.6 | 13.8 |
| | | 1990 | ... | ... | 6.9 | 57.0 | 63.9 | 9.1 | 12.7 | 14.2 |
| | | 1991 | ... | ... | 8.8 | 61.8 | 70.6 | 11.3 | 15.0 | 3.2 |
| | | 1992 | ... | ... | 9.8 | 60.6 | 70.4 | 12.2 | 14.7 | 2.7 |
| | | 1993 | ... | ... | 12.3 | 72.7 | 85.0 | 9.7 | 3.9 | 1.4 |

II.19 Current public expenditure by level of education
Dépenses publiques ordinaires par niveau d'enseignement
Gastos públicos ordinarios por nivel de enseñanza

| Country<br>Pays<br>País | Year<br>Année<br>Año | Pre-primary<br>Pré-primaire<br>Pre-primaria<br>(%) | Primary<br>Primaire<br>Primaria<br>(%) | Preprimary + Primary<br>Préprimaire + Primaire<br>Preprimaria + Primaria<br>(%) | Secondary<br>Secondaire<br>Secundaria<br>(%) | Preprimary + Primary + Secondary<br>Préprimaire + Primaire + Secondaire<br>Preprimaria + Primaria + Secundaria<br>(%) | Tertiary<br>Supérieur<br>Superior<br>(%) | Other types<br>Autres types<br>Otros tipos<br>(%) | Not distributed<br>Non réparties<br>Sin distribución<br>(%) |
|---|---|---|---|---|---|---|---|---|---|
| Tajikistan (cont) | 1995 | ... | ... | 14.4 | 67.6 | 82.0 | 10.3 | 5.5 | 2.2 |
| | 1996 | ... | ... | 14.9 | 71.2 | 86.1 | 7.1 | 5.2 | 1.6 |
| Thailand | 1970 | 0.5 | 53.5 | 54.0 | 19.5 | 73.5 | 13.8 | 0.8 | 11.9 |
| | 1975 | 0.6 | 62.5 | 63.1 | 16.2 | 79.3 | 11.1 | 2.0 | 7.7 |
| | 1981 | 0.2 | 55.1 | 55.3 | 28.3 | 83.6 | 13.3 | 1.8 | 1.3 |
| | 1985 | ... | ... | 58.4 | 21.1 | 79.5 | 13.2 | 2.2 | 5.1 |
| | 1990 | 0.2 | 56.0 | 56.2 | 21.6 | 77.8 | 14.6 | 2.3 | 5.3 |
| | 1991 | 0.6 | 53.9 | 54.5 | 21.2 | 75.8 | 16.3 | 2.4 | 5.5 |
| | 1993 | 1.7 | 53.0 | 54.7 | 20.7 | 75.4 | 15.4 | 2.3 | 7.0 |
| | 1994 | 1.8 | 51.0 | 52.8 | 21.5 | 74.3 | 16.5 | 2.5 | 6.6 |
| | 1995 | 1.4 | 49.6 | 51.1 | 23.6 | 74.6 | 19.4 | 4.3 | 1.7 |
| | 1996 | 16.4 | 33.9 | 50.4 | 20.0 | 70.3 | 16.4 | - | 13.3 |
| Turkey @ | 1981 | ... | ... | 40.0 | 26.9 | 66.9 | 25.5 | 3.7 | 3.9 |
| | 1985 | ... | ... | 45.9 | 22.4 | 68.3 | 23.9 | 3.3 | 4.5 |
| | 1993 | 1.1 | 53.1 | 54.2 | 25.1 | 79.3 | 20.7 | - | - |
| | 1994 | 0.2 | 45.2 | 45.4 | 23.0 | 68.3 | 31.7 | - | - |
| (4) | 1995 | 0.2 | 43.0 | 43.3 | 22.0 | 65.3 | 34.7 | - | - |
| Uzbekistan | 1993 | ... | ... | 16.8 | 69.9 | 86.8 | 9.7 | 0.6 | 3.0 |
| Viet Nam | 1997 | 5.0 | 38.0 | 43.0 | 26.0 | 69.0 | 22.0 | 5.0 | 4.0 |
| **Europe** | | | | | | | | | |
| Albania | 1994 | 6.7 | 57.2 | 63.9 | 20.6 | 84.5 | 10.3 | 1.9 | 3.3 |
| Austria @ | 1970 | 0.7 | 29.6 | 30.3 | 47.8 | 78.0 | 13.4 | 6.3 | 2.3 |
| | 1975 | 1.2 | 23.0 | 24.2 | 50.8 | 75.0 | 14.7 | 6.1 | 4.1 |
| | 1980 | 6.1 | 17.9 | 24.0 | 53.2 | 77.2 | 14.5 | 4.4 | 3.8 |
| | 1985 | 5.9 | 17.2 | 23.1 | 46.9 | 70.1 | 16.6 | 4.1 | 9.2 |
| | 1990 | 6.0 | 17.7 | 23.7 | 46.6 | 70.3 | 19.1 | 4.3 | 6.2 |
| | 1991 | 6.2 | 17.7 | 23.9 | 46.2 | 70.1 | 19.8 | 4.3 | 5.9 |
| | 1992 | 6.6 | 17.8 | 24.4 | 46.8 | 71.2 | 18.7 | 4.3 | 5.8 |
| | 1993 | 7.0 | 18.6 | 25.5 | 48.7 | 74.2 | 18.6 | - | 7.1 |
| | 1995 | 6.9 | 21.1 | 28.0 | 47.7 | 75.7 | 21.6 | - | 2.6 |
| | 1996 | 7.4 | 20.7 | 28.1 | 49.0 | 77.0 | 21.2 | - | 1.8 |
| Belarus | 1970 | ... | ... | ... | ... | 81.7 | 10.3 | 8.0 | - |
| | 1975 | ... | ... | ... | ... | 77.3 | 13.4 | 9.3 | - |
| | 1980 | ... | ... | ... | ... | 74.3 | 13.9 | 11.8 | - |
| | 1985 | ... | ... | ... | ... | 74.8 | 14.0 | 11.3 | - |
| | 1990 | ... | ... | ... | ... | 73.8 | 14.4 | 11.7 | - |
| | 1991 | ... | ... | ... | ... | 76.8 | 13.1 | 10.0 | - |
| | 1992 | ... | ... | ... | ... | 82.1 | 12.2 | 5.7 | - |
| | 1993 | ... | ... | ... | ... | 84.5 | 10.6 | 4.8 | - |
| | 1994 | ... | ... | ... | ... | 82.5 | 11.1 | 4.9 | 1.5 |
| | 1995 | ... | ... | ... | ... | 87.1 | 11.0 | 0.3 | 1.6 |
| | 1996 | ... | ... | ... | ... | 72.5 | 11.1 | 11.7 | 4.7 |
| Belgium @ | (2) 1970 | ... | ... | 24.7 | 51.7 | 76.4 | 13.3 | 0.8 | 9.5 |
| | (2) 1975 | ... | ... | 25.5 | 47.7 | 73.2 | 15.3 | 4.4 | 7.1 |
| | (2) 1980 | ... | ... | 25.3 | 47.3 | 72.7 | 17.3 | 6.4 | 3.7 |
| | (2) 1985 | ... | ... | 24.7 | 46.4 | 71.0 | 16.7 | 7.3 | 5.0 |
| | (2) 1990 | ... | ... | 23.3 | 42.9 | 66.1 | 16.5 | 9.3 | 8.1 |
| | (2) 1991 | ... | ... | 23.6 | 41.7 | 65.3 | 16.4 | 11.5 | 6.7 |
| | 1993 | 8.1 | 19.8 | 27.9 | 46.0 | 73.9 | 17.2 | - | 8.9 |
| | 1994 | 8.7 | 21.1 | 29.8 | 46.9 | 76.7 | 20.3 | - | 2.9 |
| | (14) 1995 | 9.3 | 20.6 | 29.9 | 46.6 | 76.5 | 20.5 | - | 3.0 |
| | (14) 1996 | 8.6 | 21.3 | 29.9 | 45.5 | 75.4 | 21.5 | - | 3.1 |
| Bulgaria | 1970 | 14.8 | ... | ... | ... | 66.3 | 14.5 | 19.2 | - |
| | 1975 | 18.5 | ... | ... | ... | 63.9 | 12.9 | 23.2 | - |
| | 1980 | 19.7 | ... | ... | ... | 65.0 | 13.6 | 21.4 | - |
| | 1985 | 19.2 | ... | ... | ... | 65.3 | 12.4 | 22.3 | - |
| | 1990 | 20.2 | ... | ... | ... | 70.7 | 13.9 | 15.4 | - |
| | 1991 | 21.1 | ... | ... | ... | 70.0 | 13.8 | 16.2 | - |
| | 1992 | 21.8 | ... | ... | ... | 75.9 | 13.7 | 10.4 | - |
| | 1993 | 21.5 | ... | ... | ... | 74.4 | 15.7 | 9.9 | - |
| | 1994 | 20.3 | ... | ... | ... | 75.3 | 15.5 | 9.2 | - |
| | 1995 | 21.4 | ... | ... | ... | 75.1 | 15.8 | 9.1 | - |
| | 1996 | 21.3 | ... | ... | ... | 73.8 | 18.0 | 8.2 | - |
| Czech Republic @ | 1992 | 9.1 | ... | ... | ... | 79.2 | 13.0 | 7.3 | 0.5 |
| | 1993 | 9.3 | 38.9 | 48.2 | 25.8 | 74.0 | 17.9 | 7.8 | 0.3 |
| | 1994 | 11.8 | 16.9 | 28.7 | 54.1 | 82.8 | 14.2 | - | 3.1 |
| | 1995 | 12.1 | 16.9 | 29.0 | 53.6 | 82.6 | 14.7 | - | 2.6 |
| | 1996 | 11.9 | 19.4 | 31.3 | 50.2 | 81.5 | 15.8 | - | 2.7 |

Current public expenditure by level of education II.19
Dépenses publiques ordinaires par niveau d'enseignement
Gastos públicos ordinarios por nivel de enseñanza

| Country / Pays / País | Year / Année / Año | Pre-primary / Pré-primaire / Pre-primaria (%) | Primary / Primaire / Primaria (%) | Preprimary + Primary / Préprimaire + Primaire / Preprimaria + Primaria (%) | Secondary / Secondaire / Secundaria (%) | Preprimary + Primary + Secondary / Préprimaire + Primaire + Secondaire / Preprimaria + Primaria + Secundaria (%) | Tertiary / Supérieur / Superior (%) | Other types / Autres types / Otros tipos (%) | Not distributed / Non réparties / Sin distribución (%) |
|---|---|---|---|---|---|---|---|---|---|
| Denmark @ | 1970 | ... | ... | ... | ... | 71.1 | 20.8 | 8.1 | - |
| | 1975 | ... | ... | ... | ... | 71.0 | 20.8 | 8.1 | - |
| | 1980 | ... | ... | ... | ... | 72.1 | 17.6 | 6.0 | 4.4 |
| | 1991 | 2.4 | 21.7 | 24.2 | 43.2 | 67.3 | 18.4 | 14.3 | - |
| | 1993 | 10.6 | 19.3 | 29.9 | 41.9 | 71.9 | 25.0 | - | 3.1 |
| | 1994 | 10.2 | 19.1 | 29.3 | 39.2 | 68.6 | 25.1 | - | 6.3 |
| | 1995 | 11.2 | 21.5 | 32.7 | 39.7 | 72.4 | 22.8 | - | 4.8 |
| | 1996 | 11.5 | 22.1 | 33.6 | 39.3 | 72.9 | 22.0 | - | 5.2 |
| Estonia | 1992 | ... | ... | 18.7 | 55.8 | 74.5 | 15.9 | 9.3 | 0.3 |
| | 1993 | ... | ... | 19.4 | 58.1 | 77.5 | 13.3 | 8.7 | 0.5 |
| | 1994 | ... | ... | 19.2 | 57.3 | 76.6 | 14.0 | 8.7 | 0.7 |
| | 1995 | ... | ... | 18.8 | 55.0 | 73.8 | 17.6 | 7.9 | 0.8 |
| | 1996 | ... | ... | 18.5 | 50.7 | 69.2 | 17.9 | 9.5 | 3.4 |
| Federal Republic of Yugoslavia | 1991 | ... | ... | ... | ... | 69.8 | 18.6 | 4.1 | 7.5 |
| | 1992 | ... | ... | 44.3 | 25.6 | 69.9 | 18.8 | 2.2 | 9.1 |
| | 1994 | ... | ... | ... | ... | 65.7 | 22.4 | 3.2 | 8.7 |
| | 1995 | ... | ... | ... | ... | 65.6 | 21.8 | 3.1 | 9.4 |
| | 1996 | ... | ... | ... | ... | 65.5 | 23.6 | 2.6 | 8.4 |
| Finland @ | 1970 | ... | ... | 35.8 | 49.5 | 85.2 | 9.8 | 3.9 | 1.1 |
| | 1975 | ... | ... | 46.1 | 31.3 | 77.4 | 12.8 | 7.6 | 2.3 |
| | 1980 | ... | ... | 31.8 | 40.7 | 72.5 | 18.9 | 8.0 | 0.6 |
| | 1985 | ... | ... | 30.8 | 41.6 | 72.4 | 18.7 | 8.4 | 0.5 |
| | 1990 | ... | ... | 27.9 | 39.4 | 67.3 | 23.9 | 8.2 | 0.6 |
| | 1991 | 2.5 | 25.5 | 27.9 | 37.9 | 65.8 | 26.1 | 7.5 | 0.7 |
| | 1992 | 2.3 | 25.0 | 27.3 | 36.8 | 64.1 | 27.6 | 7.7 | 0.6 |
| | 1993 | 8.6 | 25.2 | 33.8 | 35.4 | 69.2 | 28.7 | - | 2.1 |
| | 1994 | 9.0 | 25.3 | 34.3 | 37.7 | 72.0 | 26.1 | - | 1.9 |
| | 1995 | 8.9 | 24.5 | 33.4 | 36.1 | 69.5 | 28.8 | - | 1.8 |
| | 1996 | 8.5 | 24.5 | 33.0 | 36.2 | 69.2 | 28.9 | - | 1.9 |
| France @ | 1975 | 7.8 | 23.0 | 30.7 | 38.7 | 69.4 | 13.4 | 11.7 | 5.4 |
| | 1980 | 8.4 | 22.0 | 30.4 | 40.3 | 70.7 | 12.5 | 11.0 | 5.8 |
| | 1985 | 10.0 | 19.5 | 29.4 | 40.8 | 70.3 | 12.9 | 11.0 | 5.8 |
| | 1990 | 9.8 | 17.6 | 27.3 | 40.7 | 68.0 | 13.8 | 12.2 | 6.0 |
| | 1991 | 9.5 | 16.9 | 26.4 | 40.4 | 66.8 | 13.8 | 11.8 | 7.6 |
| | 1992 | 9.5 | 16.8 | 26.4 | 40.4 | 66.7 | 14.1 | 11.5 | 7.7 |
| | 1993 | 11.1 | 20.2 | 31.4 | 50.3 | 81.7 | 16.7 | - | 1.6 |
| | 1994 | 11.7 | 20.4 | 32.1 | 50.0 | 82.1 | 16.5 | - | 1.4 |
| | 1995 | 11.9 | 19.8 | 31.8 | 50.0 | 81.8 | 17.0 | - | 1.3 |
| | 1996 | 11.6 | 19.8 | 31.4 | 49.5 | 80.9 | 17.9 | - | 1.2 |
| Germany @ | 1993 | ... | ... | ... | ... | 73.3 | 21.4 | - | 5.3 |
| | 1994 | ... | ... | ... | ... | 73.0 | 21.8 | - | 5.1 |
| | 1995 | ... | ... | ... | ... | 72.0 | 22.6 | - | 5.4 |
| | 1996 | ... | ... | ... | ... | 72.2 | 22.5 | - | 5.2 |
| Gibraltar | 1970 | ... | ... | 40.6 | 49.7 | 90.3 | 3.0 | (3) 0.8 | 5.8 |
| | 1975 | ... | ... | 47.6 | 36.6 | 84.3 | 10.3 | (3) 0.6 | 4.8 |
| | 1980 | ... | ... | 47.6 | 40.8 | 88.3 | 5.6 | (3) 0.5 | 5.6 |
| | 1984 | ... | ... | 52.9 | 37.8 | 90.7 | 6.9 | (3) 2.4 | - |
| Greece @ | 1970 | 2.2 | 48.8 | 51.0 | 28.3 | 79.3 | 15.5 | 1.4 | 3.7 |
| | 1975 | 3.2 | 36.7 | 40.0 | 28.6 | 68.5 | 20.0 | 0.3 | 11.2 |
| | 1979 | 4.8 | 36.9 | 41.7 | 36.8 | 78.4 | 21.0 | 0.6 | - |
| | 1985 | 6.1 | 31.6 | 37.6 | 41.3 | 78.9 | 20.1 | 0.9 | 0.0 |
| | 1990 | 5.9 | 28.2 | 34.1 | 45.1 | 79.1 | 19.5 | 1.4 | ... |
| | 1991 | 5.7 | 28.1 | 33.7 | 45.3 | 79.1 | 19.6 | 1.3 | ... |
| (4) | 1993 | ... | ... | 34.4 | 39.5 | 73.9 | 26.1 | - | ... |
| (4) | 1994 | ... | ... | 32.1 | 39.7 | 71.8 | 28.2 | - | ... |
| (4) | 1995 | ... | ... | 35.9 | 40.9 | 76.8 | 22.6 | - | 0.6 |
| (4) | 1996 | ... | ... | 35.3 | 38.0 | 73.3 | 25.0 | - | 1.7 |
| Hungary @ | 1970 | 9.1 | 38.7 | 47.8 | 26.8 | 74.7 | 22.3 | 2.6 | 0.4 |
| | 1975 | 11.6 | 38.0 | 49.6 | 25.0 | 74.6 | 21.4 | 3.8 | 0.2 |
| | 1981 | 14.1 | 38.3 | 52.4 | 21.6 | 74.0 | 19.3 | 6.4 | 0.3 |
| | 1985 | 14.2 | 36.9 | 51.1 | 19.9 | 71.0 | 16.9 | 10.8 | 1.3 |
| | 1990 | 13.6 | 41.8 | 55.4 | 23.9 | 79.3 | 15.2 | 3.7 | 1.8 |
| | 1991 | 13.9 | 41.5 | 55.4 | 24.6 | 80.0 | 14.9 | 3.7 | 1.4 |
| | 1992 | 13.5 | 40.5 | 53.9 | 24.9 | 78.8 | 16.9 | 4.3 | - |
| | 1993 | 13.9 | 40.2 | 54.1 | 24.2 | 78.3 | 16.8 | 4.9 | - |
| | 1994 | 14.3 | 39.8 | 54.1 | 23.0 | 77.1 | 17.8 | 5.2 | - |
| | 1995 | 14.5 | 20.9 | 35.4 | 45.1 | 80.5 | 18.3 | - | 1.2 |
| | 1996 | 15.3 | 21.5 | 36.8 | 46.3 | 83.1 | 15.5 | - | 1.3 |
| Iceland @ | 1971 | ... | ... | ... | ... | 88.3 | 7.2 | 1.2 | 3.3 |
| | 1990 | ... | ... | 59.5 | 25.6 | 85.1 | 14.9 | - | ... |
| | 1993 | 4.6 | 27.4 | 31.9 | 39.6 | 71.5 | 24.6 | - | 3.9 |
| | 1994 | 4.8 | 28.8 | 33.6 | 40.7 | 74.3 | 21.9 | - | 3.8 |
| | 1995 | ... | ... | ... | ... | 75.5 | 20.8 | - | 3.7 |
| | 1996 | 5.1 | 30.8 | 35.9 | 41.9 | 77.8 | 17.7 | - | 4.5 |

II.19  Current public expenditure by level of education
Dépenses publiques ordinaires par niveau d'enseignement
Gastos públicos ordinarios por nivel de enseñanza

| Country<br><br>Pays<br><br>País | Year<br><br>Année<br><br>Año | Pre-<br>primary<br><br>Pré-<br>primaire<br><br>Pre-<br>primaria<br>(%) | Primary<br><br>Primaire<br><br>Primaria<br><br>(%) | Preprimary<br>+ Primary<br><br>Préprimaire<br>+ Primaire<br><br>Preprimaria<br>+ Primaria<br>(%) | Secondary<br><br>Secondaire<br><br>Secundaria<br><br>(%) | Preprimary<br>+ Primary<br>+ Secondary<br>Préprimaire<br>+ Primaire<br>+ Secondaire<br>Preprimaria<br>+ Primaria<br>+ Secundaria<br>(%) | Tertiary<br><br>Supérieur<br><br>Superior<br><br>(%) | Other<br>types<br><br>Autres<br>types<br><br>Otros<br>tipos<br>(%) | Not<br>distributed<br><br>Non<br>réparties<br><br>Sin<br>distribución<br>(%) |
|---|---|---|---|---|---|---|---|---|---|
| Ireland @ | 1970 | ... | ... | 42.8 | 40.9 | 83.7 | 13.9 | - | 2.4 |
| | 1975 | ... | ... | 35.9 | 37.0 | 72.8 | 17.7 | 2.2 | 7.3 |
| | 1980 | 8.7 | 26.1 | 34.8 | 39.2 | 74.0 | 17.6 | 6.1 | 2.3 |
| | 1985 | 10.2 | 29.1 | 39.4 | 39.7 | 79.1 | 17.7 | 0.2 | 3.0 |
| | 1990 | 8.7 | 29.0 | 37.8 | 40.1 | 77.9 | 20.4 | <— | 1.7 |
| | 1991 | 8.7 | 28.8 | 37.5 | 40.1 | 77.6 | 20.6 | <— | 1.8 |
| | 1992 | 8.6 | 28.5 | 37.2 | 39.4 | 76.6 | 20.9 | <— | 2.5 |
| | 1993 | 8.3 | 27.3 | 35.6 | 40.5 | 76.1 | 21.5 | - | 2.4 |
| | 1994 | 8.0 | 26.5 | 34.5 | 41.0 | 75.5 | 22.2 | - | 2.3 |
| | 1995 | 7.6 | 25.6 | 33.2 | 41.8 | 75.0 | 22.6 | - | 2.5 |
| | 1996 | 7.7 | 24.5 | 32.2 | 41.5 | 73.7 | 23.8 | - | 2.5 |
| Italy @ | 1970 | 2.7 | 28.4 | 31.1 | 38.1 | 69.2 | 8.8 | 4.6 | 17.4 |
| | 1975 | 4.8 | 30.0 | 34.8 | 42.4 | 77.2 | 13.3 | 3.0 | 6.4 |
| | 1979 | 6.0 | 29.2 | 35.1 | 41.0 | 76.1 | 9.1 | - | 14.8 |
| | 1985 | 7.0 | 23.0 | 30.1 | 35.5 | 65.6 | 10.2 | - | 24.2 |
| | 1993 | 7.7 | 22.0 | 29.7 | 50.0 | 79.7 | 14.5 | - | 5.8 |
| | 1994 | 7.6 | 22.8 | 30.4 | 48.5 | 78.9 | 15.7 | - | 5.4 |
| | 1995 | 7.7 | 23.4 | 31.0 | 47.5 | 78.5 | 15.0 | - | 6.5 |
| | 1996 | 8.4 | 23.6 | 32.0 | 49.2 | 81.2 | 15.1 | - | 3.7 |
| Latvia | 1980 | ... | ... | 14.4 | 56.8 | 71.2 | 11.2 | - | 17.6 |
| | 1985 | ... | ... | 15.8 | 56.2 | 71.9 | 10.3 | - | 17.8 |
| | 1990 | ... | ... | 11.2 | 56.3 | 67.4 | 11.6 | - | 20.9 |
| | 1991 | ... | ... | 12.0 | 58.7 | 70.7 | 14.0 | - | 15.3 |
| | 1992 | ... | ... | 13.4 | 65.9 | 79.3 | 14.3 | - | 6.4 |
| (4) 1993 | | ... | ... | 8.7 | 74.2 | 82.8 | 14.1 | 0.1 | 2.9 |
| (4) 1994 | | ... | ... | 8.2 | 73.1 | 81.3 | 13.3 | - | 5.4 |
| (4) 1995 | | ... | ... | 8.3 | 72.7 | 80.9 | 12.2 | 0.9 | 6.0 |
| | 1996 | ... | ... | 12.1 | 58.9 | 71.0 | 12.2 | 3.2 | 13.6 |
| Lithuania | 1992 | ... | ... | 17.8 | 51.5 | 69.3 | 21.0 | 3.9 | 5.9 |
| | 1993 | ... | ... | 16.0 | 49.5 | 65.5 | 19.1 | 4.6 | 10.8 |
| | 1994 | ... | ... | 14.1 | 51.5 | 65.6 | 19.0 | 5.2 | 10.2 |
| | 1995 | ... | ... | 14.0 | 52.2 | 66.2 | 18.0 | 5.5 | 10.3 |
| | 1996 | ... | ... | 15.1 | 50.9 | 66.0 | 18.3 | 5.3 | 10.4 |
| Luxembourg @ | 1970 | ... | ... | 45.3 | 37.3 | 82.6 | 1.8 | 3.7 | 12.0 |
| | 1975 | ... | ... | 41.9 | 40.1 | 82.0 | 2.3 | 4.2 | 11.5 |
| | 1980 | ... | ... | 49.3 | 29.1 | 78.4 | 1.5 | 19.1 | 1.0 |
| | 1986 | 9.2 | 34.3 | 43.5 | 42.7 | 86.2 | 3.3 | 8.8 | 1.7 |
| | 1989 | 10.2 | 34.2 | 44.4 | 41.9 | 86.3 | 3.3 | 7.7 | 2.6 |
| | 1995 | ... | ... | 51.9 | 43.3 | 95.2 | 4.8 | - | - |
| | 1996 | ... | ... | 51.9 | 43.4 | 95.3 | 4.7 | - | - |
| Malta | 1970 | ... | ... | 41.8 | 29.2 | 71.0 | 12.9 | 0.2 | 15.9 |
| | 1975 | ... | ... | 25.4 | 49.1 | 74.5 | 13.5 | 1.6 | 10.5 |
| | 1980 | ... | ... | 31.4 | 44.3 | 75.7 | 9.3 | 1.5 | 13.5 |
| | 1985 | 3.2 | 27.8 | 31.0 | 43.3 | 74.4 | 8.2 | 2.3 | 15.2 |
| | 1990 | ... | ... | 25.1 | 44.7 | 69.8 | 14.6 | 2.2 | 13.4 |
| | 1991 | ... | ... | 23.0 | 40.1 | 63.1 | 19.0 | 1.7 | 16.2 |
| | 1992 | ... | ... | 22.5 | 40.4 | 62.9 | 17.9 | 2.1 | 17.1 |
| | 1994 | 4.5 | 18.0 | 22.6 | 32.0 | 54.5 | 10.9 | - | 34.6 |
| Moldova | 1996 | ... | ... | 24.5 | 52.9 | 77.5 | 13.3 | 3.0 | 6.2 |
| Monaco | 1989 | 3.4 | 14.8 | 18.1 | 52.1 | 70.2 | - | 0.6 | 29.2 |
| | 1995 | 3.7 | 13.6 | 17.4 | 45.6 | 63.0 | - | 22.1 | 14.9 |
| | 1996 | 3.7 | 13.5 | 17.2 | 44.9 | 62.1 | - | 22.0 | 15.9 |
| | 1997 | 4.2 | 16.0 | 20.3 | 52.9 | 73.2 | (3) 2.7 | - | 24.2 |
| Netherlands @ | 1970 | 4.8 | 20.8 | 25.5 | 38.6 | 64.1 | 22.1 | 3.9 | 9.8 |
| | 1975 | 5.7 | 20.3 | 26.0 | 36.2 | 62.2 | 28.3 | 5.0 | 4.5 |
| | 1980 | 5.5 | 19.2 | 24.7 | 33.8 | 58.5 | 27.5 | 8.7 | 5.3 |
| | 1985 | ... | ... | 22.6 | 35.9 | 58.5 | 26.4 | 8.7 | 6.4 |
| | 1990 | 5.2 | 16.3 | 21.5 | 37.7 | 59.2 | 32.1 | 5.6 | 3.0 |
| | 1991 | 5.7 | 16.9 | 22.6 | 37.0 | 59.6 | 31.9 | 5.5 | 3.0 |
| | 1993 | 6.8 | 22.7 | 29.5 | 39.4 | 68.9 | 31.1 | - | - |
| | 1994 | 6.9 | 22.8 | 29.7 | 39.6 | 69.2 | 30.8 | - | - |
| | 1995 | 7.1 | 23.2 | 30.4 | 39.7 | 70.1 | 29.9 | - | - |
| | 1996 | 7.3 | 23.6 | 30.9 | 39.8 | 70.7 | 29.3 | - | - |
| Norway @ | 1970 | ... | ... | 47.5 | 23.4 | 71.0 | 12.2 | 6.1 | 10.7 |
| | 1975 | ... | ... | 48.8 | 24.7 | 73.5 | 13.3 | 10.9 | 2.3 |
| | 1980 | ... | ... | 47.9 | 24.3 | 72.2 | 13.6 | 8.1 | 6.0 |
| | 1985 | ... | ... | 45.2 | 28.3 | 73.5 | 13.5 | 7.6 | 5.4 |
| | 1990 | ... | ... | 39.5 | 24.7 | 64.1 | 15.2 | 8.6 | 12.0 |
| | 1991 | ... | ... | 38.3 | 26.9 | 65.2 | 16.5 | 9.1 | 9.2 |
| | 1992 | ... | ... | 36.5 | 26.1 | 62.6 | 16.9 | 10.3 | 10.3 |
| | 1993 | ... | ... | ... | ... | 65.0 | 25.9 | - | 9.1 |
| | 1994 | 11.1 | 31.2 | 42.3 | 23.0 | 65.3 | 26.0 | - | 8.8 |
| | 1995 | 7.6 | 31.3 | 38.9 | 22.8 | 61.7 | 27.1 | - | 11.2 |
| | 1996 | 8.2 | 30.5 | 38.7 | 23.0 | 61.7 | 27.9 | - | 10.4 |

Current public expenditure by level of education    II.19
Dépenses publiques ordinaires par niveau d'enseignement
Gastos públicos ordinarios por nivel de enseñanza

| Country / Pays / País | Year / Année / Año | Pre-primary / Pré-primaire / Pre-primaria (%) | Primary / Primaire / Primaria (%) | Preprimary + Primary / Préprimaire + Primaire / Preprimaria + Primaria (%) | Secondary / Secondaire / Secundaria (%) | Preprimary + Primary + Secondary / Préprimaire + Primaire + Secondaire / Preprimaria + Primaria + Secundaria (%) | Tertiary / Supérieur / Superior (%) | Other types / Autres types / Otros tipos (%) | Not distributed / Non réparties / Sin distribución (%) |
|---|---|---|---|---|---|---|---|---|---|
| Poland @ | 1970 | 6.6 | 34.1 | 40.7 | 25.8 | 66.5 | 18.0 | 14.6 | 0.9 |
| | 1975 | 7.0 | 27.6 | 34.6 | 23.4 | 57.9 | 25.4 | 15.8 | 0.9 |
| | 1980 | 8.2 | 28.7 | 36.9 | 21.0 | 57.9 | 23.6 | 17.8 | 0.7 |
| | 1985 | 10.5 | 33.7 | 44.2 | 17.9 | 62.1 | 18.2 | 19.7 | - |
| | 1990 | 9.9 | 32.9 | 42.8 | 17.5 | 60.2 | 22.0 | 17.8 | - |
| | 1991 | 12.9 | 36.5 | 49.4 | 18.5 | 67.9 | 16.5 | 15.5 | - |
| | 1992 | 11.0 | 37.9 | 48.9 | 19.5 | 68.4 | 16.9 | 14.7 | - |
| | 1993 | 10.7 | 39.0 | 49.7 | 20.5 | 70.2 | 16.0 | 13.9 | - |
| (4) | 1995 | 9.4 | 42.8 | 52.2 | 20.2 | 72.3 | 14.6 | - | 13.1 |
| (4) | 1996 | 6.5 | 31.2 | 37.6 | 15.1 | 52.7 | 11.1 | - | 36.1 |
| Portugal @ | 1975 | 0.1 | 55.1 | 55.2 | 23.8 | 79.0 | 10.6 | 0.5 | 9.9 |
| | 1980 | ... | ... | 52.8 | 25.4 | 78.2 | 10.5 | 6.0 | 5.3 |
| | 1985 | 1.2 | 49.8 | 51.0 | 30.6 | 81.6 | 12.7 | 1.6 | 4.1 |
| (2) | 1990 | 2.3 | 42.3 | 44.6 | 32.5 | 77.1 | 16.3 | 3.1 | 3.5 |
| (2) | 1991 | 2.4 | 40.5 | 42.9 | 35.1 | 78.0 | 15.0 | 3.0 | 4.0 |
| | 1992 | 2.1 | 37.4 | 39.6 | 37.5 | 77.1 | 15.5 | 3.5 | 3.9 |
| | 1993 | 2.5 | 37.6 | 40.0 | 35.4 | 75.5 | 14.2 | - | 10.3 |
| | 1994 | 2.6 | 34.5 | 37.1 | 38.8 | 75.9 | 14.9 | - | 9.3 |
| | 1995 | 2.7 | 35.2 | 37.9 | 42.7 | 80.6 | 16.4 | - | 2.9 |
| | 1996 | 2.6 | 31.6 | 34.2 | 41.6 | 75.8 | 16.4 | - | 7.8 |
| Romania | 1970 | 6.3 | 72.4 | ... | ... | 78.8 | 14.6 | 6.7 | - |
| | 1974 | 10.0 | 70.4 | ... | ... | 80.4 | 13.4 | 6.3 | - |
| | 1990 | 7.1 | 45.0 | 52.1 | 22.1 | 74.1 | 9.6 | 8.4 | 7.8 |
| (4) | 1992 | 8.4 | 36.3 | 44.7 | 24.4 | 69.1 | 15.2 | 10.8 | 5.0 |
| (4) | 1993 | 8.4 | 36.5 | 44.9 | 23.8 | 68.7 | 15.9 | 8.9 | 6.5 |
| (4) | 1996 | 8.1 | 34.6 | 42.7 | 23.8 | 66.5 | 16.0 | 8.3 | 9.1 |
| Russian Federation @(4) | 1995 | ... | ... | 23.2 | 57.4 | 80.7 | 19.3 | - | |
| San Marino | 1970 | ... | ... | 50.0 | 40.5 | 90.5 | (3) 9.5 | - | - |
| | 1975 | ... | ... | 52.0 | 33.3 | 85.3 | (3) 8.2 | - | 6.5 |
| | 1980 | ... | ... | ... | ... | 96.6 | (3) 2.7 | 0.7 | - |
| | 1990 | 19.5 | 32.2 | 51.7 | 32.1 | 83.8 | (3) 6.7 | 2.4 | 7.2 |
| | 1991 | 17.0 | 30.2 | 47.2 | 28.4 | 75.6 | (3) 17.2 | 2.6 | 4.6 |
| | 1992 | 18.6 | 32.0 | 50.7 | 30.9 | 81.5 | (3) 11.2 | 2.1 | 5.1 |
| | 1993 | 16.5 | 31.1 | 47.6 | 29.9 | 77.5 | (3) 16.3 | 2.2 | 4.0 |
| | 1994 | 17.1 | 31.6 | 48.7 | 31.7 | 80.3 | (3) 15.3 | 2.5 | 1.9 |
| | 1995 | 17.3 | 30.9 | 48.2 | 32.1 | 80.3 | (3) 14.0 | 3.0 | 2.7 |
| | 1996 | 17.6 | 30.9 | 48.6 | 32.5 | 81.1 | (3) 13.6 | 2.6 | 2.7 |
| Slovakia | 1992 | 10.1 | 28.5 | 38.6 | 18.5 | 57.1 | 15.0 | 2.7 | 25.2 |
| | 1993 | 10.0 | 28.7 | 38.7 | 19.6 | 58.4 | 14.4 | 2.8 | 24.4 |
| | 1994 | 9.8 | 29.5 | 39.3 | 19.0 | 58.3 | 14.3 | 2.7 | 24.7 |
| | 1995 | 11.3 | 35.7 | 46.9 | 12.8 | 59.8 | 16.7 | 3.5 | 20.0 |
| | 1996 | 9.9 | 30.6 | 40.5 | 28.0 | 68.6 | 12.7 | 4.3 | 14.5 |
| Slovenia | 1991 | 21.0 | 22.3 | 43.3 | 37.0 | 80.4 | 17.0 | 2.5 | 0.2 |
| | 1992 | 11.5 | 22.1 | 33.7 | 44.1 | 77.7 | 19.3 | 2.0 | 1.0 |
| | 1993 | 11.4 | 21.1 | 32.5 | 46.7 | 79.2 | 16.9 | 2.7 | 1.2 |
| | 1994 | 11.4 | 19.5 | 30.9 | 45.7 | 76.5 | 18.9 | 3.5 | 1.1 |
| | 1995 | 10.7 | 19.3 | 29.9 | 48.4 | 78.3 | 16.9 | 3.7 | 1.1 |
| Spain @ | 1970 | ... | ... | 52.3 | 23.4 | 75.8 | 18.2 | 1.3 | 4.7 |
| | 1974 | ... | ... | ... | ... | 78.7 | 14.5 | 1.5 | 5.4 |
| | 1979 | 3.5 | 58.9 | 62.4 | 19.3 | 81.7 | 14.0 | 1.7 | 2.6 |
| | 1990 | 6.0 | 23.3 | 29.3 | 45.0 | 74.2 | 15.4 | 9.9 | 0.5 |
| | 1991 | 7.3 | 22.1 | 29.4 | 44.8 | 74.3 | 16.1 | 9.1 | 0.5 |
| | 1992 | 6.4 | 22.2 | 28.7 | 46.8 | 75.4 | 16.0 | 8.2 | 0.5 |
| | 1993 | 6.8 | 22.1 | 28.9 | 53.2 | 82.2 | 15.3 | - | 2.5 |
| | 1994 | 7.7 | 22.3 | 29.9 | 53.2 | 83.1 | 14.7 | - | 2.1 |
| | 1995 | 8.1 | 24.1 | 32.3 | 50.7 | 83.0 | 15.1 | - | 1.9 |
| | 1996 | 7.3 | 26.1 | 33.3 | 47.9 | 81.3 | 16.6 | - | 2.1 |
| Sweden @ | 1970 | ... | ... | 42.7 | 17.7 | 60.4 | 14.5 | 3.7 | 21.4 |
| | 1975 | ... | ... | 38.3 | 13.3 | 51.5 | 12.3 | 6.6 | 29.6 |
| | 1980 | 0.1 | 44.6 | 44.6 | 13.6 | 58.3 | 9.3 | 16.1 | 16.4 |
| | 1985 | 0.1 | 47.9 | 48.0 | 20.1 | 68.1 | 13.1 | 11.7 | 7.1 |
| | 1990 | 0.1 | 47.6 | 47.7 | 19.6 | 67.3 | 13.2 | 18.3 | 1.3 |
| | 1991 | 0.0 | 42.1 | 42.1 | 19.0 | 61.1 | 13.9 | 23.9 | 1.0 |
| | 1992 | 0.0 | 40.7 | 40.7 | 18.3 | 59.0 | 15.8 | 23.7 | 1.4 |
| (4) | 1994 | 6.9 | 26.2 | 33.1 | 40.2 | 73.3 | 26.7 | - | - |
| (4) | 1995 | 7.2 | 25.7 | 32.9 | 39.4 | 72.3 | 27.7 | - | - |
| (4) | 1996 | 7.3 | 26.8 | 34.1 | 38.7 | 72.8 | 27.2 | - | - |
| Switzerland @ | 1970 | 1.8 | 33.2 | 35.1 | 40.2 | 75.3 | 17.5 | 0.6 | 6.6 |
| | 1975 | 3.2 | ... | ... | 77.9 | 81.2 | 17.0 | - | 1.8 |
| | 1980 | 2.8 | ... | ... | 73.7 | 76.5 | 18.6 | 2.2 | 2.7 |
| | 1985 | 3.1 | ... | ... | 73.6 | 76.7 | 18.1 | 2.9 | 2.3 |
| | 1990 | 3.6 | 46.3 | 49.9 | 25.1 | 75.0 | 19.7 | 3.3 | 1.9 |
| | 1991 | 3.6 | 45.9 | 49.5 | 25.7 | 75.2 | 19.4 | 3.5 | 2.0 |
| | 1993 | 3.8 | 27.2 | 31.0 | 47.1 | 78.1 | 19.9 | - | 2.0 |

II.19  Current public expenditure by level of education
Dépenses publiques ordinaires par niveau d'enseignement
Gastos públicos ordinarios por nivel de enseñanza

| Country / Pays / País | Year / Année / Año | Pre-primary / Pré-primaire / Pre-primaria (%) | Primary / Primaire / Primaria (%) | Preprimary + Primary / Préprimaire + Primaire / Preprimaria + Primaria (%) | Secondary / Secondaire / Secundaria (%) | Preprimary + Primary + Secondary / Préprimaire + Primaire + Secondaire / Preprimaria + Primaria + Secundaria (%) | Tertiary / Supérieur / Superior (%) | Other types / Autres types / Otros tipos (%) | Not distributed / Non réparties / Sin distribución (%) |
|---|---|---|---|---|---|---|---|---|---|
| Switzerland @ (cont) | 1994 | 3.8 | 27.0 | 30.9 | 47.0 | 77.9 | 20.0 | - | 2.1 |
|  | 1995 | 3.9 | 26.8 | 30.8 | 47.5 | 78.3 | 19.7 | - | 2.0 |
|  | 1996 | 4.1 | 26.5 | 30.6 | 48.1 | 78.6 | 19.3 | - | 2.0 |
| The Former Yugoslav Rep. of Macedonia | 1992 | ... | ... | 56.5 | 23.5 | 79.9 | 17.1 | 3.0 | - |
|  | 1993 | ... | ... | 57.1 | 21.2 | 78.3 | 19.7 | 2.0 | - |
|  | 1994 | ... | ... | 55.1 | 23.2 | 78.3 | 21.7 | - | - |
|  | 1995 | ... | ... | 54.9 | 22.8 | 77.8 | 22.2 | - | - |
|  | 1996 | ... | ... | 54.4 | 23.6 | 78.0 | 22.0 | - | - |
| Ukraine | 1970 | ... | ... | ... | ... | 66.2 | 14.1 | 19.7 | - |
|  | 1975 | ... | ... | ... | ... | 74.4 | 13.4 | 12.3 | - |
|  | 1980 | ... | ... | ... | ... | 72.6 | 14.0 | 13.4 | - |
|  | 1985 | ... | ... | ... | ... | 74.2 | 13.5 | 12.3 | - |
|  | 1990 | ... | ... | ... | ... | 69.9 | 15.1 | 15.0 | - |
|  | 1991 | ... | ... | ... | ... | 68.3 | 13.8 | 18.0 | - |
|  | 1992 | ... | ... | ... | ... | 70.3 | 12.6 | 17.1 | - |
|  | 1993 | ... | ... | ... | ... | 74.7 | 8.1 | 17.2 | - |
|  | 1994 | ... | ... | ... | ... | 73.4 | 9.8 | 16.8 | - |
|  | 1995 | ... | ... | ... | ... | 73.5 | 10.7 | 15.8 | - |
| United Kingdom @ | 1970 | ... | ... | 26.7 | 36.2 | 62.9 | 23.0 | <— | 14.1 |
|  | 1975 | ... | ... | 28.5 | 39.5 | 68.0 | 20.7 | <— | 11.3 |
|  | 1980 | ... | ... | 26.6 | 40.1 | 66.8 | 22.4 | <— | 10.8 |
|  | 1985 | 3.0 | 23.7 | 26.7 | 45.9 | 72.6 | 19.8 | 4.8 | 2.8 |
|  | 1990 | 3.6 | 26.1 | 29.7 | 43.8 | 73.5 | 19.6 | 5.1 | 1.7 |
|  | 1991 | 3.7 | 26.2 | 29.8 | 42.3 | 72.1 | 20.7 | 5.2 | 2.1 |
|  | (4) 1992 | 1.6 | 30.6 | 32.2 | 45.4 | 77.7 | 22.3 | - | - |
|  | (4) 1993 | 2.3 | 30.3 | 32.6 | 44.4 | 77.0 | 23.0 | - | - |
|  | (4) 1994 | 2.3 | 30.4 | 32.7 | 43.6 | 76.4 | 23.6 | - | - |
|  | (4) 1995 | 2.6 | 29.7 | 32.3 | 44.0 | 76.3 | 23.7 | - | - |
| **Oceania** | | | | | | | | | |
| American Samoa | 1975 | ... | ... | ... | ... | 85.4 | 14.6 | - | - |
|  | 1986 | 5.5 | 32.3 | 37.8 | 40.2 | 78.0 | 15.5 | 4.2 | 2.2 |
| Australia @ | 1980 | 1.7 | ... | ... | 67.0 | 68.7 | 22.6 | 2.7 | 6.0 |
|  | 1985 | 1.6 | ... | ... | 60.3 | 61.9 | 30.5 | 4.4 | 3.2 |
|  | 1990 | 2.2 | ... | ... | 57.4 | 59.6 | 32.0 | 4.8 | 3.6 |
|  | 1991 | 2.0 | ... | ... | 60.6 | 62.5 | 29.5 | 5.1 | 2.9 |
|  | 1992 | 1.1 | 29.7 | 30.8 | 41.6 | 72.3 | 26.6 | - | 1.0 |
|  | 1993 | 1.2 | 30.8 | 32.0 | 38.5 | 70.5 | 29.5 | - | - |
|  | 1994 | 0.7 | 29.9 | 30.6 | 39.6 | 70.2 | 29.8 | - | - |
|  | 1995 | 1.6 | 29.0 | 30.6 | 38.9 | 69.5 | 30.5 | - | - |
| Cook Islands | 1970 | ... | ... | 58.7 | 38.0 | 96.7 | 0.1 | - | 3.2 |
|  | 1981 | 1.8 | 38.9 | 40.7 | 27.5 | 68.2 | 4.5 | - | 27.3 |
|  | 1986 | 2.7 | 35.1 | 37.8 | 35.8 | 73.6 | 6.0 | - | 20.3 |
|  | 1997 | 7.5 | 53.5 | 61.0 | 38.2 | 99.1 | 0.9 | - | - |
| Fiji | 1970 | ... | ... | 65.2 | 29.5 | 94.7 | - | - | 5.3 |
|  | 1975 | ... | ... | 43.0 | 41.6 | 84.5 | 6.7 | - | 8.8 |
|  | 1981 | ... | ... | 53.0 | 45.1 | 98.1 | 1.9 | - | - |
|  | 1989 | ... | ... | 50.5 | 37.0 | 87.6 | 9.0 | 1.6 | 1.9 |
| French Polynesia | 1970 | ... | ... | 58.7 | 40.9 | 99.5 | - | 0.5 | - |
|  | 1975 | 7.7 | 28.6 | 36.3 | 61.0 | 97.3 | - | 0.8 | 2.0 |
|  | 1984 | ... | ... | 53.7 | 40.9 | 94.6 | - | 0.1 | 5.3 |
|  | (2) 1990 | 15.5 | 29.4 | 44.9 | 49.0 | 93.8 | 2.5 | - | 3.7 |
|  | (2) 1991 | 15.6 | 29.0 | 44.6 | 48.9 | 93.5 | 3.0 | - | 3.5 |
|  | (2) 1993 | 13.8 | 27.4 | 41.3 | 49.0 | 90.3 | 1.1 | 3.3 | 5.4 |
| Guam | 1970 | ... | ... | ... | ... | 85.3 | 14.7 | - | - |
|  | 1975 | ... | ... | ... | ... | 80.4 | 19.6 | - | - |
| Kiribati | 1970 | ... | ... | 32.6 | 36.5 | 69.1 | (3) 14.6 | 5.6 | 10.7 |
|  | 1975 | ... | ... | 26.9 | 58.1 | 84.9 | (3) 6.2 | - | 8.9 |
|  | 1989 | ... | ... | 50.5 | 28.7 | 79.2 | (3) 7.9 | - | 12.9 |
| New Caledonia | 1981 | ... | ... | 24.0 | 75.6 | 99.6 | 0.4 | - | - |
|  | 1986 | ... | ... | 24.8 | 74.4 | 99.2 | 0.8 | - | - |
|  | (2) 1990 | 13.0 | 29.8 | 42.8 | 53.0 | 95.8 | 1.0 | - | 3.1 |
|  | (2) 1991 | 13.1 | 27.8 | 40.9 | 50.6 | 91.5 | 1.5 | - | 6.9 |
|  | (2) 1993 | 10.8 | 21.4 | 32.1 | 53.0 | 85.1 | 1.3 | 2.5 | 11.1 |
| New Zealand @ | 1970 | ... | ... | 37.7 | 25.5 | 63.2 | 23.3 | 0.6 | 12.9 |
|  | 1975 | 1.4 | 35.6 | 37.0 | 24.3 | 61.3 | 28.8 | 2.1 | 7.9 |
|  | 1980 | 1.4 | 35.4 | 36.9 | 29.7 | 66.5 | 28.3 | 2.6 | 2.6 |
|  | 1985 | 1.5 | 36.9 | 38.3 | 28.5 | 66.8 | 28.3 | 2.2 | 2.7 |
|  | 1990 | 3.7 | 26.9 | 30.5 | 25.3 | 55.8 | 37.4 | 3.0 | 3.8 |

II.19

Current public expenditure by level of education
Dépenses publiques ordinaires par niveau d'enseignement
Gastos públicos ordinarios por nivel de enseñanza

| Country / Pays / País | Year / Année / Año | Pre-primary / Pré-primaire / Pre-primaria (%) | Primary / Primaire / Primaria (%) | Preprimary + Primary / Préprimaire + Primaire / Preprimaria + Primaria (%) | Secondary / Secondaire / Secundaria (%) | Preprimary + Primary + Secondary / Préprimaire + Primaire + Secondaire / Preprimaria + Primaria + Secundaria (%) | Tertiary / Supérieur / Superior (%) | Other types / Autres types / Otros tipos (%) | Not distributed / Non réparties / Sin distribución (%) |
|---|---|---|---|---|---|---|---|---|---|
| New Zealand @ (cont) | 1991 | 4.0 | 23.9 | 28.0 | 22.0 | 49.9 | 34.8 | 2.5 | 12.7 |
| | 1992 | 3.9 | 22.2 | 26.1 | 20.9 | 47.0 | 36.7 | 2.4 | 13.9 |
| | 1993 | 4.4 | 22.8 | 27.2 | 42.4 | 69.6 | 28.2 | - | 2.2 |
| | 1994 | 4.2 | 23.7 | 27.9 | 40.7 | 68.6 | 29.4 | - | 2.0 |
| | 1995 | 4.2 | 24.5 | 28.8 | 40.3 | 69.0 | 29.1 | - | 1.9 |
| | 1996 | 4.2 | 24.5 | 28.7 | 40.3 | 69.0 | 29.1 | - | 1.9 |
| Niue | 1975 | 0.3 | 35.1 | 35.5 | 39.3 | 74.8 | - | - | 25.2 |
| | 1980 | ... | ... | 32.2 | 48.1 | 80.3 | - | 1.1 | 18.7 |
| | 1986 | ... | ... | 36.6 | 44.5 | 81.1 | (3) 16.8 | - | 2.0 |
| Pacific Islands (Palau) | 1975 | ... | ... | 30.7 | 18.9 | 49.6 | 13.6 | 3.0 | 33.9 |
| | 1981 | ... | ... | 27.7 | 48.3 | 76.0 | 12.6 | 6.9 | 4.6 |
| Papua New Guinea | 1971 | 0.0 | 28.3 | 28.4 | 24.3 | 52.7 | 10.4 | 2.6 | 34.3 |
| | 1975 | ... | ... | 39.6 | 22.6 | 62.2 | 31.0 | 1.2 | 5.6 |
| Samoa | 1975 | ... | ... | 65.2 | 18.8 | 84.0 | - | 3.5 | 12.6 |
| | 1990 | ... | ... | 52.6 | 25.2 | 77.9 | - | | 22.1 |
| Solomon Islands | 1971 | ... | ... | 32.4 | 44.3 | 76.7 | (3) 11.3 | - | 12.0 |
| | 1979 | ... | ... | 44.1 | 42.2 | 86.4 | (3) 13.3 | 0.4 | - |
| | 1991 | 0.0 | 50.3 | 50.5 | 29.8 | 86.3 | (3) 13.7 | 0.1 | ... |
| Tokelau | 1981 | 1.4 | 26.8 | 28.3 | 71.7 | 100.0 | - | - | - |
| Tonga | 1971 | ... | ... | 51.2 | 30.3 | 81.4 | (3) 1.1 | - | 17.5 |
| | 1974 | ... | ... | 50.0 | 35.1 | 85.1 | (3) 1.3 | - | 13.6 |
| | 1980 | ... | ... | 55.0 | 25.4 | 80.5 | (3) 14.7 | - | 4.9 |
| | 1985 | ... | ... | 44.7 | 30.9 | 75.6 | (3) 17.9 | - | 6.5 |
| (4) | 1992 | ... | ... | 38.8 | 24.2 | 63.0 | (3) 7.3 | - | 29.7 |
| Tuvalu | 1990 | ... | | 35.9 | 59.0 | 95.0 | - | | 5.0 |
| Vanuatu, Republic of | 1990 | ... | ... | 59.8 | 26.6 | 86.4 | (3) 3.4 | - | 10.2 |
| | 1994 | ... | ... | 57.9 | 33.0 | 90.8 | (3) 6.4 | - | 2.8 |

## General note
For general explanations and definitions, please refer to the beginning of this chapter.

## Note générale
Pour les explications et définitions générales, prière de se référer au début de ce chapitre.

## Nota general
Para las explicaciones y definiciones generales, referirse al comienzo de este capítulo.

**Notes**

@ For countries participating in the UNESCO/OECD/Eurostat survey, expenditures given previously in the column 'other types' are distributed among the different levels of education. This is indicated by a line that separates the relevant years from the previous ones.

(1) Not including expenditure on tertiary education.

(2) Ministry of Education only.

(3) Data refer to scholarships.
(4) Including capital expenditure.
(5) Data refer to post-secondary education.

(6) Including scholarships and allocations for study abroad for all levels of education.

(7) Data on pre-primary, primary and secondary refer to expenditure on public and private ordinary schools and technical colleges.

(8) Data on tertiary education refer to expenditure on universities, technikons and teacher training.

(9) Transfers to universities and to other types of institutions as well as some types of pensions and of staff benefits are shown under the column of expenditure 'not distributed'.

**Notes**

@ Pour les pays qui participent à l'enquête de l'UNESCO/OCDE/Eurostat, les dépenses présentées antérieurement dans le colonne 'autres types' sont distribuées entre les différents niveaux d'enseignement. Ceci est indiqué par une ligne qui sépare les années concernées des années antérieures.

(1) Non compris les dépenses de l'enseignement supérieur.

(2) Ministère de l'Education seulement.

(3) Les données se réfèrent aux bourses d'études.
(4) Y compris les dépenses en capital.
(5) Les données se réfèrent à l'enseignement post-secondaire.

(6) Y compris les bourses et allocations d'études à l'étranger pour tous les niveaux d'enseignement.

(7) Les données relatives au préprimaire, primaire et secondaire se réfèrent aux dépenses des écoles publiques et privées et des collèges techniques.

(8) Les données relatives à l'enseignement supérieur se réfèrent aux dépenses des universités, des 'technikons', et des écoles normales.

(9) Les transferts de fonds aux universités et à certains autres établissements ainsi que différents types de pensions et d'indemnités sont inclus dans la colonne des dépenses 'non réparties'.

**Notas**

@ Para los países que participan en la encuesta de la UNESCO/OCDE/Eurostat, los gastos presentados anteriormente en la columna 'otros tipos' fueron clasificados en los distintos niveles de educación. Esto está indicado por una línea que separa los años correspondientes de los años anteriores.

(1) No incluyen los gastos de la enseñanza superior.

(2) Ministerio de Educación solamente.

(3) Los datos se refieren a las becas de estudio.
(4) Incluyen los gastos de capital.
(5) Los datos se refieren a la enseñanza post-secundaria.

(6) Incluyen las becas y los subsidios para los estudios en el extranjero en todos los niveles de enseñanza.

(7) Los datos relativos a la preprimaria, primaria y secundaria se refieren a los gastos de las escuelas públicas y privadas y de los colegios técnicos.

(8) Los datos relativos a la enseñanza superior se refieren a los gastos de las universidades, de los 'technikons' y de las escuelas normales.

(9) Las transferencias del gobierno a las universidades y a otros establecimientos así como diferentes tipos de pensiones y indemnizaciones del personal quedan incluidos en la columna de los gastos 'sin distribución'.

**II.19** Current public expenditure by level of education
Dépenses publiques ordinaires par niveau d'enseignement
Gastos públicos ordinarios por nivel de enseñanza

(10) Expenditure on tertiary education is included with expenditure 'not distributed'.

(11) Not including expenditure on mid-level specialised colleges and technical schools.

(12) Expenditure of the Office of Greek Education only.

(13) Including capital expenditure on tertiary education.

(14) Flemish Community only.

(10) Les dépenses de l'enseignement supérieur sont incluses dans les dépenses 'non réparties'.

(11) Non compris les dépenses relatives aux collèges spécialisés du moyen degré et aux écoles techniques.

(12) Les dépenses du bureau grec de l'éducation seulement.

(13) Y compris les dépenses en capital relatives à l'enseignement supérieur.

(14) Communauté flamande seulement.

(10) Los gastos de la enseñanza superior quedan incluidos en los gastos 'sin distribución'.

(11) No incluyen los gastos relativos a los colegios especializados de medio grado y las escuelas técnicas.

(12) Los gastos del servicio griego de educación solamente.

(13) Incluyen los gastos de capital relativos a la enseñanza superior.

(14) Comunidad flamenca solamente.

Current public expenditure by purpose II.20
Dépenses publiques ordinaires selon leur destination
Gastos públicos ordinarios segun su destino

II.20 Current public expenditure on education:
percentage of emoluments and teaching materials

Dépenses publiques ordinaires afférentes à l'éducation:
pourcentage des émoluments et du matériel pour l'enseignement

Gastos públicos ordinarios destinados a la educación:
porcentaje de emolumentos y de material educativo

| Country<br><br>Pays<br><br>País | Year<br><br>Année<br><br>Año | Emoluments / Émoluments / Emolumentos | | | Teaching materials<br><br>Matériel pour l'enseignement<br><br>Material educativo<br>(%) |
|---|---|---|---|---|---|
| | | Teaching staff<br><br>Personnel enseignant<br><br>Personal docente<br>(%) | Non-teaching staff<br><br>Personnel non-enseignant<br><br>Personal no docente<br>(%) | Total<br><br>Total<br><br>Total<br>(%) | |
| **Africa** | | | | | |
| Algeria | 1980 | 63.6 | ... | ... | 0.3 |
| (1) | 1991 | 77.0 | 13.3 | 90.4 | 0.0 |
| (1) | 1992 | 73.2 | 18.1 | 91.3 | 0.3 |
| (1) | 1995 | 73.2 | 21.5 | 94.8 | 0.2 |
| (1) | 1996 | 74.3 | 20.8 | 95.2 | 0.1 |
| Angola (2) | 1985 | ... | ... | 90.2 | 1.0 |
| | 1990 | ... | ... | 86.3 | 0.7 |
| Benin | 1970 | 70.4 | ... | ... | 0.9 |
| | 1975 | 66.5 | ... | ... | 0.5 |
| | 1995 | ... | ... | 78.6 | 4.7 |
| Botswana | 1970 | 64.9 | 2.2 | 67.2 | - |
| | 1975 | 52.8 | 6.5 | 59.3 | 12.2 |
| | 1979 | 57.6 | 5.6 | 63.1 | 16.4 |
| | 1985 | 52.3 | 6.4 | 58.7 | 3.5 |
| | 1991 | 43.3 | 8.9 | 52.2 | 4.0 |
| Burkina Faso | 1970 | 62.4 | 1.9 | 64.3 | ... |
| | 1975 | 56.3 | 2.2 | 58.5 | 5.1 |
| | 1980 | ... | ... | 61.0 | 0.4 |
| | 1985 | 52.9 | 8.1 | 61.0 | 0.1 |
| | 1989 | 54.0 | 5.8 | 59.8 | ... |
| | 1992 | ... | ... | 61.5 | 0.5 |
| | 1994 | ... | ... | 52.7 | 6.1 |
| Burundi | 1970 | ... | ... | 73.3 | 7.4 |
| | 1975 | ... | ... | 72.6 | 10.9 |
| | 1981 | ... | ... | 74.9 | 1.2 |
| | 1985 | ... | ... | 68.0 | 1.6 |
| | 1990 | 58.3 | 16.7 | 75.0 | 0.8 |
| | 1991 | 55.5 | 16.4 | 71.9 | 1.0 |
| | 1992 | 56.1 | 17.3 | 73.4 | 0.7 |
| Cameroon | 1970 | 69.6 | ... | ... | ... |
| | 1975 | ... | ... | 81.8 | ... |
| | 1981 | 65.4 | ... | ... | ... |
| Cape Verde | 1985 | 65.6 | 24.7 | 90.3 | 0.2 |
| Central African Republic | 1975 | 63.5 | 6.2 | 69.7 | - |
| | 1979 | 69.4 | ... | ... | ... |
| (2) | 1986 | 66.8 | 12.6 | 79.4 | 2.4 |
| (2) | 1990 | 68.1 | 11.5 | 79.6 | 1.3 |
| (2) | 1991 | ... | ... | 79.9 | - |
| Chad | 1970 | 61.5 | ... | ... | - |
| | 1975 | 59.2 | ... | ... | 9.9 |
| | 1991 | 58.6 | 17.8 | 76.4 | 1.4 |
| | 1994 | 64.7 | 10.2 | 74.9 | 1.0 |
| | 1996 | 64.4 | 8.9 | 73.3 | 5.1 |

II.20 Current public expenditure by purpose
Dépenses publiques ordinaires selon leur destination
Gastos públicos ordinarios segun su destino

| Country / Pays / País | Year / Année / Año | Emoluments / Émoluments / Emolumentos | | | Teaching materials Matériel pour l'enseignement Material educativo (%) |
|---|---|---|---|---|---|
| | | Teaching staff Personnel enseignant Personal docente (%) | Non-teaching staff Personnel non-enseignant Personal no docente (%) | Total Total Total (%) | |
| Comoros (2) | 1992 | 71.3 | 4.5 | 75.8 | - |
| | 1993 | 73.3 | 6.0 | 79.3 | - |
| | 1995 | 70.3 | 5.4 | 75.7 | - |
| Congo | 1970 | 74.0 | 4.8 | 78.8 | - |
| | 1980 | 70.8 | ... | ... | 5.5 |
| | 1991 | ... | ... | 85.2 | ... |
| | 1993 | ... | ... | 80.4 | 3.2 |
| | 1994 | ... | ... | 82.0 | - |
| | 1995 | ... | ... | 83.7 | - |
| Côte d'Ivoire | 1970 | 57.4 | 5.6 | 63.0 | 22.4 |
| | 1975 | 68.4 | 4.4 | 72.8 | 12.2 |
| | 1981 | ... | ... | 73.0 | - |
| | 1985 | ... | ... | 76.3 | - |
| | 1992 | ... | ... | 81.0 | - |
| | 1993 | ... | ... | 78.5 | - |
| | 1994 | ... | ... | 76.0 | - |
| | 1995 | ... | ... | 73.7 | - |
| | 1996 | ... | ... | 72.4 | - |
| | 1997 | ... | ... | 71.3 | - |
| Djibouti | 1971 | 83.7 | 2.9 | 86.6 | - |
| | 1974 | 89.9 | 1.1 | 91.0 | - |
| (2) | 1985 | ... | ... | 74.7 | 12.6 |
| | 1990 | ... | ... | 70.0 | 7.1 |
| | 1991 | ... | ... | 76.8 | 6.5 |
| Egypt | 1970 | ... | ... | 84.4 | ... |
| | 1975 | ... | ... | 81.2 | ... |
| | 1980 | ... | ... | 75.8 | 0.7 |
| | 1991 | ... | ... | 83.3 | 0.8 |
| | 1992 | ... | ... | 81.8 | 0.8 |
| | 1993 | ... | ... | 79.3 | 0.8 |
| | 1994 | ... | ... | 79.1 | 0.7 |
| | 1995 | ... | ... | 80.7 | 0.7 |
| | 1996 | ... | ... | 81.8 | ... |
| Eritrea (1) | 1993 | ... | ... | 86.9 | ... |
| | 1994 | ... | ... | 73.8 | ... |
| Ethiopia (1) | 1970 | 78.6 | 5.8 | 84.4 | - |
| | 1975 | 75.7 | 10.9 | 86.5 | 4.7 |
| | 1981 | 83.4 | 8.1 | 91.5 | 5.8 |
| | 1990 | 90.1 | 3.0 | 93.1 | 0.9 |
| Gabon | 1976 | 43.9 | ... | ... | - |
| | 1980 | 56.7 | ... | ... | ... |
| (1) | 1992 | 88.6 | ... | ... | 0.5 |
| Gambia | 1990 | 42.6 | 4.9 | 47.5 | 3.8 |
| | 1994 | ... | ... | 46.8 | 5.3 |
| | 1995 | ... | ... | 51.1 | 4.2 |
| | 1996 | ... | ... | 49.1 | 4.5 |
| Ghana | 1970 | 78.5 (3) | 10.7 (3) | 89.1 (3) | ... |
| | 1976 | 70.8 (3) | 14.0 | 84.9 | 9.0 |
| | 1984 | 53.6 | 4.2 | 57.9 | 21.6 |
| | 1990 | ... | ... | 62.7 | - |
| Guinea | 1979 | 62.8 | 8.3 | 71.1 | - |
| | 1984 | 82.5 | 9.8 | 92.3 | 2.6 |
| | 1992 | 60.4 | 9.3 | 69.6 | ... |
| | 1993 | 55.6 | 11.1 | 66.7 | ... |
| Guinea-Bissau | 1980 | 73.5 (3) | 10.8 (3) | 84.3 | ... |
| Lesotho | 1984 | 69.9 | 3.7 | 73.5 | 2.1 |
| | 1994 | 65.2 | 5.0 | 70.2 | ... |
| | 1996 | 57.6 | 5.7 | 63.3 | - |
| Liberia | 1980 | 48.9 | 9.0 | 57.8 | 8.6 |
| Madagascar | 1970 | 70.6 | 8.0 | 78.6 | ... |
| | 1975 | 77.8 | 9.9 | 87.7 | 4.5 |
| | 1980 | 81.8 | 4.6 | 86.4 | 3.1 |
| | 1985 | 76.7 | 3.8 | 80.4 | 0.3 |
| (1) | 1993 | ... | ... | 83.3 | ... |
| Malawi | 1975 | 55.4 (3) | 7.5 (3) | 62.9 (3) | 1.9 |
| | 1981 | 43.4 (3) | 12.6 (3) | 56.0 | ... |

Current public expenditure by purpose  II.20
Dépenses publiques ordinaires selon leur destination
Gastos públicos ordinarios segun su destino

| Country / Pays / País | | Year / Année / Año | Emoluments / Émoluments / Emolumentos | | | Teaching materials |
|---|---|---|---|---|---|---|
| | | | Teaching staff / Personnel enseignant / Personal docente (%) | Non-teaching staff / Personnel non-enseignant / Personal no docente (%) | Total / Total / Total (%) | Matériel pour l'enseignement / Material educativo (%) |
| Malawi (cont) | | 1985 | 45.7 | 8.5 | 54.2 | 2.0 |
| | | 1989 | 52.8 | 2.9 | 55.7 | - |
| Mali | | 1975 | ... | ... | 63.0 | 6.6 |
| | | 1980 | 51.0 | 9.7 | 60.7 | 4.2 |
| | | 1985 | 63.1 | 8.4 | 71.6 | 1.8 |
| | | 1993 | ... | ... | 57.3 | 2.7 |
| | | 1995 | ... | ... | 57.1 | 14.3 |
| Mauritania | | 1970 | ... | ... | 82.9 | ... |
| | (2) | 1993 | 51.9 | 24.4 | 76.3 | 5.9 |
| | (2) | 1996 | ... | ... | 72.1 | 1.1 |
| Mauritius | | 1970 | ... | ... | 86.0 | ... |
| | | 1990 | 53.8 | 26.5 | 80.3 | 1.6 |
| Morocco (2) | | 1970 | ... | ... | 84.9 | ... |
| | | 1980 | ... | ... | 83.4 | - |
| | | 1985 | ... | ... | 86.4 | - |
| | | 1991 | ... | ... | 88.1 | - |
| | | 1995 | ... | ... | 88.4 | - |
| | | 1006 | 78.0 | 10.4 | 88.4 | 0.5 |
| Mozambique | | 1990 | ... | | 74.5 | |
| Niger | | 1970 | 64.6 | 10.5 | 75.1 | ... |
| | | 1980 | 68.2 | ... | ... | 13.1 |
| | (1) | 1991 | 57.2 | 20.4 | 77.6 | 4.7 |
| Reunion | | 1970 | 81.5 | 4.3 | 85.8 | ... |
| | | 1980 | 71.0 | 7.1 | 78.1 | 0.2 |
| | | 1985 | ... | ... | 91.0 | 0.6 |
| | | 1990 | 83.1 | 7.6 | 90.7 | 0.7 |
| | | 1991 | 83.7 | 8.3 | 92.0 | 0.8 |
| | | 1993 | 86.2 | 8.5 | 94.7 | 0.3 |
| Rwanda | | 1970 | 73.7 | 4.7 | 78.4 | |
| | | 1975 | 74.4 | 3.6 | 78.0 | 2.9 |
| | | 1980 | 74.8 | 6.5 | 81.3 | 3.6 |
| | | 1989 | 80.7 | 3.3 | 84.0 | 1.7 |
| Sao Tome and Principe | | 1986 | ... | ... | 68.7 | - |
| Senegal | | 1975 | ... | ... | 67.8 | 9.7 |
| | | 1980 | ... | ... | 66.1 | - |
| | | 1985 | ... | ... | 74.2 | - |
| | | 1990 | ... | ... | 69.4 | - |
| | | 1991 | ... | ... | 70.4 | |
| | | 1992 | ... | ... | 66.8 | - |
| | | 1996 | ... | ... | 59.9 | - |
| | | 1997 | ... | ... | 68.9 | - |
| Seychelles | | 1970 | ... | ... (3) | 75.8 | ... |
| | | 1975 | ... | ... (3) | 84.1 | 5.7 |
| | | 1980 | 64.4 | 12.6 | 77.1 | 9.8 |
| | | 1985 | 41.8 (3) | 28.4 (3) | 70.2 | 3.4 |
| | | 1990 | ... | ... | 62.4 | 3.4 |
| | | 1992 | ... | ... | 58.0 | 6.5 |
| | | 1995 | ... | ... | 61.5 | 4.9 |
| Somalia | | 1970 | 68.1 (3) | 7.7 (3) | 75.8 | 24.2 |
| | (1) | 1980 | ... | ... (3) | 80.9 | 16.6 |
| | (1) | 1986 | ... | ... | 65.6 | 18.4 |
| South Africa | | 1986 | 69.9 | 14.0 | 83.9 | - |
| | | 1989 | 71.7 | 12.8 | 84.5 | - |
| | | 1990 | 73.3 | 12.0 | 85.3 | - |
| | | 1992 | 78.5 | 10.0 | 88.5 | 2.7 |
| | | 1993 | 76.5 | 8.9 | 85.4 | 4.4 |
| | | 1995 | 74.4 | 10.4 | 84.8 | 3.2 |
| | (1) | 1996 | 75.3 | 12.0 | 87.3 | 3.8 |
| St. Helena | | 1970 | 54.0 | 8.0 | 62.0 | - |
| | | 1975 | 49.4 | 16.5 | 65.8 | 17.7 |
| | | 1980 | 58.8 | 15.3 | 74.0 | 10.7 |
| Swaziland | | 1970 | 75.0 | ... | ... | 8.1 |
| | | 1976 | 70.6 | | | ... |
| | | 1981 | 86.5 | 6.0 | 92.5 | 7.5 |
| | | 1986 | 74.2 | 5.2 | 79.4 | ... |

II.20  Current public expenditure by purpose
Dépenses publiques ordinaires selon leur destination
Gastos públicos ordinarios segun su destino

| Country<br><br>Pays<br><br>País | Year<br><br>Année<br><br>Año | Emoluments / Émoluments / Emolumentos | | | | | Teaching<br>materials<br><br>Matériel<br>pour<br>l'enseignement<br><br>Material<br>educativo<br>(%) |
|---|---|---|---|---|---|---|---|
| | | Teaching<br>staff<br><br>Personnel<br>enseignant<br><br>Personal<br>docente<br>(%) | | Non-teaching<br>staff<br><br>Personnel<br>non-enseignant<br><br>Personal<br>no docente<br>(%) | | Total<br><br>Total<br><br>Total<br>(%) | |
| Swaziland (cont) | 1989 | 61.6 | | 3.8 | | 65.4 | ... |
| | 1993 | 51.5 | | 12.3 | | 63.8 | 2.4 |
| | 1994 | 49.0 | | 18.3 | | 67.3 | 3.1 |
| | 1995 | ... | | ... | | 71.7 | 1.7 |
| Togo | 1970 | 70.1 | | 7.3 | | 77.4 | ... |
| | 1981 | 58.5 | | 4.6 | | 63.1 | 1.3 |
| | 1986 | ... | | ... | | 64.2 | 4.6 |
| | 1990 | 54.7 | | 2.6 | | 57.3 | ... |
| | 1992 | 57.6 | | 2.4 | | 60.0 | 1.0 |
| | 1996 | 74.2 | | 3.0 | | 77.2 | 2.4 |
| Tunisia | 1980 | ... | | ... | | 81.3 | 4.9 |
| | 1985 | | | | | 84.1 | 1.0 |
| | 1993 | 76.5 | | 10.9 | | 87.4 | - |
| | 1995 | 77.0 | | 10.4 | | 87.4 | 0.0 |
| Uganda (1) | 1994 | 69.9 | | 4.5 | | 74.4 | 1.2 |
| Zambia | 1971 | 62.5 (3) | | 15.1 (3) | | 77.6 | 9.8 |
| | 1975 | 63.7 (3) | | 14.1 (3) | | 77.8 | 6.9 |
| | 1980 | 52.6 (3) | | 17.1 (3) | | 69.7 | 2.6 |
| | 1985 | ... | | ... | | 60.8 | 2.7 |
| Zimbabwe | 1975 | 74.2 | | 6.4 | | 80.6 | 0.5 |
| | 1980 | 75.2 | | 3.5 | | 78.7 | 0.5 |
| | 1986 | ... | | ... | | 83.4 | 5.8 |
| (1) | 1990 | 86.5 | | | | ... | 2.1 |
| (1) | 1991 | 89.7 | | 3.2 | | 92.9 | 3.8 |
| (1) | 1992 | 89.1 | | 3.1 | | 92.2 | 2.1 |
| (1) | 1995 | 89.2 | | 2.2 | | 91.4 | 2.0 |
| (1) | 1996 | 91.1 | | 2.4 | | 93.5 | 1.9 |
| **North America** | | | | | | | |
| Antigua and Barbuda | 1971 | 73.2 | | 7.3 | | 80.4 | 3.1 |
| | 1975 | 58.9 | | 6.1 | | 65.0 | 3.8 |
| | 1979 | 64.7 | | 3.6 | | 68.4 | 3.0 |
| Belize | 1970 | 67.0 (3) | | 11.2 (3) | | 78.1 | - |
| | 1974 | 64.7 | | 5.7 | | 70.4 | 2.4 |
| (1) | 1996 | 85.6 | | 4.6 | | 90.2 | 0.5 |
| Bermuda | 1970 | 71.9 | | 3.0 | | 74.9 | - |
| | 1975 | 79.4 | | 5.6 | | 85.0 | 2.6 |
| | 1980 | 59.7 | | 5.0 | | 64.7 | 16.6 |
| | 1984 | 68.5 | | 7.0 | | 75.5 | 5.2 |
| | 1990 | 69.8 | | 3.7 | | 73.4 | - |
| | 1991 | 66.8 | | 3.9 | | 70.7 | |
| British Virgin Islands | 1970 | 78.9 (3) | | 8.0 (3) | | 86.9 | - |
| | 1975 | 74.0 (3) | | 4.0 (3) | | 78.1 | 3.1 |
| | 1980 | 75.0 (3) | | 5.9 (3) | | 80.9 | 1.6 |
| | 1985 | ... | | ... | | 71.8 | - |
| | 1990 | ... | | ... | | 67.0 | - |
| | 1991 | ... | | ... | | 61.8 | - |
| Canada @ | 1970 | 51.9 | | 5.5 | | 57.4 | 10.6 |
| | 1975 | 54.0 | | 6.3 | | 60.3 | 10.4 |
| | 1980 | 52.2 | | 6.9 | | 59.1 | 10.0 |
| | 1985 | 51.2 | | 17.1 | | 68.3 | 7.0 |
| | 1990 | 51.9 | | 19.0 | | 70.9 | 7.2 |
| | 1991 | 51.7 | | 19.4 | | 71.1 | 6.4 |
| | 1992 | 50.6 | | 19.2 | | 69.8 | 6.0 |
| | 1993 | ... | | ... | | 80.1 | ... |
| | 1994 | 56.2 | | 21.5 | | 77.7 | ... |
| Cayman Islands | 1975 | ... | | ... | | 82.7 | 5.6 |
| | 1980 | 68.8 | | 13.1 | | 81.8 | 6.4 |
| Costa Rica | 1970 | ... | | ... | | 92.6 | - |
| | 1991 | ... | | ... | | 94.5 | - |
| | 1992 | ... | | ... | | 91.7 | - |
| | 1993 | ... | | ... | | 95.0 | - |
| | 1994 | ... | | ... | | 95.4 | - |
| | 1995 | ... | | ... | | 95.6 | - |
| | 1996 | ... | | ... | | 90.9 | - |
| Cuba | 1980 | 38.8 | | 3.8 | | 42.7 | 6.6 |
| | 1985 | ... | | ... | | 53.1 | 0.8 |
| | 1990 | ... | | ... | | 57.4 | 1.9 |
| | 1991 | ... | | ... | | 62.0 | 1.3 |

Current public expenditure by purpose
Dépenses publiques ordinaires selon leur destination
Gastos públicos ordinarios segun su destino

II.20

| Country<br><br>Pays<br><br>País | Year<br><br>Année<br><br>Año | Emoluments / Émoluments / Emolumentos | | | Teaching<br>materials<br><br>Matériel<br>pour<br>l'enseignement<br><br>Material<br>educativo<br>(%) |
|---|---|---|---|---|---|
| | | Teaching<br>staff<br><br>Personnel<br>enseignant<br><br>Personal<br>docente<br>(%) | Non-teaching<br>staff<br><br>Personnel<br>non-enseignant<br><br>Personal<br>no docente<br>(%) | Total<br><br>Total<br><br>Total<br>(%) | |
| Cuba (cont) | 1992 | ... | ... | 64.5 | 1.2 |
| | 1993 | ... | ... | 64.6 | 0.9 |
| | 1994 | ... | ... | 60.2 | 1.0 |
| | 1995 | ... | ... | 58.2 | 1.0 |
| | 1996 | ... | ... | 56.7 | 1.0 |
| Dominica | 1989 | 59.1 | 10.7 | 69.8 | 0.9 |
| Dominican Republic | 1976 | 58.3 | 5.4 | 63.7 | 3.3 |
| | 1980 | 62.2 | 6.6 | 68.8 | - |
| | 1985 | ... | ... | 76.2 | |
| | 1996 | ... | ... | 91.6 | 0.2 |
| El Salvador | 1970 | 87.3 | 7.0 | 94.2 | ... |
| | 1975 | 82.5 | 4.5 | 87.0 | 7.8 |
| Guadeloupe | 1970 | 81.2 | 4.5 | 85.7 | ... |
| | 1980 | 69.2 | 8.8 | 78.0 | 0.2 |
| | 1990 | 82.4 | 9.2 | 91.6 | 0.8 |
| | 1991 | 83.8 | 9.5 | 93.3 | 0.7 |
| | 1993 | 86.3 | 9.4 | 95.7 | 0.3 |
| Guatemala | 1970 | 82.6 (3) | 4.3 (3) | 86.8 | ... |
| | 1976 | 65.0 (3) | 7.5 (3) | 72.6 | ... |
| | 1979 | 69.1 (3) | 6.2 (3) | 75.3 | 0.5 |
| (2) | 1984 | 70.4 (3) | 7.7 (3) | 78.1 | 0.3 |
| (2) | 1995 | 62.8 | 1.6 | 64.4 | 0.3 |
| Haiti | 1976 | 85.4 | 2.9 | 88.3 | 4.4 |
| | 1980 | ... | ... | 78.2 | 2.2 |
| | 1985 | ... | ... | 88.5 | 1.3 |
| | 1990 | ... | ... | 95.3 | 0.0 |
| Honduras | 1970 | 79.8 | 3.4 | 83.2 | 1.7 |
| | 1980 | 71.1 | 6.5 | 77.6 | 2.6 |
| | 1989 | ... | ... | 78.6 | 0.3 |
| | 1994 | 58.2 | 6.6 | 64.9 | 0.5 |
| | 1995 | 67.8 | 6.7 | 74.6 | 0.2 |
| Jamaica (2) | 1974 | 69.1 | 4.3 | 73.4 | 3.2 |
| (2) | 1980 | 65.6 (3) | 12.5 (3) | 78.2 | 2.2 |
| | 1985 | 58.8 (3) | 17.1 (3) | 75.9 | 2.6 |
| (2) | 1990 | 58.3 | 6.2 | 64.5 | 0.5 |
| | 1991 | 50.5 | 9.7 | 60.2 | 0.8 |
| (2) | 1992 | 57.3 | 11.2 | 68.5 | 0.1 |
| (2) | 1994 | 57.9 | 11.0 | 68.8 | 0.7 |
| (2) | 1995 | 66.4 | 8.6 | 75.0 | 0.3 |
| (2) | 1996 | 64.1 | 12.1 | 76.2 | 0.5 |
| Martinique | 1970 | 87.2 | 4.7 | 91.9 | - |
| | 1980 | 78.0 | 9.2 | 87.1 | 0.2 |
| | 1990 | 81.6 | 10.3 | 91.9 | 0.7 |
| | 1991 | 82.8 | 10.8 | 93.6 | 0.7 |
| | 1993 | 85.0 | 10.6 | 95.6 | 0.3 |
| Mexico @ (5) | 1994 | ... | ... | 97.9 | ... |
| | 1995 | ... | ... | 89.7 | ... |
| Nicaragua | 1970 | 81.5 | 4.8 | 86.3 | - |
| | 1980 | 69.7 | 10.8 | 80.5 | 2.2 |
| | 1985 | 61.2 | 7.8 | 69.0 | 2.4 |
| (1) | 1992 | 69.6 | 10.2 | 79.8 | 0.4 |
| Panama | 1970 | 66.5 (3) | 12.7 (3) | 79.2 | ... |
| | 1975 | 69.7 (3) | 4.1 (3) | 73.8 | ... |
| | 1980 | 65.3 (3) | 13.8 (3) | 79.1 | 1.8 |
| | 1985 | 60.7 (3) | 9.3 (3) | 70.1 | 0.9 |
| | 1990 | 59.6 | 3.6 | 63.2 | ... |
| | 1991 | 57.7 | 7.3 | 65.0 | ... |
| | 1992 | 51.3 | 8.8 | 60.1 | ... |
| St. Kitts and Nevis | 1984 | 82.8 | 9.0 | 91.8 | 2.3 |
| | 1995 | 70.6 | 13.5 | 84.1 | ... |
| St. Lucia | 1971 | ... | ... | 76.9 | - |
| | 1975 | 69.3 | 4.8 | 74.1 | 3.9 |
| | 1980 | 66.9 | 7.2 | 74.1 | 2.8 |
| St. Pierre and Miquelon | 1970 | 89.7 | 0.5 | 90.2 | ... |
| | 1980 | 72.0 | 4.7 | 76.8 | 5.6 |
| | 1986 | 69.8 | 6.5 | 76.3 | 5.4 |
| | 1990 | 84.1 | 8.3 | 92.4 | 3.4 |

II.20    Current public expenditure by purpose
Dépenses publiques ordinaires selon leur destination
Gastos públicos ordinarios segun su destino

| Country<br><br>Pays<br><br>País | Year<br><br>Année<br><br>Año | Emoluments / Émoluments / Emolumentos | | | Teaching<br>materials<br><br>Matériel<br>pour<br>l'enseignement<br><br>Material<br>educativo<br>(%) |
|---|---|---|---|---|---|
| | | Teaching<br>staff<br><br>Personnel<br>enseignant<br><br>Personal<br>docente<br>(%) | Non-teaching<br>staff<br><br>Personnel<br>non-enseignant<br><br>Personal<br>no docente<br>(%) | Total<br><br><br>Total<br><br><br>Total<br>(%) | |
| St. Pierre and Miquelon (cont) | 1991 | 85.2 | 8.1 | 93.3 | 3.6 |
| | 1992 | 84.9 | 9.0 | 93.9 | 3.0 |
| | 1993 | 85.8 | 8.7 | 94.5 | 2.9 |
| St. Vincent and the Grenadines | 1986 | 86.1 | 7.5 | 93.6 | 1.5 |
| | 1990 | 82.9 | 10.2 | 93.1 | 2.8 |
| Trinidad and Tobago | 1980 | 73.2 | 7.1 | 80.2 | 4.0 |
| | 1985 | 69.5 | 6.1 | 75.6 | 2.7 |
| | 1990 | 69.7 | 4.6 | 74.3 | - |
| | 1994 | ... | ... | 66.7 | 0.1 |
| (1) | 1996 | ... | ... | 73.3 | 11.6 |
| Turks and Caicos Islands | 1975 | 74.0 (3) | 11.8 (3) | 85.9 | 4.2 |
| | 1980 | 72.7 | 3.6 | 76.3 | 7.2 |
| U. S. Virgin Islands | 1980 | 45.0 (3) | 16.7 (3) | 61.7 | 2.1 |
| United States @ (6) | 1992 | 53.0 | 22.5 | 75.5 | ... |
| (6) | 1993 | 52.9 | 22.4 | 75.3 | ... |
| | 1994 | 49.4 | 20.7 | 70.1 | ... |
| **South America** | | | | | |
| Argentina | 1980 | ... | ... | 86.7 | 7.9 |
| | 1984 | ... | ... | 89.6 | ... |
| | 1996 | 67.8 | 23.6 | 91.4 | ... |
| Bolivia | 1980 | 75.7 | 6.5 | 82.1 | ... |
| | 1996 | ... | ... (3) | 74.3 | ... |
| Brazil | 1995 | ... | | 84.5 | ... |
| Chile | 1974 | 88.0 | 3.1 | 91.1 | 0.8 |
| | 1980 | 76.8 | 2.5 | 79.2 | 5.1 |
| Colombia (2) | 1981 | 93.4 | 1.8 | 95.1 | ... |
| | 1984 | 94.5 | 0.5 | 95.0 | 0.1 |
| | 1996 | 80.8 | 4.5 | 85.3 | ... |
| Ecuador | 1970 | 76.4 | 9.0 | 85.4 | ... |
| | 1980 | 77.4 | 2.2 | 79.6 | 0.8 |
| | 1985 | 62.9 | 7.1 | 70.0 | ... |
| | 1989 | ... | ... | 81.6 | 2.0 |
| Falkland Islands (Malvinas) | 1970 | ... | ... | 58.3 | - |
| | 1975 | 48.9 | 2.9 | 51.8 | 3.6 |
| | 1979 | 56.4 | 4.9 | 61.3 | 6.9 |
| | 1996 | 39.5 | 8.5 | 48.0 | 2.6 |
| French Guiana | 1970 | 73.0 | 7.5 | 80.5 | - |
| | 1980 | 63.6 | 10.8 | 74.4 | 1.3 |
| | 1990 | 84.5 | 9.2 | 93.7 | 0.6 |
| | 1991 | 85.3 | 9.5 | 94.8 | 0.6 |
| | 1993 | 87.5 | 8.9 | 96.4 | 0.4 |
| Guyana | 1970 | ... | ... | 87.6 | - |
| | 1975 | 66.9 | 4.8 | 71.7 | 6.5 |
| | 1979 | 66.5 | 8.8 | 75.3 | 6.0 |
| | 1985 | ... | ... | 59.4 | 2.5 |
| Peru | 1975 | 65.1 | 4.9 | 69.9 | 2.7 |
| | 1980 | 59.4 | 8.4 | 67.8 | 0.9 |
| | 1985 | 55.2 | 11.4 | 66.6 | 0.3 |
| | 1996 | 40.1 | 7.2 | 47.3 | 8.6 |
| Suriname | 1980 | 41.8 (3) | 23.4 (3) | 65.2 | 7.2 |
| | 1986 | 32.5 | 11.6 | 44.1 | 2.7 |
| | 1990 | 33.4 | 13.6 | 47.0 | 4.3 |
| | 1991 | 33.2 | 13.3 | 46.5 | 5.1 |
| | 1992 | 33.1 | 12.1 | 45.2 | 5.5 |
| | 1993 | 31.8 | 12.1 | 43.9 | 5.2 |
| Uruguay | 1980 | 56.9 (3) | 20.5 (3) | 77.4 | 5.1 |
| | 1985 | 46.3 (3) | 32.0 (3) | 78.3 | ... |
| | 1990 | ... | ... (3) | 79.3 | ... |
| | 1991 | ... | ... (3) | 77.0 | ... |
| | 1992 | ... | ... (3) | 79.5 | ... |
| | 1994 | 47.4 | 22.3 | 69.7 | ... |
| | 1995 | 44.5 | 27.3 | 71.8 | ... |
| | 1996 | 41.5 | 17.2 | 58.7 | ... |

Current public expenditure by purpose  II.20
Dépenses publiques ordinaires selon leur destination
Gastos públicos ordinarios segun su destino

| Country / Pays / País | Year / Année / Año | Emoluments / Émoluments / Emolumentos | | | Teaching materials / Matériel pour l'enseignement / Material educativo (%) |
| | | Teaching staff / Personnel enseignant / Personal docente (%) | Non-teaching staff / Personnel non-enseignant / Personal no docente (%) | Total / Total / Total (%) | |
|---|---|---|---|---|---|
| Venezuela | 1970 | 70.3 | 6.1 | 76.4 | - |
| | 1980 | 60.7 | 13.7 | 74.4 | 1.0 |
| | 1984 | 60.0 | 11.0 | 71.0 | 4.5 |
| **Asia** | | | | | |
| Afghanistan | 1970 | ... | ... | 67.6 | 21.2 |
| | 1980 | 46.8 (3) | 32.8 (3) | 79.6 | 12.7 |
| Azerbaijan | 1992 | ... | ... | 72.5 | 0.2 |
| | 1995 | | | 63.1 | ... |
| | 1996 | ... | ... | 65.0 | ... |
| Bahrain | 1970 | 73.3 | 6.0 | 79.3 | 14.4 |
| | 1975 | 67.4 | ... | ... | 8.5 |
| | 1980 | 69.2 | 7.7 | 76.9 | 6.5 |
| | 1984 | ... | ... (3) | 87.5 | 6.2 |
| | 1992 | ... | ... (3) | 82.3 | 3.6 |
| | 1993 | ... | ... (3) | 83.8 | ... |
| | 1994 | 62.6 (3) | 25.3 (3) | 87.9 | 6.4 |
| | 1995 | 62.8 (3) | 25.2 (3) | 88.0 | 6.3 |
| | 1996 | 62.7 (0) | 25.4 (3) | 88.1 | 6.2 |
| Bangladesh (2) | 1986 | ... | ... | 54.8 | 1.3 |
| | 1989 | ... | ... | 55.5 | 0.2 |
| | 1991 | ... | ... | 59.0 | 0.1 |
| Bhutan | 1970 | 48.4 | 5.9 | 54.2 | - |
| | 1992 | 53.6 | ... | 58.1 | 6.2 |
| | 1993 | 53.2 | 4.6 | 57.8 | 6.3 |
| Brunei Darussalam | 1970 | 45.4 | 6.1 | 51.6 | - |
| | 1975 | 49.5 | 9.6 | 59.1 | 8.3 |
| | 1980 | 43.5 | 6.3 | 49.8 | 5.1 |
| | 1984 | ... | ... | 62.4 | 2.5 |
| | 1990 | 33.7 | 18.5 | 52.2 | ... |
| (4) | 1991 | 38.8 | 16.5 | 55.3 | ... |
| (4) | 1992 | 37.7 | 15.4 | 53.1 | ... |
| (4) | 1993 | 28.7 | 16.4 | 45.1 | ... |
| China (7) | 1980 | ... | ... | 56.1 | 4.7 |
| | 1985 | ... | ... | 55.3 | 5.8 |
| | 1990 | ... | ... | 69.7 | ... |
| | 1991 | ... | ... | 69.7 | ... |
| Cyprus (8) | 1970 | 72.0 | 5.6 | 77.6 | - |
| | 1975 | 79.1 | 6.5 | 85.7 | 3.3 |
| | 1980 | 80.0 | 0.1 | 88.1 | 2.4 |
| | 1985 | 81.9 | 10.6 | 92.5 | 1.0 |
| | 1990 | 82.3 | 9.1 | 91.4 | 0.9 |
| | 1991 | 82.7 | 8.9 | 91.6 | 0.9 |
| | 1992 | 80.8 | 8.6 | 89.4 | 1.3 |
| | 1993 | 79.7 | 9.1 | 88.8 | 2.7 |
| | 1994 | 80.7 | 9.1 | 89.8 | 1.1 |
| | 1995 | 80.2 | 9.4 | 89.6 | 1.3 |
| Georgia | 1994 | ... | ... | 52.6 | - |
| Hong Kong | 1970 | 81.2 | 6.1 | 87.2 | - |
| | 1975 | 79.4 | 4.8 | 84.2 | 1.4 |
| | 1980 | 72.9 | 15.2 | 88.1 | 1.3 |
| | 1984 | 76.5 | 10.6 | 87.1 | 1.9 |
| India | 1970 | 67.7 | 2.3 | 70.0 | - |
| | 1975 | 65.5 | ... | ... | ... |
| | 1986 | 62.5 | 9.2 | 71.8 | 1.1 |
| Indonesia (2) | 1995 | ... | ... | 84.0 | ... |
| Iran, Islamic Republic of (1) | 1976 | 64.3 | 8.8 | 73.1 | 0.3 |
| | 1996 | ... | ... | 83.2 | 1.0 |
| Iraq | 1970 | 86.9 | 5.9 | 92.8 | - |
| | 1976 | ... | ... | 81.0 | 9.4 |
| Israel @ | 1993 | ... | ... | 73.1 | ... |
| | 1994 | ... | ... | 74.7 | ... |
| Japan @ | 1992 | ... | ... | 79.8 | ... |
| | 1993 | ... | ... | 77.6 | ... |
| | 1994 | ... | ... | 79.3 | ... |

II.20  Current public expenditure by purpose
Dépenses publiques ordinaires selon leur destination
Gastos públicos ordinarios segun su destino

| Country / Pays / País | Year / Année / Año | Emoluments / Émoluments / Emolumentos | | | Teaching materials |
|---|---|---|---|---|---|
| | | Teaching staff / Personnel enseignant / Personal docente (%) | Non-teaching staff / Personnel non-enseignant / Personal no docente (%) | Total / Total / Total (%) | Matériel pour l'enseignement / Material educativo (%) |
| Jordan | 1970 | 79.8 | 5.3 | 85.1 | - |
| | 1981 | 63.6 | 8.8 | 72.4 | 2.9 |
| | 1984 | ... | ... | 77.9 | 4.3 |
| | 1989 | ... | ... | 85.1 | 2.3 |
| | 1996 | 70.4 | 10.9 | 81.3 | 5.5 |
| | 1997 | ... | ... | 85.0 | 5.6 |
| Kazakstan | 1996 | ... | ... | 45.0 | |
| | 1997 | ... | ... | 46.4 | ... |
| Korea, Republic of @ | 1970 | 79.7 | 4.1 | 83.8 | |
| | 1980 | ... | | 81.0 | ... |
| | 1985 | 69.4 | 7.8 | 77.2 | ... |
| | 1990 | 61.2 | 10.2 | 71.4 | 2.5 |
| | 1991 | 58.9 | 9.5 | 68.4 | 1.1 |
| | 1992 | 59.7 | 8.7 | 68.4 | 1.0 |
| | 1993 | 59.0 | 8.7 | 67.7 | 0.9 |
| | 1994 | ... | ... | 73.5 | 0.8 |
| | 1995 | ... | ... | 77.0 | ... |
| Kuwait | 1970 | | | 76.2 | - |
| | 1975 | ... | ... | 63.6 | 3.9 |
| | 1980 | ... | ... | 78.7 | 5.1 |
| | 1985 | ... | ... | 73.3 | 1.5 |
| Kyrgyzstan | 1993 | ... | ... | 40.9 | 0.4 |
| | 1994 | ... | ... | 51.0 | ... |
| | 1995 | ... | ... | 54.1 | ... |
| | 1996 | ... | ... | 45.6 | ... |
| Lao People's Democratic Republic | 1970 | 73.9 | 5.6 | 79.5 | ... |
| | 1992 | 65.0 | 13.0 | 78.0 | 0.4 |
| | 1996 | 75.0 | 4.3 | 79.3 | 5.5 |
| | 1997 | 67.1 | 10.6 | 77.7 | 4.0 |
| Malaysia | 1980 | 57.5 (3) | 16.4 (3) | 73.8 | 5.8 |
| | 1985 | 65.0 | 3.1 | 68.2 | 3.0 |
| | 1991 | ... | ... | 77.5 | 1.2 |
| | 1992 | ... | ... | 81.5 | 1.0 |
| | 1993 | ... | ... | 62.6 | 6.0 |
| | 1994 | ... | ... | 62.1 | 11.3 |
| | 1996 | ... | ... | 72.7 | ... |
| | 1997 | ... | ... | 81.2 | ... |
| Myanmar (2) | 1994 | ... | ... | 56.8 | ... |
| Nepal | 1980 | 59.2 | 11.7 | 70.9 | 7.1 |
| Oman | 1975 | 67.2 | 15.8 | 83.0 | 2.6 |
| | 1980 | 60.3 | 16.1 | 76.4 | 6.4 |
| | 1985 | ... | ... | 72.2 | 6.2 |
| | 1990 | ... | ... | 83.9 | 2.5 |
| | 1991 | ... | ... | 84.2 | 3.0 |
| | 1992 | ... | ... | 84.7 | 2.4 |
| | 1993 | ... | ... | 84.8 | 2.2 |
| | 1995 | ... | ... | 83.6 | 1.3 |
| | 1996 | ... | ... | 84.4 | 0.8 |
| Philippines | 1980 | ... | ... | 78.4 | 0.3 |
| | 1990 | ... | ... | 96.1 | 0.6 |
| | 1995 | ... | ... | 86.4 | ... |
| | 1997 | ... | ... | 84.9 | ... |
| Qatar | 1970 | 44.6 | 24.7 | 69.2 | 10.4 |
| | 1975 | 51.8 | 21.5 | 73.4 | 12.1 |
| | 1980 | ... | ... | 68.7 | 3.7 |
| | 1985 | ... | ... | 70.7 | 2.5 |
| | 1990 | ... | ... | 80.9 | 1.6 |
| | 1991 | ... | ... | 79.9 | 2.0 |
| | 1992 | ... | ... | 80.3 | 1.2 |
| | 1993 | ... | ... | 79.7 | 1.2 |
| | 1994 | ... | ... | 79.5 | 1.2 |
| Saudi Arabia | 1970 | ... | ... | 68.7 | ... |
| | 1974 | ... | ... | 69.5 | 8.1 |
| | 1980 | ... | ... | 65.5 | ... |
| | 1981 | ... | ... | 71.3 | ... |
| | 1984 | ... | ... | 72.6 | ... |
| | 1985 | ... | ... | 76.5 | ... |
| | 1986 | ... | ... | 76.2 | ... |
| | 1993 | ... | ... | 82.0 | ... |

Current public expenditure by purpose II.20
Dépenses publiques ordinaires selon leur destination
Gastos públicos ordinarios segun su destino

| Country / Pays / País | Year / Année / Año | Emoluments / Émoluments / Emolumentos | | | | Total | Teaching materials |
| | | Teaching staff / Personnel enseignant / Personal docente (%) | | Non-teaching staff / Personnel non-enseignant / Personal no docente (%) | | Total / Total / Total (%) | Matériel pour l'enseignement / Material educativo (%) |
|---|---|---|---|---|---|---|---|
| Saudi Arabia (cont) | 1994 | ... | | ... | | 84.2 | ... |
| | 1995 | ... | | ... | | 84.6 | ... |
| Sri Lanka | 1970 | 85.0 | | 2.9 | | 88.0 | ... |
| | 1975 | 71.7 | | 4.5 | | 76.2 | 1.6 |
| Syrian Arab Republic (1) | 1971 | ... | | ... | | 80.6 | ... |
| | 1975 | 77.0 | | 4.8 | | 81.8 | 5.9 |
| | 1980 | 85.9 | | 4.3 | | 90.2 | 2.0 |
| | 1985 | ... | | ... | | 87.3 | 2.9 |
| | 1989 | ... | | ... | | 91.1 | 2.2 |
| | 1992 | ... | | ... | | 89.0 | 3.5 |
| | 1994 | ... | | ... | | 91.5 | 3.5 |
| | 1995 | ... | | ... | | 89.8 | 4.0 |
| | 1996 | ... | | ... | | 90.3 | 4.0 |
| | 1997 | ... | | ... | | 89.3 | 4.2 |
| Tajikistan | 1993 | ... | | ... | | 61.1 | 0.8 |
| | 1995 | ... | | ... | | 63.4 | 0.6 |
| | 1996 | ... | | ... | | 60.6 | 0.7 |
| Thailand | 1970 | 65.4 | | 11.9 | | 77.4 | ... |
| | 1975 | 77.2 | | 3.8 | | 81.0 | 3.7 |
| | 1980 | 80.3 | | 4.5 | | 84.8 | 4.6 |
| | 1985 | 75.0 | | 8.6 | | 83.6 | 4.2 |
| | 1990 | 62.0 | | 18.7 | | 80.7 | 4.0 |
| | 1991 | 64.3 | | 9.6 | | 73.9 | 4.1 |
| | 1993 | 61.3 | | 10.8 | | 72.1 | 3.8 |
| | 1994 | 61.6 | | 12.1 | | 73.7 | 4.5 |
| (4) | 1995 | 68.2 | | 9.6 | | 77.8 | 3.6 |
| Turkey @ | 1971 | 74.2 | | 10.0 | | 84.2 | ... |
| | 1980 | ... | | ... | | 89.7 | 0.5 |
| | 1985 | ... | | ... | | 90.7 | 0.5 |
| | 1993 | ... | | ... | | 94.8 | ... |
| | 1994 | ... | | ... | | 86.7 | ... |
| | 1995 | ... | | ... | | 85.9 | ... |
| United Arab Emirates | 1975 | ... | | ... | | 66.4 | 3.7 |
| | 1981 | ... | | ... | | 51.9 | 11.8 |
| | 1985 | ... | | ... | | 61.3 | 5.7 |
| | 1990 | ... | | ... | | 69.7 | 1.1 |
| | 1991 | ... | | ... | | 70.5 | 0.8 |
| | 1992 | ... | | ... | | 71.7 | 0.6 |
| | 1993 | ... | | ... | | 73.6 | 0.9 |
| | 1994 | ... | | ... | | 87.0 | ... |
| | 1995 | ... | | ... | | 87.1 | ... |
| | 1996 | ... | | ... | | 74.0 | 0.9 |
| Uzbekistan | 1993 | ... | | ... | | 58.4 | 0.9 |
| Viet Nam | 1994 | 62.6 | | 6.2 | | 68.8 | 9.7 |
| | 1995 | 63.9 | | 6.3 | | 70.2 | 9.7 |
| | 1996 | 65.3 | | 6.3 | | 71.6 | 9.0 |
| | 1997 | 66.0 | | 6.3 | | 72.3 | 8.3 |
| Yemen | 1994 | ... | | ... | | 83.6 | 7.3 |
| | 1995 | ... | | ... | | 83.2 | 8.2 |
| | 1996 | ... | | ... | | 79.0 | 6.1 |
| | 1997 | ... | | ... | | 78.9 | 6.8 |
| **Europe** | | | | | | | |
| Albania | 1994 | ... | | ... | | 75.2 | 5.3 |
| Austria @ | 1970 | 51.3 (3) | | 34.9 (3) | | 86.2 | ... |
| | 1975 | 48.1 (3) | | 35.0 (3) | | 83.1 | ... |
| | 1980 | 53.1 (3) | | 32.1 (3) | | 85.2 | ... |
| | 1985 | 49.9 | | 14.5 | | 64.4 | 1.3 |
| | 1990 | 50.5 | | 15.0 | | 65.5 | 1.1 |
| | 1991 | 50.6 | | 15.2 | | 65.8 | 1.0 |
| | 1992 | 51.9 | | 15.8 | | 67.6 | 1.1 |
| | 1993 | ... | | ... | | 69.0 | ... |
| | 1994 | ... | | ... | | 67.7 | ... |
| | 1995 | ... | | ... | | 64.9 | ... |
| | 1996 | 46.8 | | 8.7 | | 55.5 | ... |
| Belarus | 1970 | ... | | ... | | 61.4 | ... |
| | 1996 | ... | | ... | | 57.8 | 1.6 |

II.20  Current public expenditure by purpose
Dépenses publiques ordinaires selon leur destination
Gastos públicos ordinarios segun su destino

| Country<br><br>Pays<br><br>País | | Year<br><br>Année<br><br>Año | Emoluments / Émoluments / Emolumentos | | | Teaching<br>materials<br><br>Matériel<br>pour<br>l'enseignement<br><br>Material<br>educativo<br>(%) |
|---|---|---|---|---|---|---|
| | | | Teaching<br>staff<br><br>Personnel<br>enseignant<br><br>Personal<br>docente<br>(%) | Non-teaching<br>staff<br><br>Personnel<br>non-enseignant<br><br>Personal<br>no docente<br>(%) | Total<br><br>Total<br><br>Total<br>(%) | |
| Belgium @ | (2) | 1975 | 72.3 | 2.8 | 75.2 | ... |
| | (2) | 1980 | 73.0 | 3.0 | 76.1 | 0.1 |
| | (2) | 1985 | 79.6 | 1.0 | 80.6 | 0.0 |
| | (2) | 1990 | 80.8 | 1.8 | 82.6 | ... |
| | (2) | 1991 | 83.0 | 3.0 | 86.0 | ... |
| | (2) | 1992 | 78.4 | 3.3 | 81.7 | ... |
| | | 1993 | 76.2 | 3.2 | 79.4 | ... |
| | | 1994 | 76.9 | 3.8 | 80.7 | ... |
| | (6) (9) | 1995 | 80.4 | 2.1 | 82.5 | ... |
| | (6) (9) | 1996 | 78.0 | 1.9 | 79.9 | ... |
| Bulgaria | | 1970 | ... | ... | 54.2 | ... |
| | | 1975 | ... | ... | 47.6 | ... |
| | | 1980 | ... | ... | 44.4 | ... |
| | | 1985 | ... | ... | 37.4 | ... |
| | | 1990 | ... | ... | 59.9 | ... |
| | | 1991 | ... | ... | 55.1 | ... |
| | | 1992 | ... | ... | 66.1 | ... |
| | | 1993 | ... | ... | 71.1 | ... |
| | | 1994 | ... | ... | 67.8 | ... |
| | | 1995 | ... | ... | 70.4 | ... |
| | | 1996 | ... | ... | 66.3 | ... |
| Czech Republic @ | | 1992 | ... | ... | 41.1 | 22.9 |
| | | 1993 | ... | ... | 32.2 | 28.1 |
| | (5) | 1994 | 40.0 | 14.4 | 54.4 | ... |
| | (5) | 1995 | 37.5 | 16.4 | 53.9 | ... |
| | | 1996 | 39.8 | 16.0 | 55.8 | ... |
| Denmark @ | | 1980 | 49.3 | 15.6 | 65.0 | 4.8 |
| | | 1991 | ... | ... | 57.8 | ... |
| | | 1993 | 52.2 | 28.9 | 81.1 | ... |
| | | 1994 | 49.3 | 27.7 | 77.0 | ... |
| | | 1995 | 50.2 | 28.3 | 78.5 | ... |
| | | 1996 | 50.1 | 29.1 | 79.2 | ... |
| Estonia | | 1992 | ... | ... | 46.0 | 1.3 |
| | | 1993 | ... | ... | 47.3 | 2.8 |
| | | 1994 | ... | ... | 50.1 | 3.2 |
| | | 1995 | ... | ... | 69.4 | 4.1 |
| | | 1996 | ... | ... | 65.9 | 3.6 |
| Federal Republic of Yugoslavia | | 1991 | ... | ... | 65.0 | 15.1 |
| | | 1992 | ... | ... | 60.2 | 11.8 |
| | | 1994 | ... | ... | 41.2 | 15.4 |
| | | 1995 | ... | ... | 40.6 | 16.2 |
| | | 1996 | ... | ... | 56.2 | 11.8 |
| Finland @ | | 1970 | 57.2 | 1.1 | 58.3 | ... |
| | | 1975 | 61.9 | 2.2 | 64.1 | 3.9 |
| | | 1980 | 50.5 | 6.3 | 56.8 | 5.7 |
| | | 1985 | 47.6 | 17.2 | 64.8 | 6.9 |
| | | 1990 | 47.7 | 16.5 | 64.2 | 6.9 |
| | | 1991 | 48.2 | 16.9 | 65.1 | 6.4 |
| | | 1992 | 47.9 | 16.5 | 64.4 | 6.3 |
| | | 1993 | 52.0 | 16.6 | 68.6 | ... |
| | | 1994 | 53.2 | 16.6 | 69.8 | ... |
| | | 1995 | 52.2 | 16.4 | 68.6 | ... |
| | | 1996 | 52.3 | 16.3 | 68.6 | ... |
| France @ | | 1975 | 68.5 | 3.3 | 71.8 | 0.1 |
| | | 1980 | 68.1 | 3.5 | 71.6 | 0.1 |
| | | 1985 | ... | ... | 71.7 | 2.0 |
| | | 1990 | ... | ... | 73.2 | 0.5 |
| | | 1991 | ... | ... | 72.5 | 0.5 |
| | | 1992 | ... | ... | 72.3 | 0.5 |
| | | 1993 | ... | ... | 76.7 | ... |
| | | 1994 | ... | ... | 77.1 | ... |
| | | 1995 | ... | ... | 77.3 | ... |
| | | 1996 | ... | ... | 77.2 | ... |
| Germany @ | (5) | 1993 | ... | ... | 82.2 | ... |
| | (5) | 1994 | ... | ... | 83.1 | ... |
| | (5) | 1995 | ... | ... | 84.1 | ... |
| | | 1996 | ... | ... | 83.9 | ... |
| Gibraltar | | 1970 | 49.7 | 3.6 | 53.3 | ... |
| | | 1975 | 52.4 | 4.8 | 57.2 | 8.1 |
| | | 1980 | 56.4 | 5.6 | 62.0 | 4.2 |
| | | 1984 | 63.6 | 4.7 | 68.3 | 3.3 |

Current public expenditure by purpose II.20
Dépenses publiques ordinaires selon leur destination
Gastos públicos ordinarios segun su destino

| Country / Pays / País | Year / Année / Año | Emoluments / Émoluments / Emolumentos | | | Teaching materials |
| | | Teaching staff / Personnel enseignant / Personal docente (%) | Non-teaching staff / Personnel non-enseignant / Personal no docente (%) | Total / Total / Total (%) | Matériel pour l'enseignement / Material educativo (%) |
|---|---|---|---|---|---|
| Greece @ | 1970 | 79.6 | 4.4 | 84.0 | ... |
| | 1975 | 74.2 | 5.6 | 79.8 | ... |
| | 1981 | 84.8 | 5.7 | 90.6 | 3.4 |
| | 1985 | 82.9 | 7.5 | 90.4 | ... |
| | 1990 | 85.2 | 6.1 | 91.3 | ... |
| | 1991 | 84.4 | 6.3 | 90.7 | ... |
| (5) | 1993 | ... | ... | 88.3 | ... |
| (5) | 1994 | ... | ... | 88.5 | ... |
| (5) | 1995 | ... | ... | 91.2 | ... |
| (5) | 1996 | ... | ... | 87.1 | ... |
| Hungary @ | 1970 | 42.8 | 0.4 | 43.2 | ... |
| | 1975 | 44.4 | 0.2 | 44.6 | ... |
| | 1980 | 45.2 | 0.3 | 45.5 | ... |
| | 1985 | ... | ... | 52.1 | ... |
| | 1990 | ... | ... | 45.2 | ... |
| | 1991 | ... | ... | 47.0 | ... |
| | 1992 | ... | ... | 42.9 | ... |
| | 1993 | ... | ... | 44.4 | ... |
| | 1994 | ... | ... | 45.7 | ... |
| (5) | 1995 | ... | ... | 73.0 | ... |
| (5) | 1996 | ... | ... | 70.8 | ... |
| Iceland @ | 1971 | ... | ... | 84.0 | ... |
| | 1990 | 53.5 | 16.6 | 70.1 | 1.5 |
| (5) | 1993 | ... | ... | 72.3 | ... |
| | 1994 | ... | ... | 73.5 | ... |
| | 1995 | ... | ... | 72.9 | ... |
| | 1996 | ... | ... | 73.8 | ... |
| Ireland @ | 1970 | 62.1 | 3.5 | 65.7 | ... |
| | 1975 | 70.4 | 3.8 | 74.2 | 2.3 |
| | 1980 | 67.6 | 4.1 | 71.7 | 0.4 |
| | 1985 | 72.9 | 3.1 | 76.0 | 0.4 |
| | 1990 | 74.9 | 8.4 | 83.3 | 0.3 |
| | 1991 | 74.3 | 8.1 | 82.4 | 0.3 |
| | 1992 | 75.3 | 8.6 | 83.9 | 0.3 |
| (5) | 1993 | 76.9 | 10.8 | 87.7 | ... |
| (5) | 1994 | 72.9 | 9.7 | 82.6 | ... |
| (5) | 1995 | 74.3 | 11.5 | 85.8 | ... |
| (5) | 1996 | 72.1 | 11.1 | 83.2 | ... |
| Italy @ | 1970 | 62.2 | 16.5 | 78.7 | ... |
| | 1975 | ... | ... | 73.4 | ... |
| | 1979 | 68.2 | 16.9 | 85.1 | ... |
| | 1985 | ... | ... | 79.0 | ... |
| (5) | 1993 | 64.4 | 18.4 | 82.8 | ... |
| (5) | 1994 | 65.7 | 18.6 | 84.3 | ... |
| (5) | 1995 | 64.8 | 20.2 | 85.0 | ... |
| (5) | 1996 | 68.0 | 17.5 | 85.5 | ... |
| Latvia | 1996 | 40.5 | 11.0 | 51.5 | 1.2 |
| Lithuania | 1993 | ... | ... | 55.4 | 1.4 |
| | 1994 | ... | ... | 65.3 | 1.3 |
| | 1995 | ... | ... | 68.1 | 1.6 |
| | 1996 | ... | ... | 69.0 | 1.4 |
| Luxembourg @ | 1975 | 80.8 | ... | ... | - |
| | 1980 | ... | ... | 87.8 | 1.0 |
| | 1986 | 73.8 | 9.7 | 83.5 | 1.6 |
| | 1989 | 72.9 | 9.7 | 82.6 | 1.2 |
| | 1995 | 92.9 | 3.6 | 96.5 | ... |
| | 1996 | ... | ... | 96.0 | ... |
| Malta | 1970 | 71.1 | 6.6 | 77.7 | - |
| | 1975 | 68.9 | 4.9 | 73.8 | 0.2 |
| | 1980 | 53.0 | 28.0 | 81.0 | 0.2 |
| | 1985 | 52.2 | 25.0 | 77.2 | 0.1 |
| | 1990 | 42.4 | 21.3 | 63.7 | 0.0 |
| | 1991 | 41.9 | 14.9 | 56.8 | 0.1 |
| | 1992 | 38.7 | 22.3 | 61.0 | 0.0 |
| Moldova | 1995 | ... | ... | 71.1 | ... |
| Monaco | 1980 | 81.3 | 3.7 | 85.1 | - |
| | 1992 | ... | ... | 83.8 | 2.7 |
| | 1995 | ... | ... | 68.2 | 1.8 |
| | 1996 | ... | ... | 68.0 | 1.8 |
| | 1997 | ... | ... | 91.0 | 2.3 |

**Current public expenditure by purpose**
Dépenses publiques ordinaires selon leur destination
Gastos públicos ordinarios segun su destino

| Country / Pays / País | | Year / Année / Año | Emoluments / Émoluments / Emolumentos | | | Teaching materials / Matériel pour l'enseignement / Material educativo |
|---|---|---|---|---|---|---|
| | | | Teaching staff / Personnel enseignant / Personal docente (%) | Non-teaching staff / Personnel non-enseignant / Personal no docente (%) | Total / Total / Total (%) | (%) |
| Netherlands @ | | 1975 | 75.5 | 2.8 | 78.3 | 0.7 |
| | | 1980 | 73.5 | 3.2 | 76.7 | 1.1 |
| | | 1985 | 71.0 | 2.1 | 73.1 | 1.9 |
| | | 1990 | 64.3 | 2.2 | 66.5 | 1.9 |
| | | <u>1991</u> | 64.7 | 2.3 | 66.9 | 2.0 |
| | | 1993 | ... | ... | 77.1 | ... |
| | | 1994 | ... | ... | 77.6 | ... |
| | | 1995 | ... | ... | 77.7 | ... |
| | | 1996 | ... | ... | 77.7 | ... |
| Norway @ | | 1970 | ... | ... | 74.8 | |
| | | 1975 | ... | ... | 71.3 | |
| | | 1980 | ... | ... | 64.3 | 6.0 |
| | | 1985 | ... | ... | 64.1 | 6.3 |
| | | 1990 | ... | ... | 61.0 | 8.3 |
| | | 1991 | ... | ... | 59.2 | 8.6 |
| | | <u>1992</u> | ... | ... | 58.7 | 8.6 |
| | (5) | 1993 | ... | ... | 77.6 | ... |
| | (5) | 1994 | ... | ... | 78.6 | ... |
| | (5) | 1995 | ... | ... | 77.8 | ... |
| | (5) | 1996 | ... | ... | 77.7 | ... |
| Portugal @ | | 1975 | 78.8 | 5.0 | 83.8 | 2.7 |
| | | 1980 | ... | ... | 82.8 | 0.8 |
| | | 1985 | ... | ... | 82.7 | 0.1 |
| | (2) | 1990 | 86.1 | 2.5 | 88.6 | ... |
| | (2) | 1991 | 85.4 | 3.0 | 88.3 | ... |
| | | <u>1992</u> | ... | ... | 85.7 | ... |
| | | 1993 | ... | ... | 83.3 | ... |
| | (5) | 1994 | ... | ... | 92.5 | ... |
| | | 1995 | ... | ... | 89.3 | ... |
| | | 1996 | ... | ... | 88.7 | ... |
| Romania | | 1990 | ... | ... | 79.3 | 2.7 |
| | | 1992 | ... | ... | 56.6 | 1.4 |
| | | 1993 | ... | ... | 80.9 | 1.2 |
| | | 1996 | ... | ... | 66.8 | 0.9 |
| San Marino | | 1970 | 79.5 | ... | ... | ... |
| | | 1975 | 79.6 | ... | ... | ... |
| | | 1980 | 84.7 | ... | ... | 2.8 |
| | | 1984 | 82.5 | ... | ... | 2.2 |
| Slovakia | | 1992 | ... | ... | 55.3 | 2.9 |
| | | 1993 | ... | ... | 59.7 | 0.6 |
| | | 1994 | ... | ... | 57.9 | 0.7 |
| | | 1995 | ... | ... | 52.1 | 0.8 |
| | | 1996 | 37.9 | 14.8 | 52.7 | 1.0 |
| Slovenia | | 1991 | 54.9 | 11.1 | 66.0 | 2.6 |
| | | 1992 | 61.9 | 11.3 | 73.2 | 1.6 |
| | | 1993 | 56.2 | 14.1 | 70.3 | 1.6 |
| | | 1994 | 58.0 | 12.6 | 70.6 | 7.5 |
| | | 1995 | 62.2 | 10.0 | 72.2 | 5.7 |
| Spain @ | | 1970 | 69.3 | 4.0 | 73.3 | 6.2 |
| | | 1976 | 83.8 | 3.8 | 87.6 | 4.5 |
| | | 1979 | 88.1 | 2.1 | 90.2 | ... |
| | | 1990 | ... | ... | 65.6 | ... |
| | | 1991 | ... | ... | 66.6 | ... |
| | | <u>1992</u> | ... | ... | 69.0 | ... |
| | | 1993 | ... | ... | 80.4 | ... |
| | | 1994 | ... | ... | 81.7 | ... |
| | | 1995 | ... | ... | 82.1 | ... |
| | | 1996 | ... | ... | 83.8 | ... |
| Sweden @ | | 1970 | 45.2 | 3.6 | 48.7 | ... |
| | | 1975 | 52.4 | 3.5 | 55.9 | ... |
| | | 1980 | ... | ... | 49.2 | 2.4 |
| | | 1985 | ... | ... | 44.9 | 2.7 |
| | | 1990 | ... | ... | 47.4 | ... |
| | | 1991 | ... | ... | 39.1 | ... |
| | | <u>1992</u> | ... | ... | 38.7 | 2.8 |
| | | 1994 | ... | ... | 62.8 | ... |
| | | 1995 | ... | ... | 57.1 | ... |
| | | 1996 | ... | ... | 57.9 | ... |
| Switzerland @ | | 1975 | 61.5 | 13.0 | 74.4 | ... |
| | | 1980 | 61.0 | 13.3 | 74.3 | 3.5 |
| | | 1985 | 61.8 | 13.2 | 75.0 | 3.1 |

Current public expenditure by purpose II.20
Dépenses publiques ordinaires selon leur destination
Gastos públicos ordinarios segun su destino

| Country / Pays / País | Year / Année / Año | Emoluments / Émoluments / Emolumentos | | | Teaching materials / Matériel pour l'enseignement / Material educativo |
| | | Teaching staff / Personnel enseignant / Personal docente (%) | Non-teaching staff / Personnel non-enseignant / Personal no docente (%) | Total / Total / Total (%) | (%) |
|---|---|---|---|---|---|
| Switzerland @ (cont) | 1990 | 61.2 | 13.8 | 74.9 | 3.2 |
| | 1991 | 60.5 | 14.2 | 74.7 | 3.0 |
| (5) | 1993 | ... | ... | 84.3 | ... |
| (5) | 1994 | ... | ... | 84.2 | ... |
| (5) | 1995 | 68.6 | 15.8 | 84.4 | ... |
| (5) | 1996 | 67.1 | 17.0 | 84.1 | ... |
| The Former Yugoslav Rep. of Macedonia | 1992 | ... | ... | 82.7 | |
| | 1993 | ... | ... | 87.2 | 0.0 |
| | 1994 | ... | ... | 82.9 | 0.1 |
| | 1995 | ... | ... | 82.5 | 0.1 |
| | 1996 | ... | ... | 83.6 | 0.2 |
| United Kingdom @ | 1980 | 52.1 | ... | ... | 3.6 |
| | 1985 | 51.6 | 17.7 | 69.3 | 3.7 |
| | 1990 | 51.4 | 16.7 | 68.1 | 5.3 |
| | 1991 | 49.9 | 15.3 | 65.2 | 4.8 |
| (6) | 1992 | 52.0 | 15.5 | 67.5 | ... |
| (6) | 1993 | 48.6 | 15.0 | 63.6 | ... |
| (6) | 1994 | 49.2 | 15.9 | 65.1 | ... |
| (6) | 1995 | 44.9 | 16.5 | 61.4 | ... |
| **Oceania** | | | | | |
| American Samoa | 1981 | ... | ... | 58.5 | 4.7 |
| | 1986 | ... | ... | 63.9 | 6.4 |
| Australia @ | 1986 | ... | ... | (3) 81.6 | ... |
| | 1990 | ... | ... | (3) 77.0 | ... |
| | 1991 | ... | ... | (3) 74.1 | ... |
| (10) | 1992 | ... | ... | 70.9 | ... |
| (10) | 1993 | ... | ... | 76.3 | ... |
| (10) | 1994 | 52.8 | 23.0 | 75.8 | ... |
| (10) | 1995 | 53.1 | 21.8 | 74.9 | ... |
| Cook Islands | 1970 | ... | ... | (3) 83.8 | ... |
| | 1981 | 72.3 (3) | 17.5 (3) | 89.8 | 10.2 |
| | 1984 | 74.5 (3) | 12.3 (3) | 86.8 | 6.9 |
| | 1991 | 61.9 | 6.2 | 68.1 | 2.3 |
| Fiji | 1974 | 58.4 | 8.4 | 66.8 | 10.6 |
| | 1979 | 76.7 | 7.9 | 84.6 | 1.1 |
| | 1989 | ... | ... | 82.2 | 3.9 |
| (2) | 1992 | ... | ... | 73.5 | |
| French Polynesia | 1970 | 69.3 | ... | ... | - |
| | 1975 | 71.4 | 1.6 | 73.0 | 3.1 |
| | 1984 | 80.2 | 7.5 | 87.7 | 5.2 |
| (2) | 1990 | 83.2 | 8.4 | 91.6 | 0.8 |
| (2) | 1991 | 83.4 | 8.6 | 92.0 | 0.7 |
| (2) | 1993 | 85.9 | 8.4 | 94.4 | - |
| Kiribati | 1970 | 46.1 | 10.7 | 56.7 | ... |
| | 1980 | 45.2 | 9.1 | 54.2 | 5.1 |
| | 1985 | 58.3 | 15.6 | 73.9 | 7.1 |
| | 1990 | ... | ... | 60.6 | 5.6 |
| | 1991 | ... | ... | 61.6 | 3.9 |
| | 1992 | ... | ... | 57.7 | - |
| | 1994 | ... | ... | 55.1 | 5.0 |
| New Caledonia | 1970 | 88.1 | 1.6 | 89.7 | - |
| | 1981 | 85.8 | ... | ... | 6.9 |
| | 1984 | 88.1 | ... | ... | 7.3 |
| (2) | 1990 | 85.9 | 5.0 | 90.9 | 1.2 |
| (2) | 1991 | 82.3 | 9.6 | 91.9 | 1.1 |
| (2) | 1993 | 79.7 | 8.2 | 87.9 | 0.8 |
| New Zealand @ | 1980 | ... | ... | (3) 84.1 | 5.6 |
| | 1985 | ... | ... | 67.2 | 5.8 |
| | 1990 | 40.4 | 1.2 | 41.6 | ... |
| | 1991 | 35.9 | 0.9 | 36.8 | ... |
| | 1992 | 34.4 | 0.8 | 35.2 | ... |
| Niue | 1970 | 65.2 | ... | ... | - |
| | 1975 | ... | ... | 87.2 | 9.7 |
| | 1980 | 74.2 (3) | 20.1 (3) | 94.3 | 2.8 |
| | 1986 | ... | ... | 73.0 | 3.1 |
| Norfolk Island | 1970 | 69.9 | 4.9 | 74.8 | ... |
| | 1975 | 74.6 | 2.9 | 77.5 | 4.8 |
| | 1980 | 76.5 | 3.3 | 79.8 | 4.5 |

II.20    Current public expenditure by purpose
Dépenses publiques ordinaires selon leur destination
Gastos públicos ordinarios segun su destino

| Country / Pays / País | Year / Année / Año | Emoluments / Émoluments / Emolumentos | | | Teaching materials |
|---|---|---|---|---|---|
| | | Teaching staff / Personnel enseignant / Personal docente (%) | Non-teaching staff / Personnel non-enseignant / Personal no docente (%) | Total / Total / Total (%) | Matériel pour l'enseignement / Material educativo (%) |
| Pacific Islands (Palau) | 1970 | 52.6 | 7.9 | 60.5 | - |
| | 1976 | 55.5 | 11.5 | 66.9 | 6.5 |
| | 1981 | 59.3 (3) | 22.7 (3) | 82.0 | 3.3 |
| Papua New Guinea | 1976 | 81.6 | 4.6 | 86.2 | 5.9 |
| Samoa | 1970 | 83.2 | 10.3 | 93.5 | ... |
| | 1975 | ... | ... | 92.4 | ... |
| | 1990 | 72.3 | 12.0 | 84.3 | 0.7 |
| Solomon Islands | 1971 | 45.2 | 10.6 | 55.8 | 17.7 |
| | 1979 | 62.9 | 5.7 | 68.6 | 8.8 |
| | 1991 | ... | ... | 72.3 | 3.9 |
| Tonga | 1971 | 64.9 | 3.3 | 68.2 | 3.5 |
| | 1975 | 68.4 (3) | 12.8 (3) | 81.2 | 1.6 |
| | 1980 | 76.6 | 2.4 | 79.0 | 3.5 |
| | 1985 | 57.8 | 9.8 | 67.6 | 2.4 |
| | 1992 | ... | ... | 70.7 | 0.4 |
| Tuvalu | 1990 | 58.1 | 2.8 | 60.9 | 5.2 |
| Vanuatu, Republic of | 1990 | ... | ... | 89.8 | - |
| | 1991 | ... | ... | 90.4 | - |
| | 1994 | 68.3 | 8.4 | 76.7 | |

**General note**

For general explanations and definitions, please refer to the beginning of this chapter.

**Note générale**

Pour les explications et définitions générales, prière de se référer au début de ce chapitre.

**Nota general**

Para las explicaciones y definiciones generales, referirse al comienzo de este capítulo.

Notes

@ For countries participating in the UNESCO/OECD/Eurostat survey, data refer to expenditure in (a) public institutions, (b) government dependent and (c) private institutions from public and private sources. This is indicated by a line that separates the relevant years from the previous ones

(1) Not including expenditure on tertiary education.

(2) Ministry of Education only.

(3) Including administration other than personnel.

(4) Not including expenditure on universities.

(5) Data refer to expenditure in public institutions only.

(6) Not including expenditure in independent private institutions.

(7) Not including expenditure on mid-level specialised colleges and technical schools.

(8) Expenditure of the Office of Greek Education only.

(9) Flemish Community only.

(10) Not including pre-primary education.

Notes

@ Pour les pays qui participent à l'enquête de l'UNESCO/OCDE/Eurostat, les données se réfèrent aux dépenses des établissements d'enseignement (a) publics, (b) privés subventionnés et (c) privés non subventionnés de sources publiques et privées. Ceci est indiqué par une ligne qui sépare les années concernées des années antérieures.

(1) Non compris les dépenses de l'enseignement supérieur.

(2) Ministère de l'Education seulement.

(3) Y compris les dépenses d'administration autres que celles du personnel.

(4) Non compris les dépenses relatives aux universités.

(5) Les données se réfèrent aux dépenses des établissements publiques seulement.

(6) Non compris les dépenses des établissements privées non subventionnées.

(7) Non compris les dépenses relatives aux collèges spécialisés du moyen degré et les écoles techniques.

(8) Les dépenses du bureau grec de l'éducation seulement.

(9) Communauté flamande seulement.

(10) Non compris l'enseignement préprimaire.

Notas

@ Para los países que participan en la encuesta de la UNESCO/OCDE/Eurostat, los datos se refieren a los gastos de establecimientos de educacíon (a) públicos, (b) privados subvencionados por el gobierno y (c) privados autónomos de fuentes públicas y privadas. Esto está indicado por una línea que separa los años correspondientes de los años anteriores.

(1) No incluye los gastos de la enseñanza superior.

(2) Ministerio de Educación solamente.

(3) Incluyen los gastos de administración otros que los del personal.

(4) No incluyen los gastos relativos a las universidades.

(5) Los datos se refieren a los gastos de los establecimientos públicos solamente.

(6) No incluyen los gastos de los establecimientos privados autónomos.

(7) No incluyen los gastos relativos a los colegios especializados de medio grado y las escuelas técnicas.

(8) Los gastos del servicio griego de educación solamente.

(9) Comunidad flamenca solamente.

(10) No incluye la enseñanza preprimaria.

Science and technology III
Science et technologie
Ciencia y tecnología

# III. Science and technology

# Science et technologie

# Ciencia y tecnología

This chapter presents three tables showing indicators and statistics by country on research and experimental development (R&D) that have been gathered through UNESCO statistical questionnaires, supplemented by data taken from official reports and publications. Certain recent data for member countries of the OECD (Organisation for Economic Co-operation and Development) have been drawn from the OECD database and are footnoted accordingly.

The definitions and classifications utilized in these tables are based on the Recommendation concerning the International Standardization of Statistics on Science and Technology (UNESCO, 1978) and the Frascati Manual (OECD, 1993).

*Research and experimental development (R&D)* is defined as any creative work undertaken on a systematic basis in order to increase the stock of knowledge, including knowledge of man, culture and society, and the use of this stock of knowledge to devise new applications.

---

Ce chapitre présente trois tableaux d'indicateurs et des statistiques par pays sur la recherche scientifique et le développement expérimental (R-D) qui ont été établis à partir des questionnaires statistiques de l'UNESCO et complétés par les données recueillies à l'aide de rapports officiels et de publications. Certaines données plus récentes concernant les pays membres de l'OCDE (Organisation de Coopération et de Développement Economiques) ont été extraites de la base de données de l'OCDE, ce qui est précisé dans ce cas par une note au bas du tableau.

Les définitions et classifications utilisées dans ces tableaux sont basées sur la Recommandation concernant la normalisation internationale des statistiques relatives à la science et à la technologie (UNESCO, 1978) et sur le Manuel de Frascati (OCDE, 1993).

La *recherche et le développement expérimental (R-D)* englobe tous les travaux de création entrepris de façon systématique en vue d'accroître la somme des connaissances, y compris la connaissance de l'homme, de la culture et de la société, ainsi que l'utilisation de cette somme de connaissances pour de nouvelles applications.

---

En este capítulo se presentan tres cuadros de indicadores y estadísticas por países sobre la investigación y desarrollo experimental (I y D) que han sido realizados a partir de los cuestionarios estadísticos de la UNESCO, completados por datos derivados de informes oficiales y publicaciones. Algunos datos recientes sobre los miembros de la OCDE (Organización para la Cooperación y Desarrollo Económicos) provienen de la base de datos de la OCDE, y se precisa en ese caso en las notas al final de cada cuadro.

Las definiciones y clasificaciones empleadas en estos cuadros han sido tomadas de la Recomendación sobre la normalización internacional de las estadísticas relativas a la ciencia y la tecnología (UNESCO, 1978) y del Manual de Frascati (OCDE, 1993).

Por *investigación y desarrollo experimental (I y D)* se entiende cualquier trabajo creativo llevado a cabo de forma sistemática para incrementar el volumen de conocimientos, incluido el conocimiento del hombre, la cultura y la sociedad, y el uso de esos conocimientos para derivar nuevas aplicaciones.

---

**III** Country tables on science and technology
Tableaux sur le science et technologie par pays
Cuadros sobre la ciencia y tecnología por países

# Country tables on science and technology

# Tableaux sur la science et la technologie par pays

# Cuadros sobre ciencia y tecnología por países

Country tables on science and technology III
Tableaux sur le science et technologie par pays
Cuadros sobre la ciencia y tecnología por países

# Notes and explanations on country tables

# Notes et explications sur les tableaux par pays

# Notas y explicaciones de los cuadros por países

### Table III.1  Selected R&D indicators
This table presents selected R&D indicators including the number of researchers and R&D technicians per million inhabitants, number of R&D technicians per researcher, R&D expenditure as percentage of GNP, and R&D expenditure per capita and per researcher in national currency. For the indication of national currencies please refer to Table III.3.
*Researchers* are professionals engaged in the conception or creation of new knowledge, products, processes, methods and systems, and in the planning and management of R&D projects.  Post-graduate students engaged in R&D are considered as researchers.
*Technicians (and equivalent staff)* comprise persons whose main tasks require technical knowledge and experience in one or more fields of engineering, physical and life sciences, or social sciences and humanities.  They participate in R&D by performing scientific and technical tasks involving the application of concepts and operational methods, normally under the supervision of researchers.  As distinguished from *technicians* participating in R&D under the supervision of researchers in engineering, physical and life sciences, *equivalent staff* perform the corresponding R&D tasks in the social sciences and humanities.
*Other supporting staff* includes skilled and unskilled craftsmen, secretarial and clerical staff participating in or directly associated with R&D projects.  Included in this category are all managers and administrators dealing mainly with financial and personnel matters and general administration, insofar as their activities are a direct service to R&D.

### Table III.2  Personnel engaged in R&D by category of personnel
This table gives the total number of researchers, R&D technicians, and other supporting staff as defined above. Data on female R&D personnel by category are also shown when available.

### Table III.3  Percentage distribution of gross domestic expenditure on R&D by source of funds
*Gross domestic expenditure on R&D (GERD)* is total intramural expenditure on R&D performed on the national territory during a given period.  It includes R&D performed within a country and funded from abroad but excludes payments made abroad for R&D.
The sources of funds for GERD are classified according to the following five categories:
*Business enterprise funds* include funds allocated to R&D by all firms, organizations and institutions whose primary activity is the market production of goods and services (other than the higher education sector) for sale to the general public at an economically significant price, and those private non-profit institutes mainly serving these firms, organizations and institutions.
*Government funds* refer to funds allocated to R&D by the central (federal), state or local government authorities. These includes all departments, offices and other bodies which furnish but normally do not sell to the community those common services, other than higher education, which cannot be conveniently and economically provided and administer the state and the economic and social policy of the community. Public enterprises funds are included in the business enterprise funds sector. These authorities also include private non-profit institutes controlled and mainly financed by government.
*Higher education funds* include funds allocated to R&D by institutions of higher education comprising all universities, colleges of technology, other institutes of post-secondary education, and all research institutes, experimental stations and clinics operating under the direct control of or administered by or associated with higher educational establishments.
*Private non-profit funds* are funds allocated to R&D by non-market, private non-profit institutions serving the general public, as well as by private individuals and households.
*Funds from abroad* refer to funds allocated to R&D by institutions and individuals located outside the political frontiers of a country except for vehicles, ships, aircraft and space satellites operated by domestic organisations and testing grounds acquired by such organisations, and by all international organizations (except business enterprises) including their facilities and operations within the frontiers of a country.

---

### Tableau III.1  Indicateurs sélectionnés de R-D
Ce tableau présente des indicateurs sélectionnés de R-D, tels que le nombre de chercheurs et de techniciens en R-D par million d'habitants, le nombre de techniciens en R-D par chercheurs, les dépenses en R-D en pourcentage du PNB, et les dépenses en R-D par habitant et par chercheur en monnaie nationale. Pour l'indication des monnaies nationales, voir le tableau III.3.
Les *chercheurs* sont des spécialistes travaillant à la conception ou à la création de connaissances, de produits, de procédés, de méthodes et de systèmes, et dans la planification et la gestion de projets de R-D. Les étudiants diplômés ayant des activités de R-D sont également considérés comme des chercheurs.
*Techniciens (et personnel assimilé)* comprend des personnes dont les tâches principales requièrent des connaissances et une expérience technique dans un ou plusieurs domaines de l'ingénierie, des sciences physiques et de la vie ou des sciences sociales et humaines. Ils participent à la R-D en exécutant des tâches scientifiques et techniques faisant intervenir l'application de principes et de méthodes opérationnelles, généralement sous le contrôle de chercheurs. Pour se distinguer des *techniciens* qui participent à la R-D sous le contrôle de chercheurs dans les domaines de l'ingénierie, des sciences physiques et de la vie, le *personnel assimilé* effectue des travaux correspondants dans les sciences sociales et humaines.
*Autre personnel de soutien* comprend les travailleurs, qualifiés ou non, et le personnel de secrétariat et de bureau qui participent à l'exécution des projets de R-D ou qui sont directement associés à l'exécution de tels projets. Sont inclus dans cette catégorie les gérants et administrateurs qui s'occupent principalement de problèmes financiers, le personnel et l'administration en général, dans la mesure où leurs activités ont une relation directe avec la R-D.

III   Country tables on science and technology
Tableaux sur le science et technologie par pays
Cuadros sobre la ciencia y tecnología por países

**Tableau III.2  Personnel employé dans la R-D par catégorie de personnel**
Ce tableau présente le nombre total de chercheurs, techniciens de R-D et autre personnel de soutien tels que définis ci-dessus. Les données sur les femmes dans le personnel de R-D par catégorie sont indiquées lorsqu'elles sont disponibles.

**Tableau III.3  Répartition en pourcentage des dépenses intérieures brutes de R-D par source de fonds**
*Dépense intérieure brute de R-D (DIRD)* est la dépense totale intra-muros afférente aux travaux de R-D exécutés sur le territoire national pendant une période donnée. Elle comprend la R-D exécutée sur le territoire national et financée par l'étranger mais ne tient pas compte des paiements effectués à l'étranger pour des travaux de R-D.
Les sources de financement pour la DIRD sont classées selon les cinq catégories suivantes :
*Fonds des entreprises* inclut les fonds alloués à la R-D par toutes les firmes, organismes et institutions dont l'activité première est la production marchande de biens ou de services (autres que dans le secteur d'enseignement supérieur) en vue de leur vente au public, à un prix qui correspond à la réalité économique, et les institutions privées sans but lucratif principalement au service de ces entreprises, organismes et institutions.
*Fonds de l'Etat* sont les fonds fournis à la R-D par le gouvernement central (fédéral), d'état ou par les autorités locales. Ceci inclut tous les ministères, bureaux et autres organismes qui fournissent, sans normalement les vendre, des services collectifs autres que d'enseignement supérieur, qu'il n'est pas possible d'assurer de façon pratique et économique par d'autres moyens et qui, de surcroît, administrent les affaires publiques et appliquent la politique économique et sociale de la collectivité. Les fonds des entreprises publiques sont comprises dans ceux du secteur des entreprises. Les fonds de l'Etat incluent également les institutions privées sans but lucratif contrôlées et principalement financées par l'Etat.
*Fonds de l'enseignement supérieur* inclut les fonds fournis à la R-D par les établissements d'enseignement supérieur tels que toutes les universités, grandes écoles, instituts de technologie et autres établissements postsecondaires, ainsi que tous les instituts de recherche, les stations d'essais et les cliniques qui travaillent sous le contrôle direct des établissements d'enseignement supérieur ou qui sont administrés par ces derniers ou leur sont associés.
*Fonds d'institutions privées à but non lucratif* sont les fonds destinés à la R-D par les institutions privées sans but lucratif non marchandes au service du public, ainsi que par les simples particuliers ou les ménages.
*Fonds étrangers* concernent les fonds destinés à la R-D par les institutions et les individus se trouvant en dehors des frontières politiques d'un pays, à l'exception des véhicules, navires, avions et satellites utilisés par des institutions nationales, ainsi que des terrains d'essai acquis par ces institutions, et par toutes les organisations internationales (à l'exception des entreprises), y compris leurs installations et leurs activités à l'intérieur des frontières d'un pays.

---

**Cuadro III.1  Indicadores seleccionados de I y D**
Este cuadro presenta indicadores seleccionados de I y D, tales como el número de investigadores y de técnicos de I y D por millones de habitantes, el número de técnicos de I y D por investigadores, el gasto de I y D como porcentaje del PNB, el gasto de I y D por persona y por investigador en moneda nacional. Para la indicación de las monedas nacionales, véase el cuadro III.3.
Los *investigadores* son profesionales que trabajan en la concepción o creación de nuevos conocimientos, productos, procesos, métodos y sistemas, y en la planificación y gestión de proyectos de I y D. Los estudiantes postgraduados que desarrollan actividades de I y D deben también considerarse como investigadores.
*Técnicos (y personal asimilado)* son personas cuyas tareas principales requieren conocimientos y experiencia de naturaleza técnica en uno o varios campos de la ingeniería, de las ciencias físicas y de la vida o de las ciencias sociales y las humanidades. Participan en la I y D ejecutando tareas científicas y técnicas que requieren la aplicación de métodos y principios operativos, generalmente bajo la supervisión de investigadores. El *personal asimilado*, siendo de distinta categoría que los *técnicos* que participan en la I y D bajo la supervisión de los investigadores en ingeniería, ciencias físicas y de la vida, realiza los trabajos en ciencias sociales y humanidades que le corresponden.
*Otro personal de apoyo* incluye a los trabajadores, cualificados o no, y al personal de secretariado y de oficina, que participan en la ejecución de proyectos de I y D o que están directamente relacionados con la ejecución de tales proyectos. Se incluye en esta categoría a todos los gerentes y administradores que se ocupan fundamentalmente de problemas financieros, personal y administración en general, en tanto que sus actividades tengan una relación directa con la I y D.

**Cuadro III.2  Personal empleado en I y D por categoría de personal**
Este cuadro presenta el número total de investigadores, técnicos de I y D y otro personal de apoyo tal como han sido definidos más arriba. Los datos sobre las mujeres en el personal de I y D por categoría se indican cuando se dispone de ellos.

**Cuadro III.3  Distribución porcentual del gasto interior bruto en I y D por origen de fondos**
*Gasto interior bruto en I y D (GERD)* es el total de gastos intramuros destinados a la realización de las acciones de I y D efectuadas en el territorio nacional, durante un periodo determinado. Se incluye la I y D realizada en el territorio nacional y financiada por el extranjero, sin incluir los pagos efectuados en el extranjero por trabajos de I y D.
Las fuentes de financiamiento del GERD se han clasificado según las cinco categorías siguientes:
*Fondos del sector de empresas* incluye los fondos destinados a la I y D procedentes de todas las empresas, organismos e instituciones cuya actividad esencial consiste en la producción mercantil de bienes y servicios (exceptuando los del sector de la enseñanza superior) para su venta al público, a un precio que corresponde al de la realidad económica, y de las instituciones privadas sin fines de lucro que están esencialmente al servicio de dichas empresas, organismos e instituciones.
*Fondos del sector de la administración* se refiere a los fondos destinados a la I y D proporcionados por las autoridades centrales (federales), estatales o locales. Estas incluyen todos los ministerios, oficinas y otros organismos que suministran, generalmente a título gratuito, servicios colectivos otros que la enseñanza superior, que no sería económico ni fácil suministrar de otro modo y que, además, administran los asuntos públicos y la política económica y social de la colectividad. Los fondos de las empresas públicas se incluyen en los del sector de empresas. El sector de la administración incluye también las instituciones privadas sin fines de lucro controladas y financiadas principalmente por la administración.
*Fondos de la enseñanza superior* incluye los fondos destinados a la I y D por los establecimientos de enseñanza superior tales como todas las universidades y centros de nivel universitario, todos los institutos de investigación, estaciones experimentales y hospitales directamente controlados, administrados o asociados a centros de enseñanza superior.
*Fondos de las instituciones privadas sin fines de lucro* son los fondos destinados a la I y D procedentes de instituciones privadas sin fines de lucro, que están fuera del mercado y al servicio del público, así como de individuos privados y de las economías domésticas.

Country tables on science and technology III
Tableaux sur le science et technologie par pays
Cuadros sobre la ciencia y tecnología por países

*Fondos extranjeros* se refiere a los fondos en I y D procedentes de instituciones e individuos que se encuentran fuera de las fronteras políticas de un país, excluyendo los vehículos, navíos, aviones y satélites utilizados por instituciones nacionales, así como bases experimentales adquiridas por esas instituciones, y de los organismos internacionales (excluyendo las empresas), donde se incluyen sus instalaciones y actividades al interior de las fronteras de un país.

III.1    Selected R&D indicators
Indicateurs sélectionnés de R-D
Indicadores seleccionados de I y D

## III.1    Selected R&D indicators

### Indicateurs sélectionnés de R-D

### Indicadores seleccionados de I y D

| Country / Pays / País | | Year / Année / Año | Personnel engaged in R&D<br>Personnel employé à des travaux de R-D<br>Personal dedicado a actividades de I y D | | | Expenditure for R&D<br>Dépenses consacrées à la R-D<br>Gastos destinados a la I y D | | |
|---|---|---|---|---|---|---|---|---|
| | | | Researchers per million inhabitants<br>Chercheurs par million d'habitants<br>Investigadores por millón de habitantes | Technicians per million inhabitants<br>Techniciens par million d'habitants<br>Técnicos por millón de habitantes | Number of technicians per researcher<br>Nombre de techniciens par chercheur<br>Número de técnicos por investigador | As percentage of gross national product (GNP)<br>En pourcentage du produit national brut (PNB)<br>En porcentaje del producto nacional bruto (PNB) | Per capita (in national currency)<br>Par habitant (en monnaie nationale)<br>Por persona (en moneda nacional) | Annual average per researcher (in national currency)<br>Moyenne anuelle par chercheur (en monnaie nationale)<br>Promedio anual por investigador (en moneda nacional) |
| **Africa** | | | | | | | | |
| Benin | | 1989 | 176 | 54 | 0.3 | ... | ... | ... |
| Burkina Faso | | 1993 | ... | ... | ... | 0.13 | 100 | ... |
| | | 1994 | ... | ... | ... | 0.07 | 67 | ... |
| | | 1995 | ... | ... | ... | 0.08 | 81 | ... |
| | | 1996 | 16 | 15 | 1.0 | 0.17 | 196 | 12 932 444 |
| | | 1997 | 17 | 16 | 0.9 | 0.19 | 240 | 14 695 807 |
| Burundi | | 1984 | (1)(2) 25 | (1)(2) 20 | (1)(2) 0.8 | 0.15 | 38 | 1 519 272 |
| | | 1989 | (1)(2) 33 | (1)(2) 32 | (1)(2) 1.0 | 0.31 | 101 | 3 154 042 |
| Central African Republic | (1) | 1984 | 78 | 66 | 0.8 | 0.25 | 268 | 3 473 424 |
| | | 1990 | 56 | 32 | 0.6 | ... | ... | ... |
| Congo | | 1983 | (3) 435 | ... | ... | (4) 0.01 | (4) 19 | (4) 42 718 |
| | | 1984 | (1) 462 | (1) 789 | (1) 1.7 | 0.01 | 14 | 29 618 |
| Egypt | | 1982 | 434 | 146 | 0.3 | ... | ... | ... |
| | | 1983 | 423 | 142 | 0.3 | ... | ... | ... |
| | | 1986 | 410 | 132 | 0.3 | ... | ... | ... |
| | | 1990 | 437 | 305 | 0.7 | ... | ... | ... |
| | | 1991 | 459 | 341 | 0.7 | ... | ... | ... |
| | | 1992 | ... | ... | ... | 0.20 | 5 | ... |
| | | 1993 | ... | ... | ... | 0.20 | 6 | ... |
| | | 1994 | ... | ... | ... | 0.22 | 7 | ... |
| | | 1995 | ... | ... | ... | 0.22 | 7 | ... |
| | | 1996 | ... | ... | ... | 0.22 | 8 | ... |
| Gabon | | 1983 | (1) 231 | (1)(5) 31 | 0.1 | ... | ... | ... |
| | | 1984 | (1) 221 | (1)(5) 30 | 0.1 | (2) 0.01 | (2) 1 | (2) 2 413 |
| | | 1985 | (1) 235 | (1)(5) 28 | 0.1 | (2) 0.01 | (2) 1 | (2) 2 256 |
| | | 1986 | (1) 255 | (1)(5) 25 | 0.1 | (2) 0.01 | (2) 1 | (2) 1 801 |
| | | 1987 | (1) 234 | (1)(5) 22 | 0.1 | ... | ... | ... |
| Libyan Arab Jamahiriya | | 1980 | 362 | 493 | 1.4 | 0.22 | 8 | 20 796 |
| Madagascar | (6) | 1980 | (1)(7) 13 | (1)(7) 42 | (1)(7) 3.3 | 0.17 | 157 | 12 427 492 |
| | (1)(8) | 1985 | 16 | 67 | 4.4 | ... | ... | ... |
| | | 1986 | 17 | 64 | 3.9 | ... | ... | ... |
| | | 1987 | 20 | 65 | 3.4 | ... | ... | ... |
| | | 1988 | 21 | 67 | 3.2 | ... | ... | ... |
| | | 1989 | 24 | 85 | 3.6 | ... | ... | ... |
| | (9) | 1994 | 12 | 37 | 3.0 | ... | ... | ... |
| | (9) | 1995 | ... | ... | ... | 0.18 | 1 636 | ... |
| Mauritius | | 1980 | 158 | 112 | 0.7 | 0.43 | 38 | 240 132 |
| | | 1981 | 187 | 109 | 0.6 | 0.54 | 54 | 287 913 |
| | | 1982 | 175 | 171 | 1.0 | 0.51 | 57 | 325 434 |
| | | 1983 | 212 | 166 | 0.8 | 0.32 | 39 | 180 569 |
| | | 1984 | 262 | 175 | 0.7 | 0.29 | 39 | 147 149 |
| | | 1985 | 263 | 188 | 0.7 | 0.17 | 26 | 97 379 |
| | | 1986 | 298 | 177 | 0.6 | 0.28 | 52 | 173 443 |
| | | 1987 | 227 | 167 | 0.7 | 0.53 | 122 | 535 043 |
| | | 1988 | 223 | 112 | 0.5 | 0.21 | 56 | 249 351 |
| | | 1989 | 185 | 165 | 0.9 | (44) 0.32 | (44) 100 | (44) 540 415 |
| | | 1992 | 361 | 158 | 0.4 | ... | ... | ... |

Selected R&D indicators III.1
Indicateurs sélectionnés de R-D
Indicadores seleccionados de I y D

| Country / Pays / País | Year / Année / Año | Personnel engaged in R&D / Personnel employé à des travaux de R-D / Personal dedicado a actividades de I y D | | | Expenditure for R&D / Dépenses consacrées à la R-D / Gastos destinados a la I y D | | |
|---|---|---|---|---|---|---|---|
| | | Researchers per million inhabitants / Chercheurs par million d'habitants / Investigadores por millón de habitantes | Technicians per million inhabitants / Techniciens par million d'habitants / Técnicos por millón de habitantes | Number of technicians per researcher / Nombre de techniciens par chercheur / Número de técnicos por investigador | As percentage of gross national product (GNP) / En pourcentage du produit national brut (PNB) / En porcentaje del producto nacional bruto (PNB) | Per capita (in national currency) / Par habitant (en monnaie nationale) / Por persona (en moneda nacional) | Annual average per researcher (in national currency) / Moyenne anuelle par chercheur (en monnaie nationale) / Promedio anual por investigador (en moneda nacional) |
| Nigeria (10) | 1983 | 24 | 140 | 5.8 | 0.24 | 2 | 77 857 |
| | 1984 | 23 | 132 | 5.9 | 0.17 | 2 | 60 371 |
| | 1985 | 19 | 87 | 4.6 | 0.12 | 2 | 58 335 |
| | 1986 | 20 | 78 | 4.0 | 0.12 | 2 | 53 582 |
| | 1987 | 15 | 76 | 5.3 | 0.09 | 2 | 75 809 |
| Rwanda | 1980 | 10 | 7 | 0.8 | ... | ... | ... |
| | 1982 | 12 | 8 | 0.7 | 0.21 | 48 | 4 228 549 |
| | 1983 | 12 | 10 | 0.9 | 0.21 | 51 | 4 436 250 |
| | 1984 | 12 | 11 | 0.9 | 0.17 | 45 | 3 778 986 |
| | 1985 | ... | ... | ... | 0.54 | 152 | 12 937 465 |
| | 1995 | 35 | 8 | 0.2 | (11) 0.04 | (11) 20 | (11) 555 564 |
| Senegal (45) | 1993 | 3 | 5 | 1.6 | 0.02 | 29 | 11 450 550 |
| | 1994 | 3 | 4 | 1.7 | 0.02 | 35 | 14 852 632 |
| | 1995 | 3 | 4 | 1.5 | 0.02 | 55 | 24 105 264 |
| | 1996 | 3 | 4 | 1.5 | 0.02 | 48 | 21 587 369 |
| | 1997 | ... | ... | ... | 0.01 | ... | ... |
| Seychelles | 1980 | 32 | 16 | 0.5 | ... | ... | ... |
| | 1981 | 32 | 16 | 0.5 | ... | ... | ... |
| | 1983 | 282 | 94 | 0.3 | ... | ... | ... |
| | 1991 | 58 | 143 | 2.5 | ... | ... | ... |
| South Africa | 1983 | 270 | 164 | 0.6 | 0.88 | 27 | 96 919 |
| | 1985 | 324 | 197 | 0.6 | 0.93 | 36 | 108 316 |
| | 1987 | 359 | 175 | 0.5 | 0.84 | 42 | 115 889 |
| | 1989 | 298 | 138 | 0.5 | 0.77 | 54 | 178 894 |
| | 1991 | 349 | 145 | 0.4 | 0.93 | 81 | 230 217 |
| | 1993 | 1 031 | 315 | 0.3 | 0.70 | 72 | 69 750 |
| Togo | 1989 | 81 | 54 | 0.7 | 0.79 | 974 | 11 985 560 |
| | 1994 | 98 | 63 | 0.6 | 0.48 | 627 | 6 395 349 |
| Tunisia | 1993 | 111 | 56 | 0.5 | 0.30 | 5 | 42 303 |
| | 1994 | 115 | 61 | 0.5 | 0.32 | 6 | 46 656 |
| | 1995 | 117 | 58 | 0.5 | 0.33 | 6 | 51 010 |
| | 1996 | 120 | 58 | 0.5 | 0.33 | 7 | 53 550 |
| | 1997 | 125 | 57 | 0.5 | 0.30 | 7 | 52 415 |
| Uganda | 1992 | ... | ... | ... | 0.58 | 887 | ... |
| | 1993 | 17 | 13 | 0.7 | 0.60 | 1 267 | 76 003 725 |
| | 1994 | 19 | 14 | 0.7 | 0.66 | 1 553 | 83 044 826 |
| | 1995 | 20 | 16 | 0.8 | 0.60 | 1 660 | 86 802 293 |
| | 1996 | 20 | 15 | 0.7 | 0.57 | 1 792 | 90 327 798 |
| | 1997 | 21 | 14 | 0.6 | ... | ... | ... |
| **North America** | | | | | | | |
| Canada | 1981 | (15) 1 573 | ... | ... | (16) 1.30 | 178 | 113 032 |
| | (17) 1982 | 1 794 | 909 | 0.5 | *1.42 | *203 | *113 086 |
| | (17) 1983 | 1 819 | 894 | 0.5 | 1.37 | 211 | 115 984 |
| | (17) 1984 | 1 919 | 945 | 0.5 | 1.41 | 235 | 122 281 |
| | (17) 1985 | 2 047 | 996 | 0.5 | 1.46 | 259 | 126 347 |
| | (17) 1986 | 2 151 | 1 013 | 0.5 | 1.49 | 275 | 127 765 |
| | (17) 1987 | 2 196 | 1 047 | 0.5 | 1.43 | 284 | 128 946 |
| | (17) 1988 | 2 246 | 1 042 | 0.5 | 1.39 | 299 | 132 795 |
| | (17) 1989 | 2 265 | 1 056 | 0.5 | 1.41 | 321 | 141 596 |
| | (17) 1990 | 2 301 | 1 004 | 0.4 | 1.51 | 347 | 150 493 |
| | (17) 1991 | 2 320 | 977 | 0.4 | 1.55 | 356 | 153 390 |
| | 1992 | ... | ... | ... | 1.57 | 361 | ... |
| | (17) 1993 | 2 648 | 1 070 | 0.4 | *1.55 | *366 | *137 950 |
| | 1994 | (15) 2 660 | ... | ... | (16) 1.69 | 411 | 154 213 |
| | 1995 | (15) 2 719 | ... | ... | (16) 1.68 | 421 | 154 838 |
| | 1996 | ... | ... | ... | 1.65 | 420 | ... |
| | 1997 | ... | ... | ... | (16) 1.66 | 446 | ... |
| | 1998 | ... | ... | ... | ... (16) | 455 | ... |
| Costa Rica | (1) 1988 | 532 | ... | ... | ... | ... | ... |
| | (19) 1989 | ... | ... | ... | 0.18 | 238 | ... |
| | (19) 1990 | ... | ... | ... | 0.17 | 275 | ... |
| | (19) 1991 | ... | ... | ... | 0.21 | 439 | ... |
| Cuba | 1980 | 581 | 676 | 1.2 | 0.55 | 10 | 17 011 |
| | 1981 | 699 | 814 | 1.2 | 0.51 | 12 | 16 333 |
| | 1982 | 761 | 819 | 1.1 | 0.57 | 14 | 17 483 |
| | 1983 | 830 | 846 | 1.0 | 0.59 | 15 | 17 363 |
| | 1984 | 953 | 883 | 0.9 | 0.64 | 17 | 17 198 |
| | 1985 | 1 019 | 914 | 0.9 | 0.68 | 19 | 17 708 |
| | 1986 | 986 | 851 | 0.9 | 0.78 | 21 | 20 348 |

III.1    Selected R&D indicators
Indicateurs sélectionnés de R-D
Indicadores seleccionados de I y D

| Country / Pays / País | | Year / Année / Año | Researchers per million inhabitants / Chercheurs par million d'habitants / Investigadores por millón de habitantes | | Technicians per million inhabitants / Techniciens par million d'habitants / Técnicos por millón de habitantes | | Number of technicians per researcher / Nombre de techniciens par chercheur / Número de técnicos por investigador | | As percentage of gross national product (GNP) / En pourcentage du produit national brut (PNB) / En porcentaje del producto nacional bruto (PNB) | | Per capita (in national currency) / Par habitant (en monnaie nationale) / Por persona (en moneda nacional) | | Annual average per researcher (in national currency) / Moyenne anuelle par chercheur (en monnaie nationale) / Promedio anual por investigador (en moneda nacional) | |
|---|---|---|---|---|---|---|---|---|---|---|---|---|---|---|
| **Cuba** (cont) | | 1987 | | 1 088 | | 869 | | 0.8 | | 0.93 | | 23 | | ... |
| | | 1988 | | ... | | ... | | ... | | 0.81 | | 21 | | ... |
| | | 1989 | | 1 145 | | 839 | | 0.7 | | 0.84 | | 22 | | 18 421 |
| | | 1991 | | 1 535 | | 893 | | 0.6 | | ... | | 18 | | 11 337 |
| | | 1992 | | 1 370 | | 878 | | 0.6 | | ... | | 23 | | 16 786 |
| | | 1995 | | 1 612 | | 1 121 | | 0.7 | | ... | | 18 | | 10 683 |
| **El Salvador** | | 1980 | (20) | 117 | | 338 | | 2.9 | | ... | | ... | | ... |
| | | 1981 | (20) | 122 | | 425 | | 3.5 | | ... | | ... | | ... |
| | | 1986 | | ... | | ... | | ... | (21) | 1.94 | (21) | 70 | | ... |
| | | 1987 | (20) | 39 | | 356 | | 9.2 | (21) | 1.79 | (21) | 74 | (21) | 1 886 725 |
| | | 1992 | (21) | 20 | | ... | | ... | (8) | 2.20 | (8) | 204 | (8) | 10 623 128 |
| **Guatemala** | | 1983 | | ... | | ... | | ... | | 0.51 | | 7 | | 16 598 |
| | (4)(5) | 1988 | | 104 | | 112 | | 1.1 | (22) | 0.16 | (22) | 4 | (22) | 37 132 |
| **Jamaica** (23) | | 1982 | | 11 | | 6 | | 0.5 | | 0.06 | | 2 | | 131 125 |
| | | 1983 | | 12 | | 9 | | 0.7 | | 0.07 | | 2 | | 149 539 |
| | | 1984 | | 11 | | 10 | | 0.9 | | 0.07 | | 3 | | 218 827 |
| | | 1985 | | 10 | | 14 | | 1.5 | | 0.04 | | 2 | | 171 667 |
| | | 1986 | | 8 | | 7 | | 0.8 | | 0.04 | | 2 | | 223 112 |
| **Mexico** | | 1984 | | 226 | | 399 | | 1.8 | | 0.58 | | 2 156 | | 9 552 791 |
| | | 1985 | | ... | | ... | | ... | | 0.44 | | 2 582 | | ... |
| | | 1986 | | ... | | ... | | ... | | 0.34 | | 3 183 | | ... |
| | | 1987 | | ... | | ... | | ... | | 0.31 | | 7 228 | | ... |
| | | 1988 | | ... | | ... | | ... | | 0.22 | | 10 926 | | ... |
| | | 1993 | | 161 | | 108 | | 0.7 | | 0.23 | | 32 | | 196 038 |
| | | 1994 | | 191 | | 106 | | 0.6 | | 0.31 | | 47 | | 244 339 |
| | | 1995 | | 214 | | 74 | | 0.3 | | 0.33 | | 63 | | 292 645 |
| **Nicaragua** | (1) | 1985 | | 191 | | 63 | | 0.3 | | ... | | ... | | ... |
| | | 1987 | | 204 | | 85 | | 0.4 | | ... | | ... | | ... |
| **Panama** | | 1986 | | ... | | ... | | ... | | 0.01 | | 1 | | ... |
| | | 1981 | | 252 | | ... | | ... | | ... | | ... | | ... |
| **United States** | (26) | 1980 | | 2 859 | | ... | | ... | (27) | 2.32 | (27) | 277 | (27) | 96 873 |
| | (26) | 1981 | | 2 973 | | ... | | ... | (27) | 2.40 | (27) | 317 | (27) | 106 649 |
| | (26) | 1982 | | 2 993 | | ... | | ... | (27) | 2.54 | (27) | 345 | (27) | 115 255 |
| | (26) | 1983 | | 3 047 | | ... | | ... | (27) | 2.58 | (27) | 375 | (27) | 123 172 |
| | (26) | 1984 | | 3 332 | | ... | | ... | | 2.72 | | 435 | | 130 497 |
| | (26) | 1985 | | 3 512 | | ... | | ... | | 2.87 | | 483 | | 137 537 |
| | (26) | 1986 | | 3 671 | | ... | | ... | | 2.87 | | 503 | | 137 090 |
| | (26) | 1987 | | 3 744 | | ... | | ... | | 2.88 | | 531 | | 141 785 |
| | (26) | 1988 | | 3 811 | | ... | | ... | | 2.84 | | *559 | | *146 708 |
| | (15) | 1989 | | 3 675 | | ... | | ... | (16) | 2.72 | | 572 | | 155 460 |
| | | 1990 | | ... | | ... | | ... | (16) | 2.77 | | 608 | | ... |
| | (15) | 1991 | | 3 743 | | ... | | ... | (16) | 2.81 | | 626 | | 167 259 |
| | | 1992 | | ... | | ... | | ... | (16) | 2.74 | | 639 | | ... |
| | | 1993 | | 3 676 | | ... | | ... | (16) | 2.61 | | 633 | | 172 042 |
| | | 1994 | | ... | | ... | | ... | (16) | 2.52 | | 639 | | ... |
| | | 1995 | | ... | | ... | | ... | (16) | 2.61 | | 688 | | ... |
| | | 1996 | | ... | | ... | | ... | (16) | 2.64 | | 720 | | ... |
| | | 1997 | | ... | | ... | | ... | (16) | 2.63 | | ... | | ... |
| **South America** | | | | | | | | | | | | | | |
| **Argentina** | | 1982 | | 363 | | ... | | ... | | ... | | ... | | ... |
| | | 1985 | | *357 | | *235 | | *0.7 | | ... | | ... | | ... |
| | | 1988 | | *351 | | *198 | | *0.6 | | ... | | ... | | ... |
| | | 1995 | | 660 | | 147 | | 0.2 | | 0.38 | | 30 | | 44 915 |
| **Bolivia** | | 1990 | | ... | | ... | | ... | | 1.30 | | 27 | | ... |
| | (12) | 1991 | (12) | 250 | (12) | 154 | (12) | 0.6 | | 1.67 | | 43 | | 168 293 |
| | | 1992 | | 158 | | ... | | ... | | ... | | ... | | ... |
| | | 1993 | | 159 | | ... | | ... | | ... | | ... | | ... |
| | | 1994 | | 164 | | ... | | ... | | ... | | ... | | ... |
| | | 1995 | | 162 | | ... | | ... | | ... | | ... | | ... |
| | | 1996 | | 172 | | ... | | ... | | ... | | ... | | ... |
| **Brazil** | (1)(13) | 1981 | | 175 | | ... | | ... | | ... | | ... | | ... |
| | (1)(13) | 1982 | | 256 | | ... | | ... | | ... | | ... | | ... |
| | (1)(13) | 1983 | | 299 | | ... | | ... | | ... | | ... | | ... |
| | (1)(13) | 1984 | | 362 | | ... | | ... | | ... | | ... | | ... |
| | (1)(13) | 1985 | | 391 | | ... | | ... | | ... | | ... | | ... |
| | | 1994 | | ... | | ... | | ... | | 0.82 | | 18 | | ... |
| | (14) | 1995 | (14) | 168 | (14) | 59 | (14) | 0.3 | | 0.84 | | 33 | | 194 140 |
| | | 1996 | | ... | | ... | | ... | | 0.81 | | 37 | | ... |

Selected R&D Indicators III.1
Indicateurs sélectionnés de R-D
Indicadores seleccionados de I y D

| Country / Pays / País | Year / Année / Año | Personnel engaged in R&D / Personnel employé à des travaux de R-D / Personal dedicado a actividades de I y D | | | Expenditure for R&D / Dépenses consacrées à la R-D / Gastos destinados a la I y D | | |
|---|---|---|---|---|---|---|---|
| | | Researchers per million inhabitants / Chercheurs par million d'habitants / Investigadores por millón de habitantes | Technicians per million inhabitants / Techniciens par million d'habitants / Técnicos por millón de habitantes | Number of technicians per researcher / Nombre de techniciens par chercheur / Número de técnicos por investigador | As percentage of gross national product (GNP) / En pourcentage du produit national brut (PNB) / En porcentaje del producto nacional bruto (PNB) | Per capita (in national currency) / Par habitant (en monnaie nationale) / Por persona (en moneda nacional) | Annual average per researcher (in national currency) / Moyenne anuelle par chercheur (en monnaie nationale) / Promedio anual por investigador (en moneda nacional) |
| Chile | (1) 1980 | 358 | ... | ... | ... | ... | ... |
| | (1) 1985 | 429 | ... | ... | ... | ... | ... |
| | (1) 1987 | 435 | ... | ... | ... | ... | ... |
| | (1) 1988 | 366 | 233 | 0.6 | ... | ... | ... |
| | (1) 1989 | 412 | ... | ... | ... | ... | ... |
| | (1) 1990 | 423 | ... | ... | ... | ... | ... |
| | (1) 1991 | 430 | ... | ... | ... | ... | ... |
| | 1992 | 433 | ... | ... | ... | ... | ... |
| | 1993 | 438 | ... | ... | 0.90 | 11 584 | 26 465 080 |
| | 1994 | 445 | ... | ... | 0.83 | 12 538 | 28 193 782 |
| | 1995 | ... | ... | ... | 0.67 | 12 017 | ... |
| | 1996 | ... | ... | ... | 0.68 | 13 879 | ... |
| Colombia | (18) 1982 | 37 | 35 | 0.9 | 0.12 | 93 | 2 543 189 |
| Ecuador | 1990 | 102 | ... | ... | ... | ... | ... |
| | 1993 | ... | ... | ... | 0.01 | 69 | ... |
| | 1994 | ... | ... | ... | 0.01 | 171 | ... |
| | 1995 | 133 | 42 | 0.3 | 0.02 | 387 | 2 921 490 |
| | 1996 | ... | ... | ... | 0.01 | 461 | ... |
| | 1007 | 140 | ... | ... | 0.02 | 1 318 | 9 273 748 |
| Guyana | (3) 1980 | 124 | 330 | 2.7 | 0.06 | 2 | 8 766 |
| | 1982 | 115 | 230 | 2.0 | 0.23 | 4 | 31 461 |
| Peru | (24) 1981 | ... | ... | ... | 0.30 | 2 | 3 954 |
| | (24) 1982 | ... | ... | ... | 0.27 | 3 | ... |
| | (24) 1983 | ... | ... | ... | 0.29 | 5 | ... |
| | (24) 1984 | ... | ... | ... | 0.25 | 9 | ... |
| | 1994 | *631 | *189 | *0.3 | ... | ... | ... |
| | (25) 1996 | 232 | 10 | ... | ... | ... | ... |
| | (25) 1997 | 233 | ... | ... | ... | ... | ... |
| Uruguay | 1987 | 687 | | | ... | ... | ... |
| Venezuela | (19) 1980 | ... | ... | ... | 0.29 | 57 | (1) 231 767 |
| | 1981 | ... | ... | ... | 0.30 | 65 | ... |
| | 1982 | ... | ... | ... | 0.35 | 73 | ... |
| | 1983 | ... | ... | ... | 0.36 | 74 | (1) 261 931 |
| | 1984 | ... | ... | ... | 0.34 | 82 | ... |
| | 1985 | ... | ... | ... | 0.32 | 83 | ... |
| | 1986 | ... | ... | ... | 0.28 | 74 | ... |
| | 1987 | ... | ... | ... | (28) 0.37 | (28) 137 | ... |
| | 1988 | ... | ... | ... | (28) 0.39 | (28) 176 | ... |
| | 1989 | ... | ... | ... | (28) 0.27 | (28) 205 | ... |
| | 1990 | ... | ... | ... | (28) 0.54 | (28) 608 | ... |
| | 1991 | *214 | *33 | *0.2 | (28) 0.49 | (28) 717 | (28) *3 361 555 |
| | 1992 | *209 | *32 | *0.2 | (28) 0.49 | (28) 960 | ... |
| **Asia** | | | | | | | |
| Armenia | 1997 | 1 485 | 177 | 0.1 | ... | ... | ... |
| Azerbaijan | 1993 | 3 302 | 268 | 0.1 | 0.55 | 127 | 38 379 |
| | 1994 | 3 103 | 197 | 0.1 | 0.32 | 886 | 285 316 |
| | 1995 | 2 850 | 180 | 0.1 | 0.19 | 3 138 | 1 101 267 |
| | 1996 | 2 791 | 188 | 0.1 | 0.21 | 4 226 | 1 514 223 |
| Bangladesh | 1993 | 51 | 32 | 0.6 | 0.01 | 1 | 7 072 |
| | 1994 | 47 | 18 | 0.4 | 0.04 | 3 | 57 981 |
| | 1995 | 52 | 33 | 0.6 | 0.03 | 3 | 45 036 |
| China | 1988 | ... | ... | ... | 0.67 | 9 | ... |
| | 1989 | ... | ... | ... | 0.67 | 10 | ... |
| | 1990 | ... | ... | ... | 0.68 | 11 | ... |
| | 1991 | ... | ... | ... | 0.68 | ... | ... |
| | 1992 | ... | ... | ... | 0.64 | ... | ... |
| | 1993 | ... | ... | ... | 0.75 | 22 | ... |
| | 1994 | 349 | ... | ... | 0.67 | 26 | 73 473 |
| | 1995 | 347 | (29) 200 | (29) 0.6 | 0.61 | 29 | 82 589 |
| | 1996 | 454 | ... | ... | 0.61 | 33 | 72 416 |
| | 1997 | ... | ... | ... | 0.66 | ... | ... |
| Cyprus | 1991 | 196 | 222 | 1.1 | 0.18 | 7 | 35 815 |
| | 1992 | 209 | 235 | 1.1 | 0.18 | 8 | 37 946 |
| India | 1980 | ... | ... | ... | 0.56 | 12 | 117 229 |
| | 1981 | ... | ... | ... | 0.59 | 14 | ... |
| | 1982 | *131 | 85 | *0.6 | *0.68 | *17 | *128 715 |

III.1    Selected R&D indicators
Indicateurs sélectionnés de R-D
Indicadores seleccionados de I y D

| Country / Pays / País | Year / Année / Año | Personnel engaged in R&D / Personnel employé à des travaux de R-D / Personal dedicado a actividades de I y D | | | Expenditure for R&D / Dépenses consacrées à la R-D / Gastos destinados a la I y D | | |
|---|---|---|---|---|---|---|---|
| | | Researchers per million inhabitants / Chercheurs par million d'habitants / Investigadores por millón de habitantes | Technicians per million inhabitants / Techniciens par million d'habitants / Técnicos por millón de habitantes | Number of technicians per researcher / Nombre de techniciens par chercheur / Número de técnicos por investigador | As percentage of gross national product (GNP) / En pourcentage du produit national brut (PNB) / En porcentaje del producto nacional bruto (PNB) | Per capita (in national currency) / Par habitant (en monnaie nationale) / Por persona (en moneda nacional) | Annual average per researcher (in national currency) / Moyenne anuelle par chercheur (en monnaie nationale) / Promedio anual por investigador (en moneda nacional) |
| **India (cont)** | 1983 | ... | ... | ... | 0.67 | 19 | ... |
| | 1984 | *134 | 97 | *0.7 | 0.78 | 24 | *177 914 |
| | 1985 | ... | ... | ... | 0.80 | 27 | ... |
| | 1986 | *137 | 90 | *0.7 | 0.84 | 32 | *226 741 |
| | 1987 | ... | ... | ... | 0.87 | 36 | ... |
| | 1988 | *146 | 100 | *0.7 | 0.86 | 41 | *281 219 |
| | 1989 | ... | ... | ... | 0.83 | 45 | ... |
| | 1990 | *151 | 114 | *0.8 | 0.80 | 50 | *326 973 |
| | 1991 | ... | ... | ... | 0.75 | 53 | ... |
| | 1992 | 133 | 112 | 0.8 | 0.73 | 57 | 425 616 |
| | 1993 | ... | ... | ... | 0.77 | 68 | ... |
| | 1994 | *149 | 108 | *0.7 | 0.73 | 75 | *499 698 |
| **Indonesia** | 1980 | ... | ... | ... | (19) 0.35 | (19) 1 064 | ... |
| | 1981 | ... | ... | ... | (19) 0.36 | (19) 1 302 | ... |
| | 1982 | (1) 110 | (1) 21 | (1) 0.2 | (19) *0.50 | (19) *1 877 | (19) *17 092 671 |
| | 1983 | ... | ... | ... | (19) 0.37 | (19) 1 682 | (19) 14 585 497 |
| | 1984 | (1) 152 | (1) 26 | (1) 0.2 | (19) 0.33 | (19) 1 701 | (19) 11 207 070 |
| | 1985 | (1) 127 | (1) 24 | (1) 0.2 | (19) 0.27 | (19) 1 447 | (19) 11 442 345 |
| | 1986 | (1) 174 | ... | ... | (19) 0.25 | (19) 1 418 | (19) 8 161 440 |
| | 1987 | (1) 176 | ... | ... | (19) 0.16 | (19) 1 031 | ... |
| | 1988 | (1) 182 | ... | ... | (19) 0.19 | (19) 1 467 | (19) 8 092 984 |
| (4) | 1994 | ... | ... | ... | 0.07 | 1 259 | ... |
| **Iran, Islamic Republic of** | 1985 | 68 | 39 | 0.6 | ... | ... | ... |
| | 1994 | 560 | 166 | 0.3 | 0.48 | 9 722 | 17 372 181 |
| **Israel** | 1984 | 4 828 | 1 033 | 0.2 | ... | ... | ... |
| | 1989 | ... | ... | ... | 2.23 | 430 | ... |
| | 1990 | ... | ... | ... | 2.15 | 499 | ... |
| | 1992 | ... | ... | ... | 2.17 | 733 | ... |
| | 1993 | ... | ... | ... | 2.21 | 831 | ... |
| | 1994 | ... | ... | ... | 2.25 | 971 | ... |
| | 1995 | ... | ... | ... | 2.14 | 1 050 | ... |
| | 1996 | ... | ... | ... | ... | *1 169 | ... |
| | 1997 | ... | ... | ... | 2.35 | ... | ... |
| **Japan** (12)(17) | 1980 | 3 778 | 745 | 0.2 | 2.19 | 44 914 | 11 891 239 |
| (12)(17) | 1981 | 3 934 | 769 | 0.2 | 2.33 | 50 824 | 12 919 126 |
| (12)(17) | 1982 | 4 048 | 769 | 0.2 | 2.42 | 55 063 | 13 602 762 |
| (12)(17) | 1983 | 4 156 | 782 | 0.2 | 2.55 | 60 150 | 14 473 153 |
| (12)(17) | 1984 | 4 425 | 809 | 0.2 | 2.63 | 65 706 | 14 849 046 |
| (12)(17) | 1985 | 4 538 | 822 | 0.2 | 2.77 | 73 573 | 16 215 806 |
| (12)(17) | 1986 | 4 737 | 839 | 0.2 | 2.74 | 75 680 | 15 979 593 |
| (12)(17) | 1987 | 4 840 | 840 | 0.2 | 2.80 | 80 596 | 16 653 078 |
| (12)(17) | 1988 | 5 016 | 840 | 0.2 | 2.83 | 86 700 | 17 284 709 |
| (12)(17) | 1989 | 5 175 | 857 | 0.2 | 2.94 | 96 004 | 18 553 968 |
| (12)(17) | 1990 | 5 395 | 844 | 0.2 | 3.03 | 105 866 | 19 625 529 |
| (12)(17) | 1991 | 5 558 | 916 | 0.2 | 2.99 | 111 081 | 19 987 873 |
| (12)(17) | 1992 | 5 671 | 869 | 0.2 | ... | ... | ... |
| | 1993 | (15) 5 138 | ... | ... | (16) 2.86 | 109 864 | 21 384 344 |
| (12)(17) | 1994 | 6 293 | 827 | 0.1 | 2.82 | 108 644 | 17 266 949 |
| | 1995 | (15) 5 368 | ... | ... | (16) 2.96 | 114 833 | 21 395 584 |
| | 1996 | (15) 4 909 | ... | ... | (16) 2.80 | 112 549 | 22 928 184 |
| **Jordan** (30) | 1981 | ... | ... | ... | *0.11 | *1 | ... |
| | 1982 | ... | ... | ... | *0.14 | *1 | *1 898 |
| | 1983 | ... | ... | ... | *0.17 | *1 | ... |
| | 1984 | *108 | *8 | *0.1 | *0.28 | *2 | *13 115 |
| | 1985 | *98 | *8 | *0.1 | *0.28 | *2 | *13 753 |
| | 1986 | ... | ... | ... | 0.27 | 2 | 13 367 |
| | 1987 | *97 | *7 | *0.1 | *0.26 | *2 | *13 249 |
| | 1988 | *96 | *9 | *0.1 | *0.26 | *2 | *13 222 |
| | 1989 | 94 | 10 | 0.1 | *0.26 | *2 | *13 230 |
| **Kazakstan** | 1993 | ... | ... | ... | 0.37 | 7 | ... |
| | 1994 | ... | ... | ... | 0.36 | 92 | ... |
| | 1995 | ... | ... | ... | 0.30 | 181 | ... |
| | 1996 | ... | ... | ... | 0.35 | 299 | ... |
| | 1997 | ... | ... | ... | 0.32 | 327 | ... |
| **Korea, Republic of** (1)(31) | 1980 | 484 | 195 | 0.4 | 0.57 | 5 554 | 11 485 660 |
| | 1981 | 536 | 228 | 0.4 | 0.64 | 7 579 | 14 148 638 |
| | 1982 | 725 | 298 | 0.4 | 0.87 | 11 664 | 16 088 600 |
| | 1983 | 808 | 490 | 0.6 | 1.00 | 15 626 | 19 358 886 |
| | 1984 | 921 | 624 | 0.7 | 1.19 | 20 685 | 22 475 110 |
| | 1985 | 1 017 | 592 | 0.6 | 1.46 | 28 309 | 27 853 206 |
| | 1986 | 1 141 | 739 | 0.6 | 1.64 | 36 921 | 32 381 256 |
| | 1987 | 1 267 | 790 | 0.6 | ... | ... | ... |

Selected R&D indicators III.1
Indicateurs sélectionnés de R-D
Indicadores seleccionados de I y D

| Country / Pays / País | Year / Année / Año | Personnel engaged in R&D / Personnel employé à des travaux de R-D / Personal dedicado a actividades de I y D | | | Expenditure for R&D / Dépenses consacrées à la R-D / Gastos destinados a la I y D | | |
|---|---|---|---|---|---|---|---|
| | | Researchers per million inhabitants / Chercheurs par million d'habitants / Investigadores por millón de habitantes | Technicians per million inhabitants / Techniciens par million d'habitants / Técnicos por millón de habitantes | Number of technicians per researcher / Nombre de techniciens par chercheur / Número de técnicos por investigador | As percentage of gross national product (GNP) / En pourcentage du produit national brut (PNB) / En porcentaje del producto nacional bruto (PNB) | Per capita (in national currency) / Par habitant (en monnaie nationale) / Por persona (en moneda nacional) | Annual average per researcher (in national currency) / Moyenne anuelle par chercheur (en monnaie nationale) / Promedio anual por investigador (en moneda nacional) |
| Korea, Republic of (cont) | 1988 | 1 344 | 849 | 0.6 | ... | ... | ... |
| | 1989 | 1 560 | 911 | 0.6 | 1.91 | 66 337 | |
| | 1990 | 1 645 | 1 000 | 0.6 | 1.88 | 78 142 | 47 513 780 |
| | 1991 | 1 762 | 250 | 0.1 | 1.95 | 96 081 | 54 535 501 |
| | 1992 | 2 032 | 350 | 0.2 | 2.10 | 114 163 | 56 205 568 |
| | 1993 | ... | ... | ... | (16) 2.32 | 139 451 | |
| | 1994 | 2 637 | 318 | 0.1 | 2.60 | 177 247 | 67 220 221 |
| | 1995 | (15) 2 235 | ... | ... | (16) 2.71 | 210 030 | 93 977 523 |
| | 1996 | (15) 2 193 | ... | ... | (16) 2.82 | 239 896 | 109 400 803 |
| Kuwait | 1993 | 205 | 63 | 0.3 | 0.27 | 11 | 53 292 |
| | 1994 | 227 | 70 | 0.3 | 0.23 | 11 | 44 791 |
| | 1995 | 232 | 72 | 0.3 | 0.20 | 10 | 42 855 |
| | 1996 | 236 | 73 | 0.3 | 0.16 | 10 | 42 353 |
| | 1997 | 230 | 71 | 0.3 | 0.16 | 11 | 45 928 |
| Kyrgyzstan | 1993 | 847 | 93 | 0.1 | ... | ... | ... |
| | 1994 | 722 | 72 | 0.1 | 0.26 | 7 | 9 233 |
| | 1995 | 718 | 71 | 0.1 | 0.31 | 11 | 14 123 |
| | 1996 | 573 | 56 | 0.1 | 0.22 | 11 | 17 787 |
| | 1997 | 584 | 50 | 0.1 | 0.20 | 13 | 22 148 |
| Malaysia (1)(31) | 1983 | 182 | ... | ... | ... | ... | ... |
| (31) | 1988 | 327 | 69 | 0.2 | ... | ... | ... |
| | 1992 | 88 | 89 | 1.0 | 0.40 | 30 | 337 233 |
| | 1994 | 117 | 42 | 0.4 | 0.35 | 32 | 267 367 |
| | 1996 | 93 | 32 | 0.3 | 0.24 | 27 | 290 069 |
| Mongolia | 1995 | 910 | 176 | 0.2 | ... | ... | ... |
| Pakistan (32) | 1981 | 59 | 74 | 1.3 | ... | ... | ... |
| | 1982 | 60 | 79 | 1.3 | 0.77 | 28 | 456 075 |
| | 1983 | ... | ... | ... | 0.77 | 33 | ... |
| | 1984 | ... | ... | ... | 0.84 | 40 | ... |
| | 1985 | ... | ... | ... | 0.83 | 42 | ... |
| | 1986 | 90 | 134 | 1.5 | 0.95 | 51 | 562 981 |
| | 1987 | ... | ... | ... | 0.92 | 52 | ... |
| | 1988 | 60 | 83 | 1.4 | ... | ... | ... |
| (33) | 1990 | 56 | 79 | 1.4 | ... | ... | ... |
| | 1997 | 72 | 13 | 0.2 | ... | ... | ... |
| Philippines | 1980 | (1) 112 | (1) 51 | (1) 0.5 | ... | ... | (1) ... |
| | 1981 | (1) 152 | (1) 68 | (1) 0.5 | 0.19 | 11 | (1) 70 615 |
| | 1982 | (1) 156 | (1) 69 | (1) 0.4 | ... | ... | (1) ... |
| | 1983 | (1) 85 | (1) 36 | (1) 0.4 | 0.15 | 10 | (1) 117 112 |
| | 1004 | (1) 91 | (1) 35 | (1) 0.4 | 0.13 | 12 | (1) 127 000 |
| | 1992 | 157 | 22 | 0.1 | *0.22 | *47 | *295 236 |
| Qatar | 1982 | ... | ... | ... | 0.05 | 50 | ... |
| | 1983 | ... | ... | ... | 0.07 | 59 | ... |
| (8) | 1984 | ... | ... | ... | 0.06 | 43 | 421 516 |
| | 1985 | ... | ... | ... | 0.03 | 20 | ... |
| | 1986 | (1) 594 | (1) 159 | (1) 0.3 | (34) 0.04 | (34) 18 | (1)(34) 29 040 |
| Singapore (31) | 1981 | 485 | 328 | 0.7 | (31) 0.30 | (31) 34 | (1) 68 651 |
| | 1984 | 908 | 514 | 0.6 | (31) 0.53 | (31) 82 | (1) 89 255 |
| | 1987 | 1 187 | 539 | 0.5 | (31) 0.87 | (31) 133 | (1) 111 485 |
| | 1990 | 1 426 | ... | ... | (31) 0.94 | (31) 212 | (1) 148 442 |
| | 1995 | 2 318 | 301 | 0.1 | (31) 1.13 | (31) 412 | (1) 177 592 |
| Sri Lanka | 1983 | ... | ... | ... | 0.18 | 14 | 112 227 |
| | 1984 | 166 | 38 | 0.2 | 0.18 | 17 | 98 053 |
| | 1985 | 174 | 44 | 0.2 | ... | ... | ... |
| | 1996 | 191 | 47 | 0.2 | 0.19 | 78 | 408 933 |
| Syrian Arab Republic | 1997 | 30 | 25 | 0.8 | 0.20 | 92 | 3 109 091 |
| Tajikistan | 1992 | 722 | ... | ... | ... | ... | ... |
| | 1993 | 666 | ... | ... | ... | ... | ... |
| Thailand | 1980 | ... | ... | ... | 0.39 | 55 | ... |
| | 1982 | ... | ... | ... | 0.40 | 68 | ... |
| | 1983 | ... | ... | ... | 0.24 | 44 | ... |
| | 1984 | ... | ... | ... | 0.34 | 66 | ... |
| | 1985 | ... | ... | ... | 0.34 | 68 | ... |
| | 1987 | 105 | 53 | 0.5 | 0.21 | 51 | 481 022 |
| | 1989 | 87 | 33 | 0.4 | 0.16 | 54 | 613 973 |
| | 1990 | ... | ... | ... | 0.18 | 68 | ... |
| | 1991 | ... | ... | ... | 0.16 | 70 | 402 795 |

III.1 Selected R&D indicators
Indicateurs sélectionnés de R-D
Indicadores seleccionados de I y D

| Country / Pays / País | Year / Année / Año | Personnel engaged in R&D / Personnel employé à des travaux de R-D / Personal dedicado a actividades de I y D | | | Expenditure for R&D / Dépenses consacrées à la R-D / Gastos destinados a la I y D | | |
|---|---|---|---|---|---|---|---|
| | | Researchers per million inhabitants / Chercheurs par million d'habitants / Investigadores por millón de habitantes | Technicians per million inhabitants / Techniciens par million d'habitants / Técnicos por millón de habitantes | Number of technicians per researcher / Nombre de techniciens par chercheur / Número de técnicos por investigador | As percentage of gross national product (GNP) / En pourcentage du produit national brut (PNB) / En porcentaje del producto nacional bruto (PNB) | Per capita (in national currency) / Par habitant (en monnaie nationale) / Por persona (en moneda nacional) | Annual average per researcher (in national currency) / Moyenne anuelle par chercheur (en monnaie nationale) / Promedio anual por investigador (en moneda nacional) |
| Thailand (cont) | 1993 | 114 | 45 | 0.4 | 0.15 | 78 | 686 844 |
| | 1995 | 118 | 41 | 0.3 | 0.13 | 89 | 749 999 |
| | 1996 | 103 | 39 | 0.4 | 0.13 | 94 | 915 558 |
| Turkey | 1984 | 202 | 128 | 0.6 | 0.59 | 2 624 | 13 000 303 |
| | 1985 | 224 | 147 | 0.7 | 0.55 | 3 823 | 17 068 553 |
| | 1990 | 221 | ... | ... | 0.34 | 23 501 | 106 610 303 |
| | 1991 | 210 | ... | ... | 0.53 | 58 252 | 278 711 668 |
| | 1992 | (15) 217 | ... | ... | (16) 0.49 | 92 037 | 426 056 924 |
| | 1993 | (15) 230 | ... | ... | (16) 0.44 | 148 194 | 645 067 196 |
| | 1994 | (15) 241 | ... | ... | (16) 0.36 | 232 259 | 967 584 385 |
| | 1995 | 259 | ... | ... | 0.38 | 481 582 | 1 861 321 749 |
| | 1996 | (15) 291 | ... | ... | (16) 0.45 | 1 070 526 | 3 688 259 065 |
| Uzbekistan | 1992 | 1 763 | 314 | 0.2 | ... | ... | ... |
| Viet Nam (19) | 1983 | ... | ... | ... | ... | 6 | ... |
| | 1984 | ... | ... | ... | ... | 9 | ... |
| | 1985 | 334 | ... | ... | ... | 9 | (3) 24 900 |
| **Europe** | | | | | | | |
| Austria | 1981 | 890 | 815 | 0.9 | 1.15 | 1 635 | 1 837 162 |
| | 1982 | ... | ... | ... | *1.20 | *1 830 | ... |
| | 1983 | ... | ... | ... | *1.21 | *1 964 | ... |
| | 1984 | 1 009 | 904 | 0.9 | *1.26 | *2 148 | *2 130 464 |
| | 1985 | ... | ... | ... | 1.27 | 2 274 | ... |
| | 1986 | ... | ... | ... | *1.31 | *2 468 | ... |
| | 1987 | ... | ... | ... | *1.32 | *2 571 | ... |
| | 1988 | ... | ... | ... | *1.31 | *2 662 | ... |
| | 1989 | 1 147 | 1 101 | 1.0 | 1.38 | 2 998 | 2 615 226 |
| | 1990 | ... | ... | ... | *1.35 | *3 152 | ... |
| | 1991 | ... | ... | ... | (16) 1.50 | (16) 3 734 | ... |
| | 1992 | ... | ... | ... | (16) 1.49 | (16) 3 880 | ... |
| | 1993 | 1 627 | 812 | 0.5 | 1.50 | 4 022 | 2 472 058 |
| | 1994 | ... | ... | ... | (16) 1.56 | (16) 4 362 | ... |
| | 1995 | ... | ... | ... | (16) 1.56 | (16) 4 500 | ... |
| | 1996 | ... | ... | ... | (16) 1.54 | (16) 4 566 | ... |
| | 1997 | ... | ... | ... | (16) 1.53 | (16) 4 732 | ... |
| | 1998 | ... | ... | ... | ... | (16) 4 985 | ... |
| Belarus | 1992 | 3 259 | 509 | 0.2 | ... | ... | ... |
| | 1993 | 2 939 | 402 | 0.1 | 1.12 | 1 060 | 360 354 |
| | 1994 | 2 517 | 345 | 0.1 | 1.03 | 17 592 | 6 990 418 |
| | 1995 | 2 288 | 302 | 0.1 | 1.12 | 127 607 | 55 780 565 |
| | 1996 | 2 248 | 266 | 0.1 | 1.07 | 184 561 | 82 128 066 |
| Belgium | 1981 | (15) 1 294 | ... | ... | ... | ... | ... |
| | 1982 | (15) 1 362 | ... | ... | ... | ... | ... |
| | 1983 | (15) 1 364 | ... | ... | (16) 1.63 | 6 773 | 4 966 779 |
| | 1984 | (15) 1 412 | ... | ... | (16) 1.65 | 7 375 | 5 224 012 |
| | 1985 | ... | ... | ... | 1.70 | 8 099 | ... |
| | 1986 | 1 592 | (29) 2 078 | (29) 1.3 | 1.69 | 8 485 | 5 331 309 |
| | 1987 | 1 624 | (29) 2 093 | (29) 1.3 | (16) 1.69 | 8 883 | (15)(16) 5 471 400 |
| | 1988 | 1 681 | (29) 2 033 | (29) 1.2 | 1.65 | 9 216 | 5 482 705 |
| | 1989 | 1 772 | (29) 2 037 | (29) 1.1 | 1.70 | 10 329 | 5 830 598 |
| | 1990 | 1 856 | (29) 2 041 | (29) 1.1 | 1.70 | 10 909 | 5 878 462 |
| | 1991 | *1 815 | (29) 2 201 | (29) *1.2 | *1.67 | *11 232 | *6 189 727 |
| | 1993 | ... | ... | ... | (16) 1.60 | 11 636 | ... |
| | 1994 | (15) 2 242 | ... | ... | (16) 1.58 | 12 074 | 5 387 226 |
| | 1995 | (15) 2 272 | ... | ... | (16) 1.60 | 12 662 | 5 573 140 |
| Bulgaria | 1980 | 4 368 | 1 183 | 0.3 | ... | ... | ... |
| | 1981 | 4 654 | 1 334 | 0.3 | ... | ... | ... |
| | 1982 | 4 792 | 1 403 | 0.3 | ... | ... | ... |
| | 1983 | 4 856 | 1 389 | 0.3 | ... | ... | ... |
| | 1984 | 5 034 | 1 393 | 0.3 | ... | ... | ... |
| | 1985 | 5 359 | 1 462 | 0.3 | ... | ... | ... |
| | 1986 | 5 186 | 1 262 | 0.2 | ... | ... | ... |
| | 1987 | 5 691 | 1 312 | 0.2 | ... | ... | ... |
| | 1988 | 5 628 | 1 409 | 0.3 | ... | ... | ... |
| | 1989 | 5 806 | 1 391 | 0.2 | ... | ... | ... |
| | 1990 | 6 034 | 1 407 | 0.2 | ... | ... | ... |
| | 1991 | 5 733 | 1 316 | 0.2 | ... | ... | ... |
| | 1992 | 4 384 | 1 247 | 0.3 | 1.67 | 383 | ... |
| | 1993 | 3 178 | 910 | 0.3 | 1.21 | 413 | 129 672 |
| | 1994 | 1 476 | 897 | 0.6 | 0.88 | 539 | 364 928 |
| | 1995 | 1 647 | 906 | 0.6 | ... | ... | ... |
| | 1996 | 1 747 | 967 | 0.6 | 0.57 | 1 083 | 620 162 |

Selected R&D indicators III.1
Indicateurs sélectionnés de R-D
Indicadores seleccionados de I y D

| Country / Pays / País | Year / Année / Año | Personnel engaged in R&D / Personnel employé à des travaux de R-D / Personal dedicado a actividades de I y D | | | Expenditure for R&D / Dépenses consacrées à la R-D / Gastos destinados a la I y D | | |
|---|---|---|---|---|---|---|---|
| | | Researchers per million inhabitants / Chercheurs par million d'habitants / Investigadores por millón de habitantes | Technicians per million inhabitants / Techniciens par million d'habitants / Técnicos por millón de habitantes | Number of technicians per researcher / Nombre de techniciens par chercheur / Número de técnicos por investigador | As percentage of gross national product (GNP) / En pourcentage du produit national brut (PNB) / En porcentaje del producto nacional bruto (PNB) | Per capita (in national currency) / Par habitant (en monnaie nationale) / Por persona (en moneda nacional) | Annual average per researcher (in national currency) / Moyenne anuelle par chercheur (en monnaie nationale) / Promedio anual por investigador (en moneda nacional) |
| Croatia | 1988 | 2 156 | 1 064 | 0.5 | ... | ... | ... |
| | 1989 | 2 224 | 1 041 | 0.5 | ... | ... | ... |
| | 1990 | 2 056 | 988 | 0.5 | ... | ... | ... |
| | 1991 | 1 920 | 874 | 0.5 | ... | ... | ... |
| | 1992 | 1 979 | 847 | 0.4 | 1.06 | 7 | 3 052 |
| | 1993 | 2 005 | 739 | 0.4 | 0.99 | 91 | 45 010 |
| | 1994 | 1 959 | 684 | 0.3 | 0.87 | 164 | 83 396 |
| | 1995 | 1 984 | 698 | 0.4 | 1.00 | 210 | 105 531 |
| | 1996 | 1 916 | 714 | 0.4 | 1.03 | 238 | 123 813 |
| Czech Republic | 1991 | ... | ... | ... | (16) 2.13 | 1 476 | ... |
| | 1992 | (15) 1 947 | ... | ... | (16) 1.84 | 1 406 | 721 918 |
| | 1993 | (15) 1 320 | ... | ... | (16) 1.36 | 1 194 | 904 088 |
| | 1994 | (15) 1 291 | ... | ... | (16) 1.26 | 1 258 | 974 334 |
| | 1995 | 1 156 | 693 | 0.6 | 1.12 | 1 355 | 1 171 563 |
| | 1996 | (15) 1 252 | ... | ... | (16) 1.11 | 1 576 | 1 258 762 |
| | 1997 | (15) 1 222 | ... | ... | (16) 1.20 | 1 891 | 1 548 283 |
| Denmark | 1981 | (15) 1 324 | ... | ... | (16) 1.14 | 872 | 658 571 |
| | 1982 | 1 417 | (29) 1 949 | (29) 1.4 | 1.19 | 1 034 | 729 566 |
| | 1983 | 1 500 | (29) 2 045 | (29) 1.4 | 1.24 | 1 192 | 794 294 |
| | 1984 | 1 589 | (29) 2 133 | (29) 1.3 | 1.28 | 1 349 | 848 948 |
| | 1985 | 1 676 | (29) 2 219 | (29) 1.3 | 1.31 | 1 505 | 897 864 |
| | 1986 | 1 794 | (29) 2 301 | (29) 1.3 | 1.38 | 1 724 | 961 069 |
| | 1987 | 1 911 | (29) 2 380 | (29) 1.2 | 1.48 | 1 942 | 1 016 164 |
| | 1988 | 2 025 | (29) 2 495 | (29) 1.2 | 1.55 | 2 131 | 1 052 465 |
| | 1989 | 2 138 | (29) 2 609 | (29) 1.2 | 1.62 | 2 319 | 1 084 839 |
| | 1990 | 2 239 | (29) 2 635 | (29) 1.2 | 1.70 | 2 529 | 1 129 596 |
| | 1991 | 2 338 | (29) 2 660 | (29) 1.1 | 1.78 | 2 736 | 1 170 222 |
| | 1992 | (15) 2 488 | ... | ... | (16) 1.81 | 2 882 | 1 158 309 |
| | 1993 | 2 635 | (29) 2 644 | (29) 1.0 | 1.86 | 3 025 | 1 147 883 |
| | 1995 | (15) 3 054 | ... | ... | (16) 1.97 | 3 549 | 1 162 280 |
| | 1996 | (15) 3 122 | ... | ... | (16) 2.08 | 3 893 | 1 246 825 |
| | 1997 | (15) 3 190 | ... | ... | (16) 1.95 | 4 121 | 1 291 650 |
| | 1998 | (15) 3 259 | ... | ... | ... | (16) 4 348 | 1 333 972 |
| Estonia (35) | 1993 | 2 494 | 452 | 0.2 | 0.60 | 86 | 34 144 |
| | 1994 | 2 153 | 563 | 0.3 | 0.73 | 144 | 66 727 |
| | 1995 | ... | ... | ... | 0.61 | 169 | 80 606 |
| | 1996 | 2 079 | 372 | 0.2 | 0.57 | 204 | 98 344 |
| | 1997 | 2 017 | 391 | 0.2 | 0.57 | 247 | 122 382 |
| Federal Republic of Yugoslavia | 1991 | 1 180 | 526 | 0.4 | ... | ... | ... |
| | 1995 | 1 099 | 515 | 0.5 | ... | ... | ... |
| Finland | 1981 | 2 025 | (29) 1 726 | (29) 0.9 | ... | ... | ... |
| | 1983 | 2 257 | (29) 1 910 | (29) 0.8 | ... | ... | ... |
| | 1984 | ... | ... | ... | *1.52 | *922 | ... |
| | 1985 | ... | ... | ... | *1.61 | *1 064 | ... |
| | 1986 | ... | ... | ... | *1.72 | *1 208 | ... |
| | 1987 | (15) 2 146 | ... | ... | (16) 1.80 | 1 376 | 641 169 |
| | 1988 | ... | ... | ... | *1.83 | *1 568 | ... |
| | 1989 | (8) 2 278 | (29)(8) 1 988 | (29)(8) 0.9 | *1.88 | *1 797 | *788 725 |
| | 1990 | ... | ... | ... | (16) 1.97 | 1 975 | ... |
| | 1991 | (8) 2 282 | (29)(8) 2 093 | (29)(8) 0.9 | 2.15 | 2 031 | 890 095 |
| | 1992 | ... | ... | ... | (16) 2.28 | 2 064 | ... |
| | 1993 | (15) 3 010 | ... | ... | (16) 2.33 | 2 110 | 701 104 |
| | 1994 | ... | ... | ... | (16) 2.44 | 2 348 | ... |
| | 1995 | 2 799 | (29)(8) 1 996 | (29) 0.7 | 2.46 | 2 529 | 903 526 |
| | 1996 | ... | ... | ... | (16) 2.70 | 2 905 | ... |
| | 1997 | ... | ... | ... | (16) 2.78 | 3 280 | ... |
| France | 1980 | 1 391 | (29) 2 994 | (29) 2.2 | ... | ... | ... |
| | 1981 | 1 580 | (29) 3 024 | (29) 1.9 | 1.97 | 1 155 | 730 667 |
| | 1982 | 1 658 | (29) 3 108 | (29) 1.9 | 2.07 | 1 377 | 830 589 |
| | 1983 | 1 698 | (29) 3 086 | (29) 1.8 | 2.12 | 1 551 | 913 388 |
| | 1984 | 1 790 | (29) 3 129 | (29) 1.7 | 2.22 | 1 753 | 979 614 |
| | 1985 | 1 855 | (29) 3 095 | (29) 1.7 | 2.27 | 1 920 | 1 035 357 |
| | 1986 | 1 893 | (29) 3 054 | (29) 1.6 | 2.25 | 2 042 | 1 079 150 |
| | 1987 | 1 961 | (29) 3 022 | (29) 1.5 | 2.28 | 2 176 | 1 109 777 |
| | 1988 | 2 053 | (29) 2 994 | (29) 1.5 | 2.29 | 2 329 | 1 134 314 |
| | 1989 | 2 135 | (29) 2 993 | (29) 1.4 | 2.34 | 2 545 | 1 192 004 |
| | 1990 | 2 186 | (29) 2 981 | (29) 1.4 | 2.43 | 2 771 | 1 267 706 |
| | 1991 | 2 267 | (29) 2 972 | (29) 1.3 | 2.43 | 2 862 | 1 262 176 |
| | 1992 | (15) 2 475 | ... | ... | (16) 2.44 | 2 958 | 1 195 237 |
| | 1993 | (15) 2 536 | ... | ... | (16) 2.48 | 3 020 | 1 190 702 |
| | 1994 | 2 583 | (29) 2 873 | (29) 1.1 | 2.40 | 3 039 | 1 176 751 |
| | 1995 | (15) 2 607 | ... | ... | (16) 2.35 | 3 087 | 1 184 090 |
| | 1996 | (15) 2 659 | ... | ... | (16) 2.33 | 3 135 | 1 179 212 |
| | 1997 | ... | ... | ... | (16) 2.25 | 3 140 | ... |

III.1 Selected R&D indicators
Indicateurs sélectionnés de R-D
Indicadores seleccionados de I y D

| Country / Pays / País | Year / Année / Año | Personnel engaged in R&D / Personnel employé à des travaux de R-D / Personal dedicado a actividades de I y D | | | Expenditure for R&D / Dépenses consacrées à la R-D / Gastos destinados a la I y D | | |
|---|---|---|---|---|---|---|---|
| | | Researchers per million inhabitants / Chercheurs par million d'habitants / Investigadores por millón de habitantes | Technicians per million inhabitants / Techniciens par million d'habitants / Técnicos por millón de habitantes | Number of technicians per researcher / Nombre de techniciens par chercheur / Número de técnicos por investigador | As percentage of gross national product (GNP) / En pourcentage du produit national brut (PNB) / En porcentaje del producto nacional bruto (PNB) | Per capita (in national currency) / Par habitant (en monnaie nationale) / Por persona (en moneda nacional) | Annual average per researcher (in national currency) / Moyenne annuelle par chercheur (en monnaie nationale) / Promedio anual por investigador (en moneda nacional) |
| Germany | 1981 | (15) 1 596 | ... | ... | ... | (16) 478 | 299 195 |
| | 1982 | ... | ... | ... | ... | (16) 515 | ... |
| | 1983 | (15) 1 684 | ... | ... | ... | (16) 542 | 321 782 |
| | 1984 | ... | ... | ... | ... | (16) 567 | ... |
| | 1985 | (15) 1 850 | ... | ... | ... | (16) 638 | 344 778 |
| | 1986 | ... | ... | ... | ... | (16) 676 | ... |
| | 1987 | (15) 2 121 | ... | ... | ... | (16) 733 | 345 620 |
| | 1988 | ... | ... | ... | ... | (16) 765 | ... |
| | 1989 | (15) 2 236 | ... | ... | ... | (16) 810 | 362 081 |
| | 1990 | ... | ... | ... | ... | (16) 841 | ... |
| | 1991 | (15) 3 029 | ... | ... | (16) 2.59 | 934 | 308 090 |
| | 1992 | (15) 2 916 | ... | ... | (16) 2.47 | 949 | 325 276 |
| | 1993 | 2 843 | 1 472 | 0.5 | 2.43 | 949 | 333 804 |
| | 1994 | ... | ... | ... | (16) 2.34 | 950 | ... |
| | 1995 | (15) 2 831 | ... | ... | (16) 2.31 | 974 | 344 051 |
| | 1996 | ... | ... | ... | (16) 2.30 | 989 | |
| | 1997 | ... | ... | ... | (16) 2.41 | 1 061 | |
| | 1998 | ... | ... | ... | ... | (16) 1 102 | ... |
| Greece | 1981 | | ... | ... | (16) 0.18 | 441 | ... |
| | 1986 | ... | ... | ... | (16) 0.28 | 1 836 | |
| | 1988 | ... | ... | ... | (16) 0.31 | 2 731 | |
| | 1989 | (15) 538 | ... | ... | (16) 0.38 | 4 035 | 7 507 435 |
| | 1991 | (15) 607 | ... | ... | (16) 0.37 | 5 790 | 9 551 044 |
| | 1993 | 773 | 314 | 0.4 | 0.47 | 9 669 | 12 510 586 |
| Hungary | 1980 | (7) 2 390 | (7)(36) 2 215 | (7)(36) 0.9 | ... | ... | ... |
| | 1981 | (7) 2 081 | (7)(36) 2 029 | (7)(36) 1.0 | 2.59 | 1 815 | 872 368 |
| | 1982 | (7) 2 056 | (7)(36) 1 718 | (7)(36) 0.8 | 2.63 | 1 986 | 965 635 |
| | 1983 | (7) 2 077 | (7)(36) 1 734 | (7)(36) 0.8 | 2.37 | 1 917 | 922 601 |
| | 1984 | (7) 2 121 | (7)(36) 1 737 | (7)(36) 0.8 | 2.42 | 2 137 | 1 007 461 |
| | 1985 | (7) 2 125 | (7)(36) 1 690 | (7)(36) 0.8 | 2.44 | 2 276 | 1 071 089 |
| | 1986 | (7) 2 181 | (7)(36) 1 689 | (7)(36) 0.8 | 2.64 | 2 606 | 1 194 960 |
| | 1987 | (7) 2 125 | (7)(36) 1 596 | (7)(36) 0.8 | 2.73 | 3 066 | 1 442 964 |
| | 1988 | (7) 2 052 | (7)(36) 1 495 | (7)(36) 0.7 | 2.34 | 3 102 | 1 512 205 |
| | 1989 | (7) 1 964 | (7)(36) 1 357 | (7)(36) 0.7 | 2.04 | 3 215 | 1 636 778 |
| | 1990 | 1 694 | 1 130 | 0.7 | 1.67 | 3 217 | 1 899 716 |
| | 1991 | 1 401 | 862 | 0.6 | 1.12 | 2 588 | 1 847 212 |
| | 1992 | 1 195 | 695 | 0.6 | 1.09 | 3 008 | 2 517 099 |
| | 1993 | (15) 1 150 | ... | ... | (16) 1.01 | 3 374 | 2 935 015 |
| | 1994 | (15) 1 146 | ... | ... | (16) 0.93 | 3 789 | 3 305 991 |
| | 1995 | (37) 1 027 | 510 | 0.5 | 0.76 | 4 029 | 3 924 183 |
| | 1996 | (15) 1 022 | ... | ... | (16) 0.68 | 4 404 | 4 312 971 |
| | 1997 | (15) 1 099 | ... | ... | ... | (16) 6 081 | 5 536 068 |
| Iceland | 1981 | 1 723 | (29) 1 498 | (29) 0.9 | 0.65 | 693 | 402 011 |
| | 1983 | 1 750 | (29) 1 539 | (29) 0.9 | 0.71 | 1 958 | 1 118 645 |
| | 1984 | ... | ... | ... | (16) 0.77 | 2 708 | ... |
| | 1985 | 2 125 | (29) 1 270 | (29) 0.6 | 0.73 | 3 507 | 1 650 391 |
| | 1986 | ... | ... | ... | (16) 0.75 | 4 757 | ... |
| | 1987 | 2 252 | (29) 1 300 | (29) 0.6 | 0.78 | 6 450 | 2 865 108 |
| | 1989 | (15) 2 719 | ... | ... | (16) 1.07 | 12 500 | 4 598 453 |
| | 1990 | (15) 2 651 | ... | ... | (16) 1.03 | 14 170 | 5 345 134 |
| | 1991 | (15) 2 663 | ... | ... | (16) 1.21 | 17 904 | 6 723 756 |
| | 1992 | (15) 2 724 | ... | ... | (16) 1.38 | 20 422 | 7 499 280 |
| | 1993 | (15) 3 099 | ... | ... | (16) 1.38 | 20 904 | 6 745 596 |
| | 1994 | (15) 3 177 | ... | ... | (16) 1.44 | 22 735 | 7 156 722 |
| | 1995 | 4 015 | (29) 1 467 | (29) 0.4 | 1.59 | 25 963 | 6 466 477 |
| | 1996 | (15) 3 351 | ... | ... | (16) 1.55 | 27 002 | 8 058 800 |
| | 1997 | (15) 4 131 | ... | ... | ... | (16) 29 843 | 7 224 328 |
| Ireland | 1981 | *766 | *410 | *0.5 | *0.74 | *25 | *31 626 |
| | 1982 | 797 | 366 | 0.5 | 0.75 | 29 | 35 191 |
| | 1983 | 920 | 378 | 0.4 | 0.74 | 30 | 32 190 |
| | 1984 | 1 025 | 378 | 0.4 | 0.82 | 36 | 34 664 |
| | 1985 | 1 054 | 378 | 0.4 | 0.89 | 42 | 39 215 |
| | 1986 | 1 088 | 380 | 0.3 | 0.96 | 48 | 43 519 |
| | 1987 | (15) 945 | ... | ... | (16) 0.96 | 52 | 54 130 |
| | 1988 | 1 804 | 367 | 0.2 | 0.92 | 53 | 29 256 |
| | 1989 | (15) 1 169 | ... | ... | (16) 0.95 | 61 | 51 772 |
| | 1990 | (15) 1 319 | ... | ... | (16) 0.97 | 68 | 51 207 |
| | 1991 | (15) 1 470 | ... | ... | (16) 1.07 | 79 | 53 622 |
| | 1992 | (15) 1 572 | ... | ... | (16) 1.19 | 93 | 58 879 |
| | 1993 | 1 855 | 506 | 0.3 | 1.37 | 113 | 60 711 |
| | 1994 | (15) 2 040 | ... | ... | (16) 1.52 | 134 | 65 569 |
| | 1995 | (15) 2 319 | ... | ... | (16) 1.61 | 155 | 66 669 |
| Italy | 1980 | 833 | 490 | 0.6 | 0.76 | 51 340 | 61 645 440 |
| | 1981 | 921 | 520 | 0.6 | 0.89 | 71 724 | 77 897 331 |

Selected R&D Indicators III.1
Indicateurs sélectionnés de R-D
Indicadores seleccionados de I y D

| Country / Pays / País | Year / Année / Año | Researchers per million inhabitants / Chercheurs par million d'habitants / Investigadores por millón de habitantes | Technicians per million inhabitants / Techniciens par million d'habitants / Técnicos por millón de habitantes | Number of technicians per researcher / Nombre de techniciens par chercheur / Número de técnicos por investigador | As percentage of gross national product (GNP) / En pourcentage du produit national brut (PNB) / En porcentaje del producto nacional bruto (PNB) | Per capita (in national currency) / Par habitant (en monnaie nationale) / Por persona (en moneda nacional) | Annual average per researcher (in national currency) / Moyenne anuelle par chercheur (en monnaie nationale) / Promedio anual por investigador (en moneda nacional) |
|---|---|---|---|---|---|---|---|
| Italy (cont) | 1982 | 1 002 | 496 | 0.5 | 0.92 | 86 819 | 86 685 560 |
| | 1983 | 1 112 | 507 | 0.5 | 0.97 | 106 338 | 95 634 868 |
| | 1984 | 1 093 | 538 | 0.5 | 1.02 | 129 094 | 118 152 133 |
| | 1985 | 1 124 | 583 | 0.5 | 1.14 | 160 873 | 143 240 986 |
| | 1986 | 1 195 | 579 | 0.5 | 1.15 | 179 333 | 150 184 822 |
| | 1987 | 1 241 | 637 | 0.5 | 1.20 | 205 688 | 165 769 531 |
| | 1988 | 1 315 | 673 | 0.5 | 1.23 | 233 366 | 177 478 974 |
| | 1989 | 1 336 | 704 | 0.5 | 1.26 | 259 821 | 194 556 209 |
| | 1990 | 1 366 | 742 | 0.5 | 1.32 | 298 147 | 218 311 431 |
| | 1991 | (15) 1 318 | ... | ... | (16) 1.26 | 309 294 | 234 685 518 |
| | 1992 | (15) 1 302 | ... | ... | (16) 1.22 | 314 171 | 241 299 052 |
| | 1993 | (15) 1 301 | ... | ... | (16) 1.16 | 307 757 | 236 628 947 |
| | 1994 | 1 322 | 798 | 0.6 | 1.08 | 303 513 | 229 640 765 |
| | 1995 | (15) 1 318 | ... | ... | (16) 1.03 | 311 555 | 236 495 195 |
| | 1996 | ... | ... | ... | (16) 1.05 | 335 543 | ... |
| | 1997 | ... | ... | ... | (16) 2.21 | 358 271 | ... |
| Latvia | 1993 | 1 531 | 408 | 0.3 | 0.49 | 3 | 1 786 |
| | 1994 | 1 169 | 367 | 0.3 | 0.43 | 4 | 2 878 |
| | 1995 | 1 211 | 398 | 0.3 | 0.53 | 5 | 4 007 |
| | 1996 | 1 137 | 341 | 0.3 | 0.48 | 6 | 4 601 |
| | 1997 | 1 049 | 351 | 0.3 | 0.43 | 6 | 5 323 |
| Lithuania | 1995 | ... | ... | ... | 0.70 | 45 | ... |
| | 1996 | 2 028 | 631 | 0.3 | ... | ... | ... |
| Moldova | 1994 | 493 | 1924 | 3.9 | 1.1 | 12.06 | 3091328 |
| | 1995 | 416 | 1554 | 3.7 | 1.1 | 16.54 | 4429295 |
| | 1996 | 250 | 1632 | 6.5 | 0.9 | 15.56 | 2388144 |
| | 1997 | 330 | 1641 | 5.0 | 0.9 | 16.43 | 3299377 |
| Netherlands | (17) 1980 | 1 869 | (29) 1 919 | (29) 1.0 | 1.87 | 449 | 240 182 |
| | (17) 1981 | 2 084 | (29) 1 968 | (29) 0.9 | 1.98 | 495 | 237 328 |
| | (17) 1982 | 2 112 | (29) 1 911 | (29) 0.9 | 1.96 | 510 | 241 512 |
| | (17) 1983 | 2 128 | (29) 1 889 | (29) 0.9 | 1.99 | 537 | 252 179 |
| | (17) 1984 | 2 173 | (29) 1 879 | (29) 0.9 | 1.95 | 545 | 250 703 |
| | (17) 1985 | 2 320 | (29) 1 917 | (29) 0.8 | 2.06 | 604 | 260 203 |
| | (17) 1986 | 2 419 | (29) 1 893 | (29) 0.8 | 2.19 | 655 | 270 440 |
| | (17) 1987 | 2 507 | (29) 1 827 | (29) 0.7 | 2.29 | 685 | 273 198 |
| | (17) 1988 | 2 544 | (29) 1 824 | (29) 0.7 | 2.24 | 689 | 270 869 |
| | (17) 1989 | 2 633 | (29) 1 843 | (29) 0.7 | 2.12 | 692 | 262 737 |
| | (17) 1990 | 2 693 | (29) 1 867 | (29) 0.7 | 2.03 | 699 | 259 563 |
| | (17) 1991 | 2 657 | (29) 1 358 | (29) 0.5 | 1.92 | 690 | 259 525 |
| | 1992 | ... | ... | ... | (16) 1.99 | 738 | ... |
| | 1993 | (15) 2 110 | ... | ... | (16) 2.01 | 763 | 361 709 |
| | 1994 | ... | ... | ... | 2.04 | 813 | ... |
| | 1995 | (15) 2 202 | ... | ... | (16) 2.09 | 857 | 388 889 |
| | 1996 | (15) 2 219 | ... | ... | (16) 2.08 | 900 | 405 458 |
| Norway | 1980 | 1 818 | (29) 1 855 | (29) 1.0 | 1.20 | 889 | 488 731 |
| | 1981 | 1 830 | (29) 1 792 | (29) 1.0 | 1.22 | 1 029 | 561 990 |
| | 1982 | 1 887 | (29) 1 816 | (29) 1.0 | *1.30 | *1 205 | *638 703 |
| | 1983 | 2 009 | (29) 1 864 | (29) 0.9 | 1.35 | 1 380 | 687 070 |
| | 1984 | 2 168 | (29) 1 997 | (29) 0.9 | *1.43 | *1 651 | *761 427 |
| | 1985 | 2 334 | (29) 2 189 | (29) 0.9 | 1.52 | 1 953 | 836 763 |
| | 1986 | 2 429 | (29) 2 285 | (29) 0.9 | *1.71 | *2 251 | *926 878 |
| | 1987 | 2 740 | (29) 2 013 | (29) 0.7 | 1.70 | 2 438 | 889 900 |
| | 1989 | 2 880 | (29) 1 910 | (29) 0.7 | 1.74 | 2 732 | 948 725 |
| | 1991 | 3 159 | (29) 1 594 | (29) 0.5 | 1.71 | 2 958 | 936 330 |
| | 1993 | (15) 3 431 | ... | ... | (16) 1.78 | 3 314 | 966 105 |
| | 1995 | 3 664 | (29) 1 842 | (29) 0.5 | 1.74 | 3 658 | 998 532 |
| | 1997 | ... | ... | ... | (16) 1.58 | ... | ... |
| Poland | 1980 | 2 615 | (39) 1 603 | (39) 0.6 | ... | ... | ... |
| | 1981 | 2 479 | (39) 1 421 | (39) 0.6 | ... | ... | ... |
| | 1982 | 2 179 | (39) 1 131 | (39) 0.5 | ... | ... | ... |
| | 1983 | 2 050 | (39) 1 011 | (39) 0.5 | ... | ... | ... |
| | 1984 | 2 032 | (39) 949 | (39) 0.5 | ... | ... | ... |
| | 1985 | 1 533 | (39) 1 452 | (39) 0.9 | 1.00 | 2 699 | 1 761 350 |
| | 1986 | (38) 1 202 | (38)(39) 1 656 | (38)(39) 1.4 | 1.25 | 4 146 | 3 449 520 |
| | 1987 | (38) 1 143 | (38)(39) 1 700 | (38)(39) 1.5 | ... | ... | ... |
| | 1988 | ... | ... | ... | (40) 1.37 | (40) 10 215 | (40) 11 363 615 |
| | 1989 | ... | ... | ... | (40) 1.15 | (40) 34 236 | (40) 40 007 631 |
| | 1990 | ... | ... | ... | (40)(41) 1.63 | (40)(41) 225 346 | (40)(41) 286 331 167 |
| | 1991 | ... | ... | ... | (40)(41) 1.10 | (40)(41) 222 507 | (40)(41) 291 445 343 |
| | 1992 | 1 081 | 1 377 | 1.3 | (40) 0.85 | (40) 249 135 | (40) 230 624 132 |
| | 1994 | (15) 1 231 | ... | ... | (16) 0.84 | 45 | 36 283 |
| | 1995 | (15) 1 307 | ... | ... | (16) 0.75 | 56 | 42 297 |
| | 1996 | (15) 1 358 | ... | ... | (16) 0.77 | 72 | 52 625 |

III.1    Selected R&D indicators
Indicateurs sélectionnés de R-D
Indicadores seleccionados de I y D

| Country / Pays / País | Year / Année / Año | Personnel engaged in R&D / Personnel employé à des travaux de R-D / Personal dedicado a actividades de I y D | | | Expenditure for R&D / Dépenses consacrées à la R-D / Gastos destinados a la I y D | | |
|---|---|---|---|---|---|---|---|
| | | Researchers per million inhabitants / Chercheurs par million d'habitants / Investigadores por millón de habitantes | Technicians per million inhabitants / Techniciens par million d'habitants / Técnicos por millón de habitantes | Number of technicians per researcher / Nombre de techniciens par chercheur / Número de técnicos por investigador | As percentage of gross national product (GNP) / En pourcentage du produit national brut (PNB) / En porcentaje del producto nacional bruto (PNB) | Per capita (in national currency) / Par habitant (en monnaie nationale) / Por persona (en moneda nacional) | Annual average per researcher (in national currency) / Moyenne anuelle par chercheur (en monnaie nationale) / Promedio anual por investigador (en moneda nacional) |
| Portugal | 1980 | 273 | 294 | 1.1 | 0.30 | 422 | 1 546 565 |
| | 1982 | 306 | 314 | 1.0 | 0.34 | 662 | 2 166 678 |
| | 1984 | 351 | 309 | 0.9 | 0.38 | 1 142 | 3 253 986 |
| | 1986 | 453 | 346 | 0.8 | 0.41 | 2 007 | 4 435 723 |
| | 1988 | 507 | 362 | 0.7 | 0.45 | 3 026 | 5 977 379 |
| | 1990 | 599 | 381 | 0.6 | 0.55 | 5 273 | 8 807 076 |
| | 1992 | (15) 959 | ... | ... | (16) 0.65 | 8 157 | 8 506 804 |
| | 1995 | 1 182 | 167 | 0.1 | 0.62 | 9 347 | 7 908 706 |
| Romania | 1987 | 2 553 | 1 837 | 0.7 | ... | ... | ... |
| | 1988 | 2 550 | 1 835 | 0.7 | ... | ... | ... |
| | 1989 | 2 575 | 1 853 | 0.7 | ... | ... | ... |
| | 1991 | 1 222 | 486 | 0.4 | 0.79 | 750 | 613 703 |
| | 1994 | 1 387 | 581 | 0.4 | ... | ... | ... |
| | 1995 | ... | ... | ... | 0.72 | 22 631 | ... |
| Russian Federation | (1) 1989 | 7 576 | 1 835 | 0.2 | ... | ... | ... |
| | (1) 1990 | 6 697 | 1 581 | 0.2 | ... | ... | ... |
| | (1) 1991 | 5 911 | 1 340 | 0.2 | ... | ... | ... |
| | 1994 | 4 192 | 880 | 0.2 | 0.86 | 34 693 | 8 276 270 |
| | 1995 | 3 503 | 685 | 0.2 | 0.76 | 82 037 | 23 423 352 |
| | 1996 | 3 801 | 656 | 0.2 | 0.88 | 131 150 | 34 504 406 |
| | 1997 | 3 587 | 600 | 0.2 | ... | ... | ... |
| Slovakia | 1992 | 2 016 | 1 058 | 0.5 | ... | ... | ... |
| | 1993 | 1 678 | 852 | 0.5 | ... | ... | ... |
| | 1994 | 1 920 | 795 | 0.4 | ... | ... | ... |
| | 1995 | 1 814 | 763 | 0.4 | 1.05 | 1 004 | 553 394 |
| | 1996 | 1 866 | 792 | 0.4 | ... | ... | ... |
| Slovenia | 1992 | 2 972 | 2 370 | 0.8 | 1.49 | 7 727 | 2 599 849 |
| | 1993 | 1 906 | 1 190 | 0.6 | 1.61 | 11 699 | 6 138 318 |
| | 1994 | 2 408 | 1 174 | 0.5 | 1.75 | 16 475 | 6 842 879 |
| | 1995 | 2 461 | 1 097 | 0.4 | 1.69 | 18 922 | 7 689 198 |
| | 1996 | 2 251 | 1 027 | 0.5 | 1.46 | 18 454 | 8 201 159 |
| Spain | 1981 | (15) 510 | ... | ... | (16) 0.44 | 1 927 | 3 778 960 |
| | 1982 | (15) 495 | ... | ... | (16) 0.50 | 2 527 | 5 111 384 |
| | 1983 | (15) 510 | ... | ... | (16) 0.49 | 2 822 | 5 535 425 |
| | 1984 | 536 | 162 | 0.3 | (42) 0.51 | (42) 3 294 | (42) 6 154 248 |
| | 1985 | 558 | 183 | 0.3 | (42) 0.56 | (42) 4 038 | (42) 7 240 317 |
| | 1986 | 635 | 197 | 0.3 | (42) 0.62 | (42) 5 115 | (42) 8 060 184 |
| | 1987 | 682 | 212 | 0.3 | (42) 0.65 | (42) 5 937 | (42) 8 710 944 |
| | 1988 | 799 | 255 | 0.3 | (42) 0.73 | (42) 7 375 | (42) 9 229 665 |
| | 1989 | 838 | 285 | 0.3 | (42) 0.76 | (42) 8 662 | (42) 10 341 476 |
| | 1990 | 955 | 299 | 0.3 | (42) 0.86 | (42) 10 776 | (42) 11 283 147 |
| | 1991 | (15) 1 032 | ... | ... | (16) 0.89 | 12 168 | 11 794 993 |
| | 1992 | (15) 1 057 | ... | ... | (16) 0.93 | 13 681 | 12 953 600 |
| | 1993 | (15) 1 098 | ... | ... | (16) 0.93 | 14 109 | 12 853 138 |
| | 1994 | 1 211 | 343 | 0.3 | *0.87 | *13 863 | *11 451 597 |
| | 1995 | (15) 1 197 | ... | ... | (16) 0.86 | 14 929 | 12 477 046 |
| | 1996 | (15) 1 305 | ... | ... | (16) 0.89 | 16 191 | 12 415 012 |
| | 1997 | ... | ... | ... | (16) 0.90 | ... | ... |
| Sweden | 1981 | 2 128 | (29) 2 948 | (29) 1.4 | (43) 2.33 | (43) 1 602 | (43) 752 713 |
| | 1983 | 2 211 | (29) 3 287 | (29) 1.5 | (43) 2.62 | (43) 2 185 | (43) 988 533 |
| | 1985 | 2 539 | (29) 3 402 | (29) 1.3 | (43) 2.96 | (43) 2 993 | (43) 1 178 727 |
| | 1987 | 2 701 | (29) 3 457 | (29) 1.3 | (43) 3.04 | (43) 3 631 | (43) 1 344 467 |
| | 1989 | 3 007 | (29) 3 473 | (29) 1.2 | 3.02 | 4 263 | 1 417 706 |
| | 1991 | 3 080 | (29) 3 147 | (29) 1.0 | 2.95 | 4 803 | 1 559 571 |
| | 1993 | 3 706 | (29) 3 166 | (29) 0.9 | 3.43 | 5 448 | 1 470 299 |
| | 1995 | (15) 3 826 | ... | ... | (16) 3.76 | 6 739 | 1 761 385 |
| Switzerland | 1981 | ... | ... | ... | (16) 2.11 | 667 | ... |
| | 1983 | ... | ... | ... | (16) 2.11 | 723 | ... |
| | 1986 | 2 262 | 1 625 | 0.7 | ... | ... | ... |
| | 1989 | 2 408 | 1 374 | 0.6 | ... | ... | ... |
| | 1992 | (15) 2 545 | ... | ... | (16) 2.51 | 1 306 | 513 270 |
| | 1996 | (15) 3 006 | ... | ... | (16) 2.60 | 1 388 | 461 752 |
| The Former Yugoslav Rep. of Macedonia | 1995 | 1 335 | 546 | 0.4 | (44) 0.31 | (44) 217 | (44) 162 150 |
| Ukraine | 1995 | 3 176 | 714 | 0.2 | ... | ... | ... |
| | 1996 | 2 883 | 713 | 0.2 | ... | ... | ... |
| | 1997 | 2 171 | 575 | 0.3 | ... | ... | ... |
| United Kingdom | 1981 | (15) 2 254 | ... | ... | (16) 2.37 | 107 | 47 430 |
| | 1982 | (15) 2 271 | ... | ... | ... | ... | ... |
| | 1983 | (15) 2 251 | ... | ... | (16) 2.19 | 119 | 52 456 |

Selected R&D Indicators III.1
Indicateurs sélectionnés de R-D
Indicadores seleccionados de I y D

| Country / Pays / País | Year / Année / Año | Personnel engaged in R&D / Personnel employé à des travaux de R-D / Personal dedicado a actividades de I y D | | | Expenditure for R&D / Dépenses consacrées à la R-D / Gastos destinados a la I y D | | |
|---|---|---|---|---|---|---|---|
| | | Researchers per million inhabitants / Chercheurs par million d'habitants / Investigadores por millón de habitantes | Technicians per million inhabitants / Techniciens par million d'habitants / Técnicos por millón de habitantes | Number of technicians per researcher / Nombre de techniciens par chercheur / Número de técnicos por investigador | As percentage of gross national product (GNP) / En pourcentage du produit national brut (PNB) / En porcentaje del producto nacional bruto (PNB) | Per capita (in national currency) / Par habitant (en monnaie nationale) / Por persona (en moneda nacional) | Annual average per researcher (in national currency) / Moyenne anuelle par chercheur (en monnaie nationale) / Promedio anual por investigador (en moneda nacional) |
| United Kingdom  (cont) | 1984 | (15) 2 283 | ... | ... | ... | ... | ... |
| | 1985 | (15) 2 314 | ... | ... | (16) 2.23 | 141 | 60 756 |
| | 1986 | (15) 2 361 | ... | ... | (16) 2.25 | 152 | 64 351 |
| | 1987 | (15) 2 353 | ... | ... | (16) 2.19 | 162 | 68 814 |
| | 1988 | (15) 2 397 | ... | ... | (16) 2.15 | 176 | 73 249 |
| | 1989 | (15) 2 319 | ... | ... | (16) 2.17 | 193 | 83 226 |
| | 1990 | (15) 2 311 | ... | ... | (16) 2.21 | 209 | 90 158 |
| | 1991 | (15) 2 217 | ... | ... | (16) 2.15 | 211 | 94 782 |
| | 1992 | (15) 2 263 | ... | ... | (16) 2.14 | 220 | 96 863 |
| | 1993 | 2 413 | 1 017 | 0.4 | 2.22 | 239 | 98 779 |
| | 1994 | (15) 2 441 | ... | ... | (16) 2.12 | 242 | 98 915 |
| | 1995 | (15) 2 504 | ... | ... | (16) 2.04 | 244 | 97 068 |
| | 1996 | (15) 2 448 | ... | ... | (16) 1.95 | 246 | 100 278 |
| **Oceania** | | | | | | | |
| Australia | 1981 | 1 661 | 834 | 0.5 | 1.01 | 106 | 63 784 |
| | 1984 | 1 881 | 906 | 0.5 | 1.15 | 157 | 83 392 |
| | 1985 | 1 944 | 950 | 0.5 | 1.18 | 176 | 90 358 |
| | 1986 | 2 205 | 1 024 | 0.5 | 1.32 | 212 | 96 081 |
| | 1987 | 2 257 | 1 024 | 0.5 | 1.28 | 229 | 101 225 |
| | 1988 | 2 408 | 1 016 | 0.4 | 1.31 | 260 | 107 740 |
| | 1990 | 2 478 | 943 | 0.4 | 1.41 | 302 | 121 606 |
| | 1992 | (15) 3 009 | ... | ... | (16) 1.66 | 374 | 124 296 |
| | 1994 | 3 185 | 797 | 0.3 | 1.72 | 413 | 129 532 |
| | 1996 | (15) 3 357 | ... | ... | (16) 1.80 | 480 | 142 768 |
| Guam | 1983 | 158 | 132 | 0.8 | (5) 0.06 | (5) 4 | (5) 21 334 |
| | 1984 | 154 | 129 | 0.8 | (5) 0.07 | (5) 4 | (5) 23 945 |
| | 1985 | 160 | 93 | 0.6 | (5) 0.06 | (5) 4 | (5) 22 000 |
| | 1986 | 156 | 91 | 0.6 | ... | (5) 5 | (5) 26 422 |
| | 1987 | 152 | 88 | 0.6 | ... | ... | |
| | 1989 | 161 | 84 | 0.5 | ... | (5) *15 | (5) *91 715 |
| | 1991 | 168 | 81 | 0.5 | ... | (5) 17 | (5) 96 305 |
| New Zealand | 1989 | (15) 1 450 | ... | ... | (16) 0.95 | 187 | 128 996 |
| | 1990 | (15) 1 457 | ... | ... | (16) 1.07 | 216 | 148 090 |
| | 1991 | (15) 1 393 | ... | ... | (16) 1.06 | 210 | 150 358 |
| | 1992 | (15) 1 699 | ... | ... | (16) 1.06 | 218 | 127 952 |
| | 1993 | 1 749 | 809 | 0.5 | 1.09 | 233 | 133 140 |
| | 1995 | (15) 1 663 | ... | ... | (16) 1.04 | 243 | 145 700 |

**General note**
For general explanations and definitions, please refer to the beginning of this chapter.
**Note générale**
Pour les explications et définitions générales, se référer au début de ce chapitre.
**Nota general**
Para las explicaciones y definiciones generales, referirse al comienzo de este capítulo.

| Notes | Notes | Notas |
|---|---|---|
| (1) Data refer to full-time plus part-time personnel. | (1) Les données se réfèrent au personnel à plein temps et à temps partiel. | (1) Los datos se refieren al personal de jornada completa y de jornada parcial. |
| (2) Not including data for the productive sector. | (2) Non compris les données relatives au secteur de la production. | (2) No incluyen los datos del sector productivo. |
| (3) Not including data for the general service sector. | (3) Non compris les données relatives au secteur de service général. | (3) No incluyen los datos del sector de servicio general. |
| (4) Data refer to the productive sector only. | (4) Les données se réfèrent au secteur de la production seulement. | (4) Los datos se refieren al sector productivo solamente. |
| (5) Data refer to the higher education sector only. | (5) Les données se réfèrent au secteur de l'enseignement supérieur seulement. | (5) Los datos se refieren al sector de la enseñanza superior solamente. |
| (6) Data refer to 4 research institutes only. | (6) Les données se réfèrent à 4 instituts de recherche seulement. | (6) Los datos se refieren a 4 institutos de investigación solamente. |
| (7) Not including personnel engaged in the administration of R&D. | (7) Non compris le personnel employé dans les services administratifs de la R-D. | (7) No incluyen al personal empleado en los servicios administrativos de la I y D. |
| (8) Not including data for the higher education sector. | (8) Non compris les données relatives au secteur de l'enseignement supérieur. | (8) No incluyen los datos del sector de la enseñanza superior. |
| (9) Data refer to the Ministry of Scientific Research only. | (9) Les données concernent le Ministère de la Recherche Scientifique seulement. | (9) Los datos se refieren al Ministerio de la Investigación Científica solamente. |
| (10) Data relate only to 23 out of 26 national research institutes under the Federal Ministry of Science and Technology. | (10) Les données concernent 23 des 26 instituts de recherche sous la tutelle du Ministère Fédéral de la Science et de la Technologie. | (10) Los datos se refieren a 23 de los 26 institutos de investigación bajo la tutela del Ministerio Federal de Ciencia y Tecnología. |
| (11) Data refer to the National University of Rwanda only. | (11) Les données se réfèrent à l'Université Nationale du Rwanda seulement. | (11) Los datos se refieren a la Universidad Nacional de Rwanda solamente. |
| (12) Data refer to full-time personnel. | (12) Les données concernent le personnel à plein temps. | (12) Los datos se refieren al personal de jornada completa. |

III.1    Selected R&D indicators
Indicateurs sélectionnés de R-D
Indicadores seleccionados de I y D

| | |
|---|---|
| (13) Not including private productive enterprises. | (13) Non compris les entreprises privées du secteur de la production. |
| (14) Data for scientists and engineers refer to researchers listed in the directory of research groups in Brazil compiled by the Conselho Nacional de Desenvolvimento Cientifico e Tecnologico (CNPq). | (14) Les données pour les scientifiques et les ingénieurs se réfèrent aux chercheurs figurant dans le répertoire des groupes de recherche brésiliens élaboré par le Conselho Nacional de Desenvolvimento Cientifico e Tecnologico (CNPq). |
| (15) Data for researchers refers to full-time equivalent. Data are from OECD. | (15) Les données concernant les chercheurs sont exprimées en équivalent plein temps. Les données sont de l'OCDE. |
| (16) Data on R&D expenditure are from OECD. | (16) Les données sur les dépenses en R-D sont de l'OCDE. |
| (17) Not including data for social sciences and humanities in the productive sector (integrated R&D). | (17) Non compris les données sur les sciences sociales et humaines dans le secteur de la production (activités de R-D intégrées). |
| (18) Not including data for the productive sector (non-integrated R&D). | (18) Non compris les données relatives au secteur de la production (activités de R-D non intégrées). |
| (19) Data refer to government funds or expenditure. | (19) Les données se réfèrent aux fonds publics ou aux dépenses publiques. |
| (20) Data refer to full-time plus part-time researchers in public enterprises. | (20) Les données concernent les chercheurs à plein temps et à temps partiel dans les entreprises publiques. |
| (21) Data refer to R&D in public enterprises. | (21) Les données se réfèrent à la R-D dans les entreprises publiques. |
| (22) Not including data for the productive sector (non-integrated R&D) and the general service sector. | (22) Non compris les données du secteur de la production (activités de R-D non intégrées) et du secteur de service général. |
| (23) Data refer to the Scientific Research Council only. | (23) Les données concernent le 'Scientific Research Council' seulement. |
| (24) Data are the budget allotment for science and technology. | (24) Les données correspondent à l'allocation budgétaire destinée à la science et la technologie. |
| (25) Data refer only to the institutions: CONCYTEC, IMARPE, INICTEL, INIA, UNMSR, and UP. | (25) Les données se réfèrent seulement aux institutions suivantes : CONCYTEC, IMARPE, INICTEL, INIA, UNMSR, et UP. |
| (26) Not including data for law, humanities and education. | (26) Non compris les données relatives au droit, aux sciences humaines et aux sciences de l'éducation. |
| (27) Not including capital expenditure in the productive sector. | (27) Non compris les dépenses en capital dans le secteur de la production. |
| (28) Data refer to scientific and technological activities (STA). | (28) Les données se réfèrent aux activités scientifiques et technologiques (AST). |
| (29) Including other supporting personnel. | (29) Y compris le personnel de soutien. |
| (30) Data refer to the East Bank only. | (30) Les données se réfèrent à la rive orientale seulement. |
| (31) Not including data for social sciences and humanities. | (31) Non compris les données pour les sciences sociales et humaines. |
| (32) Data refer to R&D activities concentrated mainly in government-financed research establishments; social sciences and humanities in the higher education and general service sectors are excluded; not including military and defence R&D. | (32) Les données se réfèrent aux activités de R-D concentrées principalement dans les établissements de recherche financés par le gouvernement ; les sciences sociales et humaines dans le secteur de l'enseignement supérieur et le secteur de service général sont exclus. Les activités de R-D de caractère militaire ou relevant de la défense nationale ne sont pas incluses. |
| (33) Data refer to the general service sector only. | (33) Les données se réfèrent au secteur de service général seulement. |
| (34) Not including social sciences and humanities in the higher education sector. | (34) Non compris les sciences sociales et humaines dans le secteur de l'enseignement supérieur. |
| (35) Not including business enterprise sector. | (35) Non compris le secteur des entreprises. |
| (36) Skilled workers are included with technicians and equivalent staff rather than with other supporting staff. | (36) Les travailleurs qualifiés sont inclus avec les techniciens et assimilés plutôt qu'avec le personnel de soutien. |
| (37) Not including scientists and engineers engaged in the administration of R&D; data for technicians include skilled workers; of military R&D, only that part carried out in civil establishments is included. | (37) Non compris les scientifiques et les ingénieurs employés dans les services administratifs de R-D ; les données pour les techniciens incluent les travailleurs qualifiés. Pour la R-D militaire, seule est considérée la partie effectuée dans les établissements civils. |
| (38) Due to methodological changes, "managerial personnel in the technical section" previously classified as researchers are now included with technicians. | (38) Suite à des changements de méthodologie, "le personnel d'administration de la section technique", auparavant classé parmi les chercheurs, sont inclus maintenant avec les techniciens. |
| (39) Not including data for technicians and equivalent staff as well as other supporting staff in the higher education sector. | (39) Non compris les données sur les techniciens et assimilé et le personnel de soutien dans le secteur de l'enseignement supérieur. |
| (40) Not including capital expenditure in the productive sector (integrated R&D) and in the higher education sector. | (40) Non compris les dépenses en capital dans le secteur de la production (activités de R-D intégrées) et dans le secteur de l'enseignement supérieur. |
| (41) Not including data for the productive sector (integrated R&D). | (41) Non compris les données du secteur de la production (activités de R-D intégrées). |
| (42) Not including data for private non-profit organizations. | (42) Non compris les données des organisations privées à but non lucratif. |
| (43) Not including social sciences and humanities in the productive and general service sectors. | (43) Non compris les sciences sociales et humaines dans le secteur de la production et dans les secteurs de service général. |
| (44) Data refer to current expenditure only. | (44) Les données se réfèrent aux dépenses courantes seulement. |
| (45) Data relate to one research institute only. | (45) Les données se réfèrent aux dépenses courantes seulement. |

(13) No incluyen las empresas privadas en el sector productivo.

(14) Los datos sobre los cientificos e ingenieros se refieren a los investigadores que figuran en el repertorio de los grupos de investigación brasileños elaborado por el Conselho Nacional de Desenvolvimento Cientifico e Tecnologico (CNPq).

(15) Los datos sobre los investigadores están expuestos en equivalente de jornada completa. Los datos son de la OCDE.

(16) Los datos relativos a los gastos en I y D son de la OCDE.

(17) No incluyen los datos de las ciencias sociales y humanas en el sector productivo (actividades de I y D integradas).

(18) No incluyen los datos del sector productivo (actividades de I y D no integradas).

(19) Los datos se refieren a los fondos públicos o a los gastos públicos.

(20) Los datos se refieren a los investigadores de jornada completa y de jornada parcial en las empresas públicas.

(21) Los datos se refieren a la I y D en las empresas públicas.

(22) No incluyen los datos del sector productivo (actividades de I y D no integradas) y los del sector de servicio general.

(23) Los datos se refieren al 'Scientific Research Council' solamente.

(24) Los datos corresponden a la asignación presupuestal destinada a la ciencia y tecnología.

(25) Los datos se refieren solamente a las instituciones siguientes: CONCYTEC, IMARPE, INICTEL, INIA, UNMSR, y UP.

(26) No incluyen los datos relativos a derecho, ciencias humanas y ciencias de la educación.

(27) No incluyen los gastos de capital en el sector productivo.

(28) Los datos se refieren a las actividades científicas y tecnológicas (ACT).

(29) Incluyen al personal de apoyo.

(30) Los datos se refieren a la orilla oriental solamente.

(31) No incluyen los datos relativos a las ciencias sociales y humanas.

(32) Los datos se refieren a las actividades de I y D concentradas principalmente en los establecimientos de investigación subvencionados por el gobierno. Las ciencias sociales y humanas en el sector de la enseñanza superior y en el sector del servicio general no se incluyen. Las actividades militares y de defensa de I y D no se incluyen.

(33) Los datos se refieren al sector de servicio general solamente.

(34) No incluyen las ciencias sociales y humanas en el sector de la enseñanza superior.

(35) No incluyen el sector de las empresas.

(36) Los trabajadores cualificados se incluyen con los técnicos y el personal asimilado en vez de con el personal de apoyo.

(37) No incluyen a los científicos e ingenieros empleados en los servicios administrativos de I y D. Los datos sobre los técnicos incluyen a los trabajadores cualificados. Para las actividades de I y D de carácter militar, solo se considera la parte correspondiente a los establecimientos civiles.

(38) Debido a cambios de metodología "el personal de administración de la sección técnica", antes incluido con los investigadores, se incluye ahora con los técnicos.

(39) No incluyen los datos relativos a los técnicos, el personal asimilado y al personal de apoyo en el sector de la enseñanza superior.

(40) No incluyen los gastos de capital en el sector productivo (actividades de I y D integradas) y en el sector de la enseñanza superior.

(41) No incluyen los datos relativos al sector productivo (actividades de I y D integradas).

(42) No incluyen los datos de organizaciones privadas sin fines de lucro.

(43) No incluyen las ciencias sociales y humanas en el sector productivo y en los sectores de servicio general.

(44) Los datos se refieren a los gastos corrientes solamente.

(45) Los datos se refieren a un único instituto de investigación solamente.

Personnel engaged in R&D by category of personnel  III.2
Personnel employé dans la R-D par catégorie de personnel
Personal empleado en I y D por categoría de personal

## III.2 Personnel engaged in R&D by category of personnel

### Personnel employé dans la R-D par catégorie de personnel

### Personal empleado en I y D por categoría de personal

Data are expressed in full-time equivalent (FTE)  
Les données sont exprimées en équivalent plein temps (EPT)  
Los datos se expresan en equivalente de jornada completa (EJC)

| Country / Pays / País | Year / Année / Año | All R&D personnel / Tout le personnel de R-D / Todo el personal de I y D | Researchers / Chercheurs / Investigadores MF | F | Technicians and equivalent staff / Techniciens et personnel assimilé / Técnicos y personal asimilado MF | F | Other supporting staff / Autre personnel de soutien / Otro personal de apoyo MF | F |
|---|---|---|---|---|---|---|---|---|
| **Africa** | | | | | | | | |
| Benin (1) | 1989 | 2 687 | 794 | 100 | 242 | 64 | 1 651 | 339 |
| Burkina Faso | 1996 | 738 | 162 | 32 | 158 | 13 | 418 | ... |
| | 1997 | 780 | 176 | 34 | 165 | 16 | 439 | ... |
| Burundi (2)(3) | 1984 | 515 | 114 | 10 | 90 | ... | 311 | ... |
| | 1989 | 814 | 170 | 17 | 168 | ... | 476 | ... |
| Central African Republic (3) | 1984 | 1 290 | 196 | ... | 166 | ... | 928 | ... |
| | 1990 | ... | 162 | 16 | 92 | 5 | ... | ... |
| Congo (3) | 1984 | 2 335 | 862 | ... | 1 473 | ... | ... | ... |
| Egypt | 1982 | 46 796 | 19 939 (3) | 11 503 | 6 678 (3) | 3 947 | 20 179 (3) | 13 487 |
| | 1983 | 46 797 | 19 941 | ... | 6 678 | | 20 178 | ... |
| | 1986 | 47 970 | 20 893 | | 6 733 | | 20 344 | ... |
| | 1990 | 89 154 | 24 599 | 8 055 | 17 150 | 1 200 | 47 405 | 25 471 |
| | 1991 | 102 296 | 26 415 | ... | 19 607 | ... | 56 274 | ... |
| Libyan Arab Jamahiriya | 1980 | 3 600 | 1 100 | ... | 1 500 | ... | 1 000 | ... |
| Madagascar (4) | 1994 | 1 047 | 159 | 45 | 483 | 175 | 405 | 85 |
| Mauritius | 1980 | 1 069 | 152 | ... | 108 | ... | 809 | ... |
| | 1981 | 1 318 | 182 | ... | 106 | ... | 1 030 | ... |
| | 1982 | 1 388 | 173 | ... | 169 | ... | 1 046 | ... |
| | 1983 | 1 191 | 211 (3) | 13 | 165 (3) | 16 | 815 (3) | 108 |
| | 1984 | 1 224 | 263 | 20 | 176 | 26 | 785 | 96 |
| | 1985 | 1 113 | 267 | 25 | 191 | 22 | 655 | 80 |
| | 1986 | 1 145 | 305 | 26 | 181 | 29 | 659 | 99 |
| | 1987 | 995 | 234 | 23 | 172 | 29 | 589 | 70 |
| | 1988 | 962 | 231 | 24 | 116 | 33 | 615 | 79 |
| | 1989 | 1 021 | 193 | 33 | 172 | 46 | 656 | 97 |
| | 1992 | 1 162 | 389 | ... | 170 | ... | 603 | ... |
| Nigeria (5) | 1983 | 18 741 | 1 702 | ... | 9 947 | ... | 7 092 | ... |
| | 1984 | 18 345 | 1 650 | ... | 9 696 | ... | 6 999 | ... |
| | 1985 | 13 924 | 1 422 | ... | 6 565 | ... | 5 937 | ... |
| | 1986 | 12 845 | 1 499 | ... | 6 005 | ... | 5 341 | ... |
| | 1987 | 12 880 | 1 338 | ... | 6 042 | ... | 5 500 | ... |
| Rwanda | 1980 | 111 | 48 | ... | 36 | ... | 27 | ... |
| | 1982 | 130 | 62 | ... | 41 | ... | 27 | ... |
| | 1983 | 149 | 64 | ... | 55 | ... | 30 | ... |
| | 1984 | 164 | 69 | ... | 60 | ... | 35 | ... |
| | 1995 | 315 | 181 | 18 | 40 | 31 | 94 | 33 |
| Senegal (40) | 1993 | 84 | 20 | 5 | 32 | 9 | 32 | ... |
| | 1994 | 83 | 19 | 6 | 32 | 8 | 32 | ... |
| | 1995 | 76 | 19 | 5 | 28 | 7 | 29 | ... |
| | 1996 | 78 | 19 | 5 | 29 | 7 | 30 | ... |
| South Africa | 1983 | 15 995 | 7 939 | ... | 4 819 | ... | 3 237 | ... |
| | 1985 | 19 510 | 9 946 | ... | 6 044 | ... | 3 520 | ... |
| | 1987 | 20 557 | 11 469 | ... | 5 600 | ... | 3 488 | ... |
| | 1989 | 18 175 | 9 919 | ... | 4 584 | ... | 3 672 | ... |
| | 1991 | 22 223 | 12 102 | ... | 5 006 | ... | 5 115 | ... |
| | 1993 | 60 464 | 37 192 | ... | 11 343 | ... | 11 929 | ... |

III.2   Personnel engaged in R&D by category of personnel
Personnel employé dans la R-D par catégorie de personnel
Personal empleado en I y D por categoría de personal

| Country<br>Pays<br>País | | Year<br>Année<br>Año | All R&D personnel<br>Tout le personnel<br>de R-D<br>Todo el personal<br>de I y D | Researchers<br>Chercheurs<br>Investigadores | | Technicians and<br>equivalent staff<br>Techniciens et<br>personnel assimilé<br>Técnicos y personal<br>asimilado | | Other supporting staff<br>Autre personnel de<br>soutien<br>Otro personal de<br>apoyo | |
|---|---|---|---|---|---|---|---|---|---|
| | | | | MF | F | MF | F | MF | F |
| Togo | | 1989 | 1 200 | 277 | ... | 183 | ... | 740 | ... |
| | | 1994 | 1 473 | 387 | ... | 249 | ... | 837 | ... |
| Tunisia | | 1993 | 3 130 | 953 | ... | 480 | ... | 1 697 | ... |
| | | 1994 | 3 324 | 1 003 | ... | 528 | ... | 1 793 | ... |
| | | 1995 | 3 476 | 1 043 | ... | 510 | ... | 1 923 | ... |
| | | 1996 | 3 589 | 1 085 | ... | 524 | ... | 1 980 | ... |
| | | 1997 | 3 680 | 1 145 | ... | 524 | ... | 2 011 | ... |
| Uganda | | 1993 | 708 | 298 | 94 | 215 | 25 | 195 | ... |
| | | 1994 | 800 | 344 | 122 | 244 | 18 | 212 | ... |
| | | 1995 | 860 | 362 | 136 | 298 | 23 | 200 | ... |
| | | 1996 | 890 | 386 | 149 | 285 | 27 | 219 | ... |
| | | 1997 | 950 | 422 | 162 | 272 | 34 | 256 | ... |
| **North America** | | | | | | | | | |
| Canada | (8) | 1981 | 78 180 | 39 060 | ... | ... | | ... | |
| | (6) | 1982 | *87 570 | *45 010 | ... | *22 790 | ... | *19 770 | ... |
| | (6) | 1983 | 89 820 | 46 110 | ... | 22 670 | ... | 21 040 | ... |
| | (6) | 1984 | 94 200 | 49 190 | ... | 24 210 | ... | 20 800 | ... |
| | (6) | 1985 | 99 840 | 53 100 | ... | 25 830 | ... | 20 910 | ... |
| | (6) | 1986 | 103 740 | 56 510 | ... (7) | 26 600 | ... | 20 630 | ... |
| | (8) | 1986 | 105 420 | 56 750 | ... | ... | | ... | |
| | (6) | 1987 | 107 680 | 58 490 | ... | 27 870 | ... | 21 320 | ... |
| | (8) | 1988 | 111 440 | 61 540 | ... | ... | | ... | |
| | (6) | 1989 | 112 020 | 62 050 | ... (7) | 28 940 | ... | 21 030 | ... |
| | (6) | 1990 | 113 550 | 63 930 | ... (7) | 27 890 | ... | 21 730 | ... |
| | (6) | 1991 | 114 500 | 65 350 | ... (7) | 27 520 | ... | 21 630 | ... |
| | (8) | 1992 | 117 330 | 70 050 | ... | ... | | ... | |
| | (6) | 1993 | 126 910 | 76 550 | ... | 30 920 | ... | 19 440 | ... |
| | (8) | 1994 | 126 660 | 77 860 | ... | ... | | ... | |
| | (8) | 1995 | 129 750 | 80 510 | ... | ... | | ... | |
| Costa Rica (13) | (3) | 1988 | 1 528 | 1 528 | ... | ... | ... | ... | ... |
| | | 1996 | 1 866 | 1 866 | ... | ... | ... | ... | ... |
| Cuba | | 1980 | 21 521 | 5 637 | ... | 6 556 | ... | 9 328 | ... |
| | | 1981 | 25 249 | 6 834 | ... | 7 959 | ... | 10 456 | ... |
| | | 1982 | 26 574 | 7 497 | ... | 8 066 | ... | 11 011 | ... |
| | | 1983 | 29 064 | 8 247 | (3) 5 089 | 8 408 | ... | 12 409 | ... |
| | | 1984 | 32 937 | 9 548 | ... | 8 843 | ... | 14 546 | ... |
| | | 1985 | 34 150 | 10 305 | ... | 9 238 | ... | 14 607 | ... |
| | | 1986 | 32 192 | 10 068 | ... | 8 687 | ... | 13 437 | ... |
| | | 1987 | 33 287 | 11 225 | ... | 8 962 | ... | 13 100 | ... |
| | | 1989 | 32 614 | 12 052 | ... | 8 830 | ... | 11 732 | ... |
| | | 1991 | 37 829 | 16 433 | ... | 9 558 | ... | 11 838 | ... |
| | | 1992 | 35 996 | 14 770 | 6 383 | 9 465 | 5 251 | 11 761 | 4 892 |
| | | 1995 | 44 119 | 17 667 | ... | 12 288 | ... | 14 164 | ... |
| El Salvador | | 1992 | 1 775 | (9) 102 | ... | (9) 1 612 | ... | 61 | ... |
| Guatemala (10) | | 1988 | 2 575 | 858 | ... | 925 | ... | 792 | ... |
| Jamaica (11) | | 1982 | 86 | 24 | ... | 13 | ... | 49 | ... |
| | | 1983 | 104 | 26 | ... | 19 | ... | 59 | ... |
| | | 1984 | 100 | 23 | ... | 21 | ... | 56 | ... |
| | | 1985 | 121 | 21 | ... | 31 | ... | 69 | ... |
| | | 1986 | 104 | 18 | 10 | 15 | 3 | 71 | 40 |
| Mexico | | 1984 | 68 972 | 16 679 | 4 319 | 29 467 | 7 631 | 22 826 | 5 911 |
| | | 1993 | 26 932 | 14 103 | ... | 9 441 | ... | 3 388 | ... |
| | | 1994 | 30 501 | 17 061 | ... | 9 437 | ... | 4 003 | ... |
| | | 1995 | 33 297 | 19 434 | ... | 6 675 | ... | 7 188 | ... |
| Nicaragua (3) | | 1985 | 1 803 | 650 | ... | 212 | ... | 941 | ... |
| | | 1987 | 2 005 | 725 | ... | 302 | ... | 978 | ... |
| United States (12) (13) | | 1980 | 658 700 | 658 700 | ... | ... | ... | ... | ... |
| | | 1981 | 691 400 | 691 400 | ... | ... | ... | ... | ... |
| | | 1982 | 702 800 | 702 800 | ... | ... | ... | ... | ... |
| | | 1983 | 722 500 | 722 500 | ... | ... | ... | ... | ... |
| | | 1984 | 797 800 | 797 800 | ... | ... | ... | ... | ... |
| | | 1985 | 849 200 | 849 200 | ... | ... | ... | ... | ... |
| | | 1986 | 896 500 | 896 500 | ... | ... | ... | ... | ... |
| | | 1987 | *923 300 | *923 300 | ... | ... | ... | ... | ... |
| | | 1988 | *949 200 | *949 200 | ... | ... | ... | ... | ... |
| | | 1993 | *962 700 | *962 700 | ... | ... | ... | ... | ... |
| **South America** | | | | | | | | | |
| Argentina | | 1980 | *22 800 | *9 500 | (3) *5 400 | *13 300 | ... | ... | ... |
| | | 1982 | 35 144 | 10 486 | (3) 6 705 | 8 124 | ... | 16 534 | ... |
| | | 1985 | *28 900 | *10 800 | ... | *7 100 | ... | *11 000 | ... |
| | | 1988 | *22 855 | *11 088 | *4 798 | *6 241 | ... | *5 526 | ... |
| | | 1995 | 32 510 | 22 927 | 10 655 | 5 092 | ... | 4 491 | ... |

Personnel engaged in R&D by category of personnel III.2
Personnel employé dans la R-D par catégorie de personnel
Personal empleado en I y D por categoría de personal

| Country / Pays / País | | Year / Année / Año | All R&D personnel / Tout le personnel de R-D / Todo el personal de I y D | Researchers / Chercheurs / Investigadores | | Technicians and equivalent staff / Techniciens et personnel assimilé / Técnicos y personal asimilado | | Other supporting staff / Autre personnel de soutien / Otro personal de apoyo | |
|---|---|---|---|---|---|---|---|---|---|
| | | | | MF | F | MF | F | MF | F |
| Bolivia | (3) | 1991 | ... | 1 681 | 700 | 1 039 | 500 | ... | ... |
| | | 1992 | ... | 1 088 | ... | ... | ... | ... | ... |
| | | 1993 | ... | 1 120 | ... | ... | ... | ... | ... |
| | | 1994 | ... | 1 180 | ... | ... | ... | ... | ... |
| | | 1995 | ... | 1 200 | ... | ... | ... | ... | ... |
| | | 1996 | ... | 1 300 | ... | ... | ... | ... | ... |
| Brazil | | 1995 | ,,, (14) | 26 754 | ... | 9 327 | | ... | ... |
| Chile | (3) | 1988 | 8 740 | 4 630 | ... | 2 940 | | 1 170 | ... |
| Colombia | | 1982 (1) | 3 709 | 1 083 | | 1 024 | ... | 1 602 | ... |
| Ecuador | | 1990 | 1 415 | 1 043 | 240 (15) | 372 | ... (15) | ./. | ... |
| | | 1995 | ... | 1 517 | 472 | ... | ... | ... | ... |
| | | 1997 | 1 874 | 1 676 | 250 (15) | 198 | ... (15) | ./. | ... |
| Paraguay | (3) | 1981 | ... | 807 | | | | 1 545 | ... |
| Peru | | 1996 | ... | 5 551 | ... | 234 | ... | ... | ... |
| | | 1997 | ... | 5 576 | ... | 34 | ... | ... | ... |
| Uruguay | (3) | 1987 | ... | 2 093 | 720 | | ... | ... | ... |
| Venezuela | | 1992 | *5 333 | *4 258 | *1 490 | *650 | *205 | *425 | *179 |
| **Asia** | | | | | | | | | |
| Armenia | | 1997 | 7 716 | 5 492 | 2 509 | 653 | 321 | 1 571 | ... |
| Azerbaijan | | 1993 | 30 555 | 24 519 | 10 448 | 1 989 | ... | 4 047 | ... |
| | | 1994 | 27 478 | 23 276 | 10 177 | 1 477 | ... | 2 725 | ... |
| | | 1995 | 25 629 | 21 547 | 8 813 | 1 356 | ... | 2 726 | ... |
| | | 1996 | 25 556 | 21 234 | 8 889 | 1 428 | ... | 2 894 | ... |
| Bangladesh | | 1993 | 16 496 | 5 843 | 664 | 3 645 | 61 | 7 008 | ... |
| | | 1994 | 15 010 | 5 418 | 568 | 2 055 | 404 | 7 537 | ... |
| | | 1995 | 16 629 | 6 097 | 851 | 3 825 | 728 | 6 707 | ... |
| China | | 1994 | 655 100 | 420 700 | ... (15) | 234 400 | ... (15) | ./. | ... |
| | | 1995 | 665 600 | 422 700 | ... (15) | 242 900 | ... (15) | ./. | ... |
| | | 1996 | 787 000 | 559 000 | ... (15) | 228 000 | ... (15) | ./. | ... |
| China, Hong Kong SAR | (36) | 1995 | 1 627 | 574 | ... | 613 | ... | 440 | ... |
| Cyprus | | 1991 | 341 | 135 | ... | 153 | ... | 53 | ... |
| | | 1992 | 366 | 147 | ... | 165 | ... | 54 | ... |
| India | (16) | 1982 | *218 995 | *93 698 | 3 276 | 60 887 | ... | 64 410 | ... |
| | (16) | 1984 | *244 049 | *100 136 | 3 653 | 72 233 | ... | 71 680 | ... |
| | | 1986 | *256 735 | *107 409 | ... | *70 233 | ... | *79 093 | ... |
| | (16) | 1988 | *286 381 | *119 027 | *5 552 | *80 956 | *4 233 | *86 398 | *8 214 |
| | (16) | 1990 | *322 977 | *128 036 (18) | 7 710 | 96 737 | 6 138 | 98 204 | 13 140 |
| | (17) | 1992 | 315 448 | 117 586 | 7 737 | 98 202 | 7 096 | 99 660 | ... |
| | (16) | 1994 | *336 589 | *136 503 | 10 505 | 98 769 | 9 333 | 101 317 | 17 411 |
| Indonesia | (3) | 1982 | 28 464 | 17 287 | ... | 3 234 | ... | 7 943 | ... |
| | | 1984 | 36 185 | 24 895 | ... | 4 125 | ... | 7 165 | ... |
| | | 1985 | ... | 21 160 | ... | 3 888 | ... | ... | ... |
| Iran, Islamic Republic of | | 1985 | (19) 5 048 | 3 194 | ... | 1 854 | ... | ... | ... |
| | | 1994 | 50 326 | 34 256 | ... | 10 104 | ... | 5 966 | ... |
| Israel | | 1984 | 26 800 | 20 100 | (3) 10 400 | 4 300 | 1 400 | 2 400 | 2 100 |
| Japan | (20)(6) | 1980 | 601 192 | 441 186 | 33 734 | 86 970 | (15) 51 924 | 73 036 | ... |
| | (20)(6) | 1981 | 629 172 | 463 062 | 34 007 | 90 426 | (15) 54 733 | 75 684 | ... |
| | (20)(6) | 1982 | 648 977 | 479 954 | ... | 91 169 | | 77 854 | ... |
| | (20)(6) | 1983 | 668 939 | 496 145 | 37 891 | 93 326 | 17 858 | 79 468 | 41 865 |
| | (20)(6) | 1984 | 710 872 | 531 612 | 41 496 | 97 074 | 18 314 | 82 186 | 42 580 |
| | (20)(6) | 1985 | 730 432 | 548 249 | 43 490 | 99 280 | 19 294 | 82 903 | 43 665 |
| | (20)(6) | 1986 | 761 650 | 575 292 | 46 187 | 101 861 | 19 453 | 84 497 | 45 167 |
| | (20)(6) | 1987 | 778 501 | 590 680 | 48 765 | 102 486 | 20 250 | 85 335 | 45 212 |
| | (20)(6) | 1988 | 803 833 | 614 854 | 55 384 | 102 950 | 20 410 | 86 029 | 46 242 |
| | (20)(6) | 1989 | 830 855 | 636 817 | 45 040 | 105 430 | 20 364 | 88 608 | 47 770 |
| | (20)(6) | 1990 | 863 382 | 666 393 | ... | 104 190 | ... | 92 799 | ... |
| | (20)(6) | 1991 | 899 286 | 688 994 | ... | 113 562 | ... | 96 730 | ... |
| | (20)(6) | 1992 | 910 051 | 705 346 | ... | 108 014 | ... | 96 691 | ... |
| | (8) | 1993 | 947 455 | 641 083 | ... | ... | ... | ... | ... |
| | (20)(6) | 1994 | 994 622 | 787 402 | ... | 103 400 | ... | 103 820 | ... |
| | (8) | 1995 | 948 088 | 673 421 | ... | ... | ... | ... | ... |
| | (8) | 1996 | 891 783 | 617 365 | ... | ... | ... | ... | ... |

**Personnel engaged in R&D by category of personnel**
**Personnel employé dans la R-D par catégorie de personnel**
**Personal empleado en I y D por categoría de personal**

| Country<br><br>Pays<br><br>País | Year<br><br>Année<br><br>Año | All R&D personnel<br><br>Tout le personnel<br>de R-D<br><br>Todo el personal<br>de I y D | Researchers<br>Chercheurs<br>Investigadores | | Technicians and<br>equivalent staff<br>Techniciens et<br>personnel assimilé<br>Técnicos y personal<br>asimilado | | Other supporting staff<br>Autre personnel de<br>soutien<br>Otro personal de<br>apoyo | |
|---|---|---|---|---|---|---|---|---|
| | | | MF | F | MF | F | MF | F |
| Jordan (21) | 1984 | *610 | *421 | ... | *29 | ... | *160 | ... |
| | 1985 | *585 | *400 | ... | *29 | ... | *156 | ... |
| | 1987 | *602 | *422 | ... | *30 | ... | *150 | ... |
| | 1988 | *609 | *423 | ... | *36 | ... | *150 | ... |
| | 1989 (19) | 463 | 422 | ... | 41 | ... | ... | ... |
| Korea, Republic of (3)(22) | 1980 | 30 473 | 18 434 | ... | 7 417 | ... | 4 622 | |
| (3)(22) | 1981 | 35 805 | 20 718 | ... | 8 815 | ... | 6 272 | |
| (3)(22) | 1982 | 46 390 | 28 448 | ... | 11 663 | ... | 6 279 | |
| (3)(22) | 1983 | 58 720 | 32 117 | 1 816 | 19 493 (15) | 5 195 | 7 110 | |
| (3)(22) | 1984 | 70 524 | 37 103 | ... | 25 153 | | 8 268 | |
| (3)(22) | 1985 | 73 516 | 41 473 | ... | 24 152 | | 7 891 | |
| (3)(22) | 1986 | 87 430 | 47 042 | 2 743 | 30 465 | 4 806 | 9 923 | 3 275 |
| (3)(22) | 1987 | 96 288 | 52 783 | ... | 32 923 | | 10 582 | ... |
| (3)(22) | 1988 | 104 737 | 56 545 | 3 670 | 35 720 | | 12 472 | |
| (3)(22) | 1989 | 119 357 | 66 220 | ... | 38 655 | | 14 482 | |
| (3)(22) | 1990 | 125 512 | 70 503 | ... | 42 841 | | 12 168 | |
| (3)(22) | 1991 | 131 983 | 76 252 | ... | 10 782 | | 44 949 | |
| (3)(22) | 1992 | 148 947 | 88 764 | 5 512 | 15 253 | | 44 930 | |
| (3)(22) | 1994 | 190 298 | 117 446 | ... | 14 141 | | 58 711 | |
| (8) | 1995 | 152 247 | 100 456 | ... | ... | | ... | |
| (8) | 1996 | 135 703 | 99 433 | ... | ... | | ... | |
| Kuwait | 1993 | 733 | 381 | ... | 117 | ... | 235 | ... |
| | 1994 | 763 | 397 | ... | 122 | ... | 244 | ... |
| | 1995 | 753 | 392 | ... | 120 | ... | 241 | ... |
| | 1996 | 763 | 397 | ... | 122 | ... | 244 | ... |
| | 1997 | 742 | 387 | ... | 118 | ... | 237 | ... |
| Kyrgyzstan | 1993 | 5 897 | 3 826 | ... | 417 | ... | 1 654 | ... |
| | 1994 | 4 552 | 2 912 | ... | 559 | ... | 1 081 | ... |
| | 1995 | 4 558 | 3 279 | ... | 323 | ... | 956 | ... |
| | 1996 | 4 126 | 2 629 | ... | 256 | ... | 1 241 | ... |
| | 1997 | 4 161 | 2 685 | 1 249 | 226 | ... | 1 250 | ... |
| Malaysia | 1992 | 4 563 | 1 633 | 501 | 1 655 | 507 | 1 275 | ... |
| | 1994 | 6 675 | 2 286 | 597 | 811 | 198 | 3 577 | ... |
| | 1996 | 4 436 | 1 893 | 509 | 654 | 146 | 1 888 | ... |
| Mongolia | 1995 | 3 599 | 2 228 | 939 | 431 | 237 | 940 | 554 |
| Pakistan (23) | 1981 | 22 922 | 5 144 | ... | 6 476 | ... | 11 302 | ... |
| | 1982 | 24 723 | 5 397 | ... | 7 138 | ... | 12 188 | ... |
| | 1986 | 40 076 | 9 325 | ... | 14 028 | ... | 16 723 | ... |
| | 1988 | 28 990 | 6 641 | ... | 9 286 | ... | 13 063 | ... |
| | 1990 | 29 040 | 6 626 | 464 | 9 314 | ... | 13 100 | ... |
| | 1997 | 36 706 | 9 977 | 859 | 1 749 | 27 | 24 980 | ... |
| Philippines | 1992 | 14 578 | 9 960 | 5 260 | 1 399 | 374 | 3 219 | 1 338 |
| Qatar (3)(24) | 1986 | 290 | 229 | 58 | 61 | 2 | ... | |
| Singapore (22) (3) | 1981 | 2 741 | 1 193 | ... | 807 | ... | 741 | |
| (3) | 1984 | 4 886 | 2 401 | *384 | 1 359 | ... | 1 126 | ... |
| (3) | 1987 | 5 876 | 3 361 | 649 | 1 526 | ... | 989 | ... |
| | 1995 | 9 497 | 7 695 | ... | 997 | ... | 805 | ... |
| Sri Lanka | 1984 (19) | 3 211 | 2 619 | ... | 592 | ... | ... | ... |
| | 1985 (19) | 3 483 | 2 790 | 667 | 693 | 188 | ... | ... |
| | 1996 (19) | 4 281 | 3 448 | 1 103 | 833 | ... | ... | ... |
| Syrian Arab Republic | 1997 | 804 | 440 | ... | 364 | ... | ... | ... |
| Tajikistan (3) | 1992 | ... | 3 974 | 1 144 | ... | ... | ... | ... |
| | | ... | 3 722 | ... | ... | ... | ... | ... |
| Thailand | 1987 | 10 621 | 5 539 | ... | 2 785 | ... | 2 297 | ... |
| | 1989 | 8 200 | 4 738 | ... | 1 763 | ... | 1 699 | ... |
| | 1993 | 12 064 | 6 513 | ... | 2 535 | ... | 3 016 | ... |
| | 1995 | 12 802 | 6 899 | 1 639 | 2 346 | 1 113 | 3 557 | 1 973 |
| | 1996 | 10 209 | 6 038 | ... | 2 303 | ... | 1 868 | ... |
| Turkey | 1984 | 27 007 | 9 914 | ... | 6 284 | ... | 10 809 | ... |
| | 1985 | 29 241 | 11 276 | ... | 7 367 | ... | 10 598 | ... |
| | 1990 (16) | 16 019 | 12 366 | ... | 1 226 | ... (17) | 2 427 | ... |
| | 1991 (16) | 14 969 | 11 948 | ... | 1 329 | ... (17) | 1 692 | ... |
| (8) | 1992 | 15 701 | 12 573 | ... | ... | ... | ... | ... |
| (8) | 1993 | 16 087 | 13 605 | ... | ... | ... | ... | ... |
| (8) | 1994 | 16 899 | 14 460 | ... | ... | ... | ... | ... |
| | 1995 (16) | 18 498 | 15 854 | ... | 1 606 | ... (17) | 1 038 | ... |
| (8) | 1996 | 21 995 | 18 092 | ... | ... | ... | ... | ... |
| Uzbekistan | 1992 | ... | *37 625 | *17 005 | *6 687 | ... | ... | ... |
| Viet Nam (37) | 1995 | ... | 20 000 | ... | ... | ... | ... | ... |

Personnel engaged in R&D by category of personnel III.2
Personnel employé dans la R-D par catégorie de personnel
Personal empleado en I y D por categoría de personal

| Country / Pays / País | | Year / Année / Año | All R&D personnel / Tout le personnel de R-D / Todo el personal de I y D | Researchers / Chercheurs / Investigadores | | Technicians and equivalent staff / Techniciens et personnel assimilé / Técnicos y personal asimilado | | Other supporting staff / Autre personnel de soutien / Otro personal de apoyo | |
|---|---|---|---|---|---|---|---|---|---|
| | | | | MF | F | MF | F | MF | F |
| **Europe** | | | | | | | | | |
| Austria | | 1981 | 18 599 | 6 712 | ... | 6 145 | ... | 5 742 | ... |
| | | 1984 | 20 161 | 7 609 | ... | 6 817 | ... | 5 735 | ... |
| | (8) | 1985 | 20 161 | 7 609 | ... | ... | ... | ... | ... |
| | | 1989 | 23 083 | 8 782 | (25) 868 | 8 434 | ... | 5 867 | ... |
| | | 1993 | 24 458 | 12 821 | 2 008 | 6 397 | 1 945 | 5 240 | 2 119 |
| Belarus | | 1992 | 52 728 | 33 685 | ... | 5 254 | ... | 13 789 | ... |
| | | 1993 | 47 524 | 30 474 | ... | 4 164 | ... | 12 886 | ... |
| | | 1994 | 39 819 | 26 141 | ... | 3 579 | ... | 10 099 | ... |
| | | 1995 | 35 858 | 23 771 | ... | 3 131 | ... | 8 956 | ... |
| | | 1996 | 34 898 | 23 324 | ... | 2 758 | ... | 8 816 | ... |
| Belgium | (8) | 1981 | 32 531 | 12 747 | ... | ... | ... | ... | ... |
| | (8) | 1982 | 33 042 | 13 410 | ... | ... | ... | ... | ... |
| | (8) | 1983 | 33 032 | 13 431 | ... | ... | ... | ... | ... |
| | (8) | 1984 | 33 390 | 13 906 | ... | ... | ... | ... | ... |
| | (8) | 1985 | 34 859 | 14 759 | ... | ... | ... | ... | ... |
| | | 1986 | 36 203 | 15 705 | ... | (15) 20 498 | ... | (15) ./. | ... |
| | | 1987 | 36 727 | 16 045 | ... | (15) 20 682 | ... | (15) ./. | ... |
| | | 1988 | 36 770 | 16 646 | ... | (15) 20 124 | ... | (15) ./. | ... |
| | | 1989 | 37 795 | 17 583 | ... | (15) 20 212 | ... | (15) ./. | ... |
| | | 1990 | 38 773 | 18 465 | ... | (15) 20 308 | ... | (15) ./. | ... |
| | | 1991 | *40 063 | *18 105 | ... | (15) 21 958 | ... | (15) ./. | ... |
| | (8) | 1994 | 37 703 | 22 552 | ... | ... | ... | ... | ... |
| | (8) | 1995 | 38 449 | 22 918 | ... | ... | ... | ... | ... |
| Bulgaria | (16) | 1980 | 72 335 | 38 706 | 16 829 | (16) 10 483 | 7 295 | (16) 23 146 | 8 335 |
| | (16) | 1981 | 78 477 | 41 378 | 19 187 | (16) 11 856 | 7 999 | (16) 25 243 | 11 550 |
| | (16) | 1982 | 81 207 | 42 756 | 19 697 | (16) 12 519 | 8 385 | (16) 25 932 | 12 074 |
| | (16) | 1983 | 83 291 | 43 462 | 19 890 | (16) 12 429 | 8 186 | (16) 27 400 | 12 894 |
| | (16) | 1984 | 87 329 | 45 125 | 21 070 | (16) 12 484 | 8 347 | (16) 29 720 | 14 022 |
| | (16) | 1985 | 90 308 | 48 008 | 22 769 | (16) 13 099 | 8 514 | (16) 29 201 | 13 589 |
| | (16) | 1986 | 91 168 | 46 329 | 20 289 | (16) 11 271 | 6 724 | (16) 33 568 | 16 346 |
| | (16) | 1987 | 96 471 | 50 585 | 22 268 | (16) 11 662 | 6 774 | (16) 34 224 | 17 443 |
| | | 1988 | 100 731 | 49 703 | ... | 12 444 | ... | 38 584 | ... |
| | | 1989 | 107 301 | 50 932 | ... | 12 201 | ... | 44 168 | ... |
| | | 1990 | 112 158 | 52 597 | ... | 12 266 | ... | 47 295 | ... |
| | | 1991 | 88 733 | 49 705 | 23 592 | 11 407 | 6 409 | 27 621 | 14 319 |
| | (26) | 1992 | 57 655 | 37 825 | 17 362 | 10 752 | 6 555 | 9 078 | 5 606 |
| | | 1993 | 41 606 | 27 292 | 12 120 | 7 811 | 4 994 | 6 503 | ... |
| | | 1994 | 23 729 | 12 608 | 5 220 | 7 665 | 5 184 | 3 456 | ... |
| | | 1995 | 25 055 | 13 990 | 5 723 | 7 697 | 5 298 | 3 368 | ... |
| | | 1996 | 26 158 | 14 751 | 6 114 | 8 169 | 5 462 | 3 238 | ... |
| Croatia | | 1988 | 20 818 | 9 716 | ... | 4 795 | ... | 6 307 | ... |
| | | 1989 | 21 008 | 10 039 | ... | 4 699 | ... | 6 270 | ... |
| | | 1990 | 19 000 | 9 286 | ... | 4 461 | ... | 5 253 | ... |
| | | 1991 | 17 216 | 8 670 | ... | 3 943 | ... | 4 603 | ... |
| | | 1992 | 17 233 | 8 928 | 3 339 | 3 818 | 2 332 | 4 487 | 3 069 |
| | | 1993 | 16 369 | 9 032 | ... | 3 328 | ... | 4 009 | ... |
| | | 1994 | 15 713 | 8 812 | ... | 3 075 | ... | 3 826 | ... |
| | | 1995 | 15 953 | 8 911 | 3 418 | 3 134 | 1 903 | 3 908 | 2 634 |
| | | 1996 | 15 787 | 8 597 | 3 364 | 3 204 | 2 033 | 3 986 | ... |
| Czech Republic | (8) | 1991 | 81 895 | ... | ... | ... | ... | ... | ... |
| | (8) | 1992 | 60 292 | 20 084 | ... | ... | ... | ... | ... |
| | (8) | 1993 | 40 793 | 13 627 | ... | ... | ... | ... | ... |
| | (8) | 1994 | 37 779 | 13 325 | ... | ... | ... | ... | ... |
| | | 1995 | 22 678 | 11 935 | ... | 7 153 | ... | 3 590 | ... |
| | (8) | 1996 | 23 373 | 12 915 | ... | ... | ... | ... | ... |
| | (8) | 1997 | 23 230 | 12 580 | ... | ... | ... | ... | ... |
| Denmark | (8) | 1981 | 16 476 | 6 785 | ... | ... | ... | ... | ... |
| | | 1982 | 17 235 | 7 255 | ... | (15) 9 980 | ... | (15) ./. | ... |
| | | 1983 | 18 142 | 7 676 | ... | (15) 10 466 | ... | (15) ./. | ... |
| | | 1984 | 19 029 | 8 123 | ... | (15) 10 906 | ... | (15) ./. | ... |
| | | 1985 | 19 914 | 8 567 | ... | (15) 11 347 | ... | (15) ./. | ... |
| | | 1986 | 20 934 | 9 171 | ... | (15) 11 763 | ... | (15) ./. | ... |
| | | 1987 | 21 953 | 9 775 | ... | (15) 12 178 | ... | (15) ./. | ... |
| | | 1988 | 23 146 | 10 369 | ... | (15) 12 777 | ... | (15) ./. | ... |
| | | 1989 | 24 339 | 10 962 | ... | (15) 13 377 | ... | (15) ./. | ... |
| | | 1990 | 25 047 | 11 505 | ... | (15) 13 542 | ... | (15) ./. | ... |
| | | 1991 | 25 756 | 12 049 | ... | (15) 13 707 | ... | (15) ./. | ... |
| | (8) | 1992 | 26 573 | 12 861 | ... | ... | ... | ... | ... |
| | | 1993 | 27 390 | 13 673 | ... | (15) 13 717 | ... | (15) ./. | ... |
| | (8) | 1995 | 30 213 | 15 954 | ... | ... | ... | ... | ... |
| | (8) | 1996 | 30 841 | 16 361 | ... | ... | ... | ... | ... |
| | (8) | 1997 | 31 467 | 16 766 | ... | ... | ... | ... | ... |
| | (8) | 1998 | 32 107 | 17 173 | ... | ... | ... | ... | ... |
| Estonia | (27) | 1996 | 4 689 | 3 047 | 1 252 | 545 | 390 | 1 097 | ... |
| | | 1997 | 4 605 | 2 956 | 1 155 | 573 | 398 | 1 076 | ... |

**Personnel engaged in R&D by category of personnel**
**Personnel employé dans la R-D par catégorie de personnel**
**Personal empleado en I y D por categoría de personal**

| Country / Pays / País | | Year / Année / Año | All R&D personnel / Tout le personnel de R-D / Todo el personal de I y D | Researchers / Chercheurs / Investigadores | | | Technicians and equivalent staff / Techniciens et personnel assimilé / Técnicos y personal asimilado | | | Other supporting staff / Autre personnel de soutien / Otro personal de apoyo | | |
|---|---|---|---|---|---|---|---|---|---|---|---|---|
| | | | | MF | | F | MF | | F | MF | | F |
| Federal Republic of Yugoslavia | | 1991 | 26 559 | 12 082 | | ... | 5 377 | | ... | 9 100 | | ... |
| | | 1995 | 25 392 | 11 611 | | 4 150 | 5 436 | | 2 950 | 8 345 | | 4 713 |
| Finland | | 1981 | 18 004 | 9 722 | | ... | 8 282 | (15) | ... | ./. | (15) | ... |
| | | 1983 | 20 218 | 10 951 | | ... | 9 267 | (15) | ... | ./. | (15) | ... |
| | (8) | 1985 | 23 550 | ... | | ... | ... | | ... | ... | | ... |
| | (8) | 1987 | 26 227 | 10 593 | | ... | ... | | ... | ... | | ... |
| | (8) | 1989 | 28 516 | ... | | ... | ... | | ... | ... | | ... |
| | (8) | 1991 | 29 575 | 14 030 | | ... | ... | | ... | ... | | ... |
| | (8) | 1993 | 30 527 | 15 229 | | ... | ... | | ... | ... | | ... |
| | (8) | 1994 | 32 331 | ... | | ... | ... | | ... | ... | | ... |
| | (8) | 1995 | 33 634 | 16 863 | | ... | ... | | ... | ... | | ... |
| France | | 1980 | 236 200 | 74 900 | | ... | 161 300 | (15) | | ... | | ... |
| | | 1981 | 249 100 | 85 500 | | ... | 163 600 | (15) | | ... | | ... |
| | | 1982 | 259 000 | 90 100 | | ... | 168 900 | (15) | | ... | | ... |
| | | 1983 | 261 200 | 92 700 | | ... | 168 500 | (15) | | ... | | ... |
| | | 1984 | 269 900 | 98 200 | | ... | 171 700 | (15) | | ... | | ... |
| | | 1985 | 273 000 | 102 300 | | ... | 170 700 | (15) | | ... | | ... |
| | | 1986 | 274 301 | 104 953 | | ... | 169 348 | (15) | | ... | | ... |
| | | 1987 | 277 921 | 109 359 | | ... | 168 562 | (15) | | ... | | ... |
| | | 1988 | 283 099 | 115 163 | | ... | 167 936 | (15) | | ... | | ... |
| | | 1989 | 289 282 | 120 430 | | ... | 168 852 | (15) | | ... | | ... |
| | | 1990 | 293 031 | 123 961 | | ... | 169 070 | (15) | | ... | | ... |
| | | 1991 | 298 592 | 129 215 | | ... | 169 377 | (15) | | ... | | ... |
| | (8) | 1992 | 311 234 | 141 710 | | ... | ... | | | ... | | ... |
| | (8) | 1993 | 314 170 | 145 898 | | ... | ... | | | ... | | ... |
| | | 1994 | 315 159 | 149 193 | | ... | 165 966 | (15) | | ... | | ... |
| | (8) | 1995 | 318 384 | 151 249 | | ... | ... | | | ... | | ... |
| | (8) | 1996 | 320 805 | 154 839 | | ... | ... | | | ... | | ... |
| Germany | (8) | 1981 | 359 419 | 124 678 | | ... | ... | | ... | ... | | ... |
| | (8) | 1983 | 368 995 | 130 843 | | ... | ... | | ... | ... | | ... |
| | (8) | 1985 | 398 328 | 143 627 | | ... | ... | | ... | ... | | ... |
| | (8) | 1987 | 419 207 | 165 616 | | ... | ... | | ... | ... | | ... |
| | (8) | 1988 | 422 500 | ... | | ... | ... | | ... | ... | | ... |
| | (8) | 1989 | 426 447 | 176 401 | | ... | ... | | ... | ... | | ... |
| | (8) | 1990 | 431 100 | ... | | ... | ... | | ... | ... | | ... |
| | (8) | 1991 | 516 331 | 241 869 | | ... | ... | | ... | ... | | ... |
| | (8) | 1992 | 487 695 | 234 280 | | ... | ... | | ... | ... | | ... |
| | | 1993 | 475 018 | 229 839 | | ... | 118 985 | | ... | 126 194 | | ... |
| | (8) | 1995 | 459 138 | 231 128 | | ... | ... | | ... | ... | | ... |
| Greece | (8) | 1989 | 9 586 | 5 461 | | ... | ... | | ... | ... | | ... |
| | (8) | 1991 | 11 059 | 6 230 | | ... | ... | | ... | ... | | ... |
| | | 1993 | 14 549 | 8 030 | | ... | 3 257 | | ... | 3 262 | | ... |
| Hungary | | 1981 | 51 512 (28) | 22 267 | (3) | 10 334 | 21 719 (29) | | ... | 7 526 (30) | | ... |
| | | 1982 | 49 236 (28) | 21 970 | (3) | 10 354 | 18 354 (29) | | ... | 8 912 (30) | | ... |
| | | 1983 | 48 740 (28) | 22 132 | | ... | 18 477 (29) | | ... | 8 131 (30) | | ... |
| | | 1984 | 49 360 (28) | 22 518 | (3) | 10 528 | 18 438 (29) | | ... | 8 404 (30) | | ... |
| | | 1985 | 48 745 (28) | 22 479 | | ... | 17 869 (29) | | ... | 8 397 (30) | | ... |
| | | 1986 | 49 148 (28) | 22 974 | (3) | 10 668 | 17 795 (29) | | ... | 8 379 (30) | | ... |
| | | 1987 | 47 227 (28) | 22 284 | (3) | 11 122 | 16 735 (29) | | ... | 8 208 (30) | | ... |
| | | 1988 | 45 069 (28) | 21 427 | (3) | 10 281 | 15 612 (29) | | ... | 8 030 (30) | | ... |
| | | 1989 | 42 276 (28) | 20 431 | | ... | 14 113 (29) | | ... | 7 732 (30) | | ... |
| | | 1990 | 36 384 | 17 550 | | ... | 11 711 | | ... | 7 123 | | ... |
| | | 1991 | 29 397 | 14 471 | | ... | 8 903 | | ... | 6 023 (30) | | ... |
| | | 1992 | 24 192 | 12 311 | | ... | 7 152 | | ... | 4 729 | | ... |
| | (8) | 1993 | 22 609 | 11 818 | | ... | ... | | ... | ... | | ... |
| | (8) | 1994 | 22 008 | 11 752 | | ... | ... | | ... | ... | | ... |
| | | 1995 | 19 585 | 10 499 | | ... | 5 207 | | ... | 3 879 | | ... |
| | (8) | 1996 | 19 776 | 10 408 | | ... | ... | | ... | ... | | ... |
| | (8) | 1997 | 20 758 | 11 154 | | ... | ... | | ... | ... | | ... |
| Iceland | | 1981 | 744 | 398 | | ... | 346 | (15) | ... | ./. | (15) | ... |
| | | 1983 | 776 | 413 | | ... | 363 | (15) | ... | ./. | (15) | ... |
| | | 1985 | 818 | 512 | | ... | 306 | (15) | ... | ./. | (15) | ... |
| | | 1987 | 877 | 556 | | ... | 321 | (15) | ... | ./. | (15) | ... |
| | | 1989 | 1 177 | 773 | | ... | 404 | (15) | ... | ./. | (15) | ... |
| | (8) | 1990 | 1 188 | 676 | | ... | ... | | ... | ... | | ... |
| | (8) | 1991 | 1 197 | 687 | | ... | ... | | ... | ... | | ... |
| | (8) | 1992 | 1 244 | 708 | | ... | ... | | ... | ... | | ... |
| | (8) | 1993 | 1 363 | 815 | | ... | ... | | ... | ... | | ... |
| | (8) | 1994 | 1 412 | 845 | | ... | ... | | ... | ... | | ... |
| | | 1995 | 1 694 | 1 076 | | ... | 393 | | ... | 225 | | ... |
| | (8) | 1996 | 1 516 | 908 | | ... | ... | | ... | ... | | ... |
| | (8) | 1997 | 1 779 | 1 130 | | ... | ... | | ... | ... | | ... |
| Ireland | | 1981 | *5 474 | *2 635 | | ... | *1 408 | | ... | *1 431 | | ... |
| | | 1982 | 5 449 | 2 773 | | ... | 1 271 | | ... | 1 405 | | ... |
| | | 1983 | 5 819 | 3 232 | | ... | 1 326 | | ... | 1 261 | | ... |
| | | 1984 | 6 193 | 3 626 | | ... | 1 336 | | ... | 1 231 | | ... |
| | | 1985 | 6 264 | 3 741 | | ... | 1 340 | | ... | 1 183 | | ... |
| | | 1986 | 6 343 | 3 861 | | ... | 1 348 | | ... | 1 134 | | ... |

III.2

Personnel engaged in R&D by category of personnel
Personnel employé dans la R-D par catégorie de personnel
Personal empleado en I y D por categoría de personal

| Country / Pays / País | | Year / Année / Año | All R&D personnel / Tout le personnel de R-D / Todo el personal de I y D | Researchers / Chercheurs / Investigadores MF | F | Technicians and equivalent staff / Techniciens et personnel assimilé / Técnicos y personal asimilado MF | F | Other supporting staff / Autre personnel de soutien / Otro personal de apoyo MF | F |
|---|---|---|---|---|---|---|---|---|---|
| Ireland (cont) | (8) | 1987 | 5 704 | 3 344 | ... | ... | ... | ... | ... |
| | | 1988 | 8 590 | 6 351 | ... | 1 291 | ... | 948 | ... |
| | (8) | 1989 | 6 328 | 4 098 | ... | ... | ... | ... | ... |
| | (8) | 1990 | 6 846 | 4 618 | ... | ... | ... | ... | ... |
| | (8) | 1991 | 8 002 | 5 161 | ... | ... | ... | ... | ... |
| | (8) | 1992 | 8 488 | 5 547 | ... | ... | ... | ... | ... |
| | | 1993 | 9 534 | 6 592 | ... | 1 797 | ... | 1 145 | ... |
| | (8) | 1994 | 10 681 | 7 307 | ... | ... | ... | ... | ... |
| | (8) | 1995 | 12 206 | 8 368 | ... | ... | ... | ... | ... |
| Italy | | 1980 | 95 803 | 46 999 | ... | 27 605 | ... | 21 199 | ... |
| | | 1981 | 102 836 | 52 060 | ... | 29 385 | ... | 21 391 | ... |
| | | 1982 | 105 927 | 56 707 | ... | 28 027 | ... | 21 193 | ... |
| | | 1983 | 112 743 | 63 021 | ... | 28 694 | ... | 21 028 | ... |
| | | 1984 | 112 884 | 61 979 | ... | 30 480 | ... | 20 425 | ... |
| | | 1985 | 117 887 | 63 759 | ... | 33 058 | ... | 21 070 | ... |
| | | 1986 | 122 352 | 67 844 | ... | 32 892 | ... | 21 616 | ... |
| | | 1987 | 128 175 | 70 556 | ... | 36 219 | ... | 21 400 | ... |
| | | 1988 | 135 665 | 74 833 | ... | 38 287 | ... | 22 545 | ... |
| | | 1989 | 140 496 | 76 074 | ... | 40 067 | ... | 24 355 | ... |
| | | 1990 | 144 917 | 77 876 | ... | 42 304 | ... | 24 737 | ... |
| | (8) | 1991 | 143 641 | 75 238 | ... | ... | ... | ... | ... |
| | (8) | 1992 | 142 855 | 74 422 | ... | ... | ... | ... | ... |
| | (8) | 1993 | 142 171 | 74 434 | ... | ... | ... | ... | ... |
| | | 1994 | 143 823 | 75 722 | ... | 45 701 | ... | 22 400 | ... |
| | (8) | 1995 | 141 789 | 75 536 | ... | ... | ... | ... | ... |
| Latvia | | 1993 | 6 552 | 3 999 | 1 593 | 1 066 | 729 | 1 487 | ... |
| | | 1994 | 5 239 | 3 010 | 1 359 | 944 | 557 | 1 285 | ... |
| | | 1995 | 5 238 | 3 072 | 1 413 | 1 008 | 603 | 1 158 | 704 |
| | | 1996 | 4 744 | 2 839 | 1 324 | 850 | 512 | 1 055 | ... |
| | | 1997 | 4 437 | 2 610 | 1 197 | 872 | 470 | 955 | ... |
| Lithuania | | 1996 | 12 569 | 7 532 | 3 129 | 2 344 | 1 546 | 2 693 | ... |
| Malta (36) | | 1988 | 46 | 34 | ... | 5 | .. | 7 | ... |
| Moldova | | 1994 | 13 142 | 2 158 | ... | 8 421 | 3 702 | 2 563 | ... |
| | | 1995 | 10 645 | 1 821 | ... | 6 802 | 2 989 | 2 022 | ... |
| | | 1996 | 10 697 | 1 096 | ... | 7 142 | 3 118 | 2 459 | ... |
| | | 1997 | 10 667 | 1 442 | ... | 7 181 | 3 250 | 2 044 | ... |
| Netherlands | (6) | 1980 | 53 560 | 26 430 | ... | (15) 27 130 | ... | (15) ./. | ... |
| | (6) | 1981 | 57 610 | 29 630 | ... | (15) 27 980 | ... | (15) ./. | ... |
| | (6) | 1982 | 57 450 | 30 160 | ... | (15) 27 290 | ... | (15) ./. | ... |
| | (6) | 1983 | 57 630 | 30 530 | ... | (15) 27 100 | ... | (15) ./. | ... |
| | (6) | 1984 | 58 400 | 31 320 | ... | (15) 27 080 | ... | (15) ./. | ... |
| | (6) | 1985 | 61 400 | 33 620 | ... | (15) 27 780 | ... | (15) ./. | ... |
| | (6) | 1986 | 62 830 | 35 250 | ... | (15) 27 580 | ... | (15) ./. | ... |
| | (6) | 1987 | 63 520 | 36 750 | ... | (15) 26 770 | ... | (15) ./. | ... |
| | (6) | 1988 | 64 420 | 37 520 | ... | (15) 26 900 | ... | (15) ./. | ... |
| | (6) | 1989 | 66 460 | 39 100 | ... | (15) 27 360 | ... | (15) ./. | ... |
| | (6) | 1990 | 68 170 | 40 260 | ... | (15) 27 910 | ... | (15) ./. | ... |
| | | 1991 | 66 710 | 40 000 | ... | 20 440 | ... | 6 270 | ... |
| | (8) | 1992 | 72 310 | ... | ... | ... | ... | ... | ... |
| | (8) | 1993 | 74 420 | 32 200 | ... | ... | ... | ... | ... |
| | (8) | 1994 | 78 980 | 34 200 | ... | ... | ... | ... | ... |
| | (8) | 1995 | 79 256 | 34 038 | ... | ... | ... | ... | ... |
| | (8) | 1996 | 80 789 | 34 482 | ... | ... | ... | ... | ... |
| Norway | | 1981 | 14 843 | 7 498 | ... | (15) 7 345 | ... | (15) ./. | ... |
| | | 1982 | 15 218 | 7 754 | ... | (15) 7 464 | ... | (15) ./. | ... |
| | | 1983 | 15 969 | 8 283 | ... | (15) 7 686 | ... | (15) ./. | ... |
| | | 1984 | 17 230 | 8 970 | ... | (15) 8 260 | ... | (15) ./. | ... |
| | | 1985 | 18 781 | 9 692 | ... | (15) 9 089 | ... | (15) ./. | ... |
| | | 1986 | 19 640 | 10 120 | ... | (15) 9 520 | ... | (15) ./. | ... |
| | | 1987 | 19 888 | 11 465 | ... | (15) 8 423 | ... | (15) ./. | ... |
| | | 1989 | 20 217 | 12 156 | ... | (15) 8 061 | ... | (15) ./. | ... |
| | | 1991 | 20 252 | 13 460 | ... | (15) 6 792 | ... | (15) ./. | ... |
| | (8) | 1993 | 22 091 | 14 763 | ... | ... | ... | ... | ... |
| | | 1995 | 23 938 | 15 931 | ... | (15) 8 007 | ... | (15) ./. | ... |
| | (8) | 1997 | 24 000 | ... | ... | ... | ... | ... | ... |
| Poland | | 1980 | (16) 240 000 | 93 000 | ... | (31) 57 000 | ... | 90 000 | ... |
| | | 1981 | (16) 221 000 | 89 000 | ... | (31) 51 000 | ... | 81 000 | ... |
| | | 1982 | (16) 188 000 | 79 000 | ... | (31) 41 000 | ... | 68 000 | ... |
| | | 1983 | (16) 176 000 | 75 000 | ... | (31) 37 000 | ... | 64 000 | ... |
| | | 1984 | (16) 174 000 | 75 000 | ... | (31) 35 000 | ... | 64 000 | ... |
| | | 1985 | (16) 181 000 | 57 000 | ... | (31) 54 000 | ... | 70 000 | ... |
| | | 1986 | (16) 177 000 | 45 000 | ... | (31)(32) 62 000 | ... | 70 000 | ... |
| | | 1987 | (16) 174 000 | 43 000 | ... | (31)(32) 64 000 | ... | 67 000 | ... |
| | (8) | 1994 | 79 248 | 47 433 | ... | ... | ... | ... | ... |
| | | 1995 | 82 852 | 49 787 | *17 695 | 19 553 | *8 628 | 13 512 | *7 381 |
| | (8) | 1996 | 83 348 | 52 474 | ... | ... | ... | ... | ... |

**Personnel engaged in R&D by category of personnel**
**Personnel employé dans la R-D par catégorie de personnel**
**Personal empleado en I y D por categoría de personal**

| Country / Pays / País | | Year / Année / Año | All R&D personnel / Tout le personnel de R-D / Todo el personal de I y D | Researchers / Chercheurs / Investigadores | | Technicians and equivalent staff / Techniciens et personnel assimilé / Técnicos y personal asimilado | | Other supporting staff / Autre personnel de soutien / Otro personal de apoyo | |
|---|---|---|---|---|---|---|---|---|---|
| | | | | MF | F | MF | F | MF | F |
| Portugal | | 1980 | 7 711 | 2 663 | ... | 2 867 | ... | 2 181 | ... |
| | | 1982 | 8 552 | 3 019 | ... | 3 100 | ... | 2 433 | ... |
| | | 1984 | 9 267 | 3 475 | ... | 3 059 | ... | 2 733 | ... |
| | | 1986 | 10 570 | 4 479 | ... | 3 419 | ... | 2 672 | ... |
| | | 1988 | 10 883 | 5 004 | ... | 3 571 | ... | 2 308 | ... |
| | | 1990 | 12 043 | 5 908 | ... | 3 755 | ... | 2 380 | ... |
| | (8) | 1992 | 13 448 | 9 451 | ... | | ... | ... | ... |
| | | 1995 | 15 589 | 11 648 | ... | 1 645 | ... | 2 296 | ... |
| Romania | | 1987 | 167 049 | 58 647 | | 42 195 | | 66 207 | |
| | | 1988 | 167 711 | 58 879 | ... | 42 362 | ... | 66 470 | ... |
| | | 1989 | 169 964 | 59 670 | 24 582 | 42 931 | 28 204 | 67 363 | 29 563 |
| | | 1991 | 60 712 | 28 302 (26) | 12 675 | 11 248 (26) | 6 085 | 21 162 (26) | 11 616 |
| | | 1994 | 59 102 | 31 672 | 14 048 | 13 272 | 7 991 | 14 158 | ... |
| Russian Federation | | 1994 | 1 264 138 | 621 790 | 256 328 | 130 452 | ... | 511 896 | ... |
| | | 1996 | 1 113 244 | 562 070 | 229 959 | 96 922 | ... | 454 252 | ... |
| | | 1997 | 1 053 013 | 532 469 | 210 662 | 89 003 | ... | 431 541 | ... |
| Slovakia | | 1992 | 30 284 | 10 681 | ... | 5 605 | ... | 13 998 | ... |
| | | 1993 | 25 094 | 8 927 | ... | 4 532 | ... | 11 635 | ... |
| | | 1994 | 17 256 | 10 249 | 3 540 | 4 244 | 2 270 | 2 763 | ... |
| | | 1995 | 16 182 | 9 711 | 3 420 | 4 081 | 2 198 | 2 390 | 1 325 |
| | | 1996 | 16 613 | 10 010 | 7 164 | 4 244 | 3 601 | 2 359 | ... |
| Slovenia | | 1992 | 12 653 | 5 789 | 1 745 | 4 615 | 2 197 | 2 249 | 1 557 |
| | | 1993 | 8 866 | 3 745 | 1 253 | 2 337 | 1 281 | 2 784 | |
| | | 1994 | 9 924 | 4 767 | 1 544 | 2 323 | 1 158 | 2 834 | |
| | | 1995 | 9 879 | 4 897 | 1 569 | 2 183 | 1 107 | 2 799 | 1 374 |
| | | 1996 | 8 882 | 4 489 | 1 486 | 2 048 | 961 | 2 345 | ... |
| Spain | (8) | 1981 | 36 221 | 19 268 | ... | ... | ... | ... | ... |
| | (8) | 1982 | 35 530 | 18 782 | ... | ... | ... | ... | ... |
| | (8) | 1983 | 36 169 | 19 450 | ... | ... | ... | ... | ... |
| | (16) | 1984 | 39 287 | 20 506 | 2 747 | 6 181 | 615 | 12 600 | 3 489 |
| | (16) | 1985 | 40 653 | 21 455 | 2 918 | 7 024 | 698 | 12 174 | 3 465 |
| | (16) | 1986 | 44 947 | 24 525 | 3 852 | 7 596 | 839 | 12 826 | 3 923 |
| | (16) | 1987 | 48 103 | 26 462 | 4 474 | 8 196 | 1 020 | 13 445 | 4 296 |
| | (16) | 1988 | 54 337 | 31 170 | (26) 7 585 | 9 914 | 1 448 | 13 253 | 4 101 |
| | (16) | 1989 | 58 025 | 32 812 | (26) 8 174 | 11 150 | 1 683 | 14 063 | 4 703 |
| | (16) | 1990 | 64 582 | 37 534 | (26) 9 907 | 11 735 | 2 007 | 15 313 | 5 210 |
| | (8) | 1991 | 72 406 | 40 642 | ... | ... | ... | ... | ... |
| | (8) | 1992 | 73 320 | 41 681 | ... | ... | ... | ... | ... |
| | (8) | 1993 | 75 734 | 43 367 | ... | ... | ... | ... | ... |
| | | 1994 | 80 399 | 47 867 | ... | 13 532 | ... | (34) 19 000 | ... |
| | (8) | 1995 | 79 988 | 47 342 | ... | ... | ... | ... | ... |
| | (8) | 1996 | 87 263 | 51 633 | ... | ... | ... | ... | ... |
| | (8) | 1997 | 89 029 | ... | ... | ... | ... | ... | ... |
| Sweden | (35) | 1981 | 42 214 | 17 696 | ... | (15) 24 518 | ... | (15) ./. | |
| | (35) | 1983 | 45 758 | 18 400 | ... | (15) 27 358 | ... | (15) ./. | |
| | (35) | 1985 | 49 599 | 21 200 | ... | (15) 28 399 | ... | (15) ./. | |
| | (35) | 1987 | 51 811 | 22 725 | ... | (15) 29 086 | ... | (15) ./. | |
| | (35) | 1989 | *55 129 | *25 585 | ... | (15) *29 544 | ... | (15) ./. | |
| | | 1991 | 53 604 | 26 515 | ... | (15) 27 089 | ... | (15) ./. | |
| | | 1993 | 59 876 | 32 288 | ... | (15) 27 588 | ... | (15) ./. | |
| | (8) | 1995 | 62 635 | 33 665 | | ... | | ... | |
| Switzerland | | 1986 | 45 200 | 14 910 | ... | 10 710 | ... | 19 580 | ... |
| | | 1989 | 51 000 | 16 300 | ... | 9 300 | ... | 25 400 | ... |
| | (8) | 1992 | 47 870 | 17 710 | ... | ... | ... | ... | ... |
| | (8) | 1996 | 50 265 | 21 635 | ... | ... | ... | ... | ... |
| The Former Yugoslav Rep. of Macedonia | | 1995 | 5 043 | 2 620 | 1 081 | 1 070 | 794 | 1 353 | 898 |
| Ukraine | | 1995 | 263 730 | 163 299 | ... | 36 687 | ... | 63 744 | ... |
| | | 1996 | 240 709 | 147 732 | ... | 36 524 | ... | 56 453 | ... |
| | | 1997 | 193 397 | 112 327 | ... | 29 725 | ... | 51 345 | ... |
| United Kingdom | (8) | 1981 | 312 000 | 127 000 | ... | ... | ... | ... | ... |
| | (8) | 1982 | 308 000 | 128 000 | ... | ... | ... | ... | ... |
| | (8) | 1983 | 303 000 | 127 000 | ... | ... | ... | ... | ... |
| | (8) | 1984 | 296 000 | 129 000 | ... | ... | ... | ... | ... |
| | (8) | 1985 | 289 000 | 131 000 | ... | ... | ... | ... | ... |
| | (8) | 1986 | 291 000 | 134 000 | ... | ... | ... | ... | ... |
| | (8) | 1987 | 288 000 | 134 000 | ... | ... | ... | ... | ... |
| | (8) | 1988 | 290 000 | 137 000 | ... | ... | ... | ... | ... |
| | (8) | 1989 | 281 000 | 133 000 | ... | ... | ... | ... | ... |
| | (8) | 1990 | 280 000 | 133 000 | ... | ... | ... | ... | ... |
| | (8) | 1991 | 261 000 | 128 000 | ... | ... | ... | ... | ... |
| | (8) | 1992 | 264 000 | 131 000 | ... | ... | ... | ... | ... |
| | | 1993 | 279 000 | 140 000 | ... | 59 000 | ... | 80 000 | ... |

Personnel engaged in R&D by category of personnel   III.2
Personnel employé dans la R-D par catégorie de personnel
Personal empleado en I y D por categoría de personal

| Country<br><br>Pays<br><br>País | Year<br><br>Année<br><br>Año | | All R&D personnel<br><br>Tout le personnel<br>de R-D<br><br>Todo el personal<br>de I y D | Researchers<br><br>Chercheurs<br><br>Investigadores | | Technicians and<br>equivalent staff<br><br>Techniciens et<br>personnel assimilé<br><br>Técnicos y personal<br>asimilado | | Other supporting staff<br><br>Autre personnel de<br>soutien<br><br>Otro personal de<br>apoyo | |
|---|---|---|---|---|---|---|---|---|---|
| | | | | MF | F | MF | F | MF | F |
| **Oceania** | | | | | | | | | |
| Australia | 1981 | | 45 211 | 24 486 | ... | 12 284 | ... | 8 441 | ... |
| | 1984 | | 51 255 | 28 967 | ... | 13 947 | ... | 8 341 | ... |
| | 1985 | | 53 798 | 30 406 | ... | 14 848 | ... | 8 544 | ... |
| | 1986 | | 60 109 | 35 029 | ... | 16 255 | ... | 8 825 | ... |
| | 1987 | | 62 442 | 36 424 | ... | 16 526 | ... | 9 492 | ... |
| | 1988 | | 66 042 | 39 471 | ... | 16 647 | ... | 9 924 | ... |
| | 1990 | | 67 796 | 41 837 | ... | 15 922 | ... | 10 037 | ... |
| | 1994 | | 86 161 | 56 520 | ... | 14 133 | ... (34) | 15 508 | ... |
| | 1996 | (8) | 90 519 | 60 890 | ... | ... | ... | ... | ... |
| Fiji (38) | 1986 | | 156 | 36 | 4 | 90 | 10 | 30 | ... |
| Guam | 1985 | (36) | 46 | 19 | ... | 11 | ... | 16 | ... |
| | 1986 | (36) | 47 | 19 | ... | 11 | ... | 17 | ... |
| | 1987 | (36) | 48 | 19 | ... | 11 | ... | 18 | ... |
| | 1989 | (36) | *52 | *21 | *4 | *11 | *4 | *20 | *2 |
| | 1991 | (36) | 55 | 23 | 5 | 11 | 5 | 21 | 1 |
| New Caledonia (39) | 1985 | | 334 | 77 | 7 | 71 | 11 | 186 | 37 |
| New Zealand | 1989 | (8) | 9 148 | 4 818 | ... | ... | ... | ... | ... |
| | 1990 | (8) | 8 808 | 4 893 | ... | ... | ... | ... | ... |
| | 1991 | (8) | 8 706 | 4 752 | ... | ... | ... | ... | ... |
| | 1992 | (8) | 0 032 | 5 903 | ... | ... | ... | ... | ... |
| | 1993 | | 10 488 | 6 198 | ... | 2 866 | ... | 1 424 | ... |
| | 1995 | (8) | 10 547 | 6 104 | ... | ... | ... | ... | ... |

## General note
For general explanations and definitions, please refer to the beginning of this chapter.

## Note générale
Pour les explications et définitions générales, se référer au début de ce chapitre.

## Nota general
Para las explicaciones y definiciones generales, referirse al comienzo de este capítulo.

### Notes

(1) Not including data for the productive sector (non-integrated R&D).

(2) Not including data for the productive sector.

(3) Data refer to full-time plus part-time personnel.

(4) Data refer to the Ministry of Scientific Research only.

(5) Data relate only to 23 out of 26 national research institutes under the Federal Ministry of Science and Technology.

(6) Not including data for social sciences and humanities in the productive sector (integrated R&D).

(7) Technicians and equivalent staff engaged in social sciences and humanities are included with other supporting staff.

(8) Data for researchers refers to full-time-equivalent Data are from OECD.

(9) Data refer to researchers and technicians and equivalent staff in public enterprises only.

(10) Data relate to the productive sector (integrated R&D) and the higher education sector only.

(11) Data relate to the Scientific Research Council only.

(12) Not including data for law, humanities and education.

(13) Data refer to researchers only.

(14) Data refer to researchers listed in the directory of research group in Brazil by the Conselho Nacional de Desenvolvimento Científico e Tecnologica (CNPq).

### Notes

(1) Non compris les données relatives au secteur de la production (activités de R-D non intégrées).

(2) Non compris les données relatives au secteur de la production.

(3) Les données se réfèrent au personnel à plein temps et à temps partiel.

(4) Les données concernent le Ministère de la Recherche Scientifique seulement.

(5) Les données concernent seulement 23 des 26 instituts de recherche nationaux sous tutelle du Ministère Fédéral de la Science et de la Technologie.

(6) Non compris les données pour les sciences sociales et humaines dans le secteur de la production (activités de R-D intégrées).

(7) Les techniciens et personnel assimilé employés dans les sciences sociales et humaines sont inclus avec le personnel de soutien.

(8) Les données relatives aux chercheurs sont exprimées en équivalent plein temps. Les données sont de l'OCDE.

(9) Les données se réfèrent aux chercheurs et techniciens et personnel assimilé dans les entreprises publiques seulement.

(10) Les données se réfèrent au secteur de la production (activités de R-D intégrées) et au secteur de l'enseignement supérieur seulement.

(11) Les données se réfèrent au 'Scientific Research Council seulement'.

(12) Non compris les données pour le droit, les sciences humaines et les sciences de l'éducation.

(13) Les données se réfèrent aux chercheurs seulement.

(14) Les données se réfèrent aux chercheurs figurant dans le répertoire du groupe de chercheurs brésiliens élaboré par le Conselho Nacional de Desenvolvimento Cientifico e Tecnologica (CNPq).

### Notas

(1) No incluyen los datos relativos al sector productivo (actividades de I y D no integradas).

(2) No incluyen los datos relativos al sector productivo.

(3) Los datos se refieren al personal de jornada completa y de jornada parcial.

(4) Los datos se refieren al Ministerio de Investigación Científica solamente.

(5) Los datos se refieren a 23 de los 26 institutos de investigación nacionales bajo la tutela del Ministerio Federal de Ciencia y Tecnología.

(6) No incluyen los datos para las ciencias sociales y humanas en el sector productivo (actividades de I y D integradas).

(7) Los técnicos y el personal asimilado empleados en las ciencias sociales y humanas se incluyen con el otro personal de apoyo.

(8) Los datos sobre los investigadores están expresados en equivalente de jornada completa. Los datos son de la OCDE.

(9) Los datos se refieren a los investigadores, técnicos y al personal asimilado en las empresas públicas solamente.

(10) Los datos se refieren al sector productivo (actividades de I y D integradas) y al sector de la enseñanza superior solamente.

(11) Los datos se refieren al 'Scientific Research Council' solamente.

(12) No incluyen los datos en derecho, ciencias humanas y ciencias de la educación.

(13) Los datos se refieren a los investigadores solamente.

(14) Los datos se refieren a los investigadores que figuran en el repertorio del grupo de investigadores brasileños preparado por el Consejo Nacional de Desenvolvimento Cientifico e Tecnologica (CNPq).

III.2    Personnel engaged in R&D by category of personnel
Personnel employé dans la R-D par catégorie de personnel
Personal empleado en I y D por categoría de personal

(15) Technicians and equivalent staff and other supporting staff are counted together.

(16) Not including technicians and equivalent staff and other supporting staff in the higher education sector.

(17) Not including data for the higher education sector.

(18) Data relating to women researchers do not include the higher education sector

(19) Not including data for other supporting staff.

(20) Data refer to full-time personnel.

(21) Data relate to the East Bank only.

(22) Not including data for social sciences and humanities.

(23) Data relate to R&D activities concentrated mainly in government-financed research establishments.

(24) Not including social sciences and humanities in the higher education sector.

(25) Not including data for the productive sector (integrated R&D).

(26) Due to methodological changes, data are not comparable with earlier years.

(27) Not including business enterprise sector.

(28) Not including personnel engaged in the administration of R&D.

(29) Skilled workers are included with technicians and equivalent staff rather than with other supporting staff.

(30) Data for other supporting staff do not include skilled workers but include security, maintenance and repair personnel.

(31) Data relating to technicians and equivalent staff refer only to those persons with a vocational education at the second level of education.

(32) Due to methodological changes "managerial personnel in the technical section" previously classified as scientists and engineers are now included with technicians and equivalent staff.

(33) Not including data for private non-profit organizations.

(34) Including technicians and equivalent staff in higher education sector.

(35) Not including social sciences and humanities in the productive and general service sectors.

(36) Data refer to the higher education sector only.

(37) Not including general service sector.

(38) Data relate to one research institute only.

(39) Data refer only to 6 out of 11 research institutes.

(40) Data relate to one research institute only.

(15) Les techniciens et personnel assimilé et les autres personnel de soutien sont comptés ensemble .

(16) Non compris les techniciens et personnel assimilé et personnel de soutien dans le secteur de l'enseignement supérieur.

(17) Non compris les données pour le secteur de l'enseignement supérieur.

(18) Les données relatives aux femmes chercheurs n'incluent pas le secteur de l'enseignement supérieur.

(19) Non compris les données pour les autres personnel de soutien.

(20) Les données se réfèrent au personnel à plein temps.

(21) Les données se réfèrent à la rive orientale seulement.

(22) Non compris les données pour les sciences sociales et humaines.

(23) Les données se réfèrent pour la plupart aux activités de R-D dans les établissements de recherche financés par le gouvernement.

(24) Non compris les sciences sociales et humaines dans le secteur de l'enseignement supérieur.

(25) Non compris les données pour le secteur de la production (activités de R-D intégrées).

(26) Suite à des changements de méthodologie, les données ne sont pas comparables avec les années précédentes.

(27) Non compris le secteur des entreprises.

(28) Non compris le personnel employé dans les services administratifs de R-D.

(29) Les travailleurs qualifiés sont inclus avec les techniciens et le personnel assimilé plutôt qu'avec les autres personnel de soutien.

(30) Les données concernant les autres personnel de soutien n'incluent pas les travailleurs qualifiés mais incluent le personnel de sécurité et d'entretien.

(31) Les techniciens et le personnel assimilé se réfèrent seulement aux personnes ayant suivi un enseignement technique dans l'enseignement secondaire.

(32) Suite à des changements de méthodologie "le personnel d'administration dans la section technique" classé auparavant parmi les scientifiques et ingénieurs est maintenant inclus avec les techniciens et personnel assimilé.

(33) Non compris les données concernant les organisations privées à but non lucratif.

(34) Y compris les techniciens et personnel assimilé dans le secteur de l'enseignement supérieur.

(35) Non inclus les sciences sociales et humaines dans le secteur de la production et le secteur de service général.

(36) Les données se réfèrent au secteur de l'enseignement supérieur seulement.

(37) Non compris le secteur de service général.

(38) Les données ne concernent qu'un institut de recherche.

(39) Les données concernent 6 des 11 instituts de recherche.

(40) Les données concernent un seul institut de recherche.

(15) Los técnicos, el personal asimilado y otro personal de apoyo están contados conjuntamente.

(16) No incluyen a los técnicos,al personal asimilado y al personal de apoyo en el sector de la enseñanza superior.

(17) No incluyen los datos para el sector de la enseñanza superior.

(18) Los datos relativos a las mujeres investigadoras no incluyen el sector de la enseñanza superior.

(19) No incluyen los datos para el otro personal de apoyo.

(20) Los datos se refieren al personal de jornada completa.

(21) Los datos se refieren a la orilla oriental solamente.

(22) No incluyen los datos para las ciencias sociales y humanas.

(23) Los datos se refieren principalmente a las actividades de I y D en los establecimientos de investigación subvencionados por el gobierno.

(24) No incluyen las ciencias sociales y humanas en el sector de la enseñanza superior.

(25) No incluyen los datos para el sector productivo (actividades de I y D integradas).

(26) Debido a cambios de metodología, los datos no son comparables con los años anteriores.

(27) No incluyen el sector de empresas.

(28) No incluyen al personal empleado en los servicios administrativos de I y D.

(29) Los trabajadores cualificados se incluyen con los técnicos y el personal asimilado más bien que con el otro personal de apoyo.

(30) Los datos referidos al personal de apoyo no incluyen a los trabajadores cualificados, pero incluyen al personal de seguridad y de mantenimiento.

(31) Los técnicos se refieren solamente a las personas que cursaron una enseñanza técnica en la enseñanza secundaria.

(32) Debido a cambios de metodología "el personal de administración en la sección técnica" antes incluido con los científicos y los ingenieros se incluye ahora con los técnicos y personal asimilado.

(33) No incluyen los datos referidos a organizaciones privadas sin fines de lucro.

(34) Incluyen a los técnicos y el personal asimilado en el sector de la enseñanza superior.

(35) No incluyen las ciencias sociales y humanas en el sector productivo y al sectore de servicio general.

(36) Los datos se refieren al sector de la enseñanza superior solamente.

(37) No incluyen el sector de servicio general.

(38) Los datos se refieren a un centro de investigación solamente.

(39) Los datos se refieren a 6 de los 11 institutos de investigación.

(40) Los datos se refieren a un único instituto de investigación solemente.

Percentage distribution of gross domestic expenditure on R&D by source of funds
Répartition en pourcentage de dépenses intérieures brutes de R-D par source de fonds
Distribución porcentual del gasto interior bruto en I y D por origen de fondos

III.3

## III.3 Percentage distribution of gross domestic expenditure on R&D by source of funds

### Répartition en pourcentage des dépenses intérieures brutes de R-D par source de fonds

### Distribución porcentual del gasto interior bruto en I y D por origen de fondos

| Country / Pays / País | Reference year / Année de référence / Año de referencia | Currency / Monnaie / Moneda | Total gross domestic expenditure on R&D / Dépenses intérieures brutes totales de R-D / Gasto interior bruto total en I y D (000) | Source of funds / Source de fonds / Origen de fondos | | | | | |
|---|---|---|---|---|---|---|---|---|---|
| | | | | Business enterprise / Entreprises / Sector de empresas (%) | Government / Etat / Sector de la administración (%) | Higher education / Enseignement supérieur / Enseñanza superior (%) | Private non-profit / Institutions privées sans but lucratif / Instituciones privadas sin fines de lucro (%) | Funds from abroad / Fonds de l'etranger / Fondos del extranjero (%) | Not distributed / Non répartis / Sin distribución (%) |
| **Africa** | | | | | | | | | |
| Burundi (1)(2) | 1989 | Franc | 536 187 | - | 39.4 | - | - | 60.6 | - |
| Central African Republic | 1996 | Franc C.F.A. (3) | 130 899 | - | 100.0 | - | - | - | - |
| Congo | 1984 | Franc C.F.A. | 25 530 | 25.5 | 68.8 | - | - | 5.7 | - |
| Madagascar (4) | 1995 | Franc | 22 477 000 | - | 8.7 | 1.7 | - | 89.7 | - |
| Mauritius | 1980 | Rupee | 36 500 | 20.5 | 34.0 | 45.5 | —> | 0.4 | - |
| | 1981 | | 52 400 | 40.8 | 24.6 | 34.2 | —> | 0.5 | - |
| | 1982 | | 56 300 | 39.1 | 29.5 | 30.9 | —> | 1.0 | - |
| | 1983 | | 38 100 | 1.3 | 49.6 | 48.0 | —> | 1.0 | - |
| | 1984 | | 38 700 | 1.6 | 41.3 | 53.2 | —> | 3.9 | - |
| | 1985 | | ... | ... | 86.2 | 5.0 | —> | 8.8 | - |
| | 1986 | | 52 900 | 1.5 | 39.5 | 53.1 | —> | 5.9 | - |
| | 1987 | | 125 200 | 0.6 | 14.7 | 23.9 | —> | 60.8 | - |
| | 1988 | | 57 600 | 1.9 | 26.4 | 63.7 | —> | 8.0 | - |
| (5) | 1989 | | 54 300 | 2.4 | 35.0 | 62.6 | —> | | - |
| (6) | 1997 | | ... | ... | 94.7 | ... | ... | 5.3 | - |
| Nigeria (7) | 1987 | Naira | 86 270 | ... | 100.0 | ... | ... | ... | - |
| Rwanda | 1984 | Franc | 260 750 | ... | 72.5 | ... | ... | 17.8 | 9.7 |
| Seychelles | 1983 | Rupee | 12 854 | - | 48.8 | - | - | 51.2 | - |
| (7) | 1991 | | 4 593 | - | 100.0 | - | - | - | - |
| South Africa | 1983 | Rand | 769 439 | 50.5 | 32.1 | 17.5 | | - | - |
| | 1985 | | 1 077 305 | 41.3 | 35.4 | 23.3 | —> | - | - |
| | 1987 | | 1 329 126 | 41.3 | 38.3 | 20.5 | —> | - | - |
| | 1989 | | 1 774 447 | 41.9 | 34.6 | 23.5 | —> | - | - |
| | 1991 | | 2 786 086 | 46.8 | 32.4 | 20.8 | —> | - | - |
| | 1993 | | 2 594 107 | 54.4 | 42.7 | 1.8 | —> | 1.0 | - |
| Togo (8) | 1995 | Franc C.F.A. | 52 737 405 | - | - | - | - | 100.0 | - |
| Tunisia | 1997 | Dinar | 60 015 | ... | 55.5 | 32.3 | ... | 4.0 | 8.2 |
| Uganda | 1996 | Shilling | 34 866 530 | 2.2 | 6.6 | 0.6 | 0.3 | 90.3 | - |
| **North America** | | | | | | | | | |
| Canada (9) | 1981 | Dollar | *4 334 000 | *36.6 | *38.7 | *16.0 | ... | *3.0 | *5.7 |
| (9) | 1982 | | 5 090 000 | 38.3 | 40.8 | 15.4 | ... | 4.0 | 1.4 |
| (9) | 1983 | | 5 365 000 | 38.6 | *43.9 | *13.4 | ... | 4.2 | 0.8 |
| (9) | 1984 | | 6 015 000 | 38.5 | 44.6 | 11.9 | ... | 4.2 | 0.8 |
| (9) | 1985 | | 6 709 000 | 40.6 | 40.5 | 11.8 | ... | 4.4 | 2.7 |
| (9) | 1986 | | 7 220 000 | 40.5 | 39.5 | 12.2 | ... | 7.3 | 0.5 |
| (9) | 1987 | | 7 542 000 | 40.9 | 37.0 | 11.2 | ... | 9.0 | 1.9 |
| (9) | 1989 | | *8 786 000 | *40.8 | *36.1 | *10.3 | ... | *10.3 | *2.5 |
| (9) | 1990 | | 9 621 000 | 41.9 | 35.8 | 12.6 | —> | 9.8 | - |
| (9) | 1991 | | 10 024 000 | 41.3 | 35.3 | 13.4 | —> | 10.0 | - |
| | 1992 | | 10 289 000 | 41.1 | 35.5 | 13.4 | —> | 9.9 | - |
| (9) | 1993 | | *10 560 000 | *41.2 | *35.5 | *13.3 | —> | *10.0 | - |
| | 1996 | | 12 564 000 | 50.7 | 30.1 | 8.4 | —> | 10.8 | - |

**Percentage distribution of gross domestic expenditure on R&D by source of funds**
**Répartition en pourcentage de dépenses intérieures brutes de R-D par source de fonds**
**Distribución porcentual del gasto interior bruto en I y D por origen de fondos**

| Country / Pays / País | Reference year / Année de référence / Año de referencia | Currency / Monnaie / Moneda | Total gross domestic expenditure on R&D / Dépenses intérieures brutes totales de R-D / Gasto interior bruto total en I y D (000) | Source of funds / Source de fonds / Origen de fondos | | | | | |
|---|---|---|---|---|---|---|---|---|---|
| | | | | Business enterprise / Entreprises / Sector de empresas (%) | Government / Etat / Sector de la administración (%) | Higher education / Enseignement supérieur / Enseñanza superior (%) | Private non-profit / Institutions privées sans but lucratif / Instituciones privadas sin fines de lucro (%) | Funds from abroad / Fonds de l'etranger / Fondos del extranjero (%) | Not distributed / Non répartis / Sin distribución (%) |
| Costa Rica (7) | 1989 | Colon | 703 100 | ... | 100.0 | ... | ... | ... | - |
| | 1990 | | 838 400 | ... | 100.0 | ... | ... | ... | - |
| | 1991 | | 1 378 600 | ... | 100.0 | ... | ... | ... | - |
| Cuba | 1981 | Peso | 111 614 | ... | (5) 74.4 | ... | ... | (5) 5.9 | 19.6 |
| | 1982 | | 131 064 | ... | (5) 74.9 | ... | ... | (5) 3.7 | 21.3 |
| | 1983 | | 143 188 | - | 98.4 | - | - | 1.6 | - |
| | 1984 | | 164 202 | - | 96.4 | - | - | 3.6 | - |
| | 1985 | | 182 478 | - | 96.9 | - | - | 3.1 | - |
| (7) | 1987 | | 236 268 | - | 100.0 | - | - | - | - |
| (7) | 1988 | | 212 796 | - | 100.0 | - | - | - | - |
| (7) | 1989 | | 222 000 | - | 100.0 | - | - | - | - |
| (7) | 1991 | | 186 291 | - | 100.0 | - | - | - | - |
| (7) | 1992 | | 247 925 | - | 100.0 | - | - | - | - |
| (7) | 1995 | | 188 731 | - | 100.0 | - | - | - | - |
| El Salvador (10) | 1980 | Colon | 202 694 | - | 56.9 | - | - | 43.1 | - |
| | 1986 | | 335 174 | - | 84.8 | - | - | 15.2 | - |
| | 1987 | | 356 591 | - | 92.1 | - | - | 7.9 | - |
| (7) | 1989 | | 290 881 | - | 100.0 | - | - | - | - |
| | 1992 | | 1 083 559 | - | 47.4 | - | - | 52.6 | - |
| Guatemala | 1988 | Quetzal | (11) 31 859 | 0.5 | 36.7 | 45.7 | —> | 17.0 | - |
| Jamaica | 1986 | Dollar | (12) 4 016 | - | 100.0 | - | - | - | - |
| Mexico | 1989 | Peso | (36) 1 050 283 | (13) 5.0 | 95.0 | ... | ... | (13) ./. | - |
| | 1995 | | 5 622 597 | 17.6 | 66.2 | 8.4 | 1.1 | 6.7 | - |
| Nicaragua | 1987 | Cordoba | (5) *988 970 | - | *80.8 | - | - | *19.2 | - |
| Panama | 1986 | Balboa | (14) 173 | - | 100.0 | - | - | - | - |
| United States | 1980 | Dollar | (15) 63 810 000 | (5) 47.6 | (5) 46.5 | (5) 3.5 | ... | ... | 2.4 |
| | 1983 | | (15) 88 992 000 | 48.1 | 45.4 | 3.4 | ... | ... | 3.1 |
| | 1986 | | (15) 122 900 900 | 48.4 | (5) 45.0 | 3.2 | ... | ... | 3.5 |
| | 1988 | | (15) 139 255 000 | 48.7 | (5) 44.6 | 3.8 | ... | ... | 2.9 |
| | 1995 | | *171 000 000 | *59.4 | *35.5 | *5.1 | —> | ... | |
| **South America** | | | | | | | | | |
| Argentina | 1988 | Peso | 3 466 700 | 8.0 | 85.0 | 5.0 | —> | 2.0 | - |
| | 1995 | | 1 029 748 | 11.3 | 84.7 | 0.6 | —> | 3.4 | - |
| Brazil (14)(16) | 1982 | Cruzeiro | *305 500 000 | *19.8 | *66.9 | *8.1 | —> | *5.3 | - |
| | 1995 | | (17) 5 770 830 | 20.8 | 43.9 | ... | ... | - | 35.3 |
| | 1996 | | (17) 5 905 020 | 40.0 | 57.2 | 2.8 | - | - | - |
| Chile | 1986 | Peso | 14 263 900 | 27.1 | 68.3 | 4.6 | ... | ... | - |
| | 1987 | | 19 979 500 | 26.0 | 69.0 | 5.0 | —> | ... | - |
| | 1988 | | 23 161 300 | 18.2 | 70.4 | 8.1 | —> | 3.3 | - |
| | 1995 | | 170 760 000 | 20.2 | 68.5 | - | - | 11.3 | - |
| | 1997 | | 207 506 800 | 15.2 | 70.7 | - | 7.6 | 6.5 | - |
| Colombia (18) | 1982 | Peso | 2 754 273 | ... | ... | ... | ... | 10.5 | 89.5 |
| Peru | 1984 | Inti | (19) 159 024 | 27.2 | 48.0 | 3.8 | - | 21.0 | - |
| | 1995 | Sol | 756 877 | - | 81.9 | 18.1 | —> | - | - |
| Venezuela (7) | 1980 | Bolivar | 851 280 | ... | 98.8 | ... | ... | ... | 1.2 |
| | 1981 | | 1 012 170 | - | 100.0 | - | - | - | - |
| | 1982 | | 1 151 820 | - | 100.0 | - | - | - | - |
| | 1983 | | 1 196 500 | - | 100.0 | - | - | - | - |
| | 1984 | | 1 361 820 | - | 100.0 | - | - | - | - |
| | 1985 | | 1 411 720 | - | 100.0 | - | - | - | - |
| | 1986 | | 1 294 930 | - | 100.0 | - | - | - | - |
| (20) | 1987 | | 2 458 200 | - | 100.0 | - | - | - | - |
| (20) | 1988 | | 3 249 900 | - | 100.0 | - | - | - | - |
| (20) | 1989 | | 3 890 200 | - | 100.0 | - | - | - | - |
| (20) | 1990 | | 11 847 000 | - | 100.0 | - | - | - | - |
| (20) | 1991 | | 14 313 500 | - | 100.0 | - | - | - | - |
| (20) | 1992 | | 19 622 000 | - | 100.0 | - | - | - | - |
| **Asia** | | | | | | | | | |
| China, Hong Kong SAR | 1995 | Dollar | (21) 2 742 000 | 2.8 | 91.0 | 5.7 | - | 0.5 | - |
| Cyprus (7) | 1980 | Pound | 707 | - | 100.0 | - | - | - | - |
| (7) | 1981 | | 802 | - | 100.0 | - | - | - | - |
| (7) | 1982 | | 937 | - | 100.0 | - | - | - | - |
| (7) | 1983 | | 1 044 | - | 100.0 | - | - | - | - |
| | 1984 | | 1 173 | - | 98.8 | - | - | 1.2 | - |

Percentage distribution of gross domestic expenditure on R&D by source of funds    III.3
Répartition en pourcentage de dépenses intérieures brutes de R-D par source de fonds
Distribución porcentual del gasto interior bruto en I y D por origen de fondos

| Country / Pays / País | Reference year / Année de référence / Año de referencia | Currency / Monnaie / Moneda | Total gross domestic expenditure on R&D / Dépenses intérieures brutes totales de R-D / Gasto interior bruto total en I y D (000) | Source of funds / Source de fonds / Origen de fondos | | | | | |
|---|---|---|---|---|---|---|---|---|---|
| | | | | Business enterprise / Entreprises / Sector de empresas (%) | Government / Etat / Sector de la administra-ción (%) | Higher education / Enseignement supérieur / Enseñanza superior (%) | Private non-profit / Institutions privées sans but lucratif / Instituciones privadas sin fines de lucro (%) | Funds from abroad / Fonds de l'etranger / Fondos del extranjero (%) | Not distributed / Non répartis / Sin distribución (%) |
| Cyprus (cont) | 1991 | | 4 835 | 14.7 | 75.5 | 7.3 | - | 2.5 | - |
| | 1992 | | 6 037 | 13.1 | 76.4 | 8.8 | —> | 1.7 | - |
| India | 1982 | Rupee (36) | 12 060 300 | 13.4 | 82.7 | ... | ... | ... | 3.9 |
| | 1984 | (36) | 18 143 200 | 13.0 | 87.0 | ... | ... | ... | - |
| | 1986 | (36) | 26 675 300 | 11.9 | 88.1 | ... | ... | ... | - |
| | 1988 | (36) | 34 718 100 | 10.5 | 89.5 | ... | ... | - | - |
| | 1990 | (36) | 41 864 300 | 12.6 | 87.4 | ... | ... | - | - |
| | 1994 | | 75 063 500 | 24.0 | 75.0 | 1.0 | —> | - | - |
| Indonesia (7)(22) | 1984 | Rupiah | 279 000 000 | - | 100.0 | - | - | - | - |
| (7)(22) | 1985 | | 242 120 000 | - | 100.0 | - | - | - | - |
| (7)(22) | 1986 | | 241 750 000 | - | 100.0 | - | - | - | - |
| | 1994 | (23) | 244 843 000 | 76.4 | 15.8 | 0.5 | - | 7.2 | - |
| Iran, Islamic Republic of (7) | 1984 | Rial | 21 527 000 | - | 100.0 | - | - | - | - |
| (7) | 1985 | | 22 010 713 | - | 100.0 | - | - | - | - |
| | 1994 | | 620 849 320 | - | 86.8 | 13.2 | —> | - | - |
| Israel | 1981 | Shekel (24) | 7 485 | 22.1 | 65.2 | 12.7 | —> | - | - |
| | 1982 | (24) | 19 217 | 23.2 | 66.5 | 10.3 | —> | - | - |
| | 1983 | (24) | 56 300 | 21.7 | 63.8 | 14.5 | —> | - | - |
| | 1990 | | 2 323 400 | 38.0 | 37.6 | 16.9 | —> | 7.5 | - |
| | 1992 | | 3 003 100 | 37.2 | 37.1 | 18.0 | > | 7.6 | - |
| | 1995 | | 5 842 000 | 35.7 | 40.7 | 10.2 | 7.0 | 6.5 | - |
| Japan (9) | 1980 | Yen | 5 246 248 000 | 72.0 | 27.9 | - | - | 0.1 | - |
| | 1981 | | 5 982 356 000 | 72.9 | 27.0 | - | - | 0.1 | - |
| | 1982 | | 6 528 700 000 | 74.4 | 25.5 | - | - | 0.1 | - |
| | 1983 | | 7 180 782 000 | 75.9 | 24.0 | - | - | 0.1 | - |
| | 1984 | | 7 893 931 000 | 77.4 | 22.5 | - | - | 0.1 | - |
| | 1985 | | 8 890 299 000 | 78.9 | 21.0 | - | - | 0.1 | - |
| | 1986 | | 9 192 932 000 | 78.6 | 21.3 | - | - | 0.1 | - |
| | 1987 | | 9 836 640 000 | 78.4 | 21.5 | - | - | 0.1 | - |
| | 1988 | | 10 627 572 000 | 80.0 | 19.9 | - | - | 0.1 | - |
| | 1991 | | 13 771 524 000 | 81.7 | 18.2 | - | - | 0.1 | - |
| Kazakstan | 1997 | Tenge | 5 369 900 | 1.0 | 40.2 | ... | 5.7 | 11.8 | 41.3 |
| Korea, Republic of (25) | 1980 | Won | 211 726 652 | 48.4 | 49.8 | - | - | 1.8 | - |
| | 1981 | | 293 131 465 | 56.4 | 41.5 | - | - | 2.1 | - |
| | 1982 | | 457 688 485 | 58.7 | 41.1 | - | - | 0.2 | - |
| | 1983 | | 621 749 314 | 72.5 | 27.3 | - | - | 0.2 | - |
| | 1986 | | 1 523 279 000 | 80.9 | 19.0 | - | - | 0.1 | - |
| | 1988 | | 2 454 152 000 | 78.3 | 17.0 | 0.4 | ... | ... | 4.4 |
| | 1990 | | 3 349 864 000 | 80.6 | 15.2 | - | ... | ... | 4.2 |
| | 1992 | | 4 989 031 000 | 82.4 | 17.2 | - | - | 0.4 | - |
| | 1994 | | 7 894 746 000 | 84.0 | 15.9 | - | - | - | - |
| Kuwait | 1984 | Dinar (20) | 71 163 | 64.3 | 34.3 | 1.4 | - | - | - |
| Kyrgyzstan | 1995 | Som | 46 309 | 29.4 | 67.3 | 1.8 | —> | 1.5 | - |
| | 1997 | | 59 467 | 24.8 | 63.3 | 3.5 | —> | 8.5 | - |
| Malaysia | 1988 | Ringgit (7) | 87 100 | - | 100.0 | - | - | - | - |
| | 1989 | (7) | 97 200 | - | 100.0 | - | - | - | - |
| | 1992 | | 550 700 | 43.0 | 53.1 | 2.1 | —> | 1.8 | - |
| | 1996 | | 549 100 | 8.3 | 13.5 | ... | ... | 1.6 | 76.6 |
| Pakistan | 1984 | Rupee (26)(7) | 3 834 287 | - | 100.0 | - | - | - | - |
| | 1987 | (26)(7) | 5 582 081 | - | 100.0 | - | - | - | - |
| Philippines | 1984 | Peso | 614 080 | 23.6 | 60.8 | 2.4 | ... | 13.0 | 0.1 |
| | 1992 | | *2 940 549 | *1.9 | *3.2 | *70.2 | —> | *24.7 | - |
| Qatar | 1986 | Riyal | 6 650 | | 100.0 | | - | - | - |
| Singapore | 1984 | Dollar (25) | 214 300 | 43.0 | 49.0 | - | - | 8.0 | - |
| | 1987 | (25)(27) | 374 700 | 59.6 | 38.8 | 1.6 | - | - | - |
| | 1995 | (25) | 1 366 570 | 62.5 | 31.4 | 2.4 | —> | 3.7 | - |
| Sri lanka | 1983 | Rupee (6) | 217 608 | (28) ./ | (28) 91.2 | ... | ... | 8.8 | - |
| | 1984 | (6) | 256 799 | ... | 83.7 | | | 16.3 | - |
| Thailand | 1985 | Baht | 3 473 000 | 13.8 | 69.6 | - | - | 16.6 | - |
| | 1987 | | 2 664 380 | 9.7 | 68.5 | 7.2 | —> | 14.5 | - |
| | 1995 | | 5 174 240 | 12.2 | 79.7 | 5.1 | —> | 3.1 | - |
| | 1996 | (29) | 5 528 135 | ... | 61.1 | 6.8 | 8.7 | 5.0 | 18.4 |
| Turkey | 1990 | Lira | 1 318 343 000 | 27.6 | 71.3 | 0.9 | - | 0.2 | - |
| | 1991 | | 3 330 047 000 | 28.5 | 70.1 | 1.3 | - | 0.2 | - |
| | 1995 | | 29 509 395 000 | 32.9 | 62.4 | 2.7 | - | 2.0 | - |

**Percentage distribution of gross domestic expenditure on R&D by source of funds**
**Répartition en pourcentage de dépenses intérieures brutes de R-D par source de fonds**
**Distribución porcentual del gasto interior bruto en I y D por origen de fondos**

| Country / Pays / País | Reference year / Année de référence / Año de referencia | Currency / Monnaie / Moneda | Total gross domestic expenditure on R&D / Dépenses intérieures brutes totales de R-D / Gasto interior bruto total en I y D (000) | Source of funds / Source de fonds / Origen de fondos | | | | | |
|---|---|---|---|---|---|---|---|---|---|
| | | | | Business enterprise / Entreprises / Sector de empresas (%) | Government / Etat / Sector de la administración (%) | Higher education / Enseignement supérieur / Enseñanza superior (%) | Private non-profit / Institutions privées sans but lucratif / Instituciones privadas sin fines de lucro (%) | Funds from abroad / Fonds de l'etranger / Fondos del extranjero (%) | Not distributed / Non répartis / Sin distribución (%) |
| Viet Nam (7) | 1983 | Dong | 331 000 | - | 100.0 | - | - | - | - |
| | 1984 | | 516 000 | - | 100.0 | - | - | - | - |
| | 1985 | | 498 000 | - | 100.0 | - | - | - | - |
| **Europe** | | | | | | | | | |
| Austria | 1981 | Schilling | 12 331 026 | 50.2 | 46.9 | 0.4 | —> | 2.5 | - |
| | 1982 | | *13 798 400 | *48.4 | *48.8 | *0.4 | —> | *2.4 | - |
| | 1983 | | *14 808 500 | *48.7 | *48.6 | *0.4 | —> | *2.3 | - |
| | 1984 | | *16 210 700 | *48.0 | *49.3 | *0.4 | —> | *2.3 | - |
| | 1985 | | 17 182 272 | 49.1 | 48.1 | 0.3 | —> | 2.5 | - |
| | 1986 | | *18 691 700 | *48.3 | *49.1 | *0.3 | —> | *2.4 | - |
| | 1987 | | *19 524 800 | *48.8 | *48.5 | *0.3 | —> | *2.4 | - |
| | 1988 | | *20 797 700 | *49.8 | *47.5 | *0.3 | —> | *2.4 | - |
| | 1989 | | 22 966 910 | 53.0 | 43.4 | 0.3 | —> | 3.2 | - |
| | 1990 | | *24 281 600 | *50.9 | *46.5 | *0.3 | —> | 2.3 | - |
| | 1993 | | 31 694 247 | 49.0 | 47.9 | 0.4 | —> | 2.6 | - |
| Belarus | 1992 | B.Rouble | 8 392 900 | 57.5 | 42.2 | 0.3 | —> | ... | - |
| | 1995 | | 1 325 959 800 | 59.5 | 40.1 | 0.4 | —> | ... | - |
| | 1997 | | 2 098 170 700 | 27.9 | 67.2 | 0.1 | —> | 4.8 | - |
| Belgium (30) | 1987 | Franc | 91 323 600 | 67.9 | 26.5 | 0.7 | —> | 1.0 | 3.9 |
| (30) | 1988 | | 91 265 100 | 71.6 | 26.7 | 0.7 | —> | 1.0 | - |
| (31) | 1990 | | 108 545 800 | 70.4 | 27.6 | 0.7 | —> | 1.3 | - |
| | 1991 | | *112 065 000 | *64.8 | *31.3 | *0.9 | —> | *3.0 | - |
| Bulgaria | 1980 | Lev | 470 800 | 62.8 | 37.2 | - | - | - | - |
| | 1981 | | 537 000 | 65.8 | 34.2 | - | - | - | - |
| | 1982 | | 631 800 | 62.4 | 37.6 | - | - | - | - |
| | 1983 | | 669 800 | 62.5 | 37.5 | - | - | - | - |
| | 1984 | | 696 900 | 63.2 | 36.8 | - | - | - | - |
| | 1985 | | 812 300 | 64.2 | 35.8 | - | - | - | - |
| | 1986 | | 856 100 | 64.4 | 35.6 | - | - | - | - |
| | 1987 | | 923 800 | 59.8 | 40.2 | - | - | - | - |
| | 1989 | | 1 042 400 | 58.4 | 41.6 | - | - | - | - |
| | 1991 | | 1 874 800 | 65.7 | 34.3 | - | - | - | - |
| | 1996 | | 9 148 000 | 60.5 | 35.1 | 3.8 | 0.4 | 0.1 | - |
| Croatia | 1992 | Kuna | 27 242 365 | 31.7 | 37.2 | 30.2 | —> | 0.8 | - |
| | 1995 | | 1 159 331 | 19.0 | 63.3 | 17.3 | —> | 0.4 | - |
| Czech Republic | 1995 | C.Koruny | 13 982 600 | 63.1 | 32.3 | 1.3 | ... | 3.3 | - |
| Denmark | 1983 | Krone | 6 097 000 | 45.6 | 48.8 | 1.5 | —> | 2.0 | 2.1 |
| | 1985 | | 7 692 000 | 48.9 | 46.0 | 3.1 | —> | 2.1 | - |
| | 1987 | | 9 933 000 | 47.6 | 45.9 | 3.8 | —> | 2.7 | - |
| | 1989 | | 11 892 000 | 46.9 | 45.5 | 4.6 | —> | 3.1 | - |
| | 1991 | | 14 100 000 | 51.4 | 39.7 | 4.6 | —> | 4.4 | - |
| | 1993 | | 15 695 000 | 49.8 | 37.9 | 5.0 | —> | 7.4 | - |
| Estonia (32) | 1995 | Krooni | 250 604 | 12.9 | 71.3 | 6.2 | - | 9.6 | - |
| | 1997 | | 369 751 | 7.7 | 67.4 | 4.7 | 5.2 | 14.9 | - |
| Federal Republic of Yugoslavia | 1995 | Dinar (5) | 424 831 | 28.2 | 54.1 | 16.8 | - | 0.8 | - |
| | 1996 | | 871 670 | 33.6 | 48.6 | 16.2 | —> | 1.6 | - |
| Finland | 1981 | Markka | 2 595 000 | 54.5 | 39.4 | 0.8 | ... | 1.0 | 4.3 |
| | 1983 | | 3 626 730 | 55.6 | 42.3 | 1.2 | ... | 0.9 | - |
| | 1987 | | 6 792 000 | 58.8 | 39.4 | 0.7 | —> | 1.0 | - |
| | 1991 | | 10 172 000 | 53.8 | 44.3 | 0.6 | —> | 1.3 | - |
| | 1995 | | 12 915 000 | 57.7 | 37.4 | 0.4 | —> | 4.5 | - |
| France | 1987 | Franc | 121 364 000 | 41.8 | 51.9 | 0.3 | —> | 5.9 | - |
| | 1988 | | 130 631 000 | 43.3 | 49.9 | 0.6 | —> | 6.2 | - |
| | 1989 | | 143 553 000 | 43.9 | 48.1 | 0.6 | —> | 7.3 | - |
| | 1990 | | 157 146 000 | 43.5 | 48.3 | 0.7 | —> | 7.5 | - |
| | 1991 | | 163 092 000 | 42.5 | 48.8 | 0.7 | —> | 8.0 | - |
| | 1994 | | 175 563 000 | 48.7 | 41.6 | 1.4 | —> | 8.3 | - |
| Germany | 1993 | Deutsche Mark | 76 721 000 | 61.4 | 36.7 | 0.3 | —> | 1.6 | - |
| Greece | 1986 | Drachma | 18 331 000 | 23.2 | 74.4 | - | - | 2.4 | - |
| | 1993 | | 100 460 000 | 20.2 | 45.8 | 3.7 | —> | 30.3 | - |
| Hungary | 1981 | Forint | 19 425 000 | 79.3 | 20.3 | - | - | 0.4 | - |
| | 1982 | | 21 215 000 | 80.2 | 19.4 | - | - | 0.4 | - |
| | 1983 | | 20 419 000 | 78.5 | 21.2 | - | - | 0.3 | - |
| | 1984 | | 22 686 000 | 78.2 | 21.4 | - | - | 0.4 | - |
| | 1985 | | 24 077 000 | 78.6 | 20.9 | - | - | 0.4 | - |
| | 1986 | | 27 453 000 | 79.6 | 19.5 | - | - | 0.9 | - |

III.3

Percentage distribution of gross domestic expenditure on R&D by source of funds
Répartition en pourcentage de dépenses intérieures brutes de R-D par source de fonds
Distribución porcentual del gasto interior bruto en I y D por origen de fondos

| Country / Pays / País | Reference year / Année de référence / Año de referencia | Currency / Monnaie / Moneda | Total gross domestic expenditure on R&D / Dépenses intérieures brutes totales de R-D / Gasto interior bruto total en I y D (000) | Business enterprise / Entreprises / Sector de empresas (%) | Government / Etat / Sector de la administración (%) | Higher education / Enseignement supérieur / Enseñanza superior (%) | Private non-profit / Institutions privées sans but lucratif / Instituciones privadas sin fines de lucro (%) | Funds from abroad / Fonds de l'etranger / Fondos del extranjero (%) | Not distributed / Non répartis / Sin distribución (%) |
|---|---|---|---|---|---|---|---|---|---|
| Hungary (cont) | 1987 | | 32 155 000 | 79.1 | 19.8 | - | - | 1.1 | - |
| | 1988 | | 32 402 000 | 76.6 | 21.1 | 1.3 | —> | 0.9 | - |
| | 1989 | | 33 441 000 | 72.5 | 25.3 | 1.5 | —> | 0.7 | - |
| | 1991 | | 26 731 000 | 56.0 | 40.0 | 2.1 | —> | 1.8 | - |
| | 1995 | | 43 767 000 | 36.3 | 49.3 | 4.0 | —> | 4.6 | 5.9 |
| Iceland | 1981 | Krona | 160 100 | 19.4 | 76.1 | 0.2 | —> | 4.3 | - |
| | 1983 | | 462 000 | 31.1 | 65.7 | 3.0 | —> | 0.2 | - |
| | 1985 | | 845 000 | 22.5 | 74.5 | - | - | 3.0 | - |
| | 1987 | | 1 593 000 | 31.0 | 66.0 | - | - | 3.0 | - |
| | 1989 | | 3 123 000 | 23.0 | 70.0 | 4.0 | —> | 3.0 | - |
| | 1995 | | 6 957 929 | 34.6 | 57.3 | 3.7 | —> | 4.4 | 6.9 |
| Ireland | 1981 | Pound | 83 332 | 34.3 | 51.7 | 1.4 | —> | 5.7 | - |
| | 1982 | | 97 582 | 37.7 | 56.5 | 1.1 | —> | 4.8 | - |
| | 1984 | | 125 691 | 43.3 | 48.5 | 1.5 | —> | 6.7 | - |
| | 1986 | | 168 025 | 48.1 | 43.8 | 1.5 | —> | 6.6 | - |
| | 1993 | | 400 201 | 63.4 | 27.8 | 0.9 | —> | 7.8 | - |
| Italy | 1980 | Lira | 2 897 274 000 | 52.1 | 45.3 | - | - | 2.6 | - |
| | 1981 | | 4 055 335 000 | 50.1 | 47.2 | - | - | 2.7 | - |
| | 1982 | | 4 915 678 000 | 48.5 | 48.5 | - | - | 3.0 | - |
| | 1985 | | 9 132 902 000 | 44.6 | 51.7 | - | - | 3.6 | - |
| | 1986 | | 10 189 139 000 | 40.3 | 55.3 | - | - | 4.4 | - |
| | 1987 | | 11 696 035 000 | 41.7 | 54.0 | - | - | 4.3 | - |
| | 1988 | | 13 281 284 000 | 43.9 | 51.8 | - | - | 4.2 | - |
| | 1990 | | 17 001 221 000 | 43.7 | 51.5 | - | - | 4.8 | - |
| | 1994 | | 17 388 858 000 | 43.7 | 50.2 | - | - | 6.1 | - |
| Latvia | 1995 | Lat | 12 307 | 20.5 | 53.0 | 3.7 | —> | 22.8 | - |
| | 1996 | | 13 060 | ... | 56.1 | 2.3 | —> | 24.0 | 17.7 |
| | 1997 | | 13 893 | ... | 59.0 | ... | ... | 26.9 | 14.1 |
| Malta | 1988 | Lira (21) | 10 | - | 100.0 | - | - | - | - |
| Moldova | 1995 | Lei | 72 357 | 0.8 | 23.2 | 63.8 | —> | 4.1 | 8.2 |
| | 1997 | | 71 941 | 51.4 | 47.8 | 0.2 | - | 0.6 | - |
| Netherlands | 1980 | Guilder (9) | 6 348 000 | 45.2 | 48.3 | 1.0 | - | 5.6 | - |
| | 1982 | (9) | 7 284 000 | 44.9 | 48.6 | 1.2 | - | 5.2 | - |
| | 1983 | (9) | 7 699 000 | 46.4 | 47.4 | 1.2 | - | 5.0 | - |
| | 1984 | (9) | 7 852 000 | 48.3 | 47.0 | 1.3 | - | 3.4 | - |
| | 1985 | (9) | 8 748 000 | 51.7 | 44.3 | 1.4 | - | 2.6 | - |
| | 1986 | (9) | 9 533 000 | 52.5 | 43.9 | 1.4 | - | 2.2 | - |
| | 1987 | (9) | 10 040 000 | 52.1 | 43.9 | 2.0 | - | 2.0 | - |
| | 1988 | (9) | 10 163 000 | 53.4 | 42.6 | 1.7 | - | 2.3 | - |
| | 1990 | (9) | 10 450 000 | 51.2 | 45.0 | 1.7 | - | 2.1 | - |
| | 1991 | (9) | 10 381 000 | 51.3 | 44.8 | 1.9 | - | 2.0 | - |
| | 1994 | | 10 486 000 | 44.7 | 43.0 | 2.6 | - | 9.9 | - |
| Norway | 1980 | Krone | 3 629 800 | 35.6 | 58.6 | 4.2 | - | 1.6 | - |
| | 1981 | | 4 213 800 | 39.4 | 57.0 | 2.2 | - | 1.4 | - |
| | 1982 | | *4 952 500 | *41.6 | *53.5 | *2.3 | - | *2.5 | - |
| | 1983 | | *5 691 000 | *44.0 | *51.0 | *2.8 | - | *2.2 | - |
| | 1984 | | *6 830 000 | 47.5 | 48.2 | 2.4 | ... | 1.9 | 0.1 |
| | 1985 | | 8 109 900 | 50.2 | 45.6 | 2.1 | - | 2.1 | - |
| | 1986 | | 9 380 000 | 50.9 | 44.5 | 2.1 | - | 2.6 | - |
| | 1987 | | 10 202 700 | 48.6 | 47.1 | 2.6 | - | 1.7 | - |
| | 1989 | | 11 532 700 | 45.6 | 50.8 | 1.3 | - | 2.3 | - |
| | 1995 | | 15 907 600 | 49.9 | 43.5 | 1.6 | —> | 4.9 | - |
| Poland | 1995 | Zloty | 2 113 000 | 31.8 | 64.4 | 2.1 | - | 1.7 | - |
| Portugal | 1980 | Escudo | 4 118 500 | 26.6 | 66.8 | 4.7 | —> | 1.9 | - |
| | 1982 | | 6 541 200 | 30.0 | 61.9 | 4.8 | —> | 3.3 | - |
| | 1984 | | 11 307 600 | 30.8 | 60.2 | 6.6 | —> | 2.4 | - |
| | 1986 | | 19 867 600 | 26.8 | 61.3 | 9.0 | —> | 2.9 | - |
| | 1988 | | 29 910 800 | 27.4 | 63.5 | 6.4 | —> | 2.7 | - |
| | 1990 | | 52 032 200 | 27.0 | 58.1 | 10.2 | —> | 4.6 | - |
| | 1995 | | 92 120 600 | 18.9 | 65.2 | 3.9 | —> | 11.9 | - |
| Romania | 1989 | Leu | 20 866 000 | 94.7 | 5.3 | - | - | - | - |
| (33) | 1991 | | 17 369 000 | (5) 54.3 | (5) 22.9 | (5) 8.1 | ... | (5) 0.7 | 14.0 |
| | 1995 | | 514 420 000 | 23.1 | 63.4 | 10.4 | - | 3.2 | - |
| Russian Federation | 1997 | Rouble | 24 449 691 200 | 15.5 | 59.6 | 0.1 | ... | 7.4 | 17.4 |
| Slovakia | 1995 | S.Koruny | 5 374 000 | 60.4 | 37.8 | 0.1 | - | 1.6 | - |
| Slovenia | 1992 | Tolar | 15 050 524 | 51.1 | 35.9 | 8.4 | —> | 4.3 | - |
| | 1995 | | 37 654 000 | 45.5 | 40.9 | 10.3 | —> | 3.3 | - |
| | 1996 | | 36 816 000 | 49.1 | 43.4 | 4.5 | 0.4 | 2.7 | - |

**Percentage distribution of gross domestic expenditure on R&D by source of funds**
Répartition en pourcentage de dépenses intérieures brutes de R-D par source de fonds
Distribución porcentual del gasto interior bruto en I y D por origen de fondos

| Country / Pays / País | Reference year / Année de référence / Año de referencia | Currency / Monnaie / Moneda | Total gross domestic expenditure on R&D / Dépenses intérieures brutes totales de R-D / Gasto interior bruto total en I y D (000) | Source of funds / Source de fonds / Origen de fondos | | | | | |
|---|---|---|---|---|---|---|---|---|---|
| | | | | Business enterprise / Entreprises / Sector de empresas (%) | Government / Etat / Sector de la administración (%) | Higher education / Enseignement supérieur / Enseñanza superior (%) | Private non-profit / Institutions privées sans but lucratif / Instituciones privadas sin fines de lucro (%) | Funds from abroad / Fonds de l'etranger / Fondos del extranjero (%) | Not distributed / Non répartis / Sin distribución (%) |
| Spain | 1981 | Peseta | 67 938 006 | 45.9 | 51.7 | 0.1 | —> | 1.2 | 1.2 |
| | 1983 | | 100 697 093 | 49.1 | 49.6 | 0.1 | —> | 1.2 | - |
| | 1984 | | 126 199 000 | 48.9 | 44.6 | ... | ... | 0.7 | 5.8 |
| | 1985 | | 155 341 000 | 47.2 | 43.0 | 0.2 | —> | 4.8 | 4.7 |
| | 1986 | | 197 676 000 | 49.3 | 44.1 | 0.9 | —> | 1.7 | 4.1 |
| | 1987 | | 230 509 000 | 46.8 | 46.6 | 1.1 | —> | 1.5 | 4.1 |
| | 1988 | | 287 688 658 | 47.5 | 48.8 | 1.1 | —> | 2.5 | - |
| | 1989 | | 339 324 489 | 47.8 | 46.7 | 0.8 | —> | 4.7 | - |
| | 1990 | (34) | 423 501 631 | 47.7 | 45.3 | 0.2 | —> | 6.8 | - |
| | 1994 | | *548 153 562 | *40.3 | *52.4 | *1.0 | —> | *6.4 | - |
| Sweden | 1983 | Krona (35) | 18 189 000 | 59.0 | 39.3 | 0.2 | - | 1.5 | - |
| | 1985 | (35) | 24 989 000 | 60.9 | 37.1 | 0.8 | - | 1.2 | - |
| | 1987 | (35) | 30 553 000 | 61.1 | 37.0 | 0.4 | - | 1.6 | - |
| | 1991 | | 41 352 000 | 60.6 | 35.7 | 2.2 | —> | 1.5 | - |
| | 1993 | | 47 473 000 | 62.9 | 31.4 | 2.4 | —> | 2.4 | 0.9 |
| Switzerland | 1980 | Franc (5) | 3 611 100 | 76.7 | 23.3 | - | - | - | - |
| | 1981 | (5) | 3 789 100 | 76.2 | 23.8 | - | - | - | - |
| | 1983 | (5) | 4 643 000 | 78.1 | 21.9 | - | - | - | - |
| | 1986 | (36) | 7 015 000 | 78.9 | 21.1 | - | - | - | - |
| | 1992 | | 9 090 000 | 67.4 | 28.4 | 2.3 | —> | 1.9 | - |
| The Former Yugoslav Rep. of Macedonia | 1995 | Dinar (5) | 876 244 | 48.4 | 41.9 | 7.5 | —> | 2.2 | - |
| Ukraine | 1995 | Hryvnais | 651 963 | 46.3 | 37.6 | 0.5 | - | 15.6 | - |
| | 1997 | | 1 113 189 | ... | 41.9 | ... | ... | 24.6 | 33.5 |
| United Kingdom (25)(37) | 1981 | Pound Sterling | 5 921 200 | 42.7 | 47.7 | 2.6 | - | (37) 6.9 | - |
| (25)(37) | 1983 | | 6 583 000 | 43.6 | 48.9 | 2.2 | - | (37) 5.3 | - |
| (37) | 1985 | | 8 198 100 | 45.8 | 40.7 | 2.2 | ... | (37) 7.9 | 3.4 |
| (37) | 1986 | | 8 945 500 | 48.6 | 37.8 | 2.3 | ... | (37) 9.4 | 1.9 |
| (37) | 1989 | | 11 531 800 | 50.4 | 36.5 | 3.2 | —> | (37) 9.9 | - |
| (37) | 1990 | | 12 136 500 | 49.4 | 35.8 | 3.3 | —> | (37) 11.5 | - |
| (37) | 1991 | | 11 905 000 | 50.2 | 34.2 | 3.8 | —> | (37) 11.7 | - |
| | 1993 | | 13 829 000 | 51.9 | 32.7 | 3.7 | —> | (37) 11.7 | - |
| **Oceania** | | | | | | | | | |
| Australia | 1981 | Dollar | 1 561 800 | 20.5 | 73.9 | 2.1 | —> | 1.0 | 2.5 |
| | 1984 | | 2 415 600 | 27.9 | 68.9 | 1.7 | —> | 1.1 | 0.3 |
| | 1985 | | 2 747 400 | 31.7 | 64.1 | 1.9 | —> | 1.3 | 1.0 |
| | 1986 | | 3 365 600 | 34.8 | 59.5 | 1.6 | —> | 0.9 | 3.3 |
| | 1987 | | 3 687 000 | 36.1 | 56.4 | 2.7 | —> | 1.0 | 3.8 |
| | 1988 | | 4 252 600 | 40.5 | 54.4 | 2.2 | —> | 1.3 | 1.5 |
| | 1990 | | 5 087 600 | 39.6 | 55.3 | 3.8 | —> | 1.3 | - |
| | 1994 | | 7 321 100 | 45.7 | 48.1 | 4.2 | —> | 2.0 | - |
| Fiji (38) | 1986 | Dollar | 3 800 | - | 73.7 | - | - | 26.3 | - |
| Guam (5)(21) | 1989 | U.S.Dollar | *1 926 | - | *88.6 | *11.4 | - | - | - |
| | 1991 | | 2 215 | - | 87.7 | 12.3 | - | - | - |
| New Zealand | 1993 | Dollar | 825 200 | 33.9 | 54.7 | 8.9 | - | 2.4 | - |

**General note**

For general explanations and definitions, please refer to the beginning of this chapter.

**Note générale**

Pour les explications et définitions générales, se référer au début de ce chapitre.

**Nota general**

Para las explicaciones y definiciones generales, referirse al comienzo de este capítulo.

Notes

(1) Not including data for the productive sector.

(2) Not including labour costs at the Ministry of Public Health.

(3) Figures in millions.

(4) Data refer to the Ministry of Scientific Research only.

(5) Data refer to current expenditure only.

Notes

(1) Non compris les données du secteur de la production.

(2) Non compris les coûts salariaux du Ministère de la Santé Publique.

(3) Chiffres en millions.

(4) Les données se réfèrent au Ministère de la Recherche Scientifique seulement.

(5) Les données se réfèrent aux dépenses courantes seulement.

Notas

(1) No incluyen los datos del sector productivo.

(2) No incluyen los costos salariales del Ministerio de Salud Pública.

(3) Cifras en millones.

(4) Los datos se refieren al Ministerio de Investigación Científica solamente.

(5) Los datos se refieren a los gastos corrientes solamente.

Percentage distribution of gross domestic expenditure on R&D by source of funds III.3
Répartition en pourcentage de dépenses intérieures brutes de R-D par source de fonds
Distribución porcentual del gasto interior bruto en I y D por origen de fondos

(6) Data refer to government funds and funds from abroad.

(7) Data refer to government funds only.

(8) Data refer to funds from abroad only.

(9) Not including data for social sciences and humanities in the productive sector (integrated R&D).

(10) Data refer to R&D activites performed in public enterprises.

(11) Not including data for the productive sector (non-integrated R&D) and the general service sector.

(12) Data relate to the Scientific Research Council only.

(13) Business enterprise funds and funds from abroad are counted together.

(14) Data refer to the central government only.

(15) Not including data for law, humanities and education.

(16) Not including private productive enterprises.

(17) In Reais.

(18) Not including data for the productive sector (non-integrated R&D).

(19) Data are the budget allotment for science and technology.

(20) Data refer to scientific and technological activities (STA).

(21) Data refer to the higher education sector only.

(22) Data refer to the general service sector only.

(23) Data refer to the productive sector only.

(24) Not including data for humanities and law financed by the universities' current budgets.

(25) Not including data for social sciences and humanities.

(26) Data refer to R&D activities which are concentrated mainly in government-financed research establishments. Social sciences and humanities in the higher education and general service sectors are not included.

(27) Not including funds from abroad.

(28) Business enterprise funds and government fund are counted together.

(29) Not including business enterprise funds

(30) Not including data from communities and regions.

(31) Including data from communities and regions.

(32) Not including business enterprise sector.

(33) Due to methodological changes in 1991 data are not comparable with previous years.

(34) Not including private non-profit organizations.

(35) Not including social sciences and humanities in the productive and general service sectors.

(36) Data refer to business enterprise and government funds only.

(37) Not including funds for R&D performed abroad.

(38) Data relate to one research institute only.

---

(6) Les données se réfèrent aux fonds publics et aux fonds étrangers.

(7) Les données se réfèrent aux fonds publics seulement.

(8) Les données se réfèrent aux fonds étrangers seulement.

(9) Non compris les données pour les sciences sociales et humaines dans le secteur de la production (activités de R-D intégrées).

(10) Les données se réfèrent aux activités de R-D dans les entreprises publiques.

(11) Non compris les données du secteur de la production (activités de R-D non intégrées) et du secteur de service général.

(12) Les données se réfèrent au 'Scientific Research Council' seulement.

(13) Les fonds des entreprises et les fonds étrangers sont comptés ensemble.

(14) Les données se réfèrent au gouvernement central seulement.

(15) Non compris les données pour droit, sciences humaines et sciences de l'éducation.

(16) Non compris les entreprises privées.

(17) En Reais.

(18) Non compris les données pour le secteur de la production (activités de R-D non intégrées).

(19) Les données se réfèrent à l'allocation budgétaire pour la science et la technologie.

(20) Les données se réfèrent aux activités scientifiques et technologiques (AST).

(21) Les données se réfèrent au secteur de l'enseignement supérieur seulement.

(22) Les données se réfèrent au secteur de service général seulement.

(23) Les données se réfèrent au secteur de la production seulement.

(24) Non compris les données pour les sciences humaines et le droit qui rentrent dans les dépenses courantes des universités.

(25) Non compris les données pour les sciences sociales et humaines.

(26) Les données se réfèrent aux activités de R-D concentrées pour la plupart dans les établissements de recherche financés par le gouvernement. Les sciences sociales et humaines dans le secteur de l'enseignement supérieur et le secteur de service général ne sont pas inclues.

(27) Non compris les fonds étrangers.

(28) Les fonds des entreprises et les fonds de l'Etat sont comptés ensemble.

(29) Non compris les fonds des entreprises.

(30) Non compris les données relatives aux communautés et aux régions.

(31) Y compris les données relatives aux communautés et aux régions.

(32) Non compris le secteur des entreprises.

(33) Suite à des changements de méthodologie en 1991, les données ne sont pas comparables avec celles des années précédentes.

(34) Non compris les organisations privées à but non lucratif.

(35) Non compris les sciences sociales et humaines dans le secteur de la production et dans le secteur de service général.

(36) Les données se réfèrent aux fonds publics et des entreprises seulement.

(37) Non compris les fonds pour les activités de R-D exécutées à l'étranger.

(38) Les données se réfèrent à un institut de recherche seulement.

---

(6) Los datos se refieren a los fondos públicos y extranjeros.

(7) Los datos se refieren a los fondos públicos.

(8) Los datos se refieren a los fondos extranjeros solamente.

(9) No incluyen los datos para las ciencias sociales y humanas en el sector productivo (actividades de I y D integradas).

(10) Los datos se refieren a las actividades de I y D en las empresas públicas.

(11) No incluyen los datos del sector productivo (actividades de I y D no integradas) y del sector de servicio general.

(12) Los datos se refieren al 'Scientific Research Council' solamente.

(13) Los fondos de las empresas y del extranjero están contados conjuntamente.

(14) Los datos se refieren al gobierno central solamente.

(15) No incluyen los datos para derecho, ciencias humanas y ciencias de la educación.

(16) No incluyen las empresas privadas.

(17) En Reais.

(18) No incluyen los datos para el sector productivo (actividades de I y D no integradas).

(19) Los datos se refieren a la asignación presupuestal destinada a la ciencia y la tecnología.

(20) Los datos se refieren a las actividades científicas y tecnológicas (ACT).

(21) Los datos se refieren al sector de la enseñanza superior solamente.

(22) Los datos se refieren al sector de servicio general solamente.

(23) Los datos se refieren al sector productivo solamente.

(24) No incluyen los datos para las ciencias humanas y el derecho que hacen parte de los gastos corrientes de las universidades.

(25) No incluyen los datos para las ciencias sociales y humanas.

(26) Los datos se refieren a las actividades de I y D concentradas principalmente en los establecimientos de investigación subvencionados por el gobierno. Las ciencias sociales y humanas en el sector de la enseñanza superior y en el sector del servicio general no se incluyen.

(27) No incluyen los fondos extranjeros.

(28) Los fondos de las empresas y del sector de la administración están contados conjuntamente.

(29) No incluyen los fondos de las empresas.

(30) No incluyen los datos relativos a las comunidades y regiones.

(31) Incluyen los datos relativos a las comunidades y regiones.

(32) No incluyen el sector de empresas.

(33) Debido a cambios de metodología en 1991, los datos no son comparables con los de los años anteriores.

(34) No incluyen las organizaciones privadas sin fines de lucro.

(35) No incluyen las ciencias sociales y humanas en el sector productivo y en el sector de servicio general.

(36) Los datos se refieren a los fondos públicos y de las empresas solamente.

(37) No incluyen los fondos para las actividades de I y D efectuadas en el extranjero.

(38) Los datos se refieren a un único instituto de investigación solamente.

Culture and communication IV
Culture et communication
Cultura y comunicación

# IV. Culture and communication

# Culture et communication

# Cultura y comunicación

This chapter comprises three summary tables and fourteen country tables showing statistics on certain types of libraries, book production, newspapers, international trade in printed matter, 'cultural paper', films and cinemas, and broadcasting receivers. Some of these statistics are compiled in accordance with definitions and classifications laid down in the Recommendations concerning the international standardization of library statistics (1970), statistics on radio and television (1976) and statistics on the production and distribution of books, newspapers and periodicals (revised version 1985). Essential extracts from these Recommendations can be found in the relevant chapters of previous editions of this Yearbook.

The reader will find below definitions, general notes, etc. regarding the individual culture and communication tables. In these tables only those countries which have reported data for at least one year following 1990 are shown.

---

Ce chapitre comprend trois tableaux récapitulatifs et quatorze tableaux par pays qui présentent des statistiques sur certaines catégories de bibliothèques, sur l'édition de livres, de journaux, sur le commerce international en matière d'imprimés, sur le "papier culturel", les films et le cinéma, et les récepteurs de radiodiffusion. Certaines de ces statistiques ont été établies conformément aux définitions et classifications élaborées dans les Recommandations concernant la normalisation internationale des statistiques relatives aux bibliothèques (1970), des statistiques sur la radiodiffusion sonore et la télévision (1976) et des statistiques sur la production et la distribution de livres, de journaux et de périodiques (version révisée de 1985). Les principaux textes de ces Recommandations peuvent être consultés dans les chapitres correspondants des éditions antérieures de cet *Annuaire*.

Le lecteur trouvera ci-dessous les définitions, les notes générales et autres remarques sur chaque tableau relatif à la culture et la communication. Dans ces tableaux, seuls sont présentés les pays pour lesquels des données sont disponibles pour au moins une année postérieure à 1990.

---

Este capítulo comprende tres cuadros recapitulativos y catorce cuadros por países que presentan estadísticas sobre ciertas categorías de bibliotecas, producción de libros, periódicos, comercio internacional de impresos, "papel cultural", películas y cines y receptores de radiodifusión. Algunas de estas estadísticas han sido establecidas de acuerdo con las definiciones y clasificaciones de las Recomendaciones sobre la normalización internacional de las estadísticas relativas a las bibliotecas (1970), estadísticas sobre radio y televisión (1976) y estadísticas sobre la edición y distribución de libros, diarios y publicaciones periódicas (versión revisada de 1985). Los textos esenciales de estas Recomendaciones se encuentran en los capítulos apropiados de las ediciones previas de este *Anuario*.

Las definiciones, notas generales, etc., referentes a los cuadros sobre la cultura y comunicación se encuentran a continuación. En estos cuadros sólo se presentan los países para los cuales se dispone de datos posteriores a 1990.

---

**IV.S**  Summary tables on culture and communication by groups of countries
Tableaux récapitulatifs sur la culture et la communication par groupes de pays
Cuadros recapitulativos sobre cultura y comunicación por grupos de países

# Summary tables on culture and communication by groups of countries

# Tableaux récapitulatifs sur la culture et la communication par groupes de pays

# Cuadros recapitulativos sobre cultura y comunicación por grupos de países

These tables provide a summary presentation of data on selected subjects in the field of culture and communication statistics. The statistics contained in these tables are shown by continent, major area and groups of countries. The subjects treated are the following: daily newspapers, newsprint paper, printing and writing paper, radio and television receivers.

---

Ces tableaux donnent une présentation générale sur les données relatives à des sujets sélectionnés dans le champ des statistiques sur la culture et la communication. Les statistiques qui figurent dans ces tableaux sont présentées par continents, grandes régions et groupes de pays. Les sujets considérés sont les suivants : journaux quotidiens, papier journal, papier d'impression et d'écriture, récepteurs de radiodiffusion et de télévision.

---

Estos cuadros dan una presentación recapitulativa de los datos sobre algunos temas seleccionados en las estadísticas relativas al área de la cultura y la comunicación. Los datos contenidos en estos cuadros se presentan por continente, grandes regiones y grupos de países. Los temas tratados son los siguientes: periódicos diarios, papel de periódico, papel de imprenta y de escribir, receptores de radio y televisión.

---

## IV.S.1 Daily newspapers: number and circulation

### Journaux quotidiens: nombre et tirage

### Periódicos diarios: número y tirada

| Continents, major areas and groups of countries / Continents, grandes régions et groupes de pays / Continentes, grandes regiones y grupos de países | Year / Année / Año | Number of dailies / Nombre de quotidiens / Número de diarios | Estimated circulation Tirage (estimation) Tirada (estimación) Total (millions) (millones) | per 1,000 inhabitants Pour 1 000 habitants Por 1 000 habitantes |
|---|---|---|---|---|
| World total | 1970 | 7 947 | 392 | 107 |
|  | 1975 | 7 300 | 448 | 110 |
|  | 1980 | 7 847 | 491 | 111 |
|  | 1985 | 8 445 | 529 | 110 |
|  | 1990 | 8 220 | 563 | 107 |
|  | 1991 | 8 096 | 557 | 105 |
|  | 1992 | 8 104 | 575 | 106 |
|  | 1993 | 8 053 | 539 | 98 |
|  | 1994 | 8 283 | 538 | 97 |
|  | 1995 | 8 291 | 537 | 95 |
|  | 1996 | 8 391 | 548 | 96 |
| Africa | 1970 | 199 | 4.0 | 12 |
|  | 1975 | 165 | 5.1 | 13 |
|  | 1980 | 169 | 7.4 | 16 |
|  | 1985 | 179 | 8.8 | 17 |
|  | 1990 | 205 | 10 | 17 |
|  | 1991 | 205 | 10 | 16 |
|  | 1992 | 207 | 10 | 16 |
|  | 1993 | 201 | 10 | 16 |
|  | 1994 | 206 | 11 | 16 |
|  | 1995 | 219 | 11 | 16 |
|  | 1996 | 224 | 12 | 16 |
| America | 1970 | 2 876 | 88 | 170 |
|  | 1975 | 2 949 | 88 | 156 |
|  | 1980 | 3 112 | 98 | 158 |
|  | 1985 | 3 051 | 102 | 153 |
|  | 1990 | 2 918 | 104 | 144 |
|  | 1991 | 2 926 | 103 | 141 |
|  | 1992 | 2 964 | 105 | 141 |
|  | 1993 | 2 785 | 104 | 138 |
|  | 1994 | 2 881 | 103 | 134 |
|  | 1995 | 2 903 | 105 | 135 |
|  | 1996 | 2 939 | 111 | 141 |
| Asia | 1970 | 1 630 | 102 | 49 |
|  | 1975 | 1 713 | 127 | 54 |
|  | 1980 | 2 090 | 149 | 58 |
|  | 1985 | 2 712 | 169 | 60 |
|  | 1990 | 2 731 | 197 | 62 |
|  | 1991 | 2 660 | 203 | 63 |
|  | 1992 | 2 661 | 210 | 64 |
|  | 1993 | 2 811 | 211 | 64 |
|  | 1994 | 2 897 | 216 | 64 |
|  | 1995 | 2 960 | 221 | 64 |
|  | 1996 | 3 010 | 229 | 66 |
| Europe | 1970 | 3 133 | 193 | 281 |
|  | 1975 | 2 352 | 221 | 304 |
|  | 1980 | 2 371 | 232 | 309 |
|  | 1985 | 2 395 | 243 | 316 |
|  | 1990 | 2 265 | 245 | 340 |
|  | 1991 | 2 200 | 235 | 325 |
|  | 1992 | 2 161 | 244 | 337 |
|  | 1993 | 2 145 | 207 | 288 |
|  | 1994 | 2 188 | 202 | 278 |
|  | 1995 | 2 101 | 194 | 267 |
|  | 1996 | 2 115 | 190 | 261 |
| Oceania | 1970 | 109 | 5.2 | 269 |
|  | 1975 | 121 | 6.3 | 297 |
|  | 1980 | 105 | 5.9 | 261 |
|  | 1985 | 108 | 5.5 | 228 |
|  | 1990 | 101 | 6.3 | 240 |
|  | 1991 | 105 | 5.9 | 227 |
|  | 1992 | 111 | 5.6 | 207 |
|  | 1993 | 111 | 5.7 | 215 |
|  | 1994 | 111 | 6.4 | 233 |
|  | 1995 | 108 | 6.3 | 232 |
|  | 1996 | 103 | 6.4 | 227 |

| Continents, major areas and groups of countries / Continents, grandes régions et groupes de pays / Continentes, grandes regiones y grupos de países | Year / Année / Año | Number of dailies / Nombre de quotidiens / Número de diarios | Estimated circulation Tirage (estimation) Tirada (estimación) Total (millions) (millones) | per 1,000 inhabitants Pour 1 000 habitants Por 1 000 habitantes | Continents, major areas and groups of countries / Continents, grandes régions et groupes de pays / Continentes, grandes regiones y grupos de países | Year / Année / Año | Number of dailies / Nombre de quotidiens / Número de diarios | Estimated circulation Tirage (estimation) Tirada (estimación) Total (millions) (millones) | per 1,000 inhabitants Pour 1 000 habitants Por 1 000 habitantes |
|---|---|---|---|---|---|---|---|---|---|
| Developing countries | 1970 | 2 681 | 75 | 29 | Eastern Asia and Oceania | 1970 | 305 | 37 | 26 |
| | 1975 | 2 775 | 96 | 32 | | 1975 | 343 | 51 | 33 |
| | 1980 | 3 359 | 122 | 37 | | 1980 | 351 | 60 | 35 |
| | 1985 | 4 049 | 145 | 40 | | 1985 | 388 | 71 | 61 |
| | 1990 | 3 991 | 170 | 42 | | 1990 | 359 | 87 | 67 |
| | 1991 | 3 873 | 198 | 48 | | 1991 | 379 | 91 | 54 |
| | 1992 | 4 063 | 244 | 58 | | 1992 | 434 | 96 | 56 |
| | 1993 | 4 022 | 257 | 60 | | 1993 | 468 | 96 | 55 |
| | 1994 | 4 206 | 257 | 59 | | 1994 | 404 | 98 | 56 |
| | 1995 | 4 324 | 257 | 58 | | 1995 | 412 | 97 | 54 |
| | 1996 | 4 419 | 272 | 60 | | 1996 | 400 | 102 | 56 |
| of which: | | | | | | | | | |
| Sub-Saharan Africa | 1970 | 157 | 2.6 | 10 | Southern Asia | 1970 | 1 013 | 9.2 | 12 |
| | 1975 | 136 | 3.3 | 10 | | 1975 | 1 046 | 12 | 14 |
| | 1980 | 134 | 4.7 | 13 | | 1980 | 1 432 | 17 | 18 |
| | 1985 | 139 | 5.2 | 12 | | 1985 | 2 055 | 23 | 22 |
| | 1990 | 159 | 5.8 | 12 | | 1990 | 2 050 | 28 | 23 |
| | 1991 | 158 | 5.7 | 11 | | 1991 | 1 952 | 29 | 24 |
| | 1992 | 159 | 5.8 | 11 | | 1992 | 1 905 | 34 | 28 |
| | 1993 | 156 | 5.9 | 11 | | 1993 | 2 056 | 35 | 28 |
| | 1994 | 161 | 6.0 | 11 | | 1994 | 2 181 | 38 | 29 |
| | 1995 | 164 | 6.2 | 11 | | 1995 | 2 249 | 42 | 32 |
| | 1996 | 168 | 7.1 | 12 | | 1996 | 2 299 | 44 | 33 |
| Arab States | 1970 | 105 | 2.1 | 17 | Least developed countries | 1970 | 158 | 1.3 | 4.5 |
| | 1975 | 108 | 3.0 | 22 | | 1975 | 160 | 1.5 | 4.6 |
| | 1980 | 107 | 4.5 | 27 | | 1980 | 158 | 1.8 | 5.0 |
| | 1985 | 125 | 6.4 | 32 | | 1985 | 183 | 2.5 | 6.2 |
| | 1990 | 129 | 8.2 | 36 | | 1990 | 172 | 3.4 | 7.7 |
| | 1991 | 129 | 12 | 52 | | 1991 | 172 | 3.0 | 6.7 |
| | 1992 | 137 | 8.9 | 38 | | 1992 | 178 | 3.1 | 6.8 |
| | 1993 | 129 | 10 | 42 | | 1993 | 184 | 3.7 | 8.0 |
| | 1994 | 127 | 9.3 | 38 | | 1994 | 180 | 4.0 | 8.6 |
| | 1995 | 135 | 9.3 | 37 | | 1995 | 182 | 3.6 | 7.5 |
| | 1996 | 140 | 9.2 | 36 | | 1996 | 172 | 3.9 | 8.0 |
| Latin America and the Caribbean | 1970 | 1 012 | 22 | 76 | Developed countries | 1970 | 5 266 | 316 | 292 |
| | 1975 | 1 052 | 23 | 70 | | 1975 | 4 525 | 353 | 292 |
| | 1980 | 1 243 | 30 | 83 | | 1980 | 4 488 | 370 | 363 |
| | 1985 | 1 257 | 34 | 85 | | 1985 | 4 396 | 383 | 342 |
| | 1990 | 1 198 | 36 | 82 | | 1990 | 4 229 | 393 | 340 |
| | 1991 | 1 233 | 37 | 82 | | 1991 | 4 223 | 359 | 303 |
| | 1992 | 1 287 | 39 | 86 | | 1992 | 4 041 | 332 | 278 |
| | 1993 | 1 120 | 38 | 83 | | 1993 | 4 031 | 281 | 233 |
| | 1994 | 1 225 | 38 | 81 | | 1994 | 4 077 | 281 | 288 |
| | 1995 | 1 262 | 42 | 88 | | 1995 | 3 967 | 280 | 230 |
| | 1996 | 1 309 | 49 | 101 | | 1996 | 3 972 | 276 | 226 |

Newsprint and other printing and writing paper
Papier journal et autre papier d'impresion et d'écriture
Papel de periódico y otro papel de imprenta y de escribir

IV.S.2

## IV.S.2 Newsprint and other printing and writing paper: production and consumption

## Papier journal et autre papier d'impression et d'écriture: production et consommation

## Papel de periódico y otro papel de imprenta y de escribir: producción y consumo

MT = Millions of metric tons          MT = Millions de tonnes métriques          MT = Millones de toneladas métricas

| Continents, major areas and groups of countries<br><br>Continents, grandes régions et groupes de pays<br><br>Continentes, grandes regiones y grupos de países | Year<br><br>Année<br><br>Año | Newsprint<br>Papier journal<br>Papel de periódico | | | Printing and writing paper<br>Papiers d'impression et d'écriture<br>Papeles de imprenta y de escribir | | |
|---|---|---|---|---|---|---|---|
| | | Production<br><br>Production<br><br>Producción<br><br>(MT) | Consumption<br><br>Consommation<br><br>Consumo<br><br>(MT) | Consumption per inhabitant<br><br>Consommation par habitant<br><br>Consumo por habitante<br>(kg) | Production<br><br>Production<br><br>Producción<br><br>(MT) | Consumption<br><br>Consommation<br><br>Consumo<br><br>(MT) | Consumption per inhabitant<br><br>Consommation par habitant<br><br>Consumo por habitante<br>(kg) |
| World total | 1970 | 21 | 21 | 6.0 | 26 | 26 | 7.2 |
| | 1975 | 20 | 21 | 5.4 | 28 | 28 | 7.0 |
| | 1980 | 26 | 26 | 6.0 | 39 | 41 | 9.4 |
| | 1985 | 28 | 28 | 6.0 | 50 | 50 | 10.6 |
| | 1990 | 33 | 33 | 6.4 | 70 | 70 | 13.5 |
| | 1991 | 33 | 32 | 6.3 | 71 | 71 | 13.5 |
| | 1992 | 32 | 32 | 6.3 | 72 | 72 | 13.6 |
| | 1993 | 33 | 32 | 6.2 | 72 | 72 | 13.0 |
| | 1994 | 34 | 34 | 6.6 | 82 | 80 | 14.4 |
| | 1995 | 35 | 34 | 6.1 | 81 | 77 | 13.8 |
| | 1996 | 35 | 34 | 6.1 | 83 | 81 | 14.2 |
| | 1997 | 36 | 35 | 6.1 | 90 | 88 | 15.1 |
| Africa | 1970 | 0.2 | 0.3 | 1.0 | 0.2 | 0.4 | 1.3 |
| | 1975 | 0.2 | 0.3 | 0.9 | 0.2 | 0.4 | 1.1 |
| | 1980 | 0.2 | 0.3 | 0.8 | 0.3 | 0.6 | 1.4 |
| | 1985 | 0.4 | 0.3 | 0.5 | 0.4 | 0.8 | 1.5 |
| | 1990 | 0.4 | 0.5 | 0.9 | 0.6 | 1.0 | 1.7 |
| | 1991 | 0.4 | 0.5 | 0.9 | 0.6 | 1.0 | 1.7 |
| | 1992 | 0.4 | 0.4 | 0.8 | 0.5 | 1.0 | 1.5 |
| | 1993 | 0.4 | 0.5 | 0.8 | 0.6 | 1.1 | 1.6 |
| | 1994 | 0.4 | 0.3 | 0.6 | 0.6 | 1.1 | 1.6 |
| | 1995 | 0.5 | 0.5 | 0.8 | 0.5 | 0.8 | 1.1 |
| | 1996 | 0.5 | 0.6 | 0.8 | 0.5 | 0.8 | 1.2 |
| | 1997 | 0.4 | 0.5 | 0.7 | 0.7 | 1.1 | 1.5 |
| America | 1970 | 11 | 11 | 22.9 | 11 | 11 | 22.1 |
| | 1975 | 11 | 10 | 19.8 | 11 | 11 | 20.4 |
| | 1980 | 13 | 13 | 21.0 | 17 | 17 | 28.7 |
| | 1985 | 15 | 14 | 21.6 | 21 | 22 | 33.4 |
| | 1990 | 16 | 15 | 20.7 | 26 | 26 | 37.2 |
| | 1991 | 16 | 14 | 22.1 | 26 | 26 | 36.5 |
| | 1992 | 16 | 14 | 21.2 | 26 | 27 | 36.9 |
| | 1993 | 16 | 14 | 21.8 | 28 | 29 | 38.5 |
| | 1994 | 17 | 15 | 22.3 | 33 | 34 | 44.3 |
| | 1995 | 17 | 14 | 18.5 | 31 | 31 | 40.4 |
| | 1996 | 16 | 14 | 17.5 | 30 | 31 | 39.2 |
| | 1997 | 17 | 14 | 18.0 | 33 | 33 | 42.0 |
| Asia | 1970 | 2.5 | 3.1 | 1.5 | 3.9 | 4.0 | 1.9 |
| | 1975 | 2.8 | 3.2 | 1.4 | 5.1 | 5.2 | 2.2 |
| | 1980 | 3.5 | 4.6 | 1.8 | 7.2 | 7.5 | 2.9 |
| | 1985 | 3.8 | 5.3 | 1.9 | 9.7 | 10 | 3.6 |
| | 1990 | 5.2 | 6.8 | 2.2 | 17 | 18 | 6.0 |
| | 1991 | 5.3 | 7.2 | 2.3 | 18 | 19 | 6.2 |
| | 1992 | 5.3 | 7.6 | 2.4 | 19 | 21 | 6.3 |
| | 1993 | 5.1 | 7.5 | 2.3 | 17 | 18 | 5.5 |
| | 1994 | 5.5 | 8.1 | 2.5 | 19 | 21 | 6.1 |
| | 1995 | 6.0 | 8.5 | 2.5 | 20 | 21 | 6.2 |
| | 1996 | 6.5 | 10 | 2.9 | 22 | 24 | 7.0 |
| | 1997 | 6.8 | 10 | 2.9 | 24 | 26 | 7.2 |

IV.S.2    Newsprint and other printing and writing paper
Papier journal et autre papier d'impresion et d'écriture
Papel de periódico y otro papel de imprenta y de escribir

| Continents, major areas and groups of countries / Continents, grandes régions et groupes de pays / Continentes, grandes regiones y grupos de países | Year / Année / Año | Newsprint / Papier journal / Pepel de periódico | | | Printing and writing paper / Papiers d'impression et d'écriture / Papeles de imprenta y de escribir | | |
|---|---|---|---|---|---|---|---|
| | | Production / Production / Producción (MT) | Consumption / Consommation / Consumo (MT) | Consumption per inhabitant / Consommation par habitant / Consumo por habitante (kg) | Production / Production / Producción (MT) | Consumption / Consommation / Consumo (MT) | Consumption per inhabitant / Consommation par habitant / Consumo por habitante (kg) |
| Europe | 1970 | 7.0 | 6.7 | 9.6 | 11 | 10 | 14.3 |
| | 1975 | 6.3 | 6.9 | 9.5 | 11 | 11 | 14.8 |
| | 1980 | 8.2 | 7.7 | 10.3 | 14 | 15 | 20.1 |
| | 1985 | 8.7 | 7.8 | 10.2 | 19 | 17 | 22.1 |
| | 1990 | 10 | 10 | 12.6 | 25 | 23 | 29.1 |
| | 1991 | 10 | 10 | 12.4 | 25 | 23 | 29.1 |
| | 1992 | 9.4 | 9.4 | 14.4 | 25 | 23 | 33.9 |
| | 1993 | 10 | 9.2 | 13.7 | 26 | 23 | 31.1 |
| | 1994 | 11 | 10 | 15.5 | 29 | 24 | 33.1 |
| | 1995 | 12 | 10 | 14.5 | 29 | 24 | 32.4 |
| | 1996 | 11 | 10 | 13.4 | 29 | 24 | 33.6 |
| | 1997 | 11 | 9.4 | 13.1 | 32 | 26 | 36.4 |
| Oceania | 1970 | 0.4 | 0.5 | 34.3 | 0.2 | 0.3 | 15.5 |
| | 1975 | 0.4 | 0.6 | 36.2 | 0.2 | 0.4 | 20.5 |
| | 1980 | 0.5 | 0.6 | 34.3 | 0.3 | 0.4 | 24.4 |
| | 1985 | 0.7 | 0.8 | 39.8 | 0.3 | 0.6 | 28.8 |
| | 1990 | 0.7 | 0.8 | 35.3 | 0.5 | 0.9 | 44.2 |
| | 1991 | 0.7 | 0.7 | 31.6 | 0.4 | 0.9 | 42.1 |
| | 1992 | 0.8 | 0.7 | 31.2 | 0.3 | 0.8 | 30.2 |
| | 1993 | 0.8 | 0.7 | 34.3 | 0.3 | 0.9 | 33.9 |
| | 1994 | 0.8 | 0.8 | 34.0 | 0.4 | 1.0 | 34.9 |
| | 1995 | 0.8 | 0.9 | 31.5 | 0.4 | 1.2 | 42.8 |
| | 1996 | 0.8 | 0.9 | 30.3 | 0.4 | 1.0 | 34.5 |
| | 1997 | 0.8 | 0.8 | 28.2 | 0.4 | 1.0 | 35.8 |
| Developing countries | 1970 | 1.1 | 2.3 | 0.9 | 2.4 | 3.2 | 1.3 |
| | 1975 | 1.2 | 2.2 | 0.8 | 3.6 | 4.2 | 1.5 |
| | 1980 | 1.6 | 3.5 | 1.1 | 5.6 | 6.4 | 2.0 |
| | 1985 | 2.4 | 4.0 | 1.1 | 7.8 | 8.7 | 2.4 |
| | 1990 | 3.2 | 5.0 | 1.3 | 11 | 13 | 3.2 |
| | 1991 | 3.2 | 5.3 | 1.3 | 12 | 13 | 3.3 |
| | 1992 | 3.4 | 5.5 | 1.4 | 12 | 15 | 3.6 |
| | 1993 | 3.4 | 5.8 | 1.4 | 10 | 13 | 2.9 |
| | 1994 | 3.8 | 6.4 | 1.6 | 13 | 15 | 3.4 |
| | 1995 | 4.4 | 7.2 | 1.7 | 13 | 14 | 3.2 |
| | 1996 | 4.8 | 8.3 | 1.9 | 15 | 17 | 3.8 |
| | 1997 | 5.0 | 8.5 | 1.9 | 17 | 19 | 4.1 |
| of which: | | | | | | | |
| Sub-Saharan Africa | 1970 | 0.2 | 0.3 | 1.1 | 0.1 | 0.3 | 1.2 |
| | 1975 | 0.2 | 0.3 | 1.0 | 0.1 | 0.3 | 0.9 |
| | 1980 | 0.2 | 0.2 | 0.7 | 0.2 | 0.4 | 1.1 |
| | 1985 | 0.4 | 0.2 | 0.5 | 0.3 | 0.5 | 1.1 |
| | 1990 | 0.4 | 0.4 | 0.9 | 0.4 | 0.6 | 1.4 |
| | 1991 | 0.4 | 0.4 | 0.9 | 0.4 | 0.6 | 1.4 |
| | 1992 | 0.4 | 0.3 | 0.7 | 0.4 | 0.6 | 1.2 |
| | 1993 | 0.4 | 0.4 | 0.8 | 0.5 | 0.6 | 1.2 |
| | 1994 | 0.4 | 0.3 | 0.6 | 0.6 | 1.1 | 1.6 |
| | 1995 | 0.5 | 0.4 | 0.8 | 0.3 | 0.5 | 0.9 |
| | 1996 | 0.5 | 0.4 | 0.8 | 0.3 | 0.5 | 1.0 |
| | 1997 | 0.4 | 0.4 | 0.7 | 0.6 | 0.8 | 1.4 |
| Arab States | 1970 | - | 0.1 | 0.5 | 0.1 | 0.2 | 1.4 |
| | 1975 | - | 0.1 | 0.6 | 0.1 | 0.2 | 1.5 |
| | 1980 | - | 0.2 | 0.9 | 0.1 | 0.4 | 2.3 |
| | 1985 | - | 0.2 | 0.9 | 0.1 | 0.5 | 2.5 |
| | 1990 | - | 0.2 | 0.8 | 0.2 | 0.6 | 2.6 |
| | 1991 | - | 0.2 | 0.9 | 0.2 | 0.6 | 2.5 |
| | 1992 | - | 0.2 | 0.9 | 0.2 | 0.6 | 2.6 |
| | 1993 | - | 0.2 | 1.1 | 0.2 | 0.7 | 3.1 |
| | 1994 | - | 0.2 | 1.0 | 0.2 | 0.7 | 2.9 |
| | 1995 | - | 0.2 | 1.0 | 0.2 | 0.4 | 2.0 |
| | 1996 | - | 0.2 | 1.0 | 0.2 | 0.4 | 1.9 |
| | 1997 | - | 0.2 | 1.0 | 0.2 | 0.5 | 2.1 |
| Latin America and the Caribbean | 1970 | 0.3 | 0.8 | 3.6 | 0.6 | 1.0 | 3.5 |
| | 1975 | 0.3 | 0.8 | 2.9 | 1.0 | 1.2 | 3.8 |
| | 1980 | 0.5 | 1.3 | 3.5 | 1.9 | 2.0 | 5.8 |
| | 1985 | 0.8 | 1.3 | 3.3 | 2.2 | 2.2 | 5.5 |
| | 1990 | 1.0 | 1.5 | 3.4 | 2.4 | 2.3 | 5.5 |
| | 1991 | 1.0 | 1.4 | 4.0 | 2.5 | 2.4 | 5.5 |
| | 1992 | 0.9 | 1.2 | 3.4 | 2.6 | 3.0 | 6.6 |
| | 1993 | 0.8 | 1.3 | 3.6 | 2.8 | 3.0 | 6.4 |
| | 1994 | 0.8 | 1.4 | 3.8 | 3.0 | 3.1 | 6.7 |
| | 1995 | 0.9 | 1.8 | 3.8 | 3.0 | 2.9 | 6.0 |
| | 1996 | 0.9 | 1.7 | 3.5 | 3.1 | 2.9 | 6.0 |
| | 1997 | 0.9 | 1.9 | 3.9 | 3.4 | 3.2 | 6.5 |

Newsprint and other printing and writing paper  IV.S.2
Papier journal et autre papier d'impresion et d'écriture
Papel de periódico y otro papel de imprenta y de escribir

| Continents, major areas and groups of countries<br><br>Continents, grandes régions et groupes de pays<br><br>Continentes, grandes regiones y grupos de países | Year<br><br>Année<br><br>Año | Newsprint<br>Papier journal<br>Papel de periódico | | | Printing and writing paper<br>Papiers d'impression et d'écriture<br>Papeles de imprenta y de escribir | | |
|---|---|---|---|---|---|---|---|
| | | Production<br><br>Production<br><br>Producción<br><br>(MT) | Consumption<br><br>Consommation<br><br>Consumo<br><br>(MT) | Consumption per inhabitant<br><br>Consommation par habitant<br><br>Consumo por habitante<br><br>(kg) | Production<br><br>Production<br><br>Producción<br><br>(MT) | Consumption<br><br>Consommation<br><br>Consumo<br><br>(MT) | Consumption per inhabitant<br><br>Consommation par habitant<br><br>Consumo por habitante<br><br>(kg) |
| Eastern Asia and Oceania | 1970 | 0.5 | 0.8 | 0.7 | 0.9 | 1.1 | 0.9 |
| | 1975 | 0.6 | 0.8 | 0.6 | 1.6 | 1.7 | 1.3 |
| | 1980 | 0.7 | 1.3 | 0.9 | 2.4 | 2.6 | 1.8 |
| | 1985 | 0.8 | 1.7 | 1.1 | 3.9 | 4.2 | 2.8 |
| | 1990 | 1.2 | 2.1 | 1.3 | 6.9 | 7.4 | 4.5 |
| | 1991 | 1.3 | 2.4 | 1.4 | 7.2 | 7.9 | 4.7 |
| | 1992 | 1.5 | 2.7 | 1.6 | 8.0 | 9.0 | 5.3 |
| | 1993 | 1.7 | 2.9 | 1.7 | 5.6 | 6.5 | 3.7 |
| | 1994 | 2.0 | 3.4 | 1.9 | 7.5 | 8.7 | 4.9 |
| | 1995 | 2.3 | 3.6 | 2.0 | 7.9 | 8.6 | 4.8 |
| | 1996 | 2.9 | 4.4 | 2.4 | 10 | 11 | 6.2 |
| | 1997 | 3.1 | 4.7 | 2.6 | 11 | 12 | 6.7 |
| Southern Asia | 1970 | 0.1 | 0.2 | 0.3 | 0.5 | 0.6 | 0.8 |
| | 1975 | 0.1 | 0.2 | 0.3 | 0.6 | 0.7 | 0.8 |
| | 1980 | 0.1 | 0.4 | 0.4 | 0.6 | 0.7 | 0.8 |
| | 1985 | 0.2 | 0.5 | 0.5 | 0.8 | 1.0 | 0.9 |
| | 1990 | 0.4 | 0.6 | 0.5 | 1.1 | 1.4 | 1.2 |
| | 1991 | 0.4 | 0.7 | 0.6 | 1.2 | 1.4 | 1.2 |
| | 1992 | 0.4 | 0.7 | 0.6 | 1.2 | 1.5 | 1.2 |
| | 1993 | 0.4 | 0.6 | 0.5 | 1.3 | 1.5 | 1.2 |
| | 1994 | 0.4 | 0.8 | 0.6 | 1.3 | 1.6 | 1.3 |
| | 1995 | 0.4 | 0.8 | 0.6 | 1.4 | 1.6 | 1.2 |
| | 1996 | 0.4 | 1.1 | 0.8 | 1.4 | 1.7 | 1.3 |
| | 1997 | 0.4 | 1.1 | 0.8 | 1.4 | 1.7 | 1.2 |
| Least developed countries | 1970 | 0.04 | 0.1 | 0.3 | 0.04 | 0.1 | 0.3 |
| | 1975 | 0.02 | 0.04 | 0.1 | 0.05 | 0.1 | 0.3 |
| | 1980 | 0.04 | 0.04 | 0.1 | 0.04 | 0.1 | 0.3 |
| | 1985 | 0.05 | 0.1 | 0.2 | 0.1 | 0.1 | 0.3 |
| | 1990 | 0.05 | 0.1 | 0.2 | 0.1 | 0.1 | 0.2 |
| | 1991 | 0.06 | 0.1 | 0.2 | 0.1 | 0.1 | 0.2 |
| | 1992 | 0.06 | 0.1 | 0.2 | 0.1 | 0.1 | 0.2 |
| | 1993 | 0.05 | 0.1 | 0.1 | 0.1 | 0.1 | 0.2 |
| | 1994 | 0.06 | 0.1 | 0.2 | 0.1 | 0.2 | 0.3 |
| | 1995 | 0.05 | 0.1 | 0.2 | 0.1 | 0.1 | 0.2 |
| | 1996 | 0.04 | 0.1 | 0.2 | 0.1 | 0.1 | 0.2 |
| | 1997 | 0.04 | 0.1 | 0.2 | 0.1 | 0.1 | 0.2 |
| Developed countries | 1970 | 20 | 19 | 18.3 | 24 | 23 | 22.0 |
| | 1975 | 19 | 19 | 17.4 | 25 | 24 | 22.1 |
| | 1980 | 24 | 23 | 20.3 | 33 | 35 | 30.9 |
| | 1985 | 26 | 24 | 21.2 | 42 | 42 | 36.2 |
| | 1990 | 30 | 28 | 23.3 | 58 | 57 | 47.5 |
| | 1991 | 29 | 27 | 22.5 | 59 | 57 | 47.7 |
| | 1992 | 29 | 26 | 24.5 | 59 | 57 | 51.3 |
| | 1993 | 29 | 26 | 20.9 | 62 | 59 | 48.7 |
| | 1994 | 31 | 28 | 25.5 | 69 | 66 | 53.8 |
| | 1995 | 31 | 27 | 23.2 | 68 | 64 | 52.2 |
| | 1996 | 30 | 26 | 21.9 | 68 | 64 | 52.7 |
| | 1997 | 31 | 27 | 21.9 | 73 | 69 | 55.8 |

IV.S.3  Radio and television receivers
Récepteurs de radiodiffusion sonore et de télévision
Receptores de radiodifusión sonora y de televisión

## IV.S.3   Radio and television receivers

### Récepteurs de radiodiffusion sonore et de télévision

### Receptores de radiodifusión sonora y de televisión

| Continents, major areas and groups of countries / Continents, grandes régions et groupes de pays / Continentes, grandes regiones y grupos de países | Year / Année / Año | Number of radio broadcasting receivers / Nombre de récepteurs de radiodiffusion sonore / Número de receptores de radiodifusión sonora | | Number of television receivers / Nombre de récepteurs de télévision / Número de receptores de televisión | |
|---|---|---|---|---|---|
| | | Total (millions/milliones) | per 1,000 inhabitants / pour 1 000 habitants / por 1 000 habitantes | Total (millions/millones) | per 1,000 inhabitants / pour 1 000 habitants / por 1 000 habitantes |
| World total | 1970 | 906 | 245 | 299 | 81 |
| | 1975 | 1 173 | 288 | 408 | 100 |
| | 1980 | 1 384 | 312 | 563 | 127 |
| | 1985 | 1 684 | 348 | 749 | 155 |
| | 1990 | 2 075 | 394 | 1 092 | 208 |
| | 1991 | 2 138 | 400 | 1 137 | 213 |
| | 1992 | 2 180 | 401 | 1 175 | 216 |
| | 1993 | 2 216 | 402 | 1 210 | 220 |
| | 1994 | 2 258 | 404 | 1 264 | 226 |
| | 1995 | 2 313 | 408 | 1 297 | 229 |
| | 1996 | 2 396 | 417 | 1 366 | 238 |
| | 1997 | 2 432 | 418 | 1 396 | 240 |
| Africa | 1970 | 33 | 93 | 1.6 | 4.6 |
| | 1975 | 44 | 108 | 2.7 | 6.8 |
| | 1980 | 61 | 131 | 8.2 | 18 |
| | 1985 | 90 | 169 | 14 | 27 |
| | 1990 | 116 | 190 | 25 | 41 |
| | 1991 | 121 | 193 | 27 | 43 |
| | 1992 | 126 | 195 | 28 | 44 |
| | 1993 | 131 | 198 | 30 | 45 |
| | 1994 | 138 | 202 | 32 | 47 |
| | 1995 | 144 | 207 | 36 | 52 |
| | 1996 | 152 | 213 | 41 | 58 |
| | 1997 | 158 | 216 | 44 | 60 |
| America | 1970 | 361 | 698 | 108 | 209 |
| | 1975 | 487 | 861 | 153 | 270 |
| | 1980 | 566 | 918 | 202 | 328 |
| | 1985 | 649 | 971 | 259 | 388 |
| | 1990 | 711 | 984 | 292 | 404 |
| | 1991 | 730 | 996 | 300 | 409 |
| | 1992 | 743 | 999 | 305 | 409 |
| | 1993 | 754 | 998 | 310 | 410 |
| | 1994 | 765 | 998 | 315 | 412 |
| | 1995 | 775 | 997 | 327 | 421 |
| | 1996 | 802 | 1 019 | 338 | 429 |
| | 1997 | 811 | 1 017 | 342 | 429 |
| Asia | 1970 | 171 | 81 | 42 | 20 |
| | 1975 | 246 | 105 | 55 | 23 |
| | 1980 | 318 | 123 | 104 | 40 |
| | 1985 | 416 | 147 | 198 | 70 |
| | 1990 | 748 | 235 | 487 | 153 |
| | 1991 | 781 | 241 | 510 | 158 |
| | 1992 | 800 | 244 | 539 | 164 |
| | 1993 | 817 | 245 | 563 | 169 |
| | 1994 | 834 | 246 | 606 | 179 |
| | 1995 | 861 | 251 | 617 | 180 |
| | 1996 | 886 | 254 | 653 | 187 |
| | 1997 | 900 | 255 | 672 | 190 |

Radio and television receivers IV.S.3
Récepteurs de radiodiffusion sonore et de télévision
Receptores de radiodifusión sonora y de televisión

| Continents, major areas and groups of countries / Continents, grandes régions et groupes de pays / Continentes, grandes regiones y grupos de países | Year / Année / Año | Number of radio broadcasting receivers / Nombre de récepteurs de radiodiffusion sonore / Número de receptores de radiodifusión sonora | | Number of television receivers / Nombre de récepteurs de télévision / Número de receptores de televisión | |
|---|---|---|---|---|---|
| | | Total (millions/millones) | per 1,000 inhabitants / pour 1 000 habitants / por 1 000 habitantes | Total (millions/millones) | per 1,000 inhabitants / pour 1 000 habitants / por 1 000 habitantes |
| Europe | 1970 | 327 | 465 | 144 | 205 |
| | 1975 | 379 | 521 | 192 | 264 |
| | 1980 | 420 | 560 | 243 | 324 |
| | 1985 | 504 | 656 | 268 | 349 |
| | 1990 | 474 | 657 | 278 | 385 |
| | 1991 | 479 | 661 | 290 | 401 |
| | 1992 | 483 | 665 | 293 | 404 |
| | 1993 | 486 | 670 | 296 | 408 |
| | 1994 | 494 | 680 | 300 | 413 |
| | 1995 | 504 | 693 | 305 | 419 |
| | 1996 | 526 | 723 | 322 | 443 |
| | 1997 | 531 | 729 | 325 | 446 |
| Oceania | 1970 | 15 | 779 | 3.6 | 188 |
| | 1975 | 17 | 811 | 5.6 | 262 |
| | 1980 | 20 | 875 | 6.8 | 300 |
| | 1985 | 24 | 974 | 8.6 | 352 |
| | 1990 | 26 | 999 | 9.9 | 378 |
| | 1991 | 27 | 1 003 | 10 | 379 |
| | 1992 | 27 | 1 009 | 10 | 384 |
| | 1993 | 28 | 1 010 | 11 | 385 |
| | 1994 | 28 | 1 009 | 11 | 387 |
| | 1995 | 29 | 1 010 | 11 | 387 |
| | 1996 | 30 | 1 065 | 12 | 425 |
| | 1997 | 31 | 1 071 | 12 | 427 |
| Developing countries | 1970 | 240 | 90 | 26 | 9.9 |
| | 1975 | 306 | 102 | 43 | 14 |
| | 1980 | 398 | 120 | 88 | 27 |
| | 1985 | 543 | 148 | 202 | 55 |
| | 1990 | 895 | 220 | 504 | 124 |
| | 1991 | 943 | 228 | 532 | 128 |
| | 1992 | 972 | 230 | 563 | 133 |
| | 1993 | 996 | 232 | 588 | 137 |
| | 1994 | 1 021 | 234 | 625 | 143 |
| | 1995 | 1 057 | 238 | 649 | 146 |
| | 1996 | 1 100 | 244 | 697 | 154 |
| | 1997 | 1 124 | 245 | 720 | 157 |
| of which: | | | | | |
| Sub-Saharan Africa | 1970 | 23 | 83 | 0.4 | 1.5 |
| | 1975 | 32 | 100 | 0.8 | 2.5 |
| | 1980 | 47 | 125 | 4.4 | 12 |
| | 1985 | 68 | 158 | 7.1 | 17 |
| | 1990 | 86 | 173 | 15 | 30 |
| | 1991 | 90 | 177 | 16 | 32 |
| | 1992 | 93 | 178 | 17 | 32 |
| | 1993 | 98 | 182 | 18 | 34 |
| | 1994 | 103 | 187 | 20 | 36 |
| | 1995 | 109 | 192 | 23 | 41 |
| | 1996 | 115 | 198 | 26 | 45 |
| | 1997 | 121 | 202 | 29 | 48 |
| Arab States | 1970 | 16 | 131 | 2.7 | 21 |
| | 1975 | 21 | 147 | 4.3 | 30 |
| | 1980 | 29 | 175 | 9.3 | 56 |
| | 1985 | 43 | 209 | 16 | 79 |
| | 1990 | 56 | 249 | 22 | 100 |
| | 1991 | 58 | 251 | 24 | 103 |
| | 1992 | 60 | 253 | 24 | 104 |
| | 1993 | 61 | 255 | 25 | 106 |
| | 1994 | 63 | 257 | 26 | 106 |
| | 1995 | 65 | 259 | 28 | 111 |
| | 1996 | 69 | 267 | 30 | 118 |
| | 1997 | 71 | 269 | 31 | 119 |
| Latin America and the Caribbean | 1970 | 56 | 196 | 16 | 57 |
| | 1975 | 69 | 216 | 23 | 70 |
| | 1980 | 94 | 259 | 35 | 98 |
| | 1985 | 126 | 314 | 55 | 138 |
| | 1990 | 153 | 347 | 72 | 162 |
| | 1991 | 166 | 370 | 76 | 170 |
| | 1992 | 173 | 378 | 78 | 171 |
| | 1993 | 177 | 380 | 80 | 172 |
| | 1994 | 181 | 383 | 83 | 175 |
| | 1995 | 184 | 384 | 91 | 190 |
| | 1996 | 200 | 410 | 100 | 204 |
| | 1997 | 204 | 412 | 101 | 205 |

IV.S.3    Radio and television receivers
Récepteurs de radiodiffusion sonore et de télévision
Receptores de radiodifusión sonora y de televisión

| Continents, major areas and groups of countries<br>Continents, grandes régions et groupes de pays<br>Continentes, grandes regiones y grupos de países | Year<br>Année<br>Año | Number of radio broadcasting receivers<br>Nombre de récepteurs de radiodiffusion sonore<br>Número de receptores de radiodifusión sonora | | Number of television receivers<br>Nombre de récepteurs de télévision<br>Número de receptores de televisión | |
|---|---|---|---|---|---|
| | | Total<br>(millions/millones) | per 1,000 inhabitants<br>pour 1 000 habitants<br>por 1 000 habitantes | Total<br>(millions/millones) | per 1,000 inhabitants<br>pour 1 000 habitants<br>por 1 000 habitantes |
| Eastern Asia and Oceania | 1970 | 114 | 97 | 3.9 | 3.3 |
| | 1975 | 146 | 111 | 8.4 | 6.4 |
| | 1980 | 180 | 126 | 26 | 18 |
| | 1985 | 223 | 144 | 96 | 62 |
| | 1990 | 490 | 293 | 346 | 207 |
| | 1991 | 505 | 297 | 362 | 214 |
| | 1992 | 516 | 300 | 384 | 223 |
| | 1993 | 523 | 300 | 398 | 228 |
| | 1994 | 530 | 301 | 422 | 239 |
| | 1995 | 538 | 302 | 428 | 240 |
| | 1996 | 549 | 305 | 449 | 249 |
| | 1997 | 558 | 306 | 461 | 253 |
| Southern Asia | 1970 | 25 | 34 | 0.7 | 0.9 |
| | 1975 | 32 | 38 | 2.4 | 2.9 |
| | 1980 | 42 | 45 | 6.1 | 6.4 |
| | 1985 | 77 | 72 | 15 | 14 |
| | 1990 | 102 | 86 | 34 | 29 |
| | 1991 | 116 | 95 | 38 | 32 |
| | 1992 | 122 | 99 | 43 | 34 |
| | 1993 | 128 | 102 | 49 | 39 |
| | 1994 | 135 | 105 | 54 | 42 |
| | 1995 | 152 | 116 | 56 | 43 |
| | 1996 | 156 | 117 | 68 | 51 |
| | 1997 | 160 | 118 | 73 | 54 |
| Least developed countries | 1970 | 17 | 56 | 0.2 | 0.5 |
| | 1975 | 23 | 66 | 0.4 | 1.0 |
| | 1980 | 31 | 79 | 1.4 | 3.5 |
| | 1985 | 45 | 100 | 2.2 | 5.0 |
| | 1990 | 57 | 112 | 6.5 | 13 |
| | 1991 | 60 | 116 | 7.4 | 14 |
| | 1992 | 63 | 118 | 7.8 | 15 |
| | 1993 | 66 | 121 | 8.5 | 16 |
| | 1994 | 71 | 127 | 9.2 | 16 |
| | 1995 | 75 | 131 | 10 | 17 |
| | 1996 | 81 | 138 | 12 | 20 |
| | 1997 | 85 | 142 | 14 | 23 |
| Developed countries | 1970 | 666 | 643 | 272 | 263 |
| | 1975 | 867 | 802 | 365 | 337 |
| | 1980 | 986 | 880 | 475 | 424 |
| | 1985 | 1 141 | 986 | 547 | 472 |
| | 1990 | 1 181 | 987 | 588 | 492 |
| | 1991 | 1 195 | 994 | 605 | 503 |
| | 1992 | 1 208 | 999 | 612 | 506 |
| | 1993 | 1 220 | 1 005 | 622 | 512 |
| | 1994 | 1 237 | 1 015 | 640 | 525 |
| | 1995 | 1 255 | 1 025 | 648 | 529 |
| | 1996 | 1 297 | 1 056 | 669 | 545 |
| | 1997 | 1 308 | 1 061 | 675 | 548 |

Country tables on culture and communication IV
Tableaux sur la culture et la communication par pays
Cuadros sobre cultura y comunicación por países

# Country tables on culture and communication
# Tableaux sur la culture et la communication par pays
# Cuadros sobre cultura y comunicación por países

The tables in this section can be grouped according to seven subjects: libraries, book production, the press, international trade in printed matter, cultural paper, films and cinemas and broadcasting.

---

Les tableaux de cette section peuvent être groupés en sept sujets : bibliothèques, édition de livres, presse, commerce international en matière d'imprimés, papier culturel, films et cinémas et radiodiffusion.

---

Los cuadros de esta sección pueden ser agrupados en siete sujetos: bibliotecas, edición de libros, prensa, comercio internacional de impresos, papel cultural, películas y cines y radiodifusión.

---

IV    Country tables on culture and communication
Tableaux sur la culture et la communication par pays
Cuadros sobre cultura y comunicación por países

# Notes and explanations on country tables

# Notes et explications sur les tableaux par pays

# Notas y explicaciones de los cuadros por países

**Table IV.1  National libraries: collections, registered users, works loaned out, current expenditure, employees**
National libraries are libraries which, irrespective of their title, are responsible for acquiring and conserving copies of all significant publications produced in a country and functioning as a *deposit* library, either by law or other arrangement, and normally compile a national bibliography.  In countries where the national library has an appreciable number of service points, it can be assumed that it has other functions in addition to those described above and also serves as a public library, which is often confirmed by the fact that the number of registered users is unusually high.

**Table IV.2  Public libraries: collections, registered users, works loaned out, current expenditure, employees**
Public (or popular) libraries are those which serve the population of a community or region free of charge or for a nominal fee; they may serve the general public or special categories of users such as children, members of the armed forces, hospital patients, prisoners, workers and employees.

**Table IV.3  Libraries of institutions of tertiary education: collections, registered users, works loaned out, current expenditure, employees**
Libraries of institutions of tertiary education are those primarily serving students and teachers in universities and other institutions of education at this level.  They may be open to the general public as well.  A distinction should be made between:
(a)    the main or central library of universities or similar degree-granting institutions, or a group of libraries which may be located separately but have one and the same director;
(b)    libraries attached to university institutes or departments which are neither under the direction of nor administered by the main or central library;
(c)    libraries of institutions of tertiary education other than universities and similar institutions.

**Table IV.4  School libraries**
School libraries are those attached to all types of schools below tertiary education and serving primarily the pupils and teachers of such schools, even though they may also be open to the general public.  Separate collections for the use of several classes in the same school should be regarded as a single library to be counted as both an administrative unit and as a service point.

**Table IV.5  Book production: number of titles by UDC classes**
This table shows the number of titles of non-periodic printed publications (books and pamphlets) published in a particular country and made available to the public.  Unless otherwise stated, statistics on titles refer to both first and re-editions of books and pamphlets.  It should be noted that in cases where the class breakdown does not add up to the total, this is due to the fact that certain types of books (children's books, school textbooks, government publications or others) included in the total are not broken down according to UDC classes.

**Table IV.6  Book production: number of copies by UDC classes**
Statistics on the number of copies refer to first and re-editions as well as to re-prints, i.e. publications that do not require a new ISBN.  For commercial and other reasons, these statistics are far less readily available than those on titles.

**Table IV.7  Book production: number of titles and copies of school textbooks**
School textbooks are non-periodic publications intended for pupils receiving primary or secondary education.

**Table IV.8  Daily and non-daily newspapers: number and circulation**
*Newspapers* are periodic publications intended for the general public and mainly designed to be a primary source of written information on current events connected with public affairs, international questions, politics, etc.  A newspaper thus defined and issued at least four times a week is considered to be a *daily* newspaper; those appearing three times a week or less frequently are considered as *non-daily* newspapers.
Despite the fact that, according to the 1985 Recommendation, the distinguishing feature between newspapers and periodicals is the content and not the periodicity, a few countries, including some demographically important ones, group any periodic publication under either dailies or non-dailies, simply according to the frequency of appearance.
*Circulation* figures show the average circulation, or the average circulation per issue in the case of non-daily publications.  These figures should include the number of copies (a) sold directly, (b) sold by subscription (c) mainly distributed free of charge both inside the country and abroad.

**Table IV.9  International trade in books and pamphlets, newspapers and periodicals.**
The data shown in this table are provided by the Statistical Division of the United Nations and correspond to those published in the *U.N. World Trade Annual*.
Books and pamphlets correspond to code 892.11 of the Standard International Trade Classification (SITC), Revision 1; newspapers and periodicals correspond to code 892.2.  Export values are f.o.b. (free on board) at the frontier of the exporting country.  Import values are c.i.f. (cost, insurance, freight) except for Canada and Australia where they are f.o.b.  Export data include, where appropriate, re-exports.
Data for Belgium include data for Luxembourg; Switzerland includes Liechtenstein; France includes Monaco and, from 1996 onwards, Guadeloupe, Martinique and French Guyana; before 1992 Ethiopia includes Eritrea; data for the United States include data for Puerto Rico and, from 1981 onwards, the United States Virgin Islands; data for South Africa refer to the Southern African Customs Union which is composed of Botswana, Lesotho, Namibia, the Republic of South Africa and Swaziland.
It should be noted that blank spaces in this and the following table signify either "data not available" or "magnitude nil".

Country tables on culture and communication
Tableaux sur la culture et la communication par pays
Cuadros sobre cultura y comunicación por países

IV

**Table IV.10  Newsprint and other printing and writing paper: production, imports, exports and consumption**

The data in this table relate to the production, importation, exportation and consumption of "*cultural paper*", i.e. newsprint and other printing and writing paper.  As in preceding years, these data have been supplied by the *Food and Agriculture Organization of the United Nations (FAO)*.  Readers needing additional information should refer to the *Yearbook of Forest Products* published by the FAO.

The term *Newsprint* (item 641.1 of the Standard International Trade Classification, Revision 2) designates bleached, un-sized or slack-sized printing paper, without coating, of the type usually used for newspapers.  Newsprint weighs from 45 to 60 grammes per square metre, at least 70 per cent of the weight of fibrous material usually being derived from mechanical pulp.

The expression *other printing* and *writing paper* (item 641.2 of the Standard International Trade Classification, Revision 2) covers paper other than newsprint in rolls or sheets, suitable for use in printing and writing.  It does not cover articles manufactured from printing and writing paper such as stationery, exercise books, registers, etc.

For countries where no separate information for the two above-mentioned categories of paper is available, the totals are shown under the category *newsprint*.

In this table, data for Belgium include data for Luxembourg.

**Table IV.11  Production of long films**

The minimum length of films classified as long (or feature) films varies considerably from country to country, ranging from less than 1,000 metres in some to more than 3,000 metres in others; a number of countries, however, have adopted the length of around 1,600 metres.  Only films produced for commercial exhibition in cinemas are shown in this table.  Consequently, films produced solely for television broadcasting are as a general rule excluded.  Figures on international co-production are usually included in the national figures of each of the countries concerned but they are also shown separately when available.

**Table IV.12  Importation of long films by country of origin**

'By country of origin' means the country which produced the film and not the country from which it was imported.  As with production, films imported solely for television broadcasting are not included.  It should also be noted that due to lack of precise information the column *Other countries* may include data for some of the principal countries of origin and the symbol ./. has been used in such cases.  It is possible that some of the films shown as being imported from the Russian Federation were produced in the former USSR.

**Table IV.13  Cinemas: number, seating capacity, annual attendance and box office receipts**

The statistics in this table refer to both *fixed cinemas* and *mobile units* used regularly for the commercial exhibition of long films.  However, in the case of mobile units it is possible that some countries also include non-commercial units.

The term *fixed cinema* applies to establishments possessing their own equipment and includes indoor cinemas (those with a permanent fixed roof over most of the seating accommodation), outdoor cinemas and drive-ins (establishments designed to enable the audience to watch a film while seated in their automobile).

*Mobile units* are defined as projection units equipped and used to serve more than one site.

The capacity figures shown are the sum of the number of seats in indoor and outdoor cinemas plus the number of places for automobiles, multiplied by a factor of 4 in the case of drive-ins.  Consequently, mobile units are not included in capacity statistics.

Cinema attendance is normally calculated from the number of tickets sold during a given year, hence the reference to commercial exhibition of films.

**Table IV.14  Radio and television receivers**

The statistics shown in this table relate to all types of receivers for radio and television broadcasts to the general public, including those connected to a cable distribution system.  Private sets installed in public places are also included as well as communal receivers.

---

**Tableau IV.1  Bibliothèques nationales : collections, usagers inscrits, documents prêtés au-dehors, dépenses ordinaires, personnel**

Les bibliothèques nationales sont des bibliothèques qui, quelle que soit leur appellation, sont responsables de l'acquisition et de la conservation d'exemplaires de toutes les publications éditées dans le pays et fonctionnant comme bibliothèques de *dépôt*, soit en vertu d'une loi, soit en vertu d'un accord particulier et qui normalement établissent une bibliographie nationale. Dans les pays où la bibliothèque nationale a un grand nombre de points de service, on peut supposer qu'elle assume des fonctions autres que celles décrites ci-dessus, fonctionnant également comme une bibliothèque publique, ce qui est souvent confirmé par le fait du très grand nombre d'usagers inscrits.

**Tableau IV.2  Bibliothèques publiques : collections, usagers inscrits, documents prêtés au-dehors, dépenses ordinaires, personnel**

Les bibliothèques publiques (ou populaires) sont celles qui servent, gratuitement ou contre une cotisation de principe, une collectivité et, notamment, une collectivité locale ou régionale, et qui s'adresse soit à l'ensemble du public, soit à certaines catégories d'usagers, telles que les enfants, les membres des forces armées, les malades des hôpitaux, les prisonniers, les ouvriers et les employés.

**Tableau IV.3  Bibliothèques d'établissements d'enseignement supérieur : collections, usagers inscrits, documents prêtés au-dehors, dépenses ordinaires, personnel**

Les bibliothèques d'établissements d'enseignement supérieur sont, en premier lieu, au service des étudiants et du personnel enseignant des universités et autres établissements d'enseignement supérieur. Elles peuvent être ouvertes à l'ensemble du public. Une distinction devrait être faite entre :

(a)  les bibliothèques principales ou centrales d'universités ou d'établissements qui délivrent des diplômes analogues ou encore un groupe de bibliothèques pouvant avoir des localisations distinctes mais placées sous la responsabilité d'un directeur unique ;

(b)  les bibliothèques d'instituts ou de départements universitaires qui ne sont ni dirigées ni administrées par la bibliothèque universitaire principale ou centrale ;

(c)  les bibliothèques d'établissements d'enseignement supérieur autres qu'universités et autres établissements analogues.

**Tableau IV.4  Bibliothèques scolaires**

Les bibliothèques scolaires sont rattachées aux établissements d'enseignement de n'importe quel type au-dessous du niveau de l'enseignement supérieur et doivent avant tout être au service des élèves et des professeurs de ces établissements, même si elles sont, par

IV  Country tables on culture and communication
Tableaux sur la culture et la communication par pays
Cuadros sobre cultura y comunicación por países

ailleurs, ouvertes au public. Les collections séparées mises à la disposition des différentes classes scolaires dans le même établissement doivent être considérées comme une seule bibliothèque et comptabilisées en tant qu'une seule unité administrative et un point de service.

**Tableau IV.5  Edition de livres : nombre de titres classés d'après la CDU**
Ce tableau présente le nombre de titres de publications non périodiques (livres et brochures) édités dans le pays et offerts au public. A moins qu'une indication contraire ne soit précisée, les statistiques sur les titres se réfèrent à la fois aux premières éditions et aux rééditions de livres et brochures. Il faut observer que dans les cas où la répartition des catégories ne concorde pas avec le total, cela est dû au fait que certains types de livres (les livres pour enfants, les manuels scolaires, les publications officielles et autres) inclus dans le total ne sont pas répartis selon les mêmes catégories que la CDU.

**Tableau IV.6  Edition de livres : nombre d'exemplaires classés d'après la CDU**
Les statistiques sur le nombre d'exemplaires se réfèrent aux premières éditions et aux rééditions, ainsi qu'aux réimpressions, c'est-à-dire aux publications qui ne nécessitent pas un nouveau numéro de ISBN. Pour des raisons essentiellement commerciales, ces statistiques sont beaucoup moins disponibles que celles portant sur les titres.

**Tableau IV.7  Edition de livres : nombre de titres et d'exemplaires de manuels scolaires**
Les manuels scolaires sont des publications non périodiques destinées aux élèves de l'enseignement primaire ou secondaire.

**Tableau IV.8  Journaux quotidiens et non quotidiens : nombre et diffusion**
Les *journaux* sont des publications périodiques destinées au grand public, qui ont essentiellement pour objet de constituer une source originale d'information écrite sur les événements d'actualité intéressant les affaires publiques, les questions internationales, la politique etc. Un journal répondant à cette définition et paraissant au moins quatre fois par semaine est considéré comme un quotidien, un journal paraissant trois fois par semaine ou moins fréquemment est classé dans la catégorie des *journaux non quotidiens*.
Malgré la Recommandation de 1985 selon laquelle la distinction principale entre les journaux et les périodiques relève du contenu et non de la périodicité, certains pays, y compris quelques uns qui sont importants au niveau démographique, regroupent les publications périodiques parmi celles quotidiennes ou non quotidiennes, en tenant compte seulement de la fréquence de leur publication.
Les chiffres concernant la *diffusion* représentent la diffusion quotidienne moyenne ou la diffusion moyenne par numéro dans le cas des publications non quotidiennes. Ces chiffres devraient comprendre le nombre d'exemplaires (a) vendus directement, (b) vendus par abonnement, (c) distribués en général gratuitement dans le pays et à l'étranger.

**Tableau IV.9  Commerce international de livres et brochures et de journaux et périodiques**
Les données présentées dans ce tableau proviennent de la Division Statistique des Nations Unies et correspondent à celles publiées dans le *U.N. World Trade Annual*.
Les livres et les brochures correspondent au code 892.11 de la Classification type pour le commerce international (CTCI), Révision 1. Les journaux et périodiques correspondent au code 892.2. Les valeurs d'exportations sont f.o.b. (franco à bord) à la frontière du pays exportateur. Les valeurs d'importations sont c.i.f. (coût, assurance, fret) excepté pour le Canada et l'Australie où elles s'expriment f.o.b. Les exportations comprennent, s'il y a lieu, les réexportations.
Les données pour la Belgique incluent le Luxembourg ; la Suisse comprend le Liechtenstein ; la France comprend Monaco et, à partir de 1996, la Guadeloupe, la Martinique et la Guyane française. Avant 1992, l'Ethiopie comprend l'Erythrée. Les données pour les Etats-Unis comprennent le Porto Rico et, à partir de 1981, les Iles Vierges américaines ; les données pour l'Afrique du Sud se réfèrent à la *Southern African Customs Union* composée du Botswana, du Lesotho, de la Namibie, de l'Afrique du Sud et du Swaziland.
Il faut noter que les espaces blancs dans ce tableau et le suivant signifient soit "données non disponibles" soit "chiffre nul".

**Tableau IV.10  Papier journal et autre papier d'impression et d'écriture : production, importations, exportations et consommation**
Les données qui figurent dans ce tableau se rapportent à la production, à l'importation, à l'exportation et à la consommation de "papier culturel", c'est-à-dire de papier journal, de papier d'impression (autre que le papier journal) et de papier d'écriture. Comme pour les années précédentes, ces données nous ont été fournies par l'*Organisation des Nations Unies pour l'Alimentation et l'Agriculture* (FAO). Les lecteurs qui souhaiteraient obtenir des renseignements complémentaires doivent se référer à l'*Annuaire des Produits Forestiers* publié par la FAO.
Le terme *papier journal* (sous-groupe 641.1 de la Classification Type pour le Commerce International, Révision 2) désigne le papier d'impression blanchi, non collé ou peu encollé, non couché, du type utilisé habituellement pour les journaux. Le papier journal a un poids de 45 à 60 grammes au mètre carré et contient en général au moins 70 pour cent en poids de matière fibreuse tirée de la pâte mécanique.
L'expression *autres papiers d'impression* et *papier d'écriture* (sous-groupe 641.2 de la Classification Type pour le Commerce International, Révision 2) désigne les différents types de papier (en feuilles ou en rouleaux) autres que le papier journal qui sont destinés à l'impression ainsi qu'à l'écriture. N'entrent pas dans cette catégorie les produits manufacturés tels que fournitures de bureau, cahiers, registres, etc.
Pour les pays qui ne distinguent pas les deux catégories de papier signalées ci-dessus, les totaux sont indiqués dans la catégorie *papier journal*.
Dans ce tableau, les données pour la Belgique comprennent les données du Luxembourg.

**Tableau IV.11  Production de films de long métrage**
La longueur minimale des films considérés comme des *longs métrages* diffère considérablement selon les pays : elle peut varier entre moins de 1 000 et plus de 3 000 mètres. Cependant, un certain nombre de pays ont adopté comme norme un chiffre voisin de 1 600 mètres. Seuls les films produits pour la projection cinématographique commerciale sont présentés dans ce tableau. Par conséquent, les films produits uniquement pour les besoins de la télévision sont exclus. Les données sur les coproductions internationales sont généralement comprises dans les données nationales de chaque pays concerné, mais elles sont aussi présentées séparément lorsque les chiffres sont disponibles.

**Tableau IV.12  Importations de films de long métrage par pays d'origine**
L'expression "par pays d'origine" se réfère au pays qui produit le film et non le pays d'où il est importé. De même que pour la production, les films importés uniquement pour la diffusion à la télévision ne sont pas inclus. Il faut noter que le symbole ./. indique que, faute d'informations précises, les données relatives à certains principaux pays d'origine peuvent être comprises dans la colonne "*autres pays*". Il est possible que quelques-uns des films présentés comme importés de la Fédération de Russie aient été produits dans l'ex U.R.S.S.

**Tableau IV.13  Cinémas: nombre d'établissements, nombre de sièges, fréquentation annuelle et recettes guichet**

Les statistiques dans ce tableau se réfèrent aux *établissements fixes* et aux *cinémas itinérants* utilisés régulièrement pour la projection commerciale de longs métrages. Cependant, dans le cas des *cinémas itinérants*, il se peut que certains pays incluent aussi des établissements non commerciaux.

Le terme *établissement fixe* désigne tout établissement doté de son propre équipement ; il englobe les salles fermées (c'est-à-dire celles où un toit fixe recouvre la plupart des places assises), les cinémas de plein air et les cinémas pour automobilistes ou *drive-in* (conçus pour permettre aux spectateurs d'assister à la projection sans quitter leur voiture).

Les *cinémas itinérants* sont définis comme groupes mobiles de projection équipés de manière à pouvoir être utilisés dans des lieux différents.

Les chiffres présentés relatifs à la capacité sont obtenus par la somme du nombre de sièges dans les salles fermées et les cinémas de plein air, plus le nombre de places d'automobiles multiplié par le facteur 4 dans le cas des *drive-in*. Par conséquent, les cinémas itinérants ne sont pas inclus dans les statistiques sur la capacité.

La fréquentation des cinémas est calculée sur la base du nombre de billets vendus au cours d'une année donnée, d'où la seule prise en compte des projections commerciales de films.

**Tableau IV.14  Récepteurs de radiodiffusion sonore et de télévision : total et nombre pour 1 000 habitants**

Les statistiques présentées dans ce tableau concernent tous les types de récepteurs qui permettent au grand public de capter les émissions de radio et de télévision, y compris ceux qui sont reliés à un système de distribution par câble. Les récepteurs privés installés dans des endroits publics sont également inclus, de même que les récepteurs communautaires.

---

**Cuadro IV.1  Bibliotecas nacionales: fondos, usuarios inscritos, documentos prestados al exterior, gastos ordinarios, personal**

Las bibliotecas nacionales, cualquiera sea su denominación, son responsables de la adquisición y conservación de ejemplares de todas las publicaciones significativas impresas en el país. Funcionan como bibliotecas de *depósito*, en virtud de una disposición legal o de otras disposiciones y normalmente elaboran una bibliografía nacional. En los países donde la biblioteca nacional tiene un gran número de puntos de servicio, se puede suponer que asume otras funciones aparte de las ya descritas y que sirve también como biblioteca pública, lo que se confirma a menudo por la gran cantidad de usuarios registrados.

**Cuadro IV.2  Bibliotecas públicas: fondos, usuarios inscritos, documentos prestados al exterior, gastos ordinarios, personal**

Las bibliotecas públicas (o populares) son aquéllas que están, gratuitamente o por una módica suma, al servicio de una comunidad, especialmente de una comunidad local o regional, para atender al público en general, o a cierta categoría de usuarios, como niños, militares, enfermos de los hospitales, prisioneros, obreros y empleados.

**Cuadro IV.3  Bibliotecas de instituciones de enseñanza superior: fondos, usuarios inscritos, documentos prestados al exterior, gastos ordinarios, personal**

Las bibliotecas de instituciones de enseñanza superior son bibliotecas dedicadas básicamente al servicio de los estudiantes y del personal docente de las universidades y demás instituciones de la enseñanza superior. Pueden estar también abiertas al público en general. Conviene distinguir entre:

(a)  la biblioteca principal o central de la universidad o de otras instituciones que conceden títulos de nivel equivalente al universitario, o incluso un grupo de bibliotecas que pueden tener locales distintos pero que dependen de un director único;

(b)  las bibliotecas de centros o de departamentos universitarios que no están dirigidas o administradas por la biblioteca universitaria principal o central;

(c)  las bibliotecas de instituciones de enseñanza superior que no forman parte de la universidad ni de instituciones similares.

**Cuadro IV.4  Bibliotecas escolares**

Las bibliotecas escolares son aquéllas que dependen de instituciones de enseñanza de cualquier categoría inferior a la enseñanza superior y que, ante todo, están al servicio de los alumnos y profesores de esos establecimientos, aunque estén abiertas al público. Los fondos separados para el uso de varias clases de la misma escuela deben considerarse como una sola biblioteca, como una sola unidad administrativa y como un solo punto de servicio.

**Cuadro IV.5  Edición de libros: número de títulos clasificados según la CDU**

Este cuadro presenta el número de títulos de publicaciones no periódicas (libros y folletos) editadas en un país particular y puestas a disposición del público. A menos que haya una indicación contraria, las estadísticas relativas a los títulos se refieren a las primeras ediciones y reediciones de libros y folletos. Debe notarse que cuando la distribución por categorías no corresponde al total, esto se debe al hecho que ciertos tipos de libros (libros de niños, libros de texto, publicaciones gubernamentales y otros) incluidos en el total no están clasificados de acuerdo con las categorías de la CDU.

**Cuadro IV.6  Edición de libros: número de ejemplares clasificados según la CDU**

Las estadísticas sobre el número de ejemplares se refieren tanto a las primeras ediciones y reediciones como a las reimpresiones, o sea, publicaciones que no necesitan un nuevo ISBN. Por razones antes que nada comerciales, se dispone mucho menos de este tipo de estadísticas que de aquéllas relativas a los títulos.

**Cuadro IV.7  Edición de libros: número de títulos y de ejemplares de libros de texto**

Los libros de texto son publicaciones no periódicas destinadas a los alumnos que reciben enseñanza primaria o secundaria.

**Cuadro IV.8  Periódicos diarios y no diarios: número y circulación**

Los *periódicos* son publicaciones periódicas destinadas al gran público y que tienen esencialmente por objeto constituir una fuente de información escrita sobre los acontecimientos de actualidad relacionados con asuntos públicos, cuestiones internacionales, política, etc. Un periódico que responda a esa definición y que se publique al menos cuatro veces por semana se considerará como un diario; un periódico que aparezca tres veces por semana o con menor frecuencia, se clasificará en la categoría de los periódicos no diarios.

**IV** Country tables on culture and communication
Tableaux sur la culture et la communication par pays
Cuadros sobre cultura y comunicación por países

A pesar del hecho que según la Recomendación de 1985, la característica principal que distingue los periódicos diarios y no diarios es el contenido y no la periodicidad, algunos países, incluyendo países importantes a nivel demográfico, reúnen cualquier tipo de publicación periódica bajo el rubro de diarios o no diarios, simplemente según la frecuencia de su aparición.

Las cifras relativas a la *circulación* expresan el promedio de difusión cotidiana, o, en el caso de las publicaciones no diarias, el promedio por número. En todo caso, las cifras correspondientes comprenden en principio el número de (a) ejemplares vendidos directamente, (b) por suscripción, y (c) principalmente distribuidos en forma gratuita tanto en el país como en el extranjero.

### Cuadro IV.9  Comercio internacional de libros y folletos y de publicaciones periódicas

Los datos de este cuadro provienen de la División de Estadística de las Naciones Unidas y corresponden a aquéllos publicados en el *U.N. World Trade Annual*.

Los libros y folletos corresponden al Código 892.11 de la Clasificación Uniforme para el Comercio Internacional (CUCI), Revisión 1 y los diarios y periódicos al Código 892.2 del CUCI. Los datos sobre las exportaciones son f.o.b. (franco a bordo) a la frontera del país exportador. Los datos sobre las importaciones son c.i.f. (coste, seguro y flete) excepto para Canadá y Australia donde son f.o.b. Los datos de exportación incluyen, cuando es el caso, las reexportaciones.

Los datos de Bélgica incluyen Luxemburgo; los de Suiza, Liechtenstein; los de Francia, Mónaco. Desde 1996 Francia incluye Guadalupe, Martinica y la Guyana francesa. Antes de 1992 Etiopía incluye Eritrea. Los datos de Estados Unidos incluyen Puerto Rico y desde 1981 las Islas Vírgenes Americanas. Los datos de Africa del Sur se refieren a la *Southern African Customs Union*, conformada por Botswana, Lesotho, Namibia, Sudáfrica y Swazilandia.

Debe notarse que los espacios en blanco en este cuadro y en el siguiente significan ya sea "datos no disponibles", ya sea "cifra nula".

### Cuadro IV.10  Papel de periódico y otro papel de imprenta y de escribir: producción, importaciones, exportaciones y consumo

Los datos que figuran en este cuadro se refieren a la producción, importación, exportación y consumo de "*papel cultural*", es decir de papel de periódico y otro papel de imprenta y de escribir. Como en años anteriores, los datos han sido proporcionados por la *Organización de las Naciones Unidas para la Alimentación y la Agricultura* (FAO). Los lectores deseosos de obtener más información deben dirigirse al *Anuario de Productos Forestales* publicado por la FAO.

El término *papel de periódico* (subgrupo 641.1 de la Clasificación Uniforme para el Comercio Internacional, Revisión 2) se refiere al papel de imprenta blanqueado, no encolado o poco encolado, no cuché, del tipo utilizado corrientemente para los periódicos. El papel de periódico tiene un peso de 45 a 60 gramos por metro cuadrado y contiene, en general, al menos un 70 por ciento en peso de materia fibrosa extraída de la pasta mecánica.

La expresión *otros papeles de imprenta y papel de escribir* (subgrupo 641.2 de la Clasificación Uniforme para el Comercio Internacional, Revisión 2) designa las diferentes clases de papel en hojas o en rollo que no sean el papel de periódico y que se destinan a la impresión y escritura. No se incluyen es esa categoría los productos manufacturados tales como material de oficina, cuadernos, libros de registro, etc. Para los países donde no se dispone de información separada para las dos categorías de papel arriba mencionadas, los totales se indican en la categoría *papel de periódico*.

En este cuadro, los datos de Bélgica incluyen Luxemburgo.

### Cuadro IV.11  Producción de películas de largo metraje

La longitud mínima de las películas consideradas de largo metraje difiere considerablemente de un país a otro. Esta puede variar de menos de 1 000 a más de 3 000 metros. A pesar de ello, muchos países han adoptado una norma de alrededor 1 600 metros. Sólo las películas destinadas a la proyección cinematográfica comercial figuran en este cuadro. En consecuencia, se excluyen por lo general las películas producidas exclusivamente para la televisión. Los datos sobre las coproducciones internacionales se incluyen generalmente en las estadísticas nacionales de cada país interesado, pero también se presentan por separado cuando están disponibles.

### Cuadro IV.12  Importación de películas de largo metraje por país de origen

"Por país de origen" se entiende el país que produce la película y no el país de donde se importa. Así como en el caso de la producción, las películas importadas para la difusión por la televisión no están incluidas. Debe notarse que el símbolo ./. indica que, a falta de informaciones precisas, los datos correspondientes a ciertos países principales de origen pueden estar incluidos en la columna "*otros países*". Es posible que algunas de las películas presentadas como películas importadas de la Federación de Rusia hayan sido producidas en la ex U.R.S.S.

### Cuadro IV.13  Cines: número de establecimientos, número de asientos, frecuentación anual y recaudación de taquilla

Las estadísticas de este cuadro se refieren a los *establecimientos fijos* y *unidades móviles* utilizados regularmente para la proyección comercial de películas de largo metraje. Sin embargo, en el caso de las unidades móviles, es posible que algunos países hayan tomado en cuenta en sus datos los establecimientos no comerciales.

El término *establecimiento fijo* designa todo establecimiento dotado de su propio equipo y comprende las salas cerradas (es decir, aquéllas en las que un techo fijo protege la mayor parte de los asientos), los cines al aire libre y los cines para automovilistas o drive-in (concebidos para que los espectadores puedan asistir a la proyección sin salir de su vehículo).

Los *cines ambulantes* se definen como unidades móviles de proyección equipados de modo que puedan utilizarse en lugares diferentes.

Las cifras presentadas relativas a la capacidad corresponden a la suma del número de asientos para el caso de cines con salas cerradas y de cines al aire libre, y al número de plazas para automóviles multiplicado por el factor 4 en el caso de los drive-in. Por lo tanto, en las estadísticas de capacidad no se toman en cuenta las unidades móviles.

La frecuentación de los cines se calcula normalmente tomando como base el número de billetes vendidos en el curso de un año dado, por lo que se refiere solamente a la exhibición comercial de películas.

### Cuadro IV.14  Receptores de radiodifusión sonora y de televisión: total y número por 1 000 habitantes

Las estadísticas presentadas en este cuadro conciernen todos los tipos de receptores que permiten al público captar las emisiones de radio y televisión, incluso a aquéllos que están conectados a un sistema de distribución por cable. También se incluyen los receptores privados instalados en lugares públicos y los receptores comunales.

## IV.1 National libraries: collections, registered users, works loaned out, current expenditure, employees

Bibliothèques nationales: collections, usagers inscrits, documents prêtés au-dehors, dépenses ordinaires, personnel

Bibliotecas nacionales: fondos, usuarios inscritos, documentos prestados al exterior, gastos ordinarios, personal

| Country / Pays / País | Year / Année / Año | Administrative unit / Unités administratives / Unidades administrativas | Service points / Points de service / Puntos de servicio | Books/Livres/Libros — Number of volumes (000) / Nombre de volumes (000) / Número de volúmenes (000) | Books/Livres/Libros — Metres of shelving / Mètres de rayonnage / Metros de estantes | Microforms / Microcopies / Microcopias | Audio-visual documents (000) / Matériels audio-visuels (000) / Materiales audio-visuales (000) | Other library materials (000) / Autres matériels de bibliothèque (000) / Otros materiales de biblioteca (000) | Registered users (000) / Usagers inscrits (000) / Usuarios inscritos (000) |
|---|---|---|---|---|---|---|---|---|---|
| **Africa** | | | | | | | | | |
| Algeria | 1971 | 1 | 1 | 754 | 16 295 | ... | ... | ... | 6.3 |
| | 1980 | 1 | 1 | 600 | 34 100 | 1 750 | 6.00 | ... | 12 |
| | 1995 | 1 | 1 | 623 | ... | ... | (1) 43 | ... | (2) 0.7 |
| Benin | 1977 | 1 | 8 | *5 | ... | ... | ... | ... | ... |
| | 1980 | 1 | 8 | *6 | ... | ... | ... | ... | ... |
| | 1986 | 1 | 8 | 6 | 165 | ... | 0.16 | ... | 0.1 |
| | 1989 | 1 | 8 | 6 | 177 | ... | 0.17 | 0.01 | 0.2 |
| | 1995 | 1 | 8 | *7 | ... | ... | 0.01 | 0.00 | 0.4 |
| Egypt | 1972 | 1 | ... | 95 | ... | ... | ... | ... | ... |
| | 1974 | 1 | 12 | 1 118 | ... | ... | ... | ... | ... |
| | 1980 | 1 | ... | 1 000 | ... | 36 000 | 21 | ... | ... |
| | 1985 | 1 | ... | 1 224 | ... | ... | ... | ... | 1 297 |
| | 1990 | 1 | ... | 2 117 | ... | ... | ... | ... | 1 798 |
| | 1991 | 1 | 52 | 2 195 | ... | ... | ... | 40 | ... |
| | 1995 | 1 | 60 | 1 154 | ... | ... | 29 | ... | ... |
| Ethiopia | 1982 | 1 | 13 | 59 | ... | ... | 0.20 | ... | ... |
| | 1986 | 1 | 10 | 100 | ... | ... | 0.39 | 6.36 | ... |
| | 1994 | 1 | 9 | 100 | ... | 365 | 1.34 | 7.53 | 0.4 |
| Gabon | 1985 | 1 | 1 | (6) 52 | ... | 200 | 0.01 | ... | ... |
| | 1992 | 1 | 1 | ... | ... | ... | 0.00 | ... | 2.4 |
| Gambia | 1980 | 1 | 1 | 3 | 220 | ... | ... | ... | 0.7 |
| | 1986 | 1 | 5 | 3 | 220 | ... | ... | 0.21 | 2.0 |
| | 1992 | 1 | 5 | 2 | 220 | 80 | 0.22 | ... | 1.4 |
| | 1995 | 1 | 5 | 2 | 220 | 50 | 0.05 | ... | 1.5 |
| Mauritius | 1971 | 1 | 1 | 49 | ... | ... | ... | ... | 2.9 |
| | 1986 | 1 | 2 | 16 | 285 | 71 | ... | ... | ... |
| | 1989 | 1 | 1 | 36 | 390 | 3 665 | ... | 2.79 | ... |
| | 1992 | 1 | 1 | 38 | 467 | 3 665 | ... | 2.80 | ... |
| Nigeria | 1977 | 2 | 3 | 158 | ... | 4 214 | ... | 0.28 | 0.6 |
| | 1980 | 1 | 8 | 251 | ... | ... | ... | ... | ... |
| | 1986 | 1 | 15 | 478 | 18 038 | ... | 76 | ... | 39 |
| | 1989 | 1 | 15 | 558 | 17 120 | ... | 90 | ... | 30 |
| | 1992 | 1 | 12 | 865 | ... | ... | ... | 0.48 | 34 |

| Annual additions / Acquisitions annuelles / Adquisiciones anuales | | Loans to users (000) | Inter-Library loans | Current expenditure / Dépenses ordinaires / Gastos ordinarios | | Library employees / Personnel des bibliothèques / Personal de las bibliotecas | | | Country | Year |
|---|---|---|---|---|---|---|---|---|---|---|
| Volumes (000) | Other materials (000) | Prêts aux usagers (000) | Prêts entre bibliothèques | Total (000) | Staff (%) | Total | Holding a diploma | Trained on the job | Pays | Année |
| Volumes (000) | Autres matériels (000) | | | Total (000) | Personnel (%) | Total | Diplômé | Formé sur le tas | | |
| Volúmenes (000) | Otros materiales (000) | Préstamos a los usuarios (000) | Préstamos entre bibliotecas | Total (000) | Personal (%) | Total | Diplomado | Formado en ejercicio | País | Año |
| | | | | | | | | | **Africa** | |
| 24 | ... | 17 | ... | 2 080 | 52 | 90 | 4 | 13 | Algeria | 1971 |
| 19 | 0.53 | 80 | 92 | 2 725 | 66 | 82 | 9 | 3 | | 1980 |
| 3.0 | 10 | (3) 2.17 | 2 408 | ... | ... | 271 | 116 | ... | | 1995 |
| 2.4 | ... | ... | ... | (4) 12 565 | ... | 24 | 2 | 3 | Benin | 1977 |
| ... | ... | ... | ... | 16 657 | 85 | 42 | 2 | 10 | | 1980 |
| 0.3 | 0.16 | 4.13 | ... | ... | ... | 30 | 9 | ... | | 1986 |
| 1.1 | ... | 1.26 | ... | 17 573 | 98 | 33 | 10 | ... | | 1989 |
| 0.4 | ... | 6.55 | ... | ... | ... | 29 | 7 | 4 | | 1995 |
| 31 | ... | ... | ... | ... | ... | 1 022 | 432 | ... | Egypt | 1972 |
| | ... | ... | ... | ... | ... | 609 | ... | ... | | 1974 |
| 24 | 7.47 | ... | ... | (5) 83 | ... | 800 | 160 | 300 | | 1980 |
| ... | ... | ... | ... | ... | ... | ... | ... | ... | | 1985 |
| ... | ... | ... | ... | ... | ... | ... | ... | ... | | 1990 |
| ... | ... | 160 | ... | ... | ... | 303 | ... | ... | | 1991 |
| ... | ... | ... | ... | ... | ... | 316 | ... | ... | | 1995 |
| 1.3 | ... | ... | ... | 311 | 78 | 70 | 20 | 10 | Ethiopia | 1982 |
| 23 | 1.11 | ... | ... | 382 | 88 | 49 | 13 | 19 | | 1986 |
| ... | ... | ... | ... | 545 | 64 | 50 | 8 | 22 | | 1994 |
| ... | 0.01 | ... | ... | 177 000 | 70 | 10 | 4 | 1 | Gabon | 1985 |
| 0.5 | ... | ... | ... | ... | ... | 5 | 2 | 3 | | 1992 |
| 0.2 | ... | ... | ... | ... | ... | ... | ... | ... | Gambia | 1980 |
| 0.0 | ... | 0.05 | ... | 147 480 | 73 | 28 | 7 | 14 | | 1986 |
| 0.3 | 0.03 | 3.00 | ... | ... | ... | 3 | 2 | ... | | 1992 |
| 0.1 | 0.05 | 3.00 | ... | ... | ... | 3 | 2 | ... | | 1995 |
| 1.0 | ... | 84 | ... | 94 | 72 | 6 | 1 | 2 | Mauritius | 1971 |
| 0.5 | 0.03 | ... | ... | (7) 88 | ... | 3 | 1 | 2 | | 1986 |
| 0.6 | ... | ... | ... | ... | ... | 2 | ... | ... | | 1989 |
| 2.6 | ... | ... | ... | 202 | 90 | 4 | 2 | 2 | | 1992 |
| ... | 4.12 | 1.13 | 210 | 1 940 | 23 | 570 | 20 | 15 | Nigeria | 1977 |
| 29 | ... | 0.31 | 11 | 3 303 | 22 | 514 | 58 | ... | | 1980 |
| 38 | 0.99 | 0.83 | 63 | 3 693 | 66 | 527 | 76 | 2 | | 1986 |
| 6.7 | 0.39 | ... | 55 | 6 108 | 52 | 614 | 101 | 52 | | 1989 |
| 16 | 6.28 | ... | ... | 15 573 | ... | 682 | 153 | ... | | 1992 |

| Country / Pays / País | Year / Année / Año | Administrative unit / Unités administratives / Unidades administrativas | Service points / Points de service / Puntos de servicio | Collections / Collections / Fondos — Books/Livres/Libros — Number of volumes (000) / Nombre de volumes (000) / Número de volúmenes (000) | Books/Livres/Libros — Metres of shelving / Mètres de rayonnage / Metros de estantes | Microforms / Microcopies / Microcopias | Audio-visual documents (000) / Matériels audio-visuels (000) / Materiales audio-visuales (000) | Other library materials (000) / Autres matériels de bibliothèque (000) / Otros materiales de biblioteca (000) | Registered users (000) / Usagers inscrits (000) / Usuarios inscritos (000) |
|---|---|---|---|---|---|---|---|---|---|
| South Africa | 1991 | 2 | 5 | ... | ... | ... | ... | ... | ... |
| Togo | 1978 | 1 | ... | 6 | 201 | ... | ... | ... | |
| | 1993 | 1 | 1 | 16 | ... | ... | 0.00 | 0.00 | 0.0 |
| | 1995 | 1 | 1 | 19 | ... | ... | ... | 0.01 | 0.5 |
| | | | | | | | | | 12 |
| Zambia | 1983 | 1 | 1 | *1 | ... | ... | ... | ... | 0.1 |
| | 1992 | 1 | 1 | 16 | ... | ... | ... | 500 | (8) 0.1 |
| Zimbabwe | 1981 | 1 | 2 | 45 | ... | 3 100 | 1.76 | 31 | ... |
| | 1988 | 1 | 1 | 80 | ... | ... | 0.01 | ... | 31 |
| | 1993 | 1 | 1 | 96 | ... | ... | ... | ... | 47 |
| **North America** | | | | | | | | | |
| Barbados | 1992 | 1 | 1 | 38 | ... | *672 | ... | *0.31 | ... |
| | 1995 | 1 | 1 | 174 | ... | 673 | 3.10 | 0.41 | 59 |
| Belize | 1992 | (9) 1 | 1 | *150 | ... | ... | ... | ... | 25 |
| Canada | 1971 | 1 | 1 | 201 | ... | ... | ... | ... | 11 |
| | 1981 | 1 | 1 | 896 | 56 656 | 1 060 015 | (10) 41 | ... | ... |
| | 1986 | 1 | 1 | 1 192 | ... | 2 794 183 | (10) 67 | (11) 2 333 | ... |
| | 1989 | 1 | 1 | 7 200 | ... | 3 500 000 | 112 | 302 | ... |
| | 1991 | 1 | 1 | ... | ... | 5 001 730 | 134 | 2 930 | 7.5 |
| | 1995 | 1 | 1 | 6 387 | ... | 5 769 774 | 180 | 3 057 | 7.0 |
| Costa Rica | 1971 | 1 | 1 | 200 | 10 227 | ... | ... | ... | *2.0 |
| | 1983 | 1 | 1 | 1 000 | ... | ... | ... | ... | ... |
| | 1995 | 1 | 1 | 763 | 37 172 | ... | 1.52 | ... | ... |
| Cuba | 1971 | 1 | 1 | 444 | ... | ... | ... | ... | 310 |
| | 1980 | 1 | 1 | 776 | ... | ... | ... | ... | 295 |
| | 1992 | 1 | 1 | 2 431 | ... | ... | 35 | 183 | 13 |
| | 1995 | 1 | 1 | 2 446 | ... | 1 995 | 4.99 | 214 | 1.0 |
| **South America** | | | | | | | | | |
| Brazil | 1971 | 1 | 1 | 2 563 | ... | ... | ... | ... | 7.8 |
| | 1974 | 1 | 1 | 2 624 | ... | ... | ... | ... | ... |
| | 1985 | 1 | 1 | 1 993 | ... | 6 724 | ... | 145 | 95 |
| | 1993 | 1 | 2 | 5 280 | 38 548 | 20 859 | 30 | 722 | 466 |
| Chile | 1974 | 1 | 1 | 2 000 | 85 000 | ... | ... | ... | 8.9 |
| | 1977 | 1 | 1 | 1 200 | 17 500 | ... | ... | ... | ... |
| | 1980 | 1 | 1 | *2 000 | ... | ... | ... | ... | ... |
| | 1984 | 1 | 3 | 2 766 | ... | ... | 0.77 | 8.56 | 1.7 |
| | 1986 | 1 | 2 | 3 480 | ... | ... | 0.83 | 14 | ... |
| | 1989 | 1 | 2 | 3 514 | ... | 5 200 | 1.24 | 14 | ... |
| | 1993 | 1 | 3 | 3 554 | ... | 10 800 | 1.24 | ... | ... |
| | 1995 | 1 | 4 | ... | 31 504 | 20 000 | 5.00 | (3) 0.90 | ... |
| Colombia | 1974 | 1 | 1 | *450 | 37 073 | ... | ... | ... | ... |
| | 1980 | 1 | 1 | 540 | 18 000 | ... | 0.66 | ... | ... |
| | 1993 | 1 | 1 | 463 | 17 534 | ... | 8.93 | (3) 0.57 | 3.7 |
| Ecuador | 1995 | 1 | 3 | 150 | ... | 160 | 0.00 | ... | ... |
| Peru | 1977 | 1 | 1 | 2 137 | 15 569 | 219 | ... | 186 | ... |
| | 1981 | 1 | 1 | 2 569 | 16 179 | 12 317 | 12 | 22 | ... |
| | 1983 | 1 | 1 | 2 690 | 19 507 | 24 166 | 10 | 36 | 40 |
| | 1986 | 1 | 1 | 4 016 | ... | ... | 8.64 | 29 | 26 |
| | 1992 | 1 | 1 | 3 890 | ... | ... | ... | 325 | 8.7 |
| Venezuela | 1971 | 1 | 1 | ... | ... | ... | ... | ... | 11 |
| | 1980 | 1 | 8 | 765 | ... | ... | 122 | ... | ... |
| | 1987 | 1 | 3 | 1 817 | ... | 10 100 | 452 | (3) 201 | ... |
| | 1989 | 1 | 3 | 1 975 | ... | 11 712 | | (3) 72 | 74 |
| | 1991 | 1 | 7 | 2 197 | ... | 15 724 | 1 900 | ... | 115 |
| | 1992 | 1 | 7 | 4 868 | ... | 16 089 | 1 925 | ... | 101 |
| | 1993 | 1 | 7 | 5 115 | ... | 17 118 | 2 051 | ... | 99 |
| | 1995 | 1 | 7 | 3 690 | ... | ... | 1 964 | 366 | ... |

| Annual additions / Acquisitions annuelles / Adquisiciones anuales — Volumes (000) | Other materials (000) / Autres matériels (000) / Otros materiales (000) | Loans to users (000) / Prêts aux usagers (000) / Préstamos a los usuarios (000) | Inter-Library loans / Prêts entre bibliothèques / Préstamos entre bibliotecas | Current expenditure — Total (000) | Staff (%) / Personnel (%) / Personal (%) | Library employees — Total | Holding a diploma / Diplômé / Diplomado | Trained on the job / Formé sur le tas / Formado en ejercicio | Country / Pays / País | Year / Année / Año |
|---|---|---|---|---|---|---|---|---|---|---|
| ... | ... | ... | ... | 6 | 71 | 253 | 70 | 9 | South Africa | 1991 |
| 0.5 | ... | ... | ... | 22 920 | 80 | 40 | 7 | 15 | Togo | 1978 |
| 0.6 | ... | 0.30 | 180 | ... | ... | 39 | 9 | 10 | | 1993 |
| 0.2 | 0.00 | 0.20 | ... | ... | ... | 37 | 5 | 3 | | 1995 |
| ... | ... | 0.85 | ... | 17 | 76 | 4 | 1 | 1 | Zambia | 1983 |
| 0.1 | ... | ... | ... | 605 | 83 | 7 | ... | 3 | | 1992 |
| 0.9 | 1.95 | ... | ... | ... | ... | 10 | 5 | 2 | Zimbabwe | 1981 |
| 1.5 | ... | 137 | 1 364 | 368 | 65 | 26 | 6 | 1 | | 1988 |
| 0.8 | ... | ... | 1 073 | 588 | 60 | ... | 14 | 2 | | 1993 |
| | | | | | | | | | **North America** | |
| 1.0 | 0.02 | ... | ... | 2 308 | 91 | ... | ... | ... | Barbados | 1992 |
| 4.5 | 0.29 | ... | 4 | ... | ... | 82 | 13 | ... | | 1995 |
| ... | ... | ... | ... | ... | ... | 24 | 3 | ... | Belize | 1992 |
| ... | ... | 64 | ... | ... | ... | ... | ... | ... | Canada | 1971 |
| 40 | 96 | 124 | 55 820 | 21 609 | 55 | 499 | 186 | ... | | 1981 |
| ... | 184 | 149 | ... | 36 243 | 60 | 521 | 199 | ... | | 1986 |
| 85 | 275 | 98 | 71 429 | 38 639 | 62 | 504 | 178 | 5 | | 1989 |
| 207 | 58 | 149 | 74 808 | (12) 23 226 | 100 | 500 | 162 | 10 | | 1991 |
| 132 | 257 | 231 | 49 355 | 33 763 | 60 | 469 | 210 | 259 | | 1995 |
| 3.6 | ... | 94 | ... | 480 | 65 | 31 | 18 | 3 | Costa Rica | 1971 |
| 41 | ... | 132 | ... | 16 454 | 55 | 98 | 27 | ... | | 1983 |
| 7.9 | 1.01 | 190 | ... | 345 000 | 69 | 89 | 24 | ... | | 1995 |
| 28 | ... | 223 | ... | ... | ... | 275 | 44 | 140 | Cuba | 1971 |
| ... | ... | 265 | ... | ... | ... | 301 | 45 | ... | | 1980 |
| 56 | ... | 53 | ... | ... | ... | 310 | 107 | 137 | | 1992 |
| 7.2 | 1.97 | 174 | ... | ... | ... | 308 | 166 | ... | | 1995 |
| | | | | | | | | | **South America** | |
| ... | ... | ... | ... | 2 734 | 100 | 400 | 88 | 1 | Brazil | 1971 |
| ... | ... | ... | ... | 4 926 | 96 | 292 | 88 | 171 | | 1974 |
| ... | ... | ... | ... | ... | ... | 279 | ... | ... | | 1985 |
| 67 | 4.41 | 62 | ... | 1 387 700 | 77 | 526 | 151 | 151 | | 1993 |
| 19 | ... | 1 000 | ... | 442 295 | 81 | 274 | 15 | 122 | Chile | 1974 |
| 3.7 | ... | ... | ... | ... | ... | 180 | 14 | 13 | | 1977 |
| 7.3 | ... | 344 | 73 | 36 558 | 81 | 190 | 23 | 6 | | 1980 |
| 8.4 | 2.83 | 507 | ... | ... | ... | 128 | 37 | 7 | | 1984 |
| 70 | 2.22 | 976 | ... | ... | ... | 143 | 40 | 5 | | 1986 |
| ... | ... | 1 309 | ... | ... | ... | 145 | 45 | 5 | | 1989 |
| ... | ... | ... | ... | ... | ... | 145 | 45 | 5 | | 1993 |
| 25 | 1.41 | 444 | ... | ... | ... | 187 | 59 | 5 | | 1995 |
| 10 | ... | ... | ... | 4 650 | 81 | 99 | 4 | ... | Colombia | 1974 |
| 26 | ... | 178 | ... | 14 750 | 82 | 100 | 10 | 40 | | 1980 |
| 13 | 2.67 | 61 | ... | 351 226 | 15 | 101 | 16 | 12 | | 1993 |
| 1.0 | ... | 240 | ... | (5) 1 500 | ... | 26 | 1 | 23 | Ecuador | 1995 |
| 71 | ... | ... | ... | 49 376 | 87 | 260 | 32 | ... | Peru | 1977 |
| 55 | 49 | 673 | ... | 232 278 | 98 | 191 | 48 | ... | | 1981 |
| 69 | 13 | 719 | ... | ... | ... | 237 | 65 | ... | | 1983 |
| 69 | 4.59 | ... | ... | (12) 127 000 | 100 | 339 | 67 | ... | | 1986 |
| 163 | ... | ... | ... | 1 139 477 | 78 | ... | ... | ... | | 1992 |
| 24 | ... | ... | ... | ... | ... | 73 | 17 | ... | Venezuela | 1971 |
| ... | ... | 152 | ... | 5 894 | 96 | 110 | 32 | 67 | | 1980 |
| (13) 158 | ... | 317 | 35 | 27 699 | 49 | 414 | 42 | 133 | | 1987 |
| 104 | ... | 272 | 65 | 161 538 | 46 | 581 | 38 | 143 | | 1989 |
| 98 | 14 | 367 | ... | ... | ... | ... | ... | ... | | 1991 |
| ... | ... | 389 | ... | ... | ... | ... | ... | ... | | 1992 |
| ... | ... | 395 | ... | ... | ... | ... | ... | ... | | 1993 |
| 92 | 43 | 827 | (15) 1 155 | 359 427 | 68 | 1 054 | 204 | 363 | | 1995 |

| Country / Pays / País | Year / Année / Año | Administrative unit / Unités administratives / Unidades administrativas | Service points / Points de service / Puntos de servicio | Collections / Collections / Fondos | | Microforms / Microcopies / Microcopias | Audio-visual documents (000) / Matériels audio-visuels (000) / Materiales audio-visuales (000) | Other library materials (000) / Autres matériels de bibliothèque (000) / Otros materiales de biblioteca (000) | Registered users (000) / Usagers inscrits (000) / Usuarios inscritos (000) |
|---|---|---|---|---|---|---|---|---|---|
| | | | | Books/Livres/Libros | | | | | |
| | | | | Number of volumes (000) / Nombre de volumes (000) / Número de volúmenes (000) | Metres of shelving / Mètres de rayonnage / Metros de estantes | | | | |
| **Asia** | | | | | | | | | |
| Armenia | 1992 | 2 | 3 | 4 094 | ... | ... | 42 | 502 | 34 |
| | 1994 | 3 | 3 | 6 714 | ... | ... | ... | ... | 74 |
| Azerbaijan | 1992 | 1 | 13 | 2 360 | ... | 52 366 | 27 | 677 | 25 |
| | 1995 | 1 | 13 | 3 684 | ... | ... | 79 | 686 | 26 |
| Bangladesh | 1989 | 1 | 1 | 15 | 328 | ... | ... | ... | ... |
| | 1995 | 1 | 1 | 14 | ... | ... | ... | 0.59 | ... |
| Cyprus | 1992 | 1 | 2 | 54 | ... | 200 | 0.12 | ... | 6.5 |
| | 1995 | 1 | 2 | 57 | 2 665 | 200 | 0.15 | ... | 6.4 |
| Georgia | 1992 | 1 | 1 | 7 524 | 90 351 | 5 591 | 26 | 1 501 | 462 |
| | 1995 | 1 | 1 | 10 114 | ... | 1 046 | ... | 3 022 | 551 |
| Iran, Islamic Republic of | 1980 | 1 | 1 | 160 | ... | ... | ... | 20 | 6.0 |
| | 1992 | 1 | 5 | 392 | 10 364 | 573 | 11 | 13 | 2.9 |
| | 1995 | 1 | 5 | 411 | 10 500 | 78 200 | 10 | 57 | 13 |
| Israel | 1995 | 1 | 1 | 3 000 | ... | 155 848 | 0.18 | 11 | 2.2 |
| Japan | 1974 | 1 | 3 | (17) 2 958 | ... | ... | ... | ... | ... |
| | 1980 | 1 | 3 | (17) 3 631 | ... | 107 868 | (18) 230 | 211 | (19) 484 |
| | 1985 | 1 | 3 | (17) 4 085 | ... | ... | ... | ... | (19) 492 |
| | 1990 | 1 | 3 | (17) 5 528 | ... | ... | ... | ... | (19) 452 |
| Jordan | 1981 | 1 | 1 | 17 | 500 | 1 | ... | (20) 2.78 | 0.4 |
| | 1986 | 1 | 1 | 40 | ... | ... | 11 | ... | ... |
| | 1992 | 1 | 1 | ... | ... | ... | 0.24 | ... | ... |
| | 1995 | 1 | 1 | 706 | ... | 282 | 0.01 | 428 | ... |
| Kazakstan | 1993 | 1 | 1 | 5 209 | ... | ... | ... | ... | 46 |
| | 1995 | 1 | 1 | 5 299 | ... | 41 366 | 22 | 92 | 43 |
| Korea, Republic of | 1974 | 2 | 3 | 728 | ... | ... | ... | ... | ... |
| | 1977 | 2 | 2 | 636 | ... | ... | ... | ... | 686 |
| | 1981 | 2 | 3 | 1 360 | ... | 4 838 | 6.07 | ... | 340 |
| | 1985 | 2 | 2 | 1 734 | ... | ... | ... | ... | ... |
| | 1986 | 2 | 4 | 1 583 | ... | 138 136 | ... | ... | 998 |
| | 1990 | 1 | 2 | 2 218 | ... | ... | ... | ... | 1 974 |
| | 1991 | 1 | 2 | 2 451 | ... | ... | ... | ... | 2 122 |
| | 1992 | 1 | 2 | *2 000 | ... | ... | ... | ... | 2 057 |
| | 1994 | 1 | 2 | 2 343 | ... | ... | ... | ... | 2 164 |
| | 1995 | 1 | 2 | 2 576 | ... | 200 961 | 74 | 374 | 2 158 |
| Kyrgyzstan | 1992 | 1 | 1 | 3 076 | ... | 304 367 | 11 | 2 510 | 33 |
| | 1995 | 1 | 1 | 2 965 | ... | 307 633 | 250 | 2 374 | 19 |
| Malaysia | 1977 | 1 | 1 | 94 | 1 875 | 1 196 | 0.18 | 0.91 | 7.8 |
| | 1980 | 1 | 2 | 194 | 4 800 | 5 103 | 0.23 | 1.73 | 8.5 |
| | 1986 | 1 | 6 | 527 | ... | 19 816 | 0.94 | 2.56 | 16 |
| | 1989 | 1 | 9 | 703 | ... | 28 244 | 6.79 | 11 | 177 |
| | 1992 | 1 | 9 | 858 | ... | 41 802 | 6.96 | 41 | 135 |
| | 1995 | 1 | 9 | 1 108 | ... | 46 115 | 28 | 47 | 176 |
| Myanmar | 1971 | 1 | 1 | 1 | ... | ... | ... | ... | ... |
| | 1985 | 1 | 1 | 3 | ... | ... | ... | 2.92 | (19) 28 |
| | 1990 | 1 | 1 | 4 | ... | ... | ... | 2.81 | (19) 11 |
| | 1995 | 1 | 1 | 4 | ... | ... | ... | 3.97 | (19) 15 |
| | 1996 | 1 | 1 | 5 | ... | ... | ... | 4.20 | (19) 15 |
| Oman | 1992 | 1 | 2 | 4 | 155 | ... | ... | ... | 0.2 |
| | 1995 | 1 | 2 | 4 | ... | ... | ... | ... | 0.2 |
| Pakistan | 1977 | 1 | 2 | 80 | ... | ... | ... | ... | ... |
| | 1980 | 1 | 1 | 28 | ... | 5 | ... | ... | ... |
| | 1983 | 1 | 2 | *40 | ... | ... | ... | ... | ... |
| | 1986 | 1 | 1 | 43 | ... | ... | 0.01 | ... | 0.3 |
| | 1992 | 1 | 1 | 78 | 621 | 2 913 | ... | 0.52 | ... |

| Annual additions — Acquisitions annuelles — Adquisiciones anuales | | Loans to users (000) Prêts aux usagers (000) Préstamos a los usuarios (000) | Inter-Library loans Prêts entre biblio-thèques Préstamos entre bibliotecas | Current expenditure — Dépenses ordinaires — Gastos ordinarios | | Library employees — Personnel des bibliothèques — Personal de las bibliotecas | | | Country Pays País | Year Année Año |
|---|---|---|---|---|---|---|---|---|---|---|
| Volumes (000) Volumes (000) Volúmenes (000) | Other materials (000) Autres matériels (000) Otros materiales (000) | | | Total (000) Total (000) Total (000) | Staff (%) Personnel (%) Personal (%) | Total Total Total | Holding a diploma Diplômé Diplomado | Trained on the job Formé sur le tas Formado en ejercicio | | |
| | | | | | | | | | **Asia** | |
| 25 | 6.77 | 71 | 3 598 | 47 534 | ... | 652 | 178 | 280 | Armenia | 1992 |
| ... | ... | ... | ... | ... | ... | 590 | ... | ... | | 1994 |
| 15 | 21 | 952 | (16) 4 919 | 1 426 | 76 | 349 | 267 | 2 | Azerbaijan | 1992 |
| ... | 4.46 | 811 | 8 621 | 345 708 | 42 | 352 | 267 | ... | | 1995 |
| ... | ... | ... | ... | 59 | 43 | 53 | 15 | ... | Bangladesh | 1989 |
| ... | ... | ... | ... | 10 000 | 23 | 16 | ... | ... | | 1995 |
| 2.1 | ... | 11 | 55 | (7) 63 | ... | 4 | ... | 4 | Cyprus | 1992 |
| 2.2 | ... | 9.27 | (15) 47 | (7) 54 | 64 | 4 | 1 | 3 | | 1995 |
| 37 | ... | 7.91 | 3 708 | 10 301 | 65 | 763 | 241 | 338 | Georgia | 1992 |
| 34 | 0.02 | ... | 9 813 | ... | ... | 763 | 531 | ... | | 1995 |
| 2.0 | 0.34 | 23 | ... | 43 000 | 59 | 60 | 4 | 45 | Iran, Islamic | 1980 |
| 18 | 0.15 | 41 | 148 | 970 000 | ... | 260 | ... | ... | Republic of | 1992 |
| 28 | 1.77 | 59 | 2 164 | 2 800 000 | 44 | 309 | 137 | ... | | 1995 |
| 35 | 7.58 | 23 | 3 138 | 24 753 | 80 | 176 | 132 | ... | Israel | 1995 |
| 92 | ... | ... | ... | 4 084 700 | 77 | 872 | 190 | 80 | Japan | 1974 |
| 137 | 34 | 449 | 18 525 | 7 384 933 | 68 | 875 | 125 | ... | | 1980 |
| 265 | ... | 432 | ... | ... | ... | ... | ... | ... | | 1985 |
| ... | ... | 409 | ... | ... | ... | ... | ... | ... | | 1990 |
| 3.0 | ... | ... | ... | ... | ... | 20 | ... | 5 | Jordan | 1981 |
| 1.2 | ... | 12 | 40 | 66 | 83 | ... | ... | ... | | 1986 |
| 1.6 | 0.09 | ... | ... | 220 | 68 | 66 | 8 | 10 | | 1992 |
| 1.4 | 0.12 | ... | ... | 229 | 65 | 68 | 12 | ... | | 1995 |
| 94 | ... | 3 243 | ... | ... | ... | 309 | 130 | ... | Kazakstan | 1993 |
| 47 | 2.53 | 3 201 | (16) 11 335 | 28 889 | 39 | 350 | 136 | 3 | | 1995 |
| 35 | ... | 483 | ... | 331 157 | 50 | 349 | 89 | 27 | Korea, Republic of | 1974 |
| 50 | ... | 562 | ... | 1 071 566 | 61 | 405 | 106 | ... | | 1977 |
| 91 | ... | 385 | 923 | 3 560 644 | 50 | 440 | 119 | 63 | | 1981 |
| ... | ... | 1 145 | ... | 7 115 374 | ... | 444 | ... | ... | | 1985 |
| ... | ... | ... | ... | 6 551 776 | ... | 347 | ... | ... | | 1986 |
| ... | ... | 3 388 | ... | 9 337 974 | ... | 512 | ... | ... | | 1990 |
| ... | ... | 3 728 | ... | 9 797 872 | ... | 510 | ... | ... | | 1991 |
| ... | ... | ... | ... | 6 477 852 | 40 | 230 | ... | ... | | 1992 |
| ... | ... | 3 531 | ... | 13 081 126 | ... | 500 | ... | ... | | 1994 |
| 215 | 38 | 5 870 | (15) 62 | 10 615 900 | 44 | 266 | 144 | ... | | 1995 |
| ... | 35 | 26 | (16) 13 200 | 53 470 | 54 | 217 | 136 | 81 | Kyrgyzstan | 1992 |
| 12 | 22 | 1 263 | (16) 9 701 | 1 958 | 60 | 227 | 136 | ... | | 1995 |
| 20 | 0.35 | ... | 791 | 1 821 | 52 | 102 | 28 | ... | Malaysia | 1977 |
| 16 | ... | 168 | 490 | 2 418 | 58 | 145 | 36 | ... | | 1980 |
| 41 | 4.25 | ... | ... | 5 825 | 46 | 232 | 70 | ... | | 1986 |
| 61 | 9.95 | 267 | ... | 6 876 | 47 | 228 | 70 | ... | | 1989 |
| 81 | 7.46 | ... | 446 | ... | ... | 250 | 75 | ... | | 1992 |
| 92 | 8.11 | 264 | 787 | 22 400 | 15 | 248 | 68 | 6 | | 1995 |
| 4.1 | ... | 65 | ... | 68 | 79 | 21 | 2 | 1 | Myanmar | 1971 |
| ... | ... | 17 | ... | ... | ... | ... | ... | ... | | 1985 |
| ... | ... | 20 | ... | ... | ... | ... | ... | ... | | 1990 |
| ... | ... | 45 | ... | ... | ... | ... | ... | ... | | 1995 |
| ... | ... | 30 | ... | ... | ... | ... | ... | ... | | 1996 |
| 0.0 | 0.02 | ... | ... | ... | ... | 3 | 1 | 2 | Oman | 1992 |
| 0.0 | 0.12 | 0.91 | ... | ... | ... | 2 | 1 | 1 | | 1995 |
| 7.7 | ... | - | 164 | 1 737 | 22 | 67 | 20 | ... | Pakistan | 1977 |
| 3.7 | ... | - | 125 | 2 455 | 6 | 18 | 4 | 3 | | 1980 |
| 4.5 | ... | - | ... | 15 849 | 9 | 90 | 16 | ... | | 1983 |
| 5.4 | ... | - | ... | 11 663 | ... | ... | ... | ... | | 1986 |
| 3.5 | ... | - | ... | 8 789 | 34 | 123 | 20 | ... | | 1992 |

| Country / Pays / País | Year / Année / Año | Administrative unit / Unités administratives / Unidades administrativas | Service points / Points de service / Puntos de servicio | Books/Livres/Libros — Number of volumes (000) / Nombre de volumes (000) / Número de volúmenes (000) | Books/Livres/Libros — Metres of shelving / Mètres de rayonnage / Metros de estantes | Microforms / Microcopies / Microcopias | Audio-visual documents (000) / Matériels audio-visuels (000) / Materiales audio-visuales (000) | Other library materials (000) / Autres matériels de bibliothèque (000) / Otros materiales de biblioteca (000) | Registered users (000) / Usagers inscrits (000) / Usuarios inscritos (000) |
|---|---|---|---|---|---|---|---|---|---|
| Philippines | 1980 | 1 | 1 | 220 | 10 072 | 2 567 | 0.21 | ... | 18 |
| | 1986 | 1 | 1 | ... | ... | 7 258 | ... | 5.41 | 123 |
| | 1989 | 1 | 1 | ... | ... | 29 014 | 2.68 | 6.33 | 217 |
| | 1993 | 1 | 4 | 902 | ... | 9 620 | ... | 2.50 | 190 |
| Qatar | 1983 | 1 | 1 | 106 | ... | | ... | | 5.5 |
| | 1985 | 1 | 1 | 128 | ... | | ... | | 6.6 |
| | 1989 | 1 | 1 | 165 | ... | 3 403 | ... | 1.82 | 7.2 |
| | 1992 | 1 | 1 | 185 | ... | 4 125 | ... | 1.82 | 6.3 |
| | 1995 | 1 | 1 | 228 | ... | 4 125 | ... | 1.82 | 6.5 |
| Saudi Arabia | 1974 | 1 | 1 | 23 | 250 | ... | ... | ... | ... |
| | 1995 | 1 | 6 | 60 | ... | ... | ... | ... | 6.5 |
| Singapore | 1974 | (9) 1 | 15 | 800 | 26 673 | ... | | ... | 276 |
| | 1980 | (9) 1 | 17 | 1 453 | ... | 17 128 | 10 | 18 | 445 |
| | 1984 | (9) 1 | 18 | 2 162 | ... | 55 206 | 45 | 21 | 716 |
| | 1989 | (9) 1 | 14 | 2 319 | ... | | (21) 187 | ... | 615 |
| | 1992 | (9) 1 | 8 | 2 891 | ... | 26 949 | 21 | 8.44 | 875 |
| | 1995 | (9) 1 | 10 | 3 252 | ... | 24 384 | 80 | 52 | 1 068 |
| Sri Lanka | 1977 | 1 | 3 | 13 | ... | ... | | ... | 4.8 |
| | 1984 | 1 | 2 | 76 | 1 000 | 103 | 0.03 | 0.59 | ... |
| | 1989 | 1 | 1 | 133 | ... | 5 275 | 1.22 | 16 | 0.1 |
| | 1993 | 1 | 1 | 157 | ... | 9 084 | ... | 17 | 0.1 |
| Syrian Arab Republic | 1977 | 1 | 1 | 74 | 1 604 | ... | 0.00 | ... | 24 |
| | 1980 | 1 | 1 | 85 | 1 689 | ... | ... | ... | ... |
| | 1986 | 1 | 1 | *100 | ... | ... | ... | ... | ... |
| | 1989 | 1 | 1 | 127 | ... | 14 895 | 9.49 | 1.810 | ... |
| | 1992 | 1 | 1 | 150 | ... | ... | ... | ... | ... |
| Tajikistan | 1995 | 1 | 16 | 1 834 | ... | 765 | 3.210 | (3) 2.21 | 23 |
| Thailand | 1974 | 1 | 6 | 882 | 2 310 | ... | ... | ... | 673 |
| | 1981 | 1 | 6 | 1 245 | 3 780 | 2 300 | 7.27 | 7.28 | ... |
| | 1983 | 1 | 9 | 1 155 | ... | 8 051 | 30 | ... | ... |
| | 1989 | 1 | 24 | 1 390 | 5 900 | 7 605 | 21 | 132 | 1 457 |
| | 1992 | 1 | 25 | 1 528 | 6 200 | 15 000 | 31 | 136 | 1 456 |
| Turkey | 1974 | 1 | 8 | 574 | 6 160 | ... | ... | ... | 2.8 |
| | 1980 | 1 | 1 | 782 | 8 230 | 9 340 | 1.98 | 41 | ... |
| | 1984 | 1 | 1 | 885 | ... | 9 376 | 2.99 | 105 | 20 |
| | 1989 | 1 | 1 | 1 016 | ... | 9 676 | 5.56 | 142 | 31 |
| | 1992 | 1 | 1 | 1 079 | ... | 9 778 | 12 | 167 | 10 |
| | 1995 | 1 | 1 | 1 146 | ... | 11 410 | 17 | 189 | 25 |
| **Europe** | | | | | | | | | |
| Albania | 1980 | 1 | 2 | 803 | ... | 5 496 | ... | ... | 9.0 |
| | 1986 | 1 | 2 | 883 | 17 049 | ... | ... | 33 | 8.7 |
| | 1995 | 1 | 2 | 965 | 24 050 | ... | ... | ... | 5.5 |
| Austria | 1974 | 1 | 1 | 2 180 | 52 659 | ... | ... | ... | 3.2 |
| | 1977 | 1 | 1 | 2 252 | 53 928 | 21 304 | 1 616 | 1 689 | ... |
| | 1980 | 1 | 1 | 2 327 | 77 600 | ... | ... | 1 511 | 3.8 |
| | 1983 | 1 | 1 | 2 435 | 58 177 | 188 568 | 2 386 | 1 583 | ... |
| | 1989 | 1 | 1 | 2 686 | ... | ... | ... | ... | ... |
| | 1991 | 1 | 9 | 2 648 | ... | ... | ... | ... | ... |
| | 1992 | 1 | 1 | 3 069 | ... | ... | ... | ... | ... |
| | 1993 | 1 | 9 | 2 743 | ... | 9 775 | 56 | 2 829 | (22) 67 |
| | 1994 | 1 | 9 | 2 974 | ... | 10 290 | 58 | 2 849 | (22) 66 |
| | 1995 | 1 | 10 | 2 838 | ... | 10 968 | 60 | 2 869 | (22) 70 |
| | 1996 | 1 | 10 | 2 884 | ... | 11 418 | 62 | 2 892 | (22) 86 |
| | 1997 | 1 | 10 | 2 933 | ... | 12 057 | 65 | 2 906 | (22) 85 |
| Belarus | 1992 | 1 | 2 | 6 868 | ... | 126 100 | 27 | 394 | 37 |
| | 1995 | 1 | 1 | 6 875 | ... | 120 000 | 29 | 318 | 37 |
| Belgium | 1974 | 1 | 1 | 2 952 | *86 000 | ... | ... | ... | ... |
| | 1980 | 1 | 1 | 3 366 | 95 000 | 15 000 | ... | ... | 8.1 |
| | 1983 | 1 | 1 | *3 000 | *90 000 | *15 000 | ... | 36 | 17 |

| Annual additions — Acquisitions annuelles — Adquisiciones anuales | | Loans to users (000) — Prêts aux usagers (000) — Préstamos a los usuarios (000) | Inter-Library loans — Prêts entre bibliothèques — Préstamos entre bibliotecas | Current expenditure — Dépenses ordinaires — Gastos ordinarios | | Library employees — Personnel des bibliothèques — Personal de las bibliotecas | | | Country — Pays — País | Year — Année — Año |
|---|---|---|---|---|---|---|---|---|---|---|
| Volumes (000) — Volumes (000) — Volúmenes (000) | Other materials (000) — Autres matériels (000) — Otros materiales (000) | | | Total (000) — Total (000) — Total (000) | Staff (%) — Personnel (%) — Personal (%) | Total — Total — Total | Holding a diploma — Diplômé — Diplomado | Trained on the job — Formé sur le tas — Formado en ejercicio | | |
| ... | ... | 162 | ... | 7 203 | 42 | 256 | 63 | 38 | Philippines | 1980 |
| 35 | 5.21 | 168 | ... | 9 243 | 57 | 242 | 48 | ... | | 1986 |
| 6.7 | 0.41 | ... | ... | ... | ... | 72 | 46 | 12 | | 1989 |
| 72 | 2.44 | ... | 15 | (7) 17 533 | ... | 156 | 69 | 10 | | 1993 |
| 4.5 | ... | 10 | ... | (5) 590 | ... | 40 | ... | ... | Qatar | 1983 |
| ... | ... | 13 | ... | ... | ... | ... | ... | ... | | 1985 |
| 9.4 | - | 15 | ... | (5) 500 | ... | 31 | ... | ... | | 1989 |
| 4.9 | - | 12 | ... | (5) 350 | ... | 39 | 6 | ... | | 1992 |
| 15 | ... | 12 | ... | ... | ... | 33 | 7 | 26 | | 1995 |
| 2.8 | ... | ... | ... | 300 | 25 | 23 | 6 | 3 | Saudi Arabia | 1974 |
| ... | ... | 36 | 35 | ... | ... | 17 | 7 | 1 | | 1995 |
| 92 | ... | 2 430 | ... | 3 145 | 60 | 268 | 36 | 34 | Singapore | 1974 |
| 134 | 5.34 | 3 612 | 2 833 | 10 023 | 43 | 331 | 58 | ... | | 1980 |
| 391 | 29 | 6 093 | 942 | 11 485 | 57 | 398 | 62 | ... | | 1984 |
| 270 | 13 | 9 318 | 1 306 | 15 430 | 53 | 393 | 95 | ... | | 1989 |
| 165 | ... | 8 974 | 1 779 | 18 500 | 57 | 373 | 60 | ... | | 1992 |
| 389 | 43 | 14 271 | 2 493 | 20 352 | 49 | 491 | ... | ... | | 1995 |
| 2.1 | ... | - | ... | 476 | 60 | 38 | 4 | ... | Sri Lanka | 1977 |
| 5.4 | 0.16 | - | ... | ... | ... | 81 | ... | ... | | 1984 |
| ... | ... | - | 7 | (7) 7 300 | ... | 114 | 8 | ... | | 1989 |
| ... | ... | - | 5 | (7) 9 100 | ... | 128 | 5 | ... | | 1993 |
| 0.2 | 0.00 | ... | ... | ... | ... | 17 | 1 | 1 | Syrian Arab Republic | 1977 |
| 2.0 | ... | 46 | ... | ... | ... | 14 | 1 | ... | | 1980 |
| 6.0 | ... | ... | ... | 1 919 | 43 | 91 | 2 | 30 | | 1986 |
| 13 | 5.53 | ... | ... | ... | ... | 150 | ... | ... | | 1989 |
| ... | ... | 1 500 | ... | 10 000 | ... | 315 | 15 | 300 | | 1992 |
| 1.5 | ... | 23 | (16) 192 | 6 | 39 | 140 | ... | ... | Tajikistan | 1995 |
| 13 | ... | ... | ... | 4 130 | 58 | 104 | 38 | 40 | Thailand | 1974 |
| 118 | 19 | ... | ... | 13 005 | 56 | 399 | 35 | 40 | | 1981 |
| ... | 24 | ... | 45 | 19 030 | 53 | 229 | 62 | 40 | | 1983 |
| 159 | ... | ... | 205 | 29 027 | 58 | 282 | 64 | 40 | | 1989 |
| 138 | 48 | 10 | 412 | 57 500 | 53 | 300 | 75 | 100 | | 1992 |
| 14 | ... | 24 | ... | 4 708 | - | 118 | 26 | 67 | Turkey | 1974 |
| 26 | 0.25 | 51 | 464 | 10 905 | 72 | 114 | 18 | 32 | | 1980 |
| 23 | 2.21 | ... | 405 | 191 629 | 38 | 188 | 22 | 119 | | 1984 |
| 26 | 3.90 | 156 | 482 | 1 878 877 | 44 | 210 | 44 | 65 | | 1989 |
| 21 | ... | 141 | 800 | 34 569 000 | ... | 193 | 39 | 82 | | 1992 |
| 22 | 4.00 | 279 | 687 | 55 551 006 | 31 | 207 | 27 | 123 | | 1995 |
| | | | | | | | | | **Europe** | |
| 22 | ... | 294 | 2 148 | ... | ... | 57 | 32 | 21 | Albania | 1980 |
| 20 | 4.00 | 160 | 1 346 | ... | ... | ... | ... | ... | | 1986 |
| 5.1 | ... | 19 | 265 | 12 449 | 60 | 100 | ... | ... | | 1995 |
| 30 | ... | 59 | ... | 50 642 | 44 | 243 | 113 | 19 | Austria | 1974 |
| 27 | ... | 56 | 10 276 | (7) 35 729 | ... | 243 | 114 | ... | | 1977 |
| 33 | ... | 48 | 7 270 | (5) 6 407 | ... | 256 | 146 | 22 | | 1980 |
| 31 | 68 | 53 | 8 297 | 43 166 | ... | 300 | 233 | 67 | | 1983 |
| 84 | ... | 306 | ... | (5) 11 532 | ... | 302 | 230 | 72 | | 1989 |
| 42 | ... | 409 | ... | ... | ... | 308 | 237 | 71 | | 1991 |
| 41 | 2.92 | 217 | ... | (5) 15 858 | ... | 308 | 237 | 71 | | 1992 |
| 44 | 1.31 | 411 | 5 359 | ... | ... | 308 | 238 | 70 | | 1993 |
| 51 | 1.82 | 370 | 5 201 | 215 787 | 78 | 300 | 233 | 67 | | 1994 |
| 44 | 1.82 | 337 | 5 099 | 221 418 | 80 | 312 | 238 | 74 | | 1995 |
| 47 | 2.73 | 339 | 5 619 | 229 062 | 77 | 308 | 237 | 71 | | 1996 |
| 48 | 3.04 | 345 | 5 957 | 234 684 | 77 | 308 | 238 | 71 | | 1997 |
| 110 | 71 | 3 100 | 10 233 | ... | ... | 520 | 431 | 35 | Belarus | 1992 |
| 66 | 19 | 2 698 | 10 600 | ... | ... | 445 | 237 | 100 | | 1995 |
| 50 | ... | ... | ... | 220 400 | 53 | 358 | 37 | 35 | Belgium | 1974 |
| 14 | ... | 220 | 21 918 | 345 952 | 58 | 265 | ... | 38 | | 1980 |
| 14 | 0.01 | 213 | 25 604 | 369 773 | 63 | 230 | 24 | 11 | | 1983 |

| Country / Pays / País | Year / Année / Año | Administrative unit / Unités administratives / Unidades administrativas | Service points / Points de service / Puntos de servicio | Collections / Collections / Fondos — Books/Livres/Libros — Number of volumes (000) / Nombre de volumes (000) / Número de volúmenes (000) | Books — Metres of shelving / Mètres de rayonnage / Metros de estantes | Microforms / Microcopies / Microcopias | Audio-visual documents (000) / Matériels audio-visuels (000) / Materiales audio-visuales (000) | Other library materials (000) / Autres matériels de bibliothèque (000) / Otros materiales de biblioteca (000) | Registered users (000) / Usagers inscrits (000) / Usuarios inscritos (000) |
|---|---|---|---|---|---|---|---|---|---|
| Belgium (cont) | 1990 | 1 | 1 | *4 278 | *57 591 | ... | *272 | ... | ... |
|  | 1991 | 1 | 17 | 4 155 | ... | 700 | ... | 21 | 13 |
|  | 1992 | 1 | 17 | 4 662 | ... | 750 | ... | 23 | 14 |
|  | 1993 | 1 | 17 | 4 872 | ... | 800 | ... | 24 | 15 |
|  | 1994 | 1 | 17 | 4 917 | ... | 850 | ... | 25 | 15 |
|  | 1995 | 1 | 17 | 5 168 | ... | 900 | ... | 26 | 16 |
|  | 1996 | 1 | 17 | 4 738 | ... | 950 | ... | 24 | 15 |
|  | 1997 | 1 | 17 | 5 000 | ... | 1 000 | ... | 25 | 15 |
| Bulgaria | 1977 | 1 | 1 | 1 352 | ... | 20 102 | ... | 471 | 31 |
|  | 1980 | 1 | 1 | 1 479 | ... | 27 087 | ... | 542 | 23 |
|  | 1986 | 1 | 1 | 2 048 | ... | 214 024 | 30 | 3 948 | 25 |
|  | 1989 | 1 | 1 | 2 161 | ... | 216 620 | 44 | 4 075 | 26 |
|  | 1991 | 1 | 1 | 2 217 | ... | 218 141 | 33 | 4 098 | 25 |
|  | 1992 | 1 | 1 | 2 239 | ... | 218 444 | 34 | 4 154 | 24 |
|  | 1993 | 1 | 1 | 2 269 | ... | 218 444 | 35 | 4 177 | 24 |
|  | 1994 | 1 | 1 | 2 320 | ... | 218 444 | 36 | 4 198 | 24 |
|  | 1995 | 1 | 1 | 2 379 | ... | 217 444 | 36 | 4 216 | 27 |
|  | 1996 | 1 | 1 | 2 431 | ... | 218 444 | 36 | ... | 27 |
|  | 1997 | 1 | 1 | 2 465 | ... | 218 444 | 38 | ... | 26 |
| Croatia | 1992 | 1 | 1 | 2 333 | 61 725 | 234 283 | 31 | 325 | ... |
|  | 1995 | 1 | 1 | 2 405 | 62 675 | 293 725 | 31 | 348 | 8.6 |
| Czech Republic | 1990 | 1 | 1 | 5 253 | ... | 180 856 | 43 | 1 281 | 28 |
|  | 1991 | 1 | 1 | 5 308 | ... | ... | ... | ... | 29 |
|  | 1992 | 1 | 1 | 5 315 | ... | ... | ... | ... | 37 |
|  | 1993 | 1 | 1 | 5 363 | ... | ... | ... | ... | 29 |
|  | 1994 | 1 | 1 | 5 410 | ... | ... | ... | ... | 43 |
|  | 1995 | 1 | 1 | 5 522 | ... | ... | ... | ... | 25 |
|  | 1996 | 1 | 1 | 5 586 | ... | ... | ... | ... | 27 |
|  | 1997 | 1 | 1 | 5 651 | ... | 14 123 | 18 | 14 | 29 |
| Denmark | 1974 | 1 | 1 | 2 100 | 70 000 | ... | ... | ... | ... |
|  | 1977 | 1 | 3 | 2 300 | 75 000 | 49 669 | 3.94 | ... | ... |
|  | 1980 | 1 | 4 | 2 300 | 75 000 | 63 191 | 4.38 | ... | ... |
|  | 1986 | 1 | 4 | 2 750 | 86 500 | 196 838 | 5.01 | ... | ... |
|  | 1991 | 1 | 4 | 4 246 | ... | 179 222 | 7.88 | 120 | ... |
|  | 1992 | 1 | 4 | 4 388 | 103 745 | 254 997 | 7.96 | 127 | ... |
|  | 1993 | 1 | 4 | 4 366 | ... | 327 838 | 4.81 | 132 | ... |
|  | 1994 | 1 | 4 | 4 439 | ... | 335 368 | 5.14 | 136 | ... |
|  | 1995 | 1 | 4 | 4 503 | ... | 341 563 | 5.31 | 139 | ... |
|  | 1996 | 1 | 3 | 4 623 | ... | 311 401 | 5.42 | 142 | ... |
|  | 1997 | 1 | 3 | 4 675 | ... | 372 236 | 5.56 | 146 | ... |
| Estonia | 1990 | 1 | 2 | 3 124 | ... | 37 386 | 16 | 384 | ... |
|  | 1991 | 1 | 2 | 3 235 | ... | 37 386 | 17 | 381 | (24) 46 |
|  | 1992 | 1 | 2 | 2 038 | ... | 37 386 | 18 | 1 169 | ... |
|  | 1993 | 1 | 2 | 2 085 | ... | 37 595 | 19 | 1 161 | (24) 374 |
|  | 1994 | 1 | 2 | 2 122 | ... | 37 351 | 20 | 1 170 | (24) 527 |
|  | 1995 | 1 | 2 | 2 162 | ... | 37 351 | 22 | 1 184 | (24) 539 |
|  | 1996 | 1 | 2 | 2 204 | ... | 18 547 | 25 | ... | (24) 609 |
|  | 1997 | 1 | 2 | 2 238 | ... | 21 836 | 26 | ... | (24) 607 |
| Faeroe Islands | 1974 | 1 | 1 | 73 | 2 085 | ... | ... | ... | ... |
|  | 1982 | 1 | 1 | 91 | ... | 196 | ... | 0.66 | 2.8 |
|  | 1983 | 1 | 1 | 91 | ... | 196 | ... | 0.66 | 2.8 |
|  | 1985 | 1 | 1 | 99 | ... | ... | ... | ... | ... |
|  | 1990 | 1 | 1 | 115 | ... | ... | ... | ... | ... |
|  | 1992 | 1 | 1 | 121 | ... | ... | ... | ... | ... |
|  | 1993 | 1 | 1 | 123 | ... | ... | ... | ... | ... |
| Federal Republic of Yugoslavia | 1992 | 3 | 3 | 5 607 | 180 272 | 125 000 | 284 | 516 | 176 |
|  | 1995 | 3 | 3 | 5 659 | 169 797 | 113 095 | 354 | 485 | 150 |
| Finland | 1974 | 1 | 3 | 1 735 | 48 700 | ... | ... | ... | ... |
|  | 1977 | 1 | 3 | 1 875 | 57 100 | 68 100 | ... | ... | ... |
|  | 1980 | 1 | 2 | 2 182 | ... | 82 500 | ... | ... | ... |
|  | 1986 | 1 | 1 | 2 563 | 72 760 | 232 488 | 35 | 1 642 | 678 |
|  | 1991 | 1 | 1 | 2 176 | ... | 350 000 | 66 | ... | (24) 150 |
|  | 1992 | 1 | 1 | 2 218 | 61 200 | 400 000 | 73 | ... | (24) 162 |
|  | 1993 | 1 | 1 | 2 252 | ... | 420 000 | 78 | ... | (24) 174 |

| Annual additions — Acquisitions annuelles — Adquisiciones anuales | | Loans to users (000) Prêts aux usagers (000) Préstamos a los usuarios (000) | Inter-Library loans Prêts entre bibliothèques Préstamos entre bibliotecas | Current expenditure — Dépenses ordinaires — Gastos ordinarios | | Library employees — Personnel des bibliothèques — Personal de las bibliotecas | | | Country Pays País | Year Année Año |
|---|---|---|---|---|---|---|---|---|---|---|
| Volumes (000) Volumes (000) Volúmenes (000) | Other materials (000) Autres matériels (000) Otros materiales (000) | | | Total (000) Total (000) Total (000) | Staff (%) Personnel (%) Personal (%) | Total Total Total | Holding a diploma Diplômé Diplomado | Trained on the job Formé sur le tas Formado en ejercicio | | |
| ... | ... | ... | ... | ... | ... | 273 | 36 | ... | Belgium (cont) | 1990 |
| 43 | ... | 196 | 3 953 | 160 950 | ... | 217 | 5 | 212 | | 1991 |
| 44 | ... | 222 | 3 566 | 180 613 | ... | 204 | 5 | 199 | | 1992 |
| 43 | ... | 240 | 2 290 | 192 965 | ... | 194 | 5 | 189 | | 1993 |
| 44 | ... | 246 | 1 524 | 207 042 | ... | 198 | 5 | 193 | | 1994 |
| 49 | ... | 237 | 1 699 | 199 395 | ... | 192 | 12 | 180 | | 1995 |
| 51 | ... | 248 | 1 738 | 239 788 | ... | 186 | 12 | 174 | | 1996 |
| 50 | ... | 248 | 1 743 | 249 781 | ... | 200 | 12 | 188 | | 1997 |
| 43 | 30 | ... | ... | 1 322 | 46 | 217 | 181 | 36 | Bulgaria | 1977 |
| 42 | 22 | ... | ... | 2 562 | 38 | 282 | 61 | ... | | 1980 |
| 40 | 44 | ... | ... | 3 740 | 32 | 318 | 257 | 61 | | 1986 |
| 37 | 44 | ... | ... | 4 334 | 44 | 398 | 371 | 27 | | 1989 |
| 29 | (23) 1.01 | 4.22 | 798 | 14 961 | 37 | 484 | 355 | 129 | | 1991 |
| 29 | (23) 0.54 | 4.52 | 127 | 20 487 | 48 | 386 | 273 | 113 | | 1992 |
| 32 | (23) 1.00 | 6.47 | 704 | 26 648 | 54 | 385 | 273 | 112 | | 1993 |
| 51 | (23) 0.20 | 10 | 138 | 41 502 | 49 | 366 | 230 | 136 | | 1994 |
| 59 | (23) 0.24 | 13 | 126 | 64 212 | 68 | 366 | 230 | 136 | | 1995 |
| 54 | (23) 0.67 | 9.76 | 89 | 119 082 | 59 | 366 | 235 | 131 | | 1996 |
| 37 | (23) 1.15 | 12 | 114 | 978 146 | 57 | 329 | 198 | 131 | | 1997 |
| 20 | 77 | ... | ... | (5) 102 255 | ... | 233 | 147 | ... | Croatia | 1992 |
| 21 | 24 | 0.25 | ... | ... | ... | 235 | 160 | ... | | 1995 |
| ... | ... | 172 | 856 | ... | ... | 547 | 441 | 106 | Czech Republic | 1990 |
| 71 | ... | 105 | 5 675 | 38 815 | 68 | 517 | 414 | 103 | | 1991 |
| 69 | ... | 94 | 5 617 | 71 165 | 39 | 505 | 405 | 100 | | 1992 |
| 70 | ... | 148 | 4 523 | 93 247 | 38 | 506 | 432 | 74 | | 1993 |
| 67 | ... | 183 | 4 242 | 109 049 | 35 | 491 | 419 | 72 | | 1994 |
| 51 | ... | 212 | 4 292 | 133 352 | 35 | 537 | 466 | 71 | | 1995 |
| 65 | ... | 172 | 4 008 | 169 177 | 33 | 479 | 447 | 32 | | 1996 |
| 66 | ... | 195 | 5 190 | 173 550 | 32 | 469 | 392 | 77 | | 1997 |
| 77 | ... | 112 | ... | 37 406 | 63 | 338 | 121 | 217 | Denmark | 1974 |
| 134 | ... | 70 | 41 768 | 46 790 | 73 | 329 | 122 | ... | | 1977 |
| 113 | ... | 67 | 53 054 | 57 589 | 75 | 357 | 142 | ... | | 1980 |
| 56 | ... | 129 | 51 807 | 87 027 | 66 | 308 | 130 | 178 | | 1986 |
| 75 | 0.09 | ... | 28 534 | 103 875 | 66 | 294 | 140 | 154 | | 1991 |
| 72 | 0.08 | 396 | 28 718 | 111 615 | 61 | 282 | 137 | 145 | | 1992 |
| 75 | 0.23 | 290 | 34 372 | 121 855 | 65 | 279 | 134 | 145 | | 1993 |
| 77 | 0.09 | ... | 38 544 | 109 097 | 72 | 285 | 133 | 152 | | 1994 |
| 81 | 0.17 | 535 | 40 901 | 125 062 | 65 | 290 | 133 | 157 | | 1995 |
| 71 | 0.11 | ... | 48 137 | 136 798 | 61 | 301 | 143 | 158 | | 1996 |
| 82 | 0.14 | ... | 46 732 | 144 123 | 62 | 309 | 149 | 160 | | 1997 |
| ... | ... | ... | 66 | ... | ... | 562 | 380 | 182 | Estonia | 1990 |
| 47 | ... | 11 | 66 | ... | ... | 636 | 432 | 204 | | 1991 |
| 49 | ... | 6.35 | 863 | 6 193 | 49 | 620 | 413 | 207 | | 1992 |
| 61 | ... | 29 | 69 | ... | ... | 664 | 435 | 229 | | 1993 |
| 49 | ... | 20 | 120 | ... | ... | 671 | 519 | 152 | | 1994 |
| 49 | ... | 15 | 2 120 | 31 444 | 51 | 587 | 443 | 144 | | 1995 |
| 48 | ... | 22 | ... | ... | ... | 541 | 471 | 70 | | 1996 |
| 40 | ... | 23 | ... | ... | ... | 518 | 428 | 90 | | 1997 |
| 2.8 | ... | 3.03 | ... | 836 | 61 | 8 | 3 | ... | Faeroe Islands | 1974 |
| 1.8 | ... | 12 | 29 | 2 000 | 72 | 10 | 6 | ... | | 1982 |
| 1.8 | ... | 12 | 29 | 2 000 | 72 | 10 | 6 | ... | | 1983 |
| ... | ... | 10 | ... | ... | ... | ... | ... | ... | | 1985 |
| ... | ... | 27 | ... | ... | ... | ... | ... | ... | | 1990 |
| ... | ... | 32 | ... | ... | ... | ... | ... | ... | | 1992 |
| ... | ... | 27 | ... | ... | ... | ... | ... | ... | | 1993 |
| 84 | 66 | 755 | ... | (5) 8 362 | ... | 477 | 205 | 272 | Federal Republic | 1992 |
| 99 | 2.54 | 515 | 13 263 | (5) 133 | ... | 448 | 169 | 279 | of Yugoslavia | 1995 |
| 37 | ... | 175 | ... | 5 138 | 72 | 161 | 69 | ... | Finland | 1974 |
| 40 | (25) 15 | 293 | 11 110 | 8 976 | 76 | 171 | 69 | ... | | 1977 |
| 34 | (26) 7.21 | 314 | ... | 7 294 | 77 | 117 | 55 | ... | | 1980 |
| 57 | 174 | 406 | 21 877 | 20 534 | 66 | 180 | 80 | ... | | 1986 |
| 48 | ... | 2.19 | 4 408 | 35 090 | 70 | 173 | 70 | 103 | | 1991 |
| 46 | 54 | 1.96 | 5 359 | 40 794 | 69 | 195 | 71 | 124 | | 1992 |
| 44 | ... | 2.98 | 2 832 | 44 855 | 64 | 212 | 82 | 130 | | 1993 |

| Country / Pays / País | Year / Année / Año | Administrative unit / Unités administratives / Unidades administrativas | Service points / Points de service / Puntos de servicio | Collections / Collections / Fondos | | | | | Registered users (000) / Usagers inscrits (000) / Usuarios inscritos (000) |
|---|---|---|---|---|---|---|---|---|---|
| | | | | Books/Livres/Libros | | Microforms / Microcopies / Microcopias | Audio-visual documents (000) / Matériels audio-visuels (000) / Materiales audio-visuales (000) | Other library materials (000) / Autres matériels de bibliothèque (000) / Otros materiales de biblioteca (000) | |
| | | | | Number of volumes (000) / Nombre de volumes (000) / Número de volúmenes (000) | Metres of shelving / Mètres de rayonnage / Metros de estantes | | | | |
| Finland (cont) | 1994 | 1 | 1 | 2 289 | ... | 478 000 | 84 | ... | (24) 251 |
| | 1995 | 1 | 1 | 2 317 | 59 550 | 489 946 | 89 | (3) 1.80 | (24) 550 |
| | 1996 | 1 | 1 | 2 066 | ... | 510 000 | 96 | ... | (24) 536 |
| | 1997 | 1 | 1 | 2 094 | ... | 524 000 | 101 | ... | (24) 501 |
| France | 1971 | 1 | 7 | 7 500 | 110 000 | ... | ... | ... | ... |
| | 1981 | 1 | 8 | 10 000 | 700 000 | ... | 400 | ... | ... |
| | 1990 | 1 | 1 | 12 350 | 182 561 | 1 337 207 | *800 | 3 639 | (27) 42 |
| | 1991 | 1 | 2 | 11 572 | ... | ... | ... | ... | (24) 989 |
| | 1992 | 1 | 2 | 11 684 | ... | ... | 1 100 | 4 300 | (24) 960 |
| | 1993 | 1 | 2 | 12 393 | ... | ... | ... | ... | (24) 1 073 |
| | 1994 | 1 | 2 | 12 544 | ... | ... | ... | ... | (24) 1 169 |
| | 1995 | 1 | 5 | 13 000 | ... | 1 400 000 | 1 511 | ... | (24) 1 272 |
| | 1996 | 1 | 2 | 12 652 | ... | ... | ... | ... | (24) 1 372 |
| | 1997 | 1 | 2 | 12 509 | ... | ... | ... | ... | (24) 1 370 |
| Germany | 1991 | (28) 9 | 13 | 28 091 | ... | ... | ... | ... | (24) 1 441 |
| | 1992 | (28) 8 | 13 | 29 438 | ... | 4 387 180 | 625 | 13 229 | (24) 1 399 |
| | 1993 | (28) 9 | 13 | 30 083 | ... | ... | ... | ... | (24) 1 563 |
| | 1994 | (28) 9 | 14 | 30 451 | ... | ... | ... | ... | (24) 1 703 |
| | 1995 | (28) 8 | 14 | 32 281 | ... | 5 617 018 | 803 | 13 912 | (24) 1 853 |
| | 1996 | (28) 9 | 14 | 30 713 | ... | ... | ... | ... | (24) 1 999 |
| | 1997 | (28) 9 | 14 | 30 366 | ... | ... | ... | ... | (24) 1 996 |
| Greece | 1986 | 1 | 1 | 2 500 | 33 000 | ... | ... | 6.00 | ... |
| | 1990 | 1 | 2 | 2 633 | 36 500 | ... | 5.00 | (3) 6.00 | ... |
| | 1991 | 1 | 2 | 2 683 | ... | ... | ... | ... | (24) 456 |
| | 1992 | 1 | 2 | 2 637 | ... | ... | ... | ... | (24) 481 |
| | 1993 | 1 | 2 | 2 591 | ... | ... | ... | ... | (24) 506 |
| | 1994 | 1 | 2 | 2 545 | ... | ... | ... | ... | (24) 531 |
| | 1995 | 1 | 2 | 2 545 | 35 400 | ... | 5.00 | (3) 5.25 | (24) 556 |
| | 1996 | 1 | 2 | 2 453 | ... | ... | ... | ... | (24) 580 |
| | 1997 | 1 | 2 | 2 407 | ... | ... | ... | ... | (24) 605 |
| Hungary | 1976 | 1 | 6 | 2 073 | ... | ... | 2 803 | ... | 13 |
| | 1980 | 1 | 7 | 2 364 | ... | ... | ... | 3 015 | 12 |
| | 1986 | 1 | 4 | 2 525 | ... | ... | ... | 4 115 | 18 |
| | 1990 | 1 | 2 | 2 471 | ... | 229 790 | 29 | 4 149 | 22 |
| | 1991 | 1 | 2 | 2 499 | ... | 233 684 | 30 | 4 196 | 23 |
| | 1992 | 1 | 2 | 2 660 | ... | ... | ... | 4 573 | 25 |
| | 1993 | 1 | 2 | 2 555 | ... | 246 434 | 37 | 4 273 | 25 |
| | 1994 | 1 | 2 | 2 583 | ... | 250 088 | 39 | 4 298 | 30 |
| | 1995 | 1 | 3 | 2 734 | ... | ... | ... | 4 688 | 34 |
| | 1996 | 1 | 3 | 2 606 | ... | 260 983 | 94 | ... | 29 |
| | 1997 | 1 | 3 | 2 771 | ... | 264 499 | 97 | ... | 30 |
| Iceland | 1971 | 1 | 1 | 295 | 6 553 | ... | ... | ... | 0.3 |
| | 1974 | 1 | 1 | 319 | 7 093 | ... | ... | ... | 0.3 |
| | 1985 | 1 | 1 | 380 | ... | ... | ... | ... | ... |
| | 1990 | 1 | 1 | 415 | 8 011 | *40 420 | 27 | 372 | ... |
| | 1991 | 1 | 1 | 423 | ... | ... | ... | ... | ... |
| | 1992 | 1 | 1 | 431 | ... | ... | ... | ... | (24) 4.9 |
| | 1993 | 1 | 3 | 466 | ... | ... | ... | (3) 14 | (24) 4.7 |
| | 1994 | 1 | 3 | 484 | ... | ... | ... | ... | (24) 5.9 |
| | 1995 | 1 | 6 | 750 | 18 000 | ... | 12 | (3) 15 | (24) 6.3 |
| | 1996 | 1 | 6 | 513 | ... | ... | ... | ... | (24) 6.9 |
| | 1997 | 1 | 6 | 521 | ... | ... | ... | ... | (24) 6.9 |
| Ireland | 1974 | 1 | 2 | 500 | 15 500 | ... | ... | ... | ... |
| | 1980 | 1 | 2 | 750 | 14 100 | 9 200 | ... | 20 | ... |
| | 1986 | 1 | 2 | 808 | 14 530 | 15 600 | ... | 24 | ... |
| | 1990 | 1 | 2 | 750 | 14 530 | 85 699 | 97 | 360 | (27) 28 |
| | 1991 | 1 | 2 | 700 | ... | ... | ... | ... | (24) 64 |
| | 1992 | 1 | 2 | 707 | ... | ... | ... | ... | (24) 62 |
| | 1993 | 1 | 2 | 750 | ... | ... | ... | ... | (24) 69 |
| | 1994 | 1 | 2 | 759 | ... | ... | ... | ... | (24) 75 |
| | 1995 | 1 | 2 | 735 | ... | ... | ... | ... | (24) 82 |
| | 1996 | 1 | 2 | 766 | ... | ... | ... | ... | (24) 88 |
| | 1997 | 1 | 2 | 757 | ... | ... | ... | ... | (24) 88 |

| Volumes (000) | Other materials (000) | Loans to users (000) | Inter-Library loans | Total (000) | Staff (%) | Total | Holding a diploma | Trained on the job | Country | Year |
|---|---|---|---|---|---|---|---|---|---|---|
| 37 | ... | 8.00 | 4 084 | 43 222 | 60 | 190 | 155 | 35 | Finland (cont) | 1994 |
| 37 | 26 | 8.51 | 4 313 | 59 051 | 46 | 195 | 147 | 48 | | 1995 |
| 34 | ... | 8.00 | 4 623 | 63 709 | 47 | 197 | 151 | 46 | | 1996 |
| 35 | ... | 8.00 | 4 315 | 66 606 | 45 | 192 | 146 | 46 | | 1997 |
| 79 | ... | ... | ... | 35 008 | 64 | 988 | 219 | 34 | France | 1971 |
| 60 | (23) 4.00 | ... | ... | 200 000 | ... | 1 300 | 300 | ... | | 1981 |
| ... | 747 | 1 256 | ... | ... | ... | 1 243 | 322 | ... | | 1990 |
| 700 | ... | 1 227 | ... | ... | ... | 1 253 | 347 | 906 | | 1991 |
| 729 | ... | 1 226 | ... | ... | ... | 1 273 | 352 | 921 | | 1992 |
| 760 | ... | 1 256 | ... | ... | ... | 1 279 | 358 | 921 | | 1993 |
| 801 | ... | 1 318 | ... | ... | ... | 1 256 | 372 | 884 | | 1994 |
| 760 | 72 | ... | 20 862 | 765 000 | 56 | 1 846 | 576 | ... | | 1995 |
| 794 | ... | 1 333 | ... | ... | ... | 1 273 | 363 | 910 | | 1996 |
| 795 | ... | 1 298 | ... | ... | ... | 1 254 | 360 | 894 | | 1997 |
| 743 | ... | 3 271 | ... | ... | ... | 3 168 | 1 162 | 2 006 | Germany | 1991 |
| 757 | 593 | 3 068 | 1 024 446 | 277 493 | 55 | 2 509 | ... | ... | | 1992 |
| 807 | ... | 3 347 | ... | ... | ... | 3 239 | 1 199 | 2 040 | | 1993 |
| 850 | ... | 3 511 | ... | ... | ... | 3 204 | 1 246 | 1 958 | | 1994 |
| 856 | 778 | 3 115 | 1 012 505 | 257 519 | 57 | 2 336 | ... | ... | | 1995 |
| 843 | ... | 3 552 | ... | ... | ... | 3 232 | 1 216 | 2 016 | | 1996 |
| 844 | ... | 3 459 | ... | ... | ... | 3 187 | 1 206 | 1 981 | | 1997 |
| 15 | 0.03 | ... | 2 000 | 150 000 | 53 | ... | ... | ... | Greece | 1986 |
| 13 | 0.60 | - | ... | 137 650 | 75 | 75 | 20 | ... | | 1990 |
| 50 | ... | 403 | ... | ... | ... | 385 | 197 | 188 | | 1991 |
| 54 | ... | 416 | ... | ... | ... | 401 | 209 | 192 | | 1992 |
| 58 | ... | 430 | ... | ... | ... | 418 | 222 | 196 | | 1993 |
| 62 | ... | 443 | ... | ... | ... | 436 | 235 | 201 | | 1994 |
| 12 | 0.31 | 0.05 | 50 | 262 000 | 80 | 70 | 4 | 60 | | 1995 |
| 70 | ... | 471 | ... | ... | ... | 469 | 260 | 209 | | 1996 |
| 74 | ... | 484 | ... | ... | ... | 486 | 273 | 213 | | 1997 |
| 48 | (29) 120 | 4.76 | ... | (5) 15 024 | ... | 840 | 231 | 131 | Hungary | 1976 |
| 32 | 87 | 5.48 | ... | (5) 5 828 | ... | 488 | 337 | ... | | 1980 |
| 30 | 126 | 7.49 | ... | (5) 8 819 | ... | 650 | 254 | 58 | | 1986 |
| ... | ... | 142 | 961 | ... | ... | 782 | 428 | 354 | | 1990 |
| 21 | ... | 195 | 938 | ... | ... | 790 | 438 | 352 | | 1991 |
| 21 | ... | ... | 772 | (5) 16 996 | ... | 661 | ... | ... | | 1992 |
| 20 | ... | 123 | 940 | ... | ... | 790 | 442 | 350 | | 1993 |
| 20 | ... | 130 | 724 | ... | ... | 779 | 436 | 343 | | 1994 |
| 20 | 63 | ... | 724 | (5) 24 100 | ... | 809 | ... | 221 | | 1995 |
| 22 | ... | ... | 1 559 | 973 599 | 61 | 577 | 356 | 204 | | 1996 |
| 26 | ... | ... | 1 506 | 1 183 872 | 61 | 540 | 336 | 204 | | 1997 |
| 9.7 | ... | 26 | ... | 11 439 | 58 | 20 | 12 | ... | Iceland | 1971 |
| 6.0 | ... | (30) 26 | ... | 24 482 | 74 | 22 | 6 | 7 | | 1974 |
| ... | ... | 26 | ... | ... | ... | ... | ... | ... | | 1985 |
| 6.9 | 0.05 | ... | ... | 45 977 | 65 | 36 | 25 | 11 | | 1990 |
| ... | ... | ... | ... | 52 864 | 64 | 39 | 27 | 12 | | 1991 |
| 7.3 | 0.28 | ... | ... | 53 841 | 66 | 40 | 26 | 14 | | 1992 |
| 9.1 | ... | 32 | ... | ... | ... | 34 | 27 | 7 | | 1993 |
| 11 | ... | 33 | ... | ... | ... | 35 | 28 | 7 | | 1994 |
| 11 | 0.86 | 78 | 6 099 | 285 | 49 | 85 | 33 | ... | | 1995 |
| 13 | ... | 34 | ... | ... | ... | 38 | 31 | 7 | | 1996 |
| 10 | ... | 33 | ... | ... | ... | 39 | 32 | 7 | | 1997 |
| ... | ... | ... | ... | 126 | 69 | 55 | 1 | 14 | Ireland | 1974 |
| 8.0 | 3.05 | ... | ... | ... | ... | 56 | 7 | 6 | | 1980 |
| 8.0 | 2.75 | ... | ... | 749 | 73 | 49 | 5 | 8 | | 1986 |
| 10 | ... | 120 | ... | ... | 73 | 57 | 15 | ... | | 1990 |
| 22 | ... | 117 | ... | ... | ... | 56 | 15 | 41 | | 1991 |
| 22 | ... | 117 | ... | ... | ... | 57 | 15 | 42 | | 1992 |
| 23 | ... | 120 | ... | ... | ... | 57 | 15 | 42 | | 1993 |
| 25 | ... | 126 | ... | ... | ... | 56 | 16 | 40 | | 1994 |
| 25 | ... | 129 | ... | ... | ... | 57 | 16 | 41 | | 1995 |
| 24 | ... | 127 | ... | ... | ... | 57 | 15 | 42 | | 1996 |
| 25 | ... | 124 | ... | ... | ... | 56 | 15 | 41 | | 1997 |

**National libraries**
**Bibliothèques nationales**
**Bibliotecas nacionales**

| Country / Pays / País | Year / Année / Año | Administrative unit / Unités administratives / Unidades administrativas | Service points / Points de service / Puntos de servicio | Books/Livres/Libros Number of volumes (000) / Nombre de volumes (000) / Número de volúmenes (000) | Books/Livres/Libros Metres of shelving / Mètres de rayonnage / Metros de estantes | Microforms / Microcopies / Microcopias | Audio-visual documents (000) / Matériels audio-visuels (000) / Materiales audio-visuales (000) | Other library materials (000) / Autres matériels de bibliothèque (000) / Otros materiales de biblioteca (000) | Registered users (000) / Usagers inscrits (000) / Usuarios inscritos (000) |
|---|---|---|---|---|---|---|---|---|---|
| Italy | 1977 | 8 | 8 | 11 782 | 272 547 | ... | 39 | 101 | 43 |
| | 1980 | 7 | 7 | 11 391 | 318 000 | 56 321 | 3.44 | 258 | ... |
| | 1983 | 7 | 7 | 13 281 | 303 205 | 52 344 | 3.89 | 251 | ... |
| | 1989 | 2 | 2 | 5 402 | 182 226 | 31 319 | 28 | 0.13 | ... |
| | 1991 | 2 | 4 | 12 141 | ... | ... | ... | ... | 780 |
| | 1992 | 2 | 4 | 12 218 | 175 346 | 142 036 | 4.03 | 3 861 | 603 |
| | 1993 | 2 | 4 | 12 295 | ... | ... | ... | ... | 530 |
| | 1994 | 2 | 4 | 12 419 | ... | ... | ... | (3) 31 | 677 |
| | 1995 | 2 | 4 | 12 561 | 180 964 | ... | ... | 62 | 813 |
| | 1996 | 2 | 4 | 12 676 | ... | ... | ... | (3) 31 | 742 |
| | 1997 | 2 | 4 | 12 804 | ... | ... | ... | (3) 31 | 786 |
| Latvia | 1990 | 1 | 1 | 2 301 | ... | 439 083 | 46 | 1 519 | 20 |
| | 1991 | 1 | 1 | 2 094 | ... | 439 696 | 47 | 2 086 | (19) 58 |
| | 1992 | 1 | 1 | 2 027 | ... | 440 009 | 48 | 2 526 | (19) 52 |
| | 1993 | 1 | 1 | 2 388 | ... | 153 694 | 48 | 1 958 | (19) 63 |
| | 1994 | 1 | 1 | 2 422 | ... | 158 533 | 49 | 2 351 | (19) 68 |
| | 1995 | 1 | 1 | 2 396 | ... | 168 924 | 51 | 2 207 | (19) 68 |
| | 1996 | 1 | 1 | 2 424 | ... | ... | ... | ... | (19) 80 |
| | 1997 | 1 | 1 | 2 414 | ... | ... | ... | ... | (19) 80 |
| Liechtenstein | 1974 | 1 | 1 | ... | 45 000 | ... | ... | ... | 6.0 |
| | 1980 | 1 | 1 | 60 | ... | 110 | ... | ... | 8.0 |
| | 1986 | 1 | 1 | 120 | ... | 100 | ... | 0.10 | 10 |
| | 1990 | 1 | 1 | 150 | 2 896 | 450 | 1.55 | 3.62 | 14 |
| | 1991 | 1 | 1 | 137 | ... | ... | ... | ... | ... |
| | 1992 | 1 | 1 | 160 | ... | 1 300 | 1.47 | ... | 16 |
| | 1993 | 1 | 1 | 150 | ... | ... | ... | ... | ... |
| | 1994 | 1 | 1 | 156 | ... | ... | ... | ... | ... |
| | 1995 | 1 | 2 | 158 | ... | ... | ... | ... | ... |
| | 1996 | 1 | 2 | 165 | ... | ... | ... | ... | ... |
| | 1997 | 1 | 2 | 168 | ... | ... | ... | ... | ... |
| Lithuania | 1990 | 1 | 16 | 3 189 | ... | 77 685 | 48 | ... | 25 |
| | 1991 | 1 | 15 | 3 256 | ... | 79 404 | 49 | ... | 22 |
| | 1992 | 1 | 16 | 3 236 | ... | 84 164 | 50 | ... | 25 |
| | 1993 | 1 | 16 | 7 115 | ... | 86 231 | 51 | 55 | 22 |
| | 1994 | 1 | 17 | 7 105 | ... | 87 796 | 52 | 56 | 24 |
| | 1995 | 1 | 17 | 6 647 | ... | 101 002 | 54 | 56 | 25 |
| | 1996 | 1 | 15 | 6 237 | ... | 103 037 | 56 | 57 | 27 |
| | 1997 | 1 | 15 | 5 878 | ... | 103 244 | 60 | 70 | 23 |
| Luxembourg | 1971 | 1 | 1 | 450 | 15 000 | ... | ... | ... | 5.9 |
| | 1977 | 1 | 1 | 580 | 17 820 | ... | 0.41 | ... | 10 |
| | 1980 | 1 | 1 | 612 | 18 640 | ... | ... | ... | 14 |
| | 1983 | 1 | 1 | 640 | 19 500 | ... | 0.64 | ... | 20 |
| | 1989 | 1 | 1 | 660 | 25 800 | 2 200 | 2.90 | 3.50 | (27) 23 |
| | 1991 | 1 | 1 | 562 | ... | ... | ... | ... | (24) 6.6 |
| | 1992 | 1 | 1 | 567 | ... | ... | ... | ... | (24) 6.4 |
| | 1993 | 1 | 2 | 601 | ... | ... | ... | ... | (24) 7.2 |
| | 1994 | 1 | 2 | 609 | ... | ... | ... | ... | (24) 7.8 |
| | 1995 | 1 | 2 | 590 | ... | ... | ... | ... | (24) 8.5 |
| | 1996 | 1 | 2 | 614 | ... | ... | ... | ... | (24) 9.1 |
| | 1997 | 1 | 2 | 607 | ... | ... | ... | ... | (24) 9.1 |
| Malta | 1974 | 1 | 1 | 338 | 6 500 | ... | ... | ... | ... |
| | 1977 | 1 | 1 | 347 | 6 600 | ... | ... | ... | ... |
| | 1980 | 1 | 1 | 351 | 6 800 | ... | ... | ... | ... |
| | 1983 | 1 | 2 | 355 | 6 950 | ... | ... | ... | ... |
| | 1984 | 1 | 2 | 355 | ... | ... | ... | ... | ... |
| | 1986 | 1 | 2 | 362 | 7 077 | 146 | 0.32 | 8.82 | ... |
| | 1992 | 1 | 1 | 373 | 6 928 | 700 | 0.69 | 8.82 | ... |
| Moldova | 1993 | 1 | 1 | 2 950 | ... | 2 000 | 27 | 172 | 17 |
| | 1995 | 1 | 3 | 2 868 | 49 600 | 4 111 | 27 | 169 | 17 |
| Monaco | 1980 | (9) 1 | 1 | 130 | 3 400 | ... | ... | ... | 1.3 |
| | 1986 | (9) 1 | 2 | 200 | 4 800 | ... | ... | ... | 6.0 |
| | 1992 | (9) 1 | 2 | 285 | 6 350 | ... | 1.31 | (3) 0.04 | 10 |
| | 1995 | (9) 1 | 2 | 300 | 6 500 | ... | 13 | (3) 0.09 | 11 |

| Annual additions / Acquisitions annuelles / Adquisiciones anuales | | Loans to users (000) / Prêts aux usagers (000) / Préstamos a los usuarios (000) | Inter-Library loans / Prêts entre biblio-thèques / Préstamos entre bibliotecas | Current expenditure / Dépenses ordinaires / Gastos ordinarios | | Library employees / Personnel des bibliothèques / Personal de las bibliotecas | | | Country / Pays / País | Year / Année / Año |
|---|---|---|---|---|---|---|---|---|---|---|
| Volumes (000) / Volumes (000) / Volúmenes (000) | Other materials (000) / Autres matériels (000) / Otros materiales (000) | | | Total (000) / Total (000) / Total (000) | Staff (%) / Personnel (%) / Personal (%) | Total / Total / Total | Holding a diploma / Diplômé / Diplomado | Trained on the job / Formé sur le tas / Formado en ejercicio | | |
| 122 | 2.54 | 60 | 5 017 | (31) 2 095 410 | ... | 1 058 | 156 | 902 | Italy | 1977 |
| 141 | 2.30 | 28 | ... | (31) 2 272 121 | ... | 1 338 | 318 | 238 | | 1980 |
| 159 | ... | 56 | ... | (31) 6 756 169 | ... | 1 444 | ... | ... | | 1983 |
| 72 | ... | 25 | ... | ... | ... | 773 | 103 | ... | | 1989 |
| ... | ... | 936 | ... | ... | ... | 774 | ... | ... | | 1991 |
| 98 | 35 | 852 | 2 852 | (31) 6 329 221 | ... | 778 | ... | ... | | 1992 |
| ... | ... | 539 | ... | ... | ... | 737 | ... | ... | | 1993 |
| ... | ... | 937 | ... | 12 798 917 | ... | 677 | ... | ... | | 1994 |
| 186 | 759 | 1 294 | 3 241 | 11 080 875 | ... | 629 | 208 | 421 | | 1995 |
| ... | ... | 1 476 | ... | 11 134 128 | ... | 630 | ... | ... | | 1996 |
| ... | ... | 1 312 | ... | 12 789 476 | ... | 609 | ... | ... | | 1997 |
| ... | ... | ... | 53 | (32) 586 | 32 | 425 | 379 | 46 | Latvia | 1990 |
| 493 | ... | 903 | 32 | (32) 586 | 35 | 455 | 408 | 47 | | 1991 |
| 509 | ... | 911 | ... | (32) 586 | 39 | 452 | 400 | 52 | | 1992 |
| 518 | ... | 967 | 95 | (32) 601 | 58 | 457 | 398 | 59 | | 1993 |
| 565 | ... | 1 033 | 49 | (32) 822 | 44 | 450 | 393 | 57 | | 1994 |
| 581 | ... | 1 070 | ... | 1 012 | 30 | 467 | 397 | ... | | 1995 |
| 565 | ... | 1 041 | ... | ... | ... | 441 | 391 | ... | | 1996 |
| 569 | ... | 1 039 | ... | ... | ... | 423 | ... | ... | | 1997 |
| 2.4 | ... | 24 | ... | 230 | 52 | 5 | 1 | 1 | Liechtenstein | 1974 |
| 3.0 | ... | 24 | ... | 340 | 59 | 2 | 2 | 4 | | 1980 |
| 3.4 | 0.15 | 30 | (15) 2 042 | 643 | 53 | 7 | 2 | 5 | | 1986 |
| 9.1 | ... | 57 | ... | 556 | 48 | 9 | 3 | ... | | 1990 |
| 0.3 | ... | 55 | ... | ... | ... | 7 | 2 | 5 | | 1991 |
| 4.5 | 0.28 | 60 | (15) 2 040 | 1 167 | 44 | 8 | 2 | 6 | | 1992 |
| 0.4 | ... | 57 | ... | ... | ... | 9 | 3 | 6 | | 1993 |
| 0.5 | ... | 60 | ... | ... | ... | 9 | 3 | 6 | | 1994 |
| 0.5 | ... | 62 | ... | ... | ... | 9 | 3 | 6 | | 1995 |
| 0.5 | ... | 61 | ... | ... | ... | 9 | 3 | 6 | | 1996 |
| 0.4 | ... | 59 | ... | ... | ... | 10 | 4 | 6 | | 1997 |
| ... | ... | 31 | 758 | ... | ... | 469 | 329 | 140 | Lithuania | 1990 |
| ... | ... | 25 | 596 | ... | ... | 463 | 323 | 140 | | 1991 |
| ... | ... | 25 | 154 | ... | ... | 599 | 429 | 170 | | 1992 |
| ... | ... | 30 | 45 | 2 625 | 36 | 598 | 429 | 169 | | 1993 |
| 64 | 1.02 | 31 | 62 | 2 806 | 51 | 607 | 432 | 175 | | 1994 |
| 91 | 1.64 | 31 | 150 | 9 935 | 27 | 623 | 407 | 216 | | 1995 |
| 62 | 1.91 | 33 | 406 | 12 177 | 31 | 610 | 375 | 235 | | 1996 |
| 92 | 4.86 | 35 | 1 237 | 13 565 | 33 | 596 | 410 | 100 | | 1997 |
| 1.6 | ... | *7.71 | ... | 7 160 | 68 | 19 | ... | 3 | Luxembourg | 1971 |
| 14 | 0.03 | 70 | 198 | 29 498 | 61 | 30 | 2 | 9 | | 1977 |
| 11 | 0.03 | 83 | (15) 122 | 34 729 | 65 | 30 | 3 | 9 | | 1980 |
| 8.5 | 0.21 | 91 | (15) 132 | 38 230 | 62 | 28 | 5 | 8 | | 1983 |
| ... | ... | 132 | ... | ... | ... | 40 | 32 | ... | | 1989 |
| 4.1 | ... | 121 | ... | ... | ... | 36 | 28 | 8 | | 1991 |
| 4.3 | ... | 121 | ... | ... | ... | 36 | 28 | 8 | | 1992 |
| 4.5 | ... | 124 | ... | ... | ... | 37 | 29 | 8 | | 1993 |
| 4.7 | ... | 130 | ... | ... | ... | 38 | 30 | 8 | | 1994 |
| 4.7 | ... | 134 | ... | ... | ... | 38 | 30 | 8 | | 1995 |
| 4.7 | ... | 132 | ... | ... | ... | 37 | 29 | 8 | | 1996 |
| 4.7 | ... | 128 | ... | ... | ... | 37 | 29 | 8 | | 1997 |
| ... | ... | 13 | ... | 18 | 77 | 18 | ... | 2 | Malta | 1974 |
| (6) 2.1 | ... | ... | 10 | 38 | 77 | 22 | ... | 2 | | 1977 |
| ... | ... | ... | 6 | 71 | 82 | 22 | ... | 2 | | 1980 |
| 1.1 | 0.04 | ... | 32 | 86 | 86 | 26 | 2 | 2 | | 1983 |
| ... | ... | ... | ... | ... | ... | ... | ... | ... | | 1984 |
| 2.4 | 0.39 | ... | 15 | 87 | 86 | 26 | 2 | 2 | | 1986 |
| 1.5 | 0.34 | ... | 45 | 300 | 87 | 43 | 3 | ... | | 1992 |
| 25 | 0.53 | 943 | 8 909 | ... | 81 | 254 | 158 | 57 | Moldova | 1993 |
| 25 | 0.71 | 905 | 8 718 | ... | 35 | 216 | 159 | ... | | 1995 |
| 3.0 | ... | 22 | 31 | 1 000 | 68 | 8 | 2 | 2 | Monaco | 1980 |
| 5.3 | 0.10 | 40 | 70 | 1 900 | 63 | 14 | ... | ... | | 1986 |
| 5.7 | 2.20 | 45 | 115 | ... | ... | 12 | 4 | ... | | 1992 |
| 5.2 | 1.84 | 44 | 103 | ... | ... | 13 | 4 | ... | | 1995 |

**National libraries**
**Bibliothèques nationales**
**Bibliotecas nacionales**

| Country / Pays / País | Year / Année / Año | Administrative unit / Unités administratives / Unidades administrativas | Service points / Points de service / Puntos de servicio | Collections / Collections / Fondos — Books/Livres/Libros: Number of volumes (000) / Nombre de volumes (000) / Número de volúmenes (000) | Books/Livres/Libros: Metres of shelving / Mètres de rayonnage / Metros de estantes | Microforms / Microcopies / Microcopias | Audio-visual documents (000) / Matériels audio-visuels (000) / Materiales audio-visuales (000) | Other library materials (000) / Autres matériels de bibliothèque (000) / Otros materiales de biblioteca (000) | Registered users (000) / Usagers inscrits (000) / Usuarios inscritos (000) |
|---|---|---|---|---|---|---|---|---|---|
| Netherlands | 1976 | 1 | 4 | 1 065 | 28 503 | 9 936 | ... | ... | ... |
| | 1980 | 1 | 4 | 1 600 | 40 400 | 55 300 | ... | ... | ... |
| | 1986 | 1 | 4 | 2 094 | 54 000 | 118 200 | 20 | 16 | ... |
| | 1990 | 1 | 4 | 2 482 | 54 000 | 106 310 | 20 | 16 | 97 |
| | 1991 | 1 | 4 | 2 318 | ... | ... | ... | ... | (24) 260 |
| | 1992 | 1 | 4 | 2 340 | ... | ... | ... | ... | (24) 252 |
| | 1993 | 1 | 4 | 2 482 | ... | ... | ... | ... | (24) 282 |
| | 1994 | 1 | 4 | 2 512 | ... | ... | ... | ... | (24) 307 |
| | 1995 | 1 | 4 | 2 434 | ... | ... | ... | ... | (24) 334 |
| | 1996 | 1 | 4 | 2 534 | ... | ... | ... | ... | (24) 360 |
| | 1997 | 1 | 4 | 2 505 | ... | ... | ... | ... | (24) 360 |
| Norway | 1974 | 1 | 3 | 3 381 | ... | ... | ... | ... | ... |
| | 1986 | 1 | 2 | 2 399 | 53 718 | 57 143 | 202 | 1 603 | ... |
| | 1990 | 1 | 2 | 1 988 | 78 800 | 34 928 | 156 | 1 736 | (27) 73 |
| | 1991 | 2 | 4 | 2 089 | ... | 34 028 | 157 | ... | ... |
| | 1992 | 2 | 3 | 2 186 | 66 377 | 42 830 | 259 | 1 619 | ... |
| | 1993 | 2 | 3 | 2 285 | ... | 41 842 | 296 | ... | ... |
| | 1994 | 2 | 4 | 2 436 | ... | 40 235 | (3) 32 | 40 | ... |
| | 1995 | 2 | 8 | (33) 2 216 | (33) 68 325 | (33) 44 712 | (33) 98 | (33) 1 484 | (33) 12 |
| | 1996 | 2 | 9 | 2 717 | ... | 111 957 | 346 | (3) 42 | ... |
| | 1997 | 2 | 9 | 2 832 | ... | 126 208 | 369 | (3) 42 | ... |
| Poland | 1977 | 1 | 21 | 1 714 | ... | 104 000 | 6.00 | ... | 3.0 |
| | 1980 | 1 | 21 | 1 850 | ... | 123 013 | 10 | ... | 5.6 |
| | 1983 | 1 | 21 | 1 934 | ... | 126 500 | 14 | ... | ... |
| | 1990 | 1 | 21 | 2 229 | ... | 146 135 | 26 | ... | 5.1 |
| | 1991 | 1 | 21 | 2 454 | ... | 148 441 | 28 | 14 | 3.4 |
| | 1992 | 1 | 21 | 2 484 | ... | 150 736 | 30 | 14 | 7.1 |
| | 1993 | 1 | 21 | 2 551 | ... | 154 938 | 33 | 14 | 12 |
| | 1994 | 1 | 23 | 2 593 | ... | 158 400 | 35 | 15 | 15 |
| | 1995 | 1 | 24 | 2 645 | ... | 164 646 | 36 | 15 | 20 |
| | 1996 | 1 | 24 | 2 707 | ... | 172 180 | 42 | 23 | 26 |
| | 1997 | 1 | 24 | 2 758 | ... | 177 039 | 43 | 23 | 33 |
| Portugal | 1977 | 3 | 4 | 3 138 | ... | ... | ... | ... | 232 |
| | 1980 | 3 | 4 | 3 263 | 32 391 | 1 283 | ... | ... | ... |
| | 1986 | 1 | 1 | 2 126 | 30 359 | 4 772 | 0.81 | 99 | (19) 71 |
| | 1990 | 1 | 1 | 2 236 | 44 785 | 8 883 | 1.37 | 84 | ... |
| | 1991 | 1 | 1 | 2 208 | ... | ... | ... | ... | (24) 184 |
| | 1992 | 1 | 1 | 2 500 | 58 576 | 11 146 | 1.37 | 158 | 64 |
| | 1993 | 1 | 1 | 2 530 | ... | ... | ... | ... | 64 |
| | 1994 | 1 | 1 | 2 393 | ... | ... | ... | ... | ... |
| | 1995 | 1 | 1 | 2 578 | 33 335 | 13 179 | 1.31 | 186 | 71 |
| | 1996 | 1 | 1 | 2 414 | ... | ... | ... | ... | (24) 268 |
| | 1997 | 1 | 1 | 2 387 | ... | ... | ... | ... | (24) 254 |
| Romania | 1975 | 2 | ... | 12 390 | ... | ... | ... | ... | ... |
| | 1980 | 2 | ... | 13 376 | ... | ... | ... | ... | 29 |
| | 1985 | 2 | ... | 14 192 | ... | ... | ... | ... | 38 |
| | 1990 | 2 | ... | 16 862 | ... | 407 246 | 97 | 4 670 | 68 |
| | 1991 | 2 | 45 | 15 959 | ... | 409 957 | 99 | 4 839 | 61 |
| | 1992 | 2 | 46 | 17 878 | ... | 415 636 | 103 | 5 247 | 57 |
| | 1993 | 2 | 46 | 20 040 | ... | 315 852 | 106 | 5 063 | 115 |
| | 1994 | 2 | 49 | 20 040 | ... | 318 452 | 108 | 5 178 | 115 |
| | 1995 | 2 | 51 | 18 860 | 154 728 | 538 363 | 699 | 1 612 | 318 |
| | 1996 | 5 | 48 | 18 559 | ... | ... | ... | ... | (24) 702 |
| | 1997 | 5 | 48 | 18 477 | ... | ... | ... | ... | (24) 702 |
| Russian Federation | 1993 | 2 | 2 | 68 271 | ... | ... | ... | 2 915 | 1 363 |
| | 1995 | 2 | 2 | 72 814 | ... | ... | 381 | (3) 440 | ... |
| San Marino | 1974 | 1 | 1 | 44 | 800 | ... | ... | ... | 0.1 |
| | 1983 | 1 | 1 | 45 | 800 | ... | ... | ... | 0.1 |
| | 1995 | 1 | 1 | 107 | 3 070 | ... | 0.38 | 1.15 | 0.6 |
| Slovakia | 1990 | 1 | 1 | 3 324 | ... | 92 239 | 22 | 1 058 | 3.1 |
| | 1991 | 1 | 1 | 3 363 | ... | 93 279 | 23 | 1 101 | 4.4 |
| | 1992 | 1 | 1 | 3 580 | ... | 95 185 | 24 | 1 202 | 4.8 |
| | 1993 | 1 | 1 | 3 608 | ... | 72 896 | 24 | 1 169 | 7.3 |
| | 1994 | 1 | 1 | 3 634 | ... | 74 086 | 25 | 1 205 | 9.7 |
| | 1995 | 1 | 1 | 5 874 | ... | ... | ... | ... | 24 |

| Annual additions / Acquisitions annuelles / Adquisiciones anuales | | Loans to users (000) / Prêts aux usagers (000) / Préstamos a los usuarios (000) | Inter-Library loans / Prêts entre biblio-thèques / Préstamos entre bibliotecas | Current expenditure / Dépenses ordinaires / Gastos ordinarios | | Library employees / Personnel des bibliothèques / Personal de las bibliotecas | | | Country / Pays / País | Year / Année / Año |
| Volumes (000) / Volumes (000) / Volúmenes (000) | Other materials (000) / Autres matériels (000) / Otros materiales (000) | | | Total (000) / Total (000) / Total (000) | Staff (%) / Personnel (%) / Personal (%) | Total / Total / Total | Holding a diploma / Diplômé / Diplomado | Trained on the job / Formé sur le tas / Formado en ejercicio | | |
|---|---|---|---|---|---|---|---|---|---|---|
| 20 | (26) 1.38 | 154 | ... | ... | ... | 162 | 37 | ... | Netherlands | 1976 |
| 48 | 17 | 130 | ... | ... | ... | 182 | ... | ... | | 1980 |
| 90 | 0.60 | 154 | 29 200 | 20 047 | 68 | 269 | 57 | 26 | | 1986 |
| ... | ... | 169 | ... | ... | ... | 219 | 86 | ... | | 1990 |
| 88 | ... | 165 | ... | ... | ... | 214 | 83 | 131 | | 1991 |
| 92 | ... | 165 | ... | ... | ... | 217 | 84 | 133 | | 1992 |
| 96 | ... | 169 | ... | ... | ... | 219 | 86 | 133 | | 1993 |
| 101 | ... | 178 | ... | ... | ... | 217 | 89 | 128 | | 1994 |
| 100 | ... | 182 | ... | ... | ... | 219 | 89 | 130 | | 1995 |
| 100 | ... | 180 | ... | ... | ... | 218 | 87 | 131 | | 1996 |
| 100 | ... | 175 | ... | ... | ... | 215 | 86 | 129 | | 1997 |
| 88 | ... | ... | ... | ... | ... | 321 | 209 | 112 | Norway | 1974 |
| 93 | 292 | 78 | 22 837 | (31) 7 490 | ... | 176 | 104 | 72 | | 1986 |
| 44 | ... | 119 | ... | ... | 88 | 138 | 66 | ... | | 1990 |
| 71 | ... | ... | ... | ... | ... | 146 | ... | ... | | 1991 |
| 98 | 171 | 95 | 54 973 | (5) 93 409 | 53 | 250 | ... | ... | | 1992 |
| 101 | ... | 123 | ... | ... | ... | 254 | ... | ... | | 1993 |
| 131 | ... | ... | 7 662 | (5) 113 966 | ... | 271 | 127 | 144 | | 1994 |
| (33) 45 | (33) 48 | (33) 146 | (33) 31 208 | (5) *112 700 | ... | (33) 137 | (33) 66 | 71 | | 1995 |
| 154 | ... | ... | 52 245 | 111 354 | ... | 320 | 166 | 155 | | 1996 |
| 115 | ... | ... | 63 171 | 131 123 | ... | 334 | 174 | 161 | | 1997 |
| ... | ... | 16 | ... | (31) 6 232 | ... | ... | ... | ... | Poland | 1977 |
| 40 | ... | 19 | ... | (31) 11 007 | ... | 450 | 96 | ... | | 1980 |
| 45 | 67 | 17 | ... | ... | ... | 754 | ... | ... | | 1983 |
| ... | ... | ... | 4 038 | ... | ... | 439 | 103 | 336 | | 1990 |
| 45 | 62 | 46 | 2 057 | ... | ... | 881 | 371 | 510 | | 1991 |
| 56 | ... | 80 | 2 869 | ... | ... | 880 | 380 | 500 | | 1992 |
| 57 | ... | 72 | 2 579 | ... | ... | 849 | 379 | 470 | | 1993 |
| 62 | ... | 95 | 3 026 | ... | ... | 925 | 462 | 463 | | 1994 |
| 69 | 54 | 97 | 3 344 | ... | ... | 992 | 408 | 584 | | 1995 |
| 62 | ... | 101 | 3 616 | 10 918 | 78 | 1 020 | 416 | 604 | | 1996 |
| 63 | ... | 121 | 4 498 | 12 771 | 84 | 994 | 405 | 589 | | 1997 |
| 24 | ... | (34) 493 | ... | (7) 45 531 | ... | 215 | ... | ... | Portugal | 1977 |
| 18 | ... | ... | ... | ... | ... | 237 | 41 | ... | | 1980 |
| 13 | 4.43 | ... | ... | 264 172 | 71 | 261 | 31 | 50 | | 1986 |
| 16 | 3.06 | ... | ... | 616 688 | 70 | 276 | 28 | 53 | | 1990 |
| 28 | ... | 247 | ... | ... | ... | 251 | 30 | ... | | 1991 |
| 39 | 3.18 | 247 | 205 | 1 605 013 | 43 | 363 | 39 | ... | | 1992 |
| 29 | ... | 253 | ... | 1 282 411 | 56 | 317 | 35 | ... | | 1993 |
| 32 | ... | 265 | ... | ... | ... | 248 | 32 | ... | | 1994 |
| 23 | 1.31 | 272 | 485 | 1 338 273 | 56 | 323 | 31 | 53 | | 1995 |
| 31 | ... | 268 | ... | ... | ... | 253 | ... | ... | | 1996 |
| 32 | ... | 261 | ... | ... | ... | 250 | ... | ... | | 1997 |
| ... | ... | 1 395 | ... | ... | ... | ... | ... | ... | Romania | 1975 |
| ... | ... | ... | ... | ... | ... | ... | ... | ... | | 1980 |
| ... | ... | 1 433 | ... | ... | ... | ... | ... | ... | | 1985 |
| ... | ... | ... | 4 193 | ... | ... | 1 151 | 753 | 398 | | 1990 |
| 163 | ... | 1 269 | 4 375 | ... | ... | 1 171 | 761 | 410 | | 1991 |
| 169 | ... | 1 630 | 3 053 | ... | ... | 1 215 | 758 | 457 | | 1992 |
| 172 | ... | 1 729 | 3 185 | ... | ... | 1 273 | 757 | 516 | | 1993 |
| 187 | ... | 1 847 | 2 589 | 7 438 | 45 | 1 257 | 749 | 508 | | 1994 |
| 192 | 20 | 1 913 | 19 743 | ... | ... | 727 | 520 | ... | | 1995 |
| 187 | ... | 1 861 | ... | ... | ... | 942 | 501 | 441 | | 1996 |
| 188 | ... | 1 858 | ... | ... | ... | 913 | 478 | 435 | | 1997 |
| 1 003 | 22 | 20 237 | 134 080 | 8 119 085 | 20 | 3 510 | 1 641 | ... | Russian Federation | 1993 |
| 722 | 100 | 21 247 | 108 000 | 88 800 700 | 21 | 3 281 | 2 657 | ... | | 1995 |
| 0.1 | ... | 0.02 | ... | 20 900 | 98 | 5 | ... | 1 | San Marino | 1974 |
| 0.1 | ... | 0.02 | ... | ... | ... | 5 | ... | 1 | | 1983 |
| ... | ... | 0.31 | 10 | 741 000 | 79 | 14 | 2 | 2 | | 1995 |
| ... | ... | 0.29 | 4 172 | ... | ... | 192 | 183 | 9 | Slovakia | 1990 |
| ... | ... | 0.12 | 3 774 | ... | ... | 196 | 187 | 9 | | 1991 |
| ... | ... | 0.12 | 3 662 | ... | ... | 188 | 180 | 8 | | 1992 |
| ... | ... | 0.69 | 4 854 | ... | ... | 186 | 179 | 7 | | 1993 |
| ... | ... | 11 | 3 639 | ... | ... | 169 | 140 | 29 | | 1994 |
| 35 | ... | 143 | 4 971 | 84 924 | 30 | 362 | 292 | 70 | | 1995 |

| Country / Pays / País | Year / Année / Año | Administrative unit / Unités administratives / Unidades administrativas | Service points / Points de service / Puntos de servicio | Collections / Collections / Fondos | | | | | Registered users (000) / Usagers inscrits (000) / Usuarios inscritos (000) |
|---|---|---|---|---|---|---|---|---|---|
| | | | | Books/Livres/Libros | | Microforms / Microcopies / Microcopias | Audio-visual documents (000) / Matériels audio-visuels (000) / Materiales audio-visuales (000) | Other library materials (000) / Autres matériels de bibliothèque (000) / Otros materiales de biblioteca (000) | |
| | | | | Number of volumes (000) / Nombre de volumes (000) / Número de volúmenes (000) | Metres of shelving / Mètres de rayonnage / Metros de estantes | | | | |
| Slovakia (cont) | 1996 | 1 | 1 | 5 909 | ... | ... | ... | ... | 31 |
| | 1997 | 1 | 1 | 5 944 | ... | ... | ... | ... | 32 |
| Slovenia | 1990 | 1 | 1 | 1 189 | ... | 33 655 | 84 | 214 | 13 |
| | 1991 | 1 | 1 | 1 213 | ... | 34 028 | 84 | 214 | 13 |
| | 1992 | 1 | 1 | 1 749 | 22 300 | ... | 84 | 211 | 9.3 |
| | 1993 | 1 | 1 | 1 309 | ... | 26 576 | 86 | 212 | 13 |
| | 1994 | 1 | 1 | 1 246 | ... | 26 983 | 88 | 215 | 13 |
| | 1995 | 1 | 1 | 1 811 | 23 705 | 550 | 87 | 239 | 11 |
| | 1996 | 1 | 1 | 1 488 | ... | ... | ... | ... | (24) 59 |
| | 1997 | 1 | 1 | 1 481 | ... | ... | ... | ... | (24) 59 |
| Spain | 1974 | 2 | 3 | 3 069 | 94 312 | | | | 6.4 |
| | 1980 | 2 | 3 | 3 507 | 126 426 | 4 408 | ... | ... | 45 |
| | 1986 | 1 | 9 | 2 427 | ... | 182 180 | 208 | 2 099 | ... |
| | 1990 | 1 | 2 | 3 500 | *71 148 | 23 818 | 258 | 1 280 | (27) 56 |
| | 1991 | 1 | 2 | 3 518 | ... | ... | ... | ... | (24) 693 |
| | 1992 | 1 | 2 | 3 552 | ... | ... | ... | ... | (24) 673 |
| | 1993 | 1 | 2 | 3 767 | ... | ... | ... | ... | (24) 752 |
| | 1994 | 1 | 3 | 5 372 | ... | 105 900 | 283 | 29 | (24) 819 |
| | 1995 | 1 | 2 | 3 694 | ... | ... | ... | ... | (24) 891 |
| | 1996 | 1 | 2 | 6 687 | ... | 117 072 | 302 | 30 | ... |
| | 1997 | 1 | 2 | 3 803 | ... | ... | ... | ... | (24) 960 |
| Sweden | 1975 | 1 | 1 | ... | 47 375 | ... | ... | ... | ... |
| | 1980 | 1 | 1 | 2 000 | 59 453 | 48 997 | ... | ... | 2.0 |
| | 1986 | 1 | 4 | 2 928 | 83 600 | 140 537 | ... | 79 | 3.1 |
| | 1990 | 1 | 4 | *3 677 | 91 915 | 170 270 | 1.00 | ... | ... |
| | 1991 | 1 | 4 | 3 125 | ... | 179 443 | 1.81 | ... | ... |
| | 1992 | 1 | 4 | 3 168 | 79 208 | 187 717 | 2.31 | 1 500 | ... |
| | 1993 | 1 | 4 | 3 212 | ... | 195 634 | 2.88 | ... | ... |
| | 1994 | 1 | 4 | 3 299 | ... | 199 930 | 3.19 | ... | ... |
| | 1995 | 1 | 4 | 3 335 | ... | 205 931 | 3.44 | ... | ... |
| | 1996 | 1 | 4 | 3 355 | ... | 217 258 | 3.73 | ... | ... |
| | 1997 | 1 | 3 | 3 571 | ... | 224 287 | 3.82 | ... | ... |
| Switzerland | 1977 | 1 | 1 | 1 182 | 26 800 | 142 | 8.37 | 228 | 17 |
| | 1980 | 1 | 1 | 1 045 | 29 870 | 4 500 | 201 | 198 | 14 |
| | 1986 | 1 | 1 | 1 300 | 37 000 | ... | 257 | 108 | 12 |
| | 1990 | 1 | 1 | 2 550 | 40 469 | 6 947 | 320 | 2 244 | (27) 7.6 |
| | 1991 | 1 | 1 | 2 445 | ... | ... | ... | ... | 129 |
| | 1992 | 1 | 1 | 2 653 | ... | 7 350 | 330 | 0.08 | (24) 123 |
| | 1993 | 1 | 1 | 2 669 | ... | ... | ... | ... | (24) 141 |
| | 1994 | 1 | 1 | 2 773 | ... | ... | ... | ... | (24) 154 |
| | 1995 | 1 | 1 | 2 852 | ... | 7 782 | 336 | 0.42 | (24) 165 |
| | 1996 | 1 | 2 | 2 936 | ... | ... | ... | ... | (24) 181 |
| | 1997 | 1 | 2 | 2 981 | ... | ... | ... | ... | (24) 181 |
| The Former Yugoslav Rep. of Macedonia | 1992 | 1 | 1 | 2 169 | 61 655 | 13 571 | 16 | 554 | 153 |
| | 1995 | 1 | 1 | 2 317 | 65 811 | ... | 242 | 392 | 158 |
| Ukraine | 1995 | 1 | 5 | 3 932 | 64 591 | 1 187 | 0.07 | 34 | 41 |
| United Kingdom | 1977 | 1 | 8 | ... | ... | 3 208 000 | ... | 19 000 | ... |
| | 1980 | 3 | 17 | 20 550 | ... | 5 967 000 | ... | 8 860 | ... |
| | 1990 | 3 | 23 | 27 500 | 790 000 | *6 600 000 | 1 086 | 15 043 | (36) 83 |
| | 1991 | 3 | 17 | 24 300 | ... | 6 700 000 | 1 100 | 4 300 | 56 |
| | 1992 | 3 | 17 | 24 800 | ... | 6 800 000 | 1 200 | 4 300 | 53 |
| | 1993 | 3 | 17 | 25 300 | ... | 6 800 000 | 1 200 | 4 300 | 54 |
| | 1994 | 3 | 18 | 25 500 | ... | 6 900 000 | 1 300 | 4 300 | 55 |
| | 1995 | 3 | 19 | 25 700 | ... | 7 100 000 | 1 300 | 4 300 | 56 |
| | 1996 | 3 | 19 | 26 400 | ... | 7 200 000 | 1 300 | 4 300 | 57 |
| | 1997 | 3 | 18 | 25 333 | ... | ... | ... | ... | *58 |
| **Oceania** | | | | | | | | | |
| Australia | 1974 | 1 | 1 | 1 400 | ... | ... | ... | ... | ... |
| | 1980 | 1 | 1 | 2 074 | ... | 1 245 000 | 1 849 | 55 | ... |
| | 1986 | 1 | 1 | 2 439 | ... | 1 710 000 | 1 513 | 127 | ... |
| | 1990 | 1 | 1 | 4 534 | ... | ... | ... | ... | ... |
| | 1991 | 1 | 1 | 4 625 | ... | ... | ... | ... | ... |
| | 1995 | 1 | 1 | 2 441 | ... | ... | 1 984 | 178 | ... |

| Volumes (000) / Volúmenes (000) | Other materials (000) / Autres matériels (000) / Otros materiales (000) | Loans to users (000) / Prêts aux usagers (000) / Préstamos a los usuarios (000) | Inter-Library loans / Prêts entre bibliothèques / Préstamos entre bibliotecas | Total (000) / Total (000) | Staff (%) / Personnel (%) / Personal (%) | Total | Holding a diploma / Diplômé / Diplomado | Trained on the job / Formé sur le tas / Formado en ejercicio | Country / Pays / País | Year / Année / Año |
|---|---|---|---|---|---|---|---|---|---|---|
| 36 | ... | 27 | 4 464 | 90 352 | 30 | 361 | 309 | 52 | Slovakia (cont) | 1996 |
| 38 | ... | 18 | 4 934 | 95 076 | 33 | 347 | 176 | 171 | | 1997 |
| ... | ... | 183 | 3 375 | ... | ... | 177 | 62 | 115 | Slovenia | 1990 |
| ... | ... | 190 | 3 375 | ... | ... | 178 | 63 | 115 | | 1991 |
| 44 | 19 | 241 | 6 345 | ... | ... | 114 | 3 | 75 | | 1992 |
| ... | ... | 193 | 3 375 | ... | ... | 179 | 64 | 115 | | 1993 |
| ... | 12 | 212 | 3 238 | ... | ... | 190 | 64 | 126 | | 1994 |
| 21 | 26 | 236 | 8 047 | ... | ... | ... | ... | ... | | 1995 |
| 35 | ... | 238 | ... | ... | ... | 106 | 3 | 103 | | 1996 |
| 36 | ... | 237 | ... | ... | ... | 105 | 3 | 102 | | 1997 |
| (6) 38 | ... | 51 | ... | 22 046 | 5 | 213 | 61 | 152 | Spain | 1974 |
| 56 | ... | 113 | 1 238 | 269 120 | 80 | 507 | ... | ... | | 1980 |
| 50 | ... | 109 | 1 243 | ... | ... | 591 | 63 | 386 | | 1986 |
| ... | 12 | *1 304 | ... | ... | ... | 604 | 320 | ... | | 1990 |
| 158 | ... | 1 136 | ... | ... | ... | 612 | 288 | 324 | | 1991 |
| 165 | ... | 1 135 | ... | ... | ... | 621 | 292 | 329 | | 1992 |
| 172 | ... | 1 163 | ... | ... | ... | 626 | 297 | 329 | | 1993 |
| 172 | ... | 314 | 4 025 | 2 978 900 | 64 | 570 | 220 | 350 | | 1994 |
| 180 | ... | 1 252 | ... | ... | ... | 631 | 309 | 322 | | 1995 |
| 197 | 14 | ... | 7 653 | 2 822 222 | 61 | 525 | 209 | 316 | | 1996 |
| 180 | ... | 1 202 | ... | ... | ... | 619 | 299 | 320 | | 1997 |
| 38 | ... | 111 | 3 389 | (5) 1 849 | ... | (35) 210 | 30 | ... | Sweden | 1975 |
| 291 | ... | 84 | 5 200 | 25 194 | 52 | 163 | 34 | ... | | 1980 |
| 328 | 8.94 | 109 | 10 093 | 41 262 | 61 | 189 | 52 | ... | | 1986 |
| ... | ... | 118 | ... | 91 753 | 50 | 209 | 138 | 71 | | 1990 |
| 42 | ... | 112 | 9 387 | 98 315 | 48 | 243 | 139 | 104 | | 1991 |
| 43 | 26 | 148 | 8 314 | 102 459 | 49 | 244 | 143 | 101 | | 1992 |
| 44 | ... | 176 | 8 801 | 100 299 | 51 | 236 | 142 | 94 | | 1993 |
| 87 | ... | 182 | 9 008 | 98 118 | 53 | 234 | 137 | 97 | | 1994 |
| 36 | ... | 163 | 8 552 | 94 508 | 58 | 233 | 135 | 98 | | 1995 |
| 13 | ... | 168 | 10 688 | 102 518 | 63 | 252 | 143 | 109 | | 1996 |
| 216 | ... | 135 | 8 147 | 163 663 | 44 | 265 | 152 | 113 | | 1997 |
| 44 | 9.70 | 126 | 11 443 | 5 105 | 79 | 83 | 21 | 6 | Switzerland | 1977 |
| 45 | 12 | 123 | 12 958 | 5 963 | 76 | 83 | 21 | 7 | | 1980 |
| 53 | 6.08 | 102 | 62 500 | 7 491 | 80 | 79 | 19 | ... | | 1986 |
| 52 | 4.19 | 100 | ... | ... | ... | 78 | 21 | ... | | 1990 |
| 42 | ... | 94 | ... | ... | ... | 60 | 15 | 45 | | 1991 |
| 52 | 5.55 | 98 | 11 226 | 11 963 | 70 | 71 | 18 | ... | | 1992 |
| 55 | ... | 97 | ... | ... | ... | 76 | 19 | 57 | | 1993 |
| 67 | ... | 102 | ... | ... | ... | 77 | 20 | 57 | | 1994 |
| 57 | 2.50 | 87 | 7 532 | 15 465 | 57 | 73 | 15 | ... | | 1995 |
| 76 | ... | 104 | ... | ... | ... | 82 | 22 | 60 | | 1996 |
| 61 | ... | 102 | ... | ... | ... | 82 | 22 | 60 | | 1997 |
| 11 | 1.11 | 1.04 | 5 137 | 9 653 | ... | 160 | 123 | 37 | The Former Yugoslav | 1992 |
| 17 | 2.39 | 1.42 | ... | (5) 1 125 | ... | 154 | 110 | 44 | Rep. of Macedonia | 1995 |
| 103 | 0.39 | 3 115 | 33 454 | 2 050 | 32 | 390 | 322 | 28 | Ukraine | 1995 |
| ... | ... | ... | 3 048 800 | 28 153 | 35 | 2 078 | 475 | ... | United Kingdom | 1977 |
| 482 | ... | ... | 2 055 505 | 48 763 | 41 | 2 650 | ... | ... | | 1980 |
| 543 | ... | 2 721 | ... | ... | ... | 2 814 | ... | ... | | 1990 |
| 274 | 44 | 5 419 | 3 396 000 | 107 676 | 45 | 2 747 | 1 115 | 1 632 | | 1991 |
| 287 | 47 | 5 374 | 3 458 000 | 117 117 | 44 | 2 800 | 1 136 | 1 664 | | 1992 |
| 321 | 45 | 5 467 | 3 699 000 | 126 652 | 43 | 2 875 | 1 167 | 1 708 | | 1993 |
| 312 | 43 | 5 796 | (37)3 920 000 | 128 726 | 44 | (36) 2 863 | 1 162 | 1 701 | | 1994 |
| 281 | 57 | 6 011 | 4 121 000 | 136 153 | 43 | 2 897 | 1 223 | 1 674 | | 1995 |
| 290 | 53 | 5 896 | 4 190 000 | 134 651 | 46 | 2 885 | 1 123 | 1 762 | | 1996 |
| 294 | ... | 5 661 | ... | ... | ... | 2 844 | 1 154 | 1 690 | | 1997 |
| | | | | | | | | | **Oceania** | |
| ... | ... | ... | ... | 7 907 | 55 | ... | ... | ... | Australia | 1974 |
| 55 | 299 | 123 | ... | 17 549 | 53 | 625 | 147 | 147 | | 1980 |
| 65 | 159 | 191 | (16) 77 443 | 28 300 | 55 | 665 | 157 | ... | | 1986 |
| ... | ... | ... | ... | ... | ... | ... | ... | ... | | 1990 |
| ... | ... | ... | ... | ... | ... | ... | ... | ... | | 1991 |
| 46 | 8.67 | 297 | 90 867 | 50 106 | 47 | 518 | 163 | ... | | 1995 |

## General note

For general explanations and definitions, please refer to the beginning of this chapter.

## Note générale

Pour les explications et définitions générales, prière de se référer au début de ce chapitre.

## Nota general

Para las explicaciones y definiciones generales, referirse al comienzo de este capítulo.

| Notes | Notes | Notas |
|---|---|---|
| (1) Data refer only to auditory and other library materials. | (1) Les données se réfèrent seulement aux matériels auditifs et autres matériels de bibliothèque. | (1) Los datos se refieren a los materiales auditivos y otros materiales solamente. |
| (2) Data refer only to researchers. | (2) Les données se réfèrent seulement aux chercheurs. | (2) Los datos se refieren solamente a los investigadores. |
| (3) Data refer only to manuscripts. | (3) Les données se réfèrent seulement aux manuscrits. | (3) Los datos se refieren solamente a los manuscritos. |
| (4) Data do not include expenditure on acquisitions. | (4) Les données n'incluent pas les dépenses pour les acquisitions. | (4) Los datos no incluyen los datos para adquisiciones. |
| (5) Data refer only to expenditure on acquisitions. | (5) Les données se réfèrent uniquement aux dépenses pour les acquisitions. | (5) Los datos se refieren solamente a los gastos para las adquisiciones. |
| (6) Data refer to number of titles. | (6) Les données se réfèrent au nombre de titres. | (6) Los datos se refieren al número de títulos. |
| (7) Data refer only to expenditure on employees and the acquisitions. | (7) Les données se réfèrent seulement aux dépenses pour le personnel et les acquisitions. | (7) Los datos se refieren solamente a los gastos de personal y de adquisiciones. |
| (8) Data refer only to the number of research workers. | (8) Les données se réfèrent seulement au nombre de travailleurs chercheurs. | (8) Los datos se refieren al número de trabajadores investigadores solamente. |
| (9) The national library also serves as the public library. | (9) La bibliothèque nationale remplit également la fonction de bibliothèque publique. | (9) La biblioteca nacional también desempeña la función de biblioteca pública. |
| (10) Data refer only to auditory materials. | (10) Les données se réfèrent seulement aux matériels auditifs. | (10) Los datos se refieren a los materiales auditivos solamente. |
| (11) Data refer only to government publications. | (11) Les données se réfèrent seulement aux publications gouvernementales. | (11) Los datos se refieren solamente a las publicaciones gubernamentales. |
| (12) Data refer only to expenditure on employees. | (12) Les données se réfèrent seulement aux dépenses pour le personnel. | (12) Los datos se refieren solamente a los gastos de personal. |
| (13) Data include manuscripts. | (13) Les données incluent les manuscrits. | (13) Los datos incluyen los manuscritos. |
| (14) Data refer to assistants and auxilaries of libraries only. | (14) Les données se réfèrent aux assistants et auxiliaires de bibliothèques seulement. | (14) Los datos se refieren solamente a los asistentes y auxiliares de bibliotecas. |
| (15) Data refer only to inter-library loan transactions on the international level. | (15) Les données se réfèrent seulement aux prêts entre bibliothèques au niveau international. | (15) Los datos se refieren a los préstamos entre bibliotecas a nivel internacional solamente. |
| (16) Data refer only to inter-library loan transactions on the national level. | (16) Les données se réfèrent seulement aux prêts entre bibliothèques au niveau national. | (16) Los datos se refieren a los préstamos entre bibliotecas a nivel nacional solamente. |
| (17) Data refer only to books. | (17) Les données se réfèrent seulement aux livres. | (17) Los datos se refieren a los libros solamente. |
| (18) Data refer only to gramophone records. | (18) Les données se réfèrent aux disques gramophones seulement. | (18) Los datos se refieren a los discos gramófonos solamente. |
| (19) Data refer only to the number of visits to reading rooms. | (19) Les données se réfèrent seulement au nombre de visites dans salles de lectures. | (19) Los datos se refieren al número de visitas a la sala de lectura solamente. |
| (20) Data include 200 files of photographs. | (20) Les données incluent 200 fichiers avec des photographies. | (20) Los datos incluyen 200 ficheros con fotografías. |
| (21) Data also include manuscripts and microforms. | (21) Les données incluent aussi des manuscrits et micropies. | (21) Los datos incluyen también manuscritos y microcopias. |
| (22) Data refer to the number of visits including exhibitions or sight-seeing. | (22) Les données se réfèrent au nombre de visiteurs incluant les expositions et visites touristiques. | (22) Los datos se refieren al número de visitantes incluyendo las exposiciones y las visitas turísticas. |
| (23) Data refer to audio-visual documents only. | (23) Les données se réfèrent au documents audiovisuels seulement. | (23) Los datos se refieren a los documentos audiovisuales solamente. |
| (24) Data refer only to the number of visits to the library. | (24) Les données se réfèrent seulement au nombre de visites de la bibliothèque. | (24) Los datos se refieren solamente al número de visitas de la biblioteca. |
| (25) Data refer only to microforms and audio-visiual documents. | (25) Les données se réfèrent aux micropies et aux documents audiovisuels seulement. | (25) Los datos se refieren a microcopias y documentos audiovisuales solamente. |
| (26) Data refer only to microforms. | (26) Les données se réfèrent aux micropies seulement. | (26) Los datos se refieren a microcopias solamente. |
| (27) Data refer only to the number of readers. | (27) Les données se réfèrent seulement au nombre de lecteurs. | (27) Los datos se refieren solamente al número de lectores. |
| (28) Data include central specialized libraries. | (28) Les données incluent les bibliothèques centrales specialisées. | (28) Los datos incluyen las bibliotecas centrales especializadas. |
| (29) Data do not include microforms. | (29) Les données n'incluent pas les micropies. | (29) Los datos no incluyen las microcopias. |
| (30) Data refer mainly to loans used in reading rooms. | (30) Les données se réfèrent principalement aux prêts utilisés dans les salles de lecture. | (30) Los datos se refieren principalmente a los préstamos utilizados en las salas de lectura. |
| (31) Data do not include expenditure on employees. | (31) Les données n'incluent pas les dépenses pour le personnel. | (31) Los datos no incluyen los gastos de personal. |
| (32) Data are shown in ECUs (European Currency Unit) expressed at 1990 constant prices. | (32) Les données sont montrées en ECUs (monnaie européenne commune) et s'expriment en valeurs constantes de 1990. | (32) Los datos se expresan en ECUs (moneda común europea), en moneda constante de 1990. |
| (33) Data do not include the national library in Rana. | (33) Les données n'incluent pas la bibliothèque nationale à Rana. | (33) Los datos no incluyen la biblioteca nacional en Rana. |
| (34) Data include books used in reading rooms. | (34) Les données se réfèrent aux livres utilisés dans les salles de lecture. | (34) Los datos se refieren a los libros utilizados en las salas de lectura. |
| (35) Library employees at the University Library of Stockholm are included with the staff of the national library. | (35) Le personnel de la bibliothèque de l'Université de Stockholm est inclus avec le personnel de la bibliothèque nationale. | (35) El personal de la biblioteca de la Universidad de Estocolmo está incluido con el personal de la biblioteca nacional. |
| (36) Data do not include the *National Library of Scotland*. . | (36) Les données n'incluent pas la *National Library of Scotland*. | (36) Los datos no incluyen la *National Library of Scotland*. |
| (37) Data refer only to the *British Library Document Supply Center (BLDSC)*. | (37) Les données se réfèrent à la *British Library Document Supply Centre (BLDSC)*. | (37) Los datos se refieren a la *British Library Document Supply Center (BLDSC)*. |

**IV.2**   Public libraries: collections, registered users,
works loaned out, current expenditure, employees

Bibliothèques publiques: collections, usagers inscrits,
documents prêtés au-dehors, dépenses ordinaires, personnel

Bibliotecas públicas: fondos, usuarios inscritos,
documentos prestados al exterior, gastos ordinarios, personal

| Country / Pays / País | Year / Année / Año | Administrative unit / Unités administratives / Unidades administrativas | Service points / Points de service / Puntos de servicio | Collections / Collections / Fondos | | | | | Registered users (000) / Usagers inscrits (000) / Usuarios inscritos (000) |
|---|---|---|---|---|---|---|---|---|---|
| | | | | Books/Livres/Libros | | Microforms / Microcopies / Microcopias | Audio-visual documents (000) / Matériels audio-visuels (000) / Materiales audio-visuales (000) | Other library materials (000) / Autres matériels de bibliothèque (000) / Otros materiales de biblioteca (000) | |
| | | | | Number of volumes (000) / Nombre de volumes (000) / Número de volúmenes (000) | Metres of shelving / Mètres de rayonnage / Metros de estantes | | | | |
| **Africa** | | | | | | | | | |
| Benin | 1986 | 18 | 22 | 38 | 1 047 | - | 1.00 | 0.09 | 1.3 |
| | 1989 | 12 | 12 | 28 | 777 | ... | 0.42 | ... | 0.7 |
| | 1995 | 12 | 12 | 37 | 1 094 | ... | 0.04 | ... | 2.6 |
| Burkina Faso | 1995 | (2) 21 | 21 | ... | 48 | ... | 0.00 | 0.09 | 0.3 |
| Egypt | 1972 | (2) 156 | 156 | 1 029 | ... | ... | ... | ... | ... |
| | 1995 | (2) 187 | 187 | *1 500 | ... | ... | 2.20 | ... | ... |
| Equatorial Guinea | 1971 | 1 | 1 | 17 | 118 | ... | ... | ... | 0.1 |
| | 1992 | 3 | 3 | *20 | ... | ... | ... | ... | ... |
| Gambia | 1974 | (2) 2 | 8 | 25 | 630 | ... | *0.10 | ... | *1.4 |
| | 1980 | (2) 2 | 5 | 67 | 760 | ... | 0.18 | ... | ... |
| | 1992 | (2) 2 | 6 | 94 | ... | ... | 0.22 | ... | ... |
| | 1995 | (2) 2 | *6 | 87 | ... | ... | 0.17 | 0.07 | ... |
| Kenya | 1974 | (2) 3 | 3 | 150 | ... | ... | ... | ... | 25 |
| | 1980 | (2) 2 | 21 | 510 | ... | ... | 0.30 | 3.03 | 98 |
| | 1995 | (2) 2 | 21 | 603 | ... | ... | ... | ... | 227 |
| Malawi | 1992 | (2) 1 | 7 | 237 | 3 000 | ... | ... | ... | 37 |
| Nigeria | 1971 | (2) 75 | 74 | 132 | ... | ... | ... | ... | 151 |
| | 1989 | (2) 12 | 92 | *0 | ... | 42 | 8.56 | 4.98 | 47 |
| | 1992 | (2) 12 | 76 | 611 | ... | 162 | ... | ... | 15 |
| Reunion | 1995 | (6) 18 | 54 | 540 | ... | ... | 21 | ... | ... |
| Senegal | 1987 | 10 | 11 | 15 | 382 | ... | ... | 0.01 | 1.0 |
| | 1995 | 26 | *30 | 7 | ... | ... | 0.03 | 0.01 | 0.5 |
| Togo | 1989 | 26 | 26 | 63 | 600 | ... | 0.00 | 0.02 | 7.7 |
| | 1996 | (8) 23 | 23 | 54 | ... | ... | ... | ... | ... |
| Tunisia | 1980 | 241 | *300 | 875 | 42 649 | ... | ... | ... | 53 |
| | 1989 | 252 | 340 | *1 000 | ... | ... | ... | ... | ... |
| | 1992 | 250 | *340 | 2 493 | ... | ... | 0.01 | ... | ... |

| Annual additions / Acquisitions annuelles / Adquisiciones anuales | | Loans to users (000) / Prêts aux usagers (000) / Préstamos a los usuarios (000) | Current expenditure / Dépenses ordinaires / Gastos ordinarios | | Library employees / Personnel des bibliothèques / Personal de las bibliotecas | | | Population served / Population desservie / Población servida | Country / Pays / País | Year / Année / Año |
|---|---|---|---|---|---|---|---|---|---|---|
| Volumes (000) / Volumes (000) / Volúmenes (000) | Other materials (000) / Autres matériels (000) / Otros materiales (000) | | Total (000) / Total (000) / Total (000) | Staff (%) / Personnel (%) / Personal (%) | Total / Total / Total | Holding a diploma / Diplômé / Diplomado | Trained on the job / Formé sur le tas / Formado en ejercicio | | | |
| | | | | | | | | | **Africa** | |
| 16 | ... | 26 | 87 632 | 11 | 46 | 3 | 5 | 5 | Benin | 1986 |
| 2.0 | 0.42 | 25 | (1) 105 000 | 100 | 31 | 4 | ... | 8 | | 1989 |
| 2.2 | ... | 57 | ... | ... | 26 | 9 | 10 | 10 | | 1995 |
| 0.4 | 0.01 | 1.84 | ... | ... | 23 | 25 | ... | ... | Burkina Faso | 1995 |
| 77 | ... | 6 780 | ... | ... | 520 | ... | ... | 4 | Egypt | 1972 |
| ... | ... | ... | ... | ... | 825 | ... | ... | ... | | 1995 |
| ... | ... | 0.91 | 400 | 75 | 4 | ... | ... | ... | Equatorial Guinea | 1971 |
| ... | ... | ... | (1) 120 | 100 | 3 | ... | ... | ... | | 1992 |
| 2.7 | ... | 21 | 23 | 86 | 14 | 1 | 3 | 7 | Gambia | 1974 |
| 4.5 | ... | 52 | 94 | 73 | 19 | 1 | 3 | 20 | | 1980 |
| 4.9 | ... | ... | 860 | 56 | 98 | 5 | 38 | ... | | 1992 |
| 2.1 | ... | ... | 664 | 54 | 36 | 2 | 16 | ... | | 1995 |
| 8.0 | ... | 22 | 69 | 58 | 45 | 11 | ... | 7 | Kenya | 1974 |
| 61 | 0.01 | 582 | (3) 835 | 28 | (4) 349 | 28 | 50 | ... | | 1980 |
| 26 | ... | 267 | 1 290 | 50 | 720 | 15 | 16 | 6 | | 1995 |
| 18 | ... | 294 | (5) 741 | ... | 96 | 10 | ... | ... | Malawi | 1992 |
| ... | ... | ... | *131 | ... | 458 | 70 | ... | 4 | Nigeria | 1971 |
| 39 | 0.91 | 169 | 6 774 | 78 | 1 597 | 248 | 135 | 4 | | 1989 |
| 25 | ... | 99 | 19 601 | 36 | 1 722 | 121 | 3 | 33 | | 1992 |
| 50 | 3.94 | ... | 34 732 | 84 | ... | ... | 90 | 90 | Reunion | 1995 |
| 1.7 | ... | ... | ... | ... | 11 | 1 | 10 | 30 | Senegal | 1987 |
| 0.6 | 0.02 | 4.18 | ... | ... | 8 | 3 | 5 | 58 | | 1995 |
| 2.0 | ... | 54 | (1) 32 888 | 100 | 26 | 1 | 25 | 5 | Togo | 1989 |
| 3.4 | ... | 138 | ... | ... | 30 | 20 | ... | 25 | | 1996 |
| 104 | ... | 1 113 | 300 | 54 | ... | ... | ... | ... | Tunisia | 1980 |
| 184 | ... | 7 943 | ... | ... | 745 | 70 | 395 | ... | | 1989 |
| 256 | 0.00 | 1 627 | (9) 530 000 | ... | 820 | 122 | 47 | 12 | | 1992 |

| Country<br><br>Pays<br><br>País | Year<br><br>Année<br><br>Año | Administrative<br>unit<br><br>Unités<br>administratives<br><br>Unidades<br>administrativas | Service<br>points<br><br>Points de<br>service<br><br>Puntos de<br>servicio | Collections / Collections / Fondos | | | | | Registered<br>users<br>(000)<br><br>Usagers<br>inscrits<br>(000)<br><br>Usuarios<br>inscritos<br>(000) |
| | | | | Books/Livres/Libros | | Microforms<br><br>Microcopies<br><br>Microcopias | Audio-<br>visual<br>documents<br>(000)<br>Matériels<br>audio-<br>visuels<br>(000)<br>Materiales<br>audio-<br>visuales<br>(000) | Other library<br>materials<br>(000)<br>Autres<br>matériels de<br>bibliothèque<br>(000)<br>Otros<br>materiales<br>de biblioteca<br>(000) | |
| | | | | Number of<br>volumes<br>(000)<br>Nombre de<br>volumes<br>(000)<br>Número de<br>volúmenes<br>(000) | Metres of<br>shelving<br><br>Mètres de<br>rayonnage<br><br>Metros de<br>estantes | | | | |
| Uganda | 1974 | 1 | 19 | 90 | ... | ... | ... | ... | 38 |
| | 1986 | 1 | 18 | *90 | ... | ... | ... | ... | *46 |
| | 1992 | 1 | 17 | 82 | ... | ... | ... | ... | 53 |
| **North America** | | | | | | | | | |
| Canada | 1971 | (2) 732 | 732 | 26 160 | ... | | 1 507 | 1 678 | ... |
| | 1980 | (2) 791 | 2 834 | 45 602 | ... | 1 205 654 | 2 320 | 931 | ... |
| | 1986 | (2) 997 | 3 101 | 56 860 | ... | 928 831 | 2 924 | 3 207 | ... |
| | 1990 | (2) 1 027 | 3 301 | 60 955 | ... | 3 042 677 | | 11 789 | ... |
| | 1995 | (2) 1 045 | 3 672 | 70 077 | ... | | | | ... |
| Greenland | 1974 | 1 | 74 | 93 | ... | ... | ... | ... | ... |
| | 1990 | 1 | *17 | 245 | ... | ... | ... | ... | ... |
| St. Pierre and Miquelon | 1974 | 3 | 3 | 15 | 314 | ... | ... | ... | 3.7 |
| | 1995 | (6) 1 | 1 | *1 | ... | ... | 0.15 | (12) 2.82 | 0.7 |
| **South America** | | | | | | | | | |
| Argentina | 1971 | 1 513 | 2 646 | 8 535 | 284 500 | ... | ... | ... | 7.0 |
| | 1995 | 1 545 | *2 700 | 13 496 | ... | 1 885 591 | 47 | ... | *8.0 |
| Bolivia | 1995 | (2) 200 | 250 | 50 | ... | ... | 1.50 | (12) 0.04 | 80 |
| Chile | 1980 | 161 | 161 | 581 | 10 616 | ... | 0.79 | ... | ... |
| | 1986 | 269 | 269 | 940 | ... | ... | 6.79 | ... | 23 |
| | 1989 | 293 | 293 | 1 054 | 48 263 | ... | 13 | ... | 27 |
| | 1992 | 289 | 289 | 1 121 | ... | ... | 15 | ... | ... |
| French Guiana | 1980 | (6) 1 | 2 | 19 | 406 | ... | ... | ... | 0.7 |
| | 1995 | (6) 1 | 2 | *25 | 11 000 | ... | 0.15 | ... | 0.8 |
| Venezuela | 1980 | 23 | 373 | 977 | 31 315 | ... | 5.98 | 4.87 | 66 |
| | 1987 | 24 | 415 | 2 235 | 55 880 | ... | ... | ... | 32 |
| | 1989 | 24 | 567 | 2 378 | ... | ... | ... | ... | 54 |
| | 1993 | 23 | 672 | 3 459 | ... | ... | ... | ... | ... |
| | 1995 | 23 | 701 | 3 293 | ... | ... | ... | ... | ... |
| **Asia** | | | | | | | | | |
| Armenia | 1994 | (2) 1 293 | *1 300 | 14 344 | ... | ... | ... | ... | 1 054 |
| Azerbaijan | 1992 | (2) 4 650 | *4 700 | 40 087 | ... | ... | 91 | ... | 3 022 |
| | 1995 | (2) 4 647 | *4 700 | 31 969 | ... | ... | ... | ... | 2 815 |
| Brunei Darussalam | 1974 | 2 | 5 | *60 | 160 | ... | ... | ... | ... |
| | 1980 | 1 | 8 | 97 | 2 205 | ... | ... | ... | 6.4 |
| | 1992 | 1 | 5 | 285 | ... | 64 | 12 | ... | 41 |
| China | 1985 | 2 344 | ... | 255 728 | ... | ... | ... | ... | ... |
| | 1990 | 2 527 | 2 527 | 290 640 | 7 721 000 | ... | ... | ... | ... |
| | 1991 | 2 536 | 2 536 | 306 140 | 7 676 000 | ... | ... | ... | ... |
| | 1992 | 2 565 | 2 565 | 311 750 | 7 478 000 | ... | ... | ... | ... |
| | 1993 | 2 579 | 2 579 | 314 100 | 7 970 000 | ... | ... | ... | 7 130 |
| | 1995 | *2 600 | *2 600 | 328 500 | 8 990 000 | ... | ... | ... | 5 400 |
| China, Hong Kong SAR | 1974 | (2)(14) 1 | 10 | 230 | 1 875 | ... | ... | ... | 28 |
| | 1980 | (2)(14) 1 | 13 | 1 030 | ... | 3 659 | 13 | ... | 851 |
| | 1989 | (2)(14) 2 | 53 | 3 774 | ... | 7 509 | 205 | 0.01 | 2 226 |
| | 1992 | (2)(14) 2 | 55 | 4 189 | ... | 11 037 | 233 | 1.07 | 2 647 |
| | 1995 | (2)(14) 2 | 56 | 4 966 | ... | 15 134 | 301 | 1.28 | 1 996 |
| Cyprus | 1971 | 116 | 116 | 253 | 5 040 | ... | ... | ... | ... |
| | 1992 | 116 | 116 | 318 | *5 100 | ... | 6.70 | ... | 43 |
| | 1995 | 117 | 117 | 391 | 13 358 | ... | 4.90 | ... | 19 |
| Georgia | 1992 | (2) 4 048 | 4 048 | 32 319 | ... | ... | ... | ... | *2 500 |
| | 1995 | (2) 3 929 | 3 929 | 31 255 | ... | ... | ... | ... | 2 474 |

| Annual additions / Acquisitions annuelles / Adquisiciones anuales | | Loans to users (000) | Current expenditure / Dépenses ordinaires / Gastos ordinarios | | Library employees / Personnel des bibliothèques / Personal de las bibliotecas | | | Population served | Country | Year |
|---|---|---|---|---|---|---|---|---|---|---|
| Volumes (000) / Volumes (000) / Volúmenes (000) | Other materials (000) / Autres matériels (000) / Otros materiales (000) | Prêts aux usagers (000) / Préstamos a los usuarios (000) | Total (000) / Total (000) / Total (000) | Staff (%) / Personnel (%) / Personal (%) | Total / Total / Total | Holding a diploma / Diplômé / Diplomado | Trained on the job / Formé sur le tas / Formado en ejercicio | Population desservie / Población servida | Pays / País | Année / Año |
| 4.5 | ... | 108 | ... | ... | 80 | 13 | 35 | ... | Uganda | 1974 |
| 7.4 | ... | 125 | ... | ... | 99 | 15 | 11 | 5 | | 1986 |
| 4.2 | ... | 147 | (5) 102 487 | ... | 87 | 16 | 71 | ... | | 1992 |
| | | | | | | | | | **North America** | |
| 1 818 | ... | 96 324 | 62 162 | 60 | (10) 5 269 | 1 156 | ... | ... | Canada | 1971 |
| 3 875 | ... | 126 893 | 253 421 | 63 | ... | ... | ... | ... | | 1980 |
| 3 948 | ... | 167 011 | 464 370 | 63 | 12 152 | 2 089 | ... | 100 | | 1986 |
| 4 800 | ... | 178 389 | 649 101 | 63 | 13 463 | 2 296 | ... | ... | | 1990 |
| ... | ... | 203 204 | 751 107 | 67 | 13 154 | 2 390 | ... | ... | | 1995 |
| 19 | ... | 116 | (11) 2 143 | 37 | 8 | 5 | ... | *96 | Greenland | 1974 |
| ... | ... | 192 | ... | ... | ... | ... | ... | *97 | | 1990 |
| 2.0 | ... | ... | 81 | 62 | 3 | 1 | 2 | 51 | St. Pierre and | 1974 |
| 0.7 | 0.75 | 15 | 797 | 60 | 2 | 1 | 1 | 17 | Miquelon | 1995 |
| | | | | | | | | | **South America** | |
| 7.4 | ... | 4 625 | ... | ... | ... | ... | ... | ... | Argentina | 1971 |
| *9.0 | ... | 8 366 | ... | ... | ... | 642 | 727 | ... | | 1995 |
| 3.5 | 0.20 | 26 | ... | ... | 35 | 6 | ... | ... | Bolivia | 1995 |
| 63 | ... | 4 239 | 51 407 | 73 | 487 | 69 | 4 | 66 | Chile | 1980 |
| 53 | ... | 4 149 | 216 647 | 69 | 808 | 92 | 2 | 55 | | 1986 |
| 42 | 1.59 | 5 224 | 332 309 | 79 | 656 | 90 | 3 | 77 | | 1989 |
| ... | ... | 5 536 | ... | ... | ... | ... | ... | *80 | | 1992 |
| 1.6 | ... | 15 | (13) 66 | ... | 6 | ... | ... | *10 | French Guiana | 1980 |
| 3.7 | 0.01 | 14 | (5) 332 | 64 | 6 | ... | ... | 12 | | 1995 |
| 87 | ... | 2 374 | 13 072 | 44 | 1 102 | 29 | 1 073 | 19 | Venezuela | 1980 |
| 358 | ... | ... | 67 850 | 57 | 2 193 | 202 | 1 178 | 82 | | 1987 |
| 237 | ... | ... | 103 756 | 58 | 2 010 | ... | ... | 74 | | 1989 |
| ... | ... | 21 654 | ... | ... | 2 664 | ... | ... | *25 | | 1993 |
| 164 | 39 | 25 751 | 1 457 275 | 26 | 2 982 | 18 | 2 057 | 40 | | 1995 |
| | | | | | | | | | **Asia** | |
| 144 | ... | ... | ... | ... | 2 970 | 1 418 | ... | ... | Armenia | 1994 |
| 1 365 | ... | 60 146 | ... | ... | 8 357 | ... | ... | ... | Azerbaijan | 1992 |
| ... | ... | ... | ... | ... | 8 435 | 5 466 | ... | 88 | | 1995 |
| 0.7 | ... | ... | 4 | ... | 24 | 4 | 6 | ... | Brunei Darussalam | 1974 |
| 9.1 | ... | 44 | 598 | 78 | 53 | 1 | ... | 67 | | 1980 |
| 23 | 0.67 | 112 | ... | ... | 128 | 19 | 109 | ... | | 1992 |
| 13 425 | ... | 189 416 | 133 933 | 17 | ... | 5 685 | ... | ... | China | 1985 |
| *6 000 | ... | 202 420 | 302 710 | ... | 40 247 | ... | ... | ... | | 1990 |
| 7 710 | ... | 133 250 | ... | ... | 41 000 | ... | ... | ... | | 1991 |
| 9 916 | ... | 126 250 | 411 320 | ... | 43 501 | ... | ... | ... | | 1992 |
| 7 900 | ... | 116 850 | 482 110 | ... | 44 367 | ... | ... | ... | | 1993 |
| 7 650 | ... | 182 980 | 740 800 | ... | ... | ... | ... | ... | | 1995 |
| 18 | ... | 476 | 949 | 84 | 72 | 3 | 9 | *60 | China, Hong Kong SAR | 1974 |
| (15) 111 | 2.51 | 4 096 | 17 200 | 52 | 237 | 1 | 18 | 73 | | 1980 |
| 492 | 34 | 12 860 | 131 070 | 59 | 717 | 50 | ... | 100 | | 1989 |
| 348 | 39 | 14 420 | 206 000 | 58 | 746 | 59 | ... | 100 | | 1992 |
| 601 | 47 | 21 497 | 434 300 | 43 | 806 | 111 | ... | *100 | | 1995 |
| 29 | ... | (16) 33 | 39 | 39 | 114 | 10 | 15 | *20 | Cyprus | 1971 |
| 21 | ... | 77 | (5) 285 | ... | 35 | 13 | 22 | 24 | | 1992 |
| 12 | 0.11 | 122 | 199 | 61 | 46 | 5 | 30 | 44 | | 1995 |
| 1 120 | ... | *900 | ... | ... | 6 320 | 3 450 | 2 870 | *50 | Georgia | 1992 |
| 958 | ... | 48 310 | (5) 26 612 | 60 | 6 234 | 3 398 | 2 836 | 40 | | 1995 |

| Country / Pays / País | Year / Année / Año | Administrative unit / Unités administratives / Unidades administrativas | Service points / Points de service / Puntos de servicio | Collections / Collections / Fondos | | | | | Registered users (000) / Usagers inscrits (000) / Usuarios inscritos (000) |
|---|---|---|---|---|---|---|---|---|---|
| | | | | Books/Livres/Libros | | Microforms / Microcopies / Microcopias | Audio-visual documents (000) / Matériels audio-visuels (000) / Materiales audio-visuales (000) | Other library materials (000) / Autres matériels de bibliothèque (000) / Otros materiales de biblioteca (000) | |
| | | | | Number of volumes (000) / Nombre de volumes (000) / Número de volúmenes (000) | Metres of shelving / Mètres de rayonnage / Metros de estantes | | | | |
| Iran, Islamic Republic of | 1980 | 385 | 385 | 2 161 | 20 000 | ... | 3.00 | ... | ... |
| | 1987 | 507 | 507 | 3 332 | ... | ... | 0.08 | 3.60 | 7 062 |
| | 1995 | 26 | 1 002 | 15 984 | ... | ... | ... | 6.94 | 29 862 |
| Israel | 1985 | 954 | 954 | 12 403 | ... | ... | ... | ... | (18) 938 |
| | 1993 | (2) 271 | 1 180 | 11 242 | ... | ... | 25 | ... | (18) 738 |
| Japan | 1971 | 917 | 1 577 | 29 609 | ... | ... | ... | ... | ... |
| | 1974 | 895 | 1 281 | 38 849 | ... | ... | ... | ... | 3 757 |
| | 1981 | 1 118 | 1 437 | 69 103 | ... | 558 000 | ... | ... | 7 520 |
| | 1986 | 1 107 | 2 264 | 124 500 | ... | ... | ... | ... | 13 184 |
| | 1990 | 1 475 | 1 950 | 161 694 | ... | ... | ... | ... | 16 038 |
| | 1993 | 2 172 | 3 561 | 195 390 | ... | ... | ... | 2 344 | 24 745 |
| Kazakstan | 1993 | 8 770 | *14 000 | 104 362 | ... | ... | ... | ... | 6 501 |
| | 1995 | 7 351 | 15 055 | 94 875 | ... | ... | ... | ... | 5 752 |
| Korea, Republic of | 1974 | 104 | 109 | 759 | ... | ... | ... | ... | 9 478 |
| | 1980 | 110 | 110 | 1 405 | ... | ... | ... | ... | ... |
| | 1985 | 157 | 157 | 3 740 | ... | ... | ... | ... | 23 970 |
| | 1990 | 238 | 238 | 5 685 | ... | ... | ... | ... | 14 964 |
| | 1991 | 266 | 266 | 6 419 | ... | ... | ... | ... | 30 526 |
| | 1992 | 277 | 277 | 8 443 | ... | ... | ... | 142 | 26 369 |
| | 1993 | 201 | 201 | 6 690 | ... | ... | ... | ... | 30 526 |
| | 1994 | 277 | 277 | 8 442 | ... | ... | ... | ... | 43 480 |
| | 1995 | 329 | 329 | 13 638 | ... | 65 944 | 239 | ... | 40 175 |
| | 1996 | 304 | 304 | 13 020 | ... | ... | ... | ... | |
| Kuwait | 1974 | 1 | 19 | 178 | 7 614 | ... | ... | ... | 7.6 |
| | 1981 | 1 | 23 | 281 | ... | 1 588 | 1.42 | 0.28 | 404 |
| | 1986 | 1 | 21 | 471 | ... | ... | ... | ... | 591 |
| | 1992 | 1 | 18 | 272 | 4 530 | ... | 3.63 | ... | ... |
| Kyrgyzstan | 1995 | 1 001 | 1 001 | 13 977 | ... | ... | ... | ... | 903 |
| Malaysia | 1974 | (2) 8 | 44 | 469 | 3 440 | ... | 5.86 | ... | 69 |
| | 1980 | (2) 18 | 84 | 2 419 | 58 060 | 12 590 | 7.95 | (12) 0.02 | 400 |
| | 1992 | (2) 13 | 350 | 8 144 | ... | 1 324 | 71 | 71 | 1 444 |
| | 1995 | (2) 14 | 471 | 10 895 | ... | ... | | | 1 920 |
| Pakistan | 1980 | 3 | 3 | 86 | 687 | ... | ... | ... | ... |
| | 1992 | 4 | 10 | 543 | 6 468 | 578 | 2.44 | 4.42 | 62 |
| Qatar | 1990 | 6 | 6 | 158 | ... | ... | ... | 0.25 | 3.7 |
| | 1991 | 6 | 6 | 164 | ... | ... | ... | 0.25 | 5.2 |
| | 1994 | 5 | 5 | 115 | ... | ... | ... | 0.20 | 3.1 |
| | 1995 | 5 | 5 | 138 | ... | ... | ... | ... | ... |
| Turkey | 1975 | 379 | *600 | 3 822 | ... | ... | ... | ... | ... |
| | 1980 | 363 | 647 | 5 044 | ... | ... | ... | ... | 502 |
| | 1986 | 206 | 836 | 6 565 | ... | ... | ... | (12) 167 | 655 |
| | 1995 | 1 171 | 1 171 | 11 170 | ... | ... | ... | (12) 169 | 1 071 |
| | 1995 | 1 171 | 1 171 | 11 170 | ... | ... | ... | (12) 169 | 1 071 |
| Viet Nam | 1986 | 4 | 571 | 22 392 | ... | ... | ... | ... | ... |
| | 1990 | 4 | 565 | 12 586 | ... | ... | ... | ... | ... |
| | 1991 | 4 | 550 | 10 945 | ... | ... | ... | ... | ... |
| | 1992 | 4 | 560 | 11 648 | ... | ... | ... | ... | ... |
| | 1993 | 4 | 566 | 12 737 | ... | ... | ... | ... | ... |
| | 1994 | 4 | 578 | 13 568 | ... | ... | ... | ... | ... |
| **Europe** | | | | | | | | | |
| Andorra | 1996 | 8 | 8 | 121 | ... | 0.3 | 3.8 | 11.1 | 13.5 |
| Austria | 1974 | 426 | 2 318 | 4 364 | 142 454 | ... | ... | ... | 635 |
| | 1980 | 2 047 | 2 047 | 5 275 | ... | ... | ... | ... | 697 |
| | 1985 | 2 292 | 2 292 | 6 890 | ... | ... | ... | ... | 798 |
| | 1990 | 1 997 | 2 374 | 8 195 | *227 520 | *119 251 | *324 | *259 | 869 |
| | 1991 | 1 035 | 2 177 | 7 798 | ... | ... | ... | ... | 827 |
| | 1992 | 922 | 2 009 | 8 428 | ... | ... | ... | ... | 889 |
| | 1993 | 882 | 1 881 | 8 029 | ... | ... | ... | ... | 857 |

| Annual additions / Acquisitions annuelles / Adquisiciones anuales | | Loans to users (000) / Prêts aux usagers (000) / Préstamos a los usuarios (000) | Current expenditure / Dépenses ordinaires / Gastos ordinarios | | Library employees / Personnel des bibliothèques / Personal de las bibliotecas | | | Population served / Population desservie / Población servida | Country / Pays / País | Year / Année / Año |
| Volumes (000) / Volumes (000) / Volúmenes (000) | Other materials (000) / Autres matériels (000) / Otros materiales (000) | | Total (000) / Total (000) / Total (000) | Staff (%) / Personnel (%) / Personal (%) | Total / Total / Total | Holding a diploma / Diplômé / Diplomado | Trained on the job / Formé sur le tas / Formado en ejercicio | | | |
|---|---|---|---|---|---|---|---|---|---|---|
| ... | (17) 2.00 | 300 | ... | ... | 900 | 20 | ... | 75 | Iran, Islamic Republic of | 1980 |
| ... | ... | ... | ... | ... | 1 500 | ... | ... | 25 | | 1987 |
| ... | ... | 15 186 | ... | ... | 2 488 | ... | ... | *80 | | 1995 |
| ... | ... | ... | ... | ... | 2 067 | 1 215 | 852 | *80 | Israel | 1985 |
| 790 | ... | 11 948 | 45 228 | 66 | 1 393 | 640 | ... | 84 | | 1993 |
| 2 616 | ... | *42 000 | ... | ... | 6 877 | 2 347 | ... | ... | Japan | 1971 |
| 4 148 | ... | 59 066 | 20 060 | 61 | 7 791 | 3 189 | ... | 62 | | 1974 |
| 8 685 | ... | 120 213 | ... | ... | 11 129 | 3 876 | 303 | ... | | 1981 |
| 12 013 | ... | 228 708 | 87 604 | 56 | 13 800 | 6 011 | ... | 78 | | 1986 |
| 15 205 | ... | 232 144 | ... | ... | 16 331 | 6 401 | 383 | ... | | 1990 |
| 17 032 | ... | 424 107 | ... | ... | 19 339 | 7 529 | 429 | ... | | 1993 |
| 5 026 | ... | 140 036 | 26 809 | ... | 16 276 | 10 450 | ... | 39 | Kazakstan | 1993 |
| 3 067 | ... | ... | 668 270 | 53 | 13 638 | 8 611 | ... | 94 | | 1995 |
| 64 | ... | 1 913 | 651 869 | 38 | 798 | 207 | ... | 13 | Korea, Republic of | 1974 |
| ... | ... | 2 336 | 2 936 695 | ... | 1 002 | ... | ... | ... | | 1980 |
| ... | ... | 8 161 | 11 111 000 | ... | 2 286 | ... | ... | ... | | 1985 |
| ... | ... | 13 778 | 39 960 630 | ... | 3 039 | ... | ... | ... | | 1990 |
| ... | ... | *15 000 | 30 467 157 | ... | 3 549 | ... | ... | ... | | 1991 |
| 1 166 | ... | 18 346 | 50 185 621 | ... | 4 092 | ... | ... | ... | | 1992 |
| ... | ... | 18 346 | 45 559 872 | ... | 3 255 | ... | ... | ... | | 1993 |
| ... | ... | 22 208 | 76 130 090 | ... | 4 092 | ... | ... | ... | | 1994 |
| 2 001 | 68 | 34 393 | 105 784 330 | ... | 4 440 | 1 802 | ... | ... | | 1995 |
| ... | ... | 36 465 | 127 919 550 | ... | 4 776 | ... | ... | ... | | 1996 |
| 27 | ... | 19 | ... | ... | 112 | 2 | 25 | 55 | Kuwait | 1974 |
| 24 | 0.90 | 75 | 790 | 64 | 170 | 8 | ... | 60 | | 1981 |
| 9.1 | ... | 95 | ... | ... | 119 | 6 | 20 | 43 | | 1986 |
| 43 | 0.32 | 800 | ... | ... | 99 | 18 | 65 | 6 | | 1992 |
| 11 | ... | ... | (1) 4 525 | 100 | 1 717 | 1 405 | ... | 30 | Kyrgyzstan | 1995 |
| 6 522 | ... | 682 | 1 214 | 47 | 141 | 12 | 8 | 20 | Malaysia | 1974 |
| ... | ... | ... | 8 289 | ... | 503 | 50 | ... | 15 | | 1980 |
| 1 006 | - | 4 223 | 26 008 | 39 | 915 | 65 | ... | ... | | 1992 |
| 838 | 11 | 6 991 | 18 027 | ... | 1 979 | 54 | ... | ... | | 1995 |
| 2.0 | ... | 0.07 | 600 | 83 | 550 | 13 | 3 | *40 | Pakistan | 1980 |
| 7.3 | 0.11 | 48 | 14 168 | 65 | 280 | 47 | 24 | 46 | | 1992 |
| ... | ... | 7.22 | ... | ... | ... | ... | ... | ... | Qatar | 1990 |
| ... | ... | 8.86 | ... | ... | ... | ... | ... | ... | | 1991 |
| ... | ... | 5.15 | ... | ... | ... | ... | ... | ... | | 1994 |
| 5.1 | ... | 4.66 | ... | ... | 42 | 6 | 36 | ... | | 1995 |
| ... | ... | ... | ... | ... | ... | ... | ... | 15 | Turkey | 1975 |
| 157 | ... | 2 140 | 558 763 | 83 | 2 675 | 115 | 714 | 30 | | 1980 |
| 258 | ... | 2 643 | ... | ... | 3 680 | 102 | 657 | 54 | | 1986 |
| 88 | ... | 4 497 | 773 266 | 75 | 3 657 | 285 | 475 | *50 | | 1995 |
| 88 | ... | 4 497 | 773 266 | 75 | 3 657 | 285 | 475 | *50 | | 1995 |
| ... | ... | ... | ... | ... | ... | ... | ... | ... | Viet Nam | 1986 |
| ... | ... | ... | ... | ... | ... | ... | ... | ... | | 1990 |
| ... | ... | ... | ... | ... | ... | ... | ... | ... | | 1991 |
| ... | ... | ... | ... | ... | ... | ... | ... | ... | | 1992 |
| ... | ... | ... | ... | ... | ... | ... | ... | ... | | 1993 |
| ... | ... | ... | ... | ... | ... | ... | ... | ... | | 1994 |
| | | | | | | | | | **Europe** | |
| 2.4 | 1.0 | 44.6 | 30 298 | 67 | 21 | 6 | 15 | 14 | | |
| ... | ... | 9 979 | 106 656 | ... | 1 159 | 631 | ... | *80 | Austria | 1974 |
| ... | ... | 12 017 | ... | ... | ... | ... | ... | *85 | | 1980 |
| ... | ... | 13 190 | ... | ... | ... | ... | ... | *90 | | 1985 |
| ... | ... | 13 900 | ... | ... | 1 131 | 120 | ... | 99 | | 1990 |
| 1 948 | ... | 13 323 | ... | ... | 4 986 | 683 | 4 303 | *99 | | 1991 |
| 1 504 | ... | 13 045 | ... | ... | 6 337 | 703 | 5 634 | *99 | | 1992 |
| 1 903 | ... | 13 765 | ... | ... | 7 190 | 747 | 6 443 | *99 | | 1993 |

| Country / Pays / País | Year / Année / Año | Administrative unit / Unités administratives / Unidades administrativas | Service points / Points de service / Puntos de servicio | Collections / Collections / Fondos | | | | | Registered users (000) / Usagers inscrits (000) / Usuarios inscritos (000) |
|---|---|---|---|---|---|---|---|---|---|
| | | | | Books/Livres/Libros | | Microforms / Microcopies / Microcopias | Audio-visual documents (000) / Matériels audio-visuels (000) / Materiales audio-visuales (000) | Other library materials (000) / Autres matériels de bibliothèque (000) / Otros materiales de biblioteca (000) | |
| | | | | Number of volumes (000) / Nombre de volumes (000) / Número de volúmenes (000) | Metres of shelving / Mètres de rayonnage / Metros de estantes | | | | |
| Austria (cont) | 1994 | 998 | 2 053 | 9 031 | ... | ... | ... | ... | 839 |
| | 1995 | 1 096 | 2 139 | 9 484 | ... | ... | ... | ... | 890 |
| | 1996 | 959 | 1 957 | 8 897 | ... | ... | ... | ... | 865 |
| | 1997 | 984 | 2 016 | 9 110 | ... | ... | ... | ... | 929 |
| Belarus | 1992 | 5 743 | 11 329 | 77 142 | ... | ... | 239 | ... | 4 297 |
| Belgium | 1977 | 2 495 | ... | 22 094 | ... | ... | ... | ... | 1 499 |
| | 1980 | 2 351 | ... | 24 140 | ... | ... | ... | ... | 1 731 |
| | 1985 | *1 020 | 1 517 | 23 267 | ... | *174 007 | 931 | ... | 1 743 |
| | 1991 | 1 180 | 1 770 | 28 624 | ... | 6 300 | 1 885 | 0.44 | 1 935 |
| | 1992 | 1 160 | 1 780 | 28 580 | ... | 6 300 | 1 884 | 0.49 | 2 011 |
| | 1993 | 1 060 | 1 690 | 28 312 | ... | 6 300 | 2 062 | 0.53 | 2 078 |
| | 1994 | 810 | 1 520 | 28 880 | ... | 6 300 | 2 188 | 0.58 | 2 154 |
| | 1995 | 810 | 1 430 | 29 305 | ... | 4 900 | 2 497 | 1.55 | 1 715 |
| | 1996 | 830 | 1 450 | 29 739 | ... | 6 300 | 2 330 | 7.91 | 2 210 |
| | 1997 | 860 | 1 490 | 30 531 | ... | 6 200 | 2 418 | 17 | 2 310 |
| Bulgaria | 1974 | 6 060 | 6 060 | *43 000 | ... | ... | ... | ... | |
| | 1977 | 5 902 | 5 902 | 44 117 | ... | 22 446 | ... | 921 | 2 320 |
| | 1980 | 5 808 | 5 808 | 48 930 | ... | 29 853 | ... | 1 085 | 2 282 |
| | 1983 | 5 664 | 5 664 | 52 977 | ... | 214 093 | ... | 1 372 | 2 225 |
| | 1986 | 5 591 | 5 591 | 56 042 | ... | 246 772 | 500 | 4 442 | 2 217 |
| | 1990 | 5 256 | 5 256 | 46 059 | ... | ... | 434 | *4 700 | 1 407 |
| | 1991 | (22) 5 046 | 5 046 | 45 022 | ... | 2 980 | (23) 506 | ... | 1 199 |
| | 1992 | (22) 4 851 | 4 851 | 44 199 | ... | 1 330 | (23) 465 | 4 671 | 1 086 |
| | 1993 | (22) 4 694 | 4 694 | 43 412 | ... | 3 074 | (23) 456 | ... | 1 033 |
| | 1994 | (22) 4 557 | 4 557 | 42 741 | ... | 3 110 | (23) 459 | ... | 993 |
| | 1995 | (22) 4 493 | 4 493 | 42 249 | ... | 2 968 | (23) 451 | 624 | 956 |
| | 1996 | (22) 4 399 | 4 399 | 41 577 | ... | 6 937 | (23) 447 | ... | 933 |
| | 1997 | (22) 4 237 | 4 237 | 40 791 | ... | 6 762 | (23) 448 | ... | 894 |
| Croatia | 1992 | 250 | 250 | 4 631 | 104 082 | 320 | 27 | 2.84 | 6 122 |
| | 1995 | 232 | 232 | 4 558 | 99 629 | 328 | 26 | 37 | 488 |
| Czech Republic | 1990 | 5 828 | 8 208 | 39 527 | ... | ... | ... | ... | (18) 1 561 |
| | 1991 | 6 224 | 8 302 | 53 750 | ... | ... | ... | 5 739 | 1 610 |
| | 1992 | (6) 6 272 | 8 131 | 50 569 | ... | ... | ... | (25) 5 759 | 1 478 |
| | 1993 | (6) 6 238 | 7 982 | 53 933 | ... | ... | ... | (25) 5 605 | 1 422 |
| | 1994 | (6) 6 249 | 7 923 | 54 331 | ... | ... | ... | (25) 4 988 | 1 429 |
| | 1995 | 6 179 | 7 786 | 53 359 | ... | ... | ... | (25) 4 348 | 1 428 |
| | 1996 | 6 133 | 7 626 | 53 762 | ... | ... | ... | (25) 4 397 | 1 411 |
| | 1997 | 6 245 | 7 435 | 53 693 | ... | ... | ... | (25) 4 463 | 1 403 |
| Denmark | 1974 | 251 | 1 351 | 32 713 | ... | ... | ... | ... | ... |
| | 1980 | 247 | *1 177 | 29 512 | ... | 1 630 | ... | ... | ... |
| | 1986 | 250 | *1 149 | 34 685 | ... | ... | ... | ... | ... |
| | 1989 | 250 | *1 057 | 34 709 | ... | ... | ... | 0.02 | ... |
| | 1991 | 250 | 989 | 32 873 | ... | ... | 2 560 | ... | ... |
| | 1992 | 251 | 963 | 32 479 | ... | ... | 2 527 | 0.05 | ... |
| | 1993 | 250 | 962 | 32 337 | ... | ... | 2 546 | ... | ... |
| | 1994 | 249 | 956 | 32 016 | ... | ... | 2 528 | ... | ... |
| | 1995 | 249 | 950 | 31 580 | ... | ... | 2 542 | ... | ... |
| | 1996 | 250 | 900 | 31 317 | ... | ... | 2 563 | ... | ... |
| | 1997 | 250 | 892 | 31 433 | ... | ... | 2 596 | ... | ... |
| Estonia | 1990 | 629 | *847 | 14 833 | ... | ... | ... | ... | 417 |
| | 1991 | 632 | 847 | (26) 11 009 | ... | ... | ... | ... | (27) 2 429 |
| | 1992 | (28) 622 | 827 | (26) 10 879 | ... | ... | ... | ... | (27) 2 617 |
| | 1993 | (29) 601 | 797 | (26) 10 717 | ... | ... | (30) 33 | 0.00 | 330 |
| | 1994 | 605 | 794 | 10 071 | ... | ... | (30) 34 | 0.02 | 345 |
| | 1995 | 604 | 773 | 10 296 | ... | ... | (30) 35 | 0.02 | 357 |
| | 1996 | 603 | 775 | 10 431 | ... | ... | (30) 37 | 0.03 | 387 |
| | 1997 | 602 | 743 | 10 563 | ... | ... | (30) 40 | 0.04 | 407 |
| Federal Republic of Yugoslavia | 1992 | 924 | 924 | 15 337 | ... | 4 809 | 50 | 41 | (18) 7 892 |
| | 1995 | (31) 270 | 800 | 13 974 | 295 093 | 3 364 | 34 | 29 | 6 639 |
| Finland | 1973 | 484 | 2 486 | 14 890 | ... | ... | ... | ... | 1 432 |
| | 1980 | 464 | 1 836 | 23 350 | ... | ... | ... | ... | 1 842 |
| | 1985 | 464 | 1 544 | 30 469 | ... | ... | ... | ... | 2 021 |
| | 1990 | *444 | 1 151 | 35 502 | ... | ... | ... | ... | 2 199 |

| Annual additions Acquisitions annuelles Adquisiciones anuales | | Loans to users (000) Prêts aux usagers (000) Préstamos a los usuarios (000) | Current expenditure Dépenses ordinaires Gastos ordinarios | | Library employees Personnel des bibliothèques Personal de las bibliotecas | | | Population served Population desservie Población servida | Country Pays País | Year Année Año |
|---|---|---|---|---|---|---|---|---|---|---|
| Volumes (000) Volumes (000) Volúmenes (000) | Other materials (000) Autres matériels (000) Otros materiales (000) | | Total (000) Total (000) Total (000) | Staff (%) Personnel (%) Personal (%) | Total Total Total | Holding a diploma Diplômé Diplomado | Trained on the job Formé sur le tas Formado en ejercicio | | | |
| 1 449 | ... | 15 430 | ... | ... | 8 258 | 719 | 7 539 | *99 | Austria (cont) | 1994 |
| 1 389 | ... | 15 859 | ... | ... | 9 227 | 794 | 8 433 | *99 | | 1995 |
| 1 393 | ... | 15 282 | ... | ... | 8 905 | 704 | 8 201 | *99 | | 1996 |
| 1 425 | ... | 15 728 | 440 929 | ... | 9 362 | 776 | 8 586 | *99 | | 1997 |
| (19) 4 061 | 34 | 83 435 | 656 400 | ... | 9 698 | ... | ... | ... | Belarus | 1992 |
| ... | ... | 39 569 | ... | ... | ... | ... | ... | ... | Belgium | 1977 |
| ... | ... | 42 060 | ... | ... | ... | ... | ... | ... | | 1980 |
| ... | ... | *48 345 | ... | ... | ... | ... | ... | ... | | 1985 |
| 1 516 | 156 | 63 262 | 6 035 040 | 65 | 3 330 | 2 170 | 1 160 | ... | | 1991 |
| 1 442 | ... | 62 676 | 6 124 070 | 66 | 3 470 | 2 260 | 1 210 | ... | | 1992 |
| 1 473 | 203 | 63 409 | 6 257 100 | 66 | 3 530 | 2 300 | 1 230 | ... | | 1993 |
| 1 438 | 201 | 66 038 | 6 372 140 | 68 | 3 710 | 2 420 | 1 290 | ... | | 1994 |
| 1 715 | 261 | 65 765 | (20)6 220 300 | 67 | 3 740 | 2 440 | 1 300 | ... | | 1995 |
| 1 598 | 248 | 66 250 | (20)6 389 300 | 69 | 3 930 | 2 540 | 1 390 | ... | | 1996 |
| 1 602 | 329 | 68 475 | (20)7 315 900 | 69 | 3 940 | 2 580 | 1 360 | ... | | 1997 |
| ... | ... | ... | ... | ... | ... | ... | ... | 26 | Bulgaria | 1974 |
| 3 003 | ... | 34 184 | 13 140 | 49 | 4 521 | 2 806 | 1 715 | 26 | | 1977 |
| 2 908 | 77 | 34 911 | 17 965 | 47 | 4 834 | 2 903 | 1 931 | 38 | | 1980 |
| 2 665 | (21) 83 | 34 361 | 20 490 | 47 | 3 298 | 2 414 | 884 | 38 | | 1983 |
| 2 286 | 139 | 34 095 | 23 124 | 50 | 7 179 | 3 240 | 3 939 | 38 | | 1986 |
| ... | ... | 35 611 | ... | ... | 4 490 | 3 055 | 1 435 | *40 | | 1990 |
| 869 | 20 | 19 261 | 46 213 | 76 | 2 482 | 2 842 | ... | *50 | | 1991 |
| 1 086 | 12 | 18 293 | 89 237 | 74 | 2 816 | 2 816 | ... | *50 | | 1992 |
| 883 | 8.93 | 18 310 | 135 265 | 79 | 2 630 | 2 630 | ... | *60 | | 1993 |
| 585 | 7.31 | 18 904 | 202 925 | 80 | 2 669 | 2 669 | ... | *70 | | 1994 |
| 448 | 5.87 | 18 619 | 282 752 | 77 | 2 638 | 2 638 | ... | 98 | | 1995 |
| 320 | 6.50 | 18 297 | 431 339 | 77 | 2 632 | 2 632 | ... | *96 | | 1996 |
| 314 | 4.11 | 18 246 | 10 148 204 | 74 | 2 474 | 2 474 | ... | *96 | | 1997 |
| 233 | 2.01 | 3.86 | (9) 122 990 | ... | 1 088 | 716 | ... | 9 | Croatia | 1992 |
| 198 | 1.23 | 2.88 | (9) 11 043 | ... | 1 014 | 741 | ... | 50 | | 1995 |
| ... | ... | 54 815 | ... | ... | ... | ... | ... | ... | Czech Republic | 1990 |
| 2 800 | ... | 56 271 | 509 645 | ... | 5 350 | 4 410 | 940 | ... | | 1991 |
| 1 995 | ... | 56 001 | 562 757 | 42 | 5 256 | 4 336 | 920 | ... | | 1992 |
| 3 628 | ... | 56 549 | 776 557 | 37 | 5 127 | 4 230 | 897 | ... | | 1993 |
| 2 277 | ... | 57 786 | 837 220 | 39 | 5 116 | 4 149 | 967 | ... | | 1994 |
| 1 613 | ... | 57 413 | 951 802 | 36 | 5 089 | 4 174 | 915 | ... | | 1995 |
| 2 912 | ... | 58 806 | 956 068 | 42 | 4 569 | 3 795 | 776 | ... | | 1996 |
| 2 152 | ... | 59 634 | 1 064 499 | 40 | 4 374 | 3 739 | 634 | ... | | 1997 |
| 3 967 | ... | 83 673 | 603 942 | 49 | 4 218 | 1 520 | ... | 100 | Denmark | 1974 |
| ... | ... | 78 996 | ... | ... | 5 605 | 2 069 | ... | *100 | | 1980 |
| ... | ... | 84 514 | 1 641 000 | ... | 5 799 | 2 286 | ... | *100 | | 1986 |
| ... | ... | 78 280 | 1 864 000 | 64 | 5 788 | 2 336 | 83 | 100 | | 1989 |
| 7 945 | 224 | 84 975 | 7 941 281 | 91 | 5 440 | 2 259 | 3 181 | *100 | | 1991 |
| 2 059 | 225 | 84 165 | 7 932 971 | 91 | 5 271 | 2 227 | 3 044 | *100 | | 1992 |
| 7 994 | 210 | 84 697 | 7 973 596 | 91 | 5 240 | 2 240 | 2 999 | *100 | | 1993 |
| 2 119 | 231 | 82 741 | 8 034 291 | 90 | 5 160 | 2 230 | 2 930 | *100 | | 1994 |
| 2 151 | 225 | 82 434 | 8 089 838 | 90 | 5 125 | 2 242 | 2 882 | *100 | | 1995 |
| 2 456 | 273 | 85 069 | 8 168 579 | 89 | 5 082 | 2 250 | 2 832 | *100 | | 1996 |
| 2 360 | 261 | 85 880 | 8 216 749 | 89 | 4 942 | 2 208 | 2 734 | *100 | | 1997 |
| ... | ... | 8 910 | ... | ... | 1 626 | ... | ... | *90 | Estonia | 1990 |
| 537 | ... | 8 149 | ... | ... | 1 602 | 1 290 | 312 | *90 | | 1991 |
| 534 | ... | 8 793 | ... | ... | 1 535 | 1 223 | 312 | *90 | | 1992 |
| 564 | 5.39 | 9 585 | 30 354 | 42 | 1 510 | 1 198 | 312 | *90 | | 1993 |
| 566 | ... | 11 086 | 55 143 | 49 | 1 500 | 1 199 | 301 | *90 | | 1994 |
| 556 | 2.71 | 12 159 | 61 419 | 48 | 1 541 | 1 217 | 324 | 100 | | 1995 |
| 463 | 2.90 | 13 643 | 88 131 | 51 | 1 589 | 1 253 | 336 | *100 | | 1996 |
| 523 | 10 | 14 549 | 116 459 | 47 | 1 468 | 1 166 | 302 | *100 | | 1997 |
| 267 | 3.57 | 14 332 | (9) 59 407 | ... | 1 788 | 570 | 1 218 | 97 | Federal Republic of Yugoslavia | 1992 |
| 255 | 3.88 | 12 273 | ... | ... | 1 836 | 655 | 1 123 | *97 | | 1995 |
| 848 | ... | 43 060 | 90 190 | 43 | 4 000 | 3 000 | ... | 30 | Finland | 1973 |
| 1 344 | ... | 72 513 | ... | ... | 4 450 | 2 300 | ... | ... | | 1980 |
| ... | ... | 80 335 | ... | ... | ... | ... | ... | ... | | 1985 |
| ... | ... | 85 714 | ... | ... | ... | ... | ... | ... | | 1990 |

| Country<br><br>Pays<br><br>País | Year<br><br>Année<br><br>Año | Administrative<br>unit<br><br>Unités<br>administratives<br><br>Unidades<br>administrativas | Service<br>points<br><br>Points de<br>service<br><br>Puntos de<br>servicio | Collections / Collections / Fondos | | Microforms<br><br>Microcopies<br><br>Microcopias | Audio-<br>visual<br>documents<br>(000)<br>Matériels<br>audio-<br>visuels<br>(000)<br>Materiales<br>audio-<br>visuales | Other library<br>materials<br>(000)<br>Autres<br>matériels de<br>bibliothèque<br>(000)<br>Otros<br>materiales<br>de biblioteca<br>(000) | Registered<br>users<br>(000)<br><br>Usagers<br>inscrits<br>(000)<br><br>Usuarios<br>inscritos<br>(000) |
|---|---|---|---|---|---|---|---|---|---|
| | | | | Books/Livres/Libros | | | | | |
| | | | | Number of<br>volumes<br>(000)<br>Nombre de<br>volumes<br>(000)<br>Número de<br>volúmenes<br>(000) | Metres of<br>shelving<br><br>Mètres de<br>rayonnage<br><br>Metros de<br>estantes | | | | |
| Finland (cont) | 1991 | 444 | 1 359 | 35 938 | ... | ... | 1 846 | 1.30 | 2 281 |
| | 1992 | 444 | 1 339 | 36 308 | ... | ... | 2 023 | 1.45 | 2 405 |
| | 1993 | 439 | 1 247 | 36 611 | | ... | 2 113 | 1.50 | 2 473 |
| | 1994 | 439 | 1 218 | 36 629 | ... | ... | 2 204 | 1.60 | 2 488 |
| | 1995 | 439 | 1 200 | 36 882 | ... | ... | 2 295 | 1.65 | 2 507 |
| | 1996 | 439 | 1 220 | 36 835 | ... | ... | 2 386 | 9.00 | 2 484 |
| | 1997 | 436 | 1 202 | 36 832 | ... | ... | 2 476 | 17 | 2 516 |
| France | 1977 | (24) 1 026 | 1 816 | 48 661 | 1 251 571 | ... | (32) 592 | ... | 3 636 |
| | 1980 | (24) 1 028 | 1 928 | 50 470 | 1 326 150 | ... | 826 | ... | 4 917 |
| | 1987 | (24) 1 462 | 2 740 | 78 474 | ... | 166 748 | 4 481 | ... | |
| | 1990 | (24) 1 641 | *2 740 | *89 049 | *1 766 675 | *965 501 | *5 155 | *3 176 | 4 605 |
| | 1991 | 1 776 | 3 257 | 91 103 | ... | ... | ... | ... | (27) 262 999 |
| | 1992 | 1 735 | 3 002 | 90 129 | ... | ... | ... | ... | (27) 265 367 |
| | 1993 | 1 692 | 2 829 | 89 899 | ... | ... | ... | ... | (27) 265 676 |
| | 1994 | 1 661 | 2 754 | 89 415 | ... | ... | ... | ... | (27) 264 041 |
| | 1995 | 1 652 | 2 684 | 89 598 | ... | ... | ... | ... | (27) 257 329 |
| | 1996 | 1 622 | 2 618 | 89 598 | ... | ... | ... | ... | (27) 255 136 |
| | 1997 | 1 620 | 2 577 | 89 766 | ... | ... | ... | ... | (27) 265 784 |
| Germany | 1990 | (33) 18 284 | 18 284 | 148 683 | ... | ... | ... | ... | 9 386 |
| | 1991 | (33) 14 998 | 14 998 | 144 629 | ... | ... | ... | ... | 8 806 |
| | 1992 | 6 760 | 16 745 | 149 807 | ... | ... | ... | ... | (27) 386 605 |
| | 1993 | 6 594 | 15 779 | 149 425 | ... | ... | ... | ... | (27) 387 055 |
| | 1994 | 6 474 | 15 359 | 148 621 | ... | ... | ... | ... | (27) 384 673 |
| | 1995 | 6 437 | 14 971 | 148 925 | ... | ... | ... | ... | (27) 374 894 |
| | 1996 | 6 322 | 14 600 | 148 925 | ... | ... | ... | ... | (27) 371 700 |
| | 1997 | 6 313 | 14 372 | 149 205 | ... | ... | ... | ... | (27) 387 212 |
| Greece | 1981 | *510 | *510 | 7 486 | ... | *194 279 | *19 | 19 | *1 170 |
| | 1986 | (34) 615 | 615 | 8 296 | 152 725 | ... | (35) 231 | (12) 15 | 1 399 |
| | 1990 | 680 | 680 | 7 400 | 151 526 | ... | 51 | ... | |
| | 1991 | 672 | 829 | 10 131 | ... | ... | ... | ... | (27) 1 722 |
| | 1992 | 672 | 829 | 9 957 | ... | ... | ... | ... | (27) 1 815 |
| | 1993 | 672 | 829 | 9 783 | ... | ... | ... | ... | (27) 1 909 |
| | 1994 | 672 | 829 | 9 610 | ... | ... | ... | ... | (27) 2 003 |
| | 1995 | 672 | 829 | 9 436 | ... | ... | ... | ... | (27) 2 097 |
| | 1996 | 672 | 829 | 9 262 | ... | ... | ... | ... | (27) 2 192 |
| | 1997 | 672 | 829 | 9 088 | ... | ... | ... | ... | (27) 2 286 |
| Hungary | 1974 | 8 297 | 8 297 | 30 583 | ... | ... | ... | ... | 2 255 |
| | 1980 | (2) 2 241 | 10 502 | 40 769 | ... | ... | (25) 984 | ... | 2 242 |
| | 1986 | 4 765 | 9 383 | 49 704 | ... | ... | ... | 1 132 | 2 268 |
| | 1990 | 7 350 | 7 350 | 51 636 | ... | ... | ... | ... | 1 856 |
| | 1991 | 3 190 | 3 987 | 39 253 | ... | ... | ... | ... | (27) 16 200 |
| | 1992 | 5 848 | 5 848 | 49 625 | ... | ... | ... | ... | 1 646 |
| | 1993 | 5 264 | 5 264 | 49 102 | ... | ... | ... | ... | 1 609 |
| | 1994 | 4 727 | 4 727 | 47 858 | ... | ... | ... | ... | 1 584 |
| | 1995 | (2) 2 956 | 4 468 | 45 265 | ... | 40 768 | 1 285 | 536 | 1 520 |
| | 1996 | (2) 2 854 | 3 566 | 42 988 | ... | ... | ... | ... | 1 360 |
| | 1997 | (2) 2 883 | 3 518 | 43 377 | ... | ... | ... | ... | 1 344 |
| Iceland | 1971 | 215 | 223 | 910 | ... | ... | ... | ... | 81 |
| | 1974 | 251 | 273 | 1 033 | ... | ... | ... | ... | 50 |
| | 1982 | 240 | 240 | 1 395 | ... | ... | ... | ... | ... |
| | 1985 | 234 | *235 | 1 557 | ... | ... | ... | ... | ... |
| | 1990 | *200 | *200 | 1 809 | ... | ... | 42 | ... | 95 |
| | 1991 | 203 | 209 | 1 803 | ... | 3 443 | 34 | 4.75 | 87 |
| | 1992 | 197 | 203 | 1 849 | ... | 3 464 | 38 | 8.82 | 78 |
| | 1993 | 197 | 204 | 1 895 | ... | 3 433 | 42 | 5.13 | 93 |
| | 1994 | 176 | 183 | 1 884 | ... | 3 458 | 44 | 8.60 | 91 |
| | 1995 | 176 | 183 | 1 946 | ... | 3 178 | 47 | 5.18 | 89 |
| | 1996 | 173 | 181 | 2 027 | ... | 3 178 | 50 | 1.37 | 72 |
| | 1997 | 187 | 194 | 1 901 | ... | ... | ... | ... | ... |
| Ireland | 1974 | (2) 31 | *370 | 5 124 | ... | ... | ... | ... | 721 |
| | 1977 | (2) 31 | *374 | 6 924 | ... | ... | ... | ... | 923 |
| | 1980 | (2) 31 | *374 | 7 399 | ... | 5 886 | 27 | ... | 719 |
| | 1986 | (2) 31 | 387 | 10 862 | ... | 7 519 | 124 | ... | 668 |
| | 1990 | (2) 31 | 359 | 10 980 | *304 827 | 9 726 | 145 | 10 | 742 |
| | 1991 | (2) 31 | 364 | 11 046 | ... | 10 016 | (30) 204 | ... | 808 |
| | 1992 | (2) 31 | 353 | 10 927 | ... | 11 445 | (30) 212 | ... | 804 |

| Annual additions / Acquisitions annuelles / Adquisiciones anuales | | Loans to users (000) / Prêts aux usagers (000) / Préstamos a los usuarios (000) | Current expenditure / Dépenses ordinaires / Gastos ordinarios | | Library employees / Personnel des bibliothèques / Personal de las bibliotecas | | | Population served / Population desservie / Población servida | Country / Pays / País | Year / Année / Año |
|---|---|---|---|---|---|---|---|---|---|---|
| Volumes (000) / Volumes (000) / Volúmenes (000) | Other materials (000) / Autres matériels (000) / Otros materiales (000) | | Total (000) / Total (000) / Total (000) | Staff (%) / Personnel (%) / Personal (%) | Total / Total / Total | Holding a diploma / Diplômé / Diplomado | Trained on the job / Formé sur le tas / Formado en ejercicio | | | |
| 2 056 | 228 | 89 240 | 1 328 230 | 53 | 4 612 | 1 725 | 2 887 | ... | Finland (cont) | 1991 |
| 1 808 | 218 | 96 387 | 1 303 482 | 53 | 4 479 | 1 657 | 2 822 | ... | | 1992 |
| 1 686 | 218 | 98 921 | 1 217 190 | 53 | 4 378 | 1 600 | 2 800 | ... | | 1993 |
| 1 596 | 214 | 101 863 | 1 198 456 | 55 | 4 280 | 1 550 | 2 770 | ... | | 1994 |
| 1 584 | 256 | 101 890 | 1 237 179 | 57 | 4 240 | 1 495 | 2 745 | ... | | 1995 |
| 1 593 | 210 | 104 176 | 1 268 155 | 57 | 4 249 | 1 500 | 2 750 | ... | | 1996 |
| 1 636 | 207 | 102 139 | ... | ... | 4 232 | 1 490 | 2 740 | ... | | 1997 |
| 2 976 | (32) 132 | 79 889 | 523 493 | 55 | 6 910 | 2 252 | ... | 89 | France | 1977 |
| 2 939 | (32) 143 | 89 878 | 846 995 | 65 | 6 984 | 2 290 | ... | *90 | | 1980 |
| 4 926 | (32) 414 | 88 155 | (5) 1 698 922 | ... | 13 029 | 4 870 | ... | *95 | | 1987 |
| 4 044 | 417 | 96 806 | ... | ... | 12 576 | 4 870 | ... | 97 | | 1990 |
| 5 018 | ... | 89 333 | ... | ... | 12 858 | 4 307 | 8 551 | *97 | | 1991 |
| 3 872 | ... | 89 033 | ... | ... | 12 886 | 4 236 | 8 650 | *97 | | 1992 |
| 4 900 | ... | 88 691 | ... | ... | 12 704 | 4 998 | 7 706 | *90 | | 1993 |
| 3 731 | ... | 88 376 | ... | ... | 12 907 | 5 017 | 7 920 | *90 | | 1994 |
| 3 577 | ... | 86 899 | ... | ... | 12 983 | 4 984 | 7 999 | 60 | | 1995 |
| 3 588 | ... | 86 503 | ... | ... | 12 804 | 4 905 | 7 899 | *60 | | 1996 |
| 3 669 | ... | 89 559 | ... | ... | 12 864 | 4 890 | 7 974 | *60 | | 1997 |
| ... | ... | 235 855 | 1 135 982 | ... | 15 885 | ... | ... | ... | Germany | 1990 |
| ... | ... | 229 759 | 1 258 275 | ... | 14 802 | ... | ... | ... | | 1991 |
| 7 418 | ... | 308 955 | ... | ... | 23 708 | 8 771 | 14 937 | ... | | 1992 |
| 9 387 | ... | 307 766 | ... | ... | 23 656 | 10 349 | 13 307 | ... | | 1993 |
| 7 147 | ... | 306 673 | ... | ... | 24 064 | 10 388 | 13 676 | ... | | 1994 |
| 6 854 | ... | 301 548 | ... | ... | 24 133 | 10 320 | 13 813 | ... | | 1995 |
| 6 873 | ... | 300 173 | ... | ... | 23 797 | 10 157 | 13 640 | ... | | 1996 |
| 7 029 | ... | 310 778 | ... | ... | 11 183 | 10 126 | 1 057 | ... | | 1997 |
| ... | ... | *958 | ... | ... | ... | ... | ... | ... | Greece | 1981 |
| 214 | 11 | 958 | ... | ... | 1 288 | 181 | 1 107 | ... | | 1986 |
| 228 | 14 | 1 285 | 2 187 675 | 82 | 1 394 | ... | ... | 35 | | 1990 |
| 188 | ... | 1 519 | ... | ... | 1 451 | 742 | 709 | ... | | 1991 |
| 203 | ... | 1 571 | ... | ... | 1 525 | 790 | 725 | ... | | 1992 |
| 218 | ... | 1 623 | ... | ... | 1 580 | 838 | 742 | ... | | 1993 |
| 233 | ... | 1 675 | ... | ... | 1 644 | 886 | 758 | ... | | 1994 |
| 248 | ... | 1 726 | ... | ... | 1 708 | 934 | 774 | ... | | 1995 |
| 263 | ... | 1 777 | ... | ... | 1 771 | 982 | 789 | ... | | 1996 |
| 278 | ... | 1 829 | ... | ... | 1 834 | 1 029 | 805 | ... | | 1997 |
| ... | ... | 56 480 | ... | ... | 3 334 | 420 | ... | 22 | Hungary | 1974 |
| 2 028 | ... | 52 170 | (8) 114 700 | ... | 4 634 | ... | ... | 100 | | 1980 |
| 1 173 | 90 | 48 766 | (9) 160 308 | ... | 5 116 | ... | ... | 100 | | 1986 |
| ... | ... | 42 624 | ... | ... | ... | ... | ... | 100 | | 1990 |
| 2 008 | ... | 36 000 | ... | ... | 4 625 | 4 625 | ... | 100 | | 1991 |
| ... | ... | 41 485 | (9) 346 837 | ... | 4 535 | ... | ... | 100 | | 1992 |
| ... | ... | 40 506 | ... | ... | ... | ... | ... | 100 | | 1993 |
| ... | ... | 41 190 | ... | ... | ... | ... | ... | 100 | | 1994 |
| ... | ... | 40 119 | (5) 549 600 | 91 | 8 363 | ... | ... | 100 | | 1995 |
| 1 537 | ... | 36 761 | 5 175 756 | 57 | 4 135 | 4 135 | ... | 100 | | 1996 |
| 1 444 | ... | 36 724 | 6 331 439 | 58 | 3 881 | 3 881 | ... | 100 | | 1997 |
| 9.4 | ... | 1 410 | 49 000 | ... | ... | ... | ... | ... | Iceland | 1971 |
| 53 | ... | 1 605 | 117 506 | ... | 289 | 8 | 9 | ... | | 1974 |
| ... | ... | ... | ... | ... | ... | ... | ... | ... | | 1982 |
| ... | ... | 2 053 | ... | ... | ... | ... | ... | ... | | 1985 |
| ... | ... | 1 702 | 320 994 | ... | ... | ... | ... | ... | | 1990 |
| 65 | 2.08 | 1 641 | ... | ... | 302 | 77 | 225 | 100 | | 1991 |
| 67 | 2.26 | 1 753 | 419 615 | 51 | 303 | 76 | 227 | 100 | | 1992 |
| 70 | 3.62 | 1 913 | 453 653 | 50 | 291 | 88 | 203 | 100 | | 1993 |
| 74 | 3.73 | 2 063 | 451 422 | 49 | 294 | 88 | 206 | 99 | | 1994 |
| 70 | 3.63 | 2 096 | 512 934 | 45 | 302 | 90 | 212 | 99 | | 1995 |
| 78 | 3.62 | 2 074 | 542 309 | 48 | 296 | 87 | 209 | 99 | | 1996 |
| 71 | ... | 1 923 | ... | ... | 295 | 88 | 207 | 99 | | 1997 |
| 384 | ... | 21 156 | 2 212 | 45 | 859 | 51 | ... | 24 | Ireland | 1974 |
| ... | ... | 25 376 | 5 917 | 46 | 979 | 200 | ... | ... | | 1977 |
| 689 | *12 | 16 910 | 9 300 | 44 | 830 | ... | ... | ... | | 1980 |
| ... | *18 | 13 819 | 22 493 | 52 | 1 417 | 265 | ... | 100 | | 1986 |
| 555 | 17 | 12 432 | 24 158 | 57 | 1 334 | 250 | 1 084 | 100 | | 1990 |
| 409 | 18 | 12 507 | 26 462 | 57 | 1 348 | 253 | 1 095 | ... | | 1991 |
| 377 | 15 | 12 914 | 25 647 | 60 | 1 343 | 249 | 1 094 | 100 | | 1992 |

| Country / Pays / País | Year / Année / Año | Administrative unit / Unités administratives / Unidades administrativas | Service points / Points de service / Puntos de servicio | Collections / Collections / Fondos | | Microforms / Microcopies / Microcopias | Audio-visual documents (000) / Matériels audio-visuels (000) / Materiales audio-visuales (000) | Other library materials (000) / Autres matériels de bibliothèque (000) / Otros materiales de biblioteca (000) | Registered users (000) / Usagers inscrits (000) / Usuarios inscritos (000) |
|---|---|---|---|---|---|---|---|---|---|
| | | | | Books/Livres/Libros | | | | | |
| | | | | Number of volumes (000) / Nombre de volumes (000) / Número de volúmenes (000) | Metres of shelving / Mètres de rayonnage / Metros de estantes | | | | |
| Ireland (cont) | 1993 | (2) 31 | 350 | 11 151 | ... | 11 945 | (30) 243 | ... | 761 |
| | 1994 | (2) 32 | 346 | 11 599 | ... | 11 733 | (30) 252 | ... | 774 |
| | 1995 | (2) 32 | 347 | 11 382 | ... | 15 422 | (30) 225 | 9.63 | 853 |
| | 1996 | (2) 32 | 346 | 11 165 | ... | 14 688 | (30) 256 | ... | 848 |
| | 1997 | (2) 32 | 351 | 11 212 | ... | ... | ... | ... | ... |
| Italy | 1981 | (36) 42 | *2 300 | 13 835 | ... | ... | ... | ... | 138 |
| | 1985 | (36) 42 | *2 300 | 16 133 | ... | ... | ... | ... | 269 |
| | 1990 | (36) *42 | *2 366 | 80 030 | ... | *1 003 031 | *4 472 | 2 798 | *6 756 |
| | 1991 | 92 | 2 724 | 42 092 | ... | ... | ... | ... | (27) 271 549 |
| | 1992 | 90 | 2 511 | 41 642 | ... | ... | ... | ... | (27) 273 994 |
| | 1993 | 88 | 2 366 | 41 536 | ... | ... | ... | ... | (27) 274 313 |
| | 1994 | 86 | 2 303 | 41 312 | ... | ... | ... | ... | (27) 272 625 |
| | 1995 | 86 | 2 245 | 41 397 | ... | ... | ... | ... | (27) 265 695 |
| | 1996 | 84 | 2 189 | 41 397 | ... | ... | ... | ... | (27) 263 431 |
| | 1997 | 84 | 2 155 | 41 474 | ... | ... | ... | ... | (27) 274 425 |
| Latvia | 1980 | 1 373 | ... | 25 000 | ... | ... | ... | ... | (18) 1 186 |
| | 1990 | 1 317 | ... | 22 900 | ... | ... | ... | ... | (18) 902 |
| | 1991 | 1 199 | ... | 21 018 | ... | ... | ... | ... | (18) 713 |
| | 1992 | 1 189 | ... | 19 996 | ... | ... | ... | ... | (18) 674 |
| | 1993 | 1 119 | ... | 18 440 | ... | ... | ... | ... | (18) 589 |
| | 1994 | 1 045 | ... | 16 991 | ... | ... | ... | ... | (18) 507 |
| | 1995 | 1 037 | ... | 16 430 | ... | ... | ... | ... | (18) 501 |
| | 1996 | 1 009 | ... | 15 628 | ... | ... | ... | ... | (18) 508 |
| | 1997 | 998 | ... | 14 948 | ... | ... | ... | ... | (18) 508 |
| Liechtenstein | 1981 | *3 | *3 | *18 | ... | *257 | *0.35 | ... | *0.1 |
| | 1986 | 3 | 3 | 21 | ... | ... | 0.35 | ... | 1.4 |
| | 1991 | 3 | 3 | 23 | ... | ... | ... | ... | (27) 128 |
| | 1992 | 3 | 3 | 24 | ... | ... | ... | ... | (27) 131 |
| | 1993 | 3 | 3 | 24 | ... | ... | ... | ... | (27) 133 |
| | 1994 | 3 | 3 | 24 | ... | ... | ... | ... | (27) 132 |
| | 1995 | 3 | 3 | 24 | ... | ... | ... | ... | (27) 134 |
| | 1996 | 3 | 3 | 24 | ... | ... | ... | ... | (27) 133 |
| | 1997 | 3 | 3 | 24 | ... | ... | ... | ... | (27) 135 |
| Lithuania | 1990 | 54 | 1 711 | 22 283 | ... | 1 198 | 258 | 745 | 930 |
| | 1991 | 55 | 1 657 | 26 890 | ... | 1 198 | 258 | 745 | 899 |
| | 1992 | 52 | 1 574 | 26 174 | ... | 1 198 | 258 | 745 | 773 |
| | 1993 | 53 | 1 526 | 25 245 | ... | 1 198 | 258 | 745 | 734 |
| | 1994 | 55 | 1 519 | 23 699 | ... | 1 198 | 258 | 745 | 731 |
| | 1995 | 58 | 1 511 | 23 500 | 411 781 | 1 198 | 259 | 746 | 750 |
| | 1996 | 61 | 1 489 | 23 378 | ... | 1 096 | 256 | ... | 761 |
| | 1997 | 61 | 1 478 | 23 168 | ... | 1 094 | 260 | ... | 779 |
| Luxembourg | 1986 | 2 | 5 | *613 | *17 015 | *6 459 | *29 | *10 | *44 |
| | 1991 | 2 | 6 | 536 | ... | ... | ... | ... | (27) 1 754 |
| | 1992 | 2 | 5 | 530 | ... | ... | ... | ... | (27) 1 770 |
| | 1993 | 2 | 5 | 529 | ... | ... | ... | ... | (27) 1 772 |
| | 1994 | 2 | 5 | 526 | ... | ... | ... | ... | (27) 1 761 |
| | 1995 | 2 | 5 | 527 | ... | ... | ... | ... | (27) 1 716 |
| | 1996 | 2 | 5 | 527 | ... | ... | ... | ... | (27) 1 701 |
| | 1997 | 2 | 5 | 528 | ... | ... | ... | ... | (27) 1 772 |
| Malta | 1980 | 1 | 30 | 154 | 3 630 | ... | 0.50 | ... | 35 |
| | 1983 | 1 | 43 | 196 | 6 500 | ... | 1.11 | ... | 61 |
| | 1990 | 1 | *60 | 237 | ... | ... | ... | ... | 102 |
| | 1992 | 1 | 61 | 331 | 4 350 | ... | ... | ... | 120 |
| | 1993 | 1 | *61 | 268 | ... | ... | ... | ... | 108 |
| | 1995 | 2 | 3 | 526 | ... | ... | ... | ... | (18) 216 |
| Moldova | 1993 | 1 598 | 3 143 | 18 874 | ... | ... | 52 | 0.10 | 1 235 |
| | 1995 | 1 601 | *3 200 | 18 969 | ... | ... | 62 | 16 | 1 158 |
| Monaco | 1995 | 2 | 2 | 15 | 220 | 6 | 0.00 | ... | 0.8 |
| Netherlands | 1974 | (2) 411 | 953 | 17 941 | ... | ... | ... | ... | 2 293 |
| | 1980 | (2) 475 | 1 360 | 30 722 | ... | ... | 1 209 | 667 | 4 008 |
| | 1985 | 482 | *1 300 | 38 753 | ... | ... | ... | ... | 4 162 |
| | 1990 | 606 | 1 265 | 41 515 | ... | *253 531 | 2 322 | *1 322 | 4 346 |
| | 1991 | 635 | 1 429 | 42 107 | ... | ... | ... | ... | (27) 69 065 |

| Annual additions — Acquisitions annuelles — Adquisiciones anuales | | Loans to users (000) — Prêts aux usagers (000) — Préstamos a los usuarios (000) | Current expenditure — Dépenses ordinaires — Gastos ordinarios | | Library employees — Personnel des bibliothèques — Personal de las bibliotecas | | | Population served — Population desservie — Población servida | Country — Pays — País | Year — Année — Año |
| Volumes (000) — Volumes (000) — Volúmenes (000) | Other materials (000) — Autres matériels (000) — Otros materiales (000) | | Total (000) — Total (000) — Total (000) | Staff (%) — Personnel (%) — Personal (%) | Total — Total — Total | Holding a diploma — Diplômé — Diplomado | Trained on the job — Formé sur le tas — Formado en ejercicio | | | |
|---|---|---|---|---|---|---|---|---|---|---|
| 434 | 17 | 12 795 | 26 423 | 60 | 1 333 | 247 | 1 086 | 100 | Ireland (cont) | 1993 |
| 578 | 25 | 12 354 | 28 572 | 59 | 1 349 | 258 | 1 091 | 100 | | 1994 |
| 503 | 25 | 12 356 | 29 111 | 57 | 1 322 | 265 | 1 057 | 100 | | 1995 |
| 629 | 30 | 12 568 | 32 572 | 59 | 1 321 | 261 | 1 060 | 100 | | 1996 |
| 488 | ... | 12 582 | ... | | 1 328 | 247 | 1 081 | 100 | | 1997 |
| ... | ... | 3 357 | ... | ... | ... | ... | ... | ... | Italy | 1981 |
| ... | ... | 3 434 | ... | ... | ... | ... | ... | ... | | 1985 |
| ... | ... | *356 516 | ... | ... | 23 371 | 6 116 | ... | 100 | | 1990 |
| 14 025 | ... | 257 311 | ... | ... | 24 417 | 5 270 | 19 147 | 100 | | 1991 |
| 10 823 | ... | 256 448 | ... | ... | 24 553 | 5 184 | 19 369 | 100 | | 1992 |
| 13 695 | ... | 255 461 | ... | ... | 23 371 | 6 116 | 17 255 | 100 | | 1993 |
| 10 427 | ... | 254 554 | ... | ... | 23 872 | 6 139 | 17 733 | 100 | | 1994 |
| 9 998 | ... | 250 300 | ... | ... | 24 010 | 6 099 | 17 911 | 100 | | 1995 |
| 10 027 | ... | 249 159 | ... | ... | 23 688 | 6 002 | 17 686 | 100 | | 1996 |
| 10 254 | ... | 257 962 | ... | | 23 840 | 5 984 | 17 858 | 100 | | 1997 |
| ... | ... | 30 200 | ... | ... | ... | ... | ... | ... | Latvia | 1980 |
| ... | ... | 22 700 | ... | ... | ... | ... | ... | ... | | 1990 |
| 429 | ... | 19 480 | ... | ... | 3 191 | 2 462 | 729 | ... | | 1991 |
| 360 | ... | 19 263 | ... | ... | 3 069 | 2 361 | 708 | ... | | 1992 |
| 421 | ... | 17 680 | 1 697 | ... | 2 557 | 2 111 | 446 | 24 | | 1993 |
| 328 | ... | 15 651 | 2 529 | ... | 2 501 | 2 051 | 450 | 22 | | 1994 |
| 309 | ... | 15 871 | 3 293 | ... | 2 377 | 1 930 | 447 | 20 | | 1995 |
| 364 | ... | 17 426 | 3 641 | ... | 2 356 | 1 920 | 436 | ... | | 1996 |
| 433 | ... | 17 806 | 4 214 | 51 | 2 315 | 1 886 | 429 | ... | | 1997 |
| ... | ... | *55 | ... | ... | ... | ... | ... | ... | Liechtenstein | 1981 |
| 1.3 | 0.01 | 21 | 87 | 30 | 1 | ... | 1 | 100 | | 1986 |
| 7.0 | ... | 71 | ... | ... | 5 | 2 | 3 | ... | | 1991 |
| 5.6 | ... | 72 | ... | ... | 5 | 2 | 3 | 100 | | 1992 |
| 6.9 | ... | 73 | ... | ... | 5 | 2 | 3 | ... | | 1993 |
| 5.4 | ... | 73 | ... | ... | 5 | 2 | 3 | ... | | 1994 |
| 5.2 | ... | 73 | ... | ... | 5 | 2 | 3 | ... | | 1995 |
| 5.2 | ... | 74 | ... | ... | 5 | 2 | 3 | ... | | 1996 |
| 5.2 | ... | 75 | ... | ... | 5 | 2 | 3 | ... | | 1997 |
| ... | ... | 18 411 | ... | ... | 4 041 | 3 449 | 592 | ... | Lithuania | 1990 |
| 538 | ... | 16 635 | ... | ... | 4 312 | 3 264 | 1 048 | ... | | 1991 |
| 523 | ... | 16 398 | ... | ... | 4 210 | 3 154 | 1 056 | ... | | 1992 |
| 548 | ... | 15 896 | ... | ... | 4 054 | 3 065 | 989 | ... | | 1993 |
| 609 | 7.15 | 16 172 | 15 539 | 51 | 4 404 | 3 506 | 988 | ... | | 1994 |
| 855 | 5.88 | 17 270 | 23 512 | 51 | 4 060 | 3 076 | 984 | 20 | | 1995 |
| 922 | 1.38 | 19 086 | 30 073 | 57 | 4 067 | 3 083 | 984 | ... | | 1996 |
| 830 | 5.07 | 20 942 | 38 636 | 58 | 4 089 | 3 105 | 984 | ... | | 1997 |
| ... | ... | *2 296 | (37)*3 138 154 | 60 | 150 | 39 | ... | 97 | Luxembourg | 1986 |
| 1.2 | ... | 1 985 | ... | ... | 157 | 34 | 123 | *100 | | 1991 |
| 0.9 | ... | 1 978 | ... | ... | 158 | 33 | 125 | *100 | | 1992 |
| 1.1 | ... | 1 970 | ... | ... | 150 | 39 | 111 | *100 | | 1993 |
| 0.9 | ... | 1 963 | ... | ... | 153 | 39 | 114 | *100 | | 1994 |
| 0.8 | ... | 1 931 | ... | ... | 154 | 39 | 115 | *100 | | 1995 |
| 0.8 | ... | 1 922 | ... | ... | 152 | 38 | 114 | *100 | | 1996 |
| 0.9 | ... | 1 990 | ... | ... | 153 | 38 | 115 | *100 | | 1997 |
| 17 | - | 544 | 44 | 53 | 24 | 1 | 1 | 13 | Malta | 1980 |
| 17 | 0.30 | *500 | 111 | 85 | 44 | 1 | ... | 70 | | 1983 |
| ... | ... | 368 | ... | ... | ... | ... | ... | *100 | | 1990 |
| 16 | ... | 835 | (9) 38 | ... | 102 | 2 | 1 | 100 | | 1992 |
| ... | ... | 425 | ... | ... | ... | ... | ... | *100 | | 1993 |
| 489 | ... | 833 | ... | ... | ... | ... | ... | ... | | 1995 |
| 1 087 | 4.01 | 22 724 | 1 429 | 90 | 2 658 | 2 097 | ... | 30 | Moldova | 1993 |
| 431 | 0.83 | ... | 5 603 | 51 | 2 671 | 2 181 | ... | 33 | | 1995 |
| 0.1 | ... | 4.79 | (13) 50 | ... | 3 | 1 | 2 | 100 | Monaco | 1995 |
| 1 602 | ... | 94 447 | ... | ... | 6 057 | 2 050 | ... | *95 | Netherlands | 1974 |
| 4 517 | 328 | 161 911 | 509 339 | 54 | 3 272 | 1 596 | ... | 96 | | 1980 |
| ... | ... | 172 636 | ... | ... | ... | ... | ... | *96 | | 1985 |
| ... | ... | 185 724 | ... | ... | 8 265 | 2 565 | ... | 97 | | 1990 |
| 3 567 | ... | 157 887 | ... | ... | 8 535 | 2 210 | 6 325 | *97 | | 1991 |

| Country / Pays / País | Year / Année / Año | Administrative unit / Unités administratives / Unidades administrativas | Service points / Points de service / Puntos de servicio | Collections / Collections / Fondos | | | | | Registered users (000) / Usagers inscrits (000) / Usuarios inscritos (000) |
| | | | | Books/Livres/Libros | | Microforms / Microcopies / Microcopias | Audio-visual documents (000) / Matériels audio-visuels (000) / Materiales audio-visuales (000) | Other library materials (000) / Autres matériels de bibliothèque (000) / Otros materiales de biblioteca (000) | |
| | | | | Number of volumes (000) / Nombre de volumes (000) / Número de volúmenes (000) | Metres of shelving / Mètres de rayonnage / Metros de estantes | | | | |
| Netherlands (cont) | 1992 | 620 | 1 317 | 41 657 | ... | ... | 2 260 | ... | (27) 69 687 |
| | 1993 | 605 | 1 241 | 41 551 | ... | ... | | ... | (27) 69 768 |
| | 1994 | 594 | 1 208 | 41 327 | ... | ... | | ... | (27) 69 339 |
| | 1995 | 591 | 1 177 | 41 411 | ... | ... | | ... | (27) 67 576 |
| | 1996 | 580 | 1 148 | 41 411 | ... | ... | | ... | (27) 67 000 |
| | 1997 | 579 | 1 130 | 41 489 | ... | ... | | ... | (27) 69 797 |
| Norway | 1973 | 445 | 1 392 | 9 361 | ... | ... | | ... | 621 |
| | 1980 | 454 | 1 377 | 14 037 | ... | ... | 88 | ... | 1 059 |
| | 1983 | 454 | 1 395 | 15 966 | ... | 32 108 | 137 | ... | 1 198 |
| | 1991 | 446 | 1 218 | 19 378 | ... | ... | 711 | 2.00 | (27) 17 979 |
| | 1992 | 439 | 1 214 | 19 839 | ... | ... | 767 | 2.00 | (27) 18 540 |
| | 1993 | 439 | 1 184 | 20 025 | ... | ... | 844 | 3.00 | (27) 19 144 |
| | 1994 | 435 | 1 183 | 20 428 | ... | ... | 931 | 3.00 | (27) 18 948 |
| | 1995 | 435 | 1 157 | 20 411 | ... | ... | 1 010 | 3.00 | (27) 20 279 |
| | 1996 | 435 | 1 136 | 20 709 | ... | ... | (30) 9 962 | 3.32 | (27) 20 332 |
| | 1997 | 435 | 1 108 | 20 508 | ... | ... | (30) 10 170 | 3.16 | (27) 19 858 |
| Poland | 1974 | 8 950 | 31 112 | 70 478 | ... | ... | ... | ... | 7 223 |
| | 1980 | 9 315 | 26 587 | 94 538 | ... | ... | 595 | ... | 7 388 |
| | 1985 | 9 900 | 23 300 | 119 700 | ... | ... | ... | ... | 7 514 |
| | 1990 | *9 900 | 17 565 | 136 641 | ... | ... | ... | ... | 7 423 |
| | 1991 | 9 936 | 10 300 | 135 688 | ... | 12 041 | 2 085 | 22 | 6 826 |
| | 1992 | 9 770 | 7 351 | 135 821 | ... | 12 695 | 2 253 | 57 | 6 613 |
| | 1993 | 9 605 | 5 692 | 135 928 | ... | 12 115 | 2 242 | 60 | 6 671 |
| | 1994 | 9 558 | 4 981 | 136 193 | ... | 12 441 | 2 318 | 64 | 6 893 |
| | 1995 | 9 505 | 4 428 | 136 694 | ... | 12 737 | 2 416 | 67 | 7 023 |
| | 1996 | 9 342 | 3 938 | 137 071 | ... | 13 251 | 2 520 | 71 | 7 176 |
| | 1997 | 9 230 | 3 565 | 135 867 | ... | 10 383 | 2 597 | 80 | 7 222 |
| Portugal | 1974 | (40) 77 | ... | 7 039 | ... | ... | ... | ... | ... |
| | 1980 | 118 | 599 | 6 284 | ... | 7 082 | ... | ... | 2 304 |
| | 1986 | 194 | 317 | 4 783 | 114 544 | 620 | 1.45 | 169 | ... |
| | 1990 | 167 | 234 | 3 371 | 96 289 | 1 249 | 6.79 | 138 | ... |
| | 1991 | 184 | 276 | 4 914 | ... | ... | ... | ... | (27) 48 812 |
| | 1992 | 179 | 255 | 4 861 | ... | ... | ... | ... | (27) 49 251 |
| | 1993 | 161 | ... | *3 910 | ... | ... | ... | ... | (27) 49 308 |
| | 1994 | 172 | 234 | 4 823 | ... | ... | ... | ... | (27) 49 005 |
| | 1995 | 191 | 237 | 7 884 | ... | 1 340 | 123 | 83 | (27) 47 759 |
| | 1996 | 206 | 274 | 8 664 | ... | 1 333 | 152 | 57 | (27) 47 352 |
| | 1997 | 168 | 219 | 4 842 | ... | ... | ... | ... | (27) 49 328 |
| Romania | 1974 | 6 575 | ... | 52 882 | ... | ... | ... | ... | 3 918 |
| | 1980 | 6 302 | ... | 59 827 | ... | ... | ... | ... | 3 911 |
| | 1985 | 6 960 | ... | 67 379 | ... | ... | ... | ... | 4 661 |
| | 1990 | 4 458 | ... | 55 841 | ... | ... | ... | ... | (18) 2 206 |
| | 1991 | 2 896 | 3 156 | 46 116 | ... | 9 515 | 242 | 72 | 1 835 |
| | 1992 | 2 899 | 3 166 | 47 005 | ... | 9 515 | 251 | 72 | 1 935 |
| | 1993 | 2 905 | 3 176 | 47 992 | ... | 9 515 | 257 | 74 | 1 976 |
| | 1994 | 2 910 | 3 194 | 48 892 | ... | 9 515 | 267 | 76 | 2 020 |
| | 1995 | 2 926 | 3 208 | 49 266 | ... | 9 515 | 277 | 77 | 2 071 |
| | 1996 | 2 936 | 3 221 | 49 489 | ... | 9 515 | 288 | 82 | 2 118 |
| | 1997 | 2 953 | 3 246 | 50 493 | ... | 9 515 | 295 | 86 | 1 994 |
| Russian Federation | 1990 | 62 600 | ... | 1 154 600 | ... | ... | ... | ... | 71 900 |
| | 1991 | 59 200 | ... | 1 083 000 | ... | ... | ... | ... | 65 400 |
| | 1992 | 57 200 | ... | 1 063 000 | ... | ... | ... | ... | 62 200 |
| | 1993 | 51 111 | ... | 884 754 | ... | ... | ... | 3 585 | 62 449 |
| | 1995 | 50 032 | 96 177 | 983 356 | ... | ... | 7 699 | ... | 54 201 |
| Slovakia | 1990 | 2 627 | 3 146 | 19 885 | ... | 5 094 | 317 | 410 | 953 |
| | 1991 | 2 806 | 3 166 | 19 438 | ... | 5 257 | 322 | 412 | 756 |
| | 1992 | 2 682 | 3 012 | 19 757 | ... | ... | ... | 414 | 715 |
| | 1993 | 2 683 | 3 007 | 19 245 | ... | 5 487 | 343 | 440 | 711 |
| | 1994 | 2 738 | 3 042 | 19 173 | ... | 5 525 | 354 | 456 | 745 |
| | 1995 | 2 710 | 2 823 | 19 514 | ... | ... | ... | ... | 760 |
| | 1996 | 2 706 | 2 723 | 19 414 | ... | ... | ... | ... | 766 |
| | 1997 | 2 713 | 2 630 | 19 354 | ... | ... | ... | ... | 758 |
| Slovenia | 1990 | 60 | 231 | 4 822 | ... | 1 078 | 115 | 304 | 314 |
| | 1991 | 60 | 232 | 4 975 | ... | ... | 61 | 317 | (41) 336 |
| | 1992 | 60 | 248 | 5 131 | ... | ... | 80 | 343 | (41) 366 |

| Annual additions / Acquisitions annuelles / Adquisiciones anuales | | Loans to users (000) | Current expenditure / Dépenses ordinaires / Gastos ordinarios | | Library employees / Personnel des bibliothèques / Personal de las bibliotecas | | | Population served | Country | Year |
|---|---|---|---|---|---|---|---|---|---|---|
| Volumes (000) | Other materials (000) | Prêts aux usagers (000) | Total (000) | Staff (%) | Total | Holding a diploma | Trained on the job | Population desservie | Pays | Année |
| Volumes (000) | Autres matériels (000) | | Total (000) | Personnel (%) | Total | Diplômé | Formé sur le tas | | | |
| Volúmenes (000) | Otros materiales (000) | Préstamos a los usuarios (000) | Total (000) | Personal (%) | Total | Diplomado | Formado en ejercicio | Población servida | País | Año |
| 2 753 | ... | 157 358 | ... | ... | 8 572 | 2 174 | 6 398 | *97 | Netherlands (cont) | 1992 |
| 3 483 | ... | 156 752 | ... | ... | 8 265 | 2 565 | 5 700 | *97 | | 1993 |
| 2 652 | ... | 156 196 | ... | ... | 8 433 | 2 575 | 5 858 | *97 | | 1994 |
| 2 543 | ... | 153 585 | ... | ... | 8 475 | 2 558 | 5 917 | *97 | | 1995 |
| 2 550 | ... | 152 885 | ... | ... | 8 359 | 2 517 | 5 842 | *97 | | 1996 |
| 2 608 | ... | 158 286 | ... | ... | 8 408 | 2 510 | 5 898 | *97 | | 1997 |
| 758 | ... | 12 661 | ... | ... | | | | 100 | Norway | 1973 |
| 644 | (38) ... | 16 159 | 242 904 | 58 | (39) 1 657 | ... | ... | 100 | | 1980 |
| 583 | 6.86 | 17 889 | 364 836 | 59 | 2 819 | | | 100 | | 1983 |
| 994 | ... | 20 080 | 635 859 | 61 | 1 805 | 860 | 940 | 100 | | 1991 |
| 788 | ... | 21 021 | 676 568 | 59 | 1 810 | 860 | 950 | 100 | | 1992 |
| 981 | ... | 21 699 | 701 245 | 59 | 1 843 | 880 | 960 | 100 | | 1993 |
| 761 | ... | 21 610 | 722 545 | 59 | 1 826 | 870 | 950 | 100 | | 1994 |
| 730 | ... | 21 954 | 755 846 | 59 | 1 924 | 920 | 1 010 | 100 | | 1995 |
| 743 | ... | 22 689 | 779 965 | 59 | 1 070 | 080 | 990 | 100 | | 1996 |
| 744 | ... | 22 204 | 802 956 | 61 | 1 870 | 909 | 962 | 100 | | 1997 |
| 4 154 | ... | 141 923 | 575 310 | 65 | 15 102 | ... | ... | 21 | Poland | 1974 |
| 6 928 | ... | 147 254 | (13) 398 203 | ... | 16 533 | 6 974 | 9 559 | 25 | | 1980 |
| ... | ... | 150 000 | ... | ... | ... | ... | ... | *50 | | 1985 |
| 5 309 | ... | 155 006 | ... | ... | ... | ... | ... | *60 | | 1990 |
| 5 934 | 161 | 168 031 | ... | ... | 18 931 | 1 873 | 17 058 | ... | | 1991 |
| 5 355 | 205 | 177 239 | ... | ... | 18 059 | 1 907 | 16 152 | 85 | | 1992 |
| 4 891 | 180 | 180 489 | ... | ... | 17 737 | 10 471 | 7 266 | *86 | | 1993 |
| 4 303 | 156 | 189 040 | ... | ... | 17 749 | 10 602 | 7 147 | *87 | | 1994 |
| 4 299 | 216 | 191 155 | ... | ... | 17 894 | 10 890 | 7 004 | 89 | | 1995 |
| 3 983 | 156 | 191 925 | ... | ... | 17 773 | 10 953 | 6 820 | *89 | | 1996 |
| 3 794 | 121 | 189 035 | ... | ... | 17 828 | 11 137 | 6 691 | *89 | | 1997 |
| ... | ... | ... | 53 514 | 84 | 599 | ... | ... | *26 | Portugal | 1974 |
| 272 | ... | 6 134 | 217 712 | 70 | 403 | 38 | ... | 52 | | 1980 |
| 151 | 5.14 | 743 | 403 819 | | 706 | 63 | 176 | ... | | 1986 |
| 179 | 16 | 886 | 793 050 | 73 | 757 | 72 | 237 | ... | | 1990 |
| 456 | ... | 1 110 | ... | ... | 769 | 193 | 576 | ... | | 1991 |
| 352 | ... | 1 107 | ... | ... | 773 | 190 | 583 | ... | | 1992 |
| 294 | 14 | 981 | 1 468 140 | 74 | 908 | 85 | 823 | ... | | 1993 |
| 339 | ... | 1 098 | ... | ... | 758 | 225 | 533 | ... | | 1994 |
| 439 | 18 | 1 439 | 2 176 762 | 79 | 1 266 | 118 | 477 | ... | | 1995 |
| 604 | 34 | 1 753 | 3 316 740 | 58 | 1 396 | 127 | 540 | ... | | 1996 |
| 334 | ... | 1 113 | . | ... | 756 | 219 | 537 | ... | | 1997 |
| 3 209 | ... | ... | ... | ... | ... | ... | ... | ... | Romania | 1974 |
| ... | ... | 41 311 | ... | ... | ... | ... | ... | ... | | 1980 |
| ... | ... | 53 101 | ... | ... | ... | ... | ... | ... | | 1985 |
| ... | ... | 27 843 | ... | ... | ... | ... | ... | ... | | 1990 |
| 1 142 | 8.79 | 27 873 | 500 501 | 61 | 4 335 | 3 893 | 442 | ... | | 1991 |
| 1 144 | 5.64 | 30 453 | 974 750 | 62 | 4 360 | 3 915 | 445 | ... | | 1992 |
| 1 261 | 11 | 32 685 | 2 560 044 | 59 | 4 439 | 3 978 | 461 | ... | | 1993 |
| 1 119 | 11 | 33 999 | 6 192 106 | 56 | 4 451 | 4 026 | 425 | ... | | 1994 |
| 1 170 | 7.47 | 35 038 | 11 567 257 | 56 | 4 704 | 4 197 | 507 | ... | | 1995 |
| 1 082 | 9.23 | 35 959 | 17 073 798 | 58 | 4 894 | 4 374 | 520 | ... | | 1996 |
| 984 | 7.19 | 37 893 | 39 455 587 | 55 | 5 014 | 4 433 | 581 | ... | | 1997 |
| ... | ... | ... | ... | ... | ... | ... | ... | ... | Russian Federation | 1990 |
| ... | ... | ... | ... | ... | ... | ... | ... | ... | | 1991 |
| ... | ... | ... | ... | ... | ... | ... | ... | ... | | 1992 |
| 52 570 | 379 | ... | ... | ... | 122 236 | 6 221 | ... | ... | | 1993 |
| 30 593 | 999 | 1 213 013 | 11 425 670 | ... | 172 499 | 84 462 | ... | 41 | | 1995 |
| ... | ... | 29 568 | ... | ... | 2 394 | 2 057 | 337 | ... | Slovakia | 1990 |
| ... | ... | 23 317 | ... | ... | 2 188 | 1 744 | 444 | ... | | 1991 |
| 588 | ... | 23 117 | 214 985 | 57 | ... | ... | ... | 14 | | 1992 |
| ... | ... | 23 979 | ... | ... | 1 990 | 1 714 | 276 | ... | | 1993 |
| ... | ... | 25 620 | ... | ... | 2 005 | 1 585 | 420 | ... | | 1994 |
| 490 | ... | 25 899 | 240 065 | 47 | 2 012 | 1 350 | 662 | 100 | | 1995 |
| 523 | ... | 25 922 | 284 488 | 45 | 2 043 | 1 230 | 813 | 100 | | 1996 |
| 391 | ... | 25 780 | 297 506 | 48 | 1 987 | 1 110 | 877 | 100 | | 1997 |
| ... | ... | 7 896 | (37) 9 789 | 46 | 1 086 | 433 | 653 | ... | Slovenia | 1990 |
| 252 | ... | 9 248 | 407 663 | 53 | 682 | 530 | 152 | ... | | 1991 |
| 221 | 32 | 11 274 | 1 185 677 | 50 | 684 | 538 | 146 | ... | | 1992 |

| Country / Pays / País | Year / Année / Año | Administrative unit / Unités administratives / Unidades administrativas | Service points / Points de service / Puntos de servicio | Collections / Collections / Fondos | | | | | Registered users (000) / Usagers inscrits (000) / Usuarios inscritos (000) |
| | | | | Books/Livres/Libros | | Microforms / Microcopies / Microcopias | Audio-visual documents (000) / Matériels audio-visuels (000) / Materiales audio-visuales (000) | Other library materials (000) / Autres matériels de bibliothèque (000) / Otros materiales de biblioteca (000) | |
| | | | | Number of volumes (000) / Nombre de volumes (000) / Número de volúmenes (000) | Metres of shelving / Mètres de rayonnage / Metros de estantes | | | | |
|---|---|---|---|---|---|---|---|---|---|
| Slovenia (cont) | 1993 | 60 | 254 | 5 285 | ... | 68 | 106 | 343 | (41) 397 |
| | 1994 | 60 | 239 | 5 473 | ... | 172 | 115 | 356 | (41) 421 |
| | 1995 | 60 | 239 | 5 710 | 132 298 | 206 | 135 | 356 | (41) 427 |
| | 1996 | 60 | 237 | 5 933 | ... | 243 | 148 | ... | (41) 426 |
| | 1997 | 60 | 239 | 6 159 | ... | 197 | 162 | ... | (41) 442 |
| Spain | 1974 | 1 435 | 1 916 | 8 745 | 209 168 | ... | ... | ... | 943 |
| | 1980 | (42) 1 396 | 1 662 | 11 730 | 279 824 | 25 877 | 17 | ... | 1 308 |
| | 1986 | 2 307 | 2 564 | 19 697 | ... | 455 844 | 493 | 78 | 3 044 |
| | 1990 | 3 285 | 3 635 | 27 208 | *755 342 | 148 301 | 1 144 | 157 | 4 089 |
| | 1991 | 3 706 | 4 550 | 33 238 | ... | ... | ... | ... | (27) 184 309 |
| | 1992 | 3 993 | 4 609 | 29 718 | ... | 191 105 | ... | 44 | 4 385 |
| | 1993 | 3 531 | 3 952 | 32 799 | ... | ... | ... | ... | (27) 186 185 |
| | 1994 | 4 301 | 4 880 | 33 839 | ... | 340 276 | 861 | (43) 52 | 5 327 |
| | 1995 | 3 447 | 3 750 | 32 689 | ... | ... | ... | ... | (27) 180 335 |
| | 1996 | 4 404 | 5 011 | 35 805 | ... | 305 736 | 992 | (43) 70 | 6 066 |
| | 1997 | 3 380 | 3 600 | 32 750 | ... | ... | ... | ... | (27) 186 260 |
| Sweden | 1972 | 598 | ... | 27 089 | ... | ... | ... | ... | ... |
| | 1975 | 415 | ... | 32 382 | ... | ... | ... | ... | ... |
| | 1980 | 408 | 2 204 | 39 031 | 1 040 827 | 121 000 | 956 | ... | ... |
| | 1985 | 394 | *2 000 | 44 699 | ... | ... | 1 430 | ... | ... |
| | 1990 | 377 | 1 975 | 47 489 | *1 318 400 | *691 016 | 2 351 | *1 498 | *172 |
| | 1991 | 375 | 2 152 | 47 203 | ... | ... | 2 291 | ... | (27) 41 484 |
| | 1992 | 286 | 1 792 | 45 547 | ... | ... | 2 155 | ... | (27) 41 858 |
| | 1993 | 286 | 1 734 | 45 147 | ... | ... | 2 223 | ... | (27) 41 907 |
| | 1994 | 332 | 1 819 | 46 114 | ... | ... | ... | ... | (27) 41 649 |
| | 1995 | 288 | 1 656 | 44 177 | ... | ... | (35) 2 321 | ... | (27) 40 590 |
| | 1996 | 324 | 1 729 | 46 208 | ... | ... | ... | ... | (27) 40 244 |
| | 1997 | 324 | 1 702 | 46 295 | ... | ... | ... | ... | (27) 41 924 |
| Switzerland | 1983 | *46 | 2 009 | 21 755 | *603 973 | 1 605 897 | 131 | 1 613 | 320 |
| | 1986 | *46 | *2 201 | 23 844 | *661 954 | 1 669 422 | 188 | 1 665 | *351 |
| | 1990 | *46 | *2 555 | 27 674 | *768 290 | *1 891 318 | *313 | *1 814 | *351 |
| | 1991 | 47 | 2 806 | 27 308 | ... | ... | ... | ... | (27) 29 353 |
| | 1992 | 47 | 2 665 | 27 492 | ... | ... | ... | ... | (27) 29 923 |
| | 1993 | 46 | 2 555 | 27 674 | ... | ... | ... | ... | (27) 30 409 |
| | 1994 | 45 | 2 498 | 27 881 | ... | ... | ... | ... | (27) 30 258 |
| | 1995 | 45 | 2 443 | 27 976 | ... | ... | ... | ... | (27) 30 677 |
| | 1996 | 44 | 2 385 | 28 200 | ... | ... | ... | ... | (27) 30 538 |
| | 1997 | 44 | 2 344 | 27 971 | ... | ... | ... | ... | (27) 30 955 |
| The Former Yugoslav Rep. of Macedonia | 1992 | 62 | 122 | 2 729 | 30 289 | ... | 0.41 | 0.10 | 987 |
| Ukraine | 1992 | 25 300 | *27 000 | 400 883 | ... | ... | *1 604 | ... | 21 692 |
| | 1995 | (2) 21 857 | *25 000 | 336 720 | ... | ... | 1 505 | ... | 20 076 |
| United Kingdom | 1980 | 160 | 16 244 | 131 338 | ... | 834 825 | (32) 3 267 | 823 | ... |
| | 1985 | 166 | 18 561 | 140 538 | ... | 1 468 027 | 4 439 | ... | 33 077 |
| | 1989 | 165 | 5 270 | 156 700 | ... | ... | 5 471 | ... | ... |
| | 1991 | 167 | 5 256 | 134 122 | ... | 5 048 000 | 6 121 | 79 | *33 430 |
| | 1992 | 167 | 5 204 | 133 023 | ... | 5 662 000 | 6 492 | 108 | *33 631 |
| | 1993 | 167 | 5 191 | 131 657 | ... | 6 339 000 | 6 812 | 139 | *33 734 |
| | 1994 | 167 | 5 167 | 129 612 | ... | 6 991 000 | 7 213 | 177 | *33 865 |
| | 1995 | 167 | 5 113 | 131 033 | ... | 7 149 000 | 7 371 | 202 | *33 981 |
| | 1996 | 177 | 5 168 | 130 634 | ... | 7 709 000 | 7 484 | 227 | *34 104 |
| | 1997 | 169 | 5 183 | 131 680 | ... | ... | ... | ... | *33 630 |

| Volumes (000) / Volúmenes (000) | Other materials (000) / Autres matériels (000) / Otros materiales (000) | Loans to users (000) / Prêts aux usagers (000) / Préstamos a los usuarios (000) | Total (000) / Total (000) / Total (000) | Staff (%) / Personnel (%) / Personal (%) | Total / Total / Total | Holding a diploma / Diplômé / Diplomado | Trained on the job / Formé sur le tas / Formado en ejercicio | Population served / Population desservie / Población servida | Country / Pays / País | Year / Année / Año |
|---|---|---|---|---|---|---|---|---|---|---|
| 222 | 26 | 11 775 | 1 711 730 | 45 | 711 | 560 | 151 | ... | Slovenia (cont) | 1993 |
| 247 | 8.50 | 11 980 | 2 198 150 | 44 | 740 | 582 | 158 | ... | | 1994 |
| 290 | 25 | 12 819 | 2 758 976 | 44 | 754 | 606 | 148 | 21 | | 1995 |
| 318 | 14 | 13 439 | 3 289 201 | 44 | 768 | 608 | 160 | ... | | 1996 |
| 331 | 14 | 14 380 | 3 828 983 | 45 | 785 | 613 | 172 | ... | | 1997 |
| 442 | ... | 5 215 | 288 108 | 58 | 2 665 | 417 | 2 248 | 57 | Spain | 1974 |
| 602 | (38) 1.72 | 6 279 | 1 226 082 | 70 | 4 648 | 805 | 3 843 | 61 | | 1980 |
| 1 511 | 41 | 14 358 | 6 270 325 | 67 | 3 081 | 405 | 1 654 | 78 | | 1986 |
| 2 121 | 98 | 18 078 | ... | ... | 7 289 | 4 822 | ... | *80 | | 1990 |
| 2 052 | ... | 18 463 | ... | ... | 6 293 | 3 645 | 2 648 | *80 | | 1991 |
| 2 045 | 32 | 18 401 | ... | ... | ... | ... | ... | *80 | | 1992 |
| 2 003 | ... | 18 330 | ... | ... | 6 616 | 4 230 | 2 386 | *80 | | 1993 |
| 1 962 | 84 | 21 053 | 17 305 540 | 67 | 5 483 | 3 695 | 1 788 | 83 | | 1994 |
| 1 463 | ... | 17 960 | ... | ... | 6 695 | 4 218 | 2 477 | *85 | | 1995 |
| 1 891 | 96 | 22 111 | 20 535 004 | 70 | 5 474 | 3 615 | 1 859 | *85 | | 1996 |
| 1 500 | ... | 18 510 | ... | ... | 6 608 | 4 139 | 2 469 | *85 | | 1997 |
| ... | ... | 61 529 | 295 180 | 49 | ... | ... | ... | ... | Sweden | 1972 |
| ... | ... | 73 693 | 470 209 | 52 | ... | ... | ... | ... | | 1975 |
| 2 330 | ... | 77 351 | 1 022 426 | 55 | 5 475 | 5 162 | 313 | 100 | | 1980 |
| ... | ... | 75 370 | 1 690 320 | 52 | 5 900 | ... | ... | 100 | | 1985 |
| 2 204 | 2 072 | 71 990 | 2 480 936 | 51 | 6 306 | 2 627 | ... | 100 | | 1990 |
| ... | ... | ... | 2 624 201 | 51 | ... | ... | ... | 100 | | 1991 |
| 2 005 | ... | 66 535 | 2 670 957 | 49 | 5 878 | 2 470 | ... | 100 | | 1992 |
| 1 863 | ... | 67 365 | 2 584 321 | 48 | 5 504 | 2 386 | ... | 100 | | 1993 |
| 1 464 | ... | 70 067 | ... | ... | 6 332 | 2 551 | 3 781 | 100 | | 1994 |
| 1 902 | ... | 70 355 | 2 655 038 | 62 | 5 523 | 2 422 | ... | 100 | | 1995 |
| 1 408 | ... | 68 582 | ... | ... | 6 265 | 2 494 | 3 771 | 100 | | 1996 |
| 1 440 | ... | 71 005 | ... | ... | 6 293 | 2 486 | 3 807 | 100 | | 1997 |
| ... | ... | 3 917 | ... | ... | 4 134 | 1 449 | ... | 100 | Switzerland | 1983 |
| ... | ... | *5 806 | ... | ... | 4 530 | 1 588 | ... | 100 | | 1986 |
| ... | ... | *5 806 | *87 045 716 | 69 | 5 258 | 1 843 | ... | 98 | | 1990 |
| 1 604 | ... | 5 635 | ... | ... | 5 401 | 1 608 | 3 793 | *98 | | 1991 |
| 1 273 | ... | 5 733 | ... | ... | 5 417 | 1 595 | 3 822 | *98 | | 1992 |
| 1 584 | ... | 5 806 | ... | ... | 5 258 | 1 843 | 3 415 | *98 | | 1993 |
| 1 229 | ... | 5 827 | ... | ... | 5 312 | 1 848 | 3 464 | *98 | | 1994 |
| 1 179 | ... | 5 815 | ... | ... | 5 442 | 1 879 | 3 563 | *98 | | 1995 |
| 1 199 | ... | 5 858 | ... | ... | 5 338 | 1 830 | 3 508 | *98 | | 1996 |
| 1 201 | ... | 5 916 | ... | ... | 5 317 | 1 841 | 3 476 | *98 | | 1997 |
| 68 | 0.03 | ... | 19 653 | ... | 389 | 295 | 94 | 48 | The Former Yugoslav Rep. of Macedonia | 1992 |
| *21 247 | ... | 465 368 | ... | ... | 49 300 | 37 300 | 12 000 | ... | Ukraine | 1992 |
| 8 510 | ... | 407 937 | ... | ... | 44 149 | 33 097 | 11 052 | 39 | | 1995 |
| 12 667 | 1 137 | 637 367 | 309 373 | 54 | 27 624 | ... | ... | 100 | United Kingdom | 1980 |
| ... | ... | 645 000 | ... | ... | ... | ... | ... | 100 | | 1985 |
| 13 697 | 1 087 | 564 525 | 634 230 | 50 | 33 594 | 9 280 | ... | 100 | | 1989 |
| 12 916 | 1 231 | 605 856 | 744 715 | 49 | 28 027 | 7 477 | 20 550 | 100 | | 1991 |
| 12 666 | 1 230 | 592 645 | 778 155 | 49 | 27 823 | 7 278 | 20 545 | 100 | | 1992 |
| 12 712 | 1 260 | 583 268 | 797 089 | 50 | 27 320 | 7 158 | 20 162 | 100 | | 1993 |
| 12 523 | 1 400 | 568 905 | 774 117 | 53 | 27 372 | 6 999 | 20 373 | 100 | | 1994 |
| 11 722 | 1 449 | (44) 551 444 | 782 417 | 54 | 27 024 | 6 873 | 20 151 | 100 | | 1995 |
| 10 913 | 1 321 | (44) 538 230 | 790 503 | 55 | 26 518 | 6 552 | 19 966 | 100 | | 1996 |
| 12 242 | ... | 573 391 | ... | ... | 26 843 | 6 552 | 20 291 | 100 | | 1997 |

## General note
For general explanations and definitions, please refer to the beginning of this chapter.

## Note générale
Pour les explications et définitions générales, prière de se référer au début de ce chapitre.

## Nota general
Para las explicaciones y definiciones generales, referirse al comienzo de este capítulo.

Notes

(1) Data refer only to expenditure on employees.

Notes

(1) Les données se réfèrent seulement aux dépenses pour le personnel.

Notas

(1) Los datos se refieren solamente a los gastos de personal.

(2) Data refer only to libraries financed by public authorities.

(2) Les données se réfèrent aux bibliothèques financées par les pouvoirs publics seulement.

(2) Los datos se refieren a las bibliotecas financiadas por los poderes públicos solamente.

(3) Of which 765,000 pounds for both the national and the public library organs of the Kenya National Library Services.

(3) Dont 765 000 pounds pour les services communs de la bibliothèque nationale et de la bibliothèque publique de la Kenya National Library Services.

(3) De los cuales 765 000 pounds para los servicios comunes de la biblioteca nacional y de la biblioteca pública de la Kenya National Library Services.

(4) Of which 300 employees for both the national and the public library organs of the Kenya National Library Services.

(4) Dont 300 employés des services communs de la bibliothèque nationale et de la bibliothèque publique de la Kenya National Library Services.

(4) De los cuales 300 empleados de los servicios comunes de la biblioteca nacional y de la biblioteca pública de la Kenya National Library Services.

(5) Data refer only to expenditure on employees and acquisitions.

(5) Les données se réfèrent seulement aux dépenses pour le personnel et les acquisitions.

(5) Los datos se refieren solamente a los gastos de personal y de adquisiciones.

(6) Data refer to municipal libraries only.

(6) Les données se réfèrent aux bibliothèques municipales seulement.

(6) Los datos se refieren a las bibliotecas municipales solamente.

(7) Data refer to number of titles.

(7) Les données se réfèrent au nombre de titres.

(7) Los datos se refieren al número de títulos.

(8) Data refer to 'préfectorales et municipales' libraries only.

(8) Les données se réfèrent aux bibliothèques 'préfectorales et municipales' seulement.

(8) Los datos se refieren solamente a las bibliotecas "préfectorales et municipales".

(9) Data refer only to expenditure on acquisitions.

(9) Les données se réfèrent aux dépenses pour les acquisitions seulement.

(9) La biblioteca nacional también desempeña la función de biblioteca pública.

(10) Data do not include maintenance staff.

(10) Les données n'incluent pas le personnel d'entretien.

(10) Los datos no incluyen al personal de mantenimiento.

(11) Data include current expenditure of the employees of the national library.

(11) Les données incluent les dépenses courantes relatives aux employés de la bibliothèque nationale.

(11) Los datos incluyen los gastos ordinarios relativos a los empleados de la biblioteca nacional.

(12) Data refer only to manuscripts..

(12) Les données se réfèrent seulement aux manuscrits.

(12) Los datos se refieren solamente a los manuscritos.

(13) Data do not include expenditure on employees.

(13) Les données n'incluent pas les dépenses pour le personnel.

(13) Los datos no incluyen los gastos para el personal.

(14) The public library serves as a national library.

(14) La bibliothèque publique remplit également la fonction de bibliothèque nationale.

(14) La biblioteca pública funciona también como biblioteca nacional.

(15) Data refer only to books.

(15) Les données se réfèrent seulement aux livres.

(15) Los datos se refieren solamente a los libros.

(16) Data refer only to 6 libraries.

(16) Les données se réfèrent seulement à 6 bibliothèques.

(16) Los datos se refieren a 6 bibliotecas solamente.

(17) Data refer only to audio-visual documents.

(17) Les données se réfèrent seulement aux documents audiovisuels.

(17) Los datos se refieren solamente a los documentos audiovisuales.

(18) Data refer only to the number of readers.

(18) Les données se réfèrent seulement au nombre de lecteurs.

(18) Los datos se refieren solamente al número de lectores.

(19) Data for 527 public libraries have not been included.

(19) Les données relatives aux 527 bibliothèques publiques n'ont pas été incluses.

(19) Los datos relativos a las 527 bibliotecas públicas no están incluidos.

(20) The expenditure on library automation is not included athough it has been important in the last years in particular.

(20) Les dépenses concernant l'informatisation de la bibliothèque ne sont pas incluses. Elles ont été très importantes au cours des dernières années en particulier.

(20) Los gastos referidos a la informatización de la biblioteca no están incluidos. Han sido importantes en el curso de los últimos años en particular.

(21) Data do not include audio-visual documents.

(21) Les données n'incluent pas les documents audiovisuels.

(21) Los datos no incluyen los documentos audiovisuales.

(22) Data include community centres and libraries in institutions of a general culture/education nature.

(22) Les données incluent les centres communautaires et les bibliothèques dans les institutions de nature culturelle/éducative à caractère général.

(22) Los datos incluyen los centros comunitarios y las bibliotecas en las instituciones culturales/educativas de carácter general.

(23) Data include other library materials.

(23) Les données incluent d'autres matériels de bibliothèque.

(23) Los datos incluyen otros materiales de biblioteca.

(24) Data refer only to municipal libraries and include those in overseas departments.

(24) Les données se réfèrent seulement aux bibliothèques municipales et incluent celles des départements d'Outre-Mer.

(24) Los datos se refieren solamente a las bibliotecas municipales e incluyen las bibliotecas de los departamentos de Ultramar.

(25) Data include manuscripts, microforms and CD-ROMs.

(25) Les données incluent les manuscrits, les microcopies et les Cd-Roms.

(25) Los datos incluyen los manuscritos, las microcopias y los CD-Rom.

(26) Data include manuscripts and audio-visual materials.

(26) Les données incluent les manuscrits et le matériel audiovisuel.

(26) Los datos incluyen los manuscritos y el material audiovisual.

(27) Data refer only to the number of visits to the library.

(27) Les données se réfèrent seulement au nombre de visites de la bibliothèque.

(27) Los datos se refieren solamente al número de visitas de la biblioteca.

(28) Eight trade union libraries, 1 collective farm library and 1 hospital library were closed down.

(28) Huit bibliothèques de syndicats, 1 bibliothèque de ferme collective et 1 bibliothèque d'hôpital ont été fermées.

(28) Ocho bibliotecas de sindicatos, 1 biblioteca de granja colectiva y 1 biblioteca de hospital fueron cerradas.

(29) Three public libraries of general use and 15 libraries of restricted use were closed down.

(29) Trois bibliothèques publiques à usage général et 15 bibliothèques à usage restreint ont été fermées.

(29) Tres bibliotecas públicas de uso general y 15 bibliotecas de uso restringido fueron cerradas.

(30) Data include CD-ROMs.

(30) Les données incluent les CD-Roms.

(30) Los datos incluyen los CD-Rom.

(31) Data refer only to independent libraries and those incorporated in enterprises.

(31) Les données se réfèrent seulement aux bibliothèques indépendantes et à celles qui ont été incorporées aux entreprises

(31) Los datos se refieren solamente a las bibliotecas independientes y a aquellas que han sido incorporadas a las empresas.

(32) Data refer only to auditory materials.

(32) Les données se réfèrent seulement aux matériels auditifs.

(32) Los datos se refieren a los materiales auditivos.

(33) Data refer to libraries under 'Deutsches Bibliotheksinstitut' only.

(33) Les données couvrent seulement les bibliothèques placées sous le 'Deutsches Bibliothekinstitut'.

(33) Los datos corresponden solamente a las bibliotecas que dependen de la 'Deutches Bibliothekinstitut'.

(34) Data include the national library and 123 special libraries.

(34) Les données incluent la bibliothèque nationale et 123 bibliothèques spécialisées.

(34) Los datos incluyen la biblioteca nacional y 123 bibliotecas especializadas.

(35) Data include microforms.

(35) Les données incluent les microcopies.

(35) Los datos incluyen microcopias

(36) Data refer to public libraries dependent on the Ministry of Culture only.

(36) Les données se réfèrent aux bibliothèques dépendantes du Ministère de la Culture seulement.

(36) Los datos se refieren a las bibliotecas que dependen del Ministerio de la Cultura solamente.

(37) Data are shown in ECUs expressed at 1990 constant prices.

(37) Les données sont montrées en ECUs et s'expriment en valeurs constantes de 1990.

(37) Los datos se expresan en ECUs en moneda constante de 1990.

(38) Data refer only to microforms.

(38) Les données se réfèrent seulement aux microcopies.

(38) Los datos se refieren solamente a microcopias.

(39) Data include part-time employees not in full-time equivalent.

(39) Les données incluent les employés à temps partiel et ne sont pas converties en équivalent plein-temps.

(39) Los datos incluyen a los empleados de jornada parcial y no han sido convertidos en equivalente de jornada completa.

(40) Data refer only to libraries with at least 5000 volumes.

(40) Les données se réfèrent seulement aux bibliothèques dotées d'au moins 5000 volumes.

(40) Los datos se refieren solamente a las bibliotecas con al menos 5000 volúmenes.

(41) Data refer to the total number of library users, i.e. library users who borrowed materials or visitors for other purposes.

(41) Les données se réfèrent à la totalité des usagers de la bibliothèque, c'est-à-dire aux usagers qui ont emprunté du matériel ou qui l'ont utilisé dans la bibliothèque, ainsi qu'aux visites liées à d'autres raisons.

(41) Los datos se refieren a la totalidad de los usuarios de la biblioteca, o sea a los usuarios que han tomado prestado material o que lo han utilizado en la biblioteca, así como a las visitas ligadas a otro tipo de razones.

(42) Data refer to 90% approximately of the total.

(42) Les données se réfèrent approximativement à 90% du total.

(42) Los datos se refieren al 90% del total aproximadamente.

(43) Data include CD-ROMs and all kinds of electronic documents.

(43) Les données incluent les CD-Rom et toutes sortes de documents électroniques.

(43) Los datos incluyen los CD-Rom y toda suerte de documentos electrónicos.

(44) Data refer only to loans of books, audio-visual items, i.e. recorded music, talking books, videos, and CD-ROMs.

(44) Les données se réfèrent seulement aux prêts de livres, de documents audiovisuels tels que l'enregistrement de musique, les livres parlés, les vidéos, etc., et les Cd-Rom.

(44) Los datos se refieren solamente a los préstamos de libros, documentos audiovisuales tales como la música grabada, los libros hablados, los vídeos, etc., y los CD-Rom.

IV.3   Libraries of institutions of tertiary education
Bibliothèques d'établissements d'enseignement supérieur
Bibliotecas de instituciones de enseñanza superior

## IV.3   Libraries of institutions of tertiary education: collections, registered users, works loaned out, current expenditure, employees

Bibliothèques d'établissements d'enseignement supérieur: collections, usagers inscrits, documents prêtés au-dehors, dépenses ordinaires, personnel

Bibliotecas de instituciones de enseñanza superior: fondos, usuarios inscritos, documentos prestados al exterior, gastos ordinarios, personal

| Country / Pays / País | Year / Année / Año | Administrative unit / Unités administratives / Unidades administrativas | Service points / Points de service / Puntos de servicio | Collections / Collections / Fondos | | | | | Registered users (000) / Usagers inscrits (000) / Usuarios inscritos (000) |
|---|---|---|---|---|---|---|---|---|---|
| | | | | Books/Livres/Libros | | Microforms / Microcopies / Microcopias | Audio-visual documents (000) / Matériels audio-visuels (000) / Materiales audio-visuales (000) | Other library materials (000) / Autres matériels de bibliothèque (000) / Otros materiales de biblioteca (000) | |
| | | | | Number of volumes (000) / Nombre de volumes (000) / Número de volúmenes (000) | Metres of shelving / Mètres de rayonnage / Metros de estantes | | | | |
| **Africa** | | | | | | | | | |
| Botswana | 1988 | (1) 8 | 8 | 9 | ... | ... | 0.04 | 1.21 | 0.7 |
| | 1996 | (3) 1 | 4 | 256 | ... | ... | ... | ... | 10 |
| Central African Republic | 1980 | 4 | 4 | 30 | ... | ... | ... | ... | 1.5 |
| | 1996 | 3 | 4 | 36 | 188 | 1 | 0.01 | 0.07 | ... |
| Egypt | 1972 | 112 | ... | 2 591 | ... | ... | ... | ... | ... |
| | 1979 | 112 | 163 | 2 755 | ... | ... | 4.00 | 18 | ... |
| | 1989 | 272 | 272 | 35 790 | ... | 9 700 | 6.70 | 58 | 66 |
| | 1996 | (1) 412 | ... | ... | ... | 36 100 | 13 | 37 | 3 178 |
| Ethiopia | 1996 | 5 | 9 | 30 | ... | ... | 0.24 | ... | 3.0 |
| Guinea | 1997 | (3) 1 | 1 | 15 | 250 | ... | ... | ... | 1.2 |
| Madagascar | 1981 | 2 | 6 | 174 | ... | 250 | 0.21 | 0.33 | 14 |
| | 1996 | 33 | 39 | 55 | ... | 411 | 0.02 | 1.60 | 6.4 |
| Morocco | 1994 | (4) 150 | ... | ... | ... | ... | ... | ... | 258 |
| Reunion | 1981 | (5) 1 | 1 | 30 | 1 665 | 120 | ... | ... | ... |
| | 1990 | 1 | 1 | 52 | 2 429 | 1 260 | ... | ... | 3.0 |
| Rwanda | 1981 | 2 | 3 | 132 | 3 786 | 1 337 | 7.41 | *2.50 | 1.4 |
| | 1996 | (3) 1 | | | 175.5 | | 0.37 | 0.06 | 0.2 |
| Senegal | 1981 | (8) 1 | 4 | 227 | 7 440 | 1 070 | 1.07 | ... | 7.1 |
| | 1994 | 7 | ... | 380 | 13 894 | 2 474 | 1.65 | 0.15 | 13 |
| | 1996 | (3) 1 | ... | 323 | 12 800 | ... | 2.00 | 0.03 | 11 |
| Seychelles | 1982 | 2 | 2 | 11 | ... | ... | ... | ... | 0.2 |
| | 1990 | 1 | 5 | 26 | 510 | ... | *0.04 | ... | *1.6 |

Libraries of institutions of tertiary education IV.3
Bibliothèques d'établissements d'enseignement supérieur
Bibliotecas de instituciones de enseñanza superior

| Annual additions / Acquisitions annuelles / Adquisiciones anuales | | Loans to users (000) Prêts aux usagers (000) Préstamos a los usuarios (000) | Inter-Library loans Prêts entre bibliothèques Préstamos entre bibliotecas | Current expenditure / Dépenses ordinaires / Gastos ordinarios | | Library employees / Personnel des bibliothèques / Personal de las bibliotecas | | | Country Pays País | Year Année Año |
|---|---|---|---|---|---|---|---|---|---|---|
| Volumes (000) Volumes (000) Volúmenes (000) | Other materials (000) Autres matériels (000) Otros materiales (000) | | | Total (000) Total (000) Total (000) | Staff (%) Personnel (%) Personal (%) | Total Total Total | Holding a diploma Diplômé Diplomado | Trained on the job Formé sur le tas Formado en ejercicio | | |
| | | | | | | | | | **Africa** | |
| 2.8 | 0.03 | 6.13 | ... | (2) 37 | ... | 5 | 2 | 2 | Botswana | 1988 |
| 28 | ... | 77 | 1 204 | 15 581 | 36 | 115 | 92 | 23 | | 1996 |
| 0.6 | ... | ... | ... | 3 750 | ... | 12 | 3 | ... | Central African | 1980 |
| ... | ... | ... | ... | ... | ... | 28 | 3 | 25 | Republic | 1996 |
| 51 | ... | 1 750 | ... | ... | ... | 805 | ... | ... | Egypt | 1972 |
| ... | ... | ... | ... | ... | ... | 1 476 | ... | ... | | 1979 |
| ... | ... | ... | ... | ... | ... | 2 413 | ... | ... | | 1989 |
| ... | ... | 7 407 | ... | ... | ... | ... | ... | ... | | 1996 |
| 9.5 | ... | 250 | ... | ... | ... | 41 | 7 | 23 | Ethiopia | 1996 |
| 0.9 | ... | 4.00 | ... | 5 420 | 100 | 12 | ... | ... | Guinea | 1997 |
| 1.3 | 0.05 | ... | 185 | 84 530 | 82 | 127 | 3 | 10 | Madagascar | 1981 |
| 1.7 | 1.89 | 18 | ... | 59 365 | 97 | 48 | 1 | 15 | | 1996 |
| ... | ... | ... | ... | ... | ... | 413 | 56 | 357 | Morocco | 1994 |
| 1.6 | ... | ... | ... | ... | ... | 13 | 4 | ... | Reunion | 1981 |
| 4.4 | ... | 27 | (6) 12 | (7) 1 158 | ... | 14 | 4 | ... | | 1990 |
| 5.2 | 0.01 | 25 | ... | 17 030 | 59 | 50 | 3 | ... | Rwanda | 1981 |
| 0.3 | ... | ... | ... | ... | ... | 4 | ... | 4 | | 1996 |
| 6.0 | 1.25 | 49 | ... | (2) 72 500 | ... | 67 | 18 | ... | Senegal | 1981 |
| 7.4 | ... | 118 | (9) 502 | (2) 75 981 | ... | 85 | 35 | 7 | | 1994 |
| 3.1 | ... | 119 | 236 | 100 670 | ... | 63 | 26 | ... | | 1996 |
| 1.1 | ... | 1.64 | ... | ... | ... | ... | ... | ... | Seychelles | 1982 |
| 2.3 | ... | 13 | ... | 322 | 66 | 10 | 2 | 7 | | 1990 |

IV.3    Libraries of institutions of tertiary education
Bibliothèques d'établissements d'enseignement supérieur
Bibliotecas de instituciones de enseñanza superior

| Country / Pays / País | Year / Année / Año | Administrative unit / Unités administratives / Unidades administrativas | Service points / Points de service / Puntos de servicio | Collections / Collections / Fondos | | Microforms / Microcopias | Audio-visual documents (000) / Matériels audio-visuels (000) / Materiales audio-visuales (000) | Other library materials (000) / Autres matériels de bibliothèque (000) / Otros materiales de biblioteca (000) | Registered users (000) / Usagers inscrits (000) / Usuarios inscritos (000) |
|---|---|---|---|---|---|---|---|---|---|
| | | | | Books/Livres/Libros | | | | | |
| | | | | Number of volumes (000) / Nombre de volumes (000) / Número de volúmenes (000) | Metres of shelving / Mètres de rayonnage / Metros de estantes | | | | |
| South Africa | 1991 | 88 | 166 | 6 883 | ... | 134 372 | ... | 631 | ... |
| Swaziland | 1996 | 36 | 13 | ... | ... | 5 720 | 2.61 | ... | 46 |
| Togo | 1982 | (3) 1 | 6 | 50 | 1 428 | ... | ... | ... | 4.9 |
| | 1996 | (4) 5 | 3 | 60 | ... | ... | 0.00 | 0.00 | ... |
| Uganda | 1993 | 5 | 10 | 1 096 | 56 300 | 734 | ... | ... | 35 |
| United Republic of Tanzania | 1996 | (10) 2 | 2 | 27 | 64 | ... | ... | 0.62 | 1.4 |
| Zimbabwe | 1982 | 10 | 10 | 485 | ... | 269 | ... | 0.14 | 7.4 |
| | 1990 | 25 | 31 | 764 | ... | 286 | 0.40 | ... | 31 |
| | 1996 | (3) 1 | 2 | ... | ... | ... | 0.01 | ... | ... |
| **North America** | | | | | | | | | |
| Barbados | 1981 | (11) 3 | 5 | 95 | ... | ... | ... | ... | 3.7 |
| | 1990 | (11) 1 | 2 | 22 | 1 357 | ... | 0.07 | 3.04 | 0.8 |
| | 1993 | (12) 1 | 1 | 29 | 365 | ... | 0.45 | 0.48 | 0.2 |
| Belize | 1990 | 1 | 1 | 6 | ... | ... | 0.02 | ... | 0.3 |
| Cayman Islands | 1982 | 1 | 1 | 20 | 900 | 3 000 | 3.03 | 0.36 | 0.2 |
| | 1990 | 1 | 1 | *30 | ... | ... | ... | 0.10 | 0.1 |
| Costa Rica | 1981 | (13) 1 | 1 | 205 | 6 714 | 5 547 | 14 | 3.03 | 16 |
| | 1990 | 4 | 4 | 633 | ... | ... | ... | ... | ... |
| Cuba | 1982 | (3) 56 | 56 | 1 438 | ... | ... | ... | ... | 205 |
| | 1990 | (3) 85 | 85 | 2 415 | ... | ... | ... | ... | 287 |
| | 1993 | (3) 86 | 86 | 2 525 | ... | ... | ... | ... | 271 |
| Dominican Republic | 1996 | 1 | 1 | 130 | 2 880 | ... | ... | ... | 2.5 |
| Guadeloupe | 1990 | 1 | 3 | 90 | 4 195 | 54 000 | ... | ... | 3.6 |
| Mexico | 1980 | (3) 257 | 257 | 2 611 | ... | ... | ... | ... | (15) 8 638 |
| | 1990 | (3) 899 | 899 | ... | ... | 348 142 | 429 | 1 294 | 1 265 |
| | 1992 | (3) 1 070 | 1 070 | 11 112 | 467 661 | 793 427 | 720 | ... | ... |
| | 1993 | (3) 1 139 | 1 139 | 12 776 | ... | 369 889 | 600 | 1 857 | 1 010 |
| | 1996 | (3) 1 187 | *1 187 | *14 000 | ... | 183 868 | 689 | 17 579 | 926 |
| Nicaragua | 1990 | 13 | 18 | 187 | ... | 1 146 | 1.39 | 1.11 | 28 |
| St. Vincent and the Grenadines | 1990 | 2 | 2 | 12 | ... | ... | ... | ... | 1.1 |
| Trinidad and Tobago | 1981 | (16) 1 | 1 | 222 | 9 707 | 4 476 | 6.39 | ... | 2.3 |
| | 1993 | (16) 1 | 10 | 305 | ... | 9 302 | 21 | 3.61 | 5.3 |
| **South America** | | | | | | | | | |
| Bolivia | 1996 | (4) 5 | 5 | 7 | 488 | ... | 0.28 | ... | 2.8 |
| Falkland Islands (Malvinas) | 1996 | (3) 1 | 1 | 18 | 499 | 300 | 0.39 | 0.05 | 0.5 |
| Guyana | 1996 | (3) 1 | 2 | 193 | 4 248 | 3 612 | 6.63 | 0.30 | 5.7 |
| Peru | 1982 | 3 | 7 | 58 | ... | ... | ... | (17) 2.34 | ... |
| | 1996 | (10) 1 | 7 | 3 870 | ... | ... | 70 | 81 | 60 |
| Suriname | 1996 | (3) 3 | 1 | 64 | ... | ... | ... | ... | 1.7 |
| Uruguay | 1971 | 4 | 9 | 132 | 5 517 | ... | ... | ... | 11 |
| | 1996 | (3) 1 | 1 | 40 | 1 500 | ... | 0.30 | ... | 1.3 |
| **Asia** | | | | | | | | | |
| Armenia | 1996 | (19) 15 | *15 | 6 592 | ... | ... | ... | ... | 54 |

Libraries of institutions of tertiary education    IV.3
Bibliothèques d'établissements d'enseignement supérieur
Bibliotecas de instituciones de enseñanza superior

| Annual additions / Acquisitions annuelles / Adquisiciones anuales | | Loans to users (000) | Inter-Library loans | Current expenditure / Dépenses ordinaires / Gastos ordinarios | | Library employees / Personnel des bibliothèques / Personal de las bibliotecas | | | Country | Year |
|---|---|---|---|---|---|---|---|---|---|---|
| Volumes (000) | Other materials (000) | Prêts aux usagers (000) | Prêts entre biblio-thèques | Total (000) | Staff (%) | Total | Holding a diploma | Trained on the job | | |
| Volumes (000) | Autres matériels (000) | | | Total (000) | Personnel (%) | Total | Diplômé | Formé sur le tas | Pays | Année |
| Volúmenes (000) | Otros materiales (000) | Préstamos a los usuarios (000) | Préstamos entre bibliotecas | Total (000) | Personal (%) | Total | Diplomado | Formado en ejercicio | País | Año |
| 168 | 6.39 | ... | ... | 20 051 | 51 | 1 827 | 648 | 153 | South Africa | 1991 |
| 0.4 | ... | ... | 440 | 701 | 72 | 170 | 61 | 41 | Swaziland | 1996 |
| 3.6 | ... | 23 | 22 | 34 383 | 68 | 41 | 7 | ... | Togo | 1982 |
| ... | ... | ... | 10 | 20 500 | ... | 70 | 6 | 5 | | 1996 |
| 9.2 | ... | 904 | ... | 484 000 | 28 | 178 | 26 | 35 | Uganda | 1993 |
| ... | ... | ... | ... | ... | ... | 8 | 1 | 2 | United Republic of Tanzania | 1996 |
| 24 | 0.01 | 304 | (9) 3 232 | ... | ... | 99 | 6 | 25 | Zimbabwe | 1982 |
| 7.6 | ... | 1 203 | (9) 2 296 | (7) 410 | ... | 224 | 121 | ... | | 1990 |
| ... | 0.01 | 28 | 80 | 240 | ... | 5 | 1 | 3 | | 1996 |
| | | | | | | | | | **North America** | |
| *5.1 | ... | 76 | ... | 9 858 | 29 | 40 | 9 | ... | Barbados | 1981 |
| 0.9 | ... | 12 | ... | ... | ... | 12 | 2 | ... | | 1990 |
| 0.6 | 0.18 | 1.98 | ... | 105 224 | 91 | 5 | 1 | 2 | | 1993 |
| ... | ... | ... | ... | 73 | 94 | 5 | 2 | ... | Belize | 1990 |
| 1.1 | ... | 4.20 | ... | 11 | 84 | 3 | ... | 3 | Cayman Islands | 1982 |
| 0.1 | 0.01 | 0.20 | ... | (7) 7 | ... | 1 | ... | ... | | 1990 |
| 15 | 5.13 | 471 | ... | 231 588 | 5 | 124 | 56 | ... | Costa Rica | 1981 |
| 25 | 0.30 | ... | (6) 1 585 | ... | ... | ... | ... | ... | | 1990 |
| 70 | ... | ... | ... | ... | ... | 314 | 95 | 131 | Cuba | 1982 |
| 4.1 | ... | 401 | ... | ... | ... | 750 | 215 | ... | | 1990 |
| (14) 2.3 | ... | 395 | ... | ... | ... | 740 | 220 | ... | | 1993 |
| ... | ... | 250 | ... | 5 294 | 37 | 31 | 3 | ... | Dominican Republic | 1996 |
| 6.5 | ... | 115 | (6) 173 | 7 849 | 46 | 23 | 11 | ... | Guadeloupe | 1990 |
| ... | ... | 11 053 | ... | 144 555 | 21 | 1 470 | ... | ... | Mexico | 1980 |
| 434 | 203 | ... | 46 006 | ... | ... | 4 604 | 994 | 3 610 | | 1990 |
| ... | ... | 54 637 | ... | ... | ... | 6 519 | 1 043 | 4 098 | | 1992 |
| 1 009 | 232 | 69 997 | (6) 252 191 | ... | ... | 7 247 | 1 515 | 5 732 | | 1993 |
| 919 | 172 | 10 496 | 146 160 | ... | ... | 6 197 | 1 187 | ... | | 1996 |
| 8.5 | ... | 168 | 43 075 | ... | ... | 97 | 10 | 33 | Nicaragua | 1990 |
| 0.6 | ... | ... | ... | 28 | ... | 4 | 1 | 3 | St. Vincent and the Grenadines | 1990 |
| 5.9 | 0.43 | 84 | 11 | 3 644 | 67 | 91 | 20 | ... | Trinidad and Tobago | 1981 |
| 6.9 | 3.91 | 284 | 265 | ... | ... | 94 | 21 | ... | | 1993 |
| | | | | | | | | | **South America** | |
| 3.2 | 0.11 | 22 | ... | 27 | 85 | 2 | 1 | 1 | Bolivia | 1996 |
| 0.8 | 0.15 | ... | ... | 32 | 52 | 2 | 1 | 1 | Falkland Islands (Malvinas) | 1996 |
| 5.0 | 0.07 | 236 | 17 | 3 758 | ... | 80 | 5 | 3 | Guyana | 1996 |
| 2.9 | (17) 0.59 | 367 | ... | (17)(18) 40 200 | ... | 41 | 1 | 14 | Peru | 1982 |
| 41 | 149 | ... | 50 | 5 000 | 50 | 112 | 50 | 48 | | 1996 |
| ... | 0.02 | 12 | 21 | ... | ... | 27 | 12 | 9 | Suriname | 1996 |
| 3.8 | ... | 53 | ... | 5 046 | ... | ... | ... | ... | Uruguay | 1971 |
| ... | ... | ... | ... | ... | ... | 7 | 3 | ... | | 1996 |
| | | | | | | | | | **Asia** | |
| 30 | ... | 0.75 | ... | ... | ... | ... | ... | ... | Armenia | 1996 |

**Libraries of institutions of tertiary education**
**Bibliothèques d'établissements d'enseignement supérieur**
**Bibliotecas de instituciones de enseñanza superior**

| Country / Pays / País | Year / Année / Año | Administrative unit / Unités administratives / Unidades administrativas | Service points / Points de service / Puntos de servicio | Collections / Collections / Fondos Books/Livres/Libros — Number of volumes (000) / Nombre de volumes (000) / Número de volúmenes (000) | Books/Livres/Libros — Metres of shelving / Mètres de rayonnage / Metros de estantes | Microforms / Microcopies / Microcopias | Audio-visual documents (000) / Matériels audio-visuels (000) / Materiales audio-visuales (000) | Other library materials (000) / Autres matériels de bibliothèque (000) / Otros materiales de biblioteca (000) | Registered users (000) / Usagers inscrits (000) / Usuarios inscritos (000) |
|---|---|---|---|---|---|---|---|---|---|
| Azerbaijan | 1997 | 40 | 80 | 9 759 | ... | 13 324 | 1.19 | ... | 108 |
| Bahrain | 1990 | (20) 1 | 1 | 35 | 790 | ... | 0.50 | ... | 1.8 |
| Brunei Darussalam | 1981 | 5 | *5 | 48 | 1 140 | ... | ... | | 0.8 |
| | 1990 | 2 | 3 | 150 | ... | 530 | 2.45 | 1.29 | 1.5 |
| China | 1990 | 1 064 | *4 500 | 356 415 | | 876 414 | 1 124 | ... | 3 244 |
| | 1993 | 1 075 | *5 000 | 406 471 | ... | 19 653 547 | 1 138 | ... | 4 272 |
| China, Hong Kong SAR | 1981 | 12 | 25 | 1 750 | 549 | 112 567 | 27 | 0.05 | 63 |
| | 1990 | 17 | 33 | 3 370 | ... | ... | 255 | | 123 |
| Iran, Islamic Republic of | 1982 | 198 | 198 | 3 993 | 33 272 | | ... | ... | ... |
| | 1994 | 113 | 168 | 2 323 | ... | | ... | ... | 281 |
| Japan | 1982 | 893 | 1 317 | 131 499 | ... | ... | ... | ... | 2 205 |
| | 1990 | (21) 507 | 704 | 181 839 | ... | ... | ... | ... | 1 370 |
| | 1991 | (21) 514 | 724 | ... | ... | | | | ... |
| Jordan | 1990 | 33 | 44 | 1 227 | | 34 105 | 11 | 2.74 | 51 |
| Korea, Republic of | 1981 | 222 | ... | 11 025 | | | | ... | ... |
| | 1990 | 305 | ... | 26 554 | ... | ... | ... | (22) 914 | 97 256 |
| | 1993 | 311 | ... | 35 423 | ... | ... | ... | ... | 86 438 |
| | 1994 | 340 | ... | 35 758 | ... | ... | ... | ... | 61 559 |
| Lebanon | 1993 | 72 | ... | *2 075 | ... | ... | ... | ... | ... |
| Malaysia | 1982 | (21) 6 | 18 | 2 040 | 16 925 | 248 206 | 126 | 31 | 50 |
| | 1990 | 48 | 73 | 3 412 | ... | 1 794 904 | 32 | 4.79 | ... |
| Mongolia | 1990 | (21) 9 | ... | 1 581 | ... | ... | ... | ... | 20 |
| Oman | 1991 | 2 | 6 | 65 | ... | 859 | 15 | ... | 6.5 |
| | 1993 | (3) 1 | 4 | 78 | 1 945 | ... | ... | ... | *6.0 |
| | 1996 | (3) 1 | 5 | 101 | ... | 1 500 | 16 | 0.07 | 6.0 |
| Pakistan | 1993 | 31 | 113 | 3 955 | 135 367 | 23 500 | 6.26 | 104 | 49 |
| Qatar | 1981 | 2 | 5 | 98 | 3 330 | 648 | ... | ... | 3.0 |
| | 1993 | 2 | 7 | 329 | ... | 23 520 | 0.67 | 2.13 | 6.0 |
| Saudi Arabia | 1993 | 21 | 65 | 4 844 | 113 849 | 741 274 | 9.33 | 138 | 484 |
| Singapore | 1981 | 4 | 15 | 1 350 | ... | 116 861 | 14 | 0.01 | 34 |
| | 1990 | 5 | 12 | 2 354 | (24) 14 865 | 255 809 | (24) 76 | (24)(25) 3.99 | 78 |
| Sri Lanka | 1990 | 11 | 36 | 829 | ... | 5 212 | 1.71 | 5.84 | 31 |
| | 1996 | 13 | 38 | 736 | ... | 585 | 1.36 | 1.81 | 26 |
| Syrian Arab Republic | 1980 | (27) 1 | 13 | 1 | ... | ... | ... | ... | 5.0 |
| | 1993 | (27) 1 | *13 | 10 | 250 | ... | ... | ... | ... |
| Thailand | 1996 | 73 | 129 | 6 274 | 121 200.41 | 189 154 | 3 211 | 195 | 544 |
| Turkey | 1993 | 212 | 212 | 5 700 | ... | ... | 74 | 216 | ... |
| | 1997 | (4) 68 | 66 | ... | ... | ... | 193 | 230 | ... |
| United Arab Emirates | 1982 | 1 | 14 | 95 | 2 380 | 1 893 | 1.93 | ... | 4.0 |
| | 1990 | 3 | 22 | 248 | 11 177 | ... | 8.56 | 0.11 | 13 |
| | 1997 | 1 | 6 | 13 | ... | 30 000 | ... | 0.03 | 20 |
| Uzbekistan | 1993 | 58 | 304 | 2 358 | 158 738 | 14 344 | 1.62 | 952 | 263 |
| Palestine | 1991 | 6 | 10 | 349 | ... | ... | 4.53 | 3.34 | 13 |
| **Europe** | | | | | | | | | |
| Austria | 1985 | *21 | *218 | 12 703 | ... | *969 665 | *232 | 1 367 | 2 342 |
| | 1990 | (29) 21 | *248 | 15 446 | ... | ... | ... | ... | 3 186 |

Libraries of institutions of tertiary education IV.3
Bibliothèques d'établissements d'enseignement supérieur
Bibliotecas de instituciones de enseñanza superior

| Annual additions — Acquisitions annuelles — Adquisiciones anuales | | Loans to users (000) Prêts aux usagers (000) Préstamos a los usuarios (000) | Inter-Library loans Prêts entre biblio-thèques Préstamos entre bibliotecas | Current expenditure — Dépenses ordinaires — Gastos ordinarios | | Library employees — Personnel des bibliothèques — Personal de las bibliotecas | | | Country Pays País | Year Année Año |
|---|---|---|---|---|---|---|---|---|---|---|
| Volumes (000) Volumes (000) Volúmenes (000) | Other materials (000) Autres matériels (000) Otros materiales (000) | | | Total (000) Total (000) Total (000) | Staff (%) Personnel (%) Personal (%) | Total Total Total | Holding a diploma Diplômé Diplomado | Trained on the job Formé sur le tas Formado en ejercicio | | |
| 65 | 2.05 | 2 540 | ... | 1 223 567 | 20 | 712 | 367 | 104 | Azerbaijan | 1997 |
| 1.3 | ... | 9.07 | ... | | | 9 | 3 | ... | Bahrain | 1990 |
| ... | | | | | | 10 | ... | 5 | Brunei Darussalam | 1981 |
| 11 | 0.34 | 65 | ... | | | 55 | 18 | 33 | | 1990 |
| 420 | | 65 802 | 80 146 | (2) 210 587 | ... | 35 208 | 21 747 | ... | China | 1990 |
| (14) 10 170 | 599 | ... | ... | (2) 316 408 | ... | 44 417 | 30 894 | ... | | 1993 |
| 80 | 23 | 1 644 | 616 | 40 279 | 66 | 412 | 73 | 1 | China, Hong Kong | 1981 |
| 225 | ... | | | 186 440 | 50 | 648 | 114 | 15 | SAR | 1990 |
| 200 | ... | 1 110 | ... | (7) 449 446 | ... | 1 196 | 156 | ... | Iran, Islamic | 1982 |
| ... | | | | ... | ... | 630 | ... | ... | Republic of | 1994 |
| 7 282 | ... | 14 871 | ... | 99 200 960 | 40 | 11 519 | ... | ... | Japan | 1982 |
| ... | | 16 928 | | ... | ... | 11 708 | ... | ... | | 1990 |
| ... | | ... | | ... | ... | 11 944 | ... | ... | | 1991 |
| 36 | 6.57 | 914 | | 1 998 | 33 | 351 | 73 | 183 | Jordan | 1990 |
| 821 | ... | ... | | 9 100 385 | | 1 969 | 462 | 483 | Korea, Republic of | 1981 |
| ... | | 21 703 | ... | 41 112 958 | 18 | 3 282 | 1 943 | ... | | 1990 |
| ... | | 27 765 | ... | 46 088 804 | ... | 3 100 | ... | ... | | 1993 |
| ... | | 45 496 | ... | 101 475 898 | ... | 3 525 | ... | ... | | 1994 |
| ... | | ... | ... | 238 | ... | 449 | 57 | ... | Lebanon | 1993 |
| 143 | 0.29 | 1 632 | 4 804 | 18 057 | 32 | 1 007 | 133 | 62 | Malaysia | 1982 |
| 384 | 115 | 2 189 | ... | ... | ... | 1 754 | 329 | ... | | 1990 |
| 1.1 | ... | ... | ... | ... | ... | 100 | ... | ... | Mongolia | 1990 |
| 12 | 0.33 | 101 | (6) 42 | ... | ... | 67 | 35 | 17 | Oman | 1991 |
| *8.9 | *5.65 | 61 | 19 | ... | ... | 68 | 35 | ... | | 1993 |
| 6.6 | 0.83 | 96 | 1 043 | 1 034 | 39 | 54 | 28 | 13 | | 1996 |
| 29 | ... | 364 | ... | 13 010 | ... | 569 | 88 | 41 | Pakistan | 1993 |
| 18 | ... | 17 | ... | 7 328 | 25 | 38 | ... | ... | Qatar | 1981 |
| 5.0 | 5.00 | ... | ... | ... | ... | 132 | 14 | 61 | | 1993 |
| 99 | 68 | ... | 9 825 | 17 865 | 32 | 512 | 161 | 117 | Saudi Arabia | 1993 |
| 60 | 5.06 | 976 | 1 643 | (23) 12 537 | (23) 70 | 262 | 47 | 20 | Singapore | 1981 |
| 137 | (26) 5.95 | 2 130 | (24) 2 104 | ... | ... | 398 | 98 | 8 | | 1990 |
| 26 | 0.01 | 462 | 421 | 110 425 | 42 | 415 | 28 | 55 | Sri Lanka | 1990 |
| 19 | 0.28 | 199 | ... | ... | ... | 325 | 23 | 25 | | 1996 |
| 0.6 | ... | ... | ... | 131 | 53 | 60 | 4 | 30 | Syrian Arab | 1980 |
| 0.0 | ... | *5.00 | ... | (28) 8 | 100 | ... | ... | ... | Republic | 1993 |
| 312 | 57 | 3 111 | 6 029 | 459 613 | 37 | 7 768 | 425 | 221 | Thailand | 1996 |
| ... | ... | ... | ... | ... | ... | 1 310 | 263 | 749 | Turkey | 1993 |
| ... | ... | ... | ... | ... | ... | 1 180 | 297 | ... | | 1997 |
| 31 | 0.42 | 37 | ... | 12 834 | 30 | 101 | 11 | 5 | United Arab | 1982 |
| 34 | 1.34 | (1) 62 | ... | (7) 7 159 | ... | 129 | 19 | 35 | Emirates | 1990 |
| 15 | 2.36 | 171 | 73 | ... | ... | 87 | 29 | 45 | | 1997 |
| 941 | 8.64 | 14 344 | (6) 935 | 3 392 | 26 | 1 602 | 1 060 | 383 | Uzbekistan | 1993 |
| ... | | ... | ... | ... | | ... | ... | ... | Palestine | 1991 |
| | | | | | | | | | **Europe** | |
| ... | ... | 1 146 | ... | ... | | ... | ... | ... | Austria | 1985 |
| 372 | ... | 1 836 | ... | (7) 214 559 | ... | 837 | ... | ... | | 1990 |

IV.3   Libraries of institutions of tertiary education
Bibliothèques d'établissements d'enseignement supérieur
Bibliotecas de instituciones de enseñanza superior

| Country / Pays / País | Year / Année / Año | Administrative unit / Unités administratives / Unidades administrativas | Service points / Points de service / Puntos de servicio | Collections / Collections / Fondos | | Microforms / Microcopies / Microcopias | Audio-visual documents (000) / Matériels audio-visuels (000) / Materiales audio-visuales (000) | Other library materials (000) / Autres matériels de bibliothèque (000) / Otros materiales de biblioteca (000) | Registered users (000) / Usagers inscrits (000) / Usuarios Inscritos (000) |
|---|---|---|---|---|---|---|---|---|---|
| | | | | Books/Livres/Libros | | | | | |
| | | | | Number of volumes (000) / Nombre de volumes (000) / Número de volúmenes (000) | Metres of shelving / Mètres de rayonnage / Metros de estantes | | | | |
| Austria (cont) | 1991 | 22 | 258 | 15 426 | ... | ... | ... | ... | (30) 2 310 |
| | 1992 | 22 | 245 | 15 378 | ... | ... | ... | ... | (30) 2 605 |
| | 1993 | 21 | 248 | 15 201 | ... | ... | ... | ... | (30) 2 485 |
| | 1994 | 22 | 227 | 15 083 | ... | ... | ... | ... | (30) 2 761 |
| | 1995 | 21 | 216 | 15 151 | ... | ... | ... | ... | (30) 3 142 |
| | 1996 | 21 | 218 | 15 262 | ... | ... | ... | ... | (30) 3 261 |
| | 1997 | 21 | 225 | 15 627 | ... | ... | ... | ... | (30) 3 637 |
| Belarus | 1990 | 33 | ... | 19 570 | ... | ... | ... | ... | 204 |
| | 1993 | 38 | ... | 20 428 | ... | ... | ... | ... | 193 |
| | 1996 | (19) 33 | ... | 19 725 | ... | ... | ... | ... | 241 |
| Belgium | 1981 | 14 | 140 | *5 988 | ... | *566 649 | *178 | 179 | *73 |
| | 1985 | 14 | 140 | *5 988 | ... | *566 649 | *178 | 179 | *73 |
| | 1990 | 16 | 140 | *5 988 | *147 413 | *566 649 | *178 | *179 | 87 |
| | 1991 | 16 | 119 | 16 497 | ... | 302 000 | 3.00 | 20 | 106 |
| | 1992 | 16 | 119 | 16 745 | ... | 302 000 | 3.00 | 20 | 110 |
| | 1993 | 16 | 118 | 17 088 | ... | 305 000 | 4.00 | 20 | 114 |
| | 1994 | 16 | 120 | 17 392 | ... | 306 000 | 4.00 | 20 | 118 |
| | 1995 | 16 | 120 | 17 676 | ... | 309 000 | 4.00 | 20 | 118 |
| | 1996 | 16 | 118 | 17 939 | ... | 309 000 | 11 | 21 | 140 |
| | 1997 | 16 | 117 | 18 301 | ... | 311 000 | 11 | 21 | 139 |
| Bulgaria | 1981 | 56 | ... | 4 949 | ... | 1 855 | ... | 410 | 120 |
| | 1990 | 56 | ... | 7 043 | ... | 10 074 | 30 | 299 | 145 |
| | 1991 | 56 | 56 | 7 171 | ... | 11 234 | (31) 42 | ... | 142 |
| | 1992 | 69 | 69 | 7 504 | ... | 9 121 | 32 | | 145 |
| | 1993 | 81 | 81 | 7 520 | ... | 11 555 | 33 | 312 | 150 |
| | 1994 | 90 | 90 | 7 885 | ... | 12 866 | 36 | ... | 171 |
| | 1995 | 93 | 93 | 8 170 | ... | 13 036 | 43 | ... | 189 |
| | 1996 | 93 | 93 | 8 268 | ... | 14 148 | 43 | ... | 211 |
| | 1997 | 92 | 92 | 8 269 | ... | 15 715 | 44 | ... | 191 |
| Croatia | 1992 | 128 | 136 | 3 433 | 75 073 | 111 | 36 | 77 | 102 |
| | 1995 | (19) 134 | 134 | 5 720 | 151 569 | 293 992 | 42 | 441 | 737 |
| Czech Republic | 1990 | 41 | 1 197 | 7 845 | ... | 413 290 | 77 | 202 | 149 |
| | 1991 | 43 | 1 078 | (32) 9 740 | ... | ... | ... | ... | 171 |
| | 1992 | 50 | 1 031 | (32) 9 626 | ... | ... | ... | ... | 176 |
| | 1993 | (3) 58 | 1 091 | (32) 8 551 | ... | ... | ... | ... | 184 |
| | 1994 | 72 | 1 057 | (32) 8 912 | ... | ... | ... | ... | 191 |
| | 1995 | 74 | 1 040 | (32) 8 591 | ... | ... | ... | ... | 230 |
| | 1996 | 65 | 986 | 9 937 | ... | 20 455 | 50 | 23 | 243 |
| | 1997 | 60 | 1 047 | 9 190 | ... | ... | ... | ... | (30) 4 041 |
| Denmark | 1981 | (34) 18 | 23 | 6 825 | 150 000 | 1 146 814 | 850 | ... | ... |
| | 1985 | 14 | 25 | 6 956 | ... | 270 198 | *255 | ... | *62 |
| | 1990 | 19 | 54 | 11 247 | 268 996 | 1 103 996 | 771 | ... | ... |
| | 1991 | 18 | 48 | 7 885 | ... | 996 540 | 779 | 37 | ... |
| | 1992 | 17 | 47 | 8 092 | ... | 1 037 841 | 763 | 52 | ... |
| | 1993 | 19 | 50 | 8 218 | ... | 1 042 763 | 775 | 60 | 117 |
| | 1994 | 19 | 48 | 8 357 | ... | 1 085 868 | 791 | 69 | ... |
| | 1995 | 19 | 43 | 8 582 | ... | 1 722 772 | 811 | 71 | ... |
| | 1996 | 19 | 45 | 8 797 | ... | 1 117 962 | 833 | 77 | ... |
| | 1997 | 20 | 43 | 8 896 | ... | 1 116 466 | 827 | 77 | ... |
| Estonia | 1990 | 13 | 27 | 4 815 | ... | 674 356 | 9.54 | 532 | 68 |
| | 1991 | 13 | 27 | 4 743 | ... | ... | ... | ... | (30) 1 265 |
| | 1992 | 13 | 27 | 4 734 | ... | ... | ... | ... | (30) 1 262 |
| | 1993 | (23) 13 | 27 | 4 815 | 95 004 | 674 356 | 9.54 | 60 | 68 |
| | 1994 | 19 | 35 | 5 465 | ... | 610 538 | 10 | 62 | 66 |
| | 1995 | 19 | 35 | 5 395 | ... | 609 742 | 23 | 65 | 63 |
| | 1996 | 20 | 35 | 5 460 | ... | 609 742 | 24 | 67 | 64 |
| | 1997 | 16 | 33 | 5 315 | ... | 356 204 | 27 | 67 | 59 |
| Federal Republic of Yugoslavia | 1992 | 166 | 310 | 7 052 | 108 242 | 1 771 | 71 | 43 | 1 745 |
| | 1995 | 3 132 | ... | 23 363 | 172 125 | 2 145 | 122 | 60 | 193 |
| Finland | 1980 | 28 | *450 | 6 140 | ... | ... | ... | ... | ... |
| | 1981 | 30 | *499 | 7 435 | ... | 636 459 | *302 | 108 | *123 |
| | 1985 | 30 | *499 | 10 512 | ... | 1 030 735 | 259 | 117 | *123 |
| | 1990 | 19 | 456 | 12 266 | 410 047 | 965 492 | 628 | 2.87 | ... |
| | 1991 | 19 | 465 | 12 724 | ... | 1 026 065 | 661 | 12 | (30) 4 248 |

Libraries of institutions of tertiary education IV.3
Bibliothèques d'établissements d'enseignement supérieur
Bibliotecas de instituciones de enseñanza superior

| | Annual additions Acquisitions annuelles Adquisiciones anuales | | Loans to users (000) Prêts aux usagers (000) Préstamos a los usuarios (000) | Inter-Library loans Prêts entre biblio-thèques Préstamos entre bibliotecas | Current expenditure Dépenses ordinaires Gastos ordinarios | | Library employees Personnel des bibliothèques Personal de las bibliotecas | | | Country Pays País | Year Année Año |
|---|---|---|---|---|---|---|---|---|---|---|---|
| | Volumes (000) Volumes (000) Volúmenes (000) | Other materials (000) Autres matériels (000) Otros materiales (000) | | | Total (000) Total (000) Total (000) | Staff (%) Personnel (%) Personal (%) | Total Total Total | Holding a diploma Diplômé Diplomado | Trained on the job Formé sur le tas Formado en ejercicio | | |
| | 479 | ... | 1 322 | ... | ... | ... | 794 | 453 | 341 | Austria (cont) | 1991 |
| | 463 | ... | 1 376 | ... | ... | ... | 734 | 438 | 296 | | 1992 |
| | 459 | ... | 1 459 | ... | ... | ... | 765 | 453 | 312 | | 1993 |
| | 440 | ... | 1 565 | ... | ... | ... | 739 | 483 | 256 | | 1994 |
| | 440 | ... | 1 554 | ... | ... | ... | 702 | 475 | 227 | | 1995 |
| | 443 | ... | 1 777 | ... | ... | ... | 706 | 485 | 221 | | 1996 |
| | 502 | ... | 1 965 | ... | ... | ... | 924 | 610 | 314 | | 1997 |
| | 1 086 | ... | ... | 4 500 | ... | ... | 1 215 | 733 | ... | Belarus | 1990 |
| | 636 | ... | ... | (6) 11 367 | ... | ... | 1 311 | 784 | ... | | 1993 |
| | ... | ... | 20 105 | 1 394 | ... | ... | 1 200 | 1 069 | ... | | 1996 |
| | ... | ... | *633 | ... | ... | ... | ... | ... | ... | Belgium | 1981 |
| | ... | ... | *633 | ... | ... | ... | ... | ... | ... | | 1985 |
| | 66 | ... | 705 | ... | ... | ... | 660 | 220 | ... | | 1990 |
| | 259 | ... | 1 002 | 00 000 | 1 404 600 | 57 | 600 | 210 | 180 | | 1991 |
| | 280 | ... | 1 072 | 85 000 | 1 451 700 | 57 | 680 | 210 | 470 | | 1992 |
| | 282 | ... | 1 073 | 84 000 | 1 521 200 | 56 | 670 | 220 | 450 | | 1993 |
| | 296 | ... | 1 172 | 84 000 | 1 618 300 | 55 | 670 | 220 | 450 | | 1994 |
| | 324 | ... | 1 262 | 93 000 | 1 655 600 | 56 | 680 | 230 | 450 | | 1995 |
| | 331 | ... | 1 271 | 106 000 | 1 756 200 | 56 | 700 | 240 | 460 | | 1996 |
| | 393 | ... | 1 293 | 110 000 | 1 859 000 | 54 | 710 | 250 | 460 | | 1997 |
| | 259 | 12 | 2 738 | ... | 3 379 | 31 | 427 | 297 | 130 | Bulgaria | 1981 |
| | 221 | 10 | 2 970 | ... | 7 792 | 35 | 530 | 395 | 135 | | 1990 |
| | 170 | 1.48 | 3 158 | ... | 13 619 | 48 | ... | 497 | ... | | 1991 |
| | 159 | 1.51 | 3 254 | ... | 43 376 | 37 | ... | 475 | ... | | 1992 |
| | 154 | 5.91 | 3 481 | ... | 64 257 | 45 | ... | 492 | ... | | 1993 |
| | 146 | 0.63 | 4 092 | ... | 110 456 | 34 | ... | 513 | ... | | 1994 |
| | 199 | 1.76 | 4 014 | ... | 120 451 | 42 | ... | 532 | ... | | 1995 |
| | 149 | 1.73 | 4 569 | ... | 241 508 | 43 | 540 | 472 | 68 | | 1996 |
| | 103 | 0.41 | 5 282 | ... | 1 905 601 | 48 | ... | 498 | ... | | 1997 |
| | 80 | 37 | 1 103 | 1 542 | (7) 179 469 | ... | 281 | 234 | ... | Croatia | 1992 |
| | 109 | 27 | 3.18 | ... | 6 769 | ... | 519 | 404 | ... | | 1995 |
| | ... | ... | 2 262 | 965 | ... | ... | 743 | 431 | 312 | Czech Republic | 1990 |
| (33) | 250 | ... | 1 536 | 16 000 | ... | ... | 505 | 280 | 225 | | 1991 |
| (33) | 217 | ... | 1 581 | 16 000 | ... | ... | 516 | 286 | 230 | | 1992 |
| (33) | 209 | ... | 1 633 | (6) 16 466 | (7) 47 988 | ... | 562 | 312 | 250 | | 1993 |
| (33) | 212 | ... | 1 398 | 16 364 | ... | ... | 611 | 338 | 273 | | 1994 |
| (33) | 219 | ... | 1 582 | 16 364 | ... | ... | 000 | 077 | 000 | | 1995 |
| | 184 | 4.67 | 2 204 | 16 537 | ... | ... | 610 | 338 | 272 | | 1996 |
| | 213 | ... | 1 656 | ... | ... | ... | 581 | 322 | 259 | | 1997 |
| | 303 | 118 | 1 431 | 244 268 | 193 796 | 62 | 864 | 385 | ... | Denmark | 1981 |
| | ... | ... | 2 370 | ... | ... | ... | ... | ... | ... | | 1985 |
| | 288 | 146 | 1 793 | 407 718 | 409 623 | 61 | 1 344 | 360 | 221 | | 1990 |
| | 206 | 23 | 2 397 | 344 541 | 297 031 | 60 | 806 | 365 | 442 | | 1991 |
| | 210 | 21 | 2 716 | 374 310 | 310 380 | 58 | 790 | 364 | 425 | | 1992 |
| | 211 | 16 | 3 065 | 402 555 | 352 886 | 56 | 759 | 370 | 389 | | 1993 |
| | 207 | 18 | 3 231 | 395 347 | 346 388 | 59 | 783 | 374 | 409 | | 1994 |
| | 233 | 20 | 3 403 | 408 285 | 371 878 | 57 | 805 | 300 | 125 | | 1995 |
| | 229 | 20 | 3 666 | 448 794 | 410 179 | 55 | 835 | 397 | 139 | | 1996 |
| | 234 | 18 | 4 065 | 506 238 | 415 642 | 58 | 853 | 404 | 449 | | 1997 |
| | ... | ... | 3 240 | 101 | ... | ... | 589 | 505 | 84 | Estonia | 1990 |
| | 105 | ... | 3 162 | ... | ... | ... | 540 | 470 | 70 | | 1991 |
| | 105 | ... | 3 156 | ... | ... | ... | 540 | 470 | 70 | | 1992 |
| | 131 | 0.35 | 3 240 | 101 | 8 879 | 38 | 546 | 471 | 75 | | 1993 |
| | 97 | 0.87 | 3 923 | 316 | 16 213 | 59 | 545 | 468 | 77 | | 1994 |
| | 88 | 1.27 | 2 152 | 67 | 26 604 | 46 | 530 | 462 | 69 | | 1995 |
| | 89 | 1.59 | 2 231 | 72 | 30 357 | 40 | 501 | 425 | 76 | | 1996 |
| | 94 | 2.28 | 1 830 | 49 | 34 250 | 49 | 482 | 407 | 75 | | 1997 |
| | 116 | 1.84 | 3 297 | ... | (7) 20 181 | ... | 443 | 261 | 182 | Federal Republic of Yugoslavia | 1992 |
| | ... | ... | ... | ... | ... | ... | 564 | 470 | ... | | 1995 |
| | ... | ... | 1 200 | ... | ... | ... | ... | ... | ... | Finland | 1980 |
| | ... | ... | 1 905 | ... | ... | ... | ... | ... | ... | | 1981 |
| | ... | ... | 2 360 | ... | ... | ... | ... | ... | ... | | 1985 |
| | 472 | ... | 2 719 | 99 600 | 194 438 | 49 | 1 052 | 408 | 645 | | 1990 |
| | 471 | ... | 3 033 | 101 679 | 228 295 | 54 | 1 041 | 408 | 633 | | 1991 |

IV.3   Libraries of institutions of tertiary education
Bibliothèques d'établissements d'enseignement supérieur
Bibliotecas de instituciones de enseñanza superior

| Country / Pays / País | Year / Année / Año | Administrative unit / Unités administratives / Unidades administrativas | Service points / Points de service / Puntos de servicio | Collections / Collections / Fondos — Books/Livres/Libros — Number of volumes (000) / Nombre de volumes (000) / Número de volúmenes (000) | Books — Metres of shelving / Mètres de rayonnage / Metros de estantes | Microforms / Microcopies / Microcopias | Audio-visual documents (000) / Matériels audio-visuels (000) / Materiales audio-visuales (000) | Other library materials (000) / Autres matériels de bibliothèque (000) / Otros materiales de biblioteca (000) | Registered users (000) / Usagers inscrits (000) / Usuarios inscritos (000) |
|---|---|---|---|---|---|---|---|---|---|
| Finland (cont) | 1992 | 19 | 427 | 13 036 | ... | 1 010 843 | 531 | 3.77 | ... |
| | 1993 | 19 | 438 | 12 979 | ... | 1 024 218 | 551 | 4.45 | (30) 5 120 |
| | 1994 | 19 | 299 | 12 166 | ... | 1 097 339 | 262 | 167 | (30) 7 157 |
| | 1995 | 19 | 261 | 13 009 | ... | 1 119 583 | 254 | 146 | (30) 8 994 |
| | 1996 | 19 | 305 | 13 546 | ... | 1 215 956 | 216 | 190 | (30) 8 117 |
| | 1997 | 19 | 304 | 13 833 | ... | 1 249 403 | 227 | 197 | (30) 8 959 |
| France | 1981 | (3)(35) 61 | 184 | 17 700 | 870 000 | 178 000 | 30 | 3 059 | ... |
| | 1985 | 61 | 185 | 18 100 | ... | *240 250 | *30 | 3 109 | 560 |
| | 1990 | (3)(35) 67 | 220 | 21 400 | 1 034 000 | 1 065 000 | ... | 4 164 | 794 |
| | 1991 | 72 | 213 | 23 196 | ... | ... | ... | ... | (30) 17 828 |
| | 1992 | 73 | 203 | 23 122 | ... | ... | ... | ... | (30) 20 104 |
| | 1993 | 70 | 205 | 22 857 | ... | ... | ... | ... | (30) 19 180 |
| | 1994 | 72 | 187 | 22 679 | ... | ... | ... | ... | (30) 21 312 |
| | 1995 | (3)(35) 85 | ... | 40 000 | ... | ... | ... | 2 600 | 1 121 |
| | 1996 | (3)(35) 95 | 324 | 23 000 | 1 189 000 | 2 355 000 | ... | ... | 1 211 |
| | 1997 | 71 | 186 | 23 497 | ... | ... | ... | ... | (30) 28 075 |
| Germany | 1990 | (36) 3 819 | ... | 118 695 | ... | 19 458 088 | 728 | 20 882 | 1 712 |
| | 1991 | 238 | ... | 119 690 | ... | ... | ... | ... | 1 704 |
| | 1992 | 232 | 882 | 117 865 | ... | ... | ... | ... | (30) 28 572 |
| | 1993 | (37) 271 | ... | 126 117 | ... | 25 978 612 | 953 | 17 510 | 1 803 |
| | 1994 | 229 | 814 | 115 603 | ... | ... | ... | ... | (30) 30 288 |
| | 1995 | 225 | 774 | 116 127 | ... | ... | ... | ... | (30) 34 465 |
| | 1996 | 225 | 783 | 116 979 | ... | ... | ... | ... | (30) 35 778 |
| | 1997 | 227 | 809 | 119 776 | ... | ... | ... | ... | (30) 39 900 |
| Gibraltar | 1996 | (3) 83 | ... | 1 941 | 82 937 | 32 057 | 29 | 6.08 | 621 |
| Greece | 1981 | *39 | *70 | *6 482 | ... | *509 297 | *160 | 803 | *128 |
| | 1985 | *39 | *70 | *6 482 | ... | *509 297 | *160 | 803 | *128 |
| | 1990 | *39 | *70 | 6 482 | *167 639 | *509 297 | *160 | *803 | *128 |
| | 1991 | 40 | 73 | 6 578 | ... | ... | ... | ... | (30) 2 940 |
| | 1992 | 41 | 69 | 6 558 | ... | ... | ... | ... | (30) 3 316 |
| | 1993 | 39 | 70 | 6 482 | ... | ... | ... | ... | (30) 3 163 |
| | 1994 | 40 | 64 | 6 432 | ... | ... | ... | ... | (30) 3 515 |
| | 1995 | 39 | 61 | 6 461 | ... | ... | ... | ... | (30) 4 000 |
| | 1996 | 39 | 62 | 6 508 | ... | ... | ... | ... | (30) 4 152 |
| | 1997 | 40 | 64 | 6 664 | ... | ... | ... | ... | (30) 4 630 |
| Holy See | 1981 | 17 | 19 | 2 675 | 63 905 | 1 099 | 0.21 | 0.01 | 15 |
| | 1990 | (21) 15 | 28 | 3 216 | 139 168 | 3 691 | 0.24 | 126 | 47 |
| Hungary | 1971 | (38) 24 | 24 | 5 097 | ... | ... | ... | ... | 54 |
| | 1982 | (39) 28 | ... | ... | ... | ... | ... | ... | 70 |
| | 1990 | 29 | 29 | 12 116 | ... | 416 373 | 78 | 1 972 | 92 |
| | 1991 | 29 | 29 | 12 473 | ... | 442 958 | 91 | 1 890 | 93 |
| | 1992 | 29 | 29 | 12 433 | ... | 458 197 | 87 | 2 171 | 104 |
| | 1993 | 29 | 29 | 12 803 | ... | 473 797 | 88 | 2 357 | 116 |
| | 1994 | 29 | 29 | 12 856 | ... | 460 307 | 91 | 2 334 | 128 |
| | 1995 | 29 | 29 | 12 856 | ... | 459 387 | 91 | 2 325 | 128 |
| | 1996 | 34 | 35 | 9 900 | ... | ... | ... | ... | (30) 3 428 |
| | 1997 | 34 | 35 | 10 015 | ... | ... | ... | ... | (30) 3 883 |
| Iceland | 1971 | 1 | ... | 161 | 4 030 | ... | ... | ... | 1.0 |
| | 1981 | *1 | *17 | *197 | ... | *200 | *3.25 | 0.87 | *1.8 |
| | 1985 | *1 | *17 | *241 | ... | *200 | *3.85 | 1.11 | *2.1 |
| | 1990 | 6 | 16 | 370 | *8 011 | *40 420 | *27 | *372 | 10 |
| | 1991 | 6 | 16 | 382 | 11 472 | ... | 0.63 | ... | ... |
| | 1992 | 2 | 16 | 301 | ... | ... | ... | ... | (30) 82 |
| | 1993 | 2 | 16 | 308 | ... | ... | ... | ... | (30) 78 |
| | 1994 | 2 | 16 | 313 | ... | ... | ... | ... | (30) 86 |
| | 1995 | 2 | 15 | 321 | ... | ... | ... | ... | (30) 99 |
| | 1996 | 2 | 15 | 329 | ... | ... | ... | ... | (30) 103 |
| | 1997 | 2 | 16 | 334 | ... | ... | ... | ... | (30) 115 |
| Ireland | 1980 | 7 | 38 | 3 918 | 109 255 | ... | ... | ... | 31 |
| | 1981 | 15 | 38 | 3 910 | ... | 202 498 | *64 | 319 | *51 |
| | 1985 | 15 | 36 | 4 440 | ... | 202 498 | *64 | 319 | *51 |
| | 1990 | *15 | 33 | 5 018 | 177 832 | *202 498 | *64 | *319 | *51 |
| | 1991 | 15 | 34 | 5 092 | ... | ... | ... | ... | (30) 1 177 |
| | 1992 | 16 | 33 | 5 076 | ... | ... | ... | ... | (30) 1 328 |
| | 1993 | 15 | 33 | 5 018 | ... | ... | ... | ... | (30) 1 267 |

Libraries of institutions of tertiary education **IV.3**
Bibliothèques d'établissements d'enseignement supérieur
Bibliotecas de instituciones de enseñanza superior

| Annual additions / Acquisitions annuelles / Adquisiciones anuales | | Loans to users (000) Prêts aux usagers (000) Préstamos a los usuarios (000) | Inter-Library loans Prêts entre biblio-thèques Préstamos entre bibliotecas | Current expenditure / Dépenses ordinaires / Gastos ordinarios | | Library employees / Personnel des bibliothèques / Personal de las bibliotecas | | | Country Pays País | Year Année Año |
|---|---|---|---|---|---|---|---|---|---|---|
| Volumes (000) Volumes (000) Volúmenes (000) | Other materials (000) Autres matériels (000) Otros materiales (000) | | | Total (000) Total (000) Total (000) | Staff (%) Personnel (%) Personal (%) | Total Total Total | Holding a diploma Diplômé Diplomado | Trained on the job Formé sur le tas Formado en ejercicio | | |
| 465 | ... | 3 559 | 106 855 | 238 303 | 54 | 1 031 | 403 | 328 | Finland (cont) | 1992 |
| 431 | ... | 4 093 | 68 414 | 231 130 | 57 | 1 055 | 413 | 642 | | 1993 |
| 373 | 9.75 | 4 920 | 136 352 | 228 164 | 56 | 1 033 | 910 | 123 | | 1994 |
| 415 | 11 | 5 613 | 140 848 | 242 727 | 54 | 1 021 | 914 | 106 | | 1995 |
| 444 | 15 | 6 380 | 147 104 | 294 658 | 49 | 1 081 | 953 | 127 | | 1996 |
| 443 | 11 | 7 400 | 150 686 | 310 469 | 48 | 1 063 | 927 | 136 | | 1997 |
| 351 | 65 | 3 576 | 239 770 | 106 126 | 6 | 3 178 | 1 233 | ... | France | 1981 |
| ... | ... | 7 679 | ... | ... | ... | ... | ... | ... | | 1985 |
| 522 | 297 | 10 346 | (6) 495 000 | 872 000 | 57 | 3 210 | 1 312 | ... | | 1990 |
| 712 | ... | 10 496 | | | | 3 153 | 1 263 | 1 890 | | 1991 |
| 688 | ... | 10 920 | | | | 2 864 | 1 222 | 1 642 | | 1992 |
| 683 | ... | 11 579 | | | | 2 993 | 1 264 | 1 729 | | 1993 |
| 654 | ... | 12 418 | | ... | | 2 768 | 1 347 | 1 421 | | 1994 |
| 839 | ... | 15 400 | (6) 610 893 | 1 360 000 | 52 | 3 864 | 975 | 712 | | 1995 |
| 900 | ... | 11 476 | | 675 000 | ... | ... | ... | ... | | 1996 |
| 747 | ... | 15 598 | | ... | | 3 446 | 1 703 | 1 743 | | 1997 |
| 3 615 | 2 891 | 44 704 | ... | 583 996 | ... | 9 010 | ... | ... | Germany | 1990 |
| ... | ... | 46 358 | | 647 083 | ... | 8 891 | ... | ... | | 1991 |
| 3 844 | ... | 43 184 | | | | 12 452 | 4 502 | 7 950 | | 1992 |
| 3 818 | 2 843 | 52 451 | | (18) 1 117 336 | 69 | 8 941 | ... | ... | | 1993 |
| 3 654 | ... | 49 110 | | | | 11 841 | 4 960 | 6 881 | | 1994 |
| 3 656 | ... | 48 787 | | | | 10 957 | 4 878 | 6 079 | | 1995 |
| 3 684 | ... | 55 767 | | | | 10 920 | 4 984 | 5 936 | | 1996 |
| 4 175 | ... | 61 687 | | | | 14 708 | 6 270 | 8 438 | | 1997 |
| 79 | 5.35 | 271 | 9 754 | 1 658 504 | 44 | 316 | 173 | 68 | Gibraltar | 1996 |
| ... | ... | *1 766 | ... | ... | ... | ... | ... | ... | Greece | 1981 |
| ... | ... | *1 766 | | | | | | ... | | 1985 |
| ... | ... | *1 766 | | | | 831 | 243 | ... | | 1990 |
| 402 | ... | 1 601 | | | | 886 | 243 | 643 | | 1991 |
| 388 | ... | 1 666 | | | | 793 | 235 | 558 | | 1992 |
| 385 | ... | 1 766 | | | | 831 | 243 | 588 | | 1993 |
| 369 | ... | 1 894 | | | | 742 | 259 | 483 | | 1994 |
| 369 | ... | 1 882 | | | | 682 | 255 | 427 | | 1995 |
| 372 | ... | 2 151 | | | | 677 | 260 | 417 | | 1996 |
| 421 | ... | 2 380 | | | | 920 | 327 | 593 | | 1997 |
| 30 | 0.19 | 78 | ... | 809 263 | 26 | 75 | 32 | 43 | Holy See | 1981 |
| 42 | 0.12 | ... | | | | 80 | 40 | 40 | | 1990 |
| 110 | ... | 977 | ... | ... | ... | 678 | 154 | 97 | Hungary | 1971 |
| | ... | 785 | | | | 803 | ... | ... | | 1982 |
| ... | ... | 970 | 972 | | | 958 | 701 | 257 | | 1990 |
| ... | ... | 1 077 | 916 | | | 934 | 698 | 236 | | 1991 |
| ... | ... | 1 080 | 1 083 | | | 926 | 690 | 236 | | 1992 |
| ... | ... | 1 200 | 1 067 | | | 926 | 690 | 236 | | 1993 |
| ... | ... | 1 400 | 1 007 | | | 926 | 690 | 236 | | 1994 |
| ... | ... | 1 400 | 1 002 | | | 926 | 690 | 236 | | 1995 |
| 357 | ... | 1 569 | ... | (7) 871 436 | ... | 826 | 651 | 175 | | 1996 |
| 418 | ... | 1 788 | ... | (7) 1 047 415 | ... | 960 | 592 | 368 | | 1997 |
| 8.2 | ... | 8.42 | ... | ... | ... | 6 | 4 | ... | Iceland | 1971 |
| ... | ... | *31 | | | | ... | ... | ... | | 1981 |
| ... | ... | *31 | | | | ... | ... | ... | | 1985 |
| 6.9 | 0.05 | 75 | | (40) 787 | 51 | 39 | 28 | 11 | | 1990 |
| 14 | ... | 75 | | | | 44 | 28 | 16 | | 1991 |
| 13 | ... | 38 | | | | 22 | 15 | 7 | | 1992 |
| 14 | ... | 42 | | | | 24 | 16 | 8 | | 1993 |
| 14 | ... | 46 | | | | 24 | 17 | 7 | | 1994 |
| 13 | ... | 50 | | | | 25 | 17 | 8 | | 1995 |
| 14 | ... | 56 | | | | 26 | 18 | 8 | | 1996 |
| 14 | ... | 58 | | | | 29 | 20 | 9 | | 1997 |
| 116 | ... | 933 | ... | 5 126 | 62 | 399 | 137 | ... | Ireland | 1980 |
| ... | ... | 932 | | | | ... | ... | ... | | 1981 |
| ... | ... | 1 077 | | | | ... | ... | ... | | 1985 |
| 113 | ... | 1 164 | | | | 441 | 125 | ... | | 1990 |
| 161 | ... | 1 055 | | | | 470 | 125 | 345 | | 1991 |
| 155 | ... | 1 098 | | | | 421 | 121 | 300 | | 1992 |
| 154 | ... | 1 164 | | | | 441 | 125 | 316 | | 1993 |

**Libraries of institutions of tertiary education**
**Bibliothèques d'établissements d'enseignement supérieur**
**Bibliotecas de instituciones de enseñanza superior**

| Country / Pays / País | Year / Année / Año | Administrative unit / Unités administratives / Unidades administrativas | Service points / Points de service / Puntos de servicio | Collections / Collections / Fondos | | Microforms / Microcopies / Microcopias | Audio-visual documents (000) / Matériels audio-visuels (000) / Materiales audio-visuales (000) | Other library materials (000) / Autres matériels de bibliothèque (000) / Otros materiales de biblioteca (000) | Registered users (000) / Usagers inscrits (000) / Usuarios inscritos (000) |
|---|---|---|---|---|---|---|---|---|---|
| | | | | Books/Livres/Libros | | | | | |
| | | | | Number of volumes (000) / Nombre de volumes (000) / Número de volúmenes (000) | Metres of shelving / Mètres de rayonnage / Metros de estantes | | | | |
| Ireland (cont) | 1994 | 15 | 30 | 4 979 | ... | ... | ... | ... | (30) 1 407 |
| | 1995 | 15 | 29 | 5 001 | ... | ... | ... | ... | (30) 1 601 |
| | 1996 | 15 | 29 | 5 038 | ... | ... | ... | ... | (30) 1 662 |
| | 1997 | 15 | 30 | 5 159 | ... | ... | ... | ... | (30) 1 854 |
| Italy | 1972 | 3 060 | ... | (41) 55 114 | ... | ... | ... | ... | 1 148 |
| | 1995 | 1 629 | 1 900 | 36 051 | ... | 659 685 | ... | 415 | 822 |
| | 1996 | 1 571 | 1 887 | 36 590 | ... | 822 412 | ... | 426 | 875 |
| | 1997 | 1 513 | 1 924 | 39 351 | ... | 1 466 678 | ... | 444 | 988 |
| Latvia | 1990 | 8 | 8 | 6 627 | ... | 111 605 | 21 | 529 | 58 |
| | 1991 | (42) 13 | 13 | 7 036 | ... | ... | ... | ... | 62 |
| | 1992 | (42) 13 | 13 | 7 109 | ... | ... | ... | ... | 57 |
| | 1993 | (42) 13 | 13 | 7 100 | ... | ... | ... | ... | 54 |
| | 1994 | (42) 14 | 14 | 7 031 | ... | ... | ... | ... | 50 |
| | 1995 | (42) 14 | 14 | 6 894 | ... | ... | ... | ... | 54 |
| | 1996 | (42) 14 | 14 | 6 880 | ... | ... | ... | ... | 56 |
| | 1997 | (42) 14 | 14 | 5 920 | ... | ... | ... | ... | 52 |
| Liechtenstein | 1981 | *1 | *1 | *30 | ... | *2 273 | *0.54 | *3.20 | *0.3 |
| | 1985 | *1 | *1 | *30 | ... | *2 273 | *0.54 | *3.20 | *0.3 |
| | 1990 | 1 | 1 | *30 | *783 | 2 252 | 0.54 | 3.15 | *0.3 |
| | 1991 | 1 | 1 | 29 | ... | ... | ... | ... | (30) 8.2 |
| | 1992 | 1 | 1 | 29 | ... | ... | ... | ... | (30) 9.3 |
| | 1993 | 1 | 1 | 30 | ... | ... | ... | ... | (30) 8.9 |
| | 1994 | 1 | 1 | 30 | ... | ... | ... | ... | (30) 9.9 |
| | 1995 | 1 | 1 | 31 | ... | ... | ... | ... | (30) 11 |
| | 1996 | 1 | 1 | 31 | ... | ... | ... | ... | (30) 12 |
| | 1997 | 1 | 1 | 32 | ... | ... | ... | ... | (30) 13 |
| Lithuania | 1990 | 13 | 46 | 10 184 | ... | 25 466 | 1.55 | 930 | 94 |
| | 1991 | 14 | 52 | 10 547 | ... | 26 824 | 1.89 | 212 | 91 |
| | 1992 | 15 | 58 | 10 590 | ... | 27 155 | 1.93 | 215 | 87 |
| | 1993 | 15 | 62 | 10 635 | ... | 27 862 | 2.19 | 218 | 84 |
| | 1994 | 15 | 65 | 10 701 | ... | 28 354 | 2.21 | 222 | 77 |
| | 1995 | 15 | 77 | 11 033 | ... | 25 654 | 2.23 | 224 | 74 |
| | 1996 | 15 | 82 | 11 285 | ... | 25 455 | 2.32 | 227 | 84 |
| | 1997 | 15 | 83 | 12 035 | ... | 25 422 | 2.39 | 237 | 86 |
| Luxembourg | 1981 | 1 | 1 | *269 | ... | *21 109 | *6.64 | 33 | *5.3 |
| | 1985 | 1 | 1 | *269 | ... | *21 109 | *6.64 | 33 | *5.3 |
| | 1990 | 1 | 1 | 269 | *7 134 | *21 109 | *6.64 | 33 | *5.3 |
| | 1991 | 1 | 1 | 273 | ... | ... | ... | ... | (30) 125 |
| | 1992 | 1 | 1 | 272 | ... | ... | ... | ... | (30) 141 |
| | 1993 | 1 | 1 | 269 | ... | ... | ... | ... | (30) 134 |
| | 1994 | 1 | 1 | 267 | ... | ... | ... | ... | (30) 149 |
| | 1995 | 1 | 1 | 268 | ... | ... | ... | ... | (30) 170 |
| | 1996 | 1 | 1 | 270 | ... | ... | ... | ... | (30) 176 |
| | 1997 | 1 | 1 | 276 | ... | ... | ... | ... | (30) 196 |
| Moldova | 1993 | 15 | ... | 5 844 | ... | ... | ... | ... | ... |
| | 1996 | 19 | 19 | 7 190 | ... | ... | ... | ... | 61 |
| Netherlands | 1981 | 690 | 1 016 | 17 536 | 500 000 | 947 200 | 788 | 729 | ... |
| | 1985 | 653 | *1 039 | 20 633 | ... | 1 208 000 | *865 | 498 | *224 |
| | 1990 | 477 | *1 039 | 24 238 | *637 000 | *1 682 000 | *962 | *720 | *224 |
| | 1991 | 475 | 981 | 24 746 | ... | ... | ... | ... | (30) 5 114 |
| | 1992 | 481 | 933 | 24 668 | ... | ... | ... | ... | (30) 5 767 |
| | 1993 | 369 | 943 | 25 266 | 721 000 | 1 754 000 | ... | ... | ... |
| | 1994 | 474 | 862 | 24 194 | ... | ... | ... | ... | (30) 6 113 |
| | 1995 | 348 | 820 | 26 488 | 792 000 | 1 844 000 | ... | ... | ... |
| | 1996 | 465 | 829 | 24 483 | ... | ... | ... | ... | (30) 7 221 |
| | 1997 | 469 | 856 | 25 068 | ... | ... | ... | ... | (30) 8 053 |
| Norway | 1981 | 82 | 281 | 7 148 | 209 481 | ... | ... | ... | ... |
| | 1985 | *86 | *200 | *7 912 | ... | *415 128 | *362 | *3 157 | *57 |
| | 1990 | 99 | 210 | 8 718 | 261 326 | 468 543 | 157 | 4 060 | 89 |
| | 1991 | 121 | 210 | 8 810 | ... | 440 640 | 279 | ... | (30) 1 182 |
| | 1992 | 119 | 205 | 8 872 | ... | 420 810 | 506 | ... | (30) 1 344 |
| | 1993 | (23) 95 | 209 | 9 412 | 267 841 | 464 807 | 430 | ... | 236 |
| | 1994 | 95 | 214 | 9 726 | ... | 449 445 | 77 | 30 | (30) 1 419 |
| | 1995 | 95 | 203 | 10 157 | ... | 464 842 | 92 | 25 | (30) 1 624 |

Libraries of institutions of tertiary education  IV.3
Bibliothèques d'établissements d'enseignement supérieur
Bibliotecas de instituciones de enseñanza superior

| Annual additions / Acquisitions annuelles / Adquisiciones anuales | | Loans to users (000) / Prêts aux usagers (000) / Préstamos a los usuarios (000) | Inter-Library loans / Prêts entre bibliothèques / Préstamos entre bibliotecas | Current expenditure / Dépenses ordinaires / Gastos ordinarios | | Library employees / Personnel des bibliothèques / Personal de las bibliotecas | | | Country / Pays / País | Year / Année / Año |
| Volumes (000) / Volúmenes (000) | Other materials (000) / Autres matériels (000) / Otros materiales (000) | | | Total (000) | Staff (%) / Personnel (%) / Personal (%) | Total | Holding a diploma / Diplômé / Diplomado | Trained on the job / Formé sur le tas / Formado en ejercicio | | |
|---|---|---|---|---|---|---|---|---|---|---|
| 148 | ... | 1 248 | ... | ... | ... | 393 | 133 | 260 | Ireland (cont) | 1994 |
| 148 | ... | 1 240 | ... | ... | ... | 360 | 131 | 229 | | 1995 |
| 149 | ... | 1 418 | ... | ... | ... | 358 | 134 | 224 | | 1996 |
| 169 | ... | 1 568 | ... | ... | ... | 486 | 168 | 318 | | 1997 |
| ... | ... | 4 216 | ... | ... | ... | 4 937 | 3 097 | 243 | Italy | 1972 |
| 539 | ... | 3 262 | ... | ... | ... | 5 061 | 3 292 | 287 | | 1995 |
| 2 761 | ... | 3 641 | ... | ... | ... | 5 435 | 3 528 | 322 | | 1996 |
| | | 5 915 | | | | | | | | 1997 |
| ... | ... | 4 609 | 261 | ... | ... | 615 | 414 | 201 | Latvia | 1990 |
| ... | ... | 4 115 | ... | ... | ... | 426 | ... | ... | | 1991 |
| ... | ... | 3 522 | ... | ... | ... | 403 | ... | ... | | 1992 |
| 221 | ... | 3 438 | ... | 223 | ... | 392 | ... | ... | | 1993 |
| ... | ... | 3 195 | ... | 432 | 40 | 407 | ... | ... | | 1994 |
| ... | ... | 3 193 | ... | 333 | 72 | 305 | ... | ... | | 1995 |
| ... | ... | 4 264 | ... | 455 | 47 | 360 | 153 | 207 | | 1996 |
| 77 | ... | 3 003 | ... | 599 | 52 | 327 | 134 | 193 | | 1997 |
| ... | ... | *9.44 | ... | ... | ... | ... | ... | ... | Liechtenstein | 1981 |
| ... | ... | *9.44 | ... | ... | ... | ... | ... | ... | | 1985 |
| ... | ... | *9.35 | ... | ... | ... | 3 | 1 | ... | | 1990 |
| 1.5 | ... | 8.11 | ... | ... | ... | 3 | 1 | 2 | | 1991 |
| 1.5 | ... | 8.51 | ... | ... | ... | 3 | 1 | 2 | | 1992 |
| 1.6 | ... | 9.35 | ... | ... | ... | 3 | 1 | 2 | | 1993 |
| 1.6 | ... | 10 | ... | ... | ... | 3 | 1 | 2 | | 1994 |
| 1.5 | ... | 11 | ... | ... | ... | 3 | 1 | 2 | | 1995 |
| 1.6 | ... | 12 | ... | ... | ... | 3 | 1 | 2 | | 1996 |
| 1.6 | ... | 13 | ... | ... | ... | 3 | 1 | 2 | | 1997 |
| ... | 0.00 | 4 009 | 1 947 | ... | ... | 686 | 509 | 177 | Lithuania | 1990 |
| 284 | 0.18 | 4 346 | 1 944 | ... | ... | 674 | 516 | 158 | | 1991 |
| 271 | 0.04 | 4 196 | 1 446 | ... | ... | 666 | 514 | 152 | | 1992 |
| 216 | 0.09 | 3 784 | 966 | ... | ... | 629 | 504 | 125 | | 1993 |
| 219 | 0.05 | 3 655 | 780 | ... | ... | 634 | 491 | 143 | | 1994 |
| 143 | 0.14 | 3 193 | 400 | ... | ... | 629 | 490 | 139 | | 1995 |
| 143 | 0.14 | 4 221 | 363 | ... | ... | 617 | 536 | 81 | | 1996 |
| 154 | 0.13 | 5 774 | 288 | ... | ... | 629 | 528 | 101 | | 1997 |
| ... | ... | *73 | ... | ... | ... | ... | ... | ... | Luxembourg | 1981 |
| ... | ... | *73 | ... | ... | ... | ... | ... | ... | | 1985 |
| ... | ... | *73 | ... | ... | ... | 5 | 1 | ... | | 1990 |
| 17 | ... | 66 | ... | ... | ... | 5 | 1 | 4 | | 1991 |
| 16 | ... | 69 | ... | ... | ... | 5 | 1 | 4 | | 1992 |
| 16 | ... | 73 | ... | ... | ... | 5 | 1 | 4 | | 1993 |
| 16 | ... | 79 | ... | ... | ... | 4 | 1 | 3 | | 1994 |
| 16 | ... | 78 | ... | ... | ... | 4 | 1 | 3 | | 1995 |
| 16 | ... | 89 | ... | ... | ... | 4 | 1 | 3 | | 1996 |
| 18 | ... | 99 | ... | ... | ... | 5 | 1 | 4 | | 1997 |
| 134 | ... | ... | (6) 1 798 | ... | ... | 201 | 114 | ... | Moldova | 1993 |
| ... | ... | ... | ... | ... | (43) | 478 | ... | ... | | 1996 |
| 642 | 15 | 3 883 | 344 900 | 37 093 | ... | 1 982 | 898 | 544 | Netherlands | 1981 |
| ... | ... | 4 095 | ... | ... | ... | ... | ... | ... | | 1985 |
| ... | ... | *4 132 | ... | ... | ... | 1 980 | 920 | ... | | 1990 |
| 698 | ... | 3 830 | ... | ... | ... | 2 078 | 919 | 1 159 | | 1991 |
| 675 | ... | 3 984 | ... | ... | ... | 1 897 | 890 | 1 007 | | 1992 |
| ... | ... | 4 782 | ... | ... | ... | 2 058 | ... | ... | | 1993 |
| 641 | ... | 4 531 | ... | ... | ... | 1 851 | 980 | 871 | | 1994 |
| ... | ... | 5 339 | 563 300 | 76 008 | ... | 2 092 | ... | ... | | 1995 |
| 647 | ... | 5 145 | ... | ... | ... | 1 737 | 985 | 752 | | 1996 |
| 733 | ... | 5 692 | ... | ... | ... | 2 307 | 1 239 | 1 068 | | 1997 |
| 286 | ... | ... | (7) 35 490 | ... | ... | 564 | 381 | 183 | Norway | 1981 |
| ... | ... | *1 005 | ... | ... | ... | ... | ... | ... | | 1985 |
| 278 | 164 | 1 072 | 205 816 | 197 432 | 50 | 788 | 372 | 416 | | 1990 |
| 289 | ... | 1 690 | ... | (7) 69 979 | ... | 653 | ... | ... | | 1991 |
| 308 | ... | 1 800 | ... | ... | ... | 669 | ... | ... | | 1992 |
| 337 | ... | 2 063 | 217 263 | (44) 288 492 | 49 | 744 | ... | ... | | 1993 |
| 348 | ... | 2 358 | 294 320 | (44) 319 850 | ... | 808 | 548 | 260 | | 1994 |
| 316 | ... | 2 760 | 326 894 | (44) 330 524 | ... | 866 | 570 | 296 | | 1995 |

IV.3 Libraries of institutions of tertiary education
Bibliothèques d'établissements d'enseignement supérieur
Bibliotecas de instituciones de enseñanza superior

| | | | | Collections / Collections / Fondos | | | | | |
|---|---|---|---|---|---|---|---|---|---|
| | | | | Books/Livres/Libros | | | Audio-visual documents (000) | Other library materials (000) | Registered users (000) |
| Country | Year | Administrative unit | Service points | Number of volumes (000) | Metres of shelving | Microforms | | | |
| Pays | Année | Unités administratives | Points de service | Nombre de volumes (000) | Mètres de rayonnage | Microcopies | Matériels audio-visuels (000) | Autres matériels de bibliothèque (000) | Usagers inscrits (000) |
| País | Año | Unidades administrativas | Puntos de servicio | Número de volúmenes (000) | Metros de estantes | Microcopias | Materiales audio-visuales (000) | Otros materiales de biblioteca (000) | Usuarios inscritos (000) |
| Norway (cont) | 1996 | 95 | 215 | 10 586 | ... | 480 975 | 99 | 33 | (30) 1 691 |
| | 1997 | 103 | 217 | 10 725 | ... | 480 471 | 115 | 35 | (30) 1 891 |
| Poland | 1971 | 3 687 | 3 687 | 23 355 | ... | ... | ... | ... | 597 |
| | 1980 | 1 064 | ... | 34 220 | ... | ... | (45) 717 | 7 404 | ... |
| | 1990 | 101 | 912 | 40 464 | ... | 1 415 081 | 349 | 9 778 | 822 |
| | 1991 | 272 | 494 | 28 473 | ... | 1 197 115 | 141 | 229 | 392 |
| | 1992 | 274 | 495 | 29 291 | ... | 1 276 495 | 141 | 222 | 411 |
| | 1993 | 266 | 485 | 29 554 | ... | 7 079 471 | 146 | 244 | 471 |
| | 1994 | 269 | 492 | 30 221 | ... | 7 080 388 | 150 | 229 | 492 |
| | 1995 | 266 | 490 | 31 340 | ... | 7 478 085 | 154 | 252 | 543 |
| | 1996 | 268 | 486 | 31 532 | ... | 1 652 751 | 158 | 241 | 599 |
| | 1997 | 273 | 511 | 33 526 | ... | 1 669 599 | 163 | 284 | 668 |
| Portugal | 1981 | 219 | 219 | 2 193 | 75 998 | 6 122 | ... | ... | (46) 818 |
| | 1985 | *171 | *171 | *1 723 | ... | *15 103 | *22 | *103 | *146 |
| | 1990 | 204 | 264 | 5 080 | 128 438 | 57 912 | 19 | 251 | 155 |
| | 1991 | 215 | 286 | 5 329 | ... | ... | ... | ... | (30) 3 283 |
| | 1992 | 217 | 272 | 5 312 | ... | ... | ... | ... | (30) 3 702 |
| | 1993 | (3) 242 | 343 | 6 279 | ... | 75 970 | 86 | 315 | 349 |
| | 1994 | 214 | 251 | 5 211 | ... | ... | ... | ... | (30) 3 925 |
| | 1995 | 210 | 239 | 5 234 | ... | ... | ... | ... | (30) 4 466 |
| | 1996 | 211 | 242 | 5 273 | ... | ... | ... | ... | (30) 4 636 |
| | 1997 | 212 | 250 | 5 399 | ... | ... | ... | ... | (30) 5 170 |
| Romania | 1979 | (49) 43 | ... | 19 072 | ... | ... | ... | ... | 252 |
| | 1980 | 43 | ... | 19 297 | ... | ... | ... | ... | 274 |
| | 1989 | 47 | ... | 29 484 | ... | ... | ... | ... | 288 |
| | 1990 | 48 | 48 | 25 011 | ... | 1 193 499 | 222 | 5 653 | 288 |
| | 1991 | 46 | 46 | 21 632 | ... | 1 252 937 | 257 | 5 347 | 284 |
| | 1992 | 60 | 60 | 25 056 | ... | 1 248 371 | 237 | 5 914 | 358 |
| | 1993 | 64 | 64 | 20 919 | 309 300 | 1 225 931 | 227 | 6 099 | 614 |
| | 1994 | 64 | 64 | 20 919 | ... | 1 132 012 | 224 | 5 739 | 614 |
| | 1995 | 64 | 64 | 20 919 | ... | 1 086 934 | 215 | 5 500 | 614 |
| | 1996 | (3) 75 | 439 | 21 276 | 782 534 | ... | 181 | 1 204 | 366 |
| | 1997 | 59 | 339 | 23 412 | ... | ... | ... | ... | (30) 10 048 |
| Russian Federation | 1990 | 491 | ... | 323 763 | ... | ... | ... | ... | 3 960 |
| | 1993 | 519 | ... | 324 696 | ... | ... | ... | ... | 3 730 |
| | 1996 | 520 | ... | 328 345 | ... | ... | ... | ... | 3 735 |
| Slovakia | 1990 | 26 | 526 | 4 874 | ... | 224 117 | 42 | 1 062 | 120 |
| | 1991 | 27 | 534 | 4 863 | ... | 235 576 | 48 | 1 005 | 112 |
| | 1992 | 27 | 547 | 4 539 | ... | 243 976 | 46 | 1 156 | 116 |
| | 1993 | (3) 33 | 546 | 4 738 | ... | ... | ... | ... | 108 |
| | 1994 | 32 | 534 | 4 579 | ... | 250 483 | 50 | 1 270 | 118 |
| | 1995 | 36 | 519 | 4 552 | ... | ... | ... | ... | 117 |
| | 1996 | 37 | 520 | 4 516 | ... | ... | ... | ... | 124 |
| | 1997 | 47 | 524 | 4 646 | ... | ... | ... | ... | 133 |
| Slovenia | 1990 | 2 | 69 | 2 705 | ... | 47 819 | 15 | (50) 376 | 211 |
| | 1991 | 67 | 67 | 2 781 | ... | ... | ... | (50) 349 | (30) 905 |
| | 1992 | 68 | 68 | 2 899 | 79 567 | ... | ... | (50) 394 | (30) 965 |
| | 1993 | 68 | 68 | 2 974 | ... | ... | ... | (50) 446 | (30) 1 094 |
| | 1994 | 68 | 68 | 3 048 | ... | ... | ... | (50) 442 | (30) 1 188 |
| | 1995 | 66 | 66 | 3 098 | ... | ... | ... | (50) 442 | (30) 1 184 |
| | 1996 | 66 | 66 | 3 089 | ... | ... | ... | (50) 417 | 141 |
| | 1997 | 68 | 68 | 3 148 | ... | ... | ... | (50) 429 | 126 |
| Spain | 1980 | (53) 326 | 600 | 7 806 | 256 370 | 12 475 | 35 | ... | 263 |
| | 1985 | 505 | 1 178 | 12 959 | ... | 52 518 | *240 | 128 | 962 |
| | 1990 | 567 | 1 028 | 16 050 | *642 005 | 435 008 | 332 | 211 | 912 |
| | 1991 | 596 | 1 085 | 16 660 | ... | ... | ... | ... | (30) 12 893 |
| | 1992 | 648 | 1 131 | 18 618 | 783 100 | 737 569 | 501 | 237 | 1 648 |
| | 1993 | 579 | 1 043 | 16 417 | ... | ... | ... | ... | (30) 13 870 |
| | 1994 | 636 | 1 087 | 21 795 | ... | 1 093 931 | 538 | (55) 61 | 2 017 |
| | 1995 | 583 | 907 | 16 363 | ... | ... | ... | ... | (30) 17 538 |
| | 1996 | 640 | 1 118 | 24 736 | ... | 1 284 689 | 612 | (55) 102 | 3 283 |
| | 1997 | 588 | 947 | 16 877 | ... | ... | ... | ... | (30) 20 303 |
| Sweden | 1972 | 6 | 6 | ... | 163 665 | ... | ... | ... | ... |
| | 1980 | 15 | ... | ... | 347 871 | 122 154 | ... | ... | ... |
| | 1985 | 15 | *134 | 15 694 | ... | *331 991 | *26 | *365 | *109 |

Libraries of institutions of tertiary education IV.3
Bibliothèques d'établissements d'enseignement supérieur
Bibliotecas de instituciones de enseñanza superior

| Annual additions — Volumes (000) / Volúmenes (000) | Other materials (000) / Autres matériels (000) / Otros materiales (000) | Loans to users (000) / Prêts aux usagers (000) / Préstamos a los usuarios (000) | Inter-Library loans / Prêts entre bibliothèques / Préstamos entre bibliotecas | Current expenditure — Total (000) | Staff (%) / Personnel (%) / Personal (%) | Library employees — Total | Holding a diploma / Diplômé / Diplomado | Trained on the job / Formé sur le tas / Formado en ejercicio | Country / Pays / País | Year / Année / Año |
|---|---|---|---|---|---|---|---|---|---|---|
| 346 | ... | 3 038 | 348 004 | (44) 365 591 | ... | 868 | 568 | 300 | Norway (cont) | 1996 |
| 335 | ... | 3 009 | 358 394 | (44) 394 787 | ... | 885 | 581 | 303 | | 1997 |
| ... | ... | 4 436 | | | | 3 746 | ... | | Poland | 1971 |
| 1 241 | ... | 6 352 | (9) 2 300 | ... | ... | 4 936 | 903 | | | 1980 |
| ... | ... | 19 767 | 1 974 | ... | ... | 5 738 | 1 933 | 3 805 | | 1990 |
| 1 333 | 473 | 6 223 | 45 463 | 8 352 | 34 | 3 840 | 2 608 | 1 232 | | 1991 |
| 1 291 | 14 | 6 751 | 39 649 | 12 072 | 43 | 3 723 | 2 546 | 1 177 | | 1992 |
| 1 385 | 318 | 7 724 | 33 290 | 17 771 | 40 | 3 875 | 2 794 | 1 081 | | 1993 |
| 1 396 | 14 | 8 209 | 36 650 | 38 781 | 48 | 3 748 | 2 714 | 1 034 | | 1994 |
| 1 408 | 14 | 9 171 | 39 126 | 45 464 | 41 | 3 872 | 2 786 | 1 086 | | 1995 |
| 1 438 | 15 | 10 489 | 50 739 | 68 141 | 45 | 3 857 | 2 798 | 1 059 | | 1996 |
| 1 843 | 14 | 11 597 | 51 860 | 103 750 | 48 | 6 601 | 4 949 | 1 652 | | 1997 |
| 54 | (47) 1.35 | (48) 265 | (6) 20 786 | 115 473 | 35 | 197 | 48 | 344 | Portugal | 1981 |
| ... | ... | *306 | ... | ... | ... | ... | ... | ... | | 1985 |
| 179 | 19 | 536 | 4 194 | 935 027 | 52 | 843 | 442 | 293 | | 1990 |
| 209 | ... | 519 | ... | ... | ... | 549 | 123 | 426 | | 1991 |
| 202 | ... | 540 | ... | ... | ... | 489 | 119 | 370 | | 1992 |
| 201 | 28 | 790 | 3 036 | 1 643 597 | 48 | 960 | 151 | 323 | | 1993 |
| 192 | ... | 614 | ... | ... | ... | 452 | 131 | 321 | | 1994 |
| 192 | ... | 610 | ... | ... | ... | 412 | 129 | 283 | | 1995 |
| 194 | ... | 697 | ... | ... | ... | 409 | 132 | 277 | | 1996 |
| 219 | ... | 771 | ... | ... | ... | 559 | 166 | 393 | | 1997 |
| ... | ... | 13 965 | ... | ... | ... | ... | ... | ... | Romania | 1979 |
| ... | ... | 14 233 | ... | ... | ... | ... | ... | ... | | 1980 |
| ... | ... | 13 950 | ... | ... | ... | ... | ... | ... | | 1989 |
| ... | ... | 7 640 | 2 787 | ... | ... | 4 201 | 2 056 | 2 145 | | 1990 |
| ... | ... | 7 173 | 2 592 | ... | ... | 4 204 | 2 078 | 2 126 | | 1991 |
| ... | ... | 7 265 | 2 951 | ... | ... | 4 041 | 2 017 | 2 024 | | 1992 |
| 494 | 48 | 8 948 | 2 762 | ... | ... | 3 843 | 1 959 | 1 884 | | 1993 |
| ... | ... | 8 948 | 2 478 | ... | ... | 3 665 | 1 872 | 1 793 | | 1994 |
| ... | ... | 8 948 | 2 371 | ... | ... | 3 531 | 1 811 | 1 720 | | 1995 |
| 429 | 1 525 | 103 | 3 967 | ... | ... | 1 561 | 1 332 | 144 | | 1996 |
| 494 | ... | 10 283 | ... | ... | ... | 559 | 368 | 191 | | 1997 |
| 16 975 | ... | 282 534 | (6) 203 101 | ... | ... | 21 825 | 6 852 | ... | Russian | 1990 |
| 12 478 | ... | 272 378 | (6) 116 748 | ... | ... | 22 118 | 15 366 | ... | Federation | 1993 |
| ... | ... | 292 132 | ... | ... | ... | 20 863 | 13 201 | ... | | 1996 |
| ... | ... | 2 169 | 523 | ... | ... | 523 | 471 | 52 | Slovakia | 1990 |
| ... | ... | 2 054 | 487 | ... | ... | 495 | 451 | 44 | | 1991 |
| ... | ... | 1 960 | 577 | ... | ... | 432 | 394 | 38 | | 1992 |
| 104 | ... | 2 085 | ... | (18) 61 830 | 53 | 504 | 455 | 95 | | 1993 |
| ... | ... | 2 043 | 548 | ... | ... | 455 | 415 | 40 | | 1994 |
| 125 | ... | 2 212 | 550 | ... | ... | 464 | ... | ... | | 1995 |
| 109 | ... | 2 275 | 6 701 | ... | ... | 469 | ... | ... | | 1996 |
| 91 | ... | 2 503 | 6 908 | ... | ... | 557 | ... | ... | | 1997 |
| ... | ... | 1 659 | ... | ... | ... | 325 | 299 | 26 | Slovenia | 1990 |
| 82 | ... | 1 591 | ... | (51) 103 082 | ... | 294 | 259 | 35 | | 1991 |
| 87 | 11 | 1 620 | (52) 56 768 | (51) 312 699 | ... | 298 | ... | ... | | 1992 |
| 83 | 11 | 1 938 | (52) 52 253 | (51) 440 831 | ... | 341 | ... | ... | | 1993 |
| 90 | 14 | 2 234 | (52) 63 333 | (51) 552 180 | ... | 322 | ... | ... | | 1994 |
| 95 | 12 | 2 217 | 33 993 | 589 833 | ... | 321 | ... | ... | | 1995 |
| 95 | 18 | 2 659 | 39 039 | 654 489 | ... | 334 | 287 | 47 | | 1996 |
| 98 | 19 | 3 123 | 47 147 | 1 831 713 | ... | 344 | 293 | 51 | | 1997 |
| 365 | (54) 5.67 | *7 396 | ... | ... | ... | ... | ... | ... | Spain | 1980 |
| | | | | | | | | | | 1985 |
| 781 | 170 | 6 604 | 332 453 | 9 396 703 | 53 | 2 887 | 982 | 875 | | 1990 |
| 1 000 | ... | 6 917 | ... | ... | | 3 325 | 2 000 | 1 325 | | 1991 |
| 959 | 226 | 7 895 | 229 703 | 13 629 351 | 58 | 3 567 | 1 163 | 1 085 | | 1992 |
| 959 | ... | 7 630 | ... | ... | | 3 214 | 2 002 | 1 212 | | 1993 |
| 1 463 | 44 | 11 209 | 152 912 | 18 995 967 | 58 | 4 204 | 2 851 | 1 353 | | 1994 |
| 919 | ... | 8 130 | ... | ... | | 2 978 | 2 098 | 880 | | 1995 |
| 1 228 | 46 | 13 889 | 209 108 | 23 281 871 | 58 | 4 774 | 3 398 | 1 376 | | 1996 |
| 1 049 | ... | 10 279 | ... | ... | | 3 919 | 2 697 | 1 222 | | 1997 |
| 192 | ... | 852 | 109 998 | (7) 6 764 | ... | 506 | 136 | ... | Sweden | 1972 |
| ... | ... | (56) 1 393 | ... | 138 652 | 72 | 1 018 | 308 | ... | | 1980 |
| ... | ... | 2 001 | ... | ... | ... | ... | ... | ... | | 1985 |

IV.3 Libraries of institutions of tertiary education
Bibliothèques d'établissements d'enseignement supérieur
Bibliotecas de instituciones de enseñanza superior

| Country / Pays / País | Year / Année / Año | Administrative unit / Unités administratives / Unidades administrativas | Service points / Points de service / Puntos de servicio | Collections / Collections / Fondos | | Microforms / Microcopies / Microcopias | Audio-visual documents (000) / Matériels audio-visuels (000) / Materiales audio-visuales (000) | Other library materials (000) / Autres matériels de bibliothèque (000) / Otros materiales de biblioteca (000) | Registered users (000) / Usagers inscrits (000) / Usuarios inscritos (000) |
|---|---|---|---|---|---|---|---|---|---|
| | | | | Books/Livres/Libros | | | | | |
| | | | | Number of volumes (000) / Nombre de volumes (000) / Número de volúmenes (000) | Metres of shelving / Mètres de rayonnage / Metros de estantes | | | | |
| Sweden (cont) | 1990 | 26 | 137 | 18 275 | 461 426 | 342 570 | 29 | 220 | ... |
| | 1991 | 25 | 117 | 18 960 | 460 619 | 2 344 762 | 30 | 306 | ... |
| | 1992 | 26 | 116 | 19 351 | ... | 2 425 670 | 31 | 311 | ... |
| | 1993 | 26 | 104 | 20 093 | ... | 3 165 266 | 32 | 315 | ... |
| | 1994 | 26 | 109 | 19 677 | ... | 3 323 961 | 34 | 360 | ... |
| | 1995 | 28 | 111 | 20 229 | ... | ... | 36 | 350 | ... |
| | 1996 | 31 | 117 | 21 159 | ... | 3 532 437 | 40 | 352 | ... |
| | 1997 | 31 | 117 | 22 356 | ... | 3 562 088 | 39 | 357 | ... |
| Switzerland | 1981 | 11 | ... | 13 035 | 309 700 | 1 340 000 | 591 | ... | (23) 115 |
| | 1985 | *12 | *263 | *15 311 | ... | *1 604 248 | *628 | *1 887 | *156 |
| | 1990 | (3) 9 | ... | 13 519 | 339 908 | 2 010 609 | 253 | 288 | 137 |
| | 1991 | 13 | 254 | 16 524 | ... | ... | ... | ... | (30) 1 887 |
| | 1992 | 13 | 246 | 16 565 | ... | ... | ... | ... | (30) 2 144 |
| | 1993 | (3) 9 | 250 | 14 427 | 362 308 | 2 274 718 | 776 | 98 | 201 |
| | 1994 | 11 | 244 | 17 232 | ... | ... | ... | ... | (30) 2 264 |
| | 1995 | 11 | 232 | 17 675 | ... | ... | ... | ... | (30) 2 591 |
| | 1996 | 11 | 241 | 18 104 | ... | ... | ... | ... | (30) 2 699 |
| | 1997 | 12 | 245 | 18 415 | ... | ... | ... | ... | (30) 3 017 |
| The Former Yugoslav Rep. of Macedonia | 1992 | 26 | 43 | 1 135 | 26 323 | ... | 18 | 1.47 | 497 |
| | 1995 | (1) 22 | 42 | 1 087 | 23 932 | ... | 2.65 | 0.13 | (57) 466 |
| Ukraine | 1997 | (3) 1 | 59 | 2 804 | 24 019 | 1 112 | 2.35 | 13 | 17 |
| United Kingdom | 1980 | (58) 554 | 937 | 24 010 | 599 447 | 736 966 | ... | ... | ... |
| | 1985 | 215 | 860 | *77 161 | ... | *3 182 376 | *1 377 | 5 064 | *1 088 |
| | 1990 | 215 | *860 | 89 832 | 1 804 000 | *3 182 376 | 1 636 | 5 064 | 1 331 |
| | 1991 | 221 | 894 | 91 163 | ... | ... | ... | ... | (30) 17 607 |
| | 1992 | 224 | 851 | 90 875 | ... | ... | ... | ... | (30) 19 855 |
| | 1993 | 215 | 860 | 89 832 | ... | ... | ... | ... | (30) 18 943 |
| | 1994 | 221 | 786 | 89 131 | ... | ... | ... | ... | (30) 21 048 |
| | 1995 | 216 | 748 | 89 535 | ... | ... | ... | ... | (30) 23 951 |
| | 1996 | 217 | 756 | 90 192 | ... | ... | ... | ... | (30) 24 863 |
| | 1997 | 218 | 781 | 92 348 | ... | ... | ... | ... | (30) 27 727 |
| **Oceania** | | | | | | | | | |
| Australia | 1994 | 43 | 231 | 33 000 | ... | 5 000 000 | 555 | 2 005 | 550 |
| Nauru | 1990 | 1 | 1 | 1 | ... | ... | 0.13 | ... | 0.1 |
| New Caledonia | 1990 | (59) 1 | 2 | 9 | 269 | 4 800 | ... | 0.52 | 0.7 |
| New Zealand | 1981 | (21) 1 | 4 | 6 | ... | ... | 0.09 | 0.10 | 0.5 |
| | 1990 | 7 | 33 | 5 910 | ... | 730 818 | 26 | 569 | ... |
| Niue | 1990 | 1 | 1 | 3 | 70 | ... | ... | ... | 0.0 |
| Papua New Guinea | 1982 | (60) 1 | 1 | 50 | ... | 110 | 1.08 | 0.58 | 2.6 |
| | 1996 | (60) 1 | 1 | 9 | 12 | 4 | ... | ... | 0.3 |

Libraries of institutions of tertiary education **IV.3**
Bibliothèques d'établissements d'enseignement supérieur
Bibliotecas de instituciones de enseñanza superior

| Annual additions Acquisitions annuelles Adquisiciones anuales | | Loans to users (000) Prêts aux usagers (000) Préstamos a los usuarios (000) | Inter-Library loans Prêts entre biblio-thèques Préstamos entre bibliotecas | Current expenditure Dépenses ordinaires Gastos ordinarios | | Library employees Personnel des bibliothèques Personal de las bibliotecas | | | Country Pays País | Year Année Año |
|---|---|---|---|---|---|---|---|---|---|---|
| Volumes (000) Volumes (000) Volúmenes (000) | Other materials (000) Autres matériels (000) Otros materiales (000) | | | Total (000) Total (000) Total (000) | Staff (%) Personnel (%) Personal (%) | Total Total Total | Holding a diploma Diplômé Diplomado | Trained on the job Formé sur le tas Formado en ejercicio | | |
| 305 | 39 | 1 366 | 436 574 | 400 478 | 62 | 1 201 | 609 | 592 | Sweden (cont) | 1990 |
| 312 | ... | 2 176 | 364 321 | 473 383 | 58 | 1 240 | 683 | 557 | | 1991 |
| 298 | ... | 2 644 | 380 122 | 495 241 | 59 | 1 262 | 698 | 564 | | 1992 |
| 294 | ... | 3 234 | 449 071 | 539 025 | 60 | 1 265 | 714 | 551 | | 1993 |
| 285 | ... | 3 677 | 466 729 | 609 528 | 55 | 1 309 | 755 | 554 | | 1994 |
| 309 | ... | 4 142 | 470 892 | 645 343 | 55 | 1 349 | 815 | 533 | | 1995 |
| 408 | ... | 4 451 | 550 836 | 750 710 | 56 | 1 417 | 911 | 506 | | 1996 |
| 503 | ... | 5 271 | 590 020 | 774 661 | 58 | 1 468 | 939 | 529 | | 1997 |
| 342 | 106 | 1 495 | | 59 824 | 64 | 661 | 204 | ... | Switzerland | 1981 |
| ... | ... | *1 315 | | ... | ... | ... | ... | ... | | 1985 |
| 294 | 102 | 1 358 | 374 385 | 98 694 | 62 | 698 | 251 | ... | | 1990 |
| 361 | ... | 1 512 | | ... | ... | 920 | 243 | 677 | | 1991 |
| 367 | ... | 1 587 | | ... | ... | 871 | 242 | 629 | | 1992 |
| 278 | 133 | 1 599 | 142 827 | 113 546 | 65 | 709 | 196 | ... | | 1993 |
| 385 | ... | 1 928 | | ... | ... | 917 | 279 | 638 | | 1994 |
| 364 | ... | 2 078 | | ... | ... | 938 | 283 | 655 | | 1995 |
| 383 | ... | 2 329 | | ... | ... | 937 | 285 | 652 | | 1996 |
| 399 | ... | 2 431 | | ... | ... | 1 091 | 325 | 766 | | 1997 |
| 7.8 | 0.49 | 0.15 | 1 061 | 37 244 | ... | 58 | 51 | 7 | The Former Yugoslav Rep. of Macedonia | 1992 |
| 13 | 0.62 | 0.010 | 824 | 6 053 | ... | 65 | 56 | 9 | | 1995 |
| 21 | | 2.15 | 610 | 259 | 78 | 166 | 38 | 98 | Ukraine | 1997 |
| 1 666 | 91 | ... | (6) 380 000 | 36 009 | 56 | 4 009 | ... | ... | United Kingdom | 1980 |
| ... | ... | *30 152 | | ... | ... | ... | ... | ... | | 1985 |
| 1 910 | 48 | 34 897 | | ... | ... | 7 858 | 2 946 | ... | | 1990 |
| 2 405 | ... | 31 636 | | ... | ... | 8 313 | 2 944 | 5 369 | | 1991 |
| 2 323 | ... | 32 912 | | ... | ... | 7 513 | 2 849 | 4 664 | | 1992 |
| 2 307 | ... | 34 897 | | ... | ... | 7 858 | 2 946 | 4 912 | | 1993 |
| 2 208 | ... | 37 428 | | ... | ... | 7 176 | 3 139 | 4 037 | | 1994 |
| 2 209 | ... | 37 181 | | ... | ... | 6 654 | 3 087 | 3 567 | | 1995 |
| 2 226 | ... | 42 501 | | ... | ... | 6 637 | 3 154 | 3 483 | | 1996 |
| 2 523 | ... | 47 013 | | ... | ... | 8 919 | 3 968 | 4 951 | | 1997 |
| | | | | | | | | | **Oceania** | |
| 1 500 | ... | 21 000 | (6) 390 000 | 361 000 | 53 | 4 785 | 1 578 | ... | Australia | 1994 |
| ... | ... | ... | ... | ... | ... | ... | ... | 1 | Nauru | 1990 |
| 3.9 | 5.32 | 6.50 | ... | 1 235 | 40 | 2 | 1 | ... | New Caledonia | 1990 |
| 2.4 | ... | | | 3 921 | 57 | 2 | 1 | 1 | New Zealand | 1981 |
| 182 | 66 | 2 578 | 53 059 | 36 239 | 39 | 592 | 119 | 133 | | 1990 |
| *0.0 | ... | *0.20 | 9 | ... | ... | ... | ... | ... | Niue | 1990 |
| 4.7 | ... | 50 | 252 | 466 | 40 | 30 | 9 | ... | Papua New Guinea | 1982 |
| 0.0 | ... | ... | ... | ... | 1 | 1 | 1 | 1 | | 1996 |

## General note
For general explanations and definitions, please refer to the beginning of this chapter.

## Note générale
Pour les explications et définitions générales, prière de se référer au début de ce chapitre.

## Nota general
Para las explicaciones y definiciones generales, referirse al comienzo de este capítulo.

**Notes**

(1) Data refer to libraries of universities and similar institutions which are not administered by the main or central library.

(2) Data do not include expenditure on employees.

(3) Data refer only to main or central university libraries.

**Notes**

(1) Les données concernent les bibliothèques d'université et d'institutions similaires qui ne sont pas administrées par la bibliothèque principale ou centrale.

(2) Les données n'incluent pas les dépenses pour le personnel.

(3) Les données concernent seulement les bibliothèques principales ou centrales.

**Notas**

(1) Los datos se refieren a las bibliotecas universitarias o de institutos similares que no están administradas por la biblioteca principal o central.

(2) Los datos no incluyen los gastos para el personal.

(3) Los datos se refieren a las bibliotecas principales o centrales solamente.

**IV.3** Libraries of institutions of tertiary education
Bibliothèques d'établissements d'enseignement supérieur
Bibliotecas de instituciones de enseñanza superior

(4) Data do not include libraries of institutions of tertiary education other than universities.

(5) All data are included in France.

(6) Data refer only to inter-library loan transactions at the national level.

(7) Data refer only to expenditure on acquisitions.

(8) All data refer to the Central University Library of Dakar only.

(9) Data refer only to inter-library loan transactions at the international level.

(10) Data refer only to libraries of institutions of tertiary education other than universities.

(11) Data do not include "Erdiston Teachers' Training College".

(12) Data refer only to the library of "Erdiston Teachers' Training College".

(13) Data refer only to the University "Carlos Monge Alfara".

(14) Data refer to number of titles.

(15) Data refer only to the number of visits to reading rooms.

(16) All data refer to the main or central library of the University of the West Indies in St. Augustine.

(17) Data refer to the University 'Santa María' only.

(18) Data refer only to expenditure on employees and acquisitions.

(19) Data do not include libraries of universities and similar institutions which are not administered by the main or central library.

(20) Data refer to "Ahmed Al-Farsi" Library (College of Health Sciences) only.

(21) Data refer to university libraries only.

(22) Data refer only to manuscripts.

(23) Data do not include expenditure on libraries of institutions of tertiary education.

(24) Data refer to only 4 libraries.

(25) Data refer only to computer files.

(26) Data refer to only 3 libraries.

(27) Data refer only to the University of Damascus.

(28) Data refer only to expenditure on employees.

(29) Data refer to 19 main or central university libraries, to an unknown number of libraries of institutes or departments and to 2 libraries of institutions of tertiary education other than universities.

(30) Data refer only to the number of visits to the library.

(31) Data include other library materials.

(32) Data refer to all documents.

(33) Data include audio-visual materials.

(34) Data do not include some 400 libraries attached to institutes or departments and 26 libraries which are not administered by the main or central university library.

(35) All data include Guadeloupe, French Guiana, Martinique and Reunion.

(36) Data do not include 33 main libraries of institutions of tertiary education that are not administered by the main library nor 3549 libraries attached to institutes or departments but which are not under the direction of or administered by the main or central library.

(37) Data refer to 235 libraries out of a total number of 271.

(38) Data refer to university libraries only, i.e. main university libraries, central libraries or a group of libraries which have premises apart, but come under the responsibility of only one director.

(4) Les données n'incluent pas les bibliothèques d'institutions de l'enseignement supérieur autres que les universités.

(5) Toutes les données sont incluses dans la France.

(6) Les données se réfèrent seulement aux prêts entre bibliothèques au niveau national.

(7) Les données se réfèrent uniquement aux dépenses pour les acquisitions.

(8) Toutes les données concernent la Bibliothèque Universitaire de Dakar seulement.

(9) Les données se réfèrent seulement aux prêts entre bibliothèques au niveau international.

(10) Les données se réfèrent seulement aux bibliothèques d'institutions de l'enseignement supérieur autres que les universités.

(11) Les données n'incluent pas le "Erdiston Teachers' Training College".

(12) Les données concernent seulement la bibliothèque du "Erdiston Teachers' Training College".

(13) Les données concernent seulement l'Université "Carlos Monge Alfara".

(14) Les données se réfèrent au nombre de titres.

(15) Les données se réfèrent seulement au nombre de visites dans les salles de lecture.

(16) Les données concernent la bibliothèque principale ou centrale de l'Université de West Indies à St. Augustine.

(17) Les données concernent l'Université "Santa María" seulement.

(18) Les données se réfèrent seulement aux dépenses pour le personnel et les acquisitions.

(19) Les données n'incluent pas les bibliothèques universitaires et d'institutions similaires qui ne sont pas administrées par la bibliothèque principale ou centrale.

(20) Les données concernent la bibliothèque "Ahmed Al-Farsi" (College of Health Sciences) seulement.

(21) Les données concernent les bibliothèques universitaires seulement.

(22) Les données se réfèrent seulement aux manuscrits.

(23) Les données n'incluent pas les dépenses destinées aux bibliothèques des établissements de l'enseignement supérieur.

(24) Les données se réfèrent seulement à 4 bibliothèques.

(25) Les données concernent les fichiers informatiques seulement

(26) Les données se réfèrent seulement à 3 bibliothèques.

(27) Les données concernent l'Université de Damas seulement.

(28) Les données se réfèrent seulement aux dépenses pour le personnel.

(29) Les données concernent 19 bibliothèques principales ou centrales, un nombre inconnu de bibliothèques d'instituts ou départements et 2 bibliothèques d'établissements de l'enseignement supérieur autres que des universités.

(30) Les données se réfèrent seulement au nombre de visites dans la bibliothèque.

(31) Les données incluent d'autres matériels de bibliothèque.

(32) Les données concernent tous les types de documents.

(33) Les données incluent le matériel audiovisuel.

(34) Les données n'incluent pas quelques 400 bibliothèques rattachées à des instituts ou départements et 26 bibliothèques qui ne sont pas administrées par la bibliothèque principale ou centrale.

(35) Les données incluent la Guadeloupe, la Guyane, la Martinique et la Réunion.

(36) Les données n'incluent pas 33 bibliothèques principales d'établissements de l'enseignement supérieur qui ne sont pas administrées par la bibliothèque principale, de même que 3 549 bibliothèques rattachées à des instituts ou départements mais qui ne sont pas sous la direction ou administrées par la bibliothèque principale ou centrale.

(37) Les données concernent 235 bibliothèques sur un nombre total de 271.

(38) Les données concernent les bibliothèques universitaires seulement, c'est-à-dire les bibliothèques universitaires principales, centrales, ou un groupe de bibliothèques dont les locaux sont séparés mais qui sont sous la responsabilité d'un seul directeur.

(4) Los datos no incluyen las bibliotecas de institutos de enseñanza superior otros que las universidades.

(5) Todos los datos se incluyen en Francia.

(6) Los datos se refieren a los préstamos entre bibliotecas a nivel nacional solamente.

(7) Los datos se refieren solamente a los gastos para las adquisiciones.

(8) Todos los datos se refieren a la Biblioteca Universitaria de Dakar solamente.

(9) Los datos se refieren a los préstamos entre bibliotecas a nivel internacional solamente.

(10) Los datos se refieren a las bibliotecas de institutos de enseñanza superior otros que las universidades.

(11) Los datos no incluyen el "Erdiston Teachers' Training College".

(12) Los datos se refieren solamente a la biblioteca del "Erdiston Teachers' Training College".

(13) Los datos se refieren solamente a la Universidad "Carlos Monge Alfara".

(14) Los datos se refieren al número de títulos.

(15) Los datos se refieren al número de visitas a las salas de lectura solamente.

(16) Los datos se refieren a la biblioteca principal o central de la Universidad de West Indies en St. Augustine.

(17) Los datos se refieren a la Universidad "Santa María" solamente.

(18) Los datos se refieren solamente a los gastos de personal y de adquisiciones.

(19) Los datos no incluyen las bibliotecas universitarias y de institutos similares que no son administradas por la biblioteca principal o central.

(20) Los datos se refieren a la biblioteca "Ahmed Al-Farsi" (College of Health Sciences) solamente.

(21) Los datos se refieren a las bibliotecas universitarias solamente.

(22) Los datos se refieren solamente a los manuscritos.

(23) Los datos no incluyen los gastos destinados a las bibliotecas de los institutos de enseñanza superior.

(24) Los datos se refieren a 4 bibliotecas solamente.

(25) Los datos se refieren a los ficheros informáticos solamente.

(26) Los datos se refieren a 3 bibliotecas solamente.

(27) Los datos se refieren a la Universidad de Damasco solamente.

(28) Los datos se refieren solamente a los gastos de personal.

(29) Los datos se refieren a 19 bibliotecas principales o centrales, a un número desconocido de bibliotecas de centros o departamentos y a 2 bibliotecas de institutos de enseñanza superior otros que las universidades.

(30) Los datos se refieren solamente al número de visitas a la biblioteca.

(31) Los datos incluyen otros materiales de biblioteca.

(32) Los datos se refieren a todo tipo de documentos.

(33) Los datos incluyen el material audiovisual.

(34) Los datos no incluyen unas 400 bibliotecas que dependen de centros o departamentos y 26 bibliotecas que no están administradas por la biblioteca principal o central.

(35) Los datos incluyen Guadalupe, Guyana, Martinica y la Reunión.

(36) Los datos no incluyen 33 bibliotecas principales de institutos de enseñanza superior que no están administradas por la biblioteca principal, así como 3 549 bibliotecas que dependen de centros o departamentos pero que no están bajo la dirección o administradas por la biblioteca principal o central.

(37) Los datos se refieren a 235 bibliotecas dentro de un total de 271.

(38) Los datos se refieren a las bibliotecas universitarias solamente, o sea las bibliotecas universitarias principales, centrales, o un grupo de bibliotecas cuyos locales están separados pero que están bajo la responsabilidad de un solo director.

Libraries of institutions of tertiary education  IV.3
Bibliothèques d'établissements d'enseignement supérieur
Bibliotecas de instituciones de enseñanza superior

(39) Data include only those main or central university libraries that are part of the national network and as such are obliged to supply statistics.

(40) Data are shown in ECUs (European Currency Unit) expressed at 1990 constant prices.

(41) Data include periodicals.

(42) Data do not include private libraries

(43) Data do not take into account the number hours of work.

(44) Data refer only to those libraries that have reported.

(45) Data include microfilms and microfiches.

(46) Data include non-registered borrowers.

(47) Data refer only to manuscripts and microforms.

(48) Data include books used in reading rooms.

(49) All data refer only to university libraries.

(50) Data refer to microforms, other library materials and CD-ROMs.

(51) Data refer to expenditure on the acquisition of books only.

(52) Data refer to the sum total of inter-library loans issued and received.

(53) Data refer to approximately 90% of the total.

(54) Data refer only to microforms.

(55) Data include CD-ROMs.

(56) Data include photocopies.

(57) Data refer to the total number of library users.

(58) Data do not include Scotland.

(59) Data refer to the one university library for the Pacific (New Caledonia and French Polynesia).

(60) Data refer only to the University of Technology.

(61) Data include periodicals.

---

(39) Les données incluent seulement les bibliothèques universitaires principales ou centrales qui font partie du réseau national et qui, en tant que telles, sont obligées de fournir des statistiques.

(40) Les données sont montrées en ECUs (monnaie européenne commune) et s'expriment en valeurs constantes de 1990.

(41) Les données incluent les périodiques

(42) Les données n'incluent pas les bibliothèques privées.

(43) Les données ne tiennent pas compte du nombre d'heures de travail.

(44) Les données concernent les bibliothèques qui ont fourni des données.

(45) Les données incluent les microfilms et les microfiches.

(46) Les données incluent les usagers non inscrits qui empruntent.

(47) Les données concernent seulement les manuscrits et les microcopies.

(48) Les données se réfèrent aux livres utilisés dans les salles de lecture.

(49) Les données concernent seulement les bibliothèques universitaires.

(50) Les données concernent les microcopies, les autres matériels de bibliothèque et les CD-Roms.

(51) Les données concernent les dépenses pour l'acquisition de livres seulement.

(52) Les données concernent la somme totale de prêts entre bibliothèques sortis et reçus.

(53) Les données se réfèrent approximativement à 90% du total.

(54) Les données se réfèrent seulement aux microcopies.

(55) Les données incluent les CD-Roms.

(56) Les données incluent les photocopies.

(57) Les données concernent l'ensemble des usagers de la bibliothèque.

(58) Les données n'incluent pas l'Ecosse.

(59) Les données concernent la bibliothèque universitaire pour le Pacifique (Nouvelle-Calédonie et Polynésie française).

(60) Les données concernent l'Université de Technologie seulement.

(61) Les données incluent les périodiques.

---

(39) Los datos incluyen solamente las bibliotecas universitarias principales o centrales que hacen parte de la red nacional y que, en tanto que tales, están obligadas de proporcionar estadísticas.

(40) Los datos se expresan en ECUs (moneda común europea), en moneda constante de 1990.

(41) Los datos incluyen los periódicos.

(42) Los datos no incluyen las bibliotecas privadas.

(43) Los datos no tienen en cuenta la cantidad de horas de trabajo.

(44) Los datos se refieren a las bibliotecas que han proporcionado datos.

(45) Los datos incluyen los microfilmes y los microficheros.

(46) Los datos incluyen a los usuarios no inscritos que hacen préstamos.

(47) Los datos se refieren a los manuscritos y microcopias solamente.

(48) Los datos se refieren a los libros utilizados en las salas de lectura.

(49) Los datos se refieren a las bibliotecas universitarias solamente.

(50) Los datos se refieren a las microcopias, otros materiales de biblioteca y CD-Rom.

(51) Los datos se refieren a los gastos para la adquisición de libros solamente.

(52) Los datos se refieren a la suma total de préstamos entre bibliotecas salidos y recibidos.

(53) Los datos se refieren al 90% del total aproximadamente.

(54) Los datos se refieren solamente a las microcopias.

(55) Los datos incluyen los CD-Rom.

(56) Los datos incluyen las fotocopias.

(57) Los datos se refieren al conjunto de los usuarios de la biblioteca.

(58) Los datos no incluyen Escocia.

(59) Los datos se refieren a la biblioteca universitaria para el Pacífico (Nueva Caledonia y Polinesia Francesa).

(60) Los datos se refieren a la Universidad de Tecnología solamente.

(61) Los datos incluyen los periódicos.

## IV.4    School libraries

## Bibliothèques scolaires

## Bibliotecas escolares

| Country<br><br>Pays<br><br>País | Year<br><br>Année<br><br>Año | Service points<br><br>Points de service<br><br>Puntos de servicio | Collections / Collections / Fondos | | | Loans to users<br><br>Prêts aux usagers<br><br>Préstamos a los usuarios | | Current expenditure total<br><br>Dépenses ordinaires total<br><br>Gastos ordinarios total<br>(000) | Total library employees<br><br>Total personnel des bibliothèques<br><br>Total personal de las bibliotecas |
|---|---|---|---|---|---|---|---|---|---|
| | | | Volumes of books (000)<br><br>Volumes de livres (000)<br><br>Volúmenes de libros (000) | Audio-visual documents<br><br>Matériels audio-visuels<br><br>Materiales audio-visuales | Other library materials<br><br>Autres matériels de bibliothèque<br><br>Otros materiales de biblioteca | | | | |
| **Africa** | | | | | | | | | |
| Congo | 1990 | 1 | 10 | ... | ... | 5 800 | | ... | 7 |
| Mauritius | 1980 | 28 | 139 | ... | ... | 358 179 | (1) | 550 | 35 |
| | 1987 | 26 | 148 | ... | ... | 183 463 | (2) | 255 | 52 |
| | 1990 | 26 | 161 | ... | ... | ... | (2) | 1 500 | 56 |
| Seychelles | 1974 | 4 | 28 | ... | ... | ... | | ... | 2 |
| | 1984 | 22 | 72 | ... | ... | 1 515 489 | (2) | 153 | 22 |
| | 1987 | 19 | 101 | ... | ... | 230 097 | (2) | 8 | 25 |
| | 1990 | 24 | 150 | ... | ... | 221 334 | | 586 | 26 |
| **North America** | | | | | | | | | |
| Cuba | 1984 | 3 261 | 13 855 | ... | ... | 8 757 700 | | ... | 4 632 |
| | 1987 | 3 860 | 15 415 | ... | ... | 10 215 000 | | ... | 5 177 |
| | 1993 | 3 800 | ... | ... | ... | ... | | ... | 5 250 |
| Dominica | 1971 | 4 | (3) 6 | ... | ... | ... | | (3) ... | 7 |
| | 1993 | 7 | 15 | ... | ... | *19 738 | | ... | 4 |
| Greenland | 1974 | 24 | 72 | ... | ... | 191 100 | | ... | 15 |
| | 1990 | 24 | 177 | ... | ... | 134 000 | | ... | ... |
| Mexico | 1981 | 1 880 | 5 403 | ... | ... | 15 224 489 | | 111 950 | 3 786 |
| | 1987 | 2 988 | 8 132 | 712 255 | 61 876 | 22 998 178 | | ... | 5 787 |
| | 1990 | 3 546 | 9 844 | 841 241 | 581 215 | 3 544 578 | | ... | 6 761 |
| | 1991 | 3 557 | 10 670 | 900 000 | ... | ... | | ... | ... |
| | 1992 | 3 838 | 12 460 | 929 930 | ... | ... | | ... | 7 844 |
| | 1993 | 4 017 | 14 260 | 939 062 | 752 214 | 45 396 723 | | ... | 8 289 |
| Nicaragua | 1987 | 412 | 595 | ... | ... | 937 812 | | 124 080 | 271 |
| | 1990 | 174 | ... | *150 | ... | *9 176 | | ... | 174 |
| St. Vincent and the Grenadines | 1990 | 3 | ... | ... | ... | ... | | ... | 2 |
| **Asia** | | | | | | | | | |
| Bahrain | 1984 | 93 | 158 | ... | ... | 310 885 | (1) | 315 | 83 |
| | 1987 | 150 | 186 | ... | ... | ... | (2) | 25 | 93 |
| | 1990 | 184 | *166 | *10 000 | ... | *11 000 | | *1 260 | 170 |
| Brunei Darussalam | 1977 | 13 | 59 | 100 | ... | ... | (4) | 128 | 18 |
| | 1981 | 15 | 191 | 139 | 20 | 20 571 | | 644 | 64 |
| | 1991 | 23 | 287 | 2 205 | 8 200 | 139 664 | | 556 | 89 |
| China, Hong Kong SAR | 1981 | 191 | 1 422 | ... | ... | 962 920 | | ... | 191 |
| | 1990 | *374 | 3 266 | ... | ... | *3 043 212 | | ... | 374 |

| Country / Pays / País | Year / Année / Año | Service points / Points de service / Puntos de servicio | Collections / Collections / Fondos | | | Loans to users / Prêts aux usagers / Préstamos a los usuarios | | Current expenditure total / Dépenses ordinaires total / Gastos ordinarios total (000) | Total library employees / Total personnel des bibliothèques / Total personal de las bibliotecas |
|---|---|---|---|---|---|---|---|---|---|
| | | | Volumes of books (000) / Volumes de livres (000) / Volúmenes de libros (000) | Audio-visual documents / Matériels audio-visuels / Materiales audio-visuales | Other library materials / Autres matériels de bibliothèque / Otros materiales de biblioteca | | | | |
| Iran, Islamic Republic of | 1993 | 4 001 | *16 068 | ... | ... | ... | | 11 645 | 22 |
| Korea, Republic of | 1974 | 3 661 | 10 632 | ... | ... | 38 849 243 | | 999 530 | ... |
| | 1981 | 3 184 | 11 912 | ... | ... | 31 623 895 | | 2 424 600 | 1 852 |
| | 1986 | 5 550 | 21 249 | ... | ... | 24 710 362 | | 4 932 873 | 1 944 |
| | 1990 | 6 468 | 27 675 | ... | ... | 25 247 532 | | 4 461 801 | ... |
| | 1993 | 7 366 | 27 440 | ... | ... | 20 480 284 | | 13 052 349 | ... |
| | 1994 | 9 117 | 29 725 | ... | ... | 13 816 913 | | ... | ... |
| Kuwait | 1974 | 254 | 1 291 | ... | ... | ... | | 599 | 417 |
| | 1984 | 446 | 2 651 | 236 | ... | ... | | 3 171 | 751 |
| | 1990 | 587 | 3 117 | 2 000 | ... | ... | | ... | 890 |
| Lebanon | 1993 | 227 | 815 | ... | ... | ... | (2) | 268 | 285 |
| Mongolia | 1990 | 530 | 3 220 | ... | ... | 3 126 000 | | ... | 500 |
| Oman | 1987 | 130 | 132 | ... | ... | 155 927 | (2) | 38 914 | 97 |
| | 1994 | 249 | 284 | 99 | ... | 201 700 | (2) | 65 000 | 271 |
| Qatar | 1974 | 69 | 154 | | ... | 57 052 | | ... | 70 |
| | 1982 | 122 | 214 | ... | ... | ... | | ... | 127 |
| | 1987 | 156 | 471 | 140 | ... | 7 927 | | ... | 157 |
| | 1994 | 162 | 465 | 1 220 | ... | 484 925 | | ... | 132 |
| Saudi Arabia | 1974 | 2 188 | 5 436 | ... | ... | 7 533 000 | | 4 500 | 386 |
| | 1993 | 5 206 | 8 698 | ... | ... | ... | | ... | 5 206 |
| Singapore | 1974 | 363 | 2 244 | ... | ... | 886 404 | | 868 | 550 |
| | 1983 | 405 | 4 087 | ... | ... | 5 012 030 | | 6 005 | 18 |
| | 1984 | 396 | 5 000 | ... | ... | 6 500 000 | (2) | 4 600 | ... |
| | 1990 | 366 | 4 640 | ... | ... | 7 671 617 | (2) | 1 758 | 14 |
| United Arab Emirates | 1990 | 290 | 667 | 11 500 | ... | ... | | 13 155 | 206 |
| | 1993 | 330 | 750 | 16 500 | ... | ... | | 13 035 | 204 |
| Uzbekistan | 1993 | 8 863 | 39 276 | ... | ... | 35 689 228 | | 64 009 | 9 571 |
| **Europe** | | | | | | | | | |
| Austria | 1990 | *432 | *2 240 | *66 553 | *3 471 | *7 299 856 | (5) | 11 469 | 444 |
| | 1991 | 436 | 2 255 | ... | ... | 7 680 156 | | ... | 244 |
| | 1992 | 434 | 2 239 | ... | ... | 7 523 588 | | ... | 270 |
| | 1993 | 432 | 2 240 | ... | ... | 7 299 856 | | ... | 444 |
| | 1994 | 436 | 2 244 | ... | ... | 7 283 423 | | ... | 400 |
| | 1995 | 438 | 2 273 | ... | ... | 7 255 009 | | ... | 413 |
| | 1996 | 439 | 2 287 | ... | ... | 7 268 300 | | ... | 413 |
| | 1997 | 434 | 2 342 | ... | ... | 7 232 427 | | ... | 390 |
| Belarus | 1990 | 5 198 | 76 281 | ... | ... | ... | | ... | 2 660 |
| | 1993 | 4 867 | 95 957 | ... | ... | ... | | ... | 3 051 |
| Belgium | 1990 | *923 | *8 578 | *183 647 | *11 241 | *26 571 344 | (5) | 43 920 | 1 384 |
| | 1991 | 932 | 8 634 | ... | ... | 27 955 629 | | ... | 753 |
| | 1992 | 927 | 8 576 | ... | ... | 27 385 723 | | ... | 836 |
| | 1993 | 923 | 8 578 | ... | ... | 26 571 344 | | ... | 1 384 |
| | 1994 | 931 | 8 593 | ... | ... | 26 511 527 | | ... | 1 244 |
| | 1995 | 936 | 8 705 | ... | ... | 26 408 103 | | ... | 1 283 |
| | 1996 | 938 | 8 758 | ... | ... | 26 456 480 | | ... | 1 281 |
| | 1997 | 927 | 8 969 | ... | ... | 26 325 903 | | ... | 1 214 |
| Bulgaria | 1977 | 3 700 | 13 224 | ... | 105 963 | 8 205 868 | | 2 079 | 567 |
| | 1987 | 3 312 | 16 179 | 43 281 | 80 556 | 9 079 856 | | 3 842 | 3 233 |
| | 1990 | 3 208 | 16 625 | 56 848 | 78 726 | 7 891 413 | | 4 757 | 5 096 |
| | 1991 | 3 154 | 16 369 | 58 710 | ... | 7 676 390 | | 12 391 | 978 |
| | 1992 | 3 097 | 16 259 | 55 601 | ... | 7 383 064 | | 23 237 | 913 |
| | 1993 | 3 062 | 16 097 | 60 994 | ... | 7 461 809 | | 31 422 | 930 |
| | 1994 | 3 011 | 16 079 | 63 740 | ... | 7 216 734 | | 42 583 | 952 |
| | 1995 | 2 986 | 16 020 | 66 633 | ... | 7 383 628 | | 63 994 | 956 |
| | 1996 | 2 961 | 15 980 | 68 391 | ... | 7 050 308 | | 102 259 | 944 |
| | 1997 | 2 876 | 15 787 | 70 247 | ... | 7 086 246 | | 912 637 | 891 |
| Croatia | 1992 | 1 127 | 5 530 | ... | 134 210 | ... | | ... | ... |
| Czech Republic | 1990 | 5 124 | 33 046 | 230 149 | 240 502 | 16 349 228 | (5) | 3 355 | 9 245 |
| | 1991 | 5 111 | 33 162 | 226 749 | 240 374 | 16 345 795 | (5) | 3 385 | 8 867 |
| | 1992 | 4 934 | 32 175 | 221 235 | 232 447 | 15 953 274 | (5) | 3 395 | 8 655 |
| | 1993 | 4 817 | 31 602 | 218 387 | 240 272 | 15 530 399 | (5) | 3 390 | 8 428 |
| | 1994 | 4 787 | 31 137 | 217 626 | 255 361 | 15 285 832 | (5) | 4 036 | 8 513 |

| Country / Pays / País | Year / Année / Año | Service points / Points de service / Puntos de servicio | Collections / Collections / Fondos | | | Loans to users / Prêts aux usagers / Préstamos a los usuarios | Current expenditure total / Dépenses ordinaires total / Gastos ordinarios total (000) | Total library employees / Total personnel des bibliothèques / Total personal de las bibliotecas |
|---|---|---|---|---|---|---|---|---|
| | | | Volumes of books (000) / Volumes de livres (000) / Volúmenes de libros (000) | Audio-visual documents / Matériels audio-visuels / Materiales audio-visuales | Other library materials / Autres matériels de bibliothèque / Otros materiales de biblioteca | | | |
| Czech Republic (cont) | 1995 | 4 728 | 30 861 | 215 124 | 252 411 | 15 128 910 | (5) 4 075 | 8 310 |
| | 1996 | 5 782 | 31 062 | 129 850 | ... | 17 826 030 | ... | ... |
| | 1997 | 4 108 | 30 858 | ... | ... | 16 732 013 | ... | ... |
| Denmark | 1990 | 1 773 | 32 235 | 597 853 | ... | 36 610 500 | 241 065 | ... |
| | 1991 | 1 790 | 20 464 | 582 927 | 327 | 34 843 876 | 258 699 | 59 |
| | 1992 | 1 754 | 20 246 | 568 266 | 453 | 33 056 198 | 253 410 | 61 |
| | 1993 | 1 756 | 20 494 | 498 302 | 840 | 29 798 239 | 262 618 | 127 |
| | 1994 | 1 766 | 19 859 | 456 072 | 1 709 | 28 987 483 | 240 575 | 124 |
| | 1995 | 1 778 | 21 216 | 432 176 | 1 039 | 27 773 455 | 252 103 | 126 |
| | 1996 | 1 783 | 21 810 | 427 720 | 1 222 | 27 560 176 | 262 112 | 136 |
| | 1997 | 1 784 | 22 197 | 410 057 | 1 328 | 27 542 884 | 271 346 | 131 |
| Estonia | 1990 | 509 | 5 540 | 6 807 | 33 874 | 3 928 136 | ... | 485 |
| | 1991 | 509 | 5 540 | 6 807 | 34 471 | 3 928 136 | ... | 485 |
| | 1992 | 572 | 5 540 | 6 807 | 33 980 | 4 192 951 | ... | 569 |
| | 1993 | 490 | 5 540 | (6) 6 807 | ... | 3 352 489 | 7 395 | 522 |
| | 1994 | 539 | 5 795 | (6) 8 571 | ... | 3 412 215 | 12 093 | 474 |
| | 1995 | 549 | 5 819 | (6) 13 990 | ... | 3 494 767 | 19 264 | 658 |
| | 1996 | 560 | 5 881 | (6) 23 329 | ... | 3 754 124 | 33 695 | 673 |
| | 1997 | 571 | 6 107 | (6) 28 976 | ... | 4 444 370 | 31 327 | 534 |
| Federal Republic of Yugoslavia | 1992 | 2 837 | 13 222 | ... | ... | ... | ... | ... |
| Finland | 1974 | 4 903 | 2 400 | ... | ... | ... | ... | ... |
| | 1983 | 5 250 | 5 700 | ... | ... | 3 200 000 | ... | ... |
| | 1990 | 5 349 | 7 428 | ... | ... | ... | (2) 31 056 | ... |
| | 1991 | 5 490 | 7 476 | ... | ... | 25 468 274 | ... | 811 |
| | 1992 | 5 462 | 7 426 | ... | ... | 24 949 076 | ... | 897 |
| | 1993 | 5 439 | 7 428 | ... | ... | 24 207 156 | ... | 1 471 |
| | 1994 | 5 484 | 7 441 | ... | ... | 24 152 661 | ... | 1 325 |
| | 1995 | 5 517 | 7 538 | ... | ... | 24 058 439 | ... | 1 366 |
| | 1996 | 5 529 | 7 584 | ... | ... | 24 102 512 | ... | 1 366 |
| | 1997 | 5 461 | 7 767 | ... | ... | 23 983 553 | ... | 1 292 |
| France | 1990 | *5 533 | *51 390 | 1 100 253 | *67 344 | *159 192 111 | (5) 263 133 | 8 295 |
| | 1991 | 5 584 | 51 725 | ... | ... | 167 485 528 | ... | 4 518 |
| | 1992 | 5 557 | 51 378 | ... | ... | 164 071 154 | ... | 5 013 |
| | 1993 | 5 533 | 51 390 | ... | ... | 159 192 111 | ... | 8 295 |
| | 1994 | 5 579 | 51 482 | ... | ... | 158 833 740 | ... | 7 457 |
| | 1995 | 5 612 | 52 155 | ... | ... | 158 214 115 | ... | 7 685 |
| | 1996 | 5 625 | 52 469 | ... | ... | 158 503 946 | ... | 7 680 |
| | 1997 | 5 556 | 53 734 | ... | ... | 157 721 645 | ... | 7 272 |
| Germany | 1991 | 6 520 | 20 225 | ... | ... | 183 651 567 | ... | 3 812 |
| | 1992 | 6 488 | 20 089 | ... | ... | 179 907 631 | ... | 4 170 |
| | 1993 | 6 460 | 20 094 | ... | ... | 174 557 653 | ... | 6 673 |
| | 1994 | 6 513 | 20 130 | ... | ... | 174 164 691 | ... | 6 050 |
| | 1995 | 6 553 | 20 393 | ... | ... | 173 485 259 | ... | 6 256 |
| | 1996 | 6 567 | 20 516 | ... | ... | 173 803 065 | ... | 6 256 |
| | 1997 | 6 487 | 21 011 | ... | ... | 172 945 255 | ... | 5 892 |
| Greece | 1990 | *974 | *9 049 | *193 728 | *11 858 | *28 029 967 | (5) 46 331 | 1 460 |
| | 1991 | 983 | 9 108 | ... | ... | 29 490 242 | ... | 795 |
| | 1992 | 978 | 9 046 | ... | ... | 28 889 051 | ... | 882 |
| | 1993 | 974 | 9 049 | ... | ... | 28 029 967 | ... | 1 460 |
| | 1994 | 982 | 9 065 | ... | ... | 27 966 866 | ... | 1 312 |
| | 1995 | 988 | 9 183 | ... | ... | 27 857 765 | ... | 1 353 |
| | 1996 | 990 | 9 239 | ... | ... | 27 908 797 | ... | 1 352 |
| | 1997 | 978 | 9 461 | ... | ... | 27 771 053 | ... | 1 280 |
| Hungary | 1977 | ... | 14 912 | ... | ... | 6 045 229 | (2) 34 997 | ... |
| | 1981 | ... | 18 153 | ... | ... | 6 457 945 | (2) 44 149 | ... |
| | 1987 | ... | 25 433 | ... | ... | 8 248 519 | (2) 67 299 | ... |
| | 1990 | ... | 26 736 | 217 606 | 227 396 | 7 506 122 | ... | 8 742 |
| | 1991 | 621 | 10 149 | ... | ... | 3 073 934 | ... | 1 760 |
| | 1992 | 621 | 10 149 | ... | ... | 3 108 475 | ... | 1 672 |
| | 1993 | 621 | 10 149 | ... | ... | 3 108 475 | ... | 1 662 |
| | 1994 | 621 | 10 149 | ... | ... | 3 108 475 | ... | 1 729 |
| | 1995 | 621 | 10 149 | ... | ... | 3 108 475 | ... | 1 867 |
| | 1996 | 621 | 10 149 | ... | ... | 3 108 475 | ... | 1 879 |
| | 1997 | 621 | 10 149 | ... | ... | 3 102 718 | ... | 1 628 |
| Iceland | 1987 | 48 | 225 | 5 247 | ... | 125 631 | (2) 7 545 | 86 |
| | 1990 | 78 | 358 | 7 753 | ... | 186 000 | ... | 71 |
| | 1991 | (7) 86 | (7) 335 | (7) 7 808 | ... | (7) 229 256 | (7) 19 051 | 25 |
| | 1992 | 111 | 537 | 11 154 | ... | 272 290 | 39 619 | 33 |
| | 1993 | 123 | 616 | 14 256 | 21 | 363 224 | 44 333 | 36 |

| Country / Pays / País | Year / Année / Año | Service points / Points de service / Puntos de servicio | Collections / Collections / Fondos | | | Loans to users / Prêts aux usagers / Préstamos a los usuarios | | Current expenditure total / Dépenses ordinaires total / Gastos ordinarios total (000) | | Total library employees / Total personnel des bibliothèques / Total personal de las bibliotecas |
|---|---|---|---|---|---|---|---|---|---|---|
| | | | Volumes of books (000) / Volumes de livres (000) / Volúmenes de libros (000) | Audio-visual documents / Matériels audio-visuels / Materiales audio-visuales | Other library materials / Autres matériels de bibliothèque / Otros materiales de biblioteca | | | | | |
| Iceland (cont) | 1994 | 133 | 614 | 14 925 | 64 | 367 955 | | 42 549 | | 39 |
| | 1995 | 137 | 659 | 16 622 | 140 | 361 767 | | 46 690 | | 39 |
| | 1996 | 139 | 653 | 33 294 | 265 | 427 727 | | 51 374 | | 41 |
| | 1997 | 151 | 677 | 32 099 | 402 | 441 097 | | 53 554 | | 44 |
| Ireland | 1990 | *453 | *4 212 | 2 784 | *7 308 | 3 410 630 | (5) | *21 566 | | 64 |
| | 1991 | 457 | 4 239 | ... | ... | 3 588 313 | | ... | | 46 |
| | 1992 | 455 | 4 211 | ... | ... | 3 515 162 | | ... | | 48 |
| | 1993 | 453 | 4 212 | ... | ... | 3 410 630 | | ... | | 64 |
| | 1994 | 457 | 4 219 | ... | ... | 3 402 952 | | ... | | 60 |
| | 1995 | 459 | 4 275 | ... | ... | 3 389 677 | | ... | | 64 |
| | 1996 | 461 | 4 300 | ... | ... | 3 395 886 | | ... | | 64 |
| | 1997 | 455 | 4 404 | ... | ... | 3 379 126 | | ... | | 59 |
| Italy | 1990 | *8 920 | *15 620 | 1 166 509 | *33 087 | 168 778 622 | (5) | *79 980 | | 8 975 |
| | 1991 | 9 003 | 15 722 | ... | ... | 177 571 466 | | ... | | 4 789 |
| | 1992 | 8 958 | 15 616 | ... | ... | 173 951 479 | | ... | | 5 314 |
| | 1993 | 8 920 | 15 620 | ... | ... | 168 778 622 | | ... | | 8 794 |
| | 1994 | 8 984 | 15 634 | ... | ... | 168 151 895 | | ... | | 7 906 |
| | 1995 | 9 033 | 15 000 | ... | ... | 167 257 062 | | ... | | 8 143 |
| | 1996 | 9 059 | 15 911 | ... | ... | 167 682 788 | | ... | | 8 142 |
| | 1997 | 8 957 | 16 333 | ... | ... | 167 219 605 | | ... | | 7 709 |
| Latvia | 1990 | 553 | 8 196 | 52 959 | 55 342 | 3 421 893 | (5) | 424 | | 2 111 |
| | 1991 | 553 | 8 196 | 53 020 | 56 206 | 3 421 893 | (5) | 424 | | 2 092 |
| | 1992 | 643 | 8 947 | 52 638 | 55 306 | 3 421 893 | (5) | 424 | | 2 162 |
| | 1993 | 570 | 8 559 | 52 892 | 58 193 | 3 257 630 | (5) | 424 | | 2 121 |
| | 1994 | 542 | 8 171 | 53 574 | 62 863 | 3 093 366 | (5) | 484 | | 2 101 |
| | 1995 | 542 | 8 171 | 53 764 | 63 083 | 3 093 366 | (5) | 484 | | 2 079 |
| | 1996 | 577 | 8 459 | ... | ... | 3 231 979 | | ... | | 743 |
| | 1997 | 569 | 8 404 | ... | ... | 3 214 538 | | ... | | 643 |
| Liechtenstein | 1991 | 2 | 9 | ... | ... | 30 749 | | ... | | 2 |
| | 1992 | 2 | 9 | ... | ... | 30 244 | | ... | | 2 |
| | 1993 | 2 | 9 | ... | ... | 29 927 | | ... | | 3 |
| | 1994 | 2 | 9 | ... | ... | 30 154 | | ... | | 3 |
| | 1995 | 2 | 9 | ... | ... | 30 008 | | ... | | 3 |
| | 1996 | 2 | 10 | ... | ... | 30 121 | | ... | | 3 |
| | 1997 | 2 | 10 | ... | ... | 29 129 | | ... | | 3 |
| Lithuania | 1990 | 2 137 | 23 358 | 78 486 | 82 017 | 9 652 504 | | ... | | |
| | 1991 | 2 215 | 23 786 | ... | ... | 9 580 575 | | ... | | 1 758 |
| | 1992 | 2 128 | 22 448 | ... | ... | 9 117 967 | | ... | | 1 565 |
| | 1993 | 2 109 | 21 797 | ... | ... | 8 114 590 | | 5 621 | | 1 519 |
| | 1994 | 2 181 | 21 626 | ... | ... | 8 224 235 | | 6 320 | | 1 682 |
| | 1995 | 2 215 | 21 242 | 3 256 | ... | 7 911 809 | | 9 020 | | 1 763 |
| | 1996 | 2 247 | 21 324 | ... | ... | 8 272 690 | | 18 250 | | 1 771 |
| | 1997 | 1 971 | 16 324 | ... | ... | 7 094 076 | | 18 500 | | 1 493 |
| Luxembourg | 1990 | *32 | *296 | 6 345 | *388 | *918 023 | (5) | 1 517 | | 48 |
| | 1991 | 32 | 298 | ... | ... | 965 849 | | ... | | 26 |
| | 1992 | 32 | 296 | ... | ... | 946 159 | | ... | | 29 |
| | 1993 | 32 | 296 | ... | ... | 918 023 | | ... | | 48 |
| | 1994 | 32 | 297 | ... | ... | 915 956 | | ... | | 43 |
| | 1995 | 32 | 301 | ... | ... | 912 383 | | ... | | 45 |
| | 1996 | 33 | 303 | ... | ... | 914 055 | | ... | | 45 |
| | 1997 | 32 | 310 | ... | ... | 909 543 | | ... | | 42 |
| Monaco | 1977 | 1 | 3 | ... | | ... | | 10 | | 2 |
| | 1981 | 7 | 12 | 96 | 1 606 | ... | | 538 | | 5 |
| | 1995 | 8 | 57 | 5 665 | | ... | (2) | 334 | | 9 |
| Netherlands | 1990 | *1 493 | 13 868 | 296 913 | *18 173 | 42 959 398 | (5) | 71 009 | | 2 239 |
| | 1991 | 1 507 | 13 958 | ... | ... | 45 197 450 | | ... | | 1 220 |
| | 1992 | 1 499 | 13 865 | ... | ... | 44 276 051 | | ... | | 1 353 |
| | 1993 | 1 493 | 13 868 | ... | ... | 42 959 398 | | ... | | 2 239 |
| | 1994 | 1 505 | 13 893 | ... | ... | 42 862 688 | | ... | | 2 013 |
| | 1995 | 1 514 | 14 074 | ... | ... | 42 695 477 | | ... | | 2 075 |
| | 1996 | 1 518 | 14 159 | ... | ... | 42 773 691 | | ... | | 2 073 |
| | 1997 | 1 499 | 14 501 | ... | ... | 42 562 580 | | ... | | 1 963 |
| Norway | 1973 | 3 467 | 3 968 | ... | ... | 5 069 505 | | 8 800 | | ... |
| | 1981 | 3 757 | 6 221 | ... | ... | 5 756 161 | (2) | 15 558 | | ... |
| | 1984 | 3 789 | 6 645 | ... | ... | 5 362 441 | (2) | 17 248 | | ... |
| | 1988 | 3 523 | 6 849 | ... | ... | 4 354 105 | | ... | | ... |
| | 1990 | 3 383 | 6 858 | ... | ... | 4 748 415 | | 26 739 | | ... |
| | 1991 | 3 330 | 7 109 | ... | ... | 4 814 312 | | ... | | 773 |
| | 1992 | 3 307 | 7 358 | ... | ... | 4 681 936 | | ... | | 889 |
| | 1993 | 3 189 | 7 616 | ... | ... | 4 696 247 | | ... | | 1 358 |

| Country / Pays / País | Year / Année / Año | Service points / Points de service / Puntos de servicio | Collections / Collections / Fondos | | | Loans to users / Prêts aux usagers / Préstamos a los usuarios | Current expenditure total / Dépenses ordinaires total / Gastos ordinarios total (000) | Total library employees / Total personnel des bibliothèques / Total personal de las bibliotecas |
|---|---|---|---|---|---|---|---|---|
| | | | Volumes of books (000) / Volumes de livres (000) / Volúmenes de libros (000) | Audio-visual documents / Matériels audio-visuels / Materiales audio-visuales | Other library materials / Autres matériels de bibliothèque / Otros materiales de biblioteca | | | |
| Norway (cont) | 1994 | 3 247 | 7 887 | ... | ... | 4 800 418 | ... | 1 255 |
| | 1995 | 3 212 | 7 928 | ... | ... | 4 717 400 | ... | 1 297 |
| | 1996 | 3 230 | 8 269 | ... | ... | 4 714 786 | ... | 1 311 |
| | 1997 | 3 075 | 7 725 | ... | ... | 4 228 024 | ... | 1 258 |
| Poland | 1973 | 29 794 | 104 177 | ... | 1 014 900 | 111 070 100 | ... | ... |
| | 1985 | ... | 133 456 | ... | ... | 90 720 700 | ... | ... |
| | 1990 | 21 538 | 157 901 | 972 571 | 1 005 712 | 87 496 306 | (5) 13 228 | 37 048 |
| | 1991 | 21 538 | 157 901 | 972 571 | 1 005 741 | 87 496 306 | (5) 13 633 | 36 495 |
| | 1992 | 20 879 | 155 014 | 972 571 | 1 005 745 | 85 474 000 | (5) 13 945 | 36 378 |
| | 1993 | 20 879 | 155 014 | 972 571 | 1 005 712 | 85 474 000 | (5) 14 179 | 36 132 |
| | 1994 | 20 879 | 155 014 | 972 571 | 1 047 982 | 85 474 000 | (5) 17 150 | 36 756 |
| | 1995 | 20 879 | 155 014 | 972 571 | 1 047 948 | 85 474 000 | (5) 17 553 | 36 801 |
| | 1996 | 21 538 | 157 901 | ... | ... | 87 496 306 | ... | 36 852 |
| | 1997 | 21 538 | 157 901 | ... | ... | 87 496 306 | ... | 33 996 |
| Portugal | 1977 | 655 | 1 554 | ... | ... | ... | ... | ... |
| | 1981 | 712 | 1 658 | ... | ... | ... | ... | ... |
| | 1984 | 677 | 2 254 | ... | ... | ... | ... | ... |
| | 1987 | 916 | 2 601 | 58 084 | 5 517 | 395 751 | ... | ... |
| | 1990 | 707 | 2 896 | 57 466 | 37 940 | 352 327 | 14 846 | 574 |
| | 1991 | 800 | 4 605 | ... | ... | 325 000 | ... | 317 |
| | 1992 | 809 | 4 608 | ... | ... | 338 523 | ... | 349 |
| | 1993 | 877 | 4 312 | 222 502 | 12 448 | 313 260 | 94 067 | 574 |
| | 1994 | 865 | 4 610 | ... | ... | 497 419 | ... | 517 |
| | 1995 | 865 | 4 903 | ... | ... | 629 115 | ... | 533 |
| | 1996 | 868 | 4 946 | ... | ... | 644 272 | ... | 533 |
| | 1997 | 900 | 5 234 | ... | ... | 680 000 | ... | 504 |
| Romania | 1975 | ... | 38 415 | ... | ... | 19 492 000 | ... | ... |
| | 1980 | ... | 47 075 | ... | ... | 23 278 000 | ... | ... |
| | 1985 | ... | 57 271 | ... | ... | 25 449 000 | ... | ... |
| | 1990 | 10 029 | 56 110 | 531 185 | 555 081 | 21 856 000 | (5) 7 743 | 21 338 |
| | 1991 | 10 246 | 59 856 | 525 312 | 556 875 | 23 227 700 | (5) 7 842 | 20 543 |
| | 1992 | 9 728 | 58 675 | 518 053 | 544 306 | 24 123 000 | (5) 7 950 | 20 267 |
| | 1993 | 9 339 | 58 912 | 518 820 | 570 812 | 24 640 000 | (5) 8 054 | 20 024 |
| | 1994 | 9 339 | 58 912 | 523 604 | 614 391 | 24 640 000 | (5) 9 710 | 20 483 |
| | 1995 | 9 339 | 58 912 | 521 130 | 611 457 | 24 640 000 | (5) 9 872 | 20 133 |
| | 1996 | 9 774 | 59 085 | ... | ... | 23 807 943 | ... | 4 742 |
| | 1997 | 9 641 | 58 696 | ... | ... | 23 679 466 | ... | 4 110 |
| Russian Federation | 1990 | 64 263 | 739 822 | ... | ... | ... | 20 000 | 33 358 |
| | 1993 | 64 318 | 1 180 774 | ... | ... | ... | ... | 39 239 |
| San Marino | 1983 | 17 | 22 | 2 056 | 635 | ... | 15 050 | 6.0 |
| Slovakia | 1990 | 5 477 | 11 130 | 129 136 | 134 945 | 2 728 328 | ... | 6 454 |
| | 1991 | 5 751 | 10 920 | 128 960 | 136 708 | 2 690 052 | ... | 6 088 |
| | 1992 | 5 878 | 10 787 | 127 549 | 134 013 | 2 491 817 | ... | 5 971 |
| | 1993 | 6 005 | 10 655 | 127 682 | 140 478 | 2 293 582 | ... | 5 839 |
| | 1994 | 6 259 | 10 390 | 128 879 | 151 225 | 1 928 891 | ... | 6 270 |
| | 1995 | 6 398 | 10 703 | ... | ... | 1 952 328 | 15 314 | 5 183 |
| | 1996 | 6 115 | 10 164 | ... | ... | 1 844 574 | 10 946 | 5 160 |
| | 1997 | 6 537 | 10 953 | 19 569 | ... | 1 849 539 | 17 044 | 4 831 |
| Slovenia | 1990 | 1 071 | 6 075 | 125 622 | 104 738 | 4 802 027 | ... | 723 |
| | 1991 | 1 071 | 6 075 | 125 622 | 104 733 | 4 802 027 | ... | 723 |
| | 1992 | 1 071 | 6 075 | 230 000 | 104 338 | 4 802 000 | 657 540 | 644 |
| | 1993 | 1 071 | 5 950 | 125 622 | 159 947 | 4 788 076 | ... | 732 |
| | 1994 | 1 071 | 5 826 | 125 622 | 216 996 | 4 774 125 | ... | 739 |
| | 1995 | 1 071 | 5 826 | 125 622 | 216 973 | 4 774 125 | ... | 739 |
| | 1996 | 1 071 | 5 970 | 115 219 | ... | 5 437 650 | 2 018 714 | 778 |
| | 1997 | 1 057 | 5 905 | ... | ... | 4 724 739 | ... | 690 |
| Spain | 1990 | *626 | *2 268 | *45 925 | *12 674 | 271 233 | ... | 4 386 |
| | 1974 | 731 | 1 807 | ... | ... | 342 372 | 40 000 | 1 277 |
| | 1981 | 626 | 2 268 | 45 925 | ... | 271 233 | 87 837 | 1 752 |
| | 1991 | 632 | 7 168 | ... | ... | 285 363 | ... | 2 211 |
| | 1992 | 629 | 7 120 | ... | ... | 279 546 | ... | 2 512 |
| | 1993 | 626 | 7 122 | ... | ... | 271 233 | ... | 4 386 |
| | 1994 | 631 | 7 134 | ... | ... | 270 622 | ... | 3 892 |
| | 1995 | 635 | 7 228 | ... | ... | 269 567 | ... | 3 990 |
| | 1996 | 636 | 7 271 | ... | ... | 270 060 | ... | 3 983 |
| | 1997 | 629 | 7 447 | ... | ... | 268 728 | ... | 3 803 |
| Sweden | 1983 | ... | 35 700 | ... | ... | 26 900 000 | ... | ... |
| | 1974 | 3 250 | 25 563 | ... | ... | 17 743 878 | ... | 282 |
| | 1990 | 5 515 | 28 580 | 849 161 | 44 287 | 16 000 000 | (5) 146 337 | 5 660 |
| | 1991 | 5 523 | 29 100 | ... | ... | 17 464 809 | ... | 3 119 |

| Country / Pays / País | Year / Année / Año | Service points / Points de service / Puntos de servicio | Collections / Collections / Fondos | | | Loans to users / Prêts aux usagers / Préstamos a los usuarios | | Current expenditure total / Dépenses ordinaires total / Gastos ordinarios total (000) | Total library employees / Total personnel des bibliothèques / Total personal de las bibliotecas |
| | | | Volumes of books (000) / Volumes de livres (000) / Volúmenes de libros (000) | Audio-visual documents / Matériels audio-visuels / Materiales audio-visuales | Other library materials / Autres matériels de bibliothèque / Otros materiales de biblioteca | | | | |
|---|---|---|---|---|---|---|---|---|---|
| Sweden | 1992 | 5 495 | 28 904 | ... | ... | 17 108 770 | | ... | 3 448 |
| | 1993 | 5 472 | 28 911 | ... | ... | 16 600 000 | | ... | 5 660 |
| | 1994 | 5 517 | 28 963 | ... | ... | 16 562 630 | | ... | 5 099 |
| | 1995 | 5 550 | 29 341 | ... | ... | 16 498 018 | | ... | 5 259 |
| | 1996 | 5 563 | 29 518 | ... | ... | 16 528 241 | | ... | 5 256 |
| | 1997 | 5 495 | 30 230 | ... | ... | 16 446 665 | | ... | 4 970 |
| Switzerland | 1990 | 361 | 1 873 | 55 655 | 2 903 | 6 104 502 | (5) | 95 912 | 371 |
| The Former Yugoslav Rep. of Macedonia | 1992 | 641 | 2 837 | ... | ... | ... | | ... | ... |
| United Kingdom | 1990 | 5 086 | 51 396 | 1 100 378 | 67 352 | 159 210 241 | (5) | 215 041 | 4 705 |
| | 1991 | 5 133 | 51 731 | ... | ... | 167 504 602 | | ... | 2 802 |
| | 1992 | 5 108 | 51 384 | ... | ... | 164 089 839 | | ... | 3 030 |
| | 1993 | 5 086 | 51 396 | ... | ... | 159 210 241 | | ... | 4 705 |
| | 1994 | 5 128 | 51 487 | ... | ... | 158 851 829 | | ... | 4 298 |
| | 1995 | 5 159 | 52 160 | ... | ... | 158 232 134 | | ... | 4 458 |
| | 1996 | 5 170 | 52 475 | ... | ... | 158 521 997 | | ... | 4 461 |
| | 1997 | 5 107 | 53 740 | ... | ... | 157 739 608 | | ... | 4 182 |
| **Oceania** | | | | | | | | | |
| Niue | 1974 | 8 | 20 | ... | ... | ... | | *4 | ... |
| | 1990 | 2 | 4 | 45 | ... | 15 000 | | 13 | 3.0 |

## General note
For general explanations and definitions, please refer to the beginning of this chapter.

## Note générale
Pour les explications et définitions générales, prière de se référer au début de ce chapitre.

## Nota general
Para las explicaciones y definiciones generales, referirse al comienzo de este capítulo.

Notes

(1) Data refer only to expenditure on employees and acquisitions.

(2) Data refer only to expenditure on acquisitions.

(3) One library and one service point only.

(4) Data do not include expenditure on acquisitions.

(5) The figure is shown in ECUs (European Currency Unit) expressed at 1990 constant prices.

(6) Data include other library materials.

(7) Schools are divided into two categories: one from 6 to 15 years and the other 16 to 20 years. Data refer to one kind of category only..

Notes

(1) Les données se réfèrent seulement aux dépenses pour le personnel et les acquisitions.

(2) Les données se réfèrent aux dépenses pour les acquisitions seulement.

(3) Pour une bibliothèque et un point de service seulement.

(4) Les données n'incluent pas les dépenses pour les acquisitions.

(5) Le chiffre est montré en ECUs (monnaie européenne commune) et s'exprime en valeur constante de 1990.

(6) Les données incluent d'autres matériels de bibliothèque.

(7) Les écoles sont divisées en deux catégories : la première va de 6 à 15 ans et la seconde de 16 à 20 ans. Les données se réfèrent à l'une des deux catégories seulement.

Notas

(1) Los datos se refieren solamente a los gastos de personal y de adquisiciones.

(2) La biblioteca nacional también desempeña la función de biblioteca pública.

(3) Para una biblioteca y un punto de servicio. solamente

(4) Los datos no incluyen los gastos de adquisiciones.

(5) La cifra se expresa en ECUs (moneda común europea), en valores constantes de 1990.

(6) Los datos incluyen otros materiales de biblioteca.

(7) Las escuelas se dividen en dos categorías: la primera va de 6 a 15 años y la segunda de 16 a 20 años. Los datos se refieren a una de las dos categorías solamente.

IV.5   Number of titles by UDC classes
Nombre de titres classés d'après la CDU
Número de títulos clasificados según la CDU

## IV.5   Book production: number of titles by UDC classes

### Edition de livres: nombre de titres classés d'après la CDU

### Edición de libros: número de títulos clasificados según la CDU

| Country / Pays / País | Year / Année / Año | | Total | Gener-alities / Généra-lités / Genera-lidades | Philos-ophy / Philo-sophie / Filo-sofía | Religion / Religion / Religión | Social sciences / Sciences sociales / Ciencias sociales | Phil-ology / Philo-logie / Filo-logía | Pure sciences / Sciences pures / Ciencias puras | Applied sciences / Sciences appl. / Ciencias aplicadas | Arts / Arts / Artes | Litera-ture / Litté-rature / Litera-tura | Geog./ history / Géogr./ histoire / Geogr./ historia |
|---|---|---|---|---|---|---|---|---|---|---|---|---|---|
| **Africa** | | | | | | | | | | | | | |
| Algeria | 1979 | | 275 | 13 | 2 | 3 | 125 | 12 | 50 | 35 | 4 | 18 | 13 |
| | 1984 | | 718 | 26 | 15 | 32 | 201 | 13 | 104 | 125 | 22 | 119 | 61 |
| | 1991 | | 494 | 14 | 17 | 82 | 91 | 15 | 97 | 55 | 19 | 52 | 52 |
| | 1992 | | 506 | 18 | 10 | 42 | 153 | 28 | 71 | 77 | 19 | 54 | 34 |
| | 1994 | | 323 | 22 | 21 | 9 | 97 | 4 | 42 | 14 | 10 | 72 | 32 |
| | 1996 | (1) | 670 | 39 | 21 | 112 | 96 | 34 | 71 | 157 | 30 | 77 | 33 |
| Angola | 1979 | (2) | 57 | 2 | - | - | 6 | - | - | - | - | 35 | - |
| | 1985 | | 47 | - | - | - | 1 | - | - | - | - | 46 | - |
| | 1995 | | 22 | - | - | - | - | - | - | - | - | 22 | - |
| Benin | 1992 | (1)(2) | 647 | 10 | 4 | - | 534 | 7 | 12 | 77 | - | - | 3 |
| | 1994 | (2) | 84 | 5 | - | 1 | 22 | 6 | 6 | 37 | 1 | 5 | 1 |
| Botswana | 1976 | | 79 | 7 | - | 1 | 50 | - | 6 | 12 | - | - | 3 |
| | 1980 | (2) | 97 | - | - | - | 67 | - | 6 | 19 | 2 | - | 3 |
| | 1991 | (2) | 158 | 8 | - | - | 125 | 1 | 10 | 11 | - | - | 3 |
| Burkina Faso | 1980 | (2) | 4 | - | - | - | 4 | - | - | - | - | - | - |
| | 1985 | (2) | 4 | - | - | - | 1 | - | - | - | - | 3 | - |
| | 1995 | (2) | 17 | 1 | - | - | 3 | - | - | - | 1 | 11 | 1 |
| | 1996 | (1)(2) | 12 | 1 | - | - | 1 | - | - | 1 | - | 9 | - |
| Democratic Rep. of the Congo | 1979 | (2) | 231 | 13 | 1 | 142 | 38 | 5 | 6 | 7 | 3 | 14 | 2 |
| | 1992 | (2) | 64 | - | 1 | 30 | 27 | - | - | 5 | - | - | 1 |
| Egypt | 1974 | | 1 765 | 41 | 40 | 382 | 434 | 141 | 145 | 151 | 42 | 277 | 112 |
| | 1985 | | 1 366 | 14 | 49 | 186 | 202 | 107 | 82 | 141 | 56 | 423 | 106 |
| | 1990 | | 2 036 | 514 | 54 | 353 | 199 | 91 | 147 | 126 | 77 | 367 | 108 |
| | 1991 | | 2 599 | 293 | 37 | 291 | 142 | 172 | 172 | 208 | 76 | 392 | 85 |
| | 1993 | | 3 108 | 289 | 58 | 329 | 220 | 238 | 190 | 280 | 118 | 378 | 176 |
| | 1995 | | 2 215 | 92 | 66 | 307 | 180 | 226 | 206 | 331 | 140 | 515 | 152 |
| Eritrea | 1993 | | 106 | - | - | - | 37 | 33 | 29 | 7 | - | - | - |
| Ethiopia | 1979 | (1) | 225 | - | - | 42 | 45 | 31 | 58 | 37 | 2 | 5 | 5 |
| | 1985 | | 227 | 18 | - | 28 | 74 | 9 | 14 | 55 | 5 | 9 | 15 |
| | 1990 | | 385 | 32 | 1 | 15 | 179 | 11 | 24 | 71 | 9 | 32 | 11 |
| | 1991 | | 240 | 36 | - | 23 | 66 | 11 | 8 | 44 | 3 | 31 | 18 |
| Gambia | 1976 | (2) | 11 | - | - | - | 11 | - | - | - | - | - | - |
| | 1985 | (2) | 72 | 2 | - | 5 | 17 | - | 7 | 36 | 4 | - | 1 |
| | 1991 | (2) | 21 | - | - | - | 15 | - | - | 5 | - | - | 1 |
| | 1994 | | 21 | - | - | 4 | 5 | 4 | 6 | 1 | - | - | 1 |
| | 1996 | (3) | 14 | - | - | - | 10 | - | - | 2 | - | - | 2 |
| Ghana | 1975 | | 344 | 144 | 1 | 90 | 43 | 8 | 4 | 14 | 12 | 19 | 9 |
| | 1980 | | 209 | 10 | 4 | 52 | 65 | 3 | 5 | 27 | 2 | 35 | 6 |
| | 1992 | | 28 | - | 1 | 6 | 7 | 3 | - | 5 | 2 | 4 | - |
| Kenya | 1976 | | 183 | 4 | - | 59 | 65 | 5 | 13 | 7 | 3 | 14 | 13 |
| | 1980 | | 232 | 17 | 4 | 18 | 34 | 66 | 16 | 29 | 2 | 24 | 22 |
| | 1986 | | 933 | 23 | 3 | 97 | 229 | 91 | 102 | 94 | 47 | 131 | 116 |
| | 1990 | | 348 | 2 | - | 115 | 47 | 56 | 26 | 41 | 12 | 23 | 26 |
| | 1991 | (1) | 239 | 7 | - | 84 | 48 | 26 | 13 | 34 | 1 | 19 | 7 |
| | 1994 | (1)(2) | 300 | 3 | 3 | 76 | 73 | 41 | 19 | 41 | 13 | 12 | 14 |
| Libyan Arab Jamahiriya | 1975 | | 129 | 7 | 3 | 2 | 26 | 16 | 21 | 2 | 9 | 39 | 4 |
| | 1994 | | 26 | - | 2 | 2 | 2 | 1 | 2 | 5 | - | 11 | 1 |

Number of titles by UDC classes
Nombre de titres classés d'après la CDU
Número de títulos clasificados según la CDU

IV.5

| Country / Pays / País | Year / Année / Año | | Total / Total / Total | Generalities / Généralités / Generalidades | Philosophy / Philosophie / Filosofía | Religion / Religion / Religión | Social sciences / Sciences sociales / Ciencias sociales | Philology / Philologie / Filología | Pure sciences / Sciences pures / Ciencias puras | Applied sciences / Sciences appl. / Ciencias aplicadas | Arts / Arts / Artes | Literature / Littérature / Literatura | Geog./history / Géogr./histoire / Geogr./historia |
|---|---|---|---|---|---|---|---|---|---|---|---|---|---|
| Madagascar | 1976 | | 228 | 3 | 5 | 41 | 73 | 13 | 11 | 18 | 5 | 47 | 12 |
| | 1980 | | 258 | 1 | 6 | 16 | 59 | 28 | 54 | 59 | 7 | 19 | 9 |
| | 1984 | | 321 | 3 | 8 | 48 | 41 | 14 | 20 | 161 | 7 | 13 | 6 |
| | 1990 | | 154 | 2 | 5 | 36 | 47 | 5 | 7 | 25 | 2 | 12 | 13 |
| | 1991 | | 46 | - | - | 23 | 9 | - | - | 6 | 1 | 3 | 4 |
| | 1992 | (2) | 85 | - | 2 | 33 | 25 | - | 1 | 13 | 1 | 7 | 3 |
| | 1993 | | 143 | 1 | 3 | 25 | 47 | 12 | 8 | 23 | - | 14 | 10 |
| | 1994 | | 114 | - | 6 | 37 | 29 | 6 | 6 | 11 | - | 11 | 8 |
| | 1995 | | 131 | 3 | 3 | 32 | 44 | 2 | 2 | 13 | 4 | 19 | 9 |
| | 1996 | | 119 | 1 | 3 | 25 | 22 | 2 | 4 | 36 | 6 | 18 | 2 |
| Malawi | 1974 | | 234 | 16 | - | 49 | 105 | 10 | 29 | 46 | 2 | 8 | 21 |
| | 1980 | | 79 | 3 | - | 26 | 30 | - | 3 | 14 | - | 1 | 2 |
| | 1984 | | 134 | 1 | - | 71 | 33 | - | 1 | 17 | 3 | - | 8 |
| | 1989 | | 141 | 11 | - | 31 | 53 | 2 | 7 | 22 | - | 11 | 4 |
| | 1992 | | 189 | 12 | - | 15 | 75 | 7 | 19 | 31 | 6 | 15 | 9 |
| | 1993 | | 206 | 12 | - | 29 | 56 | 8 | 13 | 53 | 4 | 20 | 11 |
| | 1994 | | 243 | 10 | - | 41 | 92 | 11 | 11 | 40 | 10 | 24 | 4 |
| | 1995 | | 182 | 10 | - | 44 | 81 | 5 | 5 | 18 | 5 | 14 | - |
| | 1996 | (2)(4) | 117 | - | - | 1 | 76 | 14 | 10 | 5 | 3 | - | 8 |
| Mali | 1975 | (2) | 42 | - | 3 | - | 4 | 7 | 9 | 1 | 2 | 4 | 12 |
| | 1984 | (5) | 160 | - | - | - | 98 | 19 | 17 | 23 | - | - | 3 |
| | 1995 | (1)(2) | 14 | 1 | - | - | 1 | - | - | 1 | - | 11 | |
| Mauritius | 1975 | | 49 | - | 1 | 3 | 17 | 1 | 2 | 9 | - | 8 | 8 |
| | 1980 | | 87 | - | - | 4 | 10 | 11 | 5 | 6 | 4 | 28 | 13 |
| | 1985 | | 94 | 2 | 1 | 3 | 24 | 18 | 6 | 8 | 9 | 14 | 9 |
| | 1990 | | 75 | 3 | 1 | 4 | 21 | 3 | 2 | 6 | - | 17 | 18 |
| | 1991 | | 56 | 3 | 2 | 6 | 14 | 2 | 1 | 10 | 1 | 9 | 8 |
| | 1992 | | 80 | 1 | 1 | 3 | 21 | 13 | 5 | 5 | 1 | 20 | 10 |
| | 1993 | | 96 | 1 | 1 | 2 | 24 | 30 | 7 | 5 | - | 23 | 3 |
| | 1994 | | 84 | 9 | 1 | 1 | 35 | 3 | 1 | 6 | 1 | 15 | 12 |
| | 1995 | | 64 | 4 | 1 | 3 | 20 | 6 | 1 | 4 | 2 | 18 | 5 |
| | 1996 | | 80 | 1 | 4 | 4 | 14 | 4 | 1 | 6 | 6 | 32 | 8 |
| Morocco | 1994 | (6) | 354 | 21 | 4 | 40 | 128 | ./. | 2 | 24 | 8 | 76 | 51 |
| | 1995 | | 940 | 275 | 8 | 58 | 273 | 12 | 9 | 37 | 24 | 134 | 110 |
| | 1996 | | 918 | 33 | 13 | 45 | 359 | 12 | 13 | 135 | 107 | 136 | 65 |
| Namibia | 1990 | | 106 | 7 | - | 2 | 57 | - | 2 | 18 | 2 | 14 | 4 |
| Niger | 1976 | | 78 | 11 | - | - | 32 | 5 | - | 7 | 1 | 4 | 18 |
| | 1979 | (4) | 18 | - | - | - | 6 | 2 | 3 | 4 | - | - | 3 |
| | 1991 | (2) | 5 | - | - | - | - | - | - | - | - | 5 | |
| Nigeria | 1975 | | 1 324 | 212 | 13 | 40 | 443 | 8 | 49 | 271 | 47 | 209 | 32 |
| | 1980 | | 2 316 | 130 | 42 | 52 | 856 | 140 | 104 | 470 | 104 | 188 | 230 |
| | 1985 | | 2 213 | 78 | 47 | 126 | 693 | 151 | 289 | 383 | 93 | 126 | 227 |
| | 1989 | | 1 466 | 86 | 18 | 240 | 440 | 66 | 50 | 246 | 82 | 146 | 92 |
| | 1991 | | 1 546 | 32 | 12 | 148 | 622 | 156 | 102 | 186 | 30 | 156 | 102 |
| | 1992 | | 1 562 | 55 | 14 | 142 | 733 | 104 | 71 | 196 | 30 | 148 | 69 |
| | 1994 | | 1 008 | 11 | 7 | 121 | 458 | 53 | 72 | 114 | 37 | 60 | 75 |
| | 1995 | | 1 314 | 18 | 36 | 203 | 530 | 91 | 80 | 116 | 52 | 133 | 55 |
| Reunion | 1980 | | 99 | - | - | 5 | 23 | - | 12 | 16 | 10 | 24 | 9 |
| | 1985 | | 73 | 1 | - | 6 | 15 | 2 | 2 | 12 | 4 | 18 | 13 |
| | 1992 | | 69 | 1 | - | - | 20 | - | 4 | 5 | 12 | 14 | 13 |
| South Africa | 1974 | | 3 849 | 84 | 32 | 192 | 916 | 243 | 407 | 653 | 108 | 929 | 285 |
| | 1990 | | 4 950 | 168 | 47 | 585 | 1 128 | 285 | 420 | 731 | 294 | 1 065 | 227 |
| | 1991 | | 4 836 | 154 | 37 | 638 | 1 115 | 220 | 370 | 751 | 231 | 1 082 | 238 |
| | 1992 | | 4 738 | 176 | 41 | 661 | 1 203 | 225 | 312 | 808 | 210 | 870 | 232 |
| | 1993 | | 4 751 | 123 | 35 | 584 | 1 080 | 332 | 345 | 938 | 173 | 966 | 175 |
| | 1994 | | 4 574 | 116 | 40 | 491 | 1 034 | 315 | 363 | 911 | 189 | 907 | 208 |
| | 1995 | | 5 418 | 136 | 33 | 516 | 1 262 | 566 | 330 | 1 002 | 156 | 1 227 | 190 |
| Tunisia | 1975 | | 107 | 2 | - | - | 9 | - | - | - | - | 9 | |
| | 1981 | (4) | 172 | - | 4 | 4 | 6 | 47 | 48 | 24 | - | 15 | 24 |
| | 1985 | | 540 | 14 | 15 | 152 | 140 | 13 | 32 | 39 | 9 | 95 | 31 |
| | 1992 | (1) | 1 165 | 130 | 100 | 35 | 194 | - | 68 | 108 | 20 | 310 | 200 |
| | 1993 | (1)(2) | 539 | 10 | 12 | 13 | 69 | 2 | 3 | 18 | 5 | 116 | 31 |
| | 1994 | (1) | 569 | 18 | 26 | 11 | 130 | 4 | 9 | 39 | 11 | 286 | 27 |
| | 1995 | (1) | 563 | 8 | 25 | 7 | 132 | 23 | 9 | 19 | 24 | 166 | 150 |
| | 1996 | | 720 | 24 | 18 | 14 | 138 | 6 | 4 | 38 | 23 | 338 | 111 |
| Uganda | 1974 | | 373 | - | - | 19 | 197 | - | 3 | 140 | 11 | 2 | 1 |
| | 1992 | | 162 | 4 | 2 | - | 77 | - | - | 78 | - | - | 1 |
| | 1993 | (1)(7) | 314 | - | - | 4 | 10 | 43 | 35 | 14 | - | 4 | 11 |
| | 1996 | (1) | 288 | - | - | 7 | - | 45 | 41 | 7 | - | 4 | 9 |
| United Republic of Tanzania | 1976 | | 399 | 54 | - | 66 | 158 | 27 | 15 | 36 | 13 | 16 | 14 |
| | 1980 | | 512 | 31 | 4 | 94 | 151 | 17 | 50 | 86 | 57 | 22 | - |
| | 1984 | (2) | 363 | 17 | 1 | 41 | 195 | 6 | 7 | 77 | 4 | 9 | 6 |
| | 1990 | (2) | 172 | - | 1 | 18 | 45 | 2 | 7 | 40 | 3 | 47 | 9 |

Number of titles by UDC classes
Nombre de titres classés d'après la CDU
Número de títulos clasificados según la CDU

| Country / Pays / País | Year / Année / Año | | Total / Total / Total | Generalities / Généralités / Generalidades | Philosophy / Philosophie / Filosofía | Religion / Religion / Religión | Social sciences / Sciences sociales / Ciencias sociales | Philology / Philologie / Filología | Pure sciences / Sciences pures / Ciencias puras | Applied sciences / Sciences appl. / Ciencias aplicadas | Arts / Arts / Artes | Literature / Littérature / Literatura | Geog./history / Géogr./histoire / Geogr./historia |
|---|---|---|---|---|---|---|---|---|---|---|---|---|---|
| Zimbabwe | 1980 | | 246 | 4 | 1 | 9 | 94 | 19 | 19 | 34 | 8 | 24 | 34 |
| | 1985 | | 544 | 5 | 2 | 15 | 132 | 141 | 58 | 89 | 16 | 66 | 20 |
| | 1990 | | 349 | 6 | - | 14 | 153 | 22 | 16 | 70 | 7 | 56 | 5 |
| | 1992 | | 232 | 6 | - | 15 | 107 | 15 | 3 | 48 | 7 | 24 | 7 |
| **North America** | | | | | | | | | | | | | |
| Canada | 1975 | (7) | 6 735 | 420 | 104 | 302 | 2 145 | 267 | 341 | 834 | 778 | 977 | 567 |
| | 1980 | | 19 063 | 577 | 762 | 454 | 3 853 | 485 | 1 805 | 2 641 | 1 111 | 1 763 | 932 |
| | 1993 | | 22 208 | 528 | 340 | 409 | 6 188 | 425 | 940 | 2 409 | 794 | 3 196 | 1 101 |
| | 1994 | | 21 701 | 501 | 360 | 432 | 7 278 | 362 | 944 | 2 997 | 1 457 | 4 367 | 2 064 |
| | 1995 | | 17 931 | 467 | 336 | 406 | 6 261 | 411 | 888 | 2 625 | 745 | 3 213 | 1 211 |
| | 1996 | | 19 900 | 480 | 403 | 534 | 7 902 | 503 | 911 | 3 530 | 1 171 | 2 854 | 1 612 |
| United States | 1975 | (1)(8) | 85 287 | 1 142 | 1 419 | 1 969 | 8 849 | 442 | 2 845 | 6 004 | 3 530 | 6 519 | 3 048 |
| | 1981 | (1)(8) | 76 976 | 1 448 | 1 193 | 2 086 | 8 760 | 461 | 2 850 | 7 638 | 2 793 | 2 583 | 2 673 |
| | 1985 | (9) | 50 070 | 2 905 | 1 559 | 2 564 | 10 340 | 632 | 3 304 | 9 387 | 3 063 | 8 235 | 4 280 |
| | 1990 | (9) | 46 743 | 1 760 | 1 683 | 2 285 | 9 472 | 649 | 2 742 | 7 569 | 2 524 | 8 687 | 4 200 |
| | 1991 | (9) | 48 146 | 1 886 | 1 766 | 2 389 | 10 039 | 566 | 2 710 | 8 181 | 2 646 | 8 401 | 4 451 |
| | 1992 | (9) | 49 276 | 2 153 | 1 806 | 2 540 | 10 147 | 617 | 2 729 | 8 144 | 2 851 | 8 816 | 4 329 |
| | 1993 | (9) | 49 757 | 1 870 | 1 764 | 2 633 | 10 379 | 699 | 2 678 | 8 222 | 3 063 | 8 592 | 4 388 |
| | 1994 | (9) | 51 863 | 2 208 | 1 741 | 2 730 | 11 072 | 700 | 3 021 | 8 384 | 3 146 | 8 836 | 4 704 |
| | 1995 | (9) | 62 039 | 2 751 | 2 068 | 3 324 | 12 840 | 732 | 3 323 | 9 891 | 4 238 | 11 537 | 5 657 |
| | 1996 | (9) | 68 175 | 3 027 | 2 333 | 3 803 | 14 225 | 898 | 3 725 | 10 762 | 4 245 | 13 221 | 6 583 |
| **South America** | | | | | | | | | | | | | |
| Argentina | 1975 | | 5 141 | 599 | 569 | —> | 852 | (10) ./ | 77 | 315 | 1 363 | 1 257 | 109 |
| | 1980 | | 4 698 | 231 | 715 | —> | 1 008 | (10) ./ | 141 | 731 | 630 | 1 104 | 138 |
| | 1992 | | 5 628 | 144 | 338 | 407 | 1 571 | 53 | 108 | 572 | 358 | 1 712 | 365 |
| | 1994 | (1) | 9 065 | 279 | 996 | 607 | 2 594 | 86 | 28 | 920 | 404 | 2 778 | 373 |
| | 1995 | (1) | 9 113 | 157 | 437 | 492 | 2 823 | 91 | 89 | 866 | 580 | 2 664 | 476 |
| | 1996 | (1) | 9 850 | 339 | 818 | 541 | 2 529 | 111 | 111 | 900 | 490 | 2 520 | 525 |
| Brazil | 1975 | | 12 296 | 1 212 | 409 | 1 021 | 3 055 | - | 1 330 | 1 060 | 598 | 2 902 | 709 |
| | 1984 | | 21 184 | 2 598 | 773 | 1 870 | 7 071 | 487 | 1 694 | 2 418 | 1 418 | 2 074 | 781 |
| | 1992 | (1)(11) | 27 557 | 1 749 | 1 388 | 3 175 | 5 022 | 376 | 352 | 683 | 391 | 3 037 | 721 |
| | 1993 | (1)(11) | 20 141 | 1 480 | 1 225 | 3 005 | 4 430 | 919 | 1 451 | 2 355 | 491 | 3 713 | 1 072 |
| | 1994 | (1)(11) | 21 574 | 2 013 | 2 281 | 2 823 | 5 629 | 941 | 773 | 2 341 | 1 051 | 2 358 | 1 364 |
| Chile | 1975 | (2) | 628 | 5 | 27 | 72 | 236 | 6 | 27 | 61 | 37 | 119 | 38 |
| | 1979 | | 273 | - | 7 | 27 | 75 | 12 | 12 | 20 | 14 | 62 | 44 |
| | 1985 | | 1 638 | 34 | 31 | 126 | 455 | 31 | 66 | 129 | 47 | 510 | 209 |
| | 1989 | | 2 350 | 25 | 36 | 123 | 908 | 42 | 72 | 296 | 69 | 567 | 212 |
| | 1991 | | 1 966 | 15 | 55 | 134 | 718 | 39 | 55 | 155 | 101 | 535 | 159 |
| | 1992 | | 1 820 | 13 | 59 | 127 | 587 | 34 | 58 | 183 | 43 | 548 | 168 |
| | 1995 | | 2 469 | 18 | 59 | 158 | 707 | 33 | 71 | 261 | 80 | 860 | 222 |
| Colombia | 1975 | | 1 272 | 34 | 18 | 80 | 515 | 34 | 65 | 108 | 46 | 242 | 130 |
| | 1980 | | 5 492 | 700 | 70 | 155 | 1 408 | 107 | 430 | 671 | 441 | 1 170 | 340 |
| | 1984 | | 15 041 | 1 078 | 239 | 352 | 2 784 | 290 | 1 098 | 6 067 | 997 | 1 501 | 635 |
| | 1991 | (1) | 1 481 | 141 | 28 | 88 | 570 | 43 | 40 | 243 | 52 | 216 | 60 |
| Ecuador | 1974 | (2) | 31 | 1 | - | - | 9 | 1 | - | - | 1 | 17 | 2 |
| | 1991 | | 717 | 30 | 7 | 8 | 197 | 5 | 38 | 33 | 30 | 288 | 81 |
| | 1994 | (2) | 11 | - | - | - | - | 1 | - | - | 1 | 9 | - |
| | 1995 | (2) | 12 | - | - | - | - | 1 | - | - | - | 11 | - |
| Guyana | 1976 | | 213 | 4 | 1 | 8 | 72 | 16 | 8 | 48 | 10 | 34 | 12 |
| | 1980 | (2) | 110 | - | - | 6 | 69 | 2 | 1 | 10 | 3 | 14 | 5 |
| | 1986 | | 129 | 6 | - | 5 | 81 | - | - | 13 | 2 | 17 | 5 |
| | 1989 | (2) | 46 | 1 | - | - | 29 | - | - | 4 | 3 | 4 | 5 |
| | 1994 | (2)(12) | 33 | - | - | - | 5 | 9 | 10 | 9 | - | - | - |
| | 1996 | (2) | 42 | 3 | - | 2 | 23 | - | 1 | 1 | 3 | 4 | 5 |
| Paraguay | 1993 | | 152 | 11 | 2 | 4 | 71 | 6 | 4 | 14 | 2 | 28 | 10 |
| Peru | 1975 | | 1 090 | 27 | 17 | 43 | 486 | 36 | 41 | 165 | 39 | 135 | 101 |
| | 1980 | | 766 | 6 | 10 | 43 | 314 | 19 | 31 | 117 | 10 | 142 | 74 |
| | 1985 | | 518 | 12 | 8 | 19 | 214 | 2 | 14 | 59 | 12 | 98 | 80 |
| | 1990 | | 894 | 34 | 21 | 31 | 338 | 35 | 45 | 169 | 38 | 81 | 102 |
| | 1991 | | 1 063 | 36 | 23 | 34 | 389 | 37 | 63 | 194 | 76 | 108 | 103 |
| | 1992 | | 1 657 | 52 | 39 | 45 | 540 | 47 | 86 | 316 | 130 | 222 | 180 |
| | 1993 | | 2 106 | 68 | 87 | 60 | 743 | 51 | 99 | 354 | 150 | 303 | 191 |
| | 1994 | | 1 993 | 65 | 81 | 59 | 697 | 39 | 88 | 321 | 111 | 328 | 204 |
| | 1995 | | 1 294 | 49 | 29 | 56 | 453 | 74 | 79 | 134 | 106 | 167 | 147 |
| | 1996 | | 612 | 44 | 24 | 25 | 266 | 13 | 27 | 66 | 11 | 97 | 39 |
| Suriname | 1996 | (2) | 47 | 18 | 1 | 16 | 6 | 2 | - | 2 | - | 1 | 1 |
| Uruguay | 1975 | | 481 | 99 | 12 | 14 | 102 | - | 19 | 61 | 23 | 77 | 74 |
| | 1980 | | 857 | - | 36 | 21 | 319 | 22 | 95 | 150 | 44 | 88 | 82 |
| | 1985 | | 858 | 1 | 12 | 51 | 331 | 25 | 60 | 115 | 24 | 149 | 90 |
| | 1989 | | 805 | - | 11 | 26 | 330 | 19 | 54 | 90 | 19 | 154 | 102 |
| | 1991 | | 1 143 | 6 | 68 | 35 | 340 | 17 | 81 | 205 | 33 | 276 | 82 |
| | 1996 | | 934 | 22 | 33 | 33 | 264 | 9 | 29 | 201 | 77 | 193 | 73 |

Number of titles by UDC classes  IV.5
Nombre de titres classés d'après la CDU
Número de títulos clasificados según la CDU

| Country / Pays / País | Year / Année / Año | | Total | Generalities / Généralités / Generalidades | Philosophy / Philosophie / Filosofía | Religion / Religion / Religión | Social sciences / Sciences sociales / Ciencias sociales | Philology / Philologie / Filología | Pure sciences / Sciences pures / Ciencias puras | Applied sciences / Sciences appl. / Ciencias aplicadas | Arts / Arts / Artes | Literature / Littérature / Literatura | Geog./history / Géogr./histoire / Geogr./historia |
|---|---|---|---|---|---|---|---|---|---|---|---|---|---|
| Venezuela | 1980 | | 5 201 | 190 | 72 | 119 | 1 761 | 102 | 427 | 656 | 218 | 845 | 811 |
| | 1987 | (2) | 1 202 | 34 | 64 | 83 | 355 | 30 | 64 | 281 | 66 | 195 | 30 |
| | 1990 | (2) | 3 175 | 92 | 140 | 121 | 924 | 55 | 192 | 671 | 254 | 501 | 225 |
| | 1991 | (2) | 3 461 | 97 | 182 | 122 | 873 | 58 | 186 | 667 | 288 | 710 | 278 |
| | 1992 | (2) | 3 879 | 86 | 130 | 121 | 935 | 79 | 275 | 843 | 386 | 680 | 344 |
| | 1993 | (2) | 3 934 | 129 | 147 | 86 | 1 038 | 57 | 203 | 960 | 324 | 749 | 241 |
| | 1994 | (2) | 3 660 | 147 | 141 | 138 | 1 003 | 86 | 160 | 794 | 301 | 625 | 265 |
| | 1995 | (2) | 4 225 | 229 | 217 | 186 | 1 106 | 85 | 187 | 1 032 | 243 | 636 | 304 |
| | 1996 | (2) | 3 468 | 87 | 210 | 188 | 955 | 81 | 136 | 608 | 274 | 682 | 247 |
| **Asia** | | | | | | | | | | | | | |
| Afghanistan | 1976 | | 64 | - | - | 5 | - | 16 | 27 | - | - | - | 16 |
| | 1980 | | 273 | 40 | 3 | 5 | 126 | 13 | 26 | 35 | 3 | 4 | 18 |
| | 1990 | | 2 795 | 165 | 25 | 170 | 1 045 | 30 | 125 | 680 | 95 | 200 | 260 |
| Armenia | 1994 | (2) | 224 | - | 4 | 3 | 19 | 17 | 15 | 14 | 10 | 84 | 28 |
| | 1996 | (2) | 396 | 2 | 4 | 13 | 52 | 13 | 10 | 32 | 15 | 123 | 47 |
| Azerbaijan | 1992 | | 599 | 9 | 15 | 9 | 131 | 25 | 36 | 63 | 13 | 241 | 57 |
| | 1994 | | 375 | 12 | 11 | 20 | 157 | 17 | 1 | 20 | 4 | 128 | 5 |
| | 1995 | | 498 | 10 | 11 | 22 | 144 | 13 | 12 | 44 | 17 | 176 | 49 |
| | 1996 | | 542 | 12 | 10 | 25 | 167 | 21 | 17 | 44 | 9 | 209 | 28 |
| Bahrain | 1996 | (2) | 40 | 6 | - | - | 7 | - | - | 1 | - | 14 | 12 |
| Brunei Darussalam | 1975 | | 29 | 15 | - | 0 | 0 | - | 2 | - | - | 1 | - |
| | 1980 | | 61 | 9 | - | 18 | 18 | 2 | 8 | - | 1 | 3 | 2 |
| | 1985 | (2) | 25 | 9 | - | - | 1 | - | 11 | 2 | - | - | 2 |
| | 1990 | (1)(13) | 25 | 2 | - | - | 13 | 2 | - | - | - | 8 | - |
| | 1992 | (1)(2) | 45 | 4 | 3 | 7 | 24 | 2 | 2 | 1 | 1 | - | 1 |
| China | 1980 | (6) | 19 109 | ./. | 2 091 | ./. | 2 095 | ./. | 5 715 | ./. | ./. | 3 322 | ./. |
| | 1985 | (6) | 40 265 | 970 | 514 | ./. | 9 921 | 746 | 2 360 | 7 298 | 1 489 | 4 859 | 1 757 |
| | 1990 | (1)(6) | 73 923 | 2 588 | 1 206 | ./. | 36 231 | 2 403 | 3 087 | 12 196 | 5 727 | 7 756 | 2 729 |
| | 1993 | (6) | 92 972 | 3 098 | 1 222 | ./. | 48 796 | 2 724 | 3 248 | 15 311 | 5 560 | 9 488 | 3 525 |
| | 1994 | (6) | 100 951 | 3 013 | 1 156 | ./. | 55 380 | 3 175 | 3 673 | 15 783 | 5 350 | 9 735 | 3 686 |
| Cyprus | 1975 | | 373 | 8 | 5 | 14 | 120 | 5 | 10 | 45 | 36 | 94 | 36 |
| | 1985 | (4) | 82 | - | - | - | 11 | 23 | 30 | 3 | 2 | 6 | 7 |
| | 1990 | | 692 | 25 | 5 | 35 | 173 | 72 | 39 | 130 | 34 | 112 | 67 |
| | 1991 | | 855 | 40 | 10 | 43 | 190 | 55 | 33 | 188 | 72 | 158 | 66 |
| | 1992 | | 900 | 37 | 11 | 69 | 210 | 41 | 19 | 197 | 79 | 191 | 46 |
| | 1993 | | 942 | 24 | 7 | 68 | 223 | 32 | 26 | 250 | 61 | 209 | 42 |
| | 1994 | | 1 040 | 25 | 4 | 62 | 241 | 25 | 16 | 244 | 95 | 285 | 43 |
| | 1995 | | 1 128 | 48 | 3 | 47 | 365 | 36 | 28 | 214 | 124 | 153 | 110 |
| | 1996 | | 930 | 22 | 6 | 30 | 341 | 84 | 27 | 181 | 121 | 61 | 57 |
| Georgia | 1994 | (2) | 314 | - | 11 | 12 | 41 | 30 | 16 | 33 | 9 | 137 | 25 |
| | 1995 | | 1 104 | 574 | 17 | 17 | 81 | 23 | 36 | 67 | 10 | 216 | 63 |
| | 1996 | (2) | 581 | 4 | 17 | 18 | 124 | 38 | 49 | 74 | 16 | 190 | 51 |
| India | 1975 | | 12 708 | 250 | 350 | 1 025 | 4 245 | 233 | 532 | 874 | 250 | 4 104 | 845 |
| | 1980 | | 13 148 | 159 | 427 | 773 | 3 697 | 161 | 764 | 1 708 | 267 | 4 278 | 914 |
| | 1985 | (1) | 11 660 | 278 | 403 | 915 | 3 032 | 182 | 513 | 1 190 | 289 | 3 973 | 885 |
| | 1990 | | 13 937 | 294 | 383 | 905 | 2 805 | 195 | 444 | 3 367 | 341 | 3 989 | 1 214 |
| | 1991 | | 14 438 | 214 | 449 | 807 | 3 204 | 197 | 397 | 3 864 | 331 | 3 746 | 1 229 |
| | 1992 | | 15 778 | 231 | 418 | 907 | 3 254 | 200 | 463 | 4 747 | 366 | 3 887 | 1 305 |
| | 1993 | | 12 768 | 219 | 399 | 769 | 3 399 | 196 | 543 | 1 441 | 356 | 4 309 | 1 040 |
| | 1994 | | 11 460 | 307 | 412 | 848 | 2 188 | 233 | 584 | 1 183 | 297 | 4 350 | 1 058 |
| | 1995 | | 11 643 | 382 | 377 | 948 | 2 501 | 150 | 486 | 1 278 | 274 | 4 078 | 1 169 |
| | 1996 | | 11 903 | 505 | 354 | 764 | 2 504 | 256 | 593 | 1 314 | 298 | 4 423 | 892 |
| Indonesia | 1975 | | 2 187 | 383 | 26 | 219 | 642 | 57 | 117 | 423 | 80 | 95 | 145 |
| | 1980 | | 2 322 | 242 | 83 | 129 | 846 | 35 | 131 | 426 | 115 | 178 | 137 |
| | 1992 | (2) | 6 303 | 191 | 148 | 892 | 1 192 | 294 | 186 | 788 | 64 | 231 | 246 |
| | 1996 | (3) | 4 018 | 245 | 82 | 438 | 805 | 263 | 497 | 749 | 115 | 480 | 144 |
| Iran, Islamic Republic of | 1981 | | 1 385 | 17 | 37 | 351 | 302 | 30 | 48 | 129 | 57 | 259 | 155 |
| | 1985 | (1) | 5 568 | 128 | 132 | 1 351 | 354 | 393 | 235 | 662 | 250 | 839 | 282 |
| | 1989 | (1) | 6 289 | 168 | 283 | 1 354 | 484 | 632 | 387 | 967 | 310 | 1 292 | 412 |
| | 1991 | (1) | 5 018 | 191 | 225 | 947 | 499 | 482 | 229 | 657 | 316 | 1 120 | 352 |
| | 1992 | (1) | 6 822 | 346 | 372 | 1 009 | 585 | 629 | 451 | 967 | 402 | 1 620 | 441 |
| | 1994 | | 10 753 | 341 | 404 | 1 932 | 998 | 910 | 617 | 1 319 | 439 | 1 849 | 603 |
| | 1995 | (1) | 13 031 | 384 | 383 | 2 834 | 972 | 907 | 1 021 | 1 227 | 226 | 535 | 1 189 |
| | 1996 | (1) | 15 073 | 438 | 537 | 3 293 | 1 025 | 947 | 1 244 | 1 787 | 443 | 157 | 576 |
| Israel | 1975 | | 1 907 | 12 | 25 | 255 | 385 | 40 | 82 | 147 | 49 | 512 | 116 |
| | 1979 | | 2 397 | 46 | 57 | 264 | 319 | 35 | 179 | 136 | 51 | 945 | 325 |
| | 1985 | | 2 214 | 25 | 40 | 173 | 230 | 50 | 79 | 71 | 44 | 718 | 234 |
| | 1992 | (7) | 2 310 | 22 | 53 | 182 | 263 | 92 | 101 | 85 | 31 | 638 | 173 |
| Japan | 1975 | | 34 590 | 1 076 | 604 | 773 | 9 918 | 623 | 1 672 | 8 441 | 1 997 | 6 674 | 2 812 |
| | 1981 | (1) | 42 217 | 1 340 | 1 416 | 611 | 7 512 | 3 069 | 2 735 | 6 134 | 6 195 | 10 286 | 2 919 |
| | 1985 | (1)(7) | 45 430 | 1 529 | 1 608 | 679 | 10 708 | 2 493 | 2 709 | 7 349 | 5 698 | 10 506 | 2 151 |

**Number of titles by UDC classes**
Nombre de titres classés d'après la CDU
Número de títulos clasificados según la CDU

| Country / Pays / País | Year / Année / Año | | Total | Generalities / Généralités / Generalidades | Philosophy / Philosophie / Filosofía | Religion / Religion / Religión | Social sciences / Sciences sociales / Ciencias sociales | Philology / Philologie / Filología | Pure sciences / Sciences pures / Ciencias puras | Applied sciences / Sciences appl. / Ciencias aplicadas | Arts / Arts / Artes | Literature / Littérature / Literatura | Geog./history / Géogr./histoire / Geogr./historia |
|---|---|---|---|---|---|---|---|---|---|---|---|---|---|
| Japan (cont) | 1992 | (1)(2) | 35 496 | 539 | 1 539 | 638 | 8 529 | 917 | 1 142 | 6 276 | 5 532 | 8 525 | 1 859 |
|  | 1996 | (1)(2) | 56 221 | 1 149 | 1 791 | 1 078 | 12 770 | 1 402 | 1 363 | 12 155 | 10 046 | 11 924 | 2 543 |
| Jordan | 1976 | (2) | 392 | 3 | 1 | 35 | 110 | 54 | 51 | 59 | 2 | 25 | 52 |
|  | 1991 | (1) | 663 | 5 | 1 | 64 | 186 | 3 | 100 | 14 | 20 | 200 | 53 |
|  | 1992 | (1)(2) | 790 | - | 3 | 64 | 299 | 1 | 109 | 5 | 29 | 251 | 17 |
|  | 1993 | (1)(2) | 500 | 15 | 11 | 77 | 115 | 14 | 13 | 37 | 10 | 136 | 72 |
|  | 1995 |  | 465 | 15 | 9 | 74 | 106 | 10 | 19 | 26 | 22 | 128 | 56 |
|  | 1996 |  | 511 | 25 | 8 | 60 | 122 | 16 | 39 | 45 | 21 | 116 | 59 |
| Kazakstan | 1992 |  | 1 226 | - | 21 | 16 | 293 | 85 | 117 | 313 | 23 | 304 | 54 |
|  | 1994 | (2) | 1 148 | - | 24 | 17 | 342 | 69 | 49 | 158 | 51 | 222 | 65 |
|  | 1995 |  | 1 115 | 65 | 12 | 17 | 339 | 50 | 44 | 197 | 31 | 291 | 69 |
|  | 1996 |  | 1 226 | 53 | 22 | 23 | 464 | 44 | 58 | 202 | 39 | 253 | 68 |
| Korea, Republic of | 1975 |  | 10 921 | 581 | 372 | 614 | 1 172 | 1 168 | 799 | 1 823 | 773 | 3 074 | 545 |
|  | 1980 |  | 20 978 | 1 009 | 814 | 1 934 | 2 328 | 1 282 | 820 | 1 719 | 1 326 | 8 575 | 1 171 |
|  | 1985 |  | 35 837 | 564 | 1 194 | 3 019 | 5 959 | 2 846 | 1 899 | 3 467 | 2 605 | 11 754 | 2 530 |
|  | 1990 |  | 39 330 | 3 250 | 1 005 | 3 042 | 3 983 | 2 756 | 2 918 | 3 677 | 6 153 | 9 992 | 2 554 |
|  | 1991 |  | 29 432 | 2 239 | 874 | 1 959 | 3 256 | 2 144 | 2 041 | 2 774 | 5 859 | 6 895 | 1 391 |
|  | 1992 |  | 27 889 | 3 044 | 659 | 2 063 | 2 635 | 1 741 | 1 491 | 2 880 | 5 954 | 6 270 | 1 152 |
|  | 1993 |  | 30 861 | 633 | 803 | 2 068 | 4 925 | 2 217 | 1 767 | 3 589 | 6 281 | 7 230 | 1 348 |
|  | 1994 |  | 34 204 | 579 | 640 | 1 844 | 6 584 | 2 371 | 2 025 | 3 856 | 6 315 | 8 885 | 1 105 |
|  | 1995 |  | 35 864 | 1 854 | 947 | 2 146 | 4 300 | 4 421 | 2 692 | 4 422 | 6 614 | 6 958 | 1 510 |
|  | 1996 | (1)(2) | 30 487 | 303 | 678 | 1 605 | 3 201 | 1 384 | 359 | 3 513 | 6 543 | 4 164 | 716 |
| Kuwait | 1975 |  | 48 | 20 | - | - | 10 | - | 1 | 5 | - | 12 | - |
|  | 1980 | (2) | 25 | 1 | - | - | 9 | 1 | - | 2 | 12 | - | - |
|  | 1985 | (14) | 250 | 3 | 6 | 5 | 103 | 18 | 56 | 14 | 21 | 12 | 12 |
|  | 1992 | (15) | 196 | 17 | 5 | 17 | 18 | - | 102 | 6 | 15 | 13 | 3 |
| Kyrgyzstan | 1994 |  | 328 | 31 | 2 | 3 | 193 | 16 | 3 | 29 | 5 | 46 | - |
|  | 1995 |  | 407 | 16 | 3 | 6 | 177 | 17 | 15 | 58 | 4 | 97 | 14 |
|  | 1996 |  | 351 | 11 | 5 | 3 | 176 | 16 | 19 | 25 | 8 | 73 | 15 |
| Lao People's Democratic Republic | 1976 | (2) | 31 | 2 | 6 | 1 | 7 | - | - | 3 | 1 | 10 | 1 |
|  | 1990 | (2) | 109 | - | - | 3 | 9 | 25 | 1 | 12 | - | 58 | 1 |
|  | 1991 | (1) | 58 | - | - | 1 | 31 | 2 | - | 2 | 1 | 20 | 1 |
|  | 1992 | (1)(2) | 64 | - | - | 1 | 7 | 11 | - | 6 | - | 36 | 3 |
|  | 1995 | (2) | 88 | - | - | 2 | 41 | 6 | 6 | 9 | 2 | 15 | 7 |
| Macau | 1996 |  | 67 | 2 | - | - | 44 | 3 | - | 2 | 13 | 2 | 1 |
| Malaysia | 1975 |  | 1 445 | 31 | 26 | 57 | 417 | 158 | 151 | 311 | 25 | 218 | 51 |
|  | 1980 |  | 1 948 | 41 | 20 | 145 | 471 | 200 | 276 | 270 | 48 | 338 | 139 |
|  | 1985 |  | 2 554 | 57 | 11 | 187 | 696 | 418 | 266 | 341 | 77 | 349 | 152 |
|  | 1990 |  | 4 578 | 108 | 32 | 416 | 1 018 | 766 | 620 | 433 | 94 | 856 | 235 |
|  | 1991 |  | 3 748 | 85 | 22 | 291 | 906 | 635 | 360 | 349 | 135 | 757 | 208 |
|  | 1993 |  | 3 799 | 56 | 29 | 288 | 480 | 709 | 309 | 323 | 141 | 1 292 | 172 |
|  | 1994 |  | 4 050 | 53 | 25 | 488 | 716 | 883 | 413 | 291 | 122 | 827 | 232 |
|  | 1995 |  | 6 465 | 101 | 41 | 659 | 1 259 | 748 | 530 | 598 | 190 | 2 053 | 286 |
|  | 1996 |  | 5 843 | 73 | 36 | 606 | 1 088 | 1 043 | 685 | 538 | 221 | 1 259 | 294 |
| Mongolia | 1975 | (2) | 490 | 8 | 10 | 3 | 171 | 31 | 27 | 117 | 19 | 87 | 17 |
|  | 1986 |  | 889 | - | - | - | 467 | 6 | 16 | 181 | 41 | 178 | - |
|  | 1990 |  | 717 | 49 | - | - | 300 | 2 | 45 | 103 | - | 218 | - |
|  | 1992 | (2) | 285 | 26 | 12 | 5 | 36 | 6 | 17 | 20 | 9 | 135 | 19 |
| Myanmar | 1974 |  | 1 164 | 25 | 37 | 195 | 70 | 52 | 13 | 60 | 16 | 574 | 27 |
|  | 1985 |  | 673 | 387 | 7 | 216 | 4 | 11 | 1 | 20 | 3 | - | 24 |
|  | 1991 |  | 3 509 | 8 | 92 | 780 | 42 | (10) ./. | 74 | 18 | 1 031 | 1 450 | 14 |
|  | 1992 |  | 3 785 | 11 | 78 | 720 | 18 | (10) ./. | 66 | 26 | 1 274 | 1 584 | 8 |
|  | 1993 |  | 3 660 | - | 73 | 713 | 26 | (10) ./. | 82 | 22 | 1 171 | 1 551 | 22 |
| Oman | 1992 | (1) | 24 | 1 | - | 3 | - | 9 | - | 1 | - | - | 10 |
|  | 1996 | (2) | 7 | - | - | 4 | - | - | - | 1 | - | 1 | 1 |
| Philippines | 1976 | (16) | 1 616 | 17 | 26 | 73 | 588 | 90 | 116 | 506 | 129 | 28 | 43 |
|  | 1980 |  | 1 254 | 35 | 10 | 43 | 477 | 7 | 66 | 427 | 113 | 34 | 42 |
|  | 1984 | (13) | 542 | 30 | 8 | 4 | 58 | 7 | 32 | 274 | 118 | 8 | 3 |
|  | 1990 | (1) | 1 112 | 58 | 21 | 32 | 462 | 61 | 98 | 206 | 20 | 109 | 45 |
|  | 1991 |  | 825 | 84 | 15 | 40 | 294 | 38 | 27 | 100 | 18 | 183 | 26 |
|  | 1992 |  | 1 016 | 78 | 4 | 6 | 735 | 13 | 13 | 88 | 11 | 58 | 10 |
|  | 1994 | (1) | 1 233 | 36 | 13 | 51 | 323 | 70 | 45 | 159 | 187 | 47 | 45 |
|  | 1995 | (1) | 1 229 | 65 | 23 | 47 | 290 | 51 | 31 | 157 | 18 | 199 | 14 |
|  | 1996 | (1) | 1 507 | 22 | 18 | 34 | 378 | 65 | 43 | 68 | 17 | 249 | 33 |
| Qatar | 1974 |  | 152 | - | 1 | 38 | 24 | 15 | 36 | 4 | - | 16 | 18 |
|  | 1980 |  | 337 | 15 | - | 85 | 9 | - | - | - | - | 5 | 4 |
|  | 1990 |  | 521 | 9 | 5 | 48 | 293 | 22 | 56 | 34 | 9 | 19 | 26 |
|  | 1992 | (1) | 372 | 23 | 14 | 31 | 186 | 19 | 36 | 24 | 11 | 17 | 11 |
|  | 1993 | (1) | 368 | 11 | 6 | 42 | 141 | 19 | 63 | 43 | 8 | 17 | 18 |
|  | 1994 | (1) | 371 | 23 | 6 | 26 | 149 | 15 | 60 | 41 | 4 | 11 | 36 |
|  | 1995 | (1) | 419 | 21 | 5 | 70 | 84 | 36 | 120 | 40 | 5 | 16 | 22 |
|  | 1996 | (1)(3) | 209 | 9 | 3 | 26 | 88 | 7 | 19 | 27 | 6 | 12 | 12 |

Number of titles by UDC classes IV.5
Nombre de titres classés d'après la CDU
Número de títulos clasificados según la CDU

| Country / Pays / País | Year / Année / Año | | Total / Total / Total | Gener-alities / Généra-lités / Genera-lidades | Philos-ophy / Philo-sophie / Filo-sofía | Religion / Religion / Religión | Social sciences / Sciences sociales / Ciencias sociales | Phil-ology / Philo-logie / Filo-logía | Pure sciences / Sciences pures / Ciencias puras | Applied sciences / Sciences appl. / Ciencias aplicadas | Arts / Arts / Artes | Litera-ture / Litté-rature / Litera-tura | Geog./ history / Géogr./ histoire / Geogr./ historia |
|---|---|---|---|---|---|---|---|---|---|---|---|---|---|
| Saudi Arabia | 1975 | (2)(4) | 125 | - | - | 24 | 13 | 7 | 59 | - | - | 4 | 18 |
| | 1980 | | 218 | 3 | - | 67 | 27 | 2 | 1 | 11 | 4 | 61 | 31 |
| | 1996 | (2) | 3 900 | 209 | 154 | 1 042 | 620 | 250 | 404 | 363 | 128 | 421 | 309 |
| Sri Lanka | 1975 | | 1 153 | 2 | 30 | 157 | 424 | 25 | 43 | 118 | 78 | 204 | 72 |
| | 1980 | | 1 875 | 35 | 31 | 402 | 615 | 83 | 85 | 160 | 51 | 335 | 78 |
| | 1985 | | 2 222 | 3 | 30 | 260 | 1 053 | 58 | 51 | 247 | 150 | 272 | 98 |
| | 1990 | | 2 455 | 41 | 17 | 215 | 1 232 | 65 | 47 | 173 | 102 | 400 | 163 |
| | 1991 | | 2 535 | 236 | 26 | 275 | 953 | 118 | 47 | 239 | 98 | 405 | 138 |
| | 1992 | | 4 225 | 263 | 46 | 312 | 2 209 | 179 | 71 | 400 | 75 | 531 | 139 |
| | 1993 | | 3 204 | 298 | 41 | 279 | 1 446 | 132 | 59 | 231 | 84 | 509 | 125 |
| | 1994 | | 2 929 | 218 | 32 | 251 | 1 601 | 88 | 58 | 211 | 49 | 297 | 124 |
| | 1995 | | 3 933 | 350 | 29 | 306 | 2 082 | 137 | 63 | 268 | 69 | 489 | 140 |
| | 1996 | | 4 115 | 338 | 29 | 28 | 2 505 | 139 | 55 | 390 | 33 | 483 | 115 |
| Syrian Arab Republic | 1975 | | 177 | 1 | 8 | 1 | 26 | 6 | 32 | 55 | 6 | 38 | 4 |
| | 1980 | (2) | 95 | - | 4 | - | 22 | - | 4 | 1 | 3 | 34 | 4 |
| | 1992 | (1) | 598 | 144 | 24 | 62 | 79 | 13 | 1 | 89 | 25 | 112 | 49 |
| Tajikistan | 1994 | | 231 | - | 3 | 1 | 24 | 7 | 16 | 47 | 8 | 60 | 22 |
| | 1995 | | 226 | - | 6 | 2 | 58 | 17 | 22 | 42 | 3 | 33 | 10 |
| | 1996 | (2) | 132 | - | 5 | - | 18 | 11 | 14 | 19 | 9 | 27 | 12 |
| Thailand | 1975 | | 2 419 | 266 | 64 | 268 | 1 076 | 89 | 69 | 215 | 84 | 178 | 110 |
| | 1980 | | 4 091 | 294 | 64 | 252 | 1 981 | 292 | 210 | 641 | 105 | 16 | 236 |
| | 1985 | | 7 289 | 706 | 240 | 436 | 2 704 | 237 | 512 | 1 312 | 241 | 702 | 199 |
| | 1990 | | 7 783 | 445 | 226 | 296 | 2 326 | 254 | 447 | 2 269 | 590 | 462 | 468 |
| | 1991 | | 7 676 | 429 | 198 | 273 | 2 415 | 260 | 539 | 2 271 | 411 | 477 | 403 |
| | 1992 | | 7 626 | 413 | 189 | 302 | 2 341 | 234 | 591 | 2 235 | 443 | 457 | 421 |
| | 1996 | | 8 142 | 464 | 202 | 275 | 2 456 | 259 | 617 | 2 371 | 407 | 644 | 447 |
| Turkey | 1976 | | 6 320 | 510 | 147 | 337 | 1 977 | 152 | 400 | 956 | 316 | 1 039 | 486 |
| | 1980 | | 3 396 | 65 | 82 | 302 | 843 | 94 | 158 | 437 | 109 | 1 124 | 182 |
| | 1985 | | 6 685 | 86 | 96 | 522 | 1 670 | 152 | 184 | 990 | 222 | 1 294 | 326 |
| | 1990 | | 6 291 | 557 | 267 | 520 | 1 799 | 154 | 135 | 835 | 156 | 1 458 | 410 |
| | 1991 | | 6 365 | 486 | 111 | 503 | 1 639 | 138 | 315 | 1 413 | 217 | 777 | 360 |
| | 1992 | | 6 549 | 159 | 204 | 526 | 1 591 | 176 | 140 | 811 | 236 | 1 371 | 463 |
| | 1993 | | 5 978 | 74 | 129 | 385 | 1 459 | 117 | 144 | 712 | 230 | 1 238 | 454 |
| | 1994 | | 4 473 | 332 | 143 | 309 | 1 329 | 82 | 63 | 544 | 147 | 1 237 | 287 |
| | 1995 | | 6 275 | 185 | 162 | 397 | 2 053 | 175 | 211 | 1 106 | 257 | 1 224 | 505 |
| | 1996 | | 6 546 | 128 | 231 | 636 | 1 551 | 181 | 222 | 764 | 229 | 2 035 | 569 |
| Turkmenistan | 1992 | | 565 | 47 | 5 | 6 | 147 | 21 | 72 | 74 | 18 | 136 | 39 |
| | 1994 | (2) | 450 | 1 | 5 | 7 | 150 | 23 | 46 | 60 | 20 | 121 | 17 |
| United Arab Emirates | 1979 | (2) | 6 | 1 | - | - | 3 | - | - | - | - | 1 | 1 |
| | 1990 | (4) | 281 | 6 | 3 | 37 | 16 | 86 | 104 | 17 | - | - | 12 |
| | 1992 | | 302 | 10 | 3 | 46 | 20 | 85 | 99 | 9 | 3 | - | 27 |
| | 1993 | (4) | 293 | - | 3 | 68 | 2 | 83 | 99 | 9 | 2 | - | 27 |
| Uzbekistan | 1992 | (6) | 1 267 | 4 | 150 | ./. | 72 | 86 | ./. | 188 | ./. | 407 | ./. |
| | 1993 | (6) | 1 340 | ./. | 118 | ./. | 54 | 71 | ./. | 136 | ./. | 605 | ./. |
| | 1995 | | 1 200 | 18 | 20 | 20 | 414 | 60 | 60 | 213 | 11 | 316 | 68 |
| | 1996 | | 1 003 | 8 | 7 | 22 | 367 | 44 | 42 | 158 | 10 | 277 | 68 |
| Viet Nam | 1975 | | 1 275 | - | 6 | 2 | 346 | 112 | 178 | 180 | 36 | 311 | 104 |
| | 1981 | | 1 495 | 143 | 14 | 12 | 638 | 12 | 70 | 156 | 72 | 329 | 49 |
| | 1986 | (6) | 2 285 | ./. | ./. | ./. | 301 | ./. | ./. | 364 | ./. | 556 | ./. |
| | 1990 | (6) | 2 923 | ./. | ./. | ./. | 394 | ./. | ./. | 283 | ./. | 888 | ./. |
| | 1991 | (6) | 3 429 | ./. | ./. | ./. | 444 | ./. | ./. | 395 | ./. | 979 | ./. |
| | 1992 | (6) | 4 707 | ./. | ./. | ./. | 683 | ./. | ./. | 603 | ./. | 1 024 | ./. |
| | 1993 | (6) | 5 581 | ./. | ./. | ./. | 647 | ./. | ./. | 646 | ./. | 1 502 | ./. |
| Palestine | 1996 | (2) | 114 | 3 | 2 | 8 | 47 | 3 | 12 | 21 | - | 10 | 8 |
| **Europe** | | | | | | | | | | | | | |
| Albania | 1980 | | 948 | 21 | 2 | - | 211 | 63 | 103 | 223 | 46 | 237 | 42 |
| | 1985 | | 939 | 9 | 6 | - | 189 | 75 | 159 | 281 | 42 | 139 | 39 |
| | 1991 | | 381 | 12 | - | 4 | 28 | 35 | 74 | 127 | 20 | 63 | 18 |
| Andorra | 1989 | (1)(2) | 45 | - | - | 4 | 7 | - | - | 4 | 12 | 3 | 15 |
| | 1991 | (1) | 49 | 1 | - | - | 17 | - | 1 | 2 | 14 | 6 | 8 |
| | 1992 | | 56 | 3 | - | 1 | 15 | 1 | 3 | 4 | 7 | 10 | 12 |
| | 1994 | (1) | 57 | - | - | - | 24 | - | 3 | 4 | 5 | 15 | 6 |
| Austria | 1975 | | 5 636 | 98 | 203 | 171 | 1 480 | 146 | 727 | 1 048 | 426 | 812 | 525 |
| | 1980 | | 7 098 | 153 | 270 | 255 | 1 636 | 125 | 884 | 1 277 | 566 | 1 129 | 803 |
| | 1985 | | 8 440 | 193 | 285 | 411 | 1 531 | 206 | 1 451 | 1 908 | 624 | 1 078 | 753 |
| | 1990 | | 6 258 | 328 | 132 | 298 | 2 397 | 156 | 302 | 682 | 733 | 639 | 591 |
| | 1991 | | 6 505 | 288 | 132 | 260 | 2 484 | 169 | 353 | 855 | 784 | 641 | 539 |
| | 1992 | | 4 986 | 156 | 193 | 164 | 1 552 | 124 | 449 | 501 | 528 | 919 | 400 |
| | 1993 | (8) | 5 628 | 171 | 175 | 167 | 1 813 | 167 | 585 | 613 | 585 | 908 | 444 |
| | 1994 | (8) | 7 987 | 229 | 246 | 284 | 2 758 | 229 | 847 | 703 | 922 | 1 181 | 588 |
| | 1995 | (8) | 8 222 | 406 | 255 | 239 | 2 948 | 239 | 657 | 738 | 929 | 1 208 | 603 |
| | 1996 | (8) | 8 056 | 243 | 289 | 289 | 2 851 | 209 | 651 | 682 | 963 | 1 188 | 691 |

**Number of titles by UDC classes**
Nombre de titres classés d'après la CDU
Número de títulos clasificados según la CDU

| Country / Pays / País | Year / Année / Año | Total / Total / Total | Gener-alities / Généra-lités / Genera-lidades | Philos-ophy / Philo-sophie / Filo-sofía | Religion / Religion / Religión | Social sciences / Sciences sociales / Ciencias sociales | Phil-ology / Philo-logie / Filo-logía | Pure sciences / Sciences pures / Ciencias puras | Applied sciences / Sciences appl. / Ciencias aplicadas | Arts / Arts / Artes | Litera-ture / Litté-rature / Litera-tura | Geog./history / Géogr./histoire / Geogr./historia |
|---|---|---|---|---|---|---|---|---|---|---|---|---|
| Belarus | 1975 | 2 941 | 125 | 47 | 7 | 794 | 103 | 233 | 1 187 | 105 | 268 | 72 |
| | 1980 | 3 009 | 172 | 66 | 4 | 950 | 92 | 171 | 1 144 | 78 | 286 | 46 |
| | 1985 | 3 431 | 121 | 60 | 12 | 1 143 | 94 | 190 | 1 251 | 106 | 380 | 74 |
| | 1990 | 2 823 | 116 | 94 | 8 | 792 | 112 | 181 | 953 | 148 | 349 | 70 |
| | 1991 | 2 432 | 120 | 56 | 21 | 599 | 103 | 186 | 824 | 94 | 342 | 87 |
| | 1992 | 2 364 | 112 | 41 | 27 | 665 | 123 | 140 | 674 | 80 | 418 | 84 |
| | 1993 | 2 926 | 151 | 45 | 144 | 711 | 168 | 142 | 690 | 110 | 667 | 98 |
| | 1994 | 3 346 | 161 | 68 | 184 | 790 | 169 | 187 | 792 | 77 | 813 | 105 |
| | 1995 | 3 205 | 132 | 74 | 181 | 756 | 125 | 147 | 665 | 61 | 952 | 112 |
| | 1996 | 3 809 | 214 | 84 | 153 | 930 | 146 | 182 | 776 | 100 | 1 127 | 97 |
| Belgium | 1975 | 5 848 | 175 | 136 | 214 | 1 113 | 359 | 492 | 825 | 812 | 1 204 | 518 |
| | 1980 (16) | 9 009 | 151 | 231 | 345 | 1 462 | 511 | 601 | 1 047 | 861 | 1 525 | 883 |
| | 1985 (16) | 8 327 | 169 | 240 | 480 | 1 235 | 291 | 343 | 1 153 | 890 | 2 807 | 719 |
| | 1990 (16) | 12 157 | 303 | 285 | 458 | 2 530 | 335 | 461 | 1 886 | 1 074 | 3 673 | 1 152 |
| | 1991 (16) | 13 913 | 300 | 311 | 686 | 2 847 | 478 | 817 | 2 228 | 1 325 | 3 696 | 1 225 |
| Bulgaria | 1975 | 3 669 | 118 | 67 | 15 | 974 | 116 | 267 | 1 006 | 173 | 741 | 192 |
| | 1980 | 4 681 | 198 | 43 | 14 | 1 404 | 135 | 254 | 1 206 | 222 | 975 | 230 |
| | 1985 | 5 171 | 233 | 67 | 21 | 1 502 | 246 | 291 | 1 283 | 216 | 985 | 327 |
| | 1990 | 3 412 | 104 | 47 | 18 | 766 | 112 | 308 | 936 | 146 | 781 | 194 |
| | 1991 | 3 260 | 94 | 93 | 104 | 642 | 1 | 231 | 736 | 106 | 1 070 | 183 |
| | 1992 | 4 773 | 127 | 151 | 146 | 814 | 1 | 264 | 729 | 145 | 2 191 | 205 |
| | 1993 | 5 771 | 194 | 236 | 211 | 1 016 | 157 | 275 | 821 | 154 | 2 448 | 259 |
| | 1994 | 5 925 | 252 | 270 | 165 | 1 176 | 130 | 236 | 798 | 156 | 2 445 | 297 |
| | 1995 | 5 400 | 204 | 238 | 156 | 1 045 | 162 | 276 | 765 | 154 | 2 104 | 296 |
| | 1996 | 4 840 | 155 | 256 | 156 | 1 060 | 130 | 195 | 576 | 129 | 1 935 | 248 |
| Croatia | 1993 | 2 094 | 39 | 50 | 166 | 453 | 59 | 88 | 412 | 65 | 448 | 75 |
| | 1994 | 2 671 | 44 | 94 | 220 | 679 | 68 | 102 | 463 | 158 | 608 | 58 |
| | 1995 | 2 902 | 46 | 84 | 220 | 704 | 73 | 138 | 489 | 181 | 669 | 80 |
| | 1996 | 1 718 | 7 | 41 | 68 | 329 | 30 | 55 | 170 | 31 | 317 | 21 |
| Czech Republic | 1992 | 6 743 | 330 | 178 | 244 | 1 045 | 353 | 684 | 1 107 | 423 | 1 981 | 398 |
| | 1993 | 8 203 | 299 | 252 | 267 | 1 849 | 358 | 636 | 1 111 | 382 | 2 465 | 584 |
| | 1994 | 9 309 | 302 | 283 | 331 | 1 458 | 305 | 806 | 1 164 | 511 | 3 498 | 651 |
| | 1995 | 8 994 | 314 | 283 | 321 | 1 447 | 243 | 732 | 1 178 | 524 | 3 374 | 578 |
| | 1996 | 10 244 | 187 | 363 | 289 | 1 928 | 369 | 972 | 1 471 | 662 | 3 261 | 742 |
| Denmark | 1975 | 7 068 | 211 | 190 | 242 | 1 448 | 227 | 537 | 1 403 | 513 | 1 572 | 725 |
| | 1980 | 9 256 | 264 | 275 | 277 | 1 705 | 321 | 722 | 2 139 | 593 | 2 081 | 879 |
| | 1985 | 9 554 | 180 | 345 | 260 | 1 883 | 288 | 619 | 2 273 | 614 | 2 233 | 859 |
| | 1990 | 11 082 | 232 | 479 | 328 | 2 013 | 295 | 773 | 2 732 | 722 | 2 522 | 986 |
| | 1991 | 10 198 | 234 | 358 | 259 | 1 907 | 305 | 791 | 2 416 | 643 | 2 410 | 875 |
| | 1992 | 11 761 | 271 | 510 | 316 | 2 225 | 361 | 932 | 2 723 | 773 | 2 505 | 1 145 |
| | 1993 | 11 492 | 339 | 485 | 269 | 2 188 | 339 | 891 | 2 794 | 714 | 2 367 | 1 106 |
| | 1994 | 11 973 | 403 | 503 | 332 | 2 377 | 293 | 964 | 2 859 | 767 | 2 366 | 1 109 |
| | 1995 | 12 478 | 368 | 554 | 339 | 2 509 | 328 | 913 | 3 006 | 797 | 2 432 | 1 232 |
| | 1996 | 12 352 | 233 | 536 | 294 | 2 460 | 347 | 863 | 3 036 | 923 | 2 561 | 1 099 |
| Estonia | 1991 | 1 654 | 64 | 56 | 37 | 305 | 129 | 159 | 403 | 89 | 320 | 92 |
| | 1992 | 1 557 | 63 | 42 | 73 | 320 | (10) ./. | 161 | 314 | 87 | 437 | 60 |
| | 1993 | 1 965 | 87 | 50 | 58 | 412 | (10) ./. | 174 | 290 | 140 | 631 | 123 |
| | 1994 | 2 291 | 125 | 52 | 75 | 517 | (10) ./. | 194 | 393 | 140 | 667 | 128 |
| | 1995 | 2 635 | 191 | 86 | 74 | 634 | (10) ./. | 195 | 307 | 176 | 851 | 121 |
| | 1996 | 2 628 | 181 | 92 | 93 | 571 | (10) ./. | 193 | 341 | 176 | 885 | 96 |
| Federal Republic of Yugoslavia | 1991 | 4 049 | 172 | 122 | 74 | 1 044 | 3 | 161 | 701 | 305 | 1 317 | 150 |
| | 1992 | 2 618 | 43 | 42 | 71 | 775 | 3 | 110 | 400 | 308 | 784 | 82 |
| | 1994 | 2 799 | 117 | 62 | 48 | 908 | 4 | 76 | 409 | 165 | 846 | 164 |
| | 1995 | 3 531 | 121 | 54 | 75 | 1 023 | 3 | 151 | 624 | 225 | 975 | 280 |
| | 1996 | 5 367 | 206 | 102 | 136 | 1 515 | 6 | 234 | 791 | 302 | 1 613 | 462 |
| Finland | 1975 | 4 558 | 109 | 95 | 228 | 836 | - | 465 | 796 | 273 | 1 442 | 314 |
| | 1980 | 6 511 | 297 | 165 | 365 | 1 749 | 264 | 687 | 1 469 | 252 | 956 | 307 |
| | 1985 | 8 930 | 329 | 191 | 360 | 2 345 | 347 | 940 | 2 425 | 428 | 1 129 | 436 |
| | 1990 | 10 153 | 307 | 165 | 286 | 2 359 | 368 | 1 059 | 2 330 | 659 | 1 707 | 559 |
| | 1991 | 11 208 | 335 | 189 | 339 | 2 766 | 394 | 1 146 | 2 660 | 754 | 1 979 | 646 |
| | 1992 | 11 033 | 291 | 181 | 456 | 2 603 | 403 | 1 080 | 2 774 | 761 | 1 816 | 668 |
| | 1993 | 11 785 | 319 | 245 | 319 | 2 862 | 346 | 1 108 | 3 196 | 794 | 1 738 | 858 |
| | 1994 | 12 539 | 320 | 230 | 341 | 3 066 | 405 | 1 209 | 3 167 | 828 | 1 861 | 1 112 |
| | 1995 | 13 494 | 315 | 266 | 390 | 3 385 | 438 | 1 212 | 3 537 | 870 | 1 947 | 1 134 |
| | 1996 | 13 104 | 325 | 240 | 355 | 3 189 | 411 | 1 215 | 3 477 | 807 | 1 898 | 1 187 |
| France | 1974 | 28 245 | 775 | 791 | 943 | 5 320 | 607 | 1 594 | 4 863 | 1 800 | 7 155 | 2 399 |
| | 1980 | 32 318 | 684 | 1 157 | 871 | 3 175 | 420 | 1 534 | 3 786 | 2 535 | 13 329 | 4 827 |
| | 1985 | 37 860 | 886 | 1 218 | 756 | 12 098 | 392 | 1 437 | 4 873 | 2 678 | 9 804 | 3 718 |
| | 1990 | 41 720 | 796 | 1 504 | 1 171 | 11 237 | 879 | 2 071 | 4 683 | 3 406 | 10 994 | 4 979 |
| | 1991 | 43 682 | 770 | 1 659 | 1 302 | 11 741 | 933 | 1 986 | 5 030 | 3 176 | 11 867 | 5 218 |
| | 1992 | 45 379 | 755 | 1 642 | 1 402 | 13 062 | 1 040 | 2 038 | 5 094 | 3 525 | 11 659 | 5 162 |
| | 1993 | 41 234 | 731 | 1 890 | 1 322 | 7 893 | 1 010 | 1 971 | 5 578 | 3 308 | 12 401 | 5 130 |
| | 1994 | 45 311 | 1 029 | 2 053 | 1 407 | 8 306 | 1 029 | 2 140 | 6 226 | 3 538 | 13 524 | 6 059 |
| | 1995 | 34 766 | 706 | 1 392 | 1 252 | 7 315 | 877 | 1 576 | 4 120 | 2 620 | 10 545 | 4 363 |
| Germany | 1991 | 67 890 | 5 647 | 3 173 | 3 350 | 15 177 | (10) ./. | 2 224 | 10 353 | 5 888 | 12 953 | 9 125 |
| | 1992 | 67 277 | 5 914 | 3 132 | 3 595 | 15 104 | (10) ./. | 2 141 | 9 441 | 5 734 | 13 426 | 8 790 |
| | 1993 | 67 206 | 6 126 | 3 403 | 3 620 | 14 816 | (10) ./. | 2 326 | 9 688 | 5 743 | 12 501 | 8 983 |

Number of titles by UDC classes  IV.5
Nombre de titres classés d'après la CDU
Número de títulos clasificados según la CDU

| Country / Pays / País | Year / Année / Año | Total / Total / Total | Generalities / Généralités / Generalidades | Philosophy / Philosophie / Filosofía | Religion / Religion / Religión | Social sciences / Sciences sociales / Ciencias sociales | Philology / Philologie / Filología | Pure sciences / Sciences pures / Ciencias puras | Applied sciences / Sciences appl. / Ciencias aplicadas | Arts / Arts / Artes | Literature / Littérature / Literatura | Geog./history / Géogr./histoire / Geogr./historia |
|---|---|---|---|---|---|---|---|---|---|---|---|---|
| Germany (cont) | 1994 | 70 643 | 6 255 | 3 594 | 3 815 | 16 259 | (10) ./. | 2 532 | 10 062 | 5 797 | 13 015 | 9 314 |
| | 1995 | 74 174 | 6 991 | 3 861 | 3 637 | 16 816 | (10) ./. | 2 637 | 10 410 | 6 810 | 13 571 | 9 441 |
| | 1996 | 71 515 | 6 287 | 3 580 | 3 718 | 16 210 | 3 176 | 2 756 | 10 550 | 5 921 | 9 622 | 9 695 |
| Greece | 1975 | 2 613 | 18 | 102 | 170 | 386 | 77 | 63 | 132 | 68 | 1 272 | 325 |
| | 1980 | 4 048 | 60 | 124 | 455 | 943 | 128 | 89 | 450 | 192 | 1 189 | 418 |
| | 1985 | 4 651 | 70 | 128 | 170 | 1 061 | 226 | 267 | 468 | 257 | 1 569 | 435 |
| | 1990 | 3 255 | 95 | 79 | 183 | 511 | 80 | 134 | 154 | 224 | 1 474 | 321 |
| | 1991 | 4 066 | 143 | 158 | 289 | 638 | 159 | 157 | 260 | 246 | 1 633 | 383 |
| | 1995 (1) | 4 134 | 152 | 98 | 204 | 613 | 190 | 254 | 287 | 284 | 1 598 | 454 |
| | 1996 (1) | 4 225 | 166 | 83 | 242 | 659 | 131 | 363 | 300 | 282 | 1 595 | 404 |
| Holy See | 1975 | 207 | 10 | 35 | 122 | 26 | 4 | - | - | - | 1 | 9 |
| | 1980 | 161 | 3 | 19 | 119 | 11 | 1 | - | 1 | 4 | - | 3 |
| | 1985 | 169 | 3 | 11 | 121 | 21 | 1 | 1 | 4 | 1 | 2 | 4 |
| | 1990 | 131 | - | 17 | 66 | 36 | 4 | - | - | 2 | - | 6 |
| | 1991 (3) | 196 | 4 | 40 | 111 | 28 | 8 | - | - | 2 | - | 3 |
| | 1992 (1) | 205 | 5 | 37 | 117 | 31 | 7 | - | - | - | - | 8 |
| | 1995 | 298 | - | 48 | 198 | 42 | 1 | - | - | 2 | - | 7 |
| | 1996 | 228 | - | 38 | 105 | 78 | 2 | - | - | - | 5 | - |
| Hungary | 1975 | 8 603 | 243 | 85 | 67 | 2 153 | 255 | 763 | 2 747 | 633 | 1 169 | 488 |
| | 1980 | 9 254 | 336 | 102 | 73 | 2 251 | 387 | 851 | 2 605 | 762 | 1 379 | 508 |
| | 1985 | 9 389 | 301 | 97 | 123 | 2 413 | 423 | 856 | 2 512 | 756 | 1 409 | 499 |
| | 1990 | 8 322 | 153 | 167 | 288 | 1 365 | 446 | 529 | 1 928 | 531 | 2 307 | 608 |
| | 1991 | 8 133 | 196 | 194 | 380 | 1 298 | 478 | 496 | 1 833 | 535 | 2 119 | 604 |
| | 1992 | 8 536 | 249 | 237 | 312 | 1 432 | 439 | 557 | 1 711 | 551 | 2 452 | 596 |
| | 1993 | 9 170 | 264 | 286 | 368 | 1 418 | 454 | 565 | 1 669 | 601 | 2 876 | 669 |
| | 1994 | 10 108 | 261 | 342 | 421 | 1 499 | 459 | 636 | 1 764 | 737 | 3 193 | 796 |
| | 1995 | 9 314 | 207 | 306 | 468 | 1 376 | 438 | 649 | 1 483 | 598 | 3 064 | 725 |
| | 1996 | 9 193 | 399 | 336 | 394 | 1 313 | 478 | 602 | 1 446 | 534 | 2 717 | 974 |
| Iceland | 1975 | 795 | 10 | 15 | 33 | 212 | 20 | 46 | 100 | 30 | 251 | 78 |
| | 1990 | 1 515 | 29 | 29 | 45 | 249 | 146 | 113 | 169 | 97 | 486 | 152 |
| | 1991 | 1 576 | 21 | 38 | 41 | 293 | 109 | 70 | 141 | 106 | 533 | 173 |
| | 1992 | 1 649 | 34 | 19 | 52 | 273 | 150 | 144 | 192 | 130 | 491 | 164 |
| | 1993 | 1 327 | 38 | 34 | 42 | 207 | 96 | 103 | 172 | 77 | 429 | 129 |
| | 1994 | 1 429 | 36 | 22 | 37 | 276 | 123 | 110 | 166 | 124 | 382 | 153 |
| | 1995 | 1 522 | 29 | 25 | 65 | 331 | 105 | 94 | 169 | 122 | 438 | 144 |
| | 1996 | 1 527 | 29 | 30 | 43 | 354 | 124 | 114 | 168 | 107 | 414 | 144 |
| Italy | 1975 | 9 187 | 314 | 480 | 486 | 2 090 | 201 | 476 | 1 092 | 732 | 2 594 | 722 |
| | 1980 | 12 029 | 346 | 599 | 965 | 2 822 | 322 | 614 | 1 308 | 1 283 | 2 564 | 1 206 |
| | 1985 | 15 545 | 412 | 764 | 1 085 | 3 156 | 367 | 692 | 2 665 | 1 577 | 3 515 | 1 312 |
| | 1990 | 25 068 | 704 | 1 414 | 1 477 | 5 684 | 497 | 786 | 3 085 | 2 957 | 6 124 | 2 340 |
| | 1991 | 27 751 | 813 | 1 506 | 1 661 | 5 854 | 530 | 997 | 3 735 | 3 524 | 6 660 | 2 471 |
| | 1992 | 29 351 | 880 | 1 678 | 1 752 | 6 223 | 612 | 1 042 | 3 613 | 3 620 | 7 143 | 2 788 |
| | 1993 | 30 110 | 1 107 | 1 623 | 1 767 | 6 134 | 720 | 1 111 | 3 590 | 3 459 | 7 678 | 2 921 |
| | 1994 | 32 673 | 800 | 1 751 | 2 013 | 6 039 | 824 | 1 140 | 3 687 | 3 429 | 8 978 | 4 012 |
| | 1995 | 34 470 | 783 | 2 045 | 2 041 | 6 572 | 860 | 1 265 | 3 663 | 3 609 | 9 225 | 4 407 |
| | 1996 | 35 236 | 723 | 2 146 | 2 232 | 6 698 | 763 | 1 173 | 3 898 | 4 264 | 8 539 | 4 800 |
| Latvia | 1992 | 1 509 | 67 | 50 | 74 | 169 | 72 | 64 | 283 | 66 | 361 | 77 |
| | 1993 | 1 614 | 62 | 30 | 57 | 206 | 70 | 61 | 197 | 69 | 428 | 118 |
| | 1994 | 1 677 | 49 | 59 | 77 | 222 | 53 | 36 | 144 | 50 | 529 | 66 |
| | 1995 | 1 968 | 75 | 78 | 78 | 378 | 56 | 54 | 148 | 67 | 426 | 88 |
| | 1996 | 1 965 | 91 | 63 | 87 | 414 | 67 | 54 | 166 | 87 | 364 | 65 |
| Lithuania | 1992 | 2 361 | 179 | 71 | 66 | 416 | 130 | 189 | 559 | 127 | 500 | 124 |
| | 1993 | 2 224 | 168 | 57 | 73 | 434 | 155 | 177 | 437 | 76 | 516 | 131 |
| | 1994 | 2 885 | 197 | 68 | 110 | 520 | 155 | 185 | 571 | 138 | 787 | 154 |
| | 1995 | 3 164 | 152 | 92 | 160 | 630 | 203 | 223 | 653 | 155 | 773 | 123 |
| | 1996 | 3 645 | 206 | 81 | 163 | 712 | 222 | 270 | 669 | 183 | 961 | 178 |
| Luxembourg | 1974 | 387 | 25 | 5 | 24 | 167 | 14 | 21 | 16 | 41 | 33 | 41 |
| | 1980 | 297 | 11 | 4 | 3 | 128 | 1 | 6 | 12 | 42 | 39 | 51 |
| | 1985 | 297 | 30 | 4 | 8 | 86 | 1 | 4 | 13 | 76 | 37 | 38 |
| | 1990 | 372 | 15 | 5 | 4 | 110 | (10) ./. | 15 | 14 | 81 | 64 | 64 |
| | 1991 | 503 | 58 | 8 | 6 | 196 | (10) ./. | 6 | 28 | 101 | 47 | 53 |
| | 1992 | 586 | 44 | 9 | 10 | 240 | 2 | 9 | 61 | 108 | 48 | 55 |
| | 1993 | 640 | 19 | - | 11 | 292 | 5 | 7 | 85 | 118 | 46 | 57 |
| | 1994 | 681 | 64 | 13 | 15 | 246 | 2 | 19 | 49 | 118 | 67 | 88 |
| Malta | 1975 | 135 | 4 | - | 33 | 26 | 4 | 3 | 4 | 11 | 33 | 17 |
| | 1980 | 110 | - | - | 14 | 28 | 4 | 1 | 4 | 6 | 42 | 11 |
| | 1985 | 357 | 9 | - | 81 | 130 | 8 | 1 | 16 | 27 | 62 | 23 |
| | 1990 | 460 | 7 | 6 | 69 | 200 | 14 | 5 | 11 | 55 | 59 | 34 |
| | 1992 | 395 | 9 | 7 | 76 | 155 | 17 | 6 | 17 | 22 | 34 | 52 |
| | 1993 | 417 | 8 | 11 | 80 | 163 | 18 | 4 | 16 | 29 | 41 | 47 |
| | 1995 | 404 | 4 | 6 | 78 | 159 | 8 | 4 | 13 | 28 | 47 | 57 |
| Moldova | 1992 | 802 | 24 | 13 | 12 | 174 | 27 | 57 | 204 | 20 | 225 | 46 |
| | 1993 | 354 | - | 3 | 5 | 48 | 27 | 48 | 71 | 17 | 84 | 51 |
| | 1994 | 797 | 11 | 18 | 24 | 364 | 23 | 35 | 171 | 19 | 100 | 32 |
| | 1995 | 1 016 | 41 | 19 | 48 | 385 | 37 | 47 | 272 | 19 | 109 | 39 |
| | 1996 | 921 | 52 | 9 | 22 | 456 | 21 | 27 | 165 | 15 | 124 | 30 |

**Number of titles by UDC classes**
**Nombre de titres classés d'après la CDU**
**Número de títulos clasificados según la CDU**

| Country / Pays / País | Year / Année / Año | Total | Generalities / Généralités / Generalidades | Philosophy / Philosophie / Filosofía | Religion / Religion / Religión | Social sciences / Sciences sociales / Ciencias sociales | Philology / Philologie / Filología | Pure sciences / Sciences pures / Ciencias puras | Applied sciences / Sciences appl. / Ciencias aplicadas | Arts / Arts / Artes | Literature / Littérature / Literatura | Geog./history / Géogr./histoire / Geogr./historia |
|---|---|---|---|---|---|---|---|---|---|---|---|---|
| Monaco | 1980 | 109 | 59 | 3 | 4 | 10 | - | 1 | 1 | 19 | 9 | 3 |
| | 1985 | 121 | 35 | 15 | 8 | 2 | - | 2 | 6 | 26 | 15 | 12 |
| | 1990 | 41 | 3 | - | 1 | 1 | - | 1 | 8 | 22 | 2 | 3 |
| Netherlands | 1975 | 12 028 | 233 | 431 | 488 | 1 906 | 1 699 | 1 058 | 1 158 | 582 | 3 356 | 1 117 |
| | 1980 (1) | 14 591 | 155 | 535 | 726 | 2 285 | 1 883 | 1 180 | 1 603 | 933 | 3 955 | 1 336 |
| | 1985 (1) | 12 629 | 78 | 470 | 662 | 1 300 | 157 | 502 | 1 824 | 782 | 2 634 | 993 |
| | 1990 (1) | 13 691 | 87 | 488 | 716 | 1 537 | 244 | 213 | 2 164 | 772 | 2 719 | 1 194 |
| | 1991 (1) | 16 017 | 84 | 612 | 823 | 1 615 | 307 | 351 | 2 581 | 880 | 3 082 | 1 278 |
| | 1992 (1) | 15 997 | 71 | 628 | 833 | 1 701 | 233 | 358 | 2 502 | 874 | 3 251 | 1 393 |
| | 1993 (1) | 34 067 | 70 | 710 | 788 | 1 883 | 334 | 215 | 2 310 | 2 826 | 2 950 | 1 364 |
| Norway | 1975 | 4 855 | 89 | 73 | 149 | 1 094 | 243 | 555 | 678 | 223 | 1 328 | 423 |
| | 1980 | 5 578 | 170 | 94 | 274 | 1 144 | 89 | 541 | 1 122 | 263 | 1 478 | 403 |
| | 1985 (7)(8) | 3 559 | 111 | 71 | 114 | 750 | 69 | 167 | 384 | 232 | 1 435 | 226 |
| | 1990 (7)(8) | 3 712 | 165 | 65 | 140 | 805 | 47 | 165 | 482 | 295 | 1 217 | 331 |
| | 1991 (7)(8) | 3 884 | 122 | 122 | 176 | 673 | 82 | 183 | 454 | 250 | 1 360 | 462 |
| | 1992 (7)(8) | 4 881 | 196 | 139 | 193 | 1 096 | 107 | 270 | 658 | 378 | 1 432 | 412 |
| | 1993 (7)(8) | 4 943 | 166 | 145 | 168 | 983 | 136 | 189 | 566 | 326 | 1 860 | 404 |
| | 1994 (7)(8) | 6 846 | 156 | 186 | 458 | 1 223 | 228 | 280 | 760 | 490 | 2 683 | 382 |
| | 1995 (7)(8) | 7 265 | 184 | 148 | 307 | 1 010 | 111 | 218 | 644 | 413 | 3 110 | 1 120 |
| | 1996 (7)(8) | 6 900 | 160 | 162 | 281 | 1 215 | 138 | 288 | 707 | 384 | 2 831 | 734 |
| Poland | 1975 | 10 277 | 210 | 125 | 167 | 1 977 | 389 | 1 019 | 3 628 | 556 | 1 658 | 548 |
| | 1980 | 11 919 | 597 | 180 | 245 | 2 345 | 472 | 946 | 3 839 | 811 | 1 662 | 822 |
| | 1985 | 9 649 | 318 | 165 | 413 | 1 910 | 339 | 919 | 2 589 | 533 | 1 714 | 749 |
| | 1990 | 10 242 | 148 | 213 | 482 | 2 095 | 439 | 974 | 2 527 | 588 | 1 830 | 946 |
| | 1991 | 10 688 | 161 | 212 | 437 | 1 944 | 468 | 1 102 | 2 504 | 708 | 2 267 | 885 |
| | 1992 | 10 727 | 211 | 333 | 514 | 1 801 | 423 | 1 000 | 2 147 | 631 | 2 691 | 976 |
| | 1993 | 9 788 | 157 | 354 | 684 | 1 493 | 414 | 796 | 1 753 | 495 | 2 668 | 974 |
| | 1994 | 10 874 | 212 | 342 | 566 | 1 785 | 428 | 939 | 2 190 | 479 | 2 982 | 951 |
| | 1995 | 11 925 | 238 | 382 | 900 | 1 885 | 670 | 1 083 | 2 210 | 575 | 2 895 | 1 087 |
| | 1996 | 14 104 | 265 | 456 | 1 078 | 2 958 | 616 | 1 291 | 2 654 | 678 | 2 828 | 1 280 |
| Portugal | 1975 | 5 943 | 224 | 130 | 311 | 1 806 | (10) ./ | 350 | 919 | 302 | 1 415 | 486 |
| | 1980 | 6 085 | 494 | 138 | 246 | 1 078 | (10) ./ | 424 | 1 079 | 742 | 1 400 | 484 |
| | 1985 | 10 293 | 588 | 176 | 488 | 1 296 | (10) ./ | 505 | 733 | 3 418 | 2 375 | 714 |
| | 1990 | 6 150 | 109 | 103 | 160 | 1 795 | 16 | 81 | 475 | 163 | 2 853 | 395 |
| | 1991 (11) | 6 430 | 97 | 114 | 85 | 1 031 | 31 | 115 | 348 | 220 | 1 341 | 355 |
| | 1992 (6)(11) | 6 462 | 92 | 764 | ./ | ./ | ./ | ./ | 373 | 154 | 1 974 | ./ |
| | 1993 (6)(11) | 6 089 | 286 | ./ | ./ | 830 | ./ | ./ | 410 | 159 | 2 021 | ./ |
| | 1994 (6)(11) | 6 667 | ./ | ./ | ./ | 789 | ./ | 401 | ./ | 192 | 1 934 | ./ |
| | 1996 (11) | 7 868 | 312 | 178 | 233 | 1 207 | 17 | 190 | 506 | 260 | 4 554 | 411 |
| Romania | 1975 | 7 860 | 138 | 146 | 52 | 1 395 | 361 | 1 060 | 2 346 | 398 | 1 583 | 381 |
| | 1980 | 7 350 | 101 | 137 | 67 | 1 292 | 383 | 1 039 | 2 165 | 415 | 1 411 | 340 |
| | 1985 | 5 276 | 105 | 61 | 47 | 503 | 162 | 756 | 1 881 | 250 | 1 280 | 231 |
| | 1990 | 2 178 | 54 | 38 | 44 | 134 | 93 | 318 | 749 | 112 | 549 | 87 |
| | 1991 | 2 914 | 73 | 54 | 117 | 202 | 149 | 349 | 778 | 98 | 919 | 175 |
| | 1992 | 3 662 | 71 | 83 | 133 | 254 | 201 | 382 | 758 | 118 | 1 442 | 220 |
| | 1993 | 6 130 | 109 | 167 | 255 | 490 | 350 | 694 | 1 307 | 191 | 2 237 | 330 |
| | 1994 | 4 074 | 85 | 119 | 148 | 431 | 183 | 425 | 870 | 85 | 1 534 | 194 |
| | 1995 | 5 517 | 98 | 237 | 231 | 650 | 323 | 643 | 1 161 | 120 | 1 804 | 250 |
| | 1996 | 7 199 | 213 | 275 | 301 | 913 | 431 | 989 | 1 485 | 105 | 2 182 | 305 |
| Russian Federation | 1991 | 34 050 | 3 471 | 478 | 509 | 6 179 | 768 | 3 407 | 10 025 | 1 058 | 6 873 | 1 282 |
| | 1992 | 28 716 | 3 354 | 480 | 585 | 4 550 | 722 | 2 727 | 7 681 | 690 | 6 975 | 952 |
| | 1993 | 29 017 | 1 430 | 756 | 778 | 4 630 | 817 | 2 751 | 8 661 | 624 | 7 581 | 989 |
| | 1994 | 30 390 | 2 860 | 896 | 957 | 5 965 | 995 | 2 644 | 6 849 | 704 | 7 176 | 1 344 |
| | 1995 | 33 623 | 2 968 | 1 038 | 854 | 7 719 | 988 | 2 790 | 6 783 | 685 | 7 704 | 2 094 |
| | 1996 | 36 237 | 3 362 | 1 275 | 984 | 8 801 | 1 171 | 2 869 | 7 003 | 664 | 8 493 | 1 615 |
| Slovakia | 1992 | 3 308 | 75 | 94 | 197 | 577 | 147 | 325 | 850 | 168 | 734 | 141 |
| | 1993 | 3 285 | 73 | 93 | 212 | 671 | 165 | 264 | 713 | 126 | 817 | 151 |
| | 1994 | 3 481 | 63 | 143 | 164 | 656 | 139 | 271 | 774 | 146 | 938 | 187 |
| | 1996 | 3 800 | 72 | 129 | 248 | 753 | 135 | 337 | 844 | 192 | 879 | 211 |
| Slovenia | 1990 | 1 853 | 40 | 38 | 79 | 465 | (10) ./ | 96 | 389 | 216 | 423 | 105 |
| | 1991 | 2 459 | 48 | 66 | 100 | 508 | (10) ./ | 233 | 475 | 270 | 610 | 149 |
| | 1992 | 2 136 | 94 | 60 | 83 | 517 | 86 | 234 | 327 | 235 | 354 | 146 |
| | 1994 | 2 906 | 57 | 117 | 106 | 536 | 125 | 263 | 481 | 393 | 631 | 197 |
| | 1995 | 3 194 | 72 | 119 | 123 | 623 | 117 | 295 | 461 | 400 | 763 | 221 |
| | 1996 | 3 441 | 82 | 123 | 135 | 659 | 123 | 319 | 620 | 438 | 680 | 262 |
| Spain | 1975 | 23 527 | 2 907 | 967 | 1 335 | 5 566 | 380 | 924 | 2 058 | 1 030 | 6 439 | 1 921 |
| | 1980 | 28 599 | 4 492 | 1 179 | 1 544 | 4 038 | 1 477 | 1 808 | 2 763 | 2 051 | 7 235 | 1 608 |
| | 1985 | 34 684 | 1 099 | 1 452 | 1 701 | 4 648 | 2 654 | 1 956 | 3 904 | 2 319 | 12 333 | 2 618 |
| | 1990 | 36 239 | 829 | 1 065 | 1 801 | 5 857 | 1 925 | 2 448 | 4 740 | 2 791 | 11 097 | 3 686 |
| | 1991 | 39 082 | 1 133 | 1 126 | 1 875 | 6 976 | 1 755 | 2 444 | 5 115 | 3 500 | 11 474 | 3 684 |
| | 1992 | 41 816 | 1 342 | 1 447 | 1 760 | 7 638 | 1 631 | 2 512 | 5 873 | 3 116 | 12 098 | 4 399 |
| | 1993 | 40 758 | 1 550 | 1 509 | 1 919 | 8 334 | 1 401 | 2 101 | 5 571 | 3 344 | 11 220 | 3 809 |
| | 1994 | 44 261 | 1 680 | 1 562 | 1 908 | 8 482 | 1 362 | 2 483 | 5 925 | 3 453 | 13 619 | 3 787 |
| | 1995 | 48 467 | 1 723 | 1 761 | 1 890 | 9 423 | 1 772 | 2 790 | 6 711 | 3 574 | 14 492 | 4 331 |
| | 1996 | 46 330 | 1 504 | 1 744 | 1 941 | 9 324 | 2 102 | 3 000 | 6 907 | 3 763 | 11 695 | 4 350 |

Number of titles by UDC classes IV.5
Nombre de titres classés d'après la CDU
Número de títulos clasificados según la CDU

| Country / Pays / País | Year / Année / Año | Total / Total / Total | Generalities / Généralités / Generalidades | Philosophy / Philosophie / Filosofía | Religion / Religion / Religión | Social sciences / Sciences sociales / Ciencias sociales | Philology / Philologie / Filología | Pure sciences / Sciences pures / Ciencias puras | Applied sciences / Sciences appl. / Ciencias aplicadas | Arts / Arts / Artes | Literature / Littérature / Literatura | Geog./history / Géogr./histoire / Geogr./historia |
|---|---|---|---|---|---|---|---|---|---|---|---|---|
| Sweden | 1975 | 9 012 | 222 | 173 | 285 | 1 453 | 338 | 613 | 2 078 | 372 | 2 891 | 587 |
| | 1980 | 7 598 | 179 | 95 | 245 | 1 463 | 151 | 391 | 1 190 | 296 | 2 317 | 536 |
| | 1985 | 9 532 | 227 | 194 | 377 | 339 | 260 | 465 | 1 124 | 655 | 2 899 | 833 |
| | 1990 | 12 034 | 284 | 260 | 451 | 2 104 | 393 | 747 | 2 430 | 772 | 3 509 | 1 084 |
| | 1991 | 11 866 | 272 | 314 | 379 | 2 099 | 398 | 822 | 2 497 | 710 | 3 357 | 1 018 |
| | 1992 | 12 813 | 305 | 346 | 404 | 2 451 | 405 | 912 | 2 696 | 842 | 3 222 | 1 230 |
| | 1993 | 12 895 | 336 | 271 | 502 | 2 394 | 471 | 902 | 2 894 | 826 | 3 176 | 1 123 |
| | 1994 | 13 822 | 317 | 401 | 577 | 2 722 | 428 | 919 | 3 038 | 923 | 3 226 | 1 271 |
| | 1995 | 12 700 | 332 | 313 | 464 | 2 429 | 434 | 936 | 2 823 | 817 | 3 104 | 1 048 |
| | 1996 | 13 496 | 396 | 328 | 502 | 2 685 | 464 | 900 | 3 285 | 850 | 2 876 | 1 210 |
| Switzerland | 1975 | 9 928 | 149 | 300 | 613 | 2 281 | 231 | 934 | 1 778 | 913 | 1 394 | 804 |
| | 1980 | 10 362 | 131 | 283 | 650 | 2 138 | 184 | 907 | 2 363 | 987 | 1 375 | 894 |
| | 1985 | 11 822 | 150 | 379 | 718 | 2 197 | 179 | 967 | 2 696 | 1 222 | 1 725 | 751 |
| | 1990 | 13 839 | 212 | 587 | 740 | 3 046 | 211 | 1 131 | 2 859 | 1 358 | 1 830 | 1 012 |
| | 1991 | 14 886 | 284 | 617 | 816 | 3 203 | 231 | 1 188 | 3 300 | 1 472 | 1 975 | 966 |
| | 1992 | 14 663 | 282 | 508 | 846 | 3 188 | 230 | 1 344 | 3 285 | 1 406 | 1 839 | 876 |
| | 1993 | 14 870 | 241 | 647 | 867 | 3 358 | 239 | 1 475 | 3 238 | 1 457 | 1 782 | 729 |
| | 1994 | 15 378 | 262 | 709 | 814 | 3 654 | 220 | 1 610 | 3 414 | 1 363 | 1 616 | 694 |
| | 1995 | 15 771 | 272 | 702 | 736 | 3 770 | 223 | 1 581 | 3 427 | 1 610 | 1 759 | 817 |
| | 1996 | 15 371 | 296 | 639 | 737 | 3 852 | 230 | 1 396 | 3 300 | 1 731 | 1 669 | 693 |
| The Former Yugoslav Rep. of Macedonia | 1990 | 559 | 6 | 6 | 3 | 162 | - | 13 | 29 | 41 | 279 | 20 |
| | 1994 | 672 | 11 | 10 | 5 | 363 | 12 | 18 | 45 | 23 | 151 | 34 |
| | 1995 | 885 | 7 | 12 | 7 | 365 | 14 | 23 | 72 | 58 | 248 | 79 |
| | 1996 | 892 | 24 | 13 | 31 | 400 | 14 | 40 | 49 | 39 | 245 | 37 |
| Ukraine | 1975 | 8 731 | 309 | 134 | 40 | 2 289 | 264 | 974 | 3 316 | 249 | 901 | 255 |
| | 1980 | 9 061 | 367 | 184 | 43 | 2 413 | 194 | 1 028 | 3 379 | 221 | 1 047 | 185 |
| | 1985 (17) | 8 362 | 341 | 185 | 62 | 2 348 | 163 | 708 | 2 900 | 214 | 1 172 | 199 |
| | 1990 (17) | 7 046 | 187 | 187 | 44 | 1 676 | 120 | 575 | 2 439 | 203 | 1 327 | 224 |
| | 1991 | 5 857 | 22 | 117 | 78 | 1 160 | 226 | 539 | 2 087 | 101 | 1 303 | 224 |
| | 1992 | 4 410 | 7 | 70 | 94 | 837 | 144 | 513 | 1 439 | 69 | 1 050 | 187 |
| | 1993 | 5 002 | 7 | 114 | 115 | 930 | 181 | 798 | 1 358 | 89 | 1 112 | 298 |
| | 1994 | 4 882 | 141 | 86 | 169 | 1 097 | 183 | 249 | 1 388 | 273 | 1 055 | 241 |
| | 1995 | 6 225 | 260 | 155 | 253 | 1 471 | 234 | 393 | 1 592 | 272 | 1 227 | 368 |
| United Kingdom | 1975 | 35 526 | 806 | 1 146 | 1 180 | 6 622 | 680 | 3 622 | 5 694 | 3 637 | 8 395 | 3 744 |
| | 1980 | 48 069 | 1 355 | 1 565 | 1 859 | 9 595 | 1 353 | 4 454 | 9 218 | 4 165 | 10 099 | 4 406 |
| | 1985 | 52 861 | 2 178 | 1 497 | 2 179 | 9 420 | 1 234 | 4 442 | 10 092 | 4 251 | 11 917 | 5 651 |
| | 1992 | 86 573 | 2 385 | 2 888 | 3 252 | 17 286 | 2 434 | 9 490 | 14 695 | 6 294 | 17 601 | 10 248 |
| | 1994 | 95 015 | 2 445 | 3 063 | 4 278 | 19 791 | 3 858 | 10 764 | 10 969 | 9 927 | 19 139 | 10 781 |
| | 1995 | 101 764 | 2 096 | 3 168 | 5 575 | 21 632 | 3 264 | 9 364 | 16 205 | 8 938 | 20 029 | 11 493 |
| | 1996 | 107 263 | 2 082 | 3 548 | 5 003 | 23 889 | 3 563 | 9 417 | 16 616 | 9 431 | 21 686 | 12 028 |
| **Oceania** | | | | | | | | | | | | |
| Australia | 1975 | 5 563 | 213 | 30 | 164 | 2 170 | 223 | 441 | 909 | 423 | 532 | 458 |
| | 1980 | 9 621 | 372 | 106 | 264 | 3 169 | 489 | 695 | 1 858 | 830 | 986 | 852 |
| | 1985 | 10 251 | 427 | 82 | 363 | 3 623 | 447 | 609 | 2 016 | 946 | 842 | 896 |
| | 1989 (16) | 10 723 | 353 | 135 | 333 | 3 997 | 277 | 627 | 1 753 | 966 | 1 205 | 1 077 |
| | 1994 (10) | 10 835 | 210 | 151 | 240 | 4 450 | 157 | 511 | 1 730 | 700 | 1 812 | 857 |
| Fiji | 1976 (4) | 139 | - | - | - | 50 | 16 | 47 | 24 | 2 | - | - |
| | 1980 | 110 | 3 | - | - | 4 | 31 | 19 | 26 | 11 | - | 16 |
| | 1994 (18) | 401 | - | - | - | 22 | 21 | 40 | 39 | 2 | - | 21 |
| Papua New Guinea | 1991 | 122 | 8 | - | 19 | 64 | 1 | 6 | 16 | 4 | - | 4 |

## General note

For general explanations and definitions, please refer to the beginning of this chapter.

## Note générale

Pour les explications et définitions générales, prière de se référer au début de ce chapitre.

## Nota general

Para las explicaciones y definiciones generales, referirse al comienzo de este capítulo.

Notes

(1) Not including pamphlets.
(2) First editions only.
(3) Data refer to school textbooks and government publications only.
(4) Data refer to school textbooks only.
(5) Data refer to school textbooks, government publications and university theses only.

Notes

(1) Non compris les brochures.
(2) Premières éditions seulement.
(3) Les données se réfèrent aux manuels scolaires et aux publications officielles seulement.
(4) Les données se réfèrent aux manuels scolaires seulement.
(5) Les données se réfèrent aux manuels scolaires, aux publications officielles et aux thèses universitaires seulement.

Notas

(1) No se incluyen los folletos.
(2) Primeras ediciones solamente.
(3) Los datos se refieren a los libros de texto y a las publicaciones oficiales solamente.
(4) Los datos se refieren a los libros de texto solamente.
(5) Los datos se refieren a los libros de texto, a las publicaciones oficiales y a las tesis universitarias solamente.

IV.5 Number of titles by UDC classes
Nombre de titres classés d'après la CDU
Número de títulos clasificados según la CDU

(6) Works indicated by the symbol ./. are distributed without specification among other classes for which a figure is shown.

(7) Not including government publications.

(8) Not including school textbooks.

(9) Not including pamphlets, school textbooks, government publications and university theses but including juvenile titles for which a class breakdown is not available .

(10) Data on philology are included with those on literature

(11) Including reprints.

(12) Data refer to school textbooks and chidren's books only.

(13) Data refer to school textbooks, chidren's books and government publications only.

(14) Data refer to school textbooks, chidren's books, government publications and university theses only.

(15) Government publications only.

(16) The figures do not represent the total book production, but only those actually received in the National Library.

(17) Popularization of science books for children are included in the total but not distributed.

(18) Data refer only to books published by the Ministry of Education and the Government printing department.

(6) Les ouvrages représentés par le symbole ./. sont distribués sans spécification entre les autres catégories pour lesquelles un chiffre est donné.

(7) Non compris les publications officielles.

(8) Non compris les manuels scolaires.

(9) Non compris les brochures, les manuels scolaires, les publications officielles et les thèses universitaires mais y compris les livres pour jeunes pour lesquels une répartition par catégories n'est pas disponible.

(10) Les données relatives à la philologie sont comprises avec celles de la littérature.

(11) Y compris les réimpressions.

(12) Les données se réfèrent aux manuels scolaires et aux livres pour enfants seulement.

(13) Les données se réfèrent aux manuels scolaires, aux livres pour enfants et aux publications officielles seulement.

(14) Les données se réfèrent aux manuels scolaires, aux livres pour enfants, aux publications officielles et aux thèses universitaires seulement.

(15) Publications officielles seulement.

(16) Les chiffres ne représentent pas la totalité de l'édition des livres mais seulement le nombre de titres enregistrés à la Bibliothèque Nationale.

(17) Les livres pour enfants destinés à la vulgarisation des sciences sont inclus dans le total mais ne sont pas répartis.

(18) Les données se réfèrent seulement aux livres publiés par le Ministère de l'Education et le département des publications du gouvernement.

(6) Las obras de las categorías indicadas por el símbolo ./. han sido distribuidas sin especificación entre las categorías para las cuales se ha presentado una cifra.

(7) No se incluyen las publicaciones oficiales.

(8) No se incluyen los libros de texto

(9) No se incluyen los folletos, los libros de texto, las publicaciones oficiales y las tesis universitarias pero incluyen los libros para jóvenes para los cuales no se dispone la repartición por categorías.

(10) Los datos relativos a la filología quedan incluidos con los de la literatura.

(11) Se incluyen las reimpresiones.

(12) Los datos se refieren a los libros de texto y a los libros para niños solamente.

(13) Los datos se refieren a los libros de texto, a los libros para niños y a las publicaciones oficiales solamente.

(14) Los datos se refieren a los libros de texto, a los libros para niños, a las publicaciones oficiales y a las tesis universitarias solamente.

(15) Publicaciones oficiales solamente.

(16) Las cifras no representan la totalidad de la edición de libros sino solamente el número de títulos registrados en la Biblioteca Nacional

(17) Los libros para niños destinados a la vulgarización de las ciencias quedan incluidos en el total pero no están distribuidos.

(18) Los datos se refieren solamente a los libros publicados por el Ministerio de Educación y el departamento de publicaciones del gobierno.

Number of copies by UDC classes IV.6
Nombre d'exemplaires classés d'après la CDU
Número de ejemplares clasificados según la CDU

IV.6    Book production: number of copies by UDC classes

Edition de livres: nombre d'exemplaires classés d'après la CDU

Edición de libros: número de ejemplares clasificados según la CDU

Data are presented in thousands          Les données sont présentées en milliers          Los datos se presentan en miles

| Country<br><br>Pays<br><br>País | Year<br><br>Année<br><br>Año | | Total<br><br>Total<br><br>Total | Gener-<br>alities<br>Généra-<br>lités<br>Genera-<br>lidades | Philos-<br>ophy<br>Philo-<br>sophie<br>Filo-<br>sofía | Religion<br><br>Religion<br><br>Religión | Social<br>sciences<br>Sciences<br>sociales<br>Ciencias<br>sociales | Phil-<br>ology<br>Philo-<br>logie<br>Filo-<br>logía | Pure<br>sciences<br>Sciences<br>pures<br>Ciencias<br>puras | Applied<br>sciences<br>Sciences<br>appl.<br>Ciencias<br>aplicadas | Arts<br><br>Arts<br><br>Artes | Litera-<br>ture<br>Litté-<br>rature<br>Litera-<br>tura | Geog./<br>history<br>Géogr./<br>histoire<br>Geogr./<br>historia |
|---|---|---|---|---|---|---|---|---|---|---|---|---|---|
| **Africa** | | | | | | | | | | | | | |
| Angola | 1979<br>1985 | (1) | 430<br>419 | 6<br>- | -<br>- | -<br>- | 35<br>3 | -<br>- | -<br>- | -<br>- | -<br>- | 249<br>416 | -<br>- |
| Benin | 1992<br>1994 | (1)(2)<br>(1) | 874<br>42 | 18<br>2 | 7<br>- | -<br>1 | 692<br>11 | 12<br>3 | 24<br>3 | 109<br>18 | -<br>0.0 | -<br>3 | 12<br>1 |
| Burkina Faso | 1985<br>1995<br>1996 | (1)<br>(1)<br>(1)(2) | 9<br>37<br>14 | -<br>2<br>2 | -<br>-<br>- | -<br>-<br>- | 6<br>6<br>1 | -<br>-<br>- | -<br>-<br>- | -<br>-<br>1 | -<br>2<br>- | 3<br>25<br>10 | -<br>2<br>- |
| Democratic Rep. of the Congo | 1992 | (1) | 535 | - | 6 | 240 | 232 | - | - | 50 | - | - | 7 |
| Egypt | 1974<br>1985<br>1990<br>1991<br>1993<br>1995 | | 33 120<br>37 853<br>43 149<br>127 800<br>108 042<br>92 353 | 845<br>219<br>6 966<br>9 102<br>4 185<br>632 | 145<br>284<br>373<br>495<br>586<br>1 249 | 4 472<br>3 168<br>9 261<br>11 696<br>11 196<br>13 577 | 5 411<br>3 478<br>4 317<br>4 527<br>4 605<br>2 344 | 3 597<br>5 214<br>2 226<br>10 198<br>9 417<br>16 725 | 5 565<br>8 758<br>11 020<br>15 395<br>11 538<br>19 936 | 1 872<br>2 169<br>2 618<br>7 488<br>8 571<br>17 910 | 139<br>564<br>454<br>1 813<br>3 073<br>6 681 | 8 519<br>8 901<br>2 742<br>5 154<br>2 643<br>6 750 | 2 555<br>5 098<br>3 172<br>2 316<br>2 384<br>6 549 |
| Eritrea | 1993 | | 420 | - | - | - | 85 | 229 | 93 | 13 | - | - | - |
| Ethiopia | 1985<br>1991 | | 651<br>674 | 52<br>110 | -<br>- | 84<br>69 | 217<br>158 | 27<br>33 | 39<br>22 | 145<br>129 | 15<br>9 | 27<br>91 | 45<br>53 |
| Gambia | 1976<br>1985<br>1991<br>1994<br>1996 | (1)<br>(1)<br>(1)<br><br>(3) | 17<br>45<br>7<br>20<br>10 | -<br>0.0<br>-<br>-<br>- | -<br>-<br>-<br>-<br>- | -<br>5<br>-<br>4<br>- | 17<br>12<br>3<br>2<br>7 | -<br>-<br>-<br>3<br>- | -<br>9<br>-<br>6<br>- | -<br>15<br>3<br>0.0<br>0.0 | -<br>2<br>-<br>-<br>- | -<br>-<br>-<br>-<br>- | -<br>2<br>1<br>5<br>3 |
| Ghana | 1975 | | 648 | 24 | 10 | 5 | 385 | 23 | 40 | 21 | - | 92 | 48 |
| Kenya | 1976<br>1990<br>1991 | <br><br>(2) | 2 039<br>695<br>452 | 26<br>4<br>13 | -<br>-<br>- | 249<br>230<br>155 | 1 191<br>93<br>85 | 78<br>112<br>50 | 252<br>52<br>21 | 55<br>82<br>69 | 10<br>24<br>1 | 84<br>46<br>42 | 94<br>52<br>16 |
| Libyan Arab Jamahiriya | 1975 | | 2 645 | 23 | 10 | 8 | 311 | 62 | 328 | 6 | 42 | 1 842 | 13 |
| Madagascar | 1976<br>1980<br>1984<br>1990<br>1991<br>1992<br>1993<br>1994<br>1995<br>1996 | <br><br><br><br><br>(1) | 800<br>516<br>493<br>541<br>111<br>402<br>537<br>287<br>292<br>296 | 1<br>3<br>6<br>1<br>-<br>-<br>5<br>-<br>1<br>- | 11<br>5<br>16<br>1<br>-<br>4<br>9<br>18<br>1<br>3 | 193<br>23<br>230<br>80<br>36<br>35<br>80<br>85<br>65<br>46 | 345<br>169<br>112<br>328<br>27<br>340<br>169<br>97<br>181<br>95 | 45<br>30<br>21<br>6<br>-<br>-<br>26<br>12<br>3<br>2 | 41<br>179<br>27<br>12<br>-<br>3<br>23<br>1<br>2<br>4 | 49<br>34<br>18<br>53<br>27<br>8<br>89<br>51<br>20<br>48 | 11<br>7<br>11<br>0.0<br>5<br>1<br>-<br>-<br>6<br>3 | 88<br>57<br>22<br>21<br>7<br>8<br>128<br>12<br>8<br>92 | 16<br>9<br>30<br>39<br>9<br>3<br>8<br>11<br>5<br>3 |
| Malawi | 1984<br>1996 | <br>(1)(4) | 3 105<br>9 174 | 0.0<br>- | -<br>- | 1 690<br>20 | 1 200<br>21 | -<br>4 290 | 0.0<br>1 920 | 201<br>960 | 2<br>80 | -<br>- | 12<br>1 880 |
| Mali | 1975<br>1984<br>1995 | (1)<br>(5)<br>(1)(2) | 88<br>92<br>28 | -<br>-<br>2 | 6<br>-<br>- | -<br>-<br>- | 4<br>49<br>2 | 23<br>20<br>- | 36<br>12<br>- | 1<br>10<br>2 | 2<br>-<br>- | 4<br>-<br>22 | 12<br>1<br>- |
| Mauritius | 1975<br>1980<br>1985<br>1990 | | 96<br>337<br>243<br>216 | -<br>-<br>1<br>1 | 1<br>9<br>1<br>1 | 3<br>-<br>4<br>3 | 32<br>59<br>32<br>116 | 1<br>136<br>87<br>2 | 4<br>77<br>58<br>6 | 44<br>21<br>8<br>9 | -<br>2<br>4<br>- | 6<br>21<br>18<br>17 | 5<br>12<br>30<br>61 |

Number of copies by UDC classes
Nombre d'exemplaires classés d'après la CDU
Número de ejemplares clasificados según la CDU

| Country Pays País | Year Année Año | | Total Total Total | Gener- alities Généra- lités Genera- lidades | Philos- ophy Philo- sophie Filo- sofía | Religion Religion Religión | Social sciences Sciences sociales Ciencias sociales | Phil- ology Philo- logie Filo- logía | Pure sciences Sciences pures Ciencias puras | Applied sciences Sciences appl. Ciencias aplicadas | Arts Arts Artes | Litera- ture Litté- rature Litera- tura | Geog./ history Géogr./ histoire Geogr./ historia |
|---|---|---|---|---|---|---|---|---|---|---|---|---|---|
| Mauritius (cont) | 1991 | | 157 | 3 | 3 | 5 | 99 | 1 | 6 | 15 | 1 | 11 | 13 |
| | 1992 | | 99 | 1 | 1 | 2 | 15 | 28 | 20 | 6 | 0.0 | 11 | 15 |
| | 1993 | | 135 | 1 | 1 | 2 | 31 | 45 | 9 | 7 | - | 34 | 5 |
| | 1994 | | 100 | 7 | 1 | 4 | 43 | 7 | 2 | 10 | 2 | 12 | 12 |
| | 1995 | | 116 | 7 | 2 | 4 | 43 | 11 | 1 | 10 | 3 | 28 | 7 |
| | 1996 | | 163 | 2 | 11 | 9 | 35 | 10 | 3 | 10 | 11 | 54 | 18 |
| Morocco | 1994 | (6) | 1 380 | 234 | 11 | 133 | 470 | ./. | 1 | 71 | 3 | 163 | 294 |
| | 1995 | | 2 861 | 825 | 224 | 174 | 819 | 36 | 27 | 111 | 72 | 402 | 171 |
| | 1996 | | 1 836 | 66 | 26 | 90 | 718 | 24 | 26 | 270 | 214 | 272 | 130 |
| Mozambique | 1980 | | 5 918 | - | - | - | 5 318 | - | - | - | 40 | 180 | 50 |
| | 1984 | | 3 490 | - | - | - | 3 362 | - | - | 29 | 14 | 85 | - |
| Niger | 1979 | (4) | 13.2 | - | - | - | 10.4 | 0.0 | 1.2 | 0.8 | - | - | 0.6 |
| | 1991 | (1) | 11 | - | - | - | - | - | - | - | - | 11 | - |
| Nigeria | 1975 | | 18 800 | 1 750 | 245 | 120 | 10 774 | 40 | 330 | 2 769 | 275 | 1 040 | 1 457 |
| South Africa | 1974 | | 17 474 | 69 | 30 | 963 | 4 370 | 1 113 | 1 489 | 1 607 | 251 | 5 210 | 2 370 |
| | 1990 | | 30 829 | 117 | 81 | 5 106 | 2 101 | 6 067 | 2 560 | 3 431 | 1 209 | 8 530 | 1 627 |
| | 1991 | | 34 940 | 95 | 71 | 6 514 | 2 142 | 7 176 | 2 868 | 3 427 | 1 184 | 9 707 | 1 756 |
| | 1992 | | 42 935 | 115 | 87 | 6 861 | 3 728 | 9 794 | 3 694 | 7 022 | 595 | 8 266 | 2 773 |
| | 1993 | | 36 813 | 52 | 75 | 6 104 | 2 480 | 9 151 | 3 666 | 4 308 | 462 | 8 170 | 2 345 |
| | 1994 | | 37 561 | 109 | 72 | 6 110 | 2 072 | 9 477 | 5 107 | 3 519 | 578 | 7 221 | 3 296 |
| | 1995 | | 31 349 | 86 | 101 | 4 013 | 2 129 | 7 663 | 3 460 | 3 543 | 572 | 7 108 | 2 674 |
| Tunisia | 1975 | | 1 519 | 6 | - | 15 | 10 | - | - | - | - | 38 | - |
| | 1981 | (4) | 6 000 | - | 19 | 300 | 40 | 2 850 | 1 915 | 256 | - | 250 | 370 |
| | 1992 | (2) | 94 142 | 14 900 | 3 990 | 2 848 | 13 560 | - | 15 545 | 17 355 | 1 944 | 20 500 | 3 500 |
| Uganda | 1993 | (2)(7) | 2 229 | - | - | 8 | 19 | 269 | 287 | 90 | - | 6 | 90 |
| United Republic of Tanzania | 1990 | (1) | 364 | - | 2 | 30 | 107 | 6 | 24 | 62 | 8 | 101 | 24 |
| **South America** | | | | | | | | | | | | | |
| Argentina | 1975 | | 41 450 | 11 039 | 3 294 | —> | 6 340 | (8) ./. | 461 | 3 381 | 3 380 | 12 061 | 1 494 |
| | 1980 | | 21 310 | 3 080 | 2 856 | —> | 5 547 | (8) ./. | 288 | 2 359 | 469 | 6 305 | 406 |
| | 1992 | | 49 293 | 384 | 1 587 | 3 379 | 7 173 | 418 | 356 | 1 963 | 2 559 | 10 272 | 21 202 |
| | 1994 | (2) | 48 882 | 804 | 3 832 | 4 008 | 10 363 | 937 | 70 | 3 866 | 3 926 | 17 591 | 3 485 |
| | 1995 | (2) | 51 033 | 679 | 870 | 2 092 | 22 155 | 583 | 188 | 2 631 | 1 255 | 16 450 | 1 547 |
| | 1996 | (2) | 39 663 | 1 172 | 3 135 | 2 619 | 8 490 | 626 | 186 | 2 746 | 968 | 9 565 | 2 882 |
| Brazil | 1975 | | 226 015 | 33 471 | 3 334 | 40 321 | 57 307 | - | 16 360 | 5 108 | 18 853 | 38 801 | 12 460 |
| | 1984 | | 293 102 | 61 057 | 3 206 | 46 479 | 67 762 | 14 981 | 22 930 | 27 985 | 20 760 | 16 811 | 11 131 |
| | 1992 | (2) | 189 933 | 13 102 | 3 320 | 14 402 | 12 152 | 1 119 | 4 496 | 1 571 | 979 | 11 910 | 2 569 |
| | 1993 | (2) | 131 251 | 5 051 | 2 775 | 14 935 | 14 145 | 32 007 | 30 337 | 14 542 | 2 863 | 9 573 | 5 023 |
| | 1994 | (2) | 104 397 | 10 030 | 5 490 | 9 953 | 19 673 | 21 277 | 15 828 | 6 389 | 2 166 | 5 602 | 7 989 |
| Chile | 1975 | (1) | 9 420 | 75 | 405 | 1 080 | 3 540 | 90 | 405 | 915 | 555 | 1 785 | 570 |
| | 1979 | | 4 095 | - | 105 | 405 | 1 125 | 180 | 180 | 300 | 210 | 930 | 660 |
| Colombia | 1975 | | 8 504 | 465 | 39 | 152 | 5 507 | 73 | 154 | 327 | 743 | 636 | 408 |
| | 1980 | | 22 646 | 1 200 | 105 | 515 | 6 639 | 1 535 | 2 880 | 1 607 | 1 011 | 5 945 | 1 209 |
| | 1984 | | 118 754 | 6 806 | 1 198 | 5 390 | 25 717 | 4 080 | 15 070 | 19 785 | 7 185 | 22 318 | 11 205 |
| | 1991 | (2) | 11 314 | 1 243 | 313 | 303 | 4 373 | 19 | 85 | 1 648 | 661 | 1 164 | 1 505 |
| Ecuador | 1974 | (1) | 46 | 2 | - | - | 14 | 1 | - | - | 1 | 25 | 3 |
| | 1994 | (1) | 40 | - | - | - | - | 2 | - | - | 2 | 36 | - |
| | 1995 | (1) | 19 | - | - | - | - | 2 | - | - | - | 17 | - |
| Guyana | 1994 | (1)(9) | 508 | - | - | - | 26 | 192 | 212 | 78 | - | - | - |
| Peru | 1996 | | 1 836 | 132 | 72 | 75 | 798 | 39 | 81 | 198 | 33 | 291 | 117 |
| Suriname | 1996 | (1) | 21 | 13 | 0.0 | 5 | 1 | 1 | - | 0.0 | - | 1 | 0.0 |
| Uruguay | 1989 | | 1 009 | - | 14 | 14 | 417 | 26 | 65 | 98 | 17 | 203 | 155 |
| | 1991 | | 1 970 | 8 | 54 | 50 | 546 | 36 | 136 | 370 | 64 | 544 | 162 |
| Venezuela | 1994 | (1) | 8 180 | 175 | 332 | 557 | 2 435 | 314 | 274 | 1 906 | 497 | 986 | 704 |
| | 1996 | (1) | 7 420 | 166 | 387 | 655 | 2 411 | 217 | 679 | 968 | 474 | 1 109 | 354 |
| **Asia** | | | | | | | | | | | | | |
| Afghanistan | 1976 | | 3 072 | - | - | 135 | - | 1 098 | 1 290 | - | - | - | 549 |
| | 1980 | | 3 741 | 1 128 | 38 | 7 | 465 | 1 226 | 604 | 12 | 2 | 3 | 256 |
| Armenia | 1994 | (1) | 1 739 | - | 9 | 5 | 92 | 105 | 31 | 48 | 12 | 402 | 65 |
| | 1996 | (1) | 20 212 | 120 | 21 | 365 | 765 | 128 | 58 | 301 | 410 | 1 846 | 498 |
| Azerbaijan | 1992 | | 8 954 | 25 | 185 | 99 | 2 911 | 587 | 144 | 617 | 52 | 3 356 | 978 |
| | 1994 | | 5 557 | 39 | 134 | 306 | 3 744 | 99 | 6 | 183 | 68 | 967 | 11 |
| | 1995 | | 3 592 | 27 | 70 | 149 | 2 397 | 129 | 7 | 69 | 48 | 545 | 151 |
| | 1996 | | 2 643 | 17 | 15 | 107 | 2 017 | 32 | 15 | 64 | 11 | 328 | 37 |

IV.6

Number of copies by UDC classes
Nombre d'exemplaires classés d'après la CDU
Número de ejemplares clasificados según la CDU

| Country / Pays / País | Year / Année / Año | | Total / Total / Total | Generalities / Généralités / Generalidades | Philosophy / Philosophie / Filosofía | Religion / Religion / Religión | Social sciences / Sciences sociales / Ciencias sociales | Philology / Philologie / Filología | Pure sciences / Sciences pures / Ciencias puras | Applied sciences / Sciences appl. / Ciencias aplicadas | Arts / Arts / Artes | Literature / Littérature / Literatura | Geog./history / Géogr./histoire / Geogr./historia |
|---|---|---|---|---|---|---|---|---|---|---|---|---|---|
| Brunei Darussalam | 1975 | | 145 | 64 | - | 51 | 15 | - | 10 | - | - | 5 | - |
| | 1980 | | 225 | 42 | - | 70 | 5 | 10 | 60 | - | 10 | 15 | 13 |
| | 1985 | (1) | 26 | 5 | - | - | 5 | - | 15 | 1 | - | - | 0.0 |
| | 1990 | (2)(10) | 56 | 3 | - | - | 28 | 12 | - | - | - | 13 | - |
| China | 1980 | (6) | 3 805 280 | ./. | 319 420 | ./. | 549 490 | ./. | 228 610 | ./. | ./. | 257 650 | ./. |
| | 1985 | (6) | 5 965 410 | 90 350 | 15 110 | ./. | 1 828 090 | 46 520 | 35 580 | 188 310 | 45 970 | 253 640 | 55 710 |
| | 1990 | (2) | 5 387 020 | 43 450 | 15 070 | ./. | 4 832 210 | 50 800 | 35 560 | 125 650 | 125 380 | 122 330 | 36 570 |
| | 1993 | (6) | 5 855 140 | 31 390 | 10 810 | ./. | 5 178 470 | 65 070 | 47 490 | 232 440 | 108 370 | 115 940 | 65 160 |
| | 1994 | (6) | 5 945 320 | 31 020 | 9 880 | ./. | 5 298 300 | 76 570 | 47 010 | 225 860 | 78 090 | 122 470 | 56 120 |
| Cyprus | 1975 | | 362 | 4 | 3 | 7 | 80 | 4 | 7 | 59 | 39 | 112 | 47 |
| | 1985 | (4) | 610 | - | - | - | 49 | 215 | 218 | 6 | 2 | 45 | 75 |
| | 1990 | | 1 232 | 19 | 3 | 44 | 460 | 240 | 69 | 175 | 20 | 110 | 92 |
| | 1991 | | 1 354 | 35 | 8 | 54 | 439 | 189 | 53 | 280 | 62 | 145 | 89 |
| | 1992 | | 1 359 | 33 | 5 | 80 | 468 | 145 | 31 | 303 | 80 | 149 | 65 |
| | 1993 | | 1 354 | 26 | 5 | 80 | 500 | 85 | 40 | 345 | 71 | 145 | 57 |
| | 1994 | | 1 530 | 22 | 5 | 70 | 560 | 91 | 46 | 407 | 133 | 153 | 43 |
| | 1995 | | 1 723 | 52 | 3 | 52 | 706 | 127 | 85 | 353 | 172 | 82 | 91 |
| | 1996 | | 1 776 | 23 | 7 | 34 | 753 | 290 | 79 | 306 | 186 | 35 | 63 |
| Georgia | 1994 | (1) | 1 131 | - | 37 | 76 | 237 | 117 | 30 | 76 | 12 | 476 | 70 |
| | 1995 | | 1 627 | 785 | 33 | 43 | 109 | 20 | 20 | 87 | 22 | 396 | 112 |
| | 1996 | (1) | 834 | 3 | 12 | 63 | 310 | 27 | 29 | 62 | 20 | 234 | 74 |
| Indonesia | 1996 | (3) | 8 103 | 487 | 147 | 908 | 1 534 | 732 | 1 011 | 1 272 | 243 | 1 369 | 310 |
| Iran, Islamic Republic of | 1989 | (2) | 31 565 | 523 | 1 282 | 8 245 | 1 957 | 3 082 | 1 770 | 4 405 | 1 512 | 6 363 | 2 327 |
| | 1991 | (2) | 24 310 | 613 | 809 | 5 724 | 2 586 | 2 566 | 891 | 2 669 | 1 607 | 5 138 | 1 707 |
| | 1992 | (2) | 26 275 | 1 256 | 1 302 | 4 028 | 2 227 | 2 427 | 1 574 | 3 180 | 1 858 | 6 326 | 2 097 |
| | 1995 | (2) | 87 756 | 1 343 | 1 454 | 13 213 | 3 623 | 5 003 | 4 922 | 5 168 | 933 | 2 236 | 2 184 |
| | 1996 | (2) | 87 861 | 1 466 | 2 035 | 17 953 | 3 768 | 4 881 | 6 207 | 6 065 | 2 125 | 666 | 2 204 |
| Israel | 1975 | | 11 126 | 100 | 46 | 1 474 | 964 | 383 | 359 | 511 | 175 | 2 442 | 664 |
| | 1979 | | 14 887 | 909 | 185 | 2 214 | 2 024 | 423 | 1 389 | 565 | 224 | 5 127 | 1 604 |
| | 1985 | | 8 872 | 227 | 104 | 1 485 | 530 | 973 | 818 | 314 | 265 | 2 918 | 1 209 |
| | 1992 | (7) | 9 368 | 152 | 117 | 1 273 | 1 183 | 1 084 | 1 180 | 397 | 467 | 2 648 | 812 |
| Japan | 1981 | (2) | 664 254 | 17 090 | 13 496 | 3 590 | 65 583 | 111 844 | 97 415 | 53 840 | 106 139 | 152 229 | 43 028 |
| | 1985 | (2)(7) | 717 269 | 10 930 | 16 265 | 3 350 | 276 769 | 37 324 | 34 322 | 53 842 | 59 510 | 205 832 | 19 125 |
| | 1992 | (1)(2) | 316 725 | 4 811 | 13 698 | 4 224 | 36 201 | 5 762 | 5 005 | 20 436 | 56 347 | 157 353 | 12 888 |
| | 1996 | (1)(2) | 400 013 | 6 970 | 14 175 | 4 776 | 42 519 | 6 545 | 4 573 | 51 497 | 100 078 | 157 121 | 11 759 |
| Jordan | 1976 | (1) | 2 673 | 6 | 2 | 249 | 930 | 108 | 514 | 148 | 6 | 349 | 361 |
| Kazakstan | 1992 | | 30 512 | - | 181 | 419 | 9 792 | 1 590 | 241 | 2 714 | 58 | 14 616 | 901 |
| | 1994 | (1) | 18 999 | - | 168 | 320 | 11 075 | 455 | 45 | 438 | 169 | 3 051 | 612 |
| | 1995 | | 13 051 | 226 | 23 | 209 | 9 778 | 146 | 71 | 355 | 253 | 1 515 | 475 |
| | 1996 | | 21 014 | 184 | 38 | 177 | 18 776 | 183 | 55 | 176 | 45 | 1 185 | 195 |
| Korea, Republic of | 1975 | | 129 579 | 2 948 | 6 587 | 2 775 | 26 857 | 27 652 | 26 349 | 9 820 | 18 044 | 4 704 | 3 843 |
| | 1980 | | 69 428 | 12 769 | 2 268 | 7 113 | 8 971 | 3 003 | 8 185 | 6 907 | 2 674 | 15 504 | 2 034 |
| | 1985 | | 124 122 | 5 461 | 2 796 | 9 509 | 29 922 | 15 946 | 11 736 | 6 728 | 6 620 | 28 829 | 6 575 |
| | 1990 | | 247 962 | 60 795 | 6 725 | 11 913 | 16 562 | 28 905 | 39 854 | 9 394 | 17 586 | 37 966 | 18 262 |
| | 1991 | | 160 551 | 42 063 | 3 950 | 5 104 | 10 126 | 21 973 | 31 869 | 6 182 | 12 272 | 21 082 | 5 930 |
| | 1992 | | 136 392 | 50 225 | 4 755 | 4 538 | 8 332 | 13 505 | 17 465 | 7 274 | 9 709 | 16 009 | 4 580 |
| | 1993 | | 151 344 | 9 151 | 3 617 | 43 250 | 20 270 | 15 954 | 7 943 | 12 875 | 27 385 | 5 321 |
| | 1994 | | 160 305 | 5 072 | 2 636 | 5 774 | 43 733 | 25 419 | 24 258 | 7 939 | 15 351 | 26 427 | 3 696 |
| | 1995 | | 187 252 | 5 689 | 4 371 | 6 799 | 46 556 | 40 819 | 33 877 | 9 865 | 17 959 | 17 401 | 3 916 |
| | 1996 | (1)(2) | 142 804 | 826 | 3 403 | 4 806 | 5 105 | 6 625 | 565 | 4 905 | 20 214 | 11 632 | 1 901 |
| Kuwait | 1975 | | 187 | 67 | - | - | 20 | - | 16 | 30 | - | 54 | - |
| | 1980 | (1) | 359 | 10 | - | - | 184 | 1 | 20 | 144 | - | - | - |
| | 1985 | (11) | 6 107 | 64 | 106 | 303 | 890 | 811 | 1 619 | 72 | 272 | 1 832 | 138 |
| Kyrgyzstan | 1994 | | 1 875 | 119 | 12 | 180 | 874 | 87 | 6 | 50 | 3 | 544 | - |
| | 1995 | | 1 937 | 93 | 4 | 34 | 959 | 30 | 6 | 33 | 4 | 570 | 204 |
| | 1996 | | 1 980 | 13 | 4 | 16 | 1 275 | 44 | 8 | 48 | 19 | 515 | 38 |
| Lao People's Democratic Republic | 1976 | (1) | 268 | 55 | 37 | 5 | 88 | - | - | 8 | 7 | 61 | 7 |
| | 1990 | (1) | 566 | - | - | 14 | 39 | 106 | 20 | 28 | - | 356 | 3 |
| | 1991 | (2) | 161 | - | - | 1 | 74 | 7 | - | 4 | 2 | 70 | 3 |
| | 1992 | (1)(2) | 136 | - | - | 1 | 13 | 31 | - | 10 | - | 73 | 8 |
| | 1995 | (1) | 995 | - | - | 7 | 180 | 229 | 315 | 201 | 14 | 35 | 14 |
| Macau | 1996 | | 99 | 2 | - | - | 76 | 3 | - | 4 | 10 | 2 | 2 |
| Malaysia | 1975 | | 5 511 | 13 | 46 | 158 | 1 269 | 1 154 | 1 299 | 462 | 38 | 647 | 425 |
| | 1980 | | 5 977 | 130 | 84 | 820 | 1 366 | 441 | 838 | 360 | 109 | 1 032 | 797 |
| | 1985 | | 10 468 | 135 | 27 | 766 | 1 885 | 3 426 | 1 581 | 366 | 224 | 1 217 | 841 |
| | 1990 | | 23 233 | 124 | 70 | 2 434 | 4 943 | 6 396 | 4 736 | 810 | 340 | 2 071 | 1 309 |
| | 1991 | | 13 620 | 102 | 39 | 909 | 1 968 | 4 350 | 1 630 | 1 043 | 385 | 2 202 | 992 |
| | 1993 | | 13 960 | 76 | 75 | 1 538 | 1 533 | 3 657 | 1 761 | 692 | 485 | 3 197 | 946 |
| | 1994 | | 17 424 | 81 | 114 | 1 976 | 2 667 | 5 365 | 1 987 | 788 | 518 | 2 097 | 1 831 |
| | 1995 | | 21 405 | 202 | 106 | 2 000 | 4 379 | 3 986 | 2 673 | 976 | 604 | 5 323 | 1 156 |
| | 1996 | | 29 040 | 110 | 65 | 3 213 | 5 388 | 7 642 | 4 468 | 1 644 | 820 | 3 663 | 2 027 |

Number of copies by UDC classes
Nombre d'exemplaires classés d'après la CDU
Número de ejemplares clasificados según la CDU

| Country<br>Pays<br>País | Year<br>Année<br>Año | | Total<br>Total<br>Total | Gener-<br>alities<br>Généra-<br>lités<br>Genera-<br>lidades | Philos-<br>ophy<br>Philo-<br>sophie<br>Filo-<br>sofía | Religion<br>Religion<br>Religión | Social<br>sciences<br>Sciences<br>sociales<br>Ciencias<br>sociales | Phil-<br>ology<br>Philo-<br>logie<br>Filo-<br>logía | Pure<br>sciences<br>Sciences<br>pures<br>Ciencias<br>puras | Applied<br>sciences<br>Sciences<br>appl.<br>Ciencias<br>aplicadas | Arts<br>Arts<br>Artes | Litera-<br>ture<br>Litté-<br>rature<br>Litera-<br>tura | Geog./<br>history<br>Géogr./<br>histoire<br>Geogr./<br>historia |
|---|---|---|---|---|---|---|---|---|---|---|---|---|---|
| Mongolia | 1975 | (1) | 3 829 | 22 | 44 | 6 | 684 | 877 | 526 | 455 | 272 | 711 | 232 |
| | 1986 | | 6 923 | - | - | - | 4 702 | 37 | 32 | 460 | 157 | 1 535 | - |
| | 1990 | | 6 397 | 159 | - | - | 2 507 | 12 | 334 | 492 | - | 2 893 | - |
| | 1992 | (1) | 959 | 104 | 48 | 15 | 115 | 12 | 82 | 65 | 21 | 405 | 92 |
| Myanmar | 1974 | | 4 038 | 88 | 90 | 547 | 458 | 193 | 116 | 230 | 67 | 1 348 | 148 |
| Oman | 1992 | (2) | 25 | 1 | - | 3 | - | 9 | - | 1 | - | - | 11 |
| | 1996 | (1) | 21 | - | - | 12 | - | - | - | 6 | - | 2 | 1 |
| Philippines | 1976 | (12) | 13 255 | 54 | 28 | 295 | 11 438 | 40 | 103 | 1 059 | 68 | 158 | 12 |
| | 1984 | (1)(10) | 14 718 | - | - | - | 3 925 | 5 325 | 5 219 | 249 | - | - | - |
| Qatar | 1974 | | 960 | - | 1 | 246 | 74 | 116 | 276 | 23 | - | 158 | 66 |
| | 1980 | | 2 205 | 75 | - | 554 | 29 | - | - | - | - | 10 | 4 |
| Saudi Arabia | 1975 | (1)(4) | 14 493 | - | - | 3 430 | 65 | 880 | 5 918 | - | - | 212 | 3 988 |
| Sri Lanka | 1975 | | 4 271 | 13 | 117 | 439 | 1 768 | 506 | 285 | 383 | 82 | 524 | 154 |
| | 1980 | | 9 073 | 108 | 142 | 2 099 | 2 474 | 1 216 | 1 066 | 749 | 69 | 865 | 285 |
| | 1985 | | 10 636 | 6 | 101 | 1 006 | 5 457 | 1 391 | 733 | 515 | 218 | 1 033 | 176 |
| | 1990 | | 19 691 | 180 | 129 | 725 | 14 099 | 1 249 | 690 | 475 | 174 | 1 340 | 630 |
| | 1991 | | 20 251 | 332 | 75 | 1 581 | 8 735 | 3 509 | 2 348 | 777 | 165 | 1 219 | 1 510 |
| | 1992 | | 26 777 | 734 | 176 | 1 428 | 15 348 | 2 296 | 1 289 | 1 555 | 199 | 1 445 | 2 307 |
| | 1993 | | 16 931 | 376 | 108 | 1 256 | 5 970 | 3 449 | 1 726 | 1 167 | 129 | 1 313 | 1 437 |
| | 1994 | | 15 337 | 428 | 109 | 1 030 | 5 379 | 3 045 | 1 095 | 1 120 | 87 | 1 304 | 1 740 |
| | 1995 | | 19 650 | 470 | 122 | 2 266 | 6 318 | 3 976 | 1 155 | 2 064 | 107 | 1 615 | 1 557 |
| Syrian Arab Republic | 1975 | | 349 | 3 | 20 | 1 | 82 | 9 | 57 | 76 | 17 | 76 | 8 |
| | 1980 | (1) | 310 | - | 15 | - | 64 | - | 14 | 4 | 10 | 104 | 19 |
| Tajikistan | 1994 | | 2 561 | - | 25 | 30 | 128 | 24 | 66 | 367 | 18 | 516 | 61 |
| | 1995 | | 1 902 | - | 14 | 3 | 87 | 24 | 35 | 93 | 5 | 142 | 16 |
| | 1996 | (1) | 997 | - | 165 | - | 284 | 259 | 103 | 34 | 29 | 69 | 10 |
| Turkmenistan | 1992 | | 6 604 | 159 | 24 | 180 | 2 390 | 69 | 93 | 224 | 74 | 3 209 | 182 |
| | 1994 | (1) | 5 493 | 0.0 | 63 | 177 | 2 815 | 270 | 59 | 173 | 125 | 1 706 | 105 |
| United Arab Emirates | 1979 | (1) | 35 | 10 | - | - | 15 | - | - | - | - | 5 | 5 |
| | 1990 | (4) | 4 423 | 7 | 28 | 457 | 229 | 1 541 | 1 479 | 58 | - | - | 624 |
| | 1992 | | 5 558 | 30 | 39 | 460 | 53 | 2 306 | 1 902 | 160 | 10 | - | 598 |
| | 1993 | (4) | 5 117 | - | 28 | 631 | 21 | 1 902 | 1 819 | 145 | 4 | - | 567 |
| Uzbekistan | 1992 | (6) | 47 657 | 910 | 5 355 | ./. | 887 | 588 | ./. | 3 582 | ./. | 16 490 | ./. |
| | 1993 | (6) | 44 033 | ./. | 2 054 | ./. | 414 | 923 | ./. | 2 207 | ./. | 17 451 | ./. |
| | 1995 | | 38 884 | 55 | 332 | 642 | 30 079 | 714 | 147 | 1 285 | 107 | 4 975 | 548 |
| | 1996 | | 30 914 | 39 | 39 | 406 | 24 566 | 355 | 158 | 632 | 45 | 4 355 | 319 |
| Viet Nam | 1975 | (6) | 44 618 | ./. | 29 | 6 | 7 569 | 10 887 | 11 589 | 1 608 | 242 | 7 838 | 4 850 |
| | 1981 | | 37 117 | 612 | 284 | 77 | 7 492 | 80 | 517 | 938 | 547 | 26 283 | 287 |
| | 1986 | (6) | 59 600 | ./. | ./. | ./. | 3 371 | ./. | ./. | 4 017 | ./. | 10 271 | ./. |
| | 1990 | (6) | 38 200 | ./. | ./. | ./. | 2 309 | ./. | ./. | 924 | ./. | 2 846 | ./. |
| | 1991 | (6) | 65 100 | ./. | ./. | ./. | 2 827 | ./. | ./. | 1 046 | ./. | 2 247 | ./. |
| | 1992 | (6) | 71 500 | ./. | ./. | ./. | 1 912 | ./. | ./. | 980 | ./. | 2 160 | ./. |
| | 1993 | (6) | 83 000 | ./. | ./. | ./. | 1 475 | ./. | ./. | 1 308 | ./. | 4 014 | ./. |
| Palestine | 1996 | (1) | 571 | 3 | 2 | 4 | 522 | 2 | 4 | 18 | - | 7 | 9 |
| **Europe** | | | | | | | | | | | | | |
| Albania | 1980 | | 8 005 | 25 | 27 | - | 1 707 | 1 148 | 1 400 | 946 | 79 | 2 201 | 472 |
| | 1985 | | 5 710 | 21 | 10 | - | 1 524 | 810 | 1 201 | 536 | 271 | 970 | 367 |
| Belarus | 1975 | | 34 366 | 440 | 235 | 86 | 6 801 | 2 511 | 3 668 | 4 722 | 1 471 | 11 846 | 2 586 |
| | 1980 | | 38 271 | 481 | 264 | 18 | 9 393 | 413 | 872 | 5 034 | 789 | 19 941 | 1 066 |
| | 1985 | | 53 269 | 318 | 361 | 79 | 8 071 | 207 | 462 | 9 026 | 1 008 | 32 871 | 866 |
| | 1990 | | 54 911 | 438 | 1 494 | 355 | 9 986 | 960 | 780 | 7 256 | 935 | 32 290 | 417 |
| | 1991 | | 52 911 | 799 | 1 195 | 3 656 | 11 005 | 1 950 | 715 | 7 480 | 666 | 24 023 | 1 422 |
| | 1992 | | 71 940 | 1 055 | 964 | 4 409 | 15 004 | 1 665 | 311 | 8 010 | 417 | 39 599 | 506 |
| | 1993 | | 98 351 | 3 269 | 539 | 13 946 | 17 392 | 1 813 | 294 | 11 082 | 1 086 | 47 782 | 1 148 |
| | 1994 | | 80 606 | 3 438 | 584 | 11 511 | 18 446 | 1 439 | 284 | 8 860 | 301 | 34 849 | 894 |
| | 1995 | | 62 859 | 1 247 | 790 | 8 394 | 20 494 | 890 | 1 275 | 4 117 | 411 | 24 370 | 871 |
| | 1996 | | 59 073 | 3 504 | 650 | 5 449 | 16 086 | 432 | 362 | 5 733 | 313 | 25 824 | 720 |
| Bulgaria | 1975 | | 49 099 | 185 | 516 | 56 | 5 938 | 2 737 | 5 805 | 5 171 | 1 349 | 24 758 | 2 584 |
| | 1980 | | 53 929 | 316 | 565 | 90 | 10 751 | 1 263 | 2 624 | 4 802 | 1 356 | 29 364 | 2 798 |
| | 1985 | | 63 106 | 428 | 504 | 216 | 16 563 | 1 540 | 1 503 | 7 210 | 2 150 | 30 515 | 2 477 |
| | 1990 | | 47 074 | 423 | 408 | 266 | 12 413 | 1 126 | 1 853 | 5 913 | 1 484 | 21 189 | 1 999 |
| | 1991 | | 40 880 | 1 011 | 1 717 | 1 142 | 9 032 | 0.0 | 1 560 | 4 699 | 767 | 19 599 | 1 353 |
| | 1992 | | 53 677 | 1 328 | 1 416 | 1 606 | 10 687 | 10 | 1 287 | 3 813 | 803 | 30 499 | 2 228 |
| | 1993 | | 55 356 | 2 292 | 1 714 | 1 395 | 12 613 | 1 118 | 1 740 | 4 322 | 748 | 27 359 | 2 055 |
| | 1994 | | 42 746 | 2 690 | 1 389 | 692 | 10 312 | 1 008 | 1 252 | 3 578 | 584 | 20 091 | 1 150 |
| | 1995 | | 32 085 | 2 893 | 1 095 | 485 | 10 057 | 1 138 | 1 234 | 1 969 | 568 | 11 693 | 953 |
| | 1996 | | 20 317 | 1 076 | 790 | 450 | 7 316 | 388 | 787 | 1 288 | 216 | 7 258 | 748 |

Number of copies by UDC classes **IV.6**
Nombre d'exemplaires classés d'après la CDU
Número de ejemplares clasificados según la CDU

| Country<br>Pays<br>País | Year<br>Année<br>Año | Total<br>Total<br>Total | Gener-<br>alities<br>Généra-<br>lités<br>Genera-<br>lidades | Philos-<br>ophy<br>Philo-<br>sophie<br>Filo-<br>sofía | Religion<br>Religion<br>Religión | Social<br>sciences<br>Sciences<br>sociales<br>Ciencias<br>sociales | Phil-<br>ology<br>Philo-<br>logie<br>Filo-<br>logía | Pure<br>sciences<br>Sciences<br>pures<br>Ciencias<br>puras | Applied<br>sciences<br>Sciences<br>appl.<br>Ciencias<br>aplicadas | Arts<br>Arts<br>Artes | Litera-<br>ture<br>Litté-<br>rature<br>Litera-<br>tura | Geog./<br>history<br>Géogr./<br>histoire<br>Geogr./<br>historia |
|---|---|---|---|---|---|---|---|---|---|---|---|---|
| Estonia | 1991 | 23 300 | 485 | 2 284 | 912 | 1 473 | 1 685 | 901 | 3 765 | 485 | 10 395 | 915 |
| | 1992 | 15 960 | 402 | 728 | 769 | 1 592 | (8) ./. | 589 | 2 274 | 375 | 8 811 | 420 |
| | 1993 | 12 313 | 186 | 240 | 430 | 937 | (8) ./. | 643 | 1 030 | 668 | 7 433 | 746 |
| | 1994 | 8 592 | 256 | 226 | 260 | 1 274 | (8) ./. | 798 | 772 | 530 | 3 999 | 477 |
| | 1995 | 7 930 | 205 | 256 | 139 | 1 187 | (8) ./. | 757 | 792 | 599 | 3 592 | 403 |
| | 1996 | 6 662 | 198 | 228 | 225 | 1 196 | (8) ./. | 704 | 651 | 458 | 2 776 | 226 |
| Federal Republic of<br>Yugoslavia | 1991 | 16 299 | 311 | 363 | 251 | 9 371 | 6 | 170 | 1 269 | 599 | 3 632 | 327 |
| | 1992 | 11 351 | 61 | 78 | 200 | 7 077 | 3 | 121 | 868 | 798 | 2 031 | 114 |
| | 1994 | 11 905 | 712 | 107 | 92 | 8 392 | 3 | 69 | 610 | 203 | 1 402 | 315 |
| | 1995 | 9 398 | 190 | 50 | 82 | 6 354 | 2 | 177 | 775 | 207 | 1 203 | 358 |
| | 1996 | 16 699 | 324 | 88 | 266 | 12 030 | 6 | 167 | 878 | 327 | 2 013 | 600 |
| Holy See | 1980 | 156 | 10 | 16 | 109 | 11 | 1 | - | 1 | 3 | - | 5 |
| | 1985 | 147 | 4 | 17 | 98 | 18 | 1 | 1 | 3 | 1 | 1 | 3 |
| | 1990 | 110 | - | 11 | 53 | 30 | 3 | - | - | 2 | - | 11 |
| | 1991 | (3) 161 | 4 | 33 | 90 | 19 | 11 | - | - | 1 | - | 3 |
| | 1992 | (2) 153 | 3 | 29 | 85 | 22 | 5 | - | - | - | - | 9 |
| | 1995 | 154 | - | 18 | 107 | 21 | 1 | - | - | 1 | - | 6 |
| | 1996 | 108 | - | 24 | 48 | 24 | 6 | - | - | - | 6 | - |
| Hungary | 1975 | 81 774 | 4 843 | 487 | 644 | 13 725 | 5 776 | 8 836 | 8 705 | 4 399 | 27 247 | 7 112 |
| | 1980 | 104 300 | 5 638 | 772 | 861 | 13 529 | 6 958 | 10 431 | 11 359 | 7 636 | 37 742 | 9 374 |
| | 1985 | 102 644 | 5 071 | 809 | 1 001 | 13 037 | 7 087 | 12 213 | 14 300 | 6 484 | 34 283 | 8 359 |
| | 1990 | 125 741 | 2 847 | 2 803 | 3 190 | 5 659 | 9 093 | 11 103 | 14 668 | 4 196 | 64 700 | 7 482 |
| | 1991 | 99 964 | 3 364 | 2 433 | 4 113 | 4 706 | 8 352 | 8 179 | 12 160 | 3 946 | 45 119 | 7 592 |
| | 1992 | 88 097 | 4 046 | 2 667 | 2 040 | 2 920 | 6 579 | 9 098 | 8 213 | 3 661 | 43 440 | 5 433 |
| | 1993 | 77 157 | 3 180 | 1 624 | 2 201 | 3 112 | 5 047 | 6 214 | 6 768 | 3 062 | 41 328 | 4 622 |
| | 1994 | 75 645 | 2 731 | 1 701 | 2 033 | 3 163 | 4 075 | 7 124 | 7 071 | 3 708 | 39 307 | 4 732 |
| | 1995 | 66 923 | 2 476 | 1 274 | 2 243 | 2 977 | 4 089 | 7 630 | 5 732 | 3 032 | 33 631 | 3 839 |
| | 1996 | 53 194 | 3 215 | 1 218 | 1 389 | 2 466 | 3 775 | 5 879 | 5 458 | 2 174 | 22 533 | 5 087 |
| Italy | 1975 | 144 582 | 6 520 | 4 152 | 5 713 | 24 812 | 5 560 | 7 231 | 13 366 | 8 731 | 55 708 | 12 789 |
| | 1980 | 167 123 | 10 054 | 3 468 | 9 537 | 29 293 | 6 485 | 10 736 | 16 062 | 14 862 | 48 108 | 18 518 |
| | 1985 | 140 773 | 7 098 | 2 861 | 11 601 | 26 492 | 8 166 | 11 441 | 15 496 | 10 866 | 33 023 | 13 729 |
| | 1990 | 220 956 | 9 213 | 5 718 | 13 834 | 40 553 | 9 683 | 10 551 | 22 480 | 15 706 | 72 498 | 20 720 |
| | 1991 | 215 646 | 10 016 | 7 229 | 14 547 | 35 467 | 10 139 | 11 082 | 21 908 | 19 470 | 67 762 | 18 026 |
| | 1992 | 223 655 | 11 425 | 7 645 | 14 725 | 40 797 | 7 943 | 11 005 | 18 479 | 20 205 | 72 992 | 18 439 |
| | 1993 | 251 066 | 16 788 | 10 278 | 12 118 | 37 189 | 8 837 | 11 328 | 20 261 | 17 673 | 98 794 | 17 800 |
| | 1994 | 289 100 | 19 264 | 9 737 | 15 995 | 37 891 | 9 272 | 12 942 | 19 224 | 18 658 | 118 270 | 27 847 |
| | 1995 | 289 242 | 11 237 | 9 375 | 15 289 | 39 827 | 10 402 | 11 841 | 18 742 | 22 005 | 116 860 | 33 664 |
| | 1996 | 278 821 | 8 331 | 11 340 | 16 242 | 39 981 | 8 523 | 10 923 | 20 212 | 26 355 | 108 590 | 28 324 |
| Latvia | 1992 | 21 980 | 576 | 938 | 1 358 | 810 | 375 | 60 | 2 870 | 930 | 8 314 | 576 |
| | 1993 | 14 410 | 397 | 316 | 744 | 965 | 601 | 58 | 1 386 | 339 | 4 757 | 522 |
| | 1994 | 10 835 | 298 | 365 | 395 | 575 | 324 | 64 | 749 | 179 | 3 388 | 190 |
| | 1995 | 9 550 | 254 | 193 | 285 | 1 313 | 230 | 163 | 491 | 167 | 1 945 | 211 |
| | 1996 | 7 734 | 195 | 196 | 232 | 1 231 | 218 | 55 | 506 | 129 | 1 154 | 158 |
| Lithuania | 1992 | 30 954 | 3 015 | 1 041 | 1 812 | 2 385 | 2 660 | 1 498 | 3 328 | 1 353 | 12 504 | 1 358 |
| | 1993 | 19 242 | 1 546 | 517 | 1 171 | 1 129 | 2 354 | 1 502 | 1 636 | 317 | 8 169 | 901 |
| | 1994 | 19 627 | 1 780 | 256 | 1 085 | 1 094 | 2 207 | 1 489 | 2 401 | 452 | 7 886 | 977 |
| | 1995 | 14 114 | 922 | 366 | 945 | 898 | 2 080 | 1 335 | 1 564 | 742 | 4 674 | 588 |
| | 1996 | 14 915 | 1 070 | 206 | 759 | 1 107 | 2 111 | 1 928 | 1 854 | 641 | 3 767 | 1 472 |
| Moldova | 1992 | 363 | 1 | 0.0 | 3 | 244 | 5 | 0.0 | 11 | 1 | 95 | 3 |
| | 1993 | 5 619 | - | 7 | 168 | 320 | 531 | 459 | 278 | 145 | 3 118 | 593 |
| | 1994 | 5 850 | 5 | 337 | 271 | 1 896 | 281 | 130 | 407 | 199 | 2 174 | 150 |
| | 1995 | 30 570 | 593 | 1 041 | 5 801 | 14 427 | 678 | 253 | 1 818 | 364 | 4 982 | 613 |
| | 1996 | 2 779 | 159 | 11 | 156 | 1 726 | 114 | 51 | 117 | 12 | 391 | 42 |
| Monaco | 1980 | 621 | 190 | 14 | 14 | 37 | - | 0.0 | 54 | 259 | 36 | 17 |
| | 1985 | 671 | 149 | 71 | 59 | 2 | - | 12 | 28 | 182 | 102 | 66 |
| | 1990 | 722 | 9 | - | 0.0 | 1 | - | 1 | 9 | 690 | 2 | 10 |
| Poland | 1975 | 143 871 | 597 | 862 | 1 850 | 20 549 | 10 048 | 14 501 | 19 642 | 6 786 | 58 279 | 10 757 |
| | 1980 | 147 138 | 2 458 | 1 212 | 3 014 | 12 956 | 15 582 | 13 014 | 19 781 | 10 378 | 55 509 | 13 140 |
| | 1985 | 246 321 | 1 359 | 2 386 | 8 207 | 23 541 | 16 124 | 19 297 | 33 859 | 12 784 | 106 167 | 22 597 |
| | 1990 | 175 562 | 944 | 2 240 | 8 532 | 10 036 | 17 627 | 16 094 | 19 762 | 8 455 | 68 721 | 23 151 |
| | 1991 | 125 509 | 997 | 2 328 | 5 789 | 8 768 | 14 092 | 11 319 | 13 353 | 6 832 | 52 149 | 9 882 |
| | 1992 | 125 820 | 3 487 | 3 621 | 4 427 | 6 409 | 13 606 | 15 716 | 12 841 | 5 725 | 46 983 | 13 005 |
| | 1993 | 102 533 | 1 299 | 2 075 | 5 197 | 4 686 | 9 740 | 10 547 | 10 667 | 4 455 | 44 474 | 9 393 |
| | 1994 | 98 612 | 3 809 | 1 920 | 3 190 | 4 569 | 7 926 | 11 312 | 11 178 | 5 030 | 40 631 | 9 047 |
| | 1995 | 115 634 | 4 216 | 1 710 | 4 825 | 5 026 | 14 203 | 20 182 | 9 014 | 4 243 | 42 679 | 9 536 |
| | 1996 | 80 306 | 2 158 | 1 319 | 4 238 | 7 638 | 9 474 | 10 429 | 9 557 | 3 415 | 25 345 | 6 733 |
| Portugal | 1975 | 31 139 | 1 236 | 555 | 1 573 | 16 478 | (8) ./. | 1 250 | 1 817 | 1 402 | 5 495 | 1 333 |
| | 1980 | 29 299 | 347 | 367 | 1 081 | 4 469 | (8) ./. | 623 | 7 625 | 7 752 | 5 748 | 1 287 |
| | 1985 | 67 292 | 3 915 | 375 | 1 629 | 4 014 | (8) ./. | 7 770 | 1 979 | 38 923 | 7 112 | 1 575 |
| | 1990 | (6) 24 246 | ./. | 508 | ./. | 13 279 | ./. | ./. | 1 527 | 2 626 | 5 664 | 642 |
| | 1991 | (6) 24 928 | ./. | ./. | ./. | 3 688 | ./. | 986 | ./. | 1 816 | 3 671 | 674 |
| | 1992 | (6) 24 324 | 582 | 1 507 | ./. | ./. | ./. | ./. | 429 | 374 | 2 776 | ./. |
| | 1993 | (6) 21 234 | 1 664 | ./. | ./. | 1 815 | ./. | ./. | 630 | 233 | 2 981 | ./. |
| | 1994 | (6) 26 942 | ./. | ./. | ./. | 2 285 | ./. | 869 | ./. | 369 | 3 407 | ./. |
| Romania | 1975 | 76 486 | 1 320 | 909 | 371 | 10 007 | 7 108 | 10 963 | 10 378 | 3 724 | 28 082 | 3 624 |
| | 1980 | 87 222 | 1 703 | 1 142 | 364 | 13 976 | 6 110 | 13 851 | 10 654 | 5 960 | 27 539 | 5 923 |

IV.6    Number of copies by UDC classes
Nombre d'exemplaires classés d'après la CDU
Número de ejemplares clasificados según la CDU

| Country / Pays / País | Year / Année / Año | | Total / Total / Total | Gener-alities / Généra-lités / Genera-lidades | Philos-ophy / Philo-sophie / Filo-sofía | Religion / Religion / Religión | Social sciences / Sciences sociales / Ciencias sociales | Phil-ology / Philo-logie / Filo-logía | Pure sciences / Sciences pures / Ciencias puras | Applied sciences / Sciences appl. / Ciencias aplicadas | Arts / Arts / Artes | Litera-ture / Litté-rature / Litera-tura | Geog./ history / Géogr./ histoire / Geogr./ historia |
|---|---|---|---|---|---|---|---|---|---|---|---|---|---|
| Romania (cont) | 1985 | | 69 266 | 999 | 1 031 | 276 | 6 457 | 3 616 | 8 664 | 9 452 | 2 518 | 31 079 | 5 174 |
| | 1990 | | 52 477 | 480 | 1 129 | 466 | 3 266 | 6 533 | 9 000 | 4 784 | 2 272 | 20 099 | 4 448 |
| | 1991 | | 57 272 | 707 | 821 | 1 831 | 2 625 | 5 620 | 6 984 | 2 460 | 1 549 | 28 977 | 5 698 |
| | 1992 | | 66 598 | 589 | 1 436 | 1 830 | 3 942 | 6 255 | 8 026 | 2 715 | 1 615 | 36 017 | 4 173 |
| | 1993 | | 75 907 | 949 | 1 767 | 2 513 | 4 327 | 8 276 | 8 574 | 4 600 | 2 183 | 37 558 | 5 160 |
| | 1994 | | 50 230 | 605 | 922 | 1 448 | 3 844 | 4 532 | 6 466 | 2 912 | 872 | 25 222 | 3 407 |
| | 1995 | | 34 914 | 421 | 1 129 | 1 732 | 2 650 | 5 952 | 5 999 | 2 401 | 1 142 | 10 625 | 2 863 |
| | 1996 | | 38 374 | 779 | 1 062 | 3 539 | 4 092 | 6 681 | 5 700 | 2 413 | 1 189 | 10 302 | 2 617 |
| Russian Federation | 1991 | | 1 629 960 | 58 408 | 32 260 | 41 496 | 303 253 | 19 367 | 42 540 | 178 900 | 35 828 | 881 750 | 36 158 |
| | 1992 | | 1 312 964 | 54 293 | 15 430 | 33 917 | 269 561 | 24 734 | 10 116 | 135 927 | 15 364 | 734 212 | 19 410 |
| | 1993 | | 949 861 | 29 447 | 15 632 | 34 372 | 192 883 | 12 123 | 6 074 | 91 870 | 7 171 | 546 658 | 13 631 |
| | 1994 | | 594 323 | 38 626 | 12 446 | 27 946 | 154 489 | 10 986 | 3 870 | 62 534 | 5 491 | 267 464 | 10 471 |
| | 1995 | | 475 039 | 36 181 | 8 352 | 12 350 | 175 517 | 6 976 | 4 226 | 39 653 | 3 281 | 178 526 | 9 977 |
| | 1996 | | 421 387 | 27 427 | 8 091 | 12 307 | 141 978 | 5 487 | 5 365 | 35 111 | 2 588 | 176 599 | 6 434 |
| Slovakia | 1992 | | 13 258 | 624 | 250 | 1 206 | 2 326 | 924 | 879 | 1 703 | 2 956 | 1 704 | 686 |
| | 1993 | | 8 355 | 161 | 215 | 525 | 2 060 | 637 | 1 008 | 2 026 | 496 | 865 | 362 |
| | 1994 | | 6 139 | 64 | 189 | 445 | 1 969 | 290 | 555 | 1 264 | 126 | 734 | 503 |
| Slovenia | 1990 | | 6 267 | 152 | 73 | 216 | 2 297 | (8)   ./. | 420 | 909 | 443 | 1 394 | 306 |
| Spain | 1975 | | 194 270 | 29 492 | 6 206 | 8 128 | 59 630 | 2 163 | 6 451 | 11 001 | 5 270 | 54 023 | 11 906 |
| | 1980 | | 263 229 | 58 127 | 7 194 | 11 590 | 29 132 | 17 979 | 16 709 | 16 973 | 13 511 | 76 871 | 11 916 |
| | 1985 | | 240 236 | 7 522 | 8 635 | 10 622 | 18 079 | 19 283 | 11 505 | 17 922 | 11 245 | 118 010 | 17 413 |
| | 1990 | | 184 949 | 2 839 | 4 067 | 11 441 | 22 568 | 17 567 | 14 528 | 18 680 | 13 278 | 63 766 | 16 215 |
| | 1991 | | 198 093 | 3 867 | 3 507 | 11 620 | 25 332 | 11 798 | 11 811 | 22 177 | 12 496 | 78 723 | 16 762 |
| | 1992 | | 194 785 | 4 846 | 4 335 | 9 698 | 24 787 | 11 428 | 9 798 | 19 002 | 11 372 | 79 848 | 19 671 |
| | 1993 | | 183 229 | 5 301 | 5 078 | 11 759 | 26 611 | 10 620 | 9 035 | 20 508 | 10 199 | 69 374 | 14 744 |
| | 1994 | | 180 181 | 6 273 | 4 566 | 9 232 | 23 315 | 8 832 | 10 941 | 20 341 | 10 210 | 69 626 | 16 845 |
| | 1995 | | 194 646 | 6 401 | 5 159 | 10 378 | 26 415 | 10 478 | 12 293 | 21 449 | 12 195 | 74 637 | 15 241 |
| | 1996 | | 192 019 | 5 213 | 5 345 | 10 179 | 23 313 | 13 150 | 13 850 | 24 522 | 13 592 | 66 239 | 16 616 |
| The Former Yugoslav Rep. of Macedonia | 1990 | | 1 683 | 3 | 6 | 8 | 910 | - | 11 | 48 | 138 | 536 | 23 |
| | 1994 | | 2 918 | 10 | 6 | 40 | 2 515 | 9 | 15 | 21 | 87 | 183 | 32 |
| | 1995 | | 2 832 | 4 | 11 | 40 | 2 120 | 12 | 15 | 50 | 186 | 315 | 79 |
| | 1996 | | 2 496 | 24 | 11 | 46 | 1 925 | 11 | 177 | 27 | 24 | 224 | 27 |
| Ukraine | 1975 | | 155 853 | 699 | 1 843 | 1 087 | 25 104 | 13 565 | 13 364 | 25 703 | 3 724 | 61 016 | 9 748 |
| | 1980 | | 145 094 | 1 841 | 1 055 | 859 | 46 651 | 1 066 | 1 668 | 15 035 | 2 451 | 71 117 | 3 351 |
| | 1985 | (13) | 155 476 | 1 642 | 1 059 | 1 307 | 44 736 | 489 | 1 537 | 14 917 | 2 054 | 81 693 | 2 843 |
| | 1990 | (13) | 170 476 | 995 | 4 776 | 767 | 40 871 | 1 869 | 1 706 | 19 840 | 2 248 | 91 949 | 2 983 |
| | 1991 | | 136 417 | 149 | 1 138 | 3 393 | 33 464 | 2 063 | 1 412 | 16 385 | 1 016 | 73 998 | 3 399 |
| | 1992 | | 128 471 | 233 | 645 | 3 556 | 29 807 | 2 501 | 1 533 | 16 111 | 1 087 | 70 918 | 2 080 |
| | 1993 | | 87 567 | 110 | 578 | 1 353 | 24 896 | 2 308 | 2 065 | 13 391 | 576 | 40 331 | 1 959 |
| | 1994 | | 52 855 | 607 | 670 | 3 731 | 17 080 | 2 072 | 529 | 6 397 | 1 290 | 19 132 | 1 347 |
| | 1995 | | 68 876 | 1 799 | 636 | 3 417 | 35 710 | 2 341 | 990 | 6 948 | 1 061 | 13 932 | 2 042 |
| **Oceania** | | | | | | | | | | | | | |
| Fiji | 1976 | (4) | 220 | - | - | - | 21 | 35 | 112 | 0.0 | 6 | - | - |
| | 1980 | | 273 | 19 | - | - | 7 | 110 | 29 | 55 | 8 | - | 45 |
| | 1994 | (14) | 2 256 | - | - | - | 88 | 325 | 290 | 94 | 2 | - | 148 |

## General note
For general explanations and definitions, please refer to the beginning of this chapter.

## Note générale
Pour les explications et définitions générales, prière de se référer au début de ce chapitre.

## Nota general
Para las explicaciones y definiciones generales, referirse al comienzo de este capítulo.

Notes

(1) First editions only.
(2) Not including pamphlets.
(3) Data refer to school textbooks and government publications only.
(4) Data refer to school textbooks only.
(5) Data refer to school textbooks, government publications and university theses only.
(6) Works indicated by the symbol ./. are distributed without specification among other classes for which a figure is shown.
(7) Not including government publications.

Notes

(1) Premières éditions seulement.
(2) Non compris les brochures.
(3) Les données se réfèrent aux manuels scolaires et aux publications officielles seulement.
(4) Les données se réfèrent aux manuels scolaires seulement.
(5) Les données se réfèrent aux manuels scolaires, aux publications officielles et aux thèses universitaires seulement.
(6) Les ouvrages représentés par le symbole ./. sont distribués sans spécification entre les autres catégories pour lesquelles un chiffre est donné.
(7) Non compris les publications officielles.

Notas

(1) Primeras ediciones solamente.
(2) No se incluyen los folletos.
(3) Los datos se refieren a los libros de texto y a las publicaciones oficiales solamente.
(4) Los datos se refieren a los libros de texto solamente.
(5) Los datos se refieren a los libros de texto, a las publicaciones oficiales y a las tesis universitarias solamente.
(6) Las obras de las categorías indicadas por el símbolo ./. han sido distribuidas sin especificación entre las categorías para las cuales se ha presentado una cifra.
(7) No se incluyen las publicaciones oficiales.

Number of copies by UDC classes **IV.6**
Nombre d'exemplaires classés d'après la CDU
Número de ejemplares clasificados según la CDU

(8) Data on philology are included with those on literature.

(9) Data refer to school textbooks and chidren's books only.

(10) Data refer to school textbooks, chidren's books and government publications only.

(11) Data refer to school textbooks, chidren's books, government publications and university theses only.

(12) The figures do not represent the total book production, but only those actually received in the National Library.

(13) Popularization of science books for children are included in the total but are not distributed.

(14) Data refer only to books published by the Ministry of Education and the Government printing department.

(8) Les données relatives à la philologie sont comprises avec celles de la littérature.

(9) Les données se réfèrent aux manuels scolaires et aux livres pour enfants seulement.

(10) Les données se réfèrent aux manuels scolaires, aux livres pour enfants et aux publications officielles seulement.

(11) Les données se réfèrent aux manuels scolaires, aux livres pour enfants, aux publications officielles et aux thèses universitaires seulement.

(12) Les chiffres ne représentent pas la totalité de l'édition des livres mais seulement le nombre de titres enregistrés à la Bibliothèque Nationale.

(13) Les livres pour enfants destinés à la vulgarisation des sciences sont inclus dans le total mais ne sont pas répartis.

(14) Les données se réfèrent seulement aux livres publiés par le Ministère de l'Education et le département des publications du gouvernement.

(8) Los datos relativos a la filología quedan incluidos con los de la literatura.

(9) Los datos se refieren a los libros de texto y a los libros para niños solamente.

(10) Los datos se refieren a los libros de texto, a los libros para niños y a las publicaciones oficiales solamente.

(11) Los datos se refieren a los libros de texto, a los libros para niños, a las publicaciones oficiales y a las tesis universitarias solamente.

(12) Las cifras no representan la totalidad de la edición de libros sino solamente el número de títulos registrados en la Biblioteca Nacional

(13) Los libros para niños destinados a la vulgarización de las ciencias quedan incluidos en el total pero no están distribuidos.

(14) Los datos se refieren solamente a los libros publicados por el Ministerio de Educación y el departamento de publicaciones del gobierno.

IV.7    Number of titles and copies of school textbooks
Nombre de titres et d'exemplaires de manuels scolaires
Número de títulos y de ejemplares de libros de texto

## IV.7   Book production: number of titles and copies of school textbooks

## Edition de livres: nombre de titres et d'exemplaires de manuels scolaires

## Edición de libros: número de títulos y de ejemplares de libros de texto

‡   Data for years shown with this symbol are all first editions

‡   Toutes les données relatives aux années accompagnées de ce symbole sont des premières éditions

‡   Todos los datos relativos a los años donde figura este símbolo son primeras ediciones

| Country / Pays / País | Year / Année / Año | Number of titles / Nombre de titres / Número de títulos — Books / Livres / Libros | Pamphlets / Brochures / Folletos | Total | Number of copies / Nombre d'exemplaires / Número de ejemplares — Books / Livres / Libros (000) | Pamphlets / Brochures / Folletos (000) | Total (000) |
|---|---|---|---|---|---|---|---|
| **Africa** | | | | | | | |
| Algeria | ‡ 1979 | 18 | 1 | 19 | ... | ... | ... |
| | 1984 | 39 | - | 39 | ... | - | ... |
| | 1991 | 1 | - | 1 | ... | - | ... |
| | 1992 | 15 | - | 15 | ... | - | ... |
| | 1996 | 12 | ... | ... | ... | ... | ... |
| Benin | ‡ 1992 | 6 | ... | ... | 9 | ... | ... |
| Botswana | ‡ 1991 | 4 | - | 4 | ... | - | ... |
| Democratic Rep. of the Congo | ‡ 1979 | 5 | - | 5 | ... | - | ... |
| | ‡ 1992 | 14 | - | 14 | 112 | - | 112 |
| Egypt | 1985 | 329 | 13 | 342 | 30 716 | 571 | 31 287 |
| | 1990 | 378 | 31 | 409 | 29 186 | 2 346 | 31 532 |
| | 1991 | 646 | 67 | 713 | 50 283 | 8 650 | 58 933 |
| | 1993 | 735 | 74 | 809 | 41 149 | 8 112 | 49 261 |
| | 1995 | 701 | 213 | 914 | 60 752 | 15 030 | 75 782 |
| Eritrea | 1993 | 64 | - | 64 | 323 | - | 323 |
| Ethiopia | 1985 | 60 | - | 60 | 180 | - | 180 |
| | 1990 | 42 | - | 42 | ... | - | ... |
| | 1991 | 23 | - | 23 | 69 | - | 69 |
| Gambia | 1994 | 2 | - | 2 | 6 | - | 6 |
| | 1996 | 11 | - | 11 | 8 | - | 8 |
| Ghana | ‡ 1980 | 10 | 3 | 13 | ... | ... | ... |
| Kenya | 1980 | 39 | - | 39 | ... | - | ... |
| | ‡ 1994 | 128 | ... | ... | ... | ... | ... |
| Madagascar | 1980 | 90 | 18 | 108 | 213 | 24 | 237 |
| | 1984 | 44 | 9 | 53 | 100 | 35 | 135 |
| | 1990 | 22 | 19 | 41 | 77 | 253 | 330 |
| | 1991 | 2 | - | 2 | 8 | - | 8 |
| | ‡ 1992 | 1 | - | 1 | 3 | - | 3 |
| | ‡ 1993 | 31 | 4 | 35 | 62 | 5 | 67 |
| | ‡ 1994 | 14 | 3 | 17 | 56 | 4 | 60 |
| | ‡ 1995 | 2 | 4 | 6 | 28 | 3 | 31 |
| | ‡ 1996 | 3 | 3 | 6 | 10 | 20 | 30 |
| Malawi | 1984 | 38 | - | 38 | 1 160 | - | 1 160 |
| | 1989 | 5 | 1 | 6 | ... | ... | ... |
| | 1992 | 20 | 18 | 38 | ... | ... | ... |
| | 1993 | 10 | 6 | 16 | ... | ... | ... |
| | 1994 | 8 | 12 | 20 | ... | ... | ... |
| | 1995 | 10 | 7 | 17 | ... | ... | ... |
| | ‡ 1996 | 43 | 74 | 117 | 9 171 | 0.0 | 9 171 |
| Mali | 1984 | - | 76 | 76 | - | 56 | 56 |
| Mauritius | ‡ 1980 | 15 | 3 | 18 | 268 | 4 | 272 |
| | 1985 | 23 | 5 | 28 | 153 | 29 | 182 |
| | 1990 | 5 | 1 | 6 | 17 | 37 | 54 |
| | ‡ 1991 | 2 | - | 2 | 7 | - | 7 |

Number of titles and copies of school textbooks IV.7
Nombre de titres et d'exemplaires de manuels scolaires
Número de títulos y de ejemplares de libros de texto

| Country / Pays / País | Year / Année / Año | Number of titles / Nombre de titres / Número de títulos | | | Number of copies / Nombre d'exemplaires / Número de ejemplares | | |
|---|---|---|---|---|---|---|---|
| | | Books Livres Libros | Pamphlets Brochures Folletos | Total | Books Livres Libros (000) | Pamphlets Brochures Folletos (000) | Total (000) |
| Mauritius (cont) | 1992 | 19 | 3 | 22 | 58 | 2 | 60 |
| | 1993 | 38 | 10 | 48 | 54 | 10 | 64 |
| | 1994 | 14 | 1 | 15 | 16 | 1 | 17 |
| | ‡ 1995 | 12 | 1 | 13 | 23 | 2 | 25 |
| | ‡ 1996 | 12 | - | 12 | 26 | - | 26 |
| Morocco | 1994 | ... | ... | 23 | ... | ... | 96 |
| | 1996 | 54 | 30 | 84 | 324 | 120 | 444 |
| Namibia | 1990 | 10 | - | 10 | ... | - | ... |
| Niger | 1979 | 13 | 5 | 18 | 10.4 | 2.8 | 13.2 |
| Nigeria | 1985 | 453 | 127 | 580 | ... | ... | ... |
| | 1989 | 800 | 460 | 1 260 | ... | ... | ... |
| | 1991 | 846 | - | 846 | ... | ... | ... |
| | 1992 | 340 | 67 | 407 | ... | ... | ... |
| | 1994 | ... | ... | 769 | ... | ... | ... |
| | ‡ 1995 | 166 | 30 | 196 | ... | ... | ... |
| Reunion | ‡ 1985 | - | 3 | 3 | - | ... | ... |
| | ‡ 1992 | 1 | - | 1 | ... | ... | ... |
| South Africa | 1990 | 254 | 91 | 345 | 9 646 | 522 | 10 168 |
| | 1991 | 274 | 25 | 299 | 11 797 | 400 | 12 197 |
| | 1992 | 302 | 11 | 313 | 16 714 | 908 | 17 622 |
| | 1993 | 254 | 47 | 301 | 13 234 | 1 177 | 14 411 |
| | 1994 | 215 | 57 | 272 | 16 087 | 210 | 16 297 |
| | 1995 | 237 | 48 | 285 | 11 328 | 330 | 11 658 |
| Tunisia | 1981 | 172 | - | 172 | 6 000 | - | 6 000 |
| | 1985 | 38 | 4 | 42 | ... | ... | ... |
| | 1992 | 288 | ... | ... | 30 990 | ... | ... |
| | 1994 | 49 | ... | ... | ... | ... | ... |
| | 1995 | 98 | ... | ... | ... | ... | ... |
| | 1996 | 76 | - | 76 | ... | - | ... |
| Uganda | 1993 | 94 | ... | ... | 720 | ... | ... |
| | 1996 | 99 | ... | ... | ... | ... | ... |
| United Republic of Tanzania | 1980 | 48 | 10 | 58 | ... | ... | ... |
| | ‡ 1984 | 12 | 3 | 15 | ... | ... | ... |
| | ‡ 1990 | 23 | 20 | 43 | 46 | 40 | 86 |
| Zimbabwe | ‡ 1980 | 42 | 7 | 49 | ... | ... | ... |
| | 1985 | 119 | 106 | 225 | ... | ... | ... |
| | ‡ 1990 | 17 | 14 | 31 | ... | ... | ... |
| | ‡ 1992 | 6 | 2 | 8 | ... | ... | ... |
| **North America** | | | | | | | |
| Canada | 1980 | 496 | - | 496 | ... | - | ... |
| | 1993 | ... | ... | 1 240 | ... | ... | ... |
| | ‡ 1994 | ... | ... | 1 235 | ... | ... | ... |
| | 1995 | ... | ... | 1 111 | ... | ... | ... |
| **South America** | | | | | | | |
| Argentina | 1980 | ... | ... | 406 | ... | ... | 4 113 |
| | 1992 | 736 | - | 736 | 4 720 | - | 4 720 |
| | 1995 | 530 | ... | ... | 7 701 | ... | ... |
| | 1996 | 412 | ... | ... | 3 126 | ... | ... |
| Brazil | 1992 | 2 754 | ... | ... | 73 857 | ... | ... |
| | 1993 | 4 151 | ... | ... | 45 380 | ... | ... |
| | 1994 | 5 454 | ... | ... | 82 222 | ... | ... |
| Colombia | 1980 | 527 | - | 527 | 6 800 | - | 6 800 |
| | 1984 | 2 570 | ... | ... | 25 750 | ... | ... |
| | 1991 | 44 | ... | ... | 700 | ... | ... |
| Ecuador | ‡ 1995 | 1 | - | 1 | 2 | - | 2 |
| Guyana | ‡ 1994 | 32 | - | 32 | 468 | - | 468 |
| | ‡ 1996 | 1 | - | 1 | ... | - | ... |
| Paraguay | 1993 | 25 | - | 25 | ... | ... | ... |
| Peru | ‡ 1980 | 16 | 3 | 19 | ... | ... | ... |
| | 1985 | 16 | - | 16 | ... | ... | ... |
| | 1990 | 31 | 9 | 40 | ... | ... | ... |
| | 1991 | 36 | 12 | 48 | ... | ... | ... |
| | 1992 | 13 | ... | ... | ... | ... | ... |
| | 1993 | 14 | 4 | 18 | ... | ... | ... |

Number of titles and copies of school textbooks
Nombre de titres et d'exemplaires de manuels scolaires
Número de títulos y de ejemplares de libros de texto

| Country<br>Pays<br>País | Year<br>Année<br>Año | Number of titles<br>Nombre de titres<br>Número de títulos | | | Number of copies<br>Nombre d'exemplaires<br>Número de ejemplares | | |
|---|---|---|---|---|---|---|---|
| | | Books<br>Livres<br>Libros | Pamphlets<br>Brochures<br>Folletos | Total | Books<br>Livres<br>Libros<br>(000) | Pamphlets<br>Brochures<br>Folletos<br>(000) | Total<br>(000) |
| Peru (cont) | ‡ 1994 | 34 | 5 | 39 | ... | ... | ... |
| | 1995 | 110 | 27 | 137 | ... | ... | ... |
| Uruguay | 1980 | 135 | 42 | 177 | ... | ... | ... |
| | 1985 | 62 | 11 | 73 | ... | ... | ... |
| | 1991 | 48 | 3 | 51 | 110 | 4 | 114 |
| | 1996 | 51 | 15 | 66 | ... | ... | ... |
| Venezuela | ‡ 1996 | 125 | - | 125 | ... | - | ... |
| **Asia** | | | | | | | |
| Afghanistan | 1980 | 63 | - | 63 | 3 016 | - | 3 016 |
| | 1990 | 150 | - | 150 | ... | | ... |
| Armenia | ‡ 1994 | 21 | - | 21 | 902 | - | 902 |
| | ‡ 1996 | 52 | - | 52 | 13 355 | - | 13 355 |
| Azerbaijan | 1992 | 29 | 1 | 30 | 2 276 | 98 | 2 374 |
| | 1994 | 41 | 1 | 42 | 2 807 | 150 | 2 957 |
| | 1995 | 21 | - | 21 | 2 100 | - | 2 100 |
| | 1996 | 52 | 4 | 56 | 1 735 | 68 | 1 803 |
| Brunei Darussalam | 1980 | 16 | - | 16 | 95 | - | 95 |
| | 1990 | 6 | ... | ... | 22 | ... | ... |
| China | 1980 | ... | ... | 3 440 | ... | ... | 1 895 150 |
| | 1985 | ... | ... | 6 159 | ... | ... | 2 488 460 |
| | 1990 | 11 107 | ... | ... | 2 657 140 | ... | ... |
| Cyprus | 1985 | 71 | 10 | 81 | 597 | 6 | 603 |
| | 1990 | 59 | 55 | 114 | 293 | 180 | 473 |
| | 1991 | 67 | 52 | 119 | 353 | 168 | 521 |
| | 1992 | 54 | 47 | 101 | 282 | 144 | 426 |
| | 1993 | 48 | 61 | 109 | 256 | 176 | 432 |
| | 1994 | 52 | 47 | 99 | 272 | 142 | 414 |
| | 1995 | 67 | 53 | 120 | 296 | 161 | 457 |
| | 1996 | 71 | 68 | 139 | 305 | 184 | 489 |
| Georgia | ‡ 1994 | 2 | - | 2 | 5 | - | 5 |
| | 1995 | 31 | - | 31 | 740 | - | 740 |
| | ‡ 1996 | 29 | - | 29 | 129 | - | 129 |
| India | ‡ 1980 | 567 | - | 567 | ... | - | ... |
| | 1985 | 581 | ... | ... | ... | ... | ... |
| | 1990 | 210 | 2 | 212 | ... | ... | ... |
| | 1991 | 269 | 3 | 272 | ... | ... | ... |
| | 1992 | 260 | | 260 | ... | ... | ... |
| | 1993 | ... | ... | 311 | ... | ... | ... |
| | 1994 | 191 | - | 191 | ... | - | ... |
| | 1995 | 193 | - | 193 | ... | - | ... |
| | 1996 | 187 | | 187 | ... | | ... |
| Indonesia | 1980 | 399 | 29 | 428 | ... | ... | ... |
| | ‡ 1992 | 715 | - | 715 | ... | - | ... |
| | 1996 | 731 | - | 731 | 2 296 | - | 2 296 |
| Israel | 1979 | 342 | 48 | 390 | ... | ... | 3 722 |
| | 1985 | ... | ... | 291 | ... | ... | 3 961 |
| | 1992 | ... | ... | 349 | ... | ... | 3 731 |
| Japan | 1981 | 1 778 | ... | ... | 231 585 | ... | ... |
| | 1985 | 1 589 | ... | ... | 219 169 | ... | ... |
| | ‡ 1992 | 2 512 | ... | ... | 12 190 | ... | ... |
| | ‡ 1996 | 3 401 | ... | ... | 11 999 | ... | ... |
| Kazakstan | 1996 | 164 | 20 | 184 | 15 259 | 2 526 | 17 785 |
| Korea, Republic of | 1980 | 2 598 | 243 | 2 841 | 33 902 | 2 063 | 35 965 |
| | 1985 | 3 396 | 88 | 3 484 | 50 293 | 368 | 50 661 |
| | 1990 | 3 878 | 837 | 4 715 | 106 698 | 5 965 | 112 663 |
| | 1991 | 3 840 | 713 | 4 553 | 87 990 | 5 823 | 93 813 |
| | 1992 | 3 008 | 563 | 3 571 | 93 391 | 6 588 | 99 979 |
| | 1993 | 3 139 | 696 | 3 835 | 74 141 | 15 079 | 89 220 |
| | 1994 | 3 568 | 902 | 4 470 | 72 488 | 6 864 | 79 352 |
| | 1995 | 4 106 | 1 078 | 5 184 | 77 329 | 9 308 | 86 637 |
| | ‡ 1996 | 3 908 | ... | ... | 68 831 | ... | ... |
| Kyrgyzstan | 1994 | 11 | 2 | 13 | 379 | 151 | 530 |
| | 1995 | 23 | 3 | 26 | 665 | 84 | 749 |
| | 1996 | 41 | 8 | 49 | 981 | 144 | 1 125 |
| Lao People's | ‡ 1990 | 9 | - | 9 | 180 | - | 180 |
| Democratic Republic | ‡ 1991 | 25 | - | 25 | 50 | - | 50 |
| | ‡ 1995 | 9 | - | 9 | 747 | - | 747 |

Number of titles and copies of school textbooks IV.7
Nombre de titres et d'exemplaires de manuels scolaires
Número de títulos y de ejemplares de libros de texto

| Country Pays País | Year Année Año | Number of titles Nombre de titres Número de títulos | | | Number of copies Nombre d'exemplaires Número de ejemplares | | |
|---|---|---|---|---|---|---|---|
| | | Books Livres Libros | Pamphlets Brochures Folletos | Total | Books Livres Libros (000) | Pamphlets Brochures Folletos (000) | Total (000) |
| Macau | ‡ 1996 | 10 | - | 10 | 9 | - | 9 |
| Malaysia | 1980 | 346 | 47 | 393 | 2 352 | 131 | 2 483 |
| | 1985 | 389 | 16 | 405 | 1 945 | 112 | 2 057 |
| | 1990 | 1 409 | 4 | 1 413 | 14 250 | 30 | 14 280 |
| | 1991 | 772 | | 772 | 6 029 | | 6 029 |
| | 1993 | 865 | - | 865 | 6 552 | - | 6 552 |
| | 1994 | 1 023 | | 1 023 | 7 799 | | 7 799 |
| | 1995 | 918 | - | 918 | 7 620 | - | 7 620 |
| | 1996 | 1 822 | - | 1 822 | ... | | ... |
| Mongolia | ‡ 1992 | 37 | - | 37 | 370 | - | 370 |
| Philippines | 1980 | 95 | | 95 | ... | - | ... |
| | 1984 | 175 | 10 | 185 | 14 464 | 0.0 | 14 464 |
| | 1990 | 142 | ... | 142 | ... | ... | ... |
| | 1991 | 323 | 13 | 336 | ... | ... | ... |
| | 1992 | 203 | - | 203 | ... | 0.0 | ... |
| | 1994 | 207 | | ... | ... | | ... |
| | 1995 | 184 | ... | ... | ... | ... | ... |
| | 1996 | 250 | ... | ... | ... | ... | ... |
| Qatar | 1980 | 219 | - | 219 | 1 533 | - | 1 533 |
| | 1990 | 334 | 52 | 386 | ... | ... | ... |
| | 1992 | 200 | ... | ... | ... | - | ... |
| | 1993 | 184 | - | 184 | ... | - | ... |
| | 1994 | 228 | | ... | ... | | ... |
| | 1995 | 259 | ... | ... | ... | ... | ... |
| | 1996 | 100 | ... | ... | ... | ... | ... |
| Saudi Arabia | 1975 | 125 | - | 125 | 14493 | - | 14493 |
| | ‡ 1996 | ... | ... | 140 | ... | ... | ... |
| Sri Lanka | 1980 | 30 | 14 | 44 | 1 306 | 617 | 1 923 |
| | 1985 | 71 | 14 | 85 | 3 006 | 613 | 3 619 |
| | 1990 | 138 | 35 | 173 | 9 674 | 1 819 | 11 493 |
| | 1991 | 128 | 4 | 132 | 12 365 | 76 | 12 441 |
| | 1992 | 85 | 5 | 90 | 7 718 | 560 | 8 278 |
| | 1993 | 93 | 1 | 94 | 8 502 | 100 | 8 602 |
| | 1994 | 9 | 5 | 14 | 7 695 | 1 280 | 8 975 |
| | 1995 | 81 | 9 | 90 | 8 466 | 945 | 9 411 |
| | 1996 | 94 | - | 94 | ... | - | ... |
| Tajikistan | 1994 | 21 | - | 21 | 1 210 | - | 1 210 |
| | 1995 | 20 | - | 20 | 1 451 | - | 1 451 |
| | ‡ 1996 | 2 | - | 2 | 2 | - | 2 |
| Thailand | 1980 | 280 | 22 | 302 | ... | ... | ... |
| | 1985 | 560 | - | 560 | ... | ... | ... |
| | 1990 | 579 | - | 579 | ... | | ... |
| | 1991 | 604 | - | 604 | ... | | ... |
| | 1992 | 640 | - | 640 | ... | | ... |
| | 1996 | 690 | - | 690 | ... | | ... |
| Turkey | 1980 | 159 | 7 | 166 | ... | ... | ... |
| | 1985 | 212 | - | 212 | ... | ... | ... |
| | 1990 | ... | ... | 220 | ... | ... | ... |
| | 1991 | 173 | 5 | 178 | ... | ... | ... |
| | 1992 | 503 | - | 503 | ... | | ... |
| | 1993 | 603 | - | 603 | ... | | ... |
| | 1994 | ... | ... | 355 | ... | | ... |
| | 1995 | 238 | - | 238 | ... | | ... |
| | 1996 | 530 | - | 530 | ... | | ... |
| Turkmenistan | 1992 | 27 | 1 | 28 | 1 678 | 85 | 1 763 |
| | ‡ 1994 | 29 | - | 29 | 2 103 | - | 2 103 |
| United Arab Emirates | 1990 | 281 | - | 281 | 4 423 | - | 4 423 |
| | 1992 | 270 | - | 270 | 5 490 | - | 5 490 |
| | 1993 | 293 | - | 293 | 5 117 | - | 5 117 |
| Uzbekistan | 1992 | ... | ... | 196 | ... | ... | 18 090 |
| | 1993 | | | 194 | | | 20 069 |
| | 1995 | 145 | 14 | 159 | 25 197 | 2 350 | 27 547 |
| | 1996 | 123 | 6 | 129 | 20 972 | 97 | 21 069 |
| Viet Nam | 1981 | ... | ... | 300 | ... | ... | 4 037 |
| | 1986 | ... | ... | 421 | ... | ... | 30 462 |
| | 1990 | ... | ... | 778 | ... | ... | 28 273 |
| | 1991 | ... | ... | 778 | ... | ... | 53 385 |
| | 1992 | ... | ... | 792 | ... | ... | 61 951 |
| | 1993 | ... | ... | 1 370 | ... | ... | 66 049 |

Number of titles and copies of school textbooks
Nombre de titres et d'exemplaires de manuels scolaires
Número de títulos y de ejemplares de libros de texto

| Country | Year | Number of titles Nombre de titres Número de títulos | | | Number of copies Nombre d'exemplaires Número de ejemplares | | |
|---|---|---|---|---|---|---|---|
| Pays | Année | Books Livres | Pamphlets Brochures | Total | Books Livres | Pamphlets Brochures | Total |
| País | Año | Libros | Folletos | | Libros (000) | Folletos (000) | (000) |
| **Europe** | | | | | | | |
| Albania | 1980 | 372 | 4 | 376 | 4 060 | 57 | 4 117 |
| | 1985 | 555 | 7 | 562 | 3 456 | 7 | 3 463 |
| | 1991 | 190 | 5 | 195 | 3 110 | 151 | 3 261 |
| Andorra | 1991 | 4 | ... | ... | ... | ... | ... |
| | 1992 | 5 | - | 5 | ... | - | ... |
| Austria | 1980 | 184 | 13 | 197 | ... | ... | ... |
| | 1985 | 637 | 31 | 668 | ... | ... | ... |
| Belarus | 1980 | 80 | 1 | 81 | 3 825 | 61 | 3 886 |
| | 1985 | 73 | 4 | 77 | 2 733 | 175 | 2 908 |
| | 1990 | 65 | 14 | 79 | 3 772 | 1 299 | 5 071 |
| | 1991 | 71 | 18 | 89 | 5 031 | 2 338 | 7 369 |
| | 1992 | 101 | 33 | 134 | 7 698 | 3 546 | 11 244 |
| | 1993 | 132 | 38 | 170 | 11 112 | 3 073 | 14 185 |
| | 1994 | 123 | 49 | 172 | 9 329 | 5 632 | 14 961 |
| | 1995 | 139 | 44 | 183 | 12 947 | 4 725 | 17 672 |
| | 1996 | 172 | 40 | 212 | 11 033 | 1 712 | 12 745 |
| Bulgaria | 1980 | 922 | 37 | 959 | 10 766 | 36 | 10 802 |
| | 1985 | 1 026 | 72 | 1 098 | 12 145 | 378 | 12 523 |
| | 1990 | 890 | 35 | 925 | 10 617 | 829 | 11 446 |
| | 1991 | 773 | 62 | 835 | 8 350 | 393 | 8 743 |
| | 1992 | 990 | 47 | 1 037 | 11 766 | 434 | 12 200 |
| | 1993 | 1 022 | 67 | 1 089 | 13 175 | 1 236 | 14 411 |
| | 1994 | 1 052 | 72 | 1 124 | 9 057 | 2 224 | 11 281 |
| | 1995 | 1 006 | 61 | 1 067 | 9 441 | 1 673 | 11 114 |
| | 1996 | 876 | 37 | 913 | 6 587 | 866 | 7 453 |
| Croatia | 1993 | 149 | 36 | 185 | 951 | 195 | 1 146 |
| | 1994 | 208 | 66 | 274 | ... | ... | ... |
| | 1995 | 261 | 77 | 338 | ... | ... | ... |
| | 1996 | 152 | 28 | 180 | ... | ... | ... |
| Czech Republic | 1992 | 269 | 62 | 331 | ... | ... | ... |
| | 1993 | 319 | 96 | 415 | ... | ... | ... |
| | 1994 | 337 | 74 | 411 | ... | ... | ... |
| | 1995 | 177 | 27 | 204 | ... | ... | ... |
| | 1996 | 391 | 79 | 470 | ... | ... | ... |
| Denmark | 1980 | ... | ... | 1 009 | ... | ... | ... |
| | 1985 | ... | ... | 846 | ... | ... | ... |
| | 1990 | ... | ... | 817 | ... | ... | ... |
| | 1991 | ... | ... | 721 | ... | ... | ... |
| | 1992 | ... | ... | 869 | ... | ... | ... |
| | 1993 | ... | ... | 789 | ... | ... | ... |
| | 1994 | ... | ... | 844 | ... | ... | ... |
| | 1995 | ... | ... | 773 | ... | ... | ... |
| | 1996 | ... | ... | 783 | ... | ... | ... |
| Estonia | 1991 | ... | ... | 98 | ... | ... | 1 846 |
| | 1992 | 75 | 18 | 93 | 996 | 197 | 1 193 |
| | 1993 | 112 | 39 | 151 | 1 385 | 332 | 1 717 |
| | 1994 | 167 | 59 | 226 | 1 655 | 500 | 2 155 |
| | 1995 | 170 | 66 | 236 | 1 498 | 483 | 1 981 |
| | 1996 | 162 | 68 | 230 | 1 298 | 481 | 1 779 |
| Federal Republic of Yugoslavia | 1991 | 877 | 82 | 959 | 8 635 | 103 | 8 738 |
| | 1992 | 334 | 23 | 357 | 6 274 | 161 | 6 435 |
| | 1994 | 577 | 32 | 609 | 7 777 | 160 | 7 937 |
| | 1995 | 827 | 45 | 872 | 5 959 | 120 | 6 079 |
| | 1996 | 1 090 | 82 | 1 172 | 11 206 | 329 | 11 535 |
| Finland | 1980 | 456 | 75 | 531 | ... | ... | ... |
| | 1985 | 635 | 57 | 692 | ... | ... | ... |
| | 1990 | 558 | 57 | 615 | ... | ... | ... |
| | 1991 | 541 | 49 | 590 | ... | ... | ... |
| | 1992 | 462 | 36 | 498 | ... | ... | ... |
| | 1993 | 365 | 34 | 399 | ... | ... | ... |
| | 1994 | 461 | 33 | 494 | ... | ... | ... |
| | 1995 | 508 | 44 | 552 | ... | ... | ... |
| | 1996 | 450 | 62 | 512 | ... | ... | ... |
| France | 1990 | ... | ... | 1 076 | ... | ... | ... |
| | 1991 | ... | ... | 1 100 | ... | ... | ... |
| | 1992 | ... | ... | 971 | ... | ... | ... |
| | 1993 | ... | ... | 1 041 | ... | ... | ... |
| | 1994 | ... | ... | 891 | ... | ... | ... |
| | 1995 | ... | ... | 767 | ... | ... | ... |
| Germany | 1991 | ... | ... | 3 084 | ... | ... | ... |
| | 1992 | ... | ... | 3 351 | ... | ... | ... |

Number of titles and copies of school textbooks
Nombre de titres et d'exemplaires de manuels scolaires
Número de títulos y de ejemplares de libros de texto

IV.7

| Country Pays País | Year Année Año | Number of titles Nombre de titres Número de títulos | | | Number of copies Nombre d'exemplaires Número de ejemplares | | |
|---|---|---|---|---|---|---|---|
| | | Books Livres Libros | Pamphlets Brochures Folletos | Total | Books Livres Libros (000) | Pamphlets Brochures Folletos (000) | Total (000) |
| Germany (cont) | 1993 | ... | ... | 3 311 | ... | ... | ... |
| | 1994 | ... | ... | 3 551 | ... | ... | ... |
| | 1995 | ... | ... | 3 410 | ... | ... | ... |
| | 1996 | ... | ... | 3 436 | ... | ... | ... |
| Greece | 1980 | 114 | 14 | 128 | ... | ... | ... |
| Hungary | 1980 | 787 | 72 | 859 | 21 708 | 4 275 | 25 983 |
| | 1985 | 1 064 | 61 | 1 125 | 26 208 | 3 032 | 29 240 |
| | 1990 | 1 052 | 51 | 1 103 | 20 403 | 1 511 | 21 914 |
| | 1991 | 1 088 | 47 | 1 135 | 20 883 | 1 541 | 22 424 |
| | 1992 | 1 187 | 40 | 1 227 | 24 309 | 260 | 24 569 |
| | 1993 | 1 302 | 49 | 1 351 | 17 966 | 487 | 18 453 |
| | 1994 | 1 588 | 62 | 1 650 | 18 189 | 707 | 18 896 |
| | 1995 | 1 272 | 30 | 1 302 | 17 893 | 459 | 18 352 |
| | 1996 | 1 382 | 11 | 1 393 | 16 273 | 48 | 16 321 |
| Iceland | 1990 | 194 | 126 | 320 | ... | ... | ... |
| | 1991 | 141 | 114 | 255 | ... | ... | ... |
| | 1992 | 181 | 133 | 314 | ... | ... | ... |
| | 1993 | 133 | 68 | 201 | ... | ... | ... |
| | 1994 | 156 | 120 | 276 | ... | ... | ... |
| | 1995 | 98 | 115 | 213 | ... | ... | ... |
| | 1996 | 124 | 118 | 242 | ... | ... | ... |
| Italy | 1980 | 1 032 | 52 | 1 084 | 51 224 | 1 240 | 52 464 |
| | 1985 | 1 168 | 35 | 1 203 | 45 485 | 275 | 45 760 |
| | 1990 | 1 658 | 40 | 1 698 | 55 193 | 680 | 55 873 |
| | 1991 | 1 745 | 78 | 1 823 | 49 173 | 952 | 50 125 |
| | 1992 | 1 912 | 125 | 2 037 | 50 373 | 946 | 51 319 |
| | 1993 | 1 963 | 168 | 2 131 | 45 000 | 1 607 | 46 607 |
| | 1994 | 1 967 | 198 | 2 165 | 44 671 | 1 768 | 46 439 |
| | 1995 | 2 382 | 232 | 2 614 | 50 343 | 2 384 | 52 727 |
| | 1996 | 2 179 | 194 | 2 373 | 46 385 | 1 669 | 48 054 |
| Latvia | 1992 | 77 | 41 | 118 | 1 006 | 1 030 | 2 036 |
| | 1993 | 112 | 49 | 161 | 1 346 | 854 | 2 200 |
| | 1994 | 168 | 34 | 202 | 1 819 | 495 | 2 314 |
| | 1995 | 216 | 65 | 281 | 1 810 | 837 | 2 647 |
| | 1996 | 214 | 51 | 265 | 1 868 | 594 | 2 462 |
| Lithuania | 1992 | 146 | 20 | 166 | 3 743 | 591 | 4 334 |
| | 1993 | 152 | 25 | 177 | 3 285 | 704 | 3 989 |
| | 1994 | 136 | 42 | 178 | 3 142 | 1 208 | 4 350 |
| | 1995 | 163 | 39 | 202 | 3 319 | 818 | 4 137 |
| | 1996 | 219 | 87 | 306 | 3 667 | 1 704 | 5 371 |
| Luxembourg | ‡ 1980 | 20 | 14 | 34 | ... | ... | ... |
| | 1991 | 19 | 1 | 20 | ... | ... | ... |
| | 1992 | 21 | 3 | 24 | ... | ... | ... |
| | 1993 | 38 | - | 38 | ... | ... | ... |
| | ‡ 1994 | 7 | 4 | 11 | ... | - | ... |
| Malta | ‡ 1985 | 14 | 8 | 22 | ... | ... | ... |
| | ‡ 1990 | 11 | - | 11 | ... | ... | ... |
| | ‡ 1992 | 10 | 5 | 15 | ... | ... | ... |
| | ‡ 1993 | 14 | 9 | 23 | ... | ... | ... |
| | ‡ 1995 | 14 | 13 | 27 | ... | ... | ... |
| Moldova | 1992 | 66 | - | 66 | 20 | - | 20 |
| | 1993 | 17 | - | 17 | 1 004 | - | 1 004 |
| | 1994 | 43 | - | 43 | 866 | - | 866 |
| | 1995 | 48 | - | 48 | 8 880 | - | 8 880 |
| | ‡ 1996 | 17 | - | 17 | 457 | - | 457 |
| Netherlands | 1980 | 3 032 | ... | ... | ... | ... | ... |
| | 1985 | 2 055 | ... | ... | ... | ... | ... |
| | 1990 | 2 119 | ... | ... | ... | ... | ... |
| | 1991 | 2 268 | ... | ... | ... | ... | ... |
| | 1992 | 2 196 | ... | ... | ... | ... | ... |
| | 1993 | 11 002 | ... | ... | ... | ... | ... |
| Poland | 1980 | 559 | 26 | 585 | 34 287 | 3 292 | 37 579 |
| | 1985 | 373 | 18 | 391 | 40 703 | 5 047 | 45 750 |
| | 1990 | 372 | 12 | 384 | 36 791 | 1 869 | 38 660 |
| | 1991 | 313 | 28 | 341 | 22 288 | 1 342 | 23 630 |
| | 1992 | 501 | 65 | 566 | 34 362 | 4 097 | 38 459 |
| | 1993 | 424 | 15 | 439 | 26 180 | 229 | 26 409 |
| | 1994 | 535 | 39 | 574 | 26 823 | 878 | 27 701 |
| | 1995 | 872 | 119 | 991 | 37 677 | 6 334 | 44 011 |
| | 1996 | 803 | 90 | 893 | 24 264 | 2 203 | 26 467 |
| Portugal | 1980 | ... | ... | 531 | ... | ... | 10 049 |
| | 1985 | ... | ... | 698 | ... | ... | 6 869 |
| | 1990 | ... | ... | 658 | ... | ... | 9 862 |
| | 1991 | ... | ... | 1 545 | ... | ... | 11 458 |
| | 1992 | ... | ... | 1 606 | ... | ... | 10 888 |

**IV.7**  Number of titles and copies of school textbooks
Nombre de titres et d'exemplaires de manuels scolaires
Número de títulos y de ejemplares de libros de texto

| Country<br>Pays<br>País | Year<br>Année<br>Año | Number of titles<br>Nombre de titres<br>Número de títulos | | | Number of copies<br>Nombre d'exemplaires<br>Número de ejemplares | | |
|---|---|---|---|---|---|---|---|
| | | Books<br>Livres<br>Libros | Pamphlets<br>Brochures<br>Folletos | Total | Books<br>Livres<br>Libros<br>(000) | Pamphlets<br>Brochures<br>Folletos<br>(000) | Total<br>(000) |
| Portugal (cont) | 1993 | ... | ... | 1 391 | ... | ... | 10 602 |
| | 1994 | ... | ... | 1 381 | ... | ... | 10 348 |
| | 1996 | ... | ... | 1 411 | ... | ... | 10 855 |
| Romania | 1980 | 817 | - | 817 | 28 087 | - | 28 087 |
| | 1994 | 361 | 1 | 362 | 14 885 | 10 | 14 895 |
| | 1996 | 480 | 2 | 482 | 15 112 | 18 | 15 130 |
| Russian Federation | 1991 | ... | ... | 578 | ... | ... | 163 884 |
| | 1992 | ... | ... | 629 | ... | ... | 189 621 |
| | 1993 | ... | ... | 807 | ... | ... | 143 377 |
| | 1994 | ... | ... | 1 031 | ... | ... | 108 373 |
| | 1995 | ... | ... | 1 727 | ... | ... | 133 399 |
| | 1996 | ... | ... | 2 149 | ... | ... | 100 497 |
| Slovakia | 1992 | 701 | 8 | 709 | 2 040 | 0.0 | 2 040 |
| | 1993 | 807 | 14 | 821 | 2 664 | 3 | 2 667 |
| | 1994 | 170 | 38 | 208 | 2 258 | 10 | 2 268 |
| | 1996 | 258 | 24 | 282 | ... | ... | ... |
| Slovenia | 1992 | 410 | 24 | 434 | ... | ... | ... |
| | 1994 | 437 | 44 | 481 | ... | ... | ... |
| | 1995 | 462 | 26 | 488 | ... | ... | ... |
| | 1996 | 472 | 39 | 511 | ... | ... | ... |
| Spain | 1980 | 3 408 | 335 | 3 743 | 45 237 | 6 257 | 51 494 |
| | 1985 | 2 300 | 261 | 2 561 | 28 003 | 2 956 | 30 959 |
| | 1990 | 3 003 | 376 | 3 379 | 35 293 | 4 323 | 39 616 |
| | 1991 | 2 725 | 237 | 2 962 | 28 703 | 1 779 | 30 482 |
| | 1992 | 2 338 | 102 | 2 440 | 25 908 | 676 | 26 584 |
| | 1993 | 2 282 | 63 | 2 345 | 24 787 | 341 | 25 128 |
| | 1994 | 2 285 | 61 | 2 346 | 22 286 | 265 | 22 551 |
| | 1995 | 2 599 | 78 | 2 677 | 24 688 | 567 | 25 255 |
| | 1996 | 3 213 | 141 | 3 354 | 28 692 | 863 | 29 555 |
| Sweden | 1990 | ... | ... | 496 | ... | ... | ... |
| | 1991 | 420 | 63 | 483 | ... | ... | ... |
| | 1992 | 487 | 97 | 584 | ... | ... | ... |
| | 1993 | 466 | 113 | 579 | ... | ... | ... |
| | 1994 | 488 | 75 | 563 | ... | ... | ... |
| | 1995 | 510 | 68 | 578 | ... | ... | ... |
| | 1996 | 540 | 108 | 648 | ... | ... | ... |
| Switzerland | 1980 | ... | ... | 133 | ... | ... | ... |
| | 1985 | ... | ... | 218 | ... | ... | ... |
| | 1990 | 186 | 117 | 303 | ... | ... | ... |
| | 1991 | ... | ... | 308 | ... | ... | ... |
| | 1992 | ... | ... | 344 | ... | ... | ... |
| | 1993 | ... | ... | 247 | ... | ... | ... |
| | 1994 | ... | ... | 381 | ... | ... | ... |
| | 1995 | ... | ... | 315 | ... | ... | ... |
| | 1996 | ... | ... | 282 | ... | ... | ... |
| The Former Yugoslav Rep. of Macedonia | 1990 | 178 | 6 | 184 | 810 | 50 | 860 |
| | 1994 | 358 | 44 | 402 | 2 148 | 371 | 2 519 |
| | 1995 | 166 | - | 166 | 1 032 | - | 1 032 |
| | 1996 | 235 | - | 235 | 1 264 | - | 1 264 |
| Ukraine | 1980 | 261 | 1 | 262 | 26 649 | 205 | 26 854 |
| | 1985 | 170 | 10 | 180 | 25 505 | 1 977 | 27 482 |
| | 1990 | 193 | 6 | 199 | 28 084 | 1 248 | 29 332 |
| | 1991 | 173 | 12 | 185 | 25 183 | 1 176 | 26 359 |
| | 1992 | 177 | 12 | 189 | 23 268 | 2 359 | 25 627 |
| | 1993 | 156 | 11 | 167 | 17 667 | 1 236 | 18 903 |
| | 1994 | 128 | 5 | 133 | 7 833 | 18 | 7 851 |
| | 1995 | 293 | 23 | 316 | 30 058 | 217 | 30 275 |
| United Kingdom | 1980 | 1 596 | 721 | 2 317 | ... | ... | ... |
| | 1985 | 1 346 | 478 | 1 824 | ... | ... | ... |
| | 1992 | ... | ... | 2 773 | ... | ... | ... |
| | 1994 | 2 157 | 999 | 3 156 | ... | ... | ... |
| | 1995 | 2 482 | 1 230 | 3 712 | ... | ... | ... |
| | 1996 | 2 853 | 1 190 | 4 043 | ... | ... | ... |
| **Oceania** | | | | | | | |
| Australia | 1980 | 481 | 264 | 745 | ... | ... | ... |
| | 1985 | 379 | 294 | 673 | ... | ... | ... |
| | 1989 | 487 | 391 | 878 | ... | ... | ... |
| Fiji | 1976 | 73 | 66 | 139 | 179 | 41 | 220 |
| | 1994 | 124 | 99 | 223 | 407 | 844 | 1 251 |
| Papua New Guinea | 1991 | 3 | - | 3 | ... | ... | ... |

Number of titles and copies of school textbooks  IV.7
Nombre de titres et d'exemplaires de manuels scolaires
Número de títulos y de ejemplares de libros de texto

**General note**
For general explanations and definitions, please refer to the beginning of this chapter.

**Note générale**
Pour les explications et définitions générales, prière de se référer au début de ce chapitre.

**Nota general**
Para las explicaciones y definiciones generales, referirse al comienzo de este capítulo.

IV.8    Daily and non-daily newspapers
Journaux quotidiens et non quotidiens
Periódicos diarios y no diarios

## IV.8    Daily and non-daily newspapers: number and circulation
(total and per 1,000 inhabitants)

### Journaux quotidiens et non quotidiens: nombre et diffusion
(total et pour 1 000 habitants)

### Periódicos diarios y no diarios: número y circulación
(total y por 1 000 habitantes)

| Country / Pays / País | Year / Année / Año | Daily newspapers / Journaux quotidiens / Periódicos diarios — Number of titles / Nombre de titres / Número de títulos | Daily — Circulation / Diffusion / Circulación — Total (000) | Daily — Circulation — Per 1,000 inhabitants / Pour 1 000 habitants / Por 1 000 habitantes | Non-daily newspapers / Journaux non quotidiens / Periódicos no diarios — Number of titles / Nombre de titres / Número de títulos | Non-daily — Circulation — Total (000) | Non-daily — Circulation — Per 1,000 inhabitants / Pour 1 000 habitants / Por 1 000 habitantes |
|---|---|---|---|---|---|---|---|
| **Africa** | | | | | | | |
| Algeria | 1970 | 4 | 275 | 20 | ... | ... | ... |
| | 1975 | 4 | 285 | 18 | ... | ... | ... |
| | 1980 | 4 | 448 | 24 | ... | ... | ... |
| | 1985 | 5 | 570 | 26 | ... | ... | ... |
| | 1990 | 10 | 1 274 | 51 | 37 | 1 409 | 57 |
| | 1991 | *10 | *1 270 | *50 | ... | ... | ... |
| | 1992 | *5 | *1 265 | *48 | ... | ... | ... |
| | 1993 | *5 | *1 260 | *47 | ... | ... | ... |
| | 1994 | 6 | *1 250 | *46 | ... | ... | ... |
| | 1995 | 8 | 1 440 | 51 | ... | ... | ... |
| | 1996 | 5 | 1 080 | 38 | ... | ... | ... |
| Angola | 1975 | 4 | *85 | *14 | ... | ... | ... |
| | 1980 | 4 | 143 | 20 | ... | ... | ... |
| | 1985 | 4 | 103 | 13 | ... | ... | ... |
| | 1990 | 4 | *115 | *12 | ... | ... | ... |
| | 1991 | *4 | *116 | *12 | ... | ... | ... |
| | 1992 | 4 | *116 | *12 | ... | ... | ... |
| | 1993 | *4 | *117 | *11 | ... | ... | ... |
| | 1994 | 4 | *117 | *11 | ... | ... | ... |
| | 1995 | 5 | 122 | 11 | ... | ... | ... |
| | 1996 | 5 | *128 | *11 | ... | ... | ... |
| Benin | 1970 | *1 | *1 | *0.4 | ... | ... | ... |
| | 1975 | 1 | 1 | 0.3 | (1) 4 | (1) 9 | 2.8 |
| | 1980 | 1 | 1 | 0.3 | ... | ... | ... |
| | 1985 | 1 | 1 | 0.3 | ... | ... | ... |
| | 1990 | 1 | *1 | *0.3 | ... | ... | ... |
| | 1991 | *1 | *1 | *0.3 | ... | ... | ... |
| | 1992 | 1 | 1 | 0.2 | ... | ... | ... |
| | 1993 | *1 | *1 | *0.2 | ... | ... | ... |
| | 1994 | 1 | 1 | 0.2 | 10 | *51 | *9.5 |
| | 1995 | 1 | 3 | 0.5 | 4 | *66 | *12 |
| | 1996 | 1 | 12 | 2.2 | | | |
| Botswana | 1970 | 2 | 13 | 20 | ... | ... | ... |
| | 1975 | 1 | 14 | 18 | ... | ... | ... |
| | 1980 | 1 | 19 | 21 | ... | ... | ... |
| | 1985 | 1 | 18 | 17 | ... | ... | ... |
| | 1990 | 1 | 18 | 14 | ... | ... | ... |
| | 1991 | *1 | *20 | *15 | ... | ... | ... |
| | 1992 | 1 | *25 | *18 | 4 | 61 | 45 |
| | 1993 | *1 | *33 | *24 | ... | ... | ... |
| | 1994 | 1 | 35 | 24 | ... | ... | ... |
| | 1995 | 1 | 45 | 31 | 5 | 79 | 53 |
| | 1996 | 1 | 40 | 27 | 3 | 51 | 33 |
| Burkina Faso | 1970 | 1 | 2 | 0.3 | ... | ... | ... |
| | 1975 | 1 | 2 | 0.2 | (1) 3 | (1) 5 | 0.9 |
| | 1980 | 1 | 2 | 0.2 | ... | ... | ... |
| | 1985 | 2 | 4 | 0.4 | 14 | 23 | 2.9 |
| | 1990 | 1 | 3 | 0.3 | 10 | 14 | 1.5 |

Daily and non-daily newspapers **IV.8**
Journaux quotidiens et non quotidiens
Periódicos diarios y no diarios

| Country / Pays / País | Year / Année / Año | Daily newspapers / Journaux quotidiens / Periódicos diarios | | | Non-daily newspapers / Journaux non quotidiens / Periódicos no diarios | | |
|---|---|---|---|---|---|---|---|
| | | Number of titles / Nombre de titres / Número de títulos | Circulation / Diffusion / Circulación | | Number of titles / Nombre de titres / Número de títulos | Circulation / Diffusion / Circulación | |
| | | | Total (000) / Total (000) / Total (000) | Per 1,000 inhabitants / Pour 1 000 habitants / Por 1 000 habitantes | | Total (000) / Total (000) / Total (000) | Per 1,000 inhabitants / Pour 1 000 habitants / Por 1 000 habitantes |
| Burkina Faso (cont) | 1991 | 3 | 15 | 1.6 | 58 | ... | ... |
| | 1992 | 1 | *15 | *1.6 | ... | ... | ... |
| | 1993 | *1 | *16 | *1.6 | ... | ... | ... |
| | 1994 | 4 | 16 | 1.6 | ... | ... | ... |
| | 1995 | 3 | *15 | *1.4 | 9 | 42 | 4.0 |
| | 1996 | 4 | *14 | *1.3 | ... | ... | ... |
| Burundi | 1970 | 1 | 0.3 | 0.09 | ... | ... | ... |
| | 1975 | 1 | 2 | 0.4 | 3 | 55 | 15 |
| | 1980 | 1 | 1 | 0.2 | ... | ... | ... |
| | 1985 | 1 | 2 | 0.4 | ... | ... | ... |
| | 1990 | 1 | 20 | 3.7 | ... | ... | ... |
| | 1991 | *1 | *20 | *3.6 | ... | ... | ... |
| | 1992 | 1 | 20 | 3.5 | ... | ... | ... |
| | 1993 | *1 | *20 | *3.4 | ... | ... | ... |
| | 1994 | 1 | 20 | 3.3 | ... | ... | ... |
| | 1995 | 1 | 20 | 3.2 | ... | ... | ... |
| | 1996 | 1 | 20 | 3.2 | ... | ... | ... |
| Cameroon | 1970 | 2 | 17 | 2.6 | ... | ... | ... |
| | 1975 | 2 | 25 | 3.3 | 17 | ... | ... |
| | 1980 | 2 | 65 | 7.5 | ... | ... | ... |
| | 1985 | *2 | *70 | *7.0 | ... | ... | ... |
| | 1990 | 2 | 80 | 7.0 | ... | ... | ... |
| | 1991 | *1 | *60 | *5.1 | ... | ... | ... |
| | 1992 | 1 | 50 | 4.1 | ... | ... | ... |
| | 1993 | *1 | *50 | *4.0 | ... | ... | ... |
| | 1994 | 1 | 50 | 3.9 | ... | ... | ... |
| | 1995 | 2 | 85 | 6.4 | ... | ... | ... |
| | 1996 | 2 | 91 | 6.7 | 7 | 152 | 11 |
| Cape Verde | 1975 | - | - | - | 1 | 4 | 14 |
| | 1995 | - | - | - | 6 | 21 | 55 |
| | 1996 | - | - | - | 4 | *20 | *51 |
| Central African Republic | 1990 | 1 | *2 | *0.7 | ... | ... | ... |
| | 1991 | 1 | *2 | *0.7 | ... | ... | ... |
| | 1992 | 1 | *2 | *0.6 | ... | ... | ... |
| | 1993 | 1 | 3 | 1.0 | 1 | 2 | 0.6 |
| | 1994 | 1 | *2 | *0.6 | 1 | 1 | 0.3 |
| | 1995 | 1 | *2 | *0.6 | 1 | 2 | 0.6 |
| | 1996 | 3 | 6 | 1.8 | 7 | 13 | 3.9 |
| Chad | 1970 | *1 | *2 | *0.4 | ... | ... | ... |
| | 1975 | 4 | *0.8 | *0.2 | ... | ... | ... |
| | 1980 | 1 | 1 | 0.2 | ... | ... | ... |
| | 1985 | 1 | 1 | 0.2 | 1 | 1 | 0.2 |
| | 1990 | 1 | 2 | 0.3 | ... | ... | ... |
| | 1991 | *1 | *2 | *0.3 | ... | ... | ... |
| | 1992 | 1 | 2 | 0.2 | ... | ... | ... |
| | 1993 | *1 | *2 | *0.2 | ... | ... | ... |
| | 1994 | 1 | 2 | 0.2 | ... | ... | ... |
| | 1995 | 1 | 2 | 0.2 | 2 | 10 | 1.5 |
| | 1996 | 1 | 2 | 0.2 | ... | ... | ... |
| Comoros | 1995 | - | - | - | 1 | 0.3 | 0.5 |
| Congo | 1970 | 3 | *0.5 | *0.4 | ... | ... | ... |
| | 1975 | 3 | 0.5 | 0.3 | ... | ... | ... |
| | 1980 | 1 | 3 | 1.8 | ... | ... | ... |
| | 1985 | 1 | 8 | 4.2 | ... | ... | ... |
| | 1990 | 5 | *17 | *7.7 | 3 | 139 | 63 |
| | 1991 | *5 | *18 | *7.9 | ... | ... | ... |
| | 1992 | 6 | *19 | *8.1 | ... | ... | ... |
| | 1993 | *6 | *19 | *7.9 | ... | ... | ... |
| | 1994 | 6 | *19 | *7.6 | ... | ... | ... |
| | 1995 | 6 | *20 | *7.8 | 15 | 38 | 15 |
| | 1996 | 6 | ... | ... | ... | ... | ... |
| Democratic Rep. of the Congo | 1970 | 13 | 200 | 9.9 | ... | ... | ... |
| | 1975 | 6 | *50 | *2.2 | ... | ... | ... |
| | 1980 | 5 | *60 | *2.2 | ... | ... | ... |
| | 1985 | 4 | *50 | *1.6 | 7 | ... | ... |
| | 1990 | 5 | *75 | *2.0 | 77 | ... | ... |
| | 1991 | *5 | *90 | *2.3 | ... | ... | ... |
| | 1992 | 9 | *112 | *2.8 | ... | ... | ... |
| | 1993 | *9 | *112 | *2.7 | ... | ... | ... |
| | 1994 | 9 | *112 | *2.6 | ... | ... | ... |
| | 1995 | 9 | *120 | *2.6 | ... | ... | ... |
| | 1996 | 9 | *124 | *2.7 | ... | ... | ... |

IV.8    Daily and non-daily newspapers
Journaux quotidiens et non quotidiens
Periódicos diarios y no diarios

| Country / Pays / País | Year / Année / Año | Daily newspapers / Journaux quotidiens / Periódicos diarios | | | Non-daily newspapers / Journaux non quotidiens / Periódicos no diarios | | |
|---|---|---|---|---|---|---|---|
| | | Number of titles / Nombre de titres / Número de títulos | Circulation / Diffusion / Circulación | | Number of titles / Nombre de titres / Número de títulos | Circulation / Diffusion / Circulación | |
| | | | Total (000) | Per 1,000 inhabitants / Pour 1 000 habitants / Por 1 000 habitantes | | Total (000) | Per 1,000 inhabitants / Pour 1 000 habitants / Por 1 000 habitantes |
| Côte d'Ivoire | 1970 | 3 | 44 | 8.0 | ... | ... | ... |
| | 1975 | 3 | *55 | *8.1 | (1)   2 | (1)   65 | 9.6 |
| | 1980 | 2 | 81 | 9.9 | ... | ... | ... |
| | 1985 | *2 | 90 | 9.1 | 1 | 20 | 2.0 |
| | 1990 | 2 | 90 | 7.7 | 1 | 45 | 3.9 |
| | 1991 | 4 | 118 | 9.8 | 3 | 80 | 6.7 |
| | 1992 | 4 | 118 | 9.5 | 4 | 95 | 7.6 |
| | 1993 | 4 | 118 | 9.2 | 8 | 157 | 12 |
| | 1994 | 8 | 190 | 14 | 11 | 205 | 16 |
| | 1995 | 9 | 198 | 15 | 13 | 235 | 17 |
| | 1996 | 12 | 231 | 17 | 15 | 251 | 18 |
| Djibouti | 1975 | - | - | - | 1 | 4 | 17 |
| | 1995 | - | - | - | 1 | 0.5 | 0.8 |
| Egypt | 1970 | 14 | 745 | 21 | 26 | 791 | 22 |
| | 1975 | 12 | 1 095 | 28 | 19 | 1 498 | 39 |
| | 1980 | 12 | 1 701 | 39 | 23 | 1 558 | 36 |
| | 1985 | 12 | 2 383 | 48 | 29 | 2 617 | 53 |
| | 1990 | 14 | *2 400 | *43 | ... | ... | ... |
| | 1991 | 13 | *2 400 | 42 | 35 | 1 502 | 26 |
| | 1992 | 16 | *2 426 | *41 | ... | ... | ... |
| | 1993 | 14 | *2 500 | 42 | 37 | 1 706 | 28 |
| | 1994 | 15 | 2 685 | 44 | 38 | 1 629 | 27 |
| | 1995 | 15 | 2 373 | 38 | 40 | 1 442 | 23 |
| | 1996 | 17 | *2 400 | *38 | ... | ... | ... |
| Equatorial Guinea | 1970 | *2 | *1 | *3.8 | ... | ... | ... |
| | 1975 | 2 | *1 | *5.3 | ... | ... | ... |
| | 1980 | 2 | *2 | *6.9 | ... | ... | ... |
| | 1985 | 2 | *2 | *4.8 | ... | ... | ... |
| | 1990 | 2 | *2 | *5.7 | ... | ... | ... |
| | 1991 | *2 | *2 | *4.2 | ... | ... | ... |
| | 1992 | 1 | *1 | *2.7 | ... | ... | ... |
| | 1993 | *1 | *1 | *2.6 | ... | ... | ... |
| | 1994 | 1 | *1 | *2.6 | ... | ... | ... |
| | 1995 | 1 | *2 | *5.0 | ... | ... | ... |
| | 1996 | 1 | *2 | *4.9 | ... | ... | ... |
| Eritrea | 1996 | - | - | - | ... | ... | ... |
| Ethiopia | 1970 | 8 | *40 | *1.4 | ... | ... | ... |
| | 1975 | 3 | 44 | 1.4 | 6 | 34 | 1.1 |
| | 1980 | 3 | 40 | 1.1 | ... | ... | ... |
| | 1985 | 3 | 41 | 1.0 | 7 | 262 | 6.4 |
| | 1990 | 6 | *100 | *2.1 | ... | ... | ... |
| | 1991 | *5 | *85 | *1.7 | ... | ... | ... |
| | 1992 | 4 | *70 | *1.4 | ... | ... | ... |
| | 1993 | *4 | *83 | *1.6 | ... | ... | ... |
| | 1994 | 4 | *81 | *1.5 | ... | ... | ... |
| | 1995 | 4 | *92 | *1.7 | 17 | 159 | 2.9 |
| | 1996 | 4 | 86 | 1.5 | ... | ... | ... |
| Gabon | 1975 | 1 | 3 | 5.1 | ... | ... | ... |
| | 1980 | 1 | 15 | 22 | ... | ... | ... |
| | 1985 | 1 | 20 | 25 | ... | ... | ... |
| | 1990 | 1 | *20 | *21 | ... | ... | ... |
| | 1991 | *1 | *20 | *21 | ... | ... | ... |
| | 1992 | 1 | *20 | *20 | ... | ... | ... |
| | 1993 | *1 | *20 | *20 | ... | ... | ... |
| | 1994 | 1 | *20 | *19 | ... | ... | ... |
| | 1995 | 2 | *30 | *28 | ... | ... | ... |
| | 1996 | 2 | 33 | 30 | ... | ... | ... |
| Gambia | 1985 | *2 | *1 | *1.9 | 6 | ... | ... |
| | 1990 | 2 | *2 | *1.6 | 6 | *7 | *7.6 |
| | 1991 | *2 | *2 | *1.9 | ... | ... | ... |
| | 1992 | 2 | *2 | *2.0 | ... | ... | ... |
| | 1993 | *2 | *2 | *1.9 | ... | ... | ... |
| | 1994 | 2 | *2 | *1.9 | ... | ... | ... |
| | 1995 | 1 | 1 | 0.9 | ... | ... | ... |
| | 1996 | 1 | 2 | 1.7 | 4 | *6 | *5.2 |
| Ghana | 1970 | *3 | *300 | *35 | ... | ... | ... |
| | 1975 | 4 | 500 | 51 | ... | ... | ... |
| | 1980 | 5 | *500 | *46 | ... | ... | ... |
| | 1985 | 5 | *510 | *39 | ... | ... | ... |
| | 1990 | 2 | 200 | 13 | 87 | 1 111 | 73 |
| | 1991 | *3 | *230 | *15 | ... | ... | ... |
| | 1992 | 4 | *280 | *17 | ... | ... | ... |
| | 1993 | *4 | *290 | *17 | ... | ... | ... |
| | 1994 | 4 | *310 | *18 | ... | ... | ... |

Daily and non-daily newspapers **IV.8**
Journaux quotidiens et non quotidiens
Periódicos diarios y no diarios

| Country / Pays / País | Year / Année / Año | Daily newspapers / Journaux quotidiens / Periódicos diarios | | | Non-daily newspapers / Journaux non quotidiens / Periódicos no diarios | | |
|---|---|---|---|---|---|---|---|
| | | Number of titles / Nombre de titres / Número de títulos | Circulation / Diffusion / Circulación Total (000) | Per 1,000 inhabitants / Pour 1 000 habitants / Por 1 000 habitantes | Number of titles / Nombre de titres / Número de títulos | Circulation / Diffusion / Circulación Total (000) | Per 1,000 inhabitants / Pour 1 000 habitants / Por 1 000 habitantes |
| Ghana (cont) | 1995 | 4 | *310 | *18 | ... | ... | ... |
| | 1996 | 4 | 250 | 14 | ... | ... | ... |
| Guinea | 1970 | - | - | - | 1 | 5 | 1.3 |
| | 1985 | - | - | - | 1 | 13 | 2.6 |
| | 1990 | - | - | - | *1 | *10 | *1.7 |
| | 1996 | - | - | - | 1 | 20 | 2.7 |
| Guinea-Bissau | 1970 | 1 | *5 | *9.5 | ... | ... | ... |
| | 1975 | 1 | 6 | 9.6 | ... | ... | ... |
| | 1980 | 1 | 6 | 7.5 | ... | ... | ... |
| | 1985 | 1 | 6 | 6.8 | ... | ... | ... |
| | 1990 | 1 | 6 | 6.2 | ... | ... | ... |
| | 1991 | *1 | *6 | *6.0 | ... | ... | ... |
| | 1992 | 1 | 6 | 5.9 | ... | ... | ... |
| | 1993 | *1 | *6 | *5.8 | ... | ... | ... |
| | 1994 | 1 | 6 | 5.6 | ... | ... | ... |
| | 1995 | 1 | 6 | 5.5 | ... | ... | ... |
| | 1996 | 1 | 6 | 5.4 | ... | ... | ... |
| Kenya | 1970 | 4 | 155 | 13 | ... | ... | ... |
| | 1975 | 3 | 134 | 9.8 | ... | ... | ... |
| | 1980 | 3 | 216 | 13 | ... | ... | ... |
| | 1985 | 4 | 283 | 14 | ... | ... | ... |
| | 1990 | 5 | *330 | *14 | ... | ... | ... |
| | 1991 | *5 | *340 | *14 | ... | ... | ... |
| | 1992 | 5 | *354 | *14 | ... | ... | ... |
| | 1993 | *5 | *356 | *14 | ... | ... | ... |
| | 1994 | 5 | *358 | *13 | ... | ... | ... |
| | 1995 | 4 | 264 | 9.7 | 7 | 484 | 18 |
| | 1996 | 4 | 263 | 9.4 | 7 | 524 | 19 |
| Lesotho | 1975 | 1 | 1 | 1.1 | ... | ... | ... |
| | 1980 | 3 | 44 | 33 | ... | ... | ... |
| | 1985 | 4 | 47 | 30 | ... | ... | ... |
| | 1990 | 4 | *20 | *11 | ... | ... | ... |
| | 1991 | *3 | *16 | *9.1 | ... | ... | ... |
| | 1992 | 2 | *14 | *7.8 | ... | ... | ... |
| | 1993 | *2 | *14 | *7.6 | ... | ... | ... |
| | 1994 | 2 | *14 | *7.4 | ... | ... | ... |
| | 1995 | *2 | *14 | *7.3 | ... | ... | ... |
| | 1996 | *2 | *15 | *7.6 | 7 | 74 | 37 |
| Liberia | 1970 | 2 | 7 | 5.1 | ... | ... | ... |
| | 1975 | 3 | 13 | 8.1 | (1) 8 | ... | ... |
| | 1980 | 3 | 11 | 5.9 | ... | ... | ... |
| | 1985 | 5 | *28 | *13 | ... | ... | ... |
| | 1990 | 8 | *35 | *14 | ... | ... | ... |
| | 1991 | *5 | *35 | *14 | ... | ... | ... |
| | 1992 | 8 | *35 | *15 | ... | ... | ... |
| | 1993 | *8 | *35 | *16 | ... | ... | ... |
| | 1994 | 8 | *35 | *17 | ... | ... | ... |
| | 1995 | *8 | *35 | *17 | ... | ... | ... |
| | 1996 | 6 | *35 | *16 | ... | ... | ... |
| Libyan Arab Jamahiriya | 1970 | 8 | *30 | *15 | ... | ... | ... |
| | 1975 | 2 | 41 | 17 | 5 | 94 | 39 |
| | 1980 | 3 | *55 | *18 | ... | ... | ... |
| | 1985 | 3 | *65 | *17 | ... | ... | ... |
| | 1990 | 3 | *70 | *16 | ... | ... | ... |
| | 1991 | *3 | *71 | *16 | ... | ... | ... |
| | 1992 | 4 | *71 | *15 | ... | ... | ... |
| | 1993 | *4 | *71 | *15 | ... | ... | ... |
| | 1994 | 4 | *71 | *15 | ... | ... | ... |
| | 1995 | 4 | *71 | *14 | ... | ... | ... |
| | 1996 | 4 | *71 | *14 | ... | ... | ... |
| Madagascar | 1970 | 13 | 53 | 7.7 | ... | ... | ... |
| | 1975 | *12 | *55 | *7.0 | ... | ... | ... |
| | 1980 | 6 | 55 | 6.2 | ... | ... | ... |
| | 1985 | 7 | 67 | 6.6 | ... | ... | ... |
| | 1990 | 5 | 50 | 4.3 | 27 | 105 | 9.1 |
| | 1991 | 7 | 43 | 3.6 | 36 | *115 | *9.6 |
| | 1992 | 7 | 48 | 3.9 | 37 | *168 | *14 |
| | 1993 | 9 | *55 | *4.3 | 34 | 96 | 7.5 |
| | 1994 | 7 | *55 | *4.1 | 31 | 90 | 6.8 |
| | 1995 | 6 | 59 | 4.3 | 31 | *90 | *6.5 |
| | 1996 | 5 | 66 | 4.6 | ... | ... | ... |
| Malawi | 1970 | *2 | ... | ... | ... | ... | ... |
| | 1975 | 2 | 18 | 3.4 | ... | ... | ... |
| | 1980 | *2 | *20 | *3.2 | ... | ... | ... |

IV.8 Daily and non-daily newspapers
Journaux quotidiens et non quotidiens
Periódicos diarios y no diarios

| Country / Pays / País | Year / Année / Año | Daily newspapers / Journaux quotidiens / Periódicos diarios | | | Non-daily newspapers / Journaux non quotidiens / Periódicos no diarios | | |
|---|---|---|---|---|---|---|---|
| | | Number of titles / Nombre de titres / Número de títulos | Circulation / Diffusion / Circulación | | Number of titles / Nombre de titres / Número de títulos | Circulation / Diffusion / Circulación | |
| | | | Total (000) | Per 1,000 inhabitants / Pour 1 000 habitants / Por 1 000 habitantes | | Total (000) | Per 1,000 inhabitants / Pour 1 000 habitants / Por 1 000 habitantes |
| Malawi (cont) | 1985 | 1 | *22 | *3.0 | 5 | 121 | 17 |
| | 1990 | 1 | 25 | 2.7 | ... | ... | ... |
| | 1991 | 1 | 25 | 2.6 | 3 | 125 | 13 |
| | 1992 | 1 | 25 | 2.6 | 4 | 133 | 14 |
| | 1993 | *1 | *25 | *2.6 | ... | ... | ... |
| | 1994 | 1 | 25 | 2.6 | ... | ... | ... |
| | 1995 | *1 | *25 | *2.6 | ... | ... | ... |
| | 1996 | 5 | ... | ... | 4 | *120 | *12 |
| Mali | 1970 | *1 | *2 | *0.3 | ... | ... | ... |
| | 1975 | 1 | 3 | 0.5 | (1) 1 | (1) *13 | *2.0 |
| | 1980 | 2 | *4 | *0.5 | ... | ... | ... |
| | 1985 | 2 | *10 | *1.3 | ... | ... | ... |
| | 1990 | 2 | *10 | *1.1 | ... | ... | ... |
| | 1991 | *2 | *10 | *1.1 | ... | ... | ... |
| | 1992 | 2 | *10 | *1.1 | ... | ... | ... |
| | 1993 | *2 | *10 | *1.1 | ... | ... | ... |
| | 1994 | 2 | *10 | *1.0 | ... | ... | ... |
| | 1995 | *2 | *11 | *1.1 | ... | ... | ... |
| | 1996 | 3 | *12 | *1.2 | ... | ... | ... |
| Mauritania | 1990 | 1 | *1 | *0.5 | ... | ... | ... |
| | 1991 | *1 | *1 | *0.5 | ... | ... | ... |
| | 1992 | 1 | *1 | *0.5 | ... | ... | ... |
| | 1993 | *1 | *1 | *0.5 | ... | ... | ... |
| | 1994 | 1 | *1 | *0.4 | ... | ... | ... |
| | 1995 | 1 | *1 | *0.4 | ... | ... | ... |
| | 1996 | 2 | *1 | *0.5 | ... | ... | ... |
| Mauritius | 1970 | *12 | *80 | *97 | ... | ... | ... |
| | 1975 | 12 | 82 | 91 | ... | ... | ... |
| | 1980 | 10 | 80 | 83 | ... | *40 | *39 |
| | 1985 | 7 | *70 | *69 | 8 | 75 | 71 |
| | 1990 | 7 | 80 | 76 | 24 | ... | ... |
| | 1991 | 6 | 80 | 75 | 23 | ... | ... |
| | 1992 | 6 | 80 | 74 | 25 | ... | ... |
| | 1993 | 6 | *80 | *73 | 25 | ... | ... |
| | 1994 | 6 | *80 | *73 | 28 | ... | ... |
| | 1995 | 5 | 80 | 72 | 25 | *70 | *63 |
| | 1996 | 6 | 85 | 76 | 29 | ... | ... |
| Morocco | 1970 | 14 | *300 | *20 | ... | ... | ... |
| | 1975 | 7 | *250 | *14 | 31 | ... | ... |
| | 1980 | 11 | *270 | *14 | ... | ... | ... |
| | 1985 | 14 | 320 | *15 | ... | ... | ... |
| | 1990 | 13 | *320 | *13 | ... | ... | ... |
| | 1991 | *13 | *328 | *13 | ... | ... | ... |
| | 1992 | 14 | *335 | *14 | ... | ... | ... |
| | 1993 | *14 | *340 | *14 | ... | ... | ... |
| | 1994 | 13 | 344 | 13 | ... | ... | ... |
| | 1995 | 20 | 630 | 24 | (2) 636 | 3 384 | ... |
| | 1996 | 22 | 704 | 27 | (2) 699 | 3 671 | ... |
| Mozambique | 1970 | 6 | *60 | *6.4 | ... | ... | ... |
| | 1975 | 2 | 42 | 4.0 | ... | ... | ... |
| | 1980 | 2 | 54 | 4.5 | ... | ... | ... |
| | 1985 | 2 | 81 | 6.0 | ... | ... | ... |
| | 1990 | 2 | 81 | 5.7 | ... | ... | ... |
| | 1991 | *2 | *81 | *5.5 | ... | ... | ... |
| | 1992 | 2 | 81 | 5.3 | ... | ... | ... |
| | 1993 | *2 | *81 | *5.1 | ... | ... | ... |
| | 1994 | 2 | 81 | 4.8 | ... | ... | ... |
| | 1995 | 3 | *80 | *4.6 | ... | ... | ... |
| | 1996 | 2 | 49 | 2.7 | 4 | *160 | *8.9 |
| Namibia | 1970 | 3 | *10 | *13 | ... | ... | ... |
| | 1975 | 3 | *16 | *18 | ... | ... | 7.8 |
| | 1980 | 4 | 27 | 26 | 1 | 8 | 17 |
| | 1985 | 3 | 21 | 17 | 4 | 20 | 53 |
| | 1990 | *6 | ... | ... | 18 | 71 | ... |
| | 1991 | *6 | *23 | *17 | ... | ... | ... |
| | 1992 | 4 | *25 | *18 | ... | ... | ... |
| | 1993 | 4 | *30 | *20 | ... | ... | ... |
| | 1994 | 4 | *32 | *21 | ... | ... | ... |
| | 1995 | 4 | *30 | *19 | ... | ... | 10 |
| | 1996 | 4 | 30 | 19 | 2 | 16 | ... |
| Niger | 1970 | *1 | *3 | *0.7 | ... | ... | 2.1 |
| | 1975 | 2 | 3 | 0.6 | 14 | 10 | 0.9 |
| | 1980 | 1 | 3 | 0.5 | 1 | 5 | 0.7 |
| | 1985 | 1 | 4 | 0.5 | 1 | 5 | 0.6 |
| | 1990 | 1 | 3 | 0.4 | 1 | 5 | |

Daily and non-daily newspapers    IV.8
Journaux quotidiens et non quotidiens
Periódicos diarios y no diarios

| Country<br>Pays<br>País | Year<br>Année<br>Año | Daily newspapers / Journaux quotidiens / Periódicos diarios | | | Non-daily newspapers / Journaux non quotidiens / Periódicos no diarios | | |
|---|---|---|---|---|---|---|---|
| | | Number of titles<br>Nombre de titres<br>Número de títulos | Circulation / Diffusion / Circulación | | Number of titles<br>Nombre de titres<br>Número de títulos | Circulation / Diffusion / Circulación | |
| | | | Total (000)<br>Total (000)<br>Total (000) | Per 1,000 inhabitants<br>Pour 1 000 habitants<br>Por 1 000 habitantes | | Total (000)<br>Total (000)<br>Total (000) | Per 1,000 inhabitants<br>Pour 1 000 habitants<br>Por 1 000 habitantes |
| Niger (cont) | 1991 | 1 | 3 | 0.4 | 3 | 15 | 1.9 |
| | 1992 | 1 | 3 | 0.4 | 4 | 20 | 2.4 |
| | 1993 | 1 | 3 | 0.4 | 5 | 12 | 1.4 |
| | 1994 | 1 | 3 | 0.3 | 5 | *13 | *1.5 |
| | 1995 | 2 | 4 | 0.4 | 5 | 15 | 1.6 |
| | 1996 | 1 | 2 | 0.2 | 5 | 14 | 1.5 |
| Nigeria | 1970 | 21 | 440 | 8.9 | ... | ... | ... |
| | 1975 | 12 | *650 | *11 | ... | ... | ... |
| | 1980 | 16 | *1 100 | *17 | ... | ... | ... |
| | 1985 | 19 | *1 400 | *18 | ... | ... | ... |
| | 1990 | 31 | *1 700 | *20 | ... | ... | ... |
| | 1991 | *30 | *1 800 | *20 | ... | ... | ... |
| | 1992 | 26 | *1 850 | *20 | ... | ... | ... |
| | 1993 | *26 | *1 900 | *20 | ... | ... | ... |
| | 1994 | 27 | *1 950 | *20 | ... | ... | ... |
| | 1995 | 27 | *1 950 | *20 | ... | ... | ... |
| | 1996 | 25 | *2 740 | *27 | ... | ... | ... |
| Reunion | 1970 | *2 | *23 | *50 | ... | ... | ... |
| | 1975 | 2 | 27 | 56 | ... | ... | ... |
| | 1980 | 3 | 56 | 111 | ... | ... | ... |
| | 1985 | 2 | 49 | 88 | ... | ... | ... |
| | 1990 | 3 | *55 | *91 | ... | ... | ... |
| | 1991 | *3 | *55 | *90 | ... | ... | ... |
| | 1992 | 3 | 55 | 88 | ... | ... | ... |
| | 1993 | *3 | *55 | *87 | ... | ... | ... |
| | 1994 | 3 | 55 | 85 | ... | ... | ... |
| | 1995 | 3 | *57 | *87 | ... | ... | ... |
| | 1996 | 3 | 55 | 83 | ... | ... | ... |
| Rwanda | 1970 | - | - | - | 9 | 82 | 22 |
| | 1975 | 1 | 0.2 | 0.05 | 12 | 81 | 18 |
| | 1980 | 1 | 0.3 | 0.06 | 14 | 136 | 26 |
| | 1985 | 1 | 0.3 | 0.04 | 19 | 166 | 27 |
| | 1990 | 1 | 0.5 | 0.07 | 15 | *155 | *22 |
| | 1991 | 1 | 0.5 | 0.07 | 15 | ... | ... |
| | 1992 | 1 | 0.5 | 0.07 | 15 | ... | ... |
| | 1993 | *1 | *0.8 | *0.1 | ... | ... | ... |
| | 1994 | 1 | *0.5 | *0.09 | ... | ... | ... |
| | 1995 | 1 | *0.5 | *0.1 | ... | ... | ... |
| | 1996 | 1 | ... | ... | 2 | 123 | 22 |
| Senegal | 1970 | 1 | 20 | 4.8 | ... | ... | ... |
| | 1975 | 1 | 25 | 5.2 | ... | ... | ... |
| | 1980 | 1 | 35 | 6.3 | ... | ... | ... |
| | 1985 | 3 | 53 | 8.3 | ... | ... | ... |
| | 1990 | 1 | 50 | 6.8 | ... | ... | ... |
| | 1991 | *1 | *50 | *6.6 | ... | ... | ... |
| | 1992 | 1 | 50 | 6.5 | ... | ... | ... |
| | 1993 | *1 | *50 | *6.3 | ... | ... | ... |
| | 1994 | 3 | 48 | 5.9 | 6 | 37 | 4.6 |
| | 1995 | 3 | 48 | 5.8 | 6 | 37 | 4.4 |
| | 1996 | 1 | 45 | 5.3 | ... | ... | ... |
| Seychelles | 1970 | 2 | 2 | 38 | ... | ... | ... |
| | 1975 | 2 | 4 | 61 | ... | ... | ... |
| | 1980 | 1 | 4 | 63 | 2 | 4 | 63 |
| | 1985 | 1 | 4 | 61 | 2 | 4 | 61 |
| | 1990 | 1 | 3 | 47 | 2 | 4 | 60 |
| | 1991 | 1 | 3 | 47 | 2 | 4 | 60 |
| | 1992 | 1 | 3 | 46 | 5 | 10 | 138 |
| | 1993 | 1 | 3 | 46 | 6 | 11 | 157 |
| | 1994 | 1 | 3 | 45 | 4 | 8 | 114 |
| | 1995 | 1 | 3 | 45 | 3 | 7 | 93 |
| | 1996 | 1 | 3 | 46 | 3 | 7 | 92 |
| Sierra Leone | 1970 | 5 | *30 | *11 | ... | ... | ... |
| | 1975 | 2 | 30 | 10 | 9 | 90 | 31 |
| | 1980 | 1 | 10 | 3.1 | ... | ... | ... |
| | 1985 | 1 | 10 | 2.8 | ... | ... | ... |
| | 1990 | 1 | 10 | 2.5 | ... | ... | ... |
| | 1991 | *1 | *10 | *2.5 | ... | ... | ... |
| | 1992 | 1 | 10 | 2.5 | ... | ... | ... |
| | 1993 | *1 | *10 | *2.4 | ... | ... | ... |
| | 1994 | 1 | 10 | 2.4 | ... | ... | ... |
| | 1995 | 1 | 20 | 4.8 | ... | ... | ... |
| | 1996 | 1 | 20 | 4.7 | ... | ... | ... |
| Somalia | 1970 | 2 | 5 | 1.2 | 2 | 5 | 1.4 |
| | 1975 | 1 | *3 | *0.7 | ... | ... | ... |
| | 1980 | 2 | *5 | *0.9 | ... | ... | ... |

IV.8   Daily and non-daily newspapers
       Journaux quotidiens et non quotidiens
       Periódicos diarios y no diarios

| Country<br><br>Pays<br><br>País | Year<br><br>Année<br><br>Año | Daily newspapers / Journaux quotidiens / Periódicos diarios | | | Non-daily newspapers / Journaux non quotidiens / Periódicos no diarios | | |
|---|---|---|---|---|---|---|---|
| | | Number of titles<br><br>Nombre de titres<br><br>Número de títulos | Circulation / Diffusion / Circulación | | Number of titles<br><br>Nombre de titres<br><br>Número de títulos | Circulation / Diffusion / Circulación | |
| | | | Total (000)<br>Total (000)<br>Total (000) | Per 1,000 inhabitants<br>Pour 1 000 habitants<br>Por 1 000 habitantes | | Total (000)<br>Total (000)<br>Total (000) | Per 1,000 inhabitants<br>Pour 1 000 habitants<br>Por 1 000 habitantes |
| Somalia (cont) | 1985 | 2 | *7 | *1.1 | ... | ... | ... |
| | 1990 | 1 | 9 | 1.2 | ... | ... | ... |
| | 1991 | *1 | *9 | *1.1 | ... | ... | ... |
| | 1992 | 1 | 9 | 1.1 | ... | ... | ... |
| | 1993 | *1 | *9 | *1.1 | ... | ... | ... |
| | 1994 | 1 | 9 | 1.1 | ... | ... | ... |
| | 1995 | 1 | *10 | *1.2 | ... | ... | ... |
| | 1996 | 2 | *10 | *1.2 | 2 | ... | ... |
| South Africa | 1970 | 22 | *800 | *36 | ... | ... | ... |
| | 1975 | *20 | *1 000 | *40 | ... | ... | ... |
| | 1980 | *24 | *1 400 | *51 | ... | ... | ... |
| | 1985 | 24 | 1 440 | 47 | ... | ... | ... |
| | 1990 | 22 | 1 340 | 39 | ... | ... | ... |
| | 1991 | 19 | 1 298 | 37 | 10 | 1 527 | 44 |
| | 1992 | 20 | 1 248 | 35 | ... | ... | ... |
| | 1993 | 17 | 1 272 | 35 | 48 | 1 313 | 36 |
| | 1994 | 17 | *1 346 | *37 | 49 | 1 328 | 36 |
| | 1995 | *17 | *1 300 | *35 | 46 | 1 265 | 34 |
| | 1996 | 17 | 1 288 | 34 | 48 | 1 110 | 29 |
| St. Helena | 1996 | - | - | - | 1 | 2 | 246 |
| Sudan | 1975 | 4 | *30 | *1.9 | ... | ... | ... |
| | 1980 | 6 | 105 | 5.6 | ... | ... | ... |
| | 1985 | 5 | *250 | *12 | ... | ... | ... |
| | 1990 | 5 | *610 | *25 | ... | ... | ... |
| | 1991 | *5 | *615 | *25 | ... | ... | ... |
| | 1992 | 5 | *620 | *25 | ... | ... | ... |
| | 1993 | *5 | *620 | *24 | ... | ... | ... |
| | 1994 | 5 | *620 | *24 | ... | ... | ... |
| | 1995 | 5 | *650 | *24 | ... | ... | ... |
| | 1996 | 5 | *737 | *27 | ... | ... | ... |
| Swaziland | 1970 | 1 | 4 | 9.5 | ... | ... | ... |
| | 1975 | 1 | 5 | 9.3 | ... | ... | ... |
| | 1980 | 1 | 9 | 15 | ... | ... | ... |
| | 1985 | 2 | 10 | 15 | ... | ... | ... |
| | 1990 | 3 | *11 | *15 | ... | ... | ... |
| | 1991 | *3 | *12 | *15 | ... | ... | ... |
| | 1992 | 3 | *12 | *15 | ... | ... | ... |
| | 1993 | *3 | *12 | *15 | ... | ... | ... |
| | 1994 | 3 | *12 | *14 | ... | ... | ... |
| | 1995 | 3 | *15 | *17 | ... | ... | ... |
| | 1996 | 3 | *24 | *27 | ... | ... | ... |
| Togo | 1970 | 1 | *5 | *2.5 | ... | ... | ... |
| | 1975 | 1 | 7 | 2.9 | ... | ... | ... |
| | 1980 | 3 | *16 | *6.1 | ... | ... | ... |
| | 1985 | 2 | *11 | *3.6 | ... | ... | ... |
| | 1990 | 1 | 10 | 2.8 | ... | ... | ... |
| | 1991 | *1 | *11 | *3.0 | ... | ... | ... |
| | 1992 | 2 | *12 | *3.2 | ... | ... | ... |
| | 1993 | *1 | *11 | *2.9 | ... | ... | ... |
| | 1994 | 1 | *10 | *2.5 | ... | ... | ... |
| | 1995 | *1 | *10 | *2.5 | ... | ... | ... |
| | 1996 | 1 | *15 | *3.6 | ... | ... | ... |
| Tunisia | 1970 | *2 | *100 | *20 | ... | ... | ... |
| | 1975 | 4 | 190 | 34 | ... | ... | ... |
| | 1980 | 5 | 272 | 42 | ... | ... | ... |
| | 1985 | 6 | *280 | *38 | ... | ... | ... |
| | 1990 | 6 | *345 | *42 | ... | ... | ... |
| | 1991 | *8 | *360 | *43 | ... | ... | ... |
| | 1992 | 9 | *410 | *48 | ... | ... | ... |
| | 1993 | *8 | *405 | *47 | ... | ... | ... |
| | 1994 | 7 | *403 | *46 | ... | ... | ... |
| | 1995 | 8 | 270 | 30 | 25 | 775 | 87 |
| | 1996 | 8 | 280 | 31 | 25 | 900 | 99 |
| Uganda | 1970 | 7 | *60 | *6.1 | ... | ... | ... |
| | 1975 | *3 | *46 | *4.1 | ... | ... | ... |
| | 1980 | 1 | 25 | 1.9 | ... | ... | ... |
| | 1985 | 1 | 25 | 1.7 | ... | ... | ... |
| | 1990 | 2 | 30 | 1.8 | ... | ... | ... |
| | 1991 | *5 | *50 | *3.0 | ... | ... | ... |
| | 1992 | 6 | *80 | *4.6 | ... | ... | ... |
| | 1993 | *5 | *50 | *2.8 | ... | ... | ... |
| | 1994 | 2 | *35 | *1.9 | ... | ... | ... |
| | 1995 | 2 | 40 | 2.1 | 4 | 74 | 3.9 |
| | 1996 | 2 | 40 | 2.1 | 4 | 67 | 3.4 |

Daily and non-daily newspapers IV.8
Journaux quotidiens et non quotidiens
Periódicos diarios y no diarios

| Country Pays País | Year Année Año | Daily newspapers / Journaux quotidiens / Periódicos diarios | | | Non-daily newspapers / Journaux non quotidiens / Periódicos no diarios | | |
|---|---|---|---|---|---|---|---|
| | | Number of titles Nombre de titres Número de títulos | Circulation / Diffusion / Circulación | | Number of titles Nombre de titres Número de títulos | Circulation / Diffusion / Circulación | |
| | | | Total (000) Total (000) Total (000) | Per 1,000 inhabitants Pour 1 000 habitants Por 1 000 habitantes | | Total (000) Total (000) Total (000) | Per 1,000 inhabitants Pour 1 000 habitants Por 1 000 habitantes |
| United Republic of Tanzania | 1970 | *3 | *50 | *3.7 | ... | ... | ... |
| | 1975 | 3 | 70 | 4.4 | ... | ... | ... |
| | 1980 | 3 | 208 | 11 | ... | ... | ... |
| | 1985 | 2 | 101 | 4.6 | ... | ... | ... |
| | 1990 | 3 | *67 | *2.6 | ... | ... | ... |
| | 1991 | 3 | 67 | 2.5 | ... | ... | ... |
| | 1992 | 3 | *73 | *2.7 | ... | ... | ... |
| | 1993 | 3 | 73 | 2.6 | ... | ... | ... |
| | 1994 | 3 | 55 | 1.9 | ... | ... | ... |
| | 1995 | 4 | 121 | 4.0 | ... | ... | ... |
| | 1996 | 3 | *120 | *3.9 | ... | ... | ... |
| Western Sahara | 1996 | - | - | - | ... | ... | ... |
| Zambia | 1970 | 1 | 57 | 14 | ... | ... | ... |
| | 1975 | 2 | 106 | 22 | ... | ... | ... |
| | 1980 | 2 | 110 | 19 | ... | ... | ... |
| | 1985 | 2 | 95 | 15 | 11 | 285 | 44 |
| | 1990 | 2 | 99 | 14 | ... | ... | ... |
| | 1991 | *2 | *95 | *13 | ... | ... | ... |
| | 1992 | 2 | 70 | 9.2 | ... | ... | ... |
| | 1993 | *2 | *70 | *9.0 | ... | ... | ... |
| | 1994 | 2 | 70 | 8.8 | ... | ... | ... |
| | 1995 | 3 | 107 | 13 | ... | ... | ... |
| | 1996 | 3 | 114 | 14 | ... | ... | ... |
| Zimbabwe | 1970 | 4 | 83 | 16 | ... | ... | ... |
| | 1975 | 3 | 116 | 19 | ... | ... | ... |
| | 1980 | 2 | 133 | 19 | ... | ... | ... |
| | 1985 | 3 | 203 | 24 | 4 | 233 | 28 |
| | 1990 | 2 | 206 | 21 | ... | ... | ... |
| | 1991 | *2 | *200 | *20 | ... | ... | ... |
| | 1992 | 2 | 195 | 19 | ... | ... | ... |
| | 1993 | *2 | *195 | *19 | ... | ... | ... |
| | 1994 | 2 | 195 | 18 | ... | ... | ... |
| | 1995 | 2 | 192 | 18 | ... | ... | ... |
| | 1996 | 2 | 209 | 19 | ... | ... | ... |
| **North America** | | | | | | | |
| Anguilla | 1996 | - | - | - | ... | ... | ... |
| Antigua and Barbuda | 1970 | 1 | *4 | *61 | ... | ... | ... |
| | 1975 | 1 | 4 | 71 | ... | ... | ... |
| | 1980 | 1 | 6 | 99 | ... | ... | ... |
| | 1985 | 1 | 6 | 97 | ... | ... | ... |
| | 1990 | 1 | 6 | 94 | ... | ... | ... |
| | 1991 | *1 | *6 | *93 | ... | ... | ... |
| | 1992 | *1 | *6 | *93 | 4 | ... | ... |
| | 1993 | *1 | *6 | *92 | ... | ... | ... |
| | 1994 | *1 | *6 | *92 | ... | ... | ... |
| | 1995 | *1 | *6 | *91 | ... | ... | ... |
| | 1996 | 1 | 6 | 91 | 4 | ... | ... |
| Aruba | 1990 | 12 | 53 | 839 | ... | ... | ... |
| | 1991 | *12 | *55 | *835 | ... | ... | ... |
| | 1992 | 14 | 69 | 996 | ... | ... | ... |
| | 1993 | *14 | *60 | *821 | ... | ... | ... |
| | 1994 | 14 | 52 | 676 | ... | ... | ... |
| | 1995 | 13 | 73 | 896 | ... | ... | ... |
| | 1996 | 13 | 73 | 852 | ... | ... | ... |
| Bahamas | 1970 | 3 | 28 | 162 | ... | ... | ... |
| | 1975 | 2 | 31 | 164 | ... | ... | ... |
| | 1980 | 3 | 33 | 157 | ... | ... | ... |
| | 1985 | 3 | 39 | 168 | ... | ... | ... |
| | 1990 | 3 | 35 | 137 | ... | ... | ... |
| | 1991 | *3 | *35 | *135 | ... | ... | ... |
| | 1992 | 3 | 35 | 132 | ... | ... | ... |
| | 1993 | *3 | *35 | *130 | ... | ... | ... |
| | 1994 | 3 | 35 | 127 | ... | ... | ... |
| | 1995 | *3 | *35 | *125 | ... | ... | ... |
| | 1996 | 3 | 28 | 99 | ... | ... | ... |
| Barbados | 1970 | 1 | 23 | 95 | 3 | 32 | 136 |
| | 1975 | 1 | 24 | 98 | 1 | 25 | 101 |
| | 1980 | 2 | 39 | 156 | ... | ... | ... |
| | 1985 | 2 | 40 | 158 | 4 | *80 | *317 |
| | 1990 | 2 | 30 | 117 | 4 | *95 | *369 |
| | 1991 | *2 | *35 | *135 | ... | ... | ... |
| | 1992 | 2 | 41 | 159 | ... | ... | ... |
| | 1993 | *2 | *41 | *158 | ... | ... | ... |

IV.8    Daily and non-daily newspapers
Journaux quotidiens et non quotidiens
Periódicos diarios y no diarios

| Country / Pays / País | Year / Année / Año | Daily newspapers / Journaux quotidiens / Periódicos diarios | | | Non-daily newspapers / Journaux non quotidiens / Periódicos no diarios | | |
|---|---|---|---|---|---|---|---|
| | | Number of titles / Nombre de titres / Número de títulos | Circulation / Diffusion / Circulación | | Number of titles / Nombre de titres / Número de títulos | Circulation / Diffusion / Circulación | |
| | | | Total (000) | Per 1,000 inhabitants / Pour 1 000 habitants / Por 1 000 habitantes | | Total (000) | Per 1,000 inhabitants / Pour 1 000 habitants / Por 1 000 habitantes |
| Barbados (cont) | 1994 | 2 | 41 | 157 | ... | ... | ... |
| | 1995 | *2 | *41 | *155 | ... | ... | ... |
| | 1996 | 2 | 53 | 199 | ... | ... | ... |
| Belize | 1970 | 1 | 4 | 33 | 4 | 16 | 130 |
| | 1975 | 1 | 4 | 30 | 4 | 20 | 150 |
| | 1980 | 1 | 3 | 21 | 7 | 45 | 308 |
| | 1985 | 1 | 3 | 18 | 5 | 22 | 133 |
| | 1990 | - | - | - | 7 | 37 | 197 |
| | 1996 | - | - | - | 6 | 80 | 363 |
| Bermuda | 1970 | 1 | 11 | 202 | ... | ... | ... |
| | 1975 | 1 | 11 | 215 | ... | ... | ... |
| | 1980 | 1 | 14 | 257 | ... | ... | ... |
| | 1985 | 1 | 18 | 316 | ... | ... | ... |
| | 1990 | 1 | *18 | *303 | 3 | 35 | 582 |
| | 1991 | *1 | *17 | *284 | ... | ... | ... |
| | 1992 | 1 | 16 | 265 | ... | ... | ... |
| | 1993 | *1 | *16 | *263 | ... | ... | ... |
| | 1994 | 1 | 16 | 260 | ... | ... | ... |
| | 1995 | 1 | 17 | 274 | 2 | 13 | 215 |
| | 1996 | 1 | 17 | 272 | 2 | 13 | 213 |
| British Virgin Islands | 1975 | - | - | - | 1 | 2 | 184 |
| | 1990 | - | - | - | 2 | 4 | 248 |
| | 1996 | - | - | - | 2 | 4 | 182 |
| Canada | 1970 | *100 | *4 200 | *197 | ... | ... | ... |
| | 1975 | 121 | *4 900 | *211 | 1 095 | *10 000 | *431 |
| | 1980 | 123 | 5 425 | 221 | 1 184 | 12 591 | 512 |
| | 1985 | 117 | 5 566 | 215 | 1 265 | 15 567 | 600 |
| | 1990 | 108 | 5 800 | 209 | ... | ... | ... |
| | 1991 | 106 | 5 815 | 206 | ... | ... | ... |
| | 1992 | 106 | *5 800 | *203 | ... | ... | ... |
| | 1993 | 108 | 5 537 | 191 | ... | ... | ... |
| | 1994 | 107 | *5 500 | *188 | ... | ... | ... |
| | 1995 | 107 | 4 881 | 165 | ... | ... | ... |
| | 1996 | 107 | 4 718 | 158 | *1 071 | *21 235 | *709 |
| Cayman Islands | 1990 | 1 | 6 | 209 | ... | ... | ... |
| | 1991 | *1 | *6 | *219 | ... | ... | ... |
| | 1992 | 1 | 8 | 263 | ... | ... | ... |
| | 1993 | *1 | *8 | *253 | ... | ... | ... |
| | 1994 | 1 | 8 | 243 | ... | ... | ... |
| | 1995 | *1 | *8 | *250 | ... | ... | ... |
| | 1996 | 1 | 9 | 256 | ... | ... | ... |
| Costa Rica | 1970 | 8 | 177 | 102 | ... | ... | ... |
| | 1975 | 6 | 174 | 88 | ... | ... | ... |
| | 1980 | 4 | 251 | 110 | ... | ... | ... |
| | 1985 | 6 | *280 | *106 | ... | ... | ... |
| | 1990 | 5 | *306 | *100 | ... | ... | ... |
| | 1991 | 4 | 314 | 100 | 12 | 106 | 34 |
| | 1992 | 4 | 322 | 99 | ... | ... | ... |
| | 1993 | *4 | *325 | *97 | ... | ... | ... |
| | 1994 | 5 | 333 | 96 | ... | ... | ... |
| | 1995 | *5 | *300 | *84 | *12 | 106 | 30 |
| | 1996 | 6 | 320 | 88 | ... | ... | ... |
| Cuba | 1970 | 16 | *500 | *59 | ... | ... | ... |
| | 1975 | 15 | *600 | *64 | ... | ... | ... |
| | 1980 | 17 | 1 050 | 108 | ... | ... | ... |
| | 1985 | 17 | 1 207 | 119 | ... | ... | ... |
| | 1990 | 19 | 1 824 | 172 | 4 | 36 | 3.4 |
| | 1991 | 17 | *1 300 | *121 | 17 | 922 | 86 |
| | 1992 | 17 | *1 700 | *158 | 17 | 1 121 | 104 |
| | 1993 | 17 | *1 300 | *120 | 17 | 250 | 23 |
| | 1994 | 17 | *1 300 | *119 | 17 | 173 | 16 |
| | 1995 | 17 | *1 300 | *119 | 24 | 422 | 38 |
| | 1996 | 17 | *1 300 | *118 | 24 | 456 | 41 |
| Dominica | 1970 | - | - | - | 3 | 7 | 93 |
| | 1990 | - | - | - | 2 | *7 | *98 |
| | 1992 | - | - | - | 1 | 5 | 63 |
| | 1994 | - | - | - | ... | ... | ... |
| | 1996 | - | - | - | 1 | 5 | 64 |
| Dominican Republic | 1970 | *5 | *80 | *18 | ... | ... | ... |
| | 1975 | 10 | *200 | *40 | ... | ... | ... |
| | 1980 | 7 | 220 | 39 | ... | ... | ... |
| | 1985 | 7 | 216 | 34 | 40 | ... | ... |
| | 1990 | 12 | *230 | *32 | ... | ... | ... |

Daily and non-daily newspapers    IV.8
Journaux quotidiens et non quotidiens
Periódicos diarios y no diarios

| Country / Pays / País | Year / Année / Año | Daily newspapers / Journaux quotidiens / Periódicos diarios | | | Non-daily newspapers / Journaux non quotidiens / Periódicos no diarios | | |
|---|---|---|---|---|---|---|---|
| | | Number of titles / Nombre de titres / Número de títulos | Circulation / Diffusion / Circulación | | Number of titles / Nombre de titres / Número de títulos | Circulation / Diffusion / Circulación | |
| | | | Total (000) Total (000) Total (000) | Per 1,000 inhabitants Pour 1 000 habitants Por 1 000 habitantes | | Total (000) Total (000) Total (000) | Per 1,000 inhabitants Pour 1 000 habitants Por 1 000 habitantes |
| Dominican Republic (cont) | 1991 | *11 | *250 | *34 | ... | ... | ... |
| | 1992 | 11 | *265 | *36 | ... | ... | ... |
| | 1993 | *11 | *265 | *35 | ... | ... | ... |
| | 1994 | 11 | 264 | 34 | ... | ... | ... |
| | 1995 | *11 | *264 | *34 | ... | ... | ... |
| | 1996 | 12 | *416 | *52 | ... | ... | ... |
| El Salvador | 1970 | 12 | 204 | 57 | ... | ... | ... |
| | 1975 | 10 | 211 | 51 | ... | ... | ... |
| | 1980 | 7 | 291 | 63 | ... | ... | ... |
| | 1985 | 4 | 243 | 51 | ... | ... | ... |
| | 1990 | 5 | *270 | *53 | 1 | 8 | 1.6 |
| | 1991 | 5 | 120 | 23 | 1 | 8 | 1.5 |
| | 1992 | 8 | *150 | *28 | 1 | 8 | 1.5 |
| | 1993 | 5 | 140 | 26 | 4 | 23 | 4.2 |
| | 1994 | 6 | 284 | 51 | 5 | 33 | 5.9 |
| | 1995 | *6 | *280 | *49 | 6 | 48 | 8.5 |
| | 1996 | 5 | 278 | 48 | 6 | 52 | 9.0 |
| Greenland | 1985 | - | - | - | 3 | 15 | 273 |
| | 1996 | 2 | *1 | *18 | ... | ... | ... |
| Grenada | 1970 | 2 | *4 | *42 | ... | ... | ... |
| | 1975 | 1 | *3 | *36 | ... | ... | ... |
| | 1980 | 1 | *4 | *45 | ... | ... | ... |
| | 1990 | - | - | - | 3 | ... | ... |
| | 1992 | - | - | - | 2 | *5 | *55 |
| | 1995 | - | - | - | 1 | 13 | 136 |
| | 1996 | - | - | - | 4 | 14 | 151 |
| Guadeloupe | 1970 | 2 | 24 | 76 | ... | ... | ... |
| | 1975 | 2 | 24 | 74 | ... | ... | ... |
| | 1980 | 1 | *32 | *98 | ... | ... | ... |
| | 1985 | 2 | *33 | *93 | ... | ... | ... |
| | 1990 | 1 | *34 | *87 | ... | ... | ... |
| | 1991 | *1 | *35 | *87 | ... | ... | ... |
| | 1992 | 1 | 35 | 87 | ... | ... | ... |
| | 1993 | *1 | *35 | *85 | ... | ... | ... |
| | 1994 | 1 | 35 | 84 | ... | ... | ... |
| | 1995 | *1 | *35 | *82 | ... | ... | ... |
| | 1996 | 1 | 35 | 81 | ... | ... | ... |
| Guatemala | 1970 | 8 | *200 | *38 | ... | ... | ... |
| | 1975 | 10 | 249 | 41 | 18 | 50 | 8.2 |
| | 1980 | 9 | *200 | *29 | ... | ... | ... |
| | 1985 | 9 | *250 | *32 | ... | ... | ... |
| | 1990 | 5 | 190 | 22 | ... | ... | ... |
| | 1991 | *5 | *185 | *21 | ... | ... | ... |
| | 1992 | 6 | 180 | 20 | ... | ... | ... |
| | 1993 | *5 | *200 | *21 | ... | ... | ... |
| | 1994 | 5 | 240 | 25 | ... | ... | ... |
| | 1995 | *5 | *240 | *24 | ... | ... | ... |
| | 1996 | 7 | *338 | *33 | ... | ... | ... |
| Haiti | 1970 | 7 | 79 | 17 | ... | ... | ... |
| | 1975 | 7 | 93 | 19 | ... | ... | ... |
| | 1980 | 4 | *36 | *6.6 | ... | ... | ... |
| | 1985 | 5 | *50 | *8.2 | ... | ... | ... |
| | 1990 | 4 | 45 | 6.4 | ... | ... | ... |
| | 1991 | *4 | *45 | *6.3 | ... | ... | ... |
| | 1992 | 4 | 45 | 6.2 | ... | ... | ... |
| | 1993 | *4 | *45 | *6.1 | ... | ... | ... |
| | 1994 | 4 | 45 | 6.0 | ... | ... | ... |
| | 1995 | *4 | *25 | *3.3 | ... | ... | ... |
| | 1996 | 4 | 20 | 2.5 | ... | ... | ... |
| Honduras | 1970 | *6 | *80 | *31 | ... | ... | ... |
| | 1975 | 8 | *120 | *40 | ... | ... | ... |
| | 1980 | 6 | 212 | 59 | ... | ... | ... |
| | 1985 | 7 | 293 | 70 | ... | ... | ... |
| | 1990 | 5 | 199 | 41 | ... | ... | ... |
| | 1991 | *4 | *170 | *34 | ... | ... | ... |
| | 1992 | 4 | *159 | *31 | ... | ... | ... |
| | 1993 | *4 | *200 | *37 | ... | ... | ... |
| | 1994 | 5 | *238 | *43 | ... | ... | ... |
| | 1995 | *5 | *240 | *42 | ... | ... | ... |
| | 1996 | 7 | *320 | *55 | ... | ... | ... |
| Jamaica | 1970 | *3 | *100 | *54 | ... | ... | ... |
| | 1975 | 3 | 131 | 65 | ... | ... | ... |
| | 1980 | 3 | 109 | 51 | ... | ... | ... |
| | 1985 | 4 | *138 | *60 | ... | ... | ... |

IV.8    Daily and non-daily newspapers
        Journaux quotidiens et non quotidiens
        Periódicos diarios y no diarios

| Country<br>Pays<br>País | Year<br>Année<br>Año | Daily newspapers / Journaux quotidiens / Periódicos diarios | | | Non-daily newspapers / Journaux non quotidiens / Periódicos no diarios | | |
|---|---|---|---|---|---|---|---|
| | | Number of titles<br>Nombre de titres<br>Número de títulos | Circulation / Diffusion / Circulación | | Number of titles<br>Nombre de titres<br>Número de títulos | Circulation / Diffusion / Circulación | |
| | | | Total (000)<br>Total (000)<br>Total (000) | Per 1,000 inhabitants<br>Pour 1 000 habitants<br>Por 1 000 habitantes | | Total (000)<br>Total (000)<br>Total (000) | Per 1,000 inhabitants<br>Pour 1 000 habitants<br>Por 1 000 habitantes |
| Jamaica (cont) | 1990 | 3 | *155 | *65 | ... | ... | ... |
| | 1991 | *3 | *160 | *67 | ... | ... | ... |
| | 1992 | 3 | *160 | *66 | ... | ... | ... |
| | 1993 | *3 | *160 | *66 | ... | ... | ... |
| | 1994 | 3 | *160 | *65 | ... | ... | ... |
| | 1995 | *3 | *160 | *65 | ... | ... | ... |
| | 1996 | 3 | *158 | *63 | ... | ... | ... |
| Martinique | 1970 | 2 | *25 | *77 | ... | ... | ... |
| | 1975 | 2 | 27 | 82 | ... | ... | ... |
| | 1980 | 1 | 28 | 86 | ... | ... | ... |
| | 1985 | 1 | 32 | 94 | ... | ... | ... |
| | 1990 | 1 | 32 | 87 | ... | ... | ... |
| | 1991 | *1 | *32 | *86 | ... | ... | ... |
| | 1992 | 1 | 32 | 86 | ... | ... | ... |
| | 1993 | *1 | *32 | *85 | ... | ... | ... |
| | 1994 | 1 | 32 | 84 | ... | ... | ... |
| | 1995 | *1 | *32 | *84 | ... | ... | ... |
| | 1996 | 1 | 30 | 78 | ... | ... | ... |
| Mexico | 1970 | 196 | 4 598 | 91 | 50 | 460 | 9.1 |
| | 1975 | 216 | 5 499 | 93 | 47 | 459 | 7.8 |
| | 1980 | 317 | 8 322 | 123 | 61 | 957 | 14 |
| | 1985 | 332 | 9 964 | 132 | 25 | 603 | 8.0 |
| | 1990 | *285 | 11 237 | 135 | *56 | 1 593 | 19 |
| | 1991 | 290 | 9 502 | 112 | 53 | 1 451 | 17 |
| | 1992 | 292 | 10 231 | 118 | 56 | 1 258 | 15 |
| | 1993 | 308 | 10 190 | 116 | 45 | 1 276 | 15 |
| | 1994 | 309 | 10 420 | 116 | 45 | 1 274 | 14 |
| | 1995 | 301 | 9 338 | 102 | 21 | 648 | 7.1 |
| | 1996 | 295 | 9 030 | 97 | 23 | 620 | 6.7 |
| Montserrat | 1990 | - | - | - | 2 | 2 | 201 |
| | 1996 | - | - | - | 2 | 3 | 252 |
| Netherlands Antilles | 1970 | 5 | 33 | 206 | ... | ... | ... |
| | 1975 | 5 | 55 | 328 | ... | ... | ... |
| | 1980 | 8 | *52 | *299 | ... | ... | ... |
| | 1985 | 6 | *54 | *297 | ... | ... | ... |
| | 1990 | 6 | *54 | *288 | ... | ... | ... |
| | 1991 | *6 | *53 | *278 | ... | ... | ... |
| | 1992 | 6 | 53 | 273 | ... | ... | ... |
| | 1993 | *6 | *53 | *268 | ... | ... | ... |
| | 1994 | 6 | 53 | 263 | ... | ... | ... |
| | 1995 | *6 | *53 | *258 | ... | ... | ... |
| | 1996 | 6 | 70 | 334 | ... | ... | ... |
| Nicaragua | 1970 | *5 | *80 | *38 | ... | ... | ... |
| | 1975 | 7 | *100 | *40 | ... | ... | ... |
| | 1980 | 3 | 136 | 47 | ... | ... | ... |
| | 1985 | 3 | *160 | *47 | ... | ... | ... |
| | 1990 | 6 | *180 | *47 | ... | ... | ... |
| | 1991 | *5 | *150 | *38 | ... | ... | ... |
| | 1992 | 3 | *130 | *32 | ... | ... | ... |
| | 1993 | *3 | *110 | *26 | ... | ... | ... |
| | 1994 | 4 | 130 | 30 | ... | ... | ... |
| | 1995 | *4 | *130 | *29 | ... | ... | ... |
| | 1996 | 4 | *135 | *30 | ... | ... | ... |
| Panama | 1970 | 7 | 130 | 86 | ... | ... | ... |
| | 1975 | 6 | 131 | 76 | ... | ... | ... |
| | 1980 | 5 | *110 | *56 | ... | ... | ... |
| | 1985 | 7 | 245 | 113 | ... | ... | ... |
| | 1990 | 8 | *234 | *98 | ... | ... | ... |
| | 1991 | *8 | *230 | *94 | ... | ... | ... |
| | 1992 | 8 | 223 | 90 | ... | ... | ... |
| | 1993 | *8 | *220 | *87 | ... | ... | ... |
| | 1994 | 7 | 160 | 62 | ... | ... | ... |
| | 1995 | *7 | *160 | *61 | ... | ... | ... |
| | 1996 | 7 | 166 | 62 | ... | ... | ... |
| Puerto Rico | 1970 | 4 | 495 | 182 | ... | ... | ... |
| | 1975 | 4 | 430 | 146 | ... | ... | ... |
| | 1980 | 4 | 512 | 160 | ... | ... | ... |
| | 1985 | 5 | 599 | 177 | ... | ... | ... |
| | 1990 | 3 | 456 | 129 | ... | ... | ... |
| | 1991 | *3 | *480 | *135 | ... | ... | ... |
| | 1992 | 3 | 507 | 141 | ... | ... | ... |
| | 1993 | *3 | *480 | *132 | ... | ... | ... |
| | 1994 | 3 | 475 | 129 | ... | ... | ... |
| | 1995 | *3 | *475 | *128 | ... | ... | ... |
| | 1996 | 3 | 475 | 127 | ... | ... | ... |

Daily and non-daily newspapers
Journaux quotidiens et non quotidiens
Periódicos diarios y no diarios

IV.8

| Country / Pays / País | Year / Année / Año | Daily newspapers / Journaux quotidiens / Periódicos diarios | | | Non-daily newspapers / Journaux non quotidiens / Periódicos no diarios | | |
|---|---|---|---|---|---|---|---|
| | | Number of titles / Nombre de titres / Número de títulos | Circulation / Diffusion / Circulación | | Number of titles / Nombre de titres / Número de títulos | Circulation / Diffusion / Circulación | |
| | | | Total (000) / Total (000) / Total (000) | Per 1,000 inhabitants / Pour 1 000 habitants / Por 1 000 habitantes | | Total (000) / Total (000) / Total (000) | Per 1,000 inhabitants / Pour 1 000 habitants / Por 1 000 habitantes |
| St. Kitts and Nevis | 1970 | - | - | - | 2 | 9 | 182 |
| | 1975 | - | - | - | 2 | 9 | 187 |
| | 1980 | - | - | - | 2 | 9 | 197 |
| | 1985 | - | - | - | 5 | 19 | 432 |
| | 1990 | - | - | - | 2 | 5 | 119 |
| | 1992 | - | - | - | 2 | 6 | 146 |
| | 1993 | - | - | - | 2 | 6 | 147 |
| | 1996 | - | - | - | 2 | 10 | 239 |
| St. Lucia | 1985 | - | - | - | ... | ... | ... |
| | 1990 | - | - | - | 3 | 18 | 134 |
| | 1992 | - | - | - | 3 | 18 | 130 |
| | 1995 | - | - | - | 5 | 34 | 236 |
| | 1996 | - | - | - | 5 | 34 | 233 |
| St. Pierre and Miquelon | 1990 | - | - | - | 1 | 2 | 297 |
| | 1992 | - | - | - | 1 | 2 | 294 |
| | 1996 | - | - | - | 1 | 2 | 293 |
| St. Vincent and the Grenadines | 1970 | - | - | - | 2 | 4 | 46 |
| | 1975 | - | - | - | 3 | 5 | 55 |
| | 1980 | - | - | - | 3 | 5 | 54 |
| | 1985 | - | - | - | 2 | 5 | 45 |
| | 1995 | 1 | 1 | 9.1 | 6 | 34 | 305 |
| | 1996 | 1 | 1 | 9.0 | 6 | 34 | 302 |
| Trinidad and Tobago | 1970 | 3 | 140 | 145 | ... | ... | ... |
| | 1975 | 3 | 135 | 134 | ... | ... | ... |
| | 1980 | 4 | *155 | *143 | ... | ... | ... |
| | 1985 | 4 | 173 | 147 | 2 | 160 | 136 |
| | 1990 | 2 | 95 | 78 | 5 | 125 | 103 |
| | 1991 | *2 | *120 | *98 | ... | ... | ... |
| | 1992 | 4 | 175 | 142 | ... | ... | ... |
| | 1993 | *4 | *160 | *129 | ... | ... | ... |
| | 1994 | *4 | *150 | *120 | ... | ... | ... |
| | 1995 | *4 | *150 | *119 | ... | ... | ... |
| | 1996 | 4 | 156 | 123 | 5 | *150 | *118 |
| Turks and Caicos Islands | 1990 | - | - | - | 1 | 10 | 865 |
| | 1992 | - | - | - | 1 | 10 | 799 |
| | 1996 | - | - | - | 1 | 5 | 344 |
| U. S. Virgin Islands | 1970 | 3 | 14 | 220 | ... | ... | ... |
| | 1975 | 3 | 17 | 180 | ... | ... | ... |
| | 1980 | 3 | 17 | 171 | ... | ... | ... |
| | 1985 | 3 | 21 | 214 | ... | ... | ... |
| | 1990 | 2 | 19 | 188 | ... | ... | ... |
| | 1991 | *2 | *20 | *197 | ... | ... | ... |
| | 1992 | 2 | 22 | 219 | ... | ... | ... |
| | 1993 | *2 | *23 | *231 | ... | ... | ... |
| | 1994 | 2 | 26 | 260 | ... | ... | ... |
| | 1995 | 2 | 24 | 247 | ... | ... | ... |
| | 1996 | 3 | 42 | 437 | ... | ... | ... |
| United States | 1970 | 1 763 | 62 108 | 296 | 7 696 | ... | ... |
| | 1975 | 1 775 | 60 655 | 275 | 9 589 | ... | ... |
| | 1980 | 1 745 | 62 200 | 270 | 7 696 | ... | ... |
| | 1985 | 1 676 | 62 800 | 260 | 7 328 | ... | ... |
| | 1990 | 1 611 | 62 328 | 245 | 8 999 | ... | ... |
| | 1991 | 1 586 | 60 700 | 236 | 9 120 | ... | ... |
| | 1992 | 1 570 | 60 164 | 232 | 8 855 | ... | ... |
| | 1993 | 1 556 | 59 815 | 228 | 9 816 | *71 500 | *273 |
| | 1994 | 1 548 | 59 305 | 224 | 9 728 | 70 000 | 265 |
| | 1995 | 1 533 | 58 193 | 218 | *9 728 | *70 000 | *262 |
| | 1996 | 1 520 | 56 990 | 212 | ... | ... | ... |
| **South America** | | | | | | | |
| Argentina | 1970 | 179 | *4 300 | *179 | ... | ... | ... |
| | 1975 | 164 | *3 000 | *115 | ... | ... | ... |
| | 1980 | 220 | *4 000 | *142 | ... | ... | ... |
| | 1985 | 218 | *3 940 | *130 | ... | ... | ... |
| | 1990 | 159 | *4 000 | *123 | ... | ... | ... |
| | 1991 | *180 | *4 500 | *136 | ... | ... | ... |
| | 1992 | 190 | *4 780 | *143 | *7 | *350 | *10 |
| | 1993 | 80 | 2 600 | 77 | ... | ... | ... |
| | 1994 | 187 | *4 705 | *137 | ... | ... | ... |
| | 1995 | *190 | *4 300 | *124 | ... | ... | ... |
| | 1996 | 181 | *4 320 | *123 | ... | ... | ... |
| Bolivia | 1970 | 13 | 208 | 49 | ... | ... | ... |
| | 1975 | 14 | 199 | 42 | ... | ... | ... |

IV.8   Daily and non-daily newspapers
Journaux quotidiens et non quotidiens
Periódicos diarios y no diarios

| Country / Pays / País | Year / Année / Año | Daily newspapers / Journaux quotidiens / Periódicos diarios | | | Non-daily newspapers / Journaux non quotidiens / Periódicos no diarios | | |
|---|---|---|---|---|---|---|---|
| | | Number of titles / Nombre de titres / Número de títulos | Circulation / Diffusion / Circulación | | Number of titles / Nombre de titres / Número de títulos | Circulation / Diffusion / Circulación | |
| | | | Total (000) | Per 1,000 inhabitants / Pour 1 000 habitants / Por 1 000 habitantes | | Total (000) | Per 1,000 inhabitants / Pour 1 000 habitants / Por 1 000 habitantes |
| Bolivia (cont) | 1980 | 14 | 226 | 42 | ... | ... | ... |
| | 1985 | 14 | *290 | *49 | ... | ... | ... |
| | 1990 | 17 | *400 | *61 | ... | ... | ... |
| | 1991 | *17 | *395 | *59 | ... | ... | ... |
| | 1992 | 16 | *390 | *57 | ... | ... | ... |
| | 1993 | *16 | *400 | *57 | ... | ... | ... |
| | 1994 | 17 | *410 | *57 | ... | ... | ... |
| | 1995 | *17 | *410 | *55 | ... | ... | ... |
| | 1996 | 18 | *420 | *55 | ... | ... | ... |
| Brazil | 1970 | *250 | *4 000 | *42 | ... | ... | ... |
| | 1975 | 289 | 4 653 | 43 | 836 | 2 598 | 24 |
| | 1980 | 343 | 5 482 | 45 | 1 175 | 4 530 | 37 |
| | 1985 | 322 | 6 534 | 48 | 1 297 | 4 766 | 35 |
| | 1990 | 356 | *6 400 | *43 | ... | ... | ... |
| | 1991 | *360 | *8 300 | *55 | ... | ... | ... |
| | 1992 | 373 | *8 500 | *56 | ... | ... | ... |
| | 1993 | 323 | 6 296 | 41 | - | ... | ... |
| | 1994 | 317 | *7 224 | *46 | - | ... | ... |
| | 1995 | 352 | 6 551 | 41 | 703 | ... | ... |
| | 1996 | 380 | 6 472 | 40 | 938 | ... | ... |
| Chile | 1970 | *45 | *900 | *95 | ... | ... | ... |
| | 1975 | 47 | *1 000 | *97 | ... | ... | ... |
| | 1980 | 34 | *1 200 | *108 | ... | ... | ... |
| | 1985 | *38 | *1 250 | *104 | ... | ... | ... |
| | 1990 | *45 | *1 350 | *103 | ... | ... | ... |
| | 1991 | 44 | *1 352 | *101 | 38 | 67 | 5.1 |
| | 1992 | 45 | *1 354 | *100 | 48 | 102 | 7.5 |
| | 1993 | 51 | *1 356 | *98 | 43 | ... | ... |
| | 1994 | 52 | *1 358 | *97 | 32 | ... | ... |
| | 1995 | 56 | *1 400 | *99 | 68 | ... | ... |
| | 1996 | 52 | *1 410 | *98 | 63 | ... | ... |
| Colombia | 1970 | *30 | *1 200 | *53 | ... | ... | ... |
| | 1975 | 40 | *1 450 | *57 | 8 | 125 | 4.9 |
| | 1980 | 36 | *1 400 | *49 | ... | ... | ... |
| | 1985 | *46 | *1 800 | *57 | ... | ... | ... |
| | 1990 | 45 | *2 000 | *57 | ... | ... | ... |
| | 1991 | *45 | *2 050 | *57 | ... | ... | ... |
| | 1992 | 46 | *2 100 | *58 | ... | ... | ... |
| | 1993 | 19 | *1 800 | *49 | (3) 4 | (3) 32 | 0.9 |
| | 1994 | 34 | *1 552 | *41 | (3) 4 | (3) 45 | 1.2 |
| | 1995 | *34 | *1 500 | *39 | (3) 4 | (3) 58 | 1.5 |
| | 1996 | 37 | *1 800 | *46 | (3) 5 | (3) 65 | 1.7 |
| Ecuador | 1970 | 25 | 250 | 42 | ... | ... | ... |
| | 1975 | 29 | *333 | *48 | ... | ... | ... |
| | 1980 | 18 | 558 | 70 | ... | ... | ... |
| | 1985 | 26 | *800 | *88 | ... | ... | ... |
| | 1990 | 25 | *820 | *80 | ... | ... | ... |
| | 1991 | 36 | 688 | 65 | ... | ... | ... |
| | 1992 | 36 | 688 | 64 | ... | ... | ... |
| | 1993 | *30 | *750 | *68 | ... | ... | ... |
| | 1994 | 24 | 808 | 72 | ... | ... | ... |
| | 1995 | *24 | *800 | *70 | ... | ... | ... |
| | 1996 | 29 | *820 | *70 | ... | ... | ... |
| Falkland Islands (Malvinas) | 1995 | - | - | - | 2 | 0.9 | 410 |
| | 1996 | - | - | - | 3 | 1 | 453 |
| French Guiana | 1970 | 1 | 2 | 31 | - | - | - |
| | 1975 | 1 | 2 | 26 | - | - | - |
| | 1980 | 1 | 1 | 15 | ... | ... | ... |
| | 1985 | 1 | 1 | 11 | ... | ... | ... |
| | 1990 | 1 | 1 | 8.5 | ... | ... | ... |
| | 1991 | *1 | *1 | *8.2 | ... | ... | ... |
| | 1992 | 1 | 2 | 12 | ... | ... | ... |
| | 1993 | *1 | *2 | *12 | ... | ... | ... |
| | 1994 | 1 | 2 | 11 | ... | ... | ... |
| | 1995 | 1 | 2 | 11 | ... | ... | ... |
| | 1996 | 1 | 2 | 10 | ... | ... | ... |
| Guyana | 1970 | 3 | 44 | 61 | ... | ... | ... |
| | 1975 | 2 | 50 | 68 | ... | ... | ... |
| | 1980 | 1 | 58 | 76 | ... | ... | ... |
| | 1985 | 2 | 78 | 98 | ... | ... | ... |
| | 1990 | 2 | *48 | *60 | ... | ... | ... |
| | 1991 | *2 | *46 | *58 | ... | ... | ... |
| | 1992 | 2 | *44 | *55 | ... | ... | ... |
| | 1993 | *2 | *42 | *52 | ... | ... | ... |
| | 1994 | 2 | *40 | *49 | ... | ... | ... |

Daily and non-daily newspapers IV.8
Journaux quotidiens et non quotidiens
Periódicos diarios y no diarios

| Country / Pays / País | Year / Année / Año | Daily newspapers / Journaux quotidiens / Periódicos diarios | | | Non-daily newspapers / Journaux non quotidiens / Periódicos no diarios | | |
|---|---|---|---|---|---|---|---|
| | | Number of titles / Nombre de titres / Número de títulos | Circulation / Diffusion / Circulación | | Number of titles / Nombre de titres / Número de títulos | Circulation / Diffusion / Circulación | |
| | | | Total (000) / Total (000) / Total (000) | Per 1,000 inhabitants / Pour 1 000 habitants / Por 1 000 habitantes | | Total (000) / Total (000) / Total (000) | Per 1,000 inhabitants / Pour 1 000 habitants / Por 1 000 habitantes |
| Guyana (cont) | 1995 | 2 | 39 | 47 | ... | ... | ... |
| | 1996 | 2 | 42 | 50 | ... | ... | ... |
| Paraguay | 1970 | 11 | *200 | *85 | ... | ... | ... |
| | 1975 | 8 | *140 | *53 | ... | ... | ... |
| | 1980 | 5 | *160 | *51 | ... | ... | ... |
| | 1985 | 6 | *170 | *47 | ... | ... | ... |
| | 1990 | 5 | *165 | *39 | ... | ... | ... |
| | 1991 | *5 | *163 | *38 | ... | ... | ... |
| | 1992 | 5 | 168 | 38 | ... | ... | ... |
| | 1993 | *5 | *180 | *39 | ... | ... | ... |
| | 1994 | 5 | 203 | 43 | ... | ... | ... |
| | 1995 | *5 | *200 | *41 | ... | ... | ... |
| | 1996 | 5 | 213 | 43 | ... | ... | ... |
| Peru | 1970 | 85 | *1 660 | *126 | ... | ... | ... |
| | 1975 | 49 | 1 377 | 91 | 31 | 2 799 | 185 |
| | 1980 | 66 | *1 400 | *81 | ... | ... | ... |
| | 1985 | 70 | *1 600 | *82 | ... | ... | ... |
| | 1990 | 66 | *1 700 | *79 | ... | ... | ... |
| | 1991 | *60 | *1 650 | *75 | ... | ... | ... |
| | 1992 | 59 | *1 590 | *71 | ... | ... | ... |
| | 1993 | 63 | *1 698 | *75 | ... | ... | ... |
| | 1994 | 48 | 2 003 | 87 | ... | ... | ... |
| | 1995 | *48 | *2 000 | *85 | ... | ... | ... |
| | 1996 | *74 | *2 000 | *84 | ... | ... | ... |
| Suriname | 1970 | 5 | 20 | 54 | ... | ... | ... |
| | 1975 | 7 | *35 | *96 | ... | ... | ... |
| | 1980 | 4 | *45 | *127 | ... | ... | ... |
| | 1985 | 5 | *55 | *143 | ... | ... | ... |
| | 1990 | 2 | 40 | 100 | ... | ... | ... |
| | 1991 | *2 | *41 | *102 | ... | ... | ... |
| | 1992 | 3 | *43 | *106 | 1 | *5 | *12 |
| | 1993 | *3 | *43 | *106 | ... | ... | ... |
| | 1994 | 3 | *43 | *105 | ... | ... | ... |
| | 1995 | 2 | 50 | 122 | 5 | 34 | 83 |
| | 1996 | 2 | 50 | 122 | 5 | 44 | 107 |
| Uruguay | 1970 | *25 | *750 | *267 | ... | ... | ... |
| | 1975 | 30 | *800 | *283 | ... | ... | ... |
| | 1980 | 24 | *700 | *240 | ... | ... | ... |
| | 1985 | 25 | *680 | *226 | 92 | ... | ... |
| | 1990 | 30 | *720 | *232 | ... | ... | ... |
| | 1991 | *31 | *730 | *233 | ... | ... | ... |
| | 1992 | 32 | *750 | *238 | ... | ... | ... |
| | 1993 | 32 | *750 | *236 | ... | ... | ... |
| | 1994 | 32 | *750 | *235 | ... | ... | ... |
| | 1995 | 36 | *950 | *295 | 76 | ... | ... |
| | 1996 | 36 | *950 | *293 | 62 | ... | ... |
| Venezuela | 1970 | *40 | *1 000 | *93 | ... | ... | ... |
| | 1975 | 49 | *1 300 | *102 | ... | ... | ... |
| | 1980 | 66 | 2 937 | 195 | ... | ... | ... |
| | 1985 | 55 | *2 700 | *158 | ... | ... | ... |
| | 1990 | 54 | *2 800 | *144 | ... | ... | ... |
| | 1991 | *60 | *3 500 | *175 | ... | ... | ... |
| | 1992 | 82 | *4 200 | *205 | ... | ... | ... |
| | 1993 | *85 | *4 400 | *210 | ... | ... | ... |
| | 1994 | 89 | *4 559 | *213 | ... | ... | ... |
| | 1995 | *89 | *4 500 | *206 | ... | ... | ... |
| | 1996 | 86 | *4 600 | *206 | ... | ... | ... |
| **Asia** | | | | | | | |
| Afghanistan | 1970 | 18 | 101 | 7.4 | ... | ... | ... |
| | 1975 | 15 | *80 | *5.2 | 11 | 89 | 5.8 |
| | 1980 | 13 | *90 | *5.6 | ... | ... | ... |
| | 1985 | 13 | *110 | *7.6 | ... | ... | ... |
| | 1990 | 14 | *180 | *12 | ... | ... | ... |
| | 1991 | *15 | *150 | *9.7 | 31 | ... | ... |
| | 1992 | 16 | *206 | *12 | 13 | ... | ... |
| | 1993 | 17 | *219 | *12 | ... | ... | ... |
| | 1994 | 15 | 216 | 12 | ... | ... | ... |
| | 1995 | *15 | *200 | *10 | ... | ... | ... |
| | 1996 | 12 | 113 | 5.6 | ... | ... | ... |
| Armenia | 1991 | 8 | ... | ... | 62 | *344 | *97 |
| | 1992 | *7 | *84 | *23 | 57 | *200 | *56 |
| | 1993 | *7 | *84 | *23 | ... | ... | ... |
| | 1994 | 7 | *84 | *23 | ... | ... | ... |

IV.8 Daily and non-daily newspapers
Journaux quotidiens et non quotidiens
Periódicos diarios y no diarios

| Country / Pays / País | Year / Année / Año | Daily newspapers / Journaux quotidiens / Periódicos diarios | | | Non-daily newspapers / Journaux non quotidiens / Periódicos no diarios | | |
|---|---|---|---|---|---|---|---|
| | | Number of titles / Nombre de titres / Número de títulos | Circulation / Diffusion / Circulación | | Number of titles / Nombre de titres / Número de títulos | Circulation / Diffusion / Circulación | |
| | | | Total (000) | Per 1,000 inhabitants / Pour 1 000 habitants / Por 1 000 habitantes | | Total (000) | Per 1,000 inhabitants / Pour 1 000 habitants / Por 1 000 habitantes |
| Armenia (cont) | 1995 | 7 | *85 | *24 | 83 | 268 | 75 |
| | 1996 | 11 | ... | ... | 112 | *304 | *85 |
| Azerbaijan | 1991 | ... | ... | ... | 191 | 2 656 | 366 |
| | 1992 | 6 | 427 | 58 | 273 | 3 476 | 473 |
| | 1993 | *5 | *300 | *40 | ... | ... | ... |
| | 1994 | 3 | *214 | *29 | ... | ... | ... |
| | 1995 | 3 | *210 | *28 | 238 | ... | ... |
| | 1996 | 6 | ... | ... | 251 | ... | ... |
| Bahrain | 1970 | *1 | *8 | *36 | ... | ... | ... |
| | 1975 | *1 | *10 | *37 | ... | ... | ... |
| | 1980 | 3 | *14 | *40 | ... | ... | ... |
| | 1985 | 2 | 19 | 45 | ... | ... | ... |
| | 1990 | 2 | 29 | 59 | ... | ... | ... |
| | 1991 | *2 | *35 | *69 | ... | ... | ... |
| | 1992 | 3 | *43 | *83 | ... | ... | ... |
| | 1993 | 3 | 70 | 132 | 5 | 17 | 31 |
| | 1994 | 3 | *65 | *119 | ... | ... | ... |
| | 1995 | *3 | *65 | *117 | ... | ... | ... |
| | 1996 | 4 | 67 | 117 | ... | ... | ... |
| Bangladesh | 1970 | 25 | *200 | *3.0 | ... | ... | ... |
| | 1975 | 30 | *250 | *3.3 | ... | ... | ... |
| | 1980 | 44 | 274 | 3.1 | ... | ... | ... |
| | 1985 | 60 | 591 | 5.9 | 151 | 540 | 5.4 |
| | 1990 | 52 | *700 | *6.4 | ... | ... | ... |
| | 1991 | *50 | *700 | *6.3 | ... | ... | ... |
| | 1992 | 51 | *710 | *6.3 | ... | ... | ... |
| | 1993 | *51 | *800 | *7.0 | ... | ... | ... |
| | 1994 | 51 | *950 | *8.1 | ... | ... | ... |
| | 1995 | *51 | *950 | *8.0 | ... | ... | ... |
| | 1996 | 37 | 1 117 | 9.3 | ... | ... | ... |
| Bhutan | 1992 | - | - | - | 1 | 11 | 6.0 |
| | 1996 | - | - | - | 1 | 11 | 5.5 |
| Brunei Darussalam | 1970 | *1 | *2 | *15 | 1 | 20 | 154 |
| | 1975 | *1 | *3 | *19 | 3 | 56 | 345 |
| | 1980 | *1 | *4 | *21 | 1 | 25 | 130 |
| | 1985 | *1 | *5 | *22 | 2 | 69 | 310 |
| | 1990 | 1 | 10 | 39 | 3 | 87 | 339 |
| | 1991 | *1 | *15 | *57 | ... | ... | ... |
| | 1992 | 1 | 20 | 74 | 2 | 57 | 210 |
| | 1993 | *1 | *20 | *72 | ... | ... | ... |
| | 1994 | 1 | 20 | 70 | ... | ... | ... |
| | 1995 | *1 | *20 | *68 | ... | ... | ... |
| | 1996 | 1 | 21 | 69 | 1 | 45 | 149 |
| Cambodia | 1996 | 2 | 17 | 1.7 | ... | ... | ... |
| China | 1970 | ... | ... | ... | (4) 42 | (4) 13 009 | ... |
| | 1975 | ... | ... | ... | (4) 180 | (4) 32 030 | ... |
| | 1980 | ... | ... | ... | (4) 188 | (4) 6 236 | ... |
| | 1985 | 70 | *39 000 | *36 | *628 | *152 070 | *142 |
| | 1990 | 44 | *48 000 | *42 | *729 | *67 950 | *59 |
| | 1991 | ... | ... | ... | (4) 812 | (4) 124 330 | ... |
| | 1992 | ... | ... | ... | (4) 875 | (4) 134 409 | ... |
| | 1993 | ... | ... | ... | (4) 943 | (4) 136 268 | ... |
| | 1994 | ... | ... | ... | (4) 1 015 | (4) 131 481 | ... |
| China, Hong Kong SAR | 1970 | 57 | *3 000 | *761 | 17 | ... | ... |
| | 1975 | 82 | ... | ... | 36 | ... | ... |
| | 1980 | 41 | *3 600 | *714 | ... | ... | ... |
| | 1985 | 46 | *4 100 | *751 | ... | ... | ... |
| | 1990 | 38 | *4 250 | *745 | ... | ... | ... |
| | 1991 | 45 | *4 380 | *757 | 19 | ... | ... |
| | 1992 | 49 | *4 750 | *809 | 17 | ... | ... |
| | 1993 | *45 | *4 500 | *753 | 20 | ... | ... |
| | 1994 | 43 | *4 168 | *684 | 20 | ... | ... |
| | 1995 | 46 | *4 500 | *723 | 8 | ... | ... |
| | 1996 | 52 | *5 000 | *786 | 11 | ... | ... |
| Cyprus | 1970 | 10 | 68 | 111 | ... | ... | ... |
| | 1975 | 12 | *80 | *131 | ... | ... | ... |
| | 1980 | *11 | *78 | *128 | ... | ... | ... |
| | 1985 | 10 | 83 | 128 | 35 | 118 | 182 |
| | 1990 | 11 | 78 | 114 | 31 | 128 | 188 |
| | 1991 | 9 | 77 | 111 | 30 | 132 | 191 |
| | 1992 | 9 | 77 | 109 | 30 | 133 | 189 |
| | 1993 | 10 | 77 | 107 | 29 | 132 | 184 |

Daily and non-daily newspapers
Journaux quotidiens et non quotidiens
Periódicos diarios y no diarios

IV.8

| Country / Pays / País | Year / Année / Año | Daily newspapers / Journaux quotidiens / Periódicos diarios | | | Non-daily newspapers / Journaux non quotidiens / Periódicos no diarios | | |
|---|---|---|---|---|---|---|---|
| | | Number of titles / Nombre de titres / Número de títulos | Circulation / Diffusion / Circulación | | Number of titles / Nombre de titres / Número de títulos | Circulation / Diffusion / Circulación | |
| | | | Total (000) / Total (000) / Total (000) | Per 1,000 inhabitants / Pour 1 000 habitants / Por 1 000 habitantes | | Total (000) / Total (000) / Total (000) | Per 1,000 inhabitants / Pour 1 000 habitants / Por 1 000 habitantes |
| Cyprus (cont) | 1994 | 10 | 77 | 105 | 29 | 132 | 180 |
| | 1995 | 10 | 84 | 113 | 32 | 185 | 249 |
| | 1996 | 9 | 84 | 111 | 31 | 185 | 245 |
| East Timor | 1996 | - | - | - | ... | ... | ... |
| Georgia | 1996 | - | - | - | ... | ... | ... |
| India | 1970 | *800 | *7 000 | *13 | ... | ... | ... |
| | 1975 | 835 | 9 383 | 15 | 4 146 | 7 322 | 12 |
| | 1980 | 1 173 | 14 531 | 21 | ... | ... | ... |
| | 1985 | 1 802 | 19 804 | 26 | (2) 20 846 | (2) 42 177 | ... |
| | 1990 | ... | ... | ... | (2) 25 454 | (2) 30 191 | ... |
| | 1991 | ... | ... | ... | (2) 26 728 | (2) 29 389 | ... |
| | 1992 | ... | ... | ... | (2) 28 184 | (2) 35 281 | ... |
| | 1993 | ... | ... | ... | (2) 29 597 | (2) 38 123 | ... |
| | 1994 | ... | ... | ... | (2) 31 264 | (2) 40 568 | ... |
| | 1995 | ... | ... | ... | (2) 32 702 | (2) 43 192 | ... |
| Indonesia | 1970 | *50 | *1 500 | *12 | ... | ... | ... |
| | 1975 | *60 | *2 000 | *15 | ... | ... | ... |
| | 1980 | 84 | 2 281 | 15 | ... | ... | ... |
| | 1985 | 97 | 3 010 | 18 | 67 | 1 919 | 11 |
| | 1990 | 64 | 5 144 | 28 | 94 | 4 521 | 25 |
| | 1991 | 63 | 4 851 | 26 | 91 | 3 905 | 21 |
| | 1992 | 68 | 4 591 | 24 | 92 | 3 501 | 19 |
| | 1993 | 75 | 4 691 | 24 | 87 | 3 868 | 20 |
| | 1994 | 76 | 4 775 | 25 | 89 | 3 695 | 19 |
| | 1995 | 74 | 4 701 | 24 | 93 | 3 928 | 20 |
| | 1996 | 69 | 4 665 | 23 | 94 | 4 696 | 23 |
| Iran, Islamic Republic of | 1970 | 33 | *400 | *14 | ... | ... | ... |
| | 1975 | 19 | *700 | *21 | 38 | ... | ... |
| | 1980 | *45 | *970 | *25 | ... | ... | ... |
| | 1985 | 15 | *1 250 | *26 | ... | ... | ... |
| | 1990 | 21 | *1 500 | *27 | 50 | *470 | *8.3 |
| | 1991 | *15 | *1 300 | *23 | ... | ... | ... |
| | 1992 | 13 | *1 250 | *21 | ... | ... | ... |
| | 1993 | *13 | *1 200 | *20 | ... | ... | ... |
| | 1994 | 12 | *1 154 | *19 | ... | ... | ... |
| | 1995 | 27 | 1 446 | 23 | ... | ... | ... |
| | 1996 | 32 | 1 651 | 26 | ... | ... | ... |
| Iraq | 1970 | 4 | *150 | *16 | ... | ... | ... |
| | 1975 | 7 | *230 | *21 | ... | ... | ... |
| | 1980 | 5 | *340 | *26 | ... | ... | ... |
| | 1985 | 6 | *600 | *39 | 22 | ... | ... |
| | 1990 | 6 | *650 | *00 | ... | ... | ... |
| | 1991 | *6 | *655 | *35 | ... | ... | ... |
| | 1992 | 6 | *660 | *35 | ... | ... | ... |
| | 1993 | *5 | *600 | *31 | ... | ... | ... |
| | 1994 | 4 | 532 | 27 | ... | ... | ... |
| | 1995 | *4 | *530 | *26 | ... | ... | ... |
| | 1996 | 4 | 407 | 20 | ... | ... | ... |
| Israel | 1970 | 24 | 600 | 202 | ... | ... | ... |
| | 1975 | 23 | *850 | *246 | ... | ... | ... |
| | 1980 | 36 | *1 000 | *258 | ... | ... | ... |
| | 1985 | 21 | *1 100 | *260 | 83 | ... | ... |
| | 1990 | 30 | *1 200 | *258 | ... | ... | ... |
| | 1991 | *30 | *1 220 | *253 | ... | ... | ... |
| | 1992 | 31 | *1 240 | *248 | ... | ... | ... |
| | 1993 | *32 | *1 350 | *260 | ... | ... | ... |
| | 1994 | 34 | 1 534 | 285 | ... | ... | ... |
| | 1995 | *34 | *1 500 | *269 | ... | ... | ... |
| | 1996 | 34 | *1 650 | *288 | ... | ... | ... |
| Japan | 1970 | 178 | 53 304 | 511 | ... | ... | ... |
| | 1975 | 176 | 60 782 | 545 | ... | ... | ... |
| | 1980 | 151 | 66 258 | 567 | ... | ... | ... |
| | 1985 | 124 | 68 296 | 565 | ... | ... | ... |
| | 1990 | 125 | 72 524 | 587 | ... | ... | ... |
| | 1991 | 124 | 72 536 | 585 | ... | ... | ... |
| | 1992 | 121 | 71 690 | 576 | *16 | *9 100 | *73 |
| | 1993 | 122 | 72 043 | 577 | 6 | ... | ... |
| | 1994 | 121 | 71 924 | 575 | 6 | ... | ... |
| | 1995 | 121 | 72 047 | 574 | 6 | ... | ... |
| | 1996 | 122 | 72 705 | 578 | 6 | ... | ... |
| Jordan | 1970 | 5 | 56 | 24 | 3 | 1 | 0.4 |
| | 1975 | 4 | 58 | 22 | 6 | 1 | 0.4 |

IV.8   Daily and non-daily newspapers
Journaux quotidiens et non quotidiens
Periódicos diarios y no diarios

| Country / Pays / País | Year / Année / Año | Daily newspapers / Journaux quotidiens / Periódicos diarios | | | Non-daily newspapers / Journaux non quotidiens / Periódicos no diarios | | |
|---|---|---|---|---|---|---|---|
| | | Number of titles / Nombre de titres / Número de títulos | Circulation / Diffusion / Circulación | | Number of titles / Nombre de titres / Número de títulos | Circulation / Diffusion / Circulación | |
| | | | Total (000) / Total (000) / Total (000) | Per 1,000 inhabitants / Pour 1 000 habitants / Por 1 000 habitantes | | Total (000) / Total (000) / Total (000) | Per 1,000 inhabitants / Pour 1 000 habitants / Por 1 000 habitantes |
| Jordan (cont) | 1980 | 4 | 66 | 23 | 4 | 2 | 0.7 |
| | 1985 | 4 | 155 | 38 | 4 | 2 | 0.5 |
| | 1990 | 4 | 225 | 49 | 6 | 22 | 4.8 |
| | 1991 | 4 | *230 | *48 | 6 | 22 | 4.6 |
| | 1992 | 4 | 250 | 50 | 6 | 25 | 5.0 |
| | 1993 | 4 | 250 | 48 | 7 | 27 | 5.1 |
| | 1994 | 4 | 250 | 45 | 21 | 60 | 11 |
| | 1995 | 4 | 250 | 44 | 34 | 90 | 16 |
| | 1996 | 4 | 250 | 42 | 41 | 95 | 16 |
| Kazakstan | 1996 | - | - | - | ... | ... | ... |
| Korea, Democratic. People's Rep | 1970 | *8 | *3 000 | *210 | ... | ... | ... |
| | 1975 | 11 | *3 500 | *215 | ... | ... | ... |
| | 1980 | 11 | *4 000 | *226 | ... | ... | ... |
| | 1985 | 11 | *4 500 | *238 | ... | ... | ... |
| | 1990 | 11 | *5 000 | *244 | ... | ... | ... |
| | 1991 | *11 | *5 000 | *240 | ... | ... | ... |
| | 1992 | 11 | *5 000 | *236 | ... | ... | ... |
| | 1993 | *11 | *5 000 | *232 | ... | ... | ... |
| | 1994 | 11 | *5 000 | *229 | ... | ... | ... |
| | 1995 | *11 | *5 000 | *225 | ... | ... | ... |
| | 1996 | 3 | *4 500 | *199 | ... | ... | ... |
| Korea, Republic of | 1970 | 44 | 4 396 | 138 | ... | ... | ... |
| | 1975 | 36 | 6 010 | 170 | ... | ... | ... |
| | 1980 | 30 | 8 000 | 210 | ... | ... | ... |
| | 1985 | 35 | *10 000 | *245 | ... | ... | ... |
| | 1990 | 39 | *12 000 | *280 | ... | ... | ... |
| | 1991 | *50 | *15 000 | *347 | ... | ... | ... |
| | 1992 | 63 | *18 000 | *412 | ... | ... | ... |
| | 1993 | 116 | *17 500 | *397 | ... | ... | ... |
| | 1994 | 62 | *17 714 | *398 | ... | ... | ... |
| | 1995 | *62 | *17 700 | *394 | ... | ... | ... |
| | 1996 | 60 | ... | ... | ... | ... | ... |
| Kuwait | 1970 | 5 | 20 | 27 | 10 | 100 | 134 |
| | 1975 | 8 | 180 | 179 | 10 | 140 | 139 |
| | 1980 | 8 | 305 | 222 | 10 | 240 | 175 |
| | 1985 | 8 | 380 | 221 | 10 | 340 | 198 |
| | 1990 | 9 | *535 | *250 | 21 | ... | ... |
| | 1991 | 9 | *580 | *277 | 22 | ... | ... |
| | 1992 | 9 | *600 | *301 | 24 | ... | ... |
| | 1993 | 9 | *630 | *338 | 41 | ... | ... |
| | 1994 | 9 | 655 | 374 | 46 | ... | ... |
| | 1995 | 9 | 655 | 388 | 57 | ... | ... |
| | 1996 | 8 | 635 | 377 | 78 | ... | ... |
| Kyrgyzstan | 1990 | *2 | *30 | *6.8 | ... | ... | ... |
| | 1991 | *2 | *35 | *7.9 | ... | ... | ... |
| | 1992 | *2 | *38 | *8.5 | ... | ... | ... |
| | 1993 | 2 | 39 | 8.7 | 127 | 940 | 208 |
| | 1994 | 3 | 53 | 12 | 137 | 720 | 158 |
| | 1995 | 2 | 52 | 11 | 140 | 1 092 | 239 |
| | 1996 | 3 | 67 | 15 | 146 | 896 | 195 |
| Lao People's Democratic Republic | 1970 | *5 | *10 | *3.7 | ... | ... | ... |
| | 1975 | 8 | *15 | *5.0 | ... | ... | ... |
| | 1980 | 3 | *14 | *4.4 | ... | ... | ... |
| | 1985 | 3 | *13 | *3.6 | ... | ... | ... |
| | 1990 | 3 | *14 | *3.4 | ... | ... | ... |
| | 1991 | *3 | *14 | *3.3 | ... | ... | ... |
| | 1992 | 3 | *14 | *3.2 | ... | ... | ... |
| | 1993 | *3 | *14 | *3.1 | ... | ... | ... |
| | 1994 | 3 | *14 | *3.0 | ... | ... | ... |
| | 1995 | *3 | *14 | *2.9 | ... | ... | ... |
| | 1996 | 3 | 18 | 3.7 | ... | ... | ... |
| Lebanon | 1970 | *30 | *250 | *101 | 46 | ... | ... |
| | 1975 | 33 | *300 | *108 | ... | ... | ... |
| | 1980 | 14 | *290 | *109 | ... | ... | ... |
| | 1985 | 13 | *300 | *112 | ... | ... | ... |
| | 1990 | *14 | *320 | *125 | ... | ... | ... |
| | 1991 | *15 | *400 | *153 | ... | ... | ... |
| | 1992 | 16 | *500 | *185 | ... | ... | ... |
| | 1993 | *16 | *500 | *178 | ... | ... | ... |
| | 1994 | 16 | *500 | *172 | ... | ... | ... |
| | 1995 | 14 | *330 | *110 | ... | ... | ... |
| | 1996 | 15 | *435 | *141 | ... | ... | ... |
| Macau | 1970 | 6 | *40 | *158 | ... | ... | ... |
| | 1975 | 6 | *45 | *178 | ... | ... | ... |

Daily and non-daily newspapers IV.8
Journaux quotidiens et non quotidiens
Periódicos diarios y no diarios

| Country / Pays / País | Year / Année / Año | Daily newspapers / Journaux quotidiens / Periódicos diarios | | | Non-daily newspapers / Journaux non quotidiens / Periódicos no diarios | | |
|---|---|---|---|---|---|---|---|
| | | Number of titles / Nombre de titres / Número de títulos | Circulation / Diffusion / Circulación | | Number of titles / Nombre de titres / Número de títulos | Circulation / Diffusion / Circulación | |
| | | | Total (000) | Per 1,000 inhabitants / Pour 1 000 habitants / Por 1 000 habitantes | | Total (000) | Per 1,000 inhabitants / Pour 1 000 habitants / Por 1 000 habitantes |
| Macau (cont) | 1980 | 6 | *70 | *278 | ... | ... | ... |
| | 1985 | 9 | *250 | *817 | ... | ... | ... |
| | 1990 | 8 | *240 | *645 | ... | ... | ... |
| | 1991 | 11 | *245 | *637 | ... | ... | ... |
| | 1992 | 9 | *250 | *630 | *3 | ... | ... |
| | 1993 | *9 | *250 | *613 | ... | ... | ... |
| | 1994 | 9 | *250 | *597 | ... | ... | ... |
| | 1995 | *9 | *250 | *582 | ... | ... | ... |
| | 1996 | 10 | *200 | *455 | ... | ... | ... |
| Malaysia | 1970 | 37 | 783 | 72 | ... | ... | ... |
| | 1975 | 31 | 1 038 | 85 | 10 | 828 | 68 |
| | 1980 | 40 | *810 | *59 | ... | ... | ... |
| | 1985 | 32 | *1 500 | *96 | 19 | ... | ... |
| | 1990 | 45 | *2 000 | *112 | ... | ... | ... |
| | 1991 | 32 | 2 050 | 112 | 8 | 1 490 | 81 |
| | 1992 | 39 | *2 200 | *117 | 8 | 1 530 | 82 |
| | 1993 | 33 | 1 931 | 101 | - | - | - |
| | 1994 | 44 | *2 819 | *143 | - | - | - |
| | 1995 | 44 | 2 800 | 139 | 39 | 2 500 | 124 |
| | 1996 | 42 | 3 345 | 163 | 44 | 1 424 | 69 |
| Maldives | 1970 | *1 | *1 | *8.2 | ... | ... | ... |
| | 1975 | 1 | *1 | *7.3 | 6 | ... | ... |
| | 1980 | 2 | 1 | 6.3 | ... | ... | ... |
| | 1985 | 2 | 2 | 8.2 | 15 | 5 | 25 |
| | 1990 | *2 | *3 | *12 | ... | ... | ... |
| | 1991 | *2 | *3 | *13 | ... | ... | ... |
| | 1992 | 2 | 3 | 13 | ... | ... | ... |
| | 1993 | *2 | *3 | *12 | ... | ... | ... |
| | 1994 | 2 | 3 | 12 | ... | ... | ... |
| | 1995 | *2 | *3 | *12 | ... | ... | ... |
| | 1996 | 2 | 5 | 19 | ... | ... | ... |
| Mongolia | 1970 | 2 | 133 | 106 | ... | ... | ... |
| | 1975 | 1 | 112 | 77 | ... | ... | ... |
| | 1980 | 2 | 177 | 106 | ... | ... | ... |
| | 1985 | 2 | 177 | 93 | ... | ... | ... |
| | 1990 | 1 | 162 | 73 | 55 | 1 133 | 511 |
| | 1991 | *2 | *170 | *75 | ... | ... | ... |
| | 1992 | 3 | *208 | *90 | ... | ... | ... |
| | 1993 | *2 | *207 | *88 | - | - | - |
| | 1994 | 1 | 207 | 86 | - | - | - |
| | 1995 | 3 | 70 | 29 | 39 | 233 | 95 |
| | 1996 | 4 | 68 | 27 | 30 | 137 | 55 |
| Myanmar | 1970 | 8 | *200 | *7.4 | ... | ... | ... |
| | 1975 | 7 | 319 | 10 | ... | ... | ... |
| | 1980 | 7 | *350 | *10 | ... | ... | ... |
| | 1985 | 7 | 511 | 14 | ... | ... | ... |
| | 1990 | 2 | *700 | *17 | ... | ... | ... |
| | 1991 | 4 | 325 | 7.9 | ... | ... | ... |
| | 1992 | 2 | 324 | 7.8 | ... | ... | ... |
| | 1993 | 5 | 783 | 19 | ... | ... | ... |
| | 1994 | 5 | 1 032 | 24 | ... | ... | ... |
| | 1995 | 5 | 446 | 10 | ... | ... | ... |
| | 1996 | 5 | 449 | 10 | ... | ... | ... |
| Nepal | 1970 | 16 | *29 | *2.6 | 41 | ... | ... |
| | 1975 | 29 | *110 | *8.6 | ... | ... | ... |
| | 1980 | 28 | *120 | *8.3 | ... | ... | ... |
| | 1985 | 28 | *130 | *7.9 | ... | ... | ... |
| | 1990 | 28 | *150 | *8.0 | ... | ... | ... |
| | 1991 | *25 | *145 | *7.5 | ... | ... | ... |
| | 1992 | 25 | *140 | *7.1 | ... | ... | ... |
| | 1993 | 27 | *161 | *8.0 | ... | ... | ... |
| | 1994 | 28 | *162 | *7.8 | ... | ... | ... |
| | 1995 | *28 | *160 | *7.5 | ... | ... | ... |
| | 1996 | 29 | *250 | *11 | ... | ... | ... |
| Oman | 1985 | 3 | 51 | 36 | 3 | 14 | 9.8 |
| | 1990 | 4 | 62 | 34 | 6 | ... | ... |
| | 1991 | 4 | 73 | 39 | 6 | ... | ... |
| | 1992 | 4 | 79 | 41 | 5 | ... | ... |
| | 1993 | *4 | *65 | *32 | ... | ... | ... |
| | 1994 | 4 | 63 | 30 | ... | ... | ... |
| | 1995 | 4 | 63 | 29 | ... | ... | ... |
| | 1996 | 4 | 63 | 28 | ... | ... | ... |
| Pakistan | 1970 | *100 | *850 | *13 | ... | ... | ... |
| | 1975 | 102 | *993 | *13 | ... | ... | ... |
| | 1980 | 106 | *1 032 | *12 | ... | ... | ... |

IV.8 Daily and non-daily newspapers
Journaux quotidiens et non quotidiens
Periódicos diarios y no diarios

| Country / Pays / País | Year / Année / Año | Daily newspapers / Journaux quotidiens / Periódicos diarios | | | Non-daily newspapers / Journaux non quotidiens / Periódicos no diarios | | |
|---|---|---|---|---|---|---|---|
| | | Number of titles / Nombre de titres / Número de títulos | Circulation / Diffusion / Circulación Total (000) / Total (000) / Total (000) | Per 1,000 inhabitants / Pour 1 000 habitants / Por 1 000 habitantes | Number of titles / Nombre de titres / Número de títulos | Circulation / Diffusion / Circulación Total (000) / Total (000) / Total (000) | Per 1,000 inhabitants / Pour 1 000 habitants / Por 1 000 habitantes |
| Pakistan (cont) | 1985 | 118 | 1 149 | 11 | 346 | 449 | 4.4 |
| | 1990 | 398 | 1 826 | 15 | (2) 724 | (2) 1 720 | ... |
| | 1991 | 452 | ... | ... | (2) 719 | (2) 1 957 | ... |
| | 1992 | 274 | 2 855 | 23 | ... | ... | ... |
| | 1993 | *274 | *2 840 | *22 | ... | ... | ... |
| | 1994 | 273 | 2 840 | 21 | ... | ... | ... |
| | 1995 | *223 | *2 800 | *21 | ... | ... | ... |
| | 1996 | 264 | ... | ... | ... | ... | ... |
| Philippines | 1970 | 17 | 610 | 16 | ... | ... | ... |
| | 1975 | 15 | 850 | 20 | 84 | ... | ... |
| | 1980 | 22 | 2 000 | 41 | ... | ... | ... |
| | 1985 | 15 | 2 170 | 40 | 59 | 797 | 15 |
| | 1990 | 47 | *3 400 | *56 | 306 | *610 | *10 |
| | 1991 | *45 | *3 300 | *53 | ... | ... | ... |
| | 1992 | 43 | *3 200 | *50 | ... | ... | ... |
| | 1993 | 45 | 4 395 | 67 | 218 | 472 | 7.2 |
| | 1994 | 42 | 4 286 | 64 | ... | ... | - |
| | 1995 | *42 | *4 200 | *61 | 243 | 153 | 2.2 |
| | 1996 | 47 | 5 700 | 82 | ... | ... | - |
| Qatar | 1975 | 1 | *20 | *117 | ... | ... | ... |
| | 1980 | 3 | *30 | *131 | ... | ... | ... |
| | 1985 | 4 | 60 | 168 | 1 | 6 | 17 |
| | 1990 | 5 | *80 | *165 | 1 | *6 | *12 |
| | 1991 | *4 | *75 | *149 | 1 | *7 | *13 |
| | 1992 | 4 | *70 | *136 | 1 | *7 | *13 |
| | 1993 | 4 | 80 | 152 | 1 | 7 | 13 |
| | 1994 | 4 | 80 | 149 | 1 | 7 | 13 |
| | 1995 | 4 | 80 | 146 | *1 | *7 | *13 |
| | 1996 | 5 | 90 | 161 | *1 | *7 | *13 |
| Saudi Arabia | 1970 | 5 | 60 | 10 | ... | ... | ... |
| | 1975 | 12 | *215 | *30 | ... | ... | ... |
| | 1980 | 11 | 340 | 35 | 60 | 740 | 77 |
| | 1985 | 12 | 420 | 33 | 95 | 980 | 77 |
| | 1990 | 12 | 570 | 36 | 114 | 1 350 | 84 |
| | 1991 | 12 | ... | ... | 122 | 1 950 | 118 |
| | 1992 | 13 | 729 | 43 | 143 | 1 450 | 85 |
| | 1993 | 12 | 890 | 51 | 148 | ... | ... |
| | 1994 | 12 | 940 | 53 | 159 | ... | ... |
| | 1995 | 12 | 1 060 | 58 | 168 | *2 150 | *118 |
| | 1996 | 13 | 1 105 | 59 | 185 | ... | ... |
| Singapore | 1970 | 12 | *400 | *193 | ... | ... | ... |
| | 1975 | 10 | 449 | 198 | 4 | 253 | 112 |
| | 1980 | 12 | 690 | 286 | ... | ... | ... |
| | 1985 | 10 | *706 | *261 | ... | ... | ... |
| | 1990 | 8 | 763 | 253 | ... | ... | ... |
| | 1991 | *9 | *800 | *260 | ... | ... | ... |
| | 1992 | 10 | *930 | *296 | ... | ... | ... |
| | 1993 | 8 | 971 | 303 | 2 | ... | ... |
| | 1994 | 8 | 1 027 | 315 | 7 | 1 035 | 317 |
| | 1995 | *8 | *1 000 | *301 | 2 | ... | ... |
| | 1996 | 8 | 1 095 | 324 | 2 | ... | ... |
| Sri Lanka | 1970 | 20 | 612 | 49 | (2) 137 | (2) 1 141 | ... |
| | 1975 | 15 | 480 | 35 | (2) 142 | (2) 1 077 | ... |
| | 1980 | 21 | 450 | 30 | (2) 192 | (2) 1 556 | ... |
| | 1985 | 17 | 390 | 24 | (2) 196 | (2) 1 794 | ... |
| | 1990 | 18 | *550 | *32 | 81 | ... | ... |
| | 1991 | 10 | *350 | *20 | 72 | ... | ... |
| | 1992 | 10 | *480 | *28 | 80 | ... | ... |
| | 1993 | 9 | *440 | *25 | 67 | ... | ... |
| | 1994 | 9 | *450 | *25 | 80 | 1 800 | 101 |
| | 1995 | 9 | 515 | 29 | 38 | 2 520 | 141 |
| | 1996 | 9 | 530 | 29 | 40 | 2 665 | 147 |
| Syrian Arab Republic | 1970 | 5 | *60 | *9.6 | ... | ... | ... |
| | 1975 | 6 | *77 | *10 | 6 | ... | ... |
| | 1980 | 7 | *114 | *13 | ... | ... | ... |
| | 1985 | 7 | *163 | *16 | ... | ... | ... |
| | 1990 | 10 | *210 | *17 | ... | ... | ... |
| | 1991 | 8 | 248 | 19 | 5 | 49 | 3.9 |
| | 1992 | 8 | 248 | 19 | 5 | 49 | 3.8 |
| | 1993 | 8 | 261 | 19 | 5 | 52 | 3.9 |
| | 1994 | 8 | 261 | 19 | 5 | 52 | 3.8 |
| | 1995 | 8 | 274 | 19 | 5 | 55 | 3.8 |
| | 1996 | 8 | 287 | 20 | 5 | 57 | 3.9 |
| Tajikistan | 1990 | *10 | *250 | *47 | ... | ... | ... |
| | 1991 | 13 | 289 | 53 | 80 | 87 | 16 |

Daily and non-daily newspapers IV.8
Journaux quotidiens et non quotidiens
Periódicos diarios y no diarios

| Country / Pays / País | Year / Année / Año | Daily newspapers / Journaux quotidiens / Periódicos diarios | | | Non-daily newspapers / Journaux non quotidiens / Periódicos no diarios | | |
|---|---|---|---|---|---|---|---|
| | | Number of titles / Nombre de titres / Número de títulos | Circulation / Diffusion / Circulación | | Number of titles / Nombre de titres / Número de títulos | Circulation / Diffusion / Circulación | |
| | | | Total (000) Total (000) Total (000) | Per 1,000 inhabitants Pour 1 000 habitants Por 1 000 habitantes | | Total (000) Total (000) Total (000) | Per 1,000 inhabitants Pour 1 000 habitants Por 1 000 habitantes |
| Tajikistan (cont) | 1992 | 9 | 116 | 21 | 110 | 57 | 10 |
| | 1993 | *5 | *100 | *18 | 93 | 459 | 82 |
| | 1994 | 2 | *80 | *14 | 96 | 503 | 89 |
| | 1995 | *2 | *80 | *14 | 92 | 399 | 69 |
| | 1996 | 2 | *120 | *21 | 73 | 153 | 26 |
| Thailand | 1970 | 15 | 2 320 | 65 | 29 | 480 | 13 |
| | 1975 | 22 | 2 540 | 61 | 51 | 960 | 23 |
| | 1980 | 27 | 2 680 | 57 | 88 | 1 790 | 38 |
| | 1985 | 32 | 4 350 | 85 | 116 | 2 570 | 50 |
| | 1990 | 34 | 4 500 | 81 | 302 | 1 850 | 33 |
| | 1991 | 38 | 4 650 | 83 | 360 | 1 580 | 28 |
| | 1992 | 41 | 4 820 | 85 | 395 | 1 680 | 30 |
| | 1993 | 35 | 3 530 | 61 | 385 | 2 150 | 37 |
| | 1994 | 35 | 2 766 | 48 | 250 | 1 890 | 33 |
| | 1995 | 35 | 2 700 | 46 | 280 | 1 850 | 32 |
| | 1996 | 30 | 3 800 | 64 | 320 | 2 550 | 43 |
| Turkey | 1970 | (5) *50 | *1 500 | *42 | ... | ... | ... |
| | 1975 | (5) *50 | *2 000 | *50 | ... | ... | ... |
| | 1980 | (5) *50 | *2 500 | *56 | ... | ... | ... |
| | 1985 | (5) *50 | 3 020 | 60 | 354 | ... | ... |
| | 1990 | (5) 56 | *4 000 | *71 | 872 | 1 500 | 27 |
| | 1991 | (5) 56 | *4 200 | *73 | 1 020 | ... | ... |
| | 1992 | (5) 56 | *4 500 | *77 | 1 084 | ... | ... |
| | 1993 | (5) 56 | 4 678 | 79 | 1 091 | ... | ... |
| | 1994 | (5) 57 | *5 000 | *83 | 1 100 | ... | ... |
| | 1995 | (5) 57 | 5 600 | 91 | 1 321 | *2 000 | *33 |
| | 1996 | (5) 57 | 6 845 | 110 | 1 468 | ... | ... |
| Turkmenistan | 1996 | - | - | - | ... | ... | ... |
| United Arab Emirates | 1970 | *1 | *4 | *18 | - | - | - |
| | 1975 | 2 | 10 | 20 | - | - | - |
| | 1980 | 9 | 152 | 149 | 1 | 20 | 20 |
| | 1985 | 13 | 290 | 187 | 1 | 25 | 16 |
| | 1990 | 8 | 250 | 130 | ... | ... | ... |
| | 1991 | *9 | *280 | *141 | ... | ... | ... |
| | 1992 | 11 | *335 | *164 | ... | ... | ... |
| | 1993 | 8 | 300 | 143 | ... | ... | ... |
| | 1994 | 8 | 300 | 139 | ... | ... | ... |
| | 1995 | *8 | *310 | *140 | ... | ... | ... |
| | 1996 | 7 | 384 | 170 | ... | ... | ... |
| Uzbekistan | 1991 | 12 | ... | ... | 37 | 2 680 | 128 |
| | 1992 | 12 | ... | ... | 43 | 1 279 | 60 |
| | 1993 | 4 | ... | ... | 318 | 2 586 | 119 |
| | 1994 | 4 | ... | ... | 313 | 2 422 | 110 |
| | 1995 | 3 | 84 | 3.7 | 338 | 1 507 | 67 |
| | 1996 | 3 | 75 | 3.3 | 350 | 1 404 | 61 |
| Viet Nam | 1980 | 4 | *520 | *9.7 | ... | ... | ... |
| | 1985 | 4 | *540 | *9.0 | ... | ... | ... |
| | 1990 | 5 | *560 | *8.4 | ... | ... | ... |
| | 1991 | *4 | *565 | *8.3 | ... | ... | ... |
| | 1992 | 4 | *570 | *8.2 | ... | ... | ... |
| | 1993 | *4 | *570 | *8.0 | ... | ... | ... |
| | 1994 | 4 | *570 | *7.9 | ... | ... | ... |
| | 1995 | 10 | 294 | 4.0 | 184 | 2 910 | 39 |
| | 1996 | 10 | 300 | 4.0 | 214 | 4 023 | 54 |
| Yemen | 1990 | *2 | *200 | *17 | ... | ... | ... |
| | 1991 | *2 | *210 | *17 | ... | ... | ... |
| | 1992 | 4 | 236 | 18 | ... | ... | ... |
| | 1993 | *4 | *235 | *17 | ... | ... | ... |
| | 1994 | 3 | 230 | 16 | ... | ... | ... |
| | 1995 | *3 | *230 | *15 | ... | ... | ... |
| | 1996 | *3 | *230 | *15 | ... | ... | ... |
| **Europe** | | | | | | | |
| Albania | 1970 | 3 | *130 | *61 | 20 | 52 | 24 |
| | 1975 | 2 | 115 | 47 | ... | ... | ... |
| | 1980 | 2 | 145 | 54 | 29 | 59 | 22 |
| | 1985 | 2 | 135 | 46 | ... | ... | ... |
| | 1990 | 2 | 135 | 41 | ... | ... | ... |
| | 1991 | *3 | *140 | *42 | ... | ... | ... |
| | 1992 | 4 | *165 | *50 | ... | ... | ... |
| | 1993 | *3 | *150 | *46 | ... | ... | ... |
| | 1994 | 3 | *130 | *41 | ... | ... | ... |
| | 1995 | *3 | *130 | *41 | ... | ... | ... |
| | 1996 | 5 | 116 | 37 | ... | ... | ... |

**Daily and non-daily newspapers**
Journaux quotidiens et non quotidiens
Periódicos diarios y no diarios

| Country<br><br>Pays<br><br>País | Year<br><br>Année<br><br>Año | Daily newspapers / Journaux quotidiens / Periódicos diarios | | | Non-daily newspapers / Journaux non quotidiens / Periódicos no diarios | | | |
|---|---|---|---|---|---|---|---|---|
| | | Number of titles<br><br>Nombre de titres<br><br>Número de títulos | Circulation / Diffusion / Circulación | | Number of titles<br><br>Nombre de titres<br><br>Número de títulos | | Circulation / Diffusion / Circulación | |
| | | | Total (000)<br>Total (000)<br>Total (000) | Per 1,000 inhabitants<br>Pour 1 000 habitants<br>Por 1 000 habitantes | | | Total (000)<br>Total (000)<br>Total (000) | Per 1,000 inhabitants<br>Pour 1 000 habitants<br>Por 1 000 habitantes |
| Andorra | 1992 | 3 | *4 | *69 | 4 | | *8 | *143 |
| | 1993 | *3 | *4 | *67 | ... | | ... | ... |
| | 1994 | 3 | *4 | *65 | ... | | ... | ... |
| | 1995 | *3 | *4 | *62 | ... | | ... | ... |
| | 1996 | 3 | *4 | *60 | ... | | ... | ... |
| Austria | 1970 | 32 | 2 331 | 312 | 117 | | ... | ... |
| | 1975 | 30 | 2 405 | 317 | 129 | | ... | ... |
| | 1980 | 30 | 2 651 | 351 | 142 | | ... | ... |
| | 1985 | 33 | 2 729 | 361 | 145 | | ... | ... |
| | 1990 | 25 | 2 706 | 351 | 124 | | ... | ... |
| | 1991 | 23 | 2 560 | 330 | 118 | | ... | ... |
| | 1992 | 27 | 3 108 | 398 | 117 | | ... | ... |
| | 1993 | 16 | 2 529 | 321 | 141 | | ... | ... |
| | 1994 | 16 | 2 530 | 319 | 156 | | ... | ... |
| | 1995 | 17 | 2 088 | 261 | 156 | | ... | ... |
| | 1996 | 17 | *2 382 | *296 | 153 | | ... | ... |
| Belarus | 1990 | 28 | 2 937 | 286 | 196 | | 2 786 | 272 |
| | 1991 | 21 | 2 417 | 235 | 261 | | 3 404 | 330 |
| | 1992 | 10 | 1 899 | 184 | 338 | | 4 749 | 459 |
| | 1993 | *10 | *1 899 | *183 | ... | | ... | ... |
| | 1994 | 10 | 1 899 | 183 | ... | | ... | ... |
| | 1995 | *10 | *1 800 | *173 | ... | | ... | ... |
| | 1996 | 8 | ... | ... | ... | | ... | ... |
| Belgium | 1970 | 49 | *2 200 | *228 | ... | | ... | ... |
| | 1975 | 30 | 2 340 | 239 | ... | | ... | ... |
| | 1980 | 26 | 2 289 | 232 | ... | | ... | ... |
| | 1985 | 24 | 2 171 | 220 | 2 | | 30 | 3.0 |
| | 1990 | 33 | *2 000 | *201 | 3 | | *40 | *4.0 |
| | 1991 | 33 | *1 800 | *180 | 3 | | ... | ... |
| | 1992 | 33 | 1 704 | 170 | 3 | | *40 | *4.0 |
| | 1993 | 32 | 1 710 | 170 | ... | | ... | ... |
| | 1994 | 32 | 1 691 | 168 | ... | | ... | ... |
| | 1995 | 31 | 1 628 | 161 | ... | | ... | ... |
| | 1996 | 30 | 1 625 | 161 | ... | | ... | ... |
| Bosnia and<br>Herzegovina | 1990 | *2 | ... | ... | ... | | ... | ... |
| | 1991 | 2 | ... | ... | 23 | | 3 488 | 837 |
| | 1992 | 2 | 518 | 131 | 22 | | 2 508 | 635 |
| | 1993 | *2 | *518 | *140 | ... | | ... | ... |
| | 1994 | 2 | 518 | 147 | ... | | ... | ... |
| | 1995 | *2 | *520 | *152 | ... | | ... | ... |
| | 1996 | 3 | ... | ... | ... | | ... | ... |
| Bulgaria | 1970 | 13 | 1 857 | 219 | (6) 679 | | 4 114 | 485 |
| | 1975 | 14 | 2 109 | 242 | (6) 484 | | 3 940 | 452 |
| | 1980 | 14 | 2 244 | 253 | (6) 463 | (6) | 4 152 | 469 |
| | 1985 | 17 | 2 626 | 293 | (6) 377 | (6) | 4 563 | 509 |
| | 1990 | 24 | 4 065 | 466 | (6) 516 | (6) | 8 350 | 958 |
| | 1991 | 31 | 1 358 | 157 | (6) 696 | (6) | 8 133 | 938 |
| | 1992 | 46 | 1 464 | 170 | (6) 871 | (6) | 8 992 | 1 042 |
| | 1993 | 54 | 1 417 | 165 | (6) 874 | (6) | 8 280 | 964 |
| | 1994 | 17 | 1 843 | 216 | (6) *1 000 | (6) | *8 000 | *936 |
| | 1995 | *17 | *2 200 | *259 | (6) 1 000 | (6) | 8 810 | 1 037 |
| | 1996 | 17 | 2 145 | 254 | (6) 869 | (6) | 5 791 | 685 |
| Croatia | 1990 | 9 | 232 | 51 | 563 | | 110 | 24 |
| | 1991 | 8 | *73 | *16 | ... | | ... | ... |
| | 1992 | 9 | 75 | 17 | ... | | ... | ... |
| | 1993 | 9 | *150 | *33 | ... | | ... | ... |
| | 1994 | 9 | 495 | 110 | ... | | ... | ... |
| | 1995 | 9 | 480 | 107 | 766 | | 437 | 97 |
| | 1996 | 10 | 515 | 115 | 767 | | 584 | 130 |
| Czech Republic | 1990 | *70 | *8 000 | *776 | ... | | ... | ... |
| | 1991 | 88 | 9 000 | 873 | 858 | | ... | ... |
| | 1992 | 55 | 6 000 | 582 | 600 | | ... | ... |
| | 1993 | 31 | ... | ... | 168 | | 64 | 6.2 |
| | 1994 | 23 | 2 259 | 219 | 87 | | 928 | 90 |
| | 1995 | 23 | 2 950 | 286 | 172 | | 4 241 | 411 |
| | 1996 | 21 | 2 620 | 254 | 181 | | 4 200 | 407 |
| Denmark | 1970 | 55 | 1 790 | 363 | 14 | | 1 294 | 263 |
| | 1975 | 49 | 1 723 | 341 | 11 | | 1 214 | 240 |
| | 1980 | 48 | 1 874 | 366 | 11 | | 1 237 | 241 |
| | 1985 | 47 | 1 855 | 363 | 11 | | 1 251 | 245 |
| | 1990 | 47 | 1 810 | 352 | 12 | | 1 513 | 294 |
| | 1991 | 44 | 1 727 | 335 | 12 | | 1 505 | 292 |
| | 1992 | 42 | 1 710 | 331 | 11 | | 1 490 | 288 |
| | 1993 | 42 | 1 668 | 321 | 11 | | 1 482 | 286 |

Daily and non-daily newspapers **IV.8**
Journaux quotidiens et non quotidiens
Periódicos diarios y no diarios

| Country / Pays / País | Year / Année / Año | Daily newspapers / Journaux quotidiens / Periódicos diarios | | | Non-daily newspapers / Journaux non quotidiens / Periódicos no diarios | | |
|---|---|---|---|---|---|---|---|
| | | Number of titles / Nombre de titres / Número de títulos | Circulation / Diffusion / Circulación | | Number of titles / Nombre de titres / Número de títulos | Circulation / Diffusion / Circulación | |
| | | | Total (000) | Per 1,000 inhabitants / Pour 1 000 habitants / Por 1 000 habitantes | | Total (000) | Per 1,000 inhabitants / Pour 1 000 habitants / Por 1 000 habitantes |
| Denmark (cont) | 1994 | 37 | 1 616 | 310 | 11 | 1 495 | 287 |
| | 1995 | 37 | 1 610 | 308 | 11 | 1 482 | 284 |
| | 1996 | 37 | 1 628 | 311 | 11 | 1 500 | 286 |
| Estonia | 1990 | 11 | ... | ... | 42 | 863 | 549 |
| | 1991 | 10 | ... | ... | 48 | 1 110 | 710 |
| | 1992 | 10 | 307 | 198 | 50 | 800 | 517 |
| | 1993 | 12 | 277 | 181 | 56 | 930 | 608 |
| | 1994 | 15 | 279 | 185 | 71 | 885 | 587 |
| | 1995 | 15 | 243 | 164 | 71 | 622 | 419 |
| | 1996 | 15 | 255 | 174 | 59 | 531 | 362 |
| Faeroe Islands | 1980 | - | - | - | 6 | 38 | 881 |
| | 1990 | - | - | - | 7 | 6 | 128 |
| | 1991 | - | - | - | 8 | 6 | 129 |
| | 1992 | - | - | - | 7 | 6 | 130 |
| | 1995 | 1 | 6 | 134 | ... | ... | ... |
| | 1996 | 1 | 6 | 145 | ... | ... | ... |
| Federal Republic of Yugoslavia | 1990 | 15 | 366 | 36 | 947 | ... | ... |
| | 1991 | 11 | 973 | 95 | 790 | 10 692 | 1 044 |
| | 1992 | 10 | 544 | 53 | 599 | 5 088 | 492 |
| | 1993 | 11 | 511 | 49 | 439 | 3 172 | 304 |
| | 1994 | 15 | 966 | 92 | 514 | 3 405 | 324 |
| | 1995 | 17 | 850 | 80 | 573 | 3 781 | 358 |
| | 1996 | 18 | 1 128 | 106 | 602 | 3 935 | 371 |
| Finland | 1970 | 67 | *2 000 | *434 | 173 | ... | ... |
| | 1975 | 60 | 2 100 | 446 | 223 | ... | ... |
| | 1980 | 58 | 2 414 | 505 | 240 | ... | ... |
| | 1985 | 65 | 2 661 | 543 | 353 | ... | ... |
| | 1990 | 66 | 2 780 | 558 | 382 | ... | ... |
| | 1991 | 64 | 2 770 | 553 | 180 (7) | 1 350 | 270 |
| | 1992 | 58 | 2 578 | 512 | 184 (7) | 1 287 | 256 |
| | 1993 | 56 | 2 484 | 491 | 171 | 1 143 | 226 |
| | 1994 | 56 | 2 405 | 473 | 171 | 1 095 | 215 |
| | 1995 | 56 | 2 368 | 464 | 167 | 1 045 | 205 |
| | 1996 | 56 | 2 332 | 455 | 162 | 1 006 | 196 |
| France | 1970 | (8) 106 | 12 067 | 238 | ... | ... | ... |
| | 1975 | (8) 95 | *11 000 | *209 | ... | ... | ... |
| | 1980 | (8) 90 | 10 332 | 192 | ... | ... | ... |
| | 1985 | (8) 92 | 10 670 | 193 | ... | ... | ... |
| | 1990 | (8) 79 | 11 792 | 208 | 224 | 2 895 | 51 |
| | 1991 | (8) 77 | 11 695 | 205 | 227 | 3 068 | 54 |
| | 1992 | (8) *80 | *10 000 | *175 | ... | ... | ... |
| | 1993 | (8) 85 | 9 090 | 158 | 290 | 2 894 | 50 |
| | 1994 | (8) 118 | *13 685 | *237 | 295 | 2 856 | 49 |
| | 1995 | (8) *80 | *12 200 | *210 | 278 | 1 714 | 30 |
| | 1996 | (8) 117 | *12 700 | *218 | ... | ... | ... |
| Germany | 1990 | 356 | 24 174 | 305 | 34 | 5 725 | 72 |
| | 1991 | 410 | 26 425 | 331 | 36 | 4 871 | 61 |
| | 1992 | 416 | 25 952 | 323 | 38 | 5 322 | 66 |
| | 1993 | 417 | 25 902 | 320 | 40 | 6 837 | 85 |
| | 1994 | 411 | 25 757 | 317 | 39 | 6 874 | 85 |
| | 1995 | 389 | 25 600 | 313 | 38 | 7 100 | 87 |
| | 1996 | 375 | 25 500 | 311 | 36 | 6 600 | 81 |
| Gibraltar | 1970 | 2 | 6 | 236 | 3 | 9 | 341 |
| | 1975 | 1 | 3 | 109 | 2 | 6 | 221 |
| | 1980 | 1 | 2 | 84 | ... | ... | ... |
| | 1985 | 1 | 3 | 107 | ... | ... | ... |
| | 1990 | 2 | *4 | *156 | ... | ... | ... |
| | 1991 | *2 | *4 | *157 | ... | ... | ... |
| | 1992 | 2 | *4 | *158 | *5 | *6 | *234 |
| | 1993 | *2 | *5 | *190 | ... | ... | ... |
| | 1994 | 2 | *6 | *229 | ... | ... | ... |
| | 1995 | *2 | *6 | *231 | ... | ... | ... |
| | 1996 | 2 | *6 | *233 | ... | ... | ... |
| Greece | 1970 | 117 | 705 | 80 | 510 | ... | ... |
| | 1975 | 108 | 921 | 102 | 644 | ... | ... |
| | 1980 | 128 | *1 160 | *120 | ... | ... | ... |
| | 1985 | 140 | *1 210 | *122 | 1 009 | ... | ... |
| | 1990 | 130 | 1 250 | 122 | ... | ... | ... |
| | 1991 | *135 | *1 300 | *126 | ... | ... | ... |
| | 1992 | 145 | *1 400 | *135 | ... | ... | ... |
| | 1993 | *150 | *1 500 | *144 | ... | ... | ... |
| | 1994 | 168 | *1 622 | *155 | ... | ... | ... |
| | 1995 | *160 | *1 600 | *153 | ... | ... | ... |
| | 1996 | 156 | ... | ... | ... | ... | ... |

IV.8  Daily and non-daily newspapers
Journaux quotidiens et non quotidiens
Periódicos diarios y no diarios

| Country / Pays / País | Year / Année / Año | Daily newspapers / Journaux quotidiens / Periódicos diarios | | | Non-daily newspapers / Journaux non quotidiens / Periódicos no diarios | | |
|---|---|---|---|---|---|---|---|
| | | Number of titles / Nombre de titres / Número de títulos | Circulation / Diffusion / Circulación | | Number of titles / Nombre de titres / Número de títulos | Circulation / Diffusion / Circulación | |
| | | | Total (000) / Total (000) / Total (000) | Per 1,000 inhabitants / Pour 1 000 habitants / Por 1 000 habitantes | | Total (000) / Total (000) / Total (000) | Per 1,000 inhabitants / Pour 1 000 habitants / Por 1 000 habitantes |
| Holy See | 1970 | 1 | 70 | 70 000 | ... | ... | ... |
| | 1975 | 1 | 70 | 70 000 | 6 | 45 | 45 000 |
| | 1980 | 1 | 70 | 70 000 | ... | ... | ... |
| | 1985 | 1 | 70 | 70 000 | ... | ... | ... |
| | 1990 | 1 | 70 | 85 366 | ... | ... | ... |
| | 1991 | 1 | 70 | 92 715 | ... | ... | ... |
| | 1992 | 1 | 70 | 102 639 | ... | ... | ... |
| | 1993 | *1 | *70 | *115 132 | ... | ... | ... |
| | 1994 | 1 | 70 | 128 440 | ... | ... | ... |
| | 1995 | 1 | 70 | 140 000 | ... | ... | ... |
| | 1996 | 1 | 70 | 147 059 | ... | ... | ... |
| Hungary | 1970 | 27 | 2 207 | 213 | ... | ... | ... |
| | 1975 | 27 | 2 455 | 233 | 79 | 4 791 | 455 |
| | 1980 | 27 | 2 648 | 247 | *89 | *6 202 | *579 |
| | 1985 | 28 | 2 717 | 257 | 95 | 5 607 | 530 |
| | 1990 | 34 | 2 460 | 237 | 255 | 6 278 | 606 |
| | 1991 | 35 | 2 308 | 223 | 279 | 4 603 | 445 |
| | 1992 | *33 | 2 202 | 214 | *201 | *2 027 | *197 |
| | 1993 | *30 | 2 122 | 206 | *194 | *3 058 | *297 |
| | 1994 | *34 | 1 870 | 182 | *189 | *3 350 | *327 |
| | 1995 | 41 | 2 022 | 198 | 111 | 5 914 | 578 |
| | 1996 | 40 | 1 895 | 186 | 80 | 5 826 | 572 |
| Iceland | 1970 | 5 | 86 | 421 | 63 | ... | ... |
| | 1975 | 5 | 93 | 427 | 64 | ... | ... |
| | 1980 | 6 | 125 | 548 | 56 | ... | ... |
| | 1985 | 6 | 113 | 466 | 65 | ... | ... |
| | 1990 | 6 | *130 | *510 | 66 | ... | ... |
| | 1991 | 6 | *133 | *516 | 58 | ... | ... |
| | 1992 | 5 | *135 | *519 | 72 | ... | ... |
| | 1993 | 5 | *136 | *517 | 78 | ... | ... |
| | 1994 | 5 | *137 | *516 | 77 | ... | ... |
| | 1995 | 5 | 140 | 522 | 113 | ... | ... |
| | 1996 | 5 | *145 | *535 | 84 | ... | ... |
| Ireland | 1970 | 7 | 686 | 232 | ... | ... | ... |
| | 1975 | 7 | 693 | 218 | 51 | 1 601 | 504 |
| | 1980 | 7 | 779 | 229 | ... | ... | ... |
| | 1985 | 7 | 685 | 193 | 57 | 1 725 | 486 |
| | 1990 | 7 | 591 | 169 | ... | ... | ... |
| | 1991 | *8 | *631 | *180 | ... | ... | ... |
| | 1992 | 8 | 609 | 173 | 53 | 1 571 | 445 |
| | 1993 | 8 | 583 | 164 | 53 | 1 519 | 427 |
| | 1994 | 8 | 572 | 160 | 53 | 1 491 | 416 |
| | 1995 | 7 | 546 | 151 | 55 | 1 538 | 426 |
| | 1996 | 6 | 543 | 149 | 77 | 1 561 | 430 |
| Italy | 1970 | 73 | 7 735 | 144 | ... | ... | ... |
| | 1975 | 78 | 6 497 | 117 | 111 | 2 266 | 41 |
| | 1980 | 77 | 5 697 | 101 | 299 | 5 536 | 98 |
| | 1985 | 72 | 5 511 | 97 | 286 | 2 710 | 48 |
| | 1990 | 76 | *6 000 | *105 | 217 | 1 634 | 29 |
| | 1991 | 80 | 5 805 | 102 | 188 | 1 192 | 21 |
| | 1992 | 78 | 6 068 | 106 | 230 | 1 277 | 22 |
| | 1993 | 78 | 5 845 | 102 | 226 | 1 296 | 23 |
| | 1994 | 74 | 5 985 | 104 | 231 | 1 428 | 25 |
| | 1995 | 76 | 5 722 | 100 | 274 | 2 132 | 37 |
| | 1996 | 78 | 5 960 | 104 | ... | ... | ... |
| Latvia | 1990 | *15 | *200 | *75 | ... | ... | ... |
| | 1991 | *16 | *220 | *82 | 172 | 3 594 | 1 345 |
| | 1992 | 17 | 258 | 97 | 186 | 2 717 | 1 026 |
| | 1993 | 17 | 921 | 352 | 225 | 2 944 | 1 126 |
| | 1994 | 22 | 589 | 229 | 235 | 2 683 | 1 042 |
| | 1995 | 21 | 437 | 172 | 265 | 2 478 | 977 |
| | 1996 | 24 | 616 | 247 | 228 | 1 433 | 573 |
| Liechtenstein | 1970 | 1 | 5 | 246 | - | - | - |
| | 1975 | 2 | 12 | 503 | - | - | - |
| | 1980 | 2 | 14 | 539 | - | - | - |
| | 1985 | 2 | 14 | 507 | - | - | - |
| | 1990 | *2 | *17 | *593 | ... | ... | ... |
| | 1991 | 2 | 20 | 674 | 3 | 3 | 96 |
| | 1992 | 2 | 20 | 664 | ... | ... | ... |
| | 1993 | *2 | *19 | *635 | ... | ... | ... |
| | 1994 | 2 | 18 | 593 | ... | ... | ... |
| | 1995 | 2 | 19 | 617 | ... | ... | ... |
| | 1996 | 2 | 19 | 602 | 1 | 14 | 449 |
| Lithuania | 1990 | *15 | *800 | *214 | ... | ... | ... |
| | 1991 | *16 | *820 | *219 | ... | ... | ... |

Daily and non-daily newspapers    IV.8
Journaux quotidiens et non quotidiens
Periódicos diarios y no diarios

| Country / Pays / País | Year / Année / Año | Daily newspapers / Journaux quotidiens / Periódicos diarios | | | Non-daily newspapers / Journaux non quotidiens / Periódicos no diarios | | |
|---|---|---|---|---|---|---|---|
| | | Number of titles / Nombre de titres / Número de títulos | Circulation / Diffusion / Circulación | | Number of titles / Nombre de titres / Número de títulos | Circulation / Diffusion / Circulación | |
| | | | Total (000) / Total (000) / Total (000) | Per 1,000 inhabitants / Pour 1 000 habitants / Por 1 000 habitantes | | Total (000) / Total (000) / Total (000) | Per 1,000 inhabitants / Pour 1 000 habitants / Por 1 000 habitantes |
| Lithuania (cont) | 1992 | 18 | 836 | 223 | 395 | 2 851 | 760 |
| | 1993 | 20 | 502 | 134 | 373 | 3 283 | 876 |
| | 1994 | 16 | 506 | 135 | 429 | 3 200 | 856 |
| | 1995 | 19 | 417 | 112 | 458 | 3 358 | 901 |
| | 1996 | 19 | 344 | 93 | 424 | 2 664 | 717 |
| Luxembourg | 1970 | 7 | 140 | 413 | 1 | 2 | 5.9 |
| | 1975 | 7 | 130 | 359 | 1 | 3 | 6.9 |
| | 1980 | 5 | 135 | 371 | 1 | 3 | 6.9 |
| | 1985 | 4 | 140 | 382 | 1 | 3 | 8.2 |
| | 1990 | 5 | 143 | 376 | ... | ... | ... |
| | 1991 | 5 | 143 | 371 | ... | ... | ... |
| | 1992 | 5 | 145 | 371 | ... | ... | ... |
| | 1993 | 5 | 147 | 371 | ... | ... | ... |
| | 1994 | 5 | 154 | 384 | ... | ... | ... |
| | 1995 | 5 | 135 | 332 | 5 | 32 | 79 |
| | 1996 | 5 | 135 | 328 | 5 | 70 | 170 |
| Malta | 1970 | 6 | *50 | *165 | ... | ... | ... |
| | 1975 | 6 | *55 | *181 | ... | ... | ... |
| | 1980 | 5 | *60 | *185 | ... | ... | ... |
| | 1985 | 4 | *56 | *163 | 9 | ... | ... |
| | 1990 | 3 | *54 | *152 | 6 | ... | ... |
| | 1991 | 3 | 54 | 151 | 7 | ... | ... |
| | 1992 | 3 | 54 | 149 | 8 | ... | ... |
| | 1993 | 3 | *60 | *164 | 8 | ... | ... |
| | 1994 | 3 | 64 | 172 | 10 | ... | ... |
| | 1995 | *3 | *50 | *133 | ... | ... | ... |
| | 1996 | 2 | 48 | 127 | 4 | 105 | 278 |
| Moldova | 1990 | *5 | ... | ... | ... | ... | ... |
| | 1991 | 5 | ... | ... | 211 | ... | ... |
| | 1992 | 5 | ... | ... | 212 | ... | ... |
| | 1993 | 4 | ... | ... | 179 | ... | ... |
| | 1994 | 4 | ... | ... | 157 | 1 195 | 273 |
| | 1995 | 2 | 200 | 46 | 198 | *1 300 | *297 |
| | 1996 | 4 | 261 | 60 | 206 | *1 350 | *309 |
| Monaco | 1970 | 3 | *9 | *380 | ... | ... | ... |
| | 1975 | 2 | 11 | 419 | ... | ... | ... |
| | 1980 | 2 | 10 | 388 | ... | ... | ... |
| | 1985 | 2 | *10 | *355 | ... | ... | ... |
| | 1990 | 1 | 8 | 267 | ... | ... | ... |
| | 1991 | 1 | 8 | 264 | ... | ... | ... |
| | 1992 | 1 | 8 | 261 | ... | ... | ... |
| | 1993 | 1 | 8 | 257 | ... | ... | ... |
| | 1994 | 1 | *8 | *254 | ... | ... | ... |
| | 1995 | 1 | 8 | 251 | 5 | 50 | 1 572 |
| | 1996 | 1 | ... | ... | 5 | 50 | 1 554 |
| Netherlands | 1970 | 97 | 4 153 | 319 | ... | ... | ... |
| | 1975 | 84 | 4 194 | 307 | ... | ... | ... |
| | 1980 | 84 | 4 612 | 326 | ... | ... | ... |
| | 1985 | 88 | 4 496 | 310 | ... | ... | ... |
| | 1990 | 45 | *4 500 | *301 | ... | ... | ... |
| | 1991 | *44 | *4 550 | *302 | ... | ... | ... |
| | 1992 | 44 | *4 600 | *303 | ... | ... | ... |
| | 1993 | 44 | 4 728 | 310 | (3) 63 | (3) 393 | 26 |
| | 1994 | 46 | 5 138 | 334 | (3) 64 | (3) 400 | 26 |
| | 1995 | 39 | 4 752 | 307 | (3) 63 | (3) 585 | 38 |
| | 1996 | 38 | 4 753 | 306 | (3) 63 | (3) 590 | 38 |
| Norway | 1970 | 86 | 1 539 | 397 | 73 | 271 | 70 |
| | 1975 | 80 | 1 657 | 413 | 73 | 311 | 78 |
| | 1980 | 85 | 1 892 | 463 | 79 | 376 | 92 |
| | 1985 | 82 | 2 120 | 511 | 77 | 392 | 94 |
| | 1990 | 85 | 2 588 | 610 | 65 | 347 | 82 |
| | 1991 | 81 | 2 521 | 592 | 67 | 363 | 85 |
| | 1992 | 82 | 2 600 | 607 | 66 | 358 | 84 |
| | 1993 | 84 | 2 623 | 609 | 65 | 342 | 79 |
| | 1994 | 83 | 2 623 | 606 | 69 | 366 | 85 |
| | 1995 | 83 | 2 582 | 594 | 70 | 371 | 85 |
| | 1996 | 83 | 2 578 | 590 | 71 | 367 | 84 |
| Poland | 1970 | 43 | 6 832 | 210 | 38 | 1 691 | 52 |
| | 1975 | 44 | 8 429 | 248 | 43 | 2 005 | 59 |
| | 1980 | 43 | 8 407 | 236 | 45 | 2 266 | 64 |
| | 1985 | 45 | 7 714 | 207 | 52 | 2 986 | 80 |
| | 1990 | 67 | 4 889 | 128 | 63 | 2 058 | 54 |
| | 1991 | 68 | 5 258 | 137 | 54 | 1 604 | 42 |
| | 1992 | 72 | 6 085 | 159 | 57 | 1 856 | 48 |
| | 1993 | 71 | 6 381 | 166 | 53 | 1 710 | 44 |

**IV.8** Daily and non-daily newspapers
Journaux quotidiens et non quotidiens
Periódicos diarios y no diarios

| Country / Pays / País | Year / Année / Año | Daily newspapers / Journaux quotidiens / Periódicos diarios | | | Non-daily newspapers / Journaux non quotidiens / Periódicos no diarios | | |
|---|---|---|---|---|---|---|---|
| | | Number of titles / Nombre de titres / Número de títulos | Circulation / Diffusion / Circulación | | Number of titles / Nombre de titres / Número de títulos | Circulation / Diffusion / Circulación | |
| | | | Total (000) | Per 1,000 inhabitants / Pour 1 000 habitants / Por 1 000 habitantes | | Total (000) | Per 1,000 inhabitants / Pour 1 000 habitants / Por 1 000 habitantes |
| Poland (cont) | 1994 | 66 | 5 404 | 140 | 48 | 1 880 | 49 |
| | 1995 | 63 | 4 846 | 126 | 45 | 1 268 | 33 |
| | 1996 | 55 | 4 351 | 113 | 32 | 860 | 22 |
| Portugal | 1970 | 33 | *743 | *82 | ... | ... | ... |
| | 1975 | 30 | 612 | 67 | 307 | ... | ... |
| | 1980 | 28 | *480 | *49 | ... | ... | ... |
| | 1985 | 25 | 413 | 42 | 295 | 1 580 | 160 |
| | 1990 | 24 | 446 | 45 | 328 | ... | ... |
| | 1991 | 29 | 509 | 52 | ... | ... | ... |
| | 1992 | 25 | 465 | 47 | 171 | ... | ... |
| | 1993 | 27 | 460 | 47 | 173 | 4 068 | 413 |
| | 1994 | 23 | 404 | 41 | *175 | 3 729 | 378 |
| | 1995 | 28 | 728 | 74 | 194 | *4 000 | *406 |
| | 1996 | 27 | 740 | 75 | 182 | *3 800 | *385 |
| Romania | 1970 | 55 | 3 422 | 169 | ... | ... | ... |
| | 1975 | 20 | 3 015 | 142 | 39 | 991 | 47 |
| | 1980 | 35 | 4 024 | 181 | 24 | 746 | 34 |
| | 1985 | 36 | 3 601 | 158 | 24 | 742 | 33 |
| | 1990 | 65 | 6 300 | 271 | ... | ... | ... |
| | 1991 | 83 | *6 500 | *280 | ... | ... | ... |
| | 1992 | 76 | *7 500 | *325 | ... | ... | ... |
| | 1993 | *70 | *7 000 | *305 | ... | ... | ... |
| | 1994 | 69 | *6 809 | *298 | ... | ... | ... |
| | 1995 | 93 | ... | ... | ... | ... | ... |
| | 1996 | 106 | ... | ... | ... | ... | ... |
| Russian Federation | 1990 | 328 | ... | ... | 4 420 | 60 576 | 408 |
| | 1991 | 378 | 74 550 | 502 | 4 485 | 85 674 | 576 |
| | 1992 | 339 | 57 367 | 386 | 4 498 | 86 677 | 583 |
| | 1993 | 297 | 20 551 | 138 | 4 353 | 65 690 | 442 |
| | 1994 | 293 | 19 542 | 132 | 4 233 | 66 071 | 445 |
| | 1995 | 292 | 17 919 | 121 | 4 809 | 103 542 | 699 |
| | 1996 | 285 | 15 517 | 105 | 4 596 | 98 558 | 666 |
| San Marino | 1970 | 5 | 1 | 65 | 5 | 4 | 218 |
| | 1975 | 4 | 1 | 53 | 14 | 4 | 190 |
| | 1980 | 3 | 1 | 47 | 10 | 6 | 283 |
| | 1985 | *3 | *1 | *49 | 10 | 8 | 358 |
| | 1990 | *3 | *1 | *52 | 5 | 12 | 518 |
| | 1991 | *3 | *1 | *55 | 6 | 12 | 512 |
| | 1992 | *3 | *1 | *59 | 6 | 13 | 547 |
| | 1993 | *3 | *2 | *62 | ... | ... | ... |
| | 1994 | *3 | *2 | *65 | ... | ... | ... |
| | 1995 | 3 | 2 | 72 | 8 | 12 | 482 |
| | 1996 | 3 | 2 | 71 | 8 | 12 | 476 |
| Slovakia | 1990 | *18 | *1 300 | *247 | ... | ... | ... |
| | 1991 | 18 | 1 410 | 267 | 165 | 1 317 | 250 |
| | 1992 | 21 | 1 680 | 317 | 262 | 2 091 | 395 |
| | 1993 | 20 | 1 146 | 215 | ... | ... | ... |
| | 1994 | 21 | 1 087 | 204 | ... | ... | ... |
| | 1995 | 20 | 1 051 | 196 | ... | ... | ... |
| | 1996 | 19 | 989 | 184 | ... | ... | ... |
| Slovenia | 1990 | *4 | *303 | *158 | ... | ... | ... |
| | 1991 | 5 | *306 | *158 | 204 | ... | ... |
| | 1992 | 6 | 308 | 158 | 153 | ... | ... |
| | 1993 | 6 | 322 | 164 | 156 | ... | ... |
| | 1994 | 6 | 360 | 182 | 163 | ... | ... |
| | 1995 | 7 | 390 | 196 | 156 | ... | ... |
| | 1996 | 7 | 397 | 199 | 127 | ... | ... |
| Spain | 1970 | 116 | 3 450 | 102 | 102 | 3 235 | 96 |
| | 1975 | 115 | 3 491 | 98 | 132 | 3 878 | 109 |
| | 1980 | 111 | 3 487 | 93 | ... | ... | ... |
| | 1985 | 102 | 3 078 | 80 | 62 | ... | ... |
| | 1990 | *125 | 3 450 | 88 | ... | ... | ... |
| | 1991 | *130 | *4 000 | *102 | ... | ... | ... |
| | 1992 | 148 | *4 100 | *104 | ... | ... | ... |
| | 1993 | 89 | *4 100 | *104 | (9) 20 | (9) 4 300 | 109 |
| | 1994 | 90 | 4 020 | 102 | (8) 14 | (9) 4 470 | 113 |
| | 1995 | 86 | 4 046 | 102 | (9) 14 | (9) 4 980 | 126 |
| | 1996 | 87 | 3 931 | 99 | (9) 12 | (9) 4 850 | 122 |
| Sweden | 1970 | 114 | 4 338 | 539 | 72 | 403 | 50 |
| | 1975 | 112 | 4 413 | 539 | 72 | 460 | 56 |
| | 1980 | 114 | 4 386 | 528 | 83 | 523 | 63 |
| | 1985 | 115 | 4 389 | 526 | 73 | 449 | 54 |
| | 1990 | 107 | 4 499 | 526 | 70 | 416 | 49 |

Daily and non-daily newspapers
Journaux quotidiens et non quotidiens
Periódicos diarios y no diarios

IV.8

| Country<br>Pays<br>País | Year<br>Année<br>Año | Daily newspapers / Journaux quotidiens / Periódicos diarios | | | Non-daily newspapers / Journaux non quotidiens / Periódicos no diarios | | |
|---|---|---|---|---|---|---|---|
| | | Number of titles<br>Nombre de titres<br>Número de títulos | Circulation / Diffusion / Circulación | | Number of titles<br>Nombre de titres<br>Número de títulos | Circulation / Diffusion / Circulación | |
| | | | Total (000)<br>Total (000)<br>Total (000) | Per 1,000 inhabitants<br>Pour 1 000 habitants<br>Por 1 000 habitantes | | Total (000)<br>Total (000)<br>Total (000) | Per 1,000 inhabitants<br>Pour 1 000 habitants<br>Por 1 000 habitantes |
| Sweden (cont) | 1991 | 107 | 4 442 | 516 | 69 | 392 | 45 |
| | 1992 | 104 | 4 419 | 510 | 70 | 414 | 48 |
| | 1993 | 103 | 4 232 | 486 | 70 | 447 | 51 |
| | 1994 | 102 | 4 155 | 474 | 71 | 459 | 52 |
| | 1995 | 95 | 4 096 | 465 | 71 | 447 | 51 |
| | 1996 | 94 | 3 933 | 445 | 69 | 409 | 46 |
| Switzerland | 1970 | 117 | 2 318 | 375 | 178 | 890 | 144 |
| | 1975 | 95 | 2 574 | 406 | 160 | 860 | 136 |
| | 1980 | 89 | 2 483 | 393 | 167 | 883 | 140 |
| | 1985 | 97 | 3 213 | 492 | 310 | 6 082 | 931 |
| | 1990 | 94 | 3 063 | 448 | (10) 619 | 10 523 | 1 540 |
| | 1991 | 95 | 3 256 | 472 | (10) 632 | 9 725 | 1 410 |
| | 1992 | (11) 83 | 2 635 | 379 | (11) 139 | 1 286 | 185 |
| | 1993 | (11) 80 | 2 791 | 397 | (11) 139 | 1 304 | 186 |
| | 1994 | (11) 80 | 2 920 | 412 | (11) 138 | 1 281 | 181 |
| | 1995 | 98 | 2 754 | 386 | 140 | 1 406 | 197 |
| | 1996 | 88 | 2 383 | 331 | 131 | 1 314 | 182 |
| The Former Yugoslav Rep. of Macedonia | 1990 | 2 | 55 | 29 | 110 | ... | ... |
| | 1991 | *2 | *50 | *26 | ... | ... | ... |
| | 1992 | 2 | 43 | 22 | 25 | ... | ... |
| | 1993 | 2 | 38 | 20 | 18 | ... | ... |
| | 1994 | 3 | 44 | 23 | 14 | ... | ... |
| | 1995 | 3 | 54 | 28 | 20 | 84 | 43 |
| | 1996 | 3 | 41 | 21 | 37 | 133 | 68 |
| Ukraine | 1990 | 127 | 13 026 | 251 | 1 660 | 11 893 | 229 |
| | 1991 | 115 | 10 961 | 211 | 1 776 | 15 843 | 305 |
| | 1992 | 90 | 6 083 | 117 | 1 605 | 18 194 | 351 |
| | 1993 | 42 | 4 761 | 92 | 1 676 | 30 665 | 593 |
| | 1994 | 38 | 2 530 | 49 | 1 579 | 15 363 | 298 |
| | 1995 | 36 | 2 322 | 45 | 1 728 | 16 296 | 317 |
| | 1996 | 44 | 2 780 | 54 | 2 162 | 19 934 | 389 |
| United Kingdom | 1970 | 110 | 25 186 | 453 | 1 184 | 38 056 | 684 |
| | 1975 | 109 | 24 805 | 441 | 1 142 | 35 977 | 640 |
| | 1980 | 113 | 23 472 | 417 | 1 032 | 32 734 | 581 |
| | 1985 | 104 | 22 495 | 397 | 853 | 26 270 | 464 |
| | 1990 | *103 | *22 350 | *388 | 856 | 7 100 | 123 |
| | 1991 | *102 | *22 200 | *385 | 850 | 6 700 | 116 |
| | 1992 | 101 | *22 100 | *382 | 842 | 7 100 | 123 |
| | 1993 | 98 | 19 578 | 337 | (3) 477 | (3) 7 000 | 121 |
| | 1994 | 103 | 20 372 | 350 | (3) 473 | (3) 6 700 | 115 |
| | 1995 | 100 | 20 101 | 345 | (3) 473 | (3) 6 600 | 113 |
| | 1996 | 99 | 19 332 | 331 | (3) 478 | (3) 6 220 | 106 |
| **Oceania** | | | | | | | |
| American Samoa | 1970 | 1 | 3 | 95 | ... | ... | ... |
| | 1975 | 1 | 4 | 122 | 2 | 6 | 193 |
| | 1980 | 2 | 10 | 315 | ... | ... | ... |
| | 1985 | 3 | *9 | *224 | ... | ... | ... |
| | 1990 | ... | ... | ... | 2 | 5 | 103 |
| | 1991 | *2 | *2 | *41 | ... | ... | ... |
| | 1992 | *1 | *2 | *40 | 2 | 4 | 85 |
| | 1993 | *1 | *2 | *38 | ... | ... | ... |
| | 1994 | *1 | *2 | *37 | ... | ... | ... |
| | 1995 | *1 | *2 | *35 | ... | ... | ... |
| | 1996 | 2 | 5 | 85 | 1 | 3 | 48 |
| Australia | 1970 | 58 | 4 028 | 321 | ... | ... | ... |
| | 1975 | 70 | *5 336 | *384 | 592 | ... | ... |
| | 1980 | 62 | *4 700 | *323 | ... | ... | ... |
| | 1985 | 62 | *4 300 | *275 | ... | ... | ... |
| | 1990 | 62 | *5 150 | *305 | ... | ... | ... |
| | 1991 | *65 | *4 800 | *280 | ... | ... | ... |
| | 1992 | 69 | *4 600 | *265 | ... | ... | ... |
| | 1993 | *69 | *4 700 | 183 | 94 | 378 | 22 |
| | 1994 | 69 | 5 340 | 301 | 95 | 376 | 21 |
| | 1995 | *69 | *5 340 | *298 | 96 | 379 | 21 |
| | 1996 | 65 | *5 370 | *296 | 98 | 383 | 21 |
| Cook Islands | 1970 | *1 | *0.5 | *24 | ... | ... | ... |
| | 1975 | 1 | 0.8 | 42 | ... | ... | ... |
| | 1980 | 1 | 2 | 112 | ... | ... | ... |
| | 1985 | 1 | 2 | 119 | ... | ... | ... |
| | 1990 | 1 | 2 | 109 | ... | ... | ... |
| | 1991 | 1 | 2 | 108 | ... | ... | ... |
| | 1992 | 1 | 2 | 107 | ... | ... | ... |
| | 1993 | 1 | 2 | 107 | ... | ... | ... |
| | 1994 | 1 | 2 | 106 | 1 | 1 | 53 |

IV.8   Daily and non-daily newspapers
Journaux quotidiens et non quotidiens
Periódicos diarios y no diarios

| Country<br><br>Pays<br><br>País | Year<br><br>Année<br><br>Año | Daily newspapers / Journaux quotidiens / Periódicos diarios | | | Non-daily newspapers / Journaux non quotidiens / Periódicos no diarios | | |
|---|---|---|---|---|---|---|---|
| | | Number of titles<br><br>Nombre de titres<br><br>Número de títulos | Circulation / Diffusion / Circulación | | Number of titles<br><br>Nombre de titres<br><br>Número de títulos | Circulation / Diffusion / Circulación | |
| | | | Total (000)<br>Total (000)<br>Total (000) | Per 1,000 inhabitants<br>Pour 1 000 habitants<br>Por 1 000 habitantes | | Total (000)<br>Total (000)<br>Total (000) | Per 1,000 inhabitants<br>Pour 1 000 habitants<br>Por 1 000 habitantes |
| Cook Islands (cont) | 1995 | 1 | 2 | 106 | 1 | 1 | 53 |
| | 1996 | 1 | 2 | 105 | 1 | 1 | 53 |
| Fiji | 1970 | 1 | 16 | 31 | ... | ... | ... |
| | 1975 | 1 | 20 | 35 | ... | ... | ... |
| | 1980 | 3 | 64 | 102 | ... | ... | ... |
| | 1985 | 3 | 68 | 97 | ... | ... | ... |
| | 1990 | 1 | 27 | 37 | ... | ... | ... |
| | 1991 | *1 | *27 | *37 | ... | ... | ... |
| | 1992 | 1 | 27 | 36 | ... | ... | ... |
| | 1993 | *1 | *27 | *36 | ... | ... | ... |
| | 1994 | 1 | 35 | 46 | ... | ... | ... |
| | 1995 | *1 | *35 | *46 | ... | ... | ... |
| | 1996 | 1 | 40 | 51 | ... | ... | ... |
| French Polynesia | 1970 | 4 | 10 | 91 | ... | ... | ... |
| | 1975 | 4 | 11 | 85 | 2 | 2 | 15 |
| | 1980 | 2 | *13 | *86 | ... | ... | ... |
| | 1985 | 3 | 23 | 132 | ... | ... | ... |
| | 1990 | 2 | 21 | 107 | ... | ... | ... |
| | 1991 | *2 | *22 | *110 | ... | ... | ... |
| | 1992 | 4 | *24 | *118 | ... | ... | ... |
| | 1993 | *4 | *24 | *116 | ... | ... | ... |
| | 1994 | 4 | *24 | *114 | ... | ... | ... |
| | 1995 | *4 | *24 | *112 | ... | ... | ... |
| | 1996 | 4 | *24 | *110 | ... | ... | ... |
| Guam | 1970 | 2 | 17 | 197 | ... | ... | ... |
| | 1975 | 1 | 18 | 192 | ... | ... | ... |
| | 1980 | 1 | 18 | 170 | ... | ... | ... |
| | 1985 | 1 | 18 | 152 | ... | ... | ... |
| | 1990 | 1 | 22 | 161 | ... | ... | ... |
| | 1991 | *1 | *22 | *160 | ... | ... | ... |
| | 1992 | 1 | 25 | 177 | ... | ... | ... |
| | 1993 | *1 | *25 | *173 | ... | ... | ... |
| | 1994 | 1 | 25 | 169 | ... | ... | ... |
| | 1995 | 1 | 25 | 165 | ... | ... | ... |
| | 1996 | 1 | 28 | 178 | ... | ... | ... |
| Kiribati | 1996 | - | - | - | ... | ... | ... |
| Marshall Islands | 1996 | - | - | - | 1 | 10 | 177 |
| Nauru | 1996 | - | - | - | ... | ... | ... |
| New Caledonia | 1970 | 1 | 7 | 65 | ... | ... | ... |
| | 1975 | 2 | 18 | 135 | ... | ... | ... |
| | 1980 | 1 | 15 | 105 | ... | ... | ... |
| | 1985 | 1 | 19 | 123 | ... | ... | ... |
| | 1990 | 1 | 19 | 113 | ... | ... | ... |
| | 1991 | *1 | *20 | *116 | ... | ... | ... |
| | 1992 | 3 | *23 | *130 | ... | ... | ... |
| | 1993 | *3 | *23 | *126 | ... | ... | ... |
| | 1994 | 3 | *23 | *122 | ... | ... | ... |
| | 1995 | *3 | *23 | *119 | ... | ... | ... |
| | 1996 | 3 | *24 | *121 | ... | ... | ... |
| New Zealand | 1970 | 40 | 1 058 | 375 | ... | ... | ... |
| | 1975 | 40 | *900 | *292 | 106 | ... | ... |
| | 1980 | 32 | 1 039 | 334 | ... | ... | ... |
| | 1985 | 32 | 1 057 | 325 | ... | ... | ... |
| | 1990 | 30 | *1 000 | *297 | ... | ... | ... |
| | 1991 | 29 | 913 | 267 | ... | ... | ... |
| | 1992 | 28 | *825 | *237 | ... | ... | ... |
| | 1993 | 28 | 865 | 244 | ... | ... | ... |
| | 1994 | 28 | *865 | *239 | ... | ... | ... |
| | 1995 | 25 | 828 | 226 | 8 | 384 | 105 |
| | 1996 | 23 | 804 | 216 | 9 | 385 | 104 |
| Niue | 1975 | - | - | - | 1 | ... | ... |
| | 1990 | - | - | - | 1 | 2 | 784 |
| | 1991 | - | - | - | 1 | 2 | 842 |
| | 1992 | - | - | - | 1 | 2 | 860 |
| | 1996 | - | - | - | 1 | *2 | *941 |
| Papua New Guinea | 1970 | 1 | *18 | *7.4 | ... | ... | ... |
| | 1975 | 1 | *20 | *7.3 | ... | ... | ... |
| | 1980 | 1 | 27 | 8.7 | ... | ... | ... |
| | 1985 | 2 | 45 | 13 | ... | ... | ... |
| | 1990 | 2 | 49 | 13 | ... | ... | ... |
| | 1991 | *2 | *50 | *13 | ... | ... | ... |
| | 1992 | 2 | 64 | 16 | ... | ... | ... |
| | 1993 | *4 | *64 | *16 | ... | ... | ... |

Daily and non-daily newspapers
Journaux quotidiens et non quotidiens
Periódicos diarios y no diarios

IV.8

| Country / Pays / País | Year / Année / Año | Daily newspapers / Journaux quotidiens / Periódicos diarios | | | Non-daily newspapers / Journaux non quotidiens / Periódicos no diarios | | |
|---|---|---|---|---|---|---|---|
| | | Number of titles / Nombre de titres / Número de títulos | Circulation / Diffusion / Circulación | | Number of titles / Nombre de titres / Número de títulos | Circulation / Diffusion / Circulación | |
| | | | Total (000) / Total (000) / Total (000) | Per 1,000 inhabitants / Pour 1 000 habitants / Por 1 000 habitantes | | Total (000) / Total (000) / Total (000) | Per 1,000 inhabitants / Pour 1 000 habitants / Por 1 000 habitantes |
| | 1994 | 2 | 65 | 15 | ... | ... | ... |
| | 1995 | *2 | *65 | *15 | ... | ... | ... |
| | 1996 | 2 | 65 | 15 | ... | ... | ... |
| Solomon Islands | 1996 | ... | ... | ... | 3 | 9 | 23 |
| Tonga | 1990 | 1 | *7 | *73 | ... | ... | ... |
| | 1991 | *1 | *7 | *73 | ... | ... | ... |
| | 1992 | 1 | *7 | *73 | ... | ... | ... |
| | 1993 | *1 | *7 | *72 | ... | ... | ... |
| Tonga (cont) | 1994 | 1 | 7 | 72 | ... | ... | ... |
| | 1995 | *1 | *7 | *72 | ... | ... | ... |
| | 1996 | 1 | 7 | 72 | ... | ... | ... |
| Tuvalu | 1990 | - | - | - | 1 | 0.3 | 34 |
| | 1992 | - | - | - | 1 | 0.3 | 32 |
| | 1996 | - | - | - | 1 | 0.3 | 28 |
| Vanuatu, Republic of | 1975 | - | - | - | 2 | 5 | 49 |
| | 1980 | - | - | - | 2 | 4 | 33 |
| | 1985 | - | - | - | 1 | 2 | 15 |
| | 1990 | - | - | - | 1 | 2 | 12 |
| | 1002 | - | - | - | 1 | 2 | 11 |
| | 1996 | - | - | - | 2 | 4 | 23 |

## General note
For general explanations and definitions, please refer to the beginning of this chapter.

## Note générale
Pour les explications et définitions générales, prière de se référer au début de ce chapitre.

## Nota general
Para las explicaciones y definiciones generales, referirse al comienzo de este capítulo.

Notes

(1) Data refer to rural non-daily newspapers only.

(2) Data on non-dailies include periodicals.

(3) Data refer to regional/local non-dailies only.

(4) Data on non-dailies include daily newspapers.

(5) Data do not include local newspapers.

(6) Data include regional editions.

(7) Data do not include non-daily newspapers distributed free of charge.

(8) Including DOM-TOM.

(9) Data refer to weekly newspapers only.

(10) Data include the district newspapers and the home bulletins.

(11) Data refer only to newspapers purchased and do not include satellites publications.

Notes

(1) Les données concernent seulement les journaux non quotidiens des zones rurales.

(2) Les données relatives aux journaux non quotidiens comprennent les périodiques.

(3) Les données se réfèrent aux journaux non quotidiens régionaux/locaux seulement.

(4) Les données relatives aux journaux non quotidiens comprennent les journaux quotidiens.

(5) Les données n'incluent pas les journaux locaux.

(6) Les données comprennent les éditions régionales.

(7) Les données n'incluent pas les journaux non-quotidiens qui sont distribués gratuitement.

(8) Y compris les DOM TOM.

(9) Les données ne concernent que les journaux hebdomadaires.

(10) Les données comprennent les journaux de quartier et les bulletins locaux.

(11) Les données se réfèrent seulement aux journaux payants et n'incluent pas les éditions satellites.

Notas

(1) Los datos se refieren solamente a los periódicos no diarios de las zonas rurales.

(2) Los datos relativos a los periódicos no diarios incluyen los periódicos.

(3) Los datos se refieren a los periódicos no diarios regionales/locales solamente.

(4) Los datos relativos a los periódicos no diarios incluyen los diarios.

(5) Los datos no incluyen los periódicos locales.

(6) Los datos incluyen las ediciones regionales.

(7) Los datos no incluyen los periódicos no diarios distribuidos gratuitamente.

(8) Incluyen los DOM TOM (Departamentos y Territorios de Ultramar).

(9) Los datos se refieren a los periódicos semanales solamente.

(10) Los datos incluyen los diarios municipales y boletines locales.

(11) Los datos se refieren solamente a los periódicos vendidos y no incluyen las ediciones satélites.

IV.9 International trade in books and pamphlets, newspaper and periodicals
Commerce international de livres et brochures et de journaux et périodiques
Comercio internacional de libros y folletos y de publicaciones periódicas

## IV.9 International trade in books and pamphlets, newspaper and periodicals

## Commerce international de livres et brochures et de journaux et périodiques

## Comercio internacional de libros y folletos y de publicaciones periódicas

Amounts shown are in thousands of U.S. dollars

Les montants sont exprimés en milliers de dollars des États-Unis

Los importes se expresan en miles de dólares de los Estados Unidos

| Country / Pays / País | Year / Année / Año | Books and pamphlets / livres et brochures / libros y folletos | | | Newspaper and periodicals / journaux et périodiques / publicaciones periódicas | | |
|---|---|---|---|---|---|---|---|
| | | Exports / Exportations / Exportaciones | Imports / Importations / Importaciones | Balance / Balance / Balanza | Exports / Exportations / Exportaciones | Imports / Importations / Importaciones | Balance / Balance / Balanza |
| **Africa** | | | | | | | |
| Algeria | 1970 | 122 | 5 326 | -5 204 | | 138 | - 138 |
| | 1975 | 102 | 5 606 | -5 504 | | 9 308 | -9 308 |
| | 1980 | 195 | 22 520 | -22 325 | | 9 539 | -9 539 |
| | 1985 | 268 | 30 271 | -30 003 | | 16 941 | -16 941 |
| | 1990 | 73 | 9 093 | -9 020 | 3 389 | 7 408 | -4 019 |
| | 1991 | 129 | 11 071 | -10 942 | 2 775 | 537 | 2 238 |
| | 1992 | 66 | 2 830 | -2 764 | 3 471 | 250 | 3 221 |
| | 1993 | 22 | 3 704 | -3 682 | 2 155 | 51 | 2 104 |
| | 1994 | | 3 193 | -3 193 | 700 | 71 | 629 |
| | 1995 | 15 | 8 783 | -8 768 | 3 267 | 523 | 2 744 |
| | 1996 | 16 | 10 874 | -10 858 | 1 689 | 914 | 775 |
| | 1997 | 17 | 9 717 | -9 700 | 1 410 | 584 | 826 |
| Cameroon | 1970 | 7 | 664 | - 657 | | 436 | - 436 |
| | 1975 | | 2 792 | -2 792 | | 888 | - 888 |
| | 1980 | 666 | 8 315 | -7 649 | | 3 331 | -3 331 |
| | 1990 | 59 | 94 308 | -94 249 | 2 | 9 716 | -9 714 |
| | 1995 | 12 | 3 655 | -3 643 | | 3 159 | -3 159 |
| | 1996 | 212 | 8 666 | -8 454 | | 3 124 | -3 124 |
| Central African Republic | 1970 | | 113 | - 113 | | 50 | -50 |
| | 1975 | | 420 | - 420 | | 125 | - 125 |
| | 1980 | | 228 | - 228 | | 66 | -66 |
| | 1993 | 200 | 841 | - 641 | | 999 | - 999 |
| | 1994 | 283 | 794 | - 511 | | 374 | - 374 |
| | 1995 | 119 | 1 237 | -1 118 | | 578 | - 578 |
| | 1996 | 125 | 1 401 | -1 276 | | 343 | - 343 |
| Chad | 1970 | | 162 | - 162 | | 51 | -51 |
| | 1975 | 1 | 469 | - 468 | | 73 | -73 |
| | 1995 | | 994 | - 994 | | 477 | - 477 |
| Congo | 1970 | | 32 | -32 | | 145 | - 145 |
| | 1975 | | 190 | - 190 | | 26 | -26 |
| | 1980 | 2 | 1 522 | -1 520 | | 238 | - 238 |
| | 1985 | | 1 867 | -1 867 | | 47 | -47 |
| | 1993 | | 198 | - 198 | | | |
| | 1994 | | 665 | - 665 | | 79 | -79 |
| | 1995 | 27 | 2 435 | -2 408 | | 1 461 | -1 461 |
| Côte d'Ivoire | 1970 | 18 | 1 387 | -1 369 | 5 | 487 | - 482 |
| | 1975 | 104 | 5 486 | -5 382 | 15 | 1 246 | -1 231 |
| | 1985 | 142 | 9 928 | -9 786 | 68 | 7 043 | -6 975 |
| | 1996 | | 13 258 | -13 258 | | 7 865 | -7 865 |
| Djibouti | 1985 | | 570 | - 570 | | 306 | - 306 |
| | 1990 | 4 | 1 745 | -1 741 | | 220 | - 220 |
| | 1991 | 6 | 1 533 | -1 527 | | 53 | -53 |
| | 1992 | | 1 305 | -1 305 | | 163 | - 163 |
| Egypt | 1970 | 3 692 | 1 206 | 2 486 | 812 | 845 | -33 |
| | 1975 | 9 632 | 2 350 | 7 282 | 1 798 | 2 302 | - 504 |
| | 1980 | 980 | 3 254 | -2 274 | 230 | 398 | - 168 |
| | 1985 | 4 213 | 7 127 | -2 914 | 2 505 | 5 529 | -3 024 |
| | 1990 | 7 765 | 9 903 | -2 138 | 2 070 | 2 389 | - 319 |
| | 1991 | 6 446 | 9 080 | -2 634 | 590 | 1 029 | - 439 |
| | 1992 | 5 645 | 15 882 | -10 237 | 1 398 | 2 244 | - 846 |
| | 1993 | 5 009 | 14 297 | -9 288 | 1 919 | 2 325 | - 406 |

International trade in books and pamphlets, newspaper and periodicals    IV.9
Commerce international de livres et brochures et de journaux et périodiques
Comercio internacional de libros y folletos y de publicaciones periódicas

| Country / Pays / País | Year / Année / Año | Books and pamphlets / livres et brochures / libros y folletos | | | Newspaper and periodicals / journaux et périodiques / publicaciones periódicas | | |
|---|---|---|---|---|---|---|---|
| | | Exports Exportations Exportaciones | Imports Importations Importaciones | Balance Balance Balanza | Exports Exportations Exportaciones | Imports Importations Importaciones | Balance Balance Balanza |
| Egypt (cont) | 1994 | 5 897 | 11 051 | -5 154 | 4 446 | 3 444 | 1 002 |
| | 1995 | 4 852 | 10 621 | -5 769 | 3 277 | 2 967 | 310 |
| | 1996 | 5 774 | 11 515 | -5 741 | 2 424 | 3 610 | -1 186 |
| | 1997 | 4 588 | 13 358 | -8 770 | 2 266 | 3 387 | -1 121 |
| Ethiopia | 1970 | | | | | 134 | - 134 |
| | 1975 | | 885 | - 885 | | 372 | - 372 |
| | 1980 | | | | | 97 | -97 |
| | 1985 | | | | | 86 | -86 |
| | 1990 | 23 | 2 316 | -2 293 | | 71 | -71 |
| | 1991 | 131 | 1 531 | -1 400 | | 60 | -60 |
| | 1992 | 12 | 3 705 | -3 693 | | 85 | -85 |
| | 1993 | | | | | 21 | -21 |
| | 1995 | | 4 598 | -4 598 | | 90 | -90 |
| Gabon | 1970 | | 77 | -77 | | 131 | - 131 |
| | 1975 | | 547 | - 547 | | 322 | - 322 |
| | 1980 | | 2 121 | -2 121 | | 640 | - 640 |
| | 1993 | 193 | 7 578 | -7 385 | | 4 081 | -4 081 |
| | 1994 | 229 | 5 388 | -5 159 | | 2 486 | -2 486 |
| | 1996 | 306 | 5 995 | -5 689 | | 3 439 | -3 439 |
| Ghana | 1970 | 15 | 2 520 | -2 505 | 1 | 149 | - 148 |
| | 1975 | 5 | 3 956 | -3 951 | 1 | 216 | - 215 |
| | 1980 | 1 | 4 322 | -4 321 | | 295 | - 295 |
| | 1992 | 53 | 6 671 | -6 618 | 1 | 245 | - 244 |
| Kenya | 1970 | | | | 6 | 1 910 | -1 904 |
| | 1975 | 285 | 2 818 | -2 533 | 181 | 1 384 | -1 203 |
| | 1980 | 1 559 | 8 999 | -7 440 | 33 | 1 744 | -1 711 |
| | 1985 | 614 | 5 686 | -5 072 | 142 | 992 | - 850 |
| | 1990 | 1 986 | 4 259 | -2 273 | 23 | 877 | - 854 |
| | 1991 | 1 059 | 7 212 | -6 153 | 2 487 | 997 | 1 490 |
| | 1992 | 780 | 7 544 | -6 764 | 287 | 840 | - 553 |
| | 1993 | 379 | 8 745 | -8 366 | 158 | 1 349 | -1 191 |
| | 1994 | 688 | 6 183 | -5 495 | 318 | 2 501 | -2 183 |
| | 1995 | 2 456 | 9 006 | -6 550 | 652 | 1 782 | -1 130 |
| | 1996 | 1 888 | 12 220 | -10 332 | 615 | 2 624 | -2 009 |
| | 1997 | | | | | | |
| Libyan Arab Jamahiriya | 1970 | | 1 959 | -1 959 | | 625 | - 625 |
| | 1975 | | 7 285 | -7 285 | | 1 684 | -1 684 |
| | 1980 | | 5 158 | -5 158 | | 132 | - 132 |
| | 1985 | | 21 322 | -21 322 | | 1 063 | -1 063 |
| | 1990 | 289 | 18 512 | -18 223 | | 3 360 | -3 360 |
| | 1991 | | 28 958 | -28 958 | | 64 | -64 |
| Madagascar | 1970 | 38 | 1 096 | -1 058 | | 88 | -88 |
| | 1975 | 26 | 1 543 | -1 517 | | 1 291 | -1 291 |
| | 1980 | 4 | 1 416 | -1 412 | 12 | 1 612 | -1 600 |
| | 1985 | 11 | 1 572 | -1 561 | 1 | 523 | - 522 |
| | 1990 | 1 | 2 309 | -2 308 | | 695 | - 695 |
| | 1991 | 17 | 1 604 | -1 587 | | 312 | - 312 |
| | 1992 | 16 | 1 576 | -1 560 | 1 | 696 | - 695 |
| | 1993 | 14 | 3 737 | -3 723 | | 573 | - 573 |
| | 1994 | 5 | 2 156 | -2 151 | | 718 | - 718 |
| | 1995 | 43 | 2 443 | -2 400 | | 1 204 | -1 204 |
| | 1996 | 39 | 1 524 | -1 485 | | 1 069 | -1 069 |
| | 1997 | 14 | 3 134 | -3 120 | 7 | 1 167 | -1 160 |
| Malawi | 1970 | 17 | 284 | - 267 | | | |
| | 1975 | 32 | 501 | - 469 | | | |
| | 1980 | 1 | 12 | -11 | 14 | 394 | - 380 |
| | 1985 | 57 | 869 | - 812 | | 153 | - 153 |
| | 1990 | 50 | 1 679 | -1 629 | | 407 | - 407 |
| | 1991 | 43 | 2 730 | -2 687 | | 531 | - 531 |
| | 1994 | 23 | 2 943 | -2 920 | | 687 | - 687 |
| | 1995 | 12 | 4 399 | -4 387 | | 392 | - 392 |
| Mali | 1970 | | 148 | - 148 | | 55 | -55 |
| | 1975 | | 496 | - 496 | | 123 | - 123 |
| | 1980 | | 3 758 | -3 758 | | 371 | - 371 |
| | 1990 | | 438 | - 438 | | 316 | - 316 |
| Mauritius | 1970 | | 239 | - 239 | | 75 | -75 |
| | 1975 | 7 | 840 | - 833 | 1 | 198 | - 197 |
| | 1980 | 46 | 2 794 | -2 748 | | 737 | - 737 |
| | 1990 | 257 | 5 199 | -4 942 | 8 | 1 174 | -1 166 |
| | 1991 | 253 | 5 960 | -5 707 | 17 | 1 192 | -1 175 |
| | 1992 | 354 | 8 599 | -8 245 | 6 | 1 958 | -1 952 |
| | 1993 | 284 | 8 597 | -8 313 | 16 | 3 667 | -3 651 |
| | 1994 | 750 | 9 049 | -8 299 | 15 | 2 875 | -2 860 |
| | 1995 | 762 | 9 531 | -8 769 | 1 | 4 147 | -4 146 |
| | 1996 | 1 400 | 9 642 | -8 242 | 256 | 3 519 | -3 263 |
| | 1997 | 3 005 | 8 317 | -5 312 | 2 | 3 063 | -3 061 |

IV.9 International trade in books and pamphlets, newspaper and periodicals
Commerce international de livres et brochures et de journaux et périodiques
Comercio internacional de libros y folletos y de publicaciones periódicas

| Country<br>Pays<br>País | Year<br>Année<br>Año | Books and pamphlets / livres et brochures / libros y folletos | | | Newspaper and periodicals / journaux et périodiques/ publicaciones periódicas | | |
|---|---|---|---|---|---|---|---|
| | | Exports<br>Exportations<br>Exportaciones | Imports<br>Importations<br>Importaciones | Balance<br>Balance<br>Balanza | Exports<br>Exportations<br>Exportaciones | Imports<br>Importations<br>Importaciones | Balance<br>Balance<br>Balanza |
| Morocco | 1970 | 122 | 1 932 | -1 810 | 3 | 333 | - 330 |
| | 1975 | 196 | 5 307 | -5 111 | 52 | 4 641 | -4 589 |
| | 1980 | 200 | 14 596 | -14 396 | | 13 053 | -13 053 |
| | 1985 | 426 | 11 729 | -11 303 | | 5 932 | -5 932 |
| | 1990 | 881 | 23 809 | -22 928 | 17 | 3 671 | -3 654 |
| | 1991 | 818 | 22 722 | -21 904 | 9 | 3 860 | -3 851 |
| | 1992 | 691 | 26 858 | -26 167 | | 3 472 | -3 472 |
| | 1993 | 738 | 23 264 | -22 526 | 12 | 1 959 | -1 947 |
| | 1994 | 1 275 | 23 887 | -22 612 | 17 | 4 054 | -4 037 |
| | 1995 | 1 262 | 22 580 | -21 318 | 129 | 4 985 | -4 856 |
| | 1996 | 1 131 | 23 737 | -22 606 | 211 | 13 244 | -13 033 |
| | 1997 | 860 | 21 542 | -20 682 | 8 | 13 943 | -13 935 |
| Mozambique | 1994 | | | | | 352 | - 352 |
| | 1995 | | | | | 53 | -53 |
| | 1996 | | | | | 116 | - 116 |
| Nigeria | 1970 | | | | 20 | 1 361 | -1 341 |
| | 1975 | | | | 1 | 2 850 | -2 849 |
| | 1985 | | | | | 1 108 | -1 108 |
| | 1991 | 7 | 31 217 | -31 210 | | 592 | - 592 |
| Reunion | 1970 | 13 | 863 | - 850 | 1 | 110 | - 109 |
| | 1975 | 5 | 2 047 | -2 042 | 140 | 578 | - 438 |
| | 1980 | 66 | 3 951 | -3 885 | 337 | 2 034 | -1 697 |
| | 1985 | 136 | 5 626 | -5 490 | 118 | 3 883 | -3 765 |
| | 1990 | 146 | 15 293 | -15 147 | 236 | 3 889 | -3 653 |
| | 1991 | 101 | 13 340 | -13 239 | 273 | 4 509 | -4 236 |
| | 1992 | 243 | 15 020 | -14 777 | 297 | 5 193 | -4 896 |
| | 1993 | 390 | 15 780 | -15 390 | 231 | 8 017 | -7 786 |
| | 1994 | 236 | 18 436 | -18 200 | 64 | 9 276 | -9 212 |
| | 1995 | 251 | 20 558 | -20 307 | 1 | 13 656 | -13 655 |
| Senegal | 1970 | 13 | 761 | - 748 | 7 | 286 | - 279 |
| | 1975 | 84 | 2 810 | -2 726 | 9 | 423 | - 414 |
| | 1980 | 201 | 7 398 | -7 197 | 3 787 | 982 | 2 805 |
| | 1990 | 38 | 5 353 | -5 315 | | 8 434 | -8 434 |
| | 1991 | 84 | 5 293 | -5 209 | 9 | 5 670 | -5 661 |
| | 1992 | 78 | 5 957 | -5 879 | 21 | 4 216 | -4 195 |
| | 1993 | 326 | 5 793 | -5 467 | 4 | 3 729 | -3 725 |
| | 1994 | 119 | 3 203 | -3 084 | | 1 709 | -1 709 |
| | 1995 | 7 | 4 472 | -4 465 | 4 | 1 021 | -1 017 |
| Seychelles | 1975 | | | | | 9 | -9 |
| | 1980 | | | | | 170 | - 170 |
| | 1985 | 14 | 232 | - 218 | | 125 | - 125 |
| | 1990 | 1 | 777 | - 776 | | 157 | - 157 |
| | 1991 | | 501 | - 501 | | 195 | - 195 |
| | 1992 | 1 | 1 142 | -1 141 | | 116 | - 116 |
| | 1993 | | 931 | - 931 | | 164 | - 164 |
| | 1994 | | 1 135 | -1 135 | | 273 | - 273 |
| | 1995 | | 927 | - 927 | | 389 | - 389 |
| | 1996 | 8 | 725 | - 717 | | 268 | - 268 |
| South Africa | 1975 | 887 | 29 586 | -28 699 | 1 066 | 7 061 | -5 995 |
| | 1980 | 3 806 | 55 013 | -51 207 | 1 123 | 7 133 | -6 010 |
| | 1985 | | 50 150 | -50 150 | | 6 621 | -6 621 |
| | 1992 | 6 546 | 112 706 | - 106 160 | 731 | 7 583 | -6 852 |
| | 1993 | 6 028 | 128 670 | - 122 642 | 1 075 | 7 865 | -6 790 |
| | 1994 | 7 340 | 122 352 | - 115 012 | 1 530 | 8 842 | -7 312 |
| | 1995 | 14 831 | 136 253 | - 121 422 | 2 925 | 11 106 | -8 181 |
| | 1996 | 13 406 | 133 653 | - 120 247 | 4 750 | 14 534 | -9 784 |
| Sudan | 1970 | 1 | 2 734 | -2 733 | 6 | 847 | - 841 |
| | 1975 | | 2 294 | -2 294 | 16 | 833 | - 817 |
| | 1980 | | 3 546 | -3 546 | 2 | 576 | - 574 |
| | 1985 | | 2 437 | -2 437 | | 466 | - 466 |
| | 1992 | 15 | 2 674 | -2 659 | 5 | 1 265 | -1 260 |
| | 1993 | 1 | 1 097 | -1 096 | 10 | 1 674 | -1 664 |
| | 1994 | | 2 996 | -2 996 | 29 | 1 764 | -1 735 |
| | 1995 | 3 | 872 | - 869 | 4 | 1 373 | -1 369 |
| | 1996 | 2 | 432 | - 430 | 8 | 726 | - 718 |
| Togo | 1970 | 3 | 112 | - 109 | | 3 | -3 |
| | 1975 | | 510 | - 510 | | 20 | -20 |
| | 1980 | 25 | 1 240 | -1 215 | 29 | 101 | -72 |
| | 1990 | 2 | 2 298 | -2 296 | | 930 | - 930 |
| | 1991 | 74 | 1 878 | -1 804 | | 769 | - 769 |
| Tunisia | 1970 | 114 | 1 044 | - 930 | 1 | 368 | - 367 |
| | 1975 | 498 | 3 100 | -2 602 | 8 | 240 | - 232 |
| | 1980 | 1 054 | 5 198 | -4 144 | 10 | 2 605 | -2 595 |
| | 1985 | 1 602 | 4 763 | -3 161 | 3 | 3 699 | -3 696 |
| | 1990 | 1 037 | 9 070 | -8 033 | 649 | 4 646 | -3 997 |
| | 1991 | 1 884 | 9 134 | -7 250 | 1 064 | 4 597 | -3 533 |

International trade in books and pamphlets, newspaper and periodicals IV.9
Commerce international de livres et brochures et de journaux et périodiques
Comercio internacional de libros y folletos y de publicaciones periódicas

| Country | Year | Books and pamphlets / livres et brochures / libros y folletos | | | Newspaper and periodicals / journaux et périodiques/ publicaciones periódicas | | |
|---|---|---|---|---|---|---|---|
| Pays | Année | Exports | Imports | Balance | Exports | Imports | Balance |
| | | Exportations | Importations | Balance | Exportations | Importations | Balance |
| País | Año | Exportaciones | Importaciones | Balanza | Exportaciones | Importaciones | Balanza |
| Tunisia (cont) | 1992 | 1 446 | 13 349 | -11 903 | 1 250 | 5 758 | -4 508 |
| | 1993 | 1 350 | 13 171 | -11 821 | 659 | 5 502 | -4 843 |
| | 1994 | 1 207 | 12 863 | -11 656 | 540 | 5 847 | -5 307 |
| | 1995 | 1 452 | 12 923 | -11 471 | 454 | 6 500 | -6 046 |
| | 1996 | 837 | 15 978 | -15 141 | 453 | 6 507 | -6 054 |
| | 1997 | 1 364 | 14 642 | -13 278 | 381 | 5 923 | -5 542 |
| Zambia | 1970 | | 33 | -33 | 2 | 257 | - 255 |
| | 1975 | 17 | 1 427 | -1 410 | | 541 | - 541 |
| | 1993 | 3 | | 3 | 11 | | 11 |
| Zimbabwe | 1985 | 131 | 3 179 | -3 048 | 11 | 102 | -91 |
| | 1990 | 910 | 4 716 | -3 806 | 5 | 179 | - 174 |
| | 1991 | 934 | 4 135 | -3 201 | 2 | 129 | - 127 |
| | 1992 | 1 512 | 4 436 | -2 924 | 3 | 136 | - 133 |
| | 1993 | 1 475 | 5 916 | -4 441 | 188 | 673 | - 485 |
| | 1994 | 1 126 | 15 013 | -13 887 | 88 | 2 103 | -2 015 |
| | 1995 | 888 | 11 273 | -10 385 | 37 | 2 580 | -2 543 |
| | 1996 | 1 064 | 10 649 | -9 585 | 172 | 3 846 | -3 674 |
| | 1997 | 1 310 | 13 703 | -12 393 | 158 | 3 866 | -3 708 |
| **North America** | | | | | | | |
| Aruba | 1990 | | 1 750 | -1 750 | | 759 | - 759 |
| | 1991 | | 1 811 | -1 811 | | 916 | - 916 |
| Barbados | 1970 | 10 | 407 | - 397 | 21 | 85 | -64 |
| | 1975 | 86 | 1 088 | -1 002 | 47 | 165 | - 118 |
| | 1980 | 137 | 2 229 | -2 092 | 217 | 464 | - 247 |
| | 1985 | 38 | 2 704 | -2 666 | 164 | 866 | - 702 |
| | 1990 | 387 | 5 239 | -4 852 | 667 | 1 219 | - 552 |
| | 1991 | 649 | 4 443 | -3 794 | 275 | 1 267 | - 992 |
| | 1992 | 549 | 4 095 | -3 546 | 388 | 3 675 | -3 287 |
| | 1993 | 228 | 4 003 | -3 775 | 245 | 1 134 | - 889 |
| | 1994 | 348 | 5 868 | -5 520 | 247 | 1 545 | -1 298 |
| | 1995 | 310 | 6 059 | -5 749 | 339 | 1 716 | -1 377 |
| | 1996 | 312 | 7 174 | -6 862 | 287 | 1 701 | -1 414 |
| | 1997 | 372 | 7 352 | -6 980 | 541 | 1 683 | -1 142 |
| Belize | 1980 | | 165 | - 165 | | 175 | - 175 |
| | 1985 | | 329 | - 329 | | 156 | - 156 |
| | 1990 | | 883 | - 883 | | 144 | - 144 |
| | 1992 | | 1 191 | -1 191 | | 181 | - 181 |
| | 1993 | | 1 452 | -1 452 | | 218 | - 218 |
| | 1994 | 1 | 1 560 | -1 559 | | 277 | - 277 |
| | 1995 | 1 | 1 541 | -1 540 | | 162 | - 162 |
| | 1996 | | 2 085 | -2 085 | | 125 | - 125 |
| | 1997 | 3 | 1 714 | -1 711 | | 123 | - 123 |
| Bermuda | 1975 | | | | | 316 | - 316 |
| | 1980 | | | | | 287 | - 287 |
| | 1985 | | | | | 444 | - 444 |
| | 1990 | | | | | 373 | - 373 |
| | 1991 | | | | | 501 | - 501 |
| | 1992 | | | | | 634 | - 634 |
| | 1993 | | | | | 473 | - 473 |
| | 1994 | | | | | | |
| | 1995 | | 9 038 | -9 038 | | | |
| | 1997 | | 9 368 | -9 368 | | | |
| Canada | 1970 | | 122 477 | - 122 477 | 9 919 | 63 020 | -53 101 |
| | 1975 | | 202 345 | - 202 345 | 27 786 | 116 443 | -88 657 |
| | 1980 | | 337 110 | - 337 110 | 72 571 | 243 981 | - 171 410 |
| | 1985 | | 442 994 | - 442 994 | 162 068 | 325 106 | - 163 038 |
| | 1990 | 104 070 | 802 518 | - 698 448 | 125 911 | 572 267 | - 446 356 |
| | 1991 | 112 022 | 803 084 | - 691 062 | 115 158 | 568 817 | - 453 659 |
| | 1992 | 143 996 | 854 298 | - 710 302 | 119 550 | 565 750 | - 446 200 |
| | 1993 | 173 577 | 848 428 | - 674 851 | 166 693 | 567 343 | - 400 650 |
| | 1994 | 168 400 | 922 745 | - 754 345 | 136 352 | 615 655 | - 479 303 |
| | 1995 | 202 268 | 990 642 | - 788 374 | 153 385 | 638 761 | - 485 376 |
| | 1996 | 226 188 | 955 027 | - 728 839 | 143 685 | 645 356 | - 501 671 |
| | 1997 | 263 898 | 1 040 899 | - 777 001 | 130 283 | 683 368 | - 553 085 |
| Costa Rica | 1970 | 78 | 685 | - 607 | | 222 | - 222 |
| | 1975 | 224 | 2 216 | -1 992 | | 362 | - 362 |
| | 1980 | 1 748 | 10 696 | -8 948 | | 343 | - 343 |
| | 1985 | 1 486 | 6 648 | -5 162 | 47 | 2 228 | -2 181 |
| | 1990 | 3 470 | 11 883 | -8 413 | 33 | 1 320 | -1 287 |
| | 1991 | 4 104 | 9 071 | -4 967 | 67 | 1 062 | - 995 |
| | 1992 | 5 069 | 11 877 | -6 808 | 69 | 1 219 | -1 150 |
| | 1993 | 5 801 | 16 011 | -10 210 | 136 | 1 275 | -1 139 |
| | 1994 | 5 101 | 20 861 | -15 760 | 200 | 2 668 | -2 468 |
| | 1995 | 7 346 | 16 388 | -9 042 | 132 | 3 911 | -3 779 |
| | 1996 | 6 692 | 16 916 | -10 224 | 111 | 3 562 | -3 451 |

IV.9   International trade in books and pamphlets, newspaper and periodicals
Commerce international de livres et brochures et de journaux et périodiques
Comercio internacional de libros y folletos y de publicaciones periódicas

| Country / Pays / País | Year / Année / Año | Books and pamphlets / livres et brochures / libros y folletos | | | Newspaper and periodicals / journaux et périodiques / publicaciones periódicas | | |
|---|---|---|---|---|---|---|---|
| | | Exports / Exportations / Exportaciones | Imports / Importations / Importaciones | Balance / Balance / Balanza | Exports / Exportations / Exportaciones | Imports / Importations / Importaciones | Balance / Balance / Balanza |
| Dominica | 1980 | | 203 | - 203 | | 8 | -8 |
| | 1985 | | 276 | - 276 | | 43 | -43 |
| | 1993 | | 930 | - 930 | | 84 | -84 |
| | 1994 | | 932 | - 932 | | 65 | -65 |
| | 1995 | 1 | 1 064 | -1 063 | | 74 | -74 |
| | 1996 | 3 | 1 365 | -1 362 | | 105 | - 105 |
| Dominican Republic | 1975 | 14 | 2 575 | -2 561 | 251 | 746 | - 495 |
| | 1980 | 155 | 3 459 | -3 304 | 173 | 1 816 | -1 643 |
| | 1985 | 791 | 1 110 | - 319 | 259 | 1 062 | - 803 |
| | 1992 | 439 | | 439 | 334 | | 334 |
| | 1993 | 645 | | 645 | 346 | | 346 |
| | 1994 | 1 077 | | 1 077 | 277 | | 277 |
| | 1995 | 969 | | 969 | 186 | | |
| El Salvador | 1970 | 26 | 404 | - 378 | 2 | 177 | - 175 |
| | 1975 | 464 | 1 391 | - 927 | 61 | 776 | - 715 |
| | 1980 | 174 | 1 953 | -1 779 | 2 | 1 064 | -1 062 |
| | 1985 | 60 | 2 350 | -2 290 | 6 | 721 | - 715 |
| | 1990 | 287 | 1 704 | -1 417 | 21 | 267 | - 246 |
| | 1991 | 245 | 1 937 | -1 692 | 5 | 178 | - 173 |
| | 1992 | 846 | 4 427 | -3 581 | 19 | 459 | - 440 |
| | 1993 | 1 475 | 6 730 | -5 255 | 35 | 559 | - 524 |
| | 1994 | 1 070 | 7 890 | -6 820 | 15 | 579 | - 564 |
| | 1995 | 1 315 | 9 962 | -8 647 | 15 | 883 | - 868 |
| | 1996 | 1 467 | 14 547 | -13 080 | 20 | 821 | - 801 |
| | 1997 | 1 116 | 13 232 | -12 116 | 103 | 899 | - 796 |
| Greenland | 1980 | 46 | 1 197 | -1 151 | | 37 | -37 |
| | 1985 | 22 | 865 | - 843 | | 13 | -13 |
| | 1990 | 33 | 1 418 | -1 385 | 2 | 31 | -29 |
| | 1991 | 64 | 1 578 | -1 514 | | 34 | -34 |
| | 1992 | 68 | 1 857 | -1 789 | | 7 | -7 |
| | 1993 | 78 | 1 580 | -1 502 | 1 | 4 | -3 |
| | 1994 | 117 | 1 851 | -1 734 | | 2 | -2 |
| | 1995 | 113 | 1 767 | -1 654 | 1 | 135 | - 134 |
| | 1996 | 90 | 1 632 | -1 542 | 2 | 18 | -16 |
| | 1997 | 89 | 1 788 | -1 699 | 1 | 241 | - 240 |
| Grenada | 1980 | | 250 | - 250 | | 16 | -16 |
| | 1985 | | 660 | - 660 | | 15 | -15 |
| | 1990 | | 919 | - 919 | | 14 | -14 |
| | 1991 | 1 | 1 488 | -1 488 | | 99 | -99 |
| | 1993 | 19 | 1 330 | -1 311 | | 121 | - 121 |
| | 1994 | 14 | 1 543 | -1 529 | | 250 | - 250 |
| | 1995 | 1 | 1 683 | -1 682 | | 413 | - 413 |
| | 1996 | 1 | 1 917 | -1 916 | | 350 | - 350 |
| Guadeloupe | 1970 | | 990 | - 990 | | 173 | - 173 |
| | 1975 | 22 | 1 823 | -1 801 | | 259 | - 259 |
| | 1980 | 176 | 3 961 | -3 785 | 201 | 2 241 | -2 040 |
| | 1985 | 30 | 5 371 | -5 341 | 124 | 5 363 | -5 239 |
| | 1990 | 401 | 14 814 | -14 413 | 19 | 13 407 | -13 388 |
| | 1991 | 299 | 13 667 | -13 368 | 10 | 14 894 | -14 884 |
| | 1992 | 638 | 12 156 | -11 518 | 568 | 16 834 | -16 266 |
| | 1993 | 500 | 12 630 | -12 130 | 816 | 16 434 | -15 618 |
| | 1994 | 460 | 14 900 | -14 440 | 904 | 15 185 | -14 281 |
| | 1995 | 393 | 16 551 | -16 158 | 1 879 | 15 272 | -13 393 |
| Guatemala | 1970 | 44 | 626 | - 582 | 4 | 297 | - 293 |
| | 1975 | 132 | 2 004 | -1 872 | 12 | 499 | - 487 |
| | 1980 | 220 | 6 360 | -6 140 | 2 | 216 | - 214 |
| | 1985 | 193 | 4 148 | -3 955 | 8 | 1 205 | -1 197 |
| | 1990 | 361 | 6 013 | -5 652 | 33 | 702 | - 669 |
| | 1991 | 220 | 6 993 | -6 773 | 3 | 219 | - 216 |
| | 1992 | 389 | 8 669 | -8 280 | | 98 | -98 |
| | 1993 | 220 | 8 977 | -8 757 | 1 | 167 | - 166 |
| | 1994 | 312 | 9 763 | -9 451 | 8 | 388 | - 380 |
| | 1995 | 698 | 13 538 | -12 840 | 15 | 527 | - 512 |
| | 1996 | 1 379 | 12 994 | -11 615 | 581 | 1 842 | -1 261 |
| | 1997 | 1 859 | 14 136 | -12 277 | 90 | 2 797 | -2 707 |
| Honduras | 1970 | | 792 | - 792 | | 120 | - 120 |
| | 1975 | | 972 | - 972 | | 26 | -26 |
| | 1980 | | 3 167 | -3 167 | | 65 | -65 |
| | 1985 | | 2 648 | -2 648 | | 2 583 | -2 583 |
| | 1990 | 6 | 2 669 | -2 663 | | 353 | - 353 |
| | 1991 | 7 | 2 985 | -2 978 | | 447 | - 447 |
| | 1992 | 87 | 3 123 | -3 036 | | 309 | - 309 |
| | 1993 | 23 | 4 277 | -4 254 | | 569 | - 569 |
| | 1994 | 22 | 3 537 | -3 515 | 3 | 463 | - 460 |
| | 1995 | 4 | 3 925 | -3 921 | 3 | 637 | - 634 |
| | 1996 | 130 | 4 123 | -3 993 | | 998 | - 998 |
| | 1997 | 13 | 5 357 | -5 344 | | 1 130 | -1 130 |

International trade in books and pamphlets, newspaper and periodicals    IV.9
Commerce international de livres et brochures et de journaux et périodiques
Comercio internacional de libros y folletos y de publicaciones periódicas

| Country<br><br>Pays<br><br>País | Year<br><br>Année<br><br>Año | Books and pamphlets / livres et brochures / libros y folletos | | | Newspaper and periodicals / journaux et périodiques/ publicaciones periódicas | | |
|---|---|---|---|---|---|---|---|
| | | Exports<br>Exportations<br>Exportaciones | Imports<br>Importations<br>Importaciones | Balance<br>Balance<br>Balanza | Exports<br>Exportations<br>Exportaciones | Imports<br>Importations<br>Importaciones | Balance<br>Balance<br>Balanza |
| Jamaica | 1975 | 57 | 7 655 | -7 598 | 40 | 109 | -69 |
| | 1980 | 187 | 3 525 | -3 338 | 54 | 30 | 24 |
| | 1985 | 282 | 4 642 | -4 360 | 80 | 238 | - 158 |
| | 1990 | 346 | 11 681 | -11 335 | 200 | 2 792 | -2 592 |
| | 1991 | 342 | 7 625 | -7 283 | 152 | 3 486 | -3 334 |
| | 1992 | 312 | 8 471 | -8 159 | 76 | 1 347 | -1 271 |
| | 1993 | 200 | 10 257 | -10 057 | 68 | 1 192 | -1 124 |
| | 1994 | 311 | 13 210 | -12 899 | 92 | 1 277 | -1 185 |
| | 1995 | 240 | 17 254 | -17 014 | 131 | 1 348 | -1 217 |
| | 1996 | 291 | 17 481 | -17 190 | 218 | 2 224 | -2 006 |
| Martinique | 1970 | 12 | 1 268 | -1 256 | | 2 | -2 |
| | 1975 | 38 | 2 878 | -2 840 | 3 | 989 | - 986 |
| | 1980 | 268 | 5 555 | -5 287 | 1 143 | 3 498 | -2 355 |
| | 1985 | 194 | 5 657 | -5 463 | 1 446 | 3 584 | -2 138 |
| | 1990 | 660 | 13 921 | -13 261 | 2 | 275 | - 273 |
| | 1991 | 487 | 13 930 | -13 443 | 37 | 1 104 | -1 067 |
| | 1992 | 377 | 11 893 | -11 516 | 50 | 963 | - 913 |
| | 1993 | 51 | 12 009 | -12 009 | 58 | 1 279 | -1 221 |
| | 1994 | 163 | 12 695 | -12 532 | 70 | 1 562 | -1 492 |
| | 1995 | 182 | 15 097 | -14 915 | 36 | 3 118 | -3 082 |
| Mexico | 1970 | 16 950 | 15 056 | 1 894 | 774 | 2 891 | -2 117 |
| | 1975 | 23 387 | 36 201 | -12 814 | 9 813 | 4 699 | 5 114 |
| | 1980 | 46 178 | 105 381 | -59 203 | 19 439 | 15 400 | 4 039 |
| | 1985 | 21 163 | 61 973 | -40 810 | 8 510 | 10 637 | 2 127 |
| | 1990 | 28 354 | 111 747 | -83 393 | 7 598 | 34 321 | -26 723 |
| | 1991 | 54 580 | 149 243 | -94 663 | 13 430 | 42 809 | -29 379 |
| | 1992 | 63 368 | 198 564 | - 135 196 | 15 866 | 63 696 | -47 830 |
| | 1993 | 77 833 | 250 740 | - 172 907 | 16 721 | 77 858 | -61 137 |
| | 1994 | 76 656 | 324 868 | - 248 212 | 14 529 | 93 712 | -79 183 |
| | 1995 | 98 818 | 202 859 | - 104 041 | 17 052 | 66 332 | -49 280 |
| | 1996 | 96 358 | 209 844 | - 113 486 | 21 419 | 53 614 | -32 195 |
| | 1997 | 112 829 | 247 416 | - 134 587 | 37 842 | 58 807 | -20 965 |
| Montserrat | 1975 | | | | | 2 | -2 |
| | 1993 | 2 | | 2 | | | |
| Netherlands Antilles | 1970 | | 607 | - 607 | | 284 | - 284 |
| | 1975 | | 1 387 | -1 387 | | 549 | - 549 |
| | 1980 | | 2 133 | -2 133 | | 1 029 | -1 029 |
| | 1985 | | 2 114 | -2 114 | | 1 036 | -1 036 |
| | 1990 | | 2 084 | -2 084 | | 680 | - 680 |
| | 1991 | | 2 328 | -2 328 | | 1 294 | -1 294 |
| | 1992 | | 3 437 | -3 437 | | 1 115 | -1 115 |
| | 1995 | 10 633 | 4 558 | 6 075 | | 1 859 | -1 859 |
| Nicaragua | 1970 | 17 | 655 | - 638 | | 11 | -11 |
| | 1975 | 19 | 1 388 | -1 369 | | 27 | -27 |
| | 1980 | 22 | 2 465 | -2 443 | | 60 | -60 |
| | 1985 | 6 | 4 252 | -4 246 | 6 | 57 | -51 |
| | 1990 | 9 | 1 860 | -1 851 | | 42 | -42 |
| | 1991 | 19 | 2 212 | -2 193 | | 46 | -46 |
| | 1992 | 5 | 12 995 | -12 990 | | 248 | - 248 |
| | 1993 | 34 | 4 762 | -4 728 | 6 | 351 | - 345 |
| | 1994 | 22 | 5 800 | -5 778 | 2 | 510 | - 508 |
| | 1995 | 93 | 4 567 | -4 474 | 7 | 518 | - 511 |
| | 1996 | 116 | 5 507 | -5 391 | 4 | 478 | - 474 |
| | 1997 | 69 | 9 369 | -9 300 | 4 | 842 | - 838 |
| Panama | 1970 | 2 | | 2 | 2 | 131 | - 129 |
| | 1975 | | | | 7 | 2 073 | -2 066 |
| | 1980 | | | | | 3 910 | -3 910 |
| | 1985 | | 1 902 | -1 902 | | 4 064 | -4 064 |
| | 1990 | 209 | 8 083 | -7 874 | 304 | 4 363 | -4 059 |
| | 1991 | 1 | 8 829 | -8 828 | | 4 538 | -4 538 |
| | 1992 | 9 | 10 178 | -10 169 | | 5 265 | -5 265 |
| | 1993 | 4 | 9 564 | -9 560 | 1 | 5 946 | -5 945 |
| | 1994 | 6 | 11 429 | -11 423 | | 6 864 | -6 864 |
| | 1995 | 49 | 12 871 | -12 822 | | 6 181 | -6 181 |
| | 1996 | 39 | 11 835 | -11 796 | | 5 845 | -5 845 |
| | 1997 | 7 | 12 399 | -12 392 | 33 | 6 194 | -6 161 |
| St. Kitts and Nevis | 1993 | 2 | 764 | - 762 | | 111 | - 111 |
| | 1994 | 1 | 1 019 | -1 018 | | 84 | -84 |
| | 1995 | | 865 | - 865 | | 145 | - 145 |
| | 1996 | 11 | 843 | - 832 | | 197 | - 197 |
| | 1997 | 15 | 1 164 | -1 149 | | 145 | - 145 |
| St. Lucia | 1975 | | 174 | - 174 | 1 | 31 | -30 |
| | 1980 | 10 | 695 | - 685 | | 86 | -86 |
| | 1985 | 8 | 730 | - 722 | | 162 | - 162 |
| | 1990 | 5 | 1 927 | -1 922 | | 184 | - 184 |
| | 1991 | 3 | 2 369 | -2 366 | 1 | 229 | - 228 |
| | 1992 | | 2 843 | -2 843 | 1 | 206 | - 205 |
| | 1993 | 7 | 2 265 | -2 258 | 3 | 279 | - 276 |

IV.9    International trade in books and pamphlets, newspaper and periodicals
Commerce international de livres et brochures et de journaux et périodiques
Comercio internacional de libros y folletos y de publicaciones periódicas

| Country<br><br>Pays<br><br>País | Year<br><br>Année<br><br>Año | Books and pamphlets / livres et brochures / libros y folletos | | | Newspaper and periodicals / journaux et périodiques/ publicaciones periódicas | | |
|---|---|---|---|---|---|---|---|
| | | Exports<br>Exportations<br>Exportaciones | Imports<br>Importations<br>Importaciones | Balance<br>Balance<br>Balanza | Exports<br>Exportations<br>Exportaciones | Imports<br>Importations<br>Importaciones | Balance<br>Balance<br>Balanza |
| St. Lucia (cont) | 1994 | 24 | 2 853 | -2 829 | | 323 | - 323 |
| | 1995 | 4 | 2 686 | -2 682 | | 417 | - 417 |
| | 1996 | 1 | 2 114 | -2 113 | | 564 | - 564 |
| St. Vincent and the | 1980 | 11 | 239 | - 228 | | 32 | -32 |
| Grenadines | 1993 | | 787 | - 787 | | 210 | - 210 |
| | 1994 | | 864 | - 864 | | 153 | - 153 |
| | 1995 | 1 | 790 | - 789 | | 154 | - 154 |
| | 1996 | 1 | | 1 | | | |
| | 1997 | 1 | | 1 | | | |
| Trinidad and Tobago | 1970 | | | | 91 | 154 | -63 |
| | 1975 | 277 | 3 643 | -3 366 | 200 | 275 | -75 |
| | 1980 | 212 | 10 883 | -10 671 | 70 | 954 | - 884 |
| | 1985 | 642 | 13 718 | -13 076 | 87 | 3 256 | -3 169 |
| | 1990 | 743 | 7 212 | -6 469 | 203 | 1 574 | -1 371 |
| | 1991 | 787 | 11 096 | -10 309 | 171 | 1 416 | -1 245 |
| | 1992 | 1 091 | 11 872 | -10 781 | 280 | 1 502 | -1 222 |
| | 1993 | 1 060 | 9 580 | -8 520 | 306 | 1 087 | - 781 |
| | 1994 | 1 199 | 8 701 | -7 502 | | | |
| | 1995 | 1 468 | 8 377 | -6 909 | | | |
| | 1996 | 1 145 | 9 346 | -8 201 | 332 | 895 | - 563 |
| | 1997 | 2 095 | 12 676 | -10 581 | 300 | 845 | - 545 |
| United States | 1970 | 180 768 | 91 737 | 89 031 | 76 619 | 23 681 | 52 938 |
| | 1975 | 274 885 | 146 931 | 127 954 | 140 096 | 44 020 | 96 076 |
| | 1980 | 588 686 | 314 378 | 274 308 | 242 198 | 107 020 | 135 178 |
| | 1985 | 582 084 | 590 973 | -8 889 | 394 535 | 174 287 | 220 248 |
| | 1990 | 1 490 992 | 930 827 | 560 165 | 703 304 | 193 262 | 510 042 |
| | 1991 | 1 611 479 | 939 577 | 671 902 | 744 080 | 179 220 | 564 860 |
| | 1992 | 1 754 050 | 1 031 959 | 722 091 | 761 527 | 198 235 | 563 292 |
| | 1993 | 1 783 283 | 1 046 060 | 737 223 | 764 059 | 256 435 | 507 624 |
| | 1994 | 1 832 859 | 1 109 672 | 723 187 | 823 393 | 228 482 | 594 911 |
| | 1995 | 1 964 562 | 1 288 962 | 675 600 | 855 971 | 242 448 | 613 523 |
| | 1996 | 1 990 980 | 1 354 422 | 636 558 | 847 346 | 235 990 | 611 356 |
| | 1997 | 2 095 381 | 1 406 380 | 689 001 | 898 224 | 223 918 | 674 306 |
| **South America** | | | | | | | |
| Argentina | 1970 | 12 334 | 8 437 | 3 897 | 2 370 | 1 677 | 693 |
| | 1975 | 18 162 | 11 254 | 6 908 | 4 748 | 3 227 | 1 521 |
| | 1980 | 44 003 | 70 168 | -26 165 | 5 804 | 9 265 | -3 461 |
| | 1985 | 15 698 | 5 154 | 10 544 | 2 228 | 180 | 2 048 |
| | 1990 | 21 194 | 5 774 | 15 420 | 3 056 | 2 667 | 389 |
| | 1991 | 23 330 | 9 738 | 13 592 | 3 970 | 6 768 | -2 798 |
| | 1992 | 44 605 | 22 459 | 22 146 | 7 569 | 18 618 | -11 049 |
| | 1993 | 38 288 | 35 122 | 3 166 | 12 780 | 21 478 | -8 698 |
| | 1994 | 36 132 | 52 132 | -16 000 | 17 061 | 24 156 | -7 095 |
| | 1995 | 53 198 | 77 995 | -24 797 | 33 205 | 21 205 | 12 000 |
| | 1996 | 48 216 | 66 050 | -17 834 | 32 345 | 16 439 | 15 906 |
| | 1997 | 47 634 | 91 857 | -44 223 | 34 042 | 28 300 | 5 742 |
| Bolivia | 1970 | 3 | 719 | - 716 | | 338 | - 338 |
| | 1975 | 3 | 2 699 | -2 696 | | 777 | - 777 |
| | 1980 | 5 | 7 683 | -7 678 | | 939 | - 939 |
| | 1985 | | 2 675 | -2 675 | | 505 | - 505 |
| | 1990 | 12 | 4 774 | -4 762 | | 774 | - 774 |
| | 1991 | 62 | 6 105 | -6 043 | 28 | 831 | - 803 |
| | 1992 | 50 | 4 895 | -4 845 | | 972 | - 972 |
| | 1993 | 101 | 5 307 | -5 206 | | 899 | - 899 |
| | 1994 | 369 | 6 048 | -5 679 | | 965 | - 965 |
| | 1995 | 115 | 5 842 | -5 727 | 2 | 1 115 | -1 113 |
| | 1996 | 269 | 19 600 | -19 331 | | 1 183 | -1 183 |
| | 1997 | 697 | 11 509 | -10 812 | | 1 374 | -1 374 |
| Brazil | 1970 | 841 | 9 730 | -8 889 | 1 470 | 3 243 | -1 773 |
| | 1975 | 10 081 | 21 956 | -11 875 | 4 299 | 7 507 | -3 208 |
| | 1980 | 10 255 | 36 872 | -26 617 | 11 302 | 11 705 | - 403 |
| | 1985 | 8 552 | 16 492 | -7 940 | 3 316 | 7 970 | -4 654 |
| | 1990 | 4 983 | 53 506 | -48 523 | 7 110 | 29 104 | -21 994 |
| | 1991 | 5 569 | 56 876 | -51 307 | 10 255 | 33 732 | -23 477 |
| | 1992 | 11 594 | 39 796 | -28 202 | 12 920 | 28 017 | -15 097 |
| | 1993 | 22 166 | 47 634 | -25 468 | 15 752 | 26 325 | -10 573 |
| | 1994 | 15 394 | 60 607 | -45 213 | 11 795 | 32 772 | -20 977 |
| | 1995 | 12 454 | 172 334 | - 159 880 | 9 156 | 81 780 | -72 624 |
| | 1996 | 9 422 | 217 678 | - 208 256 | 8 332 | 119 157 | - 110 825 |
| | 1997 | 12 238 | 247 475 | - 235 237 | 11 207 | 120 413 | - 109 206 |
| Chile | 1970 | 658 | 11 930 | -11 272 | 1 153 | 1 558 | - 405 |
| | 1975 | 1 171 | 11 503 | -10 332 | 810 | 1 921 | -1 111 |
| | 1980 | 727 | 12 921 | -12 194 | 3 758 | 2 969 | 789 |
| | 1985 | 2 708 | 12 398 | -9 690 | 4 397 | 1 851 | 2 546 |
| | 1990 | 10 546 | 15 639 | -5 093 | 9 061 | 3 016 | 6 045 |
| | 1991 | 16 472 | 20 064 | -3 592 | 20 545 | 3 774 | 16 771 |
| | 1992 | 21 376 | 26 749 | -5 373 | 34 266 | 5 117 | 29 149 |
| | 1993 | 25 200 | 30 767 | -5 567 | 36 167 | 6 573 | 29 594 |

International trade in books and pamphlets, newspaper and periodicals  IV.9
Commerce international de livres et brochures et de journaux et périodiques
Comercio internacional de libros y folletos y de publicaciones periódicas

| Country | Year | Books and pamphlets / livres et brochures / libros y folletos | | | Newspaper and periodicals / journaux et périodiques/ publicaciones periódicas | | |
|---------|------|---------|---------|---------|---------|---------|---------|
| Pays | Année | Exports | Imports | Balance | Exports | Imports | Balance |
| | | Exportations | Importations | Balance | Exportations | Importations | Balance |
| País | Año | Exportaciones | Importaciones | Balanza | Exportaciones | Importaciones | Balanza |
| Chile (cont) | 1994 | 35 255 | 31 538 | 3 717 | 34 272 | 8 372 | 25 900 |
| | 1995 | 55 425 | 46 885 | 8 540 | 56 591 | 9 460 | 47 131 |
| | 1996 | 46 549 | 49 035 | -2 486 | 53 679 | 9 632 | 44 047 |
| | 1997 | 54 671 | 50 517 | 4 154 | 55 817 | 10 059 | 45 758 |
| Colombia | 1970 | 1 183 | 13 559 | -12 376 | 743 | 1 200 | - 457 |
| | 1975 | 9 044 | 19 346 | -10 302 | 3 608 | 1 438 | 2 170 |
| | 1980 | 24 051 | 35 836 | -11 785 | 11 990 | 5 917 | 6 073 |
| | 1985 | 25 612 | 33 350 | -7 738 | 10 136 | 4 210 | 5 926 |
| | 1990 | 57 929 | 19 197 | 38 732 | 20 976 | 5 037 | 15 939 |
| | 1991 | 91 089 | 17 417 | 73 672 | 27 572 | 3 990 | 23 582 |
| | 1992 | 79 628 | 19 046 | 60 582 | 33 129 | 4 763 | 28 366 |
| | 1993 | 76 370 | 33 521 | 42 849 | 34 308 | 7 697 | 26 611 |
| | 1994 | 85 296 | 50 945 | 34 351 | 30 275 | 9 217 | 21 058 |
| | 1995 | 87 410 | 57 123 | 30 287 | 16 967 | 10 936 | 6 031 |
| | 1996 | 85 025 | 60 001 | 25 024 | 9 803 | 10 941 | - 1 138 |
| | 1997 | 84 825 | 66 758 | 18 067 | 10 623 | 13 142 | -2 519 |
| Ecuador | 1970 | | 324 | - 324 | | 324 | - 324 |
| | 1975 | 574 | 5 236 | -4 662 | 73 | 1 646 | -1 573 |
| | 1980 | 777 | 3 362 | -2 585 | 39 | | 39 |
| | 1985 | 32 | 22 017 | -21 985 | | 1 028 | -1 028 |
| | 1990 | 255 | 9 535 | -9 280 | | 821 | - 821 |
| | 1991 | 182 | 11 119 | -10 937 | 13 | 971 | - 958 |
| | 1992 | 1 315 | 99 631 | -98 316 | 13 | 8 666 | -8 653 |
| | 1993 | 1 262 | 59 025 | -57 763 | 78 | 4 866 | -4 788 |
| | 1994 | 574 | 40 738 | -40 164 | | 4 332 | -4 332 |
| | 1995 | 590 | 35 039 | -34 449 | 52 | 3 925 | -3 873 |
| | 1996 | 996 | 30 821 | -29 825 | 1 | 3 467 | -3 466 |
| | 1997 | 1 339 | 30 509 | -29 170 | 16 | 3 484 | -3 468 |
| French Guiana | 1970 | | 45 | -45 | | | |
| | 1975 | | 49 | -49 | | 1 | -1 |
| | 1980 | 39 | 569 | - 530 | | 4 | -4 |
| | 1985 | 6 | 578 | - 572 | | 630 | - 630 |
| | 1990 | 22 | 3 064 | -3 042 | | 1 059 | -1 059 |
| | 1991 | 153 | 2 594 | -2 441 | 617 | 1 701 | -1 084 |
| | 1992 | 87 | 3 580 | -3 493 | 72 | 2 860 | -2 788 |
| | 1993 | 58 | 2 939 | -2 881 | | 959 | - 959 |
| | 1994 | 105 | 2 975 | -2 870 | | 1 073 | -1 073 |
| | 1995 | 36 | 3 582 | -3 546 | | 1 316 | -1 316 |
| Guyana | 1970 | | | | 1 | 36 | -35 |
| | 1975 | 10 | 1 563 | -1 553 | 6 | 93 | -87 |
| | 1991 | | 622 | - 622 | | 250 | - 250 |
| | 1992 | | 1 007 | -1 007 | | 219 | - 219 |
| Paraguay | 1970 | | 66 | -66 | | | |
| | 1975 | | 188 | - 188 | | 29 | -29 |
| | 1980 | | 720 | - 720 | | 1 | -1 |
| | 1985 | | 415 | - 415 | | 7 | -7 |
| | 1990 | 1 177 | 741 | 436 | | 82 | -82 |
| | 1991 | 738 | 981 | - 243 | 4 | 68 | -64 |
| | 1992 | 1 217 | 2 079 | - 862 | | 80 | -80 |
| | 1993 | 1 227 | 2 923 | -1 696 | 5 | 160 | - 155 |
| | 1994 | 1 382 | 4 120 | -2 738 | 57 | 506 | - 449 |
| | 1995 | 1 424 | 4 746 | -3 322 | 29 | 755 | - 726 |
| | 1996 | 1 284 | 6 659 | -5 375 | | 922 | - 922 |
| | 1997 | 726 | 11 844 | -11 118 | | 712 | - 712 |
| Peru | 1970 | 98 | 8 810 | -8 712 | 3 | 2 960 | -2 957 |
| | 1975 | 402 | 11 740 | -11 338 | 37 | 5 045 | -5 008 |
| | 1980 | 1 533 | 7 738 | -6 205 | 153 | 4 972 | -4 819 |
| | 1985 | 3 170 | 18 385 | -15 215 | 28 | 3 783 | -3 755 |
| | 1990 | 708 | 22 584 | -21 876 | 4 | 2 402 | -2 398 |
| | 1991 | 1 005 | 12 806 | -11 801 | 70 | 2 664 | -2 594 |
| | 1992 | 2 684 | 11 397 | -8 713 | 104 | 3 829 | -3 725 |
| | 1993 | 894 | 11 741 | -10 847 | 95 | 4 362 | -4 267 |
| | 1994 | 1 221 | 15 987 | -14 766 | 138 | 5 115 | -4 977 |
| | 1995 | 1 078 | 21 977 | -20 899 | 342 | 5 270 | -4 928 |
| | 1996 | 1 329 | 29 806 | -28 477 | 320 | 5 470 | -5 150 |
| | 1997 | 1 577 | 34 027 | -32 450 | 285 | 5 165 | -4 880 |
| Suriname | 1990 | 8 | 2 030 | -2 022 | | 64 | -64 |
| | 1991 | 14 | 1 850 | -1 836 | | 393 | - 393 |
| | 1992 | 19 | 1 898 | -1 879 | | 157 | - 157 |
| | 1994 | 10 | 567 | - 557 | | 600 | - 600 |
| | 1995 | 3 | 1 081 | -1 078 | | 352 | - 352 |
| Uruguay | 1970 | | 86 | -86 | | | |
| | 1975 | 62 | | 62 | | | |
| | 1980 | 517 | 22 | 495 | | | |
| | 1985 | 834 | 160 | 674 | 162 | | 162 |
| | 1990 | 327 | 103 | 224 | 2 | | 2 |
| | 1991 | 125 | 208 | -83 | 329 | | 329 |
| | 1992 | 283 | 175 | 108 | 934 | | 934 |

IV.9    International trade in books and pamphlets, newspaper and periodicals
Commerce international de livres et brochures et de journaux et périodiques
Comercio internacional de libros y folletos y de publicaciones periódicas

| Country / Pays / País | Year / Année / Año | Books and pamphlets / livres et brochures / libros y folletos | | | Newspaper and periodicals / journaux et périodiques/ publicaciones periódicas | | |
|---|---|---|---|---|---|---|---|
| | | Exports / Exportations / Exportaciones | Imports / Importations / Importaciones | Balance / Balance / Balanza | Exports / Exportations / Exportaciones | Imports / Importations / Importaciones | Balance / Balance / Balanza |
| Uruguay (cont) | 1993 | 173 | 308 | - 135 | 1 248 | | 1 248 |
| | 1994 | 22 | 222 | - 200 | 1 037 | 4 | 1 033 |
| | 1995 | 25 | 256 | - 231 | 51 | 339 | - 288 |
| | 1996 | 40 | 343 | - 303 | 19 | 11 | 8 |
| | 1997 | 17 | 339 | - 322 | 3 | 13 | -10 |
| Venezuela | 1970 | 4 | 379 | - 375 | 240 | 3 246 | -3 006 |
| | 1975 | 1 995 | 14 062 | -12 067 | 73 | 6 453 | -6 380 |
| | 1980 | 1 729 | 52 356 | -50 627 | 1 871 | 27 675 | -25 804 |
| | 1985 | 3 155 | 69 548 | -66 393 | 1 511 | 29 518 | -28 007 |
| | 1990 | 3 537 | 23 707 | -20 170 | 986 | 6 154 | -5 168 |
| | 1991 | 1 724 | 30 486 | -28 762 | 1 048 | 9 435 | -8 387 |
| | 1992 | 2 325 | 39 963 | -37 638 | 1 051 | 13 086 | -12 035 |
| | 1993 | 3 228 | 41 074 | -37 846 | 1 055 | 15 871 | -14 816 |
| | 1994 | 2 717 | 32 179 | -29 462 | 1 002 | 14 917 | -13 915 |
| | 1995 | 3 042 | 38 626 | -35 584 | 638 | 14 991 | -14 353 |
| | 1996 | 2 122 | 33 071 | -30 949 | 294 | 12 205 | -11 911 |
| | 1997 | 2 079 | 46 231 | -44 152 | 267 | 15 306 | -15 039 |
| **Asia** | | | | | | | |
| Bahrain | 1970 | | | | 5 | 62 | -57 |
| | 1975 | | | | | 14 | -14 |
| | 1994 | 13 | 3 530 | -3 517 | 23 | 1 274 | -1 251 |
| | 1995 | 28 | 3 502 | -3 474 | | 1 553 | -1 553 |
| | 1996 | 23 | 4 301 | -4 278 | 1 | 1 038 | -1 037 |
| Bangladesh | 1980 | 28 | 999 | - 971 | 22 | 48 | -26 |
| | 1985 | 50 | 1 236 | -1 186 | 140 | 76 | 64 |
| | 1990 | 34 | 3 111 | -3 077 | 232 | 189 | 43 |
| | 1991 | 11 | 3 005 | -2 994 | 157 | 273 | - 116 |
| | 1992 | 36 | 2 679 | -2 643 | 84 | 353 | - 269 |
| | 1993 | 40 | 5 325 | -5 285 | | 253 | - 253 |
| | 1994 | 108 | 4 206 | -4 098 | 20 | 382 | - 362 |
| | 1995 | 44 | 5 252 | -5 208 | 8 | 516 | - 508 |
| | 1996 | 34 | 6 397 | -6 363 | 8 | 480 | - 472 |
| Bhutan | 1991 | | 230 | - 230 | | 1 | -1 |
| | 1992 | | 334 | - 334 | | 7 | -7 |
| | 1993 | | 474 | - 474 | | 15 | -15 |
| | 1994 | | 401 | - 401 | | 10 | -10 |
| Brunei Darussalam | 1970 | 4 | 260 | - 256 | 1 | 73 | -72 |
| | 1975 | 5 | 621 | - 616 | 25 | 478 | - 453 |
| | 1980 | | 1 768 | -1 768 | 30 | 855 | - 825 |
| | 1985 | | 3 893 | -3 893 | 24 | 2 919 | -2 895 |
| | 1990 | 1 | 4 249 | -4 248 | 32 | 3 946 | -3 914 |
| | 1991 | 1 | 4 616 | -4 615 | 61 | 4 261 | -4 200 |
| | 1992 | 6 | 5 480 | -5 474 | 42 | 4 525 | -4 483 |
| | 1993 | | 4 354 | -4 354 | 27 | 3 531 | -3 504 |
| | 1994 | 2 | 6 133 | -6 131 | 19 | 3 317 | -3 298 |
| China | 1990 | 19 570 | 30 895 | -11 325 | 2 295 | 27 726 | -25 431 |
| | 1991 | 22 475 | 26 654 | -4 179 | 4 127 | 22 536 | -18 409 |
| | 1992 | 34 253 | 41 768 | -7 515 | 3 549 | 26 977 | -23 428 |
| | 1993 | 49 250 | 39 972 | 9 278 | 1 763 | 10 330 | -8 567 |
| | 1994 | 56 544 | 37 499 | 19 045 | 2 188 | 8 270 | -6 082 |
| | 1995 | 72 991 | 42 204 | 30 787 | 3 547 | 22 905 | -19 358 |
| | 1996 | 100 566 | 45 349 | 55 217 | 3 795 | 16 300 | -12 505 |
| | 1997 | 136 263 | 44 888 | 91 375 | 7 849 | 30 873 | -23 024 |
| China, Hong Kong SAR | 1970 | | | | 2 485 | 758 | 1 727 |
| | 1975 | | | | 5 864 | 1 082 | 4 782 |
| | 1980 | 75 742 | 11 652 | 64 090 | 15 414 | 3 325 | 12 089 |
| | 1985 | 104 548 | 29 692 | 74 856 | 21 104 | 5 719 | 15 385 |
| | 1990 | 265 404 | 70 144 | 195 260 | 35 948 | 10 336 | 25 612 |
| | 1991 | 320 544 | 84 745 | 235 799 | 37 959 | 16 107 | 21 852 |
| | 1992 | 359 288 | 101 997 | 257 291 | 36 234 | 21 423 | 14 811 |
| | 1993 | 346 337 | 125 495 | 220 842 | 38 776 | 30 001 | 8 775 |
| | 1994 | 340 779 | 134 973 | 205 806 | 38 874 | 33 313 | 5 561 |
| | 1995 | 379 482 | 155 182 | 224 300 | 44 488 | 34 813 | 9 675 |
| | 1996 | 379 536 | 190 449 | 189 087 | 44 672 | 29 607 | 15 065 |
| | 1997 | 366 017 | 214 277 | 151 740 | 44 886 | 35 986 | 8 900 |
| Cyprus | 1970 | 68 | 861 | - 793 | 26 | 525 | - 499 |
| | 1975 | 109 | 1 245 | -1 136 | 56 | 535 | - 479 |
| | 1980 | 135 | 4 890 | -4 755 | 663 | 3 192 | -2 529 |
| | 1985 | 649 | 4 369 | -3 720 | 2 563 | 1 090 | 1 473 |
| | 1990 | 843 | 8 849 | -8 006 | 2 916 | 7 991 | -5 075 |
| | 1991 | 647 | 8 890 | -8 243 | 2 048 | 7 993 | -5 945 |
| | 1992 | 768 | 12 146 | -11 378 | 1 781 | 10 807 | -9 026 |
| | 1993 | 258 | 9 766 | -9 508 | 1 163 | 8 918 | -7 755 |
| | 1994 | 377 | 12 208 | -11 831 | 799 | 10 152 | -9 353 |
| | 1995 | 452 | 15 452 | -15 000 | 711 | 11 692 | -10 981 |
| | 1996 | 447 | 21 587 | -21 140 | 529 | 10 726 | -10 197 |
| | 1997 | 494 | 19 480 | -18 986 | 282 | 12 606 | -12 324 |

International trade in books and pamphlets, newspaper and periodicals    IV.9
Commerce international de livres et brochures et de journaux et périodiques
Comercio internacional de libros y folletos y de publicaciones periódicas

| Country / Pays / País | Year / Année / Año | Books and pamphlets / livres et brochures / libros y folletos | | | Newspaper and periodicals / journaux et périodiques/ publicaciones periódicas | | |
|---|---|---|---|---|---|---|---|
| | | Exports Exportations Exportaciones | Imports Importations Importaciones | Balance Balance Balanza | Exports Exportations Exportaciones | Imports Importations Importaciones | Balance Balance Balanza |
| India | 1970 | | | | 334 | 301 | 33 |
| | 1975 | | | | 706 | 850 | - 144 |
| | 1980 | | | | 608 | 1 900 | -1 292 |
| | 1985 | 8 483 | 38 535 | -30 052 | 5 042 | 3 525 | 1 517 |
| | 1990 | 9 964 | 45 649 | -35 685 | 6 739 | 1 774 | 4 965 |
| | 1991 | 10 279 | 24 841 | -14 562 | 5 536 | 2 905 | 2 631 |
| | 1992 | 13 109 | 39 831 | -26 722 | 5 656 | 6 000 | - 344 |
| | 1993 | 13 971 | 41 801 | -27 830 | 5 523 | 5 682 | - 159 |
| | 1994 | 17 904 | 48 778 | -30 874 | 6 435 | 5 520 | 915 |
| | 1995 | 22 563 | 56 053 | -33 490 | 7 652 | 6 001 | 1 651 |
| | 1996 | 24 707 | 35 483 | -10 776 | 11 753 | 3 898 | 7 855 |
| Indonesia | 1970 | | 1 277 | -1 277 | | 238 | - 238 |
| | 1975 | 65 | 3 807 | -3 742 | | 382 | - 382 |
| | 1980 | 40 | 3 086 | -3 046 | 2 | 640 | - 638 |
| | 1985 | 149 | 8 290 | -8 141 | 12 | 1 572 | -1 560 |
| | 1990 | 438 | 19 245 | -18 807 | 143 | 2 413 | -2 270 |
| | 1991 | 391 | 13 060 | -12 669 | 47 | 2 860 | -2 813 |
| | 1992 | 677 | 17 425 | -16 748 | 41 | 4 121 | -4 080 |
| | 1993 | 576 | 14 880 | -14 304 | 76 | 4 961 | -4 885 |
| | 1994 | 878 | 14 283 | -13 405 | 84 | 7 357 | -7 273 |
| | 1995 | 2 286 | 19 874 | -17 588 | 409 | 11 589 | -11 180 |
| | 1996 | 5 992 | 19 244 | -13 252 | 134 | 13 483 | -13 349 |
| | 1997 | 4 505 | 27 457 | -22 952 | 250 | 11 103 | -10 853 |
| Israel | 1970 | 3 976 | 1 878 | 2 098 | 1 086 | 1 688 | - 602 |
| | 1975 | 10 792 | 3 004 | 7 788 | 2 451 | 2 046 | 405 |
| | 1980 | 12 841 | 8 411 | 4 430 | 1 166 | 2 162 | - 996 |
| | 1985 | 12 769 | 13 009 | - 240 | 1 394 | 2 507 | -1 113 |
| | 1990 | 19 650 | 15 536 | 4 114 | 2 848 | 5 708 | -2 860 |
| | 1991 | 21 937 | 14 416 | 7 521 | 2 384 | 6 200 | -3 816 |
| | 1992 | 18 862 | 16 879 | 1 983 | 2 574 | 5 582 | -3 008 |
| | 1993 | 19 294 | 19 548 | - 254 | 2 396 | 5 349 | -2 953 |
| | 1994 | 19 349 | 21 962 | -2 613 | 2 268 | 6 768 | -4 500 |
| | 1995 | 21 274 | 29 665 | -8 391 | 2 027 | 8 491 | -6 464 |
| | 1996 | 23 638 | 34 892 | -11 254 | 1 667 | 9 209 | -7 542 |
| | 1997 | 23 149 | 37 335 | -14 186 | 1 936 | 8 544 | -6 608 |
| Japan | 1970 | 17 502 | 46 605 | -29 103 | 7 878 | 3 921 | 3 957 |
| | 1975 | 19 370 | 58 079 | -38 709 | 5 735 | 33 430 | -27 695 |
| | 1980 | 61 522 | 100 649 | -39 127 | 21 701 | 48 615 | -26 914 |
| | 1985 | 140 021 | 91 382 | 48 639 | 25 065 | 44 991 | -19 926 |
| | 1990 | 218 575 | 231 725 | -13 150 | 35 513 | 112 338 | -76 825 |
| | 1991 | 217 033 | 201 410 | 15 623 | 37 759 | 106 022 | -68 263 |
| | 1992 | 221 549 | 209 889 | 11 660 | 40 770 | 152 786 | - 112 016 |
| | 1993 | 207 857 | 216 292 | -8 435 | 44 430 | 142 894 | -98 464 |
| | 1994 | 200 371 | 233 875 | -33 504 | 49 017 | 156 641 | - 107 624 |
| | 1995 | 193 164 | 261 216 | -68 052 | 51 956 | 185 555 | - 133 599 |
| | 1996 | 172 191 | 270 193 | -98 002 | 43 573 | 182 383 | - 138 810 |
| | 1997 | 148 118 | 293 313 | - 145 195 | 39 824 | 150 740 | - 110 916 |
| Jordan | 1970 | 22 | 320 | - 298 | | 4 | -4 |
| | 1975 | 5 | 797 | - 792 | | 149 | - 149 |
| | 1980 | 1 047 | 3 614 | -2 567 | 1 | 540 | - 539 |
| | 1985 | 879 | 5 437 | -4 558 | 5 | 662 | - 657 |
| | 1990 | 274 | 8 949 | -8 675 | | 478 | - 478 |
| | 1991 | | | | | 455 | - 455 |
| | 1992 | 10 060 | 8 537 | 1 523 | 13 | 664 | - 651 |
| | 1993 | 18 578 | 8 791 | 9 787 | 29 | 811 | - 782 |
| | 1994 | 6 504 | 6 959 | - 455 | 20 | 309 | - 289 |
| | 1995 | 15 137 | 6 734 | 8 403 | | 320 | - 320 |
| Korea, Republic of | 1970 | 179 | 3 067 | -2 888 | 29 | 687 | - 658 |
| | 1975 | 1 083 | 3 064 | -1 981 | 104 | 1 300 | -1 196 |
| | 1980 | 3 167 | 10 409 | -7 242 | 227 | 3 733 | -3 506 |
| | 1985 | 8 473 | 11 554 | -3 081 | 767 | 7 709 | -6 942 |
| | 1990 | 29 161 | 28 182 | 979 | 1 625 | 19 388 | -17 763 |
| | 1991 | 35 407 | 28 982 | 6 425 | 1 638 | 23 479 | -21 841 |
| | 1992 | 32 183 | 31 396 | 787 | 2 276 | 26 493 | -24 217 |
| | 1993 | 34 029 | 40 205 | -6 176 | 1 787 | 29 173 | -27 386 |
| | 1994 | 36 310 | 61 351 | -25 041 | 1 776 | 31 970 | -30 194 |
| | 1995 | 45 508 | 75 036 | -29 528 | 1 757 | 33 405 | -31 648 |
| | 1996 | 45 389 | 86 790 | -41 401 | 1 990 | 39 726 | -37 736 |
| Kuwait | 1990 | 590 | 5 202 | -4 612 | 537 | 3 714 | -3 177 |
| | 1991 | | | | | 224 | - 224 |
| | 1992 | | | | 2 | 5 581 | -5 579 |
| | 1993 | | | | | 6 176 | -6 176 |
| | 1994 | | | | 270 | 4 441 | -4 171 |
| | 1995 | 785 | 8 537 | -7 752 | 330 | 5 159 | -4 829 |
| | 1996 | 699 | 8 767 | -8 068 | 291 | 5 528 | -5 237 |
| | 1997 | | | | 138 | 6 023 | -5 885 |
| Kyrgyzstan | 1995 | 47 | 371 | - 324 | | 36 | -36 |
| | 1996 | 124 | 1 085 | - 961 | 2 | 122 | - 120 |

IV.9    International trade in books and pamphlets, newspaper and periodicals
Commerce international de livres et brochures et de journaux et périodiques
Comercio internacional de libros y folletos y de publicaciones periódicas

| Country / Pays / País | Year / Année / Año | Books and pamphlets / livres et brochures / libros y folletos | | | Newspaper and periodicals / journaux et périodiques / publicaciones periódicas | | |
|---|---|---|---|---|---|---|---|
| | | Exports / Exportations / Exportaciones | Imports / Importations / Importaciones | Balance / Balance / Balanza | Exports / Exportations / Exportaciones | Imports / Importations / Importaciones | Balance / Balance / Balanza |
| Macau | 1975 | 10 | 375 | - 365 | | | |
| | 1980 | | 685 | - 685 | | 1 | -1 |
| | 1985 | 121 | 1 281 | -1 160 | | 44 | -44 |
| | 1990 | 148 | 545 | - 397 | 1 | 52 | -51 |
| | 1991 | 110 | 838 | - 728 | 7 | 22 | -15 |
| | 1992 | 75 | 937 | - 862 | 24 | 77 | -53 |
| | 1993 | 103 | 1 548 | -1 445 | 24 | 29 | -5 |
| | 1994 | 114 | 1 203 | -1 089 | 11 | 43 | -32 |
| | 1995 | 76 | 1 075 | - 999 | 9 | 32 | -23 |
| | 1996 | 57 | 1 108 | -1 051 | 8 | 395 | - 387 |
| | 1997 | 385 | 1 402 | -1 017 | 5 | 515 | - 510 |
| Malaysia | 1970 | 1 212 | 6 634 | -5 422 | 200 | 1 800 | -1 600 |
| | 1975 | 1 358 | 10 935 | -9 577 | 254 | 2 646 | -2 392 |
| | 1980 | 2 217 | 20 756 | -18 539 | 788 | 4 881 | -4 093 |
| | 1985 | 4 067 | 30 362 | -26 295 | 939 | 11 527 | -10 588 |
| | 1990 | 9 674 | 46 213 | -36 539 | 1 679 | 13 178 | -11 499 |
| | 1991 | 11 584 | 48 449 | -36 865 | 1 699 | 12 841 | -11 142 |
| | 1992 | 18 632 | 55 832 | -37 200 | 2 329 | 12 940 | -10 611 |
| | 1993 | 20 703 | 56 059 | -35 356 | 977 | 12 247 | -11 270 |
| | 1994 | 30 178 | 74 111 | -43 933 | 1 352 | 12 805 | -11 453 |
| | 1995 | 31 791 | 78 527 | -46 736 | 1 451 | 11 111 | -9 660 |
| | 1996 | 37 511 | 80 200 | -42 689 | 1 101 | 12 616 | -11 515 |
| | 1997 | 32 783 | 80 016 | -47 233 | 869 | 10 074 | -9 205 |
| Mongolia | 1996 | 1 | 219 | - 218 | | 9 | -9 |
| Myanmar | 1970 | 1 | 426 | - 425 | | 108 | - 108 |
| | 1975 | 1 | 78 | -77 | | 11 | -11 |
| | 1991 | 3 | 52 | -49 | 25 | 6 | 19 |
| | 1992 | | 106 | - 106 | 17 | 29 | -12 |
| Nepal | 1985 | 91 | 1 806 | -1 715 | | 52 | -52 |
| | 1990 | 27 | 2 823 | -2 796 | | 278 | - 278 |
| | 1991 | 8 | | 8 | | | |
| Oman | 1970 | | | | | | |
| | 1975 | | | | | 3 | -3 |
| | 1980 | | | | 14 | 1 169 | -1 155 |
| | 1985 | | | | 55 | 3 075 | -3 020 |
| | 1990 | 303 | 3 118 | -2 815 | 192 | 2 386 | -2 194 |
| | 1991 | 566 | 2 659 | -2 093 | 255 | 2 135 | -1 880 |
| | 1992 | 1 076 | 2 423 | -1 347 | 243 | 1 505 | -1 262 |
| | 1993 | 149 | 3 327 | -3 178 | 274 | 1 311 | -1 037 |
| | 1994 | 101 | 2 749 | -2 648 | 288 | 2 105 | -1 817 |
| | 1995 | 198 | 3 393 | -3 195 | 228 | 2 422 | -2 194 |
| | 1996 | 213 | 2 592 | -2 379 | 228 | 2 065 | -1 837 |
| | 1997 | 446 | 3 703 | -3 257 | 115 | 2 442 | -2 327 |
| Pakistan | 1970 | | | | 8 | 175 | - 167 |
| | 1975 | | | | 114 | 175 | -61 |
| | 1980 | | | | 162 | 305 | - 143 |
| | 1985 | 743 | 5 215 | -4 472 | 863 | 473 | 390 |
| | 1990 | 984 | 7 994 | -7 010 | 2 307 | 411 | 1 896 |
| | 1991 | 1 124 | 8 410 | -7 286 | 2 081 | 527 | 1 554 |
| | 1992 | 1 481 | 9 529 | -8 048 | 3 005 | 690 | 2 315 |
| | 1993 | 1 621 | 11 623 | -10 002 | 3 630 | 450 | 3 180 |
| | 1994 | 1 347 | 10 899 | -9 552 | 4 038 | 371 | 3 667 |
| | 1995 | 1 354 | 9 484 | -8 130 | 4 220 | 512 | 3 708 |
| | 1996 | 1 535 | 10 744 | -9 209 | 3 676 | 1 354 | 2 322 |
| | 1997 | 1 632 | 9 249 | -7 617 | 1 627 | 1 158 | 469 |
| Philippines | 1970 | 17 | 3 508 | -3 491 | 1 | 1 031 | -1 030 |
| | 1975 | 67 | 5 466 | -5 399 | 199 | 1 231 | -1 032 |
| | 1980 | 57 | 13 726 | -13 669 | 319 | 3 601 | -3 282 |
| | 1985 | 61 | 4 324 | -4 263 | 349 | 2 250 | -1 901 |
| | 1990 | 410 | 14 547 | -14 137 | 469 | 4 990 | -4 521 |
| | 1991 | 323 | 19 843 | -19 520 | 572 | 5 293 | -4 721 |
| | 1992 | 427 | 29 792 | -29 365 | 840 | 5 599 | -4 759 |
| | 1993 | 626 | 26 393 | -25 767 | 1 174 | 7 896 | -6 722 |
| | 1994 | 689 | 35 118 | -34 429 | 1 208 | 8 711 | -7 503 |
| | 1995 | 836 | 44 346 | -43 510 | 1 247 | 9 187 | -7 940 |
| | 1996 | 939 | 48 773 | -47 834 | 1 120 | 9 091 | -7 971 |
| | 1997 | 984 | 46 161 | -45 177 | 1 100 | 11 746 | -10 646 |
| Qatar | 1991 | | | | 134 | 294 | - 160 |
| | 1992 | | | | 97 | 171 | -74 |
| | 1993 | | | | | 253 | - 253 |
| | 1994 | | | | | 368 | - 368 |
| Saudi Arabia | 1975 | 25 | 7 538 | -7 513 | 1 | 731 | - 730 |
| | 1980 | 356 | 27 130 | -26 774 | 56 | 2 112 | -2 056 |
| | 1985 | 924 | 24 750 | -23 826 | | 5 932 | -5 932 |
| | 1990 | 1 794 | 26 749 | -24 955 | 53 | 1 663 | -1 610 |
| | 1991 | 653 | 25 324 | -24 671 | 4 | 692 | - 688 |
| | 1992 | 1 296 | 37 739 | -36 443 | 2 | 834 | - 832 |

International trade in books and pamphlets, newspaper and periodicals    IV.9
Commerce international de livres et brochures et de journaux et périodiques
Comercio internacional de libros y folletos y de publicaciones periódicas

| Country / Pays / País | Year / Année / Año | Books and pamphlets / livres et brochures / libros y folletos | | | Newspaper and periodicals / journaux et périodiques / publicaciones periódicas | | |
|---|---|---|---|---|---|---|---|
| | | Exports / Exportations / Exportaciones | Imports / Importations / Importaciones | Balance / Balance / Balanza | Exports / Exportations / Exportaciones | Imports / Importations / Importaciones | Balance / Balance / Balanza |
| Saudi Arabia (cont) | 1993 | 2 114 | 43 048 | -40 934 | 25 | 1 939 | -1 914 |
| | 1994 | 1 493 | 26 382 | -24 889 | 40 | 590 | - 550 |
| | 1995 | 1 517 | 27 757 | -26 240 | 4 | 908 | - 904 |
| | 1996 | 1 032 | 61 373 | -60 341 | 34 | 769 | - 735 |
| Singapore | 1970 | 6 499 | 6 023 | 476 | 737 | 2 472 | -1 735 |
| | 1975 | 19 634 | 13 790 | 5 844 | 1 824 | 5 055 | -3 231 |
| | 1980 | 44 951 | 31 770 | 13 181 | 3 207 | 14 794 | -11 587 |
| | 1985 | 58 835 | 39 292 | 19 543 | 6 015 | 15 471 | -9 456 |
| | 1990 | 171 497 | 87 884 | 83 613 | 15 643 | 21 256 | -5 613 |
| | 1991 | 208 671 | 99 965 | 108 706 | 16 520 | 23 207 | -6 687 |
| | 1992 | 231 496 | 104 435 | 127 061 | 22 757 | 25 368 | -2 611 |
| | 1993 | 249 490 | 114 466 | 135 024 | 21 022 | 26 782 | -5 760 |
| | 1994 | 310 501 | 135 829 | 174 672 | 33 698 | 27 800 | 5 898 |
| | 1995 | 419 270 | 160 410 | 258 860 | 45 300 | 28 918 | 16 382 |
| | 1996 | 402 125 | 178 092 | 224 033 | 44 029 | 28 963 | 15 066 |
| | 1997 | 367 687 | 191 225 | 176 462 | 40 556 | 35 708 | 4 848 |
| Sri Lanka | 1970 | | 205 | - 205 | | 31 | -31 |
| | 1975 | 15 | 354 | - 339 | | 73 | -73 |
| | 1980 | 11 | 1 123 | -1 112 | 1 | 130 | - 129 |
| | 1985 | 71 | 2 287 | -2 216 | 32 | 648 | - 616 |
| | 1990 | 177 | 3 362 | -3 185 | 170 | 1 772 | -1 602 |
| | 1991 | 176 | 3 890 | -3 714 | 154 | 1 028 | - 874 |
| | 1992 | 186 | 5 582 | -5 396 | 356 | 1 217 | - 861 |
| | 1993 | 347 | 5 462 | -5 115 | 491 | 911 | - 420 |
| | 1994 | 264 | 8 336 | -8 072 | 676 | 1 063 | - 387 |
| Syrian Arab Republic | 1970 | | | | | | |
| | 1975 | 66 | 215 | - 149 | | 273 | - 273 |
| | 1980 | 197 | 861 | - 664 | 4 | 11 | -7 |
| | 1985 | 94 | 342 | - 248 | 2 | 129 | - 127 |
| | 1990 | 356 | 600 | - 244 | 1 | 90 | -89 |
| | 1991 | | | | | | |
| | 1992 | 336 | 406 | -70 | 1 | 11 | -10 |
| | 1995 | 560 | 889 | - 329 | 13 | 81 | -68 |
| Thailand | 1970 | 2 | 1 942 | -1 940 | | 294 | - 294 |
| | 1975 | 49 | 2 209 | -2 160 | 9 | 194 | - 185 |
| | 1980 | 114 | 4 543 | -4 429 | 158 | 556 | - 398 |
| | 1985 | 308 | 8 167 | -7 859 | 822 | 1 562 | - 740 |
| | 1990 | 1 948 | 17 843 | -15 895 | 3 222 | 9 444 | -6 222 |
| | 1991 | 3 976 | 21 112 | -17 136 | 2 717 | 12 793 | -10 076 |
| | 1992 | 4 247 | 18 351 | -14 104 | 3 362 | 9 429 | -6 067 |
| | 1993 | 4 919 | 23 145 | -18 226 | 4 235 | 10 497 | -6 262 |
| | 1994 | 7 996 | 34 751 | -26 755 | 4 812 | 10 298 | -5 486 |
| | 1995 | 7 384 | 46 224 | -38 840 | 25 045 | 14 281 | 10 764 |
| | 1996 | 11 314 | 47 657 | -36 343 | 5 170 | 16 680 | -11 510 |
| | 1997 | 6 483 | 48 593 | -42 110 | 3 677 | 13 882 | -10 205 |
| Turkey | 1970 | 31 | 1 599 | -1 568 | 168 | 682 | - 514 |
| | 1975 | 128 | 2 992 | -2 864 | 48 | 1 189 | -1 141 |
| | 1980 | 877 | 956 | -79 | 173 | 342 | - 169 |
| | 1985 | 12 620 | 3 588 | 9 032 | 2 353 | 1 140 | 1 213 |
| | 1990 | 2 135 | 15 808 | -13 673 | 1 650 | 7 685 | -6 035 |
| | 1991 | 1 784 | 11 500 | -9 716 | 2 434 | 7 841 | -5 407 |
| | 1992 | 2 653 | 14 237 | -11 584 | 2 575 | 12 028 | -9 453 |
| | 1993 | 3 895 | 85 231 | -81 336 | 4 396 | 11 149 | -6 753 |
| | 1994 | 2 632 | 50 375 | -47 743 | 2 286 | 11 141 | -8 855 |
| | 1995 | 3 287 | 33 020 | -29 733 | 1 244 | 14 949 | -13 705 |
| | 1996 | 4 279 | 34 873 | -30 594 | 4 765 | 15 475 | -10 710 |
| | 1997 | 3 906 | 31 998 | -28 092 | 4 137 | 19 759 | -15 622 |
| United Arab Emirates | 1980 | | 2 120 | -2 120 | | 98 | -98 |
| | 1985 | | | | | | |
| | 1990 | | | | | | |
| | 1991 | | | | 1 | 119 | - 118 |
| | 1992 | | | | | 197 | - 197 |
| | 1993 | | | | 2 | 289 | - 287 |
| Yemen | 1990 | | | | | | |
| | 1991 | | 101 | - 101 | | | |
| | 1995 | 20 | 827 | - 807 | | 570 | - 570 |
| **Europe** | | | | | | | |
| Albania | 1996 | 23 | 1 534 | -1 511 | 357 | 49 | 308 |
| | 1997 | 13 | 374 | - 361 | 62 | 112 | -50 |
| Austria | 1970 | 13 620 | 13 442 | 178 | 958 | 16 835 | -15 877 |
| | 1975 | 31 943 | 45 635 | -13 692 | 2 215 | 49 198 | -46 983 |
| | 1980 | 61 473 | 129 062 | -67 589 | 18 788 | 105 448 | -86 660 |
| | 1985 | 45 798 | 97 104 | -51 306 | 22 826 | 92 739 | -69 913 |
| | 1990 | 87 496 | 248 780 | - 161 284 | 76 959 | 244 476 | - 167 517 |
| | 1991 | 91 751 | 249 078 | - 157 327 | 82 497 | 241 539 | - 159 042 |
| | 1992 | 91 138 | 269 721 | - 178 583 | 89 293 | 254 489 | - 165 196 |

IV.9  International trade in books and pamphlets, newspaper and periodicals
Commerce international de livres et brochures et de journaux et périodiques
Comercio internacional de libros y folletos y de publicaciones periódicas

| Country<br>Pays<br>País | Year<br>Année<br>Año | Books and pamphlets / livres et brochures / libros y folletos | | | Newspaper and periodicals / journaux et périodiques/ publicaciones periódicas | | |
|---|---|---|---|---|---|---|---|
| | | Exports<br>Exportations<br>Exportaciones | Imports<br>Importations<br>Importaciones | Balance<br>Balance<br>Balanza | Exports<br>Exportations<br>Exportaciones | Imports<br>Importations<br>Importaciones | Balance<br>Balance<br>Balanza |
| Austria (cont) | 1993 | 111 192 | 269 068 | - 157 876 | 81 878 | 230 571 | - 148 693 |
| | 1994 | 99 436 | 304 964 | - 205 528 | 81 903 | 250 820 | - 168 917 |
| | 1995 | 115 505 | 349 285 | - 233 780 | 114 941 | 299 434 | - 184 493 |
| | 1996 | 132 515 | 356 365 | - 223 850 | 94 441 | 255 805 | - 161 364 |
| Belgium | 1970 | 27 334 | 24 105 | 3 229 | 28 902 | 22 225 | 6 677 |
| | 1975 | 80 798 | 85 366 | -4 568 | 56 759 | 60 422 | -3 663 |
| | 1980 | 166 693 | 180 524 | -13 831 | 95 346 | 129 345 | -33 999 |
| | 1985 | 133 169 | 123 036 | 10 133 | 63 090 | 139 800 | -76 710 |
| | 1990 | 353 413 | 292 705 | 60 708 | 112 791 | 340 999 | - 228 208 |
| | 1991 | 340 014 | 289 292 | 50 722 | 125 954 | 343 029 | - 217 075 |
| | 1992 | 387 298 | 310 283 | 77 015 | 126 639 | 299 593 | - 172 954 |
| | 1993 | 310 116 | 273 551 | 36 565 | 102 648 | 333 450 | - 230 802 |
| | 1994 | 328 083 | 312 528 | 15 555 | 107 568 | 337 122 | - 229 554 |
| | 1995 | 412 665 | 346 490 | 66 175 | 157 266 | 255 622 | -98 356 |
| | 1996 | 352 971 | 405 666 | -52 695 | 144 483 | 252 256 | - 107 773 |
| | 1997 | 324 932 | 386 269 | -61 337 | 121 758 | 210 577 | -88 819 |
| Bulgaria | 1992 | | 2 787 | -2 787 | | 1 601 | -1 601 |
| Croatia | 1992 | 4 521 | 3 711 | 810 | 13 | 390 | - 377 |
| | 1993 | 3 307 | 1 726 | 1 581 | 148 | 594 | - 446 |
| | 1994 | 5 261 | 2 133 | 3 128 | 152 | 1 428 | -1 276 |
| | 1995 | 5 807 | 6 418 | - 611 | 415 | 4 507 | -4 092 |
| | 1996 | 3 361 | 7 138 | -3 777 | 794 | 2 943 | -2 149 |
| | 1997 | 4 888 | 7 886 | -2 998 | 946 | 2 362 | -1 416 |
| Czech Republic | 1993 | 24 335 | 38 223 | -13 888 | 6 822 | 14 801 | -7 979 |
| | 1994 | 24 770 | 42 870 | -18 100 | 8 592 | 18 533 | -9 941 |
| | 1995 | 35 881 | 62 848 | -26 967 | 13 835 | 25 479 | -11 644 |
| | 1996 | 32 253 | 62 471 | -30 218 | 22 937 | 29 479 | -6 542 |
| | 1997 | 34 502 | 56 943 | -22 441 | 31 027 | 27 071 | 3 956 |
| Denmark | 1970 | 4 748 | 9 332 | -4 584 | 1 612 | 3 311 | -1 699 |
| | 1975 | 15 162 | 22 573 | -7 411 | 4 706 | 7 342 | -2 636 |
| | 1980 | 38 482 | 43 074 | -4 592 | 6 984 | 7 856 | - 872 |
| | 1985 | 67 946 | 51 458 | 16 488 | 12 753 | 11 908 | 845 |
| | 1990 | 128 044 | 104 960 | 23 084 | 31 483 | 24 722 | 6 761 |
| | 1991 | 123 296 | 109 935 | 13 361 | 29 078 | 28 904 | 174 |
| | 1992 | 130 376 | 118 572 | 11 804 | 29 822 | 27 576 | 2 246 |
| | 1993 | 122 849 | 87 148 | 35 701 | 46 675 | 31 189 | 15 486 |
| | 1994 | 118 783 | 83 075 | 35 708 | 48 378 | 28 328 | 20 050 |
| | 1995 | 128 095 | 92 245 | 35 850 | 60 927 | 31 374 | 29 553 |
| | 1996 | 116 228 | 104 112 | 12 116 | 43 248 | 29 708 | 13 540 |
| | 1997 | 108 401 | 122 010 | -13 609 | 29 865 | 45 226 | -15 361 |
| Estonia | 1995 | 795 | 3 343 | -2 548 | 1 069 | 1 473 | - 404 |
| | 1996 | 831 | 4 521 | -3 690 | 917 | 3 061 | -2 144 |
| | 1997 | 1 163 | 6 672 | -5 509 | 626 | 2 058 | -1 432 |
| Faeroe Islands | 1980 | | 1 137 | -1 137 | | 18 | -18 |
| | 1985 | | 841 | - 841 | | 29 | -29 |
| | 1990 | | 1 560 | -1 560 | | 112 | - 112 |
| | 1991 | | 1 416 | -1 416 | | 928 | - 928 |
| | 1992 | | 1 277 | -1 277 | | 390 | - 390 |
| | 1993 | | 919 | - 919 | | 563 | - 563 |
| | 1994 | | 947 | - 947 | | 1 522 | -1 522 |
| | 1995 | | | | | | |
| Federal Republic of Yugoslavia | 1992 | 1 177 | 538 | 639 | 7 701 | 149 | 7 552 |
| | 1996 | 1 260 | 1 131 | 129 | 2 006 | 3 221 | -1 215 |
| | 1997 | 563 | 2 555 | -1 992 | 1 844 | 4 589 | -2 745 |
| Finland | 1970 | 2 327 | 4 714 | -2 387 | 1 632 | 1 612 | 20 |
| | 1975 | 6 419 | 11 439 | -5 020 | 5 652 | 3 480 | 2 172 |
| | 1980 | 18 856 | 21 589 | -2 733 | 25 404 | 6 549 | 18 855 |
| | 1985 | 26 149 | 19 457 | 6 692 | 23 938 | 8 209 | 15 729 |
| | 1990 | 44 314 | 54 668 | -10 354 | 51 179 | 23 695 | 27 484 |
| | 1991 | 39 273 | 52 807 | -13 534 | 53 081 | 24 941 | 28 140 |
| | 1992 | 32 323 | 51 788 | -19 465 | 57 976 | 23 349 | 34 627 |
| | 1993 | 32 447 | 38 091 | -5 644 | 55 783 | 18 639 | 37 144 |
| | 1994 | 42 478 | 40 540 | 1 938 | 83 739 | 19 100 | 64 639 |
| | 1995 | 62 288 | 45 258 | 17 030 | 152 855 | 20 871 | 131 984 |
| | 1996 | 58 775 | 48 648 | 10 127 | 172 939 | 30 437 | 142 502 |
| | 1997 | 55 990 | 46 159 | 9 831 | 156 436 | 27 507 | 128 929 |
| France | 1970 | 70 364 | 71 281 | - 917 | 55 668 | 57 718 | -2 050 |
| | 1975 | 158 653 | 147 691 | 10 962 | 117 649 | 107 362 | 10 287 |
| | 1980 | 302 666 | 327 453 | -24 787 | 209 530 | 200 091 | 9 439 |
| | 1985 | 241 496 | 228 189 | 13 307 | 186 261 | 182 336 | 3 925 |
| | 1990 | 548 272 | 600 281 | -52 009 | 387 972 | 424 850 | -36 878 |
| | 1991 | 562 002 | 617 024 | -55 022 | 378 432 | 416 739 | -38 307 |
| | 1992 | 619 532 | 636 785 | -17 253 | 400 030 | 434 636 | -34 606 |
| | 1993 | 488 034 | 509 816 | -21 782 | 386 641 | 282 976 | 103 665 |
| | 1994 | 538 379 | 546 199 | -7 820 | 386 596 | 334 316 | 52 280 |

International trade in books and pamphlets, newspaper and periodicals IV.9
Commerce international de livres et brochures et de journaux et périodiques
Comercio internacional de libros y folletos y de publicaciones periódicas

| Country<br>Pays<br>País | Year<br>Année<br>Año | Books and pamphlets / livres et brochures /<br>libros y folletos | | | Newspaper and periodicals / journaux et périodiques/<br>publicaciones periódicas | | |
|---|---|---|---|---|---|---|---|
| | | Exports<br>Exportations<br>Exportaciones | Imports<br>Importations<br>Importaciones | Balance<br>Balance<br>Balanza | Exports<br>Exportations<br>Exportaciones | Imports<br>Importations<br>Importaciones | Balance<br>Balance<br>Balanza |
| France (cont) | 1995 | 627 691 | 712 902 | -85 211 | 549 683 | 446 002 | 103 681 |
| | 1996 | 594 169 | 637 271 | -43 102 | 482 365 | 392 426 | 89 939 |
| | 1997 | 603 695 | 572 919 | 30 776 | 439 423 | 395 106 | 44 317 |
| Germany | 1991 | 930 634 | 539 405 | 391 229 | 900 599 | 266 201 | 634 398 |
| | 1992 | 992 573 | 597 465 | 395 108 | 966 677 | 264 128 | 702 549 |
| | 1993 | 894 522 | 472 516 | 422 006 | 851 411 | 249 180 | 602 231 |
| | 1994 | 918 216 | 505 203 | 413 013 | 923 803 | 308 034 | 615 769 |
| | 1995 | 980 518 | 493 264 | 487 254 | 982 361 | 318 507 | 663 854 |
| | 1996 | 996 763 | 576 950 | 419 813 | 1 085 457 | 320 789 | 764 668 |
| | 1997 | 861 691 | 474 830 | 386 861 | 819 965 | 314 139 | 505 826 |
| Greece | 1970 | 789 | 1 458 | - 669 | 816 | 940 | - 124 |
| | 1975 | 1 202 | 1 555 | - 353 | 1 028 | 1 438 | - 410 |
| | 1980 | 3 690 | 8 110 | -4 420 | 916 | 844 | 72 |
| | 1985 | 2 983 | 5 653 | -2 670 | 3 380 | 895 | 2 485 |
| | 1990 | 4 998 | 31 372 | -26 374 | 11 746 | 5 546 | 6 200 |
| | 1991 | 7 615 | 36 917 | -29 302 | 9 273 | 8 319 | 954 |
| | 1992 | 7 873 | 36 683 | -28 810 | 6 758 | 15 086 | -8 328 |
| | 1993 | 8 572 | 31 956 | -23 384 | 7 225 | 27 820 | -20 595 |
| | 1994 | 7 625 | 38 829 | -31 204 | 8 379 | 35 756 | -27 377 |
| | 1995 | 10 248 | 44 319 | -34 071 | 8 171 | 39 499 | -31 328 |
| | 1996 | 12 810 | 53 544 | -40 734 | 8 517 | 38 501 | -29 984 |
| | 1997 | 13 229 | 52 162 | -38 933 | 9 091 | 22 401 | -13 310 |
| Hungary | 1991 | | 12 624 | -12 624 | | 14 638 | -14 638 |
| | 1992 | 20 640 | 18 900 | 1 740 | 4 255 | 18 326 | -14 071 |
| | 1993 | 14 678 | 25 149 | -10 471 | 2 816 | 14 989 | -12 173 |
| | 1994 | 12 441 | 32 618 | -20 177 | 2 483 | 12 909 | -10 426 |
| | 1995 | 16 013 | 32 433 | -16 420 | 3 974 | 11 909 | -7 935 |
| | 1996 | 12 652 | 23 332 | -10 680 | 4 865 | 8 679 | -3 814 |
| | 1997 | 13 663 | 29 504 | -15 841 | 5 503 | 10 504 | -5 001 |
| Iceland | 1970 | | 294 | - 294 | | 267 | - 267 |
| | 1975 | 69 | 721 | - 652 | | 557 | - 557 |
| | 1980 | 184 | 1 938 | -1 754 | | 1 326 | -1 326 |
| | 1985 | 107 | 2 367 | -2 260 | | 1 388 | -1 388 |
| | 1990 | 200 | 5 783 | -5 583 | 31 | 2 573 | -2 542 |
| | 1991 | 355 | 7 344 | -6 989 | 27 | 2 856 | -2 829 |
| | 1992 | 348 | 7 400 | -7 052 | 32 | 2 882 | -2 850 |
| | 1993 | 814 | 5 763 | -4 949 | 142 | 2 798 | -2 656 |
| | 1994 | 779 | 5 850 | -5 071 | 77 | 2 585 | -2 508 |
| | 1995 | 751 | 5 870 | -5 119 | 1 | 3 389 | -3 388 |
| | 1996 | 673 | 6 543 | -5 870 | | 3 153 | -3 153 |
| | 1997 | 849 | 6 157 | -5 308 | 15 | 3 190 | -3 175 |
| Ireland | 1970 | | 3 200 | -3 200 | 1 533 | 6 543 | -5 010 |
| | 1975 | 3 869 | 11 822 | -7 953 | 4 089 | 12 552 | -8 463 |
| | 1980 | 6 061 | 32 265 | -26 204 | 3 596 | 31 436 | -27 840 |
| | 1985 | 20 315 | 35 093 | -14 778 | 5 911 | 24 639 | -18 728 |
| | 1990 | 31 974 | 105 431 | -73 457 | 16 827 | 60 741 | -43 914 |
| | 1991 | 38 602 | 108 684 | -70 082 | 12 798 | 67 076 | -54 278 |
| | 1992 | 43 658 | 118 572 | -74 914 | 14 775 | 90 860 | -76 085 |
| | 1993 | 45 993 | 74 248 | -28 255 | 10 271 | 62 582 | -52 311 |
| | 1994 | 52 383 | 75 743 | -23 360 | 13 934 | 75 589 | -61 655 |
| | 1995 | 64 819 | 88 213 | -23 394 | 16 498 | 78 194 | -61 696 |
| | 1996 | 101 196 | 120 127 | -18 931 | 18 664 | 69 606 | -50 942 |
| | 1997 | 75 008 | 118 191 | -43 183 | 17 743 | 91 626 | -73 883 |
| Italy | 1970 | 33 835 | 10 523 | 23 312 | 50 510 | 6 290 | 44 220 |
| | 1975 | 68 254 | 21 088 | 47 166 | 68 647 | 13 964 | 54 683 |
| | 1980 | 171 293 | 38 526 | 132 767 | 168 573 | 32 137 | 136 436 |
| | 1985 | 156 519 | 48 606 | 107 913 | 115 130 | 39 919 | 75 211 |
| | 1990 | 387 544 | 125 261 | 262 283 | 211 252 | 50 753 | 160 499 |
| | 1991 | 412 042 | 101 848 | 310 194 | 202 010 | 33 816 | 168 194 |
| | 1992 | 417 653 | 113 691 | 303 962 | 169 346 | 55 943 | 113 403 |
| | 1993 | 395 923 | 132 955 | 262 968 | 201 731 | 83 683 | 118 048 |
| | 1994 | 452 768 | 153 729 | 299 039 | 204 940 | 107 612 | 97 328 |
| | 1995 | 554 064 | 162 204 | 391 860 | 233 919 | 143 131 | 90 788 |
| | 1996 | 587 095 | 174 983 | 412 112 | 228 757 | 172 216 | 56 541 |
| | 1997 | 552 378 | 184 788 | 367 590 | 192 915 | 152 475 | 40 440 |
| Latvia | 1994 | 356 | 1 295 | - 939 | 317 | 1 911 | -1 594 |
| | 1995 | 337 | 2 083 | -1 746 | 415 | 2 826 | -2 411 |
| | 1996 | 594 | 2 801 | -2 207 | 680 | 2 276 | -1 596 |
| | 1997 | 883 | 4 343 | -3 460 | 1 936 | 2 512 | - 576 |
| Lithuania | 1993 | | | | | | |
| | 1994 | 827 | 1 998 | -1 171 | 117 | 1 161 | -1 044 |
| | 1995 | 880 | 4 997 | -4 117 | 868 | 1 694 | - 826 |
| | 1996 | 1 323 | 8 934 | -7 611 | 1 076 | 1 656 | - 580 |
| | 1997 | 1 636 | 8 710 | -7 074 | 2 676 | 2 096 | 580 |
| Malta | 1970 | 553 | 394 | 159 | 1 | 575 | - 574 |
| | 1975 | 602 | 703 | - 101 | 20 | 941 | - 921 |
| | 1980 | 1 458 | 1 786 | - 328 | 29 | 2 319 | -2 290 |

International trade in books and pamphlets, newspaper and periodicals
Commerce international de livres et brochures et de journaux et périodiques
Comercio internacional de libros y folletos y de publicaciones periódicas

| Country / Pays / País | Year / Année / Año | Books and pamphlets / livres et brochures / libros y folletos | | | Newspaper and periodicals / journaux et périodiques/ publicaciones periódicas | | |
|---|---|---|---|---|---|---|---|
| | | Exports / Exportations / Exportaciones | Imports / Importations / Importaciones | Balance / Balance / Balanza | Exports / Exportations / Exportaciones | Imports / Importations / Importaciones | Balance / Balance / Balanza |
| Malta (cont) | 1985 | 530 | 1 439 | - 909 | 18 | 1 962 | -1 944 |
| | 1990 | 1 244 | 4 930 | -3 686 | 72 | 4 393 | -4 321 |
| | 1991 | 1 809 | 5 915 | -4 106 | 137 | 4 697 | -4 560 |
| | 1992 | 1 953 | 6 062 | -4 109 | 31 | 5 659 | -5 628 |
| | 1993 | 2 613 | 6 270 | -3 657 | 34 | 5 355 | -5 321 |
| | 1994 | 2 193 | 5 614 | -3 421 | | 7 283 | -7 283 |
| | 1995 | 2 375 | 6 497 | -4 122 | 11 | 6 892 | -6 881 |
| | 1996 | 2 983 | 6 987 | -4 004 | | 8 850 | -8 850 |
| Moldova | 1994 | 1 543 | 2 964 | -1 421 | 20 | | 20 |
| | 1995 | 951 | 374 | 577 | 21 | 19 | 2 |
| Netherlands | 1970 | 30 749 | 19 782 | 10 967 | 15 350 | 14 089 | 1 261 |
| | 1975 | 73 186 | 65 040 | 8 146 | 39 227 | 18 745 | 20 482 |
| | 1980 | 166 260 | 179 161 | -12 901 | 77 031 | 51 407 | 25 624 |
| | 1985 | 144 719 | 141 948 | 2 771 | 71 875 | 39 227 | 32 648 |
| | 1990 | 332 377 | 309 595 | 22 782 | 175 286 | 93 281 | 82 005 |
| | 1991 | 337 846 | 327 560 | 10 286 | 177 759 | 95 663 | 82 096 |
| | 1992 | 379 946 | 347 445 | 32 501 | 195 893 | 98 685 | 97 208 |
| | 1993 | 292 230 | 246 681 | 45 549 | 131 880 | 114 491 | 17 389 |
| | 1994 | 299 917 | 285 574 | 14 343 | 128 828 | 118 483 | 10 345 |
| | 1995 | 269 224 | 266 319 | 2 905 | 238 717 | 116 288 | 122 429 |
| | 1996 | 234 676 | 265 760 | -31 084 | 180 429 | 112 046 | 68 383 |
| | 1997 | 183 631 | 208 531 | -24 900 | 124 945 | 95 099 | 29 846 |
| Norway | 1970 | 1 276 | 4 849 | -3 573 | 499 | 2 024 | -1 525 |
| | 1975 | 4 333 | 11 954 | -7 621 | 935 | 5 746 | -4 811 |
| | 1980 | 4 123 | 37 003 | -32 880 | 546 | 15 444 | -14 898 |
| | 1985 | 5 004 | 39 340 | -34 336 | 271 | 16 445 | -16 174 |
| | 1990 | 22 028 | 88 518 | -66 490 | 1 073 | 36 931 | -35 858 |
| | 1991 | 22 362 | 95 315 | -72 953 | 783 | 42 097 | -41 314 |
| | 1992 | 22 314 | 105 211 | -82 897 | 628 | 42 633 | -42 005 |
| | 1993 | 19 251 | 84 919 | -65 668 | 424 | 35 025 | -34 601 |
| | 1994 | 22 173 | 83 577 | -61 404 | 740 | 36 617 | -35 877 |
| | 1995 | 24 336 | 111 518 | -87 182 | 1 181 | 42 233 | -41 052 |
| | 1996 | 27 688 | 108 646 | -80 958 | 8 035 | 52 676 | -44 641 |
| | 1997 | 21 422 | 110 654 | -89 232 | 4 867 | 50 586 | -45 719 |
| Poland | 1991 | | | | | | |
| | 1992 | 6 040 | 109 561 | - 103 521 | 2 273 | 57 144 | -54 871 |
| | 1993 | 10 746 | 99 530 | -88 784 | 2 271 | 74 614 | -72 343 |
| | 1994 | 9 701 | 85 200 | -75 499 | 4 163 | 80 572 | -76 409 |
| | 1995 | 14 282 | 104 675 | -90 393 | 6 233 | 87 296 | -81 063 |
| | 1996 | 21 503 | 116 520 | -95 017 | 10 354 | 76 517 | -66 163 |
| | 1997 | 25 259 | 112 807 | -87 548 | 15 667 | 65 566 | -49 899 |
| Portugal | 1970 | 760 | 1 640 | - 880 | 59 | 846 | - 787 |
| | 1975 | 1 867 | 4 658 | -2 791 | 85 | 4 165 | -4 080 |
| | 1980 | 13 021 | 7 507 | 5 514 | 2 283 | 10 442 | -8 159 |
| | 1985 | 9 912 | 8 226 | 1 686 | 1 329 | 10 805 | -9 476 |
| | 1990 | 26 586 | 31 703 | -5 117 | 4 515 | 31 848 | -27 333 |
| | 1991 | 30 755 | 44 532 | -13 777 | 3 810 | 35 578 | -31 768 |
| | 1992 | 25 347 | 59 402 | -34 055 | 4 202 | 46 795 | -42 593 |
| | 1993 | 23 134 | 39 704 | -16 570 | 3 609 | 70 017 | -66 408 |
| | 1994 | 16 376 | 47 881 | -31 505 | 2 453 | 60 612 | -58 159 |
| | 1995 | 27 388 | 82 833 | -55 445 | 3 412 | 74 431 | -71 019 |
| | 1996 | 24 809 | 75 308 | -50 499 | 2 978 | 73 957 | -70 979 |
| | 1997 | 34 441 | 75 602 | -41 161 | 4 920 | 74 750 | -69 830 |
| Romania | 1990 | 2 662 | 5 339 | -2 677 | | | |
| | 1991 | 236 | 3 957 | -3 721 | 555 | 2 293 | -1 738 |
| | 1992 | 525 | 6 882 | -6 357 | 103 | 784 | - 681 |
| | 1993 | 389 | 8 593 | -8 204 | 146 | 657 | - 511 |
| | 1994 | 477 | 12 829 | -12 352 | 877 | 812 | 65 |
| | 1995 | 837 | 23 742 | -22 905 | 488 | 2 752 | -2 264 |
| | 1996 | 851 | 22 990 | -22 139 | 256 | 5 026 | -4 770 |
| | 1997 | 1 089 | 18 176 | -17 087 | 397 | 11 909 | -11 512 |
| Russian Federation | 1995 | | | | | | |
| | 1996 | 261 858 | 97 710 | 164 148 | 4 453 | 211 888 | - 207 435 |
| | 1997 | 303 760 | 139 382 | 164 378 | 11 305 | 220 341 | - 209 036 |
| Slovakia | 1994 | 41 844 | 15 592 | 26 252 | 15 348 | 10 675 | 4 673 |
| | 1995 | 50 355 | 18 117 | 32 238 | 19 759 | 12 606 | 7 153 |
| | 1996 | 55 205 | 27 115 | 28 090 | 28 513 | 15 238 | 13 275 |
| | 1997 | 48 341 | 26 768 | 21 573 | 34 218 | 17 661 | 16 557 |
| Slovenia | 1992 | 34 263 | 6 898 | 27 365 | 939 | 3 617 | -2 678 |
| | 1993 | 38 413 | 6 119 | 32 294 | 1 328 | 6 457 | -5 129 |
| | 1994 | 37 705 | 7 013 | 30 692 | 1 580 | 11 629 | -10 049 |
| | 1995 | 43 203 | 9 851 | 33 352 | 2 580 | 18 434 | -15 854 |
| | 1996 | 38 703 | 13 591 | 25 112 | 15 186 | 24 959 | -9 773 |
| | 1997 | 38 065 | 9 947 | 28 118 | 11 694 | 18 184 | -6 490 |
| Spain | 1970 | 55 767 | 10 026 | 45 741 | 3 013 | 4 601 | -1 588 |
| | 1975 | 129 766 | 19 829 | 109 937 | 6 346 | 12 120 | -5 774 |

International trade in books and pamphlets, newspaper and periodicals    IV.9
Commerce international de livres et brochures et de journaux et périodiques
Comercio internacional de libros y folletos y de publicaciones periódicas

| Country<br>Pays<br>País | Year<br>Année<br>Año | Books and pamphlets / livres et brochures /<br>libros y folletos | | | Newspaper and periodicals / journaux et périodiques/<br>publicaciones periódicas | | |
|---|---|---|---|---|---|---|---|
| | | Exports<br>Exportations<br>Exportaciones | Imports<br>Importations<br>Importaciones | Balance<br>Balance<br>Balanza | Exports<br>Exportations<br>Exportaciones | Imports<br>Importations<br>Importaciones | Balance<br>Balance<br>Balanza |
| Spain (cont) | 1980 | 358 768 | 31 485 | 327 283 | 20 611 | 28 382 | -7 771 |
| | 1985 | 234 631 | 30 864 | 203 767 | 23 914 | 21 590 | 2 324 |
| | 1990 | 293 001 | 141 268 | 151 733 | 65 512 | 82 186 | -16 674 |
| | 1991 | 306 874 | 161 830 | 145 044 | 81 209 | 81 893 | - 684 |
| | 1992 | 358 335 | 173 624 | 184 711 | 116 818 | 95 128 | 21 690 |
| | 1993 | 374 443 | 130 238 | 244 205 | 124 526 | 118 259 | 6 267 |
| | 1994 | 461 942 | 137 611 | 324 331 | 121 093 | 110 689 | 10 404 |
| | 1995 | 513 725 | 148 384 | 365 341 | 152 135 | 148 012 | 4 123 |
| | 1996 | 572 691 | 160 189 | 412 502 | 169 407 | 153 799 | 15 608 |
| Sweden | 1970 | 8 505 | 14 148 | -5 643 | 3 693 | 4 760 | -1 067 |
| | 1975 | 22 795 | 28 885 | -6 090 | 7 888 | 8 093 | - 205 |
| | 1980 | 35 323 | 68 593 | -33 270 | 10 654 | 24 132 | -13 478 |
| | 1985 | 37 294 | 68 631 | -31 337 | 11 051 | 25 674 | -14 623 |
| | 1990 | 73 093 | 189 538 | - 116 445 | 26 182 | 68 735 | -42 553 |
| | 1991 | 75 848 | 200 416 | - 124 568 | 24 604 | 75 415 | -50 811 |
| | 1992 | 80 058 | 214 166 | - 134 108 | 13 970 | 78 033 | -64 063 |
| | 1993 | 68 929 | 159 786 | -90 857 | 13 273 | 82 348 | -69 075 |
| | 1994 | 79 154 | 163 407 | -84 253 | 13 891 | 84 852 | -70 961 |
| | 1995 | 93 332 | 143 889 | -50 557 | 18 012 | 66 639 | -48 627 |
| | 1996 | 96 734 | 155 572 | -58 838 | 26 753 | 89 179 | -62 426 |
| | 1997 | 89 595 | 167 044 | -77 449 | 25 307 | 68 584 | -43 277 |
| Switzerland | 1970 | 35 557 | 38 261 | -2 704 | 3 477 | 28 319 | -24 842 |
| | 1975 | 79 828 | 90 772 | -10 944 | 8 368 | 63 331 | -54 963 |
| | 1980 | 146 465 | 186 976 | -40 511 | 24 871 | 119 377 | -94 506 |
| | 1985 | 80 943 | 150 122 | -69 179 | 31 883 | 118 288 | 86 405 |
| | 1990 | 145 694 | 357 513 | - 211 819 | 69 828 | 276 873 | - 207 045 |
| | 1991 | 135 222 | 362 503 | - 227 281 | 74 270 | 285 059 | - 210 789 |
| | 1992 | 141 322 | 389 169 | - 247 847 | 77 085 | 285 888 | - 208 803 |
| | 1993 | 170 317 | 391 119 | - 220 802 | 72 908 | 264 906 | - 191 998 |
| | 1994 | 211 356 | 441 349 | - 229 993 | 78 479 | 303 761 | - 225 282 |
| | 1995 | 176 311 | 498 801 | - 322 490 | 94 738 | 377 337 | - 282 599 |
| | 1996 | 154 726 | 487 232 | - 332 506 | 85 468 | 349 272 | - 263 804 |
| | 1997 | 119 226 | 413 376 | - 294 150 | 59 756 | 299 791 | - 240 035 |
| The Former Yugoslav<br>Rep. of Macedonia | 1995 | 15 | 492 | - 477 | 110 | 40 | 70 |
| | 1996 | 13 | 503 | - 490 | 70 | 26 | 44 |
| United Kingdom | 1970 | 111 197 | 49 859 | 61 338 | 42 988 | 14 060 | 28 928 |
| | 1975 | 230 127 | 111 478 | 118 649 | 63 071 | 32 056 | 31 015 |
| | 1980 | 552 655 | 288 096 | 264 559 | 99 367 | 55 948 | 43 419 |
| | 1985 | 610 037 | 338 181 | 271 856 | 105 182 | 56 516 | 48 666 |
| | 1990 | 1 298 553 | 781 777 | 516 776 | 222 085 | 214 609 | 7 476 |
| | 1991 | 1 265 822 | 770 029 | 495 793 | 236 572 | 242 962 | -6 390 |
| | 1992 | 1 359 309 | 858 322 | 500 987 | 264 585 | 255 592 | 8 993 |
| | 1993 | 1 308 988 | 792 162 | 516 826 | 414 719 | 230 745 | 183 974 |
| | 1994 | 1 465 940 | 826 013 | 639 927 | 484 091 | 160 085 | 324 006 |
| | 1995 | 1 665 820 | 995 444 | 670 376 | 600 680 | 149 237 | 451 443 |
| | 1996 | 1 786 236 | 954 851 | 831 385 | 619 018 | 173 144 | 445 874 |
| | 1997 | 1 854 699 | 998 985 | 855 714 | 673 835 | 234 502 | 439 333 |
| **Oceania** | | | | | | | |
| Australia | 1970 | 3 623 | 50 319 | -46 696 | 2 565 | 11 688 | -9 123 |
| | 1975 | 11 814 | 118 318 | - 106 504 | 7 018 | 35 016 | -27 998 |
| | 1980 | 24 152 | 198 182 | - 174 030 | 10 149 | 56 314 | -46 165 |
| | 1985 | 18 895 | 240 151 | - 221 256 | 10 804 | 72 549 | -61 745 |
| | 1990 | 47 176 | 388 335 | - 341 159 | 9 134 | 120 483 | - 111 349 |
| | 1991 | 46 184 | 377 354 | - 331 170 | 10 264 | 126 666 | - 116 402 |
| | 1992 | 62 745 | 379 445 | - 316 700 | 12 483 | 135 727 | - 123 244 |
| | 1993 | 58 536 | 340 374 | - 281 838 | 18 694 | 145 614 | - 126 920 |
| | 1994 | 67 476 | 371 200 | - 303 724 | 23 597 | 162 247 | - 138 650 |
| | 1995 | 66 805 | 383 344 | - 316 539 | 23 872 | 158 104 | - 134 232 |
| | 1996 | 73 958 | 393 059 | - 319 101 | 13 373 | 148 536 | - 135 163 |
| | 1997 | 63 533 | 399 643 | - 336 110 | 17 708 | 158 536 | - 140 828 |
| Fiji | 1970 | 5 | 422 | - 417 | | 5 | -5 |
| | 1975 | 23 | 715 | - 692 | | 11 | -11 |
| | 1980 | 121 | 996 | - 875 | | 91 | -91 |
| | 1985 | 55 | 1 397 | -1 342 | 2 | 50 | -48 |
| | 1990 | 40 | 2 088 | -2 048 | 4 | 4 | - |
| | 1991 | 86 | 1 786 | -1 700 | | 27 | -27 |
| | 1992 | 131 | 3 225 | -3 094 | 2 | 32 | -30 |
| | 1993 | 54 | 2 199 | -2 145 | 4 | 15 | -11 |
| | 1994 | 134 | 3 321 | -3 187 | 30 | 93 | -63 |
| | 1995 | | | | | | |
| | 1996 | | | | | | |
| | 1997 | | | | | | |
| Kiribati | 1995 | | 375 | - 375 | | 1 | -1 |
| New Zealand | 1970 | 704 | 16 285 | -15 581 | 77 | 5 363 | -5 286 |
| | 1975 | 1 379 | 39 041 | -37 662 | 99 | 14 175 | -14 076 |
| | 1980 | 2 672 | 63 435 | -60 763 | 2 824 | 20 662 | -17 838 |
| | 1985 | 6 561 | 63 095 | -56 534 | 2 197 | 26 598 | -24 401 |

IV.9   International trade in books and pamphlets, newspaper and periodicals
Commerce international de livres et brochures et de journaux et périodiques
Comercio internacional de libros y folletos y de publicaciones periódicas

| Country / Pays / País | Year / Année / Año | Books and pamphlets / livres et brochures / libros y folletos | | | Newspaper and periodicals / journaux et périodiques / publicaciones periódicas | | |
|---|---|---|---|---|---|---|---|
| | | Exports Exportations Exportaciones | Imports Importations Importaciones | Balance Balance Balanza | Exports Exportations Exportaciones | Imports Importations Importaciones | Balance Balance Balanza |
| New Zealand (cont) | 1990 | 3 906 | 87 378 | -83 472 | 394 | 45 773 | -45 379 |
| | 1991 | 4 397 | 84 371 | -79 974 | 809 | 44 113 | -43 304 |
| | 1992 | 5 822 | 87 054 | -81 232 | 1 045 | 44 256 | -43 211 |
| | 1993 | 6 915 | 88 416 | -81 501 | 869 | 52 097 | -51 228 |
| | 1994 | 9 305 | 99 229 | -89 924 | 1 160 | 60 336 | -59 176 |
| | 1995 | 10 687 | 103 624 | -92 937 | 1 434 | 62 197 | -60 763 |
| | 1996 | 11 614 | 108 933 | -97 319 | 751 | 65 743 | -64 992 |
| | 1997 | 10 671 | | 10 671 | 1 752 | | 1 752 |
| Papua New Guinea | 1975 | | 1 334 | -1 334 | | 389 | - 389 |
| | 1985 | 16 | 2 741 | -2 725 | | 399 | - 399 |
| | 1990 | 16 | 5 125 | -5 109 | 1 | 212 | - 211 |
| | 1991 | 5 | | 5 | | | |
| | 1992 | 26 | | 26 | | | |
| | 1993 | 12 | | 12 | | | |
| Samoa | 1980 | | | | 1 | 42 | -41 |
| | 1990 | | 285 | - 285 | | 21 | -21 |
| Solomon Islands | 1996 | | | | | 682 | - 682 |
| Tuvalu | 1980 | | 12 | -12 | | 1 | -1 |
| | 1985 | | 11 | -11 | | | |
| Vanuatu, Republic of | 1970 | | | | | 37 | -37 |
| | 1975 | | | | | 117 | - 117 |
| | 1993 | | 483 | - 483 | | 154 | - 154 |
| | 1994 | | | | | 160 | - 160 |

**General note**
For general explanations and definitions, please refer to the beginning of this chapter.

**Note générale**
Pour les explications et définitions générales, prière de se référer au début de ce chapitre.

**Nota general**
Para las explicaciones y definiciones generales, referirse al comienzo de este capítulo.

Newsprint and other printing and writing paper IV.10
Papier journal et autre papier d'impression et d'écriture
Papel de periódico y otro papel de imprenta y de escribir

## IV.10 Newsprint and other printing and writing paper: production, imports, exports and consumption (total and per 1,000 inhabitants)

Papier journal et autre papier d'impression et d'écriture: production, importations, exportations et consommation (total et pour 1 000 habitants)

Papel de periódico y otro papel de imprenta y de escribir: producción, importaciones, exportaciones y consumo (total y por 1 000 habitantes)

Production, imports, exports and consumption are expressed in metric tons; consumption per 1,000 inhabitants is expressed in kilograms.

Production, importations, exportations et consommation sont exprimées en tonnes métriques; la consommation pour 1 000 habitants est exprimée en kilogrammes.

Producción, importaciones, exportaciones y consumo se expresan en toneladas métricas; el consumo por 1 000 habitantes se expresa en kilogramos.

| Country / Pays / País | Year / Année / Año | Newsprint / Papier journal / Papel de periódico | | | | | Other printing and writing paper / Autre papier d'impression et d'écriture / Otro papel de imprenta y de escribir | | | | |
|---|---|---|---|---|---|---|---|---|---|---|---|
| | | Production / Production / Producción | Imports / Importations / Importaciones | Exports / Exportations / Exportaciones | Consumption / Consommation / Consumo | Consumption per 1,000 inh. / Consommation pour 1 000 hab. / Consumo por 1 000 hab. | Production / Production / Producción | Imports / Importations / Importaciones | Exports / Exportations / Exportaciones | Consumption / Consommation / Consumo | Consumption per 1,000 inh. / Consommation pour 1 000 hab. / Consumo por 1 000 hab. |
| **Africa** | | | | | | | | | | | |
| Algeria | 1970 | | 6 200 | | 6 200 | 451 | 23 000 | 19 000 | | 42 000 | 3 055 |
| | 1975 | | 8 900 | | 8 900 | 556 | 18 000 | 7 200 | | 25 200 | 1 573 |
| | 1980 | | 12 000 | | 12 000 | 640 | 26 000 | 3 200 | | 29 200 | 1 558 |
| | 1985 | | 15 600 | | 15 600 | 713 | 30 000 | 26 500 | | 56 500 | 2 581 |
| | 1990 | | 30 000 | | 30 000 | 1 203 | 39 000 | 26 000 | | 65 000 | 2 607 |
| | 1991 | | 29 900 | | 29 900 | 1 170 | 37 000 | 38 200 | | 75 200 | 2 944 |
| | 1992 | | 24 028 | | 24 028 | 918 | 37 000 | 20 478 | 46 | 57 432 | 2 195 |
| | 1993 | | 29 600 | | 29 600 | 1 105 | 33 000 | 26 800 | | 59 800 | 2 233 |
| | 1994 | | 22 600 | | 22 600 | 824 | 36 000 | 21 000 | | 57 000 | 2 079 |
| | 1995 | | 22 600 | | 22 600 | 805 | 35 000 | 21 000 | 21 | 55 979 | 1 995 |
| | 1996 | | 12 400 | | 12 400 | 432 | 29 000 | 41 000 | 21 | 69 979 | 2 437 |
| | 1997 | | 8 200 | | 8 200 | 279 | 34 000 | 52 000 | 21 | 85 979 | 2 925 |
| Angola | 1970 | | 100 | | 100 | 18 | 1 500 | 2 000 | | 3 500 | 626 |
| | 1975 | | 1 100 | | 1 100 | 180 | 3 000 | | | 3 000 | 490 |
| | 1980 | | 1 500 | | 1 500 | 214 | 3 000 | | | 3 000 | 427 |
| | 1985 | | 500 | | 500 | 62 | | | | | |
| | 1990 | | 100 | | 100 | 11 | | | | | |
| | 1991 | | 100 | | 100 | 10 | | | | | |
| | 1992 | | 1 300 | | 1 300 | 132 | | 2 100 | | 2 100 | 213 |
| | 1993 | | 400 | | 400 | 39 | | 2 100 | | 2 100 | 205 |
| | 1994 | | 400 | | 400 | 38 | | 1 300 | | 1 300 | 123 |
| | 1995 | | 400 | | 400 | 36 | | 1 327 | | 1 327 | 121 |
| | 1996 | | 400 | | 400 | 35 | | 300 | | 300 | 26 |
| | 1997 | | 70 | | 70 | 6 | | 1 553 | 33 | 1 520 | 130 . |
| Benin | 1975 | | 100 | | 100 | 33 | | 500 | | 500 | 164 |
| | 1980 | | 100 | | 100 | 29 | | 100 | | 100 | 29 |
| | 1985 | | 100 | | 100 | 25 | | 500 | | 500 | 124 |
| | 1990 | | | | | | | 721 | | 721 | 155 |
| | 1991 | | | | | | | 100 | | 100 | 21 |
| | 1992 | | | | | | | 560 | | 560 | 114 |
| | 1993 | | 30 | | 30 | 6 | | 848 | | 848 | 168 |
| | 1994 | | 30 | | 30 | 6 | | 648 | | 648 | 125 |
| | 1995 | | 2 | | 2 | | | 601 | | 601 | 113 |
| | 1996 | | 2 | | 2 | | | 500 | | 500 | 91 |
| | 1997 | | 48 | 14 | 34 | 6 | | 1 411 | | 1 411 | 251 |
| Burkina Faso | 1992 | | | | | | | 1 084 | | 1 084 | 113 |
| | 1993 | | | | | | | 680 | | 680 | 69 |
| | 1994 | | | | | | | 680 | | 680 | 67 |
| | 1995 | | 55 | | 55 | 5 | | 320 | | 320 | 31 |
| | 1996 | | 55 | | 55 | 5 | | 320 | | 320 | 30 |
| | 1997 | | 219 | | 219 | 20 | | 860 | | 860 | 78 |

IV.10  Newsprint and other printing and writing paper
Papier journal et autre papier d'impression et d'écriture
Papel de periódico y otro papel de imprenta y de escribir

| Country / Pays / País | Year / Année / Año | Newsprint — Papier journal — Papel de periódico | | | | | Other printing and writing paper — Autre papier d'impression et d'écriture — Otro papel de imprenta y de escribir | | | | |
|---|---|---|---|---|---|---|---|---|---|---|---|
| | | Production / Production / Producción | Imports / Importations / Importaciones | Exports / Exportations / Exportaciones | Consumption / Consommation / Consumo | Consumption per 1,000 inh. / Consommation pour 1 000 hab. / Consumo por 1 000 hab. | Production / Production / Producción | Imports / Importations / Importaciones | Exports / Exportations / Exportaciones | Consumption / Consommation / Consumo | Consumption per 1,000 inh. / Consommation pour 1 000 hab. / Consumo por 1 000 hab. |
| **Burundi** | | | | | | | | | | | |
| | 1985 | | | | | | | 400 | | 400 | 84 |
| | 1990 | | | | | | | 700 | | 700 | 128 |
| | 1991 | | | | | | | 700 | | 700 | 125 |
| | 1992 | | 18 | | 18 | 3 | | 259 | | 259 | 45 |
| | 1993 | | | | | | | 249 | 160 | 89 | 15 |
| | 1994 | | | | | | | 400 | | 400 | 66 |
| | 1995 | | 200 | | 200 | 32 | | 900 | | 900 | 146 |
| | 1996 | | 200 | | 200 | 32 | | 500 | | 500 | 80 |
| | 1997 | | 200 | | 200 | 31 | | 111 | | 111 | 17 |
| **Cameroon** | | | | | | | | | | | |
| | 1970 | | 100 | | 100 | 15 | | 1 300 | | 1 300 | 197 |
| | 1975 | | | | | | | 2 000 | | 2 000 | 266 |
| | 1980 | | 500 | | 500 | 58 | | 4 000 | | 4 000 | 462 |
| | 1985 | | 2 100 | | 2 100 | 211 | | 4 600 | | 4 600 | 461 |
| | 1990 | | 4 000 | | 4 000 | 349 | | 3 200 | | 3 200 | 279 |
| | 1991 | | 2 900 | | 2 900 | 246 | | 8 300 | | 8 300 | 704 |
| | 1992 | | 6 | | 6 | | | 6 135 | | 6 135 | 506 |
| | 1993 | | 2 727 | | 2 727 | 219 | | 7 255 | | 7 255 | 582 |
| | 1994 | | 426 | | 426 | 33 | | 6 380 | | 6 380 | 498 |
| | 1995 | | 400 | | 400 | 30 | | 3 300 | | 3 300 | 250 |
| | 1996 | | 4 000 | | 4 000 | 295 | | 2 800 | | 2 800 | 207 |
| | 1997 | | 2 500 | | 2 500 | 180 | | 8 400 | | 8 400 | 603 |
| **Cape Verde** | | | | | | | | | | | |
| | 1992 | | | | | | | 18 | | 18 | 51 |
| | 1993 | | 31 | | 31 | 85 | | 165 | | 165 | 454 |
| | 1994 | | 50 | | 50 | 134 | | 81 | | 81 | 218 |
| | 1995 | | 50 | | 50 | 131 | | 100 | | 100 | 263 |
| | 1996 | | 30 | | 30 | 77 | | 100 | | 100 | 257 |
| | 1997 | | 75 | | 75 | 188 | | 211 | | 211 | 529 |
| **Central African Republic** | | | | | | | | | | | |
| | 1970 | | | | | | | 200 | | 200 | 108 |
| | 1992 | | | | | | | 131 | | 131 | 43 |
| | 1993 | | | | | | | 200 | | 200 | 63 |
| | 1994 | | | | | | | 200 | | 200 | 62 |
| | 1995 | | | | | | | 200 | | 200 | 61 |
| | 1996 | | | | | | | 200 | | 200 | 60 |
| | 1997 | | | | | | | 100 | | 100 | 29 |
| **Chad** | | | | | | | | | | | |
| | 1975 | | | | | | | 100 | | 100 | 25 |
| | 1980 | | | | | | | 200 | | 200 | 45 |
| | 1985 | | | | | | | 100 | | 100 | 20 |
| | 1990 | | | | | | | 200 | | 200 | 35 |
| | 1991 | | | | | | | 200 | | 200 | 34 |
| | 1992 | | 33 | | 33 | 5 | | 127 | 78 | 49 | 8 |
| | 1993 | | | | | | | 163 | | 163 | 26 |
| | 1994 | | | | | | | 200 | | 200 | 31 |
| | 1995 | | | | | | | 500 | | 500 | 75 |
| | 1996 | | | | | | | 100 | | 100 | 14 |
| | 1997 | | | | | | | 88 | | 88 | 12 |
| **Comoros** | | | | | | | | | | | |
| | 1992 | | 12 | | 12 | 22 | | 83 | | 83 | 149 |
| | 1993 | | 12 | | 12 | 21 | | 215 | | 215 | 375 |
| | 1994 | | 12 | | 12 | 20 | | 412 | | 412 | 699 |
| | 1995 | | 12 | | 12 | 20 | | 412 | | 412 | 680 |
| | 1996 | | 12 | | 12 | 19 | | 412 | | 412 | 661 |
| | 1997 | | 12 | | 12 | 19 | | 412 | | 412 | 644 |
| **Congo** | | | | | | | | | | | |
| | 1970 | | | | | | | 200 | | 200 | 158 |
| | 1975 | | | | | | | 200 | | 200 | 138 |
| | 1980 | | | | | | | 100 | | 100 | 60 |
| | 1985 | | | | | | | 500 | | 500 | 260 |
| | 1990 | | | | | | | 300 | | 300 | 135 |
| | 1991 | | | | | | | 300 | | 300 | 131 |
| | 1992 | | 120 | | 120 | 51 | | 452 | | 452 | 192 |
| | 1993 | | 224 | | 224 | 93 | | 380 | 94 | 286 | 118 |
| | 1994 | | 45 | | 45 | 18 | | 192 | 94 | 98 | 39 |
| | 1995 | | 100 | | 100 | 39 | | 100 | | 100 | 39 |
| | 1996 | | | | | | | 600 | | 600 | 228 |
| | 1997 | | | | | | | 700 | | 700 | 258 |

Newsprint and other printing and writing paper  IV.10
Papier journal et autre papier d'impression et d'écriture
Papel de periódico y otro papel de imprenta y de escribir

| Country / Pays / País | Year / Année / Año | Newsprint / Papier journal / Papel de periódico | | | | | Other printing and writing paper / Autre papier d'impression et d'écriture / Otro papel de imprenta y de escribir | | | | |
|---|---|---|---|---|---|---|---|---|---|---|---|
| | | Production / Producción | Imports / Importations / Importaciones | Exports / Exportations / Exportaciones | Consumption / Consommation / Consumo | Consumption per 1,000 inh. / Consommation pour 1 000 hab. / Consumo por 1 000 hab. | Production / Producción | Imports / Importations / Importaciones | Exports / Exportations / Exportaciones | Consumption / Consommation / Consumo | Consumption per 1,000 inh. / Consommation pour 1 000 hab. / Consumo por 1 000 hab. |
| Côte d'Ivoire | 1970 | | 900 | | 900 | 163 | | | | | |
| | 1975 | | 800 | | 800 | 118 | | 4 200 | | 4 200 | 622 |
| | 1980 | | 800 | | 800 | 98 | | 4 200 | | 4 200 | 513 |
| | 1985 | | 1 400 | | 1 400 | 142 | | 8 400 | | 8 400 | 850 |
| | 1990 | | 3 200 | | 3 200 | 275 | | | | | |
| | 1991 | | 2 000 | | 2 000 | 166 | | | | | |
| | 1992 | | | | | | | 9 100 | 40 | 9 060 | 729 |
| | 1993 | | 1 424 | | 1 424 | 111 | | 9 000 | 100 | 8 900 | 694 |
| | 1994 | | 1 800 | | 1 800 | 136 | | 9 278 | 100 | 9 178 | 696 |
| | 1995 | | 5 000 | | 5 000 | 370 | | 2 000 | 100 | 1 900 | 140 |
| | 1996 | | 3 500 | | 3 500 | 253 | | 3 300 | 100 | 3 200 | 232 |
| | 1997 | | 3 500 | | 3 500 | 249 | | 3 300 | 100 | 3 200 | 228 |
| Democratic Rep. of the Congo | 1970 | | 500 | | 500 | 25 | | 2 400 | | 2 400 | 118 |
| | 1975 | | 1 000 | | 1 000 | 43 | | 2 000 | | 2 000 | 86 |
| | 1980 | | 1 000 | | 1 000 | 37 | | 2 700 | | 2 700 | 100 |
| | 1985 | | 1 000 | | 1 000 | 32 | | 4 900 | | 4 900 | 155 |
| | 1990 | | 800 | | 800 | 21 | | 2 000 | | 2 000 | 54 |
| | 1991 | | 800 | | 800 | 21 | | 1 500 | | 1 500 | 39 |
| | 1992 | | 59 | | 59 | 1 | | 1 029 | | 1 029 | 25 |
| | 1993 | | 152 | | 152 | 4 | | 5 176 | | 5 176 | 123 |
| | 1994 | | 150 | | 150 | 3 | | 9 859 | | 9 859 | 225 |
| | 1995 | | 599 | | 599 | 13 | | 898 | | 898 | 20 |
| | 1996 | | 27 | | 27 | 1 | | 10 600 | | 10 600 | 227 |
| | 1997 | | 27 | | 27 | 1 | | 2 900 | | 2 900 | 60 |
| Djibouti | 1992 | | | | | | | 149 | | 149 | 267 |
| | 1993 | | | | | | | 55 | 23 | 32 | 56 |
| | 1994 | | | | | | | 67 | 23 | 44 | 75 |
| | 1995 | | 13 | | 13 | 22 | | 3 | | 3 | 5 |
| | 1997 | | | | | | | 310 | | 310 | 503 |
| Egypt | 1970 | | 32 900 | | 32 900 | 932 | 40 000 | 5 000 | | 45 000 | 1 275 |
| | 1975 | | 40 200 | | 40 200 | 1 035 | 24 000 | 34 000 | | 58 000 | 1 493 |
| | 1980 | | 67 000 | | 67 000 | 1 531 | 66 000 | 53 600 | | 119 600 | 2 734 |
| | 1985 | | 35 300 | | 35 300 | 710 | 52 000 | 129 000 | | 181 000 | 3 638 |
| | 1990 | | 58 200 | | 58 200 | 1 033 | 73 000 | 110 900 | | 183 900 | 3 265 |
| | 1991 | | 79 400 | | 79 400 | 1 379 | 65 000 | 126 200 | | 191 200 | 3 321 |
| | 1992 | | 73 449 | | 73 449 | 1 250 | 58 000 | 171 201 | 570 | 228 631 | 3 891 |
| | 1993 | | 75 300 | | 75 300 | 1 257 | 85 000 | 170 000 | 3 263 | 251 737 | 4 201 |
| | 1994 | | 69 800 | | 69 800 | 1 143 | 75 000 | 167 300 | 1 300 | 241 000 | 3 945 |
| | 1995 | | 89 900 | | 89 900 | 1 443 | 70 000 | 37 800 | 200 | 107 600 | 1 728 |
| | 1996 | | 88 000 | | 88 000 | 1 386 | 70 000 | 36 200 | 200 | 106 000 | 1 669 |
| | 1997 | | 100 000 | | 100 000 | 1 545 | 70 000 | 36 200 | 200 | 106 000 | 1 638 |
| Equatorial Guinea | 1993 | | | | | | | 16 | | 16 | 42 |
| | 1994 | | | | | | | 16 | | 16 | 41 |
| Eritrea | 1996 | | | | | | | 100 | | 100 | 30 |
| | 1997 | | | | | | | 100 | | 100 | 29 |
| Ethiopia | 1970 | | 900 | | 900 | 31 | | 900 | | 900 | 31 |
| | 1975 | | 400 | | 400 | 12 | 3 500 | 2 800 | | 6 300 | 196 |
| | 1980 | | 2 000 | | 2 000 | 55 | 3 500 | 200 | | 3 700 | 102 |
| | 1985 | | 2 200 | | 2 200 | 53 | 8 000 | 5 700 | | 13 700 | 333 |
| | 1990 | | 2 300 | | 2 300 | 48 | 7 000 | 1 300 | | 8 300 | 173 |
| | 1991 | | 2 300 | | 2 300 | 46 | 5 000 | 1 300 | | 6 300 | 127 |
| | 1992 | | 24 | | 24 | | 2 000 | 1 654 | | 3 654 | 72 |
| | 1993 | | 644 | | 644 | 12 | 5 900 | 1 000 | | 6 900 | 132 |
| | 1994 | | | | | | 5 900 | 3 375 | | 9 275 | 172 |
| | 1995 | | | | | | 4 900 | 440 | | 5 340 | 96 |
| | 1996 | 1 300 | 1 000 | | 2 300 | 41 | 3 000 | 2 800 | | 5 800 | 102 |
| | 1997 | 1 900 | 1 000 | | 2 900 | 50 | 2 500 | 3 300 | | 5 800 | 100 |
| Gabon | 1970 | | | | | | | 100 | | 100 | 198 |
| | 1975 | | | | | | | 12 600 | | 12 600 | 21 232 |
| | 1980 | | | | | | | 1 300 | | 1 300 | 1 878 |
| | 1985 | | | | | | | 2 700 | | 2 700 | 3 362 |
| | 1990 | | | | | | | 1 500 | | 1 500 | 1 605 |
| | 1991 | | | | | | | 1 500 | | 1 500 | 1 559 |
| | 1992 | | | | | | | 1 337 | | 1 337 | 1 350 |

IV.10    Newsprint and other printing and writing paper
Papier journal et autre papier d'impression et d'écriture
Papel de periódico y otro papel de imprenta y de escribir

| Country / Pays / País | Year / Année / Año | Newsprint · Papier journal · Papel de periódico | | | | | Other printing and writing paper · Autre papier d'impression et d'écriture · Otro papel de imprenta y de escribir | | | | |
|---|---|---|---|---|---|---|---|---|---|---|---|
| | | Production / Producción | Imports / Importations / Importaciones | Exports / Exportations / Exportaciones | Consumption / Consommation / Consumo | Consumption per 1,000 inh. / Consommation pour 1 000 hab. / Consumo por 1 000 hab. | Production / Producción | Imports / Importations / Importaciones | Exports / Exportations / Exportaciones | Consumption / Consommation / Consumo | Consumption per 1,000 inh. / Consommation pour 1 000 hab. / Consumo por 1 000 hab. |
| Gabon (cont) | 1993 | | | | | | | 1 339 | | 1 339 | 1 314 |
| | 1994 | | | | | | | 897 | | 897 | 856 |
| | 1995 | | | | | | | 300 | | 300 | 278 |
| | 1996 | | | | | | | 400 | | 400 | 361 |
| | 1997 | | | | | | | 400 | | 400 | 352 |
| Gambia | 1992 | | 5 | | 5 | 5 | | 222 | | 222 | 223 |
| | 1993 | | 26 | | 26 | 25 | | 185 | | 185 | 179 |
| | 1994 | | 27 | | 27 | 25 | | 238 | 15 | 223 | 208 |
| | 1995 | | 26 | | 26 | 23 | | 53 | 5 | 48 | 43 |
| | 1997 | | 45 | | 45 | 38 | | 199 | | 199 | 167 |
| Ghana | 1970 | | 3 600 | | 3 600 | 418 | | 7 600 | | 7 600 | 882 |
| | 1975 | | 7 300 | | 7 300 | 743 | | 6 700 | | 6 700 | 682 |
| | 1980 | | 1 500 | | 1 500 | 138 | | 3 300 | | 3 300 | 305 |
| | 1985 | | 4 000 | | 4 000 | 309 | | 5 500 | | 5 500 | 425 |
| | 1990 | | 6 000 | | 6 000 | 397 | | 7 300 | | 7 300 | 483 |
| | 1991 | | 8 400 | | 8 400 | 538 | | 4 500 | | 4 500 | 288 |
| | 1992 | | 564 | | 564 | 35 | | 10 406 | 34 | 10 372 | 644 |
| | 1993 | | 2 040 | | 2 040 | 123 | | 6 077 | 4 | 6 073 | 365 |
| | 1994 | | 1 144 | | 1 144 | 67 | | 5 889 | 30 | 5 859 | 342 |
| | 1995 | | 4 500 | | 4 500 | 255 | | 1 000 | | 1 000 | 57 |
| | 1996 | | 7 600 | | 7 600 | 419 | | 1 000 | | 1 000 | 55 |
| | 1997 | | 3 400 | | 3 400 | 182 | | 8 600 | | 8 600 | 461 |
| Guinea | 1992 | | 2 | | 2 | | | 230 | | 230 | 36 |
| | 1993 | | | | | | | 294 | | 294 | 44 |
| | 1994 | | | | | | | 252 | | 252 | 36 |
| | 1995 | | | | | | | 200 | | 200 | 28 |
| | 1996 | | | | | | | 100 | | 100 | 14 |
| | 1997 | | 265 | | 265 | 36 | | 404 | | 404 | 55 |
| Guinea-Bissau | 1975 | | 100 | | 100 | 159 | | | | | |
| | 1980 | | 100 | | 100 | 126 | | | | | |
| | 1985 | | 200 | | 200 | 228 | | | | | |
| | 1992 | | | | | | | 329 | | 329 | 324 |
| | 1993 | | 5 | | 5 | 5 | | 125 | | 125 | 120 |
| | 1994 | | 5 | | 5 | 5 | | 107 | | 107 | 101 |
| | 1995 | | 5 | | 5 | 5 | | 27 | | 27 | 25 |
| | 1996 | | 5 | | 5 | 5 | | 27 | | 27 | 24 |
| | 1997 | | 2 | | 2 | 2 | | 111 | | 111 | 98 |
| Kenya | 1970 | | 5 000 | | 5 000 | 435 | | 6 900 | 100 | 6 800 | 591 |
| | 1975 | | 3 900 | | 3 900 | 284 | 8 000 | 3 000 | 400 | 10 600 | 771 |
| | 1980 | | 7 900 | | 7 900 | 475 | 19 000 | 1 900 | 8 300 | 12 600 | 758 |
| | 1985 | 7 000 | 2 600 | | 9 600 | 483 | 30 000 | 100 | 300 | 29 800 | 1 500 |
| | 1990 | 6 000 | 965 | | 6 965 | 296 | 28 000 | 5 600 | 155 | 33 445 | 1 420 |
| | 1991 | 11 000 | 965 | | 11 965 | 492 | 23 000 | 5 600 | 155 | 28 445 | 1 170 |
| | 1992 | 16 000 | 956 | 10 | 16 946 | 676 | 32 000 | 4 344 | 20 | 36 324 | 1 449 |
| | 1993 | 16 000 | 298 | | 16 298 | 631 | 32 000 | 9 545 | 105 | 41 440 | 1 605 |
| | 1994 | 13 000 | 1 006 | | 14 006 | 528 | 17 000 | 8 166 | 105 | 25 061 | 944 |
| | 1995 | 14 000 | 5 315 | 4 | 19 311 | 710 | 18 000 | 3 641 | 105 | 21 536 | 791 |
| | 1996 | 14 000 | 2 400 | | 16 400 | 589 | 18 000 | 6 700 | | 24 700 | 887 |
| | 1997 | 14 000 | 7 610 | | 21 610 | 760 | 18 000 | 12 241 | 145 | 30 096 | 1 058 |
| Liberia | 1970 | | 100 | | 100 | 72 | | 200 | | 200 | 144 |
| | 1975 | | | | | | | 450 | | 450 | 280 |
| | 1980 | | | | | | | 300 | | 300 | 160 |
| | 1985 | | 200 | | 200 | 91 | | 100 | | 100 | 46 |
| | 1990 | | 29 | | 29 | 11 | | 2 638 | | 2 638 | 1 023 |
| | 1991 | | 29 | | 29 | 12 | | 2 638 | | 2 638 | 1 055 |
| | 1992 | | 23 | | 23 | 10 | | 126 | | 126 | 53 |
| | 1993 | | | | | | | 200 | | 200 | 91 |
| | 1994 | | | | | | | 200 | | 200 | 95 |
| | 1995 | | | | | | | 200 | | 200 | 96 |
| | 1996 | | | | | | | 100 | | 100 | 46 |
| | 1997 | | | | | | | 200 | | 200 | 83 |
| Libyan Arab Jamahiriya | 1970 | | 800 | | 800 | 403 | | 1 400 | | 1 400 | 705 |
| | 1975 | | 100 | | 100 | 41 | | 8 700 | | 8 700 | 3 557 |
| | 1980 | | 800 | | 800 | 263 | | 3 500 | | 3 500 | 1 150 |

Newsprint and other printing and writing paper    IV.10
Papier journal et autre papier d'impression et d'écriture
Papel de periódico y otro papel de imprenta y de escribir

| Country / Pays / País | Year / Année / Año | Newsprint / Papier journal / Papel de periódico | | | | | Other printing and writing paper / Autre papier d'impression et d'écriture / Otro papel de imprenta y de escribir | | | | |
|---|---|---|---|---|---|---|---|---|---|---|---|
| | | Production / Production / Producción | Imports / Importations / Importaciones | Exports / Exportations / Exportaciones | Consumption / Consommation / Consumo | Consumption per 1,000 inh. / Consommation pour 1 000 hab. / Consumo por 1 000 hab. | Production / Production / Producción | Imports / Importations / Importaciones | Exports / Exportations / Exportaciones | Consumption / Consommation / Consumo | Consumption per 1,000 inh. / Consommation pour 1 000 hab. / Consumo por 1 000 hab. |
| Libyan Arab Jamahiriya (cont) | 1985 | | 2 000 | | 2 000 | 528 | | 7 400 | | 7 400 | 1 955 |
| | 1990 | | 865 | | 865 | 196 | | 5 982 | | 5 982 | 1 355 |
| | 1991 | | 865 | | 865 | 191 | | 5 982 | | 5 982 | 1 321 |
| | 1992 | | | | | | | 2 128 | | 2 128 | 459 |
| | 1993 | | | | | | | 11 300 | | 11 300 | 2 382 |
| | 1994 | | 181 | | 181 | 37 | | 4 669 | | 4 669 | 962 |
| | 1995 | | 900 | | 900 | 181 | | 1 700 | | 1 700 | 342 |
| | 1996 | | 500 | | 500 | 98 | | 1 200 | | 1 200 | 236 |
| | 1997 | | 500 | | 500 | 96 | | 1 200 | | 1 200 | 230 |
| Madagascar | 1970 | 300 | | | 300 | 44 | 3 900 | | 1 300 | 2 600 | 379 |
| | 1975 | 817 | | | 817 | 104 | 8 200 | | 800 | 7 400 | 946 |
| | 1980 | 3 500 | | | 3 500 | 394 | | 600 | | 600 | 68 |
| | 1985 | 800 | | | 800 | 79 | 6 600 | 2 300 | | 8 900 | 879 |
| | 1990 | 350 | | | 350 | 30 | 3 000 | 516 | | 3 516 | 302 |
| | 1991 | 270 | | | 270 | 22 | 3 200 | 516 | | 3 716 | 309 |
| | 1992 | 320 | 234 | | 554 | 45 | 3 000 | 509 | 35 | 3 474 | 280 |
| | 1993 | 320 | 10 | | 330 | 26 | 4 100 | 1 088 | 29 | 5 159 | 401 |
| | 1994 | 220 | 500 | | 720 | 54 | 3 700 | 1 200 | | 4 900 | 368 |
| | 1995 | 170 | 1 300 | | 1 470 | 107 | 3 100 | 1 100 | | 4 200 | 306 |
| | 1996 | 100 | 900 | | 1 000 | 71 | 2 300 | 2 500 | | 4 800 | 338 |
| | 1997 | 100 | 1 100 | | 1 200 | 82 | 2 500 | 1 100 | | 3 600 | 246 |
| Malawi | 1970 | | 200 | | 200 | 44 | | 2 500 | | 2 500 | 553 |
| | 1975 | | | | | | | 2 200 | | 2 200 | 420 |
| | 1980 | | 600 | | 600 | 97 | | 9 700 | | 9 700 | 1 569 |
| | 1985 | | 600 | | 600 | 83 | | 100 | | 100 | 14 |
| | 1990 | | | | | | | 1 548 | | 1 548 | 166 |
| | 1991 | | | | | | | 1 548 | | 1 548 | 163 |
| | 1992 | | 42 | | 42 | 4 | | 155 | 4 | 151 | 16 |
| | 1993 | | 42 | | 42 | 4 | | 312 | | 312 | 33 |
| | 1994 | | 42 | | 42 | 4 | | 429 | | 429 | 45 |
| | 1995 | | 1 161 | 61 | 1 100 | 114 | | 105 | | 105 | 11 |
| | 1996 | | 1 161 | 61 | 1 100 | 112 | | 105 | | 105 | 11 |
| | 1997 | | 1 161 | 61 | 1 100 | 109 | | 86 | 1 | 85 | 8 |
| Mali | 1970 | | 200 | | 200 | 36 | | | | | |
| | 1975 | | 100 | | 100 | 16 | | 200 | | 200 | 32 |
| | 1980 | | | | | | | 200 | | 200 | 29 |
| | 1985 | | | | | | | 300 | | 300 | 38 |
| | 1990 | | | | | | | 300 | | 300 | 34 |
| | 1991 | | | | | | | 300 | | 300 | 33 |
| | 1992 | | | | | | | 873 | | 873 | 94 |
| | 1993 | | | | | | | 652 | 160 | 492 | 52 |
| | 1994 | | | | | | | 977 | 88 | 889 | 92 |
| | 1995 | | 400 | | 400 | 40 | | 201 | 88 | 113 | 11 |
| | 1996 | | 18 | | 18 | 2 | | 900 | 88 | 812 | 80 |
| | 1997 | | 137 | | 137 | 13 | | 1 901 | 88 | 1 813 | 174 |
| Mauritania | 1992 | | 21 | | 21 | 10 | | 700 | | 700 | 327 |
| | 1993 | | 4 | | 4 | 2 | | 942 | | 942 | 428 |
| | 1994 | | 4 | | 4 | 2 | | 942 | | 942 | 416 |
| | 1995 | | 47 | | 47 | 20 | | 133 | | 133 | 57 |
| | 1996 | | 24 | | 24 | 10 | | 500 | | 500 | 209 |
| | 1997 | | 24 | | 24 | 10 | | 373 | | 373 | 152 |
| Mauritius | 1970 | | 600 | | 600 | 726 | | 800 | | 800 | 968 |
| | 1975 | | 600 | | 600 | 673 | | 1 000 | | 1 000 | 1 121 |
| | 1980 | | 500 | | 500 | 518 | | 1 600 | | 1 600 | 1 656 |
| | 1985 | | 1 400 | | 1 400 | 1 378 | | 1 700 | | 1 700 | 1 674 |
| | 1990 | | 2 800 | | 2 800 | 2 650 | | 5 200 | | 5 200 | 4 921 |
| | 1991 | | 3 700 | | 3 700 | 3 467 | | 6 600 | | 6 600 | 6 184 |
| | 1992 | | 3 656 | | 3 656 | 3 389 | | 8 619 | 44 | 8 575 | 7 948 |
| | 1993 | | 3 400 | | 3 400 | 3 116 | | 7 500 | 3 | 7 497 | 6 871 |
| | 1994 | | 4 200 | | 4 200 | 3 808 | | 8 300 | 100 | 8 200 | 7 434 |
| | 1995 | | 4 200 | | 4 200 | 3 770 | | 8 300 | 100 | 8 200 | 7 361 |
| | 1996 | | 3 100 | | 3 100 | 2 758 | | 8 800 | 100 | 8 700 | 7 741 |
| | 1997 | | 941 | | 941 | 831 | | 3 981 | 41 | 3 940 | 3 478 |
| Morocco | 1970 | | 3 100 | | 3 100 | 202 | 10 000 | 2 000 | | 12 000 | 784 |
| | 1975 | | 2 800 | | 2 800 | 162 | 16 500 | 1 300 | | 17 800 | 1 029 |
| | 1980 | | 5 400 | | 5 400 | 279 | 25 000 | 3 200 | | 28 200 | 1 455 |

IV.10  Newsprint and other printing and writing paper
Papier journal et autre papier d'impression et d'écriture
Papel de periódico y otro papel de imprenta y de escribir

| Country / Year / Pays / Année / País / Año | Newsprint / Papier journal / Papel de periódico | | | | | Other printing and writing paper / Autre papier d'impression et d'écriture / Otro papel de imprenta y de escribir | | | | |
|---|---|---|---|---|---|---|---|---|---|---|
| | Production / Production / Producción | Imports / Importations / Importaciones | Exports / Exportations / Exportaciones | Consumption / Consommation / Consumo | Consumption per 1,000 inh. / Consommation pour 1 000 hab. / Consumo por 1 000 hab. | Production / Production / Producción | Imports / Importations / Importaciones | Exports / Exportations / Exportaciones | Consumption / Consommation / Consumo | Consumption per 1,000 inh. / Consommation pour 1 000 hab. / Consumo por 1 000 hab. |
| **Morocco (cont)** | | | | | | | | | | |
| 1985 | | 4 800 | | 4 800 | 222 | 24 000 | 4 000 | | 28 000 | 1 293 |
| 1990 | | 12 100 | | 12 100 | 506 | 29 000 | 25 800 | | 54 800 | 2 290 |
| 1991 | | 14 000 | | 14 000 | 575 | 29 000 | 29 700 | | 58 700 | 2 411 |
| 1992 | | 15 828 | | 15 828 | 640 | 29 000 | 4 996 | 48 | 33 948 | 1 372 |
| 1993 | | 23 387 | 19 | 23 368 | 930 | 25 000 | 21 652 | 208 | 46 444 | 1 848 |
| 1994 | | 18 800 | | 18 800 | 736 | 29 000 | 21 400 | 800 | 49 600 | 1 942 |
| 1995 | | 17 000 | | 17 000 | 655 | 30 000 | 18 800 | 400 | 48 400 | 1 864 |
| 1996 | | 16 800 | | 16 800 | 636 | 30 000 | 14 500 | 200 | 44 300 | 1 677 |
| 1997 | | 19 000 | | 19 000 | 707 | 23 000 | 20 000 | 200 | 42 800 | 1 592 |
| **Mozambique** | | | | | | | | | | |
| 1970 | | 200 | | 200 | 21 | | | | | |
| 1975 | | 1 700 | | 1 700 | 162 | | | | | |
| 1980 | | 1 500 | | 1 500 | 124 | | 4 000 | | 4 000 | 331 |
| 1985 | | 100 | | 100 | 7 | | 100 | | 100 | 7 |
| 1990 | | 1 100 | | 1 100 | 77 | | 1 000 | | 1 000 | 70 |
| 1991 | | 800 | | 800 | 55 | | 1 000 | | 1 000 | 68 |
| 1992 | | 592 | 115 | 477 | 31 | | 487 | 53 | 434 | 28 |
| 1993 | | 261 | | 261 | 16 | | 1 542 | | 1 542 | 96 |
| 1994 | | 118 | | 118 | 7 | | 616 | | 616 | 37 |
| 1995 | | 118 | | 118 | 7 | | 616 | | 616 | 35 |
| 1996 | | 23 | | 23 | 1 | | 100 | | 100 | 6 |
| 1997 | | 25 | | 25 | 1 | | 255 | | 255 | 14 |
| **Niger** | | | | | | | | | | |
| 1975 | | 150 | | 150 | 31 | | 100 | | 100 | 21 |
| 1980 | | 100 | | 100 | 18 | | 100 | | 100 | 18 |
| 1985 | | 100 | | 100 | 15 | | 1 100 | | 1 100 | 166 |
| 1990 | | 100 | | 100 | 13 | | 600 | | 600 | 78 |
| 1991 | | 300 | | 300 | 38 | | 300 | | 300 | 38 |
| 1992 | | | | | | | 907 | 4 | 903 | 109 |
| 1993 | | 32 | | 32 | 4 | | 199 | | 199 | 23 |
| 1994 | | 122 | | 122 | 14 | | 464 | 3 | 461 | 52 |
| 1995 | | 122 | | 122 | 13 | | 142 | 3 | 139 | 15 |
| 1996 | | 16 | | 16 | 2 | | 300 | 3 | 297 | 31 |
| 1997 | | 16 | | 16 | 2 | | 300 | 3 | 297 | 30 |
| **Nigeria** | | | | | | | | | | |
| 1970 | | 17 100 | | 17 100 | 345 | 2 000 | 25 200 | | 27 200 | 548 |
| 1975 | | 23 700 | | 23 700 | 416 | 2 000 | 29 000 | | 31 000 | 544 |
| 1980 | | 29 000 | | 29 000 | 442 | 3 500 | 41 900 | | 45 400 | 692 |
| 1985 | | 14 800 | | 14 800 | 195 | 4 500 | 50 000 | | 54 500 | 719 |
| 1990 | 30 000 | 2 768 | | 32 768 | 377 | 5 000 | 70 989 | | 75 989 | 873 |
| 1991 | 15 000 | 2 768 | | 17 768 | 199 | 5 000 | 70 989 | | 75 989 | 850 |
| 1992 | 12 000 | 4 685 | | 16 685 | 182 | 5 000 | 64 614 | | 69 614 | 759 |
| 1993 | 12 000 | 7 355 | | 19 355 | 206 | | 50 053 | 19 | 50 034 | 532 |
| 1994 | 12 000 | 6 011 | | 18 011 | 187 | | 44 769 | 19 | 44 750 | 464 |
| 1995 | 13 000 | 14 735 | | 27 735 | 280 | | 8 123 | 19 | 8 104 | 82 |
| 1996 | 13 000 | 12 400 | | 25 400 | 250 | | 11 600 | 19 | 11 581 | 114 |
| 1997 | 13 000 | 8 963 | | 21 963 | 211 | | 43 158 | 19 | 43 139 | 415 |
| **Reunion** | | | | | | | | | | |
| 1970 | | 400 | | 400 | 868 | | 300 | | 300 | 651 |
| 1975 | | 500 | | 500 | 1 035 | | | | | |
| 1980 | | 1 000 | | 1 000 | 1 975 | | | | | |
| 1985 | | 3 100 | | 3 100 | 5 586 | | 1 600 | | 1 600 | 2 883 |
| 1990 | | 3 900 | | 3 900 | 6 457 | | 3 900 | | 3 900 | 6 457 |
| 1991 | | 3 900 | | 3 900 | 6 350 | | 3 900 | | 3 900 | 6 350 |
| 1992 | | 5 788 | 34 | 5 754 | 9 213 | | 7 707 | 57 | 7 650 | 12 249 |
| 1993 | | 5 730 | 12 | 5 718 | 9 006 | | 6 201 | 153 | 6 048 | 9 526 |
| 1994 | | 5 186 | 24 | 5 162 | 8 002 | | 5 574 | 12 | 5 562 | 8 622 |
| 1995 | | 7 519 | 91 | 7 428 | 11 342 | | 3 550 | 7 | 3 543 | 5 410 |
| 1996 | | 7 519 | 91 | 7 428 | 11 181 | | 3 550 | 7 | 3 543 | 5 333 |
| 1997 | | 7 519 | 91 | 7 428 | 11 030 | | 3 550 | 7 | 3 543 | 5 261 |
| **Rwanda** | | | | | | | | | | |
| 1985 | | | | | | | 400 | | 400 | 66 |
| 1990 | | | | | | | 1 200 | | 1 200 | 172 |
| 1991 | | | | | | | 3 000 | | 3 000 | 447 |
| 1992 | | | | | | | 1 418 | | 1 418 | 227 |
| 1993 | | | | | | | 244 | 10 | 234 | 41 |
| 1994 | | 100 | | 100 | 19 | | 208 | 8 | 200 | 37 |
| 1995 | | 200 | | 200 | 38 | | 200 | | 200 | 38 |
| 1996 | | 200 | | 200 | 37 | | 400 | | 400 | 73 |
| 1997 | | 86 | | 86 | 14 | | 734 | | 734 | 123 |

Newsprint and other printing and writing paper IV.10
Papier journal et autre papier d'impression et d'écriture
Papel de periódico y otro papel de imprenta y de escribir

| Country / Pays / País | Year / Année / Año | Newsprint – Papier journal – Papel de periódico | | | | | Other printing and writing paper – Autre papier d'impression et d'écriture – Otro papel de imprenta y de escribir | | | | |
|---|---|---|---|---|---|---|---|---|---|---|---|
| | | Production / Producción | Imports / Importations / Importaciones | Exports / Exportations / Exportaciones | Consumption / Consommation / Consumo | Consumption per 1,000 inh. / Consommation pour 1 000 hab. / Consumo por 1 000 hab. | Production / Producción | Imports / Importations / Importaciones | Exports / Exportations / Exportaciones | Consumption / Consommation / Consumo | Consumption per 1,000 inh. / Consommation pour 1 000 hab. / Consumo por 1 000 hab. |
| Sao Tome and Principe | 1992 | | | | | | | 3 | | 3 | 24 |
| | 1993 | | | | | | | 69 | | 69 | 544 |
| | 1994 | | | | | | | 5 | | 5 | 39 |
| | 1995 | | | | | | | 20 | 16 | 4 | 30 |
| | 1996 | | | | | | | 16 | 16 | | |
| | 1997 | | | | | | | 38 | 16 | 22 | 159 |
| Senegal | 1970 | | 500 | | 500 | 120 | | 3 300 | | 3 300 | 794 |
| | 1975 | | 1 800 | | 1 800 | 375 | | 1 200 | | 1 200 | 250 |
| | 1980 | | 900 | | 900 | 163 | | 1 800 | | 1 800 | 325 |
| | 1985 | | 1 000 | | 1 000 | 157 | | 7 000 | | 7 000 | 1 098 |
| | 1990 | | 500 | | 500 | 68 | | 4 500 | | 4 500 | 614 |
| | 1991 | | 1 900 | | 1 900 | 253 | | 1 300 | | 1 300 | 173 |
| | 1992 | | 368 | | 368 | 48 | | 3 661 | 3 | 3 658 | 474 |
| | 1993 | | 361 | | 361 | 46 | | 4 658 | | 4 658 | 588 |
| | 1994 | | 500 | | 500 | 62 | | 4 658 | | 4 658 | 574 |
| | 1995 | | 500 | | 500 | 60 | | 1 100 | | 1 100 | 132 |
| | 1996 | | 500 | | 500 | 58 | | 1 100 | | 1 100 | 129 |
| | 1997 | | 500 | | 500 | 57 | | 1 100 | | 1 100 | 125 |
| Seychelles | 1992 | | 266 | | 266 | 3 739 | | 589 | | 589 | 8 280 |
| | 1993 | | | | | | | 33 | | 33 | 459 |
| | 1994 | | 192 | | 192 | 2 642 | | 63 | | 63 | 867 |
| | 1995 | | 192 | | 192 | 2 614 | | 63 | | 63 | 858 |
| | 1996 | | 192 | | 192 | 2 587 | | 63 | | 63 | 849 |
| | 1997 | | 192 | | 192 | 2 559 | | 63 | | 63 | 840 |
| Sierra Leone | 1970 | | 200 | | 200 | 75 | | 200 | | 200 | 75 |
| | 1975 | | 100 | | 100 | 34 | | | | | |
| | 1980 | | 200 | | 200 | 62 | | | | | |
| | 1985 | | 200 | | 200 | 56 | | 200 | | 200 | 56 |
| | 1990 | | | | | | | 300 | | 300 | 75 |
| | 1991 | | | | | | | 600 | | 600 | 149 |
| | 1992 | | 39 | | 39 | 10 | | 289 | | 289 | 71 |
| | 1993 | | 325 | | 325 | 80 | | 537 | | 537 | 132 |
| | 1994 | | 70 | | 70 | 17 | | 732 | | 732 | 178 |
| | 1995 | | 213 | | 213 | 51 | | 43 | | 43 | 10 |
| | 1996 | | 1 500 | | 1 500 | 350 | | 200 | | 200 | 47 |
| | 1997 | | 3 749 | | 3 749 | 848 | | 164 | 195 | | |
| Somalia | 1970 | | 500 | | 500 | 139 | | 100 | | 100 | 28 |
| | 1975 | | 300 | | 300 | 73 | | 100 | | 100 | 24 |
| | 1980 | | 200 | | 200 | 34 | | 1 300 | | 1 300 | 222 |
| | 1985 | | 100 | | 100 | 15 | | 100 | | 100 | 15 |
| | 1990 | | | | | | | 152 | | 152 | 20 |
| | 1991 | | | | | | | 152 | | 152 | 19 |
| | 1993 | | | | | | | 27 | | 27 | 3 |
| | 1994 | | | | | | | 144 | | 144 | 18 |
| | 1995 | | 25 | | 25 | 3 | | 144 | | 144 | 18 |
| | 1996 | | 25 | | 25 | 3 | | 144 | 50 | 94 | 11 |
| | 1997 | | 198 | | 198 | 22 | | 18 | 136 | | |
| South Africa | 1970 | 160 000 | 52 500 | | 212 500 | 9 621 | 70 000 | 130 500 | 3 600 | 196 900 | 8 915 |
| | 1975 | 210 000 | 300 | 14 500 | 195 800 | 7 918 | 77 000 | 74 000 | 6 800 | 144 200 | 5 831 |
| | 1980 | 224 000 | | 70 000 | 154 000 | 5 585 | 177 000 | 92 600 | 14 400 | 255 200 | 9 255 |
| | 1985 | 325 000 | 100 | 205 000 | 120 100 | 3 910 | 256 000 | 84 000 | 56 000 | 284 000 | 9 245 |
| | 1990 | 355 000 | 51 | 75 562 | 279 489 | 8 217 | 395 000 | 69 234 | 21 596 | 442 638 | 13 014 |
| | 1991 | 350 000 | 51 | 75 562 | 274 489 | 7 909 | 395 000 | 69 234 | 21 596 | 442 638 | 12 755 |
| | 1992 | 330 000 | 1 700 | 118 195 | 213 505 | 6 031 | 335 000 | 114 933 | 32 977 | 416 956 | 11 777 |
| | 1993 | 350 000 | 1 400 | 77 450 | 273 950 | 7 588 | 400 000 | 106 037 | 46 496 | 459 541 | 12 728 |
| | 1994 | 367 000 | 5 503 | 228 400 | 144 103 | 3 916 | 380 000 | 122 727 | 24 428 | 478 299 | 12 999 |
| | 1995 | 440 000 | 4 100 | 182 300 | 261 800 | 6 987 | 301 000 | 133 700 | 9 300 | 425 400 | 11 353 |
| | 1996 | 440 000 | 4 100 | 128 000 | 316 100 | 8 291 | 301 000 | 138 000 | 9 300 | 429 700 | 11 270 |
| | 1997 | 370 000 | 3 100 | 103 000 | 270 100 | 6 968 | 546 000 | 173 000 | 22 100 | 696 900 | 17 980 |
| St. Helena | 1992 | | | | | | | 1 | | 1 | 170 |
| | 1993 | | | | | | | 6 | | 6 | 1 011 |
| | 1994 | | 15 | | 15 | 2 506 | | 48 | | 48 | 8 020 |
| | 1995 | | 15 | | 15 | 2 486 | | 48 | | 48 | 7 954 |
| | 1996 | | 15 | | 15 | 2 465 | | 48 | | 48 | 7 887 |
| | 1997 | | 15 | | 15 | 2 444 | | 48 | | 48 | 7 821 |

IV.10 Newsprint and other printing and writing paper
Papier journal et autre papier d'impression et d'écriture
Papel de periódico y otro papel de imprenta y de escribir

| Country / Pays / País | Year / Année / Año | Newsprint — Papier journal — Papel de periódico | | | | | Other printing and writing paper — Autre papier d'impression et d'écriture — Otro papel de imprenta y de escribir | | | | |
|---|---|---|---|---|---|---|---|---|---|---|---|
| | | Production / Producción | Imports / Importations / Importaciones | Exports / Exportations / Exportaciones | Consumption / Consommation / Consumo | Consumption per 1,000 inh. / Consommation pour 1 000 hab. / Consumo por 1 000 hab. | Production / Producción | Imports / Importations / Importaciones | Exports / Exportations / Exportaciones | Consumption / Consommation / Consumo | Consumption per 1,000 inh. / Consommation pour 1 000 hab. / Consumo por 1 000 hab. |
| **Sudan** | | | | | | | | | | | |
| | 1970 | | 2 700 | | 2 700 | 195 | | 3 700 | | 3 700 | 267 |
| | 1975 | | 3 400 | | 3 400 | 212 | | 5 000 | | 5 000 | 312 |
| | 1980 | | 1 500 | | 1 500 | 80 | | 7 200 | | 7 200 | 385 |
| | 1985 | | 8 500 | | 8 500 | 396 | | 6 900 | | 6 900 | 322 |
| | 1990 | | 900 | | 900 | 37 | | 3 200 | | 3 200 | 133 |
| | 1991 | | 900 | | 900 | 37 | | 3 200 | | 3 200 | 130 |
| | 1992 | | | | | | | 1 562 | | 1 562 | 62 |
| | 1993 | | 676 | | 676 | 26 | | 3 139 | | 3 139 | 123 |
| | 1994 | | 957 | | 957 | 37 | | 5 147 | | 5 147 | 197 |
| | 1995 | | 1 600 | | 1 600 | 60 | | | | | |
| | 1996 | | 1 600 | | 1 600 | 59 | | | | | |
| | 1997 | | 895 | | 895 | 32 | | 3 117 | 1 | 3 116 | 112 |
| **Togo** | | | | | | | | | | | |
| | 1985 | | | | | | | 1 800 | | 1 800 | 595 |
| | 1990 | | | | | | | 1 200 | | 1 200 | 342 |
| | 1991 | | | | | | | 1 200 | | 1 200 | 332 |
| | 1992 | | 27 | 18 | 9 | 2 | | 866 | 13 | 853 | 229 |
| | 1993 | | 54 | | 54 | 14 | | 644 | | 644 | 168 |
| | 1994 | | 400 | | 400 | 101 | | 600 | | 600 | 152 |
| | 1995 | | 700 | | 700 | 172 | | 1 400 | | 1 400 | 345 |
| | 1996 | | 100 | | 100 | 24 | | 1 700 | | 1 700 | 408 |
| | 1997 | | 300 | | 300 | 70 | | 700 | | 700 | 163 |
| **Tunisia** | | | | | | | | | | | |
| | 1975 | | | | | | 15 000 | | 3 800 | 11 200 | 1 976 |
| | 1980 | | 5 500 | | 5 500 | 853 | 18 000 | 11 100 | 100 | 29 000 | 4 498 |
| | 1985 | | 9 900 | | 9 900 | 1 350 | 26 000 | 4 700 | | 30 700 | 4 186 |
| | 1990 | | 11 100 | | 11 100 | 1 361 | 29 000 | 7 423 | | 36 423 | 4 466 |
| | 1991 | | 10 200 | | 10 200 | 1 226 | 23 000 | 2 300 | | 25 300 | 3 041 |
| | 1992 | | 13 400 | | 13 400 | 1 580 | 28 000 | 11 494 | 379 | 39 115 | 4 612 |
| | 1993 | | 5 800 | | 5 800 | 671 | 36 000 | 10 100 | | 46 100 | 5 334 |
| | 1994 | | 15 800 | 181 | 15 619 | 1 776 | 39 000 | 14 778 | 2 000 | 51 778 | 5 886 |
| | 1995 | | 16 600 | 800 | 15 800 | 1 767 | 33 000 | 9 640 | 650 | 41 990 | 4 695 |
| | 1996 | | 13 000 | 500 | 12 500 | 1 377 | 33 000 | 10 100 | 170 | 42 930 | 4 728 |
| | 1997 | | 13 000 | 500 | 12 500 | 1 357 | 34 000 | 10 100 | 170 | 43 930 | 4 770 |
| **Uganda** | | | | | | | | | | | |
| | 1970 | | 1 000 | | 1 000 | 102 | | 2 600 | | 2 600 | 265 |
| | 1975 | | 500 | | 500 | 45 | | 400 | | 400 | 36 |
| | 1980 | | 200 | | 200 | 15 | | 500 | | 500 | 38 |
| | 1985 | | 200 | | 200 | 14 | | 400 | | 400 | 27 |
| | 1990 | | 1 | | 1 | | | 1 276 | | 1 276 | 78 |
| | 1991 | | 1 | | 1 | | | 1 276 | | 1 276 | 76 |
| | 1992 | | | | | | | 733 | | 733 | 42 |
| | 1993 | | 61 | | 61 | 3 | | 2 242 | | 2 242 | 125 |
| | 1994 | | 61 | | 61 | 3 | | 2 465 | | 2 465 | 134 |
| | 1995 | | 2 482 | | 2 482 | 131 | | 972 | | 972 | 51 |
| | 1996 | | 1 000 | | 1 000 | 51 | | 100 | | 100 | 5 |
| | 1997 | | 2 277 | | 2 277 | 114 | | 4 319 | | 4 319 | 216 |
| **United Republic of Tanzania** | | | | | | | | | | | |
| | 1970 | | 1 500 | | 1 500 | 110 | | 5 100 | | 5 100 | 372 |
| | 1975 | | 4 500 | | 4 500 | 283 | | 5 000 | | 5 000 | 314 |
| | 1980 | | 3 500 | | 3 500 | 188 | | 7 000 | | 7 000 | 377 |
| | 1985 | | 2 500 | | 2 500 | 115 | | 4 200 | | 4 200 | 193 |
| | 1990 | 8 000 | 212 | | 8 212 | 322 | 6 000 | 1 163 | | 7 163 | 281 |
| | 1991 | 8 000 | 212 | | 8 212 | 312 | 6 000 | 1 163 | | 7 163 | 272 |
| | 1992 | 8 000 | 725 | 217 | 8 508 | 312 | 6 000 | 461 | 80 | 6 381 | 234 |
| | 1993 | 8 000 | 4 200 | | 12 200 | 433 | 6 000 | 1 700 | 11 | 7 689 | 273 |
| | 1994 | 8 000 | 400 | | 8 400 | 289 | 6 000 | 2 600 | 11 | 8 589 | 295 |
| | 1995 | 8 000 | 1 487 | | 9 487 | 317 | 6 000 | 313 | 11 | 6 302 | 211 |
| | 1996 | 8 000 | 1 300 | | 9 300 | 303 | 6 000 | 600 | 11 | 6 589 | 215 |
| | 1997 | 8 000 | 1 868 | | 9 868 | 314 | 6 000 | 998 | 11 | 6 987 | 222 |
| **Zambia** | | | | | | | | | | | |
| | 1970 | | 2 100 | | 2 100 | 501 | | 5 300 | | 5 300 | 1 265 |
| | 1975 | | | | | | | 4 400 | | 4 400 | 909 |
| | 1980 | | 3 000 | | 3 000 | 523 | | 6 300 | | 6 300 | 1 098 |
| | 1985 | | 3 000 | | 3 000 | 468 | 1 000 | 800 | | 1 800 | 281 |
| | 1990 | | 4 000 | | 4 000 | 553 | 900 | 3 000 | | 3 900 | 539 |
| | 1991 | | 4 000 | | 4 000 | 539 | 1 000 | 3 000 | | 4 000 | 539 |
| | 1992 | | 1 600 | | 1 600 | 210 | 1 000 | 3 300 | | 4 300 | 565 |
| | 1993 | | 1 700 | | 1 700 | 218 | 2 000 | 1 700 | 6 | 3 694 | 473 |
| | 1994 | | 1 700 | | 1 700 | 213 | 1 000 | 369 | 6 | 1 363 | 170 |
| | 1995 | | 2 500 | | 2 500 | 305 | 1 000 | 488 | 20 | 1 468 | 179 |
| | 1996 | | 2 500 | | 2 500 | 298 | 1 000 | 488 | 20 | 1 468 | 175 |
| | 1997 | | 2 500 | | 2 500 | 291 | 1 000 | 372 | 20 | 1 352 | 157 |

Newsprint and other printing and writing paper
Papier journal et autre papier d'impression et d'écriture
Papel de periódico y otro papel de imprenta y de escribir

IV.10

| Country / Year | Newsprint / Papier journal / Papel de periódico | | | | | Other printing and writing paper / Autre papier d'impression et d'écriture / Otro papel de imprenta y de escribir | | | | |
|---|---|---|---|---|---|---|---|---|---|---|
| Pays / Année | Production | Imports | Exports | Consumption | Consumption per 1,000 inh. | Production | Imports | Exports | Consumption | Consumption per 1,000 inh. |
| País / Año | Production / Producción | Importations / Importaciones | Exportations / Exportaciones | Consommation / Consumo | Consommation pour 1 000 hab. / Consumo por 1 000 hab. | Production / Producción | Importations / Importaciones | Exportations / Exportaciones | Consommation / Consumo | Consommation pour 1 000 hab. / Consumo por 1 000 hab. |
| **Zimbabwe** | | | | | | | | | | |
| 1980 | 16 000 | | | 16 000 | 2 245 | 8 500 | | | 8 500 | 1 193 |
| 1985 | 18 000 | 400 | | 18 400 | 2 194 | 4 900 | | | 4 900 | 584 |
| 1990 | 21 000 | 1 610 | | 22 610 | 2 292 | 7 600 | | | 7 600 | 771 |
| 1991 | 21 000 | 1 000 | | 22 000 | 2 177 | 7 600 | | | 7 600 | 752 |
| 1992 | 21 000 | 4 347 | 49 | 25 298 | 2 452 | 11 824 | | 290 | 11 534 | 1 118 |
| 1993 | 15 000 | 16 | 25 | 14 991 | 1 426 | 3 535 | | 7 | 3 528 | 336 |
| 1994 | 17 000 | 16 | 25 | 16 991 | 1 589 | 6 535 | | 19 | 6 516 | 609 |
| 1995 | 17 000 | 2 192 | 25 | 19 167 | 1 763 | 1 645 | | 250 | 1 395 | 128 |
| 1996 | 17 000 | 1 300 | 25 | 18 275 | 1 655 | 2 600 | | 2 000 | 600 | 54 |
| 1997 | 17 000 | 3 700 | 25 | 20 675 | 1 844 | 2 500 | | 2 000 | 500 | 45 |
| **North America** | | | | | | | | | | |
| **Anguilla** | | | | | | | | | | |
| 1992 | | | | | | | 382 | 14 | 368 | 49 047 |
| 1993 | | 2 | | 2 | 263 | | 419 | | 419 | 55 124 |
| **Antigua and Barbuda** | | | | | | | | | | |
| 1992 | | 6 | | 6 | 93 | | 90 | | 90 | 1 394 |
| 1993 | | 34 | 28 | 6 | 92 | | 167 | | 167 | 2 571 |
| 1994 | | 13 | | 13 | 199 | | 376 | 149 | 227 | 3 474 |
| 1995 | | 13 | | 13 | 198 | | 376 | 149 | 227 | 3 453 |
| 1996 | | 13 | | 13 | 197 | | 376 | 149 | 227 | 3 434 |
| 1997 | | 13 | | 13 | 196 | | 376 | 149 | 227 | 3 415 |
| **Aruba** | | | | | | | | | | |
| 1993 | | 233 | | 233 | 3 190 | | 447 | | 447 | 6 120 |
| 1994 | | 573 | | 573 | 7 415 | | 251 | | 251 | 3 248 |
| 1995 | | 573 | | 573 | 7 030 | | 251 | | 251 | 3 080 |
| 1996 | | 573 | | 573 | 6 690 | | 251 | | 251 | 2 930 |
| 1997 | | 573 | | 573 | 6 381 | | 251 | | 251 | 2 795 |
| **Bahamas** | | | | | | | | | | |
| 1970 | | 1 000 | | 1 000 | 5 891 | | 500 | | 500 | 2 946 |
| 1975 | | 600 | | 600 | 3 177 | | 200 | | 200 | 1 059 |
| 1980 | | 900 | | 900 | 4 284 | | 100 | | 100 | 476 |
| 1985 | | 400 | | 400 | 1 726 | | 100 | | 100 | 432 |
| 1990 | | 1 400 | | 1 400 | 5 488 | | 300 | | 300 | 1 176 |
| 1991 | | 1 500 | | 1 500 | 5 769 | | 900 | | 900 | 3 461 |
| 1992 | | 1 442 | | 1 442 | 5 441 | | 1 474 | 250 | 1 224 | 4 619 |
| 1993 | | 489 | | 489 | 1 811 | | 1 412 | 100 | 1 312 | 4 858 |
| 1994 | | 1 500 | | 1 500 | 5 450 | | 1 863 | 165 | 1 698 | 6 170 |
| 1995 | | 1 600 | | 1 600 | 5 706 | | 500 | 165 | 335 | 1 195 |
| 1996 | | 800 | | 800 | 2 801 | | 800 | | 800 | 2 801 |
| 1997 | | 900 | | 900 | 3 094 | | 2 100 | | 2 100 | 7 220 |
| **Barbados** | | | | | | | | | | |
| 1970 | | 900 | | 900 | 3 770 | | 500 | | 500 | 2 094 |
| 1975 | | 500 | | 500 | 2 036 | | 800 | | 800 | 3 257 |
| 1980 | | 1 500 | | 1 500 | 6 023 | | 2 800 | | 2 800 | 11 243 |
| 1985 | | 1 400 | | 1 400 | 5 539 | | 3 100 | | 3 100 | 12 266 |
| 1990 | | 1 700 | | 1 700 | 6 610 | | 800 | | 800 | 3 111 |
| 1991 | | 3 300 | | 3 300 | 12 769 | | 4 600 | | 4 600 | 17 799 |
| 1992 | | 2 780 | | 2 780 | 10 698 | | 1 684 | 1 | 1 683 | 6 476 |
| 1993 | | 2 245 | | 2 245 | 8 589 | | 3 264 | 1 | 3 263 | 12 484 |
| 1994 | | 3 844 | | 3 844 | 14 623 | | 3 151 | 1 | 3 150 | 11 983 |
| 1995 | | 3 241 | | 3 241 | 12 262 | | 416 | 1 | 415 | 1 570 |
| 1996 | | 2 300 | | 2 300 | 8 658 | | 1 200 | | 1 200 | 4 517 |
| 1997 | | 1 200 | | 1 200 | 4 496 | | 3 700 | | 3 700 | 13 863 |
| **Belize** | | | | | | | | | | |
| 1970 | | 200 | | 200 | 1 630 | | 100 | | 100 | 815 |
| 1975 | | 200 | | 200 | 1 496 | | 100 | | 100 | 748 |
| 1980 | | 200 | | 200 | 1 370 | | 300 | | 300 | 2 056 |
| 1985 | | 200 | | 200 | 1 206 | | 200 | | 200 | 1 206 |
| 1990 | | 200 | | 200 | 1 067 | | 300 | | 300 | 1 600 |
| 1991 | | 100 | | 100 | 520 | | 300 | | 300 | 1 560 |
| 1992 | | 287 | | 287 | 1 454 | | 423 | | 423 | 2 143 |
| 1993 | | 80 | | 80 | 395 | | 253 | 100 | 153 | 755 |
| 1994 | | 211 | | 211 | 1 015 | | 290 | 99 | 191 | 919 |
| 1995 | | 100 | | 100 | 469 | | 295 | 100 | 195 | 914 |
| 1996 | | | | | | | 300 | 100 | 200 | 914 |
| 1997 | | | | | | | 300 | 100 | 200 | 892 |
| **Bermuda** | | | | | | | | | | |
| 1992 | | | | | | | 858 | | 858 | 14 211 |
| 1993 | | | | | | | 1 187 | | 1 187 | 19 485 |
| 1994 | | | | | | | 987 | | 987 | 16 059 |

IV.10 Newsprint and other printing and writing paper
Papier journal et autre papier d'impression et d'écriture
Papel de periódico y otro papel de imprenta y de escribir

| Country / Pays / País | Year / Année / Año | Newsprint / Papier journal / Papel de periódico | | | | | Other printing and writing paper / Autre papier d'impression et d'écriture / Otro papel de imprenta y de escribir | | | | |
|---|---|---|---|---|---|---|---|---|---|---|---|
| | | Production / Producción | Imports / Importations / Importaciones | Exports / Exportations / Exportaciones | Consumption / Consommation / Consumo | Consumption per 1,000 inh. / Consommation pour 1 000 hab. / Consumo por 1 000 hab. | Production / Producción | Imports / Importations / Importaciones | Exports / Exportations / Exportaciones | Consumption / Consommation / Consumo | Consumption per 1,000 inh. / Consommation pour 1 000 hab. / Consumo por 1 000 hab. |
| **Bermuda (cont)** | 1995 | | 1 392 | | 1 392 | 22 452 | | 987 | | 987 | 15 919 |
| | 1996 | | 1 392 | | 1 392 | 22 262 | | 987 | | 987 | 15 785 |
| | 1997 | | 1 392 | | 1 392 | 22 077 | | 987 | | 987 | 15 654 |
| **British Virgin Islands** | 1992 | | | | | | | 6 | | 6 | 350 |
| | 1993 | | | | | | | 117 | 1 | 116 | 6 574 |
| | 1994 | | | | | | | 117 | 1 | 116 | 6 391 |
| | 1995 | | | | | | | 117 | 1 | 116 | 6 215 |
| | 1996 | | | | | | | 117 | 1 | 116 | 6 045 |
| | 1997 | | | | | | | 117 | 1 | 116 | 5 882 |
| **Canada** | 1970 | 7 996 000 | | 7 339 300 | 656 700 | 30 796 | 821 000 | 35 000 | 300 100 | 555 900 | 26 069 |
| | 1975 | 7 010 000 | | 6 348 800 | 661 200 | 28 489 | 679 000 | 146 700 | 275 600 | 550 100 | 23 702 |
| | 1980 | 8 625 000 | | 7 706 800 | 918 200 | 37 336 | 1 511 000 | 126 800 | 652 700 | 985 100 | 40 056 |
| | 1985 | 8 991 000 | | 8 274 700 | 716 300 | 27 612 | 2 141 000 | 242 300 | 731 200 | 1 652 100 | 63 685 |
| | 1990 | 9 069 000 | | 8 722 300 | 346 700 | 12 475 | 3 599 000 | 443 700 | 1 864 800 | 2 177 900 | 78 367 |
| | 1991 | 8 977 000 | | 8 561 300 | 415 700 | 14 756 | 3 564 000 | 256 700 | 1 569 700 | 2 251 000 | 79 905 |
| | 1992 | 8 931 000 | 32 082 | 8 695 745 | 267 337 | 9 365 | 3 567 000 | 504 834 | 1 938 884 | 2 132 950 | 74 717 |
| | 1993 | 9 165 000 | 14 576 | 9 029 000 | 150 576 | 5 207 | 4 194 000 | 506 166 | 2 117 000 | 2 583 166 | 89 335 |
| | 1994 | 9 321 000 | 10 000 | 9 424 000 | | | 4 444 000 | 560 000 | 2 384 000 | 2 620 000 | 89 502 |
| | 1995 | 9 226 000 | 14 000 | 9 162 000 | 78 000 | 2 634 | 4 882 000 | 595 000 | 2 744 000 | 2 733 000 | 92 277 |
| | 1996 | 9 015 000 | 7 000 | 8 608 000 | 414 000 | 13 825 | 4 689 000 | 763 000 | 2 714 000 | 2 738 000 | 91 429 |
| | 1997 | 9 205 000 | 19 000 | 8 906 000 | 318 000 | 10 509 | 4 966 000 | 738 000 | 3 142 000 | 2 562 000 | 84 664 |
| **Cayman Islands** | 1992 | | 146 | | 146 | 5 118 | | 133 | | 133 | 4 662 |
| | 1993 | | 191 | | 191 | 6 440 | | 101 | | 101 | 3 406 |
| | 1994 | | 292 | | 292 | 9 477 | | 271 | 155 | 116 | 3 765 |
| | 1995 | | 292 | | 292 | 9 125 | | 271 | 155 | 116 | 3 625 |
| | 1996 | | 292 | | 292 | 8 790 | | 271 | 155 | 116 | 3 492 |
| | 1997 | | 292 | | 292 | 8 473 | | 271 | 155 | 116 | 3 366 |
| **Costa Rica** | 1970 | | 11 100 | | 11 100 | 6 413 | | 4 000 | | 4 000 | 2 311 |
| | 1975 | | 11 200 | | 11 200 | 5 690 | | 2 800 | | 2 800 | 1 423 |
| | 1980 | | 12 000 | | 12 000 | 5 253 | | 7 600 | | 7 600 | 3 327 |
| | 1985 | | 11 000 | | 11 000 | 4 163 | | 6 100 | | 6 100 | 2 309 |
| | 1990 | | 15 000 | | 15 000 | 4 920 | | 11 000 | | 11 000 | 3 608 |
| | 1991 | | 16 800 | | 16 800 | 5 343 | | 11 500 | | 11 500 | 3 657 |
| | 1992 | | 15 392 | | 15 392 | 4 743 | | 174 498 | 100 | 174 398 | 53 742 |
| | 1993 | | 18 801 | 24 | 18 777 | 5 607 | | 25 420 | 2 | 25 418 | 7 590 |
| | 1994 | | 18 073 | 21 | 18 052 | 5 229 | | 4 800 | 148 | 4 652 | 1 347 |
| | 1995 | | 15 300 | | 15 300 | 4 305 | | 3 000 | | 3 000 | 844 |
| | 1996 | | 14 400 | 100 | 14 300 | 3 915 | | 7 400 | 200 | 7 200 | 1 971 |
| | 1997 | | 17 000 | 100 | 16 900 | 4 509 | | 15 000 | 400 | 14 600 | 3 895 |
| **Cuba** | 1970 | | 22 800 | | 22 800 | 2 676 | 20 000 | 6 500 | | 26 500 | 3 110 |
| | 1975 | | 26 700 | | 26 700 | 2 869 | 30 000 | 22 000 | | 52 000 | 5 588 |
| | 1980 | | 32 000 | | 32 000 | 3 295 | 31 300 | 15 400 | | 46 700 | 4 809 |
| | 1985 | | 43 200 | | 43 200 | 4 271 | 59 000 | 17 000 | | 76 000 | 7 513 |
| | 1990 | | 38 600 | | 38 600 | 3 632 | 39 000 | 13 200 | | 52 200 | 4 912 |
| | 1991 | | 38 600 | | 38 600 | 3 604 | 37 000 | 13 200 | | 50 200 | 4 687 |
| | 1992 | | 2 | | 2 | | 15 000 | 247 | 47 | 15 200 | 1 410 |
| | 1993 | | | | | | 14 000 | 707 | | 14 707 | 1 356 |
| | 1994 | | | | | | 14 000 | 1 315 | | 15 315 | 1 404 |
| | 1995 | | 5 100 | | 5 100 | 465 | 14 000 | 2 500 | | 16 500 | 1 505 |
| | 1996 | | 2 100 | | 2 100 | 191 | 14 000 | 1 400 | | 15 400 | 1 398 |
| | 1997 | | 5 500 | | 5 500 | 497 | 14 000 | 11 000 | | 25 000 | 2 259 |
| **Dominica** | 1990 | | | | | | | 204 | | 204 | 2 858 |
| | 1991 | | | | | | | 204 | | 204 | 2 864 |
| | 1992 | | 136 | | 136 | 1 912 | | 235 | 157 | 78 | 1 097 |
| | 1993 | | 651 | | 651 | 9 163 | | 524 | | 524 | 7 376 |
| | 1994 | | 651 | | 651 | 9 172 | | 200 | | 200 | 2 818 |
| | 1995 | | | | | | | 60 | | 60 | 846 |
| | 1996 | | | | | | | 83 | | 83 | 1 171 |
| | 1997 | | | | | | | 1 100 | | 1 100 | 15 534 |
| **Dominican Republic** | 1970 | | 4 200 | | 4 200 | 950 | | 3 600 | | 3 600 | 814 |
| | 1975 | | 6 600 | | 6 600 | 1 307 | | 5 900 | | 5 900 | 1 169 |
| | 1980 | | 12 400 | | 12 400 | 2 177 | | 25 900 | | 25 900 | 4 546 |
| | 1985 | | 7 800 | | 7 800 | 1 223 | | 23 400 | | 23 400 | 3 670 |
| | 1990 | | 15 000 | | 15 000 | 2 110 | | 31 081 | | 31 081 | 4 371 |

Newsprint and other printing and writing paper
Papier journal et autre papier d'impression et d'écriture
Papel de periódico y otro papel de imprenta y de escribir
IV.10

| Country<br>Pays<br>País | Year<br>Année<br>Año | Newsprint / Papier journal / Papel de periódico | | | | | Other printing and writing paper / Autre papier d'impression et d'écriture / Otro papel de imprenta y de escribir | | | | |
|---|---|---|---|---|---|---|---|---|---|---|---|
| | | Production<br>Production<br>Producción | Imports<br>Importa-<br>tions<br>Importa-<br>ciones | Exports<br>Exporta-<br>tions<br>Exporta-<br>ciones | Consump-<br>tion<br>Consom-<br>mation<br>Consumo | Consump-<br>tion per<br>1,000 inh.<br>Consomma-<br>tion pour<br>1 000 hab.<br>Consumo<br>por<br>1 000 hab. | Production<br>Production<br>Producción | Imports<br>Importa-<br>tions<br>Importa-<br>ciones | Exports<br>Exporta-<br>tions<br>Exporta-<br>ciones | Consump-<br>tion<br>Consom-<br>mation<br>Consumo | Consump-<br>tion per<br>1,000 inh.<br>Consomma-<br>tion pour<br>1 000 hab.<br>Consumo<br>por<br>1 000 hab. |
| Dominican Republic (cont) | 1991 | | 13 000 | | 13 000 | 1 792 | | 31 081 | | 31 081 | 4 284 |
| | 1992 | | 16 245 | | 16 245 | 2 195 | | 18 473 | 48 | 18 425 | 2 490 |
| | 1993 | | 18 403 | | 18 403 | 2 440 | | 19 936 | 67 | 19 869 | 2 634 |
| | 1994 | | 14 254 | | 14 254 | 1 855 | | 23 543 | 67 | 23 476 | 3 055 |
| | 1995 | | 12 500 | | 12 500 | 1 598 | | 3 700 | | 3 700 | 473 |
| | 1996 | | 18 100 | | 18 100 | 2 274 | 10 000 | 11 000 | | 21 000 | 2 638 |
| | 1997 | | 27 900 | | 27 900 | 3 446 | 10 000 | 13 300 | | 23 300 | 2 877 |
| El Salvador | 1970 | | 13 000 | | 13 000 | 3 613 | | 2 100 | | 2 100 | 584 |
| | 1975 | | 10 300 | 100 | 10 200 | 2 476 | | 4 100 | 400 | 3 700 | 898 |
| | 1980 | | 15 000 | | 15 000 | 3 271 | | | | | |
| | 1985 | | 12 700 | | 12 700 | 2 663 | | 2 000 | 500 | 1 500 | 315 |
| | 1990 | | 12 000 | | 12 000 | 2 348 | | 15 000 | | 15 000 | 2 935 |
| | 1991 | | 18 100 | | 18 100 | 3 476 | | 30 300 | | 30 300 | 5 819 |
| | 1992 | | 17 835 | | 17 835 | 3 356 | | 39 452 | 56 | 39 396 | 7 413 |
| | 1993 | | 25 078 | 9 | 25 069 | 4 617 | | 16 249 | | 16 249 | 2 993 |
| | 1994 | | 22 800 | 9 | 22 791 | 4 108 | | 14 300 | | 14 300 | 2 577 |
| | 1995 | | 19 100 | 500 | 18 600 | 3 281 | | 1 700 | 123 | 1 577 | 278 |
| | 1996 | 14 000 | 19 900 | 200 | 33 700 | 5 821 | 3 000 | 1 700 | 120 | 4 577 | 791 |
| | 1997 | 14 000 | 17 000 | 100 | 30 900 | 5 228 | 3 000 | 10 500 | 1 900 | 11 600 | 1 963 |
| Greenland | 1992 | | | | | | | 234 | | 234 | 4 193 |
| | 1993 | | | | | | | 517 | | 517 | 9 263 |
| | 1994 | | | | | | | 110 | | 110 | 1 972 |
| | 1995 | | 100 | | 100 | 1 792 | | 110 | | 110 | 1 971 |
| | 1996 | | 100 | | 100 | 1 791 | | 110 | | 110 | 1 970 |
| | 1997 | | 100 | | 100 | 1 789 | | 110 | | 110 | 1 968 |
| Grenada | 1992 | | 2 | | 2 | 22 | | 50 | | 50 | 548 |
| | 1993 | | 2 | | 2 | 22 | | 80 | | 80 | 874 |
| | 1994 | | 2 | | 2 | 22 | | 69 | | 69 | 751 |
| | 1995 | | 2 | | 2 | 22 | | 69 | | 69 | 749 |
| | 1996 | | 2 | | 2 | 22 | | 69 | | 69 | 746 |
| | 1997 | | 2 | | 2 | 22 | | 69 | | 69 | 744 |
| Guadeloupe | 1985 | | | | | | | 900 | | 900 | 2 535 |
| | 1990 | | | | | | | 1 300 | | 1 300 | 3 327 |
| | 1991 | | | | | | | 600 | | 600 | 1 509 |
| | 1992 | | 4 | | 4 | 10 | | 3 253 | 2 | 3 251 | 8 037 |
| | 1993 | | 85 | | 85 | 207 | | 4 849 | | 4 849 | 11 793 |
| | 1994 | | 23 | | 23 | 55 | | 1 952 | 105 | 1 847 | 4 421 |
| | 1995 | | 7 | | 7 | 16 | | 417 | 11 | 406 | 957 |
| | 1996 | | 7 | | 7 | 16 | | 417 | 11 | 406 | 943 |
| | 1997 | | 7 | | 7 | 16 | | 417 | 11 | 406 | 929 |
| Guatemala | 1970 | | 8 300 | | 8 300 | 1 583 | | 1 100 | 4 100 | | |
| | 1975 | 600 | 7 500 | | 8 100 | 1 346 | 9 000 | 1 600 | 4 400 | 6 200 | 1 030 |
| | 1980 | | 17 000 | | 17 000 | 2 493 | 14 700 | 5 600 | 13 500 | 6 800 | 997 |
| | 1985 | 100 | 7 100 | | 7 200 | 930 | 9 000 | 17 800 | 1 800 | 25 000 | 3 231 |
| | 1990 | | 13 000 | | 13 000 | 1 486 | 10 000 | 2 000 | 1 000 | 11 000 | 1 257 |
| | 1991 | | 15 000 | | 15 000 | 1 671 | | 2 200 | 700 | 1 500 | 167 |
| | 1992 | | 18 206 | 24 | 18 182 | 1 973 | | 46 000 | 90 | 45 910 | 4 983 |
| | 1993 | | 38 000 | 9 | 37 991 | 4 016 | | 25 538 | | 25 538 | 2 700 |
| | 1994 | | 21 200 | 100 | 21 100 | 2 172 | | 18 600 | 141 | 18 459 | 1 900 |
| | 1995 | | 20 500 | 200 | 20 300 | 2 035 | 2 000 | 17 600 | 71 | 19 529 | 1 958 |
| | 1996 | | 18 000 | 100 | 17 900 | 1 747 | 2 000 | 20 000 | 200 | 21 800 | 2 128 |
| | 1997 | | 22 000 | 100 | 21 900 | 2 082 | 2 000 | 20 000 | 200 | 21 800 | 2 072 |
| Haiti | 1970 | | 700 | | 700 | 155 | | 300 | | 300 | 66 |
| | 1975 | | 800 | | 800 | 163 | | 300 | | 300 | 61 |
| | 1980 | | 300 | | 300 | 55 | | 600 | | 600 | 110 |
| | 1985 | | 913 | | 913 | 149 | | 2 530 | | 2 530 | 413 |
| | 1990 | | 468 | | 468 | 68 | | 2 005 | | 2 005 | 290 |
| | 1991 | | 468 | | 468 | 66 | | 2 005 | | 2 005 | 284 |
| | 1992 | | | | | | | 115 | | 115 | 16 |
| | 1993 | | | | | | | 3 199 | | 3 199 | 438 |
| | 1994 | | 21 | | 21 | 3 | | 2 570 | | 2 570 | 346 |
| | 1995 | | 354 | | 354 | 47 | | 867 | | 867 | 115 |
| | 1996 | | 600 | | 600 | 78 | | 1 800 | | 1 800 | 234 |
| | 1997 | | 300 | | 300 | 38 | | 3 400 | | 3 400 | 435 |

IV.10 Newsprint and other printing and writing paper
Papier journal et autre papier d'impression et d'écriture
Papel de periódico y otro papel de imprenta y de escribir

| Country / Pays / País | Year / Année / Año | Newsprint / Papier journal / Papel de periódico | | | | | Other printing and writing paper / Autre papier d'impression et d'écriture / Otro papel de imprenta y de escribir | | | | |
|---|---|---|---|---|---|---|---|---|---|---|---|
| | | Production / Producción | Imports / Importations / Importaciones | Exports / Exportations / Exportaciones | Consumption / Consommation / Consumo | Consumption per 1,000 inh. / Consommation pour 1 000 hab. / Consumo por 1 000 hab. | Production / Producción | Imports / Importations / Importaciones | Exports / Exportations / Exportaciones | Consumption / Consommation / Consumo | Consumption per 1,000 inh. / Consommation pour 1 000 hab. / Consumo por 1 000 hab. |
| Honduras | | | | | | | | | | | |
| | 1970 | | 2 700 | | 2 700 | 1 042 | | 2 500 | | 2 500 | 964 |
| | 1975 | | 2 100 | | 2 100 | 696 | | 2 500 | 200 | 2 300 | 762 |
| | 1980 | | 6 500 | | 6 500 | 1 821 | | 5 400 | | 5 400 | 1 513 |
| | 1985 | | 6 400 | | 6 400 | 1 529 | | 3 100 | | 3 100 | 740 |
| | 1990 | | 4 800 | | 4 800 | 984 | | | | | |
| | 1991 | | 6 200 | | 6 200 | 1 233 | | 24 800 | | 24 800 | 4 933 |
| | 1992 | | 3 819 | | 3 819 | 737 | | 50 309 | 278 | 50 031 | 9 659 |
| | 1993 | | 7 819 | | 7 819 | 1 466 | | 12 793 | 2 | 12 791 | 2 398 |
| | 1994 | | 8 700 | | 8 700 | 1 584 | | 7 600 | | 7 600 | 1 384 |
| | 1995 | 7 500 | 7 500 | | 15 000 | 2 653 | 8 000 | 8 300 | | 16 300 | 2 883 |
| | 1996 | 7 500 | 7 700 | | 15 200 | 2 613 | 9 000 | 8 700 | | 17 700 | 3 043 |
| | 1997 | 11 000 | 11 300 | | 22 300 | 3 729 | 11 000 | 10 700 | | 21 700 | 3 628 |
| Jamaica | | | | | | | | | | | |
| | 1970 | | 8 600 | | 8 600 | 4 601 | | 4 100 | | 4 100 | 2 194 |
| | 1975 | | 8 700 | | 8 700 | 4 322 | | 6 300 | | 6 300 | 3 130 |
| | 1980 | | 3 500 | | 3 500 | 1 641 | | 6 900 | | 6 900 | 3 235 |
| | 1985 | | 4 500 | | 4 500 | 1 959 | | 3 800 | | 3 800 | 1 654 |
| | 1990 | | 8 000 | | 8 000 | 3 377 | | 5 700 | | 5 700 | 2 406 |
| | 1991 | | 8 600 | | 8 600 | 3 604 | | 8 100 | | 8 100 | 3 394 |
| | 1992 | | 4 172 | | 4 172 | 1 734 | | 9 061 | | 9 061 | 3 765 |
| | 1993 | | 9 300 | | 9 300 | 3 830 | | 9 000 | | 9 000 | 3 706 |
| | 1994 | | 7 500 | | 7 500 | 3 060 | | 9 300 | | 9 300 | 3 795 |
| | 1995 | | 11 200 | | 11 200 | 4 529 | | 8 600 | | 8 600 | 3 478 |
| | 1996 | | 12 100 | | 12 100 | 4 850 | | 6 300 | | 6 300 | 2 525 |
| | 1997 | | 12 100 | | 12 100 | 4 808 | | 6 300 | | 6 300 | 2 503 |
| Martinique | | | | | | | | | | | |
| | 1980 | | 800 | | 800 | 2 453 | | | | | |
| | 1985 | | 1 200 | | 1 200 | 3 524 | | | | | |
| | 1990 | | 3 600 | | 3 600 | 9 992 | | | | | |
| | 1991 | | 3 600 | | 3 600 | 9 885 | | | | | |
| | 1992 | | 3 192 | 24 | 3 168 | 8 609 | | 1 386 | 8 | 1 378 | 3 745 |
| | 1993 | | 5 500 | | 5 500 | 14 799 | | 1 400 | | 1 400 | 3 767 |
| | 1994 | | 4 300 | | 4 300 | 11 459 | | 2 200 | | 2 200 | 5 863 |
| | 1995 | | 3 200 | | 3 200 | 8 447 | | 400 | 100 | 300 | 792 |
| | 1996 | | 3 200 | | 3 200 | 8 370 | | 400 | 100 | 300 | 785 |
| | 1997 | | 3 200 | | 3 200 | 8 296 | | 400 | 100 | 300 | 778 |
| Mexico | | | | | | | | | | | |
| | 1970 | 40 000 | 118 800 | | 158 800 | 3 139 | 122 000 | 236 800 | | 358 800 | 7 091 |
| | 1975 | 29 000 | 185 600 | | 214 600 | 3 631 | 256 000 | 64 000 | | 320 000 | 5 415 |
| | 1980 | 116 000 | 110 000 | | 226 000 | 3 345 | 526 000 | 65 300 | | 591 300 | 8 751 |
| | 1985 | 260 000 | 37 500 | | 297 500 | 3 942 | 456 000 | 63 600 | | 519 600 | 6 885 |
| | 1990 | 398 000 | 56 600 | | 454 600 | 5 462 | 528 000 | 40 100 | | 568 100 | 6 826 |
| | 1991 | 401 000 | 92 900 | | 493 900 | 5 824 | 532 000 | 54 900 | | 586 900 | 6 921 |
| | 1992 | 289 000 | 135 152 | 2 456 | 421 696 | 4 882 | 545 000 | 198 015 | 45 065 | 697 950 | 8 079 |
| | 1993 | 216 000 | 163 300 | 333 | 378 967 | 4 308 | 462 000 | 215 000 | 24 900 | 652 100 | 7 412 |
| | 1994 | 214 000 | 228 300 | 1 700 | 440 600 | 4 919 | 402 000 | 142 300 | 400 | 543 900 | 6 073 |
| | 1995 | 265 000 | 70 300 | 26 300 | 309 000 | 3 390 | 509 000 | 106 800 | 2 000 | 613 800 | 6 734 |
| | 1996 | 265 000 | 60 500 | 24 700 | 300 800 | 3 244 | 509 000 | 91 300 | 25 700 | 574 600 | 6 197 |
| | 1997 | 305 000 | 108 000 | 22 600 | 390 400 | 4 141 | 623 000 | 101 000 | 17 000 | 707 000 | 7 499 |
| Montserrat | | | | | | | | | | | |
| | 1992 | | | | | | | 10 | | 10 | 921 |
| | 1993 | | | | | | | 4 | | 4 | 369 |
| | 1994 | | | | | | | 3 | | 3 | 278 |
| | 1995 | | | | | | | 3 | | 3 | 279 |
| | 1996 | | | | | | | 3 | | 3 | 279 |
| | 1997 | | | | | | | 3 | | 3 | 280 |
| Netherlands Antilles | | | | | | | | | | | |
| | 1970 | | | | | | | 600 | | 600 | 3 772 |
| | 1975 | | 500 | | 500 | 3 008 | | 600 | | 600 | 3 610 |
| | 1980 | | 600 | | 600 | 3 455 | | 1 100 | | 1 100 | 6 334 |
| | 1985 | | 2 100 | | 2 100 | 11 550 | | 800 | | 800 | 4 400 |
| | 1990 | | 1 200 | | 1 200 | 6 392 | | 1 400 | | 1 400 | 7 457 |
| | 1991 | | | | | | | 1 000 | | 1 000 | 5 248 |
| | 1992 | | | | | | | 1 227 | | 1 227 | 6 323 |
| | 1993 | | | | | | | 2 175 | | 2 175 | 10 987 |
| | 1994 | | | | | | | 1 701 | 795 | 906 | 4 490 |
| | 1995 | | 1 728 | | 1 728 | 8 422 | | 241 | 24 | 217 | 1 058 |
| | 1996 | | 2 800 | | 2 800 | 13 457 | | 300 | 24 | 276 | 1 326 |
| | 1997 | | 2 800 | | 2 800 | 13 299 | | 892 | 17 | 875 | 4 156 |
| Nicaragua | | | | | | | | | | | |
| | 1970 | | 3 700 | | 3 700 | 1 743 | | 2 500 | | 2 500 | 1 178 |
| | 1975 | | 4 000 | | 4 000 | 1 601 | | 1 800 | | 1 800 | 721 |

Newsprint and other printing and writing paper
Papier journal et autre papier d'impression et d'écriture
Papel de periódico y otro papel de imprenta y de escribir

IV.10

| Country / Year | Newsprint — Papier journal — Papel de periódico | | | | | Other printing and writing paper — Autre papier d'impression et d'écriture — Otro papel de imprenta y de escribir | | | | |
|---|---|---|---|---|---|---|---|---|---|---|
| Pays / Année / País / Año | Production / Production / Producción | Imports / Importations / Importaciones | Exports / Exportations / Exportaciones | Consumption / Consommation / Consumo | Consumption per 1,000 inh. / Consommation pour 1 000 hab. / Consumo por 1 000 hab. | Production / Production / Producción | Imports / Importations / Importaciones | Exports / Exportations / Exportaciones | Consumption / Consommation / Consumo | Consumption per 1,000 inh. / Consommation pour 1 000 hab. / Consumo por 1 000 hab. |
| **Nicaragua (cont)** | | | | | | | | | | |
| 1980 | | 3 000 | | 3 000 | 1 027 | | 1 900 | | 1 900 | 650 |
| 1985 | | 5 000 | | 5 000 | 1 469 | | 2 900 | | 2 900 | 852 |
| 1990 | | 6 400 | | 6 400 | 1 672 | | 1 200 | | 1 200 | 314 |
| 1991 | | 6 000 | | 6 000 | 1 525 | | 1 200 | | 1 200 | 305 |
| 1992 | | 3 966 | | 3 966 | 979 | | 6 565 | 7 | 6 558 | 1 620 |
| 1993 | | 3 300 | | 3 300 | 791 | | 2 015 | | 2 015 | 483 |
| 1994 | | 4 000 | | 4 000 | 930 | | 2 615 | | 2 615 | 608 |
| 1995 | | 2 100 | | 2 100 | 475 | | 300 | | 300 | 68 |
| 1996 | | 3 600 | | 3 600 | 791 | | 3 400 | | 3 400 | 747 |
| 1997 | | 3 500 | | 3 500 | 748 | | 1 400 | | 1 400 | 299 |
| **Panama** | | | | | | | | | | |
| 1970 | | 5 900 | | 5 900 | 3 917 | | 5 900 | | 5 900 | 3 917 |
| 1975 | | 3 400 | | 3 400 | 1 973 | | 3 200 | | 3 200 | 1 857 |
| 1980 | | 2 600 | | 2 600 | 1 334 | 3 000 | 1 800 | | 4 800 | 2 462 |
| 1985 | | 6 300 | | 6 300 | 2 907 | | 9 000 | | 9 000 | 4 152 |
| 1990 | | 9 700 | | 9 700 | 4 046 | | 10 100 | | 10 100 | 4 213 |
| 1991 | | 7 300 | | 7 300 | 2 987 | | 9 800 | | 9 800 | 4 009 |
| 1992 | | 11 450 | | 11 450 | 4 596 | | 15 855 | 50 | 15 805 | 6 344 |
| 1993 | | 11 500 | 1 700 | 9 800 | 3 861 | | 13 100 | 100 | 13 000 | 5 122 |
| 1994 | | 11 900 | 3 800 | 8 100 | 3 134 | | 10 500 | | 10 500 | 4 062 |
| 1995 | | 10 600 | 8 400 | 2 200 | 836 | | 3 400 | 100 | 3 300 | 1 254 |
| 1996 | | 12 100 | 6 800 | 5 300 | 1 980 | | 19 500 | 800 | 18 700 | 6 986 |
| 1997 | | 14 000 | 9 000 | 5 000 | 1 837 | | 13 000 | 800 | 12 200 | 4 482 |
| **St. Kitts and Nevis** | | | | | | | | | | |
| 1992 | | 10 | | 10 | 244 | | 22 | | 22 | 536 |
| 1993 | | 15 | | 15 | 369 | | 29 | | 29 | 713 |
| 1994 | | 15 | | 15 | 372 | | 146 | | 146 | 3 619 |
| 1995 | | 15 | | 15 | 375 | | 146 | | 146 | 3 650 |
| 1996 | | 15 | | 15 | 378 | | 146 | | 146 | 3 681 |
| 1997 | | 15 | | 15 | 381 | | 146 | | 146 | 3 710 |
| **St. Lucia** | | | | | | | | | | |
| 1992 | | 26 | | 26 | 188 | | 279 | | 279 | 2 021 |
| 1993 | | 45 | | 45 | 321 | | 293 | | 293 | 2 092 |
| 1994 | | 35 | | 35 | 246 | | 1 026 | | 1 026 | 7 222 |
| 1995 | | 35 | | 35 | 243 | | 1 026 | | 1 026 | 7 120 |
| 1996 | | 35 | | 35 | 240 | | 1 026 | | 1 026 | 7 021 |
| 1997 | | 35 | | 35 | 236 | | 1 026 | | 1 026 | 6 924 |
| **St. Pierre and Miquelon** | | | | | | | | | | |
| 1992 | | | | | | | 1 087 | | 1 087 | 168 371 |
| 1993 | | | | | | | 10 | | 10 | 1 547 |
| 1994 | | | | | | | 13 | | 13 | 2 010 |
| 1995 | | | | | | | 13 | | 13 | 2 008 |
| 1996 | | | | | | | 13 | | 13 | 2 003 |
| 1997 | | | | | | | 13 | | 13 | 1 998 |
| **St. Vincent and the Grenadines** | | | | | | | | | | |
| 1985 | | | | | | | 3 700 | | 3 700 | 36 348 |
| 1990 | | | | | | | 196 | | 196 | 1 853 |
| 1991 | | | | | | | 196 | | 196 | 1 838 |
| 1992 | | 7 | | 7 | 65 | | 65 | | 65 | 605 |
| 1993 | | 36 | | 36 | 332 | | 108 | | 108 | 997 |
| 1994 | | 36 | | 36 | 330 | | 51 | | 51 | 467 |
| 1995 | | 36 | | 36 | 327 | | 25 | | 25 | 227 |
| 1996 | | 36 | | 36 | 325 | | 25 | | 25 | 226 |
| 1997 | | 15 | | 15 | 134 | | 4 | | 4 | 36 |
| **Trinidad and Tobago** | | | | | | | | | | |
| 1970 | | 5 600 | | 5 600 | 5 768 | | 2 800 | 240 | 2 560 | 2 637 |
| 1975 | | 6 300 | | 6 300 | 6 226 | | 1 900 | | 1 900 | 1 878 |
| 1980 | | 5 100 | | 5 100 | 4 715 | | 4 300 | | 4 300 | 3 975 |
| 1985 | | 11 900 | | 11 900 | 10 100 | | 8 400 | | 8 400 | 7 129 |
| 1990 | | 3 700 | | 3 700 | 3 045 | | 16 100 | | 16 100 | 13 249 |
| 1991 | | 7 000 | | 7 000 | 5 721 | | 16 100 | | 16 100 | 13 158 |
| 1992 | | 9 334 | 14 | 9 320 | 7 557 | | 7 422 | 132 | 7 290 | 5 911 |
| 1993 | | 4 451 | 2 | 4 449 | 3 577 | | 7 478 | 66 | 7 412 | 5 960 |
| 1994 | | 4 400 | 2 | 4 398 | 3 508 | | 9 200 | 50 | 9 150 | 7 299 |
| 1995 | | 9 000 | 2 | 8 998 | 7 127 | | 9 100 | 50 | 9 050 | 7 168 |
| 1996 | | 6 500 | 2 | 6 498 | 5 116 | | 10 700 | 50 | 10 650 | 8 385 |
| 1997 | | 11 900 | 2 | 11 898 | 9 319 | | 12 900 | 200 | 12 700 | 9 947 |
| **Turks and Caicos Islands** | | | | | | | | | | |
| 1992 | | | | | | | 28 | | 28 | 2 238 |
| 1994 | | | | | | | 4 | | 4 | 296 |
| 1995 | | | | | | | 4 | | 4 | 286 |

**IV.10**    Newsprint and other printing and writing paper
Papier journal et autre papier d'impression et d'écriture
Papel de periódico y otro papel de imprenta y de escribir

| Country / Pays / País | Year / Année / Año | Newsprint / Papier journal / Papel de periódico | | | | | Other printing and writing paper / Autre papier d'impression et d'écriture / Otro papel de imprenta y de escribir | | | | |
|---|---|---|---|---|---|---|---|---|---|---|---|
| | | Production / Producción | Imports / Importations / Importaciones | Exports / Exportations / Exportaciones | Consumption / Consommation / Consumo | Consumption per 1,000 inh. / Consommation pour 1 000 hab. / Consumo por 1 000 hab. | Production / Producción | Imports / Importations / Importaciones | Exports / Exportations / Exportaciones | Consumption / Consommation / Consumo | Consumption per 1,000 inh. / Consommation pour 1 000 hab. / Consumo por 1 000 hab. |
| Turks and Caicos Islands (cont) | 1996 | | | | | | | 4 | | 4 | 275 |
| | 1997 | | | | | | | 4 | | 4 | 265 |
| United States | 1970 | 3 143 000 | 6 019 300 | 130 300 | 9 032 000 | 42 987 | 9 684 000 | 259 200 | 164 900 | 9 778 300 | 46 539 |
| | 1975 | 3 348 000 | 5 305 000 | 149 800 | 8 503 200 | 38 622 | 9 708 000 | 331 400 | 360 400 | 9 679 000 | 43 962 |
| | 1980 | 4 238 000 | 6 593 600 | 158 600 | 10 673 000 | 46 323 | 13 829 000 | 848 200 | 278 900 | 14 398 300 | 62 491 |
| | 1985 | 4 923 000 | 7 685 700 | 285 200 | 12 323 500 | 50 954 | 16 468 000 | 2 072 800 | 171 700 | 18 369 100 | 75 951 |
| | 1990 | 6 001 000 | 7 529 300 | 526 600 | 13 003 700 | 51 180 | 20 092 000 | 2 032 200 | 355 000 | 21 769 200 | 85 680 |
| | 1991 | 6 206 000 | 6 796 700 | 674 000 | 12 328 700 | 48 035 | 19 872 000 | 2 662 000 | 846 000 | 21 688 000 | 84 500 |
| | 1992 | 6 424 000 | 6 659 519 | 928 492 | 12 155 027 | 46 878 | 20 281 010 | 2 879 000 | 991 925 | 22 168 085 | 85 496 |
| | 1993 | 6 419 000 | 7 062 000 | 925 297 | 12 555 703 | 47 937 | 21 511 010 | 2 891 000 | 1 017 000 | 23 385 010 | 89 283 |
| | 1994 | 6 984 000 | 7 150 000 | 862 000 | 13 272 000 | 50 176 | 25 714 000 | 3 519 000 | 1 239 000 | 27 994 000 | 105 834 |
| | 1995 | 6 351 000 | 7 083 000 | 1 013 000 | 12 421 000 | 46 517 | 23 042 000 | 3 878 000 | 1 261 000 | 25 659 000 | 96 094 |
| | 1996 | 6 303 000 | 6 304 000 | 1 013 000 | 11 594 000 | 43 030 | 22 553 000 | 4 008 000 | 1 515 000 | 25 046 000 | 92 956 |
| | 1997 | 6 544 000 | 6 502 000 | 967 000 | 12 079 000 | 44 445 | 24 328 000 | 4 768 000 | 1 512 000 | 27 584 000 | 101 497 |
| **South America** | | | | | | | | | | | |
| Argentina | 1970 | 3 200 | 274 300 | 100 | 277 400 | 11 577 | 122 700 | 4 200 | 4 200 | 122 700 | 5 121 |
| | 1975 | | 148 800 | | 148 800 | 5 712 | 94 000 | 6 200 | 1 500 | 98 700 | 3 789 |
| | 1980 | 97 000 | 174 000 | 200 | 270 800 | 9 639 | 152 000 | 38 000 | 11 000 | 179 000 | 6 372 |
| | 1985 | 201 000 | 12 500 | 10 200 | 203 300 | 6 708 | 157 000 | 10 000 | 2 300 | 164 700 | 5 435 |
| | 1990 | 208 000 | 15 000 | 55 000 | 168 000 | 5 165 | 170 000 | 16 000 | 30 000 | 156 000 | 4 796 |
| | 1991 | 198 000 | 52 000 | 27 000 | 223 000 | 6 763 | 176 000 | 16 000 | 30 000 | 162 000 | 4 913 |
| | 1992 | 206 000 | 97 076 | 1 365 | 301 711 | 9 028 | 197 000 | 105 253 | 9 392 | 292 861 | 8 763 |
| | 1993 | 129 000 | 154 100 | 300 | 282 800 | 8 350 | 209 000 | 135 500 | 8 600 | 335 900 | 9 918 |
| | 1994 | 142 000 | 117 100 | 100 | 259 000 | 7 547 | 233 000 | 162 400 | 2 900 | 392 500 | 11 437 |
| | 1995 | 176 000 | 105 300 | | 281 300 | 8 091 | 246 000 | 56 500 | 2 400 | 300 100 | 8 631 |
| | 1996 | 166 000 | 64 400 | | 230 400 | 6 542 | 228 000 | 61 500 | 30 500 | 259 000 | 7 354 |
| | 1997 | 166 000 | 138 400 | 200 | 304 200 | 8 528 | 228 000 | 71 200 | 36 500 | 262 700 | 7 365 |
| Bolivia | 1970 | | 4 700 | | 4 700 | 1 116 | | 3 900 | | 3 900 | 926 |
| | 1975 | | 4 700 | | 4 700 | 988 | | 3 900 | | 3 900 | 820 |
| | 1980 | | 6 000 | | 6 000 | 1 120 | | 6 000 | | 6 000 | 1 120 |
| | 1985 | | 3 000 | | 3 000 | 509 | | 1 500 | | 1 500 | 254 |
| | 1990 | | 7 700 | | 7 700 | 1 172 | | | | | |
| | 1991 | | 7 700 | | 7 700 | 1 144 | | | | | |
| | 1992 | | 7 628 | | 7 628 | 1 107 | | 7 514 | 29 | 7 485 | 1 086 |
| | 1993 | | 9 200 | | 9 200 | 1 303 | | 9 100 | | 9 100 | 1 288 |
| | 1994 | | 9 500 | | 9 500 | 1 313 | | 13 600 | | 13 600 | 1 879 |
| | 1995 | | 11 300 | | 11 300 | 1 524 | | 2 400 | | 2 400 | 324 |
| | 1996 | | 7 800 | | 7 800 | 1 027 | | 2 100 | | 2 100 | 277 |
| | 1997 | | 7 000 | | 7 000 | 900 | | 2 100 | | 2 100 | 270 |
| Brazil | 1970 | 103 000 | 108 800 | 200 | 211 600 | 2 204 | 254 000 | 58 000 | 900 | 311 100 | 3 240 |
| | 1975 | 125 000 | 116 000 | 300 | 240 700 | 2 225 | 416 000 | 60 000 | 6 000 | 470 000 | 4 345 |
| | 1980 | 105 000 | 167 100 | 500 | 271 600 | 2 232 | 870 000 | 68 000 | 135 000 | 803 000 | 6 600 |
| | 1985 | 208 000 | 95 400 | 4 400 | 299 000 | 2 211 | 1 146 000 | 27 000 | 239 000 | 934 000 | 6 907 |
| | 1990 | 246 000 | 123 100 | 20 200 | 348 900 | 2 358 | 1 321 000 | 68 400 | 414 000 | 975 400 | 6 593 |
| | 1991 | 253 000 | 211 000 | 12 000 | 452 000 | 3 007 | 1 348 000 | 103 000 | 504 000 | 947 000 | 6 300 |
| | 1992 | 226 000 | 105 222 | 34 352 | 296 870 | 1 945 | 1 394 000 | 55 100 | 496 500 | 952 600 | 6 241 |
| | 1993 | 268 000 | 152 000 | 39 220 | 380 780 | 2 458 | 1 670 000 | 68 100 | 602 800 | 1 135 300 | 7 329 |
| | 1994 | 263 000 | 287 600 | 16 900 | 533 700 | 3 396 | 1 858 000 | 62 700 | 581 300 | 1 339 400 | 8 524 |
| | 1995 | 282 000 | 379 500 | 17 500 | 644 000 | 4 042 | 1 791 000 | 53 700 | 555 000 | 1 289 700 | 8 094 |
| | 1996 | 277 000 | 384 000 | 20 000 | 641 000 | 3 968 | 1 807 000 | 41 700 | 500 000 | 1 348 700 | 8 349 |
| | 1997 | 265 000 | 471 000 | 13 500 | 722 500 | 4 414 | 1 996 000 | 41 000 | 561 000 | 1 476 000 | 9 016 |
| Chile | 1970 | 124 400 | | 78 300 | 46 100 | 4 855 | | 7 900 | | 7 900 | 832 |
| | 1975 | 120 000 | | 78 300 | 41 700 | 4 034 | 41 000 | 3 000 | 14 000 | 30 000 | 2 902 |
| | 1980 | 131 000 | | 63 000 | 68 000 | 6 100 | 48 000 | 13 000 | 15 000 | 46 000 | 4 127 |
| | 1985 | 172 000 | | 116 000 | 56 000 | 4 649 | 63 000 | 18 600 | 10 300 | 71 300 | 5 919 |
| | 1990 | 171 000 | | 115 000 | 56 000 | 4 275 | 60 000 | 43 000 | 3 000 | 100 000 | 7 634 |
| | 1991 | 171 000 | | 114 900 | 56 100 | 4 211 | 75 000 | 43 000 | 3 500 | 114 500 | 8 595 |
| | 1992 | 161 000 | 8 556 | 111 536 | 58 020 | 4 283 | 82 000 | 79 842 | 7 916 | 153 926 | 11 362 |
| | 1993 | 185 000 | 7 211 | 145 985 | 46 226 | 3 357 | 86 000 | 82 872 | 5 304 | 163 568 | 11 877 |
| | 1994 | 186 000 | 17 000 | 151 400 | 51 600 | 3 687 | 98 000 | 75 900 | 3 400 | 170 500 | 12 184 |
| | 1995 | 206 000 | 19 000 | 136 300 | 88 700 | 6 242 | 70 000 | 66 800 | 1 000 | 135 800 | 9 556 |
| | 1996 | 198 000 | 35 000 | 138 200 | 94 800 | 6 574 | 83 000 | 59 600 | 900 | 141 700 | 9 826 |
| | 1997 | 184 000 | 22 000 | 146 000 | 60 000 | 4 103 | 83 000 | 59 600 | 900 | 141 700 | 9 689 |
| Colombia | 1970 | | | | | | 43 800 | 2 500 | 3 400 | 42 900 | 1 902 |
| | 1975 | | | | | | 44 000 | 9 200 | 900 | 52 300 | 2 061 |

Newsprint and other printing and writing paper   IV.10
Papier journal et autre papier d'impression et d'écriture
Papel de periódico y otro papel de imprenta y de escribir

| Country / Pays / País | Year / Année / Año | Newsprint — Papier journal — Papel de periódico | | | | | Other printing and writing paper — Autre papier d'impression et d'écriture — Otro papel de imprenta y de escribir | | | | |
| | | Production / Producción | Imports / Importations / Importaciones | Exports / Exportations / Exportaciones | Consumption / Consommation / Consumo | Consumption per 1,000 inh. / Consommation pour 1 000 hab. / Consumo por 1 000 hab. | Production / Producción | Imports / Importations / Importaciones | Exports / Exportations / Exportaciones | Consumption / Consommation / Consumo | Consumption per 1,000 inh. / Consommation pour 1 000 hab. / Consumo por 1 000 hab. |
|---|---|---|---|---|---|---|---|---|---|---|---|
| Colombia (cont) | 1980 | | 71 000 | | 71 000 | 2 496 | 71 000 | 24 300 | 2 500 | 92 800 | 3 262 |
| | 1985 | | 77 500 | | 77 500 | 2 448 | 106 000 | 4 700 | 5 300 | 105 400 | 3 329 |
| | 1990 | | 75 900 | | 75 900 | 2 170 | 128 000 | 4 500 | 3 600 | 128 900 | 3 686 |
| | 1991 | | | | | | 135 000 | 22 700 | 6 000 | 151 700 | 4 254 |
| | 1992 | | | | | | 187 000 | 49 921 | 26 458 | 210 463 | 5 787 |
| | 1993 | | | | | | 184 000 | 52 664 | 10 717 | 225 947 | 6 093 |
| | 1994 | | | | | | 211 000 | 57 193 | 17 665 | 250 528 | 6 627 |
| | 1995 | 1 000 | 107 400 | 600 | 107 800 | 2 797 | 197 000 | 33 800 | 38 500 | 192 300 | 4 989 |
| | 1996 | 1 000 | 81 200 | | 82 200 | 2 092 | 205 000 | 42 000 | 41 500 | 205 500 | 5 231 |
| | 1997 | | 81 200 | | 81 200 | 2 028 | 216 000 | 52 700 | 54 500 | 214 200 | 5 349 |
| Ecuador | 1970 | | | | | | | 5 900 | | 5 900 | 988 |
| | 1975 | | | | | | 3 000 | 11 000 | | 14 000 | 2 027 |
| | 1980 | | 32 600 | | 32 600 | 4 095 | 4 200 | 19 000 | | 23 200 | 2 914 |
| | 1985 | | 39 600 | | 39 600 | 4 352 | 1 000 | 28 400 | | 29 400 | 3 231 |
| | 1990 | | 24 000 | | 24 000 | 2 338 | 8 500 | 25 000 | | 33 500 | 3 264 |
| | 1991 | | | | | | 2 300 | 6 800 | | 9 100 | 867 |
| | 1992 | | | | | | 2 900 | 42 880 | 1 608 | 44 172 | 4 113 |
| | 1993 | | | | | | 2 900 | 22 167 | 1 300 | 23 767 | 2 164 |
| | 1994 | | | | | | | 23 600 | 1 900 | 21 700 | 1 934 |
| | 1995 | | 48 200 | 100 | 48 100 | 4 197 | 2 200 | 8 000 | 400 | 9 800 | 855 |
| | 1996 | | 29 000 | 100 | 28 900 | 2 470 | 2 300 | 3 200 | 200 | 5 300 | 453 |
| | 1997 | | 29 000 | 100 | 28 900 | 2 421 | 2 300 | 6 000 | 100 | 8 200 | 687 |
| Falkland Islands (Malvinas) | 1992 | | | | | | | 22 | | 22 | 10 199 |
| | 1993 | | | | | | | 19 | | 19 | 8 756 |
| | 1994 | | | | | | | 25 | | 25 | 11 457 |
| | 1995 | | 128 | | 128 | 58 314 | | 25 | | 25 | 11 390 |
| | 1996 | | 128 | | 128 | 57 997 | | 25 | | 25 | 11 328 |
| | 1997 | | 128 | | 128 | 57 658 | | 25 | | 25 | 11 261 |
| French Guiana | 1992 | | | | | | | 733 | | 733 | 5 707 |
| | 1993 | | | | | | | 300 | | 300 | 2 233 |
| | 1994 | | | | | | | 300 | | 300 | 2 136 |
| | 1995 | | 158 | | 158 | 1 077 | | 79 | | 79 | 538 |
| | 1996 | | 158 | | 158 | 1 031 | | 79 | | 79 | 515 |
| | 1997 | | 158 | | 158 | 988 | | 79 | | 79 | 494 |
| Guyana | 1970 | | 1 200 | | 1 200 | 1 692 | | 1 200 | | 1 200 | 1 692 |
| | 1975 | | 1 400 | | 1 400 | 1 908 | | 1 400 | | 1 400 | 1 908 |
| | 1980 | | 1 500 | | 1 500 | 1 976 | | 800 | | 800 | 1 054 |
| | 1985 | | 500 | | 500 | 630 | | 1 400 | | 1 400 | 1 765 |
| | 1990 | | 500 | | 500 | 629 | | 300 | | 300 | 377 |
| | 1991 | | 500 | | 500 | 625 | | 300 | | 300 | 375 |
| | 1992 | | 300 | | 300 | 372 | | 700 | | 700 | 868 |
| | 1993 | | 700 | | 700 | 860 | | 1 000 | | 1 000 | 1 228 |
| | 1994 | | 500 | | 500 | 608 | | 800 | | 800 | 973 |
| | 1995 | | 500 | | 500 | 603 | | 800 | | 800 | 964 |
| | 1996 | | 1 100 | | 1 100 | 1 314 | | 100 | | 100 | 119 |
| | 1997 | | 1 100 | | 1 100 | 1 304 | | 100 | | 100 | 119 |
| Paraguay | 1970 | | 4 100 | | 4 100 | 1 744 | | 500 | | 500 | 213 |
| | 1975 | | 3 100 | | 3 100 | 1 166 | | 1 400 | | 1 400 | 527 |
| | 1980 | | 8 000 | | 8 000 | 2 569 | 2 000 | 3 800 | | 5 800 | 1 863 |
| | 1985 | | 8 000 | | 8 000 | 2 217 | 2 000 | 3 700 | | 5 700 | 1 580 |
| | 1990 | | 10 500 | | 10 500 | 2 489 | 2 000 | 6 900 | | 8 900 | 2 110 |
| | 1991 | | 13 600 | | 13 600 | 3 133 | 2 000 | 6 900 | | 8 900 | 2 050 |
| | 1992 | | 13 264 | | 13 264 | 2 973 | | 10 959 | 163 | 10 796 | 2 420 |
| | 1993 | | 15 440 | | 15 440 | 3 370 | | 14 947 | 43 | 14 904 | 3 253 |
| | 1994 | | 15 513 | | 15 513 | 3 298 | | 16 759 | 43 | 16 716 | 3 554 |
| | 1995 | | 15 513 | | 15 513 | 3 213 | | 9 000 | 43 | 8 957 | 1 855 |
| | 1996 | | 7 300 | | 7 300 | 1 473 | | 12 200 | 600 | 11 600 | 2 340 |
| | 1997 | | 13 800 | | 13 800 | 2 712 | | 9 600 | 200 | 9 400 | 1 847 |
| Peru | 1970 | | | | | | 22 000 | 2 700 | 2 700 | 22 000 | 1 668 |
| | 1975 | | | | | | 38 000 | 4 200 | | 42 200 | 2 783 |
| | 1980 | 30 000 | 6 500 | | 36 500 | 2 107 | 42 400 | 3 200 | 400 | 45 200 | 2 609 |
| | 1985 | | 39 000 | | 39 000 | 2 001 | 49 000 | 5 800 | 900 | 53 900 | 2 765 |
| | 1990 | | 87 600 | | 87 600 | 4 061 | 45 000 | 3 100 | 900 | 47 200 | 2 188 |
| | 1991 | | | | | | 50 000 | 3 300 | 900 | 52 400 | 2 386 |

IV.10 Newsprint and other printing and writing paper
Papier journal et autre papier d'impression et d'écriture
Papel de periódico y otro papel de imprenta y de escribir

| Country / Pays / País | Year / Année / Año | Newsprint — Papier journal — Papel de periódico | | | | | Other printing and writing paper — Autre papier d'impression et d'écriture — Otro papel de imprenta y de escribir | | | | |
|---|---|---|---|---|---|---|---|---|---|---|---|
| | | Production / Producción | Imports / Importations / Importaciones | Exports / Exportations / Exportaciones | Consumption / Consommation / Consumo | Consumption per 1,000 inh. / Consommation pour 1 000 hab. / Consumo por 1 000 hab. | Production / Producción | Imports / Importations / Importaciones | Exports / Exportations / Exportaciones | Consumption / Consommation / Consumo | Consumption per 1,000 inh. / Consommation pour 1 000 hab. / Consumo por 1 000 hab. |
| Peru (cont) | 1992 | | | | | | 12 000 | 34 317 | 26 | 46 291 | 2 071 |
| | 1993 | | | | | | 12 000 | 58 253 | 1 | 70 252 | 3 089 |
| | 1994 | | | | | | 9 000 | 55 800 | 1 | 64 799 | 2 801 |
| | 1995 | 56 900 | | | 56 900 | 2 418 | 22 000 | 21 700 | 1 | 43 699 | 1 857 |
| | 1996 | 56 900 | | | 56 900 | 2 376 | 22 000 | 21 500 | 1 | 43 499 | 1 817 |
| | 1997 | 56 900 | | | 56 900 | 2 335 | 22 000 | 21 500 | 1 | 43 499 | 1 785 |
| Suriname | 1975 | | | | | | | 2 000 | | 2 000 | 5 487 |
| | 1980 | | 600 | | 600 | 1 689 | | 2 000 | | 2 000 | 5 630 |
| | 1985 | | 1 000 | | 1 000 | 2 606 | | 1 000 | | 1 000 | 2 606 |
| | 1990 | | 1 000 | | 1 000 | 2 490 | | 1 200 | | 1 200 | 2 988 |
| | 1991 | | | | | | | 1 200 | | 1 200 | 2 973 |
| | 1992 | | | | | | | 831 | | 831 | 2 050 |
| | 1993 | | | | | | | 1 555 | 3 | 1 552 | 3 817 |
| | 1994 | | | | | | | 355 | 29 | 326 | 799 |
| | 1995 | | 300 | | 300 | 733 | | 100 | | 100 | 244 |
| | 1996 | | 700 | | 700 | 1 705 | | 200 | | 200 | 487 |
| | 1997 | | 700 | | 700 | 1 699 | | 200 | | 200 | 485 |
| Uruguay | 1970 | | 20 800 | | 20 800 | 7 406 | 14 500 | 100 | | 14 600 | 5 199 |
| | 1975 | | 10 600 | | 10 600 | 3 748 | 10 800 | 800 | 1 000 | 10 600 | 3 748 |
| | 1980 | | 15 200 | | 15 200 | 5 217 | 25 400 | 4 100 | 8 400 | 21 100 | 7 242 |
| | 1985 | | 8 900 | | 8 900 | 2 958 | 15 000 | 500 | 7 300 | 8 200 | 2 725 |
| | 1990 | | 17 400 | | 17 400 | 5 603 | 16 000 | 4 900 | 5 700 | 15 200 | 4 894 |
| | 1991 | | 12 500 | | 12 500 | 3 998 | 26 000 | 6 000 | 11 100 | 20 900 | 6 684 |
| | 1992 | | 13 430 | 300 | 13 130 | 4 170 | 26 000 | 17 173 | 8 392 | 34 781 | 11 045 |
| | 1993 | | 14 943 | | 14 943 | 4 711 | 26 000 | 10 329 | 8 275 | 28 054 | 8 845 |
| | 1994 | | 15 096 | | 15 096 | 4 725 | 26 000 | 11 108 | 8 709 | 28 399 | 8 889 |
| | 1995 | | 12 514 | 3 | 12 511 | 3 888 | 28 000 | 3 890 | 949 | 30 941 | 9 614 |
| | 1996 | | 10 300 | 3 | 10 297 | 3 176 | 28 000 | 3 400 | 5 500 | 25 900 | 7 990 |
| | 1997 | | 10 300 | 3 | 10 297 | 3 153 | 28 000 | 3 400 | 5 500 | 25 900 | 7 932 |
| Venezuela | 1970 | | | | | | 26 200 | 8 800 | | 35 000 | 3 265 |
| | 1975 | | | | | | 55 700 | 5 000 | | 60 700 | 4 767 |
| | 1980 | | 141 000 | | 141 000 | 9 343 | 84 200 | 18 400 | | 102 600 | 6 799 |
| | 1985 | | 136 000 | | 136 000 | 7 936 | 103 000 | 12 700 | | 115 700 | 6 751 |
| | 1990 | | 103 500 | | 103 500 | 5 307 | 118 000 | 3 700 | | 121 700 | 6 240 |
| | 1991 | | | | | | 126 000 | 9 500 | | 135 500 | 6 783 |
| | 1992 | | | | | | 128 000 | 26 594 | 7 763 | 146 831 | 7 181 |
| | 1993 | | | | | | 118 000 | 32 744 | 9 898 | 140 846 | 6 735 |
| | 1994 | | | | | | 153 000 | 26 900 | 32 700 | 147 200 | 6 886 |
| | 1995 | | 95 400 | 100 | 95 300 | 4 363 | 145 000 | 14 900 | 7 600 | 152 300 | 6 972 |
| | 1996 | | 70 800 | 34 | 70 766 | 3 172 | 145 000 | 12 000 | 8 900 | 148 100 | 6 638 |
| | 1997 | | 70 800 | 34 | 70 766 | 3 107 | 117 000 | 37 000 | 30 000 | 124 000 | 5 444 |
| **Asia** | | | | | | | | | | | |
| Afghanistan | 1970 | | | | | | | 400 | | 400 | 29 |
| | 1975 | | 1 200 | | 1 200 | 78 | | 1 300 | | 1 300 | 85 |
| | 1980 | | 100 | | 100 | 6 | | 500 | | 500 | 31 |
| | 1985 | | | | | | | 900 | | 900 | 62 |
| | 1990 | | | | | | | 600 | | 600 | 41 |
| | 1991 | | | | | | | 600 | | 600 | 39 |
| | 1992 | | | | | | | 700 | | 700 | 42 |
| | 1993 | | 17 | | 17 | 1 | | 505 | | 505 | 29 |
| | 1994 | | 17 | | 17 | 1 | | 66 | 50 | 16 | 1 |
| | 1995 | | 17 | 16 | 1 | | | 20 | 2 | 18 | 1 |
| | 1996 | | 264 | 16 | 248 | 12 | | 17 | 2 | 15 | 1 |
| | 1997 | | 90 | 16 | 74 | 4 | | 35 | 2 | 33 | 2 |
| Armenia | 1993 | | | | | | | 3 | | 3 | 1 |
| | 1994 | | | | | | | 7 | | 7 | 2 |
| | 1995 | | | | | | | 1 | | 1 | |
| | 1996 | | | | | | | 11 | | 11 | 3 |
| | 1997 | | 660 | | 660 | 186 | | 639 | 21 | 618 | 174 |
| Azerbaijan | 1993 | | | | | | | 33 | | 33 | 4 |
| | 1994 | | | | | | | 100 | | 100 | 13 |
| | 1995 | | 236 | | 236 | 31 | | 46 | 22 | 24 | 3 |
| | 1996 | | 1 500 | | 1 500 | 197 | | 1 100 | | 1 100 | 145 |
| | 1997 | | 2 100 | | 2 100 | 275 | | 1 000 | | 1 000 | 131 |

Newsprint and other printing and writing paper  IV.10
Papier journal et autre papier d'impression et d'écriture
Papel de periódico y otro papel de imprenta y de escribir

| Country / Pays / País | Year / Année / Año | Newsprint / Papier journal / Papel de periódico | | | | | Other printing and writing paper / Autre papier d'impression et d'écriture / Otro papel de imprenta y de escribir | | | | |
|---|---|---|---|---|---|---|---|---|---|---|---|
| | | Production / Producción | Imports / Importations / Importaciones | Exports / Exportations / Exportaciones | Consumption / Consommation / Consumo | Consumption per 1,000 inh. / Consommation pour 1 000 hab. / Consumo por 1 000 hab. | Production / Producción | Imports / Importations / Importaciones | Exports / Exportations / Exportaciones | Consumption / Consommation / Consumo | Consumption per 1,000 inh. / Consommation pour 1 000 hab. / Consumo por 1 000 hab. |
| **Bahrain** | 1970 | | | | | | | 400 | | 400 | 1 822 |
| | 1975 | | | | | | | 1 500 | | 1 500 | 5 516 |
| | 1980 | | | | | | | 1 700 | | 1 700 | 4 899 |
| | 1985 | | | | | | | 2 100 | | 2 100 | 5 079 |
| | 1990 | | | | | | | 5 535 | | 5 535 | 11 297 |
| | 1991 | | | | | | | 4 900 | | 4 900 | 9 715 |
| | 1992 | | 26 | | 26 | 50 | | 2 721 | 1 | 2 720 | 5 248 |
| | 1993 | | 2 663 | | 2 663 | 5 009 | | 4 776 | | 4 776 | 8 983 |
| | 1994 | | 2 106 | | 2 106 | 3 866 | | 3 952 | 62 | 3 890 | 7 141 |
| | 1995 | | 3 327 | | 3 327 | 5 967 | | 984 | 62 | 922 | 1 654 |
| | 1996 | | 5 500 | | 5 500 | 9 646 | | 2 000 | | 2 000 | 3 508 |
| | 1997 | | 5 500 | | 5 500 | 9 441 | | 4 400 | | 4 400 | 7 553 |
| **Bangladesh** | 1975 | 20 000 | | 5 300 | 14 700 | 192 | 24 000 | | 400 | 23 600 | 308 |
| | 1980 | 37 000 | | 18 000 | 19 000 | 215 | 27 000 | | 1 000 | 26 000 | 295 |
| | 1985 | 47 000 | | 18 100 | 28 900 | 291 | 38 000 | 1 800 | | 39 800 | 401 |
| | 1990 | 46 000 | | | 46 000 | 420 | 38 000 | 8 500 | | 46 500 | 425 |
| | 1991 | 50 000 | | | 50 000 | 449 | 34 000 | 14 300 | | 48 300 | 434 |
| | 1992 | 50 000 | 180 | 4 503 | 45 677 | 404 | 34 000 | 16 293 | 16 | 50 277 | 444 |
| | 1993 | 46 000 | 213 | | 46 213 | 402 | 45 000 | 14 502 | 13 | 59 489 | 518 |
| | 1994 | 48 000 | 2 | | 48 002 | 411 | 50 000 | 37 158 | 1 | 87 157 | 747 |
| | 1995 | 40 000 | 19 680 | | 59 680 | 503 | 40 000 | 17 795 | 1 | 57 794 | 487 |
| | 1996 | 30 000 | 29 400 | | 59 400 | 493 | 30 000 | 24 600 | 1 | 54 599 | 453 |
| | 1997 | 28 000 | 50 000 | | 78 000 | 636 | 28 000 | 25 000 | 1 | 52 999 | 432 |
| **Bhutan** | 1993 | | | | | | | 100 | 36 | 64 | 36 |
| | 1994 | | | | | | | 487 | 10 | 477 | 263 |
| | 1995 | | 43 | | 43 | 23 | | | | | |
| | 1996 | | 43 | | 43 | 23 | | 23 | | 23 | 12 |
| | 1997 | | 43 | | 43 | 22 | | 3 | 82 | | |
| **Brunei Darussalam** | 1970 | | 100 | | 100 | 771 | | 200 | | 200 | 1 542 |
| | 1975 | | 200 | | 200 | 1 244 | | 200 | | 200 | 1 244 |
| | 1980 | | 200 | | 200 | 1 036 | | 500 | | 500 | 2 590 |
| | 1985 | | 400 | | 400 | 1 794 | | 1 200 | | 1 200 | 5 381 |
| | 1990 | | 500 | | 500 | 1 946 | | 1 500 | | 1 500 | 5 837 |
| | 1991 | | 500 | | 500 | 1 891 | | 1 500 | | 1 500 | 5 674 |
| | 1992 | | 233 | | 233 | 857 | | 989 | 17 | 972 | 3 575 |
| | 1993 | | 20 | 19 | 1 | 4 | | 196 | 8 | 188 | 673 |
| | 1994 | | 2 | | 2 | 7 | | 1 760 | 109 | 1 651 | 5 753 |
| | 1995 | | 6 | | 6 | 20 | | 640 | 35 | 605 | 2 055 |
| | 1996 | | | | | | | 600 | | 600 | 1 990 |
| | 1997 | | | | | | | 600 | | 600 | 1 946 |
| **Cambodia** | 1992 | | | | | | | 331 | | 331 | 36 |
| | 1993 | | | | | | | 500 | | 500 | 53 |
| | 1994 | | 600 | | 600 | 62 | | 400 | | 400 | 41 |
| | 1995 | | 500 | | 500 | 50 | | 200 | | 200 | 20 |
| | 1996 | | 200 | | 200 | 20 | | 500 | | 500 | 49 |
| | 1997 | | 200 | | 200 | 19 | | 500 | | 500 | 48 |
| **China** | 1970 | 386 000 | 13 600 | 13 000 | 386 600 | 465 | 778 000 | 2 100 | 13 300 | 766 800 | 923 |
| | 1975 | 340 000 | 51 300 | 1 900 | 389 400 | 420 | 1 260 000 | 3 600 | 21 300 | 1 242 300 | 1 339 |
| | 1980 | 373 000 | 155 500 | 700 | 527 800 | 528 | 1 769 000 | 6 700 | 34 200 | 1 741 500 | 1 743 |
| | 1985 | 452 000 | 332 200 | | 784 200 | 733 | 3 076 000 | 78 300 | 55 300 | 3 099 000 | 2 896 |
| | 1990 | 475 000 | 243 100 | 1 100 | 717 000 | 621 | 4 984 000 | 167 500 | 93 300 | 5 058 200 | 4 378 |
| | 1991 | 486 000 | 234 500 | 3 100 | 717 400 | 613 | 5 199 000 | 300 200 | 189 100 | 5 310 100 | 4 538 |
| | 1992 | 590 000 | 243 130 | 5 246 | 827 884 | 699 | 5 531 000 | 525 436 | 195 625 | 5 860 811 | 4 952 |
| | 1993 | 629 000 | 371 528 | 5 263 | 995 265 | 832 | 3 009 000 | 531 448 | 217 219 | 3 323 229 | 2 778 |
| | 1994 | 721 000 | 388 824 | 6 733 | 1 103 091 | 913 | 4 528 000 | 863 139 | 283 266 | 5 107 873 | 4 227 |
| | 1995 | 865 000 | 377 200 | 105 400 | 1 136 800 | 931 | 4 677 000 | 661 300 | 154 500 | 5 183 800 | 4 247 |
| | 1996 | 995 000 | 708 100 | 23 200 | 1 679 900 | 1 363 | 6 291 000 | 1 183 100 | 136 200 | 7 337 900 | 5 954 |
| | 1997 | 825 000 | 886 100 | 20 800 | 1 690 300 | 1 359 | 6 711 000 | 1 415 900 | 155 000 | 7 971 900 | 6 407 |
| **China, Hong Kong SAR** | 1970 | | 48 200 | 3 200 | 45 000 | 11 417 | | 53 700 | 4 300 | 49 400 | 12 533 |
| | 1975 | | 54 700 | 1 400 | 53 300 | 12 125 | | 51 100 | 4 300 | 46 800 | 10 647 |
| | 1980 | | 90 000 | 14 200 | 75 800 | 15 044 | | 117 400 | 5 000 | 112 400 | 22 308 |
| | 1985 | | 116 200 | 2 300 | 113 900 | 20 875 | | 95 400 | 1 600 | 93 800 | 17 191 |
| | 1990 | | 203 400 | 5 600 | 197 800 | 34 674 | | 380 500 | 41 600 | 338 900 | 59 409 |
| | 1991 | | 174 200 | 6 800 | 167 400 | 28 951 | | 452 900 | 75 400 | 377 500 | 65 286 |
| | 1992 | | 223 825 | 4 788 | 219 037 | 37 290 | | 526 658 | 4 195 | 522 463 | 88 946 |
| | 1993 | | 214 670 | 2 005 | 212 665 | 35 568 | | 550 626 | 6 177 | 544 449 | 91 058 |

IV.10  Newsprint and other printing and writing paper
Papier journal et autre papier d'impression et d'écriture
Papel de periódico y otro papel de imprenta y de escribir

| Country / Pays / País | Year / Année / Año | Newsprint — Papier journal — Papel de periódico | | | | | Other printing and writing paper — Autre papier d'impression et d'écriture — Otro papel de imprenta y de escribir | | | | |
|---|---|---|---|---|---|---|---|---|---|---|---|
| | | Production / Producción | Imports / Importations / Importaciones | Exports / Exportations / Exportaciones | Consumption / Consommation / Consumo | Consumption per 1,000 inh. / Consommation pour 1 000 hab. / Consumo por 1 000 hab. | Production / Producción | Imports / Importations / Importaciones | Exports / Exportations / Exportaciones | Consumption / Consommation / Consumo | Consumption per 1,000 inh. / Consommation pour 1 000 hab. / Consumo por 1 000 hab. |
| China, Hong Kong SAR (cont) | 1994 | | 257 600 | 8 600 | 249 000 | 40 844 | | 684 651 | 147 100 | 537 551 | 88 175 |
| | 1995 | | 233 400 | 14 900 | 218 500 | 35 106 | | 689 300 | 186 700 | 502 600 | 80 753 |
| | 1996 | | 270 200 | 15 600 | 254 600 | 40 016 | | 752 100 | 215 000 | 537 100 | 84 416 |
| | 1997 | | 424 000 | 16 200 | 407 800 | 62 637 | | 801 900 | 231 000 | 570 900 | 87 689 |
| Cyprus | 1970 | | 1 700 | | 1 700 | 2 764 | | 4 100 | | 4 100 | 6 667 |
| | 1975 | | 1 300 | | 1 300 | 2 134 | | 1 900 | | 1 900 | 3 119 |
| | 1980 | | 2 600 | | 2 600 | 4 256 | | 3 300 | | 3 300 | 5 401 |
| | 1985 | | 3 200 | | 3 200 | 4 944 | | 4 700 | | 4 700 | 7 261 |
| | 1990 | | 3 100 | | 3 100 | 4 555 | | 5 800 | | 5 800 | 8 522 |
| | 1991 | | 4 000 | | 4 000 | 5 783 | | 15 900 | | 15 900 | 22 987 |
| | 1992 | | 5 912 | | 5 912 | 8 390 | | 17 474 | 619 | 16 855 | 23 920 |
| | 1993 | | 5 435 | | 5 435 | 7 565 | | 15 112 | 852 | 14 260 | 19 847 |
| | 1994 | | 6 800 | | 6 800 | 9 291 | | 16 000 | 100 | 15 900 | 21 724 |
| | 1995 | | 6 000 | | 6 000 | 8 065 | | 19 300 | | 19 300 | 25 941 |
| | 1996 | | 7 900 | | 7 900 | 10 472 | | 9 200 | | 9 200 | 12 195 |
| | 1997 | | 6 000 | | 6 000 | 7 860 | | 16 400 | 1 000 | 15 400 | 20 174 |
| East Timor | 1996 | | | | | | 29 | | | 29 | 35 |
| | 1997 | | | | | | 29 | | | 29 | 34 |
| Georgia | 1993 | | | | | | | 1 | 2 | | |
| | 1994 | | | | | | | 105 | | 105 | 20 |
| | 1995 | | | | | | | 15 | | 15 | 3 |
| | 1997 | | 1 372 | | 1 372 | 268 | | 1 488 | 30 | 1 458 | 285 |
| India | 1970 | 37 300 | 144 200 | | 181 500 | 327 | 444 700 | 2 800 | 14 200 | 433 300 | 781 |
| | 1975 | 52 000 | 100 800 | | 152 800 | 246 | 504 000 | 2 700 | 100 | 506 600 | 816 |
| | 1980 | 40 000 | 270 000 | | 310 000 | 450 | 514 000 | 12 200 | 1 500 | 524 700 | 762 |
| | 1985 | 200 000 | 188 000 | | 388 000 | 505 | 680 000 | 45 000 | 200 | 724 800 | 944 |
| | 1990 | 310 000 | 85 000 | | 395 000 | 464 | 900 000 | 22 400 | 7 600 | 914 800 | 1 075 |
| | 1991 | 300 000 | 239 700 | | 539 700 | 622 | 990 000 | 6 000 | 6 900 | 989 100 | 1 140 |
| | 1992 | 320 000 | 246 701 | 680 | 566 021 | 640 | 1 060 000 | 15 145 | 19 095 | 1 056 050 | 1 194 |
| | 1993 | 320 000 | 175 673 | 740 | 494 933 | 549 | 1 085 000 | 96 259 | 841 | 1 180 418 | 1 311 |
| | 1994 | 350 000 | 159 124 | 87 | 509 037 | 555 | 1 112 000 | 65 880 | 12 994 | 1 164 886 | 1 270 |
| | 1995 | 400 000 | 170 300 | 2 200 | 568 100 | 608 | 1 150 000 | 21 900 | 4 000 | 1 167 900 | 1 251 |
| | 1996 | 400 000 | 494 100 | 2 700 | 891 400 | 938 | 1 150 000 | 92 800 | 500 | 1 242 300 | 1 308 |
| | 1997 | 400 000 | 475 000 | 2 700 | 872 300 | 903 | 1 150 000 | 116 600 | 10 800 | 1 255 800 | 1 300 |
| Indonesia | 1970 | 3 000 | 40 600 | | 43 600 | 362 | 6 000 | 44 000 | | 50 000 | 416 |
| | 1975 | | 46 700 | | 46 700 | 344 | 45 000 | 8 000 | | 53 000 | 391 |
| | 1980 | | 66 000 | | 66 000 | 437 | 121 000 | 34 700 | 7 000 | 148 700 | 985 |
| | 1985 | 63 000 | 95 400 | 1 200 | 157 200 | 939 | 201 000 | 10 500 | 28 900 | 182 600 | 1 091 |
| | 1990 | 157 000 | 13 800 | 600 | 170 200 | 931 | 504 000 | 19 100 | 81 000 | 442 100 | 2 418 |
| | 1991 | 151 000 | 22 600 | 6 300 | 167 300 | 901 | 599 000 | 19 500 | 166 400 | 452 100 | 2 433 |
| | 1992 | 169 000 | 21 965 | 79 300 | 111 665 | 592 | 735 000 | 46 326 | 202 815 | 578 511 | 3 065 |
| | 1993 | 195 000 | 8 347 | 102 626 | 100 721 | 526 | 844 000 | 50 309 | 418 254 | 476 055 | 2 484 |
| | 1994 | 239 000 | 4 200 | 67 100 | 176 100 | 905 | 992 000 | 68 016 | 395 396 | 664 620 | 3 416 |
| | 1995 | 243 000 | 4 000 | 58 000 | 189 000 | 957 | 1 061 000 | 26 400 | 442 000 | 645 400 | 3 268 |
| | 1996 | 267 000 | 37 500 | 58 000 | 246 300 | 1 229 | 1 236 000 | 37 000 | 578 000 | 695 000 | 3 468 |
| | 1997 | 422 000 | 37 500 | 58 200 | 401 300 | 1 973 | 1 587 000 | 37 000 | 578 000 | 1 046 000 | 5 143 |
| Iran, Islamic Republic of | 1970 | | 10 900 | | 10 900 | 383 | 12 000 | 99 800 | | 111 800 | 3 933 |
| | 1975 | | 32 800 | | 32 800 | 984 | 36 000 | 33 800 | | 69 800 | 2 093 |
| | 1980 | | 14 000 | | 14 000 | 357 | 45 000 | 32 000 | | 77 000 | 1 962 |
| | 1985 | | 18 000 | | 18 000 | 378 | 45 000 | 55 400 | | 100 400 | 2 108 |
| | 1990 | | 36 000 | | 36 000 | 639 | 72 000 | 219 000 | | 291 000 | 5 168 |
| | 1991 | | 40 000 | | 40 000 | 693 | 75 000 | 134 000 | | 209 000 | 3 622 |
| | 1992 | | 38 700 | | 38 700 | 656 | 60 000 | 116 000 | 10 | 175 990 | 2 985 |
| | 1993 | | 11 880 | | 11 880 | 198 | 65 000 | 66 887 | 42 | 131 845 | 2 194 |
| | 1994 | | 47 900 | | 47 900 | 783 | 85 000 | 111 300 | 45 | 196 255 | 3 206 |
| | 1995 | | 53 000 | | 53 000 | 850 | 85 000 | 125 000 | 45 | 209 955 | 3 369 |
| | 1996 | | 60 000 | | 60 000 | 945 | 85 000 | 140 000 | | 225 000 | 3 545 |
| | 1997 | | 50 520 | | 50 520 | 782 | 85 000 | 116 664 | 4 | 201 660 | 3 120 |
| Iraq | 1970 | | 3 100 | | 3 100 | 331 | | 11 100 | | 11 100 | 1 186 |
| | 1975 | | 4 900 | | 4 900 | 445 | 8 000 | 5 600 | | 13 600 | 1 234 |
| | 1980 | | 14 000 | | 14 000 | 1 076 | 9 000 | 1 500 | | 10 500 | 807 |
| | 1985 | | 20 000 | | 20 000 | 1 306 | 9 000 | 27 000 | | 36 000 | 2 350 |
| | 1990 | | 34 000 | | 34 000 | 1 881 | 16 000 | 27 000 | | 43 000 | 2 379 |
| | 1991 | | 34 000 | | 34 000 | 1 837 | 5 000 | 27 000 | | 32 000 | 1 728 |

Newsprint and other printing and writing paper
Papier journal et autre papier d'impression et d'écriture
Papel de periódico y otro papel de imprenta y de escribir

IV.10

| Country / Pays / País | Year / Année / Año | Newsprint / Papier journal / Papel de periódico | | | | | Other printing and writing paper / Autre papier d'impression et d'écriture / Otro papel de imprenta y de escribir | | | | |
|---|---|---|---|---|---|---|---|---|---|---|---|
| | | Production / Production / Producción | Imports / Importations / Importaciones | Exports / Exportations / Exportaciones | Consumption / Consommation / Consumo | Consumption per 1,000 inh. / Consommation pour 1 000 hab. / Consumo por 1 000 hab. | Production / Production / Producción | Imports / Importations / Importaciones | Exports / Exportations / Exportaciones | Consumption / Consommation / Consumo | Consumption per 1,000 inh. / Consommation pour 1 000 hab. / Consumo por 1 000 hab. |
| Iraq (cont) | 1993 | | | | | | 5 000 | 79 | | 5 079 | 264 |
| | 1994 | | | | | | 7 000 | 79 | | 7 079 | 360 |
| | 1995 | | | | | | 7 000 | 79 | | 7 079 | 352 |
| | 1996 | | | | | | 7 000 | 9 | | 7 009 | 340 |
| | 1997 | | | | | | 7 000 | 95 | | 7 095 | 335 |
| Israel | 1970 | 9 400 | 24 600 | | 34 000 | 11 432 | 31 800 | 5 100 | 1 500 | 35 400 | 11 903 |
| | 1975 | 7 000 | 30 700 | | 37 700 | 10 912 | 47 000 | 2 400 | 1 400 | 48 000 | 13 893 |
| | 1980 | 4 000 | 34 100 | | 38 100 | 9 823 | 41 000 | 10 000 | 2 300 | 48 700 | 12 556 |
| | 1985 | 1 000 | 48 700 | | 49 700 | 11 742 | 53 000 | 10 900 | 300 | 63 600 | 15 026 |
| | 1990 | 1 000 | 78 000 | | 79 000 | 16 953 | 61 000 | 32 000 | 2 000 | 91 000 | 19 528 |
| | 1991 | | 78 000 | | 78 000 | 16 198 | 69 000 | 56 600 | 4 500 | 121 100 | 25 148 |
| | 1992 | | 107 738 | | 107 738 | 21 555 | 69 000 | 73 200 | 4 822 | 137 378 | 27 486 |
| | 1993 | | 105 421 | | 105 421 | 20 291 | 61 000 | 79 426 | 1 386 | 139 040 | 26 762 |
| | 1994 | | 114 045 | | 114 045 | 21 162 | 62 000 | 86 160 | 939 | 147 221 | 27 318 |
| | 1995 | | 108 000 | 2 | 107 998 | 19 402 | 95 000 | 75 000 | 1 700 | 168 300 | 30 236 |
| | 1996 | | 128 400 | 2 | 128 398 | 22 439 | 95 000 | 54 100 | 1 600 | 147 500 | 25 777 |
| | 1997 | | 133 000 | 2 | 132 998 | 22 696 | 95 000 | 64 000 | 1 900 | 157 100 | 26 809 |
| Japan | 1970 | 1 917 000 | 88 000 | 32 000 | 1 973 000 | 18 911 | 2 410 000 | 2 000 | 191 000 | 2 221 000 | 21 288 |
| | 1975 | 2 160 000 | 29 500 | 107 300 | 2 082 200 | 18 670 | 2 772 000 | 24 500 | 194 400 | 2 602 100 | 23 332 |
| | 1980 | 2 674 000 | 126 900 | 97 500 | 2 703 400 | 23 144 | 4 137 000 | 26 300 | 247 000 | 3 916 300 | 33 528 |
| | 1985 | 2 592 000 | 330 400 | 81 000 | 2 841 400 | 23 514 | 4 746 000 | 86 000 | 320 200 | 4 511 800 | 37 338 |
| | 1990 | 3 479 000 | 434 900 | 125 500 | 3 788 400 | 30 666 | 9 250 000 | 111 400 | 254 300 | 9 107 100 | 73 719 |
| | 1991 | 3 515 000 | 461 600 | 155 400 | 3 821 200 | 30 822 | 9 727 000 | 108 800 | 299 800 | 9 536 000 | 76 917 |
| | 1992 | 3 255 000 | 544 053 | 92 153 | 3 706 900 | 29 800 | 9 610 000 | 74 000 | 243 800 | 9 440 200 | 75 890 |
| | 1993 | 2 917 000 | 550 053 | 59 297 | 3 407 756 | 27 310 | 9 543 000 | 118 000 | 184 000 | 9 477 000 | 75 948 |
| | 1994 | 2 972 000 | 536 300 | 33 600 | 3 474 700 | 27 766 | 9 805 000 | 116 800 | 194 500 | 9 727 300 | 77 730 |
| | 1995 | 3 098 000 | 580 100 | 100 500 | 3 577 600 | 28 513 | 10 565 000 | 167 700 | 195 100 | 10 537 600 | 83 984 |
| | 1996 | 3 140 000 | 637 900 | 31 100 | 3 746 800 | 29 791 | 10 812 000 | 179 000 | 140 000 | 10 851 000 | 86 277 |
| | 1997 | 3 192 000 | 628 500 | 29 000 | 3 791 500 | 30 082 | 11 112 000 | 151 000 | 195 200 | 11 067 800 | 87 813 |
| Jordan | 1970 | | 600 | | 600 | 261 | | 500 | | 500 | 217 |
| | 1975 | | 700 | | 700 | 269 | | 2 000 | | 2 000 | 769 |
| | 1980 | | 2 600 | | 2 600 | 890 | | 7 100 | | 7 100 | 2 429 |
| | 1985 | | 8 400 | | 8 400 | 2 037 | | 7 700 | | 7 700 | 1 868 |
| | 1990 | | 5 305 | | 5 305 | 1 148 | | 19 825 | | 19 825 | 4 292 |
| | 1991 | | 5 305 | | 5 305 | 1 106 | | 19 825 | | 19 825 | 4 133 |
| | 1992 | | 8 230 | | 8 230 | 1 641 | | 38 219 | 804 | 37 415 | 7 459 |
| | 1993 | | 8 887 | | 8 887 | 1 689 | | 53 446 | 4 110 | 49 336 | 9 377 |
| | 1994 | | 14 000 | | 14 000 | 2 542 | | 41 200 | 3 300 | 37 900 | 6 883 |
| | 1995 | | 10 700 | | 10 700 | 1 866 | | 29 700 | 400 | 29 300 | 5 110 |
| | 1996 | | 10 900 | | 10 900 | 1 836 | | 33 700 | 400 | 33 300 | 5 608 |
| | 1997 | | 11 400 | | 11 400 | 1 861 | | 24 900 | 400 | 24 500 | 4 000 |
| Kazakstan | 1993 | | | | | | | 189 | | 189 | 11 |
| | 1994 | | | | | | | 534 | | 534 | 32 |
| | 1995 | | | | | | | 400 | | 400 | 24 |
| | 1996 | | 16 000 | | 16 000 | 973 | | 11 700 | | 11 700 | 712 |
| | 1997 | | 11 000 | | 11 000 | 672 | | 8 400 | | 8 400 | 513 |
| Korea, Democratic People's Rep. | 1970 | | 1 300 | | 1 300 | 91 | | 2 100 | | 2 100 | 147 |
| | 1975 | | 1 300 | | 1 300 | 80 | | 2 100 | | 2 100 | 129 |
| | 1980 | | 1 300 | | 1 300 | 74 | | 2 100 | | 2 100 | 119 |
| | 1985 | | 3 200 | | 3 200 | 169 | | 3 500 | | 3 500 | 185 |
| | 1990 | | 200 | | 200 | 10 | | 1 500 | | 1 500 | 73 |
| | 1991 | | 200 | | 200 | 10 | | 1 500 | | 1 500 | 72 |
| | 1992 | | 650 | | 650 | 31 | | 5 233 | 725 | 4 508 | 213 |
| | 1993 | | 1 101 | | 1 101 | 51 | | 3 835 | 2 007 | 1 828 | 85 |
| | 1994 | | 2 966 | 4 | 2 962 | 135 | | 6 978 | 481 | 6 497 | 297 |
| | 1995 | | 1 002 | | 1 002 | 45 | | 417 | 201 | 216 | 10 |
| | 1996 | | 1 002 | | 1 002 | 44 | | 900 | 100 | 800 | 35 |
| | 1997 | | 804 | | 804 | 35 | | 2 178 | 71 | 2 107 | 92 |
| Korea, Republic of | 1970 | 101 700 | 6 600 | | 108 300 | 3 393 | 22 300 | 400 | | 22 700 | 711 |
| | 1975 | 155 000 | 4 000 | | 159 000 | 4 507 | 132 000 | 100 | 10 900 | 121 200 | 3 435 |
| | 1980 | 249 000 | 22 000 | 22 000 | 249 000 | 6 531 | 293 000 | 400 | 50 500 | 242 900 | 6 371 |
| | 1985 | 238 000 | 7 200 | 7 200 | 238 000 | 5 833 | 483 000 | 1 400 | 43 800 | 440 600 | 10 797 |
| | 1990 | 522 000 | 40 300 | 40 300 | 522 000 | 12 177 | 919 000 | 34 900 | 75 900 | 878 000 | 20 481 |
| | 1991 | 563 000 | 120 300 | | 683 300 | 15 788 | 919 000 | 78 200 | 68 900 | 928 300 | 21 448 |
| | 1992 | 613 000 | 200 278 | 65 | 813 213 | 18 609 | 1 040 000 | 51 000 | 104 000 | 987 000 | 22 586 |
| | 1993 | 743 000 | 149 121 | 16 000 | 876 121 | 19 856 | 1 116 000 | 34 000 | 171 000 | 979 000 | 22 188 |

IV.10  Newsprint and other printing and writing paper
Papier journal et autre papier d'impression et d'écriture
Papel de periódico y otro papel de imprenta y de escribir

| Country Pays País | Year Année Año | Newsprint Papier journal Papel de periódico | | | | | Other printing and writing paper Autre papier d'impression et d'écriture Otro papel de imprenta y de escribir | | | | |
|---|---|---|---|---|---|---|---|---|---|---|---|
| | | Production Production Producción | Imports Importa- tions Importa- ciones | Exports Exporta- tions Exporta- ciones | Consump- tion Consom- mation Consumo | Consump- tion per 1,000 inh. Consomma- tion pour 1 000 hab. Consumo por 1 000 hab. | Production Production Producción | Imports Importa- tions Importa- ciones | Exports Exporta- tions Exporta- ciones | Consump- tion Consom- mation Consumo | Consump- tion per 1,000 inh. Consomma- tion pour 1 000 hab. Consumo por 1 000 hab. |
| Korea, Republic of (cont) | 1994 | 874 000 | 135 400 | 29 000 | 980 400 | 22 011 | 1 350 000 | 69 900 | 308 100 | 1 111 800 | 24 961 |
| | 1995 | 948 000 | 177 000 | 11 600 | 1 113 400 | 24 770 | 1 439 000 | 123 700 | 370 800 | 1 191 900 | 26 517 |
| | 1996 | 1 305 000 | 83 300 | 61 000 | 1 327 300 | 29 271 | 1 640 000 | 158 100 | 470 400 | 1 327 700 | 29 280 |
| | 1997 | 1 592 000 | 14 100 | 279 200 | 1 326 900 | 29 015 | 1 813 000 | 112 000 | 666 000 | 1 259 000 | 27 530 |
| Kuwait | 1970 | | | | | | | 6 700 | 300 | 6 400 | 8 599 |
| | 1975 | | 4 800 | | 4 800 | 4 769 | | 12 000 | 1 200 | 10 800 | 10 730 |
| | 1980 | | 19 000 | | 19 000 | 13 819 | | 26 500 | 3 800 | 22 700 | 16 510 |
| | 1985 | | 18 000 | | 18 000 | 10 464 | | 16 000 | 1 200 | 14 800 | 8 604 |
| | 1990 | | 2 014 | | 2 014 | 940 | | 18 623 | 11 | 18 612 | 8 685 |
| | 1991 | | 2 014 | | 2 014 | 962 | | 18 623 | 11 | 18 612 | 8 887 |
| | 1992 | | 6 250 | | 6 250 | 3 139 | | 33 428 | 487 | 32 941 | 16 546 |
| | 1993 | | 17 593 | | 17 593 | 9 446 | | 22 715 | | 22 715 | 12 196 |
| | 1994 | | 20 773 | | 20 773 | 11 858 | | 27 255 | | 27 255 | 15 558 |
| | 1995 | | 6 982 | | 6 982 | 4 133 | | 4 408 | | 4 408 | 2 609 |
| | 1996 | | 14 900 | | 14 900 | 8 836 | | 9 800 | | 9 800 | 5 812 |
| | 1997 | | 14 900 | | 14 900 | 8 602 | | 9 800 | | 9 800 | 5 658 |
| Kyrgyzstan | 1993 | | | | | | | 154 | 3 | 151 | 33 |
| | 1994 | | | | | | | 23 | | 23 | 5 |
| | 1995 | | | | | | | 23 | | 23 | 5 |
| | 1996 | | 3 179 | 171 | 3 008 | 654 | | 226 | 67 | 159 | 35 |
| | 1997 | | 3 179 | 171 | 3 008 | 651 | | 226 | 67 | 159 | 34 |
| Lao People's Democratic Republic | 1970 | | 300 | | 300 | 111 | | 400 | | 400 | 147 |
| | 1975 | | 200 | | 200 | 66 | | 500 | | 500 | 165 |
| | 1980 | | 200 | | 200 | 62 | | 500 | | 500 | 156 |
| | 1992 | | 36 | | 36 | 8 | | 116 | | 116 | 26 |
| | 1993 | | 100 | | 100 | 22 | | 200 | | 200 | 44 |
| | 1994 | | 100 | | 100 | 22 | | 200 | | 200 | 43 |
| | 1995 | | 100 | | 100 | 21 | | 200 | | 200 | 42 |
| | 1996 | | 100 | | 100 | 20 | | 200 | | 200 | 41 |
| | 1997 | | 100 | | 100 | 20 | | 500 | | 500 | 99 |
| Lebanon | 1970 | | 5 100 | | 5 100 | 2 066 | | 23 500 | | 23 500 | 9 518 |
| | 1975 | | 6 300 | | 6 300 | 2 277 | | 25 400 | | 25 400 | 9 178 |
| | 1980 | | 7 000 | | 7 000 | 2 622 | | 33 200 | | 33 200 | 12 438 |
| | 1985 | | 4 700 | | 4 700 | 1 762 | | 20 900 | | 20 900 | 7 835 |
| | 1990 | | 3 068 | | 3 068 | 1 201 | | 23 843 | | 23 843 | 9 331 |
| | 1991 | | 3 068 | | 3 068 | 1 175 | | 23 843 | | 23 843 | 9 134 |
| | 1992 | | 4 444 | 21 | 4 423 | 1 639 | | 21 677 | 561 | 21 116 | 7 824 |
| | 1993 | | 4 300 | | 4 300 | 1 532 | | 44 000 | 700 | 43 300 | 15 426 |
| | 1994 | | 7 100 | | 7 100 | 2 436 | | 42 300 | 100 | 42 200 | 14 476 |
| | 1995 | | 5 300 | | 5 300 | 1 762 | | 7 100 | 100 | 7 000 | 2 327 |
| | 1996 | | 7 200 | 100 | 7 100 | 2 303 | | 42 000 | 800 | 41 200 | 13 362 |
| | 1997 | | 10 900 | 100 | 10 800 | 3 436 | | 46 800 | 200 | 46 600 | 14 827 |
| Macau | 1970 | | 3 700 | | 3 700 | 14 571 | | 2 500 | | 2 500 | 9 845 |
| | 1975 | | 2 800 | | 2 800 | 11 068 | | 1 900 | | 1 900 | 7 511 |
| | 1980 | | 6 200 | | 6 200 | 24 600 | | | | | |
| | 1985 | | | | | | | 4 900 | | 4 900 | 16 004 |
| | 1990 | | 300 | | 300 | 806 | | 5 400 | | 5 400 | 14 510 |
| | 1991 | | 1 100 | | 1 100 | 2 860 | | 5 100 | | 5 100 | 13 259 |
| | 1992 | | 2 932 | 4 | 2 928 | 7 383 | | 3 938 | 315 | 3 623 | 9 136 |
| | 1993 | | 2 961 | | 2 961 | 7 258 | | 3 536 | 300 | 3 236 | 7 932 |
| | 1994 | | 4 200 | | 4 200 | 10 024 | | 4 300 | 500 | 3 800 | 9 069 |
| | 1995 | | 4 200 | | 4 200 | 9 776 | | 300 | | 300 | 698 |
| | 1996 | | 1 900 | | 1 900 | 4 318 | | 300 | 300 | | |
| | 1997 | | 4 076 | 6 | 4 070 | 9 047 | | 4 139 | 808 | 3 331 | 7 404 |
| Malaysia | 1970 | | 38 400 | 200 | 38 200 | 3 520 | | 20 500 | 600 | 19 900 | 1 834 |
| | 1975 | | | 200 | | | 1 000 | 31 100 | 500 | 31 600 | 2 578 |
| | 1980 | | 66 000 | 100 | 65 900 | 4 788 | 1 000 | 61 700 | 100 | 62 600 | 4 548 |
| | 1985 | | 100 000 | | 100 000 | 6 379 | 3 000 | 70 000 | | 73 000 | 4 656 |
| | 1990 | | 154 000 | | 154 000 | 8 630 | 130 000 | 157 719 | 88 604 | 199 115 | 11 158 |
| | 1991 | | 191 400 | | 191 400 | 10 461 | 131 000 | 177 600 | 58 900 | 249 700 | 13 647 |
| | 1992 | | 226 863 | 3 877 | 222 986 | 11 891 | 201 000 | 212 782 | 89 824 | 323 958 | 17 276 |
| | 1993 | | 172 700 | | 172 700 | 8 991 | 201 000 | 156 800 | 20 700 | 337 100 | 17 550 |
| | 1994 | 2 000 | 211 700 | | 213 700 | 10 869 | 159 000 | 252 800 | 53 400 | 358 400 | 18 229 |
| | 1995 | 2 000 | 296 800 | 2 800 | 296 000 | 11 720 | 162 000 | 82 800 | 3 500 | 241 300 | 12 000 |
| | 1996 | 2 000 | 237 900 | 700 | 239 200 | 11 640 | 145 000 | 281 000 | 57 400 | 368 600 | 17 937 |
| | 1997 | 3 000 | 299 000 | 1 200 | 300 800 | 14 335 | 126 000 | 206 100 | 53 200 | 278 900 | 13 292 |

Newsprint and other printing and writing paper IV.10
Papier journal et autre papier d'impression et d'écriture
Papel de periódico y otro papel de imprenta y de escribir

| Country / Pays / País | Year / Année / Año | Newsprint / Papier journal / Papel de periódico | | | | | Other printing and writing paper / Autre papier d'impression et d'écriture / Otro papel de imprenta y de escribir | | | | |
|---|---|---|---|---|---|---|---|---|---|---|---|
| | | Production / Production / Producción | Imports / Importations / Importaciones | Exports / Exportations / Exportaciones | Consumption / Consommation / Consumo | Consumption per 1,000 inh. / Consommation pour 1 000 hab. / Consumo por 1 000 hab. | Production / Production / Producción | Imports / Importations / Importaciones | Exports / Exportations / Exportaciones | Consumption / Consommation / Consumo | Consumption per 1,000 inh. / Consommation pour 1 000 hab. / Consumo por 1 000 hab. |
| Maldives | 1990 | | 200 | | 200 | 927 | | 200 | | 200 | 927 |
| | 1991 | | 200 | | 200 | 900 | | 200 | | 200 | 900 |
| | 1992 | | 96 | | 96 | 420 | | 100 | | 100 | 437 |
| | 1993 | | | | | | | 2 300 | 3 | 2 297 | 9 757 |
| | 1994 | | 114 | | 114 | 471 | | 1 200 | 1 | 1 199 | 4 951 |
| | 1995 | | 114 | | 114 | 458 | | 900 | 1 | 899 | 3 610 |
| | 1996 | | 114 | | 114 | 445 | | 900 | 1 | 899 | 3 510 |
| | 1997 | | 114 | | 114 | 433 | | 900 | 1 | 899 | 3 413 |
| Mongolia | 1970 | | 2 400 | | 2 400 | 1 911 | | | | | |
| | 1975 | | 2 600 | | 2 600 | 1 796 | | 1 700 | | 1 700 | 1 175 |
| | 1980 | | 2 300 | | 2 300 | 1 383 | | 1 900 | | 1 900 | 1 142 |
| | 1985 | | 3 800 | | 3 800 | 1 991 | | 3 100 | | 3 100 | 1 624 |
| | 1990 | | 397 | | 397 | 179 | | 544 | | 544 | 245 |
| | 1991 | | 397 | | 397 | 175 | | 544 | | 544 | 240 |
| | 1992 | | 505 | | 505 | 218 | | 450 | 11 | 439 | 189 |
| | 1993 | | 275 | | 275 | 116 | | 59 | 5 | 54 | 23 |
| | 1994 | | 114 | | 114 | 47 | | 342 | 5 | 337 | 140 |
| | 1995 | | 324 | | 324 | 132 | | 77 | 5 | 72 | 29 |
| | 1996 | | 1 200 | | 1 200 | 481 | | 100 | 5 | 95 | 38 |
| | 1997 | | 411 | | 411 | 162 | | 400 | 5 | 395 | 156 |
| Myanmar | 1970 | | 15 900 | | 15 900 | 587 | 400 | 11 700 | | 12 100 | 446 |
| | 1975 | | 6 500 | | 6 500 | 214 | 7 000 | 7 400 | | 14 400 | 473 |
| | 1980 | | 4 000 | | 4 000 | 118 | 7 000 | 8 000 | | 15 000 | 444 |
| | 1985 | | 5 300 | | 5 300 | 141 | 10 000 | 5 300 | | 15 300 | 408 |
| | 1990 | | 3 300 | | 3 300 | 81 | 5 000 | 1 600 | | 6 600 | 163 |
| | 1991 | | 3 300 | | 3 300 | 80 | 5 000 | 1 600 | | 6 600 | 161 |
| | 1992 | | 8 700 | | 8 700 | 210 | 5 000 | 1 300 | | 6 300 | 152 |
| | 1993 | | 1 700 | | 1 700 | 41 | 8 000 | 1 500 | | 9 500 | 227 |
| | 1994 | | 400 | | 400 | 9 | 8 000 | 8 200 | | 16 200 | 382 |
| | 1995 | | 8 100 | | 8 100 | 189 | 8 000 | 3 700 | | 11 700 | 273 |
| | 1996 | | 7 300 | | 7 300 | 168 | 8 000 | 3 700 | | 11 700 | 270 |
| | 1997 | | 9 600 | | 9 600 | 218 | 11 000 | 5 400 | | 16 400 | 373 |
| Nepal | 1985 | | 1 200 | | 1 200 | 73 | | | | | |
| | 1992 | | 629 | 36 | 593 | 30 | | 4 481 | 115 | 4 366 | 221 |
| | 1993 | | | | | | | 59 | | 59 | 3 |
| | 1994 | | | | | | | 69 | | 69 | 3 |
| | 1995 | | | | | | | 1 429 | 61 | 1 368 | 64 |
| | 1996 | | | | | | | 7 | | 7 | |
| | 1997 | | 1 372 | | 1 372 | 61 | | 975 | 739 | 236 | 11 |
| Oman | 1985 | | 700 | | 700 | 491 | | 5 900 | | 5 900 | 4 141 |
| | 1990 | | 1 200 | | 1 200 | 672 | | 6 200 | | 6 200 | 3 474 |
| | 1991 | | 1 200 | | 1 200 | 646 | | 6 200 | | 6 200 | 3 336 |
| | 1992 | | 411 | | 411 | 213 | | 8 257 | 25 | 8 232 | 4 260 |
| | 1993 | | 1 000 | | 1 000 | 498 | | 7 900 | 100 | 7 800 | 3 888 |
| | 1994 | | 1 000 | | 1 000 | 481 | | 12 600 | 100 | 12 500 | 6 008 |
| | 1995 | | 1 100 | | 1 100 | 510 | | 1 100 | 100 | 1 000 | 464 |
| | 1996 | | 1 200 | | 1 200 | 538 | | 800 | 100 | 700 | 314 |
| | 1997 | | 1 000 | | 1 000 | 434 | | 3 971 | 100 | 3 871 | 1 679 |
| Pakistan | 1970 | | 500 | | 500 | 8 | 6 300 | 7 000 | 400 | 12 900 | 196 |
| | 1975 | | 6 700 | | 6 700 | 90 | 17 000 | 45 000 | | 62 000 | 830 |
| | 1980 | | 33 100 | | 33 100 | 388 | 28 000 | 23 200 | | 51 200 | 600 |
| | 1985 | | 40 400 | | 40 400 | 399 | 34 000 | 63 500 | | 97 500 | 963 |
| | 1990 | | 53 000 | | 53 000 | 445 | 55 000 | 45 200 | | 100 200 | 841 |
| | 1991 | | 59 000 | | 59 000 | 481 | 62 000 | 39 000 | | 101 000 | 824 |
| | 1992 | | 75 950 | | 75 950 | 603 | 55 000 | 63 064 | 47 | 118 017 | 937 |
| | 1993 | | 60 000 | | 60 000 | 464 | 52 000 | 30 000 | | 82 000 | 635 |
| | 1994 | | 129 000 | | 129 000 | 973 | 62 000 | 56 000 | | 118 000 | 890 |
| | 1995 | | 85 000 | | 85 000 | 624 | 99 000 | 50 000 | | 149 000 | 1 094 |
| | 1996 | | 61 500 | | 61 500 | 439 | 110 000 | 33 200 | | 143 200 | 1 022 |
| | 1997 | | 48 500 | | 48 500 | 337 | 120 000 | 33 900 | | 153 900 | 1 068 |
| Philippines | 1970 | 30 000 | 45 500 | | 75 500 | 2 011 | 30 000 | 10 700 | | 40 700 | 1 084 |
| | 1975 | 68 000 | 800 | | 68 800 | 1 600 | 38 000 | 11 600 | | 49 500 | 1 151 |
| | 1980 | 80 000 | 20 000 | | 100 000 | 2 070 | 58 000 | 12 000 | 200 | 69 800 | 1 445 |
| | 1985 | 56 000 | 2 000 | | 58 000 | 1 061 | 31 000 | 8 200 | | 39 200 | 717 |
| | 1990 | 52 000 | 200 | | 52 200 | 860 | 94 000 | 11 400 | | 105 400 | 1 737 |
| | 1991 | 100 000 | 100 | | 100 100 | 1 612 | 95 000 | 36 000 | | 131 000 | 2 109 |

**IV.10**   Newsprint and other printing and writing paper
Papier journal et autre papier d'impression et d'écriture
Papel de periódico y otro papel de imprenta y de escribir

| Country / Pays / País | Year / Année / Año | Newsprint / Papier journal / Papel de periódico | | | | | Other printing and writing paper / Autre papier d'impression et d'écriture / Otro papel de imprenta y de escribir | | | | |
|---|---|---|---|---|---|---|---|---|---|---|---|
| | | Production / Production / Producción | Imports / Importations / Importaciones | Exports / Exportations / Exportaciones | Consumption / Consommation / Consumo | Consumption per 1,000 inh. / Consommation pour 1 000 hab. / Consumo por 1 000 hab. | Production / Production / Producción | Imports / Importations / Importaciones | Exports / Exportations / Exportaciones | Consumption / Consommation / Consumo | Consumption per 1,000 inh. / Consommation pour 1 000 hab. / Consumo por 1 000 hab. |
| **Philippines (cont)** | 1992 | 125 000 | 2 290 | 1 128 | 126 162 | 1 983 | 144 000 | 48 857 | 366 | 192 491 | 3 026 |
| | 1993 | 110 000 | 16 800 | 238 | 126 562 | 1 941 | 103 000 | 71 000 | 100 | 173 900 | 2 668 |
| | 1994 | 110 000 | 34 800 | 500 | 144 300 | 2 161 | 103 000 | 82 100 | 400 | 184 700 | 2 766 |
| | 1995 | 138 000 | 3 100 | 9 800 | 131 300 | 1 921 | 154 000 | 72 900 | 500 | 226 400 | 3 312 |
| | 1996 | 138 000 | 11 100 | 14 600 | 134 500 | 1 924 | 154 000 | 84 100 | 100 | 238 000 | 3 405 |
| | 1997 | 138 000 | 23 600 | 43 000 | 118 600 | 1 660 | 154 000 | 84 100 | 100 | 238 000 | 3 332 |
| **Qatar** | 1970 | | | | | | | 600 | | 600 | 5 389 |
| | 1975 | | | | | | | 1 400 | | 1 400 | 8 179 |
| | 1980 | | | | | | | 3 400 | | 3 400 | 14 831 |
| | 1985 | | | | | | | 3 500 | | 3 500 | 9 784 |
| | 1990 | | | | | | | 3 970 | | 3 970 | 8 180 |
| | 1991 | | | | | | | 3 970 | | 3 970 | 7 899 |
| | 1992 | | 93 | | 93 | 180 | | 1 776 | | 1 776 | 3 439 |
| | 1993 | | 24 | | 24 | 45 | | 2 813 | 4 | 2 809 | 5 323 |
| | 1994 | | 53 | | 53 | 99 | | 1 932 | 12 | 1 920 | 3 570 |
| | 1995 | | 306 | | 306 | 558 | | 895 | 12 | 883 | 1 611 |
| | 1996 | | 900 | | 900 | 1 612 | | 800 | 12 | 788 | 1 411 |
| | 1997 | | 570 | | 570 | 1 002 | | 2 040 | 12 | 2 028 | 3 566 |
| **Saudi Arabia** | 1970 | | 500 | | 500 | 87 | | 6 700 | | 6 700 | 1 166 |
| | 1975 | | 2 300 | | 2 300 | 317 | | 12 200 | | 12 200 | 1 682 |
| | 1980 | | 13 000 | | 13 000 | 1 354 | | 45 200 | | 45 200 | 4 706 |
| | 1985 | | 28 000 | | 28 000 | 2 214 | | 51 200 | | 51 200 | 4 048 |
| | 1990 | | 7 000 | | 7 000 | 436 | | 77 279 | | 77 279 | 4 816 |
| | 1991 | | 7 000 | | 7 000 | 423 | | 77 279 | | 77 279 | 4 671 |
| | 1992 | | 10 943 | 3 | 10 940 | 645 | | 69 014 | 143 | 68 871 | 4 060 |
| | 1993 | | 29 566 | | 29 566 | 1 704 | | 106 761 | 277 | 106 484 | 6 137 |
| | 1994 | | 26 069 | 150 | 25 919 | 1 459 | | 79 347 | 1 300 | 78 047 | 4 393 |
| | 1995 | | 25 200 | 400 | 24 800 | 1 359 | | 60 000 | 800 | 59 200 | 3 243 |
| | 1996 | | 42 200 | 200 | 42 000 | 2 231 | | 32 500 | 18 | 32 482 | 1 725 |
| | 1997 | | 36 300 | 400 | 35 900 | 1 843 | | 84 000 | 18 | 83 982 | 4 311 |
| **Singapore** | 1970 | | 24 500 | 900 | 23 600 | 11 376 | | 23 600 | 3 300 | 20 300 | 9 785 |
| | 1975 | | 30 300 | 2 100 | 28 200 | 12 464 | | 28 900 | 9 600 | 19 300 | 8 530 |
| | 1980 | | 60 000 | 4 300 | 55 700 | 23 069 | | 71 100 | 17 900 | 53 200 | 22 034 |
| | 1985 | | 69 500 | 12 600 | 56 900 | 21 007 | | 121 500 | 24 600 | 96 900 | 35 775 |
| | 1990 | | 106 600 | 8 900 | 97 700 | 32 390 | | 193 300 | 30 000 | 163 300 | 54 138 |
| | 1991 | | 122 000 | 6 800 | 115 200 | 37 415 | | 199 000 | 29 000 | 170 000 | 55 213 |
| | 1992 | | 114 881 | 10 824 | 104 057 | 33 123 | | 223 689 | 41 104 | 182 585 | 58 119 |
| | 1993 | | 120 950 | 205 | 120 745 | 37 694 | | 219 127 | 11 014 | 208 113 | 64 968 |
| | 1994 | | 157 825 | 9 975 | 147 850 | 45 307 | | 317 222 | 79 828 | 237 394 | 72 747 |
| | 1995 | | 156 600 | 12 300 | 144 300 | 43 455 | | 128 600 | 38 800 | 89 800 | 27 043 |
| | 1996 | | 168 200 | 10 500 | 157 700 | 46 723 | | 104 400 | 32 400 | 72 000 | 21 332 |
| | 1997 | | 170 000 | 10 500 | 159 500 | 46 544 | | 251 900 | 32 400 | 219 500 | 64 053 |
| **Sri Lanka** | 1970 | | 18 300 | | 18 300 | 1 462 | 8 900 | 4 300 | | 13 200 | 1 055 |
| | 1975 | | 6 500 | | 6 500 | 478 | 9 000 | 6 200 | | 15 200 | 1 117 |
| | 1980 | | 8 000 | | 8 000 | 540 | 12 500 | 15 600 | | 28 100 | 1 896 |
| | 1985 | | 17 200 | | 17 200 | 1 072 | 14 000 | 6 000 | | 20 000 | 1 246 |
| | 1990 | | 22 700 | | 22 700 | 1 332 | 11 700 | 28 400 | | 40 100 | 2 353 |
| | 1991 | | 11 500 | | 11 500 | 668 | 12 300 | 28 400 | | 40 700 | 2 363 |
| | 1992 | | 19 124 | 2 | 19 122 | 1 099 | 10 700 | 38 814 | 26 | 49 488 | 2 844 |
| | 1993 | | 8 300 | | 8 300 | 472 | 15 000 | 17 706 | | 32 706 | 1 861 |
| | 1994 | | 25 548 | | 25 548 | 1 440 | 15 000 | 47 879 | 48 | 62 831 | 3 540 |
| | 1995 | | 26 200 | | 26 200 | 1 462 | 13 000 | 17 300 | 48 | 30 252 | 1 688 |
| | 1996 | | 28 700 | | 28 700 | 1 586 | 11 000 | 17 300 | | 28 300 | 1 564 |
| | 1997 | | 22 517 | | 22 517 | 1 232 | 11 000 | 17 442 | | 28 442 | 1 556 |
| **Syrian Arab Republic** | 1970 | | 1 500 | | 1 500 | 240 | | 7 200 | | 7 200 | 1 151 |
| | 1975 | | 900 | | 900 | 121 | | 12 000 | | 12 000 | 1 613 |
| | 1980 | | 3 700 | | 3 700 | 425 | | 30 000 | | 30 000 | 3 447 |
| | 1985 | | 5 600 | | 5 600 | 539 | | 24 500 | | 24 500 | 2 357 |
| | 1990 | | 7 064 | | 7 064 | 570 | | 16 678 | | 16 678 | 1 347 |
| | 1991 | | 7 064 | | 7 064 | 554 | | 16 678 | | 16 678 | 1 307 |
| | 1992 | | 3 232 | | 3 232 | 246 | | 23 235 | 3 | 23 232 | 1 770 |
| | 1993 | | 5 785 | | 5 785 | 429 | | 21 062 | 51 | 21 011 | 1 559 |
| | 1994 | | 2 588 | | 2 588 | 187 | | 33 146 | 20 | 33 126 | 2 394 |
| | 1995 | | 5 500 | | 5 500 | 387 | | 7 800 | 20 | 7 780 | 548 |
| | 1996 | | 1 700 | | 1 700 | 117 | | 12 900 | 20 | 12 880 | 884 |
| | 1997 | | 7 873 | | 7 873 | 527 | | 36 730 | 20 | 36 710 | 2 456 |

Newsprint and other printing and writing paper IV.10
Papier journal et autre papier d'impression et d'écriture
Papel de periódico y otro papel de imprenta y de escribir

| Country / Pays / País | Year / Année / Año | Newsprint / Papier journal / Papel de periódico Production / Producción | Imports / Importations / Importaciones | Exports / Exportations / Exportaciones | Consumption / Consommation / Consumo | Consumption per 1,000 inh. / Consommation pour 1 000 hab. / Consumo por 1 000 hab. | Other printing and writing paper / Autre papier d'impression et d'écriture / Otro papel de imprenta y de escribir Production / Producción | Imports / Importations / Importaciones | Exports / Exportations / Exportaciones | Consumption / Consommation / Consumo | Consumption per 1,000 inh. / Consommation pour 1 000 hab. / Consumo por 1 000 hab. |
|---|---|---|---|---|---|---|---|---|---|---|---|
| Tajikistan | 1992 | | | | | | 15 | 3 | | 12 | 2 |
| | 1993 | | | | | | 15 | 3 | | 12 | 2 |
| | 1994 | | | | | | 15 | 3 | | 12 | 2 |
| | 1995 | | | | | | 15 | 3 | | 12 | 2 |
| | 1996 | | | | | | 2 | 3 | | | |
| | 1997 | | | | | | 2 | 3 | | | |
| Thailand | 1970 | | 36 300 | | 36 300 | 1 016 | 32 000 | 12 500 | 300 | 44 200 | 1 237 |
| | 1975 | | 63 400 | | 63 400 | 1 533 | 51 000 | 2 100 | 1 800 | 51 300 | 1 240 |
| | 1980 | | 91 600 | | 91 600 | 1 961 | 73 000 | 8 800 | 300 | 81 500 | 1 745 |
| | 1985 | | 137 800 | | 137 800 | 2 694 | 103 000 | 21 500 | | 124 500 | 2 434 |
| | 1990 | | 194 900 | | 194 900 | 3 506 | 190 000 | 23 200 | 1 800 | 211 400 | 3 802 |
| | 1991 | | 238 000 | | 238 000 | 4 227 | 186 000 | 27 000 | 1 300 | 211 700 | 3 760 |
| | 1992 | | 238 809 | 296 | 238 513 | 4 189 | 224 000 | 71 869 | 2 687 | 293 182 | 5 150 |
| | 1993 | | 289 785 | 618 | 289 167 | 5 028 | 256 000 | 55 861 | 2 747 | 309 114 | 5 375 |
| | 1994 | 39 000 | 298 200 | 4 900 | 332 300 | 5 724 | 299 000 | 64 200 | 17 700 | 345 500 | 5 951 |
| | 1995 | 116 000 | 252 200 | 23 100 | 345 100 | 5 888 | 381 000 | 68 800 | 31 100 | 418 700 | 7 144 |
| | 1996 | 125 000 | 205 500 | 13 600 | 316 900 | 5 356 | 401 000 | 75 100 | 46 200 | 429 900 | 7 265 |
| | 1997 | 118 000 | 171 500 | 3 400 | 286 100 | 4 789 | 529 000 | 53 900 | 61 200 | 521 700 | 8 733 |
| Turkey | 1970 | 10 700 | 15 400 | | 26 100 | 739 | 42 400 | 4 300 | | 46 700 | 1 322 |
| | 1975 | | | | | | 72 000 | 2 400 | | 74 400 | 1 859 |
| | 1980 | 86 000 | 71 400 | | 157 400 | 3 542 | 69 000 | 2 800 | | 71 800 | 1 616 |
| | 1985 | 145 000 | 17 000 | | 162 000 | 3 218 | 91 000 | 21 300 | | 112 300 | 2 231 |
| | 1990 | 151 000 | 80 900 | | 231 900 | 4 134 | 139 000 | 65 400 | | 204 400 | 3 644 |
| | 1991 | 93 000 | 58 000 | | 151 000 | 2 641 | 125 000 | 65 400 | | 190 400 | 3 331 |
| | 1992 | 134 600 | 124 512 | 74 | 259 038 | 4 451 | 127 000 | 100 304 | 9 324 | 217 980 | 3 745 |
| | 1993 | 94 000 | 256 340 | 100 | 350 240 | 5 914 | 111 000 | 196 865 | 5 398 | 302 467 | 5 107 |
| | 1994 | 110 000 | 124 700 | 200 | 234 500 | 3 893 | 164 000 | 25 000 | 20 400 | 168 600 | 2 799 |
| | 1995 | 151 000 | 183 000 | 19 000 | 315 000 | 5 141 | 197 000 | 25 000 | 13 000 | 209 000 | 3 411 |
| | 1996 | 78 000 | 255 000 | 400 | 332 600 | 5 336 | 191 000 | 26 000 | 2 800 | 214 200 | 3 436 |
| | 1997 | 60 000 | 229 000 | 400 | 288 600 | 4 552 | 135 000 | 20 000 | 2 800 | 152 200 | 2 401 |
| Turkmenistan | 1992 | | | | | | 20 | | | 20 | 5 |
| | 1993 | | | | | | 92 | | | 92 | 23 |
| | 1994 | | | | | | 26 | | | 26 | 7 |
| | 1995 | | | | | | 26 | | | 26 | 6 |
| | 1996 | | | | | | 26 | | | 26 | 6 |
| | 1997 | | 79 | | 79 | 19 | 199 | | | 199 | 47 |
| United Arab Emirates | 1992 | | 7 266 | 128 | 7 138 | 3 493 | | 27 780 | 2 568 | 25 212 | 12 336 |
| | 1993 | | 15 900 | 300 | 15 600 | 7 422 | | 52 900 | 2 200 | 50 700 | 24 122 |
| | 1994 | | 21 000 | 200 | 20 800 | 9 642 | | 64 200 | 200 | 64 000 | 29 668 |
| | 1995 | | 21 000 | 200 | 20 800 | 9 413 | | 64 200 | 200 | 64 000 | 28 963 |
| | 1996 | | 13 400 | 200 | 13 200 | 5 842 | | 30 000 | 14 | 29 986 | 13 270 |
| | 1997 | | 13 400 | 200 | 13 200 | 5 721 | | 30 000 | 14 | 29 986 | 12 996 |
| Uzbekistan | 1993 | | | | | | | 2 786 | | 2 786 | 128 |
| | 1994 | | | | | | | 5 483 | | 5 483 | 248 |
| | 1995 | | 2 | | 2 | | | 268 | | 268 | 12 |
| | 1996 | | 400 | | 400 | 18 | | 1 000 | | 1 000 | 44 |
| | 1997 | | 400 | | 400 | 17 | | 1 000 | | 1 000 | 43 |
| Viet Nam | 1970 | | 21 700 | | 21 700 | 508 | 19 000 | 100 | | 19 100 | 447 |
| | 1975 | | 2 000 | | 2 000 | 42 | 31 000 | | | 31 000 | 645 |
| | 1980 | | 2 500 | | 2 500 | 47 | 23 000 | | | 23 000 | 428 |
| | 1985 | 5 000 | 5 000 | | 10 000 | 167 | 38 000 | | | 38 000 | 634 |
| | 1990 | 9 000 | | | 9 000 | 135 | 26 000 | | 9 300 | 16 700 | 250 |
| | 1991 | 11 500 | | | 11 500 | 169 | 58 000 | | 2 100 | 55 900 | 820 |
| | 1992 | 10 200 | 3 635 | 918 | 12 917 | 186 | 63 000 | 6 648 | 201 | 69 447 | 998 |
| | 1993 | 13 000 | 1 057 | 1 556 | 12 501 | 176 | 67 000 | 15 515 | | 82 515 | 1 161 |
| | 1994 | 16 000 | 2 755 | 1 556 | 17 199 | 237 | 48 000 | 24 241 | 1 519 | 70 722 | 975 |
| | 1995 | 18 000 | 3 398 | 392 | 21 006 | 284 | 55 000 | 16 435 | 115 | 71 320 | 966 |
| | 1996 | 18 000 | 11 600 | 200 | 29 400 | 391 | 55 000 | 22 400 | 500 | 76 900 | 1 023 |
| | 1997 | 18 000 | 3 360 | 200 | 21 160 | 277 | 55 000 | 15 109 | 545 | 69 564 | 911 |
| Yemen | 1970 | | | | | | 400 | | | 400 | 63 |
| | 1975 | | 100 | | 100 | 14 | 1 800 | | | 1 800 | 257 |
| | 1980 | | 500 | | 500 | 61 | 1 000 | | | 1 000 | 122 |
| | 1985 | | 300 | | 300 | 31 | 300 | | | 300 | 31 |
| | 1990 | | 300 | | 300 | 26 | 300 | | | 300 | 26 |

IV.10  Newsprint and other printing and writing paper
Papier journal et autre papier d'impression et d'écriture
Papel de periódico y otro papel de imprenta y de escribir

| Country / Pays / País | Year / Année / Año | Newsprint — Papier journal — Papel de periódico | | | | | Other printing and writing paper — Autre papier d'impression et d'écriture — Otro papel de imprenta y de escribir | | | | |
|---|---|---|---|---|---|---|---|---|---|---|---|
| | | Production / Producción | Imports / Importations / Importaciones | Exports / Exportations / Exportaciones | Consumption / Consommation / Consumo | Consumption per 1,000 inh. / Consommation pour 1 000 hab. / Consumo por 1 000 hab. | Production / Producción | Imports / Importations / Importaciones | Exports / Exportations / Exportaciones | Consumption / Consommation / Consumo | Consumption per 1,000 inh. / Consommation pour 1 000 hab. / Consumo por 1 000 hab. |
| Yemen (cont) | 1991 | | 300 | | 300 | 25 | | 300 | | 300 | 25 |
| | 1992 | | 226 | | 226 | 18 | | 10 428 | | 10 428 | 811 |
| | 1993 | | 900 | | 900 | 66 | | 13 416 | | 13 416 | 987 |
| | 1994 | | 900 | | 900 | 63 | | 6 151 | 13 | 6 138 | 429 |
| | 1995 | | 700 | | 700 | 47 | | 1 000 | 13 | 987 | 66 |
| | 1996 | | 400 | | 400 | 26 | | 1 400 | 13 | 1 387 | 88 |
| | 1997 | | 1 021 | | 1 021 | 63 | | 9 544 | 13 | 9 531 | 585 |
| **Europe** | | | | | | | | | | | |
| Albania | 1992 | 8 000 | 112 | | 8 112 | 2 473 | 4 500 | 601 | 802 | 4 299 | 1 311 |
| | 1993 | 8 000 | 440 | | 8 440 | 2 600 | 4 500 | 630 | 20 | 5 110 | 1 574 |
| | 1994 | 8 000 | 80 | | 8 080 | 2 518 | 4 500 | 300 | | 4 800 | 1 496 |
| | 1995 | 8 000 | 80 | | 8 080 | 2 544 | 4 500 | 300 | | 4 800 | 1 511 |
| | 1996 | 8 000 | 4 400 | | 12 400 | 3 935 | 4 500 | | | 4 500 | 1 428 |
| | 1997 | 8 000 | 4 636 | | 12 636 | 4 035 | 4 500 | 2 387 | 46 | 6 841 | 2 184 |
| Andorra | 1992 | | | | | | | 946 | 651 | 295 | 5 255 |
| | 1993 | | 20 | | 20 | 341 | | 1 295 | 37 | 1 258 | 21 426 |
| | 1994 | | 8 | | 8 | 130 | | 1 776 | 28 | 1 748 | 28 472 |
| | 1995 | | 8 | | 8 | 125 | | 1 776 | 28 | 1 748 | 27 272 |
| | 1996 | | 8 | | 8 | 120 | | 1 776 | 28 | 1 748 | 26 167 |
| | 1997 | | 8 | | 8 | 115 | | 1 776 | 28 | 1 748 | 25 138 |
| Austria | 1970 | 170 000 | 400 | 67 000 | 103 400 | 13 847 | | 8 100 | 288 100 | | |
| | 1975 | 147 000 | 4 600 | 30 800 | 120 800 | 15 939 | 523 000 | 12 100 | 409 800 | 125 300 | 16 533 |
| | 1980 | 176 000 | 1 500 | 39 100 | 138 400 | 18 333 | 618 000 | 56 700 | 562 100 | 112 600 | 14 915 |
| | 1985 | 241 000 | 6 300 | 133 000 | 114 300 | 15 124 | 850 000 | 129 400 | 890 800 | 88 600 | 11 723 |
| | 1990 | 333 000 | 38 400 | 227 000 | 144 400 | 18 740 | 1 377 000 | 241 000 | 958 000 | 660 000 | 85 655 |
| | 1991 | 397 000 | 41 000 | 287 000 | 151 000 | 19 464 | 1 447 000 | 265 000 | 1 247 000 | 465 000 | 59 940 |
| | 1992 | 395 000 | 61 624 | 103 045 | 353 579 | 45 230 | 1 546 000 | 291 026 | 1 669 218 | 167 808 | 21 466 |
| | 1993 | 387 000 | 73 635 | 26 064 | 434 571 | 55 144 | 1 574 000 | 289 468 | 1 718 020 | 145 448 | 18 456 |
| | 1994 | 403 000 | 69 000 | 6 000 | 466 000 | 58 668 | 1 728 000 | 339 000 | 1 965 000 | 102 000 | 12 842 |
| | 1995 | 380 000 | 74 100 | 63 200 | 390 900 | 48 858 | 1 764 000 | 427 000 | 1 858 000 | 333 000 | 41 621 |
| | 1996 | 361 000 | 66 000 | 257 000 | 170 000 | 21 111 | 1 787 000 | 473 000 | 1 878 000 | 382 000 | 47 438 |
| | 1997 | 397 000 | 106 000 | 306 000 | 197 000 | 24 324 | 1 826 000 | 544 300 | 1 980 000 | 390 300 | 48 192 |
| Belarus | 1992 | | | | | | | 18 | | 18 | 2 |
| | 1993 | | 13 | | 13 | 1 | | 282 | 81 | 201 | 19 |
| | 1994 | | | | | | | 400 | | 400 | 39 |
| | 1995 | | | | | | | 900 | | 900 | 87 |
| | 1996 | | | | | | | 1 600 | 34 | 1 566 | 151 |
| | 1997 | | | | | | | 6 500 | 34 | 6 466 | 625 |
| Belgium | 1970 | 95 000 | 110 300 | 25 600 | 179 700 | 18 611 | 352 000 | 208 300 | 237 400 | 322 900 | 33 442 |
| | 1975 | 77 000 | 105 400 | 20 500 | 161 900 | 16 527 | 330 000 | 155 500 | | 485 500 | 49 561 |
| | 1980 | 102 000 | 126 000 | 31 000 | 197 000 | 19 996 | 436 000 | 337 700 | 288 400 | 485 300 | 49 260 |
| | 1985 | 109 000 | 140 100 | 27 600 | 221 500 | 22 471 | 414 000 | 357 100 | 178 300 | 592 800 | 60 140 |
| | 1990 | 102 000 | 184 400 | 46 200 | 240 200 | 24 139 | 733 000 | 764 600 | 621 700 | 875 900 | 88 025 |
| | 1991 | 106 000 | 177 000 | 30 000 | 253 000 | 25 357 | 678 000 | 686 000 | 600 000 | 764 000 | 76 572 |
| | 1992 | 119 000 | 172 801 | 48 334 | 243 467 | 24 331 | 666 000 | 789 141 | 609 637 | 845 504 | 84 496 |
| | 1993 | 119 000 | 181 400 | 77 200 | 223 200 | 22 241 | 666 000 | 912 000 | 644 800 | 933 200 | 92 988 |
| | 1994 | 122 000 | 190 500 | 96 400 | 216 100 | 21 474 | 610 000 | 1 084 300 | 863 100 | 831 200 | 82 597 |
| | 1995 | 122 000 | 181 100 | 40 000 | 263 100 | 26 080 | 610 000 | 1 134 100 | 1 059 600 | 684 500 | 67 853 |
| | 1996 | 104 000 | 204 300 | 54 600 | 253 700 | 25 096 | 991 000 | 959 400 | 1 015 200 | 935 200 | 92 511 |
| | 1997 | 104 000 | 233 500 | 111 600 | 225 900 | 22 308 | 991 000 | 1 288 700 | 1 263 100 | 1 016 600 | 100 389 |
| Bosnia and Herzegovina | 1992 | | | | | | | 522 | 441 | 81 | 21 |
| | 1993 | | 5 | | 5 | 1 | | 509 | 500 | 9 | 2 |
| | 1994 | | | | | | | 98 | | 98 | 28 |
| | 1995 | | | | | | | 98 | | 98 | 29 |
| | 1996 | | | | | | | 98 | | 98 | 29 |
| | 1997 | | 3 093 | | 3 093 | 879 | | 4 968 | 24 | 4 944 | 1 405 |
| Bulgaria | 1970 | | 35 400 | | 35 400 | 4 170 | 41 000 | 9 500 | | 50 500 | 5 948 |
| | 1975 | | 49 000 | | 49 000 | 5 618 | 42 000 | 18 400 | | 60 400 | 6 925 |
| | 1980 | | 46 200 | | 46 200 | 5 214 | 36 000 | 13 400 | | 49 400 | 5 575 |
| | 1985 | | 42 300 | | 42 300 | 4 721 | 81 000 | 10 000 | | 91 000 | 10 156 |
| | 1990 | | 30 700 | | 30 700 | 3 521 | 52 000 | 6 800 | | 58 800 | 6 744 |
| | 1991 | | 30 700 | | 30 700 | 3 541 | 47 000 | 4 000 | | 51 000 | 5 882 |
| | 1992 | | 330 | 52 | 278 | 32 | 8 000 | 3 058 | 1 825 | 9 233 | 1 070 |

Newsprint and other printing and writing paper IV.10
Papier journal et autre papier d'impression et d'écriture
Papel de periódico y otro papel de imprenta y de escribir

| Country / Pays / País | Year / Année / Año | Newsprint / Papier journal / Papel de periódico | | | | | Other printing and writing paper / Autre papier d'impression et d'écriture / Otro papel de imprenta y de escribir | | | | |
|---|---|---|---|---|---|---|---|---|---|---|---|
| | | Production / Production / Producción | Imports / Importations / Importaciones | Exports / Exportations / Exportaciones | Consumption / Consommation / Consumo | Consumption per 1,000 inh. / Consommation pour 1 000 hab. / Consumo por 1 000 hab. | Production / Production / Producción | Imports / Importations / Importaciones | Exports / Exportations / Exportaciones | Consumption / Consommation / Consumo | Consumption per 1,000 inh. / Consommation pour 1 000 hab. / Consumo por 1 000 hab. |
| Bulgaria (cont) | | | | | | | | | | | |
| | 1993 | | 4 500 | 800 | 3 700 | 431 | 3 800 | 18 200 | 600 | 21 400 | 2 492 |
| | 1994 | | 7 000 | 800 | 6 200 | 726 | 4 500 | 25 900 | 700 | 29 700 | 3 475 |
| | 1995 | | 7 600 | 800 | 6 800 | 800 | 4 500 | 8 800 | 200 | 13 100 | 1 541 |
| | 1996 | | 30 500 | 500 | 30 000 | 3 551 | 4 500 | 22 200 | 800 | 25 900 | 3 066 |
| | 1997 | | 32 000 | 200 | 31 800 | 3 789 | 4 500 | 30 000 | 500 | 34 000 | 4 051 |
| Croatia | | | | | | | | | | | |
| | 1992 | | 74 | | 74 | 16 | | 5 288 | 137 | 5 151 | 1 142 |
| | 1993 | | 18 342 | 202 | 18 140 | 4 026 | 2 000 | 35 166 | 2 275 | 34 891 | 7 743 |
| | 1994 | 3 000 | 24 000 | | 27 000 | 6 001 | 3 800 | 25 000 | 300 | 28 500 | 6 335 |
| | 1995 | 1 700 | 34 100 | | 35 800 | 7 968 | 4 100 | 25 400 | 300 | 29 200 | 6 499 |
| | 1996 | 1 000 | 33 600 | 600 | 34 000 | 7 576 | 4 200 | 26 000 | 200 | 30 000 | 6 684 |
| | 1997 | 2 400 | 33 600 | 2 300 | 33 700 | 7 515 | 4 700 | 20 000 | 2 700 | 22 000 | 4 906 |
| Czech Republic | | | | | | | | | | | |
| | 1992 | | 9 800 | 5 200 | 4 600 | 446 | | 27 800 | 44 300 | | |
| | 1993 | 59 000 | 31 769 | 28 000 | 62 769 | 6 079 | 63 000 | 93 000 | 55 000 | 101 000 | 9 782 |
| | 1994 | 86 000 | 22 000 | 57 000 | 51 000 | 4 938 | 160 000 | 127 000 | 64 000 | 223 000 | 21 592 |
| | 1995 | 89 000 | 10 000 | 53 000 | 46 000 | 4 455 | 173 000 | 146 000 | 72 000 | 247 000 | 23 922 |
| | 1996 | 101 000 | 6 000 | 62 000 | 45 000 | 4 362 | 158 000 | 170 000 | 69 000 | 259 000 | 25 107 |
| | 1997 | 94 000 | 42 600 | 62 000 | 74 600 | 7 242 | 185 000 | 192 400 | 79 400 | 298 000 | 28 930 |
| Denmark | | | | | | | | | | | |
| | 1970 | | 149 200 | 200 | 149 000 | 30 231 | 71 000 | 84 600 | 10 800 | 144 800 | 29 379 |
| | 1975 | | 125 700 | 400 | 125 300 | 24 764 | 59 000 | 91 600 | 14 700 | 135 900 | 26 858 |
| | 1980 | | 153 300 | 700 | 152 600 | 29 787 | 113 000 | 135 800 | 57 600 | 191 200 | 37 322 |
| | 1985 | | 188 800 | 1 000 | 187 800 | 36 725 | 142 000 | 149 000 | 73 000 | 218 000 | 42 631 |
| | 1990 | | 217 100 | 700 | 216 400 | 42 102 | 124 000 | 232 100 | 66 900 | 289 200 | 56 265 |
| | 1991 | | 213 000 | 600 | 212 400 | 41 214 | 132 000 | 237 700 | 74 400 | 295 300 | 57 299 |
| | 1992 | | 219 026 | 866 | 218 160 | 42 195 | 117 000 | 242 098 | 70 927 | 288 171 | 55 737 |
| | 1993 | | 223 000 | 565 | 222 435 | 42 870 | 93 000 | 265 000 | 58 000 | 300 000 | 57 819 |
| | 1994 | | 267 000 | 1 300 | 265 700 | 51 026 | 93 000 | 314 000 | 76 000 | 331 000 | 63 566 |
| | 1995 | | 263 000 | 1 500 | 261 500 | 50 049 | 93 000 | 339 000 | 89 000 | 343 000 | 65 648 |
| | 1996 | | 256 000 | 500 | 255 500 | 48 749 | 93 000 | 314 000 | 79 000 | 328 000 | 62 582 |
| | 1997 | | 263 000 | 600 | 262 400 | 49 923 | 93 000 | 375 000 | 90 000 | 378 000 | 71 916 |
| Estonia | | | | | | | | | | | |
| | 1992 | | 641 | 13 | 628 | 405 | 8 700 | 10 | 4 | 8 706 | 5 621 |
| | 1993 | | 1 634 | 215 | 1 419 | 928 | 8 700 | 3 162 | 35 | 11 827 | 7 737 |
| | 1994 | | 8 000 | 300 | 7 700 | 5 110 | 8 700 | 5 900 | 500 | 14 100 | 9 357 |
| | 1995 | | 10 400 | 1 200 | 9 200 | 6 192 | 8 700 | 13 100 | 1 000 | 20 800 | 14 000 |
| | 1996 | | 10 800 | 3 100 | 7 700 | 5 253 | 20 000 | 19 200 | 5 100 | 34 100 | 23 261 |
| | 1997 | | 30 900 | 11 100 | 19 800 | 13 682 | 20 000 | 25 800 | 10 200 | 35 600 | 24 600 |
| Faeroe Islands | | | | | | | | | | | |
| | 1992 | | 381 | | 381 | 8 255 | | 301 | | 301 | 6 522 |
| | 1993 | | 396 | 206 | 190 | 4 162 | | 863 | 156 | 707 | 15 488 |
| | 1994 | | 384 | 6 | 378 | 8 378 | | 853 | 202 | 651 | 14 429 |
| | 1995 | | 384 | 6 | 378 | 8 471 | | 853 | 202 | 651 | 14 590 |
| | 1996 | | 384 | 6 | 378 | 8 555 | | 853 | 202 | 651 | 14 734 |
| | 1997 | | 384 | 6 | 378 | 8 632 | | 853 | 202 | 651 | 14 866 |
| Federal Republic of Yugoslavia | | | | | | | | | | | |
| | 1992 | | 1 856 | | 1 856 | 180 | | 10 886 | 9 300 | 1 586 | 154 |
| | 1993 | | 690 | | 690 | 66 | | 2 178 | 472 | 1 706 | 164 |
| | 1994 | | 400 | | 400 | 38 | | 1 300 | 300 | 1 000 | 95 |
| | 1995 | | 600 | | 600 | 57 | | 900 | 100 | 800 | 76 |
| | 1996 | | 18 100 | | 18 100 | 1 706 | | 19 600 | 600 | 19 000 | 1 791 |
| | 1997 | | 18 100 | | 18 100 | 1 703 | 25 000 | 19 600 | 600 | 44 000 | 4 140 |
| Finland | | | | | | | | | | | |
| | 1970 | 1 305 000 | 900 | 1 187 000 | 118 900 | 25 814 | 981 000 | 1 600 | 779 200 | 203 400 | 44 160 |
| | 1975 | 992 000 | | 776 200 | 215 800 | 45 803 | 1 340 000 | 3 000 | 1 176 800 | 166 200 | 35 276 |
| | 1980 | 1 569 000 | | 1 431 900 | 137 100 | 28 685 | 2 027 000 | 4 300 | 1 750 000 | 281 300 | 58 855 |
| | 1985 | 1 811 000 | | 1 643 400 | 167 600 | 34 189 | 3 166 000 | 9 000 | 2 756 800 | 418 200 | 85 308 |
| | 1990 | 1 430 000 | | 1 202 900 | 227 100 | 45 544 | 4 768 000 | 30 300 | 4 172 500 | 625 800 | 125 500 |
| | 1991 | 1 305 000 | | 1 159 300 | 145 700 | 29 088 | 4 778 000 | 27 000 | 4 131 000 | 674 000 | 134 557 |
| | 1992 | 1 257 000 | 2 187 | 1 146 000 | 113 187 | 22 483 | 5 045 000 | 30 000 | 4 325 061 | 749 939 | 148 964 |
| | 1993 | 1 425 000 | 19 771 | 1 250 000 | 194 771 | 38 486 | 5 567 000 | 28 000 | 4 906 000 | 689 000 | 136 145 |
| | 1994 | 1 446 000 | 17 000 | 1 252 000 | 211 000 | 41 488 | 6 159 000 | 31 000 | 5 554 000 | 636 000 | 125 053 |
| | 1995 | 1 425 000 | 18 000 | 1 099 000 | 344 000 | 67 348 | 6 457 000 | 27 000 | 5 667 000 | 817 000 | 159 951 |
| | 1996 | 1 327 000 | 30 000 | 1 051 000 | 306 000 | 59 695 | 6 014 000 | 33 000 | 5 122 000 | 925 000 | 180 450 |
| | 1997 | 1 470 000 | 39 000 | 1 211 000 | 298 000 | 57 963 | 7 317 000 | 44 000 | 6 374 000 | 987 000 | 191 978 |
| France | | | | | | | | | | | |
| | 1970 | 430 200 | 177 000 | 1 700 | 605 500 | 11 926 | 1 418 000 | 228 000 | 158 000 | 1 488 000 | 29 307 |
| | 1975 | 238 000 | 165 000 | 1 000 | 402 000 | 7 628 | 1 311 000 | 362 000 | 262 000 | 1 411 000 | 26 775 |
| | 1980 | 261 000 | 371 400 | 3 600 | 628 800 | 11 670 | 2 011 000 | 596 600 | 528 200 | 2 079 400 | 38 593 |

IV.10   Newsprint and other printing and writing paper
Papier journal et autre papier d'impression et d'écriture
Papel de periódico y otro papel de imprenta y de escribir

| Country / Pays / País | Year / Année / Año | Newsprint — Papier journal — Papel de periódico | | | | | Other printing and writing paper — Autre papier d'impression et d'écriture — Otro papel de imprenta y de escribir | | | | |
|---|---|---|---|---|---|---|---|---|---|---|---|
| | | Production / Producción | Imports / Importations / Importaciones | Exports / Exportations / Exportaciones | Consumption / Consommation / Consumo | Consumption per 1,000 inh. / Consommation pour 1 000 hab. / Consumo por 1 000 hab. | Production / Producción | Imports / Importations / Importaciones | Exports / Exportations / Exportaciones | Consumption / Consommation / Consumo | Consumption per 1,000 inh. / Consommation pour 1 000 hab. / Consumo por 1 000 hab. |
| France (cont) | 1985 | 264 000 | 317 800 | 13 500 | 568 300 | 10 301 | 1 898 000 | 851 800 | 621 600 | 2 128 200 | 38 575 |
| | 1990 | 422 000 | 497 600 | 131 500 | 788 100 | 13 895 | 2 773 000 | 1 342 400 | 981 300 | 3 134 100 | 55 258 |
| | 1991 | 509 000 | 442 300 | 222 200 | 729 100 | 12 790 | 2 827 000 | 1 363 100 | 1 061 000 | 3 129 100 | 54 893 |
| | 1992 | 670 000 | 422 233 | 349 867 | 742 366 | 12 961 | 2 948 000 | 1 803 949 | 1 407 004 | 3 344 945 | 58 401 |
| | 1993 | 802 000 | 418 000 | 476 000 | 744 000 | 12 932 | 2 936 000 | 1 792 000 | 1 363 000 | 3 365 000 | 58 488 |
| | 1994 | 844 000 | 488 000 | 525 000 | 807 000 | 13 967 | 3 268 000 | 2 095 000 | 1 592 000 | 3 771 000 | 65 264 |
| | 1995 | 890 000 | 439 000 | 535 000 | 794 000 | 13 685 | 3 096 000 | 2 102 000 | 1 536 000 | 3 662 000 | 63 116 |
| | 1996 | 783 000 | 463 000 | 489 000 | 757 000 | 12 996 | 3 141 000 | 809 000 | 558 000 | 3 392 000 | 58 231 |
| | 1997 | 783 000 | 493 000 | 605 000 | 671 000 | 11 476 | 3 141 000 | 957 000 | 559 000 | 3 539 000 | 60 525 |
| Germany | 1990 | 1 244 000 | 1 234 900 | 428 800 | 2 050 100 | 25 831 | 4 982 000 | 2 660 200 | 2 209 700 | 5 432 500 | 68 450 |
| | 1991 | 1 229 000 | 1 360 800 | 379 400 | 2 210 400 | 27 681 | 5 114 000 | 2 940 600 | 2 245 600 | 5 809 000 | 72 746 |
| | 1992 | 1 222 000 | 1 258 675 | 423 157 | 2 057 518 | 25 602 | 5 173 000 | 2 932 178 | 2 510 973 | 5 594 205 | 69 610 |
| | 1993 | 1 302 000 | 1 314 000 | 507 000 | 2 109 000 | 26 081 | 4 928 000 | 2 919 000 | 2 315 000 | 5 532 000 | 68 410 |
| | 1994 | 1 499 000 | 1 291 000 | 575 000 | 2 215 000 | 27 242 | 5 865 000 | 3 220 000 | 2 947 000 | 6 138 000 | 75 492 |
| | 1995 | 1 726 000 | 1 183 000 | 561 000 | 2 348 000 | 28 753 | 5 872 000 | 3 026 000 | 3 461 000 | 5 437 000 | 66 580 |
| | 1996 | 1 572 000 | 1 095 000 | 569 000 | 2 098 000 | 25 614 | 5 702 000 | 3 057 000 | 3 373 000 | 5 386 000 | 65 756 |
| | 1997 | 1 618 000 | 1 162 000 | 637 000 | 2 143 000 | 26 116 | 6 390 000 | 3 167 000 | 3 970 000 | 5 587 000 | 68 087 |
| Gibraltar | 1992 | | 8 | | 8 | 301 | | 197 | 7 | 190 | 7 156 |
| | 1993 | | 43 | | 43 | 1 631 | | 93 | | 93 | 3 528 |
| | 1994 | | 38 | | 38 | 1 452 | | 110 | 1 | 109 | 4 165 |
| | 1995 | | 38 | | 38 | 1 462 | | 110 | 1 | 109 | 4 195 |
| | 1996 | | 38 | | 38 | 1 473 | | 110 | 1 | 109 | 4 225 |
| | 1997 | | 38 | | 38 | 1 484 | | 110 | 1 | 109 | 4 255 |
| Greece | 1970 | | 31 600 | | 31 600 | 3 594 | 30 000 | 5 700 | | 35 700 | 4 060 |
| | 1975 | | 48 000 | 100 | 47 900 | 5 295 | 35 000 | 34 300 | 300 | 69 000 | 7 627 |
| | 1980 | 9 000 | 40 000 | 7 900 | 41 100 | 4 262 | 80 000 | 42 500 | 28 300 | 94 200 | 9 769 |
| | 1985 | 12 000 | 68 800 | 1 800 | 79 000 | 7 952 | 70 000 | 46 300 | 3 200 | 113 100 | 11 385 |
| | 1990 | 16 000 | 88 800 | 4 100 | 100 700 | 9 853 | 75 000 | 86 500 | 2 700 | 158 800 | 15 538 |
| | 1991 | 20 000 | 79 200 | | 99 200 | 9 652 | 76 000 | 64 000 | 2 700 | 137 300 | 13 360 |
| | 1992 | 20 000 | 38 429 | 1 214 | 57 215 | 5 536 | 76 000 | 121 870 | 1 047 | 196 823 | 19 045 |
| | 1993 | 9 000 | 59 552 | 947 | 67 605 | 6 507 | 125 000 | 138 739 | 1 676 | 262 063 | 25 223 |
| | 1994 | 9 000 | 59 559 | 328 | 68 231 | 6 534 | 125 000 | 119 000 | 500 | 243 500 | 23 320 |
| | 1995 | 9 000 | 35 400 | 2 800 | 41 600 | 3 966 | 125 000 | 53 200 | 2 500 | 175 700 | 16 751 |
| | 1996 | 9 000 | 43 900 | 2 800 | 50 100 | 4 757 | 125 000 | 82 400 | 1 000 | 206 400 | 19 598 |
| | 1997 | 9 000 | 96 600 | 1 800 | 103 800 | 9 821 | 125 000 | 217 700 | 2 400 | 340 300 | 32 199 |
| Hungary | 1970 | | 53 600 | | 53 600 | 5 185 | 74 200 | 35 400 | 1 200 | 108 400 | 10 486 |
| | 1975 | | 56 300 | | 56 300 | 5 346 | 101 000 | 42 700 | 19 200 | 124 500 | 11 821 |
| | 1980 | | 63 000 | 2 000 | 61 000 | 5 697 | 115 000 | 44 000 | 24 300 | 134 700 | 12 580 |
| | 1985 | | 67 500 | | 67 500 | 6 381 | 136 000 | 31 100 | 28 700 | 138 400 | 13 082 |
| | 1990 | | 51 600 | | 51 600 | 4 978 | 127 000 | 27 000 | 36 000 | 118 000 | 11 385 |
| | 1991 | | 94 600 | | 94 600 | 9 156 | 88 000 | 60 600 | 7 500 | 141 100 | 13 656 |
| | 1992 | | 24 325 | | 24 325 | 2 360 | 107 000 | 52 153 | 8 902 | 150 251 | 14 580 |
| | 1993 | | 25 909 | 60 | 25 849 | 2 514 | 64 000 | 112 955 | 3 233 | 173 722 | 16 897 |
| | 1994 | | 106 000 | 300 | 105 700 | 10 306 | 80 000 | 87 000 | 5 700 | 161 300 | 15 728 |
| | 1995 | | 91 000 | | 91 000 | 8 898 | 83 000 | 81 000 | 12 800 | 151 200 | 14 785 |
| | 1996 | | 84 000 | | 84 000 | 8 241 | 142 000 | 73 000 | 64 000 | 151 000 | 14 814 |
| | 1997 | | 85 000 | | 85 000 | 8 369 | 169 000 | 96 000 | 76 000 | 189 000 | 18 610 |
| Iceland | 1970 | | 3 100 | | 3 100 | 15 188 | | 1 800 | | 1 800 | 8 819 |
| | 1975 | | 3 000 | | 3 000 | 13 760 | | 1 800 | | 1 800 | 8 256 |
| | 1980 | | 4 000 | | 4 000 | 17 531 | | 3 200 | | 3 200 | 14 025 |
| | 1985 | | 5 800 | | 5 800 | 24 027 | | 2 800 | | 2 800 | 11 599 |
| | 1990 | | 4 800 | | 4 800 | 18 839 | | 4 200 | | 4 200 | 16 484 |
| | 1991 | | 4 800 | | 4 800 | 18 639 | | 4 200 | | 4 200 | 16 309 |
| | 1992 | | 583 | | 583 | 2 240 | | 1 195 | 4 | 1 191 | 4 576 |
| | 1993 | | 5 289 | | 5 289 | 20 109 | | 8 729 | 9 | 8 720 | 33 154 |
| | 1994 | | 5 682 | | 5 682 | 21 382 | | 8 506 | 149 | 8 357 | 31 449 |
| | 1995 | | 5 800 | | 5 800 | 21 610 | | 5 200 | 149 | 5 051 | 18 819 |
| | 1996 | | 6 000 | | 6 000 | 22 140 | | 5 400 | 100 | 5 300 | 19 557 |
| | 1997 | | 6 000 | | 6 000 | 21 934 | | 5 400 | 100 | 5 300 | 19 375 |
| Ireland | 1970 | 6 000 | 48 200 | | 54 200 | 18 350 | 10 000 | 5 300 | 1 000 | 14 300 | 4 841 |
| | 1975 | 10 000 | 47 000 | 300 | 56 700 | 17 846 | 19 000 | 8 900 | 2 100 | 25 800 | 8 120 |
| | 1980 | | 60 800 | 200 | 60 600 | 17 818 | 23 000 | 22 100 | 6 700 | 38 400 | 11 291 |
| | 1985 | | 51 400 | 400 | 51 000 | 14 358 | | 42 000 | 1 100 | 40 900 | 11 515 |
| | 1990 | | 63 000 | 1 000 | 62 000 | 17 699 | | 94 000 | 5 811 | 88 189 | 25 175 |
| | 1991 | | 63 000 | 1 000 | 62 000 | 17 659 | | 134 000 | 1 000 | 133 000 | 37 882 |
| | 1992 | | 68 112 | 1 820 | 66 292 | 18 784 | | 117 814 | 14 552 | 103 262 | 29 260 |

Newsprint and other printing and writing paper **IV.10**
Papier journal et autre papier d'impression et d'écriture
Papel de periódico y otro papel de imprenta y de escribir

| Country / Pays / País | Year / Année / Año | Newsprint / Papier journal / Papel de periódico | | | | | Other printing and writing paper / Autre papier d'impression et d'écriture / Otro papel de imprenta y de escribir | | | | |
|---|---|---|---|---|---|---|---|---|---|---|---|
| | | Production / Production / Producción | Imports / Importations / Importaciones | Exports / Exportations / Exportaciones | Consumption / Consommation / Consumo | Consumption per 1,000 inh. / Consommation pour 1 000 hab. / Consumo por 1 000 hab. | Production / Production / Producción | Imports / Importations / Importaciones | Exports / Exportations / Exportaciones | Consumption / Consommation / Consumo | Consumption per 1,000 inh. / Consommation pour 1 000 hab. / Consumo por 1 000 hab. |
| **Ireland (cont)** | | | | | | | | | | | |
| | 1993 | | 77 389 | 7 600 | 69 789 | 19 633 | | 122 000 | 9 100 | 112 900 | 31 761 |
| | 1994 | | 70 400 | 1 300 | 69 100 | 19 288 | | 132 000 | 7 300 | 124 700 | 34 807 |
| | 1995 | | 62 000 | | 62 000 | 17 178 | | 156 000 | 9 000 | 147 000 | 40 730 |
| | 1996 | | 70 000 | | 70 000 | 19 264 | | 140 000 | 12 000 | 128 000 | 35 225 |
| | 1997 | | 173 000 | 1 000 | 172 000 | 47 025 | | 126 000 | 7 000 | 119 000 | 32 535 |
| **Italy** | | | | | | | | | | | |
| | 1970 | 311 000 | 13 800 | 42 500 | 282 300 | 5 245 | 1 167 000 | 24 100 | 133 000 | 1 058 100 | 19 659 |
| | 1975 | 243 000 | 11 500 | 9 600 | 244 900 | 4 417 | 1 054 000 | 33 900 | 111 000 | 976 900 | 17 621 |
| | 1980 | 277 000 | 63 700 | 13 000 | 327 700 | 5 807 | 1 799 000 | 147 900 | 330 400 | 1 616 500 | 28 644 |
| | 1985 | 178 000 | 232 000 | 28 000 | 382 000 | 6 729 | 1 940 000 | 331 000 | 479 000 | 1 792 000 | 31 565 |
| | 1990 | 233 000 | 374 000 | 10 000 | 597 000 | 10 469 | 2 247 000 | 765 000 | 528 000 | 2 484 000 | 43 561 |
| | 1991 | 196 000 | 350 000 | 6 000 | 540 000 | 9 459 | 2 252 000 | 799 000 | 531 000 | 2 520 000 | 44 142 |
| | 1992 | 101 000 | 486 814 | 10 448 | 577 366 | 10 101 | 2 397 000 | 964 396 | 573 664 | 2 787 732 | 48 771 |
| | 1993 | 83 000 | 468 000 | 7 471 | 543 529 | 9 497 | 2 381 000 | 1 000 166 | 729 862 | 2 651 304 | 46 327 |
| | 1994 | 154 000 | 471 000 | 4 000 | 621 000 | 10 839 | 2 595 000 | 1 224 000 | 812 000 | 3 007 000 | 52 485 |
| | 1995 | 183 000 | 440 000 | 5 000 | 618 000 | 10 778 | 2 594 000 | 1 104 000 | 819 000 | 2 879 000 | 50 211 |
| | 1996 | 178 000 | 372 000 | 15 000 | 535 000 | 9 326 | 2 662 000 | 1 004 000 | 825 000 | 2 841 000 | 49 524 |
| | 1997 | 180 000 | 438 000 | 8 000 | 610 000 | 10 631 | 2 930 000 | 1 247 000 | 899 000 | 3 278 000 | 57 131 |
| **Latvia** | | | | | | | | | | | |
| | 1992 | 400 | 24 | | 424 | 160 | 2 000 | 102 | 74 | 2 028 | 766 |
| | 1993 | 3 000 | 15 000 | | 18 000 | 6 887 | 1 000 | 18 000 | 999 | 18 001 | 6 888 |
| | 1994 | 2 000 | 11 600 | | 13 600 | 5 281 | 1 000 | 10 100 | 1 300 | 9 800 | 3 806 |
| | 1995 | 2 000 | 14 300 | | 16 300 | 6 426 | 2 000 | 4 000 | 600 | 5 400 | 2 129 |
| | 1996 | 3 000 | 11 000 | | 14 000 | 5 603 | 1 000 | 25 000 | 600 | 25 400 | 10 165 |
| | 1997 | 3 000 | 12 500 | | 15 500 | 6 298 | 1 000 | 27 500 | 600 | 27 900 | 11 336 |
| **Lithuania** | | | | | | | | | | | |
| | 1992 | | | | | | | 30 | | 30 | 8 |
| | 1993 | | 16 000 | 2 133 | 13 867 | 3 702 | 1 900 | 371 | 1 710 | 561 | 150 |
| | 1994 | | 16 200 | 2 200 | 14 000 | 3 747 | 1 900 | 8 700 | 2 600 | 8 000 | 2 141 |
| | 1995 | | 15 900 | 1 000 | 14 900 | 3 999 | 1 900 | 7 000 | 5 300 | 3 600 | 966 |
| | 1996 | | 13 000 | 200 | 12 800 | 3 445 | 1 900 | 12 700 | 3 600 | 11 000 | 2 961 |
| | 1997 | | 13 000 | 200 | 12 800 | 3 455 | 1 900 | 12 700 | 3 600 | 11 000 | 2 969 |
| **Malta** | | | | | | | | | | | |
| | 1970 | | 300 | | 300 | 991 | | 2 900 | | 2 900 | 9 580 |
| | 1975 | | 200 | | 200 | 657 | | 2 400 | | 2 400 | 7 889 |
| | 1980 | | 700 | | 700 | 2 160 | | 2 300 | | 2 300 | 7 096 |
| | 1985 | | 1 500 | | 1 500 | 4 356 | | 4 200 | | 4 200 | 12 197 |
| | 1990 | | 2 600 | | 2 600 | 7 341 | | 6 400 | | 6 400 | 18 070 |
| | 1991 | | 3 100 | | 3 100 | 8 668 | | 9 100 | | 9 100 | 25 444 |
| | 1992 | | 3 100 | | 3 100 | 8 566 | | 1 700 | 29 | 1 671 | 4 617 |
| | 1993 | | 2 900 | | 2 900 | 7 912 | | 5 200 | | 5 200 | 14 187 |
| | 1994 | | 5 500 | | 5 500 | 14 823 | | 8 600 | | 8 600 | 23 178 |
| | 1995 | | 3 400 | | 3 400 | 9 066 | | 10 500 | | 10 500 | 27 998 |
| | 1996 | | 3 000 | | 3 000 | 7 929 | | 10 500 | | 10 500 | 27 751 |
| | 1997 | | 3 000 | | 3 000 | 7 870 | | 10 500 | | 10 500 | 27 545 |
| **Moldova** | | | | | | | | | | | |
| | 1992 | | | | | | | 5 | | 5 | 1 |
| | 1993 | | | | | | | 114 | | 114 | 26 |
| | 1994 | | 600 | 600 | | | | 5 100 | 3 200 | 1 900 | 434 |
| | 1995 | | 4 200 | 500 | 3 700 | 846 | | 4 600 | 1 100 | 3 500 | 800 |
| | 1996 | | 4 200 | 500 | 3 700 | 846 | | 4 600 | 1 100 | 3 500 | 800 |
| | 1997 | | 4 200 | 500 | 3 700 | 845 | | 4 600 | 1 100 | 3 500 | 800 |
| **Netherlands** | | | | | | | | | | | |
| | 1970 | 167 000 | 247 300 | 35 600 | 378 700 | 29 059 | 489 000 | 213 000 | 151 200 | 550 800 | 42 264 |
| | 1975 | 125 000 | 257 400 | 22 700 | 359 700 | 26 345 | 406 000 | 249 400 | 193 900 | 461 500 | 33 801 |
| | 1980 | 171 000 | 331 900 | 45 100 | 457 800 | 32 367 | 571 000 | 394 300 | 283 600 | 681 700 | 48 197 |
| | 1985 | 191 000 | 270 800 | 77 600 | 384 200 | 26 512 | 562 000 | 446 700 | 379 000 | 629 700 | 43 453 |
| | 1990 | 300 000 | 393 900 | 200 600 | 493 300 | 32 993 | 819 000 | 934 600 | 708 100 | 1 045 500 | 69 926 |
| | 1991 | 309 000 | 369 100 | 213 500 | 464 600 | 30 860 | 834 000 | 1 043 100 | 673 000 | 1 204 100 | 79 979 |
| | 1992 | 306 000 | 340 828 | 209 056 | 437 772 | 28 874 | 797 000 | 1 086 472 | 814 415 | 1 069 057 | 70 512 |
| | 1993 | 326 000 | 403 481 | 238 814 | 490 667 | 32 140 | 775 000 | 1 025 777 | 772 000 | 1 028 777 | 67 388 |
| | 1994 | 311 000 | 432 000 | 227 000 | 516 000 | 33 579 | 902 000 | 759 000 | 743 000 | 918 000 | 59 739 |
| | 1995 | 361 000 | 430 000 | 220 000 | 571 000 | 36 937 | 818 000 | 712 000 | 687 000 | 843 000 | 54 532 |
| | 1996 | 338 000 | 394 500 | 238 000 | 494 500 | 31 819 | 840 000 | 1 023 000 | 865 000 | 998 000 | 64 217 |
| | 1997 | 373 000 | 394 500 | 296 200 | 471 300 | 30 184 | 878 000 | 1 128 000 | 1 017 400 | 988 600 | 63 314 |
| **Norway** | | | | | | | | | | | |
| | 1970 | 554 000 | | 475 600 | 78 400 | 20 220 | 317 000 | 4 900 | 223 600 | 98 300 | 25 352 |
| | 1975 | 435 000 | | | 435 000 | 108 552 | 292 000 | 16 400 | 163 400 | 145 000 | 36 184 |
| | 1980 | 589 000 | | 522 800 | 66 200 | 16 203 | 337 000 | 52 800 | 231 300 | 158 500 | 38 795 |
| | 1985 | 877 000 | | 761 300 | 115 700 | 27 862 | 304 000 | 91 200 | 222 200 | 173 000 | 41 661 |
| | 1990 | 910 000 | | 822 300 | 87 700 | 20 677 | 339 000 | 114 400 | 309 700 | 143 700 | 33 880 |

IV.10  Newsprint and other printing and writing paper
Papier journal et autre papier d'impression et d'écriture
Papel de periódico y otro papel de imprenta y de escribir

| Country / Pays / País | Year / Année / Año | Newsprint — Papier journal — Papel de periódico | | | | | Other printing and writing paper — Autre papier d'impression et d'écriture — Otro papel de imprenta y de escribir | | | | |
|---|---|---|---|---|---|---|---|---|---|---|---|
| | | Production / Producción | Imports / Importations / Importaciones | Exports / Exportations / Exportaciones | Consumption / Consommation / Consumo | Consumption per 1,000 inh. / Consommation pour 1 000 hab. / Consumo por 1 000 hab. | Production / Producción | Imports / Importations / Importaciones | Exports / Exportations / Exportaciones | Consumption / Consommation / Consumo | Consumption per 1,000 inh. / Consommation pour 1 000 hab. / Consumo por 1 000 hab. |
| **Norway (cont)** | 1991 | 955 000 | | 794 600 | 160 400 | 37 637 | 368 000 | 119 000 | 309 600 | 177 400 | 41 626 |
| | 1992 | 934 000 | 8 551 | 751 100 | 191 451 | 44 704 | 308 000 | 122 669 | 249 811 | 180 858 | 42 230 |
| | 1993 | 1 007 000 | 11 025 | 821 600 | 196 425 | 45 635 | 495 000 | 138 423 | 436 850 | 196 573 | 45 669 |
| | 1994 | 1 007 000 | 20 000 | 770 600 | 256 400 | 59 264 | 606 000 | 156 400 | 596 000 | 166 400 | 38 461 |
| | 1995 | 973 000 | 27 000 | 780 000 | 220 000 | 50 585 | 746 000 | 192 000 | 749 000 | 189 000 | 43 457 |
| | 1996 | 913 000 | 42 000 | 761 000 | 194 000 | 44 371 | 677 000 | 197 000 | 656 000 | 218 000 | 49 860 |
| | 1997 | 798 000 | 45 900 | 834 600 | 9 300 | 2 116 | 861 000 | 177 000 | 651 600 | 386 400 | 87 905 |
| **Poland** | 1970 | 87 900 | 15 000 | 15 000 | 87 900 | 2 702 | 188 100 | 21 000 | 100 | 209 000 | 6 426 |
| | 1975 | 83 000 | 38 000 | | 121 000 | 3 557 | 210 000 | 56 000 | 2 000 | 264 000 | 7 760 |
| | 1980 | 91 000 | 36 000 | | 127 000 | 3 570 | 199 000 | 28 000 | 2 000 | 225 000 | 6 325 |
| | 1985 | 82 000 | 53 400 | | 135 400 | 3 639 | 216 000 | 17 000 | | 233 000 | 6 263 |
| | 1990 | 25 000 | 8 000 | 15 400 | 17 600 | 462 | 243 000 | 4 300 | 14 700 | 232 600 | 6 102 |
| | 1991 | 64 000 | 2 000 | 15 000 | 51 000 | 1 333 | 230 000 | 6 400 | 15 400 | 221 000 | 5 778 |
| | 1992 | 61 000 | 513 | 2 367 | 59 146 | 1 542 | 262 000 | 22 432 | 26 243 | 258 189 | 6 731 |
| | 1993 | 46 000 | 41 000 | 15 000 | 72 000 | 1 872 | 284 000 | 68 100 | 31 600 | 320 500 | 8 333 |
| | 1994 | 68 000 | 19 500 | 12 700 | 74 800 | 1 941 | 336 000 | 85 700 | 22 700 | 399 000 | 10 352 |
| | 1995 | 95 000 | 7 900 | 44 000 | 58 900 | 1 526 | 389 000 | 209 200 | 45 900 | 552 300 | 14 305 |
| | 1996 | 86 000 | 15 000 | 42 000 | 59 000 | 1 526 | 431 000 | 353 000 | 96 000 | 688 000 | 17 797 |
| | 1997 | 80 000 | 26 000 | 45 000 | 61 000 | 1 577 | 470 000 | 420 000 | 157 000 | 733 000 | 18 944 |
| **Portugal** | 1970 | 700 | 43 500 | 200 | 44 000 | 4 865 | 43 200 | 1 500 | 300 | 44 400 | 4 909 |
| | 1975 | 1 000 | 28 500 | 2 100 | 27 400 | 3 013 | 54 000 | 2 300 | 14 400 | 41 900 | 4 608 |
| | 1980 | | 41 000 | | 41 000 | 4 198 | 87 000 | 4 300 | 14 000 | 77 300 | 7 915 |
| | 1985 | | 40 300 | | 40 300 | 4 069 | 103 000 | 16 000 | 35 400 | 83 600 | 8 441 |
| | 1990 | | 54 000 | 400 | 53 600 | 5 431 | 167 000 | 79 500 | 49 100 | 197 400 | 20 003 |
| | 1991 | | 56 000 | 500 | 55 500 | 5 628 | 282 000 | 99 000 | 132 000 | 249 000 | 25 250 |
| | 1992 | | 59 185 | 1 208 | 57 977 | 5 882 | 353 000 | 104 442 | 118 264 | 339 178 | 34 410 |
| | 1993 | | 63 415 | 921 | 62 494 | 6 341 | 385 000 | 107 034 | 146 413 | 345 621 | 35 071 |
| | 1994 | | 62 000 | 200 | 61 800 | 6 271 | 435 000 | 121 000 | 292 000 | 264 000 | 26 789 |
| | 1995 | | 69 000 | 100 | 68 900 | 6 991 | 438 000 | 116 000 | 287 000 | 267 000 | 27 090 |
| | 1996 | | 79 600 | 5 300 | 74 300 | 7 536 | 486 000 | 101 400 | 300 000 | 287 400 | 29 151 |
| | 1997 | | 84 300 | 5 300 | 79 000 | 8 009 | 533 000 | 175 300 | 367 300 | 341 000 | 34 571 |
| **Romania** | 1970 | 53 000 | 9 500 | 10 800 | 51 700 | 2 553 | 123 000 | 4 000 | 45 100 | 81 900 | 4 044 |
| | 1975 | 44 000 | 12 500 | | 56 500 | 2 659 | 121 000 | 1 200 | 38 000 | 84 200 | 3 963 |
| | 1980 | 103 000 | 12 000 | 59 000 | 56 000 | 2 522 | 141 000 | | 57 000 | 84 000 | 3 784 |
| | 1985 | 90 000 | | 30 000 | 60 000 | 2 640 | 139 000 | | 46 000 | 93 000 | 4 092 |
| | 1990 | 67 000 | | 12 976 | 54 024 | 2 328 | 111 000 | | 46 000 | 65 000 | 2 801 |
| | 1991 | 57 000 | | 12 976 | 44 024 | 1 900 | 52 000 | | 46 000 | 6 000 | 259 |
| | 1992 | 57 000 | 18 | 1 837 | 55 181 | 2 390 | 52 000 | 1 169 | 7 704 | 45 465 | 1 969 |
| | 1993 | 57 000 | 65 | 1 043 | 56 022 | 2 439 | 52 000 | 9 789 | 1 348 | 60 441 | 2 631 |
| | 1994 | 57 000 | 3 500 | 5 800 | 54 700 | 2 394 | 36 000 | 14 500 | 13 400 | 37 100 | 1 624 |
| | 1995 | 47 000 | 9 500 | 6 000 | 50 500 | 2 222 | 48 000 | 23 100 | 19 000 | 52 100 | 2 292 |
| | 1996 | 31 000 | 24 900 | 2 700 | 53 200 | 2 351 | 56 000 | 25 700 | 10 500 | 71 200 | 3 146 |
| | 1997 | 42 000 | 17 500 | 10 800 | 48 700 | 2 160 | 40 000 | 28 700 | 10 000 | 58 700 | 2 603 |
| **Russian Federation** | 1992 | 943 000 | 24 | 88 869 | 854 155 | 5 744 | 845 000 | 24 216 | 6 681 | 862 535 | 5 801 |
| | 1993 | 845 000 | 1 628 | 578 000 | 268 628 | 1 808 | 665 000 | 15 950 | 12 111 | 668 839 | 4 502 |
| | 1994 | 1 038 000 | 400 | 571 300 | 467 100 | 3 149 | 430 000 | 18 900 | 66 600 | 382 300 | 2 577 |
| | 1995 | 1 457 000 | 1 000 | 1 005 000 | 453 000 | 3 059 | 486 000 | 22 400 | 221 000 | 287 400 | 1 941 |
| | 1996 | 1 245 000 | 1 000 | 868 000 | 378 000 | 2 556 | 433 000 | 44 000 | 151 000 | 326 000 | 2 205 |
| | 1997 | 1 198 000 | 1 000 | 806 000 | 393 000 | 2 662 | 440 000 | 134 000 | 193 000 | 381 000 | 2 580 |
| **Slovakia** | 1993 | 20 000 | 7 523 | | 27 523 | 5 172 | 90 000 | 15 124 | 59 338 | 45 786 | 8 604 |
| | 1994 | 20 000 | 22 000 | 1 000 | 41 000 | 7 678 | 85 000 | 25 000 | 40 000 | 70 000 | 13 109 |
| | 1995 | 20 000 | 22 000 | 1 000 | 41 000 | 7 657 | 100 000 | 30 000 | 50 000 | 80 000 | 14 940 |
| | 1996 | 5 000 | 20 500 | 2 500 | 23 000 | 4 287 | 200 000 | 36 200 | 95 300 | 140 900 | 26 262 |
| | 1997 | 1 500 | 23 800 | 700 | 24 600 | 4 579 | 214 000 | 94 000 | 113 000 | 195 000 | 36 297 |
| **Slovenia** | 1992 | 81 000 | 2 013 | 2 569 | 80 444 | 41 292 | 60 000 | 7 111 | 27 424 | 39 687 | 20 372 |
| | 1993 | 66 000 | 5 988 | 17 519 | 54 469 | 27 717 | 45 000 | 33 599 | 130 836 | | |
| | 1994 | 76 000 | 6 000 | 19 000 | 63 000 | 31 821 | 44 000 | 32 000 | 153 000 | | |
| | 1995 | 93 000 | 9 700 | 32 600 | 70 100 | 35 226 | 32 000 | 16 000 | 85 000 | | |
| | 1996 | 39 000 | 11 000 | 30 000 | 20 000 | 10 025 | 80 000 | 16 000 | 85 000 | 11 000 | 5 514 |
| | 1997 | 49 000 | 177 000 | 443 000 | | | 183 000 | 36 000 | 175 000 | 44 000 | 22 051 |
| **Spain** | 1970 | 115 000 | 78 800 | | 193 800 | 5 737 | 322 800 | 11 300 | 15 900 | 318 200 | 9 420 |
| | 1975 | 103 000 | 101 800 | 900 | 203 900 | 5 728 | 521 000 | 53 000 | 64 300 | 509 700 | 14 319 |
| | 1980 | 108 000 | 57 600 | 3 200 | 162 400 | 4 326 | 717 000 | 82 000 | 42 900 | 756 100 | 20 140 |
| | 1985 | 134 000 | 134 600 | 5 500 | 263 100 | 6 838 | 712 000 | 110 900 | 112 700 | 710 200 | 18 459 |

Newsprint and other printing and writing paper IV.10
Papier journal et autre papier d'impression et d'écriture
Papel de periódico y otro papel de imprenta y de escribir

| Country / Pays / País | Year / Année / Año | Newsprint / Papier journal / Papel de periódico | | | | | Other printing and writing paper / Autre papier d'impression et d'écriture / Otro papel de imprenta y de escribir | | | | |
|---|---|---|---|---|---|---|---|---|---|---|---|
| | | Production / Production / Producción | Imports / Importa-tions / Importa-ciones | Exports / Exporta-tions / Exporta-ciones | Consump-tion / Consom-mation / Consumo | Consump-tion per 1,000 inh. / Consomma-tion pour 1 000 hab. / Consumo por 1 000 hab. | Production / Production / Producción | Imports / Importa-tions / Importa-ciones | Exports / Exporta-tions / Exporta-ciones | Consump-tion / Consom-mation / Consumo | Consump-tion per 1,000 inh. / Consomma-tion pour 1 000 hab. / Consumo por 1 000 hab. |
| **Spain (cont)** | 1990 | 173 000 | 261 000 | 24 000 | 410 000 | 10 432 | 832 000 | 642 800 | 170 200 | 1 304 600 | 33 193 |
| | 1991 | 149 000 | 312 200 | 24 300 | 436 900 | 11 089 | 853 000 | 731 800 | 212 900 | 1 371 900 | 34 821 |
| | 1992 | 120 000 | 353 706 | 20 191 | 453 515 | 11 492 | 850 000 | 828 091 | 217 851 | 1 460 240 | 37 001 |
| | 1993 | 94 000 | 363 000 | 16 700 | 440 300 | 11 144 | 812 000 | 879 000 | 284 000 | 1 407 000 | 35 612 |
| | 1994 | 99 000 | 380 000 | 14 000 | 465 000 | 11 760 | 874 000 | 919 800 | 327 000 | 1 466 800 | 37 096 |
| | 1995 | 148 000 | 360 300 | 12 200 | 496 100 | 12 538 | 858 000 | 930 500 | 386 000 | 1 402 500 | 35 445 |
| | 1996 | 137 000 | 364 000 | 27 000 | 474 000 | 11 972 | 844 000 | 918 000 | 198 000 | 1 564 000 | 39 502 |
| | 1997 | 143 000 | 397 000 | 48 800 | 491 200 | 12 400 | 901 000 | 1 130 300 | 339 000 | 1 692 300 | 42 721 |
| **Sweden** | 1970 | 1 030 000 | | 686 600 | 343 400 | 42 696 | 537 000 | 16 100 | 283 800 | 269 300 | 33 483 |
| | 1975 | 1 213 000 | | 920 800 | 292 200 | 35 666 | 448 000 | 18 400 | 277 500 | 188 900 | 23 057 |
| | 1980 | 1 534 000 | | 1 238 400 | 295 600 | 35 570 | 998 000 | 32 700 | 510 100 | 520 600 | 62 644 |
| | 1985 | 1 594 000 | 300 | 1 352 000 | 242 300 | 29 017 | 1 364 000 | 64 600 | 679 400 | 749 200 | 89 721 |
| | 1990 | 2 273 000 | 2 900 | 1 772 100 | 503 800 | 58 863 | 1 655 000 | 111 300 | 1 289 800 | 476 500 | 55 673 |
| | 1991 | 2 063 000 | 3 000 | 1 557 000 | 509 000 | 59 117 | 1 793 000 | 108 000 | 1 418 000 | 483 000 | 56 097 |
| | 1992 | 2 124 000 | 12 751 | 1 617 733 | 519 018 | 59 915 | 1 805 000 | 118 137 | 1 480 713 | 442 424 | 51 073 |
| | 1993 | 2 325 000 | 15 766 | 1 885 000 | 455 766 | 52 305 | 1 884 000 | 114 485 | 1 524 393 | 474 092 | 54 408 |
| | 1994 | 2 415 000 | 39 000 | 2 030 000 | 424 000 | 48 401 | 2 061 000 | 131 000 | 1 798 000 | 394 000 | 44 976 |
| | 1995 | 2 046 000 | 15 000 | 1 983 000 | 378 000 | 42 955 | 2 047 000 | 123 000 | 1 538 000 | 632 000 | 71 818 |
| | 1996 | 2 283 000 | 38 000 | 1 958 000 | 363 000 | 41 102 | 2 170 000 | 111 000 | 1 848 000 | 433 000 | 49 028 |
| | 1997 | 2 411 000 | 38 000 | 2 195 000 | 254 000 | 28 681 | 2 459 000 | 130 000 | 2 153 000 | 436 000 | 49 232 |
| **Switzerland** | 1970 | 143 000 | 24 600 | 100 | 167 500 | 27 074 | 249 000 | 77 300 | 8 900 | 317 400 | 51 304 |
| | 1975 | 143 000 | 6 000 | 8 200 | 140 800 | 22 213 | 180 000 | 82 400 | 28 700 | 233 700 | 36 869 |
| | 1980 | 210 000 | 24 600 | 27 600 | 207 000 | 32 756 | 284 000 | 156 600 | 76 000 | 364 600 | 57 695 |
| | 1985 | 232 000 | 45 000 | 30 000 | 247 000 | 37 792 | 300 000 | 205 000 | 119 000 | 386 000 | 59 059 |
| | 1990 | 280 000 | 88 000 | 58 000 | 310 000 | 45 361 | 370 000 | 335 000 | 109 000 | 596 000 | 87 210 |
| | 1991 | 272 000 | 92 000 | 51 000 | 313 000 | 45 378 | 360 000 | 344 000 | 113 000 | 591 000 | 85 683 |
| | 1992 | 282 000 | 94 810 | 67 660 | 309 150 | 44 412 | 373 000 | 335 948 | 173 499 | 535 449 | 76 921 |
| | 1993 | 288 000 | 105 000 | 69 400 | 323 600 | 46 073 | 381 000 | 325 680 | 188 910 | 517 770 | 73 718 |
| | 1994 | 234 000 | 116 000 | 68 000 | 282 000 | 39 805 | 413 000 | 397 000 | 256 000 | 554 000 | 78 198 |
| | 1995 | 263 000 | 113 000 | 79 000 | 297 000 | 41 580 | 444 000 | 379 000 | 284 000 | 539 000 | 75 460 |
| | 1996 | 259 000 | 99 000 | 89 000 | 269 000 | 37 370 | 441 000 | 379 000 | 294 000 | 526 000 | 73 073 |
| | 1997 | 308 000 | 96 000 | 119 000 | 285 000 | 39 308 | 461 000 | 451 000 | 329 000 | 583 000 | 80 409 |
| **The Former Yugoslav Rep. of Macedonia** | 1993 | | 2 100 | | 2 100 | 1 081 | 4 400 | 6 100 | 300 | 10 200 | 5 249 |
| | 1994 | | 3 000 | | 3 000 | 1 536 | 2 200 | 9 100 | 200 | 11 100 | 5 683 |
| | 1995 | | 3 200 | | 3 200 | 1 630 | 2 400 | 10 100 | 300 | 12 200 | 6 213 |
| | 1996 | | 3 200 | | 3 200 | 1 620 | 1 000 | 10 100 | 300 | 10 800 | 5 469 |
| | 1997 | | 3 200 | | 3 200 | 1 611 | 1 000 | 10 100 | 300 | 10 800 | 5 437 |
| **Ukraine** | 1993 | | | | | | 5 900 | 1 200 | | 4 700 | 91 |
| | 1994 | | | | | | 5 900 | 1 200 | | 4 700 | 91 |
| | 1995 | | 800 | | 800 | 16 | 2 200 | 300 | | 1 900 | 37 |
| | 1996 | 15 000 | 64 400 | 4 800 | 74 600 | 1 455 | 30 000 | 84 000 | 9 500 | 104 500 | 2 039 |
| | 1997 | 8 000 | 60 400 | 2 500 | 65 900 | 1 291 | 29 000 | 102 000 | 7 700 | 123 300 | 2 415 |
| **United Kingdom** | 1970 | 756 900 | 789 100 | 1 800 | 1 544 200 | 27 757 | 1 145 300 | 274 700 | 69 000 | 1 351 000 | 24 285 |
| | 1975 | 319 000 | 943 000 | 4 900 | 1 257 100 | 22 358 | 952 000 | 531 000 | 58 400 | 1 424 600 | 25 337 |
| | 1980 | 363 000 | 1 076 500 | 58 400 | 1 381 100 | 24 518 | 937 000 | 814 500 | 111 800 | 1 639 700 | 29 109 |
| | 1985 | 382 000 | 1 242 000 | 63 000 | 1 561 000 | 27 571 | 965 000 | 1 342 000 | 151 000 | 2 156 000 | 38 080 |
| | 1990 | 696 000 | 1 307 600 | 145 000 | 1 858 600 | 32 289 | 1 387 000 | 2 106 200 | 476 000 | 3 017 200 | 52 417 |
| | 1991 | 672 000 | 1 327 500 | 148 600 | 1 850 900 | 32 058 | 1 478 000 | 2 021 000 | 485 600 | 3 013 400 | 52 192 |
| | 1992 | 700 000 | 1 333 360 | 156 339 | 1 877 021 | 32 420 | 1 583 000 | 2 247 095 | 575 467 | 3 254 628 | 56 214 |
| | 1993 | 741 000 | 1 354 336 | 163 033 | 1 932 303 | 33 291 | 1 675 000 | 2 155 117 | 685 673 | 3 144 444 | 54 175 |
| | 1994 | 769 000 | 1 696 000 | 202 000 | 2 263 000 | 38 898 | 1 819 000 | 2 653 000 | 672 000 | 3 800 000 | 65 316 |
| | 1995 | 873 000 | 1 553 000 | 164 000 | 2 262 000 | 38 794 | 1 766 000 | 2 619 000 | 600 000 | 3 785 000 | 64 914 |
| | 1996 | 976 000 | 1 524 000 | 188 000 | 2 312 000 | 39 568 | 1 753 000 | 2 759 000 | 574 000 | 3 938 000 | 67 396 |
| | 1997 | 1 030 000 | 1 628 000 | 252 000 | 2 406 000 | 41 097 | 1 779 000 | 3 059 000 | 671 000 | 4 167 000 | 71 177 |
| **Oceania** | | | | | | | | | | | |
| **American Samoa** | 1994 | | | | | | | 14 | | 14 | 256 |
| | 1995 | | 122 | | 122 | 2 150 | | 14 | | 14 | 247 |
| | 1996 | | 122 | | 122 | 2 070 | | 14 | | 14 | 238 |
| | 1997 | | 122 | | 122 | 1 995 | | 14 | | 14 | 229 |
| **Australia** | 1970 | 173 300 | 275 300 | 100 | 448 500 | 35 779 | 126 300 | 123 000 | 17 100 | 232 200 | 18 524 |
| | 1975 | 196 000 | 324 500 | 200 | 520 300 | 37 430 | 160 000 | 163 900 | 12 900 | 311 000 | 22 373 |
| | 1980 | 221 000 | 336 800 | 1 200 | 556 600 | 38 204 | 210 000 | 181 100 | 16 200 | 374 900 | 25 732 |

IV.10    Newsprint and other printing and writing paper
Papier journal et autre papier d'impression et d'écriture
Papel de periódico y otro papel de imprenta y de escribir

| Country / Pays / País | Year / Année / Año | Newsprint / Papier journal / Papel de periódico | | | | | Other printing and writing paper / Autre papier d'impression et d'écriture / Otro papel de imprenta y de escribir | | | | |
|---|---|---|---|---|---|---|---|---|---|---|---|
| | | Production / Production / Producción | Imports / Importations / Importaciones | Exports / Exportations / Exportaciones | Consumption / Consommation / Consumo | Consumption per 1,000 inh. / Consommation pour 1 000 hab. / Consumo por 1 000 hab. | Production / Production / Producción | Imports / Importations / Importaciones | Exports / Exportations / Exportaciones | Consumption / Consommation / Consumo | Consumption per 1,000 inh. / Consommation pour 1 000 hab. / Consumo por 1 000 hab. |
| Australia (cont) | 1985 | 354 000 | 301 900 | 4 300 | 651 600 | 41 659 | 227 000 | 249 900 | 13 600 | 463 300 | 29 620 |
| | 1990 | 371 000 | 288 100 | 400 | 658 700 | 39 004 | 406 000 | 451 400 | 36 000 | 821 400 | 48 638 |
| | 1991 | 395 000 | 188 600 | 200 | 583 400 | 34 082 | 390 000 | 425 800 | 34 000 | 781 800 | 45 673 |
| | 1992 | 404 000 | 171 860 | 6 897 | 568 963 | 32 821 | 304 000 | 424 940 | 48 238 | 680 702 | 39 266 |
| | 1993 | 433 000 | 204 700 | 5 600 | 632 100 | 36 029 | 304 000 | 541 000 | 41 800 | 803 200 | 45 781 |
| | 1994 | 426 000 | 206 000 | 2 700 | 629 300 | 35 459 | 348 000 | 581 000 | 46 000 | 883 000 | 49 755 |
| | 1995 | 444 000 | 257 100 | 1 100 | 700 000 | 39 006 | 365 000 | 781 800 | 26 500 | 1 120 300 | 62 426 |
| | 1996 | 445 000 | 281 600 | 1 900 | 724 700 | 39 947 | 351 000 | 576 800 | 25 900 | 901 900 | 49 715 |
| | 1997 | 421 000 | 250 000 | 300 | 670 700 | 36 585 | 364 000 | 625 200 | 34 700 | 954 500 | 52 065 |
| Cook Islands | 1993 | | | | | | | 42 | | 42 | 2 240 |
| | 1994 | | | | | | | 52 | | 52 | 2 763 |
| | 1995 | | 45 | | 45 | 2 381 | | 52 | | 52 | 2 751 |
| | 1996 | | 45 | | 45 | 2 368 | | 52 | | 52 | 2 736 |
| | 1997 | | 45 | | 45 | 2 353 | | 52 | | 52 | 2 719 |
| Fiji | 1970 | | 800 | | 800 | 1 538 | | 500 | | 500 | 961 |
| | 1975 | | 900 | | 900 | 1 562 | | 2 600 | | 2 600 | 4 514 |
| | 1980 | | 1 700 | | 1 700 | 2 683 | | 2 400 | | 2 400 | 3 787 |
| | 1985 | | 2 000 | | 2 000 | 2 861 | | 3 000 | | 3 000 | 4 291 |
| | 1990 | | 1 400 | | 1 400 | 1 927 | | 4 900 | | 4 900 | 6 746 |
| | 1991 | | 1 800 | | 1 800 | 2 455 | | 6 800 | | 6 800 | 9 276 |
| | 1992 | | 1 800 | | 1 800 | 2 430 | | 1 557 | | 1 557 | 2 102 |
| | 1993 | | 2 475 | | 2 475 | 3 302 | | 1 257 | | 1 257 | 1 677 |
| | 1994 | | 2 700 | | 2 700 | 3 559 | | 6 000 | | 6 000 | 7 910 |
| | 1995 | | 2 500 | | 2 500 | 3 256 | | 6 000 | | 6 000 | 7 815 |
| | 1996 | | 2 200 | | 2 200 | 2 832 | | 6 000 | | 6 000 | 7 723 |
| | 1997 | | 2 200 | | 2 200 | 2 798 | | 1 300 | | 1 300 | 1 653 |
| French Polynesia | 1980 | | 100 | | 100 | 662 | | | | | |
| | 1990 | | 1 508 | | 1 508 | 7 706 | | | | | |
| | 1992 | | | | | | | 762 | | 762 | 3 742 |
| | 1993 | | | | | | | 999 | | 999 | 4 815 |
| | 1994 | | | | | | | 1 203 | | 1 203 | 5 693 |
| | 1995 | | 1 485 | | 1 485 | 6 900 | | 413 | | 413 | 1 919 |
| | 1996 | | 600 | | 600 | 2 738 | | 300 | | 300 | 1 369 |
| | 1997 | | 600 | | 600 | 2 689 | | 1 382 | 20 | 1 362 | 6 104 |
| Guam | 1992 | | | | | | 10 000 | 11 | 4 | 10 007 | 71 172 |
| | 1993 | | | | | | 10 000 | 9 | | 10 009 | 69 459 |
| | 1994 | | | | | | 4 000 | 1 | | 4 001 | 27 105 |
| | 1995 | | 41 | | 41 | 271 | 2 000 | 1 | | 2 001 | 13 243 |
| | 1996 | | 41 | | 41 | 265 | 2 000 | 1 | | 2 001 | 12 949 |
| | 1997 | | 41 | | 41 | 260 | 2 000 | 1 | | 2 001 | 12 672 |
| Kiribati | 1993 | | | | | | | 25 | | 25 | 331 |
| | 1994 | | | | | | | 43 | | 43 | 562 |
| | 1995 | | 4 | | 4 | 52 | | 43 | | 43 | 554 |
| | 1996 | | 4 | | 4 | 51 | | 43 | | 43 | 546 |
| | 1997 | | 4 | | 4 | 50 | | 43 | | 43 | 538 |
| Marshall Islands | 1992 | | | | | | | 22 | | 22 | 446 |
| | 1993 | | | | | | | 36 | | 36 | 705 |
| | 1994 | | | | | | | 36 | | 36 | 681 |
| | 1995 | | | | | | | 36 | | 36 | 658 |
| | 1996 | | | | | | | 36 | | 36 | 637 |
| | 1997 | | | | | | | 36 | | 36 | 616 |
| Nauru | 1992 | | | | | | | | 1 | | |
| | 1993 | | | | | | | 1 | | 1 | 99 |
| | 1994 | | | | | | | 4 | | 4 | 388 |
| | 1995 | | | | | | | 4 | | 4 | 381 |
| | 1996 | | | | | | | 4 | | 4 | 374 |
| | 1997 | | | | | | | 4 | | 4 | 367 |
| New Caledonia | 1980 | | 1 300 | | 1 300 | 9 089 | | | | | |
| | 1985 | | 300 | | 300 | 1 938 | | | | | |
| | 1990 | | 1 100 | | 1 100 | 6 567 | | 1 200 | | 1 200 | 7 164 |
| | 1991 | | | | | | | 1 000 | | 1 000 | 5 819 |

Newsprint and other printing and writing paper
Papier journal et autre papier d'impression et d'écriture
Papel de periódico y otro papel de imprenta y de escribir

IV.10

| Country / Pays / País | Year / Année / Año | Newsprint — Papier journal — Papel de periódico | | | | | Other printing and writing paper — Autre papier d'impression et d'écriture — Otro papel de imprenta y de escribir | | | | |
|---|---|---|---|---|---|---|---|---|---|---|---|
| | | Production / Producción | Imports / Importations / Importaciones | Exports / Exportations / Exportaciones | Consumption / Consommation / Consumo | Consumption per 1,000 inh. / Consommation pour 1 000 hab. / Consumo por 1 000 hab. | Production / Producción | Imports / Importations / Importaciones | Exports / Exportations / Exportaciones | Consumption / Consommation / Consumo | Consumption per 1,000 inh. / Consommation pour 1 000 hab. / Consumo por 1 000 hab. |
| New Caledonia(cont) | 1992 | | | | | | | 581 | | 581 | 3 284 |
| | 1993 | | | | | | | 1 106 | | 1 106 | 6 065 |
| | 1994 | | | | | | | 1 106 | | 1 106 | 5 888 |
| | 1995 | | 1 455 | | 1 455 | 7 539 | | 240 | | 240 | 1 243 |
| | 1996 | | 3 300 | | 3 300 | 16 686 | | 500 | | 500 | 2 528 |
| | 1997 | | 3 300 | | 3 300 | 16 322 | | 2 323 | | 2 323 | 11 489 |
| New Zealand | 1970 | 213 900 | 500 | 118 600 | 95 800 | 33 976 | 29 700 | 16 900 | 400 | 46 200 | 16 385 |
| | 1975 | 219 000 | 2 300 | 106 400 | 114 900 | 37 268 | 34 000 | 12 600 | 300 | 46 300 | 15 017 |
| | 1980 | 319 000 | 300 | 241 200 | 78 100 | 25 089 | 33 000 | 26 400 | 1 600 | 57 800 | 18 568 |
| | 1985 | 298 000 | 21 100 | 187 000 | 132 100 | 40 682 | 48 000 | 58 400 | 3 500 | 102 900 | 31 690 |
| | 1990 | 295 000 | 18 700 | 224 200 | 89 500 | 26 633 | 38 000 | 81 300 | 9 000 | 110 300 | 32 823 |
| | 1991 | 321 000 | 6 000 | 240 500 | 86 500 | 25 353 | 35 000 | 83 000 | 3 000 | 115 000 | 33 706 |
| | 1992 | 379 000 | 2 305 | 279 542 | 101 763 | 29 282 | 17 000 | 101 000 | 5 989 | 112 011 | 32 231 |
| | 1993 | 369 000 | 624 | 255 509 | 114 115 | 32 193 | 10 000 | 108 170 | 6 065 | 112 105 | 31 626 |
| | 1994 | 372 000 | 100 | 251 600 | 120 500 | 33 360 | 14 000 | 65 100 | 2 900 | 76 200 | 21 096 |
| | 1995 | 396 000 | | 228 400 | 167 600 | 45 651 | 13 000 | 73 300 | 4 500 | 81 800 | 22 281 |
| | 1996 | 379 000 | | 257 300 | 121 700 | 32 711 | 13 000 | 65 400 | 4 800 | 73 600 | 19 783 |
| | 1997 | 383 000 | | 257 300 | 125 700 | 33 420 | 12 000 | 66 000 | 5 000 | 73 000 | 19 409 |
| Niue | 1994 | | | | | | | 5 | | 5 | 2 373 |
| | 1995 | | | | | | | 5 | | 5 | 2 426 |
| | 1996 | | | | | | | 5 | | 5 | 2 476 |
| | 1997 | | | | | | | 5 | | 5 | 2 524 |
| Pacific Islands (Palau) | 1992 | | | | | | | 24 | | 24 | 1 503 |
| | 1993 | | | | | | | 13 | | 13 | 794 |
| | 1994 | | | | | | | 36 | | 36 | 2 143 |
| | 1995 | | | | | | | 36 | | 36 | 2 090 |
| | 1996 | | | | | | | 36 | | 36 | 2 039 |
| | 1997 | | | | | | | 36 | | 36 | 1 990 |
| Papua New Guinea | 1970 | | | | | | | 700 | | 700 | 289 |
| | 1992 | | | | | | | 1 581 | | 1 581 | 394 |
| | 1993 | | | | | | | 1 061 | 5 | 1 056 | 257 |
| | 1994 | | | | | | | 1 592 | 5 | 1 587 | 377 |
| | 1995 | | 2 300 | | 2 300 | 535 | | 1 592 | 5 | 1 587 | 369 |
| | 1996 | | 2 700 | | 2 700 | 614 | | 800 | 5 | 795 | 181 |
| | 1997 | | 2 700 | | 2 700 | 600 | | 800 | 5 | 795 | 177 |
| Samoa | 1970 | | | | | | | 300 | | 300 | 2 076 |
| | 1985 | | | | | | | 100 | | 100 | 637 |
| | 1990 | | | | | | | 117 | | 117 | 731 |
| | 1991 | | | | | | | 117 | | 117 | 726 |
| | 1993 | | | | | | | 61 | | 61 | 372 |
| | 1994 | | | | | | | 96 | | 96 | 579 |
| | 1995 | | 83 | | 83 | 495 | | 12 | | 12 | 72 |
| | 1996 | | 100 | | 100 | 589 | | | | | |
| | 1997 | | 100 | | 100 | 581 | | | | | |
| Solomon Islands | 1992 | | | | | | | 23 | | 23 | 67 |
| | 1993 | | | | | | | 36 | | 36 | 101 |
| | 1994 | | | | | | | 74 | | 74 | 202 |
| | 1995 | | | | | | | 16 | | 16 | 42 |
| | 1996 | | | | | | | 16 | | 16 | 41 |
| | 1997 | | | | | | | 16 | | 16 | 40 |
| Tonga | 1992 | | | | | | | 10 | | 10 | 104 |
| | 1993 | | | | | | | 236 | | 236 | 2 443 |
| | 1994 | | | | | | | 126 | | 126 | 1 301 |
| | 1995 | | 35 | | 35 | 360 | | 30 | | 30 | 309 |
| | 1996 | | 2 | | 2 | 21 | | 10 | | 10 | 103 |
| | 1997 | | 2 | | 2 | 20 | | 3 | | 3 | 31 |
| Tuvalu | 1992 | | | | | | | 1 | 1 | | |
| | 1994 | | | | | | | 2 | | 2 | 201 |
| | 1995 | | | | | | | 2 | | 2 | 195 |
| | 1996 | | | | | | | 2 | | 2 | 190 |
| | 1997 | | | | | | | 2 | | 2 | 185 |

IV.10   Newsprint and other printing and writing paper
Papier journal et autre papier d'impression et d'écriture
Papel de periódico y otro papel de imprenta y de escribir

| Country / Pays / País | Year / Année / Año | Newsprint — Papier journal — Papel de periódico | | | | | Other printing and writing paper — Autre papier d'impression et d'écriture — Otro papel de imprenta y de escribir | | | | |
|---|---|---|---|---|---|---|---|---|---|---|---|
| | | Production / Production / Producción | Imports / Importations / Importaciones | Exports / Exportations / Exportaciones | Consumption / Consommation / Consumo | Consumption per 1,000 inh. / Consommation pour 1 000 hab. / Consumo por 1 000 hab. | Production / Production / Producción | Imports / Importations / Importaciones | Exports / Exportations / Exportaciones | Consumption / Consommation / Consumo | Consumption per 1,000 inh. / Consommation pour 1 000 hab. / Consumo por 1 000 hab. |
| Vanuatu, Republic of | | | | | | | | | | | |
| | 1992 | | | | | | | 4 | | 4 | 25 |
| | 1993 | | | | | | | 30 | | 30 | 187 |
| | 1994 | | | | | | | 45 | | 45 | 273 |
| | 1995 | | 8 | | 8 | 47 | | 45 | | 45 | 267 |
| | 1996 | | 1 | | 1 | 6 | | 23 | | 23 | 133 |
| | 1997 | | 1 | | 1 | 6 | | 50 | | 50 | 282 |

**General note**

For general explanations and definitions, please refer to the beginning of this chapter.

**Note générale**

Pour les explications et définitions générales, prière de se référer au début de ce chapitre.

**Nota general**

Para las explicaciones y definiciones generales, referirse al comienzo de este capítulo.

Production of long films IV.11
Production de films de long métrage
Producción de películas de largo metraje

# IV.11 Production of long films

## Production de films de long métrage

## Producción de películas de largo metraje

**Definition of data:**

P = Production completed in the year indicated

C = Approved by censor for public showing in the year indicated

S = Shown commercially for the first time in the year indicated

O = Other criteria

Length = Minimum length (in meters) which categorizes the film as a 'long film'

**Code:**

P = Production terminée dans l'année indiquée

C = Approuvé par la censure pour la projection en public dans l'année indiquée

S = Mis en exploitation commerciale pour la première fois dans l'année indiquée

O = Autres critères

Longueur = Longueur minimale (en mètres) des films considérés de 'long métrage'

**Tipo de datos:**

P = Producción terminada el año indicado

C = Aprobado por la censura para su presentación al público en el año indicado

S = Puesto en explotación comercial por primera vez en el año indicado

O = Otros criterios

Longitud = Longitud mínima (en metros) de las películas consideradas de 'largo metraje'

| Country / Pays / País | Year / Année / Año | Production of long films / Production de films de long métrage / Producción de películas de largo metraje | | | |
|---|---|---|---|---|---|
| | | Length / Longueur / Longitud | Defini-tion of data / Code / Tipo de datos | Total | of which copro-duction / dont copro-duction / de los cuales copro-ducción |
| **Africa** | | | | | |
| Algeria | 1970 | 1 600 | S | 3 | 2 |
| | 1975 | 2 000 | C | 3 | 2 |
| | 1981 | 2 400 | C | 2 | 1 |
| | 1985 | 2 600 | P | 2 | - |
| | 1990 | ... | ... | 3 | ... |
| Angola | 1979 | 1 800 | P | 1 | - |
| | 1986 | ... | ... | 1 | ... |
| Burkina Faso | 1986 | ... | S | 5 | 3 |
| Cameroon | 1975 | 3 000 | S | 1 | - |
| | 1979 | ... | P | 3 | - |
| | 1985 | 1 600 | O | 2 | - |
| Côte d'Ivoire | 1979 | ... | P | 2 | 1 |
| | 1981 | 2 400 | P | 2 | - |
| | 1993 | 2 100 | S | 2 | 2 |
| Egypt | 1970 | 2 000 | C | 47 | 1 |
| | 1975 | 2 000 | P | 90 | - |
| | 1986 | ... | ... | 103 | - |
| | 1989 | ... | ... | 59 | - |
| | 1994 | ... | C | 72 | ... |
| Ethiopia | 1990 | ... | ... | 1 | 1 |
| | 1991 | ... | ... | 1 | - |
| Ghana | 1970 | 2 000 | P | 3 | - |
| | 1975 | 2 000 | P | 1 | - |
| | 1981 | 2 400 | P | 1 | 1 |
| | 1984 | ... | P | 1 | 1 |

| Country / Pays / País | Year / Année / Año | Production of long films / Production de films de long métrage / Producción de películas de largo metraje | | | |
|---|---|---|---|---|---|
| | | Length / Longueur / Longitud | Defini-tion of data / Code / Tipo de datos | Total | of which copro-duction / dont copro-duction / de los cuales copro-ducción |
| Guinea | 1984 | 2 400 | S | 1 | 1 |
| | 1991 | ... | P | 1 | 1 |
| Libyan Arab Jamahiriya | 1975 | ... | ... | 2 | 1 |
| Mali | 1993 | 2 100 | P | 3 | 2 |
| Mauritius | 1989 | 2 700 | P | 1 | 1 |
| Morocco | 1992 | 1 900 | C | 2 | ... |
| | 1993 | 1 900 | C | 4 | ... |
| Nigeria | 1980 | 1 800 | C | 20 | 20 |
| Sierra Leone | 1970 | 2 000 | P | 2 | - |
| Sudan | 1980 | ... | ... | 1 | 1 |
| | 1989 | ... | ... | 1 | - |
| Tunisia | 1970 | ... | ... | 3 | ... |
| | 1986 | ... | P | 2 | ... |
| United Republic of Tanzania | 1986 | 2 500 | P | 1 | 1 |
| **North America** | | | | | |
| Canada | 1971 | ... | ... | 25 | ... |
| | 1975 | 2 000 | P | 41 | ... |
| | 1980 | 2 060 | P | 32 | ... |
| | 1984 | 2 060 | ... | 44 | ... |
| | 1990 | ... | P | 54 | ... |
| | 1991 | ... | ... | 39 | ... |
| | 1992 | ... | ... | 22 | ... |

IV.11  Production of long films
Production de films de long métrage
Producción de películas de largo metraje

| Country / Pays / País | Year / Année / Año | Production of long films — Production de films de long métrage — Producción de películas de largo metraje | | | |
|---|---|---|---|---|---|
| | | Length / Longueur / Longitud | Definition of data / Code / Tipo de datos | Total | of which coproduction / dont coproduction / de los cuales coproducción |
| Costa Rica | 1985 | ... | S | 2 | 2 |
| Cuba | 1970 | 2 000 | P | 1 | - |
| | 1975 | ... | P | 8 | - |
| | 1980 | ... | P | 6 | - |
| | 1985 | ... | P | 10 | 3 |
| | 1990 | ... | P | 8 | 4 |
| | 1991 | ... | P | 6 | 3 |
| | 1992 | ... | P | 6 | 3 |
| | 1993 | ... | P | 6 | 3 |
| Guatemala | 1985 | | P | 3 | - |
| Mexico | 1970 | ... | S | 124 | 2 |
| | 1975 | ... | S | 162 | ... |
| | 1980 | ... | P | 109 | 48 |
| | 1985 | ... | O | 101 | 5 |
| | 1990 | ... | P | 98 | 1 |
| | 1991 | ... | P | 32 | 1 |
| | 1992 | ... | P | 45 | 2 |
| | 1993 | ... | P | 53 | 4 |
| | 1994 | ... | C | 46 | 2 |
| | 1995 | ... | C | 14 | 1 |
| United States | 1970 | ... | ... | 236 | ... |
| | 1975 | ... | ... | 176 | ... |
| | 1980 | ... | O | 264 | ... |
| | 1985 | ... | ... | 255 | ... |
| | 1990 | ... | ... | 276 | ... |
| | 1991 | ... | ... | 260 | ... |
| | 1992 | ... | ... | 210 | ... |
| | 1993 | ... | ... | 440 | ... |
| | 1994 | ... | ... | 420 | ... |
| **South America** | | | | | |
| Argentina | 1970 | 2 000 | S | 28 | ... |
| | 1975 | 1 620 | S | 34 | 1 |
| | 1980 | 1 650 | P | 27 | - |
| | 1985 | ... | ... | 24 | ... |
| | 1990 | ... | P | 16 | 3 |
| | 1991 | ... | P | 21 | 6 |
| Bolivia | 1979 | 2 500 | S | 1 | - |
| | 1985 | 1 620 | C | 2 | - |
| | 1989 | 1 620 | P | 1 | - |
| | 1994 | ... | S | 1 | - |
| | 1995 | ... | S | 4 | 1 |
| Brazil | 1970 | ... | ... | 72 | ... |
| | 1975 | 2 000 | S | 90 | 1 |
| | 1980 | ... | P | 103 | ... |
| | 1985 | 1 645 | C | 86 | ... |
| Chile | 1992 | ... | C | 2 | ... |
| | 1993 | ... | C | 1 | ... |
| Colombia | 1975 | 2 400 | ... | 2 | - |
| | 1979 | ... | ... | 5 | 5 |
| | 1985 | 2 500 | C | 9 | 1 |
| | 1989 | ... | P | 3 | ... |
| Ecuador | 1990 | ... | S | 2 | 1 |
| | 1991 | ... | S | 1 | - |
| Guyana | 1975 | 3 230 | S | 4 | - |
| Peru | 1975 | 2 500 | ... | 1 | - |
| | 1980 | 2 000 | ... | 1 | 1 |
| | 1986 | ... | ... | 4 | 2 |
| | 1990 | ... | C | 5 | 4 |
| | 1991 | ... | C | 1 | 1 |
| Uruguay | 1979 | 2 000 | S | 2 | 1 |
| | 1985 | 1 800 | P | 1 | 1 |
| Venezuela | 1970 | 2 000 | ... | 3 | 3 |
| | 1975 | 2 600 | P | 9 | 1 |
| | 1980 | ... | S | 12 | 4 |

| Country / Pays / País | Year / Année / Año | Production of long films — Production de films de long métrage — Producción de películas de largo metraje | | | |
|---|---|---|---|---|---|
| | | Length / Longueur / Longitud | Definition of data / Code / Tipo de datos | Total | of which coproduction / dont coproduction / de los cuales coproducción |
| Venezuela (cont) | 1985 | ... | S | 16 | 1 |
| | 1990 | ... | S | 4 | 2 |
| | 1991 | ... | S | 7 | 1 |
| | 1992 | ... | S | 2 | 1 |
| | 1993 | ... | S | 4 | 2 |
| **Asia** | | | | | |
| Afghanistan | 1980 | ... | P | 2 | - |
| | 1985 | ... | P | 3 | - |
| Armenia | 1992 | 1 800 | P | 5 | 1 |
| | 1993 | 1 800 | P | 5 | 2 |
| | 1994 | 1 800 | P | 2 | 2 |
| | 1995 | 1 800 | P | 3 | 1 |
| Azerbaijan | 1992 | ... | ... | 5 | 1 |
| | 1993 | ... | ... | 4 | 1 |
| Bangladesh | 1986 | 4 000 | S | 65 | 1 |
| | 1989 | 4 000 | ... | 77 | 3 |
| China | 1975 | ... | ... | 27 | ... |
| | 1980 | ... | ... | 82 | ... |
| | 1985 | ... | ... | 127 | ... |
| | 1990 | ... | ... | 134 | 11 |
| | 1991 | ... | ... | 130 | 9 |
| | 1992 | ... | ... | 170 | ... |
| | 1993 | ... | ... | 154 | ... |
| China, Hong Kong SAR | 1970 | 2 000 | C | 137 | - |
| | 1975 | 2 400 | C | 112 | 3 |
| | 1980 | 1 600 | C | 141 | - |
| | 1990 | 1 600 | C | 247 | 8 |
| | 1991 | 1 600 | C | 239 | 3 |
| | 1994 | 1 600 | S | 267 | - |
| | 1995 | 1 600 | S | 315 | - |
| Cyprus | 1971 | 1 500 | C | 1 | - |
| | 1985 | ... | S | 2 | 1 |
| | 1992 | ... | P | 1 | 1 |
| Georgia | 1992 | 1 800 | P | 1 | ... |
| | 1993 | 1 800 | P | 5 | ... |
| India | 1970 | 2 000 | C | 396 | - |
| | 1975 | 2 000 | C | 475 | - |
| | 1980 | 2 000 | C | 742 | - |
| | 1985 | 2 000 | C | 912 | - |
| | 1990 | ... | ... | 948 | ... |
| | 1991 | ... | ... | 910 | ... |
| | 1992 | ... | ... | 838 | ... |
| Indonesia | 1970 | 3 000 | ... | 14 | ... |
| | 1975 | 3 000 | C | 41 | 3 |
| | 1980 | ... | P | 73 | - |
| | 1985 | ... | ... | 63 | 1 |
| | 1990 | ... | ... | 112 | ... |
| | 1991 | ... | ... | 85 | ... |
| | 1992 | ... | ... | 32 | ... |
| | 1993 | ... | ... | 27 | ... |
| | 1994 | ... | ... | *40 | ... |
| Iran, Islamic Republic of | 1971 | 2 000 | C | 63 | - |
| | 1975 | 2 400 | C | 68 | - |
| | 1979 | 1 900 | C | 14 | - |
| | 1985 | ... | C | 42 | - |
| | 1990 | ... | ... | 61 | ... |
| | 1991 | ... | ... | 52 | ... |
| | 1992 | ... | ... | 47 | ... |
| | 1993 | ... | ... | 50 | ... |
| | 1994 | 1 920 | ... | 45 | ... |
| | 1995 | 1 920 | ... | 62 | ... |
| Iraq | 1976 | ... | ... | 1 | - |
| | 1980 | ... | ... | 2 | - |
| | 1985 | ... | ... | 1 | - |

Production of long films IV.11
Production de films de long métrage
Producción de películas de largo metraje

| Country / Pays / País | Year / Année / Año | Production of long films / Production de films de long métrage / Producción de películas de largo metraje | | | |
|---|---|---|---|---|---|
| | | Length / Longueur / Longitud | Definition of data / Code / Tipo de datos | Total | of which coproduction / dont coproduction / de los cuales coproducción |
| Israel | 1970 | 2 000 | P | 8 | 8 |
| | 1975 | ... | C | 8 | ... |
| | 1980 | ... | C | 15 | - |
| | 1985 | ... | C | 14 | 1 |
| Japan | 1970 | 2 000 | P | 423 | ... |
| | 1975 | 2 000 | ... | 333 | ... |
| | 1980 | 1 600 | S | 320 | 1 |
| | 1985 | ... | P | 319 | 1 |
| | 1990 | 1 600 | ... | 239 | ... |
| | 1991 | 1 600 | ... | 230 | ... |
| | 1992 | 1 600 | P | 240 | 3 |
| | 1993 | 1 600 | P | 238 | 3 |
| Kazakstan | 1992 | 2 300 | ... | 23 | 6 |
| | 1993 | 2 300 | ... | 15 | 6 |
| | 1994 | 2 138 | ... | 9 | 1 |
| | 1995 | 2 138 | ... | 10 | - |
| Korea, Democratic People's Rep. | 1985 | ... | P | 37 | 1 |
| Korea, Republic of | 1970 | 2 466 | C | 224 | 6 |
| | 1975 | ... | C | 99 | 7 |
| | 1980 | 2 000 | C | 91 | 2 |
| | 1985 | 2 500 | C | 81 | 7 |
| | 1989 | 2 500 | C | 110 | - |
| | 1992 | ... | C | 96 | - |
| | 1993 | ... | C | 63 | - |
| Lebanon | 1970 | ... | ... | 6 | ... |
| | 1992 | 2 700 | P | 5 | 4 |
| | 1993 | 2 700 | P | 5 | 4 |
| Malaysia | 1970 | 3 000 | P | 4 | - |
| | 1975 | 3 000 | P | 5 | 2 |
| | 1980 | ... | ... | 14 | - |
| | 1985 | ... | ... | 1 | - |
| | 1990 | ... | ... | 14 | 1 |
| | 1991 | ... | ... | 15 | - |
| | 1992 | 2 000 | P | 12 | - |
| | 1993 | 2 000 | P | 12 | - |
| Myanmar | 1975 | 4 000 | C | 66 | - |
| | 1986 | ... | ... | 85 | - |
| Pakistan | 1970 | 3 600 | S | 141 | 1 |
| | 1975 | 3 700 | S | 120 | 1 |
| | 1979 | 3 600 | S | 95 | 1 |
| | 1990 | 4 500 | S | 84 | 1 |
| | 1991 | 4 500 | S | 91 | - |
| | 1992 | 5 000 | S | 91 | 1 |
| | 1993 | 5 000 | S | 88 | 3 |
| | 1994 | 4 000 | C | 76 | ... |
| | 1995 | 4 000 | C | 64 | ... |
| Philippines | 1975 | 2 400 | ... | 143 | ... |
| | 1984 | ... | ... | 139 | ... |
| | 1989 | 2 100 | ... | 142 | ... |
| | 1994 | ... | C | 428 | ... |
| | 1995 | ... | C | 456 | ... |
| Singapore | 1975 | 2 700 | C | 4 | 1 |
| | 1985 | 3 030 | O | 25 | 2 |
| Sri Lanka | 1970 | 3 000 | S | 25 | - |
| | 1975 | 3 000 | S | 31 | 1 |
| | 1980 | 1 664 | C | 40 | 3 |
| | 1986 | 2 800 | ... | 15 | 1 |
| | 1992 | 3 000 | C | 38 | - |
| | 1993 | 3 000 | C | 58 | 1 |
| Syrian Arab Republic | 1980 | 2 100 | ... | 1 | - |
| | 1985 | ... | ... | 1 | - |
| | 1989 | ... | ... | 1 | - |
| | 1992 | ... | ... | 3 | - |
| | 1993 | ... | ... | 2 | 1 |
| Tajikistan | 1992 | 1 800 | P | 1 | - |
| Thailand | 1975 | ... | ... | 55 | ... |
| | 1979 | ... | C | 120 | - |
| | 1985 | ... | ... | 134 | ... |
| | 1989 | 1 700 | C | 194 | - |
| Turkey | 1975 | ... | ... | 160 | ... |
| | 1980 | ... | ... | 74 | 1 |
| | 1985 | ... | C | 96 | ... |
| | 1990 | ... | ... | 127 | 17 |
| | 1991 | ... | ... | 63 | - |
| Uzbekistan | 1992 | ... | P | 8 | 1 |
| | 1993 | ... | P | 10 | 1 |
| Viet Nam | 1975 | ... | ... | 7 | - |
| | 1980 | ... | ... | 16 | ... |
| | 1984 | ... | ... | 16 | ... |
| **Europe** | | | | | |
| Albania | 1985 | ... | P | 14 | - |
| | 1989 | ... | ... | 11 | ... |
| Austria | 1970 | 2 500 | S | 7 | 4 |
| | 1975 | 2 000 | S | 6 | 2 |
| | 1980 | 2 000 | S | 8 | 2 |
| | 1985 | 2 000 | S | 18 | 9 |
| | 1990 | 1 600 | ... | 19 | - |
| | 1991 | 1 600 | ... | 11 | - |
| | 1992 | 1 600 | S | 10 | - |
| | 1993 | 1 600 | S | 15 | - |
| | 1994 | 1 600 | S | 17 | - |
| | 1995 | 1 600 | S | 22 | - |
| Belarus | 1979 | 2 300 | ... | 6 | ... |
| | 1986 | 1 800 | P | 6 | - |
| | 1994 | 1 800 | P | 4 | - |
| | 1995 | 1 800 | P | 2 | 1 |
| Belgium | 1970 | 1 800 | ... | 13 | 7 |
| | 1975 | 1 600 | C | 7 | ... |
| | 1980 | 1 600 | ... | 5 | 3 |
| | 1985 | 1 600 | ... | 7 | 2 |
| | 1990 | 1 600 | ... | 12 | 9 |
| | 1991 | 1 600 | ... | 15 | 13 |
| | 1992 | 1 600 | ... | 20 | 17 |
| | 1993 | 1 600 | O | 5 | 4 |
| | 1994 | 1 600 | O | 8 | 6 |
| | 1995 | 1 600 | O | 8 | 8 |
| Bulgaria | 1970 | 1 200 | P | 16 | 2 |
| | 1975 | 1 200 | ... | 25 | 3 |
| | 1980 | ... | ... | 31 | ... |
| | 1985 | 1 800 | P | 40 | 8 |
| | 1990 | 2 600 | ... | 32 | 1 |
| | 1991 | 2 600 | ... | 14 | 1 |
| | 1992 | ... | ... | 5 | 1 |
| | 1993 | ... | ... | 12 | 4 |
| | 1994 | 2 600 | ... | 5 | - |
| | 1995 | 2 600 | ... | 11 | 5 |
| Croatia | 1980 | ... | ... | 3 | ... |
| | 1985 | ... | ... | 6 | ... |
| | 1990 | ... | ... | 3 | ... |
| | 1991 | ... | ... | 4 | ... |
| | 1992 | ... | P | 1 | - |
| | 1993 | ... | P | 1 | 1 |
| | 1994 | 2 000 | P | 2 | 1 |
| | 1995 | 2 000 | P | 3 | - |
| Czech Republic | 1992 | 1 900 | S | 11 | 4 |
| | 1993 | 1 900 | S | 15 | 3 |
| | 1994 | 1 800 | P | 23 | 7 |
| | 1995 | 1 800 | P | 22 | 6 |

IV.11 Production of long films
Production de films de long métrage
Producción de películas de largo metraje

| Country / Pays / País | Year / Année / Año | Production of long films / Production de films de long métrage / Producción de películas de largo metraje | | | |
|---|---|---|---|---|---|
| | | Length / Longueur / Longitud | Definition of data / Code / Tipo de datos | Total | of which coproduction / dont coproduction / de los cuales coproducción |
| Denmark | 1970 | 1 800 | C | 18 | ... |
| | 1975 | 2 000 | C | 17 | 2 |
| | 1980 | 2 000 | S | 12 | - |
| | 1985 | 1 600 | S | 10 | 2 |
| | 1990 | 1 600 | S | 13 | - |
| | 1991 | 1 600 | S | 11 | 2 |
| | 1992 | 1 600 | S | 9 | 1 |
| | 1993 | 1 600 | S | 11 | 1 |
| | 1994 | 1 600 | S | 14 | ... |
| | 1995 | 1 600 | S | 12 | ... |
| Estonia | 1992 | 500 | P | 5 | - |
| | 1993 | 500 | P | 13 | 5 |
| | 1994 | 1 500 | P | 5 | 5 |
| | 1995 | 1 500 | P | 3 | 3 |
| Finland | 1970 | 1 000 | C | 13 | 8 |
| | 1975 | 1 000 | C | 5 | ... |
| | 1980 | 2 000 | S | 10 | 3 |
| | 1985 | 1 700 | S | 13 | - |
| | 1990 | 1 500 | S | 13 | 3 |
| | 1991 | 1 500 | S | 12 | - |
| | 1992 | 1 500 | S | 10 | 5 |
| | 1993 | 1 500 | S | 13 | 2 |
| | 1994 | 1 505 | S | 11 | 6 |
| | 1995 | 1 505 | S | 8 | 5 |
| France | 1970 | 1 776 | O | 138 | 72 |
| | 1975 | 1 776 | O | 222 | 62 |
| | 1980 | ... | O | 189 | 45 |
| | 1985 | 1 600 | O | 151 | 45 |
| | 1990 | ... | ... | 146 | 65 |
| | 1991 | ... | ... | 156 | 83 |
| | 1992 | ... | ... | 155 | 83 |
| | 1993 | ... | ... | 152 | 85 |
| | 1994 | ... | ... | 115 | ... |
| | 1995 | ... | ... | 141 | 67 |
| Germany | 1991 | 1 600 | S | 72 | 19 |
| | 1992 | 1 600 | S | 63 | 10 |
| | 1993 | 1 600 | S | 67 | 17 |
| | 1994 | 1 600 | S | 60 | 14 |
| | 1995 | 1 600 | S | 63 | 26 |
| Greece | 1970 | 2 000 | C | 112 | ... |
| | 1975 | 2 000 | C | 70 | ... |
| | 1980 | 2 000 | C | 27 | - |
| | 1985 | 2 000 | C | 33 | - |
| | 1990 | 1 600 | C | 6 | - |
| | 1991 | 1 600 | C | 7 | - |
| | 1992 | ... | ... | 14 | ... |
| | 1993 | ... | ... | 18 | ... |
| | 1994 | ... | ... | 25 | ... |
| Hungary | 1970 | 2 000 | P | 23 | 2 |
| | 1975 | 2 000 | P | 19 | - |
| | 1980 | 2 000 | P | 26 | 5 |
| | 1985 | 2 000 | P | 21 | - |
| | 1990 | 2 000 | P | 23 | 1 |
| | 1991 | 2 000 | P | 19 | - |
| | 1992 | 2 000 | S | 25 | ... |
| | 1993 | 2 000 | S | 19 | ... |
| | 1994 | ... | P | 17 | ... |
| | 1995 | ... | P | 12 | 1 |
| Iceland | 1980 | 2 000 | ... | 3 | - |
| | 1985 | ... | ... | 5 | - |
| | 1990 | ... | ... | 2 | - |
| | 1991 | ... | ... | 1 | - |
| | 1992 | ... | ... | 5 | ... |
| | 1993 | ... | ... | 2 | - |
| | 1994 | 2 000 | S | 2 | 2 |
| | 1995 | 2 000 | S | 7 | 6 |
| Ireland | 1970 | ... | C | 5 | ... |
| | 1975 | ... | C | 2 | ... |
| | 1981 | 1 500 | C | 2 | - |
| | 1985 | 1 500 | C | 2 | - |
| Ireland (cont) | 1990 | 1 600 | ... | 3 | - |
| | 1993 | 1 600 | ... | 17 | ... |
| | 1994 | 1 600 | ... | 17 | ... |
| Italy | 1970 | 2 000 | C | 240 | 135 |
| | 1975 | 1 600 | C | 203 | 43 |
| | 1980 | 1 600 | S | 160 | 32 |
| | 1985 | 1 600 | S | 73 | 7 |
| | 1990 | 1 600 | S | 115 | 17 |
| | 1991 | 1 600 | S | 99 | 16 |
| | 1992 | 1 600 | S | 114 | 14 |
| | 1993 | 1 600 | S | 105 | 21 |
| | 1994 | 1 600 | S | 120 | 18 |
| | 1995 | 1 600 | S | 96 | 18 |
| Latvia | 1991 | ... | ... | 12 | ... |
| | 1992 | ... | ... | 4 | ... |
| | 1993 | ... | ... | 7 | ... |
| | 1994 | 1 500 | P | 2 | ... |
| | 1995 | 1 500 | P | 2 | ... |
| Lithuania | 1992 | 1 650 | P | 2 | - |
| | 1993 | 1 650 | P | 1 | - |
| | 1994 | 1 900 | S | 2 | - |
| | 1995 | 1 900 | S | 3 | 1 |
| Luxembourg | 1989 | ... | S | 2 | 1 |
| | 1992 | ... | S | 3 | 2 |
| | 1993 | ... | S | 4 | 4 |
| Moldova | 1992 | 2 200 | P | 6 | 2 |
| Netherlands | 1970 | 1 776 | P | 3 | - |
| | 1975 | 1 776 | P | 16 | - |
| | 1980 | ... | S | 7 | - |
| | 1985 | ... | ... | 16 | ... |
| | 1990 | ... | S | 14 | - |
| | 1991 | ... | S | 12 | 2 |
| | 1993 | ... | ... | 16 | ... |
| | 1994 | ... | ... | 16 | 4 |
| Norway | 1970 | 2 000 | S | 9 | 2 |
| | 1975 | 1 000 | C | 14 | 1 |
| | 1980 | 1 000 | S | 10 | - |
| | 1985 | 2 000 | C | 12 | - |
| | 1990 | 2 000 | C | 9 | 1 |
| | 1991 | 2 000 | C | 9 | - |
| | 1992 | 2 000 | S | 8 | 4 |
| | 1993 | 2 000 | S | 9 | 3 |
| | 1994 | 2 000 | S | 13 | ... |
| | 1995 | 2 000 | S | 15 | ... |
| Poland | 1970 | 2 000 | P | 28 | - |
| | 1975 | 2 000 | P | 36 | - |
| | 1980 | 2 000 | P | 37 | 2 |
| | 1985 | 2 100 | P | 43 | 7 |
| | 1990 | 2 100 | P | 37 | 5 |
| | 1991 | 2 100 | P | 25 | 9 |
| | 1992 | 2 100 | P | 21 | 12 |
| | 1993 | 2 100 | P | 27 | 13 |
| | 1994 | ... | ... | 20 | 6 |
| Portugal | 1970 | 1 800 | C | 4 | - |
| | 1976 | 1 800 | P | 8 | ... |
| | 1980 | 1 600 | C | 9 | 1 |
| | 1985 | 1 600 | P | 5 | 2 |
| | 1990 | 1 600 | P | 8 | 3 |
| | 1991 | 1 600 | P | 9 | 4 |
| | 1992 | ... | C | 15 | 4 |
| | 1993 | ... | C | 11 | 5 |
| | 1994 | ... | ... | 13 | 7 |
| Romania | 1970 | 2 000 | P | 11 | 2 |
| | 1975 | 2 000 | P | 23 | ... |
| | 1980 | 1 800 | P | 32 | - |
| | 1985 | ... | S | 26 | ... |
| | 1990 | ... | ... | 4 | ... |

Production of long films
Production de films de long métrage
Producción de películas de largo metraje

IV.11

| Country / Pays / País | Year / Année / Año | Length / Longueur / Longitud | Definition of data / Code / Tipo de datos | Total | of which coproduction / dont coproduction / de los cuales coproducción |
|---|---|---|---|---|---|
| Romania (cont) | 1991 | ... | ... | 15 | ... |
| | 1992 | ... | S | 16 | ... |
| | 1993 | ... | S | 17 | ... |
| | 1994 | ... | S | 15 | 5 |
| | 1995 | ... | S | 9 | 5 |
| Russian Federation | 1990 | ... | P | 31 | 3 |
| | 1991 | ... | P | 23 | - |
| | 1992 | 1 800 | C | 178 | 15 |
| | 1993 | 1 800 | C | 137 | 18 |
| | 1994 | 1 250 | ... | 74 | 5 |
| | 1995 | 1 250 | ... | 46 | 2 |
| Slovakia | 1992 | ... | P | 4 | 2 |
| | 1993 | ... | P | 3 | 3 |
| | 1994 | ... | P | 2 | ... |
| | 1995 | ... | P | 4 | 7 |
| Slovenia | 1990 | ... | ... | 4 | ... |
| | 1991 | ... | ... | 4 | 2 |
| | 1992 | ... | P | 3 | - |
| | 1993 | ... | P | 1 | 1 |
| | 1994 | ... | P | 1 | - |
| | 1995 | ... | P | 2 | - |
| Spain | 1970 | 2 000 | ... | 105 | 63 |
| | 1975 | 2 000 | C | 105 | 21 |
| | 1980 | 1 650 | C | 118 | 36 |
| | 1985 | 1 620 | P | 65 | 12 |
| | 1990 | ... | C | 47 | 10 |
| | 1991 | ... | C | 64 | 18 |
| | 1992 | ... | C | 52 | 14 |
| | 1993 | ... | C | 56 | 15 |
| | 1994 | 1 640 | C | 44 | 12 |
| | 1995 | 1 640 | C | 59 | 24 |
| Sweden | 1970 | 2 000 | S | 20 | 7 |
| | 1975 | 2 000 | S | 14 | - |
| | 1980 | 2 000 | ... | 20 | 3 |
| | 1985 | 2 000 | ... | 17 | 3 |
| | 1990 | ... | S | 16 | 6 |
| | 1991 | ... | S | 30 | 10 |
| | 1992 | 1 650 | S | 20 | 11 |
| | 1993 | 1 650 | S | 29 | 16 |
| | 1994 | ... | ... | 32 | 16 |
| Switzerland | 1970 | 1 600 | ... | 5 | ... |
| | 1975 | 1 600 | S | 30 | 2 |
| | 1980 | 1 600 | S | 13 | 1 |
| | 1985 | 1 600 | S | 44 | 20 |
| | 1990 | ... | P | 31 | 12 |
| | 1991 | ... | P | 33 | 18 |
| | 1992 | ... | P | 36 | 17 |

| Country / Pays / País | Year / Année / Año | Length / Longueur / Longitud | Definition of data / Code / Tipo de datos | Total | of which coproduction / dont coproduction / de los cuales coproducción |
|---|---|---|---|---|---|
| Switzerland (cont) | 1993 | ... | P | 34 | 16 |
| | 1994 | ... | P | 37 | ... |
| | 1995 | ... | P | 37 | ... |
| The Former Yugoslav Rep. of Macedonia | 1991 | 2 000 | P | 1 | ... |
| | 1993 | 2 000 | P | 3 | 1 |
| | 1995 | 2 000 | P | 2 | - |
| Ukraine | 1990 | ... | P | 20 | - |
| | 1991 | ... | P | 13 | - |
| | 1992 | ... | ... | 28 | - |
| | 1993 | ... | ... | 15 | - |
| | 1994 | ... | ... | 7 | 1 |
| | 1995 | ... | ... | 6 | - |
| United Kingdom | 1970 | 2 000 | S | 85 | 2 |
| | 1975 | 2 000 | S | 70 | 4 |
| | 1980 | 2 000 | S | 57 | ... |
| | 1985 | ... | ... | 55 | ... |
| | 1990 | ... | ... | 53 | ... |
| | 1991 | ... | ... | 51 | ... |
| | 1992 | ... | ... | 48 | ... |
| | 1993 | ... | ... | 52 | ... |
| | 1994 | ... | P | 84 | ... |
| | 1995 | ... | P | 78 | ... |
| Federal Republic of Yugoslavia | 1990 | 2 000 | C | 15 | - |
| | 1991 | 2 000 | C | 6 | 1 |
| | 1992 | ... | P | 11 | 2 |
| | 1993 | ... | P | 11 | 1 |
| | 1994 | ... | P | 8 | 4 |
| **Oceania** | | | | | |
| Australia | 1970 | 2 000 | P | 11 | ... |
| | 1975 | 2 000 | C | 43 | ... |
| | 1979 | ... | C | 30 | ... |
| | 1985 | ... | O | 34 | ... |
| | 1990 | ... | ... | 37 | ... |
| | 1991 | ... | ... | 27 | ... |
| | 1992 | 1 800 | O | 30 | 2 |
| | 1993 | 1 800 | O | 23 | 2 |
| | 1994 | ... | O | 29 | 4 |
| | 1995 | ... | O | 18 | 1 |
| New Zealand | 1979 | ... | P | 9 | ... |
| | 1985 | ... | ... | 5 | ... |
| | 1990 | 3 780 | P | 3 | ... |
| | 1991 | 3 780 | P | 5 | 1 |
| | 1992 | 3 780 | P | 4 | 2 |
| | 1993 | 3 780 | P | 5 | 1 |
| | 1994 | ... | P | 4 | 3 |
| | 1995 | ... | P | 4 | 3 |

**General note**

For general explanations and definitions, please refer to the beginning of this chapter.

**Note générale**

Pour les explications et définitions générales, prière de se référer au début de ce chapitre.

**Nota general**

Para las explicaciones y definiciones generales, referirse al comienzo de este capítulo.

IV.12    Importation of long films by country of origin
Importations de films de long métrage par pays d'origine
Importación de películas de largo metraje por país de origen

## IV.12    Importation of long films by country of origin

## Importations de films de long métrage par pays d'origine

## Importación de películas de largo metraje por país de origen

Definition of data:

I =    Imported in the year indicated

C =    Approved by censor for public showing in
the year indicated

S =    Shown commercially for the first time in the
year indicated

O =    Other criteria

Code:

I =    Importation effectuée dans l'année
indiquée

C =    Approuvé par la censure pour la projection
en public dans l'année indiquée

S =    Mis en exploitation commerciale pour la
première fois dans l'année indiquée

O =    Autres critères

Tipo de datos:

I =    Importada en el año indicado

C =    Aprobado por la censura para su
presentación al público en el año indicado

S =    Puesto en explotación comercial por
primera vez en el año indicado

O =    Otros criterios

| Country / Pays / País | Year / Année / Año | Definition of data / Code / Tipo de datos | Total | United States % | France % | Italy % | India % | Russian Federation % | United Kingdom % | Germany % | Japan % | China, Hong-Kong SAR % | Other countries / Autres pays / Otros países % |
|---|---|---|---|---|---|---|---|---|---|---|---|---|---|---|
| **Africa** | | | | | | | | | | | | | | |
| Benin | 1985 | S | 762 | 35.3 | 18.5 | 2.4 | 21.5 | 0.7 | 0.4 | 0.3 | 0.4 | 19.3 | 1.3 |
| | 1992 | S | 183 | 36.1 | 10.9 | 8.2 | - | - | - | - | - | 24.6 | 20.2 |
| | 1993 | S | 219 | 30.6 | 4.1 | 2.7 | 34.7 | - | - | - | - | 16.4 | 11.4 |
| Congo | 1994 | I | 40 | 22.5 | 37.5 | - | 10.0 | - | 12.5 | - | - | 17.5 | - |
| | 1995 | I | 43 | 25.6 | 39.5 | - | 9.3 | - | 14.0 | - | - | 11.6 | - |
| Côte d'Ivoire | 1976 | I | 372 | 16.1 | 32.8 | 10.2 | 17.2 | ... | - | ... | ... | ... | 23.7 |
| | 1979 | I | 595 | 31.3 | 34.8 | 11.1 | 8.2 | ./. | - | - | ./. | ./. | 14.6 |
| | 1992 | S | 88 | 52.3 | 2.3 | - | 39.8 | - | - | - | - | 4.5 | 1.1 |
| | 1993 | S | 86 | 45.3 | 5.8 | - | 41.9 | - | - | - | - | 7.0 | - |
| Egypt | 1970 | ... | 323 | 48.0 | 5.9 | 23.5 | 3.4 | 7.4 | 5.6 | ... | ... | ... | 6.2 |
| | 1975 | I | 204 | 37.3 | 2.9 | 39.2 | 0.5 | 7.4 | 4.4 | 0.5 | 0.5 | - | 7.4 |
| | 1984 | I | 243 | 38.7 | 3.3 | 32.5 | 1.2 | 1.2 | 2.5 | 0.8 | 0.8 | - | 18.9 |
| | 1989 | ... | 153 | 65.4 | 0.7 | 9.8 | 3.9 | 2.0 | 1.3 | 0.7 | 1.3 | 2.0 | 13.1 |
| | 1991 | ... | 146 | 72.6 | 0.7 | 10.3 | 4.1 | 1.4 | - | - | 0.7 | 1.4 | 8.9 |
| | 1994 | C | 220 | 70.9 | 1.4 | - | 0.9 | - | - | - | - | - | 26.8 |
| Guinea | 1985 | I | 231 | 48.1 | 5.2 | 6.1 | 15.2 | 9.5 | 0.9 | - | 3.0 | 11.3 | 0.9 |
| | 1990 | I | 375 | 29.3 | 12.8 | 16.8 | 26.4 | - | - | 2.4 | 7.5 | 4.8 | - |
| | 1991 | I | 394 | 52.5 | 4.6 | 8.1 | 27.2 | - | - | 1.5 | 4.8 | 1.3 | - |
| Kenya | 1974 | ... | 165 | 20.0 | - | 17.0 | 32.7 | - | 18.8 | - | - | 11.5 | - |
| | 1992 | ... | 374 | 25.7 | - | 5.9 | 50.5 | - | 7.8 | - | - | 10.2 | - |
| | 1993 | ... | 364 | 26.4 | - | 3.3 | 51.9 | - | 8.0 | - | - | 10.4 | - |
| Madagascar | 1990 | I | 45 | 60.0 | 6.7 | 13.3 | 2.2 | - | 2.2 | - | - | 8.9 | 6.7 |
| | 1991 | I | 19 | 84.2 | 5.3 | - | - | - | - | - | - | 10.5 | - |
| Malawi | 1992 | ... | 101 | - | 58.4 | - | - | - | - | - | - | - | 41.6 |
| | 1993 | ... | 124 | - | 58.1 | - | - | - | - | - | - | - | 41.9 |
| Mauritius | 1975 | C | 393 | - | 63.4 | - | 26.5 | 0.8 | - | - | - | 9.4 | - |
| | 1985 | C | 324 | - | 78.4 | - | 21.6 | - | - | - | - | - | - |
| | 1990 | I | 59 | ... | 91.5 | - | 8.5 | ... | - | ... | ... | ... | ... |
| | 1991 | I | 62 | ... | 80.6 | - | 19.4 | ... | - | ... | ... | ... | ... |
| | 1992 | I | 41 | ... | 95.1 | - | 4.9 | ... | - | ... | ... | ... | ... |
| | 1993 | I | 50 | ... | 66.0 | - | 34.0 | ... | - | ... | ... | ... | ... |

Importation of long films by country of origin    IV.12
Importations de films de long métrage par pays d'origine
Importación de películas de largo metraje por país de origen

| Country / Pays / País | Year / Année / Año | Definition of data / Code / Tipo de datos | Total | Principal countries of origin / Principaux pays d'origine / Principales países de origen | | | | | | | | | Other countries / Autres pays / Otros países % |
|---|---|---|---|---|---|---|---|---|---|---|---|---|---|
| | | | | United States % | France % | Italy % | India % | Russian Federation % | United Kingdom % | Germany % | Japan % | China, Hong-Kong SAR % | |
| Morocco | 1976 | C | 473 | 20.9 | 28.5 | 9.5 | 11.0 | 0.6 | 2.3 | ./. | ./. | ./. | 27.1 |
| | 1985 | ... | 369 | 36.3 | 12.7 | 8.4 | 16.8 | - | 8.1 | 0.8 | 0.3 | - | 16.5 |
| | 1989 | ... | 347 | 36.3 | 19.9 | 7.8 | 16.7 | - | 9.2 | 0.6 | - | - | 9.5 |
| | 1992 | C | 361 | 38.5 | 6.4 | 10.2 | 25.8 | - | 10.5 | 0.8 | 0.6 | 0.3 | 6.9 |
| | 1993 | C | 443 | 37.2 | 8.6 | 16.0 | 21.4 | - | - | 1.1 | 0.5 | 6.5 | 8.6 |
| | 1994 | I | 325 | 45.5 | 10.2 | 9.5 | 17.2 | - | - | 0.3 | - | 1.8 | 15.4 |
| | 1995 | I | 393 | 47.1 | 7.1 | 6.4 | 20.9 | - | 3.3 | 0.5 | 0.3 | 2.3 | 12.2 |
| United Republic of Tanzania | 1976 | S | 160 | 20.0 | 2.5 | 15.6 | 32.5 | 2.5 | 6.3 | 1.3 | 1.3 | 16.9 | 1.3 |
| | 1980 | S | 178 | 28.1 | 1.1 | 6.7 | 29.2 | 0.6 | 7.9 | 1.1 | 2.8 | 21.3 | 1.1 |
| | 1986 | S | 61 | 18.0 | - | 6.6 | 45.9 | 9.8 | - | - | - | 19.7 | - |
| | 1990 | C | 63 | 28.6 | 1.6 | 3.2 | 55.6 | 6.3 | - | - | - | 4.8 | - |
| | 1991 | C | 71 | 28.2 | - | 5.6 | 62.0 | - | - | - | - | 4.2 | - |
| Zimbabwe | 1990 | ... | 204 | 87.3 | 0.5 | 0.5 | - | - | 2.9 | 0.5 | - | 3.4 | 4.9 |
| | 1991 | ... | 215 | 90.2 | 1.4 | - | - | - | 4.7 | - | - | - | 3.7 |
| **North America** | | | | | | | | | | | | | |
| Barbados | 1975 | ... | 1 083 | 57.4 | 0.8 | 11.6 | 0.1 | ... | 6.4 | 0.4 | 0.4 | 22.5 | 0.4 |
| | 1990 | C | 190 | 98.9 | - | - | - | - | - | - | - | 1.1 | - |
| | 1991 | C | 185 | 97.8 | - | - | - | - | - | - | - | 2.2 | - |
| Canada | 1970 | ... | 733 | 39.7 | 12.3 | 15.4 | ... | ... | 17.9 | ... | ... | ... | 14.7 |
| | 1975 | O | 715 | 44.1 | 17.3 | 11.0 | 3.1 | ... | 7.3 | 2.7 | ... | ... | 14.5 |
| | 1980 | O | 777 | 38.0 | 13.1 | 11.7 | 10.7 | ./. | 1.7 | 2.3 | ./. | 14.5 | 8.0 |
| | 1984 | O | 1 520 | 38.5 | 17.0 | 4.6 | ./. | ./. | 1.3 | 1.3 | ./. | 7.1 | 30.2 |
| | 1990 | I | 1 115 | 63.9 | 14.0 | ./. | ./. | ./. | 2.9 | ./. | ./. | ./. | 19.3 |
| Costa Rica | 1985 | C | 223 | 59.2 | 4.9 | 12.6 | - | - | 1.3 | 1.3 | - | 0.9 | 19.7 |
| | 1994 | I | 63 | 95.2 | 1.6 | - | - | - | 1.6 | - | - | - | 1.6 |
| | 1995 | I | 49 | 95.9 | - | - | - | - | 4.1 | - | - | - | - |
| Cuba | 1970 | ... | 124 | 8.9 | 11.3 | 6.5 | - | 21.0 | 2.4 | - | 18.5 | - | 31.5 |
| | 1980 | S | 124 | 9.7 | 8.1 | 9.7 | - | 14.5 | 9.7 | 7.3 | 0.8 | - | 40.3 |
| | 1985 | S | 125 | 14.4 | 12.0 | 7.2 | - | 18.4 | 4.0 | 0.8 | 4.0 | - | 39.2 |
| | 1990 | S | 61 | 31.1 | 3.3 | 1.6 | - | 8.2 | - | 1.6 | 3.3 | - | 50.8 |
| | 1992 | S | 44 | 25.0 | 13.6 | 2.3 | - | 6.8 | 2.3 | 4.5 | 2.3 | - | 43.2 |
| | 1993 | S | 22 | 40.9 | 9.1 | - | - | 4.5 | - | 4.5 | - | - | 40.9 |
| El Salvador | 1985 | ... | 478 | 49.8 | 9.4 | 13.2 | 0.4 | - | 1.9 | 3.1 | 0.4 | 0.6 | 21.1 |
| | 1994 | I | 210 | 56.2 | 13.8 | 1.4 | - | - | 1.0 | - | - | 0.5 | 27.1 |
| | 1995 | I | 200 | 61.0 | 14.5 | 0.5 | - | - | 2.0 | - | 0.5 | 0.5 | 22.0 |
| Mexico | 1970 | ... | 404 | 40.1 | 5.9 | 5.9 | ... | ... | 10.6 | 3.0 | 4.5 | ... | 30.0 |
| | 1975 | ... | 514 | 39.3 | 6.6 | 19.1 | ... | ... | 7.8 | 2.9 | ... | 8.0 | 16.3 |
| | 1980 | I | 504 | 63.1 | 3.8 | 9.1 | - | - | 5.2 | 4.0 | 0.2 | 2.4 | 12.3 |
| | 1985 | C | 288 | 51.4 | 2.1 | 2.4 | 0.3 | 0.7 | 5.9 | 1.4 | 1.4 | 1.7 | 32.6 |
| | 1990 | C | 317 | 53.0 | 4.7 | 9.8 | 0.6 | 0.6 | 2.8 | 3.2 | 1.6 | 6.0 | 17.7 |
| | 1991 | C | 241 | 69.3 | 0.8 | 10.0 | 0.8 | 5.8 | 4.6 | 0.8 | 0.4 | 2.5 | 5.0 |
| | 1992 | C | 353 | 59.5 | 2.8 | 5.4 | 0.3 | 0.6 | 3.7 | 0.8 | 1.1 | 3.4 | 22.4 |
| | 1993 | C | 275 | 66.2 | 2.9 | 4.4 | 5.1 | 2.2 | 2.9 | 0.4 | - | 2.2 | 13.8 |
| | 1994 | C | 293 | 61.1 | 4.1 | 11.3 | - | - | 1.4 | 1.4 | 0.7 | - | 20.1 |
| | 1995 | C | 268 | 59.3 | 6.3 | 9.3 | - | 0.7 | 2.6 | 1.5 | 0.7 | 0.4 | 19.0 |
| Trinidad and Tobago | 1992 | I | 41 | ... | 95.1 | ... | 4.9 | ... | ... | ... | ... | ... | ... |
| | 1993 | I | 50 | ... | 66.0 | ... | 34.0 | ... | ... | ... | ... | ... | ... |
| **South America** | | | | | | | | | | | | | |
| Bolivia | 1979 | S | 394 | 44.4 | 3.6 | 16.2 | 0.5 | 3.6 | 4.6 | 1.5 | 1.3 | 2.8 | 21.6 |
| | 1989 | S | 189 | 69.3 | 1.1 | 5.3 | - | - | 2.1 | 2.1 | - | 3.7 | 16.4 |
| | 1992 | S | 179 | 69.8 | 2.2 | 7.8 | - | - | 2.2 | 1.1 | - | 2.8 | 14.0 |
| | 1993 | S | 167 | 73.7 | 1.8 | 6.0 | - | - | 1.2 | 1.2 | - | 3.0 | 13.2 |
| | 1994 | S | 143 | 76.2 | 1.4 | 0.7 | - | - | 0.7 | 1.4 | - | 11.9 | 7.7 |
| | 1995 | S | 149 | 76.5 | 1.3 | 1.3 | - | - | 2.0 | 1.3 | 0.7 | 12.1 | 4.7 |
| Chile | 1992 | C | 304 | 52.0 | 6.6 | 6.6 | - | - | 5.3 | 2.3 | 3.0 | - | 24.3 |
| | 1993 | C | 220 | 59.5 | 5.0 | 6.4 | - | 0.9 | 6.4 | 1.8 | 0.9 | - | 19.1 |
| Ecuador | 1986 | S | 340 | 83.8 | 0.6 | 1.2 | 0.9 | 1.2 | 1.5 | - | - | 0.6 | 10.3 |
| | 1990 | S | 215 | 99.5 | - | - | - | - | - | - | - | - | 0.5 |
| | 1991 | S | 203 | 99.5 | - | - | - | - | - | - | - | - | 0.5 |
| Venezuela | 1975 | ... | 680 | 40.4 | 5.7 | 16.2 | ... | ... | 5.1 | ... | ... | ... | 32.5 |
| | 1980 | I | 904 | 38.3 | 6.6 | 16.3 | - | 2.0 | - | 2.4 | 1.4 | 8.7 | 24.2 |
| | 1985 | I | 807 | 73.6 | 3.5 | 16.1 | - | 0.5 | 2.5 | 1.4 | - | 2.5 | - |
| | 1990 | C | 211 | 86.7 | 0.9 | 0.9 | 0.5 | - | 2.8 | 0.9 | - | 0.5 | 6.6 |
| | 1991 | C | 203 | 84.7 | 4.4 | 1.5 | - | - | 2.5 | - | - | - | 6.9 |
| | 1992 | C | 178 | 98.3 | 1.7 | - | - | - | - | - | - | - | - |
| | 1993 | C | 171 | 80.1 | 4.1 | 1.8 | - | - | 1.2 | 0.6 | - | 2.3 | 9.9 |

Importation of long films by country of origin
Importations de films de long métrage par pays d'origine
Importación de películas de largo metraje por país de origen

| Country / Pays / País | Year / Année / Año | Definition of data / Code / Tipo de datos | Total | Principal countries of origin / Principaux pays d'origine / Principales países de origen | | | | | | | | |
|---|---|---|---|---|---|---|---|---|---|---|---|---|
| | | | | United States % | France % | Italy % | India % | Russian Federation % | United Kingdom % | Germany % | Japan % | China, Hong-Kong SAR % | Other countries / Autres pays / Otros países % |

| Country | Year | Def. | Total | US % | France % | Italy % | India % | Russian Fed. % | UK % | Germany % | Japan % | China HK SAR % | Other % |
|---|---|---|---|---|---|---|---|---|---|---|---|---|---|
| **Asia** | | | | | | | | | | | | | |
| Armenia | 1992 | I | 117 | 53.0 | 12.0 | 0.9 | 8.5 | 12.0 | 1.7 | 2.6 | - | - | 9.4 |
| | 1993 | I | 24 | 29.2 | 20.8 | - | 25.0 | 20.8 | - | - | 4.2 | - | - |
| | 1994 | I | 26 | 92.3 | - | - | - | 7.7 | - | - | - | - | - |
| | 1995 | I | 28 | 46.4 | 21.4 | 3.6 | 3.6 | 21.4 | - | - | - | - | 3.6 |
| Azerbaijan | 1992 | ... | 5 | 60.0 | - | - | 20.0 | 20.0 | - | - | - | - | - |
| | 1993 | ... | 3 | 33.3 | - | - | 33.3 | 33.3 | - | - | - | - | - |
| China, Hong Kong SAR | 1970 | ... | 563 | 27.9 | 6.9 | 13.7 | ... | ... | 10.8 | ... | 5.3 | | 35.3 |
| | 1975 | C | 517 | 31.1 | 8.3 | 16.2 | ... | ... | 8.7 | 2.3 | 3.5 | | 29.8 |
| | 1980 | C | 601 | 32.8 | 9.8 | 8.5 | 1.8 | - | 3.5 | 5.3 | 7.7 | | 30.6 |
| | 1990 | C | 1 051 | 28.9 | 9.7 | 3.7 | 0.2 | 0.4 | 5.3 | 5.4 | 23.1 | | 23.2 |
| | 1991 | C | 1 062 | 30.1 | 7.5 | 3.4 | 0.3 | 0.9 | 4.7 | 3.8 | 25.6 | | 23.6 |
| | 1994 | S | 143 | 64.3 | 2.8 | 1.4 | - | - | 1.4 | - | 6.3 | | 23.8 |
| | 1995 | S | 177 | 65.5 | 2.8 | 1.1 | - | - | 2.3 | 1.1 | 7.9 | | 19.2 |
| Cyprus | 1970 | ... | 614 | 27.9 | ... | 16.0 | | | 18.7 | ... | ... | ... | 37.5 |
| | 1975 | ... | 291 | 25.4 | 4.1 | 18.9 | - | 2.1 | 13.7 | 3.1 | - | 4.5 | 28.2 |
| | 1985 | C | 88 | 45.5 | 4.5 | 11.4 | - | - | 3.4 | 6.8 | 1.1 | 3.4 | 23.9 |
| | 1992 | C | 85 | 100.0 | - | - | - | - | - | - | - | - | - |
| | 1993 | C | 105 | 99.0 | - | - | - | - | - | - | - | - | 1.0 |
| | 1994 | C | 121 | 96.7 | 0.8 | - | - | - | 0.8 | - | - | - | 1.7 |
| | 1995 | C | 179 | 88.8 | 6.1 | 0.6 | - | - | 1.7 | - | - | - | 2.8 |
| Georgia | 1992 | S | 80 | 31.3 | 16.3 | 7.5 | 12.5 | 16.3 | 3.8 | 3.8 | 3.8 | - | 5.0 |
| | 1993 | S | 39 | 33.3 | 25.6 | 7.7 | 7.7 | 5.1 | 5.1 | - | 2.6 | - | 12.8 |
| India | 1970 | ... | 166 | 63.9 | 5.4 | 7.2 | | 3.0 | 6.6 | - | 3.0 | - | 10.8 |
| | 1980 | I | 119 | 21.0 | 0.8 | 0.8 | - | 13.4 | 8.4 | - | 0.8 | 0.8 | 53.8 |
| | 1985 | I | 182 | 59.9 | 1.6 | 5.5 | - | 6.6 | 12.6 | 2.2 | 0.5 | 4.9 | 6.0 |
| | 1990 | ... | 174 | 58.0 | 1.1 | 1.1 | - | 2.3 | 8.6 | 1.7 | 2.9 | 6.3 | 17.8 |
| | 1991 | ... | 141 | 72.3 | 0.7 | 1.4 | - | 2.1 | 11.3 | 0.7 | - | 9.2 | 2.1 |
| Iran, Islamic Republic of | 1971 | ... | 288 | 39.2 | 7.3 | 24.3 | 4.5 | 0.7 | 9.4 | ... | ... | ... | 14.6 |
| | 1975 | ... | 400 | 28.3 | 7.0 | 24.0 | 8.0 | 3.3 | 6.8 | 4.0 | ... | 3.3 | 15.5 |
| | 1980 | C | 114 | 17.5 | 4.4 | 17.5 | ./. | 26.3 | 7.9 | 1.8 | 2.6 | 0.9 | 21.1 |
| | 1990 | ... | 192 | 8.3 | 15.1 | 7.3 | - | 12.0 | - | 8.3 | 1.0 | 1.0 | 46.9 |
| | 1991 | ... | 82 | 4.9 | 19.5 | 7.3 | - | 1.2 | 1.2 | 24.4 | 6.1 | - | 35.4 |
| | 1992 | ... | 66 | 3.0 | 9.1 | 7.6 | 3.0 | 50.0 | - | 1.5 | 9.1 | - | 16.7 |
| | 1993 | ... | 54 | 7.4 | 7.4 | 7.4 | 5.6 | 38.9 | - | 1.9 | 13.0 | - | 18.5 |
| | 1994 | ... | 51 | 9.8 | 3.9 | 3.9 | 7.8 | 19.6 | - | - | 29.4 | 2.0 | 23.5 |
| | 1995 | ... | 73 | 6.8 | 1.4 | 11.0 | 6.8 | 17.8 | 1.4 | - | 24.7 | - | 30.1 |
| Israel | 1970 | ... | 417 | 35.7 | 8.9 | 22.8 | 3.1 | - | 3.8 | 1.4 | - | ... | 24.2 |
| | 1975 | ... | 439 | 29.6 | 11.4 | 13.0 | ... | - | 12.8 | 0.9 | - | 10.3 | 23.0 |
| | 1980 | C | 259 | 47.9 | 5.8 | 4.2 | 18.1 | - | 6.9 | 0.4 | 0.4 | 6.2 | 10.0 |
| | 1985 | C | 196 | 65.8 | 7.7 | 3.1 | - | 1.5 | 9.2 | 1.0 | 0.5 | - | 11.2 |
| | 1992 | ... | 189 | 62.4 | 7.4 | 4.2 | - | - | 8.5 | - | 1.1 | - | 16.4 |
| | 1993 | ... | 152 | 80.3 | 4.6 | 1.3 | - | - | 3.9 | - | 0.7 | - | 9.2 |
| Japan | 1970 | ... | 236 | 50.8 | 10.2 | 16.5 | 0.4 | 2.5 | 8.1 | 5.9 | - | ... | 5.5 |
| | 1975 | ... | 225 | 57.8 | 12.9 | 8.0 | ... | ... | 2.2 | - | - | - | 19.1 |
| | 1980 | S | 209 | 67.5 | 12.0 | 5.3 | - | 1.4 | 4.8 | 1.4 | - | 2.9 | 4.8 |
| | 1985 | C | 264 | 68.2 | 11.7 | 3.4 | 0.4 | 0.8 | 3.8 | 3.4 | - | 3.0 | 5.3 |
| | 1990 | ... | 465 | 53.3 | 11.0 | 8.4 | - | ./. | 6.9 | ./. | - | ./. | 20.4 |
| | 1991 | ... | 467 | 52.7 | 10.9 | 7.9 | ./. | 3.4 | 5.8 | ./. | - | 3.2 | 16.1 |
| | 1992 | C | 377 | 60.5 | 10.1 | 4.2 | 0.3 | 1.3 | 5.6 | 1.6 | - | 4.5 | 11.9 |
| | 1993 | C | 352 | 59.7 | 13.1 | 4.8 | - | 1.7 | 4.8 | 1.4 | - | 2.6 | 11.9 |
| Jordan | 1975 | ... | 738 | 20.3 | 4.1 | 8.1 | - | 1.4 | 7.9 | - | 2.7 | - | 55.6 |
| | 1980 | I | 590 | 13.6 | 2.5 | 44.1 | 16.9 | 1.7 | 5.1 | 3.4 | 2.5 | 10.2 | - |
| | 1989 | I | 278 | 39.6 | 0.7 | 11.9 | 15.5 | - | 1.1 | 0.7 | - | 2.9 | 27.7 |
| | 1992 | ... | 157 | 60.5 | - | 3.8 | 7.6 | - | 0.6 | 0.6 | - | 9.6 | 17.2 |
| | 1993 | ... | 153 | 63.4 | - | 3.3 | 5.2 | - | 1.3 | - | - | 11.8 | 15.0 |
| | 1994 | ... | 269 | 51.3 | 1.1 | 5.2 | 7.1 | - | 1.5 | - | 2.2 | 10.8 | 20.8 |
| | 1995 | ... | 271 | 65.7 | 0.7 | 3.3 | 6.3 | - | 0.7 | - | - | 7.0 | 16.2 |
| Kazakstan | 1992 | C | 130 | 30.8 | 5.4 | - | 13.1 | 43.1 | 2.3 | 2.3 | - | - | 3.1 |
| | 1993 | C | 94 | 44.7 | 2.1 | 1.1 | 8.5 | 35.1 | 1.1 | 2.1 | 1.1 | 1.1 | 3.2 |
| | 1994 | C | 76 | 46.1 | 3.9 | 2.6 | 13.2 | - | 1.3 | 1.3 | - | - | 31.6 |
| | 1995 | C | 51 | 49.0 | - | 3.9 | 13.7 | - | - | 2.0 | - | 3.9 | 27.5 |
| Korea, Republic of | 1970 | ... | 56 | 66.1 | 16.1 | 3.6 | ... | ... | ... | ... | ... | 10.7 | 3.6 |
| | 1975 | ... | 34 | 47.1 | 11.8 | 14.7 | ... | ... | 8.8 | ... | ... | ... | 17.6 |
| | 1980 | C | 39 | 53.8 | 10.3 | 2.6 | - | - | 15.4 | ... | - | 10.3 | 7.7 |
| | 1986 | C | 51 | 76.5 | 5.9 | - | - | - | 5.9 | - | - | 7.8 | 3.9 |
| | 1989 | C | 278 | 37.8 | 4.7 | 10.4 | 0.4 | 0.4 | 2.2 | 3.2 | - | 31.7 | 9.4 |
| | 1992 | C | 319 | 52.7 | 7.5 | 5.0 | 0.3 | 1.3 | 1.6 | 1.6 | - | 23.2 | 6.9 |
| | 1993 | C | 347 | 51.9 | 7.8 | 5.8 | - | - | 2.0 | 0.9 | - | 20.5 | 11.2 |

Importation of long films by country of origin
Importations de films de long métrage par pays d'origine
Importación de películas de largo metraje por país de origen

IV.12

| Country / Pays / País | Year / Année / Año | Definition of data Code / Tipo de datos | Total | United States % | France % | Italy % | India % | Russian Federation % | United Kingdom % | Germany % | Japan % | China, Hong-Kong SAR % | Other countries Autres pays Otros países % |
|---|---|---|---|---|---|---|---|---|---|---|---|---|---|
| Kyrgyzstan | 1994 | I | 88 | 67.0 | - | 1.1 | 15.9 | 11.4 | 1.1 | - | 2.3 | 1.1 | - |
| | 1995 | I | 65 | 76.9 | - | 1.5 | 9.2 | 12.3 | - | - | - | - | - |
| Lao People's Democratic Rep. | 1980 | ... | 113 | - | - | - | 18.6 | 80.5 | - | - | - | - | 0.9 |
| | 1990 | I | 179 | 7.3 | 1.7 | - | 3.9 | - | - | - | 0.6 | 59.2 | 27.4 |
| | 1991 | I | 112 | - | 1.8 | - | 3.6 | - | - | - | 0.9 | 72.3 | 21.4 |
| | 1992 | S | 48 | - | - | - | - | - | - | - | - | 41.7 | 58.3 |
| | 1993 | S | 36 | - | - | - | - | - | - | - | - | 27.8 | 72.2 |
| Lebanon | 1970 | ... | 441 | 35.8 | 11.8 | 17.0 | ... | 4.8 | 11.8 | ... | ... | ... | 18.8 |
| | 1992 | I | 366 | 80.6 | 7.1 | 0.8 | 0.8 | - | 1.4 | - | - | 2.2 | 7.1 |
| | 1993 | I | 277 | 83.0 | 2.2 | - | 2.5 | - | 1.1 | - | - | 2.2 | 9.0 |
| Pakistan | 1990 | C | 101 | 41.6 | 1.0 | 6.9 | - | 1.0 | 4.0 | 3.0 | - | 37.6 | 5.0 |
| | 1991 | C | 129 | 29.5 | - | 13.2 | - | 0.8 | 3.1 | 0.8 | 0.8 | 47.3 | 4.7 |
| | 1992 | C | 103 | 39.8 | - | 16.5 | - | - | 1.0 | 1.0 | 1.0 | 35.9 | 4.9 |
| | 1993 | C | 84 | 46.4 | 1.2 | 2.4 | - | - | 1.2 | - | 1.2 | 44.0 | 3.6 |
| | 1994 | C | 116 | 49.1 | - | 6.9 | - | - | 0.9 | 3.4 | - | 37.1 | 2.6 |
| | 1995 | C | 89 | 58.4 | - | 3.4 | - | - | 1.1 | 2.2 | - | 33.7 | 1.1 |
| Sri Lanka | 1975 | ... | 83 | - | 8.4 | - | 34.9 | 4.8 | 51.8 | - | - | - | - |
| | 1980 | S | 94 | 41.5 | 2.1 | 2.1 | 13.8 | - | 36.2 | - | - | 1.1 | 3.2 |
| | 1985 | I | 61 | 37.7 | - | 3.3 | 18.0 | - | 16.4 | - | - | 24.6 | - |
| | 1992 | C | 116 | 62.1 | - | - | 37.9 | - | - | - | - | - | - |
| | 1990 | O | 01 | 88.5 | - | - | 11.5 | - | - | - | - | - | - |
| Syrian Arab Republic | 1980 | ... | 155 | 20.6 | 16.8 | 13.5 | 1.3 | 16.1 | 30.3 | - | - | - | 1.3 |
| | 1985 | ... | 91 | - | - | - | 26.4 | 6.6 | - | - | - | - | 67.0 |
| | 1993 | ... | 122 | 86.1 | - | - | - | - | - | - | - | - | 13.9 |
| Tajikistan | 1992 | C | 788 | 12.8 | 6.7 | 3.8 | 15.2 | 39.3 | 0.1 | 7.6 | 1.3 | 0.6 | 12.4 |
| | 1993 | C | 530 | 15.1 | 6.0 | 3.8 | 17.2 | 36.2 | 0.4 | 6.8 | 1.5 | 0.6 | 12.5 |
| | 1994 | C | 68 | 11.8 | 8.8 | 7.4 | 25.0 | 17.6 | - | 5.9 | 4.4 | 1.5 | 17.6 |
| | 1995 | C | 66 | 6.1 | 7.6 | 6.1 | 24.2 | 19.7 | - | 6.1 | 1.5 | 1.5 | 27.3 |
| Uzbekistan | 1992 | C | 75 | 26.7 | 1.3 | - | 40.0 | 18.7 | - | 4.0 | - | - | 9.3 |
| | 1993 | C | 53 | 32.1 | 1.9 | - | 49.1 | 11.3 | - | - | - | 1.9 | 3.8 |
| **Europe** | | | | | | | | | | | | | |
| Austria | 1970 | ... | 437 | 29.3 | 9.2 | 18.3 | ... | ... | 9.6 | 24.0 | 2.3 | ... | 7.3 |
| | 1975 | S | 329 | 31.9 | 11.2 | 18.5 | ... | 0.9 | 7.3 | 14.0 | 2.4 | 5.8 | 7.9 |
| | 1980 | S | 296 | 36.1 | 13.2 | 16.9 | - | - | 3.7 | 15.5 | 0.3 | 6.8 | 7.4 |
| | 1985 | S | 366 | 52.5 | 15.6 | 4.4 | - | - | 4.9 | 13.1 | 1.1 | 0.5 | 7.9 |
| | 1990 | S | 273 | 56.4 | 8.8 | 1.8 | - | 1.5 | 6.2 | 12.1 | 0.4 | 0.7 | 12.1 |
| | 1991 | S | 261 | 57.5 | 8.4 | 3.4 | 0.4 | 1.1 | 4.6 | 10.0 | 1.1 | 0.8 | 12.6 |
| | 1992 | S | 239 | 53.1 | 10.0 | 5.4 | - | 0.4 | 7.9 | 11.3 | 0.8 | 0.4 | 10.5 |
| | 1993 | S | 234 | 56.4 | 10.3 | 1.7 | - | 0.4 | 3.8 | 12.4 | 1.3 | - | 13.7 |
| | 1994 | S | 221 | 54.8 | 8.6 | 0.9 | 0.5 | - | 7.2 | 12.7 | 0.9 | 1.8 | 12.7 |
| | 1995 | S | 219 | 58.9 | 9.1 | 1.8 | 0.5 | 0.5 | 6.8 | 9.6 | - | - | 12.8 |
| Belarus | 1992 | I | 220 | - | - | - | - | 100.0 | - | - | - | - | - |
| | 1993 | I | 235 | - | - | - | - | 100.0 | - | - | - | - | - |
| Belgium | 1985 | O | 133 | 60.9 | 24.8 | ... | ... | ... | ... | ... | ... | ... | 14.3 |
| | 1990 | S | 308 | 52.9 | 16.9 | 1.9 | - | 1.0 | 5.2 | 1.3 | 1.3 | - | 19.5 |
| | 1991 | S | 364 | 54.4 | 17.0 | 0.8 | 0.3 | 1.6 | 3.8 | 1.6 | 0.3 | - | 20.1 |
| | 1992 | S | 365 | 49.3 | 19.2 | 2.5 | - | - | 5.8 | 1.9 | - | - | 21.4 |
| | 1993 | S | 416 | 50.2 | 21.6 | 1.2 | - | - | 6.0 | 1.2 | - | - | 19.7 |
| | 1994 | S | 518 | 50.8 | 16.4 | 1.5 | - | - | 5.6 | 1.5 | - | - | 24.1 |
| | 1995 | S | 477 | 42.8 | 17.4 | 2.5 | - | - | 5.9 | 1.5 | - | - | 30.0 |
| Bulgaria | 1970 | ... | 136 | ... | ... | ... | ... | 39.7 | ... | ... | ... | ... | 60.3 |
| | 1975 | I | 162 | ... | ... | ... | ... | 34.6 | ... | ... | ... | ... | 65.4 |
| | 1980 | I | 193 | 7.8 | 3.6 | 4.7 | 2.1 | 32.1 | 1.0 | 0.5 | 1.6 | - | 46.6 |
| | 1985 | I | 191 | 6.8 | 4.7 | 3.1 | 1.0 | 29.3 | 2.6 | 0.5 | 3.7 | 0.5 | 47.6 |
| | 1990 | S | 151 | 15.9 | 4.0 | 2.0 | - | 19.2 | 1.3 | 1.3 | 1.3 | - | 55.0 |
| | 1991 | S | 123 | 43.9 | 4.9 | - | - | 13.8 | 2.4 | - | - | - | 35.0 |
| | 1992 | ... | 164 | 60.4 | 12.8 | 2.4 | - | - | - | - | - | - | 24.4 |
| | 1993 | ... | 119 | 84.0 | 6.7 | 1.7 | 1.7 | - | - | 0.8 | - | - | 5.0 |
| | 1994 | ... | 137 | 89.1 | 2.9 | 1.5 | - | - | 1.5 | - | - | 0.7 | 4.4 |
| | 1995 | ... | 134 | 88.1 | 3.7 | 2.2 | - | - | 0.7 | - | - | 0.7 | 4.5 |
| Croatia | 1992 | I | 4 | 100.0 | - | - | - | - | - | - | - | - | - |
| | 1993 | I | 17 | 94.1 | 5.9 | - | - | - | - | - | - | - | - |
| | 1994 | I | 104 | 87.5 | 3.8 | 1.0 | - | - | 3.8 | - | - | - | 3.8 |
| | 1995 | I | 33 | 60.6 | - | - | - | - | - | 24.2 | - | - | 15.2 |
| Czech Republic | 1992 | S | 139 | 79.9 | 9.4 | 2.2 | - | - | 3.6 | 1.4 | - | 0.7 | 2.9 |
| | 1993 | S | 155 | 76.8 | 4.5 | 5.8 | - | - | 5.2 | 1.9 | - | 0.6 | 5.2 |
| | 1994 | S | 135 | 83.7 | 2.2 | 3.0 | - | - | 3.7 | 2.2 | - | 0.7 | 4.4 |
| | 1995 | S | 109 | 78.0 | 8.3 | 2.8 | - | - | 3.7 | 0.9 | - | - | 6.4 |

Importation of long films by country of origin
Importations de films de long métrage par pays d'origine
Importación de películas de largo metraje por país de origen

| Country / Pays / País | Year / Année / Año | Definition of data / Code / Tipo de datos | Total | United States % | France % | Italy % | India % | Russian Federation % | United Kingdom % | Germany % | Japan % | China, Hong-Kong SAR % | Other countries / Autres pays / Otros países % |
|---|---|---|---|---|---|---|---|---|---|---|---|---|---|
| Denmark | 1970 | ... | 249 | 77.9 | 6.8 | 2.8 | ... | ... | 8.8 | 2.0 | ... | ... | 1.6 |
|  | 1975 | S | 228 | 49.1 | 1.8 | 6.6 | ... | 0.9 | 7.9 | 7.0 | ... | ... | 26.8 |
|  | 1980 | S | 249 | 55.0 | 8.0 | 5.6 | - | 0.4 | 7.6 | 2.8 | 0.8 | 0.4 | 19.3 |
|  | 1985 | S | 217 | 62.7 | 6.9 | 3.7 | - | 0.5 | 8.3 | 2.8 | - | - | 15.2 |
|  | 1990 | S | 172 | 69.8 | 2.3 | 0.6 | - | - | 2.9 | 1.2 | - | - | 23.3 |
|  | 1991 | S | 147 | 70.1 | 4.1 | 1.4 | - | - | 6.1 | 1.4 | - | - | 17.0 |
|  | 1992 | ... | 134 | 68.7 | 3.0 | 0.7 | - | - | 5.2 | - | - | - | 22.4 |
|  | 1993 | ... | 152 | 71.7 | 6.6 | 0.7 | - | - | 3.3 | 0.7 | - | - | 17.1 |
|  | 1994 | S | 151 | 67.5 | 2.6 | 0.7 | - | - | 5.3 | - | - | 2.0 | 21.9 |
|  | 1995 | S | 150 | 60.7 | 5.3 | 3.3 | - | - | 8.0 | 2.7 | - | 1.3 | 18.7 |
| Estonia | 1993 | I | 115 | 78.3 | - | - | - | 6.1 | - | - | - | - | 15.7 |
|  | 1994 | I | 146 | 58.9 | 17.1 | 2.7 | - | 11.6 | 2.1 | 0.7 | 2.7 | 0.7 | 3.4 |
|  | 1995 | I | 85 | 80.0 | 12.9 | - | - | 1.2 | 4.7 | - | - | - | 1.2 |
| Federal Republic of Yugoslavia | 1990 | I | 101 | 83.2 | 3.0 | 2.0 | - | - | 1.0 | 4.0 | 3.0 | 4.0 | - |
|  | 1991 | I | 19 | 84.2 | - | - | - | - | - | - | - | 5.3 | 10.5 |
|  | 1992 | I | 81 | 63.0 | 9.9 | 2.5 | - | - | 14.8 | 2.5 | - | - | 7.4 |
|  | 1993 | I | 44 | 75.0 | 4.5 | 2.3 | - | - | 2.3 | - | - | - | 15.9 |
| Finland | 1970 | ... | 284 | 40.5 | 15.1 | 11.3 | ... | 9.2 | 5.6 | 3.9 | ... | ... | 14.4 |
|  | 1975 | S | 217 | 34.6 | 6.9 | 6.9 | ... | 7.4 | 8.8 | 4.6 | ... | ... | 30.9 |
|  | 1980 | S | 228 | 48.7 | 2.2 | 7.9 | - | 3.5 | 9.2 | 2.2 | 0.9 | - | 25.4 |
|  | 1985 | S | 224 | 55.8 | 3.1 | 2.2 | - | 4.9 | 7.6 | 0.9 | - | - | 25.4 |
|  | 1990 | S | 156 | 70.5 | 7.1 | - | - | 3.8 | 3.8 | 1.3 | - | 0.6 | 12.8 |
|  | 1991 | S | 163 | 73.0 | 3.1 | 1.2 | - | 0.6 | 2.5 | - | 0.6 | 0.6 | 18.4 |
|  | 1992 | S | 150 | 60.7 | 5.3 | 0.7 | - | - | 4.0 | - | 0.7 | 0.7 | 28.0 |
|  | 1993 | S | 168 | 57.7 | 5.4 | 1.2 | - | - | 4.8 | - | 1.2 | 1.2 | 28.6 |
|  | 1994 | S | 141 | 68.8 | 7.1 | 1.4 | - | - | 2.8 | 2.8 | 1.4 | 0.7 | 14.9 |
|  | 1995 | S | 131 | 65.6 | 5.3 | 1.5 | - | - | 5.3 | 1.5 | - | 3.8 | 16.8 |
| France | 1980 | ... | 460 | 32.2 | - | 14.1 | 2.6 | 0.2 | 7.0 | 8.0 | 2.4 | 17.0 | 16.5 |
|  | 1985 | S | 298 | 40.6 | - | 6.7 | 9.1 | 8.1 | 8.4 | 2.3 | 1.3 | 9.7 | 13.8 |
|  | 1990 | S | 241 | 57.3 | - | 5.4 | 0.4 | 5.0 | 3.3 | 1.2 | 3.7 | 2.9 | 20.7 |
|  | 1991 | S | 298 | 53.0 | - | 3.4 | 0.3 | 2.0 | 6.7 | 2.0 | 8.4 | 1.3 | 22.8 |
|  | 1992 | ... | 219 | 54.8 | - | 4.1 | 1.4 | 3.7 | 5.5 | 1.8 | 2.7 | 1.8 | 24.2 |
|  | 1993 | ... | 226 | 55.8 | - | 2.7 | - | 1.8 | 6.2 | 4.0 | 6.2 | 2.7 | 20.8 |
|  | 1994 | ... | 249 | 58.6 | - | 2.8 | - | 0.4 | 5.2 | 2.0 | 7.2 | 0.4 | 23.3 |
|  | 1995 | ... | 235 | 57.0 | - | 3.0 | - | - | 8.1 | 3.8 | 6.4 | - | 21.7 |
| Germany | 1990 | S | 258 | 60.5 | 9.3 | 3.9 | - | 1.9 | 8.1 | - | 1.2 | - | 15.1 |
|  | 1991 | S | 264 | 61.7 | 7.2 | 3.8 | - | 1.5 | 5.3 | - | 2.7 | 1.1 | 16.7 |
|  | 1992 | S | 225 | 57.8 | 11.1 | 5.3 | - | 0.4 | 9.3 | - | 1.8 | 1.3 | 12.9 |
|  | 1993 | S | 196 | 66.3 | 10.7 | 0.5 | - | 0.5 | 7.1 | - | 0.5 | 0.5 | 13.8 |
|  | 1994 | S | 203 | 65.0 | 9.4 | 1.5 | - | - | 8.9 | - | 1.0 | 1.0 | 13.3 |
|  | 1995 | S | 197 | 68.5 | 6.6 | 2.0 | - | 1.5 | 7.1 | - | - | - | 14.2 |
| Greece | 1970 | ... | 713 | 31.8 | 9.7 | 18.7 | ... | ... | 4.3 | ... | ... | ... | 35.5 |
|  | 1975 | C | 682 | 31.4 | 13.2 | 22.4 | ... | 3.7 | 7.3 | 7.3 | ... | ... | 14.7 |
|  | 1980 | C | 462 | 33.3 | 15.2 | 18.6 | 0.2 | 1.7 | 10.6 | 3.9 | 2.4 | 4.1 | 10.0 |
|  | 1985 | C | 271 | 65.7 | 8.9 | 7.0 | - | 0.7 | 5.2 | 8.1 | 0.7 | 1.1 | 2.6 |
|  | 1990 | C | 139 | 83.5 | 2.2 | 1.4 | - | 1.4 | 4.3 | 2.2 | 0.7 | 1.4 | 2.9 |
|  | 1991 | C | 143 | 83.2 | 5.6 | - | - | - | 4.9 | 0.7 | - | 0.7 | 4.9 |
|  | 1992 | ... | 109 | 84.4 | 5.5 | 1.8 | - | - | 3.7 | 2.8 | - | - | 1.8 |
|  | 1993 | ... | 148 | 75.7 | 10.1 | 0.7 | - | - | 4.7 | 0.7 | 1.4 | 1.4 | 5.4 |
| Hungary | 1970 | ... | 150 | 16.7 | 10.7 | 6.7 | ... | 20.7 | 5.3 | ... | ... | ... | 40.0 |
|  | 1975 | I | 170 | 6.5 | 6.5 | 11.8 | - | 22.4 | 5.3 | ... | ... | ... | 47.6 |
|  | 1980 | I | 184 | 15.8 | 8.7 | 9.2 | - | 20.1 | 3.3 | 2.2 | 1.6 | - | 39.1 |
|  | 1985 | I | 186 | 23.7 | 9.7 | 5.4 | - | 15.6 | 3.8 | 2.7 | 1.1 | - | 38.2 |
|  | 1990 | ... | 227 | 55.5 | 7.5 | 5.3 | - | 4.0 | 2.6 | 3.5 | 1.3 | - | 20.3 |
|  | 1991 | ... | 199 | 58.8 | 10.6 | 5.0 | - | 1.5 | - | 4.5 | 1.0 | - | 18.6 |
|  | 1992 | S | 165 | 55.8 | 13.3 | 5.5 | - | 1.8 | 6.1 | 2.4 | 0.6 | 1.8 | 12.7 |
|  | 1993 | S | 159 | 71.7 | 8.2 | 0.6 | - | 1.3 | 8.8 | 3.1 | - | 0.6 | 5.7 |
|  | 1995 | I | 80 | 31.3 | 15.0 | 18.8 | - | - | 13.8 | - | - | - | 21.3 |
| Iceland | 1970 | ... | 391 | 68.3 | 7.7 | 3.3 | ... | ... | 10.0 | ... | ... | ... | 10.7 |
|  | 1986 | I | 203 | 74.4 | 3.9 | 3.0 | - | - | 9.4 | 1.0 | - | - | 8.4 |
|  | 1990 | S | 177 | 88.7 | 2.3 | 0.6 | - | - | 2.8 | 0.6 | - | - | 5.1 |
|  | 1991 | S | 186 | 83.9 | 3.8 | 1.1 | - | - | 2.2 | 1.6 | - | - | 7.5 |
|  | 1992 | S | 201 | 79.6 | 2.5 | 0.5 | - | - | 4.5 | 1.5 | - | - | 11.4 |
|  | 1993 | S | 201 | 81.6 | 3.5 | 1.5 | - | 0.5 | 3.5 | - | 0.5 | - | 9.0 |
|  | 1994 | S | 201 | 73.6 | 9.5 | 1.5 | - | - | 4.5 | - | - | 0.5 | 10.4 |
|  | 1995 | S | 182 | 76.9 | 6.0 | 0.5 | - | - | 8.2 | 0.5 | - | - | 7.7 |
| Italy | 1970 | ... | 271 | 51.7 | 14.8 | - | ... | ... | 9.2 | 7.0 | 7.4 | ... | 10.0 |
|  | 1975 | S | 308 | 42.9 | 13.3 | - | ... | 1.9 | 12.0 | 4.5 | - | 5.8 | 19.5 |
|  | 1980 | S | 395 | 35.7 | 25.6 | - | - | 0.8 | 4.1 | 10.1 | 3.0 | 3.3 | 17.5 |
|  | 1985 | S | 279 | 56.3 | 18.6 | - | - | 0.7 | 6.5 | 5.4 | 0.4 | 0.7 | 11.5 |
|  | 1990 | S | 380 | 67.6 | 10.0 | - | - | 0.5 | 4.5 | 2.1 | 0.3 | - | 15.0 |
|  | 1991 | S | 331 | 66.5 | 11.2 | - | - | - | 8.2 | 2.4 | 0.6 | - | 11.2 |

Importation of long films by country of origin
Importations de films de long métrage par pays d'origine
Importación de películas de largo metraje por país de origen

IV.12

| Country / Pays / País | Year / Année / Año | Definition of data Code / Tipo de datos | Total | Principal countries of origin / Principaux pays d'origine / Principales países de origen | | | | | | | | | Other countries / Autres pays / Otros países % |
|---|---|---|---|---|---|---|---|---|---|---|---|---|---|
| | | | | United States % | France % | Italy % | India % | Russian Federation % | United Kingdom % | Germany % | Japan % | China, Hong-Kong SAR % | |
| Italy (cont) | 1992 | ... | 323 | 64.7 | 9.0 | - | - | 0.6 | 9.6 | 3.1 | 0.9 | 0.3 | 11.8 |
| | 1993 | ... | 292 | 65.8 | 7.2 | - | - | 0.7 | 7.2 | 6.5 | 0.3 | 1.0 | 11.3 |
| | 1994 | ... | 253 | 66.8 | 7.5 | - | - | 0.4 | 6.7 | 2.8 | 0.8 | 0.8 | 14.2 |
| | 1995 | ... | 247 | 64.0 | 10.5 | - | - | - | 8.5 | 1.6 | 0.4 | 0.4 | 14.6 |
| Lithuania | 1992 | I | 197 | 52.8 | 7.1 | 3.6 | 7.1 | 12.7 | 3.0 | 1.5 | 0.5 | 1.0 | 10.7 |
| | 1993 | I | 140 | 60.0 | 20.7 | 2.9 | 0.7 | 9.3 | - | - | - | - | 6.4 |
| | 1994 | I | 121 | 66.9 | 9.9 | 3.3 | 2.5 | 8.3 | - | 0.8 | 1.7 | 2.5 | 4.1 |
| | 1995 | I | 70 | 57.1 | 15.7 | 5.7 | - | 5.7 | 5.7 | 1.4 | 1.4 | - | 7.1 |
| Luxembourg | 1992 | S | 184 | 55.4 | 16.8 | 3.8 | - | - | 4.9 | 3.8 | - | - | 15.2 |
| | 1993 | S | 187 | 47.1 | 18.2 | 1.1 | - | - | 7.5 | 4.8 | 0.5 | - | 20.9 |
| | 1994 | S | 145 | 66.9 | 11.7 | 1.4 | - | - | 6.9 | 4.1 | - | - | 9.0 |
| Moldova | 1992 | C | 233 | 42.5 | 12.0 | 3.9 | 6.9 | 18.0 | 0.9 | - | - | - | 15.9 |
| | 1993 | C | 265 | 43.8 | 14.7 | 3.4 | 7.2 | 19.6 | 1.1 | - | - | 0.8 | 9.4 |
| | 1994 | S | 133 | 75.2 | 6.8 | 0.8 | 2.3 | 6.8 | - | - | 0.8 | - | 7.5 |
| | 1995 | C | 108 | 73.1 | 9.3 | 2.8 | 0.9 | 2.8 | 0.9 | - | 2.8 | - | 7.4 |
| Netherlands | 1970 | ... | 358 | 31.6 | 14.2 | 15.9 | ... | 1.7 | 17.0 | 12.0 | 1.4 | ... | 6.1 |
| | 1975 | S | 309 | 35.0 | 17.8 | 10.0 | ... | ... | 13.3 | 6.1 | 2.3 | 5.5 | 10.0 |
| | 1980 | S | 329 | 42.9 | 16.7 | 7.9 | - | 1.8 | 6.1 | 8.2 | 1.5 | 6.4 | 8.5 |
| | 1990 | S | 173 | 68.2 | 3.5 | 1.2 | - | 1.7 | 7.5 | 2.3 | - | - | 15.6 |
| | 1991 | S | 173 | 76.3 | 12.1 | 1.2 | - | 0.6 | 4.6 | - | - | - | 5.2 |
| Norway | 1975 | C | 250 | 43.2 | 6.4 | 11.2 | ... | 2.0 | 22.4 | 2.0 | ... | ... | 12.8 |
| | 1980 | C | 251 | 52.2 | 4.4 | 5.6 | - | - | 13.9 | 3.6 | 0.4 | 0.4 | 19.5 |
| | 1985 | C | 256 | 58.6 | 8.2 | 1.6 | - | - | 8.6 | 2.0 | 1.2 | 0.8 | 19.1 |
| | 1990 | C | 171 | 67.3 | 5.8 | 2.3 | - | 1.8 | 4.7 | 2.9 | 0.6 | 0.6 | 14.0 |
| | 1991 | C | 189 | 60.8 | 7.4 | 1.6 | - | 3.7 | 6.3 | - | 0.5 | - | 19.6 |
| | 1992 | C | 183 | 57.4 | 9.3 | 2.7 | - | 0.5 | 6.0 | 4.9 | - | 0.5 | 18.6 |
| | 1993 | C | 182 | 61.0 | 6.6 | - | - | 0.5 | 6.0 | 1.1 | 0.5 | - | 24.2 |
| | 1994 | C | 152 | 68.4 | 8.6 | 2.6 | - | - | 4.6 | 2.6 | - | - | 13.2 |
| | 1995 | C | 171 | 60.8 | 11.1 | 2.9 | 0.6 | 0.6 | 6.4 | 2.9 | - | 1.8 | 12.9 |
| Poland | 1970 | ... | 178 | 14.0 | 9.6 | 7.3 | ... | 18.5 | 7.9 | ... | 3.4 | ... | 39.3 |
| | 1975 | S | 166 | 13.3 | 10.8 | 9.6 | ... | 23.5 | 4.2 | 1.2 | 1.8 | ... | 35.5 |
| | 1980 | S | 135 | 11.9 | 4.4 | 6.7 | - | 26.7 | 5.2 | 2.2 | 2.2 | ... | 40.7 |
| | 1985 | I | 103 | 8.7 | 5.8 | - | - | 38.8 | 1.0 | 1.0 | 1.0 | - | 43.7 |
| | 1990 | S | 124 | 70.2 | 4.8 | 0.8 | - | 2.4 | 4.8 | 3.2 | - | 0.8 | 12.9 |
| | 1991 | S | 129 | 81.4 | 7.0 | 1.6 | - | 0.8 | 3.1 | 1.6 | - | 0.8 | 3.9 |
| | 1992 | S | 103 | 85.4 | 4.9 | - | - | - | 2.9 | 2.9 | 1.0 | - | 2.9 |
| | 1993 | S | 126 | 71.4 | 6.3 | 1.6 | - | - | 4.8 | 4.8 | 1.6 | - | 9.5 |
| Portugal | 1971 | ... | 773 | 27.7 | 27.9 | 11.8 | ... | ... | 8.8 | ... | ... | ... | 23.8 |
| | 1976 | I | 380 | 21.6 | 20.5 | 24.7 | ... | ... | 6.3 | 4.7 | ... | ... | 22.1 |
| | 1980 | I | 386 | 33.9 | 15.3 | 17.1 | 7.0 | ... | 14.8 | 2.1 | 1.8 | 4.4 | 3.6 |
| | 1985 | S | 235 | 56.6 | 11.5 | 6.4 | 1.3 | 0.9 | 7.7 | 3.8 | - | 2.6 | 9.4 |
| | 1990 | ... | 230 | 55.7 | 14.3 | 6.5 | - | 0.4 | 12.2 | 3.0 | - | 3.0 | 4.8 |
| | 1991 | C | 288 | 67.4 | 6.6 | 4.5 | - | 0.3 | 11.5 | 1.0 | 0.3 | 2.8 | 5.6 |
| | 1992 | C | 229 | 73.4 | 4.4 | 4.4 | - | - | 6.1 | 0.4 | - | 3.1 | 8.3 |
| | 1993 | C | 195 | 63.1 | 4.1 | 4.6 | - | - | 16.9 | 2.1 | 0.5 | 1.0 | 7.7 |
| Romania | 1970 | ... | 169 | 10.7 | 14.2 | 6.5 | ... | 19.5 | 5.6 | ... | ... | ... | 49.1 |
| | 1976 | S | 162 | 21.0 | 4.3 | 7.4 | ... | 17.9 | 5.6 | ... | 2.5 | ... | 41.4 |
| | 1980 | I | 158 | 19.0 | 6.3 | 4.4 | 1.3 | 13.9 | 2.5 | - | 1.9 | 0.6 | 50.0 |
| | 1993 | I | 692 | 45.2 | 7.4 | 8.8 | 2.6 | 9.4 | 4.6 | 2.9 | - | 2.9 | 16.2 |
| | 1994 | S | 106 | 87.7 | 2.8 | 2.8 | 2.8 | - | - | 0.9 | - | 1.9 | 0.9 |
| | 1995 | S | 101 | 74.3 | 7.9 | 5.0 | 6.9 | - | - | - | - | 5.0 | 1.0 |
| Russian Federation | 1990 | I | 64 | 14.1 | 15.6 | 1.6 | 42.2 | - | - | - | - | - | 26.6 |
| | 1991 | I | 57 | 24.6 | 22.8 | 7.0 | 33.3 | - | - | - | - | - | 12.3 |
| | 1994 | ... | 288 | 74.3 | 4.5 | 5.2 | 1.7 | - | 0.3 | 2.1 | 1.7 | 0.3 | 9.7 |
| | 1995 | ... | 118 | 59.3 | 11.0 | 11.9 | - | - | 3.4 | - | - | - | 14.4 |
| San Marino | 1970 | ... | 369 | 41.2 | 7.3 | 35.5 | ... | ... | 7.9 | 3.3 | 1.1 | ... | 3.8 |
| | 1975 | S | 429 | 30.8 | 11.4 | 39.2 | ... | ... | 13.5 | - | - | ... | 5.1 |
| | 1980 | S | 374 | 30.5 | 12.6 | 34.0 | - | 0.3 | 11.0 | 2.7 | - | 2.7 | 6.4 |
| | 1985 | S | 280 | 43.9 | 6.1 | 32.1 | - | 1.1 | 6.1 | 2.5 | 2.5 | - | 5.7 |
| | 1990 | S | 228 | 59.2 | 7.5 | 17.1 | - | 0.4 | 4.8 | 2.2 | 2.2 | - | 6.6 |
| | 1991 | S | 165 | 55.2 | 7.9 | 18.2 | - | 1.2 | 5.5 | 1.8 | 1.2 | - | 9.1 |
| | 1992 | S | 190 | 51.1 | 11.6 | 18.4 | - | 1.6 | 4.7 | 1.6 | 4.7 | 0.5 | 5.8 |
| | 1994 | S | 146 | 61.0 | 5.5 | 16.4 | - | 1.4 | 4.1 | 2.1 | 2.7 | 0.7 | 6.2 |
| | 1995 | S | 218 | 56.9 | 7.8 | 17.9 | - | 0.5 | 6.4 | 0.9 | 1.4 | - | 8.3 |
| Slovakia | 1992 | ... | 151 | 71.5 | 7.9 | 2.0 | - | - | 4.6 | 1.3 | - | 0.7 | 11.9 |
| | 1993 | ... | 164 | 68.3 | 3.7 | 4.9 | - | - | 6.7 | 2.4 | - | 0.6 | 13.4 |
| | 1994 | I | 148 | 73.6 | 4.1 | 3.4 | - | - | 4.1 | 2.0 | - | 0.7 | 12.2 |
| | 1995 | I | 121 | 63.6 | 5.0 | 1.7 | - | 0.8 | 9.9 | 1.7 | - | - | 17.4 |

**Importation of long films by country of origin**
**Importations de films de long métrage par pays d'origine**
**Importación de películas de largo metraje por país de origen**

| Country / Pays / País | Year / Année / Año | Definition of data / Code / Tipo de datos | Total | United States % | France % | Italy % | India % | Russian Federation % | United Kingdom % | Germany % | Japan % | China, Hong-Kong SAR % | Other countries / Autres pays / Otros países % |
|---|---|---|---|---|---|---|---|---|---|---|---|---|---|
| Slovenia | 1992 | S | 88 | 85.2 | 1.1 | 1.1 | - | - | 3.4 | - | - | - | 9.1 |
| | 1993 | S | 145 | 75.9 | 3.4 | 2.1 | - | - | 8.3 | - | - | - | 10.3 |
| | 1994 | I | 134 | 76.9 | 6.0 | 0.7 | 0.7 | - | 6.0 | 0.7 | - | - | 9.0 |
| | 1995 | I | 96 | 74.0 | 8.3 | - | 1.0 | - | 5.2 | 1.0 | - | 1.0 | 9.4 |
| Spain | 1970 | ... | 311 | 30.2 | 16.1 | 17.7 | ... | ... | 11.3 | 5.1 | 1.6 | ... | 18.0 |
| | 1975 | C | 381 | 31.2 | 15.0 | 17.3 | ... | ... | 13.1 | 3.7 | ... | ... | 19.7 |
| | 1980 | C | 404 | 36.4 | 11.6 | 23.0 | - | 1.0 | 9.9 | 4.7 | 0.7 | 0.7 | 11.9 |
| | 1985 | C | 344 | 52.0 | 16.0 | 6.1 | - | 0.9 | 5.8 | 9.0 | - | - | 10.2 |
| | 1990 | ... | 297 | 58.2 | 9.4 | 5.7 | - | 0.3 | 9.1 | 3.0 | 0.7 | - | 13.5 |
| | 1991 | ... | 292 | 66.1 | 12.0 | 3.1 | - | - | 8.2 | 2.7 | 0.3 | - | 7.5 |
| | 1992 | C | 282 | 60.3 | 9.9 | 6.7 | - | 0.4 | 7.4 | 1.8 | 2.1 | 1.1 | 10.3 |
| | 1993 | C | 250 | 62.8 | 9.2 | 4.0 | - | - | 7.6 | 6.0 | 0.4 | 0.4 | 9.6 |
| | 1994 | C | 301 | 60.5 | 7.0 | 2.3 | - | - | 10.0 | 10.3 | 1.3 | 0.7 | 8.0 |
| | 1995 | C | 346 | 55.2 | 9.2 | 4.9 | 0.3 | - | 9.5 | 12.7 | 0.6 | 0.6 | 6.9 |
| Sweden | 1970 | ... | 311 | 46.9 | 2.9 | 6.4 | ... | ... | 13.2 | 3.2 | ... | ... | 27.3 |
| | 1975 | ... | 370 | 58.9 | 2.2 | 4.9 | ... | ... | 4.9 | 1.6 | ... | ... | 27.6 |
| | 1979 | C | 318 | 52.5 | 14.2 | 6.0 | - | 2.8 | 7.2 | 4.7 | - | - | 12.6 |
| | 1986 | S | 211 | 64.9 | 10.9 | - | 0.5 | 1.4 | 8.1 | 2.4 | 0.5 | - | 11.4 |
| | 1990 | S | 202 | 55.9 | 5.4 | 2.0 | - | 1.5 | 6.4 | 0.5 | 2.0 | 0.5 | 25.7 |
| | 1991 | S | 196 | 52.6 | 6.6 | 3.6 | - | 1.0 | 7.1 | 0.5 | 1.0 | - | 27.6 |
| | 1992 | S | 194 | 51.0 | 9.8 | 3.1 | - | 0.5 | 7.7 | 0.5 | 2.1 | 1.5 | 23.7 |
| | 1993 | S | 203 | 48.8 | 13.3 | 1.0 | - | 1.0 | 6.9 | - | 2.0 | 1.0 | 26.1 |
| Switzerland | 1970 | ... | 443 | 35.7 | 14.2 | 17.8 | ... | ... | 7.0 | 17.8 | ... | ... | 14.4 |
| | 1975 | I | 411 | 33.8 | 22.6 | 17.8 | ... | ... | 4.9 | 8.5 | ... | ... | 12.4 |
| | 1980 | I | 669 | 38.6 | 13.5 | 8.2 | 1.9 | 0.6 | 3.9 | 7.9 | 1.8 | 1.9 | 21.7 |
| | 1985 | I | 358 | 49.7 | 23.2 | 5.9 | - | - | 4.5 | 12.0 | - | - | 4.7 |
| | 1990 | I | 310 | 61.0 | 16.5 | 3.2 | 1.0 | 2.3 | 2.3 | 5.8 | 1.6 | 0.3 | 6.1 |
| | 1991 | I | 327 | 55.0 | 16.2 | 7.0 | 1.5 | 0.9 | 3.1 | 4.6 | 0.6 | - | 11.0 |
| | 1992 | I | 359 | 59.3 | 12.8 | 2.8 | - | 1.1 | 3.6 | 7.8 | - | - | 12.5 |
| The Former Yugoslav Rep. of Macedonia | 1993 | I | 43 | 88.4 | - | - | - | - | - | 2.3 | - | 7.0 | 2.3 |
| | 1994 | I | 34 | 97.1 | - | - | - | - | - | - | - | - | 2.9 |
| | 1995 | I | 25 | 72.0 | 8.0 | - | - | 4.0 | 4.0 | - | - | - | 12.0 |
| Ukraine | 1976 | S | 118 | 7.6 | 3.4 | 8.5 | - | - | - | 10.2 | 3.4 | - | 66.9 |
| | 1992 | ... | 264 | 52.3 | 3.8 | 1.1 | 3.8 | 31.8 | 1.5 | - | - | - | 5.7 |
| | 1993 | ... | 256 | 46.9 | 6.3 | 1.6 | 4.3 | 29.7 | 2.0 | 0.8 | - | - | 8.6 |
| | 1994 | C | 174 | 79.3 | 3.4 | 2.3 | - | 9.2 | 1.1 | 1.1 | 1.7 | ... | 1.7 |
| | 1995 | C | 164 | 66.5 | 7.9 | 3.7 | - | 12.2 | 2.4 | 0.6 | 1.2 | ... | 5.5 |
| **Oceania** | | | | | | | | | | | | | |
| Australia | 1971 | ... | 989 | 27.2 | 5.6 | 6.6 | ... | 16.2 | 39.2 | ... | ... | ... | 5.3 |
| | 1975 | I | 916 | 27.2 | 6.6 | 12.2 | ... | ... | 8.7 | 6.0 | ... | 6.9 | 32.4 |
| | 1980 | I | 1 027 | 26.6 | 6.5 | 4.1 | 2.1 | 2.6 | 6.4 | 3.1 | 3.5 | 17.5 | 27.5 |
| | 1985 | C | 819 | 32.8 | 6.2 | 2.3 | ... | 1.3 | 9.6 | 6.5 | 2.0 | 9.4 | 29.8 |
| | 1989 | C | 516 | 46.9 | 2.5 | 5.2 | 0.6 | 2.3 | 11.6 | 1.4 | 3.5 | 13.4 | 12.6 |
| | 1992 | S | 200 | 68.0 | 5.5 | - | - | - | 13.0 | - | - | - | 13.5 |
| | 1993 | S | 236 | 72.5 | 6.8 | - | - | - | 5.5 | - | - | - | 15.3 |
| | 1994 | S | 226 | 67.7 | 7.5 | - | - | - | 9.7 | - | - | - | 15.0 |
| | 1995 | S | 239 | 71.5 | 7.1 | - | - | - | 9.6 | - | - | - | 11.7 |
| New Zealand | 1976 | C | 586 | 54.3 | 7.5 | 5.8 | - | - | 14.3 | 4.8 | 1.4 | 2.9 | 9.0 |
| | 1979 | C | 564 | 49.1 | 9.6 | 3.7 | 0.2 | 1.1 | 13.3 | 6.9 | 1.6 | 2.5 | 12.1 |
| | 1985 | C | 469 | 58.2 | 7.0 | 3.4 | 0.2 | 0.6 | 12.6 | 4.7 | 1.9 | 0.2 | 11.1 |
| | 1994 | I | 118 | 82.2 | 5.1 | 2.5 | - | - | 8.5 | - | - | - | 1.7 |
| | 1995 | I | 124 | 80.6 | 5.6 | 3.2 | - | - | 8.1 | - | - | - | 2.4 |

**General note**
For general explanations and definitions, please refer to the beginning of this chapter.

**Note générale**
Pour les explications et définitions générales, prière de se référer au début de ce chapitre.

**Nota general**
Para las explicaciones y definiciones generales, referirse al comienzo de este capítulo.

| Notes | Notes | Notas |
|---|---|---|
| (1) These data include importations for 1985. | (1) Ces données comprennent les importations pour 1985. | (1) Estos datos incluyen las importaciones para 1985. |
| (2) Data on films imported from the United Kingdom and the United States are counted together. | (2) Les données relatives aux films importés du Royaume-Uni et des Etats-Unis sont comptées ensemble. | (2) Los datos relativos a las películas importadas del Reino Unido y de los Estados Unidos se cuentan conjuntamente. |

## IV.13 Cinemas: number, seating capacity, annual attendance and box office receipts

Cinémas: nombre d'établissements, nombre de sièges, fréquentation annuelle et recettes guichet

Cines: número de establecimientos, número de asientos, frecuentación anual y recaudación de taquilla

| Country / Pays / País | Year / Année / Año | | Number of Cinemas / Nombre d'établis- sements / Número de establecimientos | Seating capacity / Nombre de sièges / Número de asientos (000) | Annual attendance / Fréquentation annuelle / Frecuentación anual (000 000) | Seats per 1,000 inhabitants / Sièges pour 1 000 habitants / Asientos por 1 000 habitantes | Annual attendance per inhabitant / Fréquentation annuelle par habitant / Frecuentación anual por habitante | Gross box office receipts / Recettes brutes / Recaudación total de taquilla (000 000) | Currency / Monnaie / Moneda |
|---|---|---|---|---|---|---|---|---|---|
| **Africa** | | | | | | | | | |
| Benin | 1970 | (1) | 6 | 9.0 | 1.2 | 3.3 | 0.4 | ... | Franc C.F.A. |
| | 1985 | (1) | 10 | ... | 1.5 | ... | 0.4 | 219 | |
| | 1992 | (1) | 26 | 9.4 | 1.1 | 1.9 | 0.2 | 198 | |
| | 1993 | (1) | 23 | 9.4 | 0.7 | 1.9 | 0.1 | 116 | |
| Cameroon | 1979 | (1) | 83 | 29.0 | ... | 3.4 | ... | ... | Franc C.F.A. |
| | 1985 | (1) | 197 | 39.8 | ... | 4.0 | ... | ... | |
| | 1990 | (1) | 230 | 38.9 | ... | 3.4 | ... | ... | |
| | 1991 | (1) | 232 | 39.9 | ... | 3.4 | ... | ... | |
| Congo | 1970 | | 24 | 6.5 | ... | 5.1 | ... | ... | Franc C.F.A. |
| | 1994 | (1) | 28 | 11.2 | ... | 4.5 | ... | ... | |
| | 1995 | (1) | 30 | 4.4 | ... | 1.7 | ... | ... | |
| Côte d'Ivoire | 1992 | | 60 | 70.0 | 7.9 | 5.6 | 0.6 | ... | Franc C.F.A. |
| | 1993 | | 60 | 70.0 | 7.3 | 5.5 | 0.6 | ... | |
| Egypt | 1970 | | 238 | 214.8 | 65.4 | 6.1 | 1.9 | ... | Pound |
| | 1975 | | 246 | 213.0 | 65.2 | 5.5 | 1.7 | 7.0 | |
| | 1991 | | 149 | 126.0 | 16.5 | 2.2 | 0.3 | 23 | |
| | 1994 | | 138 | 106.0 | 12.9 | 1.7 | 0.2 | 37 | |
| Guinea | 1985 | | 29 | 61.2 | 2.6 | 12.3 | 0.5 | ... | Syli |
| | 1990 | | 88 | 46.4 | 4.4 | 8.1 | 0.8 | 897 | |
| | 1991 | | 80 | 41.0 | 3.9 | 6.8 | 0.6 | 793 | |
| Kenya | 1976 | (1) | 50 | 26.0 | 8.5 | 1.8 | 0.6 | 8.5 | Shilling |
| | 1992 | (1) | 42 | 7.0 | 8.0 | 0.3 | 0.3 | ... | |
| | 1993 | (1) | 42 | 7.0 | 5.8 | 0.3 | 0.2 | ... | |
| Madagascar | 1970 | (1) | 53 | 11.9 | 0.0 | 1.7 | 0.0 | ... | Franc |
| | 1974 | | 31 | 12.4 | 2.9 | 1.6 | 0.4 | ... | |
| | 1990 | | 20 | ... | 0.7 | ... | 0.1 | 356 | |
| | 1991 | | 11 | ... | 0.4 | ... | 0.0 | 209 | |
| Mauritius | 1975 | | 48 | 48.0 | 17.0 | 53.8 | 19.1 | ... | Rupee |
| | 1980 | | 47 | 47.0 | 7.0 | 48.7 | 7.2 | 42 | |
| | 1985 | | 44 | 40.0 | ... | 39.4 | ... | ... | |
| | 1990 | | 17 | 15.0 | 0.7 | 14.2 | 0.7 | *14 | |
| | 1991 | | 15 | 13.0 | 0.6 | 12.2 | 0.6 | *15 | |
| | 1992 | | 15 | 14.0 | 0.7 | 13.0 | 0.7 | *22 | |
| | 1993 | | 16 | 14.0 | 0.7 | 12.8 | 0.7 | *22 | |
| Morocco | 1970 | | 242 | 146.9 | 23.0 | 9.6 | 1.5 | 43 | Dirham |
| | 1975 | | 201 | 128.4 | 36.3 | 7.4 | 2.1 | 110 | |
| | 1985 | | 242 | 164.0 | 32.3 | 7.6 | 1.5 | 135 | |
| | 1989 | | 252 | 166.1 | 30.2 | 7.1 | 1.3 | 143 | |
| | 1992 | | 210 | 141.0 | 22.7 | 5.7 | 0.9 | ... | |
| | 1993 | | 203 | 138.0 | 20.4 | 5.5 | 0.8 | ... | |
| | 1994 | | 190 | 134.0 | 1.9 | 5.2 | 0.1 | 107 | |
| | 1995 | | 185 | 131.0 | 17.3 | 5.0 | 0.7 | 103 | |

| Country / Pays / País | Year / Année / Año | Number of Cinemas / Nombre d'établissements / Número de establecimientos | Seating capacity / Nombre de sièges / Número de asientos (000) | Annual attendance / Fréquentation annuelle / Frecuentación anual (000 000) | Seats per 1,000 inhabitants / Sièges pour 1 000 habitants / Asientos por 1 000 habitantes | Annual attendance per inhabitant / Fréquentation annuelle par habitant / Frecuentación anual por habitante | Gross box office receipts / Recettes brutes / Recaudación total de taquilla (000 000) | Currency / Monnaie / Moneda |
|---|---|---|---|---|---|---|---|---|
| Rwanda | 1970 | 4 | 0.8 | ... | 0.2 | ... | ... | Franc |
| | 1975 | 3 | 2.0 | 0.1 | 0.2 | 0.0 | ... | |
| | 1980 | 10 | 3.1 | 0.3 | 0.6 | 0.1 | 52 | |
| | 1985 | 34 | 9.3 | ... | 1.5 | ... | ... | |
| | 1990 | 4 | 1.9 | ... | 0.3 | ... | ... | |
| United Republic of Tanzania | 1976 | 50 | 15.8 | 3.3 | 1.0 | 0.2 | 13 | Shilling |
| | 1980 | 35 | 14.7 | 4.0 | 0.8 | 0.2 | 48 | |
| | 1986 | 31 | 16.4 | 4.2 | 0.7 | 0.2 | 167 | |
| | 1990 | 28 | 12.4 | 1.9 | 0.5 | *0.1 | 183 | |
| | 1991 | 28 | 12.4 | 1.9 | 0.5 | *0.1 | 148 | |
| Zimbabwe | 1990 | 24 | 12.3 | 1.7 | 1.2 | 0.2 | 6.7 | Dollar |
| | 1991 | 24 | 12.2 | 1.8 | 1.2 | 0.2 | 7.6 | |
| **North America** | | | | | | | | |
| Barbados | 1970 | (1) 9 | 6.2 | 1.4 | 26.0 | 5.7 | ... | Dollar |
| | 1975 | (1) 10 | 7.2 | 1.3 | 29.3 | 5.2 | 1.3 | |
| | 1990 | 3 | ... | 0.0 | ... | 0.0 | ... | |
| | 1991 | 4 | ... | 0.0 | ... | 0.0 | ... | |
| Canada | 1975 | 1 492 | 1265.3 | 97.5 | 54.5 | 4.2 (2) | 213 | Dollar |
| | 1980 | 1 298 | 1163.1 | 101.2 | 47.3 | 4.1 (2) | 306 | |
| | 1986 | 898 | 906.0 | 76.1 | 34.5 | 2.9 (2) | 305 | |
| | 1990 | 742 | 722.0 | 79.0 | 26.0 | 2.8 (2) | 439 | |
| Costa Rica | 1985 | 105 | ... | 0.2 | ... | *0.1 | ... | Colon |
| | 1994 | 38 | ... | 1.5 | ... | 0.4 | 760 | |
| | 1995 | 39 | ... | 1.7 | ... | 0.5 | 1 058 | |
| Cuba | 1970 | (1) 757 | ... | 12.9 | ... | 1.5 | ... | Peso |
| | 1975 | (1) 1 049 | ... | 33.8 | ... | 3.6 | ... | |
| | 1980 | (1) 1 207 | 275.2 | 81.0 | 28.3 | 8.3 | 26 | |
| | 1985 | (1) 1 441 | 277.5 | 76.5 | 27.4 | 7.6 | 25 | |
| | 1990 | (1) 1 079 | 243.0 | 36.3 | 22.9 | 3.4 | 13 | |
| | 1991 | (1) 1 111 | 214.4 | 29.9 | 20.0 | 2.8 | 12 | |
| | 1992 | (1) 1 021 | 192.9 | 22.1 | 17.9 | 2.1 | 14 | |
| | 1993 | (1) 903 | 187.9 | 23.8 | 17.3 | 2.2 | 6.4 | |
| Mexico | 1970 | 1 769 | 1508.9 | 253.4 | 29.8 | 5.0 | ... | Peso |
| | 1975 | (1) 2 632 | 1588.0 | 253.7 | 26.9 | 4.3 | 1 800 | |
| | 1980 | (1) 2 831 | ... | 264.0 | ... | 3.9 | 5 778 | |
| | 1985 | (1) 2 246 | ... | 450.0 | ... | 6.0 | ... | |
| | 1990 | 1 896 | ... | 54.8 | ... | 0.7 | 99 000 | |
| | 1991 | 1 658 | ... | 47.5 | ... | 0.6 | 136 000 | |
| | 1992 | 1 616 | ... | ... | ... | ... | 183 948 | |
| | 1993 | 1 415 | ... | ... | ... | ... | 233 980 | |
| | 1994 | 1 434 | 1147.0 | 82.0 | 12.8 | 0.9 | 780 | New Peso |
| | 1995 | 1 495 | 774.0 | 63.0 | 8.5 | 0.7 | 888 | |
| United States | 1970 | 13 750 | ... | 921.0 | ... | 4.4 | 1 521 | Dollar |
| | 1975 | 15 969 | ... | 1250.0 | ... | 5.7 | 2 538 | |
| | 1980 | 17 590 | ... | 1021.5 | ... | 4.4 | 2 749 | |
| | 1985 | 21 147 | ... | 1056.1 | ... | 4.4 | 3 749 | |
| | 1990 | 23 689 | ... | 1056.6 | ... | 4.2 | 5 022 | |
| | 1991 | 24 570 | ... | 981.9 | ... | 3.8 | 4 803 | |
| | 1992 | 25 105 | ... | 971.2 | ... | 3.7 | 4 650 | |
| | 1993 | 25 737 | ... | 1180.0 | ... | 4.5 | 4 980 | |
| | 1994 | 26 586 | ... | 1210.0 | ... | 4.6 | 5 250 | |
| **South America** | | | | | | | | |
| Argentina | 1970 | (1) 1 693 | 751.3 | 53.9 | 31.4 | 2.2 | ... | Peso |
| | 1975 | (1) 1 430 | 790.5 | 82.2 | 30.3 | 3.2 | ... | |
| | 1980 | (1) 1 136 | 601.0 | 59.8 | 21.4 | 2.1 | ... | |
| | 1985 | (1) 1 242 | ... | 54.0 | ... | 1.8 | ... | |
| | 1990 | 430 | 70.0 | 20.1 | 2.2 | 0.6 | ... | |
| | 1991 | 342 | 69.0 | 18.0 | 2.1 | *0.5 | ... | |
| | 1992 | 280 | ... | 7.8 | ... | 0.2 | ... | |
| Bolivia | 1989 | 79 | ... | 4.6 | ... | 0.7 | 9 905 | Boliviano |
| | 1992 | (1) 137 | ... | 2.4 | ... | *0.3 | ... | |
| | 1993 | (1) 130 | ... | 2.2 | ... | *0.3 | ... | |
| Chile | 1970 | 374 | 263.9 | 56.7 | 27.8 | 6.0 | 180 | Peso |
| | 1975 | 291 | 185.5 | 23.4 | 17.9 | 2.3 | ... | |
| | 1980 | 180 | 115.0 | 14.4 | 10.3 | 1.3 | ... | |
| | 1985 | 177 | 107.0 | 12.6 | 8.9 | 1.0 | ... | |
| | 1990 | 163 | 91.2 | 11.4 | 7.0 | 0.9 | ... | |
| | 1991 | *154 | *89.0 | 10.0 | *6.7 | *0.7 | ... | |
| | 1992 | *137 | *83.5 | 8.4 | *6.2 | *0.6 | ... | |
| | 1993 | *133 | *75.9 | 8.0 | *5.5 | *0.6 | ... | |

| Country / Pays / País | Year / Année / Año | Number of Cinemas / Nombre d'établissements / Número de establecimientos | Seating capacity / Nombre de sièges / Número de asientos (000) | Annual attendance / Fréquentation annuelle / Frecuentación anual (000 000) | Seats per 1,000 inhabitants / Sièges pour 1 000 habitants / Asientos por 1 000 habitantes | Annual attendance per inhabitant / Fréquentation annuelle par habitant / Frecuentación anual por habitante | Gross box office receipts / Recettes brutes / Recaudación total de taquilla (000 000) | Currency / Monnaie / Moneda |
|---|---|---|---|---|---|---|---|---|
| Ecuador | 1970 | 164 | ... | 22.5 | ... | 3.8 | ... | Sucre |
| | 1986 | 118 | 110.0 | 11.1 | 11.8 | 1.2 | 884 | |
| | 1990 | 161 | 77.6 | 7.8 | 7.6 | 0.8 | 3 162 | |
| | 1991 | 134 | 75.3 | 6.8 | 7.2 | 0.6 | 4 949 | |
| Venezuela | 1975 | 597 | ... | ... | ... | ... | 117 | Bolivar |
| | 1980 | 561 | ... | 45.6 | ... | 3.0 | 254 | |
| | 1985 | 455 | 169.0 | 13.2 | 9.9 | 0.8 | 157 | |
| | 1990 | 341 | 119.7 | 22.8 | 6.1 | 1.2 | 866 | |
| | 1991 | 329 | 122.5 | 20.2 | 6.1 | 1.0 | 983 | |
| | 1992 | 321 | 111.1 | 18.0 | 5.4 | 0.9 | 1 257 | |
| | 1993 | 218 | 132.0 | 18.3 | 6.3 | 0.9 | 1 896 | |
| **Asia** | | | | | | | | |
| Armenia | 1992 | (1) 579 | 119.1 | ... | 33.3 | ... | 11 | Dram |
| | 1993 | (1) 577 | 118.5 | ... | 33.1 | ... | 44 | |
| | 1994 | (1) 599 | 124.9 | ... | 34.9 | ... | ... | |
| | 1995 | (1) 599 | 124.9 | ... | 34.9 | ... | ... | |
| Azerbaijan | 1992 | 148 | 374.0 | 3.7 | 50.9 | 0.5 | ... | Manat |
| | 1993 | 100 | 348.0 | 1.9 | 46.9 | 0.3 | ... | |
| China | 1985 | (1) 182 948 | ... | 21756.4 | ... | 20.3 | ... | Yuan |
| | 1990 | (1) 140 184 | ... | 16107.3 | ... | 13.9 | 2 225 | |
| | 1991 | (1) 139 639 | ... | 14428.4 | ... | 12.3 | 2 365 | |
| China, Hong Kong SAR | 1970 | 103 | 121.3 | 79.4 | 30.8 | 20.1 | ... | Dollar |
| | 1975 | 87 | 105.7 | 54.1 | 24.0 | 12.3 | ... | |
| | 1980 | 80 | 96.8 | 64.0 | 19.2 | 12.7 | ... | |
| | 1990 | 161 | ... | ... | ... | ... | 1 428 | |
| | 1991 | 166 | ... | ... | ... | ... | 1 557 | |
| | 1994 | 186 | 99.9 | 35.0 | 16.4 | 5.7 | 1 449 | |
| | 1995 | 184 | 94.8 | 28.0 | 15.2 | 4.5 | 1 368 | |
| Cyprus | 1970 | 206 | 127.0 | 6.1 | 206.5 | 9.9 | ... | Pound |
| | 1992 | 15 | 7.6 | ... | 10.8 | ... | ... | |
| | 1993 | 17 | 8.7 | ... | 12.1 | ... | ... | |
| | 1994 | 31 | 7.6 | 0.5 | 10.4 | 0.6 | ... | |
| | 1995 | 35 | 8.4 | 0.8 | 11.3 | 1.0 | 1.8 | |
| Georgia | 1992 | (1) 469 | 161.4 | 27.9 | 29.8 | 5.2 | 98 | Rouble USSR |
| | 1993 | (1) 290 | 106.8 | 30.4 | 19.9 | 5.7 | 91 093 | Coupon of Georgia |
| India | 1975 | (1) 9 235 | 5638.0 | ... | 9.1 | ... | ... | Rupee |
| | 1980 | (1) 10 815 | 4830.0 | 4380.0 | 7.0 | 6.4 | 3 350 | |
| | 1985 | (1) 12 696 | 6034.3 | 4921.0 | 7.9 | 6.4 | 4 500 | |
| | 1990 | (1) *13 550 | *6611.4 | 4300.0 | *7.8 | 5.1 | ... | |
| | 1991 | (1) *13 448 | *6751.4 | 4300.0 | *7.8 | 5.0 | ... | |
| Iran, Islamic Republic of | 1975 | 448 | 297.3 | ... | 8.9 | ... | ... | Rial |
| | 1980 | 410 | 264.0 | 163.0 | 6.7 | 4.2 | ... | |
| | 1985 | 419 | 167.0 | 27.9 | 3.5 | 0.6 | 2 273 | |
| | 1990 | 272 | 170.3 | 81.1 | 3.0 | 1.4 | 12 074 | |
| | 1991 | 273 | 169.6 | 66.6 | 2.9 | 1.2 | 14 632 | |
| | 1992 | 276 | 169.7 | 54.0 | 2.9 | 0.9 | 15 742 | |
| | 1993 | 277 | 171.4 | 29.0 | 2.9 | 0.5 | 12 616 | |
| | 1994 | 294 | 197.0 | 56.0 | 3.2 | 0.9 | ... | |
| | 1995 | 287 | 173.0 | 26.0 | 2.8 | 0.4 | ... | |
| Israel | 1970 | 271 | 185.8 | 35.1 | 62.5 | 11.8 | 76 | Shekel |
| | 1975 | 235 | 162.3 | 28.5 | 47.0 | 8.2 | ... | |
| | 1990 | 203 | 88.6 | ... | 19.0 | ... | ... | |
| | 1991 | 218 | 75.8 | ... | 15.7 | ... | ... | |
| | 1992 | 241 | 71.1 | ... | 14.2 | ... | ... | |
| | 1993 | 256 | 63.9 | ... | 12.3 | ... | ... | |
| | 1994 | 266 | 62.5 | 10.0 | 11.6 | 1.9 | ... | |
| Japan | 1970 | 3 247 | 1463.6 | ... | 14.0 | ... | 82 488 | Yen |
| | 1975 | 2 996 | ... | ... | ... | ... | 130 750 | |
| | 1980 | 2 364 | 946.0 | 165.9 | 8.1 | 1.4 | 164 400 | |
| | 1985 | 2 137 | ... | 155.1 | ... | 1.3 | 173 688 | |
| | 1990 | 1 836 | ... | 146.0 | ... | 1.2 | 171 900 | |
| | 1991 | 1 804 | ... | 138.3 | ... | 1.1 | 163 400 | |
| | 1992 | 1 744 | ... | 125.6 | ... | 1.0 | 152 000 | |
| | 1993 | 1 734 | ... | 130.7 | ... | 1.0 | 163 700 | |
| | 1994 | 1 747 | ... | 123.0 | ... | 1.0 | 153 590 | |
| | 1995 | 1 776 | ... | 127.0 | ... | 1.0 | ... | |
| Jordan | 1975 | 43 | 22.5 | ... | 8.7 | ... | ... | Dinar |
| | 1989 | 61 | 94.0 | 1.0 | 20.9 | 0.2 | ... | |
| | 1992 | 35 | ... | 0.2 | ... | 0.0 | ... | |
| | 1993 | 35 | ... | 0.2 | ... | 0.0 | ... | |

| Country / Pays / País | Year / Année / Año | | Number of Cinemas / Nombre d'établissements / Número de establecimientos | Seating capacity / Nombre de sièges / Número de asientos (000) | Annual attendance / Fréquentation annuelle / Frecuentación anual (000 000) | Seats per 1,000 inhabitants / Sièges pour 1 000 habitants / Asientos por 1 000 habitantes | Annual attendance per inhabitant / Fréquentation annuelle par habitant / Frecuentación anual por habitante | Gross box office receipts / Recettes brutes / Recaudación total de taquilla (000 000) | Currency / Monnaie / Moneda |
|---|---|---|---|---|---|---|---|---|---|
| Kazakstan | 1992 | (1) | 8 013 | 410.4 | 56.2 | 24.5 | 3.4 | 0.2 | Tenge |
| | 1993 | (1) | 5 947 | ... | 39.4 | ... | 2.4 | 2.3 | |
| | 1994 | | 1 896 | 389.8 | 13.2 | 23.5 | 0.8 | 24 | |
| | 1995 | | 1 580 | 346.7 | 6.2 | 21.0 | 0.4 | 39 | |
| Korea, Republic of | 1970 | | 782 | 440.8 | 168.0 | 13.8 | 5.3 | ... | Won |
| | 1975 | | 610 | 359.6 | 78.1 | 10.2 | 2.2 | ... | |
| | 1980 | | 447 | 254.0 | 54.6 | 6.7 | 1.4 | 43 419 | |
| | 1985 | | 482 | ... | 48.1 | ... | 1.2 | 68 898 | |
| | 1991 | | 762 | ... | 52.2 | ... | 1.2 | | |
| | 1992 | | 693 | 223.0 | 47.1 | 5.1 | 1.1 | | |
| | 1993 | | 640 | 212.0 | ... | | 4.8 | ... | |
| Kuwait | 1970 | | 8 | 12.1 | 3.8 | 16.3 | 5.1 | ... | Dinar |
| | 1975 | | 10 | 14.1 | 4.7 | 14.0 | 4.7 | ... | |
| | 1980 | | 14 | 17.2 | 4.4 | 12.5 | 3.2 | ... | |
| | 1985 | | 14 | 18.1 | 1.1 | 10.5 | 0.6 | ... | |
| | 1990 | | 14 | 17.3 | 0.3 | 8.1 | 0.1 | ... | |
| | 1992 | | 14 | ... | 0.4 | ... | 0.2 | ... | |
| | 1993 | | 7 | ... | 0.7 | ... | 0.4 | ... | |
| | 1994 | | 6 | ... | 0.8 | ... | 0.5 | ... | |
| Kyrgyzstan | 1994 | (1) | 480 | 106.7 | 1.5 | 23.5 | 0.3 | 3.1 | Som |
| | 1995 | (1) | 385 | 87.8 | 0.6 | 19.2 | 0.1 | 2.0 | |
| Lao People's Democratic Republic | 1990 | (1) | 31 | 6.6 | 1.4 | 1.6 | 0.3 | 340 | Kip |
| | 1991 | (1) | 31 | 6.6 | 1.0 | 1.5 | 0.2 | 245 | |
| Lebanon | 1970 | (1) | 173 | 85.0 | 49.7 | 34.4 | 20.1 | ... | Pound |
| | 1992 | (1) | 78 | 26.8 | 99.2 | 9.9 | 36.7 | 691 568 | |
| | 1993 | (1) | 79 | 26.8 | 99.2 | 9.5 | 35.3 | 691 733 | |
| Malaysia | 1975 | | 648 | 250.0 | ... | 20.4 | ... | 109 | Ringgit |
| | 1989 | | 169 | 152.4 | 41.6 | 8.8 | *2.4 | *119 | |
| | 1992 | | 257 | 155.8 | 25.8 | 8.3 | 1.4 | ... | |
| | 1993 | | 261 | 157.0 | 39.4 | 8.2 | 2.1 | ... | |
| Myanmar | 1975 | | 175 | 135.6 | ... | 4.5 | ... | ... | Kyat |
| | 1986 | | 163 | 126.4 | ... | 3.3 | ... | ... | |
| | 1991 | | 163 | 127.2 | ... | 3.1 | ... | ... | |
| | 1992 | | 162 | 125.3 | ... | 3.0 | ... | ... | |
| | 1993 | | 163 | 126.0 | ... | 3.0 | ... | ... | |
| Singapore | 1970 | | 72 | 55.0 | 28.0 | 26.5 | 13.5 | ... | Dollar |
| | 1975 | | 72 | 63.8 | 42.0 | 28.2 | 18.6 | 16 | |
| | 1980 | | 81 | 80.9 | 50.1 | 33.5 | 20.7 | 76 | |
| | 1990 | | 80 | ... | 20.7 | ... | 6.8 | ... | |
| | 1991 | | 80 | ... | 20.7 | ... | 6.7 | ... | |
| | 1992 | | 80 | ... | 19.3 | ... | 6.1 | 597 | |
| | 1993 | | 80 | ... | 20.0 | ... | 6.2 | ... | |
| | 1994 | | 80 | ... | 17.9 | ... | 5.5 | ... | |
| | 1995 | | 80 | ... | 18.1 | ... | 5.5 | ... | |
| Sri Lanka | 1970 | | 297 | 142.6 | 97.8 | 11.4 | 7.8 | ... | Rupee |
| | 1975 | | 350 | 183.8 | 55.5 | 13.5 | 4.1 | 64 | |
| | 1980 | | 347 | 196.0 | 63.5 | 13.2 | 4.3 | 140 | |
| | 1985 | | 318 | 201.0 | 36.5 | 12.5 | 2.3 | 39 | |
| | 1992 | | 255 | 142.0 | 29.2 | 8.2 | 1.7 | 222 | |
| | 1993 | | 259 | 143.0 | 27.2 | 8.1 | 1.5 | 223 | |
| Syrian Arab Republic | 1970 | | 114 | 68.0 | ... | 10.9 | ... | ... | Pound |
| | 1975 | | 100 | 58.0 | ... | 7.8 | ... | 35 | |
| | 1980 | | 93 | 53.4 | 13.4 | 6.1 | 1.5 | 25 | |
| | 1985 | | 85 | 47.8 | 11.6 | 4.6 | 1.1 | ... | |
| | 1989 | | 77 | 40.0 | 7.0 | 3.3 | 0.6 | ... | |
| | 1992 | | 56 | 24.8 | 4.0 | 1.9 | 0.3 | 9.5 | |
| | 1993 | | 55 | 23.8 | 3.9 | 1.8 | 0.3 | 12 | |
| Tajikistan | 1992 | (1) | 620 | 137.6 | 15.7 | 25.0 | 2.9 | 25 | Rouble |
| | 1993 | (1) | 916 | 200.2 | 12.7 | 35.8 | 2.3 | 235 | |
| | 1994 | (1) | 514 | 108.0 | 2.5 | 19.1 | 0.4 | 3.3 | |
| | 1995 | (1) | 172 | 39.0 | 0.4 | 6.8 | 0.1 | 6.0 | |
| Turkey | 1980 | | 941 | 506.3 | 62.5 | 11.4 | 1.4 | ... | Lira |
| | 1985 | | 576 | 299.0 | 25.8 | 5.9 | 0.5 | 4 580 | |
| | 1990 | | 354 | 191.0 | 19.2 | 3.4 | 0.3 | ... | |
| | 1991 | | 341 | 178.0 | 16.5 | 3.1 | 0.3 | ... | |
| | 1993 | | 320 | ... | 15.0 | ... | 0.3 | 392 135 | |
| Uzbekistan | 1992 | | 3 357 | 669.2 | 64.2 | 31.4 | 3.0 | 130 | Rouble |
| | 1993 | | 2 777 | 609.3 | 29.0 | 28.0 | 1.3 | 1 219 | |

| Country<br><br>Pays<br><br>País | Year<br><br>Année<br><br>Año | | Number of<br>Cinemas<br><br>Nombre<br>d'établis-<br>sements<br><br>Número de<br>estableci-<br>mientos | Seating<br>capacity<br><br>Nombre<br>de sièges<br><br>Número de<br>asientos<br><br>(000) | Annual<br>attendance<br><br>Fréquentation<br>annuelle<br><br>Frecuentación<br>anual<br><br>(000 000) | Seats per<br>1,000<br>inhabitants<br><br>Sièges pour<br>1 000<br>habitants<br><br>Asientos por<br>1 000<br>habitantes | Annual<br>attendance<br>per inhabitant<br><br>Fréquentation<br>annuelle par<br>habitant<br><br>Frecuentación<br>anual por<br>habitante | Gross<br>box office<br>receipts<br><br>Recettes<br>brutes<br><br>Recaudación<br>total de<br>taquilla<br>(000 000) | Currency<br><br>Monnaie<br><br>Moneda |
|---|---|---|---|---|---|---|---|---|---|
| Viet Nam | 1970 | | 121 | 84.4 | 22.7 | 2.0 | 0.5 | ... | Dong |
| | 1975 | (1) | 914 | 119.6 | 138.4 | 2.5 | 2.9 | 32 | |
| | 1980 | (1) | 1 107 | ... | 288.9 | ... | 5.4 | ... | |
| | 1985 | (1) | 1 394 | ... | 345.8 | ... | 5.8 | ... | |
| **Europe** | | | | | | | | | |
| Austria | 1970 | (1) | 871 | 281.2 | 32.9 | 37.7 | 4.4 | ... | Schilling |
| | 1975 | (1) | 567 | 184.4 | 20.8 | 24.3 | 2.7 | ... | |
| | 1980 | (1) | 489 | 151.0 | 17.8 | 20.0 | 2.4 | 655 | |
| | 1985 | (1) | 513 | 131.0 | ... | 17.3 | ... | ... | |
| | 1990 | (1) | 390 | 81.4 | 10.1 | 10.6 | 1.3 | 591 | |
| | 1991 | (1) | 395 | 80.8 | 10.5 | 10.4 | 1.4 | 654 | |
| | 1992 | (1) | 386 | 71.9 | 9.3 | 9.2 | 1.2 | 606 | |
| | 1993 | (1) | 386 | 70.6 | 12.0 | 9.0 | 1.5 | 809 | |
| | 1994 | (1) | 394 | 72.3 | 13.0 | 9.1 | 1.6 | 906 | |
| | 1995 | (1) | 412 | 72.7 | 11.9 | 9.1 | 1.5 | 847 | |
| Belarus | 1970 | | 6 330 | ... | 131.3 | ... | 14.5 | ... | B.Rouble |
| | 1980 | | 7 143 | ... | 143.0 | ... | 14.8 | ... | |
| | 1985 | | 7 377 | ... | 140.5 | ... | 14.1 | ... | |
| | 1990 | | 6 916 | 1047.7 | 116.7 | 102.1 | 11.4 | ... | |
| | 1991 | | 5 976 | 951.5 | 94.4 | 92.4 | 9.2 | ... | |
| | 1992 | | 4 568 | 809.9 | 55.9 | 78.3 | 5.4 | 270 | |
| | 1993 | | 4 168 | 744.3 | 29.5 | 71.8 | 2.8 | 2 581 | |
| | 1994 | | 3 900 | 712.9 | 18.7 | 68.6 | 1.8 | 3 515 | |
| | 1995 | | 3 780 | 700.1 | 12.5 | 67.4 | 1.2 | 19 290 | |
| Belgium | 1970 | | 732 | 370.6 | 30.5 | 38.4 | 3.2 | ... | Franc |
| | 1975 | | 568 | 267.7 | 25.5 | 27.3 | 2.6 | ... | |
| | 1980 | | 500 | ... | 21.6 | ... | 2.2 | 2 061 | |
| | 1985 | | 445 | ... | 17.9 | ... | 1.8 | 2 358 | |
| | 1990 | | 411 | ... | 17.1 | ... | 1.7 | 2 596 | |
| | 1991 | | 390 | ... | 16.5 | ... | 1.7 | 2 690 | |
| | 1992 | | 383 | ... | 16.6 | ... | 1.7 | 2 829 | |
| | 1993 | | 409 | ... | 19.2 | ... | 1.9 | 3 247 | |
| | 1994 | | 421 | 96.8 | 21.2 | 9.6 | 2.1 | 3 989 | |
| | 1995 | | 423 | ... | 19.2 | ... | 1.9 | 3 526 | |
| Bulgaria | 1970 | (1) | 3 170 | 676.5 | 112.6 | 79.7 | 13.3 | ... | Lev |
| | 1975 | (1) | 3 689 | 736.6 | 114.3 | 84.5 | 13.1 | 26 | |
| | 1980 | (1) | 3 453 | 726.8 | 95.8 | 82.0 | 10.8 | 42 | |
| | 1985 | (1) | 3 314 | 716.9 | 96.4 | 80.0 | 10.8 | 45 | |
| | 1990 | (1) | 2 174 | 524.0 | 47.7 | 60.1 | 5.5 | 41 | |
| | 1991 | (1) | 979 | 271.0 | 25.7 | 31.3 | 3.0 | 57 | |
| | 1992 | | 383 | 135.0 | 20.3 | 15.6 | 2.4 | 94 | |
| | 1993 | | 270 | 122.0 | 11.1 | 14.2 | 1.3 | 103 | |
| | 1994 | | 247 | 115.0 | 6.6 | 13.5 | 0.8 | 123 | |
| | 1995 | | 232 | 108.0 | 4.7 | 12.7 | 0.6 | 219 | |
| Croatia | 1970 | (1) | 427 | ... | 21.4 | ... | 5.1 | ... | Kuna |
| | 1975 | (1) | 378 | ... | 20.3 | ... | 4.8 | ... | |
| | 1980 | (1) | 317 | ... | 20.2 | ... | 4.6 | ... | |
| | 1985 | (1) | 309 | ... | 20.5 | ... | 4.6 | ... | |
| | 1990 | (1) | 274 | 97.6 | 8.1 | 21.6 | 1.8 | ... | |
| | 1991 | (1) | 173 | 66.5 | 3.1 | 14.7 | 0.7 | ... | |
| | 1992 | (1) | 123 | 46.9 | 2.1 | 10.4 | 0.5 | 506 | |
| | 1993 | (1) | 132 | 52.0 | 3.7 | 11.5 | 0.8 | ... | |
| | 1994 | (1) | 139 | 54.0 | 4.5 | 12.0 | 1.0 | 55 | |
| | 1995 | (1) | 151 | 55.0 | 3.7 | 12.2 | 0.8 | 75 | |
| Czech Republic | 1992 | (1) | 1 530 | 390.0 | 30.2 | 37.8 | 2.9 | 450 | C.Koruny |
| | 1993 | (1) | 1 380 | 360.0 | 21.9 | 34.9 | 2.1 | 433 | |
| | 1994 | (1) | 1 245 | 400.0 | 12.9 | 38.7 | 1.2 | 303 | |
| | 1995 | | 940 | 330.0 | 9.3 | 32.0 | 0.9 | 255 | |
| Denmark | 1970 | (1) | 385 | 138.2 | 24.3 | 28.0 | 4.9 | ... | Krone |
| | 1975 | (1) | 375 | 127.7 | 13.9 | 25.2 | 2.7 | 204 | |
| | 1980 | (1) | 481 | 112.0 | 15.9 | 21.9 | 3.1 | 262 | |
| | 1985 | (1) | 430 | 76.0 | 11.3 | 14.9 | 2.2 | 253 | |
| | 1990 | (1) | 349 | 57.0 | 9.6 | 11.1 | 1.9 | 267 | |
| | 1991 | (1) | 337 | 55.0 | 9.2 | 10.7 | 1.8 | 271 | |
| | 1992 | (1) | 318 | 53.0 | 8.6 | 10.3 | 1.7 | 253 | |
| | 1993 | (1) | 312 | 52.0 | 10.2 | 10.0 | 2.0 | 312 | |
| | 1994 | (1) | 311 | 50.0 | 10.3 | 9.6 | 2.0 | 325 | |
| | 1995 | (1) | 315 | 50.0 | 8.8 | 9.6 | 1.7 | 289 | |
| Estonia | 1990 | | 641 | ... | 10.9 | ... | 6.9 | ... | Krooni |
| | 1991 | | 617 | ... | 7.3 | ... | 4.7 | ... | |
| | 1992 | | 453 | 69.1 | 3.4 | 44.6 | 2.2 | 3.2 | |
| | 1994 | | 250 | ... | 1.4 | ... | 0.9 | 14 | |
| | 1995 | | 220 | ... | 1.0 | ... | 0.7 | 16 | |

| Country / Pays / País | Year / Année / Año | | Number of Cinemas / Nombre d'établissements / Número de establecimientos | Seating capacity / Nombre de sièges / Número de asientos (000) | Annual attendance / Fréquentation annuelle / Frecuentación anual (000 000) | Seats per 1,000 inhabitants / Sièges pour 1 000 habitants / Asientos por 1 000 habitantes | Annual attendance per inhabitant / Fréquentation annuelle par habitant / Frecuentación anual por habitante | Gross box office receipts / Recettes brutes / Recaudación total de taquilla (000 000) | Currency / Monnaie / Moneda |
|---|---|---|---|---|---|---|---|---|---|
| Federal Republic of Yugoslavia | 1980 | (1) | 545 | ... | 32.1 | ... | 3.4 | ... | Dinar |
| | 1985 | (1) | 565 | ... | 32.5 | | 3.3 | ... | |
| | 1990 | (1) | 398 | 151.0 | 8.3 | 14.9 | 0.8 | ... | |
| | 1991 | (1) | 234 | 99.0 | 3.0 | 9.7 | 0.3 | ... | |
| | 1992 | (1) | 170 | 76.0 | 2.3 | 7.4 | 0.2 | ... | |
| | 1993 | (1) | *128 | 62.0 | 1.8 | 5.9 | 0.2 | ... | |
| | 1994 | (1) | 137 | 63.0 | 1.5 | 6.0 | 0.1 | ... | |
| | 1995 | (1) | 146 | 73.0 | 2.2 | 6.9 | 0.2 | ... | |
| Finland | 1970 | | 360 | 100.7 | ... | 21.9 | ... | ... | Markka |
| | 1975 | | 343 | 95.2 | 9.6 | 20.2 | 2.0 | 71 | |
| | 1980 | | 365 | 93.6 | 9.9 | 19.6 | 2.1 | 133 | |
| | 1985 | | 378 | 89.0 | 6.7 | 18.2 | 1.4 | 165 | |
| | 1990 | | 340 | 66.3 | 6.2 | 13.3 | 1.2 | 182 | |
| | 1991 | | 333 | 63.0 | 6.0 | 12.6 | 1.2 | 184 | |
| | 1992 | | 330 | 60.7 | 5.4 | 12.1 | 1.1 | 174 | |
| | 1993 | | 335 | 60.8 | 5.8 | 12.0 | 1.1 | 196 | |
| | 1994 | | 326 | 58.6 | 5.6 | 11.5 | 1.1 | 201 | |
| | 1995 | | 330 | 58.4 | 5.3 | 11.4 | 1.0 | 194 | |
| France | 1970 | (1) | 7 798 | 2122.5 | 187.2 | 41.8 | 3.7 | 889 | Franc |
| | 1975 | (1) | 5 766 | 1755.6 | 182.9 | 33.3 | 3.5 | 1 571 | |
| | 1980 | (1) | 4 738 | 1418.8 | 175.9 | 26.3 | 3.3 | 2 479 | |
| | 1985 | (1) | 7 142 | 1276.1 | 172.2 | 23.1 | 3.1 | 4 301 | |
| | 1990 | | 5 260 | 1012.0 | 121.9 | 17.8 | 2.1 | 3 826 | |
| | 1991 | | 5 008 | 986.8 | 117.5 | 17.3 | 2.1 | 3 880 | |
| | 1992 | | 4 785 | 972.1 | 115.4 | 17.0 | 2.0 | 3 921 | |
| | 1993 | | 4 713 | 961.7 | 132.7 | 16.7 | 2.3 | 4 519 | |
| | 1994 | | 4 295 | 909.7 | 124.4 | 15.7 | 2.2 | 4 287 | |
| | 1995 | | 4 365 | 919.2 | 130.1 | 15.8 | 2.2 | 4 523 | |
| Germany | 1990 | (1) | 3 800 | 836.2 | 102.5 | 10.5 | 1.3 | 828 | Deutsche Mark |
| | 1991 | (1) | 3 734 | 763.0 | 119.9 | 9.6 | 1.5 | 981 | |
| | 1992 | (1) | 3 671 | 725.3 | 105.9 | 9.0 | 1.3 | 891 | |
| | 1993 | (1) | 3 748 | 745.7 | 130.5 | 9.2 | 1.6 | 1 170 | |
| | 1994 | (1) | 3 803 | 741.0 | 132.8 | 9.1 | 1.6 | 1 228 | |
| | 1995 | (1) | 3 861 | 730.0 | 124.5 | 8.9 | 1.5 | 1 183 | |
| Gibraltar | 1970 | | 3 | 2.0 | 0.7 | 75.0 | 24.5 | ... | Pound Stg |
| | 1975 | | 4 | 2.4 | 0.3 | 86.9 | 11.6 | ... | |
| | 1980 | | 4 | 2.3 | 0.2 | 80.7 | 6.7 | ... | |
| Greece | 1990 | | 584 | 392.0 | ... | 38.4 | ... | ... | Drachma |
| | 1991 | | 584 | 392.0 | ... | 38.1 | ... | ... | |
| | 1994 | | 320 | ... | 6.5 | ... | 0.6 | 8 800 | |
| Hungary | 1970 | (1) | 3 879 | 607.7 | 79.6 | 58.8 | 7.7 | ... | Forint |
| | 1975 | (1) | 3 595 | 561.6 | 74.4 | 53.3 | 7.1 | ... | |
| | 1980 | (1) | 3 624 | 559.0 | 60.7 | 52.2 | 5.7 | 499 | |
| | 1985 | (1) | 3 745 | 558.0 | 70.2 | 52.7 | 6.6 | 830 | |
| | 1990 | (1) | 1 864 | 343.0 | 35.9 | 33.1 | 3.5 | 1 510 | |
| | 1991 | (1) | 1 007 | 225.0 | 21.6 | 21.8 | 2.1 | 1 220 | |
| | 1992 | (1) | 715 | 136.0 | 15.3 | 13.2 | 1.5 | 1 114 | |
| | 1993 | (1) | 633 | *134.0 | 14.8 | *13.0 | 1.4 | 1 504 | |
| | 1994 | (1) | 595 | 140.0 | 15.9 | 13.7 | 1.5 | 2 141 | |
| | 1995 | (1) | 597 | 116.0 | 14.0 | 11.3 | 1.4 | 2 311 | |
| Iceland | 1970 | | 42 | 9.5 | 1.7 | 46.5 | 8.3 | ... | Krona |
| | 1975 | | 43 | 9.4 | 2.6 | 43.1 | 11.9 | ... | |
| | 1980 | | 33 | 11.0 | 2.6 | 48.2 | 11.4 | ... | |
| | 1985 | | 21 | 6.0 | 1.4 | 24.9 | 5.8 | ... | |
| | 1990 | | 22 | 5.5 | 1.2 | 21.6 | 4.8 | ... | |
| | 1991 | | 23 | 5.6 | 1.3 | 21.7 | 5.2 | ... | |
| | 1992 | | 24 | 6.2 | 1.3 | 23.8 | 5.0 | ... | |
| | 1993 | | 24 | 6.1 | 1.2 | 23.2 | 4.7 | ... | |
| | 1994 | | 24 | 6.0 | 1.2 | 22.6 | 4.7 | 683 | |
| | 1995 | | 23 | 6.0 | 1.2 | 22.4 | 4.5 | 665 | |
| Ireland | 1985 | | 125 | 52.5 | 11.6 | 14.8 | 3.3 | 30 | Pound |
| | 1990 | | 172 | ... | 7.4 | ... | 2.1 | 19 | |
| | 1991 | | 192 | ... | 8.1 | ... | 2.3 | 22 | |
| | 1992 | | 189 | 43.0 | 8.3 | 12.2 | 2.3 | 21 | |
| | 1993 | | 184 | ... | 9.3 | ... | 2.6 | 24 | |
| | 1994 | | 191 | ... | 10.4 | ... | 2.9 | 27 | |
| Italy | 1970 | | 9 616 | ... | ... | ... | ... | 181 896 | Lira |
| | 1975 | | 8 981 | ... | 515.7 | ... | 9.3 | 362 542 | |
| | 1980 | | 8 453 | ... | 241.9 | ... | 4.3 | 401 544 | |
| | 1985 | | 4 885 | ... | 123.1 | ... | 2.2 | 500 389 | |
| | 1990 | | 3 293 | ... | 90.7 | ... | 1.6 | 607 567 | |
| | 1991 | | 3 338 | ... | 88.6 | ... | 1.6 | 657 890 | |

| Country<br><br>Pays<br><br>País | Year<br><br>Année<br><br>Año | Number of<br>Cinemas<br><br>Nombre<br>d'établis-<br>sements<br><br>Número de<br>estableci-<br>mientos | | Seating<br>capacity<br><br>Nombre<br>de sièges<br><br>Número de<br>asientos<br><br>(000) | Annual<br>attendance<br><br>Fréquentation<br>annuelle<br><br>Frecuentación<br>anual<br><br>(000 000) | Seats per<br>1,000<br>inhabitants<br><br>Sièges pour<br>1 000<br>habitants<br><br>Asientos por<br>1 000<br>habitantes | Annual<br>attendance<br>per inhabitant<br><br>Fréquentation<br>annuelle par<br>habitant<br><br>Frecuentación<br>anual por<br>habitante | Gross<br>box office<br>receipts<br><br>Recettes<br>brutes<br><br>Recaudación<br>total de<br>taquilla<br>(000 000) | Currency<br><br>Monnaie<br><br>Moneda |
|---|---|---|---|---|---|---|---|---|---|
| Italy (cont) | 1992 | 3 522 | | ... | 83.6 | ... | 1.5 | 663 084 | |
| | 1993 | 3 567 | | ... | 92.2 | ... | 1.6 | 758 829 | |
| | 1994 | 3 617 | | ... | 98.2 | ... | 1.7 | 823 727 | |
| | 1995 | 3 816 | | ... | 90.7 | ... | 1.6 | 797 396 | |
| Latvia | 1985 | 1 142 | | ... | 35.1 | ... | 13.5 | ... | Lat |
| | 1990 | 1 103 | | ... | 19.7 | ... | 7.4 | ... | |
| | 1991 | 771 | | ... | 11.6 | ... | 4.4 | ... | |
| | 1992 | 552 | | ... | 5.2 | ... | 2.0 | ... | |
| | 1993 | 420 | | ... | 1.8 | ... | 0.7 | ... | |
| | 1994 | 261 | | 58.0 | 1.6 | 22.5 | 0.6 | 0.8 | |
| | 1995 | 245 | | 54.0 | 1.0 | 21.3 | 0.4 | 0.7 | |
| Lithuania | 1992 | (1) | 360 | 66.8 | 6.6 | 17.8 | 1.7 | 48 | Talonas |
| | 1993 | (1) | 245 | 53.5 | 2.3 | 14.3 | 0.6 | 1.1 | Lita |
| | 1994 | (1) | 215 | 46.0 | 1.4 | 12.3 | 0.4 | 1.9 | |
| | 1995 | (1) | 174 | 38.2 | 0.7 | 10.3 | 0.2 | 1.4 | |
| Luxembourg | 1989 | 14 | | 3.0 | 0.5 | 8.0 | 1.4 | 80 | Franc |
| | 1992 | 17 | | 3.1 | 0.6 | 7.9 | 1.5 | 114 | |
| | 1993 | 17 | | 3.1 | 0.7 | 7.8 | 1.8 | 134 | |
| | 1994 | 17 | | 3.1 | 0.7 | 7.7 | 1.8 | 133 | |
| Malta | 1970 | 40 | | 31.0 | 3.2 | 102.4 | 10.6 | ... | Lira |
| | 1975 | 36 | | 29.1 | 3.1 | 95.7 | 10.2 | 0.7 | |
| | 1980 | 34 | | 23.0 | 2.7 | 71.0 | 8.3 | 0.9 | |
| | 1985 | 22 | | 16.0 | 1.0 | 46.5 | 2.9 | 0.4 | |
| | 1990 | 10 | | 7.0 | 0.3 | 19.8 | 0.7 | ... | |
| | 1991 | 10 | | 7.0 | 0.3 | 19.6 | 0.7 | ... | |
| | 1992 | 10 | | 7.0 | 0.3 | 19.3 | 0.8 | ... | |
| Moldova | 1992 | (1) | 106 | 41.0 | 9.0 | 9.4 | 2.0 | 0.1 | Lei |
| | 1993 | (1) | 76 | 29.9 | 4.7 | 6.8 | 1.1 | 0.4 | |
| | 1994 | (1) | 79 | 26.3 | 2.6 | 6.0 | 0.6 | 1.8 | |
| | 1995 | 68 | | 22.3 | 1.4 | 5.1 | 0.3 | 1.8 | |
| Monaco | 1970 | 4 | | 2.0 | 0.1 | 84.5 | 4.9 | ... | French Franc |
| | 1975 | 3 | | 1.4 | 0.1 | 55.9 | 4.4 | ... | |
| | 1980 | 3 | | 1.4 | 0.1 | 52.7 | 3.8 | ... | |
| | 1990 | 4 | | 1.6 | 0.1 | 53.4 | 3.7 | 3.9 | |
| Netherlands | 1970 | (1) | 424 | 201.0 | 24.1 | 15.4 | 1.8 | ... | Guilder |
| | 1975 | (1) | 432 | 169.2 | 28.3 | 12.4 | 2.1 | 124 | |
| | 1980 | (1) | 534 | 156.7 | 30.7 | 11.1 | 2.2 | 213 | |
| | 1985 | (1) | 473 | 116.5 | 15.3 | 8.0 | 1.1 | 155 | |
| | 1990 | (1) | 435 | 100.8 | 14.6 | 6.7 | 1.0 | 168 | |
| | 1991 | (1) | 430 | 98.8 | 14.9 | 6.6 | 1.0 | 182 | |
| | 1992 | 425 | | 94.7 | 13.7 | 6.2 | 0.9 | 165 | |
| | 1993 | 425 | | 92.0 | 15.9 | 6.0 | 1.0 | 188 | |
| | 1994 | 423 | | 90.6 | 16.0 | 5.9 | 1.0 | 188 | |
| Norway | 1970 | (1) | 463 | 147.1 | 18.6 | 37.9 | 4.8 | 84 | Krone |
| | 1975 | (1) | 451 | 143.3 | 18.6 | 35.8 | 4.6 | 124 | |
| | 1980 | (1) | 444 | 137.0 | 17.5 | 33.5 | 4.3 | 208 | |
| | 1985 | (1) | 472 | 125.0 | 12.9 | 30.1 | 3.1 | 298 | |
| | 1990 | (1) | 402 | 101.0 | 11.4 | 23.8 | 2.7 | 383 | |
| | 1991 | (1) | 431 | 106.0 | 10.8 | 24.9 | 2.5 | 382 | |
| | 1993 | 400 | | 96.0 | 10.9 | 22.3 | 2.5 | 410 | |
| | 1994 | 394 | | 92.6 | 11.6 | 21.4 | 2.7 | 446 | |
| Poland | 1970 | (1) | 3 285 | 624.9 | 137.6 | 19.2 | 4.2 | ... | Zloty |
| | 1975 | (1) | 2 639 | 553.1 | 140.3 | 16.3 | 4.1 | 1 274 | |
| | 1980 | (1) | 2 228 | 501.5 | 97.6 | 14.1 | 2.7 | 1 393 | |
| | 1985 | (1) | 2 057 | 473.0 | 107.1 | 12.7 | 2.9 | 5 563 | |
| | 1990 | (1) | 1 435 | 373.0 | 32.8 | 9.8 | 0.9 | 86 848 | |
| | 1991 | (1) | 959 | 270.0 | 20.9 | 7.1 | 0.5 | 117 204 | |
| | 1992 | (1) | 772 | 226.0 | 13.3 | 5.9 | 0.3 | 183 730 | |
| | 1993 | (1) | 705 | 212.0 | 14.9 | 5.5 | 0.4 | 346 466 | |
| | 1994 | (1) | 773 | 233.0 | 17.0 | 6.0 | 0.4 | 578 000 | |
| Portugal | 1970 | 485 | | 273.3 | 28.0 | 30.2 | 3.1 | 307 | Escudo |
| | 1975 | 482 | | 268.5 | 41.6 | 29.5 | 4.6 | 716 | |
| | 1980 | 423 | | 237.0 | 30.8 | 24.3 | 3.2 | 1 583 | |
| | 1985 | 360 | | 179.9 | 19.5 | 18.2 | 2.0 | 2 439 | |
| | 1990 | 276 | | 111.0 | 9.6 | 11.2 | 1.0 | 2 856 | |
| | 1991 | 240 | | 95.3 | 8.2 | 9.7 | 0.8 | 2 526 | |
| | 1992 | 209 | | 76.0 | 7.8 | 7.7 | 0.8 | 2 744 | |
| | 1993 | 187 | | 66.1 | 7.8 | 6.7 | 0.8 | 3 122 | |
| | 1994 | 263 | | 84.7 | 6.4 | 8.6 | 0.6 | 3 066 | |

| Country<br><br>Pays<br><br>País | Year<br><br>Année<br><br>Año | | Number of Cinemas<br><br>Nombre d'établis-sements<br><br>Número de estableci-mientos | Seating capacity<br><br>Nombre de sièges<br><br>Número de asientos<br><br>(000) | Annual attendance<br><br>Fréquentation annuelle<br><br>Frecuentación anual<br><br>(000 000) | Seats per 1,000 inhabitants<br><br>Sièges pour 1 000 habitants<br><br>Asientos por 1 000 habitantes | Annual attendance per inhabitant<br><br>Fréquentation annuelle par habitant<br><br>Frecuentación anual por habitante | Gross box office receipts<br><br>Recettes brutes<br><br>Recaudación total de taquilla<br><br>(000 000) | Currency<br><br>Monnaie<br><br>Moneda |
|---|---|---|---|---|---|---|---|---|---|
| Romania | 1970 | (1) | 6 275 | 218.1 | 198.8 | 10.8 | 9.8 | ... | Leu |
| | 1975 | (1) | 6 099 | 218.8 | 185.7 | 10.3 | 8.7 | ... | |
| | 1980 | (1) | 5 801 | 249.3 | 193.6 | 11.2 | 8.7 | ... | |
| | 1985 | (1) | 5 643 | 257.0 | 191.6 | 11.3 | 8.4 | ... | |
| | 1990 | (1) | 4 637 | 235.8 | 130.1 | 10.2 | 5.6 | ... | |
| | 1991 | (1) | 3 222 | 209.5 | 67.4 | 9.0 | 2.9 | ... | |
| | 1992 | (1) | 1 771 | 175.4 | 46.1 | 7.6 | 2.0 | ... | |
| | 1993 | (1) | 1 470 | 168.3 | 33.7 | 7.3 | 1.5 | ... | |
| | 1994 | (1) | 693 | 162.0 | 25.9 | 7.1 | 1.1 | ... | |
| | 1995 | (1) | 626 | 162.0 | 17.0 | 7.1 | 0.7 | ... | |
| Russian Federation | 1992 | | 2 337 | 324.6 | 845.4 | 2.2 | 5.7 | *338 000 | Rouble |
| | 1993 | | 2 282 | 285.6 | 380.7 | 1.9 | 2.6 | *190 000 | |
| | 1994 | | 2 066 | 972.5 | 389.7 | 6.6 | 2.6 | 108 475 | |
| | 1995 | | 2 016 | 875.8 | 140.1 | 5.9 | 0.9 | ... | |
| San Marino | 1970 | | 9 | 1.8 | 0.2 | 97.9 | 11.1 | ... | Lira |
| | 1975 | | 10 | 2.8 | 0.2 | 147.6 | 10.5 | 67 | |
| | 1980 | | 6 | 2.6 | 0.1 | 122.5 | 4.7 | 83 | |
| | 1985 | | 7 | 3.2 | 0.1 | 143.3 | 4.5 | 63 | |
| | 1990 | | 3 | 2.0 | 0.0 | 86.3 | 0.9 | 63 | |
| | 1991 | | 3 | 2.0 | 0.0 | 85.3 | 1.2 | 90 | |
| | 1992 | | 3 | 2.0 | 0.0 | 84.1 | 1.5 | 152 | |
| | 1993 | | 3 | 2.0 | 0.0 | 82.8 | 1.7 | 191 | |
| | 1994 | | 2 | 1.8 | 0.0 | 73.4 | 1.8 | 242 | |
| | 1995 | | 2 | 1.8 | 0.1 | 72.3 | 2.0 | 253 | |
| Slovakia | 1992 | | 526 | 157.0 | 11.9 | 29.6 | 2.2 | ... | S.Koruny |
| | 1993 | | 456 | 150.0 | 8.9 | 28.2 | 1.7 | ... | |
| | 1994 | | 430 | 92.7 | 6.4 | 17.4 | 1.2 | 134 | |
| | 1995 | | 326 | 85.0 | 5.6 | 15.9 | 1.1 | 152 | |
| Slovenia | 1990 | | 140 | 40.1 | 2.8 | 20.9 | 1.5 | ... | Tolar |
| | 1991 | | 113 | 33.4 | 1.8 | 17.3 | 0.9 | ... | |
| | 1992 | | 88 | 27.5 | 1.6 | 14.1 | 0.8 | 232 | |
| | 1993 | | 94 | 28.6 | 2.3 | 14.6 | 1.2 | 732 | |
| | 1994 | | 102 | 31.0 | 2.7 | 15.7 | 1.4 | 717 | |
| | 1995 | | 98 | 29.0 | 2.9 | 14.6 | 1.5 | 890 | |
| Spain | 1970 | | 6 917 | 4925.4 | 330.9 | 145.8 | 9.8 | ... | Peseta |
| | 1975 | | 5 076 | 2550.0 | 255.8 | 71.6 | 7.2 | 12 973 | |
| | 1980 | | 4 096 | 2690.6 | 176.0 | 71.7 | 4.7 | 22 560 | |
| | 1985 | | 3 109 | ... | 101.1 | ... | 2.6 | 25 296 | |
| | 1990 | | 1 773 | ... | 78.5 | ... | 2.0 | 28 262 | |
| | 1991 | | 1 806 | ... | 79.1 | ... | 2.0 | 30 956 | |
| | 1992 | | 1 807 | ... | 83.3 | ... | 2.1 | 36 332 | |
| | 1993 | | 1 791 | ... | 87.7 | ... | 2.2 | 40 579 | |
| | 1994 | | 1 888 | ... | 89.1 | ... | 2.3 | 43 560 | |
| | 1995 | | 2 090 | ... | 94.6 | ... | 2.4 | 48 229 | |
| Sweden | 1970 | | 1 374 | ... | 26.0 | ... | 3.2 | 178 | Krona |
| | 1975 | | 1 192 | 344.4 | 22.3 | 42.0 | 2.7 | 283 | |
| | 1980 | | 1 189 | ... | 24.0 | ... | 2.9 | 465 | |
| | 1986 | | 1 114 | 241.0 | 17.0 | 28.8 | 2.0 | ... | |
| | 1990 | | 1 171 | 223.0 | 15.7 | 26.1 | 1.8 | 787 | |
| | 1991 | | 1 176 | 218.0 | 15.6 | 25.3 | 1.8 | 847 | |
| | 1992 | | 1 163 | 216.0 | 16.0 | 24.9 | 1.8 | 848 | |
| | 1993 | | 1 169 | 214.0 | 15.7 | 24.6 | 1.8 | 860 | |
| | 1994 | | 1 177 | 209.7 | 15.9 | 23.9 | 1.8 | 906 | |
| | 1995 | | 1 176 | ... | 15.2 | ... | 1.7 | 905 | |
| Switzerland | 1970 | | 601 | 218.0 | 32.0 | 35.2 | 5.2 | ... | Franc |
| | 1975 | | 506 | 185.5 | 23.0 | 29.3 | 3.6 | ... | |
| | 1980 | | 483 | 163.6 | 20.9 | 25.9 | 3.3 | 144 | |
| | 1985 | | 437 | 128.0 | 16.4 | 19.6 | 2.5 | 144 | |
| | 1990 | | 398 | 100.6 | 14.3 | 14.7 | 2.1 | ... | |
| | 1991 | | 399 | 99.2 | 15.4 | 14.4 | 2.2 | ... | |
| | 1992 | | 397 | 97.8 | ... | 14.0 | ... | ... | |
| | 1993 | | 415 | 98.6 | 15.9 | 14.0 | 2.3 | 180 | |
| | 1994 | | 431 | 100.7 | 16.2 | 14.2 | 2.3 | 194 | |
| | 1995 | | 439 | 100.7 | ... | 14.1 | ... | ... | |
| The Former Yugoslav Rep. of Macedonia | 1991 | | 47 | 17.0 | 0.6 | 8.8 | 0.3 | 0.2 | Dinar |
| | 1992 | | 38 | 14.0 | 0.3 | 7.2 | 0.2 | 0.7 | |
| | 1994 | | 39 | 15.0 | 0.3 | 7.7 | 0.2 | 20 | |
| | 1995 | | 38 | 14.0 | 0.2 | 7.1 | 0.1 | 22 | |
| Ukraine | 1970 | (1) | 28 816 | ... | 857.0 | ... | 18.1 | ... | Karbovanets |
| | 1975 | (1) | 27 797 | ... | 834.0 | ... | 17.0 | ... | |
| | 1980 | (1) | 27 690 | ... | 809.0 | ... | 16.2 | ... | |
| | 1985 | (1) | 28 300 | ... | 802.0 | ... | 15.7 | ... | |
| | 1991 | (1) | 25 031 | ... | 415.8 | ... | 8.0 | ... | |
| | 1994 | (1) | 16 620 | 3657.0 | 54.5 | 70.9 | 1.1 | 241 726 | |
| | 1995 | (1) | 14 997 | 3298.0 | 30.8 | 64.1 | 0.6 | 567 688 | |

| Country<br><br>Pays<br><br>País | Year<br><br>Année<br><br>Año | Number of<br>Cinemas<br>Nombre<br>d'établis-<br>sements<br>Número de<br>estableci-<br>mientos | Seating<br>capacity<br>Nombre<br>de sièges<br>Número de<br>asientos<br>(000) | Annual<br>attendance<br>Fréquentation<br>annuelle<br>Frecuentación<br>anual<br>(000 000) | Seats per<br>1,000<br>inhabitants<br>Sièges pour<br>1 000<br>habitants<br>Asientos por<br>1 000<br>habitantes | Annual<br>attendance<br>per inhabitant<br>Fréquentation<br>annuelle par<br>habitant<br>Frecuentación<br>anual por<br>habitante | Gross<br>box office<br>receipts<br>Recettes<br>brutes<br>Recaudación<br>total de<br>taquilla<br>(000 000) | Currency<br><br>Monnaie<br><br>Moneda |
|---|---|---|---|---|---|---|---|---|
| United Kingdom | 1970 | 1 529 | 1465.8 | 193.0 | 26.3 | 3.5 | 59 | Pound Stg |
|  | 1975 | 1 530 | 879.0 | 116.3 | 15.6 | 2.1 | 71 |  |
|  | 1980 | 1 605 | 688.0 | 102.0 | 12.2 | 1.8 | 143 |  |
|  | 1985 | 1 271 | ... | 70.2 | ... | 1.2 | 132 |  |
|  | 1990 | 1 673 | ... | ... | ... | ... | 261 |  |
|  | 1991 | 1 777 | ... | 97.6 | ... | 1.7 | 295 |  |
|  | 1992 | 1 860 | ... | 102.9 | ... | 1.8 | 290 |  |
|  | 1993 | 1 890 | ... | 113.4 | ... | 2.0 | 343 |  |
|  | 1994 | 1 969 | 553.0 | 124.4 | 9.5 | 2.1 | 364 |  |
|  | 1995 | 2 019 | ... | 114.6 | ... | 2.0 | 384 |  |
| **Oceania** |  |  |  |  |  |  |  |  |
| Australia | 1970 | 974 | 471.5 | ... | 37.6 | ... | ... | Dollar |
|  | 1985 | 616 | ... | ... | ... | 2.4 | 160 |  |
|  | 1989 | 772 | ... | 39.8 | ... | 2.4 | 258 |  |
|  | 1992 | 906 | 296.0 | 45.5 | 17.1 | 2.6 | 323 |  |
|  | 1993 | 951 | 298.0 | 53.3 | 17.0 | 3.0 | 369 |  |
|  | 1994 | 1 028 | 312.0 | 68.0 | 17.6 | 3.8 | 476 |  |
|  | 1995 | 1 137 | 332.0 | 69.0 | 18.5 | 3.8 | 502 |  |
| New Zealand | 1970 | 227 | 143.4 | 14.3 | 50.9 | 5.1 | 7.3 | Dollar |
|  | 1975 | 228 | 125.1 | 11.9 | 40.6 | 3.9 | ... |  |
|  | 1991 | 140 | ... | 6.1 | ... | 1.8 | 34 |  |
|  | 1992 | 175 | ... | 6.6 | ... | 1.9 | 38 |  |
|  | 1993 | 211 | ... | 9.7 | ... | 2.7 | 56 |  |
|  | 1994 | 228 | ... | 13.3 | ... | 3.7 | 77 |  |
|  | 1995 | 255 | ... | 14.1 | ... | 3.8 | 82 |  |

## General note
For general explanations and definitions, please refer to the beginning of this chapter.

## Note générale
Pour les explications et définitions générales, prière de se référer au début de ce chapitre.

## Nota general
Para las explicaciones y definiciones generales, referirse al comienzo de este capítulo.

**Notes**

(1) Data on number of cinemas include mobile units used for non commercial exhibitions.

(2) Receipts do not include taxes.

**Notes**

(1) Les données sur le nombre de cinémas comprennent les cinémas itinérants non commerciaux.

(2) Les recettes ne tiennent pas compte des taxes.

**Notas**

(1) Los datos sobre el número de establecimientos incluyen las unidades móviles no comerciales.

(2) La recaudación no toma en cuenta los impuestos.

IV.14    Radio and television receivers
Récepteurs de radiodiffusion sonore et de télévision
Receptores de radiodifusión sonora y de televisión

## IV.14    Radio and television receivers: total and number per 1,000 inhabitants

### Récepteurs de radiodiffusion sonore et de télévision: total et nombre pour 1 000 habitants

### Receptores de radiodifusión sonora y de televisión: total y número por 1 000 habitantes

| Country<br>Pays<br>País | Year<br>Année<br>Año | Radio receivers<br>Récepteurs de radiodiffusion sonore<br>Receptores de radiodifusión sonora | | Television receivers<br>Récepteurs de télévision<br>Receptores de televisión | |
|---|---|---|---|---|---|
| | | Number of receivers (thousands)<br>Nombre de postes récepteurs (milliers)<br>Número de receptores (en miles) | Number of receivers per 1,000 inhabitants<br>Nombre de postes récepteurs pour 1 000 habitants<br>Número de receptores por 1 000 habitantes | Number of receivers (thousands)<br>Nombre de postes récepteurs (milliers)<br>Número de receptores (en miles) | Number of receivers per 1,000 inhabitants<br>Nombre de postes récepteurs pour 1 000 habitants<br>Número de receptores por 1 000 habitantes |
| **Africa** | | | | | |
| Algeria | 1970 | 2 500 | 182 | 400 | 29 |
| | 1975 | 3 000 | 187 | 500 | 31 |
| | 1980 | 3 700 | 197 | 975 | 52 |
| | 1985 | 4 800 | 219 | 1 500 | 69 |
| | 1990 | 5 810 | 233 | 1 840 | 74 |
| | 1991 | 5 985 | 234 | 1 900 | 74 |
| | 1992 | 6 160 | 235 | 2 000 | 76 |
| | 1993 | 6 310 | 236 | 2 100 | 78 |
| | 1994 | 6 470 | 236 | 2 150 | 78 |
| | 1995 | 6 700 | 239 | 2 500 | 89 |
| | 1996 | 6 870 | 239 | 3 000 | 104 |
| | 1997 | 7 100 | 242 | 3 100 | 105 |
| Angola | 1970 | 95 | 17 | - | - |
| | 1975 | 118 | 19 | - | - |
| | 1980 | 145 | 21 | 30 | 4.3 |
| | 1985 | 217 | 27 | 37 | 4.6 |
| | 1990 | 260 | 28 | 57 | 6.2 |
| | 1991 | 270 | 28 | 59 | 6.2 |
| | 1992 | 282 | 29 | 62 | 6.3 |
| | 1993 | 295 | 29 | 68 | 6.6 |
| | 1994 | 320 | 30 | 70 | 6.6 |
| | 1995 | 370 | 34 | 80 | 7.3 |
| | 1996 | 600 | 53 | 100 | 8.8 |
| | 1997 | 630 | 54 | 150 | 13 |
| Benin | 1970 | 85 | 31 | - | - |
| | 1975 | 150 | 49 | - | - |
| | 1980 | 230 | 66 | 5 | 1.4 |
| | 1985 | 300 | 75 | 15 | 3.7 |
| | 1990 | 415 | 89 | 23 | 4.9 |
| | 1991 | 428 | 89 | 24 | 5.0 |
| | 1992 | 442 | 90 | 25 | 5.1 |
| | 1993 | 461 | 91 | 28 | 5.5 |
| | 1994 | 480 | 92 | 30 | 5.8 |
| | 1995 | 500 | 94 | 32 | 6.0 |
| | 1996 | 600 | 109 | 50 | 9.1 |
| | 1997 | 620 | 110 | 60 | 11 |
| Botswana | 1970 | 50 | 78 | - | - |
| | 1975 | 66 | 87 | - | - |
| | 1980 | 90 | 99 | - | - |
| | 1985 | 115 | 106 | - | - |
| | 1990 | 150 | 118 | 20 | 16 |
| | 1991 | 155 | 118 | 21 | 16 |
| | 1992 | 160 | 118 | 22 | 16 |
| | 1993 | 167 | 119 | 24 | 17 |
| | 1994 | 180 | 125 | 25 | 17 |
| | 1995 | 190 | 129 | 27 | 18 |
| | 1996 | 230 | 152 | 29 | 19 |
| | 1997 | 237 | 154 | 31 | 20 |

Radio and television receivers    IV.14
Récepteurs de radiodiffusion sonore et de télévision
Receptores de radiodifusión sonora y de televisión

| Country<br><br>Pays<br><br>País | Year<br><br>Année<br><br>Año | Radio receivers<br>Récepteurs de radiodiffusion sonore<br>Receptores de radiodifusión sonora | | Television receivers<br>Récepteurs de télévision<br>Receptores de televisión | |
|---|---|---|---|---|---|
| | | Number of receivers<br>(thousands)<br>Nombre de postes<br>récepteurs (milliers)<br>Número de receptores<br>(en miles) | Number of receivers<br>per 1,000 inhabitants<br>Nombre de postes<br>récepteurs pour 1 000<br>habitants<br>Número de receptores por<br>1 000 habitantes | Number of receivers<br>(thousands)<br>Nombre de postes<br>récepteurs (milliers)<br>Número de receptores<br>(en miles) | Number of receivers<br>per 1,000 inhabitants<br>Nombre de postes<br>récepteurs pour 1 000<br>habitants<br>Número de receptores por<br>1 000 habitantes |
| Burkina Faso | 1970 | 87 | 16 | 6 | 1.1 |
| | 1975 | 100 | 16 | 9 | 1.5 |
| | 1980 | 125 | 18 | 20 | 2.9 |
| | 1985 | 150 | 19 | 37 | 4.7 |
| | 1990 | 235 | 26 | 48 | 5.3 |
| | 1991 | 245 | 26 | 49 | 5.3 |
| | 1992 | 255 | 27 | 52 | 5.4 |
| | 1993 | 265 | 27 | 54 | 5.5 |
| | 1994 | 280 | 28 | 57 | 5.6 |
| | 1995 | 290 | 28 | 60 | 5.8 |
| | 1996 | 350 | 33 | 90 | 8.4 |
| | 1997 | 370 | 34 | 100 | 9.1 |
| Burundi | 1970 | 65 | 19 | - | - |
| | 1975 | 100 | 27 | - | - |
| | 1980 | 160 | 39 | - | - |
| | 1985 | 250 | 53 | 0.3 | 0.1 |
| | 1990 | 320 | 59 | 5 | 0.8 |
| | 1991 | 340 | 61 | 5 | 0.9 |
| | 1992 | 360 | 63 | 6 | 1.0 |
| | 1993 | 375 | 64 | 9 | 1.5 |
| | 1994 | 400 | 66 | 10 | 1.7 |
| | 1995 | 410 | 67 | 12 | 1.9 |
| | 1996 | 425 | 68 | 20 | 3.2 |
| | 1997 | 440 | 69 | 25 | 3.9 |
| Cameroon | 1970 | 300 | 45 | - | - |
| | 1975 | 400 | 53 | - | - |
| | 1980 | 760 | 88 | - | - |
| | 1985 | 1 200 | 120 | - | - |
| | 1990 | 1 650 | 144 | 270 | 24 |
| | 1991 | 1 725 | 146 | 279 | 24 |
| | 1992 | 1 775 | 146 | 288 | 24 |
| | 1993 | 1 830 | 147 | 300 | 24 |
| | 1994 | 1 900 | 148 | 309 | 24 |
| | 1995 | 2 000 | 152 | 320 | 24 |
| | 1996 | 2 200 | 162 | 400 | 30 |
| | 1997 | 2 270 | 163 | 450 | 32 |
| Cape Verde | 1970 | 23 | 86 | - | - |
| | 1975 | 31 | 112 | - | - |
| | 1980 | 41 | 142 | - | - |
| | 1985 | 50 | 161 | - | - |
| | 1990 | 59 | 173 | 1 | 2.9 |
| | 1991 | 61 | 175 | 1 | 2.9 |
| | 1992 | 63 | 177 | 1 | 3.1 |
| | 1993 | 65 | 179 | 1 | 3.3 |
| | 1994 | 67 | 180 | 1 | 3.5 |
| | 1995 | 69 | 181 | 1 | 3.7 |
| | 1996 | 71 | 182 | 1 | 3.7 |
| | 1997 | 73 | 183 | 2 | 4.3 |
| Central African Republic | 1970 | 46 | 25 | - | - |
| | 1975 | 70 | 34 | - | - |
| | 1980 | 120 | 52 | 0.5 | 0.2 |
| | 1985 | 150 | 58 | 5 | 1.7 |
| | 1990 | 200 | 68 | 13 | 4.4 |
| | 1991 | 210 | 70 | 14 | 4.5 |
| | 1992 | 220 | 71 | 14 | 4.6 |
| | 1993 | 227 | 72 | 15 | 4.8 |
| | 1994 | 235 | 73 | 16 | 4.8 |
| | 1995 | 245 | 75 | 16 | 4.9 |
| | 1996 | 270 | 80 | 17 | 5.1 |
| | 1997 | 283 | 83 | 18 | 5.3 |
| Chad | 1970 | 450 | 123 | - | - |
| | 1975 | 500 | 124 | - | - |
| | 1980 | 750 | 168 | - | - |
| | 1985 | 1 150 | 225 | - | - |
| | 1990 | 1 335 | 232 | 7 | 1.2 |
| | 1991 | 1 378 | 233 | 7 | 1.2 |
| | 1992 | 1 423 | 233 | 8 | 1.2 |
| | 1993 | 1 470 | 233 | 8 | 1.3 |
| | 1994 | 1 520 | 234 | 8 | 1.3 |
| | 1995 | 1 570 | 234 | 9 | 1.3 |
| | 1996 | 1 620 | 235 | 9 | 1.3 |
| | 1997 | 1 670 | 236 | 10 | 1.4 |

IV.14    Radio and television receivers
Récepteurs de radiodiffusion sonore et de télévision
Receptores de radiodifusión sonora y de televisión

| Country<br><br>Pays<br><br>País | Year<br><br>Année<br><br>Año | Radio receivers<br>Récepteurs de radiodiffusion sonore<br>Receptores de radiodifusión sonora | | Television receivers<br>Récepteurs de télévision<br>Receptores de televisión | |
|---|---|---|---|---|---|
| | | Number of receivers<br>(thousands)<br>Nombre de postes<br>récepteurs (milliers)<br>Número de receptores<br>(en miles) | Number of receivers<br>per 1,000 inhabitants<br>Nombre de postes<br>récepteurs pour 1 000<br>habitants<br>Número de receptores por<br>1 000 habitantes | Number of receivers<br>(thousands)<br>Nombre de postes<br>récepteurs (milliers)<br>Número de receptores<br>(en miles) | Number of receivers<br>per 1,000 inhabitants<br>Nombre de postes<br>récepteurs pour 1 000<br>habitants<br>Número de receptores por<br>1 000 habitantes |
| Comoros | 1970 | 26 | 94 | - | - |
| | 1975 | 36 | 113 | - | - |
| | 1980 | 46 | 119 | - | - |
| | 1985 | 56 | 123 | - | - |
| | 1990 | 69 | 131 | 0.2 | 0.4 |
| | 1991 | 72 | 133 | 0.2 | 0.4 |
| | 1992 | 75 | 135 | 0.2 | 0.4 |
| | 1993 | 78 | 136 | 0.3 | 0.4 |
| | 1994 | 81 | 137 | 0.3 | 0.4 |
| | 1995 | 84 | 139 | 0.4 | 0.7 |
| | 1996 | 87 | 140 | 1 | 1.6 |
| | 1997 | 90 | 141 | 1 | 1.9 |
| Congo | 1970 | 95 | 75 | 2 | 1.6 |
| | 1975 | 125 | 86 | 3 | 2.0 |
| | 1980 | 150 | 90 | 4 | 2.2 |
| | 1985 | 180 | 94 | 5 | 2.8 |
| | 1990 | 250 | 113 | 13 | 5.9 |
| | 1991 | 260 | 114 | 14 | 5.9 |
| | 1992 | 270 | 115 | 14 | 6.0 |
| | 1993 | 280 | 116 | 17 | 7.0 |
| | 1994 | 290 | 117 | 18 | 7.0 |
| | 1995 | 300 | 117 | 20 | 7.8 |
| | 1996 | 330 | 125 | 30 | 11 |
| | 1997 | 341 | 126 | 33 | 12 |
| Côte d'Ivoire | 1970 | 550 | 100 | 34 | 6.2 |
| | 1975 | 715 | 106 | 110 | 16 |
| | 1980 | 1 000 | 122 | 310 | 38 |
| | 1985 | 1 300 | 132 | 500 | 51 |
| | 1990 | 1 700 | 146 | 703 | 60 |
| | 1991 | 1 765 | 147 | 730 | 61 |
| | 1992 | 1 835 | 148 | 765 | 62 |
| | 1993 | 1 905 | 149 | 795 | 62 |
| | 1994 | 1 975 | 150 | 822 | 62 |
| | 1995 | 2 100 | 155 | 850 | 63 |
| | 1996 | 2 200 | 159 | 870 | 63 |
| | 1997 | 2 260 | 161 | 900 | 64 |
| Democratic Rep. of the Congo | 1970 | 3 000 | 148 | 6 | 0.3 |
| | 1975 | 4 000 | 172 | 7 | 0.3 |
| | 1980 | 5 200 | 193 | 10 | 0.4 |
| | 1985 | 6 300 | 199 | 13 | 0.4 |
| | 1990 | 7 735 | 207 | 2 018 | 54 |
| | 1991 | 8 500 | 219 | 2 500 | 64 |
| | 1992 | 9 000 | 222 | 2 660 | 66 |
| | 1993 | 10 000 | 237 | 3 000 | 71 |
| | 1994 | 12 000 | 273 | 3 400 | 77 |
| | 1995 | 14 103 | 310 | 3 679 | 81 |
| | 1996 | 15 970 | 341 | 5 051 | 108 |
| | 1997 | 18 030 | 376 | 6 478 | 135 |
| Djibouti | 1970 | 8 | 54 | 1 | 6.8 |
| | 1975 | 12 | 59 | 3 | 15 |
| | 1980 | 21 | 75 | 5 | 18 |
| | 1985 | 30 | 77 | 12 | 31 |
| | 1990 | 41 | 79 | 22 | 43 |
| | 1991 | 43 | 79 | 23 | 43 |
| | 1992 | 44 | 79 | 24 | 43 |
| | 1993 | 46 | 80 | 25 | 43 |
| | 1994 | 47 | 80 | 25 | 43 |
| | 1995 | 48 | 80 | 26 | 43 |
| | 1996 | 50 | 82 | 27 | 44 |
| | 1997 | 52 | 84 | 28 | 45 |
| Egypt | 1970 | 4 400 | 125 | 529 | 15 |
| | 1975 | 4 900 | 126 | 620 | 16 |
| | 1980 | 6 000 | 137 | 1 400 | 32 |
| | 1985 | 12 000 | 241 | 3 860 | 78 |
| | 1990 | 17 000 | 302 | 5 700 | 101 |
| | 1991 | 17 500 | 304 | 6 100 | 106 |
| | 1992 | 18 000 | 306 | 6 250 | 106 |
| | 1993 | 18 500 | 309 | 6 550 | 109 |
| | 1994 | 18 950 | 310 | 6 700 | 110 |
| | 1995 | 19 400 | 311 | 6 850 | 110 |
| | 1996 | 20 000 | 315 | 7 500 | 118 |
| | 1997 | 20 500 | 317 | 7 700 | 119 |

Radio and television receivers IV.14
Récepteurs de radiodiffusion sonore et de télévision
Receptores de radiodifusión sonora y de televisión

| Country<br>Pays<br>País | Year<br>Année<br>Año | Radio receivers<br>Récepteurs de radiodiffusion sonore<br>Receptores de radiodifusión sonora | | Television receivers<br>Récepteurs de télévision<br>Receptores de televisión | |
|---|---|---|---|---|---|
| | | Number of receivers<br>(thousands)<br>Nombre de postes<br>récepteurs (milliers)<br>Número de receptores<br>(en miles) | Number of receivers<br>per 1,000 inhabitants<br>Nombre de postes<br>récepteurs pour 1 000<br>habitants<br>Número de receptores por<br>1 000 habitantes | Number of receivers<br>(thousands)<br>Nombre de postes<br>récepteurs (milliers)<br>Número de receptores<br>(en miles) | Number of receivers<br>per 1,000 inhabitants<br>Nombre de postes<br>récepteurs pour 1 000<br>habitants<br>Número de receptores por<br>1 000 habitantes |
| Equatorial Guinea | 1970 | 70 | 240 | - | - |
| | 1975 | 78 | 347 | 0.4 | 1.8 |
| | 1980 | 87 | 401 | 1 | 4.6 |
| | 1985 | 128 | 411 | 2 | 7.1 |
| | 1990 | 147 | 418 | 3 | 9.4 |
| | 1991 | 151 | 419 | 3 | 9.4 |
| | 1992 | 155 | 420 | 4 | 9.5 |
| | 1993 | 160 | 422 | 4 | 9.5 |
| | 1994 | 165 | 424 | 4 | 9.6 |
| | 1995 | 170 | 426 | 4 | 9.6 |
| | 1996 | 175 | 427 | 4 | 9.6 |
| | 1997 | 180 | 428 | 4 | 9.8 |
| Eritrea | 1993 | 250 | 83 | 1 | 0.3 |
| | 1994 | 300 | 97 | 1 | 0.4 |
| | 1995 | 310 | 97 | 1 | 0.4 |
| | 1996 | 330 | 100 | 1 | 0.4 |
| | 1997 | 345 | 100 | 1 | 0.4 |
| Ethiopia | 1970 | 3 200 | 111 | 8 | 0.3 |
| | 1975 | 4 300 | 133 | 20 | 0.6 |
| | 1980 | 6 100 | 168 | 30 | 0.8 |
| | 1985 | 8 000 | 194 | 70 | 1.7 |
| | 1990 | 9 300 | 193 | 180 | 3.7 |
| | 1991 | 9 590 | 194 | 200 | 4.0 |
| | 1992 | 9 890 | 194 | 210 | 4.1 |
| | 1993 | 10 200 | 194 | 220 | 4.2 |
| | 1994 | 10 550 | 196 | 230 | 4.3 |
| | 1995 | 10 900 | 197 | 250 | 4.5 |
| | 1996 | 11 300 | 199 | 300 | 5.3 |
| | 1997 | 11 750 | 202 | 320 | 5.5 |
| Gabon | 1970 | 62 | 123 | 1 | 2.0 |
| | 1975 | 80 | 135 | 7 | 12 |
| | 1980 | 105 | 152 | 9 | 14 |
| | 1985 | 132 | 164 | 22 | 27 |
| | 1990 | 165 | 177 | 43 | 46 |
| | 1991 | 171 | 178 | 45 | 46 |
| | 1992 | 177 | 179 | 46 | 46 |
| | 1993 | 183 | 180 | 48 | 47 |
| | 1994 | 189 | 180 | 49 | 47 |
| | 1995 | 195 | 181 | 51 | 47 |
| | 1996 | 201 | 182 | 60 | 54 |
| | 1997 | 208 | 183 | 63 | 55 |
| Gambia | 1970 | 18 | 103 | - | - |
| | 1975 | 59 | 108 | - | - |
| | 1980 | 73 | 114 | - | - |
| | 1985 | 105 | 141 | - | - |
| | 1990 | 148 | 161 | - | - |
| | 1991 | 155 | 162 | - | - |
| | 1992 | 162 | 163 | 0.5 | 0.5 |
| | 1993 | 169 | 163 | 1 | 1.0 |
| | 1994 | 176 | 164 | 3 | 2.8 |
| | 1995 | 182 | 164 | 4 | 3.2 |
| | 1996 | 189 | 164 | 4 | 3.5 |
| | 1997 | 196 | 165 | 4 | 3.6 |
| Ghana | 1970 | 880 | 102 | 16 | 1.9 |
| | 1975 | 1 060 | 108 | 33 | 3.4 |
| | 1980 | 1 700 | 157 | 57 | 5.3 |
| | 1985 | 2 500 | 193 | 150 | 12 |
| | 1990 | 3 420 | 226 | 246 | 16 |
| | 1991 | 3 530 | 226 | 310 | 20 |
| | 1992 | 3 645 | 226 | 465 | 29 |
| | 1993 | 3 760 | 226 | 977 | 59 |
| | 1994 | 3 880 | 226 | 1 500 | 88 |
| | 1995 | 4 000 | 227 | 1 600 | 91 |
| | 1996 | 4 250 | 234 | 1 650 | 91 |
| | 1997 | 4 400 | 236 | 1 730 | 93 |
| Guinea | 1970 | 91 | 23 | - | - |
| | 1975 | 110 | 27 | - | - |
| | 1980 | 135 | 30 | 6 | 1.3 |
| | 1985 | 180 | 36 | 8 | 1.7 |
| | 1990 | 240 | 42 | 40 | 7.0 |
| | 1991 | 252 | 42 | 42 | 7.0 |
| | 1992 | 270 | 43 | 45 | 7.1 |
| | 1993 | 290 | 44 | 48 | 7.2 |

IV.14    Radio and television receivers
Récepteurs de radiodiffusion sonore et de télévision
Receptores de radiodifusión sonora y de televisión

| Country<br><br>Pays<br><br>País | Year<br><br>Année<br><br>Año | Radio receivers<br>Récepteurs de radiodiffusion sonore<br>Receptores de radiodifusión sonora | | Television receivers<br>Récepteurs de télévision<br>Receptores de televisión | |
|---|---|---|---|---|---|
| | | Number of receivers (thousands)<br>Nombre de postes récepteurs (milliers)<br>Número de receptores (en miles) | Number of receivers per 1,000 inhabitants<br>Nombre de postes récepteurs pour 1 000 habitants<br>Número de receptores por 1 000 habitantes | Number of receivers (thousands)<br>Nombre de postes récepteurs (milliers)<br>Número de receptores (en miles) | Number of receivers per 1,000 inhabitants<br>Nombre de postes récepteurs pour 1 000 habitants<br>Número de receptores por 1 000 habitantes |
| Guinea (cont) | 1994 | 310 | 45 | 50 | 7.2 |
| | 1995 | 325 | 45 | 65 | 9.1 |
| | 1996 | 350 | 48 | 75 | 10 |
| | 1997 | 357 | 49 | 85 | 12 |
| Guinea-Bissau | 1970 | 6 | 11 | - | - |
| | 1975 | 10 | 16 | - | - |
| | 1980 | 25 | 31 | - | - |
| | 1985 | 30 | 34 | - | - |
| | 1990 | 38 | 39 | - | - |
| | 1991 | 39 | 39 | - | - |
| | 1992 | 40 | 39 | - | - |
| | 1993 | 41 | 39 | - | - |
| | 1994 | 42 | 40 | - | - |
| | 1995 | 45 | 41 | - | - |
| | 1996 | 47 | 42 | - | - |
| | 1997 | 49 | 43 | - | - |
| Kenya | 1970 | 265 | 23 | 16 | 1.4 |
| | 1975 | 400 | 29 | 38 | 2.8 |
| | 1980 | 650 | 39 | 62 | 3.7 |
| | 1985 | 1 600 | 81 | 100 | 5.0 |
| | 1990 | 2 000 | 85 | 225 | 9.6 |
| | 1991 | 2 100 | 86 | 234 | 9.6 |
| | 1992 | 2 200 | 88 | 260 | 10 |
| | 1993 | 2 300 | 89 | 280 | 11 |
| | 1994 | 2 400 | 90 | 295 | 11 |
| | 1995 | 2 600 | 96 | 500 | 18 |
| | 1996 | 3 000 | 108 | 700 | 25 |
| | 1997 | 3 070 | 108 | 730 | 26 |
| Lesotho | 1970 | 11 | 10 | | - |
| | 1975 | 22 | 19 | - | - |
| | 1980 | 33 | 25 | - | - |
| | 1985 | 44 | 29 | 0.5 | 0.3 |
| | 1990 | 56 | 33 | 10 | 5.8 |
| | 1991 | 58 | 33 | 11 | 6.0 |
| | 1992 | 60 | 33 | 11 | 6.1 |
| | 1993 | 63 | 34 | 13 | 7.1 |
| | 1994 | 65 | 35 | 20 | 11 |
| | 1995 | 75 | 39 | 25 | 13 |
| | 1996 | 100 | 51 | 50 | 25 |
| | 1997 | 104 | 52 | 54 | 27 |
| Liberia | 1970 | 195 | 141 | 7 | 5.1 |
| | 1975 | 264 | 164 | 9 | 5.6 |
| | 1980 | 335 | 179 | 21 | 11 |
| | 1985 | 475 | 217 | 35 | 16 |
| | 1990 | 580 | 225 | 47 | 18 |
| | 1991 | 600 | 240 | 49 | 19 |
| | 1992 | 622 | 264 | 51 | 21 |
| | 1993 | 645 | 293 | 53 | 24 |
| | 1994 | 670 | 319 | 55 | 26 |
| | 1995 | 675 | 323 | 56 | 27 |
| | 1996 | 715 | 325 | 60 | 27 |
| | 1997 | 790 | 329 | 70 | 29 |
| Libyan Arab Jamahiriya | 1970 | 220 | 111 | 1 | 0.5 |
| | 1975 | 340 | 139 | 85 | 35 |
| | 1980 | 480 | 158 | 186 | 61 |
| | 1985 | 800 | 211 | 235 | 62 |
| | 1990 | 1 020 | 231 | 435 | 99 |
| | 1991 | 1 060 | 234 | 465 | 103 |
| | 1992 | 1 100 | 237 | 485 | 105 |
| | 1993 | 1 140 | 240 | 504 | 106 |
| | 1994 | 1 180 | 243 | 525 | 108 |
| | 1995 | 1 250 | 252 | 550 | 111 |
| | 1996 | 1 300 | 256 | 680 | 134 |
| | 1997 | 1 350 | 259 | 730 | 140 |
| Madagascar | 1970 | 900 | 131 | 4 | 0.6 |
| | 1975 | 1 250 | 160 | 8 | 1.0 |
| | 1980 | 1 600 | 180 | 45 | 5.1 |
| | 1985 | 1 950 | 193 | 100 | 9.9 |
| | 1990 | 2 400 | 206 | 240 | 21 |
| | 1991 | 2 480 | 206 | 248 | 21 |
| | 1992 | 2 565 | 206 | 260 | 21 |
| | 1993 | 2 655 | 206 | 272 | 21 |

Radio and television receivers IV.14
Récepteurs de radiodiffusion sonore et de télévision
Receptores de radiodifusión sonora y de televisión

| Country / Pays / País | Year / Année / Año | Radio receivers<br>Récepteurs de radiodiffusion sonore<br>Receptores de radiodifusión sonora | | Television receivers<br>Récepteurs de télévision<br>Receptores de televisión | |
|---|---|---|---|---|---|
| | | Number of receivers (thousands)<br>Nombre de postes récepteurs (milliers)<br>Número de receptores (en miles) | Number of receivers per 1,000 inhabitants<br>Nombre de postes récepteurs pour 1 000 habitants<br>Número de receptores por 1 000 habitantes | Number of receivers (thousands)<br>Nombre de postes récepteurs (milliers)<br>Número de receptores (en miles) | Number of receivers per 1,000 inhabitants<br>Nombre de postes récepteurs pour 1 000 habitants<br>Número de receptores por 1 000 habitantes |
| United Republic of Tanzania (cont) | 1994 | 8 000 | 275 | 60 | 2.1 |
| | 1995 | 8 300 | 277 | 70 | 2.3 |
| | 1996 | 8 550 | 279 | 100 | 3.3 |
| | 1997 | 8 800 | 280 | 103 | 3.3 |
| Western Sahara | 1970 | 9 | 118 | 1 | 13 |
| | 1975 | 11 | 141 | 2 | 24 |
| | 1980 | 22 | 155 | 2 | 17 |
| | 1985 | 33 | 194 | 4 | 22 |
| | 1990 | 42 | 203 | 5 | 23 |
| | 1991 | 44 | 204 | 5 | 23 |
| | 1992 | 46 | 205 | 5 | 24 |
| | 1993 | 48 | 207 | 5 | 24 |
| | 1994 | 50 | 209 | 6 | 24 |
| | 1995 | 52 | 210 | 6 | 24 |
| | 1996 | 54 | 210 | 6 | 24 |
| | 1997 | 56 | 211 | 6 | 24 |
| Zambia | 1970 | 160 | 38 | 17 | 4 1 |
| | 1975 | 230 | 48 | 23 | 4.8 |
| | 1980 | 320 | 56 | 60 | 10 |
| | 1985 | 500 | 78 | 90 | 14 |
| | 1990 | 650 | 90 | 210 | 29 |
| | 1991 | 680 | 92 | 217 | 29 |
| | 1992 | 705 | 93 | 225 | 30 |
| | 1993 | 730 | 94 | 237 | 30 |
| | 1994 | 760 | 95 | 245 | 31 |
| | 1995 | 800 | 98 | 260 | 32 |
| | 1996 | 1 000 | 119 | 270 | 32 |
| | 1997 | 1 030 | 120 | 277 | 32 |
| Zimbabwe | 1970 | 145 | 28 | 50 | 9.5 |
| | 1975 | 200 | 33 | 60 | 9.8 |
| | 1980 | 240 | 34 | 73 | 10 |
| | 1985 | 500 | 60 | 178 | 21 |
| | 1990 | 832 | 84 | 260 | 26 |
| | 1991 | 860 | 85 | 270 | 27 |
| | 1992 | 890 | 86 | 280 | 27 |
| | 1993 | 920 | 88 | 290 | 28 |
| | 1994 | 945 | 88 | 297 | 28 |
| | 1995 | 1 000 | 92 | 320 | 29 |
| | 1996 | 1 100 | 100 | 350 | 32 |
| | 1997 | 1 140 | 102 | 370 | 33 |
| **North America** | | | | | |
| Anguilla | 1990 | 2 | 295 | - | - |
| | 1991 | 2 | 292 | - | - |
| | 1992 | 3 | 333 | - | - |
| | 1993 | 3 | 330 | - | - |
| | 1994 | 3 | 327 | - | - |
| | 1995 | 3 | 327 | 1 | 128 |
| | 1996 | 3 | 342 | 1 | 146 |
| | 1997 | 3 | 344 | 1 | 146 |
| Antigua and Barbuda | 1970 | 10 | 174 | 5 | 87 |
| | 1975 | 15 | 254 | 15 | 254 |
| | 1980 | 17 | 281 | 16 | 264 |
| | 1985 | 21 | 338 | 19 | 306 |
| | 1990 | 26 | 407 | 23 | 360 |
| | 1991 | 27 | 421 | 23 | 361 |
| | 1992 | 27 | 424 | 24 | 364 |
| | 1993 | 28 | 425 | 24 | 369 |
| | 1994 | 28 | 432 | 24 | 373 |
| | 1995 | 29 | 441 | 28 | 426 |
| | 1996 | 35 | 529 | 31 | 463 |
| | 1997 | 36 | 542 | 31 | 463 |
| Aruba | 1993 | 30 | 411 | 17 | 233 |
| | 1994 | 35 | 453 | 18 | 237 |
| | 1995 | 41 | 501 | 19 | 238 |
| | 1996 | 45 | 525 | 20 | 229 |
| | 1997 | 50 | 557 | 20 | 219 |
| Bahamas | 1970 | 65 | 383 | - | - |
| | 1975 | 90 | 477 | | |
| | 1980 | 102 | 485 | 31 | 148 |
| | 1985 | 120 | 518 | 51 | 220 |
| | 1990 | 137 | 537 | 58 | 225 |

IV.14   Radio and television receivers
Récepteurs de radiodiffusion sonore et de télévision
Receptores de radiodifusión sonora y de televisión

| Country<br>Pays<br>País | Year<br>Année<br>Año | Radio receivers<br>Récepteurs de radiodiffusion sonore<br>Receptores de radiodifusión sonora | | Television receivers<br>Récepteurs de télévision<br>Receptores de televisión | |
|---|---|---|---|---|---|
| | | Number of receivers<br>(thousands)<br>Nombre de postes<br>récepteurs (milliers)<br>Número de receptores<br>(en miles) | Number of receivers<br>per 1,000 inhabitants<br>Nombre de postes<br>récepteurs pour 1 000<br>habitants<br>Número de receptores por<br>1 000 habitantes | Number of receivers<br>(thousands)<br>Nombre de postes<br>récepteurs (milliers)<br>Número de receptores<br>(en miles) | Number of receivers<br>per 1,000 inhabitants<br>Nombre de postes<br>récepteurs pour 1 000<br>habitants<br>Número de receptores por<br>1 000 habitantes |
| Bahamas (cont) | 1991 | 140 | 538 | 59 | 227 |
| | 1992 | 143 | 540 | 60 | 228 |
| | 1993 | 146 | 541 | 61 | 227 |
| | 1994 | 200 | 727 | 63 | 228 |
| | 1995 | 205 | 731 | 64 | 228 |
| | 1996 | 210 | 735 | 66 | 231 |
| | 1997 | 215 | 739 | 67 | 230 |
| Barbados | 1970 | 89 | 373 | 16 | 67 |
| | 1975 | 94 | 383 | 46 | 187 |
| | 1980 | 135 | 542 | 52 | 209 |
| | 1985 | 200 | 791 | 60 | 237 |
| | 1990 | 225 | 875 | 70 | 272 |
| | 1991 | 226 | 875 | 71 | 275 |
| | 1992 | 228 | 875 | 72 | 277 |
| | 1993 | 229 | 876 | 73 | 277 |
| | 1994 | 231 | 879 | 73 | 278 |
| | 1995 | 235 | 889 | 74 | 280 |
| | 1996 | 236 | 888 | 75 | 282 |
| | 1997 | 237 | 888 | 76 | 285 |
| Belize | 1970 | 48 | 391 | - | - |
| | 1975 | 59 | 441 | - | - |
| | 1980 | 71 | 487 | - | - |
| | 1985 | 88 | 530 | - | - |
| | 1990 | 109 | 582 | 31 | 165 |
| | 1991 | 112 | 582 | 32 | 166 |
| | 1992 | 115 | 583 | 33 | 166 |
| | 1993 | 119 | 585 | 34 | 168 |
| | 1994 | 122 | 585 | 35 | 168 |
| | 1995 | 125 | 586 | 38 | 178 |
| | 1996 | 129 | 590 | 40 | 183 |
| | 1997 | 133 | 591 | 41 | 183 |
| Bermuda | 1970 | 46 | 868 | 17 | 321 |
| | 1975 | 50 | 943 | 20 | 377 |
| | 1980 | 60 | 1 110 | 30 | 555 |
| | 1985 | 68 | 1 195 | 45 | 791 |
| | 1990 | 77 | 1 289 | 56 | 944 |
| | 1991 | 78 | 1 295 | 57 | 944 |
| | 1992 | 78 | 1 299 | 57 | 946 |
| | 1993 | 79 | 1 300 | 58 | 947 |
| | 1994 | 80 | 1 302 | 58 | 950 |
| | 1995 | 81 | 1 306 | 59 | 952 |
| | 1996 | 82 | 1 303 | 66 | 1 049 |
| | 1997 | 82 | 1 296 | 66 | 1 042 |
| British Virgin Islands | 1970 | 5 | 447 | 0.3 | 30 |
| | 1975 | 5 | 460 | 0.7 | 64 |
| | 1980 | 6 | 469 | 2 | 171 |
| | 1985 | 7 | 494 | 3 | 204 |
| | 1990 | 8 | 465 | 3 | 202 |
| | 1991 | 8 | 480 | 4 | 210 |
| | 1992 | 8 | 468 | 4 | 210 |
| | 1993 | 9 | 482 | 4 | 216 |
| | 1994 | 9 | 496 | 4 | 223 |
| | 1995 | 9 | 482 | 4 | 222 |
| | 1996 | 9 | 469 | 4 | 219 |
| | 1997 | 9 | 470 | 4 | 218 |
| Canada | 1970 | 14 600 | 685 | 7 100 | 333 |
| | 1975 | 16 100 | 694 | 9 200 | 396 |
| | 1980 | 17 734 | 721 | 10 617 | 432 |
| | 1985 | 23 237 | 896 | 14 028 | 541 |
| | 1990 | 28 461 | 1 024 | 17 019 | 612 |
| | 1991 | 29 295 | 1 040 | 18 192 | 646 |
| | 1992 | 29 800 | 1 044 | 18 687 | 655 |
| | 1993 | 30 200 | 1 044 | 19 394 | 671 |
| | 1994 | 30 580 | 1 045 | 19 973 | 682 |
| | 1995 | 30 950 | 1 045 | 21 000 | 709 |
| | 1996 | 32 000 | 1 069 | 21 250 | 710 |
| | 1997 | 32 300 | 1 067 | 21 500 | 710 |
| Cayman Islands | 1970 | 3 | 248 | - | - |
| | 1975 | 4 | 283 | - | - |
| | 1980 | 12 | 690 | 2 | 103 |
| | 1985 | 19 | 897 | 4 | 188 |
| | 1990 | 24 | 911 | 5 | 196 |

Radio and television receivers   **IV.14**
Récepteurs de radiodiffusion sonore et de télévision
Receptores de radiodifusión sonora y de televisión

| Country<br><br>Pays<br><br>País | Year<br><br>Année<br><br>Año | Radio receivers<br>Récepteurs de radiodiffusion sonore<br>Receptores de radiodifusión sonora | | Television receivers<br>Récepteurs de télévision<br>Receptores de televisión | |
|---|---|---|---|---|---|
| | | Number of receivers (thousands)<br>Nombre de postes récepteurs (milliers)<br>Número de receptores (en miles) | Number of receivers per 1,000 inhabitants<br>Nombre de postes récepteurs pour 1 000 habitants<br>Número de receptores por 1 000 habitantes | Number of receivers (thousands)<br>Nombre de postes récepteurs (milliers)<br>Número de receptores (en miles) | Number of receivers per 1,000 inhabitants<br>Nombre de postes récepteurs pour 1 000 habitants<br>Número de receptores por 1 000 habitantes |
| Cayman Islands (cont) | 1991 | 26 | 930 | 5 | 197 |
| | 1992 | 27 | 932 | 6 | 198 |
| | 1993 | 28 | 934 | 6 | 199 |
| | 1994 | 29 | 935 | 6 | 200 |
| | 1995 | 30 | 938 | 6 | 200 |
| | 1996 | 35 | 1 054 | 7 | 202 |
| | 1997 | 36 | 1 030 | 7 | 202 |
| Costa Rica | 1970 | 280 | 162 | 100 | 58 |
| | 1975 | 350 | 178 | 128 | 65 |
| | 1980 | 460 | 201 | 155 | 68 |
| | 1985 | 650 | 246 | 200 | 76 |
| | 1990 | 781 | 256 | 420 | 138 |
| | 1991 | 808 | 257 | 435 | 138 |
| | 1992 | 835 | 257 | 450 | 139 |
| | 1993 | 865 | 258 | 465 | 139 |
| | 1994 | 896 | 260 | 480 | 139 |
| | 1995 | 924 | 260 | 495 | 139 |
| | 1996 | 950 | 260 | 510 | 140 |
| | 1997 | 980 | 261 | 525 | 140 |
| Cuba | 1970 | 1 330 | 156 | 400 | 47 |
| | 1975 | 1 805 | 194 | 595 | 64 |
| | 1980 | 2 914 | 300 | 1 273 | 131 |
| | 1985 | 3 282 | 324 | 1 600 | 158 |
| | 1990 | 3 650 | 343 | 1 770 | 167 |
| | 1991 | 3 693 | 345 | 1 785 | 167 |
| | 1992 | 3 732 | 346 | 1 800 | 167 |
| | 1993 | 3 768 | 347 | 1 850 | 171 |
| | 1994 | 3 800 | 348 | 1 870 | 171 |
| | 1995 | 3 850 | 351 | 2 500 | 228 |
| | 1996 | 3 870 | 351 | 2 600 | 236 |
| | 1997 | 3 900 | 352 | 2 640 | 239 |
| Dominica | 1970 | 15 | 214 | - | - |
| | 1975 | 20 | 276 | - | - |
| | 1980 | 31 | 421 | - | - |
| | 1985 | 38 | 524 | - | - |
| | 1990 | 42 | 588 | 5 | 70 |
| | 1991 | 42 | 594 | 5 | 72 |
| | 1992 | 42 | 596 | 5 | 73 |
| | 1993 | 43 | 598 | 5 | 74 |
| | 1994 | 43 | 600 | 5 | 75 |
| | 1995 | 45 | 635 | 5 | 76 |
| | 1996 | 46 | 645 | 5 | 77 |
| | 1997 | 46 | 647 | 6 | 78 |
| Dominican Republic | 1970 | 650 | 147 | 100 | 23 |
| | 1975 | 770 | 153 | 180 | 36 |
| | 1980 | 900 | 158 | 400 | 70 |
| | 1985 | 1 020 | 160 | 500 | 78 |
| | 1990 | 1 210 | 170 | 600 | 84 |
| | 1991 | 1 240 | 171 | 615 | 85 |
| | 1992 | 1 270 | 172 | 650 | 88 |
| | 1993 | 1 300 | 172 | 680 | 90 |
| | 1994 | 1 330 | 173 | 695 | 90 |
| | 1995 | 1 380 | 176 | 728 | 93 |
| | 1996 | 1 410 | 177 | 750 | 94 |
| | 1997 | 1 440 | 178 | 770 | 95 |
| El Salvador | 1970 | 850 | 236 | 92 | 26 |
| | 1975 | 1 100 | 267 | 135 | 33 |
| | 1980 | 1 550 | 338 | 300 | 65 |
| | 1985 | 1 900 | 398 | 350 | 73 |
| | 1990 | 2 125 | 416 | 600 | 117 |
| | 1991 | 2 175 | 418 | 3 500 | 672 |
| | 1992 | 2 225 | 419 | 3 600 | 677 |
| | 1993 | 2 280 | 420 | 3 700 | 681 |
| | 1994 | 2 500 | 451 | 3 800 | 685 |
| | 1995 | 2 600 | 459 | 3 900 | 688 |
| | 1996 | 2 670 | 461 | 3 910 | 675 |
| | 1997 | 2 750 | 465 | 4 000 | 677 |
| Greenland | 1970 | 9 | 194 | 2 | 43 |
| | 1975 | 12 | 242 | 3 | 61 |
| | 1980 | 15 | 299 | 4 | 70 |
| | 1985 | 19 | 357 | 7 | 132 |
| | 1990 | 23 | 405 | 11 | 198 |

IV.14    Radio and television receivers
Récepteurs de radiodiffusion sonore et de télévision
Receptores de radiodifusión sonora y de televisión

| Country<br>Pays<br>País | Year<br>Année<br>Año | Radio receivers<br>Récepteurs de radiodiffusion sonore<br>Receptores de radiodifusión sonora | | Television receivers<br>Récepteurs de télévision<br>Receptores de televisión | |
|---|---|---|---|---|---|
| | | Number of receivers (thousands)<br>Nombre de postes récepteurs (milliers)<br>Número de receptores (en miles) | Number of receivers per 1,000 inhabitants<br>Nombre de postes récepteurs pour 1 000 habitants<br>Número de receptores por 1 000 habitantes | Number of receivers (thousands)<br>Nombre de postes récepteurs (milliers)<br>Número de receptores (en miles) | Number of receivers per 1,000 inhabitants<br>Nombre de postes récepteurs pour 1 000 habitants<br>Número de receptores por 1 000 habitantes |
| Greenland (cont) | 1991 | 23 | 406 | 11 | 199 |
| | 1992 | 23 | 414 | 11 | 203 |
| | 1993 | 23 | 415 | 12 | 206 |
| | 1994 | 24 | 423 | 12 | 211 |
| | 1995 | 25 | 448 | 20 | 358 |
| | 1996 | 26 | 466 | 21 | 376 |
| | 1997 | 27 | 483 | 22 | 385 |
| Grenada | 1970 | 15 | 159 | - | - |
| | 1975 | 22 | 240 | - | - |
| | 1980 | 35 | 394 | - | - |
| | 1985 | 45 | 501 | - | - |
| | 1990 | 54 | 590 | 30 | 331 |
| | 1991 | 54 | 590 | 30 | 330 |
| | 1992 | 54 | 592 | 30 | 331 |
| | 1993 | 55 | 595 | 31 | 333 |
| | 1994 | 55 | 596 | 31 | 338 |
| | 1995 | 55 | 597 | 32 | 347 |
| | 1996 | 56 | 606 | 32 | 349 |
| | 1997 | 57 | 615 | 33 | 353 |
| Guadeloupe | 1970 | 30 | 94 | 8 | 25 |
| | 1975 | 35 | 107 | 18 | 55 |
| | 1980 | 50 | 153 | 37 | 113 |
| | 1985 | 80 | 225 | 77 | 217 |
| | 1990 | 89 | 228 | 102 | 261 |
| | 1991 | 91 | 228 | 104 | 262 |
| | 1992 | 92 | 228 | 106 | 262 |
| | 1993 | 94 | 229 | 108 | 263 |
| | 1994 | 96 | 230 | 111 | 265 |
| | 1995 | 98 | 231 | 114 | 269 |
| | 1996 | 110 | 255 | 116 | 269 |
| | 1997 | 113 | 258 | 118 | 270 |
| Guatemala | 1970 | 220 | 42 | 72 | 14 |
| | 1975 | 300 | 50 | 110 | 18 |
| | 1980 | 350 | 51 | 175 | 26 |
| | 1985 | 450 | 58 | 207 | 27 |
| | 1990 | 600 | 69 | 475 | 54 |
| | 1991 | 625 | 70 | 490 | 55 |
| | 1992 | 645 | 70 | 510 | 55 |
| | 1993 | 680 | 72 | 530 | 56 |
| | 1994 | 700 | 72 | 545 | 56 |
| | 1995 | 750 | 75 | 600 | 60 |
| | 1996 | 800 | 78 | 620 | 61 |
| | 1997 | 835 | 79 | 640 | 61 |
| Haiti | 1970 | 76 | 17 | 11 | 2.4 |
| | 1975 | 93 | 19 | 13 | 2.6 |
| | 1980 | 105 | 19 | 16 | 2.9 |
| | 1985 | 140 | 23 | 21 | 3.4 |
| | 1990 | 290 | 42 | 30 | 4.3 |
| | 1991 | 310 | 44 | 31 | 4.4 |
| | 1992 | 320 | 45 | 32 | 4.5 |
| | 1993 | 330 | 45 | 33 | 4.5 |
| | 1994 | 350 | 47 | 34 | 4.6 |
| | 1995 | 380 | 50 | 35 | 4.6 |
| | 1996 | 400 | 52 | 36 | 4.7 |
| | 1997 | 415 | 53 | 38 | 4.8 |
| Honduras | 1970 | 250 | 96 | 22 | 8.5 |
| | 1975 | 350 | 116 | 34 | 11 |
| | 1980 | 500 | 140 | 65 | 18 |
| | 1985 | 1 600 | 382 | 280 | 67 |
| | 1990 | 1 980 | 406 | 370 | 76 |
| | 1991 | 2 045 | 407 | 385 | 77 |
| | 1992 | 2 110 | 407 | 400 | 77 |
| | 1993 | 2 175 | 408 | 415 | 78 |
| | 1994 | 2 240 | 408 | 428 | 78 |
| | 1995 | 2 310 | 409 | 500 | 88 |
| | 1996 | 2 380 | 409 | 550 | 95 |
| | 1997 | 2 450 | 410 | 570 | 95 |
| Jamaica | 1970 | 500 | 268 | 70 | 37 |
| | 1975 | 550 | 273 | 110 | 55 |
| | 1980 | 800 | 375 | 170 | 80 |
| | 1985 | 920 | 401 | 215 | 94 |
| | 1990 | 1 010 | 426 | 310 | 131 |

Radio and television receivers **IV.14**
Récepteurs de radiodiffusion sonore et de télévision
Receptores de radiodifusión sonora y de televisión

| Country / Pays / País | Year / Année / Año | Radio receivers / Récepteurs de radiodiffusion sonore / Receptores de radiodifusión sonora | | Television receivers / Récepteurs de télévision / Receptores de televisión | |
|---|---|---|---|---|---|
| | | Number of receivers (thousands) / Nombre de postes récepteurs (milliers) / Número de receptores (en miles) | Number of receivers per 1,000 inhabitants / Nombre de postes récepteurs pour 1 000 habitants / Número de receptores por 1 000 habitantes | Number of receivers (thousands) / Nombre de postes récepteurs (milliers) / Número de receptores (en miles) | Number of receivers per 1,000 inhabitants / Nombre de postes récepteurs pour 1 000 habitants / Número de receptores por 1 000 habitantes |
| Jamaica (cont) | 1991 | 1 025 | 430 | 320 | 134 |
| | 1992 | 1 035 | 430 | 330 | 137 |
| | 1993 | 1 045 | 430 | 340 | 140 |
| | 1994 | 1 060 | 433 | 345 | 141 |
| | 1995 | 1 080 | 437 | 400 | 162 |
| | 1996 | 1 200 | 481 | 450 | 180 |
| | 1997 | 1 215 | 483 | 460 | 183 |
| Martinique | 1970 | 50 | 154 | 10 | 31 |
| | 1975 | 57 | 174 | 22 | 67 |
| | 1980 | 62 | 190 | 38 | 117 |
| | 1985 | 67 | 197 | 44 | 129 |
| | 1990 | 72 | 200 | 48 | 133 |
| | 1991 | 73 | 200 | 49 | 135 |
| | 1992 | 74 | 201 | 50 | 136 |
| | 1993 | 75 | 202 | 51 | 137 |
| | 1994 | 76 | 203 | 52 | 139 |
| | 1995 | 77 | 203 | 55 | 145 |
| | 1996 | 80 | 200 | 65 | 170 |
| | 1997 | 82 | 213 | 66 | 171 |
| Mexico | 1970 | 5 600 | 111 | 1 800 | 36 |
| | 1975 | 6 900 | 117 | 2 700 | 46 |
| | 1980 | 9 000 | 133 | 3 820 | 57 |
| | 1985 | 15 000 | 199 | 8 500 | 113 |
| | 1990 | 21 500 | 258 | 12 350 | 148 |
| | 1991 | 22 000 | 259 | 12 750 | 150 |
| | 1992 | 22 500 | 260 | 13 100 | 152 |
| | 1993 | 23 000 | 261 | 13 500 | 153 |
| | 1994 | 23 500 | 262 | 15 000 | 167 |
| | 1995 | 24 000 | 263 | 20 000 | 219 |
| | 1996 | 30 000 | 324 | 25 000 | 270 |
| | 1997 | 31 000 | 329 | 25 600 | 272 |
| Montserrat | 1970 | 5 | 401 | - | - |
| | 1975 | 5 | 421 | - | - |
| | 1980 | 6 | 475 | - | - |
| | 1985 | 6 | 533 | - | - |
| | 1990 | 6 | 575 | 2 | 148 |
| | 1991 | 6 | 582 | 2 | 150 |
| | 1992 | 6 | 586 | 2 | 151 |
| | 1993 | 6 | 588 | 2 | 151 |
| | 1994 | 6 | 593 | 2 | 152 |
| | 1995 | 7 | 604 | 2 | 186 |
| | 1996 | 7 | 615 | 2 | 224 |
| | 1997 | 7 | 626 | 3 | 234 |
| Netherlands Antilles | 1970 | 130 | 817 | 32 | 201 |
| | 1975 | 140 | 842 | 35 | 211 |
| | 1980 | 175 | 1 008 | 43 | 248 |
| | 1985 | 190 | 1 045 | 58 | 319 |
| | 1990 | 192 | 1 023 | 61 | 322 |
| | 1991 | 195 | 1 023 | 62 | 323 |
| | 1992 | 199 | 1 025 | 63 | 325 |
| | 1993 | 203 | 1 025 | 64 | 325 |
| | 1994 | 207 | 1 026 | 66 | 326 |
| | 1995 | 211 | 1 028 | 67 | 327 |
| | 1996 | 214 | 1 028 | 68 | 327 |
| | 1997 | 217 | 1 031 | 69 | 328 |
| Nicaragua | 1970 | 350 | 165 | 55 | 26 |
| | 1975 | 500 | 200 | 83 | 33 |
| | 1980 | 670 | 229 | 160 | 55 |
| | 1985 | 802 | 236 | 190 | 56 |
| | 1990 | 955 | 250 | 240 | 63 |
| | 1991 | 990 | 252 | 249 | 63 |
| | 1992 | 1 030 | 254 | 260 | 64 |
| | 1993 | 1 075 | 258 | 273 | 65 |
| | 1994 | 1 120 | 261 | 285 | 66 |
| | 1995 | 1 155 | 261 | 300 | 68 |
| | 1996 | 1 200 | 264 | 310 | 68 |
| | 1997 | 1 240 | 265 | 320 | 68 |
| Panama | 1970 | 215 | 143 | 130 | 86 |
| | 1975 | 260 | 151 | 185 | 107 |
| | 1980 | 300 | 154 | 225 | 115 |
| | 1985 | 400 | 185 | 350 | 161 |
| | 1990 | 540 | 225 | 400 | 167 |

IV.14   Radio and television receivers
Récepteurs de radiodiffusion sonore et de télévision
Receptores de radiodifusión sonora y de televisión

| Country<br><br>Pays<br><br>País | Year<br><br>Année<br><br>Año | Radio receivers<br>Récepteurs de radiodiffusion sonore<br>Receptores de radiodifusión sonora | | Television receivers<br>Récepteurs de télévision<br>Receptores de televisión | |
|---|---|---|---|---|---|
| | | Number of receivers (thousands)<br>Nombre de postes récepteurs (milliers)<br>Número de receptores (en miles) | Number of receivers per 1,000 inhabitants<br>Nombre de postes récepteurs pour 1 000 habitants<br>Número de receptores por 1 000 habitantes | Number of receivers (thousands)<br>Nombre de postes récepteurs (milliers)<br>Número de receptores (en miles) | Number of receivers per 1,000 inhabitants<br>Nombre de postes récepteurs pour 1 000 habitants<br>Número de receptores por 1 000 habitantes |
| Panama (cont) | 1991 | 552 | 226 | 410 | 168 |
| | 1992 | 564 | 226 | 420 | 169 |
| | 1993 | 575 | 227 | 430 | 169 |
| | 1994 | 586 | 227 | 440 | 170 |
| | 1995 | 600 | 228 | 460 | 175 |
| | 1996 | 800 | 299 | 500 | 187 |
| | 1997 | 815 | 299 | 510 | 187 |
| Puerto Rico | 1970 | 1 525 | 561 | 410 | 151 |
| | 1975 | 1 760 | 599 | 630 | 214 |
| | 1980 | 2 000 | 626 | 725 | 227 |
| | 1985 | 2 300 | 681 | 850 | 252 |
| | 1990 | 2 450 | 694 | 930 | 264 |
| | 1991 | 2 520 | 707 | 942 | 264 |
| | 1992 | 2 550 | 708 | 952 | 264 |
| | 1993 | 2 582 | 709 | 965 | 265 |
| | 1994 | 2 610 | 709 | 975 | 265 |
| | 1995 | 2 636 | 710 | 1 000 | 269 |
| | 1996 | 2 670 | 712 | 1 010 | 269 |
| | 1997 | 2 700 | 714 | 1 021 | 270 |
| St. Kitts and Nevis | 1970 | 19 | 408 | 3 | 64 |
| | 1975 | 20 | 430 | 4 | 88 |
| | 1980 | 20 | 462 | 4 | 91 |
| | 1985 | 21 | 477 | 5 | 114 |
| | 1990 | 27 | 645 | 9 | 203 |
| | 1991 | 27 | 654 | 9 | 207 |
| | 1992 | 27 | 663 | 9 | 211 |
| | 1993 | 27 | 671 | 9 | 215 |
| | 1994 | 27 | 677 | 9 | 216 |
| | 1995 | 27 | 685 | 10 | 238 |
| | 1996 | 28 | 693 | 10 | 260 |
| | 1997 | 28 | 701 | 10 | 264 |
| St. Lucia | 1970 | 58 | 573 | 2 | 15 |
| | 1975 | 70 | 647 | 2 | 16 |
| | 1980 | 81 | 701 | 9 | 80 |
| | 1985 | 92 | 733 | 17 | 134 |
| | 1990 | 100 | 746 | 25 | 186 |
| | 1991 | 102 | 746 | 25 | 187 |
| | 1992 | 103 | 749 | 26 | 187 |
| | 1993 | 105 | 750 | 27 | 189 |
| | 1994 | 107 | 753 | 27 | 190 |
| | 1995 | 109 | 754 | 30 | 208 |
| | 1996 | 109 | 745 | 31 | 212 |
| | 1997 | 111 | 746 | 32 | 213 |
| St. Pierre and Miquelon | 1970 | 2 | 296 | 1 | 241 |
| | 1975 | 2 | 356 | 2 | 288 |
| | 1980 | 4 | 583 | 3 | 533 |
| | 1985 | 4 | 633 | 4 | 600 |
| | 1990 | 4 | 649 | 4 | 602 |
| | 1991 | 4 | 650 | 4 | 606 |
| | 1992 | 4 | 649 | 4 | 607 |
| | 1993 | 4 | 650 | 4 | 607 |
| | 1994 | 4 | 651 | 4 | 608 |
| | 1995 | 4 | 652 | 4 | 610 |
| | 1996 | 4 | 663 | 4 | 613 |
| | 1997 | 4 | 669 | 4 | 615 |
| St. Vincent and the Grenadines | 1970 | 22 | 251 | 2 | 17 |
| | 1975 | 32 | 346 | 4 | 46 |
| | 1980 | 42 | 429 | 5 | 53 |
| | 1985 | 55 | 540 | 6 | 59 |
| | 1990 | 70 | 662 | 15 | 142 |
| | 1991 | 71 | 666 | 15 | 144 |
| | 1992 | 72 | 670 | 16 | 147 |
| | 1993 | 73 | 674 | 16 | 148 |
| | 1994 | 74 | 678 | 16 | 149 |
| | 1995 | 75 | 682 | 18 | 161 |
| | 1996 | 76 | 686 | 18 | 163 |
| | 1997 | 77 | 690 | 18 | 163 |
| Trinidad and Tobago | 1970 | 200 | 206 | 60 | 62 |
| | 1975 | 225 | 222 | 105 | 104 |
| | 1980 | 300 | 277 | 210 | 194 |
| | 1985 | 500 | 424 | 320 | 272 |
| | 1990 | 600 | 494 | 387 | 318 |

Radio and television receivers IV.14
Récepteurs de radiodiffusion sonore et de télévision
Receptores de radiodifusión sonora y de televisión

| Country<br><br>Pays<br><br>País | Year<br><br>Année<br><br>Año | Radio receivers<br>Récepteurs de radiodiffusion sonore<br>Receptores de radiodifusión sonora | | Television receivers<br>Récepteurs de télévision<br>Receptores de televisión | |
|---|---|---|---|---|---|
| | | Number of receivers<br>(thousands)<br>Nombre de postes<br>récepteurs (milliers)<br>Número de receptores<br>(en miles) | Number of receivers<br>per 1,000 inhabitants<br>Nombre de postes<br>récepteurs pour 1 000<br>habitants<br>Número de receptores por<br>1 000 habitantes | Number of receivers<br>(thousands)<br>Nombre de postes<br>récepteurs (milliers)<br>Número de receptores<br>(en miles) | Number of receivers<br>per 1,000 inhabitants<br>Nombre de postes<br>récepteurs pour 1 000<br>habitants<br>Número de receptores por<br>1 000 habitantes |
| Trinidad and Tobago (cont) | 1991 | 608 | 497 | 394 | 322 |
| | 1992 | 616 | 499 | 400 | 324 |
| | 1993 | 625 | 503 | 405 | 326 |
| | 1994 | 635 | 507 | 410 | 327 |
| | 1995 | 650 | 515 | 415 | 329 |
| | 1996 | 670 | 528 | 419 | 330 |
| | 1997 | 680 | 533 | 425 | 333 |
| Turks and Caicos Islands | 1970 | 2 | 430 | - | - |
| | 1975 | 3 | 480 | - | - |
| | 1980 | 4 | 534 | - | - |
| | 1985 | 5 | 527 | - | - |
| | 1990 | 6 | 493 | - | - |
| | 1991 | 6 | 499 | - | - |
| | 1992 | 6 | 500 | - | - |
| | 1993 | 7 | 500 | - | - |
| | 1994 | 7 | 500 | - | - |
| | 1995 | 7 | 501 | - | - |
| | 1996 | 7 | 502 | - | - |
| | 1997 | 8 | 504 | - | - |
| U. S. Virgin Islands | 1970 | 48 | 756 | 9 | 142 |
| | 1975 | 75 | 788 | 30 | 317 |
| | 1980 | 82 | 848 | 50 | 517 |
| | 1985 | 93 | 937 | 59 | 594 |
| | 1990 | 101 | 991 | 64 | 631 |
| | 1991 | 102 | 1 005 | 65 | 641 |
| | 1992 | 103 | 1 024 | 65 | 648 |
| | 1993 | 104 | 1 047 | 66 | 664 |
| | 1994 | 105 | 1 065 | 66 | 674 |
| | 1995 | 106 | 1 088 | 67 | 691 |
| | 1996 | 106 | 1 104 | 67 | 700 |
| | 1997 | 107 | 1 119 | 68 | 709 |
| United States | 1970 | 290 000 | 1 380 | 84 600 | 403 |
| | 1975 | 401 000 | 1 821 | 121 000 | 550 |
| | 1980 | 454 500 | 1 973 | 155 800 | 676 |
| | 1985 | 500 000 | 2 067 | 190 000 | 786 |
| | 1990 | 529 440 | 2 084 | 203 000 | 799 |
| | 1991 | 535 200 | 2 085 | 205 500 | 801 |
| | 1992 | 541 000 | 2 086 | 208 000 | 802 |
| | 1993 | 546 800 | 2 088 | 210 500 | 804 |
| | 1994 | 553 000 | 2 091 | 212 800 | 805 |
| | 1995 | 559 000 | 2 093 | 215 000 | 805 |
| | 1996 | 570 000 | 2 116 | 217 000 | 805 |
| | 1997 | 575 000 | 2 116 | 219 000 | 806 |
| **South America** | | | | | |
| Argentina | 1970 | 9 000 | 376 | 3 500 | 146 |
| | 1975 | 9 890 | 380 | 4 000 | 154 |
| | 1980 | 12 000 | 427 | 5 140 | 183 |
| | 1985 | 18 000 | 594 | 6 500 | 214 |
| | 1990 | 21 800 | 670 | 7 100 | 218 |
| | 1991 | 22 140 | 671 | 7 195 | 218 |
| | 1992 | 22 450 | 672 | 7 300 | 218 |
| | 1993 | 22 800 | 673 | 7 400 | 218 |
| | 1994 | 23 150 | 675 | 7 500 | 219 |
| | 1995 | 23 500 | 676 | 7 600 | 219 |
| | 1996 | 23 850 | 677 | 7 800 | 221 |
| | 1997 | 24 300 | 681 | 7 950 | 223 |
| Bolivia | 1970 | 1 800 | 427 | 35 | 8.3 |
| | 1975 | 2 300 | 483 | 45 | 9.5 |
| | 1980 | 2 800 | 523 | 300 | 56 |
| | 1985 | 3 675 | 623 | 420 | 71 |
| | 1990 | 4 380 | 666 | 730 | 111 |
| | 1991 | 4 490 | 667 | 755 | 112 |
| | 1992 | 4 605 | 668 | 775 | 112 |
| | 1993 | 4 725 | 669 | 800 | 113 |
| | 1994 | 4 850 | 670 | 825 | 114 |
| | 1995 | 4 980 | 672 | 850 | 115 |
| | 1996 | 5 110 | 673 | 880 | 116 |
| | 1997 | 5 250 | 675 | 900 | 116 |
| Brazil | 1970 | 20 000 | 208 | 6 100 | 64 |
| | 1975 | 26 000 | 240 | 8 400 | 78 |
| | 1980 | 38 000 | 312 | 15 000 | 123 |
| | 1985 | 49 000 | 362 | 25 000 | 185 |

IV.14    Radio and television receivers
Récepteurs de radiodiffusion sonore et de télévision
Receptores de radiodifusión sonora y de televisión

| Country<br>Pays<br>País | Year<br>Année<br>Año | Radio receivers<br>Récepteurs de radiodiffusion sonore<br>Receptores de radiodifusión sonora | | Television receivers<br>Récepteurs de télévision<br>Receptores de televisión | |
|---|---|---|---|---|---|
| | | Number of receivers<br>(thousands)<br>Nombre de postes<br>récepteurs (milliers)<br>Número de receptores<br>(en miles) | Number of receivers<br>per 1,000 inhabitants<br>Nombre de postes<br>récepteurs pour 1 000<br>habitants<br>Número de receptores por<br>1 000 habitantes | Number of receivers<br>(thousands)<br>Nombre de postes<br>récepteurs (milliers)<br>Número de receptores<br>(en miles) | Number of receivers<br>per 1,000 inhabitants<br>Nombre de postes<br>récepteurs pour 1 000<br>habitants<br>Número de receptores por<br>1 000 habitantes |
| Brazil (cont) | 1990 | 57 000 | 385 | 30 800 | 208 |
| | 1991 | 58 500 | 389 | 31 400 | 209 |
| | 1992 | 59 600 | 390 | 32 000 | 210 |
| | 1993 | 61 000 | 394 | 32 650 | 211 |
| | 1994 | 62 500 | 398 | 33 200 | 211 |
| | 1995 | 63 500 | 399 | 35 000 | 220 |
| | 1996 | 70 000 | 433 | 36 000 | 223 |
| | 1997 | 71 000 | 434 | 36 500 | 223 |
| Chile | 1970 | 1 400 | 147 | 500 | 53 |
| | 1975 | 1 700 | 164 | 700 | 68 |
| | 1980 | 3 250 | 292 | 1 225 | 110 |
| | 1985 | 4 000 | 332 | 1 750 | 145 |
| | 1990 | 4 500 | 344 | 2 700 | 206 |
| | 1991 | 4 600 | 345 | 2 780 | 209 |
| | 1992 | 4 680 | 345 | 2 850 | 210 |
| | 1993 | 4 765 | 346 | 2 910 | 211 |
| | 1994 | 4 850 | 347 | 2 960 | 212 |
| | 1995 | 4 950 | 348 | 3 050 | 215 |
| | 1996 | 5 100 | 354 | 3 120 | 216 |
| | 1997 | 5 180 | 354 | 3 150 | 215 |
| Colombia | 1970 | 2 217 | 98 | 810 | 36 |
| | 1975 | 2 808 | 111 | 1 600 | 63 |
| | 1980 | 3 300 | 116 | 2 250 | 79 |
| | 1985 | 4 000 | 126 | 2 750 | 87 |
| | 1990 | 5 600 | 160 | 3 600 | 103 |
| | 1991 | 15 000 | 421 | 3 750 | 105 |
| | 1992 | 18 600 | 511 | 3 870 | 106 |
| | 1993 | 19 200 | 518 | 3 980 | 107 |
| | 1994 | 19 800 | 524 | 4 070 | 108 |
| | 1995 | 20 200 | 524 | 4 200 | 109 |
| | 1996 | 20 600 | 524 | 4 500 | 115 |
| | 1997 | 21 000 | 524 | 4 590 | 115 |
| Ecuador | 1970 | 1 700 | 285 | 150 | 25 |
| | 1975 | 2 000 | 290 | 252 | 36 |
| | 1980 | 2 425 | 305 | 500 | 63 |
| | 1985 | 2 850 | 313 | 600 | 66 |
| | 1990 | 3 330 | 324 | 880 | 86 |
| | 1991 | 3 420 | 326 | 910 | 87 |
| | 1992 | 3 510 | 327 | 940 | 88 |
| | 1993 | 3 600 | 328 | 1 000 | 91 |
| | 1994 | 3 700 | 330 | 1 050 | 94 |
| | 1995 | 3 800 | 332 | 1 100 | 96 |
| | 1996 | 4 000 | 342 | 1 500 | 128 |
| | 1997 | 4 150 | 348 | 1 550 | 130 |
| Falkland Islands (Malvinas) | 1970 | 0.6 | 267 | - | - |
| | 1975 | 0.6 | 305 | - | - |
| | 1980 | 0.8 | 395 | - | - |
| | 1985 | 1.0 | 472 | - | - |
| | 1990 | 0.9 | 399 | - | - |
| | 1991 | 0.9 | 401 | - | - |
| | 1992 | 0.9 | 403 | - | - |
| | 1993 | 0.9 | 406 | - | - |
| | 1994 | 0.9 | 408 | - | - |
| | 1995 | 1.0 | 433 | - | - |
| | 1996 | 1 | 453 | 1 | 453 |
| | 1997 | 1 | 457 | 1 | 495 |
| French Guiana | 1970 | 10 | 203 | 2 | 49 |
| | 1975 | 14 | 244 | 6 | 108 |
| | 1980 | 30 | 441 | 11 | 162 |
| | 1985 | 61 | 674 | 17 | 184 |
| | 1990 | 74 | 632 | 20 | 171 |
| | 1991 | 79 | 640 | 21 | 175 |
| | 1992 | 82 | 642 | 23 | 176 |
| | 1993 | 86 | 643 | 24 | 179 |
| | 1994 | 90 | 643 | 25 | 180 |
| | 1995 | 95 | 647 | 27 | 181 |
| | 1996 | 100 | 649 | 28 | 183 |
| | 1997 | 104 | 650 | 30 | 188 |
| Guyana | 1970 | 200 | 282 | - | - |
| | 1975 | 266 | 362 | - | - |
| | 1980 | 310 | 408 | - | - |
| | 1985 | 355 | 448 | - | - |
| | 1990 | 387 | 487 | 28 | 35 |

Radio and television receivers **IV.14**
Récepteurs de radiodiffusion sonore et de télévision
Receptores de radiodifusión sonora y de televisión

| Country<br>Pays<br>País | Year<br>Année<br>Año | Radio receivers<br>Récepteurs de radiodiffusion sonore<br>Receptores de radiodifusión sonora | | Television receivers<br>Récepteurs de télévision<br>Receptores de televisión | |
|---|---|---|---|---|---|
| | | Number of receivers<br>(thousands)<br>Nombre de postes<br>récepteurs (milliers)<br>Número de receptores<br>(en miles) | Number of receivers<br>per 1,000 inhabitants<br>Nombre de postes<br>récepteurs pour 1 000<br>habitants<br>Número de receptores por<br>1 000 habitantes | Number of receivers<br>(thousands)<br>Nombre de postes<br>récepteurs (milliers)<br>Número de receptores<br>(en miles) | Number of receivers<br>per 1,000 inhabitants<br>Nombre de postes<br>récepteurs pour 1 000<br>habitants<br>Número de receptores por<br>1 000 habitantes |
| Guyana (cont) | 1991 | 390 | 488 | 30 | 38 |
| | 1992 | 395 | 490 | 31 | 38 |
| | 1993 | 400 | 491 | 32 | 39 |
| | 1994 | 405 | 493 | 33 | 40 |
| | 1995 | 410 | 494 | 40 | 48 |
| | 1996 | 415 | 496 | 45 | 54 |
| | 1997 | 420 | 498 | 46 | 55 |
| Paraguay | 1970 | 220 | 94 | 45 | 19 |
| | 1975 | 270 | 102 | 54 | 20 |
| | 1980 | 350 | 112 | 68 | 22 |
| | 1985 | 600 | 166 | 85 | 24 |
| | 1990 | 730 | 173 | 300 | 71 |
| | 1991 | 753 | 173 | 350 | 81 |
| | 1992 | 775 | 174 | 370 | 83 |
| | 1993 | 800 | 175 | 385 | 84 |
| | 1994 | 830 | 176 | 400 | 85 |
| | 1995 | 870 | 180 | 450 | 93 |
| | 1996 | 900 | 182 | 500 | 101 |
| | 1997 | 925 | 182 | 515 | 101 |
| Peru | 1970 | 1 748 | 132 | 395 | 30 |
| | 1975 | 2 050 | 135 | 610 | 40 |
| | 1980 | 2 750 | 159 | 895 | 52 |
| | 1985 | 4 000 | 205 | 1 500 | 77 |
| | 1990 | 5 420 | 251 | 2 080 | 96 |
| | 1991 | 5 550 | 253 | 2 140 | 97 |
| | 1992 | 5 675 | 254 | 2 200 | 98 |
| | 1993 | 5 800 | 255 | 2 260 | 99 |
| | 1994 | 5 950 | 257 | 2 310 | 100 |
| | 1995 | 6 100 | 259 | 2 500 | 106 |
| | 1996 | 6 500 | 271 | 3 000 | 125 |
| | 1997 | 6 650 | 273 | 3 060 | 126 |
| Suriname | 1970 | 92 | 247 | 28 | 75 |
| | 1975 | 110 | 302 | 34 | 93 |
| | 1980 | 189 | 532 | 40 | 113 |
| | 1985 | 230 | 599 | 45 | 117 |
| | 1990 | 265 | 660 | 55 | 137 |
| | 1991 | 270 | 669 | 56 | 139 |
| | 1992 | 275 | 679 | 57 | 141 |
| | 1993 | 280 | 689 | 58 | 143 |
| | 1994 | 285 | 699 | 59 | 145 |
| | 1995 | 290 | 709 | 60 | 147 |
| | 1996 | 295 | 719 | 62 | 151 |
| | 1997 | 300 | 728 | 63 | 153 |
| Uruguay | 1970 | 1 000 | 356 | 280 | 100 |
| | 1975 | 1 500 | 530 | 351 | 124 |
| | 1980 | 1 630 | 559 | 368 | 126 |
| | 1985 | 1 760 | 585 | 500 | 166 |
| | 1990 | 1 865 | 601 | 710 | 229 |
| | 1991 | 1 880 | 601 | 718 | 230 |
| | 1992 | 1 895 | 602 | 725 | 230 |
| | 1993 | 1 910 | 602 | 735 | 232 |
| | 1994 | 1 925 | 603 | 742 | 232 |
| | 1995 | 1 940 | 603 | 750 | 233 |
| | 1996 | 1 955 | 603 | 775 | 239 |
| | 1997 | 1 970 | 603 | 782 | 239 |
| Venezuela | 1970 | 3 800 | 354 | 950 | 89 |
| | 1975 | 4 775 | 375 | 1 284 | 101 |
| | 1980 | 5 900 | 391 | 1 710 | 113 |
| | 1985 | 7 000 | 408 | 2 250 | 131 |
| | 1990 | 8 600 | 441 | 3 100 | 159 |
| | 1991 | 8 900 | 446 | 3 200 | 160 |
| | 1992 | 9 200 | 450 | 3 300 | 161 |
| | 1993 | 9 500 | 454 | 3 400 | 163 |
| | 1994 | 9 750 | 456 | 3 500 | 164 |
| | 1995 | 10 000 | 458 | 3 700 | 169 |
| | 1996 | 10 500 | 471 | 4 000 | 179 |
| | 1997 | 10 750 | 472 | 4 100 | 180 |
| **Asia** | | | | | |
| Afghanistan | 1970 | 700 | 51 | - | - |
| | 1975 | 820 | 53 | - | - |
| | 1980 | 1 200 | 75 | 45 | 2.8 |
| | 1985 | 1 450 | 100 | 100 | 6.9 |

IV.14 Radio and television receivers
Récepteurs de radiodiffusion sonore et de télévision
Receptores de radiodifusión sonora y de televisión

| Country<br><br>Pays<br><br>País | Year<br><br>Année<br><br>Año | Radio receivers<br>Récepteurs de radiodiffusion sonore<br>Receptores de radiodifusión sonora | | Television receivers<br>Récepteurs de télévision<br>Receptores de televisión | |
|---|---|---|---|---|---|
| | | Number of receivers<br>(thousands)<br>Nombre de postes<br>récepteurs (milliers)<br>Número de receptores<br>(en miles) | Number of receivers<br>per 1,000 inhabitants<br>Nombre de postes<br>récepteurs pour 1 000<br>habitants<br>Número de receptores por<br>1 000 habitantes | Number of receivers<br>(thousands)<br>Nombre de postes<br>récepteurs (milliers)<br>Número de receptores<br>(en miles) | Number of receivers<br>per 1,000 inhabitants<br>Nombre de postes<br>récepteurs pour 1 000<br>habitants<br>Número de receptores por<br>1 000 habitantes |
| Afghanistan (cont) | 1990 | 1 720 | 117 | 137 | 9.3 |
| | 1991 | 1 820 | 117 | 147 | 9.5 |
| | 1992 | 1 940 | 118 | 160 | 9.7 |
| | 1993 | 2 080 | 118 | 172 | 9.8 |
| | 1994 | 2 230 | 119 | 185 | 9.9 |
| | 1995 | 2 400 | 122 | 200 | 10 |
| | 1996 | 2 550 | 125 | 250 | 12 |
| | 1997 | 2 750 | 132 | 270 | 13 |
| Armenia | 1990 | 620 | 175 | 600 | 169 |
| | 1991 | 800 | 224 | 795 | 223 |
| | 1992 | 810 | 226 | 801 | 224 |
| | 1993 | 820 | 229 | 805 | 225 |
| | 1994 | 825 | 230 | 810 | 226 |
| | 1995 | 830 | 232 | 815 | 228 |
| | 1996 | 840 | 236 | 820 | 230 |
| | 1997 | 850 | 239 | 825 | 232 |
| Azerbaijan | 1990 | 140 | 20 | 124 | 17 |
| | 1991 | 142 | 20 | 126 | 17 |
| | 1992 | 145 | 20 | 128 | 17 |
| | 1993 | 147 | 20 | 130 | 18 |
| | 1994 | 149 | 20 | 132 | 18 |
| | 1995 | 160 | 21 | 156 | 21 |
| | 1996 | 170 | 22 | 167 | 22 |
| | 1997 | 175 | 23 | 170 | 22 |
| Bahrain | 1970 | 65 | 296 | 13 | 59 |
| | 1975 | 85 | 313 | 30 | 110 |
| | 1980 | 125 | 360 | 90 | 259 |
| | 1985 | 210 | 508 | 170 | 411 |
| | 1990 | 269 | 549 | 208 | 425 |
| | 1991 | 278 | 551 | 215 | 426 |
| | 1992 | 287 | 554 | 222 | 428 |
| | 1993 | 296 | 557 | 230 | 433 |
| | 1994 | 305 | 560 | 236 | 433 |
| | 1995 | 320 | 574 | 260 | 466 |
| | 1996 | 330 | 579 | 268 | 470 |
| | 1997 | 338 | 580 | 275 | 472 |
| Bangladesh | 1970 | 850 | 13 | 8 | 0.1 |
| | 1975 | 1 150 | 15 | 25 | 0.3 |
| | 1980 | 1 500 | 17 | 80 | 0.9 |
| | 1985 | 4 000 | 40 | 261 | 2.6 |
| | 1990 | 4 855 | 44 | 525 | 4.8 |
| | 1991 | 4 990 | 45 | 550 | 4.9 |
| | 1992 | 5 189 | 46 | 570 | 5.0 |
| | 1993 | 5 360 | 47 | 670 | 5.8 |
| | 1994 | 5 500 | 47 | 685 | 5.9 |
| | 1995 | 5 600 | 47 | 700 | 5.9 |
| | 1996 | 6 000 | 50 | 750 | 6.2 |
| | 1997 | 6 150 | 50 | 770 | 6.3 |
| Bhutan | 1970 | 11 | 10 | - | - |
| | 1975 | 14 | 11 | - | - |
| | 1980 | 16 | 12 | - | - |
| | 1985 | 19 | 12 | - | - |
| | 1990 | 24 | 14 | - | - |
| | 1991 | 25 | 14 | - | - |
| | 1992 | 26 | 15 | - | - |
| | 1993 | 27 | 15 | - | - |
| | 1994 | 28 | 15 | - | - |
| | 1995 | 30 | 16 | 10 | 5.4 |
| | 1996 | 35 | 18 | 10 | 5.5 |
| | 1997 | 37 | 19 | 11 | 5.5 |
| Brunei Darussalam | 1970 | 15 | 116 | 5 | 39 |
| | 1975 | 24 | 149 | 14 | 87 |
| | 1980 | 41 | 212 | 26 | 135 |
| | 1985 | 55 | 247 | 45 | 202 |
| | 1990 | 68 | 265 | 60 | 233 |
| | 1991 | 70 | 266 | 62 | 235 |
| | 1992 | 73 | 269 | 64 | 236 |
| | 1993 | 75 | 270 | 66 | 236 |
| | 1994 | 77 | 270 | 68 | 238 |
| | 1995 | 80 | 272 | 70 | 238 |
| | 1996 | 90 | 299 | 75 | 249 |
| | 1997 | 93 | 302 | 77 | 250 |

Radio and television receivers    IV.14
Récepteurs de radiodiffusion sonore et de télévision
Receptores de radiodifusión sonora y de televisión

| Country / Pays / País | Year / Année / Año | Radio receivers / Récepteurs de radiodiffusion sonore / Receptores de radiodifusión sonora | | Television receivers / Récepteurs de télévision / Receptores de televisión | |
|---|---|---|---|---|---|
| | | Number of receivers (thousands) / Nombre de postes récepteurs (milliers) / Número de receptores (en miles) | Number of receivers per 1,000 inhabitants / Nombre de postes récepteurs pour 1 000 habitants / Número de receptores por 1 000 habitantes | Number of receivers (thousands) / Nombre de postes récepteurs (milliers) / Número de receptores (en miles) | Number of receivers per 1,000 inhabitants / Nombre de postes récepteurs pour 1 000 habitants / Número de receptores por 1 000 habitantes |
| Cambodia | 1970 | 420 | 61 | 19 | 2.7 |
| | 1975 | 510 | 72 | 30 | 4.2 |
| | 1980 | 600 | 92 | 35 | 5.4 |
| | 1985 | 800 | 108 | 52 | 7.0 |
| | 1990 | 942 | 109 | 68 | 7.9 |
| | 1991 | 975 | 109 | 71 | 7.9 |
| | 1992 | 1 007 | 110 | 74 | 8.0 |
| | 1993 | 1 045 | 110 | 77 | 8.1 |
| | 1994 | 1 080 | 111 | 80 | 8.2 |
| | 1995 | 1 120 | 112 | 85 | 8.5 |
| | 1996 | 1 300 | 127 | 90 | 8.8 |
| | 1997 | 1 340 | 128 | 94 | 9.0 |
| China | 1970 | 65 000 | 78 | 660 | 0.8 |
| | 1975 | 80 000 | 86 | 1 185 | 1.3 |
| | 1980 | 95 000 | 95 | 9 020 | 9.0 |
| | 1985 | 120 000 | 112 | 69 650 | 65 |
| | 1990 | 372 866 | 323 | 309 001 | 267 |
| | 1991 | 385 000 | 329 | 320 000 | 273 |
| | 1992 | 394 000 | 333 | 340 000 | 287 |
| | 1993 | 398 500 | 333 | 350 000 | 293 |
| | 1994 | 403 000 | 333 | 370 000 | 306 |
| | 1995 | 408 000 | 334 | 374 410 | 307 |
| | 1996 | 412 797 | 335 | 393 630 | 319 |
| | 1997 | 417 000 | 335 | 400 000 | 321 |
| China, Hong Kong SAR | 1970 | 1 600 | 406 | 444 | 113 |
| | 1975 | 2 200 | 500 | 837 | 190 |
| | 1980 | 2 550 | 506 | 1 114 | 221 |
| | 1985 | 3 250 | 596 | 1 275 | 234 |
| | 1990 | 3 800 | 666 | 1 550 | 272 |
| | 1991 | 3 855 | 667 | 1 600 | 277 |
| | 1992 | 3 920 | 667 | 1 630 | 277 |
| | 1993 | 4 000 | 669 | 1 660 | 278 |
| | 1994 | 4 100 | 673 | 1 700 | 279 |
| | 1995 | 4 200 | 675 | 1 750 | 281 |
| | 1996 | 4 300 | 676 | 1 790 | 281 |
| | 1997 | 4 450 | 684 | 1 840 | 283 |
| Cyprus | 1970 | 105 | 171 | 54 | 88 |
| | 1975 | 115 | 189 | 59 | 97 |
| | 1980 | 162 | 265 | 85 | 139 |
| | 1985 | 190 | 294 | 92 | 142 |
| | 1990 | 205 | 301 | 215 | 316 |
| | 1991 | 209 | 302 | 220 | 318 |
| | 1992 | 214 | 304 | 225 | 319 |
| | 1993 | 219 | 305 | 230 | 320 |
| | 1994 | 225 | 307 | 235 | 321 |
| | 1995 | 230 | 309 | 240 | 323 |
| | 1996 | 300 | 398 | 244 | 323 |
| | 1997 | 310 | 406 | 248 | 325 |
| East Timor | 1970 | 7 | 12 | - | - |
| | 1975 | 8 | 12 | - | - |
| | 1980 | 10 | 16 | - | - |
| | 1985 | 12 | 17 | - | - |
| | 1990 | 14 | 19 | - | - |
| | 1991 | 15 | 19 | - | - |
| | 1992 | 15 | 19 | - | - |
| | 1993 | 16 | 20 | - | - |
| | 1994 | 16 | 20 | - | - |
| | 1995 | 17 | 20 | - | - |
| | 1996 | 17 | 21 | - | - |
| | 1997 | 18 | 21 | - | - |
| Georgia | 1990 | 2 500 | 458 | 2 400 | 440 |
| | 1991 | 2 700 | 496 | 2 430 | 446 |
| | 1992 | 2 900 | 536 | 2 440 | 451 |
| | 1993 | 2 950 | 550 | 2 450 | 457 |
| | 1994 | 3 000 | 565 | 2 500 | 471 |
| | 1995 | 3 005 | 572 | 2 550 | 486 |
| | 1996 | 3 010 | 580 | 2 560 | 494 |
| | 1997 | 3 020 | 590 | 2 570 | 502 |
| India | 1970 | 17 000 | 31 | 28 | 0.1 |
| | 1975 | 21 000 | 34 | 515 | 0.8 |
| | 1980 | 26 000 | 38 | 3 000 | 4.4 |
| | 1985 | 50 000 | 65 | 10 000 | 13 |
| | 1990 | 67 000 | 79 | 27 000 | 32 |

IV.14    Radio and television receivers
Récepteurs de radiodiffusion sonore et de télévision
Receptores de radiodifusión sonora y de televisión

| Country<br><br>Pays<br><br>País | Year<br><br>Année<br><br>Año | Radio receivers<br>Récepteurs de radiodiffusion sonore<br>Receptores de radiodifusión sonora | | Television receivers<br>Récepteurs de télévision<br>Receptores de televisión | |
|---|---|---|---|---|---|
| | | Number of receivers (thousands)<br>Nombre de postes récepteurs (milliers)<br>Número de receptores (en miles) | Number of receivers per 1,000 inhabitants<br>Nombre de postes récepteurs pour 1 000 habitants<br>Número de receptores por 1 000 habitantes | Number of receivers (thousands)<br>Nombre de postes récepteurs (milliers)<br>Número de receptores (en miles) | Number of receivers per 1,000 inhabitants<br>Nombre de postes récepteurs pour 1 000 habitants<br>Número de receptores por 1 000 habitantes |
| India (cont) | 1991 | 80 000 | 92 | 30 800 | 36 |
| | 1992 | 85 000 | 96 | 34 900 | 39 |
| | 1993 | 90 000 | 100 | 40 300 | 45 |
| | 1994 | 95 000 | 104 | 45 700 | 50 |
| | 1995 | 111 000 | 119 | 47 000 | 50 |
| | 1996 | 113 500 | 119 | 57 700 | 61 |
| | 1997 | 116 000 | 120 | 63 000 | 65 |
| Indonesia | 1970 | 10 000 | 83 | 90 | 0.7 |
| | 1975 | 14 000 | 103 | 300 | 2.2 |
| | 1980 | 18 000 | 119 | 3 000 | 20 |
| | 1985 | 21 500 | 128 | 6 438 | 38 |
| | 1990 | 26 500 | 145 | 10 500 | 57 |
| | 1991 | 27 000 | 145 | 11 000 | 59 |
| | 1992 | 27 500 | 146 | 11 500 | 61 |
| | 1993 | 28 200 | 147 | 12 000 | 63 |
| | 1994 | 28 800 | 148 | 12 500 | 64 |
| | 1995 | 29 500 | 149 | 13 000 | 66 |
| | 1996 | 31 000 | 155 | 13 500 | 67 |
| | 1997 | 31 500 | 155 | 13 750 | 68 |
| Iran, Islamic Republic of | 1970 | 2 900 | 102 | 533 | 19 |
| | 1975 | 4 000 | 120 | 1 500 | 45 |
| | 1980 | 6 400 | 163 | 2 000 | 51 |
| | 1985 | 10 000 | 210 | 2 600 | 55 |
| | 1990 | 13 400 | 238 | 3 620 | 64 |
| | 1991 | 13 860 | 240 | 3 731 | 65 |
| | 1992 | 14 400 | 244 | 3 842 | 65 |
| | 1993 | 14 900 | 248 | 4 030 | 67 |
| | 1994 | 15 400 | 252 | 4 150 | 68 |
| | 1995 | 16 000 | 257 | 4 300 | 69 |
| | 1996 | 16 600 | 262 | 4 500 | 71 |
| | 1997 | 17 000 | 263 | 4 610 | 71 |
| Iraq | 1970 | 1 026 | 110 | 350 | 37 |
| | 1975 | 1 252 | 114 | 415 | 38 |
| | 1980 | 2 100 | 161 | 650 | 50 |
| | 1985 | 3 000 | 196 | 900 | 59 |
| | 1990 | 3 880 | 215 | 1 300 | 72 |
| | 1991 | 4 000 | 216 | 1 350 | 73 |
| | 1992 | 4 115 | 218 | 1 400 | 74 |
| | 1993 | 4 225 | 219 | 1 450 | 75 |
| | 1994 | 4 335 | 221 | 1 500 | 76 |
| | 1995 | 4 500 | 224 | 1 600 | 80 |
| | 1996 | 4 700 | 228 | 1 700 | 82 |
| | 1997 | 4 850 | 229 | 1 750 | 83 |
| Israel | 1970 | 477 | 160 | 534 | 180 |
| | 1975 | 595 | 172 | 680 | 197 |
| | 1980 | 950 | 245 | 900 | 232 |
| | 1985 | 1 800 | 425 | 1 100 | 260 |
| | 1990 | 2 180 | 468 | 1 245 | 267 |
| | 1991 | 2 270 | 471 | 1 300 | 270 |
| | 1992 | 2 400 | 480 | 1 360 | 272 |
| | 1993 | 2 510 | 483 | 1 430 | 275 |
| | 1994 | 2 610 | 484 | 1 500 | 278 |
| | 1995 | 2 700 | 485 | 1 600 | 287 |
| | 1996 | 3 000 | 524 | 1 650 | 288 |
| | 1997 | 3 070 | 524 | 1 690 | 288 |
| Japan | 1970 | 23 250 | 223 | 35 000 | 335 |
| | 1975 | 58 026 | 520 | 40 000 | 359 |
| | 1980 | 79 200 | 678 | 62 976 | 539 |
| | 1985 | 95 000 | 786 | 70 000 | 579 |
| | 1990 | 111 000 | 899 | 75 500 | 611 |
| | 1991 | 111 500 | 899 | 76 000 | 613 |
| | 1992 | 112 000 | 900 | 76 500 | 615 |
| | 1993 | 113 000 | 906 | 80 000 | 641 |
| | 1994 | 113 800 | 909 | 85 000 | 679 |
| | 1995 | 114 500 | 913 | 85 500 | 681 |
| | 1996 | 120 000 | 954 | 85 900 | 683 |
| | 1997 | 120 500 | 956 | 86 500 | 686 |
| Jordan | 1970 | 370 | 161 | 46 | 20 |
| | 1975 | 450 | 173 | 120 | 46 |
| | 1980 | 550 | 188 | 172 | 59 |
| | 1985 | 791 | 192 | 240 | 58 |
| | 1990 | 1 015 | 220 | 315 | 68 |

Radio and television receivers    IV.14
Récepteurs de radiodiffusion sonore et de télévision
Receptores de radiodifusión sonora y de televisión

| Country<br><br>Pays<br><br>País | Year<br><br>Année<br><br>Año | Radio receivers<br>Récepteurs de radiodiffusion sonore<br>Receptores de radiodifusión sonora | | Television receivers<br>Récepteurs de télévision<br>Receptores de televisión | |
|---|---|---|---|---|---|
| | | Number of receivers<br>(thousands)<br>Nombre de postes<br>récepteurs (milliers)<br>Número de receptores<br>(en miles) | Number of receivers<br>per 1,000 inhabitants<br>Nombre de postes<br>récepteurs pour 1 000<br>habitants<br>Número de receptores por<br>1 000 habitantes | Number of receivers<br>(thousands)<br>Nombre de postes<br>récepteurs (milliers)<br>Número de receptores<br>(en miles) | Number of receivers<br>per 1,000 inhabitants<br>Nombre de postes<br>récepteurs pour 1 000<br>habitants<br>Número de receptores por<br>1 000 habitantes |
| Jordan (cont) | 1991 | 1 060 | 221 | 335 | 70 |
| | 1992 | 1 120 | 223 | 360 | 72 |
| | 1993 | 1 200 | 228 | 380 | 72 |
| | 1994 | 1 265 | 230 | 405 | 74 |
| | 1995 | 1 350 | 235 | 430 | 75 |
| | 1996 | 1 600 | 269 | 480 | 81 |
| | 1997 | 1 660 | 271 | 500 | 82 |
| Kazakstan | 1990 | 4 175 | 249 | 3 700 | 221 |
| | 1991 | 6 100 | 364 | 3 740 | 223 |
| | 1992 | 6 200 | 370 | 3 750 | 224 |
| | 1993 | 6 300 | 378 | 3 845 | 231 |
| | 1994 | 6 400 | 386 | 3 860 | 233 |
| | 1995 | 6 450 | 391 | 3 870 | 234 |
| | 1996 | 6 460 | 393 | 3 870 | 235 |
| | 1997 | 6 470 | 395 | 3 880 | 237 |
| Korea, Democratic People's Rep. | 1970 | 1 150 | 81 | - | - |
| | 1975 | 1 450 | 89 | 100 | 6.1 |
| | 1980 | 1 750 | 99 | 130 | 7.4 |
| | 1985 | 2 000 | 106 | 200 | 11 |
| | 1990 | 2 600 | 127 | 330 | 16 |
| | 1991 | 2 660 | 128 | 350 | 17 |
| | 1992 | 2 750 | 130 | 400 | 19 |
| | 1993 | 2 850 | 133 | 500 | 23 |
| | 1994 | 2 940 | 134 | 1 000 | 46 |
| | 1995 | 3 000 | 135 | 1 050 | 47 |
| | 1996 | 3 300 | 146 | 1 090 | 48 |
| | 1997 | 3 360 | 146 | 1 200 | 52 |
| Korea, Republic of | 1970 | 23 000 | 720 | 600 | 19 |
| | 1975 | 30 000 | 850 | 2 500 | 71 |
| | 1980 | 36 000 | 944 | 6 300 | 165 |
| | 1985 | 41 000 | 1 005 | 7 721 | 189 |
| | 1990 | 43 350 | 1 011 | 9 000 | 210 |
| | 1991 | 43 795 | 1 012 | 11 383 | 263 |
| | 1992 | 44 250 | 1 013 | 12 000 | 275 |
| | 1993 | 44 700 | 1 013 | 13 000 | 295 |
| | 1994 | 45 300 | 1 017 | 14 408 | 323 |
| | 1995 | 46 000 | 1 023 | 15 000 | 334 |
| | 1996 | 47 000 | 1 037 | 15 258 | 336 |
| | 1997 | 47 500 | 1 039 | 15 900 | 348 |
| Kuwait | 1970 | 150 | 202 | 100 | 134 |
| | 1975 | 203 | 202 | 150 | 149 |
| | 1980 | 390 | 284 | 353 | 257 |
| | 1985 | 800 | 465 | 640 | 372 |
| | 1990 | 1 100 | 513 | 820 | 383 |
| | 1991 | 1 110 | 530 | 820 | 392 |
| | 1992 | 1 120 | 563 | 825 | 414 |
| | 1993 | 1 130 | 607 | 830 | 446 |
| | 1994 | 1 140 | 651 | 840 | 479 |
| | 1995 | 1 150 | 681 | 850 | 503 |
| | 1996 | 1 160 | 688 | 860 | 510 |
| | 1997 | 1 175 | 678 | 875 | 505 |
| Kyrgyzstan | 1990 | 460 | 105 | 70 | 16 |
| | 1991 | 470 | 106 | 80 | 18 |
| | 1992 | 480 | 107 | 100 | 22 |
| | 1993 | 490 | 108 | 110 | 24 |
| | 1994 | 500 | 110 | 130 | 29 |
| | 1995 | 510 | 112 | 150 | 33 |
| | 1996 | 515 | 112 | 200 | 44 |
| | 1997 | 520 | 113 | 210 | 45 |
| Lao People's Democratic Republic | 1970 | 220 | 81 | - | - |
| | 1975 | 280 | 93 | - | - |
| | 1980 | 350 | 109 | - | - |
| | 1985 | 430 | 120 | - | - |
| | 1990 | 520 | 125 | 22 | 5.3 |
| | 1991 | 540 | 126 | 25 | 5.9 |
| | 1992 | 560 | 127 | 28 | 6.4 |
| | 1993 | 580 | 128 | 32 | 7.1 |
| | 1994 | 600 | 129 | 40 | 8.6 |
| | 1995 | 630 | 132 | 45 | 9.4 |
| | 1996 | 700 | 143 | 50 | 10 |
| | 1997 | 730 | 145 | 52 | 10 |

Radio and television receivers
Récepteurs de radiodiffusion sonore et de télévision
Receptores de radiodifusión sonora y de televisión

| Country<br><br>Pays<br><br>País | Year<br><br>Année<br><br>Año | Radio receivers<br>Récepteurs de radiodiffusion sonore<br>Receptores de radiodifusión sonora | | Television receivers<br>Récepteurs de télévision<br>Receptores de televisión | |
|---|---|---|---|---|---|
| | | Number of receivers<br>(thousands)<br>Nombre de postes<br>récepteurs (milliers)<br>Número de receptores<br>(en miles) | Number of receivers<br>per 1,000 inhabitants<br>Nombre de postes<br>récepteurs pour 1 000<br>habitants<br>Número de receptores por<br>1 000 habitantes | Number of receivers<br>(thousands)<br>Nombre de postes<br>récepteurs (milliers)<br>Número de receptores<br>(en miles) | Number of receivers<br>per 1,000 inhabitants<br>Nombre de postes<br>récepteurs pour 1 000<br>habitants<br>Número de receptores por<br>1 000 habitantes |
| Lebanon | 1970 | 600 | 243 | 260 | 105 |
| | 1975 | 1 321 | 477 | 410 | 148 |
| | 1980 | 2 000 | 749 | 750 | 281 |
| | 1985 | 2 050 | 768 | 800 | 300 |
| | 1990 | 2 255 | 882 | 880 | 344 |
| | 1991 | 2 310 | 885 | 910 | 349 |
| | 1992 | 2 390 | 886 | 950 | 352 |
| | 1993 | 2 490 | 887 | 990 | 353 |
| | 1994 | 2 590 | 888 | 1 050 | 360 |
| | 1995 | 2 680 | 891 | 1 100 | 366 |
| | 1996 | 2 750 | 892 | 1 150 | 373 |
| | 1997 | 2 850 | 907 | 1 180 | 375 |
| Macau | 1970 | 55 | 217 | - | - |
| | 1975 | 61 | 241 | - | - |
| | 1980 | 72 | 286 | - | - |
| | 1985 | 95 | 310 | - | - |
| | 1990 | 120 | 322 | 30 | 81 |
| | 1991 | 125 | 325 | 32 | 83 |
| | 1992 | 130 | 328 | 34 | 86 |
| | 1993 | 135 | 331 | 36 | 88 |
| | 1994 | 140 | 334 | 40 | 95 |
| | 1995 | 145 | 337 | 45 | 105 |
| | 1996 | 155 | 352 | 47 | 107 |
| | 1997 | 160 | 356 | 49 | 109 |
| Malaysia | 1970 | 1 500 | 138 | 130 | 12 |
| | 1975 | 2 000 | 163 | 452 | 37 |
| | 1980 | 5 650 | 411 | 1 200 | 87 |
| | 1985 | 6 600 | 421 | 1 800 | 115 |
| | 1990 | 7 680 | 430 | 2 640 | 148 |
| | 1991 | 7 880 | 431 | 2 725 | 149 |
| | 1992 | 8 080 | 431 | 2 820 | 150 |
| | 1993 | 8 280 | 431 | 2 915 | 152 |
| | 1994 | 8 500 | 432 | 3 100 | 158 |
| | 1995 | 8 700 | 433 | 3 300 | 164 |
| | 1996 | 8 900 | 433 | 3 500 | 170 |
| | 1997 | 9 100 | 434 | 3 600 | 172 |
| Maldives | 1970 | 7 | 58 | - | - |
| | 1975 | 9 | 62 | - | - |
| | 1980 | 13 | 82 | 1 | 7.0 |
| | 1985 | 19 | 103 | 3 | 17 |
| | 1990 | 25 | 116 | 5 | 24 |
| | 1991 | 26 | 117 | 5 | 24 |
| | 1992 | 27 | 119 | 6 | 25 |
| | 1993 | 28 | 121 | 6 | 25 |
| | 1994 | 29 | 121 | 6 | 25 |
| | 1995 | 31 | 124 | 7 | 26 |
| | 1996 | 33 | 129 | 7 | 27 |
| | 1997 | 34 | 129 | 7 | 28 |
| Mongolia | 1970 | 105 | 84 | 1 | 0.8 |
| | 1975 | 125 | 86 | 4 | 2.4 |
| | 1980 | 160 | 96 | 6 | 3.4 |
| | 1985 | 200 | 105 | 45 | 24 |
| | 1990 | 289 | 130 | 85 | 38 |
| | 1991 | 297 | 131 | 92 | 41 |
| | 1992 | 306 | 132 | 93 | 40 |
| | 1993 | 315 | 133 | 96 | 41 |
| | 1994 | 322 | 134 | 105 | 44 |
| | 1995 | 330 | 135 | 110 | 45 |
| | 1996 | 350 | 140 | 115 | 46 |
| | 1997 | 360 | 142 | 118 | 47 |
| Myanmar | 1970 | 400 | 15 | - | - |
| | 1975 | 662 | 22 | - | - |
| | 1980 | 774 | 23 | 1 | 0.0 |
| | 1985 | 2 500 | 67 | 20 | 0.5 |
| | 1990 | 3 400 | 84 | 101 | 2.5 |
| | 1991 | 3 500 | 85 | 161 | 3.9 |
| | 1992 | 3 580 | 86 | 197 | 4.7 |
| | 1993 | 3 690 | 88 | 213 | 5.1 |
| | 1994 | 3 800 | 90 | 226 | 5.3 |
| | 1995 | 4 000 | 93 | 230 | 5.4 |
| | 1996 | 4 150 | 96 | 250 | 5.8 |
| | 1997 | 4 200 | 96 | 260 | 5.9 |

Radio and television receivers IV.14
Récepteurs de radiodiffusion sonore et de télévision
Receptores de radiodifusión sonora y de televisión

| Country Pays País | Year Année Año | Radio receivers Récepteurs de radiodiffusion sonore Receptores de radiodifusión sonora | | Television receivers Récepteurs de télévision Receptores de televisión | |
|---|---|---|---|---|---|
| | | Number of receivers (thousands) Nombre de postes récepteurs (milliers) Número de receptores (en miles) | Number of receivers per 1,000 inhabitants Nombre de postes récepteurs pour 1 000 habitants Número de receptores por 1 000 habitantes | Number of receivers (thousands) Nombre de postes récepteurs (milliers) Número de receptores (en miles) | Number of receivers per 1,000 inhabitants Nombre de postes récepteurs pour 1 000 habitants Número de receptores por 1 000 habitantes |
| Nepal | 1970 | 180 | 16 | - | - |
| | 1975 | 230 | 18 | - | - |
| | 1980 | 300 | 21 | - | - |
| | 1985 | 450 | 27 | 20 | 1.2 |
| | 1990 | 650 | 35 | 35 | 1.9 |
| | 1991 | 670 | 35 | 40 | 2.1 |
| | 1992 | 690 | 35 | 45 | 2.3 |
| | 1993 | 720 | 36 | 55 | 2.7 |
| | 1994 | 745 | 36 | 100 | 4.8 |
| | 1995 | 780 | 37 | 110 | 5.2 |
| | 1996 | 810 | 37 | 120 | 5.5 |
| | 1997 | 840 | 38 | 130 | 5.8 |
| Oman | 1970 | 200 | 277 | - | - |
| | 1975 | 300 | 341 | 3 | 2.8 |
| | 1980 | 550 | 487 | 35 | 31 |
| | 1985 | 800 | 561 | 900 | 632 |
| | 1990 | 1 010 | 566 | 1 130 | 633 |
| | 1991 | 1 055 | 568 | 1 185 | 638 |
| | 1992 | 1 103 | 571 | 1 240 | 642 |
| | 1993 | 1 155 | 576 | 1 300 | 648 |
| | 1994 | 1 210 | 582 | 1 375 | 661 |
| | 1995 | 1 280 | 594 | 1 450 | 673 |
| | 1996 | 1 340 | 601 | 1 520 | 682 |
| | 1997 | 1 400 | 607 | 1 600 | 694 |
| Pakistan | 1970 | 3 000 | 46 | 99 | 1.5 |
| | 1975 | 4 000 | 54 | 380 | 5.1 |
| | 1980 | 5 500 | 64 | 938 | 11 |
| | 1985 | 8 500 | 84 | 1 304 | 13 |
| | 1990 | 10 650 | 89 | 1 989 | 17 |
| | 1991 | 10 980 | 90 | 2 205 | 18 |
| | 1992 | 11 315 | 90 | 2 300 | 18 |
| | 1993 | 11 660 | 90 | 2 450 | 19 |
| | 1994 | 12 000 | 90 | 2 600 | 20 |
| | 1995 | 12 500 | 92 | 2 680 | 20 |
| | 1996 | 12 900 | 92 | 3 000 | 21 |
| | 1997 | 13 500 | 94 | 3 100 | 22 |
| Philippines | 1970 | 3 300 | 88 | 400 | 11 |
| | 1975 | 4 300 | 100 | 756 | 18 |
| | 1980 | 6 000 | 124 | 1 050 | 22 |
| | 1985 | 7 300 | 134 | 1 500 | 27 |
| | 1990 | 8 600 | 142 | 2 700 | 44 |
| | 1991 | 8 810 | 142 | 2 800 | 45 |
| | 1992 | 9 150 | 144 | 2 900 | 46 |
| | 1993 | 9 400 | 144 | 3 050 | 47 |
| | 1994 | 9 700 | 145 | 3 200 | 48 |
| | 1995 | 10 000 | 146 | 3 300 | 48 |
| | 1996 | 11 000 | 157 | 3 500 | 50 |
| | 1997 | 11 500 | 161 | 3 700 | 52 |
| Qatar | 1970 | 25 | 225 | 0.5 | 4.5 |
| | 1975 | 50 | 292 | 20 | 117 |
| | 1980 | 90 | 393 | 76 | 331 |
| | 1985 | 150 | 419 | 120 | 335 |
| | 1990 | 206 | 424 | 190 | 391 |
| | 1991 | 215 | 428 | 198 | 394 |
| | 1992 | 222 | 430 | 205 | 397 |
| | 1993 | 228 | 432 | 210 | 398 |
| | 1994 | 235 | 437 | 215 | 400 |
| | 1995 | 240 | 438 | 220 | 401 |
| | 1996 | 250 | 448 | 225 | 403 |
| | 1997 | 256 | 450 | 230 | 404 |
| Saudi Arabia | 1970 | 700 | 122 | 500 | 87 |
| | 1975 | 950 | 131 | 800 | 110 |
| | 1980 | 2 500 | 260 | 2 100 | 219 |
| | 1985 | 3 545 | 280 | 3 080 | 244 |
| | 1990 | 4 655 | 290 | 3 950 | 246 |
| | 1991 | 4 850 | 293 | 4 100 | 248 |
| | 1992 | 5 000 | 295 | 4 260 | 251 |
| | 1993 | 5 150 | 297 | 4 370 | 252 |
| | 1994 | 5 300 | 298 | 4 455 | 251 |
| | 1995 | 5 500 | 301 | 4 700 | 257 |
| | 1996 | 6 000 | 319 | 4 900 | 260 |
| | 1997 | 6 250 | 321 | 5 100 | 262 |

IV.14    Radio and television receivers
Récepteurs de radiodiffusion sonore et de télévision
Receptores de radiodifusión sonora y de televisión

| Country<br>Pays<br>País | Year<br>Année<br>Año | Radio receivers<br>Récepteurs de radiodiffusion sonore<br>Receptores de radiodifusión sonora | | Television receivers<br>Récepteurs de télévision<br>Receptores de televisión | |
|---|---|---|---|---|---|
| | | Number of receivers (thousands)<br>Nombre de postes récepteurs (milliers)<br>Número de receptores (en miles) | Number of receivers per 1,000 inhabitants<br>Nombre de postes récepteurs pour 1 000 habitants<br>Número de receptores por 1 000 habitantes | Number of receivers (thousands)<br>Nombre de postes récepteurs (milliers)<br>Número de receptores (en miles) | Number of receivers per 1,000 inhabitants<br>Nombre de postes récepteurs pour 1 000 habitants<br>Número de receptores por 1 000 habitantes |
| Singapore | 1970 | 500 | 241 | 200 | 96 |
| | 1975 | 725 | 320 | 421 | 186 |
| | 1980 | 900 | 373 | 740 | 306 |
| | 1985 | 1 550 | 572 | 850 | 314 |
| | 1990 | 1 780 | 590 | 1 020 | 338 |
| | 1991 | 1 820 | 591 | 1 043 | 339 |
| | 1992 | 1 860 | 592 | 1 070 | 341 |
| | 1993 | 1 900 | 593 | 1 095 | 342 |
| | 1994 | 1 940 | 594 | 1 150 | 352 |
| | 1995 | 2 000 | 602 | 1 200 | 361 |
| | 1996 | 2 500 | 741 | 1 300 | 385 |
| | 1997 | 2 550 | 744 | 1 330 | 388 |
| Sri Lanka | 1970 | 800 | 64 | - | - |
| | 1975 | 1 000 | 74 | - | - |
| | 1980 | 1 500 | 101 | 35 | 2.4 |
| | 1985 | 2 551 | 159 | 450 | 28 |
| | 1990 | 3 400 | 199 | 750 | 44 |
| | 1991 | 3 450 | 200 | 850 | 49 |
| | 1992 | 3 500 | 201 | 865 | 50 |
| | 1993 | 3 590 | 204 | 950 | 54 |
| | 1994 | 3 640 | 205 | 1 000 | 56 |
| | 1995 | 3 700 | 206 | 1 480 | 83 |
| | 1996 | 3 800 | 210 | 1 550 | 86 |
| | 1997 | 3 850 | 211 | 1 530 | 84 |
| Syrian Arab Republic | 1970 | 1 170 | 187 | 116 | 19 |
| | 1975 | 1 400 | 188 | 224 | 30 |
| | 1980 | 1 700 | 195 | 385 | 44 |
| | 1985 | 2 200 | 212 | 590 | 57 |
| | 1990 | 3 150 | 254 | 740 | 60 |
| | 1991 | 3 270 | 256 | 775 | 61 |
| | 1992 | 3 392 | 258 | 810 | 62 |
| | 1993 | 3 515 | 261 | 850 | 63 |
| | 1994 | 3 640 | 263 | 880 | 64 |
| | 1995 | 3 750 | 264 | 950 | 67 |
| | 1996 | 4 000 | 275 | 1 000 | 69 |
| | 1997 | 4 150 | 278 | 1 050 | 70 |
| Tajikistan | 1990 | 600 | 113 | 10 | 1.9 |
| | 1991 | 700 | 129 | 12 | 2.2 |
| | 1992 | 720 | 131 | 15 | 2.7 |
| | 1993 | 735 | 131 | 16 | 2.9 |
| | 1994 | 750 | 132 | 17 | 3.0 |
| | 1995 | 780 | 136 | 18 | 3.1 |
| | 1996 | 800 | 137 | 19 | 3.3 |
| | 1997 | 850 | 143 | 20 | 3.4 |
| Thailand | 1970 | 3 500 | 98 | 250 | 7.0 |
| | 1975 | 5 000 | 121 | 500 | 12 |
| | 1980 | 6 550 | 140 | 1 000 | 21 |
| | 1985 | 8 000 | 156 | 4 122 | 81 |
| | 1990 | 9 500 | 171 | 5 900 | 106 |
| | 1991 | 9 900 | 176 | 7 997 | 142 |
| | 1992 | 9 969 | 175 | 8 300 | 146 |
| | 1993 | 10 186 | 177 | 9 570 | 166 |
| | 1994 | 10 814 | 186 | 10 808 | 186 |
| | 1995 | 11 000 | 188 | 11 000 | 188 |
| | 1996 | 12 000 | 203 | 11 150 | 188 |
| | 1997 | 13 959 | 234 | 15 190 | 254 |
| Turkey | 1970 | 3 550 | 101 | 400 | 11 |
| | 1975 | 4 200 | 105 | 1 050 | 26 |
| | 1980 | 5 000 | 113 | 3 500 | 79 |
| | 1985 | 7 000 | 139 | 9 180 | 182 |
| | 1990 | 9 000 | 160 | 12 987 | 232 |
| | 1991 | 9 200 | 161 | 13 500 | 236 |
| | 1992 | 9 425 | 162 | 15 000 | 258 |
| | 1993 | 9 600 | 162 | 16 000 | 270 |
| | 1994 | 9 830 | 163 | 17 500 | 291 |
| | 1995 | 10 000 | 163 | 18 958 | 309 |
| | 1996 | 11 000 | 176 | 20 588 | 330 |
| | 1997 | 11 300 | 178 | 20 900 | 330 |
| Turkmenistan | 1990 | 800 | 218 | 500 | 136 |
| | 1991 | 850 | 226 | 550 | 147 |
| | 1992 | 900 | 235 | 600 | 156 |
| | 1993 | 950 | 242 | 650 | 166 |

Radio and television receivers
Récepteurs de radiodiffusion sonore et de télévision
Receptores de radiodifusión sonora y de televisión

IV.14

| Country<br><br>Pays<br><br>País | Year<br><br>Année<br><br>Año | Radio receivers<br>Récepteurs de radiodiffusion sonore<br>Receptores de radiodifusión sonora | | Television receivers<br>Récepteurs de télévision<br>Receptores de televisión | |
|---|---|---|---|---|---|
| | | Number of receivers<br>(thousands)<br>Nombre de postes<br>récepteurs (milliers)<br>Número de receptores<br>(en miles) | Number of receivers<br>per 1,000 inhabitants<br>Nombre de postes<br>récepteurs pour 1 000<br>habitants<br>Número de receptores por<br>1 000 habitantes | Number of receivers<br>(thousands)<br>Nombre de postes<br>récepteurs (milliers)<br>Número de receptores<br>(en miles) | Number of receivers<br>per 1,000 inhabitants<br>Nombre de postes<br>récepteurs pour 1 000<br>habitants<br>Número de receptores por<br>1 000 habitantes |
| Turkmenistan (cont) | 1994 | 1 020 | 255 | 720 | 180 |
| | 1995 | 1 065 | 261 | 735 | 180 |
| | 1996 | 1 200 | 289 | 800 | 192 |
| | 1997 | 1 225 | 289 | 820 | 194 |
| United Arab Emirates | 1970 | 30 | 135 | - | - |
| | 1975 | 100 | 198 | 25 | 50 |
| | 1980 | 240 | 236 | 89 | 88 |
| | 1985 | 380 | 245 | 130 | 84 |
| | 1990 | 515 | 268 | 172 | 90 |
| | 1991 | 532 | 268 | 185 | 93 |
| | 1992 | 549 | 269 | 200 | 98 |
| | 1993 | 565 | 269 | 210 | 100 |
| | 1994 | 583 | 270 | 220 | 102 |
| | 1995 | 600 | 272 | 230 | 104 |
| | 1996 | 800 | 354 | 300 | 133 |
| | 1997 | 820 | 355 | 310 | 134 |
| Uzbekistan | 1990 | 7 000 | 341 | 100 | 4.9 |
| | 1991 | 7 500 | 358 | 150 | 7.2 |
| | 1992 | 8 000 | 375 | 200 | 9.4 |
| | 1993 | 9 000 | 414 | 250 | 12 |
| | 1994 | 10 000 | 452 | 5 900 | 267 |
| | 1995 | 10 300 | 458 | 6 125 | 272 |
| | 1996 | 10 500 | 460 | 6 300 | 276 |
| | 1997 | 10 800 | 465 | 6 400 | 276 |
| Viet Nam | 1970 | 2 800 | 66 | 1 000 | 23 |
| | 1975 | 3 500 | 73 | 1 200 | 25 |
| | 1980 | 5 000 | 93 | 1 800 | 34 |
| | 1985 | 6 000 | 100 | 2 000 | 33 |
| | 1990 | 6 900 | 103 | 2 600 | 39 |
| | 1991 | 7 070 | 104 | 2 800 | 41 |
| | 1992 | 7 240 | 104 | 2 900 | 42 |
| | 1993 | 7 420 | 104 | 3 000 | 42 |
| | 1994 | 7 600 | 105 | 3 100 | 43 |
| | 1995 | 7 800 | 106 | 3 200 | 43 |
| | 1996 | 8 050 | 107 | 3 500 | 47 |
| | 1997 | 8 200 | 107 | 3 570 | 47 |
| Yemen | 1990 | 310 | 27 | 300 | 26 |
| | 1991 | 400 | 33 | 320 | 26 |
| | 1992 | 450 | 35 | 340 | 26 |
| | 1993 | 520 | 38 | 365 | 27 |
| | 1994 | 580 | 40 | 390 | 27 |
| | 1995 | 650 | 43 | 420 | 28 |
| | 1996 | 1 000 | 64 | 450 | 29 |
| | 1997 | 1 050 | 64 | 470 | 29 |
| **Europe** | | | | | |
| Albania | 1970 | 200 | 94 | 2 | 1.0 |
| | 1975 | 250 | 103 | 5 | 1.9 |
| | 1980 | 400 | 150 | 96 | 36 |
| | 1985 | 493 | 166 | 232 | 78 |
| | 1990 | 570 | 173 | 280 | 85 |
| | 1991 | 578 | 175 | 285 | 86 |
| | 1992 | 590 | 180 | 290 | 88 |
| | 1993 | 600 | 185 | 300 | 92 |
| | 1994 | 650 | 203 | 310 | 97 |
| | 1995 | 700 | 220 | 350 | 110 |
| | 1996 | 800 | 254 | 400 | 127 |
| | 1997 | 810 | 259 | 405 | 129 |
| Andorra | 1970 | 4 | 190 | 1 | 79 |
| | 1975 | 5 | 199 | 2 | 79 |
| | 1980 | 7 | 198 | 4 | 116 |
| | 1985 | 9 | 200 | 6 | 137 |
| | 1990 | 11 | 206 | 8 | 155 |
| | 1991 | 11 | 210 | 20 | 372 |
| | 1992 | 12 | 212 | 21 | 378 |
| | 1993 | 13 | 214 | 22 | 382 |
| | 1994 | 14 | 220 | 24 | 383 |
| | 1995 | 14 | 225 | 25 | 390 |
| | 1996 | 15 | 226 | 26 | 391 |
| | 1997 | 16 | 227 | 27 | 391 |

IV.14 Radio and television receivers
Récepteurs de radiodiffusion sonore et de télévision
Receptores de radiodifusión sonora y de televisión

| Country<br><br>Pays<br><br>País | Year<br><br>Année<br><br>Año | Radio receivers<br>Récepteurs de radiodiffusion sonore<br>Receptores de radiodifusión sonora | | Television receivers<br>Récepteurs de télévision<br>Receptores de televisión | |
|---|---|---|---|---|---|
| | | Number of receivers<br>(thousands)<br>Nombre de postes<br>récepteurs (milliers)<br>Número de receptores<br>(en miles) | Number of receivers<br>per 1,000 inhabitants<br>Nombre de postes<br>récepteurs pour 1 000<br>habitants<br>Número de receptores por<br>1 000 habitantes | Number of receivers<br>(thousands)<br>Nombre de postes<br>récepteurs (milliers)<br>Número de receptores<br>(en miles) | Number of receivers<br>per 1,000 inhabitants<br>Nombre de postes<br>récepteurs pour 1 000<br>habitants<br>Número de receptores por<br>1 000 habitantes |
| Austria | 1970 | 3 200 | 429 | 1 900 | 254 |
| | 1975 | 3 600 | 475 | 2 550 | 336 |
| | 1980 | 3 830 | 507 | 2 950 | 391 |
| | 1985 | 4 180 | 553 | 3 260 | 431 |
| | 1990 | 4 755 | 617 | 3 650 | 474 |
| | 1991 | 4 795 | 618 | 3 700 | 477 |
| | 1992 | 4 840 | 619 | 3 800 | 486 |
| | 1993 | 4 890 | 621 | 3 900 | 495 |
| | 1994 | 4 940 | 622 | 3 950 | 497 |
| | 1995 | 4 990 | 624 | 4 000 | 500 |
| | 1996 | 6 000 | 745 | 4 200 | 522 |
| | 1997 | 6 080 | 751 | 4 250 | 525 |
| Belarus | 1990 | 2 595 | 253 | 2 260 | 220 |
| | 1991 | 2 650 | 257 | 2 275 | 221 |
| | 1992 | 2 700 | 261 | 2 284 | 221 |
| | 1993 | 2 800 | 270 | 2 300 | 222 |
| | 1994 | 2 900 | 279 | 2 320 | 223 |
| | 1995 | 2 950 | 284 | 2 350 | 226 |
| | 1996 | 3 000 | 289 | 2 500 | 241 |
| | 1997 | 3 020 | 292 | 2 520 | 243 |
| Belgium | 1970 | 5 400 | 559 | 2 750 | 285 |
| | 1975 | 6 200 | 633 | 3 315 | 338 |
| | 1980 | 7 200 | 731 | 3 815 | 387 |
| | 1985 | 7 450 | 756 | 3 950 | 401 |
| | 1990 | 7 660 | 770 | 4 450 | 447 |
| | 1991 | 7 750 | 777 | 4 480 | 449 |
| | 1992 | 7 800 | 779 | 4 510 | 451 |
| | 1993 | 7 850 | 782 | 4 540 | 452 |
| | 1994 | 7 950 | 790 | 4 565 | 454 |
| | 1995 | 8 000 | 793 | 4 600 | 456 |
| | 1996 | 8 050 | 796 | 4 700 | 465 |
| | 1997 | 8 075 | 797 | 4 720 | 466 |
| Bosnia and Herzegovina | 1990 | 750 | 174 | 0.5 | 0.1 |
| | 1991 | 770 | 185 | 0.6 | 0.1 |
| | 1992 | 780 | 197 | 0.6 | 0.2 |
| | 1993 | 785 | 211 | 0.7 | 0.2 |
| | 1994 | 800 | 227 | 0.8 | 0.2 |
| | 1995 | 840 | 246 | 0.9 | 0.2 |
| | 1996 | 900 | 263 | 0.9 | 0.3 |
| | 1997 | 940 | 267 | 0.9 | 0.3 |
| Bulgaria | 1970 | 2 975 | 350 | 1 335 | 157 |
| | 1975 | 3 150 | 361 | 1 960 | 225 |
| | 1980 | 3 500 | 395 | 2 150 | 243 |
| | 1985 | 3 750 | 419 | 2 220 | 248 |
| | 1990 | 3 950 | 453 | 2 900 | 333 |
| | 1991 | 3 970 | 458 | 3 100 | 358 |
| | 1992 | 3 980 | 461 | 3 127 | 362 |
| | 1993 | 3 990 | 465 | 3 190 | 371 |
| | 1994 | 4 000 | 468 | 3 200 | 374 |
| | 1995 | 4 010 | 472 | 3 220 | 379 |
| | 1996 | 4 500 | 533 | 3 300 | 391 |
| | 1997 | 4 510 | 537 | 3 310 | 394 |
| Croatia | 1990 | 1 088 | 241 | 1 027 | 227 |
| | 1991 | 1 089 | 241 | 1 030 | 228 |
| | 1992 | 1 089 | 241 | 1 045 | 232 |
| | 1993 | 1 102 | 245 | 1 072 | 238 |
| | 1994 | 1 174 | 261 | 1 138 | 253 |
| | 1995 | 1 200 | 267 | 1 150 | 256 |
| | 1996 | 1 500 | 334 | 1 200 | 267 |
| | 1997 | 1 510 | 337 | 1 220 | 272 |
| Czech Republic | 1990 | 7 916 | 768 | 4 891 | 475 |
| | 1991 | 7 950 | 771 | 5 100 | 495 |
| | 1992 | 8 000 | 775 | 5 200 | 504 |
| | 1993 | 8 050 | 780 | 5 300 | 513 |
| | 1994 | 8 100 | 784 | 5 400 | 523 |
| | 1995 | 8 184 | 793 | 5 430 | 526 |
| | 1996 | 8 261 | 801 | 5 469 | 530 |
| | 1997 | 8 270 | 803 | 5 470 | 531 |
| Denmark | 1970 | 4 000 | 812 | 1 835 | 372 |
| | 1975 | 4 625 | 914 | 2 110 | 417 |
| | 1980 | 4 750 | 927 | 2 550 | 498 |
| | 1985 | 4 875 | 953 | 2 675 | 523 |

Radio and television receivers
Récepteurs de radiodiffusion sonore et de télévision
Receptores de radiodifusión sonora y de televisión

IV.14

| Country<br><br>Pays<br><br>País | Year<br><br>Année<br><br>Año | Radio receivers<br>Récepteurs de radiodiffusion sonore<br>Receptores de radiodifusión sonora | | Television receivers<br>Récepteurs de télévision<br>Receptores de televisión | |
|---|---|---|---|---|---|
| | | Number of receivers (thousands)<br>Nombre de postes récepteurs (milliers)<br>Número de receptores (en miles) | Number of receivers per 1,000 inhabitants<br>Nombre de postes récepteurs pour 1 000 habitants<br>Número de receptores por 1 000 habitantes | Number of receivers (thousands)<br>Nombre de postes récepteurs (milliers)<br>Número de receptores (en miles) | Number of receivers per 1,000 inhabitants<br>Nombre de postes récepteurs pour 1 000 habitants<br>Número de receptores por 1 000 habitantes |
| Denmark (cont) | 1990 | 5 250 | 1 021 | 2 750 | 535 |
| | 1991 | 5 270 | 1 023 | 2 780 | 539 |
| | 1992 | 5 300 | 1 025 | 2 800 | 542 |
| | 1993 | 5 345 | 1 030 | 2 850 | 549 |
| | 1994 | 5 370 | 1 031 | 2 900 | 557 |
| | 1995 | 5 400 | 1 034 | 3 000 | 574 |
| | 1996 | 6 000 | 1 145 | 3 100 | 591 |
| | 1997 | 6 020 | 1 145 | 3 121 | 594 |
| Estonia | 1990 | 680 | 433 | 520 | 331 |
| | 1991 | 700 | 448 | 550 | 352 |
| | 1992 | 705 | 455 | 555 | 358 |
| | 1993 | 710 | 464 | 560 | 366 |
| | 1994 | 720 | 478 | 565 | 375 |
| | 1995 | 730 | 491 | 570 | 384 |
| | 1996 | 1 000 | 682 | 600 | 409 |
| | 1997 | 1 010 | 698 | 605 | 418 |
| Faeroe Islands | 1970 | 14 | 348 | - | - |
| | 1975 | 15 | 366 | - | - |
| | 1980 | 18 | 403 | 4 | 92 |
| | 1985 | 22 | 483 | 9 | 197 |
| | 1990 | 24 | 507 | 11 | 244 |
| | 1991 | 24 | 511 | 12 | 247 |
| | 1992 | 24 | 518 | 12 | 251 |
| | 1993 | 24 | 526 | 12 | 256 |
| | 1994 | 24 | 534 | 12 | 266 |
| | 1995 | 25 | 549 | 14 | 314 |
| | 1996 | 25 | 573 | 14 | 317 |
| | 1997 | 26 | 582 | 15 | 343 |
| Federal Republic of Yugoslavia | 1990 | 2 850 | 281 | 1 800 | 177 |
| | 1991 | 2 900 | 283 | 1 850 | 181 |
| | 1992 | 2 950 | 286 | 1 880 | 182 |
| | 1993 | 3 000 | 288 | 1 900 | 182 |
| | 1994 | 3 060 | 291 | 2 376 | 226 |
| | 1995 | 3 080 | 291 | 2 676 | 253 |
| | 1996 | 3 100 | 292 | 2 700 | 255 |
| | 1997 | 3 150 | 296 | 2 750 | 259 |
| Finland | 1970 | 2 750 | 597 | 1 200 | 261 |
| | 1975 | 3 100 | 658 | 1 658 | 352 |
| | 1980 | 4 000 | 837 | 1 980 | 414 |
| | 1985 | 4 830 | 985 | 2 300 | 469 |
| | 1990 | 4 960 | 995 | 2 470 | 495 |
| | 1991 | 4 990 | 996 | 2 500 | 499 |
| | 1992 | 5 020 | 997 | 2 530 | 503 |
| | 1993 | 5 050 | 998 | 2 550 | 504 |
| | 1994 | 5 100 | 1 003 | 2 600 | 511 |
| | 1995 | 6 800 | 1 331 | 2 800 | 548 |
| | 1996 | 7 100 | 1 385 | 3 100 | 605 |
| | 1997 | 7 700 | 1 498 | 3 200 | 622 |
| France | 1970 | 25 000 | 492 | 12 000 | 236 |
| | 1975 | 30 000 | 569 | 15 000 | 285 |
| | 1980 | 39 900 | 741 | 19 000 | 353 |
| | 1985 | 48 000 | 870 | 21 500 | 390 |
| | 1990 | 50 370 | 888 | 22 800 | 402 |
| | 1991 | 50 800 | 891 | 31 710 | 556 |
| | 1992 | 51 100 | 892 | 32 530 | 568 |
| | 1993 | 51 450 | 894 | 33 370 | 580 |
| | 1994 | 51 740 | 895 | 34 000 | 588 |
| | 1995 | 52 000 | 896 | 34 250 | 590 |
| | 1996 | 55 000 | 944 | 34 500 | 592 |
| | 1997 | 55 300 | 946 | 34 800 | 595 |
| Germany | 1990 | 69 650 | 878 | 44 000 | 554 |
| | 1991 | 70 270 | 880 | 44 400 | 556 |
| | 1992 | 71 000 | 883 | 44 800 | 557 |
| | 1993 | 72 000 | 890 | 45 200 | 559 |
| | 1994 | 76 000 | 935 | 45 600 | 561 |
| | 1995 | 77 000 | 943 | 46 000 | 563 |
| | 1996 | 77 500 | 946 | 46 300 | 565 |
| | 1997 | 77 800 | 948 | 46 500 | 567 |
| Gibraltar | 1970 | 26 | 975 | 5 | 187 |
| | 1975 | 30 | 1 086 | 6 | 217 |
| | 1980 | 33 | 1 144 | 7 | 244 |
| | 1985 | 34 | 1 201 | 8 | 283 |

IV.14   Radio and television receivers
Récepteurs de radiodiffusion sonore et de télévision
Receptores de radiodifusión sonora y de televisión

| Country<br>Pays<br>País | Year<br>Année<br>Año | Radio receivers<br>Récepteurs de radiodiffusion sonore<br>Receptores de radiodifusión sonora | | Television receivers<br>Récepteurs de télévision<br>Receptores de televisión | |
|---|---|---|---|---|---|
| | | Number of receivers (thousands)<br>Nombre de postes récepteurs (milliers)<br>Número de receptores (en miles) | Number of receivers per 1,000 inhabitants<br>Nombre de postes récepteurs pour 1 000 habitants<br>Número de receptores por 1 000 habitantes | Number of receivers (thousands)<br>Nombre de postes récepteurs (milliers)<br>Número de receptores (en miles) | Number of receivers per 1,000 inhabitants<br>Nombre de postes récepteurs pour 1 000 habitants<br>Número de receptores por 1 000 habitantes |
| Gibraltar (cont) | 1990 | 36 | 1 340 | 10 | 363 |
| | 1991 | 36 | 1 352 | 10 | 366 |
| | 1992 | 36 | 1 363 | 10 | 369 |
| | 1993 | 36 | 1 374 | 10 | 373 |
| | 1994 | 36 | 1 387 | 10 | 375 |
| | 1995 | 36 | 1 401 | 10 | 379 |
| | 1996 | 37 | 1 415 | 10 | 384 |
| | 1997 | 37 | 1 429 | 10 | 390 |
| Greece | 1970 | 2 000 | 227 | 187 | 21 |
| | 1975 | 2 550 | 282 | 1 155 | 128 |
| | 1980 | 3 310 | 343 | 1 650 | 171 |
| | 1985 | 4 000 | 403 | 1 896 | 191 |
| | 1990 | 4 250 | 416 | 1 970 | 193 |
| | 1991 | 4 300 | 418 | 2 000 | 195 |
| | 1992 | 4 350 | 421 | 2 050 | 198 |
| | 1993 | 4 400 | 423 | 2 100 | 202 |
| | 1994 | 4 450 | 426 | 2 150 | 206 |
| | 1995 | 4 500 | 429 | 2 300 | 219 |
| | 1996 | 5 000 | 475 | 2 500 | 237 |
| | 1997 | 5 020 | 475 | 2 540 | 240 |
| Hungary | 1970 | 3 600 | 348 | 2 120 | 205 |
| | 1975 | 4 100 | 389 | 2 850 | 271 |
| | 1980 | 5 340 | 499 | 3 320 | 310 |
| | 1985 | 6 144 | 581 | 4 250 | 402 |
| | 1990 | 6 275 | 605 | 4 330 | 418 |
| | 1991 | 6 280 | 608 | 4 340 | 420 |
| | 1992 | 6 285 | 610 | 4 350 | 422 |
| | 1993 | 6 300 | 613 | 4 360 | 424 |
| | 1994 | 6 350 | 619 | 4 360 | 425 |
| | 1995 | 6 500 | 636 | 4 375 | 428 |
| | 1996 | 7 000 | 687 | 4 400 | 432 |
| | 1997 | 7 010 | 690 | 4 420 | 435 |
| Iceland | 1970 | 125 | 612 | 45 | 220 |
| | 1975 | 140 | 642 | 56 | 257 |
| | 1980 | 162 | 710 | 65 | 285 |
| | 1985 | 185 | 766 | 75 | 311 |
| | 1990 | 200 | 785 | 83 | 326 |
| | 1991 | 203 | 788 | 86 | 334 |
| | 1992 | 205 | 788 | 89 | 342 |
| | 1993 | 208 | 791 | 91 | 346 |
| | 1994 | 211 | 794 | 93 | 350 |
| | 1995 | 215 | 801 | 95 | 354 |
| | 1996 | 250 | 923 | 96 | 354 |
| | 1997 | 260 | 950 | 98 | 358 |
| Ireland | 1970 | 690 | 234 | 447 | 151 |
| | 1975 | 907 | 285 | 600 | 189 |
| | 1980 | 1 275 | 375 | 785 | 231 |
| | 1985 | 2 050 | 577 | 910 | 256 |
| | 1990 | 2 170 | 619 | 1 025 | 293 |
| | 1991 | 2 200 | 627 | 1 220 | 347 |
| | 1992 | 2 220 | 629 | 1 304 | 369 |
| | 1993 | 2 240 | 630 | 1 359 | 382 |
| | 1994 | 2 270 | 634 | 1 409 | 393 |
| | 1995 | 2 300 | 637 | 1 450 | 402 |
| | 1996 | 2 500 | 688 | 1 460 | 402 |
| | 1997 | 2 550 | 697 | 1 470 | 402 |
| Italy | 1970 | 30 500 | 567 | 12 000 | 223 |
| | 1975 | 32 500 | 586 | 15 000 | 271 |
| | 1980 | 34 000 | 602 | 22 000 | 390 |
| | 1985 | 37 000 | 652 | 23 600 | 416 |
| | 1990 | 45 500 | 798 | 24 200 | 424 |
| | 1991 | 45 650 | 800 | 24 300 | 426 |
| | 1992 | 45 734 | 800 | 24 400 | 427 |
| | 1993 | 45 800 | 800 | 24 500 | 428 |
| | 1994 | 45 850 | 800 | 25 000 | 436 |
| | 1995 | 47 000 | 820 | 25 500 | 445 |
| | 1996 | 50 000 | 872 | 30 000 | 523 |
| | 1997 | 50 500 | 880 | 30 300 | 528 |
| Latvia | 1990 | 1 400 | 522 | 800 | 298 |
| | 1991 | 1 500 | 561 | 850 | 318 |
| | 1992 | 1 600 | 604 | 900 | 340 |
| | 1993 | 1 700 | 650 | 1 000 | 383 |

Radio and television receivers **IV.14**
Récepteurs de radiodiffusion sonore et de télévision
Receptores de radiodifusión sonora y de televisión

| Country<br><br>Pays<br><br>País | Year<br><br>Année<br><br>Año | Radio receivers<br>Récepteurs de radiodiffusion sonore<br>Receptores de radiodifusión sonora | | Television receivers<br>Récepteurs de télévision<br>Receptores de televisión | |
|---|---|---|---|---|---|
| | | Number of receivers<br>(thousands)<br>Nombre de postes<br>récepteurs (milliers)<br>Número de receptores<br>(en miles) | Number of receivers<br>per 1,000 inhabitants<br>Nombre de postes<br>récepteurs pour 1 000<br>habitants<br>Número de receptores por<br>1 000 habitantes | Number of receivers<br>(thousands)<br>Nombre de postes<br>récepteurs (milliers)<br>Número de receptores<br>(en miles) | Number of receivers<br>per 1,000 inhabitants<br>Nombre de postes<br>récepteurs pour 1 000<br>habitants<br>Número de receptores por<br>1 000 habitantes |
| Latvia (cont) | 1994 | 1 710 | 664 | 1 200 | 466 |
| | 1995 | 1 720 | 678 | 1 210 | 477 |
| | 1996 | 1 750 | 700 | 1 215 | 486 |
| | 1997 | 1 760 | 715 | 1 220 | 496 |
| Liechtenstein | 1970 | 5 | 237 | 3 | 118 |
| | 1975 | 7 | 321 | 5 | 195 |
| | 1980 | 13 | 519 | 7 | 280 |
| | 1985 | 18 | 653 | 9 | 325 |
| | 1990 | 19 | 662 | 10 | 336 |
| | 1001 | 19 | 667 | 10 | 337 |
| | 1992 | 20 | 671 | 10 | 339 |
| | 1993 | 20 | 662 | 10 | 337 |
| | 1994 | 21 | 675 | 10 | 344 |
| | 1995 | 21 | 669 | 11 | 348 |
| | 1996 | 21 | 663 | 11 | 349 |
| | 1997 | 21 | 658 | 12 | 364 |
| Lithuania | 1990 | 1 500 | 401 | 1 300 | 348 |
| | 1991 | 1 550 | 413 | 1 400 | 373 |
| | 1992 | 1 600 | 426 | 1 410 | 376 |
| | 1993 | 1 650 | 441 | 1 420 | 379 |
| | 1994 | 1 700 | 455 | 1 430 | 383 |
| | 1995 | 1 800 | 483 | 1 670 | 448 |
| | 1996 | 1 850 | 498 | 1 680 | 452 |
| | 1997 | 1 900 | 513 | 1 700 | 459 |
| Luxembourg | 1970 | 157 | 463 | 71 | 209 |
| | 1975 | 179 | 494 | 87 | 240 |
| | 1980 | 200 | 549 | 90 | 247 |
| | 1985 | 229 | 624 | 92 | 251 |
| | 1990 | 240 | 630 | 141 | 370 |
| | 1991 | 244 | 633 | 144 | 374 |
| | 1992 | 247 | 634 | 147 | 376 |
| | 1993 | 251 | 634 | 150 | 379 |
| | 1994 | 256 | 638 | 153 | 381 |
| | 1995 | 260 | 639 | 156 | 383 |
| | 1996 | 280 | 679 | 160 | 388 |
| | 1997 | 285 | 683 | 163 | 391 |
| Malta | 1970 | 120 | 396 | 130 | 429 |
| | 1975 | 141 | 463 | 176 | 579 |
| | 1980 | 165 | 509 | 202 | 623 |
| | 1985 | 178 | 517 | 235 | 682 |
| | 1990 | 186 | 525 | 255 | 720 |
| | 1991 | 188 | 526 | 261 | 730 |
| | 1992 | 191 | 528 | 265 | 732 |
| | 1993 | 194 | 529 | 269 | 733 |
| | 1994 | 198 | 532 | 272 | 733 |
| | 1995 | 200 | 533 | 275 | 733 |
| | 1996 | 250 | 661 | 278 | 733 |
| | 1997 | 255 | 669 | 280 | 735 |
| Moldova | 1990 | 2 400 | 550 | 960 | 220 |
| | 1991 | 2 450 | 560 | 980 | 224 |
| | 1992 | 2 500 | 571 | 1 000 | 228 |
| | 1993 | 2 600 | 594 | 1 180 | 269 |
| | 1994 | 3 000 | 685 | 1 200 | 274 |
| | 1995 | 3 100 | 708 | 1 210 | 277 |
| | 1996 | 3 200 | 731 | 1 250 | 286 |
| | 1997 | 3 220 | 736 | 1 260 | 288 |
| Monaco | 1970 | 22 | 930 | 15 | 634 |
| | 1975 | 24 | 950 | 16 | 638 |
| | 1980 | 26 | 961 | 17 | 640 |
| | 1985 | 28 | 994 | 19 | 674 |
| | 1990 | 30 | 1 013 | 22 | 736 |
| | 1991 | 31 | 1 015 | 22 | 739 |
| | 1992 | 31 | 1 020 | 23 | 744 |
| | 1993 | 32 | 1 022 | 23 | 747 |
| | 1994 | 32 | 1 024 | 24 | 754 |
| | 1995 | 33 | 1 025 | 24 | 754 |
| | 1996 | 34 | 1 047 | 24 | 758 |
| | 1997 | 34 | 1 039 | 25 | 768 |
| Netherlands | 1970 | 7 350 | 564 | 3 086 | 237 |
| | 1975 | 7 710 | 565 | 4 230 | 310 |
| | 1980 | 9 200 | 650 | 5 650 | 399 |
| | 1985 | 12 000 | 828 | 6 700 | 462 |

IV.14    Radio and television receivers
Récepteurs de radiodiffusion sonore et de télévision
Receptores de radiodifusión sonora y de televisión

| Country<br>Pays<br>País | Year<br>Année<br>Año | Radio receivers<br>Récepteurs de radiodiffusion sonore<br>Receptores de radiodifusión sonora | | Television receivers<br>Récepteurs de télévision<br>Receptores de televisión | |
|---|---|---|---|---|---|
| | | Number of receivers<br>(thousands)<br>Nombre de postes<br>récepteurs (milliers)<br>Número de receptores<br>(en miles) | Number of receivers<br>per 1,000 inhabitants<br>Nombre de postes<br>récepteurs pour 1 000<br>habitants<br>Número de receptores por<br>1 000 habitantes | Number of receivers<br>(thousands)<br>Nombre de postes<br>récepteurs (milliers)<br>Número de receptores<br>(en miles) | Number of receivers<br>per 1,000 inhabitants<br>Nombre de postes<br>récepteurs pour 1 000<br>habitants<br>Número de receptores por<br>1 000 habitantes |
| Netherlands (cont) | 1990 | 13 550 | 906 | 7 200 | 482 |
| | 1991 | 13 650 | 907 | 7 300 | 485 |
| | 1992 | 13 755 | 907 | 7 400 | 488 |
| | 1993 | 13 865 | 908 | 7 500 | 491 |
| | 1994 | 14 000 | 911 | 7 600 | 495 |
| | 1995 | 14 500 | 938 | 7 700 | 498 |
| | 1996 | 15 000 | 965 | 8 000 | 515 |
| | 1997 | 15 300 | 980 | 8 100 | 519 |
| Norway | 1970 | 2 455 | 633 | 1 025 | 264 |
| | 1975 | 2 575 | 643 | 1 252 | 312 |
| | 1980 | 2 700 | 661 | 1 430 | 350 |
| | 1985 | 3 230 | 778 | 1 640 | 395 |
| | 1990 | 3 370 | 795 | 1 790 | 422 |
| | 1991 | 3 390 | 795 | 1 804 | 423 |
| | 1992 | 3 410 | 796 | 1 820 | 425 |
| | 1993 | 3 430 | 797 | 1 835 | 426 |
| | 1994 | 3 450 | 797 | 1 850 | 428 |
| | 1995 | 3 500 | 805 | 1 875 | 431 |
| | 1996 | 4 000 | 915 | 2 000 | 457 |
| | 1997 | 4 030 | 917 | 2 030 | 462 |
| Poland | 1970 | 7 000 | 215 | 4 640 | 143 |
| | 1975 | 9 700 | 285 | 7 120 | 209 |
| | 1980 | 10 615 | 298 | 8 750 | 246 |
| | 1985 | 12 250 | 329 | 10 400 | 280 |
| | 1990 | 16 500 | 433 | 11 640 | 305 |
| | 1991 | 16 600 | 434 | 11 685 | 306 |
| | 1992 | 16 700 | 435 | 11 755 | 306 |
| | 1993 | 16 800 | 437 | 11 820 | 307 |
| | 1994 | 16 900 | 438 | 11 890 | 308 |
| | 1995 | 17 500 | 453 | 12 000 | 311 |
| | 1996 | 20 000 | 517 | 13 000 | 336 |
| | 1997 | 20 200 | 522 | 13 050 | 337 |
| Portugal | 1970 | 1 400 | 155 | 505 | 56 |
| | 1975 | 1 530 | 168 | 860 | 95 |
| | 1980 | 1 660 | 170 | 1 540 | 158 |
| | 1985 | 2 000 | 202 | 1 765 | 178 |
| | 1990 | 2 240 | 227 | 2 950 | 299 |
| | 1991 | 2 250 | 228 | 3 050 | 309 |
| | 1992 | 2 260 | 229 | 3 100 | 314 |
| | 1993 | 2 280 | 231 | 3 150 | 320 |
| | 1994 | 2 290 | 232 | 3 160 | 321 |
| | 1995 | 2 400 | 244 | 3 200 | 325 |
| | 1996 | 3 000 | 304 | 3 300 | 335 |
| | 1997 | 3 020 | 306 | 3 310 | 336 |
| Romania | 1970 | 4 200 | 207 | 1 630 | 80 |
| | 1975 | 5 000 | 235 | 2 950 | 139 |
| | 1980 | 5 587 | 252 | 4 000 | 180 |
| | 1985 | 6 196 | 273 | 4 300 | 189 |
| | 1990 | 6 645 | 286 | 4 500 | 194 |
| | 1991 | 6 700 | 289 | 4 560 | 197 |
| | 1992 | 6 800 | 294 | 4 580 | 198 |
| | 1993 | 6 850 | 298 | 4 595 | 200 |
| | 1994 | 6 900 | 302 | 4 600 | 201 |
| | 1995 | 6 933 | 305 | 5 092 | 224 |
| | 1996 | 7 190 | 318 | 5 229 | 231 |
| | 1997 | 7 200 | 319 | 5 250 | 233 |
| Russian Federation | 1990 | 55 000 | 371 | 53 978 | 364 |
| | 1991 | 55 500 | 373 | 54 396 | 366 |
| | 1992 | 56 000 | 377 | 54 850 | 369 |
| | 1993 | 56 500 | 380 | 55 000 | 370 |
| | 1994 | 57 000 | 384 | 55 500 | 374 |
| | 1995 | 58 000 | 392 | 56 000 | 378 |
| | 1996 | 61 000 | 413 | 60 000 | 406 |
| | 1997 | 61 500 | 417 | 60 500 | 410 |
| San Marino | 1970 | 5 | 272 | 3 | 136 |
| | 1975 | 6 | 316 | 4 | 211 |
| | 1980 | 10 | 471 | 6 | 297 |
| | 1985 | 12 | 520 | 7 | 309 |
| | 1990 | 14 | 583 | 8 | 347 |
| | 1991 | 14 | 578 | 8 | 350 |
| | 1992 | 14 | 595 | 8 | 354 |
| | 1993 | 14 | 587 | 9 | 356 |

Radio and television receivers    IV.14
Récepteurs de radiodiffusion sonore et de télévision
Receptores de radiodifusión sonora y de televisión

| Country<br><br>Pays<br><br>País | Year<br><br>Année<br><br>Año | Radio receivers<br>Récepteurs de radiodiffusion sonore<br>Receptores de radiodifusión sonora | | Television receivers<br>Récepteurs de télévision<br>Receptores de televisión | |
|---|---|---|---|---|---|
| | | Number of receivers (thousands)<br>Nombre de postes récepteurs (milliers)<br>Número de receptores (en miles) | Number of receivers per 1,000 inhabitants<br>Nombre de postes récepteurs pour 1 000 habitants<br>Número de receptores por 1 000 habitantes | Number of receivers (thousands)<br>Nombre de postes récepteurs (milliers)<br>Número de receptores (en miles) | Number of receivers per 1,000 inhabitants<br>Nombre de postes récepteurs pour 1 000 habitants<br>Número de receptores por 1 000 habitantes |
| San Marino (cont) | 1994 | 15 | 604 | 9 | 357 |
| | 1995 | 15 | 603 | 9 | 358 |
| | 1996 | 16 | 614 | 9 | 359 |
| | 1997 | 16 | 610 | 9 | 360 |
| Slovakia | 1990 | 2 550 | 485 | 2 300 | 438 |
| | 1991 | 2 700 | 512 | 2 400 | 455 |
| | 1992 | 3 000 | 566 | 2 500 | 472 |
| | 1993 | 3 015 | 567 | 2 520 | 474 |
| | 1994 | 3 030 | 567 | 2 530 | 474 |
| | 1995 | 3 040 | 568 | 2 540 | 474 |
| | 1996 | 3 100 | 578 | 2 600 | 485 |
| | 1997 | 3 120 | 581 | 2 620 | 488 |
| Slovenia | 1990 | 700 | 365 | 550 | 287 |
| | 1991 | 710 | 368 | 603 | 312 |
| | 1992 | 720 | 370 | 607 | 312 |
| | 1993 | 730 | 371 | 618 | 314 |
| | 1994 | 735 | 371 | 625 | 316 |
| | 1995 | 740 | 372 | 630 | 317 |
| | 1996 | 800 | 401 | 700 | 351 |
| | 1997 | 805 | 403 | 710 | 356 |
| Spain | 1970 | 7 700 | 228 | 4 115 | 122 |
| | 1975 | 9 050 | 254 | 6 640 | 187 |
| | 1980 | 9 700 | 258 | 9 505 | 253 |
| | 1985 | 11 300 | 294 | 10 400 | 270 |
| | 1990 | 12 000 | 305 | 15 500 | 394 |
| | 1991 | 12 100 | 307 | 15 600 | 396 |
| | 1992 | 12 200 | 309 | 15 700 | 398 |
| | 1993 | 12 300 | 311 | 15 800 | 400 |
| | 1994 | 12 350 | 312 | 15 900 | 402 |
| | 1995 | 12 450 | 315 | 16 000 | 404 |
| | 1996 | 13 000 | 328 | 16 100 | 407 |
| | 1997 | 13 100 | 331 | 16 200 | 409 |
| Sweden | 1970 | 3 750 | 466 | 3 680 | 458 |
| | 1975 | 4 200 | 513 | 3 750 | 458 |
| | 1980 | 7 000 | 842 | 3 830 | 461 |
| | 1985 | 7 250 | 868 | 3 875 | 464 |
| | 1990 | 7 500 | 876 | 4 000 | 467 |
| | 1991 | 7 550 | 877 | 4 030 | 468 |
| | 1992 | 7 600 | 877 | 4 060 | 469 |
| | 1993 | 7 650 | 878 | 4 085 | 469 |
| | 1994 | 7 700 | 879 | 4 150 | 474 |
| | 1995 | 7 750 | 881 | 4 200 | 477 |
| | 1996 | 8 000 | 906 | 4 400 | 498 |
| | 1997 | 8 250 | 932 | 4 600 | 519 |
| Switzerland | 1970 | 3 700 | 598 | 1 500 | 242 |
| | 1975 | 4 500 | 710 | 2 050 | 323 |
| | 1980 | 5 140 | 813 | 2 300 | 364 |
| | 1985 | 5 426 | 830 | 2 550 | 390 |
| | 1990 | 5 682 | 831 | 2 725 | 399 |
| | 1991 | 5 743 | 833 | 2 755 | 399 |
| | 1992 | 5 805 | 834 | 2 785 | 400 |
| | 1993 | 5 870 | 836 | 2 839 | 404 |
| | 1994 | 6 000 | 847 | 2 967 | 419 |
| | 1995 | 6 100 | 854 | 3 000 | 420 |
| | 1996 | 7 000 | 972 | 3 200 | 445 |
| | 1997 | 7 100 | 979 | 3 310 | 457 |
| The Former Yugoslav Rep. of Macedonia | 1990 | 367 | 192 | 335 | 175 |
| | 1991 | 372 | 194 | 340 | 177 |
| | 1992 | 378 | 195 | 345 | 178 |
| | 1993 | 385 | 198 | 350 | 180 |
| | 1994 | 390 | 200 | 355 | 182 |
| | 1995 | 395 | 201 | 360 | 183 |
| | 1996 | 400 | 203 | 500 | 253 |
| | 1997 | 410 | 206 | 510 | 257 |
| Ukraine | 1990 | 41 000 | 790 | 16 950 | 327 |
| | 1991 | 41 300 | 796 | 17 024 | 328 |
| | 1992 | 41 500 | 800 | 17 300 | 334 |
| | 1993 | 41 700 | 806 | 17 500 | 338 |
| | 1994 | 41 800 | 810 | 17 520 | 340 |
| | 1995 | 44 300 | 861 | 17 550 | 341 |
| | 1996 | 45 000 | 878 | 18 000 | 351 |
| | 1997 | 45 050 | 882 | 18 050 | 353 |

IV.14 Radio and television receivers
Récepteurs de radiodiffusion sonore et de télévision
Receptores de radiodifusión sonora y de televisión

| Country<br>Pays<br>País | Year<br>Année<br>Año | Radio receivers<br>Récepteurs de radiodiffusion sonore<br>Receptores de radiodifusión sonora | | Television receivers<br>Récepteurs de télévision<br>Receptores de televisión | |
|---|---|---|---|---|---|
| | | Number of receivers (thousands)<br>Nombre de postes récepteurs (milliers)<br>Número de receptores (en miles) | Number of receivers per 1,000 inhabitants<br>Nombre de postes récepteurs pour 1 000 habitants<br>Número de receptores por 1 000 habitantes | Number of receivers (thousands)<br>Nombre de postes récepteurs (milliers)<br>Número de receptores (en miles) | Number of receivers per 1,000 inhabitants<br>Nombre de postes récepteurs pour 1 000 habitants<br>Número de receptores por 1 000 habitantes |
| United Kingdom | 1970 | 45 000 | 809 | 18 000 | 324 |
| | 1975 | 48 000 | 854 | 20 200 | 359 |
| | 1980 | 53 500 | 950 | 22 600 | 401 |
| | 1985 | 57 000 | 1 007 | 24 425 | 431 |
| | 1990 | 80 000 | 1 390 | 24 900 | 433 |
| | 1991 | 81 000 | 1 403 | 25 050 | 434 |
| | 1992 | 81 500 | 1 408 | 25 150 | 434 |
| | 1993 | 82 000 | 1 413 | 25 250 | 435 |
| | 1994 | 83 000 | 1 427 | 25 500 | 438 |
| | 1995 | 83 200 | 1 427 | 26 000 | 446 |
| | 1996 | 84 000 | 1 438 | 30 000 | 513 |
| | 1997 | 84 500 | 1 443 | 30 500 | 521 |
| **Oceania** | | | | | |
| American Samoa | 1970 | 20 | 733 | 2 | 73 |
| | 1975 | 26 | 878 | 5 | 169 |
| | 1980 | 31 | 957 | 6 | 171 |
| | 1985 | 38 | 968 | 7 | 178 |
| | 1990 | 45 | 958 | 10 | 212 |
| | 1991 | 47 | 958 | 10 | 210 |
| | 1992 | 48 | 958 | 11 | 212 |
| | 1993 | 50 | 959 | 11 | 213 |
| | 1994 | 52 | 959 | 12 | 214 |
| | 1995 | 54 | 959 | 13 | 220 |
| | 1996 | 55 | 925 | 13 | 221 |
| | 1997 | 57 | 929 | 14 | 221 |
| Australia | 1970 | 12 000 | 957 | 2 758 | 220 |
| | 1975 | 13 900 | 1 000 | 4 549 | 327 |
| | 1980 | 16 000 | 1 098 | 5 600 | 384 |
| | 1985 | 19 500 | 1 247 | 7 000 | 448 |
| | 1990 | 21 600 | 1 279 | 8 200 | 486 |
| | 1991 | 22 000 | 1 285 | 8 330 | 487 |
| | 1992 | 22 400 | 1 292 | 8 480 | 489 |
| | 1993 | 22 730 | 1 296 | 8 610 | 491 |
| | 1994 | 23 000 | 1 296 | 8 730 | 492 |
| | 1995 | 23 300 | 1 298 | 8 850 | 493 |
| | 1996 | 25 000 | 1 378 | 10 000 | 551 |
| | 1997 | 25 500 | 1 391 | 10 150 | 554 |
| Cook Islands | 1970 | 6 | 304 | - | - |
| | 1975 | 7 | 366 | - | - |
| | 1980 | 8 | 420 | - | - |
| | 1985 | 10 | 620 | - | - |
| | 1990 | 12 | 665 | 3 | 164 |
| | 1991 | 12 | 668 | 3 | 167 |
| | 1992 | 13 | 669 | 3 | 169 |
| | 1993 | 13 | 704 | 3 | 179 |
| | 1994 | 13 | 707 | 3 | 181 |
| | 1995 | 13 | 709 | 4 | 185 |
| | 1996 | 14 | 710 | 4 | 189 |
| | 1997 | 14 | 711 | 4 | 193 |
| Fiji | 1970 | 150 | 288 | - | - |
| | 1975 | 200 | 347 | - | - |
| | 1980 | 300 | 473 | - | - |
| | 1985 | 370 | 529 | - | - |
| | 1990 | 430 | 592 | 11 | 15 |
| | 1991 | 440 | 600 | 11 | 15 |
| | 1992 | 450 | 607 | 12 | 16 |
| | 1993 | 460 | 614 | 13 | 17 |
| | 1994 | 468 | 617 | 13 | 17 |
| | 1995 | 480 | 625 | 14 | 18 |
| | 1996 | 490 | 631 | 20 | 26 |
| | 1997 | 500 | 636 | 21 | 27 |
| French Polynesia | 1970 | 50 | 451 | 8 | 72 |
| | 1975 | 65 | 501 | 14 | 108 |
| | 1980 | 78 | 516 | 18 | 121 |
| | 1985 | 93 | 532 | 27 | 155 |
| | 1990 | 108 | 550 | 33 | 171 |
| | 1991 | 111 | 554 | 34 | 172 |
| | 1992 | 113 | 556 | 35 | 173 |
| | 1993 | 117 | 562 | 36 | 174 |
| | 1994 | 119 | 563 | 37 | 175 |
| | 1995 | 122 | 567 | 38 | 177 |
| | 1996 | 125 | 570 | 39 | 178 |
| | 1997 | 128 | 574 | 40 | 179 |

Radio and television receivers IV.14
Récepteurs de radiodiffusion sonore et de télévision
Receptores de radiodifusión sonora y de televisión

| Country / Pays / País | Year / Année / Año | Radio receivers — Récepteurs de radiodiffusion sonore — Receptores de radiodifusión sonora | | Television receivers — Récepteurs de télévision — Receptores de televisión | |
|---|---|---|---|---|---|
| | | Number of receivers (thousands) / Nombre de postes récepteurs (milliers) / Número de receptores (en miles) | Number of receivers per 1,000 inhabitants / Nombre de postes récepteurs pour 1 000 habitants / Número de receptores por 1 000 habitantes | Number of receivers (thousands) / Nombre de postes récepteurs (milliers) / Número de receptores (en miles) | Number of receivers per 1,000 inhabitants / Nombre de postes récepteurs pour 1 000 habitants / Número de receptores por 1 000 habitantes |
| Guam | 1970 | 84 | 983 | 40 | 468 |
| | 1975 | 95 | 996 | 50 | 524 |
| | 1980 | 110 | 1 032 | 63 | 591 |
| | 1985 | 150 | 1 256 | 76 | 636 |
| | 1990 | 185 | 1 381 | 88 | 657 |
| | 1991 | 190 | 1 385 | 90 | 657 |
| | 1992 | 195 | 1 387 | 93 | 658 |
| | 1993 | 201 | 1 395 | 95 | 659 |
| | 1994 | 206 | 1 396 | 97 | 660 |
| | 1995 | 211 | 1 396 | 100 | 662 |
| | 1006 | 216 | 1 398 | 103 | 667 |
| | 1997 | 221 | 1 400 | 106 | 668 |
| Kiribati | 1970 | 7 | 140 | - | - |
| | 1975 | 8 | 144 | - | - |
| | 1980 | 12 | 193 | - | - |
| | 1985 | 13 | 196 | - | - |
| | 1990 | 15 | 202 | - | - |
| | 1991 | 15 | 203 | - | - |
| | 1992 | 15 | 207 | - | - |
| | 1993 | 16 | 209 | - | - |
| | 1994 | 16 | 213 | | |
| | 1995 | 17 | 213 | 0.7 | 8.8 |
| | 1996 | 17 | 213 | 1 | 13 |
| | 1997 | 17 | 212 | 1 | 15 |
| Nauru | 1970 | 2 | 410 | - | - |
| | 1975 | 3 | 432 | - | - |
| | 1980 | 4 | 525 | - | - |
| | 1985 | 5 | 538 | - | - |
| | 1990 | 6 | 599 | - | - |
| | 1991 | 6 | 602 | - | - |
| | 1992 | 6 | 604 | - | - |
| | 1993 | 6 | 604 | - | - |
| | 1994 | 6 | 606 | - | - |
| | 1995 | 6 | 607 | 0.3 | 29 |
| | 1996 | 7 | 608 | 0.4 | 37 |
| | 1997 | 7 | 609 | 0.5 | 46 |
| New Caledonia | 1970 | 35 | 324 | 8 | 74 |
| | 1975 | 55 | 413 | 15 | 113 |
| | 1980 | 69 | 479 | 25 | 175 |
| | 1985 | 80 | 517 | 40 | 258 |
| | 1990 | 87 | 519 | 42 | 251 |
| | 1991 | 90 | 521 | 43 | 250 |
| | 1992 | 93 | 523 | 45 | 252 |
| | 1993 | 96 | 524 | 46 | 252 |
| | 1994 | 99 | 524 | 48 | 253 |
| | 1995 | 102 | 526 | 49 | 254 |
| | 1996 | 104 | 526 | 51 | 255 |
| | 1997 | 107 | 527 | 52 | 257 |
| New Zealand | 1970 | 2 400 | 851 | 790 | 280 |
| | 1975 | 2 670 | 866 | 958 | 311 |
| | 1980 | 2 755 | 885 | 1 035 | 332 |
| | 1985 | 2 950 | 909 | 1 397 | 430 |
| | 1990 | 3 130 | 931 | 1 500 | 446 |
| | 1991 | 3 200 | 938 | 1 530 | 448 |
| | 1992 | 3 340 | 961 | 1 670 | 481 |
| | 1993 | 3 410 | 962 | 1 715 | 484 |
| | 1994 | 3 480 | 963 | 1 800 | 498 |
| | 1995 | 3 550 | 967 | 1 830 | 498 |
| | 1996 | 3 700 | 995 | 1 878 | 505 |
| | 1997 | 3 750 | 997 | 1 926 | 512 |
| Niue | 1970 | 0.8 | 167 | - | - |
| | 1975 | 0.9 | 217 | - | - |
| | 1980 | 1.0 | 278 | - | - |
| | 1985 | 1 | 428 | - | - |
| | 1990 | 1 | 486 | - | - |
| | 1991 | 1 | 496 | - | - |
| | 1992 | 1 | 508 | - | - |
| | 1993 | 1 | 521 | - | - |
| | 1994 | 1 | 534 | - | - |
| | 1995 | 1 | 547 | - | - |
| | 1996 | 1 | 570 | - | - |
| | 1997 | 1 | 586 | - | - |

IV.14 Radio and television receivers
Récepteurs de radiodiffusion sonore et de télévision
Receptores de radiodifusión sonora y de televisión

| Country<br>Pays<br>País | Year<br>Année<br>Año | Radio receivers<br>Récepteurs de radiodiffusion sonore<br>Receptores de radiodifusión sonora | | Television receivers<br>Récepteurs de télévision<br>Receptores de televisión | |
|---|---|---|---|---|---|
| | | Number of receivers<br>(thousands)<br>Nombre de postes<br>récepteurs (milliers)<br>Número de receptores<br>(en miles) | Number of receivers<br>per 1,000 inhabitants<br>Nombre de postes<br>récepteurs pour 1 000<br>habitants<br>Número de receptores por<br>1 000 habitantes | Number of receivers<br>(thousands)<br>Nombre de postes<br>récepteurs (milliers)<br>Número de receptores<br>(en miles) | Number of receivers<br>per 1,000 inhabitants<br>Nombre de postes<br>récepteurs pour 1 000<br>habitants<br>Número de receptores por<br>1 000 habitantes |
| Pacific Islands (Palau) | 1970 | 5 | 525 | 1 | 126 |
| | 1975 | 7 | 605 | 3 | 278 |
| | 1980 | 8 | 615 | 6 | 492 |
| | 1985 | 9 | 650 | 8 | 570 |
| | 1990 | 10 | 630 | 9 | 596 |
| | 1991 | 10 | 642 | 9 | 597 |
| | 1992 | 10 | 645 | 10 | 601 |
| | 1993 | 11 | 647 | 10 | 603 |
| | 1994 | 11 | 661 | 10 | 604 |
| | 1995 | 11 | 662 | 10 | 606 |
| | 1996 | 12 | 663 | 11 | 606 |
| | 1997 | 12 | 663 | 11 | 608 |
| Papua New Guinea | 1970 | 80 | 33 | - | - |
| | 1975 | 110 | 40 | - | - |
| | 1980 | 180 | 58 | - | - |
| | 1985 | 230 | 67 | - | - |
| | 1990 | 280 | 73 | 9 | 2.3 |
| | 1991 | 288 | 73 | 9 | 2.3 |
| | 1992 | 298 | 74 | 10 | 2.5 |
| | 1993 | 310 | 75 | 12 | 2.8 |
| | 1994 | 320 | 76 | 12 | 2.9 |
| | 1995 | 330 | 77 | 15 | 3.5 |
| | 1996 | 400 | 91 | 40 | 9.1 |
| | 1997 | 410 | 91 | 42 | 9.3 |
| Samoa | 1970 | 75 | 519 | - | - |
| | 1975 | 85 | 563 | - | - |
| | 1980 | 100 | 644 | 3 | 16 |
| | 1985 | 125 | 797 | 5 | 32 |
| | 1990 | 150 | 938 | 6 | 39 |
| | 1991 | 152 | 943 | 6 | 39 |
| | 1992 | 155 | 954 | 6 | 39 |
| | 1993 | 160 | 976 | 7 | 40 |
| | 1994 | 165 | 996 | 7 | 40 |
| | 1995 | 170 | 1 014 | 7 | 40 |
| | 1996 | 175 | 1 031 | 10 | 59 |
| | 1997 | 178 | 1 035 | 11 | 61 |
| Solomon Islands | 1970 | 12 | 72 | - | - |
| | 1975 | 14 | 74 | - | - |
| | 1980 | 20 | 88 | - | - |
| | 1985 | 27 | 100 | - | - |
| | 1990 | 38 | 118 | - | - |
| | 1991 | 39 | 119 | - | - |
| | 1992 | 41 | 119 | 2 | 5.8 |
| | 1993 | 43 | 121 | 2 | 6.0 |
| | 1994 | 45 | 121 | 2 | 6.0 |
| | 1995 | 46 | 121 | 2 | 6.1 |
| | 1996 | 55 | 140 | 2 | 6.1 |
| | 1997 | 57 | 141 | 3 | 6.2 |
| Tokelau | 1970 | 0.7 | 384 | - | - |
| | 1975 | 0.7 | 443 | - | - |
| | 1980 | 0.8 | 477 | - | - |
| | 1985 | 0.9 | 512 | - | - |
| | 1990 | 1 | 653 | - | - |
| | 1991 | 1 | 694 | - | - |
| | 1992 | 1 | 737 | - | - |
| | 1993 | 1 | 781 | - | - |
| | 1994 | 1 | 799 | - | - |
| | 1995 | 1 | 813 | - | - |
| | 1996 | 1 | 838 | - | - |
| | 1997 | 1 | 846 | - | - |
| Tonga | 1970 | 10 | 122 | - | - |
| | 1975 | 13 | 147 | - | - |
| | 1980 | 20 | 218 | - | - |
| | 1985 | 30 | 318 | - | - |
| | 1990 | 53 | 553 | - | - |
| | 1991 | 54 | 557 | - | - |
| | 1992 | 54 | 562 | 1 | 10 |
| | 1993 | 54 | 562 | 2 | 16 |
| | 1994 | 55 | 568 | 2 | 16 |
| | 1995 | 56 | 576 | 2 | 16 |
| | 1996 | 60 | 616 | 2 | 21 |
| | 1997 | 61 | 619 | 2 | 21 |

**Radio and television receivers**  IV.14
Récepteurs de radiodiffusion sonore et de télévision
Receptores de radiodifusión sonora y de televisión

| Country<br><br>Pays<br><br>País | Year<br><br>Année<br><br>Año | Radio receivers<br>Récepteurs de radiodiffusion sonore<br>Receptores de radiodifusión sonora | | Television receivers<br>Récepteurs de télévision<br>Receptores de televisión | |
|---|---|---|---|---|---|
| | | Number of receivers (thousands)<br>Nombre de postes récepteurs (milliers)<br>Número de receptores (en miles) | Number of receivers per 1,000 inhabitants<br>Nombre de postes récepteurs pour 1 000 habitants<br>Número de receptores por 1 000 habitantes | Number of receivers (thousands)<br>Nombre de postes récepteurs (milliers)<br>Número de receptores (en miles) | Number of receivers per 1,000 inhabitants<br>Nombre de postes récepteurs pour 1 000 habitants<br>Número de receptores por 1 000 habitantes |
| Tuvalu | 1970 | 1 | 172 | - | - |
| | 1975 | 1 | 167 | - | - |
| | 1980 | 2 | 215 | - | - |
| | 1985 | 2 | 241 | - | - |
| | 1990 | 3 | 308 | - | - |
| | 1991 | 3 | 301 | - | - |
| | 1992 | 3 | 308 | - | - |
| | 1993 | 3 | 310 | - | - |
| | 1994 | 3 | 311 | - | - |
| | 1995 | 3 | 312 | - | - |
| | 1996 | 4 | 380 | - | - |
| | 1997 | 4 | 384 | - | - |
| Vanuatu, Republic of | 1970 | 11 | 120 | - | - |
| | 1975 | 13 | 127 | - | - |
| | 1980 | 23 | 196 | - | - |
| | 1985 | 36 | 268 | - | - |
| | 1990 | 43 | 286 | 1 | 9.1 |
| | 1991 | 44 | 287 | 1 | 9.1 |
| | 1992 | 45 | 287 | 2 | 9.6 |
| | 1993 | 47 | 292 | 2 | 12 |
| | 1994 | 49 | 294 | 2 | 13 |
| | 1995 | 50 | 296 | 2 | 13 |
| | 1996 | 60 | 347 | 2 | 13 |
| | 1997 | 62 | 350 | 2 | 14 |

**General note**
For general explanations and definitions, please refer to the beginning of this chapter.

**Note générale**
Pour les explications et définitions générales, prière de se référer au début de ce chapitre.

**Nota general**
Para las explicaciones y definiciones generales, referirse al comienzo de este capítulo.